musicHound

WORLD

musicHound WORLD

The Essential Album Guide

Edited by Adam McGovern
Photographs by Jack & Linda Vartoogian

Forewords by Angélique Kidjo
& David Byrne

VISIBLE
INK
PRESS

DETROIT • SAN FRANCISCO • LONDON • BOSTON • WOODBRIDGE, CT

musicHound® **WORLD**
The
Essential
Album
Guide

Published by Visible Ink Press
a division of Gale Group, Inc.
27500 Drake Rd.
Farmington Hills, MI 48331-3535

Gale Group is a trademark used herein under license.

Visible Ink Press, MusicHound, the MusicHound logo, and A Cunning Canine Production are registered trademarks of Gale Group, Inc.

Most Visible Ink Press books are available at special quantity discounts when purchased in bulk by corporations, organizations, or groups. Customized printings, special imprints, messages, and excerpts can be produced to meet your needs. For more information, contact Special Markets Manager, Gale Group, 27500 Drake Rd., Farmington Hills, MI 48331-3535. Or call 1-800-776-6265.

Cover photo of Oumou Sangare © Jack Vartoogian

Library of Congress Catalog Card Number: 99-66755

ISBN 1-57859-039-6

Printed in the United States of America
All rights reserved

10 9 8 7 6 5 4 3 2 1

musicHound CONTENTS

musicHound SIDEBARS

I HATE WORLD MUSIC

by david byrne   **ix**

I hate the term "world music." That's probably why I have been singled out to write about it. OK, I'm not stupid, I realize that it commonly refers to non-Western music of any and all sorts . . . popular music, traditional music, classical music, and any other categories that might be lying around. It ranges from the most blatantly commercial (in their terms) Hindi film music to the ultra-cosmopolitan art-pop of Brazil; from a former state-run folkloric choir with arrangements done by classically trained composers to *norteño* songs glorifying drug dealers.

This means, of course, that the term "world music" itself is inherently Euro-, even Anglocentric. The term means, to many people, anything that is not sung in English . . . or doesn't fit into the Anglo-Western pop universe this year. Next year, who knows. That's a lot of stuff. Hence the thickness of this book. In the Victorian tradition of the great dictionary makers, bizarre museum builders, and object categorizers, we are now attempting to classify all of that which we might define as music . . . from all over the world. Whew.

So, we find ourselves talking about 99 percent of the music on this planet: virtually all existing music—classical, traditional, commercial, experimental, and alternative pop—if it's not in English. That means Balinese gamelan (classical AND traditional), metal salsa (yes, it exists, and it's great!), Turkish transvestite pop singers, German techno with "exotic" samples, African guitar-pop bands, African field recordings, and Japanese formula-pop crap . . . and on and on. Virtually everything, like I said. Except English-language pop, folk, and dance music . . . although there is even some overlap there, but gimme a break; let's eliminate something!

So here we go, let's talk about . . . music.

Music is not necessarily all good. As in, not all good for you and not all made with integrity. In the first sense it can, and has, inspired a lot of wars, bloodshed, and mayhem . . . and personal psychological damage as well.

As ridiculous as they often sound, the conservative critics of rock and roll, and now of techno and rave, are not far off the mark, for music truly is, at its best, plenty subversive and dangerous. Hearing the right piece of music at the right time of your life can inspire radical change, destructive personal behavior, and fascist politics. Sometimes all at the same time. Even joy is dangerous at the right—or wrong—time. Certainly joy and ecstasy are dangerous politically, but they can be confusing personally as well.

On the other hand, music can inspire love, religious ecstasy, cathartic release, social bonding, and a glimpse of another dimension. A sense of another form of time . . . another kind of space . . . and another, better, universe. It heals a broken heart, explains and sympathizes, offers a shoulder to cry on and a friend when no one else understands.

But enough about me.

There is some terrific music being made all over the world. One would hope so . . . it would be strange to imagine, as many multinational corporations seem to, that Western pop holds the copyright on musical creativity. No, the fact is, more is probably going on outside the Western pop tradition than inside it. So much incredible noise is happening that we'll never exhaust it. For example, there are guitar bands in Africa that can be, if you let them, as inspiring and transporting as any kind of rock, pop, soul, funk, or disco you grew up with. But you must have an inkling of that, or you wouldn't be reading this. You must already have heard something that made you realize there is so much great stuff out there, that to restrict yourself to only English-language pop is like deciding to eat the same meal for the rest of your life. The "no-surprise surprise," as the Holiday Inn chain claims, which is reassuring, I guess, but lacks some kick. Sure, sometimes you just wanna watch TV and fall asleep . . .

. . . But there are other times when you want to be transported to somewhere special, with someone or by yourself, and get your mind around some stuff it never encountered before, feel feelings that you don't completely understand, and stay there for a while. Look around. Fall in love.

That's why you've picked up this book.

This interest in music not like that made in our own little villages (Dumbarton, Scotland, and Arbutus, Maryland, in my case) is not cultural tourism, because once you've let something in, let it grab hold of you, you're forever changed. Of course, you can listen and remain unaffected, unmoved—like a tourist. Your loss.

But in fact, after listening to some of this music for a while, it probably won't seem "exotic" anymore, even if you still don't understand all the words. Thinking of things as exotic is only cool when it's your sister, co-worker, or wife—it's nice to exoticize that which has become overly familiar. But in other circumstances viewing people and cultures as exotic is a distancing effect that too often allows for exploitation and racism. Maybe it's naive, but I would love to believe that once one grows to love some aspect of a culture, its music for instance, one can never again think of those people as less than oneself. I would like to imagine that if I am deeply moved by a song originating from some place other than my own hometown, then I have in some way shared an experience with the people of that culture. I can identify in some small way. Not that I will ever experience music exactly the same as those who make it. I'm not Hank Williams, or even Hank Jr., but I can still love his music and be moved by it. Doesn't mean I gotta live like him. Or get as fucked up as he did—or as much as the late, great flamenco singer Camarón de la Isla, for that matter. That's what art does; it communicates the vibe, the feeling, the attitude . . . and we don't have to go through all the shit the artist did to get it. On the other hand, I know plenty of racists who love "soul" music, rap, and R&B . . . so dream on, Dave.

The "authenticity" issue is such a weird can of worms. Westerners get obsessed with it. They agonize over which is the "true" music, the real deal. It always comes up. I myself would like to question the authenticity of some of the new-age ethno-fusion shit that's out there, but I also know that to rule out everything I personally abhor would be to rule out the possibility of a future miracle. I don't have to listen to all of it, but I don't feel a need to prohibit it either. Everybody knows the world has two types of music. My kind, and everyone else's. And even my kind ain't always so great.

What is considered authentic today was probably some kind of bastard fusion a few years ago. I don't think the Police would ever qualify as an "authentic" reggae band . . . but does it matter? An all-Japanese salsa orchestra's record was #1 on the salsa charts in the U.S.—did the *salseros* care? No, most loved the songs and were frankly amazed. So, in my humble opinion, we can make no rules as far as music goes. Fela Kuti, the great Nigerian musical mastermind, was as influenced by Miles and Coltrane as he was by African grooves. . . . OK, maybe that one seems natural. But check this: Mr. Juju himself, King Sunny Adé, namechecks country & western crooner Jim Reeves as an influence. True. Rumor has it that the famous Balinese monkey chant was coordinated and choreographed by a German! The first South African pop record I bought was all tunes with American car race themes—Indy 500 and the like. Sound effects too. So let's forget about this authenticity bugaboo. I'm sorry I even brought it up. If one is transported by the music, then knowing that the creators had open ears can only add to the enjoyment.

Maybe that's where this book comes in. I myself find that knowing a little more about the artist who wrote or recorded one of my favorite songs only intensifies the listening and dancing experience. And often a little information such as that provided here can help a fan sniff out some other sounds of interest nearby. Not by following a load of hype and marketing muscle, but by venturing further down a path of musical pleasure.

David Byrne's exploration of world musics with Talking Heads and as a solo artist gave many Americans their first taste of styles from outside the U.S. Byrne helped popularize African, Latin, and other sounds in his own work, and then went on to be a major patron of his inspirations, forming the prominent and influential Luaka Bop world-music label and helping to launch the Stateside careers of Zap Mama, Tom Zé, Margareth Menezes, Cornershop, and many more. He is one of this country's most important advocates of world music—whether he hates it or not.

WORLD MUSIC: THE REAL ALTERNATIVE

by angélique kidjo | **xi**

By definition, one would think every music made in the world is "world" music. It's not! But then, I wouldn't want people to think that world music is the music of the "rest" of the world, apart from England and America, or even that it's Third World music.

Whatever its meaning, this new label (for a genre that's not new: Miriam Makeba is a perfect example of a world-music artist from the '60s who *succeeded* in the '60s) promotes a huge variety of sounds. From griots to high-tech sound designers, all these musics prove you can be different; you don't have to be "mainstream" to express yourself and touch people all over the world.

The core of the genre is, I guess, traditional music, because that's what creates the differences between every culture and influences the style of the artists. But tradition is not an end. Critics generally want a musician from a foreign country to stick to a pure tradition; he has to be "authentic." That's not considering him as an artist but as an animal in a zoo. You would not ask Bono from U2 to sing just Irish folk music!

The most thrilling part of world music, beyond the instruments and the techniques—which *MusicHound World* presents in detail—is the personality of the artists themselves. While reading the entries you'll discover that Cesaria Evora, for example, sings in a particular language with a special kind of music, but first of all she is Cesaria: a unique human being whose voice carries an emotion that can cross any frontier.

Believe me, music in the world is so rich. When I travel in my own country, every village has its own rhythms, its own songs; imagine what it means when you're talking about so many countries and five continents. So I hope this book will help you not to get lost and to have a better idea of the diversity that is just waiting to be heard. You will find the "old school"—for instance, E.T. Mensah, the king of highlife music, who used to make me dance as a little girl—and you have the new generation like Talvin Singh. But there's so much more: imagine, in the same book you can find Antonio Carlos Jobim, Nustrat Fateh Ali Khan, and Bob Marley!

I've got one wish: I hope 10 years from now that this book, quite thick already, will double, triple in size with thousands of new artists who will emerge from every country of the world, letting us discover sounds and emotions no one could have imagined.

Angélique Kidjo is perhaps the reigning queen of world music, breaking barriers in her own art and all across the pop market. Her unique synthesis of the traditional sounds of her native Benin with state-of-the-art technology and an up-to-date spectrum of other styles has made her one of the best-regarded performers in world music—and all music. She is known to U.S. listeners for high-profile crossovers like her recent appearances on the Lilith Fair tour, and has made inroads virtually unprecedented for an African artist in America. In Kidjo world music finds one of its most eloquent ambassadors.

THE WORLD IN TUNE

by adam mcgovern | **xiii**

A popular Western commercial jingle of the Cold War years went, "I'd like to teach the world to sing/In perfect harmony." Since then, at a faster and faster pace, the world has been singing back—and the book you're holding arrives at a time when more people than ever are realizing and welcoming the fact that it takes two to teach.

Most of us can clearly remember when it wasn't so. What is now known loosely as world music was once (and still is) the multiple sound of many "old" worlds streaming amongst each other and into the "new" one, as waves of immigration and eras of colonization shaped the modern era. The voluntary and compulsory immigrants to the Americas took their music with them as a companion and comfort in an often inhospitable new land—and as their descendants moved into a later, general American society (or hoped to, or tried), this music frequently became an unwelcome reminder of even harder times. The drive for upward mobility in both the privileged and struggling classes made "world" music, music rooted in distant cultural soils, a discarded symbol of rudiments rather than a prized example of essence.

Today our ears are opening back up. As people of all backgrounds in the former colonial powers weary of strife, and ancient hostilities rage through the former colonies of both market empires and totalitarian spheres, there is a growing impulse to bolster cultural pride while encouraging cultural sharing.

MusicHound World aims to provide a roadmap to this common ground. It is first and foremost a story book, telling tales of lives you'll both recognize and marvel at, introducing legends you've never heard of and revealing the down-to-earth people at their core. It is a series of history lessons that enliven the present day, a travelogue to a world you live in but may not know. Most of all, *MusicHound World* is an *open* book: although it's a tool for expanding horizons while it shrinks distances, the directions it sets you on are all your own.

That's the value of this unwieldy but refreshingly un-limitable thing called world music. The proliferation of unfamiliar and unclassifiable sounds under that umbrella make it the truest of "alternative" musics—and unlike either the "alternative" or "classic" styles of our mainstream marketplace, in world music too many different things are going on for any rules to ever set in. True, in one way it's still a term that shuts out—"world" music can mean every music that's not by "us." But in another way it's a catch-all that allows the kind of unregimented music-loving that so many Americans yearn for in an era of rigid radio formats and Top-40 sameness. As David Byrne points out in his foreword, the "world music" menu takes in each country's pop, folkloric, classical, and other traditions—and in how many other books will you find all of *those* together nowadays?

One of the few generalizations that can be made about world music is that it takes primary inspiration from sounds that stretch back to the dawn of humanity, while often pressing forward into others never before imagined; as such it is, above all, music about eternal beginnings.

World music is a for-the-ages form being spread by up-to-the-minute technology—and yet world music is a form that suggests that if our technology didn't exist it might *not* be necessary to invent it: consider the synthesizer-like tone of the Australian Aboriginal *didgeridoo,* or (without even *any* instrument!) the miraculous "throat-singing" of Central Asian Tuva. Millennia before the stereo and the satellite dish, entertainment was communal and had to be homegrown. These are qualities that many have never stopped valuing; from the African campfire drum circle to the Canadian Celtic "kitchen party," world music has always offered do-it-yourself spectacle that engages all the senses—a built-in appeal of the "world" genre that is right in time for our modern multimedia appetites.

As traditional cultures embrace the future and younger societies dig for their roots, the two meet halfway on the world-music turntable. With this many sounds, the world may never sing in perfect harmony. But with this much to choose from, the contrast can be music to our ears.

So how do you use *MusicHound World*? Here's what you'll find in the entries, and what we intend to accomplish with each point:

• Of course there's the headline listing of artists' and bands' names and birth information, and band members (with years of service and instruments played). In this book you'll also find information on where artists are currently based and what countries all band members are from—the sometimes wide range among band members' cultures, and the distance between where individual artists come from and where they've gotten to, can tell a lot about how small the world is becoming and how far its musicians' styles are expanding. *MusicHound World* also lists each artist's or band's genre(s)—not to box and label their creativity, but to give the reader a frame of reference and a touchstone for investigating like-minded artists.

• Then there's the introductory paragraph, which will give you not only biographical information but also a sense of the artist's or band's sound and their stature and significance in the world-music—and overall music—pantheon. Next come the "buyer's guide" sections:

• **what to buy:** The album or albums that we feel are essential purchases for consuming this act. It may be a greatest hits set, or it may be a particular album that captures the essence of the artist in question. In any event, this is where you should start—and don't think it wasn't hard to make these choices when eyeballing the catalogs of Fela Kuti, Celia Cruz, Fairport Convention, or some of the other world-music titans. Note that for acts with a limited catalog, **what's available** may take the place of **what to buy** and the other sections.

• **what to buy next:** In other words, once you're hooked, these will be the most rewarding next purchases.

• **what to avoid:** This category could include albums the world would be better off without, or it may designate work that newcomers to the particular artist are better off saving for later. Checking the bone ratings (about which, more below)—and of course the writer's comments—usually makes it clear whether we're saying "avoid this forever, and cover your ears if anybody plays it in your vicinity," or merely indicating that it's "for completists."

• **the rest:** Everything else that's available for this act, beyond the most notably good, bad, and rare, rated with the Hound's trusty bone scale. Note that for some artists with sizable catalogs, we've condensed this section down to **best of the rest.**

• **worth searching for:** An out-of-print gem. A bootleg. A guest appearance on another artist's album or a film soundtrack. Work in other media (books, film, academia). Something that may require some looking but will reward you for the effort. You'll see a bit more of this section in *MusicHound World* than in many of the other books in the series, since our subject matter is so far-flung. World-music albums can go in and out of print with some rapidity, but every day more is becoming available and staying that way. This book's entries are still geared toward making it easy for you to find albums rather than lose your sanity; the series' focus is on recordings on CD, in print, and available in the USA—we just don't want you to miss any other treasures.

• ◀◀: The crucial influences on this act's music.

• ▶▶: The acts that have been influenced by this artist or group. Used only where applicable; it's a little early for Anoushka Shankar or Ricky Martin to have influenced anybody.

Speaking of not wanting you to miss any good music, in this book we've expanded the series' usual *list* of compilation albums to a whole section of reviews. Collections like these are still the best way for listeners in America to enjoy certain international stars, not to mention the *only* way to hear the great (and often anonymous) traditional musicians of many cultures. The Compilations section is organized alphabetically by region ("Africa" at the beginning, "International" at the end); albums under each heading are organized alphabetically by title (country or countries covered are handily listed right beneath the titles).

Now, you ask, what's with those bones? It's simple — 𝄞𝄞𝄞𝄞𝄞 is nirvana (not Nirvana), a **woof!** is dog food. Keep in mind that the bone ratings don't pertain just to the act's own catalog, but to its worth in the whole music realm. Therefore a lesser act's **what to buy** choice might rate no more than 𝄞𝄞𝄞; some even rate 𝄞𝄞, a not-so-subtle sign that you might want to think

twice about that act. Note that for recent releases that were not available to be reviewed before press time, "N/A" will appear instead of a bone rating.

As with any opinions, all of what you're about to read is subjective and personal. There's no such thing as bad publicity, and nothing is more boring than a critic with whom you always agree (especially if you make sure to go out and buy everything he or she hates!). Ultimately, though, we think the Hound will point you in the right direction, and if you buy the 𝄞𝄞𝄞𝄞𝄞 and 𝄞𝄞𝄞𝄞 choices, you'll have an album collection to howl about. But if you've got a bone to pick, the Hound wants to hear about it — and promises not to bite (but maybe bark a little bit). If you think we're wagging our tails in the wrong direction or lifting our leg at something that doesn't deserve it, let us know. If you think an act has been capriciously excluded — or charitably included — tell us. Your comments and suggestions will serve the greater Music-Hound audience and future projects, so don't be shy.

MusicHound World *acknowledges the many organizations that have opened the world's musical borders. After this book introduces you to the artists the international scene has to offer, you can experience them all the better through the following groups, which are among the leading ones Stateside and worldwide that present performances, publish CD/cassette catalogs, provide educational offerings and research resources, and otherwise promote the enjoyment and understanding of world music. And don't forget to check out the books, magazines, Web sites, record labels, concert venues, and radio stations in the Resources section at the back of the book.*

Midem Americas
25 Park Ave, 24th Fl.
New York, NY 10017 USA
Tel: (212) 370-7470
Fax: (212) 370-7471
Web site: www.midem.com

North American Folk Music and Dance Alliance
Washington, DC 20036 USA
Tel: (202) 835-FOLK (3655)
Fax: (202) 835-3656
e-mail: fa@folk.org
Web site: www.folk.org

WOMAD (World of Music, Arts & Dance), USA
PO Box 9750
Seattle, WA 98109 USA
Fax: (206) 281-7799
e-mail: info@onereel.org
Web sites: www.onereel.org
www.womadusa.com

WOMAD, England
Millside
Mill Lane, Box, Nr Corsham
Wiltshire SN13 8PN
UK
Tel: 44 1225 744494
Fax: 44 1225 743481
e-mail: womad@realworld.on.net
Web site: realworld.on.net/womad

WOMEX (The Worldwide Music Expo)
Carmerstr. 11
D-10623 Berlin
Germany
e-mail: info@womex.de
Web site: www.womex.de

World Music Institute
New York, NY 10001-6936 USA
Tel: (212) 545-7536
e-mail: WMI@HearTheWorld.org
Web site: www.HearTheWorld.org

Editor

Adam McGovern has written on every genre of music imaginable—and some inconceivable, which is what he likes best. He has plied this trade for *Smug, COVER, B-Side, Raygun, Yahoo! Internet Life, Rock & Rap Confidential,* the AlterWorld and Total TV Web sites, and a host of other outlets with similarly lax background checks. A childhood with more relocations than Dr. Richard Kimble gave him a lifelong taste for the rootless variety of world music. He was not raised by wolves as is widely believed, though his parents considered it regularly and still wonder if it's not too late. McGovern has published some of the earliest mainstream features in this country on major world artists like Angélique Kidjo, Zap Mama, and Boukman Eksperyans, as well as the groundbreaking Africa Fête tour. The panoramic cultural view needed for a volume on world music has been fortified by his writings on all other artforms, and his curation of international art exhibits in New York City, not to mention his effortless ability to sit back and be a Russian-German-Romanian-Irish Jew. McGovern comes to the *MusicHound World* project from baptisms by *Rock* and *Lounge* in the same series. He lives in New Jersey with his partner, Lynn, until their cat Mishka gets tired of them.

Series Editor

Gary Graff is an award-winning music journalist and series editor of the MusicHound album guides. A native of Pittsburgh, Pennsylvania, his work is published regularly by Reuters, *Guitar World, ICE,* the *San Francisco Chronicle,* the *Cleveland Plain Dealer,* the *Pittsburgh Post-Gazette,* Michigan's *Oakland Press,* SW Radio Networks, *Country Song Roundup,* and other publications. A regular contributor to the Web site Mr. Showbiz/Wall of Sound, his weekly "Rock 'n' Roll Insider" report airs on De-troit rock station WRIF-FM (101.1). He also appears on public TV station WTVS's *Backstage Pass* program and is a founding board member of the Music Critics Organization and co-producer of the annual Detroit Music Awards. He lives in the Detroit suburbs with his wife, daughter, and two stepsons.

Managing Editor

Judy Galens is a senior editor at Visible Ink Press. She edited books on such disparate subjects as baseball, inventing, weather, and food festivals before hitting her stride with the MusicHound series. She lives in the Detroit area with her husband and their son, Graham, who enjoys kicking back to the sounds of Virginia Rodrigues, the Klezmatics, and the Buena Vista Social Club.

Associate Managing Editor

Dean Dauphinais is an obsessive-compulsive senior editor at Visible Ink Press and the managing editor of several Music-Hound titles. Although he considers himself a neophyte when it comes to world music, Antonio Carlos Jobim and Djavan are two of his favorite artists. Dauphinais lives la vida loca in suburban Detroit and thinks his wife, Kathy, and two sons, Sam and Josh, are out of this world.

Photo Editors

Jack and Linda Vartoogian's planet-ranging photographic, music, and dance interests couldn't find a more appropriate platform than *MusicHound World.* Even after 35 years of living in New York City, where all things performance arrive sooner or later (and where they are staff photographers for the World Music Institute), the Vartoogians continue to search for the best of the musical, the theatrical, or the choreographed—the farther from home the better. A glance at the range of periodicals to which they regularly contribute suggests some of the breadth of their interests: the *New York Times,* the *Village Voice, Time, New York,* the *Oxford American, Pulse!, Living Blues, JazzTimes, Jazziz,* and *Dance Magazine,* to name only a few. As for books, there is Jack's *Afropop!* (Chartwell Books, 1995) as well as Jack and Linda's *The Living World of Dance* (Smithmark, 1997) and *How to Look at Dance* with Walter Terry (Morrow, 1982). Last but far from least, they have contributed to dozens of other music and dance books, including almost every MusicHound volume in print. Jack and Linda may be reached by e-mail at jack@frontrowphotos.com or linda@ frontrowphotos.com. At their Web site (www.frontrowphotos. com), soon to be operational as this book goes to print, interested readers may travel through the Vartoogian's virtual world of images on their own.

Copy Editors
Barbara Cohen, Diane L. Dupuis, Christina Fuoco, Stacy Meyn, Pamela Shelton, Devra Sladics

Publisher
Martin Connors

MusicHound Staff
Michelle Banks, Christa Brelin, Jim Craddock, Jeff Hermann, Justin Karr, Diane Maniaci, Brad Morgan, Matt Nowinski, Carol Schwartz, Christine Tomassini

Proofreading
Jane Hoehner, Terri Schell

Art Direction
Tracey Rowens, Michelle DiMercurio, Cindy Baldwin

Graphic Services
Randy Bassett, Robert Duncan, Pam Reed, Barbara Yarrow

Permissions
Sarah Chesney

Production
Mary Beth Trimper, Dorothy Maki, Evi Seoud, Rita Wimberley

Technology Wizards
Jeffrey Muhr, Wayne Fong

Typesetting Virtuoso
Marco Di Vita of the Graphix Group

Marketing & Promotion
PJ Butland, Marilou Carlin, Kim Marich, Lauri Taylor, Betsy Rovegno

MusicHound Development
Julia Furtaw

Contributors
Karen Ashbrook plays hammered dulcimer, Irish flute, and pennywhistle. She has several recordings on the Maggie's Music label; a music book from Mel Bay Publications; and an instructional book/tape set for Irish music on dulcimer from Oak Publications. Her Irish book has become a classic tutorial of the dulcimer literature in America. Karen performs and records with the Celtic women's trio Ceoltoiri, and also plays Jewish and contra dance music. Her private lessons in Silver Spring, Maryland, and week-long classes at Common Ground, Augusta Arts Center, and other camps around the country are very popular.

Robert Baird is music editor of *Stereophile Magazine* in Santa Fe, New Mexico, and a contributor to *MusicHound Country* and *MusicHound Folk.*

Andrew BeDell lives in bucolic Mahwah, New Jersey, and is a freelance writer and editor who specializes in music and popular culture. For many years he edited muckraking columnist Jack Anderson while writing his own syndicated column about TV (trying hard not to confuse fact with fiction). Most recently he worked as a feature writer and pop music reviewer for the *St. Louis Post-Dispatch.*

Ari Bendersky is an editor with JAMTv and the *Rolling Stone* Network. When he's not busy chasing down music news scoops, he can generally be found scarfing sushi, listening to the Grateful Dead, or ironically dodging city traffic on his mountain bike.

PJ Birosik (musikintl@aol.com) is owner of Musik International (the leading full-service marketing and promotion company for alternative forms of music since 1977); reviews music, video, and books for 28 publications; is the recipient of two gold records for promotion; is listed in *Who's Who in Entertainment*; is a member of NARAS and AFIM; and is a past Board of Directors member for Los Angeles Women in Music.

Philip Booth is a freelance writer, musician, and DJ (WUSF-FM) based in Tampa, Florida. He has written for *Option, Billboard, Spin,* Salon, *Down Beat, Jazziz, Guitar World, JazzTimes,* and a variety of daily and weekly newspapers. Booth gets his worldbeat fix at Reggae Sunsplash, the New Orleans Jazz and Heritage Festival, and Skipper's Smokehouse and the Tropical Heatwave festival in Tampa.

Hank Bordowitz has written about music and 'temporary culture for over two decades now. For a dozen years, he wrote the "Cosmopolitan" column in *Jazziz,* covering the noise of the world. These days, he programs the world-music channel for Music Choice digital cable radio, as well as contributing articles and reviews to dozens of magazines ranging from *Playboy* to *Brutarian*. He also authored the tome *Bad Moon Rising: The Unauthorized History of Creedence Clearwater Revival*.

Iris Brooks specializes in cultural reporting. Her musical adventures include folk drumming with untouchables on the roof of a mud hut in Benares, India; a pennywhistle serenade for penguins in Antarctica; and a "sound safari" concert with the birds of Zimbabwe while paddling down the Zambezi River. She has served as editor for *EAR* magazine, the New York Philharmonic, and the Lincoln Center Festival. Over 100 of her music and arts articles have appeared in a variety of magazines.

Ken Burke is a singer/songwriter who has contributed to several MusicHound volumes in addition to serving up reviews and features for the likes of *Blues Access, Blues Suede News, Original Cool, Little Rhino Gazette, Texas Jamboree,* and *Outer Shell*. Only one year after its debut, sales figures for Burke's album *Arizona Songs* have reached double digits!

Salvatore Caputo is a freelance music writer living in Tempe, Arizona, with his wife and three kids. His interest in world music was sparked primarily by his immigrant father's Italian record collection, and a college ethnomusicology course in which he learned to love and play Indonesian *gamelan*.

Heidi Cerrigione is a traditional musician and freelance writer from Ellington, Connecticut. She plays autoharp, hammered dulcimer, and mountain dulcimer and performs with her husband, John, as the duo Cabin Fever; with a contra dance band called Heart's Ease; and with Doofus, a non-contra band with no discernible agenda. She contributes regularly to the *Autoharp Clearinghouse Magazine* and typesets music for various publications. She recently published her first book, *30 Old Time Songs and Tunes for Autoharp and Mountain Dulcimer,* co-written with her partner in Doofus, Neal Walters.

Thor Christensen is the pop music critic for the *Dallas Morning News* and has written for *Spin, Billboard,* and other music publications. He blows a lame blues harmonica.

Martin Connors has contributed to a variety of MusicHound and VideoHound books, and he is especially fond of Celtic music and that country/folk/alternative/guitar-strumming/ high-lonesome sound emanating from a lot of places, but especially Texas. He is thankful for the Ark in Ann Arbor, Michigan; his access to Canadian radio and television; and great record stores on land and on the Web.

Cary Darling is an entertainment editor at the *Orange County Register,* where he writes a weekly world and dance music column.

Jim DeRogatis is the pop music critic at the *Chicago Sun-Times* and the author of *Kaleidoscope Eyes: Psychedelic Rock from the '60s to the '90s* and a forthcoming biography of the late rock critic Lester Bangs.

Kerry Dexter is a freelance writer/editor, photographer, and television and radio producer. Her work has appeared in *Dirty Linen, Bluegrass Unlimited, Crossroads, Tapestry,* and other print and electronic media. She is based in Florida.

Josh Freedom du Lac was born on Haight Street three years and two full seasons after the Summer of Love and has grown to hate patchouli oil, drum-n-space music, questions about his middle name, and one-dimensional wines. The co-editor of *MusicHound R&B* and a budding cork dork, du Lac has been the pop music critic for the *Sacramento Bee* since 1994—incidentally, a great year for California Cabernet Sauvignon.

Daniel Durchholz is co-editor of *MusicHound Rock* and writes for numerous magazines, newspapers, and Web publications. He lives in St. Louis with his wife and four children.

Michael Eldridge teaches literature and culture "behind the redwood curtain" at Humboldt State University in Arcata, California—where a crack local steelband and a nearby village named Trinidad don't quite compensate for the fact that classes start before Labor Day, making it virtually impossible to attend Brooklyn Carnival.

Bill Ellis is music writer for the *Memphis Commercial Appeal* daily newspaper. He has a master's degree in classical guitar performance from the University of Cincinnati—College Conservatory of Music, and is a professional acoustic blues guitarist with several recordings; his latest is *The Full Catastrophe*. Bill also performs with his father, banjo player and former Bill Monroe sideman Tony Ellis. Bill spent over five years in Japan teaching English, writing for the *Japan Times*, and playing gigs. He has traveled extensively as a musician and tourist, including visits to Indonesia, Egypt, New Zealand, a USIA tour of Central America, and a recent month-long stay in Morocco for his newspaper.

Banning Eyre has been writing about music, especially African music, since 1988. His work has appeared in the *Boston Phoenix, Billboard, Guitar Player, Rhythm* magazine, *Folk Roots,* and *Sing Out!* as well as on National Public Radio's *Afropop Worldwide* and *All Things Considered*. He is the co-author of *Afropop! An Illustrated Guide to African Music*

(Chartwell, 1995), and the author of *In Griot Time: An American Guitarist in Mali* (Temple University Press, 2000). He is presently at work on a cultural biography of Thomas Mapfumo and the Blacks Unlimited from Zimbabwe.

John C. Falstaff once lived across the canal from the National Stadium in Dublin, where he frequently seized the opportunity to see acts such as Thin Lizzy, Horslips, Alan Stivell, and even Focus, but drew the line at Slade and Status Quo. Despite this, he went on to live a productive life in Atlanta, where he now hosts Georgia's only Celtic music radio show, on WRFG Atlanta (89.3 FM), and writes on all sorts of music for *Creative Loafing* locally and *Dirty Linen* nationally. Globally he can be read at http://www.pd.org/~jcf, and complained to at jcf@pd.org.

Christina Fuoco, the former music writer for the *Observer & Eccentric* newspapers in Livonia, Michigan, is now the senior content producer for Detroit.CitySearch.Com. She's addicted to working on MusicHound books and also freelances for Allstar, Michigan's *Flint Journal,* and CDnow.

Lawrence Gabriel is a Detroit-based writer, poet, and musician who is also editor of Detroit's *Metro Times.*

David Galens is the editor of the Gale Group's *Drama for Students* and *Study Guides to Great Literature* print series. He is also a freelance journalist and the guitarist/composer for the Detroit-based band the Civilians.

Ron Garmon is a music and film critic living in Los Angeles. He is consulting editor of *RetroVision* and his work has appeared in *The Tracking Angle, Cult Movies,* and *Scarlet Street,* among other publications. He claims no moral authority whatsoever.

Helen Giano is a music writer for *Smug* magazine.

Andrew Gilbert is a Bay Area–based writer who contributes regularly to the *San Diego Union-Tribune, Contra Costa Times, East Bay Express,* and the online magazine Salon. His writing on jazz has also appeared in the Los Angeles *Reader,* the Los Angeles *View,* the San Jose *Metro,* the Santa Cruz *County Sentinel, Musician,* and *Jazziz.* Born and raised in Los Angeles, Gilbert was first exposed to jazz at the Kuumbwa Jazz Center in Santa Cruz, California. For two years in the mid-'90s he was manager of the Jazz Bakery Performance Space in L.A. He is currently working on a documentary on the singer Weslia Whitfield. He can be reached at jazzscribe@aol.com.

Simon Glickman is the lead singer and lyricist for the L.A. band Spanish Kitchen. He has written for *MusicHound Rock, MusicHound R&B, MusicHound Folk, Contemporary Musicians, Uncommon Heroes, Entertainment Today, Rockrgrl,* and other

publications, and served as co-editor of *Native North American Biography.*

Gary Pig Gold, a proud contributor to *MusicHound Rock, MusicHound Country, MusicHound R&B, MusicHound Folk, MusicHound Swing,* and even *MusicHound Lounge,* divides time in his Hoboken, New Jersey, home between writing his syndicated-all-over-the-place "Pigshit" column; running his own little record company; producing power-pop records for Shane Faubert and the Dave Rave Conspiracy; performing in his "maximum rhythm 'n' bluegrass" combo the Ghost Rockets; and listening intently to how very much Robert Plant actually sounds just like that one-and-only diva of Arabic song, Umm Kulthum.

Alex Gordon is a contributor to *MusicHound Lounge,* a former associate editor of *Inside Sports* magazine, and the co-author of the book *College: The Best Five Years of Your Life,* published by Hysteria Press and available in finer bookstores.

Gary Graff is the creator and series editor of MusicHound (see above).

David Greenberger has been publishing *The Duplex Planet* since 1979. His commentaries and music reviews are heard regularly on National Public Radio's *All Things Considered.*

Ben Greenman is a journalist whose work has appeared in *Rolling Stone, Wired,* the *Village Voice, TimeOut New York, Miami New Times,* the *Chicago Reader, Yahoo! Internet Life* (where he is now executive editor), and other publications. He is also the author or co-author of 10 books, including *NetMusic: Your Guide to the Music Scene in Cyberspace* (Michael Wolff and Company), and a contributor to *Alt.Culture: An A-to-Z Guide to the '90s* (HarperCollins).

Jason Gross, the short version: Freelance scribe for the *Village Voice, Spin,* and other rags; editor/perpetrator of Perfect Sound Forever online magazine (http://www.furious.com/perfect); besieged by CDs from every record company on God's earth (and other places); desperately in need of sleep and/or ammo. Any questions?

William Hanson works for the Mott Foundation in Flint, Michigan.

Craig Harris has been writing about non-mainstream music since 1971. His work appears regularly in the *Boston Globe,* the *Middlesex News, Dirty Linen,* and *Folk Roots.* The author/photographer of *The New Folk Music,* published by White Cliffs Media in 1991, he is also an accomplished percussionist, and has appeared with Rod MacDonald, Geoff Bartley, Anni Clark, Chuck Brodsky, Dewey Burns, Ellis Paul, Merl Saunders, and

Rick Danko. Harris's photographs have been featured on CD and video covers for Robin Williamson, Greg Greenway, Barbara Kessler, the Jazz Futures, and the Greenwich Village Folk Festival. He is a music teacher at the Somerville Charter School in Somerville, Massachusetts.

Alex Henderson is a Philadelphia-based journalist, entertainment critic, and technical writer whose work has appeared in *Billboard, Spin, Pulse!, Jazziz, HITS, CD Review, JazzTimes, Cash Box,* and many other national publications. His taste in music ranges widely, and he has written liner notes and/or bios for Rhino, Island, MCA, Concord Jazz, Del-Fi, and countless other labels. Henderson now divides his time between music criticism and technical writing; in addition to contributing over 3,000 reviews to the *All Music Guide* since 1996, he has written many press releases for Vision X Software and Big Mouth Media (http://visionx.com/bigmouth), a company specializing in public relations for software developers.

Geoffrey Himes writes about music on a regular basis for the *Washington Post, Replay, New Country,* and *Country Music.* He contributed to *The Blackwell Guide to Recorded Country Music, The Rolling Stone Jazz & Blues Album Guide,* and *The Country Music Foundation Encyclopedia.* He has also written about music for *Down Beat, Request,* National Public Radio, *No Depression, Fi Magazine, Crawdaddy!, Musician, Sing Out!,* the *Baltimore Sun,* and the Patuxent Newspapers. He lives in Baltimore with his wife, Elizabeth Cusick.

Steve Holtje is co-editor of *MusicHound Jazz* and an editor at CDnow.

Aaron Howard is the Arts & Entertainment writer for the *Jewish Herald-Voice,* a contributing writer for *Houston Sidewalk,* and the former music editor of *Inside Houston* magazine. He is able to indulge his keen interest in both Jewish and Indian culture at the city's only kosher Indian restaurant. Who would have guessed that deep in the heart of Texas is a huge immigrant community that supports an amazing diversity of live ethnic musics?

Stephen Ide is a graphic designer who in his spare time is a writer, photographer, guitarist, and harmonica player. He pens a monthly folk records review column for the *Patriot Ledger* in Quincy, Massachusetts; contributes articles, reviews, and photographs to publications including the *New England Folk Almanac, Dirty Linen,* and *Bluegrass Unlimited*; and is the webmaster for the Rose Garden Coffeehouse in Mansfield, Massachusetts.

Jazzbo is Joseph Monish Patel, a San Francisco–based music journalist and writer who contributes to several print and Inter-

net publications, including *Rap Pages, The Source, URB, Raygun,* and Mr. Showbiz.

Isaac Josephson is communities manager at Tunes.com; producer of Downbeatjazz.com; and the co-founder of Centerstage Chicago. In his spare time he avoids his past, incurs parking fines, and spends his money in bicycle shops.

Chris King (brodog@hoobellatoo.org) teaches African literature; writes about world music, literature, politics, and folklore; plays in an eclectic folk band, Three Fried Men; observes the Native American ritual ways of prayer; and works with a documentary collective, Hoobellatoo, specializing in the work of overlooked world elders (check out his field recordings of merchant marine songsters, tribal drummers, and Missouri spirit mediums at www.hoobellatoo.org and www.skunty.com). He has been called "dog" *and* "chief" in two African languages.

Steve Kiviat is an Alexandria, Virginia–based contributor to the *Washington City Paper* and other publications.

Steve Knopper, editor of *MusicHound Lounge* and *MusicHound Swing,* knows one non-English expression: "Il y a un cheval sur la table." It's French. He has written for *Rolling Stone, George, Musician, Newsday, Billboard, Request,* the *Chicago Tribune,* and many other publications.

Nancy Ann Lee is enjoying a second career as a freelance music journalist and photographer. She co-edited and contributed some photos to *MusicHound Jazz* and has written for *MusicHound Swing* and the forthcoming *MusicHound Classical.* Lee regularly reviews world-music, classical, and jazz albums for the CDnow Web site. For more than a decade she has been a regular *JazzTimes* reviewer, and has written about music for various other magazines and local alternative weekly newspapers. She is based in Cleveland.

Marty Lipp writes a world-music column for *Newsday* and has written for the *New York Times, Details, New York* magazine, the *Beat, Rhythm* magazine, and the Rootsworld.com Web site. He is currently working on his first novel.

Bret Love is the managing editor at *INsite Magazine,* where he dreams of one day visiting all the countries whose music he writes about. In addition to spending what little spare time he has as a freelance writer and photographer who has contributed to Rolling Stone Online, *Drink,* and *Jezebel,* he's also an amateur musician, and wishes like hell that he could play a fraction of the exotic instruments he collects.

John Lupton is a native of Wilmington, Delaware. In addition to his work as a contributing writer for *Sing Out!* magazine, he is a longtime board member and current president of the Brandywine Friends of Old Time Music, a Delaware-based organization that sponsors concerts and festivals, including the Delaware Valley Bluegrass Festival and the now-defunct Brandywine Mountain Music Convention. He is also a board member of the Green Willow Folk Club, which specializes in presenting Celtic and British artists in the Delaware area. Since 1989, he has been co-host of *Rural Free Delivery,* a weekly radio show featuring bluegrass, country, and old time music, broadcast over WVUD-FM 91.3, the non-commercial station owned and operated by the University of Delaware. Professionally, he works in computer network management and administration at the University of Pennsylvania in Philadelphia.

Elizabeth Lynch is an Evanston, Illinois, writer and novelist who has written for *MusicHound Country, MusicHound Folk, MusicHound Rock,* the *Chicago Sun-Times,* the *Fort Lauderdale Sun-Sentinel,* and *Replay* magazine.

Garaud MacTaggart is a Buffalo, New York–based freelance writer and editor whose first exposure to world music came from the old 78 rpm records played by his parents—"Blue Bells of Scotland" by his father and "Finlandia" by his mother. Since he took accordion lessons during his youth, MacTaggart also has a perverse interest in all manner of squeezeboxes. He worked for nearly two decades in music retail before deciding to write for a living. He is co-editor of the forthcoming *MusicHound Classical,* and is glad his wife Claudia doesn't think he can ever have too many albums.

Brian Mansfield has co-edited *MusicHound Country* and *MusicHound Folk.* He lives in Nashville, Tennessee, and is a senior editor for CDnow and the Nashville correspondent for *USA Today.* Mansfield writes regularly for *ICE* and CountryNow.com. His work has also appeared in *Request, Pulse!, Country America,* and *Daily Variety.*

Lynne Margolis has spent most of her career writing about music and other art forms. She created the pop music beat at the *Tribune-Review* in Pittsburgh before being named as the paper's first TV and radio writer. After realizing writing about TV turns one's brain into mush, she decided to go back to the music and is now a contributing editor at MusicDirect.com; a twice-weekly columnist at RadioDigest.com; and contributor to the *Christian Science Monitor,* the Creative Loafing Network, and other outlets. In other words, a freelancer. A happy one. She has contributed to *MusicHound R&B, MusicHound Lounge, MusicHound Folk, MusicHound Swing* and *MusicHound Rock.*

Sandy Masuo has written about a bewildering variety of music for a wide range of publications, including the *Boston Phoenix,* the *Los Angeles Times, Musician, Rolling Stone, Raygun,* and several online publications, including Allstar, MTV Online, and Launch. She is the associate editor at *Request* magazine and lives in Los Angeles with her anti-social cat, Spot.

Michaelangelo Matos is a freelance critic whose work can be read regularly in Minneapolis's *City Pages, NY Press, Chicago Reader, Request, Creative Loafing Atlanta, Pulse of the Twin Cities,* and *Crawdaddy!.* His "Monthly Mixtape" column can be accessed at Perfect Sound Forever online: www.furious.com/perfect/mixtape.html.

Cliff McGann is a Massachusetts-based musician, freelance writer, and folklorist. He gained a deep respect for Gaelic culture during the summers he spent on his grandparents' Nova Scotia farm. His love of traditional music led him to the Celtic Studies department at St. Francis Xavier University in Antigonish, Nova Scotia, and eventually to the Folklore department at Memorial University in Newfoundland, where he is completing his thesis on Cape Breton fiddler Dan R. MacDonald. He is a regular contributor to *Celtic Heritage* magazine and the *Boston Irish Reporter.*

Andre McGarrity is a 1995 screenwriting graduate from New York's prestigious School of Visual Arts, where he won the school's coveted Dusty Award for best screenplay. He currently works as creative editor for impact! interactive! inc., a Southfield, Michigan–based new-media company specializing in providing content for the Internet.

TJ McGrath is a co-founder of and contributing editor to *Dirty Linen,* a magazine featuring folk and world music. He also wrote and edited *Fairport Fanatics,* the first American newsletter devoted to English folk-rock and artists such as Fairport Convention, Sandy Denny, Richard Thompson, Nick Drake, and Iain Matthews. His freelance writing has also appeared in the magazines *Trouser Press* and *Guitar Extra.* He has written liner notes for albums by Jackson C. Frank and Scott Appel. He lives in a drafty cottage in Connecticut called Mole's End with his wife, four boys, and a cat named Lulu.

Chris Meloche is a jazz music fan, freelance writer, and struggling musician.

Kevin Meyer is a freelance writer (and frustrated wannabe drummer) who lives vicariously through the music he collects. A one-time college-rag music editor, Meyer is today a blues and roots-rock devotee who dreams of a Wilco/Dave Alvin collaboration and still pines for Luther Allison and the Long Ryders.

Stacy Meyn (spceltd@aol.com) is a media maven, covering music, movies, and martial arts for a plethora of magazines and

Web sites. In addition to favoring alliteration, she is also an editor, DJ, record producer, and radio programmer, as well as an investigative reporter of health issues. She resides in Alameda, California, where they used to keep the "nuclear wessels."

Sandy Miranda is a native of San Francisco who produces the popular *Music of the World* show on Wednesday mornings for KPFA-FM Pacifica Radio in Berkeley (and on www.kpfa.org). She is also a producer for *Global Village,* which is heard across Canada on CBC Radio One, at www.cbc.ca, and by shortwave all over the USA, Latin America, and the Caribbean. She is especially fond of old-time Hawaiian music, and you can often find her running around with a tape recorder at traditional music events in the islands (when she's not swimming around with the honu, a.k.a. green sea turtles). She has been known to write about music and culture for the *San Francisco Chronicle, Rhythm* magazine, *Folk Roots,* online music mags, and other nefarious publications, and has a handsome tabby named Elvis who likes to sing along with the Tuvans. Sandy likes to play guitar and Congolese goat-skin drums, but the shaker egg seems to be her one true instrument.

Jo Hughey Morrison is a Celtic harper and freelance writer whose work has appeared in *MusicHound Folk, Folk Tales, Rambles,* and the *Folk Harp Journal.* She has played harp at the Smithsonian, the U.S. Capitol, and Mount Vernon, and has taught popular harp classes at Common Ground. She released her debut solo recording, *The Three Musics,* in 1998.

Jeffrey Muhr is a freelance writer and musician who plays keyboards, drums, and guitar. His experiences in the latter field include training in Javanese music with the Friends of the Gamelan in Chicago, and a musical tour of Java and Bali. To pay the bills, he manages databases at the Gale Group and serves as Technology Wizard for the MusicHound series.

Chris Nickson is English and lives in Seattle, where he writes about roots music, both in print and online. He preaches the gospel of good beer and believes in the power of Leeds United.

Meredith Ochs is a writer/editor at *Guitar World* magazine, and slings a mean Telecaster for the twang-pop band Candy Jones. She has contributed to *New York,* the *New York Press,* the *Boston Phoenix,* and Salon, and hosts a weekly roots music program on legendary freeform radio WFMU (91.1 FM/www.wfmu.org).

David Okamoto is the music editor for the *Dallas Morning News* and a contributing editor to *ICE* magazine. His work has also appeared in *CD Review, Rolling Stone,* and *Jazziz.* In between writing for *MusicHound Rock, MusicHound Lounge, MusicHound Folk, MusicHound Country,* and *MusicHound Jazz,* he

helped produce a compilation of Martin Mull's music for Razor & Tie Records. Really.

Allan Orski has written extensively for the MusicHound series, as well as Rolling Stone Online and a number of other publications, many of which have mysteriously gone belly-up shortly after Allan began writing for them. This, of course, is mere coincidence.

Dan Ouellette is a contributing writer for *Down Beat, Stereophile,* and the *San Francisco Chronicle,* and features editor for *Schwann Spectrum.*

Michael Parrish is associate professor of biological sciences at Northern Illinois University, with research focusing on dinosaurs and other extinct reptiles. He is also a freelance music writer who contributes to, among other publications, the *Chicago Tribune, Dirty Linen,* and *Sing Out!*

David Paul is a freelance journalist who has contributed interviews and articles on contemporary and world music to *Performing Arts Journal, Seconds* magazine, *All Music Guide,* and the *Eugene Weekly.*

Bob Paxman is a Nashville-based entertainment journalist whose works have appeared in *MusicHound R&B, MusicHound Folk, Country Weekly, Billboard, TV Host,* and numerous other publications.

Rick Petreycik lives in Bridgeport, Connecticut, and has written for *Guitar Player, New Country, Keyboard, Musician,* and *Live.* He was also a contributor to *The Comprehensive Country Music Encyclopedia, MusicHound Country,* and *MusicHound Folk.*

Randy Pitts is a contributor to *MusicHound Country* and *MusicHound Folk* who has labored in the vineyards of traditional music in various circumstances for nearly 20 years, most recently as artistic director of the Freight and Salvage in Berkeley, California, where he worked from 1989 until 1996.

Gary Plochinski is an advertising copy editor at the Bozell agency in suburban Detroit, and was a founding member of the Polish Muslims.

j. poet is older than rock 'n' roll, but younger than your parents. He has been interested in folk and world music since he heard Olatunji's *Drums of Passion* album, more years ago than he'd care to remember. He has worked as a political organizer, cook, poet, editor, and freelance writer. His world-music column for *Pulse!* magazine was the first nationally distributed one of its kind for the current world music boom. He is a frequent contributor to more magazines, newspapers, and Web sites than will fit in this space, including *Pulse!, Rhythm, Folk Roots, In-*

dian Artist, Salon, *Drum,* and the New York Times Syndicate. He lives in a Victorian flat in San Francisco with his partner, Leslie, a rabbit named Flannel, and two birds. He loves tropical climates, hot music, and spicy food, and believes that while you can be too thin, you can't have too much money or garlic. poet was the lead singer and songwriter for the folk/punk band the Young Adults, and is considering a return to the stage to mine the riches of his extensive back catalog. He also writes poetry and dark fiction, and has finished several novels that will eventually make some adventurous publisher fabulously wealthy.

David Poole, a traveler to more than 50 countries, has written about music for *Artforum, Detour,* and *TimeOut New York* magazines, as well as *MusicHound Soundtracks,* in addition to writing on Turkey for Fodor's travel guides.

Sam Prestianni is an unrepentant music junkie, writer, teacher, musician, and music journalist/critic. He has published widely for the past 12 years in dozens of magazines and newspapers, including *Option, Raygun,* and *Alternative Press.* He currently pens features and reviews for the San Francisco *Weekly,* San Francisco *Sidewalk, Speak, Soma,* and other freelance outlets. He is also the "Outside/In" columnist for *Jazziz.* Contact him at: johnnycritic@earthlink.net.

Richard Price, bored by being house-bound with chicken pox in 1985, studied *Digital Audio's* editorial style and submitted his first album review. The publication bought it and asked for more—proving that anyone who puts his mind to it can be a music writer. He has since contributed hundreds of articles, reviews, and columns on rock, country, jazz, classical, new-age, avant-garde, and world music to leading audio publications including *High Fidelity, CD Review, BAM (Bay Area Music),* the *Schwann CD Catalog,* and Amazon.com's music site.

Barry M. Prickett is a Sacramento, California–based freelance music writer, editor of children's books, and drummer (thus not a musician). He enjoys counting past four, battling sucker MCs, and posing for muscle mag covers in his spare time.

David Prince's words on music have appeared as album liner notes and in a number of publications including the *Boston Phoenix,* Santa Fe *Reporter, Cadence, Raygun, Stereophile, Schwann/Spectrum,* the Albuquerque *Tribune,* and the *Village Voice.* He has produced and hosted jazz and freeform radio programs at both commercial and community stations in Santa Fe, New Mexico, as well as for Albuquerque's NPR affiliate, KUNM-FM. He can be reached via e-mail at Flight505@aol.com.

Doug Pullen is the music and media writer for the *Flint Journal* (Michigan) and Booth Newspapers. He is a contributor to

MusicHound Rock, MusicHound Country, MusicHound R&B, MusicHound Blues, and *MusicHound Folk.*

Derek Rath has been writing on music for 24 years, with a focus on world music since the mid-'80s. He has been published on four continents and has made radio contributions to the BBC, KCRW (Santa Monica), and KPFK (Los Angeles). Born in Britain, he resides in Southern California where he can at least starve in the sunshine.

Dennis Rea is a guitarist/composer/writer who plays with ambient-improv group LAND and in numerous collaborative projects in Seattle. He is co-director of the Seattle Improvised Music Festival, co-editor of the *Tentacle,* and author of the forthcoming *Live at the Forbidden City,* an account of his experiences performing music in China and Taiwan. His company, Nunatak Press and Music, can be found on the Web at http://www.wolfenet.com/~nunatak/.

Bryan Reesman is a graduate of NYU's Tisch School of the Arts with a B.F.A. in film; a former story analyst for Miramax Films, New Line Cinema, and Imagine Entertainment; and an aspiring drummer. He currently freelances for music publications nationwide. He writes regularly for *Gig, Goldmine, Keyboard, Magnet, Mix, Mixmag,* Allstar, and MTV Online, and has also been published in *Bikini,* the *Boston Phoenix, Detour, Guitar Player,* the *Improper Bostonian, Requestline,* and numerous other publications.

Bob Remstein writes on popular music for several Web sites (Wall of Sound, E! Online) as well as for less high-tech media (*Musician* magazine). An active keyboardist and composer, his "Theme for the Children" can be found on the Qwest/Warner Bros. album *Love Shouldn't Hurt.*

Chris Rietz is the manager of Elderly Music in Lansing, Michigan, and a freelance writer and folk music aficionado.

Cynthia Rogers works as a freelance editor in New York City.

Ken Roseman is proud to announce that he sent in all of his *MusicHound World* assignments via e-mail and is thus no longer a *complete* Luddite. The related communication with music experts in Germany, Denmark, Spain, Scotland, Finland, Israel, England, and elsewhere has even made him feel like something of a global citizen, and that beats plane fare. Ken is a deep fan of cultural fusions, and says a hearty "Go Huskies!" to any alumni of Robert E. Peary High School who may be reading this. (No, there isn't any connection!)

Leland Rucker is the editor of *MusicHound Blues* and co-author of *The Toy Book: A Celebration of Slinky, G.I. Joe, Tinkertoys,*

Hula Hoops, Barbie Dolls, Snoot-Flutes, Coonskin Caps, Slot Cars, Frisbees, Yo-Yos, Betsy Wetsy and Much Much More (Alfred Knopf, 1992). He lives in Boulder, Colorado.

Christopher Scanlon is the former editor of *The Video Source Book* and a MusicHound contributor. He has a master's degree in social work.

Bruce Schoenfeld writes from his Colorado home on topics ranging from wine to bullfighting for the *New York Times Magazine*, *Outside*, *Travel & Leisure*, and other national publications. While writing, he often listens to the new-wave and power-pop albums of the late '70s and early '80s that helped transform him from an unsteady youth to a sober, sophisticated adult—as well as Puccini, Dean Martin, and Blue Rodeo. It gives his work a certain edge.

Joel Selvin has covered pop music for the *San Francisco Chronicle* since 1970 and is the author of several books on the subject. He co-produced Dick Dale's *Tribal Thunder* album.

Todd Shanker's deep and diverse music collection is known to Chicagoans as the Shanksonian Institution (library cards are available). His work has appeared in *Pulse!*, *Option*, the *Beat*, *Alternative Press*, and many other publications. His "House of Stylus" column for Chicago's *I.E.* covers new and vintage vinyl-available soul, jazz, indie, hip-hop, funk, punk, reggae, garage rock, and more. By day he is a dedicated public defender who has argued victoriously in the Illinois Supreme Court and flashed stunning James Brown–like moves while avoiding judge-hurled gavels.

Tim Sheridan is a playwright and music fan who never met a genre he didn't like. He has contributed to *Entertainment Weekly*, Launch, *Down Beat*, the *All Music Guide*, *Mojo*, the *Chicago Reader*, and his two children. He lives in Oak Park, Illinois.

Clea Simon writes a weekly column about radio for the *Boston Globe*. She is the author of *Mad House: Growing Up in the Shadow of Mentally Ill Siblings* (Doubleday), and has contributed to the *Boston Phoenix*, *Ms.*, the *New York Times Book Review*, *Rolling Stone*, and Salon, among other publications.

Jared Snyder is a graduate of Boston University who currently lives in Philadelphia. He has published articles on music from the United States, the Caribbean, and Africa. His current project is a book of historic images of accordion players from around the world. He plays diatonic accordion and electric guitar professionally in the Philadelphia area.

Denise Sofranko is a freelance writer.

David Sokol, senior editor at *Disney Magazine*, served as music editor and production manager of the Advocate Newspaper chain in Massachusetts and Connecticut from 1977 to 1993. He was hired as editor-in-chief to launch *New Country* magazine in November 1993 and quickly turned it into the most respected and objective monthly in the field of country music. His writing appears in *MusicHound Country*, *MusicHound Folk*, and in numerous other publications including *Stereophile* and Launch Online.

Steven Stancell writes the "Alternative Discs" column for the *New York Beacon*, and in 1996 authored the first biographical encyclopedia on rap music, *Rap Whoz Who*, which received a Ralph J. Gleason Music Book Award nomination. Stancell's earlier literary pieces have appeared on WBAI-FM's *Radio Unnamable with Bob Fass*, and his play *Neighborhood Disrupted* was produced by the American Theater of Actors in 1984. He is also a multi-genre musician, composer, and record producer, responsible for the co-production (with Strafe) of Shaman's 1985 single "This Is Not a Jungle, This Is a Zoo."

Wif Stenger is bicoastal—that is, dividing his time between the eastern seaboard and Finland's south shore. He covers cultural phenomena for *Billboard*, the *International Herald Tribune* (Paris), *Discover Africa*, Radio Finland, Public Radio International, and other unlikely outlets.

Mario Tarradell is the country music critic for the *Dallas Morning News*. His work has also appeared in *MusicHound Country*, *MusicHound Folk*, and *Replay* and *New Country* magazines.

Tom Terrell is a freelance music journalist based in New York who claims to know everything about pop music since 1955—and remembers it all despite a longtime backstage association with George Clinton and Funkadelic.

Suzy Rothfield Thompson grew up in the Northeast, studied classical music as a child, and apprenticed in Louisiana with master fiddler Dewey Balfa under an NEA fellowship. In 1981, Suzy helped form the Blue Flame Stringband, which evolved into the California Cajun Orchestra. Suzy has performed and recorded with those bands, Any Old Time, Klezmorim, and Eric Thompson. She has recorded as a side musician with jazz violinist Darol Anger, bluegrass fiddler/singer Laurie Lewis, the Savoy-Doucet Cajun Band, Sukay, and others. She appears briefly in the film *J'ai Etais Au Bal* (aired on PBS as *French Dance Tonight*), playing fiddle with D.L. Menard and Danny Poullard. In 1994, she represented the USA on a Masters of Folk Violin tour in England and Scotland. She has taught fiddle at Augusta Heritage Center (Elkins, West Virginia); Festival of American Fiddle Tunes (Port Townsend, Washington); Lark in the Morning (Mendocino, California); and Ashokan Fiddle & Dance Camp (New York). She is also a music reviewer for the *Old Time Herald.*

Philippe Varlet is a performer and teacher of Irish traditional music as well as an ethnomusicologist doing research on many aspects of that tradition. In particular, he specializes in the history of early recordings of Irish music, which he collects and of which he has produced several CD anthologies, including *From Galway to Dublin* (Rounder), *Milestone at the Garden* (Rounder), and *Joe Derrane—Irish Accordion* (Rego/Copley). Varlet resides near Washington, D.C., where he performs regularly at local *ceilis* (Irish communal dances) and concerts and provides private instruction on Irish fiddle playing. His name is familiar to members of Internet Irish music lists who seek assistance in identifying tunes and their sources. He has a master's degree in composition from Catholic University and studied ethnomusicology at the University of Maryland.

Jack and Linda Vartoogian are *MusicHound World*'s photo editors (see above).

Stephen Vilnius was born in Grosse Pointe, Michigan, raised in Orange County, California, and now resides in Ferndale, Michigan, where he plays fretless bass in the pop band Brilliant. He is the nephew of Jose Feliciano.

Neal Walters is a veteran folk-music performer, teacher, critic, and collector, and the co-editor of *MusicHound Folk.*

Mara Weiss and Nego Beto write the "Brazil Beat" column for *The Beat* magazine.

Sam Wick not only contributed to *MusicHound Lounge,* but is editor-in-chief of *Lounge* magazine, which is credited with

spurring the sputnik ascension of the so-called "cocktail nation." In addition to penning books, Wick is a frequent contributor to *Drink, Grammy,* and just about every bartender's pension plan.

Steve Winick is a talented writer about all kinds of music. He particularly loves English and Celtic folk, and writes prolifically about the artists that fall into that category.

Pamela Murray Winters is the author of a forthcoming biography of Sandy Denny. In addition to her contributions to *MusicHound World* and *MusicHound Folk,* she has written about music for *Dirty Linen, Relix, femme musique, Folk Tales,* and the *Washington Review.* She is a native of the Washington, D.C., area, an occasional vegetarian, an enthusiastic steering-wheel percussionist, and a library school dropout. She can sing in seven languages, but not very well.

Art Wojtowicz is a Detroit-based freelance copywriter, folk singer-songwriter, and recording studio owner and operator. His writing credits include a successful Broadway-style musical, an album of original piano music, and numerous pieces of political satire and poetry. His upcoming CD will present a loving and humorous look at the heroes of everyday life on this planet earth. Art's greatest accomplishment is finding continuing peace and happiness. His life's goal—to be a kid again.

Josh Zarov is the project manager for Ticketmaster Multimedia. He is also a contributor to Live Vibes Online.

Tony Ziselberger is the manager of a White Castle in Jacksonville, Mississippi. He has loved folk music since he was in his mother's womb and has been writing about it since the 1970s.

musicHound ACKNOWLEDGMENTS

Befitting its global-village aspirations, this book was truly a community effort. My first thanks must go to the contributors, who served as invaluable consultants and comrades from the book's formative stages through its completion, offering advice on content, sharing crucial information, and providing indispensable encouragement. Their labors of love are a joy instantly taken up by the reader, and there could be no greater testament to their talent or gift to this project.

Of particular note is j. poet, with his unparalleled knowledge of the shape of world music today and insight into the shape this book should take, and his limitless familiarity with (and generosity in sharing) the contacts essential to making this book come about—not to mention writing more of it than anyone!

It's also hard to imagine *MusicHound World* existing without two colleagues, Jack and Linda Vartoogian, who made some excellent written contributions in the miraculously obtained spare time from their vital duties as photo editors. Not only did they supply the all-important visual accompaniment that does so much to make the music come alive, but they were pivotal advisers and constant supporters, making sure that many of the book's principal benefactors—from some of its finest contributors, to its most important sponsors, to its stellar foreword essayists—were initially reached and steadily encouraged, and bringing their seemingly boundless awareness of world music and affection for its practitioners to every facet of the book we all envisioned and now hold in our hands.

The *MusicHound World* contributors' honor roll certainly extends especially to those who stepped in at crucial junctures to take seconds—or even thirds and fourths—on their assignment loads; supply background scholarship; and do emergency rewrites as we raced (calmly!) to keep up with the ever-evolving world-music phenomenon and bring you the most up-to-date and comprehensive reading of its contours. The champions I'm talking about include PJ Birosik, Kerry Dexter, Michael Eldridge, John C. Falstaff, Marty Lipp, Bret Love, Stacy Meyn, David Poole, and Todd Shanker.

With a lineup like the one described above, I must give undying gratitude to the publishers, publicists, and other professionals who sent some of the top talent in world-music writing my way. I am particularly indebted to Andrew Seidenfeld of No Problem! Productions; Paul Hartman of *Dirty Linen*; Sarah Weinstein Dennison of Palm Pictures; CC Smith of *The Beat*; Jimi Schultz, formerly of In-Media and now of the *Aquarian Weekly* and *East Coast Rocker*; and Cliff Furnald of the Rootsworld Web site. The artists whose stories we strive to tell, and we the storytellers, could have no allies more conscientious and kindred than these.

Of course, the fortunate union of expert writers with a project perfect for them was also but one of many services performed by the staff at Visible Ink Press, a dream team from the perspectives of editorial excellence, interpersonal accommodation, and every other standpoint I can think of. The thoughtful insight, thorough care, tireless vigilance, and inexhaustible patience of the two editors who tag-teamed around a maternity leave over the course of the project, Judy Galens and Dean Dauphinais, made for the kind of literary relationship every writer/editor wishes to have, and the kind of honor he hopes to earn. The managerial vision and judicious receptivity of publisher Marty Connors; the creativity and determination of marketer Kim Marich and publicist Marilou Carlin; the expertise and wisdom of computer magician Jeff Muhr (who made the book happen both technically and textually, contributing scores of exceptional entries); the attentiveness and organizational flair of VIP Managing Editor Christa Brelin; the perceptiveness and devotion of the copy editors—particularly Barbara Cohen, Diane Dupuis, Christina Fuoco, Pamela Shelton, and Devra Sladics—and the wit and savvy of copywriter PJ Butland, all added up to an atmosphere of the utmost openness, professionalism, and genuine sense of shared mission to rely on and live up to.

And there could be no thanks more imperative and heartfelt than those offered to the person who made it possible for me to work with such an unsurpassable outfit on such an important project to begin with: Gary Graff, who primarily conceived the MusicHound format, gave me an early break as a writer in its inaugural volume, and, in recommending me for this book, showed a belief in me for which full repayment is impossible but gratitude inexhaustible. To justify his support and uphold the tradition he brought about would be my greatest accolade.

One of the many gifts Gary bestowed was that of advice, not only from his own considerable reserve of experience and imagination, but also from series veterans with whom he put me in touch. It is another dearly held hope that the honesty expressed and enthusiasm conveyed—not to mention hours of valuable time donated—by *MusicHound Lounge* and *MusicHound Swing* editor Steve Knopper, *MusicHound Blues* editor Leland Rucker, and *MusicHound Rock* co-editor Daniel Durchholz—three of this book's best writers in addition to being three of the series' most distinguished standard-bearers—will be honored by this compendium that couldn't have come about without their counsel.

MusicHound World was blessed by the involvement of many such impeccable reputations, perhaps never more prominently and generously than with our from-heaven foreword writers, David Byrne and Angélique Kidjo. Their graciousness in giving of their time, authority, and good names; their eloquence in expressing the nature and value of this vast and to many still new thing called world music; the patience they applied to the process and the quality they bequeathed the finished work, are all true treasures.

Special thanks for stewarding these two crucial contributions must go to the artists' representation: for Angélique, the team at Annie Ohayon Media Relations, especially Reyna Mastrosimone and Annie herself; and for David, the team at Todo Mundo and Luaka Bop, especially Kara Finlay. Their persistence, diplomacy, and expertise changed the course of this project everlastingly for the better. And once that was accomplished, Jeff Kaye, also at Luaka, was essential in building on it with the media to gain a priceless public ear for the book and its mission.

Combining with the forewords to literally bookend *MusicHound World*'s appeal to the world-music connoisseur and newcomer alike, the bonus CD from Wicklow Entertainment is a prized survey of some of world music's most enjoyable and influential voices, made possible by one of its most prestigious new presenters. The generosity, receptivity, belief in the project, and true dedication to artist and audience shown in the realization of this collaboration by Label Manager John Voigtmann (now International Marketing Manager for RCA Records), A&R Manager Ian Menzies, special projects coordinator Ethan Crimmins, and, of course, label founder Paddy Moloney, commends their enterprise and enriches this one.

Wicklow showed particular enthusiasm in the promotion of the book, as did *Rhythm* magazine, America's definitive chronicle of the world's music. The effort and imagination of *Rhythm*'s publisher Alecia Cohen especially ensured the maximum meeting between our endeavor and the public, both veteran and new, that will enjoy it—not to mention making it more possible for that public to seek out the artists profiled here by furnishing our book's Concert Venues appendix.

Way before these priceless finishing touches were put on the book, getting that far was assured through a miraculous computer resuscitation by Kiyomasa Toma; an automotive laying on of hands by Bill Brunskill that kept me mobile (back when I could still leave the house!); an emergency transfer of recordings and background material by Shomik Roy to a needy contributor; and a last-minute editing assist on the longest two letter-sections of the artist entries by Stacy Meyn. Thanks to all for saving me from myself.

In addition to all these singular supporters are the legions of other publishers, publicists, institutions, scholars, and artists themselves to whom I and the contributors extend our gratitude, just some of whom include: Klaus Adolphi of Horch; everyone at Almo Sounds; Ian Anderson of *Folk Roots*; Ana Araiz of LusAna Productions; Bess at Shanachie; Jane Blumenfeld of In-Media; Sandy Brechin; Lellie Capwell at Vanguard; Michelle Carter, Munsie Davis, and Bob Haddad at Music of the World; Greg Cohen; Jason Consoli at TVT; Andrew Cronshaw; Matt Darriau; Brenda Dunlap at Smithsonian Folkways; Jacob Edgar, David Hazan, Dawn Richardson, Dan Storper, and Dave Weinberg of Putumayo; Fortuna; Baruch Friedland of Zikidisc; Adrian Jeffries, formerly of Tinder Records; Dominic Kanza; Judy Kerr et al. at Capitol; Cynthia Kirk at syn•tax; Svend Kjeldsen of Roots

Music Agency; Stephanie Levine at Tuff Gong International; David Lewiston; Fredric Lieberman; Fiona MacKenzie; Talitha MacKenzie; Tess Magnum at Alula; Shiley Menard; Hilda Mendez at Arhoolie; Heather Mount at the Knitting Factory; Eduardo Muszcat of MCD World Music; Tom Muzquiz at Rhino Records; Stuart Oravetz at Sony; Margareta Paslaru; Aliza Rabinoff at Shore Fire Media; Christina Roden; Cynthia Rogers at Traditional Crossroads; Lisa Samper at Narada; Sue Schrader at RealWorld; Ronnie Simpson at Lismor/Iona; Chandra Smith at Triloka; Huston Smith; Joanna Spindler at Silverwave; Karen Strom; Brita Toivonen at Finlandia Records; Peter Uhlmann of Tanz Folkfest Rudolstadt; Terri Williamson and Ann Brumbaugh at Celestial Harmonies; and Rainer Zellner at akku disc.

Still more thanks are owed to the other employers who held my place and egged me on as this tome pulled farther away from deadline and closer to perfection—or at least perfectionism—especially my *other* best editor, Cree McCree at *Yahoo! Internet Life.*

An equally admirable waiting game was played by the friends and loved ones who agreed to retain that designation for the duration of my self-imposed exile to the keyboard, including but not limited to Salvatore DiSalvio; Peter Killeen; Elke Claus; Laura Firman and Kiyo Toma; Beth Ann Vogel; Rhonda DiMascio; Lora and Fred Blake; Bill and Marge Selden; Mary Van Bodegon and family; and Inge and Stephen Brunskill. I'm done, guys, and I promise it was worth it! . . . Uh, *Adam,* remember?

Speaking of loved ones, thanks go to my parents, Vivienne and Frank, who first opened my eyes to the world, and love goes to my nephew, Dylan, who sees it through fresher eyes.

Ultimately, all thanks go to the most wise and creative person I've ever known and the love of my life, Lynn Brunskill. She's both my destiny and my true beginning, and met her most selfless of many challenges yet as my long hours stretched to long months and CDs piled up everywhere but the damn refrigerator. (Oh—so THAT's where that one got to! . . . Sorry, King Sunny!) Anyway, honey, I'm home.

On a more uncharacteristically somber note, as world music endlessly renews itself, some spirits sadly have to make way, and this book is dedicated to the memory of the artists who, over the course of its completion, passed from life into legend, among them Dennis Brown, Junior Braithwaite of the Wailers, Mahlathini, Rose Kaohu Moe, Augustus Pablo, and Aldus Roger.

A book of this scope, on a subject of this importance, is rightfully the accomplishment of many, and its completion is deservedly the pride of all who are listed above. If there is anyone I left out, you have my sincerest apologies, my blanket recommendation, and my assurance that you will be mentioned in the second edition by myself or my executor, as necessary!

Adam McGovern

A

Najat Aatabou
Berber popular music

Born May 19, 1960, in Khémisset, Morocco. Based in Casablanca, Morocco.

Najat Aatabou sang from an early age and had her "accidental" debut in 1983. During a family celebration, a friend made a tape of her singing "J'en ai Marre (I'm Sick of It)," a song she'd composed that detailed the dissatisfaction a woman felt with her traditional place in society. The friend took the tape to Hossein Dobala, a producer in Casablanca. A few days later Dobala visited Aatabou and asked her to make a cassette of "J'en ai Marre." Afraid of her parents' reaction, Aatabou put the song out under an assumed name, but her powerful voice was instantly recognizable to anyone who knew her. The song became a smash hit, selling almost half a million copies, and Aatabou left her home town of Khémisset for the metropolis of Casablanca, another untraditional move for a single woman. Her next single, "Shouffi Rhirou," was also a hit, even though the traditional media—radio, TV, and concert halls—ignored her, at least at first. Aatabou's sound stays true to her Berber heritage; she uses Berber musicians and sings in a folky style using straightforward lyrics that have made her a favorite with the common people.

what's available: *The Voice of the Atlas* 🎵🎵🎵 (Globestyle England, 1991, prod. Hossein Dobala) is a compilation of Aatabou's many album and cassette releases from 1984 to 1987. The band is a small acoustic unit, mostly just *oud* (lute) and percussion, but the rhythms are relentless and Aatabou's driving, soulful vocals are incredibly affecting. The two tracks with a full orchestra were hailed on their release for taking Aatabou in an exciting new direction.

influences:
 Jil Jilala, Lem Chaheb

j. poet

Abana Ba Nasery
Omutibo dance music

Formed 1964, in Mwilonje, Kenya. Based in Bunyore, Kenya.

Studio band: Shem Tube (Kenya), guitar, vocals, leader; Justo Osala Omufila (Kenya), guitar, vocals; Enos Okola (Kenya), Fanta bottle, vocals. Touring band: The above musicians plus Lee (England), drums; Chopper (England), bass; Alan Prosser (England), viola, violin; Hijaz Mustapha (England), banjo, dobro-bass, melodeon; Ron Kavana (Ireland), bouzouki, banjo; Thomás Lynch (Ireland), uilleann pipes; Expen$ive Mustapha (England), trumpets.

Two acoustic guitars, three singers, and a percussionist rubbing out rhythms on an empty Fanta bottle: As odd as it sounds, those are the ingredients of *omutibo,* a traditional style of dance music from western Kenya. But when the Nursery Boys, as they are called in English, start to play their richly syncopated, polyrhythmic style of guitar picking, they rock the house, be they in Bunyore or London. Omutibo, a social music for funeral ceremonies and gatherings of beer-drinking older men, was usually played on the *litungu* (Ugandan harp) and *siriri* (a one- or two-stringed fiddle) until soldiers returning from World War II introduced the guitar to Kenya. At first, omutibo was played on a single guitar, but players like Shem Tube added a second and began using the rhythms of *sukuti,* a style usually played at Saturday night dances for young people.

Tube's family was poor and he only had five years of schooling, but when he got interested in music in the late '50s, he taught himself to play guitar. He met Omufila in 1964 and they began playing local dances in the Kakamenga district. In 1968, record producer Manasse Omwoma recorded them under the name Abana Ba Nasery—Nursery Boys—because of Tube's diminutive stature. They recorded regularly until 1972, when they formed an electric dance band called Mwilonje Jazz, which mutated into Les Bunyore and Super Bunyore. These outfits played a slightly urbanized form of omutibo, but were recording projects only—due to the high cost of electric instruments—and the Nursery Boys configuration has continued intermittently instead. Unhappily, because of the economic situation in Kenya, neither Tube nor Omufila owns a guitar. Tube, who makes his living as a farmer, says he works on a song in his head, until "it's good enough for recording."

what to buy: The tunes on *Abana Ba Nasery* 𝄞𝄞𝄞𝄞𝄞 (Globestyle, 1989, prod. Manasse Omwoma) were taken from singles the band recorded between 1968 and 1972, and they still sound as fresh and exciting as the day they were recorded. The guitar work is subtle and sublime, proving again that less is more; the Fanta rhythms have a faint Cuban trace that adds a touch of tropical grace to the playing.

what to buy next: When *Abana Ba Nasery* was released in England, it caused a sensation and led Ben Mandelson, head of the Globestyle label, to track down the trio and offer them a mini-tour of England and Europe. The result was *Nursery Boys Go Ahead* 𝄞𝄞𝄞𝄞 (Xenophile, 1992), a recording that proves traditional music doesn't have to be updated to be exciting. The backing tracks add a bit of folk-rock muscle to the band, creating what may be the first sessions of Afro Celtic fusion, but the main attraction remains the amazing fretwork of Tube and Omufila. The duo hasn't lost its chops, despite the dire economic straits; this is another low-key masterpiece.

influences:
◀◀ George Mukabi, Bunyore Band
▶▶ Samite, Victoria Kings, Shirati Jazz

j. poet

Dimi Mint Abba
Iggawin (Moorish music of Mauritania)
Born 1958, in Mauritania. Based in Mauritania and Dakar, Senegal.

Harsh history and geography underlie the plaintive, soulful songs of Dimi Mint Abba. The northwest African nation of Mauritania has seen centuries of struggle among Berber, Arab, Sudanese, Bambara, Tuareg, Wolof, Peul, French, and other peoples. Trumping all those forces has been the ever-encroaching desert, which has driven three-fourths of the once-nomadic population into cities, especially the crowded coastal capital, Nouakchott, where old cultures have collided and new ones continue to be forged. Abba and her husband/collaborator Khalifa Ould Eide both come from musical families and so began their careers early. Abba's spectacular voice brought her to national attention when she was just 16. At 17, she represented her country at the prestigious Umm Kulthum festival in Tunisia. Moorish *iggawin* tradition is loaded with ancient complexities, and young Dimi had to learn dance and percussion before approaching music theory and the formidable 14-string *ardin* harp. The iggawin system of modes specifies three "ways" of playing: the "black way," the "white way," and the "spotted way." While these rules and disciplines survive, the realities of modern Nouakchott have inevitably lead to extensions and experiments. No surprise, then, that Khalifa sports an electric guitar and Dimi's contemporary band includes electric keyboards alongside traditional Moorish instruments. Her central appeal remains her voice, which has the power to float on air, flutter through it bird-like, or tear it with the ragged precision of a chain saw.

what's available: *Khalifa Ould Eide & Dimi Mint Abba: Moorish Music from Mauritania* 𝄞𝄞𝄞𝄞 (World Circuit, 1990, prod. Nick Gold, John Hadden) is the only full-length album in circulation. Luckily, it's a gem. The mostly acoustic backing supports Dimi's nightingale voice with the evocative, jangling textures of the North African desert.

influences:
◀◀ Centuries of Moorish tradition
▶▶ Ali Farka Touré, Malouma

Banning Eyre

Abdelli
Berber worldbeat fusion
Born Abderrahmane Abdelli, in Algeria. Based in Belgium.

The love of that sprawling thing called "world music" contains utopian aspirations that can find many hasty and misguided expressions, from reckless cultural oversimplification to attempts at stuffing the whole world onto a single disc. A little selectivity can actually better reveal the far-flung cultural affinities for which the well-meaning one-worldists are looking. Eschewing the proverbial kitchen sink and lots more, Algerian native Abderrahmane Abdelli and Belgian producer Thierry Van Roy zeroed in on the sonic similarities of Abdelli's own Berber (Kabyl tribe) roots and those of some crack South American and Eastern European players for an ear-opening debut album. The Berbers are the indigenous people of pre-Islamic North Africa, and their music has a distinctive syncopation that

Dimi Mint Abba

nonetheless finds a sympathetic echo in Latin rhythms, and a sweet string sound that converses well with the Ukrainian *bandura* (zither) a little closer across the globe. "Discovered" by a Belgian official just hours away from deportation to the strife he'd left in Algeria, Abdelli lucked upon patrons who shared his taste for cultural mixing more than many non-Berbers back home or Europeans at the time—and listeners the world over would soon realize that the fortune was theirs as well. He hasn't been much heard from since, but his debut album remains essential, and very much in-demand and in-print.

what's available: *New Moon* ♫♫♫ (RealWorld, 1995, prod. Thierry Van Roy) is an album of understated brilliance, soothing but never soporific, and sophisticatedly energized at all the right points. Geographically distant styles synchronize invigoratingly, and in a nervy effort to preserve the immediacy and naturalism of Abdelli's vocals, they were recorded *before* the instruments, surprisingly with no loss to the finished product's organic, intimate feel. Pleasurable but purposeful, accommodating but individualistic, this is music for a new moon, and the new dawn after that.

influences:

◀◀ Berber tradition, Radio Tarifa, Abed Azrié, Thierry Van Roy

▶▶ Rasha

Adam McGovern

Abel & Kaninerna

Worldbeat

Formed 1989, in Gothenburg, Sweden. Based in Gothenburg, Sweden.

Bo Ingvarsson, guitar, vocals; Carita Jonnson, accordion, clarinet, keyboards, Swedish bagpipe, flute, vocals; Pelle Bolander, fiddle, vocals; Benke Stanlén, bass, vocals; Tommy Johansson, drums, percussion. (All members are from Sweden.)

Bo Ingvarsson began looking for musicians to fulfill his skewed visions in 1989. The current Abel and Kaninerna lineup fell into place in 1990; they recorded their eponymous debut in 1993, an international hootenanny of folky and ethnic flavors. The Swedish press has compared them to the Pogues and that's a good starting place—at least attitude-wise—but their mix of ska, metal, rock, reggae, klezmer, Balkan and Swedish folk music, tangos, Gregorian chants, and just about everything else is a bit more far-reaching than their Irish counterparts. Judging from the vocal inflections, the lyrics are probably as off-the-wall as the band's musical excesses.

what's available: A bitch's brew of influences, solid arrangements, and vocals that sputter with snotty attitude make *Sömnlösa Nätter och Hemmagjord Vodoo (Sleepless Nights and Homemade Voodoo)* ♫♫♫♫ (Slask Sweden, 1994, prod.

Stefan Pettersoon) a solid outing; a great blend of Swedish folk, worldbeat, and pure rock insolence.

influences:

◀◀ Lars Danielson, Gryningen, Ricard Wolff

j. poet

Rabib Abou-Khalil

Arabic jazz

Born 1957, in Beirut, Lebanon. Based in Cologne, Germany.

Abou-Khalil grew up listening to classical Arabic music, Sinatra, Zappa, and Monk. He started playing *oud* (a Middle Eastern lute) at six, and studied that instrument and flute in Beirut, before his parents moved to Munich to escape the civil war. In Germany he studied Western classical flute, but the oud kept calling him back. As he developed his oud technique, he began exploring his own system of notation, based partially on Arabic music, which "follows the human voice," and partially on Western compositional theory. Equally drawn to jazz and Arabic music, Abou-Khalil found a way to do both. His first album, *Between Dusk and Dawn,* was self-produced and caused a sensation in the Arabic world. Since then he has gone from strength to strength, recording with heavies like Glen Velez, Steve Swallow, Nabil Khaiat, and Glen Moore.

what to buy: Arabic blues sound like an anomaly? Check out *Odd Times* ♫♫♫♫ (Enja, 1997, prod. Rabib Abou-Khalil) for Howard Levy's blues harp on "The Sphinx and I ..." and "One of Those Days" before coming to a hasty conclusion. Levy's harp and the amazing sounds of Nabil Khaiat's frame drum provide the icing, but the cake is still the subtle yet driving oud of Abou-Khalil.

what to buy next: The words "world jazz" are tossed around with reckless abandon these days, but on *Blue Camel* ♫♫♫♫ (Mesa, 1992, prod. Rabib Abou-Khalil) as elsewhere, Rabib Abou-Khalil's music lives up to the name. He effortlessly fuses Arabic classical modes, or his approximations of them, with touches of flamenco, jazz, rock, and South Indian percussion. The compositions on *Blue Camel* show us the best of all possible worlds, one where traditions blend without losing their individual authentic flavor.

the rest:

Al-Jadida ♫♫♫♫ (Enja, 1991)
Tarab ♫♫♫♫ (Enja, 1993)
The Sultan's Picnic ♫♫♫♫ (Enja, 1994)
Arabian Waltz ♫♫♫♫ (Enja, 1995)

influences:

◀◀ Mohammed Abdel Wahab, Wadih Al-Safi, Fairuz

j. poet

Camara Aboubacar

Manding pop music

Born mid-1950s, in Guinea. Based in Paris, France.

Camara Aboubacar is a young singer, guitarist, and player of the *kora,* the 21-string harp-lute important to the music of West Africa's *griots* and *jalis* (oral historians). His name sets him up to be confused with one of Guinea's greatest vocalists, Aboubacar Demba Camara of Bembeya Jazz, who died in 1973. Perhaps that's one reason the young kora man uses the convention of putting his surname before his given name. Aboubacar started out as a guitarist raised on urban music, and became a protégé of singing kora innovator Jali Musa Jawara. Jawara took Aboubacar to Paris and used him on some of his acclaimed 1980s recordings. Following Jawara's roots-pop lead, Aboubacar then took up the kora himself. In Paris, he recorded two CDs for the international market, and made something of a name for himself back home. Decidedly not a traditionalist, Aboubacar backs his kora and vocal with keyboards, electric guitar, *balafon* (wooden xylophone), bass, and electronic drums. His second international release, *Téléphone,* is the one that deservedly got the U.S. press's attention, and opened ears for the certain accomplishments to come.

what's available: *Téléphone* ♪♪♪♪ (Celluloid/Melodie, 1994) is a fine example of electric griot pop. Aboubacar blends his fleet kora lines gracefully into energized grooves, and sings like an angel.

influences:

◀◀ Mory Kanté, Sekouba "Bambino" Diabate

see also: *Bembeya Jazz*

Banning Eyre

Nathan Abshire

Cajun

Born June 27, 1913, in Gueydan, LA, USA. Died May 13, 1981, in Basile, LA, USA.

"The good times are killing me" was painted on the side of Nathan Abshire's accordion case and was his motto in life. He started playing at the age of six, learning from both his parents, who were well-known accordionists in their own right. As a young teenager he played dances with his longtime friend, fiddler Lionel Leleux, sometimes walking 10 miles each way with his accordion over his shoulder. Legendary accordionist Amédée Ardoin regularly used friendly coercion to have the young Abshire substitute for him at dances. When Abshire finally recorded, for Bluebird in 1934, his sides reveal an extremely bluesy kind of Cajun accordionist. However, the instrument would come to fall from favor until the 1950s—but one of

the records that helped bring it back was Abshire's "Pine Grove Blues." The song was a massive regional hit, and continues to be extremely popular among Cajuns and Creoles. Abshire's singing was just as soulful and bluesy as his accordion playing and he continued to produce regional hits, including "Bayou Teche Waltz," "Musician's Life," and a Cajun version of "The Games People Play." The good times may have killed him, but good songs stand as his epitaph.

what to buy: *French Blues* ♪♪♪♪ (Arhoolie, 1993, prod. Chris Strachwitz) brings together everything Abshire made for the Koury label. Forget about the funky recording quality; these are the real deal—a soulful Cajun sound with Abshire's accordion cutting through the sawing fiddle of Will Kegley and a swooping steel guitar. Abshire's playing has a lot in common with the Cajun delicacy of "cracklin's" (fried pork skin): Hot like his blues, crisp on the outside like his two-steps, and liquid fat on the inside like his waltzes.

what to buy next: *The Legendary Jay Miller Sessions* ♪♪♪♪ (Flyright, 1990, prod. Ray Templeton) is a little cleaner than *French Blues,* but there's still plenty of soul in these recordings, which include the superb fiddling of Dewey Balfa. The collection also spotlights several of Miller's production experiments, such as the horse clops on the "Mardi Gras Song" and the pairing of Abshire's bluesy accordion with the sound of blues harpist Lazy Lester on "La La Blues."

the rest:

The Good Times Are Killing Me ♪♪♪♪ (Swallow, 1986)
Cajun Tradition: Volume 1 ♪♪♪♪ (La Louisianne, 1990)
Cajun Tradition: Volume 2 ♪♪♪♪ (La Louisianne, 1990)
Cajun Fais Do Do ♪♪♪♪ (Arhoolie, 1996)
(Various Artists) *Les Haricots Sont Pas Salés: Legendary Masters of Cajun and Creole Music* ♪♪♪♪ (Cinq Planetes, 1998)

worth searching for: The compilation of classic Cajun 78s *Le Grand Mamou: A Cajun Music Anthology: The Historic Victor/Bluebird Sessions 1928–1941* ♪♪♪♪ (Country Music Foundation, 1990, prod. Country Music Foundation) includes "One-Step de Lacassine" by a young Nathan Abshire and the Rayne-Bo Ramblers. On this one-chord vamp Abshire surges past the string band with his bluesy riffs, almost tipping over the group as they bear down to keep up. This appears to be the only one of Abshire's early songs that he never recorded in the later part of his career.

influences:

◀◀ Amédée Ardoin, Alphonse "Bois Sec" Ardoin

▶▶ Balfa Brothers, Michael Doucet, Buckwheat Zydeco

see also: *Amédée Ardoin, Balfa Brothers*

Jared Snyder

The Abyssinians
Roots reggae

Formed 1968, in Kingston, Jamaica; disbanded 1980; reunited 1989; disbanded 1990; reunited 1999. Based in Kingston, Jamaica.

Bernard Collins, vocals; Donald Manning, vocals; Lynford Manning, vocals. (All members are from Jamaica.)

Under the definition of roots reggae, you will find the Abyssinians. Identified by the ancient name of Ethiopia and the primeval pit that represents the void between what is, what should be, and what will be, the Abyssinians were one of the very first Jamaican vocal groups to give passionate voice to the Rastafarian faith and express pride in their African cultural roots. "Satta Massa Ganna" (1969) and "Declaration of Rights" (1971) stand today as two of the most important, influential, and utterly moving songs in the history of Jamaican music. With Bernard Collins's pristine, spiritual lead vocals clasped tightly with the blood-oath-close harmonies of brothers Donald and Lynford Manning, the group took listeners to Satta's "faraway land" and implored black people to "get up and fight for your rights" over intricate *nyabinghi* (ritual Rasta) drumming long before such proclamations became *de rigueur* in the mid-to-late '70s. The first historic recording of "Satta" was made but shelved by Clement Dodd, which motivated the Abyssinians to start their own Clinch imprint and purchase the master back from Dodd in 1971. After "Satta" and "Declaration of Rights" rocked the very soul of Jamaica, the group followed up with a series of inspiring singles, including "Y Mas Gan," "Leggo Beast," "Reason Time," and a version of Satta called "Mabrak," which featured them "toasting" (reggae-rapping) biblical passages. Their debut album, *Forward on to Zion* (1976), contained recut versions of many of their greatest songs backed by the most inspiring of Jamaican musicians, including the Heptones's Leroy Sibbles, Sly Dunbar and Robbie Shakespeare, and guitarist Earl "Chinna" Smith. The follow-up *Arise* was released in England by Virgin, but never saw the light of day in Jamaica and did not sell well elsewhere. Nonetheless, it constituted their second straight masterpiece. In 1980, the American blues-based label Alligator released the virtually flawless *Forward,* which combined hypnotic new material—most notably "Forward Jah," "Prophesy," and "Praise Him"—with rarities like "Mabrak" and the flipside to the limited first pressing of "Satta," the righteous ska-tinged meditation "Jerusalem." Sadly, infighting that pitted the brothers Manning against Collins led to a breakup in the early '80s. Though they reunited briefly toward the end of the decade and recorded new songs of the same stunning quality as their early classics (most notably "Come Along" and "Do Good"), the feud between the factions continued, with both sides separately recording under the same name for most of the '90s. Another reunion and tour as this book went to press was a guarded celebration for true reggae believers everywhere. Though their catalog is relatively small, the hefty satchel of songs the band has released is of a singularly high quality and stands alone as uniquely heavyweight *and* heavenly. The Abyssinians are an essential cornerstone in the foundation of reggae music.

what to buy: *Satta Massa Ganna* &&&& (Heartbeat, 1993, prod. the Abyssinians) is a rerelease of the essential-as-oxygen *Forward on to Zion* &&&& (Blue Moon, 1976, prod. the Abyssinians) with the added bonus of digital clarity and four rare singles. If this interdimensional vocalizing doesn't send you, then you are incapable of uplift. The lack of sales for *Arise* &&&&& (Blue Moon, 1976, prod. the Abyssinians) had everything to do with music-business bullshit and nothing to do with the music, which is as lush, exotic, and meaningful as can be found anywhere. *Forward* &&&& (Alligator, 1982/Musidisc, 1996, prod. the Abyssinians) is imbued with the passion of captive Old Testament prophets vocalizing a longing for freedom with sage knowledge of faith's reward. Visionary cuts like "Forward Jah" and the hauntingly dread "This Is Not the End" are packaged with rare treasures "Mabrak," "Jerusalem," and "Peculiar Number."

the rest:
1995 + Tax &&&& (Self-released, 1995)
Declaration of Dub &&&& (Heartbeat, 1998)
Reunion &&& (Artists Only!, 1998)
Satta Dub &&&& (Tabou, 1998)
Last Days &&& (Tabou, 1999)

worth searching for: The superb roots-reggae documentary *Rockers* is hard to find but is available on video. The opening scene alone, where the Abyssinians sing "Satta Massa Ganna" *a cappella* with Ras Michael, is reason enough to begin your search now.

influences:
◀◀ Carlton & His Shoes, Count Ossie, Marcus Garvey

▶▶ Burning Spear, Culture, Junior Byles, Keith Hudson, The Twinkle Brothers, Wailing Souls

see also: *Sly & Robbie*

Todd Shanker

Ad Vielle Que Pourra
French/Canadian folk

Formed 1985, in St. Patrice de Beaurivages, Québec, Canada. Based in Montréal, Québec, Canada.

Daniel Thonon (1987–1997), vocals, hurdy-gurdy, harpsichord, accordion, piano, guitar, shakuhachi, Jew's harp, bouzouki; Alain Leroux (1987–1993/1995–1996), vocals, violin, mandola, bouzouki, mandocello; Clément Demers (1987–1990), accordion; Luc Thonon (1987–1995), Flemish pipes, recorder, flute, saxophone, accordion, bagpipes; Gilles Plante (1987–1994), vocals, flute, recorder, bagpipes, bombarde, tarragoto; Jean-Louis Cros (1990–1993/

1995–1996), guitar, guitarelle, bass guitar; Éric Mercier (1989–1990), bagpipes, oboe, shawm, bombarde; Pierre Imbert (1995–1997), vocals, hurdy-gurdy, tambourine, kalimba. (Members are from Belgium, France, and Canada.)

Ad Vielle Que Pourra is a French pun building on *vielle à roue* (the term for hurdy-gurdy) and its similarities to the phrase *advienne que pourra* ("come what may"). It's also the name of a French-Canadian band that has played Breton Celtic-tinged songs, on and off, since 1987. Unlike their Québecois contemporaries La Bottine Souriante, Ad Vielle Que Pourra tend to perform original works within an adapted historical framework, rather than arrangements of traditional tunes. Their music also has more of a European focus than a Québecois one, no doubt owing in part to the recent roots of their principal personnel. Belgian-born Daniel Thonon, a skilled luthier (stringed instrument maker) and hurdy-gurdy player, was at the center of the outfit from its beginnings. The other co-founder and major figure within the band was Alain Leroux, a French fiddler who had previously started Ar Skloferien, one of the best-known Breton Celtic groups of the 1970s. This duo, along with accordionist Clément Demers, flautist Gilles Plante, and the skilled multi-instrumentalist Luc Thonon, formed the initial lineup for Ad Vielle Que Pourra shortly after meeting at a festival in Québec. Their edition of the group released *New French Folk Music* in 1989, a well-constructed, lively batch of original tunes done in typical Breton style. Demers was the first member to leave, and he was replaced by Jean-Louis Cros by the time *Come What May* was released in 1991. When *Musaïque* was recorded in 1993 Cros had already left, and mounting creative tensions between remaining members were straining the band's future. Leroux also departed after that album's sessions and, with Cros, formed a new duo, Alter Fgo. They later joined forces with Demers and Éric Mercier (who had played briefly with Ad Vielle Que Pourra but never recorded with them) to create yet another new ensemble. The result was Korventenn, a group that billed itself as "the one and only North America-based band playing authentic traditional Celtic dance music and songs from Brittany." Before this band went on the road, however, Daniel Thonon, Leroux, and Cros had joined up with Pierre Imbert (former hurdy-gurdy player with Lo Jai) to put out one more Ad Vielle Que Pourra album, *Ménage à quatre*. The end always seemed to be in sight for this outfit, but none had been definitively announced at this writing.

what to buy: *New French Folk Music* ♪♪♪♪ (Green Linnet, 1989, prod. Daniel Thonon, Alain Leroux) was surprisingly sophisticated for a first release, with both swinging and atmospheric instrumental arrangements and clean vocals. Daniel Thonon and Leroux wrote all the music heard here, with the former contributing a clever batch of new dance tunes and the later

the bagpipe

A bagpipe is known for one fundamental thing—continuous sound. In order to achieve this, a bag is inflated and squeezed, supplying the pipes with the air required to let them sing. There are two basic types of bagpipes: mouth-blown and bellows-blown. With mouth-blown pipes the instrumentalist provides the air, while in the bellows-blown air is pumped from a bellows, held under one arm. Bellows-blown pipers like to claim that given a table and a straw, they can drink beer while playing their pipes. Ancient shepherds are credited with independently inventing the bagpipe in a variety of areas, from India to Ireland to Hungary, creating the bag from an animal's hide or stomach and connecting hollow sticks or bones to it as pipes. The best-known bagpipes in the United States are Celtic in origin: the Scottish Great Highland Bagpipes, commonly heard at parades and funerals, and the Irish uilleann pipes, as played by the Chieftains. Bagpipes vary in sound based on the type of reeded pipes attached to the bag. Most bagpipes incorporate a steady drone as their sonic backdrop, produced by pipes also called "drones." The number of drones varies, and they may all have the same pitch or be tuned at varying intervals. The other pipe attached to the bag is the "chanter," similar to a reeded recorder, which is used to play the melody.

—*Jo Hughey Morrison*

dwelling more on balladry. Standouts include Thonon's "Schottische du Stockfish" and Leroux's "Fillettes des Campagnes."

what to buy next: All through *Musaïque* ♪♪♪♪ (Green Linnet, 1994, prod. Daniel Thonon, Alain Leroux) the playing was uniformly interesting, the production was solid, and the tunes were of fairly high quality. But the increasing antipathy between Thonon and Leroux, both of whom were talented composers and performers, was probably starting to become a factor. "La Complainte des Rengaines," the very last cut on the disc, is a wistful ballad by Thonon lamenting hit songs and their eventual relegation to the dustbins of memory, perhaps foretelling the band's demise. *Ménage à quatre* ♪♪♪♪ (Green Linnet/Xenophile, 1996, prod. Daniel Thonon) introduced the two-hurdy-gurdy attack of Thonon and Imbert, making a good attempt at recreating the magic of earlier days—but a list of who wrote what reveals this as essentially Thonon's show. Leroux was only credited with arranging two songs while Thonon tallied 10 compositions, a fact that upset the writing balance present in their previous projects.

the rest:
Come What May ♫♫♫ (Green Linnet, 1991)

worth searching for: Alter Ego's *Mémoires d'Outremer* ♫♫♫ (Green Linnet/Xenophile, 1995, prod. Alain Leroux and Jean-Louis Cros) is a very pleasant set of performances. Leroux's "Fillettes des Campagnes" (a remake from Ad Vielle's first album) is a welcome revival, though the rest of the material sounds a bit like a Pentangle project sung in French.

influences:
◄◄ Alan Stivell, Ar Skloferien, Lo Jai

►► Korventenn

Garaud MacTaggart

Adaro
"Medieval crossover"

Formed 1997, in Stuttgart area, southern Germany. Based in Stuttgart area, southern Germany.

Christoph Pelgen, lead vocals, bombarde, gong, Spanish shawm, German bagpipes; Konstanze Kulinsky, vocals, electric and acoustic hurdy-gurdy; Jürgen Treyz, vocals, guitars, MIDI guitar, keyboards, loops; Ulli Stotz, drums, electric percussion; Davide Piai (Italy), bass, vocals (1998–present). (All members are from Germany except where noted otherwise.)

In only two years of existence, Adaro has made quite a mark. Its blend of medieval and folk sounds with heavy-metal dynamics and high-tech dance/pop grooves is quite attention-getting, with a lasting intrigue beyond its initial novelty. The band uses authentic "early music" and folk instruments, and goes back to centuries-old texts for inspiration. So far, the group's catalog numbers two: the full-length CD *Stella Splendens* (1997) and a four-cut EP, *Words Never Spoken* (1999).

what's available: *Stella Splendens* ♫♫♫♫ (akku disk, 1997, prod. Jürgen Treyz) is a fantastic fusion of medieval, folk, heavy metal, "prog," and other influences. Imagine a cranked-up Steeleye Span (elegant, precise multi-part vocal harmonies over a full electric band) singing in venerable and sometimes obsolete non-English languages, and you'll be as prepared as you're gonna get. Most of the selections on *Stella Splendens* are adaptations of material from two medieval song cycles: the *Cantigas de Santa Maria* from 13th century Spain (sung in Gallego Portuguese) and the *Llibre Vermell* from the Montserrat cloister of 14th-century Spain (sung in Latin and Catalan). Loud electric guitars, drums, bass, and keyboards mix with hurdy-gurdy, bagpipes, and medieval crumhorn to create a fantastic wall of sound buried in the dim past and unearthed in the unforeseeable future. The four pieces on *Words Never Spoken* ♫♫♫♫ (akku disk, 1999, prod. Jürgen Treyz, Davide Piai, Rainer Zellner) continue down the same winding sonic path—with some inevitable differences. For one thing, Jürgen Treyz wrote the music for three of the four cuts. What's more, each track is a mini-suite with several shifts of rhythm, texture, and melody. For example, "Sanctus Dominus" (with more 13th-century lyrics plus music by Treyz) starts off softly with voice, violin, and acoustic guitar. Then there's an abrupt shift as a mini-choir sings the title phrase repeatedly over an aggressive rhythm section. Then another softer passage begins and the pattern repeats. "Der Totden Dantz," an instrumental composed entirely by Treyz, begins as a fast Middle-Ages thrash that then gets even faster! But the pace quiets down for a lovely acoustic hurdy-gurdy interlude. But then an even more bombastic mix of medieval sounds, heavy metal, and grandiose prog-rock begins. Adaro tramples all boundaries and that keeps its music fascinating.

influences:
◄◄ Steeleye Span, Gryphon, Malicorne, Jethro Tull, Horch

►► Horch, U.L.M.A.N., Radio Tarifa

Ken Roseman

Obo Addy
Afro-Beat

Born 1936, in Ghana. Based in Portland, OR, USA.

Obo Addy was drawn to drumming by the power he heard from infancy; his father was a shaman who used drumming to heal the sick. After learning the drumming rituals of his own tribe, the Ga, Addy moved to the city and played with the Joe Kelly Band—and after learning English, became the band's lead singer. In 1957 there was a heady post-colonial vibe in Ghana, and Addy was invited to join the Arts Council of Ghana, a group that was using music as a method to smooth over intertribal rivalries. The experience enabled Addy to learn from master drummers from all over the country. In 1969 Addy and his brothers moved to London, where they put together Oboade, a highlife band that toured Europe, Japan, and Australia. When the group broke up in 1977 Addy came to Seattle, but soon moved to Portland, thinking it would be easier to make his mark in that town's smaller scene. His first American band, Kukrudu, included Africans and Americans and played jazz, African rock, and "worldbeat." "People have the impression that African music must be traditional to be authentic," Addy says. "But in Ghana we grew up listening to American music as well as African music." Kukrudu has released several well-received albums on Avocet, Portland's premiere avant jazz label. In 1989, Addy also created Okropong, a company he trained to sing, dance, and play the traditional music of Ghana. He stays busy as an educator (teaching African drumming and culture to high school and university students) and as a composer (the Kronos Quartet commissioned "Wawshishijay" for their *Pieces of Africa* album) in addition to performing with his groups.

what to buy: *Okropong* 𝄞𝄞𝄞 (Earthbeat!, 1990, prod. Obo Addy) is a percussion showcase for Addy, who plays and sings everything on the album, mostly traditional material from various regions of Ghana. The production is minimal and the drums have a full, warm sound.

what to buy next: On *The Rhythm of Which a Chief Walks Gracefully* 𝄞𝄞𝄞 (Earthbeat!, 1994, prod. Obo Addy, Denis Carter) Addy mixes Ghanaian tradition with his own compositions. Some of the vocal backgrounds have a new-agey feel, but the drumming throughout is powerful and crisply produced.

worth searching for: While not as strong as his traditional recordings, Addy's worldbeat albums are worth tracking down. *Let Me Play My Drums* 𝄞𝄞𝄞 (Burnside, 1988, prod. Obo Addy, Chris Baum) is on CD, and probably easiest to find. *Obo* 𝄞𝄞𝄞 (Avocet, 1984) and *African American* 𝄞𝄞𝄞 (Flying Heart, 1986) both came out on small labels before the advent of digital technology.

influences:

◄◄ African Brothers, Highlife International, O. J. Ekemode

►► Kotoja

see also: *Yacub Addy, Kronos Quartet*

j. poet

Yacub Addy /Odadaa!

Traditional Ghanaian music, Tsimo
Formed 1982, in USA. Based in Troy, NY, USA.

Rotating membership across more than a decade and a half, consistently led by Yacub Addy (born 1931, in Avenor, Ghana).

Promoting authentic traditional African culture to uninitiated audiences is an enterprise rich in opportunities for failure—and attempts to "modernize" these roots to broaden their appeal usually end up so homogenized that little interest is retained. Remarkably, traditional artist Yacub Addy, senior among the widely known Addy clan of musicians and dancers, has managed just such a melding of past and present, in America, since 1982.

Born in 1931 in Avenor, a village outside Ghana's capital, Accra, Addy was raised in the ways of old Africa: his father practiced

Yacub Addy of Odadaa!

traditional medicine with the help of Addy's mother, who sang in the ceremonies associated with her husband's practice. At the same time, Ghana's airwaves, not to mention Africa's in general, were thick with the sound of American swing and, later, be-bop. Addy, already having learned the traditional drumming and music of his Ga tribal heritage, also fell in love with the music of greats such as Louis Armstrong, Count Basie, and Louis Jordan.

Profound as these outside influences were, young Addy's aim was to preserve and present the music of his culture in a newly liberated Ghana where, as early as the first year of independence, 1957, he organized the first staged performances of traditional Ghanaian music and dance. By 1963 he and his brothers were touring Europe, and not long thereafter were performing in America, where he settled.

Invoking the name of a traditional rhythm, Addy founded Odadaa!, a company of U.S.-based Ghanaian (and some African-American) performers, in 1982. Now headquartered in Troy, New York, where Addy is a lecturer in African drumming at both Rensselaer Polytechnic Institute and Skidmore College, Odadaa! continues to tour the United States and abroad. In performance, emphasis is on drum-centered traditional music and dance, but

King Sunny Adé

other instruments are incorporated as appropriate. Of special interest, though, is the wide variety of drums at the heart of the ensemble—tall, short, round, square, upright, handheld, even sat-upon. Calabash shakers, flutes, bells—an iron bell provides the essential beat to follow—and voices complete the musical ensemble, which is then complemented with several dance pieces. The accent again is on the traditional, but Addy's love of American jazz is evident not only in his own compositions, but also in the group's collaborations with such jazz/world-music trailblazers as Randy Weston and his longtime associate, saxophonist Talib Kibwe, who bring their principal genre's phrasings to Odadaa's work while properly subsuming their performance into the group's structure. Such ongoing partnerships hold the continued promise of preserving musical styles and cultural forms that might otherwise quickly disappear.

what to buy: Credited to "Yacub Addy's Odadaa!," *Children of the Ancients* &&&& (Aku Music, 1999, prod. Yacub Addy, Amina Addy)—not to be confused with the similarly titled release below—nicely presents the engaging mix of traditional and modern which defines Odadaa!. Only the dancing is missing, though this studio album recreates the sound and feel of the outfit's live performances surprisingly well. Of the disc's seven tracks, three are traditional Ga pieces, including the exuberant "Kolomashi"—literally "Colonialists will leave," or perhaps "Colonials go home!"—a processional from the '40s and '50s independence struggle. The remaining four tracks are Addy compositions that meld traditional Ghanaian and more modern Western elements in a fusion he calls "Tsimo" (pronounced "chee-mo"), from a Ga word meaning "powerful" or "heavy" (it's also a phrase exchanged between Ga drummers when their playing reaches a particularly energized level).

the rest:
(With Oboade) *Kpanlogo Party* &&&& (Tangent 1973/Lyrichord)
Yacub Addy, Master Drummer of Ghana: Blena Bii—Children of the Ancients &&&& (Makossa International, 1982)

influences:
◀ Okonfo Akoto, Akua Hagan, Tetteh Coblah Addy (a.k.a. Attafio Tetteh), Louis Armstrong, Count Basie, Louis Jordan

▶▶ Obo Addy, Mustapha Tettey Addy

see also: *Obo Addy, Randy Weston*

Jack Vartoogian

King Sunny Adé

Juju
Born 1946, in Oshogbo, Nigeria. Based in Lagos, Nigeria.

In addition to his hereditary crown, Nigeria's King Sunny Adé wears many hats—including businessman, nightclub owner,

record company president, and film director—but it's his work as a master guitarist and bandleader of the New African Beats that has brought him international attention. His innovative brand of *juju,* a rich, polyrhythmic music that features multiple guitarists each playing different yet harmonious leads, includes pedal steel, congas, synthesizers, reggae-style dub effects, and a shimmering tidal wave of multi-layered percussion. It has made him a superstar at home and one of Africa's leading musical ambassadors to the world.

Adé was born to a royal family in the Yoruba tribe, but like many musicians of different means, he dropped out of grammar school and left home in search of fame and fortune. "Ja Funmi," a tune from Adé's first American album, tells of his struggle to gain respect from his family. "I was in love with music from my youth, but my family didn't want me to be in the music world. 'Ja Funmi' means 'my head fights for me.' The head controls your body and connects you to God; your head gives you the power to fight for what you believe in." Adé's first gig was in the other popular dance-music form of "highlife," with the band Moses Olaiya and his Rhythm Dandies—but he was increasingly drawn to juju, and, in the early '60s, joined the band of Tunde Nightingale, one of the sound's earliest pioneers.

Juju traces its roots back to various forms of traditional Yoruba guitar playing that include, but are not limited to, Christian *aladura* church music, traditional *ashiko* styles, and a Nigerian "blues" form. Ethnomusicoligist Chris Waterman says that the earliest forerunner of juju was probably a variant of the rural "palm wine" guitar style of Sierra Leone, as practiced by the large Leonian and Brazilian communities in Nigeria's capital, Lagos. In the '20s, as cheap gramophones became available there, players added elements drawn from American country music (especially the picking of Jimmy Rodgers), Hawaiian and Cuban pop music, and the British music-hall tradition. In the late '40s, the African talking drum became an integral part of the lineup, and the music took a giant leap in complexity and popularity. King Sunny Adé would bring it to an even higher level of sophistication and worldwide acceptance some 20 years later.

Adé formed his first juju band, the Green Spots, in 1967. Seven years later, after already recording 12 highly successful albums, he grew tired of the Nigerian music industry's hassles, broke his contract, changed the band's name to the African Beats, and formed his own label (Sunny Aladé, associated with London's Decca Records). Since then, he has released more than 100 albums for the home and international market.

While some Nigerian songwriters have used their music to address the country's mounting social problems, Adé's lyrics tend to try to influence the fray by being seemingly above it. "If I was political, I'd vibe my music to one side or the other, the rich side or the poor side, the oppressive side or the powerless side, the white side or the black side. Some people are creative, while others build weapons to destroy; that is my concern always. That is why I took a line of preaching love. If we talk heart to heart, and don't hide anything from ourselves, [everything would be] simple. The moment you love your brother as yourself, peace will be there."

what to buy: *Juju Music* 🎜🎜🎜🎜🎜 (Mango, 1982, prod. Martin Meissonnier) is the album that introduced African pop to international audiences, and it couldn't be any stronger. Adé revamped several of his biggest Nigerian hits for the global market, and recorded them with just enough studio polish to make them come alive for ears unfamiliar with the complexities of the juju style. This album should be in any serious music collection.

what to buy next: 13 years after his international debut, Adé produced another masterwork with *E Dide—Get Up!* 🎜🎜🎜🎜 (Mesa, 1995, prod. Sunny Adé, Andrew Frankel). There are a couple of tunes in English, and the tempos are faster, but the underlying groove is as deep and powerful as ever.

the rest:

Synchro System 🎜🎜🎜🎜 (Mango, 1983)
Aura 🎜🎜🎜🎜 (Island, 1984)
Return of the Juju King 🎜🎜🎜🎜 (Mercury, 1987)
Live Live Juju 🎜🎜🎜 (Rykodisc, 1988)
Live at the Hollywood Palace 🎜🎜🎜 (Hemisphere, 1994)
Odù 🎜🎜🎜🎜 (Mesa, 1998)

worth searching for: With more than 100 albums on vinyl and cassette, it's virtually impossible to do justice to Adé's output, but anything you come across in the collector's bins is probably worth your time.

influences:

◀◀ Ebenezer Obey, I. K. Dairo, Dele Abiodun

▶▶ Talking Heads, Shina Adewale & Superstars International, Dele Taiwo

j. poet

Adioa

African reggae
Formed 1986, in Paris, France. Based in Paris, France.

Maxidilick Adioa (Sidibe Mame Malick), vocals, percussion; Falman Bazuka (Etienne Fall), vocals, bass; Tony Harey Koy, vocals, drums, rhythm programs; Charly Winter, vocals, guitar; Dave Kynner, vocals, keyboards; Natti Kynner, vocals, synthesizer.

In Senegal's Soninke language Adioa means "progress" or "advance," and the reggae sound of these players from that country, Martinique, and Guadeloupe was quite progressive for its time. The band originally formed to back up the Paris-based reggae artist Jah Ark, with whom they toured Europe extensively before beginning to play their own music in 1986. Maxidilick, the band's vocalist and main songwriter, was born in Dakar, Senegal, and played in a trio called the Free Fires Band; he also worked briefly with Alpha Blondy. He met Falman Bazuka in the early 1980s, while playing with the band Apartheid Not. Bazuka was also briefly a member of Tshala Muana's backing band. The duo moved to Paris, and after breaking away from Jah Ark forged their own sound, a combination of reggae, *zouk*, funk, and jazz, with a touch of *mbalax* drumming added to the usual reggae one-drop riddims. The band's first single, "Toubab Bi Le," told the story of an infamous massacre of Africans by French troops in the days immediately after World War II. "Buma Done Yene," their second single, was a broad-based political protest: "If I were you, I would never get involved in politics. Culture should be shared worldwide. . . ." Their mixture of styles appeared fresh when they cut *Soweto Man* for Mango in 1989, and Maxidilick has the required high tenor and forceful delivery, but little has been heard from them since.

what's available: Hard riddims, sweeping synths, sharp rock guitar, and inventive percussion make *Soweto Man* 🎜🎜🎜 (Mango, 1989, prod. Adioa, Paul "Groucho" Smykle) a solid reggae outing, in a roots reggae stylee.

influences:

◀◀ Alpha Blondy, Sonny Okosun, Kassav'

see also: *Alpha Blondy, Tshala Muana*

j. poet

Africando

Salsa, charanga
Formed 1992, in Senegal. Based in Senegal.

Pape Seck (Senegal, died February 2, 1995), vocals; Médoune Diallo (Senegal), vocals (1992–present); Nicolas Menheim (Senegal), vocals (1992–present); Ronnie Baró (USA), vocals (1995–present); Gnonnas Pedro (Benin), vocals (1996–present).

Ever since the 1930s the sultry Caribbean rhythms of Cuba and Puerto Rico—cultivated by the islands' musically fertile if socially troubled mix of African, Latin, and Native cultures—have returned to Africa via records, tapes, and radio broadcasts, making a huge impression on many indigenous bands. In Senegal, the Cuban *charanga* style with its violins and flutes was especially influential, and Cuban bands like Orquesta Aragon and the more recent Orquesta Ritmo Oriental still have their adherents. Where many of the Senegalese charanga-style bands differed from their Caribbean cousins was in taking the parts written for violin and flute and transferring them to the guitar. The 1960s saw further innovations in the form with the advent of the Star Band de Dakar, the first of the great African charanga bands to blend the *jali* traditions of Senegal and Gambia with Afro-Cuban rhythms. In 1971 another group, the Orchestre Baobab, helped complete the transition by incorporating Mandinka and Wolof lyrics into the equation. Pape Seck, one of the lead vocalists for the Star Band de Dakar, and Medoune Diallo, a singer with the Orchestre Baobab, were to form the vocal heart of Africando. The group itself came together when the legendary African producer Ibrahim Sylla was convinced by Boncana Maiga—a flautist from Mali with extensive experience in Cuba and in New York-based salsa bands—to combine some of Senegal's finest singers with a hand-picked batch of Latin musicians for a few sessions. The resulting dates mixed Seck, Diallo, and Nicolas Menheim (a singer in Youssou N'Dour's band) with salsa veterans whose partial résumés included work in bands led by Tito Puente, Mongo Santamaria, Cachao, Cal Tjader, Tito Nieves, and Johnny Pacheco. Ronnie Baró, the former lead vocalist with Orquesta Broadway, was initially in the chorus during the recording sessions but ended up singing lead on the title tune for the first album. After the gruff-voiced Seck died of liver cancer, Baró was brought into the band as a regular member. Just before the band recorded its third album, Gnonnas Pedro, a strong singer in the Afro-Cuban tradition from Benin, was added to the mix, giving Africando a legend-worthy front line of vocalists.

what to buy: Africando's initial release, *Vol. 1—Trovador* 𝄞𝄞𝄞𝄞 (Stern's, 1993, prod. Ibrahim Sylla), is chock full of rhythm and glorious vocals. The band organized by Boncana Maiga plays his arrangements with such verve that it's difficult to keep your feet still. Nicolas Menheim opens things up with "Doley Mbolo," a Wolof version of El Gran Combo's "La Eliminacion de los Feos," but the album enters immortality when Pape Seck's gruff yet supple singing puts "Lakh Bi" into hyperdrive. From then on *Vol. 1—Trovador* is nigh unbeatable. That "nigh" is necessary because the outtakes from the session form the heart of *Vol. 2—Tierra Tradicional* 𝄞𝄞𝄞𝄞 (Stern's, 1994, prod. Ibrahim Sylla), the perfect place to start one's acquaintance with Africando. Medoune Diallo is heard to great effect on "Xale Bile" but the heart of the album once again belongs to Seck, the power behind "Yay Boy," a huge favorite of New York City's Latino community when the album first hit the airwaves. The group's version of "Sabador (La Bamba)" is another killer cut.

what to buy next: *Gombo Salsa* 𝄞𝄞𝄞𝄞 (Stern's Africa, 1996, prod. Ibrahim Sylla) is more of a straight-ahead salsa album than the first two releases, though the blend of African and Spanish languages is still at the lyrical heart of the songs. Most of the musicians from the first two discs play on these sessions, ensuring high-quality instrumental continuity. There is also a batch of

major-league Latin and African music stars helping out, including flute wizard José Fajardo and vocalist Tabu Ley Rochereau.

the rest:
Balboa! 𝄞𝄞𝄞𝄝 (Stern's Africa, 1998)

worth searching for: Pape Seck was involved with the outfit Starband Number One in 1972. Besides Seck the lineup also boasted Maquette N'Diaye, a singer prized for his Latin stylings. *No. 1 de No. 1.* 𝄞𝄞𝄞𝄞 (Dakar Sound, 1996, compilation prod. Ted Jaspers) documents this band, with various studio sessions and three live performances recorded at the Sahel nightclub where they regularly performed. It also includes the original version of "Maccaki," later recorded on the first Africando album as "Mathiaky."

influences:
◀◀ Orchestra Aragon, Eddie Palmieri, Johnny Pacheco

see also: *Sékouba "Bambino" Diabaté, Boncana Maiga, Tshala Muana, Orchestra Baobab, Gnonnas Pedro, Tabu Ley Rochereau*

Garaud MacTaggart

Afro Celt Sound System
Anglo-Celtic/Afro pop fusion
Formed 1995, in England. Based in England.

Ever-rotating membership, which has principally included: Simon Emmerson (England), guitars, programming; Myrdhin (Brittany, France), Celtic harp; Kauwding Cissokho (a.k.a. Kaouding Cissoko, Senegal), kora (1995–98); Massamba Diop (Senegal), talking drums (1995–98); Jo Bruce (U.K., died October 8, 1997), keyboards; James McNally (England), bodhrán, accordion, low whistle, keyboards; Martin Russell (England), keyboards, programming, engineering; N'Faly Kouyate (West Africa), vocals, kora, balafon (1998–present); Moussa Sissokho (West Africa), talking drum, djembe (1998–present).

The man behind the boards for many of Senegalese superstar Baaba Maal's tribal/Celtic crossover experiments, Simon Emmerson was eventually inspired to specialize in this surprising but successful hybrid with his own outfit, the Afro Celt Sound System. After collaborating on one such project of similar sensibility with Maal—prophetically, in a studio that happened to be decorated in Celtic symbols painted by artist Jamie Reid—Emmerson sent Reid a tape of the finished work, mentioning that he'd "recorded a collaboration between West African and Irish musicians and that [he'd] thought the studio atmosphere had been brilliant." In reply, Reid sent Emmerson an artwork titled "AfroCelts—Sound Magic Music from the Light Continent," along with a note stating, "Here's the sleeve for the album you are going to make." This set a predestined tone that would carry through in 1995 at a British WOMAD (World of Music, Arts and Dance) festival, where Afro Celt Sound System took the stage for the first time under that name, before they'd ever stepped into a studio—not a bad limbering-up exercise for the type of sound-assembly project that could easily succumb to the syndrome of being able to produce the goods but not deliver them live. There would be no worry of that, though; another thing this band was destined to do was transplant the creative disorder of the concert setting into the recording one. After launching at WOMAD, Emmerson, Jo Bruce, and Ron Aslan laid down debut backing tracks at RealWorld studios (like the festival, another Peter Gabriel-associated endeavor) during the all-star 1995 sound summit "RealWorld Recording Week," thus gaining access to a host of stellar participants—including French Celtic harpist Myrdhin, who'd played on some of the Maal recordings, and two members of Maal's band, Kauwding Cissokho (*kora* or African harp-lute) and Massamba Diop (*tama* or "talking drum"). A strong Celtic flavor came from vocalist Iarla O'Lionáird, multi-instrumentalist Ronan Browne (uilleann pipes, flute, mandolin, harmonium), and members of the Scottish avant-garde folk/rock/dance band Shooglenifty. The first Afro Celt Sound System disc, *Volume 1: Sound Magic,* was released in 1996; the follow-up, *Volume 2: Release,* in 1999. All along and still ongoing, much performance and a revolving cast of co-conspirators have kept up the circulation of fresh ideas and happy accidents that make the System's destiny as fulfilling for the listener as it is for the band.

what to buy: *Volume 1: Sound Magic* ♪♪♪♪ (RealWorld, 1996, prod. Simon Emmerson, Ron Aslan) puts the "multi" in multicultural, combining Anglo-Celtic and African roots with late '90s high-tech dance/pop grooves. Faster cuts like "Whirl-Y-Reel 1" lay melody lines played by uilleann pipes, harp, kora, whistles, and flute over chugging, dance-demanding rhythm tracks. Gaelic singer Iarla O'Lionáird's selections sound like slow airs, with the vocal taking the main melody while percussionists set down a steady rhythm and keyboard washes give the arrangements a haunting, symphonic effect. But there are even a few numbers with basically acoustic textures, like "Dark Noon, High Tide," in which the uilleann pipes are joined by acoustic guitar and percussion for a softer (if no less energetic) version of the System's characteristic sound. The evolution continues on *Volume 2: Release* ♪♪♪♪ (RealWorld, 1999, prod. Simon Emmerson, Martin Russell), the main difference being that each track has more of an individual identity, and O'Lionáird's vocals are more prominent. His authentic Gaelic vocalizing works equally well on a slow, contemplative piece or a rousing dance number. As is already an Afro Celt trademark, several unexpected guests keep the party hearty; invited this time are Sinéad O'Connor, who gets the haunting Gaelic vibe perfectly on "Release," and uilleann pipers Ronan Browne (on a return appearance from *Volume 1*) and Michael McGoldrick, who contribute well to the project's distinctive Celtic flavor.

solo outings:
Kaouding Cissoko:
Kora Revolution ♪♪♪♪ (Palm Pictures/Yoff, 1999)

influences:
◄◄ Fripp & Eno, Kraftwerk, techno, electronica, Baaba Maal, Mouth Music, Moving Hearts, Capercaillie, Alan Stivell

►► Talitha MacKenzie, Shooglenifty, Peatbog Faeries

see also: *Baaba Maal, Ayub Ogada*

Ken Roseman and Adam McGovern

Mahmoud Ahmed
Ethopian soul
Born in Addis-Ababa, Ethiopia. Based in Addis-Ababa, Ethiopia.

In Ethiopia traditional music and popular music exist side by side, and most performers have two repertoires, one traditional, one pop. But the evolution of Ethiopian pop music has had an uphill battle. Thirty years of civil war, followed by 17 years of military dictatorship, put the brakes on the nightclub scene and made recording difficult. The last records were issued in 1978, and songs on cassettes were often banned for their "subversive" lyrics. Ahmed's father died when he was a child, and the family became homeless. Ahmed survived by shining shoes, often singing to the delight of his customers. He was expelled from grammar school and began singing seriously, hoping to make a living with music. During the years of the civil war, the only modern bands were those of the army and police. He auditioned for the army band, but was told he'd have to enlist to make the grade. Instead he got a job as a painter, carpenter and busboy at the Arizona, one of the few nightclubs in Addis-Ababa. One day he approached the bandstand during a rehearsal and asked for an audition. Gima Hadgue, the bandleader, let him sing; at the end of the number the applause signified the birth of a new star. Ahmed next joined the Imperial Bodyguard band as singer, and stayed there for 11 years. By the 1980s Ahmed owned his own record store and nightclub. With no formal music business, performers depend on hundreds of record-store labels for their bread and butter. Ahmed has recorded for them all, and with the end of the dictatorship and beginnings of democracy, performs regularly on the nightclub circuit.

what's available: Ahmed recorded *Soul of Addis* ♪♪♪ (EarthWorks, 1997, prod. Mahmoud Ahmed) in the mid-1980s, and it's a solid effort. Ahmed sings *tixta,* which he calls the "Ethiopian blues," although to American ears it sounds like a cross between reggae, deep fried Southern soul, and Arabic R&B. Like many soul shouters, Ahmed has a big, emotional voice, with instrumental tracks that maintain a slow, satisfying simmer and feature a familiar backbeat and wailing, blues-drenched horn charts.

James McNally (l) & N'Faly Kouyate of Afro Celt Sound System

worth searching for: The recording on *Ere Mela Mela* 🎜🎜🎜 (Crammed Discs, 1986, prod. Mahmoud Ahmed, Francis Falceto) isn't the best, and it's mixed with Ahmed's voice (and occasionally the sax) way out front, but this collection of cassette singles from 1975–1978 gives you a good idea of what Ethiopian street music sounds like.

influences:

◄◄ Imperial Bodyguard Band, Tlahoun Gessesse

►► Aster Aweke, Ephrem Tamru, Kuku Sebsebe, Neway Debebe

j. poet

Pierre Akendengue

Pan-African pop

Born 1944, in Port Gentil, Gabon. Based in Port Gentil, Gabon and Paris, France.

Gabon is home to almost 50 ethnic groups, and until the ascent of Pierre Akendengue, most Gabonese recordings concentrated on this vast reservoir of folk and traditional music. In the wake of Akendengue's success, a Gabonese sound is starting to develop, but much of the country's music is still dominated by that of its powerful neighbors, Congo and Cameroon. That said, Akendengue is one of Africa's most creative and visionary musicians, and Gabon's reigning musical genius. He is an internationally recognized singer, composer, poet, playwright, and musician who spent seven years of his life in exile because of his outspoken political opinions.

By the age of 14 Akendengue's songs were being played on national radio. He moved to Paris when he was 20 to study literature in Caen and psychology at the Sorbonne. Unfortunately, he was also going blind, and he returned to Gabon, where his opposition to the government forced him into exile. He began releasing albums in 1974, and from the first they revealed a singular vision, combining music, poetry, traditional and electric instruments, political lyrics, and a diverse style. The latter melded influences from Caribbean to Latin, from North American (funk, bluesy guitars) to African, with an emphasis on inventive percussion arrangements. In 1993 Akendengue recorded *Lambarena,* one of the most startling African albums ever made.

Subtitled "Johann Sebastion Bach in Africa," Akendengue mixed a baroque chamber orchestra with an African rhythm section to play Bach. He arranged choral works for African voices, adapted African traditional music for baroque instrumentation, and had his drummers work changes on Bach's cantatas and partitas. Today, he continues to confound, following dance-happy excursions with dark, introspective outings full of sighing choral work and low-key yet relentless percussion.

what to buy: _Lambarena_ 𝄞𝄞𝄞𝄞 (Celluloid/Melodie France, 1993, prod. Akendengue) is the first African concept album, recorded as a tribute to Albert Schweitzer, another lover of Bach, and named after the town Schweitzer lived and worked in. Akendengue finds the Africanisms in Bach, and the Baroque "influences" in African music, to create a work of rare beauty and stunning originality. _Maladalite_ 𝄞𝄞𝄞𝄞𝄲 (Celluloid/Melodie France, 1995, prod. Akendengue) is an African singer/songwriter album that once again combines classic European influences with Latin rhythms and traditional African touches.

the rest:
Awana W'Africa 𝄞𝄞𝄞𝄞 (Celluloid/Melodie France, 1983)
Reveil de L'Afrika 𝄞𝄞𝄞𝄞 (Celluloid/Melodie France, 1984)
Piroguier 𝄞𝄞𝄞𝄞 (Melodie France)
Silence 𝄞𝄞𝄞𝄞 (Celluloid/Melodie France)

influences:
◀◀ Gabonese folk music, J. S. Bach

▶▶ Kassav', Missema

j. poet

Farid al-Atrash

Arabic pop
Born c. 1915, in Jabal al-Duruz, Syria. Died December 26, 1974, in Beirut, Lebanon.

Farid al-Atrash was known as "The King of the _Oud_" (Arabic lute), but he was also a gifted composer and singer. Like his Egyptian counterpart, Mohamed Abdel Wahab, al-Atrash often blended non-Arabic styles (including flamenco, tango, and waltz rhythms) into his tunes, forever broadening the Middle Eastern musical palette. In 1924 al-Atrash's mother Aliyah Husayn moved her three children from Syria to Egypt, escaping the fighting that was going on between the French forces of occupation and the Druze rebels (among them Prince Fahd al-Atrash, Farid's father). Aliyah sang and played the oud on the radio and in various venues around Cairo to support her family. Farid heard her practicing around the house but started his formal musical education by singing in the choir at a local Christian-sponsored school. Legend has it that an instructor was unimpressed by Farid's pleasant but innocuous vocals, finally advising him to "cry" as a way of expressing feelings that audi-

ences could react to. This advice worked and al-Atrash was later known for the "tear" in his voice when singing the poignant lyrics that helped shape his popularity. After graduation al-Atrash worked for a while in Ibrahim Hammoudeh's group before enrolling at the Institute of Arabic Music, where he studied oud performance with Riyad al-Sunbati. His career took off during the '30s when he started singing and playing on the Egyptian state-run radio network. By 1941 al-Atrash had added "film star" to his resume when he acted, along with his sister Amal (an incredibly popular singer known professionally as Asmahan), in a movie called _Intisar Ichabab_. He also wrote all the music for it, something he was to do for most of the remaining 30-plus films in his cinematic career. Even though al-Atrash was creating an artistically fulfilling oeuvre, his personal life had its playboy aspects, which would alienate his mother even as it created the raw material for his songs. Toward the end of his life al-Atrash had homes in Beirut and Cairo and had written more than 300 songs, plus a substantial number of works that stressed his instrumental prowess. When he died there were rumors that his family refused to let him be buried in the ancestral homeland due to his profligate behavior, but his will supposedly stressed his wish to be buried in Egypt where his career had first taken root.

what to buy: There are more than 20 different CDs available featuring Farid al-Atrash, but all are imports and none are especially easy to find in mainstream stores. Almost every one of them pairs the artist and an Arabic orchestra, with violins stroking a minor mode as percussion floats around the vocals. _An Evening with the King of the 'Oud'_ 𝄞𝄞𝄞𝄞 (Voice of Lebanon, 1992) is a good place to start since one of his biggest hits, "al-Rabi," is included. _Super Belly Dance, Volume 1_ 𝄞𝄞𝄞𝄞 (Voice of Stars, 1978, prod. Daniel der Sahakian) is an exciting album of instrumental music with nary a reflective tune among its five.

what to buy next: With the exception of al-Atrash's soundtrack music, most of his available albums are taken from concerts. The eponymous (given the variations in his name's spelling in different countries) _Farid El Atrache_ 𝄞𝄞𝄞𝄞 (Voice of Lebanon, 1990), with its dramatic "Baa Ayez Tensani" and the somewhat lighter-textured "Gara Eih Ya Ossalna," is one of the best studio albums available. It is fairly well engineered, with an emphasis on the vocal rather than the instrumental. _King of the Oud_ 𝄞𝄞𝄞𝄲 (Voice of Lebanon, 1990) is part concert recording and part studio effort. Most of al-Atrash's performances started with _taqâsîm_ (an improvisational discipline based on a complex set of preestablished rules and conventions) that demonstrated his formidable technique on the oud before commencing the vocal portion of his show. The first cut on this album displays al-Atrash's instrumental artistry but is cobbled together from various concerts, with the audience(s) getting a bit

Ishtar of Alabina & Los Ninos de Sara

exuberant at times. The other piece on the disc is a studio version of "Kelmet Itaab," an astonishing virtuoso piece for oud and singer, sans orchestra, that is worth the price of the album.

best of the rest:
Super Belly Dance, Vol. 2 🎵🎵🎵🎵 (Voice of Lebanon, 1980)
Baa Ayez Tensani 🎵🎵🎵🎵 (Voice of Lebanon, 1990)
Les Archives (1930) 🎵🎵🎵🎵 (Voice of Lebanon, 1993)

worth searching for: Soundtrack recordings are the best place to hear how al-Atrash attempted to blend Western musical idioms with Arabic modes. *Original soundtrack recordings from "Rissala Men Imraa Majhoula" and "Youm Bila Ghad"* 🎵🎵🎵 (Voice of Lebanon, 1992) contains eight tunes that run the gamut from flamenco to waltz to traditional Arabic melodies, with a little Cuban *clave* rhythm tossed in for percussive spice. If all else fails, there is a well-recorded collection by Hossam Ramzy called *Best of Farid al-Atrash* 🎵🎵🎵 (Arc Music, 1993, prod. Hossam Ramzy) that will give you a sense of how al-Atrash might have sounded.

influences:
◀◀ Riyad al-Sunbati

▶▶ Hossam Ramzy, Fawzi Sayeb, George Abyad

see also: *Hossam Ramzy, Mohamed Abdel Wahab*

Garaud MacTaggart

Alaap
Bhangra
Formed c. 1982, in London, England. Based in London, England.

Channi Singh, leader, singer, composer, toombi; Pandit Dinesh, dholak, tabla, chanda, bass, keyboards, drum programs, percussion; Stephen Luscombe, sound effects, live keyboard mixing; Errol Reed, keyboards; Arvind, keyboards; Paul Inder, guitar, bass; Sunil, tabla, dholak, dhol; Johny, dhol; Sumeet, keyboards; Claudio, sax. (All members are from England.)

Bhangra is a genuine worldbeat sound, created to serve a community that calls two far-flung countries home. In the Punjab (now part of Pakistan), where one of the main crops is hemp, or *bhang,* there are yearly harvest festivals driven by the relentless beat of the *dhol,* a doubled-headed folk drum. After the massive immigration to England that followed in the wake of

World War II, the new Indian communities began looking for their own cultural expressions, a quest that Channi Singh of Alaap would eventually take up. When he realized the bhangra beat fit neatly into the 4/4 of Western pop, the band began adding western drum kits and electric instruments to the traditional lineup of dohls, dholak, and tablas. The result was an explosion of creativity that eventually led to new beats like "jungle." Singh formed Alaap in the early 1980s, and the band's updating of bhangra for a new generation made them a sensation, although Alaap has stayed closer to the music's traditional (and acoustic) roots than many.

what to buy: *Hits of Alaap* ♪♪♪♪ (Multitone, 1991, prod. various) collects the hits that started the bhangra craze in Britain; Punjabi folk music given a modern spin. Multitone recently folded, but most Indian import stores will be able to supply you with all the Alaap titles you need.

the rest:
Teri Chunni De Sitare ♪♪♪♪ (Multitone, 1978)
Best of Alaap ♪♪♪♪ (Multitone, 1990)
Gold ♪♪♪♪ (Multitone, 1991)
Simply Alaap ♪♪♪♪ (Multitone, 1993)

influences:
◀◀ Punjabi folk music

▶▶ Heera, Premi, Holle Holle, Safri Boys

j. poet

Alabina

Egyptian-flamenco dance music
Formed 1997, in Paris, France. Based in Paris, France.

Ishtar (Egypt), vocals; Tonio, guitar, vocals; Coco, percussion, vocals; Santi, guitar, vocals; Ramon, guitar, vocals. (All members are from Spain unless otherwise noted.)

Alabina may be the only group that crosses Egyptian and Spanish styles, and they have certainly struck a popular chord with their passionate, accessible sound, making the world-music charts in France, Denmark, England, and the States. The band came together when Ishtar, the group's alluring vocalist, did some recording sessions with Los Ninos de Sara, a group of four cousins who played a driving, listener-friendly blend of flamenco and other gypsy music. The musicians decided to work together more permanently, and chose as their name a modified version of their song titled "Yallabina (Let's Go)." Their two CDs to date have blended Egyptian and Spanish vocals, and crossed traditional gypsy instrumentation with bright, contemporary pop production.

what's available: *Alabina* ♪♪♪♪ (Astor Place, 1997), the group's debut album, is its best, and showcases the wonderful contrasts between Tonio's deep vocals in Spanish and Ishtar's sultry vocals in Egyptian. When they alternate lines, as on the slow, soulful "Linda Maria," the sound they produce is exquisite. On churning dance tunes like "Espreso," Ishtar proves that she is a strong contender for diva-of-the-moment. *Alabina 2* ♪♪♪ (Astor Place, 1998) continues in the same vein, but with a bigger, more layered instrumental sound. Smooth ballads, driving flamenco, and bouncy pop tunes are all attired in keyboards and percussion designed to maintain a strong dance groove.

influences:
◀◀ Gipsy Kings, Celine Dion

Michael Parrish

Chava Alberstein

Folk, worldbeat
Born 1946, in Szczecin, Poland. Based in Israel.

Chava Alberstein has been called "the first lady of Israeli song," and since the recording of her self-titled debut in 1964, she has released more than 50 albums in her adoptive homeland. A native of Poland, Alberstein moved with her family to northern Haifa, Israel, at the age of four. She acquired a love of Yiddish and Hebrew—along with her innate affinity for music—equally early on. Alberstein's public debut came with a popular Israeli radio show appearance in 1963 with her clarinetist brother Alex. Still a teenager, she spotlighted the range that would become her trademark as she performed a black gospel tune in English, a folk song in Spanish, a *chanson* in French, and a song in Yiddish. The positive reception prompted a swift step up to the even more widely heard show, *Moadon Hazemer*.

When CBS launched an Israeli branch in 1964, Alberstein became one of the first artists signed. Her debut album, which included four songs in Yiddish, was recorded in two hours, simply featuring Alberstein on vocals and guitar. She recorded the follow-up, an all-Hebrew effort, a month later. Drafted into the Army shortly afterward, Alberstein spent two years entertaining the Israeli troops. Upon her release, she recorded an album backed by an orchestra and her first collection of children's music. Maintaining this busy and diverse schedule, she performed a one-woman show and two children's musicals, and also played with a jazz band, Hoplatina.

Alberstein sought still other outlets for her talents: In addition to hosting a weekly children's television show for two years, she appeared in several feature films including *Joseph and the Amazing Technicolor Dream Coat,* and authored a children's book, *I Am Not Perfect*. A book of Alberstein's songs, *Sher Bementana (A Gift of Songs),* was the first of its kind to be published in Israel.

Chava Alberstein

Alberstein's broad tastes and ambitions were underscored by a 1996 tour with Argentinian songstress and activist Mercedes Sosa, which served to accentuate not only Alberstein's persistent social consciousness but her international appeal. That popularity finally spread to America in 1998, as she introduced herself with a look back and a bold new move, each in the same year: the retrospective *Crazy Flower: The Collection,* and a collaboration with innovative 21st-century klezmer band the Klezmatics.

what's available: *Crazy Flower: The Collection* ♪♪♪♪ (Shanachie, 1998, prod. various) surveys Alberstein's lengthy career and includes tracks from her Israeli albums. *The Well* ♪♪♪♪ (Xenophile, 1998, prod. Ben Mink) combines Alberstein's soulful vocals, uplifting musical accompaniment by the Klezmatics, and the spirited words of 20th-century Yiddish poets.

influences:

◀◀ Leonid Utyosov, Moshe Beregovsky

▶▶ The Klezmatics, Muzsikás

see also: *The Klezmatics*

Craig Harris

Albita

Son, guajira

Born Albita Rodriguez, 1962, in Havana, Cuba. Based in Miami, FL, USA.

Albita performs *guajira,* a form of Cuban "country" music that many young Cubans consider corny, but since she and her band came to the United States in 1993 they've created the biggest buzz Miami's Cuban community has ever witnessed. She was immediately signed to Emilio Estefan's Crescent Moon label, had a video directed by Madonna's brother Chris Ciccone, posed for photo spreads in the fashion pages of magazines like *Detour* and *Mirabella,* and started doing turn-away business at Centro Vasco, where she and her band of expatriates churned out a "pure" brand of neo-classical Cuban music. "I grew up listening to *punto guarijo,*" Albita says. "That mixture of Africa and Spain was inspirational. I wanted to do pure Cuban music, but the younger generation wasn't interested, which made it hard to stay authentic." Albita began playing guitar at 14, hoping to become a songwriter. Her forceful alto made her a favorite of Castro, but Havana wasn't wild about her "old school" style. "Because of the embargo,

Albita

North American music (especially rock) has an exotic appeal," she explains. "Music needs roots to stay strong, but authentic music isn't hip [in Cuba]. I had to leave home for my artistic survival." In 1993, Albita and her band decided to defect. They'd gotten a four-year gig in Colombia, but after two years they flew to Mexico for a bogus "recording session." They took taxis across the border at El Paso. A friend put her in touch with Emilio Estefan, who helped the band with a place to stay and a recording contract. The rest is history in the making.

what to buy: *No Se Parece A Nada* ♪♪♪♪ (Crescent Moon/Epic, 1995, prod. Juan R. Marquez), like the new land in which the band found itself, is as good a place to start as any. Albita is an expressive vocalist, with a rough-hewn alto that grabs you by the ears and gives you a good shake. The power of her band and the strength of the arrangements makes you realize how bland most *salsa romantico* is. Although that band is a crack unit, Estefan augmented the group with some of the top Latin musicians in the world for this album. Cachao Lopez played bass on a few tracks, and Ruben Blades did some arranging for a set that spins around you like a storm from the heart of West Africa. "I like that

elemental feeling," the singer says. "Jazz, bolero, guaguanco, African drums, and syncopation, that's what keeps the music strong." *Una Mujer Como Yo* ♪♪♪♪ (Crescent Moon/Epic, 1997, prod. Kike Santander, Roberto Blades, Julia Sierra, Albita) is another pure energetic jolt from Albita and her band.

worth searching for: *Habra Musica Guajira* ♪♪♪♪ (EGREM, 1988) is Albita's debut for Cuba's state-run record label, the set that made her a "contenda."

influences:
◄◄ Celia Cruz

see also: *Ruben Blades, Cachao, Gloria Estefan*

j. poet

Haris Alexiou
Laiko, rembetiko
Born in Greece. Based in Greece.

Haris Alexiou's sultry vocals, personal lyrics, and tales of heartache have situated her as one of Greece's most admired contemporary artists, continually evoking the passion in everyday life through the *rembetiko* (Greek urban blues) style. Even as Alexiou does a great job of recording *rembetika* (the slightly different term for "rembetiko songs"), her *laika,* or pop songs, have managed to remain honest and simple—a feat that has eluded many modern-day recording artists in Greece. While the bulk of her work has been released in the past decade, few remember that Alexiou has been recording since 1973, when she appeared on Apostolos Kaladias's seminal rembetiko revival album *Mikra Asia* ("Asia Minor"). Her big break came with the single "Dimitroula" (from her album *Laika Tragoudia*), one of Greece's most popular hits throughout the 1970s. A versatile artist, Alexiou has sung in French and Arabic as well as Greek. Her rapturous songs about love continue to both break and heal the heart.

what to buy: *Mikra Asia (Asia Minor)* ♪♪♪♪ (1973) is a marvelous evocation of the oriental influence carried over to Greece through the city of Smyrne, which is now known as Ishmir, part of Turkey. Matching Alexiou with such other heavyweights-to-be as George Dalaras, this album helps trace the roots of rembetiko. Alexiou came into her own with the solo debut *Laika Tragoudia* ♪♪♪♪ (Mercury, 1975), which established the commercial success and commanding vocals that would make her one of the preeminent acts in Greece. Collaborating with musicians like Manu Katché and Pino Palladino, Alexiou released *To Pehnidi tis Kardias (Games of the Heart)* ♪♪♪♪♪ (Mercury, 1988, prod. Haris Andreadis), writing her own lyrics—a challenge few female artists have tackled in popular Greek music—and matching the poignancy of her most popular work, with a newly personal dimension.

what to buy next: *Odos Nefelis* ♪♪♪♪ (Mercury, 1995, prod. Haris Andreadis) is Alexiou's first plunge into full songwriting, in which she acquits herself admirably while lending her characteristic interpretive insight to the album's one cover, François Bernheim's "Les Hommes qui Passent." The recent *Di Efkon* ♪♪♪ (Mondo Melodia, 1998, prod. Haris Andreadis) has given Alexiou more presence on an international level, but lacks the warmth of her previous efforts.

the rest:
Ta Tslilika ♪♪♪ (Mercury)

worth searching for: *Ena Fili to Kosmo (A Kiss to the World)* ♪♪♪♪ (Mercury, 1997, prod. Haris Andreadis) is Alexiou's live album. Complete with a booklet surveying her career, this collection showcases her prowess as a performer; highlights include a 1993 set in Athens with spiritual singer/songwriter Petros Gaitanos.

influences:

◄◄ George Dalaras, Apostolos Kaladias, Mikis Theodorakis, Arletta

►► Anna Visi

Helen Giano

Jerry Alfred & the Medicine Beat

Native folk-rock
Formed 1993, in Yukon, Canada. Based in the Northern Tutchone Nation, Yukon, Canada.

Jerry Alfred, guitar, traditional drums, lead vocals; Bob Hamilton, electric and acoustic guitar, mandolin, bouzouki, vocals; Andrea McColeman, keyboards, accordion, marimba, vocals; Marc Paradis, drums, percussion; Marie Gogo, vocals. (All members are from Canada.)

Jerry Alfred is the song keeper of his nation, a position of great importance to a people whose traditions are passed down orally through song and poetry. "Our music was dying out," Alfred said. "The people in my tribe that lived in areas with the longest contact with Europeans had a lot of their culture missing, and the young kids were ashamed of singing with a drum. Our language was mostly spoken by middle-aged people." Alfred couldn't help but notice how acclimated young Indians were to the rhythms of rap and rock, so he decided to use pop music as a means of awaking them to the beauty of their own culture. Alfred teamed with producer and guitarist Bob Hamilton in a largely exploratory fashion for a first album, *Etsi Shon.* It won the Canadian Juno award for best Aboriginal Album in 1995, and became a pop hit as well, which led Alfred and Hamilton to create a band to take their show on the road. The album's title track was included on the United Nations' 50th Anniversary CD, and provided part of the soundtrack for the Native American Photo Exhibit at the Atlanta Olympics. Its success has also made the younger people of the Tutchone Nation start seeking out their elders to learn their native language. Alfred said the album's popularity surprised him—but not totally. "A medicine man told my father, when I was young, that I'd be a singer and bring back the old songs to my people. I think a lot of (non-Native) people are searching for that connection to the land and the old ways, the feeling that we have in our blood. Maybe when this music came out, people could sense how it stretches back in time to those deep feelings."

what's available: *Etsi Shon: Grandfather Song* ♪♪♪ (Red House, 1996, prod. Bob Hamilton) is an album of timeless beauty. Hamilton's atmospheric guitar fills the background with sustained notes that shimmer like the northern lights. There are touches of rock, American and Canadian folk, blues, and Acadian (French Canadian) folk in the mix, but it's Alfred's plaintive singing and drumming that hook you. *Nendaä: Go Back* 𝄞𝄞𝄞 (Red House, 1996, prod. Bob Hamilton), recorded after the Medicine Beat had a year of touring under its belt, is comparatively polished and mainstream, sounding more folky than Native at times.

influences:

◀ The Band, Gordon Lightfoot, Bob Dylan, Neil Young

j. poet

Lillian Allen

Reggae, dub poetry

Born in Jamaica. Based in Toronto, Ontario, Canada.

Lillian Allen is a seminal figure in dub poetry, the reggae-based verse that was a forerunner of rap and kin to calypso in its political content. For the past 20 years she's become particularly well-known for live performances at festivals, where she reads from her many books of poetry (including *Women Do This Every Day,* 1993) and performs with an always-stellar band. An eloquent wordsmith, Allen never shrinks from controversy, but in her revolution everyone dances.

worth searching for: At this writing all of Allen's recordings are out of print Stateside, so grab whichever one you find. *Nothing but a Hero* 𝄞𝄞𝄞𝄞 (Redwood, 1991) is a children's album of energetic charm, with a great title track saluting Harriet Tubman ("You didn't just sit there on your bum bum bum/Waiting for your freedom to come come come") and a number of other songs to entertain and educate children and adults. *Revolutionary Tea Party* 𝄞𝄞𝄞𝄞 (Redwood, 1986) was named by *Ms.* magazine as a "Landmark Album of the Past 20 Years" in 1991. *Conditions Critical* 𝄞𝄞𝄞𝄞 (Redwood, 1988) is equally powerful.

influences:

◀ Sister Carol

▶ Lauryn Hill

see also: *Benjamin Zephaniah*

Pamela Murray Winters

Herb Alpert

"Ameriachi"

Born March 31, 1935, in Los Angeles, CA, USA. Based in Los Angeles, CA, USA.

Widely derided for stuffing the pop charts of the 1960s with a slew of Mexicali-lite instrumental hits, Alpert and his band the Tijuana Brass, in their own insidious way, actually did more than any other recording group to expose the Latin sound to legions of unsuspecting listeners the world over. From his very first chart success in 1962 (a rearrangement of Sol Lake's "Twinkle

Star" scored as a trumpet duet and rechristened "The Lonely Bull"), Alpert's easy-listening, south-of-the-border renditions of everything from Beatles to Bacharach quickly ingrained themselves into everything from TV game shows to motion picture soundtracks. Along with business partner Jerry Moss, Alpert produced and released each of these hits on his very own A&M Records label, which also launched several other Mexican-styled instrumental combos during the '60s, and would long reign as one of the most successful independent recording organizations in the world. In his own decidedly understated manner, Alpert to this day continues to take his trumpet into hitherto uncharted musical realms—recent collaborators include such diverse artists as South African great Hugh Masekela, pop-reggae hitmakers UB40, and dance-music superproducer Jimmy Jam. He's also got as good an impresario's ear as ever, now heading the label Almo Sounds and breaking visionary Latin acts—like Ozomatli—with the critical credibility that's eluded Alpert himself. And while he would be the first to admit he's hardly an innovator in league with, say, Quincy Jones, his Tijuana Brass sound remains an inescapable ingredient of soft jazz, Latin music . . . and, yes, TV game shows.

what to buy: From the overabundance of greatest hits packages available, *Foursider* 𝄞𝄞𝄞𝄞 (A&M, 1973, prod. Herb Alpert, Jerry Moss) and *Classics, Volume 20* 𝄞𝄞𝄞 (A&M, 1987, prod. various) together provide a suitable overview of Alpert's work, both with the Brass and beyond.

what to buy next: The classic original *Whipped Cream and Other Delights* 𝄞𝄞𝄞 (A&M, 1965, prod. Herb Alpert, Jerry Moss) is the quintessential Alpert: from its crossover wallop of covers ("Lemon Tree," the monster hit "A Taste of Honey," and even Leiber & Stoller's "Love Potion #9") to its sleeve (of a whipped-cream-drenched, finger-licking young bride), this album was no less than the *Sgt. Pepper* of the MOR set in its day.

the rest:

Lonely Bull 𝄞𝄞𝄞 (A&M, 1962)
Christmas Album 𝄞𝄞𝄞𝄞 (A&M, 1968)
Greatest Hits 𝄞𝄞𝄞𝄞 (A&M, 1970)
Greatest Hits, Volume Two 𝄞𝄞𝄞𝄞 (A&M, 1973)
Rise 𝄞𝄞𝄞 (A&M, 1979)
Classics, Volume One 𝄞𝄞𝄞𝄞 (A&M, 1987)
Keep Your Eye on Me 𝄞𝄞 (A&M, 1987)
North on South Street 𝄞𝄞 (A&M, 1991)
Midnight Sun 𝄞𝄞𝄞 (A&M, 1992)
Second Wind 𝄞𝄞 (Almo Sounds, 1996)
Passion Dance 𝄞𝄞𝄞 (Almo Sounds, 1997)
Coleccion Mi Historia 𝄞𝄞𝄞𝄞 (PolyGram Latino, 1997)
Herb Alpert and Colors N/A (Almo Sounds, 1999)

influences:

◀ Chet Baker, Louis Prima, Carlos Arruza

▶▶ Sergio Mendes, Baja Marimba Band, Chuck Mangione

see also: *Ozomatli*

Gary Pig Gold

Altan

Irish traditional

Formed 1987, in Gaoth Dobhair, County Donegal, Ireland. Based in Dublin, Ireland.

Mairéad Ní Mhaonaigh, fiddle, vocals; Frankie Kennedy (died 1994), flute, whistle, vocals; Ciarán Curran, bouzouki; Mark Kelly, guitar, vocals; Paul O'Shaughnessy, fiddle (1988–92); Cíarán Tourish, fiddle, whistle, vocals (1990–present); Dáithí Sproule, guitar, vocals (1992–present); Dermot Byrne, accordion (1994–present). (All members are from Ireland.)

As sure as Planxty and the Bothy Band were the Irish supergroups of the 1970s, Altan has dominated the traditional scene since the end of the 1980s. What is somewhat unusual about Altan is that its music is deeply rooted in the Donegal tradition, one that had received little attention before the band's commercial success popularized the Gaelic songs and Scottish-tinged highlands, strathspeys, and reels that comprise the unique Altan sound. From the start, the two main ingredients at the core of that sound were the dynamic interplay of the flute and fiddle played by husband and wife Frankie Kennedy and Mairéad Ní Mhaonaigh, and Ní Mhaonaigh's magical soprano. These were first captured on disc on the couple's 1983 *Ceol Aduaidh,* made at a time when few people had ever heard of Irish "Germans" (a type of Donegal barndance) or mazurkas. Ciarán Curran was one of the accompanists, and so was keyboardist Eithne Ní Bhraonáin, better known today as Enya. Indeed, Ní Mhaonaigh grew up in Gaoth Dobhair (Gweedore) in West Donegal, just a few miles away from Enya's family, whose band Clannad had started performing their brand of traditional music and jazz fusion in the early 1970s.

By the mid-1980s Ní Mhaonaigh and Kennedy had begun touring the United States with Curran and guitarist Mark Kelly, when they caught the attention of Green Linnet. As Dónal Lunny and Mícheál Ó Domhnaill had in the Bothy Band a decade earlier, Curran and Kelly were crafting highly inventive accompaniments for the foursome's instrumentals and songs. Their first album on the new label, released in 1987, was simply called *Altan* after Loch Altan, the name of a lake near Ní Mhaonaigh's home—as well as that of a reel she composed and played on the album. The title stuck and became the name of the band. By the time they recorded their next album, *Horse with a Heart,* in July 1988, the quartet had become a quintet with the addition of Dublin fiddle player Paul O'Shaughnessy, and the same ensemble made *The Red*

the bouzouki

Originally a Greek folk instrument belonging to the family of long-necked lutes, the bouzouki was introduced into Irish traditional music in the early 1970s by Johnny Moynihan, who was then a member of the band Sweeney's Men, and later of Planxty, De Dannan, and Arcady. Now made by local craftspeople, the bouzouki and its relations—alternately called octave mandolins, citterns, or (improperly) mandocellos, and typically strung with four or five courses—have collectively become the instrument of choice for accompanying traditional music throughout the British Isles, Ireland, and further afield. Early Irish exponents who contributed to its success include De Dannan's Alec Finn, who still plays a three-course, bowl-back Greek instrument; Andy Irvine, formerly with Sweeney's Men and Planxty, and now with Patrick Street; and Dónal Lunny, of Planxty and Bothy Band fame, who introduced the five-course *blarge* (i.e., "bouzouki large," covering a wider range) during the second Planxty period, and the electric solid-body bouzouki while a member of Moving Hearts. The instrument is generally tuned an octave below the mandolin (GDAE) or in related open tunings (GDAD, ADAD), and can be used to pick melodies or counter-melodies; strum chords; or play combinations of all of the above.

see also: Arcady, Bothy Band, De Dannan, Andy Irvine, Dónal Lunny, Moving Hearts, Patrick Street, Planxty, Sweeney's Men

—Philippe Varlet

Crow in 1990. Because O'Shaughnessy could not commit to constant touring, yet another musician, Inishowen fiddle player Cíarán Tourish, was added to the lineup, bringing his fiery playing into the mix on the band's highly successful 1992 *Harvest Storm.* Not too long after, O'Shaughnessy was obliged to leave the band for good. Donegal-born singer and guitar player Dáithí Sproule, a longtime friend of Ní Mhaonaigh and Kennedy who lives in Minneapolis, had been called upon on occasion to substitute for Mark Kelly; his status as a full-fledged member was made official on the band's next album, *Island Angel.*

That 1993 release was to be the band's last original recording for Green Linnet. These were trying times for Altan, most of all because of Frankie Kennedy's ongoing battle with cancer, one he ultimately lost in September 1994. By then, another long-time musical friend, accordionist Dermot Byrne, from Bridgend in North Donegal, had joined the ranks. Eventually, the band signed with Virgin and in 1996 released *Blackwater,* a rather disappointing mixture of somewhat uninspired instrumental medleys and overproduced vocal tracks, possibly a result of the transition to a major label. Their latest album, *Runaway Sunday,* is in a similar vein but with more exciting instrumental work. This work gives us hope that, to paraphrase a song they have done in eulogy of Kennedy, they will indeed carry on.

what to buy: Although not an Altan album strictly speaking, *Ceol Aduaidh* 𝄞𝄞𝄞𝄞 (Gael-Linn, 1983/Green Linnet, 1994, prod. Nicky Ryan) is the first commercial recording made by Mairéad Ní Mhaonaigh and Frankie Kennedy. However, the magical sound of their fiddle and flute duets and of Ní Mhaonaigh's singing, already accompanied by Ciarán Curran's cittern, are just as you hear them on later albums by the group. *Altan* 𝄞𝄞𝄞𝄞 (Green Linnet, 1987, prod. Dónal Lunny), the first official band album, is very similar in some ways, but the accompaniments and the song arrangements in particular have become quite sophisticated thanks to the addition of Mark Kelly's guitar. It is the magnificent *Horse with a Heart* 𝄞𝄞𝄞𝄞𝄞 (Green Linnet, 1989, prod. Phil Cunningham), though, that truly established Altan as a new force on the Irish traditional music scene. As with the Bothy Band's *1975* album, instrumental medleys such as the opening reel set "The Curlew" and the jig "The Road to Durham" were learned and repeated at many a session in the early 1990s. Other, quieter moments of the album, like Ní Mhaonaigh's achingly beautiful vocals on "The Lass of Glenshee" or Kennedy's flute solo on Tommy Peoples's air "An Feochán," are likely to be remembered as well. Throughout, the production by ex-Silly Wizard Phil Cunningham, who also contributes under-stated keyboards and whistle parts, is exemplary. Although recorded with the same lineup and later given a NAIRD award (or Indie Grammy), *The Red Crow* 𝄞𝄞𝄞 (Green Linnet, 1990, prod. P. J. Curtis) is not quite as strong an album as *Horse with a Heart*. Still, Ní Mhaonaigh's singing on the County Down song "The Flowers of Magherally" and on "Mallaí Chroich Shlí," as well as the instrumental renditions of Jerry Holland's now universally known reel "Brenda Stubbert's," Ní Mhaonaigh's own reel "The Red Crow," and the charming "Tommy Bhetty's Waltz," give the album its share of highlights. The addition to the lineup of yet another fiddler, in the person of Ciarán Tourish, could have been a mixed blessing, but the opening track of *Harvest Storm* 𝄞𝄞𝄞𝄞 (Green Linnet, 1992, prod. P.J. Curtis) dispels all doubts. The powerful sound of the band's three fiddles on the reel medley "Pretty Peg" is simply breathtaking. This is followed by one of the very best vocal tracks recorded by the band, the song "Dónal Agus Mórag,"

featuring beautiful guitar work by Kelly and haunting vocal harmonies. With the presence of guest musicians like Dónal Lunny, Hothouse Flowers' Liam o' Maonlaí, and ex–Stockton's Wing percussionist Tommy Hayes, there is some experimentation with new instrumental sounds, like that of the bass *bodhrán* (Irish frame drum) and the Australian *didgeridoo,* but P.J. Curtis's production keeps things nicely balanced. *Island Angel* 𝄞𝄞𝄞𝄞 (Green Linnet, 1993, prod. Brian Masterson, Altan) continues in the same vein. The band got around to recording some tunes Ní Mhaonaigh and Kennedy had been performing for years, like their friend Fintan Mc-Manus's reel, known to many as "The Guns of the Magnificent Seven." Ironically in view of sad events to come, Kennedy's flute playing is heard very strongly, as on his own reel "Humours of Andytown," or on the bittersweet "Island Angel," a piece composed for him by Ní Mhaonaigh. Ní Mhaonaigh's voice shines on "Bríd óg Ní Mháille" and the children's song "Dúlamán," with superb vocal harmonies that evoke the sound of Clannad (who recorded the song in 1976). There are two well-produced anthologies available, *The First Ten Years, 1986–1995* 𝄞𝄞𝄞𝄞 (Green Linnet, 1995, prod. Dónal Lunny) and *The Best of Altan* 𝄞𝄞𝄞𝄞 (Green Linnet, 1997, prod. various), both based on the band's first five albums. The latter includes a bonus CD containing eight tracks recorded live in Germany in 1989 by the *Horse with a Heart* lineup and first released as part of the collection *Ireland* 𝄞𝄞𝄞𝄞 (WDR, 1993, prod. Christian Scholze, Jean Trouillet, Jan Reichow). The sonics are quite good and one gets a chance to experience the strength of the band's live sound. The last track, a medley of reels concluding with the essential Donegal one "The Gravel Walk," has not been recorded on any of the band's studio albums.

what to buy next: The band's latest, *Runaway Sunday* 𝄞𝄞𝄞 (Virgin, 1997, prod. Altan, Alastair McMillan), is not quite in the same vein as Altan's early work but is a step up from the previous *Blackwater*. Obviously, the sound of Kennedy's flute is missed on the instrumental tracks. This time around, though, they include some mighty tunes, among them "John Doherty's Reels," the two Con Cassidy jigs in "Australian Waters," and a version of "Scots Mary" with a third part that came from Doherty as well. As on *Blackwater,* however, the song arrangements often sound suspiciously mainstream, as if Ní Mhaonaigh were being promoted as the next great Irish folk vocalist. Still, it is hard not to fall under the spell of her heartrending "Time Has Passed," seemingly an acknowledgment of the trauma caused by her husband's death and of what the last three years must have been like—"Time has passed/You are gone/Your tune is played/I must carry on."

what to avoid: *Blackwater* 𝄞𝄞 (Virgin, 1996, prod. Altan, Brian Masterson) was the band's first album after Frankie Kennedy's untimely death. What may have been a cathartic experience for the musicians did not necessarily translate into their best work.

Mairéad Ní Mhaonaigh of Altan

The instrumental tracks, while missing the unique tone color to which Kennedy's flute contributed, still feature some superior lead playing by Ní Mhaonaigh, Tourish, and new band member Dermot Byrne on accordion. However, the vocal tracks suffer from overproduction, with the addition of everything from Brendan Power's harmonica, to Dónal Lunny's popish keyboards, to a string quartet on "Blackwaterside." The album concludes on Ní Mhaonaigh's somber "Tune for Frankie."

the rest:
Altan ♫♫♫♪ (K-Tel, 1996)

worth searching for: The most devoted fans of Mairéad Ní Mhaonaigh's playing and singing may want to look for the first LP recorded by the Irish all-women band Macalla, *Mná na héireann (Women of Ireland)* ♫♫♫♫ (Gael-Linn, 1984, prod. Nicky Ryan), featuring, alongside Ní Mhaonaigh, Paul O'Shaughnessy's mother Pearl on fiddle, and a host of other terrific musicians.

influences:
◀◀ John Doherty, Con Cassidy, Proinsias ó Maonaigh, Tommy Peoples, Clannad, Planxty, the Bothy Band, Macalla

▶▶ Four Men and a Dog, Déanta, Dervish, Craobh Rua

see also: *Clannad, Phil Cunningham, John Doherty, Enya, Dónal Lunny, Tommy Peoples, Silly Wizard, Trian*

Philippe Varlet

Amampondo
Traditional folk
Formed 1981, in Cape Town, South Africa. Based in South Africa.

Dizu Zungulu Plaatjies, lead vocals, percussion, dance; Mzwandile Qotoyi, bass and piccolo marimba, African drums, percussion, dance; Simpiwe Matole, soprano marimba, vocals, dance, acrobatics; Michael "Nkululeku" Ludonga, drums, tenor marimba, vocals, dance; Mandla Lande, African drums, percussion, vocals, dance/acrobatics; Blackie Zandisile Mbizela, bass marimba, percussion, vocals; Lulu Lungiswa Plaatjies, lead and backing vocals, percussion, dance; Nondzondeleo Fancy Galada, lead and backing vocals, percussion, dance; Mantombi Matotiyane, lead and backing vocals; Mandosini Marquinei, lead and backing vocals, umrhubbe, isitolototolo, uhadi, dance; Nonhtle Sylvester, percussion, dance, vocals. (All members are from South Africa.)

This delightful 11-person ensemble from South Africa was founded by Dizu Plaatjies, who originally started it as a drums-and-marimba-based street-musician troupe. Eventually, though, a move up from the street into a concert venue elevated them even higher, to the world stage. An extended engagement at Johannesburg's exclusive Market Theater led to them being sent overseas as musical ambassadors of the Republic of South Africa. After returning and playing Nelson Mandela's 70th birth-

day concert, the group was banned from general public performance for four years by the dissident African National Congress (having hit two countries not participating in the anti-apartheid boycott while on tour). During this period, they taught music and performed in schools, until the ban was lifted with the intervention of Archbishop Desmond Tutu, only to be imposed again shortly thereafter. But with Nelson Mandela's release from prison in 1992, the ANC's edict was permanently lifted, and the group has since toured widely, both within and outside South Africa. Their self-titled debut release merges their ebullient vocal, marimba, and percussion sound with rhythmic traditions from elsewhere in Africa and the Americas.

what's available: *Drums for Tomorrow* ♫♫♫♫ (M.E.L.T. 2000, 1998, prod. B. Wassy), Amampondo's international debut, is a sensuous blend of layered percussion, joyful vocal harmonies, and melodic marimba textures as danceable as it is unique. With contemporary production by Cameroonian drummer Brice Wassy, the disc incorporates non-percussive instrumentation including trumpets and saxophones, and features many guest world-music notables including Brazilian percussionist Airto Moreira and Cuban guitarist Jose Luis Quintana.

worth searching for: The visual element is vital to Amampondo's performances, and the video *Africa 2000* (M.E.L.T. 2000 Video, 1998) affords a fuller experience of the contributions made by the troupe's dancers and acrobats.

solo outings:
Dizu Plaatjies and Mzwandile Qotoyi:
Qotoyi N/A (DZM)

influences:
◀◀ Ladysmith Black Mambazo, Juluka

see also: *Airto Moreira*

Michael Parrish

Amina
Arabic worldbeat
Born in Morocco. Based in Paris, France.

Amina Annabi, a Moroccan singer based in Paris, sings in Arabic, French, and English and mixes traditional Arabic rhythms, funk 'n' roll, romantic Parisian pop, and modern dance beats with the sounds of *saz* (lute), *ney* (flute), and electric guitar. As the child of immigrant parents, she scandalized the older generation with her rapid assimilation and choice of music as a career. She began her career singing backup and dancing on stage with various Franco-Arabic bands in Paris, and, after hooking up with producer Marlin Meissennier, began exploring a fusion of Arabic, French, and international pop. On "Belly Dance," for example (one of her biggest hits), the singer rode a sample taken from James Brown's "Cold Sweat" to deliver a sexy message that must have outraged the folks back home. Amina and Meissennier also collaborated with Senegal's Wasis Diop on "C'est le Dernier Qui a Parlé Qui a Raison (It Is the Last One Who Speaks Who Is Right)," the winner of the Eurovision Song Contest in 1991. Diop's music for the tune combined an Arabic melody with a hip-hop rhythm, Baroque string charts, and a French chord progression; an approach that's typical of much of the world fusion music coming out of the studios of Paris.

what's available: *Yalil* 🎵🎵🎵 (Island France, 1989, prod. Marlin Meissennier) is a slick yet soulful outing that showcases Amina's smooth, sensuous alto and Meissennier's understated production; there's a bit of R&B, some smooth Afropop (two tracks are co-produced by Wasis Diop), and lots of low-key Western pop. An American printing of *Yalil* exists, but for some reason it's missing "C'est le Dernier Qui a Parlé Qui a Raison (It Is the Last One Who Speaks Who Is Right)," one of the set's most affecting ballads.

influences:

◀◀ Umm Kulthum, Najat Aatabou

▶▶ Yosefa Dahari

see also: *Wasis Diop*

j. poet

Anam

Pan-Celtic

Formed 1992, in Dublin, Ireland. Based in Edinburgh, Scotland.

Brian Ó hEadra (Ireland), guitar, vocals; Myles Farrell (Ireland), bouzouki, (1992–95); Steve Larkin (Ireland), fiddle (departed; dates of service unknown); John Connolly (Ireland), button accordion (departed; dates of service unknown); Treasa Harkin (Ireland), button accordion (1995–present); Aimée Leonard (Orkney Islands, Scotland), bodhrán, vocals (1994–98); Neil Davey (Cornwall, England), bouzouki, mandolin (1997–present); Fiona MacKenzie (Scotland), vocals, bodhrán (1998–present); Anna Wendy Stevenson (Scotland), fiddle (1998–present).

The Best New Band at France's trend-setting Festival Inter-Celtique de Lorient in 1993 and, by way of numerous personnel changes, a virtually new band for each album since, Anam's stylistic survey of the Celtic world provides a fine welcome for listeners new to it, and a rich experience even for those more familiar with the terrain. Currently a quintet, the band toured North America in early 1999, and was completing a new album—with, to the surprise of few, two new members—as this book went to press.

what to buy: *Riptide* 🎵🎵🎵 (Green Linnet, 1998, prod. Calum Malcolm) is a fine showcase for the acoustic-based yet pop-oriented approach of this young Pan-Celtic band. Anam's sound is very smooth and easy on the ears; Ó hEadra and Leonard provide lush, polished vocal harmonies on several tracks that are surprisingly reminiscent of Simon & Garfunkel. And the group's instrumental selections, generally featuring accordion backed by mandolin, bouzouki, and percussion, also have a fairly soft texture. To be sure, though, what the band lacks in aggressiveness they *don't* lack in inventiveness. For example, on their arrangement of "An Blew Treghys," a selection of Cornish *gavottes* (a centuries-old traditional dance style), accordion plays the lead melody line while guitar, bouzouki, and *bodhrán* (Irish frame drum) kick in with lively syncopated rhythms. "Aird a Chuamhaing," a lovely Gaelic song of lament for the homeland from the emigrant's perspective written by Sean Mac Ambrois, starts off with more full vocal harmonies, and finishes up with a neat instrumental passage that has a vaguely Middle Eastern flavor. *First Footing* 🎵🎵🎵 (JVC, 1996, prod. Gerry O'Beirne), title notwithstanding, is Anam's third album, recorded by the trio of Ó hEadra, Leonard, and Harkin (augmented by several guest players). There's a jazzy version of "Sally Free and Easy" that's a bit reminiscent of Scottish folk-rockers Pentangle, but overall *First Footing* doesn't chart a lot of new territory; it's simply a collection of unaffected, well-played songs and instrumentals. It'll be interesting to see how the latest new members change Anam's sound, but as of now it is a group that folks previously not too involved with Celtic music can go to for a good first taste; those with more experience will enjoy Treasa Harkin's deft accordion work and the group's subtle incorporation of contemporary influences.

the rest:

Anam 🎵🎵🎵 (Ceirnini Anam, 1994)
Saoirse 🎵🎵🎵 (Ceirnini Anam, 1996)

worth searching for: It's a shame there probably won't be any more albums by Seelyhoo, Anam vocalist MacKenzie's former band, but the two that were made are a great mix of Scottish folk ballads and instrumentals with a strong touch of jazzy swing. *Leetera* 🎵🎵🎵🎵 (Greentrax, 1998, prod. Seelyhoo), Seelyhoo's second album, is more confident than its predecessor, *The First Caul* 🎵🎵🎵🎵 (Greentrax, 1995, prod. Seelyhoo, Roy Ashby, Adie Bolton), but both are recommended. MacKenzie is a fine Gaelic singer, and Jennifer Wrigley (fiddle) and Sandy Brechin (accordion) are bloody hot instrumentalists!

solo outings:

Fiona MacKenzie:

Camhanach 🎵🎵🎵 (Macmeanmna, 1997)

influences:

◀◀ Altan, the Bothy Band, Capercaillie, Pentangle, Simon & Garfunkel

▶▶ Dervish, Deaf Shepherd, Show of Hands

Ken Roseman

Robin Adnan Anders

Sufi percussion, shamanic drums, trance music, sacred world music
Born in Minnesota, USA. Based in McGregor, MN, USA.

Sufi Muslim master-drummer Robin Adnan Anders is a renowned soloist who believes that "a drum is a home therapy kit in a box." He is considered a virtuoso of percussion, being equally proficient on the rhythm instruments of numerous cultures including the *doumbek, tar, rik, tupan, tabla, dourbakee, muzhar, daire,* and more, as well as trap set and keyboards. His non-profit corporation Arts for Life (3208 W. Lake St., Ste. 84, Minneapolis, MN 55405) affirms the common spirit of humanity, using communications technology in an unprecedented way. Recognizing the need for the world to see itself as a global community, and also to put state-of-the-art technology to a positive use, Arts for Life organizes worldwide satellite and Internet-linked drum jams and celebration dances. Anders's other "world"ly excursions have included duties as percussionist with the Grammy-nominated 3 Mustaphas 3; drummer with the award-winning Boiled in Lead; member of the Electric Arab Orchestra with Egyptian pop singer Anoushka; and teacher of Sufi drumming around the world, in addition to his work in soundtracks (National Geographic's *The Great Barrier Reef*); video (the interactive drum piece *Voices of the Doumbek,* co-created in partnership with Interworld Music); the folk, rock, and world-music festival circuit (too prestigious to ignore but too numerous to mention); and concert appearances on public broadcasting services the world over. Most recently he hosted a contingent to the annual Sacred World Music Festival in Morocco, noting that "in many cultures, there is a belief that the sound of the drum actually rearranges matter and spirit on the atomic level—correcting imbalances in emotion by bringing into balance those feelings that require release. It is not surprising, then, that the drum has been the tool of the shaman for all recorded time."

what to buy: Seemingly destined to be a modern mystic, Anders reveals, "I began my career as a bell-ringing altar boy for the Catholic church. I guess you could say I spent a lot of my childhood immersed in ritual." This early interest in the otherworldly eventually led him to a Washington, D.C., workshop given by an Iraqi Sufi master. "It was a transcendent experience that changed my entire life. He helped me realize that my music could only be as good as the quality of my life. After that, I began exploring disciplines from all over the world like Zen and transcendental meditation, deliberately looking for inspiration and joy on a daily basis." This search for a very personal, deeply profound sense of sacred ecstasy permeates all of Anders's work and is most evident on *Omaiyo* 𝄞𝄞𝄞𝄞 (Candescence/Rykodisc, 1998, prod. Robin Adnan Anders), which boasts enough healing trances, sacred dances, and mystical rhythms to satisfy both straining body and yearning soul. His transfiguration of rhythm into devotion is positively spellbinding, highlighted by tracks such as "Tourra" and "Kadar," a 14-minute extended journey into altered consciousness led by tabla and clay-top dourbakee drum. *Omaiyo* starts out with gentle chanting voices, melodic percussion, and tuned instruments (saxophone, violin, guitar), then slowly removes the layers until only the sound of a Laotian jaw harp remains; it is nothing less than a masterpiece celebrating the union of spirit through percussion. (True to its purpose, proceeds from the album benefit the Sufi Foundation of America.)

what to buy next: The seeds for *Omaiyo* are sewn on Anders's debut solo effort, *Blue Buddha* 𝄞𝄞𝄞𝄞 (Interworld, 1993, prod. Robin Adnan Anders), another inspired alchemy of inner quest and celestial expression.

worth searching for: Robin Adnan Anders and Antonio H. Albarran are legendary in nomadic circles as the pashas of pulse, the sadus of swing, the bards of boom, the sultans of smoke—or, as it says on their debut duo CD cover, the Darbuki Kings. The Darbuki Kings' *Lawrence of Suburbia* 𝄞𝄞𝄞𝄞 (Darbuki Records, 1998, prod. Robin Adnan Anders, Matthew Davidson) may have been recorded with tongue firmly in cheek, but its seven syncopated selections display pyrotechnic playing and a wealth of sassily sensuous rhythms from all over the Middle East and North Africa. What started as a joke ends up as a treasure trove of sizzling instrumentals seriously worth seeking out.

influences:

◀◀ Hossam Ramzy, Fez Sacred World Music Festival performers

▶▶ Electric Arab Orchestra

PJ Birosik

Laurie Anderson

Experimental music and performance
Born June 5, 1947, in Chicago, IL, USA. Based in New York, NY, USA.

It's inaccurate to call Laurie Anderson a "world" artist because almost nobody can determine which world she's from. But Anderson, in her eclectic mix of rock 'n' roll, spoken-word poetry, strange unnamed sound effects, film, sculpture, slides, and mime, has occasionally used non-Western styles to great effect. "Monkey's Paw," one of her best songs, complements the vocalist's spooky, deep-chanting voice with South African guitarist Ray Phiri and bassist Bhakithi Khumalo (both of whom appear on this and several other songs from Anderson's *Strange Angels* as well as Paul Simon's *Graceland*). Anderson was elated to discover in the South African musicians a kindred, literally offbeat rhythmic sense that she had thought was just one more sound she alone could hear, and the album may be the epitome of her unostentatious but effective incorporation of "world" textures—an approach that goes to structural roots rather than settling for surface sonic garnish. Seeming satires of the latter kind of tourism appear regularly in her work as well (albeit with a wicked stylistic accuracy), from the pseudo-Scottish "Sweaters" and would-be Weimar "Example #22" on *Big Science,* to the approximately Japanese "Kokoku" on *Mr. Heartbreak,* to the Cold War–surplus Eastern European textures of *Bright Red,* not to mention her habit of having all or part of her wry monologues be spoken in various tongues. Anderson's other worldbeat influences are indirect: she taught Egyptian architecture in the early '70s at City College of New York, and her Tibetan near-death mountain-climbing experience inspired *Bright Red.* Still best known among pop audiences for her 1982 hit "O Superman," she continues to tour, displaying her spiky haircut, droll political wisdom, and bizarre special effects.

what to buy: For *Strange Angels* 𝄢𝄢𝄢𝄢 (Warner Bros., 1989, prod. Laurie Anderson, Roma Baran), Anderson stopped treating her voice with electronic effects and incorporated her deep tone into South African and other kinds of music. The experiment works: The monotone "Monkey's Paw" is as spooky as most hoodoo blues songs about mojos and black cat bones, and many Anderson fans consider this her best album.

what to buy next: Anderson's only hit, the #2 "O Superman," is on her debut *Big Science* 𝄢𝄢𝄢𝄢 (Warner Bros., 1982, prod. Laurie Anderson, Roma Baran), which is eclectic and jittery but satisfying even after more than 15 years. At four CDs, *United States Live* 𝄢𝄢𝄢 (Warner Bros., 1984, prod. Laurie Anderson, Roma Baran) is a big project even for devoted Anderson fans—especially given its emphasis on spoken-word material—but more than anything else it's hilarious; she could have made it in comedy if the music world hadn't reached her first. The *all* spoken-word disc *The Ugly One with the Jewels* 𝄢𝄢𝄢𝄢 (Warner Bros., 1995, prod. Laurie Anderson) belongs in this book by way of its subject matter; its bemused tales of Anderson's international travels soften culture clash with an affectionate skepticism and self-deprecation. If "world music" is diversity's soundtrack, this is its laughtrack.

what to avoid: *Mister Heartbreak* 𝄢𝄢 (Warner Bros., 1984, prod. various) is overproduced and contains none of the accessible charm of its predecessor, *Big Science.* Of course, that's just how many Anderson fans like it.

the rest:
Home of the Brave 𝄢𝄢𝄢 (Warner Bros., 1986)
Bright Red 𝄢𝄢𝄢 (Warner Bros., 1994)

worth searching for: One of Anderson's earliest recordings, 1978's "Song from America on the Move"—on which she uses a gadget called the harmonizer for the first time—shows up on the out-of-print *Cash Cow: The Best of Giorno Poetry Systems* 𝄢𝄢𝄢 (East Side Digital, 1993, prod. various). Other arty, deliberately non-mainstream artists here include William S. Burroughs (a friend and primary influence for Anderson), the punk band Hüsker Dü, Frank Zappa, Patti Smith, and ex-Blondie singer Debbie Harry.

influences:

◀◀ William S. Burroughs, Lenny Bruce, Captain Beefheart, Philip Glass, Frank Zappa, Lou Reed

▶▶ Talking Heads, Henry Rollins, Jello Biafra

Steve Knopper and Adam McGovern

Leny Andrade

Samba, jazz
Born in Rio de Janeiro, Brazil. Based in Rio de Janeiro, Brazil.

Singer Leny Andrade is a master. Affectionately called "Brazil's Ella Fitzgerald" and "the first lady of Brazilian jazz," Andrade's full, throaty voice and emotive delivery wrap themselves around classic and contemporary Brazilian music and jazz standards alike. Indeed, her unique phrasing and scat style do rival Ella's (with a Portuguese accent). Renowned and respected as a musician's singer well beyond the Brazilian jazz community, until recently Andrade had been largely undiscovered by U.S. listeners. That's changing, and although she has rarely recorded in English, she makes an emotional connection which itself makes translation unnecessary.

what's available: Andrade has been recording since 1961, so it's hard to believe that *Maiden Voyage* 𝄢𝄢𝄢𝄢 (Chesky, 1994, prod. David Chesky, Fred Hersch) is her first album made in the United States. Accompanied by Fred Hersch on piano (he also arranged), David Dunaway on bass, and Helio Schiavo on drums, Andrade delivers an eclectic selection—this time largely in English—ranging from evergreens like "This Can't Be Love," "I've Got You Under My Skin," and "My Funny Valentine" to Stevie Wonder's "Ribbon in the Sky" and Herbie Hancock's "Maiden Voyage." The sampling of Brazilian staples includes a tasty reading of Jobim's classic bossa nova "Dindi," and a new perspective on Luis Bonfá's familiar samba "Manha de Carnaval." On *Cartola 80 Anos* 𝄢𝄢𝄢𝄢 (1987, Pandisc), Andrade celebrates the songs of Brazilian samba composer Cartola in a simpatico pairing of singer and music.

influences:

◀◀ Luis Bonfá, Antonio Carlos Jobim, João Gilberto, Ella Fitzgerald

▶▶ Cassandra Wilson, Abbie Lincoln

Andrew BeDell

Leny Andrade

Maya Angelou

Calypso, poetry, spoken-word

Born Marguerite Johnson, April 4, 1928, in St. Louis, MO, USA. Based in Winston-Salem, NC, USA.

Decades before she read poetry at President Clinton's inauguration, Angelou made a pretty fair living as a calypso singer. Her gospel-trained voice, cute songs, and dramatic presentation made a powerful impact on the cabaret circuit. Working an extended gig at the Purple Onion in San Francisco, Angelou drew rave reviews and steady crowds of college kids who viewed calypso as the ultimate rhythmic folk music. Her success in clubs led to a featured role in the off-Broadway musical *Calypso Heat Wave,* as well as its 1957 film version. However, not many artists—outside of Harry Belafonte—were able to use calypso as a springboard to lasting Stateside fame. When the fad dissipated, Angelou began her career as a historian, screenwriter, poet, and character actress. She didn't abandon music, though. Angelou wrote songs for Sidney Poitier's *For the Love of Ivy,* as well as tunes for soul singer Roberta Flack. A Pulitzer Prize-nominated author, Angelou has found time to earn a Tony nomination for *Look Away,* and make well-received appearances in films such as *How to Make an American Quilt.* In recent times, she's better known as Dr. Maya Angelou—a professor at Wake Forest University.

what to buy: Angelou wrote nearly half the songs on *Miss Calypso* 𝄞𝄞𝄞 (Liberty, 1956/Scamp, 1996, reissue prod. Ashley Warren), a fine reproduction of her lone musical LP. The bongo-and-conga patterns perfectly accent Tommy Tedesco's guitar work, and Angelou's vocals are first-rate.

what to buy next: The best audio introduction to this artist's poetry can be found on *Black Pearls: The Poetry of Maya Angelou* 𝄞𝄞𝄞 (GWP, 1969/Rhino Word Beat, 1998, original prod. Paul Robinson, reissue prod. Elizabeth Pavone), which intertwines 33 atmospheric and streetwise recitations with occasional jazz interludes. Many tracks are informed by the Black Power sensibilities of the late '60s and are the basis for a number of her audiobooks.

what to avoid: Angelou's collaboration with Ashford and Simpson, *Been Found* 𝄞𝄞 (Ichiban, 1996, prod. Jimmy Simpson, Logan Anderson), attempts to blend the soul duo's sensual R&B with the famed poet's readings. The result is an uneasy mix that never quite jells or satisfies. For hardcore fans only.

best of the rest:

On the Pulse of Morning 𝄞𝄞𝄞𝄞 (Random House Audio Books, 1993)
I Know Why the Caged Bird Sings 𝄞𝄞𝄞𝄞 (Random House Audio Books, 1996)

worth searching for: Angelou contributes solid vocals to Herbie Mann's excellent jazz disc *Evolution of Mann* 𝄞𝄞𝄞𝄞 (Atlantic, 1960/Rhino, 1992, prod. Herbie Mann, Frank Socolow, Pat Rebilot). You completists out there should know that Angelou also makes guest appearances on *The Electric B. B. King—His Best* 𝄞𝄞𝄞𝄞 (MCA, 1968/1998, reissue prod. Andy McKaie), *Bobby Jones & New Life with the Nashville Super Choir* 𝄞𝄞𝄞 (Gospo-Centric, 1998, prod. Derrick Lee), and the eponymous debut of Branford Marsalis's genre-crossing band project *Buckshot LeFonque* 𝄞𝄞𝄞 (Columbia, 1994, prod. various).

influences:

◀◀ Harry Belafonte, Mahalia Jackson

▶▶ Cicely Tyson, Rita Dove, Roberta Flack

see also: *Herbie Mann*

Ken Burke

Anggun

Worldbeat, pop

Born Anggun Cipta Sasmi, April 29, 1974, in Djakarta, Indonesia. Based in Paris, France.

Thanks to world-music journalists, missionaries, multinational record labels, and (never forget) MTV, the music universe has shrunken in the two and a half decades Anggun has breathed air on the planet. Even a far-flung country with as strong and cen-turies-old a culture as Indonesia is caught up in the yin/yang pleasure principles of Western R&B, rock, and pop. Anggun was raised in a home full of paintings, sculptures, and a breakfast-to-bed soundtrack of all kinds of music (*gamelan* to classical to the Police). Encouraged by Moms and Pops, Anggun sang, danced, and played piano before she learned to tie her shoes. At the age of nine, Anggun made her recording debut with a self-penned children's album. Overnight, the precocious kidlet became a star. In 1986, Anggun hooked up with Ian Antonio, the biggest pro-ducer in Indonesian pop. Over the next seven years, the duo pro-duced six award-winning/mega-selling albums. Anggun had the Total Package: youth, beauty, hooky songs, rock-star charisma (Pat Benatar lungs, Jon Bon Jovi moves, and Chrissie Hynde cheek). At 19 she was flush—German sports car, big bank, and her own record company. But Anggun wanted more; she wanted the world. In 1995 the singer relocated to Paris. Falling in with the movers and shakers of the city's world-music underground, Anggun was inspired to create pop music more reflective of her culture. Within a year, she was introduced to hot Parisian pro-ducer/songwriter Erick Benzi (Celine Dion, Khaled, Johnny Hally-day). Over the next 18 months, the pair would collaborate and lay down tracks for the album that became her international debut. While *Snow on the Sahara* rocked the European and Asian charts, it barely registered on the Stateside Richter. Still, a series of U.S. club dates proved Anggun to be an engaging singer/pianist in the Kate Bush-esque vein of Sarah McLach-lan—and she's gotta have *something* left to look forward to!

what's available: Though it begins and ends smashingly (the Deep Forest-y bounce of the title tune, the achingly exalted cover of Bowie's "Life on Mars"), *Snow on the Sahara* ♪♪♪♪ (Epic, 1998, prod. Erick Benzi) is a frustratingly uneven blend of radio cheese ("Valparaiso," "Dream of Me"), Lilith Fair patchouli ("By the Moon," "A Rose in the Wind"), Peter Gabrielesque honey ("Secret of the Sea"), and Indo-soul-sistah buttah ("My Sensual Mind"). More international pop than world music for sure.

influences:

◄◄ Stevie Nicks, Kate Bush, Peter Gabriel, Everything but the Girl

▶▶ Ashley Maher, Sarah McLachlan, Alanis Morissette

Tom Terrell

Anitas Livs

World, blues

Formed 1993, in Stockholm, Sweden. Based in Stockholm, Sweden.

Anita Livstrand, leader, drums, percussion, vocals; Lise-Lottte Nore-lius, drums, percussion, vocals; Monica Äslund, drums, percussion, vocals. (All members are from Sweden.)

Anitas Livs is a trio of art-damaged Swedish female singer/per-cussionists. Founder Anita Livstrand has played with Don Cherry, Lise-Lotte Norelius plays African percussion and sam-plers, and Monica Äslund is also a dancer. The trio uses hand drumming, sampled sounds, and studio magic to make music that's both commercial and impenetrable. Strangely enough, their vocal sound owes much to the early blues stylings of Bessie Smith and Ma Rainey, while their percussion is heavily rooted in West African traditions. They also delve into Sami (formerly Laplander) *joiking* (a form of traditional *a cappella* singing), Indian *ragas,* and American gospel.

what's available: *World Wide Web* ♪♪♪♪ (Slask, 1995, prod. Michael Blair) opens with the Stones/Robert Johnson tune "No Expectations," then kicks into gear with a polyrhythmic Swedish walking tune and a couple of Sanskrit hymns. They also pull off an all-percussion arrangement of Sam Cooke's "GoodTimes," a Tibetan folk song, a dance from the Italian Re-naissance, and their own eclectic compositions with equal aplomb. The band's debut, *Ugh!* ♪♪♪♪ (Slask, 1993, prod. Ani-tas Lives, Thomas Mera Gartz), shows their eclectic vision al-ready in place with a bit of joiking, blues, and Gospel all given the big beat treatment.

influences:

◄◄ Don Cherry, Jan Johansson, Bessie Smith

j. poet

Annabouboula

Greek folk-rock

Formed 1986, in New York, NY, USA. Based in New York, NY, USA and Athens, Greece.

Anna Paidoussi, vocals; George Sempepos, guitar, synthesizer, drum programs; Chris Lawrence, drum programs, clarinet. (All members are from USA.)

The three principals behind Annabouboula (Greek for "all mixed up") got together when Lawrence, a Texan of Greek de-scent, returned to New York after a stint in Greece, where the Anglo-Americanisms of the Greek rock scene had caused him some distress. The trio got together to try playing a rock 'n' roll version of "In the Baths of Istanbul," an old Greek belly danc-ing tune. Sempepos and Paidoussi had both dabbled in Greek traditional music during their youth, and the latter already had a reputation as a *rembetiko* singer. Rembetiko, a mournful, minor-key music often called the Greek blues, became the foundation of Annabouboula—but having grown up with rock, funk, reggae, and the other world beats that filter into the un-conscious of all New Yorkers, this band's brand of rembetiko has an arty, experimental edge that sometimes makes them sound like a Greek-American Talking Heads.

Marc Anthony

what's available: The trio is still working on its conception with *In the Baths of Constantinople* 🎵🎵🎵 (Shanachie, 1990, prod. George Sempepos, Chris Lawrence), but the culture clash makes for some compelling music. Paidoussi's passionate vocals and the creative sparks her partners are tossing off make this sound inspired and inspiring. The rock approach gives the material a peculiar, edgy feel. On *Greek Fire* 🎵🎵🎵 (Shanachie, 1990, prod. George Sempepos, Chris Lawrence) Talking Heads are the obvious analogy; the Middle Eastern and Greek flavors are given a funky, rhythmically quirky spin that's straight out of New York's downtown club scene.

influences:

◀◀ Roza Eskenazi, Georges Dalaras, Talking Heads, Cargo Cult

j. poet

Marc Anthony

Salsa, Latin hip-hop

Born Marco Antonio Muniz, early 1970s, in Brooklyn, NY, USA. Based in New York, NY, USA.

Marc Anthony is one of the most commercially successful vo-calists in the history of salsa, with four out of four albums each reaching the top of the *Billboard* Latin charts, regularly sold-out concerts, and a 1999 Grammy for Best Tropical Latin Performance (for *Contra La Corriente*). To match his marketplace acceptance, Anthony has also acquired a reputation as the most artistically serious of the performers fueling the late-century Stateside "Latin Pop" phenomenon. Indeed, most Anglos first heard of him when he made entertainment headlines by post-poning an almost certain pop ascendancy to tackle the sophis-ticated realm of Broadway as a star of Paul Simon's musical *The Capeman*. It was an overall commercial and critical failure in which Anthony nonetheless gave an acclaimed performance, emerging with his reputation only enhanced. To be sure, Anthony is now "popping" on his own terms, though his professional roots are in more generally mainstream soil. In his early teens he and his sister sang on numerous demo tapes and commercial jingles; his first break as a songwriter came when his tune "Boy, I've Been Told" was covered by dance floor diva Sa-Fire. He subsequently sang backup vocals on Sa-Fire's self-titled debut album, and other discs by the Latin Rascals and Menudo. Anthony's own debut CD, *When the Night Is Over*, was more of a hip-hop effort than his later salsa-inspired recordings, though he is now a standard-bearer—in praise if not always practice—for more traditionally based music during a "crossover" boom that some Latino observers fear will lead to cultural homogenization. Anthony himself has kept his roots secure while keeping his options open, acting in such films as *Hackers, Big Night, The Substitute,* and *Bringing Out the Dead;* recording high-profile duets with Jennifer Lopez and Maxwell; singing (with Australian star Tina Arenas) the theme song for *The Mask of Zorro;* and, at this writing, working on a highly anticipated English-language album.

what to buy: Anthony's salsa expertise is reflected on his second release, *Otra Nota* 𝄢𝄢𝄢 (Soho, 1993, prod. Sergio George).

what to buy next: With guest appearances by Latin-jazz greats Tito Puente and Eddie Palmieri, Anthony's debut *When the Night Is Over* 𝄢𝄢𝄢 (Atlantic, 1991, prod. "Little" Louie Vega) is dance-inspiring hip-hop with a difference.

the rest:
Todo A Su Tiempo 𝄢𝄢𝄢 (Soho, 1995)
Contra La Corriente 𝄢𝄢𝄢 (Soho, 1997/RMM, 1998)

influences:
◀◀ Tito Puente, Eddie Palmieri, Jose Feliciano

▶▶ Sa-Fire, Tina Arenas

see also: *Jennifer Lopez*

Craig Harris and Adam McGovern

Anúna

Irish traditional and neo-traditional choral music
Formed in Dublin, Ireland. Based in Dublin, Ireland.

Variable membership led by director Michael McGlynn (born 1964, in Dublin, Ireland).

Anúna is a highly innovative choir masterminded by singer and composer Michael McGlynn, whose goal is to take a form normally associated almost exclusively with church music and bring it to a broader public. McGlynn has succeeded in exposing younger, nontraditional audiences to a dazzling variety of ancient, medieval, and modern choral music from Ireland (and beyond), performed with style and considerable discipline by his 16-member ensemble. In pursuing his vision, McGlynn displays a zeal and energy that remind one of the Chieftains' Paddy Moloney—and if his sense of marketing and eye for publicity prove to be half as sharp as Moloney's, the world may be hearing a lot more of Anúna in the years ahead.

Though many first encountered Anúna singing Bill Whelan's compositions for *Riverdance,* the phenomenal 1995 stage

the didgeridoo

Variously spelled "didgerido," "didjeridu," and "didjeridoo," and locally known as a *yadaki* or *yidaki* in addition to its most widely used spelling, the *didgeridoo*'s mysterious origins predate written history by many thousands of years; natives of Australia's Northern Territories claim its use for over 40,000! This ancient legacy contrasts an increasingly popular sound which is easily mistaken for that of a synthesizer. The traditional instrument is made from a tree branch that has been hollowed out by termites; in recent years, didgeridoos made from dried cactus branches, sliced pieces of wood, and plastic resin compounds have appeared. The "didg," as it is popularly dubbed, is a simple tube with no finger holes or fitted mouthpiece. Beeswax is used to coat the rim that touches the lips, and instruments vary substantially in length depending upon the diameter available and tone desired by the player. Sounds—continuous, hypnotic, pulsing drones; deep, rumbling vibrations; and sharp, ear-piercing blasts—are created by using a combination of lip movement, throat vocalization, and tongue manipulation. Unlike most Western woodwind players, the didg performer does not need to break the cycle of sound to breathe; masterful performers can breathe in through one nostril and out the other, ensuring a consistent pattern of sound for hours. The use of the didgeridoo is essential in Aboriginal spiritual ceremonies, many of which find several performers playing for eight- to 12-hour stretches without interruption. In some tribal clans of northern Australia only men are allowed to play the instrument, and the didgeridoos used in several traditional ceremonies are frequently destroyed afterward because of the enormous power invested in them. Didgeridoo instrumentals can be traditional compositions or improvisations, inspired by real-life events, deep emotions, or visions. Usually, didgeridoos are decorated by the craftsman with natural ochre and designs pertaining to the season and heritage of the individual instrument, though it is becoming more common for plain ones to be sold and customized by the purchaser.

PJ Birosik

show, video, and Grammy-winning album of which they were an integral part, the choir's origins go back much further. McGlynn, who by the mid-'80s had earned degrees in both English and music from University College Dublin, composed several pieces in diverse styles before deciding to specialize in choral and vocal works and, in 1987, founding the choir An Uaithne—named after the collective term for the three ancient forms of Irish music: *Suantraí* (lullaby), *Geantraí* (pleasant music), and *Goltraí* (lament). By 1992, the ensemble had opted for the simplified spelling (and similar pronunciation) of "Anúna," and were starting to incorporate some theatrical movements into their stage act, with McGlynn's identical twin brother John serving as production designer. McGlynn credits the voice of classical-rock institution Renaissance's Annie Haslam with providing the blueprint for the female sound of Anúna, and points out that Irish trad/rock legend Clannad's *Dulaman* and *Magical Ring* albums were also hugely influential on the choir's impressionistic, introspective style.

In 1993, Anúna's self-titled, largely *a cappella* debut album appeared. Its temporal span—including texts from the 6th, 9th, 12th, 17th, and 20th centuries—and great range of styles proved to be hallmarks of the Anúna sound. This was also the year they performed live as part of a much larger choral unit for Bill Whelan's ambitious *The Spirit of Mayo* suite. When Whelan was commissioned to come up with the "interval" (intermission) music for the 1994 Eurovision Song Contest spectacular, broadcast live from Dublin to a huge European TV audience, it was Anúna he picked for the resulting song and dance number called "Riverdance." Katie McMahon's sweet and haunting performance fronting the choir captivated all who saw it, and within a year a full stage show of the same name was born, with Anúna in the forefront on four sumptuous songs.

By the time *Riverdance* the show hit the boards, Anúna had already released their second album *Invocation* (featuring more instrumental accompaniment than its predecessor), but found themselves touring as part of the extraordinarily successful stage production for over a year, not only singing but also taking on some modest theatrical and dancing roles. This introduced them to new audiences in cultural capitol stops like London and New York, and also forced them to draw on a larger pool of singers, many of whom had day jobs they were not ready to quit. In a swirl of unprecedented opportunities and obstacles, Anúna managed to do their own live shows as the hectic *Riverdance* schedule would permit, and issued a third album, *Omnis*. Soloists including Katie McMahon, Monica Donlon, and Eimear Quinn played a prominent role in the Anúna sound at this point; Quinn also won the 1996 Eurovision Song Contest for Ireland with a solo outing called "The Voice."

With no end in sight for *Riverdance*—at this writing let alone at the time—McGlynn decided to pull Anúna out so the group could focus on its own goals. But while the choir officially became disassociated with the show, most of its vocalists (including McMahon) stayed on under the new name, the Riverdance Singers. This forced McGlynn to do some fancy footwork of his own to get the depleted ranks back up to the numbers and standards to which he had become accustomed. *Deep Dead Blue* was recorded and released in Ireland in 1996, titled after the rare Elvis Costello (words)/Bill Frisell (tune) composition which opens it and shows just how broad this group's range is, but the album has yet to receive a widespread release. *Omnis,* on the other hand—rerecorded the same year, with the new Anúna line-up—was issued internationally in 1997. One further album, *Behind the Closed Eye,* which sees the choir accompanied by the Ulster Orchestra, was released just in Ireland in 1997, and also awaits broader distribution.

McGlynn and the aforesaid Paddy Moloney have already crossed paths, the latter having invited Anúna to contribute to several recent Chieftains albums. They back Sting on *The Long Black Veil* (1995), and actress Brenda Fricker (reciting a Yeats poem) on the opening track to *Tears of Stone* (1999); their finest such collaboration is with Elvis Costello on *Long Journey Home* (1998).

After many years of researching the few extant fragments of Irish medieval music to be found in libraries and using them as starting points for arrangements and compositions, McGlynn has more recently taken to writing all-new songs with great vigor. He has also written a specially commissioned piece for saxophone and piano for Northern Irish classical saxophone virtuoso Gerard McChrystal, part of which can be found on McChystal's *Meeting Point* (Silva Classics, 1996). He has even written songs with country stars Rodney Crowell ("I'm Tied to You") and Delbert McClinton ("Waiting for You"). McGlynn's own "Dulaman" from *Omnis* has been recorded by the renowned all-male choir Chanticleer on their *Wondrous Love* (Teldec, 1997). Few artists have survived either reversals or success like McGlynn, and he seems fit to continue bringing new life to both ancient and current genres with an end that isn't near.

what to buy: *Invocation* ♪♪♪♪ (Celtic Heartbeat, 1995, prod. Michael McGlynn, Brian Masterson) is in many ways the most balanced of the group's three international releases. Declan Masterson's piping provides great drama on the opening "Rising of the Sun," Anne-Marie O'Farrell's harp sparkles on several other tracks, and Noel Eccles is as brilliant as ever on percussion—even the humble *bodhrán* (Irish frame drum). The material is quite varied, going back as far as the 6th century, but also including Thomas Moore's 19th-century "Last Rose of Summer" and McGlynn's own setting of "Lake Isle of Innisfree" by William Butler Yeats.

what to buy next: *Anúna ♫♫♫* (Celtic Heartbeat, 1993, prod. Michael McGlynn) is an impressive debut, with some startling juxtapositions between polytextual pieces drawing on ancient Irish, English, and Latin sources; new settings of medieval poems; church music displaying Byzantine influence; lullaby and unaccompanied "mouth music" from Scotland; and Irish songs ranging from Thomas Moore's "Silent O Moyle" to a revival of the humorous "An Poc ar Buile" (popularized by Seán Ó Riada and Ceoltoiri Chualann in the 1960s). A dozen of the 15 tracks on *Omnis ♫♫♫* (Celtic Heartbeat, 1997, prod. Michael McGlynn, Brian Masterson) are rerecordings of songs from the original Irish album of same name from 1995. 12th-century visionary Hildegard von Bingen is represented once more, as is the earlier St. Godric. McGlynn takes the solo spot himself on a stunning version of the beautiful Northern Irish love song "The Flower of Maherally."

worth searching for: Look for Anúna's performance of the song "Deep Dead Blue" on *Bespoke Songs, Lost Dogs, Detours & Rendezvous (Songs of Elvis Costello)* (Rhino, 1999), whose sleeve notes include Costello crediting McGlynn with helping him overcome his reluctance to master written musical notation. The choir can also be found on *Dawn of a New Century* (Phllips, 1999) by duo Secret Garden, who first came to fame by winning the Eurovision Song Contest for Norway in 1995, in Ireland, the year after the original "Riverdance" had been the interval music. This Windham Hill-sounding album also includes Irish accordionist Mairtín O'Connor, Scotland's Karen Matheson (of Capercaillie), and fellow-Norwegian jazz-guitar legend Terje Rypdal. French Celtic treasure Dan Ar Braz performs Anúna's "Diwanit Bugale" on the compilation *L'Imaginaire Irlandais—Suite* (Keltia Musique, 1997), while Eimear Quinn—with Anúna—performs his Eurovision entry from the year *he* won the contest.

influences:

◄ Machaut, Purcell, Debussy, Howells, Ligeti, Seán Ó Riada, Bill Whelan, David Bowie, Renaissance, Clannad, David Sylvian

►► Bill Whelan, Ars Nova, Ronan Hardiman, Medieval Babes

see also: *Bill Whelan*

John C. Falstaff

Apache Indian

Ragga, bhangra, jungle
Born 1968, in Hansworth, England. Based in Hansworth, England.

Apache Indian (his stage name; a play on his parents' Asian birthplace) fell in love with reggae at an early age, but he was also exposed to British pop and dance music, as well as the traditional Indian sounds his parents played at home. As *bhangra* (a form of Indian immigrant popular music based on a traditional homeland rhythm) began to take off, Apache joined other Asian DJs in forging a combination of reggae, bhangra, and pop. "It may sound odd, but I grew up hearing Jamaican patois in school, English on the radio, and Hindi at home." Apache Indian uses all three languages in his music, as well as beats drawn from roots reggae, bhangra, Jamaican dancehall and ragga, and jungle and other English club beats. His singles, including "Arranged Marriage" (a controversial attack on Indian tradition) and parables about safe sex, have made him one of Britain's leading Asian pop stars, and also driven his albums to the top of the charts in India. In the late 1990s, the majors gave up on pushing bhangra to a larger non-Indian audience, and Apache was dropped by Island. Apache created his own label, Sunset, and has released two albums for them, *Real People* and *Wild East.*

what's available: *No Reservations ♫♫♫* (Mango, 1993, prod. Simon & Diamond) is not particularly innovative, nor as interesting as Bally Sagoo's Asian/dancehall experiments, but the album does contain an interesting mix of bhangra, reggae, and dance club beats. *Make Way For the Indian ♫♫♫* (Island, 1993, prod. Simon & Diamond) became a monster seller behind the "Boom Shak a Lak" single, but it's more formulaic and less interesting than *No Reservations. Wild East ♫♫♫* (Sunset, 1998) features remixes of the best tracks on *Real People,* a frenzied mix of bhangra, Bengali folk, techno, house, and dancehall.

influences:

◄ Alaap, Bally Sagoo, Bob Marley, Super Cat, Shabba Ranks

j. poet

Dan Ar Braz /Dan Ar Bras

Celtic
Born in Brittany, France. Based in Brittany, France.

A melodic and expressive approach to acoustic and electric guitar has made Dan Ar Braz (a.k.a. Ar Bras) one of the most influential musicians from Brittany, the Celtic area of France. First prominent in Cliff Richards's early-'60s pop/rock band the Shadows, Ar Braz went on to inspire scores of Celtic guitarists when he collaborated with Celtic harp-, bagpipe-, and flute-player Alan Stivell between 1967 and 1976, recording such landmark albums as 1972's *The Renaissance of the Celtic Harp.* Following the breakup of Stivell's band, Ar Braz continued to explore the emotional qualities of his instrument. Although he temporarily replaced Richard Thompson in English folk-rock colossus Fairport Convention, Ar Braz remained with the band for only six months and failed to produce any recordings (he does appear, however, on their 1998 live retrospective *The Cro-*

predy Box). He formed a tradition-rooted acoustic/electric Celtic band in 1977, but made his next significant mark as a solo artist in the '80s. Beginning his full switch to acoustic guitar, Ar Braz produced a series of atmospheric solo recordings including the declaratorily titled *Acoustic* in 1985, and *Music for the Silences to Come* the following year. Ar Braz's work in the '90s has included two groundbreaking albums with his 50-piece band L'Heritage Des Celtes: Their self-titled 1994 studio debut, recorded at U2's Windmill Lane facility in Dublin, established Ar Braz as a superstar in France, with the excitement of the ensemble's live shows captured that same year on the album *En Concert*. It was an even busier time for Ar Braz than this implies; he also reunited with Stivell for 1994's *Again*.

what to buy: A revelation to his fans and a breakthrough for the artist himself, Ar Braz's first attempt at an all-acoustic album, the sensibly named *Acoustic* 𝄢𝄢𝄢𝄢 (Green Linnet, 1985, prod. Dan Ar Braz), is a memorable outing accompanied by keyboard player Benoit Wildemann. *Music for the Silences to Come* 𝄢𝄢𝄢𝄢 (Keltia Musique, 1986, prod. Dan Ar Braz) continues Ar Braz's aural exploration and personal expression of acoustic Celtic music, this time complemented by saxophonist Daniel Paboeuf.

the rest:
Douar Nevez 𝄢𝄢𝄢𝄢 (Hexagone, 1977)
Allez Dire à la Ville 𝄢𝄢𝄢𝄢 (Hexagone, 1978)
The Earth's Lament 𝄢𝄢𝄢𝄢 (Hexagone, 1979)
Borders of Salt 𝄢𝄢𝄢𝄢 (Keltia Musique, 1992)
Les Iles de la Memoire 𝄢𝄢𝄢𝄢 (Keltia Musique, 1992)
Reve de Siam 𝄢𝄢𝄢𝄢 (Keltia Musique, 1992)
Xavier Grall Chante Por Dan Ar Braz 𝄢𝄢𝄢𝄢 (Keltia Musique, 1992)
En Concert 𝄢𝄢𝄢𝄢 (Keltia Musique, 1994)
L'Heritage Des Celtes 𝄢𝄢𝄢𝄢 (Keltia Musique, 1994)
Septembre Blue 𝄢𝄢𝄢𝄢 (Keltia Musique, 1994)
Songs 𝄢𝄢𝄢𝄢 (Keltia Musique, 1994)
Theme for the Green Lands 𝄢𝄢𝄢𝄢 (Keltia Musique, 1994)
Kindred Spirit 𝄢𝄢𝄢𝄢 (Keltia Musique, 1995)

influences:
◄◄ Richard Thompson, John Renbourn, Bert Jansch, Dick Gaughan

►► Pierre Bensusan, Gabriel Yacoub, Malicorne

see also: *Fairport Convention, Maddy Prior, Alan Stivell*

Craig Harris

Ar Log
Traditional Celtic
Formed 1976, in Wales. Based in Wales.

Varying lineup over more than two decades, including original members David Burns, mandolin, guitar, bodhrán, vocals; Ialo Jones, fiddle, recorder; Dayfydd Roberts, triple harp, flute; Gwyndof Roberts, knee harp. (All members are from Wales.)

Ar Log is dedicated to preserving and expanding the musical traditions of Wales. Singing in their native language and accompanying themselves on traditional instruments like the triple harp and knee harp, the group has brought a fresh vision to their centuries-old repertoire. Ar Log, whose name translates as "on hire," originally came together to represent Wales at a Celtic music festival. In the early 1980s, they backed Welsh singer-songwriter, label founder, folk preservationist, and nationalist politician Dafydd Iwan on his *Rhwng Hwyl A Thaith* and *Yma O Hyd* albums (released in 1982 and 1983, respectively, and reissued in part on Iwan's *Yma O Hyd* in 1993). Although Ar Log has slowed down its touring and experienced numerous personnel changes through the years, the group continues to perform periodically in its native country.

what to buy: *Ar Log II* 𝄢𝄢𝄢 (Dingles, 1982, prod. Ar Log) captures the Welsh band at their best, harmonizing in their native language and showcasing their uplifting instrumental talents. Their technical skills are spotlighted even more on the all-instrumental album *Meillonen* 𝄢𝄢𝄢 (Dingles, 1982, prod. Ar Log).

the rest:
Ar Log 𝄢𝄢𝄢 (Dingles, 1978)
Ar Log III 𝄢𝄢𝄢 (Dingles, 1982)
Pedawar 𝄢𝄢𝄢 (Ar Log, 1985)
Ar Log V 𝄢𝄢𝄢 (Sain, 1988)

influences:
◄◄ Welsh tradition, Dafydd Iwan

►► Merc Stevens, Cilmeri, Robin Huw Bowen

see also: *Crasdant*

Craig Harris

Arawak Mountain Singers
Powwow drum
Formed 1987, in Staten Island, NY, USA. Based in Staten Island, NY, USA.

Al Bold Eagle, drum, vocals; Louie Tureyguard, drum keeper, drum, vocals; Jorge Baracutey, drum, vocals; Cliff Standing Bear, drum, vocals; Tonee Robles, drum, vocals; Lizzy Sarobey, vocals; Joan Henry, vocals; Tree Ceibo Rivas, drum, vocals; Ray Elk Silva, drum, vocals. (All members are from USA.)

Al Bold Eagle, leader and head drummer of the Arawak Mountain Singers, is a traditional man who lives in New York City. The Arawaks, traders known for their gold, silver, and turquoise, originated in the Amazon basin, ranged throughout the Caribbean, and established outposts as far north as Virginia. Bold Eagle is a drum man, singer, and historian; his group sings songs of northern and southern plains tribes including the Comanche, Kiowa, Tonka, and Otoe. "The spirit of a tree once told us; 'Hollow a piece of me out and make an instrument. With this instrument you will liven the hearts of those that are sick; those that are sad will be happy. The ground will tremble when you beat on this instrument, this drum. It is the heartbeat of your nation. Take care of it and it will take care of you.' That is what we believe."

Bold Eagle says the first Arawak drums were hollow logs with tongues cut in their sides, similar to the slit drums Africans were playing at about the same time; some so big it took four people to play them. "We also use circle drums—the rim was a single piece of hollowed-out cedar, covered with a skin of cowhide, deer, or buffalo. If you're going to use it for healing or spiritual purposes, you paint a design on the skin to put good medicine into it. The drum is female, the drumstick is male, and the throbbing sound the drum makes is the heartbeat of the nation. Every time we set up the drum to play, each person honors the drum with a spiritual herb like sage or tobacco. When we're not playing, the drum is covered with a blanket and carried away. If we see a drum left unattended, we can ask an elder or a medicine man to take the drum away from the owner, that's how sacred the drum is."

White people often say that Native American drumming and chanting sounds monotonous, but Bold Eagle says that Native music has its own logic. Since the songs come to humans from the spirit world, they never change, and improvisation is not encouraged. "Our drumming isn't as diverse as African drumming; there are no cuts [breaks], but the drumming gets louder, faster, or slower, and every song has a meaning and origin. Songs have a spirit, the way a person has a spirit." Despite 500 years of colonial interference, most Native American drum styles have remained pure. "There are songs that were sung before Columbus was born that are still being sung today, passed down in an unbroken oral chain for generations. Before the whites came, my people were living in Boriken (Puerto Rico) and the lands now known as Florida, Venezuela, Guyana, and Brazil. As a result our music has African and Afro-Caribbean influences, with songs sung in English, Spanish, and Native tongues. Africans and Native people mixed all over the Caribbean to create rhythms like the samba, *plena, bomba,* and *guajira;* the original music of the land we call America."

what's available: On *Honoring the Ancient Ones* 🎵🎵🎵 (SOAR, 1994, prod. Al Bold Eagle) there is one song partially in English—"Soldier Boy Fought Hard"—which makes it easier for non-Native ears to track the melody. There is also an instrumental—"Cry of the Manati"—on which Bold Eagle recreates the drumming style the Arawaks may have been playing a hundred years ago; part Native, part Latin, part African. *Feel the*

Thunder 🎵🎵🎵 (SOAR, 1995, prod. Arawak Mountain Singers) is another rewarding outing.

influences:

◀◀ Rocky Boy Singers, Black Lodge Singers, White Eagle Singers

▶▶ Otter Trail

j. poet

Arcady

Irish traditional and contemporary
Formed 1988, in Dublin, Ireland. Based in Ireland.

Johnny Moynihan, bodhrán; Frances Black, vocals (1988–94); Niamh Parsons, vocals (1994–97); Patsy Broderick, piano; Brendan Larrisey, fiddle; Nicolas Quemenar, guitar, flute, whistle; Jackie Daly, accordion (1990–95); Conor Keane, accordion (1995–present). (All members are from Ireland.)

Named for the land in ancient Greece where poets and artists came together, the group Arcady does indeed represent the coming together of many of Ireland's top traditional musicians. Anchored by founder Johnny Moynihan's *bodhrán* (Irish frame drum) and the outstanding piano playing of the underrated Patsy Broderick, Arcady plays a rhythmic, straightforward Irish style with a few world music elements (harmonica and Australian *didgeridoo* among them) thrown in for spice. Like Moynihan's earlier band De Dannan, Arcady features English-language songs by talented, accessible vocalists such as Frances Black and Niamh (pronounced "Neeve") Parsons. A constant fixture on the concert scene, Arcady has managed to fashion an identifiable sound despite a tremendous amount of turnover in personnel. Sharon Shannon, Sean Keane, Cathal Hayden, and Tommy McCarthy are a few of the people who have briefly passed through the band during its history.

what's available: *Many Happy Returns* 🎵🎵🎵🎵 (Shanachie, 1995, prod. Johnny McDonough) is a tribute to the tunes and songs that form the backbone of traditional Irish music. Each of the musicians knows this material inside and out from years of playing it in sessions and competitions, and they give it their all in the studio. The band's adventuresome yet tasteful arrangements, using nontraditional instruments like didgeridoo and harmonica, keep these well-known pieces sounding fresh and contemporary. Accordion player Conor Keane in particular must be singled out for a driving, exuberant style that keeps the energy level high from the album's very first tune. The vocals are handled by Niamh Parsons, whose husky, Dolores Keane–like alto breathes new life into songs that have been sung literally millions of times. Anyone wishing to play Irish music would receive a crash course in the standard repertoire with a few listens to this album. *After the Ball* 🎵🎵🎵

(Shanachie, 1991, prod. P. J. Curtis) is Arcady's debut album: a solid, pleasant collection of traditional and contemporary material from Ireland and beyond. Singer Frances Black brings her sweet voice to pop-folk songs by Bill Staines, Stan Rogers, Andy Stewart, and Dan Seals, and the instrumentalists attack a variety of tunes from Ireland, Brittany, and the U.S. The playing, while always solid, lacks a little of the fire that shines so brilliantly on *Many Happy Returns*.

influences:

◄ De Dannan, Planxty, Joe Cooley

► Sharon Shannon, Four Men and a Dog

see also: *Frances Black, the Black Family, Jackie Daly, De Dannan, Four Men & a Dog, Dolores Keane, Niamh Parsons, Planxty, Sharon Shannon, Sweeney's Men*

Tony Ziselberger

Alphonse "Bois Sec" Ardoin

Creole, Cajun

Born November 16, 1927, in Duralde, LA, USA. Based in Duralde, LA, USA.

"Bois Sec" (translation: "dry wood") grew up playing triangle behind his uncle, the legendary Creole accordionist Amédée Ardoin. He rapidly learned to play accordion himself, and teamed up with fiddler Canray Fontenot. It was a partnership that would survive until Fontenot's death in 1995; across its long heyday their duets of fiddle and accordion would come to be augmented by Bois Sec's sons and, eventually, grandsons. The sound was always funky and loose, with a great beat and an engaging originality, and the syncopated accordion of Ardoin and soaring fiddle of Fontenot were its heart and soul. Bois Sec continues to play and to influence whole new generations of young Cajun and zydeco musicians; his 1998 collaboration with Balfa Toujours shows him alive and well and playing as spryly as ever into his eighth decade of life.

what to buy: *The Ardoin Family Band with Dewey Balfa: A Couple of Cajuns* ♫♫♫♫ (Sonet, 1987, prod. Samuel Charters) is the best recording of the Ardoin Family band. They swing and swoop around Bois Sec and guest fiddler Dewey Balfa; Lawrence Ardoin kicks the drums the way his son Sean does now in Double Clutchin'; and Russell Ardoin's bass bounces off the beat like a superball. Balfa gives some of his most blues-inspired playing with this group, showing a looser, funkier side than his own recordings reveal. Bois Sec is the focus that holds it all together, with the gentle croak of his singing and an accordion style that constantly shifts beats and accents.

what to buy next: *Les Blues du Bayou* ♫♫♫♫ (Melodeon, 1967, prod. Richard Spottswood) is just duets between Canray and

Bois Sec, with triangle contributed by Revon Reed or Isom Fontenot. Recorded at a studio in Washington, D.C., fresh from an appearance at the Newport Folk Festival, the playing is crisp and marvelous. The pair played with a loose kind of telepathy, in which both musicians knew the melody for the tune but rarely played it, preferring to play around it. Fontenot's fiddle, gliding high, cries over the bouncing, rhythmic playing of Bois Sec. The compilation *Les Haricots Sont Pas Salés: Legendary Masters of Cajun and Creole Music* ♫♫♫♫ (Cinq Planetes, 1998, prod. various) includes classic performances by Ardoin and Fontenot backed by the Balfa Brothers. As if to accentuate Bois Sec's influence on entire dynasties of other players in his genre, *Allons Danser* ♫♫♫♫ (Rounder, 1998) sees him backed by the Balfas' next generation Balfa Toujours, with Steve Riley (on drums) further fleshing out the all-star Cajun cast paying tribute and keeping pace.

the rest:

Louisiana Cajun French Music from the Southwest Prairies, Vol. 2: 1964–1967 ♫♫♫♫♪ (Rounder, 1976/1985)

worth searching for: *La Musique Creole* ♫♫♫♫ (Arhoolie, 1997, prod. Chris Strachwitz) features recordings of the Ardoin Family band from Morris Ardoin's Cowboy Club, and more duets by Canray and Bois Sec made in 1970 and '71. There is almost no overlap with the above recordings, and even when there is you'll barely notice; these guys never play a tune the same way twice.

influences:

◄ Amédée Ardoin, Dennis McGee

► Chris Ardoin, Keith Frank, Geno Delafose, Tasso, Beausoleil

see also: *Amédée Ardoin, Chris Ardoin & Double Clutchin', Balfa Brothers, Balfa Toujours, Canray Fontenot, Steve Riley & the Mamou Playboys*

Jared Snyder

Amédée Ardoin

Cajun

Born c. 1896, in L'Anse Rougeau, LA, USA. Died November 4, 1941, in Pineville, LA, USA.

The heart and soul of traditional Cajun music is Amédée Ardoin, an artist who can be considered the true father of modern Cajun and zydeco music alike. His virtuoso accordion playing and emotionally charged singing continues to be highly respected by both black and white musicians. He refined and adapted traditional Cajun and Creole songs that had been played on the fiddle or the diatonic accordion. His music was a major influence on both Clifton Chenier and Iry Lejeune, as well as the primary influence on the "bluesy" fiddling and singing of Michael Doucet and the accordion of Marc Savoy.

Alphonse "Bois Sec" Ardoin

Born the seventh of seven brothers, he was raised in L'Anse Rougeau near the town of Basile, where he became friends with fellow accordionist Adam Fontenot (father of Canray). He met Cajun fiddler Dennis McGee while sharecropping in 1921, and the two rapidly became extremely popular at dances in the Eunice area. Their partnership eventually led to three seminal recording sessions. These, combined with Ardoin's final session, form a canon for modern Cajun and zydeco music in the same way the recordings of Robert Johnson do for the blues or the Bristol Sessions do for country music. His last years were spent at the state sanitarium in Pineville, where he had been committed after what some sources say was a brutal racist beating, while others claim he was poisoned by a jealous musician.

what to buy: *I'm Never Comin' Back: The Roots of Zydeco* 𝄞𝄞𝄞𝄞 (Arhoolie, 1995, prod. Chris Strachwitz) contains all of Ardoin's second, most of his third, and all of his fourth recording sessions. It's full of classic performances, but the sound is somewhat harsh for those not used to it. "Les Blues de Crowley," which is reissued for the first time on this CD, is clearly the first zydeco recording, just needing some juiced-up bass and drums behind it to make it a current dance hall hit. Almost every song on this CD has been rehashed and rerecorded by other Cajun and Creole performers.

what to buy next: The compilation *Cajun Music: Fais Do-Do* 𝄞𝄞𝄞𝄞𝄞 (Columbia, 1994, prod. Lawrence Cohn) contains the six truly classic recordings of Ardoin and McGee that are not found on the Arhoolie release, and represents Ardoin at his best. All of these songs continue to be found in the repertoire of Cajun and zydeco bands throughout Louisiana, including "Eunice Two-Step," "Quoi Faire," and "Madame Atchen."

worth searching for: *Louisiana Cajun Music, Vol. 6: Amade Ardoin: The First Black Zydeco Recording Artist* 𝄞𝄞𝄞𝄞 (Old Timey, 1983, prod. Chris Strachwitz) is a fine collection. (In the credits of his early recordings, Ardoin's first name was spelled "Amade.") An earlier, vinyl compilation of Ardoin can also be found on Old Timey, and covers the recordings on *Cajun Music: Fais Do-Do* and many of the tunes on *I'm Never Comin' Back: The Roots of Zydeco*.

influences:

◄◄ Dennis McGee, Joe Falcon

►► Clifton Chenier, Alphonse "Bois Sec" Ardoin, Michael Doucet, Iry LeJeune

see also: *Nathan Abshire, Alphonse "Bois Sec" Ardoin, Chris Ardoin & Double Clutchin', Beausoleil, Clifton Chenier, Canray Fontenot, Iry Lejeune, Savoy-Doucet Cajun Band*

Jared Snyder

Chris Ardoin & Double Clutchin'

Zydeco

Formed 1995, in Lake Charles, LA, USA. Based in Lake Charles, LA, USA.

Chris Ardoin, one-row accordion, three-row accordion, vocals; Sean Ardoin, drums, vocals; Tammy Ledet, frattoir, vocals; Derek Dee Greenwood, bass, vocals; Bobby Broussard, guitar; Nathan Fontenot, guitar.

Chris and Sean Ardoin have one serious zydeco pedigree. They are sons of zydeco musician Lawrence "Black" Ardoin, grandsons of the celebrated Alphonse "Bois Sec" Ardoin, and great grandnephews of the legendary Amédée Ardoin. They are also part of a very young generation of new zydeco players who are reshaping the music based on their strong family traditions and contemporary musical influences. They can mix together funk and hip-hop with a Creole tinge, or play revved-up versions of traditional two-steps and waltzes. At this writing, Chris was only 16 years old, with four albums already under his belt. As Steve Riley's done with Cajun music, the Ardoin brothers have added three-part vocal harmonies to zydeco, and that's just for starters. In every way, theirs is a new and fresh approach to zydeco that still has roots back out in the countryside.

what to buy: In the first minute of "Lake Charles Connection" on *Gon' Be Jus' Fine* 𝄞𝄞𝄞𝄞 (Rounder, 1997, prod. Scott Billington), you get all the elements that make up the Double Clutchin' sound: the double bass drum beat as popularized by Beau Jocque, mixed with the slinky bass guitar and chippy minor-key rhythm guitar, the virtuoso accordion playing of Chris Ardoin, and the clean three-part harmonies. The vocals are mostly in English, with the constant interjections and asides sometimes straying to French. This sound seems to work best on the aforesaid song, "When I'm Dead and Gone," and "I Don't Want What I Can't Keep." The family tradition is represented by the frantic "Ardoin Two Step" and by Sean's reading of his grandfather's "Dimanche Apres Midi." A solid and different-sounding record.

what to buy next: The Ardoin brothers continue to grow and develop on *Turn the Page* 𝄞𝄞𝄞𝄞 (Rounder, 1998, prod. Scott Billington). You can hear more of a rap and R&B influence than on *Gon' Be Jus' Fine* ; meanwhile they play Canray Fontenot's "Barres de la Prison," a blues waltz that Fontentot performed for 50 years with their grandfather Bois Sec! There's no shortage of dance grooves on this record, though maybe because it follows such an ambitious predecessor it doesn't seem quite as fresh or innovative, just smoother and more polished.

the rest:

That's Da Lick 𝄞𝄞𝄞 (Maison De Soul, 1995)

worth searching for: *Lick It Up!* ♫♫♫ (Maison de Soul, 1995, prod. Lawrence Ardoin) features the early sound of a very young—or should we say younger—Chris Ardoin. The also-youthful zydeco band with him shows they can bust a groove with the best of their seniors.

influences:

◄◄ Alphonse "Bois Sec" Ardoin, Beau Jocque, Canray Fontenot

►► Keith Frank, Geno Delafose

see also: *Alphonse "Bois Sec" Ardoin, Amédée Ardoin*

Jared Snyder

Frankie Armstrong

English folk

Born in Workington, Cumbria, England. Based in England.

Frankie Armstrong is one of the classic voices of the English folk-song revival. A social worker who has aided the blind and the addicted, Armstrong brings a strong sense of justice and concern for humanity to the songs she sings. She came to the attention of the listening public in 1966, on two songs from *The Bird in the Bush,* a thematic album compiled by the leading folklorist of the revival, A. L. Lloyd. During the same period, she joined the Critics Group, a collective of young singers that gathered to discuss and explore folksong and the revival, under the direction of Ewan MacColl. She released several albums with the Critics Group during the late 1960s, and in 1971 began her career as a solo artist. In 1975, Lloyd wrote that Armstrong was "the outstanding woman singer in the folk revival," no small praise from such an eminent critic and authority. Lloyd also pointed out that Armstrong's great strength lies in her combination of "a distinctive approach to traditional ballads with a discriminating ear for contemporary songs." Unfortunately, the numerous solo albums she recorded during the 1970s and '80s, all of which are marvelous examples of these talents, are out of print, though plans are afoot to reissue at least one of them. During the late '80s and early '90s, Armstrong concentrated on areas of life other than her recording career. She was, for example, running singing workshops at which she helped others liberate their own voices. Therefore, the only CD release during this period was an album that she shared with Dave Van Ronk. During the late '90s, however, she decided to strike a different balance between teaching and recording, which led to an outpouring of three releases in a six-month period during late 1996 and early '97.

what to buy: *Till the Grass O'ergrew the Corn* ♫♫♫♫ (Fellside, 1996, prod. Paul Adams, Frankie Armstrong) features Armstrong singing her favorite traditional British ballads. Accompanied on many tracks by John Kirkpatrick on accordion or melodeon, and on a few by Maddy Prior's vocal harmonies, Armstrong treats the listener to 12 magical and mysterious ballads from the "Child Ballad" canon of earlier folk preservationist Francis Child. Her voice on this recent release is as strong as ever, and the hairs on the back of one's neck are apt to stand up while listening to her sing these old songs. Most of Armstrong's ballads deal with relations between the sexes, from husbands rescuing their kidnapped wives ("Young Orphy") to incest and murder between brothers and sisters ("Fair Lizzy"). The most powerful of them are the ones she sings *a cappella,* including "Lady Diamond" and the 11-minute "Child Waters," whose hair-raisingly cruel storylines are enhanced by the starkness of unaccompanied performance. Similarly frightening are the ballads "The Well below the Valley," a story of incest and rape in which the victim takes the blame, sung by Armstrong with harmony vocals by Prior; and "Clerk Colvin," the story of a two-timing rogue whose mermaid lover does him in, to which Kirkpatrick adds ominous accordion drones and noises. A few of the ballads are lighter-hearted, including "The Broomfield Hill," "John Blunt," and, in an unusual version told from a woman's point of view, "Hares on the Mountain." These do a lot to add levity to the otherwise gloomy feeling of the album. Erudite liner notes by Brian Pearson, who is clearly better-read and more knowledgeable about ballads than many professional folklorists, add the finishing touch to this fine package.

what to buy next: *Ways of Seeing* ♫♫♫ (Harbourtown, 1996, prod. Charlie Grey) is a recording made live at London concerts. It's a diverse collection of material, including Eastern European songs, a translation of a Gaelic croon, and many modern works. Armstrong is backed by a chorus of female singers on a number of cuts, and on the rest sings unaccompanied. Some highlights include the Sydney Carter song "Girl in a Garden," on which Armstrong does incredible things with her voice; "Low Ground," a song by David Craig about the Norse in Britain; and "I Only Believe in Miracles," a tribute to one of Armstrong's friends. The album, including its title, makes frequent and poignant references to Armstrong's blindness. *The Fair Moon Rejoices* ♫♫♫ (Harbourtown, 1997, prod. Gordon Jones) also contains a wide variety. Two of the highlights are poems by William Blake set to music by Mike Westbrook. Others include songs from plays, poems set to music, original compositions, and several tunes by songwriter Leon Rosselson. Accompaniments are provided by Peter Stacey on saxophones and bagpipes, Ben Lawrence on African *djembe* drum and cello, and Geoff Haynes on piano. The overall feeling of many of the pieces—due to Armstrong's emotional and dramatic singing and the jazz/classical arrangements—is that of theater music, but inflected by the folksong movement. *Let No One Deceive You: Songs of Bertholt Brecht* ♫♫♫ (Flying Fish, 1989, prod. Gary Cristall) was an inspired idea. The politics and poetry of Brecht were a spur to many in both the American and the British folksong revivals, and this album brings together a giant of the American movement, Dave Van Ronk, with one of the British. Armstrong's contributions are among her most powerful, enraged, defiant, and sometimes gentle recorded performances. Van Ronk's beefy growl is equally riveting.

the rest:
I Heard a Woman Singing 𝄞𝄞𝄞 (Flying Fish, 1998)

worth searching for: Armstrong has recorded numerous solo albums over the years, all of which are worth hearing. Some highlights of her career include *Lovely on the Water* 𝄞𝄞𝄞𝄞 (Topic Records, 1972), her debut album, and *Songs and Ballads* 𝄞𝄞𝄞𝄞 , a 1975 collection of traditional songs that was issued in the U.S. on the Antilles label. Her collaboration with Brian Pearson and Blowzabella to create the song cycle and LP *Tam Lin* 𝄞𝄞𝄞𝄞 (Plant Life, 1980) is also a fascinating piece of work. Finally, several LPs that she recorded with the Critics Group are worth hearing, especially *The Female Frolic* 𝄞𝄞𝄞𝄞 (Argo, 1968), on which she was joined by Sandra Kerr and Peggy Seeger to sing traditional songs from a feminist perspective.

influences:

◀◀ A. L. Lloyd, Ewan MacColl

▶▶ June Tabor

see also: *Blowzabella, A. L. Lloyd, Ewan MacColl, Maddy Prior*

Steve Winick

Desi Arnaz

Latin pop and jazz
Born Desiderio Alberto Arnaz y de Acha III, March 2, 1917, in Santiago, Cuba. Died December 2, 1986, in Del Mar, CA, USA.

Best known as hotheaded Ricky Ricardo, the Latin bandleader with the wiseacre wife on the beloved sitcom *I Love Lucy,* Arnaz's frequent musical numbers on television were largely responsible for introducing the blazing sounds of conga and mambo to Middle America. Before his days as a sitcom star and studio mogul—he and his real-life wife, Lucille Ball, headed up Desilu Productions—Arnaz was an accomplished musician and bandleader. His first break came in 1938, when well-known Latin-jazz bandleader Xavier Cugat caught the Cuban emigre's act in Miami and asked him to join his band as a vocalist. A year later, Arnaz struck out on his own, heading the Desi Arnaz Orchestra. Audiences adored his band's infectious if somewhat goofy numbers, and Arnaz's charisma led to a role in the Broadway musical and movie *Too Many Girls,* in which he met co-star Ball. The two married in 1940. After a stint in the army for World War II, Arnaz resumed his musical career, recording most of his signature songs for Victor in the late 1940s before turning his at-

tention full-time to *Lucy.* After 20 somewhat acrimonious but profitable years of "'splaining," Arnaz and Ball divorced in 1960. Arnaz, however, had left music permanently behind and lived in semi-retirement until his death from lung cancer in 1986.

what to buy: *The Best of Desi Arnaz: The Mambo King* 𝄞𝄞𝄞𝄞 (RCA, 1992, prod. various) is a rollicking good time, including the raucous call-and-response "El Cumbanchero" and the melodic smash hit "Babalu."

what to buy next: Focusing on songs from 1946 to 1949, *Babalu (We Love Desi)* 𝄞𝄞𝄞𝄞 (RCA, 1996, prod. Paul Williams) covers the hits and includes some rarer tracks.

the rest:
Big Bands of Hollywood 𝄞𝄞 (Laserlight, 1992)

worth searching for: *Lucy* aficionado "Weird" Al Yankovic, who paid homage to Arnaz with his early 1980s parody hit "Ricky," produced a collection of songs culled from *I Love Lucy* and Arnaz's 1951 radio show *Your Tropical Trip. Babalu Music: I Love Lucy's Greatest Hits* 𝄞𝄞𝄞 (Columbia, 1991, prod. "Weird" Al Yankovic) is fun, but overall the collection is weighed down by novelties like a duet with Bob Hope on "Nobody Loves the Ump" and a cast version of "Jingle Bells" dominated by Ball's signature shrill.

influences:

◀◀ Machito, Tito Puente, Xavier Cugat, Perez Prado, Les Elgart, Juan Garcia Esquivel

▶▶ Buster Poindexter, Gloria Estefan, "Weird" Al Yankovic

Alex Gordon

Arrow

Soca
Born Alphonsus Cassell, 1955, in Montserrat. Based in Brooklyn, NY, USA.

It was a case of déjà vu all over again when Buster Poindexter (née David Johansen) hit with "Hot, Hot, Hot" in 1987. The tune, which is the de facto national anthem of *soca* (the Caribbean's popular contraction of SOul and CAlypso), had already sold more than two million copies, topped the charts in dozens of countries in Europe and South America, and made its composer, Arrow, one of the few modern calypsonians known outside the islands. Arrow recalls singing along to the James Brown and Elvis Presley records he heard over the radio since childhood, and also absorbing the rhythms of calypso and French and African music played by his neighbors. By the time he was 16 he was competing in Montserrat's Calypso King contests, but he wasn't considering a career in music until he made his first album, *On Target,* in 1974. The response was overwhelming, and it set Arrow on a "road march" (to put it in calypso terms) from which he has never looked back. Due to the nationalistic nature of the Carnival in Trinidad and Tobago, calypso artists from other islands are not permitted to compete for the coveted (and commercially important) King of Carnival crown, but if he can't have Trinidad, Arrow will settle for the rest of the world.

"There's an irresistible beat to soca music, but some producers of calypso are content to sell 5,000 records a year," Arrow says. "They're happy if they break even, but they're complacent and the music is getting left behind. When Buster Poindexter had a hit with 'Hot, Hot, Hot,' it should have been a clue that people will accept calypso, if they only hear it. When I do my records, I always earmark 10 percent of the budget for promotion; you have to let people know you're out there." To that end, Arrow and his band, which includes rock guitarist Chris Newland, stay on the road for most of the year, playing Europe, South America, Africa, and the Caribbean. "Every album I make is more diverse," Arrow rightfully boasts. "When I'm in Colombia, I add a bit of cumbia, when I'm in England, I may have Chris play more guitar, when I'm in Africa, the drums step out, and those experiences affect the way I compose the next song."

A great controversy rages in the Caribbean about the origin of soca. About 20 years ago the major calypso artists simplified their often complex songwriting structure, toning down the political content and adding exhortations to "parr-tayy"; they also added beats borrowed from Haiti's *cadence* and *compas,* Cuba's rumba, the influential band Kassav"s *zouk,* and a taste of North American funk. The result was a dance music that has had an international impact. In recent years rap, reggae, and various Latin rhythms have also crept in, as well as *bhangra* contributed by Trinidad's sizable Indian minority. At first calypsonians dismissed the form as a dilution of the calypso tradition, but after Kitch, Sparrow, and Arrow had major hits with the new beat, they changed their minds. Since the mid-1980s, various calypso singers have stepped forward to claim they invented soca.

When Poindexter channeled Arrow's song into a hit, the author finally landed a major label contract with Mango, the world-music division of Island Records at the time. After three albums and despite constant touring that grabbed raves from the critics, Arrow was dropped. Back on his own indie label, he continues to release album after album of classic party jams.

what to buy: Arrow's major label debut *Knock Dem Dead* ♫♫♫♫♫ (Mango, 1988, prod. Arrow) features eight strong songs with plenty of rock guitar and a smattering of international beats. "Groove Master," which kicks off the album, has become another signature tune for the artist. *Soca Savage* ♫♫♫♫♫ (Arrow Records, 1984, prod. Arrow) is a great early album with "Colombia Rock," a Latinized track that was a smash throughout the Caribbean.

best of the rest:
Instant Knock Out ♫♫♫♫ (Charlie's, 1980)
Soca Dance Party ♫♫♫♫♫ (Mango, 1990)
Zombie Soca ♫♫♫♫ (Arrow, 1991)
Model de Bam Bam ♫♫♫♫ (Arrow, 1992)
Phat ♫♫♫♫ (Arrow, 1995)

influences:
◀◀ Sparrow, Kitch, James Brown

▶▶ Burning Flames, Brother Resistance

see also: *Lord Kitchener, the Mighty Sparrow*

j. poet

Joe Arroyo
Salsa, tropical, Pan-Latin, cumbia
Born Alvaro José Arroyo Gonzalez, November 1, 1955, in Cartagena, Colombia. Based in Colombia.

Joe Arroyo began his singing career at the age of eight, performing in strip joints in Cartagena. By the time he was a teenager he joined the historic Fruko y sus Tesos. That band was led by Julio Ernesto Estrada Rincon, or, more popularly, "Fruko," also known as Colombia's "Godfather of Salsa"—fittingly, since Arroyo would come to be its favorite son. In 1981 he founded his own group, La Verdad ("The Truth"), whose distinction was Arroyo's sometimes abrasive tenor and his fusion of salsa with his native land's *cumbia* dance music, Cuba's rhythmic *son,* and Haitian *compas* pop to create a sound so unusual it was given its own name: "Joe-son." His work is heard in every corner of Latin America, and the cross-cultural blend he's created has influenced *salseros* since the early 1980s.

what's available: Arroyo has an extensive discography on labels distributed in Latin America. One of the most readily available examples is *Deja Que Te Cante* ♫♫♫ (Sony International, 1998, prod. Joe Arroyo), which showcases Arroyo's cohesive fusion of sounds.

influences:
◀◀ Fruko

▶▶ Grupo Niche

Kerry Dexter

Karen Ashbrook
Hammered dulcimer, Celtic
Born April 28, 1959, in Columbus, OH, USA. Based in the Washington, DC area, USA.

Known for her delicate touch and natural affinity for Irish music, Karen Ashbrook has made a unique mark in the hammered dulcimer world. After spending five years traveling the globe and studying its music, she settled in the Washington, D.C. area, where she has become a celebrity. Her in-depth knowledge of a wide variety of styles and traditions has made her an extraordinary all-around musician. Besides her exquisite hammered dulcimer playing, she also plays a mean pennywhistle and wooden flute. She studied flute with celebrated flautist Chris Norman, and has worked with several groups, including Ceoltoiri, King David's Harp, and Celtic Naught. Ashbrook began learning how to play the hammered dulcimer the week after building one as a high school project. Her love of the instrument is reflected in her nationally acclaimed instruction book and cassette, *Playing the Hammered Dulcimer in the Irish Tradition*. Ashbrook teaches at festivals and arts institutions across the country, including Common Ground in Westminster, Maryland, and Augusta Heritage Arts Center in Elkins, West Virginia. Notable Ashbrook performances have included appearances at the Smithsonian Institution and on National Public Radio, and a request to play for part of the festivities surrounding the marriage of Prince Charles and Lady Diana.

what's available: Ashbrook's debut recording *Knock on the Door* ♪♪♪♪ (Fools-Cap Pub., 1988/Maggie's Music, 1995, prod. Karen Ashbrook) has been digitally remastered. On this delightful collection of Irish and Breton tunes, Ashbrook works with many other talented musicians to display her first-hand understanding of Irish music, creating an upbeat and enjoyable recording. On *Hills of Erin* ♪♪♪♪ (Maggie's Music, 1994, prod. Bob Read), Karen is joined by a host of excellent musicians, including David Scheim on piano, Bob Read on reeds, Carolyn Surrick on viola da gamba, and Sue Richards on harp. The result is a rich tapestry of Irish music, taking the listener on a magic carpet ride to the emerald island. The choice of tunes ranges from the slow and haunting "The Osprey" to the jolly and jocular "The Cabin Boy." Karen displays her versatility and passionate expression with a rendition of J. S. Bach's "Prelude to the First Suite for Unaccompanied Violincello" on hammered dulcimer.

influences:

◀◀ J. S. Bach, the Bothy Band, Alasdair Fraser, the Irish Tradition, Nick Blanton, David James

▶▶ Jody Marshall, Maggie Sansone

see also: *Ceoltoiri*

Jo Hughey Morrison

Ashkabad

Turkmenistanian folk music

Formed c. 1990, in Ashkabad, Turkmenistan. Based in Ashkabad, Turkmenistan.

Atabai Tsharykuliev, vocal, tar; Gassan Mamedov, violin; Sabir Rizaev, clarinet, soprano sax, serp, nagara; Kurban Kurbanov, accordion, piano; Khakberdy Allamuradovm, dep, serp, nagra. (All members are from Turkmenistan.)

Much Turkmenistanian folk music centers around wedding celebrations, and all the members of Ashkabad have played their share of weddings. Atabai Tsharykuliev, the band's singer, used to tape other wedding singers to emulate. At the end of the 1970s the (then Soviet) government tried to suppress wedding music because it was "too religious" (i.e. Islamic). Tsharykuliev kept singing, and was briefly confined to an asylum, but since 1985 he's been able to work again. Three of the band's other four members honed their chops at weddings too, and while Sabir Rizaev was classically trained, he sometimes did such gigs with them and played in rock and jazz bands with Mamedov before the two joined their friends in Ashkabad.

what's available: *City of Love* ♪♪♪♪ (Realworld, 1993, prod. John Leckie) shows how this folkloric group incorporates bits of music from Iran, Turkey, and the United States into their highly traditional style. The percussion sounds Arabic, the clarinet and accordion could have come from a klezmer band, and the fiddling has a melancholy Russian feeling.

influences:

◀◀ Alem Kossimov, Rustavi Choir, Hafezi

j. poet

Ashkaru

Worldbeat

Formed early 1990s, in Toronto, Canada. Disbanded mid-1990s.

Celina Carroll, lead and backing vocals, hand percussion; Carlo Cesta, congos, bongas, timbales, percussion; Yared Tesfaye, lead and backing vocals, guitars; Chip Yarwood, keyboards, midi woodwind, flute, tin whistle, guitar, mbira, backing vocals. (Members are from Canada and Ethiopia.)

Ashkaru was a talented worldbeat outfit from Canada, and one that, though it had only two releases before dissolving in the mid-'90s, really helped put the genre on the map in North America. Originally known as Mother Tongue, the band's Canadian/Ethiopian lineup brought a fresh sound to the Great White North, which earned them a Juno (Canadian Grammy) and hefty sales right out of the box. Barred from using their million-dollar name in the Lower 48 due to a trademark challenge from a U.S. band going by the same, they adopted the alias Ashkaru and released their well-liked international debut—titled *Mother Tongue*, thus displaying the kind of sass their music could have used a bit more of.

what's available: Given the dynamic friction when genres collide in the work of more daring fusionist favorites like Baaba Maal and Angélique Kidjo, Ashkaru's one-world melange is a bit too harmonious a bit too often. But if you like the low-impact world-vibe of Henri Dikongué (and millions do), you'll probably like *Mother Tongue* 𝅘𝅥𝅘𝅥𝅘𝅥 (Triloka, 1995, prod. various).

influences:

⏪ Poi Dog Pondering, Osibisa

⏩ Henri Dikongué

Adam McGovern

Badi Assad

Brazilian, jazz, new age, worldbeat, classical guitar
Born in São João de Boa Vista, São Paulo, Brazil. Based in USA.

Badi Assad's first musical instrument was a small electronic keyboard. "It was made for kids," she says, "and when my hands outgrew the keys, I stopped playing altogether." Not for long, though—soon the teenager took up guitar, which was natural for a family in which her two older brothers, Sergio and Odair, were already on their way to professional careers as classicists on that instrument. Though she studied the classical repertoire, Badi soon started looking into other genres, among them jazz, Brazilian rhythms, the music of her Middle Eastern heritage, and related forms of expression including percussion and dance. Gradually she began to incorporate all these elements into her own work. She has continued to explore possibilities and ignore boundaries, earning praise for her guitar technique and creative blending of musical styles.

what to buy: *Chameleon* 𝅘𝅥𝅘𝅥𝅘𝅥𝅘𝅥 (PolyGram, 1998, prod. various) is an acoustic-based advancement of Assad's quest after musical combinations in touch with cultural roots. On this disc she sings in English as well as Portuguese, and shows she knows how to blend her voice as another instrument in her palette of sounds. *Solo* 𝅘𝅥𝅘𝅥𝅘𝅥𝅘𝅥 (Chesky Jazz, 1990, prod. various) is Assad's international debut, demonstrating her technique and imagination on works by classical composers including her countryman Heitor Villa-Lobos.

the rest:

Rhythms 𝅘𝅥𝅘𝅥𝅘𝅥𝅘𝅥 (Chesky, 1995)
Echoes of Brazil 𝅘𝅥𝅘𝅥𝅘𝅥𝅘𝅥 (Chesky, 1997)

influences:

⏪ Duo Assad, Heitor Villa-Lobos, Jeff Scott Young

Kerry Dexter

Aswad

Reggae
Formed 1974, in London, England. Based in England.

Variable membership over two-plus decades; current lineup includes: Brinsley "Dan" Forde, rhythm guitar, vocals; Angus "Drummie Zed"

flutes worldwide

Krishna, Pan, and the Pied Piper all played flutes, and some variation of the instrument appears in almost every culture. A flute's range depends on its length, from pipsqueaks like Ireland's tin whistle to giants like the six-foot-long, sacred bamboo Sepik flute of Papua New Guinea. The timbre is determined by material and shape, be it wood, bamboo, metal, clay, plastic, stone, or bone; tubular or globular. Flutes may be side-blown (transverse) or end-blown; blown in pairs (double flute) or a series (panpipes).

Just as the instrument varies greatly, the performers' styles are even more diverse. The *embouchure,* or placement of the lips, tongue, and teeth on or near the mouthpiece, is crucial; whether gently piping or overblowing, the musician defines the sound. Flutes are constantly surprising—whether in mesmeric Indian songs, China's wistful melodies, lively Andean panpipe tunes, the overblowing of American free jazz, the simplicity of fife and drum, or the birdsong of Vivaldi's concertos, the flute is an extraordinarily versatile instrument capable of exquisite expression.

David Poole

Gaye, drums, vocals; Tony "Gad" Robinson, bass. (All members are from England.)

Infectious melodies and heartfelt vocal harmonies have made Aswad one of the most successful reggae bands in England. And though firmly rooted in reggae, Aswad has incorporated dancehall, funk, hip-hop, and club influences. Once dubbed "the young Wailers" by no less than Bunny Wailer of Bob Marley's real thing, Aswad's sound has continued to grow closer to Motown-like pop. The band first came together in the Ladbroke Grove section of London as a quintet. Named after the Arabic word for "black," they created a dance-inspiring blend of jazz, soul, and jazz-fusion layered over a straight-ahead reggae beat. Aswad's early singles became fixtures of London dance clubs, and as an even surer stamp of approval, the group was invited to accompany visiting Jamaican performers Bob Marley and Black Uhuru. Aswad's debut single, "Back to Africa," was released in 1976 and reached the top slot on the British reggae charts. The band then achieved international acclaim in 1988,

Aster Aweke

with their reggae interpretation of the Luther Ingram and Tina Turner tune "Don't Turn Around." *Rise and Shine,* released in 1994, earned Aswad their first Grammy nomination; the album spent four weeks at #1 on the CMJ college music charts. The band has experienced a number of personnel changes through the years, but clearly has a lot of life left in it.

what to buy: In addition to sampling tracks from Aswad's earlier albums, *Roots Rocking: The Island Anthology* 🎵🎵🎵 (PGD/Poly-Gram, 1997, prod. Aswad) includes five tunes—"Tuff We Tuff," "Not Satisfied," "Roots Rocking," "Drum and Bass Line," and "African Children"—recorded live and otherwise unavailable.

what to buy next: With the release of *New Chapter of Dub* 🎵🎵🎵 (CBS, 1982, prod. Michael "Reuben" Campbell), Aswad successfully returned to their original sound, with dub versions of songs from their commercially disappointing album *New Chapter.*

the rest:
Aswad 🎵🎵🎵 (Island, 1976)
Hulet 🎵🎵🎵 (Grove Music, 1979)
New Chapter 🎵🎵🎵 (CBS, 1981)
Showcase 🎵🎵🎵 (Island, 1981)
Not Satisfied 🎵🎵🎵 (CBS, 1982)
Live and Direct 🎵🎵🎵 (Island, 1983)
Rebel Souls 🎵🎵🎵 (Island, 1984)
To the Top 🎵🎵🎵 (Simba, 1986)
Distant Thunder 🎵🎵🎵 (Island, 1988)
Renaissance: 20 Crucial Tracks 🎵🎵🎵 (Stylus, 1988)
Too Wicked 🎵🎵🎵 (Island, 1990)
Rise and Shine 🎵🎵🎵 (Mesa, 1994)
Dub: The New Frontier 🎵🎵🎵 (Mesa, 1995)
Rise and Shine Again 🎵🎵🎵 (Mesa, 1995)
Big Up 🎵🎵🎵 (WFA/Atlantic, 1997)

worth searching for: The film soundtrack *The X-Files: Fight the Future* (OST, 1998) includes Sting and Aswad's rendition of the Police tune "Invisible Sun."

influences:
◀◀ Bob Marley & the Wailers, Toots & the Maytals, the Skatalites

▶▶ Third World, the Specials, Elvis Costello

see also: *Burning Spear, Maxi Priest*

Craig Harris

Natacha Atlas
See: Transglobal Underground

Julian Avalos & Afro-Andes
Andean folk, modern Afro-Peruvian
Formed 1993, in New York, NY, USA. Based in New York, NY, USA.

Julian Avalos (born in Laredo, Peru), guitar, vocals, leader; Arch Thompson (USA), flute, sax, rap; Cesar Ferreyra (Peru), congas, bongo, campana, vocals; Pedro Alalos (Peru), timbales, castañuelas, vocals; Juan Aguilar (Peru), bass.

Julian Avalos grew up in Laredo, a coastal town in northern Peru surrounded by sugar plantations. He remembers singing and dancing for enjoyment when he was a boy, "but I had no thoughts of seriously studying music, or doing it for a living. It was mostly to entertain my parents." For Avalos the real passion was soccer, and although his parents wanted him to stay in school and go to university, he eventually became a professional soccer player. "When I was on the juvenile teams it was a very Spartan life," Avalos said. "No smoking, no drinking, lots of hard work, like being in the military; but when we would get out to play games, it was different. The other guys on the team, the macho men, pushed me to drink, but I saw that my body would not work with alcohol." Avalos dropped out of the drinking competitions and went back to his guitar, forming a duo with a friend. "We played for fun, to get girls and help pay the rent. When I realized I wouldn't get too far with soccer, I got serious about the guitar." Cafe Con Leche, the first group Avalos formed, caused a sensation by combining the traditional music of his youth with Cuban and other Latin American strains. "I'm mixed; I have Indian, Spanish and African blood, and grew up with music from Colombia, Ecuador, Bolivia and other Spanish-speaking countries, so all these influences go into the music." Avalos eventually moved to New York, where he leads his new band, Afro-Andes. "I call the band Afro-Andes because the Andes are like the spine of the continent of South America, and although most of [our] music is original, it includes styles from the city, traditional music from the countryside, some Afro-Peruvian rhythms, some salsa from New York. Some of the music is not commercial, but my aim is to present a good mixture of songs from all of the cultures of Latin America."

worth searching for: The self-produced *The Sound of Afro-Andes* 🎵🎵🎵 (JA, 1995, prod. Julian Avalos) may be hard to find, but it offers a unique Peruvian brand of salsa, including an Afro-Andean take on the merengue.

influences:
◀◀ Los Incas, Inti-Illimani

j. poet

Aster Aweke
Ethiopian soul
Born 1961, in Gondar, Ethiopia. Based in Washington, DC, USA.

Aweke is an Ethiopian "soul singer" akin to Mahmoud Ahmed. She grew up listening to both traditional music and Western pop, and loved Aretha and James Brown. She began singing as a child, and was performing by 1977. Following a couple of successful cassettes she joined the Roha Band, but left the country soon after due to political unrest upon the demise of Haile Selassie. She first moved to San Francisco but relocated to D.C., where there was a large Ethiopian expatriate community that supported her forward-looking music, which was a blend of funk, Ethiopian soul, and R&B. When one of her demo tapes found its way to Iain Scott and Bunt Stafford Clarke—owners of Triple Earth Records and producers of Indian-music synthesist Najma's first crossover album—they flew to the states to catch her show and subsequently signed her up. Columbia released two of her Triple Earth recordings—*Aster* and *Kabu*—with a barrage of hype, but they were unable to work the albums successfully and dropped her. Triple Earth hopes to get her back into the studio for a new album soon.

what to buy: On *Aster* ♫♫♫♫ (Columbia, 1990, prod. Iain Scott, Bunt Stafford Clarke) Aweke sings against the beat, which gives her music a startling edge on first listen. After you get accustomed to it, you notice Aweke's rugged vocals and know why she's been compared to Aretha and Billy Holiday. She leaps over the language barrier and jabs you in the heart with the ferocity of her emotional attack, while the band's Ethiopian groove puts a new twist on familiar soul-music stylings. The two folk tunes Aweke sings only with *kra* (Ethiopian harp) accompaniment are show stoppers. On *Live in London* ♫♫♫♫ (Triple Earth, 1996, prod. David White) Aweke and her band cut loose with extended versions of tunes selected from her first two albums.

the rest:
Kabu ♫♫♫ (Columbia, 1991)

influences:
◀◀ Mahmoud Ahmed, Najma

see also: *Mahmoud Ahmed*

j. poet

Abed Azrié

Classical Arabic music
Born 1945, in Aleppo, Syria. Based in Paris, France.

Azrié grew up listening to Arabic folk music, as well as the Western and Latin pop he heard on the radio. His hometown of Aleppo is an ancient crossroads, and Azrié was also exposed to Greek, Turkish, Iranian, Egyptian, Kurdish, and Armenian music. As a teenager he commuted between Aleppo and Beirut in Lebanon, listening to Italian, French, Spanish, and American songs while studying Arabic literature at the Lebanese University. He moved to Paris to study European classical music in 1967. Dismayed by the population's ignorance of Arabic culture despite the city's large Arabic community, he began translating Arabic poetry—including the Sumerian "Epic of Gilgamesh" (probably the oldest complete poem known to humanity)—into

French in an effort to "take the jewels of Arabic culture and put them into everybody's hands." He has lived and worked in Paris ever since, producing an impressive amount of poetry, music, and literature.

what to buy: The lyrics on *Aromates* ♫♫♫♫♫ (Nonesuch, 1990, prod. Abed Azrié) are taken from poems by noted Syrian, Lebanese, and Palestinian poets, and the subtle, almost ambient settings were composed by Azrié, who sings them in his own hypnotic style. He barely lifts his voice above a whisper, but still his vocals have an undeniable authority. The accompaniment is bare-bones—only *qanun* (zither), *nay* (flute), percussion, and subtle synthesizer washes—but the effect is powerful.

what to buy next: During the Arabic occupation of Spain, music and art flourished. A new Euro-Arabic fusion developed, perhaps the first "worldbeat" style to have wide influence. This Arabo-Andalusian form is at the root of flamenco, Cuban rumba, and much of the classical music of Morocco, and it's explored on *Suerte* ♫♫♫♫♫ (Harmonia Mundi France, 1994, prod. Abed Azrié). Once again Azrié borrows his lyrics from the poets, this time the 11th century bards who worked in the *muwashshahat* tradition, a multi-rhyming, multi-metric style that's similar to the troubadour songs that arose at about the same time. Azrié's music combines Arabic, Spanish, and Arabo-Andalusian rhythms to navigate the common ground these cultures continue to share. His vocals are complemented here by the work of Pedro Avedo, a flamenco singer whose florid, passionate style is the polar opposite of Azrié's quiet murmur.

the rest:
New Song of Arabic Poets ♫♫♫♫ (Chant de Monde, France, 1970)
Wajd ♫♫♫♫ (Chant de Monde, France, 1973)
The Sufis ♫♫♫♫ (CDA France, 1983)
Epic of Gilgamesh ♫♫♫ (Auvidis, 1994)
Suerte Live ♫♫♫♫♫ (L'Empreinte Digitale, 1998)

influences:
◀◀ Umm Kulthum, Mohamed Abdel Wahab

j. poet

Susana Baca

Afro-Peruvian, traditional and popular
Born in Chorrillos, Peru. Based in Lima, Peru.

Susana Baca grew up in a black, working-class neighborhood of Chorrillos, on Peru's northwestern coast. She says she was sur-

Susana Baca

rounded by music as long as she can remember, but it wasn't until 1980 that she began her professional career as a world-music diva and folklorist. Centuries before, Spanish conquerors had brought West African slaves to Peru, but avoided importing large numbers of any one ethnic group, knowing a common language could foster resistance to slavery as it did in Cuba. The slaves of Peru were slowly integrated into their new country, but the rhythms of Africa still dominated their music. Black Peruvians combined elements from Spain, Africa, and the indigenous Andean cultures to produce the unique Afro-Peruvian sound. They also invented several percussion instruments, including the *licajón,* a wooden box held between the legs and played with the hands, and the *liquijada de burro,* a burro's jawbone with loosened teeth that sounds like the Cuban *güiro.*

"There was always discrimination against Negroes," Baca says. "Being black meant being a slave, being lazy or having 'rhythm in your blood.' As economic conditions improved, people didn't want to be considered black, and many Afro-Peruvians didn't want to talk about the old slave songs. For this reason, a lot of the music was lost." In the '60s the Black Consciousness movement reached Peru and Afro-Peruvian artists began to revive their roots music. The band Peru Negro created an Afro-Peruvian dance craze in the mid-'70s that still resonates in Lima's nightclubs. "Peruvian radio is dominated by foreign music," Baca said. "Growing up, I was surrounded by black music, but I never heard it on the radio, and I could find no mention of Afro-Peruvians in history books. When I started singing, I wanted to know more about my own culture and began searching for my roots, speaking to older people in my city and documenting what I heard."

As Baca got deeper into the songs and stories the elders gave her, she began documenting the history of Afro-Peru. After seven years of research, she produced the groundbreaking book-and-CD historical document *Del Fuego y Del Agua,* the success of which led to the creation of Negro Continuo, a foundation Baca started to preserve this heritage. The word spread farther when ex–Talking Head and world-music label founder David Byrne happened to see a homemade video of Baca singing in her garden. Byrne traveled to Peru, met Baca, and put together *The Soul of Black Peru,* a compilation of Afro-Peruvian music that introduced the genre to the world. To help promote the album, Baca came to the States for a couple of concerts, followed by her U.S. label debut. "These albums are an ongoing work," Baca explains. "So we chose the rhythms and tempos that haven't been explored commercially yet. I look for traditional songs; also songs that will capture the interest of the youth, so this tradition will not die out."

what's available: "People were entranced by her performance," David Byrne has remarked of Baca's first Stateside

tour. "She is elegant and the music was basic, yet very moving. When we decided to do an album with her, that was the approach we agreed on." The result was *Susana Baca* 𝄢𝄢𝄢𝄢 (Luaka Bop, 1997, prod. Greg Landau), a very roots-based outing marked by driving percussion and Baca's sophisticated vocals. The material includes traditional Afro-Peruvian songs and newer compositions that draw on Latin American poetry for their lyrics. There are elements of Brazilian music and Cuban *son* mixed with rhythms like the traditional Afro-Peruvian *lando* and the Peruvian *vals* (waltz).

worth searching for: *Del Fuego y Del Agua* 𝄢𝄢𝄢𝄢𝄢 (Tonga, 1997) is the limited U.S. edition of the limited Peruvian edition, a beautifully designed box that includes a 150-page book of historical and folkloric articles about Afro-Peruvian music and history, and a 16-track CD containing examples of Afro-Peruvian music that range from simple acoustic treatments to current synthesizer-driven dance-club hits. *Vestida de Vida* 𝄢𝄢𝄢𝄢 (Kardum France, 1997), released in Peru in 1991, showcases Baca's interpretations of black music in the Americas and includes selections from Puerto Rico, Cuba, Brazil, and the United States (Gershwin's "Summertime"). Baca's "Maria Lando" is one of the highlights of the various-artists collection *The Soul of Black Peru* 𝄢𝄢𝄢𝄢 (Luaka Bop, 1995), which is also reviewed in this book's Compilations section.

influences:
◄◄ Peru Negro, Nicómedes Santa Cruz

j. poet

Bad Brains /Soul Brains

Hybrid punk
Formed 1979, in Washington, DC, USA. Based in USA.

H.R. (born Paul D. Hudson, a.k.a. Joseph I), vocals (1979–83, 1986–87, 1988–89, 1994–95, 1999–present); Dr. Know (born Gary Wayne Miller), guitar (1979–95, 1999–present); Darryl Aaron Jenifer, bass (1979–95, 1999–present); Earl Hudson, drums (1979–83, 1986–87, 1989, 1994–95, 1999–present); Israel Joseph-I (born Dexter Pinto, in Trinidad), vocals (1992–94); Mackie Jayson, drums (1983–86, 1988–89, 1992–93). (All members are from USA unless noted otherwise.)

Bad Brains are the most influential band in hardcore, often overlooked due to an all-black lineup that's out of synch with punk stereotype. But the band's pioneering mix of that genre with reggae also makes it an unusual giant of world music, and a founder of the barrier-breaking aesthetic that has overtaken all late-century art forms. The Brains' explosive sound has the creative tension of cultures actually facing each other for the first time—call it Hard World. The band's sensibility stems from an upbringing in the ghettos around the capital of the free world; it embodies the past shame and future promise of American multiculturalism—bassist Darryl Jenifer even traces his lineage to a slave-owning signer of the Constitution. Reversing rock's usual trend, Bad Brains were not amateurs who gradually built up their sound, but fusion-jazz types who learned the value of simplicity from the late-'70s punk revolution. When they discovered the beliefs and music of Rastafarianism, the Brains set their cultural blender on high and threw away the knob. The creative energies involved make for a volatile brew, and since 1983 the band has literally made albums between breakups, with vocalist H.R. and his brother Earl Hudson departing regularly to pursue more straightforward reggae recordings. Narrowly marketed to the punk audience, portrayed more as historical figures than contemporary players, and eclipsed by violent incidents involving an unbalanced H.R., the Brains were cast into limbo after their most recent album in 1995. But the regular unearthing of vital archival sessions—and an early-1999 reunion tour with the band "positively" rechristened the Soul Brains—keep the future open and the legend alive.

what to buy: The debut, *Bad Brains* ⨯⨯⨯⨯ (ROIR, 1982/1996, prod. Jay Dublee), is not only the quintessential hardcore album, but the standard by which all nonconformist music can be measured. With oddly melodic power chords and vocal wails, polyphonic noise guitar, unpredictable acrobatics of rhythm and tempo, and precociously expert reggae, the Brains transcended a genre even as they defined it. On *I Against I* ⨯⨯⨯⨯⨯ (SST, 1986, prod. Ron St. Germain), the band grounds metal-leaning rock with the syncopation of funk, takes pop to blistering extremes, and keeps its playing tight while ambitiously stretching out its song structure. H.R. turns in his best lyrics and inflects his singing with a rich soul texture (after a drug bust, the vocals for "Sacred Love" were resourcefully recorded by phone from prison). The stunning *Quickness* ⨯⨯⨯⨯⨯ (Caroline, 1989, prod. Ron St. Germain) shifts genres within individual songs. The prodigal H.R. returned to create the lyrics and vocal melodies in one night; some remnants of his *a cappella* demos contrast the otherwise fat production sound with a fabulous rawness. His sometimes macho lyrics, and a few repeated musical ideas from *I Against I,* are the only things that qualify the album's success. Released after 17 years as *Black Dots* ⨯⨯⨯⨯ (Caroline, 1996, prod. Bad Brains), the Brains' first-ever, live-in-the-studio recording session instantly took its place among the definitive documents of rock essence.

what to buy next: *God of Love* ⨯⨯⨯ (Maverick, 1995, prod. Ric Ocasek) slows the pace of experimentation a bit and may seem to lack the other albums' visionary sweep. But it marks the band's most decisive same-song synthesis of hard rock and reggae yet, and features the must-have ambient reggae

odyssey "How I Love Thee" and the metal-gospel/country & western prayer call (believe it!) of "Thank JAH." The Brains' first multi-track recording session, laid down in 1980 but released much later as the EP *Omega Sessions* ⨯⨯⨯ (Victory, 1997), is an intriguing artifact of a studio polish the band would sand off before its debut album. *Live* ⨯⨯⨯⨯ (SST, 1988, prod. Phil Burnett) is a sterling example of the Brains on stage.

what to avoid: Even a bad album for the Brains would be a good one for many other bands. But *Rock for Light* ⨯⨯⨯ (PVC, 1983/Caroline, 1991, prod. Ric Ocasek) is packed with inferior versions of songs from the (then-rare) first album.

the rest:
Bad Brains ⨯⨯⨯ (Alternative Tentacles EP, 1982)
I and I Survive/Destroy Babylon ⨯⨯ (Important EP, 1982)
Attitude: The ROIR Session ⨯⨯ (ROIR/Important, 1989)
The Youth Are Getting Restless: Live in Amsterdam ⨯⨯⨯⨯ (Caroline, 1990)
Spirit Electricity ⨯⨯⨯⨯ (SST EP, 1991)
Rise ⨯⨯⨯ (Epic, 1993)

worth searching for: The soundtrack for *Pump Up the Volume* ⨯⨯⨯ (MCA, 1990, prod. various) features the then-headless band's cover of the MC5's "Kick Out the Jams" with Henry Rollins on vocals.

solo outings:
H.R.:
Anthology ⨯⨯⨯ (SST, 1998)

influences:
◀◀ Bob Marley, Parliament-Funkadelic, the Sex Pistols, the Clash, the Damned, the Ramones, Mahavishnu Orchestra, Return to Forever

▶▶ Living Colour, Beastie Boys, Consolidated, Bad Religion, Cornershop, Goldfinger, Sting, Babe the Blue Ox, Spearhead, Skunk Anansie, the Urge

Adam McGovern

Badawi
/Sub Dub

Experimental dub/Middle Eastern fusion
Born Reuel Mesinai, 1973, in Jerusalem, Israel. Based in New York, NY, USA.

Although he was born and primarily raised in Israel, "Raz" Mesinai's family moved back and forth to New York City on a regular basis before settling there in 1988, which explains quite a bit about the multicultural style he'd later be known for. As a child, Mesinai sought out the sounds of hip-hop and dub reggae, and his first record purchase, reggae great Burning Spear's *Garvey's Ghost,* would prove to be a lasting influence.

Interestingly, though, what convinced Mesinai to become a musician himself wasn't an album at all, but the soundtrack to the film *The Emerald Forest*—music that's not too incompatible with the pop-culture cut-and-paste aesthetic of the other styles he admired, or with the cinematic sound-textures he would one day achieve. By the time he reached his teens, having started to seriously embrace his Jewish heritage, traditional Hasidic music provided yet another formidable influence. Teaching himself to play exotic percussion instruments like the Persian *zarb,* various frame drums, and the Turkish *darabuka,* Mesinai began fusing elements of real-time performance (he had also studied piano) with his growing affection for dub. After an impressive debut under his solo pseudonym Badawi, he teamed up with bassist John "JDubs" Ward to form the experimental ensemble Sub Dub, which lasted for two critically acclaimed albums. Surprisingly, Badawi's latest efforts seem to be moving away from dub towards a more mature, fully realized Middle Eastern/Moroccan fusion that incorporates strings, piano, *santur* (Persian/Indian hammered dulcimer), *kalimba* (African thumb piano), and live percussion, and uses almost no samples. A compelling artist to watch for in coming years.

what to buy: *The Heretic of Ether* ♪♪♪♪♪ (Asphodel, 1999, prod. Raz Mesinai) is an ethno-ambient masterpiece—a conceptual work of sorts, serving as the imagery-filled soundtrack to a story unfolded in three lushly rendered "chapters." Dub plays only a minor role here, as Badawi fully pursues his interest in Arabic music for the first time, proving himself remarkably adept for a self-taught percussionist. Credit must also be given to cellist Erich Schoen-Rene and violinist Ralph Farris, whose luscious string textures lend the proceedings a romantic air of melancholy as Badawi's intricate rhythms drive the music toward a climactic ending that simply begs for an accompanying film. All the powerful emotional dynamics of an epic like *The English Patient,* and not a single word uttered throughout!

what to buy next: For a glimpse of Badawi's more "traditional" dub side, it simply doesn't get any better than Sub Dub's *Dancehall Malfunction* ♪♪♪♪ (Asphodel, 1997, prod. Sub Dub), an extremely eclectic outing that takes the form to its outer limits of aural experimentation. You can hear echoes of dub deities King Tubby and Mad Professor's whacked-out influence reverberating through these 11 instrumental tracks, with John Ward's basslines holding down the fort as Badawi adds layer upon layer of live percussion and samples, until the whole thing is a heady sonic brew best imbibed with headphones on and lights off.

the rest:
Badawi:
Badawi Presents Bedouin Sound Clash ♪♪♪♪ (ROIR, 1996)

Sub Dub:
Sub Dub ♪♪♪♪ (Instinct, 1996)

influences:
◀◀ Burning Spear, King Tubby, Lee Perry, Hossan Tehrani, Hossam Ramzy

see also: *Burning Spear, King Tubby, Mad Professor*

Bret Love

Aly Bain
See: The Boys of the Lough

Baka Beyond
Worldbeat
Formed 1992, in the Baka Forest, Cameroon. Based in London, England.

Martin Cradick (U.K.), guitar, mandolin, sampling; Paddy Le Mercier (France), violin, flute; Su Hart (U.K.), vocals; Baka Forest people (Cameroon), drums, vocals, waterdrums; Tom Green (U.K.), keyboards, programming (1995); Sagar N'Gom (Senegal), African hand drums (1995); Mark Pinto (U.K.), bass (1995–present); Alassana N'Gom (Senegal), vocals (1998); Nii Tettey Tetteh (Ghana), percussion (1998); Addoteh Richter (Ghana), percussion (1998); Annor Asanioah (Ghana), percussion (1998).

The story behind the Baka Beyond recordings, a collaboration between the Baka pygmies of Cameroon and British folk musician Martin Cradick, is tailor-made for the big screen, an epic adventure that spans continents and cultures. In his years of traveling, busking, and playing concerts, itinerant folk musician Cradick had picked up bits of reggae, Celtic, rock, flamenco, Caribbean, South American, Arabic, and West African influence, and played with musicians from all over the world, mixing and matching traditions as the spirit moved him. In 1988 he met *didgeridoo* player Graham Wiggins, who had an equally eclectic approach. Wiggins had played jazz, Cuban jazz, and modern dance music in addition to the didgeridoo, which he taught himself by listening to recordings of Aboriginal players. The duo began playing as Outback in 1989, later recruiting Senegalese percussionist Sagar N'Gom and trap drummer Ian Campbell. Cradick first heard the music of the Baka pygmies on a BBC television documentary and was so captivated by what he heard that he named the first Outback album *Baka* in their honor. He began dreaming of the pygmies, and within three years, after a strange series of coincidences, Cradick and his wife Su Hart found themselves in the jungles of Cameroon living with the Baka. Cradick has said that the Baka don't believe in coincidence, and greeted him and his wife as if they'd been expecting them. Cradick brought along a tent, drawing and recording gear, a camera, and a guitar and mandolin, but other than that he and Hart lived as the Baka lived, hunting, gathering, and playing music with their new friends. Cradick has recorded two collaborative CDs with the Baka, *Spirit of the Forest* and *The Meeting Pool*. All royalties due the Baka go into a fund to help preserve their forest and way of life, currently under attack from logging and farming interests.

what to buy: On *Spirit of the Forest* ✍✍✍ (Hannibal, 1993, prod. Martin Cradick), Cradick's tinkling mandolin, the chirping of forest insects, and the jaunty Baka rhythms flow together as naturally as the water in a jungle stream. *The Meeting Pool* ✍✍✍ (Hannibal, 1995) has more Celtic music, but half the tracks are still based on Baka singing and drumming to continue this pioneering Afro Celtic exploration. For *Journey Between* ✍✍✍ (Hannibal, 1998), Cradick and company team up with members of Ghana's Kakatsitsi instead, resulting in another solid Afro Celtic fusion with charming vocals by Su Hart and compelling percussion by the drummers of Kakatsitsi.

solo outings:
Outback:
Baka ✍✍✍ (Hannibal, 1990)
Dance the Devil Away ✍✍✍ (Hannibal, 1992)

influences:
◄◄ Outback, Battlefield Band
►► Afro Celt Sound System

see also: *Dr. Didg*

j. poet

The Balfa Brothers /Freres Balfa

Cajun
Formed 1946, in Basile, LA, USA. Disbanded 1978.

Will Balfa (died 1978), fiddle, vocals; Rodney Balfa (died 1978), guitar, vocals; Dewey Balfa, fiddle, guitar, harmonica, vocals; Harry Balfa, guitar; Burkeman Balfa, percussion; Nelda Balfa, vocals; Hadley Fontenot, accordion; Marc Savoy, accordion, fiddle; Nathan Abshire, accordion. (All members are from USA.)

The Balfa Brothers' style was based around the lonesome twin fiddles of Will and Dewey Balfa and the rock-solid guitar of Rodney Balfa. The two fiddles were not the sweet sound of the western swing that moved east into Louisiana after World War II, but a hearkening back to the rawer sound of the Cajun house-dance, prior to the introduction of the accordion. At those dances, one fiddle played lead while the other had to provide the dancing rhythm on the low strings. Taking that as their starting point, the Balfas did add a sophistication from their exposure to swing and country music, and created a new/old sound. Though the fiddle dominated, they worked

with the finest of Cajun accordionists, including Hadley Fontenot, Nathan Abshire, and Marc Savoy. Dewey's singing was always passionate, but Rodney's tenor seemed to hit the hardest. To go with it, their song choices were always superb, drawn from deep within the Cajun tradition—often their own family's. The thoughtful arrangements respected the occasional extra bar or beat that is the hallmark of music passed down from generation to generation.

The band had begun performing in 1946 with just Will and Dewey's two fiddles and a friend on guitar. Dewey also recorded with Elsie Deshotel in the early 1950s for the Koury label, while the band continued to play locally. It was Dewey's experience as a last-minute substitute, playing guitar accompaniment with Gladius Thibodeaux and Louis Lejeune, at the 1964 Newport Folk Festival that changed the course of the Balfa Brothers' career. His wildly well-received performance led to Dewey's triumphant return three years later with a band that included brothers Rodney and Will, daughter Nelda, and Hadley Fontenot. Dewey had come away from the earlier festival with a sense of the value of traditional Cajun music and the uniqueness of the Balfas' rich family tradition. This new awareness would guide him through a sterling career in the genre, both within and out of the band. In the latter category, he had a long performing and recording run with master accordionist Abshire, accompanying him on records from the 1950s onward. Meanwhile, the Balfas participated in folk festivals throughout the U.S., Canada, and France, while continuing to live fairly nondescript lives in Louisiana. Both the concerts and the quiet life came to a tragic end in 1978 when Will and Rodney were killed in a car accident outside of Bunkie, Louisiana. Dewey continued to perform, with the help of friends like Tracy Schwarz and Robert Jardell and a new generation of musicians that included his own daughter Christine, who later rededicated the family legacy with her aptly named ensemble Balfa Toujours—Balfa forever.

what to buy: *The Balfa Brothers Play Traditional Cajun Music, Vols. 1 & 2* ✍✍✍✍ (Swallow, 1987, prod. Floyd Soileau) is the *Rubber Soul* of Cajun music. The Balfas put away the drums and bass and play in an all-acoustic setting, long before the "unplugged" vogue. What you get is superbly soulful fiddle and voice, song after song. Many of these tracks are standards that have since been covered by groups like the Savoy-Doucet Cajun Band, Steve Riley & the Mamou Playboys, and Balfa Toujours.

what to buy next: On *J'ai Vu le Loup, le Renard et la Belette* ✍✍✍✍ (Rounder, 1988, prod. Gerard Dole), producer Dole has the Balfas play a mix of traditional waltzes and two-steps along with some "house-dance" music like a Cajun version of "Casey Jones" and an old contra dance, "La Vieille Danse a Balfa." The charming title track shows the place where Cajun and French folk music meet.

the rest:
New York Concerts 🎵🎵🎵 (Swallow, 1980)
Les Haricots Sont Pas Salés: Legendary Masters of Cajun and Creole Music 🎵🎵🎵🎵 (Cinq Planetes, 1998)

worth searching for: *Louisiana Cajun French Music from the Southwest Prairies: Vol. 1, 1964–1967* 🎵🎵🎵 (Rounder, 1976, prod. Ralph Rinzler) features the earliest recordings of the Balfa Brothers.

influences:
◄◄ Lawrence Walker, Dennis McGee, Leo Soileau

►► Steve Riley, Balfa Toujours, Marc & Ann Savoy, Tracy Schwarz, Michael Doucet

see also: *Nathan Abshire, Alphonse "Bois Sec" Ardoin, Balfa Toujours, Steve Riley & the Mamou Playboys, Rockin' Dopsie, Savoy-Doucet Cajun Band*

Jared Snyder and Randy Pitts

Balfa Toujours
Cajun
Formed 1992, in Basile, LA, USA. Based in La Pointe, LA, USA.

Christine Balfa, guitar, triangle, vocals; Dirk Powell, fiddle, accordion, vocals; Kevin Wimmer, fiddle, vocals; Mike Chapman, drums; Nelda Balfa, vocals, triangle; Tony Balfa, drums, bass; Peter Schwarz, fiddle, bass, vocals. (All members are from USA.)

Christine Balfa is the guitarist, singer, songwriter, and heart of Balfa Toujours (Balfa forever). She carries on the tradition of her father Dewey, her uncles Will and Rodney, and their legendary Balfa Brothers ensemble. Christine and her older sister Nelda both write and sing; the elder Balfas' lonesome double fiddle sound is recreated by Kevin Wimmer (a protégé of Dewey) and Christine's husband Dirk Powell (who is also a brilliant accordionist). The lineup rotates, but the legacy moves directly forward.

what to buy: Sometimes you just want to get down on your knees and thank the Lord for bringing the right band together with the right producer, and *La Pointe* 🎵🎵🎵🎵 (Rounder, 1998, prod. Peter Schwarz) is certainly such a case. Peter Schwarz has succeeded in making a truly down-home record with Balfa Toujours—literally, as a matter of fact, on analog equipment at the Balfa home in La Pointe. Maybe it's the ancestral setting and the old-fashioned methods; maybe it's the band's recent work with other tradition-bearers like Octa Clark, Eddie Le-Jeune, Alphonse "Bois Sec" Ardoin, and Geno Delafose that

has changed their approach. Whatever it is, this is their best so far, a balanced mix of old and new.

what to buy next: *A Vieille Terre Haute* 🎵🎵🎵🎵 (Swallow, 1995, prod. Balfa Toujours) is the band's second effort and was their finest before *La Pointe*. The addition of Mike Chapman on drums revs up the traditional sound without detracting from it, the quality of the musicianship is uniformly high, and by this point Christine Balfa has grown into a strong and passionate singer. Her songwriting in collaboration with Powell has matured also: "Les Fleurs du Printemps" stacks up with just about any traditional Cajun song for its lyrical imagery, and the last four tracks qualify as almost a mini-tribute to the Balfa Brothers, while showing how Balfa Toujours is developing their own sound, building gracefully on that heritage. *Deux Voyages* 🎵🎵🎵 (Rounder, 1996, prod. Tim O'Brien) suffers from the warm sheen in which Tim O'Brien wraps the group; it takes away some of the buzz and wheeze that's integral to the naturalistic appeal of Cajun music. Still, listening to Christine do that upward glide on Canray Fontenot's "La Valse à Canray," or to her passionate reading of the Balfa standard "La Valse à Grand Père," will convince anyone of her skills as a singer. The fidelity with which she and Powell evoke the musical and lyrical essence of old-time Creole music with songs like "Le Canard à Bois Sec" demonstrates their advancing development as writers.

the rest:
Pop, Tu Me Parles Toujours 🎵🎵🎵 (Swallow, 1993)
(With Alphonse "Bois Sec" Ardoin) *Allons Danser* 🎵🎵🎵🎵 (Rounder, 1998)

worth searching for: *The American Fogies, Volume 1* 🎵🎵🎵🎵 (Rounder, 1996, prod. Ray Alden) is an anthology of regional American groups that includes a track of Balfa Toujours kicking it through "Duson Two Step."

influences:
◄◄ Dennis McGee, Marc and Ann Savoy, Lawrence Walker, the Balfa Brothers, Dewey Balfa, Tracy Schwarz, Steve Riley

►► Tasso, Magnolia Sisters, Kristi Guillory

see also: *Alphonse "Bois Sec" Ardoin, the Balfa Brothers, Steve Riley & the Mamou Playboys, Tracy Schwarz/Tracy Schwarz Cajun Trio*

Jared Snyder

Patrick Ball
Celtic harp and storytelling
Born March 27, 1950, in San Francisco, CA, USA. Based in Sebastopol, CA, USA.

A dynamic performer, Patrick Ball combines his loves of Irish music and history to bring passionate shows to his audiences.

His unique touch on the wire-strung harp creates a bell-like tone of great beauty, neither as percussive nor as strident as many of his contemporaries on the instrument. This allows his music to sing more intimately and more freely, creating a magical and expressive sound. Combined with this technique, true genius emerges in his arrangements, which take traditional melodies and allow them to shine their brightest through the use of simple-yet-full accompaniment that never obstructs the essence of the tune. Given his musical accomplishments, it is surprising to note that he grew up expecting to follow in his father's footsteps as a lawyer, a plan that persisted through college law studies and up to his father's untimely death—after which Bell soon switched to a graduate degree in history. This led to a trip to Ireland, where he quickly fell in love with the Irish oral tradition. After another trip there he realized he wanted to combine his training with his love of Irish music into what would become his life's career. Before long, he had taught himself the harp and began weaving his magic spell with stories and songs for widespread audiences. His talents most recently culminated in the completion of a one-man play, *O'Carolan's Farewell to Music,* which he wrote in collaboration with Peter Glazer. Ball plays the title role—of Turlough O'Carolan, the legendary 18th-century harper who contributed a staggering oeuvre to the Irish musical canon—with intensity and insight.

what to buy: *Fiona* 🎵🎵🎵🎵 (Celestial Harmonies, 1993, prod. Patrick Ball) features a delightful collection of beautifully arranged Celtic tunes. Ball displays his highly evocative and emotional use of the harp, occasionally joined by Tim Britton on uilleann pipes and tin whistles and Kevin Carr on fiddle. The arrangements have a simplicity and clarity without sounding empty or hollow. Album highlights include a bewitching "She Moved through the Fair" and the heartfelt Scottish "Farewell to the Land of Mist." *Christmas Rose* 🎵🎵🎵🎵 (Fortuna, 1990, prod. Patrick Ball) won a 1991 Indie Grammy for Best Seasonal Recording and contains sprightly arrangements of upbeat carols like "Bring a Torch, Jeanette Isabella," and haunting renditions of more somber ones like the little-known Appalachian number "Jesus, Jesus, Rest Your Head." This is an unusual holiday recording not to be missed.

what to buy next: On *The Music of Turlough O'Carolan* 🎵🎵🎵🎵 (Fortuna, 1983, prod. Dan Drasin), Ball manages to make solo harp remain vibrant through an entire album without any accompaniment to add variety; a rare talent indeed. It is a wonderful collection, including 15 outstanding melodies written by the famous blind harper O'Carolan. Ball's love of the composer's music radiates in his playing. Containing more O'Carolan as well as a number of other Irish tunes, *Secret Isles* 🎵🎵🎵🎵 (Fortuna, 1985, prod. Dan Drasin) also displays Ball's remarkable talents with elegance and liveliness. Particularly

lovely on this album is a Manx set, with "Song of the Water Kelpie" and "The Sheep under the Snow" paired beautifully. With a caveat to those who prefer the musical to the spoken, Ball is a master storyteller, and he shows his talent well on the album *Storyteller: Gwilan's Harp and Other Celtic Tales* 🎵🎵🎵 (Celestial Harmonies, 1995, prod. Patrick Ball). It is the stories that take center stage here, backed by the joyous sounds of Ball's harp. The tales are hauntingly told, and the album won an Indie for Best Spoken Word Recording in 1995. *Finnegans Wake* 🎵🎵🎵 (Celestial Harmonies, 1997, prod. Patrick Ball) is a more ambitious effort; here Ball reads passages from James Joyce's well-known and highly enigmatic work. The excerpts are chosen with an ear for the musicality of the words themselves and brought further alive through interwoven harp playing (though also quite intermittent, music lovers).

the rest:
From a Distant Time 🎵🎵🎵 (Fortuna, 1983)
O'Carolan's Dream 🎵🎵🎵 (Fortuna, 1989)

influences:
◀ Turlough O'Carolan, Derek Bell, Alan Stivell

▶ Carol Thompson, Wendy Stewart

Jo Hughey Morrison

Bamboleo
Timba
Formed February 1995, in Havana, Cuba. Based in Havana, Cuba.

Lázaro Moisés Valdés, keyboards; Julio Pincheiro, keyboards (1995–97); Haila Monpié, vocals (1995–98); Vannia Borges, vocals; Osvaldo Chacon, vocals (1995–97); Rafael Leberra, vocals; Alejandro Barrero, vocals; Manuel Pelayo, tenor saxophone (1995–97); Wilfredo Cardosa, tenor saxophone; Juan R. Larrinaga, alto saxophone (1995–97); Abel Fernández, alto saxophone; Pavel Diaz, trumpet (1995–97); Omar A. Peralta, trumpet (1995–97); Junior Romero, trumpet; Ulises Texidor, bongos; Luis A. Abreu, tumbas (1995–97); Andrés Gonzalo Gavilán, tumbas; Gilberto Moreaux, drums (1995–97); Ludwig Nuñez, drums; Rafael Varges, bajo; José Espinosa, timbales. (All members are from Cuba.)

Four decades of U.S.-imposed embargo have kept Cuba jailed in near-total isolation. We've seen all the footage of decaying buildings, bedraggled slum kids, ration queues . . . but that's only yang. What you can't see is the indomitable yin-force that enriches, uplifts, and chills out the Cuban soul 24-7: all the music. The rapturous drums of *Santería* rituals, the humble lilt 'n' sway of country *son* and its sophisticated cousin *danzon*, the sweaty rushes of mambo, cha-cha-cha, rumba, Afro-Cuban salsa—the people's spiritual flashlight cutting through a century's worth of dark times. The mango curtain has not only enshrouded that rich legacy but also obscured outside-the-Western-Hemisphere supergroups like Irakere, Los Van Van, and NG La Banda. But since '95, the trickle of Cuban youngbloods whose sounds had reached these shores has become a deluge thanks to Ry Cooder's landmark album *Buena Vista Social Club*. Fortuitously swept in with the tide was Bamboleo, the hottest band in Cuba. Along with other new jacks like David Calzado & La Charanga Habanera, Bamboleo rocks the street-fresh *timba* sound. Timba freaks old-school salsa with '70s-funk horn riffs and keyboard vamps, R&B bang, rap slang, and D.C. go-go–style extended percussion breakdowns. Whether on tape or in the dancehall, Bamboleo's timba is a rawer, looser, funkier, juicier cipher than the competition. Ironically, Bamboleo's rapid ascension to Cuban-pop superstardom is due more to Monpié and Borges's street juice than the music. Near-bald, dark-complexioned, charismatic, and confident lead divas, these sistahs rendered all the ingrained stereotypes obsolete—in Cuba that's way deeper impact than a Madonna or a Lauryn Hill. At the end of the day, Bamboleo is the first modern Cuban band with the Total Package: two rock-star icons with attitude, cool tunes/hotter albums, mackadacious band, and houserockin' show. From Havana to Lincoln Center to Montreux, Bamboleo is all-world-certified. The wheel having been reinvented in '95, the atom was split in mid-'98, with Monpié and chief songwriter/now-ex-Bamboleo manager L. Limonte leaving with half the band to form Azucar Negra; at presstime, a reconstituted Bamboleo records album *numero tres*.

what to buy: Mostly written by Limonte (seven out of nine songs) and absolute when sung by Monpié ("Cuentales," "Con Un Canto En El Pecho," title track), *Yo Me Parezco A Nadie ♪♪♪♪* (Ahi-Nama Music, 1998, prod. Lázaro Moisés Valdés) is two exhilarating steps forward, one gloriously bittersweet look backward at the greatest-timba-band-you-never-saw-and-will-never-see-again.

what to buy next: The sound of a band in evolutionary transition, Bamboleo's debut *Te Gusto O Te Caigo ♪♪♪♪* (Ahi-Nama Music, 1997, prod. Lázaro Moisés Valdés) is a glop of Los Van Van/NG La Banda old-school here ("Circulame"), a pinch of African *soukous* (rumba) there ("Bamboleo y Meleza"), a whiff of timba-to-come all over ("Bemba Colora"). Roots-positive, next-level prescient.

influences:

◀◀ Irakere, Los Van Van, NG La Banda, Earth, Wind & Fire, Kool & The Gang, Sugarhill Gang

▶▶ David Calzado & La Charenga Habanera, Issac Delgado, Manolín, El Médico De La Salsa, Azucar Negra, Aldaberto Alvarez

see also: *Ry Cooder, Manolín, El Médico de la Salsa*

Tom Terrell

Bana
Morna
Born in Mindelo, Sao Vicente, Cape Verde. Based in Lisbon, Portugal.

Bana is considered the finest singer of *morna* (the melancholy Verdean style sometimes compared to blues), a man who has influenced most of the singers to come after him. Bana began singing at an early age and left high school to travel West Africa and Europe in search of a career, but finally returned to Cape Verde and the morna. Early in his career, Bana, who is over six feet tall and quite muscular, used to physically carry B. Leza, one of the great morna composers, to his gigs. By the 1950s Bana was developing his own style of singing and became quite popular with the expatriate Verdean communities in America and West Africa. In 1965 he moved to Rotterdam, Holland, and formed A Voz de Cabo Verde with Luis Morais, Toi De Bibla, Jean Da Lomba, Morgadinho, and Frank Cavaquinho. The band caused a revolution in the sound of Verdean music that continues to reverberate today. In 1975, after Cape Verde became independent, Bana was accused of collaborating with the colonial government and fled to Lisbon where he continued his career, playing at his own restaurant and operating a music shop. In 1982 the Cape Verde government issued a formal apology, and in 1992 the Portuguese government awarded him the Medal of Grand Merit for his contribution to Portuguese culture.

what's available: *Chante la Magie du Cape-Vert ♪♪♪♪*◊ (Melodie France, 1993) is a beautiful and moving collection of mornas, with a couple of mid-tempo *coledeiras* thrown in for good measure. Bana's aching sincerity and rueful delivery make each tune drip with longing and sorrow. There is no information on the CD, but the backing band of acoustic virtuosos and the low-key production give the session a classic feeling. *Ritmos de Cabo Verde ♪♪♪♪* (Movieplay) is a set of upbeat Congolese *soukous* tunes played in a Cape Verdean style, with vocals by a master singer in rare high spirits.

influences:

◀◀ B. Leza, Eugenio Tavares

▶▶ Cesaria Evora, Nando, Masa Abrantes

see also: *Cesaria Evora, Fantcha*

j. poet

Buju Banton
Ragga, roots dancehall
Born Mark Myrie, 1973, in Kingston, Jamaica. Based in Kingston, Jamaica.

Buju Banton is one of the most celebrated and controversial artists in dancehall and *ragga* (digital) reggae, a still-young man who has both reaped the rewards and felt the sting of a highly public growing-up. Banton is descended from a rebellious family of Maroons who escaped the British slavery system of the 17th century into the rugged vastness of the Jamaican countryside, using any means necessary to defend their freedom. He was raised in the poverty-stricken Denham Town and nicknamed "Buju," meaning "breadfruit," due to his chubby appearance as a child. He later took his stage surname from the undervalued Buro Banton, a deejay beloved in Jamaica but virtually unknown beyond the island. Buju began his career by deejaying on the Sweet Love and Rambo Mango sound systems (dance-ready mobile turntable, mic, and amplification set-ups) at age 13, and the same year released his presciently titled debut single, "The Ruler." With the passing of puberty, his voice matured into a cavernous growl, and in 1991, when he teamed with Penthouse producer Donovan Germain and the studio's forward-thinking engineer, Dave Kelly, Banton's star began its rise, though controversy courted him almost instantly. Despite infuriating many dark-complected sistren, his ode to light-skinned black women "Love Mi Browning" included a blistering digital rhythm that made it a dancehall hit. A string of fashion-defining smashes followed, including "The Bogle," which inspired a trendy dance and was titled after Paul Bogle, the black Baptist preacher who led the Morant Bay rebellion against British military law in 1865. On Kelly's own Madhouse imprint, Banton released the scorching "Big It Up" and "Batty Rider," the latter a keen, er, observation on the skin-tight, extremely skimpy shorts worn in the dancehalls by women called "donettes," which in turn fueled the eye-popping uniform's popularity. "The Only Man" was another surging and influential dancehall hit, this one propelled by Kelly's ingenious "Arabian" rhythm. By now, Banton had enough hit singles to release two full-length albums, *Mr. Mention* and *Stamina Daddy*. An early example of his ability to articulate the frustrations of ghetto life—and examine the have-and-have-not dynamics that keep the underclass under—came on "How Massa God World A Run." Banton also breathed life into his Cell Block 321 label, which released fine singles from Frisco Kid ("Video Light") and the vocal duo Brian & Tony Gold ("Searching for the Light"), not to mention Banton's own uncompromising "Rampage."

His forward momentum hit some self-inflicted turbulence, however, with the appearance of "Boom Bye Bye" on the Shang imprint, a tune which apparently encouraged the murder of "batty boys"—ragga slang for homosexuals—over Mad Cobra's white-hot "Flex" rhythm: "Boom bye bye inna batty boy head/Rude-boy haffi know say nasty man fe dead." In the ensuing storm of protest Banton was coldly unapologetic. Many Jamaicans admired his backbone during the controversy, and some journalists even described his stance as a matter of principle in a land deeply hostile to the gay lifestyle. Stateside, opinion was split between outright condemnation of an attitude then finally starting to go into decline, and tempered condemnation cog-

nizant of past American rushes to judge Third World cultures—each position a sign of progress in some way. Years later, the file on this 19-year-old's transgression seems to have been sealed, through a combination of the standard public attention span and perhaps some realization of his youth and inexperience at the time. To acknowledge his musical vision is not necessarily to sanction his past lyrical myopia, and indeed, Banton's conversion to Rastafarianism soon after and his socially conscious songs since indicate a reformed outlook. His most recent releases, the phenomenally rootsy *'Til Shiloh* and *Inna Heights,* have spurred a fascinating self-examination by his genre's "massive" (public), and his single "Murderer" was a devastating plea to cease the violence in the dancehall after the brutal shootings of talented performers like Dirtsman, Nitty Gritty, and Banton's own close friend Pan Head. Banton also brought back an exhilarating sonic vitality by reintroducing the organic rhythms of studio musicians to the standard digital beats that had dominated the dancehall since the mid-'80s. It's a sensory symbol of the genuineness he now seeks—when he was still a teen in the hurricane of criticism, few could have predicted that Banton would reach and know his own "inna heights" and transform himself into one of contemporary reggae's most important worldwide spiritual ambassadors.

what to buy: Despite its Grammy nomination and not because of it, *Inna Heights* ♪♪♪♪ (V.P., 1997, prod. Donovan Germain, Buju Banton) is one of the most thoughtful and cohesive albums to ever shake the soul of the dancehall, and includes Banton's excellent collaborations with Jah Mali ("Mother's Cry"), Beres Hammond ("My Woman Now"), the legendary Toots Hibbert ("54/46"), and deejay progenitor "The Ugly One"—*selecta* King Stitt ("Small Axe"). Whether backed by live rhythms or digital beats, Banton proves adept at succor-drenched singing ("Hills and Valleys," "Destiny") and rock-stone deejaying ("Redder Than Red," "Love Dem Bad"). *'Til Shiloh* ♪♪♪♪ (PolyGram, 1995, prod. various) is a similarly ambitious, Rasta-themed album with "conscious" lyrics, particularly on the watershed hits "'Til I'm Laid to Rest" and "Untold Stories," the latter recalling Marley's "Redemption Song" with its spare acoustic guitar and hungry-bellied wail. Banton also demonstrates his hydroelectric microphone flow over delightfully rude rhythms on a remix of "Champion" (with a sample of Ice Cube's "You Know How We Do") and the first album appearance of the fiery "Murderer." A lush, healing cover of the late Garnett Silk's "Complaint" provides a further sign of Banton's raised consciousness and concurrent lack of loftiness.

what to buy next: *Voice of Jamaica* ♪♪♪ (Mercury, 1993, prod. various) marked his shift into strictly cultural concerns and is his most underrated album by far, including "Tribal War," a cutting plea for peace between Kingston's then-warring political factions. Equally compelling is Banton's dissection of the repressive police-instituted curfew laws on "Operation Ardent." Elsewhere he collaborates with singer Wayne Wonder on the pensive "Commitment" and "Searching," the latter a lyrical gateway into a rapidly opening and maturing mind.

the rest:

Stamina Daddy ♪♪ (Payday, 1991)
Mr. Mention ♪♪♪ (I1s, 1991)
Bogle ♪♪ (Mango, 1992)
Quick N/A (Exworks, 2000)

influences:

◀◀ Buro Banton, Clement Irie, Tony Rebel, Garnett Silk, Winston Riley, Bunny Lee, Red Dragon, Brian & Tony Gold, Tenor Saw, King Stitt, Bob Marley, Dave Kelly, Mad Cobra

▶▶ Jigsy King, Capleton, Frisco Kid, Chevelle Franklin

see also: *Beenie Man*

Todd Shanker

Carlos Barbosa-Lima

Classical, South American folk
Born December 17, 1944, in São Paulo, Brazil. Based in Brazil and USA.

One of the foremost classical guitar players in the world, Carlos Barbosa-Lima is also a pretty good jazz guitarist. His understanding of, and versatility in, both genres has made him one of the most formidable technical players around. It should come as no surprise that Barbosa-Lima has authored at least eight books on classical, jazz, and Brazilian technique in addition to serving as a faculty member at the Manhattan School of Music. Much of Barbosa-Lima's jazz performing and recording has been in the company of Charlie Byrd and the late Laurindo Almeida, two marvelous guitarists and influential aficionados of Brazilian jazz. He has also recorded with Byrd as part of the Washington Guitar Quintet. Barbosa-Lima's playing is characterized by precision but, within the context of Brazilian repertoire, also possessed of a remarkable sense of swing, which makes him equally at home with the music of a Joplin, Gershwin, or Jobim.

what to buy: Barbosa-Lima's performances of the aforesaid three composers, while recommendable in their own way, don't have the sheer *joie de vivre* of the solo recital *Plays the Music of Luiz Bonfá & Cole Porter* ♪♪♪♪♪ (Concord Concerto, 1984, prod. Carl E. Jefferson, Charles E. Brown). Bonfá composed such wonderful songs as "Manha de Carnaval" and "Samba de Orfeu" and toured the States with Stan Getz during the height of the bossa nova craze. Cole Porter was the composer of witty standards like "Night and Day," "Love for Sale," and "In the Still of the Night," which hundreds of jazz musicians have used as a road map for improvisation. Barbosa-Lima does a great job with both oeuvres.

what to buy next: *Plays the Music of Antonio Carlos Jobim & George Gershwin* ♪♪♪ (Concord Concerto, 1982, prod. Carl E. Jefferson) in some ways is more of a classical recording than a jazz one, but Barbosa-Lima excels in each mode, with no loss of vigor in either direction. The playing is lovely and these are some of the most memorable tunes of the 20th century.

best of the rest:

(With Sharon Isbin) *Brazil, with Love* ♪♪♪♪ (Concord Picante, 1987)
(With Sharon Isbin) *Rhapsody in Blue/West Side Story* ♪♪♪ (Concord Concerto, 1988)
(With Laurindo Almeida and Charlie Byrd) *Music of the Brazilian Masters* ♪♪♪♪♪ (Concord Picante, 1989)
(With the Washington Guitar Quintet) *Charlie Byrd & the Washington Guitar Quintet* ♪♪♪♪ (Concord Concerto, 1992)
(With the Washington Guitar Quintet) *Aquarelle* ♪♪♪♪ (Concord Jazz, 1994)

worth searching for: *Chants for the Chief* ♪♪♪♪ (Concord Picante, 1991) also leans more toward Brazilian-flavored classical music than jazz, but the rhythms and percussive effects give the works a flexibility and third-world swing that most classical just doesn't have. Barbosa-Lima and composer/percussionist Thiago DeMello perform the 10-movement title work, and then the headliner plays six solo guitar pieces by various Brazilian composers who use folk melodies as their starting point.

influences:

◀◀ Andres Segovia, Atahualpa Yupanqui

▶▶ Sharon Isbin, Manuel Barrueco

see also: *Luiz Bonfá, Antonio Carlos Jobim*

Garaud MacTaggart

The Barra MacNeils

Celtic fusion
Formed 1986, in Sydney Mines, Cape Breton, Canada. Based in Cape Breton, Canada.

Sheumas MacNeil, piano, keyboard, vocals; Kyle MacNeil, violin, acoustic guitar, electric guitar, mandolin, vocals; Stewart MacNeil, vocals, accordion, keyboards, whistle, flute, electric guitar; Lucy MacNeil, vocals, bodhrán, Celtic harp, backing vocals, viola, violin. (All members are from Canada.)

Growing up together in a home where musicians would casually drop by for a jam session, the Barra MacNeils had it made when it came to a nurturing environment for their future career. Each of the four had appeared on TV and radio by the time they were 10, and they were touring during school breaks as they grew up. Each is an outstanding multi-instrumentalist, and they frequently switch roles from one piece to the next. All four also have rich, evocative voices, which blend to create memorable mouth music (an unaccompanied form of Scots Gaelic dance singing) or modern harmonies. While drawing on their Maritime roots, this quartet has forged ahead into a world of modern visions, giving listeners a shower of styles and sounds on their eight albums, rapidly switching from traditional folk to jazz, pop, and even punk. It is this lack of a single category to define them which has itself been the defining factor in the Barra Mac-Neils' success. Never seeming satisfied with having grasped any one genre, they keep reaching for others, combining as they go. Fusing pop, folk, and worldbeat, they strive to see where music might take them.

what to buy: *The Traditional Album* 🎜🎜🎜🎜 (Iona, 1994) is considered a classic of its type. Entirely instrumental, the album shows the Barra MacNeils at their best, with fiery reels and jigs galore. A must-have for traditional music fans.

what to buy next: *Until Now* 🎜🎜🎜 (1997) showcases much of the material that has made the group famous, with heavy leanings on their traditional Scottish heritage. *The Barra MacNeils* 🎜🎜🎜 (Polydor, 1986) introduced them to the world, with a rich variety of traditional music beautifully presented.

what to avoid: Fans will either love or hate *The Question* 🎜🎜 (Mercury/Polydor/PolyGram, 1995, prod. Nick Griffiths), which lives up to its name by leaving the listener wondering what type of music the band really plays. Bordering on punk, jazz, and worldbeat at times, the album shows almost nothing of the traditional roots for which the Barra MacNeils are renowned.

the rest:
Rock in the Stream 🎜🎜🎜 (Polydor/PolyGram, 1989)
TimeFrame 🎜🎜🎜 (Polydor/PolyGram, 1992)
Closer to Paradise 🎜🎜🎜 (Polydor, 1993)
Timespan 🎜🎜🎜 (Iona Records, 1996)

worth searching for: The band burns a second hole in the CD with their title-says-it-all rendition of "Rattlin' Roarin' Willie" on the Chieftains' all-star Canadian Celtic invitational, *Fire in the Kitchen* 🎜🎜🎜 (BMG Classics, 1998, prod. Paddy Moloney).

influences:

◀◀ The Rankin Family, Buddy MacMaster

▶▶ Mouth Music

Jo Hughey Morrison and Neal Walters

Ray Barretto

Salsa, hispanic pop, jazz
Born April 29, 1929, in Brooklyn, NY, USA. Based in USA.

During the late 1940s Ray Barretto, fresh from his tour of duty with the army, was hanging out in Harlem and partaking in the famous jam sessions that went on at Minton's and the Apollo

frame drums worldwide

One of the three main types of drums worldwide (along with cylindrical drums and kettle drums), the family of frame drums is remarkable not only for its nearly universal distribution, but also for its longevity—the basic instrument's history began more than 4,000 years ago in the Middle East, then spread throughout the Mediterranean world. Visual representations of frame drums appear in ceremonial scenes from ancient Mesopotamia, on Greek vases with women dancing and drumming, and in Italian Renaissance paintings featuring angels playing tambourines. In stark contrast to our modern world, where men are usually the drummers, in antiquity frame drums were most commonly associated with women. Frame drums come in a wide variety of shapes and sizes. Most are round, but some are square or triangular; all have shallow frame depths, though heads can measure from six to more than 30 inches across. Some frame drums are played with a stick, as in the shamanic traditions of Native America and Central Asia, but most are played with the hands. The most well-known frame drum in the Western world is the *bodhrán,* the traditional drum of Ireland popularized by the Chieftains. But nearly every culture has its own variation on this simple instrument, from the Moroccan *bendir* (which features twine stretched across the inside of the goatskin head to produce a buzzing effect) and the South Indian *kanjira* (a lizardskin drum with a single set of jingles), to the Brazilian *pandeiro* (a lively drum with rows of jingles) and the increasingly popular North African *tar* (a lightweight, physically and tonally deeper tambourine). For a fascinating introduction to the wondrous and ancient art of frame drumming, check out the music of Glen Velez, who is widely considered the world's finest frame drum virtuoso.

see also: Glen Velez

Bret Love

Bar. Playing alongside such members of the bop elite as Sonny Stitt and Charlie Parker inspired the career path Barretto was to take. From there he went on to play in Latin bands led by José Curbelo and Tito Puente (for whom he replaced Mongo Santamaria). After Barretto recorded with Red Garland on *Manteca,* receiving special-guest-artist billing on the album cover, he became the first choice for jazz musicians looking for a bit of Latin percussion. These have included Lou Donaldson, Gene Ammons, Dizzy Gillespie (an early influence along with Chano Pozo), and Sonny Stitt, though as a crack session man Barretto has also played on the pop side of the street with the Rolling Stones and Bette Midler, to name just a few. While working the jazz scene has always been special to Barretto, a lot of his recordings and commercial successes have come from the Latin arena. In 1961 he recorded a novelty tune for Tico Records, "El Watusi," that became a big hit in 1963, lasting seven weeks in the *Billboard* magazine Top 40. Seminal salsa label Fania Records was his next major recording home. While there he recorded several groundbreaking albums including *Acid,* which worked in elements of jazz, Latin, and soul and capitalized on the *bugalú* craze of the moment. Barreto has also been a key member of the Fania All-Stars since their founding in 1968. In 1990 his collaboration with salsa queen Celia Cruz, *Ritmo En El Corazón,* won a Grammy Award. His more recent albums have swung back towards his jazz beginnings (albeit in a decidedly Latin-influenced mode), with 1994's *Taboo* and 1996's *My Summertime* receiving Grammy nominations for Best Latin Jazz Performance.

what to buy: Barretto's outfit New World Spirit is in the running for most interesting Latin jazz group of the 1990s. The personnel has stayed fairly consistent over the years, but the lineup on *Taboo* 𝄞𝄞𝄞𝄞 (Concord Picante, 1994, prod. Allen Farnham) is even more exceptional for featuring Latin trumpet legend Ray Vega soaring over the keyboard fantasies of Colombian-born pianist Hector Martignon, with Barretto's always-inventive percussion binding the whole together. Martignon is an interesting composer as well, with his sensuous mid-tempo "Guajirita" sustaining rhythmic tension where a lesser group of musicians would probably want to sprint for the finish instead of enjoying the ride. Barretto's songs, including "Bomba-riquen" and "Montuno Blue," are also notable, as is his choice of covers, among them McCoy Tyner's "Effendi" and Nat Adderly's always-welcome "Work Song." *My Summertime* 𝄞𝄞𝄞𝄞 (Blue Note, 1996, prod. Jean-Jacques Pussiau) is another fine mix of covers and originals from Barretto and the band. Trumpeter Michael Philip Mossman, though relatively young, is already a veteran of the Latin jazz world, having appeared on the final two albums by genre pioneer Mario Bauzá in addition to playing with such jazz stars as Gene Harris, Horace Silver, and Toshiko Akiyoshi. Pianist Martignon and bassist Jairo Moreno

have been part of Barretto's band for years and help form the rhythmic core along with drummer Vince Cherico. Barretto is his usual superb self on congas.

what to buy next: *Handprints* 𝄞𝄞𝄞 (Concord Picante, 1991, prod. Ray Barretto, Eric Kressmann) is definitely a percussion album. Barretto and drummer Ed Uribe wrote 40 percent of it and provide a percolating rhythm bed for their bandmates to float improvisations over. This early edition of New World Spirit was already a pretty happening band, a lot of which owes to Barretto's guidance and virtuosity—along with his ability to attract young, high-caliber talent (and, in the case of the aforesaid Martignon and Moreno, to keep it). Saxophonist Steve Slagle is the other major player on the album and contributes three fine songs, with the leadoff tune "Tercer Ojo" taking high honors.

best of the rest:
Carnaval 𝄞𝄞𝄞 (Fantasy, 1962)
La Cuna 𝄞𝄞𝄞𝄞 (Epic, 1979)
Rican/Struction 𝄞𝄞𝄞𝄞 (Fania/Charly, 1979)
(With Celia Cruz) *Ritmo En El Corazón* 𝄞𝄞𝄞𝄞 (Fania/Charly, 1988)
Latin Gold Collection 𝄞𝄞𝄞𝄞 (PolyGram Latino, 1995)

worth searching for: Red Garland's album *Manteca* 𝄞𝄞𝄞𝄞 (Prestige, 1958, prod. Bob Weinstock) was Barretto's first big break as a jazz sideman. The same year Garland's trio once again gave Barretto featured billing on *Rojo* 𝄞𝄞𝄞 (Prestige, 1958, prod. Bob Weinstock).

influences:
◀◀ Chano Pozo, Mongo Santamaria, Tito Puente

▶▶ Giovanni Hidalgo

see also: *Mario Bauzá, Celia Cruz, Larry Harlow, Tito Puente, Mongo Santamaria*

Garaud MacTaggart

Dr. Sikuru Ayinde Barrister
Fuji

Born 1948, in Abadan, Nigeria. Based in Staten Island, NY, USA, and Nigeria.

Sometimes the reason you haven't heard much from a major African star is that he's so popular and successful at home that seeking international fame isn't worth the trouble. Until recently, that was certainly the case with Dr. Sikuru Ayinde Barrister, the greatest living exponent of Nigeria's percussion-based *fuji* style. Barrister started out singing *were* music, Muslim songs used to wake the faithful for their pre-dawn meal during Ramadan. By 1965, Barrister had adapted the form considerably, adding in elements of percussive *apala* music and a philosophical Muslim song style known as *sakara*. That was the

Dr. Sikuru Ayinde Barrister (center)

year he began calling his sound fuji, after Japan's Mt. Fuji, the "mountain of love."

In the 1970s, fuji vied for standing against Nigeria's leading pop style, *juju,* championed by King Sunny Adé and Chief Commander Ebenezer Obey. Fuji gained slowly, and by the mid-'80s, it had become the dominant recreational music among the Yoruba majority in the Nigerian capitol, Lagos. Barrister and his biggest fuji rival Kollington Ayinla had arrived. Whereas juju was predominantly Christian and incorporated electric guitars and keyboards, fuji had a Muslim identity and used only percussion and vocals. Barrister's all-night concerts were more like ceremonies, in which wealthy Lagos socialites competed to "spray" the star with money. A night's take typically reached or exceeded $10,000. Barrister did tour in Europe and the U.S. occasionally, bringing as many as 35 musicians with him. But he tended to play for Nigerian audiences, and largely missed out on the public adulation among Americans that Adé received. The spraying continued, of course, but given the expenses of touring, earnings could hardly compete with those available in Lagos.

In the mid-'90s, though, things began to change. Barrister's 1993 cassette *The Truth* got him in trouble with Nigeria's military leaders, and as governance there declined steadily, so did the income of musicians. Now, Barrister has moved to Staten Island, New York, where he has gradually reassembled his band and is poised for a full-scale assault on the U.S. market.

what to buy: *New Fuji Garbage* ♪♪♪♪ (GlobeStyle, 1991, prod. GlobeStyle) takes its name from an earlier Nigerian cassette in which Barrister played on black American lingo wherein "bad" means "good." The release is a classic, bubbling with dense, lively percussion. Barrister's voice is powerful and passionate, quite a contrast to the understated near-whisper of the top juju singers.

what to buy next: Look for Barrister's two recent U.S. releases, *Precaution/Canadian Fuji American Version* ♪♪♪♪ (New Genesis Promotion, 1996, prod. various) and *Mr. Fuji* ♪♪♪♪ (New Genesis Promotion, 1998, prod. Aare (Dr.) S.S. Balogun, a.k.a. Barry Black). These newer recordings introduce occasional keyboards and Hawaiian guitar, but the percussion-rich fuji sound palette and Barrister's ripping voice remain absolutely intact.

Waldemar Bastos

worth searching for: The Nigerian artists who contributed to Barrister's musical education are mostly unknown and unrecorded. You can get some idea of those origins, though, by listening to the historic compilation *Yoruba Street Percussion* ♫♫♫ (Original Music, 1995).

influences:

▶▶ Adewale Ayuba

see also: *King Sunny Adé, Ebenezer Obey*

Banning Eyre

Waldemar Bastos

Angolan Afro-pop
Born 1954, in São Salvador do Congo, Congo. Based in Paris, France.

Singer/guitarist Bastos, though born in Congo, was raised in Angola and became inextricably associated with its culture, both to his fans and to himself. Like so many artists of his adoptive land before and after him, he had to leave this nation—racked first by colonialism (he was imprisoned as a teenager by the Portuguese political police), then civil war, then a new set of oppressions starting in 1974—to find free expression. Over the ensuing decades, he took refuge in Brazil, a much-changed Portugal, and finally France. He made several albums overseas before recording his major-label debut in New York. Bastos is that rare breed of artist in whose hands the acoustic guitar manages to sound fresh and stimulating. His sole U.S. album so far is a fine Pan-African snapshot that synthesizes many styles from all over the continent (and beyond), fronted by a plaintive, heartfelt voice.

what's available: On *Pretaluz [blacklight]* ♫♫♫ (Luaka Bop, 1998, prod. Arto Lindsay), carefully balanced acoustic and electric guitars combine with loping bass and keys for a smooth canvas against which Bastos sings pleas for peace, love, and understanding. There is a quiet dignity and authority in songs such as "Sofrimento (Suffering)," "Muxima (Heart)," and "Kuribota (Evil Tongue)," and an overall sense of warmth and forgiveness, but also an unflinching documentation of some bloody aspects of Angola's troubled recent history. Musically, the album ranges from the Portuguese *fado* style of lament on "Sofrimento (Suffering)," to the African *semba* (basis for the Brazilian samba) of "Querida Angola," to the Caribbean *zouk*-inflected "Menina (Girl)." On the Brazilian-influenced "Minha Familia (My Family)," a delightfully dirty electric guitar unexpectedly joins the proceedings briefly. It's one of the few hints that this was recorded so far away from the source of its inspiration.

influences:

◀◀ Bonga, Youssou N'Dour

John C. Falstaff

Ashwan Batish

Indian traditional and fusion
Born November 1951, in Bombay, India. Based in Santa Cruz, CA, USA.

The sitar was freed from its traditional Indian repertoire by Bombay-born and Santa Cruz–based multi-instrumentalist Ashwan Batish. On his groundbreaking 1987 album *Sitar Power,* Batish electrified his sitar and incorporated elements of rock, jazz, and calypso into his dance-inspiring music. Batish continued his progressive experiments with the 1994 sequel, *Sitar Power #2.*

Batish inherited his love of music from his father, Pandit Shiv Dayal Batish, a renowned Indian musician who played on the Beatles' album *Help!* Just as his father influenced British rock in this capacity, the young Ashwan was in turn heavily influenced by British rock when he and the family moved to London in 1962. He continued to grow as a musician after another family move to the United States in 1973. Music, however, remained a pastime, second to Batish's dreams of working in aeronautics. These dreams were shattered with the mass factory closings by aviation giant Boeing, and Batish shifted his academic pursuits to accounting. Finally, however, though he earned a bachelor's and a master's degree in that field, Batish returned to music in the late 1970s.

Batish's first three albums were rooted in the traditional music of India. His 1980 debut effort, *Morning Meditations,* was a collaboration with his father. His second album, *The Third Stream,* released the following year, was a type of fusion recording with an acoustic-guitar accompanist. *In Concert,* released in 1984, moved him back toward the traditional, with rhythmic accompaniment by Zakir Hussain on *tabla* drum. That album's follow-up, *Om Shanti Meditation,* showcased the *swarmandal,* a four-octave Indian harp more often used for accompanying singers. This gravitation back away from tradition became a hard swerve with *Sitar Power,* following the release of which Batish married and cut down on his touring to focus on raising a family. A master instructor at his own Batish Institute of Music and Fine Arts in Santa Cruz, he also founded the label Batish Records, and has produced several concert videos as well as instructional videos on sitar, tabla, and harmonium playing.

what to buy: *Sitar Power* ♫♫♫♫ (Shanachie, 1987, prod. Ashwan Batish) is an electrified demonstration of the previously unexplored flexibility of the sitar. Accompanied by a hard-rocking rhythm section, Batish blends Indian *ragas* with jazz, rock, and calypso influences.

what to buy next: The experimentation continues on *Sitar Power #2* ♫♫♫ (Batish, 1994, prod. Ashwan Batish).

the rest:
Morning Meditation ♫♫♫ (Batish, 1980)

The Third Stream ♫♫♫ (Batish, 1981)
In Concert ♫♫♫♪ (Batish, 1984)
Om Shanti Meditation ♫♫♫ (Batish, 1985)

influences:
◀◀ Pandit Shiv Dayal Batish, Ravi Shankar, George Harrison, John McLaughlin

see also: *Zakir Hussain*

Craig Harris

Battlefield Band
Scottish traditional and contemporary
Formed 1969, in Glasgow, Scotland. Based in Scotland.

Alan Reid, keyboards, guitar, vocals; **Brian McNeill**, fiddle, viola, mandolin, vocals (1969–90); **John McCusker**, fiddle, vocals (1990–present); **John Gahagan**, concertina, whistle (1977–78); **Jamie McMenemy**, cittern, guitar, mandolin, vocals (1977–79); **Pat Kilbride**, guitar, cittern, vocals (1978); **Jenny Clark**, dulcimer, guitar, vocals (1978); **Ged Foley**, guitar, vocals (1980–84); **Alistair Russell**, guitar, cittern, vocals (1984–97); **Davy Steele**, guitar, cittern, bodhrán, vocals (1997–present); **Duncan McGillivray**, bagpipes (1979–83); **Dougie Pincock**, bagpipes (1984–90); **Iain MacDonald**, bagpipes (1990–97); **Mike Katz**, bagpipes (1997–present).

Named for a suburb of Glasgow, Battlefield Band, along with the Tannahill Weavers and Silly Wizard, has been at the very heart of the Scottish folk revival of the last three decades. Hard-driving and energetic, the band has built a loyal and sizable audience by fusing traditional Scottish music with elements from jazz and rock 'n' roll. Although their current albums sound traditional when compared to the likes of Shooglenifty or recent Capercaillie, their experiments with synthesizers and pop music were revolutionary for their day. The band's early recordings were indeed more traditional, with the sparing use of synthesizer adding a slight modern touch. During the early 1980s, they developed a larger, more aggressive sound and produced their two defining albums, *Home Is Where the Van Is* and *There's a Buzz,* which established the band as a favorite in both Scotland and the U.S. These recordings were marked by modern arrangements using electric keyboards; a brace of traditional songs; a few compositions by band members; and, most important, great bagpiping and fiddling. After wholesale personnel changes in the mid-'80s, the band developed a more political sound, but kept the energy just as high with the fine *Anthem for the Common Man* and two instrumental albums with harper Alison Kinnaird. By the late '80s, however, the band seemed to be losing steam. Although they finally recorded *Home Ground,* a much-needed live album, releases from this period represent a low point in their history and a distinct decrease of drive. The replacement of Brian McNeill with fiddler John McCusker brought

some youthful energy and ideas back to the band, and by 1997's *Across the Borders* they were once again playing solid Scottish music mixed with outside influences—in this case the playing of Irish master flutist Seamus Tansey. More sweeping changes in late '97 ushered in yet another new sound, this time with former Ceolbeg members Davey Steele and Mike Katz joining John McCusker and Alan Reid.

what to buy: *Home Is Where the Van Is* ♫♫♫♫ (Temple, 1980, prod. Robin Morton) made Battlefield Band's reputation; it's a collection of traditional instrumentals and songs given a jolt through the addition of electric bass, synthesizer, and some imaginative arrangements. Alan MacGillavry's killer bagpiping sent kilts flying, and guitarist Ged Foley's tasteful playing filled in all the gaps. Featuring a strong set of tracks, including one original by Brian MacNeil ("The Lads o' the Fair"), the group proved that the tradition could take some updating without losing its soul. They've never been better than when they featured this lineup, and *There's a Buzz* ♫♫♫♫ (Temple, 1982, prod. Robin Morton) made two in a row. Highlights include Robert Louis Stevenson's "Shining Clear," set to music by Reid, and a sweet set of instrumentals beginning with "The Presbyterian Hornpipe." *Anthem for the Common Man* ♫♫♫♫ (Temple, 1984, prod. Robin Morton) saw Dougie Pincock pick up the piping mantle and singer Alistair Russell replace Foley. The lyrics became more political, featuring a great cover of Richard Thompson's "The Old Changing Way." Any worries about a loss of energy were dispelled by the opening track, "The Four-Minute Warning," featuring the new man, Pincock, more than holding his own on the pipes.

what to buy next: Battlefield Band is at its best in concert, and *Home Ground* ♫♫♫♫ (Temple, 1989, prod. Robin Morton) accurately captures its entertaining stage show. Jammed with more than 70 minutes of music, the album shows the band working through an exuberant run of songs and dance tunes. Particular highlights are the two sets featuring Dougie Pincock's solo piping and the nine-minute tour de force "Band of a Thousand Chances," in which the group combines Scottish classics with ones by Wilson Pickett and the Beatles. Like the archetypal American mail carrier, the quintessential Scottish band will not let *Rain, Hail or Shine* ♫♫♫♫ (Temple, 1998) deter their momentum—as this first studio CD from their yet-again-reconfigured roster proves; not with a vengeance (the sound changes are not all that radical), but with a confidence that's infectious (they still hold their own with any outfit of their kind). For the true believer, this one comes enhanced with some video interviews and photos.

what to avoid: *Quiet Days* ♫♫ (Temple, 1992, prod. Robin Morton) is a little too long, has no great numbers, and reveals a band looking for direction. The subsequent *Threads* and *Across the*

Borders (listed below) found them with new life and ideas; when filling out your Battlefield Band collection skip ahead to these.

the rest:
Battlefield Band ♪♪♪♪ (Topic, 1977/Temple, 1994)
At the Front ♪♪♪♪ (Topic, 1978/Temple, 1994)
Music in Trust ♪♪♪ (Temple, 1986)
On the Rise ♪♪♪ (Temple, 1986)
After Hours ♪♪♪♪ (Temple, 1987)
Celtic Hotel ♪♪♪ (Temple, 1987)
Music in Trust 2 ♪♪♪ (Temple, 1988)
New Spring ♪♪♪ (Temple, 1991)
Opening Moves ♪♪♪♪ (Topic, 1993)
Threads ♪♪♪ (Temple, 1995)
Across the Borders ♪♪♪♪ (Temple, 1997)
Celtic Folk: Live ♪♪♪♪ (Munich, 1998)

influences:

◀◀ Tannahill Weavers, Silly Wizard

▶▶ Shooglenifty, Tartan Amoebas, Runrig

see also: *Capercaillie, Ceolbeg, House Band, Alison Kinnaird, Kornog, Ossian, Patrick Street, Shooglenifty, Silly Wizard, Tannahill Weavers*

Tony Ziselberger

Mario Bauzá

Mario Bauzá

Cuban jazz
Born April 28, 1911, in Havana, Cuba. Died July 11, 1993, in New York, NY, USA.

Mario Bauzá was involved in two of the major jazz and Latin trends of the 1930s and '40s. He was responsible for introducing Dizzy Gillespie to conga legend Chano Pozo and for bringing the standard Cuban rhythm section into line with the big band sound of Cab Calloway and Chick Webb. The meeting of Gillespie and Pozo was influential in the development of a hybrid known as Cubop which included among its proponents Stan Getz and Charlie Parker. The blending of big band arrangements with Cuban rhythms made Bauzá's brother-in-law Machito (Frank Grillo) the leader of what was arguably the most influential Latin-flavored band in the first half of this century. Bauzá's first instruments were the clarinet and the bass clarinet, which he played in the Havana Philharmonic. In 1930, shortly after coming to the United States, Bauzá joined Cuarteto Machin playing trumpet, an instrument he learned in the two weeks preceding his initial job with the band. His first major jazz gig was with Chick Webb in 1933 and from there Bauzá worked briefly with bands led by Don Redman and Fletcher Henderson before joining Cab Calloway's outfit in 1939. In 1940 Bauzá made the move to Machito's newly formed band as the musical director, and there he stayed until 1976.

During the late '70s and early '80s Bauzá and Graciela (his sister-in-law and former vocalist with Machito) recorded a couple albums for small labels, which have since turned into prized collector's items. He then made a recording in 1992 featuring Chico O'Farrill's arrangement of "Tanga," a landmark tune originally written by Bauzá back in 1943, and this led to a gratifying, deserved, and none-too-soon resurgence of his career in the last year of his life.

what to buy: *Tanga* ♪♪♪♪ (Messidor, 1992, prod. Mario Bauzá, Götz A. Wörner) is by a truly big band, something like 24 pieces not counting vocalists and special guest Paquito D'Rivera. Things could get messy when arrangers work with an ensemble this large, but everyone involved in the project is top-notch. Special honors go to Chico O'Farrill, whose transformation of Bauzá's "Tanga" into the subtitled "Afro-Cuban Jazz Suite in Five Movements" is a masterpiece. There is not a weak moment in the whole album. The end result is not only a paean to the spirit of Latin jazz but a celebration of one of its cardinal figures, Mario Bauzá. *My Time Is Now* ♪♪♪♪ (Messidor, 1993, prod. Mario Bauzá, Götz A. Wörner) is another splendid album from one of the most important musicians in Latin jazz history. The band romps through Cuban classics by Arsenio Rodríguez

("La Vida Es Un Sueño") and Moíses Simons ("El Manisero," otherwise known as "The Peanut Vendor") in addition to rearranging Kurt Weill's "Moritat" into a Latin version of "Jack the Knife" (no, that's not a typo). Many *Tanga* alumni show up here, including such major participants as vocalist Rudy Calzado, drummer Bobby Sanabria, and mythic conga player Carlos "Patato" Valdéz.

what to buy next: Two months before he died, Bauzá was actively at work recording what would be his swan song. On *944 Columbus* ♫♫♫♫ (Messidor, 1994, prod. Mario Bauzá, Götz A. Wörner) the writing, arranging, and playing are still at a remarkably high level from all involved, but the spark of genius that informed the previous two efforts was starting to fade along with the leader. There are still crucial performances on this disc, however, and it is tempting to read a valedictory feel into Bauzá's pieces as well as compositions by Dizzy Gillespie and about Chano Pozo. For those who only want to dip into Bauzá's work, the compilation *Messidor's Finest, Volume One* ♫♫♫♫♫ (Messidor, 1997, prod. Mario Bauzá, Götz A. Wörner) includes selections from all of the above, though it shouldn't stop you from exploring them in their equally rewarding fullness.

worth searching for: One of the albums Bauzá recorded with Graciela after Machito's death in 1984 was *Afro-Cuban Jazz* ♫♫♫♫ (Caiman, 1984), which features a dream-team lineup including Paquito D'Rivera, Claudio Roditi, Daniel Ponce, and Jorge Dalto.

influences:

◄◄ Antonio Machin, Don Apiazo, Cab Calloway

►► Dizzy Gillespie, Tito Puente

see also: *Paquito D'Rivera, Machito, Patato, Arsenio Rodríguez*

Garaud MacTaggart

Bayou Seco
/Bayou Eclectico

American roots

Formed 1978, in Louisiana, USA. Based in Silver City, NM, USA.

Jeanie McLerie, fiddle, guitar; Ken Keppeler, fiddle, accordion, harmonica. (Both members are from USA.)

Jeanie McLerie began singing in French at age five and took up the ukulele at age eight. For those familiar with Bayou Seco, that might sound like things haven't changed very much. McLerie and Ken Keppeler have been researching and playing the music of the Southwest—from the Mississippi River to the deserts of Arizona—for 20 years. McLerie got interested in folk forms during the 1950s and learned to play Travis-style guitar

in time to show a young James Taylor how to do it one summer on Martha's Vineyard. In 1962, she went to France to study at the Sorbonne and got ever more involved with the folk scene. While in France, she met future husband Sandy Darlington, and the two eked out a living busking the movie theater queues. In 1964, the couple moved to England to perform in its folk clubs and became acquainted with most of the traditional and revival singers—later-legend Maddy Prior even served as their roadie for a time. They returned to the U.S. in 1967 to play the Newport Folk Festival and settled in the Berkeley, California area. McLerie published *Grow Your Own,* a book on organic gardening that was subsequently picked up by Random House and sold over 180,000 copies. In 1971, they moved to New Mexico, though they separated in 1973.

Keppeler, a fourth-generation Southwesterner, came from a musical family; his father played harmonica and was a very good singer, his maternal great-grandfather was a fiddler and pump organ player. He began to play guitar in high school and often hung out at the old Ash Grove where he would hear such acts as the Kentucky Colonels, Doc Watson, and Clifton Chenier. In 1978, he met McLerie in Louisiana and they began a long association with Cajun music, learning directly from a host of renowned practitioners including Michael Doucet, Dennis McGee, Canray Fontenot, and Alphonse "Bois Sec" Ardoin. During the late '70s, McLerie worked with Ann Savoy and Jean Broussard in a group called the Magnolia Sisters and recorded *Music from the Old Timey Hotel* with Franny Leopold. In 1979, she joined Alice Gerrard and Irene Herrmann as the Harmony Sisters and they toured extensively until 1983, when she and Keppeler moved to Santa Fe, New Mexico. As artists-in-residence, they visited every nook and cranny of New Mexico to learn music and songs from cowboy, Hispanic, and Navajo sources. Keppeler also became a sought-after craftsman of violins and mandolins.

McLerie and Keppeler developed strong ties to traditional musicians in New Mexico. Over the years they met and encouraged Cleofes Ortiz, a traditional Hispanic fiddler, and Max and Antonia Apodaca, two other traditional musicians whose work they brought to public attention and who taught them many of the tunes that have since become Bayou Seco staples. Similarly, they discovered the music of the Gu-Achi Fiddlers of the Tohono O'odham people of southern Arizona. Through fiddler Elliott Johnson of Cababi, Arizona, they learned much of the old-style material that was rapidly being forgotten. They continue to share the music and dances they were taught by these old masters, touring extensively in Europe and throughout the Southwest from their home in Silver City, New Mexico. McLerie recently started a school for fiddle instruction called the Fiddling Friends, which focuses on an international repertoire of styles and emphasizes the sources, including contact with traditional musicians. Keppeler continues to make fine violins. All of these experiences and influences have combined to form the Bayou Seco sound, which has been described as "delightfully danceable Chilegumbo with a spicy bite and delicious aftertaste." Bayou Seco recordings are available from Bayou Seco, P.O. Box 1393, Silver City, NM 88061, or by e-mail from bayouseco@aol.com. Of interest to fans present and future, a new CD titled *Use It Again* is due out at this writing, set to feature rerecorded versions of tunes from the otherwise-rare *Songs of New Mexico and Beyond*. Also look for the Harmony Sisters to re-form and release a CD compilation of their two Flying Fish LPs plus a few live recordings from the early '80s.

what to buy: *Following in the Tune Prints* 🎜🎜🎜🎜 (UBIK Sound, 1995, prod. Ken Keppeler, Jeanie McLerie, Manny Rettinger) finds Bayou Seco in fine form, presenting a program of "old music in the new West . . . desert stomps, Cajun romps, and songs for modern cowgirls and *vaqueros*." The CD mixes genres shamelessly, but allows the group to salute the old masters they've learned from while pursuing their own eclectic yet delightful musical tastes. The sound is not slick and is most definitely authentic, blending elements of Cajun, Tex-Mex *norteño*, Native American "chicken scratch," and zydeco into a down-home composite sketch of the Southwest. Also check out a couple of anthologies that feature one or more cuts by the group: *Old Time Music on the Air, Vol. 2* 🎜🎜🎜🎜 (Rounder, 1996, prod. Old Time Music on the Radio) and *The American Fogies, Vol. 1* 🎜🎜🎜🎜 (Rounder, 1996, prod. Ray Alden), each filled with very generous selections of great music.

what to buy next: The cassette-only *Songs of New Mexico and Beyond* 🎜🎜🎜🎜 (UBIK Sound, 1991, prod. Ken Keppeler, Jeanie McLerie, Manny Rettinger) is another eclectic batch of Cajun, New Mexican, Navajo, original, and only-they-know-what-else. If you crave a less mixed-bag approach, *Memories in Cababi: Tunes of the Tohono O'odham* 🎜🎜🎜 (UBIK Sound, 1995), also cassette only, is a real treat; delightful tunes in a style that deserves the exposure.

the rest:
No Borders 🎜🎜🎜 (UBIK Sound, 1986) (cassette only)
Orquesta Cleofonica 🎜🎜🎜 (UBIK Sound, 1987) (cassette only)
Recuerdos de Rociada 🎜🎜🎜 (UBIK Sound) (cassette only)

worth searching for: *Cactus Gumbo and Alligator Enchiladas* 🎜🎜🎜 (Blue Guitar Productions, 1983, prod. various) is the one Bayou Seco album that is out of print and unavailable. It's certainly worth grabbing if you come across it.

solo outings:
Jeanie McLerie:

(With Franny Leopold) *Music from the Old Timey Hotel* 🎜🎜🎜 (UBIK Sound, 1994)

Harmony Sisters:
Harmony Pie 🎜🎜🎜🎝 (Flying Fish, 1980)
Second Helping 🎜🎜🎜🎝 (Flying Fish, 1983)

influences:
◀◀ The Balfa Brothers, Dennis McGee, Cleofes Ortiz, Elliott Johnson

▶▶ Balfa Toujours, Delta Sisters

see also: *Gu-Achi Fiddlers, Savoy-Doucet Cajun Band*

Neal Walters

Keola Beamer /Keola and Kapono Beamer /Nona Beamer

Slack-key guitar

Born Keolamaikalani Breckenridge Beamer, February 18, 1951, in Hawaii, USA. Based in Hawaii, USA.

One of Hawaii's most popular contemporary musicians, Keola Beamer can trace his island history back to the 15th century. Many of those ancestors were musicians too: his great-grandmother, Helen Desha Beamer, was a noted songwriter and performer, and his mother teaches dancing and music, and occasionally records. Beamer's available output is perhaps more far-reaching than any other artist in his homeland's distinctive, open-tuned "slack-key guitar" style; it incorporates elements of chants and other traditional Hawaiian sounds, as well as the influence of soft Western pop. Through the years he has recorded as a solo artist, with his brother Kapono Beamer, and with his mother Nona Beamer.

what to buy: The gorgeous *Mauna Kea: White Mountain Journal* 🎜🎜🎜🎜 (Dancing Cat, 1997, prod. George Winston) is Beamer's finest moment on record, an instrumental album that features him playing both electric and acoustic guitar. Beamer does many of the tunes solo, overdubbing a few; George Winston occasionally joins on guitar as well. Beamer's arrangements of "Kaula 'ili" and "Hi'ilawe," songs associated with slack-key legends Sonny Chillingworth and Gabby Pahinui respectively, are both exquisite. *Moe'Uhane Kika (Tales from the Dream Guitar)* 🎜🎜🎜🎜 (Dancing Cat, 1995, prod. George Winston) is of similar quality, only here Beamer's the only player, sometimes adding a nylon-string acoustic or electric overdub.

what to buy next: A rare recording with a full band, *Wooden Boat* 🎜🎜🎜 (Dancing Cat, 1994, prod. George Winston) has a more contemporary sound than most of its label's other albums. Producer George "Keoki" Winston plays guitar on several tracks (including the duets "Kalena Kai" and "He Aloha no 'O Honolulu (Beloved Is Honolulu)"), and piano on the instrumental "No Ke Ano Ahiahi (In the Evening Time)."

what to avoid: Though Keola & Kapono Beamer's *Honolulu City Lights* 𝄪𝄪 (Paradise, 1987, prod. Teddy Randazzo) is considered one of the most successful albums ever recorded in Hawaii, it will have more value to tourists and honeymooners than slack-key aficionados. Both it and *Pure Hawaiian Magic* 𝄪𝄪 (Paradise, 1991, prod. Tom Moffatt), a second duo album, contain some fine slack-key picking, but the songs and arrangements are saccharine and overly romanticized.

the rest:

Hawaiian Slack Key Guitar in the Real Old Style 𝄪𝄪𝄪 (Music of Polynesia, 1972)

Sweet Maui Moon 𝄪𝄪 (Paradise, 1989)

Kolonahe: From the Gentle Wind 𝄪𝄪𝄪𝄪 (BMG/Windham Hill/Dancing Cat, 1999)

worth searching for: Beamer has released an instructional video, *The Art of Hawaiian Slack Key Guitar,* and published a book-and-cassette package, *Guitar Playing Hawaiian Style.*

solo outings:

Nona Beamer:

The Golden Lehua Tree 𝄪𝄪𝄪 (Starscape, 1997)

influences:

◄◄ Sonny Chillingworth, Gabby Pahinui

►► Ozzie Kotani

see also: *Sonny Chillingworth, Gabby Pahinui*

Brian Mansfield

Beausoleil

Cajun

Formed 1975, in Lafayette, LA, USA. Based in USA.

Michael Doucet, fiddle, vocals; David Doucet, guitar; Billy Ware, percussion; Tommy Alesi, drums (1977–present); Jimmy Breaux, accordion (1988–present); Al Tharp, bass, banjo, fiddle, backing vocals (1990–present); Errol Verret, accordion (1975–87); Tommy Comeaux, bass, mandolin (1975–90); Robert Vignaud, bass (1982–84). (All members are from USA.)

Led by fiddler, singer, and Cajun-culture zealot Michael Doucet, Beausoleil is not only Louisiana's premier Cajun band, but during the past decade or so has also become the best-known "world-music" band from North America. When Europeans, for example, think of Cajun music, they inevitably think of Beausoleil. Based in the acoustic version of their genre—a fiddle and accordion–led style that generally follows two forms, the waltz and the two-step—Beausoleil has consistently had the

vision and skill to add elements of New Orleans R&B, blues, folk, jazz, and country to their very vital take on traditional French music from Louisiana.

A Cajun heritage enthusiast since he was a teenager, Doucet made a trip to France in 1973 that convinced him of the value of his native culture. He returned to Louisiana determined to play the string music that had come to that state from France via the Acadian people of eastern Canada. Combining musical history and infectious dance music, Beausoleil—which borrowed the nickname of Acadian resistance leader Joseph Broussard—was initially the alter ego of a regionally famous cosmic Cajun band called Coteau. Fronted by Michael Doucet and known locally as "the Cajun Grateful Dead," Coteau lasted until 1977, when it broke up and its Beausoleil incarnation continued on. The fledgling group recorded its first album for Pate Marconi/EMI in France in 1976. The second disc, *The Spirit of Cajun Music,* was made in the U.S. for Louisiana-based Swallow Records in 1977. The band signed with Arhoolie Records during the early 1980s and in the fashion of that label released a number of traditional recordings, one of which, the soundtrack to the film *Belizaire the Cajun,* won a Grammy nomination. Constant touring and a revival of interest in all things Cajun (thanks in large part to New Orleans chef Paul Prudhomme) aided and abetted Beausoleil's growing popularity; in 1986 the band members quit their day jobs and committed to music full-time. In that same year they released four albums: the *Belizaire the Cajun* soundtrack, *Allons a Lafayette, Christmas Bayou,* and *Bayou Boogie,* the last of which was the band's first disc for Rounder Records—and the first time they recorded with electric instruments. In this period they also made several appearances on radio's definitive roots-music showcase, *Prairie Home Companion,* and were invited to play Carnegie Hall. In 1990 Beausoleil signed with Rhino Records' RNA imprint (later renamed Forward Records). Three consecutive Beausoleil albums won Grammy nominations in the Best Contemporary Folk category: 1989's *Bayou Cadillac,* 1991's *Cajun Conja,* and 1993's *La Danse de la Vie.* In 1991 Mary Chapin Carpenter won a Grammy for "Down at the Twist and Shout," a song she'd written about the band. When she performed the song during the Grammys telecast, they joined her onstage, a feat repeated at the 1997 Super Bowl. Beausoleil has even come to the attention of the rock community, with *Rolling Stone* referring to them as "the best damned dance band you'll ever hear." Having performed at two presidential inaugurations—Jimmy Carter's in 1977 and Bill Clinton's in 1993—Beausoleil continues to tour over 200 nights a year.

what to buy: *Bayou Deluxe: The Best of Michael Doucet & Beausoleil* 𝄪𝄪𝄪𝄪 (Rhino, 1993, prod. various) is probably the best place to jump into Beausoleil's ever-expanding catalog. Upbeat tunes like "Vieux Crowley" mix with slower, more introspective numbers like "Je M'Endors." Drawn from eight different albums and two compilation discs, this collection is a generous slice of the many sides to this traditional-music powerhouse.

what to buy next: Choosing any one album by a band that has yet to make even a mediocre disc is nearly impossible. *Bayou Cadillac* ♫♫♫ (Rounder, 1989, prod. Michael Doucet, Ken Gorz, Ken Irwin) gets the nod on the strength of classic Louisiana tunes like "Bon Temps Rouler" and great Doucet originals like "Valse Bebe." Add to that the band stretching into a successful medley of "Bo Diddley" and "Iko Iko" and you have one of their best. Again though, this is strictly a matter of taste: *Cajun Conja* ♫♫♫ (Rhino, 1991, prod. Al Tharp, Michael Doucet) and *La Danse de la Vie* ♫♫♫ (Rhino, 1993, prod. John Jennings, Michael Doucet, Beausoleil) are very close seconds.

the rest:
Spirit of Cajun Music a.k.a. *Louisiana Cajun Music* ♫♫♫ (Swallow, 1977)
Michael Doucet dit Beausoleil ♫♫♫ (Arhoolie, 1981/1994)
Zydeco Gris Gris ♫♫♫ (Swallow, 1985)
Allons a Lafayette & More with Canray Fontenot ♫♫♫ (Arhoolie, 1986)
Christmas Bayou ♫♫♫ (Swallow, 1986)
Bayou Boogie ♫♫♫ (Rounder, 1986)
Belizaire the Cajun ♫♫♫ (Arhoolie, 1986)
Hot Chili Mama ♫♫♫ (Arhoolie, 1988)
Live! From the Left Coast ♫♫♫ (Rounder, 1989)
Deja Vu ♫♫♫ (Swallow, 1990)
Parlez-Nous a Boire ♫♫♫ (Arhoolie, 1991)
L'Echo ♫♫♫ (Forward, 1994)
L'Amour ou la Folie ♫♫♫ (Rhino, 1997)
The Best of Beausoleil ♫♫♫ (Arhoolie, 1997)
Cajunization ♫♫♫ (Rhino, 1999)

worth searching for: *Vintage Beausoleil* ♫♫♫ (Music of the World, 1995, prod. Bob Haddad) collects live performances from 1986–87 in New York City. Several are from a rain-delayed Central Park concert where the band is responding to the enthusiasm of the muddy, dedicated crowd. For even *more* vintage Beausoleil, *Arc de Triomphe Two Step* ♫♫♫ (EMD/Blue Note, 1997) unearths and retitles *La Nuit,* the band's long-lost France-only debut studio release. Another disc worth hunting down is *Le Hoogie Boogie* ♫♫♫ (Rounder, 1992), a charming children's record of Cajun music featuring Michael Doucet, his wife Sharon Arms Doucet, and the members of Beausoleil.

solo outings:
Michael Doucet:
Michael Doucet & Cajun Brew ♫♫♫ (Rounder, 1988)
(With Alison Krauss, Seamus Connolly, Kenny Baker, Claude Williams, and Joe Cormier) *Master of the Folk Violin* ♫♫♫ (Arhoolie, 1989)
Beau Solo ♫♫♫ (Arhoolie, 1990)

David Doucet:
Quand J'ai Parti ♫♫♫ (Rounder, 1990)

influences:
◄◄ Amédée Ardoin, Dewey Balfa, Canray Fontenot
►► Filé, Balfa Toujours

see also: *California Cajun Orchestra, Savoy-Doucet Cajun Band, Jo-El Sonnier*

Robert Baird

Francis Bebey
Makossa, rumba, classical
Born July 15, 1929, in Douala, Cameroon. Based in Paris, France.

One of West Africa's artistic elder statesmen, Francis Bebey has long been a champion of African culture, introducing it to the world through his music, poetry, novels, theater works, and film. As a boy, though, Bebey was alienated from this culture by his Westernized upbringing and the colonial educational policies of France. His early training in piano and guitar, Bebey has said, "schooled [me] to ignore, and even to detest, traditional African styles." But by his teens he had come under the spell of African traditional music, as well as local pop, Cuban rumba, and American jazz. Then, while a student at the Sorbonne in the 1950s, he first heard the classical guitar of Andres Segovia, a watershed in Bebey's understanding of music that changed his approach to guitar technique and composition. Before the decade was out he wrote his first important guitar piece, *Lake Michigan Summer,* during communications studies in the U.S.

Bebey's two academic paths converged in an early career as a radio journalist and disc jockey, leading the world traveler to a job with the information service of UNESCO in Paris in 1961— and, eventually, to the leadership of its traditional music section. His role during this period brought him back to Africa frequently to study its regional styles and to perform. Meanwhile, his creative abilities in both music and literature were coming into bloom; his first novel, *Agatha Moudiou's Son,* was published in 1968, and his first LP appeared the following year. Bebey has since released roughly 25 albums, mostly on the French Ozileka label, and has over a dozen books to his credit, including poetry collections, novels, and musical studies such as the popular *African Music: A People's Art.* Much of his work has certain themes in common: a focus on social issues relevant to Africans; a commitment to the integrity of African culture in the post-colonial era; and an effort to make African art meaningful to the world at large. On this point Bebey stresses that "African music . . . must first be made accessible to all men everywhere . . . and allowed to take root, germinate, and flower in their cultural understanding. "

As accomplished in his art's execution as in its conception, Bebey can be ranked among the greatest African guitarists. His instrumental style, which combines elements of European classical music with traditional Latin and African rhythms, is a powerfully emotive synthesis that transcends self-conscious "fusion." Bebey's compositions move seamlessly between the folkloric and urbane, and he masterfully employs native African instruments like the *sanza* thumb piano and his trademark pygmy flute alongside pop instruments including the saxophone, rhythm box, organ, and synthesizer. For any given release, it's hard to predict what Bebey will put together, but it's nearly a certainty that the result will have a humor and sincerity that few contemporary musicians can equal.

what to buy: When buying Bebey's albums keep in mind that, like a West African *griot* (oral historian), he enjoys revisiting favorite tunes from time to time, so don't be surprised to hear a few songs repeat between releases. With help from his sons, Bebey makes some of his most polished music on *Dibiye* ✍✍✍✍ (Pee Wee, 1998, prod. Vincent Mahey), a sometimes buoyant, sometimes melancholy set imbued with his gentle wisdom. *Djanjo Preface* ✍✍✍✍ (Ozileka, 1992, prod. Francis Bebey) is a fine selection of works for guitar. "Fond D'Ivresse" displays Bebey's genius at merging the elegance and technique of European classical music with the rhythmic flair and soul of African forms, while on "Guitar Makossa" he unforgettably interprets Cameroon's dominant *makossa* pop style.

what to buy next: *Sourire De Lune (Moon's Smile)* ✍✍✍✍ (Ozileka, 1995, prod. Francis Bebey) is a pleasant mixed bag of styles in which rhythm box, sanza, synth, and guitar all somehow work together.

what to avoid: Virtually every tune on *Mwana O* ✍✍✍ (Ozileka, 1994) can also be found on *Moon's Smile*, which has twice as many cuts.

the rest:
Amaya #2 (Ozileka, 1987)
La Condition Masculine ✍✍✍ (Ozileka, 1991)
Travail Au Noir ✍✍✍✍ (Ozileka, 1997)

worth searching for: Two releases from the sadly defunct Original Music label are worth tracking down. The breathtakingly beautiful *Akwaaba* ✍✍✍✍ (Original Music, 1986, prod. Francis Bebey, John Storm Roberts) marks a return to traditional roots, featuring sanza, pygmy flute, percussion, and some stunning vocal techniques. The lovingly assembled *Nandolo: Works 1963–1994* ✍✍✍✍ (Original Music, 1995, prod. Francis Bebey, John Storm Roberts) compiles some of Bebey's best material and includes a new performance of the classic guitar solo "Magic Box." The biographical liner notes are excellent.

influences:
◀◀ Andres Segovia, Jean Bosco Mwenda, many African traditional styles

Jeffrey Muhr

Tom Bee
See: Xit

Robby Bee & the Boyz from the Rez
Native American rap
Formed 1987, in Albuquerque, NM, USA. Based in Albuquerque, NM, USA.

Robby Bee (born 1971, in Albuquerque NM, USA), vocals, keys, samples; Michael D., vocals; Doug S., vocals. (All members are from USA.)

Robby Bee is a producer/singer/rapper/performer, one of the most progressive Native American artists of the current generation. His father Tom is the president and founder of SOAR (Sound of America Records), the country's only Native-owned and -operated label. The elder Bee was also the founder of Xit, the first all-Native rock band. Like his father, Robbie Bee gives good interview and is tireless in his efforts to promote Indian music. "To most whites, Indians are like unicorns, creatures that exist in legends, not real life; but there are as many Native Americans in L.A., riding the concrete prairie, as there are on any reservation." In an effort to change the stereotypical ideas of what Native music is, Bee created the Boyz from the Rez, an integrated Native/African American rap group. Bee is the group's producer, writer, and spokesperson. "After Columbus, 95 percent of my people were wiped out, so most people think about us in stereotypical images they got from Hollywood movies. That's what we're trying to change with our music. Native music is an expression of a living tradition; to keep it alive you've got to honor the old ways, but you have to leave room for contemporary expression too. We have to draw people in and educate them about the things Native culture has to offer."

what's available: *Reservation of Education* ✍✍✍ (Warrior, 1993, prod. Robbie Bee) gives you a good idea of the sounds Native youth find appealing; there's powwow drumming and chanting, rock guitar, and streetwise lyrics that detail the joys and trials of everyday life, pulled together by the group's solid hip-hop beats.

influences:
◀◀ Xit, Redbone, Run-D.M.C., Litefoot
▶▶ Natay

see also: *Xit*

j. poet

Beenie Man

Ragga

Born Anthony Moses Davis, August 22, 1972, in Kingston, Jamaica. Based in Kingston, Jamaica.

"Beenie" is Jamaican patois for "tiny." And that's what Beenie Man was when he started toasting (reggae-rapping) as a precocious five-year-old and released his first album five years later—appropriately titled *The Invincible Beenie Man: The Ten-Year-Old DJ Wonder*. Not so today. After woodshedding in relative obscurity with the Black Star Sounds outfit for a number of years after his novelty status waned with puberty, the adult-size Beenie Man is now a star as massive as the crowds that pack the dancehalls to hear him.

Beenie Man's microphone redemption began in 1989 when he started a long and prosperous association with the Shocking Vibes label and producer Patrick Roberts. This gave him the sounds, but as with professional wrestlers and boxers, a little controversy and an avowed enemy are sure-fire ways to build your hard-core fanbase. In the footsteps of Derrick Morgan's famed feud with Prince Buster in the '60s, Beenie Man took aim at Bounty Killer and his gun-celebrating lyrics with Beenie's 1994 "No Mama, No Cry," a moving elegy to slain deejay Pan Head. When the two engaged in a microphone clash on *Face to Face*, both benefited from the battle.

Since then Beenie Man has released more #1 hits than any artist in Jamaican music history. The 1995 single "Slam," a bawdy tribute to the sexual power and mystique of the "real ghetto gal," was the most popular song in Jamaica for nearly two years, and to this day sends women of all skin shades and classes onto the dancefloor for some serious winding and grinding. For the guys, 1996's boastful "Nuff Gal" celebrated male promiscuity in a surprisingly clever fashion for an otherwise juvenile topic, and was another huge hit. In '97, Beenie Man voiced the scorching theme song to the critically acclaimed Jamaican film *Dancehall Queen*. It too reached and held the #1 spot, and Beenie Man was named the top deejay in Jamaica for the third straight year. In '98, Beenie's success was surprising even to him. He recorded the single "Who Am I? (Sim Simma)" at Jeremy Harding's "beenie" 2 Hard studio/apartment in Kingston. The record was the unlikely indie success story of the year, reached #1 in Jamaica (of course!), and became the first independently produced and marketed ragga (digital reggae) cut to blitz into the American Top 40.

what to buy: *The Many Moods of Moses* 𝄃𝄃𝄃𝄃 (V.P., 1998, prod. Patrick Roberts) is his greatest work and without a doubt one of the most fully realized ragga albums ever made. On top of the aforementioned "Who Am I?" it includes the wicked "Woman A Sample" with Buju Banton; "Steve Biko," an uplifting tribute to the slain anti-apartheid activist; and "Ain't Gonna

hammered dulcimers worldwide

Fortunately for those who have never seen a hammered dulcimer (also called "hammer dulcimer"), it is a relatively simple instrument to describe. It consists of metal strings stretched horizontally across a shallow wooden box, generally trapezoidal in shape, which acts as a resonator. The strings vary in length and are struck with wooden mallets (hammers) to produce tones that vary in pitch. A typical hammered dulcimer has two or three strings per course, tuned in unison, similar to a piano. The word "dulcimer" comes from the Greek *dulce*, or "sweet," and the Latin *melos*, or "song." The hammered dulcimer has a well-documented history in America, dating back to colonial times, and its European-Asian relatives include the German *hackbrett*, the Hungarian *cimbalom*, the Greek *santouri*, the Arabic *santir*, and the Indian *santoor*. Some of the hammered dulcimer's virtuosos include the USA's Karen Ashbrook and India's Shiv Kumar Sharma.

see also: Karen Ashbrook, Shiv Kumar Sharma

Heidi Cerrigione

Figure It Yet," a country song recorded in Nashville! Also ambitious and deserving of big ups is *Maestro* 𝄃𝄃𝄃𝄃 (V.P., 1996, prod. Patrick Roberts), which ranges from fist-pumping roots-conscious anthems ("Africans," "Jerusalem"), to horny dance-hall barnburners ("Nuff Gal"), all the way to the utterly singular "Blackboard," which makes striking use of mariachi trumpets and groovealicious percussion.

what to buy next: Beenie Man's comeback album *Cool Cool Rider* 𝄃𝄃𝄃 (V.P., 1993, prod. Patrick Roberts) was also the release that made Shocking Vibes (the disc's Jamaican label and production crew) one of the hottest properties on the island. His heavyweight championship bout with Bounty Killer on *Face to Face* 𝄃𝄃𝄃 (V.P., 1994, prod. Patrick Roberts) provides consistently enthralling chat action. And his brief flirtation with a major label resulted in the mic-ripping *Blessed* 𝄃𝄃𝄃 (Island, 1995, prod. various), with "Slam" as its centerpiece.

the rest:

The Ten-Year-Old DJ Wonder 𝄃𝄃 (Bunny Lee, 1981)

(With Triston Palmer and Dennis Brown) *Three Against War* 𝄃𝄃𝄃 (V.P., 1994)

Beenie Man Meets Mad Cobra 🎵🎵🎵 (V.P., 1995)
All the Best 🎵🎵🎵 (Jamaican Authentic Classics, 1995)
Dis Una Fi Hear 🎵🎵 (Hightone, 1995)
Defend It 🎵🎵🎵 (V.P., 1995)
(With Spragga Benz) *Best of 2 Badd DJs* 🎵🎵🎵 (V.P., 1997)
The Doctor N/A (V.P., 1999)

worth searching for: Based on his notorious hit "Slam," Beenie Man recorded a hilarious and controversial radio jingle called "Nuff Slam," promoting a condom named after said hit and packaged with the words "Slam Country" printed over the Jamaican flag. The usual "patriotic" protests were registered; bootleg tapes of the ditty are in circulation.

influences:

◄◄ Louise "Miss Lou" Bennett, U-Roy, Wayne Smith, Yellowman, Cassius Clay/Muhammed Ali

►► Red Rat, Goofy, Kid Kurrupt

see also: *Buju Banton, Dennis Brown, Barrington Levy*

Todd Shanker

Jay Begaye

Traditional Native American
Born in Steamboat Canyon, AZ, USA. Based on the Chopaka Reserve, British Columbia, Canada.

Jay Begaye is a Navajo Din'e singer, songwriter, artist, sculptor, and founder of the Cathedral Lakes Singers, one of the best-known drum groups on the powwow trail. Although he grew up in a traditional manner, Begaye didn't get interested in singing and performing until he attended a powwow in Salt Lake City in 1981. The power of the drum groups he saw that day inspired his first song and led him to found the Cathedral Lakes Singers. In 1987 Begaye moved with his wife to the Chopaka Reserve in British Columbia, where he has developed a style that links American and Canadian Native traditions. Begaye is also a well-known artist and sculptor.

what's available: A mostly solo recording of Native praise songs, *Honoring Our Ways* 🎵🎵🎵 (SOAR, 1995, prod. Tom Bee) allows non-Indians to appreciate the beauty of Native melodies and the simple power of Native singing styles. On *The Beauty Way* 🎵🎵🎵 (SOAR, 1997, prod. Steven Butler), Begaye's double-tracked tenor has a pure, clear quality that makes these songs quietly appealing. A small drum is used on a few songs, and one, the love song "Dearest Sweetheart," features the Cathedral Lakes Singers.

influences:

◄◄ A. Paul Ortega, Snake River Singers

j. poet

M'Bilia Bel

Soukous
Born January 10, 1959, in Kinshasa, Zaire (now Congo). Based in Paris, France.

M'Bilia Bel rose from backup dancer to most popular woman singer in French-speaking Africa in the 1980s. Her mentor was the Congolese legend Tabu Ley Rochereau, who picked her out when she was dancing behind the *soukous* (African rumba) singer Abeti Masekini. Masekini was a successful band leader and the creator of the "sakossa" rhythm, and Bel had been working with her for four years. Under Rochereau's tutelage she developed her singing while performing with his band Afrisa. He first introduced her to audiences by singing duets with her and eventually letting her front the band. In 1983, still under the firm control of Rochereau, she released her first solo record. Her songs brought a woman's perspective to controversial topics like divorce and polygamous marriages. When her first child was born she took time off from solo recording but continued to collaborate with Rochereau, eventually completing seven albums with him. Their creative partnership came to an end in 1988. Since then she has followed the path of many Francophone African musicians and relocated to Paris, where she has worked with guitar giant Rigo Star. Between 1988 and 1990 she toured throughout the U.S., Europe, and West Africa. More recently she has experimented with different combinations of Western elements and the soukous sound, with varied results.

what to buy: Originally released in 1988, *Phenomene* 🎵🎵🎵🎵 (IMA, 1996, prod. Rigo Star, M'Bilia Bel) is the declaration of independence, full blown, with swingin' singin' and rich dance grooves. It's a little less wound-up than most of the soukous records of the time, and there is a sweetness reminiscent of the genre's late, lamented luminary M'Pongo Love.

what to buy next: *Bameli Soy* 🎵🎵🎵🎵 (Shanachie, 1987, prod. M'Bilia Bel, Tabu Ley Rochereau), recorded near the end of her work with Rochereau, gives a good idea of what their collaboration was like, though it is essentially a solo work. The band is crisp and tight and Bel's voice lilts over the groove. Another great set, this one from longer before her solo breakout, is *Tabu Ley et M'Bilia Bel* 🎵🎵🎵🎵 (Shanchie, 1984, prod. Tabu Ley Rochereau)—something on the order of George Jones/Tammy Wynette or maybe Porter Wagoner/Dolly Parton, only backed by a tight soukous orchestra.

the rest:

Eswi Yo Wapi 🎵🎵🎵🎵 (GEN, 1983)
Loyenghe 🎵🎵🎵 (Sonodisc, 1984)
Boya Ye 🎵🎵🎵🎵 (GEN, 1985)
Beyanga 🎵🎵🎵 (Sonodisc, 1986)
Ba Gerants Ya Mabala 🎵🎵🎵 (Sonodisc, 1986)
8/10 Benedicta 🎵🎵🎵🎵 (Sonodisc, 1987)

M'Bilia Bel

Contre Ma Volonte 🎵🎵 (Sonodisc, 1987)
Kenya/Cadence Mudanda 🎵🎵🎵 (Sonodisc, 1994)

influences:

⏪ Abeti Masekini, Bora Uzima, Yenga Moseka

see also: *Tabu Ley Rochereau, Rigo Star*

Jared Snyder

Harry Belafonte

International folk

Born Harold George Belafonte, March 1, 1927, in New York, NY, USA. Based in USA.

Whether you consider him primarily a singer, an actor, or a humanitarian, there's no disputing that Harry Belafonte is one of the most beloved entertainers of the 20th century. A native New Yorker, he spent his formative years in Jamaica, where he was exposed to the Caribbean folk music he later made hugely popular across the globe. While Belafonte is forever identified by his signature tune "Day-O (The Banana Boat Song)," several other songs associated with him ("Matilda," "Jamaica Farewell") have also become standards in both the folk and easy-listening canons. Belafonte first came to singing via acting. After his U.S. Navy service in World War II, he studied theater and started landing singing roles. His voice caught the attention of a club owner, and soon Belafonte was touring the nation as a nightclub singer with a pop repertoire. In the early 1950s, Belafonte lent his diverse talents to a number of projects, while further embracing folk standards. He won a Tony in 1953, but it wasn't until the incredible success of his 1956 albums *Belafonte* and *Calypso* that he became a household name. In fact, *Calypso*, a collection of songs from the West Indies, was lodged at the top of the *Billboard* album charts for 31 weeks, ending up as the first million-seller by a single artist. Belafonte refused to be typecast as a calypso singer, though, releasing pure calypso albums only at five-year intervals, in 1961, '66, and '71. In the years between, Belafonte explored a mind-boggling range of musical styles, tackling blues, chaingang hymns, Gershwin standards, Christmas carols, cowboy ballads, and Hebrew love songs. He also continued acting, becoming the first African American to win an Emmy in 1960 and appearing in numerous films. Though his output and commer-

Harry Belafonte

cial appeal slowed somewhat by the late '60s (his last Top 40 album was in 1964), he continued to be an influential performer as well as a tireless humanitarian and activist. Belafonte was one of the prime movers behind the USA for Africa recording session that led to 1986's inescapable "We Are the World" single. An appearance on the Marlo Thomas–organized *Free to Be You and Me* album and special in 1972 (a '70s elementary school staple), and Winona Ryder's lip-synching to "Jump in Line (Shake, Shake Senora)" in 1989's *Beetlejuice* have further introduced him to new audiences.

what to buy: The album that made Belafonte's name synonymous with its title genre, *Calypso* 𝄢𝄢𝄢𝄢 (RCA, 1956, prod. various) is an unadulterated joy, from the fun drumbeat of "Day-O" to the poignant pennywhistle of "Jamaica Farewell" to the surprisingly feminist sentiment of "Man Smart (Woman Smarter)." *All-Time Greatest Hits, Vols. 1–3* 𝄢𝄢𝄢𝄢 (RCA, 1987, prod. various) is an even more definitive package of over 50 Belafonte classics, highlighting his ability to seamlessly and successfully cross genres. *Belafonte at Carnegie Hall* 𝄢𝄢𝄢𝄢 (RCA, 1959, prod. Bob Bollard) captures the artist

in legendary form on what was the first commercially successful live album.

what to buy next: *Belafonte Returns to Carnegie Hall* 𝄢𝄢𝄢𝄢 (Mobile Fidelity, 1960) marks a triumphant homecoming to the venerable concert hall for what was scheduled to be its last event. On his second all-calypso album, *Jump Up Calypso* 𝄢𝄢𝄢𝄢 (RCA, 1961, prod. Bob Bollard), Belafonte proves that his earlier foray into the music of the islands was no fluke. His most recent collection of original material, *Paradise in Gazankulu* 𝄢𝄢𝄢𝄢 (EMI America, 1988, prod. Hilton Rosenthal), finds Belafonte newly recharged, recording anti-apartheid music in Johannesburg with South African musicians.

what to avoid: As charming as he is, Belafonte's *To Wish You a Merry Christmas* 𝄢𝄢 (RCA, 1962), a compilation of 19 holiday classics, grates on the nerves.

best of the rest:
Three for Tonight (O.S.T.) 𝄢𝄢𝄢 (RCA, 1955)
Evening with Belafonte/Mouskouri 𝄢𝄢𝄢 (RCA Victor, 1966)
Island in the Sun 𝄢𝄢𝄢𝄢 (Pair, 1990)

An Evening with Harry Belafonte ♪♪♪ (PolyGram, 1997)
With Miriam Makeba & Odetta ♪♪♪♡ (A World of Music, 1998)

worth searching for: An out-of-print set of folk standards, *Midnight Special* ♪♪♪♡ (RCA, 1962) is notable for being the first album to feature a 20-year-old harmonica player named Bob Dylan, who played on the title track, then quit after clashing with Belafonte.

influences:

◀◀ Leadbelly, Woody Guthrie

▶▶ The Kingston Trio, Peter, Paul & Mary, the Chad Mitchell Trio, Bob Dylan, Bob Marley

see also: *Irving Burgie, Miriam Makeba, Hugh Masekela*

Alex Gordon

Derek Bell

Irish traditional
Born 1935, in Belfast, Northern Ireland. Based in Ireland.

If one were to assess the short, soft-spoken, sixtysomething, vaguely rumpled Derek Bell by his appearance, you'd guess he was perhaps a professor of some sort—as indeed he is. You'd be less likely to picture him consorting with Mick Jagger, Van Morrison, and most of the notable cats in Nashville, or opening for the Pope in Dublin—but that's just the beginning of his resume as a member of the Chieftains, Ireland's musical ambassadors to the world. Perhaps uniquely, that country's chief symbol—the image that appears on the flag and the currency—is a musical instrument: the harp, for which Bell has also become famous. However, although he was the son of a fiddler and received a thorough and formal musical education as a youngster, Bell didn't start to play the harp until he was well into his 30s. He played piano and xylophone in his youth and eventually trained on oboe and English horn, graduating from London's Royal College of Music in 1957 and, two years later, earning a degree from Trinity College in Dublin. Despite such deep musical training (or perhaps because of it), and despite the fact that he'd been captivated by the sound of the Irish harp all his life, Bell's career took him elsewhere, leaving the harp as "a reward for goodness to be played in heaven!" But his life-long love for this ancient folk instrument remained unquenched, and one day he borrowed one from the North of Ireland Arts Council and started lessons; by 1965 he had joined the BBC in Belfast as solo harper for its Northern Ireland Orchestra. He eventually became Harp Professor at the Belfast Academy, a position he still holds; but the course of his future was secured in 1972, when he joined an aggregate of folk instrumentalists who called themselves the Chieftains. Bell signed on just as they were about to record their fourth album, a critical point in their early history. It was the first evidence on record of founder and musical director Paddy Moloney's ultimate dream for the band: to mold a repertoire of traditional Irish work into a unique, almost chamber-music ensemble. Indeed, such a group would be unthinkable without a harp player, and Derek Bell has been with the celebrated Chieftains ever since.

what to buy: *Carolan's Receipt* ♪♪♪♪ (Shanachie, 1992, prod. Paddy Moloney) may well be the best of many recordings devoted to the music of Turlough O'Carolan, the 18th-century Irish bardic figure and beloved composer of harp tunes. Here Bell plays the more commonly heard harp strung with nylon or gut strings, but also devotes much of the program to the more ancient wire-strung harp, an instrument with an entirely different timbre and technique. Various members of the Chieftains guest on this delightful album, providing welcome variety among the solo tracks. O'Carolan wrote at a time when the English suppression of Irish culture was relatively relaxed; in those days the indigenous music was popular, as well as the classical music of Italy and the rest of the European continent. His music was characterized by a distinctive blending of these two sensibilities, and it's hard to imagine a more perfect modern interpreter than Derek Bell, in whose nimble fingers the music of the academy and the pub converge.

what to avoid: Unfortunately, Bell forgot the winning formula used on his first collection of O'Carolan's music, and the second, *Carolan's Favourite* ♪ (Shanachie, 1989, prod. Paddy Moloney), perhaps in an ill-advised attempt to distinguish itself from its predecessor, buries the tang and spontaneity of the composer's music in an over-gentrified, orchestral sugar-coating. Even the stuff without the Belfast Orchestra, while appealing enough, suffers from the curse of all sophomore outings: it's material that wasn't chosen for the first album.

the rest:
Derek Bell's Musical Ireland ♪♪♪ (Shanachie, 1989)
Ancient Music for the Irish Harp ♪♪♪♡ (Claddagh, 1996)
Mystic Harp ♪♪♪ (Crystal Clarity, 1996)
A Celtic Evening ♪♪♪♪ (Clarity Sound & Light, 1998)
Mystic Harp 2: Sailing the Blue ♪♪♪ (Clarity Sound & Light, 1999)

influences:

◀◀ Sheila Larchet-Cuthbert, Seamus Ennis

▶▶ Patrick Ball, Kim Robertson, Sheila Woods, Maire Ní Chathasaigh

see also: *The Chieftains*

Chris Rietz

Bembeya Jazz

Manding swing dance orchestra
Formed 1961, in Beyla, Guinea. Disbanded 1991.

Large rotating membership over several decades, principally including: Aboubacar Demba Camara (died 1973), lead vocals; Sekou "Bem-

beya" Diabaté, guitar; Sekouba "Bambino" Diabaté, lead vocals (1980s). (All members are from Guinea.)

Following its independence from France, Guinea became a vital center for the emerging dance music of post-colonial West Africa. No band contributed more to the new genres than Orchestre Bembeya Jazz, named for a river in eastern Guinea where the group formed, far from the capitol of Conakry. The prevailing models for dance bands at the time were Cuban *son* and Congolese rumba outfits. But Guinea's fiercely nationalistic leader, Sekou Touré, insisted that local bands find ways to incorporate indigenous African music into their styles, and Bembeya Jazz proved an inspired trailblazer. The group managed to adapt many sounds, especially the gusty, majestic vocals and hypnotically cycling melodies of the Manding *griots* (oral historians), traditional praise singers and musical virtuosos since ancient times.

Bembeya sacrificed none of the dance drive of Latin rhythms, while delivering distinctly Guinean music with an emotional depth that resonated far beyond the country's borders. Not only did Bembeya soon begin winning national Biennale talent festivals, but in 1963 the group performed in that mecca of musical influence from and on Africa, Cuba, where local singing star Abelardo Barroso is said to have cried upon hearing the voice of Bembeya's lead singer, Aboubacar Demba Camara. After a sensational 12-year run, Bembeya was devastated when Camara died in a car accident while returning from a concert in Dakar, Senegal. As the group revived in the late '70s, the spotlight fell more and more squarely on its sensational lead guitarist, Sekou "Bembeya" Diabaté, also dubbed "Diamond Fingers" for his fleet fretwork.

Following Sekou Touré's death in 1984, Guinea liberalized and Bembeya managed to tour some in Europe and once in the U.S., in 1988. But during the '90s big bands became less and less economically feasible, and one by one, all the remaining orchestras of Conakry folded. Some Bembeya alumni have gone on to solo careers. Diamond Fingers continues to record and perform in various formations, and Sekouba "Bambino" Diabaté, who began as a talented young vocalist in Bembeya's late-'80s edition, is now a strong contender for the title of Guinea's most popular living singer.

what's available: *Bembeya Jazz National* 🎵🎵🎵🎵 (Sonodisc, 1993) offers a richly varied sampling of the final formation of this historic band. Big horns, liquid electric guitar, and an excellent cross-section of Guinea grooves.

worth searching for: Any 1970s recordings from Guinea's Bolibana label that you can find on vinyl or reissue CDs are worth owning. Sonodisc has released some over the years, though few remain in print. Sekou "Bembeya" Diabaté's *Diamond Fingers* 🎵🎵🎵🎵 (Dakar Sound, 1995) offers a beautiful acoustic set—gorgeous guitar; no vocals. *Samba Gaye* 🎵🎵🎵

(Dakar Sound, 1997), featuring accomplished *jalimuso* (female *jali* or griot) Djanka Diabaté, is Diamond Fingers' play at being a star by Guinea's new rules—i.e. without a regular band. Not up to classic Bembeya Jazz, but a respectable effort.

influences:
◗◗ Sekouba "Bambino" Diabaté

see also: *Sekouba "Bambino" Diabaté*

Banning Eyre

Jorge Ben
/Jorge Ben Jor
Samba, "suingue"
Born Julio Duilio Lima Menezes, March 22, 1945, in Rio de Janeiro, Brazil. Based in São Paulo, Brazil.

At 18 Jorge Ben still couldn't decide if he wanted to be a soccer player or a singer. It didn't matter, though. It was the mid-'60s, Rio was the most beautiful city on earth, and between the beach by day and the bohemian haunts by night, the budding artist exuded the free-spirited nonconformism of the times. He composed sambas, drawing freely from bossa nova and from close associations with the *Tropicalismo* (protest song) and *Jovem Guarda* (rock) movements. He added electric guitar to the traditional samba rhythms, and when samba musicians couldn't keep up, he began working with jazz players. His unique approach was dubbed *samba esquema novo*, meaning "new style samba," and his first full-length record of the same name was an instant hit, featuring the song "Chove Chuva" (immensely popular to this day). The 1970s found Jorge Ben very prolific, gleaning influences from Brazil's varied regional sources and gulping down American funk. It was sometime in the '70s that the term *suingue* was coined. This Portuguese version of "swing" has nothing to do with the American music genre. In Brazil, if someone has rhythm, knows how to dance, and is generally at home around music, he or she is said to have suingue. The suingue that matured with Jorge Ben in the '70s could be described as samba-funk—an exhilarating dance beat and energetic vocals, often dipping into a spoken singing style reminiscent of the Northeastern *repente* (not to mention the later Stateside rap). In the '80s Jorge Ben hit the American charts with "Mais, Que Nada" (sung by Sergio Mendes), sued Rod Stewart for ripping off the song "Taj Mahal" (and turning it into "Do Ya Think I'm Sexy?"), and changed his name. He became Jorge Ben Jor in 1989 after discovering royalties lost to American singer George Benson over confusion between their names. With his new identity came a series of highly acclaimed records and a sudden mass popularity that bordered on frenzy, etching his songs into the Brazilian psyche as eternal dancefloor standards.

what to buy: For all his universal appeal, it is disappointing to find but a few of Jorge Ben Jor's 40 albums readily available in the U.S. *Live in Rio, Vols. I and II* ♫♫♫♫ (Warner-Latin, 1992, prod. Pena Schmidt) showcases his sheer power as an entertainer. Old and new classics like "W/Brasil," "Pais Tropical," and "Salve Simpatia" weave seamlessly together, and the audience steps up as the unofficial chorus. A historic recording session in 1975 with Gilberto Gil rendered *Gil e Jorge* ♫♫♫♫ (Verve, 1994). The two masters kicked it for an afternoon and evening and just let the tape roll; the result is at once intimate and expansive, largely acoustic.

what to buy next: The other extreme, *World Dance* ♫♫♫♫ (Warner-Latin, 1994, prod. Ricky Peterson) paired Ben Jor up with Paisley Park Studios. Some have criticized this album as Americanized, remixed, and remastered to death. We like it though, and Ben Jor's music certainly lends itself to technical enhancement. For a fresh listen, try *23* ♫♫♫♫ (Warner-Latin, 1994, prod. Pena Schmidt), featuring the original tight, brassy executions of "Engenho de Dentro" and "Alcohol."

best of the rest:
Big Ben ♫♫♫♫ (Philips, 1965)
Jorge Ben ♫♫♫♫♫ (Philips, 1969)
Ben ♫♫♫♫♫ (Philips, 1972)
A Tabua Da Esmeralda ♫♫♫♫♫ (Philips, 1974)
Africa Brasil ♫♫♫♫♫ (Philips, 1976)
Tropical ♫♫♫♫ (Philips, 1977)
A Banda Do Ze Pretinho ♫♫♫♫ (Som Livre, 1978)
Salve Simpatia ♫♫♫♫♫ (Som Livre, 1979)
Ben Vinda Amizade ♫♫♫♫♫ (Som Livre, 1981)
Dadiva ♫♫♫♫♫ (Som Livre, 1983)
Ben Jor ♫♫♫♫♫ (Warner, 1989)
Homosapiens ♫♫♫♫♫ (Sony/CBS, 1995)

worth searching for: *Samba Esquema Novo* ♫♫♫♫♫ (Philips, 1963) is largely a bossa-nova album, a privileged glimpse into Ben Jor's beginnings, and almost impossible to find outside of Brazil. Features "Por Causa de Voce, Menina."

influences:
◄◄ João Gilberto, Wilson Simonal, Bezerra da Silva
►► Carlinhos Brown, Fernanda Abreu

see also: *Gilberto Gil*

Mara Weiss and Nego Beto

Mary Bergin
/Dordan

Celtic

Born September 13, 1949, in Dublin, Ireland. Dordan formed 1991, in Galway, Ireland. Based in Galway, Ireland.

Mary Bergin, flute, whistle, fiddle; Kathleen Loughnane, harp, synthesizer; Dearbhaill Standun, fiddle, viola, spoken word; Martina Goggin, vocals, percussion, guitar (1996–present). (All members are from Ireland.)

Mary Bergin is the undisputed queen of the Irish tin whistle. Her astounding technique and beautiful repertoire have defined tin whistle playing in Irish music for the past 30 years and have set a new standard for the instrument. Born in Dublin, she grew up hearing traditional music both at home and on family vacations in the west of Ireland, where she fell under the spell of legendary musicians like Willie Clancy and Junior Crehan. She began playing as a young girl and soon developed her own unique style, winning the All-Ireland title while in her late teens. After playing briefly with Ceoltoiri Laighean, a group that melded traditional and classical music in the manner of the Chieftains, she moved to Galway, married, and pursued a solo career. Her debut album, *Feadoga Stain,* was an instant classic, redefining the role of the tin whistle and propelling her to the front of the traditional music scene in Ireland. Since that time she has toured as a solo artist, with De Dannan, and with Joe and Antoinette McKenna of Sean Nua. She has also recorded a second solo album. In 1991 Bergin became a founder of her own ensemble, Dordan. Playing a combination of baroque pieces and Irish dance tunes, the group has recorded three albums and toured in Ireland, England, and the U.S. Bergin continues to perform and record both solo and with Dordan, and can often be found teaching tin whistle at music camps in the U.S. and Ireland.

what to buy: *Feadoga Stain* ♫♫♫♫♫ (Gael-Linn, 1976/ Shanachie, 1992, prod. Michael O'hEidhin) is a classic of Irish music and should be among the first albums purchased by anyone with a serious interest in the tradition. At the time of this album's original release, there had been only a few full-length recordings of tin whistle music, the instrument being taken somewhat less seriously than its cousins the flute and the uilleann pipes. Bergin's debut album changed forever the whistle's status in the genre. Driving, lyrical, and tasteful, *Feadoga Stain* set a new standard for tin whistle playing, exploring different keys and pushing the simple instrument to its limits. Bergin rips through reels and jigs with awesome grace and precision at a breakneck speed, and pulls every bit of soul out of a pair of ancient airs. Accompanied by De Dannan's Ringo McDonough and Alec Finn, Bergin plays Irish music on this recording with as much power, elegance, and style as anyone before or after.

what to buy next: *Feadoga Stain 2* ♫♫♫♫ (Shanachie, 1992, prod. Mary Bergin) shows Bergin is still an awesome musician 15 years later. The guest list is a little bigger this time, with appearances by the McKennas and Dordan. The sound is a little fuller as well, with uilleann pipes, guitar, and even bass on a few tracks. The whistle playing, of course, is at the same high standard, with her exquisite taste in tunes and arrangements always on display. *The Night Before . . . A Celtic Christmas* 🎜🎜🎜 (Narada, 1997/1998, prod. Dordan) is Dordan's third album and their first holiday collection, as well as their first to feature vocals. The group's mix of classical and traditional styles works to great effect on Christmas material, remaining tasteful without sinking into safe holiday dullness. Their selection—several originals mixed with some traditional Irish holiday music—is well chosen and arranged to allow each of the members to show off their considerable skills (especially on Tommy Coen's reel, "Christmas Eve.") Guests Steve Cooney and Johnny Connolly, on guitar and accordion respectively, provide some extra punch, and the addition of Goggin's warm alto voice brings a new dimension to the group's sound.

what to avoid: *Irish Traditional and Baroque* 🎜🎜🎜 (Shanachie, 1991, prod. Jackie Small) is Dordan's debut album. A pleasant collection that introduced the group's syncretic blend of baroque and traditional music to the world, the record features some tasty individual playing but never really cuts loose. Some standard works by Handel, Bach, and Purcell, among others, are presented alongside traditional Irish tunes and one piece composed by the group. This was a solid premiere, making explicit the links between the two genres, but it has been overshadowed by the group's subsequent releases.

the rest:
Dordan:
Celtic Aire N/A (Narada, 1999)

worth searching for: *Jigs to the Moon* 🎜🎜🎜 (Gael-Linn, 1994, prod. Dordan) was Dordan's second album and a deeper, more successful exploration of the common ground between baroque and Irish music. The group plays a German *chaconne*, a *sonatina* by the Czech composer Dussek, and a whole bunch of Turlough O'Carolan tunes in conjunction with a few traditional waltzes, reels, and jigs. Highlights include a stately version of Jerry Holland's beautiful waltz, "My Cape Breton Home," and a set of polkas drawn from English, Irish, and Austrian sources. Unfortunately, it seems that the band's sound, part Irish, part classical, falls between the marketing cracks in the U.S. Perhaps considered too traditional for the classical market, too reserved for the Irish tunehead crowd, and too serious for the new-agers, this album has yet to see release in the States.

influences:
◀◀ Willie Clancy, Tom McHaile, Seamus Ennis
▶▶ Sean Ryan, Kevin Crawford, Hesperus

see also: *De Dannan, Seán Ó Riada, Sean Nua*

Tony Ziselberger and Kerry Dexter

Maria Bethânia

Tropicalismo, MPB (Brazilian Popular Music)
Born Maria Vianna Telles Veloso, 1946, in Santo Amaro da Purificaco, Bahia, Brazil. Based in Salvador, Bahia, Brazil.

If not for a little brotherly nepotism, Brazil would have lost Maria Bethânia—one of its most beloved, influential, and enduring singers—to the theater stage. Although Moms and Pops Veloso were professional singers and sibling Caetano a guitar/songwriting prodigy, the teenaged Maria's only dream was to be a famous dramatic actress. Her budding theatrical career brought her to Salvador in 1963. Two years later, Caetano persuaded her to join the cast of a musical he was scoring. Bethânia's show-stopping rendition of his "Carcara" won her critical accolades; the single version made her an overnight national sensation. Ever the iconoclast, Bethânia refused to play the pop-star game, opting instead for the life of the cult musician. In the late '60s the two siblings hooked up with like-minded hippie freaks Gilberto Gil and Gal Costa. Together, the quartet revolutionized Brazilian pop music with a sound they called Tropicalismo. Conceived in a nation under military rule, Tropicalismo was a provocative mix of Beatles-baroque arrangements, jazzy mood swings, and allusions to social injustices subversively cloaked in "love" and "party" lyrical metaphors. A feel-good radio music that soon sparked a status-quo-defying youth movement, Tropicalismo was summarily banned by the government, and its male stars (Veloso and Gil) went into European exile. Back home Maria continued to sing Tropicalismo . . . in her own way. Gifted with an emotionally expressive, sensuously intimate, warmly burnished contralto, she cunningly made her political statements through visual symbolism (the flowing hair, simple ankle-length dresses, and barefoot humility of the common folk), dramatic gesture, and vocal nuance. In 1978, despite all attempts at dodging commercial acceptance, Bethânia's album *Alibi* made her a major star. A collection of intense love songs written by the likes of Chico Buarque and Djavan, *Alibi* not only became Brazil's first million-selling album by a female artist, it's also the *numero uno* MPB disc of all time. Today with more than 30 albums' worth of masterful interpretative songs in her discography, Maria Bethânia is still standing tall, stone immaculate.

what to buy: Even though most of Bethânia's albums are either out of print or unavailable in the States, *Ambar* 🎜🎜🎜🎜 (Metro Blue, 1996, prod. Guto Graça Mello) is the pick of the domestic litter. There's not a duff cut in the total mix; absolutely, totally essential.

what to buy next: Though recorded in Los Angeles, *As Canções Que Você Fez Pra Mim* 🎜🎜🎜 (PolyGram Latino, 1994, prod. Guta Graça Mello) is nevertheless a satisfying Bethânia-does–Sarah Vaughan experience . . . once you surrender to the orchestral strings/slick brass overkill. *Simply the Best of Maria Bethânia* 𝄞𝄞𝄞 (Verve, 1990, prod. various) is a compilation of the singer's earliest hits (1971–85, including "Alibi"). The roots of a living legend.

worth searching for: A near-invisible French import, *Maria* 𝄞𝄞𝄞𝄞 (Ruda Records, 1985, prod. Nancy Ypsilants) is subsumed in Africa-to-Brazil rhythms and spirits. Showcasing some of her most exquisite vocals, the album is essential for "A Terra Tremeu/Ofa"—her *Candomblé*-meets-Zulu gospel duet with Ladysmith Black Mambazo—alone.

influences:

◀ Gal Costa, Sarah Vaughan, Clara Nunes, Edith Piaf

▶ Virginia Rodrigues, Marisa Monte

see also: *Jorge Ben, Gal Costa, Djavan, Gilberto Gil, Caetano Veloso*

Tom Terrell

V.M. Bhatt
/Vishwa Mohan Bhatt

North Indian classical/fusion

Born 1952, in Rajasthan, India. Based in Rajasthan, India.

Vishwa Mohan Bhatt is the younger brother of Ravi Shankar's early pupil Shashi Mohan Bhatt, and thus uncle to the older Krishna Bhatt, an accomplished sitar player. Vishwa, his sister Manju, and Krishna all eventually followed in Shashi's footsteps and learned from the same legendary guru. V.M. (as he is widely known) began studying sitar at the age of five, but in 1967, after 10 years on that instrument and several on violin, his father bought him his first guitar from a visiting German musician at the institute where his father taught, and V.M. never looked back. Soon after, he and Krishna started their own "orchestra," the Bhatt Brothers, in which they played a variety of popular, classical, and Rajasthani folk music—a harbinger of the illustrious, musically diverse career to come. Thinking that the guitar sounded flat compared to the rich, warm tones created by the sitar's sympathetic strings, Bhatt began experimenting with making his own instrument, which eventually came to be known as the Mohan Vina. He modified the guitar by adding several drone strings and eight sympathetic strings, playing it like a Hawaiian slide guitar to allow for the sustained, sliding notes common to the vocal style of Indian classical music. In keeping with his history of radical innovation, the 1990s have seen V.M. Bhatt become a favorite collaborator among fusion-friendly Western musicians, including Béla Fleck, Jerry Douglas, Taj Mahal, and Ry Cooder, with whom he won a Best World Music Album Grammy for 1993's *A Meeting by the River*.

what to buy: As Bhatt's work can be divided into two distinct categories—Indian classical and genre-bending fusion—your first choice depends largely on which style suits you best. If you're the more purist, traditional type, check out *Guitar a la Hindustan* 𝄞𝄞𝄞𝄞 (Magnasound/OMI, 1992, prod. Daman Sood), a dazzling collection of four classical *ragas* featuring nimble accompaniment from *tabla* drum virtuoso Ustad Sabir Khan. If, however, you've got a fever for the flavor of fusion, there are two must-have collaborations that should top your to-buy list. The aforementioned *A Meeting by the River* 𝄞𝄞𝄞𝄞 (Water Lily Acoustics, 1993, prod. Kavichandran Alexander) is a doozy, with Bhatt's ragas matching Cooder's blues slide-for-slide to create a remarkably fluid East-West connection. *Saltanah* 𝄞𝄞𝄞𝄞 (Water Lily Acoustics, 1996, prod. Kavichandran Alexander), Bhatt's meeting of the minds with Arabic *oud* (lute) master Simon Shaheen, is somehow even better, with dizzying solos that point out the inherent similarities in their two musical traditions.

what to buy next: Only slightly less essential is *Bourbon & Rosewater* 𝄞𝄞𝄞 (Water Lily Acoustics, 1995, prod. Kavichandran Alexander), Bhatt's strangely endearing Bengali-gone-bluegrass experiment with New Grass pioneers Jerry Douglas and Edgar Meyer. It's a collaboration that few would expect to work, but once those lightning-fast fingers start picking away at chord progressions that seem to originate in some nether region halfway between Nashville and nirvana, all preconceptions are blown right out the window. An imaginative masterpiece.

what to avoid: Although not a bad album per se, *Mumtaz Mahal* 𝄞𝄞 (Water Lily Acoustics, 1995, prod. Kavichandran Alexander) sounds somewhat forced, with Bhatt's distinctive sound vastly overshadowed by that of legendary bluesman Taj Mahal. It's an okay outing for hard-core blues fans or diehard Mahal devotees, but Bhatt's talents are mostly wasted, as he is essentially relegated to the role of sideman. An ultimately disappointing effort.

the rest:

Easter Sunday Recital 𝄞𝄞𝄞 (Raga, 1990)
Bihag Desh 𝄞𝄞𝄞 (Raga, 1991)
(With Tarun Bhattacharya and Ronu Majumdar) *Song of Nature* 𝄞𝄞𝄞𝄞
  (Magnasound/OMI, 1992)
Saradanabu (Water Lily Acoustics, 1992)
Gathering Rain Clouds (Water Lily Acoustics, 1994)
(With Béla Fleck and Jie-Beng Chen) *Tabula Rasa* 𝄞𝄞𝄞 (Water Lily
  Acoustics, 1996)

worth searching for: Like most Indian classical musicians, Bhatt has released at least one album back home for every one he has released abroad, so a scouring of local Indian music shops is likely to turn up numerous inspired classical imports, a standout among standouts being *The Brilliance of Guitar* 𝄞𝄞𝄞𝄞 (EMI India, 1994).

Asha Bhosle

influences:

 Shashi Mohan Bhatt, Ravi Shankar, Ali Akbar Khan

Vijay Arun, U. Srinivas

see also: *Tarun Bhattacharya, Jie-Beng Chen, Ry Cooder, Simon Shaheen, Ravi Shankar*

Bret Love

Tarun Bhattacharya

North Indian classical

Born 1952, in West Bengal, India. Based in Calcutta, India.

Among the most respected figures in the current wave of Hindustani musicians, Tarun Bhattacharya is considered one of India's greatest masters of the *santur* (a.k.a. *santoor*), the 100-stringed hammered dulcimer popularized by Shiv Kumar Sharma (and only recently accepted in Indian classical music through his efforts). Trained at an early age by his sitarist father Robi, Bhattacharya went on to hone his skills under the tutelage of Dulal Roy and the aforesaid Sharma. His biggest in-

fluence, however, is Ravi Shankar, with whom he has studied for the past 17 years. In addition to expanding Bhattacharya's scope to include the *karnatak* traditions of South India, Shankar gave the young virtuoso his first big break in 1988, when he asked Bhattacharya to perform with a stellar Indian ensemble at Shankar's historic concert inside the Kremlin. In the last few years, Bhattacharya has primarily collaborated with *tabla* drum master Bikram Ghosh, and in 1996 the two received standing ovations for their set during the centennial of England's beloved performance series and patriotic event the Promenade Concert. When not recording or touring, Bhattacharya looks after the music academy established by his father in Calcutta.

what to buy: *Kirvani* 𝄞𝄞𝄞𝄞𝄞 (Music of the World, 1996, prod. Bob Haddad) is an awe-inspiring performance worth purchasing just for the 35-minute opening track, "Rag Kirvani." Starting with a host of innovative santur techniques, including finger-plucked chords and a variable pitch made possible by the addition of a lower string, which he presses down and releases to create otherwise impossible glides and sliding sounds, the epic track builds to a mindblowing climax featuring Bhattacharya and Ghosh trading dazzlingly complex riffs. Arguably one of the greatest Indian classical *ragas* ever captured on tape.

what to buy next: Although his near-telepathic improvisational relationship with Ghosh is sorely missed, *Sargam* ♪♪♪ (Music of the World, 1995, prod. Badal Roy, Bob Haddad) is a fine outing, pairing Bhattacharya's heavenly santur melodies with the wailing notes of Daya Shankar's *shehnai* (a double-reeded oboe) and Shashank Bakshi's able, if relatively pedestrian, tabla.

the rest:
(With Ravi Shankar) *Inside the Kremlin* ♪♪♪ (Private Music, 1989)
Imaginations ♪♪♪ (Magnasound, 1996)
(With Bikram Ghosh) *Talking Tabla* ♪♪♪ (Music of the World, 1997)
(With Ravi Shankar) *Chants of India* ♪♪♪ (Angel, 1998)

worth searching for: Bhattacharya has put out a host of albums that are available only on import, all of which reward a search—especially his collaborations with fellow Ravi Shankar protégés V.M. Bhatt and Ronu Majumdar.

influences:
◀◀ Robi Bhattacharya, Dulal Roy, Shiv Kumar Sharma, Ravi Shankar

see also: *V.M. Bhatt, Bikram Ghosh, Ravi Shankar, Shiv Kumar Sharma*

Bret Love

Asha Bhosle

Filmi music
Born 1932, in India. Based in Bombay, India.

Along with her sister, Lata Mangeshkar, Asha Bhosle has been one of the most enduring pop vocalists in the history of Indian music. She has lent her voice to thousands of songs that have appeared in thousands of movies, as well as recording light classical and traditional folk material.

Bombay, India's film capital, produces over 1,000 films a year, each usually containing at least five songs. Even today, Indian films follow traditional ideas about theater and entertainment and there is no distinction between a musical, an adventure epic, or a love story. The principals are as likely to break into song as stage a car chase. Films often rise and fall on the success of their music, so a system of musical directors and playback singers arose in the early days of the industry. Musical directors compose and arrange the music, hire the lyricist, and present their tunes with elaborate production numbers (the first music videos?). And since many actors don't sing, a parallel system of "playback singers" developed, and the singers who dub the vocals for the film stars have also become stars.

harps worldwide

Along with the flute and the drum, the harp is a truly global instrument that is found, in some form, in almost every culture worldwide. Harps are also very ancient, and have been discovered in sites as old as Mesopotamian burial chambers that date back to the third millennium B.C. Most familiar, of course, are the European harps, which come in a plethora of sizes, string numbers, and tunings, from the relatively small wire-strung Celtic folk harp (the *clarsach*), to the giant pedal harp that has returned to vogue in Euro/American classical circles in the last few decades. Harps were a central fixture of Irish and Scottish culture from 1000–1400 A.D. Though they were also suppressed in Ireland from the 14th to the 16th century by an increasing English presence, they flourished in Scotland during the same time. Much of traditional Celtic music was originally written for the instrument, including the prolific work of the blind harpist Turlough O'Carolan. The *crwth*, or Welsh folk harp, dates back to at least the 11th century, and may once have been played with some kind of bow, but is plucked today. In Latin America, the harp has also spread far and wide. Historically, folk harps have been an important part of Andean ensembles, though their popularity has waned somewhat in recent years. Harps are integral as well to the traditional *son* ensembles of Mexico, which form the foundation for much of that nation's music. The Ethiopian harp, or *krar*, is another small, handheld instrument that resembles a classical lyre, with five or six strings. Throughout the Middle East and on into Asia are found harp variants such as the *santoor*, which is played flat with hammers and was brought into Europe as the hammered dulcimer.

see also: Turlough O'Carolan (sidebar)

Michael Parrish

Asha Bhosle began singing professionally in the 1940s, when she was only 10, but for years she labored in the shadow of her more famous older sister. Often the best songs by the best directors went to Mangeshkar. The turning point came in the 1950s when the musical director O.P. Nayyar began using

Bhosle exclusively and was rewarded with a string of major hits. This opened the doors for Bhosle's collaborations with R.D. Burman, one of the greatest music directors of the 1950s. Bhosle has said that her work with Burman made her dig deeper into her own feelings and made her a better, more emotional singer. In her lengthy career, Bhosle has recorded over 11,800 songs for films, but in recent years, she has stepped back from the highly competitive soundtrack scene to begin recording classical and devotional material. Still straddling as many musical genres as the "Bollywood" films do thematic ones, in 1996 she came to San Francisco to cut a devotional album with Ali Akbar Khan, and she's also done some vocals for club remix projects.

what to buy: Bhosle has thousands of CDs, cassettes, and albums in print, making a farce of any attempt to put together a comprehensive list. The following releases—some new material, some reissued classics—barely scratch the surface, but they're all in print: *Songs to Remember* 𝄃𝄃𝄃𝄃 (EMI India); *Tribute to R.D. Burman* 𝄃𝄃𝄃𝄃 (Multitone U.K.); *Bala Main Bairagan Hungi* 𝄃𝄃𝄃𝄃 (EMI India); *Dil Padosi Hai—Hindi Love Songs* 𝄃𝄃𝄃𝄃 (EMI India); *Legacy* 𝄃𝄃𝄃𝄃𝄃 (AMMP, 1996, prod. Ali Akbar Khan). Many Westerners will only know Bhosle by reference, from the name-check in the Indian fusionist band Cornershop's alterna-pop hit "Brimful of Asha." Now learn what moved them to begin with.

influences:
◀◀ Lata Mangeshkar, Geeta Dutt

see also: *Ali Akbar Khan*

j. poet

Bhundu Boys

Jit

Formed 1980, in Harare, Zimbabwe. Based in Harare, Zimbabwe.

Biggie Tembo (died late 1980s), lead guitar, vocals; Rise Kagona, lead guitar, vocals; Shakie Kangwena (died late 1980s), keyboards, vocals; David Mankaba, bass, vocals; Kenny Chitsvatsva, drums, vocals; Shakespear Kangwena, guitar, keyboard, percussion (1993–96); Washington Kavhai, bass, percussion, vocals (1993–present); Kuda Matimba, keyboard, vocals (1997–present); Gordin Mapika, drums, vocals (1997–present). (All members are from Zimbabwe.)

Bhundu means "bush" or "jungle." When Zimbabwe won its freedom from Britain after a long, vicious war in 1980, many men came home from the bush. It was in an implicit tribute to these freedom fighters that the Bhundu Boys took their name. "We started the band in 1980, the year our country started. We were just boys who wanted to have fun and play cover versions of the music we loved," Shakle Kangwena once said. "We liked

the Rolling Stones and hard rock, even though it was the music of a culture that had been imposed upon us from the outside. Even so, there is an element of humanity in all music, so we took from that culture and combined it with our own music."

The Bhundus built their following by taking the more traditional guitar styles of *chimurenga* made popular by Thomas Mapfumo ("In Zimbabwe we look up to him the way Americans look up to the Beatles," Biggie Tembo said), adding some English/American-style finger-picking and a heavy disco-like bass drum beat, and playing with a lilting, rhythmic swing that's part highlife and part Congolese rumba. Although the songs are sung in Shona, they're constructed around short, rapid-fire bursts of guitar magic, and most of them clock in at around four minutes, making them perfect for radio play or dance-floor aerobics. This hybrid of traditional *mbira* (thumb piano) music and Western rock was called "jit," and in the early 1980s it was Zimbabwe's dominant pop music.

After their first albums exploded throughout Africa, the Bhundus were signed by Island Records for international distribution, and many people expected them to become the first African guitar heroes to make a dent in the British and American marketplace. In 1987 Scottish booker Gordon Muir brought the Bhundu Boys to the U.K., where they knocked audiences for a loop. With British music-industry heavies like Elvis Costello touting them to the press and with Madonna in their corner, they were soon duplicating the feat in American clubs. But as good as their live shows were, the American music business still rises and falls on hit "product," and with no radio support, save the few local niche-market world-music programs on smaller stations, the promise of the Bhundu Buys soon faded. In the late 1980s Tembo, the band's exuberant leader, and Shakie Kangwena died of AIDS, and while a revamped lineup is still playing clubs and releasing albums in Zimbabwe, the band's glory days are sadly passed.

what to buy: The Bhundus' first album, *Shabini* 𝄃𝄃𝄃𝄃𝄃 (Disc-Afrique France, 1986, prod. Steve Roskilly), is an amazing blast of African rock 'n' roll energy; there's not a single weak track. Their global debut, *True Jit* 𝄃𝄃𝄃𝄃𝄃 (Mango, 1988, prod. Robin Millar), has slick production values, but the band's energy still kicks serious international butt.

the rest:
Pamberi! 𝄃𝄃𝄃 (Mango, 1989)
Friends on the Road 𝄃𝄃𝄃 (Cooking Vinyl, 1993)
Muchiyedza 𝄃𝄃𝄃 (Cooking Vinyl, 1997)

worth searching for: The second Bhundu Boys album from Zimbabwe, *Tsvimbodzemoto* 𝄃𝄃𝄃𝄃𝄃 (DiscAfrique, 1987), is as good as their first; if it's not available on CD, look for cassette or vinyl.

Biggie Tembo of the Bhundu Boys

influences:

◀◀ Thomas Mapfumo, the Rolling Stones, the Beatles

j. poet

Theodore Bikel

International folk

Born March 2, 1924, in Vienna, Austria.

With a treasure-trove of folksongs and a mastery of 11 languages, Theodore Bikel was one of the originators of "world music." An internationally renowned actor too, Bikel made his deep voice and benevolent bear-like presence felt in many classic films and the original stage production of *The Sound of Music,* the album from which sold millions of copies. One of folk music's most eclectic performers, Bikel signed with Elektra in the mid-1950s and recorded such thematic albums as *From Bondage to Freedom, Yiddish Theater and Folk Songs, Songs of the Russian Gypsy,* and *Folk Songs from Just About Everywhere.* A native of Austria, Bikel moved with his family to Palestine in 1938. He first learned to speak English in hopes of becoming a linguist, then worked for a time on a collective farm, after which his destiny in performing became ever more apparent, with involvement in the Habimah Theater in Tel Aviv, a role in organizing the Tel Aviv Chamber Theater in 1943, and study at the Royal Academy of Dramatic Arts in London. Moving to New York in 1955, he continued a run of memorable film and stage roles for many years, his contributions acknowledged—but thankfully far from completed—with an appointment to the National Council for the Arts in 1977.

what to buy: *Best of Theodore Bikel* ♫♫♫ (Elektra, 1962) includes cuts from Bikel's earlier albums and showcases his full-bodied vocals and diverse repertoire.

the rest:

Actor's Holiday ♫♫ (Elektra, 1956)
Folk Songs from Just About Everywhere ♫♫♫ (Elektra, 1959)
Bravo Bikel ♫♫♫ (Elektra, 1959)
The Sound of Music ♫♫♫♫ (Columbia, 1960)
From Bondage to Freedom ♫♫♫ (Elektra, 1961)
On Tour ♫♫♫ (Elektra, 1962)
Folksinger's Choice ♫♫♫ (Elektra, 1964)
Yiddish Theater & Folk Songs ♫♫♫ (Elektra, 1965/Bainbridge, 1991)
Folk Songs of Israel ♫♫♫ (Elektra, 1966)
Songs of the Russian Gypsy ♫♫♫ (Elektra, 1967)
New Day ♫♫♫ (Reprise, 1969)
(With various artists) *A Taste of Passover* ♫♫♫ (Rounder, 1998)

influences:

◀◀ Leadbelly, Burl Ives, Pete Seeger

▶▶ Oscar Brand, Will Ackerman

Craig Harris

Bio Ritmo

Salsa, swing

Formed 1991, in Richmond, VA, USA. Based in Richmond, VA, USA.

Jim Thompson, bongos, vocals; Jorge Negrón, vocals, maracas (1991); Reinaldo González, vocals, clave (1991); Justin Riccio, timbales, tambora, vocals; Charles Kilpatrick, piano; Shade Wilson, bass; Gabriel Tomasini, congas; René Herrera (Cuba), trombone, lead vocals, arranger; Gary Jones, sax, flute (1991); Bob Miller, trumpet (1997–present); Mathew Paddock, saxes (1997–present). (All members are from USA unless otherwise noted.)

Bio Ritmo is Richmond, Virginia's hottest salsa band. "We're actually the only salsa band in town," confessed Jim Thompson, one of the band's percussionists. "We're probably the only Afro-Cuban group between New York and Miami." Bio Ritmo was a happy accident, started when Thompson was jamming with a couple of Puerto Rican friends. "We played Latin percussion to open a science fair, which led to gigs in rock clubs. We attracted a pianist, some horns, and suddenly had a salsa combo." Although they learned their Afro-Cuban licks off records, the band had a solid Latin groove on their eponymous debut for their own small label. Then René Herrera arrived on the scene. "I'd just come from Cuba," Herrera recalled. "When somebody told me there was a salsa band in town, I thought they were joking." Herrera contacted Thompson and was soon Bio Ritmo's main composer, arranger, and lead singer. "I could see their potential," Herrera said. "But Cuban music has a lot of rules, and they didn't really know what they were doing." With Herrera in charge, Bio Ritmo began a period of explosive growth, culminating in a major label deal with Triloka/Mercury. "*Rumba Baby Rumba* was recorded live, in a large studio, so we could play off each other, and we're happy with the results," says Thompson of the band's latest album. "We cut 'Tequila' as a mambo, had René give Mozart's 'Nachtmusik' a Latin tinge and even did a few tunes with English lyrics. What happens next is up to the fans."

what's available: *Que Siga La Música* ♫♫♫ (Shameless, 1995) is a steaming helping of post-punk salsa that proves you don't have to know what you're doing to have a good time. *Salsa Galactica* ♫♫♫ (Permanent, 1997, prod. Bio Ritmo) is a solid collection of tunes by René Herrera that shows the band flexing its considerable muscle, although it lacks the unbridled energy of its predecessor. *Rumba Baby Rumba* ♫♫♫ (Triloka, 1998) is slicker and more commercial as befits a major label debut, with a few swing tunes sung in English added to the mix, perhaps in hopes of latching onto the current (in 1998) swing-band fad.

influences:

◀◀ Tito Puente, Ray Baretto, Joe Cuba, Willie Colon

j. poet

Tony Bird

Worldbeat

Born February 18, 1945, in Malawi, Africa. Based in New York, NY, USA.

The creative traditions and environmental settings of southern Africa combine with Western influences in the music of white Malawian Tony Bird. His songs have successfully alternated between exposés of racism and celebrations of a childhood spent amongst monkeys and mango trees. Recorded while he was still living in Africa, Bird's first two albums, *Tony Bird* and *Bird of Paradise,* predated Paul Simon's more commercial attempts at incorporating Africa's music with Western sensibilities by a decade or more. Despite a long struggle with a muscular disorder, Bird, who moved to New York in 1979, has continued to perform in folk coffeehouses throughout the world. His 1991 album, *Sorry Africa,* featured musicians from Simon's *Graceland* sessions. Bird has been working on the follow-up, *Precious Africa,* for several years. Initially intended as an acoustic project, the album has expanded into a full-band recording with backing vocals furnished by South African superstars (and *Graceland* alumni) Ladysmith Black Mambazo.

what to buy: *Sorry Africa* 𝄢𝄢𝄢𝄢𝄢 (Rounder, 1991, prod. Morris Goldberg, Tony Bird) is one of the all-time classic worldbeat albums, capturing the sounds and lifestyle of Bird's homeland. With heavyweights from the continent collaborating with him to blend African and Western musical influences, Bird recalls the struggles and joys of his youth. A personal view of racism is hauntingly expressed in the ballad "Ahalone Incident," which tells of being stranded at night in a black township in South Africa, while the title track is an apology for apathy. "Mango Time" and "Rift Valley" offer more optimistic recollections of the Motherland.

what to buy next: Predating Paul Simon's *Graceland* by nearly a decade, *Bird of Paradise* 𝄢𝄢𝄢 (Columbia, 1978, prod. Tony Bird) looks back fondly at the Africa of Bird's youth with tunes including "Zambezi Zimbabwe," "There's a Bright Dawn," "The Cape of Flowers," and "The Mynah Birds." On an album as carefully balanced as ever, "Black Brother" provides a chilling indictment of apartheid.

the rest:

Tony Bird 𝄢𝄢𝄢 (Columbia, 1974)

influences:

◄◄ Hugh Masekela, Johnny Clegg

►► Paul Simon

see also: *Ladysmith Black Mambazo, Paul Simon*

Craig Harris

Frances Black

Irish pop, Celtic

Born in Ireland. Based in Ireland.

Frances Black began singing professionally with her brothers and sisters as the Black Family, and went on to join the group Arcady, with whom she recorded for several years. Solo tracks on the international best-selling anthology *A Woman's Heart* (reviewed in this book's Compilations section) opened the way for Frances to begin her headlining career. She's successfully forging her own identity away from the shadow of her sister Mary (long one of Ireland's top female vocalists and rapidly becoming an international music force). Frances's voice is a bit lighter than Mary's and quite distinctive. So far she's chosen material in the country and pop vein (she's covered many songs by American writer Nanci Griffith, for example), with which she's had great success in Ireland and on international tours.

what's available: *Talk to Me* 𝄢𝄢𝄢 (Celtic Heartbeat, 1995, prod. Pearse Dunne) includes Black's interpretations of a number of Nanci Griffith's songs. Griffith herself and Frances's sister Mary are among the backing vocalists. *Sky Road* 𝄢𝄢𝄢 (Uptown/Universal, 1997, prod. Pearse Dunn) shows Black venturing more into the light pop vein, while *The Smile on Your Face* 𝄢𝄢𝄢 (Dara, 1996) produced a platinum-selling single in "When You Say Nothing at All," a hit on the U.S. country charts for American singer Keith Whitley almost a decade ago. Black has signed with Sony Music and has plans to work with Declan Sinnott, who produced several of Mary's records.

influences:

◄◄ The Black Family, De Dannan, Mary Black, Nanci Griffith

see also: *Arcady, the Black Family, Mary Black*

Kerry Dexter

Mary Black

Celtic, contemporary

Born May 22, 1955, in Ireland. Based in Ireland.

Singing in an emotionally rich soprano brogue, Mary Black is one of the preeminent Irish vocalists. A member of the Black Family, General Humbert, and De Dannan before her phenomenal solo career took center stage, Black has successfully bridged the musical traditions of her native country and the lyrical poetics of modern singer-songwriters. Black grew up surrounded by music, by way of a fiddler father and music-hall-singing mother. Taught to sing folk songs herself at the age of eight by a brother, she performed with her siblings in Dublin, eventually recording with them. Later, after departing for two albums with the tradition-rooted Irish band General Humbert, Black released a self-titled debut album in 1982. Produced by

8/6 *mary black*

Mary Black

Declan Sinnott, it reached #4 on the Irish music charts. Next joining one of Ireland's most successful bands, De Dannan, she performed in the United States and sang (as did Maura O'Connell) with the band for three years, recording several albums including *Anthem,* winner of a National Association of Independent Record Distributors (NAIRD) award for Best Irish Album of 1983 (one of many NAIRD honors). Black balanced these collaborations with her own work, releasing the solo albums *Collected* and *Without the Fanfare* in 1984 and '85. Shortly after being named Irish Entertainer of 1986, she left the band to concentrate on her own career. Her subsequent solo effort, *By the Time It Gets Dark,* attained multi-platinum status, and she was voted Ireland's Best Female Artist of both 1987 and '88. Her album *No Frontiers* remained in the Irish Top 30 for more than a year, while *Babes in the Wood* spent six months on the U.S. adult alternative charts. Then in 1993 *The Holy Ground* was voted Best Irish Album of the Year and Black expanded her following with several cuts on the million-selling showcase of female Celtic singers, *A Woman's Heart* (reviewed in this book's Compilations section). In the spring of 1995 Black joined Joan Baez at New York City's legendary Bottom Line club to record

duet versions of the title track of Baez's *Ring Them Bells* and Black's own beloved "Song for Ireland." The pairing was just one of many confirmations of a stature to which Black will add years more evidence.

what to buy: On *Babes in the Wood* 🎵🎵🎵🎝 (Gift Horse, 1991, prod. Declan Sinnott), Black turns songs by Richard Thompson ("Dimming of the Day"), Joni Mitchell ("Urge for Going"), and Noel Brazil ("Golden Mile," "Might As Well Be a Slave," and the title track) into very personal statements.

what to buy next: *Collected* 🎵🎵🎵 (Gift Horse, 1984, prod. Declan Sinnott) spotlights Black's ability to make traditional Irish tunes, including "She Moved through the Fair," sound thoroughly contemporary.

the rest:
(With General Humbert) *Dolphin* 🎵🎵 (Gael-Linn, 1975)
(With General Humbert) *II* 🎵🎵🎝 (Gael-Linn, 1978)
Mary Black 🎵🎵🎝 (Gift Horse, 1982)
Without the Fanfare 🎵🎵🎝 (Gift Horse, 1985)
By the Time It Gets Dark 🎵🎵🎝 (Gift Horse, 1987)
No Frontiers 🎵🎵🎝 (Gift Horse, 1989)

The Holy Ground ♫♫♥ (Gift Horse, 1993)
Circus ♫♫♥ (Grapevine, 1995)
Looking Back ♫♫♥ (Curb, 1995)
Shine ♫♫♥ (Curb, 1997)
Song for Ireland ♫♫♫♥ (Gift Horse, 1998)

influences:

◄◄ Sandy Denny, Billie Holiday, Bonnie Raitt

►► Maura O'Connell, Tríona Ní Dhomhnaill, Nanci Griffith

see also: *The Black Family, Frances Black, De Dannan, Maura O'Connell*

Craig Harris

The Black Family
/Shay, Michael,
and Martin Black

Folk, Celtic traditional and contemporary
Formed 1965, in Dublin, Ireland. Based in California, USA, and Ireland.

Mary Black, vocals; Shay Black, vocals, guitar, piano, synthesizer; Michael Black, vocals, tenor banjo, guitar; Martin Black, vocals, fiddle, bouzouki, tenor banjo; Frances Black, vocals. (All members are from Ireland.)

Hailing from Dublin, the Black Family ranks with the Clannad/Enya Brennans on the scale of Ireland's most successful musical clans. As kids, Mary, Shay, Martin, and Michael Black absorbed music from their household. Their father was a fiddle player from Rathlin Island off the coast of Antrim, and their mother was a Dublin-born singer of traditional and music-hall songs. Although neither parent was a full-time musician, they played and sang with passion and passed that passion on to their children. Four of the children performed together around Dublin in their teen years, but the family act was broken up in 1977 when Mary went professional with the group Terrace. Terrace later changed its name to General Humbert and recorded two albums that are now out of print. Mary's career then took her to De Dannan, one of Ireland's top traditional bands, in 1983. After several albums with them, she left the band in 1986. As she concentrated on an already successful solo career, Mary also took the opportunity to revive the family group with an album and a tour. For this version of the Black Family, Mary's youngest sibling, Frances, also participated. By 1989, with Mary's solo career having made her a household name in Ireland and keeping her too busy for multiple projects, the Black Family continued as a quartet again, though their second album was recorded with harmony vocals and production assistance from Mary. Frances's initial success with the Black Family led her to a gig with the traditional folk group Arcady, a track on the best-selling anthology *A Woman's Heart*

(reviewed in this book's Compilations section), and ultimately her own successful solo career. By 1995 she too was a household name in Ireland, with big-selling albums and sold-out tours. Still, both she and Mary found time to contribute harmony vocals to the 1995 album of Shay, Michael, and Martin Black, the trio that remained of the Black Family. These days, Michael and Shay live in the San Francisco area while their three siblings remain in Ireland. The family rarely gets a chance to sing together anymore, though all five siblings did reunite for a concert at Milwaukee's famed Irish Fest in the summer of 1997, to raise money to restore the house on Rathlin Island where their father was born.

what to buy: *The Black Family* ♫♫♫♫♥ (Dara, 1986, prod. Declan Sinnott) was the group's debut, and it is a truly terrific album. It features quite a variety, from ballads to Bob Dylan, from sea chanteys to sweet love songs, and from political commentary to Victorian music-hall silliness. The songs on which Mary takes lead vocals show why she's the most famous singer of the lot; "James Connolly" and "Will Ye Gang, Love" are exactly the kind of achy-breaky material she excels at, and she nails both of them beautifully. Frances's turns at the mic are cast in a similar vein, sad and full of longing. The men, on the other hand, sing energetic sea chanteys and music-hall songs along with a few melancholy numbers like Michael's "Broom of the Cowdenknowes." Musical accompaniment is provided by the Black brothers, as well as by members of Mary's touring band.

what to buy next: *What a Time* ♫♫♫♫ (Dara, 1995, prod. Máire Breatnach) is the first recording credited to the trio of Shay, Michael, and Martin Black. It's about a 50-50 mix of traditional material and contemporary songs by Jez Lowe, Ron Kavana, Kieran Goss, Bob Franke, and others. As an added attraction, the boys' mother Patty sings lead on one silly music-hall ditty, in which a young woman's boyfriend dumps her for her widowed mother; the song's title is the bitter observation "Now I Have to Call Him Father." A lot of the traditional songs, in fact, are anonymous pieces of amusing doggerel from the Victorian music-hall stage, performed with audible good humor by the Blacks. The contemporary songs deal with Ireland's past and present, but also with the universal theme of love: long-distance love, true love, and the fear of losing love. The brothers' sharp nasal voices suit most of these songs quite well, especially the working-class tough-guy tunes "Down Our Street," "London Danny," and "The Recruiting Sergeant." The instrumental backing is by the Blacks, with accompanists including Máire Breatnach on fiddle, Mairtin O'Connor on accordion, and Noel Eccles on percussion. The singing and arrangements are full of ebullient energy, making this a fun listen. *Time for Touching Home* ♫♫♫ (Dara, 1989, prod. Declan Sinnott, Mary Black) was recorded by the quartet of Shay, Michael, Martin, and

Frances, with harmony vocals and production assistance by Mary. It features a panoply of contemporary folk from Irish, North American, and British songwriters, including Nanci Griffith, Jimmy McCarthy, Jez Lowe, Leon Rosselson, Stan Rogers, and Dougie MacClean. In this it marks a shift away from their earlier traditional material, but also includes a few old sea chanteys and a version of "Peat Bog Soldiers" from the Irish folk cannon. The backing ensemble includes such prominent Irish traditional musicians as Máire Breatnach (fiddle) and Peter Brown (uilleann pipes), along with the Black brothers and members of Mary's band. All the arrangements are tastefully done, and the voices, as always, shine.

influences:

◀◀ Nanci Griffith, Jez Lowe, Ron Kavana

▶▶ Mary Black, Frances Black

see also: *Arcady, Frances Black, Mary Black, Máire Breatnach, Clannad, De Dannan*

Steve Winick

Black 47

Hybrid Celtic

Formed 1989, in New York, NY, USA. Based in New York, NY, USA.

Larry Kirwan, guitar, keyboards, percussion, lead vocals; Chris Byrne, uilleann pipes, tin whistle, bodhrán, vocals; Fred Parcells, trombone, tin whistle, vocals; Geoffrey Blythe, saxophone, clarinet; Thomas Hamlin, drums, percussion; Andrew Goodsight, bass (1995–present); Kevin Jenkins, bass (1993–95); David Conrad, bass (1989–93). (Members are from Ireland and USA.)

Black 47 is a New York Irish outfit combining the attitude of the Big Apple with the pride of the Emerald Isle. Essentially an extremely rowdy bar band in the best sense, Black 47 is so named for the peak year of the Irish famine during the 19th century. Larry Kirwan, erstwhile playwright from the old sod itself, and Chris Byrne, a New York City cop with a passion for Irish traditional as well as rap and punk, shared several pints at the hole-in-the-wall pub Paddy Reilly's while complaining about the dismal state of modern music. At some point that evening, Black 47 was born, and soon thereafter Paddy Reilly's became the band's home. Kirwan and company's reputation for original music and a confrontational attitude soon attracted a loyal following. Kirwan's songs, crowded with lyrics and ecstatic horn arrangements, tend toward the rousing anthem as the band wails like a Memphis soul unit trapped in the bodies of an Irish folk combo. Their first recording was a self-produced indie release that was basically sold by hand as they toured Irish hot spots around the country, always landing back at Paddy's. After catching the show one evening, Cars veteran Ric Ocasek volun-

teered to polish that first album, and *Fire of Freedom* was completed in a mere three weeks. Soon the band found itself a rising star, while still fulfilling its dates at Paddy's. Ex–Talking Head Jerry Harrison arrived for production duty on the second album, and appearances on *The Tonight Show* and other national media led to more widespread recognition. Black 47 recently released their third major-label album—keeping their lifeline to street credibility and the juice of the barley with a still-regular slot at Paddy's.

what to buy: The essential Black 47 album is their first one. *Fire of Freedom* ♫♫♫ (SBK Records, 1992, prod. Ric Ocasek, Larry Kirwan) is Celtic to the core, while still strongly suggesting the band's American roots. Songs range from the swing of "Funky Ceili" to the rabble-rousing pint-raising of "James Connelly." While the production seems a bit crowded and thin, the band's exuberant personality is well captured.

what to buy next: *Green Suede Shoes* ♫♫♫ (SBK Records, 1996, prod. Larry Kirwan) returns to the band's pub roots, supplying a sweaty, passionate sound to support the usual free-the-Irish-or-we'll-really-bang-on-the-bodhrán anthems (e.g. "Bobby Sands MP").

the rest:

Home of the Brave ♫♫ (SBK Records, 1994)
Live in New York City ♫♫♫ (Gadfly, 1999)

influences:

◀◀ The Pogues, Enemy Orchard, Them, Bruce Springsteen, Booker T. & the MG's

▶▶ Goats Don't Shave

Martin Connors

Black Lodge Singers

Powwow drum

Formed c. 1982, in White Swan, WA, USA. Based in White Swan, WA, USA.

Thomas Scabby Robe, singing, drumming; Kenny Scabby Robe Jr., singing, drumming; Elgin Scabby Robe, singing, drumming; Erwin Scabby Robe, singing, drumming; Kenneth Scabby Robe Sr., singing, drumming; Louise Scabby Robe, singing; Myron Scabby Robe, singing, drumming; Darwin Scabby Robe, singing, drumming; William White Grass, singing, drumming; Keith Kicking Woman, singing, drumming; Lonnie Sammaria, singing, drumming; Shaen Old Mouse, singing, drumming. (All members are from USA.)

In pre-Columbian America, Black Lodge was the name of a Black Feet warrior society. The members stayed to themselves and had their own ceremonies, apart from the rest of the tribe. They were known by their black (or black and white) lodges or teepees. The elders of this society passed on the name Black

Black Stalin

Lodge to Kenny Scabby Robe, inspiring him to form this drum group. All members of the drum group conduct themselves in a traditional Indian way, observing strict drum etiquette. But the group is also dedicated to taking drum music out of the Indian community and into the white world, hence their recent album *Kid's Pow Wow Songs,* a collection that interpolates familiar tunes like "Twinkle Twinkle Little Star" and the theme from "The Flintstones." They perform Northern Style singing, where the voices have a high, almost falsetto quality.

what to buy: The subtle qualities of powwow music are difficult for non-Indian ears, but the tunes and phrases on *Kid's Pow Wow Songs* ♪♪♪ (Canyon, 1996, prod. Robert Doyle, Steven Butler) should be familiar to mainstream listeners and give you a clue as to how the drummers and singers develop a melody.

the rest:
Intertribal Pow Wow Songs, Live in Arizona ♪♪♪ (Canyon, 1996)
Live at White Swan ♪♪♪ (Canyon, 1996)
Round Dance Tonight ♪♪♪ (Canyon, 1997)

influences:
◀◀ Native American tradition

j. poet

Black Stalin
/Stalin

Soca, calypso, kaiso
Born in Trinidad. Based in Trinidad and Brooklyn, NY, USA.

Black Stalin, four-time winner of the Calypso Monarch crown, is one of the *soca* (SOul + CAlypso) style's most militant lyricists, and a practicing Rastaman. "In the Caribbean everyone is aware of Marcus Garvey," Stalin says from his Brooklyn home. "My parents collected newspaper articles about his work, so my Rastafarian faith is an inheritance from them." Stalin was born in Trinidad and "grew up poor, poor, poor. But there was always music. I lived near a pan yard [a social club where a steel band rehearses] and I was infatuated by *kaiso* from an early age. [Stalin prefers the traditional name for calypso, which implies social criticism and an ability to turn in on-the-spot lyrical improvisations.] Fortunately I had a gift for it." Stalin first performed for assemblies in grammar school; by high school he was a street musician and freelance calypsonian. "I would hang out in the calypso tents, and in '67 I met Kitchener. He taught me the fine points of the trade, how to write a lyric and aspects of presenting a whole show." Stalin competed for years before taking the crown in '79, but his winning (and first) album *Caribbean Man* is one of soca's greatest. Stalin's lyrics of Pan-African unity are full of militant fire, and the tunes ride monstrous, sweat-inducing groves. "There was criticism because [it] was so political, but politics affect every decision we make in our lives, and a calypsonian is the people's messenger. Like the old African storytellers who went from village to village to spread the news, a calypsonian should be a serious educator."

what to buy: The compilation *Roots, Rock, Soca* 𝄞𝄞𝄞𝄞 (Rounder, 1991, prod. various) includes most of *Caribbean Man* —one of the greatest soca albums ever waxed, on a par with Bob Marley's *Burnin'* for its impact on Caribbean culture. Stalin, like Sparrow, has never made a bad album and seldom cuts a weak tune. The production on *Rebellion* 𝄞𝄞𝄞 (Ice, 1994, prod. Eddy Grant) is a bit slick, but Stalin's missionary spark always shines through.

best of the rest:
You Ask for It 𝄞𝄞𝄞𝄞 (CCP, 1984)
I Time 𝄞𝄞𝄞𝄞 (B's, 1986)
To De Master 𝄞𝄞𝄞𝄞 (WB, 1989)

worth searching for: *In Ah Earlier Time* 𝄞𝄞𝄞𝄞 (Makossa, 1981) may not be on CD yet, but it stands with *Caribbean Man* as a stunning example of soul-stirring, militant music-making.

influences:
◄◄ Lord Kitchener, Pretender, Sparrow, Attila the Hun
►► David Rudder

see also: *Lord Kitchener, the Mighty Sparrow*

j. poet

Black Uhuru
Reggae
Formed 1974, in Kingston, Jamaica. Based in Kingston, Jamaica.

Derrick "Duckie" Simpson, vocals; Rudolph "Garth" Dennis, vocals (1974–76; 1989–96); Don McCarlos (a.k.a. Don Carlos), vocals (1974–76; 1989–96); Michael Rose, vocals (1977–84); Errol Nelson, vocals (1977); Sandra "Puma" Jones (USA, died January 28, 1990), vocals (1978–86); Delroy "Junior" Reid (1985–89); Janet "Olafunke" Reid, vocals (1986–88); O'Neill Beckford (a.k.a. Andrew Bees), vocals (1998–present); Jennifer Connally (a.k.a. Jenifah Nyah), vocals

(1998–present). (All members are from Jamaica except where noted otherwise.)

The first reggae group to win a Grammy award (for their 1984 album *Anthem*), Black Uhuru are one of the most successful bands in their genre and country; *Rolling Stone* referred to them as "Jamaica's premier post–Bob Marley reggae outfit."

Formed in the ghettos of Kingston in 1974 by vocalists Duckie Simpson, Don Carlos, and Garth Dennis under the name Uhuru (Swahili for "freedom"), the band initially released a beautiful but commercially disappointing version of the Impressions' "Romancing to the Folk Song." After Carlos departed and Dennis joined the Wailing Souls, hints of Black Uhuru's later preeminence could be heard on their excellent 1977 debut LP *Love Crisis* (later reissued as *Black Sounds of Freedom*), which featured new members Michael Rose and Errol Nelson (formerly of the Jayes). Rose's anguished lead vocals injected a rapt intensity into the majestic "I Love King Selassie" and a spiritually uninhibited interpretation of Bob Marley's "Natural Mystic." Rose had previously released the stellar single "Born Free" and the original version of "Guess Who's Coming to Dinner," which was based on the Sidney Poitier film and later became a hit for Black Uhuru on their 1979 *Showcase* album.

In 1978, Nelson rejoined the Jayes and was replaced by the gifted African American Puma Jones, a former social worker who journeyed to Jamaica to trace her African cultural roots and subsequently became a *nyah* (ritual Rasta) dancer with Ras Michael & the Sons of Negus. Along with the addition of reggae dynamic duo Sly Dunbar and Robbie Shakespeare as producers and instrumentalists (though not official members), it was Puma's eerie soprano harmonies, in combination with Rose's distinctively dread lead vocals and Simpson's deep bass harmonies, that solidified the band's signature sound. During this politically outspoken period Black Uhuru released a succession of Sly & Robbie productions—most notably the singles "Plastic Smile" and "General Penitentiary" and the aforesaid Jamaican hit album *Showcase* —which lead to a contract with Island records. A series of uncompromising modern roots albums followed, including *Sinsemilla, Red, Chill Out,* and *Anthem*; compilations of their early singles were issued on *Black Uhuru* and *Guess Who's Coming to Dinner.*

In late 1984, Rose left the group to run a coffee plantation, which in turn spurred Sly & Robbie's departure. The domino effect continued when Island decided not to re-sign the band. However, a new era for Black Uhuru began with the recruitment of another exciting lead vocalist: Junior Reid. Raised in the infamously impoverished Waterhouse district and with performance skills steeped in Kingston's intensely competitive dancehalls, Reid was a singer who made up in rhythmically concussive impact what he may have lacked in expressiveness.

After the Grammy-nominated *Brutal,* the band issued two stunning and rare singles on Reid's newly inaugurated JR Productions imprint, "Pain on the Poor Man's Brain" and "Nah Get Rich and Switch." In 1986, Jones fell ill and was replaced by Janet "Olafunke" Reid; sadly, Puma died of cancer in 1990 at the age of 37. Junior Reid left the group in 1989, soon after the release of *Live in New York City.*

The original lineup of Simpson, Carlos, and Dennis then reunited. Their comeback album *Now,* released in 1990, reached the #2 position on the *Billboard* world-music chart, bringing the legend back to life. After recording a number of albums together throughout the '90s, the trio broke up in 1996, and the blood was bad; Simpson sued Carlos and Dennis for the rights to the Black Uhuru name in what would be a bitterly contested lawsuit. In 1998, Simpson won the court clash, re-formed the band with newcomers Andrew Bees and Jenifah Nyah, and recorded the recently released *Unification.*

what to buy: Black Uhuru's culture-proud defiance, visually arresting appearance, supernatural vocal arrangements, and impressive roster of richly conceived songs have ensured a legacy as powerful and absorbing as a spell cast by a St. Ann's Parish sorcerer. Befitting one of the great international reggae bands, *Liberation* 𝄢𝄢𝄢𝄢 (PolyGram, 1993, prod. various) is a terrific anthology of the group's best and boldest work for Island records, with the inimitable Michael Rose on lead vocals and including the amazing title cuts from *Sinsemilla* and *Chill Out* ; both "Youth of Eglington" and "Sponji Reggae" from *Red* ; and "Black Uhuru Anthem," "Solidarity," and "Botanical Roots" from *Anthem.* After Junior Reid joined the group, Black Uhuru continued their culturally and politically radical stance with *Brutal* 𝄢𝄢𝄢𝄢 (RAS, 1986, prod. Black Uhuru, Doctor Dread). Featuring several tracks recorded at the Lion and Fox studios in Washington, D.C., the album spotlights the harmonic vocals of what some fans argue is the band's finest lineup: Junior Reid, Duckie Simpson, and Puma Jones. *Brutal* was successfully redone dub-style on *Brutal Dub* 𝄢𝄢𝄢𝄢 (RAS 1986, prod. Black Uhuru, Doctor Dread).

what to buy next: *Black Sounds of Freedom* 𝄢𝄢𝄢𝄢 (Prince Jammy's, 1977/Shanachie, 1982, prod. Prince Jammy)—originally titled *Love Crisis* —is Black Uhuru's debut, and strong proof that music and spirituality have always been inextricably linked for this band. Besides the aforementioned devotional classic "I Love King Selassie" and the tight, whorling cover of Marley's "Natural Mystic," there is Rose's achingly resonant vocals on "Hard Ground" and the gorgeous "African Love," which sweeps cultural roots, slavery, religion, and even jazz and blues into an uncommon Rastafarian repatriation song. To top it off, the backing band is exquisite and includes Sly & Robbie and future Roots Radics Bingy Bunny (guitar) and Style Scott (syndrums).

the rest:
Showcase 𝄢𝄢𝄢 (Taxi, 1979)
Sensimilla 𝄢𝄢𝄢 (Island, 1980)
Black Uhuru 𝄢𝄢𝄢 (Virgin, 1981/Island, 1987)
Red 𝄢𝄢𝄢𝄢 (Island, 1981)
Tear It Up 𝄢𝄢𝄢𝄢 (Island, 1981)
Chill Out 𝄢𝄢𝄢 (Island, 1982/1992)
Guess Who's Coming to Dinner 𝄢𝄢𝄢𝄢 (Heartbeat, 1983)
The Dub Factor 𝄢𝄢𝄢 (Island, 1983/1993)
Anthem 𝄢𝄢𝄢𝄢𝄢 (Island, 1984/1989)
Reggae Greats 𝄢𝄢𝄢𝄢 (Island, 1985)
Positive 𝄢𝄢𝄢 (RAS, 1987)
Positive Dub 𝄢𝄢 (RAS, 1988)
Live in New York City 𝄢𝄢 (Rohit, 1989)
Now 𝄢𝄢𝄢 (Mesa, 1990)
Now Dub 𝄢𝄢𝄢 (Mesa, 1990)
Iron Storm 𝄢𝄢𝄢 (Mesa, 1991)
Iron Storm Dub 𝄢𝄢 (Mesa, 1992)
Mystical Truth 𝄢𝄢𝄢 (Mesa, 1992)
Mystical Truth Dub 𝄢𝄢𝄢 (Mesa, 1993)
Strongg 𝄢𝄢𝄢 (Mesa, 1994)
Strongg Dub 𝄢𝄢 (Mesa, 1994)
Love Dub 𝄢𝄢 (Culture Press, 1994)
20 Greatest Hits 𝄢𝄢𝄢 (Sonic Sounds, 1994)
Live 𝄢𝄢𝄢 (Sonic Sounds, 1995)
RAS Portraits 𝄢𝄢𝄢 (RAS, 1997)
Unification 𝄢𝄢 (Five Star General, 1998)

worth searching for: Filmed at London's Rainbow Theatre in 1981, *Tear It Up—Live!* (PolyGram Video, 1991) is the best available document of a Black Uhuru show at the band's performing peak. Combining stadium rock's spectacle with reggae's entrancing mysticism, the set features Rose's ferocious vocals on bedrock Uhuru hits like "General Penitentiary," "Plastic Smile," and "Youth of Eglington," all backed by Sly & Robbie's penetrating and propulsive rhythms. Puma Jones adds otherworldly harmonies and spellbinding African dance to this galvanic performance.

influences:
◀◀ Bob Marley & the Wailers, Curtis Mayfield & the Impressions, Wailing Souls, Peter Tosh, Sly & Robbie, Mikey Chung

▶▶ UB40, U Brown, African Headcharge, Dub Syndicate

see also: *Roots Radics, Sly & Robbie, Wailing Souls*

Todd Shanker and Craig Harris

Black Umfolosi

Ndebele a cappella music
Formed 1982, in Bulawayo, Zimbabwe. Based in Bulawayo, Zimbabwe.

Thomeki Dube, vocals; Bornface Mlilo, vocals; Lucky Moyo, vocals; Morgen Moyo, vocals; Sotsha Moyo, vocals; Noah "Mike" Ncube, vo-

Black Umfolosi

cals; **Benia Phuti, vocals; Taurai Tichareva, vocals. (All members are from Zimbabwe.)**

The South African vocal technique known as "bombing"—for its low bursts of unison bass voices—started as a competitive entertainment form in the mining hostels of South Africa. Ladysmith Black Mambazo brought this and other South African *a cappella* styles to a global audience, but they are hardly the only practitioners. Across the border in Zimbabwe, the Ndebele people are closely related to South Africa's Zulus, and the music of Black Umfolosi testifies to that closeness. Though Black Umfolosi perform a wide range of Southern African styles, their concerts and their one international release mostly rely on rich, rhythmic layerings of male voices, very much in keeping with the classic mining-hostel sound. The group's name refers to a river in South Africa where the chief Mzilikazi fought Zulu warlord Shaka Zulu early in the 19th century. Mzilikazi and his followers then moved north to become today's Ndebele in Zimbabwe. Three of Black Umfolosi's eight singers are brothers, which may help to explain their easy, unified sound. Lead singer Sotsha Moyo has a rougher timbre than Ladysmith's silky-

smooth frontman Joseph Shabalala; Sotsha's growl complements his own group's lush, controlled vocal mix. In performance, the members of Black Umfolosi often wear warriors' pelts and dance with gusto. They also feature a version of the "gumboots dance"—not unfamiliar to Ladysmith fans—in which a synchronized line of hopping, coiling men slap the sides of their high, rubber boots in tight, earthy rhythms.

what's available: *Festival~Umdlalo* ♫♫♫ (World Circuit/Rounder, 1993), the group's only recording to reach the international market, swings and stomps. It lacks the ultimate intensity of Ladysmith in their prime, but if you love those deep harmonies, you won't be disappointed. The group has made other albums before and since this one, but none is available outside Zimbabwe.

influences:
◀◀ Ladysmith Black Mambazo, other South African choral groups

see also: *Ladysmith Black Mambazo*

Banning Eyre

Ruben Blades

Ruben Blades

Salsa

Born July 16, 1948, in Panama City, Panama.

A Harvard-trained lawyer and movie star, Ruben Blades the singer emerged with the mid-'70s Fania label, which popularized much of the New York salsa scene. After a stint with trombonist Willie Colon, Blades worked with the band Son (a.k.a. Seis) Del Solar, eschewing the jazz influence in salsa for a more pop-oriented sound incorporating synthesizers. Blades's music is hugely popular among Latin Americans due to his lyrical examination of some of the sadder realities of life in that community; he's closer to the *nueva cancion* ("new song") movement of Latino leftists than to the exuberant party salsa of New York. For non–Spanish speakers Blades always provides translations of his songs with the albums. Major movie roles in *Crossover Dreams, The Milagro Beanfield War,* and others, as well as an acclaimed turn on stage in Paul Simon's less-than-acclaimed musical *The Capeman,* have given Blades a public profile well beyond the music world. And his social concerns have taken him further than that; Blades came in second in the 1994 elec-

tions for Panama's presidency (which is better than Joe Walsh ever did in his periodic campaigns to run the U.S.).

what to buy: Blades took a piercing look at hard lives on *Buscando America (Searching for America)* ♫♫♫♫ (Elektra, 1984, prod. Ruben Blades). "Decisions" spotlights a pregnant teenage girl and a philandering husband. "Disappearances" depicts loved ones searching for disappeared family members, and the title song despairs that the promise of America has been kidnapped by dictators. Throughout, Blades avoids preachiness by letting his characters tell their own stories. The Colon-Blades collaboration *Siembra* ♫♫♫♫ (Fania, 1978, prod. Willie Colon) is a more traditional salsa scorcher, with the Fania crew providing grooves and Colon's trombone adding a jazzy touch. This disc is legendary among salsa fans. *Greatest Hits* ♫♫♫ (WEA Latina, 1996, prod. various) is as good a place as any for Blades novices to begin, though it's skimpy at only 10 tracks.

what to buy next: *Nothing but the Truth* ♫♫♫♫ (Elektra, 1988, prod. various) is Blades's first all-English outing, with songs written by Sting, Lou Reed, and Elvis Costello. Not one for the salsa fans, but it merits listening.

what to avoid: *Agua de Luna (Moon Water)* ♫♫ (Elektra, 1987, prod. Ruben Blades) features unmemorable arrangements and conceptual lyrics that seldom feel lived in by the songs' characters.

best of the rest:
Crossover Dreams (Soundtrack) ♫♫♫ (Elektra, 1986)
Antecedente ♫♫♫ (Elektra, 1988)
Amor y Control ♫♫♫ (Sony Discos, 1992)
La Rosa de Los Vientos ♫♫♫ (Sony Tropical, 1996)
Fabulosos Calavera ♫♫♫ (BMG U.S. Latin, 1997)

worth searching for: *Ruben Blades and Son de Solar . . . Live* ♫♫♫ (Elektra, 1990, prod. Ruben Blades) is a smoking dance set driven by the salsa ethos of his earlier work.

influences:
◀◀ Celia Cruz, Fania All Stars

▶▶ Victor Manuel, Jon Secada, Robbie Robertson

see also: *Albita, Willie Colon, Little Steven, Paul Simon, Yomo Toro*

Lawrence Gabriel

Edward "Eddie" Blazonczyk

Polka

Born 1941, in Chicago, IL, USA. Based in Bridgeview, IL, USA.

Blazonczyk's polka pedigree is relatively spotless. Although he did pull a stint playing bass guitar for his own rock group (Eddie Bell and the Hill Boppers) and with Bill Haley, Blazonczyk grew up in the bosom of the genre. His mother, Antonia Blazonczyk, ran a couple of Chicago-area banquet halls (starting with Pulaski Village in 1948 and the Club Antoinette in 1967) that featured polka music. A host of genre giants passed through the clubs, including Frankie Yankovic, Eddie Zima, and Li'l Wally Jagiello. Her role in providing performance space and sustenance for the art and its practitioners would later earn her a spot in the I.P.A. (International Polka Association) Polka Hall of Fame. In 1963, Blazonczyk gave up his rock 'n' roll dreams to re-dedicate himself to polka music. His first album, *Polka Parade,* was released that year on his own Bel-Aire label and helped establish the young bandleader as a force to be reckoned with in the genre. While Blazonczyk's own style has its roots in the pulsing, energetic beat of Li'l Wally Jagiello and the smooth, cultured vocal stylings of Marion Lush, he is a trailblazer within his chosen field. He sought to broaden his fan base by blending polka rhythms with American-style country music on groundbreaking albums like *All American Country Polkas* and *Country Flavored Polkas,* and mixing English lyrics with the Polish-language tunes favored by the older members of his constituency. As a result, he influenced generations of aspiring young talent. In concert,

his clear tenor vocals cut through crowd noise with ease, and his band, the Versatones, is a sharply honed outfit that has served as a training ground for many current stars touring the polka circuit. With the Versatones, Blazonczyk has released over 50 albums on Bel-Aire and other labels, and won over 100 different awards from the three main organizations promoting polka in the United States (the International Polka Association, the United States Polka Association, and the United Polka Boosters). Notwithstanding his influence as a bandleader, Blazonczyk's activities promoting polka are arguably even more important. He runs his own record label, recording studio, and record store, produces radio shows, promotes concerts and festivals (including Polka Fireworks in Champion, Pennsylvania, and Bel-Aire Polka Days in Chicago), and is one of the founding members of the I.P.A.'s Polka Hall of Fame (in 1968). In recognition of Blazonczyk's efforts on behalf of polka music a resolution honoring him was read into the Congressional Record in 1997, and he received a National Heritage Fellowship from the National Endowment for the Arts (NEA) in 1998.

what to buy: Neophytes to the Blazonczyk experience should start with *Polkatime: 20 of the Best from Eddie Blazonczyk and the Versatones* ♫♫♫♫ (Cleveland International, 1996, compilation prod. Eddie Blazonczyk, Pamela Popovich) and/or *Greatest Hits, Volume II* ♫♫♫♫ (Cleveland International, 1997, compilation prod. Eddie Blazonczyk). Both volumes select English- and Polish-language hits that Blazonczyk recorded for Bel-Aire Records from 1968 to 1994, but the second release contains only 12 tracks compared to 20 on the first album. Both discs feature a fair number of early rock and roll standards ("Tweedle Dee," "Hey Joe," "Apples, Peaches, Pumpkin Pie") and country music tunes ("Talk Back Trembling Lips," "Talkin' to the Wrong Man," "Today's Teardrops") that Blazonczyk adapted for the polka market, but they also include more idiomatic polka classics. The second set is shorter in length but still deserving of its bone rating. Longtime fans may carp about tunes not included ("Potato Chip Polka" for one) but that just hints at how deep the man's catalog is for those wishing to explore it further.

what to buy next: While Blazonczyk has been nominated for a polka Grammy ten times (and counting), he has won it only once. That disc, *Another Polka Celebration* ♫♫♫♫ (Bel-Aire, 1985, prod. Eddie Blazonczyk), managed to tie in the voting with Jimmy Sturr's *I Remember Warsaw* for the top spot in 1986. The most interesting of Blazonczyk's recent albums is *Shakin' Not Stirred* ♫♫♫♫ (Bel-Aire, 1998, prod. Eddie Blazonczyk Jr.), where he continues to assault the preconceptions many folks have about polka music. There are a batch of country music mutants ("Someone Cares for You" and "'Scuse Moi My Heart"), a cajun-inflected fiddle tune ("Cajun Polka Queen"), and an interesting treatment of a Stephen Foster classic ("After

Eddie Blazonczyk (l) and Eddie Jr. (center) with the Versatones

the Ball") mixed in with straightforward Chicago-style polkas and *obereks* (another favorite dance rhythm at polka festivals).

best of the rest:
Polka Fireworks 🎵🎵🎵 (Bel-Aire, 1984)
Let's Celebrate Again 🎵🎵🎵 (Bel-Aire, 1986)
Good Ol' Days 🎵🎵🎵 (Bel-Aire, 1989)
Everybody Polka 🎵🎵🎵 (Bel-Aire, 1989)
All Around the World 🎵🎵🎵 (Bel-Aire, 1990)

worth searching for: Blazonczyk has influenced a host of current polka practitioners so it isn't surprising that a tribute album has been released. Frankie Liszka and TBC put out *Our Polka Hero* 🎵🎵🎵 (Ethnic World Records, 1997, prod. TBC), featuring a batch of hits associated with Blazonczyk. Numerous polka luminaries assist the boys in the band, including Dave "Scrubby" Seweryniak, Larry Trojak, and Mark Trzepacz from the Dynatones and former Versatone Lenny Gomulka.

influences:
◀◀ Antonia Blazonczyk, Eddie Zima, Steve Adamczyk, Li'l Wally Jagiello, Marion Lush

▶▶ The Dynatones, Lenny Gomulka & Chicago Push, Brave Combo, the Polka Family Band, Frankie Liszka & TBC, Toledo Polkamotion, Eddie Blazonczyk Jr.

Garaud MacTaggart

Alpha Blondy
African reggae
Born Seydou Kone, January 1, 1953, in Dimbo Kora, Cote d'Ivoire. Based in Cote d'Ivoire.

Radical politics are fused with African folk music and Bob Marley–inspired reggae by Ivory Coast–born Alpha Blondy. Accompanied by his 12-piece band Solar System, Blondy has used music to speak out against police brutality and racial oppression and to encourage revolution and African unity. Sung in a number of African, Middle Eastern, and European languages, Blondy mainstays like "Apartheid Is Nazism", "Bloodshed in Africa," and "Interplanetary Revolution" leave no doubt about his views.

A member of the Jula tribe, Blondy was raised by his grandmother. A rebellious child, Blondy (meaning "bandit") took the

Alpha Blondy

other half of his stage name from the first letter of the Greek alphabet (fully conscious of its Biblical associations). Although as a youth he listened to Western rock bands including Deep Purple, Led Zeppelin, and the Beatles, Blondy initially set his sights on becoming not a musician but a teacher. After traveling to the U.S. to study English at Hunter College and Columbia University in New York, Blondy began performing Bob Marley songs in Harlem clubs. His recording debut might have come soon after when he made six songs produced by Clive Hunt, but Hunt quickly disappeared with the master tapes.

It was part of a cycle of anger, justified and otherwise, that has consistently gotten Blondy into trouble with the authorities. Returning to the Ivory Coast, he was arrested for threatening the Ivorian ambassador in New York. Arriving at the police station, he slapped an officer. He subsequently spent a week in jail and a short stay at the Bingerville Asylum in Abidjian. Blondy's fortunes took their first upswing after a well-received performance on the Ivory Coast TV talent show *Premier Choice.* On the strength of this break he released his debut album, *Jah Love,* in 1983, and he's been making his own breaks ever since.

what to buy: A heavily political collection, *The Best* 𝄞𝄞𝄞𝄞 (Shanachie, 1990, prod. Alpha Blondy) reprises 10 tunes from Blondy's early albums, including "Cocody Rock" and "Jerusalem" (recorded with none other than the Wailers), and "Apartheid Is Nazism," "I Love Paris," and "Come Back Jesus" (recorded with the Solar System).

what to buy next: *Jerusalem* 𝄞𝄞𝄞𝄞 (Tuff Gong, 1984/Shanachie, 1988, prod. Alpha Blondy) is a true cultural exchange, with the rhythms of the Motherland and the diaspora finding hallowed common ground. Recorded at Bob Marley's Tuff Gong studios in Jamaica, the album backs Blondy's gutsy vocals and hard-hitting lyrics with accompaniment from that definitive complement of reggae royalty, the Wailers.

the rest:
Jah Love 𝄞𝄞𝄞 (Tuff Gong, 1983)
Cocody Rock 𝄞𝄞𝄞𝄞 (Tuff Gong, 1984/Shanachie, 1986)
Revolution 𝄞𝄞𝄞 (Tuff Gong, 1987/Shanachie, 1989)
Apartheid Is Nazism 𝄞𝄞𝄞 (Shanachie, 1988)
Masada 𝄞𝄞𝄞 (EMD/Blue Note, 1992)
Dieu 𝄞𝄞𝄞 (EMD/Blue Note, 1995)

The Best of Alpha Blondy 🎵🎵🎵🎵 (World Pacific, 1996)
Prophets 🎵🎵🎵🎵 (EMI, 1998)

influences:
◄◄ Bob Marley, Peter Tosh, Aswad, Black Uhuru

see also: *Bob Marley*

Craig Harris

Bloque
Rock en Español
Formed 1997, in Bogotá, Colombia. Based in Colombia.

Ivan Benavides, vocals, guitar; Ernesto "Teto" Ocampo, guitar, vocals; Mayte Montero, maraca, gaitas, vocals; Carlos Ivan Medina, piano, vocals; Luis Angel Pastor (el Papa), bass; Pablo Bernal, drums; Alex Martinez, bongos, bell, tambora; Gilbert Martinez, congas, cymbals, side drum, plastic bag, chequere, guiro. (All members are from Colombia.)

Just as "Rock en Español" was becoming clichéd shorthand for Spanish-speaking bands that sounded like the Police and made barely a dent in the U.S. pop psyche, Bloque came along to box a few uninformed ears and reveal just how fresh and inventive this genre could be. Bloque's two principals—frontman Ivan Benavides and guitarist Ernesto Ocampo—had already made a mark as band members and co-writers for techno-traditional Latin superstar Carlos Vives, with whom they field-tested the kind of roots 'n' horizons music they'd later push further as Bloque. Recruiting six additional players, Benavides and Ocampo went about crafting a style that eschewed both fashion and trend: "Something in this world stinks and it's not the sewers/So much concern with image, so much makeup," they sing in "El Hedor (The Stench)." Instead, Bloque effects a strong synthesis of sounds, embracing jazz, hip-hop, and crunching electric guitar riffs along with the traditional African-derived polyrhythms of its homeland. Benavides calls the result "psychotropical funk," and by any other label it's an arresting brew that's immediately pushed Bloque to the forefront of the world pop movement.

what's available: *Bloque* 🎵🎵🎵🎵 (Luaka Bop/Warner Bros., 1998, prod. Ivan Benavides, Ernesto Ocampo) starts with a song called "Damage in the Bathroom" and closes with Benavides's declaration that "We're partying/And the world is crumbling." Well, when your john and the world is in trouble, why not throw down a little? And on its debut, Bloque throws down a lot. "Nena" fuses hard-rock guitar with salsa rhythms, while the politically charged "Rap del Rebusque" offers horn-fueled hip-hop. Jazz flavors roll through "La Pluma"—a tribute to Colombian guitar hero Peregoyo—and Southern Baptist organ riffs dance around the Afropop licks of "Ay Donde Andara." As with much of Rock en Español, the meaning is sometimes lost

lutes worldwide

L ute" is a general term describing an extremely large family of diverse musical instruments, the most well-known being the guitar. This family can be divided into long, short, and bowed lutes, but all consist of two parts: a neck (or fingerboard) and a body (or resonator). Lutes have at least one string, but usually more, attached to the body and running across a bridge to the end of the neck, where they connect to some sort of tuning device.

Long lutes have long necks and proportionally smaller bodies, and are generally plucked; archaeology shows that they existed in ancient civilizations in Mesopotamia, Egypt, Greece, and Rome, and they're still popular today throughout much of the non-Western world. Among the more well-known long lutes are the Asian *tar* (not to be confused with the North African frame drum of the same name); the Indian *sitar* and *tambura*; the Turkish *saz*; and the Japanese *shamisen.*

Short lutes have necks that are shorter than their bodies, which, in the case of the guitar and violin, is compensated for by running the fingerboard down onto the resonator. These lutes can be seen in Central Asian artwork dating back to the 8th century B.C. The most important short lute is arguably the *oud* (or *'ud*), which originated in the Middle East around the 7th century A.D. and served as the prototype for nearly all of the European plucked instruments—including the guitar, which evolved from the Spanish *qitara*. Other variations include the Ukrainian *balalaika* and the Chinese *pipa.*

Bowed lutes, usually referred to by the generic term "fiddle," come in a broad variety of shapes and sizes, but their precise origins remain unknown. Before the 9th century there is no mention of bowed lutes to be found, yet by the 10th century they were common from Europe and North Africa to Eastern Asia. Modern instruments of this family include the Arabic *rabab*; the Greek *lyra*; the Bulgarian *gadulka*; the Indian *sarangi*; and, of course, the European violin.

see also: The Bouzouki (sidebar)

Bret Love

in translation, but you don't need a lyric sheet in any language to understand the passion and fire of these 12 songs.

influences:

Tito Puente, Peregoyo, Carlos Vives, Led Zeppelin, Jimi Hendrix, Ruben Blades, Grandmaster Flash

see also: *Carlos Vives*

Gary Graff

Blowzabella

British and Celtic folk fusion

Formed 1978, at the London College of Furniture, London, England. Disbanded c. 1990.

Original members: Jon Swayne, bagpipes, woodwinds; Bill O'Toole, bagpipes, woodwinds; Sam Palmer, hurdy-gurdy; Dave Armitage, melodeon, percussion. Final lineup: Andy Cutting, melodeons, percussion; Nigel Eaton, hurdy-gurdies, cello, percussion; Jo Freya, vocals, saxophone, clarinet; Paul James, soprano saxophone, bagpipes, rauschfeife; Ian Luff, guitars, cittern; Jon Swayne, saxophones, bagpipes.

A far cry from the typical folk music produced in England, the gone-but-never-forgotten Blowzabella's distinctive sound was carried on the base of a drone. Using bagpipes and hurdy-gurdy to establish it, the group explored this driving and primal sound to its fullest through the interweaving of dance melodies. The result was hypnotic and extremely unusual, sounding almost as much Middle Eastern as English and drawing on a variety of roots, from England to Ireland to Eastern Europe. The original group—a bunch of musical instrument craftsmen—set out, with great success, to combine the drone with traditional dance tunes; the band's later incarnations explored this further with the use of original material and other harmonic sounds. Blowzabella's members still perform in various configurations, and are a vital link in a chain giving tradition a future.

what's available: The only Blowzabella album currently to be had on an American label, *Vanilla* ♫♫♫ (Green Linnet, 1990, prod. Paul James) represents the band at its pinnacle. Exciting and highly danceable, the group explores more complex harmonies in its instrumentals and, through vocalist Jo Freya, displays strong emotion in its songs. The result is one of Blowzabella's most varied, highly textured albums, while still spotlighting their drone-based trademark.

worth searching for: *Compilation* ♫♫♫ (Osmosys, 1995) chronicles the history of the band, featuring two or three cuts from each of their six original albums. *A Richer Dust* ♫♫♫ (Osmosys, 1988) includes "Wars of the Roses Suite," which was written on a grant from a local arts council to commemorate the 500th an-

niversary of the Battle of Stoke Field. This piece marked a major turning point for the band, after which their confidence in their own material soared and they began to explore music of a new seriousness and complexity.

influences:

John Kirkpatrick, Ashley Hutchings, Roger Nicholson

Tanteeka

see also: *Frankie Armstrong*

Jo Hughey Morrison

Mari Boine
/Mari Boine Persen

Modern joik, worldbeat

Born 1956, in Gamehhisnjarga, Norway. Based in Voss, Norway.

Mari Boine is a Sami (the indigenous people of Northern Finland), but she was raised without any connection to her heritage. "At school we learned Sami culture was worthless," Boine said. "I was ashamed of being Sami." Boine began singing in a Christian church. Unknown to her at the time, there was a Sami influence at work even then. Though the hymns she sang had Christian lyrics, the tunes were adapted from Sami folksongs and *joiks* (a Sami spiritual form). As her confidence as a performer grew, she began to revisit Sami culture, particularly the joiking tradition, which offers singers unlimited freedom to discover their own voices. She dove into her own background and began developing her own style of joiking, one that included jazz, rock, and world music, particularly the rhythms of the Andes and Africa. Her first album, 1987's *Jaskatvouda Manna,* brought her to the attention of Peter Gabriel, who signed her to RealWorld. *Gula Gula,* her international debut, introduced most of the world to Sami music and included tunes about racial discrimination and sexism as well as celebrations of the natural world. Since 1993 she has been recording for Verve World in Europe. Coming full circle in her exploration of personal roots and global affinities, her current project is a combination of Christian hymns and Sami shamanistic music.

what's available: Her latest American release, *Radiant Warmth* ♫♫♫ (Antilles, 1997, prod. Mari Boine and band), is a compilation of two Verve albums from Norway. Boine's eclectic musical bag includes African and Arabic rhythms, jazzy fiddling, and the impressive bass playing of her musical partner, Roger Ludvigsen, but it's Boine's joiking—full of grace notes, falsetto shrieks, growls, and unexpected ululations—that really grabs your ear, and chills you to the bone. Boine's major-label debut, *Gula Gula* ♫♫♫ (RealWorld, 1989), was a reissue of her second album (cut for the indie Sami label Iduit), with a few overdubs to make it more friendly to Western ears. It's more folky and less eclectic than *Radiant Warmth,* but still worth owning if you like her style.

worth searching for: Boine's Norwegian albums include *Jaskatvouda Manna* (Iduit), *Goaskinviellja (Eagle Brother)* (Verve World, 1993), and *Leahkastin (Unfolding)* (Verve World, 1995).

influences:
◄◄ Girls of Angeli

►► Ulla

j. poet

Yami Bolo

Reggae
Born Rolando McLean, 1970, in Kingston, Jamaica. Based in Jamaica.

One of the least "slack" (sexually explicit) of the younger reggae performers, Yami Bolo also might be one of the most experienced. Performing since his early teens, he set out on a prestige-by-association track early, performing and recording with heavyweight after heavyweight in his genre. He worked with Sugar Minott's Youth Promotion Crew in the late '70s alongside such notables as Tony Rebel and the late Garnett Silk, and cut his first side for Winston Riley in 1985. One of the young singers not totally caught up in the present-day *ragga* (digital reggae) style, he performs cultural, positive music with a strong "rocksteady" (proto-reggae) beat but lots of modern sounds as well. Bolo's voice stands up with the best, reminiscent of a tougher Michael Rose (the storied Black Uhuru vocalist). He also throws a tasteful cover version onto nearly every album.

what to buy: *Up Life Street* ♫♫♫ (Heartbeat, 1992, prod. T. Douglas, RE McLean) is a throwback to the days of vinyl, when one side might say one thing, and the flipside might present another. In this case, the first "side" is a set of tunes with a streetwise political perspective on life in Kingston. From the opening sirens of "Blood a Run," Bolo rails melodically against Babylon. Later he switches gears, starting with an outstanding cover of the Philly International standard "Life Is a Song Worth Singing." With the exception of "Jah Jah Loving," a more spiritual tune, this "side" stands up with any lovers' rock (the romantic, soul-inspired reggae variant from England) out there.

what to buy next: On the reality tip, *Fighting for Peace* ♫♫♫ (RAS, 1994, prod. Yami Bolo, Leggo) includes Bolo's big hit "Glock War, Gun War." On the other, it has an absolutely wonderful version of "Nature Boy." That's depth.

the rest:
He Who Knows It, Feels It ♫♫♫ (Heartbeat, 1991)
Yami Bolo Meets Lloyd Hemmings ♫♫ (Rockers International/RAS, 1995)
Born Again ♫♫♫ (RAS, 1996)

influences:
◄◄ Black Uhuru, Sugar Minott

see also: *Black Uhuru, Sugar Minott, Garnett Silk, the Techniques*

Hank Bordowitz

Luiz Bonfá

Brazilian jazz, samba, bossa nova
Born October 17, 1922, in Santa Cruz, Brazil. Based outside of Rio de Janeiro, Brazil.

Brazilian jazz, bossa nova, samba—who comes to mind? Probably Antonio Carlos Jobim and João Gilberto. Both are brilliant musicians and composers who did much to define Brazilian jazz as we know it today. But another looms large: guitarist and composer Luiz Bonfá. Arguably as influential as either Jobim or Gilberto, Bonfá spent his early years honing his impeccable guitar playing and songwriting in the clubs and casinos around Rio de Janeiro. He moved to New York in the late 1950s and, along with Jobim, Gilberto, and saxophonist Stan Getz, helped take bossa nova international in the early '60s. Bonfá is perhaps most famous as the co-composer (with Jobim and Vinícius de Morães) of the score for Marcel Camus's landmark film *Black Orpheus,* which included the theme "Manhã De Carnaval" (one of the most-recorded songs of all time). In an idiom where subtlety is key, Bonfá is a king. Throughout his career, Bonfá has made more than 30 albums, but sadly, most are out of print and not available on CD. He can, however, be readily heard on the bossa nova recordings of Stan Getz, for which he was such an integral participant and inspiration.

what's available: *Non Stop to Brazil* ♫♫♫♫ (Chesky, 1989, prod. David Chesky) captures Bonfá at his most intimate. Accompanied by renowned Brazilian percussionist Café on all tracks and by New York musician Gene Bertoncini as second guitarist on three, Bonfá retraces some of his classics, including "Manhã De Carnaval," "Gentle Rain," "Passeio No Rio," and "Sambolero."

worth searching for: Stan Getz's bossa nova recordings are a sure thing for any jazz collector and provide an excellent opportunity to hear Bonfá in a small group setting. The CDs include *Jazz Samba* ♫♫♫♫♫ (Verve, 1963, prod. Creed Taylor) and the five-disc boxed set *The Bossa Nova Years* ♫♫♫♫♫ (Verve, 1964/1989, prod. Richard Seidel, Seth Rothstein, Phil Schaap).

influences:
◄◄ Isaias Savio

►► Antonio Carlos Jobim, João Gilberto, Charlie Byrd, Laurindo Almeida

see also: *João Gilberto, Antonio Carlos Jobim*

Andrew BeDell

Bonga

Semba, fado, political

Born Barcelo de Carvalho, 1943, in Luanda, Angola. Based in Lisbon, Portugal.

Born in the working-class outskirts of the Angolan capital and renowned for his feats on the soccer field and the Portuguese national track team, Barcelo de Carvalho forfeited official approval for a leadership role in the Angolan independence movement. He became Bonga Keunza after an arrest warrant was issued in his original name by the Portuguese authorities. Seeking to revive the indigenous music that had fallen into disrepute in his then-colonized homeland, Bonga recorded his first album, *Angola 72,* soon after going into political exile in the Netherlands. His eloquent rasp of a voice, spotlit by spare instrumentation, made the record an instant classic on two continents, considered as profound a turning point for contemporary African music as Bonga had tried to effect for Angolan society. The follow-up, *Angola 74,* was equally well received. Bonga continues to record and support a variety of human-rights causes, his dream perhaps deferred but his hope undiminished.

what to buy: Rousing, tender, and deeply emotional, *Angola 72* ♪♪♪♪ (Morabeza, 1972/Tinder, 1997, prod. Bonga) is still Bonga's main claim to history's attention. His favored style here is the *semba,* an ancient African folk form that became the *samba* when exported via the slave ships from what is now Angola to Brazil. Banned on Angolan radio (but widely played on stations throughout Central and East Africa), the album became a touchstone and manifesto for the burgeoning liberation movement in the singer's homeland. Even to the most calcified of English-only ears, the music speaks a language of pride and better times ahead.

what to buy next: With a larger contingent of session players and a commercial dance beat, *Angola 74* ♪♪♪♪ (Morabeza, 1974/Tinder, 1997, prod. Bonga) extended Bonga's activist concerns into more accessible sonic territory. If the previous album was his *Plastic Ono Band,* this is his *Imagine.* Bonga's voice is even stronger here, with a firmer grip on the emotional demands of each song. To extend the Western pop metaphor, *74* really most resembles *There's a Riot Goin' On,* with Bonga matching Sly Stone's exhilarating message and graceful command of mood and form. For the moment at least, these are the only two albums available in America by this hugely influential performer.

influences:

◀◀ James Brown, Patrice Lumumba

▶▶ Waldemar Bastos

Ron Garmon

Cedella Marley Booker

Gospel, reggae, calypso, pop

Born Cedella Malcolm, 1926, in Nine Miles, St. Ann's Parish, Jamaica. Based in Miami, FL, USA.

Everyone knows Bob Marley's legacy lives on—in the person of his also-acclaimed life partner and spiritual executor Rita and the couple's talented children—but how many people know his *heritage* lives on too, through the recordings of his musical mom? Cedella Marley Booker–"Mother Booker" to her relatives and widespread admirers—lived a quiet life for most of her now 70-plus years, running a grocery shop in the hill country of St. Ann and later living with young Robert Nesta Marley in the government housing of Kingston before settling in the U.S. without fanfare. But her voice was never quiet, nurtured by an upbringing around a musician father and uncle, and apprenticed, to local acclaim, in the gospel choirs of her home parish. Years afterward, the son she saw rise to fame would promise to one day produce a gospel album with Mother Booker singing in front of his legendary band the Wailers. But destiny intervened, and Booker ended up succoring her son on his deathbed with the songs that grew into her first album, chronicling their mutual ordeal and serving as one of many heartfelt epitaphs he continues to receive. Song became Bob's immortality and Mother Booker's survival, and though her body of work remains small, it retains the rare uplift of music not driven by the market but moved by the spirit.

what's available: This living madonna of reggae's holy family never fails to draw a pantheon of other music luminaries to her side for her infrequent recordings. For instance, *Awake Zion* ♪♪♪♪ (ROIR, 1990, prod. Aston "Family Man" Barrett, Cedella Booker, Sporty), originally released in 1984 as *Redemption Songs* with one less track, features nearly all of the prophesied Wailers as its backing band. In both sound quality and style, the album's first few songs recall budget compilations of 1940s Stateside pop and country entertainers, but stick with it; inspiration hits in due course. "Stay Alive" stands out with impassioned vocals and real-deal reggae production; gospel meets girl-group and Booker revels in her roots on the exuberant "You've Got to Move." The singer transcends "Mother Don't Cry"'s odd Nashville-reggae arrangement with an emotion-brimming, life-force vocal and a moving, insightful spoken dedication to the bereaved. She then acquits herself admirably on a gospel-ized version of Marley's "Put It On (Lord I Thank You)." The sensational "Something in a Something" (the one track added for the album's '90s release) contrasts a raw live choral recording with slick late-'80s pop-reggae production for a cinematic sound-pan from Booker's church-house roots to her studio reign. Living up to her nickname in yet another way, Mother

Booker does an unlikely diva turn on a children's album, *Smilin' Island of Song* 🎝🎝🎝 (Music for Little People/Warner Bros., 1994, prod. Leib Ostrow, Taj Mahal), which features jubilant Caribbean traditionals, some Booker originals penned with Ronald Asher, and one Marley song. Once again, an extended family of musical admirers convenes around her, including boundary-less bluesman Taj Mahal, string virtuoso and world-music patron David Lindley, and Trinidadian multi-percussionist Kester Smith. Booker is in fine, full voice; the tracks are by and large delightful; and though the loose between-song narrative is more for kids than grown-ups, its overall message of intercultural welcome is nourishing and deft, its end-of-disc instrument identification guide is illuminating and succinct, and Booker's background stories on the songs are a folkloric gem. Mahal lends his smoldering vocals to a sweet, singular "Banana Boat Song"; prime reggae and calypso rhythms abound; Booker's own "Jah Wanna Dance" and her cover of Marley's "Three Little Birds" work beautifully; and spry, imaginative arrangements guarantee as much substance for the adults as there is fun for the target audience—especially on a dread, cautionary "Ooey Gooey the Silly Worm" (stop laughing, youl).

influences:

◀◀ Omeriah Malcolm, Shiloh Apostolic Church

▶▶ Bob Marley, Rita Marley

see also: *Taj Mahal, Bob Marley, Rita Marley, Ziggy Marley & the Melody Makers, Bunny Wailer*

Adam McGovern

Boom Shaka

Reggae
Formed 1986, in Los Angeles, CA, USA. Based in Los Angeles, CA, USA.

Trevor "Trevy" Felix (Dominica), lead vocals, guitar; Lesterfari Simbarashe (USA), lead guitar; Ra Bassie (Dominica), bass, vocals.

Boom Shaka plays roots reggae—with touches of dancehall, rock, and funk, as befits a band trying to make it in L.A.'s club scene. "Trevy" Felix, originally from Dominica, came to the U.S. in 1978 to join his brother Ra Bassie in a quest for fame and fortune in the music business. They tried several styles but finally fell under the spell of the militant message and Caribbean groove of reggae. In 1986 they met Lesterfari Simbarashe, an L.A. native who'd played with Black Uhuru, and things clicked. With the help of a couple of side men, they recorded *Creation* for their own Baga Style label, but a strong local buzz led to national distribution by Moving Target, Celluloid's reggae subdivision. They tour their high-energy show endlessly, and although the music does have traces of funk

and dancehall in the riddims, they are serious about maintaining a roots-reggae vibe, and eschew technology in favor of live musicians. In 1998 they signed a three-record deal with Shanachie, which should take them another step closer to national recognition.

what to buy: *Best Defenses* 🎝🎝🎝 (Liberty, 1992, prod. Ron Terry) is a solid roots-reggae set highlighted by a touch of Motown and a decided Afro-Jamaican *funde* groove. On *Rebel-Lion* 🎝🎝🎝 (Shanachie, 1998, prod. Fabian Cooke) the band's strong original material is supplemented by a couple of tasty covers, including a reggae-ized version of Prince's "Sign o' the Times."

the rest:
Creation 🎝🎝🎝 (Moving Target, 1988)
Freedom Now! 🎝🎝🎝 (Stone Mountain, 1996)

influences:
◀◀ Steel Pulse, Black Uhuru

see also: *Black Uhuru*

j. poet

Jimmy Bosch

Salsa, Latin jazz
Born 1962, in Hoboken, NJ, USA. Based in New York, NY, USA.

Jimmy Bosch is the preeminent trombone player in Latin music. Renowned for his highly lyrical style, Bosch has worked with such genre leaders as Eddie Palmieri, Marc Anthony, Celia Cruz, Ray Barretto, Ruben Blades, and Manuel Orquendo. A student of the trombone from age 11, Bosch first attracted attention with a local merengue band, Arcoires. Shortly after enrolling in the classical music department of New Jersey's Rutgers University in 1978, Bosch began playing with Orquendo's Salsa band Y Libre. Notwithstanding his ascent as a much in-demand session player, he stayed with this musical mentor until the mid-1990s. Then, after years as one of Latin music's most illustrious faces in the crowd, Bosch successfully stepped into the spotlight with the formation of his own band, the Masters, in 1996, releasing his debut solo album two years later.

what's available: With Bosch's Latin-flavored trombone playing accompanied by such influential honored guests as Cuban trumpeter Chocolate Armenteros and vocalist Pete Rodriquez, *Soneando Trombon* 🎝🎝🎝🎝 (Ryko Jazz, 1998, prod. Jimmy Bosch) is an excitingly auspicious solo debut.

influences:
◀◀ Ruben Blades, Willie Colon, Manuel Orquendo

▶▶ Marc Anthony, Cachao, La India

see also: *La India*

Craig Harris

Jimmy Bosch

The Bothy Band

Irish traditional
Formed February 1975, in Dublin, Ireland. Disbanded August 1979.

Dónal Lunny, bouzouki, guitar, bodhrán, synthesizer, vocals; Paddy Glackin, fiddle (1975); Paddy Keenan, uilleann pipes, whistles; Matt Molloy, flute, whistles; Mícheál Ó Domhnaill, guitar, vocals; Tríona Ní Dhomhnaill, vocals, clavinet, harmonium, electric piano; Tommy Peoples, fiddle (1975–76); Kevin Burke (England), fiddle (1976–79). (All members are from Ireland except where noted otherwise.)

When Dónal Lunny left Planxty and formed his record company Mulligan, he also began to work with a select group of musicians, Matt Molloy (flute), Paddy Keenan (pipes), and Paddy Glackin (fiddle), who had been performing with Tony MacMahon (accordion) for radio broadcasts. The five were joined soon afterwards by siblings Mícheál Ó Domhnaill (guitar, vocals) and Tríona Ní Dhomhnaill (vocals, clavinet), whose songs from the Donegal *sean-nós* ("old-style") tradition had brought them recognition with the band Skara Brae. They had indeed previously recorded with Lunny, Molloy, and Donegal fiddle player Tommy Peoples on Mick Hanly's 1974 *Celtic Folkweave,* and

Tríona had also played and recorded with Molloy, Peoples, piper Peter Browne, and singer Liam Weldon in 1973 under the name Sixteen Ninety-One. The configuration that would come to be known as the Bothy Band was initially called Seachtar ("seven" in Gaelic) and was short-lived, MacMahon being forced to leave early on because of his work as a TV and radio producer. With a name change, the six remaining musicians made their debut at Trinity College, Dublin, on February 2, 1975. Only a few months later, Glackin was replaced by Peoples, with whom the band made its first recording, simply called *The Bothy Band 1975.* The impact of that album was tremendous, and many of the tunes and songs on it became instant classics, played and replayed to this day at sessions in and out of Ireland. After Kevin Burke replaced Peoples as the band's fiddle player, the Bothy Band recorded two equally memorable studio albums in 1976 and '77, then released a live recording made in Paris in 1978. By then, the strain of constant touring and financial mismanagement had taken its toll, and band members were starting to pursue other projects. The Bothy Band made its final appearance at the Ballysadare festival in August 1979. While hopes of a reunion have not materialized so far, all former members have continued to be major creative forces in the Irish traditional music scene and beyond.

what to buy: From the very first chord strummed by Lunny and Ó Domhnaill—with Keenan's drones adding their low buzz before he and Molloy launch into "The Kesh Jig"—to the last echoes of the reel "The Sailor's Bonnet," *The Bothy Band 1975* ♪♪♪♪♪ (Mulligan, 1975/Green Linnet, 1983, prod. Dónal Lunny, Mícheál Ó Domhnaill) is a monumental album that set the scene for much of what has happened since in the world of Irish traditional music. The sound quality may not be quite as good as what listeners would expect today, and the lead instruments may be slightly out of tune on a couple of tracks; still, this is the quintessential Bothy Band recording. Peoples's razor-sharp, urgent fiddle playing gives the band unmatched raw sound and energy, while Lunny and Ó Domhnaill's inventive chord progressions and tightly matched accompaniment patterns propel the music forward. Last but not least, the Domhnaills' thrilling songs in English and Gaelic perfectly balance the band's instrumental virtuosity. *Old Hag You Have Killed Me* ♪♪♪♪ (Mulligan, 1976/Green Linnet, 1982, prod. Dónal Lunny, Mícheál Ó Domhnaill) is the band's mature album. With Kevin Burke's flowing and bluesy Sligo- and Clare-tinged fiddle playing replacing Peoples's hard-edged sound in the mix, the band may have lost some of its grittiness, but none of its energy. The production is first-rate and one gets a sense that the band is graduating from its experimental phase and taking charge of its sound. The players achieve a near-perfect balance between breathtaking instrumentals, like the fiddle-driven "Farewell to Erin" or the dramatic "Michael Gorman's," and striking vocal tracks, like the piece of Scottish "mouth music" "Fionnghuala" and Ní Dhomhnaill's lilting "16 Come Next Sunday." The group's third album, *Out of the Wind into the Sun* ♪♪♪♪ (Mulligan, 1977/Green Linnet, 1985, prod. Dónal Lunny, Mícheál Ó Domhnaill), while still packing a punch, did not quite achieve that same balance. Although they are classics, Ní Dhomhnaill's songs (she is the only vocalist on this one) are all pretty much in the same vein. On the other hand, the band's instrumentals are as powerful as ever, especially the reel marathon "Rip the Calico," Kevin Burke's setting of the classic pipe tune "The Hag at the Churn," and the amazing closing set of slides. By the time the live album *Afterhours* ♪♪♪♪ (Mulligan, 1978/Green Linnet, 1984, prod. the Bothy Band) was recorded in Paris, the band was reportedly falling apart, a victim of the pressures of the road. Yet the performance is as good as one might hope for—and there are even a few surprises, like some songs that did not appear on any of the studio albums, particularly "The Death of Queen Jane" and "The Heathery Hills of Yarrow."

what to buy next: *The Best of the Bothy Band* ♪♪♪♪ (Green Linnet, 1988) is an appealing collection of 12 tracks taken from the band's four original albums. When rumors started circulating about new Bothy Band recordings about to be released, they generated a considerable amount of anticipation. As it turns out, the 16 tracks on *Live in Concert* ♪♪♪♪ (Windsong, 1994/Green Linnet, 1996, prod. Pete Dauncey) were selected from two BBC-sponsored concerts that took place in 1976 and 1978. Although perhaps not as impressive as *Afterhours*, the album has its moments. The first batch of tracks is somewhat curious because sitting in for Paddy Keenan is piper Peter Browne, formerly associated with some of the "Bothies" in the band Sixteen Ninety-One. Browne is not nearly the piper Keenan is, but his presence may be the cause of changes in the instrumental medleys that will keep the listeners attentive. Keenan's pipe solo, from the 1978 concert, may also sound odd but will make sense to anyone who has met this moody genius or heard him perform. There is still plenty of exciting music throughout, as the crowd's reactions during the closing "Rip the Calico" medley will attest.

worth searching for: As obscure albums go, one could hardly beat the two Breton-produced LPs mixing tracks by Sixteen Ninety-One with recordings by the Castle Ceili Band of Dublin. On *Irish Music* ♪♪♪♫ (Escalibur, c. 1973) and *Chants et Danses d'Irlande* ♪♪♪♫ (Folk Loisirs, c. 1973), which were combined on the more recent CD release *Irish Traditional Pub Music* (Arfolk), Bothy Band fans can hear the emergence of some of the ideas that shaped the band's sound a few years later. A prototype version of the famous track "Green Groves" has Molloy's flute introducing the tune, soon joined by Tommy Peoples's fiery fiddling, with Tríona Ní Dhomhnaill's now-classic clavinet accompaniment taking it up a notch on "Flowers of Red Hill." While the mix is often rough, there are some nice surprises, particularly with Tríona's songs, which include the unaccompanied "Rinne Me Smaointeadh Im Intinn" and a version of "The Banks of Claudy," which her brother recorded with Mick Hanly on the LP *Celtic Folkweave* ♪♪♪♪ (Polydor, 1974, prod. Dónal Lunny). There is also hope that the Domhnaills' work on *Skara Brae* ♪♪♪♪ (Gael-Linn, 1971/Shanachie, 1983) will eventually reappear on CD, but for now one must search the used LP bins for it.

influences:

◄◄ Ceoltóirí Cualann, Sweeney's Men, Planxty, Skara Brae, Sixteen Ninety-One, Seachtar

►► Touchstone, Moving Hearts, Nightnoise, the Dónal Lunny Group, Altan, Dervish

see also: *Kevin Burke, Patrick Cassidy, Paddy Glackin, Dónal Lunny, Matt Molloy, Maighread Ní Dhomhnaill, Tríona Ní Dhomhnaill, Nightnoise, Tommy Peoples, Planxty, Trian*

Philippe Varlet

Boukan Ginen

Mizik rasin

Formed 1990, in Port-au-Prince, Haiti. Based in Port-au-Prince, Haiti.

Eddy François, vocal, guitar, bass; Vladimir Jean-Félix, lead guitar, bass; Richard Laguerre, bass; Bedy Andre Eugene, guitars; Milot Eliassant, keyboards; Evens Seney, hand drums; Myrtho Exavier, hand drums; Dieseul Liberus, hand drums; Jude Sanon, hand drums; Jean E. Dorvil, lead vocals. (All members are from Haiti.)

Eddy François, Evens Seney, and Jean E. Dorvil were early members of Boukman Eksperyans and helped that band revolutionize Haitian music by returning the African rhythms of the *Vodou* ritual to the soundscape of the island's carnival forms. *Mizik rasin* (roots music) soon became the island's most notable artistic export since the heyday of Tabou Combo, with Boukman spawning a number of clones and worthy competitors. In 1990, François, Seney, and Dorvil left Boukman over the usual "creative differences" and founded Boukan Ginen. Happily, the split has produced two great bands, with Boukan Ginen quickly finding its own artistic voice. Boukan's literal voice, though, sings—like Boukman's—in Creole, the "language of the poor," which was frowned upon during the days of the Duvalier regime. Their songs are full of breakneck rhythms, soul-stirring vocal harmonies, blazing hand drumming, and militant lyrics—still a potent and sometimes dangerous mix, even under the current, allegedly democratic government.

what to buy: *Jou a Rive* ♪♪♪♪ (Xenophile, 1995, prod. Yvon Ciné) is a blast of pure energy that'll shake you to the core. The African vibe is palpable, not only in the bouncy drum rhythms, but also the deep Ladysmith-like vocal harmonies. Vladimir Jean-Félix adds some shredding rock guitar to the mix, but it's the supersonic basslines and supercharged drumming that make this music cook.

what to avoid: *Rèv an Nou* ♪♪♪ (Xenophile, 1996, prod. Boukan Ginen) is a relative disappointment after the blistering energy of the band's debut. The production is softer, with the electric kick drum bringing to mind the smooth pop of the Afro-Parisian session heavies. There are traces of Cuba and Jamaica in the band's sound, and "Move Fanmi" and "Ma Doute" will definitely get you moving, but overall this is a rather laid-back excursion.

influences:

◀◀ Boukman Eksperyans, Groupo Mackandal

▶▶ Ram

see also: *Boukman Eksperyans, Tabou Combo*

j. poet

Boukman Eksperyans

Mizik rasin (roots music), rara, Vodou, worldbeat

Formed 1979, in Ouanaminthe, Haiti. Based in Port-au-Prince, Haiti.

Théodore "Lôlô" Beaubrun Jr., lead and backup vocals, keyboards, piano, tambou; Mimerose "Manze" Beaubrun, lead and backup vocals; Daniel "Dady" Beaubrun, lead and backup vocals, lead guitar, rhythm guitar, bass, keyboards, drum programming, percussion (member until the late 1990s); Marjorie Beaubrun, lead and backup vocals, percussion (1992–late 1990s); Eddy "Samba Agau" François, lead and backup vocals, rhythm guitar, bass (member until 1990); Evens Seney, backup vocals, maman tambou (member until 1990); Gary Seney, backup vocals, tambou, kata, maman tambou, percussion; Frantz "Ti Crab" Seney, backup vocals, percussion (member until 1992); Patrick St. Val-Demorcy, backup vocals, percussion (member until 1992); Maguy Jean-Louis, lead and backup vocals, percussion (member until the late 1990s); Henri B.D. Pierre Joseph, backup vocals, katabou, tambou, percussion; Michel Melthon "Olicha" Lynch (died 1994), backup vocals, maman tambou, percussion (1992–94); Hans "Bwa Gris" Dominique, maman tambou, bamboo, percussion (1992–present); Mackel "Ti Bazol" Jean-Baptiste, lead guitar, bass (1995–present); Ted Gabriel Beabrun, percussion, keyboards (1998–present); Jean Paul Coffy, keyboards (1998–present); Alexis Raymond, drums, percussion (1998–present); Hubert Sévère, bass, vocals (1998–present). (Published spellings of names and instruments vary; all members are from Haiti.)

Lots of bands inspire passionate pros and cons, but they've got nothing on Boukman Eksperyans. "One time some military guys at a concert tried to shoot on us, but other military pulled their guns out also, and said to them, 'If you shoot on the people of Boukman we're going to shoot on you.'" Co-leader Lôlô Beaubrun is recalling one of many times the band has found itself on a dictatorship's literal hit parade. "And these colonels, captains, majors, told us to leave the stage, and gave us security to go home. And they were risking their lives at that time, but no reaction ever came." That time was 1990, shortly before Boukman's Carnival anthem "Ke'-m Pa Sote" ("My Heart Doesn't Leap/I'm Not Afraid") became the theme song of those who swept the dictator Prosper Avril from power; and the place was Haiti, where rock 'n' roll rebellion is more than a figure of speech.

"Boukman" was the name of a prominent figure in Haiti's original liberation struggle with France, but Boukman the band's first revolution was musical. They dared a back-to-the-future-ism common to many of the most lauded "Third World" bands—those who revive indigenous genres frowned upon by their nations' West-courting elites, and endow their music with a distinctness and originality that ends up catching more of the international community's attention than ever before. In Boukman's case the progression from underground to global sensation drew on the misunderstood religion of *Vodou*, the springtime street-festival rhythms of *rara*, and the vernacular language of

Creole, mixed with a range of modern influences that the band adopted audaciously rather than accepting meekly. Their simultaneous seizing of outside possibilities and reclaiming of their roots was both rewarded as an instant musical hit and embraced as a validation of the common people after a long suppression of their identity and ambitions by a succession of U.S.-supported regimes. That period was actually still at full force when Boukman formed, and not quite over when the band's first album appeared in the historical minefield between the fall of the Duvalier dynasty and the unprecedented free election of Jean Bertrand Aristide. The international attention and intense homefront support garnered by Boukman's blend of alternately impassioned and unearthly vocals and alternately insistent and reassuring rhythms no doubt helped keep them alive, as song after song was banned from broadcast and performance and physical threats were made on members. But Lôlô also attributes the band's longevity to fans in higher places.

"A guy came to our concert with an Uzi and tried to shoot on us, but something was happening that night and he never really could do the act—and we were just in front of him. The real reason," Lôlô recalls with relieved laughter, "I think it was God—God really helped us a lot during that time." There was an earlier time when at least some of the members of Boukman might not have needed quite so much help. The Beaubrun brothers were born into celebrity and relative comfort as sons of one of their country's all-time favorite entertainment personalities, Theodore Beaubrun, "The Bill Cosby of Haiti." But rather than presenting a materialistic lure, the range of cosmopolitan influences this upbringing exposed them to seems to have just instilled a keener sense of the global machinations hindering their nation, and of how much more that nation could have. Time and again the band has thrown in with the masses, never relocating abroad and running very real risks in the process.

Then again, the powers with a stake in Haiti's most desperate hour—the period of military rule that for several years left Aristide in exile—had other ideas about the relocation part. At one point midway through an early-'90s tour of Europe and America, Boukman became a band without a country, as their British visas ran out, an executive order barring non-resident Haitians from entering the U.S. went into effect, and an ongoing U.S. embargo kept them from returning to their own land. (That same blockade, while not appreciably affecting the U.S.-trained dictator Raoul Cédras, did fatally delay medications to their ailing bandmate Michel Melthon "Olicha" Lynch). With scant hours left on their legal status in any country, Island Records had them flown to a safe house in then-CEO Chris Blackwell's adoptive home of Jamaica, where, out of the most adverse circumstances of their lives, they forged the most up-

beat and energizing album of their career, *Libète (Pran Pou Pran'l!)/Freedom (Let's Take It!)*.

Eventually both Boukman and Aristide got back to Haiti, the latter with mixed results that the band, though once a scourge of his enemies, has not hesitated to critique. The experience of being outcasts in the eyes of both the junta and the "land of the free" solidified their healthy skepticism of all people in power, while the absurdity of that situation seems to have fortified, rather than undermined, their sense of humor. "The day after the 1990 Carnival, the people got on the street against President Avril, and were singing our song ['Ke'-m Pa Sote'] at every occasion, and he left power 10 days after—and then, you know, all the politicians, on the right and left, took the song also at their rallies," Lôlô chuckles, "to show the people they're on their side—you know those guys!"

At least give Haiti's political hacks credit for having better taste in music than our own '70s-MOR-loving leaders. And rest assured that they're no more able to strip a great song of its meaning than the car-commercial producers up here. "Ke'-m Pa Sote" is the tip of a very large and unstoppable iceberg of electrifying Boukman music; the opening chord in one of the Western hemisphere's most durable artistic success stories. Its advent in 1990 was an exhilarating epilogue for an often brutally neocolonialist decade, and to hear that song ring out from both stage and audience amidst a mostly Haitian concert crowd is to feel possibility personified.

Neither the feel-good performances nor the mad-as-hell subject matter have subsided in the years since. Boukman's themes range from devotional invocations to folkloric anecdote to, in hefty proportion, denunciations of outside military intervention and monetary manipulation in their homeland. It's mostly sung in Creole so non-Haitians don't have to listen to the message if they don't want to—but its unquenchable optimism and indomitable groove is something you couldn't resist if you tried. Boukman Eksperyans stand as an unpretentious legend of late-20th-century music and politics, both survivors of the worst that human nature is capable of, and prophets of the best it has to offer.

what to buy: *Libète (Pran Pou Pran'l!)/Freedom (Let's Take It!)* ♪♪♪♪♪ (Mango, 1995, prod. Clive Hunt, Daniel Beaubrun, Theodore Beaubrun Jr.) may just be world-music's *Sgt. Pepper*, catchy but never compromised, multi-influenced but the product of an unmistakably singular vision. Boukman have never cracked the live-in-the-studio code better than with the soulful percussion-and-voice album opener "Legba," and never at a better time—the song is an invocation of the Vodou deities. Holed up as renegades from both their would-be assassins and supposed saviors, they must have felt they needed divine intervention, and divine inspiration is what they deliver, from the if-you're-not-dancing-you're-dead festivity of "Rara te Celia (Little Celia's Rara)," to the substantive pop balladry of "Ki Moun (Who Will)," and from the soul-synth diva turn of "Zili," to the urgent, exhilarating Carnival rallying cries of "Peye Pou Peye (You Must Pay)" and "Jou Mallè (Day of the Shock)." The band digs deep for the best vocals of their career, and the spirits of dub reggae hang over the Jamaican studio to guide a humanistic yet mystical electronics sound they haven't yet surpassed. Sharp songwriting, pristine but gutsy production, and an ecstatic resolve in the face of crushing obstacles yield up a true masterwork. Boukman achieve a stunningly organic sound on *Kalfou Danjere/Dangerous Crossroads* ♪♪♪♪ (Mango, 1992, prod. Eric Clermontet), with tight musicianship and serene melodicism that ingeniously evoke both the tension the band was facing after the overthrow of Aristide and the composure with which they met it. The dominant acoustic instruments are recorded in the most rich and immediate way, and the electric and electronic ones are deployed with maximum restraint, impact, and atmosphere. This is the Boukman album that hews most consistently to the folkloric continuum of sounds, yet offers a wealth of variety within it, from the rolling, pastoral rhythms of "Kouman Sa Ta Ye (What Would It Be Like)" or "Vodou Adjae," to the galloping tempo of the Carnival-theme title song, to three breathtaking, chorally chanted Vodou invocations, "Badè Zile," "Fèy (Leaf)," and "Mayi A Gaye." As striking an album in its depth as *Libète* is in its breadth.

what to buy next: On their debut, *Vodou Adjae* ♪♪♪♪ (Mango, 1991, executive prod. Claude Duvall Jr.), Boukman take a while to hit their trademark stride of balancing vital traditional acoustics with catchy modern electronics, and the wait takes its toll with some well-written songs dampened by prettified production ("Se Kreyo'l Nou Ye (We're Creole)"; "Nou La (We're Here)"). But "Plante (Plant)"'s driving coda hints at the visionary abandon to come, as does a pretty faithfully incendiary reading of the legendary "Ke'-m Pa Sote," whose inclusion alone makes this an important purchase. "Nou Pap Sa Bliye (We Won't Forget This)" gets the mix very right, and then we're off into the breathtaking vocal showcases "Wet Chen (Get Angry, Break the Chains)" and "Mizike A Manze' (Song for a Woman)." Though the syrupy "Tribilasyon," unavailable on cassette versions of the album, is enough to make you lament the advent of CDs, the other disc-only track, "Mizere'Re' (Misery Follows You)" is anomalous in a *good* way; an intriguing Haitian/hard-rock hybrid that a less eclectic band could easily mine a whole career out of. The album ends on a strong if haunting note with the compelling, ominous "Pwazon Rat (Rat Poison)," which manages to be at once syncopated and somber.

what to avoid: Comings and goings are to be expected in a band of Boukman's mini-orchestra size, but *Revolution* ♪ (Tuff

Gong International, 1998, prod. Theodore "Lôlô" Beaubrun Jr., Mimerose "Manze" Beaubrun) shows the band's most profound membership shake-up yet not to be a change for the better. Co-founders Lôlô and Manze Beaubrun stayed and their long-time partners Daniel and Marjorie Beaubrun departed, seemingly taking at least half the band's muse with them. Cheesy synths, justly uncredited hack guitar heroics, melodramatic melodic clichés, and a general shortage of momentum predominate. The rara "Peye Loa Yo" effects a nice spontaneity and replication of on-site street sonics, though it's not their most memorable exploration of the style; the Carnival tune "Tipa Tipa" starts out energetic but, as too often occurs on this album, the band gets into a good groove that soon turns into a rut. The album has its moments; unfortunately, they seldom last for the length of any one song, Exhibit A being the Carnival tune "Gran Bwa Karnival," a nine-minute heap of very good ideas and not-so-good ones that has all the scope of Boukman's past entries into this genre, but none of the resolution. Hope for the band's artistic fate is confirmed by the fact that the album's most promising track is the one furthest from its trademark sounds: "Nou Se Limye," a poignant yet amorphous pop ballad with a notable, haggard, torch-song vocal by Manze. Let's just say they're between masterpieces at the moment.

the rest:
Boukman Eksperyans—Live at Red Rocks N/A (Tuff Gong International, 1999)

influences:
◀◀ Bob Marley, Kassav'
▶▶ Boukan Ginen, Spearhead

see also: *Boukan Ginen*

Adam McGovern

Robin Huw Bowen

Welsh harp

Born June 7, 1957, in Liverpool, England. Based in Wales.

Robin Huw Bowen is on a mission to reinvigorate the tradition of the triple harp in Wales. The triple harp is a very unusual variety, with three rows of strings. It is the only truly chromatic harp extant, and it opens up a whole new repertoire. When the Welsh discovered it in the 16th century, they adopted it as their national instrument, thereby helping to maintain the tradition of harping in Wales long beyond that in the neighboring Celtic countries. Although the Welsh eventually turned to the pedal harp, there were some proponents of the triple harp to keep its legacy alive; these included the Gypsy harpers and later a few dedicated individuals who learned from the last of them. Bowen studied several of the standard-bearers' work and in his

Boukman Eksperyans

quest has developed an amazing virtuosity, surpassed by none. His mastery of his instrument and love of his ancestral roots have allowed him to give a special gift to the harping community. In 1987 he published a book of some 200 Welsh hornpipes that he collected, edited, and arranged for the triple harp; his in-depth understanding of the Welsh form of theme-and-variation is demonstrated in these arrangements. He now tours the world, introducing the magic of the triple harp to audiences wherever he goes.

what to buy: Bowen usually shines in concert in a way that doesn't quite translate to the studio. On *Greet the Harp* ✧✧✧✧ (Sain, 1988), he is joined by a few other musicians on fiddle, banjo, and guitar. Their presence adds a depth and variety that is lacking on all his other solo efforts. This is Bowen's first recording, and unquestionably his best. His rendition of "The Bells of Aberdyfi" sparkles, and his arrangement of "Ruddlan Marsh/Cuckoo's Nest" is vibrant. There are fun sets of both jigs and polkas, and this is an enjoyable, high-quality collection overall.

what to buy next: Bowen's other solo outings lack his live vivacity and his debut release's variety; he also has an unfortunate habit of repeating material among albums. But much of his choicest solo work is combined on *Harp Music of Wales* ✧✧✧ (Saydisc Records, 1995, prod. Gef Lucena). A wide scope of Welsh music is represented here, from the well-known "Ash Grove" and "All through the Night" to Gypsy tunes like "Polca Saiforella." Alongside the traditionals, two modern Welsh compositions are included: "Sailing Home," a beautiful, wistful air; and "The Thread of Life," an amazingly seductive piece clearly written for the harp. *The Sweet Harp of My Land* ✧✧✧ (Flying Fish, 1991, prod. Steve Howard, Dai Shell) has a few special gems on it, including "The Swan Song."

what to avoid: Unless you find you are a particular aficionado of Welsh Gypsy music, *Hunting the Hedgehog* ✧✧ (Firebird, 1994, prod. Steve Howard) is likely to sound very repetitive by the third or fourth listen. The toe-tapping is unrelenting, though the music is brilliantly performed, with unbelievable speed and accuracy.

the rest:
Hen Aelwyd/Old Hearth ✧✧✧ (Sain, 1999)

worth searching for: Bowen's group outings have all been strong. Particularly wonderful is Cusan Tan's *Kiss of Fire* ✧✧✧✧ (Fflach, 1992/Firebird, 1994), a rich example of what present-day Wales has to offer. Here Bowen teams up with Ann Morgan Jones and Sue Jones Davies to create new and invigorating Welsh music in the traditional vein. Lush open vocals, deep resonant cello, and soaring flute lines accompany Bowen's exquisite harp. Check out Mabsant's *Through the Wire* ✧✧✧ (Sain, 1987) if you'd like to hear Welsh music with an even more mod-

ern twist. Combining triple harp with vocals, guitar, synthesizers, and other contemporary instruments, this group explores a variety of musical styles with a political slant. Fiery and elegant, Bowen's latest band project, the Celtic supergroup Crasdant, is discussed at more length in its own entry in this book.

solo outings:
Cusan Tan:
Esgair—The Ridge ✧✧✧ (Sain, 1995)

influences:
◀ Alan Stivell, Nansi Richards, Ar Log

▶ Siwsann George

see also: *Crasdant*

Jo Hughey Morrison

David Bowie

Experimental pop

Born David Robert Jones, January 8, 1947, in London, England. Based in Switzerland and New York, NY, USA.

The around-the-world-in-12-inches approach of international folklorists like Harry Belafonte and Theodore Bikel established them as the 1950s' great precursors of what would come to be known as "world music"; late-'70s rock audiences were given a similar taste for the world's broad palette by David Bowie's *Lodger* album. The Beatles and Simon & Garfunkel had zeroed in on Indian and Andean sounds, respectively, but it was Bowie and collaborator Brian Eno (and, roughly simultaneously, Stevie Wonder with his *Secret Life of Plants* album) who reintroduced the globe-trotting aesthetic we now recognize as worldbeat. With his well-established rep for being one of rock's most impressionable impresarios, Bowie's adoption of this among many musical guises evaded the charges of piracy that have trailed other first-world culture-crossers (Peter Gabriel, David Byrne, Paul Simon) who actually delved much deeper. The sound of *Lodger* has long since been superseded by its sources—no doubt to Bowie's delight—but there was a time when it helped set a lot of Westerners on the road to the real World.

what to buy: The self-described "sketch pad" of *Lodger* ✧✧✧✧ (RCA, 1979/Rykodisc, 1991, prod. David Bowie, Tony Visconti) includes aural portraits of Africa, Asia, the Caribbean, and the Mediterranean, most fully realized on "Yassassin"'s unexpectedly successful synthesis of reggae rhythms and Turkish modalities. On "African Night Flight" hear Bowie try to invent rap but not quite know how! For an even more influential (though less readily apparent) application of Third World sources to global-pop advances, check out the disciplined but amorphous sound paintings of *Low* ✧✧✧✧ (RCA, 1977/Rykodisc, 1991, prod. David Bowie, Tony Visconti) and *"Heroes"*

♪♪♪♪♪ (RCA, 1977/Rykodisc, 1991, prod. David Bowie, Tony Visconti), whose ambient instrumentals, while seldom recognizably ethnic—save for the odd *koto* here (*"Heroes"*'s "Moss Garden") and polyrhythm there (*Low*'s "Weeping Wall")—are clearly informed by the structure and soundscapes of Indian *raga* and Indonesian *gamelan*.

what to buy next: Bowie's sax makes a most unconvincing run at Arabic charts all over *Black Tie White Noise* ♪♪♪♪ (Savage, 1993/Virgin, 1995, prod. David Bowie, Nile Rodgers), but the "Yassassin" approach scores him another worldbeat winner in "Miracle Goodnight," a weirdly workable mesh of hip-hop beat, reggae bass, highlife guitar, and electronic fugue with Euro-pop vocals. Bowie's two flirtations with "straight" reggae on the title track of *Tonight* ♪♪♪ (EMI, 1984/Virgin, 1995, prod. David Bowie, Derek Bramble, Hugh Padgham) and "Don't Look Down" are two too many, but "Tumble and Twirl"'s respectable salsa/flamenco simulation—and some lush yet vaguely troubled Western art-pop—make this album worth the cutout-bin prices at which you're likely to find it.

influences:

◄◄ Lindsay Kemp, Anthony Newley, Bob Dylan, Lou Reed, Iggy Pop, Kraftwerk, Brian Eno, Iman, Goldie

►► Grace Jones, Gary Numan, Siouxsie Sioux, Duran Duran, Little Steven, Trent Reznor, the entire "alternative" era

Adam McGovern

Boyoyo Boys

Mbaqanga, sax jive
Formed 1969, in Soweto, South Africa. Based in Soweto, South Africa.

Vusi Xhosa, lead guitar, leader; Vusi Knosi, bass; Lucas Pelo, sax; Philippe "Mle" Mziza, rhythm guitar; Boyoyo, drums (before the band's recording career), manager; Archie Mohlala, drums (1972–1984); Vusi Mashinini, drums (1987–present). (All members are from South Africa.)

According to record-company legend, it was a Boyoyo Boys tape that first sparked Paul Simon's interest in South African music. The Boys began playing as a unit in 1969, but all members had been musically inclined since they were children. Leader Vusi Xhosa began teaching himself to play on instruments he'd made from recycled materials. Finally, he stole some money and bought a guitar; his parents found out and punished him, but let him keep the guitar. Xhosa found Vusi Knosi at school and taught him to play bass. Lucas Pelo and Philippe "Mle" Mziza were recruited from rival bands. The new outfit's first name was the Mabhoko Band, with Boyoyo, a yo-yo fanatic, on drums. After a name change to the T-Bones they cut "Boyoyo," dedicated to their now-manager. It was a big hit, and the band changed its name for the third and last time. This

appalachia

The Appalachian mountains of the eastern United States have produced a rich interweave of English, Irish, Scottish, and African roots with regional folk traditions—for a sound that is distinctly American. "Old-time" (Appalachian country) music, unaccompanied ballad singing, the beginnings of bluegrass, and much of the nation's most familiar traditional folk repertoire can be traced to this region, as can the incorporation of both the banjo and the fiddle into American popular music. Shape note singing, a starkly beautiful form of sacred choral music that incorporates archaic harmonies and melodies, also came from the Appalachian region. The principal reason that Appalachia developed so many singular styles probably lies in the relative isolation in which most communities there existed. Because of this, even though ballads may have been passed from county to county, each area would over time develop its own unique version of the song. Similar diversity can be found in instrumental techniques, including picking and bowing styles as well as tunings. As the technology for field recording improved, regional variations in Appalachia became well preserved through the efforts of ethnomusicologists like Alan Lomax, Ralph Rinzler, and Mike Seeger. Among the best-documented Appalachian instrumentalists are banjo player Dock Boggs, fiddler Hobart Smith, and guitarist Doc Watson. Among the many ballad singers from the region, Aunt Molly Jackson, Sarah Ogan Gunning, and Jean Ritchie are some of the best represented.

see also: Cecil Sharp (sidebar)

Michael Parrish

proved to be such a good idea that at one point there were several different Boyoyo Boys recording in South Africa, where the producer often ends up with the rights to a band's name. You'll find the recommended albums from the original here.

what's available: The Boyoyo Boys are noted for their innovative drum patterns, thumping bass lines, snaky, syncopated guitars, and the searing, fatback sax of Lucas Pelo. *Back in Town* ♪♪♪♥ (Rounder, 1987, prod. Clive Risko) is an energetic, non-stop sampling of stomping Zulu rock 'n' roll, guaranteed to wake the dead and rattle the bones of the living. On *TJ Today* ♫♫♫ (Rounder, 1988, prod. Clive Risko) the band is joined by sax player Thomas Phale, the man who taught Pelo how to blow sax over 20 years ago. The production here is a bit smoother than on *Back in Town*, but the groove still predominates.

influences:

◄◄ Thomas Phale, Lulu Masilela, Wilson "King Force" Silgee

►► Mahlathini & Mahotella Queens, Dark City Sisters, Yvonne Chaka Chaka

j. poet

The Boys of the Lough

Pan-Celtic

Formed 1967, in Belfast, Northern Ireland.

Aly Bain, fiddle (1971–present); Cathal McConnell, flute, tin whistle, vocals; Dave Richardson, mandolin, cittern, English concertina, button accordion (1974–present); Christy O'Leary, uilleann pipes, tin whistle, mouth organ, vocals (1985–98); Chris Newman, guitar (1995–98); John Coakley, piano, guitar (1985–95); Robin Morton, vocals, Anglo concertina, bodhrán (1967–79); Dick Gaughan, guitar, vocals (1972–74); Tich Richardson (died 1983), guitar (1979–83); Mike Whellans, vocals, guitar (1971–72); Tommy Gunn (1967). (Members are from Ireland, Scotland, and England.)

The Boys of the Lough formed in Belfast as a trio of Northern Irish musicians: Cathal McConnell and Tommy Gunn, both of County Fermanagh, and Robin Morton from County Armagh. That lineup fell apart quite quickly, and the Boys of the Lough ceased to exist for a short period, but McConnell and Morton continued to perform as a duo. At the 1969 Falkirk folk festival they met Shetland fiddler Aly Bain and singer/guitarist Mike Whellans, who were playing on the Scottish folk circuit. They played a set together at the festival and left with the hope of teaming up again. Their opportunity came in 1971, and soon thereafter the band was officially re-formed, this time as a hybrid Irish/Scottish outfit. Dick Gaughan of Glasgow replaced Whellans in 1972, when the band was most of the way through recording its first LP. Interestingly, they scrapped the original takes and redid all the tracks to include Gaughan, which suggests a "lost" Boys of the Lough album somewhere, waiting to be issued—though it probably never will be. Gaughan was replaced after two years and one LP by Dave Richardson of Northumberland, completing the group's "internationalization" by the addition of its first Englishman. The four-piece lineup of McConnell, Bain, Richardson, and Morton lasted for six years, touring widely in Europe and America and releasing six albums. Robin Morton left in 1979 to found Scotland's Temple Records. He was replaced by Dave Richardson's brother, Tich, on guitar.

This grouping survived until 1983, when Tich was killed in a car accident. Although they recorded three albums, none of them is currently in print. After two years of recuperation, the band came together again in 1985, with new members Christy O'Leary and John Coakley. That configuration survived 10 years, until Coakley was replaced by jazzy English guitarist Chris Newman in 1995. The latest news from the Boys of the Lough is that both O'Leary and Newman have left the band due to contractual disputes; no replacements are known as of this writing.

what to buy: The title track of *Farewell and Remember Me* ♫♫♫♫ (Shanachie, 1987, prod. Peter Harris, Boys of the Lough), a sad emigration song sung by McConnell, is only one highlight of the Boys of the Lough's best available CD. Mostly an album of Irish music, this features two songs each from McConnell and O'Leary, the best being O'Leary's rendition of the Gaelic ballad "An Spailpin Fanach." It also contains tunes played on a historically fascinating set of uilleann pipes, made by Taylor of Philadelphia in about 1890, and later owned by the piper William Hanafin. The rest of the album is as solid a collection of Irish and Scottish dance music as you'll find.

what to buy next: *To Welcome Paddy Home* ♫♫♫ (Shanachie, 1985, prod. Peter Harris, Boys of the Lough) is only a slight step down from *Farewell and Remember Me*. The first album after the devastating car accident that killed Tich Richardson, it reflects the new band's predominant makeup with lots of material from Ireland. Mostly a terrific album of jigs, reels, and hornpipes, this also features two songs, of which the title track is the most affecting. *Sweet Rural Shade* ♫♫♫ (Shanachie, 1988, prod. Boys of the Lough, Peter Harris) is very much in the mold of the previous two albums by this lineup—mostly traditional Irish music; mostly strong, textured arrangements of dance music—with impeccable musicianship on fiddle, flute, pipes, mandolins, and other instruments. It also has a couple of songs for good measure. *Live at Passim* ♫♫♫ (Philo, 1975, prod. Boys of the Lough) captures an early version of the band, complete with Robin Morton, and is the only CD release to feature Morton's singing and sense of humor. One of his songs here, a humorous ballad/recitation/ vaudeville act, is a hilarious account of trying to care for an uncooperative baby. Other highlights include a set of Shetland fiddle tunes (including perennial favorite "The Day Dawn"); a "piece," or descriptive tone poem, from the piping tradition; and some lovely songs sung by McConnell. The group's other concert document currently available on CD is *Live at Carnegie Hall* ♫♫♫ (Sage Arts, 1992, prod. Boys of the Lough, Peter Harris, Matthew Sutton). Although it was recorded in 1988, 14 years after *Live at Passim*, the group includes another version of "Flower of Magherally," which has changed remarkably little since its earlier incarnation. This album preserves a good but short Boys of the Lough set, one at which they played support to Bill Monroe and the Blue Grass Boys. Perhaps to highlight the connections between their own music and Monroe's, they performed a high proportion of Scottish music, almost none of it from Bain's native Shetland. Jigs, reels, and polkas galore fill up this album; it has only two songs besides "Flower of Magherally," one of which is a very silly untitled number introducing the band, written and sung by emcee Garrison Keillor. *A Midwinter Night's Dream* ♫♫♫ (Blix Street, 1994, prod. Boys of the Lough) is the Boys of the Lough's Christmas album. With driving rhythms from guest guitarist Chris Newman and guest pianist Henning Sommero, the four-piece group of O'Leary, Bain, McConnell, and Richardson performs a lot of beautiful dance music from Ireland and Shetland. They also sing two carols and a heartbreaking ballad. Interesting twists include some Swedish tunes and one that is said to have come from Yaki Eskimos. Bain's strong fiddling, a preponderance of Shetland selections (including the well-known "Da Day Dawn," "Christmas Day in the Morning," "The Papa Stour Sword Dance," "Da Trowie Burn," and "Da Fields of Foula," all of which have appeared on previous Boys of the Lough albums), and a long section in the notes about "Yule in Shetland" make this an album focused on Bain's native islands. It was released in the U.K. as *The Day Dawn*.

what to avoid: *Good Friends—Good Music* ♫♫ (Philo, 1977) isn't really a Boys of the Lough CD. It's really "members of the Boys of the Lough play in duets and trios with friends who are not in the band." While this can be diverting, and isn't by any means bad, it isn't what most people will want to hear when they sit down to listen to the actual band.

the rest:
The Fair Hills of Ireland ♫♫♫ (Sage Arts, 1992)

worth searching for: Two albums, *Lochaber No More* ♫♫♫ (Philo, 1976, prod. Boys of the Lough) and *The Piper's Broken Finger* ♫♫♫ (Philo, 1976, prod. Boys of the Lough), are both available on cassette only. The band's debut, *The Boys of the Lough* ♫♫♫♫ (Shanachie, 1973, prod. Boys of the Lough), features Dick Gaughan, later to become one of the great voices of the Scottish folk scene. His renditions of several ballads are unforgettable and are very much worth buying if you can find an old LP copy; the album was available on vinyl in the U.S. for many years.

solo outings:
Aly Bain:
Aly Bain & Friends (Greentrax, 1994)
(With Phil Cunningham) *The Pearl* ♫♫♫ (Green Linnet, 1995)
Lonely Bird (Green Linnet, 1996)
(With Phil Cunningham) *The Ruby* ♫♫♫ (Green Linnet, 1998)

influences:
◄◄ The Chieftains, Tom Anderson

►► Craobh Rua

see also: *Phil Cunningham, Connie Dover, Dick Gaughan, Andy M. Stewart*

Steve Winick

Paul Brady

See: Kevin Burke, Jackie Daly, Andy Irvine, James Keane, Andy McGann, Mick Moloney, Tommy Peoples, Planxty

Anouar Brahem

Arabic classical, jazz
Born 1957, in Tunis, Tunisia. Based in Tunisia.

Music in the Islamic world generally places a higher premium on the human voice than it does on any instrument. Even such wizards of the *oud* (lute) as Farid al-Atrash and Mohammed Abdel Wahab were valued more for their vocal and songwriting abilities, respectively, than their instrumental skills. Despite this cultural bias, there is a performer from Tunisia whose gifts as a player, composer, and improviser are such that it is hard to ignore him.

Anouar Brahem started studying the oud at the Tunis National Conservatory of Music when he was 10 or 11 years old (sources differ). His primary instructor was one of Tunisia's most distinguished and accomplished performers, Ali Sriti, who taught Brahem the traditional ways of playing including the art of *taqâsîm* (an improvisational discipline based on a complex set of preestablished rules and conventions). After his musical apprenticeship, Brahem began writing his own pieces and performing in solo concerts. It was also about this time that he started working closely with percussionist Lassad Hosni.

At age 24 Brahem left Tunis for a four-year stint in Paris, where he was exposed to the music of other cultures and vice versa. He started writing music for film during these years and has since composed scores for over a dozen movies. In 1985 Brahem headed back to Tunis to continue his music research and promote some of the ideas he had picked up during his Paris sojourn. By 1987 he had been appointed to head the Musical Ensemble of the City of Tunis, a group which he proceeded to revamp. Brahem started breaking the ensemble up into smaller units and blending new compositions (some with jazz influences) into its typically traditional repertoire. He also started writing songs, departing slightly from the instrumental focus that had been the hallmark of his earlier efforts. When Brahem finally left Tunis to tour North America, he was already being touted as one of the Arab world's most adventurous musicians. It was shortly after his return from touring that Brahem met Manfred Eicher of ECM Records, who was to produce and release Brahem's albums from then on. Since that time the artist has continued an active touring schedule, hitting Europe and Japan in addition to occasional forays in North America, the Middle East, and his native North Africa. His onstage and studio associates have included a host of talents from a variety of disciplines including Jan Garbarek, Kudsi Erguner, Dave Holland, Manu Dibango, Manu Katché, and Fareed Haque.

what to buy: The best-recorded, best-sounding, best-played oud album you are ever likely to own is Brahem's *Barzakh* 🎵🎵🎵🎵 (ECM, 1991, prod. Manfred Eicher). Joined by violinist Bechir Selmi and longtime associate Lassad Hosni on percussion, the oud master has created a beautiful aural document with solo, duo, and trio arrangements that show off each performer's exceptional skills.

what to buy next: Brahem's next album, *Conte de l'incroyable amour* 🎵🎵🎵🎵 (ECM, 1992, prod. Manfred Eicher), marked a slight break from the more traditional *Barzakh*. Here is where Brahem started mixing music from Turkey and Tunisia by playing with Barbaros Erkose (clarinet), Kudsi Erguner (*ney* flute), and Lassad Hosni (percussion). The reed instruments of Erkose and Erguner provide an interesting sonic backdrop for Brahem's oud that presaged later recordings he would make with Jan Garbarek and John Surman.

the rest:
Madar 🎵🎵🎵🎵 (ECM, 1994)
Khomsa 🎵🎵🎵🎵 (ECM, 1995)

worth searching for: Brahem's *Thimar* 🎵🎵🎵🎵 (ECM, 1998, prod. Manfred Eicher) is an intriguing cross-cultural chamber-music session with master bassist Dave Holland and reed virtuoso John Surman on bass clarinet and soprano saxophone. In its classic austerity this European-only release comes closer to *Barzakh*'s haunting beauty than just about anything else Brahem has done.

influences:
◀◀ Ali Sriti

see also: *Farid al-Atrash, Kudsi Erguner, Mohammed Abdel Wahab*

Garaud MacTaggart

Brave Combo
Worldbeat
Formed 1979, in Denton, TX, USA. Based in USA.

Carl Finch, vocals, accordion, guitar; Bubba Hernandez, bass, vocals; Jeffrey Barnes, saxophone, clarinet, percussion.

A self-described "nuclear polka" band, Brave Combo is often shortchanged as a novelty act since its frenetic live shows zig-

zag from stampede-inducing romps through "Who Stole the Kishka" and "The Happy Wanderer" all the way to a surf version of "Oh, What a Beautiful Morning." But over the years the Combo—a revolving six-piece built around the nucleus of Finch, Hernandez, and Barnes—has evolved into a versatile outfit capable of being both faithful and funky: they've developed a startling command of traditional folk music from Greece, Israel, and Mexico while retaining the infectious, dance-frenzy enthusiasm that makes them a favorite at weddings, bar mitzvahs, Oktoberfests, and alternative-rock clubs. Once a band to simply get wrecked to, Brave Combo is now a group to be reckoned with.

what to buy: *No, No, No, Cha Cha Cha* 🎵🎵🎵🎵 (Rounder, 1993, prod. Brave Combo) focuses on the group's Latin influences and boasts a seamless medley of the Rolling Stones' "Satisfaction" and Ringo Starr's "No No Song," a festive salsa version of Cher's "The Way of Love," and a boss bossa-nova rendition of "Fly Me to the Moon." *Polkas for a Gloomy World* 🎵🎵🎵🎵 (Rounder, 1995, prod. Brave Combo) is their Grammy-nominated return to straight-ahead polka, mixing jaunty originals like "Flying Saucer" with traditional Mexican, Russian, and German polkas. *Group Dance Epidemic* 🎵🎵🎵🎵 (Rounder, 1997, prod. Brave Combo) collects studio versions of such live favorites as "The Chicken Dance," their Devo-like demolition of "The Hokey Pokey," and other vintage tunes designed for conga lines and bunny-hop parades. The band's warped genius is revealed on its cover of Van McCoy's "The Hustle," in which it uncovers the melodic thread connecting the disco hit with Lou Reed's "Walk on the Wild Side."

what to buy next: *Girl* 🎵🎵🎵 (Rounder, 1996, prod. Brave Combo, Bucks Burnett), a surprisingly listenable collaboration with Tiny Tim, demonstrates the depth of Brave Combo's musical vocabulary and its astounding ability to make anyone sound good. Check out the hepcat-jazz version of "Stairway to Heaven" and the "Wooly Bully"–like reworking of "Bye Bye Blackbird."

what to avoid: *Musical Varieties* 🎵🎵 (Rounder, 1988, prod. Brave Combo) is a compilation of pre-Rounder tracks from the early '80s. Although hardly horrid, they lean toward predictable gimmickry ("People Are Strange" and "Sixteen Tons" as polkas), sideswiping genres the band would eventually tackle head-on.

the rest:
Polkatharsis 🎵🎵🎵 (Rounder, 1987)
Humansville 🎵🎵🎵 (Rounder, 1989)
A Night on Earth 🎵🎵🎵🎵 (Rounder, 1990)
It's Christmas, Man! 🎵🎵🎵🎵 (Rounder, 1992)
Mood Swing Music 🎵🎵🎵 (Rounder, 1996)
Polka Party with Brave Combo 🎵🎵🎵 (Easydisk/Rounder, 1998)

worth searching for: *The Hokey Pokey* 🎵🎵🎵 (denTone, 1994, prod. Brave Combo), a self-released EP, features early versions of several tunes on *Group Dance Epidemic* as well as the otherwise unavailable concert favorite "The Hava Nagila Twist." *Kiss of Fire* 🎵🎵🎵 (Watermelon, 1996, prod. Brave Combo) is a sublime collaboration with Lauren Agnelli, formerly of folk trio the Washington Squares, on torch songs ranging from the French *chansons* of Edith Piaf and Francoise Hardy to the fiery tangos of Carlos Gardel.

influences:

◄◄ You name it, from Xavier Cugat to Astor Piazzolla

►► The New Orleans Klezmer All Stars

David Okamoto

Brave Old World

Contemporary klezmer
Formed 1989. Members live in New York, NY, USA; Chicago, IL, USA; Berkeley, CA, USA; and Berlin, Germany.

Michael Alpert, vocals, fiddle, guitar, percussion; Alan Bern, accordion, piano; Kurt Bjorling, clarinet, bass clarinet; Stuart Brotman, bass, tsimbl (cimbalom), tilinka, percussion; Joel Rubin, B-flat and C clarinets (1989–1991).

Even though Brave Old World's members live across the U.S. and, in one case, Europe, they've managed to arrange enough quality time for three albums and numerous tours all over their two home continents. But those aren't the only ways they happen to run into each other—Brave Old World also present workshops and educational programs on such topics as "Dancing to the Ceiling: Traditional East European Jewish Dance"; "The Whole World Is in These Songs: Jewish Life in Yiddish Folk and Popular Song"; and "Making Klezmer Music: Jewish Instrumental Traditions." Forging ahead from history as their name implies and forging cultures together as their lineup embodies, Brave Old World may have attained their highest public profile with the PBS documentary *In the Fiddler's House,* in which they and other klezmer youngbloods accompany old-school classicist Itzhak Perlman on his journey into Jewish roots.

what to buy: *Blood Oranges* 🎵🎵🎵🎵 (Pinorrek Records, 1997, prod. Frank Dostal) is a magnificent showcase for Brave Old World's distinctive style, which combines the discipline and richness of classical music with jazz-like improvisation. The longer instrumental selections include tempo and texture shifts agile enough to impress though not abrupt enough to overpower—an exceptional inter-player empathy lends a nimbleness to material that in other hands might come off as empty virtuosity or fall disastrously short of its ambitions. Meanwhile, lighthearted tracks like the jaunty, *a cappella* "Welcome" and the self-deprecating "The Band" keep the ensemble's serious musicianship from getting *too* serious. *Beyond the Pale* 🎵🎵🎵🎵 (Rounder, 1994, prod. Frank Dostal) is worth it alone for the instrumental showstopper "Basarabye"'s accordion-and-clarinet klezmer inferno, courtesy of Bern and Bjorling respectively. But there's much more that makes the album worthwhile, particularly the opener and closer "Berlin Overture" and "Berlin 1990," Alpert's emotional accounts of being Jewish and performing in Germany at the end of the 20th century. *Klezmer Music* 🎵🎵🎵🎵 (Flying Fish, 1991, prod. Brave Old World) is remarkable for its inclusion of "Chernobyl," which matches Alpert's original lyrics with an upbeat traditional Ukrainian/Jewish melody and a self-consciously schmaltzy vocal for a levity at odds with the subject matter—but not with the all-too-experienced Jewish tradition of fatalistic humor.

worth searching for: Look for the band on the recorded documents of Perlman's brave expedition to his own Old World, *In the Fiddler's House* 🎵🎵🎵🎵 (Angel, 1995, executive prod. Jac Venza) and *Live in the Fiddler's House* 🎵🎵🎵🎵 (Angel, 1996, prod. Steven Paul).

influences:

◄◄ Klezmer Conservatory Band, Naftule Brandwein, Dave Tarras, Andy Statman, Bronya Sakina, Leon Schwartz, the Chieftains

►► Naftule's Dream, the Klezmatics

see also: *Itzhak Perlman*

Ken Roseman

Máire Breatnach

Irish traditional and neo-traditional
Born 1956, in Dublin, Ireland. Based in Dublin, Ireland.

Violinist, composer, and occasional singer and keyboardist Máire Breatnach was brought up in Dublin, in a bilingual family that cherished traditional Irish music. Classically trained on violin, in the '80s she played in various traditional conglomerations, sometimes alongside her flutist brother Cormac. The '90s have seen her write, arrange, and record three albums of new music in a traditional vein, inspired by ancient Irish legends. While her work has solid Irish roots, it also displays the influence of 20th-century pastoral composers Peter Warlock, Arnold Bax, and Ralph Vaughan Williams. She was a featured soloist in the original *Riverdance* stage-show and soundtrack album in 1995, and has done session work—both as violinist and singer—for artists ranging from Mary Black and Sharon Shannon at home to Alan Stivell and John Renbourn overseas. Though recent recordings have indicated more consolidation than experimentation, the very track record she's consolidating is that of keeping one foot on firm traditional ground and one foot on the cutting edge.

what to buy: For both *Angel Candles* ♫♫♫ (Starc, 1993/Blix Street, 1995, prod. Máire Breatnach) and *The Voyage of Bran* ♫♫♫♫ (Starc, 1995/Celtic Heartbeat, 1995, prod. Máire Breatnach), Breatnach enlisted accordionist Sharon Shannon, piper Ronan Browne, singer and keyboardist Liam Ó Maonlaí, guitarist Steve Cooney, and percussionist Tommy Hayes for a bounty of sprightly jigs, reels, and slides, as well as dignified polkas and waltzes. She accompanies her own violin with keyboards on some delightful airs and elegiac tone poems. A few charming and unusual songs are included with the instrumentals; Breatnach and Ó Maonlaí's voices sound wonderful together.

what to buy next: *Celtic Lovers* ♫♫♫ (Starc, 1996/Blix Street, 1997, prod. Máire Breatnach) also contains some fine writing and playing, but shows little progression from the earlier albums. It slides dangerously close to the slough of new-age at times, and the lack of vocals leads to a certain monotony. Oddly, the musicians (including accordionist Máirtín O'Connor) are not credited on the U.S. issue.

worth searching for: The complex and delicate fiddling on the original Irish release of Bill Whelan's soundtrack for *Riverdance* was all Breatnach; the second, better-known *Riverdance* ♫♫♫♫ (Celtic Heartbeat, 1995) includes all of Breatnach's work plus two newer tunes featuring fiddler Eileen Ivers instead.

influences:
◄◄ Nollaig Casey, Bill Whelan

see also: *The Black Family, Eileen Ivers, Sharon Shannon, Bill Whelan*

John C. Falstaff

Jean Binta Breeze
/Breeze
/Sister Breeze

Dub poetry

Born Jean Lumsden, 1956, in Patty Hill, Hanover, Jamaica. Based in Jamaica and London, England.

The patronizing tag often bestowed upon Breeze by the boys' club of the reggae industry—"Jamaica's leading female dub poet"—doesn't begin to do her justice. Acclaimed in Britain, Europe, and the Caribbean but woefully overlooked in the U.S., she is one of the most important artists in dub poetry (the reggae form of "spoken-word"), *period,* not to mention one of the leading figures in contemporary Caribbean literature. A virtuosic stage performer equally at home in Jamaican Creole and BBC English, Breeze broke through on the Reggae Sunsplash tour of

1983, after training with fellow dub-poet luminaries Oku Onuora and Mikey Smith at the Jamaican School of Drama in the late 1970s, then retreating to the countryside for several years to work as a Rastagrarian and hone her art. Even her early, more sloganeering poems, whether denouncing "slack" (sexually explicit) deejays' denigration of women ("Get Back") or decrying the IMF's ravaging of Third World economies ("Aid Travels with a Bomb"), were animated by an understanding of theater in which the spoken word is integrally fused with elements of music and dance. By the time Breeze arrived in London in 1985 (at the urging of the genre's acknowledged giant Linton Kwesi Johnson), she'd begun to break free of the syntactic spareness and metrical monotony of some early dub poetry, dramatically modulating a range of rhythms and tones (and themes) with a vocal versatility that never fails to leave audiences rapt and electrified. Breeze's voice is uncommonly expressive, capable of great emotional range, depth, and complexity; her poems are by turns forceful and fragile, soft-spoken and deep-throated, passionate and playful. And while she can chant down Babylon with the best of them, as a homegrown feminist she's always emphasized the politics of the personal, deftly foregrounding the everyday experience of women as mothers, lovers, workers, and fighters against a backdrop of geopolitics and neocolonial economics.

worth searching for: Sadly, little of Breeze's work is currently available on CD in the U.S., though all of it is worth seeking out. Her debut album (as "Sister Breeze"), *Riddym Ravings* ♫♫♫ (ROIR, 1987, prod. Delroy Thompson, Breeze), remains in print, though on cassette only. Many of the tunes—a Rastagrarian marching song, a *Nyabinghi* (ritual Rasta) anthem, a parodic street-hustler skank—are simple though lively and rootsical. But the album is worth buying solely for Breeze's famous dramatic monologue "Riddym Ravings (The Mad Woman's Poem)," a breathtaking tour de force about urban alienation and the redemptive promise of the reggae beat that signaled a quantum leap in her performance skills. Prior to this album, Breeze had contributed two poems ("To Plant" and "Aid Travels with a Bomb") to the seminal compilation *Word Soun' 'Ave Power: Reggae Poetry* ♫♫♫ (Heartbeat, 1983, prod. Mutabaruka)—reissued with added dub versions in 1994 as *Word Soun' 'Ave Power: Dub Poets and Dub*)—and two more ("Get Back" and "Reality") to the worthier follow-up compilation *Woman Talk: Caribbean Dub Poetry* ♫♫♫ (Heartbeat cassette, 1986, prod. Mutabaruka). Her best recorded work, though, is undoubtedly *Tracks* ♫♫♫♫ (LKJ Records, 1990/Shanachie, 1991, prod. Dennis Bovell, Linton Kwesi Johnson), deleted from the Shanachie catalog but available on import from LKJ. Six short, evocative, unaccompanied poems alternate with six others set to sublime arrangements by the peerless Dennis Bovell and backed by the Dub Band. Standouts include an ebullient ska prophecy ("Confusion") and the bluesy, bittersweet dirge of a woman worn down by the tedium of domestic routine ("Ordinary Mawning"). Completists may want to search out the 12" single *Slip* ♫♫♫ (The Poets, 1982/Heartbeat, 1982, prod. Mutabaruka). Finally, a newer cassette, *Riding on de Riddym: Selected Spoken Works,* featuring unaccompanied readings of 30 poems, is available from 57 Productions, 57 Effingham Road, Lee Green, London SE12 8NT, England. Breeze's printed work has been much anthologized; her own collections are *Answers* (1983), *Riddym Ravings* (Race Today, 1988), *Spring Cleaning* (Virago, 1992), and *On the Edge of an Island* (Bloodaxe, 1997).

influences:

◄◄ Louise Bennett ("Miss Lou"), Michael Smith

see also: *Linton Kwesi Johnson, Oku Onuora*

Michael Eldridge

Anne Briggs

See: A.L. Lloyd

Michael Brook

Electronica

Born in Toronto, Canada. Based in Canada.

Though he started his career playing conventional rock and blues with various bands in his native Toronto, including a stint with the noted act Martha and the Muffins, Michael Brook nurtured his love of experimental and minimalist music by studying with masters like La Monte Young, Jon Hassell, and Hindustani classical vocalist Pandit Pran Nath. The effort paid off, eventually leading to Brook recording with ambient-music pioneer Brian Eno and his protégé Daniel Lanois; releasing like-minded albums of his own; and producing a number of extraordinary world-music/electronica collaborations with artists like Nusrat Fateh Ali Khan, Djivan Gasparyan, and U. Srinivas. Brook has also scored films such as *Captive, Albino Alligator,* and the IMAX release *The Fires of Kuwait,* and become a sure hand behind the boards for world-music and pop artists alike.

what to buy: For those who like electronic atmospheres spiced with exotic sounds from distant lands, Brook may be the quintessential artist. His album with Indian mandolinist U. Srinivas, *Dream* ♫♫♫ (RealWorld, 1995, prod. Michael Brook), began as a straight production job but turned into a full-scale collaboration, including contributions from British cellist Caroline Lavelle, Brazilian percussionist Nana Vasconcelos, and fellow Canadian avant-gardist Jane Siberry. Brook achieves a similar effect in a different musical direction with Albanian *duduk* (oboe) player Djivan Gasparyan on *Black Rock* ♫♫♫ (RealWorld, 1998, prod. Michael Brook). Among Brook's most celebrated collaborations, however, is his album with Pakistani *qawwali* (devotional song) master Nusrat Fateh Ali Khan on *Night Song* ♫♫♫♫ (RealWorld, 1996, prod. Michael Brook). Some of its tracks were remixed (with varying success) by Talvin Singh, Asian Dub Foundation, and Joi on *Nusrat Fateh Ali Khan & Michael Brook: Remixed* ♫♫♫ (RealWorld, 1997, prod. Michael Brook).

what to buy next: Brook's dreamy and textured solo work is the perfect vehicle for his effects-laden "infinite guitar," which he plays over minimalist backing on *Cobalt Blue* ♫♫♫ (4AD, 1992, prod. Michael Brook), a gorgeous mating of music and machinery. He explores some of the same material in unaccompanied solo performance on *Live at the Aquarium, London Zoo 21 May 1992* ♫♫♫ (4AD, 1993, prod. Michael Brook).

the rest:

(With the Edge) *Original Soundtrack: Captive* ♫♫♫ (Virgin, 1987/Blue Plate, 1994)
(With Pieter Nooten) *Sleeps with the Fishes* ♫♫♫ (4AD, 1987)
(With Daniel Lanois and Brian Eno) *Hybrid* ♫♫♫ (E.G. Editions, 1990)
Albino Alligator ♫♫♫ (4AD, 1997)

worth searching for: If you like the sound Brook achieves on his own records, it's worthwhile checking out some of his many fine production jobs as well. On the world-music front, they include Nusrat Fateh Ali Khan's *Mustt Mustt* ♫♫♫♫ (RealWorld, 1991, prod. Michael Brook) and *Shahbaazz* ♫♫♫♫ (RealWorld, 1991, prod. Michael Brook), and Youssou N'Dour's *Set* ♫♫♫♫ (Gold Rush, 1996, prod. Michael Brook); on the pop side, the Pogues' *Waiting for Herb* ♫♫♫ (Chameleon, 1993, prod. Michael Brook) and Mary Margaret O'Hara's exquisite *Miss America* ♫♫♫♫ (Bar/None, 1996, prod. Michael Brook).

influences:

◄◄ Jon Hassell, Brian Eno, La Monte Young, Robert Fripp, Pandit Pran Nath

►► The Orb, Talvin Singh

see also: *Brian Eno, Djivan Gasparyan, Nusrat Fateh Ali Khan, Daniel Lanois, Pandit Pran Nath, Youssou N'Dour, the Pogues, Talvin Singh, U. Srinivas, Nana Vasconcelos*

Daniel Durchholz

Carlinhos Brown

See: Timbalada

Dennis Brown

Reggae, lovers' rock, dancehall

Born 1957, in Kingston, Jamaica. Died July 1, 1999, in Kingston, Jamaica.

Bob Marley's favorite singer, Dennis Brown was best known for his reggae-ized versions of pop love songs. Beginning with his first hit, "No Man Is an Island"—recorded in 1968 at age 11—Brown became one of Jamaica's most successful reggae acts. The child prodigy had indeed honed his skills from the age of nine, by singing in tourist clubs in Jamaica and the West Indies. As a teenager, Brown was befriended and guided by influential reggae bandleader Byron Lee. Though Brown's earliest recordings were produced by Coxsone Dodd, he reached his commercial peak during his years with producer Joe Gibbs, 1977 to '82. The upswing began in earnest in 1978, when Brown attracted attention with his appearance in the live concert film *Heartland Reggae*. The following year, Brown's rerecording of "Money in My Pocket" reached #14 on the British music charts and helped catapult him to international acclaim. Following a tour throughout Europe in 1980, Brown was signed to his first major label, A&M. His subsequent North American hits included "Foul Play" and "If I Ruled the World." Too in-demand to be restricted to his own albums, Brown's vocals can be heard on recordings by Big Youth, Junior Delgado, Aswad, Gregory Isaacs, and Mutabaruka; as a sought-after producer as well, Brown oversaw albums by John Holt and the Mortals. His death in 1999 was as premature as his rise had been precocious, and was a profound loss to the reggae community.

what to buy: Despite many omissions, *Love Hate: The Best of Dennis Brown* ♪♪♪♪ (VP, 1996, prod. Robbie Shakespeare, David Harriott & the Giants) surveys the full length of Brown's recorded career.

what to buy next: The power of Brown's early concerts is documented on *Live in Montreux* ♪♪♪♫ (Laser, 1979/Magnum America, 1995, prod. Joe Gibbs) (a.k.a. *Live at Montreux*). Brown's love and message songs are accompanied by such legend-renewing colleagues as the Roots Radics on the recent *Tribulation* ♪♪♪♫ (Heartbeat, 1999, prod. Alvin "G.G." Ranglin).

best of the rest:
Super Hits ♪♪♪♫ (Trojan, 1972)
Just Dennis ♪♪♪ (Trojan, 1975)
Visions ♪♪♪ (Shanachie, 1977)
Westbound Train ♪♪♪ (Third World, 1978)
Words of Wisdom ♪♪♪ (Shanachie, 1979)
Love Has Found Its Way ♪♪♪ (Laser, 1982)
The Best (Magnum, 1982)
Satisfactory Feeling ♪♪♪ (A&M, 1983)
Money in My Pocket ♪♪♪ (Tads, 1983)
Collection ♪♪♪ (Dennis Ting, 1984)
Judge Not ♪♪♪ (Trojan, 1984)
Walls & Letters ♪♪♪ (Shanachie, 1984)
Love's Got a Hold of Me ♪♪♪ (Joe Gibbs, 1984)
Reggae Superstars Meet ♪♪♪ (Joe Gibbs, 1985)
20 Greatest Reggae Tracks ♪♪♪ (Meteor, 1985)
Halfway Up, Halfway Down ♪♪♪ (Live & Love, 1986)
Greatest Hits ♪♪♪ (Rohit, 1988)
My Time ♪♪♪ (VP, 1989)

No Contest ♪♪♪ (Rohit, 1989)
Go Now ♪♪♪ (VP, 1991)
Victory Is Mine ♪♪♪ (Rohit, 1991)
Some Like It Hot ♪♪♪ (VP, 1991)
Another Day in Paradise ♪♪♪ (Heartbeat, 1992)
Classic Hits ♪♪♪ (Sonic Sounds, 1992)
Blazing ♪♪♪ (Shanachie, 1992)
Friends in Life ♪♪♪ (Shanachie, 1992)
Live in Montego Bay ♪♪♪ (Shanachie, 1992)
Cosmic Force ♪♪♪ (Heartbeat, 1992)
Unforgettable ♪♪♪ (VP, 1993)
Light My Fire ♪♪♪ (Rounder, 1994)
20 Magnificent Hits ♪♪♪ (Sonic Sounds, 1994)
Blood Brothers ♪♪♪ (RAS, 1994)
Visions of a Reggae King ♪♪♪ (VP, 1994)
Early Days ♪♪♪ (Sonic Sounds, 1994)
The Best: Vol. 1/Africa ♪♪♪ (Lagoon, 1995)
Temperature Rising ♪♪♪ (VP, 1995)
Dennis Brown & Friends ♪♪♪ (JA, 1995)
Love Light ♪♪♪ (Blue Moon, 1995)
Milk & Honey ♪♪♪ (Trojan, 1996)
Could It Be ♪♪♪ (RAS, 1996)
Songs of Emmanuel ♪♪♪ (VP, 1996)
Dennis ♪♪♪ (World, 1996)
Lovers' Paradise ♪♪♪ (Burning Sounds, 1996)
Got to Have Loving ♪♪♪ (M.I.L. Multime, 1997)
RAS Portraits ♪♪♪ (RAS, 1997)
He's One of a Kind ♪♪♪ (Rooney, 1998)
The Pine ♪♪♪ (Music Club, 1998)
Bless Me Jah N/A (RAS, 1999)

influences:
◀◀ Marvin Gaye, Bob Marley, Sam Cooke

▶▶ Aswad, Gregory Isaacs

see also: *Beenie Man, Freddie McGregor, the Roots Radics*

Craig Harris

Buckwheat Zydeco
Zydeco
Born Stanley Dural Jr., in Lafayette, LA, USA. Based in Lafayette, LA, USA.

Although Stanley Dural Sr. was a respected *La-La* (pre-zydeco) accordionist, his son Stanley Jr. rebelled and took up the piano. By age nine he had gone professional; he put together his first R&B band in 1971 and worked the busy Lafayette scene. During the late '70s he began playing organ with zydeco king Clifton Chenier's Red Hot Louisiana Band. Chenier lectured Dural on the importance of Creole culture and music, causing a deflection in his career trajectory. By 1979 "Buckwheat" had learned the piano accordion and left to start his own zydeco band, Ils Sont Partis. His combination of traditional and more contempo-

Buckwheat Zydeco (r) with his father, Stanley Dural Sr.

rary sounds has given Buckwheat accessibility to listeners far outside the normal zydeco audience. He has been able to attract major-label interest and spread the zydeco gospel worldwide. His bands have a reputation for being extremely well-rehearsed yet spontaneously danceable.

what to buy: *100% Fortified Zydeco* 🎵🎵🎵🎵 (Black Top, 1985, prod. Hammond Scott, Nauman S. Scott) shows Buckwheat and his band rocking away. It has the mix—from the very rural and funky to the very urbane—that packs the floor at El Sido's in Lafayette.

what to buy next: When Buckwheat steps up with just the drums behind him and drives the music with his accordion, you hear how good this man can be—it's the litmus test for all good zydeco bandleaders. He passes it on *Waitin' for My Ya-Ya* 🎵🎵🎵🎵 (Rounder, 1988, prod. Scott Billington), which comes close to striking the golden balance between his talent and his desire to please a diverse audience.

the rest:
On a Night Like This 🎵🎵🎵 (Island, 1987)

Buckwheat's Party 🎵🎵🎵 (Rounder, 1987)
Turning Point 🎵🎵🎵 (Rounder, 1988)
Taking It Home 🎵🎵🎵 (PolyGram, 1988)
Ils Sont Partis 🎵🎵🎵 (Blues Unlimited, 1988)
Buckwheat's Zydeco Party 🎵🎵🎵🎵 (Rounder, 1988)
Where There's Smoke There's Fire 🎵🎵🎵 (Island, 1990)
Menageri: Essential Zydeco 🎵🎵🎵🎵 (Mango/Antilles, 1993)
Five Card Stud 🎵🎵 (Island, 1994)
Choo Choo Boogaloo 🎵🎵🎵🎵 (Warner Bros., 1994)
Trouble 🎵🎵🎵 (Atlantic, 1997)
The Buckwheat Zydeco Story N/A (Tomorrow Recordings, 1999)

influences:

⏮ Clifton Chenier, Boozoo Chavis, Amédée Ardoin

⏭ Nathan Williams, Lynn August, Zydeco Force

see also: *Clifton Chenier, Jesse Cook*

Jared Snyder

Buena Vista Social Club

See: Ry Cooder, Rubén González

Bukken Bruse

See: Annbjørg Lien

Bŭlgari

Bulgarian folk music

Formed 1993, in Bulgaria. Based in Bulgaria and Chapel Hill, NC, USA.

Georgi Doichev, gaida, vocals; Georgi Andreev, gadulka, vocals; Dimiter Lavchev, gadulka, tupan; Georgi Zeliazov, kaval, vocals; Anton Tsambov, tambura; Radostina Kaneva, vocals. (All members are from Bulgaria.)

Formed and led by Georgi Doichev, the premier bagpipe player in Bulgaria and a former lecturer in the Department of Ethnomusicology at the University of California, this sextet features some of Bulgaria's leading musicians playing authentic interpretations of traditional Bulgarian folk. All of the group's members are graduates of Bulgaria's Musical High School and Conservatory; Zeliazov, Tsambov, and Andreev are currently soloists in the orchestra of the Bulgarian National Ensemble—of which Andreev is a director; and Kaneva, one of the top singers in Bulgaria, is a soloist in the world-famous Bulgarian National Radio and Television Choir (a version of which is known and loved by many in the West as Le Mystère des Voix Bulgares). While deeply rooted in tradition, Bŭlgari's music is gleefully inventive and arranged in a way that allows the small ensemble to sound as full and robust as a large orchestra. They're at their best in a live setting (where they've been known to churn through a killer Bulgarian version of Dave Brubeck's "Take Five") and had already played more than 100 concert dates across the U.S. and Canada in their first year as part-time Americans, gaining the national prestige platform of a two-night stint at the Kennedy Center in June of 1999.

what's available: The group's only Stateside release to date, *Bulgarian Folk Music ♪♪♪♪* (Music of the World, 1999, prod. Bŭlgari), doesn't quite compare with the visceral impact of their live performances, but it's a stirring taste of traditional Eastern European folk nonetheless. Dimiter Lavchev lays down syncopated rhythms on the booming *tupan* drum as Anton Tsambov plays rhythm riffs on his 8-string *tambura* (a Bulgarian lute not to be confused with the Indian drone instrument the *tamboura*), providing a rock-solid foundation for the dazzling melodic interplay between Georgi Doichev's piercing *gaida* (bagpipes), Georgi Zeliazov's soothing *kaval* (flute), and Georgi Andreev's lightning-fast runs on his *gadulka* (a bowed, violin-like instrument). Add the enchantingly mysterious Bulgarian voice of Radostina Kaneva and you have one heck of an American debut.

influences:
◀◀ Bulgarian Radio Women's Choir, Trio Bulgarka, Trakiiskata Troika, Trio Karadzhovska

see also: *Le Mystère des Voix Bulgares*

Bret Love

Sandy Bull

World-folk

Born 1941, in New York, NY, USA. Based in Nashville, TN, USA.

Long before "world music" was a marketing term, way before Paul Simon discovered there was gold in Graceland, Sandy Bull was mixing and matching musical cultures like a hundred-CD carousel with a broken "random" button. Originally stirred by the black drum corps at the nearby Florida high school but forbidden from drumming by his dad, he turned to the guitar and moved back to his professional-harpist mother in New York at age 11, getting exposed to a wide range of musical influences from her record collection and her cabaret act, "From Bach to Boogie Woogie." At 14 he started learning both bagpipes and banjo, and in Greenwich Village he met Pete Seeger, Odetta, Ramblin' Jack Elliott, and others of some musical repute. At 16 he was already undertaking paid gigs and at 18 began studying bass and composition at Boston University College of Music—as well as playing the odd coffeehouse with Joan Baez. But he soon dropped out to return to a professional music career in New York, right in time for the booming folk revival. His expertise let him stand out in a very crowded crowd, and he was soon signed to the prestigious Vanguard label. His first album, *Fantasias,* ran the American folkloric gamut, but its real treat was "Blend," which took up an entire LP side and had him playing with jazz drummer Billy Higgins on stretched-out music that ranged from Appalachia to India.

The next level was a departure for Europe and study with *oud* (Arabic lute) master Hamza El Din. After a few months he returned to the U.S., this time California. His quickly following 1964 album *Inventions* saw him stretching out still further, adding oud, electric bass, and electric guitar to his arsenal and playing Brazilian, classical, jazz, Indian, and Middle Eastern musics, as well as his somewhat meditative take on Chuck Berry's "Memphis"—nothing if not eclectic. The follow-up *E Pluribus Unum* appeared four years later, and both justified and explained the wait with two ambitious side-length tracks, each again Cuisinarting everything into a quite delicious gumbo. His next album (and last for Vanguard), 1971's *Demolition Derby,* took it all at least two steps further.

That would be the last anyone would hear of Sandy Bull on record for some time. The experimental spirit of the '60s had passed, and no label wanted to know about his ideas. In addition, the substance-abuse problems of the '70s had arrived and would take him a while to resolve. Each spell was broken by the time of his next album, *Jukebox School of Music,* way over in the year 1987. His hiatus notwithstanding, the record was as adventurous as anything he'd done, reunited him with Higgins, and arrived at a point when the times were finally beginning to catch up with him. The carousel started spinning again and hasn't paused yet.

what to buy: *The Vanguard Sessions* ♪♪♪♪ (Vanguard, 1998, prod. various) collects from those early Vanguard years, when Bull was at his most experimental.

the rest:
Fantasias ♪♪♪ (Vanguard, 1963)
Inventions ♪♪♪ (Vanguard, 1964/Timeless Recording Society, 1996)
E Pluribus Unum ♪♪♪♪ (Vanguard, 1968)
Demolition Derby ♪♪♪ (Vanguard, 1972)
Jukebox School of Music ♪♪♪ (ROM, 1987)
Vehicles ♪♪♪ (Timeless Recording Society, 1991)
Steel Tears ♪♪♪ (Timeless Recording Society, 1996)

influences:
◀◀ Hamza El Din, Staple Singers, Pete Seeger

▶▶ Van Morrison, everyone who's ever heard him

see also: *Hamza El Din*

Chris Nickson

Jane Bunnett

Jazz, Latin jazz
Born 1955, in Toronto, Ontario, Canada. Based in Paris, France; New York, USA; Toronto, Canada; and Cuba.

Bunnett was originally trained as a classical pianist but had to take another career path when tendinitis made it too difficult for her to play. Traveling to San Francisco to recoup her energies, Bunnett heard a series of concerts by Charles Mingus that inspired her to change her instrumental focus to the flute. She is also a gifted soprano saxophone player, having studied with Steve Lacy and won a couple of *Down Beat* polls for the instrument. Another crucial landmark in her musical history—particularly for readers of this book—was her discovery of Cuban rhythms and musicians. Before that encounter, she was a fairly straight-ahead post-bop player with interesting, if conventional, ideas. Bunnett's exposure to Cuban music has opened up new vistas in her playing and widened her compositional palette.

what to buy: The definitive disc for world-music fans is the artist's own recorded initiation in that vein. Although Bunnett became a fan of Latin rhythms prior to her first trip to Cuba, it was this physical journey that introduced her to some of the most talented musicians in the genre and helped make possible the wonderful *Spirits of Havana* ♪♪♪♪ (Messidor, 1991, prod. Guillermo Barreto, Danny Greenspoon). Bunnett's flute solo over the percussion ensemble Grupo Yoruba Andabo on

"Hymn" is squarely in the tradition of such Cuban masters as Fajardo and Filiberto Rico, while the group's take on Thelonious Monk's "Epistrophy," with Bunnett on soprano saxophone, has interesting rhythms percolating beneath the surface courtesy of pianist Gonzalo Rubalcaba and a slew of percussion. The focus of the album is on the group sound, though there are spaces for soloists. Other participants in the sessions include pianist Hilario Durán, vocalist Merceditas Valdes, bassist Kieran Overs, trumpeter Larry Cramer, and timbales player Guillermo Barreto, to whom the album is dedicated.

the rest:
New York Duets ♪♪♪ (Denon/Music & Arts, 1989)
Live at Sweet Basil ♪♪♪ (Denon/Music & Arts, 1991)
The Water Is Wide ♪♪♪ (Evidence, 1994)
Rendez-Vous Brazil/Cuba ♪♪♪ (Justin Time, 1995)
Jane Bunnett & the Cuban Piano Masters ♪♪♪ (World Pacific, 1996)
Chamalongo ♪♪♪ (Blue Note, 1998)

influences:
◀◀ Charles Mingus, Steve Lacy, Guillermo Barreto

Garaud MacTaggart

Sharon Burch

Navaho singer/songwriter
Born in Gallop, NM, USA. Based in Santa Rosa, CA, USA.

Burch is the daughter of a German father and a Navaho mother; for her, growing up bi-cultural was a blessing—figuratively and literally. "My grandfather was a Navaho healer who followed the Blessing Way," Burch says, in reference to a sacred healing ritual. "He brought my mother up to respect Indians and non-Indians, and taught us not to be afraid of what happens in this life, because in the final account, everything turns back to beauty." In her music Burch has kept to the Blessing Way, managing to balance Navaho traditions with the demands of the modern non-Indian world. She has recorded three albums for Canyon Records, including *Touch the Sweet Earth,* winner of the 1996 Indie Grammy for Best Native American Recording; and while her music pays respect to her traditional Navaho childhood, it also reflects her bicultural outlook, combining Navaho words and melodies with western guitar styles. "I grew up traveling with my mom and granddad to the ceremonies my grandfather conducted. They tell me I joined in the singing as a child, and although I don't remember that, I do remember the sound of the music, bouncing off of the walls of the hogans and surrounding me." In college Burch began singing at folk festivals, and a meeting with A. Paul Ortega, the Apache godfather of Native singer/songwriters, led to her recording debut. "I sing in Navaho to pay respect to my family, the earth and the language I was raised in," Burch sums up. "Having a German father and

Native mother helped me understand that a human can relate to all people, not just your own kind. The whole planet is ours; there should be no boundaries."

what to buy: Burch finds a perfect balance between Navaho tradition and American folk music on her solo debut, *Yazzie Girl* 🎵🎵🎵🎵 (Canyon, 1989, prod. Robert Doyle). It includes traditional chants set to music by Burch, as well as her own full compositions. Her honey-soaked alto and spare guitar accompaniment make the album a treat for both Navaho and non-Indian ears. *Touch the Sweet Earth* 🎵🎵🎵🎵 (Canyon, 1993, prod. Robert Doyle) continues in the same low-key vein with a collection of traditional ballads and lullabies.

what to buy next: *The Blessing Ways* 🎵🎵🎵 (Canyon cassette, 1984) is a duet album with Ortega that sparked Burch's own songwriting career, drawing largely on the teachings of her grandfather. Ortega and Burch sing both traditional songs and Ortega's compositions with flute and drum accompaniment.

influences:
◀ A. Paul Ortega, Buffy Sainte-Marie

see also: *A. Paul Ortega*

j. poet

John Burgess

Scottish traditional

Born 1934, in Aberdeenshire, Scotland. Based in Invergordon, Scotland.

It is not for nothing that many in his native Scotland know John Burgess as "King of the Highland Pipers"—it's more like for everything. His first tutoring on the Great Highland Bagpipes came very early in life at the hands of his father; upon the family's move to Edinburgh Burgess began taking lessons with Pipe Major Willie Ross, the resident piper at Edinburgh Castle. It wasn't long before the child prodigy was dominating the world of Highland piping competitions, and at the ripe age of 16 he won a gold medal at the Argyllshire Gathering in Oban. Observers had hardly had a chance to absorb the fact that this made Burgess the youngest piper ever to win a gold medal, when he took a second gold at the Northern Meeting in Inverness the same year. Over the next three decades he would arguably come to be Scotland's most prodigiously decorated piper, winning more than 200 gold and silver medals. Taking care to replenish the tradition in another way, he became the piping instructor for the Easter Ross–area school system in the Scottish Highlands from the mid-'60s to 1996. Burgess has also, as Highland pipers go, been quite prolific in his recorded output, releasing at least 12 U.S. and U.K. albums over the course of his busy career.

what's available: *King of the Highland Pipers* 🎵🎵🎵🎵 (Topic, 1993, prod. Tony Engle, A.L. Lloyd) is a compilation culled from Burgess's first two albums for the Topic label, originally recorded in the 1970s. This must-have collection for fans of the Great Highland Bagpipes runs the gamut of Scottish music, including *piobaireachd* (the classical form for the Highland pipes, also known as *ceol mor* or "big music"), and teeming as well with fine examples of the more informal genre of the pipes, *ceol beag* or "small music," represented by some magnificent airs, reels, jigs, marches, strathspeys, and hornpipes. *The Piping Centre 1996 Recital Series—V. 2* 🎵🎵🎵 (Temple, 1996, prod. Robin Morton) was, as the title reveals, recorded as part of a concert series at Glasgow's Piping Centre featuring some of the world's finest practitioners. This volume focuses on Burgess for half of the recording, and on his contemporary Donald MacPherson, who is every bit as legendary in piping circles, for the other half. The youthful vibrancy of each man's playing belies his widely held elder-statesman status, even as the expertise displayed confirms it.

worth searching for: If further investigation into the Life of Burgess intrigues you, *John D. Burgess—A Piping Legend* is a wonderful film that documents his extraordinary career and lifelong dedication to his craft.

influences:
◀ Willie Ross, Robert Brown, Robert Nicol

▶ 78th Fraser Highlanders, Dougie Pincock, Gordon Duncan

Cliff McGann

Irving Burgie
/Lord Burgess

Calypso

Born 1924, in Brooklyn, NY, USA. Based in USA.

In the forgotten mid-'50s prehistory of the British Invasion, a brief calypso boom ruled the American airwaves, set sales records, and, some suggest, sowed the seeds of later mass success for artists with an island beat like Bob Marley and Gloria Estefan. The Stateside calypso king was Harry Belafonte, but the power behind the throne was the man who wrote his most famous songs: Irving Burgie.

A native New Yorker born to parents from the Caribbean (like Belafonte), Burgie heard many island songs while growing up and visited his mother's home country of Barbados. But this background didn't always inform his own music. Burgie began singing in chapel services while stationed in the China/Burma/India theater during World War II, and the response from his fellow soldiers convinced him to seek a music career after the war. At first he took opera training at the Juilliard School of Music, the University of Southern California, and the University of Arizona. But by the mid-'50s, with a gathering folk revival giving American roots music currency again, Burgie was inspired to look to his own heritage to compose songs and began a performing career under the name of Lord Burgess. The jazz-club audience for calypso was fast converging with the growing following for folk, so Burgie met with ready acceptance. He then met with Belafonte, after a writer for the latter's TV show caught a Burgie concert in New York. Soon Belafonte recorded eight of Burgie's songs for *Calypso* —the first album in the United States to sell over a million copies. In the wake of that success Burgie decided to concentrate on writing rather than performing, and a number of his songs have become standards in both the calypso genre Burgie and Belafonte aspired to and the lounge one many now perceive them in—each form, at the turn of the millennium, more popular in the Americas than ever.

what's available: Recently Burgie resurfaced to record his own hits and make them available to new audiences as *Island in the Sun: The Songs of Irving Burgie* 𝄞𝄞𝄞 (Angel, 1996, prod. Irving Burgie). The standards are all accounted for, including "Day-O," "Yellowbird," "Island in the Sun," "Jamaica Farewell," and the one with lyrics perhaps most evocative of the islands, "Kingston Market." The distinct Caribbean flavor is here, and so is the smooth pop sensibility of the '50s.

worth searching for: Irving Burgie's songs (sometimes credited to "Lord Burgess") appear on many albums in Harry Belafonte's extensive catalog. The original million-seller *Calypso* 𝄞𝄞𝄞𝄞 (RCA, 1956, prod. Herman Diaz Jr.) is still in print. Decades later, Burgie's staying power as a songwriter is proven with Jimmy Buffett's cover of "Jamaica Farewell" on his *Feeding Frenzy* 𝄞𝄞𝄞 (MCA, 1990, prod. Nina Avarmunde-Berducat).

influences:

◄ Sir Lancelot, Pete Seeger

►► Harry Belafonte, the Kingston Trio, Jimmy Buffett

see also: *Harry Belafonte*

Kerry Dexter

Kevin Burke

Irish traditional

Born June 9, 1950, in London, England. Based in Portland, OR, USA.

As the child of parents with roots in Sligo, Ireland, Kevin Burke grew up on the music of the Sligo master fiddlers of the 1920s and '30s: Michael Coleman, James Morrison, Paddy Killoran. As a budding fiddler himself, he was also exposed to the playing of the many expatriate Irish musicians who lived in London during the 1950s and '60s; hence the unmistakable blend of influ-

bollywood

A potpourri of Indian *raga* and *ghazal*, international jazz, orchestral, and pop, and almost every other style imaginable, Indian film music is the most alluring, bizarre, and exotic of sounds. It's also certainly the largest body of recorded work in any genre, with more than 1,000 soundtracks produced every year in Bombay ("Bollywood" to film fans), and a history dating back to the first Indian movie with sound, 1931's *Alam Ara*.

Most Indian films are romantic musicals, watched as much for the songs as for the plot. Actors lip-synch to the voices of "playback singers." The nasal treble common to female playback singers is an acquired taste for Westerners, but, once it's warmed to, possesses a delightful bite that cuts through the accompanying man's warm tenor and the loping beats of the *tabla* drum.

Many Indian communities in American towns sell this "filmi" music through Indian video stores, delis, and restaurants. In India the cassette is still the dominant medium, and typically in the U.S. soundtrack tapes cost two to three dollars, with reissues often featuring two scores on one cassette (though CDs are becoming increasingly available). The selection is often dauntingly vast, but titles and credits are written in English, and by following a few of the classic playback singers or directors you can't go wrong.

Especially look for the gorgeous voice of Lata Mangeshkar on *Mughal-E-Azam/Goonj Uthi Shehnai* 𝄞𝄞𝄞𝄞 (The Gramophone Co. of India)—or on any of her 2,000 other soundtracks if this one doesn't turn up. Next ask for the latest best-seller; it changes almost daily. An alternate search for those far away from Indian communities is the deleted *Golden Voices from the Silver Screen, Vols. 1–3* 𝄞𝄞𝄞𝄞 (Globestyle U.K.), or the also recently discontinued *Asia Classics 1: Dance Raja Dance: The South Indian Film Music of Vijaya Anand* 𝄞𝄞𝄞𝄞 (Luaka Bop/Sire, 1992), which surveys the new-generation music director whose postmodern pastiche of anything from bluegrass to funk is particularly sophisticated.

see also: Asha Bhosle, Post-Soca (sidebar)

David Poole

Kevin Burke (r) and Johnny Cunningham

ences, mainly from Sligo and Clare, which would come to characterize his style. A chance encounter with Arlo Guthrie during Willie Clancy Week in Milltown Malbay led to an invitation to record with Guthrie in the United States. This was a turning point for Burke, after which he made his decision to become a professional musician; it was during this first visit to the States that he also recorded his own debut album, *Sweeney's Dream,* for Folkways. Back in Dublin, Burke was playing in Christy Moore's backup band when he was approached to replace Tommy Peoples in the Bothy Band in 1976. With Moore's blessing, he jumped at the chance of joining the best Irish band then on the scene. During his time with them, he would do the odd gig with one or two of the other members if the venue could not accommodate the full lineup. He especially liked to work with Mícheál Ó Domhnaill, and the two of them collaborated on Burke's album *If the Cap Fits* in 1978, then made the very successful *Promenade* as a duet the following year. After the Bothy Band officially called it quits in 1979, Burke and Ó Domhnaill decided to try their luck in America and ended up based in Portland, Oregon, where local guitar and mandolin player Paul Kotapish had set up some gigs for them. Their equally successful

second duet album, the fittingly titled *Portland,* was recorded for Green Linnet in 1982. Shortly thereafter, Ó Domhnaill having broken away for headlining work, Burke found guitarist Gerry O'Beirne as a replacement and recorded *Up Close* with him in 1984. Meanwhile, Kerry accordionist Jackie Daly, who had appeared on *If the Cap Fits* and with whom Burke had recorded *Eavesdropper* in 1979, had left De Dannan, yet another of the many Irish-traditional supergroups that seem to somehow cross paths with Burke sooner or later. Burke, Daly, and former Planxty member Andy Irvine toured together, with guitarist Arty McGlynn soon joining in, and the band Patrick Street was born in 1987. Burke also kept in touch with Kotapish, who had introduced him to singer and harmonica player Mark Graham (both appeared on *Up Close*), who, in turn, introduced them to dancer Sandy Silva—and this quartet was soon touring the Pacific Northwest as an additional band setting for the prolific and eclectic Burke, Open House, which started to record for Green Linnet in 1992. A further musical venture with which Burke became associated during that period was the Celtic Fiddle Festival, a tour first organized in 1992 and bringing together the talents of Burke, Scotland's ex–Silly Wizard fiddler Johnny Cunningham, and Brittany's ex-Kornog member Christian Lemaître. This project has led to two well-received live albums thus far. One of today's best-known and busiest Irish musicians, Kevin Burke continues to appear solo as well as with Patrick Street, Open House, and the Celtic Fiddle Festival at concert venues and festivals throughout the United States and abroad.

what to buy: Although recorded early on, Burke's *If the Cap Fits* ♫♫♫♫ (Mulligan, 1978/Green Linnet, 1981, prod. Dónal Lunny) remains one of the quintessential Irish fiddle albums. The repertoire is Burke's typical mixture of Sligo and Clare tunes, with a few Kerry polkas learned from accordion player Jackie Daly, who appears on a couple of tracks. The debt to the Bothy Band is clear, Burke's main two accompanists being that band's alumni Dónal Lunny and Mícheál Ó Domhnaill. Yet there are new ideas too, like the double- and triple-tracking of the fiddle to vary the texture, which Burke continues to exploit on later recordings. The most spectacular experiment on the album has to be the relentless, 16-minute-long medley of reels that occupied most of side two of the original LP, in which Burke keeps going from tune to tune while the instrumental combinations vary with each change. *Promenade* ♫♫♫ (Mulligan, 1979/Green Linnet, 1981, prod. Gerry O'Beirne, Mícheál Ó Domhnaill) is a somewhat quieter affair, and a different kind of album since it is a duet with Ó Domhnaill, even if the fiddle instrumentals outnumber the songs. Burke performs some of his classic tune medleys, like the reels "Pigeon on the Gate" and "Lafferty's," in his characteristically fluid and lilting style. Ó Domhnaill's songs include the now-famous ballad "Lord Franklin," relating the events of Franklin's doomed expedition of 1845–47 to the Northwest Passage. By contrast, *Eavesdropper* ♫♫♫ (Mulligan, 1981/Green Linnet, 1981, prod. Kevin Burke, Jackie Daly), a duet album made in 1979 with Kerry accordion and concertina player Jackie Daly, is entirely instrumental. It features some of the closest duet playing one is likely to hear, with sparse guitar or piano accompaniment or none at all, and an eclectic repertoire of lesser-known tunes. Among the latter, a beautiful arrangement with guitar of an uncommon version of "The Blackbird" stands out. Cork flute player Conal Ó Gráda guests on a few tracks, and so does Paul Brady on piano. The excellent *Portland* ♫♫♫♫ (Green Linnet, 1982, prod. Kevin Burke, Mícheál Ó Domhnaill), the first album made by Burke and Ó Domhnaill in the United States, follows the same formula as *Promenade* but the result is even more exciting. Burke's renditions of Ed Reavy's "Maudabawn Chapel," the jig set "The Rolling Waves," and the final reel medley starting with "Tom Morrison's" and "The Beare Island Reel" have inspired many a fiddle player. Ó Domhnaill's love songs in Gaelic provide a melancholic counterpoint to the dance tunes, and the piece of Scottish mouth music (unaccompanied singing for dances) "S'iomadh Rud a Chunnaic Mi" fits perfectly in the set of instrumental flings. The entirely instrumental *Up Close* ♫♫♫ (Green Linnet, 1984, prod. Gerry O'Beirne) is the product of Burke's later association with guitarist Gerry O'Beirne. The fiddle playing is as inspiring as ever—for instance on the opening "Lord Gordon's Reel" or on Bill Monroe's "Jerusalem Ridge"—and O'Beirne's distinctive accompaniments complement it well. The participation of musical guests like ex–Bothy Band flute player Matt Molloy, Galway accordionist Joe Burke, and the amazing harmonica-playing Murphy family from Wexford brings variety to the album, even if it ends up sounding a bit piecemeal.

what to buy next: *Sweeney's Dream* ♫♫♫ (Folkways, 1973) was Burke's debut, recorded while he was on his first visit to the U.S. Still available from Folkways through the Smithsonian Institution, Washington, D.C., it has also been issued on compact disc by the Irish label Ossian (1989). Burke's selections lean heavily towards the Sligo repertoire, with famous medleys from the 78s of Coleman and Killoran and quite a few tunes that he would record again later, solo or with the Bothy Band. The accompaniment on guitar, five-string banjo, mandolin, and autoharp gives some of the tracks an American string-band sound. Burke's contributions to *The Celtic Fiddle Festival* ♫♫♫♫ (Green Linnet, 1993, prod. Johnny Cunningham) include two unaccompanied solos, the Clare jigs "Garrett Barry's" and "Cliffs of Moher," and a reprise of the "Pigeon on the Gate" medley from *Promenade*. These and the remarkable trio ensemble on other tracks make the album well worth a listen. Also look for Burke on two superior multi-act live albums, *My Love Is in America—The Boston College Irish Fiddle Festival* ♫♫♫♫ (Green Linnet, 1991, prod. Mícheál Ó Súilleabháin) and *Dear Old Erin's Isle—Irish Traditional Music from America* ♫♫♫♫ (Nimbus, 1992, prod. Mícheál Ó Súilleabháin, Robin Broadbank), the latter of which was recorded on the occasion of the 8th annual Éigse na Laoi festival of traditional music at University College, Cork.

the rest:
(With Johnny Cunningham and Christian Lemaître) *Celtic Fiddle Festival Encore* ♫♫♫ (Green Linnet, 1998)

worth searching for: Burke was one of four fiddle players featured on the LP *An Fhidil Sraith II (The Fiddle, Volume II)* ♫♫♫♫ (Gael-Linn, 1980, prod. Paddy Glackin), an outstanding collection of unaccompanied traditional fiddle playing. Of the several albums on which Burke has been a guest fiddler, few rival the classic *Andy Irvine, Paul Brady* ♫♫♫♫ (Mulligan, 1976/Green Linnet, 1981, prod. Dónal Lunny). Although the focus of the album is vocal, there are some dance tunes on which Burke's playing can be savored, particularly the jig "The Blarney Pilgrim" and the reel medley of "Fred Finn's" and "Sailing into Walpole's Marsh." One of Burke's most curious guest appearances, though, would have to be on Arlo Guthrie's *Last of the*

Brooklyn Cowboys 𝄡𝄡𝄡 (Warner Bros., 1973, prod. John Pilla, Lenny Waronker), on which the fiddler performs two short reel medleys, one with Guthrie on banjo and Ry Cooder playing bottleneck guitar.

influences:

◀◀ Michael Coleman, Paddy Killoran, Michael Gorman, Bobby Casey, Martin Rochford, Paddy Fahy

▶▶ Martin Hayes, Dale Russ, Randal Bays

see also: *The Bothy Band, Ry Cooder, Johnny Cunningham, Jackie Daly, Andy Irvine, Kornog, Matt Molloy, Open House, Patrick Street, Planxty, Silly Wizard*

Philippe Varlet

Burning Bridges

Worldbeat

Formed 1985, in San Diego, CA, USA. Based in San Diego, CA, USA.

Andrew Vereen (USA), vocals, guitars, keyboards, mandolin, flute, accordion, percussion; Cynthia Antillon (USA), vocals, percussion; Don Story (USA), guitars, vocals, percussion; Rick Nash (USA), bass, percussion; Robert Montoya (Mexico), drums, percussion; Marcos Fernandes (Portugal), drums, vocals, percussion.

Vereen, Fernandes, and Montoya, vets of San Diego's local music scene, formed Burning Bridges in 1985 to play their own brand of "inauthentic world music." After the usual round of personnel changes, the band settled into its current lineup and began plugging away at local clubs. Despite their tongue-in-cheek description of their music, the band's considerable chops serve them well as they navigate a course through an array of styles that might have seemed bewildering only a few short years ago. "Worldbeat is pop music," Fernandes says. "American music has always had traces of African, Arabic, Latin and Cuban sounds. We're presenting it in a somewhat less diluted form, but it's still pop music. Once you open your ears, you can't help but like it." Still, the Bridges found local crowds somewhat resistant, so they branched out to play coffeehouses, fashion shows, universities, and gallery openings. In 1992 the band created their own label, Accretions, and began sending out promos of their first CD, *From Benny's Tiki Room and Ammo Dump*. The album did well and led to a tour of Japan and a front page rave in *Billboard*. The success of *From Benny's . . .* has allowed Accretions to become a small full-service label, offering a home for other genre-bending bands.

what's available: The Bridges' second album, *Feast of Fools* 𝄡𝄡𝄡𝄡 (Accretions, 1996, prod. Burning Bridges, Randy Fuelle), is a quantum leap forward; a 16-track cornucopia of border-smashing styles that places the band's music at the top of the current worldbeat hit parade. Here they range from Warren

Zevon–esque folk-rock tunes to bits of Zulu jive, soca, and chimurenga, all played with plenty of attitude. They originally called their music "world rock," which may be a more apt label for their hard-hitting sound. The band was still trying to unify that sound on *From Benny's Tiki Room and Ammo Dump* 𝄡𝄡𝄡 (Accretions, 1992, prod. Burning Bridges, Randy Fuelle), which makes the program seem somewhat more diverse with distinct samplings of Arabic, African, and Caribbean styles. The low-key production gives the tunes a pleasingly folky character.

influences:

◀◀ Looters, Jungular Grooves, Kotoja

j. poet

Burning Flames

Soca, Caribbean funk

Formed 1984, in Antigua. Based in Antigua.

Toriano Edwards, vocals, guitar; Clarence Edwards, vocals, keyboards; David Edwards, vocals, bass; Rone Watkins, drums, vocals. (All members are from Antigua.)

The Edwards brothers grew up listening to the local Caribbean sounds of *soca*, salsa, reggae, and *zouk*, as well as the rock 'n' roll they heard on the radio. While still in their teens they were playing for tips on the street. In their 20s the brothers separated for a while: Toriano and David got gigs on cruise ships, while Clarence hooked up with leading calypsonian Arrow during his "Hot, Hot, Hot" period. Eventually Clarence brought his brothers and cousin Rone into Arrow's organization, where they formed the core of his backing band for three years. In 1984 they decided to strike out on their own, and since (as off-islanders) they are unable to compete in Trinidad's Carnival calypso contests, they created a more eclectic kind of soca (the modern sensation named after SOul and CAlypso) that they dubbed "C-funk." After six best-selling Caribbean albums, they were signed to Island in 1991 for their only international release, *Dig*, produced by Lawrence Dermer, Joe Galdo, and Rafael Virgil, a team known for its work with Gloria Estefan.

what's available: The Flames have a pleasing blend of funk, pop, reggae, and soca, and have been one of the top bands in the Caribbean for most of the 1990s. The album/compilation *Dig* 𝄡𝄡𝄡 (Island, 1991, prod. Lawrence Dermer, Joe Galdo, Rafael Virgil) includes reworkings of some of their biggest hits including "Island Girl," "Chook and Dig," and "Workey Workey," one of the best-selling soca singles of the '90s.

worth searching for: Most of the Flames' best work is found on smaller labels with limited distribution. Titles to look for are *Left to Right, Burning Flames Rule, Session Pwyle, Rysh and Dutty,* and their 1998 release *Fan de Flames.*

Burning Spear

influences:

◄◄ Arrow, Nelson, Taxi

see also: *Arrow*

j. poet

Burning Spear

Reggae, dub
Formed 1968, in Jamaica. Based in Jamaica.

Winston Rodney, lead vocals; Rupert Willington, bass vocals (1975–76); Delroy Hines, tenor vocals (1975–76). (All members are from Jamaica.)

The oppression of slavery and the mysticism of Rastafarianism are recurring themes for reggae's Burning Spear—at one time a group, but primarily a solo pseudonym for vocalist Winston Rodney. Taking his name from the self-description of Jomo Kenyatta, Kenya's first leader after independence, Rodney started working in the late 1960s. He recorded several singles for the prestigious producer Clement "Sir Coxsone" Dodd, but commercial success proved elusive—though the

singles "Marcus Garvey" and "Slavery Days," released in 1974 and '75 respectively, attracted international attention. Tellingly, only in 1977, after Burning Spear reverted to a Rodney solo project after a brief trio configuration, did the biggest commercial breakthrough come—with the album *Live,* which captured the dynamic energy and mystical, trance-like spirit of Rodney's concerts. Today Rodney burns on in both his creative passions and social concerns, balancing the musical career with work as a cultural history teacher at the Marcus Garvey Youth Group in Jamaica.

what to buy: With more than 30 tracks, the two-CD overview *Chant Down Babylon: The Island Anthology* 🎜🎜🎜🎜 (Island, 1986, prod. Burning Spear) surveys Burning Spear's history from its struggling beginnings, to its brief but eventful tenure as a group, to Rodney's influential later solo recordings. In addition to such best-selling tunes as "Marcus Garvey" and "Jah No Dead," the collection features 12-inch mixes and dub versions.

what to buy next: Regrouped and rededicated as a solo act, Rodney/Burning Spear (accompanied by English reggae stalwarts Aswad) declared the ongoing vitality of his art with the

David Byrne

simply but fittingly titled *Live* 🎵🎵🎵♪ (Mango, 1977, prod. Winston Rodney).

best of the rest:
Marcus Garvey 🎵🎵🎵♪ (Mango, 1976)
Garvey's Ghost 🎵🎵🎵♪ (Mango, 1976)
Man in the Hills 🎵🎵🎵♪ (Mango, 1976)
Harder Than the Best 🎵🎵🎵🎵 (Mango, 1979)
Hail H.I.M. 🎵🎵🎵♪ (Radic, 1980)
Farover 🎵🎵🎵🎵 (Heartbeat, 1982)
The Fittest of the Fittest 🎵🎵🎵🎵 (Heartbeat, 1983)
Resistance 🎵🎵🎵♪ (Heartbeat, 1984)
People of the World 🎵🎵🎵♪ (Slash, 1988)
Mek We Dweet 🎵🎵🎵♪ (Mango, 1990)
The World Should Know 🎵🎵♪ (Heartbeat, 1993)
Social Living 🎵🎵🎵🎵 (Blood & Fire, 1995)
Rasta Business 🎵🎵🎵♪ (Heartbeat, 1998)
Appointment with His Majesty 🎵🎵🎵🎵 (Heartbeat, 1998)

influences:
⏪ The Wailing Souls, Pablo Moses, Bob Marley

⏩ Third World, Augustus Pablo

see also: *Aswad*

Craig Harris

David Byrne
Art pop, worldbeat
Born May 14, 1952, in Dumbarton, Scotland. Based in New York, NY, USA.

Quirky pop and suave samba may seem worlds apart, but David Byrne has proven big enough to encompass them both. Besides writing and performing music, Byrne's far-reaching talents include video direction, screenwriting, photography, and record production, as well as heading his own label. A restless creative spirit, Byrne studied at the Rhode Island School of Design for one year in the early '70s; there he met Chris Frantz and Tina Weymouth, with whom he formed Talking Heads in 1975. Of all the bands that got their break (and, in this case, initially got miscategorized) in the late-'70s New York punk explosion, Talking Heads showed the most propensity for growth. Its eccentric first release revealed a taste for angular rhythms, and the band gradually warmed up its music with American funk and African polyrhythms. Byrne recorded two outside ventures while with the band, *My Life in the Bush of Ghosts,* a 1980 collaboration with then-frequent Heads producer Brian Eno; and *The Catherine Wheel,* the 1981 score for his Broadway collaboration with choreographer Twyla Tharp. Although Talking Heads was technically still together when Byrne released *Rei Momo* in 1989, an early-'90s retrospective set was all that would ever again bear

the band's name. Byrne was off on a musical world tour, its first stop being *Rei Momo*'s catalog of Latin rhythms.

As a "first worlder" navigating third-world waters, he was accused of having hijacked Latin music for his own purposes. However, he transcended tourism with concert spotlights for Latin musicians (including Brazil's Margareth Menezes, who legendarily "blew me off the stage"), and the formation of Luaka Bop, a label that has done much to put "world" artists on the world map—especially its commercially crucial but notoriously cautious Stateside longitudes. As a producer, Byrne compiled a number of Luaka Bop collections that serve as American primers on Cuban and Brazilian music. The label also introduced such artists as Zap Mama, Cornershop, Tom Zé, Susana Baca, Bloque, Os Mutantes, and many others to U.S. audiences, and has offered collections of Asian and African music. Even more than his own international explorations, Luaka Bop may constitute Byrne's greatest and most enduring contribution to world music.

what to buy: Reviving a practice not seen much since the days of 78 rpm discs, Byrne labeled each of the songs on *Rei Momo* 🎵🎵🎵🎵 (Luaka Bop/Sire, 1989, prod. Steve Lillywhite, David Byrne) with its rhythmic/dance style. He included sambas, cha cha chas, merengues, and rumbas, as well as styles less well-known to the American mainstream. His intellectual whimsy ("Independence Day") and paranoia ("The Dream Police") blend surprisingly well with the Latin musics' hip-swiveling ethos. The horn-whipped ride of "Make Believe Mambo" is itself worth the price of the album.

what to buy next: To some extent Byrne had submerged his own musical personality into the styles explored on *Rei Momo*. *Uh-Oh* 🎵🎵🎵🎵 (Luaka Bop/Sire, 1992, prod. Nick Launay) is more like a reassertion of his Talking Heads aesthetic with the help of Latin horns and percussion. When *My Life in the Bush of Ghosts* 🎵🎵🎵🎵 (Sire, 1981, prod. David Byrne, Brian Eno) was released, it was unusual for an album in the pop bins to include such staples of the avant-garde as found sounds—here including Egyptian songs and Islamic chants. With the advent of digital sampling, such elements have become commonplace, but that doesn't diminish the door-opening feel of this album.

what to avoid: Byrne's grasp is broad, but he hasn't figured out how to make "experimental" theater music palatable, as *The Catherine Wheel* 🎵🎵 (Sire, 1981, prod. David Byrne) and *The Forest* 🎵♪ (Luaka Bop/Sire, 1991, prod. David Byrne) reveal.

the rest:
David Byrne:
Music for the Knee Plays 🎵🎵🎵 (ECM, 1985)
David Byrne 🎵🎵🎵🎵 (Luaka Bop/Sire, 1994)
Feelings 🎵🎵🎵🎵 (Luaka Bop, 1997)

Talking Heads:

Talking Heads 77 🎵🎵🎵 (Sire, 1977)
More Songs about Buildings and Food 🎵🎵🎵🎵 (Sire, 1978)
The Name of This Band Is Talking Heads 🎵🎵🎵🎵 (Sire, 1982)
Little Creatures 🎵🎵🎵🎵 (Sire, 1985)
True Stories 🎵🎵🎵 (Sire, 1986)
Naked 🎵🎵🎵 (Sire, 1988)
Popular Favorites, 1976–1992: Sand in the Vaseline 🎵🎵🎵🎵 (Sire, 1992)

worth searching for: These Talking Heads recordings are not hard to find, but among the band's output they are the ones most interesting from a world-music standpoint: *Fear of Music* 🎵🎵🎵🎵 (Sire, 1979, prod. Brian Eno, Talking Heads) spiked its definitive art-pop with the then-uncharacteristic Fela Kuti–derived Africanesque track "I Zimbra"; *Remain in Light* 🎵🎵🎵🎵 (Sire, 1980, prod. Brian Eno, Talking Heads) was the band's first full-blown excursion into African forms; *Speaking in Tongues* 🎵🎵🎵🎵 (Sire, 1983, prod. Talking Heads) took the journey in more stylistically diverse and melodically engaging directions; and *Stop Making Sense* 🎵🎵🎵🎵 (Sire, 1984, prod. Talking Heads) records the innovative and funk-fueled tour that would turn out to be their last. These releases cover the period when the band reached its top polyrhythmic form, before less-inspired albums signaled their dissolution. The Heads themselves seemed to share this assessment by de-emphasizing the mid-period, American-roots-oriented albums *Little Creatures* and *True Stories* in their retrospective, but these (and the worldbeat swansong *Naked*) may suit some tastes.

influences:

◀◀ Celia Cruz, Willie Colon, Brian Eno, John Cage, Parliament-Funkadelic, Captain Beefheart

▶▶ Beck, Big Audio Dynamite, Love & Rockets

see also: *Brian Eno, Fela Kuti, Selena, Talking Heads*

Salvatore Caputo

Cachao

Cuban jazz
Born Israel Lopez, September 14, 1918, in Havana, Cuba. Based in USA.

Israel Lopez, a bassist and composer-arranger (who also plays trumpet, piano, celesta, and bongos), is better known as Cachao, a central figure in the development of Cuban music for a substantial portion of the 20th century. He, along with his brother Orestes, presided over the mutation of *danzón* (a Cuban ballroom dance in rather staid rondo form) into the mambo, with the arrangements they wrote for bandleader/flautist Antonio Arcaño Betancourt and his group, Arcaño y Sus Maravillas. The Latin jam session known as a *descarga* might not have evolved into the vital training ground for young Latin jazz players it later became if Cachao hadn't encouraged his compatriots to be more daring in their improvisations. Pianist Bebo Valdes has been quoted as saying, "if Cachao and Arsenio Rodriguez had never been born, the Cuban music of the '50s—and perhaps the last 30 years—would have sounded like the music of the '30s." After a series of ground-breaking *descarga* albums for the Panart, Maype, and Bonita lapels, Cachao moved to New York City where he worked with Charlie Palmieri, Tito Rodriguez, and Eddie Palmieri before finally settling in Miami. Throughout the 1960s, 1970s, and 1980s he appeared on albums with musicians/fans such as Hubert Laws, Mongo Santamaria, Eddie Palmieri, and Grupo Niche, while concertizing with Tito Puente, José Fajardo, and Alfredo "Chocolate" Armenteros. He has even played with the Miami Symphony Orchestra.

what to buy: There is a long story behind the 12-tune album *Master Sessions, Vol. 1* 🎵🎵🎵🎵 (Crescent Moon/Epic, 1994, prod. Andy Garcia). That tale deals with the years of neglect and poor-paying gigs endured by one of the major figures in Latin music history, and it has been made into an award-winning video by actor Andy Garcia that is making new fans for Cachao's music. The albums around which the video revolves have also won awards, and their content is an awesome tribute to the man and his music. From the opening notes of "Al Fin Te Vi," a duet between Cachao's bowed bass and Paquito D'Rivera's clarinet, the album rolls through a sublime primer in the art of Afro-Cuban music. There can be no standout performances when everything is this good.

what to buy next: On *Master Sessions, Vol. 2* 🎵🎵🎵🎵 (Crescent Moon/Epic, 1995, prod. Andy Garcia), 24 of the 30 songs cut during one historic week with Cachao have been released. Each of the Master Sessions albums is so impressive that the next question a listener should ask after hearing both CDs is, "When are the other six tunes coming out?" The sidemen include many greats from the Latin music community, including trumpeter Armenteros, reed man extraordinaire D'Rivera, and flautist Nestor Torres. The percussion section has so many time signatures going on that it's a good thing the melody players are used to floating with a polyrhythmic pulse. An earlier release that helps show off the reason why Cachao made such a marked impact on the Latin music community is *Descargas Cubanas, Vol. 1: Jam Session with Feeling* 🎵🎵🎵🎵 (Maype, 1962). It includes a great version of Ernesto Lecuona's classic "Siboney" and some fine *tres* (small guitar) playing on Orestes Lopez' "La Floresta." Much of this material is duplicated on *Descargando* 🎵🎵🎵🎵 (Musica del Sol, 1996), with

Cachao

somewhat better mastering and 14 tunes as opposed to the dozen found on the other album.

best of the rest:

Latin Jazz Descarga, Part I 🎵🎵🎵 (Tania, 1985/1994)
Maestro de Maestros 🎵🎵🎵 (Tania, 1986)
Cuban Jam Session, Vol. II, Descargas Cubanas 🎵🎵🎵 (Rodven, 1987)

worth searching for: Check out the companion documentary video to the Master Session albums, *Cachao … Como Su Ritmo No Hay Dos (Like His Rhythm There Is No Other)*, available from Epic Music Video, for an intriguing, well-constructed view of Latin music from the inside.

influences:

◀◀ Sexteto Habanero, Arsenio Rodriguez

▶▶ Machito, Mario Bauzá, Chico O'Farrill, Tito Puente

see also: *Albita, Paquito D'Rivera, Charlie Palmieri, Eddie Palmieri, Tito Puente, Arsenio Rodriguez, Tito Rodriguez, Mongo Santamaria, Bebo Valdes*

Garaud MacTaggart

Café Tacuba

Rock en Español, worldbeat
Formed c. 1990, in Mexico City, Mexico. Based in Mexico City, Mexico.

Anónimo, vocals; Emmanuel del Real, keyboards; Joselo Rangel, guitar; Enrique Rangel, bass. (All members are from Mexico.)

Café Tacuba, one of the leading bands of Mexico's "rocanrol" movement, have managed to reinvent rock music to suit their own needs, something that's evaded British and American bands for decades. In the process they've become demigods in Mexico and may become the first Mexican "alterlatino" band to cross over to the U.S. market without singing in English. Named after a local hangout that was once the mecca for *mestizo* (Mexican, Indian, and North American) culture, Café Tacuba began as a series of all-night discussions between four friends who had gathered to solve the problems of the world. One night they discussed the way Mexican rock was being shaped by what U.S. and U.K. bands were doing. The inspiration was coming down from the record companies and radio stations, not up from the streets, and despite Mexico's immense musical and cultural diversity, no rock band had ever built their sound on the various

Café Tacuba lead singer Anónimo

styles of Mexican folk music. That's the task Café Tacuba set for itself. The band "went acoustic" and began cranking out tunes based on traditional motifs. The group's eponymous 1992 debut rocked the nation and in '94 it released *Re,* a 20-song collection that went even deeper into its roots. *Re* was a success, even though it lacked a "pop" flavor. Tacuba's most recent outing, *Avalancha de Exitos (Avalanche of Hits),* which has become one of the first Latin rock albums to break onto the playlists of Anglo radio stations, showed the band moving in a new, more eclectic direction. The songs are all covers of well-known Latin American hits, arranged in settings that combine techno, tango, rock, *cumbia,* ska, bolero, punk, *huapango, Tejano,* and more.

what to buy: By covering well-known tunes and recasting them in a variety of Latin American forms on *Avalancha de Exitos* ♫♫♫♫ (WEA Latina, 1997, prod. Café Tacuba), Café Tacuba has created a worldbeat sound based on the Latin continuum, thereby breaking new stylistic ground. It's a major creative leap for the band's members, but their chops have muscle to spare and every track is a little gem. *Re* ♫♫♫♫ (WEA Latina, 1994, prod. Café Tacuba) is slightly less eclectic, but still impressive. For the

band to move away from the hard-core sound of its debut and take on the Mexican folk tradition was a real risk, but the result has created a revolution in Mexico's rock underground.

the rest:
Café Tacuba ♫♫♫ (WEA Latina, 1992)

influences:
◀◀ Los Tigres del Norte, Los Camperos de Valles, Juan Reynoso

j. poet

Caifanes /Jaguares

Rock en Español
Formed 1985, in Mexico City, Mexico. Disbanded 1995.

Saul Hernandez, vocals; Alfonso Andre, drums; Alejandro Marcovich, guitar. (All members are from Mexico.)

With all the hype surrounding today's crop of Rock en Español imports, the shadow that the legendary Caifanes cast is growing even longer. Caifanes had the luck of coming together right at the time when Mexican rock began to evolve from covers of American and English artists and seek its own voice. While the government still discouraged the rock movement in Caifanes's day, a generation of musical forbears like El Tri and Ritmo Peligroso had at least paved a path for them. Caifanes initially gained fame as one of the earliest Mexican rock bands signed to an American label. Their first big hit soon followed: "La Negra Tomasa," a modern reworking of classic *cumbia* rhythms. It wasn't long before Caifanes shook off the Cure comparisons that dogged them in their formative period to deliver a string of four multi-platinum albums. Tall, lanky, and exotically tattooed, frontman Saul Hernandez was what the Lizard King always should have been: both sex symbol and social leader to a generation craving a spokesman. When Caifanes split up Hernandez formed a new band, Jaguares, which continued to captivate the nation.

what to buy: Caifanes's last release, *El Mervio del Volcan* ♬♬♬♬ (BMG, 1994, prod. Greg Ladanyi, Caifanes), is easily their best. Hernandez's paganistic lyrics turn introspective as the band still manage to integrate the pop hooks that brought them to fame. This album shows why Caifanes has remained one of the models of the Rock en Español movement.

the rest:
Caifanes ♬♬♬ (BMG, 1985)
El Diabolito ♬♬♬♬ (BMG, 1990)
El Silencio ♬♬♬♬ (BMG, 1992)

worth searching for: It seemed only fitting that when Hernandez formed a new band after the breakup of Caifanes, he would call it Jaguares ("the jaguars"). Many fans saw him as an artistic shaman whose spokesman status made him an extension of the Aztec Gods of old—gods who legend has it could turn themselves into jaguars. Formed with fellow Caifanes alum Alfonso Andre in 1996, Jaguares drew on the duality of the animal, combining spirituality with sensual danger while continuing the members' musical growth. The band's first album, *El Equilibrio de los Jaguares* ♬♬♬♬ (BMG, 1996, prod. Don Was, Ed Cherney, Jaguares), picked up right where Caifanes' acclaim had left off.

influences:
◄ El Tri, Ritmo Peligroso

►► Meldita Vecindad, Café Tacuba, Mana, Molotov

Sam Wick

California Cajun Orchestra

Cajun, Creole
Founded 1982, in San Francisco, CA, USA. Based in San Francisco, CA, USA.

Danny Poullard, accordion, vocals; Eric Thompson, guitar; Suzy Thompson (Germany), fiddle, vocals; Sam Siggins, bass; David Hy-

mowitz, drums. Past members have included: Kevin Wimmer, fiddle; Alan Senauke, guitar. (All members are from USA except where noted.)

Danny Poullard is one of the finest Cajun accordionists anywhere. Born in Eunice, Louisiana, he grew up hearing his father play the instrument with his grandfather, a fiddler. Like many Creole south Louisianans, he relocated to the San Francisco Bay region. Once there, he began playing with John Simien's Louisiana Playboys at the same Creole Catholic church dances where Queen Ida got her start. When Simien died Poullard took over the band for a time. By the early 1980s he was being backed by the Blue Flame stringband, which included Eric and Suzy Thompson (then Rothfield). Suzy had studied with Dewey Balfa through an N.E.A. grant and visited such other traditional Cajun and Creole fiddlers as Dennis McGee, Wallace "Cheese" Read, and Canray Fontenot. The band evolved from steady dance work into the performing and recording unit now known as the California Cajun Orchestra. The group has an exceptionally extensive repertoire, and has garnered regular regional airplay in the Cajun heartland of South Louisiana.

what to buy: On *Nonc Adam Two-Step* ♬♬♬♬ (Arhoolie, 1995, prod. Bob Shumaker, Jody Stecher) you can hear how well the years have served this band—Poullard's playing continues to get ever better. He rips through a whole group of Iry LeJeune tunes, the standard against which every Cajun accordionist is measured. But it is the Creole tunes in particular, such as "John Pollard's Two-Step" and the title track, that are absolutely unique for current Cajun or zydeco recordings, evoking the old-time Creole music of Canray Fontenot and Alphonse "Bois Sec" Ardoin.

what to buy next: *Not Lonesome Anymore* ♬♬♬♬ (Arhoolie, 1991, prod. various) was the band's debut, showing them in good form and demonstrating the breadth of repertoire they pull from. Using four different vocalists brings an additional richness to the recording. Suzy Thompson wails through a version of the Shorty LeBlanc hit "Sugar Bee," while Charlie St. Mary sings Canray Fontenot's "Jolie Bassette." Guest Andrew Carriere contributes the vocals to old chestnuts like "Valse Crimenelle" and "L'anse Paille," and Danny Poullard gets to sing "Monsieur Leonard," written by his old bandleader John Simien.

worth searching for: Michael Doucet, Danny Poullard, and Alan Senauke's *Cajun Jam Session* ♬♬♬♬ (Arhoolie, 1983, prod. Chris Strachwitz) is a somewhat raw recording of a live radio program aired on KPFA in Berkeley, California, and hosted by Chris Strachwitz of Arhoolie Records. The music has a loose quality, but through Doucet and Poullard is graced by two true masters of the genre.

solo outings:
Eric & Suzy Thompson:
Adam & Eve Had the Blues ♬♬♬♬ (Arhoolie, 1989)

influences:

◀ Tracy Schwarz, Dewey Balfa, Canray Fontenot

▶ Steve Riley, Balfa Toujours

see also: *Alphonse "Bois Sec" Ardoin, Balfa Brothers, Beausoleil, Canray Fontenot, Iry LeJeune, Queen Ida*

Jared Snyder

Calypso Rose

Calypso, soca

Born McCartha Lewis, in Trinidad. Based in Port of Spain, Trinidad and Brooklyn, NY, USA.

Since breaking onto the scene during Carnival 1963, Calypso Rose has maintained a high writing and performing standard. One of the few women in *soca*—that pop phenomenon that takes its name from SOul and CAlypso—her compositions tend to deflate the usual sexual braggadocio of the male, but she's not above a racy double entendre when it suits her purpose. She was the first woman to win the Calypso King competition, making 1978 the year of the first Calypso Monarch. Her gruff delivery and straightforward performing style give her albums and live dates an intimate feeling.

what to buy: Smooth production lends *Soca Diva* ♫♫♫♫ (Ice, 1993, prod. Eddy Grant) plenty of pop sheen, but Rose's lyrics and no-nonsense stance come through loud and clear. "Columbus"—an indictment of colonial mentality—and "You No Need Dem"—a parable about cheating spouses—are particularly strong.

worth searching for: Rose was at a peak just before the takeover of CDs, and much of her older material has yet to find its way to that format. Look for *Pan in Town* ♫♫♫♫ (Straker's), *Trouble* ♫♫♫♫ (Straker's, 1984), and *Leh We Punta* ♫♫♫♫ (Straker's, 1987).

influences:

◀ Sparrow, Melody, Duke

▶ Singing Francine, Denyse Plummer

j. poet

Camarón de la Isla

Flamenco

Born Jose Monge Cruz, 1950, in San Fernando, Cadiz, Spain. Died July 2, 1992, in Barcelona, Spain.

Camarón de la Isla was one of the most influential vocalists in the history of flamenco. Only 41 when he died of a heroin overdose in 1992, he had been setting the pace with his exquisite, high-pitched vocals for nearly 30 years. An obituary published by the Madrid newspaper *El Pais* noted that "Camarón revolutionized flamenco from the point of absolute purity." The second of eight children born to a family of gypsy blacksmiths, Camarón

(whose nickname translates as "shrimp of the island") began singing professionally at the age of eight. His debut album, recorded in 1968, featured accompaniment by virtuoso guitarist Paco de Lucia. Although he temporarily retired in 1979, Camarón returned the following year with one of his most successful albums, *La Leyenda De Tiempo*. Toward the end of his life, Camarón worked with guitarist Tomatito. They performed their final concert together in Madrid, Spain, on January 25, 1992.

what to buy: With the release of *La Leyenda De Tiempo* ♫♫♫♫ (Philips, 1980, prod. Ricardo Pachon, Flamenco Viva), Camarón elevated flamenco music to new heights, incorporating rock and jazz influences as well as such non-flamenco instruments as Fender piano, moog, electric guitar, bass, drums, and zither.

what to buy next: *Autoretrato* ♫♫♫♫ (Alex, 1992, prod. various) samples tracks spanning Camarón's lengthy career and chronicles his evolution from flamenco roots to fusion with a variety of musical influences.

the rest:

Al Verte Las Flores Lloran ♫♫♫ (Alex, 1969/1993)
Cada Vez Que Nos Miramos ♫♫♫ (Alex, 1970/1993)
Canastera ♫♫♫ (Philips, 1972)
Son Tus Ojos Dos Estrellas ♫♫♫♫ (Alex, 1973/1993)
Arte Y Majestad ♫♫♫ (Alex, 1975/1993)
Rosa Marca ♫♫♫ (Alex, 1976/1993)
Calle Real ♫♫♫ (Alex, 1983/1993)
Como El Agua ♫♫♫ (Alex, 1984/1993)
Vivire ♫♫♫ (Alex, 1984/1993)
Te Lo Dice Camarón ♫♫♫ (Alex, 1986/1993)
Flamenco Vivo ♫♫♫♫ (Alex, 1987/1993)
Soy Gitano ♫♫♫ (Philips, 1989)
Camanito De Totana ♫♫♫ (Alex, 1993)
Una Leyenda Flamenca, Vol. 1 ♫♫♫ (Philips, 1993)
Una Leyenda Flamenca, Vol. 2 ♫♫♫ (Philips, 1994)
Lo Mejorde Camarón ♫♫♫ (PolyGram, 1994)
Grandes Canteores ♫♫♫♫ (Alex, 1995)
Nuestra Camarón ♫♫♫♫ (Alex, 1996)

influences:

◀ Manolo Caracol, Pastora Pavon

▶ Enrique Morente, Carmen Linares, El Potito

see also: *Paco de Lucia*

Craig Harris

Ian Campbell Folk Group /Ian Campbell

British folk

Formed 1960, in Birmingham, England. Disbanded 1977.

Ian Campbell, vocals; Lorna Campbell, vocals; Brian Clark, guitar, vocals; Johnny Dunkerly (died April 25, 1977), banjo, accordion, guitar,

autoharp, vocals; Dave Swarbrick, fiddle, viola, mandolin, mandola, vocals (1960–66); George Watts, flute, clarinet (1966–69); Dave Pegg, double bass, bass, mandolin (1967–69).

The Ian Campbell Folk Group were one of the finest and most influential outfits of their kind ever to come out of Britain, and are only now starting to make a belated appearance on the CD reissue market. In many ways they explored the same kind of terrain the Clancy Brothers and more particularly the Dubliners did in Ireland during the same crucial phase of the folk revival movement. Their sound remained remarkably consistent over their lifespan, in an age when rapid change was the norm, and their popularity on the folk-club circuit was not hurt by the fact that they tempered their unmistakably pro-worker politics with healthy doses of humor.

The Campbells' repertoire ranged from songs of Scottish or nautical origin—many learned from singers-revivalists A.L. (Bert) Lloyd, Ewan MacColl, and Hamish Henderson—to Australian and American items, to spirited instrumentals for fiddle and banjo, to their own original material. Ian Campbell's anti-nuclear "The Sun Is Burning" from 1963 has been covered by Simon & Garfunkel, the Dubliners, Christy Moore, and Kate Wolf.

Like Martin Carthy, another of the prominent younger pioneers of the British folk revival, the Campbells first wet their feet in the mid-'50s skiffle scene with the Clarion Skiffle Group. As the '50s gave way to the '60s, brother and sister Ian and Lorna, whose family hailed from Aberdeen, Scotland, roped in guitarist Brian Clark (who would later marry Lorna), fiddle and mandolin maestro Dave "Swarb" Swarbrick, and banjoist Dunkerly. The ICFG soon secured a residency at the Jug of Punch folk club in Birmingham, issued a live EP from there, and appeared on national radio and TV. By the time they turned professional in 1963, following the warm reception they received at that year's Edinburgh Folk Festival, they had already topped the bill at the Royal Albert Hall. More importantly, they had attracted the attention of legendary folk producer and arranger Bill Leader. With an occasional nod to Pete Seeger and Bob Dylan—the Campbells were one of the first U.K. acts in any genre to cover a song by His Zimmerness ("The Times They Are a'Changin'," in early 1965)—the ICFG left an indelible mark on the U.K. folk scene, with relentless touring and a large, impressive catalog of singles, EPs, and LPs. To date, only the LPs have started to resurface on CD.

Swarb left in 1966, working as a duo with Martin Carthy before opting for life with folk-rock pioneers Fairport Convention. George Watts was drafted to replace his distinctive fiddle with flute, but Swarb also guested on some Campbell releases up to 1969. In 1967 the ICFG finally hired a full-time bassist in the form of Dave "Peggy" Pegg—he too migrated to Fairport by 1970. As it turned out, it's been Swarb (throughout the '70s)

and Peggy (ever since) who have effectively led that folk-rock institution for the past three decades. The influence of the Campbells on Fairport is undeniable: many of the instrumentals (and a few of the songs) popularized by the band in electric form date from Swarb and Peggy's days with the Campbells.

The ICFG soldiered on (and off) well into the '70s, despite the changing musical fashions, and disbanded following Dunkerly's sad death at age 33 of Hodgkin's disease. They appeared on stage again many years later as part of Swarb's and Peggy's (separate) 50th birthday celebration concerts, and are featured on the resulting CDs. Ian Campbell issued a solo album of all original songs in 1993, on which he was joined by sister Lorna, sons David, Duncan, and Robin, and nephew Angus Clark. If the name Robin Campbell rings a bell, it may be on account of his long involvement with pop reggae/ska band UB40, led by his brother Ali: the Campbell family legacy has touched more aspects of the U.K. music scene than many realize.

what to buy: *The Ian Campbell Folk Group/Across the Hills* 🎵🎵🎵🎵 (Transatlantic, 1963/1964, Castle Communications, 1996, prod. Bill Leader) is hard to beat: the first two LPs united on one CD (although one instrumental from the second LP is inexplicably omitted). The eponymous debut includes classics such as "The Drover's Song," "Down in the Coalmine," "The Jute Mill Song," and "The Bells of Rhymney," as well as a couple of spirited fiddle/banjo instrumental medleys. *Across the Hills* is noticeably smoother, with Ian and Lorna sounding particularly wonderful singing Leon Rosselson's title track together. Lorna makes "Gypsy Rover" her own, and the entire group joins forces at the microphone for an impressive *a cappella* "Cho Cho Losa," a Johannesburg mining song learned from South African group the Manhattan Brothers. *Contemporary Campbells/New Impressions* 🎵🎵🎵 (Transatlantic, 1966/Castle Communications, 1996, prod. Nathan Joseph) teams up two later LPs. The first, with Swarb, contains many cover songs (including four by Ewan MacColl) and a stately "Battle of the Somme" on fiddle; the second, with Swarb's replacement George Watts on flute, has more group originals, and a great arrangement of "New York Girls." Both lead off with Sydney Carter songs ("Marilyn Monroe" and "Lord of the Dance," respectively).

what to buy next: *Something to Sing About* 🎵🎵🎵🎵 (Pye, 1972/Wooded Hill, 1997) was produced in conjunction with an extensive TV series about the changes in social life brought on by the industrial revolution. The album stands up surprisingly well today, and is mercifully devoid of the kind of dated, trend-conscious "let's prove we've moved with the times" sound that so many others of their ilk succumbed to during that period (something this band had gotten out of its system back in 1967–68). Ian Campbell's *And Another Thing* 🎵🎵🎵 (Celtic Music, 1993) shows the singer/writer's talents undulled by years of relative inactivity. The songs, some of which were written over the previous decade-and-a-half for stage shows and TV programs, tackle everything from politics, capitalism, and the environment to artsy pretensions and women's issues. The treatments vary from the distinctive stripped-down British folk ensemble sound that Campbell helped to define decades earlier, to the decidedly world-music colorations of son Duncan's multi-layered vocals on a song about South African politics.

worth searching for: *Traditions of an Aberdeen Family* (Topic, 1965/Ossian, 1994), credited to the Singing Campbells, saw Ian and Lorna as the younger generation's representatives in a large family celebration. The ICFG also appears on *New Electric Muse* (Castle Communications, 1996), a various-artists collection. Ian and Lorna join up with Peggy for an ICFG reunion on Swarb's 50th-birthday-bash memento *Folk on 2: Dave Swarbrick* (Cooking Vinyl, 1995), while Ian, son Duncan, Brian Clark, and Swarb do the same for Dave Pegg's *Birthday Party* (Woodworm, 1998).

influences:

◀◀ A.L. (Bert) Lloyd, Ewan MacColl, Peggy Seeger, Pete Seeger, Bob Dylan, the Dubliners, the Clancy Brothers

▶▶ The Dubliners, the Clancy Brothers, Fairport Convention, UB40

see also: *Fairport Convention, A.L. Lloyd, Ewan MacColl, Dave Swarbrick*

John C. Falstaff

Capercaillie

Scottish traditional and fusion
Formed 1984, in Oban, Scotland. Based in Scotland.

Original lineup: Karen Matheson, vocals; Donald Shaw, accordion, keyboards; Marc Duff, recorder, whistles; Joan MacLachlan, fiddle, vocals; Shaun Craig, guitar, bouzouki; Martin Macleod, bass, fiddle. **Later members include:** Mánus Lunny, bouzouki; Charlie McKerron, fiddle; John Saich, bass; Fred Morrison, bagpipes, whistles; Wilf Taylor, percussion; David Robertson, percussion.

Capercaillie rose to stardom almost overnight, forming in 1984 and recording their first album, *Cascade,* in three days. They rapidly developed a local reputation for strong live performances in their home town of Oban, Scotland. By 1988 they were being courted to compose the soundtrack for a documentary about the history of the Gaelic Scots. The resulting album, *The Blood Is Strong,* shot to platinum in Scotland, and soon the group was on tour around the world. Continuing this trend, they swiftly recorded several award-winning albums. In 1995 they appeared in the film *Rob Roy,* adding to their fame and association with Scottish culture. However, though known as a

Scottish band, Capercaillie is truly an ethnic mix. The lineup includes two Scots, one Canadian, one Irishman, and two Englishmen. Traditional Scottish music is, nonetheless, the source from which they draw much of their material—albeit with an increasing modernization of instrumentation and broadening of ethnic inspirations. The group's strongest asset has to be the supernatural voice of Karen Matheson, who inspired Sean Connery to remark that she had "a throat surely touched by God."

what to buy: Perhaps the best overview of Capercaillie's style is *Get Out* ♫♫♫ (Survival/BMG, 1992, prod. Capercaillie, Iain Morrow, Dónal Lunny), which contains some live tracks and several previously recorded ones. This album displays the basic Scottish feel that made the group so popular, while capturing a bit of the modern sound that causes frequent comparisons to the Irish group Clannad. A beautiful rendition of "Fear a' Bhàta" from *The Blood Is Strong* and a live version of their rhythmic take on the 400-year-old *waulking* (Gaelic for "washing") song "Coisich a' Rùin," which skyrocketed to the U.K.'s Top 40, are highlights of the album.

what to buy next: *Sidewaulk* ♫♫♫ (Green Linnet, 1989, prod. Dónal Lunny) captures the essence of what the group sounds like in performance, though it itself contains no live tracks. Highly traditional in nature, the driving reels and jigs make listeners want to get up and dance. *Crosswinds* ♫♫♫ (Green Linnet, 1987, prod. Capercaillie) is also filled with traditional material. There are several very moving songs here, including "Am Buachaille Ban."

what to avoid: *Beautiful Wasteland* ♫♫ (Survival, 1997) takes a much more modern approach, further electrifying the sound and combining African rhythms into the mix. It's an interesting experiment, but seems to lose completely the tradition the group originally set out to reclaim. If you like your genres spliced, however, you might be inclined to switch the ratings given here for this album with those given to their more characteristic work.

the rest:
The Blood Is Strong ♫♫♫ (Green Linnet, 1988)
Delirium ♫♫♫ (BMG, 1991)
Secret People ♫♫ (Survival/BMG, 1993)
Capercaillie ♫♫ (Survival/BMG, 1994)
To the Moon ♫♫ (Green Linnet, 1997)

worth searching for: *Cascade* ♫♫♫ (Greentrax, 1984) displays the raw energy that initially got the group off the ground.

influences:

◀◀ Na h-Oganaich, Christine Primrose, Flora MacNeill

▶▶ Clannad, Silly Wizard, Altan, Poor Clares

see also: *Andy M. Stewart*

Jo Hughey Morrison

Milton Cardona

Salsa, Latin jazz
Based in New York, NY, USA.

It seems a shame that one of the most talented conga players of our time has only released one album under his own name. Milton Cardona's skills as a percussionist have made him an in-demand session player for a variety of artists including pop stars Paul Simon and David Byrne, jazz players J.J. Johnson and Michael Brecker, and Latin-music royalty Cachao, Celia Cruz, Rubén Blades, and Willie Colon. The Colon connection has been especially fruitful for both parties, with a recorded association that dates back to Colon's 1972 album *El Juicio*. Other frequent employers include Manny Oquendo, Kip Hanrahan, and Dave Valentin, but Cardona is also a member of Conjunto Classico, a New York City–based group dedicated to the old Cuban format pioneered by Arsenio Rodríguez and others. With Conjunto Classico Cardona gets to display his often-underrated vocal talents as well, showing off a clear, fluid tenor that weaves around the beat.

what's available: Cardona's only solo album is a landmark recording of a *Santería* ceremony, *Bembé: A Recording of the Songs and Rhythms of 10* Orishas *(Deities) of Santería in New York* 𝄢𝄢𝄢𝄢 (American Clave, 1994, prod. Kip Hanrahan). Santería, like *Vodou* (formerly known to whites as "voodoo"), is a syncretic (hybrid) religion associating the African deities brought to the West by slaves with the Christian saints they encountered once they got there, Santería having a Cuban twist while Vodou has a Haitian slant. The pulse of Santería is at the heart of this album and Cardona—like fellow Santería high priest Tito Puente—is an expert at calling forth a particular "saint's" rhythm. He is ably abetted by fellow drummers Hector Hernandez, Steve Berrios, and Jose Fernandez as well as a set of female vocalists chorusing behind Cardona's invocation in a glorious call-and-response pattern.

worth searching for: Putting Cardona together with fellow *congasero* Daniel Ponce was a wonderful idea. The twist is that Ponce composes most of the tunes—and plays fiery congas and *bata* drums on all the cuts—while Cardona is one of the featured singers on all but two of them. The resulting collaboration, *Chango Te Llama* 𝄢𝄢𝄢𝄢 (Mango, 1991, prod. Oscar Hernandez), smokes from beginning to end. The Santería underpinnings of *Bembé* are repeated somewhat, but in a format that places a less overt emphasis on the religious aspects of the music.

influences:

◄ Cortijo

►► Giovanni Hidalgo

Garaud MacTaggart

border music: tex-mex

Although musical traditions develop everywhere, some of the most intriguing ones represent hybrids that originate on the borders between regions, or when immigrants bring styles from elsewhere to blend with those already present in an area. One of the most dramatic examples of this has occurred along and near the U.S./Mexico border, principally in Texas, where European, American, and Mexican roots have entwined to inspire *conjunto, norteño, Tejano,* and other "Tex-Mex" musical mergers. Blues, country, and jazz were contributed from the American canon. The most significant European ingredient was the introduction of polka styles and the accordion from the dance bands of Eastern European immigrants who moved into southern Texas in the early 20th century. The polka beat formed the backbone of the seminal conjunto sound, with the rhythmic orientation and lyrical structure coming from traditional and contemporary Mexican music. The result was a unique new strain that blended an irresistible dance beat with passionate vocals, sensuous melodies, and virtuoso musicianship.

In the 1930s two pioneers, Narciso Martinez and Don Santiago Jimenez, were the first accordion players to lead conjunto ensembles. In the '50s and '60s the popularity of this music, which had become centered in the San Antonio area, was cemented by the work of bandleaders like Tony de la Rosa and Paulino Bernal. Steve Jordan and later Flaco Jimenez took the accordion to new ground and broader audiences. Jimenez's work with Ry Cooder and others brought this musical hyphenate to the rock and country constituencies, and paved the way for the wide cross-cultural popularity of the Texas Tornados and Los Lobos.

see also: Conjunto Bernal, Ry Cooder, Tony de la Rosa, Don Santiago Jimenez, Flaco Jimenez, Esteban "Steve" Jordan, Los Lobos, Narciso Martinez, the Texas Tornados

Michael Parrish

Carreg Lafar

Welsh traditional
Formed 1993, in Cardiff, Wales. Based in Cardiff, Wales.

Linda Owen Jones, vocals; Antwn Owen Hicks, vocals, whistle, pibgorn (Welsh hornpipe), Welsh bagpipes, drum, bodhrán; Rhian Evan Jones, violin, cello, keyboards; James Rourke, flute, whistle; Nick Dowsett, 12-string acoustic guitar, vocals (1993–95); Simon O'Shea, acoustic guitar, mandola. (All members are from Wales.)

Carreg Lafar (meaning "Echo Stone") is a new Welsh band whose young members hail from all over: Wrexham in the north, Swansea on the south coast, and the valleys of southeast Wales. While much of their material is based on carefully researched old sources and sung in their native Welsh language, they inject it all with a lusty vibrancy which sets them apart from many of their peers. They first toured the U.S. in 1997, and are starting to make a mark on the festival circuit with their infectious, energetic live shows. Owen Jones exudes a feisty, indomitable spirit on stage, whether singing or egging-on her bandmates, and Owen Hicks is equally charismatic on pipes, percussion, and vocals. The band has occasional Gypsy overtones, and also sounds positively medieval at times. They show more interest—not to mention aptitude—for bringing traditional Welsh music to the great unwashed masses than most others of their generation.

what to buy: *Ysbryd y Werin (Spirit of the People)* ♪♪♪ (Sain, 1995/Blix Street, 1995, prod. Emyr Rees) is an impressive debut; its U.S. release on Blix Street features welcome translations of the mysterious song titles, as well as the helpful annotations of the original on Sain. It's mostly a high-octane romp through songs of mothers-in-law, henpecked husbands, the wonders of nature and the seasons, and the usual stuff of peasant life (hard work, dreams of romance), all sung and played with great gusto. When they do slow down, as on two tracks concerning a love of Welsh culture and on the stunning closing song (a woman's affirmation of her love for a departed sailor husband), they reveal a welcome sensitive side.

what to buy next: The band's second release, *Hyn (This)* ♪♪♪ (Sain, 1998, prod. Lawson Dando)—recorded shortly after the *British Medical Journal* reported a study of villagers in South Wales valleys that concluded that men who have more orgasms live longer—shows their energy levels undiminished. A dejected spinster finds love and marriage in the frantic opening song, which is followed by a carefully paced "If My Love Will Come." Actually, the tempos on many of the songs here are slowed down quite a bit compared to the earlier release, and there is a greater variety of musical textures and vocal harmonies.

influences:
◀◀ Ar Log

John C. Falstaff

Chubby Carrier
/Chubby Carrier
& the Bayou Swamp Band

Zydeco
Formed 1990, in Lawtell, LA, USA. Based in Lafayette, LA, USA.

Chubby Carrier (born J.R. Carrier Jr., July 1, 1967, in Lafayette, LA, USA), one-row and three-row accordion, piano accordion, vocals; John Gaar, guitar; Lance Ellis, saxophone; Tray Landry, drums; Corey Duplechain, bass; Mike Chaisson, frattoir, percussion. Past members have included: David Lejeune, guitar; Rodney Dural, bass. (All members are from USA.)

Chubby Carrier is part of an extended family of musicians from the Lawtell/Mallet area of Louisiana. His father, Roy Carrier Sr., is a well-respected zydeco musician and club owner who leads his own band, the Night Rockers. Chubby got his break filling in for Roy at the Offshore Lounge on nights when the elder Carrier was out working an oil rig in the Gulf of Mexico. Roy encouraged Chubby to develop his own style, and introduced him to Clifton Chenier and blues performers like Bobby "Blue" Bland and B.B. King. He got his start away from dad's band playing drums with Terrance Simien and the Mallet Playboys. Like Simien, he puts a lot more guitar solos in his music than most other zydeco bands. He also uses a lot more rock 'n' roll rhythms—there's even a tribute to the Grateful Dead's Jerry Garcia!—which makes him more accessible to the mainstream audience, if less appealing to the zydeco scene's hard core. This is not to disparage Chubby, though; he's a fine performer on the one- and three-row accordions right out of the Rockin' Dopsie school of tough zydeco licks, and his experience as a drummer shows in his always-tight grooves.

what to buy: On *Who Stole the Hot Sauce?* ♪♪♪ (Blind Pig, 1996, prod. Michael Freeman) Carrier shows not just his roots—with a cover of Clifton Chenier's classic version of the traditional "Zydeco Sont Pas Sale"—but the more contemporary influence of Beau Jocque as well, with his own remake of War's "The Cisco Kid." Fans of his rock 'n' roll side will want to check out the zydeco version of Pete Townshend's suitably titled "Squeezebox" to hear how a rock song can be turned into a South Louisiana dance number.

what to buy next: No one is denying that Carrier can wail on the three-row, or that the man can sing and lead a band, but *Dance All Night* ♪♪♪ (Blind Pig, 1993, prod. Chubby Carrier, Edward Chmelewski, Jerry Del Giudice) may not satisfy south Louisiana–sound purists. Still, a piquant version of the Texas Playboys' "Stay a Little Longer" is especially fun if you're familiar with Bob Wills's original. And Carrier passes the litmus test for zydeco accordionists by soloing over just the drums and rubboard on "Old Time Zydeco," and pays his respects to Clifton Chenier wlth a high-speed cover of "Tout le Temps en Temp."

the rest:

Boogie Woogie Zydeco 🎵🎵🎵 (Flying Fish, 1991)

influences:

⏪ Roy Carrier, Rockin' Dopsie, Clifton Chenier

⏩ Keith Frank, Chris Ardoin, Geno Delafose

see also: *Roy Carrier, Clifton Chenier, Beau Jocque, Rockin' Dopsie, Terrance Simien*

Jared Snyder

Roy Carrier /Roy Carrier & the Night Rockers

Zydeco

Formed 1961, in Lawtell, LA, USA. Based in Lawtell, LA, USA.

Roy Carrier, one-row and three-row button accordions, vocals; Kevin Carrier, guitar; Troy Dickie Carrier, drums; Paul Newman, bass; Kevin Brousard, frattoir; Gerard St. Julien Jr., drums. (All members are from USA.)

Roy Carrier's Offshore Club is the place for zydeco music in the small town of Lawtell, Louisiana, where the Carrier family has a deep tradition of music-making. Uncles Bebe and Eraste Carrier were playing dances in the area almost as far back as the turn of the twentieth century, and the Lawtell Playboys of Calvin Carrier and Delton Broussard also played the area for years. Roy grew up in this rich culture; he started to play the rubboard at age six and would sneak his father's accordion out to the barn to learn that instrument as well. Despite the whipping he got when his father found out, he was determined to learn accordion, and by age 14 had formed the Night Rockers with his brother. A farm accident took half of Roy's index finger on his right hand, but like Django Reinhardt and other musicians he used the adversity to his advantage, developing a "cross chord" technique that is unique among zydeco players. Roy's style has a diatonic push-pull and syncopated scratch that hearken back to the rural zydeco of the Lawtell Playboys. This is balanced by his love of blues performers like Bobby "Blue" Bland and B.B. King, as well as the influence of zydeco king Clifton Chenier. Preserving the family tradition in more ways than one, Roy is the father of the "Jimi Hendrix of the Accordion," Chubby Carrier.

what to buy: It's axiomatic that zydeco bands are always much better live than on record, and that's certainly true in this case. However, *Zydeco Strokin'* 🎵🎵🎵 (Paula, 1995, prod. Lee Lavergne) gives a good taste of what to expect when you go out and get dancing to the Night Rockers. Any good zydeco recording has to have a tune where the accordionist/leader solos over just the *frattoir* (rubboard) and drums to prove that he can drive

the band without the benefit of guitar and bass, and this album is no exception. Carrier plays a kicking version of Clifton Chenier's "Baby Do Right" over the rhythm section, and the overall mix emphasizes the drums, frattoir, and accordion over the guitar and bass. While many of the tunes are slight rewrites of current zydeco material, you also get the band riffing off on Clarence Carter's R&B hit "Strokin'," keeping just enough of the original to see where they're coming from. Carrier's strong blues influence shines on "My Baby Wants to Leave Me," and the obligatory zydeco novelty cover is, in this case, a rocking version of "Tequila." Not as good as a night at the Offshore, or seeing Carrier at your local dance hall, but it's a nice record. Don't make this your first zydeco purchase, though.

what to buy next: The same reservations stated above apply to *Offshore Blues and Zydeco* 🎵🎵🎵 (Chubby Dragon, 1997, prod. Ray Alden). Carrier ain't gonna win any awards as the poet of his generation, but that's not the point with this genre. Lots of Carrier's songs are built around a zydeco riff and call-and-response singing. His "Kansas City Blues" sounds like Wilbert Harrison lost in the fog on Highway 190 somewhere between Lawtell and Swords, and his "Living in the USA/Shake, Rattle and Roll" medley sounds like something he pulls out for LSU frat parties. Still, the man can drive a band with his accordion: check out his "My Baby Don't Wear No Shoes," done in the old house-dance style, and his cover of Chenier's "Blake Snake Moan." This one is only available by mail order—from Chubby Dragon Productions, 124 Quaker Bridge Rd, Croton-on-Hudson, NY 11052; Phone: (914) 941-8536—but it has some of Carrier's nicest playing.

the rest:

At His Best 🎵🎵🎵 (Zane, 1996)
(With Joe Walker) *Soulful Side of Zydeco* 🎵🎵 (Zane, 1996)

influences:

⏪ Clifton Chenier, Boozoo Chavis, Rockin' Dopsie

⏩ Chubby Carrier, Chris Ardoin

see also: *Chubby Carrier, C.J. Chenier, Clifton Chenier*

Jared Snyder

Liz Carroll

Irish traditional

Born September 19, 1956, in Chicago, IL, USA. Based in Chicago, IL, USA.

We have Sister Francine to thank in part for Liz Carroll's contribution to Irish traditional fiddle music. As Carroll was growing up and becoming involved in Irish dancing and music-making in her native Chicago, she first started playing on her father's three-row accordion, only later to be inspired to take up the fiddle by Sister Francine's violin teaching at school. Fortunately for Carroll, the 1960s were a time of cultural reawakening for Chicago's Irish community and, under the aegis of the city's Irish Traditional Musicians Association, she was soon playing and learning alongside veteran practitioners like Mayo piper Joe Shannon and Chicago-born fiddler John McGreevy. By 1973 Carroll's playing had become impressive enough for visiting accordionist Paddy Gavin to encourage her to compete in the All-Ireland competitions on the emerald isle itself. Although that year she was second to future De Dannan frontman Frankie Gavin in the under-18 category, she won first place in 1974, and went on to a stunning victory in the senior division the very next year, with a title in the duet competition to boot. It wasn't long before Carroll was asked to join in Mick Moloney's Green Fields of America tours, and to record for New York City–based world-music label Shanachie. Two early LPs, the first being a duet album with Offaly accordion player Tommy Maguire, were followed by a number of guest appearances on recordings by fellow Green Fielders Mick Moloney and Jimmy Keane as well as ethnomusicologist and folk-rock artist Lawrence McCullough. Carroll has since made another solo album, consisting mostly of her own compositions, and has been touring and recording since 1991 with the group Trian, alongside accordionist Billy McComiskey and singer/guitar player Dáithí Sproule. In 1994 Carroll was presented with a prestigious National Heritage Fellowship award from the National Endowment for the Arts.

what to buy: On the strength of her All-Ireland success, Carroll recorded her debut duet album, *Kiss Me Kate* &♪♪♪ (Shanachie, 1978, prod. Daniel Michael Collins, Richard Nevins), with accordion player Tommy Maguire—himself an All-Ireland winner in 1964—and Jerry Wallace on piano. The album abounds in impressively tight playing of the often-complex melodies which the notoriously tune-hungry Carroll seems to favor. However, her true musical personality really unfolds on her first solo album, *A Friend Indeed* ♪♪♪♪ (Shanachie, 1979, prod. Richard Nevins, Daniel Michael Collins), recorded a year later with Marty Fahey on piano. Here, Carroll demonstrates not only her awe-inspiring command of the instrument and the idiom—sometimes spicing things up with quirky, American-sounding licks—but showcases her talents as a composer as well. It took Carroll almost 10 years before she made her next solo album, but the result was worth the wait. *Liz Carroll* ♪♪♪♪ (Green Linnet, 1988, prod. Liz Carroll, Dáithí Sproule) is a dazzling display of her superior musicianship and compositional genius, all but six of the tunes coming from her pen. Besides her work with the group Trian, there are a few tracks by Carroll on a number of anthologies worth seeking. She recorded an uncommon setting of "Miss McLeod" followed by a couple of her own compositions on *Cherish the Ladies: Irish Women Musicians in America* ♪♪♪♪ (Shanachie, 1985, prod. Mick Moloney), the original album resulting from Mick Moloney's ef-

forts to promote the female side of Irish-American music. This also featured Eileen Ivers, recently of *Riverdance* fame. Carroll also appears on the live recording *My Love Is in America: The Boston College Irish Fiddle Festival* ♪♪♪♪ (Green Linnet, 1991, prod. Mícheál Ó Súilleabháin), a fabulous collection every Irish fiddle-music lover should have on their shelf; as well as on the recently released and equally worthwhile *Gaelic Roots* ♪♪♪♪ (Kells Music, 1997, prod. Séamus Connolly), also recorded live at Boston College. Finally, she can be heard playing solo on two more of her own compositions, and in one duet with accordionist Billy McComiskey, on *Dear Old Erin's Isle: Irish Traditional Music from America* ♪♪♪ (Nimbus, 1992, prod. Mícheál Ó Súilleabháin, Robin Broadbank), recorded live on the occasion of the eighth annual Éigse na Laoi festival of traditional music at University College, Cork.

worth searching for: *Irish Traditional Instrumental Music from Chicago, Vol. 2* ♪♪♪ (Rounder, 1976, prod. Miles Krassen, Larry McCullough) and *Ed Reavy* ♪♪♪♪ (Rounder, 1979, prod. Mick Moloney), the latter album devoted to the compositions of the famous County Cavan fiddle player, are two of the LP collections that featured Carroll's early playing; one Carroll track from the former and two from the latter were recently reissued on the easier-to-find compilation *Jigs and Reels from Ireland* ♪♪♪ (Rounder, 1998). On *Fathers and Daughters from Cherish the Ladies* ♪♪♪ (Shanachie, 1985, prod. Mick Moloney), the follow-up to the original *Cherish the Ladies* album and as yet not reissued on CD, Carroll appears on two tracks along with her father Kevin on accordion.

influences:

◀◀ Kevin Carroll, Martin Byrne, Joe Shannon, John McGreevy, Eleanor Neary, Terry Teahan

▶▶ Eileen Ivers, Cherish the Ladies, Kathleen Collins

see also: *Cherish the Ladies, Déanta, De Dannan, James Keane, Mick Moloney, Trian*

Philippe Varlet

Eliza Carthy /Waterson:Carthy

English folk, folk-rock, and fusion
Waterson:Carthy formed c. 1994, in England. Based in England.

Eliza Carthy (born 1975, in Yorkshire, England), fiddle, vocals; Norma Waterson (born August 15, 1939), vocals; Martin Carthy (born May 21, 1940), guitar, vocals; Saul Rose, melodeon (1999–present). (All members are from England.)

Eliza Carthy was born into one of the most musically gifted and important families in England. Her father is the noted guitarist and singer Martin Carthy—distinguished by service in Steeleye

Span, the Albion Country Band, Brass Monkey, the Martin Carthy & Dave Swarbrick duo, the Watersons, and Waterson:Carthy as well as by his solo work—and her mother is sublime vocalist Norma Waterson, of the latter two bands. Starting out, Eliza played guitar and mandolin; it wasn't until 1990, when she partnered in a duo with Nancy Kerr, that she picked up the fiddle as well, in that instrument (and her own vocals) finding the vehicle with which she would carry forth the family tradition in phenomenal form. In a short career that has already included work as one half of the aforesaid duo and the other third of the above-mentioned Waterson:Carthy, as well as two of her own outfits, Eliza Carthy & the Kings of Calicutt and the Eliza Carthy Band, Carthy has shot into the music firmament as one of the hottest stars of the English folk scene's '90s generation.

what to buy: *Heat, Light & Sound* ♪♪♪♪ (Topic, 1996, prod. Eliza Carthy, Ray Williams, Tony Engle) boasts exciting arrangements of traditional instrumentals and songs. Carthy's voice is charmingly untutored and sweet. The plaintive "Ten Thousand Miles/Bacca Pipes" exemplifies the best of what the English music tradition has to offer. Two years later Carthy released a unique package consisting of two complete CDs—*Red* ♪♪♪♪ (Topic, 1998, prod. Niall Macauley) and *Rice* ♪♪♪♪ (Topic, 1998, prod. Eliza Carthy, "the rest of the world")—in one box. On *Red* Carthy takes English ballad and instrumental traditions into the 21st century with startling new arrangements of centuries-old works. On "Billy Boy," accordion-led English folk-rock meets dub reggae. What makes the track even more fascinating is that Carthy's unadorned folk-singing style fits just fine with the decidedly different instrumental backing. There's also a refreshingly blues-and-jazzed-up version of "Greenwood Laddie," complete with scintillating syncopated piano riffing by Martin Green. Several of the instrumental selections are English counterparts to the approach of avant-garde Scottish folk bands like Shooglenifty and Peatbog Faeries, in which ancient dance tunes meet modern rhythm grooves and high-tech production techniques. For contrast, *Rice* is a stripped-down acoustic set that shows Carthy equally powerful singing or playing fiddle, backed only by guitar or accordion.

what to buy next: The guiding spirit of the Waterson:Carthy project is Eliza's mother Norma Waterson, whose deep, resonant voice suggests centuries of toil and more than a little pleasure. *Waterson:Carthy* ♪♪♪♪ (Topic, 1994, prod. Tony Engle) spotlights her strong lead vocals, though the Carthy father and daughter each get their turn at the mic. Eliza's fiddle blends well with her father's guitar on "Ye Mariners All," which Martin Carthy sings. *Common Tongue* ♪♪♪♪ (Topic, 1997, prod. Tony Engle), a more specifically English album

than its predecessor, is helped by the presence of various Watersons on backing vocals. The melodeon of Saul Rose (recently made a full-fledged member) duetting with Eliza Carthy's fiddle on "Valentine Waltz" is a sweet addition to the first track.

the rest:
(With Nancy Kerr) *Eliza Carthy & Nancy Kerr* ♪♪♪♪ (Mrs. Casey Records, 1993)
shape of scrape ♪♪♪♪ (Mrs. Casey Records, 1995)
(With the Kings of Calicutt) *Eliza Carthy & the Kings of Calicutt* ♪♪♪♪ (Topic, 1997)

worth searching for: Norma Waterson's solo effort, *Norma Waterson* ♪♪♪♪ (Rykodisc, 1996, prod. John Chelew), includes Martin and Eliza Carthy, as well as Roger Swallow (percussion), Danny Thompson (bass), and Richard Thompson (guitar). It emphasizes the work of a wide range of songwriters, including the latter Thompson, Jerry Garcia, Robert Hunter, Billy Bragg, and Lal Waterson. The mother-daughter vocal harmonies on "There Ain't No Sweet Man That's Worth the Salt of My Tears" are exquisite.

influences:
◀◀ Martin Carthy, the Watersons, Copper Family, Shirley Collins, Maddy Prior

▶▶ Kate Rusby, Shooglenifty, Peatbog Faeries

see also: *Martin Carthy*

Pamela Murray Winters and Ken Roseman

Martin Carthy
British folk
Born May 21, 1940, in Hatfield, Hertfordshire, England. Based in England.

There's nary a significant development in the British folk music of the past 30 years that singer-guitarist Martin Carthy can't claim to have impacted. He taught British-folk standards like "Scarborough Fair" to Paul Simon; he played with British-folk revolutionaries like Steeleye Span and Dave Swarbrick; he influenced definitive British-folk guitarists like Richard Thompson, Martin Simpson, and Stephen Fearing; he married into the British-folk institution the Watersons. Carthy's first recording came out in 1963, and he has shone ever since as an understated singer, a superbly sensitive guitarist, and a scholar of folk music noted for his respect for the original material. Today he shares the spotlight in bands like Waterson:Carthy with his spouse and daughter (Norma Waterson and Eliza Carthy), and basks in a bit of his own with such honors as his 1998 receipt of an M.B.E. (Member of the British Empire) award for his contributions to British culture.

what to buy: *The Martin Carthy Collection* ♫♫♫♫ (Green Linnet, 1993) is an obvious starting point for learning about the artist. With traditional songs; a Carthy composition ("Company Policy," about the Falklands conflict); and "Palaces of Gold" by Leon Rosselson, one of Britain's best-known political songwriters, it highlights Carthy's socially conscious side, as well as his fondness for reworking older sources.

what to buy next: Martin Carthy and Dave Swarbrick's CD *Life and Limb* ♫♫♫♫ (Topic/Green Linnet, 1991, prod. John Chelew) includes the beautifully creepy "Bows of London" and one of many versions of "The Begging Song." Swarbrick fiddles beautifully on "Carthy's March/The Lemon Tree," tunes he wrote for Carthy and Trevor Lucas, respectively.

best of the rest:
Martin Carthy ♫♫♫♫ (Topic, 1965)
Byker Hill ♫♫♫♫ (Topic, 1967)
Crown of Horn ♫♫♫♫ (Topic, 1976)
Out of the Cut ♫♫♫♫ (Rounder, 1982)
(With Dave Swarbrick) *Skin and Bone* ♫♫♫♫ (Green Linnet, 1992)

worth searching for: Carthy joins bride Norma's family on the Watersons' *For Pence and Spicy Ale* ♫♫♫♫ (Shanachie, 1975, prod. Tony Engle), which contains wassails, work songs, and other traditional fare. The presentation is *a cappella,* in a style similar to that of vocal pioneers Young Tradition, though more elaborate. The reissue also includes some tracks by individual Watersons.

influences:
◀ A.L. Lloyd, Davey Graham, Ravi Shankar, the Watersons

▶ Simon & Garfunkel, Bob Dylan, Martin Simpson, Eliza Carthy

see also: *Eliza Carthy, Ashley Hutchings, Steeleye Span, Dave Swarbrick*

Pamela Murray Winters

John Carty
Irish traditional
Born in London, England. Based in Boyle, County Roscommon, Ireland.

Born in London in the early 1960s of Irish parentage, John Carty began his self-professed addiction to Irish traditional music in the early '70s under the tutelage of Clare-born musician Brendan Mulkere. Carty went on to enter the annual Fleadh competitions of Irish music, in which he achieved success at all levels, culminating in his Senior All-Ireland banjo championship title in 1982. 1983 saw Carty travel to Australia, where he spent a year teaching and playing music. Upon returning to London in 1984 he became a fixture in the vibrant London Irish session scene until 1991, when he finally moved to Ireland itself. Carty settled in Boyle, County Roscommon—the area from which his father came—and has lived there with his own family ever since. A multi-instrumentalist, Carty is best known for his fiery banjo and fiddle playing but is also a fine flute player. His unabashed love for the true greats of Irish traditional music and his reverence for that style is a breath of fresh air at a time when frequent experimentation with Irish tradition seems to be the norm—though in Carty's imaginative hands the legacy is definitely a living one.

what to buy: *Last Night's Fun* ♫♫♫♫ (Shanachie, 1996, prod. Daniel Michael Collins) is a brilliant collection of Irish traditional music. It also features several of Carty's frequent musical partners, including pianist Brian McGrath and guitarist Francis Gaffney. The liner notes poke fun at Carty's lack of celebrity as a fiddle player by saying the recording could have been called "Out of the Blue" or "They Laughed When I Sat Down to Play." You won't be doing much laughing when you sit down to listen to *Last Night's Fun,* though it will cause you to stand up and take notice of his brilliance. *At the Racket* ♫♫♫♫ (Racket, 1997, prod. Garry O'Briain) is the eponymous debut of a remarkable band put together by Carty, McGrath, Garry O'Briain, and Seamus O'Donnell. The outfit is modeled after Irish traditional bands of the '20s and '30s like the Flanagan Brothers, from whose recording "Flanagan at the Racket" this band takes its name. The album is slyly innovative and preservationist at the same time in its use of the saxophone within a traditional idiom—uncommon today, though during the Irish dance-band heyday being evoked it was the norm rather than the exception. Overall excellence and inventiveness, O'Donnell's sax coupled with Carty's banjo, and a couple of vocal cuts thrown into the mix of mostly instrumentals make this recording a must-have for fans of Irish music with a sense of history and an eye on the future.

what to buy next: *The Cat That Ate the Candle* ♫♫♫ (Cló Iar-Chonnachta, 1994, prod. John Carty, Brian McGrath) is a marvelous recording that showcases Carty's banjo-playing side, along with his frequent musical partner McGrath. Carty's *At the Racket* cohort holds down the fort with subtle piano accompaniment while Carty lets loose on banjo. The one track that features his superb fiddling as well is what led Shanachie Records to ink Carty for a multi-album deal.

worth searching for: *Across the Waters* ♫♫♫ (Nimbus, 1994, prod. Mícheál Ó Súilleabháin, Robin Broadbank) was recorded live at University College of Cork, Ireland, as part of an annual concert series featuring music from various parts the Celtic world—including many of the finest exponents of Irish traditional music from England. While Carty's vibrant banjo playing is only featured on one track, the recording deftly illustrates the fertile Irish music scene in London from which Carty emerged.

influences:

⏮ Brendan Mulkere, Lad O'Beirne, the Flanagan Brothers, Micheal Coleman, Paddy Killoran

Cliff McGann

Karan Casey

See: Solas

Casper

Reggae, Native American

Born Casper Loma-Da-Wa (a.k.a. Lomayesva) in Winslow, AZ, USA. Based in Scottsdale, AZ, USA.

Casper grew up on the Hopi Reservation, where his father and paternal grandparents had a big influence on him. His mother was Navajo and his father Hopi; when his parents broke up Casper would get to experience both cultures. "I was raised on traditional music," he once explained. "In Hopiland, every weekend there would be ceremonies and my grandparents and father brought me into the traditional ways. They taught me to live in harmony with the Great Spirit." In high school Casper listened to pop and rap, and considered putting his poetry to music, but it was reggae that really rocked his world. "Reggae is a big thing in Hopiland," Casper explained. "Hopis went down to all the big reggae shows in Flagstaff, and eventually we started Culture Connection, a group that began bringing bands onto the rez, and I'm talking Wailers, Dennis Brown and Steel Pulse. Seeing those people on stage made me hungry. Something in the rhythm connected with the traditional music I'd been raised on. And the message of awareness and responsibility made me open my eyes." In the spirit of this heightened social consciousness, Casper continued, "What happens on the rez isn't too different from what happens to people of color everywhere, but people don't realize Hopiland isn't a reservation. We've never been relocated. One of our villages is one of the oldest continually inhabited villages in the world. I stress that in the music. We aren't imported people, we've been here a long time, and to be considered second-class citizens is absurd."

what's available: Casper speaks out strongly, both musically and lyrically, on his self-produced debut *Original Landlord* ♫♫♫♩ (Third Mesa, 1997, prod. Casper Lomayesva). He sings in a convincing Jamaican patois and the one-drop riddims of his band crackle with energy; the music is a potent blend of roots reggae, dancehall, and Native American styles. Joyous celebrations of love and music like "Love Me, Love Me" and "Nuff Dread Dem Come" complement tough political tracks like "Hundred Years of Redemption" and "Roadblock," which pays an implicit compliment to Marley's "Rebel Music (3 O'Clock Roadblock)."

influences:

⏮ Bob Marley, Gladiators, Culture

j. poet

Patrick Cassidy

Irish traditional and classical

Born 1956, in Claremorris, County Mayo, Ireland. Based in Ireland and Los Angeles, CA, USA.

Harp-player and composer Patrick Cassidy grew up in a large bilingual family in the west of Ireland, dabbling with rock music in the late '70s and early '80s while growing increasingly fascinated with piano and harp. Entirely self-taught as a composer and arranger, and inspired by the example of Irish-heritage standard-bearer Seán Ó Riada, he blossomed in his 30s on a series of albums recorded with some of the top names in classical and Irish music. At first drawing on the legacy of the great 18th-century Irish harper Turlough O'Carolan, by the '90s Cassidy had turned to ambitious large-scale orchestral and choral works based on ancient Irish historical and mythical subject matter, distinguished by librettos in the Irish language, and often incorporating uilleann pipes. While Shaun Davey in Ireland had first married pipes and orchestra in the late '70s, and Breton harper Alan Stivell had written and recorded a *Celtic Symphony* a few years later, Cassidy's vision seems quite different: to take a familiar Baroque form and imbue it with distinctively Irish colorations.

what to buy: *Famine Remembrance* ♫♫♫♫ (Windham Hill, 1997, prod. Patrick Cassidy) features operatic soloists and the Choir and Orchestra of Saint Patrick's Cathedral, NYC, on a dignified and rather somber requiem written and released for the 150th anniversary of the Great Irish Famine, which led to mass emigrations to America. Original pieces for orchestra are placed alongside choral arrangements of "St. Patrick's Breastplate" (in Irish), "De Profundis" (in Latin), and two settings of poems (in English) about the famine published in the late 1840s by "Speranza," better known as the mother of Oscar Wilde. Ex-Bothy Band piper Paddy Keenan joins in for the stately closing "Funeral March."

what to buy next: *The Children of Lir* ♫♫♫♩ (Son, 1993/Celtic Heartbeat, 1994, prod. Patrick Cassidy) was Cassidy's first oratorio, recorded by the London Symphony Orchestra, the Tallis Chambre Choir, and former Planxty piper Liam O'Flynn. The libretto (in Irish) is based on an 1883 manuscript, and the scoring is strongly reminiscent of the works of Händel and Haydn. Cassidy's song cycle *Deirdre of the Sorrows* ♫♫♫♩ (Windham Hill, 1998, prod. Patrick Cassidy) was recorded by the London Symphony Orchestra and the Tallis Chambre Choir in 1995, its release being delayed to allow *Famine Remembrance* a timely issue. Three unrelated O'Carolan pieces, recorded with the

Dori Caymmi

Dublin Philharmonic Orchestra and featuring Cassidy on harp, are appended to this CD.

worth searching for: On the Irish-only *Cruit* (Gael-Linn, 1988, prod. Patrick Cassidy) Cassidy, on harp, leads a Baroque chamber ensemble in his own arrangements of O'Carolan melodies.

influences:

◀◀ Georg Friedrich Händel, Joseph Haydn, Seán Ó Riada, Shaun Davey, Alan Stivell

see also: *Bothy Band, Shaun Davey, Liam O'Flynn, Seán Ó Riada, Planxty, Alan Stivell*

John C. Falstaff

Dori Caymmi

Brazilian pop-jazz, samba
Born 1943, in Brazil. Based in Brazil and Los Angeles, CA, USA.

The son of the late bossa nova icon Dorival Caymmi, Dori Caymmi is a Brazilian pop-jazz singer, acoustic guitarist, and composer who is known for his subtlety, softness, and restraint.

In addition to being greatly influenced by the bossa nova movement of the 1960s, Caymmi has been an ardent admirer of U.S. jazz and pre-rock pop. His vocals and acoustic guitar playing are airy, caressing, and light, yet never lightweight. Being the son of an artist who was so famous in Brazil in the '60s and '70s could have been daunting, but Dori Caymmi is a great artist in his own right. Caymmi was only 17 when he started writing music for commercials, and he went on to play or record with artists ranging from Sarah Vaughan and Toots Thielemans to Johnny Mathis. Since the early '90s, Caymmi has been recording for Quincy Jones's Qwest label with generally rewarding results.

what to buy: Although all of Caymmi's Qwest CDs are worth hearing, the best albums to start out with are *Brazilian Serenata* ♫♫♫♫ (Qwest, 1991, prod. Dori Caymmi) and *Kicking Cans* ♫♫♫♫ (Qwest, 1991, prod. Dori Caymmi). Caymmi sings in both English and Portuguese on *Brazilian Serenata,* his first recording for Qwest, and he is amazingly soulful on such introspective treasures as "Mercador de Siri," "The Colors of Joy," and "Flower of Bahia." Equally impressive and just as introspective is *Kicking Cans,* which finds him joined by John Patitucci, Billy

Childs, Branford Marsalis, and other jazz greats. Whether he's providing lyrics or wordless scat-singing, Caymmi's vocals never fail to be personal.

what to buy next: *If I Ever . . .* ♫♫♫ (Qwest, 1994, prod. Dori Caymmi) gets off to a fine start with Caymmi's gentle interpretation of Stephen Sondheim's "Send in the Clowns," and he demonstrates that he is a sensitive and poignant composer himself on heartfelt originals like "Homesick for Old Rio (Saudade Do Rio)" and "We Can Try Love Again."

influences:

◀◀ Antonio Carlos Jobim, João Gilberto, Milton Nascimento

Alex Henderson

Celtic Fiddle Festival

See: Kevin Burke, Johnny Cunningham

Ceolbeg

Scottish traditional and neo-traditional
Formed 1988, in Edinburgh, Scotland. Based in Scotland.

Peter Boond, vocals, flute, whistle, cittern; Davy Steele, lead vocals, guitar, bouzouki (1988–95); Katie Harrigan, vocals, clarsach, electroharp (1988–91); Andy Thorburn, vocals, keyboards (1988–91); Gary West, vocals, Highland pipes (1988–92); Wendy Stewart, vocals, electroharp, concertina (1991–present); Colin Matheson, vocals, keyboards (1991–95); Mike Katz, Highland pipes (1994–97); Rod Paterson, lead vocals, guitar (1995–present). (All members are from Scotland.)

In the Gaelic language of the Scots, *Ceol Beag* (KALE-beg) translates literally as "small music" and refers to the jigs, reels, and strathspeys of traditional Scottish music, while *Ceol Mor* ("big music") describes the booming classical sound of the Highland bagpipe. Over the last 20 years and more, a number of such Scottish outfits as the Battlefield Band, the Tannahill Weavers, and Wolfstone have combined traditional music, modern acoustic and electric instrumentation, and the Ceol Mor to produce what many have called "bagpipe rock," drawing large numbers of new fans into the world of folk music in the process. Missing from these bands in many instances, though, was the delicacy and variety of the Ceol Beag. From their formation during the late 1980s (Peter Boond is the sole remaining original member), Ceolbeg set out to prove that the harp and Highland pipes could be brought together in a format both traditional and contemporary to produce music that is anything but "small"—and as many critics and reviewers have commented throughout the history of Ceolbeg, the band's name is a misnomer; they're big.

Part of Ceolbeg's secret has been the uncommon ability of pipers Gary West, and later Mike Katz, to moderate the High-

land pipes and achieve a sound that one publication described as "fluency with firepower." Combined with the electroharp—particularly when played in Wendy Stewart's distinctive percussive style—as well as with keyboards and Boond's flute and cittern work, the effect has been described as "an atmospheric mist of swirling instrumentation." Yet Ceolbeg is much more than an instrumental phenomenon; much of their appeal can be traced to the powerful, emotional lead vocals of Davy Steele, a singer widely considered to be an interpreter of modern and traditional Scottish music in the same league with his close friends Andy M. Stewart and Dick Gaughan. Steele left the band in 1995, replaced by Rod Paterson, and as of September 1997 had joined the Battlefield Band to replace the departing Alistair Russell. Mike Katz has also signed on with the Battlefield Band, with his replacement in Ceolbeg yet undetermined. In more recent years Ceolbeg has added a drummer and percussionist in the person of Jim Walker, who appears on their most recent album. Their recorded output is of uniformly high quality, but from their earliest days Ceolbeg have believed themselves to be at their best when performing live—they even regard their longtime sound man Adie Bolton as a full-fledged band member. In 1991 the *Scottish Folk Gazette* recounted, with accuracy and enthusiasm, that "Ceolbeg bring to their audiences not only musical virtuosity and dynamic performances, but also a great deal of humour and repartee." Luckily, on their fine albums you can listen for yourself.

what to buy: All three of Ceolbeg's generally available releases on the Greentrax label are of consistently good quality. The one to start with is their most recent, *An Unfair Dance* ♫♫♫♫ (Greentrax, 1993, prod. Roy Ashby), if for no other reason than it contains the most music—60 full minutes. Their trademark treatments of reels and strathspeys are satisfying, and Steele's vocals are powerful, whether delivering a Burns ballad ("My Love Is like a Red, Red Rose") or one of his own songs, such as the emotion-packed "The Collier's Way," which deals with his father's experiences as a miner. It's a gripping song that deserves mention in the same breath as American mining classics like Merle Travis's "Dark as a Dungeon" and Jean Ritchie's "Blue Diamond Mine." While Steele's voice is reminiscent of pop-rock icon Sting, his singing is much richer and more expressive, and totally devoid of pretension. The unusual instrumental combination of Highland war pipes with Wendy Stewart's harp style (described by some as "bubbling") brings to mind the "bull in a china shop" metaphor, but Gary West's piping is well modulated to allow each band member's contributions to be clearly heard and appreciated.

what to buy next: Both their debut album, *Not the Bunnyhop* ♫♫♫♫ (Greentrax, 1990, prod. Phil Cunningham), and their second release, *Seeds to the Wind* ♫♫♫♫ (Greentrax, 1992, prod.

Dick Gaughan), feature the same entertaining mix of instrumental and vocal accomplishment. Highlights on *Not the Bunnyhop* include Andy M. Stewart's "Queen of Argyll" and Steele's "The High and Mighty." On *Seeds to the Wind* Steele shines on material like "Johnnie Cope" and Robert Burns's "A' the Airts," while the interplay between Stewart's harp and West's piping makes both recordings worthwhile additions to any collection.

solo outings:
Wendy Stewart:
About Time ♪♪♪♪ (Greentrax, 1992)
About Time, Vol. 2 ♪♪♪ (Greentrax, 1997)

Davy Steele:
Chasing Shadows ♪♪♪♪ (Temple, 1997)

influences:
◄◄ Capercaillie, Silly Wizard, Clan Alba, Dick Gaughan, Andy M. Stewart

►► Battlefield Band, Tannahill Weavers, Old Blind Dogs

see also: *Battlefield Band, Dick Gaughan, Andy M. Stewart, Tannahill Weavers, Wolfstone*

John Lupton

Ceoltoiri
Celtic
Formed as a duo in 1983, in the Washington, DC, area, USA. Based in the Washington, DC, area, USA.

Karen Ashbrook, hammered dulcimer, pennywhistle, boxwood flute; Sue Richards, Celtic harp; Connie McKenna, vocals, guitar (1987–present).

Ceoltoiri, the Irish Gaelic word for musicians, is the perfect name for this band, which was originally formed as a Celtic harp and hammered dulcimer duo, combining two traditional sounds that were obviously made to go together. Karen Ashbrook's virtuoso melodies combine with Sue Richards's haunting harp lines to create a rich texture of sounds, and then they switch roles, keeping the tunes fresh and interesting. It is sometimes hard to believe they can create such lush sounds with so few instruments. Occasionally described as "chamber folk," Ceoltoiri selects traditional tunes with great soul and then arranges them in a theme-and-variations format. The result is dynamic. The group was joined by guitarist Connie McKenna in 1987, after she guested on their first recording. Following Irish tradition, Connie studied *sean-nós* singing, a particular style of unaccompanied, highly ornamented vocal work, and brought an elegant classical guitar background and a rich sense of Irish vocals to the group, adding spice to an already flavorful mix.

what to buy: *Silver Apples of the Moon* ♪♪♪♪ (Maggie's Music, 1992, prod. Charlie Pilzer) combines the best these musicians have to offer, all on one recording. From delightful duets by Karen and Sue, such as "Flowing Tide/New Claret," to Connie's evocative *a cappella* sean-nós singing on "The Plain Girl's Lament," the tracks offer something different at every turn. The darkly beautiful "Death of Queen Jane" alone is worth whatever price you pay for this CD.

what to buy next: The original duo shows their stuff on *Celtic Lace* ♪♪♪ (Foolscap, 1989/Maggie's Music, 1992). This recording amply demonstrates the perfect blend that Celtic harp and hammered dulcimer can create. *Women of Ireland* ♪♪♪♪ (Maggie's Music, 1998, prod. Charlie Pilzer) features some heartwrenching ballads, beautifully delivered. The rendition of Dougie MacLean's "Caledonia" is a standout. Guests include Trian's Billy McComiskey on accordion and Kieran O'Hare on uilleann pipes. Harper and pianist Carol Rose Duane, a regular performing guest with the group, also joins them here.

influences:
◄◄ Maggie Sansone, Magical Strings

►► Ironweed, Jody Marshall

see also: *Karen Ashbrook, Trian*

Jo Hughey Morrison

Dr. Krishna Chakravarty
North Indian classical, Hindustani
Born in Benares, India. Based in Benares, India.

Dr. Krishna Chakravarty is from Benares, a city that has produced such well-known artists as Bismillah Khan and Ravi Shankar. Chakravarty, who studied with Shankar himself in the 1970s, is associate professor of sitar at Benares Hindu University and has taught in the U.S. She's a relative newcomer to the scene, with a CD debut in 1987. Shankar's passionate, bravura performing style has clearly influenced Chakravarty, and she carries on the tradition very capably.

what to buy: *Circular Dance* ♪♪♪♪ (Celestial Harmonies, 1998, prod. David Parsons, Ram Chakravarty) is Chakravarty's third recording, but her second solo effort. She is accompanied by Vinod Gangadhar Lele on *tabla* drum and an unidentified *tamboura* (stringed drone instrument) player on "Raga Hemant," "Raga Lalit," and "Bhairavi Dhun," the last a folk melody played in a lyrical, light classical style.

what to buy next: *Dancing to the Flute* ♪♪♪♪ (Celestial Harmonies, 1997, prod. David Parsons, Ram Chakravarty) is a collaboration between music faculty members of Benares Hindu University recorded for an art gallery exhibition. The album features *karnatak* (South Indian) and *dhrupad* (unembellished classical) singing (on the famous "Rag Darbari" of Emperor

Akbar's court); a *shehnai* (double-reed pipe) ensemble; *sarangi* (bowed string instrument); tamboura; and various percussion instruments. Chakravarty plays a *ragamala* (medley of classical *ragas*) on "Raga Mishra Khamaj," accompanied by Lele on tabla. Perhaps this composite raga is a tribute to her illustrious teacher and his penchant for the same.

the rest:
Ananda 𝄢𝄢𝄢𝄢 (Fortuna, 1987)

influences:
◄◄ Ravi Shankar

David Paul

Sheila Chandra

Cross-cultural vocal
Born March 14, 1965, in England. Based in England.

Indians living in Britain face an automatic culture clash, but Sheila Chandra, born of Indian parents and raised in England, has continually vaulted the cultural border with accuracy and enthusiasm. She started out firmly on mainstream ground as an actress in the British teen show *Grange Hill,* then moved closer to the precipice with the early-'80s band Monsoon, which was attempting to fuse Asian sounds with pop, initially quite successfully. When it all fell apart she inched back a bit stylistically, while still advancing personally as a now-solo artist, working with former musical partner (and future life partner) Steve Coe. From that point, a series of albums released on the Indipop label between '83 and '85 shows how quick Chandra's progress was. Over the course of four records she moved from what was essentially pop/rock (*Out on My Own*) into much more creative and sometimes experimental areas (*Nada Brahma*), with a couple of intriguing detours along the way—including one record entirely without lyrics (*Quiet*); a daring step for a singer. Then, with an already notable body of work at the venerable age of 20, she departed the music business for five years, finally re-emerging with a mature recording, *Roots and Wings,* that made it seem at once as if she hadn't ever been gone and as if she was an entirely new artist. Chandra had seen how the vocalizations of the Celtic and Indian worlds were connected, and she explored their dynamic differences and surprising similarities while also experimenting with traditional Indian patterns of *konnakkkol,* a form of "vocal percussion" with its own revelatory relationship to late-20th century rhythmic vocal genres. For all these innovations *Roots* was largely a transitional disc, the approach of which came to further fruition—with a strong spiritual element added—on Chandra's move to the prestigious RealWorld label with *Weaving My Ancestors' Voices.* Two years later *The Zen Kiss* took this route almost as far as it could go— albeit in more than one direction simultaneously; her version of

"A Sailor's Life," for instance, came close to eclipsing that of English folk-rock synonyms Fairport Convention. With this artist, though, there always seems to be more road to travel: the essential sound of the drone and all its possibilities, including the overtones she could hear in it, had long fascinated Chandra, and she explored that on *ABoneCroneDrone,* six abstract pieces that truly tested her abilities. At this writing she's no doubt ready for yet another next step—and perhaps even the world is.

what to buy: *Weaving My Ancestors' Voices* 𝄢𝄢𝄢𝄢 (RealWorld, 1992, prod. Steve Coe) is a daring day-trip among cultures, connecting their vocal similarities—which turn out to be many. In *Quiet* 𝄢𝄢𝄢𝄢 (Caroline, 1983, prod. Steve Coe) Chandra experiments with no lyrics, and effectively presages many new-age ideas while still containing plenty of substance.

the rest:
Out On My Own 𝄢𝄢𝄢 (Caroline, 1983)
The Struggle 𝄢𝄢𝄢𝄢 (Caroline, 1985)
Nada Brahma 𝄢𝄢𝄢𝄢 (Caroline, 1985)
Roots and Wings 𝄢𝄢𝄢𝄢 (Caroline, 1990)
The Zen Kiss 𝄢𝄢𝄢𝄢 (RealWorld, 1994)
ABoneCroneDrone 𝄢𝄢𝄢𝄢 (RealWorld, 1996)
Moonsung N/A (RealWorld, 1999)

influences:
◄◄ Bollywood, classical Indian music, international drones

Chris Nickson

Chateau Neuf Spelemannslag

Norwegian folk-rock
Formed 1992, in Oslo, Norway. Based in Oslo, Norway.

Carl Petter Opsahl, leader, clarinet; Eline Monrad Vistven, sax; Mikael Nyberg, sax (1992–97); Eivind Sognnæs, sax; Elisabeth Vatnl, clarinet; Tori Snerte, flute, selje flute; Linn Korsjøen, vocals; Line Nilsen, vocals; Gine Heien, vocals; Ingrid Forthun, vocals; Siri Rude, vocals; Ragnhild Mo, fiddle, hardanger fiddle; Håkon Asheim, fiddle, hardanger fiddle; Hans Hinrich Thedens, fiddle, hardanger fiddle; Randi Rosendahl Moland, keyboard; Ronny Yttrehus, guitar; Åsmund Reistad, bass; Ingar Zach, drums, percussion. (All members are from Norway.)

Chateau Neuf (the band's U.S. releases drop the "Spelemannslag" from their name) ironically bill themselves as "Norway's most popular big folk band"—ironic because most Norwegian folk music is played on solo fiddle. Chateau Neuf was formed by students at the University of Oslo to explore Norwegian folk music on "non-traditional" instruments like the guitar, piano, and woodwinds. According to Carl Petter Opsahl, the band's director, "We don't traditionally have bands in Norway, only solo playing—which makes tuning a lot easier! Fiddlers tune their instruments in different ways and if a musician knows many tunings, he is considered to be good. All the tunings have different names, often indicating a certain mood ("the blue tuning," "the light tuning")—about 30 different tunings are known."

Norway's national instrument is the hardanger fiddle, which is similar to a violin, but has four or five extra strings under the fingerboard. They resonate when the instrument is played, and are usually tuned to the key of the melody. The bridge is also flatter, allowing fiddlers to bow two or three stings at once. "The hardanger fiddle is played in the south and west of Norway (Telemark, Hardanger, Voss, and Valdres are the main areas), the ordinary fiddle in all other areas (Gudbrandsdalen, Østerdalen, Trøndelag, and the northern part of Norway)," Opsahl says. "The structure of typical hardanger fiddle tunes [is] short motifs, one or two bars, which are repeated and varied, a so-called additive structure. These tunes give a tonal center, but not any sense of harmonic development. Many of these tunes have a minor feeling, sometimes they can switch from minor to major and sometimes it's hard to tell. Also the tonality can differ from each region and from each fiddler. It has been said that there are no scales in Norwegian folk music, which is not correct, but what *kind* of scale is very complicated. In Chateau Neuf Spelemannslag we try to adapt to the fiddlers, but we mostly play what is comfortable with the tempered instruments. And we don't always mind if it's slightly out of tune."

Chateau Neuf first recorded on the two volumes of *Sweet Sunny North,* the Henry Kaiser/David Lindley investigation of Norwegian folk music, and have since released two albums of their own. While much Norwegian and Swedish folk has a slightly gloomy vibe, Chateau Neuf's sprightly music-making is guaranteed to cure the blues and put a bounce in your step.

what's available: *Stolen Goods* ♫♫♫ (NorthSide, 1998, prod. Roger Valstad) is a dizzying mixture of sprightly female vocals, mellow woodwinds, and bouncy folk/pop melodies. The women singers have a bright, cheery sound that instantly warms the heart; they bring to mind the babes in Värttinä, while the combination of woodwinds and strings gives the backing tracks a big, lush sound. The arrangements sparkle, with every tune sporting a catchy melody, a strong vocal hook, or both.

influences:
◄◄ Kjetil Løndal, Olav Heggland, Anund Roheim

j. poet

Hari Prasad Chaurasia

North Indian classical music
Born 1938, in Allahabad, India. Based in India.

Hari Prasad Chaurasia is a first-generation musician. That's not an easy path in Indian classical music, where son-follow-father

professional expectations are nearly inviolable. *His* father was a professional wrestler, and began training the young Hari to follow in his footsteps. But Chaurasia loved music and began studying in secret with a neighbor. At age 19 he got a job with All-India Radio. He might have been nothing more than a musical journeyman except that he practiced the Indian *bansuri* flute for 12 hours a day, and took the opportunity to learn everything he could when accompanying big-name musicians at their concerts. It wasn't until 1966 that Chaurasia acquired a musical guru. But his single-minded devotion to the bansuri paid off with the release of the groundbreaking *Call of the Valley* in 1967. Not only did it place Chaurasia and collaborator Shiv Kumar Sharma on the musical map, but it also validated the bansuri flute as a legitimate classical instrument. The bansuri is recognized in Indian tradition as Krishna's instrument, but because it is played with the lips it was considered somewhat impure by classical musicians. Chaurasia changed all that and took the bansuri to the next level. With his extraordinary breath control he is able to make the flute do everything from whisper to roar.

what to buy: *Call of the Valley* ♫♫♫♫ (Hemisphere/EMI, 1967, prod. G.N. Joshi) is the closest thing to a "concept album" you'll find in classical Indian music. The five movements of the principal piece tell the story of a day in the life of two lovers in a Kashmiri valley. Hard-core classical music fans were wowed by the new colors that the bansuri, the *santoor* (hammered zither), and the guitar brought to Hindustani music. Non-classical fans appreciated the accessible folk melodies this classically oriented work incorporated, and the direct way the music seemed to tell a story. The album is an ideal introduction to Indian classical music for the new listener, and has long held the interest of connoisseurs as well.

what to buy next: *The Valley Recalls* ♫♫♫♫ (Navras, 1996, prod. Vibhaker Baxi) documents a landmark reunion of Chaurasia and Sharma. Their history-making 1995 concert, recorded at Delhi's Nehru Centre, was originally released as two separate albums. Of the two collected here, particularly impressive is *Peace, Love & Harmony,* a series of *alaaps* and *gats.* The alaap is the slow, meterless, introductory movement of a classical *raga;* the gat is the second, medium-slow movement. Taken as a whole, the CD is perfect for those who prefer a dreamy, meditative type of Indian music. Chaurasia has not been as active as others of his genre in exploring cross-cultural meetings with Western artists, one notable exception being *Making Music* ♫♫♫♫ (ECM, 1987, prod. Manfred Eicher), a successful session that features improvisations with John McLaughlin on acoustic guitar, Jan Garbarek on alto and soprano saxophones, and Zakir Hussain on *tabla* drum.

worth searching for: Well-stocked Indian music stores will carry 50 or more of Chaurasia's releases. Some of the better ones include *Rag Lilit* 𝄞𝄞𝄞𝄞 (Nimbus, 1988), *Maestro's Choice* 𝄞𝄞𝄞𝄞𝄞 (Music Today, 1991), *Raga Darbari Kanada* 𝄞𝄞𝄞𝄞 (Nimbus, 1993), *Live at Shivaji Park* 𝄞𝄞𝄞𝄞 (Navras, 1993), and *Possession* 𝄞𝄞𝄞𝄞 (Pan, 1995).

influences:
◀◀ Panna Lal Ghosh

see also: *Zakir Hussain, Shakti, Shiv Kumar Sharma*

Aaron Howard

Boozoo Chavis

Creole, zydeco
Born Wilson Anthony Chavis, October 23, 1930, in Lake Charles, LA, USA. Based in Lake Charles, LA, USA.

Born and raised in Lake Charles, Louisiana, the son of a tenant farmer, Boozoo Chavis began playing the accordion in his teens. His father played the accordion too, as did a cousin, the legendary Sidney Babineaux. Chavis regularly practiced his craft at his mother's dance hall, where he would sit in with no less a zydeco deity than Clifton Chenier. In 1954 he recorded "Paper in My Shoe," which despite its very raw sound was a major regional hit—and certainly the first zydeco hit. Still, Chavis left music to pursue a more lucrative career as a horse trainer, but began a real comeback in 1984. His style remains raw, funky, and loose. His one- and three-row button accordion playing gets to the heart of a groove, and the band and dancers can't help but follow suit. The always-intense response to Chavis's music is what inspired later luminaries like Beau Jocque and Keith Frank.

what to buy: *Zydeco Trail Ride* 𝄞𝄞𝄞𝄞𝄞 (Maison de Soul, 1989, prod. Floyd Soileau) brings together the best of Boozoo's 45s from the Maison de Soul label. Each of these songs is in its way a classic that almost every zydeco band has in its repertoire, whether they give credit to Chavis or not. Check the Chavis standards like "Motor Dude Special," "Dog Hill," and "Leona Had a Party"; the band locks into a kicking groove and Chavis's no-nonsense accordion and singing charge along on top. There is a cleaned-up version of his "Deacon Jones," which was released in an X-rated version on 45. There's also a remake of Smokey Robinson's "Harlem Shuffle" that's still a very popular line dance in southwest Louisiana. And though the recordings here only hint at what it's like to hear Chavis *in* a dance hall, every one is indispensable.

what to buy next: *The Lake Charles Atomic Bomb* 𝄞𝄞𝄞𝄞 (Rounder, 1990, prod. Eddie Shuler) contains Chavis's early recordings on the Goldband label, and there is little music out there as wild or as raw. Imagine Ornette Coleman's uncle playing zydeco or Captain Beefheart backing up Amédée Ardoin. A

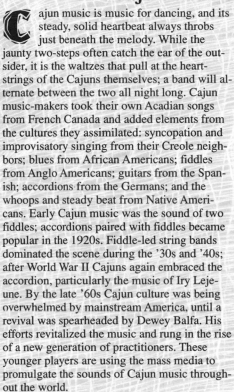

cajun music

ajun music is music for dancing, and its steady, solid heartbeat always throbs just beneath the melody. While the jaunty two-steps often catch the ear of the outsider, it is the waltzes that pull at the heartstrings of the Cajuns themselves; a band will alternate between the two all night long. Cajun music-makers took their own Acadian songs from French Canada and added elements from the cultures they assimilated: syncopation and improvisatory singing from their Creole neighbors; blues from African Americans; fiddles from Anglo Americans; guitars from the Spanish; accordions from the Germans; and the whoops and steady beat from Native Americans. Early Cajun music was the sound of two fiddles; accordions paired with fiddles became popular in the 1920s. Fiddle-led string bands dominated the scene during the '30s and '40s; after World War II Cajuns again embraced the accordion, particularly the music of Iry Lejeune. By the late '60s Cajun culture was being overwhelmed by mainstream America, until a revival was spearheaded by Dewey Balfa. His efforts revitalized the music and rung in the rise of a new generation of practitioners. These younger players are using the mass media to promulgate the sounds of Cajun music throughout the world.

Jared Snyder

version of Chavis's historic hit "Paper in My Shoe" is here, along with much more. Legends abound about the players not knowing the tunes or having had way too much to drink; nevertheless, the music has an unadulterated power like no other. From the alchemical mix of the band's immediate sound and Shuler's strange production techniques emerges something that feels very primitive and very modern at the same time. "Hamburgers and Popcorn" is one of those tracks that just has to be heard to be described.

the rest:
Louisiana Zydeco Music 𝄞𝄞𝄞 (Maison de Soul, 1986)
Boozoo Zydeco 𝄞𝄞𝄞𝄞 (Maison de Soul, 1987)
Live at Richard's 𝄞𝄞𝄞 (Rounder, 1988)

Zydeco Homebrew 🎵🎵🎵 (Maison de Soul, 1988)
Boozoo, That's Who! 🎵🎵🎵🎵 (Rounder, 1993)
Live! at the Habibi Temple 🎵🎵🎵🎵 (Rounder, 1994)
Hey Do Right 🎵🎵🎵🎶 (Discovery, 1997)
Who Stole My Monkey 🎵🎵🎵🎵🎶 (Rounder, 1998)

worth searching for: On *Boozoo Chavis* 🎵🎵🎵🎵 (Elektra/Nonesuch, 1990, prod. Terry Adams) NRBQ's Terry Adams got Chavis to play a bunch of his signature songs, including a magnificent version of the Creole classic "Bernedette." It's indisputable from listening to this music: Chavis can swing, and that's one thing most of his would-be heirs have failed to pick up from him. You can feel it on hard-core Chavis tunes like "Gilton," where the band caresses a beat while Boozoo's accordion just glides on top.

influences:
◀◀ Amédée Ardoin, Alphonse "Bois Sec" Ardoin

▶▶ Keith Frank, Beau Jocque, Geno Delafose

see also: *Clifton Chenier, Beau Jocque*

Jared Snyder

Chayanne
Latin pop, dance-pop, tropical, salsa
Born June 28, 1968, in Puerto Rico. Based in USA.

Chayanne is a once-and-future next-big-thing in the mainland USA, and an elder statesman of Latin dance-pop back home in Puerto Rico—though by no means an elder. He began singing on the radio on his native island at age 10, and racked up a range of music and stage experience throughout his teens on the way to his self-titled debut album in 1988. The "stage" part came in handy for his flourishing parallel career as an actor, at first in Spanish-language *telenovelas* (soap operas) and more recently at the movies, appearing opposite Vanessa Williams in *Dance with Me*. That film and its male lead may have missed something by being too soon for the Stateside "Latin pop" phenomenon that broke out a year later, but the tide is still in and when the next wave comes, Chayanne's musical craft is particularly seaworthy.

what to buy: *Volvera a Nacer* 🎵🎵🎵🎶 (Sony, 1996, prod. Manny Benito) and the Grammy-nominated *Atado a Tu Amor* 🎵🎵🎵🎶 (Sony, 1998, prod. Ronnie Foster) give the best picture of Chayanne's tropical dance blend of pop, rock, and salsa. *Influencias* 🎵🎵🎵 (Sony, 1994, prod. R.E. Martinez) also offers interesting melodies. The soundtrack album *Dance with Me* 🎵🎵🎵 (Sony, 1998, prod. various) puts Chayanne's music in context with that of such Latin-pop peers as Gloria Estefan and Elvis Crespo.

the rest:
Chayanne 🎵🎵🎶 (Sony, 1988)

Tiempo del Vas 🎵🎵🎶 (CBS, 1990)
Provocame 🎵🎵🎶 (CBS, 1992)

influences:
◀◀ Gloria Estefan, Emilio Estefan, Luis Gomez Escolar

see also: *Elvis Crespo, Gloria Estefan*

Kerry Dexter and Adam McGovern

Jie-Bing Chen
Traditional Chinese, contemporary Chinese, jazz
Born in Shanghai, China. Based in USA.

Jie-Bing Chen is a virtuoso player of the *erhu* (sometimes spelled "erh-hu"), a two-stringed, bowed instrument with a small resonation cavity at its base. Dating back over 2,000 years, it's somewhat similar to a violin—which is one reason Chen's been called "the Itzhak Perlman of the Far East"—but is held vertically, with the resonator in the player's lap. Lacking a fingerboard, it allows for considerable intonational expression, which an interpreter of Chen's gifts realizes to the fullest. Chen was a prodigy whose first performance came at age six, and who won two national competitions prior to graduating from the Shanghai Conservatory of Music in 1982. She was noted for incorporating her instrument into a symphonic context. Moving to the United States in 1989 and earning a master's degree in music theory from the State University of New York at Buffalo, she has since involved herself in an even broader range of musical activities than before, including jazz recordings with pianist/composer Jon Jang.

what to buy: Though Chen has recorded more than a dozen albums, most are unavailable in the U.S., but *Spirit on Two Strings, Vol. 1 (Traditional)* 🎵🎵🎵🎵 (Solar/Wind, 1993, prod. Sheng-di Wang), recorded after Chen's move to the States, has distribution here. She's accompanied here by Yang-qin Zhao on *yang-chin*, a multi-stringed, plucked instrument that sounds like a zither. Playing traditionally oriented music ranging from folk melodies to 20th-century compositions, Chen imbues the highly melodic, pentatonic material (having little or no harmonic content) with soulful expressiveness through precise manipulation of her instrument's timbres. Harder to find, *Spirit on Two Strings, Vol. 2 (Contemporary)* 🎵🎵🎵 (Solar/Wind, 1993, prod. Sheng-di Wang) also pairs her with Zhao on yang-chin.

what to buy next: *Tabula Rasa* 🎵🎵🎵 (Water Lily Acoustics, 1996, prod. Kavichandran Alexander) is a collaborative album by Chen, *mohan vina* (Indian guitar) player V.M. Bhatt, and banjo star Bela Fleck, with the rest of the band including P. Srinivasan (*mridangam* drum), S. Shankar (violin), and R. Majumdar (*bansuri* flute). As if the multi-culti intent weren't clear enough just from the lineup, the album's dedicated to Ravi Shankar and Earl Scruggs.

worth searching for: Jon Jang's *Two Flowers on a Stem* ♫♫♫♫ (Soul Note, 1996, prod. Jon Jang) is a masterful fusion of jazz and traditional Chinese music that puts Chen into a jazz group with the leader on piano, James Newton on flute, David Murray on tenor sax and bass clarinet, Santi Debriano on bass, and Jabali Billy Hart on drums. There is traditional Chinese material (the famous "Butterfly Lovers Song"), a famous jazz tune by Charles Mingus ("Meditations on Integration"), and Jang's highly creative original material.

influences:

◀◀ A-Bing, Zhong-yue Wei, Wen-ming Sun

see also: *V.M. Bhatt, Jon Jang*

Steve Holtje

Sisi Chen

Yangqin (Chinese hammered dulcimer)
Born in China. Based in Chicago, IL, USA.

Sisi Chen began studying the *yangqin,* a.k.a. yang-chin (Chinese hammered dulcimer), when she was 10. The yangqin has been a part of Chinese music for about 500 years as both a supporting and solo instrument, and Chen brings out all of its richness in her performance.

what's available: On *Tides and Sand* ♫♫♫♫ (Henry Street, 1996, prod. Peter K. Siegel) Chen interweaves traditional melodies and her own embellishments into a marvelously evocative work, with strong echoes of nature.

influences:

◀◀ Chinese tradition

Pamela Murray Winters

C.J. Chenier

Zydeco
Born September 28, 1957, in Port Arthur, TX, USA. Based in Lafayette, LA, USA.

C.J. Chenier's father, the legendary Clifton Chenier, was based in Lafayette, Louisiana, and toured constantly. The younger Chenier was able to see his father only a couple times a year. Growing up in Texas, he rarely heard zydeco, let alone Clifton's music. Instead, he studied piano and alto saxophone and took an interest in jazz and R&B. His favorites at this time included Miles Davis, John Coltrane, James Brown, and the Commodores. He eventually earned a music scholarship to Texas Southern University. In 1978 his father called him to play saxophone. The experience was a jolt: Chenier wasn't familiar with the beat and didn't know any of the songs. By the early 1980s C.J. began to learn accordion from a then-ailing Clifton, who, it was clear by then, could

not continue to tour much longer. He had to sit down to perform, and often left it to son C.J. to finish the show. When the senior Chenier died in 1987 C.J. took over the band and has come into his own as an accordionist, singer, and all-round performer. He continues as a fitting standard-bearer of his father's and Creole music's legacy—which to many are synonymous.

what to buy: The version of the Red Hot Zydeco band on *My Baby Don't Wear No Shoes* ♫♫♫♫ (Arhoolie, 1988, prod. Chris Strachwitz, C.J. Chenier) still featured Clifton's brother Cleveland on *frattoir* (rubboard), and there is a feel throughout the record of the torch being passed to the next generation. That doesn't get in the way of excellent zydeco music, though, for there's a moving reading of Clifton's "I'm Comin' Home" here, a song he often performed at the end of his life with tears in his eyes.

what to buy next: Slash Records was the home of the Blasters and Los Lobos, and *Hot Rod* ♫♫♫♫ (Slash, 1990, prod. C.J. Chenier) was their effort to branch out into zydeco music. On an excellent recording that just failed to cross into the mainstream market, Roy Carrier replaces Cleveland Chenier on frattoir, but the band doesn't miss a beat, while C.J.'s accordion playing continues to blossom.

the rest:
I Ain't No Playboy ♫♫♫ (Slash, 1992)
Too Much Fun ♫♫♫ (Alligator, 1995)
Big Squeeze ♫♫♫ (Alligator, 1996)

influences:

◀◀ Rockin' Dopsie, Clifton Chenier, Buckwheat Zydeco

▶▶ Nathan Williams, John Delafose, Lynn August

see also: *Roy Carrier, Clifton Chenier, Steve Riley & the Mamou Playboys*

Jared Snyder

Clifton Chenier

Zydeco, blues
Born June 25, 1925, in Opelousas, LA, USA. Died December 12, 1987, in Lafayette, LA, USA.

Clifton Chenier took a backwoods form of Cajun folk music called *zodico,* hyped it up with elements of jump blues, R&B, and early rock 'n' roll, and created what we know today as zydeco. A versatile musician as well as a gifted interpreter, Chenier was proficient on guitar and harmonica, but his lasting fame came via the accordion, an instrument he rescued from perpetual ridicule and made cool once again. Besides being a prolific writer of his own music, Chenier was the ultimate stylist; he could take a song from any genre, recast it with French patois, Creole, or English lyrics, and transform it into a foot-stomping Mardi Gras party jam. Chenier cut his first sides for the Elko label in 1954, but his first burst of national fame came at Specialty Records the following year. While "Ay-Te Te Fee" and "Boppin' the Rock" featured Chenier's stinging guitar work and achieved respectable chart positions, Specialty was putting all its efforts into the burgeoning rock 'n' roll scene and, as a result, Chenier's work was lost in the shuffle. He label-hopped for a few years, cutting excellent tracks for Argo, Checker, Zynn, and Crazy Cajun among others. In 1960 Chenier signed with Arhoolie (though he also leased material to the Bayou, Home Cooking, Blue Star, GNP/Crescendo, and Caillier labels), where he recorded his greatest, most influential body of work and established a base for his growing cult appeal. Along with "Louisiana Stomp" and "Squeeze Box Boogie," he scored dozens of regional hits with his danceable hybrid music and toured constantly, playing folk festivals and R&B revues and opening for rock acts both at home and abroad. In later years diabetes forced the partial amputation of his right foot and sapped his energies, but despite his illness, he is said never to have given a bad show. In his last years Chenier recorded quality sides for Maison de Soul and Alligator, his debut for the latter winning him a Grammy award. Chenier died just as the music he pioneered achieved true national prominence, but he remains the undisputed King of Zydeco.

what to buy: Chenier's best sides for Specialty, Argo, Elko, Bayou, Arhoolie, and Maison de Soul have been collected on *Zydeco Dynamite: The Clifton Chenier Anthology* ???? (Rhino, 1993, compilation prod. James Austin, Greg Durst), an amazing 40-track, two-disc set with a fine, informative booklet to boot. Nearly all facets of Chenier's remarkable talent are joyously on display here, and this batch is guaranteed to drive away the baddest hoodoo and bring on good times galore.

what to buy next: The cream of Chenier's Arhoolie work is deftly compiled on three sensational discs: *60 Minutes with the King of Zydeco* ???? (Arhoolie, 1988, prod. Chris Strachwitz) collects his finest house-rockin' sides from the mid-'60s through the late '70s; *Louisiana Blues & Zydeco* ???? (Arhoolie, 1965/1991, prod. Chris Strachwitz) gives equal space to the traditional sounds of zydeco and gut-bucket blues, at which Chenier was also a master; and *Sings the Blues* ???? (Arhoolie, 1992, prod. Roy C. Ames, Chris Strachwitz) is a potent two-LPs-on-one-disc collection featuring the title album from 1969 and *Clifton Chenier & His Red Hot Louisiana Band* from 1977. All three collections are as tasty and satisfying as pepper gravy on rice. Mon Dieu!

what to avoid: Chenier does not sing with Rockin' Dopsie on *Clifton Chenier & Rockin' Dopsie* ??? (Paula, 1992, prod. various), so for the price of this two-disc set, you could easily purchase fuller, more satisfying packages by either artist.

the rest:
Zydeco Sont Pas Sale ???? (Arhoolie, 1964/1997)
Black Snake Blues ???? (Arhoolie, 1966/1994)
King of the Bayous ???? (Arhoolie, 1970/1993)
Live at Saint Marks ??? (Arhoolie, 1971/1988)
Out West ???? (Arhoolie, 1974/1991)
Bogalusa Boogie ???? (Arhoolie, 1975/1993)
The King of Zydeco Live at Montreux ???? (Arhoolie, 1975/1991)
And His Red Hot Louisiana Band in New Orleans ??? (GNP, 1979/Crescendo, 1990)
Frenchin' the Boogie ???? (Verve, 1979/1994)
Classic Clifton ???? (Arhoolie, 1980/1993)
Bon Ton Roulet ???? (Arhoolie, 1981/1991)
I'm Here ???? (Alligator, 1982/1993)
Country Boy Now Grammy Award Winner ??? (Maison de Soul, 1984/1989)
Live ??? (Arhoolie, 1985/1993)
Live at the Long Beach & San Francisco Blues Festivals ??? (Arhoolie, 1985/1993)
Boogie & Zydeco ??? (Maison de Soul, 1987/1994)
On Tour ?? (EPM, 1989/1996)
Zydeco Legend ??? (Maison de Soul, 1989/1993)
Zodico Blues & Boogie ???? (Specialty, 1993)
We're Gonna Party ??? (Collectables, 1994)
I'm Coming Home ??? (Magnum America, 1996)

worth searching for: Hit the import racks for *Bayou Soul: The Crazy Cajun Recordings* ???? (Edsel, 1999, prod. Huey P. Meaux), an unusually strong mix of R&B and foot-stompin' zydeco recorded with the legendary producer Huey P. Meaux. Also, Chenier can be seen performing live on *King of Zydeco* (Arhoolie Video, 1995), a videotaping of a concert from late in his career.

influences:
◀◀ Amédée Ardoin, Izeb Laza, Professor Longhair, Louis Jordan, Lowell Fulson

▶▶ C.J. Chenier, Buckwheat Zydeco, Rockin' Sydney, Lonnie Brooks, the Zydeco Hurricanes

see also: *C.J. Chenier, Canray Fontenot, Rockin' Dopsie*

Ken Burke

Cherish the Ladies
Celtic
Formed 1983, in New York, NY, USA. Based in USA.

Joanie Madden, flute, whistle, vocals; Cathie Ryan, vocals, bodhrán; Aoife Clancy, vocals, guitar; Siobhan Egan, fiddle, whistle, bodhrán; Maureen Doherty Macken, button accordion, flute, whistle; Mary Coogan, guitar, tenor banjo, mandolin; Mary Rafferty, button accordion, flute, whistle; Donna Long, piano, fiddle, vocals.

The original idea behind Cherish the Ladies was simple: a series of concerts highlighting the contributions of women to Irish music in America. In 1983 folklorist and musician Mick Moloney had a brainstorming session with the directors of New York's Ethnic Folk Arts Center, Martin Koenig and Ethel Raim. Moloney drew their attention to the extraordinary number of young American women involved in Irish traditional music, and the three organizers created a concert series featuring some of these women. The resulting performances left audiences and critics roaring their approval. In 1985 Moloney convinced the National Endowment for the Arts (NEA) to fund an album, *Cherish the Ladies*. Like the concerts, it featured instrumental soloists with a few duos and trios, plus singing in the Irish language. Like the concerts, it included more than a dozen women, two of whom (flute player Joanie Madden and guitarist Mary Coogan) are still a part of the Cherish the Ladies band today. Like the concerts, the LP was a tremendous success, chosen by the Library of Congress as one of the best folk albums of 1985. The NEA knew a good thing when they saw it and decided to sponsor a Cherish the Ladies tour. The paring down of dozens of musicians and singers to a manageably sized touring ensemble was a big step in the group's evolution. The first lineup included Madden, Coogan, and Maureen Doherty Macken, as well as singer Cathie Ryan and fiddlers Siobhan Egan and Eileen Ivers. The group has been through a few more personnel changes since. First, Ivers was replaced by Winifred Horan. Eventually, Horan, too, left the band, as did Doherty Macken and Ryan; the three were replaced by Donna Long, Mary Rafferty, and Aoife Clancy, respectively. Despite the changes, though, their commitment to high-quality music and high-energy fun has never wavered.

what to buy: Cherish the Ladies' sound has never been more confident than it is on *Now Day Dawning* 🎵🎵🎵🎵 (Green Linnet, 1996, prod. Johnny Cunningham). The lineup changes that ensued between their second disc and this one resulted in no missteps, just a new repertoire of material and a renewed sense of direction. Strong playing from all the lead instrumentalists is matched by a newfound power in the accompaniments; Donna Long's piano fills out the sound beautifully, and Aoife Clancy's guitar playing leaves Mary Coogan freer to play banjo and mandolin without hurting the bottom end. She rises to the occasion marvelously on a set of polkas learned from her father. Clancy's polished voice interprets several lovely traditionals and a few other numbers by such songwriters as Dougie MacLean, Pete St. John, and even Robert Burns. The result is as fresh and appealing a set as you're likely to find in Irish music.

what to buy next: *The Back Door* 🎵🎵🎵 (Green Linnet, 1992, prod. Mick Moloney), recorded after the ensemble's establishment as an ongoing band, demonstrated the new group ethic and established the outfit as a major presence on the American Irish music scene. It features an excellent selection of instrumentals and songs, played with finesse on flute, fiddle, and accordion (with the occasional whistle or banjo), accompanied always by Mary Coogan's expert guitar and often by Cathie Ryan's *bodhrán* (Irish frame drum). The sources Ryan looked to for the songs she sings—Jimmy Crowley, Joe Heaney, Frank Harte—indicate her impeccable taste, while her one original—the title track itself—indicates her own songwriting talent. Her lovely, clear voice ensures a real treat for the listener; her vocals are sincere and expressive, and the spirit of the song always comes through. The second album, *Out and About* 🎵🎵🎵 (Green Linnet, 1993, prod. Johnny Cunningham), contains material near and dear to the group's heart: a polka and several waltzes written in a French style commemorate a trip to Brittany. Ryan's second song about Irish emigration, "Missing Pieces," shows that the sincerity and depth of feeling in her songwriting has continued to grow. This was the last album before the major lineup change. Finally, if solos and duets, rather than a full band sound, appeal to you, you'd appreciate *Cherish the Ladies* 🎵🎵🎵 (Shanachie, 1985, prod. Mick Moloney), featuring Madden, Maureen Doherty, Mary Coogan, Eileen Ivers, Liz Carroll, and others. Nicely played instrumentals, plus a few songs; note that only a few of these artists wound up in the band version of Cherish the Ladies.

the rest:
One and All: The Best of Cherish the Ladies 🎵🎵🎵🎵 (Green Linnet, 1998)
Threads of Time 🎵🎵🎵 (BMG/RCA Victor, 1998)
At Home N/A (RCA Victor, 1999)

influences:
◀ Mick Moloney, Liz Carroll

▶ Solas

see also: *Liz Carroll, Eileen Ivers, Joanie Madden, Mick Moloney, Cathie Ryan, Solas, Paul Winter*

Steve Winick

The Chieftains

Irish traditional
Formed 1963, in Dublin, Ireland. Based in Dublin, Ireland.

Paddy Moloney, uilleann pipes, tin whistle, bodhrán; Martin Fay, fiddle, bones; Sean Potts, tin whistle, bones, bodhrán (1963–79); Michael Tubridy, flute, tin whistle, concertina (1963–79); Dave Fallon, bodhrán (1963–64); Peadar Mercier, bodhrán, bones, vocals (1966–75); Sean Keane, fiddle, tin whistle (1968–present); Derek Bell, harp, tiompán (hammered dulcimer), keyboards, oboe (1973–present); Kevin Conneff, vocals, bodhrán, (1976–present); Matt Molloy, flute, tin whistle (1979–present). (All members are from Ireland.)

The Chieftains are without a doubt the single most important group to come out of Ireland: more important than the Clancy Brothers and Tommy Makem, and more important than U2.

Their impact on people's awareness—and perception—of Irish music has been incalculable. Over decades of playing together, their carefully honed blend of fiddle, flute, whistle, and harp, propelled by Paddy Moloney's signature sound on the uilleann pipes and fueled by numerous high-profile, boundary-crossing collaborations, has made them a household name in many corners of the globe.

As the best-known Irish act in the music business, whose friends and admirers—and collaborators—range from Paul McCartney, Mick Jagger, and Roger Daltrey to Chet Atkins, Willie Nelson, and Jackson Brown, the Chieftains have no peers. While pursuing a hectic musical career whose modest beginnings date back to 1963, they have incidentally done more to boost Irish tourism than most government agencies in Dublin. They also brought Breton (French Celtic) music to the attention of Irish audiences very early on, often sneaking in a few Scottish, Welsh, and Manx items too. Later, they devoted entire albums to Breton and Galician (Spanish Celtic) music.

Moloney, Fay, Tubridy, and Potts had all served in Ceoltoiri Chualann, the innovative ensemble led by visionary Irish composer and folk-tradition revivalist Sean Ó Riada, before forming their own group to record *The Chieftains* (1963), which was planned as a one-off album for fledgling Irish traditional label Claddagh. Indeed they continued to play and record with Ó Riada's group on and off throughout the '60s, as well as gigging around Ireland under their own heading as their day jobs permitted. Along the way, Mercier and Keane also made the transition from Ceoltoiri to Chieftains. Even this early on, it was clear that piper Moloney, who won his first All Ireland title for his instrument in 1952 at the age of 14, was the engine driving the group: he did the lion's share of the arranging and handled the booking and accounts. He also ended up running Claddagh Records, the label that helped put the band of the map. Today it is largely his energy, ambition, and focus—not to mention savvy marketing skills and keen eye for publicity opportunities—that have ensured the band's seldom-matched survival over three-and-a-half decades, though perhaps even he couldn't have foreseen it during the six years it took the Chieftains to issue a second album.

The band went back into the recording studio in 1969, and again in 1971, gradually hitting their stride and getting noticed by the public-at-large in Ireland. As they unknowingly climbed the stairs of fame and fortune, they were hardly typical star material: a bunch of family men in suits and ties, most of whom had learned their craft back in the '50s and looked like they had day jobs in banking, accountancy, engineering, and architecture—which they did! Along the way, they fleshed out their sound by seducing harper Derek Bell away from the stability of the BBC's Northern Ireland Orchestra. A series of excellent releases thrust them into the front ranks of Irish traditional music, and they sur-

prised everybody, including themselves, by selling out London's Royal Albert Hall on St. Patrick's Day, 1975. And so, after five albums and a dozen years of playing together more for fun than profit, the Chieftains turned professional. Film director Stanley Kubrick then hired them to contribute "Mná na hÉireann (Women of Ireland)"—which dated back to their Ó Riada days—as the love theme for the soundtrack of *Barry Lyndon,* which helped open doors in the USA. It wouldn't be too long before it was Carnegie Hall they played on St. Patrick's Day.

Ireland is a nation of begrudgers, and while the natives can be very supportive of struggling artists trying to make it big at home, once that happens and acts start to get accolades abroad, a certain cynicism invariably sets in. The level of success earned by the Chieftains outside Ireland, like that later enjoyed by U2, Clannad, Enya, and *Riverdance,* is often assumed by some elements to be a sure sign of having "sold out." One person who felt that way about the Chieftains in the mid-'70s was Dublin singer and *bodhrán* (Irish frame drum) player Kevin Conneff. An invitation to partake in the recording of *Bonaparte's Retreat* in 1976—with its attendant opportunity to actually sit down and listen to the band—forced Conneff to reevaluate. He subsequently became the group's only full-time vocalist, and found out firsthand what it meant to "sell out" as a member of one of the most successful traditional acts in the world. Matt Molloy (ex–Bothy Band) joined in 1979 to replace the flute of departing Michael Tubridy, and the band's lineup has not changed in the 20 years since.

The '80s saw the Chieftains scale back their recording schedule and spend more time on the tour circuit. Commissions for film scores came Moloney's way, which led to several albums of Irish-inspired music for the group with orchestra. In 1983 the Chieftains pulled off an amazing coup in the midst of the cold war by touring China and playing alongside local musicians. Parts of this extraordinary expedition were documented on album and video. By mid-decade—well before the *Riverdance* craze—they were livening up their concerts with dancing, most notably thanks to the abundant talents of the flamboyant Irish-American champion dancer Michael Flatley, who would come to know a thing or two about said phenomenon.

In 1987 the band issued *Celtic Wedding,* an entire album of Breton music—selected with the help of folklorist Polig Monjarret (a longtime friend of Moloney's), but recorded in their own inimitable style—as well as the first of two releases teaming them with Belfast-born classical flute maestro James Galway. A highly anticipated collaboration with another son of Belfast, Van Morrison, followed soon after in the form of *Irish Heartbeat,* while a fourth Belfast-related project, *The Celtic Harp—A Tribute to Edward Bunting,* recorded with Janet Harbison's Belfast Harp Orchestra in 1992, was inspired by the bicentenary of the historic 1792 Harp Festival in that city.

Paddy Molonoy of the Chieftains

The '90s have seen the Chieftains stretch even further, into projects that involve American country music stars and British rock icons, with predictably mixed results. More interestingly, they took another young and then-unknown Irish-American dancer named Jean Butler on tour with them (the one who, along with Flatley, would later take the world by storm in *Riverdance*), and they championed Canadian wildman Ashely MacIsaac, whose occasionally unorthodox Cape Breton fiddle and dance routines turned quite a few heads among the more traditional-minded at the time, though he is acquiring respectability as a modern master today.

The spirit of adventure they encouraged in others has continued in their own work. With the help of many coconspirators, the Chieftains tackled the music of Galicia in Spain—and the Galician diaspora in Cuba and the U.S—on *Santiago* (1996), with Linda Ronstadt (a mainstream brand name but no stranger to other Latin-influenced musics) acquitting herself quite nicely. The soundtrack to *Long Journey Home* (1998), a PBS documentary series that attempts to chart the convoluted history of Irish emigrants to the U.S. over 250-plus years, also works, though the group took a back seat to such guests as Van Morrison, Mary Black, Sinéad O'Connor, Vince Gill, Mick Moloney, Eileen Ivers, Elvis Costello, and the choral group Anúna. Oddly, the Chieftains are not credited on the cover of *Fire in the Kitchen* (1998), a collection of tracks showcasing Canadian Celtic performers, though their presence is quite noticeable. *Tears of Stone* (1999) is an album of mostly Irish love songs (from a female perspective) whose all-star cast includes singers Bonnie Raitt, Natalie Merchant, Joni Mitchell, the Rankins, the Corrs, Sissel, Akiko Yano, Sinéad O'Connor, Mary Chapin Carpenter, Loreena McKennitt, Joan Osborne, and Diana Krall, as well as fiddlers Máire Breatnach, Eileen Ivers, Natalie McMaster, and Annbjørg Lien. The album has much greater coherence than the rock-star-themed *The Long Black Veil* from a few years earlier. To expand on all these explorations, in the late '90s Moloney founded the high-profile world-music label Wicklow to promote an even wider range of international styles than the Chieftains have approached themselves.

As the century draws to a close one indisputable fact remains: the stature of diminutive Paddy Moloney and the group he shepherded through so many changes in musical fashion—not to mention the stature of Irish music in general—has never been higher worldwide. The carefully rehearsed spontaneity which now so often characterizes the Chieftains' live shows masks the fact that this is a group of consummate professionals, with all the baggage that brings with it. Those who complain about the Chieftains' recent propensity for all-star albums (with guests both appropriate and otherwise) should bear in mind that the band has more than paid its dues, and the public

is still free to listen to their early gems—or any other traditional music for that matter. Highly successful middle-aged musicians who spend much of their working lives on arduous world tours tend to have lifestyles somewhat removed from the bubbling cauldron of inspired sessions that first spewed them forth, and this is certainly true for several members of the Chieftains. Cutting-edge music naturally emerges from younger players—but many of these, and no doubt others yet to arise, are still inspired by the examples set by the Chieftains.

what to buy: *Chieftains 3* 𝄢𝄢𝄢𝄢𝄢 (Claddagh, 1971/Shanachie, 1980s, prod. Ioan Allen) and *Chieftains 4* 𝄢𝄢𝄢𝄢𝄢 (Claddagh, 1973/Shanachie, 1980s, prod. Paddy Moloney), along with the first Planxty album from the same era, are defining moments in Irish traditional music as heard by the record-buying public, and were destined to have enormous influence on a whole generation of young players. Virtually every tune on these two great albums—and many of the arrangements too—became standards soon after they were unleashed on the masses. Not that "Carolan's Concerto," "March of the King of Laois," "Lord Inchiquin," "Drowsy Maggie," "The Morning Dew," or Sean Ó Riada's "Carrigfergus" and "Mná na hÉireann (Women of Ireland)" were exactly obscure to begin with; many of them were already firm favorites from Moloney and friends' days with Ceolteoiri Chualann. *Chieftains 4* was Derek Bell's first outing with the group, and the addition of his harp was most welcome. *Chieftains 5* 𝄢𝄢𝄢𝄢𝄥 (Claddagh, 1975/Shanachie, 1987, prod. Paddy Moloney) and the oddly titled *Bonaparte's Retreat* 𝄢𝄢𝄢𝄢𝄥 (Claddagh, 1976/Shanachie, 1987, prod. Paddy Moloney) are close behind their two illustrious predecessors. The inclusion of a set of Breton tunes on the former is noteworthy, as is the 15-minute title track on the latter that features a very young Dolores Keane as guest vocalist. *Bonaparte's* closing "Round the House and Mind the Dresser" also includes future Chieftain Kevin Conneff on vocals, and live dancers stomping their stuff alongside the musicians.

what to buy next: Many first encounter the Chieftains via one of their numerous all-star collaborations, and while none of these is worth selling your grandmother for (despite the occasional Grammy that has come their way), each has its moments. *The Long Black Veil* 𝄢𝄢𝄢 (RCA/BMG, 1995, prod. Paddy Moloney) gained the group more attention and a wider audience than their previous albums, which was probably the main idea. However, it's clearly more a showcase for Famous People Paddy Moloney Knows than a real album: Sting sounds ridiculous (and uncomfortable, in both Irish *and* English) on the opening "Mo Ghile Mear" (arrangement borrowed from Peadar Ó Riada?); Mark Knopfler and Ry Cooder are definitely out of place (and arguably out of their depth) here; and the half-hearted attempt at a studio marriage of the Chieftains with old pals the Rolling Stones on "Rocky Road to Dublin" is just laughable. On the upside, Van Morrison's "Have I Told You Lately?" is good; the title track sounds like it was written for singer Mick Jagger; and Sinéad O'Connor does a credible job on "The Foggy Dew." The much-vaunted *Irish Heartbeat* ♫♫♫♪ (Mercury, 1988, prod. Van Morrison, Paddy Moloney) sees the band unite with Morrison for a partially satisfying album of (mostly) standards. Morrison's stamp on the material is unmistakable, his coproduction coming through loud and clear. *Another Country* ♫♫♫ (RCA/BMG, 1992, prod. Paddy Moloney) delivers rather less than its stellar lineup (Ricky Skaggs, Emmylou Harris, Willie Nelson, et al.) promises, but Sean Keane's laconic take on Elvis Presley's "Heartbreak Hotel" is worth hearing. Featuring dancer Jean Butler, *An Irish Evening—Live at the Grand Opera House Belfast* ♫♫♫♪ (RCA/BMG, 1992, prod. Paddy Moloney) is a bit more spirited. Roger Daltrey's "Behind Blue Eyes" almost works, and Nanci Griffith is acceptable if a little coy.

the rest:

Chieftains 1 ♫♫♫♫ (Claddagh, 1963/Shanachie, 1988)
Chieftains 2 ♫♫♫♫ (Claddagh, 1969/Shanachie, 1988)
Chieftains Live! ♫♫♫ (Claddagh, 1976/Shanachie, 1988)
Chieftains 7 ♫♫♫ (Claddagh, 1977/Columbia, 1978)
Chieftains 8 ♫♫♫♪ (Claddagh, 1978/Columbia, 1979)
Chieftains 9—Boil the Breakfast Early ♫♫♫ (Claddagh, 1979)
Chieftains 10—Cotton-Eyed Joe ♫♫♫♪ (Claddagh, 1981/Shanachie, 1991)
The Year of the Frenchies ♫♫♫ (Claddagh, 1982/Shanachie)
The Chieftains in China ♫♫♫ (Claddagh, 1985/Shanachie, 1985)
Ballad of the Irish Horse ♫♫♫♪ (Claddagh, 1986/Shanachie, 1986)
Celtic Wedding ♫♫♫♪ (RCA/BMG, 1987)
(With James Galway) *In Ireland* ♫♫♫♪ (RCA/BMG, 1987)
A Chieftains Celebration ♫♫♫ (RCA/BMG, 1989)
(With James Galway) *Over the Sea to Skye* ♫♫♫♪ (RCA/BMG, 1990)
The Bells of Dublin ♫♫♫♫ (RCA/BMG, 1991)
Reel Music—The Filmscores ♫♫♪ (RCA/BMG, 1991)
The Best of the Chieftains ♫♫♫♪ (Columbia, 1992)
The Celtic Harp—A Tribute to Edward Bunting ♫♫♫♫ (RCA/BMG, 1993)
Film Cuts ♫♫♪ (RCA/BMG, 1995)
Santiago ♫♫♫♪ (RCA/BMG, 1996)
Long Journey Home ♫♫♫♪ (Unisphere/BMG, 1998)
Fire in the Kitchen ♫♫♫♪ (RCA/BMG, 1998)
Tears of Stone ♫♫♫♪ (RCA/BMG, 1999)

worth searching for: Both *Ó Riada sa Gaiety* ♫♫♫♫ (Gael-Linn, 1969) and *Ó Riada* ♫♫♫♫ (Gael-Linn, 1972) by Sean Ó Riada and Ceoltoiri Chualann feature Moloney, Fay, Potts, Tubridy, and Mercier on live recordings of material subsequently popularized by the Chieftains. For another slice of musical history, try Van Morrison, Sinéad O'Connor and the Chieftains on a severely under-rehearsed live take of "Have I Told You Lately?" from *Live on Letterman* ♫♫♫ (Reprise, 1997). After one verse, Van hands the song over to Sinéad, who apparently didn't know all of the words! Moloney and friends manage to hold it all together.

influences:

◀◀ Sean Ó Riada, Ceoltoiri Chualann, Turlough O'Carolan, Peadar Ó Riada, Alan Stivell, Polig Monjarret, Milladoiro

▶▶ Planxty, Horslips, Alan Stivell, Whistlebinkies, Altan, Cherish the Ladies, Milladoiro, Craobh Rua, Moving Cloud

see also: *Derek Bell, Bothy Band, Ry Cooder, James Galway, Dolores Keane, James Keane, Matt Molloy, Sinéad O'Connor, Sean Ó Riada, Planxty, Linda Ronstadt, Alan Stivell*

John C. Falstaff

Toni Childs

Folk, blues, worldbeat
Born 1958, in Orange, CA, USA. Based in USA.

Singer-songwriter Toni Childs grew up in small towns all over the U.S.; her parents, missionaries for the Assemblies of God, moved the family on a regular basis, preaching their beliefs to as many as possible—and not letting much popular culture into the household. It's no wonder Toni became a bit rebellious. After spending three months in prison on a drug charge Childs moved first to London, then to Los Angeles, where she met David Ricketts of David + David. *Union* chronicles Childs and Ricketts's broken romance, and examines the broader issues of love. After a slight letdown on the follow-up, *House of Hope*, Childs offered *The Woman's Boat*, a concept album that takes the listener on a spiritual journey through life from a woman's point of view, all done in Childs's unique style of rock and world music. The album features guest appearances by Peter Gabriel, Karl Wallinger of World Party, Robert Fripp, and the late master of Pakistan's devotional *qawwali* music, Nusrat Fateh Ali Khan.

what to buy: Childs's seamless fusion of blues, folk, pop, and world music on *Union* ♫♫♫♫ (A&M, 1988, prod. David Tickle, David Ricketts) is an amazing achievement, featuring such memorable tunes as "Don't Walk Away," "Hush," and "Let the Rain Come Down."

the rest:
House of Hope ♫♫♫ (A&M, 1991)
The Woman's Boat ♫♫♫♪ (DGC, 1994)

influences:
◀◀ Peter Gabriel, Joni Mitchell, David + David

Joshua Zarov

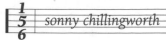
Sonny Chillingworth
Slack-key guitar
Born July 14, 1932, in Oahu, Hawaii (now USA). Died August 24, 1994.

Along with Gabby Pahinui, Sonny Chillingworth is considered one of the greats of Hawaiian slack-key guitar, a style named for its retuning (or "slacking") of the guitar's strings. Fittingly for multicultural Hawaii, the slack-key style is influenced by the music of many different cultures, most importantly that of Mexico and Portugal. Chillingworth, who counted English, Irish, and Hawaiian among his ancestry, fits easily into this melting-pot tradition. He was also part of the Purdys, one of the great *paniolo* (Hawaiian cowboy) families, and his music drew strongly on that tradition during his four-decade career. He made his first recordings around 1954, and performed with such artists as Gabby Pahinui and the Sons of Hawaii. Chillingworth was so highly regarded in his homeland that he was given the Bank of Hawai'i's Na Hoku Lifetime Award for Slack-Key Guitar in 1992. He played on more than 30 albums, but made his only solo-guitar recordings shortly before his death in 1994.

what to buy: *Sonny Solo* ♪♪♪♪ (Dancing Cat, 1994, prod. George Winston), released just months before Chillingworth's death, was many people's introduction to his music and to slack-key guitar. Chillingworth's voice imbues the love ballads and paniolo songs with all his 60-plus years of experience, and his smoothly flowing picking is both beautiful and deceptively simple.

what to avoid: The poor sound quality on *Sonny* ♪♪♥ (Mahalo, 1995, compilation prod. John Aeto) sometimes lends Chillingworth's voice an otherworldly tone that's not unpleasant, but this posthumously released compilation hardly gives Sonny's talent its due.

the rest:
Waimea Cowboy ♪♪♪ (Lehua, 1998)
Endlessly ♪♪♪♪ (BMG/Windham Hill/Dancing Cat, 1999)

influences:
◀◀ Aunty Vickie I'i Rodrigues, Gabby Pahinui

▶▶ Ozzie Kotani, the Kahumoku Brothers, Rev. Dennis Kamakahi

see also: *Gabby Pahinui*

Brian Mansfield

Chirgilchin
Throat singing/overtone singing/höömeï
Formed 1996, in Tuva. Based in Tuva.

Ondar Mongun-ool, vocals, morin-khuur, doshpulur (plucked lute), chantzy (three-stringed fiddle); Aidysmaa Kandan, vocals, tungur (shaman's drum); Tamdyn Aldar, vocal, igil (two-stringed horse-hair fiddle). (All members are from Tuva.)

Formed in the wake of a minor "throat-singing" craze in world-music circles that began in the early 1990s and was galvanized by the group Huun-Huur-Tu, Chirgilchin are a young band of throat-singers from the tiny Central Asian steppe land of Tuva, an isolated region controlled by the Soviet Union prior to that government's collapse. Throat-singing, also known as "overtone" singing or *höömeï*, is an amazing vocal technique employed by Asian peoples in regions such as Mongolia, Tibet, and Tuva. By carefully forming the mouth and tongue into certain configurations, throat-singers are able to produce two or more tones at one time, sounding out what is in essence an entire chord without instrumental aid. The result ranges from low abdominal growls to high, clear, whistling overtones with an exhilarating, disembodied quality. Chirgilchin's first CD, *The Wolf and the Kid,* assisted by Huun-Huur-Tu member Alexander Bapa on guitar and production duties, is a promising debut, but whether it turns out to be a one-time artifact of the throat-singing fad remains to be seen.

what's available: The only Chirgilchin recording to date, *The Wolf and the Kid* ♪♪♪♪ (Shanachie, 1996, prod. Alexander Bapa), embodies the simple animist spirit and love of the natural world that make Tuvan music so appealing. "Teve-Khaya (Camel Rock)" and "Kara Duruya (Black Crane)," like many Tuvan songs, express love for a special place in the landscape or reverence for the domestic and wild creatures that are still an important part of Tuvan life. Some tracks, like "Darlaashkkyn (Freedom Song)," with its minimalist, staccato string backing, or the eponymous "Chirgilchin (Mirage)," with an unusual chanted vocal, have a slightly modern flavor, while others, like "Majalykta chylgymny (Lyric Song)," have a folk-song melodic structure that seems to date from the Soviet era.

influences:
◀◀ Huun-Huur-Tu, Russian folk music

see also: *Huun-Huur-Tu*

Jeffrey Muhr

Stella Chiweshe
Mbira
Born c. 1946, near Harare, Zimbabwe. Based in Harare, Zimbabwe and Berlin, Germany.

Stella Chiweshe plays the *mbira* (thumb piano), an instrument that has deep spiritual and cultural meaning for the Shona people of Zimbabwe. When Chiweshe was born, Zimbabwe was still under British colonial rule and called Rhodesia. Colonial authorities, with the aid of Christian missionaries, had banned the mbira, and people who played it publicly were persecuted. Chiweshe also had to deal with the chauvinism of male musicians who insisted that the mbira and the drum were "men's instruments." Luckily, Chiweshe had an uncle who was an mbira master, and when he saw how serious she was about the music, he taught it to her. The mbira is used chiefly in possession rituals—where the voices of the dead communicate with the living through its music—as well as weddings, funerals, dances, processions, political gatherings, and parties. In recent times the mbira has also moved onto the international concert circuit. Before Chiweshe, female musicians got little respect and were seldom paid, but her success and that of others led to the formation, in 1990, of the Women Musician's Advisory Group.

In 1974, during the war of liberation, Chiweshe released her first single, a song to help bolster the spirit of the freedom fighters. In the next six years she released 24 popular singles, including "Kasahwa," which went gold. She also played at all-night ceremonies while holding down a day job as a housekeeper. After independence in 1980, she became a full-time musician and performer with the National Dance Company of Zimbabwe, touring Africa, Asia, Australia, and Europe. She was a special guest artist on Thomas Mapfumo's first European tour, and soon put together her own group, Earthquake, which included marimbas, electric bass, and a Western drum kit. In 1984 she began recording for the world market with Germany's Piranha label, and sometimes adds electric guitars and keyboards to her sound. She has gotten some criticism for combining secular and sacred music, and for her commercial success overseas, but with the possible exception of Thomas Mapfumo and the Bhundu Boys, Chiweshe remains Zimbabwe's best-known musical ambassador.

what to buy: The British version of Chiweshe's first Piranha album, *Ambuya?* 🎻🎻🎻🎻 (Globestyle, 1988, prod. Hijaz Mustapha), is easier to find than the German version, and despite the backing of worldbeat irregulars 3 Mustaphas 3's rhythm section—Sabah Habas Mustapha, bass; Houzam Mustapha, drums—it's a solidly traditional set. The mbira and marimba lines are mesmerizing, and Chiweshe's poignant vocals float above the mix like the calming voice of a departed ancestor. A solid overview of Chiweshe's recording career, the compilation *The Healing Tree* 🎻🎻🎻🎻 (Shanachie, 1998, prod. Hijaz Mustapha, Colin Bass, Michael Kurzawa, Stella Chiweshe) includes tracks from her four Piranha albums.

the rest:
Chisi 🎻🎻🎻🎻 (Piranha, 1988)
Kumusha 🎻🎻🎻🎻 (Piranha, 1989)
Shungu 🎻🎻🎻🎻 (Piranha, 1990)

influences:
◄ Dorothy Masuka

see also: *3 Mustaphas 3*

j. poet

Harry Choates
Cajun, western swing
Born December 26, 1922, in Rayne, LA, USA. Died July 17, 1951, in Austin, TX, USA.

Cajun music during the 1920s and early 1930s was dominated by the sounds of the diatonic accordion. But the strains of hillbilly, swing, and western swing that were coming in over the airwaves began changing that. Fiddler Harry Choates rode the crest of this changing taste right out of the bayous to the Grand Ole Opry. His light, fiddle-based style slowly evolved from traditional Cajun tunes to a sound indistinguishable from western swing. The move away from Cajun music meant the increased use of English lyrics, and a much wider audience than any prior Cajun musician had found. Choates was a groundbreaker who prepared the way for later Cajun crossover artists like Jimmy C. Newman and Doug Kershaw.

what to buy: *Fiddle King of Cajun Swing* 🎻🎻🎻🎻 (Arhoolie, 1993, prod. Chris Strachwitz) contains the classic recordings of Cajun and western swing Choates made for Goldband records. It does not include his 1946 hit "Jolie Blon," but it has just about every other one he scored. His band features the wonderful steel work of Julius "Papa Cairo" Lamperez, a true Cajun original.

the rest:
Original 1946–1949 Recordings 🎻🎻🎻 (Arhoolie, 1982)
Five-time Lobster 🎻🎻🎻 (Krazy Kat, 1990)

influences:
◄ Dennis McGee, Bob Wills, Hackberry Ramblers, Wallace Cheese Read

►► Jimmy C. Newman, Doug Kershaw

Jared Snyder

Emma Christian
Manx traditional
Born 1972, on the Isle of Man. Based on the Isle of Man.

The Isle of Man is an independent island nation of 70,000 people situated in the Irish Sea between Ireland, Scotland, and England, whose *Tynwald* (parliament) boasts an impressive 1,000-year history. The wild and beautiful Manx landscape—as seen in the film *Waking Ned Devine*—has inspired many people over the centuries, from the original Celtic inhabitants, to the later Norse/Viking invaders who settled there, right up to today's descendants of these earlier peoples.

The Manx language, which is quite similar to Irish and Scots Gaelic, came close to extinction in the 1970s, but is now enjoying a revival and is finally being taught in the schools again. The island's best-known exports include the Bee Gees (via Australia) and folk-rock diva Christine Collister, each from the more modern end of the musical spectrum, but traditional Manx music is also undergoing a healthy period of rediscovery in recent years. Singer, harper and recorder player Emma Christian has been instrumental in getting the traditional voice of Man heard once more, both on the island and overseas.

Born and raised in a remote farming community in the north, Christian grew up in an environment conducive to her future career, her storytelling father's family being one of the big musical dynasties of the island. She learned many songs from her mother as a child, and her grandfather made her simple wooden pipes from samplings growing in the wetlands. She took up the recorder with a passion, and left Man as a teenager to spend five years at Chetham's School of Music in Manchester, England. Christian went on to earn a degree in Anglo-Saxon, Norse, and Celtic from Cambridge University in 1993. By the following year she had taken up the harp to accompany her singing. She'd always sung for fun—under the influence of her mother and island elders like Walter Clarke, as well as Scottish Hebridean singers—but that year, she gave her first professional concert and released her album *Beneath the Twilight*. Soon, she was performing in such locations as Edinburgh Castle and the medieval Palace at the Tower of London. Over the years candle-lit concerts at castles, churches, cathedrals, and even caves have become one of her fortes.

While recorder and harp are less common on the Isle of Man than, say, fiddle, Christian has adapted her chosen instruments to Manx music, rather than the other way around. Her alternately mournful and sprightly recorder-playing recalls both wooden flute and tin whistle. While her amazing voice and harp have been compared to Loreena McKennitt, that's a superficial association at best: Christian comes from within the tradition, and her spiritual and meditative performances, inspired by the Manx landscape as much as by any particular singer, have an assured authority all their own. In 1996 Christian cofounded the Isle of Music Festival, a showcase for Celtic and roots music held at the spectacular Peel Castle, on an islet off the west coast of Man, during the annual Tynwald Weekend in early July. This festival draws top musicians from around the Celtic diaspora and as far away as South Africa. She also hosts a radio show of the same name on Manx Radio, which goes out live over the internet (http://www.manxradio.com).

worth searching for: Available as an import, *Beneath the Twilight* 🎵🎵🎵🎵 (Manx Celtic, 1994, prod. Steve Coren) is the only full album Christian has released so far. It's a nicely annotated, artfully constructed tapestry of voice, harp, and recorder, surveying 18 beautiful Manx songs and instrumentals. All of the singing is in Manx, but Christian has no problem overcoming language barriers when it comes to communicating feeling. Within a few listens, several of the songs (e.g., "Ushag Veg Ruy (Little Red Bird)") sound like timeless classics one has always known. For more instant gratification in the domestic record bins, four tracks from this release can also be found on *Celtic Voices: Women of Song* (Narada, 1996), and one is on the compilation *The Celtic Lullaby* (ellipsis arts . . . , 1997), which is reviewed in this book's Compilations section. Christian's appearances unavailable elsewhere can be found on other albums with less-than-optimal production values: She contributed four new tracks to *Celtic Christmas* (Saydisc, 1996, prod. Gef Lucena), five new tracks to *Celtic Songs of Love* (Beautiful Jo, 1997, prod. Tim Healey), and one live performance to *Celtic Music—Live from Mountain Stage* (Blue Plate, 1997).

influences:
⏮ Clannad, Enya, June Tabor

John C. Falstaff

Kaouding Cissoko

See: Afro Celt Sound System, Baaba Maal, Ernest Ranglin

The Clancy Brothers & Tommy Makem /Tommy Makem & Liam Clancy /Robbie O'Connell

Irish traditional and neo-traditional
Formed March 17, 1956, in New York, NY, USA. Disbanded 1990.

Pat Clancy, vocals; Tom Clancy (died 1990), vocals; Liam Clancy, vocals, guitar, concertinas (1956–75); Tommy Makem, vocals, banjo, guitar, whistle (1956–69); Bobby Clancy, vocals (1975–90); Robbie O'Connell, guitar, vocals (1975–90). (All members are from Ireland.)

The Clancy Brothers and Tommy Makem, along with Sean Ó Riada and the Chieftains, are the most important figures in the renaissance of Irish folk music over the last half century. They have spawned thousands of imitative groups, sold millions of recordings, and sparked a renewed interest in Anglo-Irish folk song both in America and in Ireland. Tom and Pat Clancy, from Carrick-on-Suir, in Tipperary, were out-of-work actors during the early 1950s, living in Cleveland and looking for a new start somewhere else. After deciding their old car wouldn't make the trip to California, they headed for New York City instead and hooked up with both younger brother Liam and Tommy Makem, a fine singer from Armagh and the son of legendary vocalist Sarah Makem. They formed a group and began performing at late-night coffee houses in Greenwich Village—their first gig was on St. Patrick's Day, 1956—and were soon making a name for themselves in New York's nascent folk scene. With a style firmly based on the Weavers' lusty sing-along arrangements and a natural stage presence from their time in the theater, the musicians became favorites at concert appearances and released two albums on their own Tradition label. Following a now-legendary appearance on *The Ed Sullivan Show* in 1961 (they played for 16 minutes when a scheduled guest took ill), they were signed to Columbia Records and soon became icons among the Irish both in the U.S. and back home. Their natural warmth and easy, singable versions of Irish folk songs earned them converts everywhere they performed. They were soon touring extensively and recording constantly, becoming the best-known exponents of Irish traditional music in the world. Their early albums consisted almost entirely of Irish standards presented in a lusty style with simple accompaniment. Later, the group began to feature their own songs and a more produced sound which didn't always work but sometimes resulted in music that was among their best. After 13 years of records and tours Makem left the group in 1970 to pursue a solo career. Liam left in 1975, replaced by youngest brother Bobby, and the outfit sank to the level of an oldies group, recording for smaller labels and returning to the Irish pubs they had left behind 15 years before. Although the original group reunited for occasional tours and an album during the 1980s, their days at the forefront of Irish music were long-since over. The death of oldest brother Tom in 1990 signaled the final end, though occasional versions of the Clancy Brothers still record and tour today.

Tommy Makem and Liam Clancy formed a duet during the mid-'70s, releasing several albums together. The duo performed fewer of the traditional Irish songs that had made the Clancy Brothers famous, instead concentrating on the work of young lesser-known songwriters. These tasteful albums were very popular with fans of the older group, and introduced such then-unknown songwriters as David Mallett, Eric Bogle, and Gordon Bok, among others, to a new generation of folk fans. Carrying the family tradition to another generation in his own way, Clancy nephew Robbie O'Connell (a latter-day member of the original group) established a well-received solo career, bridging old and new Irish music's audiences and stylistic tastes.

The Clancy Brothers & Tommy Makem reintroduced traditional Irish music, sung honestly, to Irish-American audiences. Before their *Ed Sullivan* appearance Irish music in the U.S. was for the most part a syrupy, idealized view of "dear old Ireland" written by Tin Pan Alley hacks and bearing little relation to the real thing—which carried somewhat painful associations for Irish Americans seeking to assimilate. The Clancys and their success made true Irish culture acceptable again in the American branch of the diaspora, and led the way for the great revival of Irish music in the U.S. during the '70s and '80s. The group's commercial acceptance across the Atlantic carried weight in Ireland, where people inspired by the Clancys began to look more closely at their own musical heritage. The later explorations of deeply traditional Irish music by Sean Ó Riada, the Chieftains, and those who followed them was made easier by the Clancy

cape breton music

Cape Breton music is characterized by an almost frenetic urgency, an ornate and driving beat, and strong and genuine feeling. There is a distinct sense of the people's roots that comes across in their music, drawing on their Scottish heritage. Distinguished by the strong bowing of the fiddlers and the emotional delivery of the singers, Cape Breton stands alone in its musical "guts." This is likely influenced strongly by Cape Breton step dancing— also believed to have Scottish roots, and a tradition so alive and well that no musician in the area would dream of learning to play without also learning to dance. The beats of the dance and the pulse of the music go hand-in-hand.

Cape Breton gets thrown in with Celtic culture, based on the people's origins in northwestern Nova Scotia or "New Scotland"—so named because its Scottish settlers found the landscape so hauntingly familiar. These immigrants were highly secluded from the influences of outsiders, which has created a geographical time-capsule, presenting a glimpse of what Scotland might be like had it not been constantly invaded and affected by the English, the Scandinavians, and others. Some scholars believe that Cape Breton music is much closer to that of the original Scottish culture than what is found in Scotland today.

Jo Hughey Morrison

Brothers & Tommy Makem's pioneering efforts. There are many things the group did poorly or didn't do at all. They were mediocre musicians at best, and they largely ignored the great traditions of Irish-Gaelic song and traditional dance music. But despite these criticisms, they have done more to raise the profile of traditional Irish music than any other group of the last 50 years, and for that they deserve high praise.

what to buy: The Clancys' live recordings from the early 1960s found them in full flower. Relaxed and comfortable in front of audiences and brimming with good songs, the group made a number of great concert albums during their classic early period. *In Person at Carnegie Hall* ♪♪♪♪ (Columbia, 1964/1991, prod. Robert Morgan) is as good a starting point as any. Featuring Dominic Behan's moving "Patriot Game," a great children's

Tommy Makem, sometime member of the Clancy Brothers

medley, and plenty of up-tempo favorites like "Reilly's Daughter" and "Johnson's Motor Car," the album captures the group at their accessible best. The recording is available as an individual CD and in a package with *In Concert* 🎵🎵🎵 (Columbia, 1991) and *Luck of the Irish* 🎵🎵🎵 (Columbia, 1992, prod. various), two other fine early-1960s albums. *The Makem and Clancy Collection* 🎵🎵🎵 (Shanachie, 1980/1992, prod. Archie Fisher) is a well-chosen compilation of Tommy Makem and Liam Clancy's post-Clancy Brothers recordings. Featuring the two Eric Bogle songs "No Man's Land" (called "Willie McBride" on the album) and "The Band Played Waltzing Matilda," as well as a haunting version of "Ar Eirinn ne Neosainn Ce Hi" sung by Liam, this is a good introduction to the duo's 1970s folk albums.

what to avoid: *Irish Drinking Songs* 🎵 (Columbia, 1993, prod. Lawrence Cohn) is a compilation that manages to reduce both the Clancys and the Dubliners to a bunch of drunken buffoons. Yes, both groups sang drinking songs, and both groups are closely identified with the juice of the barley, but to present solely that side of their music is to resurrect a stereotype that has haunted the Irish for centuries both at home and abroad.

Folklorist Mick Moloney, to his credit, deals somewhat with the ambivalence of many Irish towards drink in his liner notes, but by and large the compilation is a celebration of boozing that seems more than a little heavy-handed in the 1990s. That and the harsh, abrasive sound quality on about half the tracks make for an eminently avoidable listening experience.

the rest:
Come Fill Your Glass with Us 🎵🎵🎵🎵 (Tradition, 1957/1998)
Clancy Brothers & Tommy Makem 🎵🎵🎵 (Tradition, 1958/1996)
The Rising of the Moon: Irish Songs of Rebellion 🎵🎵🎵🎵 (Tradition, 1959/1998)
Lark in the Morning 🎵🎵🎵 (Tradition, 1960/1996)
(With Lou Killen) *Greatest Hits* 🎵🎵 (Vanguard, 1973)
(With Robbie O'Connell) *Clancy Brothers with Robbie O'Connell* 🎵🎵🎵 (Vanguard, 1982/1991)
Reunion 🎵🎵🎵 (Shanachie, 1984)
Greatest Hits (Vanguard, 1987)
Live! (Vanguard, 1987)
(With David Hammond) *Irish Traditional Folk Songs* (Legacy, 1993)
Irish Songs 🎵🎵🎵 (LaserLight, 1993)
Irish Songs of Rebellion 🎵🎵🎵 (LaserLight, 1993)

(With Tommy Makem) *Irish Songs of Drinking and Rebellion* (Legacy, 1994)

Tunes 'n' Tales of Ireland ♪♪ (Folk Era, 1994)

(With Tommy Makem) *Best of the Clancy Brothers* (Legacy, 1994)

Wrap the Green Flag ♪♪♪ (Columbia, 1994)

Ain't It Grand Boys: Unissued Gems ♪♪♪ (Columbia, 1995)

(With Tommy Makem) *Greatest Irish Hits* (Sony, 1995)

Older but No Wiser ♪♪ (Vanguard, 1995)

(With Tommy Makem) *Home to Ireland: 28 Irish Favorites* (Madacy, 1996)

(With Tommy Makem) *28 Irish Pub Songs* (Madacy, 1996)

(With David Hammond) *The Clancy Brothers and David Hammond* (K-Tel, 1996)

(With David Hammond) *Irish Folk Song Favorites* (Madacy, 1996)

Christmas with the Clancy Brothers ♪♪♪♪ (Columbia, 1997)

(With Tommy Makem) *Songs of Ireland and Beyond* (Columbia, 1997)

Finnegan's Wake ♪♪♪ (Sounds of the World, 1998)

(With David Hammond) *The Great Clancy Brothers and David Hammond* ♪♪♪ (Goldies, 1998)

Irish Revolutionary Songs ♪♪♪ (Legacy, 1999)

worth searching for: *A Spontaneous Concert Performance* ♪♪♪♪ (Columbia, 1961, prod. Robert Morgan) was the Clancys' Columbia debut and is currently available only on cassette. A solid set, featuring accompaniment by Bruce Langhorne and Pete Seeger on guitar and banjo respectively, the album introduced a number of songs that would be longtime favorites for the Clancy Brothers and their fans. "Finnegan's Wake," "Reilly's Daughter," and "Jug of Punch," all Clancy standards, make their first appearance on this record. The atmosphere is relaxed, the audience in fine voice, and the performers comfortable before an audience made up largely of their friends. This is an essential album and would be in the "what to buy" section were it currently available on CD. *Home Boys Home* ♪♪♪♪ (Columbia, 1968, prod. Teo Macero) matched the Clancys with Columbia's great producer Teo Macero (whose prestigious credits also include Miles Davis's *Kind of Blue*), finally allowing their songs to be framed in less rudimentary settings. This is a landmark collection of Clancy material, featuring the first appearance of Tommy Makem's classic "Four Green Fields" as well as his beautiful version of "The Bard of Armagh." Macero's use of harp, concertina, and fiddle shades these songs beautifully, providing a subtlety that the Clancy Brothers never had again. It's out of print, regrettably, but used copies are available.

solo outings:
Liam Clancy:

Liam Clancy ♪♪♪ (Vanguard, 1989)

The Dutchman ♪♪♪♪ (Shanachie, 1993)

Irish Troubador ♪♪♪♪ (Vanguard, 1999)

Tommy Makem and Liam Clancy:

Tommy Makem and Liam Clancy ♪♪♪ (Blackbird, 1976/Shanachie 1992)

We've Come a Long Way ♪♪♪ (Shanachie, 1989)

Live at the National Concert Hall ♪♪♪ (Shanachie, 1991)

Two for the Early Dew ♪♪♪ (Shanachie, 1992)

In Concert ♪♪♪ (Shanachie, 1993)

Robbie O'Connell:

The Love of Land ♪♪♪♪ (Green Linnet, 1989)

Never Learned to Dance ♪♪♪♪ (Green Linnet, 1993)

Close to the Bone ♪♪♪ (Green Linnet, 1977)

Humorous Songs Live! ♪♪♪ (Celtic Media, 1997)

Clancy, O'Connell & Clancy:

Clancy, O'Connell & Clancy ♪♪♪♪ (Helvic, 1998)

Moloney, O'Connell & Keane:

Kilkelly ♪♪♪♪♪ (Green Linnet, 1992)

There Were Roses ♪♪♪♪ (Green Linnet, 1992)

influences:

◀◀ The Weavers, Sarah Makem

▶▶ The Dubliners, Wolfe Tones, Fureys, the Pogues

see also: *The Dubliners, Joanie Madden, Tommy Makem, Mick Moloney, Áine Uí Cheallaigh*

Tony Ziselberger

Clannad
Celtic/New Age
Formed late 1960s, in County Donegal, Ireland. Based in Ireland.

Máire Brennan, vocals, harp, keyboards; Ciaran Brennan, vocals, basses, guitar, piano/synth; Paul Brennan, vocals, flute, whistles (1970–89); Padraig Duggan, mandolin, harmonica, guitar, vocals; Noel Duggan, guitar, vocals; Enya Brennan, keyboards, vocals (1980–82). (All members are from Ireland.)

Clannad took their act to Ireland, and later the U.S., in a totally unconventional way. Siblings Máire, Ciaran, and Paul Brennan teamed up with their twin uncles Padraig and Noel Duggan to form a band. They wanted to play music that echoed the sounds they had grown up hearing in their corner of Ireland. The Brennans' father owned a tavern where he performed, and would send them onstage to give him a break between acts. They sang in Gaelic, which was not at all popular with the locals back then. And they took traditional tunes and arranged them for an entire band—also not the "thing to do" at that time. Their big break came when they won first place (and a contract with Philips Records) at the local Letterkenny Folk Festival in 1970. It took several years to complete the album, however, because of a disagreement over the use of Gaelic lyrics on it. The group won out in the end, and thus a legend in contemporary traditional music was born.

Clannad's music has gone through substantial changes over the group's lifetime. Working together, experimenting with new instrumentations and sounds, they evolved a new-age style (winning a Grammy in that category for 1998's *Landmarks* and once including in their ranks *the* Enya), visiting various pop and rock stops in between. Their best-known song in the U.S. is "Theme from Harry's Game," which first appeared on a British TV show during the early '80s, later won *Billboard*'s World Music Song of the Year award, and was picked up for the movie *Patriot Games*. Despite the group's changes over the years, you can still hear the rugged hills and warring political factions of their homeland through the music's dark tone and spiritual melodies.

what to buy: For those unfamiliar with Clannad's music, the best place to start is *Magical Ring* ♪♪♪ (Tara, 1983, prod. Richard Dodd). This is where the group makes the biggest transition from the "traditional" to the contemporary, largely with their original "Theme from Harry's Game," which combines voices and synthesizers in a modern and wholly original sound. *Macalla* ♪♪♪♪ (RCA, 1985, prod. Steve Nye) is a lush musical offering of mostly original compositions, while more traditional material can be found on *Dulaman* ♪♪♪♪♪ (Blackbird, 1976/Shanachie, 1988, prod. Nicky Ryan), a recording with rich Gaelic songs and delightful Irish rhythms. *Clannad 2* ♪♪♪♪♪ (Blackbird, 1974/Shanachie 1988, prod. Dónal Lunny) is steeped in wonderful Irish tradition.

what to buy next: Clannad also has a plethora of compilations, all of which, of course, include "Harry's Game." The best of these is *Celtic Collections: Clannad* ♪♪♪♪ (K-Tel, 1996), which truly shows Clannad's wide scope, from the classic traditional "Nil Sen La" to the highly synthesized "In a Lifetime." The main problem with this album is the lack of liner notes or information about the group, leaving new fans to find their own way to more by Clannad. A better presentation can be found on *Rogha: The Best of Clannad* ♪♪♪ (RCA/BMG, 1997, prod. Ian Kimmer), which is a nice retrospective, though it only covers material from *Magical Ring* to the present. *Clannad in Concert* ♪♪♪♪♪ (Blackbird, 1979/Shanachie, 1982, prod. Nicky Ryan) is an excellent live recording from the early era.

what to avoid: Whether you are a fan of Clannad's earlier or more contemporary style, *Sirius* ♪♪ (RCA/BMG, 1988, prod. Greg Ladanyi, Russ Kunkel) is an Americanized rock departure for the band; only folk fans with heavy rock leanings are likely to appreciate it. Unless you are interested only in samplings of Clannad's music—or, conversely, want to collect everything in print—the other compilations aren't worth the money. *PastPresent* ♪♪ (RCA/BMG, 1989, prod. various) spans the time from their first modern venture with *Magical Ring* to *Sirius*. *Themes* **woof!** (Celtic Heartbeat, 1995, prod. various) combines a large assortment of movie and TV music Clannad has recorded over the years, including a very sappy version of Joni Mitchell's "Both Sides Now" and the overly dramatic love song from the latest *Last of the Mohicans*

film, "I Will Find You." Neither *Clannad: The Ultimate Collection* ♪♪♪ (BMG, 1997) nor *Clannad: An Díolaim* ♪♪♪ (Music Club, 1998) holds anything of interest that isn't found somewhere else.

the rest:
Crann Ull ♪♪♪♪ (Tara, 1980)
Fuaim ♪♪♪ (Tara, 1982)
Legend ♪♪♪ (RCA, 1984)
Atlantic Realm ♪♪ (BBC, 1989)
Anam ♪♪ (RCA, 1991)
Banba ♪♪ (BMG, 1993)
Lore ♪♪♪ (Atlantic, 1996)
Landmarks ♪♪♪ (Atlantic, 1998)

worth searching for: Lovers of Clannad's more traditional work will enjoy the live album *Ring of Gold* ♪♪♪♪ (Celtic Music, 1986). If anyone finds the out-of-print *Clannad* ♪♪♪♪ (Philips, 1973), buy it even if you don't want it! It is a collector's item, as the original master tapes have reportedly been lost.

solo outings:
Máire Brennan:
Máire ♪♪ (Atlantic, 1992)
Misty Eyed Adventures ♪♪ (Mesa, 1995)

influences:
◀◀ Pentangle, Bothy Band

▶▶ Enya, Loreena McKennit, Sarah McLachlan, Capercaillie

see also: *Enya*

Jo Hughey Morrison

Johnny Clarke
Roots reggae
Born January 1955, in Kingston, Jamaica. Based in Kingston, Jamaica.

Johnny Clarke has one of the purest, most moving tenor voices in reggae, and his music, be it a cover of Peter Tosh's "I'm the Toughest" or his own anthemic hits like "Rockers Time Now" and "Prophesy a Fulfilled," is always rich with sweet soul and deep sufferation. During the late 1970s Clarke was just as popular in Jamaica as Bob Marley, Gregory Isaacs, and Dennis Brown, though he is almost unknown in the United States and only developed a cult following in England. Clarke grew up in Whitefield Town, a rough black neighborhood in Kingston, and dropped out of school at 17 to pursue a recording career. His first single, "God Made the Sea & Sun," wasn't a hit, but he did have luck in a series of local talent shows, appearing with other soon-to-be-stars like the Mighty Diamonds. Producer Rupie Edwards heard him at a show in Bull Bay and cut several tunes with him, including "Don't Go" and "Everyday Wondering," which were fairly successful in the U.K.. When Edwards left Jamaica for England shortly thereafter, Clarke began recording for Bunny Lee, who was looking for a singer to give Dennis Brown some competition. Clarke's first hit, "None Shall Escape the Judgment," was an accident. He was supposed to sing backing vocals on the track, which was written and performed by Earl Zero (Earl Johnson). But when it arrived for mixing, Zero's vocals had been somehow erased, so it was quickly re-cut with Clarke singing lead. The tune's fast rise was due both to this switch and to the drumming of Carlton "Santa" Davis, whose prominent hi-hat cymbal riddims Lee manipulated to produce a spacey, sci-fi sound.

Clarke followed up "None Shall Escape" with dozens of his own roots rock compositions and well-received covers of other R&B and rocksteady standards. In 1975 he took a shot at international success by signing with Virgin Frontline and recording *Rockers Time Now* and *Authorized Version,* two of the strongest roots rock albums of the 1970s. Clarke's records swamped the competition in Jamaica, but did poorly in England. In the late '70s, when Bunny Lee began concentrating on getting a British distribution deal for his back catalog, he neglected his singers, including Clarke. Clarke himself briefly lived in England in the 1980s, recording for Mad Professor, Jah Shaka, and Fashion, without notable success. He retired from the music biz for a while, but staged a comeback in 1992 with *Rasta Nuh Fear.* This time out he has concentrated more on the performing side, and his appearances at clubs and festivals have been getting raves from both critics and fans. His latest CD is 1997's *Rock with Me.*

what to buy: The stunning *Authorized Rockers* 🎵🎵🎵🎵 (Virgin Frontline, 1991, prod. Bunny Lee) includes all the tracks from the landmark *Rockers Time Now* and *Authorized Version* albums. Lee's production is amazing, with the riddim section of drummer Carlton "Santa" Davis and bassist Robbie Shakespeare pushing the envelope on every track. Clarke's voice has never sounded sweeter or purer than it does on these albums, which are packed with roots rock classics that rival the militant fire and melodic power of Marley's best work.

what to buy next: *Dreader Dread 1976–78* 🎵🎵🎵🎵 (Blood & Fire, 1998, prod. various) is a fine compilation of Clarke's early work, but lacks the cohesive power of the Virgin sets.

the rest:
Moving Out 🎵🎵🎵 (Total Sounds, 1975)
Johnny Clarke 🎵🎵🎵 (Clock Tower)
Rock with Me Baby 🎵🎵🎵 (Clock Tower)
No Woman No Cry 🎵🎵🎵 (Total Sounds, 1975)
Don't Stay out Late 🎵🎵🎵 (Paradise)
Rock with Me 🎵🎵🎵 (1997)
Enter into His Gates with Praise 🎵🎵🎵 (Trojan Sounds)

influences:
◀◀ Bob Marley, Dennis Brown, Slim Smith

▶▶ Cocoa Tea

see also: *Sly & Robbie*

j. poet

Claudia

Traditional Mestizo-Zapotecan song
Born in Mexico. Based in Mexico.

Claudia's musical experience started early, beginning at age nine with study in a small percussion orchestra under Maestro Cesar Tort. Next came an apprenticeship singing—as well as playing Mexican and South American pop music on guitar—with Maestra Esther Echevarria. Claudia then studied at the Centro de Arte Guitarristico (School of Guitar Art), and participated in the workshops of Mario Arturo Ramos and Amparo Rubin, with the latter of whom she composed and produced the music for *El Abuelo y Yo,* a Mexican television series. Little of this extensive training and accomplishment could have helped predict the exploration of her homeland's native peoples with which she would eventually gain her most widespread acclaim. Now internationally respected, Claudia has recorded a well-received album of traditional music freshly interpreted, and recently performed live at 1998's prestigious MIDEM Festival in Cannes, France.

what's available: From Mexico comes the lovely, mud-covered Claudia on the cover of her debut album *Xquenda* 🎵🎵🎵🎵 (Milan Entertainment, 1997, prod. Claudia), pronounced "sh'kenda" and translating as "my other me." The album contains indigenous Mexican melodies about life and death from the Isthmus of Oaxaca, Mexico. Claudia and company thrill with a variety of these traditional songs, including a fragment of a lullaby that has almost been forgotten today ("Gasisi Nana"), a Zapotecan song for survivors to bid deceased loved ones farewell ("Guendanabani Xhianga Sicaru"), and even a wedding song with an analogy (meant to go over children's heads!) of the lost virginity and hidden sexual relations of a couple before their marriage ("Pora Gule Bicu Huiini"). Liner notes transcribe the lyrics in phonetic renditions of the Zapotecan language, with Spanish, English, and French translations. Each musician has formidable chops and the trio (Claudia on vocals, Ángel Chacón on guitars, and Rafael Gonzáles on percussion) work together in passionate and plaintive manners, creating an outlet for tradition to survive in the modern word. Claudia's voice is clear and strong, and there are overdubs enabling her to harmonize with herself. The guitars are lush and lovely, making you want to question the number of fingers Señor Chacón possesses. Percussion is spare but intense, popping up as rhythmic punctuation to set the pace of a story. Claudia sums up the combination: "In a very fortunate union, the guitar weaves a mantle with the sounds of the earth, to cover us with the voice of the heart, which, once again, appears as a most valuable instrument."

Johnny Clegg

worth searching for: Claudia states that *Xquenda* was inspired by an investigation of the ethnomusicological holdings at Mexico's National Institute of Anthropology and History. One reference used is Violeta Torres Medina's research project "Songs of Life and Death in the Isthmus of Oaxaca," the catalog number of which, if you happen to be planning a vacation to the archives of Mexico, is Serie Inah 025.

influences:

Maestro Cesar Tort, Maestra Esther Echevarria, Mario Arturo Ramos, Amparo Rubin, Botellita de Jerez

Stacy Meyn

Johnny Clegg & Savuka /Juluka

Zulu- and mbaqanga-influenced pop

Johnny Clegg born June 7, 1953, in Rochdale, England. Based in South Africa.

Johnny Clegg & Savuka (1986–95): Johnny Clegg, vocals, guitar, mouth bow; Steve Mavuso, keyboards; Keith Hutchinson, keyboards, saxophone, flute; Derek De Beer, drums, percussion; Solly Letwaba, bass; Dudu Zulu, percussion. **Juluka (1979–85, 1996):** Johnny Clegg, vocals, guitar, mouth bow; Derek De Beer, drums, percussion; Sipho Mchunu, vocals, guitar, concertina; Gary Van Zyl, bass, percussion (1981–85); Scorpion Madondo, flute, saxophone (1982–85); Cyril Mnculwana, keyboards (1983–85); Glenda Millar, keyboards (1982–85).

Born in England but raised in Zimbabwe and South Africa, Johnny Clegg learned Zulu dancing at an early age and, depending on which version of the story you believe, he met Sipho Mchunu either when Mchunu heard about this white boy who could dance like a Zulu, or when Clegg, already a lecturer in anthropology, was sought out by Mchunu because of Clegg's reputation as a hotshot guitarist. The first story maintains that the two met as teenagers around 1970 and worked together for nine years before hooking up with producer/impresario Hilton Rosenthal. The second one likely would indicate that they had only worked together for a little while before they started making records in 1979. Either way, the idea of a white man and a black man coleading a South African band was a political statement in itself, and in some ways became more important than their novel melding of South African *mbaqanga* or "township" music, Western pop/rock, and Zulu chants. By 1981 the duo had put together a backup band, and before long Juluka's colorful and energetic performances made it a hot concert draw—and brought its members into direct conflict with the racist practices of South Africa's apartheid government. By 1982 the band was wowing audiences in Britain, and soon after, Juluka was signed to a major U.S. label. Commercial success never came, and after the group broke up, Clegg returned as sole leader of a new ensemble, Savuka. Blander and more formulaic than Juluka, Clegg and Savuka also became a serious concert attraction worldwide, but their albums never really rose above the level of stylish professionalism, and the group was dropped by Capitol after 1993's *Heat, Dust & Dreams*. Meanwhile, Clegg and Mchunu have at one point reunited for some concerts and are reportedly planning a new Juluka album.

what to buy: Both groups are the subject of greatest-hits compilations. *A Johnny Clegg & Juluka Collection* 𝄢𝄢𝄢𝄢 (Putumayo, 1996, compilation prod. Dan Storper) provides a nice initiation to Clegg's international pop style. *In My African Dream: The Best of Johnny Clegg & Savuka* 𝄢𝄢𝄢𝄢 (Priority, 1994, prod. various) contains 16 tracks, several previously unreleased. More energetic and a bit more focused than Clegg and Savuka's earlier work, their *Cruel, Crazy, Beautiful World* 𝄢𝄢𝄢𝄢 (Capitol, 1989, prod. Hilton Rosenthal, Bobby Summerfield) in some ways parallels the rising tide of optimism that was about to overtake South Africa when the album was released.

what to buy next: Highlighted by Juluka's South African breakthrough hit, "Impi," *African Litany* 𝄢𝄢𝄢𝄢 (Rhythm Safari, 1982/1991, prod. Hilton Rosenthal) offers a view of the earlier band just as it was about to make the jump from national to international status.

Jimmy Cliff

what to avoid: Tame and somewhat disappointing coming after the breakup of Juluka, Savuka's debut, *Third World Child* 🎵🎵 (Capitol, 1987/Gold Rush 1996, prod. Hilton Rosenthal), is fairly pleasant but unremarkable.

the rest:
Juluka:
Ubuhle Bemvelo 🎵🎵 (Rhythm Safari, 1982/1991)
Scatterlings 🎵🎵🎵 (Warner Bros., 1983)
Stand Your Ground 🎵🎵🎵 (Warner Bros., 1984)

Johnny Clegg & Savuka:
Shadow Man 🎵🎵🎵 (Capitol, 1988)
Heat, Dust & Dreams 🎵🎵🎵 (Capitol, 1993)

Johnny Clegg:
Anthology N/A (Connoisseur/Stern's, 1999)

influences:
◀◀ Mahlathini & Mahotella Queens, Ladysmith Black Mambazo, the Police, Men at Work, Aswad

▶▶ Paul Simon (circa *Graceland*), Dave Matthews Band, Rusted Root

Bob Remstein

Jimmy Cliff
Reggae
Born April 1, 1948, in St. James, Jamaica. Based in Jamaica.

Jimmy Cliff shot to international stardom in 1971 with his lead role in the movie *The Harder They Come* and his contributions to its all-star soundtrack, which still stands as one of the primary textbooks of Reggae 101. However, he had been recording since the early 1960s, making some of the first reggae sounds heard outside of Jamaica. Working with famed producer Leslie Kong, Cliff had a handful of hits on the island, leading to more far-reaching success with "Wonderful World, Beautiful People" in 1969. After *The Harder They Come* Cliff was ostracized by the Jamaican community, perhaps jealous over his newfound stardom or merely insulted by his conversion from Rastafarianism to Islam. The sad truth is that for all the liberating forces at play during Cliff's moment in the sun, he's never been able to translate them into consistent music or attain that level of success again. Instead, he opted for a light MOR pop-soul approach that culminated in a two-album collaboration, *The Power and the Glory* and *Cliff Hanger,* with Kool & the Gang during the first half of the 1980s. Besides nabbing a Grammy for *Cliff Hanger* (so keyboard-laden it could be the *Footloose* soundtrack), Cliff appeared in *Club Paradise* with Robin Williams and added seven songs to its soundtrack in 1986, although neither generated a wider audience for the singer.

what to buy: Perhaps the best quick indoctrination into 1970s reggae, *The Harder They Come* 𝄞𝄞𝄞𝄞 (Island, 1972, prod. various) is Cliff's crowning glory—a taut and yearning soundtrack filled with top-notch performances from all artists involved. Cliff's efforts on the title track, "Sitting in Limbo," "You Can Get It If You Really Want," and, most of all, "Many Rivers to Cross," remain timeless and moving as all classics do.

what to buy next: One of his more consistent studio albums, *Wonderful World, Beautiful People* 𝄞𝄞𝄞 (A&M, 1970, prod. Larry Fallon, Leslie Kong) paved the way to superstardom with its title track, the protest of "Vietnam" (which drew high praise from Bob Dylan), and the foreboding "Time Will Tell."

what to avoid: Cliff's records of late have a disturbing lightness, and although *Hanging Fire* 𝄞𝄞 (Columbia, 1988, prod. Khalis Bayyan, I.B.M.C., Jimmy Cliff) is really not much better or worse than the bulk of his more recent releases, there's a sinking feeling that he may break into "Let's Hear It for the Boy" at any moment. Such mediocrity might not be so unsettling had he not once reached such greatness.

the rest:
In Concert: The Best of Jimmy Cliff 𝄞𝄞𝄞 (Reprise, 1976)
Special 𝄞𝄞 (Columbia, 1982)
The Power and the Glory 𝄞𝄞𝄞 (Columbia, 1983)
Reggae Greats 𝄞𝄞𝄞 (Mango, 1985)
Cliff Hanger 𝄞𝄞 (Columbia, 1985)
Images 𝄞𝄞𝄞 (Cliff, 1991)
Struggling Man 𝄞𝄞𝄞 (Mango, 1993)
Live 1993 𝄞𝄞𝄞 (Lagoon Reggae, 1993)
Samba Reggae 𝄞𝄞 (Lagoon Reggae, 1995)
Super Hits 𝄞𝄞𝄞𝄞 (Columbia Legacy, 1997)
Live & in the Studio 𝄞𝄞𝄞 (Jamaican Gold, 1998)
Humanitarian (PGD/Eureka, 1999)

worth searching for: Although it's a hit-and-miss soundtrack, *Marked for Death* 𝄞𝄞𝄞 (Delicious Vinyl, 1990) contains some stirring Cliff numbers. The ominous "John Crow" is stronger than anything he's done during the past 10 years. *Shout for Freedom* 𝄞𝄞𝄞 (BMG/Milan, 1999), an intriguing reworking of earlier material with star *soukous* bands from Central Africa, is an ambitious stylistic realization of reggae's oft-prophesied Motherland reunion. Unfortunately, substandard recording quality doesn't fulfill the listener nearly as well.

influences:
◀◀ Toots & the Maytals, Desmond Dekker, Bob Marley
▶▶ UB40, Third World, General Public, Pinchers

see also: *Joe Higgs*

Allan Orski

Cocoa Tea

Dancehall reggae, ragga
Born Calvin Scott, 1960, in Clarendon, Jamaica. Based in Kingston, Jamaica.

In Jamaica's competitive dancehalls, the shelf-life of most performers is two to three years at best. Cocoa Tea has survived and thrived for over 15, primarily due to his captivatingly sweet voice and his much-admired ability to ride rough *ragga* (digital-reggae) rhythms like a rodeo champ. To be sure, his creamy-smooth melodies are an oddity in a market where intensely percussive chat is the norm. His debut, *Rocking Dolly,* barely predated the digital age and is a rare document of his gifted vocals backed by a live band—the terrific Roots Radics. In 1989 Cocoa's reputation spread beyond the island when he teamed with Home T and Shabba Ranks on "Pirate's Anthem," which became an underground London danceclub hit. After London's longtime pirate radio station KISS-FM was granted a broadcast license, the song was the first one played on the air and became an "anthem" too for this progressive broadcaster. Cocoa's collaborations with cutting-edge ragga producers like Philip "Fatis" Burrell, Gussie Clarke, Steely & Clevie, and most recently Bobby Digital (no relation to Stateside rapper RZA's alter-ego) have consistently been received with enthusiasm in the dancehall, though a reluctance to travel has no doubt limited his audience. Still a bit of a roots throwback with his dreadlocks and devotion to Rastafarianism, Cocoa Tea's songs have always been more informed by his faith and his vision of justice than most artists of his genre. In 1991 his thoughtful opposition to the Gulf War manifested itself in "No Blood for Oil," from *Riker's Island.* Given the title, the song is surprisingly subtle and logical in its protest, and—perhaps more important to the dancehall "massive" who made it a hit—it makes you rock so! Cocoa has also distinguished himself by rarely engaging in "slackness," ragga slang for sexually explicit lyrics—a staple in today's dancehalls. He is without a doubt one of the most enduring and purely melodic singers of reggae's digital age.

what to buy: *Rocking Dolly* 𝄞𝄞𝄞𝄞 (RAS, 1985, prod. Henry "Junjo" Lawes) includes the two hits that launched Cocoa's career—the title cut and "I Lost My Sonia." The Roots Radics prove that organic rhythms—in particular *their* rhythms—kick the computer's ass. On the other hand, over a decade later, Cocoa Tea proves he can conquer even the toughest, tensile digital beats on the exceptional *Israel's King* 𝄞𝄞𝄞 (V.P., 1996, prod. Philip "Fatis" Burrell), which also features Dean Fraser's vital tenor saxophone work.

what to buy next: With Home T and renowned deejay Shabba Ranks along for the ride, *Holding On* 𝄞𝄞𝄞 (V.P., 1989, prod. Augustus "Gussie" Clarke) is one of the finest examples of "combo"-style ragga—sound clashes between soulful singers and hard-core, gravel-voiced deejays. This set includes "Pirate's Anthem" and an adrenaline-pumped version of MFSB's Philly-soul hit "Your Body's Here with Me."

the rest:

Sweet Sweet Cocoa Tea 🎵🎵🎵 (Blue Mountain, 1986)

The Marshall 🎵🎵🎵 (Jammy's, 1986)

Cocoa Tea 🎵🎵🎵 (Firehouse, 1986)

(With Tenor Saw) *Clash* 🎵🎵🎵 (Witty, 1987)

Riker's Island 🎵🎵🎵 (V.P., 1991)

(With Home T and Cutty Ranks) *Another One for the Road* 🎵🎵🎵 (Greensleeves U.K., 1991)

20 Tracks of Cocoa Tea 🎵🎵🎵 (Sonic Sounds, 1991)

Authorized 🎵🎵🎵 (Shanachie, 1992)

I Am the Toughest 🎵🎵 (V.P., 1992)

Kingston Hot! 🎵🎵 (RAS, 1992)

One Up 🎵🎵🎵 (V.P., 1993)

Tune In 🎵🎵🎵 (Greensleeves U.K., 1994)

Can't Live So 🎵🎵🎵 (Shanachie, 1994)

Sweet Love 🎵🎵 (RAS, 1995)

Come Love Me 🎵🎵🎵 (V.P., 1995)

Good Life 🎵🎵🎵 (V.P., 1996)

Ras Portraits 🎵🎵🎵 (RAS, 1997)

Early Days 1984–1986 🎵🎵🎵 (Corner Stone, 1999)

worth searching for: Available only as an import, *Come Again* 🎵🎵🎵🎵 (Dynamic, 1987, prod. Henry "Junjo" Lawes) is all uplifting melodies and heavy beats. Cocoa ingeniously integrates the tune of "Santa Claus Is Coming to Town" on the joyous title cut. Roll back the rug and prepare to rub-a-dub!

influences:

◀ Ken Boothe, Alton Ellis, Freddie McGregor, Brook Benton, King Sporty

▶ Finley Quaye, Home T

see also: *Luciano, Freddie McGregor, the Roots Radics, Shabba Ranks*

Todd Shanker

Robert Tree Cody

Native American flute and song

Born in USA. Based in AZ, USA.

Usually made from cedar, the Native American flute is an ancient instrument used by indigenous cultures of the American plains and woodlands. Called *siyotanka* by the Lakota people, this flute was used by young men to court the affections of young ladies in camp. It was also played to provide soothing music during times of quiet and relaxation. R. Carlos Nakai, Al Jewer, Andy Vasquez, and other Native flutists have risen to prominence in the past 20 years for their unmatched ability to use the flute to emulate the human voice in tone and character, expressed in sweet pitch and slow-to-sprightly tempo. Robert Tree Cody is an artist well worthy of their company. Born of Dakota-Maricopa heritage, Cody has appeared throughout the United States and Europe as a dancer,

celtic music in brief

Celtic music encompasses a wide geography, including Scotland, Wales, Ireland, Nova Scotia, Brittany, Galicia, Cornwall, and the Isle of Man. The ancient Celts or their ancestors settled these lands, making a home and a heritage in each. This one historical link has led to the contemporary cultural association of these areas in the mind of the masses. But it is perhaps unfortunate that the strong musical traditions of the Celtic world are tossed into one stylistic melting pot, for each area's traditional music has its own distinctive flavor. Welsh music, for instance, is characterized by strong vocal harmony and the love of theme and variation, while the Irish tradition includes a strong melodic line and a tendency to ornament this melody heavily. So it is actually difficult to describe what makes Celtic music "Celtic." There is a common pool of instruments, including bagpipes, harp, and fiddle. But above all it is probably the people's still-shared history; a deeply emotional connection to their heritage shines through the music of the Celts.

Jo Hughey Morrison

singer, and flutist. A prize-winning traditional dancer and an honored whistle carrier, he is well-known on the powwow circuit as Tree Cody Red Cedar Whistle. As a counselor and educator, Cody has taught students at all levels about the folklore, crafts, music, and traditional ways of the Native American people, and participates in the artist-in-residence programs of the Arizona Commission on the Arts. He is married to noted Assiniboine-Yankton Sioux-Mohave singer Marlene Cody, and has four boys.

what to buy: While almost anybody can produce some type of sound from a cedar flute, it is notoriously difficult to play really well. Native American flutists must achieve a clarity of mind, purity of heart, and singleness of purpose before picking up the instrument, as it is the depth and breadth of emotion found in the music produced that ranks a player as either gross amateur or artiste. It is clear from his recordings that Cody is one of this century's most talented players in the latter category. *Dreams from the Grandfather: Native American Songs for Flute & Voice* 🎵🎵🎵🎵 (Canyon, 1993, prod. Robert Doyle) artistically demonstrates the close relationship between singing and instrument as inspired by Kokopelli, a mysterious figure of legend whose hunchbacked, flute-playing form decorates hundreds of rock walls and ruins throughout the Southwest. Featuring Lakota lullabies, an adaptation of a Cherokee stomp dance, and the joyful prayer "Zuni Dawn," this album also includes a version of "Sky City," an homage to the song's legendary original recording by the great Navajo singer Ed Lee Natay in 1951. A gorgeous melding of voice and flute, it describes the celestial wonders of the titular Acoma pueblo and its people.

what to buy next: In collaboration with non-Native artists Rob Wallace (synthesizer) and Will Clipman (percussion), Cody brings to life the legend of the *White Buffalo* ♫♫♫ (Canyon, 1996, prod. Robert Doyle): Long before the Europeans invaded North America, a drought reduced animal populations and the indigenous peoples were starving. Two hunters seeking food for their people met a beautiful young woman who floated as she walked. One hunter attempted to defile her and was turned to a pile of bones; the other returned to his camp to announce her coming. The mysterious woman gave the people a sacred pipe, showed them how to pray, and taught them about the value of women, children, and buffalo. Before she left, she told the people she would return; as she walked away, she rolled over four times and eventually transformed into a white buffalo. Shortly after Cody, Wallace, and Clipman began working on this album, Miracle, the first white buffalo in over six decades, was born in Janesville, Wisconsin. For many Native peoples this was a powerful and positive sign of great portent, as well as the fulfilled promise of the legend. The music is therefore both suitably reverent and celebratory, an aural portrait of a people whose past has been renewed through spirit so that humankind and nature can again come into harmony.

the rest:
Young Eagle's Flight ♫♫♫ (Canyon, 1991)
(With Rob Wallace & Tony Redhouse) *Maze* ♫♫♫ (Canyon, 1998)

influences:
◀◀ Doc Tate Nevaqueya of the Comanche, Ed Lee Natay of the Navajo

PJ Birosik

Shirley Collins
/Shirley & Dolly Collins
/Etchingham Steam Band

English folk

Shirley Collins born July 5, 1935, in Hastings, Sussex, England. Dorothy (Dolly) Collins born March 6, 1933, in Hastings, Sussex, England; died September 22, 1995, in Balcombe, West Sussex, England. Etchingham Steam Band formed c. 1974, in Etchingham, Sussex, England; disbanded c. 1975. Shirley Collins based in Brighton, East Sussex, England.

Etchingham Steam Band: Shirley Collins, vocals, hobby horse; Vic Gammon, vocals, concertina, melodeon, banjo; Ian Holder, accordion; Ashley Hutchings, acoustic bass guitar, vocals, tambourine; Terry Potter, mouth organ. (All members are from England.)

Shirley Collins is one of Britain's greatest folk singers. Her lilting, wavering soprano epitomizes the spirit of British folk music: unpolished but full of magic and grace. Collins first gained attention as a singer when she worked with seminal folklorist Alan Lomax on his collection of southern U.S. ballads, many of which have antecedents in Great Britain and Ireland. Her own debut album, *False True Lovers,* was released in 1959. Sister Dolly joined her as accompanist and arranger for *The Sweet Primeroses,* released in 1967. Shirley's work on Harvest, a label known for progressive rock, indicated the growing fusion of traditional and contemporary elements in British music. It was a fusion to which she herself contributed directly by recording with (and marrying) traditionalist/trailblazer Ashley Hutchings. After their divorce she retired from music, only to reappear during the late 1980s. Collins has both reinforced and pushed the bounds of tradition throughout her career, singing parodies with Les Barker's Mrs. Ackroyd Band, introducing early instruments in work with David Munrow and Phil Pickett, and collaborating with Davey Graham on the landmark folk fusion album *Folk Roots, New Routes.*

what to buy: Shirley Collins & the Albion Band's *No Roses* ♫♫♫♫ (BBC, 1971/Mooncrest, 1991) is unquestionably a folk-rock album, thanks largely to the presence of such Fairporters and Steeleyes as Richard Thompson, Simon Nicol, Maddy Prior, and Dave Mattacks. In fact, 25 of Britain's best musicians of the time worked on the album, making it essential for any fan of the genre. The most chilling selection is "Murder of Maria Marten," based on the same 19th-century case that inspired Tom Waits's "Murder in the Red Barn." For an unplugged experience, try the eponymous *Etchingham Steam Band* ♫♫♫♫ (Fledg'ling, 1995). In the liner notes to this lone album from the band, Collins recounts how she simulated the sound of English traditional morris dancers onstage by sewing bells to her children's hobby horses and shaking them (losing many bells per performance). This band was formed during the power cuts of the mid-1970s as a low-tech performing outfit; their one album brings together recordings from various concerts and is a lighthearted ramble through Britain's thicket of dance music, ballads, and wassails.

worth searching for: Collins, then "Shirley Hutchings," is an important part of the group effort *Morris On* ♫♫♫♫ (Island, 1972/Hannibal, prod. John Wood). She sings on two tracks, "The Willow Tree" and "Staines Morris," adding class and delicacy to an otherwise rollicking, testosterone-fueled collection. Phil Pickett, sending liner-note readers to the unabridged dictionary, plays such artifacts of the modern and medieval arsenals as recorders, shawms, curtal, cornett, and cittern on Shirley and Dolly Collins' *For As Many As Will* ♫♫♫♫ (Topic, 1978/Hokey Pokey, 1993, prod.

Tony Engle), but one of the best tracks is a moving cover of Richard Thompson's "Never Again" with Shirley on vocals and Dolly on piano. This album, available as an import from U.K.-based Fledg'ling Records, was the last of the three the Collins sisters did together, and it's a fitting tribute to Dolly's sensitive keyboard work and arrangements. Other out-of-print gems from the sisters include *Love, Death, and the Lady* 𝄢𝄢𝄢𝄢 (EMI, 1974) and *The Sweet Primeroses* 𝄢𝄢𝄢 (Topic, 1967). At present the best place for the Collins catalog—and a great source for British folk in general—is the aforesaid Fledg'ling Records, P.O. Box 547, London SE26 4BD, United Kingdom; beekeeper@fledgling.demon.co.uk.

influences:

◀ Jean Ritchie, Young Tradition

▶▶ Kate Rusby, Eliza Carthy

see also: *Fairport Convention, Ashley Hutchings, Steeleye Span*

Pamela Murray Winters

Willie Colon

Salsa, Latin jazz

Born April 28, 1950, in Bronx, NY, USA. Based in Mexico City, Mexico.

You could say trombone player, bandleader, and producer Willie Colon is an institution, but that suggests a resting on laurels that he doesn't ever stay still long enough for—think of him more as a foundation, continually reinvesting in and reinvigorating the New York salsa and Latin jazz scenes of which he's been in the forefront for more than three decades. To the Anglo masses just beginning to "discover" Latin music at century's end, Colon is perhaps best known for his high-profile work on David Byrne's career-redefining 1989 Latinesque album *Rei Momo.* But to his legions of Spanish-speaking fans and longtime international music listeners he's known as the recipient of more than 11 Grammy nominations and counting, with sales of over 10 million to his credit worldwide—not to mention his prestigious Chubb fellowship from Yale University in 1995, and his citation as one of *Hispanic Business* magazine's Most Influential Hispanics in the United States the following year.

The grandson of Puerto Rican immigrants, Colon was taught his earliest songs by his grandmother. Though he studied trumpet at the age of 12, he switched to the trombone within two years. After directing the 14-piece Latin Jazz All-Stars, Colon signed a recording contract with seminal salsa label Fania in 1967. His debut album, *El Malo,* featured vocalist Hector Lavoe and included the hits "Jazzy" and "I Wish I Had Watermelon." These successes portended the acclaim and stature to come, as Colon went on to record with such influential artists as New York-born percussionist Tito Puente, Cuban songstress Celia Cruz, Puerto Rican *cuatro* (folk guitar) player Yomo Toro, and

Panamanian vocalist Ruben Blades. In general it's an international pantheon Colon was inducted into with the same seeming effortlessness displayed in his impassioned playing and incisive compositions and arrangements. In particular, Blades makes a fitting partner; not only have he and Colon recorded together periodically—winning a Grammy for *Canciones del Solar de los Aburriodos* in 1982—but Blades's outspoken activism (including his almost-successful run at the Panamanian presidency in 1994) finds a kindred spirit in Colon.

Colon's songs were banned by Nicaraguan president Samoza in the 1970s and he was arrested several times in Central and South America for his political views. Unbowed by these hostilities, he has remained civically involved Stateside. In 1993, after performing at President Clinton's inauguration, Colon turned down an invitation to become a member of the President's Committee on the Arts and Humanities in order to devote his attention to running in the New York state primary for a congressional seat in the 17th District. A former chairperson of the Association of Hispanic Arts, Colon was the first minority to serve on ASCAP's national board. To the sorrow of his many hometown fans—and perhaps the delight of many public officials—he announced his relocation to Mexico City at a 1998 concert in Central Park. Enthusiasts can keep in touch via www.williecolon.com, through which the ever forward-looking Colon has begun to give some albums their initial, exclusive release.

what to buy: Discarding the Eddie Palmieri–influenced two-trombone sound of his early albums, Colon took a dynamic, hard-bopping approach with *The Good, the Bad, the Ugly* 𝄢𝄢𝄢𝄢 (Fania, 1975, prod. Willie Colon). Colon's last album with vocalist Hector Lavoe, it created a uplifting, youth-oriented direction for modern salsa.

what to buy next: Colon's first collaboration with future Latin superstar Blades, *Matiendo Mano* 𝄢𝄢𝄢𝄢 (Fania, 1977, prod. Willie Colon) not only represents a historic meeting of musical minds but remains a dance-inspiring masterpiece.

best of the rest:

Guisando 𝄢𝄢𝄢𝄢 (Fania, 1969)
Asalto Novideno 𝄢𝄢𝄢𝄢 (Fania, 1972)
The Big Break 𝄢𝄢𝄢𝄢 (Fania, 1976)
Siembra 𝄢𝄢𝄢𝄢 (Fania, 1978)
Solo 𝄢𝄢𝄢𝄢 (Fania, 1980)
Canciones del Solar de los Aburridos 𝄢𝄢𝄢𝄢 (Fania, 1983)
Top Secrets 𝄢𝄢𝄢𝄢 (Fania, 1989)
Illegal Aliens 𝄢𝄢𝄢𝄢 (Fania, 1990)
Color Americano 𝄢𝄢𝄢𝄢 (CBS, 1990)
Honra y Cultura 𝄢𝄢𝄢𝄢 (CBS, 1991)
El Malo 𝄢𝄢𝄢𝄢 (Fania, 1991)
49 Minutes 𝄢𝄢𝄢𝄢 (Fania, 1992)
Altos Secretos 𝄢𝄢𝄢𝄢 (Fania, 1992)

Willie Colon

Corazon Guerrero 🎵🎵🎵 (Fania, 1992)
Deja Vu 🎵🎵🎵 (Fania, 1992)
El Baquine de Angelitos Negros 🎵🎵🎵 (Fania, 1992)
Last Fight 🎵🎵🎵 (Fania, 1992)
The Best 🎵🎵🎵🎵 (Sony, 1992)
Grandes Exitos 🎵🎵🎵 (Fania, 1992)
Super Exitos 🎵🎵🎵 (Fania, 1992)
Hecho in Puerto Rico 🎵🎵🎵 (Fania, 1993)
Willie & Tito 🎵🎵🎵🎵 (Vaya, 1993)
Best, Vol. 2 🎵🎵🎵🎵 (Sony, 1994)
Lo Mato 🎵🎵🎵 (FNA, 1994)
El Juicio 🎵🎵🎵 (FNA, 1994)
Trans la Tornenta 🎵🎵🎵 (Sony, 1995)
Brillantes 🎵🎵🎵 (Sony, 1996)
Fania All-Stars 🎵🎵🎵🎵 (Sony, 1997)
Mi Gran Amor 🎵🎵🎵🎵 (Madacy, 1999)

influences:

◀◀ Mongo Santamaria, Tito Puente, Eddie Palmieri, Gato Barbieri

▶▶ Ruben Blades, Yomo Toro

see also: *Ruben Blades, Celia Cruz*

Craig Harris

The Congos

Roots reggae
Formed 1975, in Kingston, Jamaica. Disbanded 1983. Re-formed 1995. Based in New York, NY, USA.

Cedric Myton, vocals (1975–83; 1995–present); Roydel "Congo Ashanti Roy" Johnson, vocals (1975–80; 1997–present); Watty Burnett, vocals (1976–80; 1995–present); Devon Russell, vocals (1983); Lindbergh Lewis, vocals (1995–97). (All members are from Jamaica.)

The Congos' hauntingly beautiful lyricism casts an array of mystical beams and shadows which together reveal spectral glimpses of Jamaica and Rastafari's past and future. Add Lee Perry's sweltering, funky, jungle-dense production on the group's 1977 masterpiece, *Heart of the Congos*, and the mighty vocal potion of Cedric Myton (falsetto), Roydel Johnson (tenor), and Watty Burnett (baritone) conjures up a musical and cultural index of both the history and potential of the African diaspora. *Heart of the Congos* is that exceedingly rare album that is both timeless and forever timely.

Myton began his career with the Tartans, a vocal group in the proto-reggae rocksteady style that had one hit, "Dance All Night" (1967) on the Merritone label. The group's ensuing singles, "Coming on Strong" (Caltone) and "Far beyond the Sun" (Treasure Isle), were equally moving but not big sellers. Myton then recorded some sides with fellow ex-Tartan Devon Russell, including "What a Sin Thing" and "Short up Dress." From there, he

formed the Royal Rasses with the great Prince Lincoln Thompson; the group's superb "Kingston 11" is a radiant musical journey into Jamaican ghetto life. In 1975 the cultural deejay Big Youth introduced Myton to Roydel Johnson. At the time, Johnson's rich textural chanting was a key element of both Ras Michael's legendary *nyahbingi* (ritual Rasta) band/commune the Sons of Negus, and the undervalued Brother Joe & the Rightful Brothers, with whom Johnson recorded the devout Rasta anthem "Go to Zion" in 1973. The Congos formed soon after Myton and Johnson's meeting, the band's classic core almost completely in place.

With the help of producer Lee "Scratch" Perry—Johnson's old elementary school friend—the Congos released their hungry and heavy first single, "At the Feast." In 1976 Watty Burnett's reverberating baritone was added to the Congos' soulful and sepulchral choir. A year later Perry was at the height of his powers after releasing a series of distinctive albums recorded at his candle-lit, graffiti-emblazoned Black Ark studio—including Max Romeo's *War inna Babylon,* the Upsetters' *Super Ape,* and the Heptones' *Party Time,* all for Island Records. However, just as Scratch prepared to record the Congos' long-planned and painstakingly conceived debut, Island refused to release his wonderfully weird and walloping solo album, *Roast Fish, Collie Weed, and Cornbread.* Scratch's revenge was to withhold *Heart of the Congos* from Island and release it on his own Black Art label. Meanwhile, the group believed that Perry had deprived them of money and recognition, so they signed a multi-record deal with CBS's French subsidiary. Unfortunately, the Congos' subsequent series of albums sounded uninspired compared to their challengingly intense debut. Ironically, the fact that *Heart of the Congos* was widely considered to be Perry's most awe-inspiring production—combined with the record's lack of major-label distribution and the inferior mix on at least five different small-label reissues—rapidly led to international demand for the original pressing. And when Perry set the Black Ark ablaze in the midst of a nervous breakdown, reducing his sanctified studio to nothing but glowing embers and smoking ashes, reggae lovers' search for the already-fabled Black Ark production only intensified.

Johnson left the Congos in 1980 and released a number of solid albums under the name Congo Ashanti Roy. Myton re-formed the group in the mid-'90s with Burnett and ex-Tartan Lindbergh Lewis. In 1997 Johnson sang backup on the group's *Natty Dread Rise Again,* and returned as a full-fledged member for the recently released *Revival.* Truth be told, the Congos have never come close to equaling their astonishing debut. *Heart of the Congos* is virtually unmatchable because the soaring, majestic vocals—emanating from the Black Ark's Temple of Zoom, as Perry occasionally called it—were seemingly moored to this planet not by gravity, but by will, as if the Congos' magnificent shibboleths had emerged from another realm to provide inspiration to the earthbound.

what to buy: The essential issue of *Heart of the Congos* ♪♪♪♪♪ (Black Art, 1977/Blood & Fire, 1996, prod. Lee "Scratch" Perry) contains definitive, restored mixes of Congos classics such as "Fisherman," "Congoman," and "Ark of the Covenant," alongside the equally divine "La La Bam-Bam" (with unforgettable background harmonies by the Heptones and Gregory Isaacs), "Children Crying," and "Solid Foundation." A bonus disc features a mind-expanding remix of "Congoman" along with a wicked dub version called "Congoman Chant," both of which were originally released on the obscure 12" EP *Island Black Swan*; also included on the extra disc are "Bring the Macka Back" and "Noah Sugar Pan"—the amazing dubs of "Fisherman" and "Ark of the Covenant"—which were originally released as B-sides on Scratch's Upsetter and Black Art labels, respectively. Throughout both discs Perry's Echoplex reverb unit, Mutron phase-shifter, and way-out mooing-cow samples provide hallucinatory smoke-and-mirror effects. The backing band is simply outstanding: the Meditations provide multiple additional layers of vocal harmonizing; Ernest Ranglin lavishes his mesmerizing lead guitar onto nearly every song; and the terrific Upsetters are the rhythmic foundation undergirding the vocals, with Sly Dunbar on drums, Boris Gardiner on bass, and Winston Wright on organ. But ultimately, it is the Congos' meticulous tone shading, intricate melodic ornamentation, and subtly bent pitches that prove that Scratch was—despite his wont to cultivate sonic anarchy—a man who loved the human voice. His passionately detailed aural choreography indicates that he knew he was working with some of the finest singers he would ever have the privilege of recording. The blended timbral magic on *Heart of the Congos* is vocal artistry at its finest.

what to avoid: *Natty Dread Rise Again* **woof!** (RAS, 1997, prod. Cedric Myton, Yvonne Myton) is a reggae disaster area to be avoided by everyone but crazed Congos completists. Most of the songs are musically featherweight, with sappy, virtually meaningless, new-agey lyrics. And on the cuts that could have been vital, obnoxious synthesizers continually intrude like fluorescent Magic Marker scrawlings on an otherwise exquisite Impressionist painting. Also steer clear of a less expensive but inferior version of *Heart of the Congos* (Black Art, 1977/V.P., 1995), minus the bonus CD and plus abhorrent sonics.

the rest:
Image of Africa ♪♪♪ (CBS, 1979/V.P., 1994)
Congos Ashanti ♪♪♪ (CBS, 1980/V.P., 1995)
Face the Music ♪♪ (CBS, 1983/V.P., 1995)
Revival ♪♪♪ (V.P. 1999)

worth searching for: *Arkology* ♪♪♪♪♪ (Island, 1997, prod. Lee "Scratch" Perry) is a three-disc compilation of Perry's work inside the Black Ark studio and is a must-own for any reggae enthusiast. For Congos fans there's the added bonus of "Don't

Blame on I" and "Feast of the Passover," two great cuts by the group rendered with the eerie passion of doomed spirits wailing dread prophecies in the night, and which are otherwise as rare as the cinders of the torched Black Ark. Perry's *Open the Gate* ♪♪♪♪ (Trojan, 1989, prod. Lee "Scratch" Perry) is stuffed with swashbuckling Black Ark rarities and only a cut or two overlaps with *Arkology*. Besides the inclusion of Scratch's riveting account of the depression that eventually led him briefly into pyromania, "City Too Hot," Congos lovers will rejoice, as the double-disc collection includes a funhouse-mirror version of "Nicodemus" and two outstanding vocal performances from Watty Burnett: "Open the Gate" and "Rainy Night in Portland."

solo outings:
Congo Ashanti Roy:
Sign of the Star ♪♪♪ (Pre, 1981)
Dub X Perience ♪♪♪ (On U Sound, 1981)
Level Vibes ♪♪♪ (Sonic Boom, 1985)
Big City ♪♪ (Red Arrow, 1994)
Light up the City ♪♪ (Jah Power, 1995)

influences:

◄ The Abyssinians, Lee Perry, Ras Michael & the Sons of Negus, Big Youth, Prince Lincoln Thompson, Bob Marley, the Maytals

► Adrian Sherwood, Dub Syndicate, African Headcharge, Bim Sherman, Annette Brisset, Black Uhuru, Culture, Mikey Dread, Gregory Isaacs, Jah Shaka, Linton Kwesi Johnson, Prince Allah

see also: *Gregory Isaacs, the Meditations, Lee "Scratch" Perry, Ernest Ranglin, Sly & Robbie*

Todd Shanker

Conjunto Alma Jarocha
Jarocho
Formed in Mexico. Based in Mexico.

Isidoro Gutiérrez Ramon, jarana, lead vocals; Tirso Velásquez Córdoba, harp; Emilio Córdoba Córdoba, jarana; Inez Rivas Herrera, jarana, lead vocals; Rufino Velásquez Córdoba, harp; Daniel Valenica, requinto. (All members are from Mexico.)

People of the fertile, naturally rich area of Mexico's main port of Veracruz are known as the *jarochos*. The historical role Veracruz plays as the gateway to Spain made the jarochos one of the Mexican regional groups most tied to old-world Hispanic culture. Their music was developed by nonprofessionals in the 1920s. Played mostly by full-time musicians today, it reflects the influences of Spain in its choice of instruments, language, harmonic and rhythmic framework, verse types, and song forms. But the music is definitely Mexican, forged to suit the players' own preferences. Conjunto Alma Jarocha leader Isidoro Gutiérrez Ramon was a resident of the small town of Boca del Rio, just south of Veracruz. The son of a musician, he worked as a carpenter and fisherman before following in his father's footsteps. His musical partners are neighbors, friends, or cousins from nearby towns.

what's available: Despite some severe liner-note confusion over personnel, the string and vocal performances on *Conjunto Alma Jarocha: Sones Jarochos* 𝄢𝄢𝄢𝄢 (Arhoolie, 1979/1994, prod. Chris Strachwitz, Dan Sheehy) hold a quaint charm. These are farmers, charcoal-makers, ranchers. Their confident vocals and instrumentals are practiced and polished as they draw from Spanish influences (heard particularly in the guitar playing) and Mexican call-and-response vocal style. Valencia's solo performance on "El Pajaro Carpintero" shows his masterful technique on the guitar-like *requinto*; he's both flamboyant and skilled, simultaneously picking melody and accompanying bass notes. Another delight is Rufino Velásquez Córdoba's fast-picked, swirling harp solo on "Siquisrí." If you haven't heard music from this part of Mexico before, it's a rare, ear-pleasing treat—especially their version of one of the oldest songs in the canon, a widely popular number you might be familiar with: "La Bamba." Should you want to sing along, Spanish-English translations are included in the 23-page liner booklet.

influences:

◄◄ Lino Carillo, Táchin Córdoba

►► Ritchie Valens

Nancy Ann Lee

Conjunto Bernal

Conjunto, norteño
Formed c. 1955, in Texas, USA. Disbanded late 1970s.

Paulino Bernal, vocals, accordion; Eloy Bernal, vocals, 12-string guitar; Ruben Perez, vocals, bass, drums. (All members are from USA.)

Conjunto Bernal is considered one of the best bands in the history of Tex-Mex music. Born and raised in dire poverty in the town of Raymondville, deep in south Texas, group founder Paulino Bernal was an accomplished accordionist by the time he had to quit school in the seventh grade to help his family survive. His parents divorced and Bernal's mother moved to Kingsville, where Paulino, his brothers, and three sisters were forced into migrant farm work to support the family. Paulino's first instrument was a guitar his mother bought for the boys. Teaching himself to play, he earned enough money performing in the cantinas to help buy food for the family. Inspired by accordionists of the '40s and '50s he heard on the radio, Paulino dreamed of playing that instrument as well, and began practicing on one his friend received as a gift. His brother Eloy was given a 12-string guitar

and the brothers soon launched their musical careers together in 1952, when they and a drummer friend were hired to play at a dance in a nearby town. Well-received, they were invited back repeatedly and began playing other towns in the area—including Alice, home of the influential Ideal Records, which through the recommendation of producer Armando Marroquin first recorded the band as backup session players.

The Bernals got their chance as headliners in March 1955, on a career-launching 78 rpm single that included the country song "Mujer Paseada (Traveled Woman)" on the front and the romantic bolero "Desprecio" on the flipside. Afterward, El Conjunto Bernal made numerous recordings for Ideal between 1955 and 1960. They toured the Southwest and beyond, playing to packed houses. Inspired by Arizona bandleader Pedro Bugarian, who featured El Conjunto Bernal with his *orquesta,* Paulino branched out from the simple *ranchera* style of *conjunto* (a name for Tex-Mex music as well as a general term for Latin ensembles) to a more sophisticated, arranged orchestral form. Around 1960 Marroquin terminated his relationship with Ideal Records, but El Conjunto Bernal remained with him as he recorded them for his new label, Nopal. The band soon relocated to McAllen in the Lower Rio Grande Valley, across the border from Mexico. Paulino began working with Victor Gonzalez, cofounding the label Bego and releasing some of Conjunto Bernal's most innovative work. In the late 1960s Paulino sold his interest in Bego to Gonzalez and founded Bernal Records, which produced many hits. However, by this time Paulino had given up performing to handle the administrative duties of show business: running the record company and hosting a regional TV music show. Other accordionists would carry on his tradition of excellence, while Paulino's problems with alcohol and drugs affected his career until 1972 when he became a born-again Christian. Clean and sober, he resumed his career as an accordionist. In the service of his faith, he started Bernal Christian Records, under which he continued to develop his style.

what to buy: Two delightful albums from the Arhoolie label, part of their Tejano Roots series, are available in the U.S. and best represent the Conjunto Bernal during their Ideal years. The biggest value is *Mi Unico Camino (My Only Path)* 𝄢𝄢𝄢𝄢 (Arhoolie, 1992, reissue prod. Chris Strachwitz). Jam-packed with 24 vocal and instrumental tracks, the album brightly showcases the talents of Conjunto Bernal's musicians. Their well-blended harmonies and happy-time melodies in the Tex-Mex tradition display the finesse of their peak recording years for Ideal, when they made hits such as "Mi Unico Camino" (a tune included here and featured as the opening song in the John Sayles film *Lone Star*) and "Sentimiento y Rencor." Paulino's deft accordion playing is prominently featured throughout, but is especially notable as he expertly navigates hastened polkas. Just as enjoyable are the swooping, two-step tempos of the ranchera-style songs such as "Mi Borrachera," and the nicely blended vocals on about half of the tunes. Original LP-release numbers and dates are given, but alas no lyrics or title translations. However, such omissions shouldn't detract from your enjoyment of this splendid, roots-rich music.

what to buy next: Without repeating any of the tracks from *Mi Unico Camino*, *16 Early Tejano Classics* ΔΔΔΔ (Arhoolie, 1997, reissue prod. Chris Strachwitz) beguiles the listener with more ranchera-style songs, polkas, and boleros recorded for Ideal. Featuring the Bernal brothers with additional vocal accompaniment on some tracks, this album is an equally high-quality and engaging CD that kicks off on the first two tracks (the ranchera title tune and "Neto's Polka") with Paulino Bernal in vocal duets with singer Carmen Marroquín. Paulino's accordion prevails throughout on melodies, and while Eloy gets no solo moments in the spotlight, he provides stable rhythmic support on guitar and joins his brother for some charming vocal duets. The Bernal polkas are evocative, and their boleros—especially the catchy "Por La Misma Senda"—a jolt.

influences:

◀◀ Narciso Martinez, Don Santiago Jimenez, José Alfredo Jimenez

▶▶ Los Tigres del Norte, Los Cadetes del Norte, Linda Ronstadt, Vicente Fernandez, Chavela Vargas

Nancy Ann Lee

Conjunto Céspedes

Son, Afro-Cuban jazz
Formed 1981 as Trio Céspedes in Oakland, CA, USA. Based in Oakland CA, USA.

Gladys "Bobi" Céspedes (Cuba), vocals, clave; Guillermo Céspedes (Cuba), tres, piano, arranger; Jesús Díaz, percussion; Rahsaan Federicks, bass, percussion; Wayne Wallace, trombone (1991–95); Raul Navarrete, trombone; Chris Cooper, violin, guitar; Eric Rangel, timbales; Mara Fox, trombone; Julius Meléndez, trumpet; Jeff Lewis, trumpet; Oscar Soltero, bongos; Rob Holland, bass (1991–95). (All members are from USA unless otherwise noted.)

Conjunto Céspedes—a family-run Afro-Cuban dance band fronted by Gladys "Bobi" Céspedes and her brother Guillermo—were one of Oakland's best-kept secrets until they signed with Xenophile Records in 1993. Xenophile's muscle launched the band's international career, establishing Bobi as a diva to watch and Guillermo as a world-class composer and arranger. Guillermo began his musical training on the violin at age seven, while he was still in Cuba. "I was more drawn to the classical guitar," he says, "but everyone in the family played guitar, so it wasn't considered a 'real' instrument." When he was 11, Guillermo

and Bobi were shipped off to the States to escape Castro's revolution. He finally revisited Cuba in 1979, and when he played some of the songs he'd been composing for friends, the reaction was so positive that he moved to Oakland to join his sister Bobi, who was already singing in Cuban folkloric groups. They started Trio Céspedes with their uncle Luis, and again the reaction was positive. Within a year, the group had added horns, percussion, and piano. "We play *son*, a working-class kind of dance music, but with a more African slant than many bands, although it's not a conscious part of what we do," Guillermo says. "These rhythms came from Africa, and were passed down for generations, but it's not something we think about when we play, although that connection is an important part of what we are, both as musicians as well as personally. We stay true to the folkloric brand of son and rumba, like the rhythms of los Muñequitos de Matanzas. I don't like to criticize other musicians, but the rhythms of *salsa romantico* are predictable. We like complicated melodies and rhythms that will challenge the dancers."

what to buy: While none of the Conjunto's albums captures the incredible energy of their concerts, *Vivito y Coleando* ΔΔΔΔ (Xenophile, 1995, prod. John Santos) comes closest with its deep African percussion and raw live energy.

the rest:
Una Sola Casa ΔΔΔ∇ (Xenophile, 1993)
Flores ΔΔΔΔ (Xenophile, 1998)

influences:
◀◀ Beny Moré, Los Muñequitos de Matanzas, Arsenio Rodriquez, Celia Cruz, Los Van Van

j. poet

Ry Cooder /Buena Vista Social Club

Rock, blues, folk, worldbeat
Born March 15, 1947, in Los Angeles, CA, USA. Based in California, USA.

Ry Cooder's guitar-playing contemporaries—Jimmy Page, Jeff Beck, and Eric Clapton among them—progressed in typical directions, alternating between blues, pop, and rock as they grew older. Cooder turned instead to other civilizations, collaborating throughout the '90s with Indian musician V.M. Bhatt, West African guitarist Ali Farka Touré, and a group of Cuban artists known as the Buena Vista Social Club. Cooder, who started his career playing blues and folk songs in the early '60s, never intended to become a rock 'n' roll superstar; he slowly developed his skills and built his reputation as a thorough musicologist and reputable session musician. He was in a few bands early on, including one with soul singer Jackie DeShannon, another with fellow blues fanatic Taj Mahal (the short-lived but influential Rising Sons), and a third with the musical mad genius Captain Beefheart around 1967. (He also sat in on the Rolling Stones' *Let It Bleed* sessions, claiming to have come up with the famous "Honky Tonk Women" riff.) Cooder's many solo albums, particularly 1976's *Chicken Skin Music* and 1974's *Paradise and Lunch,* have a raw, refreshing sense of humor, and they're almost always rooted in '50s rockabilly and harder-than-they-sound guitar licks. Never willing to stick to one style for very long, though, Cooder's interests have lurched from said rockabilly, to Tex-Mex, to Hawaiian "slack-key" guitar music, and he's expanded his breadth with each new incarnation.

what to buy: Cooder didn't just experiment with exotic styles on *Buena Vista Social Club* 🎵🎵🎵🎵 (World Circuit/Nonesuch, 1997, prod. Ry Cooder), or even incorporate them into his own music the way Paul Simon did on *Graceland*. Instead, he submerged himself in Cuban culture, plugging into an impeccable group of Cuban musicians including singer-guitarist Santiagueran Eliades Ochoa, singer Ibrahim Ferrer, and pianist Ruben Gonzalez. Cooder barely even gives himself top billing on the album, obviously preferring to showcase his peers' talents and the group's quality as a whole. He picked the right time to defer the spotlight, as some of the Social Club's banner members were only breaking through still-frosty U.S./Cuban relations to become Stateside stars in their '70s and '80s. This project rode the crest from a floodgate opened in that cultural wall by slightly earlier showcases for too-long silenced greats like the Afro-Cuban All-Stars, and to the delight of music lovers the tide hasn't been turned back since. The Club's triumphant follow-up, featuring most of the first disc's players but focusing on a particular virtuoso vocalist, was subsequently released as *Buena Vista Social Club Presents Ibrahim Ferrer* 🎵🎵🎵🎵 (World Circuit/Nonesuch, 1999, prod. Ry Cooder). Cooder's collaborations with Bhatt on *A Meeting by the River* 🎵🎵🎵🎵 (Water Lily Acoustics, 1993, prod. Kavichandran Alexander) and with Touré on *Talking Timbuktu* 🎵🎵🎵🎵 (Hannibal, 1994 prod. Ry Cooder) were his first major explorations of world music. The latter album, in a still-unsurpassed success story, reigned for 25 weeks at #1 on the *Billboard* world-music chart, and earned a Grammy.

what to buy next: Cooder's early solo albums are much more conventionally Western than his recent material, but many of them are impeccably played and surprisingly funny. *Paradise and Lunch* 🎵🎵🎵🎵 (Reprise, 1974, prod. Lenny Waronker, Russ Titelman) includes the heartwarming "Mexican Divorce" and a fun, definitive version of "Ditty Wa Ditty." *Chicken Skin Music* 🎵🎵🎵🎵 (Reprise, 1976, prod. Ry Cooder) predated Simon's *Graceland* by incorporating Tex-Mex accordion hero Flaco Jimenez (who helps with a killer "Stand by Me") and Hawaiian slack-key guitarist Gabby Pahinui into Cooder's more American-sounding rock 'n' roll. Both *Into the Purple Valley* 🎵🎵🎵 (Reprise, 1972, prod. Lenny Waronker, Jim Dickinson), with its Johnny Cash,

Woody Guthrie, and Jackie Wilson songs, and *Bop till You Drop* 🎵🎵🎵 (Warner Bros., 1979, prod. Ry Cooder), with the brilliantly weird "Down in Hollywood," showcase Cooder's fun-loving history-of-rock side. The two-disc *Music by Ry Cooder* 🎵🎵🎵🎵 (Warner Bros., 1995, prod. Ry Cooder, Joachim Cooder) is a thorough collection of Cooder's movie music, so it saves you the trouble of combing through his uneven soundtrack albums.

what to avoid: Cooder's experiments and ambitions occasionally backfire, especially on the tedious *Jazz* 🎵🎵 (Warner Bros., 1978, prod. Ry Cooder, Joseph Byrd), which has interesting ideas—like a cover of the 1880 folk song "The Dream"—but nothing else to recommend it. He sounds plain bored on *Get Rhythm* 🎵🎵 (Warner Bros., 1987, prod. Ry Cooder), despite the presence of old friend Jimenez and the always-unusual Van Dyke Parks. Also not up to snuff is his solo debut, *Ry Cooder* 🎵 (Reprise, 1970, prod. Van Dyke Parks, Ry Cooder).

the rest:
Boomer's Story 🎵🎵🎵 (Reprise, 1972)
Show Time 🎵🎵🎵 (Warner Bros., 1977)
Borderline 🎵🎵 (Warner Bros., 1980)
The Slide Area 🎵🎵 (Warner Bros., 1982)
Alamo Bay 🎵🎵 (Slash, 1985)
Blue City 🎵🎵 (Warner Bros., 1986)
Geronimo: An American Legend 🎵🎵🎵 (Warner Bros., 1993)
Trespass 🎵🎵🎵 (Sire, 1994)

worth searching for: Check the video stores for Wim Wenders's by-turns sensitive and sizzling documentary, *Buena Vista Social Club*. The film includes superb concert performances, fascinating footage of present-day Cuba, and affecting portraits of these stars' late-blooming artistic vindication. In a related note, Cooder's soundtracks go in and out of print quickly; the better collections are *Paris, Texas* 🎵🎵🎵 (Warner Bros., 1984, prod. Ry Cooder), *Johnny Handsome* 🎵🎵🎵 (Warner Bros., 1989, prod. Ry Cooder), *The Long Riders* 🎵🎵🎵 (Warner Bros., 1980, prod. Ry Cooder), *The Border* 🎵🎵🎵🎵 (Backstreet, 1981)—featuring interesting collaborations with John Hiatt, Freddie Fender, and the long-lost Sam Samudio—and the much-maligned *Crossroads* 🎵🎵🎵 (Warner Bros., 1986, prod. Ry Cooder), a terrible movie that nonetheless features great pure-blues slide work with Cooder and fellow string enthusiast and world-music impresario David Lindley.

solo outings:
Eliades Ochoa:
Sublime Illusion N/A (Higher Octave, 1999)

Omara Portuondo:
(With Chucho Valdés) *Desafíos* 🎵🎵🎵🎵 (Nubenegra/Alula, 1997/1998)

influences:
◀◀ Elmore James, Charlie Christian, Mississippi Fred McDowell, Tampa Red, Rolling Stones, Jimi Hendrix, Buddy Guy, Taj Mahal

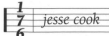

▶ Sonny Landreth, Bonnie Raitt, Rory Block, Daniel Lanois, Robbie Robertson

see also: *V.M. Bhatt, Kevin Burke, the Chieftains, Ruben Gonzalez, Flaco Jimenez, Shoukichi Kina, Gabby Pahinui, Pahinui Brothers, Ali Farka Touré*

Steve Knopper

Jesse Cook
New flamenco, new age
Born November 28, 1964, in Paris, France. Based in Toronto, Ontario, Canada.

Flamenco is usually thought of as an art for the mature, developed musician, but Jesse Cook began playing in the style at age three, following along with his mother's records on a toy guitar. The family lived in France and Spain when Jesse was young, and there he was exposed to an atmosphere rich in art, music, and varied cultures. Though when the family moved back to Canada Cook began formal music studies (first in Toronto, then in New York and Boston), the flamenco music of his childhood haunted him, and he returned to Spain to seek out and learn from the guitar masters of Andalusia and Cordoba. But his hybrid instincts seemed to assert themselves in contrast to whatever setting he'd place himself in; not content to become "just" a master of classical flamenco style, he returned again to Canada and found employment as a composer for dance, multimedia, and television, working in genres ranging from classical to rap. And sure enough, he then felt the pull of what would be his true love: compositions melding the structure and soul of flamenco (or, more precisely, Cook's own hybrid concept and term "rhumba flamenca") with world percussion. In a truly 20th-century development, this new flamenco music was selected to be played as background on the Canadian TV Guide Channel. Response to that exposure was so great that Cook decided to record his first album.

what to buy: Two qualities separate Cook's recordings from the pack of new flamenco artists currently filling the new-age charts: his strong melodic sense, which he uses in the service of musical adventure, and his ability and willingness to integrate technology into his work. He also continues his quest to introduce "rhumba flamenca" to other aspects of world music, assisted on *Vertigo* ⅃⅃⅃⅃⅃ (Narada, 1998, prod. Jesse Cook) by the contributions of guests like jazz vocalist Holly Cole, zydeco master Stanley Dural Jr., a.k.a. Buckwheat Zydeco, and classical cellist Ofra Harnoy. The thing that keeps Cook's music fresh and outstanding is his expansive vision of folk tradition, which is evident on his earlier albums, *Tempest* ⅃⅃⅃⅃ (Narada, 1995, prod. Jesse Cook) and *Gravity* ⅃⅃⅃⅃ (Narada, 1996, prod. Jesse Cook). He explains it this way: "Though sometimes the music produced is a completely new hybrid, my goal is always to make these unions sound so organic that they're almost familiar, as if a lost folk tradition was rediscovered."

influences:
◀◀ Peter Gabriel, Al de Mieola, Paco de Lucia

see also: *Buckwheat Zydeco*

Kerry Dexter

Andy Cooney
Traditional Irish, country, pop, devotional
Born in Long Island, NY, USA. Based in northeastern USA and Nashville, TN, USA.

A youthful singer/songwriter with a warm, assured delivery and boyish good looks, Andy Cooney is a major attraction on the Irish-American music circuit. One of nine children and a performer at family and church gatherings from the age of five, he turned professional at 17 and fronted for Paddy Noonan's band until launching a solo career in the late '80s. Cooney's music is a lushly produced, carefully wrought synthesis of traditional Hibernian balladry, American pop, Catholic mysticism, and (lately) big-hat country. His sad and wistful self-penned tunes evoke much Irish spirituality without the compensating grace of Irish humor. Hailed by the *New York Times* as "Irish-America's native son," Cooney is a busy live performer who tours steadily and plays cruises, weddings, and festivals throughout the U.S.

what to buy: Cooney's latest, *Irish Influence* ⅃⅃⅃ (Shanachie, 1997, prod. Michael Smith, Randy Hauser), demonstrates his maturing vocal range and a new infatuation with country music. Recorded with Catherine Coates, the album's highlights are "Galway to Graceland," a Richard Thompson cover; and "Immaculate Heart," a delicate common-man prayer to the Blessed Virgin done with light country overtones. Devotees of old-school Irish sentimentality should check out *Boston Rose and Other Irish Favorites* ⅃⅃⅃ (Rego, 1989, prod. Noel Healy, Andy Cooney), which contains Cooney's stylings of songs like "Rose of Tralee," "I Will Take You Home Again, Kathleen," and "Danny Boy."

what to buy next: Cooney's collaboration with noted composer/songwriter Phil Coulter should have resulted in a better album than *Home Away from Home* ⅃⅃⅃ (Rego, 1994, prod. Phil Coulter, Andy Cooney, Joanie Madden). Still, Cooney does do yeoman work with such Coulter originals as the title track and "Wait till the Clouds Roll By," and at least one couplet from "The Town I Loved So Well" ("There was music there/In the Derry air") is howlingly funny—all the more so (if a cruel, guilty pleasure) for its composer's unsuspectingly tear-jerking intentions.

the rest:
Vows, Prayers, and Promises ⅃⅃⅃ (Rego, 1991)
A Collection of Irish Hits ⅃⅃⅃ (Rego, 1992)
The Auld Christmas Waltz ⅃⅃⅃ (Shanachie, 1996)

influences:

◀◀ Phil Coulter, Garth Brooks, Bono

see also: *Phil Coulter*

Ron Garmon

J.P. Cormier
Cape Breton fiddle and song
Born January 23, 1969, in Cape Breton, Nova Scotia, Canada. Based in eastern Canada.

In both his words and his music, J.P. Cormier evokes the sea and the wind of his birthplace: Cape Breton, on the Atlantic coast of Canada. However, he is one of those artists who had to leave his home to find it. After a childhood learning bluegrass guitar, Cormier started playing the fiddle when he was 16. He also moved to the southern U.S. and began a successful career as a country sideman, working with some of that genre's most respected names, including Travis Tritt, Hal Ketchum, Pam Tillis, and Mark O'Connor. While living in Nashville, J.P. and his wife, noted traditional piano player Hilda Chiasson Cormier, recorded *Return to the Cape,* an album of Cape Breton fiddle music. It reopened a need in J.P. to express his cultural identity in music, which led him and Hilda to move back to Cape Breton. Going home enabled J.P. to further his own songwriting, and concentrate on the music he grew up with.

what's available: Cape Breton is a place where many cultures mix—French, Scots, Irish, English, and Miqmak Indian. All are concerned with wresting a living and a life from the sea, their constant challenge and companion. Though *Another Morning* ♪♪♪♪ (Borealis, 1997, prod. Paul Mills, Bill Garrett) is not specifically a maritime album, you can almost hear the creak of the wood and feel the salt tang of the coastal wind as you listen to Cormier's words and fiddle evoke tales of life on northern shores. There is a noteworthy guest appearance by Canadian folksinger and producer Sylvia Tyson singing harmony on "The Blackbird."

influences:
◀◀ Joe Cormier, Tony Rice, Winston Fitzgerald, Chet Atkins, Doc Watson

Kerry Dexter

Sheryl Cormier
Cajun
Born March 15, 1945, in Grand Coteau, LA, USA. Based in Crowley, LA, USA.

Although Cleoma Breaux Falcon had recorded back in the 1920s, there were still no female Cajun band leaders. While it was not uncommon for women to play music at home or to know the old traditional ballads, it is only recently that a woman could both play accordion and lead a popular band. The woman who epitomizes this change is Sheryl Cormier. She was the oldest of four children and started playing the Cajun accordion at age seven. Her father, Andrew Guilbeau, was the leader of the Sunset Playboys and her mother was the drummer. Sheryl occasionally played with the group, but gave it up when she married Russell Cormier. But even after her son was born she got back to sitting in and playing a little on weekends with different bands. Her own initial band included her husband on vocals and her son Russell Jr. on drums. This is the outfit on her first album, *La Reine de Musique Cadjine (The Queen of Cajun Music)*. Not satisfied with leading a group of male musicians, she also put together the first all-female Cajun band. Regardless of gender, her sound is that of the classic Cajun dance band and her popularity continues unabated.

what to buy: *La Reine de Musique Cadjine (The Queen of Cajun Music)* ♪♪♪♪ (Swallow, 1990, prod. Lee Lavergne) was Cormier's first LP, and has additional cuts added for the CD release. There's a solid dance sound and a strong Aldus Roger influence, which you can particularly hear on "Louisiana Waltz" by Roger himself. "Laccasine Special" and "Valse de Pont d'Amour" demonstrate that Cormier has the chops to handle tunes associated with the seminal Iry Lejeune. Her husband Russell shares the vocal duties with Ivy Dugas.

what to buy next: *Sheryl Cormier and Cajun Sounds* ♪♪♪ (Swallow, 1992, prod. Lee Lavergne) exhibits more of the real Cajun dance sound that Cormier can get out of a band. There are standards like "Bosco Stomp" and tunes with a more country sound, which is not uncommon in the repertoires of modern Cajun groups. A solid record to dance around the living room to.

influences:
◀◀ Aldus Roger, Sundown Playboys, Paul Daigle

▶▶ Kristi Guillory, Magnolia Sisters

see also: *Joseph Falcon & Cleoma Breaux Falcon, Iry LeJeune, Aldus Roger*

Jared Snyder

Cornershop
Punjabi pop
Formed 1992, in London, England. Based in London, England.

Tjinder Singh, vocals, guitar; Ben Ayres, guitar; Avtar Singh, guitar; Anthony Saffery, sitar, keyboards; Nick Simms, drums; Pete Hall, percussion. (All members are from England.)

Musical innovation these days is all about pastiche, and which styles a band chooses to blend is sometimes more critically important than how well they blend them. Illustrating this phenomena nicely is Cornershop, whose attempted fusion of Indian music (sitars, wind instruments, lyrical chants) and contemporary pop has legions of rock writers all in a tizzy. In truth, "Brimful of Asha," the band's only hit single to date, is bereft of those highly touted subcontinental soundscapes (though it does pay tribute to Asha Bhosle, diva of "Bollywood" soundtracks and darling of those same hipster critics). Cornershop does two things well: writing solid pop songs and spacing out on sitar drones. Though it's getting better at both, the group has yet to fully integrate the two ideas. Initially known more for its strong anti-racist politics than its music, Cornershop enjoyed a rise that was, at the start, a sign of the times. British pop culture was entering into a minor infatuation with Eastern culture in general (the screen adaptation of *The Buddha of Suburbia* aired on the BBC during the fall of 1993), creating a somewhat sympathetic ear and nurturing atmosphere. The band eventually improved enough to catch the notice of the patron saint of polyethnic music, David Byrne, who signed them to his Luaka Bop label in 1995. But in the wake of newfound outsider stardom, band leader Tjinder Singh spoke about concentrating more on a dance-music side project called Clinton. Go figure.

what to buy: *When I Was Born for the 7th Time* 🎷🎷🎷🎷 (Luaka Bop, 1997, prod. Tjinder Singh) was a critical favorite of 1997 largely due to the unbelievable leap in tightness and tonality it took from its predecessor. The album moves nimbly between mid-fi jangle pop and polyrhythmic sitar drones, all laced with DJ scratches, synthesizer swells, and electronic dubs to mark the times. "Sleep on the Left Side" and "Brimful of Asha" are irresistible singles, and "When the Light Appears Boy" features the poetry and the voice of Allen Ginsberg. But Singh's cover of "Norwegian Wood," sung in Punjabi, is more of a novelty than a visceral experience.

what to avoid: *Woman's Gotta Have It* 🎷🎷 (Luaka Bop, 1996, prod. Tjinder Singh) veers abruptly between sitar drones with Punjabi rants laid over funky rhythmic tracks, and angry lo-fi guitar rock. "Wog" gets the best of both worlds, combining great percussion with muted guitar jangles. "Looking for a Way Out" comes off like a simple, solid indie-pop song with stripped-down melodies. Most of the album's vocals are not in English.

worth searching for: *Hold on It Hurts* (Merge, 1995, prod. Tjinder Singh) is an out-of-print album on an independent label that shows early signs of what Cornershop would become.

influences:

◀◀ George Harrison, David Byrne, the Velvet Underground

Isaac Josephson

Gal Costa

MPB (Brazilian Popular Music)

Born 1945, in Santo Amaro, Bahia, Brazil. Based in Bahia, Brazil.

With the ever-present flower at her temple, Gal Costa led her generation in discreetly questioning political authority, and became the voice of the protest songs and the offbeat poetry and psychedelia that was the *Tropicalismo* movement. Born in the town of Santo Amaro, Bahia, she became fast friends with schoolmates Caetano Veloso and Maria Bethânia. When Caetano met Gilberto Gil, the foursome formed a circle of intense creativity that soon had them touring Brazil as the Doces Barbaros. They played to a generation that was hungry for freedom, ignoring the censure of the military government. When Veloso and Gil were exiled, Costa interpreted the lyrics they sent home.

As a solo artist Costa sought out new songwriters and fresh ideas. She was first to discover the talent of Luiz Melodia, recorded Roberto and Erasmo Carlos, and maintained strong ties to the *Jovem Guarda* rock movement. Over all, though, she embraces her Bahian roots; her renditions of Dorival Caymmi's ballads and of Carnival hits like Morais Moreira's "Festa do Interior" were instant classics, and have stayed with her throughout her career. Costa's rich, unforgettable voice, with its expansive range, is at once mysterious and personable. This voice is not the understated elegance of the bossa nova divas, but an exuberant celebration of the dark and the light, the full range of emotion that is *Musica Popular Brasileira*. Expressing the buoyant innocence of "Baby" or the haunting remoteness of "Vapor Barato," it will never cease to electrify.

what to buy: A quick intro to Costa's music can be obtained in an album that recaps many of her greatest hits—*Acustico* 🎷🎷🎷🎷 (BMG Brazil, 1997, prod. Mazzola) is from the MTV Brazil *Unplugged* series, and extracts near-perfect sound from the exquisite live performance.

what to buy next: *Tropical* 🎷🎷🎷🎷 (PolyGram, 1979, prod. Guilherme Araujo, Roberto Menescal) was for a long time considered her greatest album. It includes, among other crucial tracks, the *chorinho* dance tune "Noites Cariocas" by Jacob do Bandolim. Her older material tends to be preferable, but her recent records (often more easy to find) also provide a complex and sensitive listening experience. *Sorriso do Gato de Alice* 🎷🎷🎷🎷 (BMG Brazil, 1993, prod. Jaques Morelenbaum) has some wonderful ballads, including Djavan's "Serene" in English. Funk and acoustic samba alternate to give downtown dissonant touches. On *Mina de Agua No Meu Canto* 🎷🎷🎷🎷 (BMG Brazil, 1994, prod. Arto Lindsay) Gal interprets songs by Chico Buarque and Caetano Veloso; it has

Gal Costa

sublime moments as well as some over-the-top string-section stuff. *Aquele Frevo Axe* ♪♪♪♪ (BMG Brazil, 1998, prod. Celso Fonseca) draws from her two main homegrown cultural influences (as the title's listing of styles suggests), North-eastern and Bahian. The title track is actually a drop-dead-beautiful samba.

best of the rest:

(With Caetano Veloso) *Domingo* ♪♪♪♪ (PolyGram Brazil, 1967)

Gal ♪♪♪♪ (PolyGram Brazil, 1969)

Legal ♪♪♪♪ (PolyGram Brazil, 1970)

Fatal–Gal a Todo Vapor ♪♪♪♪♪ (PolyGram Brazil, 1971)

Cantar ♪♪♪♪ (PolyGram Brazil, 1974)

Gal Canta Caymmi ♪♪♪♪ (PolyGram Brazil, 1975)

Doces Barbaros ♪♪♪♪♪ (PolyGram Brazil, 1976)

Caras E Bocas ♪♪♪♪ (PolyGram Brazil, 1977)

Agua Viva ♪♪♪♪ (PolyGram Brazil, 1978)

Tropical ♪♪♪♪ (PolyGram Brazil, 1979)

Aquarela do Brasil ♪♪♪ (PolyGram Brazil, 1980)

Fantasia ♪♪♪ (PolyGram Brazil, 1981)

Baby Gal ♪♪♪ (PolyGram Brazil, 1983)

Profana ♪♪♪ (PolyGram Brazil, 1984)

Bem Bom ♪♪♪♪ (BMG Brazil, 1986)

Meu Nome E Gal/My Name Is Gal ♪♪♪♪♪ (Verve, 1990)

Rio Revisited ♪♪♪♪♪ (PolyGram Brazil, 1992)

Gal ♪♪♪ (BMG Brazil, 1992)

Lua de Mel Como o Diabo Gosta ♪♪♪ (BMG Brazil, 1994)

Brazilian Collection ♪♪♪♪ (PolyGram Latino, 1998)

worth searching for: As rereleases get more prevalent, any of the above-mentioned albums may suddenly become more available. Definitely also watch for *Gal Costa* ♪♪♪♪ (PolyGram Brazil, 1968), her first solo album. The arrangements, daring for the time, showcase a voice that is still not totally polished, but bursting with energy. *India* ♪♪♪♪♪ (PolyGram Brazil, 1973) was censored for Gal's skimpy clothing in the cover photo. The songs validate the folkloric in bright, sparse arrangements. Vinyl only, but it is available through the internet.

influences:

▶▶ Daniela Mercury

see also: *Maria Bethânia, Djavan, Gilberto Gil, Caetano Veloso*

Mara Weiss, Nego Beto, and Marty Lipp

Phil Coulter

Celtic, new age, pop, easy listening
Born February, 1942, in Derry, Northern Ireland. Based in Bray, Ireland.

Arguably one of the most beloved and multidimensional musicians to emerge from Ireland, Phil Coulter has made his mark as a wide-ranging songwriter, producer, arranger, and performer. In 1965 Coulter penned his first hit, "Terry," for the Irish pop band Twinkle. He also wrote several songs for the Irish rock band Them—early musical home to a singer of some passing repute himself named Van Morrison. In the late '60s Coulter formed a writing partnership with Bill Martin and wrote perhaps his most famous work, "Puppet on a String," for nowadays not-so-famous singer Sandy Shaw. In the '70s Coulter wrote and produced several hits for Scottish bubblegum band and ex-next-Beatles the Bay City Rollers, including "Summerlove Sensation," "All of Me Loves All of You," and "Remember (Sha La La)." Notwithstanding these high-profile, low-concept endeavors, Coulter has throughout his career continued to work in the traditional Irish folk vein as well. In the '80s and '90s he recorded a slew of amazingly uniform discs that might best be called traditional Celtic new-age mood music. Well-respected behind the scenes—as producer, songwriter, and pianist—Coulter has worked with such artists as Sinéad O'Connor, Morrison, the Chieftains, the Furey Brothers, and James Galway. With the last-named he has of late been making some of his most serious bids for authentic Irish-traditional posterity.

what to buy: *Phil Coulter & His Orchestra: The Live Experience* 𝄫𝄫𝄫𝄫 (Shanachie, 1996, prod. Phil Coulter) captures Coulter the entertainer at his most electric, eclectic, and indulgent. Recorded live at the Concert Hall in Limerick, Ireland, Coulter and his orchestra play an unusual MOR mix of traditional Irish folk, popular standards, and the artist's own compositions. Represented are sentimental arrangements of "The Derry Air," "The Ballad of William Bloat/I'll Tell Me Ma," and "Mo Ghile Mear." Coulter's own tunes include "The Town I Loved So Well," "Scorn Not His Simplicity," "The Old Man," and "Steal Away." In the middle of that Coulter runs through a strange medley of Henry Mancini pieces ("The Pink Panther," "Moon River," "Baby Elephant Walk") as well as Aaron Copeland's "Hoedown."

what to buy next: *Celtic Horizons* 𝄫𝄫𝄫 (Shanachie, 1996, prod. Phil Coulter) is only one of several Coulter collections (see below) that spotlight his cozy interpretations of traditional music, be it Irish, Scottish, American, or some derivation thereof. Here the tunes are Irish and include "Planxty Irwin," "Tears on the Heather," "The Road to Glenaan," and "Toward the Mist."

the rest:
Scottish Tranquility 𝄫𝄫𝄫 (Shanachie, 1984)
Sea of Tranquility 𝄫𝄫𝄫 (Shanachie, 1984)
Christmas 𝄫𝄫𝄫 (Shanachie, 1985)
Classic Tranquility 𝄫𝄫𝄫 (Shanachie, 1989)
Serenity 𝄫𝄫𝄫 (Shanachie, 1989)
Forgotten Dreams 𝄫𝄫𝄫 (Shanachie, 1989)
Words and Music 𝄫𝄫𝄫 (Shanachie, 1990)
Peace and Tranquility 𝄫𝄫𝄫 (Shanachie, 1990)
Touch of Tranquility 𝄫𝄫𝄫 (Shanachie, 1992)
Recollections 𝄫𝄫𝄫 (Shanachie, 1993)
American Tranquility 𝄫𝄫𝄫 (Shanachie, 1994)
Celtic Collections 𝄫𝄫𝄫 (Shanachie, 1997)
(With James Galway) *Legends* 𝄫𝄫𝄫𝄫 (BMG/RCA Victor, 1997)
(With James Galway) *Winter's Crossing* 𝄫𝄫𝄫𝄫 (BMG/RCA Victor, 1998)

influences:

◀◀ Irish traditional music, Tin Pan Alley, the Clancy Brothers

▶▶ Planxty, the Furey Brothers, Van Morrison, Sinéad O'Connor, the Chieftains

see also: *Andy Cooney, James Galway*

Andrew BeDell

Coupé Cloué

Cuban-influenced compas
Born Jean Gesner Henri, c. 1925, in Haiti. Died January 29, 1998, in Port-au-Prince, Haiti.

During a remarkable career as a professional soccer player, Jean Gesner Henri earned the nickname Coupé Cloué, which translates roughly as "cut and nail," a tribute to his speed and prowess. After his soccer-playing days were over, his guitar-playing and singing days began, with Trio Sélect. Coupé Cloué took the dance-band *compas direct* style of the popular Nemours Jean-Baptiste and compacted it by using more percussion and no horns, creating some of the most African-sounding music to come out of the Caribbean. During the rule of the Duvaliers, he delivered many sly messages about the life of the average Haitian that made him a hero of the common people, despite his also being a favorite of the *tontons macoutes* (when the police asked you to play, you played). With his shaved head and regal bearing, he became known as Roi Coupé, the king of compas. More acoustic and tropical than later artists who followed his lead, Coupé Cloué's music remains very popular with older Haitians—and anyone with a sense of history.

what to buy: *L'Essentiel* 𝄫𝄫𝄫𝄫 (Mini, 1990, prod. Fred Paul) is full of acknowledged classics like "Fem'm Kolokinte" and other characteristic loping jams with the long spoken-word sections that wryly and ribaldly endeared him to Creole speakers (and will make you wish you were one if you aren't already).

what to buy next: *Et Ensemble Sélect* 𝄫𝄫𝄫𝄫 (Mini, 1998, prod. Fred Paul) sounds almost Cuban at times, with a strong line of rumba accentuated by hand drums and intricate call-and-re-sponse vocals. Just try to keep from moving when this one's on!

best of the rest:
The Preacher ♪♪♪ (Mini, 1989)
The World of Coupé Cloué ♪♪♪ (Mini, 1991)
Absolument ♪♪♪ (Mini, 1997)
Back to Roots: Le Roi Coupé En Cote D'Ivoire ♪♪♪ (Mini, 1998)

worth searching for: Most of the material on the English import *Maximum Compas from Haiti* ♪♪♪♪ (Earthworks, 1992, prod. various) is on the albums listed above—but not necessarily in the same versions. A rewarding listen, compiled with the label's signature care.

influences:
◀◀ Nemours Jean-Baptiste

▶▶ Rara Machine

see also: *Nemours Jean-Baptiste*

Hank Bordowitz

Coyote Oldman
International flute
Formed 1981, in Oklahoma City, OK, USA. Based in USA.

Michael Allen, flute, composer; Barry Stramp, flute, composer, engineer. (Both members are from USA.)

The duo Coyote Oldman began when Michael Allen met Barry Stramp at a crafts fair in Oklahoma, before widespread demand for Native flute music had been sparked by the recordings of R. Carlos Nakai and Kevin Locke. To pool their shared musical interests they formed the group, the name of which is a transposition of that of a Native American trickster spirit, Oldman Coyote. Allen had studied ancient Native flutes in museums and often built his own, while Stramp was experienced not only in traditional flute but also electronic processing of music. Both men have studied and performed on other kinds of flutes as well, including the Japanese *shakuhachi*. While they still often employ flute styles of other regions, their work as Coyote Oldman is Native American-based. Allen is the traditionalist, often performing on decades-old instruments, while Stramp will manipulate the sound electronically to add another dimension to the duo's work. Stramp has also recorded a solo album and played with the group Satori, in which he performs on Eastern styles of flute.

what to buy: *In Beauty I Walk: The Best of Coyote Oldman* ♪♪♪♪ (Hearts of Space, 1997, prod. Coyote Oldman) gathers past and current explorations by the duo, with a strong selection of Native American-flavored tunes. There's also a collaboration with Chinese singer Hui Cheng, and a percussion-driven electronic meditation performed on bass flutes—which, as the

most recent track on the album, may suggest the direction of the band's next experiment.

the rest:
Tear of the Moon ♪♪♪ (Coyote Oldman, 1987)
Landscape ♪♪♪ (Coyote Oldman, 1988)
Thundercloud ♪♪♪♪ (Hearts of Space, 1990)
In Medicine River ♪♪♪♪ (Coyote Oldman, 1992)
Compassion ♪♪♪ (Perfect Pitch, 1993)
The Shape of Time ♪♪♪ (Coyote Oldman, 1995)

influences:
◀◀ Ancient Native American flute builders

▶▶ Cuzco

Kerry Dexter

Steven Cragg
Worldbeat, didgeridoo, trance music
Born in Brighton, Sussex, England. Based in England.

Steven Cragg notes that "I do not especially consider myself a musician, but more of a collager of sound." His earliest musical experiences included banging drums around a campfire; he tried playing sitar but "it had too many notes." He now performs primarily on *didgeridoo*—the ancient Aboriginal Australian tubular drone instrument easily mistakable for a synthesizer—"with percussion and a variety of studio instruments thrown in for good measure." Cragg has been playing the "didg" for 10 years, drawing inspiration from investigations into indigenous spirituality, the paranormal, and aboriginal world culture; this has included living in a cave in the French Pyrennees—considered sacred sites steeped in Cathar and Templar history—for three months. Cragg regularly visits other such sites around the world to "absorb the magic that is," playing his didgeridoo "to invoke the spirits." While busking on European street corners in the late 1980s Cragg produced two homespun demos of his didg improvisations, leading to many festival, stage, radio, and television appearances. Since emerging from obscurity, Cragg has organized the internationally recognized Glastonbury Festival's Didgeridoo Convention for four consecutive years, with participation growing from five to over 70 players; he helpfully reports that "last year, the stage was bending under the combined weight of us all . . . and was wet from dribble too!" Cragg quips that he used to rave a lot, but since the scene has died down in the U.K. he has to make his own scenes. Many contemporary dance groups have used his music to accompany performances, and Cragg has contributed his talents to an ad shown in British movie theaters that benefits the nonprofit anti-fur group Lynx. He tours constantly as a solo act and, with frequent collaborator Phil Thornton, has performed at the Isle of Man's Greenpeace Week celebration. His good works include participation in other nonprofit concerts and recordings; a percentage of his royalties from the *Tibetan Horn* album is contributed to Tibetan people's organizations. He has also performed in crop circles at the request of internationally renowned circle-phenomena investigators, noting that "I ended up making corn cookies" as a result of trying to duplicate the complicated grain patterns through sonic vibrations produced on the didg. Crossing over to music as therapy, he has given didgeridoo sound massages, "which are also powerful to receive . . . a completely different experience of the instrument." To help promote awareness and understanding of the potential of his chosen instrument, Cragg presents countless demonstrations and workshops to both adults and children around the world.

what to buy: Cragg explains that "didgeridoo playing means that one is constantly chanting, performing an aspect of [the spiritual concept of] 'pranayama' and being vibrated down to a cellular level along with the hypnotic sound we all love. The didg is a voicebox that amplifies who you are." Nowhere is this more evident than on Cragg's solo debut, *Discovery* ♪♪♪♪ (New World Music, 1997, prod. Steven Cragg). On it he utilizes Australian didgeridoo, Tibetan horn and crystal bowls, African talking drum, Native American rainmaker, a variety of Asian gongs and bells, other ethnic percussion, and minimal electronics to sound-sculpt a compelling and transcendent aural excursion into the ancient future. Punctuated with aboriginal chant by the Bayaka Pygmy peoples of Africa, the sheer variety of tones and rhythmic patterns Cragg produces from a termite-hollowed tree branch are amazing in their own right, let alone in comparison to the synthesized sounds they readily recall. The song "Summerstreams" begins with slow galactic waveforms and liquid-toned cycles that gradually transmute into a consciousness-expanding tool of unparalleled proportions; unbelievably as it seems, this track was created solely on the didg. Finally, let's not forget *Discovery*'s trippy cover art; a friend suggested it looked like Cragg was taking a hit from the biggest bong in the world—but it's a giant didgeridoo!

what to buy next: Early in his career Cragg was invited to participate on Thornton's *Initiation* ♪♪♪ (New World Music, 1990, prod. Phil Thornton), and the duo's resulting chemistry sparked a series of shared projects, including the international best-selling album *Tibetan Horn* ♪♪♪♪ (New World Music, 1992, prod. Phil Thornton). After its release, *Tibetan Horn* was turned into a performance-art theater show which ran in London from 1993–94; at another end of the cultural spectrum, several tracks from the album helped launch the

1994 Spring-Summer Flyte Ostell collection during British Fashion Week festivities. Sure to enthrall but as-yet unavailable for review, Cragg's second solo outing, *En-Trance* (New World Music, 1999, prod. Steven Cragg), features deep trance rhythms from around the world interpreted for didgeridoo and ethnic instruments.

worth searching for: The two 1990 self-released demos that Cragg first used to catch the ear of musical powers-that-be, *Tales of the Eucalyptus Tree* and *Chant of the Eucalyptus,* are worth discovering by you, too.

influences:

◄◄ Steven Kent, Peter Gabriel "and all of his RealWorld recordings"

►► British techno, jungle, and ambient

PJ Birosik

Craobh Rua

Irish traditional

Formed 1985, in Belfast, Northern Ireland. Based in Belfast, Northern Ireland.

Brian Connolly, banjo; Desy McCabe, uilleann pipes, whistles (1985–91); Michael Cassidy, fiddle (1986–present); Frankie Totten, guitar, vocals (1986–89); Jim Byrne, guitar, vocals (1989–97); Jim Delaney, bodhrán (1989–91); Mark Donnelly, uilleann pipes, whistles (1992–97); Diarmaid Moynihan, uilleann pipes, whistles (1997–99); Patrick Davey, flute, uilleann pipes, whistles (1999–present); Aaron Jones, bouzouki, guitar, vocals (1997–present). (All members are from Ireland.)

Craobh Rua started life as a duo in the mid-1980s in Belfast, and by the time their first album appeared at the start of the '90s, they had expanded to feature a classic mix of pipes, whistle, fiddle, banjo, mandolin, vocal, guitar, and *bodhrán* (Irish frame drum). They were very much in the mold of some of the Irish traditional supergroups of the '60s and '70s, and their youth, energy, passion, and feeling for the material gained them a sizable following far from home, especially in Scotland, Brittany, and Italy. Within a few years they had also cracked some of the main festival circuits in the USA. By carefully pacing their development—an approach born of both artistic discretion and persistent day jobs—Craobh Rua turned out three further albums of stellar piping, fiddling, and banjo picking on a fine array of instrumentals and songs, mostly in Irish with the occasional Scots item thrown in for good measure. Jim Byrne's warm, engaging vocals and guitar seemed effortless and perfectly complemented the instrumental work. Following the release of their fourth album in 1997, the band's extensive activities were putting increasing demands on members' time, and both Byrne and piper Donnelly bowed out. Singer Aaron Jones (ex-Seelyhoo) and Cork piper/composer Diarmaid Moynihan soon joined Connolly and Cassidy to reconstitute the quartet. If Craobh Rua can maintain the musical authority it established for itself during the '90s, it deserves to be one of the better-known Irish acts in the business.

what to buy: Both *Soh It Is* ⅃⅃⅃⅃ (BTB/Lochshore, 1997, prod. Brian Connolly, Jim Byrne) and the wonderfully titled *No Matter How Cold & Wet You Are as Long as You're Warm & Dry* ⅃⅃⅃⅃ (BTB/Lochshore, 1995, prod. Brian Connolly, Jim Byrne) are superb examples of an Irish style somewhere between the Chieftains (way back when they were still passionate) and the Bothy Band, with consummate Dubliners-influenced banjo and Andy Irvine-reminiscent vocals as the icing on the cake. The recording and production are also first rate.

what to buy next: *The More That's Said the Less the Better* ⅃⅃⅃ (BTB/Lochshore, 1992, prod. Brian Connolly, Jim Byrne) and *Not a Word about It* ⅃⅃⅃ (BTB, 1990) provide more of the same, with perhaps a little less polish and maturity.

worth searching for: The band also appears on the early '90s albums *The Shetland Sessions Vol. I* (Lismor) and *The Shetland Sessions Vol. II* (Lismor).

influences:
◀◀ The Dubliners, the Chieftains, Planxty, the Bothy Band

John C. Falstaff

Crasdant

Welsh traditional
Formed 1998, in Wales. Based in Wales.

Robin Huw Bowen (England), triple harp; Andy McLauchlin (England), flute, whistle, pibgorn (Welsh hornpipe); Stephen Rees (Wales), fiddle, accordion, whistle, pibgorn; Huw Williams (Wales), acoustic guitar, stepping.

Crasdant is a new folkloric supergroup that sees legendary triple harp ambassador Robin Huw Bowen and guitarist Huw Williams team up with longtime North Wales resident Andy McLauchlin and former Ar Log member Stephen Rees for lyrical and articulate all-instrumental explorations of traditional Welsh music. A good part of their mission is to help highlight the virtues of instrumental music in a market so often dominated by singers. Williams—best known outside Wales as part of a singer-songwriter partnership with brother Tony that has supplied English folk-rock heavyweights Fairport Convention and many others—is also a leading exponent of Welsh step dancing, being the author of the only book in print on the subject, and here he lets his feet as well as fingers do the talking. Rees is a lecturer in music at the University of Wales in Bangor, and McLauchlin has been playing in local folk and dance bands for years. The group is a welcome

addition to the growing ranks of artists who succeed in artfully blending step-dance with music, both on stage and in the studio.

what's available: *Crasdant* ⅃⅃⅃⅃ (Sain, 1999, prod. Bryn Jones, Crasdant) is a true delight: lovely lacey textures of harp, accordion, flute, whistle, and fiddle interweave effortlessly around a fine collection of hornpipes, marches, slip jigs, and slow airs, occasionally augmented by sprightly step dancing. Grace and charm are the order of the day here, and great notes are provided on the tunes, which is hardly surprising considering the scholarship of the bandmembers.

influences:
◀◀ Ar Log, Kevin Burke's Open House

see also: *Ar Log, Robin Huw Bowen*

John C. Falstaff

Elvis Crespo

Merengue, salsa, tropical, Latin dance
Born July 30, 1971, in New York, NY, USA. Based in Puerto Rico.

Elvis Crespo was born in New York City, but so much of his time since has been spent in Puerto Rico that he recently found it wise to take brush-up English lessons as his star began rising in the international market. Crespo first performed as a member of the popular Grupo Mania. Now, as a solo artist during a Stateside "Latin pop" boom that has many Spanish-speaking or bilingual stars moving more toward English vocals, Crespo has set sales records internationally with original songs performed entirely in Spanish. Many of these buyers are Spanish speakers, of course, but others who don't understand the lyrics respond to the driving merengue/salsa blend of the melodies. Recently he recorded a Spanglish version of his hit song "Suavemente" for the soundtrack of the U.S. film *Dance with Me* (because, Crespo says, that's the way the kids talk these days), and more English-language excursions seem to be in his future. Either way, that future seems to be bright.

what's available: *Pintame* ⅃⅃⅃⅌ (Sony, 1999, prod. Luis A. Cruz) and *Suavemente* ⅃⅃⅃⅌ (Sony, 1998, prod. Luis A. Cruz) are lively snapshots of Crespo's original, merengue-based style, and he gets songwriting credit for all the songs on both albums. Club dance remixes with accentuated bass, performed in a slightly slower tempo than traditional Latin merengue, have been done for *Suavemente* and are likely in the offing for *Pintame* as well. The soundtrack album *Dance with Me* ⅃⅃⅃ (Sony, 1998, prod. various) also provides a different look at Crespo's music.

influences:
◀◀ Grupo Mania

Kerry Dexter

Andrew Cronshaw

Anglo-Celtic/International fusion

Born April, 18, 1949, in Lytham St. Annes, Lancashire, England. Based in London, England.

Andrew Cronshaw is a true renaissance man. First, he records and tours in his own right as a virtuoso adept in the instruments of many lands, including electric and acoustic chord zithers, *marovantele, kantele, gu-cheng,* clavichord, flutes, *ba-wu,* concertina, whistle, shawm, and steel pans. (This instrumental diversity has its stylistic counterpart on his albums, which feature distinctive and radical reworkings of traditional material from England, Scotland, Ireland, Galicia [the Celtic area of Spain], and Finland.) Second, he is a coveted accompanist, having guested on sessions for albums by Suede, B.J. Cole, Scott Walker, Pascal Gaigne, and D. Hall & Rain. Third, he's appeared on the soundtracks for *G.I. Jane* and *The Dybbuk of the Holy Apple Field.* And last but not least, he's also developed an excellent reputation as a producer, with credits including *Abyssinians* by June Tabor; *The Wild West Show* by English singer-songwriter Bill Caddick of Home Service; *No More to the Dance* by the Silly Sisters (Tabor and Maddy Prior); and *The Man in the Moon Drinks Claret* by Pyewackett. But it doesn't stop even there. Cronshaw's musical work—particularly his attendant exploration of several regions' folk traditions—has led him down yet another avenue: journalism. He's contributed to the required-reading English magazines *Folk Roots* and *Gramaphone,* and has completed the Nordic, Portuguese, and Baltic sections for the second edition of the highly regarded *Rough Guide to World Music.* In the '90s Cronshaw developed an especial interest in Finland, producing albums by two Finnish artists, Salamakannel and Nikolai Blad, and using several Finnish musicians on his own 1993 recording *The Language of Snakes.* Cronshaw has begun work on his next CD, which will consist entirely of Finno-Ugrian material (that body of culture including parts of Hungary and Russia as well as Finland), and is being recorded in the country which has of late inspired him so much.

what's available: *The Language of Snakes* 🎵🎵🎵🎵 (Special Delivery, 1993, prod. Andrew Cronshaw) is filled with Cronshaw's distinctive arrangements of tunes from various traditions. He uses unusual combinations of instruments, and changes original rhythms to create his unique musical visions. For example, "Baile de Procesion" (from Galicia) starts off with a shimmering zither, then the bass clarinet joins in while fiddles fill out the middle. Harmonica adds yet another texture to the overall mix. Very atmospheric. Cronshaw gets funky with the clavichord on the Scottish piece "Do Chrochaidh A Thoill Thu" while sprightly fiddle and bass clarinet wail away in unison! There's also a simple but beautiful arrangement of the Irish air "Apple Praties" wherein Cronshaw plays the main melody on whistle and is backed by Ric Sanders on violins. The helpfully titled *The Andrew Cronshaw CD* 🎵🎵🎵🎵 (Topic, 1989, prod. Andrew Cronshaw, Gary Lucas) compiles the entire *The Great Dark Water* LP and all but two tracks of *Till the Beasts Returning,* thus preserving two fine but rare albums. This set proves that Cronshaw's approach, while adding new influences over the years, has remained consistent. Again you'll find unusual arrangements of traditional source material, such as the radical version of "The Blacksmith," which is basically a theme-and-variations treatment of the song's main melody line. Tempos shift, different instruments carry the tune, and there's a wild passage where the principal theme is played by zither and fiddle while a piano adds rhythm accents. You'll find no other version of "The Blacksmith" like this, guaranteed!

influences:

◀◀ Robert Fripp, Brian Eno, the Chieftains, Alan Stivell, numerous traditional folk sources

▶▶ Loreena McKennitt

see also: *Home Service, Maddy Prior*

Ken Roseman

Celia Cruz

Salsa

Born in Havana, Cuba. Based in Cuba, Mexico, and USA.

Celia Cruz is the quintessential singer in her genre, considered by many to be the "Queen of Salsa," a feminine icon in a notoriously macho fleld. She has been performing for well over four decades, but just how many years past those two-score is a matter that remains Cruz's well-guarded secret. Her voice transcends age, however, and while not quite as flexible in the 1990s as it was during her artistic heyday in the early '50s, Cruz has proven that she still carries surprising vocal power. In 1950 Cruz became the lead singer for la Sonora Matancera, one of the leading Cuban orchestras of the day. This was the start of her "classic" period, when she was cementing her reputation as the most popular female singer in Cuba. Her recordings from the time she spent with that band (until 1965) were originally released through Seeco Records and some have been reissued through Palladium and PolyGram Latino. It was also during her tenure with Sonora Matancera that Cruz and the band left Cuba for a tour that never made it back to their homeland, applying for residency in the U.S. when they were able to secure a long-term gig at the Hollywood Palladium. Ironically, Cruz fell somewhat from commercial favor from the mid-1960s through the early '70s as her audience turned to newer Latin styles like *bugálu.* But by the mid-1970s she was making the climb back into popularity, with a performance at Carnegie Hall in 1973 and a series of releases with Johnny Pacheco that were big sellers in the Hispanic community. By the late 1980s her role as "Queen of Salsa" was the real deal. She received an honorary doctorate in music from Yale in 1989, and her album with Ray Barretto *Ritmo en el Corazón* won a Grammy Award in 1990, the same year her star appeared on the Hollywood Walk of Fame. Continuing the high profile since, she has also been seen in the films *The Mambo Kings* and *The Perez Family.* Cruz's later albums on RMM still carry some Latin-jazz punch, but in general they target salsa fans—and in her case there are as many to be targeted as ever.

what to buy: *Canciones Premiadas* ♪♪♪♪ (Palladium, 1994) is a collection of Cruz's classic performances with la Sonora Matancera, originally released on Seeco. She is in marvelous voice and the band is an amazingly flexible instrumental ensemble. Certain aspects of the music may sound dated but, to keep things in perspective, so do the early Ella Fitzgerald sides with Chick Webb—which don't have nearly as much raw power and assurance as is heard from this top Latin act at the height of its popularity. Cruz has managed to remain the ruling diva of salsa by changing her style just enough to accommodate the latest recording techniques and keep pace with the younger singers in today's market. *Irrepetible* ♪♪♪♪ (RMM, 1994, prod. Willy Chirino) was a 1996 Grammy nominee for Best Tropical Latin Performance, and is a pretty good sample of Cruz's recent recordings. The material is more pop-oriented in some ways, but the musicians and arrangers working with her are more than capable of making Cruz sound contemporary without dampening the vocal fire that makes her "The Queen." The rhythm riffs on "La Guagua" and "Cuando Cuba Se Ababe de Liberar" still have the deep Afro-Cuban roots that no amount of production work can weaken. Recorded between 1951 and 1965, *100 Percent Azucar: The Best of Celia Cruz con la Sonora Matancera* ♪♪♪♪ (Rhino, 1997, prod. Rogelio Martinez) covers roughly the same time period as *Canciones Premiadas* ♪♪♪♪ (1994, Palladium), but, due to Rhino/Atlantic's wide distribution network, is more likely to be found in stores. The former's sonics have been well mastered and it includes more material, another reason some listeners may turn to this collection as a primer for Cruz. The liner notes by Nina Lenart (who coproduced the compilation with Alan Geik from the original sides by Martinez) are informative. Another recent album by the Queen, *Mi Vida Es Cantar* ♪♪♪♪ (RMM, 1998, prod. Isidro Infante), leads off with a blast and settles into a high-speed—forgive the pun—cruise. It simmers and rocks with nary a note hinting of the Social Security payments the singer might be receiving. *Timbales* player Luisito Quintero is magnificent throughout, as are the arrangements of producer/pianist Infante.

what to buy next: *La Dinamica Celia Cruz* ♪♪♪♪ (Palladium, 1991) features yet more material from the Seeco vaults with Sonora Matancera accompanying Cruz. From the first song

chinese classical music

China's classical music is significant for its long heritage (some 3,000 years), its austere beauty, and its radical differences from Western orchestral music. Unfortunately, it is also characterized by its increasing absence, as the generations alive prior to the cultural purges of 1911 and 1949 pass away. The introduction of European scales and the standardization of the music, along the lines of the Russian forms to which China once looked to "modernize" its orchestras, have sped up the demise of a vast and precious art.

What does remain of the indigenous version may jar on ears unfamiliar with the pentatonic scale, odd time signatures, and different pitches. Unlike the Western pursuit of dense harmonies and instrumental interplay, the Chinese perform as a group of individuals. Each player tells a musical story. They improvise and explore subtle timbres and pitches, adding their own idiosyncratic embellishments to traditional compositions. Typical instruments include variations on the *qin* (Chinese zither) and *dizi* (bamboo flute), and large percussion ensembles. Previously supported by royalty, classical musicians are now paid by the state and provided steady university jobs. Good examples of their work are offered by *China: Time to Listen* ♪♪♪♪ (ellipsis arts . . . , 1998) and *The Hugo Masters: An Anthology of Chinese Classical Music* ♪♪♪♪♪ (Celestial Harmonies, 1992) (each reviewed in this book's Compilations section), and a variety of collections on the French label Ocora.

Opera has had an easier time surviving, despite a mere eight operas—or ballets—being permitted performance between 1966 and '76, the years of the "cultural revolution." Opera is popular enough that the Chinese enjoy reciting their favorite excerpts. An extensive repertoire and hundreds of regional styles exist, the most famous being that of Beijing.

David Poole

("Tamborilero"), this album is a primer on Afro-Cuban rhythms, with mambos, rumbas, merengues, sones, and even a cha-cha-cha generating heat. The sound is a bit cheesy but the music is loads of fun. Cruz swears she's a devout Roman

Celia Cruz

Catholic but she somehow recorded *Homenaje a los Santos* ♪♪♪ (PolyGram Latino, 1994), an album for Seeco that uses texts from the Afro-Cuban *Santería* faith in praise of the various *Orishas* (deities). It's an aural curiosity that works, because recognizing the basic Yoruba rhythms behind the music is the ticket to a fuller understanding of Latin jazz and salsa. Pairing Cruz with other Latin music superstars is a commercial no-brainer, but *Duets* ♪♪♪ (RMM, 1997, prod. Ralph Mercado) succeeds artistically too, and reflects positively on the professionalism and creativity of all involved. Guests include Willie Colon, Tito Puente, Oscar D'Leon, and Johnny Ventura, but the most interesting twists combine Cruz with the Hispanic rock group Los Fabulosos Cadillacs ("Vasos Vaclos") and Brazilian singer/ songwriter Caetano Veloso ("Soy Loco por ti America").

best of the rest:
(With Ray Barretto) *Ritmo en el Corazón* ♪♪♪ (Fania/Charly, 1988)
The Best of Celia Cruz ♪♪♪ (Sony, 1994)
Las Guaracheras de la Guaracha ♪♪♪ (PolyGram Latino, 1994)
Mi Llaman la Reina (They Call Me the Queen) ♪♪♪ (Laserlight, 1996)
Fania All-Stars with Celia Cruz ♪♪♪ (Sony, 1997)

influences:
◄◄ Graciela

►► Gloria Estefan, India

see also: *Ray Barretto, Willie Colon, Oscar D'Leon, Wyclef Jean, Los Fabulosos Cadillacs, Johnny Pacheco, Patato, Tito Puente, Caetano Veloso*

Garaud MacTaggart

Joe Cuba
Mid-century Cuban-American dance pop
Born Gilberto Calderon, 1931, in New York, NY, USA. Based in USA.

Joe Cuba led a Cuban jazz sextet in New York in the late 1950s, recording several best-sellers based on the arrangements of Nick Jimenez and fueled by the vocals of Cheo Feliciano. The vibraphone was the group's dominant instrument as they played danceable mambo and bolero sounds identified with the pre-eminent New York Latin music of the decade.

what's available: *Joe Cuba Sextet* ♪♪♪ (Tico) may be difficult to find, but it's an authentic example of the group's typical—and very popular—sound.

influences:

◄◄ Tito Puente, Eddie Palmieri

Kerry Dexter

Cuba L.A.

Salsa

Formed 1998, in Los Angeles, CA, USA. Based in Los Angeles, CA, USA.

Danilo Lozano, flute, director; Luis Conte, congas; Harry Kim, trumpets; Raymundo Olivera, trumpet; Carlos Puerto, bass; Orestes Vilato, timbales; Ilmar Gavilan, violin; Alberto Salas, piano; Mitch Sanchez, bongos. (Members are from Cuba and USA.)

"The richness of Cuban music is in the rhythm, and the basis of the rhythm is the drum," says Danilo Lozano, flautist and "leader" of the sessions that produced *Cuba L.A.* Unlike many salsa albums recorded primarily for the Anglo market, the percussion on this work is way out front, putting *timbalero* Orestes Vilato, *bongero* Mitch Sanchez, and *conguero* Luis Conte on an equal footing with the rest of the band. "When Narada contacted me about this project, they said they wanted it done 'live,'" Lozano says. "Which is what we did." Lozano picked compositions everyone knew, and inspiration flowed freely throughout the short, three-day session. "What was most affecting to me is that we had three generations of Cubans and Cuban Americans, guys who have lived here all their lives and guys who just came over in the last couple of years, and we made beautiful music, each of us probing the roots in our own way."

Lozano's own roots go deep. His father, Rolando Lozano, recorded with Orquesta Aragon in the '50s, and after coming to the U.S. played with Tito Puente, Mongo Santamaria, and Cal Tjader. Lozano Jr. is a musician, musicologist, folklorist, and teacher of ethnomusicology at Whittier College in L.A., balancing his playing with his day job. "It's important to remember the contribution of folkloric and popular artists is not less important than the music conceived for the concert hall. Cuban culture is extremely musical. There is popular dance music, but there's also folkloric forms, guitar music, a whole panorama of regional and local styles that have emerged and developed, many of them in danger of dying out. With musical education programs taking the beating they're taking at present, it's important to be at an institution of higher learning, so I can give something back to the community, and help preserve the roots for the next generation."

what's available: "We were all in the studio together, and there were no arrangements, just a pure *descarga* [jam session]," Lozano recalls of the charged sessions which produced *Cuba L.A.* 🎵🎵🎵🎵 (Narada, 1998, prod. Danilo Lozano, Rich Denhart). "Sometimes we'd start with an idea, like on 'El Manisero,' which is led by Llmar Gavilan [on violin]. Nobody's ever played

violin on that before, so he took the lead and we all followed. And on 'Almendra' we tuned Luis Conte's congas so he could play the melody as well as the rhythm. It's a *danzon* [dance number], but we dropped the introduction and went right into the *montuno* [call-and-response] section." The sweet, swingin', non-stop jam session he's describing is well-captured on *Cuba L.A.*, which should put to rest the notion that L.A.'s salsa scene is in any way softer than New York's.

influences:

◄◄ Orquesta Aragon, Tito Puente, Mongo Santamaria

see also: *Orquesta Aragon, Tito Puente, Mongo Santamaria*

j. poet

¡Cubanismo!

Afro-Cuban jazz, son

Formed 1995, in Havana, Cuba. Based in London, England, and Havana, Cuba.

Rotating recording and touring lineups which have included: Jesús Alamañy, trumpet, arranger; Alfredo Rodríguez, piano; Tata Guines, percussion; Miguel Aurelio Diaz, percussion; Orlando Valle, flute; Carlos Puerto Jr., bass; Efraim Rios, tres, coros; Jorge Luis Rojas, lead vocals; Yosvany Terry Cabrera, sax; Emilio Del Monte, timbales; Carlos Alvarez, trombone; Carlos Godines, percussion; Leonardo Castellini, sax; Luís Alamañy Jr., trumpet; Luis Varzaga, coros; Julian Oviedo, bongos; Manuel Mirabal, trumpet; Roberto Guillot, percussion; Dave Pattman, bongos; Fernando Ferrer, lead vocals; Rolo Martinez, lead vocals; Adalberto Lara, trumpet; Youre Muñiz, trumpet; Ignacio Herrera, piano; Sergio Luna Longchamp, trombone; Alfredo Thomson, tenor sax; César López, alto sax; Pancho Amat, tres, coros; Adalberto Hernandez, bongos; Tómas Ramoz Ortiz, congas; Yaura Muñiz, trumpet; Javier Zalba, sax, baritone sax; Fernando Juan de la Cruz, lead vocals; Lázaro Miguel Rodriguez, coros; Manuel Rojas, coros; Davide Giovannini, coros; Félix Baloy Jr., coros. (All members are from Cuba.)

Jesús Alamañy, arranger and leader of iCubanismo!, has been playing trumpet since he was a child; he studied at Cuba's Conservatorio Amadeo Roldan at 13 and joined the brass section of Sierra Maestra, the group credited with invigorating the traditional Cuban *son*, at 16. "I learned to play traditionally with Lazaro Herera, the oldest trumpeter in Cuba, and already had a lot of experience in nonprofessional bands, so I was not intimidated," Alamañy says. For over a decade his fiery trumpet was part of the Sierra Maestra sound, and their popularity awakened a new generation of Cuban musicians to their musical heritage. "Sierra Maestra was both classical and nostalgic," Alamañy explains. "The *son* is the root of Cuban music, but it had been forgotten. We kept the original ideas and rhythms, but opened it up, creating a new era of dancing music." In 1992 Alamañy left Sierra Maestra and Cuba to pursue his own music in London. In December of '94, he organized a *descarga* (jam session) in Paris for conga legend Patato Valdez, inviting the cream of Cuba's session players. Hannibal Records head Joe Boyd attended and was impressed enough to invite Alemañy to produce a descarga in Havana; the sessions were recorded and became the first ¡Cubanismo! album. It was so successful that Alamañy was able to take most of the band on the road, where—between subsequent triumphant albums and member-shufflings—they've been searing dance floors and blowing minds ever since.

what to buy: Of *Jesús Alamañy's ¡Cubanismo!* ᛏᛏᛏᛏ (Hannibal, 1996, prod. Joe Boyd) Alamañy remembers, "The recording was all acoustic, to achieve the traditional sound of the *son-montuno, guaracha-son* and other traditional styles. Although we had never played together before, and didn't have time to rehearse, we worked like a family from the first." Alamañy arranged the tunes, but left room for his bandmates to shine, with the percussive attack of pianist Alfredo Rodriquez and Carlos Puerto Jr.'s staccato bass lines particular standouts. "I had a sound that had been in my head since I was a child," Alamañy says. "A balance of what's happening on the street with the rhythmic, harmonic, and melodic strengths of my Cuban cultural identity." The recorded result is blazing musicianship from start to finish, with three generations of Cuban masters.

what to buy next: The band's third outing, *Reencarnacion* ᛏᛏᛏᛏ (Hannibal, 1998), kicks off with a searing percussion-driven cover of Electro Rosell's "El Plantanal de Bartolo" and never lets up. The two descargas "Jamming in Nijmegen" and "En Las Delicias" show the band at its fiery best, but there isn't a single weak track in the set.

the rest:
Malembe ᛏᛏᛏᛏ (Hannibal, 1997)

influences:
◀◀ Harry James, Maynard Ferguson, Septeto Nacional, Sierra Maestra, Son 14, Beny Moré

see also: *Patato, Sierra Maestra*

j. poet

Culture
Roots reggae
Formed 1975, in Kingston, Jamaica. Based in Kingston, Jamaica.

Joseph Hill, lead singer; Albert Walker, harmony vocals; Kenneth Days, harmony vocals. (All members are from Jamaica.)

Joseph Hill, one of the great roots reggae singers, started drumming and doing backup vocals with Studio One session band the Soul Defenders in 1969. His first single as a lead singer, produced by Coxsone Dodd in the early 1970s, was a solo outing called "Take Me Girl," though it was released under the name the Neptunes. He also cut "Behold the Land" for

Dodd, but grew disillusioned by the music business. He dropped out and joined a Rastafarian commune in the hills outside of Kingston. In 1976 his cousin Albert Walker visited him and suggested they form a singing group. Vocal trios like the Mighty Diamonds, the Pioneers, the Heptones, and Justin Hinds & the Dominoes were setting the charts on fire, so Hill took the bait. With Walker's brother Kenneth Days they began rehearsing; Hill sang lead and wrote the songs, while Walker and Days provided sweet, soulful harmonies. They auditioned for Joe Gibbs as the African Disciples, but Morris Wellington, one of Gibbs's top arrangers, suggested the more Rastafarian name of Culture, a reference to the African roots all Rastas feel are the basis of their religion. The band's first session, backed by Sly Dunbar, Robbie Shakespeare, Tommy McCook, and other now-famous studio heavies, produced a sizable hit with "See Dem a Come," an expression of militant defiance. But the best was still ahead. Hill had an apocalyptic vision of the final judgment that inspired the lyrics of "When Two Sevens Clash," the next single and title track of Culture's first album. People took Hill's vision so seriously that on July 7, 1977, the day the sevens clashed, Kingston ground to a halt, with many people staying home awaiting the final judgment. The album was a major hit; Warner Bros. released it in England and by the time Shanachie brought it out in the U.S. in 1988 it was legendary, a reggae milestone seldom duplicated.

This success led to international tours, a deal with Virgin's Front Line logo, and *Harder Than the Rest,* another militant classic. Joe Gibbs also began releasing outtakes from the *Two Sevens* sessions, flooding the market with titles by the band, but they all did well and the trio played to sold-out houses in Europe and England. By the early 1980s the music biz was changing, and in Jamaica dancehall's computerized riddims and rap vocals had supplanted roots reggae as the dominant force. Front Line crashed and burned, and when a Hill solo outing went unreleased, the group threw in the towel. But in 1986 Hill decided to reform the group. The trio teamed up with Sly & Robbie and the Roots Radics band, taking some of the more popular dancehall riddims and recasting them in a roots mold for *In Culture,* a strong comeback effort. While it's unlikely they will ever record another set with the impact of *Two Sevens Clash,* the trio continues to produce standout roots albums, marked by killer riddims (played by real musicians), solid lyrics, smooth harmonies, and Hill's still soul-stirring vocals.

what to buy: Simply put, *Two Sevens Clash* ᛏᛏᛏᛏ (Shanachie, 1988, prod. Joe Gibbs, Errol Thompson), originally released in Jamaica on Gibbs's JGR label in 1976, is one of the greatest reggae albums ever recorded. Hill's apocalyptic visions and militant lyrics are driven by his scratchy tenor, a voice that's instantly recognizable for its soul and sufferation. Walker and

Days provide angelic harmonies, and the killer production of Gibbs and Thompson, full of echo, delay, and dubwise mixing, gives the music the impact of an atom bomb.

what to buy next: *Combolo* 𝄞𝄞𝄞𝄞 (Shanachie, 1988, prod. S.E. Pottinger) is one of Culture's best post-reunion sets. "Mrs." Pottinger, although not widely recognized outside of Jamaica, is one of the island's best producers, known for her booming bass sound and inventive percussion tracks. Hill is in fine voice here, with a selection of strong tunes marked by his usual passion and the band's sharp, understated backing.

best of the rest:
'Nuff Crisis 𝄞𝄞𝄞𝄞 (Shanachie, 1988)
Good Things 𝄞𝄞𝄞 (RAS, 1989)
In Culture 𝄞𝄞𝄞 (Jamaica Gold, 1990)
International Herb 𝄞𝄞𝄞 (Shanachie, 1990)
Harder Than the Rest 𝄞𝄞𝄞𝄞 (Shanachie, 1992)
Baldhead Bridge 𝄞𝄞𝄞𝄞 (Shanachie, 1993)

influences:
◀◀ The Wailers (pre-Island Records), Delphonics, Justin Hinds & the Dominos, Mighty Diamonds

▶▶ Black Uhuru, Wailing Souls, Ziggy Marley & the Melody Makers

see also: *The Roots Radics, Sly & Robbie*

j. poet

Johnny Cunningham

Scottish folk, rock, new age
Born August 27, 1957, in Portobello, Scotland. Based in Boston, MA, USA.

Johnny Cunningham is among the most talented and exciting artists in contemporary Scottish music. He has, over the past 25 years, infused this somewhat hidebound style with a much-needed burst of energy and creativity. After a brief childhood in a musical family where he was surrounded by accordionists and pipers, Cunningham left home at age 14 to make his way as a professional musician. Moving from one squalid Edinburgh flat to another, he met up with like-minds Gordon Jones and Bob Thomas and the trio eventually formed Silly Wizard. After several personnel changes and years of destitution, the band took off, becoming a mainstay of the Scottish folk revival and performing all over the world. Their driving dance tunes and sweet songs helped to shake the cobwebs off of Scottish music during the '70s and '80s, and led to a long run of tours and albums. Since leaving Silly Wizard Cunningham has performed with Relativity, Nightnoise, and the rock band Raindogs. He has toured as a solo artist and as a member of the Celtic Fiddle Festival, in addition to production work for numerous artists. Largely self-taught, he draws inspiration from those he grew up around and has avoided the Scottish fiddle scene with its restrictive emphasis on written collections and classical techniques. When pressed to choose a musical influence, Cunningham names Tommy Potts, the Irish fiddler who, on his album *The Liffey Banks,* pulled, pushed, and stretched traditional Irish music as far as it would go without breaking. Cunningham is the same type of musician, well schooled in the traditional roots but carrying the music forward to new places.

what to buy: *Peter and Wendy* 𝄞𝄞𝄞𝄞 (Alula, 1997, prod. Johnny Cunningham) is by far the most important, serious, and developed work of Cunningham's career. Written as the music for the Mabou Mines Theater Company's production of the 1911 J.M. Barrie novel of the same name, Cunningham's music successfully weds the sound of traditional Scottish music to the dramatic stage. Although the score is all original, the foundation of Cunningham's composition is strongly traditional, liberally borrowing forms, progressions, and even whole sections of tunes from the repertoire. In order to bring his musical ideas to their fullest fruition, Cunningham surrounded himself with the cream of Irish-America's musicians including Seamus Egan, Solas accordionist Mick McAuley, harpist Jay Ansill, and heavenly singer Susan McKeown. The result is a masterful soundtrack at once contemporary and venerable, full of beautiful playing and heartfelt singing. Sold in an attractive box with a lavish full-color book inside, the packaging reflects the exceptional care and effort that went into this production.

what to buy next: Kevin Burke, Cunningham, and Christian LeMaître's *The Celtic Fiddle Festival* 𝄞𝄞𝄞 (Green Linnet, 1993, prod. Johnny Cunningham) features Cunningham alongside Irish master Burke and Breton fiddler LeMaître. In a program split between solos and group playing, the three push each other forward, all showing off their awesome technique and mastery of related yet different styles. Highlights include Burke's set of three reels from County Clare; Cunningham's sweet "Mist-Covered Mountains of Home"; and the trio's ferocious attack on two French-Canadian reels, "The Dionne" and "The Mouth of the Tobique." The tasteful accompaniment by guitarist John McGann allows each of the fiddlers to shine to the fullest. This is a great album for any fan of the instrument, and an excellent introduction to its many sounds and styles for the fan-to-be. *Fair Warning* 𝄞𝄞𝄞 (Green Linnet, 1983, prod. Johnny Cunningham, Vincent Moos) is a fine Scottish fiddle album, featuring some nice reel sets and a few beautiful slow airs. Accompanied by uilleann piper Tim Britton and guitarist Zan McLeod among others, Cunningham's playing is always solid but lacks a little of the fire of his Silly Wizard days. The highlights are the slow air "Logan Water" and the closing set of reels.

what to avoid: *The Soul of Christmas: A Celtic Music Celebration with Thomas Moore* 🎵🎵 (Upaya, 1997, prod. Johnny Cunningham) is a two-CD set containing one disc of new-age guru Thomas Moore discussing the nature of Christmas and one disc of some well-known carols performed in a Celtic/new-age style. The musical passages feature Cunningham and many of the same musicians from the *Peter and Wendy* album as well as Kathy Mattea, Cathie Ryan, and vocalist Liam Tiernan. The songs are warm and comfortable but wanting for vigor, especially those from Tiernan, whose languid delivery slows everything it touches to an uncomfortable, glacial crawl. The instrumental settings are also slow and new-agey for the most part, allowing only rare flashes of brilliance from some usually stunning performers (the one exception being a somewhat rousing "In Exelcis Deo" featuring, refreshingly but not surprisingly, Cunningham on fiddle). The most conspicuous tracks have to be Cunningham's vocal (!) rendition of the carol "I Saw Three Ships," and his recitation of a couple of poems. Notwithstanding its sub-par overall musical quality, the set is handsomely packaged in a thick book containing Moore's discussion in essay form with some attractive, homey illustrations.

the rest:

(With Kevin Burke and Christian LeMaître) *The Celtic Fiddle Festival: Encore* 🎵🎵🎵 (Green Linnet, 1998)

worth searching for: Cunningham's first solo album, *Thoughts from Another World* 🎵🎵🎵 (Shanachie, 1982), is now out of print. It's a slightly surreal recording, but indicative of his musical restlessness and willingness to experiment.

influences:

◀◀ Aly Bain, Chuck Fleming, Tommy Potts

▶▶ Old Blind Dogs, Shooglenifty, Alisdair Fraser

see also: *Kevin Burke, Phil Cunningham, Kornog, La Muscagña, Susan McKeown, Tríona Ní Dhomhnaill, Nightnoise, Cathie Ryan, Silly Wizard, Solas*

Tony Ziselberger

Phil Cunningham

Scottish traditional and contemporary

Born January 27, 1960, in Portobello, Scotland. Based on the Isle of Skye, Scotland.

Phil Cunningham is a tremendous musician, composer, arranger, and producer who has been at the very center of Scottish music for close to 30 years. An outstanding accordionist, whistle player, and keyboardist, Phil got his start with Silly Wizard, which produced the high-energy recordings of traditional jigs, reels, and songs that jump-started Scottish music in the '70s and '80s. After that group's demise, Phil and his brother John joined with Micheal Ó Domhnaill and Triona Ní Dhomhnaill to form Relativity, the sedate, somewhat experimental sound of which would be a precursor to many of the more ethereal Celtic bands of the 1990s. Since Relativity's break-up, Phil has recorded and toured as a solo artist and with Shetland fiddler Aly Bain; written his first classical composition, *The Highlands and Islands Suite*; and produced countless albums for artists ranging from folk-rockers Wolfstone to singer Connie Dover to Irish-traditional giants Altan. He currently lives on the Isle of Skye where he and his wife Donna run a recording studio.

what to buy: Cunningham's second solo project, *The Palomino Waltz* 🎵🎵🎵 (Green Linnet, 1989, prod. Phil Cunningham), is a wonderful display of his writing and playing skills. He claims composer's credits on six of the album's nine tracks and writes variations for another. Among his outstanding originals are the beautiful "Donna's Waltz"—now a standard at sessions everywhere—and the sad slow air "The Ross Memorial Hospital." A lyrical album with three other slow airs and a set of waltzes to recommend it, the CD showcases Cunningham's underrated whistle playing alongside his justly admired accordion work. For fans of the latter on killer dance tunes, there are a few sets of reels and some tricky strathspeys in which his accordion dazzles. This is a well-produced album, with tasteful electric keyboards—also played by Cunningham—augmenting but not upstaging the tunes, and some nice guest appearances from fiddler Bain and piper Finlay MacRae.

what to buy next: *Airs and Graces* 🎵🎵🎵 (Green Linnet, 1984, prod. Phil Cunningham, Neil Ross) was Cunningham's first solo recording, and shows off his awesome accordion playing to great effect. Another platform for Cunningham's own tunes, this one features his famous air "Miss Rowan Davies" and a whole bunch of memorable reels, among them "Andy Stewart's" and "Hogtie's Reel." In addition to the accordion, instruments played by the multitalented Cunningham include whistle, keyboards, guitar, and cittern. The accompaniment is a little more traditional than on his second recording, with the synthesizer used more selectively and sparingly, and the piano and guitar filling the gaps.

what to avoid: As any connoisseur of Scotch whiskey will tell you, there's something to be said for blends, but the true treasures are found among the single malts where the individual character of the whiskey stands out. So it is with duets between Bain and Cunningham. When this unprecedented pair recorded *The Pearl* 🎵🎵🎵 (Green Linnet, 1995, prod. Phil Cunningham) expectations ran high. After all, here were two of the kings of Scottish music working together, pushing each other to greater and greater heights. Shetland-born Bain is a master fiddler with a host of rare tunes who can alternately rev it up on the reels and make you cry with the airs. Cunningham also stirs it up or tones it down with the best of 'em, plays everything, and writes all those beautiful tunes of his own. So how come this record never gets going? The reels are all solid, the slow pieces are pretty, but outside of a reprise of "The Pearl," which Phil wrote and recorded back in his Silly Wizard days, nothing stands out. These guys are both masters, but they seem to hold each other back, settling for a pleasant middle ground when they could have truly pushed the edges. As is the case with fine Scotch whiskey, stick with the solos and leave this disappointing blend alone.

the rest:
(With Aly Bain) *The Ruby* 🎵🎵🎵 (Green Linnet, 1998)

worth searching for: *Against the Storm* (Shanachie, 1984) is a now-out-of-print album featuring Phil and his brother John. It sports some tasty playing, and Shanachie's reluctance to reissue it is a mystery. Phil also has a tunebook, *The Phil Cunningham Collection, Vol. 1,* which includes many of his fine compositions.

influences:
◀◀ Jimmy Shand

▶▶ Shooglenifty, Wolfstone, Old Blind Dogs, Karen Tweed

see also: *Altan, the Boys of the Lough, Johnny Cunningham, Triona Ní Dhomhnaill, Silly Wizard, Andy M. Stewart, David Wilkie*

Tony Ziselberger

Cusan Tan
See: Robin Huw Bowen

Dadawa
Chinese classical, new age
Born 1970, in Guangzhou City, China. Based in Shanghai, China.

Dadawa's *Sister Drum* was one of the fastest-selling Mandarin albums in the history of mainland China, and the first CD from the People's Republic to be released internationally. The global reception may have seemed a direct reply to the singer's own diverse tastes. "At seven, I auditioned for the National Choir and performing with them exposed me to a lot of different music," she explains. "In the '80s pop music from Taiwan and Hong Kong entered China, and later music from America and England. I loved that influence, especially the blues and rock. Whatever I could find, I listened to."

In 1990 Dadawa entered the Fourth Grand Prize Young Singers TV Contest, winning with the song "A True Story." But Dadawa

was not satisfied with the life of a pop celebrity. "People come from all over China, and winning is seen as the path to stardom, but for me, singing was a labor of love, so even though I won, I didn't want to sign with any of the government- or privately owned record companies. I decided to seek my own path." For Dadawa that path led to the back roads of China, where she traveled on her own to sample "different ways of life." Her decision puzzled the local press. "They wrote stories that said 'Famous Singer Disappears,'" Dadawa recalls. When Dadawa returned from the sojourn she contacted the composer He Xuntain, whom she'd met after winning the contest. Along with his brother Xunyou they recorded *Yellow Children,* "a mix of pop and classical, Chinese and Western." The album did well, but the musicians wanted to try something more adventurous.

"[He Xuntain] had always been interested in Tibet. He had collected hundreds of Tibetan folk songs, and his brother had lived and worked in Tibet for many years. They asked me to travel to Tibet with them. We were looking for inspiration, and didn't intend to document or incorporate any Tibetan music into what we did. Many artists use Chinese folk music and folk art and try to mix it into pop music. That was not our intention, but when I visited there, it opened something in me. It created a sound, a feeling that I knew I would have to express." That feeling evolved into the seven songs on *Sister Drum* through two years of intense trial-and-error studio work. "When we came back from Tibet, each of us wrote one song. We tried to work without following any particular technique. We recorded many sample songs, some of them using nearly one hundred tracks, but to preserve the quality of the human voice the singing was recorded without editing." *Sister Drum* was released on the mainland in 1995 but was largely ignored by the official, government-run newspapers until the album began selling overseas. Then there were cautious articles praising the singer, while sidestepping the issue of China's ongoing efforts to destroy the people and culture of Tibet, the land Dadawa and her collaborators unhesitantly stated was their inspiration.

Since her Chinese name of Zhu Zheqin is difficult for most non-Chinese people to pronounce, Dadawa decided to create an enigmatic nom de musique that has "no translation. It doesn't belong to any language. In every country they think it means something different. In Japan and Taiwan there are words that sound like it, but 'dada' is a basic sound in every language. In every race everybody can pronounce this. I'm very sensitive to sound, but there's no explanation for how I made this name. Dadawa symbolizes the concept of going back to basics, before there is a language barrier or preconceptions to get in the way of communication."

what's available: The soaring soundscapes and lush textures of *Sister Drum* 🎵🎵🎵🎵 (Nonesuch, 1996, prod. He Xuntain) mix ambient/new age synth drones, neo-Classical melodies (both Western and Chinese), and an almost subliminal bass throb that slowly connects listeners to the meditative pulsation of the Universal Heart. He Xuntain has devised his own system of musical notation, different from both classical Chinese and Western music, although eminently listenable. The album has a big, open feel, with thundering percussion and angelic overdubbed harmonies that are symphonic in tone. The critic who described Dadawa as "a Chinese Enya" wasn't far off the mark. *Voices from the Sky* 𝄞𝄞𝄞𝄞 (Nonesuch, 1998, prod. He Xuntain) is more folky and less self-conscious—and less Western-sounding—than its predecessor, though one of the instrumental interludes on "Seven Drums" could have come straight out of the Blue Ridge Mountains.

influences:
◄◄ Cui Jian, Tan Dun

j. poet

Ustad Zia Mohiuddin Dagar /Z.M. Dagar

North Indian Classical, Hindustani
Born March 14, 1929, in Udaipur, India. Died September 28, 1990, in Bombay, India.

At his death, Zia Mohiuddin Dagar was the preeminent performer on the ancient *rudra vina* and a master of *dhrupad,* the centuries-old chant practiced by Dagar's ancestors in the Mughal courts. Though steeped in the tradition of his 19-generation musical family, Dagar broke with that tradition by reviving and performing solo on the vina, an instrument previously used only for accompanying singers. Dagar was known also for redesigning the neck, strings, and gourds of the vina, a precursor to the sitar, for enhanced sound and greater tonal stretch. Dagar's playing style was contemplative and deeply mesmerizing, based as it was on slow-moving dhrupad, and he generally performed only with *tambouras* (four-stringed drone instruments), adding a sense of austerity to his timeless sound world.

what to buy: *Todi, Ahir Lalit, Panchamkauns* 𝄞𝄞𝄞𝄞 (Raga Records, 1998, prod. John Wilton) is a live recording of Dagar with two tamboura players at the University of Washington in 1981. In "Todi" and "Ahir Lalit" Dagar adheres to his usual slow development and very, very gradual acceleration, but he ends both pieces playing at a slightly faster tempo than usual. *Raga Shudda Todi* 𝄞𝄞𝄞𝄞 (Nimbus Records, 1994, prod. Robin Broadbank) is classic Z.M. Dagar; slow, patient, and endless in a wash of tamboura drone. A relaxing, steady pulse gradually develops in the *Jor* and *Jhala* movements of this late-morning raga, bringing it to a close.

the rest:
Raga Yaman 𝄞𝄞𝄞 (Nimbus Records, 1991)

influences:
◄◄ Dabir Khan, Sadaq Ali Khan
►► Bahauddin Dagar, Nancy Lesh

David Paul

I.K. Dairo

Juju
Born Isaiah Kehinde Dairo, 1930, in Offa, Nigeria. Died February 7, 1996, in Efon-Alaiye, near Akure, Nigeria.

Multi-instrumentalist and vocalist I.K. Dairo was one of the fathers of modern *juju,* a heavily percussive, phenomenally popular dance music of Nigeria. Adding accordion and talking drum to the traditional juju lineup and incorporating vocal harmonies from Nigeria's Christian churches, Dairo created his own unique style.

The son of a carpenter, Dairo first played on a drum built for him by his father. Although in adult life he would work as a barber, construction worker, and clothes merchant, Dairo was a frequent performer with juju bands in the early 1950s. Forming his own outfit, Morning Star Orchestra (later known as the Blue Spots), Dairo—who played talking drum, guitar, and accordion—recorded his first singles in 1958. The original members of the group—which included a guitarist, bass player, three singers, and four drummers—stayed together throughout Dairo's career.

The artist reached his peak in the 1970s, when his recordings in the aftermath of the Nigerian Civil War established juju as the dominant sound in his native country. Dairo was even awarded an MBE (Member of the British Empire) from the Queen of England, the only African musician ever to receive this distinction. In the late '70s, Dairo retired from performing to manage clubs and hotels in Lagos; during the '80s, he served a ministry in the Cherubim and Seraphim churches; and in 1990, he recorded his first album in 15 years, *I Remember.* By the time he left this world six years later, he had returned to music in a way that well honored the legacy he had established, and added to the one he would leave behind.

what to buy: Dairo's comeback album *I Remember* 𝄞𝄞𝄞𝄞 (Music of the World, 1991, prod. I.K. Dairo) reunited him with the Blue Spots, and despite the long hiatus, he showed he was still capable of producing dance-inspiring music.

what to buy next: Dairo's early recordings are sampled on the anthology *The Glory Years* 𝄞𝄞𝄞𝄞 (Original Music, 1991, prod. I.K. Dairo).

the rest:
Definitive Dairo 𝄞𝄞𝄞𝄞 (Xenophile, 1971/1996)
Ju Ju Master MBE 𝄞𝄞𝄞𝄞 (Original Music, 1990)

I.K. Dairo

I.K. Dairo & His Blue Spots 🎵🎵🎵 (Original Music, 1991)
Ashiko 🎵🎵🎵 (Xenophile, 1994)

influences:

◀◀ Ojoge Daniel, Oladele Oro

▶▶ King Sunny Adé, Ebenezer Obey

Craig Harris

George Dalaras

Rembetiko, laiko
Born in Pireaus, Greece. Based in Pireaus, Greece.

George Dalaras has risen to become Greece's first modern-day music heavyweight. Born into his vocation (Dalaras's father was a bouzouki player), his love of music came from the *rembetiko* style—a Greek urban-blues form that endured censorship from the 1930s through the 1970s to emerge as a national standard-bearer—which he admired from an early age. He was discovered at the *still* early age of 16 playing guitar and singing in Athens, and in 1969 released his self-titled debut album. Since then, Dalaras's repertoire has grown to enormous proportions, in both solo work and collaborations with national and international artists. He has recorded with the likes of Al Di Meola, Paco de Lucia, and Nana Mouskouri, and has shared the stage with Peter Gabriel and Bruce Springsteen. Upon the fall of dictatorship in the 1970s, Dalaras, free of censorship, released his groundbreaking double album *Ta Rembetika (The Rembetiko Songs)*, which was the first "official" record of the genre to go platinum. Throughout his career, Dalaras has revived the styles of traditional Greek folk with a modern edge; incorporating *laiko* (the term for popular music) into his works, he has managed to appeal to a mass audience. In addition to putting his own words to music, Dalaras has worked with renowned poets such as Yannis Ritsos and Odysseus Elytis (a practice common in the rembetiko style), elevating the spoken word with his guitar playing. His passionate vocals speak of the hardships of the underdog, a theme woven into the fabric of Greek society. His active social awareness, prominently including his crusade to expose the invasion of Cypress by Turkey in 1974, won him the John F. Kennedy prize in 1994. His tireless recording and renowned live performances have earned him the title "the Bruce Springsteen of Greece." He has forever changed the landscape of modern Greek music, enjoying a crossover success rivaled only by Nana Mouskouri and projecting a youthful spirit second to none.

what to buy: George Dalaras started making his many significant contributions even before he became a star in his own right. He was one of the vocalists on composer Apostolos Kaladias's *Mikra Asia* 🎵🎵🎵🎵 (1973), which helped usher in mass acceptance for the rembetiko style. Following Kaladias's footsteps, Dalaras released *Ta Rembetika* 🎵🎵🎵🎵 (EMI/Minos, 1975), a double album filled with a passion many feel is still un-surpassed. His sorrowful vocals make this a must-have for any Dalaras fan. Moving toward a broader thematic palette, Dalaras's acute awareness of social and political issues came to fruition with *To Radar* 🎵🎵🎵🎵 (EMI/Minos, 1981). This release also marked a stylistic change for Dalaras, who here expanded his choice of instruments and made his music more up-to-date and accessible. The later progression of Dalaras's musical modernization can be heard on *Min Milas Min Gelas Kindinevi Ellas* 🎵🎵🎵🎵 (EMI/Minos, 1989), on which his band adds keyboards and various percussion instruments. The title track is politically charged, warning Greece not to forget about the hardships of war and never to make light of them. Dalaras's tour in support of this album was one of his most successful. The retrospective *A Portrait* 🎵🎵🎵 (Hemisphere, 1998, prod. various) serviceably surveys the artist's hits while steering clear of his experiments.

what to buy next: Some of Dalaras's most impressive releases have been collaborations. Working with world-renowned artists, he has brought the influence of Greek culture to the international masses. *Live Recordings with Paco de Lucia* 🎵🎵🎵🎵 (EMI, 1986) is beautiful, with Dalaras accompanying this amazing flamenco musician well. Dalaras also matched instruments with renowned guitarist Al Di Meola on *Latin* 🎵🎵🎵 (EMI, 1987); their subtle and competent duet work embodies the soul of Latin culture and achieves a most unusual and impressive collaboration.

what to avoid: Dalaras's discography is extensive, with variations in sound quality to match; beware of "best of" compilations not put out by the EMI/Minos label.

worth searching for: *Y Ta Tragoudia K' Ego Fteo* 🎵🎵🎵🎵 (EMI/Minos, 1993) is a must-have reissue of Dalaras's early 7-inches plus unreleased tracks. The recording quality may not be up to par with the better-produced albums that would follow, but the artistic quality and amazing historical value make this essential. Also worth searching for is Dalaras's work with poet Yannis Ritsos on *Ta Deca-Octo Llanatragouda Tis Pikris Patridas* 🎵🎵🎵 (EMI/Minos, 1974). His collaboration with modern Greek poet Nikos Kavadias transports the listener to exotic lands and times through sailors' voyages of the 19th century on *Grammes Ton Orizondon* 🎵🎵🎵 (EMI/Minos). Another of Dalaras's cross-cultural albums worth owning is his work with Argentinean composer Ariel Ramirez, *Missa Criola* 🎵🎵🎵 (1989), recorded live in the Catholic Church of Athens and delivering a powerful liturgy. Dalaras's interpretations of Greek life from the 1930s through the 1950s are beautifully expressed on *Vammena Kokkina Mallia* 🎵🎵🎵 (EMI/Minos, 1993). The title of the album—in English, "Dyed Red Hair"—is taken from a popular TV series of same name. And last but not least, Dalaras accompanies poet Odysseus Elytis while he recites his epic "Axion Esti," which has become one of the seminal works of modern Greek culture, on *Sinavlia Ston Palas* 🎵🎵🎵🎵 (EMI/Minos 1988).

influences:

◀◀ Stavros Kouyountzi, Mikis Theodorakis, Christos Nicopolous

▶▶ Dimitris Mitroopanos, Haris Alexiou, Pavlos Sitheropoulos

see also: *Paco de Lucia*

Helen Giano

Dalom Kids

See: Daniel Tshanda

Jackie Daly

Traditional and modern Irish folk

Born June 22, 1945, in Kanturck, County Cork, Ireland. Based in Ireland.

Accordionist Jackie Daly is among the most widely known performers in the distinctive Sliabh Luachra style of Irish music. Closely associated with the wild, hilly region between Counties Kerry and Cork, the Sliabh Luachra style is music for set dancing, marked by strongly rhythmic fiddle and box playing and a reliance on polkas and slides, as opposed to the reels and jigs more common to the rest of Ireland. Daly grew up in this region, learning music from his father and from local masters Jim Keefe and Sean Lynch. He developed a rhythmic accordion method well suited to the Sliabh Luachra style, and won the All-Ireland title in 1974. After a short stint playing with fiddler Seamus Creagh, he was asked to join the folk supergroup De Dannan in 1975. He toured with them for close to 10 years, appearing on some of the storied band's finest recordings. Then, in 1986, he joined Kevin Burke, Andy Irvine, and Arty McGlynn to form Patrick Street, with whom he continues to tour and record. Daly has also been a member of Arcady and has toured widely with fiddle player Maire O'Keefe.

what to buy: Although the music of Kerry is now well known to Irish music fans, this was by no means the case in 1977, the year *Music from Sliabh Luachra* 🎵🎵🎵🎵 (Topic, 1977/Green Linnet, 1992, prod. Tony Engle) was originally issued. Here was a revelation: a powerful young box player with a collection of tunes largely unknown outside of his hometown, playing with verve and drive in a style different from every other accordion player of the time. Featuring a great collection of slides and polkas from his native Sliabh Luachra, along with some fine slow airs, the album has lost none of its appeal in the intervening decades, and was rightly among the first four titles issued by Green Linnet in its Celtic Classics series. For serious fans of Irish music this is required listening.

what to buy next: *Eavesdropper* 🎵🎵🎵 (Mulligan, 1981/Green Linnet, 1981, prod. Kevin Burke, Jackie Daly), a duet album made with Kevin Burke in 1979, features some of the closest duet playing one is likely to hear, with sparse guitar or piano accompaniment (or none at all) and an eclectic repertoire of lesser-known tunes. Among the latter, a beautiful arrangement

ethno-techno

It's no surprise that certain types of techno have earned the subgenre moniker "trance," for the cathartic rhythms of this modern sound recall the ancient roots of that healing state of mind in the music of tribal cultures spanning the globe. Although the developing trend of fusing ethnic traditions with techno's hypnotic beat has only recently begun to gain steam in the mainstream, the movement's beginnings can be traced to the landmark 1981 album *My Life in the Bush of Ghosts,* which merged future Luaka Bop label founder David Byrne's fascination with world music and Brian Eno's technocentric bag of tricks, creating a dense, danceable mixture of the ancient and the futuristic. Artists ranging from Peter Gabriel to Bill Laswell and former PiL bassist Jah Wobble would dabble in ethno-techno experiments in the late '80s and early '90s, but the first group to make such fusions their *raison d'etre* was Transglobal Underground, whose sound borrowed liberally from African, Indian, Middle Eastern, Jamaican, and Latin music traditions, while focusing primarily on getting bodies onto the dance floor. A variety of like-minded artists soon followed suit, including Loop Guru, Dr. Didj, Trance Mission, Banco De Gaia, and Talvin Singh, but it was a more mainstream French studio project, Deep Forest, that produced the first Top 40 ethno-techno hit back in 1992 by combining pulsating tribal beats with pygmy chants. Now a staple sound that can be heard everywhere from film soundtracks to television commercials, ethno-techno promises to draw the Global Village closer together in the new millennium, bringing George Clinton's dream of "One Nation under a Groove" to fruition at last.

see also: Badawi, David Byrne, Deep Forest, Dr. Didg, Brian Eno, Peter Gabriel, Bill Laswell, Talvin Singh, Abdel Ali Slimani, Trance Mission, Transglobal Underground, Jim Wilson (sidebar)

Bret Love

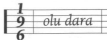
with guitar of an uncommon version of "The Blackbird" stands out. Cork flute player Conal ó Gráda guests on a few tracks, and so does Paul Brady on piano.

worth searching for: *Jackie Daly & Seamus Creagh* ♪♪♪♪ (Gael-Linn, 1977, prod. Jackie Daly, Seamus Creagh) is another outstanding album from Daly, this time playing duets with the fine fiddler who shares its title. Ably accompanied by *bodhrán* (Irish frame drum) player Colm Murphy, the boys tear through another prime set of instrumental dance tunes and one song. This is a great collection of music, and for fans of the Sliabh Luachra style, it is essential. When you've recorded a classic in your first attempt in the studio, and then you join De Dannan for *The Mist Covered Mountain* and *The Star Spangled Molly*—arguably the two finest albums that group has made—and then you go and form Patrick Street, and finally join Arcady, what happens if you next make an album that's just okay? Well, *Many's a Wild Night* ♪♪♪ (Gael-Linn, 1995, prod. Jackie Daly) is the answer. It's not a bad collection of tunes; the playing is good, if a little lacking in fire, and the production is the best of any of his solo albums. It's a solid effort that merely pales a bit in comparison with the formidable competition discussed above. Both *Jackie Daly & Seamus Creagh* and *Many's a Wild Night* are imports, but they can occasionally be found on this side of the Atlantic.

influences:

◀◀ Dennis Murphy & Julia Clifford, Padraig O'Keefe, Johnny O'Leary

▶▶ The Smoky Chimney, Sliabh Notes, Maire O'Keefe

see also: *Arcady, Kevin Burke, De Dannan, Alec Finn, Andy Irvine, Patrick Street*

Tony Ziselberger

Olu Dara

World-inflected jazz and blues

Born 1941, in Natchez, MS, USA. Based in New York, NY, USA.

Olu Dara is a genuine American artist, and a treasure. An estimable and earthy cornetist, singer, guitarist, songwriter, and musical theater composer, he has recorded and performed with such diverse talents as Art Blakey's Jazz Messengers, Brian Eno, James Blood Ulmer, Taj Mahal, Material, and Cassandra Wilson. Dara grew up in Natchez, Mississippi, and began performing at the age of 7, playing trumpet for women's clubs. He also immersed himself in painting, drawing, dancing; anything to do with the arts. At 18 he left college and joined the navy, traveling the world. He played in every kind of outfit the navy had to offer—marching bands, small jazz groups, big bands—on duty and off. And, of course, he picked up on the music of all the countries he visited throughout Europe, Africa, and the Caribbean. In 1963 Dara landed in New York City. He set music aside for a while, but

got the bug again and joined up with Art Blakey and the Messengers, touring nonstop. In the 1970s he fell into the downtown music scene and played and recorded with such avant garde musicians as David Murray, Sam Rivers, Henry Threadgill, and Julius Hemphill. In the 1980s Dara formed his own outfits, the seven-piece Okra Orchestra and the four-piece Natchezsippi Dance Band. Not to be tethered to one artistic outlet, Dara also works extensively in African American theater and dance, serving as composer and musical director for such acclaimed dramas as August Wilson's *The Piano Player*. He also continues to work on projects based on the life of writer Zora Neale Hurston. After performing and recording for more than 35 years and appearing on more than 50 albums by other artists, Dara finally made one of his own in 1998—and it was worth even this long a wait.

what's available: *In the World: From Natchez to New York* ♪♪♪♪♪ (Atlantic, 1998, prod. Yves Beauvais, Olu Dara) is Olu Dara's first album, believe it or not. And it's darn near perfect. Dara is a sophisticated yet down-home chef, combining Delta blues, jazz, calypso, reggae, rap, Nigerian *juju,* and other American, African, and Caribbean spices for one flavorful, subtle dish. Dara and his band—Kwatei Jones-Quarty and Ivan Ramirez on guitars, John Abrams on sax, Rudy Herbert on Hammond B-3 organ, Alonzo Gardner on bass, Richard James on congas, and Greg Bandy on drums—recorded it all in three days, creating an experience that's not often captured on record. The opening track, "Okra," is an old favorite from Dara's live shows, as is "Harlem Country Girl." Dara romps through the sensuous but funny "Your Lips" with the refrain "Your lips, your lips, your lips . . . are juicy." Numbers from his theatrical work include "Young Mama" and "Rain Shower." On the topical song "Jungle," Dara is joined on vocals by his son Nas, the famous hip-hop artist.

influences:

◀◀ Robert Johnson, Louis Armstrong, Bessie Smith, Ornette Coleman, Art Blakey, Dizzie Gillespie, James Blood Ulmer

▶▶ Taj Mahal, Cassandra Wilson, Nas, Madeleine Peyroux

Andrew BeDell

Alan Dargin /Reconciliation

Didgeridoo fusion, worldbeat

Dargin born in Northeast Arnhem Land, Australia. Reconciliation formed 1992, in Australia. Based in Toronto, Ontario, Canada.

Alan Dargin, didgeridoo, Celtic horn, clap sticks; Simon O'Dwyer, Celtic horn; Phillip Conyngham, didgeridoo, Celtic horn, clap sticks; Maria Cullen, bodhrán, pennywhistle. (All members are from Ireland except where noted otherwise.)

Dargin was born and raised in an Aboriginal tribe in Northeast Arnhamland, Australia. When he was five years old, his grandfather began teaching him *didgeridoo* (the now world-popular droning blown instrument) and eventually passed his own on to his grandson. "My grandfather's didgeridoo is 107 years old," Dargin says. "It's made from a variety of bloodwood that has been extinct for 80 years." Traditionally the didgeridoo is made from a branch of a tree that has been naturally hollowed out by ants. It is played in tribal ceremonies and social gatherings to accompany singers. "I learned many secrets from my grandfather," Dargin says, "but you can only be taught so much by others. You also have to listen and learn by yourself. I've taken a traditional instrument and adapted it to modern music. I play [the didgeridoo] like a jazz horn, playing in any beat or rhythm. It has a very powerful bass tone, and in an ensemble it can fill up all the holes and make the sound full, which is probably why it has so much potential for world music." Dargin has toured Australia, Europe, Asia, and the U.S., both as a solo artist and as a member of Reconciliation, a group he cofounded with Simon O'Dwyer and Maria Cullen to combine Celtic and Aboriginal music. In 1988 O'Dwyer had discovered that the Bronze Age Celtic horn, an instrument long thought "unplayable," could in fact be played with the same techniques as the didgeridoo. O'Dwyer had three horns made, based on ones in the collection of the National Museum of Dublin. In 1992, while touring Australia to demonstrate the Celtic horn, he met Dargin, and after an evening of experimentation, they decided on an ongoing collaboration.

what's available: On *Reconciliation* 𝄢𝄢𝄢 (Natural Symphonies, 1993, prod. Reconciliation) Cullen's *bodhrán* (Irish frame drum) and Dargin's clap sticks lay the foundation for extended improvisations on didgeridoo and Celtic horn. There are jigs and reels played with an Aboriginal slant, and some traditional Aboriginal tunes given a Celtic treatment. The Celtic horns have an eerie high end that's a perfect counterpart to the booming bottom of the didgeridoo. *Bloodwood* 𝄢𝄢𝄢 (Natural Symphonies, 1993, prod. Michael Atherton) features Dargin's didgeridoo, the guitar and synth of Michael Atherton, and a few guests on occasional sax, bass, and drums. The music is ambient, funky, and folky by turns, but mostly a showcase for Dargin's amazing chops.

influences:

◀◀ Yothu Yindi

▶▶ Trance Mission

j. poet

Dark City Sisters

Late marabi, early mbaqanga

Formed mid-1950s, in Johannesburg, South Africa. Disbanded mid-1960s (original lead singer still occasionally performs in Johannesburg with all-new lineup). Based in Johannesburg, South Africa.

Rotating, largely undocumented membership, principally including Joyce Mogatusi, lead vocals.

In late-'50s Johannesburg, the jazz-inspired *marabi* style still lit up the illegal township nightspots known as *shebeens*. This was the heyday of the Dark City Sisters, perhaps the country's most popular vocal group prior to the 1964 dawn of the Mahotella Queens. Late-marabi acts like the Dark City Sisters continued to imitate American swing jazz, but they had dropped pianos and banjos in favor of electric guitars, and where a scarcity of horns had once forced bands to use pennywhistles—in the style called *kwela*—postwar bands took full advantage of an influx of new instruments, and any outfit worth its salt had a swinging horn section.

The Dark City Sisters—named for Alexandra Township, the "dark city"—began as session singers at EMI, but came to be a solid unit with a distinct sound. At the start of their hit "Sekusile," a rooster crows, followed by a gentle, brush-driven swing groove with an unadorned guitar riff, and then the bell-clear voice of the group's leading lady Joyce Mogatusi. The tune heats up with doo-wop–like backing vocals—in Zulu, of course. All the elements of the coming *mbaqanga* style can be found in this group's songs—the deep, downbeat pulse, the sunny female vocal harmonies, and the chattering double-stop guitar outings. Mbaqanga guitar pioneer Marks Mankwane called the Dark City Sisters' lead guitarist Armand Memele "my guitar hero." Mahlathini, the famed "groaner" who would go on to serve 30-plus years with the Mahotella Queens, started out with the Dark City Sisters. And Ray Phiri, founder of Stimela and guitarist on Paul Simon's *Graceland,* got his start as a boy dancing for the Dark City Sisters. This is history, no doubt about it, but the work still stands up well, evidence of an enormously creative period in one of Africa's most productive musical capitols.

what to buy: *Dark City Sisters and Flying Jazz Queens* 𝄢𝄢𝄢𝄢 (Earthworks, 1993) is the only collection of Dark City Sisters tunes you're likely to find. Luckily, it's a gem, fascinating for what it reveals about township music's roots, and just plain delightful to hear.

influences:

◀◀ Spokes Mashiyane, Alexandra Black Mambazo

▶▶ Mahlathini & Mahotella Queens

see also: *Mahlathini & Mahotella Queens*

Banning Eyre

Krishna Das

Worldbeat kirtans

Born in USA. Based in Los Angeles, CA, USA.

The belief that chanting the name of God can dissolve the boundaries between the mundane and the transcendental is shared by many cultures. In India, the singing of *mantras* and *kirtans* is an art form, and each devotee is encouraged to bring his or her own musical knowledge to this practice. Das grew up with the typical American interest in jazz, blues, and rock, but a meeting with Ram Dass in 1969 opened his eyes and heart to a different way of being. Das left his old life and went to India where he lived with his guru, Neem Karoli Baba, from 1970 to 1973. While he was studying with Baba he met Mitchell Markus and Jai Uttal, and began discussing the possibility of bringing some spiritual light into the American music business. Although it took almost 20 years, the result of those conversations was Triloka Records, which was founded in the summer of 1990 and has since become a leader in the world-music and Native American genres. In between producing, playing, and singing on various ethno/techno/trance recordings, Das has found time to record his own brand of multi-culti devotional music.

what to buy: On *One Track Heart* 𝄞𝄞𝄞𝄞 (Triloka, 1996, prod. Krishna Das, Jai Uttal, Jim Wilson), Das has created mellow musical settings for some of the oldest poems known to (wo)man by combining Indian *ragas* and Western scales, sitars and twangy surfadelic guitar. Some tracks are fairly traditional, but turning "Hara Mahadeva Shaambo" into a smooth bit of Indian Motown and playing the "Hare Krishna" mantra as a loping country & western ballad are acts of quirky genius.

the rest:
Pilgrim Heart 𝄞𝄞𝄞 (Triloka, 1998)

influences:
◄◄ George Harrison, Tulku

see also: *Jai Uttal*

j. poet

Paban Das Baul & Sam Mills

Traditional Baul folk music, worldbeat
Formed 1990, in London, England. Based in London, England.

Paban Das Baul (born 1961, in West Bengal, India), vocals, percussion, samples; Sam Mills (born 1963, in London, England), keyboards, guitar, samples, vocals.

Bauls are traditional wandering musicians, known to be holy men, gurus, and poets. Their songs have been handed down for generations and are said to awaken people to their own inner light. Paban began singing and playing music as a child and wandered with his father, a martial arts champion who would wrestle strangers for money. He was initiated into the oral traditions of the Baul brotherhood at age 14 by Subol Das Baul. As a young man he met and played with black American artists who were visiting India, including Clarke Terry and Big Joe Williams. In 1980 Paban began traveling through Europe singing on the streets, in clubs, and at festivals. Mills was born

in London and got his first professional exposure in 23 Skidoo, a rock band that became so progressive they left rhythm and melody behind. When Mills first heard Baul music it turned his head around and he wound up traveling to and living in Bengal for several years. He met Paban in 1988 and in 1990 they began experimenting together, leading to the recordings on *Real Sugar.* "Baul music has never been confined to a single caste," Mills says. "It stands outside classical Indian tradition but has a motivating, rhythmic way of reaching across boundaries and creating a resonance for anyone receptive to it, regardless of their background."

what's available: On *Real Sugar* 𝄞𝄞𝄞𝄞 (Island, 1997, prod. Paban Das Baul, Sam Mills, Fritz Catin, Mimlu Sen), Paban's gruff vocals highlight nine smooth tracks that combine Indian rhythms and instruments with elements drawn from calypso, modern rock, and dance clubs.

solo outings:
Sam Mills:
(With Tama) *Nostalgie* N/A (RealWorld/Narada, 1999)

influences:
◄◄ Shelia Chandra, Fun-Da-Mental, Najma

see also: *23 Skidoo*

j. poet

Daude

MPB (Brazilian Popular Music)
Born Maria Walderlurdes Costa de Santana Dutilleux, in Salvador da Bahia, Brazil. Based in Rio de Janeiro, Brazil.

Like those in the bossa nova and *Tropicalismo* movements before her, Daude has synthesized "foreign" rhythms with Brazilian ones. Often tagged as a Brazilian rapper, Daude sees herself simply as a maker of pop music who happens to come from Brazil. "I want my music to be known all over the world, not as world music but as Daude," she said in one interview. On the other hand, she is quick to point out that she is Brazilian and that that goes a long way toward defining her music. On her self-titled first album, for example, she performs a rap-like duet with Miguel Bezerra on "Quatro Meninas." But it is not really rap; it is an updated version of the northeastern style called *repente*—albeit with some electronic muscle behind it. Daude's musical education began during her childhood in the Candeal neighborhood of Salvador da Bahia. Her father was in the military but had another, more creative side, as a music teacher and saxophone player. He was, in Daude's words, "very serious but very irreverent—crazy, but in a good way." Her father was responsible for exposing her to a wide array of music: samba, soul, big-band jazz—and he was also a mentor to a young boy

Daude

in the neighborhood who would later change his name to Car-linhos Brown and found the innovative group Timbalada. Daude's name was given to her by her brother, who couldn't pronounce her real name of Walderlurdes. After her family moved to Rio, Daude took music lessons, then went into musical theater. The first time she hit the stage, she recalls, "I thought: 'This is exactly what I want to do.'" Well, not exactly. She would eventually begin singing in small clubs, developing a repertoire and a network of music-business connections. One of the most important ones she made was Celso Fonseca, who plays guitar with Gilberto Gil. He introduced Daude to her Brazilian record company and went on to produce her first album and, with Soul II Soul's Will Mowat, part of her second. Daude eventually signed with the California-based Tinder Records to distribute her albums outside Brazil; then, with tours of the U.S., Japan, and Europe, she began laying the foundation for her dream of becoming known around the globe.

what to buy: *Daude* 𝄢𝄢𝄢 (Tinder, 1997, prod. Celso Fonseca) is heavily influenced by hip-hop, reggae, and dance music, though several songs use Brazilian rhythms as a foundation.

the rest:
Veu Vava: Remixes by Will Mowat 𝄢𝄢 (Tinder, 1997)
Daude 2 N/A (Tinder, 1999)

influences:
◀◀ Carlinhos Brown, Gilberto Gil, Soul II Soul, David Bowie

see also: *Timbalada*

Marty Lipp

Shaun Davey

Irish traditional, neo-traditional, and orchestral
Born 1948, in Belfast, Ireland. Based in Dublin, Ireland.

Keyboardist and self-taught composer Shaun Davey has been writing for TV, film, and theater since the mid-'70s, starting with advertising jingles but soon turning to the concert orchestra as a vehicle for some grander visions. Drawing on significant events in Irish history for subject matter, and using prominent Irish soloists—especially uilleann piper Liam O'Flynn and singer Rita Connolly—Davey has written a series of ambitious large-scale works that have been performed throughout the concert halls of Europe, North America, and Australia, including the prestigious Royal Festival Hall and Albert Hall in London and the Sydney Opera House.

It all started with *The Brendan Voyage* (1980), a landmark suite for orchestra and uilleann pipes, based on intrepid English sailor Tim Severin's book of the same name. It tells the tale of St. Brendan and his rumored sixth-century voyage in a small leather-covered boat (represented by ace piper O'Flynn) across the Atlantic (represented by the orchestra) to the New World. While Severin had just demonstrated the possibility of such a daunting trip via the icy waters surrounding the Faroes, Iceland, and Newfoundland, with this innovative score Davey demonstrated the possibilities of combining traditional Irish instruments with a concert orchestra via warm, evocative writing.

The Pilgrim (1984) was decidedly Pan-Celtic, and concerns the spread of Christianity throughout the Celtic regions during the Dark Ages. It uses a large cast: orchestra, traditional musicians, solo singers, and Welsh and Cornish choirs. As first released it was edited down from the larger *Lorient Festival Suite,* commissioned for the 1983 Lorient Festival in Brittany; getting all of this onto a single LP was not easy, even with the help of talented coproducer Bill Whelan. The CD from 1991 presents a longer, totally different recording taken from a 1990 concert in Glasgow and sees the suite substantially reorganized and improved.

Granuaile (1985) also features O'Flynn, Connolly, and orchestra, and tackles the tale of the extraordinary 16th-century female chieftain and sea captain Granuaile (Grace O'Malley), who ruled the waves off the west of Ireland in the time of Elizabeth I. Davey returned closer to home for his next opus, *The Relief of Derry Symphony* (1990), commissioned by the Derry City Council to commemorate the infamous 1689 siege of that city, in which 15,000 people died. While the siege only served to cement divisions among the people of the north of Ireland—divisions which persist to this day—the symphony was conceived as an attempt to depoliticize this aspect of shared history, and performers from both sides of the community came together for its debut in Derry city.

As a producer Davey has worked on numerous solo recordings by Connolly (the pair married in the 1980s) and O'Flynn, as well as sessions by Sonny Condell, Stockton's Wing, and others. His extensive theater writing includes music for productions at Dublin's Abbey and Gate Theatres and the Royal Shakespeare Company in Britain, and he has done film scores for Irish and British TV, as well as the big screen, the latter putting him on the world map like never before with his soundtrack for the recent *Waking Ned Devine.*

what to buy: *The Brendan Voyage* 𝄢𝄢𝄢 (Tara, 1980, prod. Shaun Davey) was a true parting of the waters in Irish music: Liam O'Flynn's exquisite piping takes on a full orchestra for an imaginative recounting of a small boat's long journey through hostile seas in search of a distant land. This was a bold new idea—both for Sr. Brendan and for Davey—and much of the writing (like the trip, no doubt) is memorable. One minor complaint: the occasional bass guitar and drum accompaniment sounds awkward and dated today. *Granuaile* 𝄢𝄢𝄢 (Tara, 1985, prod. Shaun Davey) was written to showcase the talents of Rita Connolly, whose lovely voice is joined here by piper O'Flynn, a 22-piece chamber orchestra, Helen Davis on harp, Dónal Lunny on bouzouki and *bodhrán* (Irish frame drum), and Noel Eccles on percussion. "Ripples in the Rockpool" (which Connolly has also rerecorded on a solo album) is one of several highlights; the song is now in the official Irish school syllabus.

what to buy next: *The Pilgrim* 𝄢𝄢𝄢 (Tara, 1991, prod. Shaun Davey) on CD is a new recording of a suite originally issued on LP in 1984. Diverse Celtic images are conjured up by Irish and Welsh harps, a Scottish pipe band, uilleann pipes (O'Flynn), Galician (Spanish Celtic) pipes, Breton (French Celtic) *bombardes* (bagpipes), a 120-member choir, and the same solo singers who were on the original release, Iarla O Lionaird and Rita Connolly. The mature and dignified *Relief of Derry Symphony* 𝄢𝄢𝄢 (Tara, 1990, prod. Shaun Davey, Brian Masterson) is performed by the Ulster Orchestra and various pipe bands, with Davey's usual collaborators, Connolly and O'Flynn, each making one contribution. Perhaps the least traditional of Davey's albums, it is also one of the finest orchestral works to emerge in Ireland for some time. The soundtrack to *Waking Ned Devine* 𝄢𝄢𝄢 (London, 1998, prod. Shaun Davey), like the film itself, is light, lively, and lots of fun. With a crack team that includes fiddler Nollaig Casey, piper/whistler John McSherry, guitarist Arty McGlynn, and singers Connolly, Liam O'Maonlai, and the Voice Squad, Davey romps through a clutch of traditional-sounding tunes that can easily stand on their own apart from the film, even if several of them *do* bear a distinct resemblance to the work of *Riverdance* composer Bill Whelan. The main theme from the film, the Waterboys' "Fisherman's Blues," is also on the CD.

worth searching for: The *High Kings of Tara* (Tara, 1980) compilation contains the rare Davey track "Pride of the Herd," featuring a very young Connolly.

influences:

◀◀ Seán Ó Riada, the Chieftains, Planxty, Liam O'Flynn, Alan Stivell, Bill Whelan

▶▶ Rita Connolly, Bill Whelan, William Jackson

see also: *Dónal Lunny, Liam O'Flynn, Bill Whelan*

John C. Falstaff

Davka

Klezmer

Formed 1993, in Berkeley, CA, USA. Based in Berkeley, CA, USA.

Daniel Hoffman, violin; Moses Sedler, cello; Adam Levenson, doumbek, zarb, Remo frame drum. (All members are from USA.)

This trio of conservatory-trained musicians uses klezmer music as a foundation but is taking it in exciting new directions by emphasizing stringed instruments and adding Arabic percussion to their playing. Their blend of Jewish music, classical romanticism, jazzy improvisation, and driving Arabic rhythm makes them unique in the ranks of modern klezmer-inspired musicians. Daniel Hoffman, one of the group's founding members, has been interested in Jewish cultural music since he began playing. He formed the San Francisco Klezmer Experience for the American Conservatory Theater's production of *Schlemiel the First,* has played with many other artists including the Flying Bulgar Klezmer Band and Alicia Svigals, and directs the Traveling Jewish Theater's Wednesday-night Jewish Music series. Cellist Moses Sedler is a long-time member of Ancient Future, one of the oldest world-music/new age instrumental ensembles, while percussionist Peter Maund has studied Indian *tabla* drum at the Ali Akbar College of Music in Marin, as well as folklore and ethnomusicology at UC Berkeley. The trio that became Davka got together to jam on Jewish melodies and Arabic rhythms and slowly developed their own style of improvised music. The pace is usually slow to mid-tempo, giving much of the material a pensive feeling, but the musical interchange is lively and they've been known to break into a hora on occasion.

what's available: Playing klezmer-esque melodies with an Arabic backbeat as the band does on *Davka* ♪♪♪ (Interworld, 1994, prod. Ben James) shows how close the roots of these musical traditions are. All three players are classically trained, and their versatility and restraint gives this set plenty of melancholy tension. Their second set, *Lavy's Dream* ♪♪♪ (Interworld, 1996, prod. Ben James), is more energetic and free-ranging than the debut, an album full of dark colors and somber soul.

influences:
◄◄ Epstein Brothers, Klezmorim

see also: *Ali Akbar Khan, the Klezmatics*

j. poet

De Dannan /De Danann

Irish traditional

Formed 1974, in Spiddal, County Galway, Ireland. Based in Galway, Ireland.

Frankie Gavin, fiddle, viola, flute, tin whistle, piano, vocals (1974–present); Alec Finn, bouzouki, guitar, keyboards (1974–present); Charlie Piggot, banjo, melodeon, tin whistle (1974–82); Johnny "Ringo" McDonagh, bodhrán, bones (1974–present); Dolores Keane, vocals, flute (1974–75, 1985–88); Johnny Moynihan, vocals, bouzouki, mandolin, tin whistle (1976–79); Jackie Daly, accordion (1980–82); Maura O'Connell, vocals (1981–82); Mary Black, vocals (1983–87); Martin O'Connor, accordion (1983–88); Caroline Lavelle, cello (1987–88); Eleanor Shanley, vocals (1988–92); Aidan Coffey, accordion (1988–94); Colm Murphy, bodhrán, bones (1988–present); Adele O'Dwyer, cello (1988–90); Tommy Flemming, vocals (1994–present); Derek Hickey, accordion (1996–present). (All members are from Ireland.)

If Planxty and the Bothy Band could be called the Beatles of Irish traditional music, then De Dannan would have to be its Rolling Stones. For not only has this Galway-based band been extremely prolific and adventurous in its choice of repertoire and its arrangements, it has also shown remarkable longevity for a folk outfit, rivaling the Chieftains as an Irish musical institution. Over a quarter-century and counting, De Danann (now spelled De Dannan) has gone through numerous changes in its lineup, in the process launching the careers of several of today's best-known Irish folk vocalists. Yet the band has kept the straight-ahead, live-session sound of its beginnings. All along, fiddle player extraordinaire Frankie Gavin and subtle bouzouki accompanist Alec Finn have remained the driving force behind that sound. Raised in a musical family, Gavin was a precocious fiddle and flute virtuoso who was still in school when the band came together at Galway-area sessions. Yorkshire-born Finn was involved in the Dublin blues scene in the 1960s before he moved to Spiddal, County Galway, and was given a bouzouki with which he started to frequent local Irish music sessions. There he met Gavin, Kerry banjo and melodeon player Charlie Piggot, and master of the *bodhrán* (Irish frame drum) and bones (like it sounds) Johnny "Ringo" McDonagh. When a few professional engagements came their way, the lads became a band. They recorded their first album in 1975 with the help of singer Dolores Keane, a neighbor of Gavin. However, Keane left soon after the album came out to perform with her husband John Faulkner. Former Sweeney's Men and Planxty member Johnny Moynihan became the band's singer for a time, appearing on its second LP, *Selected Jigs, Reels and Songs*, in 1978. By the time *The Mist Covered Mountain* came out two years later, the band had again lost its frontperson—the album's vocal tracks were of traditional Connemara singers—but gained a great instrumentalist in the person of Kerry accordion player Jackie Daly. It wasn't long before the band members were able to talk singer Maura O'Connell into joining, just in time to record *The Star Spangled Molly*, their first truly successful album. True to form, however, the band soon lost half of its lineup when Piggot, O'Connell, and Daly left in rapid succession. Piggot was disabled in a freak accident and could no longer play, O'Connell was more interested in pursuing a career in country music, and Daly needed a change. Gavin and Finn found accordion wizard Martin O'Connor and singer Mary Black to replace them, and the new lineup produced the memorable *Song for Ireland* in 1983. When they recorded *Anthem* two years later, they asked Dolores Keane if she would sing "Let It Be" on it. Somehow she ended up recording a duet with Black and was back in the band in no time. This may well have been the band's finest lineup, yet it proved to be an embarrassment of riches. There was too much talent to go around, both instrumentally and vocally, and not enough time in concert sets to accommodate it all. Black left the band in 1987. At about the same time, Gavin recruited cellist Caroline Lavelle after a chance encounter on the streets of London, and the band went on to release the nostalgic *Ballroom,* using the new spelling "De Danann" for its name. Another major change in the lineup occurred the very next year, as the band recorded *A Jacket of Batteries* in 1988 with Leitrim singer Eleanor Shanley, Aidan Coffey on accordion, Colm Murphy on bodhrán and bones, and cellist Adele O'Dwyer replacing Lavelle. Minus O'Dwyer, the same band recorded *1/2 Set in Harlem* in 1991, continuing their experimentation with contemporary songwriters' material and adding gospel and klezmer musicians to their unlikely stew. Although De Dannan's fate has seemed uncertain since, as various members dropped out or pursued solo projects, the band toured extensively in 1994 with a new singer, Tommy Flemming, and a new cassette entitled *World Tour 1994—Studio & Live Recordings.* In 1996, with Coffey replaced by accordionist Derek Hickey, De Dannan put out *Hibernian Rhapsody,* named after the band's intricate instrumental arrangement of Queen's rock anthem "Bohemian Rhapsody." However epic, it doesn't seem to be a finale just yet.

what to buy: As De Danann was without a designated singer when *The Mist Covered Mountain* 𝄞𝄞𝄞𝄞 (Gael-Linn/Shanachie, 1980, prod. De Danann) was recorded, the band opted to include vocal tracks by two prominent exponents of Connemara *sean-nós* ("old-style") singing, Seán Ó Conaire and Tom Pháidín Tom, the latter just months before his death at age 85. Despite good intentions, the juxtaposition of their typically unaccompanied, rhythmically free style of singing with the band's bouzouki and whistle accompaniments often sounds at odds. However, the strength of the album is in the exciting instrumentals spun by Gavin, Piggot, and newly recruited Kerry accordionist Jackie Daly. The spectacular opening and closing sets of jigs into reels and the arrangement of seminal 18th-century composer Turlough O'Carolan's "Mr. O'Connor" are among the best instrumental tracks of the band's recorded output. *The Star Spangled Molly* 𝄞𝄞𝄞𝄞 (Ogham/Shanachie, 1981, prod. De Danann, Nicky Ryan) is De Danann's salute to Irish American music of the 1920s and 1930s and to Gavin's favorite performers of the period, the Flanagan Brothers and Sligo fiddler James Morrison. Despite Maura O'Connell's reservations about per-

forming Irish songs, this album established her as a powerful singer and her name is forever associated with the delightful Irish American stage songs "Maggie" and "My Irish Molly-O." Frankie Gavin also sings on "I'm Leaving Tipperary," one of the more joyous Irish emigration songs, borrowed from a 78 by the Boston-based Dan Sullivan's Shamrock Band. The instrumental tracks, featuring once again the tight playing of Gavin and Daly, are as energetic as ever. In the Flanagan Brothers' "New Irish Barn Dance," the instrumentation, adding piano accompaniment and hammered dulcimer touches, brilliantly captures the tune's music-hall character, while other medleys of reels and jigs echo performers of long ago: John McKenna, P.J. Conlon, John Kimmel. Oddly enough, probably the best-known track on the album, even if totally irrelevant to its theme, would have to be De Danann's famous arrangement of the Beatles' "Hey Jude," in which the melody gets transformed into a hornpipe. The die-hard De Danann fan may want to acquire the CD version recently put out by K-Tel Music as *De Danann* (K-Tel, 1996), as it includes two additional tracks, one instrumental and one vocal, which were originally released just as a single. The stunning voice of Mary Black is one reason *Song for Ireland* 𝄞𝄞𝄞𝄞 (Cara/Sugar Hill, 1983, prod. Nick Bicât, De Danann) remains one of the band's most memorable albums. Black shines on the much-copied title song, Stephen Foster's classic "Hard Times," and "Live Not Where I Love," while Gavin is the vocalist on the Irish American stage song "Barney from Killarney." There are gems as well among the instrumentals, most of which were recorded while Daly was still in the band. Of the ones to which Daly's successor, Martin O'Connor, contributed, the opening "Arrival of the Queen of Sheba (In Galway)," based on Handel's sinfonia from his oratorio *Solomon,* is such a rollicking tour de force that one may start thinking the composer would have enjoyed it that way. *The Best of De Danann* 𝄞𝄞𝄞𝄞 (Shanachie, 1987) is an excellent anthology based on the band's first four albums. In particular, it includes some tracks from De Danann's first two LPs, *De Danann* and *Selected Jigs, Reels and Songs,* both no longer available.

what to buy next: On *Anthem* 𝄞𝄞𝄞 (Dara, 1985, prod. John Dunford, Alec Finn, Frankie Gavin), Mary Black and Dolores Keane share vocal duties, and, not surprisingly, this is the first De Danann album to give equal time to vocal and instrumental tracks. Black's voice is perfectly suited for the emotionally charged "Johnny I Hardly Knew Ye" and "Paddy's Lamentation." On the strength of their earlier success with "Hey Jude," the band asked Keane to sing on another Beatles classic, "Let It Be." Gavin and O'Connor continue to work their instrumental magic on medleys of traditional dance tunes, noteworthy new-but-stylistically-traditional compositions like Gavin's own three-part jig "The Wren's Nest," and "Ríl an Spidéal," a set of reels by Leitrim fiddle and piano player Charlie Lennon. A sequel of sorts to *The Star Spangled Molly, Ballroom* ♪♪♪♪ (WEA/Green Linnet, 1987, prod. De Dannan) celebrates the music of the Irish and Irish American dancehalls of earlier decades. Pioneer musicians like John Kimmel and Eleanor Neary are remembered through dance tunes they recorded or composed, while Dolores Keane invites us to the waltz with her renditions of classics like "Teddy O'Neill," "The Sweet Forget-Me-Not," and the closing medley starting with "The Stone Outside Dan Murphy's Door." A touch of exoticism is provided by a medley of "Jewish Reels," learned from New York klezmer musician Andy Statman. *A Jacket of Batteries* ♪♪♪ (Harmac/Green Linnet, 1988, prod. various) introduced us to a new group of talented musicians: accordionist Aidan Coffey, who proves a worthy successor to Daly and O'Connor; singer Eleanor Shanley; and drummer Colm Murphy. For better or for worse, it also gave a definite impression that the band had settled on a formula: throw in a few jigs and reels, a piece of classical music ("The Rambles of Bach"), a Beatles song ("Eleanor Rigby"), and a mixture of traditional and contemporary songs. Still, there are good moments, for instance the reel medley of "Sailing In" (Charlie Lennon) and "Alice's Reel" (Frankie Gavin), or Shanley's passionate rendition of the classic "Carrigfergus." De Dannan's latest, *Hibernian Rhapsody* ♪♪♪ (The Bee's Knees, 1995/Shanachie, 1996, prod. De Dannan), shows that despite the passing of years Finn and Gavin can still find talented musicians—this time accordionist Derek Hickey and singer Tommy Flemming—willing to join the band. Hickey proves up to the task as Gavin's new "straight man," although the band's virtuosic but pointless instrumental arrangement of Queen's "Bohemian Rhapsody" is among the least interesting tracks. The intense singing style of Tommy Flemming suggests a comparison with that of Mary Black, but recent live appearances by the band show that the new combination works better there than on record. It's worth noting that the Bees Knees release and the Shanachie release are slightly different; the former contains the songs "The Water Is Wide" and "Fios Na Siochanna" and the instrumental "Do It in Jig Time," but does not have the song "Captain Jack" (composed by Meg Davis but not credited) and the instrumental "Sean McGuire's," which are on the U.S. version. So the Irish version has 16 tracks, the U.S. 15.

what to avoid: *1/2 Set in Harlem* ♪♪ (The Bee's Knees/Green Linnet, 1991, prod. Arty McGlynn, Frankie Gavin, Alec Finn), which follows to some extent the formula of *A Jacket of Batteries,* is De Dannan's most adventurous album to date. However, the inclusion of gospel singers on tracks like "Operator" and of klezmer-style clarinet and horn on a set of Irish hornpipes ends up sounding more incongruous than dynamic.

worth searching for: The first two De Danann albums, *De Danann* ♪♪♪♪ (Polydor, 1975, prod. Dónal Lunny) and *Selected Jigs, Reels and Songs* ♪♪♪♪ (Decca, 1978, prod. Carsten Linde, Nicky Ryan, De Danann), are not currently available. They remain among the band's very best and are well worth searching for. On *De Danann,* which was available on CD from Polydor for a short while, classic instrumental tracks like the jig medley "Tripping up the Stairs," featuring Finn's fine bouzouki harmonies, or Gavin's fiddle solo on "The Gold Ring," are almost eclipsed by Dolores Keane's sean-nós vocals on songs like "The Rambling Irishman" or "The Shores of Lough Bran." *Selected Jigs, Reels and Songs* had a similar effect to that of the Bothy Band's *1975* album in that musicians would learn each and every tune on it to play at live sessions. The opening set of jigs into reels, "Tom Billy's"; the medley of Wren tunes played on three whistles; and the beautifully crafted counterpoint of bouzoukis and mandolins on "Carolan's Draught" are among the most memorable instrumental moments of this album. Johnny Moynihan's contribution will be remembered for his wonderful renditions of songs like "The Flower of Sweet Strabane" and "Barbara Allen." A few live tracks recorded in Germany in 1989 by the *Jacket of Batteries* lineup can be found on *Ireland* ♪♪♪♪ (WDR, 1993, prod. Christian Scholze, Jean Trouillet, Jan Reichow), perhaps more interesting for its recordings of Frankie Gavin with piper Liam O'Flynn and of the band Altan.

solo outings:

Alec Finn:
Blue Shamrock ♪♪♪♪ (Cross Border Media/Celtic Heartbeat, 1994)

Jackie Daly:
Jackie Daly and Séamus Creagh ♪♪♪♪ (Gael-Linn, 1977)
Music from Sliabh Luachra ♪♪♪♪ (Topic, 1977/Green Linnet, 1992)
(With Kevin Burke) *Eavesdropper* ♪♪♪♪ (Mulligan/Green Linnet, 1981)
Many's a Wild Night ♪♪♪♪ (Gael-Linn, 1995)

Martin O'Connor:
The Connachtman's Rambles ♪♪♪♪ (Mulligan, 1979)
Perpetual Motion ♪♪♪♪ (Claddagh, 1990)
Chatterbox ♪♪♪♪ (Dara, 1993)

Colm Murphy:
An Bodhrán ♪♪♪♪ (Gael-Linn, 1996)

influences:

◀◀ The Flanagan Brothers, James Morrison, John McKenna, Dan Sullivan's Shamrock Band, Planxty

▶▶ Arcady, Altan, Dervish, Patrick Street, Four Men and a Dog, Skylark

see also: *Arcady, Mary Bergin, Mary Black, the Black Family, Jackie Daly, John Faulkner, Alec Finn, Frankie Gavin, Dolores Keane, Maura O'Connell, Planxty, Andy Statman, Sweeney's Men*

Philippe Varlet

Tony de la Rosa
/El Conde (The Count)

Conjunto

Born 1931, in Sarita, TX, USA. Based in southern Texas, USA.

Tony de la Rosa began playing the accordion in a country band in south Texas before he was 14, but he soon saw that *conjunto,* that danceable mix of Spanish, Mexican, German, and American country music that pervades the border region, was his calling. In the 1950s, de la Rosa revolutionized conjunto and shaped much of its post–World War II sound by adding drums and electrifying the *bajo sexto* (12-string bass guitar) in his group. This sparked a new dance, the *tachuachito,* and led to conjunto bands playing larger rooms with a now-amplified sound. De la Rosa semi-retired some years ago, but he still tours the dancehalls and festivals of south Texas when his health permits—with some extra energy no doubt supplied by a 1998 National Heritage Fellowship from the National Endowment for the Arts, recognizing his lifetime contribution.

what's available: Three discs of Tony de la Rosa's music are readily available: *Atotoniclo* 𝄞𝄞𝄞 (Arhoolie, 1964/1995, prod. Chris Strachwitz), *Así Se Baila en Tejas* 𝄞𝄞𝄞 (Rounder, 1991, prod. Carl Finch), and *Es Mi Derecho* 𝄞𝄞𝄞 (Rounder, 1995, prod. Carl Finch). Each of them contains recordings of the lively dance-directed music de la Rosa enjoys and in which he became a pioneer. During his heyday in the 1950s and '60s, more than 75 discs bearing de la Rosa's name were issued on regional labels, and at this writing there is talk of reissuing some of these. Tony de la Rosa's work is also represented in a number of collections, including Arhoolie's *Tejano Roots* series and Rounder's *Conjunto! Texas-Mexico Border Music,* each of which is reviewed in this book's Compilations section.

influences:

◄◄ Narciso Martinez

►► Flaco Jimenez

Kerry Dexter

Paco de Lucia

Flamenco

Born Francisco Sanchez Gomez, December 21, 1947, in Algeciras, Cadiz, Spain. Based in Spain.

A melodic fluidity has placed Paco de Lucia in the forefront of contemporary flamenco. In addition to more than a score of solo albums, de Lucia has recorded with such world-renowned guitarists as Al Di Meola, John McLaughlin, and Larry Coryell. According to McLaughlin, de Lucia "just might be the world's most inspired guitarist."

Born in Algeciras, a small town on the Mediterranean Sea in southern Spain, de Lucia inherited his love of music from his father, Antonio, and older brother, Ramon. Under his father's training, de Lucia spent much of his childhood studying flamenco guitar. Making his professional debut on Radio Algeciras at the age of 12, de Lucia placed first in a major competition at the Festival Concurso Internacional Flamenco de Jerez de la Frontera two years later. In 1962, de Lucia and his brother received a special award at the same festival for their duet "Los Chiquitos de Algeciras." The following year, de Lucia became a featured accompanist for Jose Greco's dance company.

Moving with his family to Madrid in 1964, de Lucia began performing regularly at a flamenco club opened by his father. Together with his brother and Ricardo Modrego, de Lucia recorded two albums in 1965. He also recorded with singer Fernandez Diaz and saxophonist Pedro Iturralde. In 1967, de Lucia toured with Festival Flamenco Gitano and recorded his first solo album, *Fabulosa Guitarra de Paco de Lucia.* After traveling to Brazil, de Lucia began incorporating elements of the bossa nova into his highly skilled style of flamenco. Released in 1969, *Fantasia Flamenco* showcased de Lucia's unique musical hybrid.

Performing his American debut concert at Carnegie Hall in 1970, de Lucia joined with American jazz guitarists Al Di Meola (Return to Forever), John McLaughlin (Mahavishnu Orchestra, Shakti), and Larry Coryell to record two groundbreaking guitar albums in the late 1970s. After forming a sextet in 1981, de Lucia balanced appearances with the band, trio performances with J.M. Banders and J.M. Canizores, and collaborations with American jazz pianist Chick Corea. In 1989, de Lucia teamed with operatic tenor Placido Domingo as well. De Lucia's sextet was expanded in 1991 with the addition of dancer and percussionist Manuel Soler. De Lucia recorded an album, *Concierto De Aranjuez,* with Orquesta de Cadaques the same year, and has also composed and performed on such film soundtracks as *Sevillanas, Carmen, The Hit,* and *La Sabina.*

what to buy: Recorded 15 years after their first collaboration, *Guitar Trio* 𝄞𝄞𝄞𝄞 (PolyGram, 1996, prod. Paco de Lucia, John McLaughlin, Al Di Meola) reflects the continued evolution of de Lucia and American guitarists Di Meola and McLaughlin. Sharing solos and offering one another an unwavering accompaniment, the three guitarists explore the full vocabulary of their instruments.

what to buy next: De Lucia successfully returned to the pure Flamenco sounds of his earliest work on *Sirocco* 𝄞𝄞𝄞 (Verve, 1987/Polydor, 1991, prod. Paco de Lucia).

best of the rest:

Fabulosa Guitarra de Paco de Lucia 𝄞𝄞𝄞𝄞 (Verve, 1967/1984)

Castro Marin 𝄞𝄞𝄞 (PolyGram, 1981)

Paco de Lucia

Entre Dos Aguas ♪♪♪♪ (Polydor, 1986)
Solo Quiero Caminar ♪♪♪♪ (Polydor, 1986)
Los Mejores Guitarras ♪♪♪♪ (Kubaney, 1990)
En Vivo ♪♪♪♪ (Alex, 1991)
Zyryab ♪♪♪♪ (Verve, 1992)
Concerto de Aranjuez ♪♪♪♪ (PolyGram, 1993)
Live in America ♪♪♪♪ (Philips, 1994)
Dos Guitarras Flamencas En America Latina ♪♪♪♪ (PolyGram, 1994)
Duende Flamenco ♪♪♪♪ (PolyGram, 1994)
Hispanoamerica ♪♪♪♪ (PolyGram, 1994)
Anthology of Flamenco Songs ♪♪♪♪ (Iris, 1996)
Anthology of Flamenco Songs, Vol. 2 ♪♪♪♪ (Iris, 1996)
Anthology of Flamenco Songs, Vol. 3 ♪♪♪♪ (Iris, 1996)

worth searching for: Released in Japan, *4 CD Box Set* ♪♪♪♪ (Alex, 1987, prod. Paco de Lucia) is a compendious and satisfying anthology of previously released tracks.

influences:

◄◄ Egberto Gismonti, Baden Powell, Antonio de Lucia

►► The Gipsy Kings, Al Di Meola

see also: *George Dalaras, Camarón de la Isla*

Craig Harris

Dead Can Dance
Gothic/world fusion
Formed 1983, in London, England. Disbanded 1998.

Lisa Gerrard (Australia), vocals, yang ch'in, percussion; Brendan Perry (England), vocals, guitars, whistles, bouzouki, percussion; Robert Perry (England), bagpipes, whistles, bouzouki, percussion (1987–98); John Bonnar (Wales), keyboards, vocals, percussion (1987–98); Ronan O'Snodaigh (Ireland), percussion, vocals (1993–98); Lance Hogan (Ireland), guitars, percussion, vocals (1993–98); Peter Ulrich (England), percussion (1995–98).

Few bands have undergone such drastic stylistic evolutions as Dead Can Dance did over the course of a 15-year career. Usually associated with the modern gothic scene, the group was one of the first signed to Ivo Watts Russell's elite 4AD label, and along with similar groups like Cocteau Twins and Clan of Xymox, the synth-driven moodiness of their early work would ultimately help to establish 4AD's distinctive sound. But by the late '80s, the group's core members, Lisa Gerrard and Brendan Perry, had begun to shrug off the gothic stereotypes, incorporating a number of unique influences into their style, including French poetry (their second album, *Spleen and Ideal,* was directly inspired by Charles Baudelaire), baroque instrumentation, Eastern European chants, and medieval madrigal songs. As they reached the end of their first decade together, the duo began taking an even broader interest in the traditional music of various world cultures, and 1993's *Into the Labyrinth* found them using a wide variety of ethnic instrumentation, with Gerrard's ethereal vocals showing increasingly strong Arabic and Indian influences. By 1994, Dead Can Dance had found a way to resolve all of these disparate artistic elements into a remarkably seamless whole, with Gregorian-style chants and European folk nestling comfortably against Middle Eastern melodies and throbbing tribal percussion, sometimes all within the same song. Unfortunately, as Perry and Gerrard continued to evolve artistically, Dead Can Dance's releases became ever more sporadic, thanks in large part to the sheer geographical distance between them—Perry had relocated to an island off the coast of Ireland, while Gerrard had returned to her Australian homeland. In 1995, Gerrard emerged with her first solo album, *The Mirror Pool,* and although the band would go on to one more album and tour in 1996, the release of her second solo effort in 1998 ultimately spelled the end of one of music's most exotic and eclectic partnerships.

what to buy: Despite its radical stylistic changes over the years, the quality of Dead Can Dance's releases remained remarkably consistent, but their last album together, *Spiritchaser* ♫♫♫♫ (4AD, 1996, prod. Brendan Perry, Lisa Gerrard), is a paradoxically great place to start. Their most collaborative effort ever, these eight epic compositions reference everything from Native American poetry and *Vodun* (Haitian "voodoo") invocations to the Beatles' "Within You without You," all flowing together to create a hypnotic, transcendental masterpiece that seems to exist in its own time and place, evoking the best of heaven and earth simultaneously. Nearly as rapturous is *Toward the Within* ♫♫♫♫ (4AD, 1994, prod. Guy Charbonneau), an exquisitely beautiful concert recorded live at Santa Monica's Mayfield Theatre, featuring fan favorites like "Yulunga (Spirit Dance)" and "The Wind That Shakes the Barley" alongside spellbinding new (and largely improvised) compositions like "Rakim" and "Desert Song," plus a chilling cover of Sinéad O'Connor's "I Am Stretched on Your Grave."

what to buy next: Although it doesn't boast the myriad ethnic influences of their later work, *Aion* ♫♫♫♫ (4AD, 1990, prod. Dead Can Dance) highlights the band's artistic progression from gothic/baroque scene-leaders to willfully experimental in-

novators with strong medieval ties. With far less reliance on synthesizer sounds than most of their mid-'80s efforts, the field chants, maypole dances, and stunning vocal arrangements of this, their fourth album, were harbingers of even greater things to come for the pan-cultural duo.

the rest:
Dead Can Dance ♫♫♫ (4AD, 1984)
Spleen and Ideal ♫♫♫♫ (4AD, 1985)
Into the Realm of a Dying Sun ♫♫♫♫ (4AD, 1987)
The Serpent's Egg ♫♫♫♫ (4AD, 1988)
Into the Labyrinth ♫♫♫♫ (4AD, 1993)
A Passage in Time ♫♫♫♫ (Rykodisc, 1994)

worth searching for: The 77-minute *Toward the Within* live concert video may be a little difficult to track down these days, but with 14 beautiful songs and interview footage with both Gerrard and Perry, it's a must-have for any Dead Can Dance devotee. Also worth searching for is the program from their 1996 world tour to support *Spiritchaser,* with an inserted CD single called "Sambatiki," which would ultimately prove to be the group's last recording together.

solo outings:
Lisa Gerrard:
The Mirror Pool ♫♫♫♫ (4AD, 1995)
(With Pieter Bourke) *Duality* ♫♫♫♫ (4AD, 1998)

influences:
◀ Cocteau Twins, Bauhaus, Le Mystère des Voix Bulgares, Gregorian chants, Mickey Hart

▶ Enya, Deep Forest, Enigma, Adiemus, Miranda Sex Garden

Bret Love

Déanta

Irish traditional
Formed 1987, in Portglenone, County Antrim, Northern Ireland. Disbanded 1998.

Kate O'Brien, fiddle, viola (1987–98); Eoghan O'Brien, guitar, harp (1987–98); Mary Dillon, vocals, harp, keyboards, guitar (1987–98); Clódagh Warnock, bouzouki, fiddle, bodhrán, percussion (1987–98); Paul Mullan, flute, tin whistle (1987–94); Deirdre Havlin, flute, tin whistle (1994–98); Rosie Mulholland, keyboards, fiddle (1994–98). (All members are from Ireland.)

Déanta (meaning "done" or "complete" in Gaelic) is one of a handful of bands from Northern Ireland to have gained some recognition in the Irish traditional music scene. They came together in the early 1980s, when the O'Briens, Clódagh Warnock, and a few others entered the Gael-Linn Slógadh competitions—also a launchpad for the famous Donegal band Clannad some years before. As Déanta, they began to attract attention during a tour of the United States shortly after the release of their first, eponymous album in 1990. At the core of the band were siblings Kate and Eoghan O'Brien, who anchored the instrumental sound, and lead singer Mary Dillon, whose stunning voice won her two All-Ireland titles. Warnock contributed to the texture of the accompaniments with bouzouki and percussion, while flute players Paul Mullan (on the first album) and Deirdre Havlin (on the next two) joined in with fiddler Kate O'Brien for the instrumentals. An unusual aspect of the band is that its members all held day jobs and remained part-time musicians, touring very little and playing instead at large festivals now and then. Unfortunately, the unavoidable pressures of such an arrangement seemed to have finally taken their toll when the band announced its breakup early in 1998. This ending was all the more unhappy in that, despite their part-time status, Déanta had become one of Green Linnet's best-selling bands. The delightful music they created together makes this a surprise but no mystery. Their material was carefully chosen and brilliantly arranged, often composed by band members as with most of the dance tunes on their final album, *Whisper of a Secret*. And even when they played such dance tunes, these musicians seemed more interested in bringing out beauty and refinement than going for speed and drive. A most pleasing change of pace, literally.

what's available: *Déanta* ♫♫♫ (Spring, 1990/Green Linnet, 1992, prod. Steven Cooney, Déanta) is a short CD with only nine tracks, but most of them are gems. Dillon sings beautifully on "The Green Fields of Canada" and "Dark Iniseoghain," but it is the band's arrangement as well as her performance that makes "Willie Taylor" the essential track on this album. Instrumentals like the energetic "Flight of the Termite," featuring Kate O'Brien's own "Katie's Reel," or the elegant "Harp Airs," composed by Dillon and Eoghan O'Brien, are especially enjoyable. *Ready for the Storm* ♫♫♫ (Green Linnet, 1994, prod. Neil Martin) was Déanta's first album for Green Linnet and featured the two then-new members—Deirdre Havlin, a most worthy successor to Paul Mullan, on flute and whistle, and Rosie Mulholland on keyboards and fiddle. They give a great boost to the instrumentals by increasing the possibilities for timbral and textural shadings. Once again, the emphasis is on new compositions, by band members and other respected musicians like Chicago fiddler Liz Carroll or Sligo/Roscommon flute player Josie McDermott. Although Dillon does well on Dougie MacLean's "Ready for the Storm" and on "The Lakes of Pontchartrain"—a courageous choice considering the song was previously recorded by none other than Planxty and Paul Brady—her singing of Alastair McDonald's "Culloden's Harvest" and the traditional "The Benedy Glen" are the album's showstoppers. Déanta's latest, *Whisper of a Secret* ♫♫♫ (Green Linnet, 1997, prod. Neil Martin), continues very much in the same vein but takes it up a

gamelan

In Java and Bali, each village used to have its own percussion orchestra, or *gamelan*. These ensembles, some still extant today, consist of up to 40 musicians playing a variety of drums, metallophones, gongs, and other instruments to create a rich tapestry of sound quite unlike that of any other large orchestra. Those instruments are themselves collectively referred to as a gamelan, and its elements are generally all similar in design and fashioned from the same materials, usually bronze and wood. In addition to the percussion instruments, which are tuned to a uniform pitch, the orchestra's musical texture is filled out by wooden flutes, zithers, and fiddles, and typically joined by vocalists and dancers. The gamelans originated in Java prior to the 15th century, reaching their heyday in the 19th century when they were a prominent fixture of the Javanese royal courts. The orchestras' importance diminished following the nation's independence in 1945, but they still play at festivals and music schools, on the radio, and in several of the remaining royal courts. Performances usually take place in conjunction with drama, dance, and other forms of artistic expression.

Gamelan spread to Bali in the 15th century, when many of the rulers of Java fled there after the Muslim conquest of their land. In Bali, the form has taken two rather different courses. The *kecak* includes a chorus of vocalists chanting and dancing in imitation of the island's monkey population. A more widespread manifestation of Balinese gamelan is in the Hindu temples, with some manner of the music performed in the religious ceremonies of almost every village.

In recent years, interest and participation in gamelan has diminished as the youth of both countries have discovered Western rock and pop. Too often, contemporary gamelan performances are done for tourist groups, and the original cultural and religious significance of the practice is neglected. Consult the Compilations section of this volume for some gamelan recordings of good fidelity—both sonic and social—to the genuine article.

Michael Parrish

notch. Havlin's flute playing has become even more impressive, and her duets with Kate O'Brien are all the stronger for it. The two continue to produce superb new tunes—including "Beaujolais in Boston" and "Jimmy's Trip to Clonmel" from the opening track—and perform them at an appropriately relaxed pace for melodies that deserve savoring. Mary Dillon's singing is as exquisite as ever, particularly on "Willie and Mary" and on Andy Stewart's "Where Are You," and is well served by the band's sparse but intensely musical arrangements.

influences:

◀◀ Ann O'Brien, the Chieftains, Planxty, the Bothy Band, Clannad

▶▶ Altan, Dervish

Philippe Varlet

Deep Forest
Worldbeat
Formed 1992, in Paris, France. Based in France.

Eric Mouquet, keyboards, programming; Michel Sanchez, keyboards, programming.

Not a band, per se, Deep Forest is the work of two French musicians who sample ethnic music and then combine these exotic sounds into world-music/dance hybrids. At times their CDs can be fascinating to hear, but they carry with them a stigma that no politically responsible listener can, or should, ignore. Just because these two Western Europeans bought the rights to the vocal samples they manipulate doesn't make their cut-and-paste modernizations any less odious. And just because their own press materials acknowledge that Deep Forest albums aren't intended to be "ethnically correct" doesn't make their inherent disrespect toward the cultures they sonically plunder any more forgivable. In defense of Deep Forest, it must be noted that some of the vocal parts they employ were recorded specifically for their CDs. It's up to the listener to decide what's most important.

what to buy: Although the group's debut is not as consistent or varied as its third album, *Deep Forest* ♪♪♪ (Epic, 1992, prod. Dan Lacksman) is the one to buy first, largely because it includes two "hits," the Peter Gabriel–influenced title track and the alluring "Sweet Lullaby."

what to buy next: The group's most accomplished musical collage, *Comparsa* ♪♪♪♪ (550 Music/Sony, 1998, prod. Deep Forest) uses more Latin American vocal samples than African ones. As always with Deep Forest, however, let your conscience be your guide.

what to avoid: Despite the vocal contributions of Hungarian folk star Márta Sebestyén, *Boheme* ♪♪ (550 Music/Sony, 1995,

prod. Eric Mouquet, Michel Sanchez) embodies the worst aspects of designer world music. It won a Grammy, but that says more about the Grammys than it does about the album.

influences:

◀◀ Enigma, Peter Gabriel, African Pygmy folk melodies

see also: *Márta Sebestyén*

Bob Remstein

Desmond Dekker
Rocksteady
Born Desmond Decres, July 16, 1943, in Kingston, Jamaica. Based in Jamaica.

Desmond Dekker became one of Jamaica's best-selling performers with his song "Israelites," an international hit in 1969. Dekker's compelling vocals and the rocksteady (proto-reggae) rhythms of his band, the Aces, made the song Jamaica's first gold record. The younger brother of George Decres, who recorded with the Pioneers, and Sister Pauline, who joined with vocalist Derrick Morgan on the hit duet "You Never Miss Your Water," Dekker sang with a church choir as a youngster. Although he had realized a calling to music, Dekker was unable to interest a record company until demanding an audition with producer and label owner Leslie Kong in 1962. Kong was so impressed by Dekker's audition that he quickly contracted Dekker to record the single—and prompt Jamaican hit—"Honor Your Father and Your Mother." Dekker penned several songs, including "Rude Boy Train" and "Intensified," that later proved fruitful for other artists, and he was instrumental in getting Bob Marley to sign with Kong's label. Although Dekker continued to work with Kong through the 1960s, problems arose when Kong became absorbed with the career of Barbadian vocalist Jackie Opel. Shortly after Marley left to work with Clement "Sir Coxsone" Dodd, Dekker agreed to work with Duke Reid. Their collaboration, however, was never consummated, as Dekker succumbed to Kong's pleading that he return.

Dekker's first international hit was not in fact "Israelites," but "007 (Shanty Town)," which reached the top of Jamaica's charts in 1967. Released in England, the song went to #12 on the British hit parade (and was later featured in the legendary reggae film *The Harder They Come*). Dekker extended his success the following year, when his "Intensified" placed first in Jamaica's annual Independence Festival song competition. "Israelites" itself was initially released as "Poor Me, Israelites" in 1968. When the song failed to reach the charts, Graeme Goodall, Kong's U.K. representative and the managing director of Pyramid Records, remixed the master tapes and reissued the result as the "Israelites" the world would know and love—and send to the top of the charts in England, Canada, Sweden, West

Germany, Holland, and South Africa, and the #9 position in the U.S. (The song would later be known to even more people through the films *Drugstore Cowboy* and *Miami Blues*.)

Although Dekker's followup single, "A It Mek," failed to chart in the U.S., it reached #7 in England. Dekker's last chart entry, "You Can Get It If You Really Want," reached #2 in the U.K. but failed to break the top 100 Stateside. Nonetheless, following the success of "Israelites," Dekker disbanded the Aces. Although he continued to tour as a soloist, he faded into obscurity as reggae replaced rocksteady as Jamaica's dominant sound. His career suffered further in the aftermath of Kong's death in 1971, but in the late '70s it was temporarily buoyed by the British ska revival (which harkened back to yet another stylistic predecessor of reggae). Signing with Stiff Records, Dekker released two albums—*Black and Dekker* in 1980 and *Compass Point* in 1981—and later joined forces with British ska band the Specials for *King of Ska* in 1991 and *King of Kings* in 1994, a legend of reggae's beginnings and some giants of its aftermath respectively enjoying a third and second wave.

what to buy: Twenty of Dekker's recordings are reprised on *Rockin' Steady: The Best of Desmond Dekker* ⨍⨍⨍ (Rhino, 1992, prod. Leslie Kong). In addition to the hit version of "Israelites," the album spans from Dekker's first single, "Honor Your Father and Mother," in 1963, to early-'70s favorites like "You Can Get It If You Really Want" and "Reggae Recipe."

what to buy next: Recorded at the height of the British ska revival, *Black and Dekker* ⨍⨍⨍ (Stiff, 1980, prod. Robert Palmer), Dekker's first album on the Stiff label, featured turbo-charged, punk-inspired renditions of his best-known tunes.

the rest:
This Is ⨍⨍⨍ (Trojan, 1969)
Israelites ⨍⨍⨍ (UNI, 1969)
You Can Get It ⨍⨍⨍ (Trojan, 1970)
Double Dekker ⨍⨍⨍ (Trojan, 1974)
Sweet 16 Hits ⨍⨍⨍ (Trojan, 1978)
Compass Point ⨍⨍⨍ (Stiff, 1981)
Profile ⨍⨍⨍ (Teldec, 1981)
Original Reggae Hitsound ⨍⨍⨍ (Trojan, 1985)
20 Golden Pieces ⨍⨍⨍ (Bulldog, 1987)
Official Live & Rare ⨍⨍⨍ (Trojan, 1987)
Greatest Hits ⨍⨍⨍ (Street Life, 1988)
The Best of & the Rest Of ⨍⨍⨍ (Action Replay, 1989)
(With the Specials) *King of Ska* ⨍⨍⨍ (Trojan, 1991/Varese Sarabande, 1998)
Music Like Dirt ⨍⨍⨍ (Trojan, 1992)
Shanty Town Original ⨍⨍⨍ (Drive Archive, 1994)
Action! ⨍⨍⨍ (Lagoon, 1994)
(With the Specials) *King of Kings* ⨍⨍⨍ (Trojan, 1994)
Moving Out ⨍⨍⨍ (Trojan, 1996)

Archive ⨍⨍⨍ (Rialto, 1996)
First Time for a Long Time ⨍⨍⨍ (Trojan, 1997)
The Original Rude Boy ⨍⨍⨍ (Music Club, 1997)
Intensified ⨍⨍⨍ (Lagoon, 1997)
Israelites: 20 Greatest Hits ⨍⨍⨍ (Sound Solution, 1997)
Writing on the Wall ⨍⨍⨍ (Trojan, 1998)

influences:
◄◄ The Skatalites, Jimmy Cliff, Bob Marley
►► The Specials, Third World, UB40, the English Beat

see also: *The Specials*

Craig Harris

Dan Del Santo
Worldbeat
Born in TX, USA. Based in Austin, TX, USA.

Del Santo, a longtime Austin bandleader, claims to have invented the term "worldbeat" (though he's not the only one). His big band, founded in the late 1980s, combines various Latin, African, and Caribbean strains into tunes with solid grooves and politically charged lyrics.

what's available: *Off Your Nyash* ⨍⨍⨍ (Flying Fish, 1990, prod. Dan Del Santo, Slim Heilpern) was an early example of the coming worldbeat boom, including tunes that touch on reggae, Zimbabwean *chimurenga,* and other international styles.

influences:
◄◄ Joe Higgs, Thomas Mapfumo
►► Looters, Paul Simon

j. poet

Geno Delafose
Cajun, creole, zydeco
Born February 6, 1971, in Eunice, LA, USA. Based in Duralde, LA, USA.

Geno Delafose started playing *frattoir* (washboard) in his father John's band the Eunice Playboys—joining older brothers Tony and John Jr.—at the age of seven. As time went by Geno graduated to drums and then to warming up the crowd on accordion before his father came on. By 1992 he was sharing much of the on-stage accordion time with his father, and when John Sr. died in 1994, Geno was ready to take over leadership of the band. He plays in a more tuneful and traditional style than almost any of his peers, with definitely less of a rock influence and more of a Cajun one. Having been the Playboys' drummer and frattoir player both, he knows what constitutes a great beat—and with the help of his cousin Germaine Jack's excellent drum work, the band always provides.

Geno Delafose

what to buy: The music on *La Chanson Perdue* ♫♫♫♫ (Rounder, 1998, prod. Scott Billington) is like Geno himself: tall, well-mannered, and graceful. No other young zydeco musician comes to mind who would be willing to explore his Creole roots as deeply as Delafose does on this record. Old-time Creole music revolves around the interplay between button accordion and fiddle; for this recording Geno recruited fiddlers Steve Riley and Dirk Powell to duet with him on several tracks. A number of the album's selections, like "Jolie Bassette/Quo Faire" and "Chere Ici, Chere la Bas," are famously associated with the Creole musicians Canray Fontenot and "Bois Sec" Ardoin. Geno brings these tunes to life and shows that they have a role to play into the new century. Geno's other band, French Rockin' Boogie, refreshes the remaining half of the CD, proving that you can look forward and look back at the same time.

what to buy next: Although it's rare for a studio recording of zydeco music to capture the passion and feeling of the live band experience, *That's What I'm Talking About!* ♫♫♫♫ (Rounder, 1996, prod. Scott Billington) comes very close. This may not be the hottest zydeco in terms of sales, but it is about as good as unadulterated Creole zydeco music gets. From the

opening of "Geno's Two Step," this band just kicks. They acknowledge the popularity of the newer sounds, like Beau Jocque's, but stay very much in the Eunice Playboys tradition Geno grew up in; they do, however, evoke some of the Creole swing that Boozoo Chavis seems to pull off so effortlessly. This CD covers several of John Delafose's tunes and all are excellent; even Geno's obligatory soulful ballad "Teardrops" (complete with B3 organ) fits right in. There are no frills and no wasted notes here—just the pure sound of this band doing what they do best. *French Rockin' Boogie* ♫♫♫ (Rounder, 1994, prod. Scott Billington) tries too hard to be more than it needs to be. Maybe it's the horns, or maybe it's just Geno feeling his way out from the long shadow of his father on this first solo effort. This is still a very good zydeco record, maybe just not a great Delafose record.

influences:

◀◀ Clifton Chenier, Amédée Ardoin, Marc Savoy

▶▶ Keith Frank

see also: *John Delafose & the Eunice Playboys, Steve Riley & the Mamou Playboys*

Jared Snyder

John Delafose
& the Eunice Playboys

Zydeco
Formed 1980, in Eunice, LA, USA. Based in Eunice, LA, USA.

John Delafose (born April 16, 1939, in Duralde, LA, USA; died September 17, 1994, in Lawtell, LA, USA), accordion, vocals, frattoir; Geno Delafose, drums, accordion, vocals; Tony Delafose, bass; John Delafose Jr., frattoir, drums; Charles Prudhomme, guitar; Joseph Prudhomme, bass; Germaine Jack, drums, frattoir. (All members are from USA.)

John Delafose and the Eunice Playboys played zydeco the way it's meant to be played—with a hard-driving, stripped-down beat that makes you wish you were in a smoky dancehall in south Louisiana with a bunch of other crazies whose feet can't stop. As with many other zydeco outfits, the Eunice Playboys are family. A big name since the mid-'70s, John Delafose formed the band with sons Geno, John Jr., and Tony and cousin Germaine Jack (in addition to the guitar and bass combination of Charles and Joseph Prudhomme—brothers, though not of John's). A certifiable accordion legend, John played a traditional style not unlike the better-known Clifton Chenier. The Playboys' repertoire runs from the customary French-sung waltzes, to wild dance numbers with nasty grooves, to country heartbreakers.

what to buy: *Pere et Garcon Zydeco* ♫♫♫♫ (Rounder, 1992, prod. Scott Billington) is a great collection of Delafose-penned numbers, new takes on zydeco classics, and a couple of country tunes thrown in for a lagniappe. John and Geno split accordion duties on this disc, recorded live in the studio. The roughness of some of the cuts doesn't take away from the fun, it only adds to the immediacy. The set includes the traditional "Mon Coeur Fait Mal," "Watch That Dog," "Down in Texas Way," and "Grand Mamou"; John's originals range from "My Little Dog" (a classic itself) to "Go Back Where You Been" and "Friday Night Waltz"; and the Playboys give a whole new spin to Don Gibson's "I Can't Stop Loving You." *Blues Stay Away from Me* 𝄞𝄞𝄞𝄞 (Rounder, 1993, prod. Scott Billington) is worthwhile just for the Linda Barry cover art. The Eunice Playboys swing across this record, showing that great Creole music is about subtle syncopation and moving the beat around—not the bone-crunching double-clutching that dominates now. The album features John Delafose's fiddle on a couple of tunes, with the accordion duties again shared between himself and Geno.

what to buy next: *Joe Pete Got Two Women* 𝄞𝄞𝄞𝄞 (Arhoolie, 1988, prod. Chris Strachwitz) contains the classic title track and several other of Delafose's genre-defining tunes. It features an earlier version of the Eunice Playboys, when Geno and Tony enthusiastically drove the music on drums and frattoir, the always-solid Prudhomme brothers locked into tight grooves, and John Delafose laid out the accordion and vocal lines on top. It might slip and sway a little, but it always swings.

the rest:
Zydeco Man 𝄞𝄞𝄞𝄞 (Arhoolie, 1980)
Uncle Bud Zydeco 𝄞𝄞𝄞𝄞 (Arhoolie, 1982)
Heartaches & Hot Steps 𝄞𝄞𝄞𝄞 (Maison de Soul, 1984)
Zydeco Excitement! 𝄞𝄞𝄞𝄞 (Maison de Soul, 1984)

worth searching for: Delafose and the boys appear prominently on some live zydeco compilations, including *Zydeco Live! Vol. 2* (Rounder, 1989) and *Stomp Down Zydeco* (Rounder, 1992). On *Tribute to John Delafose* (Deep South Records, 1995, prod. Tony Delafose), directed by John's son Tony, a number of zydeco stars take turns interpreting and honoring his father's music, including C.J. Chenier, Buckwheat Zydeco, and Terrance Simien.

influences:

◀◀ Alphonse "Bois Sec" Ardoin, Amédée Ardoin, Clifton Chenier, Boozoo Chavis, Canray Fontenot

▶▶ Chris Ardoin, Buckwheat Zydeco, Chubby Carrier, Geno Delafose, Keith Frank, Zachary Richard

see also: *Geno Delafose, Willis Prudhomme*

Jared Snyder and Andrew BeDell

Issac Delgado

Timba, salsa
Born 1963, in Havana, Cuba. Based in Havana, Cuba.

Every young vocal music needs a Marvin Gaye . . . a cat who can ride the rhythm, change the beat, swagger and cry, get deep and slyly wink. In the go-for-yours immediacy of today's *timba* (next-generation Cuban salsa) youth, vocalist Issac Delgado is an oasis of verdant emotionality. Gifted with the same sharp, piquantly Everyman tenor as Stateside salsa greats Hector Lavoe and Rubén Blades, Delgado definitely keeps the Cuban hometown crew starvin' fo' mo' like Marvin. Raised in a family of music professionals—his mother Lina Ramirez founded the *descarga* ("jam session") band Las Mulatas De Ramme—Delgado's formative years were full of exposure to Frank Emilio Flynn and other pioneers of '50s *filin* (bolero amped by the blues); *salsero* Tito Gomez; and, from up north, recordings by NYC's Fania All-Stars, Cheo Feliciano, and Willie Colón. In 1978, Delgado had his first-ever professional gig—with childhood spar/now-acclaimed pianist Gonzalo Rubalcaba—in the band Proyecto. Steadily clocking props via residences with the Panchito Alonso Orquesta, Grupo Galaxia, and the Cabaret Tropicana (the Cotton Club of tourist Cuba), the vocalist cashed in big-time in '88 when he joined super group NG La Banda. Both sides were the better after the brief, three-year association—Delgado-sung hits bigged-up the band's profile; he became a pop star. Since venturing out with his own *orquesta* in '91, he's become the premier male vocalist in contemporary Cuban music. Politically banned from U.S. airwaves for most of the decade, Delgado's voice was still heard, ironically, through hit covers of his songs by *el Norte*–based Dons like El Canario, Johnny Rivera, and Ray Sepulveda. Gradually, through a stream of U.S.-indie-licensed compilations, a new recording on Stateside Latin powerhouse label RMM (*Otra Idea*), and two instantly legendary NYC summer-of-'97 concerts, Issac Delgado cracked the mango curtain on his own merit. This is the next major voice in international salsa.

what to buy: Just because it's closest to where he's at right now, *Otra Idea* 𝄞𝄞𝄞𝄞 (RMM, 1997) is the first-priority purchase. A potentially risky hook-up of Puerto Rican *salseros* and Cuban *timberos*, *Otra Idea* is svengali-ed into transcendence by Issac's charismatic chants on burners like "Pá Que Te Salves."

what to buy next: Recorded in Caracas, Venezuela, in '93, *Con Ganas* 𝄞𝄞𝄞𝄞 (QBADISC, 1994, prod. Gonzalo Rubalcaba) is wall-to-wall with Issac Delgado Moments like the subtle whisper-to-a-croon catharsis midway into "Dime Tu Lo Que Sabes." For those who like their Cuban soul unsweetened.

the rest:
Donde La Hora 𝄞𝄞𝄞𝄞 (QBADISC, 1994)
El Año Que Viene 𝄞𝄞𝄞𝄞 (QBADISC, 1996)

influences:

◄ Tito Gomez, Cheo Feliciano, Pete "El Conde" Rodriguez

► Adalberto Alvarado, Manolín, El Médico de la Salsa

see also: *NG La Banda*

Tom Terrell

Sandy Denny

Folk, Anglo-Celtic folk-rock, singer-songwriter

Born January 6, 1947, in London, England. Died April 21, 1978, in London, England.

Sandy Denny may have been the greatest female pop vocalist England ever produced. It's especially sad, then, that her career path was uneven and cut short. Denny began singing in London folk clubs in the mid-1960s during the "folk revival" that also spawned Simon and Garfunkel, the various Steeleyes and Fairports, and many others. Her repertoire then blended traditional English and Irish folk songs like "The Handsome Cabin Boy" with covers of songs by friends like Paul Simon and Jackson C. Frank. Her clear, bold voice brought her gigs as a member of the Strawbs (formerly the Strawberry Hill Boys) and later Fairport Convention. She may be best remembered for her music with Fairport, though she was in the group for less than 4 years (1968–69, 1974–75). Her work alongside Trevor Lucas (later her husband) in the band Fotheringay produced one excellent album and swelled her following to the point that *Melody Maker* readers twice voted her Britain's top "girl singer." She was a gifted composer with a keen ear for poetry; like Joni Mitchell, she undoubtedly influenced many singer-songwriters of the confessional/cryptic school, for better or worse. Her best-known and most often covered composition is "Who Knows Where the Time Goes?," recorded by Judy Collins among others. Pulled between the quiet joys of home and the love of performing, between solo and group work, and between the gusts of her own moody spirit, Denny never received the acclaim she deserved in her lifetime. Her death at 31, from a cerebral hemorrhage, solidified her legend. Still, her music at its best transcends the clichés of her era and the limits of her iconic status.

what to buy: *The North Star Grassman and the Ravens* ☝☝☝☝ (Island, 1971, prod. Sandy Denny, Richard Thompson, John Wood) has an enigmatic cover photo showing Sandy as an alchemist—and indeed, on this album, everything she touches has a glimmer of gold. Some of her finest compositions are here, including the antiwar song "John the Gun"; the stirring, strange "Late November"; and the eerie "Next Time Around," which may have been written about ex-lover Jackson Frank. It also shows Denny having fun: dueting with Richard Thompson on Dylan's "Down in the Flood" and taking a rockabilly turn on "Let's Jump

the Broomstick." The album also includes one of Sandy's few non-Fairport- or Fotheringay-related recordings of a traditional song, "Blackwaterside," with Thompson on accordion.

what to buy next: Check out *The Best of Sandy Denny* ☝☝☝☝ (Hannibal, 1987, prod. Joe Boyd, Trevor Lucas) to decide where to go next in your exploration of Denny's music; it's a good overview of her all-too-brief career. Either of her other two in-print solo albums, *Like an Old Fashioned Waltz* ☝☝☝☝ (Island, 1973, prod. Trevor Lucas, John Wood) and *Rendezvous* ☝☝☝☝ (Island, 1977, prod. Trevor Lucas), is a good bet. The former album has some charming big band–era covers and "Solo," one of her finest compositions, while the latter includes "Gold Dust," a California rock–style song that suggests that, had Sandy lived, her music may have taken on a more American sound. To more fully appreciate yet another worthy purchase, it's best to first discuss one you should avoid: while *One Last Sad Refrain* ☝☝☝ (Nixed) documents Denny's final major concert in 1977, the dismal technical quality saps all of the nuances from what should be a rich, intriguing listening experience. A better choice is the recent release of the same show as *Gold Dust: Live at the Royalty* ☝☝☝☝ (Island, 1998, prod. Trevor Wyatt), although fans have complained about the "enhancements" made by adding additional backing vocals and electric guitar. (In the interest of full disclosure: I like the liner-note essay in this CD, but then again, I wrote it.)

the rest:

Sandy Denny and the Strawbs ☝☝☝☝ (Sonet Dansk Grammofon A/S, 1973/Hannibal, 1991)
The Original Sandy Denny ☝☝☝☝ (Mooncrest, 1978/1991)
Who Knows Where the Time Goes? ☝☝☝☝☝ (Island, 1985)

worth searching for: At presstime, Denny's finest album, *Sandy* ☝☝☝☝☝ (Island, 1972, prod. Trevor Lucas), was out of print in the U.S. It's the one that ought to have made Denny a star, a classic singer/songwriter–style collection, with peerless vocals capped by Denny's *a cappella* rendition of the Richard Farina composition "The Quiet Joys of Brotherhood." *The BBC Sessions 1971–73* ☝☝☝☝ (Strange Fruit, 1997) was available for four months by mail order before being pulled. It's Denny at the peak of her powers and in stripped-down settings that showcase her songwriting and singing without any distracting production touches. It's flawed; it's uneven; it's brilliant. *The Attic Tracks, 1972–1984* ☝☝☝☝ (Raven, 1995, prod. various), credited to "Sandy Denny, Trevor Lucas & Friends," is a wonderfully eclectic collection of Denny rarities, including a marvelous cover of Little Feat's "Easy to Slip"; a portion of the proceeds from this album goes to Denny's heirs.

influences:

◄ Anne Briggs, Dave Swarbrick, Bob Dylan, Joni Mitchell

▶▶ Linda Thompson, Natalie Merchant, Mary Black, Dolores Keane, Vikki Clayton, Susan McKeown, Lisa Moscatiello

see also: *Fairport Convention, Trevor Lucas, Richard Thompson*

Pamela Murray Winters

Dervish

Irish traditional
Formed 1988, in Sligo, Ireland. Based in Sligo, Ireland.

Liam Kelly, flute, tin whistle (1988–present); Shane Mitchell, accordion (1988–present); Martin McGinley, fiddle, viola (1988–90); Brian McDonagh, mandolin, mandola, bouzouki, guitar (1988–present); Michael Holmes, bouzouki, guitar (1988–present); Cathy Jordan, vocals, bodhrán (1990–present); Shane McAleer, fiddle, viola (1990–present). (All members are from Ireland.)

With an unlikely name that conjures the Middle East rather than rollicking jigs and reels, Dervish is one of the most exciting traditional bands to emerge from Ireland in years. It combines the amazing instrumental virtuosity of precursors like the Bothy Band, De Dannan, or Altan with tastefully arranged and beautifully sung Irish- and English-language songs reminiscent of Planxty. One particularly appealing aspect of the Dervish sound is its members' remarkable tightness, resulting from years of playing together at informal pub sessions—or, in the case of flute player Liam Kelly and accordionist Shane Mitchell, playing together since childhood. When the pair were in high school, they formed a band called Poitín and had a moment of fame when they won first place at a festival and subsequently appeared on the popular Irish TV program *The Late Late Show.* While in college, they linked up with bouzouki player Michael Holmes and later met Brian McDonagh, a former member of the band Oisín during the late 1970s. At the request of the Sligo-based Sound Records label, the foursome agreed to cut an album, for which they secured the services of fiddle player Martin McGinley. Released in 1989, their debut under the name Dervish, *The Boys of Sligo,* started getting attention, and what was supposed to be a one-time deal began to look more promising. The band decided to add a singer to the lineup and contacted Roscommon-born Cathy Jordan, whom they knew to be terrific even though she hadn't had much exposure to traditional music. Jordan has proven herself up to the task and become one of the most respected singers on the Irish traditional music scene. Not long after her arrival, County Tyrone fiddle player Shane McAleer replaced McGinley, who was working with another band as well as for the BBC. The new lineup's first release, *Harmony Hill,* won critical acclaim and quickly made Dervish one of the most sought-after bands in Ireland. Despite an intensive touring schedule, the band managed to bring out another album, *Playing with Fire,* which topped the Irish folk music charts for several months. The release of Dervish's albums in the United States in 1995 was followed by several American tours, with appearances at major festivals. A fourth album the following year, *At the End of the Day,* was named the *Hot Press* Trad/Folk Album of the Year. Dervish's latest, a fantastic double-CD recorded live in Palma, Majorca, attests to the band's superior musicianship and performing abilities—and even more hearteningly, to their staying power.

what to buy: *Harmony Hill* 𝄞𝄞𝄞𝄞 (Whirling Discs, 1993/Kells Music, 1995, prod. Brian McDonagh) is puzzling in an unusual way: it is difficult to believe that a lineup's first album can be so good. But this one is dazzlingly so, from the first set of jigs, "Apples in Winter," to the great reel set "The Green Mountain," to Jordan's brilliant renditions of songs as diverse as the lilting "The Ploughman" and the heartbreaking "A Stór Mo Chroí." On the very aptly titled *Playing with Fire* 𝄞𝄞𝄞𝄞 (Whirling Discs/Kells Music, 1995, prod. Brian McDonagh), Dervish continues its superlative brand of traditional music, so much so that it's difficult to recommend some tracks over others. Jordan is once again astonishingly good, and equally comfortable on songs in Gaelic like "Maire Mhor" and "Pheigin Mo Chroi" (the band's designated sing-along in concert), sad tales of love and loss like "Johnny and Molly," or the amusingly grandiloquent poetry of "Cailin Rua." Each instrumental track is as exciting as the next, played with all the fire one could ever ask for.

what to buy next: The cover artwork of *At the End of the Day* 𝄞𝄞𝄞𝄞 (Whirling Discs/Kells Music, 1996, prod. Brian McDonagh), a striking panoramic photograph of a pub with the musicians having a session in the corner, pulls you in irresistibly for yet another magnificent album. The instrumental work is as good as ever, with Swedish band Väsen appearing as guests on one of their compositions. This time around, Jordan's selection of songs leans more toward the slower and melancholic, as with "For Ireland I Won't Tell Her Name," and even the tragic, as with the famine song "Lone Shanakyle"—all performed from the heart. Dervish's latest, *Live in Palma* 𝄞𝄞𝄞𝄞 (Whirling Discs, 1997/Kells Music, 1998, prod. Brian McDonagh), is an outstanding collection of 22 tracks (plus introductions) on two CDs, featuring the band's best songs and instrumental medleys from its previous three studio albums, performed at a concert in Palma, Majorca.

worth searching for: Dervish's all-instrumental first album, *The Boys of Sligo* 𝄞𝄞𝄞 (Sound, 1989, prod. Jim Lockhart), is well worth looking for. McGinley's fiddle playing, more straightforward than McAleer's in some ways, has that same northern energy and crispness to it. And while there are still rough edges, one can hear the pieces falling into place, particularly the band's ideas about varying the texture by changing the combinations of lead and accompanying instruments.

influences:

◀◀ Planxty, the Bothy Band, Oisín

▶▶ De Dannan, Altan

see also: *Väsen*

Philippe Varlet

Det Syng
Scandinavian folk

Formed 1987, in Norway. Based in Norway.

Eli Storbekken, vocals; Sinikka Langeland, vocals; Halvor Håkanes, vocals; Agnes Buen Garnås, vocals; Anne Marit Jacobsen, vocals. (All members are from Norway.)

A group of well-known Norwegian folk singers got together to record tunes that have "wandered"; all their songs can be found in the traditions of several Nordic countries.

what's available: The world-music genre is particularly rich in albums that showcase the wonders of the human voice, and *Ballader På Vandring* ♪♪♪ (Grappa Norway, 1997) is one of them. There is some spare *kantele* (zither), but most of the songs are *a cappella* showcases for the four women and one man in the group. There are ghostly cries that sound like wives calling out for dead husbands, slow mournful ballads, sprightly dance tunes, lullabies, and laments.

influences:

◀◀ Slinkombas, Tone Hulbaekmo, Arve Moen Bergset

j. poet

D'Gary
Malagasy folk and popular music

Born 1961, in Tananarive, Madagascar. Based in Betroka, Madagascar.

D'Gary is one of Madagascar's most important folk musicians. He bases his style on the traditional music of the island's southern ethnic groups, the Bara, Atandroy, Vezo, and Masikoro. By traveling throughout the nation and collecting songs usually played on traditional instruments like the *valhia, marovany, kabosy,* and *lokanga* and transposing them to guitar, he developed an unusual and highly individual style. D'Gary uses 11 different tunings and plays only with the thumb and index finger of his right hand. Even more amazingly, D'Gary learned to play on borrowed instruments, too poor to buy his own. After he participated in the sessions for *A World Out of Time,* a groundbreaking collection recorded by Henry Kaiser and David Lindley to introduce Madagascar's artists to more of the world, Kaiser sent D'Gary his first guitar as a gift. His impressive playing on that album led to recording deals with several European and American labels, who all marveled at his

technical brilliance. D'Gary would like to make a living as a professional musician, but in a culture where everyone plays music, and everyone is poor, this transition may prove difficult.

what to buy: On *Horombe* ♪♪♪♪ (Stern's, 1995, prod. D'Gary) D'Gary's folk/dance band, Jihé, turns in a pleasing set marked by the leader's shimmering lead guitar and a subtle rhythm section. The music is definitely Malagasy (the adjectival form of Madagascar), but every so often a hint of Hawaii or Louisiana floats through the mix to give you an unexpected jolt. D'Gary shows his traditional side on *Mbo Loza* ♪♪♪♪ (Indigo, 1992, prod. Label Bleu), a set that features his immense fretboard skills, supported by a small female chorus.

solo outings:

Dama & D'Gary:

The Long Way Home ♪♪♪♪ (Shanachie, 1993)

influences:

◀◀ Mama Sana, Rakoto Frah, Voninavoko

j. poet

Abdoulaye Diabaté
Bambara traditional pop

Born 1952, in Cinzana Gare, Mali. Based in Koutiala, Mali.

When young Abdoulaye Diabaté was coming of age in the 1960s, his native Mali was bursting with musical activity. The country's communist-leaning government took a strong interest in culture, and supported the development of local bands and artists through biannual national music contests and state-funded ensembles. Diabaté was born to a family of *griots*—traditional praise singers and musicians—and though his parents did not play music professionally, he learned to sing at his mother's side, and played drums at weddings and other ceremonies from boyhood.

In 1974, he began his professional career singing in a series of bands, including the Orchestre Regionale de Segou and Coule Star, a band from Sikasso that distinguished itself in the 1976 biannual competition. Diabaté's keening voice and energized stage presence earned him plenty of notice, and inevitably, in 1986, he began making his own recordings and leading his own band. Mali's local music scene had long been dominated by the music of the Manding people, one of the most pervasive ethnic groups in West Africa. From the start, Diabaté decided to emphasize the rhythms, melodies, and stories of the Bambara people. In terms of language and culture, similarities outweigh differences between the two groups, but their musical traditions are quite different, owing to the Bambara reliance on a five-note (pentatonic) scale. Diabaté's rocking, bluesy compositions have served him well with the public ever since. His band puts on an exceptional stage show featuring guitars, horns, percussion, and athletic dance routines, sometimes performed in full hunter's regalia.

Diabaté has recorded in various settings, acoustic and electric. In 1996, after releasing a highly produced session recorded in Paris, he pledged to get back to roots, and made his next record in the Malian capitol, Bamako. "We've forgotten something," he said at the time. "Malian music has been tending towards modernism, and it has lost some of its real African color and originality. I needed to return to the source, and valorize the real African music, not add too many electronics. Our power is our folklore. The people in the bush need to accept what we do." The resulting record has yet to be released internationally, but whatever marketing is to follow, musically, at least, Diabaté has come home.

what's available: *Djiriyo* ♫♫♫♪ (Stern's Africa, 1995) compiles tracks from three local Malian cassette releases. The selection includes both acoustic tracks and rather slick electric ones. Overall, a great introduction to a significant West African artist. *Kassikoun* ♫♫♫ (Syllart/Melodie) represents earlier work recorded in Paris. Production tames the music too much at times, but there are still a number of worthwhile tracks.

influences:

◀◀ Rail Band, Super Biton

▶▶ Lobi Traore

Banning Eyre

Sékouba "Bambino" Diabaté

Manding pop music
Born 1963, in Siguiri, northern Guinea. Based in Paris, France, and Conakry, Guinea.

Sékouba "Bambino" Diabaté has one of the purest, strongest singing voices in Africa. Raised squarely in the tradition of the Manding people's *griots* (oral historians), Diabaté learned to sing the stories and lineages of all the families in his region with a voice that could unlock the deepest of emotions in his listeners. In 1972, when Guinea's popular music scene benefited from a government bent on promoting culture, Diabaté moved from ceremonial settings to fronting pop bands. Earning so much attention at such a young age, he was soon tagged with the name "Bambino," and it stuck.

In the 1980s, Diabaté began singing for Bembeya Jazz, the most popular and influential of all Guinea's great dance bands. This job took him all over Africa, to seven European countries, and, in 1989, to the U.S. He became a headliner in 1990, and his second solo record, *Le Destin,* sold 160,000 copies in Guinea during its first three months on the market. Diabaté has

irish step dancing

An unmistakable part of Irish folk culture is step dancing, the fast-paced, joyous, and athletic style that provides stunning visual accompaniment to speedy musical performances of jigs, reels, and hornpipes. Step dancing derives its name from the eight-measure musical phrases, also called "steps," that are tied to the repeated movements within the dance. Although written records of Irish dances only date back to the 1500s, it seems likely that they originated much earlier, and the styles we are familiar with today are an amalgam of steps that are also common to French, Scottish, and British dancing.

In the mid-18th century, the tradition of roving dance masters teaching their own distinctive tunes and steps began. During that century and the next, step dancing flourished and diversified, with dancing schools being established for the first time in Counties Kerry, Cork, and Limerick. The form was boosted further at the end of the 19th century, when the Gaelic League was founded with the intention of perpetuating Irish culture.

In the 20th century step dancing has advanced and evolved, with more elaborate costumes and steps appearing. Once a primarily male activity and the purview of adults, step dancing gradually became much more common among females and began to be taught to young children. Dancers were initially barefoot, adopting soft shoes in the early part of the century. Use of hard-tipped shoes, resulting in the now-familiar percussive tapping generated by a speedy practitioner, has only become widespread in the last 30 years or so.

Today step dancing is a mainstay of Irish culture both in the motherland and the U.S., where schools are burgeoning and new steps and styles have rapidly developed. With the advent of Michael Flatley and *Riverdance,* the form has "stepped" out of its cultural confines to be embraced by just about everyone.

Michael Parrish

made a specialty of singing about the problems and concerns of lovers, hardly surprising fare for a pop singer. But for a griot, expected to draw lessons from the great events of history, plain love songs would never do. Diabaté has garnered a fanatical following with his probing explorations of delicate areas of social custom, particularly in questioning the restrictions on marriage in his society.

In 1996, Diabaté was invited to sing two guest spots on an album by Africando, a group combining veteran West African singers with some of the best New York Latin musicians. His very personal update of the Manding/Latin connection (stemming from the African continent's longstanding admiration of Cuba and Puerto Rico's once-removed African music) brought him new attention, and the next year, he recorded his most varied and elaborately produced album to data, *Kassa*. Its enthusiastic reception made Diabaté one of the most closely watched West African singing stars worldwide.

what's available: *Le Destin* ⅍⅍⅍⅍ (popular african music, 1992, prod. Sabine Froese) proved a groundbreaking recording in Guinean pop, in that it defied increasingly electronic production norms and relied mostly on traditional instruments. *Kassa* ⅍⅍⅍⅍ (Stern's Africa, 1997, prod. Syllart) finds Diabaté moving ahead stylistically, while leaving none of his traditional chops behind. Five producers and a number of foreign collaborators liven the mix.

worth searching for: Africando's *Gomba Salsa* ⅍⅍⅍⅍ (Stern's Africa, 1996, prod. Alain Josse, Ibrahima Sylla) features Diabaté's sensational Latin-ized version of a modern Manding classic—one that accentuates the advancement of tradition he embodies: "Apollo," a griot song honoring the '60s space missions.

influences:

◄◄ Sory Kandia Kouyaté, Bembeya Jazz, Mory Kanté, Salif Keita

see also: *Africando, Bembeya Jazz*

Banning Eyre

Toumani Diabaté

Malian kora instrumental music
Born 1965, in Bamako, Mali. Based in Bamako, Mali.

Toumani Diabaté's father, Sidiki Diabaté, was known as the "king of the *kora*" (21-string harp-lute). He left his birthplace in the Gambia—the spiritual center of West African kora music—and moved to Mali some time before that country's independence in 1960. There, amid the crush of cultural activity that blossomed in the new nation, Sidiki played a key role in shaping modern Malian kora music. Toumani was born to this legacy, and by the age of five, had begun to play a seven-string version of the instrument. At 13, Toumani performed on the full-

sized kora with the Koulikoro Ensemble at Mali's biannual musical competition, and the group was judged the best traditional orchestra.

From there, Toumani cut his own road. He made his first professional recording, *Kaira,* in London in 1987. The record broke with convention by including no singer and no other instruments. This raised eyebrows, but it also revealed Toumani as a phenomenal player by any standard. The following year, he recorded with the Spanish "new flamenco" group, Ketama. Filled out with British bassist Danny Thompson, the resulting ensemble, Songhai, explored connections between flamenco and Toumani's ancestral Manding styles that made their first album a hit in the world-music market. They recorded a follow-up in 1994. In between those efforts, Toumani recorded with a Japanese string section and heavy electronics in a formation dubbed the Symmetric Orchestra, while, back in Bamako, he launched an instrumental trio featuring masters of the other major melodic instruments in the arsenal of his *griot* (oral historian) heritage—Basekou Kouyaté on the banjo-like *ngoni*, and Keletigui Diabaté on the wooden-slatted, xylophone-like *balafon*. Despite many projects and an obviously busy schedule back home, Toumani joined Malian superstar Salif Keita in the North American Africa Fête touring festival in the summer of 1998, and returned to do the same with world-blues adventurer Taj Mahal in 1999. Toumani is, without a doubt, one of the most talented and adventurous instrumentalists in Africa.

what to buy: *Kaira* ⅍⅍⅍⅍ (Hannibal/Rykodisc, 1988) is Toumani's calling card. His personalized solo kora renditions of Manding classics are both technically masterful and abundantly musical. *Djelika* ⅍⅍⅍⅍ (Hannibal/Rykodisc, 1995) features the instrumental trio of Toumani Diabaté, Basekou Kouyaté, and Keletigui Diabaté. It meanders some, but at its best, it does show the fire this outfit is capable of delivering.

what to buy next: *Songhai* ⅍⅍⅍⅍ (Hannibal/Rykodisc, 1990) captures the spontaneous exuberance of a great musical meeting—the Manding kora and flashy new flamenco. *Songhai 2* ⅍⅍⅍⅍ (Hannibal/Rykodisc, 1994) is more sophisticated than the original, but not quite as inspired.

the rest:
(With Taj Mahal) *Kulanjan* ⅍⅍⅍⅍ (Hannibal, 1999)
(With Ballake Sissoko) *New Ancient Strings* N/A (Hannibal, 1999)

influences:

◄◄ Sidiki Diabaté, Batourou Sekou Kouyaté, Amadou Bansang Jobarteh

►► A generation of young, mostly unrecorded kora players

see also: *Taj Mahal*

Banning Eyre

Diblo Dibala

Alpha Yaya Diallo

Pan-African pop

Born in Conakry, Guinea. Based in Vancouver, B.C., Canada.

With acclaimed musicianship as his passport, composer, singer, and guitarist Alpha Yaya Diallo has tread the international stage and now leads one of Canada's most popular worldbeat outfits. Diallo's father was a traveling doctor who exposed his son to the various tribal rhythms of Guinea, as well as the music of Cape Verde, Senegal, Cameroon, and Cuba. When Diallo began playing, all these currents flowed effortlessly into his music, giving his style a bright cosmopolitan feel. During Diallo's teen years, his father was based in the Malinke region of Faranan, one of Guinea's most musically diverse subcultures. It was there he started teaching himself the guitar, imitating the rippling sounds of the *kora* (African harp-lute) and the Arabic-influenced flute melodies of his own Fula tribe. He was soon sitting in with bands like Bembeya Jazz National and Cameroon Stars. He also learned *balafon* (xylophone), drums, and flute. In 1989 Diallo moved to Finland and hooked up with Fatala, a band from Guinea that had just been signed to Peter Gabriel's RealWorld label. Diallo toured the globe with Fatala, winning raves for his flashy guitar work. When the band played in British Columbia, Diallo jumped ship and started his own.

what's available: *Aduna—The World* 𝄢𝄢𝄢𝄢 (Tinder, 1998, prod. Alpha Diallo), Diallo's American debut, combines the best tracks of his two Juno-nominated Canadian albums. Diallo uses both acoustic and electric guitars, and his playing is always subtle and understated, each note ringing clear as a bell—even when playing the percussive syncopated leads that mark the fretwork of most African guitarists. This impressive disc includes "Gogha," on which Diallo plays his guitar with the gentle quality of a *kalimba* (thumb piano); "Dewe," which combines the rhythms of black and Arabic Africa; and "Debo," a quiet acoustic guitar showcase that mixes bluesy bent notes with subtle flamenco flourishes. The Pan-African pop groove of *The Message* 𝄢𝄢𝄢𝄢 (Wicklow, 1999, prod. Kevin Finseth) shows an artist who's fully capable of giving Senagalese worldbeat titan Baaba Maal a run for his money, with Diallo having the advantage of a North American home base. Indeed the Senegalese influence is more noticeable here, and there are touches of *soukous* (African rumba), *mbalax* (the electrified Afro-Caribbean fusion popularized by Youssou N'Dour), and Cuba in the mix. The production has a tougher edge than *The World,* and every track hits with plenty of power, from horn-driven rave-ups like "Africa" to the more folkloric "Fatumata Diallo" and "Duniya," both of which feature kora master Boubacar Diabaté.

worth searching for: As captured on *Fatala: Gongoma Times* ♫♫♫ (WOMAD, 1988/RealWorld, 1993, prod. Yacouba "Bruno" Camara), Diallo's former musical family—though unfortunately not including him on this particular release—were a percussion ensemble with the young soprano voice of Mabinty Sahko adding luster to the dense poly-rhythms of talking drum, goblet drum or *djembe,* and balafon. Here they kick up a feisty party noise, distinct from much Guinean pop by the lack of guitar, or even kora, which may surprise fans of other exemplars like Mory Kanté or Bembeya Jazz. Fatala's only string instrument is the *bolon,* a harp arched over three strings. Formed in 1981 by percussionist/vocalist Yacouba "Bruno" Camara, who left Guinea for Paris in the '60s—introducing many Europeans to the delights of African percussion while no doubt broadening his style—the ensemble draws on traditional Guinean folk music, but with the Pan-African palette of their famous alumnus Diallo. This remains their only recording, and it rewards a search.

influences:
◄◄ Mory Kanté, Jali Musa Jawara, Fatala

j. poet and David Poole

Diblo Dibala /Loketo /Matchatcha

Soukous

Dibala born in Balupa Kasay, Congo (formerly Zaire). Loketo formed 1986; disbanded 1991. Matchatcha formed 1992. Based in Paris, France.

Loketo: Diblo Dibala, lead guitar; Aurlus Mabele, vocals; Mimi Kazidonna, second lead guitar; Mack Macaire, drums; Konba Belklow, percussion; Miguel Yamba, bass. Matchatcha: Diblo Dibala, lead guitar, leader; Komba Mafwala Bellow, drums; J.P. Kinzaki (France), second lead guitar; Miguel Yamba, bass (studio); Felico, bass (touring band). (All members are from Congo except where noted.)

Diblo Dibala is one of the finest players on the Afro-Parisian world-music scene, a guitarist, songwriter, arranger, and producer of prodigious proportions. Since he burst onto the African pop music landscape in the early '70s, sharing lead guitar chores with Franco in the legendary band TPOK Jazz, Diblo has been a trendsetter. Besides the dozens of albums he's recorded with his own outfits Loketo and Matchatcha, he has written, produced, and played on more than 60 albums for other artists and with the Kanda Bongo Man band. Currently he's interested in adding new sounds to his palette, including the folkloric music of Balupa Kasay (the region of his birth) and some of the licks he's heard from the American rock and blues artists he's been listening to.

Diblo speaks little English, but his friend and manager Alex Boicell fills in the blanks. "*Soukous* is the most popular dance music in Congo, and most of West Africa," Boicell says. "It's based on traditional music and drum patterns from Zaire, Cuban music—especially the rumba—and other African and American black music styles. Cuban music was, of course, founded on the African rhythms the slaves brought to the New World."

As John Storm Roberts documents in his book *The Latin Tinge* (Oxford University Press, 1979), the rumba returned to Africa in the '50s, mostly on early 78 rpm records, and it caused a sensation. Since the mixture of Cuban and West African rhythms that had evolved in the Caribbean wasn't tied to any particular West African country or ethnic group, it had potential for universal appeal. Pre-independence Congolese bands started out playing covers of Cuban hits with their own rhythmic adaptations, but the introduction of the electric guitar in the early '60s really accelerated the evolution of the music. The Africans combined the phrasing of the Cuban horn sections with local folkloric techniques to come up with the flowing improvisations that remain the music's trademark.

Until the '80s, an African rumba would start with a slow vocal and instrumental prelude; then the tempo would increase until the music got very hot, very fast. "When Diblo began playing with Kanda Bongo Man," Boicell says, "they decided to drop the introduction and go right into the hot section, the kind of music now called soukous." Young people, who were beginning to find musicians like Franco a bit old-fashioned, made Diblo one of Congo's most popular musicians.

"Diblo got interested in the guitar when he was 12," Boicell says. "His next-door neighbor took [Diblo] under his wing, and after a couple of lessons he consumed every book on guitar playing he could find. At 15 he was leading a small band, and his playing attracted Franco, Congo's top guitarist and band leader. In Congo they have contests where players can challenge each other to duels. Franco challenged Diblo—who was just a boy, remember—and he was so impressed that he offered him a job in his band."

In 1979 Kanda Bongo Man lured Diblo away from Franco. They relocated to Paris and Kanda's success there can be traced in part to Diblo's sparkling fretwork. Boicell recalls: "The first record they cut together was *Iyole.* When the DJs in Kinshasa heard it they went crazy; nobody had ever played that fast before." Even though his guitar playing had made him a near-legend in Paris and most of Africa, Diblo wasn't content. In 1986 he left Kanda Bongo Man and formed Loketo with singer Aurlus Mabele. "When Diblo and Aurlus put the band together, they wanted to do something modern, but they didn't want to lose the traditional flavor, so the music remained pure. Even with [Diblo's latest project] Matchatcha there are always tunes based on folk songs and proverbs; songs about what is happening in the village, songs that speak to the needs of the people."

One of the main criticisms of soukous is that "it all sounds the same," a cliché that Boicell says is partially true for two reasons. One is that the albums are mixed to appeal to the DJs back home, so the kick drum is put so far out in the mix that it often obliterates the intricate rhythmic patterns the drummer is laying down. The other reason is that musicians like Rigo Star, Diblo, and Matchatcha drummer Komba Mafwala Bellow are so popular that many bands hire them to produce and play on their sessions. "Some musicians have a 'fast food' mentality," Boicell said. "Rather than develop their own style, they hire Diblo or Rigo. But when it comes to reproducing the sounds of their record in public, they have to hire someone else to copy what these players did for them in the studio."

what to buy: The Afro-Parisian scene turns out a dizzying amount of music, and available releases by Diblo and the other top session players/producers come and go like the tides. *Matchatcha* ♫♫♫♫ (AfricMusic France, prod. Diblo Dibala), the first album by Diblo's new band, was an instant and major hit, showcasing his amazing chops and the breakneck rhythms of his partners. The album has also been seen under the title of *Laissez Passer,* one of its biggest hits. Kanda Bongo Man's *Amour Fou* ♫♫♫♫ (Hannibal, 1988, prod. Kanda Bongo Man) is the album that introduced Diblo to the world; a first-rate collection by one of the Congo's great vocalists, backed by the new king of the soukous guitar.

the rest:

Loketo:

Super Soukous ♫♫♫♫ (Shanachie, 1989)
Soukous Trouble ♫♫♫♫ (Shanachie, 1990)
Extra Ball ♫♫♫♫ (Shanachie, 1991)

influences:

◀◀ Franco, Tabu Ley Rochereau, Johnny Bokelo, Zaiko Langa Langa

▶▶ Rigo Star

see also: *Franco, Juan Luis Guerra, Pépé Kallé, Kanda Bongo Man, Rigo Star*

j. poet

Manu Dibango

Jazz, makossa, worldbeat

Born February 10, 1934, in Cameroon. Based in Cameroon and Paris, France.

In the 1940s and '50s, jazz gained popularity across Africa through prized recordings and the visits of Louis Armstrong, Duke Ellington, and Dizzy Gillespie. Numerous jazz bands sprang up from Algiers to Johannesburg, but it wasn't until 1960, when an exciting alto saxophonist named Manu Dibango propelled the band African Jazz out of Zaire (now Congo), that respect was gained. Within six years, Dibango was playing to a small but loyal following of natives and expatriates in Paris. In 1972, Atlantic released his album *Soul Makossa* in the U.S., and the title tune instantly became an anthem, dominating America's pop/soul airwaves as well as the discotheques. "Soul Makossa" was truly massive; though more of a jazz-funk jam than a *makossa* (Cameroonian pop) beat, the song also had a major influence on the emerging salsa scene (check out Dibango with the Fania All Stars on their 1976 album *Live at Yankee Stadium, Vol. 2*). Since Dibango's 1974 Atlantic swan song *Makossa Man,* he has played jazz festivals, toured the world many times, and released more than 20 albums on both import and domestic labels (scoring another international hit with 1985's "Abele Dance"). Today, the seemingly ageless Manu Dibango is still starring on the global stage, and his retirement seems a blessedly long way off.

what to buy: *Soul Makossa* ♫♫♫ (Atlantic, 1972) is Dibango's declaration of world conquest. In addition to the burning title tune, it boasts exotic moods and grooves aplenty ("New Bell" is a funky example). *Gone Clear* ♫♫♫♫ (Mango, 1980, prod. Geoffrey Chung) is a beguiling mix of African, R&B, and reggae grooves thanks to the presence of folks like Sly & Robbie, Jocelyn Brown, Crusher Bennett, and Randy Brecker.

what to buy next: *Electric Africa* ♫♫♫ (Celluloid, 1985, prod. various) includes "Abele Dance" and is Manu *al electrique,* kinda like computer makossa funk. *Live 91* ♫♫♫♥ (Stern, 1991, prod. Manu Dibango) is a bumping set recorded at Paris's legendary Olympia. From the spirited cover of Serge Gainsborough's reggae-fied "La Marseillaise" spoof, "La Javanaise," to MC Mello's hip-hop freestyle flow on "Jam Rap Makossa," Dibango and crew are on fire.

what to avoid: The guest list on *Wakafrika* ♫♫ (Giant, 1994, prod. George Acogny) is impressive—Peter Gabriel, Youssou N'Dour, Sinéad O'Connor, Ladysmith Black Mambazo—but they steal too much focus from Dibango's performance.

the rest:

Afrijazzy ♫♫♫♥ (Enemy, 1994)
Bao Bao ♫♫♫ (MIL Multimedia, 1996)

Manu Safari N/A (Tinder, 1999)
Come Closer N/A (Tinder, 1999)

worth searching for: Dibango's outstanding guest appearance on the Fania All Stars' *Live at Yankee Stadium, Vol. 2* ♪♪♪♪ (Fania, 1976) has to be heard. He also makes a worthwhile visit on Angélique Kidjo's *Logozo* ♪♪♪♪ (Mango, 1991/1992).

influences:

◀◀ Wes Montgomery, John Handy, Junior Walker

▶▶ Fela Kuti, Eddie Palmieri, Hugh Masekela

see also: *Les Go de Koteba, Johnny Pacheco*

Tom Terrell and Gary Graff

Diga Rhythm Band

Worldbeat

Formed as Tal Vadya, 1973, in San Rafael, CA, USA. Re-formed as Diga Rhythm Band, 1975. Re-formed as Rhythm Experience, 1984. Based in San Rafael, CA, USA.

Zakir Hussain (India), tabla, folk drums, tar; Mickey Hart (USA), traps, gongs, timbales, timpani; Jim Loveless (USA), marimbas; Jordan Amarantha, congas, bongos; Vince Delgado (USA), dumbek, tabla, talking drum; Ray Spiegal (USA), vibes; Tor Dietrichson (USA), tabla; Aushim Chaudhuri (India), tabla; Arshad Syed (India), duggi tarang, nal; Joy Schulman (USA), tabla; Peter Carmichael (USA), tabla.

Zakir Hussain put together a drum group at the Ali Akbar College of Music in 1973. The troupe was called Tal Vadya and gave students a chance to perform in public. Mickey Hart joined in 1975, and the outfit changed its name to Diga Rhythm Band. They recorded one classic self-titled album in 1976.

what's available: The 1976 date documented on *Diga Rhythm Band* ♪♪♪♪ (Rykodisc, 1988, prod. Mickey Hart) was digitized by Mickey Hart in 1988, and the sound is breathtaking. Hart brings his Afro/Arabic/rock influences—and his buddy Vince Delgado—to the group, and the result is a shimmering web of percussion with the tensile strength of a suspension bridge cable.

influences:

◀◀ Olatunji, Ustad Alla Rakha, Ray Baretto

▶▶ Balafon Marima Ensemble

see also: *Mickey Hart, Zakir Hussain, Ali Akbar Khan*

j. poet

Henri Dikongué

Pan-African pop

Born c. 1968, in Cameroon. Based in Paris, France.

Henri Dikongué has already made a big impact in Europe, where his album *C'est La Vie* hit #1 on the world-music chart. Back home in Cameroon, he's not only famous, he's notorious. His debut album, *Wa (You),* tossed verbal and musical darts at Cameroon's military regime and dealt with weighty matters like racism and the day-to-day hardships of post-colonial life brought on by economic imperialism. "I was frustrated—an angry young man—when I wrote my first album," Dikongué says. "Even today, many musicians from the older generation are chained to the past. They live in a self-imposed ghetto of dance music and happy lyrics, partially because in most African nations you risk so much criticizing the government. My generation was born in Africa, but we live all over the world, so we have a more international outlook." Dikongué's own global outlook influences his musical approach as well as his lyrical stance. Like many of the sounds being created by a new generation of African pop artists that includes Sally Nyolo, Ismaël Lô, and Wasis Diop, *C'est La Vie* tips its hat to the international cadences of the African Diaspora by embracing reggae, samba, salsa, soul, and jazz as well as the expected Cameroonian rhythms of *makossa* and *bikutsi.* Dikongué's music isn't all up-tempo, however; it's evenly balanced between smooth dance grooves and ballads. Dikongué's use of tempos that balance traditional African rhythms with classical European harmonies and structure make his slower material sound like a breath of fresh air. Tunes like "Ndotu (Sorrow)" and "Na Tem Ité Idaba (In My Dreams)" showcase Dikongué's acoustic guitar and ride understated rhythm tracks that combine African, American, and European elements in a way that takes them in a subtle new direction—perhaps the first inklings of what the international pop of the next century will sound like.

what's available: Dikongué's international debut, *C'est La Vie* ♪♪♪♪ (Tinder, 1998, prod. Gilles Fruchaux), kicks off with "Ndol'asu," a Latin-flavored tune that includes a fiddle passage that could be Stephane Grappelli sitting in with a *charanga* band. "Na Teleye Owa Ngea" combines the swing of Caribbean *soca* and the hard rhythms of bikutsi (Cameroon's brand of rock 'n' roll), while "A Muni (Man)" addresses spousal abuse with an ironic lyric and a melange of West African dance styles including makossa, high life, and *soukous.*

worth searching for: *Wa (You)* ♪♪♪♪ (Buda Musique France, 1995), Dikongué's first album, is full of solid grooves and scathing political commentary; it made him a cause célèbre back home, and a rising star on the French world-music scene.

influences:

◀◀ Sam Fan Thomas, Francis Bebey, Les Veterans

j. poet

Vieux Diop

Afro-jazz fusion

Born in Senegal. Based in New York, NY, USA.

Vieux Diop emigrated from Senegal to New York in 1983 and

brought along the music of his homeland with a missionary fervor. Though his sonic-ambassador role was self-appointed, there isn't an audience since that hasn't granted him diplomatic recognition on the spot. In addition to memorable work as a sideman holding his own with such historic world-music names as Babatunde Olatunji and Youssou N'Dour, he has racked up impressive credentials in the free-jazz realm with the Myth World Rhythm Troupe and in the worldbeat registry with Spirit Ensemble. Perhaps his biggest of many contributions to the Stateside appreciation of international sounds is as a popular world-music radio personality, a university lecturer/performer, and an outreach artist for New York City's public schools, introducing thousands of young people to the music of Africa through the prestigious Juilliard Performing Arts Program for Schools at New York's Lincoln Center. Somehow he also found time to record a well-regarded solo album in the mid-'90s.

what's available: *Vieux Diop (Via Jo)* ♪♪♪♪ (Triloka, 1995, prod. Brian Keane)—helpfully subtitled with the approximate English pronunciation of the composer/lead-singer/multi-instrumentalist's name—is a tasteful and listenable debut, melding American jazz and African polyrhythm in supple and pleasantly surprising ways, with pastoral detours that show how the "ambient" aesthetic was at work on the continents of color long before it acquired the terms or technology we know today.

worth searching for: Diop recorded an earlier band project of Caribbean-flavored West African music, *Deeso* (Alebrije, 1994), on a local label before the majors got the message.

influences:
◄◄ Youssou N'Dour, Babatunde Olatunji, Miles Davis

Adam McGovern

Wasis Diop

Pan-African pop
Born in Dakar, Senegal. Based in Paris, France.

Composer/guitarist Wasis Diop may be Senegalese, but he considers himself an international musician and uses African, Caribbean, Arabic, Asian, black American, and European elements in a seamless manner that will appeal to listeners no matter where they come from—musically or geographically. Diop's use of international colors (a bagpipe here, a vocalist singing in the style of classical Japanese opera there) has produced a smooth, cosmopolitan version of Afropop.

"In this life, nothing is static," Diop says. "The only danger is to not adapt, to not travel, to stay in one spot, musically or spiritually. Despite the history of colonization, Africa has stayed open to Western ideas. When we listened to Black American music,

for example, we listened to it as if it came from our culture, from our lost cousins. When I grew up, Black American music was the most listened-to music, and after loving it for years, we're sending this music back to America, so now maybe Americans will lend an ear to Africa, and it will give them new ideas."

"Growing up, music was the only game we had," Diop continues. "So everybody played music; every child was a musician. But the day you decide to be a professional musician things change. My family didn't accept it. There is a proverb they used to tell me: 'He who has a noble spirit listens to music, but doesn't play it.' So I was a young man before I began my career." After moving to Paris—allegedly to go to university—Diop put together a band called West African Cosmos, a jazzy instrumental combo that toured Europe several times and recorded one album for CBS France. "Eventually we hired a singer who was into reggae, which got me interested in going to Jamaica." On his first day there, Diop met famed dub auteur Lee Perry. "Lee Perry came up to me and said that he could tell I was from Africa. He asked me to come to his studio, the Black Ark, to play on some of the dub tracks he was working on. Every morning he would read to me from the Bible, and tell me stories about Africa. I added guitar to some of the songs, but every night there were deaths on the road outside—it was difficult to live with that."

In 1990, Diop began working with Amina Annabi, a pop singer with strong roots in her Moroccan culture. He wrote "C'est le Dernier Qui a Parlé Qui a Raison (It Is the Last One Who Speaks Who Is Right)" for her and the song won the Eurovision Song Contest in 1991. Amina's manager introduced Diop to Tasuaki Shimizu, a Japanese sax player who was moving in the direction of high-concept international pop à la Ryuichi Sakamoto. Diop played on Shimizu's album, joined his band, and toured Japan for two years. After returning from Japan, Diop's career went into overdrive. "My brother, Djibril Diop Mambety, directed a film called *Hyenes,* an adaptation of Friedrich Durrenmatt's *La Visite de la Vielle Dame*." Durrenmatt's play is a scathing indictment of the way the capitalist system breeds greed, corruption, and class warfare. PolyGram released Diop's soundtrack for *Hyenes* before the film, feeling the music could stand on its own. They also signed Diop as a solo artist.

"When I write, I'm inspired by the traditions of Africa. In each region the melodies are completely different from the next region, and sometimes it's difficult to transpose the melodies I'm hearing in my head; trying to resolve these difficulties can produce a new sound. In the end, everything I do is based on something I've heard before; but in music, the past, the present, and the future can exist in the same moment. Musicians never invent anything new, but reassemble sounds they've heard before to let them survive, to carry them on. That's the alchemy of the artist."

what's available: On *No Sant* ♫♫♫ (Triloka, 1995, prod. Wasis Diop, Yasuaki Shimizu), Diop's alchemical inventions include Afro-Parisian blues, South African doo-wop, Senegalese reggae skank, and a ritual song performed by Yande Kodou Sene, one of Senegal's most respected traditional female singers. The basic groove is undeniably African, but Diop's interest in Jamaican, Japanese, North American, and European music gives the proceedings a decidedly international slant. *Toxu* ♫♫♫♫ (Triloka, 1998) is another fine Afropop album that features Diop's transformation of Talking Heads' "Once in a Lifetime" into a traditional African chant, as well as "Father to Son," which combines Senegalese and Afrikaans (white South African) folk music for an implicit message of universal brotherhood.

worth searching for: The *Hyenes* ♫♫♫♫ (Mercury France, 1993) soundtrack combines synthesizer washes, hand drumming, and traditional singing to create a deep, dream-like atmosphere.

influences:

◀ Youssou N'Dour, Talking Heads, E.T. Mensah

▶ Sally Nyolo, Henri Dikongué

see also: *Amina, Lee "Scratch" Perry*

j. poet

Dissidenten

Arabic worldbeat
Formed 1980, in Berlin, Germany. Based in Berlin, Germany.

Uve Mullrich, guitar, bass, sitar, keyboards; Marlon Klein, keyboards, bass, djembe, percussion; Freido Josch, sax, flute. (All members are from Germany.)

Mullrich, Klein, and Josch, the key trio of the ever-shifting musical collective known as Dissidenten, first collaborated in the 1970s group Embryo. They played avant garde jazz/rock, ran their own indie label, and staged many large, free (in both senses of the word) music festivals. In 1983 the trio spent a year living and working at the palace of Maharaja Bhalkrishna Bharti of Gondagoan in Madya Pradesh, India; it was there that they laid plans for their first album, *Sahara Electric*, a collaboration with Algerian *rai* singer Cherif M. Lamran. This fusion of rai (Algerian pop) and rock became one of the first worldbeat "hits" in Europe. As for the band's strategy of recording in Arabic, Mullrich explains: "Much of the world loves American and British pop, yet doesn't understand the words, so why not make music in Arabic? This is the language you find around the corner in Paris or Berlin. In Berlin there are 200,000 Turks alone, and their relationship to European music is analogous to the influence blacks had on American rock and roll. Anywhere in the world, you can put on a radio and hear Bulgarian chants, rai, Celtic folk, Greek bouzouki music, funk, John Coltrane. There's no reason to limit yourself."

what to buy: The idea of fusing rock and rai is a good one—both styles thrive on attitude and confrontation—but the band is clearly still feeling its way on *Sahara Electric* ♫♫♫ (Shanachie, 1988, prod. Marlon Klein). The production is minimal, which gives the music an unfinished quality that's part of its appeal. Basing their world fusion on the Arabic continuum, rather than the African, shows promise, but this is still more Western than Eastern.

what to buy next: The dissidents take an interesting side trip to India for one of their most polished albums, *Jungle Book* ♫♫♫♫ (Triloka Worldly, 1993, prod. Marlon Klein). The production is glossy, and members of the Karnataka College of Percussion add considerable authenticity to the rhythm tracks.

best of the rest:
Live at the Pyramids ♫♫♫ (Shanachie, 1989)
Out of This World ♫♫♫ (Sire, 1989)
Instinctive Traveler ♫♫♫ (Blue Jackel, 1998)

influences:

◀ 3 Mustaphas 3, Khaled

see also: *Karnataka College of Percussion*

j. poet

Djavan

Brazilian, worldbeat
Born Djavan Caetano Viana, 1950, in Maceio, Alagoas, Brazil. Based in Rio de Janeiro, Brazil.

Djavan is one of the most popular singer/songwriter/guitarists in Brazil and was noted for his "global pop" sound even before the term gained currency outside of his country. His unique jazz-tinged phrasing, unexpected melodic shifts, and willingness to tackle Brazil's social and racial inequalities in his lyrics have made him a unique artist: a singer who doesn't fit neatly into any one category.

Djavan began singing and playing guitar in primary school, inspired by American pop music. "I began singing along to the records of Elvis, Sinatra, Billie Holliday and Duke Ellington. I got a guitar for a gift and taught myself. The first time I sang in public was for a school show. I did a song by Augostinho Dos Santos." Djavan ran away from home at the age of 16, when his parents told him he was going to be shipped off to a military academy. "My father was a soldier," Djavan says. "He said he wouldn't support me if I was going to play music." Djavan was able to make his way to Rio de Janeiro, where he began playing in nightclub bands "doing tourist music." He was also composing his own songs, getting some session work and contributing music to several *novelas*—wildly popular Brazilian TV soap operas—which helped him get his compositional chops up to speed.

After placing a few tunes with artists like Roberto Carlos and Maria Bethânia, Djavan landed a contract with Sigla and recorded his first album, *A Voz E O Violao De Djavan* (The Voice and Guitar of Djavan). Even at this early stage, his work was full of global influences. "I used all the music I loved; folkloric, classical, African, jazz, the Beatles." The success of *A Voz E O Violao De Djavan* led to a contract with EMI Brazil, for which he recorded three albums—*Djavan, Alumbaramento,* and *Seduzir* —with three hit singles, prompting a jump to Sony Brazil. His first two outings for that label, *Luz* and *Lilas,* continued his winning streak; the latter was one of the biggest import albums of 1984 in the U.S. The two recordings also elevated Djavan to superstar status in his home country, though his financial success didn't shield him from all the vagaries of that country's social structure. "Brazilians say the society is color blind, but people of African descent still have more social and economic problems and less access to education. After I had became popular, I went into a music store in Sao Paulo to buy a piano. When I told them I would pay for the instrument with cash, they called the police, who asked me where I got the money. They wanted to see my papers and refused to believe a 'nigger' could make that much money playing music."

what to buy: *Flor de Lis* ✍✍✍✍ (Sound Wave, 1990, prod. Guto Graça Mello) is 1976's landmark *A Voz E O Violao De Djavan* with a new title and cover art. It's a romp from start to finish, with all the elements that made Djavan a star—sharp melodies, wonderful phrasing, and percolating Afro-Brazilian rhythms—already in place.

what to buy next: The compilation *Djavan* ✍✍✍ (Columbia, 1985) contains tracks from the two Brazilian albums that boosted Djavan's star even higher, *Luz* and *Lilas.* Rather than culling the best songs from each album, however, the record company apparently chose to pull the tracks they thought were most likely to catch the ear of the American public. A good introduction, but the material flows better on the originals, which can easily be found in the import section of most large record stores.

best of the rest:
Seduzir ✍✍✍✍ (EMI Brazil, 1981)
Bird of Paradise ✍✍✍ (Columbia, 1987)
Djavan & Alumbaramento ✍✍✍ (World Pacific, 1992)

influences:
◄ Gilberto Gil, Caetano Veloso, Martinho Da Vila
►► Marisa Monte, Daniela Mercury

see also: *Virginia Rodrigues*

j. poet

Djur Djura
Traditional Berber, worldbeat
Born c. 1945, in Ifigha, Algeria. Based in Paris, France.

Djur Djura takes her name from Mount Djurdjura, a landmark near her village of Kabylia in Algeria. Djura is a noted writer and filmmaker, a compelling singer/composer, and an outspoken supporter of women's rights. Unhappily her fame does not sit well with her family, and she has endured several life-threatening physical attacks by her brother, who has vowed to kill her for breaking with Berber tradition.

Djura has faced hardship all her life. Her mother, who had wanted a boy child, left the baby to starve. One of Djura's grandfather's wives took her in and nursed her. Djura's family is Berber. They have their own language and customs, including a tendency to "protect" women against the secular world. This mindset has caused her many problems over the years.

In 1950 Djura's father took the family to Paris to seek work. He was imprisoned for supporting the Algerian Liberation Movement, and after his release he beat Djura and her mother. Djura enrolled in a performing arts school, where she was offered a role in an upcoming TV series, but her father refused his permission. To escape her father's wrath (and an arranged marriage), Djura fled to Algiers with her brother, Mohand. But when she was offered a job as a journalist with Algerian radio and television, he locked her in a room for five months. Mohand was also afraid that his sister was becoming too intimate with his friend Oliver. Djura's father arrived in Algeria and moved her back to her home town of Ifigha, where she immersed herself in Berber folklore and music with the aid of the village women. Her father next moved her back to Paris, where she was kept locked up until Oliver helped her escape. She worked days and went to film school nights, and she eventually persuaded her mother to leave her father, which led to her brother Mohand's threat to kill her. Mohand attacked her and slashed her face shortly thereafter.

In 1976 Djura began doing readings of some of the poems she'd written about her life, and, encouraged by the response, formed a group with two of her sisters and musicians from North Africa, France, and America. Her music, while based on the Berber songs and chants she grew up with, also contains European and Anglo/American pop flourishes.

what's available: The collection *Voice of Silence* ✍✍✍✍ (Luaka Bop, 1993, prod. Hervé Lacroix), compiled by David Byrne, includes material from four French albums, *Asirem, Groupe de Femmes Algériennes, Groupe de Femmes Algériennes: A Yemma,* and *Le Défi.* The band, put together with the help of Boudjema Merzak, conductor of the Algerian Radio and Television Orchestra, has been trained in Berber music and provides

Oscar D'Leon

a beautifully understated accompaniment to Djura's fragile vo-cals. The music ranges from the singing and handclapping styles common to Berber women's music to more classically or-chestrated pieces. The lyrics usually deal with the day-to-day realities of women's lives.

influences:
◄◄ Cheikha Remitti

j. poet

Oscar D'Leon

Salsa, tropical
Born c. 1950, in Venezuela. Based in Caracas, Venezuela.

Oscar D'Leon spent years as a part-time musician in Caracas, Venezuela, working in a car factory and driving a cab, saving his money to fund a full-time music career. In the early '70s he had his first hit, "Pensando en Ti," with a band he had organized, Di-mension Latina. Subsequently he founded the group Salsa Mayer and then created Oscar D'Leon y su Orquesta. Today that 19-piece group (which now includes D'Leon's sons as well) per-forms often in the U.S., where a highlight of the show is D'Leon's energetic playing of his white baby grand piano.

what's available: *En New York* ♫♫♫♪ (Musart, 1998) is a live recording with the band's current configuration, aptly illustrat-ing why it's said of D'Leon that he was born a Venezuelan with a Cuban soul. *Exitos con la Critica* ♫♫♫ (Musart, 1996) offers a trip through D'Leon's history as an arranger and bandleader, spotlighting his trademark use of a trombone-section backline and his agile singing style. *Navidad con Oscar D'Leon* ♫♫♫ (Musart, 1994) is salsa music for an island holiday.

influences:
◄◄ Beny Moré, Celia Cruz, Cuban salsa

see also: *Celia Cruz, Tito Puente*

Kerry Dexter

Dr. Didg

Experimental dance-rock
Formed 1993, in London, England. Based in London, England.

Graham Wiggins, didgeridoo, keyboards, melodica, percussion; Mark Revell, guitar (1993–98); Dave Motion, guitar (1998–present); Ian Campbell, drums, percussion. (All members are from England.)

Dr. Didg is the nickname of Dr. Graham Wiggins, who earned the sobriquet by testing out the *didgeridoo*—Aboriginal Aus-tralia's now-famous droning tubular instrument, organically de-rived but sonically synthesizer-like—in his physics lab. While playing the didgeridoo for money on the streets of England to support his education at Oxford, Wiggins met another local busker, guitarist Martin Cradick, and the two joined forces to form Outback, a relatively influential world-music fusion group noted for introducing the didgeridoo to Western audiences. When that band broke up in 1993, Wiggins and Outback drum-mer Ian Campbell began experimenting in a live context with a technique known as "live sampling," in which Wiggins per-forms a riff on didgeridoo, samples it, then loops it on digital delay, gradually adding more layers to create a trippy effect well-suited to Dr. Didg's eclectic brand of ethnic-influenced dance/rock fusion. Although much less traditional in nature than Martin Cradick's current project, Baka Beyond, Dr. Didg is far more accessible, exploring an improvisational sound that will appeal equally to fans of the Grateful Dead (with whom Wiggins was invited to perform in 1993) and Aboriginal rockers Yothu Yindi.

what's available: Although less organic than the group's debut, *Seritonality* ♫♫♫♪ (Hannibal, 1998, prod. Graham Wiggins) is the more fully realized effort, with hypnotic, multi-layered grooves whose danceable appeal is difficult to deny. Guitarist Mark Rev-ell is in fine form on songs like the live "Son of Tut," his melodies providing a nice modern contrast to the primal power of Wiggins's phenomenal didg work. *Out of the Woods* ♫♫♫♪

(Hannibal, 1994, prod. Graham Wiggins) is an equally enjoyable excursion that more accurately reflects the group's beginnings as street performers, with fewer effects, samples, and synthesizers and more straightforward songwriting.

influences:

⏪ David Hudson, Yothu Yindi, Grateful Dead, Material

see also: *Baka Beyond*

Bret Love

Doctor Ganga

See: Orlando Owah

Dr. Loco's Rockin' Jalapeño Band

Tejano rock, worldbeat

Formed 1987, in Palo Alto, CA, USA. Based in San Francisco, CA, USA.

Dr. Loco (José Cuéllar), sax, lead vocals, leader; Glenn Appell, lead trumpet, flugelhorn; Carlos Camplis, timbales (1987–94); Mario Barrera, timbales (1994–present); Chris Gonzalez Clarke, guitar, tres; Jesus Covarrubias, keys, accordion (1987–94); Hadley Louden, keyboards (1994–97); Daniel Martinez, keyboards (1997–present); Carlos Montoya, bass; David Stephens, trombone trump; Dean Boysen, trumpet; Mark Rendón, drums, congas (1987–94); Joe Brigandi, drums (1994–present); Sammy Dries-Daffne, congas (1987–94). (All members are from USA.)

José Cuéllar, alias Dr. Loco, the crazy Chicano with the sweet swingin' sax and ultraviolet smile, leads one of the tightest, hardest party bands in the San Francisco Bay Area. With a cannon that spans six decades and several continents, the Jalapeños provide the uninitiated with an introduction to the Latin styles that have become the building blocks for much North American pop music, at times sounding like the soundtrack for a course in Latin Music 101—a fantasy that isn't far from the truth. "In the early '80s, I was teaching at Stanford University and put together a lecture I called 'The History of Chicano Music.'" Cuéllar's stage grin isn't an act and is even more infectious when he's talking to you, one-on-one; he smiles and bobs his head in time to an invisible music that only he can hear and fills in his story with expressive hand gestures and peals of delighted laughter. "I played records by Benny Moré, the first great Cuban superstar of the '40s and '50s; *Tejano* hits; things by Santana and Los Lobos; Freddy Fender's early stuff; everything. It went over so well, I had to repeat it and began wondering what it would be like to play some of this stuff live, so the students could get a real feel for it."

Cuéllar asked around campus and found plenty of students and teachers with musical chops to spare. His first group, Dr. Loco's Original Corrido Boogie Band, played everything from '60s Te-

japan: the taiko tradition

The *taiko* (both a specific instrumental name and a general genre heading) is the traditional drum of Japan, and can range in size from small, hand-held snares to the huge *o-daiko,* which is typically carved from the largest tree that can be found and often weighs more than 1,000 pounds. The taiko's most prominent proponent is the Japanese ensemble Kodo, whose name literally means "heartbeat"; it is said that the sound of the taiko resembles a mother's heartbeat as felt in the womb, and that babies are often lulled to sleep by the drum's thunderous vibrations. Before 1981, when Kodo began its mission to introduce the taiko to audiences around the world, the instrument was little-known outside of Japan, where it was primarily used in formal ceremonies and royal court performances. The latter is easy to understand, as taiko presentations are usually elaborately organized, with just as much importance placed on the visual as the musical. Now that Kodo has received worldwide acclaim for its seemingly eternal "One Earth Tour," taiko drums are experiencing a small surge of popularity in America, where some university ensembles are beginning to experiment with their primal, powerful sound.

see also: Kodo

Bret Love

jano classics to merengue and covers of Santana's acid-drenched Latin hits. By the time Cuéllar, who has a Ph.D. in anthropology, was offered a job as head of the Chicano studies program at San Francisco State, most of his band mates had graduated and they moved north with him. With a few changes in the lineup, the group was reborn as Dr. Loco's Rockin' Jalapeño Band. "We devised a five year plan, to see how far we could go," Cuéllar says. "And we've been able to do what we set out to do, which is to preserve, explore, and expand upon our bilingual, bicultural experience as Mexican Americans. We do songs in English, Spanish, and Spanglish, although most of our tunes are bilingual. Growing up in San Antonio, I knew from an early age how creative you can be with two languages at your disposal. It allows you to derive many meanings from the same word, to pun in two languages and to create new words. The kids I hung with would invent words, then try to get our friends to use them, to see how far they'd go. In a sense that's what I'm still doing with the band, combining cultures, mixing politics and dance music into a postmodern potpourri that everyone can relate to."

what to buy: *Barrio Ritmos & Blues* ♫♫♫♫ (Loco, 1998, prod. Greg Landau) is Loco's latest, and, in line with his earlier releases, a solid primer of Chicano styles—Latino R&B ballads, *corridos*, blues, funk, salsa, and the Neville's "Look-ka Py Py," played with a Latin twist to the second line rhythms. Contact Loco at P.O. Box 410023, San Francisco, CA 94141-0023, locoline@drloco.com. Loco's funky and folky approach to the Latino songbag provides plenty of street grit to *Puro Party!* ♫♫♫♫ (Flying Fish, 1995, prod. Wayne Wallace).

the rest:
Movimiento Music ♫♫♫♫ (Flying Fish, 1992)

influences:
◀◀ Bob Wills, Bill Dogget, Thee Midniters, Little Joe, Santana, Los Lobos

j. poet

Dr. Nico
Soukous
Born Nicholas Kasanda in Zaire (now Congo). Died 1985, in Brussels, Belgium.

Buckaroo Banzai's credo "No matter where you go, there you are" is in full effect when you talk about the African Diaspora sector of world music. Check the scenario: Over time, African slaves in the Caribbean and the Americas remake/remodel ancient rhythms, melodies, and instruments in their New World images. Twentieth-century recording technology becomes the linkage free-zone where Brazilian *samba,* African American blues/jazz, Cuban *son/rumba/mambo,* and Trinidadian calypso meet, discover common roots, share secrets, make new magic. Said recordings flip back to the Motherland, inspiring new hybrids of music: jump blues into highlife, James Brown into Fela Kuti, Cuban rumba into Congolese *soukous.* . . . No matter where you go, there you are indeed.

The rumba equation is a particularly apt example of the theory. It's a no-brainer, really: Congo is the former "Belgian Congo"; in slavery days many Congolese were shipped to Cuba; '40s and '50s rumba records rocked Congo's radios, parties, and bands because it was an amped-up/jazzed-up reincarnation of traditional Congolese *maringa* music. By the end of the '50s, every successful dance band in Kinshasa (the capital city) played mostly cha-cha-chas, *boleros,* and rumbas. Original material was a commercial no-no until Le Grand Kalle (Joseph Kabasele)

& African Jazz brought on the New Sound with their 1960 megahit "Independence Cha Cha." Fittingly, this tribute to the brand-new nation of Zaire also introduced a new Zairian dance music—soukous. In soukous (literally, "shake"), rhythm shifts, melodic flow, lyrical nuance, chromatic extrapolation, jam improvisation, *everything* is centered around the guitarist's groove/mood swings. "Independence Cha Cha" was soukous's Big Bang, and when the smoke cleared, African Jazz's teenage prodigy Dr. Nico stood chilling in a French-cut suit, the undisputed grand architect of soukous guitar. A lyrically ethereal, melodically balletic, rhythmically whimsical, throw-breakdowns-to-the-break-a-dawn kinda guy, Nico blew up. Mid-decade he formed his own band, Africa Fiesta. Now a top-ranking solo act, Nico raised the bar and topped the charts when he hired singer/composer Tabu Ley Rochereau. By the time Rochereau split in the early '70s, Dr. Nico's stuff signified as old-school square, no match for either the P-Funk-like 20-piece rockestra viscerality of Franco and TPOK Jazz or the exuberantly over-the-top soukous soul of Rochereau's Afrisa International. Dr. Nico continued to record albums (mostly two-to-four tracks of extended jams) into the early '80s, but he never got back to the Big Show. In 1985, Dr. Nico died of AIDS in a Brussels hospital.

what's available: Unless you have access to an African music store, 1-800-find-a-CD, or the Internet, Dr. Nico recordings are gonna be tough to come by. That said, these imports are kinda sorta available: *1966/1967/1968* ♫♫♫♫ (African Music, 1995); *L'African Fiesta Vol. 1* ♫♫♫♫ (Sonodisc, 1994); *L'African Fiesta Vol. 2 (1962–1963)* ♫♫♫♫ (Sonodisc, 1994); and *L'African Fiesta, Vol. 4 (1967–1969)* ♫♫♫♫ (Sonodisc, 1994).

influences:
◀◀ Guy Warren, Bola Sete, Le Grand Kalle & African Jazz
▶▶ Kanda Bongo Man, Loketo (Diblo Dibala), Papa Wemba

see also: *Franco, Tabu Ley Rochereau*

Tom Terrell

John Doherty
Irish traditional
Born c. 1895, in Ardar, County Donegal, Ireland. Died January 23, 1980, in Ballyshannon, Ireland.

If any one musician can be said to embody the traditional music of his native area, John Doherty would be that musician for Donegal. The youngest of nine children, Doherty's earliest musical influences came from his father, Micker Mór, as well as his uncles of the McConnell family. Because of Donegal's proximity to Scotland, Doherty was also exposed to the strong fiddle traditions of J. Scott Skinner and William Murdoch. His virtuosity was recognized at an early age, subsequently making him much sought after to play for local dances while still in his teens. Since the early nineteenth century the Dohertys had been widely regarded as one of the main families of traveling musicians in Northern Ireland, and John was no exception. At a time when tinsmithing and fiddling were two fortunate traits to possess in the villages of Donegal, he excelled at both, and was a welcome addition to each community in which he would stop. According to most accounts of Doherty's life, he traveled a regular route, staying in each locale a week or two. By day he would ply his trade as a tinsmith, and at night he would teach tunes and play local dances and house parties. Part of John Doherty's fame owed to a recording career more prolific than many of his contemporaries—a career all the more impressive for the fact that he rarely left his native Donegal. Almost without exception the recordings of Doherty were made by folklorists who came to Donegal seeking him. By the early '50s Doherty had become well known not only for his repository of fiddle music but also for his rich wealth of local folklore. American Alan Lomax came calling in 1951, followed by Peter Kennedy in 1953, and the Irish Folklore Commission in 1957. When the '60s came around and the Donegal of Doherty's youth began to change, he traveled less frequently, choosing to stay in the places most familiar to him. Doherty's overall geographic preference led many to mischaracterize his playing as being definitive of the Donegal tradition. But Doherty's style was more unique, his frequent travels introducing him to a wide variety of community-based fiddling forms from which he kept elements he liked while discarding those that he didn't. His playing featured equal parts Scottish and Irish influences, but rolled into a style so individualistic that it even differed from that of members of his own family. His death in 1980 left a hole in Irish fiddling that will never be filled—but a legacy from which a whole new musical generation takes inspiration and from which all listeners can take comfort.

what to buy: *The Floating Bow—Traditional Fiddle Music from Donegal* ♪♪♪♪ (Claddagh, 1996, prod. Dermot McLaughlin) is culled from recordings of Doherty made between 1968 and 1974. As if more than 50 minutes of wonderfully vibrant fiddling weren't enough, the 32-page booklet includes a comprehensive career history, two pages of photographs, and detailed notes on each track. As is Doherty's trademark, this is all solo unaccompanied fiddle music, albeit running the gamut from flowing reels like "Bonnie Kate" to a masterful imitation of the highland pipes on "The Eniskillen Dragoons." Doherty's brilliance is especially captured on the final track, his fiddle going from the lonesome Gaelic air "Maidin Fhómhair" into a lyrically vibrant rendition of "Miss McLeod's Reel," which, in his hands, is pure magic.

what to buy next: *John Doherty—The Celebrated Recordings* ♪♪♪♪ (Shanachie, 1997, prod. David Hammond) is a vivacious collection of Doherty's music recorded at an informal 1974 session that took place in Glencolmcille, Donegal. The over-67-minute recording is full of Doherty's distinctive unaccompanied fiddling, replete with the triplets and double stopping for which he was renowned in his native country. *Bundle and Go* ♪♪♪♪ (Topic, 1984/Green Linnet, 1993, prod. Tony Engle) was recorded when Doherty was well into his 80s, a fact only significant for understanding how brilliant this man's fiddling was even at such an advanced age. Still, while by no means a bad recording, this doesn't stand up to the quality of music and rich liner notes of *The Floating Bow*.

worth searching for: Several of Doherty's better recordings are either only available on cassette or LP or are out of print entirely, but all are well worth tracking down. His self-titled album on the Comhaltas Ceoltóirí Éireann label, as well as *The Star of Donegal* and *Pedlar's Pack,* both on the Bristol, England–based Folktracks label, rate among his finest works. Doherty was also featured in two television documentaries. The first, *Fiddler on the Road,* was made by Ulster Television, and the second, simply titled *John Doherty,* features American folk icon Pete Seeger and was made by Folktracks. For a comprehensive look at the fiddling tradition in Donegal—including a detailed history of the Doherty family—Caoimhín MacAoidh's book *Between the Jigs and the Reels* (Drumlin Publications, Nurc, Manorhamilton, County Leitrim, Ireland) is an insightful examination into a rich musical culture.

influences:

◄◄ Mickey McConnell, Alec McConnell, J. Scott Skinner

►► Altan, Paddy Glackin, Robbie Hannan, Liz Doherty, Vincent Campbell, Tommy Peoples

see also: *Paddy Glackin*

Cliff McGann

Felix Dolan

Irish traditional
Born March 13, 1937, in Bronx, NY, USA. Based in New York, NY, USA.

If you were to track down any Irish musician in the New York area and ask who would be his or her choice of a piano player, Felix Dolan is the name you'd almost always hear. Dolan began playing the instrument at age 14, though by then he was already well accustomed to the Irish tunes he had heard from his mother, an accordion player from County Mayo. Dolan had also learned that instrument from her and would play it at local sessions. As his experience with the piano increased, he was encouraged by other musicians to accompany them. The piano displaced the accordion in his life, and he soon had a regular gig as the accompanist for two of New York's finest, Paddy Killoran and Frank McCarthy. By the time the 1960s rolled around Dolan was a prominent member of the now-famed New York Ceili Band, in which his piano was the musical cement for fiddlers Andy McGann, Paddy Reynolds, and Larry Redican, as well as Paddy O'Brien's accordion and Jack Coen's flute. He remains an active accompanist and session man, and has played with nearly every great Irish musician to have lived in or passed through New York City in the last century.

what to buy: *Warming Up* ♫♫♫♫ (Green Linnet, 1993, prod. Seamus Connolly, Martin Mulhaire) is a brilliant recording of straightforward Irish traditional instrumentals from accordionist Martin Mulhaire, fiddler Seamus Connolly, and flute player Jack Coen, in the East Galway–East Clare style. The three musicians combine for some inspired solos, duets, and trios, all brilliantly backed by the unequaled piano playing of Dolan. *Give Us Another* ♫♫♫♫ (Green Linnet, 1994, prod. Joe Derrane) was the long-awaited return to recorded Irish music for Boston-based accordionist Joe Derrane. Derrane, responsible for some of the century's most influential tracks of Irish accordion while still a teenager in the '40s and '50s, had virtually disappeared from Irish music altogether. On his triumphant comeback, Derrane's only choice for musical accompaniment was Felix Dolan's brilliantly understated piano playing.

what to buy next: *A Tribute to Michael Coleman* ♫♫♫♫ (Shaskeen, 1966/Green Linnet, 1994, prod. various) was originally recorded in 1965. Featuring button accordionist Joe Burke, fiddler Andy McGann, and Dolan, this homage to arguably the most influential Irish fiddler ever to have lived has become one of the classics of the genre. *Traditional Flute Music in the Sligo-Roscommon Style* ♫♫♫♫ (Cló Iar-Chonnachta, 1996) is a fine recording featuring Dolan accompanying Irish flute player Catherine McEvoy.

worth searching for: The documentary film *From Shore to Shore* (Cherry Lane Productions) gives a magnificent look at the musical context within which Dolan has spent most of his life. Its examination of Irish traditional music in New York City through the use of archival footage and black-and-white photos is simply phenomenal, and it gives a panoramic survey of the legacy's current heirs through appearances by New York–based musicians like Eileen Ivers, Andy McGann, and Jerry O'Sullivan as well as Dolan.

influences:

◄◄ Paddy Killoran, Michael Coleman, Dan Sullivan

►► Brendan Dolan, Donna Long

see also: *Eileen Ivers, James Keane, Andy McGann*

Cliff McGann

Dordan
See Mary Bergin

Connie Dover /Scartaglen
Celtic folk
Born in USA. Based in USA.

Scartaglen was an acoustically oriented American band that performed ballads and instrumentals from Ireland, Scotland, and England, as well as original compositions that were heavily inspired by Anglo-Celtic traditions. They released three albums, all of which are now out of print. During a band hiatus in 1991, Connie Dover traveled to Scotland and recorded her first solo album with a cast of great Scottish and Irish musicians. Since Scartaglen's demise, Dover has continued to develop her solo career. She recorded two more solo albums with Phil Cunningham (formerly of Silly Wizard) producing, and she performs live in a duo with fellow Scartaglen alum Roger Landes, with guest spots on public radio's famed *A Prairie Home Companion* being just one chapter in their emerging success story.

what to buy: Since all three Scartaglen albums are out of print, Dover's and the others' solo efforts will have to do, but they do well. Dover's three recordings—*Somebody* ♫♫♫♫ (Taylor Park Music, 1991, prod. Phil Cunningham), *The Wishing Well* ♫♫♫♫ (Taylor Park Music, 1994, prod. Phil Cunningham), and *If Ever I Return* ♫♫♫♫ (Taylor Park Music, 1997, prod. Phil Cunningham)—are all fairly similar in tone. Cunningham surrounded Dover with a fine cast of sympathetic musicians, including himself on keyboard and pennywhistles, Aly Bain of Boys of the Lough on fiddle, Christy O'Leary on uilleann pipes, and Manus Lunny on guitar, bouzouki, and *bodhrán* (Irish frame drum). Most of the selections are traditional ballads from Scotland or Ireland, with occasional surprises like the lovely French song "La Fontaine" on *If Ever I Return*.

worth searching for: *Scartaglen* ♫♫♫ (Kicking Mule, 1984, prod. Scartaglen), *The Middle Path* ♫♫♫♫ (Castle Island, 1987, prod. Scartaglen), and *Last Night's Fun* ♫♫♫ (City Spark Records, 1992, prod. Tom Mardikes) are all nice recordings and worth searching out. Band members Michael Dugger and Roger Landes have kept busy with *At Early Dawn* ♫♫♫♫ (Lopitha, 1996) and *Dragon Reels* ♫♫♫♫ (Ranger Music, 1997), respectively.

influences:

◄◄ Maddy Prior, Phil Cunningham, Silly Wizard, Planxty, Boys of the Lough, Dwight Yoakam

►► Loreena McKennitt, Dervish, Seelyhoo, Altan

see also: *The Boys of the Lough, Silly Wizard*

Ken Roseman

Mikey Dread

Reggae, dub, deejay

Born Michael Campbell, 1948, in Port Antonio, Jamaica. Based in Kingston, Jamaica.

Combining righteous Rasta messages with love songs and a wry sense of humor, deejay Mikey Dread changed the sound of Jamaican radio and went on to apply his distinctive style to his own recordings. Listening to the island airwaves in the late '70s, you might have heard the goofy dreadlocked deejay also known as Michael Campbell playing heavily mixed versions of roots-rock reggae winners like "Parrot Jungle," "Robbers Roost," and "African Anthem." Toasting over the instrumental mix, Campbell added catchy lines like "You don't steal/you don't gamble/talking 'bout mankind/Michael Campbell." His show featured "cultural" music, that is, home-grown reggae with Rastafarian themes that stood out from the American music then dominating Jamaica's broadcast time. The show was hot, and Campbell soon started recording singles for producer Lee Perry with the same improvised feel. Though Campbell still occasionally releases his own music, he has come full-circle as an impresario of emerging talent with his own label, Dread at the Controls.

what to buy: For a taste of the radio shows that made Campbell famous, check out *African Anthem Dubwise* ⨠⨠⨠⨠ (Dread at the Controls, 1978/Big Cat, 1997, prod. Michael Campbell), a bizarre deejay mix with Campbell chanting over instrumental tracks, which he mutates along with his voice, using heavy reverb. The radio jingles, goofy samples, and boasts have been kept intact, with women attesting "You make me feel so gooooood." *Beyond World War III* ⨠⨠⨠⨠ (Dread at the Controls, 1979/Heartbeat, 1989/Big Cat, 1997) offers one-love Rasta anthems like "Break Down the Walls" interspersed with spoken prophecies like "World War III," in which Campbell's pacifist warnings sound disorientingly like Barry White.

what to buy next: Once you've come through the zany world of Campbell's radio persona, you can explore his love songs on the twofer *S.W.A.L.K./Rockers Vibration* ⨠⨠⨠⨠ (Heartbeat, 1989, prod. Michael Campbell), where the bearded Casanova sings about losing his girl on the title track (which stands for "sealed with a loving kiss"), while *Rockers Vibration* spotlights his production skills on positive songs by Sugar Minott, Michael Israel, and the Ovationz. Campbell's calls to action always sound uplifting and empowering, and *Pave the Way* ⨠⨠⨠⨠ (DEP, 1985/Heartbeat, 1990, prod. Michael Campbell) balances socially conscious commands like the title one with sound advice like "Relax Enjoy Yourself." Lorna Dawkins's sexy jingles typify *Come to Mikey Dread's Dub Party* ⨠⨠⨠ (ROIR, 1995, prod. Michael Campbell), a more light-hearted album than earlier releases, with vocals playfully cut up and mixed among synthe-sizer effects, only slightly compromised by unimaginative drum-machine programming.

what to avoid: *African Anthem Revisited* ⨠⨠ (RAS, 1991, prod. Michael Campbell) is a second-rate dub mix by Jim Fox of the similarly named album above, not to be confused with the excellent original.

influences:

◀◀ Lee "Scratch" Perry, King Tubby, Jah Stitch

▶▶ Bounty Killer

see also: *Sugar Minott, Junior Murvin, Lee "Scratch" Perry*

David Poole

Paquito D'Rivera

Afro-Cuban jazz

Born June 4, 1948, in Havana, Cuba. Based in USA.

If there is a singular musician carrying on the legacy of Dizzy Gillespie's pioneering mid-'40s melding of Afro-Cuban rhythms and jazz, it is bandleader and reeds player Paquito D'Rivera. In Cuba, he was influenced by his father, a classical saxophonist who introduced his son to the recordings of Charlie Parker. Inspired at a young age by the music of American jazz musicians Parker, John Coltrane, and Lee Konitz, D'Rivera later added rhythms from his native Cuba and blended them into bopped-up, romantic, salty, sensuous sounds. The young prodigy entered the Havana Conservatory in 1960 to pursue classical studies and by his mid-teens was playing professionally. D'Rivera joined the Orquesta Cubana de Música Moderna in 1967, and with some of its members formed Irakere, an 11-piece band that played a sizzling mixture of jazz, rock, classical, and traditional Cuban music. Irakere performed in the U.S. at the 1978 Newport Jazz Festival as well as others worldwide, causing a sensation that resulted in a historic March 1979 concert in Cuba that featured an array of American pop artists performing alongside the island's best musicians. The event was documented on two albums, *Havana Jam* and *Havana Jam II*. More albums with Irakere followed in 1979 and 1980. While on tour in Spain with them in 1980, D'Rivera defected. He eventually settled in New York and within three years was playing in the most prestigious clubs and concert halls and touring Europe with Dizzy Gillespie himself. Throughout the 1980s he continued performing, recording, and touring globally with his own groups; his first albums as leader, *Paquito Blowin'* in 1981 and *Mariel* in 1982, solidified his reputation in the United States. As well as recording as a sideman with McCoy Tyner, Hendrik Meurkens, Claudio Roditi, Arturo Sandoval, Bobby Sanabria, Richie Cole, the Caribbean Jazz Project, and many others, he has chalked up a significant number of richly diverse albums as a leader for Columbia, Chesky, Messidor, Candid, and TropiJazz. D'Rivera's broad-based performances and recordings continue to brilliantly straddle the fence between his native Cuban rhythms and modern American music. After performing regularly in Gillespie's United Nation Orchestra (UNO), founded in 1988, D'Rivera took over the band's leadership upon its originator's death in 1993. D'Rivera has also made several recordings with his Havana–New York Music Ensemble, of which Danilo Perez (another UNO member) is pianist/musical director.

what to buy: *Paquito D'Rivera Presents: Forty Years of Cuban Jam Session* 𝄢𝄢𝄢𝄢 (Messidor, 1993, prod. Götz A. Wörner, Paquito D'Rivera, Brenda Feliciano), a gathering of 23 Cuban players from all over the world, developed from a party to honor two veteran Cuban-jazz reed players, Gustavo Mas and José "Chambo" Silva. Not only do you get a broad sampling of Cuban rhythms and melodies, but the liner booklet contains a brief history of the origin of American jazz and its impact on Cuban rhythms. This 11-selection Cuban *descarga* (jam session), recorded in Miami in February 1993, features leader D'Rivera playing clarinet and alto saxophone on six tunes, accompanied by a flexible rhythm section that includes Horacio Hernández and Rogelio Rivero (drums, timbales), and Rigo Herrera and Victor Valdés (percussion). Among many fine soloists is trombonist Leopoldo "Pucho" Escalante, who shines on "Despojo (Exorcism)," a powerful Yoruba-inspired percussive number performed with the full ensemble. This is a wonderfully loose and captivating album that loyally retains a musical tradition. D'Rivera and trumpeter Arturo Sandoval, former members of the groundbreaking Orquesta Cubana de Música Moderna and the innovative Irakere, mix it up with exciting side players on *Reunion* 𝄢𝄢𝄢𝄢 (Messidor, 1991, prod. Götz A. Wörner, Uwe Feltens). Fluent in Afro-Caribbean rhythms, bassist David Finck, guitarist Fareed Haque, percussionist Giovanni Hidalgo, pianist Danilo Perez, and drummer Mark Walker add panache to this nine-tune session. D'Rivera soars, Sandoval singes. It's a scorching session all the way, featuring Mario Bauza's classic Cubop number "Tanga" as well as tunes by Chucho Valdes (leader of Irakere) and members of this group. Haque contributes two parts (and solos elegantly) on a sweet, three-part Latin-American suite that also highlights D'Rivera's fluid clarinet mastery. *A Night in Englewood* 𝄢𝄢𝄢𝄢 (Messidor, 1993, prod. Götz A. Wörner, Paquito D'Rivera, Brenda Feliciano) finds D'Rivera at the helm of the UNO on an excellent session featuring his strong arrangements of nine Afro-Cuban jazz selections. Some of the best soloists in the business are spotlighted, and ensemble playing is topnotch, tight, and gorgeously textured. Guest artists on this fiery tribute to Dizzy Gillespie include Claudio Roditi (trumpet), Slide Hampton (trombone), Dave Samuels (marimba, vibraphone), and Raul Jaurena (bandoneón). Filling Gillespie's shoes is not an easy task, yet on this disc, under

D'Rivera's leadership, the band carries on the Afro-Cuban jazz tradition with matchless vitality and inventiveness. D'Rivera's clarinet artistry predominates on *Tico! Tico!* 𝄢𝄢𝄢𝄢 (Chesky, 1989, prod. David Chesky, Paquito D'Rivera), a session with his Havana–New York Music Ensemble that often expands the traditional Cuban rhythms and themes with modern thrusts. D'Rivera's clarinet playing is gorgeously romantic, and his alto and tenor sax improvs allow him to occasionally erupt into the fiery explosiveness for which he's noted. Latin-jazz pros Danilo Perez (piano), David Finck and Nilson Matta (both bass), Portinho (drums), and others assist in various small group settings. D'Rivera's excellent reading of the title tune, made famous by Carmen Miranda in the 1940s, stands out but isn't the only highlight among 12 originals by Leo Brouwer, D'Rivera, Perez, and other composers. There are many peak moments. Percussively flavored throughout, *Havana Café* 𝄢𝄢𝄢𝄢 (Chesky, 1992, prod. David Chesky, Paquito D'Rivera) is a jaunty, modern meld of Afro-Cuban rhythms and jazz improvisations built in 10 tunes mostly by band members. Former Dizzy Gillespie associates Ed Cherry (guitar) and Danilo Perez (piano) enhance this magnificent 1991 studio session with the Havana–New York Music Ensemble. Featuring bassist David Finck, guitarist Fareed Haque, drummer Jorge Rossy, and percussionist Sammy Figueroa, it remains one of D'Rivera's freshest sounding, most vigorous CDs, with everyone adding fiery flair to cohesive, edgy proceedings that lean more toward the modern than the traditional.

what to buy next: After two Heads Up recordings with the Caribbean Jazz Project, D'Rivera makes his solo debut for the label with *100 Years of Latin Love Songs* 𝄢𝄢𝄢𝄢 (Heads Up, 1998, prod. Bob Belden), a collection of 10 sweet songs of Latin American origin featuring the leader at his melodious, mellow best, playing clarinet and saxophones often accompanied by strings. The enhanced CD includes historical background on each song, a video of D'Rivera's recording sessions, and a "tour" revealing fascinating facts about each Latin American nation represented in the music. Along with the educational and entertaining CD-ROM aspects, this is an elegant, must-own session designed for laid-back listening, for slow dancing to south-of-the-border rhythms, or as music to enhance romancin'. A jazz tribute to the Cuban tradition, *Portraits of Cuba* 𝄢𝄢𝄢𝄢 (Chesky, 1996, prod. David Chesky, Carlos Franzetti) features D'Rivera collaborating with arranger Carlos Franzetti, who conducts a 14-member orchestra enhanced by guest soloists. Rivera shines in the spotlight playing clarinet and soprano and alto saxophones. Franzetti's familiarity with D'Rivera's stylings empowers him to create elaborate, dense, Gershwin-like charts full of excitement, dreamy colors, and the beauty and passion of Cuba. *A Taste of Paquito D'Rivera* 𝄢𝄢𝄢𝄢 (Columbia, 1981–86/Legacy, 1994, prod. various) is a 12-tune compilation from D'Rivera's Columbia albums after he settled in the United States, featuring tracks that demonstrate his fluent, fervid expressions on both alto saxophone and clarinet. In a mix of standards and originals, he is assisted by a who's-who of Afro-Cuban jazz, including bassist Eddie Gomez, drummer Ignacio Berroa, trumpeter Claudio Roditi, pianist Hilton Ruiz, and other specialists who play with flawless ardor. The modern orchestral version of Gillespie's "Manteca" features D'Rivera playing both alto sax and clarinet and also spotlights Claudio Roditi (trumpet) and Michel Camilo (piano). *The Caribbean Jazz Project* ✍✍✍✍ (Heads Up, 1995, prod. Caribbean Jazz Project) showcases a collaborative unit led by Dave Samuels, D'Rivera, and Andy Narell, all veteran jazz players/composers. An invigorating session of 11 originals by the co-leaders, this album features a range of music from modern contemporary jazz with Caribbean beats to a seductive, traditional *bolero*. D'Rivera (clarinet, alto saxophone), Samuels (vibraphone/marimba), and Narell (steel pans) add spicy Caribbean flavor to their jazz, energized by a solid rhythm section and creative percussionists.

what to avoid: If you're not a huge jazz fan and desire more authentic Cuban rhythms, avoid *Paquito D'Rivera & the United Nation Orchestra Live at Manchester Craftsmen's Guild* ✍✍✍ (Blue Jackel, 1997, prod. Marty Ashby, Jay Ashby). This 10-tune disc features mostly unknowns, captured at a live February 14, 1997, performance. Unfortunately, it lacks the sparking energy of the UNO *Englewood* date.

the rest:
Manhattan Burn ✍✍✍✍ (Columbia, 1987)
La Habana-Rio Conexion ✍✍✍✍ (Rounder, 1992)
(With Bebo and Chucho Valdes) *Cuba Jazz* ✍✍✍✍ (TropiJazz, 1996)
(With Caribbean Jazz Project) *Island Stories* ✍✍✍✍ (Heads Up, 1996)

worth searching for: To hear how well D'Rivera works with a singer/pianist in a small group setting, seek out *Come on Home* ✍✍✍✍✍ (Columbia, 1995, prod. Frank Zuback), a robust nine-tune CD by pianist Valerie Capers and her trio. D'Rivera guests on four tracks of this pleasing album, weaving his alto sax lines around Capers's piano melodies or her vocals, and adding particular passion to her torchy love ballad "Out of All (He's Chosen Me)." He also joins leader-pianist Bebo Valdes on *Bebo Rides Again* ✍✍✍✍ (Messidor, 1995, prod. Paquito D'Rivera), a tribute to the many other talented musicians who have fled Cuba. Valdes was an important figure in Cuban music before his own flight in 1960, and this November 1994 German studio session was his first recording in 34 years. The 11 tunes—mostly varied, danceable Cuban originals by Valdes—are performed by 10 musicians who deliver a unified, bubbling Cuban-jazz session, with stand-out solos from D'Rivera, trumpeter Diego Urcola, *conguero* Patato, and guitarist Carlos Emilio Morales. Bebo was 76 when this session was recorded and his piano technique remains vibrant (one can hear where

his son, pianist Chucho Valdes, got his chops). An exciting sampler containing "the finest contemporary Latin music" (no lie!), *United Rhythms of Messidor* ✍✍✍✍ (Messidor, 1994, prod. various) features 13 tracks, compiled by Michael Barth, from albums by the label's top performers in Latin jazz: D'Rivera, the late band leader Mario Bauzá, flutist/soprano saxist Jane Bunnett, the late bandoneón player Astor Piazzolla, jazz pianists Gonzalo Rubalcaba and Jesus "Chucho" Valdes, percussionist Giovanni Hidalgo, and more. There's no question about the caliber and authenticity of the Latin beats from these musicians. D'Rivera performs on "Tanga," "Blues for Astor," and "Despojo." If you're into Latin jazz, you've probably heard some of the tunes before or already own the albums; if not, then this enjoyable CD, covering a broad cross-section of Latin styles, serves as a fine entree.

influences:
◀◀ Mario Bauzá, Bebo Valdes, Chico O'Farrill, Benny Goodman, Charlie Parker, Dizzy Gillespie, John Coltrane, Lee Konitz

see also: *Mario Bauzá, Jane Bunnett, Cachao, Irakere, Patato, Astor Piazzolla, Tito Puente, Arturo Sandoval, Bebo Valdes, Chucho Valdes*

Nancy Ann Lee

The Drummers of Burundi

East African drumming
Formed in Burundi. Based in Burundi.

Baranshakaje Antime, percussion; Ntirandekura Côme, percussion; Mpfayokurera Joachin, percussion; Nkunzimana Nazaire, percussion; Mbazumutima Adelin, percussion; Bacanamwo Joseph, percussion; Ncurira Laurent, percussion; Sindaharaye Dinatien, percussion; Masabarakiza Joseph, percussion; Mpitabavuma Juvénal, percussion; Nahimana Placide, percussion; Congera Alchedes, percussion; Ndayarinze Aquilin, percussion; Cimpaye Déogratias, percussion; Ntakarutimana Benoît, percussion; Mboninyeretse Diminique, percussion; Habonimana Marc, percussion; Mpitabakana Vital, percussion; Nyambikiye Pasteur, percussion; Mpitabakana Marc, percussion. (All members are from Burundi.)

The Drummers of Burundi are not so much a contemporary band as an ongoing national institution, which has been performing in Burundi for centuries and around the world since the 1960s. In Burundi, drums are much more than mere musical instruments; they're viewed as sacred objects and were once reserved solely for ceremonial use, such as proclaiming important events and celebrating the planting or harvesting of the crops. Perhaps through these close ties with the country's primary industry, agriculture, the drums have acquired a symbolic association with fertility—the skin is equated with a baby's cradle, the tuning pegs with the mother's breast, the body of the

Drummers of Burundi

drum to the womb. But although the origins of Burundi's musical traditions remain shrouded in mystery, the Drummers' awe-inspiring live performances today carry less ritualistic significance and are seen more as an exuberantly expressive form of entertainment. In the '80s the "Burundi Beat" was co-opted by a number of Western musicians, most prominently Adam Ant, so it seemed appropriate when Peter Gabriel signed the Drummers of Burundi to his RealWorld label in 1992. These days, the Drummers are rivaled only by Japan's Kodo as the world's most powerful and invigorating live performers.

what's available: The Drummers of Burundi are first and foremost an in-person experience; with jerky movements, fantastic leaps, and war-like stomping, their performances are as much showcases for acrobatic agility as forums for exhilarating music. But their only Western release, *Les Tambourinaires Du Burundi* ♪♪♪♪ (1992, RealWorld, prod. Yorrick Benoist), is a fine document of the audio portion, capturing 30 uninterrupted minutes of sound and fury. Made up of 41 traditional rhythms augmented only by ecstatic shouts of enthusiasm, this extremely intense recording is unlikely to be fully appreciated by

anyone unimpressed by the visceral power of thunderous drumming. Percussion fans, however, will find the trance-like rhythmic syncopation invigorating.

influences:
▶▶ Adam Ant, Bow Wow Wow, Mickey Hart

Bret Love

Lucky Dube
African reggae
Born 1967, in Ermelo, Eastern Transvaal, South Africa. Based in South Africa.

Lucky Dube is one of South Africa's most successful artists. With a multi-octave voice and a high-spirited dancing style inspired by the Zulu culture, Dube has adopted the reggae of Jamaica for songs that lash out against political and social oppression and celebrate spiritual inspiration.

Born to an unwed mother in Ermelo, a small village near Johannesburg, Dube was raised by a grandmother, an aunt, and an

Lucky Dube

uncle. His talents for music were obvious from an early age, and by the time he reached his ninth birthday Dube was singing regularly in church, school, and bars. After forming a high-school rock band, Sky Way, Dube raised money to buy instruments by writing and performing a stage play. Though the group enjoyed a regional hit, "Zulu Soul," they soon disbanded. Dube's first break came when he joined the Love Brothers, a *mbaqanga* (South African traditional/rock township music) band in which he met his future manager and producer, Richard Siluma. When this band broke up too, Dube began performing as a soloist, with a debut album, *Lengane Ngeyetha,* released in 1983.

In time Dube switched from the mbaqanga music of his homeland to a Bob Marley– and Peter Tosh–influenced reggae. Although he played most of the instruments on his early albums, Dube formed a band, the Slaves, featuring nine musicians and three singers, shortly after releasing a rap single, "Help My Krap," in 1986. The following year, Dube's album *Think about the Children* became the first South African reggae recording to be certified gold. His next album, *Slave,* sold more than 300,000 copies in 1989. A year later, Dube's album *Prisoner* achieved double platinum status. After having toured Europe and the U.S. in 1989, Dube performed in Australia and Japan as the opening act for Peter Gabriel in '91, and in '92 became the first South African to play the definitive Reggae Sunsplash Festival in Jamaica. Dube was featured in a semi-biographical film, *Getting Lucky,* in 1984, and at this rate his life and career will provide ample material for a sequel.

what to buy: In addition to Dube's greatest hits, *Serious Reggae* ♪♪♪♪ (Shanachie, 1996, prod. Richard Siluma) includes alternate takes and new tunes, including a reggae-ized treatment of Foreigner's mid-'80s pop hit, "I Want to Know What Love Is"(!).

what to buy next: *Taxman* ♪♪♪♪ (Shanachie, 1997, prod. Richard Siluma) showcases Dube at his most romantic. While the hard reggae sounds of his earlier albums are softened by the addition of a pianist and female chorus, Dube's soulful vocals remain effective.

the rest:
Slave ♪♪♪ (Shanachie, 1989)
Prisoner ♪♪♪ (Shanachie, 1990)
Captured Live ♪♪♪ (Shanachie, 1991)
House of Exile ♪♪♪ (Shanachie, 1992)
Victims ♪♪♪ (Shanachie, 1993)
Serious Reggae Business ♪♪♪ (Shanachie, 1996)
Trinity ♪♪♪ (Polydor, 1996)

influences:
◀◀ Bob Marley, Peter Tosh

▶▶ Burning Spear, Third World

Craig Harris

The Dubliners
Modern and traditional Irish folk
Formed 1962, in Dublin, Ireland. Based in Ireland.

Ronnie Drew, vocals, guitar (1962–74; 1979–96); Luke Kelly (died 1984), vocals, guitar, banjo; Barney McKenna, tenor banjo, mandolin, vocals; Ciaran Bourke, vocals, guitar, tin whistle (1962–74); John Sheahan, fiddle, tin whistle, concertina (mid-1960s–present); Eamonn Campbell, guitars, mandolin, vocals (late 1980s–present); Sean Cannon, vocals, guitar (1984–present); Jim McCann, vocals, guitar (1974–79); Bobby Lynch, vocals, guitar (mid-1960s); Paddy Reilly, vocals, guitar (1996–present). (All members are from Ireland.)

In the history of Irish music, no group has created and maintained its niche as effectively as the Dubliners. At the beginning of "the ballad boom," that heady time during the early '60s when the Clancy Brothers made "folk songs" a meaningful category that ordinary people could relate to and take pride in, the Dubliners began their own career. While the Clancys were well-scrubbed returned Yanks from rural Tipperary, decked out in matching white Aran sweaters, the Dubliners were hard-drinking backstreet Dublin scrappers with unkempt hair and bushy beards, whose gigs seemed to happen by accident in between fist fights. But their street credibility, their undeniable talent, and their honest love of the music has kept them going and made them some of the most famous Irishmen in the world.

The Dubliners started in 1962 as the Ronnie Drew Group. Drew had recently returned to Ireland from Spain, where he had been teaching English and learning to play the guitar. He brought this new musical talent to bear on the Irish song tradition, and gathered around himself a core of terrific entertainers and musicians. Barney McKenna, a great tenor banjo picker, provided instrumental firepower. All-around showman Ciaran Bourke added second guitar, sweet creaky vocals, and tin whistle. And Luke Kelly, an intense singer and five-string banjo player who had served his time on the English folk club scene, was the band's most impressive vocalist. Kelly suggested the band's name be changed to the Dubliners. After a single Dubliners album for the Transatlantic label, Kelly departed for England. He was replaced by Bobby Lynch, who also brought along his musical partner, fiddler John Sheahan. When Kelly returned to replace Lynch in 1966, Sheahan stayed on as the group's most impressive traditional instrumentalist. This five-piece lineup of Drew, Kelly, Bourke, McKenna, and Sheahan became famous in 1967 through a song called "Seven Drunken Nights," originally recorded for an album called *A Drop of the Hard Stuff,* which was later re-titled *The New Dubliners,* and later still re-christened *Seven Drunken Nights* (it first appeared on the Major Minor label). "Seven Drunken Nights" was released as a single, but when the official media banned it for bawdiness it looked ready to languish in obscurity for good. Luckily for the Dubliners, it was picked up by the pirate station Radio Caroline and given saturation airplay, shooting to #5 on the British pop charts, launching the Dubliners to stardom, and making them a household word across Ireland, Britain, and the world.

The *Seven Drunken Nights* lineup lasted eight years, and despite always being on the verge of breaking up (Drew, Kelly, and McKenna fell out every other night or so), it was only severed by a major tragedy: in 1974, Bourke suffered a brain hemorrhage on stage that left him unable to perform. Bourke's condition, and a doctor's warning, caused Drew to examine his lifestyle and decide to leave the Dubliners as well. Drew was replaced by Jim McCann, and the band continued to perform all over the world. Drew did eventually return to the group (in 1979), and all went smoothly until tragedy struck again in 1984. Luke Kelly, whose soaring vocals defined the Dubliners' sound as surely as anything, died that year of a brain tumor. He was replaced by Galway singer Sean Cannon, who had been filling in off and on during Kelly's illness. A few years later, Eamonn Campbell signed on, playing guitars and mandolin. In 1987, this lineup of the Dubliners teamed with the Pogues to record "The Irish Rover," which became their biggest hit ever and introduced them to a whole new generation.

The latest change in the Dubliners was the departure (once again) of Ronnie Drew, in 1996. He was replaced by the great entertainer Paddy Reilly. One thing to take note of regarding this important band: the Dubliners have made many studio albums and many live albums, and have repeated the same "greatest hits" with some frequency in their recordings. Because of international licensing arrangements, many of their albums have been released more than once, by different labels, under different titles, and bearing different covers. In addition, an enormous number of Dubliners compilation albums have appeared, drawing on most of the original material. The result is that, especially where CD reissues are concerned, there are a lot of different albums with a relatively narrow selection of songs, and it's often difficult to tell the origin of any given track. Always compare any Dubliners album you contemplate buying with ones that are already in your collection, or you will quite likely wind up taking home the same songs over and over.

what to buy: *Original Dubliners, 1966–1969* 𝄞𝄞𝄞𝄞 (EMI, 1993) captures the excitement of the best-known Dubliners lineup. It collects four albums from the Dubliners' early days onto two CDs. Typically, the four original LPs were released at various times with various titles, but their best-known monikers were *Seven Drunken Nights, Seven Deadly Sins, More of the Hard Stuff,* and *Whiskey on a Sunday.* It should be said that, contrary to what the sleeve notes claim, these were not the first albums the Dubliners recorded, but it was these albums that established the Dubliners as an enduring presence and not a one-hit

wonder. The EMI set includes memorable and influential interpretations of many great songs, including Kelly's renditions of traditionals like "Whiskey in the Jar," "The Rising of the Moon," "Black Velvet Band," "Poor Paddy on the Railway," "A Nation Once Again," and "Gentleman Soldier." Kelly also sings three songs by his friend and mentor Ewan MacColl, "The Traveling People," "Shoals of Herring," and "Net Hauling Song," as well as many Scottish songs that he picked up during his years in Britain. For his part, Drew contributes some of the racier, bawdier, boozier material: "Seven Drunken Nights," "Poor Old Dicey Riley," "Quare Bungle Rye," "Whiskey on a Sunday," "The Parting Glass," and "A Pub with No Beer" are all supplied by him. Bourke sings a few as well, though his voice was weaker and creakier than those of his bandmates. "Darby O'Leary," "All for Me Grog," "Drink It Up, Men," "Mrs. McGrath" (a parody of the traditional song, based on his own life), and "The Limerick Rake" are all sung by Bourke. Many sets of instrumentals, including a memorable version of "O'Carolan's Concerto," are led by McKenna and/or Sheahan. All of these are classic tracks that would irrevocably change the way the world saw Irish music. In the collection of any lover of the genre, there will always be room for these albums—albums that in many ways started it all.

what to buy next: The Dubliners' 1992 anniversary double CD, *30 Years a-Greying* 𝄞𝄞𝄞𝄞 (RTE, 1992, prod. Eamonn Campbell, Phil Coulter), features the then-current lineup of Drew, McKenna, Sheahan, Cannon, and Campbell, along with guest musicians ranging from Rory Gallagher to the Hothouse Flowers. Even the famous Scottish comedian Billy Connolly, who got his start as a banjo-wielding folkie, does a lead vocal on the album, singing his own ironic and effective song "I'm Asking You Sergeant, Where's Mine?" A similar release from 1987, *Celebration* 𝄞𝄞𝄞 (Baycourt, 1987, prod. Eamonn Campbell), teams the Dubliners up with the Pogues, Paddy Reilly, Christy Moore, and others. It contains the hit single "The Irish Rovers" by the Dubliners and the Pogues. One of the best LPs from the Jim McCann years, *A Parcel of Rogues* 𝄞𝄞𝄞 (ARC, 1976, prod. Earl Gill), is available on CD. It's quite short but features some beautiful songs, including McCann's rendition of "Kellyburn Brae," a humorous (if misogynistic) ballad. Luke Kelly brings in a lot of his Scottish-influenced folk-club material and shows his debt to Ewan MacColl on the title track. One curious note: although most sources suggest that Ciaran Bourke did not perform on this album, he is pictured on the front cover. Since the CD reissue contains no list of the musicians or notes of any kind, the question is open to interpretation. If you want to hear a good live Dubliners show, *Live in Carre, Amsterdam* 𝄞𝄞𝄞 (Spectrum, 1985, prod. Reinoud Weidema, Rob Smaling, Tom Steenbergen) captures a lovely concert during Luke Kelly's final tours with the group. An unusual touch is that this disc features both Kelly and Sean Cannon, who filled in for Kelly during his illnesses and replaced him permanently after he died. Some of the nicest songs on this disc, like "The Waterford Boys," come from Cannon. Kelly, while his fatigue and illness are perceptible, still sings strongly and communicates beautifully with the audience. Castle Communications recently released a compilation made from Transatlantic's early Dubliners material (these *were* the Dubliners' very first albums) entitled *The Definitive Transatlantic Collection* ♪♪♪ (Castle, 1997, prod. Nathan Joseph). The tracks, most of which were recorded live, sound a little tentative compared to the EMI recordings, but they're very much worth having. Many of the songs did not appear on the band's later EMI outings or their live LPs, so this is some of the more unusual material out there. For the self-respecting fanatic, a compilation called *Complete Dubliners* ♪♪♪♪ (Earache, 1997, prod. Nathan Joseph) collects their *entire* Transatlantic output onto two CDs.

what to avoid: Two budget-priced CDs are available from K-Tel Records, *The Dubliners* ♪♪ (K-Tel, 1996) and *The Best of the Dubliners* ♪♪ (K-Tel, 1996). These are decent collections, but you get what you pay for; they're so short that both together would have fit on a single CD.

influences:

◀◀ The Clancy Brothers and Tommy Makem, Ewan MacColl

▶▶ The Johnstons, Planxty, the Pogues, Christy Moore

Steve Winick

The Dynatones
/The Dyna-Tones

Polka

Formed 1968, in Buffalo, NY, USA. Based in Buffalo, NY, USA.

Key members have included: Dave "Scrubby" Seweryniak (1968–present) vocals, concertina, accordion; Larry Trojak (1968–82, 1986–89) vocals, drums; Mark Trzepacz (1980–81, 1990–present), vocals, trumpet, cornet, keyboards. (All members are from USA.)

"The Dynatones" is a pretty popular name for a band. As this book goes to press, a blues-based group, a wedding band, and a polka ensemble all play proudly under the same banner, with not a copyright lawsuit in sight. The Buffalo, New York–based Dynatones of this entry came together while drummer/founder Larry Trojak was still a student in high school. The original members knew each other from playing in various wedding groups and formed an ensemble known as the Casinos specifically to play polkas instead of the usual nuptial material. Back then, though, they *did* have to change their name because of another, more established "Casinos." Taking inspiration from a then-defunct polka group that used to record on Lil' Wally

Jagiello's Jay-Jay Records and that was in less of a position to raise a fuss, they rechristened themselves the Dyna-Tones (losing the hyphen somewhat later) and released *Larry Trojak's Dyna-Tones* on Eddie Blazonczyk's Bel-Aire Records.

The other main member of the band, concertina player Dave "Scrubby" Seweryniak, joined just before their first gig and quickly became the focus for the manic synergy that evolved between the Dyna-Tones and their audience. While Blazonczyk was Trojak's hero and the band tried to copy the classy professionalism of Blazonczyk's Versatones, Scrubby's admiration for Lil' Wally's controlled abandon added an edge to the Dyna-Tones that helped differentiate them from the rest of the competition. Scrubby's line of patter and raucous antics on stage have attained legendary status, and he is the only member of the band to be elected to the I.P.A. (International Polka Association) Hall of Fame.

Under the dual leadership of Trojak and Seweryniak, the Dyna-Tones became one of the hottest young acts on the polka circuit. They also became known for their willingness to expand the boundaries of the form, much as Blazonczyk had before them. Concept albums were all the rage in pop music during the late 1970s, and Trojak decided to write something similar. The result was *Chapter VII,* an album that took the life of Christ and gave it a polka spin. While he has since been praised for his groundbreaking efforts, Trojak was later told by an official of the album's label that it was perhaps the worst-selling LP they'd ever released.

Nonetheless the Dyna-Tones' overall popularity remained high, but despite this they were still a part-time band, with most of the members having to hold down day jobs. Trojak wanted to make the group a full-time affair but didn't feel he was receiving the necessary commitment from the rest of the band, and, in 1982, left the group he had founded. A tumultuous series of lineup permutations, departures, and rejoinings settled down into the unhyphenated band's current incarnation, led by Mark Trzepacz. In their post-Trojak era, the Dynatones are a straight-ahead polka band, delving less into the kind of experimentation that characterized earlier editions of the group. This version of the band still includes Scrubby as the prime focus for audiences, but their more mainstream approach to the genre has led to a Grammy nomination (for *When the Band Plays a Polka* in 1991) and increased bookings. Trojak is now living in a suburb of Minneapolis, Minnesota, where he has a business doing public relations writing for industrial accounts.

what to buy: Most of the early Dyna-Tones albums are only available on tape or vinyl, which makes *Vintage Dynatones* ♪♪♪♪ (World Renowned Sounds, 1995, compilation prod. Ron Schafer) such an important release. Its 23 cuts include material from *Live Wire, Down at the Friendly Tavern,* and others—practically every noteworthy early project but Larry Trojak's religious magnum opus *Chapter VII.* Charles Keil, in his book *Polka Happiness,* called *Live Wire* 𝄢𝄢𝄢𝄢 (World Renowned Sounds, 1982, prod. the Dyna-Tones) "the polka equivalent of B.B. King's *Live at the Regal.*" This album, available only on cassette and vinyl, captures the Dyna-Tones in concert playing some of their most popular (and requested) songs, including "Zosia Polka," "Life of a Drunk Polka," and the "Kuku Oberek." It was also named Album of the Year in 1982 by the I.P.A., and remains Dynatones fans' all-time favorite.

what to buy next: Undoubtedly the most unique recording in the Dynatones catalog, and Larry Trojak's most ambitious experiment, is *Chapter VII* 𝄢𝄢𝄢𝄡 (World Renowned Sounds, 1980, prod. the Dyna-Tones), the polka concept album about the life of Christ. A spoken prologue and epilogue bracket lyrics about Jesus' birth, crucifixion, and resurrection with side trips for "John the Baptist" and "The Last Supper." While the polka mass is now a standard feature at polka festivals, this album rarely got the airplay its surprisingly lively tunesmithing deserved. *Where's Your Portki?/Where's Your Pants?* 𝄢𝄢𝄢𝄢 (Ethnic World Records, 1998, prod. the Dynatones) features one of the best lineups the group has had in a while, with Scrubby and Trzepacz alternating on lead vocals. The title tune was a big hit on polka radio shows around the country, but the band's new version of "Scrubby's Polka," though solid, is lacking the drive of the classic rendition heard on *Vintage Dynatones.*

best of the rest:

Six Million Dollar Band 𝄢𝄢𝄢𝄢 (World Renowned Sounds cassette, 1975)
Down at the Friendly Tavern 𝄢𝄢𝄢𝄢 (World Renowned Sounds cassette, 1976)
When the Band Plays a Polka 𝄢𝄢𝄢𝄢 (World Renowned Sounds cassette, 1990)
25th Anniversary Tour 𝄢𝄢𝄢𝄡 (Sunshine, 1993)

worth searching for: The Dynatones act as accompanists on *Ania Meets the Dynatones* 𝄢𝄢𝄢𝄡 (Sunshine, 1995, prod. Ania Piwowarczyk, Mark Trzepacz), which pairs them with Ania Piwowarczyk, a vocalist/composer from Hamilton, Ontario, Canada. On *Live at Holy Toledo Polka Days '97* 𝄢𝄢𝄢𝄢 (Sunshine, 1997, prod. Joe Zalewski), Scrubby plays concertina on three tunes, and he and Trzepacz appear as guest vocalists with Toledo Polkamotion. Although not as ecstatic a live date as the Dyna-Tone's *Live Wire,* this album is a lot of fun and perhaps the best 1990s example of a polka show in full swing. Scrubby's on-stage banter before "Raz Dwa Trzy" is a stone gas, and totally reflective of how this charismatic frontman can corral a concert audience.

influences:

◄◄ Eddie Blazonczyk, Ray Budzilek, L'il Wally Jagiello, Marion Lush

►► Brave Combo, City Side, Toledo Polkamotion

see also: *Edward "Eddie" Blazonczyk*

Garaud MacTaggart

Eastern Eagle Singers

Powwow

Formed in Nova Scotia, Canada. Based in Nova Scotia, Canada.

Brian Knockwood, drum, vocals; **Ivan Knockwood,** drum, vocals; **Gary Knockwood,** drum, vocals; **Colin McDonald,** drum, vocals; **Mark McDonald,** drum, vocals; **Jason McDonald,** drum, vocals; **Billy Joe Meuse,** drum, vocals; **David Meuse,** drum, vocals; **Mike Sack,** drum, vocals; **Nathan Sack,** drum, vocals; **Sam Greer,** drum, vocals; **Simon Nevis,** drum, vocals; **Darren Myo,** drum, vocals; **Scott Taylor,** drum, vocals; **Jonathan Marshall,** drum, vocals. (All members are from Canada.)

Founded by Brian Knockwood, the Eastern Eagle Singers are one of the youngest drum groups on the powwow trail. Some of the older singers criticize them for playing what traditionalists call "rock 'n' roll powwow music"—that is, incorporating modern elements into traditional Indian singing and drumming. The Eastern Eagle Singers do sound modern and somewhat "less Indian" than their predecessors, and write some tunes with a verse/chorus structure that makes them more accessible to mainstream ears than the oldtimers, but non-Natives won't confuse them with the latest alt.rock rave.

what's available: *Traditionally Yours* 𝄢𝄢𝄢𝄢 (SOAR, 1996, prod. Douglas Spotted Eagle) offers powerful drumming and singing, most of it with a Western verse/chorus structure that makes this a good beginner's album for non-Natives who want to understand powwow music.

influences:

◄◄ Grayhorse Singers, Assiniboine Jr., Black Lodge Singers

j. poet

Echoes of Incas

Andean folk, Latin American, worldbeat

Formed in Los Angeles, CA, USA. Based in Los Angeles, CA, USA, and in Mexico.

Cesar Regino, bombo, shakers, percussion; **Rigoberto Delgado Castillo,** zamponas, quenas, quenachos, mosenos, ronrroco, charango; José Delgado Castillo, chango, ronrroco, ocarinas, percussion; Alejandro Mora, electric bass; Emmanuel Mora, acoustic guitar; Eduardo Avila Costa, acoustic guitar; Arturo Garcia Orozco, guitar, flute, samponas, percussion; Gilberto Reyes, Peruvian box; Gregorio Bobadilla, quena, samponas; Kambiz Pakandam, guitar; Long John Oliva, congas, bongos; Cesar Hernandez, electric bass, sonajas; Konrad Rhee, guitar, charango, flute; Roberto E. Duenas, flute, samponas, charango; Luis Felipe Gonzales, acoustic and electric bass.

Echoes of Incas is a general banner that unites a rotating honor roll of some of Latin America's best players, with only a few of the above-listed members playing on more than one release. Rather than creating a weakness, the band's shifting roster of members hailing from Mexico, El Salvador, Peru, Venezuela, and Cuba—not to mention Iran and the USA—makes for a complex and heady blend of influences that uniquely flavors the outfit's primary Andean folkloric focus. Formed in the early 1990s in Southern California to play festivals, fairs, and university gigs, the band also shares members with a similar performing group, Ah-Kin.

what to buy: Peruvian flute-and-percussion albums have been solid sellers at museum shops, nature stores, and record chains for many years, but often the music is amateurishly produced, uses low-quality instruments, and features strident, discordant blasts of sound unfriendly to the untrained ear. Not so on *Sacred Valley* ♪♪♪♪ (EarthTone, 1996, prod. Arturo G. Orozco), in which Echoes of Incas present compelling ritual dances drawn from traditional Andean spiritual practices. Focusing on the traditional bamboo pan flutes commonly called *sikus*, the multi-tempoed tunes are thematically linked to the natural world by use of environmental sounds. Supporting arrangements for Latin ethnic guitars and percussion add color, rich textures, and uplifting beats. With foot-tapping appeal, the whirling rhythms and enthusiastic melody lines beckon one to join in the celebration.

what to buy next: Nothing revitalizes a group more than recording a new album after a lengthy tour; it's as if the energy of the audience has been magically transferred to the musicians, and then on to tape for all to enjoy. *Andean Nights* ♪♪♪♪ (EarthTone, 1998, prod. Cesar Regino) features electrifying performances on a variety of pan flutes, Latin guitars, and ethnic percussion instruments, mixed with sounds of nature. Of particular note is the breathless "Cabalgando," which captures the heady joys of galloping on horseback across the high mountain plains. The soaring, shamanic rhythms of "Mujer Aguila (Eagle Woman)" and the intriguing dance of "Caminto a Nazca (Road to Nazca)" are also admirable examples of how traditional influences and contemporary sounds can meld successfully into a wondrous listening experience.

the rest:
Ventana al Sol ♪♪♪ (EarthTone, 1995)

influences:
◀◀ Los Incas
▶▶ Ah-Kin

PJ Birosik

Eden's Bridge

Pop Celtic, contemporary Christian and devotional
Formed late 1990s, in Yorkshire, England. Based in northern England.

David Bird, guitar; Sarah Lacy, vocals; Richard Lacy, bodhrán; John Large, bass. (All members are from the U.K.)

A forensic psychologist, a recording engineer, a city planner, and an industrial chemist—this doesn't seem a very likely set of backgrounds for a quartet who create contemporary Celtic Christian music. However, driven by their wish to combine their Celtic pride with their Christian faith, these four joined together as the group Eden's Bridge.

what's available: *Celtic Psalms* ♪♪♪ (StraightWay/EMI Christian, 1997, prod. Richard Lacy) and *Celtic Worship* ♪♪♪ (StraightWay/EMI Christian, 1997, prod. Richard Lacy) both display an interesting pop/Celtic/Christian fusion and, in the original tunes and arrangements, skillfully evoke the basic Celtic-music sense of place and style. The wavelength this band is on provides an interesting contrast and complement to that of the groundbreaking various-artists collection *Celtic Spirit,* which is reviewed in this book's Compilations section.

influences:
◀◀ Michael Card, Amy Grant, the Chieftains

Kerry Dexter

Eek-a-Mouse

Reggae
Born Ripton Hylton, 1957, in Kingston, Jamaica. Based in Jamaica.

With the ability to incorporate a wide variety of vocal effects into his singing, and a passion for draping witty costuming on his 6'6" frame, Eek-a-Mouse was one of the originators of "sing-jay" or "toasting," the reggae hybrid that mixed singing and dee-jaying. The *Boston Globe* referred to him as "the Al Jarreau of Reggae," while the *Village Voice* compared his unique, self-described "bong gong giddy mem giddy hoy" style of singing to "a tonal roller coaster." A native of Kingston's Trenchtown neighborhood, Eek-a-Mouse, who took his name from a race horse, began singing in elementary school. By his teens he had acquired a reputation as talented vocalist. Although he recorded his debut singles in 1974, he didn't score his first hit until 1981, when his tune "Wa Do Dem" reached the top of the U.K. charts. Performing an unscheduled opening slot at the Reggae Sunsplash Festival the same year, he took the event by storm, earning fan fervor, a two-night booking for the following year, and his first American record contract in 1982. Eek-a-Mouse made his movie debut in the 1991 film *New Jack City,* and remains a favorite with connoisseurs of clever word-play and serious waist-windin'.

what to buy: *The Best of Eek-a-Mouse* ♫♫♫ (Greensleeves, 1987, prod. various) is a thorough examination of his greatest hits, while the *Live at Reggae Sunsplash* ♫♫♫ (Genes, 1984) collection captures Eek-a-Mouse during his groundbreaking performance at reggae's premier music festival.

the rest:
Skidip ♫♫♫ (Shanachie, 1982)
Wa Do Dem ♫♫♫ (Shanachie, 1982)
The Mouse and the Man ♫♫♫ (Shanachie, 1983)
Assassination ♫♫ (RAS, 1984)
Mouseketeer ♫♫♫ (Shanachie, 1984)
The King & I ♫♫♫ (RAS, 1985)
The Very Best ♫♫♫ (Shanachie, 1987)
Mouse-A-Mania ♫♫♫ (RAS, 1988)
Eek A Nomics ♫♫♫ (RAS, 1988)
U Neek ♫♫♫ (Island, 1991)
Black Cowboy ♫♫♫ (Explicit, 1996)
RAS Portraits ♫♫♫ (RAS, 1997)

influences:
◄◄ Black Uhuru, Yellowman
►► Half Pint, Maxi Priest

Craig Harris

Seamus Egan

See: Solas

Hamza El Din

Nubian folk and classical music
Born 1929, in Nubia (now Egypt). Based in Oakland, CA, USA.

Hamza El Din is a giant; an international emissary of Nubian culture and an artistic pioneer in the recording of world music. His 1963 Vanguard album *Music of Nubia* was the first recording of Afro-Arabic music to be distributed to the Western market, and he is widely acknowledged as the planet's premiere player of the *oud* (the prototypical lute). He also created modern Nubian music, while preserving his people's ancient traditions.

Hamza El Din grew up in a family that would be called middle class by American standards. He was raised in the countryside, but received city schooling when he was a boy. Nubia, the kingdom once called "The Gateway to Africa" by Westerners, today lies underwater in Southern Egypt and Northern Sudan, flooded by the Aswan High Dam. "When I got to Cairo to study

klezmer

Originating in Eastern Europe, klezmer was a form of Jewish folk music including fast dance tunes and more reflective pieces. It was influenced by the music of Jewish prayer and of other Eastern European cultures. Klezmer was brought to North America in the late 19th and early 20th centuries by immigrant musicians who continued to ply their trade in their new home. In fact, klezmer recordings were issued by U.S. companies from the 1910s through the '50s, though the genre's prominence declined as Jews' enthusiasm to assimilate into the broader culture grew. But in the '70s a serious klezmer revival began when young musicians discovered these older recordings. Since then the klezmer movement has developed in several distinct strands. There have been bands like the Klezmorim and Kapelye, who prefer a traditional approach with the old records as their springboard. The 11-member Klezmer Conservatory Band takes a more theatrical tack, featuring dramatic vocalizing by Judy Bressler. And then there's the progressive wing, led by New York City's marvelous Klezmatics, who fuse traditional klezmer styles with modern jazz, rock, and world-music influences. Other bands charting new directions include (regardless of their name!) Brave Old World, who incorporate jazzy improvisation and classical music's finesse into their sound, and the New Orleans Klezmer All-Stars, whose klez-rock is guaranteed to get a party started. For a superb picture of klezmer and its evolution, check out *In the Fiddler's House* ♫♫♫ (Angel, 1995), a collaboration between violin master Itzhak Perlman and kindred klezmer re-discoverers from a younger generation; *Klezmania: Klezmer for the New Millennium* ♫♫♫ (Shanachie, 1997), a sampler of new-school klezmer tracks; and *Klezmer Music: A Marriage of Heaven & Earth* ♫♫♫ (ellipsis arts . . . , 1996), a lush package with cuts by performers from the United States, Germany, and Canada.

Ken Roseman

engineering, I realized my country would vanish when the High Dam was built." El Din felt the need to warn his people, "and since we were an oral culture, I picked up the oud." At first El Din composed in the Arabic style, "to write songs about the Dam and the effect it would have," but "Middle Eastern music didn't fit the taste of my people, so I began to collect traditional music. That's how modern Nubian music came out."

El Din couldn't read or write music, so he made up his own system of notation. He spent the next three years wandering his homeland collecting traditional music. "I owned an oud, a saddle, a pair of saddlebags, and a donkey. Half of the saddlebag had papers and pens, the other side donkey food." Despite the difficulty, El Din found the work a joy, "because of the great variety of music. I discovered a lullaby for a child is even different between two sisters in the same family." El Din returned to Cairo to study classical Arabic music, "but when I played for my people they said 'You sound like an Egyptian.' So I learned to play for the Nubian taste." Despite his growing interest in music and Nubian folklore, El Din was still considering an engineering career when he experienced an inspirational and pivotal moment. "I was sitting alone on a sand dune with my oud, and a soft wind of the desert hit the strings. Behind me, in the distance, I could hear a singer, and the wind hit the strings of the oud just so, and made a chord that was in harmony with his voice, like the echo of a music from far away. I said to myself, I've got to see how far I can follow this invisible music."

El Din continued his studies in classical Arabic music, and after graduation was offered a scholarship at the Academy of St. Cecelia in Rome. It was there that El Din began his life's work, a synthesis of Arabic, Nubian, and Western music. "From Western music I learned to create sophisticated compositions; from the East, rhythms, scales, and improvisation; but I don't use Western or Eastern techniques as much as I use their philosophy to aid my own compositions, which are in Nubian style." Near the end of his schooling in Rome, El Din met Gino Foreman, who maintained connections in New York City's folk world. "In New York Gino introduced me to Bob Dylan and Joan Baez. Joan took a recording I had made to Vanguard." *Music of Nubia,* El Din's first album, is credited with creating modern Nubian music.

"By the time I got back home," El Din says, "the Aswan High Dam had been built and I was homeless, so I took the world as my village. Because of the records, I graduated to teacher, to lecturer in Arabic and Nubian music, as well as performer. I have gone from Nubia to Japan to Vienna to California. I never stay in one place very long, but when I do, my address is the Bay Area, California." El Din also has strong ties to Japan. "In the East, the Japanese *biwa* is a descendant of the oud, as is the Chinese *pipa.* I planned to spend a year in Japan studying

the biwa, but found Japanese culture so interesting I stayed 15 years." El Din's wife, who doubles as his business and road manager, is Japanese, and he has made many recordings for Japanese labels. These include *Muwashshah,* a tribute to the legendary Ziryab, an African slave who escaped from the court of Baghdad to become one of the most influential composers in the history of Arabic music. "Ziryab lived in the time of Harona Rashid in Baghdad," El Din explains. "He was owned by a court musician named Abrihim el Musoly, and employed as a slave companion to his son. Ziryab sat there while el Mosoly's son had his lessons, and became educated. In time, el Musoly's son became the court musician, but he knew Ziryab was an even better musician, so he gave him a choice: to be a slave and stop playing music, or play music and die. Ziryab escaped to Spain, and became the most important musician of the court in Andalusia. He founded the Arab Music Conservatory in Cordoba, and invented *muwashshah* ('the veil'), which swept through the Arabic world, even Iraq. Muwashshah is a short song form that teaches the student how to sing *maquims,* the scales Arabic music is based on; they're used to warm up the voice before concerts. That's why it's called muwashshah, a veil before the voice, like the hand you use to cover your mouth when you yawn."

Although his career began when he lost his home, El Din embraced the world and became a citizen of the planet, a musician who has played with symphony orchestras and composed for radio, television, and the concert stage, tireless in his efforts to keep the traditions of his beloved Nubia alive. "If you ask my nationality I say I'm Nubo-Egypto-Italio-Americano-Japanese, because I've lived in all those countries long enough to love them. I lost the sense of security you have when you're home—when you're in a strange land you walk on a thin wire if you want to stay safe—but I gained a lot. There is a Nubian proverb, 'Who lives sees, who walks sees more,' and my work has given me friends in every city around the world."

what to buy: *Escalay—The Water Wheel* 🎵🎵🎵🎵 (Nonesuch, 1968, prod. Robert Garfias) is an early world-music classic, reissued on CD in 1997, showcasing El Din's unique oud style. The album contains three lengthy improvisations: the title track by El Din; "I Remember," a song Mohamed Abdel Wahab composed for Umm Kulthum; and "Song with Tar," a traditional Nubian folk melody. At the time of its release, *Escalay* summed up the past, present, and future of Nubian music.

what to buy next: *Muwashshah* 🎵🎵🎵🎵 (JVC, 1996, prod. Hamza El Din, Tohru Ueda, Soh Fujimoto) is another album that proves good music is universal; El Din and three of his Japanese students create the sound of an Egyptian string orchestra by tuning down a synthesizer and overdubbing a few violin parts. ("When I played this music for an Egyptian conductor I know,

Hamza El Din

he refused to believe the musicians were Japanese," El Din laughs.) The album is marked by El Din's understated oud playing, warm vocals, and strong symphonic sense of melody.

the rest:
Eclipse ♫♫♫ (Rykodisc, 1988)
A Wish ♫♫♫ (Sounds True, 1999)

influences:
◄◄ Traditional Nubian folk music

see also: *Sandy Bull*

j. poet

El-Funoun

Palestinian folk
Formed 1979, in Ramallah in the occupied West Bank. Based in Ramallah in the occupied West Bank.

Muhammed Ata, artistic director; Muhsen Subhi, buzuq, oud, percussion; Thafer Al-Tawil, qanun; Mohammed Amin, bass, percussion; Raid Al Kobary, nay; Abu Ashraf, shabbabah; Abu Steif, mijwiz; Najah Atiyeh, vocals; Safa Tamish, vocals; Nidaa Hajali, vocals; Ali Awad, vocals; Mohammed Yacoub, vocals. (All members are Palestinian.)

Recently introduced to Western audiences by noted world-music aficionado Dan Rosenberg, who discovered their music while visiting the West Bank to write a story on the Palestinian arts scene, El-Funoun—whose full name in Arabic means "Palestinian Popular Arts Troupe"—is a group of singers, dancers, and musicians dedicated to reviving regional folklore as an affirmation of Palestinian identity. The popular ensemble has managed to thrive for 20 years under the most adverse conditions, including travel restrictions, border closings, frequent arrests of its members, and bans on its public performances, at times rehearsing in whispers to avoid detection by Israeli patrols. The Israeli government has long considered El-Funoun's Arab-influenced work subversive, and even some Palestinians protested against the group, claiming that their contemporary topics defied Palestinian traditions. Still, as the group's artistic director Muhammed Ata has said: "Despite the suffering and the pain, music and dance must continue . . . to express our emotions, resistance, and hopes."

what's available: Because of the political struggles in their native land, only one of El-Funoun's recordings has been made available in the United States. *Zaghareed* ♫♫♫ (Sounds True, 1999, prod. El-Funoun), whose title means "ululations," or wails of joy, uses the music of a traditional Arab ensemble to tell the tale of a woman who dreams of being able to choose her own lover despite her parents' plans for an arranged marriage. The 17 folksy tracks walk us through this decidedly modern story, from the villagers' pleading with the bride's father to

accept her choice of a husband, to the final adornment of the bride. It's a spellbinding musical journey, and a compelling introduction to a little-known culture rich in historic traditions.

worth searching for: Although the album was later banned by the Israeli government, in 1988 El-Funoun made *Sharar* (Arabic for "spark"), a tape of songs dedicated to the Palestinian uprising, with lyrics that reflected various aspects of the struggle and its martyrs. Despite the arrest of the group's then-artistic director Suheil Khouri and the confiscation of thousands of contraband cassettes, the songs became underground anthems of defiance for Palestinians, and you may still be able to find bootleg copies in select Arabic music stores.

influences:
◄◄ Mustapha Al Kurd, Al Ashiqeen, Fairuz, Marcel Khalifa

Bret Love

Eliane Elias

Brazilian and international jazz
Born March 19, 1960, in Sao Paulo, Brazil. Based in New York, NY, USA.

Eliane Elias is a powerful two-handed linear pianist whose fleeting lines are punctuated with chords and varied by altering dynamics, diverse phrasing ideas, and a wide range of moods and emotions. She's also a soft-toned singer in the style of Astrud Gilberto, an earlier Brazilian vocalist who first gained notice in the 1960s for her cool-tone singing in seminal jazz-samba groups led by Stan Getz, Antonio Carlos Jobim, and João Gilberto. Elias began classical piano studies in Brazil at age 10, and two years later was considered an accomplished classical pianist. She pursued further studies at a school run by the jazz-oriented instrumental group the Zimbo Trio, the Centrol Livre de Apremdizagem Music, or Free Center of Music Apprenticeship. She began as a student and wound up teaching by the age of 15. Inspired by jazz pianists Herbie Hancock and Chick Corea, she began blending Brazilian rhythms with jazz, performing simultaneously in local jazz and bossa nova clubs. Bassist Eddie Gomez heard Elias play in Paris and recommended she move to New York, which she did in 1981. Elias became a member of the group Steps Ahead two years later. After leaving that outfit in 1984, Elias performed and recorded with her husband, jazz-fusion trumpeter Randy Brecker. She made her debut as a leader in 1986, signed with the Blue Note label in 1989, and toured with her trio. Elias not only understands how to make great music, but has the wisdom, confidence, and perseverance to keep it happening.

what to buy: There's no question that Elias knows her Jobim, and three albums of Jobim music are among her best from a world-music perspective. Artfully mining her native rhythms makes *The Three Americas* ♫♫♫♫ (Blue Note, 1997, prod.

Eliane Elias

Eliane Elias) one of her most authentic ventures after 10 mostly jazz-focused albums. Elias takes new chances on 10 originals and two Jobim classics, melding influences of Central and South America with North American jazz. She's a powerful lyrical pianist who has demonstrated on previous recordings that she can imaginatively stretch out. On this disc, Elias displays her keyboard prowess (and occasionally sings in cool bossa style) as she artfully merges and shifts among various Brazilian beats, Cuban rhythms, Argentinean *nuevo tango,* and straight-ahead jazz—sometimes in the same tune! Such diversity is served well by Elias's cohesive core companions, bassist Marc Johnson and drummer Satoshi Takeishi, and her special guests, flutist Dave Valentin, accordionist Gil Goldstein, violinist Mark Feldman, guitarist Oscar Castro-Neves, and percussionists Manolo Badrena and Café, among others. On *Eliane Elias Sings Jobim* 𝄽𝄽𝄽𝄽𝄽 (Blue Note, 1998, prod. Eliane Elias) Elias's gentle, sweet, *sotto voce* singing is reminiscent of Astrud Gilberto (especially on the Gilberto-associated "Girl from Ipanema"). With great artistry and intimacy, Elias delivers 16 lush Jobim classics, accompanied by musicians familiar with Brazilian rhythms (and jazz): Michael Brecker (tenor saxophone), Oscar

Castro-Neves (acoustic guitar), Marc Johnson (acoustic bass), Paulo Braga (drums and bongos), and guest percussionist (on one tune) Café. The musicians perform in varied settings, including two especially lovely guitar-voice duet tracks, "Falanda de Amor (Speaking of Love)" and "Pois é" (starring Elias and Castro-Neves); trios (the best of which is the romantic, straight-ahead jazz ballad "Forgetting You"); and quintets (including "A Felicidade," featuring Brecker). If you adore the graceful, lilting rhythms of the Stan Getz "jazz samba" era, Elias's soothing vocals, and Jobim's gorgeous songs, you'll find this album a most satisfying listen.

what to buy next: In the company of bassist Gomez, drummer Jack DeJohnette, and percussionist Nana Vasconselos, Elias leads a stunning all-instrumental tribute to Jobim on *Eliane Elias Plays Jobim* 𝄽𝄽𝄽𝄽 (Blue Note, 1990, prod. Eliane Elias, Randy Brecker), an 11-tune album that ranks among her best. Merging her jazz sensibilities with native Brazilian rhythms, Elias eloquently performs Jobim classics such as "Agua de Beber," "Passarim," "Dindi," "One-Note Samba," and more. Gomez is gorgeously in his element, and DeJohnette is painterly in his expressions. This is an engaging and memorable album, worth the price for the leader's lush version of "Don't Ever Go Away" alone.

what to avoid: As with many of her early albums listed in the "best of the rest" section below, Elias brilliantly leans more to the jazz side of improvisation. So don't be misled by the titles of *Fantasia* ♪♪♪♪⁷ (Blue Note, 1992) and *Paulistana* ♪♪♪♪⁷ (Blue Note, 1993, prod. Eliane Elias). Both of these albums, while holding allure for die-hard jazz fans, offer little to attract those seeking concentrated Brazilian themes. Even the latter album, with a track featuring Brazilian composer Ivan Lins singing a duet with Elias on his smooth, modern ballad "Illuminandos," doesn't tender the appeal of her most recent recorded tributes to Jobim.

best of the rest:

Cross Currents ♪♪♪⁷ (Denon, 1988)
So Far So Close ♪♪♪♪ (Blue Note, 1989)
Illusions ♪♪♪ (Denon, 1990)
A Long Story ♪♪♪⁷ (Blue Note, 1991)
Solos and Duets ♪♪♪♪ (Blue Note, 1995)
Best of Eliane Elias ♪♪♪ (Denon, 1995)

influences:

◀◀ Bud Powell, Keith Jarrett, Art Tatum, Herbie Hancock, Chick Corea, Ivan Lins, Antonio Carlos Jobim

Nancy Ann Lee

Alton Ellis

Reggae, rocksteady, ska
Born 1944, in Kingston, Jamaica. Based in London, England.

Alton Ellis is one of the most expressive and distinctive singers Jamaica has ever produced. With nearly 40 years in music, Ellis displays versatility so impressive that he is widely known as the godfather of rocksteady *and* reggae. Ellis began his career during the formative years of ska in the late '50s. He became one of the first singers ever to be recorded in Jamaica when he voiced a handful of tracks with Eddie Perkins for producer Clement "Coxsone" Dodd. Most notable of these sides was the hit "Muriel," a doo-wop/*mento* (Jamaican roots-music) prison ballad backed by the superb Clue J. and the Blues Blasters. In the early '60s Ellis recorded such ska-rchers as "Rum Bumpers" (with a young John Holt) and "Ska Beat" for producer Vincent "Randy" Chin.

But as the charging, horn-pumped rhythms of ska relaxed into the more seductive, spare, bass-heavy music called rocksteady, Ellis's voice moved to the forefront. Some claim Ellis's "Cry Tough" and "Girl I've Got a Date" were the first rocksteady songs; at the very least, his "Do the Rocksteady" was the first song title to use the genre's label. All three are classics. This was a time when ratchet-wielding "rude-boys" were wreaking

havoc at soundsystem dances across Kingston. While many artists voiced admiration for the fearlessness of the "rudies," Ellis opposed the violence from the very beginning in "Cry Tough" and "Dance Crasher." In doing so, Ellis experienced an artistic and personal revelation that led to some of the most elegant and alluring music ever made in Jamaica. As he explains in the essential text *Reggae Routes*: "I [decided to] . . . go back to more loving sounds. . . . I was always personally inclined to be a more loving type of person. . . . I feel it more and express it more. I think it's in my nature. . . . And most of these songs are a story I'm telling about my life—it's personal."

Ellis's epochal mid-'60s recordings for Duke Reid at his acoustically vibrant Treasure Isle studios were the cream of the rocksteady era. Backed by the cool, sublime sounds of ex-Skatalite Tommy McCook and his band the Supersonics, Ellis proved he was one of the keenest observers of romance and heartbreak on such hits as "Just Another Girl," "Can't Stand It," "Ain't That Loving You," "Breaking Up," and his goose-bump-raising cover of the Delfonics' "La La Means I Love You." Ellis was so inspired during this period that he would compose late into the night, often falling asleep at the studio piano. He also recorded stellar sides at the equally legendary Studio One, including "I'm Just a Guy," "Can I Change My Mind?," "Let Him Try," and "Willow Tree."

As the sweet melodies and "gidgy gidgy boom" of rocksteady (as the Heptones' Leroy Sibbles described it) changed into reggae's faster, chugging beats, cavernous basslines, and yearning lyrics, Ellis proved his mettle: 1970's *Sunday Coming* is one of the pivotal albums in reggae history. Ellis's emotional wounds from past love lost brought a more soulful, profoundly melancholy ache to his vocals, which were punctuated with astonishing falsettos. Simply put, the album captures longing personified. Ellis also recorded two influential culture-conscious roots-reggae anthems with producer Lloyd "The Matador" Daley—"Back to Africa" and "Deliver Us"—both backed by the glorious harmonies of the Heptones. Throughout the decade Ellis continued to record hit songs for producers such as Prince Buster ("Since I Fell for You"), Clancy Eccles ("Feeling Inside"), Henry "Junjo" Lawes, Winston Riley ("I'll Be Waiting"), Joe Gibbs, and Keith Hudson ("Big Bad Boy"). In the '80s, Ellis relocated to London and recorded some fine and quite rare singles with King Jammy and Fashion Sounds. In 1994, the Jamaican government recognized his estimable contributions to the island's music by awarding him, on National Heroes Day, the Order of Distinction.

what to buy: The indispensable *Cry Tough* ♪♪♪♪♪ (Heartbeat, 1993, prod. Duke Reid and Sonia Pottinger) is a remastered version of Ellis's *Mr. Soul of Jamaica* ♪♪♪♪⁷ (Treasure Isle, 1975), which itself was a compilation of almost all of his sweet rocksteady sides for Duke Reid. This is rocksteady defined—captivating melodies and sensual bass-heavy rhythms made for dancing, singing along, and if you're lucky, falling in love. *Sunday Coming* 𝄞𝄞𝄞𝄞 (Heartbeat, 1995, prod. Clement Dodd) is a cleaned-up reissue of the stunning Studio One release from 1970. This is reggae before it became a music designed for chanting down Babylon or listening amidst a cloud of ganja smoke. Beyond the slew of gorgeous Ellis originals, there are intensely personalized covers of Brenda Holloway's "You Make Me So Very Happy," the Guess Who's "These Eyes," and the Royalettes' "Gonna Take a Miracle." The entire album is backed by Sound Dimension, the amazing Studio One session band that included such reggae luminaries as ex-Skatalite Roland Alphonso, Leroy Sibbles, and one of this globe's greatest guitarists, Ernest Ranglin.

what to buy next: Because it contains Ellis's finest rocksteady sides for Studio One, *Sings Rock & Soul* 𝄞𝄞𝄞𝄞 (Studio One, 1966, prod. Clement Dodd) is a perfect counterpart to the Treasure Isle hits on *Cry Tough.* It includes classics like "I'm Still in Love with You" (which became the basis for Althea & Donna's "Uptown Ranking") and "I'm Just a Guy" (versioned wonderfully by Michigan & Smiley as "Rub a Dub Style" in the early '80s). *The Best of Alton Ellis* 𝄞𝄞𝄞𝄞 (Studio One, 1968, prod. Clement Dodd) is the man at his reggae prime. This album collects such hits as "Set a Better Example," "Still Trying," and "Breaking Up Is Hard."

the rest:
Still in Love 𝄞𝄞𝄞 (Trojan, 1977)
Showcase 𝄞𝄞 (Studio One, 1980)
My Time Is Right 𝄞𝄞𝄞 (Trojan, 1990)
Soul Groover 𝄞𝄞𝄞𝄞 (Trojan, 1990)
(With his sister Hortense Ellis) *At Studio One* 𝄞𝄞𝄞 (Heartbeat, 1993)
Reggae Valley of Decision 𝄞𝄞𝄞 (House of Reggae, 1997)

worth searching for: *Randy's—17 North Parade* 𝄞𝄞𝄞𝄞 (Pressure Sounds, 1997, prod. Clive Chin) contains one of the hardest-to-find Ellis singles—his hypnotic and nearly unrecognizable cover of the Cornelius Brothers' and Sister Rose's "It's Too Late (To Turn Back Now)." With conviction that would be rare for anyone but Alton Ellis, he reveals that he is so deeply in love that—as the powerlessness of the freefall takes hold—he is feeling a disturbing sense of regret. To top it off, he's backed by the dynamo Now Generation rhythm section. And in case you're wondering, the rest of this collection of Clive Chin–produced reggae is top-notch and chock full of rarities.

influences:

◀◀ Curtis Mayfield, Jackie Edwards, Owen Gray, Sam Cooke, Lord Creator, the Delfonics

▶▶ Lloyd Charmers, Freddie McGregor, Cocoa Tea, Junior Brown, Maxi Priest

see also: *Jackie Mittoo, Ernest Ranglin, the Skatalites*

Todd Shanker

Emilio
See: Emilio Navaira

The English Beat /General Public
Two-tone, ska
Formed 1978, in Birmingham, England. Disbanded 1983.

The English Beat (1978–83): Andy Cox, guitar; Everett Morton, drums; David Steele, bass; Dave Wakeling, guitar, vocals; Ranking Roger, vocals, percussion (1979–83); Saxa, saxophone (1979–82). **General Public (1984–87, 1994–present):** Dave Wakeling; Ranking Roger; Micky Billingham, keyboards, vocals (1984–87); Horace Panter, bass (1984–87); Kevin White, guitar (1984–85); Stoker, drums (1984–85); Gianni Minardi, guitar (1986–87); Mario Minardi, drums (1986–87); Michael Railton, keyboards, programming, vocals (1994–present); Wayne Lothian, bass (1994–present); Dan Chase, drums (1994–present); Norman Jones, percussion, vocals (1994–present).

One good thing to come out of the racial strife that engulfed England during the late '70s and early '80s was the two-tone movement, a cluster of racially mixed bands dedicated to uniting British youth through song and dance. Followers of the music, which was a hybrid of punk rock and Jamaican ska, sported black-and-white clothing and short hair, as did the musicians. Among the best and most important of these bands was the English Beat, known simply as the Beat everywhere but in America due to trademark concerns. The Beat, which formed in 1978, released its first single in 1979, Smokey Robinson's "Tears of a Clown," on the 2-Tone record label owned by another key band in the movement, the Selecter. The single went to #6 on the British charts and featured the frenetic saxophone work of veteran Jamaican musician Saxa, who had played with the Beatles and the ska stars Desmond Dekker and Prince Buster. Saxa later joined the band full time, as did Ranking Roger, a young Birmingham percussionist whose specialty was toasting (melodic chanting). The Beat generated a string of U.K. hits, including "Hands Off . . . She's Mine," "Mirror in the Bathroom," "Best Friend," and the politically charged "Stand Down Margaret," which pleaded for "peace, love, and unity" as well as the departure of the British prime minister. The Beat enjoyed a loyal following in the U.S., too, scoring its biggest hits with 1982's "I Confess" and "Save It for Later." The band broke up in 1983, resulting in two new outfits. Cox and Steele formed Fine Young Cannibals, while Wakeling and Ranking Roger became General Public. Wakeling and Roger split up in 1988 after a falling out but have since re-formed General Public, enjoying a hit remake of the Staple Singers' "I'll Take You There" in 1994, when it was featured in the film *Threesome.*

what to buy: *I Just Can't Stop It* 𝄞𝄞𝄞𝄞 (Sire, 1980, prod. Bob Sargeant) is the English Beat's debut album and one of the best records of the '80s. Mixing Chuck Berry–like guitar sounds, Beach Boyish harmonies, sizzling sax lines, and Caribbean rhythms, this spellbinding record sounds as good today as it did two decades ago. *Special Beat Service* 𝄞𝄞𝄞𝄞 (I.R.S., 1982, prod. Bob Sargeant) is the English Beat's third record and features the band's best-known singles in the U.S., "Save It for Later" and "I Confess," as well as the verbal acrobatics of Ranking Roger and guest Pato Banton in the delightful "Pato and Roger Ago Talk."

what to buy next: Wakeling and Roger's first effort as General Public, . . . *All the Rage* 𝄞𝄞𝄞𝄞 (I.R.S., 1984, prod. General Public, Gavin MacKillop, Colin Fairley), has harder edges than anything the Beat did. The two excellent singles from the record, "Tenderness" and "Never You Done That," have a distinctly Motown feel.

what to avoid: The English Beat compilation *What Is Beat?* 𝄞𝄞𝄞 (I.R.S., 1983, prod. Bob Sargeant, the English Beat, Mike Hedges, David Peters) provides some answers to that question, but earlier records offer a clearer picture.

the rest:
The English Beat:
Wha'ppen 𝄞𝄞𝄞𝄞 (I.R.S., 1981)

General Public:
Hand to Mouth 𝄞𝄞𝄞 (I.R.S., 1986)
Rub It Better 𝄞𝄞𝄞 (Epic, 1995)

The International Beat:
The Hitting Line 𝄞𝄞𝄞 (Triple X, 1986)
Dance Hall Rockers 𝄞𝄞𝄞 (Magnum America, 1996)

worth searching for: *The Beat Goes On* (I.R.S., 1991) features some of the English Beat's biggest hits as well as songs by Fine Young Cannibals, Wakeling, Ranking Roger, and the International Beat.

solo outings:
Ranking Roger:
Radical Departure 𝄞𝄞𝄞 (I.R.S., 1988)

Dave Wakeling:
No Warning 𝄞𝄞𝄞 (I.R.S., 1991)

influences:
◀◀ Prince Buster, Desmond Dekker, Smokey Robinson, Sly & the Family Stone

▶▶ Barenaked Ladies, Dave Matthews Band, Rancid, Sublime, Save Ferris, No Doubt

William Hanson

Séamus Ennis

Irish traditional
Born May 5, 1919, in Jamestown, County Dublin, Ireland. Died October 5, 1982, in Naul, County Dublin, Ireland.

A colorful and charismatic personality, a masterful performer on the Irish uilleann pipes, a singer, storyteller, and collector, Séamus Ennis was a father-figure to a generation of Irish pipers and a giant of Irish traditional music. Like other traditional players, Ennis was raised into the music. His father, James, was a piper who performed on radio broadcasts and records with the Fingal Trio in the early 1930s, and the Ennis house in Jamestown was often visited by musician friends. Although not through formal training, Séamus learned his piping from his father. After spending a few years with Colm Ó Lochlainn's Three Candles Press, Ennis was hired by the Irish Folklore Commission in the early 1940s to collect songs in the west of Ireland. In 1947, he moved on to work for Radio Éireann, then for the BBC in London in 1951, traveling all over Britain and Ireland to record traditional music for his show *As I Roved Out*. By all accounts, Ennis was very successful in establishing a strong rapport with traditional players and singers, who saw him as one of their own. While in London, Ennis recorded his first album, *The Bonny Bunch of Roses*, for the American label Tradition. Also from that period, a couple of recordings of Ennis's piping are included on the 1965 Folkways album *Irish Music in London Pubs*. By 1958, his work with the BBC having ended, Ennis returned to Ireland and resumed his collecting for Radio Éireann. He continued to travel and perform throughout the 1960s, appearing at the Newport Folk Festival in 1964. In the early 1970s, as the Irish folk music revival came into full swing, Ennis and fellow piper Liam O'Flynn, soon to become famous as a member of the group Planxty, were sharing an apartment in Dublin. Visiting Ennis there was American folksinger Patrick Sky, who had become enamored with the pipes and who later produced *Forty Years of Irish Piping*, an album containing recordings Ennis made at that time. During that period, Ennis's piping was also featured on the Topic LP *The Wandering Minstrel* and on two LPs produced for Tara, *The Pure Drop* and *The Fox Chase*. By the late 1970s, Ennis returned "home" to North County Dublin. Despite health problems, he continued to make regular appearances to the end, even playing at the Willie Clancy Summer School a few months before his death.

what's available: On the pioneering *The Bonny Bunch of Roses* 𝄞𝄞𝄞 (Tradition, 1959/Rykodisc, 1996, prod. Robin Roberts), recently reissued on CD, Ennis presents an excellent selection of airs and dance tunes—played on pipes or whistle—and songs learned during his collecting trips. Ennis's instrumental Tara LPs, reissued as the two-CD set *The Best of Irish Piping* 𝄞𝄞𝄞𝄞 (Tara, 1995, prod. Séamus Ennis), are a monument to the art of Irish piping. Of particular interest is Ennis's 13-minute rendition of "The Fox Chase," a descriptive piece complete with galloping horses and barking hounds. From the same period, *The Wandering Minstrel* ♫♫♫♫ (Topic, 1974/Green Linnet, 1993, prod. Tony Engle) is also entirely devoted to the pipes.

worth searching for: *Irish Music in London Pubs* ♫♫♫ (Folkways, 1965, prod. Ralph Rinzler, Barry Murphy), recorded live in the London pubs frequented by Irish musicians, is still available on tape from the Smithsonian Institution in Washington, D.C. Although Séamus Ennis only appears on two tracks and the sound quality is less than optimal, the album is interesting for the presence of Sligo fiddle player Michael Gorman and street singer Margaret Barry. The first album released on the Green Linnet label, *Forty Years of Irish Piping* ♫♫♫ (Green Linnet, 1977, prod. Patrick Sky) is a poorly documented collection of disparate recordings from various times and sources, yet remains a classic well worth searching for. Available from Radio Telefis Éireann (RTE) in Dublin, *The Séamus Ennis Story* ♫♫♫ (RTE, 1988, prod. Julian Vignoles) assembles on two cassettes four radio broadcasts featuring interviews of Ennis's friends and relatives, as well as music from the master. From the same source, the recent *The Return from Fingal* ♫♫♫♫ (RTE, 1997, prod. Peter Browne) is an outstanding collection of recordings made by Radio Éireann and RTE over a 40-year period. Especially interesting are several renditions of *sean-nós* ("old-style") melodies, both sung and played on the pipes.

influences:

◄◄ James Ennis (Séamus Mac Aonghusa), Mary McCabe, Patsy Touhey, Nicholas Markey, Patrick Ward

►► Liam O'Flynn, Willie Clancy

see also: *Liam O'Flynn, Planxty*

Philippe Varlet

Brian Eno

Art rock, ambient, minimalism, electronica, world fusion

Born Brian Peter George St. John le Baptiste Eno, May 15, 1948, in Suffolk, England. Based in St. Petersburg, Russia.

Best known as the father of "ambient" music, that once-derided form of aural wallpaper that is now embraced by a new generation of electronic auteurs and their growing legions of fans, Brian Eno has also been present at some pivotal moments in world-music history. Equally influenced by a rock 'n' roll-broadcasting American Armed Forces Radio station in childhood, and a conceptual-art education in young adulthood, Eno made the first of many highly visible marks merging these two muses in the art-rock ensemble Roxy Music. He kept

his hand in the avant-pop game with his eccentric and visionary solo recordings, and collaborations with Robert Fripp, John Cale, and many others. Some of those others were U2—whose acclaimed, best-selling albums *The Unforgettable Fire, The Joshua Tree,* and *Achtung Baby* also furthered Eno's own experimental agenda in the mass marketplace—and David Bowie and Talking Heads, with each of whom he helped usher in the "worldbeat" era. The American mainstream's appreciation of international musics—such as it yet is—can be largely traced to the snapshot multiculturalism of Bowie and Eno's *Lodger* album in 1979, which in turn inspired Eno to plunge into the global sidestream with David Byrne (on the Africa-sampling *My Life in the Bush of Ghosts*) and then with all the Talking Heads (on the heavily Africa-influenced *Remain in Light,* recorded afterwards but released first). The rest—with Byrne's eventual founding of the Luaka Bop label to promote more and more of the "real thing"—has been worldbeat history in the making. Eno has sustained his fascination with and advocacy of cultures outside his own (he once notoriously defined European classical as "music minus Africa"), producing and collaborating with such artists as Geffery Oryema and Baaba Maal and providing a Foreword to the world-music tome *Rhythm Planet,* in between lecturing on conceptualism, collaborating with Laurie Anderson and Peter Gabriel on a postmodern theme park, publishing the memoir-of-sorts *A Year with Swollen Appendices,* designing screen-savers, and generally holding his place for the First Renaissance Man of the 21st Century award.

what's available: Eno and Byrne's *My Life in the Bush of Ghosts* ♫♫♫♫ (Sire, 1981, prod. Brian Eno, David Byrne) is the one from Eno's headline-billed albums that you want to start with for world-music purposes, though any of the production/co-creation jobs with Bowie and the Heads mentioned above is an essential—if, from some standpoints of "authenticity," controversial—purchase. For a more sweeping overview of *all* the worlds Eno has visited, try the two-box retrospective helpfully titled *Box I* ♫♫♫♫ (Virgin, 1993, prod. Brian Eno) and *Box II* ♫♫♫♫ (Virgin, 1993, prod. Brian Eno). *Box I* surveys art-meets-pop songs from throughout Eno's solo career, including such witty masterpieces as "Seven Deadly Finns," "Baby's on Fire," and "No One Receiving," and tracks from the previously unreleased album *My Squelchy Life. Box II* focuses on Eno's minimalist and ambient instrumentals.

influences:

◄◄ The Velvet Underground, John Cage, Lamonte Young, Baaba Maal

►► Talking Heads, David Byrne, David Bowie, Jah Wobble, Geffery Oryema, Baaba Maal, U2, the Contortions, the Orb, Mogwai

see also: *David Bowie, Michael Brook, David Byrne, Farafina, Baaba Maal, Geffery Oryema, Talking Heads*

Adam McGovern and Craig Harris

Luis Enrique

Salsa romantico
Born 1962, near Managua, Nicaragua. Based in Miami, FL, USA.

Luis Enrique was 16 when he moved to Los Angeles from a small Nicaraguan agricultural community. "At that time, there was a lot of terrorism, on both sides. No young man was safe, no matter what his politics." L.A. proved a shock to a country boy from Nicaragua, but Enrique learned fast. "I realized two things: some people didn't like Latinos, but everybody loves you if you're in a band." In his teen years Enrique sang and played drums in local bands as he devoured music: records by the Fania All-Stars, be-bop, American rock, R&B, country music, even the Bee Gees—all the sounds that show up in his own compositions. Enrique's first professional group, Mañana Es Hoy, "played acoustic instruments. We took poems from the great Latin poets and created melodies for them. We took the music we knew, from Cuba, Peru, Bolivia, or wherever, and mixed them together." Enrique moved on to a *charanga* band called Versailles; when that distinctive violin and flute-driven style became popular on the East Coast in the late '70s, the band moved to Miami. After Versailles broke up, Enrique put together a demo of his own material to shop around, and signed with Sony Discos. His first album was a commercial disappointment, but his next, *Amor y Alegría,* went platinum. Enrique's salsa is propelled by sizzling Afro-Caribbean rhythms, while his singing combines the soulfulness of an R&B singer with the smoothness of a pop balladeer. In 1990 Enrique's *Mi Mundo* earned Latin-category Grammys for Best Single, Best Song of the Year, Best Album of the Year and Best Male Vocalist—an unprecedented quadruple sweep—and his next, *Una Historia Diferente,* topped the Latin charts for another three months. In the early 1990s Enrique reigned as the king of *salsa romantico,* and though younger *salseros* and the *Rock en Español* movement have eclipsed his dominance, he continues to record compelling albums.

what to buy: *Mi Mundo* ♫♫♫♫ (Sony Discos, 1989, prod. Luis Enrique), Enrique's best album and the one that installed him as a superstar, offers strong production, a solid selection of material, and kicking rhythm tracks. This is also one of the albums that defined the romantico style.

the rest:
Amor de Medianoche ♫♫♫ (Sony Discos, 1987)
Amor y Alegria ♫♫♫♫ (Sony Discos, 1989)
Luces del Alma ♫♫♫♫ (Sony Discos, 1990)
Una Historia Diferente ♫♫♫♫ (Sony Discos, 1991)
Dilema ♫♫♫♫ (Sony Discos, 1993)
Luis Enrique ♫♫♫ (Sony Discos, 1993)
Genesis ♫♫♫♫ (Sony Discos, 1996)

influences:
◀◀ Ruben Blades, Hector "Lavoe" Perez, Cheo Feliciano

j. poet

Enya

Celtic ambient vocal
Born Eithne Ní Bhraonain, May 17, 1961, in Gweedore, County Donegal, Ireland. Based in Ireland.

"Heavenly" is the best way to describe Enya's ethereal voice. The Irish singer/songwriter/instrumentalist paints wide-open soundscapes reminiscent of the New Age genre, but more melodic, and heavily based in the Celtic folk music that formed much of her early singing career. After her start in the Irish band Clannad—which featured her older brothers and sisters—Enya hooked up with producer Nicky Ryan and lyricist Roma Ryan to write several film and television scores for the BBC. This trio reached the pinnacle of pop success in 1988 with the CD *Watermark,* selling more than four million copies worldwide. On the four successful CDs that followed, Enya's dreamy arrangements float alongside musical imagery, lyrical poetry, and mesmerizing vocals. Enya has created a new instrument with her voice—and, appropriately, her fans have made her one of the most successful recording artists of all time.

what to buy: *Watermark* ♫♫♫♫♫ (Reprise, 1989, prod. Nicky Ryan) presents a superb collection of tone poems interwoven with ethereal vocal lines sung in Gaelic, Latin, and English. The dreamy instrumental title piece overdubs piano with lush orchestration. "Storms in Africa" carries the listener to a far-away country, while the Gaelic "Na Laetha Geal Moige" exudes the warmth of home. In "Exile," Enya defines a spiritual journey: "My light shall be the moon, my path/the ocean, my guide the morning star." This is high-quality music by a distinctive artist, compelling countless replays. *The Celts* ♫♫♫♫ (Reprise, 1992, prod. Nicky Ryan) draws on Enya's twin Catholic and Celtic heritages to present an instrumental soundtrack with lingering historical and spiritual overtones. "The Sun in the Stream" is inspired by the legend of the Salmon of Knowledge, in the grove of nine wise hazel trees where the sacred River Boyne flowed. The gentle nuances of "Fairytale" tell the story of the fairy king Midir and his love for the beautiful princess Etain: a dreamy ambiance reflects the characters' great love, jealousy, and endurance. "Boadicea," meaning "Victorious," portrays the queen of the Iceni tribe who led a successful rebellion against the Romans, but eventually poisoned herself following a military defeat. Enya's use of her voice as a musical instrument is particularly strong in this collection, and the historical liner notes direct the listener's impressionistic response. *Paint the Sky with Stars: The Best of Enya* ♪♪♪♪ (Reprise, 1997, prod. Nicky Ryan) showcases the artist's greatest hits along with two new tracks: "Only If" and the title song. Most notably, "Caribbean Blue" assimilates yet another cultural paradigm into Enya's style, the exuberance of the tropics—a pleasant change of taste in an already eclectic artistic palette. This worthwhile collection provides a good opportunity to sample Enya's portfolio.

what to buy next: *Shepherd Moon* ♪♪♪ (Reprise, 1991, prod. Nicky Ryan) utilizes the same basic formula of trance and mysticism as *Watermark,* but somehow seems less engaging. Nonetheless, the tranquillity of "Angeles," "Evacuee," and "Marble Halls" will soothe the seasoned listener. Awash in synth strings, "Caribbean Blue" is this album's gigantic worldwide pop hit, while "How Can I Keep from Singing?" is Irish folk music at its best. Numerous songs in Gaelic lend additional mystery to this worthy collection. *The Memory of Trees* ♪♪♪♪ (Reprise, 1995, prod. Nicky Ryan) engages Enya's trademark style, but again lacks the spark of *Watermark.* Perhaps her preexisting popularity explains this CD's Grammy for Best New Age Album. Notably, though, "Anywhere Is" is a joyous, spiritual anthem to confusion and indecision. And Enya's lyrics, in English, Spanish, Latin, and Gaelic, leave much room for personal interpretation by her mono-lingual American followers.

worth searching for: Although the Canadian import *Enya Collection* ♪♪♪♪ (MSI/WEAC, 1986, prod. Nicky Ryan) is a three-CD set repackaging previous recordings, its 64-page booklet will entice the avid follower. *Frog Prince Soundtrack* ♪♪♪ (Karussell, 1989, prod. Nicky Ryan) is a British import recalling Enya's professional roots in television and movie scores. The EP *Oíche Chiun (Silent Night)* ♪♪♪♪ (Reprise, 1992, prod. Nicky Ryan) features three tracks (10 minutes total): "Silent Night" sung in Gaelic, "Oriel Window," a characteristically ethereal piano instrumental, and "S Fagaim Mo Bhaile," a Gaelic song. If the holiday season finds you dreaming of a dreamy Christmas, check out the Canadian import *Christmas EP* ♪♪♪ (MSI/WEA, 1986, prod. Nicky Ryan). Finally, *Interview* (BAKTABAK, 1986, prod. Nicky Ryan) is another British import—without the distraction of melody and harmony—for those seriously interested in Irish Catholicism, Celtic mysticism, and pop idolatry.

influences:

◄◄ Claude Debussy, Erik Satie, Clannad

►► Mary Black, Loreena McKennitt, Dee Carstensen, Björk, Brian Eno, the Cranberries

see also: *Altan, Clannad*

Art Wojtowicz

Epstein Brothers Band

Klezmer, Hasidic dance music

Formed 1940s, in New York, NY, USA. Based in Miami, FL, USA.

Max Epstein, clarinet; William Epstein, trumpet; Julius Epstein, drums; Isidore "Chi" Epstein (died 1986), sax; Danny Rubinstein, sax; Peter Sokolow, piano; Pat Merola, bass. All members are from the USA.

The Epstein Brothers were klezmer superstars before most people ever heard of the former term and before the latter even existed. All the brothers were born on the Lower East Side of New York City, and all played music from an early age, although their Russian émigré parents were not themselves musical. Max was a professional fiddler by age 12, earning money playing along with films in silent movie houses, and later taught himself clarinet and sax. His music leaned toward the traditional and he was one of the few American-born players who could sit in with the senior klezmorim from the Old World. Many of the tunes he knows were learned from elder European Jewish musicians. In the 1930s, Max attended NYU and earned a degree in music education while working for the Warner Bros. studio band and playing nightclub gigs. Willie turned pro at 15, playing in "show bands" in the Catskill resorts north of New York. By the 1950s he was subbing in Jewish theater bands and recording with his brother "Chi," backing comedians like Micky Katz and Benny Bell. Julie was playing with Max by the time he was 17, but also played in Dixieland bands and swing orchestras. At the height of his career he was performing 40 jobs a week for 20 different bandleaders. The Epsteins began playing klezmer in earnest after WWII, when Holocaust survivors flooded into New York City. They formed the Epstein Brothers Orchestra in the late '40s to great acclaim. By the early '70s the brothers had retired and moved to southern Florida, although Max still practiced every day and Julie started his own big show band to play at Jewish retirement homes. Strangely enough, it was interest from a German label specializing in Jewish music that brought the Epsteins together to play and record klezmer again. The revival led to their acknowledgment as elder statesmen by the current generation of young klezmorim—and a National Heritage Fellowship from the National Endowment for the Arts in 1998.

what's available: The Epsteins and their sidemen count more than three centuries of experience among them, but on *Kings of Frelekh Land* ♪♪♪♪ (Wergo/Weltmusik, 1995 prod. Joel Rubin, Rita Ottens) they play like young lions who've just discovered the power of music; these guys were tearing the roof off the sucker before George Clinton was a twinkle in his father's father's eye.

influences:

◄◄ Naftule Brandwein, Dave Tarras, Sholem Secunda, Abe Schwartz Orchestra

▶▶ The Klezmorim, Klezmatics, Andy Statman

j. poet

Kudsi Erguner

Ottoman classical, Turkish Sufi, Turkish fusion
Born February 4, 1952, in Istanbul, Turkey. Based in Paris, France.

One of Turkey's most prolific recording artists, Kudsi Erguner is widely recognized among Western audiences as a master of the Turkish *ney,* the reed flute that steers the languorous, hypnotic music of the Mevlevi Sufis, best known for their ecstatic whirling dervish ceremonies. Born in 1952, Kudsi is the eldest son of Ulvi Erguner, the last great master in a line of ney players and Mevlevi disciples stretching from Kudsi's grandfather, Suleyman Erguner (d. 1953), back to Seyh Yusuf Dede (d. 1670). During the long reign of the Ottoman Empire, *tekkes,* or Mevlevi houses, in Istanbul, Konya, and elsewhere functioned as schools for the best Ottoman art-musicians and repositories of compositions and techniques refined over generations by Sultans and Sufis alike. Kudsi and his brother Suleyman, also an excellent ney player, are the direct heirs to this remarkable cultural legacy. Both also learned from some of the great post-Ottoman musicians who flowed in and out of the government-run Istanbul Radio Orchestra—modern Turkey's secular answer to the *tekke* and *seraglio* (Sultan's palace)—which Ulvi Erguner directed for many years. Instrumentalists and singers famous for their improvisational finesse, such as Yorgo Bacanos, Udi Hrant, Necdet Yasar, and Necati Tokyay, all spent long evenings playing in the Erguner home, a private salon environment that still produces and preserves some of the best Turkish music—to the consternation of tourists in search of good live performances in Istanbul.

Kudsi absorbed Mevlevi Sufi traditions at a young age by performing with his father in dervish ceremonies. Unlike more orthodox forms of Islam, Mevlevi Sufism embraces the spiritual power of music and dance, teaching that the soul, encumbered by earthly flesh and thus separated from God, can achieve a mystical reunion with the divine through meditative rituals: the whirling of the dervish, whose every body movement is aligned with the stars; the long music cycles with their Pythagorean bearings; the slow rhythm of frame-drums; and above all the transporting sounds of the ney, heavy with breath, which the poet Rumi compared to "the words of a wise man and a lover of God." Even without its spiritual gloss, this is haunting, powerful music, and Kudsi Erguner has for over 20 years performed on or produced many of the best recordings of Mevlevi Sufi music available. In 1975, after a five-year stint as an Istanbul Radio musician, Kudsi moved to Paris, where he studied architecture and musicology, and in 1981 founded Mevlana, an institute for the study of Sufi classical music and teachings. Envisioning himself as an archivist rather than a guru, Kudsi set out to recreate the rich Ottoman historical context in which Sufi culture had flourished before being cut at the roots by the revolutionary fiats of Turkish nationalists in the 1920s.

Mevlevi music and music of the court (both seraglio and harem) were the spiritual and secular counterparts in Ottoman art-music, and historically inseparable until the 18th century. Both were centered in Istanbul among the pan-ethnic, scholarly Ottoman elite. Mevlevi and court composers, several of whom were Vienna-sieging Sultans, mutually contributed to the development of extraordinary music cycles or *fasils* made up of delicate preludes (*pesrevs*), art songs (*sharkis,* a.k.a. *sarkis*), improvisations (*taksims*), and codas (*saz semais*), memorized and regenerated decade after decade. Ottoman music drew on an enormous variety of rhythmic cycles (from two to 120 beats) and offered one of the most elaborate and sustained developments of the modal system, known as the *makam.* Based on the use of untempered intervals (as many as 53 notes to an octave), a given mode or *makam* provides a melodic pattern of notes with its own characteristic ascending and descending motifs that course through an entire fasil. Developed in performance, where their vitality depended on the unique interpretations of each ensemble musician, makams historically were rarely written down. Thus the paradoxical fate of modern efforts to revive Ottoman music, which had been suppressed, along with Sufi brotherhoods, by nationalist government officials in the 1920s: on the one hand, attempts to preserve older compositional forms were hampered by a lack of written texts, and on the other hand the very insistence on having musicians learn and perform from notated scores (in Western-style conservatories and radio orchestras) smothered the improvisational genius underlying Turkey's musical forms. How to reconnect Turkey's music to its past without the ingrained ties of familial, religious, and imperial genealogy—such is the dilemma of many musicians in Turkey today. Ulvi Erguner responded to this problem in the 1950s by transcribing forgotten makams and fasils and by pushing for recognition of older classical repertoire at Istanbul Radio. Kudsi's work has been equally determined. In 1988 he founded the Fasl Ensemble, later named the Kudsi Erguner Ensemble, which through numerous recordings and concerts has striven to resuscitate both authentic Ottoman performance practice, with its fluid interplay of refined composition and improvisation, and a broad range of repertoire, from the songs of the 13th-century Sufi poet Yunus Emre to works of the late-19th-century Armenian composer Kemani Tatyos.

In the last few years several ensembles based in Istanbul have also turned their attention to the vast canvas of Ottoman art-music, but the Kudsi Erguner Ensemble, recording most often on accessible French, German, and American labels, has done the most to expose Western listeners to an astounding classical music heritage quite unlike their own. Not simply a purist, Kudsi has been a key player in the cross-cultural world-music scene as well, contributing to the soundtracks of Peter Brook and Peter Gabriel; performing ney solos in various operas, ballets, and theater pieces; and most recently recording a fusion album with European jazz musicians.

what to buy: Kudsi Erguner has performed on more than 40 CDs and LPs. Quintessential among these, and one of the best introductions to the ney and Sufi music generally, is *Sufi Music of Turkey* ♪♪♪♪ (CMP, 1990, prod. Kurt Renker, Walter Quintus), featuring the spare, haunting sound of ney and framedrum, performed by Kudsi (both instruments) and his younger brother Suleyman Erguner (the former one). Suleyman is an extraordinary ney player in his own right, an Istanbul Radio musician with an extensive discography, and he brings out the most inspired playing in Kudsi. Listen for the taut weave of the two neys, the way a subtle line of notes falls away from one and is instantly echoed and reworked by the other. Such musical telepathy, along with the intricate solo taksims, make other ney and dervish recordings seem academic by comparison. *Fasl: Musique de l'Empire Ottoman* ♪♪♪♪ (Auvidis Ethnic, 1990, prod. Kudsi Erguner) features the Kudsi Erguner Ensemble and includes the ney, *kemenche* (spiked fiddle), *ud* (lute), *kanun* (plucked zither), and *def* and *bendir* drums, as well as a male and female chorus. This is one of the best recorded reconstructions of an entire Ottoman music suite (fasil), an assembly of musical forms (pesrevs, sharkis, and saz semais to name a few) unified within the itinerary of a single makam (mode)—here, *hidjaz houmayoun*. Though the anti-Ottoman meddling of Turkish music nationalists sealed their fate, the continuity of such interwoven suites had already begun to erode as early as the 18th century, with the beginnings of Westernization. Further weakened by the popularity of light urban music in the 19th century, such cycles finally imploded as the gramophone swept the Middle East, with its attention span the size of a wax cylinder. The fasil was never so much a pure form as an accretion of styles and composers centuries apart. Here composers range from the Mevlevi Veli Dedi and Sultan Abdoul Aziz to the great 20th-century singer Sadettin Kaynak, who succeeded Kudsi's great-grandfather as the *muezzin* (one who calls the faithful to prayer) of the Yevus Selim mosque in Istanbul. *Tatyos Efendi* ♪♪♪♪ (Traditional Crossroads, 1996, prod. Harold Hagopian) showcases the classical repertoire of a single great composer, Kemani Tatyos, whose late-19th-century pesrevs and saz semais have become standards of the classical literature. In keeping with the infiltration of Western instruments in 19th-century ensembles,

here the violin replaces the kemenche and the clarinet is introduced. Their capacity for flashy brilliance is put to good use on this album, with its hearty sampling of short taksims by Kudsi and Suleyman Erguner and other Istanbul musicians drawn from the Radio Orchestra. The short, lyrical violin taksims of Baki Kemanci (tracks 5 and 13) are well worth the price of the entire CD. The taksims are equally stunning on *Tatyos Efendi: Vocal Masterpieces* ♪♪♪♪ (Traditional Crossroads, 1996, prod. Harold Hagopian), particularly the opening ney improvisation, as elegiac and yearning as in any dervish ceremony. Tatyos's superb sharkis—love songs that became the most popular of high art forms in Turkey—are passionately interpreted by the female vocalist Melihat Gülses. The very first collection of sharkis recorded with period instruments is another wonderful Erguner Ensemble production, *Sharki: Love Songs of Istanbul* ♪♪♪♪ (CMP, 1991, prod. Kurt Renker, Walter Quintus). Featuring difficult works of 19th- and 20th-century composers, this is a less immediately accessible album, but the ardent voice of Nesrin Sipahi, one of the initiators of the return to Turkish classical music in the 1950s, fluently expresses the deranged and devotional sorrow of lost love. *Gazel: Classical Music of the Ottoman Empire* ♪♪♪♪ (CMP, 1991, prod. Kurt Renker, Walter Quintus) focuses on the elegant, multi-lingual poetic form known as the *gazel,* a vehicle for love poems throughout the Middle East that was adapted by the Sufis and their Sultan devotees for the expression of spiritual love. The three passionate singers heard here are all Imams in various Istanbul mosques.

what to buy next: *Psaumes de Yunus Emré* ♪♪♪♪ (Al Sur, 1996, prod. Michel Pagiras) resurrects compositions inspired by the 13th-century Sufi poet Yunus Emre and offers a minimalist but dramatic treatment of Sufi lyricism, featuring only ney, drum, and a male vocalist. *L'Orient de l'Occident* ♪♪♪♪ (Al Sur, 1994, prod. Festival d'Ete de Barcelone) claims to be an exploration of the historical connection between Eastern and Western styles—Ottoman Sufi and flamenco music—in the Andalusian region of modern Spain. But this seems like a thin archival patina on what is fundamentally a popular world-fusion album that stands up well without any pretexts. One is most likely to come away noting the difference between the tones of protest and supplication in flamenco and Ottoman vocal styles, both of which are powerfully represented here. *Peshrev & Semai of Tanburi Djemil Bey* ♪♪♪♪ (CMP, 1991, prod. Kurt Render, Walter Quintus) pays homage to one of the first and greatest Turkish musicians whose compositions were disseminated and dissected through recordings. Djemil (a.k.a. Cemil) Bey's virtuosity on the *tanbur* (long-necked, fretted Turkish lute), captured on over 100 cylinder recordings and 78s before his death in 1918, has been the benchmark for countless modern musicians. The Kudsi Erguner Ensemble is well-staffed for this production and the solos are especially strong.

Gloria Estefan

what to avoid: With its canonical title and picture of Kudsi Erguner on the cover, *Ottoman Classical Music* ♫ (Al Sur, 1992, prod. Niglo des Chants) would seem like an obvious Erguner project to pull from the bin, but this duet album is dominated by the amateur playing of one of Kudsi's French students, the tanburist Gilles Andrieux. Far better to seek out the legendary tanbur recordings of Djemil Bey for a satisfying experience of that instrument, or the mesmerizing ney collaborations of Kudsi and his brother for the cream of Kudsi's duet work.

best of the rest:
The Turkish Ney ♫♫♫♪ (Auvidis/UNESCO, 1990)
Whirling Dervishes from Turkey ♫♫♫♪ (Arion, 1991)
Oriental Dreams ♫♫♪ (Playasound, 1991)
Chemins ♫♫♫ (Al Sur, 1997)
Sufi Flutes ♫♫♫♫ (JVC, 1997)
Le Concert de Nanterre ♫♫♫ (Al Sur, 1998)
Ottomania: Sufi-Jazz-Project N/A (Act, 1999)

worth searching for: For serious ney devotees, two Kudsi Erguner recordings issued only on LP are consistently mentioned as some of his best work: *Meditation on the Ney* (Philips, 1978),

a solo album featuring a series of taksims, and *Sufi Music & Unrecorded Songs of the 15th Century* (GREM, 1980), which recreates part of a Sufi invocation ceremony. For the casual listener who likes the ney but doesn't give a wit about Ottoman music, there are the atmospheric soundtracks to several movies, good and bad, set against generic Middle Eastern backdrops. *Mahabahrata* ♫♫♫♪ (RealWorld, 1990, prod. Peter Brook) draws the Turkish ney (along with the Aboriginal Australian *didgeridoo* drone instrument and the Japanese *taiko* drums) into a retelling of the Hindu epic. A potentially disjointed concept actually becomes a very thoughtful, creative world-fusion album, without the electronic overkill of so many RealWorld records. *Passion Sources* ♫♫♫♫ (RealWorld, 1993, prod. Peter Gabriel) is in essence the commercial sampler of the musicians heard on the Peter Gabriel–masterminded soundtrack for Martin Scorsese's *The Last Temptation of Christ. The Sheltering Sky* ♫♫♫ (Virgin, 1991, prod. Ryuichi Sakamoto) is basically a continuous film score with exotic flute sounds thrown in, and is likely to disappoint Erguner fans as much as the movie disappoints fans of the novelist Paul Bowles; it's much more worthwhile to hunt down the best video store in town and rent Peter Brooks's *Meetings* with *Remarkable Men,* filmed in Afghanistan in 1976, which not only includes some sharp ney playing but features Kudsi Erguner himself in a cameo role.

influences:

◀◀ Ulvi Erguner, Yorgo Bacanos, Udi Hrant, Necdet Yasar, Sadettin Heper

see also: *Anouar Brahem, Udi Hrant*

Cynthia Rogers

Victor Essiet

See: The Mandators

Gloria Estefan /Miami Sound Machine

Latin pop

Born Gloria Fajardo, September 1, 1957, in Havana, Cuba. Based in Miami, FL, USA.

Simply put, Gloria Estefan has terrific pipes that were co-opted—with consent—away from Miami's Cuban dance scene into the blander but phenomenally successful realm of middle-of-the-road pop. The Cuban native, who fled that country's revolution with her family and moved to the U.S. when she was two, started out fronting the Miami Sound Machine, a former wedding band led by her husband, Emilio Estefan Jr., whose south-of-the-equator polyrhythms provided an interesting mainstream pop alternative during the mid-'80s. It didn't last long; as Estefan's voice grew from chirpy to assured, the Miami Sound Machine moniker gradually disappeared from the album covers in order to showcase the singer. In 1990, when a tractor-trailer hit Estefan's tour bus, she suffered a fractured vertebrae that required months of rigorous rehabilitation; but a year later, she was back in action, singing "Coming out of the Dark," a song inspired by the accident, to #1. Give Estefan this much: she's no producer's tool, writing many of her own lyrics and checking off on the creative decisions. If only one of those decisions would be a return to the those irresistible club grooves . . . .

what to buy: *Eyes of Innocence* 𝄢𝄢𝄢 (Epic, 1984/1989, prod. Emilio & the Jerks) contains only one minor hit, "Dr. Beat," but the Miami Sound Machine's debut is an intoxicating blend of Caribbean rhythms. You won't find anything from that album on *Greatest Hits* 𝄢𝄢𝄢 (Epic, 1992, prod. Emilio Estefan) but you do get her best, a largely upbeat collection that includes "Conga," "Rhythm Is Gonna Get You," and "Get on Your Feet."

what to buy next: *Gloria!* 𝄢𝄢𝄢 (Epic, 1998, prod. various) brings back some of the percolating spirit of the early Miami Sound Machine, blending Caribbean rhythms with South Beach disco beats, though with nary a hint of industrial or techno styles. But "Don't Release Me," her collaboration with Wyclef Jean of the Fugees, shows she's not ignorant of current musical affairs.

what to avoid: Estefan can probably sing lots of songs very well. Why'd she pick the ones on *Hold Me, Thrill Me, Kiss Me* 𝄢𝄢 (Epic, 1994, prod. various)?

the rest:

Into the Light 𝄢𝄢 (Epic, 1981)
Primitive Love 𝄢𝄢𝄢 (Epic, 1985)
Let It Loose 𝄢𝄢𝄢 (Epic, 1987)
Cuts Both Ways 𝄢𝄢𝄢 (Epic, 1989)
Mi Tierra 𝄢𝄢𝄢 (Epic, 1993)
Christmas through Your Eyes 𝄢𝄢𝄢 (Epic, 1993)
Abriendo Puertas 𝄢𝄢𝄢 (Epic, 1995)
Destiny 𝄢𝄢 (Epic, 1996)

worth searching for: Estefan's guest vocal on the song "Africa" from Arturo Sandoval's *Dayon* (GRP, 1994, prod. Arturo Sandoval, Richard Eddy) is terrific.

influences:

◀◀ Carmen Miranda, Tito Puente, Herb Alpert & the Tijuana Brass, Aretha Franklin, Donna Summer

▶▶ Debbie Gibson, Celine Dion

see also: *Albita, Chayanne, Arturo Sandoval*

Gary Graff

The Ethiopians

Roots reggae

Formed 1966, in Kingston, Jamaica. Based in Kingston, Jamaica.

Leonard Dillon, vocals (1966–present); Stephen Taylor, vocals (1966–1975); Aston "Charlie" Morris, vocals (1966–1968); Melvin "Mellow" Reid, vocals (1968–1977). (All members are from Jamaica.)

Leonard Dillon is the wisdom-blessed seer of roots-reggae pioneers the Ethiopians. Impressed by the cushioned warmth of Dillon's expressive voice, Bob Marley bandmate and later solo legend Peter Tosh introduced Dillon to producer Coxsone Dodd in 1965. Even on his earliest Wailers-backed singles with Dodd ("Sufferers on the Land," "Beggars Have No Choice," "Icewater," and "Bullwhip"), recorded under the name King Sparrow, Dillon exhibited an expansive vision of music, a vision that embraced the ideals of united humanity in his Rastafarian faith. At the same time, Dillon's folksy, proverb-fortified songs were the essence of the hard-working man's struggle to grasp joy and knowledge from even the toughest of situations.

Given that the Ethiopians influenced an entire era of Jamaican roots music, perhaps it is the humble, understated nature of Dillon's voice and lyrics that has kept this group from receiving the recognition they deserve. Whatever the case, the Ethiopians' catalog is one of the sweetest, most utterly enjoyable in all of reggae. After the group formed, their first sides included the exceptional "Gonna Take Over Now" and "(I'm a) Free Man" for Dodd. In 1967, Dillon himself produced "Train to Skaville," a tune that, despite the title, was really a grooving rocksteady classic that surprisingly charted in the U.K. That same year, the group recorded two rare singles for Lee Perry—"Cut Down" and "Not Me." The band's work for Sonia Pottinger's Gayfeet label is rocksteady as fine as it comes, with "Do It Sweet," "The Whip," "Stay Loose Mama," and the wonderful "Train to Glory" all scoring big on the island. Evoking the classic children's story *The Little Engine That Could* and committing themselves to the long haul, Dillon and company released the never-give-up anthem "Engine 54" with Lloyd "The Matador" Daley. This led to a fruitful association with Carl "Sir J.J." Johnson and a string of reggae gems, including "Well Red," "Everything Crash," "Hong Kong Flu," and "Hang On, Don't Let Go." The group also recorded superior reggae sides for a number of other top-notch producers, including Duke Reid ("Pirate," "Mother's Tender Care"), Derrick Harriott ("No Baptism"), Vincent Chin ("Sad News," "Rim Bam Bam"), Rupie Edwards ("Solid as a Rock"), and Bob Andy ("The World Is Love"). This relentless string of strong tunes ceased when Stephen Taylor was killed in a car accident in 1975. After a period of heavy mourning, Dillon returned with the traditional, Rastafarian-themed *Slave Call*, a fine record propelled by intricate *nyahbingi* ritual drumming and subtly imbued with echo and reverb by eccentric producer Niney the Observer.

Under the unwavering guidance of Dillon, the Ethiopians still occasionally record, and many of their rare singles have been reissued on various outstanding compilations. Dillon's frail, graceful, deeply soulful voice, perceptive lyrics, unerring ability to structure elaborate harmonies, and consistent flow of important ideas gleaned from his own and his country's experiences, have assured the Ethiopians a lasting legacy—and one that should be explored by any music lover. Leonard Dillon and the Ethiopians are truly the embodiment of the Jamaican maxim, "Who feels it, knows it."

what to buy: *Engine 54—Let's Ska and Rocksteady* ♪♪♪♪ (Jamaican Gold, 1968, prod. various) is one of the most celebrated rocksteady albums. The metaphor of the train as a strong engine for the unity and progress of disenfranchised, ghetto-suffering people the world over is used by Dillon on a holy trinity of classic cuts—the title song, "Train to Skaville," and "Train to Glory." The entire album is backed in cool, elegant fashion by Tommy McCook and the Supersonics, and the vintage liner notes include instructions on how to do the "rocksteady" dance and fall "under the spell" of this enchanting, exultant music. *The Original Reggae Hitsound* ♪♪♪♪ (Trojan, 1986, prod. vari-

ous) and *The World Goes Ska* ♪♪♪ (Trojan, 1992, prod. various) are two superlative compilations with no overlap. Together, they provide an awe-inspiring musical documentary of the Ethiopians and include all of the above "train" hits alongside such favorites as "Rim Bam Bam," "Do It Sweet," and "Stay Loose Mama." Also highly reggae-mended are *Clap Your Hands* ♪♪♪♪ (Lagoon, 1992, prod. Carl Johnson) and *Sir J.J. and Friends* ♪♪♪♪ (Lagoon, prod. Carl Johnson). These collections of prized Sir J.J. Johnson–produced songs include the marvelous "Everyday Talking," "Well Red," "The Selah," and "Everything Crash" (one of the best musical documents of Jamaica's internal chaos just a few years after independence, and the first song without sexually suggestive lyrics to be banned from airplay on the island).

what to buy next: Along with Count Ossie's *Grounation,* the aforementioned *Slave Call* ♪♪♪♪ (Heartbeat, 1977, Winston "Niney the Observer" Holness) is one of the best recorded examples of Rastafarian nyahbingi drumming, featuring a dense six-drum congregation that provides intricate rhythmic lattice-work. Dillon's "Ethiopian National Anthem," "Obeah Book," and "Nuh Follow Babylon" marked his triumphant return to form after nearly two years of seclusion. *Owner Fe De Yard* ♪♪♪♪ (Heartbeat, 1994, prod. various) is an object lesson on how to reissue music. This is a collection of nearly 20 years of top-drawer Ethiopians rarities like "One Heart" (1969), "So You Look Pon It" (1974), and "Let Me Blow My Smoke" (1985), with the added bonus of detailed liner notes, including a recent informative interview with Leonard Dillon that sheds much light on this gentle soul.

the rest:
Reggae Power ♪♪♪♪ (Trojan, 1969)
Woman Capture Man ♪♪♪♪ (Trojan, 1970)
Everything Crash ♪♪♪♪ (Studio One, 1980)
Open the Gate of Zion ♪♪♪ (G.G., 1980)
Dread Prophecy ♪♪♪ (Nighthawk, 1986)
Leonard Dillon on the Road Again ♪♪♪ (Heartbeat, 1991)
Tuffer Than Stone ♪♪♪♪ (Roots & Culture, 1999)

influences:

◄◄ Peter Tosh, Drumbago, Laurel Aitken, Owen Gray, Derrick Morgan, Toots Hibbert, Lee Perry.

►► Culture, the Gladiators, the Mighty Diamonds, Burning Spear, Black Uhuru, Junior Byles, the Congos, Junior Murvin, Garnett Silk

Todd Shanker

Étoile de Dakar

Senegalese rumba, mbalax
Formed 1960, in Dakar, Senegal. Based in Dakar, Senegal.

Youssou N'Dour, vocals; El Hadji Faye, vocals; Eric M'Backe N'Doye, vocals; Alla Seck, vocals, maracas; Badou N'Diaye, solo guitar; Alpha

Senyni Kanta, rhythm guitar, Kabou Gueye, bass; Assane Thaim, tama (Senegalese talking drum); Matar Gueye, tumbas; Abdou Fall, timbales, Rane Diallo, saxes; Diogomaye, sax; Marc Sambat, trumpet. (All members are from Senegal.)

It is not an exaggeration to say that modern Senegalese pop music would not have existed without the band that evolved into Youssou N'Dour's Étoile de Dakar. Over the course of its two-decade heyday, it was the training ground for dozens of famous musicians. Étoile de Dakar transformed the Cuban music that had been at the root of Senegalese pop before Liberation and turned it into something uniquely Senegalese, and vastly different from the African rumba of the Congo, *soukous*.

Étoile de Dakar began as the Star Band in 1960, created by Ibra Kasse, owner of Dakar's Miami Club, when he combined and hired the best musicians from two rival bands—Guinea Band de Dakar, who played mostly Cuban covers, and Star Band de Senui, known for their powerful electric guitar work. Senegal had just gained independence from France, and the musicians were looking for a sound that would be truly Senegalese. They began to add indigenous rhythms and folk instruments to the lineup, including the *tama* and *sabar*, Senegalese talking drums. As the group sound developed and began attracting listeners, musicians splintered off to form variants (Super Star Band and Star Number One), but the original Star Band soldiered on.

In 1975, a 16-year-old Youssou N'Dour joined the Star Band, and his musical vision transformed their sound. In 1978 they recorded an album with N'Dour on lead vocals, and soon after that N'Dour broke away from the Miami Club, taking several members of the band with him, including tama player Assane Thiam, the man whose innovative drumming laid the foundation for N'Dour's later success. When N'Dour translated the band's name back into French, they became Étoile de Dakar, and began calling their music *mbalax*, the word for rhythm in N'Dour's tribal tongue, Wolof. In Senegal the music business was still evolving, and cassettes, the main recorded medium, were manufactured quickly, mainly to draw crowds to a band's live gigs, where they made the majority of their money. N'Dour and Étoile de Dakar recorded a series of cassettes and albums that made them so popular, in 1983 N'Dour moved the group to Paris, where he began to pursue his international career.

what to buy: The sound on the reissued *Absa Gueye* 𝄞𝄞𝄞𝄞 (Stern's Classics, 1993, prod. Étoile de Dakar) is spotty, but there's no denying the power of the music; the Cuban and Congolese influences are present, but every so often they fall away to give you a hint of what N'Dour soon accomplished.

what to buy next: The final disc in the classic Étoile series, *Khaley Étoile* 𝄞𝄞𝄞𝄞 (Stern's Classics, 1998, prod. Touba Auto Cassette), cut in 1982, presents Youssou N'Dour and guitarist

music as healing

Though the idea of music as a healing tool is associated with the current new-age movement, it is in fact a relatively universal belief, with roots dating back thousands of years to a number of ancient cultures. According to Pat Moffitt Cook, a musicologist and expert on the subject, "Throughout the ages, by trial and error, selected sounds and rhythms developed into tools for diagnosing and curing illness. Sophisticated breathing patterns evolved together with prayerful chants and sacred healing songs. The songs cure, petition benevolent deities, invite spirit possession, and induce states of ecstasy." Today, similar healing traditions are still practiced in a variety of cultures, including the *ojhas* of India, the *Ayahuasca* shamen of Peru, the peyote shamen of Mexico, the medicine men of various Native American tribes, the *jhankri* of Nepal, and the priestesses of Haitian *Vodou*. Perhaps the most well-known of these rituals is the *leela*, a serene healing ceremony practiced by the Gnawa of Morocco, wherein music is used to purge a spirit that has brought on illness, infertility, or other affliction. These ceremonies typically last for seven days, and as the percussion-heavy music drones in repetition, participants may enter a trance as they find themselves possessed by healing spirits—a startling but impressive sight. This phenomenon could explain why some people in the West seem to feel a particular natural high while dancing to the similar serial rhythms of techno. To hear a variety of trance-music traditions from around the world, check out Cook's fantastic collection *Shaman, Jhankri & Néle* 𝄞𝄞𝄞𝄞 (ellipsis arts . . . , 1997), or the equally fascinating compilations *Trance 1* 𝄞𝄞𝄞𝄞 (ellipsis arts . . . , 1995) and *Trance 2* 𝄞𝄞𝄞𝄞 (ellipsis arts . . . , 1995).

Bret Love

Badou Gueye in full command of their powers; N'Dour's vocals are superb, Gueye's guitar constantly amazes, and the band has moved out of the shadow of Cuban music to establish the sound that dominated Senegalese music for the rest of the 1980s.

the rest:
Lay Suma Lay ♫♫♫ (Stern's Classics, 1994, Prod. Étoile de Dakar)
Thiapathioly ♫♫♫ (Stern's Classics, 1996, Prod. Étoile de Dakar)

influences:
◀◀ Guinea Band de Dakar, Star Band de Senui

▶▶ Youssou N'Dour, Baaba Maal, Étoile 2000, Star Band One, Super Star de Dakar

see also: *Youssou N'Dour*

j. poet

Eunice Playboys
See: John Delafose & the Eunice Playboys

Cesaria Evora
Morna, coladeira
Born August 27, 1941, in Mindelo, Sao Vicente, Cape Verde. Based in Cape Verde.

Cape Verde was essentially a bunch of rocks off the coast of Africa until the Portuguese transformed it into a depot for the slave trade in the 15th century. Over time the commerce in human flesh declined and the colony fell victim to cycles of famine and drought. By the mid-20th century, Cape Verde was extremely poor, and many of its people were migrating to other countries in search of work. It is against this backdrop that Cesaria Evora grew up. Her father and his cousin (Francisco Xavier da Cruz, a.k.a. B. Leza) used to tour the bars of Mindelo singing for tips. At the heart of their material were the indigenous *mornas* and *coladeiras,* which blend elements of bluesy Portuguese *fado* with subtle African rhythms. The morna is slower-paced and employs more fatalistic lyrics, while the comparatively up-beat coladeira is, in some ways, akin to the Brazilian samba. Evora was joining her father and his cousin on their circuit of dives when she was in her early teens, and by 1961 had made a number of successful appearances on local radio shows. She stopped singing during the early 1970s to raise a family.

Evora didn't return to music until 1985, when she was invited to Portugal by the singer Bana and a women's association to make her first record, *Tchitchi Roti.* But her career didn't really take off until 1988, when a young Frenchman with Cape Verdean bloodlines, José da Silva, convinced Evora to come to Paris where she recorded *La Diva aux Pieds Nus* for his label, Lusafrica. The album and her concerts were a small success with the Cape Verdean expatriate community in Paris, which made it possible for 1990's *Distino di Belita. Mar Azul* was then released in 1991 and marked the beginning of a definite up-ward swing for Evora. French radio stations started playing the album, her concerts throughout France began selling out, and the French press raved about her roughly honeyed voice. By

the time the spectacularly successful *Miss Perfumado* came out in 1993, Evora had toured France, Belgium, and Portugal, and her career as an international star was in full swing by the end of 1995. Her concert tours spanned the globe, her album *Cesaria Evora* was nominated for a Grammy (an honor she has now received three times), and Pol Cruchten cast her as the mother of the protagonist in his film *Black Dju.* The government of Cape Verde was so pleased by her success as their unofficial ambassador that they even awarded her a diplomatic passport.

what to buy: It's easy to see why *Miss Perfumado* ♫♫♫♫ (Lusafrica, 1992/Nonesuch, 1998, prod. José da Silva) is Cesaria Evora's best-selling album internationally and her third Grammy-nominated one Stateside. "Sodade" was the big hit, and deservedly so, but the political message behind "Cumpade Ciznone," the wry humor of Ramiro Mendes's "Angola," and the worldly-wise narration of "Barbincor" prove that there is more to morna and coladeira than the stereotypical infinite personal sadness.

what to buy next: The title tune for *Mar Azul* ♫♫♫ (Lusafrica/Melodie, 1991/Nonesuch, 1999, prod. José da Silva) was writ-ten by B. Leza and remains one of the most exquisite perfor-mances in Evora's repertoire. Paulino Viera's harmonica and Luis Morais's clarinet playing bring to the song echoes of smoky nights in Paris cafes, which may explain why French au-diences were so receptive to her concerts and this album. The rest of the disc meets the high expectations this song raises. When Evora's album *Cabo Verde* ♫♫♫ (Lusafrica/Nonesuch, 1997, prod. José da Silva) earned her second Grammy nomina-tion in three years, it signaled that the American record indus-try was taking note of her ability to sell product. Happily, the album was worth the honor and more. The personnel for the sessions is consistent with the rest of Evora's catalog, except-ing jazz wizard James Carter, who contributes tenor saxophone riffs to "Coragem Irmon."

the rest:
La Diva aux Pieds Nus ♫♫♫ (Lusafrica/Melodie, 1988)
Distino di Belita ♫♫♫ (Lusafrica/Melodie, 1990)
Les Plus Belles Mornas de Cesaria ♫♫♫ (Lusafrica/BMG France, 1994)
Cesaria Evora ♫♫♫ (Lusafrica, 1994/Nonesuch, 1995)
Café Atlantico N/A (BMG/RCA Victor, 1999)

worth searching for: Live albums sometimes present sonic drawbacks, but they also can capture the loving give-and-take between a gifted performer and her audience. *Cesaria Evora Live à l'Olympia* ♫♫♫ (Lusafrica/Melodie, 1996, prod. José da Silva) is well-recorded, and the song selection covers material from *La Diva aux Pieds Nus* through *Miss Perfumado,* with a few rarities tossed in.

Cesaria Evora

influences:

◄◄ Cabo Verde Show, Amália Rodrigues

►► Fantcha

see also: *Bana, Fantcha*

Garaud MacTaggart

Chaba Fadela

Rai

Born February 5, 1962, in Algeria. Based in Paris, France.

Despite the difficulties of being a female artist in a conservative Muslim country, Chaba Fadela carved out a successful niche for herself in the early days of pop-*rai*. Rai (a rebellious vernacular music) had always been controversial, with the older generation of Bedouin singers, both male and female, singing improvised verses about sex, alcohol, and street life. By the late 1970s producer Rachid Baba Ahmed, who had a 24-track studio in Tlemcen, was revolutionizing the style's sound by recording with synthesizers, drum machines, and electric guitars, and adding elements of funk, reggae, dub, and eventually hip-hop to the mix. When he connected with Chaba Fadela he found the passionate voice he needed to take the music to the next level. Fadela had already become well known for her performances at clubs and weddings as a featured member of Boutaïba S'ghir's group, with a rugged and emotional style that was perfect for the rough-and-tumble songs she was singing. When Fadela cut "Ana Ma H'Lali Ennoum (I Don't Like to Sleep)" in 1979, rai hit a new level of popularity and technical excellence. Fadela became the first star of the modern rai era and brought the music to international attention when she cut "N'sel Fik (You Are·Mine)," a duet with her husband Cheb Sahraoui, in 1983. "N'sel Fik" became the most popular song in the history of the genre; it was also the lead track of *Rai Rebels,* the 1988 EarthWorks compilation that introduced rai to the West, and was the title track of an album Fadela and Sahraoui cut for Island U.K. that same year. In the late 1980s, as political and religious violence in Algeria escalated (Rachid Baba Ahmed and another hit rai vocalist, Cheb Hasni, were eventually both gunned down for making music some considered sacrilegious), Fadela and Sahraoui fled to Paris with their children, where they have continued to perform as a duo and spread the gospel of rai.

what to buy: On *You Are Mine* ♪♪♪♪ (Mango, 1988, prod. Rachid Baba Ahmed), Ahmed, the Phil Specter of rai, comple-

ments Fadela's dramatic vocals with serpentine keyboard lines, funky backbeats, and synth accents that give these performances a relentless rhythmic drive.

what to buy next: Ahmed's production balances the traditional and the modern on *Hana Hana* ♪♪♪♪ (Mango, 1989, prod. Rachid Baba Ahmed), making this duet album by Fadela and Sahraoui another high-water mark of pop-rai.

the rest:

(With Cheb Sahraoui) *Walli* ♪♪♪♪ (Rounder, 1997)
(With Cheb Sahraoui) *Manich Mana* ♪♪♪♪ (Blue Silver, 1997)

influences:

◄◄ Cheikha Remitti

j. poet

Fairport Convention

English folk-rock

Formed 1967, in London, England. Disbanded 1979. Re-formed 1985. Based in the "folk-rock belt" near Banbury, Oxfordshire, England.

Primary but not complete list includes: Simon Nicol, guitar, vocals; Ashley Hutchings, bass, vocals (1967–69); Judy Dyble, recorder, autoharp, vocals (1967–68); Richard Thompson, guitar, vocals (1967–71); Iain Matthews, guitar, vocals (1967–68); Martin Lamble (died 1969), drums (1967–69); Sandy Denny (died April 21, 1978), piano, vocals (1968–69, 1974–75); Dave Swarbrick, fiddle, vocals (1969–79); Dave Mattacks, drums, keyboards (1969–74, 1985–98); Dave Pegg, bass, mandolin, vocals (1970–present); Jerry Donahue (USA), guitar, vocals (1972–75); Trevor Lucas (Australia) (died February 4, 1989), guitar, vocals (1972–75); Bruce Rowland, drums (1974–75); Martin Allcock, guitar, bouzouki, keyboards, vocals (1985–97); Ric Sanders, fiddle (1985–present); Chris Leslie, guitar, fiddle, vocals (1997–present). (All members mentioned are from England, except where otherwise noted.)

One of Fairport Convention's traditional songs, "Sir Patrick Spens," tells of a man who gets reluctantly pressed into service as a seaman and drowns. Conversely, the story of Fairport Convention is the story of a group of misfits, geniuses, and drinking buddies who manage to become a band—and stay afloat for 30 years and counting. The saga began when some London schoolboys got together at Simon Nicol's parents' house, which was called Fairport, and decided to start a band. They invited a couple of other local characters to join, including librarian Judy Dyble. The band was "discovered" when Joe Boyd, an American impresario who ran the UFO Club in London, heard them and was staggered by the skill of the teenage guitarist, Richard Thompson, on an extended solo during "East West." After the band made its first album, Dyble left and Ashley Hutchings brought in another girl singer, the folk circuit's Sandy Denny. It was Denny who brought the first folk influences to the band; she had many arrangements into which the boys were able to work themselves, and such songs as "A Sailor's Life" began making electrified appearances on Fairport set-lists. The band enjoyed modest success until a 1969 van crash killed the drummer, Martin Lamble, and left the remaining members physically and emotionally wounded. They found a new drummer, Dave Mattacks (who played jazz and knew nothing about folk music), brought in traditional fiddler Dave Swarbrick, and retired to a country house, where in a few months *Liege and Lief* was born.

The resultant concerts were a massive success; the sound Fairport achieved on that album, strongly grounded in English traditional music, was radical and highly intriguing. However, *Liege and Lief* split the band. Hutchings left to delve more deeply into traditional sources, while Denny left to concentrate on songwriting. The remaining members continued on the satisfying, if highly uncommercial, folk-rock path, through various personnel changes (including Thompson's departure and Denny's return). By the end of the 1970s, Swarbrick, the only remaining early member, was nearly deaf from his electric violin. The band (which was then, and briefly, called simply "Fairport") was laid to rest. When the reunions started, a strange thing happened: the returning members found that they really enjoyed their own music. By 1985, Fairport Convention was back. The band still holds a yearly reunion at Cropredy, Oxfordshire, near the homes of many members. Numerous other outfits, including Fairport contemporaries Steeleye Span, Pentangle, and the Incredible String Band, have combined rock and folk elements with great success; in North America, Bob Dylan and the Band have followed similar muses. Few, if any, have been able to generate the long-term affection and spirit that Fairport created and sustains.

what to buy: *What We Did on Our Holidays* ♫♫♫♫ (Hannibal, 1968, prod. Joe Boyd) brings together the band's past and future. It's a microcosm of their interests, with compositions by Denny ("Fotheringay") and Thompson ("Tale in Hard Time" and "No Man's Land"); covers of Bob Dylan ("I'll Keep It with Mine") and Joni Mitchell ("Eastern Rain"); electric arrangements of traditional songs ("Nottamun Town" and "She Moved Through the Fair"); middle-of-the-road pop ("Book Song"); an instrumental (Simon Nicol's coda "End of a Holiday"); and best of all an anthem (the Thompson-penned "Meet on the Ledge") that's sung at nearly every Fairport concert. Each member is in top form, and Denny is dazzling. *Liege and Lief* ♫♫♫♫ (A&M, 1969, prod. Joe Boyd) is perhaps Fairport's most significant album, for it most fully developed the electric folk format for which the band is best known. Thompson and Swarbrick's "Crazy Man Michael" caps off the album brilliantly; it's a song for the ages. *Jewel in the Crown* ♫♫♫ (Green Linnet, 1995, prod. Fairport Convention) is the best offering from Fairport's longest-lived lineup (Nicol/Pegg/Mattacks/Allcock/Sanders).

Chaba Fadela

what to buy next: *House Full* ♫♫♫♫ (Hannibal, 1986, prod. Joe Boyd, Frank Kornelussen) documents Fairport's first all-male lineup on its American tour, where the band members allegedly drank so much they ended up owing money to the venues rather than being paid. Thompson's timid vocals are touching in light of the powerhouse he's become. Swarbrick is front and center with deft fiddling and charming singing. *Expletive Delighted!* ♫♫♫ (Varrick, 1986) showcases the instrumental wizardry of the Nicol/Pegg/Mattacks/Allcock/Sanders lineup.

best of the rest:
Fairport Convention ♫♫♫ (Polydor, 1968)
Unhalfbricking ♫♫♫♫ (Hannibal, 1969)
Full House ♫♫♫♫ (Hannibal, 1970)
Gladys' Leap ♫♫♫ (Varrick, 1985)
Heyday ♫♫♫♫ (Hannibal, 1987)
Five Seasons ♫♫♫ (Rough Trade, 1990)
Who Knows Where the Time Goes (Green Linnet, 1998)

worth searching for: *Rising for the Moon* ♫♫♫ (Island, 1975, prod. Glyn Johns) is largely a Sandy Denny album, and it contains three of her finest compositions: "Stranger to Himself," "After Halloween," and "One More Chance." Swarbrick and Donahue provide outstanding support. *The Cropredy Box* ♫♫♫

(Woodworm, 1998, prod. Dave Pegg, Simon Nicol) is essential for completists and provides a flavor of the Cropredy reunion festivals. Recorded live in 1997, the three-disc set offers a chronology of the band's development, with present and former members (including the Breton singer Dan Ar Braz) and a variety of guest performers (including an audience of 20,000 on "Danny Boy"). Fans will enjoy the unexpurgated recording of a notorious April Fool's phone prank—which results in the album's warning label: "Parental Guidance: Explicit Swarbrick." The video documentary *It All Comes 'Round Again* (1987, prod. Paul Kovit) tells the band's story through the late 1980s. Wonderful historical footage shows the early lineup on *Top of the Pops,* the highly hirsute *Full House* boys with "Now Be Thankful," and the Trevor Lucas–fronted band singing "Polly on the Shore." Interview sequences deftly reveal the personalities associated with the band: diffident, introspective Thompson; imperious, eloquent Hutchings; former fan Sanders; and droll Pegg, cigarette always at the ready. The documentary also includes the only video footage of Sandy Denny that is commercially available.

influences:

◀◀ The Byrds, Jefferson Airplane, the Band, Bob Dylan, the Watersons

▶▶ New St. George, Mad Pudding

see also: *Dan Ar Braz, Ian Campbell Folk Group, Shirley Collins, Sandy Denny, Ashley Hutchings/Albion Band, A.L. Lloyd, Trevor Lucas, Ralph McTell, Steeleye Span, Dave Swarbrick, Richard Thompson*

Pamela Murray Winters

Joseph Falcon & Cleoma Breaux Falcon

Cajun
Formed in Louisiana, USA.

Joseph Falcon (born September 28, 1900, in Rayne, LA, USA; died November 29, 1965, in Crowley, LA, USA), one-row diatonic accordion, drums, vocals; Cleoma Breaux Falcon (born May 27, 1906, in Crowley, LA, USA; died April 9, 1941, in Crowley, LA, USA), resonator guitar, vocals.

Joe Falcon and Cleoma Breaux went into the temporary recording studio that Columbia had set up in a downtown New Orleans hotel on April 27, 1928, and made the first commercial recordings of Cajun music. His "Allons a Lafayette" was played on Victrolas in the streets of the small prairie towns of Southwest Louisiana. Cleoma is the only Cajun woman musician who recorded in the 1920s and early '30s. The combination of her resonator guitar and his solid button accordion created a sen-

sation, and both were excellent singers as well. Cleoma is reported to have been the creator of the most famous Cajun song, "Jolie Blonde," having taught it to her brother Amédée Breaux for his recording session.

what to buy: A compilation of remastered recordings of early Cajun music, *Abbeville Breakdown* ♫♫♫♫ (Columbia, 1990, prod. Lawrence Cohn) was released as part of Columbia Records' Roots and Blues series. This collection includes two great performances by Cleoma Breaux: "Prenez Courage," which is a rewrite of the Hawaiian standard "Aloha Oe," and the bluesy "Quand Je Suit Partis pour Texas." Joe Falcon is represented by "Poche Town" and the great unaccompanied "Aimer et Perdre." There are also excellent recordings of Cleoma's brothers, the Breaux Freres.

what to buy next: *Cajun Dance Party: Fais Do Do* ♫♫♫♫ (Columbia, 1994, prod. Lawrence Cohn) is the second release of old Cajun material in the Roots and Blues series. It has four excellent sides of Cleoma Falcon, including the extremely influential "Mon Coeur T'Appelle," which may be the best-known song among Cajuns after "Jolie Blonde." "Le Vieux Soulard et Sa Femme" was the first recording of an ancient French song about a drunk and his wife that has continued to be recast and recorded by everyone from Dewey Balfa to Boozoo Chavis.

the rest:
Live at a Cajun Dance ♫♫♫♫ (Arhoolie, 1997)

worth searching for: The LP *Cleoma B. Falcon: A Cajun Music Classic* ♫♫♫♫ (Jadfel, 1983, prod. Johnnie Allen) brings together many of the important records that Cleoma Falcon recorded with Joe Falcon. Listen to her growl through "Leve Tes Fenetreas Haut" sounding like a Cajun Bessie Smith, or her own "Crowley Waltz," written after almost drowning in the Hudson River. Powerful music from a pioneer woman musician.

influences:

◀◀ Dennis McGee, Leo Soileau

▶▶ Michael Doucet, Iry LeJeune, Mark and Ann Savoy, the Magnolia Sisters

Jared Snyder

Fania All-Stars
See: Johnny Pacheco, Larry Harlow

Fantcha
Morna, coladeira
Born Francelina Durão Almeida October 14, 1965 in Mindelo, Sao Vicente, Cape Verde. Based in New York, NY, USA.

Fantcha was born in the neighborhood of Mindelo called Laginha, which is also home base for superstar Cesaria Evora. Her family was musical and as a child she began singing with her brothers, who played homemade guitar and *cavaquinho* (a ukulele-like instrument). Her father had deserted the family, so she was working by the age of 10, when she was invited to join the Flores de Mindelo Carnival company. As in Brazil, Carnival is an important social event; companies often practice all year for their Carnival performances. Ti Goi (Gregorio Goncalves), a well-known Verdean composer, was the musical director of Flores de Mindelo and recognized Fantcha's talent. He provided free singing lessons to encourage her. A few years later, he introduced Fantcha to Cesaria Evora. Evora invited the younger singer to visit her home, where she learned much about style and technique. When a club named The Piano Bar opened in Laginha, it became a favorite hangout for Evora and one night she invited Fantcha to open a show for her. This experience made Fantcha even more determined to become a singer. In 1988 she traveled to Lisbon to record with Bana, who was also the first producer to record Evora, but when the album came out Bana retained all the rights to it; Fantcha made nothing. Soon after that, Evora invited Fantcha to open for her again, on a tour of Holland and France; Jose da Silva, Evora's manager and head of her record label, invited Fantcha to continue the pairing on a further tour of the USA. Fantcha decided that the large Cape Verdean community in America offered her the best opportunities, and she settled in New York City. Her 1998 debut, *Criolinha,* was widely praised by critics in America, Europe, and Cape Verde, and her future as an important artist seems assured.

what's available: *Criolinha* 🎵🎵🎵🎵 (Tinder, 1998, prod. Bau) was produced by Cesaria Evora's musical director, and his arrangements add a sparkling polish to the recording. Fantcha tends to favor *coladeiras,* tunes with a bouncy, calypso-like rhythm, but she also tries her hand at a couple of *mornas,* and when her tear-soaked vocals wash over you, it's easy to see why her earnest soulfulness captured Evora's attention.

influences:
◀◀ Cesaria Evora, Bana

see also: *Bana, Cesaria Evora*

j. poet

Farafina

African traditional and contemporary
Formed 1978, in Bobo-Dioulasso, Burkina Faso (formerly Upper Volta). Based in Burkina Faso.

Mahama Konaté, balafon (xylophone), vocals (1978–93); Paco Yé Adama, djembé (goblet drum), drums, vocals (1987–93); Soungalo Coulibaly, flute, maracas, drums, vocals (1987–present); Tiawara Keita, tama ("talking drum"), soukou (violin), doudoum'ni, kora (1987–98); Seydou Ouattara, bara (calabash) (1987–93); Yaya Ouattara, djembé, vocals (1993–present); Beh Palm, bara (1987–98); Baba Diarra, balafon, doudoum'ba (bass drum) (1987–present); Souleyname Sanou, dance, maracas, doudoum'ni, doudoum'ba, vocals (1987–present); Bakari Traoré, balafon, kora, bara, vocals (1993–98); Seydou Zon, soukou, vocals (1993–98); Mamadou Diabate, kora, vocals (1998–present); Harunna Koita, keyboards, vocals (1998–present); Dedougou Dambele, tama, kenke'ni, bara (1998–present); Salif Kone, balafon, djembé, bara (1998–present). (All members are from Burkina Faso.)

Playing in the tradition of the ensembles that backed the *griots* (oral historians) in West Africa for centuries, Farafina is a polyrhythmic percussion outfit that builds its pulsating sound with a pair of *balafons* (xylophones) and a variety of drums and shakers. Formed in 1978 by Mahama Konaté, Farafina's members come from Bobo-Dioulasso, the musical center of southern Burkina Faso. The group had already toured quite a bit in Europe before their first recorded work—*Flash of the Spirit,* a collaboration with trumpeter John Hassell—was released in 1988. Shortly after, they recorded their first album on their own, *Bolomakoté.* Between occasional follow-ups, Farafina has continued to tour extensively and, in the experimental spirit that informs their work along with the traditional one, to contribute to such atypical projects as Ryuichi Sakamoto's *Beauty* and the Rolling Stones' *Steel Wheels.*

what to buy: Ironically, Farafina's first recording represented a radical departure from their basic sound. *Flash of the Spirit* 🎵🎵🎵🎵 (Intuition, 1988/1995, prod. Daniel Lanois, Brian Eno, John Hassell) builds a compelling "ambient" atmosphere that is subdued yet invigorating. Made in collaboration with avant-garde composer and horn player Hassell, the disc finds Farafina creating a backdrop for his processed trumpet explorations, while electronic pioneer Brian Eno builds a shimmering soundscape using the group's rhythms as a palette. Farafina's first album alone, *Bolomakoté* 🎵🎵🎵🎵 (Intuition, 1988, prod. Michael Schaer, Paco Yé Adama, Vera Brandes), captures the thundering strength of their music, with visceral and complex interlocking rhythms and percussive melody pounded out on the balafons. This is nowhere better captured than on "Patron Mousso," an instrumental with showcase solos that moves with incredible speed and intensity.

what to buy next: *Faso Denou* 🎵🎵🎵 (RealWorld, 1993, prod. Bill Cobham, Daniel Lanois, Heinz Dill) is a bit more relaxed and subdued than *Bolomakoté.* On *Nemako* 🎵🎵🎵 (Intuition, 1998, prod. Michael Schaer, Thierry van Roy), the group moves into a pop context, adding electronic keyboards, guitar, and bass. While the drumming still shows plenty of vigor and style, the addition of elements from outside the band's accustomed arena really does not add much to the overall effect.

influences:
◄◄ African drumming tradition

see also: *Brian Eno, Ryuichi Sakamoto*

Jeffrey Muhr

Majek Fashek
African reggae
Born Majekodunmi Fasheke in Benin City, Nigeria. Based in Lagos, Nigeria.

Many African artists have taken reggae's message of unity and spiritual revolution to heart. The work of Bob Marley in particular has become a touchstone for those wishing to send a clear message to the powers that be; many Africans see reggae as a link in a worldwide chain joining the people of the African Diaspora. Nigeria's Majekodunmi Fasheke, known to his fans as Majek Fashek, took up Marley's challenge to become one of Africa's most popular reggae singer-songwriters. Fashek's mother said her son was "born with rhythm." After graduating from college, he formed his first band Jah Stix, but it was Fashek's charisma that brought in the crowds. In 1988 he became a "solo" performer and put together a backing group called Prisoners of Conscience, modeled on the Wailers; in concert the band's six percussionists add multi-layered Pan-African accents to the music, dropping bits of *juju,* highlife, and *zouk* to the basic reggae beat. "In Nigeria we call this music *kpangolo* music, not reggae," Fashek said in a recent interview. "It's similar to a rhythm children beat out on tin cans in Nigeria, so I consider it African music." In 1989 Fashek's solo debut, *Prisoner of Conscience,* won the Nigerian version of the Grammys for Best Reggae Artist, Best Artist, Best LP, and Best Musical Track. The album has sold more than 250,000 copies in Nigeria and two singles from it, "Send Down the Rain" and a cover of Bob Marley's "Redemption Song," stayed in the Top 10 for more than a year. According to legend (and press kit), Fashek ended a year-long drought in Nigeria when he performed "Send Down the Rain" at a benefit for struggling farmers and brought forth a thundering rainstorm. Since his debut, Fashek has recorded two more albums, *Spirit of Love* (which he calls "a mix of reggae and African rock 'n' roll") and *Rainmaker* (which has a slight hip-hop influence).

what to buy: *Spirit of Love* ♫♫♫♫ (Interscope, 1991, prod. Little Steven) was recorded in New York and Los Angeles, perhaps with visions that Fashek could replace Marley in the hearts of the record-buying public. The band is solid, with sharp horn arrangements and killer drumming that mix the best of Jamaica and Nigeria. Fashek's Marleyisms have never sounded better, and Little Steven supplies an unobtrusive rock 'n' roll polish. *Prisoner of Conscience* ♫♫♫♫ (Mango, 1989, prod. Lemmy Jack-

son) is reggae inna African stylee, with plenty of percussion accents that underscore the African origins of the familiar reggae one-drop riddims; a landmark set.

the rest:
Rainmaker ♫♫♫♫ (Tuff Gong, 1991)

worth searching for: *I and I Experience* ♫♫♫♫ (CBS, 1990), recorded between American record deals, is widely considered one of his best. Look for it on cassette in specialty record shops if you visit the continent.

influences:
◄◄ Bob Marley, Sonny Okosun, Lucky Dube

j. poet

Fatala
See: Alpha Yaya Diallo

John Faulkner
Irish traditional
Born 1943, in Oxford, England. Based in Kinvara, County Galway, Ireland.

John Faulkner might be best known as the musical partner of Irish singer Dolores Keane, but he is a formidable musician in his own right whose talent is vastly underrated. In the 1960s Faulkner was a member of Scottish folksinger Ewan MacColl's Critics Group, with whom he toured extensively (as he also did with Irish group De Dannan, formerly known as De Danann, and with Keane, to whom he was also married for some time). The multi-talented Faulkner is a master of stringed instruments (including the guitar, Irish bouzouki, and fiddle), and plays a wide array of others as well, including the hurdy-gurdy. While still quite active in Irish music circles, his main work consists of composition and production for both the record industry and for film and television through his Kinvara-based studio, Absolute Music.

what to buy: The fine recording *Kind Providence* ♫♫♫♫ (Green Linnet, 1986, prod. John Faulkner) displays Faulkner's multi-instrumental skills as he plays everything on the album, including bouzouki, guitar, fiddle, and hurdy-gurdy. His lovely voice is also featured on this inspired collection of songs from the British Isles and beyond.

what to buy next: *Nomads* ♫♫♫♫ (Clo-Iar Connachta, 1992, prod. John Faulkner) is on a wonderful Irish label known for its great recordings of *sean-nós* ("old-style") Gaelic song. Half of the recording is a concept album concerning the infamous Highland Clearances of Scotland (forced evacuations of peasantry by landowners in the 18th and 19th centuries that led to mass emigration). *Brokenhearted I'll Wander* ♫♫♫♫ (Green Linnet, 1979,

Ulali

prod. P.J. Curtis) and *Farewell to Eirinn* ♫♫♫ (Green Linnet, 1981, prod. John Faulkner, Dolores Keane, Seumas O'Neill, Carsten Linde) are two of the best recordings from the fruitful musical partnership of Keane and Faulkner. On *Brokenhearted I'll Wander* they are joined by fiddler Kieran Crehan and piper Éamonn Curran for an excellent collection of songs and instrumentals. *Farewell to Eirinn* is another remarkable set dealing specifically with the subject of Irish emigration to America.

the rest:
Solid Ground ♫♫♫ (Shanachie, 1993)
Sail Og Rua ♫♫♫ (Green Linnet, 1995)

worth searching for: Faulkner's work in television led to his involvement with the two-part 1975 documentary *Passage West,* a joint BBC and CBC television production. It examines the endless wave of emigration from the British Isles to North America in the 19th century, and Faulkner's music is featured prominently.

influences:
◀ Joe Heaney, Tommy Peoples, Mairtin Byrnes, Willie Clancy, Ewan MacColl

▶ Sean Keane

see also: *De Dannan, Dolores Keane, Ewan MacColl*

Cliff McGann

Pura Fé /Ulali

Native American vocal
Pura Fé born in USA. Ulali formed in North Carolina, USA. Based in North Carolina, USA.

Pura Fé (Tuscarora/Cherokee), vocals; Soni Moreno-Primeau (Aztec/Maya), vocals; Jennifer Kreisberg (Tuscarora/Cherokee), vocals.

Pura Fé is Native American, a member of the Tuscarora and Cherokee tribes of the southeastern United States. She comes from a family of singers, with her grandmother singing gospel and her mother and sister performing opera. Politically, she's been active on Native American and women's issues. She appears often to lend her music and that of her group, Ulali, to conferences and festivals. The three women of Ulali share Native American background as well as wide experience in the arts. Fé is a dancer who has studied with Martha Graham, Moreno-Primeau has acted on Broadway, and Kreisberg has studied music at Hartford College.

what's available: *Caution to the Wind* 𝄞𝄞 (Shanachie, 1995, prod. James McBride, Danny Weiss, Gerard Harris) is Pura Fé's first solo disc. She's got an expressive voice, and one of her interests is incorporating the connections among jazz, blues, and African American music with her Native background. Musically, she does this successfully, but lyrically her songs on this disc don't succeed, reaching neither the bluesy sincerity of Rita Coolidge's work or the insightful cultural intertwining of Tish Hinojosa's pop songs. She's forging her own path, not following either of these artists, but she has not yet found the way to make her original statement of roots connect in the pop genre as they have. With Ulali, Fé's work, while often fusing elements of other musics, is usually more strongly Native-focused. She writes many of the songs the group performs, and they frequently appear on soundtracks such as *Smoke Signals* 𝄞𝄞𝄞 (TVT, 1998, prod. Beth Rosenblatt) and in compilations such as Smithsonian Folkways' *Heartbeat: Voices of First Nations Women* (reviewed in this book's Compilations section). Their albums include two 1997 self-produced releases, *Mahk Jchi* and *Lessons from the Animal People.* A highly regarded performance was also captured on the cassette *Ladies Choice* by the American Indian Community House of New York.

influences:
◀◀ Rita Coolidge

see also: *Robbie Robertson*

Kerry Dexter

Jose Feliciano

Latin pop
Born September 10, 1945, in Lares, Puerto Rico. Based in USA.

Blind at birth from congenital glaucoma, Feliciano became a pop sensation in the late 1960s. Moving easily between flamenco, soul, jazz, and softer pop, between English-language and Spanish-language recording, Feliciano has been a notable performer for more than three decades. Born in Puerto Rico, Feliciano came with his family to Spanish Harlem in the early '50s. His first "instrument" was a tin cracker can which he used to back up his also-musical uncle. A prodigy, Feliciano taught himself to play the concertina at age six and effortlessly moved on to accordion and guitar soon afterward. When he first heard rock 'n' roll, he was inspired to add singing to his talents. To help support the family, Feliciano quit school at age 17 and spent the remainder of his teenage years busking at the same Greenwich Village coffeehouses that produced Bob Dylan. After

an appearance at the Newport Jazz Festival, he released a pair of albums that showcased his supple vocals and flamenco-influenced fretwork—*The Voice and Guitar of Jose Feliciano* and *The Fantastic Feliciano* —and then a set of Spanish-language LPs. But Feliciano's name first loomed truly large in 1968, when his cover of the Doors' "Light My Fire" hit #1, and his stylized version of the national anthem at the World Series in Detroit stirred controversy. The following year, his "Light My Fire" seemed to be everywhere, and Feliciano was everywhere else, releasing three new albums, charting with a cover of Tommy Tucker's "Hi Heeled Sneakers," and netting a Grammy for Best New Artist.

Continuing to release English- and Spanish-language albums, Feliciano recorded the holiday standard "Feliz Navidad," hit the charts occasionally (most notably with the theme song to the Freddie Prinze sitcom *Chico and the Man*), and guested on records by performers as diverse as Michael Nesmith, Joni Mitchell, Minnie Riperton, and John Lennon. Then, in 1998, Feliciano enjoyed an echo of his heyday, seeing his album *Senor Bolero* go platinum and its first single, "Me Has Echado Al Olvido," hit #1 in New York. An overdue resurgence in a career that's far from over, these honors merely contributed to the stats on Feliciano's 40+ gold and platinum records, 16 Grammy nominations (most recently, in fact, for *Senor Bolero*), six Grammys, and five-time placement as *Guitar Player* magazine's annual Best Pop Guitarist. The only artist to win Grammys in two languages and an icon to culture-crossing successors like Ricky Martin, Feliciano has a PBS special, a documentary, an instructional guitar video, a line of custom-made Jose Feliciano Model guitars, and the first Jose Feliciano's restaurant (in Las Vegas) in the works. Still, the majority of his more than 50 albums are out of print, leaving mostly greatest-hits collections readily available—but there's a lot to fill them with, and material for more no doubt on the way.

what to buy: *Feliciano!* 𝄞𝄞𝄞𝄞 (RCA, 1968, prod. Rick Jarrard) is the album that took the nation by storm, proving that Feliciano's Latin-jazz take on pop standards (including "Light My Fire," "California Dreaming," "Don't Let the Sun Catch You Crying," and a pair of Beatles songs) had mass-market appeal.

what to buy next: *Souled* 𝄞𝄞𝄞 (RCA, 1969) is almost the equal of its illustrious predecessor, with a smash cover of Tommy Tucker's "Hi Heeled Sneakers" (which Feliciano had originally recorded on his 1964 debut) and a jaunty take on Bob Dylan's "I'll Be Your Baby Tonight." . . . *On Second Thought* 𝄞𝄞𝄞 (32 Records, 1996) is a greatest-hits collection with a twist—rather than simply compiling Feliciano's biggest and best, it includes rerecordings of 25 of his best-known songs.

what to avoid: *Escenas De Amor* 𝄞𝄞 (Motown, 1982) is typical of Feliciano's lesser '80s work—it's soft Latin pop, overtly romantic, with none of the strength and power of his best albums.

best of the rest:

El Sentimiento, La Voz Y La Guitarra ♪♪♪♪ (RCA, 1967/RCA International, 1991)

The Christmas Album ♪♪♪♪ (RCA, 1970)

Tu Inmenso Amor ♪♪♪ (EMI, 1987/EMI Capitol, 1996)

All Time Greatest Hits ♪♪♪ (BMG/RCA, 1988)

Light My Fire ♪♪♪♪ (BMG/RCA, 1992)

Mis Mejores Canciones—17 Super ♪♪♪ (EMD/EMI Latin, 1993)

Americano ♪♪♪♪ (PGD/Rodven, 1996)

Exitos Y Recuerdos (EMI Special Products, 1996)

Passion of Feliciano ♪♪♪ (BMG, 1997)

Senor Bolero ♪♪♪♪ (BMG/U.S. Latin, 1998)

El Amor De Mi Vida—Masterpieces ♪♪♪ (Fuel 2000, 1998)

worth searching for: Joni Mitchell's *Court and Spark* ♪♪♪♪♪ (Asylum, 1974, prod. Joni Mitchell) is one of the folk singer's finest albums, and her best-selling effort. It also has a raft of guest stars, including Robbie Robertson, David Crosby, Joe Sample, and Felicano, who contributes electric guitar.

influences:

◄ Carlos Puebla, the Beatles, Bob Dylan, Tito Puente, João Gilberto, Laurindo Almeida

►► War, Santana, Gloria Estefan, Ricky Martin, any other Latino act of the last several decades

Ben Greenman, Christina Fuoco, and Stephen Vilnius

Fernhill

Contemporary Anglo-Celtic folk
Formed 1996, in Wales. Based in Wales.

Julie Murphy (England), vocals; Andy Cutting (England), button accordions; Ceri Rhys Matthews (Wales), guitar, clarinet; Jonathan Shorland (Wales), pastoral oboes, flutes, whistle, clarinets, bagpipe.

Though only together for a short time as yet, Fernhill have already made quite a splash. Not only is their musicianship impeccable, but their mix of Welsh, English, French, and Breton (French Celtic) influences is exceptional. They've recorded two full-length CDs and toured in England and Wales—and, more excitingly from the 21st century fusion standpoint, in Norway, East Africa, and Southern Africa. On their 1996 visit, Fernhill collaborated with native musicians in Uganda; in 1998 they played in Swaziland and Mozambique. The busy members of Fernhill are also involved with several side projects—vocalist Murphy is working on a solo CD featuring duets with Martin Simpson (guitar), Nigel Eaton (hurdy-gurdy), and fellow Fernhillians Cutting and Matthews; Matthews and Shorland have recorded two albums of Welsh pipe music; and Cutting has recorded with the Two Duos Quartet and is working on a solo album.

what's available: *Ca'nos* ♪♪♪♪ ("Night Field") (Beautiful Jo, 1996, prod. Tim Healey, Fernhill) shows how dynamic and rich a

native american pop

N̲ative American music has experienced phenomenal growth in the past decade, due in part to a tribal population boom, and in part to mainstream interest in traditional flute music sparked by the new-age crossover of R. Carlos Nakai, Kevin Locke, and Robert Mirabal.

The first Native American recordings were made in the early part of the 20th century, as folklorists began using Thomas Edison's invention to document the music of "primitive" people for the general society. Native musicians themselves saw the new media's potential for cultural bonding, and began making recordings aimed at Native listeners. There have long been Native artists in the mainstream—jazzman Don Cherry was half Cherokee, as was Jimi Hendrix, and the Band's Robbie Robertson is Mohawk—but they usually worked within the confines of what Nakai ironically calls "the greater culture." Today Native people are visible in every aspect of the music business, making music that's distinctly Indian.

Walela (Rita Coolidge, Priscilla Coolidge, and Lisa Satterfield), Sharon Burch, and Joanne Shenandoah combine Native, rock, and folk influences in a way that makes traditional Native sounds more accessible to non-Native ears. Joy Harjo, a saxophonist, best-selling poet, and professor at the University of New Mexico, has created a style that could easily fit onto the playlists of lite-jazz, Native, worldbeat, and Americana broadcasts. Casper Loma-Da-Wa (a.k.a. Lomayesva), a Hopi from Arizona, sings in a Jamaican patois as thick as a jungle vine and mercilessly indicts Babylon for its sins with a powerful combination of roots reggae, dancehall skanking, and Native chanting. There are also Native rappers like Litefoot and Robbie Bee; rockers like Kashtin, an Innuit duo that sounds a bit like R.E.M.; singer-songwriters like Jay Begaye and A. Paul Ortega; and ritual peyote ceremony singers like Primeaux & Mike. With today's music buyers' expanding interest in inter-cultural exchange, the time is right for Native artists to finally start getting the respect, and commercial recognition, they deserve.

j. poet

purely acoustic recording can be. Cutting's accordion and Shortland's woodwinds interweave brilliantly on the instrumental passages while Matthews's guitar provides rhythmic accents. And Murphy has an incredible voice; she fits in with the players as easily on fast numbers as slow ones, and sounds great singing in Welsh, English, French, or Breton. She also brings a jazzy exuberance to many of the faster songs. But on Fernhill's second CD *Llatai* ♫♫♫♫ (Beautiful Jo, 1998, prod. Fernhill) Murphy really wails, particularly on "Pontypridd." The Breton influence has also become more fully integrated into the total Fernhill sound; several tracks mix Breton dance rhythms with Welsh lyrics and melodies for a surprisingly good fit. "Gladez and Katell," an original composition by Shorland, is purely instrumental and serves mostly as an accordion/clarinet duet until guitar joins in for a little added rhythmic pulse. *Llatai* also includes a version of the English ballad "Blacksmith" that's quite distinct from the well-known Steeleye Span arrangement. Fernhill take the song a lot slower, and the acoustic setting (accordion, guitar, flute) creates a completely different, more reflective mood.

influences:

◀◀ Sandy Denny, Maddy Prior, Blowzabella, Alan Stivell

▶▶ Tanteeka

Ken Roseman

Filé

Cajun

Formed 1983, in Lafayette, LA, USA. Based in Lafayette, LA, USA.

Members have included: Ward Lormand, accordion, vocals; David Egan, piano, vocals; D'Jalma Garnier, fiddle, guitar, banjo, vocals; Kevin Shearin, bass; Peter Stevens, drums. (All members are from USA.)

The waltzes and two-steps of southwest Louisiana's Cajun music are given a modern twist by accordionist and lead vocalist Ward Lormand and his band Filé. While its roots are in the same squeezebox-and-fiddle tradition as the Balfa Brothers and Beausoleil, the group has incorporated elements of rock, R&B, and New Orleans jazz. Its best-known tune remains the 1989 Cajun-ized interpretation of Richard Thompson's "Two Left Feet." Lormand, who grew up in Ossun, a small French-speaking town northwest of Lafayette, and bassist Kevin Shearin, a native of New York State, formed Filé shortly after leaving the Cajun-rock band Cush-Cush in 1983. Filé's debut album was literally a live one—*Live at Mulate's,* recorded during a performance at the Cajun nightclub. The expressive fiddling of Minnesota-born D'Jalma Garnier, a former student of Cajun fiddler Canray Fontenot, has been an important part of Filé's sound since the early 1990s, and the band continues to

be anchored by drummer Peter Stevens, who joined in 1984, and pianist David Egan, a member since 1991.

what to buy: The title track of *2 Left Feet* ♫♫♫ (Flying Fish, 1989, prod. Eugene Foster, Filé) is a Cajun-polka treatment of Richard Thompson's tune and remains Filé's claim to fame.

what to buy next: Filé's latest effort, *La Vie Marron* ♫♫♫ (Green Linnet, 1996), was dedicated to the memory of Cajun fiddler Canray Fontenot, who not only inspired the band in general, but taught the idiosyncrasies of Cajun music to Filé's Garnier.

the rest:

Cajun Dance Band ♫♫♡ (Flying Fish, 1987)

influences:

◀◀ Beausoleil, the Balfa Brothers, Richard Thompson

▶▶ Wayne Toups & ZydeCajun, the Basin Brothers

see also: *Balfa Brothers, Beausoleil, Canray Fontenot*

Craig Harris

Film Orchestra of Shanghai /Film Symphony Orchestra

Chinese orchestral music, Buddhist music, Taoist music, Chinese healing music

Formed in Shanghai, China. Based in Shanghai, China.

Chen Da-Wei, producer; other musicians uncredited.

Working as the senior composer of the Film Symphony Orchestra, Chen Da-Wei has written music for movies, television, and dozens of recordings. Among his works, *The Flying Fairy* and *The Great River Flows to the East* were awarded the second and third prizes respectively in the 1984 National Music Contest in China. Members of the Film Orchestra of Shanghai (a name used interchangeably with the outfit's other one) also perform in the Shanghai Chinese Traditional Orchestra.

what to buy: The Film Symphony Orchestra is perhaps best known for its Buddhist Series, in which it performs what is known as "Sanskrit music," a form of Indian sacred chant accompanied by simple ceremonial instruments to glorify and eulogize Buddha and Bodhisattvas. In this vein, *The Sound of Bell Emitted in the Evening from an Ancient Temple* ♫♫♫♡ (Wind Records, 1991, prod. Chen Da-Wei) won the Mainland China Ethnic Music Award in 1991. The music itself is of utmost tranquillity, uplifting mind and spirit. After being introduced to and accepted by the Chinese, these Buddhist forms made much impact on Chinese traditional music.

what to buy next: The Film Orchestra of Shanghai as led by Mr. Chen has also recorded several albums of Chinese Taoist music; this is best exemplified by *Three Purities* ♫♫♫♫ (Wind

Records, prod. Chen Da-Wei). Taoist music is strongly influenced by regional folk music, and serves an important role in ceremonial rituals. The function of Taoist music is to stimulate sympathy and pity from the myriad gods and heavenly rulers through the playing of bells, sonorous stones, drums, pipes, string instruments, and wooden temple blocks carved in the shapes of fishes. In the six-volume Therapeutic Music series, Mr. Chen was influenced by the famous Yellow Emperor's Classic of Internal Medicine; written between the first and third centuries B.C., it is the earliest tome to recommend healing of ailments through music, thus forming the basis for all sound-healing work now gaining popularity in the West. *An Dun/Calming the Emotions* ♫♫♫♫ (Wind Records, 1991, prod. Chen Da-Wei) is an excellent example of the potent effect music has on the subtle energies of the human body.

the rest:

Jing Zhe/Awakening Insects—Spring ♫♫♫ (Wind Records)
Mang Zhong/Beard of Wheat—Summer ♫♫♫ (Wind Records)
Bai Lu/Frosty Dew—Autumn ♫♫♫ (Wind Records)
Da Xue/Great Snow—Winter ♫♫♫ (Wind Records)
Sheng Hua/Invigorating the Spirit ♫♫♫ (Wind Records)
The Jeweled Hall of Great Hero ♫♫♫♫ (Wind Records)
The Verse of Repentance ♫♫♫♫ (Wind Records)
Bowing and Making Vow Through Reciting the Name of Buddha ♫♫♫♫ (Wind Records)
Welcoming Guests from Heaven ♫♫♫♫ (Wind Records)

influences:

◀◀ Buddha, Yellow Emperor

▶▶ Shanghai Sanskrit Orchestra, Shanghai Sanskrit Chorus

PJ Birosik

Alec Finn

Irish traditional
Born in Yorkshire, England. Based in Spiddal, County Galway, Ireland.

A long-time resident of Ireland's west coast, Yorkshire-born Finn moved to Dublin in the early '60s, where he became involved in that city's vibrant blues scene. Upon moving to Spiddal in County Galway, Finn began to play the Greek bouzouki at local traditional Irish sessions. Out of these informal sets grew the nucleus of the seminal Irish band De Dannan, formerly known as De Danann, which also included Frankie Gavin, one of Ireland's most talented fiddlers. Gavin and Finn have been and remain the nucleus of a band that has seen its fair share of personnel changes over the years, including a host of great female vocalists like Dolores Keane, Mary Black, Maura O'Connell, and Eleanor Shanley. Finn's innovative use of the Greek bouzouki within De Dannan has influenced a whole generation of young accompanists, and helped bring widespread accep-

tance of the instrument within the tradition. Over the years he has also recorded with a lengthy who's who of Ireland's finest traditional musicians.

what to buy: De Dannan's *Mist Covered Mountain* ♫♫♫♫ (Shanachie, 1980) is the band's earliest recording still in print, and demonstrates the instrumental prowess of Gavin, Charlie Piggot, and accordionist Jackie Daly, all backed by Finn's subtle bouzouki. *Frankie Gavin & Alec Finn* ♫♫♫♫♫ (Shanachie, 1994, prod. Richard Nevins, Daniel Micheal Collins) was Gavin's first recording outside of De Dannan, and was recorded in Greenwich Village while the band was on a U.S. tour. Like much of Shanachie's *Masters of Irish Music* series this CD reissue, originally recorded in 1977, isn't up to today's sound standards, and the length is a paltry 31 minutes. Despite that, Gavin's fiddling is brilliant and Finn's trademark bouzouki accompaniment is represented in all its glory. *Feadóga Stáin* ♫♫♫♫♫ (Shanachie, 1992, prod. Mícheál Ó Héidhin) is the debut solo recording by Ireland's first lady of the tin whistle, Mary Bergin. It features some of Finn's finest work as an accompanist and that, factored in with Bergin's brilliance on her instrument, makes this one of the seminal works in Irish traditional music.

what to buy next: *Blue Shamrock* ♫♫♫ (Celtic Heartbeat, 1994, prod. John Faulkner, Alec Finn) is Finn's 1994 solo debut, and a beautifully evocative collection of 10 traditional Irish airs played on guitar and bouzouki. While enjoyable for its lush arrangements and new-age sensibility, it does not stylistically typify the superb work Finn has done as a member of De Dannan or as the accompanist for Bergin, Gavin, and others.

influences:

◀◀ Planxty, Johnny Moynihan

▶▶ Niall Ó Callanáin, Ciaran Curran, Roger Landes, Robin Bullock

see also: *Mary Bergin, Mary Black, Jackie Daly, De Dannan, Frankie Gavin, Dolores Keane, Maura O'Connell*

Cliff McGann

Firewater

Indie rock, klezmer
Formed 1995, in New York, NY, USA. Based in New York, NY, USA.

Tod Ashley, vocals; Duane Denison, guitar; Yuval Gabay, drums; Kurt Hoffman, saxophone, accordion; Jennifer Charles, vocals; Jim Kimball, drums; Dave Ouimet, piano; Hahn Rowe, violin. (All members are from USA.)

Firewater stands out from the alternative pack by its use of world music, dabbling just enough to open the ears of a rock audience without alienating them. The fusion is often seamless, with styles from klezmer to tango well adapted to the indie genre. Firewater is overflowing with alt.rock alumni—from Jesus Lizard, Soul Coughing, Jon Spencer Blues Explosion, Mule, Laughing Hyenas, Hugo Largo, and Foetus—who seem to be having a lot of fun exploring styles other than rock. Frontman "Tod A." from Cop Shoot Cop sings in a hoarse and boozy rasp on most tracks; imagine the Pogues' Shane MacGowan interpreting the Nirvana songbook. A.'s vivid metaphors evoke a seedy underworld populated by desperate, lonely characters; "going down like a pederast in a boy's school," "creeping like a spy on broken glass," you get the idea. And the musical idea is quite general indeed, with a mix of American gospel and Celtic jig on "Knock 'Em Down," a German-style brass band on "El Borracho," and the adaptation of a Soft Cell electrobeat (!) on "So Long Superman," while "Another Perfect Catastrophe" envisages a klezmer band tangoing around A.'s invitation to a life of crime. Hopefully, as the post-grunge audience grows older, its curiosity will be sated by more ensembles as eclectic and accessible as Firewater.

what's available: Its debut *Get off the Cross (We Need the Wood for the Fire)* ♫♫♫ (Jet Set, 1996, prod. Doug Henderson, Tod A.) is more straight-ahead indie rock with a Celtic flavor. The follow-up *The Ponzi Scheme* ♫♫♫♫ (Cherry/Universal Records, 1998, prod. Doug Henderson, Tod A.) draws on wider-ranging influences. From the opening saxophone of "Ponzi's Theme" you're into a klezmer take on James Bond.

influences:

◀◀ The Pogues, Oyster Band, Klezmatics, Talking Heads, Soft Cell, Nirvana

David Poole

Archie Fisher

Scottish folk
Born in Glasgow, Scotland. Based in Scotland.

The product of a musical household, Archie Fisher has become one of the seminal figures of the Scottish folk revival. He was born in Glasgow, to a Gaelic-speaking mother and a police inspector father, both of whom sang all the time. He has seven sisters, who acted, he says, as "a catchment area for fellow musicians," but also as an audience and as singing partners. During the early 1960s, Archie and his sister Ray spent some time in a skiffle band before recording their first sides of Scottish music in 1963. They were joined by their parents and sisters on a 1965 release credited to "The Fisher Family." When Ray married and moved away, Archie began to establish himself as a top songwriter, guitarist, and vocalist. By the late 1960s, he had made many appearances on television shows, including the popular *Here and Now,* and on BBC Schools Radio, where his original songs were used as illustrations of themes of in-

dustrialization. Many of his compositions became part of the Scottish folk repertoire through these appearances. During the 1970s he toured with Irish performers Tommy Makem and Liam Clancy, and arranged and produced several of their albums. During the 1980s, he toured and recorded as a duo with Canadian singer and instrumentalist Garnet Rogers. In addition to his career as a performer, Fisher has been an important organizer and presenter of traditional music. From 1988 to 1992 he directed the Edinburgh Folk Festival. He produced radio features and documentaries for BBC Radio Tweed in southern Scotland, and eventually launched the BBC show *Traveling Folk,* which he has hosted for more than a decade.

what to buy: *Sunsets I've Galloped Into* ♫♫♫♫ (Red House, 1988, prod. Garnet Rogers) is a collection of recently written songs, some from Fisher's pen and some from others'. Fisher's own pieces include "The Shipyard Apprentice," a song he wrote during the 1970s, and "The Black Horse," a recitation, or, as he puts it, a "song without a melody." Songs by others include Graham Miles's "Yonder Banks," Kieran Goss's "All That You Ask Me," and Stewart MacGregor's "The Presence," all fine tunes that sound great in Fisher's smooth baritone. A few traditional songs round out the package. The sound is fuller and more produced than on Fisher's previous albums, owing to the presence of piano, bass, and synthesizers as well as guitars, flute, and fiddle, played by accompanists Garnet Rogers and David Woodhead.

what to buy next: The landmark LP *The Man with a Rhyme* ♫♫♫♫ (Folk-Legacy, 1977/1997, prod. Sandy Paton) has recently been reissued on CD. It features mostly traditional songs and a few new ones written in the traditional mold. It contains Fisher's classics "The Witch of the West-Mer-Lands" and "Dark-Eyed Molly," which were made famous in folk circles by Stan Rogers. Among the traditional songs, "The Wounded Whale," which Fisher put together from versions noted in whalers' logbooks, is particularly interesting, as are the two Jacobite songs "Twa Bonnie Maidens" and "Welcome Royal Charlie." The love song "Helen of Kirkconnell Lea" was recorded at the original sessions but did not fit on the LP version; it is included here as a bonus track. In addition to his own guitar, Fisher is accompanied by the Ladies of the Lake: Wendy Grossman (concertina, banjo, dulcimer), Kathy Westra (cello), Lani Herrmann (fiddle), Ann Mayo Muir (flute), and Lorraine Lee (dulcimer). Fisher's Topic LP from 1976, *Will Ye Gang, Love* ♫♫♫♫ (Topic, 1976/Green Linnet, 1993, prod. Tony Engle, Tony Russell), has been reissued in the Green Linnet Celtic Classics series. It too features Fisher's gentle voice and guitar performing traditional songs of various types as well as songs he wrote himself. Among the former, one song was learned from Jeannie Robertson, but most seem to have drawn on the great collections of

Gavin Greig and Dean Christie. An especially interesting one is a work song once sung by oyster-dredgers, the lyrics of which are obtuse but beautiful. Among the originals, "Lindsay" is one of Fisher's best-known "traditionalesque" numbers, while "Men O' Worth" deals with the contemporary problems of the shift from a farming and fishing economy to an industrial one in Northeast Scotland. In addition to Fisher's guitar, Allan Barty plays fiddle and mandola, and John Tams adds melodeons.

the rest:
Archie Fisher 🎝🎝🎝 (Celtic Music, 1968)

worth searching for: *The Fisher Family* 🎝🎝🎝🎝 (Topic, 1965) is a collector's item, an LP featuring Archie and his sisters Ray, Cilla, and Audrey, as well as his parents. *Off the Map* 🎝🎝🎝🎝 (Snow Goose Songs, 1986) is a live album of Archie with Garnet Rogers, and it's one of his best collections of traditional and original songs.

influences:
◀◀ Ewan MacColl

▶▶ Stan Rogers, Garnet Rogers, Ray Fisher, Cilla Fisher

see also: *The Clancy Brothers and Tommy Makem/Tommy Makem and Liam Clancy*

Steve Winick

Frank Emilio Flynn
20th-century Cuban jazz, folkloric and popular music
Born April 13, 1921, in Havana, Cuba. Based in Havana, Cuba.

No dis to Buena Vista Social Club elder Reuben Gonzalez, but pianist/composer Frank Emilio Flynn is the last living link to the glory days (1930s–'50s) of the Cuban *descarga* (jam session), the *orquesta típicas* (small eight-to-10-piece bands), and the birth of Cuban jazz. Blessed with perfect pitch and big ears, precocious Emilio taught himself how to play piano at the age of 10. In 1932, he won an amateur contest held at the Teatro Nacional de la Habana (now Gran Teatro García Lorca, the equivalent of Carnegie Hall). Just as the piano opened up a new world to him, another world—of sight—closed in his 13th year. Undaunted, young Flynn assumed a double identity: music student-teacher at the Cuban Association for the Blind by day, leader of an islandwide orquesta típica broadcast on CMBG radio each night. Flynn's divine schizophrenia ended with his contributions to the early '50s *filin* ("feeling") movement. The filin pioneers reasoned that if you added blues harmonics to the 3/4 time of the bolero, you'd get an evolutionary cipher that could open up Cuban music as well as build a bridge to American jazz. Leading this new vanguard were the Frank Emilio Flynn Quintet and Loquibambia (which he directed). As the decade waned, Frank Emilio took concert stage. A renowned interpreter of Cuban classicists Ignacio Cervantes,

Ernesto Lecuona, and Manuel Saumell, the pianist hit a career peak with his '64 performance of Gershwin's *Rhapsody in Blue* and *Concerto in F* in front of the National Symphonic Orchestra. From the mid-'60s to today, Flynn has continued to make music, still part of history and the future.

what to buy: Frank Emilio Flynn has released three excellent albums on Milan Latino between '97 and '98. *A Tiempo de Danzón* 🎝🎝🎝🎝 (Milan Latino, 1998, prod. Jesus Flynn) gets a slight edge over the other two. It's basically Frank Emilio's lithe, fluid piano deftly guiding your archetypal *danzón* orchestra—two flutes, two violins, bass, kettledrum, *guiro* (scraper)—through fervid variations on classic jammies like Armando Romeu's "Cuba Mia" and Coralita Lopez's "Isora Club." Intoxicating memories of old-time danzón intensified by post-filin vapors . . . in simple terms, the old is young again. *A Tiempo de Danzón* seduces completely.

what to buy next: Featuring contemporary Cuban masters Miguel Angá, José Luis "Changuito" Quintana, and Orlando "Maraca" Valle (on *tumbadora* drum, bongo, and flute, respectively), *Babarisimo* 🎝🎝🎝🎝 (Milan Latino, 1997, prod. Sylvia Rodriguez Rivero) showcases the most recent edition of Flynn's Los Amigos outfit. A spirited collection of self-penned song ("Gandinga, Mondongo y Sandunga"), filin-ized bolero ("Mi Ayer"), cha cha cha ("Scheherezada"), and sophisticated mambo ("Tony y Jesusito"), *Barbarismo* is both validation of Flynn's prescience and a passing of the descarga to the next generation of Cuban musicians. Just as illuminating is his solo-piano *Tribute to Ersnesto Lecuona* 🎝🎝🎝🎝 (Milan Latino, 1997, prod. Frank Emilio Flynn). Arguably the greatest of Cuban composers (851 vocal, piano, stage, symphonic, and film works), Lecuona (1895–63) epitomizes the Cuban music spirit—Spain, Africa, Americas. (Fellini copped his "Siboney" for *Amarcord* and Nat King Cole rocked "Noche Azul" and "Estás en mi corazón".) In Flynn's piano you can hear past Iberian majesty ("Córdova"), and feel the faint memory of African paradise lost ("Danza Lucumí").

influences:
▶▶ Chucho Valdes, Gonzalo Rubalcaba

Tom Terrell

Folk Scat
Vocalese, Bulgarian style
Formed 1989, in Stara Zagora, Bulgaria. Based in Stara Zagora, Bulgaria.

Kiril Todorov, director, vocals, fiddle, percussion; Mariana Vlaeva, soprano; Antoaneta Krumova, soprano; Diana Georgieva, alto; Todor Gerdjikov, tenor. (All members are from Bulgaria.)

Folk Scat was founded by Kiril Todorov, a renowned Bulgarian composer and conductor who had previously worked with

Fong Naam

everything from large chamber orchestras to small vocal ensembles. With songs consisting mainly of exquisitely arranged *a cappella* vocals and minimal musical accompaniment primarily in the form of traditional Bulgarian folk instruments, the group's most prominent influence seems to be the vocalese sound of jazz artists like Lambert, Hendricks & Ross, and Bobby McFerrin. But you can also hear Todorov's classical music background factored into the equation, as well as alto Diana Georgieva and soprano Antoaneta Krumova's backgrounds in Bulgarian folk music. Fans of *Le Mystère des Voix Bulgares* will hear similar sounds at work here, but Folk Scat's masterful modern compositions and dazzling harmonic arrangements of traditional folk songs fall much easier on Western ears.

what's available: *Folk Scat* ♫♫♫♫ (Nomad, 1996, prod. Bob Haddad) is the group's only international recording to date, but it's a doozy, with spellbinding original tunes like "Ianinku" and "Chompilche" interwoven with bold arrangements of traditional Bulgarian songs like "Bre Petrunko," and even a frisky scat take on Beethoven's "Fur Elise" that would've had Ludwig swinging like a hepcat. Simply a must-have for fans of *a cappella* vocal music.

influences:
◄◄ Bulgarian Radio Women's Choir, Ladysmith Black Mambazo, Manhattan Transfer, Lambert, Hendricks & Ross

►► Zap Mama

see also: *Le Mystère des Voix Bulgares*

Bret Love

Fong Naam
Pi phat, pinpeat, mahori
Formed c. 1982, in Thailand. Based in Thailand.

Boonyong Ketkhong, renat thum, renat ek (wood xylophones); Bruce Gaston (USA), khong wong yai (large gong circle); Lamoon Phuakthongkham, renat ek, renat kaeo (glass xylophone); Suwit Kaewkramon, pi ny (oboe), khlui (flute); Prasarn Wongwirojruk, grajapi (lute), khong wong lek (small gong circle), kim (dulcimer), saw duang (fiddle); Phin Ruangnon, glong kaek, glong song na, tapone, glong yao

(percussion); Somcharn Bunkert, glongtat, glong kaek, glong yao (percussion); Kaiwan Tilokavichai, percussion; Anant Narkong, percussion; Wirad Songkroh, vocals, saw sam sai (fiddle), grap (wood clappers). (All members are from Thailand unless otherwise noted.)

Perhaps Thailand's best "classical" music ensemble, Fong Naam is a guardian of Thai culture, its members brilliant instrumentalists and daring innovators. Founded by *renat* xylophonist Boonyong Ketkhong and American expatriate Bruce Gaston in the early 1980s, Fong Naam has helped to revitalize interest in traditional Thai music both within and outside the country through its stirring, expert performances in the *pi phat* and *mahori* configurations. These ancient ensemble forms, played in Thailand, Cambodia and Laos, use a seven-note equidistant scale and are percussion-based, with instruments like the *ranat* wood xylophone and the *khong wong* gong circle playing a central role, though the mahori ensemble puts more emphasis on the use of stringed instruments. Gaston, a music theorist, composer, and teacher who moved to Thailand in the early 1970s, has expanded "serious" Thai music by creating classically rooted compositions that draw upon regional Thai styles, Western classical and jazz music, while Ketkhong's rhythmic innovations with the renat have become a major influence on Thai orchestras.

what to buy: Almost as much for Gaston's useful notes on Thai music theory as for the quality of the music, the two-volume *Fong Naam: Ancient-Contemporary Music from Thailand* 𝅘𝅥𝅘𝅥𝅘𝅥 (Celestial Harmonies, 1995, prod. Bruce Gaston) is the best introduction to the group and to Thai music in general. In addition to typical pi phat tunes, some regional and unusual styles are included, such as the gentle floating strains of a northern Thai string ensemble on "Prasat Wai." We also hear an extended piece performed with the rare glass renat, an instrument which Fong Naam helped reintroduce to the musical scene. *Jajakan: Music from New Siam* 𝅘𝅥𝅘𝅥𝅘𝅥 (Nimbus, 1996, prod. Robin Broadbank, Bruce Gaston) finds the group in an experimental mode, using Western orchestral instruments and even synthesizer to produce a compelling hybrid. Lamoon showcases his mastery of the xylophone on the tremendous "Cherd Nawk."

worth searching for: Two very nice CDs, *The Sleeping Angel* 𝅘𝅥𝅘𝅥𝅘𝅥𝅮 (Nimbus, 1991) and *The Nang Hong Suite* 𝅘𝅥𝅘𝅥𝅘𝅥𝅮 (Nimbus, 1992), have unfortunately gone out of print but are certainly worth finding. The encyclopedic six-volume survey *Siamese Classical Music* 𝅘𝅥𝅘𝅥𝅘𝅥 (Marco Polo) covers the history of various ensembles, especially the pi phat, in scrupulous detail. In print but difficult to find, it's probably easiest to order directly from the distributor, Naxos (please see this book's Record Labels appendix).

solo outings:

Bruce Gaston (with Takako Nishizaki):

Indra's Paradise: The Essence of Thai Music (Marco Polo, 1997)

Jeffrey Muhr

Canray Fontenot

Cajun, Creole, zydeco

Born October 22, 1922, in L'Anse Rougeau, LA, USA. Died July 29, 1995, in Welch, LA, USA.

With steel-blue eyes and a smile that could melt any heart, Canray Fontenot played the finest traditional Creole fiddle in Louisiana. Son of legendary accordionist Adam Fontenot, Canray grew up in a house that was constantly full of the area musicians coming to visit with his father. His wiry, bluesy fiddling deeply influenced the playing styles of later luminaries like Dewey Balfa, Michael Doucet, and Edward Poullard. He began working with the nephew of Amédée Ardoin, accordionist Alphonse "Bois Sec" Ardoin, but during the 1940s and early '50s led a string band that shared the stage with a very young Clifton Chenier. It was Chenier who persuaded Fontenot to return to music in the mid-'60s when he had given up on it. His songs "Les Barres de la Prison," "Bonsoir Moreau," and "Joe Pitre a Deux Femmes," among others, are still played in updated versions by many young zydeco bands.

what to buy: *Louisiana Hot Sauce, Creole Style* 𝅘𝅥𝅘𝅥𝅘𝅥𝅘𝅥𝅘𝅥 (Arhoolie, 1992, prod. Chris Strachwitz) is a compilation of Canray in a variety of settings, including duets with Michael Doucet, the Ardoin family, the Poullard Brothers, Freeman Fontenot, and Beausoleil.

what to buy next: Canray and Bois Sec stopped off in Washington, D.C., after a successful performance at the Newport Folk Festival and recorded *Les Blues du Bayou* 𝅘𝅥𝅘𝅥𝅘𝅥𝅘𝅥𝅘𝅥 (Melodeon, 1965, prod. Richard Spottswood). It catches them in their prime. The two never played a tune the same way twice, but there is no lack of authority in their execution.

the rest:

Louisiana Cajun French Music from the Southwest Prairies Vol. 2, Recorded 1964–1967 𝅘𝅥𝅘𝅥𝅘𝅥𝅮 (Rounder, 1976)

Cajun Fiddle Styles, Vol. 1: The Creole 𝅘𝅥𝅘𝅥𝅘𝅥 (Arhoolie, 1988)

La Musique Creole 𝅘𝅥𝅘𝅥𝅘𝅥𝅘𝅥 (Arhoolie, 1997)

Les Haricots Sont Pas Salés: Legendary Masters of Cajun and Creole Music 𝅘𝅥𝅘𝅥𝅘𝅥𝅘𝅥 (Cinq Planetes, 1998)

worth searching for: Side Two of *The Cajuns Vol. 1* 𝅘𝅥𝅘𝅥𝅘𝅥 (Gazell, 1973, prod. Sam Charters) features the Ardoin Brothers Orchestra with Canray Fontenot. These are the only recordings of Canray playing with Gustave Ardoin (son of Bois Sec), who died in a tragic accident. Canray considered his work with Gustave to be some of his finest.

influences:

◀◀ Amédée Ardoin, Dennis McGee

▶▶ Michael Doucet, Clifton Chenier, Balfa Brothers

Canray Fontenot

see also: *Alphonse "Bois Sec" Ardoin, Amédée Ardoin, Balfa Brothers, Beausoleil, Clifton Chenier, Michael Doucet, Filé*

Jared Snyder

Juan Carlos Formell

Cuban son, changui, bolero
Born 1964, in Havana, Cuba. Based in New York, NY, USA.

Though he's the son of a storied Cuban-music pioneer—the similarly named Juan Formell, leader of the legendary Los Van Van—when Juan Carlos Formell began seeking his own creative voice, he found that his country's political regime wouldn't allow him to express his folkloric roots as he wished. Reaching back to days before his father's groundbreaking style, the younger Formell's pre-Castro tastes were denounced as decadent—and Formell himself branded as subversive for his practice of yoga! Still, he managed to work as a well-respected sideman to Cuban greats Gonzalo Rubalcaba and Emiliano Salvador, and he appeared with the leading vocal group Cuarteto Tiempo. But he needed more for his music to be truly his. On a

concert trip to Mexico he seized a slim chance and swam across the Rio Grande to the United States. At first his career in the new land consisted mainly of playing music for tips around the subway stops of New York City, but whatever the struggle, he was able to realize his artistic vision of Cuba as never before. Soon his talent was recognized and he began to get club gigs, formed the band cubalibre, and was signed to the adventurous U.S. world-music label Wicklow by its founder, Paddy Moloney of the Chieftains, who characterized Formell's work as "the roots of what we find so irresistible in Cuban music."

what's available: *Songs from a Little Blue House* 𝄢𝄢𝄢𝄢𝄢 (Wicklow/BMG, 1999, prod. John Fischbach) is named for the abode of Formell's grandmother in the Oriente province of Cuba (an area as rich in cultural history for the nation as it is in family history for the artist). The disc's original songs evoke an earlier time in Cuban music, using voice, percussion, and strings (rather than jazz-style horns) to conjure images of Cuban life. It's newly composed music in a timeless style. To hear Formell's pre-exile work with Cuarteto Tiempo, look for *Cigar Music—Tobacco Songs from Old Havana* 𝄢𝄢𝄢 (Traditional Crossroads, 1996, prod.

Harold G. Hagopian, Rachel Faro), a collection of songs about—and sung by the workers of—Cuba's most famous industry, including tunes written by the beloved Beny Moré.

influences:

Juan Formell, Orquesta Aragon, Los Van Van

see also: *Los Van Van, Beny Moré*

Kerry Dexter

Fortuna

Modern and traditional Ladino

Born Fortuna Safdié, October 22, 1957, in São Paulo, Brazil. Based in São Paulo, Brazil.

In the U.S., "theatrical" rockers have often faced a steep slope toward being accepted as musicians, but since much world music is based on (or still functions as) communal ritual—religious, social, etc.—neither its practitioners nor its publics subscribe to this schism between the visual and the aural. Fortuna, whose album sets are conceived as revues in her native Brazil, is no exception—but she is exceptional in every other way. Dressed like a bejeweled medieval icon come to life to deliver stately music of that period, and eventually costume-changing down to red-velvet eveningwear for torridly syncopated finales, Fortuna's shows are highly theatrical, while bracingly simple in their physical affects. Fortuna realizes that if you come to see a band at all, you might as well have something to see—but for much of the world, which hasn't yet had a chance to meet this should-and-will-be-famous diva in person, it's the music that has to mesmerize, and it does. Fortuna's fascination with her subject matter is infectious, introducing international listeners to the little-known Ladino sound. Ladino is the music of the Sephardic Jews of medieval Spain and Portugal (and their later diaspora throughout the Mediterranean, North Africa, and beyond), which offers another historical link in the cultural chain between the Middle East and the Iberian Peninsula—and a lively strain of "worldbeat" that's stood the test of centuries. Fortuna first encountered it while on a tour of Israel, reconnecting her with her roots and changing the course of her career. The sound is just the synthesis of hypnotic melodies, slow-build percussion and understated, sexy guitar you'd expect—but in Fortuna's hands it's still full of surprises.

what to buy: On *La Prima Vez* ♪♪♪♪ (Fortuna Produções Artísticas, 1993) Fortuna performs Ladino songs from Turkey, Morocco, Greece, the Balkans, and Spain (as well as a few of her own attentive compositions in the Ladino tradition), mostly in a sparse but quietly spectacular instrumental setting of woodwinds and flamenco guitar, with occasional accordion and sparing, atmospheric keyboards. In 21 songs over a mere 47 minutes, the band exhibits a bracing energy and maintains an impressive elegance, with Fortuna's bell-like voice equally capable

of soulful soaring and melismatic pathos. True to the title song's theme of first love, this album brims with an exultant creativity and heart. A world-music classic which demands discovery. *Cantigas* ♪♪♪♪ (Fortuna Produções Artísticas, 1994) expands the odyssey to Yugoslavia and Syria, along with more masterworks from Morocco, Turkey, Greece, and Fortuna's own pen. Fortuna's vocals and original compositions have grown even further in assurance, and the album experiments with more insistent percussion; tasteful, evocative electronics; and revelatory, intertwined multi-tracked voices. *Cantigas* progresses from *La Prima Vez*'s exuberance to a lofty gravitas and seductive intensity, but is just as compelling in its own way. It is a testament to the breadth of both the Ladino canon and Fortuna's musical tastes that such a diversity of feeling can be achieved between albums drawn primarily from a finite repertoire.

what to buy next: *Mediterrâneo* ♪♪♪ (Fortuna Produções Artísticas, 1996) is sometimes a bit slower-paced than its predecessors, but always in a contemplative rather than lethargic way which may well appeal to those seeking a gutsier alternative to new-age music. One or two melodies veer toward sentimentality, but Fortuna's voice is never less than heavenly, and smokers like "Ay madre!", "Desde hoy la mi madre," "Dame tu fuerza," and "Me vaya kappará" are worth the price of the album—as is the Turkish/Balkan fusion "Bre Sarika, bre." (The latter area proves to be a particularly rich vein for this album's musical research, as also heard on "Yo hanino tu hanina" and "A la nana y a la buba.")

the rest:

Canções e Orações (Songs and Prayers) N/A (Fortuna Produções Artísticas, 2000)

worth searching for: You owe it to yourself to track down the above discs—the two current U.S. distributors are SISU Music c/o Chaim, (212) 779-1559, sisuent@earthlink.net; and Harmony Ridge c/o Mr. Jack Sutton, (800) 611-4698, www.hrmusic.com, hrmusic@hrmusic.com—but if you really can't wait, two killer tracks from *Mediterrâneo* appear on Putumayo World Music's splendid compilation *Women of Spirit* and its pretty-darn-good one *Romantica*. (The former is reviewed in this volume's Compilations section.)

influences:

Enya, Loreena McKennitt, Madredeus, Bill Douglas

Adam McGovern

Four Men & a Dog

Irish traditional, contemporary folk

Formed 1990, in Ireland. Disbanded 1997.

Cathal Hayden, fiddle, backup vocals; Kevin Doherty, guitar, lead vocals, backup vocals (1993–97); Gino Lupari, percussion, lead vocals,

backup vocals; Gerry O'Connor, fiddle, banjo, backup vocals (1993–97); Mick Daly, guitar, banjo, vocals (1990–93); Donal Murphy, accordion (1990–92); Brian McGrath, banjo, mandolin, piano (1990–93). (All members are from Ireland.)

Four Men & a Dog were the unexpected highlight of the 1990 Belfast Folk Festival. Coming seemingly out of the blue, the newly formed group phenomenally blended the traditional dance music of Ireland with a diverse host of influences including bluegrass, swing, jazz, and rap. The band's initial incarnation included singer Mick Daly, accordionist Donal Murphy, and banjo player Brian McGrath. All three departed around 1993 and were replaced by Gerry O'Connor and singer Kevin Doherty. The instrumental core for the band's entire existence was fiddler Cathal Hayden, who had left the more traditional Arcady to join Four Men & a Dog, but with the addition of O'Connor they acquired arguably the finest banjo player to ever have emerged from Ireland. Also leading the way for the group since its heyday was bodhrán player/vocalist Gino Lupari, whose larger-than-life onstage presence was partially responsible for the band's success. Four Men & a Dog's final two recordings saw them gain increasing popularity in the U.K., which was due in part to their continual move away from their traditional Irish roots. Both *Doctor A's Secret Remedies* and *Long Roads* feature members of the Band, and were actually recorded in upstate New York at Band drummer Levon Helm's studio. Doherty's announcement that he would be leaving Four Men led the other members to take an extended hiatus and eventually call it quits in 1997. Doherty and O'Connor continue to play together, while Lupari has started a new London-based band called Beware of the Dog.

what to buy: *Shifting Gravel* ♫♫♫ (Green Linnet, 1994, prod. Arty McGlynn) marked the addition of singer Kevin Doherty to the band following the departure of vocalist and folk stalwart Mick Daly. Doherty's songs brought a country influence, and although still overpowered by the fiery instrumental work of Hayden and O'Connor, his song styling had a cohesiveness to it that the band's debut album had been sorely missing.

what to buy next: The band's debut *Barking Mad* ♫♫♫ (Topic, 1992, prod. Arty McGlynn) was voted Best Album by the English magazine *Folk Roots* in 1991, making Four Men the first Irish group ever to win the award. Much of their success was based on the instrumentals, which are stellar and make the already mediocre vocal songs seem even more so. Despite some shortcomings this is an interesting album, and a successful blend of a variety of influences.

worth searching for: *Doctor A's Secret Remedies* ♫♫♫ (Transatlantic, 1995) and *Long Roads* ♫♫♫ (Castle Communications, 1996, prod. Aaron Hurwitz) are both available in the United States as imports. As previously mentioned, on these final two albums the band showed a marked migration from their early Irish roots to a more modern, folk-influenced sound.

solo outings:
Cathal Hayden:
Handed Down ♫♫♫ (Rainbow Records)

Gerry O'Connor:
Time to Time ♫♫♫♫ (Mulligan, 1991)
Myriad ♫♫♫ (Myriad Media, 1998)

influences:
◀◀ Planxty, the Bothy Band, Paddy O'Brien, Seumas Connoly

see also: *Arcady*

Cliff McGann

Frå Senegal Til Setesdal

Worldbeat, international folk
Formed 1996 in Setesdal, Norway. Based in Setesdal, Norway.

Kirsten Bråten Berg (Norway), vocals, jews harp; Solo Cissokho (Senegal), vocals, kora; Kouame Sereba (Côte d'Ivoire), vocals, drums; Bjørgulv Straume (Norway), vocals, jews harp.

Most "worldbeat" we're familiar with relies on a fusion of various African styles with familiar Anglo-American ones that were drawn from the music that came to North America with the slaves—blues, rock, funk, rap, samba, *son*, and rumba. But this worldbeat quartet is half African and half Norwegian, and its sound is based on a fusion of Norwegian and Senegalese folk music, which sounds jarring—but, to ears raised on British and American folk styles, jarring in a pleasing way. Kirsten Bråten Berg got interested in folk music in 1970 and since then has been collecting and performing it all over Norway, both solo and as a member of the Arild Andersen Group. In 1995 she met two African musicians—Sereba from Côte d'Ivoire, and Cissokho from Senegal—who were now living in Norway, and suggested a collaboration. Bjørgulv Straume, another folk singer from Setesdal, completed the lineup. Frå Senegal Til Setesdal has become very popular on the folk circuit, performing at festivals and concert halls to rave reviews. All the members also have solo careers.

worth searching for: The mostly vocal *Frå Senegal Til Setesdal* ♫♫♫♫ (Grappa Norway, 1997, prod. Hallvard Kvåle) introduces a new kind of worldbeat to Anglo-American ears. Norwegian folk singing has a swinging syncopation that's vaguely familiar to those of us raised on Celtic music, but it's also totally unique. The Norwegians sing some African songs, and the Africans arrange the Norwegian tunes, adding spare hand drum accents. The jews harps and African mouth bows supply an odd buzzing backbeat. This album is hard to find in the United States, but worth tracking down.

influences:

◄◄ Myllarguten, Slinkombas, Hans W. Brimi

j. poet

Franco
Soukous

Born L'Okanga La Ndju Pene Luambo Makiadi, 1938, in Sona-Bata, Congo; died 1989.

Franco was a singer, composer, and bandleader, but it was his guitar playing that made him a legend ("The Sorcerer of the Guitar"), possibly the most important African musician of the 20th century. In his four-and-a-half decades in the limelight he cut hundreds of albums, singles, and cassettes with his mighty OK Jazz Band, and founded a whole new style of Congolese rumba.

Congo was under the colonial heel of Belgium when Franco was born in 1938, and the music of the country was undergoing a rapid transformation from rural folk forms to more internationally influenced popular music. Christian missionaries had introduced the idea of harmony singing, although some tribal groups had been using harmony in their vocal music for centuries. There was also a strong tradition of composing topical songs to deal with the trials of everyday life, a tradition Franco later drew on when composing his lyrics. Modern *soukous* began evolving in the 1940s when the international record companies started releasing Cuban albums in West Africa. The rumba, which was based on rhythms African slaves had carried to the New World, was particularly popular, and when it was reintroduced to Congolese musicians, they began incorporating its syncopation and Latin rhythms into their own styles of dance music. The horn sections and flutes of the rumba and *charanga* bands were replaced by guitars, and soukous was born.

Franco had shown interest in music from an early age, and his first guitar was a self-made conglomeration of tin cans and electrical wire. His father passed when Franco was 10 and he had to leave school to help his mother support his brothers and sisters. He got his first real instrument at the age of 11, and by the time he was 15 he was a popular session musician with a finger-picking style that amazed his peers and brought him lots of attention from the young women. Because of his popularity, Franco was able to persuade the owners of the studio he worked for to let him and his bandmates practice at home. (The studios at that time owned the instruments and jealously guarded their session players.) In 1956 Franco and a few of his friends left the recording studio to play at the OK Club. He called his new band OK Jazz, and within a year they were rivaling Dr. Nico's African Jazz band for chart supremacy. In fact, most modern Congolese guitarists owe a stylistic debt to one or both of these giants.

In 1960 Congo attained independence, and after a period of bloody civil war became one of the most stable and prosperous nations in Black Africa. Franco and OK Jazz became one of its most successful bands along with Dr. Nico's L'Orchestre Fiesta Sukisa and Rochereau's Fiesta National. As Africa threw off colonialism, Europe became hungry for authentic African culture and Franco, Rochereau and others began touring Europe and taking advantage of the power electric guitars gave them. International beats from the Caribbean and Europe also started creeping into the music, making soukous popular throughout the African continent and winning new converts in Europe as well. Franco's success enabled him to start his own music business empire. He employed hundreds of musicians, singers, and dancers, and encouraged them to get involved with side projects and spinoff bands—so long as they recorded for the master's record company, a not-unreasonable request since he paid for their food, clothes, instruments, and housing. An amazing number of people began their careers with Franco including Sam Mangwana, Mose Fan Fan, and Papa Noel, to name but a few.

During the turbulence of the 1960s Franco often sang about political issues, and his satirical takes on the ruling class were often banned (which only added to his popularity). In one case he was actually jailed, but the international outcry by his fans had him back on the streets in three days. In the 1970s Franco began writing more about interpersonal relationships, promoting a strict moral code, although he often used bawdy humor and double entendres to make his points about faithless husbands, wife beaters, and those who abused alcohol. He remained popular at home, but never was able to make the same leap abroad, partially because he'd become involved with the ruling clique and whenever they had a problem they asked Franco to compose a tune to help smooth things over. He also began composing songs about his favorite products and tributes to his richest fans, and while the themes smack of opportunism, the musical quality remained high. In 1987 Franco returned to social commentary with one of his most important songs "Attention na SIDA (Beware of AIDS.)" He died in 1989 after a long sickness that was rumored to be AIDS-related, an allegation his organization vehemently denies.

what to buy: There's not much info on the CD booklet, but the two-disc, 11-track *20e Anniversaire* 𝄞𝄞𝄞𝄞 (Sonodisc) was originally released in 1976, during one of the creative peaks of OK Jazz. Incredible guitar work, angelic vocals, and slick production make this one a good starting place.

what to buy next: *Originalité* 𝄞𝄞𝄞𝄞 (RetroAfric, 1990) is the first disc of a six-part retrospective that tracks the career of Franco and his band from the mid-1950s to the early 1960s. Tunes are taken from 78 rpm discs and old LPs, but whatever the sonic limitations, the music remains transcendent.

worth searching for: Franco and OK Jazz recorded hundreds of albums, and provided backing tracks for dozens of singers like Sam Magwana. In the decade since his death, labels have been tracking down Franco's hits and rare tracks for release on CD. He and OK Jazz rarely made a poor recording, so almost anything with his name on it is worth owning. This list barely scratches the surface: *Le Grande Maitre Franco* 🎻🎻🎻 (Celluloid, 1991); *Tres Impoli* 🎻🎻🎻🎻 (Sonodisc, 1984); *Franco Joue avec Sam Mangwana* 🎻🎻🎻🎻 (Grace); *A L'Ancienne Belgique* 🎻🎻🎻🎻 (Grace, 1984); *For Ever* 🎻🎻🎻🎻 (Melodie); *Lettre à Monsieur le Directeur Général* 🎻🎻🎻🎻 (Melodie); *Merveilles du Passé 1957-1958-1959* 🎻🎻🎻🎻 (Sonodisc); *Live in Europe* 🎻🎻🎻🎻 (Sonodisc); *En Colere: 1979/1980* 🎻🎻🎻🎻 (Sonodisc); *Attention na SIDA* 🎻🎻🎻🎻 (Sonodisc, 1987); *Cooperation: 1980–1982* 🎻🎻🎻🎻 (Sonodisc, 1982); *Disques d'Or et Maracas d'Or* 🎻🎻🎻🎻 (Sonodisc).

influences:

▶▶ Tabu Ley Rochereau, Diblo Dibala, Pablo, Quatre

see also: *Diblo Dibala, Dr. Nico, Sam Mangwana, Tabu Ley Rochereau*

j. poet

Alasdair Fraser

Scottish fiddle
Born May 14, 1955, in Clackmannan, Scotland. Based in Scotland.

Alasdair Fraser is one of the most well-traveled and sought-after fiddlers Scotland has ever produced. His fingers soar over the strings with finesse, while his bowing produces a sound so expressive you could almost swear his fiddle is singing. His great love of Scotland's traditional music shines through as he plays familiar reels, strathspeys, and airs that delight listeners around the world. Saying Fraser is an award-winning fiddler hardly does him justice. He won the Open Competition of the Scottish National Mod Fiddle Championship two years in a row, and has since won similar national Scottish-fiddling competitions abroad, including the United States' and Canada's. He has appeared on television programs such as *CBS Sunday Morning,* been heard on radio's *A Prairie Home Companion,* and played on the soundtracks of such movies as *The Last of the Mohicans,* and *The Spitfire Grill.* Fraser has performed and recorded with a variety of virtuosos, including Chris Norman, Tim Gorman, Jean Redpath, Itzhak Perlman, Twila Paris, and Derek Bell. He also excels at composition, as is especially evident on his album *Dawn Dance.* And he teaches his gift to a new generation of musicians at his two summer fiddle programs and his workshops at numerous Scottish festivals. In passing on the art of Scottish fiddling, Fraser uses his deeply felt Scottish heritage, his wry sense of humor, and his amazing ability to encourage others.

what to buy: On *Dawn Dance* 🎻🎻🎻🎻 (Culburnie, 1995), Fraser displays his amazing flair for composition. Made up entirely of originals, this is that rare album of new, traditionally based music that stands with the best of its models. Fraser is joined by a host of other excellent players, including Eric Rigler on bagpipes and Chris Norman on flutes, who perform beautifully together. Particularly inspired is "Independence Trail/Galen's Arrival," commemorating the birth of his son. This album won the INDIE Award for "Celtic Album of 1995."

what to buy next: *The Driven Bow* 🎻🎻🎻 (Culburnie, 1988, prod. Alasdair Fraser, Jody Stecher) is a delightful collection of traditional tunes from Scotland and Nova Scotia. Fraser teams up with guitarist Jody Stecher to recreate a portion of Scottish and Cape Breton history which invites listeners to get up and dance. Fraser surrounds himself with other standouts (including Rigler and Norman again) in the wonderful ensemble Skyedance. Their album *Way Out to Hope Street* 🎻🎻🎻 (Culburnie, 1997) features a delightful selection of mostly original tunes, beautifully arranged for fiddle, pipes, flutes, keyboards, bass, and percussion.

what to avoid: *The North Road* 🎻🎻 (Sona Gaia, 1989, prod. Billy Oskay, Alasdair Fraser, Paul Machlis) has more of a new-age feel than any of Fraser's other work, leaving it feeling a little hollow, despite some excellent tunes and performances.

the rest:
Portrait of a Scottish Fiddler 🎻🎻🎻 (Brownrigg, 1984/Culburnie, 1996)
Skyedance 🎻🎻🎻 (Culburnie, 1986)

influences:

◀◀ Farquhar MacRae, Hector MacAndrew, Buddy MacMaster, Willie Fernie

▶▶ Bonnie Rideout, Natalie MacMaster, Ashley MacIsaac

see also: *Derek Bell, Itzhak Perlman, Jean Redpath*

Jo Hughey Morrison

Peter Gabriel

Experimental pop, world fusion
Born May 13, 1950, in Cobham, England. Based in England.

In many ways, Peter Gabriel stands as one of worldbeat's main mentors. You won't actually find it in the bulk of his music, but as one of the benefactors behind both WOMAD (the World of Music, Arts, and Dance organization) and the RealWorld label, he's been a driving force in making world music accessible. It all began after he left Genesis in 1975 and started releasing his successful solo albums. In 1980 there was "Biko," the anthem to slain South African activist Stephen Biko (which eventually appeared on a compilation for Amnesty International, an organization with which Gabriel has remained active). In the middle of 1982, he and WOMAD director Thomas Brooman organized that group's first festival in England—and came close to losing shirt, shoes, and service, only to have Gabriel's former Genesis mates step in and restore solvency with a surefire one-off reunion concert. The year 1986 saw the inauguration of Gabriel's RealWorld studios in Box, near Bath, and a year later the RealWorld label got underway, with then-unknown but eventually renowned signings like Nusrat Fateh Ali Khan. One artist who didn't appear on the label but received massive boosts from Gabriel was Senegal's Youssou N'Dour, who toured and recorded with him. In 1989 Gabriel provided the soundtrack to Martin Scorsese's *The Last Temptation of Christ,* which in album form was titled *Passion.* This disc took all manner of world music as its source, as was acknowledged later the same year with a compilation of tracks from the artists and musics that had inspired it (*Passion Sources*). Gabriel has always been one to give credit where credit is due, and he did so again in 1993 when following up his successful *Us* album with the multi-artist *Plus from Us* collection. His tours have long featured world artists as both opening acts (like Papa Wemba) and band members (like Manu Katche), and he's used his name to draw people to WOMAD festivals around the world—although he's now stopped doing that, WOMAD having decisively regained and kept its shirt as a stand-alone brand. But perhaps more than anything else, it's the RealWorld label, in whose operation he's heavily involved, that is his biggest legacy. RealWorld has introduced many great acts from around the globe, taken chances, and helped propel people like the late Nusrat to international fame. In his own quiet way, Gabriel has been, and remains, a true champion of world music.

what to buy: He'd whetted the popular appetite with African/pop syntheses on *Peter Gabriel* 𝄞𝄞𝄞𝄞 (a.k.a. *Security*) (Geffen, 1982, prod. Peter Gabriel, David Lord), and *Passion* 𝄞𝄞𝄞𝄞 (Geffen, 1989, prod. Peter Gabriel) was where Gabriel really brought his obsession with—and knowledge of—world music into the open, whipping it smoothly into an atmospheric whole through clever use of the studio. *Passion Sources* 𝄞𝄞𝄞𝄞 (RealWorld, 1989, prod. various) is the more real side of the coin, showcasing the music sources that he used for *Passion* and fully acknowledging the artists. *Plus from Us* 𝄞𝄞𝄞𝄞 (RealWorld, 1993, prod. various) does the same job, but covers slightly more Eurocentric territory.

the rest:
Peter Gabriel 𝄞𝄞𝄞𝄞 (Atlantic, 1977)

Peter Gabriel (l) with Angélique Kidjo

Peter Gabriel 𝄞𝄞𝄞𝄞 (Atlantic, 1978)
Peter Gabriel 𝄞𝄞𝄞𝄞 (Geffen, 1980)
Plays Live 𝄞𝄞𝄞 (Geffen, 1983)
Music from Birdy 𝄞𝄞𝄞 (Charisma, 1985)
So 𝄞𝄞𝄞 (Geffen, 1986)
Shaking the Tree 𝄞𝄞𝄞𝄞 (Geffen, 1990)
Us 𝄞𝄞𝄞𝄞 (Geffen, 1992)
Secret World Live 𝄞𝄞𝄞 (Geffen, 1994)

influences:
◀◀ Otis Redding

▶▶ Youssou N'Dour, virtually every world-music fusion artist

see also: *Manu Dibango, Youssou N'Dour*

Chris Nickson

James Galway
International pop, classical, Irish traditional
Born December 8, 1939, in Belfast, Ireland. Based in Ireland.

Galway's accomplishments in the classical milieu are many and varied. Unfortunately, the world of classical music has a rather limited commercial appeal, and those musicians who rise to the top in it often feel compelled to reach out to pop audiences. But the refined style of such artists and their tendency to prefer well-groomed popular music usually means they have more resonance in the lounge sector than anywhere else. Galway's efforts outside the classical arena are interesting when they afford him the opportunity to display his playing prowess. Alas, not all of his pop offerings really do him justice and he often seems to sacrifice musical integrity for soothing pleasantries. His work with traditional Irish musicians such as the Chieftains shows off the down-to-earth side of his talent in the beautiful lyrical quality of the sad songs and the joyous spirit of more upbeat dance numbers. When Galway tackles film music, increasingly popular in his pop repertoire, he often generates new nuances and fresh interpretations (as on the excellent *In the Pink* album, which paired him with Henry Mancini). But in recent years he has demonstrated an unfortunate tendency to veer into the schlocky show-tune world of Andrew Lloyd Webber and straight-up adult-contemporary pop. The general lack of character in these milieus doesn't provide him with the substantive material that pushes his playing into top form, and his flute ends up sounding like a fluttering garnish atop the cloying, cloddish quasi-rock arrangements. To balance this less weighty material, there's always Galway's increasing forays into straighter Celtic music, and his selection (along with pianist/composer Phil Coulter) to perform at the ceremony where Irish leader John Hume received his Nobel Peace Prize for the accord in Northern Ireland.

what to buy: For purposes of this book, you want Galway's solid and growing catalog of Celtic-rooted outings. On *In Ireland* ♪♪♪♪ (RCA, 1987, prod. Ralph Mace, Paddy Moloney), a collaboration with Ireland's celebrated traditionalists, the Chieftains, Galway gracefully delivers such classics as "Danny Boy" and "When You and I Were Young, Maggie." The album was apparently recorded live with dancers participating, and the spirit of the dance is apparent. It's a pity there aren't more complete liner notes detailing the origins of these songs. *Over the Sea to Skye* ♪♪♪♪ (RCA Victor, 1990, prod. Ralph Mace, Paddy Moloney), a second collaboration with the Chieftains, is fiery and dreamy by turns; it's a vibrant musical history lesson, with a few links to Scotland—and one to China. Evocative of the desperation and hope on either side of past generations' mass emigration from Ireland to America, Galway's collaboration with Phil Coulter, *Winter's Crossing* ♪♪♪♪ (BMG/RCA Victor, 1998), is a widely loved musical quest along the roots and branches of the Celtic diaspora. *Legends* ♪♪♪♪ (BMG/RCA Victor, 1997), by the same duo, is a pleasant and sentimental runthrough of best-known Celtic standards, from "Danny Boy" to "Riverdance."

what to buy next: For the best of Galway's pop output, go with the film-score survey *In the Pink* ♪♪♪♪ (RCA, 1984, prod. Ralph

Mace), on which Galway interprets Henry Mancini beautifully with themes as whimsical, poignant, distinctive, and colorful as the characters they complemented. Among the stand-outs: "The Pink Panther" and "Baby Elephant Walk," amusingly rendered by Galway on the petite pennywhistle. Galway's highbrow side is served well on *The Lark in the Clear Air* ♪♪♪♪ (RCA Victor, 1994, prod. Ralph Mace), which finds him reunited with Japanese synthesizer-meister Hiro Fujikake, who generally restrains the new-agey tendencies that proved such an annoyance on Galway's previous collaborations with him. Primarily classical selections, these tracks offer simple, uncluttered vehicles for Galway—a reminder of his prowess as a classical player. And for a bit of everything, *Greatest Hits* ♪♪♪♪ (RCA Victor, 1988, prod. various) is a convenient 20-track collection that neatly covers the range of Galway's pop repertoire, from film themes to traditional tunes, plus Rimsky-Korsakov's "Flight of the Bumblebee" and the Bee Gees' "I Started a Joke."

what to avoid: On *The Wind beneath My Wings* ♪♪ (RCA Victor, 1991, prod. Ralph Mace) Galway does the show-tune routine. The saccharine quotient is a bit high—"Send in the Clowns," "Memory," and "The Windmills of Your Mind" all on one album—and all the "nice" vibes make for a pleasant mood but don't really challenge him. *The Enchanted Forest—Melodies of Japan* ♪♪ (RCA Victor, 1990, prod. Ralph Mace) is a fanciful excursion that combines contemporary airs with traditional Japanese melodies. Unfortunately, the arrangements (heavy on synthesizers) lack the earthy feel of traditional instrumentation and often lapse into a kind of spacey new-age blandness.

the rest:
The Wayward Wind ♪♪♪ (RCA, 1982)
Greatest Hits, Vol. 2 ♪♪♪♪ (RCA Victor, 1992)
Beauty and the Beast: Galway at the Movies ♪♪♪♪ (RCA Victor, 1993)
Wind of Change ♪♪ (RCA Victor, 1994)
The Celtic Minstrel ♪♪♪ (RCA Victor, 1996)
Seasons ♪♪♪ (RCA Victor)
Greatest Hits, Vol. 3 ♪♪♪ (RCA Victor, 1998)

influences:
◄◄ Jean-Pierre Rampal

►► Ian Anderson

see also: *The Chieftains, Phil Coulter*

Sandy Masuo

Gamelan Son of Lion

Indonesian, new music
Formed 1974, in Piscataway, NJ, USA. Based in New York, NY, USA.

The lineup has been very fluid over the years. A musicians' collective, they exchange instrumental roles within the group. The current mem-

bers are: Barbara Benary; Daniel Goode; Mark Steven Brooks; David Demnitz; Patrick Grant; Darryl Gregory; Jody Kruskal; Laura Liben; Larry Simon.

After ethnomusicology studies in Indonesia, Barbara Benary built her own *gamelan* (tuned percussion) orchestra in 1974 out of materials that included steel keys, cans, and hubcaps. Although the instruments—a set of metallophones tuned to Indonesian *slendro* and *pelog* scales—looked as though they stepped out of a Harry Partch or John Cage fantasy, they reproduced the sound of their more elegantly fashioned Indonesian prototypes. Gamelan Son of Lion began as a student ensemble, an outgrowth of the ethnomusicology classes Benary went on to teach at Rutgers University's Livingston College in New Jersey. Fellow Livingston faculty members and contemporary composers Daniel Goode and Phil Corner joined in, and Gamelan Son of Lion became a professional, independent outfit in 1976.

Although Gamelan Son of Lion had primarily played traditional Indonesian compositions during its student ensemble days, Benary also added originals by her students to the programs. The professional ensemble still performs some traditional compositions, but the group's focus, both in performance and recording, has been on new music. Gamelan Son of Lion has debuted more than 100 pieces since its inception. In general, the pieces don't adhere to Indonesian compositional patterns and rhythms, but capitalize on the exotic (to Western ears) sound of the Indonesian scales and the liquid, trance-inducing sound of the hammers striking various keys and gongs. Indonesian flutes, electronic music, and Western instruments such as the clarinet and guitar are also added to the fusion. The group has performed music by experimental composers from Indonesia as well. Gamelan Son of Lion played at Expo '86 in Vancouver as guests of the Indonesian government, and visited Java in 1996. The group performs about a half-dozen to a dozen times a year, and its side ventures include collaborations with dance companies and other performance troupes.

what's available: Approaching its 20th year, Gamelan Son of Lion documented the diversity of pieces in its repertoire with *New Gamelan/New York* 𝄞𝄞𝄞𝄞 (GSOL Records, 1995, prod. Mark Steven Brooks). It comes very close to including the kitchen sink. David Simons's "Kebyar Leyak" uses an electronic sample of a wine goblet struck by a pencil to create a digital gamelan in order to evoke both Balinese poltergeists (*leyak*) and UFOs. Goode somehow reproduces the *slendro* scale with clarinet on the appropriately titled "Slendro Clarinet"—and subverts any Western expectations of music on that instrument. The title of *Gamelan as a Second Language* 𝄞𝄞𝄞 (GSOL Records, 1996) sums up the intent of these six compositions by David Demnitz, a pidgin of new music and Indonesian instruments but not quite as eclectic as the earlier release. Both recordings are

newfoundland music

Like its geographical location, the traditional music of the Canadian island province of Newfoundland has always been somewhat on the periphery. Settled by a wide variety of ethnic groups, Newfoundland produces music heavily reflective of its strong ties to the British Isles. The Avalon Peninsula on Newfoundland's eastern edge possesses strong Irish roots, while French traditions commingle with Scottish Gaelic ones on the island's west coast. The English song heritage remains Newfoundland's most vibrant attribute of folk culture, and was a drawing card for many well-known folksong collectors. The instrumental music of Newfoundland is social music, for dancing, and the button accordion reigns supreme. The island's modern fiddle tradition is based upon the playing of two main pioneers, Rufus Guinchard and Emile Benoit. During the 1960s and early 1970s, English folk-revival bands like Fairport Convention influenced the Newfoundland scene and, in the spirit of that seminal ensemble, outfits like Figgy Duff and the Wonderful Grand Band merged the traditional instrumental and vocal music of their own island with a rock 'n' roll sensibility. The influence of Figgy Duff in particular is readily apparent in the commercial success of Newfoundland's more contemporary Celtic-rock bands like the Punters and Great Big Sea.

see also: Great Big Sea, Jim Payne, Kelly Russell

Cliff McGann

available through Gamelan Son of Lion, 167 Spring St., New York, NY 10012 USA.

worth searching for: Gamelan Son of Lion has rarely recorded, but their older releases are currently all available on cassette. The best place to start is with *Gamelan in the New World, Vol. 1* 𝄞𝄞𝄞𝄞 (Smithsonian Folkways, 1979) and *Gamelan in the New World, Vol. 2* 𝄞𝄞𝄞𝄞 (Smithsonian Folkways, 1980). Featuring compositions by Corner, Goode, Benary, Peter Griggs, and others, these collections, originally on vinyl, established the focus of Gamelan Son of Lion's Indonesian/new music fusion. Another two cassettes, *Pieces for Gamelan Son of Lion* 𝄞𝄞𝄞𝄞

(New Wilderness Audiographics, 1984) and *Gamelan Son of Lion* 𝄞𝄞𝄞𝄞 (New Wilderness Audiographics, 1985), are available from the group. The former consists of six pieces by Benary, and the latter is another eclectic assortment featuring works by Benary, Goode, Corner, Demnitz and others, as well as the ensemble composition "Gamelan NEA."

influences:

◀◀ John Cage, Pauline Oliveiros, Karlheinz Stockhausen

▶▶ Robert Fripp, Steve Reich, Rahayu Supanggah

Salvatore Caputo

Garcia Brothers

Traditional Native American

Formed c. 1965 in San Juan Pueblo, NM, USA. Based in San Juan Pueblo, NM, USA.

Jerry Garcia, drums, gourd rattles, bells, vocals; Santiago Garcia, drums, gourd rattles, bells, vocals; Peter Garcia, drums, gourd rattles, bells, vocals; Cipriano Garcia, drums, gourd rattles, bells, vocals. (All members are from USA.)

San Juan Pueblo is one of the oldest communities in North America. When the Spanish arrived in the 16th century, the Tewa people had already been living there for hundreds of generations. The invaders from Spain and later the United States tried to stamp out all Tewa cultural expression, which drove the Tewa to practice their ceremonies in secret, preserving them to this day. The Garcia Brothers are known as great singers and composers, and they have created ceremonial songs for most of their adult lives.

what's available: The stark beauty of the Tewa ceremonial songs on *Songs of My People* 𝄞𝄞𝄞𝄞 (Music of the World, 1994, prod. Bob Haddad, James Lascelles) is captured with state-of-the-art equipment, both live in the field and in the studio. Peter Garcia and Dr. Linda Goodman have written detailed liner notes that provide social and musical insights into Tewa ceremonial traditions.

influences:

◀◀ Traditional Tewa music

j. poet

Carlos Gardel

Tango

Born Charles Romauld Gardés, December 1890, in Toulouse, France. Died June 24, 1935, in Colombia.

While the history of the great 20th-century musics is fraught with dynamic paradoxes, few are as deliciously ironic as the genesis of Argentine tango—and the story of why and how an expatriate French singer carried it from the barrios and bordellos of Buenos Aires to high-society ballrooms, cinema, and the great concert halls of Europe.

First of all, tango is immigrant music. Ten years before Carlos Gardel was born, Buenos Aires was inundated by thousands of poor folk from Spain, Italy, France, and Germany (in fact, German citizen Heinreich Band invented the accordion-like *bandoneón,* tango's core instrument). You can imagine the sociocultural malaise: fetid, overcrowded tenements, mean streets, ancient enemies nose-to-nose, violence, fear, paranoia, circle-of-poverty-forever-unbroken. In this shunned City of the Dead and Dying, the life-affirming hedonism of the brothel was a deeper saving grace to the pissed-off immigrants than any Sunday morning at Mass. The bordellos were free-zones of sex, drugs, and tango (the rock 'n' roll of its time). A roughneck rhythm mutation of Argentine *milonga* stateliness and dusky Cuban *habanera* roil, tango's original function was to inspire and accompany the strutting, slashing, pelvis-to-pelvis *pas de deux* macho-foreplay dances of the johns.

This was the netherworld that greeted French immigrant Mademoiselle Gardés and her three-year-old son Carlos when they docked in 1893. It was a hard-knock life that forced Carlos to hustle small change while most kids were in school. As he got older, the waif found steady odd-job work in bordellos. Drawn to the tango music, he began to hang out with the musicians. Soon, he joined in, rocking some very bawdy folk songs with a near-operatic, fervidly sensuous, emotionally transcendent baritone voice. This fusion of soul and body was crucial to tango's evolution. B.G. (Before Gardel), tango was a low-class, tawdry instrumental genre. A.G. (1917, the year of his first recording), tango ascended to universal soul music. Gardel's tango was indeed sexy, but it was also noble, humble, poetic, romantic, and urbane. From 1917 on, Gardel and tango never looked back.

As well as being a prolific writer of hit songs, the charismatic Gardel was the first real pop culture icon—proto-Valentino profile, gangster fedora, tailored suit, lounge-lizard cigarette—to blow up outta South America. In 1925 the prodigal son dazzled his homies from Gay Paree to Marseille. A bona fide superstar, Gardel reached global immortality after his 1934 acting/scoring Hollywood debut *Tango on Broadway* (his four previous films were Argentine). Sensing that 1935 would be his year of tango world domination, Gardel acted in and scored back-to-back flicks (*El Dia Que Me Quieras* and *Tango Bar*) and binge-recorded eight of his greatest songs (March 19–20, 1935). Three months and four days later, Gardel and his co-composer Alfredo Le Pera died in a plane crash over Colombia (ironically—and historically—Gardel's teenage protégé Astor Piazzola missed the flight). The tragedy only hastened his beatification as the patron saint of tango.

what to buy: Even though the majority of Gardel's catalog is currently import-only, the domestically released *The Best of*

Carlos Gardel 𝄞𝄞𝄞𝄞 (Hemisphere, 1998) pretty much renders that situation moot. By cherry-picking 20 songs (including last-session gems "Volver," "El Dia Que Me Quieras," and "Amargura") from the master's peak era (1926–1935), this disc is pretty much his definitive one.

influences:

▶▶ Astor Piazzola, Dino Saluzzi, Pablo Zeigler

see also: *Astor Piazzolla*

Tom Terrell

Garmarna

Modern Swedish folk
Formed 1990, in Sweden. Based in Sweden.

Stefan Brisland-Ferner, violins, viola, hurdy-gurdy, bowed harp, jew's-harps, background vocals, rhythm; Emma Hardelin, vocals, violin, flute; Jense Hoglin, drums, percussion; Gotte Ringqvist, lute, violin, bowed harp, jew's-harps, background vocals, rhythm; Rickard Westman, bouzouki, guitars.

Believe it or not, a Swedish performance of *Hamlet* was the inspiration for Garmarna. The traditional Swedish score planted a seed with Westman, Ringqvist, and Brisland-Ferner, and a week later the band was born. Within a year they were playing festivals and had added Hoglin to the band. In 1992, recording their first EP *Garmarna,* they brought in their friend Hardelin to expand the vocal possibilities. At first she was just a guest, then became a full-time member in 1993. On the strength of the EP the band toured Scandinavia. To that point the musicians had been playing traditional music on traditional instruments. Now they decided to incorporate samples into their sonic spectrum, mixing the very old and the very new in a dark marriage. The year 1994 saw the release of their debut album *Vittrad (Crumbling Away),* which was widely hailed as a true breakthrough in Swedish folk music, as if a subdued Nine Inch Nails had been transported back to the Middle Ages. The roots were decidedly Nordic, barren, and windswept, but the technology of loops and samples behind fiddles and hurdy-gurdies was something quite new, a folk-rock for the 1990s. It was a start, and the American release brought them attention in the United States and elsewhere. However, the walls really came down with the 1996 album *Gods Musicians* —which even made the charts in Sweden! Darker yet than its predecessor, if that were possible, it put all the pieces together in a still more organic way, highlighting the stark intensity of Hardelin's voice. The traditional base remained vital in the sound, but a number of the tracks were original compositions, ranging from the gorgeous to the very, very scary in the way that Garmarna seems to have established as its own.

what to buy: *Vittrad (Crumbling Away)* 𝄞𝄞𝄞𝄞 (Omnium, 1994, prod. Nicklas Holmgren, Hans Lebanzski, Garmarna) is a revelation of sound; this is where Ingmar Bergman's medieval vistas met cyberpunk. *Gods Musicians* 𝄞𝄞𝄞 (Omnium, 1996, prod. Sank) capitalizes on the magic—or sorcery as the case may be—lyrically dripping with gore as all the best folk music should. No big changes in the sound, but it all works even more smoothly. Further perfecting that sound on *Vengeance* 𝄞𝄞𝄞 (NorthSide, 1999), the band proves the end of the world still has quite a bright future.

solo outings:
Triakel (Emma Hardelin)
Triakel 𝄞𝄞𝄞 (NorthSide, 1998)

influences:
◀◀ Traditional Swedish music

Chris Nickson

Djivan Gasparyan

Armenian folk
Born 1928, in Solag, Armenia. Based in Yerevan, Armenia.

Gasparyan is a master of the *duduk,* an Armenian double-reed wind instrument that has a sound similar to an oboe and is carved from apricot wood, which is said to give the instrument its unique timbre. He is self-taught, inspired by the folk music he heard in his youth. By age 20 he was playing with the Tatul Altounian National Song and Dance Ensemble. Gasparian became one of Armenia's best-known musicians after contributing to Peter Gabriel's soundtrack for *The Last Temptation of Christ.* Since then he has toured extensively and collaborated with the Kronos Quartet. He also teaches duduk at the Yerevan Conservatory.

what to buy: *Apricots from Eden* 𝄞𝄞𝄞 (Traditional Crossroads, 1996, prod. Harold G. Hagopian) offers the fruits of traditional folk music from Armenia, played on duduk with *dan duduk* (drone) and *d'hol* (drum) accompaniment. These are dance tunes and slow folk songs, played with a melancholic minor-key bluesy-ness that's countered by Levon Arshakung's subtle percussion.

what to buy next: *Ask Me No Questions* 𝄞𝄞𝄞 (Traditional Crossroads, 1991, prod. Harold G. Hagopian) is a moving solo album of Armenian folk tunes drawn from the country's Christian and pagan traditions.

the rest:
(With Michael Brook) *Black Rock* 𝄞𝄞𝄞 (RealWorld, 1998)

influences:
◀◀ Muradian Ensemble

j. poet

Djivan Gasparyan

Dick Gaughan

Scottish, Celtic

Born May 17, 1948, in Leith, Scotland. Based in Edinburgh, Scotland.

A handful of singers come to mind who just have "it," that elusive ability to resonate with the soul through the sheer sound of their voice. Nusrat Fateh Ali Khan, Sarah Carter, Umm Kulthum, Robert Johnson . . . certainly a list of this type must also include Dick Gaughan. Any discussion of the man's talents must begin with the voice. His fierce passion for Scotland and its people must follow a close second. After that one can list his skills as a composer, his devotion to the fight for social justice, his gift for finding and interpreting the songs of others, and his accomplishments as a guitarist.

Gaughan grew up in a close-knit community in the town of Leith (now part of Edinburgh). His father, an immigrant from Ireland, was a fiddler and speaker of the Irish language; his mother was a Scot, with a repertoire of songs from the highlands in both English and Gaelic. It was in this household steeped in song that Gaughan was raised. He began working as a professional musi-cian in 1970. He was an early member of the Boys of the Lough and appears on their first album. He was a founding member of the Scottish folk-rock group Five Hand Reel. More recently he founded and produced the group ClanAlba. Gaughan is also interested in formal composition and has written music for several BBC TV films. As a passionate singer who wears his love of land on his sleeve, he is clearly the finest interpreter of traditional Scottish ballads known as the "Muckle Sangs" (the big songs). To them he bestows a power, warmth, and immediacy that brings life to these songs of great antiquity. He is also a master interpreter of Scotland's national poet, Robert Burns. His deep commitment to social justice is always present in his music, which has profoundly influenced younger performers such as Billy Bragg.

what to buy: *Handful of Earth* 🎵🎵🎵🎵 (Green Linnet, 1981, prod. Dick Gaughan) is simply a landmark recording. Gaughan is in perfect voice, and the balance between truly superb political commentary and traditional Scottish music is stunning. The incredible beauty Gaughan brings to Burns's "Now Westlin Winds" is enough to make the recording a must-have, but listen to the passion in "The Snows They Melt the Soonest" if you need a further example of Gaughan's gift. His versions of Leon Rossellon's "The World Turned Upside Down" and Ed Picket's "Workers Song" are as powerful performances of politically conscious material as you can find.

what to buy next: *A Different Kind of Love Song* ♫♫♫♫ (Appleseed, 1997, prod. Dick Gaughan, Carsten Linde) is not of the magnitude of *Handful of Earth,* simply because it does not contain the traditional Scottish pieces to offset the social commentary. But so what? This is Dick Gaughan, and he could be singing "The Best of the Carpenters" and it would still be superb music. The passion is there throughout, from the amazing "Stand Up for Judas" through his introspective interpretation of Joe South's "The Games People Play." The Appleseed people have added a bonus version of "The World Turned Upside Down" and a great Scot love song, "Lassie Lie Near Me," that helps to bring a little balance for those overwhelmed by the overt political material.

the rest:
More Forever ♫♫♫ (Leader, 1972)
Gaughan ♫♫♫ (Topic, 1978)
Andy Irvine and Dick Gaughan: Parallel Lines ♫♫♫ (Green Linnet, 1983 /Appleseed, 1997)
Live in Edinburgh ♫♫♫ (Celtic Music, 1985 /Appleseed, 1994)
True and Bold: Songs of the Scottish Miners ♫♫♫ (Struc, 1986)
Call It Freedom ♫♫♫ (Celtic Musicm, 1989)
Sail On ♫♫♫ (Appleseed, 1996)
Redwood Cathedral ♫♫♫♫ (Appleseed, 1998)

The Boys of the Lough
The Boys of the Lough ♫♫♫ (Shanachie, 1973)

worth searching for: And now for something completely different—a Dick Gaughan instrumental record: *Coppers and Brass* ♫♫♫♫ (Topic/Green Linnet, 1977, prod. Tony Engle). This record shows us just what a skilled musician lies beneath that magnificent voice. It sets his string playing in a very traditional context, as Gaughan blazes through a set of reels, jigs, hornpipes, and marches.

influences:
◄◄ Bill Broonzy, Woody Guthrie, Bert Jansch, Luke Kelley, Ewan McColl

►► Mary Black , Billy Bragg, Silly Wizard

see also: *The Boys of the Lough, Andy Irvine*

Jared Snyder

Frankie Gavin

Irish traditional

Born 1956, in Corrandulla, County Galway, Ireland. Based in Galway, Ireland.

Raised in a musical family of Northeast County Galway, just across Lough Corrib from the Connemara *Gaeltacht* (Gaelic-speaking area), Frankie Gavin grew up surrounded by traditional music to become one of Ireland's finest fiddle players. He is a supreme technician and can produce the most complex and intense fiddle music while remaining absolutely at ease on the instrument. One of his main sources of inspiration is the music of emigrant Irish performers who recorded in the United States during the 78 rpm era. In particular, Gavin credits Galway piper Patsy Touhey, Sligo fiddle player James Morrison, Leitrim flute player John McKenna, and the Flanagan Brothers, originally from Waterford, for expanding, through their recordings, his repertoire of techniques and tunes as well as the general flavor of his music. A remarkable solo artist, Gavin is perhaps better known as one of the founders of the long-lived Irish group De Danann (or De Dannan, as they spell it now). Gavin was still of school age when the band came together during the early 1970s in music sessions held around Spiddal, County Galway, then home of Gavin's longtime partner-in-crime, *bouzouki* player Alec Finn. After coming to the United States for the first time in 1976 to participate in the extraordinary festivities surrounding the bicentennial celebration in the nation's capital, the band toured again the following year, and on that occasion, Gavin recorded his first solo album for the New York label Shanachie. Being an outstanding flute and whistle player as well, Gavin was inspired to make a flute album, *Croch Suas É—Up and Away,* in 1983. His accompanist this time was Leitrim fiddle and piano player Charlie Lennon, whose excellent compositions in traditional style have become well known through Gavin's performances; in 1985 Gavin participated in the recording of Lennon's *The Emigrant Suite,* and again in his second suite, *Island Wedding,* recorded in 1991 for Radio Telefis Éireann (RTE). In the interim, Gavin produced one of his best albums and a landmark of Irish music when he recorded *A Tribute to Joe Cooley* in 1986 with accordionist Paul Brock. Gavin and Brock had first met Cooley and each other in 1973, shortly before the legendary accordionist's untimely death. Another outstanding solo album, *Frankie Goes to Town,* followed in 1991. That same year, Gavin was touring in France with an offshoot of De Dannan—accordion player Aidan Coffey and guitarist Arty McGlynn—when the trio was recorded during a concert in Paris. This exceptional document, released in 1994 as *Irlande* by the French world-music label Ocora, as well as the few 1984 tracks from German festivals made available on *Ireland,* show the kind of powerhouse performances De Dannan audiences have been rewarded with all these years. Although the full band released a new album in 1996, it appears Gavin is busy nowadays with all kinds of solo ventures. But as long as Gavin and Finn continue to play music together, no one will be surprised to see De Dannan get on the road once again.

what to buy: *Traditional Music of Ireland* ♫♫♫♫ (Shanachie, 1977, prod. Richard Nevins, Daniel Michael Collins) was Gavin's first solo album, recorded during a De Dannan tour in the United States. The recording may show its age in the less-than-stellar sound quality, but Gavin's fiddle playing is riveting, and Alec Finn's trademark bouzouki accompaniment is just what's needed. *Frankie Goes to Town* ♪♪♪♪ (The Bee's Knees, 1989/Green Linnet, 1991, prod. Frankie Gavin), the first album to be released on Gavin's own label, could not be more aptly titled. Gavin, often performing duets with himself by doubling on second fiddle, viola, or flute, plays up a storm on a variety of old and newer tunes. Among the latter are some of Gavin's own compositions, as well as a good number of tunes by his favorite composer, Charlie Lennon, who happens to be his piano accompanist for most of the album. *Irlande* ♪♪♪♪ (Ocora, 1994, prod. Radio France, Association Culture et Musique Irlandaises), available through Harmonia Mundi, is a live recording made in France in 1991 and featuring Gavin with Aidan Coffey (accordion) and Arty McGlynn (guitar). The pace is furious, yet the performance is incredibly tight, and the interplay between the musicians will make your head spin. This is truly superior musicianship at work, of the kind that can be heard whenever De Dannan appears in concert. And Gavin's opening remarks on styles of vocal encouragement to the musicians are priceless, even if probably lost on the original French audience.

what to avoid: *An Irish Christmas* ♪♪ (The Bee's Knees, 1992/Shanachie, 1996, prod. Frankie Gavin, Carl Hession), retitled *Shamrocks and Holly—An Irish Christmas Celebration* and credited to Frankie Gavin with the Carl Hession Orchestra for its U.S. release, contains very little Irish traditional music—namely, Tommy Coen's great reel "Christmas Eve"—and a lot of rather cheesy arrangements of Christmas standards.

worth searching for: Although only available in the United States as imports, Gavin's two albums on the Gael-Linn label are must-haves for Irish music devotees. *Croch Suas É—Up and Away* ♪♪♪♪ (Gael-Linn, 1983, prod. Frankie Gavin, Charlie Lennon, Jackie Small) is officially Gavin's "flute album," even though he also plays fiddle, tin whistle, and even accordion on it—combining all of them on one track credited to "Frankie Gavin's Irish Orchestra"—with Charlie Lennon (piano) and Johnny "Ringo" McDonagh (bodhrán) accompanying. The playing is as good as it gets and the material reflects Gavin's main sources of inspiration: old tunes from the 78 rpm era and new compositions like those of Charlie Lennon. *A Tribute to Joe Cooley* ♪♪♪♪ (Gael-Linn, 1986, prod. Frankie Gavin) proves, if needed, that Gavin takes after James Morrison in more ways than one and that, like the great Sligo fiddler of the 1920s, he is an awesome duet player. His partner here is accordionist Paul Brock, of recent Moving Cloud fame, who shares with Gavin a passion for early recordings of Irish and Irish-American music, and their accompanist on piano is none other than Charlie Lennon, one of the best in the business. As it

should be for a tribute to Joe Cooley, the famous accordion player from Peterswell, County Galway, the pace of the music is relaxed, so that the interplay of the two lead instruments can be savored in all its intricacies. Gavin was one of the guest musicians on Andy Irvine's excellent *Rainy Sundays . . . Windy Dreams . . .* ♪♪♪♪ (Tara, 1980, prod. Dónal Lunny). Gavin's performance of Tommy Coen's reel "Christmas Eve" is definitely one of the highlights of the album, as is the Bulgarian "Paidushko Horo" on which he plays fiddle and flute. *Ireland* ♪♪♪♪ (WDR, 1993, prod. Christian Scholze, Jean Trouillet, Jan Reichow), a collection of live recordings made in Germany, includes five tracks featuring Gavin solo or with Belfast flute player Desi Wilkinson and master uilleann piper Liam O'Flynn.

influences:

◀◀ Flanagan Brothers, John McKenna, James Morrison, Patsy Touhey

▶▶ John Carty, Paddy Glackin, Seán Kane, Tommy Peoples

see also: *De Dannan, Alec Finn, Andy Irvine, Moving Cloud, Liam O'Flynn*

Philippe Varlet

Gazoline

Zouk

Formed 1982 in Paris, France. Based in Paris, France.

Pier Rosier (Martinique), lead vocals, leader; Marc L'Mira, bass, synthesizers, percussion, vocals; Alain Cebarec, vocals; Jerico Boura, drums, percussion; Philip Aubou, drums; Alain Joseph, guitar; Jean-Francois Kellner, guitar, vocoder; Frederic Legall, synthesizer; Jean-Cristophe Prudhomme, keyboards; Laurent Albert, percussion; Edith Lefel, vocals; Nicolas Guerret, tenor sax; Mark Sims, trombone; Christian Martinez, trumpet; Alain Hato, sax; Denis Leloup, trombone; Jean-Louis Damant, trombone; Eric Jiausserand, trumpet; Philipe Slominsky, trumpet.

Gazoline's founder, Pier Rosier, was born in Lamentin, Martinique, and grew up playing a style of Carnival music called *Chouval Bwa*. He moved to Paris to pursue his career, and when Kassav' took off in 1982 with a variation on Carnival music they called *zouk*, he put together Gazoline to play a less-produced, more-traditional version.

what to buy: *Zouk Obsession* ♪♪♪♪ (Shanachie, 1990, prod. Pier Rosier) is a greatest-hits compilation from one of the few bands that's been able to challenge Kassav'"s domination of the zouk market. These six tracks are brimming over with energy, but the collection clocks in at a short 35 minutes.

the rest:

Pier Rosier ♪♪♪♪ (Sonodisc Frace, 1997)
Bidongaz ♪♪♪♪ (Melodie France, 1988)

Ghazal

influences:

◄◄ Vikings of Guadeloupe, K Percussion, Kassav', Experience 7

►► Malavoi, Kwak

j. poet

Ghazal
/Kayhan Kalhor

Indo-Iranian fusion

Ghazal formed 1996 in New York, NY, USA; Kalhor born 1963 in Tehran, Iran. Based in New York, NY, USA.

Kayhan Kalhor (Iran), leader, kamancheh (Iranian spike fiddle); Shujaat Hussain Khan (India), sitar; Swapan Chaudhuri (India), tabla.

Kayhan Kalhor, a traditionally minded Iranian musician, is a master of the *kamancheh,* a fiddle-like instrument with four strings believed to be the ancestor of all Arabic and European fiddles. He was born in Tehran, Iran, and began studying the instrument at the age of seven. He mastered Iran's formal classical music at an early age, including the system of *radif* and *dastgahs,* which resemble and are thought to predate the Indian system of *ragas.* He won national competitions of the kamancheh throughout high school, but after the Islamic Revolution he relocated, first to Italy and then to Canada. In 1990 he founded the Dastan Ensemble with vocalist Shahram Nazeri and two other young Persian musicians and has toured widely with them, performing folk, devotional, and classical music from Iran. The group won first prize at the 1991 Sacred Music Festival in Fez, Morocco. In the mid 1990s Kalhor moved again, to New York City, where he began a solo recording career. He also got the idea of forming a world-music fusion group after a performance by Shujaat Hussain Khan of India. When he was introduced to Khan by a mutual friend, they began rehearsing and were amazed at how seamlessly the two traditions fit together. Their debut album *Lost Songs of the Silk Road* received critical raves, and their performances together, with Swapan Chaudhuri lending his support on tabla, have been widely praised. At presstime they had just completed an as-yet untitled follow-up recording, planned for January 2000 release.

what to buy: Kalhor and Khan developed the pieces on *Lost Songs of the Silk Road* ⅃⅃⅃⅃ (Shanachie, 1997, prod. Brian Cullman,

Kayhan Kalhor) in the studio, starting with a single melodic phrase and exploring its possibilities according to the rules of their respective cultures. The music spins off into incredibly complex yet subtle directions, driven by the daring improvisations of the three soloists. *As Night Falls on the Silk Road* ♪♪♪♪ (Shanachie, 1998, prod. Brian Cullman) is another tour de force journey from three master musicians. By plucking the strings of the kamancheh below the bridge, Kalhor is able to produce single notes that often provide a brilliant counterpoint to Shujaat Khan's sitar.

what to buy next: *Scattering Stars Like Dust* ♪♪♪♪ (Traditional Crossroads, 1998, prod. Harold Hagopian) is a "solo" outing by Kalhor, supported by the *tombak* (Iranian clay drum) of Pejman Hadadi. The piece is based on the *dastgah chahargah* and incorporates elements drawn for Persian classical and folkloric tradition. The enclosed booklet includes detailed notes on Persian music and its history.

influences:

◄◄ Ostad Ali A. Bahari, Baqer Khan, Hoisen Khan, Ravi Shankar

j. poet

Bikram Ghosh

North Indian classical

Born 1966, in Calcutta, India. Based in India.

Ghosh is one of the most promising young *tabla* (double hand drum) virtuosos on the scene today. He was born into a musical family and taught by his father, respected tabla player Pandit Shankar Ghosh, who in the 1960s was one of the first Indian musicians to travel to the United States (to perform with Ali Akbar Khan at the Ali Akbar College of Music). Spending part of his childhood in San Rafael, California, Bikram absorbed a variety of Western influences, and in addition to Indian classical music his training included playing in school bands and dabbling in non-Indian percussion instruments like the congas. But despite an interest in fusing Western and Indian musical forms, Ghosh's output has been primarily rooted in North Indian classical traditions, although he has also become noted as one of the few tabla players to master the South Indian *karnatak* style of drumming, thanks to his 11 years studying under *mridangam* virtuoso Pandit S. Shekhar. A nimble tabla player with a brilliant penchant for improvisation, Ghosh has become a favorite accompanist for Indian music legends like Ravi Shankar, Ali Akbar Khan, and Viswa Mohan Bhatt in recent years. But his most frequent collaborator is *santur* (hammered dulcimer) master Tarun Bhattacharya, with whom he has recorded several impressive albums.

what's available: *Talking Tabla* ♪♪♪♪ (Music of the World, 1997, prod. Bob Haddad, Randy Friel) may be of limited interest to those who aren't spellbound by masterful percussive feats, as the simple musical backdrops on these relatively short com-

positions grow fairly repetitive at times. But as a rare solo tabla recording, the album is simply stunning from a rhythmic standpoint, showcasing lightning-quick fingertips and a flawless knack for improvisation that led no less knowledgeable a critic than Ravi Shankar himself to proclaim, "I have not heard tabla so beautiful as Bikram's for a long, long time."

the rest:
(With Tarun Bhattacharya) *Kirvani* ♪♪♪♪ (Music of the World, 1996)
(With Ravi Shankar) *Chants of India* ♪♪♪♪ (Angel, 1997)
(With Anoushka Shankar) *Anoushka* ♪♪♪♪ (Angel, 1998)

worth searching for: Over the years, Ghosh has recorded a variety of hard-to-find and cassette-only releases with V.M. Bhatt, Ajoy Chakraborty, and Tarun Bhattacharya. Suffice it to say that every recording featuring any of these Indian music masters is well worth owning.

influences:

◄◄ Gyan Prakash Ghosh, Shankar Ghosh, Zakir Hussain, Ali Akbar Khan, S. Shekhar

see also: *V.M. Bhatt, Tarun Bhattacharya, Ali Akbar Khan, Anoushka Shankar, Ravi Shankar*

Bret Love

Gilberto Gil

Brazilian pop

Born Gilberto Passos Gil Morreira, June 26, 1942, in Salvador, Bahia, Brazil. Based in Rio de Janeiro.

Gilberto Gil has been at the forefront of Brazil's popular music since the mid-1960s. A skilled guitar player and expressive vocalist, Gil has brought the pop sounds of his native country to international success. Gil was raised by his mother and her family, and the sounds of local bands, street singers, and accordion player Cinezio had a profound effect on him as a youngster. By the age of three, he was already determined to become a musician. Originally pursuing this dream at an accordion academy, Gil switched to the guitar after hearing a bossa nova recording by João Gilberto on the radio. He then went on to perform with the band Os Desafinados (The Out of Tune), in addition to writing advertising jingles and appearing on local television.

As his musical career grew, Gil remained committed to his academic pursuits. Although he studied business administration at Bahia University, Gil was inspired by a music seminar he attended to branch into songwriting in a less anonymous genre than the ad tune. His first success came when Tris Baianas recorded his song "Bem Devagar (Very Slowly)" in 1962. The following year, Gil recorded a double EP, *Sua M'Sica, Sua Interpretarro (His Music, His Interpretation)*. In 1964 he joined with Caetano Veloso, Maria Bethânia, Gal Costa, and Tom Zé to perform a revue, *Nus, Por Ex-*

Gilberto Gil

amplo (Us, For Example), at the Vila Velha Theater in Salvador. Gil presented his first solo show, *Invent rio,* a year later.

Following his graduation from Bahia University, Gil accepted a job as a customs inspector for Gessy Lever in Sao Paulo. For the next few years, Gil worked during the day and hung out at night in music clubs. After meeting lyricist Capinan Torquato Neto, Gil agreed to a songwriting partnership. Reuniting with Veloso, Costa, Bethânia, and Zé, he also performed in another revue, *Arena Canta Bahia.* Gil then went on to become a regular presence on Brazilian television. In 1966 he appeared on *O Fino Da Bossa,* a show hosted by singer Elis Regina. Gil's performance of his song "Louvaca (Praise)" was so potent that he was offered a recording contract by the Philips label. Moving to Rio de Janeiro with his wife Belina and daughter Nora in 1966, Gil placed first in a prestigious International Song Festival with his tune "Minha Sinhora (My Lady)." Following the release of his debut album, *Louvacao,* in 1967, Gil was chosen to host a television show, *Ensaio Geral.*

In the late 1960s, Gil separated from his wife and began living with vocalist Nana Caymmi. Although the protest songs he was then writing made him popular amongst Brazil's *Tropicalia* move-ment (a Western-influenced groundswell of tradition-based rock), Gil's political stance upset the military dictatorship then in power. In 1969 he was arrested along with Veloso and imprisoned until being granted exile in England. While there, Gil was befriended by the country's leading rock artists. Able to return to his native country in 1972, he responded with an album, *Expresso 2222,* that included two Brazilian hits—"Back in Bahia" and "Oriente."

Gil collaborated and recorded a duo album with Brazilian vocalist Jorge Ben, *Gil & Jorge,* in 1975. The following year, he briefly resumed his partnership with Veloso, Costa, and Bethânia. With the release of his solo albums *Realce* (1978) and *Nightingale* (1979), Gil was acclaimed as a leading Brazilian jazz artist; his groundbreaking performance at the Montreux Jazz Festival was featured on the two-CD set *Gil in Montreux* in 1978. Although he based his sound on traditional Brazilian music and the bossa nova, Gil has consistently incorporated other influences. His rendition of Bob Marley's reggae classic "No Woman, No Cry," for instance, reached the top of Brazil's music charts and sold over 700,000 copies. The following year, he joined with reggae great Jimmy Cliff for a tour of Brazil. The pair later performed at the 1982 Montreux Jazz Festival, and Gil even recorded an album with accompaniment by Bob Marley and the Wailers, *Raca Humana,* which was made one year before Marley's death but released three years after. Gil's greatest hit came with the disco tune "Polio" in 1982, and a Best World Music Album Grammy was awarded him in 1999 for *Quanta: Live Ao Vivo.*

what to buy: Recorded in Los Angeles, *Realce* 🎵🎵🎵 (Elektra, 1978, prod. Mazola) reinforced Gil's place in contemporary jazz and included his reggae-infused hit version of Bob Marley's "No Woman, No Cry." The softer, more intimate side of Gil's musical persona was showcased on *Acoustic* 🎵🎵🎵🎵 (Atlantic, 1994, prod. Gilberto Gil).

the rest:
Gil & Jorge 🎵🎵🎵🎵 (Verve, 1975)
Nightingale 🎵🎵🎵🎵 (Elektra, 1979)
Extra 🎵🎵🎵 (WEA Latino, 1983)
Dia Dorim Noite Neon 🎵🎵🎵🎵 (WEA Latino)
Ao Vivo En Toquiro 🎵🎵🎵 (Braziloid, 1988)
Soy Loco Por Tu America 🎵🎵🎵 (Braziloid, 1988)
O Eterno Deus Mu Dansa 🎵🎵🎵🎵 (WEA Latino, 1989)
Realce 🎵🎵🎵🎵 (WEA Latino, 1989)
Parabolic 🎵🎵🎵 (WEA Latino, 1991)
Minha Historia 🎵🎵🎵 (Philips, 1993)
Concerto 🎵🎵🎵 (Westwind, 1995)
Esoterica: Live in U.S. 1994 🎵🎵🎵🎵 (Whirlwind, 1995)
Gil/Bethânia/Veloso 🎵🎵🎵🎵 (Iris, 1995)
Oriente: Live in Japan 🎵🎵🎵🎵 (Westwind, 1995)
En Concerto 🎵🎵🎵🎵 (WEA Latino, 1996)
Gente Precia Ver O Mar 🎵🎵🎵 (WEA Latino, 1996)
Luar 🎵🎵🎵 (WEA Latino, 1996)
Mestres Da MPB 🎵🎵🎵🎵 (WEA Latino, 1996)
Mestres Da MPB, Vol.2 🎵🎵🎵🎵 (WEA Latino, 1996)
Rafavela 🎵🎵🎵 (WEA Latino, 1996)
Indigo Blue 🎵🎵🎵🎵 (Terrascope, 1997)
Quanta 🎵🎵🎵 (Atlantic, 1997)
Quanta: Live Ao Vivo 🎵🎵🎵🎵 (Atlantic, 1998)

influences:
◄◄ Sergio Mendez, Milton Nascimento, Flora Purim

►► Jorge Ben, Ivan Lins

see also: *Maria Bethânia, Gal Costa, Marlui Miranda, Elis Regina, Caetano Veloso, Tom Zé*

Craig Harris

Astrud Gilberto

Bossa nova
Born March 30, 1940, in Bahia, Brazil. Based in Brazil.

Gilberto is Brazilian music's Lana Turner, the accidental star. Married to the bossa-nova singer and guitarist João Gilberto, she was serving as an unofficial interpreter during a studio session for the legendary 1963 jazz album *Getz/Gilberto,* when a chorus of English was needed on Antonio Carlos Jobim's "The Girl from Ipanema." Her wistful evocation of Norman Gimbel's lyric supplanted her husband's Portuguese vocals on the single version—and made her an international sensation. At her best, she doesn't sound like a trained vocalist so much as a dreamy amateur, artless yet seductive. She had the same kind of sensual, South American appeal that mid-1960s National Airlines commercials were able to tap into, and is equally evocative of that era. She's most effective singing in her native Portuguese, especially the handful of songs—including "Corcovado" and "Vivo Sonhando"—written for her by Antonio Carlos Jobim and Gene Lees. In her later work much of that innocence is lost, and so is much of her allure. Her adaptations of show tunes and pop standards such as Tony Hatch's "Call Me" are to be avoided.

what to buy: Of her solo work, *Verve Jazz Masters 9* 🎵🎵🎵🎵🎵 (PolyGram/Verve, 1994, prod. Creed Taylor) artfully combines studio sessions and live performances from 1964 and 1965, mostly off the mid-1960s LPs *A Certain Smile a Certain Sadness, Look to the Rainbow,* and *The Astrud Gilberto Album with Antonio Carlos Jobim.* It includes the haunting Carnegie Hall performance of "Ipanema" from October 9, 1964; an appealingly spare studio version of "Take Me to Aruanda" with Don Sebesky's orchestra; and an ethereal adaptation of Sammy Cahn's "Day by Day." *Getz/Gilberto (20-Bit Master)* 🎵🎵🎵🎵🎵 (Verve, 1963/1987, prod. Creed Taylor) is the master session of the largest-selling jazz album ever recorded, a collaboration between jazzman Stan Getz and Gilberto's husband João, although Astrud's presence is limited. The sequel, *Getz/Gilberto, Vol. 2* 🎵🎵🎵🎵 (Verve, 1964/1993, prod. Creed Taylor), was recorded at the 1964 Carnegie Hall concert.

what to buy next: *Compact Jazz: Astrud Gilberto* 🎵🎵🎵🎵 (PolyGram/Verve, 1987, prod. Creed Taylor) duplicates *Jazz Masters 9*'s versions of many of Gilberto's better-known songs. It omits the lilting "Frevo," though, replacing it with "Summer Samba (So Nice)" from her Englewood Cliffs 1966 session with organist Walter Wanderley and others. The album also provides studio versions of "Ipanema" and "Corcovado" in place of the Carnegie Hall concert.

what to avoid: *Beach Samba* 🎵🎵 (PolyGram/Verve, 1993) has some cuts of interest, but it's not worth braving Gilberto as the Brazilian Vikki Carr, singing "It's a Lovely Day Today," "You Didn't Have to Be So Nice" (with her six-year-old son), and "Misty Roses."

best of the rest:
Plus James Last Orchestra 🎵🎵 (Verve, 1969)
Look to the Rainbow 🎵🎵 (Verve, 1987)
The Silver Collection: The Astrud Gilberto Album 🎵🎵🎵🎵 (Verve, 1987)
Astrud Gilberto with Stanley Turrentine 🎵🎵 (CBS, 1988)
Jazz 'Round Midnight: Astrud Gilberto 🎵🎵🎵 (Verve, 1996)

João Gilberto

worth searching for: *The Girl from Ipanema: The Antonio Carlos Jobim Songbook* ♫♫♫ (PolyGram/Verve, 1995, prod. various) includes the talents of Sarah Vaughan, Billy Eckstine, Ella Fitzgerald, Oscar Peterson, and Dizzy Gillespie, among others. Gilberto's contributions—the original album release of "Ipanema" and the standard versions of "Dindi" and "Agua de Beber"—hold their own among offerings by such luminaries.

influences:

◀◀ Rosemary Clooney , Antonio Carlos Jobim, Walter Wanderley

▶▶ Ann-Margret, Sade, Suzanne Vega

see also: *João Gilberto, Antonio Carlos Jobim*

Bruce Schoenfeld

João Gilberto

Bossa nova
Born June 1931, in Juazeiro, Brazil. Based in Brazil.

João Gilberto became interested in samba rhythms and American jazz while still a teenager. After moving to Rio de Janeiro in the early 1950s, he played on sessions for a variety of artists while working with Antonio Carlos Jobim to create the style of music later known as "bossa nova." (Gilberto's 1958 single of Jobim's "Chega de Saudade [No More Blues]" is considered the first song in the genre.) This "new wave" variation on samba reduced the crowded percussion work typical of the style in a manner similar to the development of "cool jazz" as a reaction to harder bop mannerisms. The main innovation contributed by Gilberto to this budding form were a style of guitar playing called *violão gago*, or "stammering guitar," and a simple, soft, intimate singing style in direct contrast to the powerful emoting in vogue at the time. By syncopating his voice with the rhythms generated by his guitar and a small rhythm section, Gilberto was able to build new harmonic patterns akin to chord progressions used in jazz. It was the latter development, no doubt in tandem with Jobim's sophisticated compositions, that made bossa nova so seductive to jazz musicians like Stan Getz and Charlie Byrd. After changing the face of Brazilian music forever in 1959 with the hugely influential album that included the Jobim masterpieces "Chega de Saudade" and "Desafinado (Out of Tune)," Gilberto, Jobim, and Gilberto's wife, Astrud, came to the States in 1963 so the latter two could record with Getz. The version they cut of Jobim's "The Girl from Ipanema," with Astrud as its inspired last-minute vocalist, was a massive hit in America, starting a U.S. bossa nova craze that lasted for a couple of years. The album they recorded with Getz is still a steady seller.

what to buy: The performances compiled on *The Legendary João Gilberto* ♫♫♫♫ (World Pacific, 1990, compilation prod. Ron McMaster, Matt Pierson) are at the core of a music revolution. The combination of Gilberto's gentle, somewhat restricted vocal range and his rhythmically sophisticated guitar playing with Jobim's songs and arrangements is beguiling, to say the least. The CD contains 38 songs in 75 minutes, in decent sound, from Gilberto's first three albums. First performances of masterpieces fill it: "Desafinado," "Samba de Una Nota Sô (One Note Samba)," and "Insensatez (How Insensitive)" are just a few. Except for a somewhat out-of-place version of "I'm Looking over a Four-Leaf Clover," which gives a foretaste of crimes committed in the name of bossa nova, this collection is solid. *Getz/Gilberto* ♫♫♫♫♫ (Verve, 1963/1987, prod. Creed Taylor) isn't the first bossa nova–influenced jazz album released in the United States, but it is the most influential—and quite deservedly so.

what to buy next: The music is marvelous, the performance is good, and (although this could be a drawback for some listeners) the audience is enthusiastic for *Live in Montreux* ♫♫♫♫ (Elektra Musician, 1987, prod. João Gilberto). Luckily, they generally wait until these gently swaying classics have run their course before leaping into the participatory fray with appreciative applause. Gilberto recorded this concert in 1985, nearly three decades after the revolution Jobim and he had popularized. The material holds up well and the intimacy achieved by Gilberto and his guitar are pluses, but the performance is valedictory rather than revelatory. The wonders of modern recording technology paved the way for *João* ♫♫♫ (Verve, 1991, prod. Mayrton Bahia, Carmela Forsin). Gilberto recorded the vocals and guitar parts in Brazil while the orchestration by Clare Fischer was added in Los Angeles. Had the folks at Verve left Gilberto alone to play his guitar backed up by some idiomatic percussion, this album might score higher. Fischer attempts to duplicate some of Jobim's orchestration from Gilberto's earlier albums, but the result is often a bit over the top. The finest touches place the vocals and rhythm over marvelous arrangements featuring clarinets and alto saxophones (as in "Little Rose"), where darkly wooded sounds highlight the lightness of Gilberto's singing. When Fischer drops his coverlet of strings over Gilberto's softly swinging vocals (as in "Malaga"), the songs verge on easy listening instead of art. Still, there is more than enough good stuff here to recommend, albeit with the orchestral caveat.

what to avoid: Gilberto's name is prominently featured on the cover of *Brazil Samba Jazz, Vol. 1* ♫♫ (Orfeon), and the album can usually be found listed under his name in stores, but it is a collection of performances by more than just him. It isn't that bad a disc once you get over the disappointment of realizing it's not quite a Gilberto album, but the other groups found in the package (Tamba No. 4, Trio Orfeo Negro, and Octavio Henrique) are definitely not up to Gilberto's standards. By the way, he only has two cuts on this album, and the 17-song medley that closes it out is uncredited but definitely not sung by Gilberto.

the rest:
João Gilberto ♫♫♫ (Verve, 1973)
Amoroso/Brasil ♫♫♫ (Warner Bros., 1993)
Personalidade ♫♫♫♫ (Verve, 1993)
Eu Sei Que Vou Te Amar: Ao Vivo ♫♫♫ (Sony Latin Jazz, 1995)
Mi Historia ♫♫♫♫ (PolyGram Latino, 1997)

influences:

◀◀ Elizete Cardozo, Miles Davis, Vinícius de Morais, Gerry Mulligan, Noel Rosa

▶▶ Chico Buarque, Charlie Byrd, Stan Getz, Gilberto Gil, Milton Nascimento, Caetano Veloso

see also: *Luiz Bonfá, Astrud Gilberto, Antonio Carlos Jobim, Herbie Mann*

Garaud MacTaggart and Marty Lipp

The Gipsy Kings

Flamenco, world fusion
Formed 1986, in southern France. Based in France.

Current members include: Nicolas Reyes, guitar, vocals; Andre Reyes, guitar, background vocals; Diego Baliardo, guitar, handclapping; Jacques "Paco" Baliardo, guitar; Tonino Baliardo, guitar; Jahloul "Chico" Bouchiki, guitar, handclapping; Marc Chantareau, percussion; Dominique Perrier, synthesizer; Gerard Prevost, synthesizer, bass. (All members are from France.)

With their powerfully strummed multi-guitar rhythms and enthusiastic singing in the Gitane dialect of southern France, the Gipsy Kings are one of the most successful world-music groups. In a little over a decade, they've sold more than 13 million records worldwide. The band is a joint labor of love by the Reyes Brothers, sons of famed flamenco vocalist Jose Reyes, and their cousins, the Baliardo brothers, sons of flamenco bandleader Manitas de Plata. These players fuse Spain's flamenco tradition with a contemporary vision and high-energy approach. The result is an irresistible dance music that critics have called "rumba flamenco."

Despite their strong musical heritage, the Reyes and Baliardo brothers grew up in poor Gypsy communities in Arles and

Nicolas Reyes of the Gipsy Kings

Montpelier, France. Their climb out of poverty began in the early 1980s when they performed traditional Gypsy music as Los Reyes. Although they released two albums, neither was commercially successful. Their first real break came when they teamed up with producer Claude Martinez and adopted a more modern approach. Their 1987 singles "Bamboleo" and "Djobi Djoba" established the Gipsy Kings as an international phenomenon. Signed by Sony in 1988, the group's self-titled debut under their new name reached the Top 10 in more than a dozen countries and spent 40 weeks on the U.S. charts. And the band's popularity has only continued to grow. Their retrospective, *The Best of the Gipsy Kings,* reached the top position on *Billboard*'s world-music chart in 1995, and they've become perennial winners of the magazine's awards as Best World Music Artist and Best Latin Pop Artist. Now into their second decade of music-making, the band are seemingly everywhere; their song "Sin Ella" was featured in the 1993 film *Restless,* and they've starred in two programs produced by PBS: the 1996 documentary *Tierra Gitana,* and a 1997 video document of their performance at Washington, D.C.'s prestigious Wolf Trap venue.

what to buy: With 19 tracks from their earlier albums, *The Best of the Gipsy Kings* 🎵🎵🎵🎵 (Columbia, 1995, prod. various) is a thorough look at the evolution of the Gipsy Kings' music. Recorded during their 1991 "Este Mundo" tour, *Live* 🎵🎵🎵🎵 (Elektra, 1992, prod. Gerard Prevost, Claude Martinez) captures the excitement of the Gipsy Kings' shows.

the rest:

Gipsy Kings 🎵🎵🎵🎵 (Elektra, 1988)
Allegria 🎵🎵🎵 (Elektra, 1989)
Luna de Fuego 🎵🎵🎵 (Elektra, 1989)
Mosaique 🎵🎵🎵 (Elektra, 1989)
Este Mundo 🎵🎵🎵 (Elektra, 1991)
Los Reyes 🎵🎵🎵 (FNA, 1994)
Love & Liberte 🎵🎵🎵🎵 (Elektra/Nonesuch, 1994)
Tierra Gitana 🎵🎵🎵🎵 (Nonesuch, 1996)
Compass 🎵🎵🎵🎵 (Atlantic, 1997)

influences:

◄◄ Paco de Lucia, Pastora Pavon, Manitas de Plata

►► Ry Cooder, Al Di Meola

Craig Harris

Regis Gisavo

Girls of Angeli
/Angelin Tytöt
/Annel Nieddat

Modern joik
Formed 1982, in Angeli, Finland. Based in Angeli, Finland.

Ursula Länsman, vocals, drums; Tunni Länsman, vocals, drums; Ulla Pirttijärvi, drums, vocals (1982–1992). (All members are from Finland.)

The Girls of Angeli are Sami, formerly known as Laplanders or Lapps. The Sami are the indigenous people of northern Finland, Sweden, Norway, and Russia, a culture probably descended from the people who came into the area after the last ice age, about 5,000 years ago. Most Sami hunt and fish, raise reindeer, and migrate according to the seasons, although there are Fjeld Sami who farm (a fjeld is a round, treeless mountain that was left behind by the retreat of the ice-age glaciers), and Sea Sami who fish and farm. Sami have maintained settlements for centuries. The Sami have spiritual beliefs, but no word for "religion," which usually refers to the Christianity that was imposed on them. They believe in an alternate world,

saivo, where everything is better than in the material world and where the dead continue to live. In our own plane, it is believed, everything is alive and has a soul, so people are expected to treat all life and every object with respect. The Sami believe some people can see into the future and visit the saivo to bring back the wisdom of the other world. The Sami have a vocal music called *joiking* that isn't singing, speaking, or chanting, but has qualities of all three, depending on the joik. Joiking is a method of purifying the self and creating harmony between the world we can see and the saivo, and it sounds at times like the singing of the Northern Plains tribes of North America.

The Girls of Angeli take their name from their home region in northern Finland. In 1982, after their class sang at a Sami festival in Utsjoki, the Länsmans and Pirttijärvi got serious about singing and bringing their traditional music to a wider audience. The Girls of Angeli have created new forms, including the joik-song, but also perform traditional joiks *a cappella* or with simple drum accompaniment. In 1992, after the trio released *Dolla,* Pirttijärvi left to pursue a solo career. Ursula and Tunni Länsman continued as a duo combining traditional joiking with rock, rap, and techno beats, hoping to introduce the world to their unique and beautiful culture.

what to buy: *The New Voice of North* 𝄞𝄞𝄞𝄞 (Finlandia Finland, 1998, prod. Sari Kaasinen), a selection from the three albums they recorded under the name Annel Nieddat, gives an excellent overview of the group's career. There are a couple of tracks with modern-rock-type embellishments, including the obligatory "rap" interlude, but most of this is more traditional, concentrating on the group's beautiful harmonies, call-and-response vocals, and indigenous drumming. There's an occasional bit of ambient window dressing à la Deep Forest, but it doesn't distract from the chilling strangeness of the joiks.

what to buy next: On *Skeaikit* 𝄞𝄞𝄞𝄞 (Mipu Finland, 1995, prod. Kajasto) the Länsmans collaborate with guitarist Alfred Hakkinen and producer Kajasto for a collection that includes a bit of hip-hop, a blast of techno, some nice singer/songwriter–style acoustic guitar, and plenty of unearthly vocals by the principals.

the rest:
Dolla 𝄞𝄞𝄞𝄞 (Mipu Finland, 1992)
Giitu 𝄞𝄞𝄞𝄞 (Mipu Finland, 1993)

influences:
◀◀ Nils-Aslak Valkeapää
▶▶ Wimme

j. poet

Regis Gisavo

Malagasy traditional, jazz
Born in Tulear, Madagascar. Based in Paris, France.

Regis Gisavo learned to play the accordion as a child in Tulear, in the southwestern part of the island of Madagascar. Born into relative poverty among 12 siblings, Gisavo took to the instrument by the age of six and became so obsessed with it that his father destroyed his first one. Gisavo absorbed a variety of traditional and European styles through listening to other musicians and the radio. By his late teens he was touring in Madagascar and playing with established musicians like guitarist D'Gary. After winning a national music competition in 1990, Gisavo bought his own accordion and moved to Paris, where he began playing with jazz outfits like Bohe Combo. He pursued an impressively broad spectrum of musical opportunities, working with African ethno-punk bands like Les Têtes Brulées and eventually joining the wildly popular Corsican pop group O Muvrini. Although Gisavo was certainly enough of a musical virtuoso to blend into these cosmopolitan styles, he felt a certain lack of direction. A conversation with jazz accordionist Richard Galliano inspired Gisavo to revisit his Malagasy (the adjectival

polkas worldwide

The irresistible oompah beat of the dance music we have come to know as polka has proved a durable and hardy transplant to a variety of cultural landscapes, though it has found its most fertile soil in the United States. At first a pastime of Eastern European immigrants, polka grew to become one of the most popular music and dance styles in the American heartland. Through similar Eastern European migrations into Texas, it also became the backbone of *conjunto* music and several related Tex-Mex styles. Today polka is a diverse and rapidly evolving form, with such notable variants as the speedy Eastern style (144 beats per minute), and the slower Chicago style (only 120 beats per minute!) that originated with bandleader Walter "Lil' Wally" Jagiello. The unfortunately named "honky" style, which features concertina and horns, is an even slower variation on the Chicago mode. The Slovenian style—adopted by one of the music's biggest stars, the late Frankie Yankovic—built in twin accordions and saxophone. Another contemporary version, popularized by the Polka Family, is Massachusetts style, which incorporates Latin percussion touches and New Orleans–esque trumpet and clarinet ornamentations. Alternative polka comes from Denton, Texas's wild and wacky Brave Combo, who once recorded an album with Tiny Tim. The group blends rock and a galaxy of other styles in their unpredictable performances, but also plays straight polkas that would bring a tear to the eye of the most conservative purist. From its origin in Eastern Europe several centuries back, polka has gone on to become an enduring, worldwide phenomenon. The joyful strains of the music, the fast-paced, athletic steps, and the conviviality of the dances have captured the hearts (and feet) of an increasingly large and diverse audience.

see also: Edward "Eddie" Blazonczyk, Brave Combo, the Dynatones

Michael Parrish

form of "Madagascar") roots. Gisavo began recording and performing in a stripped-down setting with masterful percussionist David Mirandon. The duo's performances are a showcase for Gisavo's jaw-dropping accordion technique and his deep, emotive vocals, with a repertoire emphasizing traditional Malagasy tunes and Gisavo originals.

what's available: A splendid blend of traditional Malagasy soul and smooth European jazz-pop, *Mikea* ♫♫♫ (Shanachie, 1997) mostly features just Gisavo and percussionist David Mirandon. Gisavo's driving playing and deep, otherworldly vocals make for a haunting, unique musical experience.

influences:
◀◀ D'Gary, Rossy

Michael Parrish

Egberto Gismonti
Classical/tribal/bossa nova fusion
Born 1947, in Carmo, Brazil. Based in Brazil.

Egberto Gismonti is a classically trained pianist, having studied in France with Nadia Boulanger and Jean Baralaque. Moving to Rio de Janeiro in 1968 brought Gismonti into contact with Antonio Carlos Jobim and the guitar music of Baden Powell, which firmed up the young artist's resolve to make a living with his music. He taught himself how to play a standard six-string guitar but soon found it to be inadequate for his musical vision. Gismonti moved on to a seven-string instrument before discovering that an eight-string guitar (for which he had to devise a whole new way of playing) would enable him to cover the wide range of sounds he wanted to employ. His latest recordings find Gismonti using 10- and 12-string guitars with unique tunings. In 1977 Gismonti, while working on a film project in the Amazon basin, was exposed to the music of the Xingu tribes. This had a profound effect on his future work. The combination of a classical European background, tribal music, and the urban Brazilian sounds of samba and bossa nova have made him one of the most unique performers in the world. Gismonti has recorded more than 50 albums in a wide variety of instrumental settings. He is also a well-known producer in Brazil, in addition to writing music for film, television, theater, ballet, orchestra, and chamber ensembles.

what to buy: ECM's selection of tracks for *Works* ♫♫♫♫♪ (ECM, 1994, prod. Manfred Eicher) gives you an interesting sample of Gismonti's prolific, wide-ranging catalog. There are cuts featuring his superb piano playing in a group or solo setting, as well as performances with Gismonti on guitar, again in group or solo presentations. The musicians appearing on this disc include saxophonist Jan Garbarek, percussionist Nana Vasconcelos, bassist Charlie Haden, and Gismonti's long-time associate,

bassist Zeca Assumpção. *Sanfona* ♫♫♫♫ (ECM, 1981, prod. Manfred Eicher), a superb two-CD set, contains some of Gismonti's most beguiling and accessible music. The first disc features Gismonti and supporting trio Academia de Dança playing five longish tunes and one four-part suite. There is a lot of Gismonti's piano work, certainly more than one hears on his recent recordings. His keyboard style here hovers between Chick Corea and the sound clusters of Henry Cowell, with a little Villa-Lobos tossed in for good measure. The second CD focuses on Gismonti as a solo guitarist. With aural colors and lines weaving an impressive tapestry of sound, Gismonti's playing reveals some of his debt to Baden Powell's pioneering performances of the 1960s and early '70s, even as he breaks new ground with his specially built guitars.

what to buy next: *Dança Das Çabecas* ♫♫♫♫ (ECM, 1977, prod. Manfred Eicher) is the album that introduced Gismonti to U.S. audiences. Essentially a duet album with percussionist Nana Vasconcelos, *Dança Das Çabecas* was impressive for the sheer number of musical sounds the duo brought into play in what was essentially a Brazilian jazz album. With songs like "Quarto Mundo + 1" and the 12-minute "Tango," it was no wonder the record was nominated for album of the year by *Stereo Review*. Almost 10 years after their initial duet release, Gismonti and Vasconcelos recorded yet another fine album, *Duas Voces* ♫♫♫♫ (ECM, 1985, prod. Manfred Eicher). Gismonti's flute playing on "Tomarapeba" shows the influence of his studies of Amazon aboriginal music, an element not heard in the earlier recording.

what to avoid: Gismonti arranged some music by the Brazilian composer Heitor Villa-Lobos on *Trem Caipira* ♫ (EMI-Odeon, 1985, prod. Egberto Gismonti), but to little worthwhile effect. His piano playing on "Bachiana No. 5" is fine but the rest of the album could have been done by Isao Tomita or Wendy Carlos. The electronic trappings Gismonti drapes around this intriguing music give it the air of a kitschy soundtrack.

best of the rest:
Solo ♫♫♫♪ (ECM, 1979)
(With Charlie Haden and Jan Garbarek) *Folk Songs* ♫♫♫♪ (ECM, 1980)
(With Charlie Haden and Jan Garbarek) *Magico* ♫♫♫ (ECM, 1980)
Dança Dos Escravos ♫♫♫♪ (ECM, 1989)
Infancia ♫♫♫♪ (ECM, 1991)
Zig Zag ♫♫♫♪ (ECM, 1996)
Meeting Point ♫♫♫♪ (ECM, 1997)

influences:
◀◀ Baden Powell, Claude Debussy, João Gilberto, Antonio Carlos Jobim, Maurice Ravel, Heitor Villa-Lobos

see also: *Nana Vasconcelos*

Garaud MacTaggart

Gjallarhorn

Finnish-Swedish folk

Formed 1994, in Vaasa, Finland. Based in Vaasa, Finland.

Jenny Wilhelms, lead vocals, fiddles; Christopher Öhman, viola, fiddle, mandola, vocals; Jakob Frankenhauser, didgeridoo, percussion (1994–95); Tommi Mansikka-aho, didgeridoo, percussion (1995–present); David Lillkvist, percussion (1995–present). (All members are from Finland.)

Gjallarhorn hails from a Swedish-speaking region of western Finland, which means their main cultural heritage is Swedish. They sing in Swedish, and their overall sound is closer to that of edgy Swedish folk bands like Garmarna and Väsen (particularly because of the heavy beat supplied by two percussionists) than it is to Finnish groups like Värttinä. Most of Gjallarhorn's material is from traditional sources; in fact Wilhelms spends a lot of time researching old ballads at the Finlands Folkmusikinstitut in Vaasa. And like many ancient British Isles ballads, the Nordic songs performed by Gjallarhorn feature supernatural motifs like fairies, trolls, and witches. The name Gjallarhorn itself is taken from Nordic mythology—specifically, the horn belonging to the god Heimdal, through which messages were sent from the gods of Asgard to the human beings living on "Midgard."

what's available: *Ranarop—Call of the Sea Witch* ♫♫♫♫ (Finlandia, 1997, prod. Vincent Högberg, Gjallarhorn) is Gjallarhorn's only release so far. What's most striking about it is the incredibly powerful sound produced by a comparatively sparse lineup of voices, percussion, fiddles, mandola, and Australian didgeridoo. Most of the tracks on *Ranarop* have an incredible rhythmic drive provided by various kinds of hand percussion (no conventional drum kit is used), while voices and fiddles carry the melody lines. The effect of arrangements featuring full multipart vocal harmonies over percussion and didgeridoo, as on "Herr Olof," is remarkable—it's an unusual combination of softer and harsher sounds that grabs the listener right away. Wilhelms also serves as solo lead vocalist on most of the selections, and it's amazing to hear such a delicate soprano hold its own over the joyful apocalyptic din.

influences:

◀◀ Hedningarna, Steeleye Span

▶▶ Garmarna, Väsen

Ken Roseman

Paddy Glackin

Irish traditional

Born 1954, in Dublin, Ireland. Based in Dublin, Ireland.

With his strong County Donegal roots, it isn't a coincidence that Paddy Glackin is one of the finest practitioners of the northern style of fiddling, yet stylistically he goes beyond those roots to incorporate the influence of other great musicians he heard growing up in Dublin. Glackin's father was a fine fiddler himself, and because of that, Paddy's youth was filled with visits from some of Ireland's best musicians. One of them who had a profound effect on the boy's later career was renowned fiddler John Doherty, whom Paddy met when he was only 11—after which the fiddle seemed to dominate his life. As the popularity of traditional Irish music began to rise in the 1970s, so did Paddy's star within Irish-music circles. He was a member of the highly regarded Ceoltóirí Laighean and also became the first fiddler for the Bothy Band, arguably one of the most influential Irish outfits of the last 40 years. Even so, his time in the Bothy Band was short-lived, and he moved on to work on the esteemed Radio Telefís Éireann (RTÉ) radio program *The Long Note*. His work with RTÉ led him to be named Traditional Music Officer with the Dublin Arts Council, and he has continued, since leaving that position, to promote the music of his native Ireland through education and brilliant fiddle playing.

what to buy: The collaboration with piper Robbie Hannan *The Whirlwind* ♫♫♫♫ (Shanachie, 1995, prod. Paddy Glackin, Robbie Hannan), originally released in Ireland under the title *Séideán Sí*, is a brilliant recording of some of the finest uilleann pipe and fiddle duets ever documented. There is nothing to stand in the way of these two master musicians, playing without further accompaniment. Both give stellar performances as they take solo turns between fiery duets, giving each musician time to showcase his singular talents. Hannon's very tight, very syncopated playing is full of ornamentation and stylistically brilliant. The "Dispute at the Crossroads/Jolly Tinker" set will leave listeners in awe of the duo's virtuosity.

what to buy next: *In Full Spate* ♫♫♫♫ (Gael-Linn, 1991, prod. Dónal Lunny) owes a lot to Glackin's love of northern musicians like fiddler John Doherty, but also illustrates the host of influences Glackin received growing up in Dublin. The omnipresent Dónal Lunny accompanies Glackin on *bouzouki* and *bodhrán,* and he is joined on one track by his brothers Seumas and Kevin—two fine fiddlers in their own right—and on another by his frequent musical partner Hannan.

worth searching for: *Doublin* ♫♫♫♫ (TARA) is a masterful duo recording featuring another frequent Glackin partner (and former Bothy Band–mate), uilleann piper Paddy Keenan. Tunes like the "Dublin Reel/Women of the House" set are musically out of this world, while Keenan gets to show his full command of his instrument on the slow air "Rosin Dubh." A lovely recording if you can find it.

influences:

◀◀ John Doherty, John Joe Gardiner, Tom Glackin, Frank O'Higgins

▶▶ Liz Doherty, Kevin Glackin, Seumas Glackin

see also: *The Bothy Band, John Doherty, Robbie Hannan, James Keane, Dónal Lunny, Sean Ó Riada*

Cliff McGann

Gladiators
/Albert Griffiths

Reggae
Formed 1967, in Kingston, Jamaica. Based in Kingston, Jamaica.

Albert Griffiths, leader, lead vocals, guitar; David Webber, vocals (1960s); Errol Grandison, vocals (1960s); Clinton Fearon, vocals, bass (1970s–1980s); Gallimore Sutherland, vocals, guitar (1970s–1980s). (All members are from Jamaica.)

Albert Griffiths grew up singing and playing guitar, inspired by the records of Elvis and Chuck Berry as well as the talents of his uncle Aaron, who also played guitar and sang. Griffiths began his professional career as a backup vocalist for his friend David Webber. That combination didn't work, but a few years later Griffiths formed a harmony trio with Webber and Errol Grandison, and the Gladiators were born. Griffiths, Webber, and Grandison were working as stonemasons at the time, and they borrowed money from their boss to finance their first recording, "You Are the Girl." They were able to lease the track to WIRL Records, and the company put it out as the B-side of "Train to Skaville" by the Ethiopians. The Ethiopians' track became a smash and brought the Gladiators to the attention of Treasure Isle, but their songs for that label were only modestly successful.

In 1968 the band began recording for Coxsone Dodd's Studio One and cut "Hello Carol," the hit which established the Gladiators as a major act and Griffiths as a powerful new songwriter. In between recording his own tunes with his trio, Griffiths became a guitarist in the Studio One band, appearing on recordings by the Manchesters, Stranger Cole, and Burning Spear. In the early 1970s, Griffiths began exploring other options, cutting singles for Clive Chin and Lee Perry as well as Dodd. "Bongo Red," a smash hit from 1975, brought the Gladiators to the attention of Virgin Records, which was hoping to cash in on Island's success with Bob Marley. An alliance with that label yielded *Trenchtown Mix Up,* a roots reggae classic standing up to the best work of Marley, Culture, and other roots radicals. But in 1980, at the insistence of the label, the band recorded *The Gladiators,* a crossover attempt produced by Eddy Grant that fell flat. The next year Marley died, and without his charisma, the major labels decided that reggae's commercial viability was past. In the aftermath, the Gladiators and dozens of other artists lost their label deals. Undaunted, the band kept touring and releasing singles and albums for the Jamaican market. In the mid-1980s the Gladiators signed with Rounder's reggae subsidiary Heartbeat, and these musicians continue to make compelling music in a roots reggae stylee.

what to buy: The excellent compilation *Dreadlocks the Time Is Now* ♫♫♫ (Virgin Frontline, 1990, prod. Tony Robinson, Gladiators) makes the band's best work for Virgin in the 1970s available on CD for the first time. It includes nine tracks from their classic *Trenchtown Mix Up* set, as well as strong material from *Proverbial Reggae, Naturally, Sweet So Till,* and the "Pocket Money" single. Griffiths's soaring tenor and the band's tough riddims give these tracks a timeless quality.

what to buy next: While Griffiths never matched the militant fire of his early output, his more recent efforts are still filled with worthwhile music. *A Whole Heap* ♫♫♫ (Heartbeat, 1989, prod. Tony Robinson, Gladiators) includes all the tracks from *Country Living* and *In Store for You* and gives you a solid indication of where the band was at in the late 1980s.

best of the rest:
On the Right Track ♫♫♫ (Heartbeat, 1989)
Bongo Red ♫♫♫ (Heartbeat, 1998)

worth searching for: Most of *Trenchtown Mix Up* is preserved on *Dreadlocks the Time Is Now,* but the band's second Virgin outing, *Proverbial Reggae* ♫♫♫♫ (Virgin Frontline, 1978), is just as strong and has yet to get the digital treatment.

influences:
◄◄ Burning Spear, Culture, Bob Marley, Mighty Diamonds

►► Abyssinians, Black Uhuru, Wailing Souls

j. poet

Ben Goldberg

Progressive jazz and klezmer
Born August 8, 1959, in Sycamore, IL. Based in California, USA.

Recipient of numerous National Endowment for the Arts (NEA) grants and a 1993 Goldie Award (the *San Francisco Bay Guardian*'s annual creative-music honor), clarinetist Ben Goldberg is one of the leaders of the jazz/improv community in the Bay Area. He has led a variety of combos, including New Klezmer Trio, Junk Genius, Snorkel, and Brainchild (an undocumented but phenomenal large ensemble based on Goldberg's "spontaneous composition" concept of minimally directed, collective improvisation). His efforts have attracted NYC heavyweights like John Zorn and Marty Ehrlich. Tours abroad and appearances on the festival circuit, with a couple of showcases at the distinguished Vancouver Jazz Fest, have begun to spark an international buzz. While Don Byron is popularly credited as the most adept and adventurous clarinetist in contemporary jazz, a simple comparison of discographies casts Goldberg in a far more progressive light. With New Klezmer Trio, Goldberg was exploring "Radical Jewish Culture" long before Zorn coined the term for his Tzadik imprint (and Byron delved into the *Music of Mickey Katz*). His Junk Genius quartet reworks bebop classics with an up-to-the-minute approach that pushes toward the future. And a handful of new recordings in trio, quartet, and sextet configurations reveals an innovative composer/bandleader at the vanguard of creative improvised music. Jumping off from a deceptively simple notion — "Don't improvise, just play the song . . . do what needs to be done" — the clarinetist cuts to the core of what great jazz is all about.

what to buy: *Masks & Faces* ♫♫♫♫ (Nine Winds, 1991/Tzadik, 1996, prod. Ben Goldberg), the debut recording of New Klezmer Trio (with drummer Kenny Wollesen and bassist Dan Seamans) introduced the creative merger of traditional klezmer and forward-pushing jazz. Pre-Masada, pre-Byron-does-Katz, it marks a pivotal moment in the evolution of the art form. From the leader's "Statement of Themes on Contra-alto Clarinet," the sextet on *Twelve Minor* ♫♫♫♫ (Avant, 1997, prod. Ben Goldberg) dives into more than an hour's worth of frighteningly incisive extrapolation. Rob Sudduth is a melodic monster on tenor, and Miya Masaoka and Carla Kihlstedt have to be heard to be believed. On-edge arrangements explode the bebop handbook while respecting the essence of the songs of *Junk Genius* ♫♫♫♫ (Knitting Factory Works, 1996, prod. Ben Goldberg). An almost post-punk energy pumps locomotive tracks like "Tempus Fugit," "Koko," "Shaw Nuff," and the definitive "Bebop." To be sure, this ain't no Wynton Marsalis rehash. *Here by Now* ♫♫♫♫ (Music and Arts, 1997, prod. Ben Goldberg) is a vivid look at how Goldberg's tune-based aesthetic soars in the company of like-minded collaborators. Simple melodies are transformed with ingenuity and intensity without a superfluous note in the lot.

what to buy next: New Klezmer Trio's *Melt Zonk Rewire* ♫♫♫♫ (Tzadik, 1995, prod. Ben Goldberg) expands the equation introduced on *Masks & Faces*. The mondo-"grunge" of Seamans's bass on "Feedback Doina" and Goldberg's clarinet blasted through a Fender amp on "Gas Nine" give klezmer's serpentine melodicism a welcome shock of hard-rock electricity. *Light at the Crossroads* ♫♫♫♫ (Songlines, 1997, prod. Marty Ehrlich, Ben Goldberg) is worth checking out if only for the tone of the woodwinds. Powerful improvising from all members of the quartet. Compositions are split between Ehrlich and Goldberg, with a nod to Wayne Horvitz on "Ask Me Later."

best of the rest:
What Comes Before ♫♫♫ (Tzadik, 1997)

worth searching for: With a deliriously punchy "Salt Peanuts" anticipating Junk Genius, Goldberg and Kenny Wollesen's *The Relative Value of Things* ♫♫♫♫ (33 1/4, 1992, prod. Ben Goldberg), a series of inspired duets self-released on Goldberg's literally in-house "label," offers a nascent glimpse of the Goldberg-Wollesen inventions to come.

influences:
◀◀ Ornette Coleman, Steve Lacy, Thelonious Monk, Charlie Parker

▶▶ John Zorn's Masada

see also: *Klezmorim, Masada*

Sam Prestianni

Gonzaguinha

Brazilian pop, samba
Born Luiz Gonzaga Jr., in Rio de Janeiro, Brazil. Died 1991, in Parana, Brazil.

In Brazilian pop, Luiz Gonzaga Jr., a.k.a Gonzaguinha, occupied a place that could be compared to that of Ziggy Marley in reggae. Gonzaguinha's father, the late Luiz Gonzaga Sr., is considered the godfather of *forró* music (the accordion-led dance style from northeastern Brazil), and commanded the type of reverence in Brazil that Bob Marley enjoyed in Jamaica — and just like Ziggy Marley, Gonzaguinha was destined to be compared to his seminal father when he chose to follow in his footsteps. But Gonzaguinha, who himself died in a car crash in the Brazilian state of Parana on April 9, 1991, was very much his own man, and his melodic, jazzy style of Brazilian pop was as recognizable as his father's forró. Born in Rio de Janeiro, Gonzaguinha grew up in one of the city's poor *favelas* or shantytowns. The singer/guitarist/composer knew just how rough the lives of Brazil's poor could be, and his more sociopolitical lyrics often focused on their struggles with great insight and sensitivity. But Gonzaguinha wasn't strictly a political artist — he wrote and sang about love and sexuality as passionately as he did about the issues. He was incredibly popular in Brazil in the 1980s, and his songs were covered by major Brazilian vocalists such as Gal Costa, Fagner, and Maria Bethânia. Gonzaguinha recorded extensively in Brazil, but unfortunately only a few of his albums have been released in the United States. Those albums include 1990's *E* on World Pacific and *Mestres Da MPB*, which WEA Latina released Stateside in 1996.

what's available: *E* ♫♫♫♫ (World Pacific, 1990, prod. Gonzaguinha), Gonzaguinha's U.S. debut, left the whole North American continent hungry for more. Gonzaguinha sings in Portuguese, but World Pacific provides English translations that show us just how sensitive and poetic a lyricist he can be. Some of the songs are quite issue-oriented (especially "Magica" and "Coracones Marginais"), and Gonzaguinha's reflections on the struggles of Brazil's underclass are quite poignant. But he is equally compelling when he sings about romance and sexuality on "Rai," "Tudo," and "Qualquer Situacao de Amor."

Of course, one doesn't need any liner notes to appreciate the richness of his singing—Gonzaguinha's charisma is hard to miss even if you don't understand a word of Portuguese.

influences:

⏪ Gilberto Gil, Luis Gonzaga, Caetano Veloso

Alex Henderson

Celina Gonzaléz

Afro-Cuban, salsa

Born 1928, in Jovellanos, Cuba. Based in Havana, Cuba.

Celina Gonzaléz grew up in a rural area of Cuba where traditions and musical rhythms brought to the island by African slaves remained strong. The young musician took in both of the island's major influences, blending Afro-Cuban musical patterns and Spanish lyrical forms in her work. With her husband, Reutillio Domiguez, she played *musica campesina,* a Cuban rural or country music–style salsa. Before the Cuban revolution, the duo developed a large following based on their strong vocal harmonies and basic guitar-and-percussion instrumentation. Their subjects were strongly populist (interspersed with music derived from Gonzaléz's devotion to the *Santería* faith). This caused them political problems at the time, but did not stop the couple from performing with a wide range of musicians and becoming known throughout the island and, eventually, in the rest of the Caribbean, New York, and South America. Gonzaléz was and remains a strong supporter of the ideals of the revolution, despite isolation from off-island performing opportunities imposed by Castro's government until recent years. Realignment of her career after her husband's death in 1971 saw Gonzaléz performing more often among larger ensembles, including trumpets and violins (particularly with her son's band, Campo Alegre). Although she maintains her Afro-Cuban and Santería base of ideas, Gonzaléz has evolved her sound to serve her cause of presenting the music in frameworks attractive to contemporary listeners.

what's available: The compilation *Que Viva Chango* 𝄞𝄞𝄞𝄞 (Qbadisc, 1993) offers many examples of why Gonzalez's voice and style have made her an influential international musician. *Santa Barbara* 𝄞𝄞𝄞𝄞 (Fonocaribe, 1996) is a reissue of an earlier recording. The title track is one of the earliest pieces Gonzaléz wrote (which became a salsa hit for Celia Cruz), celebrating the Christian saint who is also venerated by those who follow Santería.

influences:

⏪ Afro-Cuban slave chants and songs

⏩ Campo Alegre, Celia Cruz, Reutillio Domiguez Jr., Gloria Estefan

Kerry Dexter

Rubén González

Son

Born 1920, in Havana, Cuba. Based in Havana, Cuba.

After a decades-long embargo on all things Cuban, America is opening its ears once again to the *rumba,* the *son,* and best of all, the talent of Havana's old guard. These musicians have decades of experience and instrumental virtuosity that has only recently been set to record. First among Havana's freshly discovered treasures is the agile piano playing of Rubén González . How many musicians make it big at age 78? Rubén González is one, and he owes this not simply to his immense talent, but also to recognition by Ry Cooder and to the current resurgence of classic Cuban *son*. In fact, compared to his guitarist, Compay Segundo, González is a spring chicken—Segundo is enjoying his revival at 90. González 's career began in 1943 when he recorded with Cuban legend Arsenio Rodriguez; he later played for over 25 years with Enrique Jorrin. Arthritis put his career on hold at the end of the 1970s until the landmark Afro-Cuban All Stars project in 1996 introduced a new generation to the island's musical riches, at the hands of many of its greatest living practitioners. Gourmet stylistic omnivore Ry Cooder was so impressed that he called on González for the *Buena Vista Social Club* album the following year, and Cooder singled González out for a solo recording soon afterwards. Astounded at the results, Cooder described González as the greatest piano soloist he had ever seen. "I felt I had trained all my life for this experience," he remarked at the time. "The best record I have ever been involved in."

what to buy: The 78-year-old's solo debut *Introducing Rubén González* 𝄞𝄞𝄞𝄞 (World Circuit, 1997, prod. Nick Gold) features marvelous piano improvisation with tumbling scales on a par with Thelonious Monk, covering Cuban dance styles from *son* to rumba.

what to buy next: The best-selling brainchild of Cuba-phile Ry Cooder, *Buena Vista Social Club* 𝄞𝄞𝄞𝄞 (World Circuit, 1997, prod. Ry Cooder, Nick Gold) features all the septuagenarian greats of Havana kicking up danceable rhythms. The first such project was *The Afro-Cuban All Stars: A Toda Cuba Le Gusta* 𝄞𝄞𝄞𝄞 (World Circuit, 1997, prod. Nick Gold, Juan de Marcos González), a scintillating recording of *guarachas, sons,* and *guajiras.* "La piano con Rubén González!" intones vocalist Manuel Licia as González sashays into his distinctive solo keywork.

influences:

⏪ Enrique Jorrin, Arsenio Rodriguez

⏩ Ry Cooder, generations of Cuban musicians

see also: *Ry Cooder, Arsenio Rodriguez*

David Poole

Jerry Gonzalez
& the Fort Apache Band

Afro-Cuban, Afro-Caribbean, jazz
Formed 1980, in New York, NY, USA. Based in USA.

Jerry Gonzalez (born January 5, 1949), trumpet, flugelhorn, percussion; Andy Gonzalez, bass; John Stubblefield, tenor saxophone; Joe Ford, alto/soprano saxophones; Larry Willis, piano; Steve Berrios, percussion; Carter Jefferson, saxophone.

Trumpeter/percussionist Jerry Gonzalez leads one of today's most popular Afro-Cuban jazz outfits, the six-member Fort Apache Band. The multitalented Gonzalez and his brother, bassist Andy, grew up in the Bronx surrounded by eclectic musical influences. Jerry drew his earliest inspiration as a percussionist from Mongo Santamaria, and he began playing conga drums in contests in the parks and around the projects where he lived. Attending NYC's High School of Music and Art, Jerry met pianist Llewelyn Matthews and they both earned scholarships to New York City College of Music, where they met Kenny Dorham and formed a Latin jazz quintet. In addition to other gigs, Jerry played trumpet in Ray Barretto's band, and he occasionally subbed for the leader on congas. In 1970 he joined Dizzy Gillespie, playing congas and recording on the trumpeter's album *Portrait of Jenny*. Next, Jerry joined Eddie Palmieri's band for four years, applying his knowledge of Cuban music and developing a seasoned and unique conga style. The Gonzalez brothers joined with Manny Oquendo to co-found Conjunto Libre and the all-star Grupo Folklorico y Experimental Nuyorquino. Jerry continued to organize his own Latin jazz units with his brother and other top players, and with the musicians who would solidify into Fort Apache, he made his recording debut as a leader in 1980 with *Ya Yo Me Cure*.

While both brothers continued to work as sidemen with various sympathetic jazz players (such as Steve Turre), their 30 years of experience is best brought to fruition within the tight-yet-flexible Fort Apache Band. As one of the best-sounding ensembles arising from New York's Latin scene, the Fort Apache Band generates seamless, spontaneous shifts between scintillating Afro-Cuban rhythms and straight-ahead, bebop-influenced jazz. Starting out as a flexible entity of 10–15 pieces in the early 1980s, by the end of the decade the group had trimmed down to a quintet featuring the Gonzalez brothers with Steve Berrios (drums), Larry Willis (piano), and Carter Jefferson (saxophone). Their first two albums were recorded live at European jazz festivals. They gained wider notice in the United States after their 1989 recording *Rumba Para Monk* was cited as Jazz Record of the Year by the French Academie du Jazz. That recording consolidated their musical concept and led to a citation in the 55th Annual *Down Beat* magazine readers' poll as the top band in

the "World Beat" category. In 1991 saxophonist Joe Ford joined the group; following Carter Jefferson's death in 1993, tenor saxman John Stubblefield, who'd previously guested, became a regular member. Gonzalez and his band, often augmented by guest soloists, have continued to build on their successes, releasing a stream of albums for Sunnyside, Milestone, and Enja. Originally launched with more salsa players, Fort Apache now contains musicians equally well versed in jazz, resulting in a nicely balanced sound that smoothly straddles the fence between the two musical genres and contributes to the band's uniqueness.

what to buy: To establish a reference point for Gonzalez's development, check out his debut recording, *Ya Yo Me Cure* ♪♪♪♪ (American Clavé, 1979/Sunnyside, 1996, prod. Jerry Gonzalez, Kip Hanrahan). Although this recording doesn't feature the band that became known as Fort Apache, Gonzalez plays trumpet, flugelhorn, and percussion instruments with an array of Latin-jazz all-stars, including brother Andy on bass, pianist Hilton Ruiz, trombonist Steve Turré, and tenor saxophonist Mario Rivera. Containing a mix of seven lively tunes by Frankie Rodriguez (who also sings lead vocals and plays percussion), Duke Ellington, Thelonious Monk, and others, this varied session is not quite as refined, densely textured, and tight-sounding as forthcoming Fort Apache dates. Still, it's an engaging Latinate listen that gives you a sense of where the leader is headed. This album was originally released on vinyl (AMCL 1001) and later as a CD on Sting's short-lived Pangea label. Recorded live in Berlin in 1982, *The River Is Deep* ♪♪♪♪ (Enja, 1982/1996) features Jerry Gonzalez & the Fort Apache Band as a 12-member unit that artfully connects musical influences from Africa, the Caribbean, South America, and North America. Heavily laden with percussion (from Steve Berrios, Gene Golden, Hector "Flaco" Hernandez, and Nicky Marrero), the seven tracks include a rousing version of the title tune — translated back into Spanish, that is — "Rio Esta Hondo," a rumba in the mid-paced, African-rooted *guaguanco* drum form, featuring vocals by Frankie Rodrigues. Pulsating hand drums predominate throughout the album, and splendid Latin-jazz tunes are earmarked by blazing horn-section playing, intelligent improvisation, and skillful solos from everyone. Making their Milestone debut on *Crossroads* ♪♪♪♪ (Milestone, 1994, prod. Todd Barkan), Gonzalez and Fort Apache perform mostly original music from band members on their boldest album to date. This well-produced 12-tune session best merges jazz with Afro-Cuban rhythms and features cutting-edge solos from all members. Tenor saxman Stubblefield, a former Fort Apache guest, returns to assume full-time duties.

what to buy next: Recorded live at the 1988 International Jazz Festival in Zurich, *Obatalà* ♪♪♪♪ (Enja, 1989, prod. Matthias

Winckelmann) impresses the listener with how much Gonzalez is influenced by Dizzy Gillespie's small-ensemble Afro-Cuban jazz explorations. The balance leans more to the jazz side, but also prominently features a tantalizing percussion team (Berrios, Hernandez, Marrero, and Milton Cardona) backing the horns on exhilarating versions of Wayne Shorter's "Nefertiti," the Monk tunes "Evidence" and "Jackie-ing," and Cardona's title tune, plus four more numbers. If you like your Thelonious Monk with a Latin twist, you'll want to add *Rumba Para Monk* ♪♪♪♪ (Sunnyside, 1989/1995, prod. Jerry Gonzalez) to your CD collection. This cool-toned, tasteful Latin-jazz tribute to Monk finds Gonzalez's band pared down to the five members who would become the first Fort Apache—the Gonzalez brothers, percussionist Steve Berrios, tenor saxophonist Carter Jefferson, and pianist Larry Willis. Masterfully innovative yet faithful to Monk's pensive side (especially on the 10-minute version of "Misterioso"), this is the splendid eight-tune session that won the French equivalent of a Grammy. Jerry's horn playing had been seasoned to a new level by the time of this recording, and he delivers an especially tender improvised flugelhorn solo on the ballad "Ugly Beauty," accompanied only by Willis. *Moliendo Café* ♪♪♪♪ (Sunnyside, 1992, prod. Todd Barkan, Satoshi Harano) finds the group having achieved a well-balanced, cohesive Latin-jazz sound and bridging the divide between hard-bop and Latin grooves with great success on traditional songs such as "Obsession" and the title track, as well as on popular standards such as "Stardust" and "Summertime."

the rest:
Pensativo ♪♪♪♪ (Milestone, 1995)
Earth Dance ♪♪♪♪ (Sunnyside, 1996)
Fire Dance ♪♪♪♪♪ (Milestone, 1996)

influences:

◀◀ Mario Bauzà, John Coltrane, Miles Davis, Paquito D'Rivera, Dizzy Gillespie, Machito, Eddie Palmieri, Charlie Parker, Wayne Shorter

see also: *Ray Barretto, Milton Cardona, Charlie Palmieri, Eddie Palmieri*

Nancy Ann Lee

Steve Gorn

North Indian classical bansuri bamboo flute music, international ethno-jazz winds
Born May 23, 1944, in New York, NY, USA. Based in Kingston, NY, USA.

Steve Gorn is a New Yorker who has played bamboo flutes, clarinet, and soprano saxophone on five continents. Long recognized for his artistry on the Indian *bansuri* bamboo flute, his acceptance as a performer in India is rare for an American. But Gorn has transcended the ethnicity of his birth and has expressively embraced the ancient traditions of North Indian classical music. He is a disciple of the late Sri Gour Goswami. In addition to popularizing Indian music in the United States, Gorn has worked as a featured soloist with the New York City Ballet in Paris; with legendary jazz drummer Jack DeJohnette in Senegal; and as an arts coordinator in Bali. He has performed at an Indian music festival in Calcutta; at Mayan ruins in Mexico; and at a Maori long house in New Zealand. It's easy to see why David Amram calls him a "true world musician." Gorn mixes the vocabulary of Indian music with jazz and improvisation, creating a new globe-spanning aesthetic. He works with small ensembles and a variety of collaborators, including Tony Levin, Nana Vasconcelos, Peter Kater, and Glen Velez. Gorn has performed at such diverse venues as Lincoln Center, the Metropolitan Museum of Art, Ali Akbar College of Music, Naropa Institute, and a cave in upstate New York! He also composes for dance, theater, storytelling, performance art, television, and film. His scores are written for live instruments yet also explore "ethno-tech," the interface of world music with MIDI electronics.

what to buy: Steve Gorn has four primarily solo albums that feature North Indian classical music. He could charm humans or snakes with his unaccompanied *Luminous Ragas* ♪♪♪♪ (Interworld, 1994). The music—like its title—is translucent. It's also perfect for yoga or meditation. Gorn's newest release, *Parampara!* ♪♪♪♪ (Haus der Kulturen der Velt/Wergo & Harmonia Mundi [distributors], 1998, prod. Peter Pannke) is accompanied by *tabla* drum virtuoso Samir Chatterjee. This album is a bit stiff and could use a better-balanced mix, but has excellent liners and musical notation of the scales.

what to buy next: A compilation on which Gorn is included, *World Flutes 1* ♪♪♪♪ (EarthSea Records, 1997, prod. Peter Kater), is a treat for flute lovers. In addition to Gorn's bansuri solo accompanied by a Kurzweil K-2000, the cuts featuring Kazu Matsui on the Japanese *shakuhachi*, Joannie Madden on tin whistle, and R. Carlos Nakai on Native American flute are especially beautiful and contemplative. Gorn's other early Indian music albums include *The Indian Bamboo Flute: Two Masters in Tradition* ♪♪♪ (Lyrichord, 1992, prod. Steve Gorn) and *The Bansuri Bamboo Flute* ♪♪♪ (Music of the World/Latitudes, 1983/1997, prod. Bob Haddad).

what to avoid: The eclectic various-artists compilation *Live at the Knitting Factory 2* ♪ (A&M, 1989, prod. Robert Appel) doesn't flow and is poorly recorded, with the flute sounding unnecessarily breathy.

the rest:
(With Badal Roy) *Yantra* ♪♪♪ (Music of the World, 1987/1997)
(With Glen Velez) *Doctrine of Signatures* ♪♪♪♪ (CMP, 1991)
(With Nana Simopoulos) *Gai's Dream* ♪♪♪ (B&W, 1992)
(With Jai Uttal) *Monkey* ♪♪♪♪ (Triloka, 1992)

(With Layne Redmond) *Since the Beginning* ♪♪♪ (Interworld, 1992)

(With storyteller Laura Simms) *Making Peace—Heart Rising* ♪♪♪♪ (Earwig, 1993)

(With Nana Vasconcelos, Badal Roy, and Mike Richmond) *Asian Journal* ♪♪♪♪ (M.O.W., 1994)

(With Jai Uttal) *Beggars and Saints* ♪♪♪♪ (Triloka/Worldly, 1994)

(With Priscilla Herdman) *Forever and Always* ♪♪♪ (Flying Fish, 1994)

(With Natraj) *Meet Me Anywhere* ♪♪♪♪ (Dorian, 1994)

(With I Giullari di Piazza) *Earth, Sun, and Moon* ♪♪♪ (Lyrichord, 1995)

(With Najma) *Forbidden Kiss* ♪♪ (Shanachie, 1996)

(With Noirin Ní Riain) *Celtic Soul* ♪♪♪♪ (Living Music/Earth Music Productions, 1996)

(With Jack DeJohnette) *Dancing with Nature Spirits* ♪♪♪♪ (ECM, 1996)

(With Randy Crafton) *Duologue* ♪♪♪ (Lyrichord, 1996)

(With Akira Sataki) *Cooler Heads Prevail* ♪♪♪ (Alula, 1997)

(With Tony Levin) *From the Caves of the Iron Mountain* ♪♪♪ (Papa Bear, 1997)

(With Badal Roy) *One in the Pocket* ♪♪♪♪ (Music of the World, 1997)

(With Jai Uttal) *Shiva Station* ♪♪♪♪ (Triloka, 1997)

(With Ray Spiegel) *Sum and Kali* ♪♪♪ (Simla, 1997)

(With Warren Senders) *Wings & Shadows* ♪♪♪♪ (Bamboo Ras Productions, 1997)

(With Deepak Chopra) *A Gift of Love* ♪ (Tommy Boy/RaSa, 1998)

worth searching for: Gorn's flute soars with lilting melodies above frame drum master Glen Velez on both *Seven Heaven* ♪♪♪♪ (CMP, 1987, prod. Kurt Renker, Walter Quintus) and *Assyrian Rose* ♪♪♪♪ (CMP, 1989, prod. Kurt Renker, Walter Quintus). It's not easy to find these early recordings on the now-defunct CMP label, but they are worth searching for to hear the inventive collaborations of Gorn and Velez on their original repertoire. Mail order is possible from Framedrum Music in New York at (800) 595-7415.

influences:

◀◀ John Coltrane, Pannalal Ghosh, Charles Lloyd

see also: *Badal Roy, Jai Uttal, Nana Vasconcelos, Glen Velez*

Iris Brooks

Eddy Grant

Worldbeat

Born 1948 in Guyana. Based in St. Philip, Barbados.

Eddy Grant, a Caribbean one-man band and record company head, has sold 20 million albums worldwide, had 21 hit singles (mostly in England and Europe), and produced and recorded more than 20 solo releases. Since the mid-1980s, when his interest in *soca* (modern-day calypso) led him to acquire the back catalogs of artists like Sparrow, Kitchener, and Melody and start getting involved in the yearly fray for Carnival King, he's also produced and co-written albums for Calypso Rose, Stalin, Sparrow, and Gabby.

Grant was born in Guyana, but he moved with his family to northern London when he was still a child. He formed his first band, the Equals, in the late 1960s. The Equals may have been the first integrated pop group in British history. They recorded a string of albums and singles and finally hit with "Baby Come Back," a smooth ska/rock hybrid that showed the direction Grant would follow for the rest of his career. The stress of "the Biz," however, led to a heart attack, despite Grant's alcohol-free vegetarian lifestyle. He retired from the Equals and built a house and recording studio, and after years of experimentation, Grant emerged with his first solo album, *Message Man*, which he released on his own label, Ice. His second effort, *Walking on Sunshine*, was picked up by Columbia U.K. for distribution, and its success put Grant and Ice on the map. His mixture of rock, reggae, and dance music made him an early worldbeat star, and he may have inspired the Police's tinkering with pop-reggae (it definitely influenced the earlier, more scholarly dabblings of the Clash, who recorded Grant's "Police on My Back" to no small notice). Grant moved to Barbados in 1981, where he built Blue Wave Studios and began another period of musical experimentation. Columbia finally provided American distribution for *Killer on the Rampage,* and its first single, "Electric Avenue," pushed the album to gold status. Grant's next, *Going for Broke,* included "Romancing the Stone," the theme from the hit Michael Douglas/Kathleen Turner/Danny DeVito movie, but it failed to match the sales of *Killer.* Columbia stopped distributing Grant, but he struck a deal with the indie label Enigma, which distributed two of his most musically adventurous albums to date, *Barefoot Soldier* and *Paintings of the Soul.*

As Grant's interest in soca intensified, he put his own career on the back burner. He opened an office in New Jersey and was about to embark on a campaign to reissue and market his back catalog, as well as the work of legends like Sparrow, Roaring Lion, and Kitchener, to world-music fans in the States. But just then he was blindsided by his former business manager, who attempted to wrest control of Ice Records and Ice Publishing away from Grant. After a nasty legal battle, the courts found in Grant's favor, but Ice hasn't yet recovered.

what to buy: *Barefoot Soldier* ♪♪♪♪ (Ice, 1990, prod. Eddy Grant) is one of Grant's strongest latter-day albums. There's a bit of soca in the mix now, which keeps Grant's pleasing blend of reggae, rock, and dance music sounding fresh. He's also more overtly political, and tunes like the anti-apartheid "Gimme Hope Jo'anna" and "Youth Tom Tom" show that he hasn't lost his touch for catchy, commercial melodies.

what to buy next: The record that introduced Grant to the rest of the world, *Killer on the Rampage* ♪♪♪♪ (Epic, 1982, prod. Eddy Grant), still sounds tough, and in light of today's world-music boom, it's easy to see this as a harbinger of the intercultural music-making to follow.

best of the rest:
Walking on Sunshine ♫♫♫ (Epic, 1979)
Going for Broke ♫♫♫ (Epic, 1984)
Living on the Frontline ♫♫♫ (Epic, 1984)
File under Rock ♫♫♫ (Ice, 1988)
Paintings of the Soul ♫♫♫ (Ice, 1992)

influences:
◀◀ Bob Marley, the Rolling Stones, Sparrow
▶▶ Clash, Angélique Kidjo, Looters, the Police, UB40

j. poet

Grayhorse Singers

Powwow drum
Formed c. 1968, in the Kiowa Nation, OK, USA. Based in Oklahoma, USA.

Jack Anquoe, vocals, drums; Redcloud Anquoe, vocals, drums; Jim Anquoe, vocals, drums; Rick Anquoe, vocals, drums; Warren Anquoe, vocals, drums; Jimmy Anquoe, vocals, drums; Louis Sheridan, vocals, drums; Jason Good Blanket, vocals, drums; Jimmy Reeder, vocals, drums; La Verne Little Calf, vocals, drums. (All members are from USA.)

Jack Anquoe is considered one of the finest traditional singers and drummers on the powwow circuit. The Grayhorse Singers perform in the Southern Style, with deep, almost guttural vocals from the singers and a forceful drum attack. They are one of the most successful drum ensembles in their field.

what to buy: *Shake It Up* ♫♫♫♫ (SOAR, 1993, prod. Tom Bee) is native "shake" music, as played during powwows. The drums accompany dancers, who get points every time their left feet hit the ground on the down beat, and part of the competition is the friendly rivalry between the dancers and drummers. Drums often shift tempo or add a beat, trying to literally trip up the dancers. The varied tempos and powerful singing make this album a bit more accessible to non-Indian ears.

the rest:
Gourd Talkers ♫♫♫♫ (SOAR, 1991)
Spirits Who Dance ♫♫♫♫ (SOAR, 1996)

influences:
◀◀ Haumpy and Gertie, O-ho-mah Lodge Singers

j. poet

Great Big Sea

Celtic pop
Formed 1991, in St. John's, Newfoundland, Canada. Based in St. John's, Newfoundland, Canada.

Alan Doyle, guitar, vocals, keyboard; Séan McCann, bodhrán, tin whistle, guitar, vocals; Darrell Power, bass, acoustic guitar, vocals; **Bob Hallett, fiddle, accordion, mandolin, concertina, bouzouki, vocals. (All members are from Canada.)**

Great Big Sea is the bastard child of Newfoundland folk music and modern pop radio. The group started with the sole purpose of taking the great old folk songs from the Newfoundland outports and melding them with the influences the band members grew up with watching cable television and listening to FM radio. Few bands boast a repertoire ranging from hundred-year-old folk songs to covers of Slade and R.E.M. Diverse though the sources may be, the band blends them into a pop-inflected folk music both infectious and substantial. On the heels of its highly successful indie debut in 1992, the band was signed to Warner Music Canada, leading to the inaugural major-label effort *Up* in 1995. *Up* was an instant best-seller in Canada, as was the 1996 follow-up, *Play*. Great Big Sea's success in Canada drew the attention of Sire records in the United States, which released what in essence is a greatest-hits collection of the band's two previous Canadian discs. The group's original compositions are less interesting than the traditional material at which it excels, but band members have shown steady growth as songwriters over the course of their recordings. Great Big Sea is really in its element in a live setting, and the group brings its Newfoundland kitchen party to more than 200 venues a year.

what to buy: *Rant and Roar* ♫♫♫♫ (Sire, 1998, prod. Danny Greenspoon) is Great Big Sea's U.S. debut and features tracks culled from two previous Canadian releases. It is a lively collection of traditional Newfoundland-inspired folk music with a pop sensibility. The Scottish traditional song "Mari-Mac" is given a frantic, almost punk treatment, while the cover of R.E.M.'s "It's the End of the World As We Know It" is fraught with a modern Celtic feel thanks to some sprightly mandolin.

what to buy next: *Great Big Sea* ♫♫♫♫ (NRA Productions, 1992, prod. Pat Janes) is the independent debut that made Warner Music take notice and sign the group to a multi-album deal. *Up* ♫♫♫♫ (Warner Music, 1995, prod. Danny Greenspoon) and *Play* ♫♫♫♫ (Warner Music, 1996, prod. Danny Greenspoon) are both easily available in the United States as imports, but due to the proportion of each culled on *Rant and Roar,* only diehard fans will want to seek them out.

worth searching for: Prior to joining forces in Great Big Sea, three of the members were in the group Rankin Street. That band recorded a live set at a local St. John's, Newfoundland, pub which was later released on cassette. It shows the early inklings of what would become Great Big Sea. The blending of traditional material like the sea chantey "General Taylor" with modern pop songs like Johnny Otis's "Willie and the Hand Jive" has become this band's trademark, and it all started here. More recently, the full-blown Great Big Sea gives one of many spirited performances on the Chieftains' all-star Canadian Celtic invitational collection *Fire in the Kitchen* ♫♫♫ (BMG, 1998).

influences:

◀◀ Emile Benoit, Figgy Duff, Spirit of the West, Van Halen

▶▶ The Punters

see also: *Oyster Band*

Cliff McGann

The Green Fields of America

See: Mick Moloney

Sylvan Grey

New age
Born in USA. Based in USA.

Grey plays the *kantele,* the Finnish national instrument, which looks like an autoharp without chord bars. Her kantele has 36 strings and has a sustain that allows individual notes to build up plenty of harmonic overtones.

what's available: *Recurring Dream* ♫♫♫ (Fortuna, 1989, prod. Sylvan Grey, Dan Hersch) is a soothing, new-age excursion, with enough virtuosity to keep you awake for the length of the performance. On *Ice Flowers Melting* ♫♫♫ (Fortuna, 1988, prod. Lou Judson), Grey sounds more folky, in the American sense, and less Finnish, but the album is still a low-key charmer. It's only available on cassette.

influences:

◀◀ Martti Pokela

j. poet

Marcia Griffiths

Ska, reggae, dancehall
Born 1954, in Kingston, Jamaica. Based in Kingston, Jamaica.

The queen of reggae music, Marcia Griffiths has prospered in a male-dominated industry since the 1960s and is still going strong. You have probably heard her voice as one of the I-Threes backing Bob Marley on any of his albums after *Natty Dread,* but her best work has been as a solo artist. Discovered singing in the street during her teens by star producer Clement Dodd, Griffiths recorded ska tunes for his Studio One records. She moved on to international success with rocksteady music and covers of soul classics for producer Sonia Pottinger in 1969. The collaboration with Pottinger yielded strong albums throughout the 1970s. Her partnership with singer Bob Andy, as half of Bob & Marcia, resulted in *Young, Gifted and Black,* a #5 album in the U.K. Griffiths has been the backing vocalist of choice in reggae, and her distinctive, sweet soprano can be

the pygmies

I t's strange and sad to think that a people who have influenced world-music stars from Zap Mama to Deep Forest to the Grateful Dead's Mickey Hart are themselves in danger of extinction thanks to bureaucracy, deforestation, and international ignorance. In some small compensation, the Pygmy culture scattered throughout Africa has been well documented on CD. Depicting a society that doesn't revolve around modern conveniences—you don't see Pygmy bands marching off into studios or on extravagant world tours—these albums are true windows on their lives, field recordings done in their villages. Recurring features are complex mass chants and, occasionally, homemade flutes and makeshift percussion—clapping hands, slapping water— from nomadic peoples who don't transport elaborate instruments. Since this music is recorded in the great outdoors, don't expect polished audio, but do expect fascinating glimpses into the Pygmy cultures, encompassing their initiation rituals, stories, and everyday casual songs. Though hunting is important to the tribes (and the basis of many songs), pygmies essentially lead a peaceful lifestyle with close-knit families and little private ownership. They see themselves as part of the nurturing forest they inhabit, and have little contact with the world outside it. The animals, the wind, and the rivers are all as much a part of their songs as their own vocals, which consist of phonetic sounds rather than words— the tribes see this as coming from spirits of the forest, which they channel. Recommended CDs and the countries they cover include *Mbuti Pygmies of the Ituri Rainforest* ♫♫♫♫ (Smithsonian/ Folkways)—Congo; *Heart of the Forest* ♫♫♫♫ (Hannibal)—Cameroon; and *Anthology of World Music, Africa: The BaBenzélé Pygmies* ♫♫♫ (Rounder)—Central African Republic/Congo/ Cameroon. Even more scholarly are two collections from the ellipsis arts . . . label, each of which includes extensive notes and photos: *Echoes of the Forest* ♫♫♫♫ compiles recordings of Central African Pygmies from several sources, and Louis Sarno's amazing *Bayaka* ♫♫♫♫ (also focused on the BaBenzélé tribe) comes with a comprehensive 93-page booklet.

see also: Baka Beyond, Zap Mama

Jason Gross

heard on hundreds of other people's records. She has moved with the times, from ska and soul, to Marley's roots reggae, to her current smooth dancehall love songs.

what to buy: Griffiths began her career at Studio One in the mid-1960s. To be present at the creation, check out *The Original (at Studio One) Marcia Griffiths* ✍✍✍✍ (Studio One, 1997, prod. Clement Dodd). Coming full circle, the diva recently revisited Studio One to cover her early hits on *Truly* ✍✍✍✍ (Studio One, 1999, prod. Clement Dodd). Not only does the new recording of "My Ambition," where Griffiths sings "something keeps pushing me on," sum up the stunning drive of this inimitable singer, but her voice is fuller, more assured, and the quality of her performance is even better than in the original. Griffiths's years with producer Sonia Pottinger produced outstanding work that compares favorably with Aretha Franklin's output during the same years. Check out *Best of 1969–1974: Put a Little Love in Your Heart* ✍✍✍✍ (Trojan, 1993, prod. Sonia Pottinger), with classic soul covers like Nina Simone's "Young, Gifted and Black" and Curtis Mayfield's "Gypsy Man." Two more strong albums followed with Pottinger: the esteemed *Steppin'* ✍✍✍ (High Note 1979/Shanachie 1991, prod. Sonia Pottinger) features roots originals; *Naturally* ✍✍✍✍ (High Note JA/Sky Note U.K., 1978/Shanachie, 1992, prod. Sonia Pottinger) revisits earlier hits and is worth the price simply for her version of Bunny Wailer's "Dreamland," in which she wistfully lilts, "There is a land that I have heard about/so far across the sea."

what to buy next: Griffith's latest incarnation as a dancehall diva of smooth love songs is heard on *Indomitable* ✍✍✍ (Penthouse, 1993).

the rest:
Marcia ✍✍ (RAS, 1989)
Carousel ✍✍✍ (Mango, 1990)

influences:
◀◀ Bob Andy, Phyllis Dillon, Aretha Franklin, Miriam Makeba, Bob Marley, Nina Simone, Dionne Warwick

▶▶ Lady Saw, J.C. Lodge, Sister Carol

see also: *Rita Marley, Judy Mowatt*

David Poole

Groupa

Swedish folk music
Formed 1980 in Sweden. Based in Sweden.

Mats Edén, fiddle, viola, accordion, leader; Tina Johansson, percussion; Jonas Simonsson, flute, bass, sax; Rickard Åström, keyboards; Hållbus Totte Mattson, lute, guitars (1982–90); Bill McChesny, recorder, bass clarinet (1982–90); Lena Willemark, vocals (1989–90); Leif Stinnerbom, viola (1982–87). (All members are from Sweden.)

"In Sweden, formal study of folk music started at the beginning of the 19th Century, with the first folk festivals organized in 1906," says Mats Edén, the leader of Groupa, one of Sweden's most successful folk bands. "The union movement of the '40s used folk music to organize people, like in the U.S. In the '60s there was a split in the folk community; one faction wanted to play traditionally and explore old manuscripts and local traditions that had been forgotten; one went into folk/rock." That split still exists today, although Edén tries to reconcile it with Groupa, a band that plays "traditional music in a modern way." Groupa's music has echoes in the virtuosic fiddling of Ireland and the American South, and if ethnomusicologists are correct about European folk music traveling westward, Scandinavian music may be the root of America's mournful mountain ballads. During its 19-year history, some of Sweden's most famous musicians have passed through Groupa's ranks, including Totte Mattson (who went on to form Hedningarna, one of Sweden's most commercially successful folk bands), Lena Willemark (the singer and fiddler with Nordan Project), and Ale Möller (the band's producer and co-founder of Nordan Project).

what's available: The compilation *15 Years* ✍✍✍✍ (NorthSide, 1998, prod. Ale Möller) collects tracks from five of the band's Swedish albums. Hear one of that country's most important folk outfits, one that tries to stay true to the traditional sources of the music without slavishly imitating the sounds of yesteryear.

influences:
◀◀ Hjort Anders, Jan Johansson

▶▶ Garmarna, Hedningarna, Hoven Droven

see also: *Hedningarna, Nordan Project*

j. poet

Gu-Achi Fiddlers

Tohono O'odham fiddle music
Formed late 1970s, in Gu-Achi, AZ, USA. Based in Gu-Achi, AZ, USA.

Gerald Leos Sr., snare drum; Lester Vavages, fiddle; Tommy Lopez, bass drum; Wilfred Mendoza, guitar; Elliot Johnson, fiddle. (All members are from USA.)

The Gu-Achi Fiddlers are members of the Tohono O'odham Nation of Arizona. The notion of fiddling Indians may seem odd, but this tradition dates back to the mid-19th century, when Spanish Catholic missionaries began teaching Indians to play European instruments so they could provide music for the mass. In their spare time, the Indians adapted polkas, *schottishces,* mazurkas, and other European dances to their own devices. Fiddle dances were popular in many Indian communities, and even when the style was updated with sax and electric instruments in the 1950s (à la Southern Scratch), the fiddle remained popular in many isolated communities. The Gu-Achi Fiddlers, the first Indian fiddle band to record, have been playing together for decades, and you can hear traces of *norteño*, mariachi, and other Latin forms in their unique brand of "Indian swing band music."

what's available: The tempos are laid back on *Old Time O'odham Fiddle Music* ♪♪♪ (Canyon, 1988/1997, prod. Ray Boley), but the swing's still the thing. The Library of Congress gave the original release a citation for Outstanding Album of Folk, Ethnic, and Traditional Music.

worth searching for: The cassette-only *O'odham Fiddle Music, Vol. 2* ♪♪♪ (Canyon, 1989) offers more low-key charm from these old-timers.

influences:

◄◄ Bob Wills

►► El Conjunto Murrietta, Joaquin Brothers Band, Southern Scratch

see also: *Bayou Seco, Southern Scratch*

j. poet

Juan Luis Guerra
Merengue

Born September 8, 1961, in the Dominican Republic. Based in Santo Domingo, Dominican Republic.

Juan Luis Guerra and his band 4.40 sold more than five million copies of *Bachata Rosa* in the first three years of its release, figures that kept the album on the Latin charts for almost two years and earned a Grammy, not to mention a multimillion-dollar endorsement deal with Pepsi. Guerra's 1993 concert tour of the United States was one of the longest and most successful North American ventures ever undertaken by a Latin artist, and although he refuses to sing in English, many major labels are eager to take a chance on his successful combination of *merengue, bachata,* and *salsa romantico.*

Guerra may be the biggest international star in Latin music's history. He was born to a middle-class family in the Dominican Republic and graduated from Boston's prestigious Berklee College of Music. He formed his first version of 4.40 in 1984 (the number refers to the wavelength of standard concert pitch, A above middle C, the "perfect" note in the Western musical system). But their first album, a mixture of Latin jazz and big band music influenced by Ellington, Mingus, and Basie, proved unsatisfying both commercially and artistically. "Something was missing," Guerra told Miami's *New Times.* "I wanted to get back to the African roots of our music. Everyone here is brown or black; we can trace our roots back to Africa as well as Spain, and I wanted to work on this in all its aspects."

Guerra took the merengue—an indigenous rhythm that mixes faster-than-light African drumming, jazzy interlocking horn charts, and intricate vocal harmonies—and blended it with rock, romantic Latin pop, salsa, and bachata, another lesser-known Dominican rhythm. The bachata comes from the island nation's back country, a music that draws on Native as well as African and Spanish elements. Literally translated, it means "garbage" or "trash," and until Guerra revitalized it, it was considered too low-class, too untamed for polite consumption. By calling an album *Bachata Rosa* ("Trashy Rose" or "Pink Garbage"), Guerra made an ironic comment on the illusions of normalcy that the island's ruling class tries to maintain, since clean drinking water, electricity, and a living wage are impossible for most workers to attain. Guerra's other contribution was the addition of lyrics that deal with the day-to-day reality of the island's underclass. A follower of the Latin *nueva canción* movement, Guerra isn't afraid to write tunes that take the powers that be to task for their sins. On the title song of 1987's *Ojala que Llueva Cafe (May It Rain Coffee),* Guerra put himself in the place of a campesino trying to feed his family. "I heard a farmer in a small town say this. There are many who die without knowing they are poets, so I took his phrase and made a song about it. He was desperate when he wrote this; wishing it would rain coffee, bread, all the things he needed."

Guerra's social concerns, as well as his international vision, are in evidence on his most recent albums, *Areíto* and *Fogaraté,* where he collaborates with Congolese guitar ace Diblo Dibala for some sizzling Latin *soukous.* "I'm not going to sing in English," Guerra insists. "Spanish is the way I know, the way I feel. When I was young I loved the Beatles, even though I couldn't understand the words. People understand rhythm and harmony, even when they don't get anything else. Lyrics are important, but even if you don't understand, you can dance."

what to buy: While its sales figures are not as massive as those for *Bachata Rosa, Fogaraté* ♪♪♪ (Karen, 1994, prod. Juan Luis Guerra) is another breakthrough album. There are two collaborations with Diblo, making explicit the African roots of merengue, and of Caribbean music in general; a traditional backwoods merengue composed by, and featuring, accordion master Francisco Ulloa; "La Crimosa," a love song with a melody lifted from Mozart's "Requiem"; and, despite his assurances to the contrary, a Beatle-esque pop tune sung in English.

what to buy next: *Ojalá que Llueva Café* ♪♪♪♪ (Karen, 1987, prod. Juan Luis Guerra) is the disc that made Juan Luis a star; it's more up-tempo and less slick than his later efforts, but no less exciting. Merengue, bachata, salsa romantico, a touch of *soca,* and Guerra's passionate political poetry add up to a perfect party album, one that moves your heart as well as your feet.

the rest:
El Original 4.40 🎵🎵 (Karen, 1984)
Mudanza y Acarreo 🎵🎵 (Karen, 1986)
Mientras Más lo Pienso . . . Tú 🎵🎵🎵 (Karen, 1988)
Bachata Rosa 🎵🎵🎵🎵 (Karen, 1990)
Areito 🎵🎵🎵🎵 (Karen, 1992)

influences:
◀◀ Francisco Ulloa, Wilfrido Vargas, Johnny Ventura

▶▶ Luis y Javier, Proyecto Uno

see also: *Diblo Dibala*

j. poet

The Guo Brothers & Shung Tian

Traditional Chinese folk and classical songs (the Chinese do not differentiate between these two genres)
Guo Brothers born in Beijing, China. Shung Tian formed in Beijing, China. Based in England.

Guo Yue, Chinese bamboo flutes; Guo Yi, sheng (hand-held mouth-blown organ); Wang Shun Xin, Chinese oboe; Guo Xiaun, vocals; Guo Liang, zheng (harp); Zhao Zheng Ren, yang qin (dulcimer), Chinese drums; Chang Gui Duo, da ruan (bass guitar); Pól Brennan (Ireland), keyboards and percussion (gongs, woodblock, Chinese hand cymbals, chimes). (All members are from China unless otherwise specified; note that the Chinese list their surname first.)

Their father being an established singer and *erhu* (Chinese two-stringed violin) player, the Guo Brothers seemed destined for music careers. Circumstances assured it, as the Cultural Revolution sent their mother away before their father's death landed them in what was then called the Peking Musician's Compound, where music professionals lived and worked together. Fighting extreme poverty, the brothers would pay for music lessons in cooking oil.

Yue was in the Army Orchestra of the People's Republic of China, traveling by train and on horseback to remote areas to play for troops. Yi became part of the Peking Film Orchestra at 15, and within three years he was on the soundtracks of over 200 films. Heading to England to further their studies, the brothers were asked by David Byrne (formerly of Talking Heads and an accomplished world-music producer and performer) to contribute to the soundtrack for *The Last Emperor.* Eventually, the members of Shung Tian (former colleagues of Yi's in the Peking Film Orchestra) were able to get to England—one of the few groups to leave China without state support. In the lineup was Guo *sister* Xiaun, a famous Chinese opera singer.

what's available: *Yuan* 🎵🎵🎵🎵 (RealWorld Records, 1990, prod. Pól Brennan) translates as "to be far away," and that is the situation in which the Guo Brothers and the members of Shung Tian found themselves, as they were studying and recording worlds removed from China. Producer Brennan, a former member of Clannad, heard a tape of the Guo Brothers while working at RealWorld Studios and recognized that despite cultural differences, there was a musical affinity between himself and the Guos. Both brothers are masters of their instruments, breathing life into them as the songs of *Yuan* tell tales about the everyday experiences of villagers ("Step by Step"), soldiers ("Three Kingdoms"), royalty ("The Dream of the Red Mansion")—every kind of "folk." Songs are arranged by the brothers, and Shung Tian provides the balance of the magical instrumental potpourri that is Chinese classical/folk music. Guo Xiaun is gifted with a voice that is equally comfortable soloing in a simple folk song or soaring in arias over a full orchestra. *Yuan* can be pared down and focused at one moment and turn into a controlled traffic jam of sounds the next. These are consummate performers giving one of the best examples of Chinese music.

worth searching for: Of course, the soundtrack to *The Last Emperor* (EMD/Virgin, 1987) is a must-listen. Several compilations contain Guo Brothers tracks, along with a wealth of other fine world music: the four-CD box set *Global Meditation* 🎵🎵🎵🎵 (ellipsis arts . . . , 1993), which is reviewed in this book's Compilations section; *Imaginary Landscapes—A Brief History of Ambient, Vol. 2* 🎵🎵🎵🎵 (EMD/Virgin, 1994), which is an excellent ambient starter kit; and the ultra-pleasant *Bliss* (EMD/RealWorld, 1998), which is also reviewed in this book's Compilations section.

influences:
◀◀ Traditional Chinese music

Stacy Meyn

Trilok Gurtu

World-jazz fusion
Born 1951 in Bombay, India. Based in Hamburg, Germany.

Born into a highly musical family (his grandfather was a noted sitar player and his mother, Shobha, remains a popular classical singing star), percussionist Trilok Gurtu began studying *tabla* with Ahmed Jan Thirakwa at the age of six. By the mid-1960s, he and his brother were leading their own group in Bombay, and greatly influenced by the groundbreaking music of Miles Davis and John Coltrane, he soon turned to jazz, teaching himself to play drums, percussion, and congas. By 1973 he had left for Europe with an Indian jazz-rock group, and in 1976 he moved to America, where he began his longstanding association with jazz saxophonist Charlie Mariano. By the late 1970s and early 1980s, Gurtu was touring and recording with a veritable Who's Who in jazz fusion, including a two-year stint with multicultural trumpeter Don Cherry, a four-year association with Ralph Towner's group Oregon, and several years with Mahavishnu Orchestra founder John McLaughlin. In 1988 Gurtu recorded *Usfret,* his debut as a bandleader and the album that established his trademark sound—a seamless, highly improvisational blend of jazz, rock, and a variety of ethnic traditions. Since that time, he has alternated between appearing as a sideman with a diverse range of artists including Joe Zawinul, Pat Metheny, Bill Laswell's Material, and Pharoah Sanders, and creating his own multicultural masterpieces, many of which have featured these same stellar musicians. Now considered one of the world's finest master drummers in any musical genre, Gurtu won *Down Beat* magazine's critics poll for best percussionist in 1995, 1996, and 1997.

what to buy: Gurtu's latest album, *The Glimpse* 𝄞𝄞𝄞𝄞 (Silva Screen, 1997, prod. Trilok Gurtu, Walter Quintus, Kurt Renker), is also easily his best—a brilliant blend of musical styles paying tribute to the drummer's dearly departed friend, Don Cherry. Guest musicians—including Morocco's Jaya Deva (who performed with Cherry), India's Geetha Ramanathan Bennett, and Bulgaria's Teodosii Spassov—make this Gurtu's most ethnically diverse album yet. Nearly every track is a standout, from the rollicking Moroccan groove of "Cherry Town" and the dazzling Indian *konnakkol* (spoken percussion) of "1-2 Beaucoup" to the melancholy blues balladry of Ornette Coleman's "Law Years." A must-have for fans of world-jazz fusion.

what to buy next: *The Trilok Gurtu Collection* 𝄞𝄞𝄞 (Silva Screen, 1997, prod. Trilok Gurtu, Walter Quintus, Kurt Renker) is a fine overview of the virtuosic drummer's career, with 10 tracks culled from his six albums, many of which are now very difficult to find. Gurtu's sound has remained surprisingly consistent over the years, from his work with Cherry, Ralph Towner, and L. Shankar on 1988's "Shobharock" up through his most recent efforts, although his excursions into jazz-funk fusion aren't quite as memorable as his more ethnically influenced compositions. Look for impressive appearances by Shobha Gurtu, Nana Vasconcelos, saxophonist Jan Garbarek, and even Pink Floyd guitarist David Gilmore (!), all of whom contribute to Gurtu's distinctive sound without overwhelming it with their own dynamic personalities.

the rest:
Usfret 𝄞𝄞𝄞 (CMP, 1988)
Living Magic 𝄞𝄞𝄞 (CMP, 1991)
Crazy Saints 𝄞𝄞𝄞 (CMP, 1993)
Believe 𝄞𝄞𝄞 (CMP, 1994)
Bad Habits Die Hard 𝄞𝄞𝄞 (CMP, 1996)

influences:

◄◄ Don Cherry, John Coltrane, Shobha Gurtu, Pandit Kamalesh Maitra

►► Cornershop, Talvin Singh

see also: *Bill Laswell, Pandit Kamalesh Maitra, L. Shankar, Nana Vasconcelos*

Bret Love

The Gyuto Monks
Buddhist chant
Formed 1474, in Lhasa, Tibet. Based in Bomdile (a.k.a. Bomdi-La or Bomdilla), India.

Rotating membership over the course of more than five centuries, recently including: Kalsang Dhundup; Kalden Tsering; Dakpa Gyaltsen; Lobsang Dhundup; Ngawang Sherab; Lobsang Jungney; Tenzin Norgyal; Tupten Jigme; Tashi Namgyal; Lobsang Tsering; Ken Rinpoche; Sonam Thargyal; Samten Tharchen; Tenzin Norbu; Tsering Norbu; Karma Phunstok; Tupten Chodak; Tupten Donyo; Tsultim Tashi; Tupten Sherap.

The Gyuto Tantric University is one of about a half-dozen colleges of advanced Buddhist studies that thrived in Tibet for hundreds of years before the 1949 Chinese invasion. After a particularly bloody purge of Buddhist culture in 1959, 90 of the Gyuto Monks fled with the Dalai Lama to the northern border of India, where they re-established the college. Every monk who attends the Gyuto college learns the unique style of multiphonic chanting that has been part of its rituals for 500 years, in which each participant produces a *full chord*, not just a single note. Until recently, outsiders weren't permitted to observe these rituals—they weren't hidden out of secrecy, but because of the conviction that one must be properly initiated to safely contend with the powers that are released. World-traveling ethnologists may have recorded the Gyuto Monks' chanting prior to World War II, but even if you could find the cylinder recordings or 78 rpm discs, their poor fidelity would obscure the monks' extraordinary voices. The earliest known recordings of the Gyuto Monks were made in Dalhousie, India, by religious scholar Huston Smith in 1964, followed by ethnomusicologist David Lewiston in 1972. Although these albums were well received in academic circles and among aficionados of psychophysical phenomena, they received little mainstream attention.

The monks were still largely unknown in 1985 when the Grateful Dead's Mickey Hart organized a benefit concert and recorded *Tibetan Tantric Choir* for Windham Hill Records. (Benefits remained the standard for subsequent tours, which were organized and supported by volunteer Grateful Dead technicians and staff. Over the years, these concerts have raised enough funds to construct a new monastery/school for the lineage in exile.) Although Windham Hill was busy with the new-age music boom and lacked the interest and experience to market the monks, the album reportedly sold more copies than all of Lewiston's releases combined. During a 1988 U.S. tour, Hart recorded *Freedom Chants from the Roof of the World* for Rykodisc, and the label enthusiastically promoted the album as part of its new Hart-produced series, *The World*. In the 1990s, the monks contributed to the critically acclaimed film soundtracks for *Kundun* and *Seven Years in Tibet*; toured as emissaries of the Tibetan culture, religion, and nation; and recorded little-known albums on obscure labels. Hart added samples of their chants to his albums and protested when the Beastie Boys used unauthorized samples, asking that they contribute to the monks' charitable fund as compensation.

what to buy: You can't go wrong with any of the Gyuto Monks' titles—their chanting is arguably the most profound sacred music on the planet. Even albums with less than ideal fidelity present uniquely powerful listening experiences. *Tibetan Buddhism: Tantra of Gyuto: Sangwa Düpa and Mahakala* ♫♫♫ (WEA/Elektra/Nonesuch, 1988, prod. David Lewiston) combines material from two LPs that David Lewiston recorded on his 1972 expedition: *Tantras of Gyuto—Mahakala* (Nonesuch, 1973) and *Tantras of Gyuto—Sangua Düpa* (Nonesuch, 1975). These are the oldest Gyuto Monks recordings readily available. The *a cappella* track "Sangwa Düpa" is a 41-minute portion of a 7 1/2-hour recitation that features the potent resonance of 40 monks—perhaps the largest assemblage of Gyuto Monks ever recorded. On the 18-minute "Mahakala," the chant of a dozen monks provides a background drone for the majestic bellowing of six-foot-long trumpets and the clattering of percussion instruments. The recordings were made nearly 30 years ago in a tin-roofed shed that served as a shrine room, which accounts for the brittle edginess in the soundscape. *Tibetan Tantric Choir* ♫♫♫♫ (Windham Hill, 1987, prod. Mickey Hart) features two penetrating chants by the 11 monks who constituted the 1985 traveling troupe. "Guhyasamaja Tantra, Chapter II" is a recitation of Buddhist texts that is laden with overtone harmonics; "Melody for Mahakala" adds powerful drums, bells, cymbals, brass horns, and conch shells to the chanting. The sound quality is a bit hard and thin. At press date, Windham Hill could not confirm that this recording is still in print, but many distributors report having the title in stock. *Freedom Chants from the Roof of the World* ♫♫♫♫ (Rykodisc, 1989, prod. Mickey Hart) features similar chanting and instrumentation, but advances in recording technology, superior studio space, and the presence of almost double the number of monks produce a CD that is far more intense and clear than the Windham Hill volume. The finale, "#2 for Gaia," is a musical offering to the monks by Hart, Kitaro, and Philip Glass—which seems mundane and extraneous after two extended pieces of highly focused chanting. But

then, the monks are a tough act to follow. Remarkable stereo separation, rich fidelity, and the 53-minute length of the only cut, "Sangwa Duepa," make *Buddhist Chant II: Tibet* ♫♫♫♫ (JVC World Sounds, 1990, prod. Soh Fujimoto) a riveting listen. The CD is part of a far-ranging series of world-music titles; beware of different covers on American and Japanese editions that feature the same material.

the rest:
Tibetan Gyuto Monks Live (Keytone Records, 1997)
Music for Meditation: The Gyuto Monks Live on Tour, Featuring Chris Hinze (Keytone Records, 1998)
(With Chris Hinze) *Tibet Impressions Volume II* (Keytone Records, 1998)
Voices of the World (Full Circle Music)

worth searching for: *The Music of Tibet: The Tantric Rituals* ♫♫♫♫ (Minuteman, 1968, prod. Huston Smith) is Smith's 1964 mono album that spawned all of the interest in the Gyuto Monks, and it remains a powerful, penetrating listen. The 13 short selections emphasize the variety of the Gyuto Monks' styles rather the absorbing quality of one or two long, stately tracks. When the Minuteman label folded long ago, Smith took possession of the master tapes, which he dubs and sells by mail order. This pivotal piece of music history may be purchased for $10 from Huston Smith, 1151 Colusa Avenue, Berkeley, CA 94707 USA. Proceeds benefit Tibetan relief efforts. Narrated by Francis Huxley, the 52-minute film *Tantra of Gyuto: Sacred Rituals of Tibet* (Mystic Fire Video, 1974) contains Tibetan Buddhist ceremonies performed by the Gyuto Monks, plus rare footage of Tibet from the 1920s to the 1950s. The video is available from Mystic Fire Video, P.O. Box 422, New York, NY 10012-0008 USA; (800) 292-9001. Also available on video, *Requiem for a Faith* (Hartley Productions, 1986) is Huston Smith's excellent survey of Tibetan Buddhism, featuring examples of Gyuto Monks chanting multiphonically. The film was shot mainly at the Gyuto Monastery in Dalhousie, India. Written by Robert Thurman and narrated by Martin Sheen, Margot Kidder, and Mickey Hart, the documentary *Timeless Voices: The Gyuto Monks at St. John the Divine* (Society for Gyuto Sacred Arts, 1989) features footage from assorted Gyuto Monks concerts, including the performance that concluded their 1988 tour. (All profits from videotapes purchased from Grateful Dead Merchandising, (800) 225-3323, support the Gyuto College.) Because, due to length considerations, only 18 minutes of the LP *Tantras of Gyuto—Mahakala* (Nonesuch, 1973) appear on the *Tantra of Gyuto* CD, the balance of the original album must be considered out of print, its entirety unheard by many and worth searching for by all. The sampler *Around the World (for a Song)* (Rykodisc, 1991) includes "Yamantaka (Edit)"—a fragment from the *Freedom Chants* CD. The Beastie Boys' *Ill Communication* (Grand Royal/Capitol, 1994) reportedly contains uncredited samples of the Gyuto Monks on "Shambala" and "Bodhisattva

Vow." Authorized samples of the monks may be heard in "Only the Strange Remain" on *Mickey Hart's Mystery Box* (Rykodisc, 1996), and in "Angola" on *Mickey Hart's Planet Drum: Supralingua* (Rykodisc, 1998). In a single year, the Gyuto Monks appeared on two soundtrack albums that were nominated for Golden Globe Awards: John Williams's *Seven Years in Tibet* (Sony, 1997) and Philip Glass's *Kundun* (WEA/Atlantic/Nonesuch, 1997); naturally, the films themselves also feature the monks' performances.

influences:

▶▶ The Beastie Boys, Philip Glass, the Grateful Dead, Mickey Hart, Chris Hinze, David Hykes, Kitaro, Pauline Oliveros, Terry Riley, John Williams

see also: *Mickey Hart, Yungchen Lhamo*

Richard Price

Idjah Hadijah

Jaipongan

Born in Sunda, West Java, Indonesia. Based in Sunda, West Java, Indonesia.

Idjah Hadijah evokes visions of sweltering tropical days and steamy, languid nights, even as she cools and calms the listener with her low, gentle voice, and subtle, reserved presence. She sings in Sundanese, a language similar to but distinct in tone and style from her home island's dominant Javanese, and very different from Bahasa Indonesia, the common, national language that unites that sprawling country of 13,000-plus islands, 600-plus languages, and three time zones. Best known in the West for *Tonggeret,* her exquisite 1987 album on Icon/Nonesuch, and especially for its title track, Hadijah was famous early on as a singer in the traditional *wayang golek* Sundanese rod-puppet theater. Her performances with the famous puppeteer R. Cecep Supriadi, her husband, brought her to the attention of Gugum Gumbira Tirasonjaya, an important figure in the development of *jaipongan* (Indonesian popular music). Earlier Gugum had, like much of Indonesian youth, taken an intense interest in rock 'n' roll, but had to abandon it in the face of President Sukarno's early-1960s banning of things Western and "encouragement" of things Indonesian. Turning to the local culture of Sunda, Gugum and others developed jaipongan as a musical and dance style based on indigenous forms. In the 1970s they began to present a popular music and dance of far-reaching importance, one of a very few

such genres worldwide with virtually no Western influence or instrumentation.

At Hadijah performances, one hears echoes of the very sophisticated and refined traditional court and folk theaters of Java and Sunda. Overlaid are the far earthier, sensual tones and movements of the older Sundanese village genre of *ketuk tilu*—gamelan (tuned percussion ensemble) performances that featured professional female singer/dancers, frequently prostitutes, who danced with local men for pay. Nowadays, the jaipongan gamelan is still composed of various gongs and drums, not to mention the ubiquitous, reedy-sounding *rebab* (a two-stringed upright spike-tip fiddle), but the singers and dancers have been relieved of their extracurricular activities. What remains are haunting, lyrical songs of love and money, regal gongs, the droning rebab, intervals of drumming and whooping by the band . . . and a style that became a nationwide dance craze, no electric guitars allowed.

what's available: You want all of *Tonggeret* 𝄡𝄡𝄡𝄡 (Icon/Nonesuch Explorer, 1987, prod. Gugum Gumbira Tirasonjaya) for an introduction to a unique style by an unforgettable practitioner, though the landmark title track is also included on the worthy compilation *Global Divas* 𝄡𝄡𝄡𝄡 (Rounder, 1995, prod. Brooke Wentz). Probably the only other jaipongan recording easily available in the West is *Jaipongan Java* 𝄡𝄡𝄡𝄡 (GlobeStyle, 1990, prod. Gugum Gumbira Tirasonjaya) by the equally extraordinary Euis Komariah, with the Jugala Orchestra. For those willing to search the import bins or able to visit Indonesia itself, Hadijah recorded dozens of albums on Gugum's Jugala label in the 1980s.

influences:

◀◀ Traditional music and dance of Java and Sunda

Jack Vartoogian

Richard Hagopian

Armenian folk and dance music

Born 1937, in Fowler, CA, USA. Based in Visalia, CA, USA.

The Fresno, California, area is home to one of the most important communities in the Armenian diaspora. It is here that *oud* (lute) virtuoso Richard Hagopian has spent his life learning the Armenian musical heritage from masters such as Kanuni Garbis Bakirgian and Udi Hrant, collecting traditional music and dances and preserving a style of Armenian/Anatolian-Turkish music that has died out in Armenia and Turkey. Following the murder of two million Armenians in the Turkish Genocide of 1915, hundreds of thousands of Armenians fled to the United States. Although Armenians had played a major role in classical and popular Ottoman music, many Armenians refused to listen to Turkish music from that point onward. But when

Idjah Hadijah

Hassan Hakmoun

Richard Hagopian began studying the oud in 1947, he was attracted to the older music. Originally, each area of the Anatolian plateau had a distinct style, all of them related by *maqam* (mode) and timing; historians believe the music's roots go back to the 13th-century Armenian church. Hagopian learned much of this repertoire from old vinyl recordings and still-living first-generation performers in the United States. Since the Hagopian family was at home in both the Turkish and Armenian languages, Richard embraced the full canon without prejudice—and regardless of the Turkish connection, Armenians' important contribution to that country's classical music made him unwilling to abandon both parts of his cultural identity. Hagopian has traveled to Armenian communities all over the United States playing this music. At a time when there was almost no interest in the old music and dance among Armenian Americans, Hagopian preserved the traditions. Now many young second- and third-generation Armenians (including his own children) have rediscovered their roots. Musicians and scholars from Turkey, where Ottoman traditions have been replaced by modern and popular Turkish music, have journeyed to California to hear Hagopian play the old repertoire they can

only hear on recordings from early in the century. In recognition of such successes at sparing an entire culture's musical legacy from extinction, Hagopian received a National Heritage Fellowship from the National Endowment for the Arts in 1989.

what to buy: Although it is impossible to condense all of Armenian musical history in one volume, *Armenian Music through the Ages* ♪♪♪♪♪ (Smithsonian Folkways, 1993, prod. Harold Hagopian) contains a sprinkling of wedding, toasting, and love songs; dance music; a *taksim* (oud improvisation); and instrumentals from the Ottoman repertoire. The music has similarities to Turkish, Arab, Greek, and Persian forms, reflecting what ethnomusicologists refer to as "mixed traditions within a Pan-Islamic style."

what to buy next: *Gypsy Fire* ♪♪♪♪♪ (Traditional Crossroads, 1995, prod. Harold Hagopian) is a re-creation of the Eighth Avenue Middle Eastern club scene in New York in the 1950s. For the better part of that decade, Middle Eastern–themed nightclubs, with belly dancers and live bands playing a blend of Greek, Turkish, Israeli, Arab, and Armenian standards, were very popular in places like New York and Las Vegas. Hagopian

Richard Hagopian

is joined by a virtuoso band that includes Omar Faruk Tekbilek on the oboe-like *zurna* and *ney* (flute), and Yuri Yunakov on the *saz* (another form of lute) in a recreation of that repertoire.

worth searching for: *Kef Time* 𝄞𝄞𝄞𝄞 (SaHa, 1968/Traditional Crossroads, 1994) is a collection of Armenian dance tunes from the repertoire of The Kef Time Band, the group Hagopian played with for five years in Las Vegas as part of the Cleopatra Review. Further exploration of these styles will be rewarded by the British import *Best of Armenian Folk Music* (Arc Music, 1992).

influences:

◄◄ Kanuni Garbis Bakirgian, Udi Hrant

►► Harold Hagopian

see also: *Udi Hrant, Omar Faruk Tekbilek*

Aaron Howard

Hassan Hakmoun

Traditional Gnawa, worldbeat
Born 1963 in Marrakech, Morocco. Based in New York, NY, USA.

Although found in cities throughout North Africa, the Gnawa are a traditional people, probably originally from sub-Saharan Black Africa, known for their talents as entertainers and healers. Hakmoun began singing, dancing, and learning his people's healing traditions at the age of seven. While still a child he was accompanying master musicians to Spain and France and throughout Morocco. He was performing in his own group at 14, and made his American debut in 1987 as part of the Trio Gna, a folkloric ensemble. As in the rest of the world, rock 'n' roll swept over Morocco in the 1960s and ignited the youth with ideas of political freedom and social justice. Two rock bands that mixed traditional Islamic music with Western instruments and attitude became popular: Nass El Ghiwan and Jiljilala. Both were created by Gwana musicians who were friends and relations of Hakmoun, so it was natural for him to start his own band—Zahar—and try blending Arabic, Berber, Gnawa, funk, and rock into his own style. In 1986 he moved the band to New York, where he still resides.

what to buy: *The Fire Within* 𝄞𝄞𝄞𝄞 (Music of the World, 1995, prod. Robert Browning, Bob Haddad) is a recording of traditional Gwana *nugsha* music, played during the dedication of ceremonial robes to induce a trance-like state that will please all participants, human and invisible. Hakmoun plays the *sintir*, a three-string bass/guitar that has a pleasing low-end sound. His vocals are impassioned, and have a deep, bluesy feel that effortlessly combines Arabic and Black African styles.

what to buy next: *Hassan Hakmoun and Zakar* 𝄞𝄞𝄞 (Realworld, 1993, prod. Simon Emmerson) is a skillful worldbeat

outing, but Hakmoun's Gwana impulses are mostly submerged under the Western influences.

the rest:
Gift of the Gwana 𝄞𝄞𝄞 (Flying Fish, 1987)
Life around the World 𝄞𝄞𝄞 (Alula, 1998)

influences:

◄◄ Master Musicians of Jajouka, Don Cherry, Nass El Ghiwan, Jiljilala

see also: *Adam Rudolph*

j. poet

Robbie Hannan

Irish traditional
Born in Holywood, County Down, Ireland. Based in County Down, Ireland.

Only in his 30s, Robbie Hannan has quickly become one of Ireland's finest exponents of the traditional bellows-blown uilleann pipes. His distinctive style of playing owes much to his deep love for the traditional music of Donegal, an area in the northwest of Ireland well known for its fiddling, which draws equally upon Scottish and Irish style and repertoire. While Donegal's fiddle tradition remains vibrant, its piping tradition had been on a downswing since the early 1900s. Hannan's innovation in adapting the Donegal fiddle style to the uilleann pipes has elevated both him and his chosen instrument to a more deserved prominence. Hannan continues to perform throughout Ireland, and is curator of musicology at the Ulster Folk and Transport Museum, where he has dedicated his life to his craft.

what to buy: The collaboration with Donegal fiddler Paddy Glackin *The Whirlwind* 𝄞𝄞𝄞𝄞𝄞 (Shanachie, 1995, prod. Paddy Glackin, Robbie Hannan), originally released in Ireland under the title *Séideán Sí*, is one of the most brilliant recordings in either artist's oeuvre, or indeed in either instrument's canon. A stellar performance of solo and duo virtuosity, with an electrifying, unaccompanied immediacy. *Traditional Irish Music Played on the Uilleann Pipes* 𝄞𝄞𝄞𝄞 (Claddagh, 1990) is Hannan's wonderful solo recording. It features such great lively tunes as the "Salamanca/Jenny's Welcome to Charlie" set, but also showcases his beautifully evocative playing of slow airs like "Dark Lochnagar."

what to buy next: *The Drones & the Chanters, Vol. 2* 𝄞𝄞𝄞𝄞 (Claddagh, 1995) is a magnificent collection of uilleann piping from seven of the most talented Irish pipers you will find anywhere. Hannan's performances are spirited and, coupled with great sets by Ronan Browne, Gay McKeon, Joseph McLaughlin, Micheal O Briain, Liam O'Flynn, and Sean Potts, make this recording well worth seeking.

worth searching for: *The Piper's Rock* ♪♪♪♪ (Mulligan Records) is a sprightly collection of uilleann piping that features Hannan as well as *Riverdance* piper Davy Spillane, Eoin Ó Riabhaigh, Mícheál Ó Briain, Gay McKeon, Máire Ní Ghráda, and James O'Brien-Moran. While a little harder to locate than some of the other recordings of Hannan, true diehard fans of his work, and of piping and Irish music in general, will want to seek it out.

influences:
◄◄ John Doherty, Liam O'Flynn, Seumas Ennis, Willie Clancy, Tommy Reck

see also: *Paddy Glackin, Liam O'Flynn*

Cliff McGann

Joy Harjo & Poetic Justice
Spoken-word Native American Latin jazz-reggae
Formed 1990, in Albuquerque, NM, USA. Based in Albuquerque, NM, USA.

Joy Harjo (born May 9, 1951, in Tulsa, OK, USA), poetry, alto sax, soprano sax; John L. Williams, bass, guitar, keyboards, strings, congas, bongos, woodblock, sequencing/synthesizer; Susan M. Williams, drums, percussion; William Bluehouse Johnson, guitar, drums, percussion; Frank Poocha, drums, percussion, keyboards, tribal singing; Richard Carbajal, guitar, effects; Shkeme, vocals (1998); Charlie Baca, guitar (1998). (All members are from USA.)

A standout in both the long tradition of poets-turned-performers (Leonard Cohen, Patti Smith, John Trudell) and the burgeoning genre of "spoken word" (Henry Rollins, Maggie Estep, Me'Shell Ndegéocello), Joy Harjo has also achieved one of the most seamless syntheses of disparate world-music sounds with her band Poetic Justice. Harjo was already perhaps the hardest-working woman in American letters (and Native American advocacy) when she took up the saxophone and began her collaborations with the future members of Poetic Justice. It was a leap for which her previous progression from a painting and theater education to a writing career had well prepared her, and which would serve as a model and metaphor for the culture-bridging the band was after in its music. Finding connections between sometimes far-flung dialects in the worldwide musical language of rhythm and resistance, the band's sophisticated but dynamic style successfully melds Native American ceremonial songs and beats, reggae rhythm, occasional Latin melodic and percussive inflections, and Harjo's supple jazz sax. Though Poetic Justice's 1996 debut album *Letter from the End of the Twentieth Century* remains its only one, a followup is being recorded at this writing, and the band's tours are perpetually booked two years in advance (between Harjo's much-in-demand poetry readings and educational work, and other members' day jobs

as teachers, tribal officials, and high-powered Native-rights lawyers). Meanwhile, an increasing number of compilation appearances both reflects and fuels the demand for this exceptional and far-from-over band.

what's available: *Letter from the End of the Twentieth Century* ♪♪♪♪ (Red Horses/Silverwave, 1996, prod. Joy Harjo, Susan M. Williams, John L. Williams) is that rare album that is at once endlessly experimental and instantly catchy. Harjo's lyrics possess a fascinating insight into the construction of myth—both the sustaining cultural and misleading political varieties—and her delivery is the music's perfect rhythmic foil, at times declaiming with an arresting but quiet drama, at times downright New Wave in its swooping, dissociative intonation. Highlights (on an album of them) include the incantatory, empowering "Fear Poem"; the languid, Latinized "The Real Revolution Is Love"; the title track's poignant, politicized ghost story; and the moving Native-jazz hybrid, "The Myth of Blackbirds."

worth searching for: The one Poetic Justice compilation track not yet available elsewhere ("The Musician Who Became a Bear: A Tribute to Pepper") can be found on Smithsonian Folkways' *Heartbeat 2: More Voices of First Nations Women*, the second in a comprehensive and engrossing series reviewed in this book's Compilations section. The band is featured in the film documentary *Rockin' Warriors*, which is unfortunately not known to have a video distributor at this time. Keep track of Harjo's prolific literary and academic undertakings (and the band's next whereabouts in person and on disc) at the Joy Harjo & Poetic Justice Web site, http://www.hanksville.org/PJ/.

influences:
◄◄ Jim Pepper, John Coltrane, Bob Marley, John Trudell

Adam McGovern

Larry Harlow
Salsa
Born Lawrence Ira Kahn, March 20, 1939, in USA. Based in Brooklyn, NY, USA.

Larry Harlow is recognized as one of the leading figures in the popular Latin music field of salsa. Though born in the USA, he moved to Cuba in the mid-1950s to study the forms that inspired his adopted genre. Working primarily as a keyboardist, Harlow also plays the oboe, flute, English horn, bass, vibraphone, and percussion, and is noted for helping to create the internationally known group Fania All Stars, of which he was a member and producer for 15 years. He also composed the first salsa opera, *Hommy*. In 1994 he collaborated with another giant in the field, percussionist Ray Barretto, to form the Latin Legends Band, who recorded an album of the same name.

what to buy: *Hommy: A Latin Opera* ♫♫♫♫ (Fania, 1972, prod. Larry Harlow) is a fine example of Harlow's ambitious stretching of salsa into other music realms while not straying too far from the Latin base. *Live in Quad* ♫♫♫♫ (Fania, 1974, prod. Larry Harlow) shows that for all the studio proficiency associated with the genre, nothing beats the sound of salsa musicians interacting in a live setting. *La Raza Latina: A Salsa Suite* ♫♫♫♫ (Fania, 1977, prod. Larry Harlow) was nominated for a Grammy, and is another prime example of Harlow bringing salsa music into other compositional formats. All three of these albums were released on the Fania label, a legendary salsa standard-bearer where Harlow has done much of his best work.

what to buy next: Harlow's second recording period for Fania lasted two years and two albums: *Our Latin Feeling* ♫♫♫ (Fania, 1981, prod. Larry Harlow) and *Yo Soy Latino* ♫♫♫ (Fania, 1982, prod. Larry Harlow), each of which tries to revive the Fania spirit of the 1960s and '70s while catching the modern verve, all with good success.

best of the rest:
Heavy Smokin' ♫♫♫ (Fania, 1966)
Bajandote ♫♫♫ (Fania, 1966)
El Exigente ♫♫♫ (Fania, 1967)
Harlow Presents Miranda ♫♫♫ (Fania, 1968)
Me and My Monkey ♫♫♫ (Fania, 1969)
Electric Harlow ♫♫♫ (Fania, 1969)
Abram Paso ♫♫♫ (Fania, 1970)
Arsenio ♫♫♫ (Fania, 1971)
Harlow's Harem ♫♫♫ (Fania, 1972)
La Oportunidad ♫♫♫ (Fania, 1972)
Salsa ♫♫♫ (Fania, 1973)
El Judío Maravilloso ♫♫♫ (Fania, 1975)
Con Mi Viejo Amigo ♫♫♫ (Fania, 1976)
Best of Harlow and Miranda ♫♫♫ (Fania, 1976)
New York Latin All Stars ♫♫♫ (Nippon Phonogram, 1976)
Belmonte ♫♫♫ (Nippon Phonogram, 1976)
El Jardinero del Amor ♫♫♫ (Fania, 1977)
Latin Fever ♫♫♫ (Fania, 1977)
El Alvino Divino ♫♫♫ (Fania, 1978)
Rumbambola ♫♫♫ (Fania, 1978)
La Responsabilidad ♫♫♫ (Fania, 1979)
The Sweet Smell of Success ♫♫♫ (Fania, 1979)
Asi Soy Latino ♫♫♫ (Coco, 1980)
Senor Salsa ♫♫♫ (Tropical Buddah, 1985)
Flamingo Rouge ♫♫♫ (Razmataz, 1987)
Salsa Brothers ♫♫♫ (Songo, 1989)
My Time Is Now ♫♫♫ (Cache, 1991)
Los Tres ♫♫♫ (Caiman, 1997)

influences:
◀◀ The Afro-Cuban tradition

see also: *Ray Barretto, Yomo Toro*

Steven Stancell

George Harrison
Rock
Born February 25, 1943, in Liverpool, England. Based in England.

George Harrison has had an illustrious career; in addition to playing lead guitar, singing, and writing songs as the youngest member of the Beatles, Harrison has been on the cutting edge of world music. The first musician to play sitar on a pop record— "Norwegian Wood"—Harrison, who studied the complex Indian stringed instrument under Ravi Shankar, later played it on his own Beatles compositions, including "Within You Without You" and "Love You To." At Shankar's urging, Harrison produced and performed at two benefit all-star concerts for famine relief in Bangladesh at New York's Madison Square Garden in 1971. The second show was later released as a million-selling triple album and documentary film. Harrison's self-penned single "Bangladesh" became a Top-20 pop hit. A devotee of the Hari Krishna movement, Harrison was responsible for the Beatles' 1967 trip to India to study under the Maharishi Mahesh Yogi, and although the other Beatles became disenchanted, Harrison has remained spiritually connected to Eastern thought.

what to buy: Harrison's greatest moment may have come with the Concert for Bangladesh. In addition to performing songs from the three-disc post-Beatles masterwork *All Things Must Pass* and a memorable version of "Something," Harrison made major contributions to sets by Bob Dylan and Billy Preston. Harrison's Indian-music mentor Ravi Shankar was along for the occasion. The resulting document, *Concert for Bangladesh* ♫♫♫♫ (Apple, 1972, prod. Phil Spector, George Harrison), another three-album set, captures the historic evening. "Norwegian Wood" from the Beatles' *Rubber Soul* ♫♫♫♫♫ (Parlophone, 1965), is inescapable, but the harder Harrison went into Indian music, the less well-known the results become. That doesn't mean they're not worthy of discovery; the epic "Within You Without You" from *Sgt. Pepper's Lonely Hearts Club Band* ♫♫♫♫♫ (Parlophone, 1967, prod. George Martin) and especially the driving "Love You To" from *Revolver* ♫♫♫♫♫ (Parlophone, 1966, prod. George Martin) are prime examples of a Westerner who blazed trails into world music earlier than most—and approached it with a deference that would be emulated by few.

influences:
◀◀ Carl Perkins, Chuck Berry, Ravi Shankar
▶▶ Eric Clapton, Ashwan Batish

see also: *Ali Akbar Khan, Ravi Shankar*

Craig Harris and Adam McGovern

Mickey Hart
Rock, world fusion
Born September 11, 1943, in Long Island, NY, USA. Based in Marin County, CA, USA.

Grateful Dead percussionist/drummer Mickey Hart has had a major influence on world music over the past decade. After more than 20 years of visiting, recording, and studying with percussionists and ethnic musicians in nearly every corner of the globe, he began sharing what he'd learned. Since signing a distribution deal with Rykodisc in 1983, Hart has released a series of albums recorded during his ethnomusicological trips abroad, and another, *Drums of Passion: The Invocation,* that he produced for world-renowned Nigerian master drummer Babatunde Olatunji. Hart has simultaneously served as a music director at Smithsonian/Folkways and has been instrumental in the release of many new folk and ethnic recordings. His own albums have ranged from the pre-natal sound study *Music to Be Born By,* to multicultural collaborations like the Diga Rhythm Band's eponymous album and *Planet Drum,* recorded with a band he assembled from some of the world's best percussionists.

Hart was the son of a drummer, but was raised by his mother on New York's Long Island. By the time he was reunited with his father on the West Coast in the mid-1960s, Hart was already on his way to becoming a master percussionist, soon acquiring a solid reputation as a drum instructor and innovative player. When one of his students, Bill Kreutzmann, became a founding member of the Grateful Dead, Hart began to frequent the band's shows, often jamming with them onstage. He "officially" joined the band in 1967, and on his debut solo album *Rolling Thunder* Jerry Garcia and Kreutzmann made guest appearances, along with Indian percussionist Allha Rakha and members of the Jefferson Airplane and Quicksilver Messenger Service. In 1975 Hart joined the Diga Rhythm Band, which featured such world-music luminaries as Zakir Hussain and Vince Delgado, and which released one legendary album the following year. Hart has written two books; while *Drumming at the Edge of Magic* is an insightful autobiography, *Planet Drum* is a scholarly study on the history and use of percussion around the world.

what to buy: Hart's collaboration with some of the world's greatest drummers including Babatunde Olatunji and Sikiri Adepoju of Nigeria, Airto Moreira of Brazil, Zakir Hussain of India, and Giovanni Hidalgo of Puerto Rico, *Planet Drum* ♪♪♪♪ (Rykodisc, 1996, prod. Mickey Hart) is an essential summit meeting of percussive virtuosity. Hart resurrected the concept for the double CD *Supralingua* ♪♪♪♪ (Rykodisc, 1998, prod.

Mickey Hart), featuring a percussion ensemble composed of Adepoju, Hidalgo, Hussain, Bakithi Kumalo, and David Garibaldi, and numerous vocalists including the Gyuto Monks Tantric Choir, Rebeca Mauleon, and Bobi Cespedes.

best of the rest:
Rolling Thunder ♪♪♪ (Grateful Dead, 1976)
(With Diga Rhythm Band) *Diga* ♪♪♪ (Round, 1976/Rykodisc, 1988)
Rhythm Devils: The Apocalypse Now Sessions ♪♪♪ (Rounder, 1983)
(With Airto Moreira and Flora Purim) *Däfos* ♪♪♪ (Reference, 1985/ Rykodisc, 1988)
(With Taro Hart) *Music to Be Born By* ♪♪♪ (Rykodisc, 1990)
At the Edge ♪♪♪♪ (Rykodisc, 1991)
Mickey Hart's Mystery Box ♪♪♪♪ (Rykodisc, 1996)

influences:
◀◀ Buddy Rich, Airto Moreira, Babatunde Olatunji

▶▶ Billy Cobham, Ginger Baker

see also: *Diga Rhythm Band, Gyuto Monks, Zakir Hussain, Ali Akbar Khan, Airto Moreira, Babatunde Olatunji, Flora Purim, T.H. "Vikku" Vinayakram*

Craig Harris

Hawk Project
Jazz, Native American
Formed 1994 in Woodstock, NY, USA. Based in Shandaken, NY, USA.

Dennis Yerry, flute, trumpet, piano, Native percussion; Ken Littlehawk, flute, percussion, vocals; Gus Mancini, bass clarinet, sax, synthesizer; Steve Rust, bass; Ken Lovelett, trap drums, percussion. (All members are from USA.)

"Mixing traditional Native music with contemporary jazz can be difficult at times," says Hawk Project's leader and spokesman Dennis Yerry. "But this band creates music as an evolving group improvisation, with traditional rhythms in mind." The idea for the band came to Yerry, a Haudenosaunee (Iroquois), while he was working with filmmaker Ken Burns on the music for the PBS documentary *The West.* Yerry was musical director for a theater piece called *Black Elk Speaks* and took the drummers from that show, as well as Ken Littlehawk, to record the music for *The West.* Burns also asked Yerry and company to do incidental music for his *Lewis and Clark* documentary. After those projects they decided to make the collaboration an ongoing project, and recorded *Let Us Put Our Minds Together.* They're also the house band for *Woodstock Roundtable,* a radio show that also uses their music for its opening and closing themes. The band is working on its second album.

what's available: On *Let Us Put Our Minds Together* ♪♪♪ (Hawk, 1997, prod. Dennis Yerry, Gus Mancini), the music ranges from traditional jazz like "May You Walk in Balance," a lovely ballad played by Yerry on acoustic piano, to "Creator of Hearts," a stormy free-jazz excursion that incorporates a traditional Lakota encouragement song sung in both Lakota and English. Most of the music was recorded "live," although some traditional vocal parts were later overdubbed.

influences:

Jim Pepper, Black Elk, Don Cherry, R. Carlos Nakai, Thelonious Monk, Wilma Mankiller, Paul Robeson

j. poet

Ofra Haza

Ethnic, world-disco, Yemenite dance music
Born late 1960s, in Halika, Israel. Based in Israel.

The ancient musical traditions of the Jewish Yemenite community in Israel are updated by Ofra Haza. With her songs sung in Hebrew, Arabic, and English and set to danceable Euro-tech arrangements, Haza has brought the sounds of her homeland to the contemporary pop charts. Haza, who grew up in Tel Aviv, first attracted attention as a teenager in the early 1980s. Her international debut, *Fifty Gates of Wisdom: Yemenite Songs,* became the first Israeli album to sell a million copies in Europe and included Haza's hit "Galbi," which was later sampled by rap stars Eric B. and Rakim on their single "Paid in Full," and by M/A/R/R/S on "Pump Up the Volume." Haza has also sung on a lengthy list of albums by American and European artists including Paula Abdul and Thomas Dolby.

what to buy: The pop-minded production of Don Was inspired Haza to her greatest performance on *Kirya* 𝒥𝒥𝒥𝒥 (Shanachie, 1992, prod. Don Was). A successful blend of Yemenite traditions and modern dance rhythms, the album includes the percussive tune "Take 7/8," co-written with American multi-instrumentalist David Amram, and a unique rendition of the traditional American folksong "Do Not Forsake Me." Guest appearances range from saxophonist David McMurray and percussionist Itzha Levy to Iggy Pop and Lou Reed.

what to buy next: *Desert Wind* 𝒥𝒥𝒥𝒥 (Sire, 1989, prod. Bezalel Aloni), though it included more songs sung in English, thematically continued to reflect Haza's Yemenite heritage.

the rest:

Fifty Gates of Wisdom: Yemenite Songs 𝒥𝒥𝒥 (Shanachie, 1988/Cleopatra, 1998)
Shaday 𝒥𝒥𝒥𝒥 (Sire, 1988)

influences:

Yemenite music, European techno-disco

Paula Abdul, Natacha Atlas, Yosefa, modern ethno-techno

Craig Harris

scandinavian folk and beyond

The Scandinavian countries are currently experiencing a folk boom that is also revitalizing their pop and world-music scenes. Sweden's folk revival mirrors that of the United States during the 1960s. By the end of the 1950s, the Swedish folk tradition had almost been wiped out by the influence of European pop. Then the counterculture discovered folk music, leading to a rebirth of interest in traditional fiddling. The music got another jolt when Groupa began recording in the 1980s. They played traditionally, but promoted themselves like a pop band. Many of today's folkies started with Groupa, including Hallbus Totte Mattsson, founder of Hedningarna, whose electric approach brought folk music to the rock audience.

Finland's folk boom began in the 1970s with Konsta Jylha, a traditional fiddler from Kaustinen. In the mid-'70s, Piirpauke, arguably the world's first global fusion band, blended Finnish roots music with Arabic, Eastern European, Latin American, and African influences. Värttinä, the band that led the "Finnish Invasion" of the 1980s, came to their international fame almost by accident. The group's second album, *Oi Dai,* was one of the best-selling in the history of Finland—because the songs dealt with bawdy sex. Värttinä's success created worldwide interest in Finnish music; albums by Kaustinen fiddling group JPP, accordion ace Maria Kalaniemi, and mystical acoustic-rockers Gjallarhorn have all done well on the international market.

Norway's population is small, and the lack of nationwide commercial exploitation has allowed many unique regional styles to flourish. Traditional fiddler Annbjørg Lien uses Arabic and African beats in her compositions; Ym:Stammen play a dark, brooding kind of folk-rock that's perfectly suited to long winters and broken hearts; and Chateau Neuf Spelemannslag, billed as "Norway's biggest folk band," have a sprightly sound that should appeal to anyone who likes Värttinä.

j. poet

Hedningarna

Industrial Swedish-Finnish folk

Formed 1990s, in Sweden. Based in Sweden.

Core members: Anders Stake, hardingfele, electric violin, keyed harp, Swedish bagpipe, buckhorn, hurdy-gurdy, baseharp, stringharp, flutes, jew's harp, slide guitar, synthesizer; Björn Tollin, frame drums, keyed harp, stringdrum, percussion, programming, sampling; Hallbus Totte Mattson, teord, lute, electric violin, mashallute, hurdygurdy. (All members are from Sweden.)

It's as if someone, through the magic of time travel, found a place where the ideas of rave culture could happily co-exist with the creakiness of medieval music. That's really about the only way to describe Hedningarna (though for additional help, the name translates as "the heathens"). Whatever they've been putting in the water in Sweden has had an effect on its bands, who seem to be able to effortlessly mix past and future into some magical, mystical present. The core of Stake, Tollin, and Mattson got together in the early part of the '90s to mix up folk music, and that's what they succeeded in doing—so well that it's hard to tell the traditional material from their own compositions. After an eponymous debut album, they brought in two Finnish female vocalists, Sanna Kurki-Suonio and Tellu Paulasto, whose voices seemed to work in perfect harmony with the music. Then they took it all a step further with lots of sampling and programming on the follow-up *Kaski!,* a sort of 808 State meets early Fairport Convention in Macbeth's castle. One thing missing (but not missed) was the electric guitar, since guitar had never had much place in Swedish culture. Instead it was the fiddle, the keyed harp, and the hurdy-gurdy that lent instrumental textures. A third album, *Tra,* built on the second, with the quintet becoming a bit more electric though never losing its acoustic base. The year 1997 found Suonio and Paulasto back in Finland and Hedningarna recording as a trio again on *Hippjokk,* taking it all back to acoustic basics without ever losing the edge that electricity had given them. *Joiker* Wimme (an unearthly chant vocalist from the Northern Scandinavian Saami tradition) guested on the record. By 1998, vocalist Anita Lehtola had replaced Paulasto in yet another configuration of the band for its latest album.

what to buy: *Tra* ♫♫♫♫ (NorthSide, 1997, prod. Dag Lundquist, Hedningarna) initiates you into the magic. As rustic as a wagon-wheel stuck in mud, but still as modern as lasers in a dance club, there was nothing wasted; every note means something, and usually a lot. *Hippjokk* ♫♫♫♫ (NorthSide, 1997, prod. Dag Lundquist, Hedningarna) is just the core trio, and while it misses the female singers, it burns as steadily as a candle in the winter night, never failing to find a groove.

what to avoid: *The Heathens—Fire* ♫♫ (Sony, 1996) can hardly be terrible, as a compilation of Hedningarna's early work, but it does them little justice; stylistically mixed-up, with precious little information.

the rest:
Kaski! ♫♫♫ (NorthSide, 1998)
Karelia Visa N/A (NorthSide, 1999)

worth searching for: *Hedningarna* ♫♫♫ (Silence, 1990) is the first outing, newly hatched and curious.

influences:
◀ Traditional Swedish and Finnish folk music

see also: *Nordan Project, Wimme*

Chris Nickson

Joe Higgs

Reggae

Born 1940, in Kingston, Jamaica. Based in Jamaica.

Joe Higgs was one of the greatest influences on the development of reggae. Despite releasing only six solo albums, Higgs was a direct inspiration on Bob Marley & the Wailers, Jimmy Cliff, and Toots & the Maytals as a vocal coach, arranger, and guitar instructor. Replacing Bunny Wailer in the Wailers in 1973, Higgs also toured throughout the United States and Europe in 1975 as opening act, band director, and percussionist for Jimmy Cliff, who later recorded a song that Higgs wrote during the tour, "Sons of Garvey."

Higgs inherited his love of singing from his mother, who sang in a church choir. In the late 1950s and early 1960s, Higgs performed in a duo with Delroy Wilson. In 1959 they scored a major hit, "Oh, Manny, Oh," produced by future Jamaican prime minister Edward Seaga. After Wilson emigrated to the United States Higgs continued to perform on his own, his first solo hit, "There's a Reward," being produced by the legendary Coxsone Dodd at his storied Studio One. Years later, Higgs brought the Wailers to Dodd's attention, and got him to produce the group's early singles.

A high school music teacher, Higgs devoted most of his attention to that profession, and to coaching young reggae singers. The music sessions that he hosted nightly in the yard of his Trenchtown home served as a training ground for such future artists as Bob Marley. In 1972 Higgs placed first in a song competition sponsored by the Jamaican Tourist Board with his original tune, "Invitation to Jamaica." One of the prizes—a trip to New York—resulted in his becoming one of the first reggae artists to perform in the United States. After the 1973 and '75 tours with Marley & the Wailers and Cliff, Higgs resumed his solo career. His debut album, *Life of Contradiction,* was released in 1976, and in 1980 he had a hit in Jamaica with his song "Talk to That Man," recorded for Bunny Wailer's Solomonic label. Higgs worked with influential reggae guitarist Earl "Chinna" Smith in 1983, by which time he had established a stature in the field that rivaled his famed protégés and collaborators.

what to buy: After releasing two memorable albums in Jamaica, Higgs showed American listeners what they had missed with his first United States release, *Triumph!* ♪♪♪♪ (Alligator, 1985, prod. Joe Higgs, Earl "Chinna" Smith). Higgs displays his soulful vocal approach and heartfelt lyricism, accompanied by stellar Jamaican musicians including bassist Family Man Barrett, guitarists Junior Murvin and "Chinna" Smith, keyboardist Augustus Pablo, saxophonist Dean Fraser, and harmony singers Janice Pendarvis and Sonia Higgs. The peak of the album comes with a remake of his tune "Sound of the City." Originally recorded as a duet with Jimmy Cliff, the song is redone with Higgs overdubbing all the vocals himself.

what to buy next: His second American release, *Family* ♪♪♪♪ (Shanachie, 1988, prod. Edgy Lee, Lee Jaffe), is a further demonstration of Higgs's vocal mastery. Although the line-up of backing musicians is not as awe-inspiring as on *Triumph!,* the album sparkles with Rastafarian vision.

the rest:
Life of Contradiction ♪♪♪♪ (Grounation, 1976)
Unity Is Power ♪♪♪♪ (Elevation/Island, 1979)
Blackman Know Yourself ♪♪♪ (Shanachie, 1990)
Roots Combination ♪♪♪ (Macola, 1995)

influences:

◀◀ Count Ossie & His Mystic Revelers of Rastafari, King Tubby, the Skatalites

▶▶ Bob Marley & the Wailers, Jimmy Cliff, Toots & the Maytals

see also: *Jimmy Cliff, Barrington Levy, Bob Marley, Junior Murvin, Augustus Pablo, Toots & the Maytals, Wailing Souls, Bunny Wailer*

Craig Harris

Tish Hinojosa

Singer/songwriter, contemporary folk, Mexican-American
Born December 6, 1955, in San Antonio, TX, USA. Based in Austin, TX, USA.

Tish Hinojosa is a woman of the *frontera,* the border region of the southwestern United States and northern Mexico. The daughter of immigrants, she began her journey in music listening to the radio of both countries in her mother's kitchen as a child in San Antonio, Texas. She started her performing career singing folk music along San Antonio's Riverwalk, but soon decided she needed a change to develop her music, and moved to northern New Mexico. While absorbing the different cultures of that area, she encountered people who exposed her to the country rock of musicians Chris Hillman and Rodney Crowell, as well as the heartfelt mountain music of singers like Hazel Dickens. As she played in dance bands and for tourists, Hinojosa began to put these elements together in songs of her own. "My whole career up until that time had been doing other people's music," she recalls. "I realized that I had this whole bag of experiences I'd dragged around with me, going back to that Mexican kitchen radio, that I'd never heard addressed in song." An award-winning songwriter soon after, Hinojosa toured nationally on the college and folk club circuit. After several years of that life she made a move to country music center Nashville, Tennessee, where she got a job as an in-house demo singer for several companies. But it wasn't long before she found that her style of songwriting didn't fit the needs of Music City. "They liked my voice, but when I played my songs for them they'd look at me like I was from Mars!" she says. "And I'd hear the kind of things they were tossing back and forth. . . . It's an art, I guess, but I thought, 'This is too easy. This is not a challenging kind of songwriting.' Pretty soon we knew it was time to leave."

With her husband and young family, she moved back to New Mexico. Sorting through her Nashville experience, Hinojosa realized that after 10 years as a performer she still didn't have a recording to call her own, so she set out to make one. *Taos to Tennessee* was her calling card both to audiences and record executives. After a move to Austin, Texas, Hinojosa was approached by two major record labels, one that wanted to market her as a singer and ignore her writing, and another that wanted her for a new singer/songwriter series. She made the difficult choice to take the less lucrative deal with the greater creative control. Though Hinojosa's contract was bought out in a corporate restructuring and only produced one album, *Homeland,* that recording did bring her to another level of national exposure, prompting media comparisons to Nanci Griffith, Emmylou Harris, and Joan Baez. Her next album, *Culture Swing,* though delayed by the need to find a new record label, won a number of awards in the folk music genre. Several well-received records on independent labels followed, giving Hinojosa the chance to produce her own work, and to record two roots-oriented projects she'd long wanted to explore: a bilingual children's album and an all-Spanish disc of traditional and original music of the border. Though these projects were satisfying to the artist, and she continued an active touring career, her determination was still to reach a wider mainstream audience with her unique perspective in song. That led her back to Nashville to sign with Warner Progressive, a division of the label that also handles such genre-crossing musicians as Take 6 and Beth Nielsen Chapman. There she has so far released two discs: *Destiny's Gate,* which displays the many sides of her musical talent from poetic bilingual love songs to themes of social justice to up-tempo country shuffles; and a more introspective collection, *Dreaming from the Labyrinth/Soñar del Laberinto,* which explores the search for life's meaning.

what to buy: Tish Hinojosa is a multifaceted artist, an iconoclast like Bob Dylan and Emmylou Harris, unafraid to take risks with her music and to venture into new areas with each recording. "The light and dark colors of the border, the whole panorama of where I'm from, that's what I want to show in my music," she says. *Dreaming from the Labyrinth/Soñar del Laberinto* ✍✍✍✍ (Warner Bros., 1996, prod. Tish Hinojosa, Jim Ed Norman, Craig Barker) is a thought-provoking collection of songs exploring loss, love, and spiritual growth framed in the southwestern landscape images of Hinojosa's imagination. All the songs but one are bilingual, yet the words reference each other, rather than being translations. Both lyrically and musically it's a major creative achievement expressed in a group of very accessible and listenable songs—which seem to have missed everybody's radio playlist. There is an all-Spanish version as well, *Soñar del Laberinto* ✍✍✍✍ (Warner Bros., 1997, prod. Tish Hinojosa, Jim Ed Norman, Craig Barker). Though the songs are basically the same, it's intriguing to follow the progression of ideas laid out all in one language. A good introduction to Hinojosa's range of expression is *Destiny's Gate* ✍✍✍✍ (Warner Bros., 1993, prod. Tish Hinojosa, Jim Ed Norman), comprising English, Spanish, and bilingual love songs, country dance shuffles, and songs in the activist tradition. The title tune (which is reprised in an unlisted Spanish version at the end of the disc) is an example of Hinojosa's ability to write an economical and fresh love song, no matter what the style.

what to buy next: *Frontejas* ✍✍✍✍ (Rounder, 1995, prod. Tish Hinojosa) is a lively album containing original and traditional songs of the border, all in Spanish (except one guest appearance by Asleep at the Wheel's Ray Benson), which could find a home on the playlist of any progressive *Tejano* station. *Culture Swing* ✍✍✍✍ (Rounder, 1992, prod. Tish Hinojosa) delivers what the title promises, a trip through and between cultures, marked by a river journey ("By the Rio Grande"), a love song from a traveler ("Louisiana Road Song"), and a tribute to the last of the Spanish cowboys ("Chanate El Vaquero"). *Cado Niño/Every Child* ✍✍✍✍ (Rounder, 1996, prod. Tish Hinojosa, Craig Barker) is a bilingual children's album with lyrics and stories in both languages for sharing with the next generation.

the rest:
Taos to Tennessee ✍✍✍✍ (Watermelon, 1987)
Memorabilia Navideña ✍✍✍ (Watermelon, 1991)
Aquella Noche ✍✍✍✍✍ (Watermelon, 1991)
Best of the Sandia: Watermelon, 1991–1992 ✍✍✍✍ (Watermelon, 1997)

worth searching for: Hinojosa scored and narrates the television documentary *Rio Grande: La Frontera,* which shows up occasionally on U.S. public television stations, particularly in the southwest. She's seen performing several songs from *Frontejas* and one unrecorded song. She also done music and narration for a National Park Service film used at the San Antonio missions. She has appeared as guest vocalist on albums by many of her Austin/San Antonio/New Mexico musical friends, including Ray Wylie Hubbard, and Bill and Bonnie Hearne.

influences:
◄◄ Linda Ronstadt, Joan Baez, Guy Clark

Kerry Dexter

Fred Ho
Afro-Asian jazz fusion
Born in USA. Based in New York, NY, USA.

Wind player and composer Fred Ho is one of the leading figures in the Asian-American jazz movement, along with pianist Jon Jang, violinist Jason Hwang, and bassist Mark Izu. As leader of the multi-ethnic Asian-American Art Ensemble/Afro-Asian Music Ensemble, Ho has made it his mission to unite the disparate legacies of jazz-based improvisation and East Asian traditional music, achieving mixed results. His compositions and arrangements owe a clear debt to Duke Ellington, and they work best when not attempting to force a marriage of Asian- and African-American musics. The inclusion of traditional Chinese instruments like the *erhu* (two-stringed fiddle) and the oboe-like *suona* is sometimes inspired, sometimes mere exotica, and frequently deflects attention from his considerable gifts as a jazzman. Ho is also highly politicized, favoring compositions that address issues of Asian-American identity. Unfortunately, his agitprop grows wearisome upon repeated listenings, and he should let his music speak for itself—for there is much to appreciate in his intelligent ensemble writing and tasty work on saxophones and flute.

what to buy: *Tomorrow Is Now* ✍✍✍ (Soul Note, 1985) contains precision ensemble work and pithy soloing framed by Ho's finely crafted, wide-ranging charts.

what to avoid: As the title presages, on *We Refuse to Be Used and Abused* ✍✍ (Soul Note, 1987, prod. Giovanni Bonandrini) Ho's preachy diatribe on identity politics smothers what is otherwise commendable music.

the rest:
Bamboo That Snaps Back ✍✍✍ (Finnadar, 1985)
The Underground Railroad to My Heart ✍✍✍ (Soul Note, 1993)
Fred Ho and the Monkey Orchestra: Monkey: Part One ✍✍ (Koch Jazz, 1996)
Fred Ho and the Monkey Orchestra: Monkey: Part Two ✍✍ (Koch Jazz, 1997)
Turn Pain into Power ✍✍✍ (OO Discs, 1997)
Yes Means Yes No Means No (Koch Jazz, 1998)

influences:

◀◀ Duke Ellington, Charles Mingus, Charlie Haden's Liberation Music Orchestra

▶▶ Jon Jang, Jason Hwang, Francis Wong, Mark Izu

Dennis Rea

Hoelderlin Express /Hölderlin Express

"Electric Body Folk"
Formed 1992, in Tuebingen, Germany. Based in Tuebingen, Germany.

Elke Rogge, hurdy-gurdy; Joergen W. Lang, guitar, low whistle; Johannes Mayr, accordion (1992–94); Olav Krauss, six-string electric violin (1992–97); Ralf Gottschald, percussion (1994–present); Guray Atalay (Austro-Turkish), bass (1998–present). (All members are from Germany unless otherwise noted.)

Hoelderlin Express blends German roots and other folk traditions with jazz and rock. The group has been through a series of personnel changes that affected its always-evolving sound, but the core of Elke Rogge and Joergen Lang has remained intact. Hoelderlin's first rush to fame came when it won the German Folk Newcomers Prize at the 1993 Tanz & Folkfest Rudolstdat. Since then, it has toured all over Europe and released two full-length CDs, *Hölderlin Express* (1994) and *Electric Flies* (1996).

what's available: Despite the band's folkloric bent, *Hölderlin Express* ♪♪♪♪ (akku disk, 1994, prod. Heinrich von Kalnein) consists entirely of original compositions written by band members. Many are mini-suites, containing passages with varying rhythms, textures, and melodies. Each player in this first incarnation of Hoelderlin Express was an able lead instrumentalist, and all got their chance to shine. For instance, the hurdy-gurdy and fiddle trade hot riffs over a pulsing jazzy rhythm, and there's some snarling electric guitar mixed in as well. Johannes Mayr cuts loose with hot accordion licks on his original composition "Für Moritz." When it came time to record Hoelderlin Express's second CD *Electric Flies* ♪♪♪♪ (akku disc, 1996, prod. Heinrich von Kalnein), the membership had changed. Mayr had left (first to join the one-off band the Rolling Drones and then to try his hand in a new duo) and was replaced by percussionist Ralf Gottschald (who'd served as a session guest on the first recording). So the textures morphed and the overall sound became more aggressively rhythmic. Also, Elke Rogge's hurdy-gurdy came more to the fore; Hoelderlin Express is now a band in which the buzzing instrument isn't just used to color the arrangements, but actually plays lead melodies! Another departure from the debut album is a Middle Eastern flavor that pops up on several tracks. This is really brought out by Gottschald's dynamic playing. Lang gets to show off his acoustic guitar talents on his composition "A Win-

Fred Ho

ter's Day," a quieter number whose arrangement recalls the pioneering folk/jazz blend of England's Pentangle.

influences:

◀◀ Pentangle, Blowzabella, Pyewackett, Lo Jai

▶▶ Radio Tarifa, Shooglenifty, Tayfa

Ken Roseman

Home Service

English folk-rock
Formed 1981, in London, England. Disbanded early 1990s.

John Tams, vocals, guitar; Bill Caddick, vocals, dobro, guitar (1981–85); Jonathan Davie, bass guitar, chorus vocals; Howard Evans, trumpets, flugelhorn; Steve King, keyboards, accordion; Graeme Taylor, guitars, vocals; Roger Williams, trombone; Andy Findon, flutes, clarinets, tenor and soprano saxophones (1984–86). (All members are from England.)

Home Service, the most quintessentially English of all the major folk-rock bands, arose from one of genre pioneer Ashley Hutchings's Albion Band line-ups that had been providing music for stage productions at London's National Theatre. Ironically, Home Service wound up spending most of its all-too-

3/2/2 *home service*

brief career there as well. Home Service's first recording, a single featuring "Doing the Inglish" b/w "Bramsley," was released on August 7, 1981. No more recordings appeared until 1984, when *The Home Service,* the group's first full-length album, was released by Jigsaw. There had been occasional concert and festival appearances, and then, also in 1984, Home Service provided the music for *The Mysteries,* three contemporary adaptations of medieval plays based on the life of Jesus Christ. Band members also acted in the production, which was performed at the National Theatre and then moved to the Lyceum for a 12-week run the following year; an album featuring musical highlights from it was released at that time. Bill Caddick left Home Service in July 1985, and *Alright Jack,* the last of Home Service's trilogy of studio recordings, was issued in 1986. By then, the band had basically called it a day, though a slightly different line-up—Bill Caddick, Jonathan Davie, Alan Dunn (accordion, keyboards), Howard Evans, Andy Findon, Sebastian Guard (drums, percussion), Pete Murray (keyboards), Ralph Salmins (drums, percussion), Graeme Taylor, and Roger Williams—played a few live dates in 1992. *Wild Life,* released in 1995, features recordings of that incarnation, culled from gigs at the Half Moon in Putney, London; the Sidmouth Festival; and the Purcell Room (again at the National Theatre).

what to buy: *Early Transmissions* 🎵🎵🎵🎵 (Jigsaw, 1984/Road Goes on Forever, 1996, prod. Robin Black, Home Service) contains some of John Tams and Bill Caddick's finest original songs. Tams specialized in hymn-like anthems such as "Don't Let Them Grind You Down," while Caddick compositions such as "She Moves among Men" (a trenchant description of a waitress's lot) and "Never Gonna Be a Cowboy Now" (an eloquent lament about dashed dreams) were more reflective. Also included is a distinctive arrangement of the traditional ballad "Peat Bog Soldiers," given added majesty by the Home Service brass section. As a bonus, this reissue of Home Service's first album (originally released eponymously) collects the two songs issued as a debut single in 1981: "Doing the Inglish," a jaunty reggae/skiffle tune listing all sorts of things associated with England; and the semi-medieval dance instrumental "Bramsley," with modern brass instruments playing the sort of melody line crumhorns and shawms would have done hundreds of years ago. The basic Home Service band was augmented by several guests including Linda Thompson (vocals), Phil Langham (fiddle, accordion, vocals), Eve Matheson (backing vocals), and Phil Pickett (recorders, shawm, *rauschpfeife*) to record the "soundtrack" album for *The Mysteries* 🎵🎵🎵🎵 (CODA, 1985/Fledg'ling, 1997, prod. David Roach, John Tams). It's unlikely that the show (at least with this cast) will ever be performed live again, so think of this recording as a magnificent souvenir. There's a stunning version of the traditional "Wondrous Love," arranged by Graeme Taylor and featuring choir-like vocals backed by the full electric band—an ab-

solutely mesmerizing blend! You'll also a hear a powerful rendition of Richard Thompson's "We Sing Allelujah" and a fine Bill Caddick original, "Cain and Abel: Don't Be an Outlaw." For Linda Thompson fans, her *a cappella* styling of "All in the Morning" is a special treat. Last in the trilogy of Home Service studio recordings is *Alright Jack* 🎵🎵🎵🎵 (Making Waves/Hobson's Choice, 1986/Fledg'ling, 1997, prod. Home Service). A mini-suite of Home Service arrangements of traditional ballads set by Percy Grainger is this album's centerpiece. The instrumental passages really show what the brass section could do, and the inventive arrangements even sound like what George Gershwin might have done had he ever heard some English folk ballads. John Tams contributes two more of his stirring modern broadsides—the title song and "Scarecrow"—and his interpretation of "Rose of Allendale" is lovely. As a coda to Home Service's career (and a hint of what might have been), *Wild Life* 🎵🎵🎵🎵 (Fledg'ling, 1995) contains live recordings culled from performances by a short-lived '90s incarnation of the band. As might be expected *Wild Life* contains a few brassy march-like numbers, and there are live versions of such Home Service standards as "She Moves among Men," "Never Gonna Be a Cowboy Now," and "Scarecrow." But there are also songs not available on any other Home Service album, which is why completists will want this. Bill Caddick's "Lili Marlene Walks Away" has a Brecht-Weill mood, and "Rainbow Waistcoat" mixes a little rough bluesiness with the regal brass. The lads even try some honky-tonk on "One More Whiskey," a bit of a departure from the very English nature of most of Home Service's repertoire. To sum up, Home Service left us with only four full albums, but two were masterpieces and the others not far behind. The band was virtually unique in integrating brass into a solidly folk/traditional context, rivaled in this only by fellow Brits Brass Monkey—who were completely acoustic. And when John Tams sings one of his anthems, it's as if he personifies the spirit of England.

worth searching for: After he left Home Service, Tams concentrated on his acting career, appearing in films and television programs. *Over the Hills & Far Away—The Music of Sharpe* 🎵🎵🎵🎵 (Virgin, 1996, prod. John Tams, John McCusker, Dominic Muldowney), a soundtrack album for the *Sharpe's Rifles* television series (in which he also appeared as an actor), contains his latest studio recordings.

solo outings:
Bill Caddick:
Winter with Flowers (Fledg'ling)
The Wild West Show 🎵🎵🎵🎵 (Topic, 1986)

influences:
◀◀ The Copper Family, Steeleye Span, church hymns, silver bands, Percy Grainger, Ashley Hutchings/Albion Band, Susato, Ralph Vaughan Williams

▶ John Kirkpatrick Band, Brass Monkey, Jennifer Cutting/The New St. George (U.S.), La Bottine Souriante

see also: *Ashley Hutchings/Albion Band, Richard Thompson*

Ken Roseman

Sol Hoopii

Hawaiian jazz, blues, swing
Born 1902 in Honolulu, HI (now USA); died 1953.

Although mostly unknown by non-musicians, Hoopii is one of the most influential guitarists of the 20th century. His combination of Hawaiian music and jazz created a new, almost one-man genre, and he wrote the book of licks on which most dobro (Hawaiian guitar) and pedal steel players still rely. His experiments with open tunings influenced a generation of pickers, and a variation on his C# minor tuning is still used by today's session players in Nashville. Hoopii was born in Honolulu, the youngest of 21 children. He played guitar from his early teens, and at 17 stowed away on a liner bound for San Francisco. Legend has it that he was discovered by the crew, but when he whipped out his guitar and played for the other passengers, they were so enchanted they paid his way to the mainland. Hoopii settled in Los Angeles and formed a trio—guitar, ukelele, and Hoopii on dobro—that performed jazz and blues tunes featuring Hoopii's hot improvisations, and sounded like a stripped-down Hawaiian version of the Quintet of the Hot Club of France. Hoopii began recording in 1925 and helped kick off a Hawaiian music craze that led to his appearance in motion pictures both as a musician and actor, including Bing Crosby's *Waikiki Wedding* and parts in the Charlie Chan series. He was a much in-demand musical director, session player, and band leader until 1938, when he became a born-again Christian. For the next 10 years he traveled the Gospel circuit preaching and playing religious music, some of which he recorded for various small labels. He returned to secular music briefly for a 1948 tour of Hawaii, but continued preaching until his death in 1953.

what's available: Hoopii is at his best in the 1926 to 1930 sessions collected for *Master of the Hawaiian Guitar* 𝄢𝄢𝄢𝄢 (Rounder, 1977, prod Robert F. Gear). For years, early players "borrowed" these solos note for note, but Hoopii's sides remain as original as on the day they were cut. The tracks on *Sol Hoopii, Volume 2* 𝄢𝄢𝄢𝄢 (Rounder, 1987) from Hoopii's middle and late years are as cool, crisp, and inventive as his early work.

influences:
▶ Leon McAulliffe (Texas Playboys), Jimmy Helms (Hank Williams Band)

j. poet

Horch

Medieval/Baroque folk-rock fusion
Formed 1981, in Halle, Germany. Based in Halle, Germany.

Andreas Fabian, flute, recorders, shawm, crumhorn, vocals; **Klaus Adolphi,** vocals, guitars, mandolin, mandolin-cello, recorders, percussion, crumhorn; **Stefan Wieczorek,** basses, guitars, mandolin, recorders, bombardon, crumhorn, vocals; **Rainer Christoph Dietrich,** violin, viola, violin cello, synthesizer, vocals; **Ralph Schneider,** drums, percussion, vocals. (All members are from Germany.)

Reminiscent of the English band Gryphon and French band Malicorne, Horch plays a fusion of medieval, folk, and rock styles. Often, band members compose new music for centuries-old texts they've discovered. Founded in 1981, Horch went professional in 1984 and has released six full-length albums, beginning with *The Luteplayer* in 1987. Horch has played at concert halls, nightclubs, and major festivals, including Fairport Convention's annual bash in Cropredy, Oxfordshire, England (1994), and Germany's Tanz & Folkfest Rudolstdat (1991 and 1997). Horch's latest CD, *Schock Schwere Not,* was released in late 1998.

what to buy: *Schock Schwere Not* 𝄢𝄢𝄢𝄢 (Noise Art, 1998, prod. Adolphi, Ole, Horch) is the most forceful of Horch's recordings. Both the vocals and rhythm section are tougher and more aggressive than on earlier albums. "Das Testament," for example, uses a "heavy rock" beat and lead vocalist Klaus Adolphi adopts a gruff tone. The buzzing noises provided by crumhorns and other ancient instruments add to the distinctive sound. In fact, the crumhorn is played as a lead instrument on Andreas Fabian's composition "Jungfernsprung" and the bloody thing rocks as hard as any electric guitar! Like Steeleye Span, the Horch men are aces at singing full, precise harmonies over chugging electric "folk 'n' roll" instrumentals—check out "Die Dicke Margot" for proof. *Schock Schwere Not* closes with a surprising adaptation of Edgar Allan Poe's "The Raven." The band presents a grandiose version that starts off softly but, just a verse in, transforms Poe's lament into something verging on arena rock. I can hear the multitudes shouting along to the "Nevermore" chorus now. Those who'd prefer softer sounds might want to begin with *Barbaren* 𝄢𝄢𝄢𝄢 (Noise Art, 1996, prod. Adolphi, Ole, Horch), in which flutes and recorders play a more prominent role and the rhythms are less rocky. There's also the completely acoustic *Brantteweyn nebst Mägdeleyn* 𝄢𝄢𝄢𝄢 (Noise Art, 1995), which has a more folksy, sing-along flavor.

the rest:
The Luteplayer (1987)
Maria durch ein Dornwald ging (Amiga, 1988/ BMG, 1992)
Mittelalternativ (1991)

solo outings:
Klaus Adolphi:
Adolphi & Amigos 𝄢𝄢𝄢𝄢 (Metrix, 1993)

influences:

◀◀ Steeleye Span, Gryphon, Malicorne, Jethro Tull

▶▶ Adaro, U.L.M.A.N.

Ken Roseman

Horslips

Celtic rock

Formed 1970, in Dublin, Ireland. Disbanded 1980.

**Barry Devlin, vocal, bass; Charles O'Connor (England), vocal, con-
certina, fiddle, mandolin, guitar; Jim Lockhart, vocal, keyboards,
flute, whistle, pipes; Eamon Carr, drums, bodhrán, percussion, vocal;
Gus Guest, guitar (1970–71); Declan Sinnott, guitar (1971–72); Johnny
Fean, guitar, banjo, vocal (1972–80). (All members are from Ireland
unless otherwise noted.)**

Horslips were the first Celtic-rock band to come out of Ireland,
forging a unique brand of melodic modern music infused with
traditional tunes. They also broke the mold by insisting on succeeding in Ireland first, on their own record label (Oats), rather
than trying to get signed to a London major like their Irish rock
contemporaries. Their place in the history books was guaranteed by their first two albums, *Happy to Meet, Sorry to Part*
(1972) and *The Táin* (1973), which earned them considerable
acclaim at home and across the Irish Sea in Britain. These utilized rocked-up Irish tunes—several learned from Chieftains albums—with traditional words in both English and Irish on
Happy to Meet, and their own songs (based on a historical
saga) on *The Táin.*

After two other less overtly traditional albums came *Drive the
Cold Winter Away* (1975), an acoustic Christmas project, and
The Book of Invasions—A Celtic Symphony (1976), another concept album based on ancient Irish history. For the remainder of
their career the band opted for a decidedly rock-sounding approach, with Lockhart's flute unmistakably echoing Jethro Tull's
Ian Anderson, and sole English member O'Connor largely for-
saking his trademark mandolin, fiddle, and concertina for electric rhythm guitar. They toured North America to promote their
last few albums, which explored themes of emigration and
alienation, before calling it a day with a final fling at Whitla Hall
in Belfast in 1980 (immortalized on *The Belfast Gigs*).

Horslips' music is all distinguished by tasteful, fluid guitar
lines, inventive keyboards, a snappy rhythm section, sure-
footed post-Beatles harmonies, and a great sense of humor.
Their innovative use of Irish tunes—both plugged-in traditionals and brand-new rock songs about Irish history and legend—
was way ahead of its time. The best of their work stands up
surprisingly well after all these years; indeed much of what
today's Celtic-rock bands are doing, Horslips did 20 years earlier. The secret of their success may have been that they never

took themselves too seriously: after a night of rocked-up Irish
historical epics they were known to emerge for the encore
dressed like a cross between the Dubliners (identical long
bushy beards) and the Clancy Brothers (white Aran sweaters)
and tear into "Johnny B. Goode."

what to buy: The double-CD retrospective *Horslips Collection*
♪♪♪♪ (Outlet, 1985, prod. various) provides two-and-a-half
hours of album highlights and key non-LP singles. Belfast label
Outlet is getting good distribution in North America now.

what to buy next: *Happy to Meet, Sorry to Part* *♪♪♪* (Oats,
1972/Outlet, 1995, prod. Alan O'Duffy, Horslips) was recorded
at their own expense on the Rolling Stones' mobile studio, and
showcases a clever mix of acoustic traditional music, dazzling
electrified attacks on the same, and a style of original rock
song that fits comfortably alongside the rest. *The Táin* *♪♪♪♪*
(Oats, 1973/Outlet, 1989, prod. Alan O'Duffy, Horslips) is a rock
setting of an ancient Irish legend, and works perfectly well as a
tight progressive-rock album even if the listener is unaware of
the tunes' traditional sources (which are acknowledged in the
original sleevenotes). Like the Beatles' *Sergeant Pepper,* the
first side is a flawless suite of songs, but the album loses focus
on side two. The charming (if tentative-sounding) *Drive the
Cold Winter Away* *♪♪♪* (Oats, 1975/Outlet, 1995) was an all-
acoustic affair (their only such effort), and can claim to be one
of the very earliest Celtic Christmas albums. It is notable for the
incorporation of some English and Manx material. On *The Book
of Invasions—A Celtic Symphony* *♪♪♪* (Horslips, 1976/Outlet,
1995, prod. Alan O'Duffy, Horslips), the band tried to repeat the
success of *The Táin*: a suite of rock songs (again based on Irish
tunes) telling an ancient historical saga. It works quite well,
and was their last clearly tradition-based album. *Tracks from
the Vaults* *♪♪♪* (Horslips, 1977/Outlet, 1995, prod. various)
rounds up early singles and other oddities, the best of which
are also on *Horslips Collection.*

the rest:

Dancehall Sweethearts *♪♪♪* (Oats, 1974/Outlet, 1995)
The Unfortunate Cup of Tea! *♪♪♪* (Oats, 1975/Outlet, 1995)
Horslips Live *♪♪♪* (Horslips, 1976/Outlet, 1995)
Aliens *♪♪♪* (Horslips, 1977/Outlet, 1995)
The Man Who Built America *♪♪♪* (Horslips, 1978/Outlet, 1995)
Short Stories/Tall Tales *♪♪♪* (Horslips, 1979/Outlet, 1995)
The Belfast Gigs *♪♪♪* (Horslips, 1980/Outlet, 1989)

worth searching for: For completists only: Fean, O'Connor, and
Carr joined forces (using the moniker "Host") for another concept album, *Tryal* (Changeling, 1982), based on the true story of
a late-19th century "witch burning" in Ireland. Devlin issued
Breaking Star Codes (Starcode, 1983), a suite of songs based
on the 12 signs of the Zodiac, with the help of old pal Lockhart.

influences:

◀◀ The Chieftains, the Dubliners, the Beatles, Fairport Convention, Steeleye Span, Jethro Tull

▶▶ Alan Stivell, Moving Hearts, the Corrs, Leahy

see also: *Moving Hearts*

John C. Falstaff

The House Band

English/Celtic folk-pop fusion
Formed 1984, in England. Based in USA and England.

Ged Foley, vocals, acoustic and electric guitars, mandolin, Northumbrian pipes; Chris Parkinson, melodeons, keyboards, accordion, harmonica, vocals; Iain MacLeod, 10-string mandolin, guitar, vocals (1984–86); Jimmy Young, smallpipes, flute, whistles (1984–86); Brian Brooks, bouzouki, keyboards, whistle, vocals (1986–88); John Skelton, flutes, whistles, bombardes, bodhrán (1986–present); Roger Wilson, fiddle, guitar, viola, vocals (1995–present).

Ged Foley's trademark slow renditions of popular bar songs, Chris Parkinson's rhythmic accordion with a Cajun twist, and John Skelton's Breton (French Celtic) dance tunes on wooden flute—interspersed with shocking in-your-face *bombarde* (bagpipe) leads—make up the core of this unusual English/Celtic band. They have so much drive and variety in their arrangements it's easy to forget that for many years they were a three-piece. Foley played with both the Battlefield Band and Jez Lowe for several years before starting the House Band. Skelton played in London with an Irish band called Shegui, which also did Breton material. His driving flute-playing, European repertoire, and dry wit were a natural complement to Foley and Parkinson. Foley and Skelton have married Americans and now live in the States; Parkinson comes over to tour and teach with the band at least every other year. On more recent releases the House Band has added Mark Hellenberg on *bodhrán* and *dumbek* drums. Continually developing new material, they seem to come out with another CD every couple of years. In the musical chairs of the close-knit Irish-band scene, Foley can now also be found playing on and producing Patrick Street's latest endeavors.

what to buy: *Another Setting* 🎵🎵🎵🎵 (Green Linnet, 1994, prod. House Band) has the addition of Roger Wilson on fiddle. "Jig-jazz," as the title implies, stretches the concept of "jig" into a lighthearted, contemporary context. In good humor, there are echoes of Jamaica's Jolly Boys on "African Marketplace." The CD would be remiss without Ged singing a mellow Irish bar song. In this case, "Rocky Road to Dublin" takes on an ominous overtone in a sober rendition.

what to buy next: *Rockall* 🎵🎵🎵 (Green Linnet, 1996) is named after a desolate island north of the Hebrides that is associated with the BBC Shipping Forecast. Much of the music is from the north of England and on maritime topics. The band includes two moving songs about dying industries. There is a brilliant transition from "The Flat Cap," an unusual 3/2 English piece, into "Sgean Dhu," an old Scots 6/8 jig. The album ends with a spirited, contemporary Breton *bagad* (pipe band) march. *Stonetown* 🎵🎵🎵🎵 (Harbourtown/Green Linnet, 1991) received the British Retailers Association's award for Best Folk Album of 1992. *Groundwork* 🎵🎵🎵🎵 (Green Linnet, 1993, prod. House Band, David Kenny) is a partial compilation of the House Band's first two recordings, *The House Band* 🎵🎵🎵🎵 (Topic, 1985, prod. House Band, David Kenny) and *Pacific* 🎵🎵🎵🎵 (Topic, 1987, prod. House Band, David Kenny); both of the original recordings are out of print.

the rest:
Word of Mouth 🎵🎵🎵 (Green Linnet, 1989)
October Song 🎵🎵🎵 (Green Linnet, 1998)

worth searching for: John Skelton's recordings with the band Shegui, *All Around the World* (Green Linnet) and *In the Wind* (Highway, 1984), are worth seeking out. Chris Parkinson also has some obscure solo recordings he has produced himself.

influences:

◀◀ Battlefield Band, Shegui, Blowzabella, Kornog

▶▶ Rankin Family, Arcady

see also: *Battlefield Band, Patrick Street*

Karen Ashbrook

Hoven Droven

Swedish folk-rock
Formed 1989, in Östersund, Sweden. Based in Sweden.

Gustav Hylen, trumpet, flugelhorn, Härjedal-flute, congars (1989–97); Janne Strömstedt, organ (1997–present); Bo Lindberg, guitars; Björn Höglund, drums, percussion; Kjell-Eriok Eriksson, fiddle; Pedro Blom, bass; Jens Comén, saxophones. (All members are from Sweden.)

Hoven Droven is a Swedish folk-rock band with a mission to perform traditional material with a guitar-heavy sound.

what to buy: *Groove* 🎵🎵🎵🎵 (NorthSide, 1997, prod. various) is an excellent, hard-hitting instrumental compilation of two of the band's best Swedish albums, *Hia Hia* and *Grov*. The music is hard folk-rock that veers between the extremes of almost-heavy-metal and pastoral Swedish folk.

influences:

◀◀ Groupa, Hedningarna, Urban Turban

j. poet

3
2
6

david hudson

Ledward Kaapana of Hui Ohana

David Hudson

Australian Aboriginal

Born in North Queensland, Australia. Based in North Queensland, Australia.

A member of the Tjapukai tribe in Kurunda, northern Queensland, David Hudson mastered the *didgeridoo* (droning blown instrument) and interpretive dances of his people at an early age. Regarded as one of the world's finest "didg" players, Hudson first became known for his command of traditional styles and techniques, but eventually earned acclaim for his groundbreaking experiments in the instrument's creative possibilities—which included fitting one PVC pipe inside another to create a synthetic didg on which he could modulate the pitch, much like a trombone slide. Through his longstanding collaboration with American composer/producer Steve Roach, Hudson is credited with taking the art of the didgeridoo to a whole new level, using innovative techniques and modern compositional structures to move the ancient instrument boldly into the future. Helping to ensure that the original Australians' legacy is as long as their heritage is rich, in the late '80s Hudson co-founded the Tjapukai Dance Company, which has become one of Australia's premiere Aboriginal tourist attractions and recently developed the country's first Aboriginal theme park.

what to buy: If you're unfamiliar with Australian Aboriginal music in general or Hudson in particular, his greatest-hits collection *The Art of the Didjeridu: Selected Pieces 1987–1997* ♫♫♫♫ (Black Sun, 1997, prod. Steve Roach) is a great place to start. With 11 cuts culled from a variety of solo and collaborative albums, plus two previously unreleased tracks, this fantastic compilation is both a brilliant overview of Hudson's artistic development, and a stunning how-to lesson from one of the world's greatest didg masters.

what to buy next: *Gunyal* ♫♫♫♫ (Black Sun, 1998, prod. Steve Roach) is a fascinating concept album of sorts, transporting listeners back to a primordial time when Australia was an untamed land populated by an array of giant marsupials, reptiles, and birds. The vivid imagery of Roach's ambient textures combines organically with percussion, chants, and Hudson's hypnotically droning didg, producing a transcendental sound unlike anything you've ever heard.

the rest:
(With Steve Roach) *Dreamtime Return* 🎵🎵🎵 (Fortuna, 1988)
(With Steve Roach) *Australia: Sound of the Earth* 🎵🎵🎵 (Fortuna, 1990)
Woolunda 🎵🎵🎵🎵 (Celestial Harmonies, 1993)
Rainbow Serpent 🎵🎵🎵🎵 (Celestial Harmonies, 1994)
(With Michael Askill) *Free_Radicals* (Black Sun, 1996)

influences:
◀◀ Yothu Yindi, Gondwanaland, Blek Bela Mujik

see also: *Steve Roach, Synergy*

Bret Love

Hui Ohana /Ledward Kaapana

Hawaiian traditional and pop
Formed 1970s, in Hawaii, USA. Disbanded c. 1990.

Ledward Kaapana (born 1948, in Hawaii, USA), guitar, vocals; Nedward Kaapana, bass, vocals; Dennis Pavao, vocals, rhythm guitar. (All members are from USA.)

"Hui Ohana" is Hawaiian for "family group," a fitting name for a trio consisting of a set of twins and their cousin. This was one of the most successful of Hawaii's local groups during the 1970s and '80s. They recorded 14 albums before disbanding around 1990, though only a relative handful are still available—and mostly on local labels requiring a diligent search. When Hui Ohana broke up, guitarist Ledward Kaapana joined another group called I Kona, with which he recorded five albums. All three members of Hui Ohana have gone on to make solo albums as well, though Ledward's are the only ones to receive significant national distribution.

what to buy: Though it's atypical of the Hui Ohana sound, Ledward Kaapana's *Led Live Solo* 🎵🎵🎵🎵 (Dancing Cat, 1994, prod. George Winston) is certainly one of the easiest albums by any member of this group to find on the mainland. Recorded at an intimate venue, the album features not only Kaapana's wonderful guitar playing, but also his yodeling and informative between-song patter. *Kika Kila Meets Kihoalu* 🎵🎵🎵🎵 (BMG/Windham Hill/Dancing Cat, 1997) is a tasteful traditional duo outing by Ledward and mainland Hawaiian music patron Bob Brozman.

what to buy next: Hui Ohana's sound is marked by Ledward's deft picking—usually on electric guitar—and his cousin Dennis Pavao's ethereal falsetto, and *Hui Ohana* 🎵🎵🎵 (Paradise, 1987) serves as a fine introduction to the group's Hawaiian-pop style. Perhaps fittingly because of their falsetto trio harmonies, the title for *Live—Tahiti Come On Over* 🎵🎵🎵 (Paradise, 1989, prod. Tom Moffatt) comes from a Bee Gees tune. The group also arranges "Stars and Stripes Forever" Hawaiian-style, though

sean-nós singing

Sean-nós, or "old-style," singing refers to a specifically Irish tradition, generally of songs performed solo, without accompaniment, and in a rhythmically free and melodically decorated style. Not surprisingly, sean-nós singing has survived mainly in those areas of Ireland, known as *Gaeltacht,* where Irish Gaelic is still spoken, the principal centers being Donegal, Connemara (County Galway), and the southwest (Kerry and Cork). Although the singing of each region exhibits subtle stylistic differences, particularly in the manner of ornamentation, one main characteristic remains: sean-nós singing is about telling a story, often one that has special significance for the singer's audience, as it may relate actual events that have affected persons present or their relatives. Therefore, the melodic material is typically altered, through the introduction of ornaments or the use of elongated notes, to express the story as it unfolds verse after verse and as each singer sees fit to "tell" it—the songs may be venerable and are certainly familiar; it is the *way of singing* in which the sean-nós practitioner is encouraged, differentiated, and prized. Sean-nós has an instrumental parallel in slow airs, melodies borrowed from the sean-nós repertoire and performed on folk instruments like the uilleann pipes, the fiddle, or the flute, in a style consistent with the vocal tradition.

Philippe Varlet

elsewhere they settle into a more traditional sound on this live date from 1988. Less traditional but still intriguing is Ledward's album of collaborations with country and western musicians, *Waltz of the Wind* 🎵🎵🎵 (BMG/Windham Hill/Dancing Cat, 1998).

the rest:
Hui Ohana:
Volume I—Best of Hui Ohana 🎵🎵🎵 (Lehua, 1997)
Volume II—Best of Hui Ohana 🎵🎵🎵 (Lehua, 1997)
Hana Hou 🎵🎵🎵 (Lehua, 1998)
Kalapana to Waikiki 🎵🎵🎵 (Lehua, 1998)
Ke Kolu 🎵🎵🎵 (Lehua, 1998)
Live at Sounds Hawai'i 🎵🎵🎵 (Lehua, 1998)
Young Hawai'i Plays 🎵🎵🎵 (Lehua, 1998)

worth searching for: *Hawaiian Style Guitars* ♪♪♪ (Lehua, 1997, prod. Bill Murata, Charles Bud Dant) features alternating tracks by Hui Ohana and steel-guitar master Jerry Byrd.

influences:

◀◀ Fred Punahoa, Gabby Pahinui, Sonny Chillingworth

▶▶ George Kuo, Ozzie Kotani

Brian Mansfield

Zakir Hussain

Indian classical and popular music, world fusion
Born March 9, 1951, in Bombay, India. Based in India.

Zakir Hussain is not only a master of the *tabla,* an Indian hand drum capable of producing a range of tones, but he's acquired a full command of such older Indian percussion instruments as the *dhol, kho, duggi, dholak,* and *nal.* Best known for his work with the Grateful Dead's Mickey Hart in the Diga Rhythm Band and Planet Drum, and with jazz fusion guitarist John McLaughlin in Shakti, Hussain has consistently widened the musical traditions of his homeland. He inherited his musical aptitude from his father, Alla Rakha, a long-time tabla player for sitarist Ravi Shankar. Mastering the tabla as a youngster, Hussain made his U.S. debut as a sideman for Shankar during his concert at New York's Fillmore East in 1970. Three years later, Hussain took over the Tal Vadya Rhythm Band. The group evolved into the Diga Rhythm Band and, later, into Zakir Hussain and the Rhythm Experience. The Diga Rhythm Band's self-titled 1976 album marked Hussain's first recorded collaboration with Mickey Hart; he later performed on Hart's albums *Rolling Thunder, At the Edge,* and the *Apocalypse Now!* soundtrack. Hussain also toured and recorded with Hart's all-star percussion ensemble, Planet Drum, in 1991. In the mid-1970s, Hussain joined with Indian violinist L. Shankar and British guitarist John McLaughlin to form the acoustic world fusion band Shakti. Hussain was a featured musician on Ancient Future's 1990 album *World without Walls.* Since launching his own record label, Moment!, the same year, Hussain has collaborated with such Indian musicians as Pandit V.G. Jog, Ustad Sultan Kahn, Ustad Amjad Ali Kahn, and Girija Devi.

what to buy: Recorded during Hussain's concert with his father, Alla Rakha, at Ramkrishnan Mission Auditorium in Bombay, *Memorable Tabla Duet* ♪♪♪♪ (Chhanda Dhara, 1991, prod. Zakir Hussain) is a master class in Indian hand drumming.

what to buy next: The excitement of Hussain's performances with his band the Rhythm Experience is captured on *In Concert, Vol. 1: Live in Vancouver* ♪♪♪♪ (Eternal Music, 1997, prod. Zakir Hussain) and *In Concert, Vol. 2: Live in Vancouver* ♪♪♪♪ (Eternal Music, 1997, prod. Zakir Hussain).

the rest:

Tabla Duet ♪♪♪♪ (Chhanda Dhara, 1986)
Girija Devi & Zakir Hussain ♪♪♪ (Moment, 1988)
Ustad Amjad Ali Khan & Zakir Hussain ♪♪♪ (Moment, 1989)
Pandit V.G. Jog & Zakir Hussain ♪♪♪ (Moment, 1990)
Ustad Sultan Khan & Zakir Hussain ♪♪♪ (Moment, 1990)
Zakir Hussain & the Rhythm Experience ♪♪♪♪ (Moment, 1991)
Elements: Space ♪♪♪ (Music Today, 1994)
Sambandh ♪♪♪ (Terrascape, 1996)
Making Music ♪♪♪♪ (ECM, 1997)
Magical Moments of Rhythm ♪♪♪ (Eternal, 1998)
Essence of Rhythm ♪♪♪ (PolyGram, 1998)

influences:

◀◀ Alla Rakha, Ravi Shankar

▶▶ John McLaughlin, Mickey Hart

see also: *Hari Prasad Chaurasia, Diga Rhythm Band, Mickey Hart, Ali Akbar Khan, Bill Laswell, G.S. Sachdev, Shakti, L. Shankar, Ravi Shankar, Shiv Kumar Sharma, T.H. "Vikku" Vinayakram*

Craig Harris

Ashley Hutchings /The Albion Band

English folk and folk-rock
Born January 26, 1945, in Southgate, Middlesex, England. Based in England.

Elton John was recently knighted. If the British are serious about honoring musical heroes, Ashley Hutchings's time is long overdue. No one person has done more to re-invigorate and popularize English folk traditions than "the Guv'nor." Like many teens of his generation, Hutchings fancied himself a rock 'n' roll star and even led a series of rock 'n' roll bands in the mid-1960s. But his initial claim to fame would come as a bassist with folk-rock pioneers Fairport Convention. It was during his later Fairport days that he discovered traditional music, and he was one of the driving forces behind Fairport's landmark *Liege and Lief* set, one of the first recordings to blend Anglo-Celtic folk music with rock. That project altered Hutchings's career forever. He left Fairport in 1969 to more seriously pursue the goal of revitalizing traditional music, and the first step on this career path was the formation of Steeleye Span, with whom he recorded three albums. Since leaving Steeleye in 1971, Hutchings has concentrated on expanding his vision of a specifically English-rooted contemporary music by leading numerous incarnations of the Albion Band (a.k.a. the Albion Country Band, the Albion Dance Band), and producing a series of one-time-only projects such as *Morris On* (new arrangements of tunes from the British morris folk dance tradition), *The Compleat Dancing Master* (new

Zakir Hussain

arrangements of different kinds of dance tunes with readings), and even a romantic song cycle (*By Gloucester Docks I Sat Down and Wept—A Love Story*). Hutchings went so far as to star in a one-man stage production called *An Evening with Cecil Sharp and Ashley Hutchings,* in which he portrayed himself and the famed song researcher. He has amassed quite a collection of tapes from all of his projects, and some of this fascinating archival material is now available for all to hear on the four-CD set *The Guv'nor.* At the 1997 Cropredy festival, Hutchings narrated the Fairport Convention "oldies" set and led the opening number: his song "Wings," which looks back fondly on the growth of English folk-rock. A full studio version of "Wings" appears on *Happy Accident,* the CD that marked the Albions' return to an electric format after several years as an acoustic band. The year 1999 saw the release of *Before Us Stands Yesterday,* the first Albion Band CD to feature vocalist Gillie Nichols as a full member. At presstime Hutchings had begun recording music for a new television series, *The Ridgeway Riders,* with Phil Beer and Chris While, both of whom had participated in earlier Albion Band line-ups. With this ongoing legacy in all media, no traditionalist ever had his eyes more on the future.

what to buy: Phil Pickett's collection of "early music" instruments added a distinctive color to the arrangements of traditional dance tunes featured on *The Prospect Before Us* 𝄞𝄞𝄞𝄞 (EMI/Harvest, 1976/Hannibal, 1996, prod. Ashley Hutchings, Simon Nicol). *Rise Up Like the Sun* 𝄞𝄞𝄞𝄞 (EMI/Harvest 1978, prod. Joe Boyd, John Tams), credited to the Albion Band, was not as dance-oriented, and John Tams's role in the band had become much more prominent. He served as co-producer, did a lot of the lead singing, and brought in many of the songs. Among the Albion classics included on this album are "Ragged Heroes" (a Tams composition), "Poor Old Horse," and Richard Thompson's "Time to Ring Some Changes."

what to buy next: *Battle of the Field* 𝄞𝄞𝄞𝄞 (Island, 1976, prod. John Wood) features a never-to-be-duplicated line-up: Hutchings, Martin Carthy, John Kirkpatrick, Sue Harris, and Roger Swallow. *Twangin' n' a-Traddin* 𝄞𝄞𝄞 (Wildcat, 1995, prod. Ashley Hutchings), something completely different, was credited to a unit called the Ashley Hutchings Big Beat Combo. It's an unlikely pairing of morris and surf music—but who could resist an album that (one) credits Richard Thompson with playing electric guitar and pennywhistle and (two) includes a swingin' little tune called "Twistin' Welsh Girls"? It's a fitting reminder that Hutchings, now revered as a traditionalist, started out as a rock and rollin' Duane Eddy fan. For a comprehensive overview, completists will want *The Guv'nor* 𝄞𝄞𝄞𝄞 (HTD, compilation prod. Ashley Hutchings, Tim Woodward), a four-CD set that includes previously unreleased material from all periods of Hutchings's career. The Albions' latest full-length recording, *Be-*

fore Us Stands Yesterday 𝄞𝄞𝄞𝄞 (HTD, 1999, prod. Albion Band), demonstrates that Ashley Hutchings and Ken Nicol have become an effective songwriting team, creating memorable nouveau folk ballads with a certain English stateliness. Gillie Nichols is the latest to join the long line of ace female vocalists who've recorded with the Albions, a distinguished list that includes Shirley Collins, Cathy Lesurf, Polly Bolton, Chris While, and Julie Matthews.

best of the rest:
(With the Albion Band) *In Concert* 𝄞𝄞𝄞𝄞 (Windsong, 1993)
(With the Albion Band) *Acousticity* 𝄞𝄞𝄞𝄞 (HTD, 1993)
(With the Ashley Hutchings Dance Band) *A Batter Pudding for John Keats* 𝄞𝄞𝄞𝄞 (HTD, 1996)
The Best of '89/'90 𝄞𝄞𝄞𝄞 (HTD, 1998)

worth searching for: *Lark Rise to Candleford* (Charisma, 1979), credited to Keith Dewhurst and the Albion Band, contains music (and some spoken excerpts) from the stage production. The core of the Albion line-up involved—including John Tams—went on to form the magnificent Home Service.

influences:
◀◀ Fairport Convention, Steeleye Span, Cecil Sharp, Mr. Fox

▶▶ Home Service, Oyster Band, Jennifer Cutting/The New St. George (U.S.)

see also: *Martin Carthy, Shirley Collins, Fairport Convention, Home Service, Trevor Lucas, Cecil Sharp (sidebar) Steeleye Span, Richard Thompson*

Pamela Murray Winters and Ken Roseman

Huun-Huur-Tu
Tuvan traditional, khöömei (throat-singing)
Formed 1992, in Kyzyl, Tuva. Based in Kyzyl, Tuva.

Kaigal-ool Khovalyg, vocal, throat-singing (khöömei, sygyt, kargyraa), igil, khomuz; Anatoly Kuular, vocal, throat-singing (barbangnadyr), byzaanchi, khomuz, amyrga, ediski (birchbark reed); Sayan Bapa, vocal, throat-singing (kargyraa, khöömei), doshpuluur, marinhuur, guitar, synthesizer; Alexei Saryglar, vocal, throat-singing (sygyt), tuyug (horse hooves), xapchyk (bull testicles), tungur (shaman drum), igil, konguluur (1997–present); Albert Kuvezin, voice, guitar (1992–94); Alexander Bapa, tungur, dazhaanning khavy, amarga, bells (1993–96). (All members are from Tuva.)

The remote Siberian republic of Tuva boasts a unique musical tradition of overtone singing called *khöömei,* with obscure relations to Tibetan chant. This rustic singing of herders and hunters, accompanied on horse-hoof and bull-testicle percussion, horse-hair fiddles, Tuvan banjos, and other instruments, is best represented by Huun-Huur-Tu, the name depicting both the refraction of sunlight in the Tuvan countryside and the "re-

Kaigal-ool Khovalyg of Huun-Huur-Tu

fraction of sound" in throat-singing. Khöömei is practiced by dividing the mouth into separate cavities and adjusting the harmonic resonance of each to produce a polytonal sound. Huun-Huur-Tu takes the style into new territory by using non-Tuvan instruments like guitar and synthesizer and collaborating with non-Tuvans, including performers from Scotland, Bulgaria, and Russia. Despite this flexibility, the integrity and power of their music somehow remains intact. Huun-Huur-Tu's style alternates equally between a mesmerizing shamanic drone sometimes resembling Native American music, and an easygoing, cantering folk melody sometimes reminiscent of cowboy music. One of the most interesting groups in world music, Huun-Huur-Tu must be heard to be believed.

what to buy: You might start with their first recording, *60 Horses in My Herd* ✍️✍️✍️✍️ (Shanachie, 1993, prod. Alexander Bapa), to get a sense of what Huun-Huur-Tu does. It contains the masterpiece "Fantasy on the Igil," an absolutely indispensable piece of music. *The Orphan's Lament* ✍️✍️✍️✍️ (Shanachie, 1994, prod. Alexander Bapa) contains the amazing "Prayer," a Tibetan chant–like piece that can also be heard in various arrangements for mixed Tuvan and Bulgarian singers on *Fly, Fly My Sadness* and *Deep in the Heart of Tuva* ✍️✍️✍️ (ellipsis arts . . ., 1996, compilation prod. Ralph Leighton), which is reviewed in this book's Compilations section.

what to buy next: *Fly, Fly My Sadness* ✍️✍️✍️✍️ (Shanachie, 1996, prod. Ulrich Balss, Mikhail Alperin) is a beautiful recording, and it shows the group's adaptability. Former members of the Bulgarian State Television Female Vocal Choir (perhaps better known as Le Mystère des Voix Bulgares) join Huun-Huur-Tu for a stunning combination of two of the world's most unique singing styles. Recorded in the Netherlands, *If I'd Been Born an Eagle* ✍️✍️✍️✍️ (Shanachie, 1997, prod. Sayan Bapa) mixes pure Tuvan music with various influences. "Don't Frighten the Crane" is a particularly beautiful Tuvan folk song. *Where Young Grass Grows* ✍️✍️✍️ (Shanachie, 1999, prod. Niall Macaulay, Alexander Bapa) shares some material with *Tuva, Among the Spirits: Sound, Music and Nature in Sakha and Tuva* ✍️✍️✍️✍️ (Smithsonian Folkways Recordings, 1999, prod. Ted Levin, Joel Gordon), and highlights their musical connection to animals and the Tuvan countryside.

the rest:
(With the Bulgarian Voices Angelite and Moscow Art Trio) *Mountain Tale* ✍️✍️✍️ (Zebra Acoustic Records, 1999)

worth searching for: *Much Better* ✍️✍️✍️ (GreenWave, 1998, prod. Vladimir Volkov) is an interesting recording by the jazzy Russian ensemble the Volkov Trio, assisted by Kaigal ool-Khovalyg and others, including sometime Huun-Huur-Tu collaborator Sergey Starostin on various instruments. Starostin and Arkady Shilkloper are from the Moscow Art Trio, which also ap-

pears on *Mountain Tale*. Other musicians on *Much Better* include Igor Butman, Mola Sylla, and Olivier Ker-ourio. Styles range from bluesy fusion to Tuvan drone. Khovalyg's *igil* (two-stringed fiddle) and khöömei are accompanied on one track by an Australian didgeridoo-like alphorn. Khovalyg and Anatoly Kuular also appear on Frank Zappa's *Civilization Phaze III* ✍️✍️✍️✍️ (Barking Pumpkin Records, 1994), and the Kronos Quartet's *Night Prayers* ✍️✍️✍️✍️ (Nonesuch Records, 1994) and *Early Music (Lachrymae Antiquae)* ✍️✍️✍️✍️ (Nonesuch Records, 1997).

influences:
◀◀ Indigenous Tuvan music

see also: *Chirgilchin, Kronos Quartet, Le Mystère des Voix Bulgares, Yat-Kha*

David Paul

Abdullah Ibrahim /Dollar Brand

Jazz

Born Adolph Johannes Brand, October 9, 1934, in Cape Town, South Africa. Based in New York, NY, USA.

The rhythms of Africa are combined with the improvisations of post-bop jazz by South Africa–born pianist, composer, and bandleader Abdullah Ibrahim. A disciple of Duke Ellington who initially recorded as "Dollar Brand," Ibrahim has been a major influence on modern jazz for more than three decades.

The son of a church choir leader and the grandson of a church pianist, Ibrahim began learning to play piano at the age of seven. In addition to being influenced by the music he heard in Cape Town—which included traditional African dance music, hymns, and carnival songs as well as American and British pop and R&B—Ibrahim was inspired by the playing of jazz pianists Meade Lux Lewis and Fats Waller.

Beginning his professional music career as a vocalist with the Streamline Brothers, Ibrahim switched to piano after joining the Tuxedo Slickers. In 1959 Ibrahim, along with saxophonist Kippie Moketsi and trumpet player Hugh Masekela (the first giant of African music with whom he would be associated), formed the Jazz Epistles. Although the group became popular in South Africa, Ibrahim and his wife-to-be, Sathima Bea Benjamin, left the continent in spring of 1962 to live in a variety of locales in Europe. Settling in Switzerland for a year, Ibrahim performed regularly in a coffeehouse in Zurich. A turning point came when Duke Ellington toured the country, and, at the urging of Benjamin, listened to Ibrahim's playing. Four days later, he was invited to record with Ellington in Paris.

Following successful appearances, with a trio, at the Antibes Jazz Festival in 1964, Ibrahim began composing arrangements for a large orchestra, including the five-part suite "Anatomy of a South African Village." Ibrahim continued to work in a small format as well, recording several trio albums with fellow expatriates Johnny Gertze and Makaya Ntshako. In 1965, Ibrahim performed his debut American concert at Carnegie Hall, and appeared at the Newport Jazz Festival. While in the United States, he played piano for five East Coast performances by the Ellington Orchestra. The following year, Ibrahim collaborated on albums with the Elvin Jones Band and saxophonist Gato Barbieri.

Converting to Islam and adopting his current name in 1968, Ibrahim recorded several free-jazz albums in Europe and Canada. Although he temporarily settled in Swaziland in 1971, he spent most of his time on tour throughout Europe and North America. In 1973, Ibrahim recorded a big-band album, *African Space Program*, in New York, featuring jazz musicians Sonny Fortune, Cecil McBee, and John Stubblefield. Returning to his homeland in 1974, Ibrahim recorded several tunes with South African musicians, including "Mannenburg" (a.k.a. "Soweto Is Where It's At"), which became a theme song of the post-Soweto uprising in 1976. Angered by the oppression of apartheid, Ibrahim again left South Africa in 1976 and moved to New York. After launching his own production company, Ekapa/RPM, he recorded duo albums with Archie Shepp, Max Roach, and Johnny Dyani. Ibrahim continued a prolific output, releasing more than two dozen albums between 1973 and 1983. In 1991, he returned to his country yet again and recorded with South African musicians for the first time in 15 years. The resulting album, *Mantra Mode*, remains one of his most expressive recordings.

what to buy: Recorded live during a trio concert at Copenhagen's Cafe Montmartre, *Anatomy of a South African Village* ♫♫♫♫ (Black Lion, 1965, prod. Alan Bates) recalls Ibrahim's homeland with an expressive five-part suite. In addition to a six-tune suite dedicated to the influence of Fats Waller, Duke Ellington, and Thelonious Monk, *Sangoma* ♫♫♫♫ (Sackville, 1973, prod. Dollar Brand) features several compositions that capture the spirit and atmospheric sounds of South Africa.

best of the rest:
African Sketchbook ♫♫♫♫ (Enja, 1963)
Duke Ellington Presents the Dollar Brand Trio ♫♫♫♫ (Warner Bros., 1963)
Soweto ♫♫♫♫ (Chiaroscuro, 1965)
Cape Town Fringe ♫♫♫♫ (Chiaroscuro, 1965)

Round Midnight at the Montmartre ♫♫♫♫ (Black Lion, 1965)
African Piano ♫♫♫♫ (ECM, 1969)
African Portraits ♫♫♫♫ (Sackville, 1973)
Ancient Africa ♫♫♫♫ (Sackville, 1973)
Good News from Africa ♫♫♫♫ (Enja, 1973)
African Space Program ♫♫♫♫ (Enja, 1973)
Echoes from Africa ♫♫♫♫ (Enja, 1979)
African Marketplace ♫♫♫♫ (Elektra, 1979)
Montreux in '80 ♫♫♫♫ (Enja, 1980)
African Dawn ♫♫♫♫ (Enja, 1982)
Zimbabwe ♫♫♫♫ (Enja, 1983)
South Africa ♫♫♫♫ (Enja, 1986)
African Sun ♫♫♫♫ (Kaz, 1989)
Voice of Africa ♫♫♫♫ (Kaz, 1989)
African River ♫♫♫♫ (Enja, 1989)
Anthem for the New Nations ♫♫♫♫ (Denon, 1991)
Mantra Mode ♫♫♫♫ (Enja, 1991)
African Horns ♫♫♫♫ (Castle, 1994)
South African Ambassador ♫♫♫♫ (Jazzfest, 1997)
Cape Town Flowers ♫♫♫♫ (Tip Toe, 1997)

influences:

◀◀ Duke Ellington, Fats Waller, Thelonious Monk

▶▶ Hugh Masekela, Chris McGregor

see also: *Hugh Masekela*

Craig Harris

Immigrant Suns

Balkan-inspired rock
Formed 1992, in Detroit, MI, USA. Based in Detroit, MI, USA.

Doug Shimmin, strumstick, melodica, banjo, trumpet, bouzouki, baritone ukulele, mandolin, guitar, accordion, vocals; Ben Temkow, violin, balalaika, euphonium, accordion, pennywhistle, mbira, piano, vocals; Joel Peterson, bass, cello, clarinet, vocals; Mark Sawasky, doubek, tar, talking drum, riqq, bongos, conga, ghatam, traps, euphonium, vocals; Djeto Juncaj, qytelli, cello, guitar, accordion, tenor banjo, toy marimba, toy flute, vocals. (All members are from the USA.)

The Immigrant Suns met as members of various Detroit-area rock bands looking for other realms to explore. Djeto Juncaj, who was born in Montenegro, was seeking to experiment with the *qytelli* (a small, two-stringed lute native to Albania) in a rock context. Because the other folks in his regular band didn't want to blend Juncaj's qytelli into the mix, he ended up jamming with another ensemble that included Doug Shimmin and Mark Sawasky. The next member to join the budding group was Joel Peterson and he, in turn, brought Ben Temkow into the fold. This was the quintet that, in 1992, became the Immigrant Suns. His desire to create a hybrid form made Juncaj the initial focus of the band, but the other members contributed ideas from their own ethnic backgrounds. Greek and Polish elements crept into the music as did Armenian, Arabic, Hispanic, Hungarian, Gypsy, and klezmer influences. The results are reminiscent of the international esoterica that David Lindley's '60s-era rock group Kaleidoscope used to drench its tunes in.

what's available: Their first effort, *Montenegro* ♫♫♫ (Pho-net-ic Records, 1994, prod. Frank Pahl, the Immigrant Suns), still holds up to repeated listening, but the band was just developing an artistic identity and it was obvious that better things were possible if it could just stay together. The song titles tend toward youthful irreverence ("Blue Moons and Flying Pigs" and "Creamy Italian" being two memorable examples), but their musical vision adapts Balkan-oriented folk sounds to rock sensibilities with surprising success, foreshadowing the band's next release, *Back from Durbecca* ♫♫♫♫ (Pho-net-ic Records, 1996, prod. the Immigrant Suns). "Serpentine," the first song on the album, is a stunningly idiomatic instrumental draped in Balkanisms. The rest of the disc takes off from there to visit a wry lyricism upon space-age belly dance rhythms and the occasional Spanish tinge ("Muchacha" and "El Toro"). As a bit of inspired (yet directed) eclecticism, this set created a standard for their third album, *More Than Food* ♫♫♫♫♫ (Pho-net-ic Records, 1998, prod. the Immigrant Suns). Although it was recorded at six different studios, *More Than Food* is surprisingly unified. On this disc, the Immigrant Suns are solidifying their aesthetic, converging on a style that lets them take a subversive approach to Lennon & McCartney's "Girl" without sacrificing the ethnic element. Hits here include the darkly dancing "Gifikás" and "Kafé Turké," with a bizarro Dick Dale-ish "Surfin' Albania" tossed in for good measure.

influences:

◄ Kaleidoscope, Simon Shaheen, Muzikás

Garaud MacTaggart

Impact All Stars

Dub reggae
Active 1972–75, in Kingston, Jamaica.

The only permanent members of the Impact All Stars were: Errol "ET" Thompson, engineering, mixer; Clive Chin, producer, arranger. (Both members from Jamaica.)

Randy's Studio 17—run by Vincent "Randy" Chin—was open for business from 1968–77 and during its run hosted producers from Bunny Lee to Niney the Observer to Lee "Scratch" Perry to—most importantly for our story here—the great Clive Chin. The studio's resident engineer was Errol "ET" Thompson, considered one of the island's best-ever mixers. More than anything, the name "Impact All Stars" refers to Thompson's steady, inventive hand at the control board, for the Impact All Stars

weren't a group so much as a name given to the various musicians who worked at Studio 17 during the 1972–75 period under Clive Chin's production. The tracks were dubbed up by ET and compiled first on the Impact! label's *Randy's Dub* in 1975—total pressing: 200—and then on Blood & Fire's 1998 reissue of that album (with bonus tracks), *Forward the Bass: Dub from Randy's 1972–75*.

what's available: *Forward the Bass: Dub from Randy's 1972–1975* ♫♫♫♫ (Blood & Fire, 1998, reissue prod. Steve Barrow) is wonderful: although not as wild as the dub that King Tubby and Scratch were turning out at the time, it makes up for the kind of liberal sound-painting so beloved of dub freaks by concentrating its psychedelic efforts on drums and bass, which get blurry but never lose their way beneath single instruments dropping in and out of the mix. Following five tough, naked instrumentals utilizing almost no studio effects, the rhythms get blurrier while up top we're treated to rewinding tape solos, echoing vocals, and, on the best track, "Easy Come Dub," a pealing piano kneeling on your lobes and caressing your inner ear. *Forward the Bass* is a welcome addition to any dub collection, and a good place to begin one.

worth searching for: Although the Impact All Stars never recorded anything under that name until the songs compiled on *Forward the Bass,* fans of the album are urged to find a copy of *Rebel Rock Reggae—This Is Augustus Pablo* ♫♫♫♫ (Heartbeat, 1986), produced at Randy's by Clive Chin. Similarly basic and deceptively simple, this is one of the great reggae albums.

influences:

◄ Upsetters, King Tubby, Skatalites

►► Spring Heel Jack, Mad Professor, Badawi

see also: *King Tubby, Augustus Pablo, Lee "Scratch" Perry*

Michaelangelo Matos

Indigenous

Blues rock
Formed 1994, on the Yankton reservation in SD, USA. Based in Marty, SD, USA.

Mato Nanji, guitars, vocals; Wanbdi, drums, vocals; Pte, bass, vocals; Horse, percussion, vocals. (All members are from USA.)

This Native American group—two brothers, a sister, and a cousin—grew up together on a South Dakota reservation. Nurtured by a father/uncle who played in a '60s and '70s band called the Vanishing Americans and who introduced them, via his extensive record collection, to blues and soul, the quartet began playing when its members were pre-teens and never stopped. After a couple of self-produced discs, they hit the rock circuit, sharing the stage with Jonny Lang, Keb' Mo', and Chris

Duarte and crossing the country with their high-energy blues/rock stage show—heavy on the drums/percussion rhythm section and fronted by Nanji's explosive guitar pyrotechnics, which rarely stray from the Carlos Santana/Jimi Hendrix/Stevie Ray Vaughan axis.

what's available: *Things We Do* ♪♪♪ (Pachyderm, 1998, prod. Brent Sigmeth, Indigenous) is full of the same kind of Stratocaster braggadocio that underpins their stage show. Nanji's voice and guitar generally tend toward Vaughan-inspired excess, but the album is balanced by several songs that derive from the leaner, more economical approach of "Big Head" Todd Park Mohr.

influences:
◀◀ Stevie Ray Vaughan, Carlos Santana, Buddy Guy, Albert King, Big Head Todd and the Monsters

Leland Rucker

Inkuyo
Andean fusion
Formed 1987, in USA. Based in USA.

Gonzalo Vargas (Bolivia), quena, quenacho, sikus, antara; Enrique Coria (Chile), guitar tiple; Salmon Perez (Bolivia), charango, bandurria, drums, vocals; Danile Zamorra (Chile), bass (1993–94); Pamela Darington (USA), vocals, guitar, percussion (1987–94).

The region of South America once inhabited by the Incas—the mountain areas of Peru, Ecuador, Bolivia, Chile, and Argentina—has its own distinct musical tradition, defined more by the culture of the highlands than by national boundaries. This flute-and-percussion-based music is the source of Inkuyo's compositions, and indeed they have recorded many songs based on traditional tunes while investigating other influences. The varied backgrounds of the group's members, and their residence in the United States, have exposed them to elements of *nueva canción* (the activist, folkloric "new song" movement), *decima* (a popular structure for often-improvised poetry), and rock 'n' roll which they've begun to incorporate into their music while maintaining strong identification with and respect for Andean folklore.

what to buy: *Ancient Sun* ♪♪♪♪ (Celestial Harmonies, 1996, prod. Gonzalo Vargas), which shows the strongest influences of musics beyond the Andes, is a good listen for the current direction of the group. *Land of the Incas* ♪♪♪♪ (Fortuna, 1990, prod. Inkuyo) is a lively collection of originals which give the feeling of a journey though the mountains, stopping to share celebrations and insights along the way. Both include liner notes with useful information on the structure and background of the music.

the rest:
Temple of the Sun ♪♪♪♪ (Fortuna, 1990)

Double Headed Serpent ♪♪♪♪ (Celestial Harmonies, 1993)
Art from Sacred Landscapes ♪♪♪♪ (Celestial Harmonies, 1995)
Window to the Andes N/A (Celestial Harmonies, 1998)

influences:
▶▶ Sukay

Kerry Dexter

Inti-Illimani
Andean, Latin American, folklorico, nueva canción
Formed 1967, in Santiago, Chile. Based in Chile.

Horacio Salinas, music director, guitar, cuatro, tiple, charango, percussion, vocals; Jose Seves, guitar, quena, sikis, rondador, Mexican guitarron, congas, Peruvian cajon, vocals; Jorge Coulon, guitar, tiple, harp, hammered dulcimer, rondador, vocals; Marcelo Coulon, guitar, quena, piccolo, bass, flute, Mexican guitarron, vocals; Horacio Duran, charagno, cuatro, violin, percussion, vocals; Max Berru, bombo, caja, maracas, clave, bongo, guiro, guitar, vocals (1967–96); Pedro Villagra, saxophone, flute, piccolo, congas, sikis, clarinet, mandolin, vocals; Efren Manuel Viera, congas, bongo, timbales, baritone saxophone, clarinet. (All members are from Chile.)

The musical traditions of Chile's Andes Mountains are resurrected through the vocal harmonies and virtuoso musicianship of Inti-Illimani. Although the group continues to be rooted in venerable sounds, its enthusiastic approach adds a new dimension to its music. Formed by students at the Technical University in Santiago, Chile, the group's name translates as "Sun God" in the Aymaran Indian language of the Andean highlands. During the 1970s Inti-Illimani became leaders of the folkloric, activist *nueva canción* (new song) movement. Their outspoken lyrics made them targets of Chile's political oppression, and they were exiled from their homeland from 1973 to 1988. Although it was based in Rome for that time, the band toured practically non-stop and spread its musical message throughout the world. In addition to performing with such artists as Pete Seeger, Mikis Theodorakis, Mercedes Sosa, and John Williams, Inti-Illimani participated in the Amnesty International tour of 1988 and appeared with Sting, Bruce Springsteen, Tracy Chapman, and Peter Gabriel. Since returning to Chile that same year, Inti-Illimani has remained among the country's best-regarded performers. With the retirement of Max Berru in 1996, the band has continued to perform as a septet. The group was honored with a Human Rights award from U.C. Berkeley in 1997. Unfortunately, though the band has recorded more than 30 albums, only a few are available in the United States.

what to buy: Recorded during a 1990 concert in Germany, *Leyenda (Legend)* ♪♪♪♪ (CBS-Sony, 1990, prod. Inti-Illimani) reprises tunes spanning the band's first 23 years. Flamenco

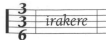

guitarist Paco Peña and classical guitarist John Williams add a further dimension to the band's tradition-rooted sound. Inti-Illimani reflected on its exile with the powerful album *Arriesgare La Piel (I Will Risk My Skin)* 🎵🎵🎵 (Xenophile, 1996, prod. Inti-Illimani), which focuses on the sorrow of lovers and families torn apart by political repression.

the rest:
Fragmento De Un Sueno 🎵🎵🎵 (CBS-Sony, 1987)
Andadas (Wanderings) 🎵🎵🎵 (Xenophile, 1993)
Lejania 🎵🎵🎵 (Xenophile, 1998)

worth searching for: Released in Italy and available in the United States only as an import, *The Best of Inti-Illimani* 🎵🎵🎵 (Inti-Illimani, 1994, prod. Inti-Illimani) is a thorough sampling of its most influential tunes.

influences:
◀◀ Traditional music of Latin America
▶▶ Flor De Cana, Forteleza

see also: *Paco Peña, Mikis Theodorakis, Mercedes Sosa*

Craig Harris

Irakere
Afro-Cuban jazz
Formed 1973, in Havana, Cuba. Based in Havana, Cuba.

Jesus "Chucho" Valdes, arranger, composer, keyboards; Arturo Sandoval, trumpet, flugelhorn, valve trombone, vocals (1973–81); Paquito D'Rivera, saxophones (1973–80); Carlos Emilio Morales, electric guitar; Enrique Pla, drums; Jorge Varona, trumpet, flugelhorn (1973–96); Oscar Valdes, vocals, percussion (1973–96); Armando Cuervo, vocals, percussion (1973–96); Carlos Averhoff, saxophones, piccolo, flute (1973–96); Carlos del Puerto, bass; Jorge "El Nino" Alfonso, congas; Jose Luis Cortez, flute (1981–88); Juan Munguia, trumpet, flugelhorn (1987–95); Miguel Diaz, percussion (1995–96); Mayra Caridad Valdes, vocals (1993–present); Mario Fernandez, trumpet (1995–present); César López, alto saxophone (1995–present); Alfredo Thompson, tenor saxophone (1995–present); Andres Miranda, congas (1995–present); Jose Miguel Melendez, timbales (1998–present); Orlando Valle, flute, keyboards (1995–96); Adalberto Ore Lara, trumpet (1995–96). (All members are from Cuba.)

Cuba has always played a part in the evolution of jazz, with pre-embargo American band leaders borrowing liberally from Afro-Cuban sounds like rumba, mambo, and cha-cha-cha. After more than a decade of Cuba's ongoing political and cultural isolation had passed, musical innovations once again began to percolate up from the island courtesy of Irakere. Born out of Orquesta Cubana de Musica Moderna, a state-sponsored collective of musicians that included Chucho Valdes, Arturo Sandoval, and Paquito D'Rivera, Irakere is credited with being in the forefront of the Latin-jazz sound's development. The group blends *songo* sounds—rhythmic structures centered around congas, *bata* drums, and *checkeré* shakers, supplemented by electric bass, keyboards, and piano—with a tight be-bop style reminiscent of Dizzy Gillespie and Charlie Parker. Before Sandoval and D'Rivera defected to the United States in the beginning of the '80s, Irakere enjoyed international acclaim as the first Castro-era Cuban band to tour and record abroad. (Their 1978 U.S. debut album won a Grammy—which they even got to collect, 15 years later.) "Irakere" means "the forest" in Yoruba, the language of Cuban slaves in the 19th century. It's a term that best describes the group's sound in its heyday (before Sandoval and D'Rivera's defections). The dense polyrhythms served as an underbrush teeming with a million different lifeforms, and the frenetic explorations of Sandoval's trumpet, Valdes's piano, D'Rivera's saxophone, and Morales's guitar evoked visions of powerful but invisible beasts calling out from behind the timber. But Irakere was more an ensemble than a showcase for individual talent, and its real niche lay in its ability to never let listeners miss "Irakere"—the forest—for the trees.

what to buy: Recorded during a brief break in the Cuban embargo, *The Best of Irakere* 🎵🎵🎵 (Columbia, recorded 1979, released 1994) is a 75-minute snapshot of the band's repertoire at that time. Two high points of this record are a mind-blowing live version of the 17-minute "Misa Negra" (The Black Mass) with its three distinct movements, and the delightful Afro-Cuban treatment of "Adagio on a Mozart Theme." On the downside, *The Best* contains a touch of disco/fusion to mark the times.

what to buy next: *Yemaya* 🎵🎵 (Blue Note, 1999) might as well be a Chucho Valdes solo record. There are some ensemble passages, but the meat of the album—and possibly the only visceral element that pokes through all the slick production—is Chucho's fiery piano lines.

worth searching for: *Irakere* (CBS, 1979) and *Live at Ronnie Scott's* (World Pacific, 1993) are two must-have live albums that are out of print. Most of the core had left by the time *Tierra En Trance* (EGREM, 1985) was released, but it's still one of the group's more consistent and sizzling works. *Bialando Asi* (Babacan, 1987) is chock-full of salsa merengue stylings. *Misa Negra* (Messidor, 1992) is a classic mostly due to the title track. Irakere is as inconsistent as it is innovative, so don't fret too much if you are unable to track down any of its many other out-of-print recordings.

influences:
◀◀ Dizzy Gillespie, Charlie Parker, Rahsaan Roland Kirk, Machito, Los Van Van, Eddie Palmieri, Silvio Rodriguez

▶▶ NG La Banda, Arturo Sandoval, Paquito D'Rivera, Chucho Valdes

see also: *Paquito D'Rivera, Arsenio Rodriguez, Arturo Sandoval, Chucho Valdes*

Isaac Josephson

Irish Rovers

Celtic folk
Formed 1964, in Calgary, Alberta, Canada. Based in Dublin, Ireland.

Jimmy Ferguson (died October 8, 1997), vocals; Joe Millar, accordion, bass; Wilcil McDowell, accordion; Will Millar, vocals, guitar, banjo (1964–present); Wallace Hood, banjo, mandolin, whistle, vocals; John Reynolds, banjo; George Millar, guitar; Kevin McKeown, percussion. (All members are from Ireland.)

The Irish Rovers have been entertaining audiences for more than 30 years with their blend of Celtic folk, barroom novelties, and poignant parables. The Rovers' exuberant, untutored sound bolsters their image as a group of friends who travel the countryside sharing stories, jokes, and songs with their extended family of fans and admirers. The Rovers allow each individual member a moment in the spotlight, and their live show is a guaranteed good time for young and old alike. After moving to Canada from Northern Ireland, brothers George and Will Millar saw the Clancy Brothers with Tommy Makem on *The Ed Sullivan Show* and were inspired to start their own group. They scuffled in the nascent Celtic scene for a few years before signing with Decca Records in 1967. The following year they scored their lone Top 10 U.S. hit with the Shel Silverstein–penned classic "The Unicorn," a mythical novelty that remains popular to this day. Several lesser hits followed, such as "Whiskey on a Sunday," "The Puppet Song," "The Biplane Evermore," "Lily the Pink," and "Did She Mention My Name"—which were more popular in Canada than in the States, and led to the Rovers starring in their own weekly TV variety show on CBC from 1971 through 1974. The group switched to Epic Records in 1980, where their ode to alcoholic excess "Wasn't That a Party" reached #37 on the pop charts and the country music Top 10, followed by their last chart records "Mexican Girl," "Pain in My Past," and "No More Bread and Butter." Will Millar eventually left the group to be replaced by Wallace Hood from Pat's People and Kevin McKeown of Emerald Express. In recent years, the Celtic music boom combined with the *Riverdance* craze has revived interest in the Irish Rovers, and the group have formed their own label, releasing new material as well as fresh versions of their classic hits. When Jimmy Ferguson (whose powerful vocal illuminates "Wasn't That a Party") died, the Rovers dedicated their entire 1998 world tour to their beloved late partner.

what to buy: All their early hits plus several fan favorites reside happily on *Irish Rovers' Greatest Hits* ♪♪♪♪ (MCA, 1981/1997,

prod. various), a 20-track compilation, though some may prefer the digitally remastered *The Best of the Irish Rovers* ♪♪♪♪ (MCA, 1999, prod. various), which features extensive notes and interviews with the band's members.

what to buy next: The two-LPs-on-one-tape reissue *The First of the Irish Rovers/The Unicorn* ♪♪♪♪ (MCA, 1980/1991, prod. various) gives you a lot of prime Rovers material in one budget offering. Nice.

what to avoid: The guys are in good voice and the production values are top-notch, but be forewarned: *The Irish Rovers Celebrate Their First 30 years* ♪♪♪ (Spinner/Rovers Records, 1996, prod. Irish Rovers) features re-recordings of their best-known songs. Seek out the original classics whenever possible.

the rest:
On the Shores of Americay ♪♪♪ (MCA, 1971/1991)
The Unicorn ♪♪♪ (MCA, 1971/1991)
The First of the Irish Rovers ♪♪♪ (MCA, 1971/1991)
Years May Come & Years May Go ♪♪♪ (MCA, 1985/1993)
Celtic Collection: The Next 30 Years ♪♪♪ (Rovers Records, 1995)
Ramblers & Gamblers ♪♪♪ (Carlton Sounds, 1997)

worth searching for: For a jaunty good time seek out *Irish Rovers Live* ♪♪♪♪ (MCA, 1972, prod. various), a solid set of laughs and great tunes in front of an enthusiastic live audience.

influences:
◀◀ Clancy Brothers & Tommy Makem, Dubliners

▶▶ Scaffold, Chieftains

Ken Burke

The Irish Tradition /Brendan Mulvihill & Billy McComiskey

Celtic
Formed 1975, in Washington, DC, USA. Disbanded 1987.

Brendan Mulvihill (born July 12, 1954, in Northampton, England), fiddle; Billy McComiskey (born December 21, 1951, in New York, NY, USA), button accordion; Andy O'Brien (Ireland), guitar, vocals.

Both as individuals and collectively, the members of the Irish Tradition stand out as some of the most talented and influential artists in the recent history of Irish music. From its first appearance in 1975, the trio's technical virtuosity and great musical rapport created a surge of interest in Irish music in the Washington, D.C., area, and led to the development of an outstanding local music scene. Some of the D.C.-area artists influenced, inspired, or taught by the Irish Tradition include Celtic Thunder, Maggie Sansone, Lisa Moscatiello, Grace Griffith, and Ceoltoiri, among many others. The group's two albums on Green Linnet, both classics, were consistently that label's biggest sellers during its early years and provided a base from which the now-mighty label could expand to its present lofty heights. Finally, Brendan Mulvihill and Billy McComiskey, as teachers, have introduced new musicians to playing of the highest caliber, and have kept the standards for traditional music high in both Washington, D.C., and New York City.

Mulvihill is an explosive fiddler with tremendous power, grace, and sensitivity in his playing. Growing up in England and New York City, he learned his music from his father, legendary fiddler and music teacher Martin Mulvihill, as well as from the many outstanding musicians he met in both New York and Birmingham, England. Mulvihill won the All-Ireland senior fiddle title in 1974, and moved to Washington, D.C., the following year. He has appeared all over the world, and has influenced many of today's top young musicians, including Eileen Ivers, Joannie Madden, and Natalie MacMaster. McComiskey is an incredibly talented accordionist with a deep sense of what makes traditional music work and an incredible virtuosity on his instrument. While growing up in New York City, he learned his music from family members and from the great local box player Sean McGlynn. McComiskey won the All-Ireland in 1986 and has appeared throughout the United States and Ireland as a solo performer and with his current group, Trian. He is a prolific composer of tunes and an outstanding teacher, having instructed or influenced performers as diverse as Celtic harpist Sue Richards, box players John Nolan, Colm Gannon, and Mary Rafferty, and piper Jerry O'Sullivan.

what to buy: The Irish Tradition's *The Corner House* ♫♫♫♫ (Green Linnet, 1978, prod. Mick Moloney) features some of the most beautiful note-for-note playing of Irish dance music ever recorded. Billy and Brendan had been performing together every night for years when they recorded this album, and it shows in their tight, tasty duet playing. In addition to backing the other two on their virtuoso flights, Andy O'Brien contributes four sweet songs. Finally, the trio's setting of "The Dark-Eyed Sailor" shows how powerful and moving a simple song arrangement can be in the hands of master musicians.

what to buy next: McComiskey's *Makin' the Rounds* ♫♫♫♫ (Green Linnet, 1981 prod. Mick Moloney, Billy McComiskey) makes a very convincing case that the button accordion, in the right hands, can be as beautiful, expressive, and moving as any other instrument in traditional Irish music. Moving from tunes he learned in his youth from friends and heroes to his own compositions, many of which are now standards, Billy shows the past and present of Irish music. He rocks with the best of them on sets like "Leave My Way" and "The Chicago Reel," and brings a classical refinement to the slow set dance "Planxty Davis." This album is a tour de force of box playing. Mulvihill and Donna Long's *The Morning Dew* ♫♫♫♫ (Green Linnet, 1992, prod. Joe

Wilson, Julia Olin) allows the musical genius to strut his stuff, ably backed by one of the finest piano players around today. Mulvihill's playing ranges from the ferocious to the elegant, and the sound is as good as any in Green Linnet's history.

the rest: *The Times We've Had* ♫♫♫♫ (Green Linnet, 1985)

worth searching for: Mulvihill and Long's self-produced cassette *The SteepleChase* ♫♫♫ (SteepleChase, 1990, prod. Donna Long, Brendan Mulvihill) was the first recording for the pair. The Irish Tradition's first recording, *Catchin' the Tune* (self-released, 1976, prod. Irish Tradition), is long out of print.

solo outings:
Brendan Mulvihill:
The Flax in Bloom ♫♫♫▽ (Green Linnet, 1979)

influences:
◀◀ Martin Mulvihill, Paddy O'Brien, Andy McGann, Jack Coen

▶▶ Cherish the Ladies, Jerry O'Sullivan

see also: *Ceoltoiri, Eileen Ivers, Joannie Madden, Natalie MacMaster, Maggie Sansone, Trian*

Tony Ziselberger

Andy Irvine
Celtic
Born June 14, 1942, in London, England. Based in Dublin, Ireland.

Andy Irvine has the most bittersweet voice in Celtic music. It has that feel of Irish whiskey poured into a glass of hot tea with a couple large dollops of sugar to sweeten it up—whether he's singing his own compositions or his arrangements of traditional pieces, it just washes over you hot and sweet and then you feel that bite that lurks underneath. After you get past that voice you notice that he is an instrumental perfectionist, whether playing harmonica, mandolin, or the Irish bouzouki. Finally you'll notice that he is also an excellent songwriter, and has produced several tunes which have become standards of Irish repertoire, most notably "West Coast of Clare." His impeccable taste and talent have made him the core of three important Irish groups, Sweeney's Men, Planxty, and Patrick Street.

Born in London, Irvine was a child actor before developing an interest in jazz and classical music. Like many other musicians in the British Isles, it was through the skiffle craze that he got interested in traditional music, particularly Woody Guthrie. By the early 1960s he was playing in the folk scene in Dublin, where his first group, Sweeney's Men, was formed in 1966. They made several recordings and lasted until he left for Eastern Europe in the turbulent summer of 1968. He spent over a year and half there, busking and absorbing the local music. The influence of that experience began to surface in the music of his next group, Planxty. That band first came together in 1972 while recording an album under Christy Moore's name. They rapidly became extremely popular both in Ireland and elsewhere in Europe, and lasted in one form or another until 1975, making several excellent recordings along the way. After Planxty Irvine worked for a while with Paul Brady, making one highly acclaimed album and touring Europe and the States with him. Shortly after that he began to work with the musicians who comprise his most current group, Patrick Street. While nowhere near the groundbreaking group Planxty was, Patrick Street instead makes its mark with the extremely high quality of craftsmanship it brings to traditional Irish music. Irvine's more adventurous side can be found in his solo efforts and his collaborations with Dick Gaughan, Davy Spillane, and others.

what to buy: *Andy Irvine and Paul Brady* ♪♪♪♪♪ (Mulligan/ Green Linnet, 1976, prod. Dónal Lunny) is perhaps the finest single record of Irish music available. These recordings were made after the demise of the groundbreaking Planxty, with Christy Moore's replacement in that band, Brady. The arrangements here are grittier than the earlier band, with Kevin Burke's fiddle replacing the role piper Liam O'Flynn played in the Planxty sound. There are more of the Balkan elements that Irvine had begun to introduce in Planxty, like the 7/8 break that transforms the middle of "The Plains of Kildare." Brady's innovative open-tuned guitar work is highlighted throughout, nowhere more than on his show-stopping "Arthur McBride." But the real magic of this record is the contrast between the voices of the two men. Irvine's bittersweet voice curls around songs like a fog, while Brady's full-throated charge never sounded better than on these recordings.

what to buy next: *Rude Awakening* ♪♪♪♪ (Green Linnet, 1991, prod. Bill Whelan) spotlights Irvine's songwriting—a sometimes-rare treat given the focus on his instrumental prowess and traditional singing in settings like Patrick Street. This is a concept album, with Irvine selecting his favorite heroes and anti-heroes to write about. His talent at putting traditional words and music into a contemporary context are still here, both in "James Connolly" and "Allan Mclean"—though on the whole, his heroes are of a more international lot: "Woody Guthrie," "Raoul Wallenberg," "Zapata." The combination of the topical and traditional is reminiscent of Dick Gaughan, someone with whom Irvine had recorded several years earlier.

the rest:
Andy Irvine and Dick Gaughan: Parallel Lines ♪♪♪♪♪ (1983, Green Linnet)
Andy Irvine/Davy Spillane: East Wind ♪♪♪♪ (1991, Tara)
Andy Irvine and Dick Gaughan ♪♪♪♪♪ (1997, Appleseed)
Rainy Sundays Windy Dreams ♪♪♪♪ (1997, Wundertüte)

shibuya: the japanese underground

Despite an early-'80s fashion craze, a growing cult of *manga* and *anime* (Japanese comics and cartoons), and a national love-hate relationship with Yoko Ono (a spiritual godmother of the bands discussed in this essay), Japanese artists haven't fared too well on the U.S. record charts (1963's "Sukiyaki," by Kyu Sakamoto, is their lone #1 hit). However, American and European influences abound in Japan. Most would point to the avant-garde electronic stew of the 1970s' Yellow Magic Orchestra as the starting point of whatever awareness the States had of contemporary Japanese music, but in Japan itself the most popular genre would remain J-Pop, a bland form of balladry fronted by teen idols and TV stars. Since the '80s, though, a steady string of cosmopolitan artists has emerged from the hip quarter of Tokyo known as Shibuya. The best-known include Pizzicato Five, United Future Organization, and Towa Tei, all of whose sounds blend lounge, jazz, and club music into an immediately consumable cocktail that, in its mix if not its ingredients, is uniquely Japanese. The cuddly, infectious pop of Shonen Knife made them the first of the underground bands to make waves Stateside when a string of their albums connected with the college crowd. In the mid-'90s U.S. audiences got their first steady taste of the burgeoning scene when domestic labels like Grand Royal and Matador began releasing the music en masse. The sights and sounds of Shibuya now encompass a vast landscape. From the Phil Spector–esque genius of Cornelius, to the crunchy loud guitars of Buffalo Daughter, to the breezy bossa-rock of Kahimi Karie and Cibo Matto, the Japanese underground is continually making the world its own.

Sam Wick

solo outings:
Sweeneys Men:
Rattlin' & Roarin' Willy ♪♪♪ (Transatlantic, 1968)
Sweeneys Men ♪♪♪♪ (Transatlantic, 1968)
Tracks of Sweeney ♪♪♪♪ (Transatlantic, 1969)

Legend of Sweeney's Men ♫♫♫ (Demon, 1988)

Planxty:
Planxty ♫♫♫♫ (Shanachie, 1972)
Well below the Valley ♫♫♫♫ (Shanachie, 1973)
Cold Blow and the Rainy Night ♫♫♫♫♫ (Shanachie, 1974)
After the Break ♫♫♫♫ (Tara, 1979)
Woman I Loved So Well ♫♫♫♫ (Tara, 1980)
Words & Music ♫♫♫♫ (Shanachie, 1983)
Planxty Collection ♫♫♫♫ (Shanachie, 1986)

Patrick Street:
All in Good Time . . . ♫♫♫♫ (Green Linnet, 1986)
Patrick Street ♫♫♫♫ (Green Linnet, 1986)
No. 2 Patrick Street ♫♫♫♫ (Green Linnet, 1988)
3 Irish Times 3 ♫♫♫♫ (Green Linnet, 1990)
Corner Boys ♫♫♫♫ (Green Linnet, 1996)
Made in Cork ♫♫♫♫♫ (Green Linnet, 1997)
Live from Patrick Street ♫♫♫♫♫ (Green Linnet, 1999)

influences:

 Woody Guthrie, Davey Graham, Seamus Ennis

▶▶ The Pogues, Eileen Ivers, Seamus Egan

see also: *Kevin Burke, Dick Gaughan, Frankie Gavin, Dónal Lunny, Liam O'Flynn, Patrick Street, Planxty, Maddy Prior, Sweeney's Men, Bill Whelan*

Jared Snyder

Gregory Isaacs

Reggae, lovers' rock
Born 1948, in Kingston, Jamaica. Based in Jamaica.

Silken vocals, romantic lyrics, and irresistible reggae rhythms have combined to make Gregory Isaacs the king of "lovers' rock." One of reggae's most prolific artists, Isaacs has recorded over 500 songs and more than 70 albums. According to the *St. Louis Dispatch,* Isaacs's music "practically massages your whole body into a state of total relaxation." Isaacs cut his first singles as a member of Jamaica-based band the Concords in the late 1960s. Although his debut solo single, "Another Heartache," was on Wirl, a small label owned by former Jamaican prime minister Edward Seaga, Isaacs released most of his 1970s singles on his own labels, African Museum and Cash & Carry. Isaacs's first hints of success came with a series of Alvin Ranglin–produced singles including "My Number One" and the politically edged "The Border." Isaacs's two-volume retrospective, *Best Of,* features some of these tracks. Following the release of his third album, *Extra Classics,* which included the minor hits "Rasta Business" and "Loving Pauper," Isaacs joined forces with top-ranked reggae rhythm section/production team Sly (Dunbar) and Robbie (Shakespeare). Over the next few years, the collaboration yielded a string of ground-breaking albums including *Sly & Robbie Present Gregory Isaacs* and *Call Me Collect.* After releasing his most commercially successful album, *The Night Nurse,* in 1987, Isaacs signed with the RAS label and hooked up with producer Gussie Clarke.

what to buy: Isaacs reached his creative apex with the recordings produced by Sly and Robbie for their Taxi label. Several of these tracks, along with Isaacs's 1987 single "I'm Coming Home," are included on *Sly & Robbie Present Gregory Isaacs* ♫♫♫♫ (RAS, 1988, prod. Sly Dunbar, Robbie Shakespeare). Spanning Isaacs's recording career, *Looking Back* ♫♫♫♫ (RAS, 1996, prod. various) features 14 tunes including "Write Myself a Letter," "Loneliness," and "Conversation."

best of the rest:
The Night Nurse ♫♫♫♫ (PGD/Mango, 1987)
The Best of Gregory Isaacs ♫♫♫♫ (Music Club, 1988)
Private Beach Party ♫♫♫♫ (RAS, 1988)
Call Me Collect ♫♫♫♫ (RAS, 1990)
State of Shock ♫♫♫♫ (RAS,1992)
Classic Hits, Vol. 2 ♫♫♫♫ (Sonic Sound, 1994)
Live in France ♫♫♫♫ (Sonic Sound, 1994)
20 Classic Hits ♫♫♫♫ (Sonic Sound, 1994)
One Man against the World: The Best of Gregory Isaacs ♫♫♫♫ (VP, 1996)
Hard Core Hits ♫♫♫♫ (Multimedia, 1997)
Greatest & Latest ♫♫♫♫ (Cleopatra, 1998)
Live at Maritime Hall ♫♫♫♫ (2BL, 1998)

influences:

◀◀ Jackie Edwards, Bob Marley, Toots & the Maytals

▶▶ UB40, Third World

see also: *The Congos, Sly & Robbie*

Craig Harris

Israel Vibration

Roots reggae
Formed 1976, in Kingston, Jamaica. Based in Kingston, Jamaica.

Cecil "Skeleton" Spence, vocals; Albert "Apple" Craig, vocals; Lascelles "Wiss" Bulgrin, vocals. (All members are from Jamaica.)

The deeply spiritual roots-reggae trio Israel Vibration is still together playing its individualistic Rastafarian take on ghetto life more than 20 years after its debut. Few institutions are this reliable in Jamaica's tradition of one-hit wonders. What is more remarkable is that Israel Vibration's music is as strong today as in reggae's golden age of the '70s.

The story of how Israel Vibration formed is an extraordinary one. At the age of three, Albert Craig woke one day to find his lower body paralyzed. In hospital they told him he had polio—and it was in polio rehab that Craig met his future partners in Israel Vibration. Their paths crossed as they were shuffled between various institutions. At 14 Craig left the confines of Alpha Boys School for a grueling life on the streets where he refused to steal, and got by on scraps of food. Rastafarian Baba Douse provided shelter for Craig in the form of a dray cart in his back yard, and bought the boy his first pair of pants and shoes. Craig's Rasta lyrics were no doubt inspired by Bible readings with the elder.

Meanwhile, as a teen, Cecil Spence was a member of the Jamaican wheelchair basketball team, traveling as far as Germany to represent his country. When Spence grew dreadlocks and adopted the Rasta lifestyle, he was thrown off the team and out of school along with colleague Lascelles Bulgrin. They gathered with Craig where he had holed up in the bush beside a football field on the campus of the University of the West Indies. The trio smoked herb, read from the Bible, and sang in harmony where crowds gathered to hear it, encouraging the as-yet unnamed group to set its singing to record.

The name Israel Vibration was devised by Craig. As he explains, "One day we sit together alongside a building near the bush we lived in, and I say, 'We never hear of a group that disclose the children of God, which is Israel.'" The name stuck, and the trio still records with long-time backing band the Roots Radics. Despite a temporary break-up in the '80s, they have been generating positive vibrations ever since.

what to buy: The best starting point is their now-classic debut *The Same Song* 🎵🎵🎵🎵 (Talent, 1978/RAS, 1996, prod. Tommy Cowan). An edition on Pressure Sounds adds the rare single "Crisis." For a career overview, check out *RAS Portraits* 🎵🎵🎵🎵 (RAS, 1997, prod. Doctor Dread, Israel Vibration). The band has remained consistently strong long enough to see its rootsical vibe come back into fashion; its latest, *Free to Move* 🎵🎵🎵🎵 (RAS, 1996, prod. Doctor Dread, Israel Vibration), features vivid social messages like "System Not Working" and "Livity in the Hood."

what to buy next: Israel Vibration is a great live band, as is evident on *Live Again!* 🎵🎵🎵🎵 (RAS, 1997, prod. Doctor Dread, Israel Vibration), which features tracks from all but its latest album, recorded at stellar shows in California and Arizona.

what to avoid: Israel Vibration's first two albums are available in reasonably good dub versions by Errol Brown and Paul Davidson. They can be found on one CD as *Israel Dub* 🎵🎵🎵🎵 (RAS, 1996, prod. Tommy Cowan). However, the rest of the catalog was remixed by the band's engineer, Jim Fox, whose weak dub skills make the original studio albums a safer bet. Fox's most recent effort to steer clear of is *Dub the Rock* 🎵🎵 (RAS, 1995, prod. Doctor Dread, Israel Vibration); earlier ones are *Dub Vibration* 🎵🎵 (RAS, 1990, prod. Doctor Dread, Israel Vibration) and *I.V.D.U.B.* 🎵🎵 (RAS, 1994, prod. Doctor Dread, Israel Vibration).

best of the rest:
Why You So Craven 🎵🎵🎵 (RAS, 1991)
Vibes Alive 🎵🎵🎵 (RAS, 1993)
Feeling Irie 🎵🎵🎵🎵 (RAS, 1996)

worth searching for: The Israel Vibration video *Reggae in Hollywood* (RAS) is worth a look.

influences:

◄◄ Bob Marley

►► Buju Banton

see also: *The Roots Radics*

David Poole

The Itals

Roots reggae
Formed 1976, in Jamaica. Based in Jamaica.

Keith Porter, vocals; Ronnie Davis, vocals (1976–95); Lloyd Ricketts, vocals (1976–85); Donovan Brisset, vocals (1985); Kada, vocals (1997–present). (All members are from Jamaica.)

Rastafarian-inspired lyrics are set to complex but soulful vocal harmonies by roots reggae band the Itals. Although lead singer and songwriter Keith Porter is the only original member still with the group, its vision has remained consistent.

The spark of the Itals was kindled when Porter and vocalist Ronnie Davis sang together in the early-'70s reggae band the Westmorlites. Although the group recorded a single, "Hitey Titey," Davis left to perform with the Tennors, while Porter launched a solo career on Jamaica's rural hotel and small club circuit. Planning to record again, Porter returned to Kingston and fortuitously ran into Davis. Two days later, the duo recorded a single, "In A Dis Ya Time." Encouraged by the results, they agreed to pool their resources. With the addition of a third singer, Lloyd Ricketts, Porter and Davis formed the first incarnation of the Itals (taken from a Jamaican term for "purity" or "lack of pollution"). After recording several singles, the Itals hooked up with the renowned Roots Radics as their backing band (an association which would become frequent throughout their career). Their debut album, *Brutal Out Deh,* released in 1981, is still their strongest recording.

The Itals hit some legal difficulties when they were sued by a similarly named band from Cleveland, Indiana. After a lengthy court battle, the Jamaican trio was granted ownership of the name, with the Cleveland band morphing into the "Itals U.S.A." In 1985, the Itals underwent their first personnel change when Rickets ran afoul of the law and was arrested and jailed. His replacement, Donovan Brisset, only remained with the group for two months before emigrating to the United States. Porter and

Davis continued to perform temporarily as a duo before adding harmony singer Kada in 1997. Although *Easy to Catch,* released in 1991, and *Modern Age,* released in 1998, incorporated electric instruments and modern production techniques, the Itals' musical roots remained intact.

what to buy: The Itals' debut album, *Brutal Out Deh* ♪♪♪♪♪ (Nighthawk, 1982, prod. the Itals, Jodie Pierson), is a harmonic roots reggae masterpiece. In addition to Rastafarian-influenced original songs including "Rastafari Chariot," "Herbs Pirate," and "Smile Knotty Dread," the album includes a unique rendition of Bob Marley's "Time Will Tell." *Early Recordings: 1971–1979* ♪♪♪♪ (Nighthawk, 1984, prod. the Itals, Lloyd Campbell) surveys the band's groundbreaking singles including "Don't Wake the Lion," "Brutal," "Living in the Ghetto," and the original recording of "Smile Knotty Dread."

the rest:
Give Me Power! ♪♪♪ (Nighthawk, 1983)
Coal & Dread ♪♪♪ (Nighthawk, 1984)
Rasta Philosophy ♪♪♪♪ (Nighthawk, 1987)
Easy to Catch ♪♪♪ (Priority, 1991)
Modern Age ♪♪♪♪ (RAS, 1998)

influences:
◄◄ Bob Marley, Peter Tosh

►► Burning Spear, Gregory Isaacs, Culture

see also: *The Roots Radics*

Craig Harris

Eileen Ivers

Celtic traditional and experimental
Born 1965, in the Bronx, NY, USA. Based in USA.

No sooner had Eileen Ivers established herself as one of the finest traditional Irish fiddlers of her generation than she transcended that circumscribed field to tour the world, first with Hall & Oates and then with the *Riverdance* stage musical. Ivers grew up in the Bronx, where she studied with the legendary Irish fiddler Martin Mulvihill; she was only 14 when she first recorded, on an anthology of Mulvihill's students. She went on to win seven All-Ireland Championships on the fiddle, including the coveted Senior Championship in 1984. She was a member of the all-female Irish folk band Cherish the Ladies, and accompanied many of the top Irish-American folk musicians, including Mick Moloney and Seamus Egan. She recorded a duet album with accordionist John Whelan in 1987. In 1990 she was recruited to play on Hall & Oates's *Change of Season* album, and to accompany them on the subsequent tour. She released her debut solo album in 1993; collaborated with composer Mícheál Ó Sáilleabháin on his Irish TV series *River of Sound;*

joined the New York Celtic rap-rock band Paddy a Go-Go; and became a featured soloist in *Riverdance.* In every venture, Ivers's trad-fiddle virtuosity has been evident, but she has not been reluctant about combining her Irish roots with African drums, hip-hop rhythms, Broadway orchestration, and anything else that might catch her fancy.

what to buy: The best introduction to Ivers's work is the single-CD anthology *So Far: The Eileen Ivers Collection, 1979–1995* ♪♪♪♪ (Green Linnet, 1997, prod. Kevin Yatarola), which features tracks from both solo albums, the duo album with Whelan, and the Mulvihill School album, as well as her appearances on the *Riverdance* soundtrack, a Cherish the Ladies album, a multiple-artist concert recording, and Jerry O'Sullivan's *The Invasion.* It's a wonderfully diverse assemblage of music, but Ivers's surpassing technique and fearless chance-taking are evident throughout. The debut album *Eileen Ivers* ♪♪♪♪ (Green Linnet, 1994, prod. Gabriel Donohue, Eileen Ivers) finds the fiddler in transition between her traditional training and her bold experiments into the future of the Celtic fiddle, and she excels at both.

To hear the experimentation part in full bloom, catch up with Ivers's latest, *Crossing the Bridge* ♪♪♪♪ (Sony Classical, 1999, prod. Brian Keane), on which she realizes much of the Celtic/world fusion she's been hinting at. The huge cast includes regulars John Doyle, Seamus Egan, Jerry O'Sullivan, Joanie Madden, and Tommy Hayes alongside jazz guitarist Al Di Meola, trumpeter Randy Brecker, South African bassist Bakithi Kumalo, drummer Steve Gadd, percussionist Alex Acuña, and many more. There are some exciting tracks here, convincingly mixing Irish music with salsa, hip-hop, jazz, and Spanish forms. Ivers also reunites with Riverdancers Colin Dunne, Maria Pagés, and Tarik Winston—themselves representing three distinct cultures—but like *Riverdance* composer Bill Whelan, somehow she makes it all work. In addition to the impressive Irish chops she's most famous for, Ivers displays an equal fondness for the fiddle stylings of jazz-fusion pioneer Jean-Luc Ponty and folk-rock veteran/Fairport Convention stalwart Dave Swarbrick in his electric wah-wah peddle mode. On the down side, consistency still isn't her strong suit, and some of the cuts here do meander a bit.

what to buy next: *Wild Blue* ♪♪♪♪ (Green Linnet, 1996, prod. Tom "T-Bone" Wolk, Eileen Ivers) is named after the varnished color and uninhibited sound of Ivers's violin. Ivers experiments with all sorts of drums, bass, and keyboards, but she never loses her foundation in traditional Celtic forms and pure violin tone. *Fresh Takes* ♪♪♪ (Green Linnet, 1987, prod. Mick Moloney) is a lovely, all-instrumental album built around the musical dialogues between Ivers's fiddle and John Whelan's button accordion, though the Bothy Band's Triona Ní Dhomhnaill adds synthesizer and clavinet to half the cuts.

Eileen Ivers

influences:

◄◄ Martin Mulvihill, Brendan Mulvihill, Eugene O'Donnell

►► Natalie MacMaster

see also: *Bothy Band, Máire Breatnach, Cherish the Ladies, Felix Dolan, the Irish Tradition, Joanie Madden, Mick Moloney, Triona Ní Dhomhnaill, Bill Whelan, Paul Winter*

Geoffrey Himes

J

Jaguares
See: Caifanes

Jon Jang
Chinese/jazz fusion
Born March 11, 1954, in Los Angeles, CA. Based in USA.

Jon Jang didn't begin playing piano until he was 19, but he must've known where he was headed right from the start. By the time his initial Soul Note recording was released in 1992, he'd done five independently produced albums, *and* the ideas and/or material for the next two projects were already in place.

what to buy: Of the readily available offerings—that is, those on Soul Note—it's the thematic *Tiananmen!* ♫♫♫♫ (Soul Note, 1993, prod. Jon Jang) that's Jang's towering achievement as of yet. Featuring his medium-sized Pan-Asian Arkestra (named after Horace Tapscott's Pan-Afrikan People's Ark, but spiritually connected to Sun Ra's Arkestra as well), this concert-length piece is a moving tone poem–cum-meditation on the 1989 Chinese student uprising. Instruments drawn from China's folk and classical heritage blend with the more usual Western assortment in creating a rich, earthy, and truly international musical language, with fabulous playing all around.

what to buy next: *Self Defense!* ♫♫♫♫ (Soul Note, 1992, prod. Jon Jang), recorded during a 1991 Arkestra recital, is nearly as good as the above recording, with a heaven-storming "Night in Tunisia" and Jang's lengthy, layered "Concerto for Jazz Ensemble and Taiko" as bookended high points. *Two Flowers on a Stem* ♫♫♫♫ (Soul Note, 1996, prod. Jon Jang) is a sextet with James Newton, David Murray, Jie-Bing Chen (on *erhu* or Chinese fiddle), Santi Debriano, and Jabali Billy Hart that's as dense and beautiful as its predecessors; it's centered around "Meditations on Integration" by Charles Mingus, with Newton's flute and Murray's bass clarinet taking the parts of Roland Kirk and

Eric Dolphy, respectively. As always, a version of the popular Chinese ballad "Butterfly Lovers Song" is also included.

the rest:
Jang ♫♫♫♪ (RPM, 1982)
Are You Chinese or Charlie Chan? ♫♫♫♪ (RPM, 1984)
Island: The Immigrant Suite Number I ♫♫♫♪ (Soul Note, 1997)

worth searching for: Jang's albums on the AsianImprov label, which he helped start, have to be searched out. Adding the most to the overall picture are *The Ballad or the Bullet* ♫♫♫♪ (AsianImprov, 1987, prod. Jon Jang, Francis Wong), which is credited to Jon Jang and the 4-in-One Quartet; *Jangle Bells* ♫♫♫♪ (AsianImprov, 1988, prod. Jon Jang); and *Never Give Up!* ♫♫♫♪ (AsianImprov, 1989, prod. Jon Jang). It may not be an unfair characterization to say these albums are looser and more fun than the increasingly serious Soul Note releases.

influences:

◄◄ Duke Ellington, Charles Mingus, Horace Tapscott's Pan-Afrikan People's Arkestra

►► Fred Ho's Afro-Asian Music Ensemble

see also: *Jie-Bing Chen*

David Prince

The Japanese Koto Consort
Sankyoku
Formed in Japan. Based in Japan.

Kofu Kikusui (Japan), shakuhachi; Noriko Noda (Japan), kotos, shamisen; Yayoi Nishimura (Japan), kotos.

The Japanese Koto Consort play *sankyoku* or "music for three instruments"—ensemble pieces for *shamisen* (a three-stringed banjo-like instrument), *koto* (a 13-string flat harp), and *shakuhachi* (bamboo flute). They are students of the *Ikuta-ryu*, one of the three schools of koto playing, this one using square picks and kotos longer than the usual six-foot size. The songs are of the late-17th-century Edo Period, when the koto began to be played in concert with the shamisen and shakuhachi. Kotos were originally the domain of well-bred, marriage-seeking Japanese girls. All the sankyoku instruments have Chinese prototypes.

what's available: *Japanese Koto Consort* ♫♫♫♫ (Lyrichord) features sankyoku and solos of the three instruments. In sankyoku, the shamisen is the dominant part, known as the "bone" of the performance; the koto is the "meat"; and the shakuhachi the "skin." The seven tracks are regal performances, each instrument complementing the others and standing alone as needed. Songs include famous classical pieces such as "Yachiyo Jishi" (also adapted for Kabuki music), the children's song "Kyo No Warabeuta," and several folk songs, among them the well-known folk melody "Kojo No Tsuki."

worth searching for: If you enjoy this music, related collections include *Gagaku* (Lyrichord), title translation: "elegant music," which includes koto performances played the way they were at the Japanese Imperial Court; *Japanese Koto Orchestra* (Lyrichord); *Japanese Masterpieces for Shakuhachi* (Lyrichord); and *The Soul of the Koto, Vols. 1 and 2* (Lyrichord).

influences:

◀◀ Ikuta Kengyo (founder of sankyoku), Kengyo Fujinaga, Kengyo Yoshizawa, Katsuko Tsukushi, Tsutomu Sakamoto, Rentaro Taki

Stacy Meyn

Victor Jara

Chilean nueva canción
Born in Loquen, Chile. Died September 14, 1973, in Santiago, Chile.

At first a seminary student, then a soldier, then an actor and theater director—and before that a young man growing up with a mother who taught him guitar and the folksongs of Chile—Victor Jara became a political songwriter in a time and place when politics was a matter of life and death. The Chile of the late '60s and early '70s was the scene of struggle and change. Jara used his songwriting talent and gentle voice to express concerns of the left-wing people's movement. For this he was brutally murdered by the right-wing military in 1973. The courage shown in his music has gone on to inspire many writers and workers for change since that time.

what's available: It isn't easy to find Jara's music in the United States, though the Plane label is reported to be in the process of issuing a four-disc retrospective to be called *Victor Jara Complete* that will contain music from many currently scarce albums. The Monitor label has several thematic compilations, some only on tape. On CD there are *Te Recuerdo Amanda* 𝄞𝄞𝄞 (Dom, 1998) and *Unfinished Song* 𝄞𝄞𝄞 (Redwood, 1990).

influences:

◀◀ Violetta Parra, Mercedes Sosa, Armando Tejado Gomez

▶▶ Daniel Vigletti, Silvio Rodriguez, Joán Baez, Tish Hinojosa

Kerry Dexter

Wyclef Jean

Hip-hop
Born Nelust Wyclef Jean, 1970, outside Croix-des-Bouquets, Haiti. Based in USA.

When the Fugees dropped *The Score* in 1996, alternative hip-hop finally got the breakthrough album it had been looking for. But it also got much more. A native of Haiti who grew up in Brooklyn and now operates out of New Jersey, Wyclef Jean burst onto the scene as the architect of the Fugees' sound—as well as of their concept. The band's very name is short for "refugees"; a reference to Haiti's blighted culture, but also to anyone who's ever been cast adrift in the search for hearth and home, literally or figuratively. Each of the group's members has released a solo album, and while Lauryn Hill's hit the biggest and Prakazrel Michael spun his off into a movie project, Jean turned his abilities into a cottage industry. In recent times he's worked as a producer, songwriter, performer, and/or remixer for the likes of Whitney Houston, Canibus, the Neville Brothers, Sparkle, Gloria Estefan, Earth, Wind & Fire, Simply Red, and Carlos Santana, and worked on the *South Park* soundtrack. Under his own billing, he's also toured his guest-heavy solo album as a kind of world-music impresario. All of a sudden, he seems to be everywhere, and that's not a bad thing.

what's available: *Wyclef Jean Presents the Carnival Featuring Refugee Allstars* 𝄞𝄞𝄞𝄞 (Ruffhouse/Columbia, 1997, prod. various) is a straight-up hip-hop album, but the island rhythms of Clef's youth and the highly politicized sentiments of his refugee program weave themselves sinuously throughout. Jean emphasizes street rhymes on "We Tryin' to Stay Alive," but on tracks like "Sang Fézi," "Yelé," and "Jaspora" he raps and sings in the French patois of his homeland. "Gunpowder" addresses the rising tide of violence, and is strongly reminiscent of the work of Jean's hero Bob Marley. There's plenty of nonsense on the album—the skits, and the vapid "To All the Girls"—but there's also the heart-tugging "Gone till November" and "Guantanemera," which features the legendary salsa diva Celia Cruz. Indeed, there's something here for almost everyone.

worth searching for: The Fugees' *The Score* (Ruffhouse/Columbia, 1996, prod. various) took hip-hop to another level, even as it looked back to heroes such as Bob Marley, whose "No Woman No Cry" the group covers here. Original tracks such as "Fu-Gee-La," "Family Business," and "Ready or Not" show that Jean & Co. learned their lessons well, but have plenty of ideas of their own to offer.

influences:

◀◀ Bob Marley, De La Soul, Arrested Development

Daniel Durchholz

Nemours Jean-Baptiste /Ensemble Nemours Jean-Baptiste

Compas direct
Born 1918, in Haiti. Based in Port-au-Prince, Haiti.

With his ardent fans, the founder of the modern *compas* style (which he called "compas direct"), sax player Nemours Jean-

Baptiste, engaged in a vicious rivalry throughout the 1960s with Webert Sicot, the founder of another French Antillean pop sound, *cadence rampa*. (By sheerest coincidence, Sicot was a former bandmate of Jean-Baptiste in Conjunto International). This rivalry rose to the level of a national obsession in Haiti and made the Beatles/Stones competition of the same period seem like a gentlemanly squabble. Jean-Baptiste had come up through the orchestras of Port-au-Prince. In 1953 he gathered his own octet for the opening of Aux Calebasses, the newest nightclub of the day in Carrefour (the "red-light district" just outside the city proper). They enjoyed a huge audience, toured America, and opened another club in Port-au-Prince, the Palladium, at which point they took the name Super Ensemble Compas Direct de Nemours Jean-Baptiste, or ENJD for short. By the '80s Jean-Baptiste was blind, broke, and bandless, though a late-decade revival of his so-seminal music helped his fortunes a mite.

what to buy: *Musical Tour of Haiti* 🎵🎵🎵🎵 (Ansonia, prod. Nemours Jean-Baptiste) is, appallingly, the only title available in the United States by this groundbreaking Caribbean artist. That's sort of like citing Shakespeare as a seminal writer, but only having *Titus Andronicus* as evidence. Like many Caribbean albums from the '60s, the spirit outweighs the sonic niceties like recording balance or horns being in tune, but these songs represent a major revolution in Haitian music. They took the hotel big bands and brought them home, with big rhythms from both Haiti and Cuba. What is most evident are the mind-bending, ultra-catchy hooks built into the horn parts.

what to buy next: *Fanatiques Compas (The Mini All-Stars)* 🎵🎵🎵🎵 (Earthworks/Sterns, 1997, prod. Fred Paul) is not strictly a Nemours Jean-Baptiste album, as the Mini All-Stars—some of Haiti's finest expatriates, led by Fred Paul, co-producer of the groundbreaking Stateside compilation *Konbit: Burning Rhythms of Haiti*—play the tunes, but Baptiste composed everything. The band is fronted by ENJD vocalists Carlo Claudin and Willy Lacroix, it must be noted, and features the prodigious accordion work of Richard Duroseau ("The Charlie Parker of the Accordion," if you believe the back of the jewel box). Compared to earlier recordings the horns are punchier, the overall sonics worlds better, and the players genuinely sound as if they love this music.

influences:

◀ Septentrional, Les Jazz des Jeunes, Jazz Guignard, Tipico Cibaeño

▶ Nearly every band from the Francophone Caribbean in his wake.

Hank Bordowitz

Don Santiago Jimenez

Norteño, conjunto, Tex-Mex
Born April 25, 1919, in San Antonio, TX, USA. Died December 18, 1984, in San Antonio, TX, USA.

Simply put, Don Santiago Jimenez, along with Narciso Martinez, virtually invented the style of *conjunto* music popular today. Indigenous to South Texas, this conjunto combines elements of the European music enjoyed by early Texas immigrants with native Mexican *rancheras* (urban songs) and other *norteño* (Northern Mexican) forms. Jimenez started playing the accordion at the age of 10, learning from his father, Patricio, a popular accordionist around San Antonio. Santiago accompanied his father when he played at dances and parties throughout South Texas. To please his fans—descendants of German and Moravian immigrants—Patricio performed the waltzes, mazurkas, and polkas they loved from their homeland. The exposure to this variety of music helped form the basis of the style and sound Santiago was to later develop.

A quick read on the two-button accordion, Santiago, nicknamed "El Flaco" (the skinny one), began playing professionally by the 1930s, cutting records and performing live on the radio in South Texas; by the 1940s, he was famous throughout the Southwest. Because of his success, other conjunto accordionists throughout the region began to copy his unique style. Not content to just play the classic tunes from his father's era, Santiago became a gifted songwriter as well, the first to combine classic ranchera duet singing with the polka beat of his two-button accordion. Most of his own compositions are considered classics today. They include "La Dueña de la Llave," "El Primer Beso," "Ay Te Dejo en San Antonio," and "Margarita, Margarita," among others. This blending of old and new became the foundation of present-day conjunto. Another element that set Santiago's style apart was his very use of the old-fashioned two-button; even later on, when most of his contemporaries and younger players were using the three-button version, Santiago continued with the trusty model he'd used to revolutionize the music.

Throughout the 1940s and 1950s Santiago recorded and performed extensively. In the 1970s he went into semi-retirement and moved to Dallas, playing music only occasionally. In 1978 he moved back to San Antonio, playing a regular weekly gig until his death in 1984. Santiago passed down his estimable musical gifts to his two sons, both influential and talented in their own right. Flaco Jimenez is perhaps the most famous of all contemporary conjunto accordion players today, updating the sound to include rock, country, R&B, and blues. His list of collaborators is extensive and includes Ry Cooder, Linda Ronstadt, Stephen Stills, and Los Lobos. Today he is a member of the Tex-Mex band the Texas Tornados, which includes Freddie Fender,

Doug Sahm, and Augie Meyers. Santiago Jimenez Jr. is the more traditional of the two siblings. His playing is more reminiscent of his father, with a repertoire leaning toward the classic style.

what to buy: *Don Santiago Jimenez, His First and Last Recordings: 1937 & 1979* ♪♪♪♪ (Arhoolie, 1994, prod. Chris Strachwitz) is a must for fans of classic Tex-Mex music. The first dozen cuts of this 25-song disc were recorded in 1979 in San Antonio, and, indeed, ended up being Santiago's last recordings. He plays accordion and sings, and is accompanied by son Flaco on *bajo sexto* (12-string bass guitar) and vocals, and by Juan Viesca on string bass. The exuberance here is evident as father and son play and sing classics like "La Dueña De La Llave," "Ere Un Encanto," "Los Gallineros" and "Antonia De Mis Amores." The second half of the disc is composed of songs culled from Don Santiago's early recordings, circa 1937–38. Although the selections were pulled from old 78s, the music sounds as vital and energetic as that recorded 40 years later. (It's interesting to note that like most accordion players of the time, Don Santiago did not sing: the music was played for dancing.) Mostly polkas, the early cuts include "Dices Pescao," "La Tunas," "Marfa, Gran Polka Moderna," and "Las Madera."

worth searching for: Once again, since he did most of his recording more than 40 years ago on now-defunct small labels, you'll have do some digging to find records by this master. Aside from *First and Last Recordings,* Arhoolie offers several excellent compilations of artists from the early accordionists to the conjuntos popular today. Two featuring Don Santiago Jimenez, Narciso Martinez, and other seminal figures are *Mexican American Border Music Volume III: Norteño & Tejano Accordion Pioneers* (reviewed in this book's Compilations section), and *Tex-Mex Fiesta.*

influences:

◀◀ Patricio Jimenez

▶▶ Flaco Jimenez, Santiago Jimenez Jr., Esteban "Steve" Jordon, Los Lobos, countless others.

see also: *Flaco Jimenez, Santiago Jimenez Jr., Los Lobos, Narciso Martinez, Texas Tornados*

Andrew BeDell

Flaco Jimenez

Conjunto, norteño, Tex-Mex fusion
Born March 11, 1939, in San Antonio, TX, USA. Based in Texas, USA.

The undisputed king of *conjunto* music and son of the influential Don Santiago Jimenez, Flaco Jimenez is a squeezebox master who plays a rousing mix of American folk and country and Mexican *rancheras* and polkas. In addition to his own records, his colorful accordion work and straightforward vocals have graced albums by Ry Cooder (who helped introduce Jimenez to the rest of America), the Mavericks, Dwight Yoakam, and the Rolling Stones. A Tex-Mex music veteran of more than three decades, Jimenez has branched out into American country both as a solo act and as a member of the Texas Tornados alongside Freddy Fender, Doug Sahm, and Augie Meyers. Some of Jimenez's many Grammys have been with that outfit, all four members of which were also involved in 1998's instant-sensation Latin-rock all-star project Los Super Seven—which, in turn, snagged Jimenez one of two additional Grammys in 1999 alone.

what to buy: Jimenez's most accessible solo work has been with Arista Texas, which released his best Tex-Mex album, *Flaco Jimenez* ♪♪♪ (Arista Texas, 1994, prod. Bill Halverson). It includes the Grammy-winning "Cat Walk" and features contributions from the Mavericks' Raul Malo, as well as from country music stars Lee Roy Parnell and Radney Foster.

what to buy next: *Buena Suerte, Senorita* ♪♪♪ (Arista, 1996, prod. Cameron Riddle, Flaco Jimenez) leans more heavily toward updating the Mexican side of his music. The rollicking *Partners* ♪♪♪ (Warner Bros., 1992, prod. Bill Halverson) features some big-name friends, including Linda Ronstadt, Emmylou Harris, Dwight Yoakam, and Los Lobos.

the rest:
El Senido de San Antonio ♪♪♪ (Arhoolie, 1980)
Ay Te Dejo en San Antonio y Mas ♪♪♪ (Arhoolie, 1986)
Flaco's Amigos ♪♪♪ (Arhoolie, 1987)
Arriba el Norte ♪♪♪ (Rounder, 1988)
Entre Humor & Batellas ♪♪♪ (Rounder, 1989)
San Antonio Soul ♪♪♪ (Rounder, 1991)
Un Mojado sin Licencia (A Wetback without a Green Card) ♪♪♪ (Arhoolie, 1993)
Flaco's First ♪♪♪ (Arhoolie, 1995)
One Night at Joey's N/A (Sony Discos, 1999)

influences:

◀◀ Don Santiago Jimenez

▶▶ Ry Cooder, Doug Sahm

see also: *Ry Cooder, Don Santiago Jimenez, Los Fabulosos Cadillacs, Los Super Seven, Texas Tornados*

Doug Pullen

Santiago Jimenez Jr.

Conjunto, norteño
Born April 8, 1944, in San Antonio, TX, USA. Based in San Antonio, TX, USA.

Santiago Jimenez Jr. is surrounded by greatness on the family tree. First there's his father, Don Santiago Jimenez, one of the greatest *conjunto* (Tex-Mex) accordionists in San Antonio's his-

Santiago Jimenez Jr.

tory and the person for whom the younger Jimenez was named. Then there's his older brother, Leonardo "Flaco" Jimenez, a world-renowned accordionist who has played with everyone from Ry Cooder to the Texas Tornados. While Flaco is considered an innovator within the genre, bringing rock and blues elements to a conjunto setting, Santiago Jr. (also an accordionist) upholds the tradition by playing his father's compositions and advocating for the *rancheras,* polkas, and *huapangos* of an earlier era. Santiago started his recording career in the early 1960s, cutting 45 rpm discs for regional companies like Corona, Lira, Del Bravo, Discos Grandes, and D.L.B. He also worked as a school janitor before jumping into the music profession full-time in 1981. He has since toured North America and Europe, been nominated for two Grammy Awards, and received funding from the National Endowment for the Arts and the Texas Folklife Resources organization, enabling him to pass on his experiences and love for the music he plays to yet another generation.

what to buy: *El Mero, Mero de San Antonio* ♫♫♫♫ (Arhoolie, 1990, compilation prod. Chris Strachwitz) should be on the shortlist of classic, "old-style" conjunto recordings. Jimenez's vocals are strong throughout and his playing on the two-row accordion is fluid, rolling over the songs' bones like a river of chords and single-note runs. Juan Viesca, the *tololoche* (string bass guitar) player who used to perform with the senior Jimenez and in the Trio San Antonio alongside the great accordionist Fred Zimmerle, adds just the right mix of virtuosity and authenticity to Jimenez Jr.'s recording. "California Polka" is a case in point, as accordion flurries swirl over popping basslines and a steady, rhythmic underpinning from the unnamed *bajo sexto* (12-string bass guitar) player.

what to buy next: Most of Jimenez's albums feature his singing over his playing, but *Purely Instrumental* ♫♫♫ (Arhoolie, 1998, prod. Chris Strachwitz) puts Jimenez the accordionist at center stage, where he acquits himself well. Bassist Mark Rubin (of the Bad Livers) anchors the record, while Hugo Gonzalez (bajo sexto) and Rufus Martinez (drums) help make up one of the best bands Jimenez has had since the Viesca days. The junior Jimenez's most direct tribute to Jimenez senior, *Canciones de Mi Padre* ♫♫♫ (Watermelon, 1994, prod. Santiago Jimenez Jr.)

is an old-fashioned trio date with accordion, bajo sexto, and tololoche playing tunes written by his father. It's also his very first self-produced album.

best of the rest:

Familia y Tradicíon 🎵🎵🎵 (Rounder, 1989)
El Gato Negro 🎵🎵🎵 (Rounder, 1990)
Corazón de Piedra 🎵🎵🎵 (Watermelon, 1992)
Musica de Tiempos Pasados, del Presente, y Futuro 🎵🎵🎵 (Watermelon, 1995)
Al Mirar Tu Cara 🎵🎵🎵 (Hacienda, 1998)
Corridos de La Frontera 🎵🎵🎵 (Watermelon, 1998)

influences:

◄◄ Don Santiago Jimenez, Fred Zimmerle, Juan Lopez, Narciso Martinez

►► Ben Tavera King, Carl Finch

see also: *Don Santiago Jimenez, Flaco Jimenez*

Garaud MacTaggart

Antonio Carlos Jobim
Bossa nova
Born January 25, 1927, in Rio de Janeiro, Brazil. Died December 8, 1994, in New York, NY, USA.

Antonio Carlos Jobim has had a tremendous influence on the development of Brazilian jazz both in the United States and around the globe. Classically trained and a musician since childhood, Jobim started recording in 1954 with a 78 rpm release on Brazil's Continental label. Gifted as a composer and proficient as a guitarist, pianist, and vocalist, Jobim—originally bound for a career as an architect—gained a high profile in his home country when singer João Gilberto released a single of Jobim's "Chega de Saudade" in 1958. By the early 1960s, collaborating with Gilberto and others—like Luiz Bonfá and Vinicius de Moraes, with whom he earned an international reputation in 1959 for the soundtrack to *Orfeo Negro (Black Orpheus)*—Jobim became the leading force of a new trend in music. Not content to simply reiterate the sounds of the popular samba, Jobim distilled the style, toning down its loud and brash qualities and adding harmonic and melodic complexity. One of his main inspirations at the time came from America's West Coast cool-jazz sounds being created by musicians like Chet Baker and Gerry Mulligan. Jobim's music was also augmented by the harmonic sensibilities of French classical composer Claude Debussy, and from this hybrid of influences came what was called the *bossa nova* or "new wave." As the growing Brazilian record industry began to export to the United States, Jobim's music started attracting the attention of jazz artists like Charlie Byrd, who first heard the bossa nova sound while on tour in Brazil in 1961 and upon his return

recorded an album with Stan Getz that included Jobim's "Desafinado." Although Jobim included "The Girl from Ipanema" on his own 1963 Verve album *The Composer of Desafinado Plays,* it is the vocal version featuring Astrud Gilberto on the 1964 Stan Getz/João Gilberto record *Getz/Gilberto* that remains the most popular rendition. Jobim's invitation to be included in a showcase of Brazilian musicians in New York City in 1962 gained him international recognition and helped catapult him to stardom as the leader of the new musical movement. Byrd and Getz became big fans of the musical style and recorded many of Jobim's compositions in the early 1960s. Countless other jazz artists continue to perform and record Jobim compositions, and his ineradicable contributions continue even after his death.

what to buy: *The Man from Ipanema* 🎵🎵🎵🎵🎵 (Verve, 1995, prod. Creed Taylor) is a deluxe three-CD set that covers the best of Jobim's career, especially such classics as "Desafinado," "Corcovado," "The Girl from Ipanema," "Dindi," and others. The first disc is made up of vocal works, the second features instrumentals, and the third contains numerous alternate takes on many of his most popular tunes. This is an essential collection that includes a 60-page booklet with biographical information as well as an interview with the artist. Lovingly assembled, it's a treat for both the ears and eyes. *Volume 13: Verve Jazz Masters* 🎵🎵🎵🎵 (Verve, 1993, prod. various) is a briefer introduction to Jobim's oeuvre distilled onto one CD, yet provides another excellent introduction to his music.

what to buy next: *The Composer of Desafinado Plays* 🎵🎵🎵 (Verve, 1963, prod. Creed Taylor) is Jobim's original album featuring "The Girl from Ipanema" (sans Astrud Gilberto's vocals). Smooth, slick, and brimming with the hallmarks of Jobim's ideas, *Wave* 🎵🎵🎵🎵 (A&M, 1967/1989, prod. Creed Taylor) and *Tide* 🎵🎵🎵🎵 (A&M, 1970/1996, prod. Creed Taylor) are two albums almost always considered as a pair. *Urubu* 🎵🎵🎵 (Warner Bros., 1976/1996, prod. Claus Ogerman) is an often-overlooked album, yet it's a showcase for Jobim's more serious music, featuring arrangements by producer Ogerman.

best of the rest:

Stone Flower 🎵🎵🎵 (CTI, 1971/Sony, 1990)
Terra Brasilis 🎵🎵🎵 (Warner Bros., 1980/1996)
Passarim 🎵🎵🎵 (Verve, 1987)
Personalidade 🎵🎵🎵 (Verve, 1987/1993)
Antonio Carlos Jobim: Composer 🎵🎵🎵 (Warner Bros., 1996)

worth searching for: *Francis Albert Sinatra & Antonio Carlos Jobim* 🎵🎵🎵🎵 (Reprise, 1967/1988, prod. Sonny Burke) pairs Jobim with the Chairman of the Board. It's a divine album, falling short of perfection only because it clocks in at a measly 28:33.

influences:

◄◄ Gerry Mulligan, Chet Baker

►► Stan Getz, Charlie Byrd, Cal Tjader, Sergio Mendes, Herbie Mann, Flora Purim, Airto Moreira

see also: *Luiz Bonfá, Astrud Gilberto, João Gilberto, Herbie Mann*

Chris Meloche and Nancy Ann Lee

Beau Jocque

Zydeco

Born Andrus Espre, 1956, in Kinder, LA, USA. Died September 10, 1999, in Kinder, LA, USA.

Beau Jocque was a big man with a big voice and a taste for tight, funky music. When an industrial accident left him partially paralyzed in 1987, he learned to play his father's button accordion during his 10-month recovery. He found himself drawn to the hypnotic music of Boozoo Chavis. Jocque used Chavis's one-chord vamps as the launchpad for a more modern style with a more contemporary beat. This combination of the most primitive Creole sounds with the most up-to-date rhythms created a sensation that is still reverberating in Louisiana and beyond. Dance floors were filled to overflowing when Beau Jocque played, and every other band jumped in to try and create their version of his sound. The Beau Jocque revolution cut as wide a swath across the zydeco landscape as Sherman's army burning their way to the sea—only this march met with no resistance.

what to buy: *Pick Up on This!* ✍✍✍✍ (Rounder, 1994, prod. Scott Billington) gives the full effect of the Beau Jocque style without too much of his more current rock and hip-hop influences. Those qualities are here, but so is a real Creole Louisiana sound. Imagine a van carrying the old Sugar Hill rhythm section of Keith LeBlanc and Doug Wimbish getting lost on their way to the jazz festival and ending up at Beau Jocque's door as he's preparing to put his band together. Whether Jocque was responsible for the double bass beat that became his trademark, or the super-deep slinky bass of Chuck Bush, both are clearly identified as part of the patented sound. Producer Billington understands this and jacks up Chuck Bush's five-string bass unlike any zydeco record made before that time. "Give It to Me" starts with the band deep in the minor-key, double-clutched groove and Beau Jocque sounding like he and Mahlathini have genetically identical vocal chords. The process repeats itself song after song, even on the relatively straight blues of "Do Right Sometime" and the waltz "Chere Migonne." This record will leave the dancers completely worn out and ready to put their feet up. *Beau Jocque Boogie* ✍✍✍✍ (Rounder, 1993, prod. Scott Billington) is the groundbreaking record that started the Beau Jocque phenom in zydeco country. From the opening beat of "Richard's Club," this record just sounded different from what had been

around before. "Give Me Cornbread" was the first big Beau Jocque hit and lead to him being obligingly pelted with the golden snack at some of the local festivals. "Damballah" may be the first zydeco tribute to a Haitian *Vodou* god ever recorded—okay, maybe just the best-known! And then there's *Check It Out, Lock It Up, Crank It Out* ✍✍✍✍ (Rounder, 1998, prod. Scott Billington). Yeah, he's portrayed as a dancehall superhero on the cover and he's playing the kind of five-row button accordion normally reserved for romantic Russian music—he's still Beau Jocque, so look out! His penchant for covering oldies continues with South Louisiana jukebox favorites like "Tequila" and "Tighten Up," but yesterday or today this may be the tightest band in the whole country, and the disc is just packed with groove-filled music.

the rest:

My Name Is Beau Jocque ✍✍✍ (Paula/Flyright, 1995)
Nursery Rhyme ✍✍✍ (Beau Jocque, 1995)
Get It, Beau Jocque ✍✍✍✍ (Rounder, 1995)
Gonna Take You Downtown ✍✍✍✍ (Rounder, 1996)
Beau Jocque & the Zydeco Hi-Rollers ✍✍✍✍ (Rounder, 1997)

influences:

◄◄ Amédée Ardoin, Alphonse "Bois Sec" Ardoin, Boozoo Chavis

►► Keith Frank, Chris Ardoin, Geno Delafose

see also: *Boozoo Chavis*

Jared Snyder

Linton Kwesi Johnson

Dub poetry

Born August 24, 1952, in Chapelton, Jamaica. Based in Brixton, England.

Linton Kwesi Johnson, or "LKJ" as he is more familiarly known to his fans, was born poor and grew up on his grandmother's farm in the Jamaican countryside. He learned how to read by studying the Bible with his grandmother, and had his heart set on becoming a writer from an early age. When he was 11 years old he went to live with his mother in the ghetto of Brixton, where he still lives and works. In 1963 Britain was in upheaval with labor strikes, the advent of the fascist National Front and the Black Power movement, and the first rumblings of worldwide youth uprising. Johnson dropped out of high school because of the racism that surrounded him, although later in life he returned to the University of London and earned a degree in sociology.

"I experimented with prose, but verse seemed more powerful," Johnson explained. "I discovered *The Souls of Black Folk* by W. E. B. DuBois and, through John Leroux (a Trinidadian publisher and radical political thinker), black writers from all over the world. That made me want to explore the experiences of my generation, black youths who were growing up in racist British society." Johnson joined the British Black Panther Youth League and organized a writer's workshop. When he performed his poems, people told him they were powerfully rhythmic and suggested that he put them to music. Inspired by the Last Poets, he began working with a Rasta drum group calling themselves Rasta Love.

In 1974 Johnson published his first book of poetry, *Voices of the Living and the Dead*. His second book, *Dread Beat and Blood*, got rave reviews that praised him as an important new voice. Since he was describing the experiences of the black West Indian underclass, Johnson used their own language, a patois that had little to do with the King's English, but was undeniably powerful. The crowds at his readings began to grow rapidly; Johnson also read his poems on BBC-TV to further raves. In the late 1970s Johnson started working with Dennis Bovell, already a force in British reggae due to his work with his band Matumbi. Matumbi had provided backing tracks for a number of lover's rock and roots reggae artists, and scored several hits on its own. After some original members split, Bovell reconfigured the group as Dennis Bovell & the Dub Band and began an ongoing partnership with Johnson. Their first collaboration, also titled *Dread Beat and Blood,* virtually created a new genre—dub poetry—by matching Johnson's revolutionary rhetoric with Bovell's equally inventive rhythms. "I first called it dub poetry during a newspaper interview," Johnson recalled. "What the DJs [rappers] were doing was improvised poetry, spontaneous expressions of culture." Since Bovell was born in Barbados, his reggae visions were not limited by traditional Jamaican notions of what the music should sound like, and he brought many international flourishes to the settings he and Johnson created for Johnson's poems, including jazz, ska, calypso, blues, and rock.

Bovell and Johnson's second collaboration, *Forces of Victory,* was a quantum leap forward, both musically and lyrically, a blistering attack on British racism that galvanized the new generation of white punks as well as the new generation of militant black youth. Johnson followed *Forces of Victory* with three more hard-hitting albums, but as dancehall reggae slowly began to gain dominance he cut back his touring and recording to produce and promote new artists on his LKJ label and self-publish his poetry.

what to buy: *Independent Intavenshan: The Island Anthology* 🎵🎵🎵🎵 (Island, 1998, prod. Dennis Bovell, LKJ) is a solid anthology of Johnson's best work for Island, including most of *Forces of Victory* and *Bass Culture* as well as tracks from *LKJ in Dub* and *Making History*.

what to buy next: *Dread Beat and Blood* 🎵🎵🎵🎵 (Heartbeat, 1981, prod. LKJ, Dennis Bovell), first released in Great Britain in 1978, created dub poetry and is still a chilling musical and political statement almost 20 years later.

the rest:
Forces of Victory 🎵🎵🎵🎵 (Island, 1979)
Bass Culture 🎵🎵🎵🎵 (Island, 1980)
LKJ in Dub 🎵🎵🎵 (Island, 1980)
Making History 🎵🎵🎵🎵 (Island, 1984)

influences:
◄◄ Dillinger, U Roy, I Roy
►► Mutabaraka, Michael Smith, Jean Binta Breeze

see also: *Oku Onuora, Benjamin Zephaniah*

j. poet

The Johnstons

See: Mick Moloney

Jolly Boys

Mento, calypso
Formed 1935, in Port Antonio, Jamaica. Based in Port Antonio, Jamaica.

Moses Deans (Jamaica), banjo, vocals; Noel Howard (Jamaica), guitar, vocals; Joseph Bennet (Jamaica), rumba box, vocals; Allan Swymmer (Jamaica), lead vocals, bongos.

If they ever give a Grammy for longevity and perseverance, Jamaica's Jolly Boys will win it without a contest. They play a rootsy brand of folk music called *mento,* and they've been at it since even before the late '40s (when they first became world-famous as the house band at the extravagant parties Errol Flynn threw in their hometown of Port Antonio). Mento refers not only to the music, but also to the dance that is done with it, and the lyrical style of dealing with topical situations in a satirical or humorous way. (Many folkloric scholars are looking for the common root that they feel links mento with Trinidad's calypso tradition.) Although they're not "boys" (guitarist Noel Howard is the youngest at 49, while the surviving original member of the band, banjo player Moses Deans, admits to 72), the Jolly Boys' sound is youthful, or more accurately, timeless. The music, a mix of calypso, Jamaican folk, and the jazz and R&B sounds the band has picked up from the recordings of tourists, is anchored by booming *funde* drumming and the African percussion of the group's rumba box—a suitcase-sized kalimba, or thumb piano—and driven by the band's tinkling Jamaican folk guitar and banjo licks, as well as Allan Swymmer's rum and honey vocals. For the past 20 years or so, the Jolly Boys have played six nights a week at the Trident Hotel in Port Antonio for the amusement of the international jet set. This exposure has honed the band's music to a fine edge; they play like a single entity with a seamless professionalism that's slick and funky at the same time.

In 1986 singer/songwriter Jules Shear was vacationing in Port Antonio; he heard the Jolly Boys and was blown away. A few

Esteban "Steve" Jordan

months later he was back with a two-track DAT machine in hand to record the tapes that became *Pop 'n' Mento*. The album did unexpectedly well and by the time Shear went back to the island to talk about a second one, the Jolly Boys could even afford new guitar strings. "They make a living," Shear says, "and have the respect of the community, but by our standards they're not wealthy by any means. When I was down there they showed me a technique they have for tying broken guitar strings together, 'cause, as they say, 'Strings are very dear, mon.'" This time Shear brought the band to New York City, and while the sound of their second album *Sunshine 'n' Water* may be 'cleaner,' it's no less funky. "We did 20 tunes in four hours," Shear said, "all on the first take, so the spontaneity is still there."

what's available: The Jolly Boys make a living playing for tourists, so although the music is down-home funky and steeped in tradition, it's also bright and user-friendly. Many of the tunes on *Pop 'n' Mento* ♫♫♫ (First Warning, 1989, prod. Jules Shear) will be familiar to lovers of calypso and Caribbean folk, with most of the material heavy on the double entendres.

Sunshine 'n' Water ♫♫♫ (First Warning, 1991, prod. Jules Shear) is another worthwhile purchase.

influences:

◄◄ Blind Blake, Growling Tiger, Attila the Hun

►► Sparrow, Explainer, Ras Michael & the Sons of Negus, Lord Melody

j. poet

Esteban "Steve" Jordan

Conjunto, Tejano
Born 1938, in Elson, TX, USA. Based in South Texas, USA.

Among modern accordionists performing in the major Tex-Mex styles of *conjunto* and *Tejano,* perhaps none have been more innovative or accomplished than Esteban Jordan. While in his teens in the late 1950s, Jordan made traditional conjunto music with his brothers, Bonnie and Silver. Throughout the 1960s Los Hermanos Jordan cut several singles for regional labels such as Cima and Falcon. Once called the Jimi Hendrix of the accordion,

Jordan freely improvised, introducing phase-shifters and other guitar-oriented electronica previously unused in Tex-Mex music, let alone on the button accordion. Nicknamed "El Parche" for the patch he wears over one eye, Jordan, with his shaggy hair flying, looks the part of the rocker, flailing away on his keyboard. With his respect for the traditional music of the border and his innovations in the modern realm, you might better compare Jordan to Keith Richards of the Rolling Stones—who, like Jordan, returns to his roots (in Richards's case, the blues) to find new inspiration. Today, Jordan remains wildly popular on the conjunto circuit and at festivals throughout the Southwest.

what to buy: *The Many Sounds of Steve Jordan* ♪♪♪♪♪ (Arhoolie, 1990, prod. Chris Strachwitz) captures El Parche and his *conjunto* (which is also Spanish for "group") at their best. The CD covers Jordan's career from his traditional treatment of *rancheras* and polkas of the early '60s to his more rocking cuts of the '70s and beyond. Among the 20 cuts is Jordan's classic "El Corrido de Jhonny El Pachuco," as well as "Midnight Blues," "Las Coronelas," and a wild cover of Buck Owens's "Together Again." Jordan's then-wife Virginia Martinez joins on vocals for many of the early cuts.

what to buy next: Both *El Huracan* ♪♪♪ (Rounder, 1989) and *Return of El Parche* ♪♪♪ (Rounder, 1984) offer about a dozen cuts apiece culled from recordings made by Jordan during the late '70s and into the mid-'80s. Both offer many tunes not included on *The Many Sounds of Steve Jordan.*

worth searching for: Jordan has cut many, many records throughout his long career, recording on at least seven labels. Fans in the Southwest, especially in South Texas and Southern California, should have no trouble finding Jordan's 45s and LPs in mainstream Latin record shops. Others may have to dig a little deeper.

influences:

◀◀ Narciso Martinez, Don Santiago Jimenez, Valerio Longoria

▶▶ La Mafia, Los Palominos, Los Lobos, Emilio Navaira

Andrew BeDell

Joyce
Brazilian jazz
Born January 31, 1948, in Rio de Janeiro, Brazil. Based in Brazil.

The Brazilian jazz vocalist/guitarist widely known only as Joyce has been thrilling audiences in her native country for 30 years. She's also a composer whose more than 200 original jazz/samba songs have been recorded by popular countrymen and women such as Milton Nascimento, Flora Purim, and the late Elis Regina. Joyce began her career in the late 1960s with a

slack-key guitar

Slack-key is an indigenous Hawaiian style of finger-picking solo acoustic guitar, the name of which refers to the instrument's open tunings (in the native Hawaiian tongue, slack-key is called *ki ho' alu*, literally, "loosen the key"). The tunings, though usually based in major chords, vary from player to player and may be kept secret. Slack-key developed from the Hawaiian cowboy tradition, after other cowboys (or "vaqueros") from Mexico, California, Spain, Portugal, and many South American countries introduced the guitar—and the Western concept of melody—to the islands during the 1830s. The guitar as a solo instrument came into its own in Hawaii in the 1940s and '50s with the recordings of such artists as Gabby Pahinui and Sonny Chillingworth, and gained further prominence in the '70s as those guitarists influenced a new generation of players. The selection of slack-key albums available on the mainland is still limited, with the easiest to find coming from pianist George Winston's Dancing Cat label, which began recording some of the best contemporary practitioners, including Keola Beamer and George Kuo, in 1994.

see also: Keola Beamer, Sonny Chillingworth, George Kahumoku, Moses Kahumoku, Rev. Dennis Kamakahi, Ray Kane, George Kuo, Leonard Kwan, Gabby Pahinui, the Pahinui Brothers

Brian Mansfield

self-titled debut album for Philips. Writing songs from a feminist perspective in Brazil's repressive political climate probably slowed her growing popularity in the 1970s, but still she prevailed during two decades of stifling military dictatorship, when every recording had to be reviewed and approved by government censors. After a couple of albums she left Philips to front the short-lived group "A Tribo" with Nelson Angelo, Toninho Horta, Novelli, and Nana Vasconcelos, releasing one album for EMI. In 1975 a European tour with Vinicius de Moraes (co-composer with Antonio Carlos Jobim of the Brazilian classic "Girl from Ipanema") led to extended stays in Europe and the United States before Joyce returned to Brazil in 1978. She signed a new contract with EMI in 1980, releasing her personal favorite album, *Feminina,* which contained the hit lullaby "Clareana," a dedication to her daughters that has become a national classic in her native country. The album was released 15 years later in England and Japan, where Joyce retains popularity among jazz/dance club fans. Throughout the 1980s and 1990s Joyce continued to record, including the self-produced 1984 album *Tardes Cariocas,* which was chosen as "Album of the Year" in Brazil and was later reissued worldwide in 1997. Her popularity in Brazil led to a record contract with Verve USA in 1990. Her first release for them, *Music Inside,* brought Joyce wider recognition up north, as did the follow-up *Language and Love,* while tours of Europe, Japan, and the States in 1994 heightened her international profile even further. *Ilha Brasil* followed; like many musicians who believe that recording with a string orchestra somehow elevates their original compositions, Joyce considers this 1996 album one of her best works. In 1997 the U.K.-based Mr. Bongo Records released a retrospective, *The Essential Joyce: 1970–1996.* Her 20th album as leader, *Astronauta: Songs of Elis* was recorded in New York for Blue Jackel in 1998. Like predecessors such as Astrud Gilberto, Purim, and Regina, Joyce is one of the few contemporary Brazilian singers who possess natural jazz sensibilities. It's unfortunate for fans that only about half of her albums are available in the United States.

what to buy: For the best introduction to Joyce, the chronological compilation *The Essential Joyce 1970–1996* ♫♫♫♫ (Mr. Bongo, 1997, compilation prod. Bongo) is a most fulfilling listen. The 23 tracks, recorded for EMI-U.K., Pointer, and other labels, span Joyce's career from the age of 19, demonstrating her versatility in beautiful melodies, catchy rhythms, and tantalizing original songs (including her lullaby classic "Clareana" and her spirited "Samba de Gago"). With various (unlisted) accompanists, the more than 76 minutes of music provide an appealing overview of one of Brazil's favorite divas. This is a must-own import CD and if you can't find it in your local record store, you'll find it online at several CD-sales Web sites. Joyce's label debut for the Huntington, New York–based Blue Jackel, *Astronauta: Songs of Elis* ♫♫♫♫ (Blue Jackel, 1998, prod. Kazuo Yoshida, Rodolfo Stroeter) is a graceful dedication to the late Elis Regina. On the 14 songs, Joyce embraces the singer's memory with tender, velvety vocals and rosy-toned acoustic guitar accompaniment. Ranging from traditional bossa nova to pop-oriented Musica Popular Brasileira ("Brazilian Popular Music" or "MPB"), the tunes highlight lively, swaying Brazilian classics by composers Milton Nascimento, Ary Barroso, Dori Caymmi, Nelson Motta, and Gilberto Gil as well as two Joyce originals and more songs Regina made famous during the '60s and '70s. Among the featured instrumentalists are Romero Lubambo (guitar), Rodolfo Stroeter (bass), Tutty Moreno (drums), Joe Lovano (saxophone), and pianists Mulgrew Miller and Renee Rosnes. The album is a more somber affair than Joyce's others, yet a heartwarming listen nonetheless.

what to buy next: A buoyant 14-song session and among Joyce's most jazzy, *Ilha Brasil* ♫♫♫♫ (Capitol, 1996, prod. Kazuo Yoshida) finds the singer backed by an array of talented Brazilian musicians in settings that include full orchestra and (usually) her Quarteto Livre, a modern group highly conversant in both jazz and Brazilian music. Featuring pianist Mozar Terra, drummer Tutty Moreno, bassist Sizão Machado, and Teco Cardoso playing reeds and flutes, the Livre (and various guests) support Joyce with innovative flair on this album, which straddles the fence between improvised jazz and Brazilian themes. In fact, but for Joyce singing in Portuguese, the straight-ahead jazz piece "Sexy Silvia" is reminiscent of a chic, swinging tune by Diane Schuur. One of the prettiest songs, "Viola de Prata," features Joyce with only piano and guitar accompaniment. This CD is a widely diverse, satisfying showcase for Joyce's original music, and a hip affair that blends the best of both worlds.

best of the rest:
Music Inside ♫♫♫ (Verve Forecast, 1990)
Language & Love ♫♫♫ (Verve Forecast, 1991)
Sings Jobim & Moraes ♫♫♫ (Iris, 1996)

influences:
◀◀ Elis Regina, Astrud Gilberto, Flora Purim

▶▶ Badi Assad, Lani Hall, Milton Nascimento

Nancy Ann Lee

JPP
/Järvelän Pikkupelimannit
Finnish folk, tango
Formed 1980, in Järvelä, Kaustinen, Finland. Based in Finland.

Arto Järvelä, fiddle (1980–present); Jouni Järvelä, string bass, fiddle (1980–93); Mauno Järvelä, fiddle (1984–present); Jarmo Varila, fiddle (1980–93); Juha Varila, fiddle (1980–93); Timo Alakotila, harmonium (1980–present); Janne Virkkala, string bass (1984–97); Matti Mäkelä, fiddle (1992–present); Tommi Pyykönen, fiddle (1992–present); Timo Myllykangas, string bass (1997–present); JPP String Orchestra: Anni Järvelä, Antti Järvelä, Riikka Järvelä, Siiri Järvelä, Ville Kangas, Tuija Myllykangas, Turo Myllykangas, Jarmo Varila, and Mika Virkkala, fiddles. (All members are from Finland.)

Järvelän Pikkupelimannit means "Little Folk Musicians of Järvelä," and it was the original name for JPP, who would soon show themselves to be not so little at all. Their current moniker was acquired in 1988 when the leading daily newspaper in Finland, *Helsingin Sanomat,* shortened their name. That was the year they received Album of the Year honors from that very newspaper, in addition to carting home the "Tunnustus Prize" from the Finnish Radio Corporation. The group's first recorded project was *Laitisen Mankeliska,* a 1986 EP that featured traditional Finnish melodies in addition to works written by Finnish folk legends Konsta Jylhä and Viljami Niittykoski, as well as the band's own Timo Alakotila and Arto Järvelä. The group's mix of exciting polkas, waltzes, and tangos made an impact with their audiences, both on the dance floor and on the festival stage. By 1989 the buzz about JPP was formidable and they began touring Europe. They also made their first domestic television appearance that year, while their international reputation was further solidified in 1992 with their inaugural North American tour and the release of their first video, an eight-minute clip called "Puikkoristikko."

Arto Järvelä, who was only 17 when the group first started, is a graduate of the illustrious Folk Music Department at the Sibelius Academy in Helsinki. It was there that he met and performed with accordion virtuoso Maria Kalaniemi in a variety of groups, including the legendary Niekku. Their association continues to this day, with mutual guest appearances on disc. Järvelä has also become a lecturer at his alma mater, in addition to playing fiddle, mandolin, and *kantele* (the Finnish zither) with a variety of other ad hoc or formal groups—including the Helsinki Mandoliners, Koinurit, Salamakannel, Ampron Prunni, and Pinnin Pojat—and releasing his own solo album, *Polska Differente*. His uncle and fellow JPP member Mauno Järvelä passes on the fiddle tradition of their native Kaustinen by (in conjunction with Alakotila) teaching young musicians in a variety of ensembles including Järvelän Näppärit and Mulukka. The elder Järvelä once worked with Kankaan Pelimannit, another pioneering fiddle group that released the album *Suvitunnelma* while JPP was still in its infancy. Alakotila, the other major force behind JPP, also teaches harmonium and improvisation at the Sibelius Academy's Folk Music Department, but still finds time to play in a variety of non-JPP settings.

what to buy: *String Tease* ♫♫♫♫ (NorthSide, 1998, prod. Timo Alakotila, Arto Järvelä) is exemplary of how JPP keep adding to the folk tradition even as they pay homage to it. The pioneering Swedish folkies of Väsen arranged a waltz and a polka for this album and mesh their instrumental talents with JPP on those two tunes, but—with the exception of Erik Hokkanen's "Finnish Gypsies"—everything else on the album was either written or arranged by band members, chiefly Timo Alakotila and Arto Järvelä. The album preceding *String Tease* was *Kaustinen Rhapsody* ♫♫♫♫ (Olarin Musiikki Oy/Green Linnet, 1994, prod. Timo Alakotila, Arto Järvelä), which introduced JPP's musical adjuncts, the JVPP (JPP String Orchestra), on three tunes. *Kaustinen Rhapsody* proves that just because JPP's string section is, at times, almost as massive as one would find in a classical ensemble, doesn't mean that it can't turn on a metaphysical dime. Rhythms sparkle and the tune selection can amaze (as it does on "Texas Blues") and get feet moving (as it does on "Kalmari Special" and "Tango for Marsha").

what to buy next: Unleashing the power of dance, JPP's third album, *I've Found a New Tango* ♫♫♫♫ (Olarin Musiikki Oy, 1990, prod. JPP), gave a whole 'nother treatment to the jazz-age standard "I've Found a New Baby" and meshed that with waltzes, polkas, and a batch of tangos that could have Argentines working up a sweat.

the rest:
Devil's Polska ♫♫♫ (Olarin Musiikki Oy/Green Linnet, 1992/1994)

worth searching for: JPP's first full-length album, the self-titled *JPP* ♫♫♫ (Olarin Musiikki Oy, 1988, prod. JPP), holds up pretty well over time. Blending traditional melodies with original tunes from Timo Alakotila and Arto and Mauno Järvelä, this project provided the essential blueprint that all future JPP albums would be built on.

influences:
◀◀ Konsta Jylhä, Viljami Niittykoski
▶▶ Järvelän Näppärit, Mulukka

see also: *Maria Kalaniemi, Väsen*

Garaud MacTaggart

Jungular Grooves
Worldbeat
Formed 1987, in Oakland, CA, USA. Based in Oakland, CA, USA.

Reggie Benn, vocals, guitar; Holly Elder, steel drums; Robert James Haven, saxophone; Michael Corbett, drums; Wendell Rand, bass. (All members are from USA.)

Reggie Benn's Jungular Grooves is an aptly named organization. The band digs deep into the international roots of the African Diaspora to create a sound that blends strains of jazzy improvisation, hot Latin rhythms, languid reggae skanks, sharp R&B horn lines, rippling steel-pan melodies, and various West African and North American guitar styles into a seamless whole that defies categorization. Like the San Francisco Bay Area bands in the first worldbeat wave of the late '70s and early '80s, Jungular Grooves bases its sound on a wide variety of African and Afro-Caribbean styles, but they've succeeded where others have failed. They may, especially on their original compositions, conjure up enticing memory traces of half a dozen cultures, but they're impossible to pin down. "What we play now goes back to my childhood," Benn says. "I had a heavy dose of West Indian–flavored music from my father, who was originally from Barbados. The family played and sang calypsos on holidays, as well as that straight-up choral harmony thing we got from church. [My family] gave me a broad understanding of music, but at the time I just thought of [it all] as records, same as what I heard on the radio. I went by tunes, not by the styles."

Salman Ahmad of Junoon

"There was a bunch of 14-, 15-year-olds who used to do the doo-wop thing outside my house," Benn continues. "They'd sing 'Sil-houettes,' or whatever, and it had a romantic aspect, going to sleep at 8 p.m., hearing these kids singing and talking outside my window. It made me associate music with freedom and the wild-ness that's out there in the dark under the street lights." Although he'd always loved music, Benn didn't think about picking up a gui-tar until he landed at Stanford University in the early '70s. "I'm a big guy, and the guitar was so small, and you have to play the strings one at a time, but I got captured by B. B. King and Marv Tarplin, the cat that played behind Smokey. Once I could play, I couldn't avoid getting work." At Stanford Benn hooked up with Tuck Andress, later of Tuck & Patti fame, and played with him for several years in various jazz and soul bands. After Benn finished with school, he migrated to the Bay Area and played with a variety of Cuban, African, and worldbeat acts including Hedzoleh Soundz, Sooliman Rogie, Cool Breeze, and Karma Kanics, a short-lived but musically exciting East Bay worldbeat organization. As Benn was honing his international chops, he was also writing tunes and thinking about starting his own band. "Since nobody who makes a living as a musician has time to rehearse, I got into a folkloric

thing, and built tunes around a sing-song hook or a simple bass line, the kind of tunes you can play instantly. Worldbeat should flow, which is a quality that was lacking in most of the bands." Benn feels that some African musicians are too rigid in their ap-proach, while Americans who try playing Afro-Caribbean styles often sound rhythmically stilted. Somehow, perhaps because of Benn's lifelong familiarity with both African American and Afro-Caribbean music, Jungular Grooves is able to avoid both extremes to present a driving, danceable multicultural sound that stretches listeners' musical imaginations, rather than aiming for the least common denominator. In a perfect world the Jungulars would have a major label deal and be traveling the globe playing their unique hybrid. Until that happens, you can dance along by tracking down their two excellent independent CDs.

what's available: Benn's gruff vocals have a unique quality, and the band includes some of the Bay Area's best world-music players. *J. Grooves* 𝄞𝄞𝄞𝄞 (International Soul, 1996, prod. Reg-gie Benn) has solid songwriting, with plenty of hooks and a groove that's as deep and steamy as the band's name implies. Why they aren't better known is a mystery. The debut *Jungular*

Grooves 🎵🎵🎵 (International Soul, 1992, prod. Reggie Benn) has a rougher edge than *J. Grooves,* but is still a charmer. "Magic," an ode to a certain basketball player, could be a big hit with a little bit of promo muscle behind it.

influences:

◀◀ Karma Kanicks, Looters, Sparrow, doo-wop

▶▶ Henri Dikongué, Alpha Yaya Diallo

j. poet

Junoon

Rock

Formed 1990, in Karachi, Pakistan. Based in Karachi, Pakistan.

Ali Azmat (Pakistan), vocals; Salman Ahmad (Pakistan), guitar; Brian O'Connell (USA), bass.

Pakistan is seldom thought of as a rock 'n' roll capital. But Junoon has blended the rich traditions of their native land, a passionate political stance, and the instrumental power and broad appeal of Western arena rock to become Pakistan's first superstars in the genre. The long-haired, hard-rocking trio was founded by guitarist and songwriter Salman Ahmad, vocalist Ali Azmat, and bassist Nusrat Hussain. When Hussain's full-time job as a pilot caused him to leave, the group was rounded out by bassist Brian O'Connell, whom Ahmad had met when living for a time in New York as a teenager. Junoon's sound was unique in the Pakistani/Indian music scene of the early '90s, and its pointedly partisan lyrics immediately won fans and severe critics. "Junoon" means passion in Pakistani, and the group is aptly named. Wildly popular at home and in India, Junoon has offended the governments of both countries by advocating cooperation rather than the stockpiling of arms. The trio's criticism of Pakistan's nuclear tests resulted in tapped phones and canceled concerts. Relatively unknown in the West, Junoon nonetheless has enough commercial clout that its most recent recording, *Azadi,* went platinum in only four weeks, despite—and in part probably because of—being banned by Pakistani television. Earlier, its song "Ehtesaab" ("Accountability") and the accompanying video were instrumental in removing former Pakistani leader Benazir Bhutto from office.

what to buy: The group's breakthrough fifth album, *Azadi* 🎵🎵🎵 (EMI, 1997, prod. Alec Raubeson, Salman Ahmad, Brian O'Connell), was the highest-selling pop album in both India and Pakistan in 1998. It includes the trio's scorching single "Sayonee," which topped the charts in Asia and the Middle East and features Azmat's deep, passionate vocal over O'Connell's burbling bass and driving hand percussion. Other tracks, such as the haunting "Saeen," feature Ahmad's unique blend of fiery acoustic and electric guitar textures (imagine a cross between Ravi Shankar and Jimmy Page).

worth searching for: Junoon's first four albums, despite being released on EMI and racking up impressive sales, are not readily available outside of Pakistan. *Kashmakash* (EMI, 1997, prod. Salman Ahmad, Brian O'Connell) contains the group's groundbreaking political commentary "Ehtesaab"; others worth hearing are *Inquilaab* (EMI, 1996, prod. Salman Ahmad, Brian O'Connell), *Talash* (EMI, 1992, prod. Salman Ahmad, Brian O'Connell, T.G), and *Junoon I* (1990, prod. Salman Ahmad).

influences:

◀◀ Led Zeppelin, U2

Michael Parrish

 K

Ledward Kaapana

See: Hui Ohana

George Kahumoku Jr.

Slack-key guitar

Born early 1950s, in HI, USA. Based in Honolulu, HI, USA.

Like many of Hawaii's slack-key guitarists (practitioners of a distinctive open-tuned style), George Kahumoku Jr. comes from a family of pickers, most notably his father, George Sr., and younger brother, Moses. Also like many slack-key guitarists, music isn't his only profession: Kahumoku doubles as a self-employed farmer with degrees in sculpture and agriculture. A player, singer, and composer, Kahumoku began his professional career at age 13 with Hawaiian singer-songwriter Kui Lee; he also performed with Moses as the Kahumoku Brothers during the 1970s and '80s.

what's available: The 12-string guitar that Kahumoku uses throughout *Drenched by Music* 🎵🎵🎵 (Dancing Cat, 1997, prod. George Winston, George Kahumoku Jr.) gives this album a fuller guitar sound than most of the other releases on the same label. The occasional vocal is sung in Hawaiian. Steel guitarist Bob Brozman joins Kahumoku on the duet "Hanohano Hawai'i," and Hawaiian singer Diana Aki contributes vocals to "Kaulana O Kawaihae (Famous Is Kawaihae)," a song also performed by Ledward Kaapana and his group Hui Ohana.

influences:

◀◀ Sonny Chillingworth, Gabby Pahinui, Ledward Kaapana, Leonard Kwan, Ray Kane

⏩ Moses Kahumoku

see also: *Hui Ohana, Moses Kahumoku*

Brian Mansfield

Moses Kahumoku

Slack-key guitar
Born 1953, in Honolulu, HI, USA. Based in HI, USA.

Moses Kahumoku is known in his home region for more than just his music. True, he's noted as a guitarist in the unique open-tuned "slack-key" style, and as one half of the popular Kahumoku Brothers with older sibling George Kahumoku Jr. But he's also a prominent activist working for Hawaiian sovereignty, as well as a fisherman and farmer. Though he does compose, he's more highly regarded as an interpreter and improviser on his instrument.

what's available: Kahumoku sings on only four of the 14 tracks on *Ho'okupu (The Gift)* ✍✍✍ (Dancing Cat, 1995, prod. George Winston), freeing up the rest of the album to focus on his singular instrumental style, which is marked by its arpeggiated melodies, single-note runs, and flamenco influence. This collection includes a couple of familiar Hawaiian songs, "Hawai'i Aloha" and "Kaula 'Ili," the latter associated with the great Sonny Chillingworth, who died shortly before the album's release.

influences:

◀◀ Sonny Chillingworth, Gabby Pahinui, Ledward Kaapana, Leonard Kwan, Ray Kane

⏩ George Kahumoku Jr.

see also: *Sonny Chillingworth, George Kahumoku Jr.*

Brian Mansfield

Kalama's Quartet

Hawaiian quartet with steel guitars
Formed 1927. Disbanded 1932. Based in New York, NY, USA.

Mike Hanapi (died 1959), tenor and falsetto voice, steel guitar; William Kalama, tenor voice, ukulele; Bob Nawahine, bass voice, harp-guitar; Dave Kaleipua Munson, baritone voice, guitar; Bob Matsu, voice, steel guitar. (All members are from Hawaii.)

Although Kalama's Quartet only cut records for five years, their songs contain some of the most beautiful Hawaiian falsetto singing and steel duets ever recorded. There is a deep, almost eerie spiritual quality to their unforgettable four-part harmonies, and no other group has ever come close to sounding like them. Their songs are so full of musical inventiveness, humor, and intense emotion that they are truly in a class by themselves, singing about the balmy trade winds, beautiful women, and places that they love. This is what the Hawaiians call "chicken skin" music, with a down-home, soulful sound that really makes you swoon. The group's leader, Mike Hanapi, moved from Honolulu to the mainland in 1912, and at age 14 he and his brother worked the Chicago Exposition. Hanapi probably learned to play the steel guitar around that time. Later he got vocal training at the New York Conservatory of Music. In 1938, he moved back to Hawaii and became a member of the Royal Hawaiian Band, playing saxophone until his death in 1959.

what's available: The original 78 rpm recordings of this group on the OKeh and Victor labels are extremely rare, and *Kalama's Quartet: Early Hawaiian Classics, 1927–1932* ✍✍✍ (Arhoolie Folklyric, 1993, prod. Chris Strachwitz, Bob Brozman) contains almost everything that remains of those gorgeous songs recorded seven decades ago. Some of the tunes, like "Medley of Hulas" and "Mama E," contain lyrics that date back to the 1800s. The oldest piece, "Kawika," is an accurate example of pre–European contact Hawaiian chant. Although the recording is very interesting historically, the sheer emotion of the music is what's important here. The state-of-the-art sound restoration of the old 78s on this release is outstanding, and several of the records "cleaned up" for the project are the only copies in existence. This one is essential for anyone interested in the roots of Hawaiian music.

worth searching for: Several releases, though not Kalama's albums as such, are not hard to find, and are essential to the band's surviving oeuvre. *Hawaiian Steel Guitar Classics, 1927–1938* ✍✍✍✍ (Arhoolie, 1993, prod. Chris Strachwitz) has two more cuts by Kalama's Quartet, and is a treasure trove of other early island gems. *Na Leo Hawai'i Kahiko: The Master Chanters of Hawai'i/Songs of Old Hawai'i* ✍✍✍ (Mountain Apple, 1997, prod. Bishop Museum) contains a 1927 recording of Kalama's Quartet's sex chant for King Kalakaua, along with some other early 20th century recordings from the archives of the Bishop Museum in Honolulu. *Vintage Hawaiian Music: The Great Singers, 1928–1934* ✍✍✍ (Rounder, 1989, prod. Bob Brozman, Chris Strachwitz) contains three Kalama's tracks, and other classics by Mme. Riviere's Hawaiians (featuring Tau Moe), Sol Hoopii Trio, Sol K. Bright Hollywaiians, and others.

influences:

◀◀ Richard Tully's Bird of Paradise Review (1904), Tau Moe Family, King Bennie Nawahi, Sol Hoopii, Sol K. Bright

⏩ Bob Brozman, Ry Cooder, Ledward Kaapana, George Kahumoku Jr.

Sandy Miranda

Maria Kalaniemi

Finnish folk

Born May 27, 1964, in Helsinki, Finland. Based in Finland.

In most people's minds, the accordion is not an instrument synonymous with cutting-edge music. But a few artists can change that perception in one sitting—Pauline Oliveros, Astor Piazzola, Guy Klusevsek, and, don't forget, Maria Kalaniemi. Kalaniemi is a versatile technical sorceress with the five-row button accordion, capable of improvising sonic wonders for the avant-garde and then playing tradition-minded polkas, waltzes, and tangos for folk dancers. When she was 19 Kalaniemi won the "Golden Accordion" at a national contest, and this led to the recording of her first album (a batch of traditional Finnish dance tunes) under the auspices of the Accordion Institute of Ikaalinen. She also joined the fledgling folk music department at the Sibelius Academy as a student, studying not only the accordion but the mandolin, violin, and *kantele* (a Finnish member of the zither family). Excited by instructor Heikki Laitinen's teaching methods, Kalaniemi and four other female students formed the first of the academy's important folk groups, Niekku. This group—made a quintet with the inclusion of fiddler Arto Järvelä, later of JPP—played traditional tunes and original songs using a variety of arrangements that pointed toward a new direction in Finnish folk music. Before finally graduating in 1990, Kalaniemi spent some time in France studying with the renowned jazz and musette accordionist Marcel Azzola. She also started examining the classical technique of using her left hand to play free-bass melody lines. These experiences helped make her next album—the one that most people regard as her first—a significant advance in both composition and performance. Kalaniemi started touring Europe and North America along with JPP and other members of the New Finnish Folk movement. In 1996 the accordionist and her band Aldargaz were the first folk musicians to win the Prize of Finland, given by its minister of education for artistic excellence. In these and many other ways, Kalaniemi has proven to be a persuasive advocate for her instrument. Not only has she returned to the Sibelius Academy in the role of an accordion lecturer, she has played with other accordionists in such outfits as Andetagen (alongside Lars Hollmer and Kimmo Pohjonen), the Helsinki Melodeon Ladies (a quintet that also features Riitta Kossi of Värtinnä), and, perhaps most notoriously, the Accordion Tribe with Guy Klucevsek, Lars Hollmer, Bratko Bibic, and Otto Lechner. In addition, she organized and performed in 1998's Harmonikka accordion festival, which featured players from around the world, further confirming her global status as a musician.

what to buy: While not technically her first album, *Maria Kalaniemi* 𝄞𝄞𝄞𝄞 (Olarin Musiikki Oy, 1992/Green Linnet, 1994, prod. Timo Alakotila) is the first release associated with Kalaniemi to make an impact with international audiences. Produced by JPP's Alakotila, this album bounces out of the gate with "Hermannin Riili" and continues on through polkas and tangos, aided by the cream of the New Finnish Folk movement. This is an absolutely stunning disc and deserves to be on the shelves of every world-music aficionado.

what to buy next: Kalaniemi's next release, *Iho* 𝄞𝄞𝄞𝄞 (Olarin Musiikki Oy, 1995/Hannibal, 1997, prod. Timo Alakotila), is more of a band affair, with Kalaniemi leading Aldargaz (basically the same musicians on another fine recital), but with a little more room for the supporting cast to make notable contributions. In addition to a solid handful of Kalaniemi compositions there are three tunes from Alakotila's pen, a few traditional Finnish songs in new arrangements, and a stunning take on Carlos Gardel's classic tango "Sus Ojos Se Cerraron," in which the accordionist does her best approximation of an Argentine virtuoso.

worth searching for: The only full-length representation of the groundbreaking Niekku that can be found on CD is a Finnish import, *Niekku 3* 𝄞𝄞𝄞𝄞 (Olarin Musiikki Oy, 1989, prod. Timo Tuovinen). Kalaniemi contributes one song, the atmospheric "Mene Myöten Myöty Neiti," with swirling kantele chords forming the backdrop for her minor-key musings and, near the end, her discordant, experimental riffing. Her most intriguing work for *Niekku 3*, however, can be found on "Kymmenellä Rivillä," an avant-garde, classically oriented piece for multi-tracked, free-bass button accordion composed by her mentor at the Sibelius Academy, Heikki Laitinen. She also contributes her accordion playing to five cuts on *Oi Miksi* 𝄞𝄞𝄞𝄞 (Riverboat/Olarin Musiikki Oy, 1994, prod. Heiki Laitinen), a superb project by her Niekku cohort, vocalist/kantele player Anna-Kaisa Leides. A more traditional outing by Kalaniemi can be heard on the album by Finnish fiddler Jussi Tarkkanen, *Ameriikan polkka* 𝄞𝄞𝄞 (Teosto, 1996, prod. Jussi Tarkkanen).

influences:

◄◄ Heikki Laitinen, Marcel Azzola

►► Petri Ikkelä, Minna Luoma, Pale Saarinen, Riitta Potinoja

see also: *JPP, Värttinä*

Garaud MacTaggart

Kayhan Kalhor

See: Ghazal

Pépé Kallé

Soukous

Born 1951, in Kinshasa, Congo. Died 1998, in Kinshasa, Congo.

Pépé Kallé and his band Empire Bakuba used to divide their time between Paris and Kinshasa, regularly topping both the

Maria Kalaniemi

African and world-music charts with a high-octane sound driven by lead guitarists Boeing Kananga and Doris Ebuya, and Kallé's own distinctive vocals. With his multi-octave range and unmistakable rumble, Kallé showed himself to be one of Congo's most powerful and innovative vocalists and songwriters.

Pépé Kallé was born in Kinshasa in 1951, and went to a Catholic grade school and high school. Like many singers, he got his start in the church choir. Kallé said that the bittersweet, almost bluesy quality of his vocals was partly a result of years of hymn singing. In high school Kallé sang with small vocal groups, usually local youths like himself playing homemade instruments. In the mid-'6os Kallé met Joseph Kabasele, a.k.a. Le Grande Kalle. Le Grande Kalle turned the Congolese music scene on its head in the late '5os by playing a re-Africanized version of the rumba and samba. His bands were a proving ground for musicians like Manu Dibango, Dr. Nico, and Rochereau. Pépé Kallé never actually played with Le Grande Kalle, but he lived and worked at Kabasele's house for several years, in exchange for vocal and music lessons. Kallé began writing his own songs at this time, and Kabasele recorded several of them, which gave Kallé some credibility when he started his own career. He would credit his sense of melody and a large part of his vocal style to the training he received from Kabasele.

Pépé Kallé's professional career began in the '7os with the band Bella Bella, where he shared singing chores with Nyboma, who went on to fame with Sam Magwana's African All Stars. Their twin lead vocals created some of the most memorable moments in Congo's musical history. Zaiko Langa Langa, the nation's leading "new wave" *soukous* (African rumba) band, was introducing the guitar pyrotechnics and galloping rhythms that have marked the music ever since, and Pépé Kallé wanted to be part of this revolution. He created Empire Bakuba, which became one of the most popular and long-lived bands in Congo. In an ever-shifting musical scene, Empire Bakuba (named after one of Congo's great warrior tribes) was also one of the few bands to remain stable, introducing several new dance crazes and winning over African, European, Japanese, and North American audiences along the way. At the time of his death in November of 1998, Kallé was collaborating with guitar giant Rigo Star on a new album and preparing another extensive North American tour.

what to buy: *Gigant-Afrique* 𝄞𝄞𝄞𝄞 (Globestyle, 1990), a compilation of Kallé's singles from the late 1980s, was put together by Ben Mandelson (a.k.a. Hijaz Mustapha of 3 Mustaphas 3) and offers a connoisseur's selection of Empire Bakuba at the height of their popularity, the legendary Diblo Dibala sitting in on three tracks.

what to buy next: *Pon Moun Paka Bouge* 𝄞𝄞𝄞𝄞 (Celluloid, 1991, prod. Pépé Kallé) is a short (30 minutes) but solid set featuring the chiming guitar of Diblo and a real drummer, which is increasingly rare on the slick soukous albums coming out of Paris.

the rest:
Larger Than Life 𝄞𝄞𝄞 (Stern's, 1992)

worth searching for: Many of Kallé's best singles, available on cassette and various European compilation CDs, are also collected under the name of his band, Empire Bakuba. Titles include *La Belle Étoile* 𝄞𝄞𝄞 (Rhythmes y Musique, 1985), *Trop C'est Trop* 𝄞𝄞𝄞 (Rhythmes y Musique, 1985), *Adieu Dr. Nico* 𝄞𝄞𝄞 (Syllart 1986), and *Cherie Ondi* 𝄞𝄞𝄞 (Rhythmes y Musique).

influences:

◀◀ Franco, Le Grande Kallé, Tabu Ley Rochereau, Zaiko Langa Langa

▶▶ Rigo Star

see also: *Diblo Dibala, Manu Dibango, Dr. Nico, Sam Mangwana, Tabu Ley Rochereau, Rigo Star, 3 Mustaphas 3, Zaiko Langa Langa*

j. poet

Rev. Dennis Kamakahi
Slack-key guitar
Born 1953, in Honolulu, HI, USA. Based in HI, USA.

A popular and prolific Hawaiian songwriter, the Rev. Dennis Kamakahi has recorded only rarely as a frontman or solo performer. The son and grandson of slack-key guitarists (players in his homeland's singular open-tuned style) and a direct descendant of Maui's last chief, Kamakahi grew up with a deep love and respect for Hawaiian musical history, which remains evident in his own work. He formed the popular group Na Paniolo during the 1960s, and in 1973 replaced Gabby Pahinui as the slack-key guitarist in the Sons of Hawaii, a group with which he continues to play. He is an ordained, but rarely practicing, Episcopalian minister.

what's available: When *Pua'ena (Glow Brightly)* 𝄞𝄞𝄞 (Dancing Cat, 1996, prod. George Winston) came out, it marked Kamakahi's first recording session in more than a decade and his first ever as a solo slack-key artist. Sung mostly in Hawaiian, the music is soothing and often romantic in nature, with tracks split between Kamakahi's originals and songs by 19th-century Hawaiian royalty. Kamakahi's stylistic and literal legacy is carried forth on *Ohana (Family)* 𝄞𝄞𝄞 (BMG/Windham Hill/Dancing Cat, 1999), an unassuming but affecting set with his son, vocalist and ukulele player David Kamakahi.

influences:

◀◀ Sons of Hawaii, Gabby Pahinui, Sonny Chillingworth, Leonard Kwan, Raymond Kane

▶ George Kuo, Hawaiian Style Band

see also: *Gabby Pahinui*

Brian Mansfield

Ini Kamoze

Dancehall, ragga
Born Cecil Campbell, October 9, 1957, in Port Maria, Jamaica. Based in Kingston, Jamaica.

Unlike most successful singers and deejays in Jamaica today, Ini Kamoze established himself by eschewing live, improvised dancehall performances for solitary, studied songwriting. Kamoze's witty and astute lyrics are often inextricably coiled with his mission to challenge ghetto youth to bolster their self-respect *and* culture-respect by resisting the diversions powerful outsiders use to divide them—easily accessible guns, politically instigated "tribal" factionalism, and the territorial, predatory drug trade. For a then-relative unknown, it's no wonder that Kamoze's first singles in the early '80s—"World of Fears" and "Trainers Choice" on the Mogho Naba imprint—were ignored by dancehall patrons. Luckily, his subsequent six-song demo tape fell into the hands of reggae legend Jimmy Cliff, who immediately passed it on to drummer-extraordinaire—and, with bassist Robbie Shakespeare, studio miracle-worker—Sly Dunbar, emphatically praising Kamoze's strangely commanding, pinched tenor; odd, zig-zagging timbre; and simultaneously useful and museful songwriting. Sly & Robbie, as they are better known, whisked Kamoze into a recording session, eventually issued in 1983 as the *Ini Kamoze* mini-album. Backed by Dunbar's complex, metallic syn-drum patterns and Shakespeare's solar-plexus-rumbling bass, the six-song EP is one of the finest and most influential dancehall records of that decade. Yet Kamoze's proclamation of the beginning of "Operation Roots & Culture" in the terrific "General" fell on deaf ears, as the dancehall was quickly mutating into a more party-hardy space where patrons' everyday misery was checked at the door for the night. Kamoze was in essence an island of conscious reality in a choppy sea of unconscious escapism. As a result, his follow-up albums, *Statement* and *Pirate,* were met with indifference, though Kamoze's galvanizing performance at 1984's Reggae Sunsplash festival did much to enhance his reputation as a live performer. After *Shocking Out* was released in 1988, the title cut—riding a savagely punchy rhythm churned by digital visionaries Steely & Clevie—became a hit single in Jamaica. Kamoze next created the Selekta label, soon releasing the popular sampler *Selekta Showcase '89,* which included another hit of his own, "Stress." In the early '90s his releases were few and far between, but always interesting and fresh. Then in late '94, Kamoze struck gold with a recut of his 1990 Jamaican hit "Here Comes the Hotstepper." Featured in Robert Altman's movie *Ready to Wear* and on MTV with a heavy-rotation video, "Hotstepper" rose to #1 on the *Billboard* pop charts and led to a recording contract with Elektra. While his first major-label release, *Lyrical Gangsta,* kowtowed to the rap crowd, back in Jamaica Kamoze released a series of singles with Philip "Fatis" Burrell (producer of the original "Hotstepper") that were as singular and riveting as his early dancehall work, including "Jah Never Fail I" (1995) and "No Watch No Face" (1996), both on the Sounds Klik label. The question remains: will Kamoze try to transform himself into the dreadlocked rapper that Elektra seems to want, or will he stay true to himself and continue tapping his deep reservoir of cultural sounds and concerns? Here's hoping for the latter.

what to buy: *Here Comes the Hotstepper* ♪♪♪♪ (Columbia, 1995, prod. Sly Dunbar, Robbie Shakespeare) is a fine compilation of Kamoze's early singles on Sly & Robbie's Taxi label, along with Salaam Remi's combustible remix of "Hotstepper," which includes a healthy sample of Chris Kenner's rollicking 1963 New Orleans R&B hit "Land of a 1,000 Dances" and a raw, fonky, old-school hip-hop rhythm that would make Fab 5 Freddy beam. That said, the highlight is the presence of three of the six cuts from Kamoze's debut EP, *Ini Kamoze* ♪♪♪♪♪ (Island JA, 1983, prod. Sly Dunbar, Robbie Shakespeare), including the uniquely empathetic and provocative "Trouble You a Trouble Me"; the profound, conscience-agitating "General" ("Listen keenly . . . if you hurt one, you hurt yourself too"); and "World-a-Music," a loving tribute to the crescendoing dancehall-reggae vibe, which at its peak is a pressure-cooker of adrenaline, guts, and euphoria. The entire brazen *Ini Kamoze* EP—including the rare "Hail Mi Idren," a must-have for fans—is available as an import from Ernie B's Reggae, PO Box 5019, El Dorado Hills, CA 95762 (Phone: (916) 939-0691; e-mail: ErnieB@calweb.com).

what to buy next: His first foray into computer-generated rhythms, *Shocking Out* ♪♪♪ (RAS, 1988, prod. Ini Kamoze, the One Two Crew) represents Kamoze's daring attempt to bring flesh-and-blood passion into the digital realm—with surprising success. He and good-friend Mutaburuka collaborate on "Revolution," a groovesome gasp of word-and-sound poetry that, despite its title, is devoid of wrathfulness and instead brimming with *nyahbingi* (Rasta ritual) mystic power. "Cool It Off" is a cogent plea to end the "arms race" from the common "sufferah"'s perspective, and ironically, over a decade later, is again ablaze with relevance as the U.S. seems primed to spend billions on a missile defense system while millions of its citizens can't afford health care.

the rest:
Statement ♪♪♪ (Island, 1984)

Pirate 𝄞𝄞𝄞 (Island, 1986)
16 Vibes of Ini Kamoze 𝄞𝄞𝄞𝄞 (Sonic Sounds, 1992)
Lyrical Gangsta 𝄞𝄞 (East West, 1995)

influences:

◀◀ Sly Dunbar, Robbie Shakespeare, Bob Marley, Horace Andy, Philip "Fatis" Burrell, Mikey Dread, Mutaburuka

▶▶ Buju Banton, Mutaburuka, Ninjaman, Super Cat, Tony Rebel

see also: *Mutaburuka, Sly & Robbie*

Todd Shanker

Kanda Bongo Man

Soukous

Born 1955, in Inongo, Zaire (now Congo). Based in Paris, France.

A unique, dance-inspiring style of Congo's *soukous* (African rumba) was created by Paris-based vocalist and showman Kanda Bongo Man. Incorporating elements of Cuban salsa, American R&B, and traditional African music into his turbo-charged, groove-filled sound, he has continued to allow his music to evolve. Describing one of his performances, the *New York Times* wrote, "music that couldn't seem more infectious subtly gathers a force, then leaps into a new groove that's even catchier." Kanda Bongo Man developed his distinctive style as a sideman for numerous soukous bands in Congo. Upon emigrating to Paris in 1979, he hooked up with guitarists Diblo Dibala and Rigo Star to create his enthusiastic musical hybrid. At least three legends were enlarged in the process, all of which are adding new chapters to this day.

what to buy: Originally recorded for a broadcast of Ned Sublette and Sean Barlow's NPR/BBC Radio 5 program *Afropop Worldwide, Soukous in Central Park* 𝄞𝄞𝄞𝄞 (Hannibal/Carthage, 1993, prod. Ned Sublette, Sean Barlow) captures the excitement and hypnotic grooves of Kanda Bongo Man's concerts.

what to buy next: *Kwassa Kwassa* 𝄞𝄞𝄞𝄞 (Hannibal, 1988, prod. Kanda Bongo Man) was Kanda Bongo Man's last album with guitarist Diblo Dibala, who embarked on his own landmark band projects afterwards. It combines two prized Paris releases, *Lela Lela* and *Sai*.

the rest:

Amou Fou/Crazy Love 𝄞𝄞𝄞 (Hannibal/Carthage, 1987)
Sai-Liza 𝄞𝄞𝄞 (Melodie, 1988)
Kanda Bongo Man 𝄞𝄞𝄞 (Globestyle, 1990)
Isambe-Monie 𝄞𝄞𝄞 (Melodie, 1990)
Zing Zong 𝄞𝄞𝄞 (Hannibal/Carthage, 1991)
Songo (Melodie, 1992)
Les Rendez-vous Des Stades 𝄞𝄞𝄞 (Melodie, 1993)
Non Stop, Non Stop 𝄞𝄞𝄞 (Globe Style, 1994)
Welcome to South Africa 𝄞𝄞𝄞 (B. Mas Productions, 1995)

influences:

◀◀ Dr. Nico, Franco, Joseph Kabasele

▶▶ Papa Wemba, Tabu Ley Rochereau

see also: *Diblo Dibala, Rigo Star*

Craig Harris

Ray Kane /Raymond Kane

Slack-key guitar

Born 1925, in 'Ele'ele, Kaua'i, HI, USA. Based in HI, USA.

One of the oldest slack-key guitarists still performing regularly, Ray Kane grew up the son of a fisherman and traded fish for guitar lessons as a youngster. He didn't begin playing seriously until after a stint in the armed services, making his first recordings in 1961 and his first full-length album more than a dozen years later. Though he was the first player in this distinctive indigenous style to give a full-length solo recital, he made his living as a welder through most of his career. In 1987 Kane received a National Endowment for the Arts National Heritage Fellowship award for his preservation and advancement of traditional music, which he continues with frequent recording and tours.

what's available: Kane relishes his role as one of the elder statesmen of slack-key, and half the charm of the live *Master of the Slack Key Guitar* 𝄞𝄞𝄞 (Rounder, 1988, prod. Robert Mugge) is the history lessons Kane offers with the performance. For a more purely musical experience, there's *Punahele* 𝄞𝄞𝄞𝄞 (Dancing Cat, 1994, prod. George Winston). It features a version of Kane's most popular tune, the title one (written in 1938), and vocals on four tracks, including "Hawai'i Aloha." Still making history, Kane's *Wa'ahila* 𝄞𝄞𝄞 (BMG/Windham Hill/Dancing Cat, 1998) finds him in fine instrumental and vocal form, in early-'90s sessions of his rich solo turns and sweet duets with his wife, Elodia, here making her recording debut.

worth searching for: Kane recorded two albums for the Hawaiian Tradewinds label: *Nanakuli's Raymond Kane* (Tradewinds, 1974), which featured a backing band, and *Slack Key* (Tradewinds), which contained a half-dozen tracks recorded by Kane in 1961, along with six cuts from the legendary Leonard Kwan.

influences:

◀◀ Sonny Chillingworth, Gabby Pahinui

▶▶ Rev. Dennis Kamakahi, George Kuo

see also: *George Kuo, Leonard Kwan, Richard Thompson*

Brian Mansfield

Kanda Bongo Man

Cisse Diamba Kanoute

See: Baaba Maal

Mory Kanté

Traditional Manding, worldbeat
Born c. 1950, in Kissidougou, Guinea. Based in Paris, France.

Kanté grew up in a family of *griots,* traditional praise singers and holders of historic songs and stories. His first instrument was the *balafon,* the West African marimba, but he was sent to Mali at age seven to study *kora* (harp-lute) at the School of Oral Tradition. When Salif Keita left the Super Rail Band for a solo career as legendary as that outfit's, Kanté was hired to replace him. When Kanté was exposed to Western music, it set off a creative explosion for the young player. He was soon incorporating funk, salsa, and other dance beats into his compositions, and the Rail Band's popularity soared. But despite this success, making ends meet was hard, so Kanté moved to Côte d'Ivoire, where he put together a troupe of more than 30 musicians and dancers to play his own brand of international pop. His singular kora style meshed perfectly with the hand drumming and synth lines of the band, and they went on to wide acclaim all across West Africa. In 1980 Kanté moved to Paris and created a new group, Les Milieus Branches, to play all African-based music, be it hip-hop, salsa, rock, samba, funk, or traditional. He has since released a series of amazingly successful worldbeat albums, including 1987's *Akwaba Beach,* which spawned the hit single "Yé Ké Yé Ké," one of the first African tunes to crack the French pop charts.

what to buy: On *Tatebola* 𝄢𝄢𝄢𝄢 (Misslin, 1996, prod. Mory Kanté), Kanté's music is slick and funky, but retains a sharp African edge. His unique kora style and propulsive balafon lines fit perfectly into the funk, house, and even techno beats that sometime drive his music. If exploring African pop is still a daunting idea, Kanté will blow away your preconceptions and rock your world.

what to buy next: It's not as slick as *Tatebola,* but Kanté's first hit album, *Akwaba Beach* 𝄢𝄢𝄢𝄢 (PolyGram, 1987, prod. Mory Kanté), stands up well and sets a shining example for those who would integrate traditional African rhythms into a global pop format.

best of the rest:
Touma 𝄢𝄢𝄢𝄢 (Island, 1991)
N'Diarabi 𝄢𝄢𝄢 (Island, 1991)
10 Cola Nuts 𝄢𝄢𝄢 (Island, 1991)

influences:
◄◄ Super Rail Band, Bembeya Jazz

►► Ibro Diabate, Camera Aboubacar

see also: *Kante Manfila, Rail Band, Talking Heads*

j. poet

Mory Kanté

Dominic Kanza & the African Rhythm Machine

Hybrid soukous
Formed 1990, in New York, NY, USA. Based In Brooklyn, NY, USA.

Dominic Kanza (born 1964, in Zaire [now Congo]), guitar, vocals; Fernand Tchikounzi (Congo), vocals; Maggie Tchikounzi (Congo), vocals; Jojo Kuo (Ghana), drums; Urban Sanchez (Puerto Rico), percussion; Mbuyiselo Mgwandi (South Africa), bass; Mark Adams (USA), keyboards.

One of world music's most distinguished behind-the-scenes talents, Dominic Kanza has recently stepped into the spotlight with pleasing results. A sought-after sideman with top-shelf international artists from Papa Wemba to Paul Simon, and the composer of one of *The Oprah Winfrey Show*'s theme songs, he released his first album as a headliner in 1999, thereby letting more of the world in on what concert throngs in his adoptive hometown of Brooklyn have long known. Born in Congo, bred in England, resident in the U.S., and at home across the world, Kanza's globalist tastes are reflected in his multi-influenced music (from Congo's bubbly, skipping *soukous* style—a variant of rumba—to rap and jazz), and his international band, whom he takes glee in introducing as various heads of state—and by the end of a typical concert, they can count on every audience member's vote.

what's available: *Congo!* ♪♪♪♪ (DKMusic, 1999, prod. Dominic Kanza) is the kind of sheer delight for the listener that belies painstaking craft on the part of the musicians. But judging from the jubilation of the end product, they seem happy to do it. Kanza's ebullient guitar work makes no fuss about his agile virtuosity, and the African Rhythm Machine's energy befits their name while their fluidity goes way beyond it. Kanza's lyrics may lack distinction, but hardly dampen *this* party. On CD you can't see the unit's impressive dancing, but you'll be busy enough doing your own.

influences:
◄◄ Papa Wemba, Carlos Santana

Adam McGovern

Kaoma

Worldbeat
Formed 1987, in Paris, France. Based in Paris, France.

Jean-Claude Bonaventure, keyboards, leader; Michel Abhissira, drums; Jacky Arconte, guitar; Chico Roger Dru, bass, percussion; Loalwa Braz, lead vocals; Monica Nogueira, vocals; Fania Niang, vocals.

World-music fans tend to be a serious lot, so it's good that every so often an act like Kaoma comes along to break the balloon. Kaoma, simply put, was an Afropop version of the Monkees. In 1986 Jean Krakos, then head of Celluloid Records, got wind of a new rhythm from Brazil. "Llorando se fue," a hit by a Bolivian folk band called K'Jarkas, had been "samba-ized" and the result was dubbed the lambada. Krakos sold Celluloid and used the money to acquire the copyrights of hundreds of tunes that used the lambada rhythm. Back in Paris, Krakos put together Kaoma from a group of African and Brazilian session players. The band's recording of "Lambada," actually a watered-down version of "Llorando se fue," was used for an Orangina commercial and the single exploded, sparking a worldwide phenomenon that died out as fast as it started. Epic picked up the single, and later the album, for U.S. release, but the fad was already over before the album hit American record bins. Check out the *Creadores de Lambada* compilation (Rodven, 1989) if you want a sample of the real thing.

what to avoid: Happily, Kaoma's counterfeit *World Beat* **woof!** (Epic, 1989, Prod. Jean-Claude Bonaventure) didn't catch on, proving that consumers are capable of exhibiting bouts of good taste. File it with your old Milli Vanilli album.

influences:
◄◄ The Monkees, new-age mush

see also: *Touré Kunda*

j. poet

Kapelye

Klezmer
Formed 1979, in Brooklyn, NY, USA. Based in NY, USA.

Henry Sapoznik, banjo, vocals; Eric Berman, tuba; Lauren Brody, accordion, vocals; Adrienne Cooper, vocals; Pete Sokolow, keyboards, vocals. (All members are from USA.)

Led by banjo player, vocalist, and folklorist Henry Sapoznik, Kapelye is one of the spearheads of the revival of klezmer, the traditional music of Eastern European Jews. The founder and director of both the YIVO Max and Frieda Weinstein Archives of Recorded Sound and the Yiddish Folk Arts Institute, and a music critic for National Public Radio, Sapoznik has used Kapelye as an outlet for the Yiddish songs he's researched and collected. While Sapoznik remains the guiding force of the band, Kapelye is a group effort with each member contributing years of experience. Lead vocalist Adrienne Cooper has been singing all her life. The latest of four generations of singers, Cooper holds degrees in history from Hebrew University and the University of Chicago, and acquired her musical training at the Rubin Academy of Music in Israel. A co-founder of the Yiddish folk arts program KlezKamp (on the faculty of which Sapoznik and Sokolow serve) and the Joseph Papp Yiddish Theater, Cooper appeared in the off-Broadway show *Song of Paradise* and has sung on numerous albums, including the Grammy-nominated soundtrack to the documentary *Partisans of Vilna* and recordings by the Klezmatics and the Flying Bulgar Klezmer Band. She also recorded a duo album, *Dreaming in Yiddish*, with Joyce Rosenzweig. Accordionist and vocalist Lauren Brody has been singing and playing traditional Yiddish—as well as Bulgarian and Macedonian—music since the late 1970s. She has performed with such groups as Pitu Guli, Aman, Trio Svetlana, Novo Selo, and the Joel Rubin Klezmer Band. Tuba player Eric Berman is a veteran of numerous orchestras, including the San Antonio Symphony, not to mention having operated a successful practice as an entertainment lawyer. Clarinetist Ken Maltz holds degrees in music education, theory, composition, and performance from Hofstra University, C.W. Post College, and Yale University. Keyboard player and vocalist Pete Sokolow has performed with such klezmer legends as Dave Tarras, Sid Beckerman, and the Epstein Brothers, in addition to the Klezmer Plus! band with Sapoznik. He also orchestrated eight albums for Chaba (Lubavitch) Nigunim, two albums for Shlomo Carlebach, the off-Broadway show *The Golden Land,* and the *Partisans of Vilna* score.

what to buy: Combining archival radio transcripts and new recordings, *On the Air: Old Time Jewish American Radio* ♪♪♪♪ (Shanachie, 1995, prod. Henry Sapoznik) recreates the old-world charm of Yiddish radio shows from the 1930s and '40s.

what to buy next: Kapelye's debut album, *Future and Past* ♪♪♪ (Flying Fish, 1983, prod. Kapelye), set the framework for the band's subsequent recordings, with its combination of traditional Yiddish music and contemporary-minded instrumental virtuosity.

the rest:
Kapelye's Chicken ♪♪♪ (Shanachie, 1987)
Levine & His Flying Machine ♪♪♪ (Shanachie, 1987)

influences:

◄◄ Eastern European Jewish musical tradition, Dave Tarras

►► Klezmer Conservatory Band, Don Byron's Bug Music, Klezmorim

see also: *The Klezmatics, Klezmer Plus!, Dave Tarras*

Craig Harris

Karnataka College of Percussion

South Indian classical music
Formed c. 1965, in Bangalore, India. Based in Bangalore, India.

K. Raghavendra, vina; T.A.S. Mani, mridangam; Mrs. R.A. Ramamani, vocals, konnakkol (rhythmic speaking); R.A. Rajagopal, konnakkol, mridangam, ghatam; T.N. Shashikumar, konnakkol, mridangam, kanjira, tavil; M.V. Sampathkumar, morsing, tambora; M.S. Govindaswamy, violin; V.K. Raman, flute. (All members are from India.)

Dr. Krishna Raghavendra, who also teaches at his own school in Bridgewater, Massachusetts, U.S., has been playing music all his life, and is a senior member of the faculty at Karnataka College of Percussion. The school trains people in percussion and music, and has fielded a touring performing troupe since the late 1970s. When you listen to South Indian classical music the last thing you expect is a jew's-harp, but an Indian jaw harp called the *morsing* is one of the featured instruments on KCP's one album to date, *River Yamuna*, a collection of classical and traditional pieces. For this album, Raghavendra "wanted to present as many percussion instruments as I could. There is *ghatam*, a cylindrical clay pot open at one end; *kanjira*, a lizard-skin tambourine; *dholak*, a folkloric drum with a distinctive ringing sound; and more. The drums play solo, in ensemble, and accompany the music and singing." Discovering new sounds is always a kick, and hearing the morsing and kanjira, either solo or supporting Raghavendra's sharp, subtle, sitar-like *veena* playing, is a treat.

what's available: The drummers and singers on *River Yamuna* ♪♪♪ (Music of the World, 1997, prod. K. Raghavendra, Bob Haddad) take us into many areas of Indian folk and classical music that have been largely unrecorded in the West. The frame drum and jew's-harp duets are especially unique and inventive.

influences:

◄◄ Alla Rakha, Ali Akbar Khan

see also: *Dissidenten*

j. poet

Kashtin

Innu pop, singer/songwriter
Formed 1989, in Maliotenam Reserve, Quebec, Canada. Based in Maliotenam Reserve, Quebec, Canada.

Claude McKenzie, guitar, vocals; Florent Vollant, guitar, vocals. (Both members are from Canada.)

Claude McKenzie and Florent Vollant are Montagnais Indians from the Maliotenam Reserve on Quebec's North Shore. They speak and sing in Innu, a language spoken by less than 12,000 people, but their music, a melodic jangle of electric guitars and straightforward rock rhythms with a hint of Cajun and Canadian folk music, struck a chord with the Canadian public. When McKenzie and Vollant met, they were already in other bands, but when they began playing together, the sparks flew. "It was like a tornado," Vollant says in retrospect, and indeed "kashtin" is Innu for "tornado." *Innu,* the band's debut album, went gold and led to sold-out tours all across Canada and western Europe, including a week at the St-Denis Theater in Paris. The band's second album, *Akua Luta,* went gold in six weeks; then disaster struck. McKenzie, who'd been living the expected irresponsible rock-star life, had a car accident on the Maliotenam reserve that seriously injured an 11-year-old girl. He pleaded guilty to drunk driving and spent nine months in jail. After his release, he went solo and recorded *Innu Town,* an album full of brooding ballads (including one in English, "I Got a Taste of Tears," that some think relates directly to the accident). McKenzie and Vollant recently put together a new version of Kashtin, and are touring with McKenzie as opening act.

what's available: *Innu* ♪♪♪ (Tristar/Sony, 1991, prod. Guy Trépanier, Claude Ranger) is a low-key charmer that mixes Native music, pop, blues, and folk into a smooth package. The duo share satisfyingly contrasting lead vocal chores, with Vollant having a smooth country tenor and McKenzie a darker, John Fogerty–esque rasp. As befits a second album after a mega-selling debut, the production values on *Akua Luta* ♪♪♪ (Tristar/Sony, 1994, prod. Kashtin, Toby Gendron) are much higher, which is especially noticeable on the rhythm tracks. That said, the duo's pleasing mix of Native, blues, singer/songwriter, and bright 1960s pop influences remains intact. On his solo outing, *Innu Town* ♪♪♪ (Groupe Concept, 1996, prod. Guy Trépanier), McKenzie trys a simpler, folkier sound. The album has a "young country" polish, which supplies a good counterbalance to McKenzie's tortured vocals.

$\frac{3}{6}{8}$ *kassav'*

Kassav'

influences:
⏪ The Louvin Brothers, Gordon Lightfoot, Ian & Sylvia, Creedence Clearwater Revival, R.E.M.

see also: *Robbie Robertson*

j. poet

Kassav'

Zouk
Formed 1979, in Paris, France. Based in Paris, France.

Pierre-Edouard Decimus, bass, founder; Georges Decimus, bass; Jacob Desvarieux, guitar; Jean-Claude Naimro, keyboards, vocals; Jocelyn Beroard, vocals; Patrick Saint-Eloi, vocals; Jean Philippe Marthely, vocals; Claude Vamur, drums; Jacques Douglas Mbida, keyboards; César Durcin, percussion; Freddy Havsepian, trumpet; Jean-Pierre Ramirez, trumpet; Claude Thiurifays, sax; Hamid Belhocine, trombone. (All members are from Guadeloupe.)

From the late 1950s to the advent of Kassav', the music of Guadeloupe and Martinique had been dominated by Haitian forms, especially *cadance* and *compas*. With the exception of a few bands like Exile One and Vikings de Guadeloupe, the Antillean music scene consisted of groups doing covers of Haitian hits. "Until the 1970s, the Haitians dominated our music," explains Jocelyn Beroard, Kassav's lead female vocalist. "Many Haitians lived and recorded in New York, and the studio sound they had was very slick. The studios back home weren't as technologically advanced, so the local albums didn't sound so good." In 1978 Pierre-Edouard Decimus, one of the founders of the Vikings, had grown disillusioned with the struggle to establish credibility for his band and decided to leave the music business. He moved to Paris, where many African and Caribbean expatriates were beginning to experiment with the kind of intercultural music that would soon make that city one of the planet's most important world-music hubs. Before calling it quits, Decimus wanted to put out one last record, a disc that would draw on the traditional *gwo ka* drum styles of Guadeloupe, American funk, French folk music, and Haitian pop. For the project he enlisted the help of his brother George, guitar ace Jacob F. Desvarieux, and an 11-piece percussion section. They called the project

Kassav', in honor of the cassava, the Antillian tuber that's a staple of the Caribbean diet.

The first Kassav' LP, *Love and Ka Dance* ("Ka Dance" is a play on "cadance," a friendly jibe at Haitian music's then-dominance on the Antillian charts), was a sensation and made Decimus re-think his decision to leave the music business. "At first Kassav' was a studio band," said Beroard. "Edouard had certain ideas about the music; everything was written down, the musicians came in and played what he had written." But after a few stu-dio efforts, Kassav' was so popular that a touring band became a necessity. Decimus called up the best players he could find—from Paris and back home—and asked them to join the band. "At first we were reluctant," Beroard said. "We all had solo ca-reers, but we realized we could help our own careers by joining this band. And since many of us wrote songs, Kassav' became more democratic, and more improvisational."

Kassav' was so popular that it spawned a new genre, *zouk*—a Creole word that means both "party" and "sweat," an apt de-scription of Kassav"s high-voltage sound. Their mix of *soukous,* cadance, compas, highlife, reggae, and rock, combined with a theatrical performance style, revolutionized Caribbean dance music, and had such an impact on Congo that many bands there incorporated *zouk* into their own soukous music and called the new fusion "zoukous." Until 1982 Kassav' commuted between Guadeloupe and Paris, but since the studios were better in Eu-rope, the band finally relocated to Paris en masse. From their Parisian base, Kassav' redefined the music of the Antilles, spawning dozens of imitators, both good and bad. "Before Kas-sav' most bands didn't play live," Beroard explained. "The scene was small, and many bands were made up of different combinations of the same musicians. Since our success, many new musicians have come along to play zouk. Also, before Kas-sav', there were not many women in music. Today many women are making a career of performing." During their 15-odd years on stage (the band went on what seems to be a permanent hia-tus in 1994), Kassav' evolved at a rapid pace. "We had musi-cians from all over the world," Beroard says. "Algeria, Cameroon, Martinique, Guadeloupe, France—all over the world, and we always kept our sound fresh. And in most bands, you have at most two or three people who write songs. In Kassav' we have eight or nine, so if you get a song on an album, you're really lucky. But it also keeps the quality high."

Over the course of their career, the core of Kassav' (listed above) was fairly stable, but many artists passed through their ranks on the way to becoming stars in their own right. And when Beroard or Patrick Saint-Eloi put out a solo album, they usually recorded with their Kassav' compatriots, and with Desvarieux or one of the Decimus brothers producing. At their height, the band was cranking out close to a dozen albums a year under

tuvan throat-singing

In 1921, in the ring of mountains where Siberia meets Outer Mongolia, a group of nomadic herdsmen founded a new country: the Shepherd's Republic of Tannu Tuva. Aside from being the region where Genghis Khan once came to recruit his horsemen, the country is best known for its primary musical form, Tuvan throat-singing. This distinctive sound comes from a tightening of the singer's throat, which screens out all but a few overtones and amplifies those that remain, resulting in as many as four distinctly audible notes at once. There are three basic styles of throat-singing: *sygyt,* which is said to be an imitation of the gentle breezes of summer and the songs of birds; *höömeï,* which evokes the sound of wind swirling among rocks; and *kargyraa,* which sounds like the howling winds of winter. There are also four common embellishments of these styles: *borbangnadyr,* a trilling of the lips or tongue; *ezenggileer,* a pulsating sound that evokes images of horseback riding; *chylandyk,* which is a cricket-like combination of sygyt and kargyraa; and *dymzhuktaar,* which produces overtones with the mouth closed via throat-humming. The most noteworthy current practi-tioner of the genre is Kongar-ool Ondar, who holds the title of "People's Throat-Singer" in Tuva and was awarded the title "National Artist of Russia" by Boris Yeltsin after serenading the Russian president in 1994. Throat-singing is historically associated with adult males, but re-cent years have seen the form growing in popu-larity among Tuvan women and children. Even outside cultures are beginning to catch on: in 1995, American bluesman Paul "Earthquake" Pena went to Tuva to learn the throat-singing technique, and wound up winning first place in the kargyraa division at the second International Throat-Singing Festival, "Höömeï '95." A film about Pena's Tuvan adventures, *Genghis Blues,* won the Sundance Film Festival's Audience Award for Best Documentary in early 1999.

see also: *Chirgilchin, Huun-Huur-Tu, Kongar-ool Ondar, Sainkho, Shu-De, Yat-Kha*

Bret Love

various names, all crammed with their trademark rhythms and punchy horn charts. Their first concert album, *Live au Zenith,* recorded right after they signed with CBS International, is one of the greatest live sets ever released. Although they're still relatively unknown in the U.S., the international success of Kassav' laid the groundwork for today's world-music explosion.

what to buy: *Zouk Is the Only Medicine We Have* ♫♫♫♫♫ (Greensleeves U.K., 1988, prod. Jacob Desvarieux, Pierre-Edouard Decimus), a compilation of Kassav''s early hits, is one of the most satisfying world-music albums extant, a non-stop orgy of rhythm and melody accented by the band's incredible lead singers. Kassav''s first album under the international CBS deal, *Vini Pou* ♫♫♫♫♫ (Columbia, 1987, prod. Jacob Desvarieux), captures them at the height of their creative powers. There isn't a weak track, and the balance between raw rhythm and studio polish is at its apex.

best of the rest:
Kassav' ♫♫♫ (Celluloid, 1980)
Passeport ♫♫♫ (Polydor France, 1983)
Live au Zenith ♫♫♫♫♫ (Columbia, 1986)
Tekit Izi ♫♫♫♫ (Columbia, 1987)
Majestik Zouk ♫♫♫♫ (Columbia, 1989)

worth searching for: Jocelyne Beroard's two "solo" albums, *Siwo* ♫♫♫♫♫ (Sonodisc, 1986, prod. Jacob Desvarieux) and *Milans* ♫♫♫♫♫ (Columbia, 1991, prod. Jacob Desvarieux), were recorded at the creative height of Kassav', and they're both killers.

influences:
◄◄ Vikings de Guadeloupe, Exile One

►► Experience 7, Zouk Machine, Simon Jurad, Zouk Allstars, Francky Vincent

j. poet

Dolores Keane
Celtic
Born in Caherlistrane, County Galway, Ireland. Based in County Galway, Ireland.

Keane's family has lived at Caherlistrane in County Galway for generations and are justifiably famous for their singing and musicianship. Her own talent blossomed early: "Learning songs and tunes was like learning to walk," she says. A neighbor of fiddle master Frankie Gavin, she appeared with him on Irish-folk supergroup De Dannan's first album. By that time she was already a mesmerizing presence on the Irish traditional music scene. She left the band to perform with her husband, John Faulkner, reunited with De Dannan for a time (including a memorable performance of "Let It Be" dueting with Mary Black), and then eventually began to pursue a solo career. She is, as folk great Nanci Griffith describes her, "the voice of Ireland."

what to buy: *The Best of Dolores Keane* ♫♫♫ (Dara, 1997, prod. various) compiles 16 of the finest songs in Keane's catalog. In addition to selections from her previous solo albums, it includes collaborations with Emmylou Harris, De Dannan, Liam Bradley, and Mick Hanly. Keane's best material is traditional and she can be compelling at it, as her work with De Dannan and husband John Faulkner attests. Her last several solo albums have been more contemporary in nature, as she tries to follow in the commercially successful footsteps of Mary Black and others. Fortunately this retrospective stays primarily in a traditional vein, with only a nod toward these more recent efforts.

what to buy next: Keane's solo album *There Was a Maid* ♫♫♫♫ (Claddagh, 1978) and her collaborations with John Faulkner contain some great material; any of several releases are worthwhile. Try *Farewell to Eirinn* ♫♫♫ (Green Linnet, 1981, prod. various), *Broken Hearted I'll Wander* ♫♫♫ (Green Linnet, 1981, prod. P.J. Curtis), or *Sail Óg Rua* ♫♫♫♫ (Green Linnet, 1984, prod. Dolores Keane, John Faulkner). You can't miss with any of them.

the rest:
Dolores Keane ♫♫♫ (self-released)
Lion in a Cage ♫♫♫ (Rings End Road, 1989)
Solid Ground ♫♫♫ (Shanachie, 1993)

influences:
◄◄ Sarah Keane, Rita Keane

►► Niamh Parsons, Eleanor McEvoy, Karan Casey

see also: *The Chieftains, De Dannan, John Faulkner, Frankie Gavin*

Neal Walters

James Keane
Irish traditional
Born February 7, 1948, in Drimnagh, Dublin, Ireland. Based in New York, NY, USA.

While James Keane's achievements may have been somewhat overshadowed by those of his older fiddle-playing brother, Chieftains member Seán Keane, they are impressive nevertheless, and Keane must be counted among Ireland's top exponents of the B/C button accordion. Keane is first and foremost a "reel man": he can play reel after reel for hours with the same great drive and energy, a penchant which one can undoubtedly trace back to his days with the Castle Ceili Band of Dublin. Keane was born into a musical family. His mother and father were both fiddle players, from Longford and Clare respectively, and they made sure to expose Seán and James to as much traditional music as they could find, taking them to the Dublin Pipers' Club and to the many local and national *fleadhs* (music festivals). Being a bit of a rebel, James went against the family tradition and became interested in the accordion, starting at age six when he began toying with a small instrument his uncle Mick Keane had left at his parents' house. As soon as he started showing promise, his father got him his own instrument. When asked about his early influences, Keane names musicians like Clare piper Willie Clancy and accordion players Joe Cooley (whom he met again years later in San Francisco), Sonny Brogan, and Bill Hart. By age 11 Keane was entering competitions, and by the time he was 16 was a member of the famous Castle Ceili Band alongside such performers as Clare fiddle players John Kelly and Joe Ryan, flute players Michael Tubridy and Mick O'Connor, and piano player Bridie Lafferty. It was during the mid-1960s that Keane accomplished the unprecedented feat of winning three consecutive All-Ireland senior titles on the accordion: in 1964, 1965, and 1966.

In 1967 he came to the United States on a three-week tour with the Loughrea Ceili Band, composed of Joe Burke (accordion), Kathleen Collins (fiddle), and Paddy Carty (flute). As soon as he returned to Ireland, Keane began making plans for another trip. He was back in New York the very next year to start performing at the John Barleycorn, a well-known Manhattan "ballad pub," with Dublin-born singer Michael "Jesse" Owens. This was a quite a change of pace for Keane, who could no longer just play the traditional jigs and reels but mostly had to accompany songs. However, in the early 1970s he recorded two instrumental albums, one of them the 1971 release *Sweet and Traditional Music of Ireland,* which also featured Longford fiddler Paddy Reynolds and New York–born accordionist Charlie Mulvihill. (The album has now been partially reissued as *Atlantic Wave,* with newly recorded tracks by Keane.) Before he left Dublin, Keane had shared an apartment with two members of the famous Johnstons, Paul Brady and Mick Moloney, both of whom credit Keane with their introduction to traditional Irish music. During the 1970s Moloney would also find himself in the United States, working towards a Ph.D. in folklore and producing recordings of Irish traditional music. Keane was one of the artists recorded for *Irish Traditional Instrumental Music from the East Coast of America, Volume I,* an anthology Moloney produced for Rounder Records in 1977. In 1980, soon after Keane moved to Canada to join the band Ryan's Fancy, he was invited by Moloney to record for Green Linnet. The result was Keane's powerful *Roll Away the Reel World,* with brother Seán playing fiddle on a few tracks. Settling back in New York in 1983, Keane resumed his musical activities in the city and renewed his collaboration with Moloney, touring with the Green Fields of America and appearing on Moloney's 1984 duet album *Uncommon Bonds* alongside fiddler Eugene O'Donnell. In 1991 Keane appeared with many other Irish performers at an event organized to bring at-

tention to the plight of Joseph Doherty, an Irish patriot held in a U.S. jail, a recording of which was released as *The Rights of Man.* Keane's long-awaited second solo album, *That's the Spirit,* finally came out in 1994, with a little surprise for his fans—the preceding year, Keane had switched from his trademark Paolo Soprani accordion to a Castagnari box, the difference in sound being quite noticeable on the recording. Keane's most recent release is *With Friends Like These.* It features legendary musicians like Tommy Peoples, Matt Molloy, Liam O'Flynn, Paddy Glackin, and Kevin Conneff, all of whom Keane met around 1962 and 1963, when traditional music sessions were taking off in Dublin. For his latest project, tentatively called *Sweeter As the Years Roll By* and soon to be released on the Shanachie label, Keane has come full circle, collaborating with younger artists—particularly members of the group Turas, who are the children of musicians with whom he performed in the Castle Ceili Band in the 1960s.

what to buy: *Roll Away the Reel World* ♪♪♪♪ (Green Linnet, 1980, prod. Mick Moloney) is the classic James Keane recording. The duets of the two Keane brothers are especially good, as on the reels "The Tempest/Sean Frank," but Keane's accordion playing is nowhere better than on the opening reel medley "Crossing the Shannon" or on "Master Crowley's," one of his favorite sets. *That's the Spirit* ♪♪♪♪ (Green Linnet, 1994, prod. Gabriel Donahue, James Keane) is Keane's first album recorded with his new Castagnari accordion. This, as well as the aggressive guitar and *bodhrán* (Irish frame drum) accompaniments, account for the album's somewhat different sound. However, the gain in precision that the new instrument allows, as Keane explains in the notes, well serves his energetic style and easily makes up for whatever raw edge from the old Paolo Soprani may have been lost in the transition. Listen to him play Martin Mulhaire's reel "Carmel Mahoney Mulhaire," which he had recorded as "O'Mahoney's" on the previous album, and you'll be convinced. *With Friends Like These* ♪♪♪♪ (Shanachie, 1998, prod. Garry O'Briain, Greg Anderson) is Keane's "going home" album, recorded with the musicians with whom Keane used to play back in Dublin when a teenager. They also happen to constitute a virtual "who's who" of Irish traditional players: Tommy Peoples and Paddy Glackin (fiddles), Matt Molloy (flute), Liam O'Flynn (uilleann pipes), and Kevin Conneff (bodhrán, vocals), with Garry O'Briain (keyboards, guitar, mandocello) providing the accompaniments.

what to buy next: Although *Atlantic Wave* ♪♪♪♪ (Kells Music, 1997, prod. Tom Horan, Paddy Noonan) is a reissue of sorts, half of it being from *Sweet and Traditional Music of Ireland* ♪♪♪♪ (Rego, 1971, prod. Paddy Noonan), Keane's tracks are brand new. The producers and performers were uncomfortable with the electric bass part on the original recordings, and Keane, who already had re-recorded some of his original tunes for later solo albums, asked to redo his tracks entirely, although still with piano great Felix Dolan as the accompanist. Keane's accordion would be easy to miss in the ensemble sound of *The Rights of Man: The Concert for Joseph Doherty* ♪♪♪♫ (Green Linnet, 1991, prod. Mick Moloney), but he plays a long and fiery solo on the excellent *Gaelic Roots* ♪♪♪♫ (Kells Music, 1997, prod. Séamus Connolly), recorded live at Boston College during the festival of the same name.

worth searching for: Keane's great solo on the reels "Within a Mile of Dublin/The Spike Island Lassies" is only one of 22 reasons to look for *Irish Traditional Instrumental Music from the East Coast of America, Volume I* ♪♪♪♪ (Rounder, 1977, prod. Mick Moloney), an anthology of some of the best Irish musicians in contemporary America.

influences:

◀◀ Willie Clancy, Joe Cooley, Sonny Brogan, Bill Harte

▶▶ Joe Burke, Bobby Gardiner, Billy McComiskey, John Whelan

see also: *Liz Carroll, the Chieftains, Felix Dolan, Paddy Glackin, Matt Molloy, Mick Moloney, Liam O'Flynn, Tommy Peoples*

Philippe Varlet

Salif Keita

Afropop

Born 1949, in Djoliba, Mali. Based in Paris, France.

The singing styles of Mali are set to a blend of traditional West African music, jazz, and pop by Salif Keita. A member of Mali's popular Rail Band in the early 1970s, Keita has continued to evolve his complex dance music as a soloist and a bandleader in his own right. Keita's 1992 album, *Amen,* was an international success that led to his becoming the first African bandleader nominated for a Grammy. The third of 13 children, the artist is descended from 13th-century emperor Soundiata Keita. Despite the occupational obstacle of limited eyesight and the cultural stigma of albino skin, Keita showed an aptitude for music since childhood. His family, however, had little regard for his talents, entertainment careers being considered unacceptably beneath someone of his lineage. Nonetheless, Keita left home for Mali's capital city, Bamako, where he performed as a street singer. His break came when he joined the Rail Band, a government-sponsored ensemble that fused Cuban, Congolese, and Malian influences. In 1972, with Guinean guitar great Kanté Manfila, Keita left the Rail Band for Les Ambassadeurs and an inter-band rivalry that riveted the region for some years to follow. His second band's great success notwithstanding, Keita set off on a solo career in the 1980s. Shortly after relocating to Paris in 1987, he released his debut solo album, *Soro,* produced by respected West African hitmaker Ibrahim Sylla. After paying homage to

the jazz-fusion band Weather Report on his second album, 1989's *Ko-Yan,* Keita teamed with Weather Report keyboardist Josef Zawinul, who produced his third recording, *Amen.* Keita's 1995 release, *Folon . . . The Past,* was rated one of the year's 10 best albums by *Tower Pulse!* In 1999 he finally released *Papa,* another groundbreaking (but long delayed) album with a top-flight African/American band and production by avant-rocker Vernon Reid. He previewed this music on the well-received 1998 edition of the Africa Fête touring revue, all-the-more confirming his stature and building anticipation for his next move.

what to buy: *The Mansa of Mali: A Retrospective* ♪♪♪♫ (Mango, 1994, prod. various) samples tunes from Keita's first three albums—*Soro, Ko-Yan,* and *Amen* —and includes a previously unreleased live version of Keita and Les Ambassadeurs' hit "Mandjou," as well as three songs from the soundtrack of *L'Enfant Lion,* a French film in which Keita performs.

what to buy next: *Amen* ♪♪♪♪ (Mango, 1992, prod. Josef Zawinul) is Keita's most creatively successful recording. An acoustic album, *Amen* remains rooted in the folkloric sounds of Keita's native country. Complementary guest performers from beyond it include Carlos Santana and Wayne Shorter. The next millennium of Pan-African music begins a year or two early on the entrancing *Papa* ♪♪♪♪ (Metro Blue, 1999, prod. Salif Keita, Vernon Reid, Souleymane Doumbia), where the innovators of two continents meet.

the rest:

Soro ♪♪♪♫ (Mango, 1987)
Ko-Yan ♪♪♪ (Mango, 1989)
Les Ambassadeurs International ♪♪♪♫ (Rounder, 1992)
Folon . . . The Past ♪♪♪♫ (Mango, 1995)
Seydou Bathili ♪♪♪ (Sonodisc, 1997)

influences:

◀◀ Fanta Damba, Mory Kanté

▶▶ Oumou Sangare, Boukman Eksperyans

see also: *Kanté Manfila, the Rail Band*

Craig Harris

Doug Kershaw
/Rusty & Doug

Cajun

Doug Kershaw born January 24, 1936, in Tiel Ridge, LA, USA. Rusty Kershaw born February 2, 1938, in Tiel Ridge, LA, USA. Rusty & Doug formed 1954. Disbanded 1964.

Rusty Kershaw, guitar, vocals; Doug Kershaw, fiddle, vocals.

With his fancy fiddling and on-stage flamboyance, Doug Ker-

Salif Keita

shaw was the first major artist to provide Cajun music with exposure to a wide audience that included college students and mainstream country fans. In 1948 Doug and his younger brothers Rusty and Pee Wee became part of the Continental Playboys, and in 1953 they hosted their own regional TV show. Rusty and Doug had their first hit record in 1955 with "So Lovely Baby," and in 1957 they cracked the charts again with "Love Me to Pieces." Their watershed year was 1961, when Doug's composition "Louisiana Man" exploded onto the regional and national charts. To this day, the song remains a Cajun and country standard. The duo split up in 1964, and Doug recorded a few mildly interesting albums for Warner Bros.

what to buy: *The Best of Doug Kershaw & Rusty Kershaw* 𝄢𝄢𝄢𝄾 (Curb, 1991) comes from the recordings the duo made for Roy Acuff's Hickory label during the 1950s and '60s. The album contains the hit versions of "Louisiana Man" and "Diggy Diggy Lo," which Doug Kershaw would re-record throughout his career. There are also versions of Hank Williams's "Kaw-Liga" and "Why Don't You Love Me" that the sparse instrumentation, sibling harmonies, and heavy slapback turn into an odd Cajun hillbilly rock. Strangely, the album doesn't include two of the duet's biggest hits from that time, "So Lovely Baby" and "Love Me to Pieces," but it's still a heck of a lot of fun.

what to buy next: *The Best of Doug Kershaw* 𝄢𝄢𝄢𝄾 (Warner Bros., 1989, prod. various) contains versions of Doug's breakthrough hits from the 1960s, including "Louisiana Man" and "Diggy Diggy Lo," as well as spicy remakes of Hank Williams's "Jambalaya (On the Bayou)" and Fats Domino's "I'm Walkin'."

the rest:
The Cajun Way 𝄢𝄢𝄾 (Warner Bros., 1969)
Alive & Pickin' 𝄢𝄢𝄾 (Warner Bros., 1975)
The Louisiana Man 𝄢𝄢𝄾 (Warner Bros., 1978)
(With Rusty Kershaw) *Now and Then* 𝄢𝄢 (Domino, 1992)

worth searching for: *The Ragin' Cajun* 𝄢𝄢𝄢 (Warner Bros., 1976) doesn't let up for a second. A great party album.

influences:
◀◀ Iry LeJeune

▶▶ Charlie Daniels, Beausoleil, Wayne Toups, Zachary Richard

Rick Petreycik and Brian Mansfield

Khac Chi Ensemble

Vietnamese folk music
Formed 1982, in Vietnam. Based in Vancouver, British Columbia, Canada.

Ho Khac Chi, dan bau; Hoang Ngoc Bich, k'longput, t'rung, tam thap; Le To Quyen, vocals; Nguyen Hoai Chau, percussion; Randy Raine-Reusch, ken be, vocal, senh tien. (All members are from Vietnam.)

Ho Khac Chi was born in 1950 in Nghe An, Vietnam. His parents

were both musicians, and he entered the National School of Music when he was eight and studied *dan bau* (one-string box zither) for 10 years. After graduation he became an instructor and traveled throughout the country playing and collecting folk music. When the school reorganized he became one of the first recognized master folk musicians and conductor of the Traditional Music Orchestra. In 1982 he formed his ensemble, one of the first groups to feature the traditional instruments of Vietnam's highlands. In 1992, after an international tour, Ho Khac Chi and his wife Hoang Ngoc Bich settled in Vancouver, British Columbia. Hoang Ngoc Bich was born in 1964 and studied dan bau at the Hanoi School of Arts. At the Hanoi Music Conservatory she also studied *k'longput* (clapping tubes), *t'rung* (marimba), and *tam thap* (hammered dulcimer). She was the first woman to perform on the *ko ni* (fiddle), and has toured internationally on her own and as a member of the Khac Chi Ensemble.

what's available: Vietnamese music is incredibly diverse and, in some instances, strangely familiar to Western ears. The dan bau, for example, sounds like a pedal steel guitar, and on "Highland Dance" from *Moonlight in Vietnam* 𝄢𝄢𝄢𝄢 (Henry St., 1997, prod. Randy Raine-Reusch) you wouldn't be surprised if Bob Wills popped up saying "Get it boy." The t'rung on "Forest Love" supplies a beat that would be at home in any disco, while the *ve ve* (percussive buzzers) and *khen be* (16-reed bamboo mouth harp) make "Mountain Cave" sound like a frolic for a gang of cartoon ghosts. The music is all acoustic and has a mellow, dreamlike quality that listeners should find instantly appealing.

influences:
◀◀ Quy Bon Family Vietnamese Folk Theater

j. poet

Khaled
/Cheb Khaled

Rai
Born February 29, 1960, in Sidi-El-Houri, Oran, Algeria. Based in Paris, France.

With his rugged tenor, charismatic stage presence, and thousand-watt smile, Khaled is King of Rai, a title he may have adopted in homage to Elvis Presley, one of his early idols. Since he burst out of Algeria in 1988, Khaled has kept himself on the leading edge of the rai revolution, ever expanding his stylistic horizons while keeping his music firmly based on the Bedouin traditions that give it its vitality. It's no wonder that EarthWorks chose a photo of Khaled to grace the cover of its 1988 compilation *Rai Rebels*. To many people, rai is Khaled.

Rai in Arabic means "opinion," and in the current Algerian political climate, having an opinion is dangerous. Rai is

Khaled

based on a combination of Bedouin traditional music and the more secular influences of the cities, in particular Oran, a port town where Spanish, Moroccan, French, and black Arabic traditions have a long history of cross-pollination. Cheikha Remitti, one of the earliest rai singers and still a powerful performing force at age 75, combined Bedouin music with a more modern attack, including the use of brass, electric guitars, and accordions in place of flutes and violins. In the 1960s, as rock culture swept the world, funk and rock began seeping into the music, and in the 1970s reggae also made an impact. By the late 1970s, rai had become Algeria's rock, with parents and clerics denouncing it for its Westernized energy and raw lyrics—singing about smoking, drinking, and sex in an Islamic country caused a sensation. The singers started calling themselves Chebs and Chabas—the masculine and feminine of a term meaning "youth" or "kid," a send-up of the traditional Cheikh and Cheikha title won by being a respected elder.

Khaled himself began singing as a youth and was drawn to the freedom of rai and its implied lifestyle while still a teenager. A local producer heard the young singer at a wedding and asked him to make a record; "Trigh Lycée," a song about cutting class and chasing girls, became a smash. Khaled left his parents' home for the life of a musician, and with a band he called the Five Stars began playing parties, weddings, and clubs. In order to further his career, Khaled made a batch of hastily recorded cassettes, which expanded his reputation as a top singer. In the mid-1980s Khaled met Rachid Baba Ahmed, the man who became the Phil Spector of rai, and together they cut a stunning succession of tunes that laid the foundation of modern "pop rai."

In 1985 Khaled relocated to Paris, partially to escape Algeria's growing sectarian violence. (Rachid, Cheb Hasni, and other singers and producers have been murdered for their pop-music "blasphemy.") Khaled's first Western album was *Kutche,* a jazz/rock take on rai that did nothing to convey the singer's forceful vocal style. Since then, Khaled has returned to a more traditional form of rai, although not without Western influences. His last two albums, *N'ssi N'ssi* and *Sahra,* have both launched singles into the French pop—not world—charts, making him Algeria's first true international pop star.

what to buy: On *N'ssi N'ssi* 𝄞𝄞𝄞𝄞 (Mango, 1993, prod. Don Was, Philippe Eidel), Khaled's voice rides a wave of Arabic funk, backed by an Egyptian string orchestra, hot rock guitar, Latin keyboards, honkin' R&B sax, and *juju*-style pedal steel guitar. Happily, the international touches serve to magnify Khaled's Algerian soul, making this the best possible kind of crossover music.

what to buy next: About half the tracks on *Sahra* 𝄞𝄞𝄞𝄞 (Island, 1996, prod. Don Was, Philippe Eidel, Clive Hunt, Jean-Jacques Goldman) were recorded in Jamaica at Groove Yard studios with the island's top session players, and their reggae/rai fusion is smooth and satisfying.

the rest:
Kutchie 𝄞𝄞𝄞 (Intuition, 1989)
Khaled 𝄞𝄞𝄞𝄞 (Barclay, 1992)

worth searching for: The European albums above are all polished studio efforts, but Khaled put out dozens of cassettes before the move to France. Some of this material can be found on various compilations, including *Young Khaled* 𝄞𝄞𝄞 (Buda, 1993), *Best of Cheb Khaled* 𝄞𝄞𝄞 (Blue Silver), *El Marsem* 𝄞𝄞𝄞 (Editions Bouarfa), and *Serbi Serbi* 𝄞𝄞𝄞 (Editions Bouarfa).

influences:

◄◄ Cheikha Remitti, Cheikh Hamada, Cheikh Madani, Cheb Hamid

►► Cheb Mami

see also: *Cheikha Remitti, Alan Stivell*

j. poet

Ali Akbar Khan
North Indian classical, Indian fusion
Born April 14, 1922, in Shibpur (a.k.a. Shivpur), East Bengal (Bangladesh). Based in San Anselmo, CA, USA.

Ali Akbar Khan is routinely acclaimed as a genius and the greatest living performer on the *sarod,* a 25-string, lute-like Indian instrument. The celebrated violinist Lord Yehudi Menuhin has called him "the greatest musician in the world." He has been designated a National Living Treasure in India, where he has been awarded the nation's highest honors: the President of India in 1963 and the Padma Vibhusan (Lotus Jewel) in 1988. In America, Khansahib (as he is respectfully called) has been recognized with a MacArthur Foundation "Genius Grant" in 1991, the Bill Graham Lifetime Achievement Award in 1993, a National Heritage Fellowship from the National Endowment for the Arts in 1997, and five Grammy Award nominations. And yet, beyond these material measures of success, it's the passion to teach his beloved music that has directed and defined his life.

Born in 1922 in East Bengal (now Bangladesh), Khansahib was the only son of Allauddin Khan, a multi-instrumentalist who traced his lineage through Mian Tansen, a legendary court musician of the 16th-century Moghul Emperor Akbar. The senior Khan—who lived to be 110—defied the rigid conventions of his day by integrating the techniques and styles of many instruments and regions; today, he is widely revered as India's greatest musician of the 20th century. Khansahib's father trained him from the age of three and, for the next 20 years, increased his regimen until he was studying and practicing 18 hours a day. Allauddin Khan withheld food if the young musician didn't live up to expectations, and forbade his son to waste precious energy in ordinary conversation. "During my childhood," Khansahib reflects, "up to age 16 or 17, I had not been allowed to say anything except 'yes' and 'no.' And if I said 'no,' my father would beat me." While abusive, the senior Khan's methods were effective—he imparted his instinct, passion, and desire to spread the family's musical heritage to the rest of the world.

Ali Akbar Khan performed his first concert at the age of 14 and became a court musician for the Maharaja of Jodhpur when he was still in his early 20s. In 1955, Yehudi Menuhin invited Khansahib and his brother-in-law, Ravi Shankar, to Europe and the United States to introduce Indian music to Western audiences. When Shankar canceled at the last minute, Khansahib embarked upon the journey only because his friends literally pushed him onto the plane. During the trip, Khansahib made the first American television performance of Indian music (on Alistair Cooke's *Omnibus* program) and the first Indian music recording ever on a long-playing record. In 1956, he established the Ali Akbar College of Music (AACM) in Calcutta. In the following years, Khansahib returned to Europe and America many times to perform and teach. At the invitation of the American Society of Eastern Art, Khansahib taught courses in Berkeley, California, in 1965 and 1966. Encouraged by the students' interest and sincerity, he founded an American Ali Akbar College of Music in Berkeley in 1967—the same year that Ravi Shankar enthralled flower children at the Monterey International Pop Festival. (Four years later, the two gave perhaps the West's most famous Indian music performances during George Harrison's Concert for Bangla Desh benefit at Madison Square Garden.) In small classroom settings, Khansahib has personally taught between 7,000 and 10,000 students, including Mickey Hart, Carlos Santana, Darby Slick, Lisa Moskow, Matthew Montfort, and Jai Uttal. Eminent *tabla* drum player Pandit Swapan Chaudhuri is AACM's Director of Percussion, the position that was previously held by tabla wizard Zakir Hussain. Guest faculty members—including Ravi Shankar, V.G. Jog, Vilayat Khan, Hussain and his father Alla Rakha, G.S. Sachdev, and Laxmi (a.k.a. Lakshmi) Shankar—have taught master classes and helped students with technique on a one-on-one basis. AACM also has established branches in Basel, Switzerland, and Fremont, California.

In addition to his classroom, performance, and recording activities, Khansahib is still transcribing his father's notes, which only he can decipher. He has also archived 30 years of his classroom lessons and thousands of performances on audio tape. As this book goes to press he is engaged in a stunning or-chestral composition for Indian and Western instruments, which may be recorded and released in the next year or two. You may contact the Ali Akbar College of Music at 215 West End Avenue, San Rafael, CA 94901; (415) 454-6264; http://www.nbn.com/~aacm/. (If you are interested in purchasing Indian music or instruments, the College Store—(415) 454-0581—is a fabulous resource.) You may contact Khansahib's family-run record label, Alam Madina Music Productions, at 74 Broadmoor Avenue, San Anselmo, CA 94960; (415) 456-5963; http://www.ammp.com/records.html.

what to buy: Ali Akbar Khan has either released or appeared on more than 120 recordings on LP, 45 rpm, cassette, and CD—and there were probably EPs and 8-track tapes along the way—so there is much to find, but the following surveys are the most essential. The Grammy-nominated *Then and Now* ♪♪♪♪♪ (AMMP, 1995, prod. Mary J. Khan) is an ideal introduction to the sarod maestro. Disc one includes the entirety of Khansahib's landmark 1955 recording *Music of India: Morning & Evening Ragas* (Angel, 1955), complete with spoken introductions by Yehudi Menuhin. Disc two features a stellar 1994 concert of Khansahib and tabla virtuoso Zakir Hussain. Contrasting performances four decades apart underscore Khansahib's fundamental brilliance for melody and timing, demonstrate how his picking style has become more aggressive, and showcase the maturation of both his emotional focus and his interplay with his accompanist. Also nominated for a Grammy, *Passing on the Tradition* ♪♪♪♪♪ (AMMP, 1996, prod. Mary J. Khan) features two classical *ragas* that are all the more breathtaking for their challenging natures. "Raga Marwa" presents an eloquent *alap* (contemplative, expressive introduction to a raga) that ranges in emotion from devotional yearning to epic heroism. This heartfelt passion continues in the improvisations of Khansahib and tabla master Pandit Swapan Chaudhuri in a 45-minute excerpt of the late-night raga "Puriya Kalyan" (pieces in this classical form are composed in synch with specific times of day and their associated moods). *Ustad Ali Akbar Khan Plays Alap* ♪♪♪♪♪ (AMMP, 1993, prod. Mary J. Khan) is Khansahib's solo exploration of the raga—without either accompaniment or the finale that he sometimes calls "Coca Cola": that is, fast-paced and flashy. Khansahib's meditative probing reaches within while longing for God—and is all conveyed with conviction and great artistry. Yet another Grammy nominee, *Legacy* ♪♪♪♪♪ (AMMP, 1996, prod. Ali Akbar Khan, Mary J. Khan, Tim White) pairs Khansahib with vocalist Asha Bhosle (best known as the definitive diva of Indian movie music, but committed to classicism as well) on 16th–18th century songs from the court of the Moghul Emperor Akbar. Vocal, sarod, sitar, *sarangi* (bowed string instrument), harmonium, and cello timbres coalesce magnificently, balanced by brief but breathtaking solos. The vision, skillful performances, and careful attention to detail make this recording a gem.

what to buy next: The four-volume *Signature Series* presents Connoisseur Society recordings of Ali Akbar Khan (sarod) and Pandit Mahapurush Misra (tabla) from the 1960s, which Alam Madina Music Productions (AMMP) remastered with great care for CD release. *Volume 1* ♫♫♫ (Connoisseur Society, 1966/AMMP, 1990), originally released under the title *Master Musician of India,* is known as the Ali Akbar Khan record that everyone bought and wore out in the '60s. It contrasts the much-beloved "Raga Chandranandan" with "Raga Gaur Manjari" (which includes a leisurely exploration of the alap's melodic pattern) and an evocation of heart-breaking yearning, "Raga Jogia Kalingra." *Volume 2* ♫♫♫♫ (Connoisseur Society, 1960s/AMMP, 1990) showcases Khansahib's command of a variety of styles: the meditative serenity of "Raga Medhavi" is complemented by the subdued rhythmic accompaniment of Misra's tabla; they give the very traditional "Khammaj" a rather surprisingly lyrical treatment; and "Rag Bhairavi Bhatiyar" interweaves two contrasting ragas to achieve a tonal robustness not heard in either composition individually. *Volume 3* ♫♫♫♫ (Connoisseur Society, 1960s/AMMP, 1994, prod. Mary J. Khan) is the high-water mark of the series. "Raga Marwa" is a marvelous exposition (with an extended alap) of the Rajput dynasty's princely valor in all its rich and grave complexity. Khansahib curves notes around one another to elicit a palpable serenity in "Raga Misra Shivaranjani," his adaptation of a traditional piece, with tabla accompaniment from Pandit Shankar Gosh. Khansahib's student Pandit Nikhil Banerjee was one of the foremost sitar players of India. The clarity of his technique is quite unmatched and is well revealed on *Volume 4* ♫♫♫ (Connoisseur Society, 1960s/AMMP, 1994, prod. Mary J. Khan). "Raga Manj Khammaj" and "Raga Misra Mand" are both "light" classical ragas, displaying the freedom and playfulness usually associated with them. Before Khansahib established his own label, *Artistic Sound of the Sarod* ♫♫♫♫ (Chhanda Dhara, 1985) was the recording that he would give as a present, feeling that it was a good example of his work. Although not representative of Khansahib's music, *Journey* ♫♫♫ (Triloka, 1990, prod. Jai Uttal) is an engaging worldbeat recording. Taking a cue from producer Uttal's East/West hybrids, the album blends Indian classical and Western pop instruments and styles in short, catchy songs. For years, National Public Radio used an excerpt from "Come Back My Love" for news program segues.

what to avoid: The eight volumes of *All India Radio Archival Releases* ♫♫ (All India Radio, 1997) feature excellent performances from 1956 to 1965 and can be found for about half the price of Khansahib's classic releases. The rub is that the CDs were slapped together to make a quick rupee, without any at-

tempt to deliver high fidelity. This is particularly galling since All India Radio issued quite decent LPs in the past. *Volume 5* **woof!** is virtually unlistenable. With so much sonically superior material available, these should be the last Ali Akbar Khan CDs you consider. A three-minute fragment of "Rag Chandranandan" was licensed from AMMP's *Signature Series, Vol. 1* for the score to Bernardo Bertolucci's 1994 film *Little Buddha.* But the soundtrack album's label (BMG/Milan) cut, pasted, and over-dubbed the original 22-minute rag into an 11-minute cut which it re-used without AMMP's knowledge or permission in a "unique collection of Tibetan music," *Wisdom & Compassion* **woof!** (BMG/Milan, 1997). The results are predictably deplorable. Perhaps its for the best that Khansahib's and Mahapurush Misra's names are mangled in the credits.

worth searching for: The two-volume *Live in Amsterdam* ♫♫♫♫♫ (Mozes and Aaronchurch, 1985, prod. John Eijlers) was one of the first attempts to extend playing time beyond LP constraints and deliver high fidelity via real-time copying onto audio cassettes. These performances of Khansahib (sarod) and Swapan Chaudhuri (tabla) sent their audience reeling with delight over the nuances of their playing, their repartee, and their exchange of musical challenges. At last word, Water Lily Acoustics still had not released its audiophile-caliber Ali Akbar Khan titles on CD, but the LPs of *Ustad Ali Akbar Khan* ♫♫♫♫ (Water Lily Acoustics, 1984, prod. Kavi Alexander), *Maihar* ♫♫♫♫ (Water Lily Acoustics, 1989, prod. Kavi Alexander), and *Indian Archetexture* ♫♫♫♫ (Water Lily Acoustics, 1992, prod. Kavi Alexander) are worth searching out. Khansahib's *Book One: Introduction to the Classical Music of North India, Volume One—The First Year's Study* is based upon a typical first-year program of study at the Ali Akbar College of Music. The three-volume *Book Two: Evening Ragas of Asawari That* introduces the reader to the theoretical basis of ragas and includes compositions for several instruments. These books, as well as the 1988 concert video *The Summer Solstice,* are available from AMMP (415-456-5963) and the AACM store (415-454-0581).

influences:

◀◀ Acharya Baba Allauddin Khansahib, Aftabuddin Khan

▶▶ Asha Bhosle, Swapan Chaudhuri, Pandit Hariprasad Chaurasia, Ry Cooder, the Grateful Dead, John Handy, Mickey Hart, Ustad Zakir Hussain, Pandit V.G. Jog, Henry Kaiser, Yehudi Menuhin, Matthew Montfort (of Ancient Future), Lisa Moskow, Ustad Alla Rakha, G.S. Sachdev, Carlos Santana, L. Subramanian, Jai Uttal

see also: *Asha Bhosle, Mickey Hart, Zakir Hussain, Ustad Vilayat Khan, G.S. Sachdev, Santana, Lakshmi Shankar, Ravi Shankar, Jai Uttal*

Richard Price

Ali Akbar Khan

Badar Ali Khan

Qawwali

Born March 1964, in Pakistan. Based in Pakistan.

The younger cousin of the late Nusrat Fateh Ali Khan (the man who introduced the devotional song form *qawwali* to the Western world), Badar has already released 22 albums in Pakistan. His voice is formidable, and he is an early and major contender for Nusrat's vacated crown.

what to buy: Badar takes a giant leap of faith by leading off his Western debut album, *Lost in Qawwali* ♪♪♪ (Triloka, 1997, prod. Baba Varma), with a shredding version of "Qalander Mast Mast," a tune memorably associated with one of Nusrat's acclaimed collaborations with Michael Brook. Badar buries Nusrat's laid-back version with his big, booming vocals and the fierce attack of his party. His scat improvisations rival his cousin's for their forceful invention. This is an impressive debut.

what to buy next: *Lost in Qawwali II* ♪♪♪ (Triloka, 1998, prod. Baba Varma) is another solid set from Badar and his band; the man sounds like a contenda. He also borrows a page from the Nusrat/Bally Sagoo playbook by presenting a funky, club-ready remix of "Qalander Mast Mast."

worth searching for: *Good Karma 1* ♪♪♪♪ (Baba, 1997) is the album that made Badar a superstar in Pakistan, and was credited with modernizing qawwali and taking it to a younger, more secular audience. It may be available in your local Indian cassette shop.

influences:
◄◄ Nusrat Fateh Ali Khan, the Sabri Brothers

see also: *Michael Brook, Nusrat Fateh Ali Khan, Bally Sagoo*

j. poet

Nusrat Fateh Ali Khan

Qawwali

Born 1948, in Pakistan. Died August 16, 1997.

Nusrat Fateh Ali Khan made *qawwali*—a Sufi devotional music that sings the praises of Allah and was almost unknown outside the Pakistani community—into one of the most exciting genres of world music. A *qawwal* is known for his vast knowledge of mystic poetry and his ability to weave these texts into a trance-inducing performance. Like Native American and African shamans, qawwals often use repetition and vocables—meaningless syllables and shouts of joy—to express the inexpressible ecstasy of communion with Allah. Nusrat was one of the great qawwals, and perhaps the most impressive singer, in any genre, of the late 20th century. He regularly moved audiences to tears, even those who spoke no Arabic or Farsi, with the sheer emo-

tional power of his voice. The West discovered Nusrat after Peter Gabriel invited him to sing on the soundtrack for *The Last Temptation of Christ.* Nusrat has hundreds of cassettes available on numerous labels, but it was his work for Gabriel's RealWorld imprint that brought him world acclaim, especially *Musst Musst* and *Night Song,* collaborations with Canadian ambient guitarist Michael Brook. The combination of dance beats and religious poetry struck many traditionalists as sacrilegious, but Nusrat's abiding faith in Allah shines through even his most secular compositions. Nusrat suffered from diabetes, and was on his was to the States for a kidney transplant when he died of renal failure.

what to buy: Hailed by fans and critics as one of 1996's best world-music albums, the Nusrat Fateh Ali Khan/Michael Brook collaboration *Night Song* ♪♪♪♪ (RealWorld, 1996, prod. Michael Brook) proves that crossover music can still preserve its integrity in the hands of a master. Nustrat's always breathtaking vocals are complemented by Brook's lush yet understated orchestrations. If you've never heard Nusrat before, this is a good place to start, and if you're a fan you won't be disappointed.

what to buy next: When you're ready for the real deal, the five-disc *En Concert a Paris* ♪♪♪♪ (Ocora Radio France, 1995, prod. Jean-Pierre Lunkner, Pascal Besnard) delivers in spades. Almost six hours of transcendental music from Nusrat and his party. The import price is hefty, but worth it. If you can't afford the whole box, *Vol. 1* and *Vol. 2* are sold separately.

best of the rest:
Qawwali: The Vocal Art of the Sufis I ♪♪♪♪ (JVC Japan, 1987)
Qawwali: The Vocal Art of the Sufis II ♪♪♪♪ (JVC Japan, 1987)
Devotional & Love Songs ♪♪♪♪ (RealWorld, 1988)
Shahen-Shah ♪♪♪♪ (RealWorld, 1989)
Mustt Mustt ♪♪♪♪ (RealWorld, 1990)
The Last Prophet ♪♪♪♪ (RealWorld, 1994)
Shabaaz ♪♪♪♪ (RealWorld, 1995)
The Supreme Collection, Vol. I ♪♪♪♪ (Caroline, 1997)
The Greatest Hits ♪♪♪♪ (Shanachie, 1997)
The Greatest Hits, Vol. 2 ♪♪♪♪ (Shanachie, 1998)

worth searching for: Nusrat has more than 200 cassettes, CDs, and albums in print, many of which can be found in the Hindi delis and music shops you'll find in most major cities. Many are pure qawwali, but his crossover albums with Hindi producers, like *Magic Touch* ♪♪♪♪ (Oriental Star, 1989, prod. Bally Sagoo) and *Must Must II* ♪♪♪♪ (Oriental Star, 1995, prod. Noor Jehan), are every bit as good as his better-known *Night Song.*

influences:
◄◄ The Sabri Brothers
►► Badar Ali Khan

see also: *Michael Brook, Badar Ali Khan, Bally Sagoo*

j. poet

Nusrat Fateh Ali Khan

Salamat Ali Khan

Updated Indian classical vocal music

Born 1934, in the Punjab, India. Based in the Punjab, India.

Salamat Ali Khan is one of the most recognized of classical Indian vocalists. Since he began performing in the 1960s with his brother Nazakat as the Ali Brothers, Salamat has been one of the few artists in his particular genre to break through to a popular international audience. His diverse recordings include world-music fusions and very traditional classical pieces recorded with his sons.

what to buy: On *Voices of Spheres* ♫♫♫ (Xdat, 1997, prod. Richard Michos), Salamat Ali Khan and his sons, Shaqfat Ali Khan and Sharafat Ali Khan, layer Western and Eastern instrumental textures over traditional *ragas* to form a hybrid of purist Indian classical music and contemporary trance sounds, augmented by the contributions of *didgeridoo* (Aboriginal Australian drone instrument) master Stephen Kent and *santur* (hammered zither) player Alan Kushan.

what to buy next: The Khans (in this case Salamat and Shaqfat) join noted Bay Area vocalist Lakshmi C. Saxena for a program of classical ragas on *Aina: Reflections* ♫♫♫ (SD, 1994). *Breath of the Rose* ♫♫♫ (Water Lily Acoustics, 1994) is a pristine audiophile recording featuring Khan performing the ragas "Rageshwari," "Bhupali," and "Mishra Khamaj" with sons Sharafat and Shaqfat. A moving tribute to his late brother, the classical program of *Salamat Remembers Nazakat* ♫♫♫♫ (Omi, 1997) emphasizes material from the pair's duet work of the 1960s and '70s.

influences:

◀◀ Nazakat Ali Khan

▶▶ Shaqfat Ali Khan

Michael Parrish

Ustad Imrat Khan

North Indian classical, Hindustani

Born 1935, in Calcutta, India. Based in St. Louis, MO, USA.

Ustad Imrat Khan, primary exponent of the bass sitar known as the *surbahar,* comes from an illustrious family of sitar players who trace their roots from the *Ustads* ("maestros") of the 16th-century Mughal courts. With his older brother Vilayat Khan, Imrat, who sang as a child, introduced the *gayeki ang* or "vocal style" of instrumental playing to North Indian classical music. This style involves a great deal of pitch-bending—up to an octave on the surbahar—to produce fluid, note-to-note continuity. The surbahar's deep resonance is ideal for slower, introspective music (the *dhrupad* style in general, and the arrhythmic *alap* section of the lengthy and complex classical pieces known as *ragas*), and Imrat Khan records this material without accompaniment. He showcases his virtuoso sitar technique in more up-tempo, extroverted movements accompanied by one or more of his sons on *tabla* drum, sitar, surbahar, and *sarod* (north Indian lute).

what to buy: It's hard to go wrong with Imrat Khan—all the U.S. recordings are first-rate. *Rag Darbari, Rag Chandra Kanhra* ♫♫♫♫ (Nimbus Records Inc., 1988, prod. Robin Broadbank) is a good place to start, with the dignified, courtly "Rag Darbari" credited to Tansen, the 16th-century Emperor Akbar's leading musician. Imrat plays surbahar on this raga, and on "Rag Chandra" he plays sitar accompanied by his son Shafaatullah on tabla. *Raga Puriya Dhanashri* ♫♫♫♫ (India Archive Music, Ltd., 1991, prod. Lyle Wachovsky) is a demanding 72-minute raga, with the introductory slow section played on solo surbahar, the instrument invented by Imrat's great-grandfather Sahibdad Khan. Imrat picks up the sitar for the second half, and Shafaatullah Khan joins him on tabla. *Rag Madhur Ranjani* ♫♫♫♫ (Music of the World, 1992, prod. Bob Haddad) is a minor-key raga composed by Imrat Khan himself and performed on sitar with Shafaatullah Khan playing tabla. Irshad Khan plays *tamboura* (four-stringed drone instrument) only intermittently, allowing the silence between notes to be heard. *Ajmer* ♫♫♫♫ (Water Lily Acoustics, 1991, prod. Khavichandran Alexander, Jayant Shah) features a slow 27-minute surbahar solo in the major-scale morning raga "Alhaiya Bilaval," followed by a sitar raga of Imrat Khan's invention with tabla accompaniment.

what to buy next: The two pieces featured on *Rag Miya ki Todi, Rag Bilaskhani Todi* ♫♫♫ (Nimbus Records Inc., 1989, prod. Robin Broadbank) are morning ragas. "Miya ki Todi" shows the surprising speed and intensity that can build in a solo surbahar performance. *Raga Marwa* ♫♫♫ (Nimbus Records Inc., 1992, prod. Robin Broadbank) is a complex sunset raga featuring 40 minutes of surbahar introduction followed by a sitar and tabla with two tambouras. *Rag Jhinjoti, Rag Pilu* ♫♫♫ (Nimbus Records Inc., 1989, prod. Robin Broadbank) presents Imrat's sitar in *jugalbandi* (duet) with sarod played by Vajahat Khan, accompanied by tabla and tamboura drone.

the rest:

Indian Music for Sitar and Surbahar for Meditation and Love ♫♫♫ (Lyrichord)

influences:

◀◀ Ustad Vilayat Khan

▶▶ Nishat Khan, Irshad Khan, Vajahat Khan, Shafaatullah Khan

see also: *Ustad Vilayat Khan*

David Paul

Ustad Vilayat Khan

North Indian classical, Hindustani

Born 1926, in Gauripur, now Bangladesh. Based in Princeton, NJ, USA.

Sitarist Ustad Vilayat Khan was born into a distinguished line of legendary musicians, the Imdadkhani *gharana* (or regional school), tracing their lineage back centuries to the great Mughal courts, out of whose patronage much Hindustani music developed. Older brother and mentor to Imrat Khan, Vilayat is known for initiating an instrumental style of playing called *gayaki ang*, which emulates the human voice. Generally speaking, gayaki ang involves bending the string several times after plucking it, allowing for note-to-note continuity. Already well known as a child prodigy by the age of 10, the widely imitated Vilayat Khan has influenced sitar design and playing styles by conceiving new tunings and construction materials for greater resonance and volume. An incorruptible spirit, he claims he has never compromised or diluted his artistic ideals and once refused an award, claiming that the judges were unfit arbiters!

what to buy: *Raga Bhairavi* 𝄞𝄞𝄞 (India Archive Music, Ltd., 1991, prod. Lyle Wachovsky) is a thrilling performance accompanied by his son Hidayat Khan on *tamboura* (four-stringed drone instrument). Instead of producing a characteristically continuous drone, though, Hidayat plays behind the sitar in an extremely quiet, four-note pattern. *Raga Bhankar* 𝄞𝄞𝄞 (India Archive Music, Ltd., 1997, prod. Lyle Wachovsky) is a rarely heard dawn *raga* (the extensive classical pieces tailored to different temporal atmospheres). Hidayat Khan accompanies on a very quiet tamboura during the 38-minute free-form introductory *alap* movement. Akram Khan then joins on *tabla* drum for an extended 16-beat *gat* movement. As always with this label, very informative liner notes (three essays on Vilayat's interpretation, one on the raga itself, and one on Vilayat) are great if you want to thoroughly explore the origins and structure of the artist's music. *Raga Jaijaivanti* 𝄞𝄞𝄞𝄞 (India Archive Music, Ltd., 1991, prod. Lyle Wachovsky) is a substantial evening raga, brimming with ideas that Vilayat develops masterfully over the course of 74 minutes. This is a very rich, very exciting piece.

worth searching for: You won't be disappointed by Vilayat and others' skillful performances on the compilation *The Rough Guide to the Music of India and Pakistan* 𝄞𝄞𝄞𝄞 (World Music Network, 1996).

influences:

◄◄ Ustad Inayat Khan, Imdad Khan, Barkatullah Khan, Hyderhusain Khan, Alagh Khan, Hamid Khan, Rameshwar Pathak, Balram Pathak, Waliullah Khan, Faiyaz Khan, Alladiya Khan, Abdul Karim Khan, Bhaskarbua, Baba Allaudin Khan, Amir Khan, Bade Ghulam Ali Khan, Samta Prasad.

►► Shujaat Khan, Hidayat Khan, Budhaditya Mukherjee, Shahid Pervez, Ustad Imrat Khan, Nishat Khan, Irshad Khan, Vajahat Khan, Shafaatullah Khan

see also: *Ali Akbar Khan, Ustad Imrat Khan*

David Paul

Khenany

Traditional Central and South American folk

Formed 1981, in Mexico. Based in Ciudad Obregon, Sonora, Mexico.

Alberto Luna, woodwinds, stringed instruments, percussion, vocals; Guspavo Hernandez, woodwinds, stringed instruments; Rafael Covarrubio Soto, vocals, stringed instruments, percussion; Hector Ramirez G., percussion, fretted instruments; David Espinoza Morales, fretted instruments, woodwinds, percussion; Concepcion Garcia L. ("Conchita"), vocals, stringed instruments, percussion; Antonio Hernandez Mosqueda ("Tono"), vocals, percussion, stringed instruments, woodwinds. (All members are from Mexico.)

Khenany, a lively septet from Sonora, Mexico, started out in 1981 as teenagers playing traditional music of the Andes. As their popularity and virtuosity grew, the band expanded their horizons to incorporate a variety of Latin American styles and rhythms, including the music of their native region. A particular interest is reviving South American music that predates the Spanish invasion. They now tour throughout North America and have developed a devoted following, particularly among Andean music fanatics. The group's name, indeed, comes from a folk tale of that culture about an ill-fated romance between Andean princess Khenany and a Spanish conquistador. To avoid being killed, the pair were transformed by the bird god Lambayeque into musical instruments—Khenany into a bamboo shoot and her lover into an armadillo shell—which then continued their romance through the ages literally making music together. The group members themselves play over 30 traditional instruments. In addition to an extensive Spanish-language repertoire, they also sing selections in Quechua, the language of the ancient Incas, and Yaqui, which is a familiar language in their home province. They have three self-distributed CDs, which can be obtained by mail-order or on the web, and which have led to a successful Stateside debut.

what to buy: *Volume IV* 𝄞𝄞𝄞 (Celestial Harmonies, 1998) is the group's most polished effort to date as well as its U.S. label debut. In addition to the traditional sounds and ancient themes of the band's previous releases, this recording incorporates contemporary influences including jazz, salsa, and bossa nova.

worth searching for: The group has three independently produced recordings that can be ordered online at http://www.khenany.com. A standout is *Volume I* 𝄞𝄞𝄞 (Khenany, 1986), the

Ustad Vilayat Khan

group's debut, which mixes familiar numbers like "El Condor Pasa" with rewarding yet less-known ancient Andean pieces.

influences:

◀◀ Inti Illimani, Malka de los Andes

Michael Parrish

Kid Creole & the Coconuts /Dr. Buzzard's Original Savannah Band

Latin and Caribbean disco and swing

Kid Creole & the Coconuts formed 1980, in New York, NY, USA. Dr. Buzzard's Original Savannah Band formed 1974, in New York, NY, USA. Based in New York, NY, USA.

Kid Creole: Thomas August "Kid Creole" Darnell Browder, vocals; Andy "Coati Mundi" Hernandez, vibes, percussion (1980–87); Peter Schott, keyboards; Cheryl Poirier, vocals. Dr. Buzzard's Original Savannah Band: Stoney Browder Jr., guitar, piano (1974–79, 1984); Thomas August "Kid Creole" Darnell Browder, bass (1974–79); Mickey Sevilla, drums (1974–79, 1984); "Sugar Coated" Andy Hernandez, vibes, marimba, accordion (1974–79); Corey Daye, vocals (1974–79, 1984); Don Armando Bonilla, percussion (1974–76); Mark Josephsberg, vibes (1984); Michael Almo, horns (1984); Roland Prince, guitars (1984); Michael Boone, bass (1984); Mark Radice, bass (1984).

Decades before swing music became hip again in the late 1990s, Dr. Buzzard's Original Savannah Band brought '30s big band sounds to the disco era with a witty edge, scoring a hit with "Cherchez La Femme" on 1976's *Dr. Buzzard's Original Savannah Band* and enjoying moderate success for a few years. The group broke up In 1980, though It resurfaced in 1984, minus August Darnell and Andy Hernandez, for the badly conceived *Calling All Beatniks*. Kid Creole, on the other hand, based its sound in disco, with Latin and Caribbean rhythms added. That unique mixture was enhanced by Darnell's often tongue-in-cheek lyrics and his Caribbean Cab Calloway image, as well as the party-hearty stage show featuring the beautiful Coconuts as backup singers and break dancing by Coati Mundi. With a sound that defies categorization, Kid Creole has more of a cult following than a widespread appeal, although the music itself presaged salsa's popularity in U.S. pop circles. The band achieved some greater exposure when it backed Barry Manilow on a cut from his 1987 release *Swing Street,* and it has been featured in the films *Against All Odds, Car 54 Where Are You?,* and *The Forbidden Dance.* Darnell has also distinguished himself as a producer.

what to buy: *In Praise of Older Women and Other Crimes* 𝄃𝄃𝄃𝄃 (Sire, 1985, prod. August Darnell) finds the band in funky and fun form with "Endicott," a cry of independence from

vodou

ne of the most misunderstood, and irrationally feared, of cultural institutions is the Haitian *Vodou* religion (known by such other names as *voudun, voudou,* and *voodoo*). A hybrid of the West African Yoruba culture brought to the islands by the slaves and the French Catholic traditions brought there by the colonizers, Vodou involves polytheistic worship (camouflaged within the personae of Western saints), animal sacrifice, and a belief that practitioners can be possessed by the various deities. Although established in Haiti, Vodou has spread up to the southern United States, down to South America, and back to Benin in Africa, where the spiritual culture originated. An important part of Vodou ceremonies is the percussion-heavy music—once, as with slaves in the U.S., a coded means of master-evading mass communication—and accompanying dance. Key to any type of Vodou music are hand drums, and these vary in size and construction throughout Haiti. The percussion figures and call-and-response songs common to the religion have been adopted by many popular Haitian groups, none more visible than the internationally renowned Boukman Eksperyans, who take their name from the Vodou priest prominent in Haiti's independence struggle at the beginning of the 19th century. Horn-and-guitar-driven dance bands like Tabou Combo and Rara Machine have brought their Vodou-based sound to the U.S., largely through Haitian immigrant communities in New York. Several fine anthologies of Vodou music are available, perhaps most notably *Rhythms of Rapture: Sacred Music of Haitian Voudou* 𝄃𝄃𝄃𝄃 (Smithsonian Folkways, 1995).

see also: Boukan Ginen, Boukman Eksperyans, RAM, Rara Machine, Tabou Combo

Michael Parrish

a henpecked husband and the group's best-known tune Stateside. The cry becomes the coo of doo-wop on "Particul'y Interested" and soulful on "Name It." The band even takes a break from its usual party mode for musically successful stabs at social concerns on "Caroline Was a Dropout" and "Dowopsalsaboprock (We're Fighting Back)." In an earlier Caribbean party mode, *Wise Guy* 𝄞𝄞𝄞 (Sire, 1982, prod. August Darnell) landed Top 10 hits in the U.K. with "Annie, I'm Not Your Daddy" and "I'm a Wonderful Thing, Baby."

what to buy next: Both of these bands feature strong musicianship and production, and *Dr. Buzzard's Original Savannah Band* 𝄞𝄞𝄞 (RCA, 1976, prod. Sandy Linzer) is a well-played, disco-style delight.

what to avoid: *Calling All Beatniks* **woof!** (Passport, 1984, prod. Sandy Linzer) features bad 1950s-style rock by Dr. Buzzard minus Darnell and Hernandez. It proves the fire in this group really came from Darnell.

the rest:
Kid Creole & the Coconuts:
Fresh Fruit in Foreign Places 𝄞𝄞𝄞 (Sire, 1981)
Doppelganger 𝄞𝄞𝄞𝄞 (Sire, 1983)
I, Too, Have Seen the Woods 𝄞𝄞𝄞𝄞 (Sire, 1987)
You Should Have Told Me You Were . . . 𝄞𝄞𝄞 (Columbia, 1991)
Kid Creole Redux 𝄞𝄞𝄞 (Sire, 1992)
To Travel Sideways 𝄞𝄞𝄞 (Atoll, 1994)

Dr. Buzzard's Original Savannah Band:
Dr. Buzzard's Original Savannah Band Meets King Penett 𝄞𝄞𝄞 (RCA, 1978)

worth searching for: *Off the Coast of Me* (Antilles, 1980, prod. August Darnell) is the transitional album from Dr. Buzzard to the Coconuts. The Kid steps out front with his humor, but he hasn't dropped the big-band feel yet.

solo outings:
The Coconuts:
Don't Steal My Coconuts 𝄞𝄞𝄞 (EMI, 1983)

influences:
◀◀ Machito & His Afro-Cubans, Cab Calloway, Desi Arnaz
▶▶ Gloria Estefan, Buster Poindexter, Squirrel Nut Zippers

Lawrence Gabriel

Angélique Kidjo
Worldbeat
Born 1960, in Ouidah, Benin. Based in Paris, France.

Angélique Kidjo is one of world music's most popular and controversial figures. Her hard-edged hybrid of Beninese tribal sources and funk-rock inflections has landed her on the high-profile Lilith Fair tour and, even more important, in the coveted "general rock" bins of some major U.S. record chains. Kidjo first came to prominence with the 1991 Afro-dance hit "Batonga." But she really started turning American heads the following year on the original Stateside version of Paris-based en-

trepreneur Mamadou Konte's Africa Fête package tour (where, in a particularly triumphant moment, Peter Gabriel came onstage as *her* guest). Kidjo's following has grown from the start, as has the criticism that she dilutes African culture (interestingly, a complaint that seems to be leveled at her more forcefully than at figures like Gabriel himself). What the critics are missing is the uncompliant way in which all Kidjo's "crossovers" are made into the least ingratiating areas of modern music (heavy rock, driving electronica), and the way in which elliptical, chant-based tribal melodies recur in her work, their unsuppressibility all the more accentuated for the contrast to her Euro-club instrumental settings. Not to mention the fact that her unlikely hit albums are almost exclusively sung not in the English of the global marketplace or even the French of her adoptive country, but the Fon of her homeland. Whether critics get it or not, Kidjo seems primed to be speaking the language of the listening public for years to come.

what to buy: *Logozo* 𝄞𝄞𝄞𝄞 (Mango, 1991, prod. Joe Galdo) is the one that made her a star, with remarkably sensual techno-pop surrounding acoustic and *a cappella* gems of a rootsier nature—plus some sizzling sax by Branford Marsalis for you Americans. The sunny but substantive *Ayé* 𝄞𝄞𝄞𝄞 (Mango, 1994, prod. D.A. "Jumbo" Vanrenen, David Z, Will Mowat) went a step beyond *Logozo*'s singles-collection feel, with inventive compositions extended in structure but no-ways dissipated in impact—especially the striding Afro-jazz of "Lon Lon Vadjro." Kidjo made her most triumphant march on the mainstream yet with *Oremi* 𝄞𝄞𝄞𝄞 (Island, 1998, prod. Peter Mokran), a well-received repositioning of the artist as an international pop giant who happens to be from Benin. With the hybrid music she'd helped pioneer now a household marketing term, Kidjo's time had come, and even the critics were kind to this rock 'n' soul 'n' jazz 'n' electronica–flavored tribal testament. A deft Jimi Hendrix cover ("Voodoo Child") and guest spots by Marsalis and Cassandra Wilson place Kidjo in a prestige pantheon she vaults into with seeming ease.

what to buy next: Kidjo rose to fame in Benin despite a traditional low tolerance for women performers; she then practically fled the country in the days of an authoritarian regime. But now she returns regularly, gathering musical ideas from the countryside. This process is most directly evident on *Fifa* 𝄞𝄞𝄞 (Mango, 1996, prod. Jean Hebrail), where field recordings are woven into Kidjo's high-tech studio mix. Surprisingly, that mix was her most standard-radio-friendly one yet, with compact tunes that might seem slight but are nonetheless cleverly infectious—and were an impressively early premonition of the Western world's Hanson-era pop resurgence.

worth searching for: Kidjo's major-label debut, the import-only *Parakou* 𝄞𝄞𝄞 (Mango U.K., 1989), blueprints the ambition and imagination the world would soon be ready for.

Angélique Kidjo

Kíla

Irish traditional and fusion
Formed 1994, in Dublin, Ireland. Based in Dublin, Ireland.

**Rónán O Snodaigh, vocals, bodhrán, percussion; Rossa O Snodaigh,
bouzouki, mandolin, low whistle, percussion; Colm O Snodaigh, flute,
tin whistle, saxophone, clarinet, acoustic guitar, vocals; Eoin Dillon,
uilleann pipes, low whistle; Dee Armstrong, fiddle, accordion, hammer dulcimer; Lance Hogan, guitars, bass, hammer dulcimer, percussion; Brian Hogan, bass, guitars. (All members are from Ireland.)**

This Dublin septet of trendy upstarts has succeeded in making
a tradition-based musical stew hip for a young audience back
home in Ireland, where they've just issued their third album in
five years. Having already earned a reputation as a formidable
live act, they're finally getting a chance to make an impression
across the Atlantic with the recent North American release of
their second album. Often hailed as a belt of fresh air in the
Celtic crossover market, it doesn't take a musicologist to realize that Kíla owes a considerable debt to the pioneering Moving
Hearts from the early '80s, not to mention the Andy Irvine/Bill
Whelan/Davy Spillane *East Wind* project from a decade later,
and the *Riverdance* phenomenon that grew out of that. Swirling
pipes and mournful low whistle; horns and demonic cross-
rhythms borrowed from jazz, the Balkans, the Caribbean, and
Dónal Lunny; slithery, sensuous bass guitar; and great big gobs
of percussion everywhere, all unashamedly echo Moving
Hearts. Still, the group has more than that to offer, in particular
a quirky style of song, mostly in Irish, which defies categorization but has managed to get them into the old sod's singles
charts. What Kíla lacks in originality, it seems to make up for in
street credibility with an audience too young or uninformed to
know where they get half their ideas. More power to them—if
Tory Amos can take Kate Bush's career to the arenas, Kíla deserves a bit of action too.

what's available: Kíla's second album, *Tóg é go bog é* 𝄞𝄞𝄞𝄞
(Key, 1997/Green Linnet, 1999, prod. Lance Hogan, Kíla)—in superior remixed and resequenced form for its American version—
leads off with "Gwerzy," an energetic instrumental that unmistakably conjures the ghost of Moving Hearts, thanks to Spillane-
drenched pipes and low whistle and an abundance of diverse
rhythms. The album moves on to the band's funky and charming
Irish chart hit "Ón taobh tuathail amach" ("Inside Out") and
then stretches out with the lengthy "Rusty Nails," which starts

with a gentle Eastern European Gypsy feel (and odd hints of
Zorba the Greek!) before dissolving into a frenzied Altan/Hearts
hybrid and then quietly going out as it came in. On "Oh to Kiss
Katie," "Jasmine," and "Ríl a Dó," we are firmly back in Moving
Hearts territory, while the eight-minute "Dusty Wine Bottle" has
some lovely fiddle and tin whistle. Dillon plays it straight (and
solo) on the pipes on "The Siege of Carrickfinn International Airport," the only piece that (its title notwithstanding) sounds truly
traditional. Despite a lack of accordion, "Double Knuckle Shuffle" recalls Sharon Shannon and Dónal Lunny ("Cavan Pot-
holes," anyone?). The *a cappella* "Leanfaidh Mé" ("Follow Me")
has a distinctively South African flavor.

influences:
◄◄ Moving Hearts, Davy Spillane, Dónal Lunny, Sharon Shannon, Altan, Bill Whelan

John C. Falstaff

Jin Hi Kim

Korean, avant-garde
Born February 6, 1957, in Inchon, Korea. Based in Connecticut, USA.

Kim, though also a composer, is most noted as a player of the
komungo. Supposedly the oldest Korean instrument—it dates
back to the fourth century—the komungo is a five-foot-long,
six-stringed zither with 16 frets, played by striking the twisted
silk strings with a bamboo stick. Kim got a degree in traditional
Korean music at Seoul National University, then moved to the
U.S. and added an MFA in electronic music and composition
from Mills College. She has consistently stretched the contexts
available to her, combining traditional Korean music with the
avant-garde—a strategy that works well since, in their emphasis on pure sound rather than harmony, the two genres are
fairly close to begin with. Her adventurous streak has not only
led her to play with jazz and avant-garde improvisers—ranging
from guitarists Derek Bailey, Bill Frisell, Elliott Sharp, and Eugene Chadbourne; to wind players Oliver Lake, James Newton,
and partner Joseph Celli; to the experimental chamber group
Kronos Quartet—but also inspired her to help design the
world's only electric komungo.

what to buy: Kim and partner Joseph Celli, who plays oboe,
English horn, *piri* (Korean oboe-like instrument), and MIDI
breath controller, go the serial collaboration route on *No World
(Trio) Improvisations* 𝄞𝄞𝄞𝄞 (O.O. Discs, 1992, prod. Joseph
Celli), with Adam Plack (Aboriginal Australian *didgeridoo*),
Shelley Hirsch (voice), Alvin Curran (synthesizer and computer
samplers), Mor Thiam (African percussion), and Malcolm Goldstein (violin) joining for one track each. Plack and Thiam come
from the world-music scene, while Hirsch, Curran, and Goldstein are avant-gardists, giving the disc a nice balance. In a way

Jin Hi Kim

it's the epitome of Kim's approach; certainly it offers a good cross-section of her creative impulses, featuring her on both traditional and electric komungo. The free improvisations on *KomunGuitar* 🎵🎵🎵 (Nonsequitur, 1993, prod. Jin Hi Kim, Steve Peters) pair Kim with a series of guitarists from the avant-garde: Elliott Sharp (doubling on saxophone), Derek Bailey, Henry Kaiser, Eugene Chadbourne (playing banjo, actually), Hans Reichel, and David First. Sometimes her louder collaborators steal the spotlight from the softer komungo, but usually the pieces are effective studies in timbral contrast.

what to buy next: *Living Tones* 🎵🎵🎵 (O.O. Discs, 1995, prod. Joseph Celli, Jin Hi Kim) again offers differing contexts, but emphasizes Kim the composer. The four long pieces here—none shorter than 11 minutes—construct lean sonic sculptures in which every gesture is multiply nuanced and fraught with meaning. "Nong Rock" is for komungo and string quartet, but Kim doesn't play on her compositions "Tchong," for *daegum* (bamboo flute, by Hong Jong-Jin) and flutes (by Robert Dick); "Yoeum," for traditional Korean *kagok* singer (Whang Kyu-Nam) and baritone vocalist (Thomas Buckner); and "Piri Quartet," for three piri players and oboe/English horn (Celli).

the rest:
No World Improvisations 🎵🎵🎵 (O.O. Discs, 1990)
Komungo Permutations 🎵🎵🎵 (Nonsequitur, 1990)

worth searching for: The rare *Komungo 'Round the World* 🎵🎵🎵 (Korean Music Source cassette/Seoul Records CD, 1994, prod. Jin Hi Kim) is another album with rotating duet partners, getting its name from their international character: Adam Plack playing the didgeridoo, Rahul Sariputura of India on sitar, Hideaki Kuribayashi of Japan on bass *koto* (Japanese zither), and Mor Thiam on *djembe* and *dogodrum* (West African hand drums). Kim appears on Celli's *Video Ears Music Eyes* 🎵🎵🎵🎵 (O.O. Discs, 1995, prod. Joseph Celli), on the substantial 15:41-long track "36 Strings" for komungo and five channels of video. With the video obviously absent from the CD listening experience, this ironically is Kim heard in the most traditional mode of any of her recorded work, the piece building from spareness to density in the manner of classical Korean court music.

influences:
⏮ Kim Su-chol

Steve Holtje

Shoukichi Kina

Okinawan folk-rock, worldbeat
Born 1948, in Koza, Okinawa. Based in Koza, Okinawa.

Kina, the son of famous songwriter/singer Shoei Kina and a player of the *shamisen* (three-string guitar/banjo), formed his band Champloose in 1973. The U.S. military had controlled Okinawa since the end of WWII, and American culture had dominated most of the island's commercial music. Kina changed that by singing in Uchinaguchi (Okinawan) and basing his playing on traditional *katcharsee* rhythms, the folk dance forms that remained popular despite the American influence. The band's first single, "Haisai Ojisan," was a hit both at home and, more surprisingly, in Japan, which still considers Okinawa something of a cultural backwater. Its success inspired some Japanese musicians to investigate Okinawan culture and eventually led to a rebirth of interest in that culture by the island's own younger generation, which now tends to incorporate traditional folksongs into rock 'n' roll. The U.S. military still owns 30 percent of Okinawa, and since they left the rest of it Japan has been reasserting its ownership and trying to eradicate the Okinawan language, which they consider a dialect of Japanese. By singing in Okinawan, Kina has been helping to keep his homeland's unique culture vital. But Kina has an international musical vision as well. In 1980 he invited Ry Cooder to help out on his *Blood Line* album, was the leader of a large Earth Day celebration on Okinawa in 1990, played at John Lennon's 50th birthday bash at the Tokyo Stadium in 1991, and in 1993 hosted and organized the Miraikanai Festival, a congress of indigenous people from around the world that featured four days of political meetings and concerts. Kina is also something of a loose cannon. At one point he was known to be a fearsome drinker and drug taker, and a near OD led him to a breakdown that caused him to retire from music for seven years. During his time off he traveled the world. He met with and explored the folklore of the Ainu, Japan's indigenous people, lived with guerrillas in the Philippines, studied with spiritual seekers in India, and hung out with ecological activists in the U.S. In 1990 he returned home and resumed touring and recording, adding touches of *zouk,* calypso, and African music to his already eclectic style.

what to buy: *The Music Power from Okinawa* 🎵🎵🎵🎵🎵 (Globestyle, 1991, prod. Koki Miura) is a reissue of a 1977 live album recorded at Kina's Mikado club in Koza. The katcharsee rhythms sound amazingly similar to Texas swing, making this extremely easy on Western ears. The music is bouncy, bright, and energetic; translations and cultural notes are included in the enclosed booklet.

what to buy next: The *Peppermint Tea House* 🎵🎵🎵🎵 (Luaka Bop, 1994, prod. Koki Miura) compilation was put together by David Byrne and features half of the *Blood Line* album with Ry Cooder, as well as recent singles and album cuts. The tracks that hew closest to Okinawan tradition are the most interesting, but there are also credible excursions into American country and western, Celtic folk, modern rock, Asian reggae, and R&B. Kina's shamisen

Shoukichi Kina (seated rear) and Champloose

can sound like a *koto* (Japanese zither), electric guitar, or banjo, and the female backing vocals always add unexpected flourishes.

worth searching for: Kina's Okinawan albums may be available at local world-music stores. Titles include *Celebration* (Nichion, 1982), *Earth Spirit* (Nichion, 1991), *Blood Line* (1980), *Nirai Kanai* (1990), and *Rainbow Movement* (1993).

influences:
◀◀ Shoei Kina

▶▶ Rinken Teruya, Rinkenband, Shang Shang Typhoon

see also: *Ry Cooder*

j. poet

Diana King

R&B/hip-hop/dancehall reggae
Born 1972, in Spanish Town, Jamaica. Based in Jamaica.

Diana King is one of reggae's hottest crossover stars, owing in no small part to the *stylistic* crossover she innovated. Bred both on the riddims of her homeland and the sweet soul waft-ing down the airwaves from America, King decided to try the vocal style of the latter with the instrumental sound of the for-mer and quickly became a sensation. Determined to crack the not all-male, but, in her view, too-male realm of reggae, and with a new musical twist to spin, she perceived an open niche and leapt into it—and don't think it wasn't a daredevil jump. Her mother refused the teenaged King a singing career, so the precocious diva snuck away to the clubs of Kingston, conve-niently 10 miles away, and secretively sang for two years. King notes a broader acceptance of performers on the basis of tal-ent rather than age in Jamaica as opposed to the U.S.—but has stressed to interviewers that the bar owners "had no idea I was 13"! Mature session work would follow, starting in 1990 with Ju-nior Tucker on his song "Stop to Start" from his *Don't Test* album. King began to get stand-alone notice with her own sin-gle "Change of Heart," before nabbing the honor of touring with the high-profile Shabba Ranks in 1994. After this, she cov-ered Bob Marley's "Stir It Up" as heard on the soundtrack *Cool Runnings,* signing on for the related Stir It Up/Cool Runnings Tour with a Jamaican-music who's-who including Jimmy Cliff, Worl-A-Girl, and others. What really helped her bomb her way into the Stateside mainstream, though, was a reggae-fied cover of Bacharach and David's "I Say a Little Prayer" from the soundtrack to *My Best Friend's Wedding*. While still perhaps best known for this and other sturdy remakes, King's strongest material is inventive originals like "Shy Guy" and "Love Triangle," also deserving hits. Her continuing knack with them shows that, though to most Yankees she probably seemed to come from nowhere, she's here to stay.

what's available: *Tougher Than Love* ♬♬♬ (Columbia/Chaos, 1994, prod. Handel Tucker, Andy Marvel, Matthew Scott Noble) best displays King's vocal style and was certified gold in 1995 along with its single "Shy Guy." Also included is the follow-up single "Ain't Nobody," originally by Chaka Khan. *Think Like a Girl* ♬♬♬ (Work Group, 1997, prod. Andy Marvel, Handel Tucker), a kind of womanist concept album, sustains King's savvy for recognizing and deploying pop hooks and keeps the hits coming back with covers like "I Say a Little Prayer" and Culture Club's "Do You Really Want to Hurt Me."

influences:

◀◀ Junior Tucker

Adam McGovern and Steven Stancell

King Changó

Latin ska

Formed 1995, in New York, NY, USA. Based in New York, NY, USA.

Mike Wagner, trombone, guitars; Glenda Lee, bass; Luís Jésus Ruíz, drums, percussion; Miguel Oldenburg, guitars, backing vocals; Blanquito Man (born Andrew Blanco), vocals, percussion, moves; Fernando Vélez, percussion; Martín Adrian Cunningham, tenor saxophone; Luís Eduardo Blanco, keyboards, accordion, cuatro, percussion, backing vocals. (Members are from Venezuela and USA.)

Like Haiti's Boukman Eksperyans and the U.S.'s Spearhead, the Venezuelan/American King Changó's style is an exhilarating cultural whirlwind that sweeps from Argentina to the Arctic, recognizing no national or musical borders along the way. The path it carved in the English-only wasteland of U.S. rock was wide enough to let Ozomatli, Los Amigos Invisibles, Bloque, and a gathering host of others charge through, prying open the cracks made by Santana and Los Lobos on previous attempts. Changó's music switches from Latin ska to African funk to bluesy rock and beyond like a stuck satellite channel-changer, on a wavelength scrambled to none: If you don't understand the often-Spanish lyrics, you will, as Boukman's Lôlô Beaubrun once remarked to this writer, "understand the music with your body." Changó has a sophisticated but spontaneous sense of what makes people jump the world over, and unlike the Anglo-dance flavor of the minute, their arsenal includes something other than inebriation and volume. After mightily bringing forth much of the mid-'90s

AlterLatino revolution, even they needed a day of rest, studio-wise—but at presstime the three years they gave everyone else to catch up was about to end with the summer-'99 *Return of El Santo*. Consider yourself warned—and be there early.

what to buy: The neon/anime/carnival/wrestling-ring graphics and genre-fissioning music of *King Changó* ♬♬♬ (Luaka Bop, 1996, prod. José Andrés Blanco, King Changó) marks one of those historic pop moments when you don't know what hit you and are too dazzled to care. And listening back, the effect of "God Damn Killers" and "Don't Drop Your Pants"' political punch, "Melting Pot" and "Revolution/Cumbia Reggae"'s lilting multicultural overtures, and "Latin Ska" and "Melting Pot Intro"'s poly-jazz workouts doesn't wear off. The band runs such an idea surplus that even the end-of-disc "secret" tracks—some kickin' low-tech basic chants—have a rare reason for existing, with only the stalker-y "So Sweet" to threaten their Best New Band of '96 status. An album that put "Alter-Latino" not just on the map, but all over it.

the rest:

Return of El Santo N/A (Luaka Bop, 1999)

worth searching for: The Latin-ska masters honor some Anglo-reggae precursors with "Venezuelan in New York" on *Outlandos D'Americas: A Rock en Español Tribute to the Police* (EMD/Ark 21, 1998).

influences:

◀◀ Los Fabulosos Cadillacs, Tropicalia, Bad Brains

▶▶ Bloque

Adam McGovern

King Tubby

Reggae, dub

Born Osbourne Ruddock, 1941, in Kingston, Jamaica. Died February 1989, in St. Andrew, Jamaica.

Producer and engineer King Tubby is credited with inventing dub music, the instrumental mix featured on the flip side of any reggae single. These mixes have become a genre unto themselves and are regularly collected on CD. Casual listeners could find the repetitive beats and lack of vocals irritating; fans of dub, however, are transported, even mesmerized, by the deep bass and mind-bending reverb. In the 1950s, Tubby was already noodling with audio equipment, repairing radios and DJ sound systems. As an engineer at Duke Reid's Treasure Isle label, Tubby began experimenting with remixes—a totally new concept at the time—in which he dropped the vocal track and boosted the rhythm, adding effects like echo and delay. Thus dub was born. Songs had a second life when released in a dub version. Crowds became ecstatic at heavier rhythms than they

Blanquito Man (Andrew Blanco, left) & Glenda Lee of King Changó

had ever heard. Throughout the '70s and '80s Tubby ran his own studio, releasing some of the most psychedelic reggae mixes Jamaica has known. King Tubby was murdered in 1989, cutting short the life if not the legend of one of Jamaican music's greatest icons. His legacy has been well preserved on countless collections and through a host of faithfully adventurous protégés.

what to buy: Tubby hit his stride as mixer for Bunny Lee's in-house band, the Aggrovators. His mixes of their ska rhythms are documented on *King Tubby's Special, 1973–1976* ♫♫♫♫ (Trojan, 1991). With Augustus Pablo, Tubby recorded his most recognizable mix, the title track to the impeccable *King Tubby Meets Rockers Uptown* ♫♫♫♫ (Clocktower, 1977).

what to buy next: As suggested by the above, most of the 100 or so collections of Tubby's dubs focus on his mixes of a particular artist. The eight available on Blood & Fire Records are beautifully presented and are generally a safe bet. *The Dreads at King Tubby's, 1974–1977: If Deejay Was Your Trade* ♫♫♫♫ (Blood and Fire, 1994) features deejays toasting over hit songs brought in and out of the mix by Tubby. Tappa Zukie's "Jah Is My Shining Star" is heartbreaking, with Zukie virtually crying the

lyrics over snippets of "You Are My Shining Star." These are proto-dancehall tracks, a harbinger of the trend that later ruled the Jamaican charts. While not strictly a Tubby record, as only five of the 22 tracks are his mixes, *Dub Explosion* ♫♫♫♫ (Trojan, 1996, prod. Chris Prete) is a great compilation with heavy dubs of roots-reggae classics. In general, there is a lot of confusing overlap in Tubby's catalog, with the same material released under different names. The most important thing to watch for when buying a King Tubby compilation is what original material he uses. If you like Yabby You, then you will probably enjoy King Tubby's remixes of Yabby You (or, perhaps more precisely, if you like a particular rhythm section used by Yabby You, since the rhythmic elements are often all that's left once a song is stripped down for a dub mix).

what to avoid: Not so much a specific warning as a helpful rule of thumb: There is a surfeit of material attributed to King Tubby, with his nom de dub tacked on like a familiar brand name to any number of compilations that often bear only a loose connection to his work at the mixing desk. As noted above, Tubby had many excellent engineers and protégés active in his studio, including

Prince Jammy, Prince Phillip, and Scientist, so often a "King Tubby" mix only means that he supervised its creation.

best of the rest:

Glen Brown and King Tubby: Termination Dub, 1973–1979 ♪♪♪♪ (Glenmore Brown, 1973–79/Blood and Fire, 1996)

Morwell Unlimited Meet King Tubby's: Dub Me ♪♪♪♫ (Morwell, 1975/Blood and Fire, 1997)

King Tubby and Prince Jammy in Fine Style: Dub Gone 2 Crazy ♪♪♪♪ (Bunny Lee, 1975–1979/Blood and Fire, 1996)

Yabby U: King Tubby's Prophecy of Dub ♪♪♪ (Prophet, 1976/Blood and Fire, 1995)

King Tubby & Soul Syndicate: Freedom Sounds in Dub ♪♪♪♪ (Freedom Sounds, 1976–1979/Blood and Fire, 1996)

Dub Gone Crazy: The Evolution of Dub at King Tubby's, 1975–1979 ♪♪♪♫ (Blood and Fire, 1994)

Yah Congo Meets King Tubby and Professor at Dub Table ♪♪♪ (ROIR, 1995)

Greenwich Farm Rub-A-Dub ♪♪♪ (Blood & Fire, 1996)

worth searching for: These selections are only the tip of the iceberg. Rare dubs by King Tubby are being unearthed and compiled every week to sate an ongoing demand. Companies that have been active in this field are the French label Lagoon, with collections including *Roots & Society, Shining Dub,* and *Creation Dub.* Greensleeves, Clocktower, Burning Sounds, Munich, Musicrama, and Shanachie have also all released King Tubby compilations.

influences:

◀◀ Duke Reid

▶▶ Prince Jammy, Scientist, Aphex Twin, Bill Laswell, Teo Macero, Mad Professor

see also: *Oku Onuora, Augustus Pablo, Roots Radics, Tappa Zukie, Yabby You*

David Poole

Alison Kinnaird

Scottish harp

Born April 30, 1949, in Edinburgh, Scotland. Based in Scotland.

Young Alison Kinnaird seemed on track to pursue a career as a cellist until, at age 14, she discovered the *clarsach*—the small, diatonic, traditional knee-harp or folk harp of Scotland. A protégé of the late Jean Campbell, she learned enthusiastically and quickly, and played well enough to start winning competitions, including Scotland's National Mod and the first-ever Pan-Celtic Festival in Killarney, Ireland. But Kinnaird soon grew dissatisfied with what was then the standard repertoire. In the absence of a current tradition, much Scottish harp music was scavenged from the repertoires of other instruments or culled

from printed collections, which were themselves often edited by pianists or concert harpists. She undertook the task that was to suffuse her musical career from then on: to resurrect (or, if necessary, reinvent) a truly traditional, Scottish repertoire and performance style for the Scottish harp—a process that was to culminate in the beginning of her recording career in 1978 with the release of her first LP, *The Harp Key.*

what to buy: If you're going to get just one, the obvious choice is *The Scottish Harp* ♪♪♪♪ (Temple, 1988, prod. Robin Morton), which is a compendium of her first two solo albums, a splendid duet album with U.S.-born wire-strung harper Ann Heymann, a couple of National Trust folk archive projects she did with the Battlefield Band, and three newly recorded tracks. The 52-plus minutes herein represent the very best of an awfully good batch of recordings.

what to buy next: Kinnaird and Christine Primrose's *The Quiet Tradition* ♪♪♪♪ (Temple, 1990, prod. Robin Morton) is a duet album with one of Scotland's premier traditional singers and represents the culmination of many years of touring and making music together. Rarely do a singer and an instrumentalist seem so well matched; it's a tribute to Kinnaird's success in rekindling the clàrsach heritage that her playing blends so adeptly with a rigorous traditionalist like Primrose.

the rest:

The Harp Key ♪♪♪♪ (Temple, 1978)

(With the Battlefield Band and Robin Morton) *Music in Trust* ♪♪♪ (Temple, 1986)

(With the Battlefield Band) *Music in Trust 2* ♪♪♪ (Temple, 1988)

(With Ann Heymann) *The Harper's Land* ♪♪♪♪ (Temple, 1992)

The Harper's Gallery ♪♪ (Temple, 1992)

influences:

◀◀ Jean Campbell

▶▶ Wendy Stewart, Sileas, Cheryl Ann Fulton, Robin Williamson

see also: *Battlefield Band*

Chris Rietz

The Klezmatics

Klezmer

Formed 1986, in New York, NY, USA. Based in New York, NY, USA.

Alicia Svigals, violin; Lorin Sklamberg, accordion, keyboards, vocals; Paul Morrissett, bass, tsimbl; Frank London, trumpet, keyboards; David Licht, drums; Matt Darriau, clarinet, saxophone. Other members have included: David Krakauer, clarinet. (All members are from USA.)

The Klezmatics play radical Jewish roots music for the 21st century, combining their identity as Jews with a postmodern mysticism and progressive politics. This innovative ensemble has shared stage and studio with classical superstar Itzhak Perl-

The Klezmatics

man, avant garde dude John Zorn, alternative rock band Ben Folds Five, transsexual cabaret singers, the Moroccan Master Musicians of Jajouka, and most recently Israeli folk icon Chava Alberstein. Their collaboration with virtuoso violinist Itzhak Perlman, *In the Fiddler's House,* topped both world music and classical music charts internationally, becoming one of the top-selling folk albums of all time. The Klezmatics' music is by turns ecstatic, angry, elegiac, frenetic, and exquisite. Standout musicians in the group include violinist Alicia Svigals, whose mesmerizing fiddling swirls with echoes of ancient Greek and Turkish modes (combined with judicious use of MIDI, jazz stylings, and classical technique); and the compelling vocalist Lorin Sklamberg, who infuses all his songs with intense emotion. But every musician in the Klezmatics is a wizard, able to switch gears instantly between the scholarly approach of re-creating an older traditional sound, and an innovative modern perspective often informed by jazz, rock, and avant-garde influences.

what to buy: *Possessed* 𝄞𝄞𝄞𝄞 (Xenophile, 1997, prod. Robert Musso) reaffirms the Klezmatics' position as the premier post-modern klezmer band, as they march into the new millennium with a progressive agenda encompassing Jewish mysticism, gay rights, racial equality, and legalization of marijuana, all of which are given the celebratory treatment formerly reserved for sacraments such as weddings. The album starts in straightforward fashion, with Lorin Sklamberg's emotion-dripping vocals on the gypsy song "Shprayz Ikh Mir" lavishly backed by an expanded ensemble including the members of the Canadian group Moxy Früvous. The album soon veers from the traditional into the exotic with the clamorous "Moroccan Game," featuring a jazzy, skittering group improvisation. "Mizmor Shir Lehanef (Reefer Song)" reflects the Klezmatics' involvement in the struggle to create honest public discourse about drugs in the U.S. Unlike their earlier work, *Possessed* includes numerous songs in English, drawn from the Klezmatics' score for playwright Tony Kushner's *A Dybbuk: Between Two Worlds* (an adaptation of the classic turn-of-the-century Yiddish drama *The Dybbuk*).

what to buy next: A collaboration with the dusky-voiced Israeli folk diva Chava Alberstein, *The Well* 𝄞𝄞𝄞𝄞 (Xenophile, 1998, prod. Ben Mink) features Yiddish poems set to music by Alberstein, with luscious arrangements by the Klezmatics and producer Ben Mink (of k.d. lang fame). The provocatively titled *Jews with Horns* ♫♫♫ (Xenophile, 1995, prod. Hijaz Hirsh-leyb Mustapha, the Klezmatics) is another fine example of how the Klezmatics use their virtuosity to seamlessly integrate traditional Yiddish and avant-garde influences. Transcendent tenor singing, mind-boggling displays of violin technique, modernistic clarinet, and jazz-drenched horn playing are used to update arrangements of traditional material, including the 19th-century Yiddish labor song "In Kamf"; the rushing, tumbling "Man in a Hat"; and the heart-wrenching vocal harmonies of "Es Vilt Zikh Mir Zen."

the rest:
Shvaygn = Toyt (Silence = Death) ♫♫♫ (Piranha, 1988)
Rhythm & Jews ♫♫♫ (Rounder, 1992)
(With Itzhak Perlman) *In the Fiddler's House* ♫♫♫ (EMI Classics/Angel, 1995)
(With Itzhak Perlman) *Live in the Fiddler's House* ♫♫♫ (EMI Classics/Angel, 1996)

worth searching for: The Klezmatics appear on the following compilations (the first three of which are also reviewed in this book's Compilations section): *Klezmer: A Marriage of Heaven & Earth* ♫♫♫ (ellipsis arts . . . , 1996), *Festival of Light* ♫♫♫ (Six Degrees/Island, 1996, prod. Robert Duskis, Bob Appel), *Klezmania: Klezmer for the New Millennium* ♫♫♫ (Shanachie, 1997, prod. Henry Sapoznik), and *A Tribute to the Skatalites* ♫♫♫ (Shanachie, 1997). *Fidl* ♫♫♫♫ (Traditional Crossroads, 1997, prod. Hugo Dwyer) is Alicia Svigals's amazing solo album, a truly stunning showcase for her talents.

solo outings:
Matt Darriau's Paradox Trio:
Matt Darriau's Paradox Trio ♫♫♫ (Knitting Factory, 1995)
Flying at a Slant ♫♫♫ (Knitting Factory, 1997)
Source ♫♫♫ (Knitting Factory/Jam, 1999)

influences:
◀◀ Schloimke Beckerman, Naftule Brandwein, Dave Tarras
▶▶ Flying Bulgar Klezmer Band, Brave Old World, Budowitz, Kapelye, Don Byron

see also: *Chava Alberstein, Margareta Paslaru, Itzhak Perlman*

Suzy Rothfield Thompson

Klezmer Conservatory Band
Klezmer
Formed 1980, in Boston, MA, USA. Based in Boston, MA, USA.

Hankus Netsky, alto saxophone, accordion, piano; Judy Bressler, vocals, tambourine, poyk; Gary Bohan, cornet; James Guttmann, bass; Mark Hamilton, trombone; Robin Miller, flute, piccolo; Miriam Rabson, violin; Javier Perez Saco, piano; Grant Smith, drums, percussion; Ilene Stahl, clarinet; Jeff Warschauer, mandolin, guitar, tenor banjo,

background vocals. Other members have included: Don Byron, clarinet; David Brody, violin; Merryl Goldberg, soprano, alto, and baritone saxophones; Evan Harlan, piano, accordion; Frank London, cornet, alto horn; Ingrid Monson, cornet; Steve Netsky, tenor banjo, guitar, mandolin; Marvin Weinberger, violin.

Known for their shimmering performances of traditional and contemporary-tinged Yiddish music, the members of the Klezmer Conservatory Band have been international ambassadors of their high-spirited and infectious dance music since Hankus Netsky assembled the group in 1980. Multi-instrumentalist and composer Netsky, who is chairman of the jazz studies department at the New England Conservatory of Music in Boston, got his introduction to Yiddish music from an uncle and a grandfather who played in Philadelphia klezmer bands during the '20s and '30s. Although klezmer music, also dubbed "Jewish jazz," faded in popularity in the United States after the 1940s, when immigrant Jews tended to want to blend into American culture, recent years have seen a strong renaissance, thanks in part to the efforts of Netsky and the KCB. The 11-piece powerhouse breathes new life into this passionate music, which dates back to medieval Europe and incorporates a gumbo of Greek and Romanian dance rhythms, Dixieland swing, ragtime, and classical elements. The band was featured in 1988's *A Jumpin' Night in the Garden of Eden*, a documentary about Yiddish music, and in the acclaimed film *Enemies, a Love Story*. The KCB, which now regularly tours Europe, made its debut abroad in the spring of 1990 when it played several concerts in Germany and brought down the house at the first International Yiddish Festival in Krakow, Poland. The group has also been featured in Joel Gray's Yiddish music revue *Borschtcapades '94*, and in the PBS special *In the Fiddler's House* with violinist Itzhak Perlman. Recorded in New York and Krakow, the latter traced the klezmer roots of Perlman's brilliant career. Besides the ever-present high-octane spirit in their songs, the KCB's album notes include translations and/or transliterations, giving an added dimension to this life-affirming, irresistibly toe-tapping music.

what to buy: The band calls *Live! The 13th Anniversary Album* ♫♫♫ (Rounder, 1993, prod. Hankus Netsky, George B. Hicks) its Bar Mitzvah album, and like that joyous coming-of-age milestone, this record, recorded at the Berklee Performance Center in Boston on May 2, 1993, teems with celebration, energy, and excitement. Highlights include "Lena from Palesteena," an "early oriental fox-trot" first recorded by the Original Dixieland Jazz Band in 1921; "The Epsteins," a raucous, cascading, traditional New York–style wedding dance originally recorded by the Epstein Brothers Orchestra in the mid-'50s; and "Rumenye, Rumenye (Romania, Romania)," which shows off singer Judy Bressler's vocal gymnastics in a multilingual rendition of a song that's been sung by Billy Crystal and danced to by John Belushi.

Throughout the album, the energy level is just short of delirious, and the concert setting notches things up even tighter than usual. With its songs and stories, *Oy Chanukah!* ♪♪♪♪ (Rounder, 1987, prod. Martin Miller) bristles with the spirit of one of the most joyous celebrations of the Jewish year. The added "Oy" in the title—the liner notes describe this multi-purpose exclamation as "a lament, a protest, a cry of dismay, a reflex of delight"—is indicative of the band's omnipresent spunk and the record's historic reflections.

what to buy next: *Dancing in the Aisles* ♪♪♪ (Rounder, 1997, prod. Hankus Netsky, George B. Hicks) is guaranteed to whisk all but the most lead-footed on a tour of show tunes, swing tunes, wedding music, and more. In addition to the group's instrumental savvy, vocalist Bressler has never sounded better. One of the album's most unusual tracks is "Freylekh Fantastique," which features excerpts from Beethoven, Mozart, Tchaikovsky, Grieg, and Mendelssohn. Roll back the rug!

the rest:
Klez! ♪♪♪♥ (Vanguard, 1988)
A Jumpin' Night in the Garden of Eden ♪♪♪♪ (Rounder, 1988)
Old World Beat ♪♪♪♥ (Rounder, 1991)
Yiddishe Renaissance ♪♪♪♥ (Vanguard, 1992)
A Touch of Klez! ♪♪♪♥ (Vanguard, 1998)

influences:
◀◀ Jewish tradition, Seymour Rechtzeit, Miriam Kressyn

▶▶ The Klezmatics, Brave Old World

see also: *Epstein Brothers Band, Itzhak Perlman*

David Sokol

Klezmer Plus!
Klezmer
Formed 1984, in New York, NY, USA. Based in New York, NY, USA.

Sid Beckerman, clarinet; Howie Leess, tenor sax; Pete Sokolow, piano; Ken Gross, trumpet; Tommy Abruzzo, bass; Si Salzburg, drums; Henry Sapoznik, tenor banjo. (All members are from USA.)

This is one of the few American klezmer bands that can boast an actual physical connection to the genre's old Eastern European tradition: clarinetist Sid Beckerman is the son of klezmer trailblazer Shloimke Beckerman, one of the three great pioneer clarinet players in the form (along with Dave Tarras and Naftule Brandwein). Sid started playing with his father at age 14 and made a living as a full-time musician until 1954. But after taking a full-time postal job, he played only sporadically at weddings and bar mitzvahs and for *shtetl* (Jewish community) associations for several years, before stopping entirely. In 1984, as he was retiring from the post office, Beckerman was recruited by Pete Sokolow and Henry Sapoznik solely on the strength of his father's name. What the band got was a first-class musician, a teacher to more than 100 students, and a mentor to an entire generation of young players. Actually, the other members of the band aren't slackers either! Saxophonist Howie Leess played with several big-name regional swing bands and the Rudy Tepel Hassidic Orchestra, the most important traditional Jewish band in New York in the 1950s. Pete Sokolow and Henry Sapoznik are in the vanguard of klezmer music research and are on the faculty of the YIVO Institute's Yiddish folk arts program, KlezKamp. Although the band has made just one recording, Klezmer Plus! and its individual members are a major influence in a venerable and—thanks largely to them—ongoing tradition.

what to buy: One of the few examples of pre-revival klezmer music, *Klezmer Plus!* ♪♪♪♪ (Flying Fish/Rounder, 1991, prod. Henry Sapoznik) features a clarinet, saxophone, and trumpet front line. The combination produces a very dance-oriented, big band–influenced sound, typical of the klezmer outfits that played this music in the Orthodox community during the 1950s.

worth searching for: Band members have produced two important songbooks for would-be klezmer musicians. *The Klezmer Plus! Folio* features transcriptions from the band's CD. *The Compleat Klezmer* by Henry Sapoznik and Pete Sokolow is probably one of the most important books on the subject. In addition to 23 tunes from the classic klezmer repertoire, the book features history, discography, bibliography, and performance tips.

influences:
◀◀ Shloimke Beckerman, Dave Tarras, Naftule Brandwein, Rudy Tepel Hassidic Orchestra

▶▶ The Klezmatics, Kapelye, Mazeltones, Metropolitan Klezmer

see also: *Kapelye, Dave Tarras*

Aaron Howard

The Klezmorim
Klezmer
Formed 1975, in Berkeley, CA, USA. Disbanded 1994.

David Julian Gray, B-flat & E-flat clarinets, piano, mandolin, mandocello, lauto, violin, harmonica (1975–86); Lev Liberman, flute, alto and soprano saxophones (1975–88); Kevin Linscott, trombone (1978–88); John Raskin, percussion, xylophone (1978–83); Donald Thornton, tuba (1978–95); Brian Wishnefsky, trumpet (1977–84); Ben Goldberg, B-flat clarinet (1986–88); Christopher Leaf, trumpet (1985–94); Ken Bergmann, percussion (1985–87); Tom Stamper, drums, percussion (1983–85); Steve Saxon, trumpet (1984–85); David Skuse, violin (1975–80); Greg Carageorge, double bass (1975–77); Laurie Chastain, violin (1975–76); Rick Elmore, bass trombone, tuba,

bass drum, cymbals (1976–78); Nada Lewis, tsambal mik, baraban, accordion (1977–78); Susie Rothfield (Germany), violin (1976–78); Miriam Dvorin, violin, vocals (1978). (All members are from USA except where noted otherwise.)

The Klezmorim occupy a pivotal place in the overall history of klezmer music, for it was their first album that ushered in the currently burgeoning klezmer revival. The Klezmorim described their music as "the rollicking, vodka-soaked sound of a steam calliope gone mad." They blended the group improvisation of Dixieland jazz with the rougher sounds of the unschooled ensembles that once roamed the villages of Eastern Europe, and added a good measure of New Vaudeville theatrics. The result was a loose, roaring, funky brass sound, different from the more classical approach of the Klezmer Conservatory Band or the modern technical virtuosity of the Klezmatics.

Today klezmer is enjoying a renaissance, with active ensembles in every city. Sometimes dubbed "Jewish jazz," klezmer first became popular in America during the 1920s, when musicians were in the midst of merging the Russian and Romanian dance music of their homelands with the newer sounds of early jazz. However, by the mid-1970s, the form had been practically defunct for decades, a casualty of immigrant Jews' desire to assimilate into American mainstream culture.

The resurrection of klezmer began in 1975 in an unlikely spot: Berkeley, California, where flutist Lev Liberman had unearthed a cache of 78 rpm discs in a Jewish museum, fell in love with this Yiddish soul music, and plunged into an exhaustive study of klezmer (a mind-boggling task at the time, since none of the source material was readily available). Clearly the next step was to form a band in order to revive this all-but-moribund musical genre. At first, that band was string-based, with violinist David Skuse playing a key role in choosing repertoire and arrangements. By 1978 the string players had dropped out, and the Klezmorim became a horn ensemble, which they remained until disbanding in 1994. Encouraged by new Klezmorim member Rick Elmore (also a member of roots-pranksters the Cheap Suit Serenaders and a seasoned street musician in his one-man-band alter-ego, Professor Gizmo), the Klezmorim began to move away from their previous scholarly approach, incorporating elements from the New Vaudeville movement into their stage show. The band toured incessantly, both nationally and internationally, and their success inspired other musicians in other cities to take up the banner of klezmer, with bands first emerging in Boston (the Klezmer Conservatory Band) and New York (Kapelye). In 1983–84, the Klezmorim collaborated on a theatrical production with superstar jugglers the Flying Karamazov Brothers, whose bizarre humor left a permanent mark; the band went on to develop their own theatrical presentation combining slapstick comedy, melodrama, and, oh yes, klezmer, which be-

came very successful—especially in Europe, where *Jazz Babies of the Ukraine,* the audio document of this you-had-to-be-there spectacle, was recorded. But as a rich body of recorded work shows, there was more to the Klezmorim than met the eye.

what to buy: Recorded live at the Great American Music Hall, *Metropolis* ♫♫♫ (Flying Fish, 1981/1993, prod. Stuart Brotman) captures the stirring, celebratory, and occasionally maniacal energy of the Klezmorim at their peak. "Constantinople," "Hot Dishes," and "The Good Soldier" showcase the Klezmorim's evocative re-creation of a Russian military marching band from the turn of the century; the outfit is rhythmically relaxed yet cohesive, sounding as if they have been playing together for decades. David Julian Gray's frenzied clarinet solos on "Kramtweiss Steps Out" and "Heyser Bulgar" feature the laughs, whoops, and swoops associated with klezmer, giving the pieces an authentic village flavor. Not all the tunes are as frenetic; the sinuous "Moldovanke" is more contemplative, and the beautiful "Tuba Doina" creates a unique texture, combining a slow, Middle Eastern–sounding tuba solo by Donald Thornton with the tinkling delicacy of the xylophone. For a look at the very earliest stirrings of the klezmer revival, *First Recordings* ♫♫♫ (Arhoolie, 1977–78/1988, prod. Chris Strachwitz, the Klezmorim) contains highlights of the Klezmorim's original two albums, including gems from their short-lived opening era as a string-based ensemble. "Fidl Volach," featuring David Skuse's exotic violin, and "Cintec De Dragoste/Hora Lui Damian," with Lev Liberman's lovely flute playing, both serve as reminders of the connection between Balkan folk-dance music and klezmer. Another high point is what the liner notes dub "The 'Turkey in the Straw' of Eastern Europe," "Yoshke Yoshke." From the Klezmorim's second album come the sprightly "Firen Di Mekhutonim Aheym" and one of the band's greatest hits, "Di Zilberne Khasene." *First Recordings* also boasts a charming cover (originally from the second album, *Streets of Gold*) by the comic-book genius Robert Crumb, which pictures the band on the deck of a ship, with the Statue of Liberty in the background. *Jazz Babies of the Ukraine* ♫♫♫ (Flying Fish, 1987, prod. Gilles Hugo) gives a sampling of the music from the stage show for which the Klezmorim became best known. It is unfortunately incomplete without the visuals: picture six dark-haired bearded men performing in fezzes, tossing rubber chickens into the crowd, leaping about like circus acrobats, and conducting a mock Socialist rally, a holy-roller revivalist meeting, and kabuki drama onstage. Lev Liberman sums it up by saying, "It's true that Ken Bergmann used plastic Halloween bones as drumsticks. Yes, I did solo on the HarpoMarxophone. And it is indisputable that we stole our moves from Betty Boop."

worth searching for: *Notes from the Underground* ♫♫♫ (Flying Fish, 1984, prod. Bernie Krause) is a clear evolutionary step toward *Jazz Babies of the Ukraine* and a precursor to later modern klezmer groups like the Klezmatics, Flying Bulgar Klezmer Band, and New Orleans Klezmer All Stars. The excellent incarnation recorded here includes Tom Stamper on drums/percussion and Steve Saxon on trumpet, both experienced jazz players who bump the general musicianship of the group up considerably. Highlights include Duke Ellington's "The Mooche" and the "oriental foxtrot" "Egyptian Ella," based on a late-'20s Ted Lewis recording with a teenage Benny Goodman on clarinet. Another standout is the brilliant tuba solo on "Stambul Tants," originally recorded by the Ukrainian accordion player and bandleader Kornienko.

influences:

◄◄ Naftule Brandwein, Abe Schwartz Orchestra, Dave Tarras, Danny Elfman's "Mystic Knights of the Oingo Boingo," Duke Ellington, Fleischman Brothers cartoon music

►► Kapelye, the Klezmatics, Brave Old World

see also: *Ben Goldberg*

Suzy Rothfield Thompson

Kodo

Japanese taiko drumming
Formed 1981, on Sado Island, Japan. Based on Sado Island, Japan.

Motofumi Yamaguchi, artistic director, flute; Ryutaro Kaneko, musical director, percussion; Yoshikazu Fujimoto, O-daiko drum; Takeshi Arai, drums, percussion; Yoko Fujimoto, drums, percussion; Kazuki Imagai, drums, percussion; Sachiko Inoue, drums, percussion; Yasukazu Kano, drums, percussion; Tomohiro Mitome, drums, percussion; Tetsuro Naito, drums, percussion; Akira Nanjo, drums, percussion; Ayako Onizawa, drums, percussion; Eiichi Saito, drums, percussion; Hideyuki Saito, drums, percussion; Takuro Susaki, drums, percussion; Michiko Yanagi, drums, percussion. (All members are from Japan.)

The Japanese characters for Kodo mean "heartbeat," and that's the perfect analogy for the primal pulse of this dynamic ensemble's percussion-heavy compositions. The group was founded in 1981 by a community of people who'd come together 10 years earlier to dedicate themselves to the study of the traditional Japanese *taiko* drum, and have since gone on to worldwide acclaim thanks to their seemingly endless "One Earth Tour." Indeed, it's in a live context that Kodo is at its best, with an artful approach to performance that lends a fantastic visual element to devastating drum assault. Just imagine: 15 drummers in traditional Japanese regalia, many of them stripped to the waist, sinewy muscles bulging as they pound out monstrous rhythms on drums weighing up to 1,000 pounds with sticks the size of a small tree branch. It's mighty powerful stuff, but while the ritualistic approach may be rooted in Japanese tradition, Kodo has always been open to experimentation and has collaborated with artists ranging from American fusionist

world music in film

Because world music suffers from a lack of commercial radio exposure, the movie industry has long been one of the premier ways for it to reach new audiences—from the bossa nova craze stirred by *Black Orpheus* (1958) to the increased profile of French rap generated by *La Haine* (1995). Indeed, world music has been a part of the movies almost from the start. The "Chiquita Banana" girl Carmen Miranda and the "Sparrow of Paris" Edith Piaf were just two of the early world-music stars whose fame increased with their film careers. Much later, Pakistani devotional singer Nusrat Fateh Ali Khan solidified his growing overseas renown through his duet with multi-platinum rocker Eddie Vedder for *Dead Man Walking* (1995). And it isn't just artists who have benefited from movies, but entire genres. For example, the samba owes at least part of its Stateside success to Walt Disney, whose studio's short film *Watercolor of Brazil* introduced a nation to the samba-ing parrot Jose Carioca. Instrumental film scores provided another outlet for world music, though typically it was "sanitized" for American consumption. Composers like Henry Mancini drew on the Third World to pepper soundtracks like that of the John Wayne safari film *Hatari* (1962). World music can be integral to a film's storyline, as with the Gypsy tale *Latcho Drom* (1993), or solely window dressing, as with Les Negresses Vertes in the Parisian romantic comedy *French Kiss* (1995). America is a mecca for world music in film, and wealths of material come from abroad, including the yearly 1,000-plus films—most of them musicals—from India alone. Sometimes compromises are involved in transit to the States. Still, with the studios' power and audiences' thirst for new sounds, budding world artists and the movies can make beautiful music together.

see also: Bollywood (sidebar)

Sam Wick

Bill Laswell to Peruvian folk group Kusillaqta. Dedicated to promoting international artistic exchange, in 1988 Kodo established the "Earth Celebration," an annual three-day percussion

Yoshikazu Fujimoto of Kodo

and arts festival that brings performers from all around the world to the group's home base on Sado Island.

what to buy: Most of the group's previous material had essentially been self-produced and financed, but with the help of producer Bill Laswell, *Ibuki* 𝄞𝄞𝄞𝄞 (TriStar Music, 1997, prod. Bill Laswell) is their most impressive and accessible outing to date. It's an impeccable recording, with Laswell's crystalline mix putting the listener right at the heart of Kodo's thunderous beats and prominent usage of *kakegoe*, or shouts of encouragement, adding even more of a visceral thrill to 10 already powerful compositions.

what to buy next: For evidence of the gripping drama inherent in Kodo's dynamic sound, check out *The Hunted—Original Motion Picture Soundtrack* 𝄞𝄞𝄞 (TriStar Music, 1995, prod. Kei-ichi Nakamura), which features 15 imagery-filled songs, many of which were specifically composed for the Japanese-themed thriller. Motofumi Yamaguchi's serene flute strains provide nice counterpoint to the group's often overpowering percussive attack. With most of their earlier recordings now long out of print, *Best of Kodo* 𝄞𝄞𝄞 (TriStar Music, 1993, prod. Kei-ichi Nakamura) is a valuable document of the group's 1988–92 recorded output, primarily focused on capturing the energetic essence of Kodo's live sound.

what to avoid: Although its bold attempts to match Kodo's throbbing rhythms with the beat-happy trance of the techno scene are somewhat interesting, *Sai-So—The Remix Project* 𝄞𝄞 (Red Ink, 1999, prod. Archie Meguro, Paul DeGooyer) is a flawed experiment that loses too much of Kodo's heart and soul, despite the best efforts of remixers including Laswell, Strobe, and DJ Krush.

the rest:
(With Isao Tomita) *Nasca Fantasy* 𝄞𝄞𝄞𝄏 (TriStar Music, 1994)
Live at ACROPOLIS, Athens, Greece 𝄞𝄞𝄞 (TriStar Music, 1995)

worth searching for: Kodo released six albums between 1988 and 1992, all of which are well worth owning but are currently out of print in the United States. If you see them in your local record shop (or, more likely, in the group's native Japan), snatch 'em up, then send me a copy! If the group's appearances in films like *The Hunted* and *Rising Sun* have whetted your appetite for a full-on Kodo concert experience, but you don't want to wait for the next leg of their ongoing One Earth Tour, check out the live performance video *Kodo* (TriStar Music Video, 1992) for a sumptuous documentation.

influences:
◄◄ The taiko drumming tradition

►► Askill, Cleworth, Lagos & Piper

see also: *Bill Laswell*

Bret Love

Habib Koité & Bamada
Pop danssa
Formed 1988, in Mali. Based in Mali.

Habib Koité (born 1958, in Mali), guitar, vocals; Baba Sissoko, tama, ngoni, balafon, caragnan; Boubacar Sidibé, guitar, harmonica, vocals; Souleymane Ann, drums, calebasse, vocals; Abdoul Wahab Berthé, bass guitar, kamalengoni. (All members are from Mali.)

Raised among *griots* (musical oral historians) in Mali, Koité taught himself the guitar to accompany his mother. He sometimes plays in Western tunings, and sometimes tunes his instrument like traditional Malian ones such as the *ngoni* (proto-banjo) or *kamalengoni* (six-stringed harp). Schooled at the Malian National Institute of Arts, he stayed on after graduation as a guitar instructor. He brought together Bamada in 1988 as a fusion of Malian sensibilities and instruments like the *balafon* (xylophone) and ngoni with Western sensibilities and instruments like the guitar, bass, and drum kit. The group won the Voxpole Festival in France, allowing them to record two songs, one of which became a West African hit. Another prize from French radio made it possible to tour. Through it all, Koité has been slowly building up to international acceptance and acclaim. *Ma Ya,* his second album and American debut, has fulfilled both.

what's available: *Ma Ya* 𝄞𝄞𝄞𝄞 (Putumayo, 1999, prod. Habib Koité), finds Koité consciously working to build a contemporary world music. His sound speaks to Western consciousness with its clean sound and middle-of-the-road rhythm section of electric bass and kit drum. It speaks to world consciousness with its polyglot of languages spoken in Mali, a continental crossroads. It speaks to African consciousness as only a griot can.

influences:
◄◄ The griot tradition, Khalilou Traore

Hank Bordowitz

Alhaji Bai Konteh
Manding traditional
Born 1920, in West Gambia. Died 1983, in Gambia.

Most Americans have seen the late Alhaji Bai Konteh, they just don't know it. The popular TV mini-series *Roots II* introduced the world to Konteh, who played the village elder who tells author Alex Haley the story of his ancestor Kunta Kinte. Konteh was from a caste of musicians in Manding society called *jalis,* similar to West Africa's other well-known oral historians, the *griots.* He was also a master of the 21-string *kora,* an African harp-lute. It is said to have originated in the Mandinka kingdom of Kaba about six centuries ago. Konteh's ancestors were from what is now Mali, but followed the fortunes of the empire, moving first to Kaabu in present-day Guinea-Bissau, then to Casamance in southern Senegal, before finally settling in Gambia. Because of his diverse background Konteh was equally at home with the stately, intricate Malian style of kora playing and the more dance-oriented rhythms of the Gambian style. Gambian music allowed for more individualistic expression, and Konteh's mastery of his instrument led him to create virtuoso performances. Konteh, with members of his family including son Dembo, toured Europe, Russia, and the U.S., bringing much of the world its first taste of the dignity and beauty of Manding music.

what's available: *Kora Melodies from the Republic of Gambia, West Africa* ♫♫♫♫ (Rounder, 1979, prod. Marc D. Pevar) is the only readily available recording, and it is a classic. In the early 1970s there were few commercial albums of African music to be found in the U.S. Most were compilations of field recordings or drum ensembles that had toured with national dance companies; when Rounder released this, it was the first full-length record of a solo traditional performer. Konteh's enormous talent is shown in a fine light throughout, on a record of beauty and clarity.

worth searching for: Pierre Dørge went to Gambia and studied with Konteh, learning much about concepts of time in Sahel African music. You'll hear the influence on *Brikama* ♫♫♫♫ (SteepleChase, 1984, prod. Pierre Dørge), credited to Pierre Dørge & New Jungle Orchestra—particularly on Dørge's tribute to his teacher, "To Alihaji Bai Konteh."

influences:

⏩ Dembo Konteh, Malamini Jobarteh, Kausu Kouyate

Jared Snyder

Kornog

French Celtic

Formed 1981, in Brittany, France. Disbanded 1987.

Christian Lemaître, fiddle; Jean-Michel Veillon, flute, bombard, whistle; Söig Sibéril, guitar; Jamie McMenemy (Scotland), mandolin, bouzouki, cittern, vocals. (All members are from France except where otherwise noted.)

After helping to found the Battlefield Band and making three albums with them, Jamie McMenemy moved to France, where he joined with guitarist Söig Sibéril, fiddler Christian Lemaître, and flautist Jean-Michel Veillon to form Kornog. This quartet of musicians all had experience within the Celtic boomlet begun by Irish trendsetters the Chieftains, but the French trio could also look to Alan Stivell for inspiration when adapting Breton traditions to the larger Celtic blueprint. Kornog's first, eponymous album was released in 1983, and the mix of McMenemy's broad Scottish

brogue with stellar musicianship from the rest of the band made them a force to be reckoned with on the Breton music scene. Their next album, *Premiére,* was recorded while on tour in North America and remains the high point of their catalog. By the time they broke up they'd made a total of four albums, including the finale, *IV,* eccentrically released only on vinyl. Since the demise of the band McMenemy has gone on to perform with Mauve Taxi and Orion, while Sibéril, Veillon, and Lemaître helped start another fine (and influential) Breton-based band, Pennou Skoulm. Sibéril and Veillon next performed in yet another group, Den, while Lemaître joined Barzaz. Lemaître is also one of the three principals (along with Johnny Cunningham and Kevin Burke) in the Celtic Fiddle Festival.

what's available: Most of Kornog's first American release, *Premiére* ♫♫♫♫ (Green Linnet, 1984, prod. Herschel Freeman), was recorded in one night at the Coffeehouse Extempore in Minneapolis, Minnesota, during a U.S. tour. It may very well be the definitive Kornog album because the performances have the excitement of a live concert without any of the glitches. "Dans An Dro" reveals Sibéril to be the finest Breton guitarist since Dan Ar Braz of Malicorne. There are some nice things to be heard on *Ar Seizh Avel (On Seven Winds)* ♫♫♫ (Green Linnet, 1985), especially "Ronds de St. Vincent," which shows off Veillon's skill on the wooden flute, and "Dans Plinn," with superb interplay between McMenemy's *bouzouki* (Greek lute) and Sibéril's guitar. McMenemy's work on a Bulgarian dance piece, "Varbishka Tarchenitza," foreshadows some of the material he would later perform with the Belgian Baltic/Celtic hybrid group Orion.

worth searching for: Christian Lemaître is an extremely talented fiddler who can stand up to the inter-band competition he finds in *The Celtic Fiddle Festival* ♫♫♫♫ (Green Linnet, 1995, prod. Johnny Cunningham). His awesome work alongside fellow fiddlers Johnny Cunningham and Kevin Burke (as well as guitarist John McGann) is the kind of thing that causes jaws to drop. This group's Kornog quotient doubled when McGann was replaced by Söig Sibéril in their follow-up release, *Encore* ♫♫♫♫ (Green Linnet, 1998, prod. Johnny Cunningham). A series of British concerts provided the material for the album, which really shows off all the players in duets and group settings. Lemaître and Sibéril's two duets amply display the long-standing empathy between these superb musicians.

influences:

⏪ Alan Stivell, Gwerz, Battlefield Band

⏩ Pennou Skoulm, Den, Kemia, Orion

see also: *Dan Ar Braz, the Battlefield Band, Kevin Burke, Johnny Cunningham, Alan Stivell*

Garaud MacTaggart

Kotoja
/Ken Okulolo

Afropop
Formed 1985, in Oakland, CA, USA. Based in Oakland, CA, USA.

Ken Okulolo (Nigeria), bass, vocals, drum programs, leader; Babatunde Williams (Nigeria), trumpet; Avi Bortnick (USA), guitar; Jeff Essex (USA), keyboards; Peck Allmond (USA), sax, trumpet; Ken Brooks (USA), tenor sax; Marty Wehner (USA), trombone; Paul Henson (USA), tenor and alto sax; Danjuma Adamu (Nigeria), percussion; Sikiru Adepoju (Nigeria), talking drum; Lemul Barrow (USA), drums; Joe Brigandi (USA), drums; Jasmine Walker (USA), vocals; Chisa Tayari (USA), vocals; Elouise Burrell (USA), vocals.

Kotoja, loosely translated, means "let us be friends," a fitting name for a band that has the vibe of an extended family. Kotoja was founded by bass player Ken Okulolo, who once played in Joni Haastrup's Monomono, a Nigerian rock band that was legendary in its homeland. Okulolo also has played with King Sunny Adé and Victor Olaiya's Highlife Band; produced records for other artists; and put out his own album for EMI Nigeria, *Talking Bass Experience*. In the early 1980s Okulolo was recruited by O.J. Ekemode for his Nigerian All Stars. Ekemode, an Afro-Beat pioneer, had relocated to California and was putting together a band of Nigeria's top players for a proposed American tour. When they reached Oakland, the tour fell apart and Okulolo and several other All Stars jumped ship to form Kotoja. The band picked up many of the Bay Area's best young jazz and funk players, as well as several expatriate Nigerians with impressive credentials. Kotoja was an immediate favorite with the worldbeat fans who were jamming clubs for the Looters, Big City, Mapenzi, Zulu Spear, and other like-minded bands. But while most of these outfits played music closer to the rock side of the equation, Kotoja was able to mix and match styles with an authentic African vibe. They could jump from *juju* to highlife to Afro-Beat (all popular Nigerian dance-music forms), often dropping in a bit of funk, Trinidadian/Barbadian *soca*, Cuban *son*, Antillean *zouk*, or other Afro-Caribbean textures to keep dancers, and listeners, guessing. As the first wave of interest in worldbeat began subsiding, Okulolo diversified into three simultaneously operating units, including Kotoja. He put together the West African Highlife Band with four other Nigerian expatriates, all of whom got their first professional experience in the highlife bands of the early '60s. He is also one half of the Nigerian Brothers, a duo that performs traditional and contemporary Nigerian acoustic guitar music.

what to buy: *Sawalé* ♫♫♫ (Mesa, 1992, prod. Ken Okulolo, Patrick Coughlin) is a non-stop dance party; the band combines juju, highlife, and Afro-beat with funk, soca, son, and other Caribbean textures for an intoxicating brew.

what to buy next: *Freedom Is What Everybody Needs* ♫♫♫ (Mesa, 1991, prod. Ken Okulolo, Jim Dean) was an impressive debut from a band already known for packing dance floors and inspiring boogie-mania with their solid Afro-funk groove.

the rest:
Super Sawalé Collection ♫♫♫ (Mesa, 1992)

influences:
◀ O.J. Ekemode, Sunny Adé, Sunny Okosuns, Fela Kuti, Monomono

▶ West African Highlife Band, Nigerian Brothers

j. poet

The Kronos Quartet

Classical, new age, world, jazz, chamber music, string quartet
Formed 1973, in San Francisco, CA, USA. Based in San Francisco, CA, USA.

David Harrington, violin; John Sherba, violin; Hank Dutt, viola; Joan Jeanrenaud, cello. (All members are from USA.)

David Harrington was inspired to form the Kronos Quartet by the joy he felt in discovering and playing new music. True to this calling, in recent years the Quartet has made a specialty of discovering and commissioning works from composers around the globe, including Foday Musa Suso, Tan Dun, Philip Glass, and Sofia Gubaidulina. Though all of the members are classically trained, they often favor avant garde and dissonant pieces over the melodic work usually associated with classical string quartets. They've received a Best Contemporary Composition Grammy for *Winter Was Hard* and several nominations in other categories, and have made a trademark of performing before equally diverse audiences. "That's not only fun, but it's challenging, and I like to hear our work in different settings," Harrington once told an interviewer, in reflection on a week that had included Kronos appearances at a jazz festival, a rock concert, and an opera house. More truly than for many outfits, to the Kronos Quartet, all the world's a stage.

what to buy: The Quartet's most outstanding contribution to world music thus far is *Pieces of Africa* ♫♫♫♫ (Elektra/Nonesuch, 1992, prod. Richard Horowitz), a fascinating combination of chamber music with a variety of songs and stories by African composers. The liner notes are illuminating, too. Venturing in another direction, they explored the music of tango great Astor Piazzolla in *Tango Sensations* ♫♫♫ (Elektra/Nonesuch, 1991, prod. Judith Sherman). *Released 1985–1995* ♫♫♫ (Elektra/Nonesuch, 1995, prod. Judith Sherman) is a two-disc retrospective that includes excerpts from the group's distinctive explorations in rock, classical, early

The Kronos Quartet with guest Foday Musa Suso (center)

music, and avant garde compositions. They have an extensive discography, all on Elektra/Nonesuch, of work more concerned with classical, rock, and jazz experiments than with world music. Because this oeuvre is so diverse, there's not really one disc that could be said to be representative (the wide-ranging *Released 1985–1995* comes closest), but *Winter Was Hard* ♫♫♫♫ (Elektra/Nonesuch, 1988, prod. Judith Sherman) is a good choice for understanding their non-world-music interests.

what to avoid: *Ghost Opera* ♫ (Elektra/Nonesuch, 1997, prod. Judith Sherman) is the Kronos Quartet's take on Chinese operatic style in compositions by Tan Dun. Yes, they like dissonance, and yes, they're good at it, but some of the music on this record takes it in painful—or worse, boring—directions.

influences:
◀◀ George Crumb, Steve Reich

see also: *Obo Addy, Huun-Huur-Tu, Pandit Pran Nath, Astor Piazzolla, Foday Musa Suso, Wu Man*

Kerry Dexter

krosfyah
Soca
Formed (as Crossfire) December 1989, in Barbados. Based in Barbados.

Edwin Yearwood, lead vocals; Anthony Bailey, guitar, vocals; Michael Agard, keyboards, vocals; Felix Forde, bass; Sherwin King, drums (1993–present); Leslie Lett (Antigua), keyboards, vocals (1993–present); Henderson Quimby, vocals (1993–97); Margaret Bovell ("Miss B"), vocals (1995); Cameron Quintyne, trumpet (1996–present); Mark Husbands, trombone (1997–present); Leonard Griffith, keyboards, vocals (1998–present); Ray Armstrong, vocals (1998–present). (All members are from Barbados unless otherwise noted.)

At the forefront of a new Bajan (Barbadian) generation including Coalishun and Square One, krosfyah is currently the hottest—not to mention the most musically talented and lyrically accomplished—young soca ("SOul" + "CAlypso") band recording in the Caribbean. After cutting their teeth for several years as a ho-hum hotel band, "Crossfire" gave themselves a conceptual facelift and memorable misspelling, and re-emerged rather quickly as regional superstars. The fireworks started in 1995, when lead singer and

krosfyah, with lead singer Edwin Yearwood (r)

composer Edwin Yearwood turned a hat trick, taking all three crowns (Party Monarch, Road March Monarch, and Pic-O-De-Crop) on the Barbados calypso festival scene—and thereby earning inevitable comparisons with his illustrious Trinidadian role model, David Rudder. After being named "Band of the Year" in Barbados's Nation Entertainment Awards, krosfyah then steamrollered through the rest of the Caribbean, stopping to conquer Trinidad carnival (as part of the "Bajan Invasion") the following year. Since then, there have been fresh triumphs throughout the world: pop charts in Australia, gold records in Canada, Road March crowns in Holland, Summerstage in Central Park. (Yearwood was also named "World Soca Monarch" of 1998.) krosfyah is first and foremost a tightly wound soca band renowned for its high-energy stage shows, but part of the group's crossover appeal is its largely unstudied eclecticism. Principal songwriters Yearwood and Tony Bailey manage to bend the soca genre without breaking it, skillfully incorporating elements of Antillean *zouk,* Jamaican dancehall, and American soul. On stage and disc, krosfyah can heat it up with white-hot, whistle-blowing road marches, then cool it down with mellow, smoldering dance tunes—and still casually toss in a traditional-sounding ballad or protest calypso for seasoning.

what to buy: *Ultimate Party—Pump Me Up* ♪♪♪♪♪ (Crossfire Entertainment, 1995/Kalinago, 1997, prod. Nicholas Brancker) is unavoidable. It's the album that made krosfyah's reputation, a near-perfect collection that in terms of songcraft, production values, and arrangements far transcends standard soca fare. A monster hit both in and out of the Caribbean—it currently holds the all-time album-sales record for the genre—*Ultimate Party* is chock-full of frenzied party socas and other superb songs like the exuberant "Obadele," a lively, melodic tribute to Barbadian champion sprinter Obadele Thompson. But its centerpiece is what's become the band's signature tune, "Pump Me Up," whose much-imitated formula mixes an infectious guitar riff; a loping, laid-back tempo (underlaid with an Indian-influenced chutney-tassa groove); "positive" lyrics; and liberal doses of Yearwood's winsome, trademark interjection, "Oh Gawsh!"

what to buy next: *Hot Zone* ♪♪♪ (Kalinago, 1998, prod. Nicholas Brancker, Chris Allman), the band's latest release, is a collection of mainly solid but (by krosfyah standards) unexceptional tunes, with a preponderance of pared-down, bass-heavy dancehall socas and by-the-numbers entries in the "Pump Me Up" mode. The Haitian *cadence*-flavored "Calor" really *is* hot, and the single-entendre ragga (deejay) soca "Woody Wood Pecker" is both catchy and witty.

worth searching for: *Aim High* ♫♫♫ (Crossfire Entertainment, 1996/Kalinago, 1996, prod. Nicholas Brancker) is nominally a "various artists" compilation, but the lion's share of the efforts are by krosfyah and its members. In the manner of *Hot Zone,* it's slightly marred by one ill-begotten foray into drecky, Boyz-II-Men–style '90s soul, but other tunes like the exhilarating peace anthem "Down de Road" and the euphorically sexy "Wet Me" more than compensate. *Aim High* has recently gone out of print, as has the splendid EP *Fyuh Riddums* ♫♫♫♫ (Kalinago, 1997, prod. Nicholas Brancker), which features the Road March winner "Highway Robbery" and the gospelly "Redemption of Me" in addition to several more songs in krosfyah's feel-good strong suit. Happily, both albums are soon to be combined and reissued under the title *Aim and Fyuh,* also on the Kalinago label. Truly dedicated fans will want to find the 1997 holiday album *Fyahside Christmas* (Kalinago, 1997, prod. Nicholas Brancker) and the 1994 cassette version of *Ultimate Party* (for the three tunes that didn't make it onto the similarly named '95 CD).

influences:
◀◀ David Rudder

Michael Eldridge

Ali Hassan Kuban

Nubian Pop
Born 1929, in Gotha, Egypt. Based in Cairo, Egypt.

Nubia, the kingdom once called "The Gateway to Africa" by Westerners, today lies underwater in Southern Egypt and Northern Sudan, flooded by the Aswan High Dam, but Nubian musical and cultural traditions can be traced back at least 5,000 years. Ali Hassan Kuban first sang for bargemen plying the Nile at age seven, later played in traditional bands at weddings and other social functions, and finally became one of the first to synthesize Nubian folk with Sudanese and Egyptian music, creating a modern urban style that is both folkloric and progressive. It is said that he decided to add brass to his band after standing outside a Cairo jazz club. Although he turns 70 this year, Kuban still leads the band and sings the hits that have made him famous.

what to buy: Many of Kuban's early hits were released on cassettes recorded in one take, into one mike, the whole band in one room. The tunes on *From Nubia to Cairo* ♫♫♫♫

(Shanachie, 1991, prod. Delta Sound), including "Sukker, Sukker, Sukker" and "Amira," were mega hits in the Arabic world, selling millions. The music features electric guitars, organs, and sax, as well as *oud, tar,* and *darabouka* (Arabic tabla). The recording quality is not the best, but the irresistible groove carries the day.

what to buy next: *Nubian Magic* ♫♫♫♫ (Mercator, 1994, prod. Bibi Hammond) is a recent album with incredible playing and top-notch production. The 65-year-old Kuban is still kicking serious butt, with a funky bass player and horn charts that sound like an Arabic version of the Famous Flames. The album includes a disco remix of "Maria-Maria," one of Kuban's latest hits, that will cause serious damage to any dance floor.

influences:
◀◀ Umm Kulthum

▶▶ Hamza El Din, Hussein Bashir, Bahr Abu Greisha

see also: *Salamat*

j. poet

Kukuruza

Bluegrass
Formed 1990s, in the former Soviet Union. Based in USA.

Irina Surina, vocals; Michael Venikov, guitar; George Palmov, mandolin, harmonica, vocals; Sergei Moslov, fiddle, vocals; Alexeui Aboltynsh, bass; Dmitri Krichevsky, drums. (All members are from the former Soviet Union.)

Kukuruza is a group of Russian musicians who fell in love with the high-lonesome sound of American bluegrass. They play familiar English-language bluegrass songs and Russian-language originals in the style. True to the heartland that drew them from their homeland, the group's name is derived from the Russian word for "corn"—no double entendre intended!

what's available: *Endless Story* ♫♫♫ (Gadfly, 1998, prod. Andrei Zachesov) is the group's furthest venture into mainstream repertoire, with tracks including "Red Haired Boy," "Crazy," and "Bird on the Wire." *Crossing Borders* ♫♫♫ (Sugar Hill, 1993, prod. Keith Case, Chris Cioffi) shows a bit more of the Russian version of high-energy bluegrass and includes guest appearances by Maura O'Connell and Jerry Douglas. Their first release, *Kukuruza: A Russian Bluegrass Band,* is out of print.

influences:
◀◀ Bill Monroe, Jerry Douglas

see also: *Maura O'Connell*

Kerry Dexter

Umm Kulthum

Arabic and Egyptian modern and traditional

Born May 4, 1904, in Tammay al Zahayrah, Egypt. Died February 3, 1975, in Cairo, Egypt.

Imagine if Bessie Smith hadn't been killed in that car crash in Mississippi, but rose to be the type of symbol of American culture that Louis Armstrong became. Combine that with the continuous musical growth that Armstrong's contemporaries Coleman Hawkins or Earl Hines maintained, and you have some idea of the incredibly pervasive influence of Umm Kulthum on almost 50 years of Egypt's history.

She arose from humble beginnings, the daughter of the imam of a small town in the Nile delta. Her father, who supplemented his income at the mosque by singing at weddings and other celebrations in the community, taught his sons his songs, but it was his daughter, eavesdropping on the sessions, who learned the lessons best. At one performance, when her brother Khalid fell ill, she stood in, and it was clear from then on that she was gifted with an exceptionally strong and vibrant voice. She became the lead singer, accompanied by the chorus of her brothers and father. In 1923 the family relocated to Cairo to capitalize on her increasing popularity. When she got there she was initially viewed as talented but unschooled in the skills that a great singer needed. To rectify this she studied Arabic poetry and began to perform with more accomplished musicians. Her repertoire moved from the religious songs of her father to new love songs composed for her. Her clothes changed to match the manners and dress of the sophisticated upper-class women of the city. She began to make recordings and perform on the radio. Eventually she broadcast every Thursday night, bringing much of the Arab world to a halt for "Umm Kulthum Night." Her popularity was so great that it allowed her the freedom to have complete control of her career. Throughout most of that career she would act as her own agent and producer. Eventually she was also elected the president of the Egyptian Musicians' Union.

The 1940s through 1950s are said to be her "golden age," when her artistic vision had reached full maturity. She commissioned composers to write for her in the style of the day, moving from an Egyptian sound, to a more classical Arabic sound, to the heady times after the 1952 revolution when she championed the modern compositions of Mohamed Abdel Wahab, which utilized Western instruments and musical concepts. By the 1960s she had moved past stardom to become "the voice and face of Egypt." This was especially true after the 1967 war, when she traveled throughout the Arab and Muslim world on behalf of her country. Her death literally brought Egypt to a halt. Millions filled the streets of Cairo to mourn her passing. Her fame had become so great that it in some ways overshadowed the magnificence of her voice, but it is the power of that voice that still sells recordings around the world. Though even in death Kulthum continues to have an impact on much of the globe comparable to Caruso, Elvis, Streisand, and Madonna all in one, you'll have to scout the import bins and Arab American shops for her material in this country. Each release is "worth searching for"; this entry covers some of the best and easiest to find.

what to buy: If you haven't heard Umm Kulthum before, nothing can quite prepare you for the music on *Al Atlaal* ♪♪♪♪♪ (Sono Cairo). Kulthum's voice in its prime is beyond compare, but picture the power of Aretha Franklin with the total control of Maria Callas. A sonic banquet for connoisseurs of the human voice.

what to buy next: *Vol. 2: 1926–1927–1928* ♪♪♪♪ (Artistes Arabes) is an excellent compilation of the great early recordings. Though remastered from old 78 rpm discs, the sound is pretty good. The selection chronicles the slow movement from a religious repertoire into a more popular form, from the world of her father into the almost art-song world of Cairo. The singing is full of youth and soul, backed with small traditional ensembles.

the rest:
Umm Kulthum, Vol. 1: 1926 ♪♪♪♪ (Artistes Arabes)
Hajrik ♪♪ (Sono Cairo)
Rubayeat el-Khayyam ♪♪♪ (Sono Cairo)
Faat el-Mi'ad ♪ (Sono Cairo)
The Twinkling Star ♪♪♪ (Voix De L'orie)
In the Old Tradition ♪♪ (Sono Cairo)
Hakam Alena Al-Hawa ♪♪♪♪ (Sono Cairo)
Loilil Hub ♪ (Sono Cairo)
Zalamouni El-Nass ♪♪♪ (Cairophone)
Ana Fi Intizarak ♪♪♪♪ (Sono Cairo)
Shams Al-Aseel ♪♪♪♪ (Sono Cairo)
Nasheed Al-Amal ♪♪♪♪ (Sono Cairo)
Sahran Lewahdi ♪♪♪♪ (Sono Cairo)
Zalamouni Ennas/Ya Ein Ya Ein ♪♪♪♪ (Sono Cairo)

worth searching for: The 1997 film documentary *Umm Kulthum, A Voice Like Egypt* is an uneven but extremely interesting look at the singer and her career. The performance snippets are not long enough and some of the interviews are too perfunctory, but still there is nothing else like it to give you an initial idea of the power and sway of this great woman.

influences:
▶ Ahmad Adaweer, Hassan el Asmar, Shabaan Adul Raheem, Shaabeeni an Talaat, Sami Ali

see also: *Mohamed Abdel Wahab*

Jared Snyder

George Kuo

Slack-key guitar

Born November 17, 1955, in Hawaii, USA. Based in Hawaii, USA.

Hawaii's unique open-tuned slack-key guitar style is not only a national treasure, but, usually, a family affair: George Kuo comes from a distinguished line of practitioners. For example, his grand-uncle Albert Kawelo taught slack-key great Ray Kane during the 1930s. With all that history behind him, Kuo developed a very traditional style of playing. He has recorded on his own, with steel-guitar player Barney Isaacs, and as a member of the Kipapa Rush Band and Eddie Kamae's Sons of Hawaii, which he joined in 1986.

what's available: *Aloha No Na Kupuna—"Love for the Elders"* ♫♫♫ (Dancing Cat, 1996, prod. George Winston) is a beautiful example of traditional slack-key playing. The influence of seminal acts Sonny Chillingworth and the Sons of Hawaii is readily heard here: two of the songs Kuo plays appear on a 1971 Sons album. Carrying forth such legacies in fine form, *Aloha No Na Kupuna* won a "Kuo a Nâ Hôkû Hanohano" award for Instrumental Album of the Year from the Hawaiian Academy of Recording Arts in 1997. Barney Isaacs's masterful steel-guitar playing gives his and Kuo's *Hawaiian Touch* ♫♫♫ (Dancing Cat, 1995, prod. George Winston) a more easily distinguishable Hawaiian sound (for mainlanders). The liner notes claim that this is the first album of acoustic-guitar/steel-guitar duets in Hawaiian history. Whether or not that's true, it's a prime collection for aficionados of the music or the instruments.

influences:

◄◄ Rev. Dennis Kamakahi, Ray Kane, Gabby Pahinui

see also: *Sonny Chillingworth, Ray Kane*

Brian Mansfield

Fela Kuti

Afro-Beat

Born Fela Anikulapo Ransome-Kuti, October 15, 1938, in Abeokuta, Nigeria. Died August 2, 1997, in Lagos, Nigeria.

In Africa and worldwide, Fela Kuti is renowned as a musician, political irritant, and supporter of Pan-Africanism. Afro-Beat, the musical hybrid he created, combines elements of dance-band highlife (via Ghana), soul (à la James Brown), and jazz for a potent rhythmic force, to which he adds lyrics decrying government corruption sung in either Yoruba or pidgin English. He got his performance baptism as a vocalist with trumpeter and highlife superstar Victor Olaiya. In 1958 Fela (as he is known to a world of fans) went to London and studied at Trinity College of Music. While there he formed a highlife band known as Koola Lobitos. After studying trumpet and music theory for four

years, he returned to Nigeria, where he re-formed Koola Lobitos. Between 1963 and '68 Fela unveiled the first version of "Afro-Beat," but it was his trip to the United States in 1969 that helped crystallize his musical ideas. He lived and recorded in Los Angeles for most of the year, absorbing lessons in black history and Black Power through an impressive reading regimen that helped develop his political consciousness. He also rethought his approach to music, telling an interviewer that he had been "using Jazz to play African music, when really I should be using African music to play Jazz." The horn-section work from James Brown's funk band also made an impression on Fela at this time. In 1970 he was back in Nigeria with a newly minted evolution of Afro-Beat, a band (Africa 70), and a vision of social justice that endeared him to much of the African populace while marking him as a gadfly to the ruling establishment. From that time forward Fela released more than 40 albums; was harassed, beaten up, and imprisoned by Nigerian governments; renamed his band Egypt 80; and through it all remained as popular with the African masses as ever. Fela was rumored to be ill months before his actual death, and some of the local newspapers reported his passing prematurely. One of his brothers, Olikoye Ransome-Kuti, later announced that Fela had died due to heart failure and complications from AIDS. His transparent casket was displayed at a funeral attended by thousands of fans and dignitaries. At this writing the sprawling recorded legacy he left behind was set to become easier for Americans to discover with an extensive reissue program on MCA Records, beginning with a "Best Best Best Of" retrospective (and that's no typo!) in 2000.

what to buy: After his release from prison in 1986 (he had been falsely charged with money-laundering by the ruling Nigerian junta), Fela reclaimed his band, enlarged it to 40 pieces, and jumped back into the musical fray. *O.D.O.O. (Overtake Don Overtake Overtake)* ♫♫♫ (Shanachie, 1990, prod. Fela Anikulapo-Kuti, Sodi) shows a strengthening of his composing, arranging, and playing skills. There are only two tracks on the album, each hovering around the half-hour mark, and both contain fiery solos within the context of Fela's rhythm and polemic. *Black Man's Cry* ♫♫♫ (Shanachie, 1992, compilation prod. Fela Anikulapo-Kuti) is probably the best single-volume Fela sampler now available, binding together six of his most popular performances from the mid-to-late '70s. The version of "Black Man's Cry" comes from a 1975 recording that Kuti made with rock drummer Ginger Baker, while "Zombie," with its constantly moving rhythm accents, post-Masekela trumpet, and Maceo Parker–inspired sax playing, is a true Afro-Beat classic.

what to buy next: In the early days of Afro-Beat, drummer Tony Allen defined the jazz-oriented rhythm that would drive Fela's music. The songs on *Open & Close* ♫♫♫ (Stern's African Clas-

Fela Kuti

sics, 1971, prod. Fela Ransome Kuti) were breaking the five-minute barrier that many of Fela's pre-Africa 70 songs had hovered near, and Allen's flexible stick work and sophisticated cymbal splashing provided the constant push needed to enhance the leader's horn charts. "Gbagada Gbagada Gbogodo Gbogodo" gives ample evidence of Allen's importance to this edition of the band, while the title tune, purporting to provide instruction for a brand new dance, is one of the last apolitical works Fela recorded.

best of the rest:

Original Sufferhead 🎵🎵🎵🎜 (Shanachie, 1981)
Beasts of No Nation 🎵🎵🎵🎜 (Shanachie, 1989)
Volumes 1 & 2 🎵🎵🎵🎵 (M.I.L. Multimedia, 1996)

worth searching for: A biography of Fela written by Carlos Moore, *Fela: This Bitch of a Life* (Allison & Busby), maintains a similar contact with reality to that of Charles Mingus's autobiography, *Beneath the Underdog*. In other words, there are fantasy sequences woven through the text that may or may not illuminate episodes in the subject's life. Included are interviews with the musician and some of his many wives (who numbered 27 at that time).

influences:

◀◀ Victor Olaiya, Guy Warren, Miles Davis, John Coltrane, Thad Jones, James Brown

▶▶ Femi Kuti, Sonny Okosun

see also: *Femi Anikulapo Kuti, Bill Laswell*

Garaud MacTaggart

Femi Anikulapo Kuti

Afro-Beat
Born 1962, in Great Britain. Based in Nigeria.

Femi Kuti is one of Fela Kuti's numerous children from countless liaisons, but he is also the first (and so far only) one to score a recording contract. He was born in Great Britain but grew up in Nigeria. Femi (like his father, known to fans by his first name) quit school when he was 16 and joined Fela's band Egypt '80, in which he played alto saxophone. By the time the

dissident Fela was imprisoned on spurious money-laundering charges in 1984, Femi was accomplished enough to lead the band in the interim. After his father's release in 1986, Femi formed his own group, the Positive Force. Show-biz legend holds that Femi got the chance to record when a team of Motown executives came to Lagos in hopes of negotiating a contract with the senior Kuti. Exasperated by a recalcitrant Fela, the record company folks went off to his club, the Shrine, where they caught Femi leading his own band in a torrid set. They ended up signing Femi and left town just before Fela changed his mind. Since that time, the young saxophonist has also led his band in a series of international tours that hit Africa, Europe, and North America.

worth searching for: Femi's one domestically available solo album, the eponymous *Femi Kuti* ♪♪♪♪ (Tabu/Motown, 1995, prod. Andy Lyden, Femi Anikulapo Kuti), is currently out of print. The songs, arrangements, and performances owe an awful lot to his father but the production values are relatively lean and clear, something that could rarely be ascribed to the old man. Femi is a pretty interesting alto soloist, even considering his lineage, with a lighter tone but more technical chops than the better-known Kuti. "Survival" seems to be the most individual cut on the album. Even though the massed horns of the Positive Force are prominent à la Fela, the intro and "B" sections experiment with lighter textures than Fela probably would have attempted, including a jazzy Korg solo that sounds like a vibraphone. Drummer Jude Amarikowa, the other major player on the album, is a find. For completists there is also the various-artists collection *Africa Fête 3* ♪♪♪ (Mango, 1995), which includes "No Place," a tune not found on Femi's full-length debut.

influences:
◄◄ Fela Kuti

see also: *Fela Kuti*

Garaud MacTaggart

Leonard Kwan

Slack-key guitar
Born 1931, in Honolulu, HI, USA. Based in Hawaii, USA.

Along with Sonny Chillingworth and Gabby Pahinui, Leonard Kwan is widely considered to be one of history's three most influential artists in Hawaii's signature open-tuned slack-key guitar style. He began around age 10, and by the end of the 1940s was playing the Hawaiian style of *ki ho'alu* (or slack-key) on the mainland. A talented musician who could play a bit of piano, ukulele, bass, and saxophone as well as guitar, Kwan worked in dance and big bands as well as in Hawaiian combos with Chillingworth and others. He made his first single in 1957 and recorded occasionally for the next two decades, retiring tem-

porarily from public life during the '80s. Shortly before his return to recording with George Winston's Dancing Cat label, Kwan was given the Bank of Hawaii Ki Ho'alu Award from the Hawaii Academy of Recording Arts, and named a Living Treasure of Honolulu.

what's available: Kwan hadn't recorded in 20 years when he made *Ke'ala's Mele* ♪♪♪♪ (Dancing Cat, 1995, prod. George Winston), but he obviously hadn't lost any of his touch. His goal was to document the music of his whole career, so the album contains many Kwan originals, including "Ki Ho'alu Chimes," a song from his first single. Recorded acoustic and solo (for the only time in Kwan's oeuvre), this album of instrumentals reveals a player with a confident style and a deep, resonant sound.

influences:
◄◄ Sonny Chillingworth

▶▶ Rev. Dennis Kamakahi, Ledward Kaapana, George Kuo

see also: *Sonny Chillingworth, Gabby Pahinui*

Brian Mansfield

Forward Kwenda

Traditional Shona mbira music
Born 1969, in Buhera, Zimbabwe. Based in Berkeley, CA, USA.

Kwenda was born in rural Zimbabwe, and began playing drums and gourd rattles at age 10. He picked up the *mbira* (thumb piano) at 14, and taught himself how to play by listening to music on the radio. He moved to Harare, the capital of Zimbabwe, in 1984, and soon formed his own group to play gigs and Shona (traditional Zimbabwean) ceremonies. In 1985, Kwenda began exploring new ways of playing and improvising that astounded the older, more traditional practitioners. In 1991 he met Erica Azim, an American who had traveled to Zimbabwe to study traditional Shona music. They began playing together and have since formed a strong musical partnership.

what's available: Kwenda's debut, *Svikiro* ♪♪♪♪ (Shanachie, 1997, prod. Erica Azim, Forward Kwenda), features meditative pieces from Shona tradition as well as his own compositions. Traditionally the music is used for healing, and for soothing the relationships between humans and nature. Shona music almost sounds baroque, with an endless series of evolving melodic and rhythmic improvisations that slowly lead listeners into a deeply spiritual space. Kwenda's soothing vocals add another serene element to the already dreamy ambiance.

influences:
◄◄ Thomas Mapfumo, Ephat Mujuru

j. poet

L

La India

Salsa nueva

Born Linda Caballero, Bronx, NY, USA. Based in Manhattan, NY, USA.

As salsa new-jacks Marc Anthony, Ricky Martin, and DLG (Dark Latin Groove) pull the music into the light of the new millennium, it's hard to believe that, not even nine years ago, the youngbloods just didn't want to hear that "old-folks music." The script was flipped in 1992 the moment a Latin House diva named India hooked up with salsa piano genius Eddie Palmieri to record *Llegó La India via Eddie Palmieri*. A fervid collection of some of Palmieri's freshest arrangements and most exuberant playing in years, *Llegó La India* got its real rush from India's raw, aggressive soprano. At first the old-schoolers dissed her—she was too loud; trampled all over the groove—but their kids heard one of their own, heard *their* groove. They bought her records and packed her shows. Egged on by a backing band of young Latin all-stars (like Jimmy Bosch and Alfredo Valdes Jr.), India's lung power could overload the house PA one minute and spray soft wet soul kisses over the dance floor the next. Part Latina soul shake and part salsa caliente, India revealed herself to be the next incarnation of Celia Cruz and La Lupe. Thanks to remixes by her husband "Little" Louie Vega—and the old schoolers finally checking in—India became the first *salsera* since back in the day to gain commercial parity with the men, and 1994's near-platinum *Dicen Que Soy* made her a bona fide superstar. She faltered for a second with an ill-advised Tito Puente big-band swing album, but came back strong in 1997–98 with her tour de force vocal hit "Runaway" on the *Nuyorican Soul* compilation, once again making the future what it used to be.

what to buy: Years after it shook Latin music, *Llegó La India via Eddie Palmieri* 𝄞𝄞𝄞𝄞𝄢 (Sony Discos, 1992, prod. Eddie Palmieri, "Little" Louie Vega) still feels wickedly brand new. Given a crash course in "old-folks music" by Palmieri and then thrown into the fire, India goes for the jugular on every song—fighting the rhythm ("Vivir sin Ti"), seducing the clave ("Soledad"), deep-housing a rumba ("Mi Primera Rumba"). It's the sound of youthful arrogance, innocence, and exuberance. It's the sound of the prodigal daughter, home at last.

what to buy next: Chock full of radio/club hits ("Nunca Voy a Olvidarte," "I Just Want to Hang around You," "Vivir Lo Nuestro," and the title track), *Dicen Que Soy* 𝄞𝄞𝄞𝄞𝄞 (Soho Latino, 1994, prod. Sergio George) was a stylistic quantum leap for India. Produced and arranged by the most influential names in

zydeco

The essential core of any zydeco band is the combination of accordion and rubboard (a.k.a. washboard, or, locally, *frattoir*). The accordionist pumps out the melody and is typically the leader and singer. The rubboard acts as the foil, providing the steady scraping rhythm that also makes for zydeco's distinctive sound. During any night's performance, the band will "drop out," leaving just the accordion and rubboard to hold up the rhythm and keep the dancers moving—the true litmus test of all zydeco bands. The genre's lyrics are still often sung in the French of its home region, though more and more commonly in English as well. The repertoire consists of Creole tunes, waltzes, and two-steps shared with the neighboring Cajun canon; Louisiana R&B standards; "swamp pop" hits; blues; and whatever else can help a band win popularity on the dance floor. Zydeco, a music indeed for and about dancing, often sounds like it's coming more from the north end of the Caribbean than from the deep South of the United States. With flourishing national visibility, zydeco has become a source of pride in the Creole community, its unique contribution to the American musical landscape.

Jared Snyder

salsa nueva (DLG, Anthony, Martin), *Dicen Que Soy*'s hip-hop/R&B-ified salsa was tailor-made for India's vocal free-for-all-ing. This is the New Style.

the rest:
India Mega Mix 𝄞𝄞𝄞𝄢 (RMM, 1996)
Sobre el Fuego 𝄞𝄞𝄞𝄢 (RMM, 1997)

worth searching for: "Runaway" on the various-artists *Nuyorican Soul* (GRP/Blue Thumb, 1998) rejoins the La India saga in advanced progress.

influences:

◄◄ Celia Cruz, La Lupe, Jocelyn Brown, Lisa Lisa

►► Brenda K. Starr, Marc Anthony

see also: *Jimmy Bosch, Eddie Palmieri*

Tom Terrell

La India

Lá Lugh

Celtic

Formed 1991 in Dublin, Ireland. Based in Dublin, Ireland.

Gerry O'Connor, fiddle; Eithne Ní Uallacháin, voice, flute, whistle. (Both members are from Ireland.)

Historically, County Louth took its name from the pre-Christian god Lugh Lámfhada, or "Long-handed Lugh." Lugh was the grandson of Balor of the Evil Eye from Tory Island, Country Donegal, and father of Cúchulainn, the central figure in the great Ulster epic *Táin Bó Cuailnge* (*The Cattle Raid of Cooley*) — the setting for which was the Cooley Mountains of north County Louth, where Gerry O'Connor and Eithne Ní Uallacháin live. O'Connor was born in Dundalk, the principal town in County Louth, while Ní Uallacháin moved there as a child. Historically, most of the county was part of Old Ulster. North Louth and the adjacent parts of South Armagh and County Monaghan were Irish-speaking areas within living memory. Ní Uallacháin, whose first language is Irish, draws her singing from that tradition. O'Connor's people have been fiddle players for generations and he first made his mark as the fiddler in the group Skylark, which released two fine albums on the Claddagh label (and on Green Linnet and Shanachie In the States). He was also part of the band Kinvara. He was taught by his mother, Rose, and was fortunate to be in close contact with older players still alive during the 1960s, notably great Sligo fiddler John Joe Gardiner. Ní Uallacháin is an exceptional flute and whistle player but is perhaps best known for her outstanding voice, which London's *Time Out* magazine described as "clear and brittle as hand-blown crystal."

what to buy: *Lá Lugh* ♪♪♪♪ (Claddagh, 1991, prod. various) is a stunning debut album filled primarily with sparkling instrumentals, although Ní Uallacháin's singing stands out. "The Emigrant's Song" is the most beautiful and haunting, and is alone worth the price of the CD.

what to buy next: *Brighid's Kiss* ♪♪♪ (Claddagh, 1996, prod. Eithne Ní Uallacháin, Gerry O'Connor, Shaun Wallace) is dedicated to Brighid, whose name means "high or exalted one" and who was the most powerful female religious figure in Irish history. She was a triple goddess—a virgin mother, a lawmaker, a saint—and a folk image whose shadows still move over Ireland. On Brighid's Day, February 1, she is said to breathe life into the mouth of the dead winter. Lá Lugh celebrates this folk tale with another solid album of hot fiddle and flute instrumentals and songs. The only thing wrong with this one is that it doesn't have "The Emigrant's Song" on it!

the rest:
Senex Puer N/A (Sony, 1999)

worth searching for: *Cosa Gan Bhróga* ♪♪♪ (Gael-Linn, 1987) is the earliest recorded effort by the duo, who are joined by Belfast flute player Dessie Wilkinson, but it's long out of print and exceptionally hard to find.

influences:
◄◄ Altan, Arcady

►► John Joe Gardiner, Kevin Burke

Neal Walters

La Mafia

Tejano

Formed 1980, in Houston, TX, USA. Disbanded December 1998.

Oscar De la Rosa, vocals; Leonard Gonzales, guitar; David de la Garza, keyboards; Tim Ruiz, bass; Michael Aguilar, drums; Mando Lichtenberger Jr., accordion, keyboards. (All members are from USA.)

Before Selena, most Americans had never heard of *Tejano* music—but before Selena there was La Mafia. Think of Tejano as a kind of Tex-Mex country music, folding in Mexican *ranchera* balladry and European polka styles, all electrified for the modern pop market's sonic tastes. Until La Mafia's breakout, Tejano was confined to the ethnic neighborhoods of Houston, San Antonio, and the Rio Grande River Valley, too country for the salsa markets of New York and Miami, too cowboy for California tastes, and too provincial for the Mexican and Latin American markets. But then La Mafia made it to the top of Tejano music—and for their next trick, did something no other U.S. band has done. La Mafia set out to conquer the huge Spanish-speaking audience outside the United States—which they did, with their sure-fire, roots-based, market-savvy pop. As a top Tejano band, La Mafia's albums sold 50,000 units; as an international pop band, the formula was good enough to boost that figure to two million units per title. At the top of their game in December 1998, the band suddenly announced they were breaking up to pursue solo projects. It's hard to imagine any of the current Tejano bands succeeding at such a level, but then nobody expected La Mafia could do it a decade ago.

what to buy: La Mafia's *Estas Tocando Fuego* ♪♪♪♪ (Sony, 1991, prod. Mando Lichtenberger Jr.) successfully combines Tejano tracks with *cumbia* dance music and pop ballads to reach a Spanish-speaking audience in Mexico and Central America. Purists in Texas gave the band heat for selling out. On the other hand, this was the album that demonstrated how to transcend Spanish musical ghettos.

what to buy next: *Eufora* ♪♪♪♪ (Sony, 1998, prod. Mando Lichtenberger Jr.) is full of power-pop tunes and lush *bolero* ballads, a state-of-the-art Pan-Spanish musical spectrum. Like it says,

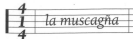

la muscagña

La Mafia: Hits de Coleccion 🎵🎵🎵 (Sony, 1998, prod. Mando Lichtenberger Jr.) is a collection of the group's more recent hits, heavy on the pop side.

the rest:
1986 🎵🎵🎵 (CBS International, 1986)
A Todo Color 🎵🎵🎵 (CBS International, 1986)
La Mafia Live 🎵🎵 (CBS International, 1987)
Amame 🎵🎵🎵 (CBS International, 1987)
Xplosiv 🎵🎵🎵 (CBS International, 1989)
Enter the Future 🎵🎵🎵 (CBS International, 1990)
Con Tanto Amor 🎵🎵🎵 (CBS International, 1990)
Ahora y Siempre 🎵🎵🎵 (Sony, 1992)
Vida 🎵🎵🎵 (Sony, 1994)
Exitos en Vivo 🎵🎵🎵 (Sony, 1995)
Un Million de Rosas 🎵🎵🎵 (Sony, 1996)
En Tu Manos 🎵🎵🎵 (Sony, 1997)

worth searching for: La Mafia's early material is not available on CD. However, EMI is reportedly planning to release some of the group's albums originally recorded for the Discos Cara label. In the meantime, search out the cassette-only *Carino* if you want to hear the group's R&B- and rock-influenced Tejano phase, or *15 Hits* if you want to know how La Mafia first got to the top of the Tejano genre.

influences:
◀◀ Rod Stewart, the Eagles, Freddy Fender

▶▶ Los Palominos, La Differencia

see also: *Selena*

                                          Aaron Howard

La Muscagña

Spanish folk
Formed 1986, in Castile, Spain. Based in Spain.

José Mari Clement, fiddle, Spanish bagpipes (1986–93); Rafa Martín, hurdy-gurdy (1986–93); Enrique Almendros, gaita charra y tamboril (three-holed flute and drum), Spanish bagpipes, percussion (1986–present); Carlos Beceiro, bass, cittern, guittara, hurdy-gurdy (1987–present); Jamie Muñoz, flutes, clarinet, accordion, percussion (1987–present); Luis Delgado, percussion, hammered dulcimer, oud, keyboards (1993–96). (All members are from Spain.)

Spanish folk music is far more diverse than many people might think. Images of quick-picked guitars, rolling castanets, and flamboyant, heel-stomping dances are not the only evidence of roots music in Spain. Looking beyond flamenco and its gypsy beginnings, past the Gaelic influences of the northern provinces, and away from the Arabic colors found in the southern region leaves one with the music of the Castillan

heartland, the birthplace of the band La Muscagña. Enrique Almendros, Rafa Martín, and José Mari Clement were all interested in Castillan music, but they came to it by way of the Irish roots-music boom of the early '80s. Almendros (whose first instrument was the dulcimer) was turned on to Castillan tradition when he heard a radio broadcast of *gaita charra y tamboril* (three-holed flute and drum) that he thought was Irish pennywhistle and bodhrán. His liking for the latter led him to explore the music of the Spanish heartland once he realized that was what he was hearing. Martín and Clement had similar experiences, and eventually the three got together to play music influenced by Castillan traditions. Through field research—partially inspired by the example of folklorist Joaquin Diaz—and by working with indigenous musicians, the nascent band became well versed in traditional performance styles. In 1987 they added flautist Jamie Muñoz and bassist Carlos Beceiro and started working on their first album. That album, *El Diablo Cojuelo,* was released in 1988, but its dulcimer-and-flute-laden songs had more of a new age tincture than the rootsy, explosive style La Muscagña favored in concert. Still, they won the Spanish National Folk Award for Young Performers and forged on to a second release, *El paso de la estantigua,* which began to present a truer picture of their musical identity.

what's available: La Muscagña have released only two albums in the United States. Like the Chieftains, this band is essentially an instrumental ensemble with vocals usually provided by a variety of guest artists. *Lubicán* 🎵🎵🎵🎵 (Green Linnet, 1993), their third album overall and their first U.S. issue, was a wonderful introduction to the band that never took off saleswise. Even though the songs were meticulously researched, the boring taint of academia was well obscured by Beceiro's funkified bass lines and Almendros' spunky presence on the gaita charrà y tamboril. *Las Seis Tentaciones* 🎵🎵🎵 (Green Linnet, 1995, prod. La Muscagña) is a solid effort made up of 13 dance tunes with nary a vocal to deflect attention from the band's wonderful musicianship, though it's not quite as exciting overall as *Lubicán.*

worth searching for: La Muscagña's finest album is not yet available as a U.S. release. Compiled from three days' worth of concerts in Madrid and Barakaldo, Spain, *En Concierto* 🎵🎵🎵🎵 (Resistencia, 1997, prod. Johnny Cunningham) features the basic trio of Almendros, Beceiro, and Muñoz plus former members Delgado and Martín, producer Cunningham on fiddle, and a small crowd of vocalists and other instrumentalists. The results are simply stunning.

influences:
◀◀ The Chieftains, Joaquin Diaz, José Ramón Cid, Isidra Camacho, Ismael Álvarez

▶ Candeal, Aljibe

see also: *Johnny Cunningham*

Garaud MacTaggart

La Sonora Dinamita
Cumbia
Formed 1960, in Colombia. Disbanded 1963. Re-formed 1975, in Colombia. Based in Colombia.

Julio Ernesto Estrada "Fruko" Rincon, bandleader; various additional performers.

Sonora Dinamita is one of the definitive Colombian *cumbia* groups. Its current version was created in 1975 by Julio Ernesto Estrada Rincon, a.k.a. "Fruko," musical director for the Discos Fuentes label. Fruko was asked by Discos Fuentes to resuscitate the group, which had run its course between 1960 and 1963 playing horn-heavy *cumbias*. With its moderate tempo and straightforward steps, cumbia—an African-rooted style from the Atlantic coast of Colombia—is the most popular dance throughout Central America and Mexico. For the Sonora Dinamita records Fruko uses mainly members of his own group Frukos y Sus Tesos—Colombia's most popular salsa band and the house band for Discos Fuentes. The dominant characteristics of this new, 10-piece incarnation are the trumpets and the high, girlish female vocal parts. The band has remained popular in Colombia's interior even though cumbia has clearly been challenged by the rural-styled *vallenata* as the most popular Colombian music. Perhaps this is due to the current Dinamita line-up's own rootsy approach.

worth searching for: If you live where you can buy Latin records you'll be able pick up some of Dinamita's classic albums; otherwise some easier-to-find various-artists anthologies will provide a good first taste of both the band and its genre. *Cumbia, Cumbia: Cumbias de Oro de Colombia* 🎵🎵🎵🎵 (World Circuit, 1989, prod. Nick Gold) is a superb compilation featuring a prime track by Sonora Dinaminta, "Se Me Perdio La Cadenita." This is one of the greatest dance compilations of all time, with excellent fidelity—and *Cumbia, Cumbia, Vol. 2* 🎵🎵🎵🎵 (World Circuit, 1993, prod. Nick Gold) may be even better. Same great variety of tunes, same high-fidelity remixes of classic cumbias. This one features "Ritmo de Tambo" by the group.

influences:
▶ Joe Arroyo, Carlos Vives

see also: *La Sonora Meliyara*

Jared Snyder

La Sonora Matancera
See: Celia Cruz

La Sonora Meliyara
Cumbia
Formed 1991, in Colombia.

La India Meliyara, lead vocals; Hugo Fernandez, trumpet; Nestor Agudelo, trombone; Ismael Gomez, trombone; Enrique Carrillo, keyboards; Hugo Molinares, guitars, keyboards; Rodrigo Morales, guitars; Neil Benitez, percussion; Rafel Benitez, percussion; Enrique Cuao, percussion; Alvaro "Macondo" Pava, backing vocals. (All members are from Colombia.)

Melinda Yara Yanguma, a.k.a. La India Meliyara because of her Native American features, has a booming voice full of spunk and fire. She has been singing since she was eight, at first with her father's trio doing traditional music—*porro, paseo, vallenato,* and *cumbia*—and later as the first woman singer with La Sonora Dinamita, the supergroup that has made the cumbia one of the best-known Latin rhythms. Meliyara left Dinamita in 1991 to form La Sonora Meliyara.

what's available: *La India Meliyara* 🎵🎵🎵🎵 (Riverboat, 1992, prod. Yemab) proves that with more exposure La India Meliyara would be known as one of world-music's top divas. Her larger-than-life voice is full of emotion—she can purr like a kitten and roar like a lioness—and her backing band cuts a deep, syncopated groove. Her lyrics tend to have a feminist slant and often poke fun at the macho posturing affected by most male artists.

influences:
◀ Peregoyo y su Combo Vacuna, Los Corraleros de Majagual, La Sonora Dinamita

see also: *La Sonora Dinamita*

j. poet

Ladysmith Black Mambazo
Zulu a cappella
Formed 1965, in Ladysmith, South Africa. Based in South Africa.

Variable membership, including: Joseph Shabalala, lead vocals; Abedrigo Mazibuko; Albert Mazibuko; Geophrey Mdletshe; Russell Methembu; Jabulane Mwelase; Inos Phungula; Ben Shabalala; Headman Shabalala (died 1992); Jockey Shabalala. (All members are from South Africa.)

The *a cappella* tones of one alto, one tenor, and seven bass vocalists with lead singer Joseph Shabalala are set to well-choreographed dancing by Ladysmith Black Mambazo. Although the South Africa-based outfit attracted international attention when its was chosen to sing on Paul Simon's Grammy-winning album *Graceland* and on Simon's subsequent world tour, it was already South Africa's leading singing group, with more than 25 albums to its credit. As one of the group's producers puts it, Ladysmith's music is like "a mixture of Stephen Foster meeting doo-wop at the roots of Soweto."

The group's unique style of voice and dance was first conceived in a dream by Joseph Shabalala in 1964. A native of the poor South African village of Ladysmith, Shabalala had traveled to the city of Durban as a teenager to work six days a week in a factory. While there, he discovered *iscathamiya,* the traditional singing style of South Africa's miners. After joining a local singing group, the Blacks, Shabalala became one of South Africa's most promising performers. His dream coincided with his conversion to Christianity, which would be as persistent an influence on his music as its Zulu roots. Although Shabalala attempted to teach his style to the Blacks, his efforts proved futile. After the Blacks disbanded he assembled several of his brothers and cousins to form Ladysmith Black Mambazo (Zulu translation: "The Black Axe of Ladysmith"). After winning nearly every local singing competition and appearing on an influential South African radio show in 1970, the group signed its first recording contract in 1973. Ladysmith's debut, *Amabutho,* was Africa's first gold record with 25,000 copies sold—and many times that since. It was 10 years later that the group's first internationally distributed album, *Induku Zethru,* was released, soon after which its collaboration with Simon made it one of the success stories of the 1980s. The group's Simon-produced *Shaka Zulu* went on to win the Grammy for best traditional folk recording in 1987.

On the world stage, Ladysmith Black Mambazo provided a musical accompaniment to the changes in South Africa during the twilight of apartheid and the dawn of freedom. In 1993 the group appeared in Oslo, Norway, as outgoing South African President F. W. de Klerk and African National Congress leader Nelson Mandela received a joint Nobel Peace Prize. The following year Ladysmith performed at the inauguration of Mandela as South Africa's first black president. It gained its largest audience ever during the opening ceremonies of the Olympic Games in Atlanta in 1996. In addition to appearing on the perennial TV favorite *Sesame Street,* Ladysmith has performed in a romantic musical, *Nomathema,* written by Shabalala, director Eric Simonson, and U.S. playwright Ntozake Shange, and in a morality play, *The Song of Jacob Zulu,* as well as being featured on the soundtracks of such films as *Moonwalker, A Dry White Season,* and *Coming to America,* and singing on albums by such diverse artists as Stevie Wonder, the Wynans, and Dolly Parton. Ladysmith Black Mambazo continues to spread its inclusive musical message in as many ways as there are listeners to hear it.

what to buy: *Classic Tracks* ♫♫♫♫ (Shanachie, 1992, prod. various) compiles 14 songs from Ladysmith's South Africa-released albums of the 1970s. Following the group's participation on

Simon's *Graceland* album and world tour, it showed its new global audience it could stand on its own with *Shaka Zulu* ♫♫♫♫ (Shanachie, 1987, prod. Paul Simon). A high-spirited recording, the album features several songs, including "Hello My Baby" and "How Long?" sung in English.

the rest:
Induku Kethu ♫♫♫ (Shanachie, 1983)
Ulwandle Oluncgwele ♫♫♫ (Shanachie, 1984)
Inala ♫♫♫ (Shanachie, 1985)
Journey of Dreams ♫♫♫ (Warner Bros., 1987)
Two Worlds One Heart ♫♫♫ (Warner Bros., 1988)
Umthombo Wamanzi ♫♫♫♫ (Shanachie, 1988)
How the Leopard Got His Stripes ♫♫♫ (Windham Hill, 1989)
The Best of Ladysmith Black Mambazo ♫♫♫ (Shanachie, 1990)
Inkanyezi Nezazi ♫♫♫ (FLTRCD, 1991)
Liph' Iqiniso ♫♫♫ (Shanachie, 1992)
Gift of the Tortoise ♫♫♫ (Earthbeat!, 1994)
Star and the Wiseman ♫♫♫ (Flame Tree, 1994)
Thuthukani Ngoxolo (Let's Develop in Peace) ♫♫♫ (Shanachie, 1994)
Heavenly ♫♫♫♫ (Shanachie, 1996)

influences:
◄ Reuben Caluza's Double Quartet, Solomon Linda's Original Evening Birds

► Paul Simon, Mahotella Queens

see also: *Black Umfulosi, Manu Dibango*

Craig Harris

Mary Jane Lamond
Traditional and technofied Cape Breton Celtic
Born November 5, 1960, in Kingston, Ontario, Canada. Based in Cape Breton, Nova Scotia, Canada.

Nova Scotia's Mary Jane Lamond is one of the young artists turning traditional music on its head. On *Suas e!* her vocals are layered over rhythms and electric guitar samples, backing tracks and synth effects. None of these detract from the essential purity of her songs (all well-researched and rediscovered classics of Canadian Celtic folklore) or voice (she sings in a pretty historical style, albeit with a contemporary soulfulness and bite); it's the settings that are shaking traditionalists. Fellow northern renegade Ashley MacIsaac, who's dubbed Lamond "Cape Breton's disco diva," guests on both of her albums; Lamond returned the favor by providing vocals for "Sleepy Maggie" on MacIsaac's superhit *Hi How Are You Today?*

Lamond grew up in Quebec and Ontario but traveled often to Cape Breton to visit her grandparents. The teenage punk fan ultimately enrolled in the Celtic studies program at Saint Francis Xavier University in Antigonish, Nova Scotia. She sings exclu-

Joseph Shabalala (l) with Ladysmith Black Mambazo

sively in Gaelic these days and is one of a relative few who are keeping the language alive.

what's available: *From the Land of the Trees (Bho Thír Nan Craobh)* ♫♫♫ (B&R, 1994, prod. Al Bennett) reveals a sweet-voiced young woman singing traditional Gaelic songs from Canada. The emphasis on rhythm in the milling songs might have prepared listeners for what was to follow, but her next album is still surprising. *Suas e!* ♫♫♫♫ (A&M, 1997/Wicklow, 1998, prod. Philip Strong, Laurel MacDonald) slips across centuries on fleet and graceful feet. One minute Lamond is singing against synthesizers; the next, she's duetting with the craggy voice of an elderly woman, Margaret Maclean. "Suas e!" roughly translates as "Go for it!"

worth searching for: On the Chieftains' who's-who showcase for Cape Breton musicians, *Fire in the Kitchen* ♫♫♫ (BMG Classics, 1998, prod. Paddy Moloney), Lamond brings over a cup of gasoline with a simmering "A Mháiri Bhóidheach" that bursts into a traditionally arranged "Dhòmhnall mac'ic lain" as scorching as *Suas e!*'s computerized version. And no folkloric futurist's collection is complete without Lamond's one-song Celt-funk coming-out party, "Sleepy Maggie," on Ashley MacIsaac's sensational *Hi How Are You Today?* ♫♫♫♫ (A&M, 1995).

influences:
◄◄ Ashley MacIsaac, Mouth Music, Sex Pistols

see also: *Ashley MacIsaac*

Pamela Murray Winters

Daniel Lanois
Art-rock/roots-rock hybrid
Born September 19, 1951, in Gaineau, Quebec, Canada. Based in Canada.

Daniel Lanois is an artist of exceptional ambition, musical vision, and lyrical depth. He also produced some of the most important albums of the 1980s and 1990s. While foremost a musician, he began his professional career as a producer/recording engineer at Grant Avenue Studio, which he owns with his brother. While there Lanois met ambient rock pioneer Brian Eno and the two struck up a long personal and working relationship. Eno brought Lanois to the attention of a number of prominent artists, most notably U2, who hired him to co-produce (with Eno) their landmark 1984 album *The Unforgettable Fire*. From there, Lanois collaborated with Peter Gabriel, the Neville Brothers, and Bob Dylan (including Dylan's critically acclaimed *Oh Mercy* and Grammy-winning *Time out of Mind*). During the late 1980s Lanois turned his attention to an artist of utmost importance: himself. Drawing on his French-Canadian ancestry and his love of blues and rock, he forged a unique sound that is the sum of his knowledge and a hallmark of his prodigious talents.

what's available: Lanois's second album, *For the Beauty of Wynona* ♫♫♫♫ (Warner Bros., 1993, prod. Daniel Lanois), is a work of stunning majesty and emotional complexity. Drawing on elements as diverse as Cajun music, guitar-rock, blues, and traditional French-Canadian balladry, Lanois crafts a sound that is greater than the sum of its parts, a style that transcends musical alchemy in its seamless fusion. Lanois's debut, *Acadie* ♫♫♫♫ (Opal/Warner Bros., 1989, prod. Daniel Lanois), is a quiet work that showcases his dedication to his French-Canadian roots, with songs populated by characters who seem to have sprung directly from history.

influences:
◄◄ Brian Eno, Nils Lofgren, Lindsey Buckingham, Clifton Chenier

►► U2, Don Was, Peter Gabriel, Morphine

see also: *Michael Brook*

David Galens

Bill Laswell /Material
Multi-genre fusion
Born February 12, 1955, in Salem, IL, USA. Based in West Orange, NJ, USA.

An incredibly prolific producer, bassist, composer, and multiple-label entrepreneur, Bill Laswell has made an astonishing career out of juggling roles, responsibilities, and musical genres. Although he remains almost invisible on the mainstream music radar, Laswell nonetheless seems capable of being everywhere at once, experimenting in jazz, funk, rock, hip-hop, noise, spoken-word, dub, ambient, drum 'n' bass, and a broad variety of world-music forms—sometimes all within the same album. He is perhaps best known as a producer, having worked with an intriguingly diverse variety of artists ranging from the Ramones, Mick Jagger, and White Zombie to Herbie Hancock, the Last Poets, and Yellowman. But he began his career as a formidable jazz/funk fusion bassist, co-founding the chameleon-like ensemble Material with drummer Fred Maher and keyboardist Michael Beinhorn in the late '70s. When a diverse cast of guest musicians was brought in for 1982's *Memory Serves* the group's future modus operandi was set, and with the exception of Laswell, the lineup has been in a state of constant evolution ever since. In the mid-'80s, Laswell was working with the *creme de la creme* of New York's avant garde jazz scene, producing and playing bass on Herbie Hancock's influential fusion album *Future Shock* and forming Last Exit with Sonny Sharrock, Peter Brötzmann, and Ronald Shannon Jackson. By the late '80s, Laswell had developed a fascination with a variety of world-music forms, and Material's groundbreaking 1989 album *Seven Souls* featured a number of influential artists who would go on to become regular collaborators, including L. Shankar, Sly Dunbar, Aiyb Dieng, Simon Shaheen, and Foday Musa Suso. In fact, this may be among Laswell's most admirable skills—the ability to find, nurture, and foster ongoing working relationships with some of the world's most remarkable musical talents. In 1990 Laswell formed the first of his many independent labels, Axiom Records, devoted to being "the ultimate vehicle and outlet for projects that consistently challenge beliefs in various networks and levels of the status quo." Although he would go on to form the Black Arc label for funk and rock projects, the Subharmonic/Submeta label for experimental electronic music, and the Meta label for spoken-word recordings, Axiom provides a home for Laswell's most personal explorations, including albums by world-music luminaries ranging from Shankar, Shaheen, and Talip Ozkan to the Master Musicians of Jajouka and Suso's Mandingo. Aside from Peter Gabriel, few people have done so much to expose the exceptional music of artists like these to Western audiences. The early and mid-'90s saw Laswell establishing himself as a trailblazing force in hip-hop, ambient music, and drum 'n' bass, with albums of varying quality featuring his name in one role or another seemingly released every other week. Eventually, however, a distinctive, genre-bending Bill Laswell "sound" began to emerge: as the late, great music critic Robert Palmer once wrote, "In contrast to the kind of reductionist thinking that separates music into discreet categories with their own record-store bins, Laswell hears the music whole, as a complex, dynamic system in which the components are distinct but always subtly related." As we move into the new millennium, Laswell—artistically rejuvenated thanks to Axiom's new distribution deal through Chris Blackwell's Palm Pictures label—remains light-years ahead, and with a broad variety of projects constantly being juggled in his capable hands, he shows no signs of slowing down to let the rest of the world catch up.

what to buy: For a glimpse of world-music fusion at its finest, it simply doesn't get any better than Nicky Skopelitis's *Ekstasis* ♪♪♪♪♪ (Axiom, 1993, prod. Bill Laswell, Nicky Skopelitis), an outstanding ensemble effort featuring the Meters' Ziggy Modeliste, Can's Jaki Liebezeit, Jah Wobble, Zakir Hussain, Bachir Attar, Simon Shaheen, and Foday Musa Suso, among others. It may be guitarist Skopelitis's name above the title, but this is truly a masterful group effort combining elements of jazz, rock, funk, dub, and ambient music with an emphasis on transcendent world-music textures. Don't think your mainstream-music-lovin' buddies can get down with world music's exotic sounds? Put on hypnotic tracks like "Heretic" and "One Eye Open" at your next party and count the conversions. Slightly more traditional in nature is the equally mesmerizing *Nagual Site* ♪♪♪♪

(Wicklow, 1998, prod. Bill Laswell), one of the first releases from head Chieftan Paddy Moloney's new label. A breathtakingly original Indian/ambient fusion, this gorgeously textured album prominently features the stunning vocal talents of Gulam Mohamed Khan and Sussan Deyhim, as well as subtle contributions from frequent Laswell co-conspirators like Skopelitis, Wobble, Hussain, Badal Roy, and Bernie Worrell. Remarkably seamless and organic, this is one of Laswell's most heady stylistic brews.

what to buy next: One of Laswell's most interesting fusion experiments, Possession + African Dub's *Off World One* ♪♪♪♪ (Submeta, 1996, prod. Bill Laswell) is a deliciously hallucinogenic excursion into the outer limits of dub experimentation pairing Laswell's subterranean bass lines and hypnotic ambient textures with African sounds supplied by Gambia's Foday Musa Suso, Mali's Fousseny Kouyate, and Senegal's Aiyb Dieng. Even in the seemingly endless canon of dub reggae, there's nothing else that sounds quite like this. Although it's far less about world music than *otherworld* music, the two-CD set *Axiom Ambient: Lost in the Translation* ♪♪♪♪ (Axiom, 1994, prod. Bill Laswell) is a must-have for anyone who appreciates the spirituality inherent in meditative forms. With input from all of the usual suspects, as well as contributions from ambient knob-twiddlers like the Orb, Terre Thaemlitz, and Tetsu Inoue, Laswell creates a contemplative epic blending a number of the label's finest compositions into a seamless flow that touches on funk, electronic, Indian, Moroccan, and Asian music, as well as jazz. Especially moving is the tender ballad "Peace," a loving tribute to Laswell's late friends Sonny Sharrock and Eddie Hazel, featuring saxophonist Pharoah Sanders. For an in-depth retrospective of Laswell's early career, check out *Deconstruction: The Celluloid Recordings* ♪♪♪♪ (Metronome/Restless, 1993, prod. Bill Laswell), another two-disc compilation featuring radically disparate tracks by Material, Massacre, Last Exit, Timezone, the Last Poets, Fab Five Freddy, Fela Kuti, Ginger Baker, and Touré Kunda, among others.

what to avoid: In any body of work as extensive as Laswell's there's bound to be a few stinkers, and this musical jack-of-all-trades has certainly had his fair share. Material's *Live from Soundscape* ♪ (DIW, 1991, prod. Verna Gillis) is rambling, free-form improvisation that offers little more than brief, sporadic moments of relatively soulless instrumental wizardry. And staying far, far away from the mindlessly repetitive, monolithically pounding noise of Chaos Face's *Doom Ride* ♪ (Subharmonic, 1994, prod. Bill Laswell) is strongly recommend.

the rest:
Baselines ♪♪♪ (Celluloid/Elektra Musician, 1983)
(With Peter Brötzmann) *Lowlife* ♪♪♪♪ (Celluloid, 1987)
Hear No Evil ♪♪♪♪ (Venture/Virgin, 1988)

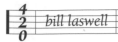

(With Ryuichi Sakamoto and Yosuke Yamashita) *Asian Games* 🎵🎵🎵 (Verve, 1994)

(With Tetsu Inoue) *Cymatic Scan* 🎵🎵🎵 (Subharmonic, 1994)

(With Pete Namlook) *Psychonavigation* 🎵🎵🎵🎵 (Subharmonic, 1994)

(With M.J. Harris) *Somnific Flux* 🎵🎵🎵🎵 (Subharmonic, 1995)

(With Terre Thaemlitz) *Web* 🎵🎵🎵 (Subharmonic, 1995)

Axiom Funk: Funkronomicon 🎵🎵🎵🎵 (Axiom, 1995)

(With Nicholas James Bullen) *Bass Terror* 🎵🎵🎵 (Sub Rosa, 1995)

Silent Recoil: Dub System One 🎵🎵🎵 (Low, 1996)

Oscillations 🎵🎵 (Subharmonic, 1996)

(With Klaus Schulze and Pete Namlook) *Dark Side of the Moog IV* 🎵🎵🎵🎵 (Ger. Fax, 1996)

Sacred System Chapter One: Book of Entrance 🎵🎵🎵 (ROIR, 1996)

Dark Massive/Disengage: Ambient Compendium 🎵🎵🎵 (M.I.L. Multimedia, 1996)

Altered Beats: Assassin Knowledges of the Remanipulated 🎵🎵🎵🎵 (Axiom, 1996)

(With Jonah Sharp) *Visitation* 🎵🎵🎵🎵 (Subharmonic, 1996)

(With Style Scott) *Dub Meltdown* 🎵🎵🎵 (WordSound, 1997)

Sacred System Chapter Two 🎵🎵🎵🎵 (ROIR, 1997)

City of Light 🎵🎵🎵🎵 (Sub Rosa, 1997)

Dreams of Freedom: Ambient Translations of Bob Marley in Dub 🎵🎵🎵🎵 (Axiom, 1997)

Panthalassa: The Music of Miles Davis 🎵🎵🎵🎵 (Columbia, 1998)

Oscillations 2 🎵🎵🎵 (Sub Rosa, 1998)

(With Sacred System) *Imaginary Cuba: Deconstructing Havana* N/A (Wicklow, 1999)

Material:

Temporary Music 🎵🎵🎵 (Celluloid, 1981/Restless 1993)

Memory Serves 🎵🎵🎵🎵 (Celluloid/Elektra Musician, 1981/Restless, 1992)

One Down 🎵🎵🎵🎵 (Celluloid/Elektra, 1982/Restless, 1992)

Red Tracks 🎵🎵🎵 (Red, 1985)

Seven Souls 🎵🎵🎵 (Virgin, 1989)

The Third Power 🎵🎵🎵 (Axiom, 1991)

Live in Japan 🎵🎵 (Restless, 1993)

Hallucination Engine 🎵🎵🎵🎵 (Axiom, 1994)

Intonarumori 🎵🎵🎵 (Axiom, 1999)

Massacre:

Killing Time 🎵🎵🎵🎵 (Celluloid, 1982)

Shango:

Shango Funk Theology 🎵🎵🎵🎵 (Celluloid, 1984)

Deadline:

Down by Law 🎵🎵🎵 (Celluloid, 1985)

Last Exit:

Last Exit 🎵🎵 (Enemy, 1986)

The Noise of Trouble: Live in Tokyo 🎵🎵🎵🎵 (Enemy, 1987)

From the Board a.k.a *Cassette Recordings '87* 🎵🎵🎵 (Celluloid, 1988/Enemy, 1995)

Headfirst into Flames 🎵🎵🎵🎵 (MuWorks, 1993)

SXL:

Live in Japan 🎵🎵🎵 (CBS/Sony Japan, 1987)

Outlands 🎵🎵🎵 (Celluloid/Pipeline, 1988)

Painkiller:

The Guts of a Virgin 🎵🎵🎵🎵 (Earache, 1991)

Buried Secrets 🎵🎵🎵🎵 (Earache, 1993)

Execution Ground 🎵🎵🎵🎵 (Subharmonic, 1994)

Complete Studio Recordings 🎵🎵🎵🎵 (Tzadik, 1998)

Praxis:

Transmutation (Mutatis Mutandis) 🎵🎵🎵🎵 (Axiom, 1992)

Sacrifist 🎵🎵🎵🎵 (Subharmonic, 1993)

Metatron 🎵🎵🎵🎵 (Subharmonic, 1994)

Divination:

Ambient Dub Vol. I 🎵🎵🎵🎵 (Subharmonic, 1993)

Ambient Dub Vol. II: Dead Slow 🎵🎵🎵🎵 (Subharmonic, 1994)

Akasha 🎵🎵🎵🎵 (Subharmonic, 1995)

Distill 🎵🎵🎵🎵 (Sub Meta, 1996)

Third Rail:

South Delta Space Age 🎵🎵🎵🎵 (Verve/Antilles, 1995)

Arcana:

The Last Wave 🎵🎵🎵🎵 (DIW, 1996)

Arc of the Testimony 🎵🎵🎵🎵 (Axiom, 1997)

Somma:

Hooked Light Rays 🎵🎵🎵 (Low, 1996)

Equations of Eternity:

Equations of Eternity 🎵🎵🎵 (WordSound, 1996)

Vevé 🎵🎵🎵 (WordSound, 1998)

Ekstasis:

Wake Up and Dream 🎵🎵🎵🎵 (CyberOctave, 1998)

worth searching for: Because Laswell's extensive discography has him frequently recording for labels that seem to pop up out of nowhere and then vanish without a trace, a number of his albums are especially difficult to track down . . . some of them deservedly so. But well worth the effort are Automaton's *Jihad* and *Dub Terror Exhaust,* two intriguing dub experiments with Gabe Katz and Sly Dunbar, and Death Cube K's *Dreamatorium,* an outlandish guitar noise-fest pairing Laswell with enigmatic axe-grinder Buckethead; all three albums were on Laswell's now-defunct Strata label. Also worth a listen is *Second Nature,* a lushly layered ambient excursion with Tetsu Inoue and Atom Heart released on the defunct Submeta label.

influences:

◀◀ John Coltrane, Jimi Hendrix, Can, Brian Eno, Miles Davis, Lee "Scratch" Perry, Parliament-Funkadelic

▶▶ John Zorn, the Orb, Buckethead, DJ Spooky, Golden Palominos, Talvin Singh, Transglobal Underground

see also: *Trilok Gurtu, Zakir Hussain, Kodo, Fela Kuti, Master Musicians of Jajouka, Talip Ozkan, Shabba Ranks, Badal Roy, Ryuichi Sakamoto, Simon Shaheen, L. Shankar, Sly & Robbie, Liu Sola, Foday Musa Suso, Touré Kunda, T.H. "Vikku" Vinayakram, Wu Man*

Bret Love

Latin Playboys

Rock
Formed 1994, in Los Angeles, CA, USA. Based in USA.

David Hidalgo, guitar, vocals; Louie Perez, drums; Mitchell Froom, keyboards; Tchad Blake, bass. (All members are from the USA.)

An East L.A. group that combined vital bar-band rock with the traditional tunes of their Mexican American upbringing, Los Lobos took a sonic side trip with 1992's *Kiko,* an album of inspired experimentation that turned out to be their masterpiece. Rather than doom the band commercially, guitarist/vocalist/songwriter David Hidalgo and drummer/lyricist Louie Perez decided to reserve their more outré tendencies for a side project. As the Latin Playboys, the pair joined with *Kiko*'s aural architects, producer/keyboardist Mitchell Froom and sound engineer/bassist Tchad Blake. The results have been spectacular, if sporadic—the debut album graced many critics' year-end Top 10 lists, but the follow-up was delayed by a Lobos/Playboys label switch. In the stolen moments between band projects and his own production work (Sheryl Crow, Richard Thompson, Suzanne Vega) Froom recorded a "solo" album, which provided avant-garde musical settings for guest performers—including usual suspects Hidalgo, Crow, and Vega—to write lyrics for and sing over.

what to buy: An album that exists in some netherworld where phantom movie music, Latin pop, soul, and avant-rock come together in secret and slip off into the night, *Latin Playboys* ♫♫♫♫ (Slash/Warner Bros., 1994, prod. Latin Playboys) astonishes in a different way every time you hear it. The culture clash of so many different styles, found sounds, and collage techniques is transporting on tracks such as "Viva La Raza," "Lagoon," and "Manifold de Amour," while "Ten Believers" operates more or less like a conventional rock song (albeit a terrific one) and "Chinese Surprize" and "New Zandu" charge forward atop excoriatingly raw guitar riffs. Elsewhere, "Rudy's Party" sounds like an ancient field recording; "If," a menacing blues; and "Same Brown Earth," a honking R&B number from outer space. This is music from dreams, but ones that are half-remembered and unsettling.

what to buy next: Picking up where they'd left off five years before, *Dose* ♫♫♫♫ (Atlantic, 1999, prod. Latin Playboys) contains similarly brilliant inventions, though the element of surprise has worn off. The Playboys attempt to push their sonic experiments even further, making some of these pieces enticingly (or

forbiddingly) raw, depending on your point of view. Still, tracks like "Fiesta Erotica" dazzle with Hidalgo's soaring guitar solos, and "Locoman" is deliciously disturbing.

worth searching for: If you're intrigued by the Playboys' unusual sound, you might as well check out the album that started the bandmembers down this twisted path. Los Lobos' *Kiko* (Slash/Warner Bros., 1992, prod. Mitchell Froom) was their break with the conventional post-Santana-ism they'd been cultivating for many years. But it was also their first brush with genius. Industrial rhythms, found sounds, and dreamy sonic landscapes take this album to a level that few bands ever achieve.

solo outings:
Mitchell Froom:
Dopamine ♫♫♫ (Atlantic, 1998)

influences:
The Band, Jimi Hendrix, Ry Cooder, Tom Waits

see also: *Los Lobos, Los Super Seven*

Daniel Durchholz

Le Mystère des Voix Bulgares /Bulgarian State Radio and Television Female Vocal Choir /Bulgarian State Female Vocal Choir /Bulgarian State Vocal Choir /Ensemble Trakia /Ensemble Pirin

Modern Bulgarian folk music
Bulgarian State Radio and Television Female Vocal Choir formed 1952, in Sofia, Bulgaria. Based in Sofia, Bulgaria.

Various uncredited members; all from Bulgaria.

The saga of the Mystère des Voix Bulgares is partially a tale of record-company hype and partially an example of the unlikely triumph of traditional music. The original Bulgarian State Radio and Television Female Vocal Choir was created in 1952, following the lead of Philip Koutev, who founded the State Ensemble for Folk Music and Dance. At that time, many folk traditions were dying out and in response Koutev began collecting folk tunes and arranging them for female choirs by adding counterpoint, additional vocal lines, and shifts in tempo and timbre. Other composers followed suit, and many female choirs blossomed. Recordings of various choirs and trios made their way to the States as early as 1960, but the tidal wave began when the 4AD label picked up a recording of various folkloric groups under the

Le Mystère des Voix Bulgares

title *Le Mystère des Voix Bulgares* for British distribution in 1987. Nonesuch grabbed the U.S. rights, and the album became a surprise best-seller, leading to *Le Mystère des Voix Bulgares, Vol. 2* a year later. At least one of the groups touring under the name Le Mystère des Voix Bulgares has no connection at all to the Nonesuch album, which is itself a compilation of work by the original Bulgarian State Radio and Television Female Vocal Choir as well as Ensemble Trakia, Ensemble Pirin, and various soloists and quartets. The liner notes on all the albums are skimpy, with individual singers getting little if any credit.

what to buy: *Le Mystère des Voix Bulgares* 𝄢𝄢𝄢𝄢 (Nonesuch, 1987, prod. Marcel Cellier) is a classic recording that shows the incredible range of the unaccompanied human voice. The choir's trills, octave swoops, shouts, and soaring harmonies are completely captivating.

what to buy next: *Le Mystère des Voix Bulgares, Vol. 2* 𝄢𝄢𝄢𝄢 (Nonesuch, 1988, prod. Marcel Cellier) is another fine sampling of Bulgarian vocal music.

what to avoid: *From Bulgaria with Love* 𝄢𝄢 (Mesa, 1992) is credited to "Le Mystère des Voix Bulgares," although the small print says it's the Bulgarian State Vocal Choir. The singing is first rate, but TranceFormation, Steve the B., and other dance-crazy producers are along for the ride to add assorted beats to the recordings. Some of the experiments work better than others, but if you really want ethno/techno trash, you're better off plunking down your money for Deep Forest or Tulku, who don't make any pretense about being "authentic."

influences:
⏮ Bisserov Sisters

see also: *Bŭlgari, Huun-Huur-Tu*

j. poet

Leahy
Celtic folk-rock
Formed 1997, in Lakefield, Ontario, Canada. Based in Lakefield, Ontario, Canada.

Donnell Leahy, fiddle; Erin Leahy, piano, keyboards; Siobheann Leahy, bass; Maria Leahy, acoustic guitar, mandolin; Frank Leahy,

drums; **Agnes Leahy,** stepdancing; **Doug Leahy,** fiddle; **Angus Leahy,** fiddle. (All members are from Canada.)

The story of Leahy is definitely a family affair. Frank and Julie Leahy, the clan's Ontario- and Cape Breton-born father and mother, taught their children fiddle music and step-dancing, respectively. The lessons took root in this talented bunch, who went on to perform part-time as the Leahy Family and, even at this early stage, saw a film documentary about them, titled *The Leahys: Music Most of All,* win a 1985 Oscar for Best Foreign Student Film. After some of the siblings dropped out, the remaining brothers and sisters revamped the act as Leahy. Their eponymous debut CD was released in the States in 1998; they appeared in the half-hour PBS special *Leahy in Concert*; and, in the most decisive case of their rising star being hitched to an even bigger one, country-pop phenom Shania Twain invited them to be the opening act on her first U.S tour. And whenever a wider audience gets a look at them, the band's in-concert magic does the rest; the exuberant stepdancing and infectious fiddle tunes make a fantastic combination that resembles a scaled-down yet equally effective version of the *Riverdance* spectacular.

what's available: *Leahy* 𝄞𝄞𝄞𝄞 (Narada, 1998, prod. Lance Anderson), the band's auspicious debut, is entirely instrumental, and focuses mostly on their original arrangements of traditional dance tunes from Ireland, Cape Breton, Scotland, and French Canada. Donnell's fiddle takes the leads on most selections and he's definitely a dynamic player. Piano adds some funky counterpoints on a few others, and the rhythm section gives everything an energetic, syncopated swing—on several cuts augmented by the sounds of stepdancing for an added "kick." Leahy's stompin' Celtic grooves will get even the most hardened "I can't dance" types out of their chairs, guaranteed.

influences:

◀◀ Frank Leahy, Julie Leahy, Moving Hearts, Jean Carignan, Denis Lanctot

▶▶ Shooglenifty, *Riverdance,* Natalie MacMaster, La Bottine Souriante

Ken Roseman

Eddie LeJeune

Cajun

Born August 20, 1951, in Lacassine, LA, USA. Based in Louisiana, USA.

Although Iry LeJeune died too young to have much direct influence on his son, the music of Eddie LeJeune deeply echoes that of his father. The younger LeJeune has the same virtuoso quality about his accordion playing and the high-lonesome LeJeune tinge in his singing. You can hear it most when he launches into

tunes associated with his father, like "Lacassine Special." The accordion runs spill over the bar lines, almost capsizing the band, and the vocals make you imagine the singer with tears streaming down his face. LeJeune is an ardent traditionalist and records with all acoustic instruments and no drums. Not that the loss of a drum matters much; there is plenty of rhythm in his singing and playing.

what to buy: *It's in the Blood* 𝄞𝄞𝄞𝄞 (Rounder, 1991, prod. Ken Irwin) may be the most traditional Cajun album recorded in the last 20 years. LeJeune's deeply rootsy singing and playing is accompanied by late great Cajun fiddler Lionel Leleux, who started playing with Nathan Abshire in the early 1930s. LeJeune and Leleux are in turn accompanied by the "freight train" guitar playing of Hubert Maitre and the steady triangle of Eddie LeJeune Jr. The whole album is beautifully recorded and beautifully played.

what to buy next: *Cajun Soul* 𝄞𝄞𝄞𝄞 (Rounder, 1988, prod. Ken Irwin) is LeJeune in the stellar company of D.L. Menard on guitar and the great Ken Smith on fiddle. This was Eddie's first recording, and he squeezes every ounce of soul from his old accordions that he can get. As beautiful and sincere an acoustic-music experience as you'll find anywhere.

the rest:

Cajun Spirit 𝄞𝄞𝄞𝄞 (Rounder, 1998)

worth searching for: *Le Trio Cadien* 𝄞𝄞𝄞𝄞 (Rounder, 1992, prod. Ken Irwin) finds the same three musicians who played on *Cajun Soul* brought together as equals. With the vocals split between D.L. and Eddie, the result is two great Cajun singers and instrumentalists accompanied by the most tasteful Cajun fiddler around.

influences:

◀◀ Nathan Abshire, Amédée Ardoin, Iry LeJeune

▶▶ Steve Riley, Tasso, Balfa Toujours, Horace Trahan

see also: *Nathan Abshire, Iry LeJeune, D.L. Menard*

Jared Snyder

Iry LeJeune

Cajun

Born October 28, 1928, in Church Point, LA, USA. Died October 8, 1955, near Eunice, LA, USA.

Young Cajuns had pretty much lost interest in the old-fashioned, accordion-based music by the time World War II rolled around. The airwaves were dominated by the western swing–influenced sounds of Harry Choates and Leo Soileau. But when the G.I.s returned after the war they wanted the comfort of those good old-time tunes, and they found it in a nearly blind farm boy who sang his heart out. Iry LeJeune was too sight-impaired to work, and spent much of his youth hanging out at his uncle Angelas's home. The older LeJeune was a superb accordionist who let his nephew listen and learn from his recordings of the great Amédée Ardoin. Iry was mightily influenced by Ardoin's virtuoso accordion and high, passionate singing. He eventually recorded his interpretations of many of Ardoin's songs, as well as those of his uncle. He in turn had enormous influence on a whole generation of Cajun musicians who learned Ardoin's songs from LeJeune's recordings.

what to buy: *Cajun's Greatest: The Definitive Collection* 𝄞𝄞𝄞𝄞𝄞 (Ace, 1994, prod. Eddie Shuler, John Broven) is the one and only record to get. The people at Ace have tried valiantly to clean up the sound as much as possible; LeJeune was often taped at home on a primitive portable recorder, and the studio mixing techniques of the originals did little to enhance these documents and much to muddle them. But it is all here: the heartbreaking vocals, the breathtaking fast accordion runs overwhelming the music. If they listen to Cajun music in heaven, this is it.

what to avoid: *The Legendary Iry LeJeune* 𝄞𝄞 (Goldband, 1991, prod. Eddie Shuler) has much of the same music as the Ace CD, except that there's an electric bass dubbed onto the original recordings, mixed to sound as if the bassist is accompanying a record player in the studio. Stick with the warts-and-all version; it actually has less warts than this.

influences:

◀ Nathan Abshire, Amédée Ardoin

▶▶ Steve Riley, Marc & Ann Savoy

see also: *Amédée Ardoin, Harry Choates, Eddie LeJeune, Leo Soileau*

Jared Snyder

Ray Lema

Afropop, worldbeat
Born in 1946, in Kinshasa, Congo. Based in Paris, France.

Rebels are a dime a dozen in the rock world, even if the appellation is usually self-applied and extremely self-aggrandizing. Not so with Ray Lema, who has been one of Africa's most innovative and controversial musicians since he broke on the international scene in the late '70s with his band Ya Tupas, a jazz/rock/*soukous* fusion project that garnered equal proportions of praise and hate mail.

Lema was born in Kinshasa in 1946 and began a classical music education in a Catholic seminary, where he seriously considered studying for the priesthood. His first public appearance took place in church, where he played Beethoven's "Moonlight Sonata" on the organ. Music called ever more insistently, and he quit the seminary and began playing soukous (the popular Congolese adaptation of rumba) in the bands of legends like Tabu Ley, Abeti, and Papa Wemba. But Lema also loved rock 'n' roll, and eventually surprised everyone—and infuriated some—by forming a band that combined it with Congolese music. In 1974 the government asked Lema to organize a national ballet company. For the next few years he traveled throughout Congo collecting folk music and dance styles from the country's 250 ethnic groups. He chose Congo's best singers and dancers to form the National Ballet of Zaire (as the country was then called), and in the process became an expert on Zairian music. Lema's next project was Ya Tupas, and while touring to support their debut album, Lema decided to settle in Washington, D.C., to explore the R&B, jazz, funk, and soul music he'd always loved. In 1982 he dropped the band and recorded his first solo album, *Koteja,* released on the Paris-based Celluloid label. This was followed by *Kinshasa—Washington, D.C.—Paris* and another move, this time to the last-named city. Lema continued to explore his cross-cultural vision in the '80s with a series of albums for Celluloid, and later for Island's world-music imprint Mango. He also lent his considerable chops and musical expertise to projects by Manu Dibango, the Mahotella Queens, and Stewart Copeland, former drummer of the Police. During the '90s Lema put his stamp on what could be called concept albums—the most notable being his work with Congolese pygmy music on *Un Touarag S'est Marié avec une Pygmée* and with members of a Bulgarian women's choir on *Ray Lema & Professor Stefanov.*

what to buy: When *Ray Lema & Professor Stefanov* 𝄞𝄞𝄞𝄞 (Buda, 1992/Tinder Gold, 1997, prod. Ray Lema, Philippe Jupin) was released in France in 1992 it became an instant classic. Lema and Stefanov, the leader and composer for a woman's vocal troupe called L'Ensemble Pirin, collaborate on tunes that feature the choir's soaring harmonies backed by Lema's deeply funky music, a mixture of African, Jamaican, and North American rhythms.

what to buy next: If you're expecting the usual Afropop product, *Gaia* 𝄞𝄞𝄞𝄞 (Mango, 1990, prod. Ray Lema, Paul "Groucho" Smykle) isn't the place to start. Lema's idiosyncratic work sounds unlike anything else you've ever heard. There's pop, rock, African and American folk, techno, *zouk,* reggae, and more, all held together by Lema's broad musical vision and some of the most inventive rhythm tracks in his field.

best of the rest:
Kinshasa—Washington, D.C.—Paris 𝄞𝄞𝄞 (Celluloid, 1983)
Medecine 𝄞𝄞𝄞 (Celluloid, 1985)
Nangadeef 𝄞𝄞𝄞 (Mango, 1989)

Euro-African Styles 🎵🎵🎵 (Buda, 1992)

Un Touarag S'eet Marié avec une Pygmée 🎵🎵🎵 (Celluloid, 1993)

influences:

◀◀ Franco, Tabu Ley Rochereau, Dr. Nico

▶▶ Kotoja, Henri Dikonque, Zap Mama

see also: *Le Mystère des Voix Bulgares*

j. poet

Ricardo Lemvo & Makina Loca

African rumba

Formed 1990, in Los Angeles, CA, USA. Based in Los Angeles, CA, USA.

Ricardo Lemvo (Congo), vocals, leader; Niño Jésus Alejandro Pérez (Cuba), tres, flute, maracas, vocals; Louis Wasson (USA), guitar; Charlie Biggs (USA), trumpet; Nengue Hernández (USA), percussion.

Ricardo Lemvo was born and raised in Kinshasa, the capital city of Zaire (now Congo) and the hotbed of *soukous,* a Zairian-style rumba that swept Africa in the '60s to become a mainstay of Africa's musical vocabulary from Kenya to Capetown. As John Storm Roberts explains in his book *Black Music in Two Worlds,* the rhythms African slaves brought with them to Cuba mixed with Spanish and indigenous music to create the rumba, one of the most influential rhythms ever created. Cuban records—mostly 78 rpm discs carried back to the Motherland by sailors and traders—caused a sensation in Africa in the late '50s and heavily influenced the popular music of Mali, Senegal, and what was then also called the Congo. Africans may have heard the echoes of their own music in those Cuban records, and created soukous to reply to this strangely familiar message from their cousins in the New World. But as Lemvo pointed out in a recent interview, "Zairian rumba is not Cuban rumba. In Cuba, rumba is the drum; in Zaire there is an almost waltz-like feeling. And there were no horns in Africa, so the horn lines got translated into electric guitar lines."

In Kinshasa, Lemvo got his musical start in an R&B cover band, singing in phonetic English, but Cuban music was always in the back of his mind. He had a cousin with an extensive collection of Cuban records, and he soaked up the Cuban sounds blasting out of the local radio stations, along with those of soukous giants like Grand Kalle, who incorporated the pure rumba. Lemvo moved with his father to Los Angeles when he was 12, and by the time he was 22 he had met keyboardist/vocalist/arranger Niño Jésus Pérez and was singing in Cuban bands. (He taught himself Spanish, and also speaks English, French, and Lingala.) With Jésus and Cameroonian guitarist Louis Wasson, Lemvo finally began working on his long-time dream, a fusion of soukous and Cuban music. Makina Loca, a conscious misspelling of the Cuban words "maquina loco"—crazy machine—got going

the kora and west african griot

A hybrid type of instrument sometimes called a "harp-lute"—because it combines the neck and body of a lute with the playing technique of a harp—the *kora* is made by stretching animal skin across a large calabash gourd resonator, with 21 to 23 nylon strings divided into two parallel rows and attached at varying lengths to a long, round neck mounted perpendicular to the sound table. The main instrument of the *griot* tradition of West Africa (known in some ethnicities as *jali* culture; *griotte* or *jalimuso* in the feminine), the kora is said to date back to the 13th century, but it came into its own internationally in the 20th century. Griots are artisans responsible for keeping the time-honored traditions of the past alive through music and storytelling, creating narratives that may be passed down orally to future generations. Accompanying themselves on the kora (or the less-popular *balafon* xylophone or *koni* 4- or 5-stringed lute), the griots spin songs praising friends, recalling epic battles, or relating important historical moments. In many ways, the griot tradition can be seen as the most ancient roots of rap: while the beautiful, harp-like sounds of the kora and the buoyant vocal melodies of the griots may seem to have little in common with the rhythm-heavy beats of modern hip-hop on the surface, the lyrical lineage connecting the two is undeniable. Thanks to modern adaptations like tuning pegs and contact pick-ups for electric amplification, artists like Toumani Diabaté, Amadu Bansang Jobarteh, and Foday Musa Suso have successfully introduced the kora to Western audiences (Suso, in particular, has collaborated with a variety of artists ranging from fusionists Bill Laswell and Don Cherry to avant-classicists the Kronos Quartet), ensuring that the griot legacy will continue to evolve and thrive for centuries to come.

see also: The Talking Drum (sidebar), West African Drumming and the Soul of Rock 'n' Roll (sidebar)

Bret Love

about seven years ago, and includes L.A. players with Cuban, African, and Chicano backgrounds. Their monthly Luna Park gigs have created quite a buzz, and their first album, *Tata Masambo*, with prestigious guests like Sam Mangwana and Bopol Mansi-amina, catapulted them into the international spotlight.

what's available: Lemvo's desire to fuse the rumba of Cuba and Congo comes one step closer to fruition on his second album, *Mambo Yoyo* ♪♪♪♪ (Putumayo, 1998, prod. Niño Jésus Pérez). The styles flow freely, with the aggressive Cuban edge a perfect foil for the mellow Congolese-style singing and guitar playing. The music kicks and Lemvo is an impressive singer, but the tunes on *Tata Masamba* ♪♪♪ (Mopiato, 1996, prod. Niño Jésus Alejandro Pérez) sound Cuban or Congolese, not Cuban *and* Congolese as they do on the second album. The record can be ordered from the Mopiato label through P.O. Box 3503, South Pasadena, California 91031.

influences:

◄◄ Franco, Pepe Kalle, Tabu Ley Rochereau, Africando

j. poet

Les Go de Koteba

Mandingo and Pan-African pop, worldbeat
Formed 1991, in Abidjan, Côte d'Ivoire. Based in Abidjan, Côte d'Ivoire.

Maate Keita (Guinea), vocals; Awa Sango (Mali), vocals; Naima Kante (Guinea), vocals.

Les Go de Koteba are marketed as an African Spice Girls, which just gives Ginger, Posh, Blitzen, and Dopey one more band to suffer in comparison to, 'cuz *this* spice is no flavor of the month. In a way, it's the flavor of at least 25 years, which is how long L'Ensemble Koteba d'Abidjan, the internationally revered performance troupe of which Les Go is a branch, has been receiving acclaim. The Ensemble was formed by Souleymane Koly in 1974 with the aim of preserving the culture of the Mandingo ethnic group among immigrants from Mali, Guinea, and Burkina Faso in the major metropolis of Abidjan in Côte d'Ivoire. Since then it's become a world-respected institution by carrying forth tradition and forging bold cultural syntheses in music, dance, and theater. In 1991 three talented young women who had been with the troupe since childhood, learning not only performance skills but also reading, writing, and their own proud history, branched off as a unique ambassadorial cell of Koteba, gaining converts through the international language of irresistible pop. "Koteba" translates roughly as "knowledge" (with a connotation of ongoing heritage and future legacy); "Go" is Côte d'Ivoire slang for "girl" (with a connotation of hip trendiness). And on their debut disc these "girls" show they know a lot, with a savvy sound sturdily rooted in African tradition but open and attentive to what

clicks around the world. It's a delicate but taut style spun from the crystalline notes of the *kora* (African harp-lute), the driving *djembe* drum, hard-pop guitar and keyboards, and the super sax of Cameroonian jazz giant Manu Dibango. Their high-energy shows were already the stuff of budding legend when their first disc was cut, and after, they became increasingly in demand as on-stage guests of roots-music powerhouses like Sweet Honey in the Rock, and as collaborators with buzz-binned choreographers like Ron Brown. It can't be long 'til they make it to your local record store and concert hall—and by then they won't have to tell you what you really, really, *really* want.

what's available: Les Go's first album, alternately known as *Les Go de Koteba* and simply *Les Go* ♪♪♪♪ (Juna/Stern's, 1997), is a blast of fresh air from world-music's next superstars. Dip in anywhere and be delighted, from "Wari"'s Latin tinge, to "Kalabante"'s striking Islamic melisma, to "ABCD"'s intriguing meld of Salif Keita's driving sound with that of relaxed jazz fusion, to the sultry sax-pop and marvelously moody, Baaba Maal-esque vocal of "Nanibali." The girls' voices are assured and versatile and rivet the attention throughout, with the multi-textured "Bara" giving a particularly good showcase for their unique yet compatible solo stylings.

influences:

◄◄ Mahotella Queens, Zap Mama, Souleymane Koly

Adam McGovern

Les Têtes Brulées

Bikutsi rock
Formed 1986, in Yaoundé, Cameroon. Based in Yaoundé, Cameroon.

Jean-Marie Ahanda, vocals; Theodore Epeme (died 1988), lead guitar, vocals; André Afata, drums, vocals; Martin Maah, bass; Roger Bekongo, rhythm guitar; Georges Essono, keyboards. (All members are from Cameroon.)

Because of their rock 'n' roll energy, body paint, shaved heads, and wild on-stage costumes, critics dubbed Cameroon's Les Têtes Brulées ("Hot Heads") the first African punk band. According to the band's founder, Jean-Marie Ahanda, that judgment isn't far from the mark. "The cultural establishment in Cameroon is very conservative," he says. "When we appeared on TV in 1987 kids went out and shaved their heads, which hardly pleased their parents and the authorities. There was a reaction against us that was very violent." Ahanda and Les Têtes play in a highly complex, multi-rhythmic, aggressive guitar-band style that's based on *bikutsi*, the traditional music of the Beti tribe from Cameroon's western rainforests. "Bikutsi is roots music—ignored in Cameroon for being peasant music. It's not chic, so it was the perfect style to use against the overly slick *makossa* [Cameroon's main pop form] musicians.

Les Têtes Brulées

Cameroon doesn't have a strong musical tradition like Mali or Senegal. Rock, salsa, and pop have been part of makossa for 20 years. The problem is not one of the past, it's in the present; the same artists keep making the same records over and over again. That's what we were rebelling against."

Their new approach made Les Têtes a sensation. A few days after their first, electrifying TV appearance, Laurent Viguíe, Salif Keita's manager, sent Ahanda a ticket to Paris in preparation for a European tour and an album. On the first date of their European tour, Les Têtes met film director Claire Denis, who decided to take a crew along and document the Têtes tour. "We got some idea of what was in store when she asked us to get back on a plane and get off again, because she hadn't got the shot of us coming down right." By late '88, Les Têtes had a feature film, *Man No Run,* and an LP in the can, but then disaster struck. Théodore "Zanzibar" Epeme, the band's amazing lead guitarist, committed suicide. "Zanzibar was very ill when we were recording. He had many complex personal problems, and he had to have injections every day," Ahanda says. "He was very depressed when he came home, and his death hit us all very hard. Luckily, the record company was understanding and held back the release of the record so it wouldn't seem like we were cashing in on his death, which was headline news all over France." After a year of soul searching, Les Têtes decided to go on. The record *Hot Heads* was released to unanimous raves, and auditions began for a new guitarist. "We couldn't replace Zanzibar, so we chose Georges Essono [a well-known local bandleader and master keyboard player]. He was not our first choice, but we tried out several guitarists and none of them worked out. Bringing in keyboards was a risk, but he brought new color and melody into the band." On the *Hot Heads* disc, Epeme's guitar crackles like lightening, and the rolling thunder of the bass and drums have a definite rock 'n' roll edge. While Ahanda expected his music to go over well among non-Africans, the thumbs-up he received from his fellow Africans came as a surprise. Unhappily, as good as Essono was on keyboards, he couldn't match the manic creative energy of Epeme's guitar, and the group never lived up to its potential. They still tour, but the torch has been passed to younger, hungrier bikutsi groups.

what's available: *Hot Heads* ♫♫♫♫♫ (Shanachie, 1990, prod. Andy Lyden, Jean-Marie Ahanda) is perhaps the greatest African rock 'n' roll album ever made, crammed with fierce guitar playing and a relentless rhythmic drive. There are still moments of inspiration on *Bikutsi Rock* ♫♫ (Shanachie, 1991), but without Epeme's guitar it comes off sounding rather generic.

influences:
◄◄ Anne-Marie Nzie, Los Camaroes

►► Mbarga Soukous, Jimmy Mvondo Mvelé

j. poet

Dan Levenson & Kim Murley /Blue Rose

Old-time string-band/bluegrass/Chinese fusion
Formed 1995, in Evart, MI, USA. Disbanded 1997.

Dan Levenson, banjo; Kim Murley, yang qin. (Both members are from USA.)

The son of an old-time square-dance caller from the Midwest, Dan Levenson heard U.S. folk music from an early age. He went on to learn guitar, banjo, and fiddle, as well as becoming a dancer with a clogging group, and a national magazine poll voted him one of the country's best banjo players in the traditional "clawhammer" style. Meanwhile, Kim Murley had taken up hammered dulcimer at the age of 13, and after graduating from college in Colorado moved to Taiwan and later Shanghai, where she spent several years studying Chinese versions of the instrument. Levenson and Murley met at a folk festival in the Midwest and later teamed up after Murley challenged Levenson to play one of her Chinese compositions. They liked the result, and banded together for about a year of touring and presenting workshops.

what's available: During their year together Levenson and Murley made one recording, *New Frontier* ♫♫♫♫ (Blue Rose, 1996, prod. Dan Levenson, Kim Murley), which may be the only *yang qin* (Chinese dulcimer) and clawhammer banjo album to date. The unlikely combination of influences and instruments almost demands a fresh approach to the tunes they cover, and the original music is strong as well. Like Navajo flutist R. Carlos Nakai's project with a Japanese string ensemble, *Island of Bows,* Levenson and Murley's collaboration shows that unexpected meetings of traditions can produce more than the sum of their parts. (Help in locating this self-released album may be found at Levenson's website, http://www.folknet.org/dan.)

influences:
◄◄ Wade Ward, Tommy Jarrell, the Chicken Chokers, Kevin Enoch, Richie Sterns, the Silk and Bamboo Players of Shanghai

Kerry Dexter

Barrington Levy

Dancehall reggae, ragga
Born in 1964, in Kingston, Jamaica. Based in Clarendon, Jamaica.

In the early '80s, as the dancehall music craze swept Jamaica, deejays exceeded singers in popularity for the first time. Live performance over rhythm-track acetates or "dub plates," as amplified through powerful sound systems, became the preference of the "massive"—the downtown, working-class crowds that packed the venues ("dancehalls") that showcased the new sound. One of the few exceptions to the preeminence of the deejay was Barrington Levy, a gripping, edgy-voiced singer who began his career with a few forgettable singles as a member of the Mighty Multitudes. However, like the Mighty Diamonds' "rockers" sound debut with the Revolutionaries five years earlier, Levy's 1979 debut LP *Bounty Hunter* was the first shot in a genre coup d'etat. Providing the template for the coming dancehall era in Jamaica, the record introduced the world to the tenacious Levy and the phenomenally heavy Roots Radics band. The 15-year-old Levy scored big with "Shaolin Temple," "Shine Eye Gal," and "Looking My Love" (a.k.a. "It's Not Easy"), and quickly became the favorite of Jamaican youth.

After a few rushed, substandard records created only to cash in on Levy's popularity, he came back in 1985 with the rootsy "Prison Oval Rock" (driven by the Wailing Souls' "Firehouse Rock" rhythm) and "Hammer," a cut that smartly played off of Johnny Osbourne's "Lend Me the 16." Bolstered by the killer rhythm section of Sly Dunbar and Robbie Shakespeare, singles like "Suffer the Little Children" (a.k.a. "Praise His Name") and "Money Move" (over the international-hit "One Step Beyond" riddim) further established Levy's name. With the help of producer Jah Screw, Levy reached a global audience when *Here I Come* was licensed by London Records and both the title cut and the ganja-praising chant "Under Mi Sensi" blew up charts around the world. In the early '90s Levy revisited the songcraft of one of his strongest influences, the great Bob Andy. Exhilarating covers of Andy's Studio One hits "Too Experienced" and "My Time" reignited interest in Levy. But he really revived his career a few years later by recutting some of his biggest hits in "combo" style with the premier ragga (digital) deejays. These collaborations were collected on *Duets* along with a new song, the huge hit "Living Dangerously" with Bounty Hunter. A wild British remix of Levy's version of "Under Mi Sensi" with Beenie Man—"Under Mi Sensi X Project Jungle Spliff"—savaged the U.K. charts and was one of the first songs to ignite the post-techno jungle craze in London. Levy then released the unique and funky single "Work" with Jigsy King, which became a celebratory anthem for the East Indian population and an instant floor-filler at *bhangra* (Indian-folk-based electronic pop) dances. Levy continues to write and record in Jamaica and seems destined to "mash down" the dancehall for years to come.

what to buy: *RAS Portraits* ✯✯✯✯ (RAS, 1997, prod. various) provides an excellent overview of Levy's sterling career and includes the wicked and wild "Living Dangerously," the rare, early dancehall classic "Robber Man," and the spliff-launching anthem "Under Mi Sensi." *Bounty Hunter Wanted* ✯✯✯✯ (Jah Life, 1983, prod. Myron "Jah Life" Wright) compiles many of the finest singles from Levy's powerhouse debut *Bounty*

Hunter along with some riveting lesser-known material from the same era. *Englishman/Robin Hood* ✯✯✯ (Greensleeves, 1980, prod. Henry "Junjo" Lawes) combines Levy's two excellent 1980 LPs, both of which are fortified with the tremendous rhythms and creative arrangements of the Roots Radics. The songs from *Englishman* later provided the musical structure for the *Scientist v. Prince Jammy* LP, a colossal example of '80s dub.

what to buy next: *Duets* ✯✯✯ (RAS, 1995, prod. Jah Screw) features the aforementioned "Living Dangerously" along with pumped-up versions of previous hits, performed by Levy in tandem with the live deejay jive of Beenie Man ("Under Mi Sensi"), Mega Banton ("Here I Come"), and many others of the ragga royalty. *Reggae Vibes* ✯✯✯ (Rocky One, 1983, prod. Joe Gibbs) features all of Levy's finest work for producer Gibbs, including "Wife and Sweetheart a Friend" and "My Woman," both mixed with bravado by engineering maestro Errol Thompson.

the rest:
21 Girls Salute ✯✯ (Jah Life, 1983)
Poor Man Style ✯✯✯ (Trojan U.K., 1983)
Making Tracks (a.k.a. Lifestyle) ✯✯✯ (Rhino U.K., 1983)
Teach Me Culture ✯✯✯ (Live & Learn, 1983)
Barrington Levy Meets Frankie Paul ✯✯✯ (Ariwa U.K., 1984)
Barrington Levy ✯✯✯ (Clocktower, 1984)
Here I Come ✯✯✯ (RAS, 1985)
Hunter Man ✯✯ (Burning Sounds U.K., 1988)
Love the Life You Live ✯✯✯ (VP, 1988)
Open Book ✯✯ (Tuff Gong, 1988)
Prison Oval Rock ✯✯✯ (RAS, 1989)
Broader than Broadway: Best Of ✯✯✯ (Profile, 1990)
Divine ✯✯ (RAS, 1991)
The Collection ✯✯✯✯ (Greensleeves U.K., 1991)
Turning Point ✯✯ (Greensleeves U.K., 1992)
Twenty Vintage Hits ✯✯✯ (Sonic Sounds, 1992)
Barrington ✯✯ (MCA, 1993)
Time Capsule ✯✯✯ (RAS, 1996)
Too Experienced: Best Of ✯✯✯✯ (V.P. 1997)
Living Dangerously ✯✯✯ (Breakaway, 1998)

worth searching for: *Shine Eye Girl* ✯✯✯ (Burning Sounds U.K., 1979, prod. Henry "Junjo" Lawes) contains the much-sought-after early Levy singles "Ah Yah Weh Deh" and "Collie Weed."

influences:
◀◀ Bob Andy, Wailing Souls, Jacob Miller, Morwells

▶▶ Yami Bolo, Apache Indian, Louchie Lou and Michie One, Mikey General

see also: *Beenie Man, Joe Gibbs, Mighty Diamonds, the Roots Radics, Sly & Robbie, Wailing Souls*

Todd Shanker

Yungchen Lhamo

Tibetan devotional song

Born in Lhasa, Tibet. Based in Australia.

Tibetan soprano and songwriter Yungchen Lhamo is far more than a public relations tool of the chic Free Tibet crowd. She is an outstanding performer and artist. The soaring tones of her voice are delightfully exotic to the ear. Her name means "Goddess of melody and song," yet she is modest on stage, in her tidy traditional pink and black brocade: "When I sing I am visualizing that I am making an offering of song to all the highest spiritual beings, and, pleased by it, they shower down blessings on everyone who actively listens to the songs. I hope that the blessings can inspire people to think of their own spirituality—something that many people tend to forget about and ignore. That is why I sing."

Lhamo suffered the brutality that followed the Chinese Cultural Revolution, as her wealthy family was punished and forced to endure poverty. Working in a factory until the age of 19, Lhamo fled Tibet in 1989, the same year the Dalai Lama received the Nobel Peace Prize. With a few friends she trekked perilously through the Himalayas to India, driven by her resolve to meet him. "To Tibetans, His Holiness is a living Buddha. There is no greater experience in life than to meet him and receive his blessings. I thought even if I was to die trying to see him, my life would have meaning." Having fulfilled her dream, Lhamo migrated to Australia, where she established the Yungchen Lhamo Foundation to build women's health centers and venues for adult education, targeting women suffering the same hardships she herself faced while growing up. As much a success in the world-music field as in life, Lhamo is a sought-after recording guest of top mainstream artists like Natalie Merchant, and a marquee performer at high-profile events like New York's Tibetan Freedom Concerts.

what's available: *Tibet Tibet* 🎵🎵🎵🎵 (RealWorld, 1996, prod. Richard Evans, Sam Doherty) is a delight. Lhamo describes the desired effect of her music when she sings, "I weave each note into a chain of flowers for you/I'll offer this in the hope that it will soothe and ease both body and mind." And so it does. The recording features mandolin, *dranyem* (a Tibetan stringed instrument), and the distinctive chants of the monks of both Drepung Ngakpa Monastery and the Gyuto Tantric College. On *Coming Home* 🎵🎵🎵 (RealWorld, 1998, prod. Hector Zazou) Lhamo ditches the monks in favor of a new-age studio treatment. Unfortunately, the poignancy of her *a cappella* performances is lost amidst the string section, looped samples, and multi-tracked vocal effects. The exotic element in new-age music is often little more than spice on a bland dish. In this case Lhamo's voice and her singing in Tibetan spice up producer Hector Zazou's familiar, meditative string arrangements.

But notwithstanding its production, the music is above par, and playfully experimental—Daniel Yvinec hints at the bassline to the Bond theme on "Per Rig Chog Sum"—while Lhamo's voice is becoming increasingly confident.

worth searching for: Look for her hard-to-find first album *Tibetan Prayer* (1994), winner of Australia's equivalent of the Grammy. For a live version of *Tibet Tibet*'s "Lama Dorje Chang" check out *Lilith Fair* (Arista, 1998).

influences:

◀ The Tibetan devotional tradition

▶ Dadawa

see also: *Gyuto Monks*

David Poole

Lhasa

Mexican, Spanish, Gypsy

Born Lhasa de Sela, 1972, in Big Indian, NY, USA. Based in Paris, France, and Montreal, Canada.

Born in the Catskills to a U.S. actress-photographer mother and a Mexican professor father, Lhasa lived a nomadic, close-knit family life as a youngster, but one filled with art, letters, and music. Because her father was a traveling teacher of Spanish and literature of the conquest, the family roamed between the United States and Mexico in a converted school bus. Growing up without TV, Lhasa and her sisters read a lot, listened to music, and sang and entertained each other in nightly performances. Lhasa lived in Mexico for eight years as a young girl, and eventually settled in Montreal (which she still considers home) in 1992 after a visit there the previous year, during which she met multi-instrumentalist Yves Desrosiers. They began working together, ultimately performing throughout Canada with bassist Mario Légaré. By 1996 Lhasa and Yves had started to work on the music that would become her debut album, *La Llorona*. The group then toured steadily for two years, performing their original music at Lilith Fair '97 and '98, where they gained wider appeal before their album came out in the States. At this writing, Lhasa is on extended stay outside of Paris, France, where she is working with her sisters, European circus entertainers, on developing a new act. Lhasa's powerfully intimate, passionate singing style draws on the influence of Billie Holiday, Chavela Vargas, Tom Waits, Bratsch, and Jacques Brel. Though she sings in Spanish on her debut, she is equally fluent in French and English. Critics worldwide have hailed that debut, already a top-seller in Canada and Europe before its U.S. release, as the work of world-music's next destined diva.

what's available: Belying her age, Lhasa's flowing Spanish lyrics—part whispered, part sung—sound ancient and dark on

Annbjørg Lien

her stunning debut recording, *La Llorona* 🎻🎻🎻🎻 (Atlantic, 1998, prod. Yves Desrosiers), titled after the mythological Mexican figure who seduces men with sad melodies and turns them into stone with a kiss. Though she sometimes sounds like the grandmotherly Cape Verdean *morna* singer Cesaria Evora, Lhasa's voice and perspective are uniquely original for her generation. Her alto has a dusky quality that oozes raw emotion in 11 songs about love and loss, enhanced with sparse, Gypsy-flavored accompaniment from Desrosiers (guitars, lap steel bass, accordion, banjo, percussion), Légaré (bass), Francois Lalonde (drums and percussion), and various guest artists playing clarinet, accordion, violin, and sousaphone. From the first, violin-laden notes of their lilting original "La Celestina," the songs by Lhasa and her musical companions are totally captivating. Lhasa's stated goal was to make the most beautiful music possible, and it's been achieved; there's not a dull track on the album.

influences:

◄◄ Billie Holiday, Chavela Vargas, Tom Waits, Bratsch, Jacques Brel

Nancy Ann Lee

Annbjørg Lien /Bukken Bruse

Modern Norwegian folk music

Lien born 1971, in Norway. Bukken Bruse formed 1993, in Oslo, Norway. Lien and Bukken Bruse based in Oslo, Norway.

Bukken Bruse: Annbjørg Lien, hardanger fiddle, nyckelharpa, vocals; Arve Moen Bergset, fiddle, hardanger fiddle, vocals; Steinar Ofsdal, flutes, jew's-harp, vocals; Bjørn Ole Rasch, keyboards. (All members are from Norway.)

Annbjørg Lien was introduced to the world-music community by her work on *Sweet Sunny North,* the compilation/adventure put together by Henry Kaiser and David Lindley to explore the folk music of Norway. She is a talented multi-instrumentalist—playing Swedish bagpipes, mandolin, flute, organ, and Swedish *bouzouki* in addition to the *hardanger* fiddle—and composes tunes that draw on a variety of international styles ranging from the Middle East to Ireland. Lien began playing a conventional violin, switching to the hardanger fiddle as soon as she was big enough to hold it. The instrument is larger than the regular violin, and has a set of sympathetic strings under the fretboard

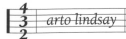

arto lindsay

that give it its distinctive sound. Lien's father played hardanger fiddle and teaches folk music, so she was surrounded by a traditional repertoire from an early age. She began playing professionally at 13, and has won numerous prizes at folk festivals. She plays regularly with her own band, as a solo artist, and as a member of Bukken Bruse, a Norwegian folk supergroup.

what to buy: The hardanger fiddle's sympathetic strings give its high end a bright, treble-filled sound that's quite unique. On *Prisme* 𝄞𝄞𝄞𝄞 (Shanachie, 1997, prod. Annbjørg Lien, Bjørn Ole Rasch), Lien's band includes Swedish bagpipes, percussion and Bukken Bruse keyboard player Bjørn Ole Rasch. The material ranges from traditional *hallings* (dance tunes that sound quite Celtic), to her own brand of Arabic music and achingly beautiful solo pieces.

what to buy next: *Felefeber: Norwegian Fiddle Magic* 𝄞𝄞𝄞 (Shanachie, 1995), another solid collection, won wide praise from the Norwegian folk community for its innovative treatment of traditional material as well as Lien's original compositions. Norse folk music can sound Celtic, but there's an even deeper sense of melancholy, perhaps due to the fact that the sun vanishes for a long stretch every winter. On the Bukken Bruse album *Steinstolen* 𝄞𝄞𝄞𝄞 (Grappa, 1998, prod. Bukken Bruse), the blue feeling is almost overwhelming. Even the up-tempo tunes produce an unsettling sense of sadness. Lien's fiddle moans, Rasch fills the background with dark, unsettling chords, and Bergset's forlorn vocals can break your heart.

influences:

◀◀ Hans W. Brimi, Andris Dahle

▶▶ Chateau Neuf Spellmannslag

j. poet

Arto Lindsay

Tropicalismo, no wave

Born May 28, 1953, in Richmond, VA, USA. Based in New York, NY, USA.

Though born in Virginia, guitarist and producer Arto Lindsay spent his childhood in Brazil which gave him a lifelong passion for the samba and *Tropicalismo* styles of that country. The contagious rhythm of samba percolates through all of Lindsay's guitar work, from his noisy beginnings in New York's no-wave scene, to his heady periods of experimental jazz, to his more blatantly Brazilian-influenced recent oeuvre. Over a trilogy of albums with the Ambitious Lovers, Lindsay mixed the dense, discordant improvisation standard among Lower East Side noise bands with his love of samba. He also contributed to the faux jazz of the Lounge Lizards and the eclectic pop of the Golden Palominos. Lindsay's latest recordings are a trilogy of lyrical albums embracing Brazilian music more wholeheartedly than at any time in his

career, with an international band from that land and others, and much singing in Portuguese. It's the fruition of a lifetime love and a thriving dual career which has seen Lindsay produce records by giants of Brazilian music like Caetano Veloso and Tom Zé, while remaining a fixture of the Downtown New York art-music scene, equal in influence and output to David Byrne and John Zorn, if not yet in name-recognition.

what to buy: Lindsay's most recent trilogy is also his strongest, with songs in Portuguese where Lindsay's voice recalls a young Antonio Carlos Jobim, snippets of drum 'n' bass, and lush guitar. The best of the best is the poetic musings of *Mundo Civilizado* 𝄞𝄞𝄞𝄞 (Bar/None, 1997, prod. Arto Lindsay, Andres Levin, Camus Celi), which was reimagined by DJ Spooky, DJ Mutamassik, and other Downtown mixologists on *Hyper Civilizado (Remixes)* 𝄞𝄞𝄞𝄞 (Gramavision, 1997, prod. Andres Levin, Camus Celi) and is bookended beautifully by *O Corpo Sutil/Subtle Body* 𝄞𝄞𝄞𝄞 (Bar/None, 1996, prod. Arto Lindsay, Patrick Dillett, Vinicius Cantuaria) and *Noon Chill* 𝄞𝄞𝄞𝄞 (Bar/None, 1998, prod. Arto Lindsay, Andres Levin, Melvin Gibbs).

what to buy next: Lindsay found a balance between the skronk of his first band, DNA, and the Brazilian pop of his youth with the Ambitious Lovers' thematic trilogy of *Envy* 𝄞𝄞𝄞 (Editions EG, 1984), *Greed* 𝄞𝄞𝄞𝄞 (Virgin, 1988), and *Lust* 𝄞𝄞𝄞 (Elektra, 1991). Most effective is *Greed*. . . but, er, who are we to judge?

worth searching for: Another long-time Lindsay collaborator is jazz and improvisation guru John Zorn, whose *Big Gundown* 𝄞𝄞𝄞𝄞 (Nonesuch, 1984, prod. Yale Evelev) is an excellent riff on Ennio Morricone's Spaghetti Western soundtracks—listen for Lindsay's Spanish guitar. In addition, Lindsay's *Aggregates 1–26* 𝄞𝄞𝄞 (Knitting Factory, 1995, prod. Arto Lindsay) reveals his strong skills as a jazz guitarist.

influences:

◀◀ Antonio Carlos Jobim, Caetano Veloso, Jorge Ben, Gilberto Gil, Tom Zé, João Gilberto, Squarepusher, the Stooges, MC5, Pere Ubu

▶▶ Gastr Del Sol, DJ Spooky, Marisa Monte

see also: *Antonio Carlos Jobim, Masada, Marisa Monte, Caetano Veloso, Tom Zé*

David Poole

Little Joe

Tejano

Born, October 17, 1940, in Temple, Texas, USA. Based in Temple, Texas, USA.

Jose Maria de Leon Hernandez, the man known to millions of *Tejano* fans by his stage name, Little Joe, was born in 1940 in Temple, a West Texas town rich in Hispanic culture. Since 1956,

Arto Lindsay

when Joe and his brothers Jesse and Johnny joined their cousin David Coronado to form their first group, David Coronado & the Latinairres, Hernandez has been at the forefront of popular Chicano music in Texas. Joe, the seventh of 13 children, grew up in a strong family unit, but in the '50s Texas held few opportunities for Mexican Americans. "I'd see my mom out pulling a cotton sack along, pregnant, with my brothers and sisters," Hernandez recalled in a recent interview. Joe's father worked odd jobs, including smuggling jars of liquor into dry counties like Lubbock; he also had a small marijuana dealership that got him a four-year stretch in prison. At the time his father was busted, Joe was 15 and he became the man of the house. It was while his father was away that Joe asked his mother for the money to buy a guitar. She gave him 15 dollars for his first instrument. The next year he was in the Latinairres. The band cut its first album in 1964, and as Joe's importance as a singer and writer grew, the name became Little Joe & the Latinairres, later Little Joe y La Familia. The band called their sound "La Onda Chicana," the Chicano Wave, a genre-breaking blend of traditional *norteño* ballads and polkas, big-band swing a la Bob Wills, rock 'n' roll, blues, and hard C&W honky-tonk, seasoned

with lyrics that give listeners realistic insights into daily Chicano life. The mix was a hit, and Hernandez has never looked back except to celebrate anniversaries of his decades in the music business. He's cut more than 40 LPs (including *Timeless,* a record that stayed on *Billboard*'s Latin chart for more than a year); had several Grammy nominations; and crusades tirelessly for causes including AIDS education, ecology, Vietnam vets and the National Hispanic Scholarship Fund.

Most recently Little Joe has been concentrating on expanding his share of the Anglo market. He's recorded *Tu Amigo,* an English-language album that featured several duets with Texas pal Willie Nelson; gotten onto the country charts with "You Belong to My Heart" (an English version of the Mexican ballad "Solamente Una Vez"); and been scoring large gigs outside the Hispanic market, including Farm Aid II and a series of co-headlining shows with Nelson. In 1991 he became the first Tejano artist to win a Grammy, when *16 de Septiembre* won the award for Best Latin Album. In 1992 he started his own label, Tejano Records. "Minorities are in a difficult position in this country," Hernandez has said. "When I play in Mexico, they call me an

American artist, but because I sing in Spanish people [in the States] consider me Mexican. There are lots of Mexican influences in cowboy and country music; if people listen to our stuff they'll recognize it once they get past the language problem."

what to buy: If the English-language tunes on *Timeless* 𝄞𝄞𝄞𝄞 (Sony Discos, 1986, prod. Robert Gallarza Jr.), like "Redneck Meskin' Boy" and the cryin'-in-yer-beer honky tonk classic "To Kill a Memory," hook listeners, the Mexican stuff will reel them in. "Siempre Mi Heroe," a tune Joe wrote in honor of his father, is guaranteed to tear your heart out, even if you speak no Spanish.

what to buy next: The collection of early hits *15 Exitos de Oro, Vol. II* 𝄞𝄞𝄞𝄞 (SRP, 1984) will knock you out with its '50s low-fi feel and its gritty garage-band energy.

best of the rest:
25th Silver Anniversary 𝄞𝄞𝄞 (Freddy, 1984)
25th Silver Anniversary—Live in Concert 𝄞𝄞𝄞 (Sony, 1985)
Aunque Pasen Los Años 𝄞𝄞𝄞 (Sony, 1988)
Tu Amigo 𝄞𝄞𝄞𝄞 (Sony, 1990)
16 de Septiembre 𝄞𝄞𝄞𝄞 (Sony, 1991)
Que Paso 𝄞𝄞𝄞 (Tejano, 1992)

worth searching for: Joe recorded at least 40 cassettes and LPs—excluding greatest hits repackages—for Tejano labels like Freddy, Scorpio and others. Your local Latino record store should have enough midline titles to keep you rocking till the millennium.

influences:
▶▶ Los Lobos, the Blazers

j. poet

Little Steven

International pop, classic rock
Born Steven Van Zandt, November 22, 1950, in Boston, MA, USA. Based in USA.

Known mostly as the ex-Springsteen guitarist with the ridiculous wardrobe, "Little Steven" Van Zandt also authored some of the '80s' sharpest and catchiest political pop (at a time when any pop without the politics of *Rambo* was in for rough going), and made a concerted stab at the international hybrid-rock movement well before there was much of one to join. In the early '80s Van Zandt broke away from guaranteed legend status with the E Street Band to be a way-too-young classic rocker of moderate interest and success. But soon he was stretching himself with socially conscious tunes that didn't draw much attention on his sophomore solo album *Voice of America,* but got everyone's notice when he organized the anti-Apartheid all-star benefit anthem "Sun City," the least

feel-good of an often smarmy mid-'80s genre. Thematically if not sonically, it would lead to his crowning achievement to date, the multicultural *Freedom—No Compromise* album, on which he consciously set out (as he explained in interviews at the time) to address the non-Anglo markets then usually written off by the U.S. music-industry monolith. His world-ly leanings were enough to attract African reggae star Majek Fashek to enlist him as producer on the latter's 1991 *Spirit of Love* album, and though Van Zandt's own output has been sporadic since, *Freedom* remains one of the most listenable and least ulterior of the whiteguy worldbeat albums that were beginning to proliferate at the time.

worth searching for: Recently revived as an import, *Freedom—No Compromise* 𝄞𝄞𝄞𝄞 (EMI/Manhattan, 1987/Conn, 1998, prod. Little Steven) is a rollickin' good relic of parallel-universe revolution-pop from a repressive era, one of many blows against the empire that didn't connect back when only Ronald Reagan and (luckily) U2 could speak their minds freely. That doesn't mean it wasn't well aimed, and this relatively clever and definitely danceable collection shoulda been a conscious-rock contenda. Its draws for world-music fans are the songs integrating styles of the African and Latin diasporas and Stevie Wonder-esque stretches of lyrics in South African and Native American languages. "Pretoria" is an affecting apartheid testimony with a pick-up South African choir; "Bitter Fruit" a Latinized lament of U.S. military intervention duetted with Ruben Blades, who also released a Spanish-language version; "Native American" a skankin' ethnic-pride anthem (this was rather early for a white guy to recognize reggae's popularity on the rez). Round it out with some more lyrical bulletins from the Central American and Native-rights fronts, and some then-vanguard integration of hip-hop technique that doesn't unduly muscle into its source's territory, and your search is rewarded well.

influences:
◀◀ Southside Johnny, Bruce Springsteen, Bob Marley, Ruben Blades

see also: *Ruben Blades, Majek Fashek*

Adam McGovern

A.L. Lloyd

English, Australian, Scottish, and international folklore
Born February 29, 1908, in London, England. Died 1982.

A.L. Lloyd was born into a working-class London family. By the time he was 15, most of that family had died of tuberculosis. Unable to find work in London, he arranged passage to Australia to work on sheep stations. It was during his nine years there that Lloyd first became interested in traditional songs. He began to sing, and he kept the words of the songs he knew in composition books; unfortunately, he lost the books, which would have been an invaluable document of Australian song in the 1920s. During these years, Lloyd also began a program of self-education that would last the rest of his life; he discovered a system whereby bush workers could borrow library books by mail, and devoured as many as he could. When he returned to England in the early 1930s, he was a budding intellectual and a confirmed Marxist. He had several jobs, but also spent part of the decade unemployed. Rather than remain idle, he visited the British Museum reading room where he began to study folk music seriously. Finally, his financial situation became so bad that he signed onto the factory ship *Southern Empress,* and spent a season as a whaler. As always, he took the opportunity to learn whatever songs he could, and he later traced some of his seafaring songs to his season at sea. Upon returning to land Lloyd had the idea of writing a radio documentary about sailors' lives. The piece, which made Lloyd's Marxist beliefs obvious, was well received. He followed it with several more radio programs for the BBC, including their first folk-song field recordings, but was ultimately let go because of his communist beliefs; ironically, it was an anti-Hitler documentary, broadcast in 1938, that probably did him in. After leaving the BBC he worked as a journalist, but by 1950 the cold war had made self-avowed communists into pariahs in the journalism trade. Lloyd decided to become a freelance folklorist.

Lloyd's activities in the 1950s were diverse, but always came back to folk songs. He became one of the editors of the *Folk Music Journal,* joined the English Folk Dance and Song Society, and founded a band called the Ramblers with Ewan MacColl and Alan Lomax. He compiled a book of coal-mining songs, founded folk clubs, collaborated with singer/activist MacColl on recording and performing projects, and generally established himself as Britain's leading expert on folk songs. He appeared in John Huston's 1956 film *Moby Dick,* playing the part of the ship's singer or shantyman. Most importantly, he was appointed artistic director of Topic Records, a company dedicated both to folklore and to Marxist causes. Although he had already recorded for many labels in Britain and Australia, most of Lloyd's recording projects from that time on would be for Topic. During the 1960s and 1970s, politics were less of a problem for him, and his status as an authority on folk music made him once again desirable to the BBC. He continued making radio documentaries on folk music, and later made the transition to television. At the same time he was in demand as a scholar. He toured many of the world's universities as a visiting lecturer, and wrote folk music articles for the *Encyclopedia Britannica.* He published his most important book, *Folk Song in England,* in 1967. During the folk boom, when many younger singers and groups began performing professionally, Lloyd became an elder statesman and teacher, providing advice, encouragement, and songs to all the important artists of the younger generation. More than anything else, that influence has been his legacy.

what to buy: Although he never considered himself a performer, Lloyd did leave behind many recordings. A few compilations have been released on CD. *Classic A.L. Lloyd* ✍✍✍✍ (Fellside, 1994, prod. Paul Adams) was collected from 11 records in the Topic catalog, as well as several unreleased tapes. It includes 24 songs representing a cross-section of Lloyd's recorded work. From his several albums of Australian songs, the compilation includes "The Cockies of Bungaree" and "Flash Jack from Gundagai," the latter of which features Fairport Convention/Fotheringay/Redgum singer Trevor Lucas on concertina. From Lloyd's forays into maritime music, *Classic A.L. Lloyd* features several fine sea chanteys and "fo'c's'le" songs (referring to the "forecastle" structure of a merchant ship, in which the crew is housed). The rest of the tracks on *Classic A.L. Lloyd* were selected from some of his general albums of English folk songs. It is here that his influence on the folk revival is most apparent. If you want to hear versions of "The Weaver and the Factory Maid," "John Barleycorn," "Skewball," "Jack Orion," "Byker Hill," "The Widow of Westmoreland's Daughter," "Two Magicians," and "Reynardine" that are curiously reminiscent of those recorded by such groups as Steeleye Span and Fairport Convention, this is the place. It's particularly interesting to hear Dave Swarbrick's fiddle accompanying Lloyd on "Jack Orion," a song that Swarbrick would later sing and play with Fairport Convention. For the most part, though, it's simply enjoyable to hear Lloyd's voice, once described as "unmistakably creaky," interpreting a slew of magnificent songs. Although Lloyd was not gifted with a strong, clear voice, he had an unaffected, often tender delivery that makes each song delightful, each ballad an instance of masterful storytelling. Lloyd is accompanied on some tracks by Swarbrick on fiddle, Alf Edwards on concertina, Steve Benbow on guitar, and several other musicians and vocalists. The recording quality is inconsistent, due to the different sources used, but the singer and the songs are uniformly excellent.

what to buy next: *The Bird in the Bush* ✍✍✍✍ (Topic, 1996, prod. Tony Engle) is a reissue of a 1966 compilation LP that focused on the theme of "erotic songs." The performers on the original release included Lloyd, Anne Briggs, and Frankie Armstrong; the CD version contains several cuts by Armstrong that were not on the original LP, as well as material from Louis Killen and Norman Kennedy. First and foremost, this is an excellent recording of brilliant singers and great songs. Armstrong and Briggs were two of the revival's most sublime voices and their contributions are outstanding. In particular, Armstrong's rendition of the title track is a masterful performance of a rarely heard song with a haunting and unusual melody, and Briggs's version of the comic "Stonecutter Boy" is a gentle tale of seduction sung to a richly ornamented tune. Killen sings three songs, including a beautiful reading of "The Cock" and a lively, jocular piece called "One May Morning." Kennedy's one number is the well-known Scottish "Night Visiting Song" that begins, "I must away, love, I can no longer tarry." Almost half of the songs are sung by Lloyd. On some tracks he is joined by Swarbrick on fiddle and Edwards on concertina, but several are unaccompanied. Due to his influence on a whole generation of English singers, many of Lloyd's versions were featured on well-known albums by other artists; his "Widow of Westmoreland's Daughter" and "Bonny Black Hare," both on this disc, made it into Fairport Convention's repertoire via Swarbrick. As on *Classic A.L. Lloyd,* listening to the master here will be a revelation to anyone with an interest in tracing the English folksong revival. The intellectual impetus for this recording also came from Lloyd, and he edited the original album. In the liner notes, he disguises his personal preferences as academic judgments, justifying his own choice of tender, loving erotic songs over bawdy or sexually explicit material by the principle that a "downright pornographic song with its proliferation of gross sexual detail is very rare in folk tradition proper." His reasoning here is unsound, based first and foremost on a romantic idea of "the folk" as happy peasants busy communing with nature and with the delights and fruitfulness of their own bodies; in the notes to individual songs, he makes facile arguments connecting sexual lyrics to ancient fertility rituals. But despite the specious commentary (which he himself came to view as outdated and naive by the time he died), *The Bird in the Bush* remains an essential album. *English and Scottish Folk Ballads* ♫♫♫ (Topic, 1996, prod. Tony Engle) is also a classic that deserved its CD release. Like *The Bird in the Bush,* this 1964 LP was beefed up with new tracks for its digital debut. The new version features many of the same performers as *The Bird in the Bush,* including Lloyd, Briggs, Killen, and Kennedy. In addition, it includes tracks by Mike Waterson and the late great Ewan MacColl. The accompanists are also mostly the same as on *Bird* : Edwards on concertina and Swarbrick on fiddle, with the addition of Briggs and Johnny Moynihan, who both play bouzouki on one track. The Scottish material, sung by MacColl and Kennedy, includes stories of warfare among clans ("The Baron o' Brackley" and "Hughie Graeme," both sung by MacColl) and bothy (itinerant farmworker) songs (Kennedy's "Drumdelgie"), as well as various broadside ballads and the great old "Lord Randall," delivered superbly by MacColl. Once again, Lloyd's distinctive voice dominates the English material, providing a third of the CD's tracks. Among them is the classic "Jack Orion," which Lloyd re-wrote from seminal folksong collector Francis Child's ballad "Glasgerion." This too would later be performed, much as Lloyd wrote it, by Fairport Convention, the link again being Swarbrick, who accompanies Lloyd on the track. "The Bitter Withy," another of Lloyd's ballads, could potentially offend Christians (which was why it was left out of Child's canon); it's about the child Jesus causing serious mischief and getting punished with a serious

spanking. More English ballad material is provided by Briggs ("Reynardine," "Willy O' Winsbury"), Waterson ("The Cruel Ship's Carpenter"), and Killen ("The Bramble Briar," "Young Edwin in the Lowlands"). *The Old Bush Songs* ♫♫♫ (Larrikin, 1994, prod. Warren Fahey) is a compilation of Lloyd's Australian songs and the only CD besides *Classic A.L. Lloyd* filled entirely with Lloyd's charmingly tentative singing. On it, Lloyd interprets a variety of songs, from the quintessentially Australian "Waltzing Matilda," "Bold Jack Donahue," and "The Kelly Gang" to Australian versions of older British folk songs like "Rocking the Cradle" and "The Derby Ram." Accompanists vary; on some tracks Edwards's concertina and Swarbrick's fiddle are the main instruments, while others feature Peggy Seeger's guitar and Ralph Rinzler's mandolin. In general, the experienced and professional musicians who back Lloyd do a fine job of providing the mostly upbeat and light environments in which his singing flourishes. Unfortunately, at 48 minutes, the CD is too short; it could easily have held five or six more songs. Lloyd did record a number of other fascinating and funny bush ballads, notably an outback version of "Seven Drunken Nights." For the sake of both interest and posterity, more of such recordings could have been included. *Blow Boys Blow* ♫♫♫ (Tradition, 1996, prod. Patrick Clancy) is a reissue of an old LP of sea chanteys recorded by Lloyd and MacColl. The dramatic interpretations of seafaring material are stirring, and backing is once again provided by Edwards, Rinzler, and other instrumentalists. The only drawback is, once again, the length; since this was originally a single LP, it clocks in at only 35 minutes. Still, priced low, it's definitely worth the purchase. Interestingly, Frank Zappa once commented on how much he liked this album; unfortunately, he loaned it to Captain Beefheart, who never returned it!

influences:

◀◀ Ernest Lloyd, Harry Cook, Phil Lumpkin

▶▶ Sandy Denny, Dave Swarbrick, Trevor Lucas, Martyn Wyndham-Read, Warren Fahey, Martin Carthy, Maddy Prior, Roy Harris, Frankie Armstrong, Ashley Hutchings, John Kirkpatrick, Louis Killen, Anne Briggs, Watersons, Shirley Collins, Fairport Convention, Steeleye Span, Albion Band, New St. George

see also: *Frankie Armstrong, Fairport Convention, Trevor Lucas, Ewan MacColl, Steeleye Span, Dave Swarbrick*

Steve Winick

Cheikh Lô

African pop

Born in 1955, in Bobo Dioulasso, Burkina Faso. Based in Dakar, Senegal.

When Cheikh Lô's international debut release appeared in 1996, he became one of the hottest commodities in African pop virtually overnight. Though he was born and spent his boyhood in the West African interior, in Burkina Faso, Lô is Senegalese, and he developed his highly original sound in the teeming cultural crossroads of Dakar. Mostly singing in the Senegalese language of Wolof, his sound is readily identifiable with that country, but like the best modern African musicians he transcends any simple classification. Lô's professional career started in his hometown with Orchestre Volta Jazz, a kind of variety band that did Cuban and Congolese hits and a few pop adaptations of Burkinabe folklore. After moving to Senegal in 1978 Lô played drums and percussion with Ouza, a progressive singer in the *mbalax* style popularized by Youssou N'Dour (itself an Afro-Caribbean fusion heavily influenced by Wolof tradition, though in an electrified setting), and then with the house band at the Hotel Savana. Once again, he found himself immersed in international variety. By then the Zairian sound was in full flower, Cameroonian *makossa* was coming on strong, and reggae had entered the mix. Lô absorbed everything. In 1985 he was given his first guitar, and began writing songs. He soon released his first cassette, which lead to well-received appearances on Senegalese television. Lô then spent two years in Paris working with a variety of groups and artists, including Zaire's Papa Wemba, whom Lô admired and recognized as a singer in the tradition of his boyhood idol, Tabu Ley. With all this experience under his belt, Lô returned to Dakar and began to concentrate on his solo career again. He wanted to create his own take on the tough Senegalese mbalax sound, make it softer, more acoustic, and accentuate the Latin rhythms and feeling in the music. In 1995, with the help of Senegal's preeminent pop star N'Dour himself, Lô got his chance; together they produced his international debut, *Ne La Thiass*.

To the many critics and listeners worldwide who acclaimed it at first listen, the phenomenon seemed sudden, but it was an outgrowth of a deeply held dedication that's second nature to Lô. For Lô is a Baye Fall, a member of a mystical brotherhood within the larger Islamic sect of the Mourides. The Mourides' founder, Cheikh Amadu Bamba, helped Senegal to embrace Islam by putting its teachings into terms that Wolof and other Senegalese peoples could accept. "His philosophy enveloped everything," says Lô. "He said, 'Pray to God as if you were going to die tomorrow, because if you think you are going to die tomorrow, you will pray a lot today.' Then he said, 'Work as if you were never going to die.'" In the summer of 1998 Lô had a chance to do just that as part of Africa Fête, a showcase of top African groups that made an extensive and grueling tour of the United States and Canada. With the success of these appearances still resonating, he set to work on his second international release.

what's available: *Ne La Tiasse* 🎵🎵🎵🎵 (World Circuit/Nonesuch, 1997, prod. Youssou N'Dour, Cheikh Lô) is a landmark for African pop. Lô's voice is rougher than that of his superstar producer N'Dour, but his sound is light and sensuous, an inspired reinterpretation of the African-Latin connection.

influences:
⏪ Youssou N'Dour, Papa Wemba, Orchestre Baobob

see also: *Tabu Ley Rochereau, Youssou N'Dour, Papa Wemba*

Banning Eyre

Ismaël Lô

Afropop

Born in 1956, in Niger. Based in Dakar, Senegal, and Paris, France.

Like many Africans who got their first Western exposure during the early worldbeat wave of the late 1970s, Ismaël Lô's career has been plagued by misunderstandings, the greatest of which may be his tag as the "Bob Dylan of Africa"—a label Lô finds laughable. "I was the first African to play harmonica and guitar at the same time, like Bob Dylan once did, so that was an easy label for those who were unfamiliar with my music," he says. Lô's enthusiasms don't really lie in the singer/songwriter area, but rather in exploring new ways of blending traditional Afropop (i.e., music made for the African market before the 1980s) with more recent Western pop forms.

Lô was born in Niger to Senegalese parents who moved back to Dakar when he was two months old. Like many teens he drove his parents crazy with his stereo, mixing the sounds of James Brown, Otis Redding, and Johnny Halliday with more African fare like the *kora* playing of Soudioulou Cissoksho, a Senegalese *griot*. Lô's mother says he was born singing, but the family wanted him to pursue a more academic course, so Lô's first guitar was an instrument he built for himself out of fishing line, an oil can, and some scrap wood. In order to learn the guitar, Lô would sneak into town and stand outside the clubs he was too young to get in to. "Sometimes I'd find empty crates and stack them up under a window, so I could climb up and see what the guitarists were doing with their fingers," Lô recalled. "It was 10 years before I had enough money to buy a real guitar." Lô learned by borrowing the instruments of friends, and put together his first band, Ngalam ("Gold"), while still a teen. After appearing on local TV, Lô was approached by Omar Pene, who was just starting Super Diamono. Lô joined the fledgling band and stayed with them during their meteoric climb to the top of the Senegalese charts. "People often ask why I joined them, and one reason was because I know the limits of one person and one guitar. I wanted to be in a band and play with other musicians."

During his time with Super Diamono Lô learned to play drums, percussion, and keyboards, and honed his electric guitar chops. Eventually, Lô's vision of his own brand of international pop made him leave Diamono and start a new group. Lô went on to record 16 albums with his own band, including hits like *Xalat, Natt, Xunbeul,* and *Waliour.* In 1990 he signed with Mango and his first release was an eponymous collection of Senegalese hits revamped for the international market. In 1996 Triloka picked up his option and his first album for the label was *Jammu Africa,* which added even more Western touches to his sound. The single "Without Blame," a duet with Marianne Faithful, got airplay on some modern rock stations, but Lô's crossover dreams have yet to some true. "All music comes from Africa, and returns to Africa," Lô says. "Most people don't know [the history of the music], but most Western music has the African feeling in it. It may be called soul, rumba or funk, but it's African. Music is a universal language, and the different rhythms are like different dialects, but the root of the rhythm is from Africa. For me music has no frontiers. I don't want to make African, or French, or American music, I just want to make music."

what's available: *Jammu Africa* ♫♫♫ (Triloka, 1996, prod. Bouya Ndoye, Nicolas Gautier) is the easiest album to find, and a fairly good representation of where Lô wants to take his music. The set includes songs from his two Mango albums *Ismaël Lô* and *Iso,* further refined and polished. *Natt* ♫♫♫ (Melodie, 1987, prod. Ibrahima Sylla) includes selections from Lô's first three albums, *Natt, Xiif,* and *Xalat,* and proves that he can make pop music without loosing the harder edge present in his Senegalese albums but missing from his more recent work. This is Afropop with its roots intact, full of grit and fire.

influences:

◄◄ Youssou N'Dour, Xalam, Mory Kante, Baaba Maal

j. poet

Kevin Locke

Native American flute and hoop dancing

Born in 1954, in South Dakota, USA. Based in Standing Rock Reservation, SD, USA.

Among Native North American performers, none is more acclaimed than Kevin Locke, a Lakota dancer and indigenous flute player. A member of the Standing Rock Sioux Nation (Hunkpapa Band of Lakotas) and resident of the sovereign Standing Rock Reservation in South Dakota, he spent his teen years with an elderly uncle whose first language was Lakota. It was from this uncle, Abraham End of Horn, that Kevin received his first training in the traditions of his culture, though he is quick to point out that he learned much from many others in the community. Among those teachers were Arlo Good Bear, Ben Black Bear Sr., Charles Wise Spirit, William Horn Cloud, and Margaret One Bull. Locke also holds a master's degree in educational administration from the University of South Dakota, where he was admitted to law school before realizing that music and dance were his destiny. Locke is an exquisite player of the indigenous cedarwood flute. Many older Lakota

say he is even better than those they remember from long ago. He is certainly a musical hero and role model to indigenous youth across North America, and younger players are frequently waiting backstage, eager to ask questions. Befitting this guiding role, Locke's Lakota name is Tokeya Inajin, "The First to Arise."

That a musician of such skill could also be a famous dancer may seem improbable, but it is so. Locke originally came to national attention as a hoop dancer, a brilliant performer in another ancient and honorable Lakota tradition. In this amazingly complex and acrobatic dance, the dancer whirls within twirling hoops, explicating the Native view of the world as hoops intersect and grow into ever more revealing designs that show the way of life. Locke was awarded a National Heritage fellowship by the National Endowment for the Arts in 1990. His performances draw from a rich repertoire of story, song, flute music, and dance. Prominent are his songs and stories of the eagle because of the qualities it is seen to possess: nobility, loftiness, and serenity. In Locke's words, "These are qualities that each one of us has by our birthright. The power we have, on our wings, is much more powerful than that of the eagle. We have the wings of our minds and thoughts. We have the wings of our heart. As we exercise them, they will carry us upward. How often do we send our children into the world with only one wing? We must exercise our hearts as well. Young eagles must have two strong wings." Locke's performances conclude with the hoop dance which reflects his belief in the unity of humankind. Using 28 hoops to tell a story, Locke depicts such things as flowers, butterflies, stars, the sun, and an eagle. The hoops represent unity, while the four colors of the hoops—black, red, yellow, and white—represent the four directions, four seasons, four winds, and four complexions of people's skin. At the end of the dance all 28 hoops have been interlocked in a spherical shape as fragile as the balance he works for in human affairs.

what to buy: *Open Circle* ♫♫♫ (Makoché, 1996), one of Locke's most recent releases, is a fine introduction to the power in his performances.

what to buy next: *Dream Catcher* ♫♫♫ (EarthBeat!/Warner Bros., 1992) and *Love Songs of the Lakota* ♫♫♫ (Indian House, 1982/1995) are calming collections of natural sounds and flute songs of the Lakota, Dakota, and Meskwaki peoples that portray Locke's subtle artistry. Included are ancient and contemporary love songs and laments, including a selection by famed Indian leader Chief Sitting Bull, who was renowned within his tribe as an honored composer and singer.

the rest:

Wopile, the Giveaway ♫♫♫ (Yellow Moon Press, 1993)
The Flood ♫♫♫ (Parabola Books, 1993) (storybook & tape)
Keepers of the Dream ♫♫♫ (EarthBeat!/Warner Bros., 1994)

Kevin Locke

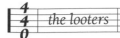

The Flash of the Mirror 🎵🎵 (Meyer Creative Productions/Makoché, 1996)

worth searching for: Several of Locke's releases are either available on cassette only or are currently out of print entirely, including *Lullaby* 🎵🎵🎵 (Music for Little People, 1994), *Lakota Wiikijo Olowan, Vol. II* 🎵🎵🎵 (Featherstone, 1986), *Journey to the Spirit World* 🎵🎵🎵 (Tatanka, 1983), *Lakota Wilkijo Olowan, Vol. I* 🎵🎵🎵 (Featherstone, 1983), *"make me a hollow reed . . ."* 🎵🎵🎵 (Kevin Locke/Meyer Creative Productions, 1990), *Lakota Love Songs & Stories* 🎵🎵🎵 (Kevin Locke/Meyer Creative Productions, 1990), and *The Seventh Direction* 🎵🎵🎵 (Kevin Locke/Meyer Creative Productions, 1990), the latter three of which are cassette-only releases. He has also appeared on the various-artists compilations *Tribal Voices* 🎵🎵🎵 (EarthBeat!/Rhino, 1996) and *Tribal Winds* 🎵🎵🎵 (EarthBeat!/Warner Bros., 1995).

influences:

◀ Richard Fool Bull, Arlo Good Bear, Ben Black Bear

Neal Walters

The Looters
Worldbeat

Formed 1984, in San Francisco, CA, USA. Disbanded 1993.

Mat Callahan, guitar, lead vocals; Joe Johnson, guitar, vocals; Jim Johnson, bass, vocals; Fred Cirillo, keyboards, vocals; Ahaguna G. Sun, drums, vocals; Akal Fillinger, keyboards (1984–87). (All members are from USA.)

The foundation of the Looters can be traced back to late-night conversations between Mat Callahan and Akal Fillinger. One night, while Fillinger played Callahan some tunes by his favorite reggae and calypso artists, an idea formed. They envisioned a band that could perform the same kind of journalistic function in this country that calypso and reggae play in the Caribbean. A band that could create exciting dance music with challenging lyrics; songs designed to raise the important social questions. "I don't buy that line that goes 'Hey, I'm only a musician, I'm not a politician,'" Callahan says. "In a manner of speaking everything is political, and we have a duty to confront the issues that effect our lives. I may not have all the answers, or any of the answers for that matter, but I have a lotta questions, and I'm gonna keep bringing 'em up." The Looters were as good as their word and built a hard-hitting international sound with elements of African, Caribbean and North American styles, gaining a reputation as one of the Bay Area's most exciting live bands.

On the business side, however, things were different. The band was turned down by the majors because their songs were too political, too controversial, and too in-your-face. Undaunted, they put out an eponymous EP on Jello Biafra's Alternative Tentacles label. Chris Blackwell, then head of Island Records, heard the EP in London's Rough Trade record shop, called the number on the back of the record, and signed the band. Blackwell gave the Looters total artistic control, and the result was *Flashpoint,* a collection of the agitprop dance tunes the band had been playing live for the past five years. Despite rave reviews from the rock press, and a sold-out tour to support the LP, the album sank without a trace and the Looters returned home a sadder but wiser band. Happily, they'd used their Island advance to build their own recording studio, so when the major-label deal went belly-up they returned home to cut *Jericho Down,* another powerful collection of tunes. The Looters' studio became the focus of Komotion International, a communal effort run by a collective of poets, musicians, and activists; in return for free studio time people would trade off on the floor-sweeping, postering, painting, and other jobs essential to keep the operation running smoothly. Although eventually closed by the police, who objected to the crowds of young, politically active people the space attracted, Komotion was a major focus for San Francisco's new bohemian generation for years. After another album, *Imago Mundi,* the Looters fell apart. Callahan went back to driving a cab, although he often surfaces with his new Gospel/R&B project the Wild Bouquet.

what to buy: *Flashpoint* 🎵🎵🎵🎵 (Island, 1988, prod. Ken Kesse) is an amazing explosion that melds hard rock with calypso, reggae, and other Caribbean beats without sounding forced or derivative. The Looters are the great lost worldbeat band.

what to buy next: A slight change of direction found the band producing an album that could be the soundtrack for a worldbeat noir flick, *Jericho Down* 🎵🎵🎵🎵 (Monster Music, 1991, prod. Mat Callahan, Fred Cirillo). The disc is full of tough playing and tunes that cut deep, both poetically and politically.

the rest:
Imago Mundi 🎵🎵🎵 (Monster Music, 1992)

influences:

◀ Sparrow, Bob Dylan, Victor Jara, Groupo Mancotal

▶ Angélique Kidjo

j. poet

Jennifer Lopez
Latin pop

Born July 24, 1970, in the Bronx, NY, USA. Based in USA.

Well before her 30th birthday, Jennifer Lopez had established herself as an actor of talent and presence—working with such prestigious directors as Oliver Stone, Francis Ford Coppola, and Steven Soderbergh—and, with her Latin heritage, she is considered by many to be the face of the 21st century. It was her portrayal of one of the leading Latin faces of the 20th that inspired Lopez to revive a childhood interest in singing: her starring role in the biopic about slain *Tejano* icon Selena Quintanilla. Though she lip-synched to Selena's own vocals in the film, the experience of being involved with music again led Lopez to pursue releasing her own album. At this writing, she still intends to make acting her first focus but is enjoying the fact that her debut album is climbing both the Latin and rock charts.

what's available: *On the 6* ♪♪♪ (WORK, 1999, prod. Corey Rooney, Jennifer Lopez) is a group of tunes that seem to hit all the pop/Latin dance genres, from techno-influenced to tropical to ballad. Lopez's Puerto Rican heritage comes through with Latin guitar riffs and tropical percussion patterns in many of the songs, as well as two mixes of a Spanish-language duet with salsa prince Marc Anthony. But can she sing? Yes, and quite well. She also makes tasteful if not wildly original use of Latin musical motifs in her English-language tunes. The songs themselves are clearly meant more for dancing than listening, and at that they succeed; now it would be interesting to see what Lopez could do with more substantial material, in English or Spanish.

worth searching for: Though she doesn't sing in the film *Selena!* Lopez gives a convincing and powerful performance that provides insight into the life of this lost phenomenon.

influences:
◄◄ Rita Moreno, Madonna

see also: *Marc Anthony, Selena*

Kerry Dexter

Lord Kitchener
/Kitch

Calypso, soca

Born April 18, 1922, in Arima, Trinidad. Based in Port of Spain, Trinidad, and Brooklyn, NY, USA.

Aldwyn Roberts, a.k.a. Lord Kitchener (or "Kitch" as he is commonly called today), is one of the greatest living calypso singers, a man who can trace his career back to the earliest days of the genre. Kitch was just 14 when both his parents died, and although he was an excellent student, he was forced to neglect his studies and work to support himself. Luckily, his father, who was a blacksmith by trade, was also an amateur musician, and he'd taught Kitch the basics of guitar playing and composition. His first gig was singing for roadside laborers, and the songs he made up about their economic plight were so well received that he decided to try calypso as a full-time career. In 1938, one of his early tunes, "Shops Close Too Early," became a local hit, and in 1943 he moved down to Port of Spain where he sang with the Roving Brigade. In 1944 he was invited to join the Victory Tent, a

the talking drum

The "talking drum," also known as the *tama,* is one of the three primary drums of the Manding people of West Africa (along with the *djembe* and the *doundoun,* or "djun djun"). The smallest of the three, the tama is an hourglass-shaped drum with strings or leather thongs stretched from the rim of one head to the other. Usually holding the tama between one arm and the body, the player can squeeze its strings to increase or decrease the tension of the drumhead as he strikes it with an L-shaped stick, allowing for distinctive bent-tone percussive sounds with melodic ranges that can exceed one octave. In the hands of masters like Material's Aiyb Dieng and Mickey Hart's Planet Drum ensemble's Sikiru Adepoju, the instrument not only "talks" but seems to sing in a rhythmic language all its own. Although most commonly identified with West African music, the tama has counterparts in a variety of cultures around the world, including the *dundun* of Ghana (no relation to the doundoun mentioned above); the *udukkai* of Kerala in India; and the *chang go,* which is virtually the national drum of Korea.

see also: The Kora and West African Griot (sidebar), West African Drumming and the Soul of Rock 'n' Roll (sidebar)

Bret Love

top calypso venue, and he met Growling Tiger, one of the music's early legends. One of his first tunes thereafter, "Green Fig," a double entendre about a man who knows his wife is cheating on him, became a sensation, and Growling Tiger dubbed the young Aldwyn Lord Kitchener, after Field Marshal Lord Kitchener, England's former secretary of war.

In 1947 Kitch started his own tent, with a number of the younger singers like Lord Melody, Spoiler, Viking, and Lord Pretender. They had a more progressive sound and introduced a stronger horn section as well as Latin, Brazilian, and North American rhythms. This "Young Brigade" was quite popular with the American troops stationed on the island during WWII, and their approval inspired the singers to drop some of the political lyrics and go for a sexier, dance-happy style. Soon after, Kitch left Trinidad for England. He wanted to take his music to the interna-

4
4
2   *lord melody*

tional market and make records. His albums for Parlophone and Melodisc continued to explore new musical ground, and he experimented with a jazzier arranging style. When his records appeared back home they were big hits, although they didn't do as well internationally as Kitch had hoped. He also experienced the racism of England first-hand and returned to political lyrics, penning the classics "Africa My Home" and "Black and White (If You're Not White You're Considered Black)."

After a decade in Europe Kitch returned to Trinidad, where he began to win Road March and Calypso King Crowns regularly. In the 1970s when calypso turned into *soca* by incorporating funk, rock, and reggae into its rhythms and accelerating its tempo, Kitch was one of the first oldtimers to jump on the bandwagon; at one point he even claimed to have invented the form. At 77, Kitch still maintains a hectic touring schedule and his yearly releases are full of spunk and fire.

what to buy: The solid survey *Klassic Kitchener, Volume One* 🎵🎵🎵🎵 (Ice, 1992, reissue prod. Eddy Grant) starts with Kitch's early British sides from the 1950s and continues through his steel-pan-driven hits of the mid-1960s. Includes "Tie Tongue Mopsy," one of his earliest double-entendre hits, and "Steel Band Music," a swinging tribute to one of Trinidad's unique contributions to the musical world.

what to buy next: *Klassic Kitchener, Volume Three* 🎵🎵🎵🎵 (Ice, 1993, reissue prod. Eddy Grant) covers hits from the mid-to-late 1970s, just as calypso was transforming itself into soca. Lyrics deal mostly with sex and good times; the rhythms are simpler and the tempos faster, but Kitch is still in excellent voice.

best of the rest:

Lord Kitchener 🎵🎵🎵🎵 (Melodisc Reissue)
Kitch—King of Calypso 🎵🎵🎵🎵 (Melodisc Reissue)
Kitchener Goes Soca 🎵🎵🎵🎵 (Charlie's, 1980)
Roots of Soca 🎵🎵🎵🎵 (Charlie's, 1983)
Master at Work 🎵🎵🎵🎵 (Kalico, 1987)
100% Kitch 🎵🎵🎵🎵 (B's, 1988)
Klassic Kitchener, Volume Two 🎵🎵🎵🎵 (Ice, 1993)

influences:

◀◀ Growling Tiger, Roaring Lion, Atilla

▶▶ Sparrow, Swallow, Arrow

j. poet

Lord Melody /Melody

Calypso
Born 1926, in Trinidad. Died 1988, in Trinidad.

Although best known to many listeners for writing "Mama Look a Boo Boo" and "Juanita," which both became hits for

Harry Belafonte, Melody had a long and varied career, both before and after the North American calypso craze of the 1950s. Like calypso legend Kitchener, who was a friend and mentor, Melody's parents died while he was young and he partially grew up in an orphanage. He began building his name during the war years with tunes like "Berlin on a Donkey" (a scathing look at Hitler and his policies), and "Boo Boo Man" and "Creature from the Black Lagoon" (in both of which he poked self-effacing fun at his own ugliness). When Belafonte rearranged "Boo Boo Man" as "Mama Look a Boo Boo," the song became an international smash and gave Melody a degree of financial security. He even toured with Belafonte briefly. In the 1970s he had a few more hits, but his cancer cut down his touring and recording activity. He died in 1988 at the age of 62.

what to buy: The compilation *Precious Melodies* 🎵🎵🎵🎵 (Ice, 1994, reissue prod. Eddy Grant) collects 20 of Melody's better-known hits, including some of the insults he traded with calypso great Sparrow during the mid-1950s. Melody has a warm, playful tenor, perfectly suited to his woeful tales of love.

what to buy next: *Lola* 🎵🎵🎵🎵 (B's, 1982, prod. Earl Rodney), one of Melody's last records, is a satisfying and soulful soca romp.

worth searching for: Melody passed early in the CD revolution, leaving his oeuvre currently awaiting large-scale reissue. Most of his work was put out in limited numbers by the indie calypso labels in New York, but Cook Records was recently acquired by the Smithsonian Institution, so his Cook albums, *Calypso 1962, Again!!* and *Through the Looking Glass,* may soon be available on CD. If you can't wait, the Smithsonian/Folkways office will make you a custom CD of these titles. Contact them at www.si.edu/folkways for details.

influences:

◀◀ Growling Tiger, Atilla, Roaring Lion

▶▶ Machel Montano, Taxi, Nelson

j. poet

Los Amigos Invisibles

Latin jazz/Brazilian dance/space-age bachelor pop
Formed 1995, in Caracas, Venezuela. Based in Venezuela.

Armando Figueredo, keyboards; Juan Manuel Roura, drums; Julio Briceno, vocals; Jose Luis Pardo, guitars; Jose Rafael Torres, bass; Mauricio Arcas, percussion. (All members are from Venezuela.)

The amazing thing about the Venezuelan sextet Los Amigos Invisibles is how cohesive it sounds, even when a hard-funk electric-piano dance song leads into a lounge-y instrumental with soft percussion and murmured vocals. A bunch of fun-loving young men who were frustrated when the Venuezelan discos closed after the oil-booming '70s, the Amigos like their funk tongue-in-cheek (or tongue-out-of-mouth: The cover photo of the band's debut has all six members unashamedly ogling a woman in a bikini near a hotel pool). Like fellow international lounge-funk artist Dimitri from Paris, the more disparate elements they mix together, the more everything fits into a tinkly, catchy sound. "Otra Vez" begins as a smoky bossa-nova ballad, and occasionally explodes as sharply as the James Brown–style opening song, "Ultra-Funk."

what's available: The band's debut, *The New Sound of the Venezuelan Gozadera* ♪♪♪♪ (Luaka Bop/Warner Bros., 1998, prod. Andres Levin), is primo space-age bachelor-pad music—complete with congas and bongos. Bands like Combustible Edison have been trying to achieve this sound, which attempts to capture the feel of *The Jetsons* in music, for years. But a Latin sense of humor is more effective than an American sense of kitsch, and the Amigos' party spirit turns "El Disco Anal" into the dance workout the title implies, and "Otra Vez" into a spacey, high-tech instrumental.

influences:

◄◄ Combustible Edison, Antonio Carlos Jobim, Astrud Gilberto, James Brown, Juan Garcia Esquivel, Perez Prado, Xavier Cugat

Steve Knopper

Los Camperos de Valles

Sones de Huasteca

Formed 1972, in Ciudad Valles, San Luis Potosí, Mexico. Based in Huasteca, Mexico.

Heliodoro Copado, violin; Marcos Hernández, guitarra quinta, vocals; Gregorio Solano, jarana, vocals. (All members are from Mexico.)

Los Camperos de Valles play music for dancing. For years they made extra income by performing at various civic and private functions, but their recordings have spread their music around the world. Now they add to that local cash flow with tours that have taken them from their home base in Mexico's Huasteca region the United States and Europe. While it may be tempting to describe their music as a downsized version of *mariachi*, that would be doing a disservice to the listener as well as the band. Los Camperos de Valles play fiery *huapango* dance music, specifically a type of *son* (Mexican style) peculiar to Huasteca. It features Heliodoro Copado's violin riffs floating above the rhythms of Hernández's *guitarra quinta* (similar in size to the *bajo sexto* 12-string bass used in Tex-Mex groups) and Gregorio Solano's *jarana,* a smaller six-stringed guitar. Soaring with the violin are high falsetto vocals from Marcos Hernández and Solano telling tales grounded in myth and village realities.

what's available: At present there are only two albums available by Los Camperos de Valles, *El Triunfo* ♪♪♪♪ (Corasón/Música Tradicional, 1992, prod. Eduardo Llerenas) and *The Muse* ♪♪♪♪ (Discos Corasón, 1995, prod. Eduardo Llerenas). Both are very well recorded and played; *El Triunfo* has a wider range of material while the music on *The Muse* is constructed around lyrics by local legend and spinner of tales, Serapio "El Güero" Nieto.

influences:

◄◄ Serapio "El Güero" Nieto, Los Cantores del Pánuco

►► Perla Tamaulipeca, Los Caimanes

Garaud MacTaggart

Los de Abajo

Ska, rock en Español, worldbeat, salsa, cumbia, funk, Mexican

Formed 1992, in Mexico City, Mexico. Based in Mexico City, Mexico.

Liber Terán, vocals; Yocupitzio Arrellano, drums; Carlos Cuevas, keyboards; Carlos Cortez, bass; Gabriel Elias, percussion; Vladimir Garnica, guitar; Damián Portugal, saxophone. (All members are from Mexico.)

Los de Abajo came together by way of both the musical fusion increasingly appealing to young Latin listeners and the ideological melange of contemporary Mexican politics. The name of the band—which it took from a modern novel about a footsoldier's political disillusionment—reflects its members' beliefs that change must come from below. After studies at Mexico's National University, the gang's first thought was simply to put together a ska/rock band. But their focus soon became using rhythm and lyrics as tools to comment on and help change what they see as a corrupt society and government. This led them to become involved in political theater as well as musical events. "We're not a mosaic but a kaleidoscope of Mexican life," says drummer Yocupitzio Arrellano.

what's available: *Los de Abajo* ♪♪♪♪ (Luaka Bop, 1998, prod. Greg Ladanyi, Hans Mues) shows the group's ability to marry lyrics of pointed social commentary to highly danceable and listenable tunes. The subject matter puts it outside the mainstream of rock in Mexico itself, but this international release is exposing the group's music to a wider audience.

worth searching for: Before signing with Luaka Bop, Los de Abajo produced two self-released cassettes which it sold at concerts in Mexico.

influences:

◄◄ Ruben Blades, Willie Colon

Kerry Dexter

Los Fabulosos Cadillacs

Ska, rock en Español

Formed c. 1984, in Buenos Aires, Argentina. Based in Buenos Aires, Argentina.

Gabriel "Vicentico" Fernandez Capello, vocals, accordion; Flavio Cianciarulo, bass; Sergio Rotman, sax; Ariel Sanzo, guitar; Daniel Lozano, trumpet; Fernando Albareda, trombone; Fernando Ricciardi, drums; "Toto" Rotblat, bongos, percussion; Mario Siperman, piano, organ. (All members are from Argentina.)

Los Fabulosos Cadillacs formed while most of the members were still in their teens to play a Latin version of ska, a style then sweeping the world thanks to the "two-tone" groups—the Specials, the Selector, and the Beat. They began touring outside of Argentina in the wake of their first album, *Bares y Fondas,* released in 1986. Since then they have become one of the leaders of the "rock en Español" movement, a style they may have created themselves with their wide-ranging approach. Unlike many rockers, they have an omnivorous aesthetic more in line with worldbeat bands. Albums have included rap, Brazilian *Candomblé* drumming, blistering guitar-driven punk, the *norteño* accordion of Flaco Jimenez, vocals by Celia Cruz, psychedelic pop with Debby Harry, and revolutionary funk with Mick Jones of the Clash and Big Audio Dynamite. After the implosion of the Argentinean economy in the early 1990s the band faced some tough times, but their growing international reputation has enabled them to carry on. In 1994 they took home the Latin Video of the Year award from MTV Latin for "Matador"; in 1998 they won the Latin Rock Grammy for their *Fabulosos Calavera* album.

what to buy: The band's Grammy signaled their former label to put out the comprehensive double-CD retrospective *20 Grandes Exitos* ♫♫♫ (Sony Latino, 1998, prod. various). It includes "Matador," a worldwide hit, as well as rare B-sides, demo versions of early songs, and other stuff of interest to fans. The older, single-disc collection *Vasos Vacios* ♫♫♫♫ (Sony Latino, 1994) is less comprehensive, but its 17 tracks have far less fat.

what to buy next: The Grammy-winning *Fabulosos Calavera* ♫♫♫ (BMG, 1997, prod. Karl Cameron Porter) shows a band that's willing to explore in any direction the music takes it— hardcore punk, lounge instrumentals, surf guitar, country & western, mariachi, *son,* blue beat, and more all rub elbows for an exhilarating musical blend.

the rest:
Bares y Fondas ♫♫♫ (Sony Latino, 1986)
El Satanico Dr. Cadillac ♫♫♫ (Sony Latino, 1989)
El Leon ♫♫♫ (Sony Latino, 1992)
Rey Azucar ♫♫♫ (Sony Latino, 1995)

influences:
◀◀ Sui Generous
▶▶ Dance Hall Crashers

see also: *Celia Cruz, Flaco Jimenez*

j. poet

Los Incas /Urubamba

Andean folk music

Formed c. 1952, in Paris, France. Based in Paris, France.

Jorge Milchberg; Carlos Arguedas; Julio Arguedas; Emilio Arteaga Quintana; Jorge Cumbo; Juan Dalera; Alfredo de Robertis. (All members are from Peru.)

The *zampoñas*—Andean pan pipes—and the *charango,* the double-stringed Andean "mandolin" made from the shell of an armadillo, are familiar all over the world. The shrill, mournful sound of the pipes seems to touch something deep in the human soul, no matter what language one speaks, and is a perfect compliment to the muted tones of the charango. The roots of Andean music go back to the Inca Empire that once included most of Ecuador, Peru, Bolivia, Chile, southern Colombia, and northern Argentina. Traditionally, each set of pipes had only a partial scale, which made any performance a cooperative venture, with a lot of musical give and take that produced interesting harmonies and overtones. Accounts from the time of the Spanish Conquest praised the hypnotic and soothing effects of the music, particularly the way the melody would bounce and shift as it was tossed back and forth between musicians. Stringed instruments were unknown before the arrival of the Spaniards, but the charango fit perfectly with the rhythms of the pan pipe, and since many songs are still composed in languages derived from the unwritten Inca tongue it's impossible to differentiate between Native and imported rhythms, although the influence of Latin jazz can be heard in most of today's professional groups.

During the '50s Paris became the center for a large community of expatriot Bolivians and Peruvians. After establishing themselves there, Jorge Milchberg y Los Incas achieved worldwide fame when the title track of their 1963 album *El Condor Pasa* became an international hit. In 1965 Paul Simon wrote English lyrics for the tune and invited the band to record it with Simon & Garfunkel. "El Condor Pasa" reached the top of the U.S. charts, and the group, then called Urubamba, after a river in their native Peru, later toured with Simon and played on his first solo album. After almost 50 years of music-making, Los Incas are still going strong and pushing boundaries. "La Chinita," from their recent *Alegria* album, is, according to musical director and composer Milchberg, "a continuation of an interior journey that explores the gods and demons that have filled the history of our people; an attempt to make music unlimited by frontiers."

what to buy: Even before Paul Simon discovered it, *El Condor Pasa* 🎵🎵🎵🎵 (Philips, 1963, prod. Jorge Milchberg) had been a massive seller. This is a beautiful recording of traditional tunes from Argentina, Peru, Bolivia, Venezuela, and even Cuba; an early world-music classic.

what to buy next: *Urubamba* 🎵🎵🎵 (Columbia, 1974, prod. Paul Simon) was recorded before the Paul Simon tour that introduced the band to a new generation of fans. It's just over 20 minutes in length, but every tune is a tiny, sparkling gem.

worth searching for: *Alegria* 🎵🎵🎵🎵 (Buda France, prod. Jorge Milchberg) is one of the few Los Incas discs that doesn't include repackagings of "El Condor Pasa" and other early hits. There is no information on the booklet, but it's a bright, compelling listen.

influences:
◀ Inca tradition
▶ Paul Simon, Susana Baca, Inti-Illimani

see also: *Paul Simon*

j. poet

Los Lobos

Latin/rock fusion, experimental pop
Formed 1974, in Los Angeles, CA, USA. Based in Los Angeles, CA, USA.

David Hidalgo, guitar, vocals; Conrad Lozano, bass, vocals; Cesar Rosas, guitar, vocals; Louie Perez, drums, guitar, vocals; Steve Berlin, saxophone, keyboards (1984–present). (All members are from USA.)

One could argue that "La Bamba" was the best thing that ever happened to Los Lobos. Not because their spunky 1987 cover of the Ritchie Valens hit gave this Los Angeles act its 15 minutes of Top 40 fame, but because fear of being labeled a Chicano version of Sha Na Na challenged them to put their own weird, wobbly spin on the festive fusing of blues, R&B, rockabilly, and Mexican folk music that originally established them as roots-rock torchbearers. Such twangy T-Bone Burnett–produced efforts as *By the Light of the Moon* and *How Will the Wolf Survive?* introduced a tight garage band that would be happy if it never left the barrios or the bars. But in 1990, prodded by Larry Hirsch and Mitchell Froom, Los Lobos transformed into one of rock's most experimental acts. Fuzz, feedback, distortion, and dense percussion blended with lead singer David Hidalgo's soulful tenor and Froom's quirky production techniques to create the intoxicating cross-section of rhythms and textures behind *The Neighborhood* and 1992's jaw-dropping *Kiko*. The band that once amazed listeners by deftly handling a variety of genres now blurs the lines so much that it's hard to figure out where they're going next, which is something that can't be said about most roots-rock bands. Meanwhile solo projects for Hidalgo and Cesar Rosas, and band offshoots like the critically acclaimed Latin Playboys and the commercially phenomenal Los Super Seven, have multiplied the directions.

what to buy: Of the early efforts, *How Will the Wolf Survive?* 🎵🎵🎵 (Slash/Warner Bros., 1984, prod. T-Bone Burnett, Steve Berlin) holds up the best. It's a roots-rock primer ranging from savage blues ("Don't Worry Baby") to engaging country-rock ("A Matter of Time," "Will the Wolf Survive?") and traditional Tex-Mex ("Serenata Norteña"). The band begins flexing its experimental muscles on *The Neighborhood* 🎵🎵🎵🎵 (Slash/Warner Bros., 1990, prod. Larry Hirsch, Mitchell Froom, Los Lobos), a rich, riveting effort driven by guest drummer Jim Keltner and a mesmerizing mix of the band's raunchiest ("Jenny's Got a Pony," "Georgia Slop") and prettiest ("Little John of God," "Be Still"). All rules go out the window on *Kiko* 🎵🎵🎵🎵 (Slash/Warner Bros., 1992, prod. Mitchell Froom, Los Lobos), an ambitious, atmospheric patchwork of the Beatles, Tom Waits, New Orleans jazz, country, and blues that never lapses into avant garde pretension. More important, Hidalgo and Louie Perez's songs—which tackle death (the lovely "Saint behind the Glass"), homelessness ("Angels with Dirty Faces"), child abuse ("Two Janes"), and domestic violence ("Reva's House")—are their hardest hitting to date.

what to buy next: *La Pistola y el Corazon* 🎵🎵🎵 (Slash/Warner Bros., 1988, prod. Los Lobos) is a delightful Spanish-language romp through traditional Mexican music played on accordions, nylon-string guitars, upright bass, *bajo sextos,* and other folkloric instruments.

what to avoid: Once you make the album to end all albums with *Kiko,* what do you do for an encore? The bluesy, noisy *Colossal Head* 🎵🎵🎵 (Slash/Warner Bros., 1996, prod. Mitchell Froom, Tchad Blake, Los Lobos) buckles under the pressure of topping its predecessor, sounding more contrived than created.

the rest:
. . . And a Time to Dance 🎵🎵🎵 (Slash/Warner Bros., 1983)
By the Light of the Moon 🎵🎵🎵 (Slash/Warner Bros., 1987)
Just Another Band from East L.A.: A Collection 🎵🎵🎵🎵 (Slash/Warner Bros., 1993)
This Time 🎵🎵🎵🎵 (Hollywood, 1999)

worth searching for: The soundtrack to Paul Bartel's black comedy *Eating Raoul* (Varese, 1982, prod. Scot Holton, Tom Null) features the then-unknown band rampaging through "Diablo con Vestido," a Spanish version of "Devil with a Blue Dress."

solo outings:

Latin Playboys:
Latin Playboys ♫♫♫ (Slash/Warner Bros., 1994)
Dose ♫♫♫♫ (Atlantic, 1999)

Los Super Seven:
Los Super Seven ♫♫♫♫ (RCA, 1998)

Houndog (David Hidalgo and Mike Halby):
Houndog (Columbia Legacy, 1999)

Cesar Rosas:
Soul Disguise (Rykodisc, 1999)

influences:

◀◀ Ritchie Valens, Sir Douglas Quintet

▶▶ The Blazers, rock en Español

see also: *Latin Playboys, Los Super Seven*

David Okamoto

Los Muñequitos de Matanzas

Traditional rumba
Formed 1952, in Matanzas, Cuba. Based in Matanzas, Cuba.

Jesus Alfonso; Gregorio Diaz; Agustin Diaz; Victoriano Espinosa; Israel Berriel Jiménez; Diosdado Ramos; Barbaro Ramos; Vivian Ramos; José Luis Montoya, drums, clave, percussion; Ana Paréz; Ricardo Llorca; Alberto Romero; Rafael Navarro Pujada; Israel Berriel Gonzalez; Luis Ramos, singing, percussion, clapping. (All members are from Cuba.)

Los Muñequitos de Matanzas play rumba—a rhythm that has become a building block of international music—but in a stripped-down form emphasizing rhythmic complexity and musicianship over show-biz flash. The band includes three drummers; five singers who double on *congas, cata,* and *shakere*; and five dancers; as well as Luis Ramos, the 10-year-old grandson of the group's director, Diosdado Ramos. Rumba was outlawed by the Spanish slave-masters who understood its power as a cultural tool. When they banned drumming, slaves began pounding out rhythms on packing crates to keep the music alive. When Los Muñequitos was founded in 1952 there was only one other group—Vive Bien—dedicated to preserving the traditional roots of the music. Originally called Guaguanco Mantancero, the band was an informal gathering of fathers, sons, and in-laws who played on weekends and at fiestas, but when "Los Muñequitos de Matanzas," a song about the characters in the comics section of the Sunday newspapers, became an unexpected hit, the band got a new name. Although the last original member died several years ago, Los Muñequitos remain vital, passing on the old songs and rhythms from father to son—and, since Vivian Ramos joined the band, to daughter as well.

what to buy: If you come to *Vacunao* ♫♫♫ (Qbadisc, 1995, prod. Ned Sublette) expecting salsa, you've come to the wrong place. This is raw, propulsive Afro-Cuban folk music, driven by sharp drumming and gruff, earthy vocals; it's music stripped down to its essentials, but full of a primal power.

what to buy next: *Cantar Maravilloso* ♫♫♫♫ (Globestyle, 1990, prod. Ben Mandelson) is the album that introduced Los Muñequitos to the world, recorded after their performance at the Suave Cuban Festival in London in 1989. Another disc full of bedrock drumming and relentless rhythm.

the rest:
Congo Yambumba ♫♫♫♫ (Qbadisc, 1994)
Oyellos de Nuevo ♫♫♫♫ (Qbadisc, 1994)

influences:
◀◀ Vive Bien

▶▶ Most of the Latin and West African bands since

j. poet

Los Pleneros de la 21

Plena, bomba
Formed 1983, in Bronx, NY, USA. Based in Bronx, NY, USA.

Miguel Barcasnegras, lead vocals; Alberto Cepeda, panderetas, bombas, cuá, percussion, vocals; Johnny Kenton, vocals; José Lantigua, piano, keyboards; Juan José Gutiérrez-Rodríguez, leader, panderetas, bombas, cuá, percussion, vocals; Aris Martinez, vocals; Ray Martinez, bass; Héctor Matas, panderetas, maracas, güiro, vocals; Edgardo Miranda, cuatro, guitars; Jose Rivera, lead vocals, panderetas, bombas, cuá, percussion; Nellie Tanco, lead vocals; Sam Charles Tanco, lead vocals. (All members are from USA.)

The *plena* is one of the main folkloric rhythms of Puerto Rico, a highly charged, often political and quite satiric musical form halfway between calypso and Dominican merengue. The rhythm in its current form is about a hundred years old, and came from the working-class barrios of San Juan where it was also known as *el periódico cantando* ("the sung newspaper"). Plena is an urban form, based on the *bomba,* which developed directly from the slave community's memories of Africa. Plena also includes traces of Taino (Native American) culture, *jobaro* (mountain music), Spanish-Arabic rhythm, *mento* (a Jamaican roots music), and European pop. Plena drums, or *panderetas,* are played in sets of three (*seguidor, segundo, requinto*) and are tuned to the major chord of the melody.

The name Los Pleneros de la 21 ("The Plena Players from Bus Stop 21") refers to Santurce, the San Juan barrio that includes Stop 21. The group was created by Juan José Gutiérrez after coming to New York City, as a way of preserving his roots. Gutiérrez had been a drummer in Puerto Rico, where the music scene—be it classical, salsa, or folkloric—is much more integrated. In New York classical

Los Muñequitos de Matanzas

drummers don't sit in with salsa bands, so Gutiérrez tracked down some of the older traditional players in his neighborhood to form Los Pleneros. In addition to playing their supercharged music in clubs and concert halls, the band also does quite a bit of outreach in the city's public school system, teaching children about Puerto Rico's rich combination of cultures—Native American, African, European, and refugees from other Caribbean islands.

what's available: *Somos Boricuas—We Are Puerto Rican* 🎵🎵🎵🎵 (Henry Street, 1996, prod. Peter K. Siegel) is guaranteed to give you a blast of pure adrenaline. The group's four percussionist/drummers and five lead singers lay down a solid foundation for the improvisatory flights of *cuatro* (Puerto Rican folk guitar) player Edgardo Miranda and pianist José Lantigua. The lyrics (translations provided) are full of furious humor and serious social commentary.

influences:
◄◄ Marcial Reyes Arvelo

see also: *Eddie Palmieri*

j. poet

Los Super Seven
Tex-Mex, Tejano
Formed 1998, in Austin, TX, USA. Based in the western and southwestern USA.

David Hidalgo, vocals, guitar, drums, bass, percussion, requinto, hidalguera; Rick Trevino, vocals, guitar; Flaco Jimenez, vocals, accordion; Cesar Rosas, vocals, six-string bass, guitar, guitarron, jarana; Freddy Fender, vocals, acoustic bass; Ruben Ramos, vocals; Joe Ely, guitar, vocals. (All members are from USA.)

Inspired to record traditional Mexican music after a night of acoustic bliss at the 1997 South by Southwest festival with the likes of the Texas Tornados, Doug Sahm, Joe Ely, Rick Trevino, and Rosie Flores, talent manager Dan Goodman set out to assemble Tex-Mex devotees old and new. With original recordings by genre pioneers like Valerio Longoria and Lydia Mendoza in hand, Goodman and producer Steve Berlin brought living *Tejano* legends Freddy Fender, the Tornados' Flaco Jimenez, and Ruben Ramos together with Los Lobos bandmates David Hidalgo and Cesar Rosas, Texas bar-rocker Ely, country idol Rick Trevino, and guest players from north and south of the border to join in an exploration of seminal Mexican roots music.

The addition of the Lobos to the mix, Goodman hoped, would allow "the Super Seven" to transcend what easily could have been a Tex-Mex cliché. The pride of East Los Angeles, Los Lobos journeyed through the West Coast club scene with a mix of Mexican folk, electric blues, and accordion-laced *norteña* that won over punkers and roots-rockers alike. With 1988's *La Pistola y el Corazon*, a set of traditional Mexican folk tunes performed on authentic period instruments, and 1992's avant garde masterpiece *Kiko,* the "Wolves" have displayed an extraordinary range of influences—with an extraordinary range of audiences to match. Fender, whose surname "Huerta" was supplanted by one Freddy liked at the end of a fretboard, is to Tejano what B.B. King is to the blues—its best-known practitioner. Known on the U.S. charts for crossover hits like "Vaya con Dios," "Wasted Days and Wasted Nights," and "Before the Next Teardrop Falls," Fender and Jimenez—the multi-Grammy-winning accordion master whose playing has graced more than 40 albums including sessions with the Rolling Stones, Bob Dylan, and Linda Ronstadt—founded the Texas Tornados. Fellow Tornados Doug Sahm (Sir Douglas Quintet) and Lone Star rocker Augie Meyers play supporting roles on the debut disc *Los Super Seven*. Current country star Trevino, son of a Tejano player, and Texas favorite Ely provide ballast and some pop influences for this excursion in Mexican-American music.

The noble experiment *Los Super Seven* completed a brilliant but brief three-city tour (snapshot for posterity on two U.S. TV appearances) to launch its release. While no word has been forthcoming about the group's future, their American peers responded strongly to the effort, awarding *Los Super Seven* a 1999 Grammy for Best Mexican-American Music Performance. An additional track from the sessions, "Wildwood Flower," was expected to appear on an upcoming tribute to country/folk pioneers the Carter Family on Bob Dylan's label in late 1999. The Grammy win and its inevitable sales boost, coupled with a growing appreciation of Hispanic culture, could demand a "Super" return.

what's available: Like any journey, *Los Super Seven* ♪♪♪♪ (RCA, 1998, prod. Steve Berlin) has many fine moments. The ever-inventive Hidalgo inspires awe as an amazing vocalist and instrumentalist. Fender and Jimenez dazzle effortlessly; their collective and individual talents shine. Ramos sets the heart free with his own impassioned yet controlled vocal contributions. A proud and stellar effort.

worth searching for: Explore the worlds from which the Supers came. Los Lobos' *La Pistola y el Corazon* ♪♪♪ (Slash/Warner Bros., 1988, prod. Los Lobos) offers a peek into the band's soul, while *Just Another Band from East L.A.: A Collection* ♪♪♪♪♪

(Slash/Warner Bros., 1993, prod. various) is a broad brush that effectively portrays why they're one of America's most important units. *Texas Tornados* ♪♪♪♪ (Warner Bros., 1990, prod. Bill Haverson, Texas Tornados) won the group *their* Grammy for best Mexican-American performance.

influences:
◄◄ Lydia Mendoza, Valerio Longoria

see also: *Flaco Jimenez, Los Lobos, Texas Tornados*

Kevin Meyer

Los Tigres del Norte
Tejano, norteña
Formed 1969, in south TX, USA.

Jorge Hernandez; Raul Hernandez; Hernán Hernandez; Eduardo Lara; Oscar Lara.

Los Tigres choose particularly Mexican American subjects for their lively, often humorous, even cynical songs about modern-day working-class life along the Texas/Mexico border. *Hispanic* magazine's characterization of the Tigres as the inventors of "*Tejano* gangsta rap" is a bit overstated—the group has too much of a sense of humor for that comparison. The infectious sibling harmony and lively dance beat of their tunes often allow a more bittersweet commentary on the realities of life along the *frontera* than a straight-ahead ballad singer could get away with—and that accounts in part for the group's continuing popularity.

what's available: *30 Nortenas de Oro* ♪♪♪♪ (Fonovisa, 1998) is a definitive three-disc set that includes upbeat dance tunes, songs about the realities of working-class life, and pieces featuring the group's wry humor and deft use of sound effects (bells, telephones, autos, and the like). The only thing missing from this otherwise comprehensive collection is the liner notes. For such an ambitious and useful archive of music, it's a disappointment that the printed material barely includes a list of the 30 tracks and their songwriters.

influences:
◄◄ Mariachi Vargas

►► Mazz, Intocable, Los del Rio, Selena, Laura Canales

Kerry Dexter

Los Van Van
Songo
Formed December, 1969, in Havana, Cuba. Based in Havana, Cuba.

Juan Formell, director, bass, vocals; Cesar Pedroso, piano; Hugo Morejon, trombone, synthesizer; Alvaro Collado, trombone; Edmundo Pina, trombone, percussion; Angel Bonne, alto sax, vocals; Gerardo

Los Van Van

Miro, violin; Fernando Leyva, violin; Jesus Linares, violin; Orlando Canto, flute, maracas; Samuel Formell, drums, pailas; Jose "Changuito" Quintana, congas, tumbas; Manuel Labarrera, congas, tumbas; Julio Norona, guiro; Pedro Calvo, bongo, choruses; Mario Rivera, bongo, choruses. (All members are from Cuba.)

You can't funk with this: Los Van Van single-handedly changed the course of Cuban contemporary music history. Here's how it happened. . . . The legend of Los Van Van begins with the 1942 birth of Juan Formell in a Havana hospital. Somewhat of a guitar prodigy, Juan turned pro at the age of 16. His rising career as a bar-hopping troubadour was interrupted by his conscription into Fidel Castro's National Police Band. It was a blessing in disguise: as the Police Band mostly played state functions, Juan had to master all of the traditional Cuban songs and rhythms—mambo, bolero, rumba, son, danzon—very quickly. Ears wide open, the rookie would listen to the nightly R&B/rock/pop broadcasts emanating from Miami on the barracks short-wave. Back on the block, Formell gained more experience via gigs with the orchestras of Guillermo Rubalcaba, Peruchin, and Carlos Faxas. In 1967, he was hired to play bass in Elio Revé's Orquesta Revé. Encouraged by the leader, Formell soon rose to director/arranger by

virtue of his mutating the band's rumbling changui (country son rhythm) into the hot salsa zone by simply throwing electric guitars and bass into the mix. When Orchestra Revé's "El Changui '68" sparked a new dance craze, Formell became a star. In 1969 he formed Los Van Van. Formell had un gran idea: if he took a traditional charanga band—flute, violin, piano, güiro (scraper)—and bumrushed in the horns/electric-bass/drums/chorus constellation, bits of jazz-improv, call-and-response Afro-Cuban conga breakdown, and R&B do-it-fluid, and immersed the whole cipher in hot, dripping sweat—he could create a totally new music. He was right. Los Van Van's new songo sound not only turned Cuba's beat around, it became the root from which three generations of big bands have sprung. Los Van Van continues to rock the Cuban soul and ram dancefloors worldwide.

what to buy: Both *Los Van Van: La Colección Cubana* ♪♪♪♪ (Music Club, 1998) and *Dancing Wet* ♪♪♪♪ (World Pacific, 1993) compile tracks Los Van Van recorded for EGREM Records during their absolute peak period (mid-'80s to early '90s). Two hour-plus albums, no duplicate tracks, all killah/no fillah. Know why the revolution was songo-ized.

what to buy next: A crisp recording of a 1994 performance at Havana's Salón Rosado de La Tropical, *Lo Ultimo en Vivo* 𝄞𝄞𝄞𝄞 (QBadisc, 1995) is positively steamroller. Feel the molten *timba* (next-generation Cuban salsa) bubbling up in the middle of sweaty tracks like "Hierbero, Ven" and "Un Socio." *Best of Los Van Van* 𝄞𝄞𝄞 (Milan, 1997) is mostly drawn from the band's early-'90s output for EGREM. Cohesive but relatively tame.

influences:

◄ Orquesta Aragón, Beny Moré, Orquesta Revé

► NG La Banda, Jesús Alemañy & ¡Cubanismo!, David Calzado & La Charanga Habanera

see also: *Juan Carlos Formell*

Tom Terrell

Trevor Lucas

Folk, folk-rock

Born December 25, 1943, in Melbourne, Australia. Died February 4, 1989, in Epping, Australia.

Trevor Lucas had a deep, mellow voice that was featured to fine effect on several albums by Fairport Convention, but he made his greatest musical mark as a producer. He started out as a folk singer on the Melbourne club circuit before traveling to England, where he was prized for his ethnicity. He worked on two albums of traditional music with folklorist A.L. Lloyd, as well as his only solo album, *Overlander* (long out of print), before forming the aptly named Eclection with Mike Rosen, Georg Hultgren (later known as George Kajanus), Gerry Conway, and Kerrilee Male. He left that band in 1970 to join his girlfriend Sandy Denny in Fotheringay, a short-lived band that melded Fairport Convention–style English folk-rock with the North American roots-folk sound favored by Eclection. Fotheringay, featuring Lucas, Denny, Conway, Jerry Donahue, and Pat Donaldson, was a promising band that lasted scarcely a year. Lucas moved into production work and helped create Denny's finest album, *Sandy*. He married Denny in 1973, not long after joining Fairport Convention, the band she'd left three years before, as vocalist and rhythm guitarist. With Fairport, Lucas recorded *Nine, Rosie, Fairport Live Convention* (also known as *A Moveable Feast*), and *Rising for the Moon* before leaving the band. He produced his wife's last two solo albums. After her death, Lucas returned to Australia, where he went on to produce and work with a number of Australian bands, notably Redgum, the Bushwackers, and Goanna. He died of a heart attack, far too young, at 45.

what to buy: Lucas's fondness for the Band is much in evidence on *Fotheringay* 𝄞𝄞𝄞𝄞 (Island, 1970, prod. Joe Boyd), a fitting souvenir of a band with a very short life and a surfeit of tal-

ented members. Some of Sandy Denny's best-known songs are here, including "The Pond and the Stream" and "The Sea," but the album's greatest charms are in the songs led by Lucas, including Bob Dylan's "Too Much of Nothing" and "The Ballad of Ned Kelly," a Lucas composition often mistaken for a traditional Australian ballad.

worth searching for: *Rock On* 𝄞𝄞𝄞 (Carthage, 1972, prod. Trevor Lucas) by the Bunch was Lucas's first foray into production work. Prized among fans of Fairport Convention, it includes various members of the Fairport family (Lucas, Denny, Richard Thompson, Ashley Hutchings, etc.) covering classic rock 'n' roll songs. Lucas provides lead vocals on "Don't Be Cruel." The album can be found on vinyl, but don't hold your breath for a CD release. Credited to "Sandy Denny, Trevor Lucas & Friends," *The Attic Tracks 1972–84* 𝄞𝄞𝄞𝄞 (Raven, 1995, prod. various) includes an alternate take of "The Ballad of Ned Kelly" and Lucas's cover of Bob Dylan's "Forever Young." A portion of the proceeds from this album goes to Lucas's heirs.

influences:

◄ Bob Dylan, the Band, Sandy Denny, Ralph McTell, Gordon Lightfoot

► Redgum, Goanna, the Bushwackers

see also: *Sandy Denny, Fairport Convention, Ashley Hutchings, A.L. Lloyd, Richard Thompson*

Pamela Murray Winters

Luciano

Roots reggae

Born Jepther Washington McClymont, December 20, 1964, in Clarendon, Jamaica. Based in Kingston, Jamaica.

Luciano is being hailed as the savior of roots reggae. In 1994, with producer Fattis Burrell, he cut four of the strongest roots tunes to hit the market since the heyday of Bob Marley: "Forward to Africa," "Black Survivors," "One-Way Ticket" and "Jah Is Alive." These singles, along with other album tracks, were rushed out in the U.S. on a variety of small labels, leading to a worldwide deal with Island Records. Luciano grew up in a single-parent family with his mother and eight siblings. To help support the family he dropped out of high school, moved to Kingston, and worked at various odd jobs until he became an apprentice to an upholsterer. His early experience with a singing group composed of himself and his sister and brother-in-law went nowhere, and when he got a finger caught in a crosscut saw he gave up playing guitar. But music was always on his mind. In 1992 he recorded his first singles (as "Luciana") for Mau Mau Productions, and also worked with New Name Records' Castro Brown as well as Freddie McGregor before signing on with Burrell's Xterminator Productions. With the Xterminator crew—Sly and Robbie, Dean Frazier, and other session heavies—and Burrell's 1990's approach, Luciano clicked and began turning out the hits that have sparked a rebirth of interest in spiritual roots reggae, a welcome trend after decades of carbon-copy dancehall hits full of sex and gunplay.

what to buy: On *The Messenger* 🎵🎵🎵🎵 (Island, 1997, prod. Fattis Burrell) Burrell and Luciano are a perfect pair; Burrell produces slamming riddim tracks without all the blurps and buzzes of the dancehall, and Luciano's pure, straightforward tenor infuses each tune with soul and sufferation.

what to buy next: *One-Way Ticket* 🎵🎵🎵 (VP, 1995, prod. Fattis Burrell) contains the early singles that made Luciano a force to be reckoned with, produced by Burrell and featuring guests like Cocoa Tea, Charlie Chaplin, and Lady G. The set includes hits like "Raggamuffin" and "Turn Your Life Around."

the rest:
Moving Up 🎵🎵🎵 (RAS, 1993)
Where There Is Life 🎵🎵🎵🎵 (Island, 1996)

influences:
◀◀ Bob Marley, Garnett Silk, Dennis Brown, Burning Spear

see also: *Cocoa Tea, Sly & Robbie*

j. poet

Dónal Lunny

Celtic

Born in Ireland. Based in Ireland.

Guitar and bouzouki player Dónal Lunny has been called "the Quincy Jones of Irish music" for his multiple roles as musician, producer, organizer, presenter, and catalyst for high-quality musical collaborations. After beginning his career as the drummer in a high school rock band, Lunny discovered the guitar and got hooked on music in earnest. A couple of years ahead of him at school in Newbridge was a young man named Christy Moore, with whom Lunny teamed up to form a singing group, the Rakes of Kildare. The music they played, he says, was a pretty close copy of the Clancy Brothers, but they had the advantage of a nearby pub where real traditional music was played. Before long the idea of combining the ballad-group sound of singing and guitar with the traditional tunes he heard in the pub began to dawn on him. When he finished school, Lunny went to Dublin to study art. There he met up with new friends, some of whom shared his musical ideas. He played in a group called the Emmet Folk with Mick Moloney, who later joined the Johnstons. Lunny then ran a folk club with Andy Irvine, who had played with Sweeney's Men. All of these groups had one thing in common: the desire to blend the more accessible style of the ballad groups with the lyrical beauty of real traditional music. All of them were successful to an extent, but none fulfilled this dream as thoroughly as Lunny's next group, Planxty. Planxty grew out of the sessions for Christy Moore's 1972 LP, *Prosperous*. Moore was returning to Ireland after a stint on England's folk club circuit, and he wanted this album to be a celebration; he asked eight musical friends to come to Downing's Pub in Prosperous, the same pub where Lunny first experienced traditional music. There they arranged and recorded the LP. When it was done, Lunny, Moore, Irvine, and Liam O'Flynn, who had worked out many of the arrangements together, decided to form Planxty, a new kind of Irish band. At the time Lunny was supporting himself by making jewelry, but he quit this job to pursue his musical career with Planxty. In 1975 he left the band to join another group that never got off the ground. His career, however, bounced back nicely, in an outfit that was first known as Seachtar and then as 1691. After Lunny joined, they changed their name to the Bothy Band, and quickly gained a reputation as the most phenomenal group ever on the Irish folk scene. While Planxty had delivered sweet lyricism, the Bothy Band traded in pure power; the combination of driving flute, fiddle, and uilleann pipes accompanied by guitar, bouzouki, and keyboards left audiences absolutely stunned. Lunny toured with the Bothy Band and recorded four albums with them. When the Bothy Band broke up, Planxty took the opportunity to reunite, and several tours plus three more albums ensued. From the last version of Planxty, Lunny and Moore built Moving Hearts, an Irish traditional/rock fusion group. Moving Hearts also involved Declan Sinnott (later Mary Black's musical director), Declan Masterson, and Davy Spillane. Lunny remembers it as a time of powerful performances as well as a great learning experience, combining bass and drums with traditional music in new ways. Since Moving Hearts broke up in the early 1980s, Lunny has been more active as a producer, organizer, and presenter than as a musician. He has produced records by many of the top groups in Ireland and Scotland, including Altan, Capercaillie, and Sharon Shannon. He has served as musical director for many television series, including two documentary series about traditional and contemporary Irish music. He has in recent years put together a group and toured, while recording under his own name only sporadically. Lunny's name as a musician, compiler, or producer, however, virtually assures a high-quality album.

what's available: *Dónal Lunny* 🎵🎵🎵 (Gael-Linn, 1987, prod. Dónal Lunny) is really not a solo album, but a live ensemble record of Lunny's 1987 band. Lunny's collaborators include Arty McGlynn (guitar), Nollaig Casey (fiddle), Cormac Breatnach (flute), and Sean Og Potts (uilleann pipes). It's all great, high-energy music, expertly played and produced. There's only one problem: it's just 27 minutes long, and priced like a full album. If you're willing to pay, it's a fine set. If not, you're better off exploring Lunny's exemplary work as a band member and producer—or picking up the recent return to solo-billed recording, *Coolfin* 𝄞𝄞𝄞 (Emd/Blue Note, 1998), which continues in just as musically satisfying—and more chronologically acceptable—fashion.

influences:

◄◄ Christy Moore, Andy Irvine, Mick Moloney

►► Planxty, Bothy Band, Moving Hearts, Altan, Capercaillie, Sharon Shannon

see also: *Altan, Bothy Band, Shaun Davey, Paddy Glackin, Andy Irvine, Matt Molloy, Mick Moloney, Christy Moore, Moving Hearts, Liam O'Flynn, Sean Ó Riada, Patrick Street, Tommy Peoples, Planxty, Tommy Sands, Sharon Shannon, Sweeney's Men*

Steve Winick

Baaba Maal

Worldbeat, traditional and modern African folk, experimental pop
Born in Podor, Senegal. Based in Podor and Dakar, Senegal.

Baaba Maal has been a new sensation for over 15 years, and there's no end in sight. One of the most charismatic and adventurous performers in any genre, he has introduced many to world music with a sound that is unshakably indigenous in character while embracing a staggering range of other influences. The intricate rhythms and keening vocals of Maal's style may be an acquired taste for some Western ears, but it's acquired quickly and irreversibly, especially if it's first encountered at one of his not-infrequent North American concerts; kinetic, colorfully garbed events almost shamanic in their intensity. Maal's style is based around the crystalline notes of the *kora* (African harp-lute), the compelling rhythms of the human voice–like talking drum, and the rich reverberations of the *hodu* (an ancestor of the banjo)—not to mention deft and delicate guitar, Celtic pipes, Latin brass ensembles, and high-tech synths. The sounds of his homeland are mixed with those of the West in an infectious but never ingratiating way.

Maal has been crossing lines and winning converts all his life. Born into the Hapulaar ethnic minority (better known to English-speakers as the Fulani), his acceptance as a performer was by no means assured—and within his own people it was barely even allowed. Born outside the caste of *griots* (musical oral

historians who exalt great figures and events, and reflect on the weighty issues implicit in their stories), Maal's talents might have gone decisively unencouraged if not for support from his mother, who had also defied tradition as a musician. Maal's ambition came from her, and his voice itself came from his father, a fieldworker who called the Muslim faithful to prayer, and who can no doubt be heard echoing in Maal's inspirational, clarion-like vocals today. The broader world was taking note of Maal's gifts from early on, as reflected in musical scholarships first to the Senegalese capital, Dakar, and then to Paris. Between the two moves, Maal and Mansour Seck, his family's griot and his own best friend from childhood, went on a year-long odyssey to absorb the village music of Hapulaar people from Maal's birthplace in northern Senegal, to southern Mauritania, and beyond to Mali. In France, Maal and Seck entertained the immigrant Hapulaar community and booked various small recording studios to cut the tracks that would become the classic *Djam Leelii* album. Upon returning to Senegal they formed the band Daande Lenol ("Voice of the People") and built on that album's phenomenal success.

With determination and sincerity, Maal would then continue an unbroken upsurge in popularity, critical acclaim, and cultural significance—a new kind of griot who extols not just the glories of the past but the possibilities of the future. An emissary for the culture of his home region Fouta Toro (where the world-traveling Maal still resides), he is also a ceaseless advocate of African and global unity and a vocal supporter of women and youth, making him that rare artist who has not just an audience, but a constituency. With a higher international profile than ever and a new label of his own (Yoff) to promote other Senegalese artists and become the kind of benefactor he sings about, Maal is a bona fide giant of 21st century music—a fact for which we already have ample recorded evidence today.

what to buy: Restlessly creative, Maal is a different artist with each release, so you can take your pick and you can't go wrong. *Djam Leelii: The Adventurers* 𝄞𝄞𝄞𝄞 (Palm Pictures, 1998, prod. Baaba Maal, Mansour Seck) is the long-awaited reissue of what is perhaps Maal's most-loved work, a haunting session recorded in Paris with Mansour Seck (who shares billing) in 1984, which made the pair transcontinental stars upon their debut. Stylistically, this unforgettable evocation of Maal and Seck's homeland is resolutely traditional, although sonically, electric if not electronic instruments have always been part of the plan. Distinguished with the subtitle *The Adventurers* to denote the addition of three essential contemporaneous bonus tracks to the original version, this is a bolt to the brain cells and a balm to the blood pressure, a warm and rootsy soundscape that feels like a homecoming no matter how unfamiliar you may be with its style. The best artists are creative gamblers who attain a certain level of mastery and then venture into a new state of uncertainty. Before Maal embarked on the creative gamble of a rapidly accelerated dialogue with Western forms, *Baayo (The Orphan)* ♪♪♪♪ (Mango, 1991, prod. Baaba Maal) was just such a plateau—the pinnacle of his mostly acoustic, strictly folkloric phase. Reflective in tone but vigorous in delivery, this album offers one joy after another, from the striking asymmetrical guitar harmonies on the title track, to the stunning asymmetrical *a cappella* vocal ones on "Diahowo," to the mesmerizing Malian tinge of "Mariama" and "Yero Mama" and beyond. With a remarkable freshness to the arrangements and confidence in the vocals, you'll need a 12-step program to stop listening to this one. *Lam Toro (King of Toro)* ♪♪♪♪ (Mango, 1993, prod. Baaba Maal, Simon Booth, Eric Clermontet) was Maal's first crack at the international market on its own terms as well as his own, and the experiment paid off in immediate worldwide stardom without impoverishing his African core. It's easy to see why—a blast of optimism and energy, this album speaks in a musical language that everyone can understand and no one could resist. The indestructible beat of Fouta Toro comes through loud and clear, and what Westernizations there are, are sparing, well-selected, and dynamic. (Astute ears will not be surprised by the presence of Joe Galdo, an early Angélique Kidjo producer, among the credits for many of the songs.) The album is brilliantly sequenced between moving laments like "Daniibe" and dead-waking celebrations like "Toro" and "Olele"; ominous dramas like "Daande Lenol" and pastoral ballads like "Sy Sawande." Maal is in astoundingly joyous, booming good voice throughout. The decision to bookend the set with two mixes of the somewhat pointless "Hamady Bogle/Hamady Boiro" (in which, at record-label suggestion, Maal's vocal track is overpowered by a B-level reggae toaster) makes it easy to avoid both without even touching the program button. On the much-admired *Firin' in Fouta* ♪♪♪♪♪ (Mango, 1994, prod. Simon Emmerson) Maal's music explodes into several continents' worth of new stylistic landscapes, while quite literally maintaining ties to the homeland with field-recorded vignettes of Senegalese village life woven through the mix. On the feminist anthem "African Woman" Maal and band convincingly evoke the Latin sounds that are beloved throughout West Africa as the New World's rhythmic cousin to the mother continent's culture—and as confirmation of the influence and indomitability of the African voice. On the brooding yet sultry "Sama Duniya" Maal beats moody European trance-pop at its own game. A global African style summit is staged in "Salimoun," a jubilantly jazzy, hip-hop-driven and kora-sweetened song of praise to the mother Maal reveres. The epically orchestral "Tiedo" ends the set on the last of many high points. The album's commercial production touches occasionally seem to get the upper hand, but what's a gamble without something being risked? *Nomad Soul* ♪♪♪♪ (Palm Pic-

tures, 1998, prod. various) is perhaps Maal's most ambitious project yet—nearly 70 minutes of stylistic sojourning that befits the title. "Souka Nayo (I Will Follow You)" is a landmark in the already-burgeoning Afro Celt genre and a prime example of Maal's uniquely transcendental pop, in which the hits are not just upbeat but uplifting. The solo-kora concert fave "Cherie" is given a dynamic Latin/rap/choral makeover, and '70s retro reaches its peak with the almost mystically groovy "Douwayra." Meanwhile, the dream-like "Guelel" achieves an effect similar to *Djam Leelii,* albeit through far-removed electronic means. Some of the most arresting moments in Maal's career have been provided by his near–*a cappella* readings, and the sparsely accompanied Maal/Brian Eno/Howie B/Jon Hassell improv "Lam Lam," which closes the album, is no exception. Maal's concerts are hard-core organic jams that burn away his music's studio sheen to the raw essence of its roots, and *Live at the Royal Festival Hall* ♪♪♪♪ (Palm Pictures, 1999, prod. Trevor Wyatt) presents enthralling documentation. The phenomenal voice you hear on those studio recordings is proven here to be the real thing, and the band is as tight in musicianship as it is sprawling in number. This disc's version of "African Woman" will make you forget all about the original—no mean feat—with the intensity and authenticity of its Latin chops and the audacity of its melodious, live-electronica denouement. Only musical masters can navigate from a workout like that track to a laid-back stretch like "Koni," and Maal, Daande Lenol, and guest-soloist Ernest Ranglin (the legendary guitarist and ska innovator) are up to it. The latter song's stunning delicacy, complete with nutritious solos by Ranglin and bassist El Hadji Niang, gives way to a radical—and priceless—reworking of "Douwayra," metamorphosized from its techno-dance origins to a rhythmically complex showcase for the percussionists and hodu soloist Barou Sall that's just as compelling. *Live* is marketed as an EP, but at some 42 minutes it's only not a full-fledged album by CD-era standards, and by any measure is an essential purchase.

what to buy next: "Souka Nayo" is an instant classic, but it's up to you to decide whether you need to buy it six times. If so, you get your chance on the maxi-single *Souka Nayo (I Will Follow You)* ♪♪♪ (Palm Pictures, 1998, prod. various), which includes five remixes of varying essentiality. Maal's such a stylistic shape-shifter to begin with that the laboratory treatment is kinda redundant; the main attraction of this release is the insight into the bare bones of his process offered by occasional unadorned vocal tracks that either didn't appear or competed with thick arrangements in the original.

worth searching for: Like many world-music artists, Maal's career has more than one history—different releases aimed at the homeland and international markets, as well as specific continents abroad, can show a fascinatingly divergent stylistic progression than the one traced in the artist's major-label canon. Maal's African and European releases offer just such fascination; a particularly good one, *Wango* ♪♪♪♪ (Syllart, 1985/Stern's, 1988, prod. Ibrahima Sylla), is a relaxed, jubilant, live-in-the-studio-sounding set that will come as a surprise but not a disappointment to listeners familiar with the grandeur and gravity of his international recordings. Other import-onlys that reward a search are *Taara* (Syllart/Melodie, 1987), *Tono* (Studio 2000-Dakar, 1994), *Sunagal* (Studio 2000-Dakar, 1995), and *Nouvelle Generation* (Studio 2000-Dakar, 1991). Casting his eyes on another new tradition, Maal's DVD *Live at the Royal Festival Hall*—the entire concert from which the EP of same name was excerpted—presents one of the first live shows documented with this medium in mind. Until you can see him in the flesh, this does a good job of catching his spirit. On the George Gershwin centennial tribute/AIDS benefit disc *Red Hot + Rhapsody* ♪♪♪♪ (Antilles/Verve, 1998, prod. various), Maal joins the many generations of great black artists who've made historic music out of Gershwin's fantasy of black life, *Porgy and Bess*, with an out-of-this-world rendition of "Bess, You Is My Woman Now." On Ernest Ranglin's *In Search of the Lost Riddim* ♪♪♪♪ (Palm Pictures, 1998, prod. Ira Coleman, Ernest Ranglin, Bart Fermie) Maal lends vocals to "Minuit" and "Haayo," two of his compositions that are otherwise unavailable Stateside, while Ranglin jazzes up "Cherie" and various members of Daande Lenol beautify the soundscape throughout the album. Maal makes a superhuman vocal contribution to Daande Lenol kora player Kaouding Cissoko's solo debut, *Kora Revolution* ♪♪♪♪ (Palm Pictures/Yoff, 1999, prod. Ira Coleman), a landmark recording for Maal's Yoff label that also features the Next Voice of World Music, 15-year-old phenomenon Cisse Diamba Kanoute (who made her debut on the Ranglin album). Maal's other guest appearances are numerous, and can be tracked through the web discography "Africa" at http://biochem. chem.nagoya-u.ac.jp/~endo/africa.html; log on and have fun trying to figure out where he finds the 25th hour in a day!

influences:

⏮ Mansour Seck, Omar Tall, Ahmadou Bamba, Orchestra Baobob, Youssou N'Dour

⏭ Afro Celt Sound System, every succeeding generation of Senegalese musicians

see also: *Afro Celt Sound System, Ernest Ranglin, Mansour Seck, Spearhead, Tarika*

Adam McGovern

Mabsant

See: Robin Huw Bowen

Sipho Mabuse /Harare

Afropop, worldbeat

Born c. 1945, in Soweto, South Africa. Based in Johannesburg, South Africa.

Mabuse—a singer, composer, producer, drummer, and keyboard player—has been making strong, Afrocentric crossover music for more than 30 years. With his 1984 album for South Africa's Gallo label, *Burn Out,* he achieved superstar status in his homeland, becoming one of the first African musicians to create international pop that still retained a deep connection to the *kwela, mbaqanga,* and African soul music he grew up on. Mabuse was born in Soweto, one of South Africa's poorest yet most culturally vital townships. He was musically omnivorous from an early age, soaking up the sounds of the Beatles and Stones along with that of local groups like the Skylarks and Manhattan Brothers, both of which featured the young Miriam Makeba. Mabuse started out as a drummer, and by high school was leading his own band, the Beaters, through sets that included tunes by the Beatles and other Anglo/American rockers. When soul music hit South Africa, Mabuse added that element to his band and began writing original tunes that combined rock, soul, and South African music. The Beaters eventually recorded an album called *Soul a Go Go,* but Mabuse wasn't satisfied with it and moved the band to Harare, in Zimbabwe (then Rhodesia). In Rhodesia, Mabuse became more serious about his Afropop vision. He changed the band's name to Harare, and although the music was still heavily influenced by American funk, tunes like "It Takes Time" and "Party" showed a growing interest in Pan-African rhythms. Harare cut two well-received albums before breaking up in 1984.

After Harare, Mabuse returned to school to study law, but music called him back, this time as a solo artist/producer. His first single, "Rise," fused African music with international club beats and became a hit. This led to his first album under his own name, *Burn Out,* which spawned two monster singles, the title track and "Jive Soweto," which sounds remarkably like the music Paul Simon would be making on *Graceland* soon after. "Burn Out" was so successful that CBS licensed the track abroad (along with "Jive Soweto" and "Zanzibar") and rushed out an EP, hoping to make the tune an international club hit. While the *Burn Out* EP didn't become the success the label had hoped for, it did pave the way for *Sipho Mabuse,* one of the first genuine Afropop albums. Unluckily, *Sipho Mabuse* came out almost a year after Simon's *Graceland* and went largely unnoticed despite its pumping rhythms and Mabuse's excellent songwriting and production skills. By the time *Chant of the Marching* came out in 1989, South African music was "dead" as far as the international press was concerned, and the album

Baaba Maal

sank without a trace, though it did respectable business back home. Mabuse continues to record and produce other artists but hasn't had an international release in over a decade.

what to buy: *Sipho Mabuse* ✍✍✍✍ (Virgin, 1987, prod. Sipho Mabuse) is an uneven album, but the high points are as good as anything on *Graceland*. Mabuse's smooth international blend of funk, pop, kwela, and mbaqanga still sounds fresh today, and his vocals have a gritty authority that Simon lacks.

what to buy next: *Chant of the Marching* ✍✍✍✍ (Virgin, 1989, prod. Nick Patrick) could have been an international hit for Mabuse, if anyone had given it one-tenth the airplay Simon got. The strong tunes, slick production, and masterful playing mark it as one of the lost masterpieces of South African music.

worth searching for: Mabuse and Harare have many African recordings that never saw international release but may be available from import services or African specialty shops. *Best of Sipho Mabuse* ✍✍✍✍ (Gallo, South Africa) includes the big hits from the late 1980s. Vinyl junkies may be able to track down some of his LPs; try *Harare* ✍✍✍ (A&M, 1981) and the EP *Burn Up* ✍✍✍✍ (Columbia, 1985).

influences:

◀◀ Miriam Makeba, Hugh Masekela, Soul Brothers, Stimela

▶▶ Yvonne Chaka Chaka, Splash, Brenda Fassi

j. poet

Ewan MacColl

English and Scottish folk

Born Jimmy Miller, 1915, in Auchterarder, Perthshire, Scotland. Died October 22, 1989.

Ewan MacColl was one of the main forces behind the folk revival that swept Britain in the 1950s and '60s. Born Jimmy Miller in Scotland, he was brought up in Salford, greater Manchester. At the age of 15 he changed his name to Ewan MacColl, memorializing a little-known 19th-century Lallans poet. He became a poet himself, as well as a laborer, working at various menial jobs while indulging in his first love, the theater. In 1931 he founded a street theater company called the Red Megaphones, and in 1934 he formed the influential Theatre in Action. MacColl's activities in this field continued through the postwar period. In 1945 he wrote his first full-length play and was ultimately hailed by George Bernard Shaw as "the only significant post-war British dramatist."

However, he was also becoming more and more interested in folk music. Both of his parents sang traditional Scottish songs, exposing him to the form at an early age. By the time of his adulthood, he had long collected and sung traditional material, and the success of jazz clubs in the 1950s gave him a new venue

for the songs he loved. He began to appear at them, a practice that accelerated during the skiffle craze of 1956–57. Because of the skiffle bands' reliance on American material, MacColl felt there was not enough native British music being sung among the younger generation. He began to advocate a policy whereby English singers would sing English songs, Scottish singers would sing Scottish songs, and so forth. MacColl found many ways to spread his ideas about folk song during the 1950s. In 1953 he began a venue—the Ballads and Blues Club—that became the model for the English folk-club phenomenon. He later founded the Singer's Club, which was organized on socialist principles, and the Critics Group, a collection of young singers who met regularly to discuss folk songs and who also performed and recorded. This group nurtured many important performers of the younger generation, including Sandra Kerr, John Faulkner, Frankie Armstrong, and Brian Pearson. During the same period, MacColl created a series of radio programs that utilized folk songs, under the rubric *The Radio Ballads*. These programs and others frequently teamed him up with singers including A.L. Lloyd. They were a great success and made MacColl relatively famous despite the same socialist politics that had harmed Lloyd's radio career. For these programs, he began to write songs, becoming accomplished at that trade as well. Throughout the 1960s, '70s, and '80s, MacColl was an influential force. He provided encouragement and advice to all manner of performers, from folk-rock stars like Maddy Prior, whose band Steeleye Span performed many songs she learned from MacColl, to Elvis Costello, whose first public appearance was a floor spot at a Ewan MacColl concert. MacColl continued to perform and record, releasing over 150 albums in his lifetime. He provided both traditional songs and ones of his own to generations of folk performers, from the Johnstons and the Dubliners in the '60s to the Pogues in the '80s. In the '70s, "The First Time Ever I Saw Your Face," which MacColl wrote for his third wife and musical partner Peggy Seeger, was recorded by Elvis Presley and also by Roberta Flack. Flack's version topped the U.S. pop charts and won a 1972 Grammy. MacColl continued to perform until shortly before his death on October 22, 1989.

what to buy: *The Real MacColl* ✍✍✍✍ (Topic, 1993, prod. Tony Engle) was compiled from five original albums recorded for Topic between 1958 and 1966. The songs it presents reflect MacColl's varied relationships with song traditions. Selections include older Child ballads, Jacobite ballads, modern songs of industrial disasters, and original MacColl compositions. Notable tracks include a detailed version of "Van Dieman's Land," an excellent "Minorie" (a.k.a. "The Two Sisters"), and a wonderful take on Hamish Henderson's World War II song "Farewell to Sicily." MacColl's wife, Peggy Seeger, accompanies him on many numbers, playing guitar and five-string banjo. The accompaniments are generally subtle, tasteful, and unobtrusive, and many of the most effective tracks—like the devastating "Bramble Briar"—are sung unaccompanied in MacColl's supple and unique voice. Of MacColl's original songs, the best-known included on *The Real MacColl* is "Dirty Old Town," his ode to Salford, which has been covered by a whole stable of folk artists including the Pogues. The traditional material includes the original recordings from which Steeleye Span learned "Rogues in a Nation," "Sheepcrook and Black Dog," and "Come Ye o'er Frae France," testifying to MacColl's influence on the generation that followed him.

what to buy next: *Black and White* ₰₰₰₰ (Green Linnet, 1991, prod. Neill MacColl, Calum MacColl) is a CD compiled by Mac-Coll's family from privately owned studio and live tapes. It gathers together a good number of MacColl's favorite traditional songs, such as the "Highland Muster Roll," which he used at the beginning of concerts to test the hall's acoustics and his own voice. It also features many of his best-known originals, including "Dirty Old Town," "The First Time Ever I Saw Your Face," "The Ballad of Accounting," "The Shoals of Herring," and "Kilroy Was Here." One of his first songs, "The Manchester Rambler," is given a particularly spirited arrangement by MacColl and many of his friends and family, including his daughter, pop star Kirsty MacColl. This is an excellent and unusual album— qualities matched by *Ewan MacColl and Peggy Seeger: Folk on Two* ₰₰₰₰ (Cooking Vinyl, 1996, prod. Geoffrey Hewitt). The latter is not primarily an album of MacColl's singing. Instead, it is better seen as an album about MacColl, featuring some vocals by him and many more by his friends and disciples. The first six tracks come from a 1986 concert in honor of MacColl's 70th birthday. Singers include Ian Campbell, Belle Stewart, Ray Fisher, Peggy Seeger, and MacColl himself, who sings only one of these tracks. The other five songs are from another concert honoring MacColl, this one from 1987. Here, Seeger sings two songs and MacColl three. "Joy of Living," the closing number, is a loving farewell to the world from a man nearing the end of his life; the fact that MacColl died only a few years later makes it a poignant moment. The album concludes with a fascinating 10-minute interview in which MacColl speaks about the origins of the British folk revival. *Classic Scots Ballads* ₰₰₰₰ (Tradition, 1997, prod. Anton Glovsky), a reissue of a 1959 LP recorded by MacColl and Seeger, contains another fine selection of songs from the duo; MacColl sings and Seeger provides vocal harmonies and guitar, banjo, concertina, and Appalachian dulcimer backup. This album focuses exclusively on traditional songs, and on ones sung in the Lowland Scots tongue; selections include "Aikendrum," "The Maid Gaed Tae the Mill," "Hughie Graeme," and "I Loved a Lass." The arrangements are tasteful and low-key, and allow MacColl's expressive voice as much freedom as it needs. Although it is short, this CD has the advantage of state-of-the-art sonic restoration, which makes it sound bet-

west african drumming and the soul of rock 'n' roll

Think rock 'n' roll is the devil's music? Blame it on the drums. The roots of rock can be traced all the way back to the throbbing tribal percussion of the Yoruba and Dahomean peoples, whose traditions stretched several hundred miles along the West African coast, from western Nigeria into Benin and Togo. As the natives of this region were sold into slavery, their traditions spread throughout the "new" world, with Haitian *Vodou*, Brazilian *Candomblé*, Cuban *Santería*, and Trinidadian *Shango* all originating from the same sources and all connected via the transatlantic slave trade. Though each of these religions developed its own instruments and styles of rhythmic syncopation, all had in common the ritualistic use of hypnotic percussion as the basis for transcendental (and often trance-inducing) songs of praise. As frightened slave-owners in the Americas began to recognize the role of the drums in non-Christian forms of worship and illicit means of communication (after all, they don't call it the "talking drum" for nothing!), the slaves were largely forced to abandon both their religious practices and the use of the drums. But even as they developed a totally new form of praise-song—the spiritual—the enslaved Africans found ingenious ways to hold on to their ancient musical traditions, with the swing of an ax or a hammer done in time to the singing to keep the ever-important beat. With the abolition of slavery, African Americans soon added instruments like the guitar to turn the spiritual into the blues, the blues into jazz, then R&B, then rock 'n' roll, and later hip-hop. Now, several hundred years after its importation, still the beat goes on.

see also: The Kora and West African Griot (sidebar), the Talking Drum (sidebar)

Bret Love

ter than most of the duo's reissues. *The Jacobite Rebellions* ♪♪♪ (1962) was one of the albums from which *The Real MacColl* was compiled; it has also been reissued as a stand-alone CD, and features many stirring performances not found on *The Real MacColl*. Most of the well-known Jacobite ballads appear on this album—unsurprisingly; they are well known partly because they appeared on this album. MacColl's rich voice was one of the revival's defining sounds, and his sense of drama informs such songs as "Come Ye o'er Frae France" and "Donald MacGillivray." The deep loss and unfulfilled longing of much of the form is expressed beautifully here, as on "Wae's Me for Prince Charlie" and "Bonnie Moorhen." MacColl is, in customary fashion, accompanied by Seeger on guitar and banjo and also sings many songs unaccompanied. *Bothy Ballads of Scotland* ♪♪♪ , on the other hand, is an entirely unaccompanied affair. It contains songs of the rural laborers of the 19th century, which were sung in the "bothy" or farm barracks. Most of the songs are therefore about farm life, farm work, and love among the fields. Many of them show hired laborers in direct conflict or at least disagreements with their employers, a frequent theme of the genre. Others treat the classic themes of folk song in general: unrequited love, premature death, good whiskey, and bawdy fun. MacColl is in fine voice on this disc, which suffers only from being relatively short and rather lo-fi.

the rest:
(With Peggy Seeger) *Lover's Garland* ♪♪♪ (Pye, 1962)
(With Peggy Seeger) *At the Present Moment* ♪♪♪ (Rounder, 1973)
Songs of Robert Burns ♪♪♪ (Ossian, 1996)
Scottish Traditional Songs ♪♪♪ (Ossian, 1996)
Traditional Songs and Ballads of Scotland ♪♪♪ (Ossian, 1996)

worth searching for: MacColl made more than 150 LPs, so used record bins are bound to have some of his material. One set that was particularly important was the nine-LP *The English and Scottish Popular Ballads* (Riverside, 1956, prod. Kenneth Goldstein), which was produced and annotated by folklorist Kenneth S. Goldstein and featured both MacColl and A.L. Lloyd. MacColl is also the main performer on about 20 Folkways albums, all of which are available as custom cassettes or CDs from Smithsonian Folkways Records at the Smithsonian Institution.

influences:
◀ Betsy Miller, Jeannie Robertson, Belle Stewart

▶▶ Dolores Keane, John Faulkner, Sandra Kerr, Brian Pearson, Frankie Armstrong, Mick Moloney, the Johnstons, the Dubliners, the Clancy Brothers, Steeleye Span, Archie Fisher, Ray Fisher, Cilla Fisher, the Tannahill Weavers, Dick Gaughan

see also: *Frankie Armstrong, Ian Campbell Folk Group, John Faulkner, A.L. Lloyd, Steeleye Span*

Steve Winick

Laurel MacDonald
Avant-garde multiculturalism
Born in Halifax, Nova Scotia, Canada. Based in Toronto, Ontario, Canada.

A distinctive vocalist/composer whose tremendous range and experimental approach invite stylistic comparisons to Laurie Anderson and former Dead Can Dance chanteuse Lisa Gerrard, this Nova Scotia native is perhaps best-known for co-producing *Suas e!,* the Wicklow Records debut of singer/songwriter Mary Jane Lamond, who is not only MacDonald's label-mate but also her cousin. However, even before MacDonald's own Wicklow debut, *Chroma,* was released in early 1999, she was a favorite on the Canadian music scene. Soon after her first album, 1995's *Kiss Closed My Eyes,* gained widespread critical acclaim, her songs found their way onto the *Here & Now: A Celebration of Canadian Music* anthology, British journalist David Toop's *Crooning on Venus* compilation, and the soundtrack to the film *The Hanging Garden.* Her music has also been incorporated into a number of ballet and modern dance performances in Canada, New York, and Paris, and the singer's inroads in the Lower 48 proceeded with a recent profile on the Bravo! TV network.

what's available: *Chroma* ♪♪♪ (Wicklow, 1999, prod. Philip Strong), MacDonald's first U.S. release, is a compelling mixture of haunting lullabies, hypnotic chanting, and existential excursions into avant-garde surrealism. At times a little too reminiscent of Laurie Anderson's alien artistry, MacDonald occasionally seems to be trying too hard, her eclectic mannerisms and stylistic eccentricities coming off as contrived rather than improvised. But for the most part, the album is filled with ethereal, lushly layered soundscapes that perfectly match her intensely evocative vocal style. From the medieval influences of "Agnus Dei" to the throbbing tribal percussion of "Òran na h-Eala" to the genteel Irish balladry of "Seek Ye the Lambs," MacDonald's aural experiments are always intriguing, even when they don't quite work. *Wingspan* ♪♪♪ (Wicklow, 1999, prod. various) is a six-song EP featuring versions of MacDonald's single "A Wing and a Prayer" remixed by techno luminaries including Bill Laswell, Transglobal Underground, and Canadian groove collective Mo Funk.

worth searching for: MacDonald's first album, *Kiss Closed My Eyes,* was a Canadian release praised as "densely textured and exquisitely woven" by *Billboard,* so you may still be able to track it down in new-age record stores here in the U.S.

influences:
◀ Laurie Anderson, Lisa Gerrard, Kate Bush, Steve Reich, Celtic folk

▶▶ Mary Jane Lamond

see also: *Mary Jane Lamond*

Bret Love

Machito

Cuban jazz

Born Frank Grillo, February 16, 1915, in Havana, Cuba. Died April 15, 1984, in London, England.

In 1937 Machito arrived in New York City, where he sang and played with Las Estrellas Habaneras, Noro Morales, Xavier Cugat, and Orquesta Siboney. By 1940 he had formed his own band, Machito's Afro-Cubans, and when his brother-in-law, Mario Bauzá, joined the group as musical director, the foundation for one of the greatest Latin bands of all time was laid. Bauzá worked with arrangers like A.K. Salim, John Bartee, and Rene Hernandez to blend Cuban percussion and rhythms with jazz for a sound that revolutionized Latin music. One of Machito's young percussion players from this time, Tito Puente, later took these innovations and polished them still further, but he was probably the only "name" musician to develop from the early 1940s-era bands. Most of the players were originally hired as ensemble members, not spectacular soloists, and the emphasis was on the aggregate, not the individual. The music of Machito's band became a major influence on Stan Kenton and Dizzy Gillespie, while other jazz players like Charlie Parker, Johnny Griffin, Herbie Mann, and Cannonball Adderley either played or recorded with Machito at one point in their careers. During the 1950s Machito's popularity started to slide with the general public, although he continued to make albums through the early '80s.

what to buy: *Mucho Macho Machito* 🎵🎵🎵🎵 (Pablo, 1991, prod. various) is a fine collection of Machito's material from the cusp of the '50s with one of his best bands. The sound has been cleaned up considerably, and songs like "Babarabatiri" and "Asia Minor" cook from beginning to end. Machito is aided by his stalwart trio of arrangers (Bauzá, Salim, and Hernandez) and the addition of jazz players Doc Cheatham, Joe Newman, and Adderley in producing *Kenya* 🎵🎵🎵🎵 (Palladium), some of the finest playing ever released under Machito's name. Their cover of "Tin Tin Deo" is superb, and the underrated Salim's charts for "Oyeme" and "Conversation" are a real treat. The percussion work of Jose Mangual, Candido, and "Patato" Valdes follows the tradition laid down by Chano Pozo and precedes efforts by Ray Barretto and Giovanni Hidalgo, among others. This album has been released under other names, including *Latin Soul Plus Jazz* on Tico and, most recently, *Afro Cuban Jazz* on La Mejor Musica. The latter album is a mid-price release that changes the sequencing, gets the writing credits wrong, eliminates any liner notes, deletes "Tururato," and adds four tunes from other sessions, including Chico O'Farril's "Mambo Parts 1 & 2."

what to buy next: Other than not having any liner notes or personnel listings, *This Is Machito and His Afro-Cubans* 🎵🎵🎵🎵 (Polydor, 1978, prod. various) is a fine collection of Machito's more jazz-oriented recordings. "Christopher Columbus" is a classic Chuck Berry riff that benefits from the Cubop treatment, while mambo cuts like "Sentimental Mambo," "Relax and Mambo," and the fun if slightly cheesy "Dragnet Mambo" show why Machito's band was such a hit at legendary dance halls like New York's Palladium.

the rest:
1983 Grammy Award Winner 🎵🎵🎵 (Impulse!, 1983)
Cubop City (1949–50) 🎵🎵🎵 (Tumbao Cuban Classics, 1992)
Tremendo Cuban (1949–52) 🎵🎵🎵 (Tumbao Cuban Classics, 1992)

influences:
◀◀ Arsenio Rodriguez

▶▶ Dizzy Gillespie, Stan Kenton, Herbie Mann, Tito Puente

see also: *Ray Barretto, Mario Bauzá, Patato, Tito Puente*

Garaud MacTaggart

Ashley MacIsaac

Celtic/Canadian fiddle

Born February 24, 1975, in Creignish, Cape Breton, Nova Scotia, Canada. Based in Nova Scotia, Canada.

Young Ashley MacIsaac's success in the music industry shouldn't come as much of a surprise. The fiddle phenomenon has been exposed to music all his life; his father, another fiddler, would play around the house, and MacIsaac himself got a rather early start, learning to stepdance at age five and beginning formal fiddle instruction at age nine. A fast learner and then some, he began touring Canada as well as U.S. cities like Detroit and Boston by the time he was 13 and has filled venues ranging from local Cape Breton sites to New York's Carnegie Hall. Does the term "prodigy" come to mind? MacIsaac has won numerous honors, including Best Live Act at the 1995 East Coast Music Awards and both Best New Solo Artist and Best Roots and Traditional Album/Solo at the 1996 Juno Awards. He was the subject of a major-label feeding frenzy while still in his teens. A&M won out.

what to buy: MacIsaac's major-label debut megahit, *Hi How Are You Today?* 🎵🎵🎵🎵 (A&M, 1995, prod. Michael Phillip Wojewoda, Pete Prilesnik), reflects both his Celtic/Canadian heritage and his youthful exuberance in its driving, aggressive instrumentation. It is a perfect, if unlikely, combination of ancient Celtic folk songs with punk-rock arrangements and attitude.

the rest:
Fine Thank You Very Much 🎵🎵🎵🎵 (Unisphere, 1998)

worth searching for: MacIsaac's fiery fiddle does a funky slow burn on "Bòg a'Lochain" from Mary Jane Lamond's *Suas e!* 🎵🎵🎵🎵🎵

(A&M, 1997/Wicklow, 1998, prod. Philip Strong, Laurel MacDonald), the breakout album from the vocalist who shared MacIsaac's acclaim on *Hi How Are You Today?*'s "Sleepy Maggie." The fiddler shows traditional chops as riveting as his experimental ones on "My Home/The Contradiction/Julia Delaney" from the Chieftains' all-star Canadian Celtic revue *Fire in the Kitchen* ♪♪♪♪ (BMG Classics, 1998, prod. Paddy Moloney). MacIsaac's Canadian releases, *Close to the Floor* (Unisphere, 1992) and *A Cape Breton Christmas* (1993), are available as imports.

influences:

◀◀ The Chieftains, the Clash, Charlie Daniels

▶▶ Leahy

see also: *Mary Jane Lamond*

                                              Christopher Scanlon

Talitha MacKenzie

Celtic, Scottish, worldbeat
Born April 3, 1956, in Oceanside, NY, USA. Based in Edinburgh, Scotland.

Talitha MacKenzie first heard traditional Gaelic singing at the age of seven and has been fascinated by it ever since. In order to perform it herself, MacKenzie studied field recordings and a "Teach Yourself Gaelic" textbook. She was interested in other cultures as well and studied French, Russian, Spanish, German, and Italian in school and still more languages on her own. But her future career path became clear during her college years. She started out as a Russian major at Connecticut College, but then switched gears and actually graduated from the New England Conservatory of Music with a degree in Music History/Ethnomusicology. During the 1970s MacKenzie was involved with various dance troupes (Renaissance, Baroque, Balkan, Celtic) and also worked as a "shantyman" and deckhand on "tall ships" where she developed an appreciation for heavily rhythmic work-related music. In the early and mid-1980s MacKenzie recorded an album with the Boston-based Irish band St. James Gate and then made her solo debut, *Shantyman*. She also toured across America for several years performing "mouth music" (unaccompanied vocals to accompany Scottish dances) with Scottish bands. In 1987 MacKenzie took the leap of moving to Scotland itself, where she immediately began working with the folk ensemble Drumalban. In 1988 she founded an outfit of her own with Scottish film and TV director Martin Swan: Mouth Music, which experimented with traditional Gaelic songs given high-tech Afro-pop dance-beat arrangements. MacKenzie kept developing that concept under her own name after resuming her solo career. Her first recording thereafter, *Sòlas,* featured original arrangements of mouth music and *waulking* (washing) songs, along with a lullaby and a sea chantey. For her next album, *Spiorad* (Spirit), MacKenzie broadened her focus by including material from Brittany, Serbia, and Bulgaria. She also wrote original texts for several of the traditional selections adapted for the album. Currently MacKenzie is teaching voice and has begun working on her fourth solo CD, *Global Sequence*. This next work will cast an even wider range than MacKenzie's earlier recordings; she plans to include adaptations of ethnic material from Cherokee, Sephardic, Persian, Brazilian, African American, and Australian Aboriginal cultures as well as her trademark Celtic sources.

what to buy: *Mouth Music* ♪♪♪♪ (Rykodisc, 1991, prod. Chic Medley) can be viewed as the first installment of a trilogy focusing on modern treatments of traditional Gaelic songs. The high-tech arrangements—utilizing keyboards and electronic percussion—that supported MacKenzie's straightforward singing style were actually fairly sparse and abstract. By the time she came to record *Sòlas* ♪♪♪♪ (Shanachie, 1994, prod. Iain McKenna, Chris Birkett, Talitha MacKenzie), she'd developed a more organic style. Although electronic instruments still predominate on most of the arrangements, the album's sound has more of a band feel, with instrumental support more sympathetic to MacKenzie's voice. And the traditional Gaelic pieces truly adapt well to their modernizations. The waulking songs are inherently rhythmic; the electric instruments only sharpen their already-strong beats. Traditional instruments like fiddles and pipes join in on several tracks to add even more colors to these fascinating arrangements. On *Spiorad* ♪♪♪♪ (Shanachie, 1996, prod. Chris Birkett) MacKenzie's voice takes on more of a pop sheen and exuberance, particularly on the opener "Fill Iu O," a waulking song for which MacKenzie wrote timely new lyrics. Then she sounds like a Gaelic reggae toaster (rapper) on "Fionnaghuala." A taste of MacKenzie's forthcoming multi-ethnic *Global Sequence* project is provided by her treatments of the Bulgarian dance tune "Hopa!" with its nifty accordion-like synth part; "Ajde Jano," a Serbian dance song whose approach here is reminiscent of the Finnish band Värttinä; and "Changerais-Tu?" a Breton (French Celtic) dance song given a jaunty reggae-fied rhythm. It fits! The dense poly-ethnic groove then opens out into "Fear A' Bhata," a lament in which MacKenzie's voice is supported only by recorder and keyboard drone. Beautiful. MacKenzie is one of those performers who takes traditional folk styles and updates them without losing the sources' soul—along the way revealing refreshing relationships between seemingly unrelated traditions.

influences:

◀◀ Field recordings of Mary Morrison (Barra), Calum Johnston (Barra), and Mrs. Archie MacDonald (South Uist), printed sources, Incredible String Band, Steeleye Span, Harry Belafonte

▶▶ Mary Jane Lamond, Afro Celt Sound System, Shooglenifty, Peatbog Faeries, Loreena McKennitt, Paul Mounsey/Nahoo, Capercaillie, Massive Attack, Angélique Kidjo

see also: *Mouth Music*

Ken Roseman

Dougie MacLean
Scottish folk
Born 1954, in Perthshire, Scotland. Based in Scotland.

Heralded as Scotland's premier folk-singing troubadour, Dougie MacLean writes finely crafted songs that are inspired by self-discovery, nature, love, and Gaelic history. Whether he's singing about the Australian outback in "Singing Land" or coming to grips with self-doubt in "Ready for the Storm," his lilting melodies are bright and beautiful lullabies in these troubled times. An exceptional performer who tours the world, MacLean's concerts are highlighted by his enthusiasm and knack for storytelling between songs. Born a gardener's son in a family where his father played fiddle and his mother mandolin, MacLean was busking around Scotland in his teens when he was picked to be a member of the Tannahill Weavers, a popular traditional folk group. MacLean, anxious to perform more of his own compositions, teamed up with Alan Roberts, a Scottish guitarist, for two albums, *Caledonia* and *C.R.M.* (the latter also with Alex Campbell). Looking to broaden his playing skills further, MacLean joined Silly Wizard, another notable Scottish folk group, and spent six months touring Europe and America with the band. Since 1983 he has been releasing his own songs on his own label, Dunkeld Records, and enjoying immense popularity as a consummate performer who champions issues such as Scottish independence and protecting the environment. Dunkeld Records can be described as promoting Scotland's "new heritage" music, and the roster of folk musicians signed to the label include Hamish Moore, Sheena Wellington, Freda Morrison, Gordon Duncan, and Blackeyed Biddy. In 1989 and '90, MacLean toured the States and did concerts for the popular public radio series *Thistle & Shamrock*. He also played the Shetland and Orkney music celebrations and was a featured performer at the Edinburgh Festival. In 1993 the BBC presented *The Land: Songs of Dougie MacLean* on television. In the last few years he has made Nashville an important spot on his itinerary, performing in concert with country star Kathy Mattea and co-producing her *Time Passes By* album. At the other extreme, 1996 saw one of his songs, "The Gael," given the techno/dance treatment by Galleria and played in discos in Europe. MacLean shows a special knack in drawing large crowds and devoted fans to his concerts who seem to know every word of every song he's written, and his live appearances are memo-

rable events for all. With the release of the highly successful *Riof* in 1997, MacLean's popularity only seems to grow. Just about all of his albums since 1983 are now available in stores or can be mail-ordered through Dunkeld Records, Cathedral Street, Dunkeld, Perthshire PH8 OAW Scotland; telephone: (01350) 727686; fax: (01350) 728606. His website, www.dunkeld.co.uk, is divided into "The Studio," "The Gallery," "The Office," and "The Store," with other sites that explain his guitar tunings, tour dates, and guitar and fiddle preferences. There is also an excellent newsletter called *Contact* (available at the address above), which keeps Dougie fans updated with news and album information.

what to buy: The best sampling of MacLean material can be found on *Putamayo Presents the Dougie MacLean Collection* ♫♫♫♫ (Putamayo, 1995, prod. Dan Storper), which surveys songs from seven MacLean albums. *Singing Land* ♫♫♫♫ (Dunkeld Records, 1986, prod. Dougie MacLean, Jennifer MacLean) is the ultimate MacLean experience; it best represents his stylistic brilliance with songs teetering between pure joy ("This Love Will Carry") and destruction ("Guillotine's Release"). Another heavy hitter for best MacLean album would be *Riof* ♫♫♫♫ (Dunkeld, 1997, prod. Dougie MacLean, Graeme Hughes, Jennifer MacLean), a fine mix of haunting instrumentals, finely crafted traditional songs, and contemporary numbers that whisk you away to the Scottish Highlands in the blink of an eye. Also quite good and highly recommended are *Real Estate* ♫♫♫ (Dunkeld, 1988, prod. Dougie MacLean, Jennifer MacLean), *Indigenous* ♫♫♫ (Dunkeld, 1991, prod. Dougie MacLean, Graeme Hughes), and *Whitewash* ♫♫♫ (Dunkeld, 1990, prod. Dougie MacLean, Jennifer MacLean).

what to buy next: *The Plant Life Years* ♫♫♫ (Osmosys, 1995, prod. Nigel Pegrum) is a compilation of songs taken from MacLean's early records *Caledonia, C.R.M.,* and *Snaigow,* and demonstrates MacLean's fondness for traditional tunes. If you're looking for mainly instrumentals with the MacLean magic touch, then you can't go wrong with *Fiddle* ♫♫♫ (Dunkeld, 1984, prod. Dougie MacLean, Jennifer MacLean), *The Search* ♫♫♫ (Dunkeld, 1990, prod. Dougie MacLean, Graeme Hughes), and *Sunset Song* ♫♫♫ (Dunkeld, 1993, prod. Dougie MacLean, Graeme Hughes). All three are rooted in traditional Scottish folklore, and provide plenty of opportunities for MacLean's masterfully played guitar and fiddle to shine. If you like Scottish poets Robert Burns, Neil Gow, and Robert Tannahill, then you'll enjoy MacLean's wonderful song interpretations on *Craigie Dhu* ♫♫♫ (Dunkeld, 1983, prod. Dougie MacLean, Roy Ashby) and *Tribute* ♫♫♫ (Dunkeld, 1995, prod. Dougie MacLean, Graeme Hughes, Jennifer MacLean). Don't forget to wear the tartan! Then again, if you want to hear more of Dougie's own passionate early songwriting in the style of

Riof, you should buy yourself *Butterstone* ♫♫♫ (Dambuster, 1989, prod. Richard Digance) and *Marching Mystery* ♫♫♫ (Dunkeld, 1994, prod. Dougie MacLean, Graeme Hughes, Jennifer MacLean).

what to avoid: If you're thinking of hearing a lot of MacLean on the soundtrack of *The Last of the Mohicans* (Morgan Creek, 1992, prod. Michael Mann), forget it. With only 10 minutes of music by MacLean, there's far too much symphonic trembling to contend with to make it worth the money.

worth searching for: Four MacLean albums are rare and quite worth the treasure hunt. The wonderful *Caledonia* ♫♫♫ (Plant Life, 1978, prod. Nigel Pegrum) features the original version of the title song, which was later made into a megahit by Frankie Miller and which is the nearest thing to a new Scottish national anthem in the last 20 years. This early edition uses the swirling sounds of the Delme String Quartet to offset MacLean's homesick longing for the mother country. The album is firmly rooted in tradition but has the familiar MacLean trademarks: jangling guitar and passionate voice. Ace guitarist Alan Roberts is featured throughout. *C.R.M.* ♫♫♫ (Plant Life, 1979, prod. Nigel Pegrum) is a spirited and rollicking romp with Scottish music legends Alex Campbell and (again) Alan Roberts. More of a Celtic hootenanny than other MacLean efforts, *C.R.M.* has a pub-like feel on numbers like "Rattlin' Roarin' Willie" and "Leis a Lurighan." *Snaigow* ♫♫♫ (Plant Life, 1980, prod. Nigel Pegrum) and *On a Wing and a Prayer* ♫♫♫ (Plant Life, 1981, prod. Nigel Pegrum) showcase MacLean's early songwriting talents as he refines his personal style.

influences:

◄◄ Jackson Browne, James Taylor, Joni Mitchell, Cat Stevens, Frazer McGlen & His Scottish Country Dance Band

►► Kathy Mattea, David Wilcox, Martin Simpson, Dick Gaughan

see also: *Silly Wizard, Andy M. Stewart, Tannahill Weavers*

TJ McGrath

Natalie MacMaster

Cape Breton Scottish fiddle music

Born June 13, 1972, in Cape Breton, Nova Scotia, Canada. Based in Nova Scotia, Canada.

Natalie MacMaster is at the top of a talented class of young musicians bringing the traditional Scottish fiddle music of Cape Breton, Nova Scotia, to the world. An excellent young fiddler and dancer with undeniable charisma and stage presence, MacMaster is well known to audiences in the United States from frequent performances at festivals and on tours. She has appeared with the Celtic Fiddle Festival, the Chieftains, Carlos Santana, and others. She grew up in a musical family, getting her first fiddle at age

three and learning to play from some of the greats of Cape Breton music, including her uncle, legendary fiddler Buddy MacMaster. She recorded her first album at age 16 and soon after was performing at major festivals in Canada and the States. MacMaster's career has continued to develop over countless concert appearances, more albums, and several awards from the Canadian music industry. She is among Canada's best-known traditional performers and has a great future ahead of her.

what to buy: What you want from MacMaster's small catalog depends on your tastes. For someone just beginning to explore Cape Breton's music, *No Boundaries* ♫♫♫ (Rounder, 1997, prod. Chad Irschick) would serve as a fine introduction. A mixed bag of instrumentals and songs from Cape Breton and beyond, set in both traditional and contemporary settings, this record was released in Canada by Warner Bros. and was designed to bring Natalie's music to as wide an audience as possible. As with all of her recordings the playing is flawless and filled with energy, particularly when she works with long-time partners Dave MacIsaac and Tracey Dares. Although some of the contemporary arrangements strain a little too hard at a Sharon Shannon-ish crossover style, Natalie's good taste keeps things pretty well under control. Rounding out the collection are two songs, one sung by Cookie Rankin of the Rankin family, and one by Cape Breton songwriter Bruce Guthro, that provide a nice change of pace from the fiddle tunes. For those music fans who like their coffee black, their scotch neat, and their fiddle music straight, *Fit As a Fiddle* ♫♫♫♫ (Rounder, 1997, prod. Glen Meisner, Dave MacIsaac) is the recording to choose. MacMaster powers through a solid set of traditional Cape Breton dance music, accompanied by MacIsaac and Dares. The arrangements are simpler than on *No Boundaries* and the forays into outside styles less adventuresome. This is a simple, powerful album showcasing Natalie at what she does best, Cape Breton fiddling with a lot of drive, swing, and power; an awesome technique wedded to great taste and a thorough understanding of the tradition.

what to buy next: Previously available only in Canada, *A Compilation* ♫♫♫ (MacMaster Music, 1996/Rounder, 1998, compilation prod. Paul MacDonald) is a reissue of selected tracks from MacMaster's first two albums, *Four on the Floor* and *Road to the Isle,* both originally on cassette and now out of print. Natalie was just a teenager when she made these strong, self-assured recordings. Her playing is excellent as always, with great swing and lift on the dance tunes and a solid touch on the slow airs. Although she has since matured as a musician, the qualities that make her stand out were all there from the beginning, as this fine CD shows.

the rest:

In My Hands N/A (Rounder, 1999)

influences:
◀◀ Buddy MacMaster, Brendan Mulvihill, Jerry Holland

▶▶ Ashley MacIsaac, Richard Wood

Tony Ziselberger

Mad Lion
Ragga/hip-hop
Born in London, England. Based in Brooklyn, NY, USA.

Like a fierce jungle cat, Mad Lion has a roar that can be heard for miles. The London-born, Jamaican-raised, Brooklyn-living *ragga* (digital reggae) MC sprang up from the Boogie Down Productions camp and quickly captured the hip-hop scene with the song "Shoot to Kill" (which so aptly used the slick backing track from KRS-One's "Black Cop"). Originally called Medallion, Mad Lion got his new name from ragga forbear Super Cat, whom he met while visiting Super Power Records in Flatbush, Brooklyn. It was at that same store where Mad Lion met KRS-One, which led to his BDP membership. Even while releasing albums and underground singles, Mad Lion also found time to earn his Certified Public Accountant's degree—just in case his career as a musician roars to a close.

what to buy: After the B-side single "Shoot to Kill" infected the underground rap-club scene, Mad Lion released the dark and menacing "Take It Easy" (another KRS-One production), and it looked as if he could do no wrong. Unfortunately, his debut album, *Real Ting* ⚜⚜ (Weeded, 1994, prod. KRS-One), couldn't sustain that same raw energy for its entirety, though Mad Lion did come through with notable songs like the title track and "Double Trouble."

the rest:
Ghetto Gold and Platinum Respect ⚜⚜ (Nervous, 1997)

worth searching for: Mad Lion is in full growl on "Friends," an all-star ragga-hop track with Queen Latifah on Salt 'n' Pepa's *Brand New* ⚜⚜⚜ (London, 1997, executive prod. Cheryl "Salt" James, Sandra "Pepa" Denton).

influences:
◀◀ Super Cat, Nicodemus, Shabba Ranks, KRS-One

Jazzbo

Mad Professor
/Neil Fraser
Dub, dub poetry, reggae, lovers' rock
Born in Guyana. Based in London, England.

Jamaican producers have not released many dub treatments (the studio-manipulated, often-instrumental versions of reggae recordings) since the heyday of the 1970s, but dub has maintained a strong following in London, where a trio of prolific producers—Adrian Sherwood, Jah Shaka, and Neil Fraser, a.k.a. Mad Professor—have been releasing new spins on traditional dub techniques since the early '80s.

Neil Fraser concocts heavy roots dub mixes, while moonlighting as a producer of lovers' rock, a British phenomenon that floats romantic soul vocals over a reggae bass line. His Ariwa Sound studios in Peckham, South London, are home to roots acts like Macka B, the current output of the legendary Lee "Scratch" Perry, and also the sweet love songs of Sandra Cross and Kofi. Alongside Adrian Sherwood's modern On-U Sound and Jah Shaka's traditionally rootsy Shaka Music, Fraser's Ariwa Sound is the heart of British dub.

Fraser's in-house team of session players includes some of London's finest reggae musicians, all of whom are multi-instrumentalists, including Black Steel, William the Conqueror, Errol the General, Dennis Nolan, and Mafia. They each seem equally adept at keyboard, guitar, bass, drums, and vocals. Most recordings—particularly the more recent efforts—have featured guest appearances by titans in the industry like the late Augustus Pablo, Yabby You, Lee "Scratch" Perry, Jah Shaka, and Horace Andy. In 1995 Fraser experimented with the state-of-the-art electronic "jungle" style, working with Douggie Digital and Juggler to remix their fast breakbeats with heavy dub rhythms—check out *Mazaruni: The Jungle Dub Experience* (Ariwa/RAS 1995); *Rupuni Safari: Steaming Jungle* (Ariwa/RAS 1995); and (with Lee Perry) *Super Ape Inna Jungle* (Ariwa/RAS 1995).

While it is as a producer that Fraser will continue to have the most profound effect on British reggae (he remains a magnet for talent from Bristol, Birmingham, Kingston, and London), his own recordings both set standards for new mixing techniques and reflect the changing socio-political concerns at the heart of London's Jamaican community—a role for which Fraser is paradoxically but perceptively positioned as a sympathetic but South America–born outsider.

what to buy: For career overviews check out *It's a Mad, Mad, Mad Professor* ⚜⚜⚜ (RAS, 1994) or the slightly more up-to-date *RAS Portraits* ⚜⚜⚜⚜ (RAS, 1997). Mad Professor's *Dub Me Crazy* series is currently on Part 12, but the highlights are the zany debut *Dub Me Crazy* ⚜⚜⚜⚜ (Ariwa 1982) and *Who Knows the Secret of the Master Tape? Dub Me Crazy Part Five* ⚜⚜⚜ (Ariwa, 1990). Professor's remix of Massive Attack's *Protection* is perhaps his greatest work: *No Protection* ⚜⚜⚜⚜ (Circa/Gyroscope, 1994, prod. Massive Attack, Nellee Hooper), a labor of love with cascading beats and rippling reverb for the group that spawned electronic trailblazer Tricky.

what to buy next: Fraser works in a variety of prolific series. The aforesaid *Dub Me Crazy* is the longest running in dub, with at least 12 diverse volumes recorded over 16 years. Most of these releases work from loosely defined concepts that serve as his central themes: black politics, Rastafarianism, Africa, love, *Vodou,* the Caribbean, psychedelia, and the Bible. But Fraser does not stick rigorously to the concept and can freely mix his pet subjects on any one album. The *Black Liberation* series is more overtly political and features samples of speeches by Jesse Jackson and Louis Farrakhan. These and other recordings are detailed in the following section; let the ratings be your guide in navigating a body of work with much of worth to discover. The list, not comprehensive for such a fertile artist even at this length, focuses on solo albums rather than Fraser's excellent collaborations with Perry and Macka B, or his vast catalog of production work on lovers' rock records.

best of the rest:

Beyond the Realms of Dub: Dub Me Crazy Part 2 𝄐𝄐𝄐 (Ariwa/RAS, 1982)

Jah Shaka Meets Mad Professor 𝄐𝄐𝄐 (Ariwa/RAS, 1984)

Negus Roots Meets Mad Professor 𝄐𝄐𝄐 (Ariwa/RAS, 1984)

Escape to the Asylum of Dub: Dub Me Crazy Part 4 𝄐𝄐𝄐 (Ariwa/RAS, 1990)

Schizophrenic Dub: Dub Me Crazy Part 6 𝄐𝄐𝄐 (Ariwa/RAS, 1990)

Adventures of a Dub Sampler: Dub Me Crazy Part 7 𝄐𝄐𝄐 (Ariwa/RAS, 1990)

Experiments of the Aural Kind: Dub Me Crazy Part 8 𝄐𝄐𝄐 (Ariwa/RAS, 1990)

Science & the Witchdoctor: Dub Me Crazy Part 9 𝄐𝄐𝄐 (Ariwa/RAS, 1990)

Psychedelic Dub: Dub Me Crazy Part 10 𝄐𝄐 (RAS, 1990)

A Feast of Yellow Dub 𝄐𝄐𝄐 (RAS, 1990)

Mad Professor Captures Pato Banton 𝄐𝄐 (Ariwa/RAS, 1990)

Mad Professor Recaptures Pato Banton 𝄐 (Ariwa/RAS, 1990)

Hi-jacked to Jamaica: Dub Me Crazy Part 11 𝄐𝄐𝄐 (Ariwa/RAS, 1991)

Dub Maniacs on the Rampage: Dub Me Crazy Part 12 𝄐𝄐𝄐 (Ariwa/RAS, 1992)

True Born African Dub 𝄐𝄐𝄐 (Ariwa/RAS, 1992)

The Lost Scrolls of Moses 𝄐𝄐𝄐 (Ariwa/RAS, 1993)

The African Connection: Dub Me Crazy Part 3 𝄐𝄐𝄐𝄐 (Ariwa/RAS, 1995)

Black Liberation Dub Chapter One 𝄐𝄐𝄐𝄐 (Ariwa/RAS, 1995)

Anti-Racist Dub Broadcast: Black Liberation Dub Chapter Two 𝄐𝄐𝄐 (Ariwa/RAS, 1995)

In a Rub a Dub Style 𝄐𝄐𝄐 (Ariwa/RAS, 1995)

Evolution of Dub: Black Liberation Dub Chapter Three 𝄐𝄐𝄐𝄐 (Ariwa/RAS, 1996)

New Decade of Dub 𝄐𝄐𝄐 (Ariwa/RAS, 1996)

Dub Take the Voodoo out of Reggae 𝄐𝄐𝄐𝄐 (Ariwa/RAS, 1996)

Caribbean Taste of Technology 𝄐𝄐𝄐𝄐 (Ariwa/RAS, 1996)

Under the Spell of Dub: Black Liberation Dub Chapter Four 𝄐𝄐𝄐𝄐 (Ariwa/RAS, 1997)

Dub You Crazy with Love 𝄐𝄐𝄐 (Ariwa/RAS, 1997)

At Checkpoint Charlie 𝄐𝄐𝄐 (Ariwa/RAS, 1998)

influences:

◄◄ King Tubby, Lee "Scratch" Perry, Bob Andy, Marcia Griffiths

►► The Orb, Massive Attack, Tricky, Bush Chemists, Dub Syndicate, New Age Steppers, Renegade Soundwave

see also: *Lee "Scratch" Perry*

David Poole

Mad Pudding

Anglo-Celtic folk-rock, Canadian folk

Formed 1989, in Vancouver, British Columbia, Canada. Based in Vancouver, British Columbia, Canada.

Amy Stephen, vocals, accordion, pennywhistle; Andy Hillhouse, vocals, guitar, mandolin, bouzouki; Cam Wilson, fiddle, vocals; Richard Ernst, fretless bass, vocals (1989–96); Boris Favre (France), electric bass, piano, vocals, pieds (feet) (1996–present); John Hildebrand, drums, percussion (1993–97); Allan Dionne, drums, percussion (1997–present). (All members are from Canada except where noted otherwise.)

Mad Pudding revolves around Andy Hillhouse, Amy Stephen, and Cam Wilson, who met as college students at the University of British Columbia in the late 1980s. Hillhouse and Stephen had begun playing as a duo but expanded when they met Wilson, who brought with him Ottawa Valley fiddle tunes he'd learned from his father. Original bassist Richard Ernst joined in 1989, but the band really decided to "get serious" when drummer Hildebrand completed the quintet in 1993. With Hildebrand, Mad Pudding became a full tilt Anglo-Celtic/Canadian-roots folk-rock band whose repertoire included traditional and self-penned material. That lineup completed two albums and toured throughout Canada, also visiting the U.S. and Great Britain. Eventually Ernst left the band and was replaced by French-born Boris Favre, whose interest in the folk music of his culture is reflected on Mad Pudding's third album, *Rattle on the Stovepipe,* which includes his original song "Le Beaujolais Nouveau"—a celebration of the arrival of the new Beaujolais wine. It's not essential, but you may enjoy the music more with a glass of same in hand.

what to buy: Mad Pudding's eclectic tastes are well showcased on *Rattle on the Stovepipe* 𝄐𝄐𝄐𝄐 (Iona, 1997, prod. Bill Vorndick), which includes hot fiddle- and accordion-led instrumentals, Amy Stephen's "Punjabi Marker"—which sounds like a centuries-old British ballad—and even two catchy pop-country numbers, "Rowena" and "Where Were You." Favre and Hildebrand form a swingin', funky rhythm section, and Stephen's and Hillhouse's vocals are more assured than before—great harmonies. This album also proves that Mad Pudding is a band whose exuberant live presence can be captured in the studio!

the rest:

Bruce's Vegetable Garden ↗↗↗↗ (Fiendish Records, 1994)
Dirt & Stone ↗↗↗↗ (Fiendish Records, 1995)
Grand Hotel N/A (Sliced Bread, 1999)

influences:

◀◀ Capercaillie, Stan Rogers, Silly Wizard, Spirit of the West, Moving Hearts

▶▶ Seelyhoo, James Keelaghan, Sharon Shannon, Kathryn Tickell

Ken Roseman

Joanie Madden

Irish whistle and flute
Born May 26, 1965, in NY, USA. Based in NY, USA.

Best known in her role as leader of the group Cherish the Ladies, Joanie Madden is rapidly developing a reputation as a fine solo artist as well. Her strong and compelling Irish whistle and flute performances have inspired many to take up the instruments, her outstanding energy and creative improvisation earning her plaudits as one of the leading flute players in the Irish canon. Born to Irish parents in America, Madden has called on her heritage when creating her own sense of musicality. She studied whistle with Jack Coen and had soon earned the title of World Champion on both whistle and concert flute. In 1984 she won the Senior All-Ireland Championship, the first American ever to do so. Despite her youth, she is already recognized as a prime mover in preserving Irish heritage in America and has won the Wild Geese award and been inducted into the Irish-American Musicians Hall of Fame. She has appeared as a guest on numerous recordings, including ones by such artists as Sinéad O'Connor, Sheila Noonan, Pete Seeger, and Eileen Ivers.

what's available: *Song of the Irish Whistle* ↗↗↗↗ (Hearts of Space, 1996, prod. Brian Keane) is an exciting collection of Irish tunes performed with passion by Madden. Filling the album with a wide variety of textures, she is joined by fine musicians Jerry O'Sullivan on uilleann pipes, Carol Thompson on Celtic harp, Brian Keane on guitars and keyboards, and others. From the evocative "Women of Ireland" to the fantastically rhythmic "The Legacy Jig/Tar Road to Sligo," Madden has created a picture of Ireland as varied as the landscape itself. Though this is predominantly a whistle recording, Madden does pick up her flute for a lilting Turlough O'Carolan tune. *Song of the Irish Whistle 2* ↗↗↗↗ (Hearts of Space, 1999, prod. Brian Keane) is the continuation. On her earlier album *A Whistle on the Wind* ↗↗↗↗ (Green Linnet, 1994, prod. Joanie Madden, Gabriel Dono-

hue), Madden's flute and whistle front a wide array of instruments, including accordion, guitar, cello, and fiddle. The title track, "A Whistle on the Wind/The Jug of Punch/The Dogs among the Bushes," combines three terrific tunes into one exciting medley. Madden's personal version of O'Carolan's "Blind Mary" is quite inspired. She ends the album accompanying a touching story-poem recited by Liam Clancy.

influences:

◀◀ Joe Madden, Jack Coen, Mike Rafferty

▶▶ Emer Mayock

see also: *Cherish the Ladies, the Clancy Brothers, Steve Gorn, Paul Winter*

Jo Hughey Morrison

Madness

Two-tone, ska, pop
Formed 1978, in London, England. Disbanded 1986.

Lee Thompson, saxophone; Chris Foreman, guitar; Mike Barson, keyboards; Dan Woodgate, drums; Mark Bedford, bass; Graham "Suggs" McPherson, vocals; Chas Smash (born Cathal Smythe), emcee, trumpet; others.

Maybe it's the fashions, or maybe the music itself, but there are some trends that Americans just seem destined not to get. Thus is was with the ska revival that swept England in the late '70s and early '80s. Purists by no means, Madness crossed all sorts of musical boundaries, from ska and gritty R&B to contemporary pop and near-novelty music for a mix that was anarchic and endlessly entertaining. All of Europe thought so, anyway, making Madness the toast of the Continent for a while, and rightfully so, considering how throughly the group broke down barriers of race, age, and attitude among audience members. Alas, the band's U.S. fortunes were much more modest. Here it's remembered as a new wave one-hit wonder for its pleasant pop song "Our House." The group disbanded in 1986, though some members later tried a comeback as *the* Madness, but by then the group had run its course. Now, a decade later, with another ska revival in full swing, Madness is finally being appreciated for the groundbreaking act it was.

what to buy: *Total Madness: The Very Best of Madness* ↗↗↗ (Geffen, 1997, prod. various) offers a good introduction to the band, with "Our House," "One Step Beyond," and "Michael Caine," but it suffers for lack of the band's early Stiff singles. The compilation *Madness* ↗↗↗ (Geffen, 1983/1993, prod. various) fills in a little more of the story, but there are still some essential tracks missing, and both sets could be longer.

the rest:

Keep Moving ↗↗↗ (Geffen, 1984/1997)

4/6/6 madredeus

Mad Not Mad ♫♫ (Geffen, 1985/1997)

worth searching for: Currently unavailable, the group's first two albums, *One Step Beyond* (Stiff, 1979/Sire, 1980) and *Absolutely* (Stiff/Sire 1980), set a very high entertainment quotient for the band to maintain.

influences:

◄◄ Prince Buster, the Skatalites

►► No Doubt, Save Ferris, Hepcat, Barenaked Ladies

Daniel Durchholz

Madredeus

Portuguese pop-folk

Formed 1987, in Lisbon, Portugal. Based in Lisbon, Portrugal.

Pedro Ayres Magalhães, guitar; Teresa Salgueiro, vocals; Rodrigo Leão, keyboards (1987–94); Gabriel Gomes, accordion (1987–97); Francisco Ribeiro, cello (1987–97); José Peixoto, guitar (1993–present); Carlos Maria Trindade, keyboards (1994–present); Fernando Júdice, bass (1997–present). (All members are from Portugal.)

According to the group's founder Pedro Ayres Magalhães, Madredeus expresses the mood summed up by the Portuguese expression "saudede": "Saudede is a state in which a person allows himself to experience contradictory feelings or cultivate non-linear thoughts about love, life, and time. For Madredeus saudede is the key and the reason we make music." Magalhães and Leão started the group as a guitar-and-synthesizer duo. They decided to expand the sound, and so accordionist Gomes and cellist Ribeiro were recruited. The inaugural lineup was complete when Magalhães and Leão discovered Salgueiro singing *fado* (a kind of cabaret urban folk-blues from Lisbon) in a bar and asked her to join. Throughout the spring of 1987 the band rehearsed in an old church in the Lisbon neighborhood of Madre de Deus, from which they would take their name. *Os Dias da MadreDeus,* their debut CD, was recorded live in the church several months later. *Existir,* the follow-up, was released in the spring of 1990 and included the #1 Portuguese hit "O Pastor." Next to come was the double live set *Lisbon,* recorded at the Coliseu Dos Recreios in that city on April 30, 1991 (though actually released in 1992). Then there was *O Espirito da Paz.* Madredeus's subsequent project, *Ainda,* came about because German director Wim Wenders decided to use their music in his on-location film *Lisbon Story*; the band not only recorded new songs for the soundtrack, but members also appeared in the film itself. No more recordings followed until 1997's *O Paraíso.* The personnel had shifted; accordionist Gomes, cellist Ribeiro, and keyboardist Leão had all left and were replaced by new keyboardist Carlos Maria Trindade and Fer-

nando Júdice on acoustic bass guitar. The ensemble sound became a little sparser and more guitar-based, with Salgueiro's remarkable voice even further to the fore. In early 1999 Madredeus released another double-CD live set, *O Porto,* featuring selections from *O Paraíso* along with five previously unrecorded songs.

what to buy: *O Paraíso* ♫♫♫♫ (Metro Blue, 1997, prod. Pedro Ayres Magalhães) is the only studio recording to date by the present Madredeus lineup, and showcases the group's current vocal-and-guitar-oriented sound. Teresa Salgueiro contributes more of her effortlessly beautiful singing, a sound that has the grandeur but not the stylization of operatically trained voices. *O Paraíso* also includes several of Magalhães's most unforgettable songs—"Os Dias são à Noite," "O Fim da Estrada," and the graceful "A Praia do Mar." *O Espirito da Paz* ♫♫♫♫ (metro blue, 1994, prod. Pedro Ayres Magalhães) is arguably the most confident of Madredeus's earlier recordings. With accordionist Gomes, the instrumental arrangements are a little more colorful. The album also includes a moving anti-war lament, "Os Senhores Da Guerra (The War Lords)."

the rest:

O Dias da MadreDeus ♫♫♫♫ (Metro Blue, 1987/1997)
Existir ♫♫♫♫ (Metro Blue, 1990/1997)
Lisbon ♫♫♫♫ (Metro Blue, 1992/1997)
Ainda ♫♫♫♫ (Metro Blue, 1995)
O Porto ♫♫♫♫ (Metro Blue, 1999)

influences:

◄◄ Pentangle, fado, Amália Rodrigues, Ofra Haza

►► Cassandra Wilson, Yosefa

Ken Roseman

Magnum Band

Compas

Formed 1976, in Miami, FL, USA. Based in Miami, FL, USA.

Rotating membership centered around Andre "Dadou" Pasquet and Claude "Tico" Pasquet.

After playing with the influential Haitian outfit Tabou Combo from the age of 16, guitarist Andre "Dadou" Pasquet and his brother Claude "Tico" Pasquet put together this veteran *compas* (Haitian dance pop) group in 1976. The band recorded many albums in the ensuing years and became a tremendous live attraction both in the Caribbean and among expatriate Caribbeans—not to mention fans of more exotic music everywhere.

what to buy: At once funky, spunky, and soooo Caribbean, the Magnum Band could stretch out on record, though not nearly as relaxed and sprawled as they could play live. *Anthology 3* ♪♪♪♪ (Antilles Mizik, 1997, prod. various), the third volume of Antilles Mizik's retrospective of the band—which comprises the only recordings in print by this diverse and deep-rooted outfit—captures them at their most paradoxical: While regarded as the standard-bearers of compas, they toss Latin salsa, Antillean *zouk,* and even reggae into the mix. Though known among Haitians as being in the front rank of their genre's lyric-writing, one of the best tracks here, "Cosmic," is an instrumental. "Libete" (in a much better mix than the one known from the groundbreaking anthology *Konbit: Burning Rhythms of Haiti*) has some of the most amazingly varied horn charts ever recorded, yet the band's leader plays guitar. All the juxtapositions create some remarkable artistic tension.

what to buy next: Rife with strong grooves and cool tropical melodies, tracks like "Best in Town" on *Anthology 1* ♪♪♪♪ (Antilles Mizik, 1997, prod. various) define the sound of modern compas. Dadou's guitar leads the way—though the horns and percussion are not far behind. At times he sounds as if he's playing *soukous* (Congolese rumba); at others the guitar parts would not sound out of place on an album by the '70s Stateside dance band Chic. Nonetheless, some songs, like the variegated "Moun Sa," just don't match the level of the Magnums' strongest material. While still a wonderfully played album, the songs on *Anthology 2* ♪♪♪ (Antilles Mizik, 1997, prod. various) seem to exacerbate some of the excusable flaws of the other volumes; for instance, "Ashadei" is marred by out-of-tune vocal harmonies and horn sections that would have sounded better if they'd been recut. But when the parts gel, as on the sexy, jazzy "Aux Cayes" and the guitar-driven "Adoration," it doesn't come much better.

influences:

◄◄ Nemours Jean-Baptiste, Tabou Combo

►► Rara Machine

see also: *Tabou Combo*

Hank Bordowitz

Taj Mahal

Blues, world music

Born Henry St. Claire Fredericks, May 17, 1942, in New York, NY, USA. Based in USA.

Although he grew up in Brooklyn and went to college in Massachusetts, Taj Mahal extends his hands to other musical cultures and soaks them up like a sponge. His father was a jazz musician, his mother a gospel singer, and his 30-plus years of exploring blues, ragtime, and Caribbean rhythms show those and many other influences. If his music seems like a history lesson

brazil: bahia

Known as "a little piece of Africa," the state of Bahia and its capital Salvador are places of cultural profusion and musical riches. The slave trade made Bahia home to diverse ethnic groups, the most numerous being the Yoruba and Ewe peoples from what is today Nigeria, Mali, and Ghana. Identification with Africa continues strongly through the religion *Candomblé,* the martial-art/dance *capoeira,* and the drums that are ever-present in Bahian music. Carnival has always been a showcase for the best of that music. As early as 1895, groups called *afoxés* paraded through the streets beating out dense polyrhythms and wearing African costumes. After decades of repression, Afrocentric organizations like Ilê Ayê, Filhos de Gandhi, Muzenza, Malé de Balé, and dozens of others returned to prominence in Carnival and in the life of Salvador.

The Afro-Brazilian rhythms of afoxe, *ijexá,* and *samba-de-roda* spawned the heavy, captivating *samba-reggae* sound. The group Olodum crossed over from roots into pop and laid the samba-reggae foundation for today's stylistically expansive *axé* phenomenon. That movement's other major influence was the *trios eletricos.* Dodo and Osmar, two guitarists in the Northeastern *frevo* style, got up on top of a moving truck with their amplifiers in the Carnival of 1950, and the crowd followed behind—as they did the next year, when an accordion completed the "trio." Now trios eletricos are multimillion-dollar ventures, huge sound trucks that lead hundreds of thousands of partiers, keep them dancing for upwards of 12 hours, and exceed the absurd in decibel output. Artists and bands like Margareth Menezes, Daniela Mercury, Chiclete com Banana, Banda Mel, É O Tchán, and Carlinhos Brown's community-based Timbalada keep Carnival cooking with ever-new music drawing on international as well as indigenous sources. This trademark blend is epitomized by PercPan, a global percussion festival conceived by Brazilian pop icon Gilberto Gil and master percussionist Nana Vasconcelos, which every year rallies the people around the drums and stirs new ideas into the great melting pot that is Bahia.

Mara Weiss and Nego Beto

at times, these didactic leanings are offset by his boundless enthusiasm and a formidable instrumental versatility. Mahal's journey began during the mid-1960s with the equally eclectic Ry Cooder in a short-lived assemblage called the Rising Sons. Mahal's first albums dug into standard blues in a manner that presented him as a guardian of tradition, after which he promptly swerved toward African rhythms, reggae, and even children's music before venturing into the then-untested waters of worldbeat. Uncharacteristically quiet during the 1980s, Mahal has returned to a blues-based approach since the turn of that decade. Whether he's with a full band playing pop arrangements or on his own playing stripped-down roots, Mahal has asserted himself yet again as both a keeper of the faith and a still-vital force that heads past the horizon.

what to buy: In the alterna-capitol of Athens, Georgia, Mahal merges the musical forces of Mississippi and the Motherland on *Kulanjan* 🎵🎵🎵🎵 (Hannibal, 1999, prod. Joe Boyd, Lucy Duran), a historic collaboration with *kora* (African harp-lute) master Toumani Diabaté—not the first time either man has crossed cultural borders to bring back artistic gold. This album marks a fuller fruition of the *Mali to Memphis* collection (see below), on which Mahal appears and which drew a fascinating but more side-by-side than syncretic comparison between the blues' branches and its roots. The disc starts out assured and perhaps a mite too relaxed, but from the menacing third track "Ol' Georgie Buck" onward, the delicate but never ephemeral interplay between kora and guitar, honky-tonk piano and African *balafon* (xylophone), and soaring *jali* and *jalimuso* (male and female oral historian/troubadour) tones of Diabaté's vocalists and Mahal's own elemental smolder-and-growl makes this not only one of the most important albums of the turn of the century, but also one of the most satisfying. The groundbreaking American/African ensemble recorded here shared their landmark moment with Stateside crowds on the 1999 Africa Fête festival tour. *Mumtaz Mahal* 🎵🎵🎵🎵 (Water Lily Acoustics, 1995, prod. Kavichandran Alexander), a jam session with master Indian string musicians V.M. Bhatt and Narasimhan Ravikiran, offers more strong evidence that all blues didn't come from the Delta. The comfort with which Mahal slips into third-world rhythms is disarming, as the easy-fitting reggae beats of *World Music* 🎵🎵🎵🎵 (Columbia Legacy, 1993, prod. Lawrence Cohn) demonstrate. Since it contains nearly all of the *Mo' Roots* album plus other tracks in remastered form, this gets the slight edge over *Mo' Roots* itself. *Sacred Island* 🎵🎵🎵🎵 (Private, 1998) hops Mahal's blues from one tropics to another, with the roots of the American South, Hawaii, and the Caribbean intermingling elegantly.

what to buy next: Two albums on one disc, *Giant Step/De Old Folks at Home* 🎵🎵🎵🎵 (Columbia, 1969, prod. David Rubinson)

toss up distinctively different sides of the blues coin, the former lightly rocking with a down-home band while the rural solo blues of the latter reveal a surprisingly adept multi-instrumentalist and vocalist. For a harder-edged entry into Mahal's early work, *Taj's Blues* 🎵🎵🎵🎵 (Columbia Legacy, 1992, prod. David Rubinson, Taj Mahal) is a handy sampler of some of his more celebrated moments, such as the classic stomper "Statesboro Blues" and "Dust My Broom." In a welcome paradoxical twist, the Grammy-winning *Phantom Blues* 🎵🎵🎵🎵 (Private Music, 1996, prod. John Porter) deserves the attention it received. Save for the rolling country soul of the opening cut, Mahal didn't pen a single tune, instead paying a charging homage to mentors like Fats Domino and Ray Charles, his vocals as muscular as ever and his clear love for the material giving an extra shot of energy.

the rest:
Mo' Roots 🎵🎵🎵 (Columbia, 1974)
Best of Taj Mahal, Vol. 1 🎵🎵🎵 (Columbia, 1981)
Shake Sugaree—Taj Mahal Sings and Plays for Children 🎵🎵🎵 (Music for Little People, 1988)
Like Never Before 🎵🎵🎵 (Private Music, 1991)
Mule Bone 🎵🎵🎵 (Gramavision, 1991)
Dancing the Blues 🎵🎵🎵 (Private Music, 1993)
The Rising Sun Collection 🎵🎵🎵 (Just a Memory, 1994)
Taj 🎵🎵🎵 (Gramavision, 1994)
(With Cedella Marley Booker) *Smilin' Island of Song* 🎵🎵🎵🎵 (Music for Little People/Warner Bros., 1994)
An Evening of Acoustic Music 🎵🎵🎵 (Ruf, 1996)
Live at Ronnie Scott's, London 🎵🎵🎵 (DRG, 1996)
Senor Blues 🎵🎵🎵 (Private Music, 1997)
(With Eric Bibb, Linda Tillery, and the Cultural Heritage Choir) *Shakin' a Tailfeather* 🎵🎵🎵🎵 (Rhino, 1997)
(With Howard Johnson & Gravity) *Right Now! Featuring Taj Mahal* 🎵🎵🎵 (Verve, 1998)
An Evening of Acoustic Music 🎵🎵🎵🎵 (House of Blues, 1998)
In Progress & In Motion: 1965–1998 🎵🎵🎵🎵 (Sony, 1998)
Blue Light Boogie 🎵🎵🎵 (Private, 1999)

worth searching for: Mahal is part of the American delegation on one-half of the compelling compilation *Mali to Memphis: An African-American Odyssey* 🎵🎵🎵🎵 (Putumayo, 1999, compilation prod. Dan Storper), which surveys the musical conversation between bluespeople at two ends of the diaspora. (The disc is also reviewed in this book's Compilations section).

influences:
◀◀ Robert Johnson, Fats Domino, Howlin' Wolf, Ray Charles
▶▶ Robert Cray, Eric Clapton, Ry Cooder

see also: *V.M. Bhatt, Cedella Marley Booker, Ry Cooder, Toumani Diabaté, Ali Farka Touré, Vinx*

Allan Orski and Adam McGovern

Mahlathini
& Mahotella Queens
/Makgona Tsohle Band

Mbanqanga, Zulu jive

Mahlathini born January 1, 1937, in Alexandra Township, South Africa; died July 28, 1999, in Johannesburg, South Africa. Mahotella Queens formed c. 1960, in Alexandra Township, South Africa. Makgona Tsohle Band formed 1965, in Pretoria, South Africa. Based in Johannesburg, South Africa.

Mahlathini (Simon Nkabinde), lead vocals. Mahotella Queens: Hilda Tloubatla, lead and harmony vocals; Nobesuthu Shawe, lead and harmony vocals; Mildred Faith Mangxola, lead and harmony vocals. Makgona Tsohle Band: West Nkosi (died 1998), sax, pennywhistle, leader; Marks Mankwane, lead guitar; Joseph Makwela, bass; Lucky Monama, drums; Vivian Ngubane, rhythm guitar. (All members of all bands are from South Africa.)

The Makgona Tsohle Band, led by the late, legendary sax player/record producer West Nkosi, was formed in 1965 when the band members quit their day jobs in hopes of becoming famous musicians. They struck it rich soon afterward by hooking up with Mahlathini & Mahotella Queens on a hit single called "Orlando Train." The single went gold, and Nkosi and his band became one of the country's most important session groups and an internationally known touring band. "Makgona Tsohle means 'Jack-of-all-trades,'" West Nkosi once said. "We know everything, we can do anything. Our *mbaqanga* is a blend of traditional style with modern instruments, a music anyone can relate to." Nkosi was born in Nelspruit, a township about three miles east of Johannesburg, and he grew up in "a very poor Swazi family with lots of brothers and sisters, but I was the only one with music in me." Nkosi's uncle was the famous sax jive player "Zacks" Nkosi, one of the musicians who moved mbaqanga toward a more urban sound while retaining its folkloric roots. "My uncle didn't give me music lessons," West Nkosi said, "but he did introduce me to the record company people who gave me my first recording contract. There were no music books available in my country, and no schools to go to if you're poor and black. I got my start playing on street corners, and in the musical theaters in the black neighborhoods. It was just a collection of shacks where people went to have a good time and try to relax, not theaters like you have in the States, but it was a place where we could play and meet other musicians." The musicians in Makgona Tsohle had been playing together "since we were boys on the street corner. We are like brothers." So when Nkosi got signed by Gallo Records he brought the rest of the band along.

Luckily, the band was teamed with Mahlathini & Mahotella Queens, and the rest, as they say, is history. Mahlathini, a.k.a. King of the Groaners and the Lion of Soweto, began singing pro-

fessionally when he was 15, with Aaron Lerole's Alexandra Black Mambazo, an *mbube* (a cappella) choir. (This group was a big influence on Joseph Shabalala, who later formed Ladysmith Black Mambazo.) When he was 17, Mahlathini's voice began to deepen, eventually settling into his unique baritone growl. "At first, my mother thought there might be something wrong with my throat, so she took me to the doctor, but he said it was my normal tone, so everyone relaxed." In the late 1950s, after Miriam Makeba left South Africa for a self-imposed exile, the mbaqanga style she had championed, a more jazzy and less rootsy form of the music, was replaced by a more traditional one, with hard-driving rhythms and vocals that were closer to rural tribal styles. Mahlathini's rumbling basso became the trademark of this new sound and many singers began emulating him in hopes of cashing in on his success. He first sang with the Dark City Sisters, but when he was teamed with the Mahotella Queens and Makgona Tsohle in 1965, the resulting unit became one of South Africa's most popular black dance bands. The Mahotella Queens retired to raise families in the mid-1970s, but Mahlathini continued on with a new group dubbed the Queens and the Mahlathini Guitar Band. In the 1980s, disco-ized versions of mbanqanga began to dominate the charts, but Mahlathini stayed his course. "Some record company people suggested that I try to make a hit, but I stuck to my roots. If my children came to me in 10 years and asked me what I had contributed to the [anti-apartheid] struggle, what would I say if I had done that kind of music? Our culture has no price."

Meanwhile, the Makgona Tsohle Band had become a force on their own. After a few years in the studio working for others, Nkosi took over as producer and from that time on had a hand in the careers of over 300 groups including Ladysmith Black Mambazo and Paul Simon. Taking stock of this accomplishment, he described his philosophy: "In our culture there is no difference between a traditional player and a 'professional' musician. We don't have those categories for music. We see it as cultural music, even if it has electric instruments. Some people think that mbaqanga sounds like soul music, or rock music, but that's mostly because the bass and guitars are [suited to] the European market. You're familiar with the way they sound, but the way we use them is our own. I hear some similarity in the rhythms, but that's the feeling that every African person has inside of themselves. Black Africans, no matter where they were born, no matter how long they've been away from home, have that feeling when they play. I hear it in reggae music too."

In 1986, in the wake of Paul Simon's *Graceland*, Mahlathini reunited with the Mahotella Queens and the Makgona Tsohle Band and began playing the burgeoning world-music circuit. Once again people heard the roar of the Lion of Soweto (a rumbling tone that many critics compared to the primal growl of

Mahlathini (r) and Mahotella Queens

Howlin' Wolf), the heavenly harmonies of the Mahotella Queens, and the relentless rhythm of Makgona Tsohle. Their international recognition ignited homefront fans and their reunion album, *Thokozile*, became a major hit both at home and abroad. Despite the untimely death of West Nkosi in a 1998 auto accident, Mahlathini and his cohorts maintained a grueling touring schedule up until Mahlathini's death in mid-1999. Though back in South Africa their roots-rock style of mbanqanga would give way in people's favor to the more international beat of "bubblegum" artists like Dan Tshanda, and the surviving musicians' professional future was unknown at presstime, their legendary status is assured.

what to buy: *The Lion of Soweto* 𝄞𝄞𝄞𝄞 (Earthworks, 1987, prod. C.B. Matawane), a compilation of hits from the mid-1970s, was put together by Trevor Herman and Jumbo Vanrenen, the white South Africans who started Earthworks to gain black South African music the worldwide attention it deserved. Despite the lengthy liner notes, there is scant information on the backing musicians, but Mahlathini's bone-chilling moan is in fine form, and every track explodes with primal energy.

what to buy next: *Thokozile* 𝄞𝄞𝄞𝄞 (Earthworks, 1988, prod. West Nkosi) reunited Mahlathini, the Mahotella Queens, and the Makgona Tsohle Band for the first time in a decade and propelled them to international stardom. The recording is crisp and clear, and the music combines the best mbaqanga of the 1950s, 1960s, and 1980s for a mini-history of the style. Mahlathini and the Queens have never sounded this exuberant.

best of the rest:
The Lion Roars 𝄞𝄞𝄞𝄞 (Shanachie, 1989)
Mbaqanga 𝄞𝄞𝄞 (Shanachie, 1989)
Rhythm & Art 𝄞𝄞𝄞𝄞 (Shanachie, 1989)
Best of Mahlathini and the Mahotella Queens 𝄞𝄞𝄞𝄞 (Kaz, 1990)
King of the Groaners 𝄞𝄞𝄞𝄞 (Earthworks, 1993)

Mahotella Queens
Izibani Zomgqashiyo 𝄞𝄞𝄞𝄞 (Shanachie, 1989)
Marriage Is a Problem 𝄞𝄞𝄞𝄞 (Shanachie, 1990)
Women of the World 𝄞𝄞𝄞𝄞 (Shanachie, 1993)

influences:
⏮ Manhattan Brothers, Skylarks, the Queens, Dark City Sisters

▶▶ Johnny Clegg, Paul Simon, Stimela

see also: *Dark City Sisters, Miriam Makeba, Daniel Tshanda*

j. poet

Boncana Maiga
West African, Central African, and Afro-Cuban pop
Born 1943, in Gao, Mali. Based in Paris, France, and Abidjan, Côte d'Ivoire.

Boncana Maiga is a pioneer in the arts of music production and arranging in Africa. He was born in Gao, in remote northern Mali. After that country's independence in 1960, the new government began sponsoring official local bands around the country, and Maiga, a young saxophonist at the time, found himself leading Le Negro Band de Gao. In 1963 he was selected for an exchange program in which he would study music in Havana, Cuba. During what became a nine-year stay in that country, Maiga switched from sax to transverse flute and played everything from Mozart to classic Cuban *charanga*. He started another band, Las Maravillas de Mali, playing Cuban music.

Maiga returned to Mali in 1974 and for a while continued with Las Maravillas. Within a few years, however, he left the band and went to work in Abidjan, Côte d'Ivoire, the blossoming center of music production for all of West Africa. There he flourished as an arranger, helping to shape the sounds of many path-breaking African artists, including Alpha Blondy and Aicha Koné (both from Côte d'Ivoire), Tata Bambo Kouyaté, Abdoulaye Diabaté, and Nahawa Doumbia (all from Mali). He also recorded and released music of his own, though it was never as successful as the work he arranged for others.

Then, in 1992, Maiga teamed up with West Africa's most powerful record producer, Ibrahima Sylla of Senegal, to create his most successful project to date: Africando. The idea was to take the great surviving singers of Senegal who had made their careers doing adaptations of Cuban music, and put them together with the top Latin session players in New York. Four sensational releases and a number of tours on three continents followed over the next five years. The project expanded to include singers from Togo and Guinea and the music has remained excellent, a multi-lingual reaffirmation of the classic Cuban sound with lots of room for adventurous updates.

what to buy: Nahawa Doumbia's *Didadi* 𝄞𝄞𝄞𝄞 (Shanachie, 1989, prod. Ibrahima Sylla) is a fine example of Maiga's ability to arrange rootsy Malian music and give it a pop sheen, as is Ami Koita's *Songs of Praise* 𝄞𝄞𝄞𝄞 (Stern's Africa, 1993). *Africando: Volumes 1–4* 𝄞𝄞𝄞𝄞 (Stern's Africa, 1992–97, prod. various) encompasses several trailblazing classics.

what to avoid: Despite some hot playing, a sampling of Maiga's own work, *Boncana Maiga: Jingles Danses et Musiques Instru-*

mentales 𝄞𝄞 (Melodie/Celluloid 1990), is extremely commercial—everything from drippy ballads to hyperactive Caribbean *zouk*. The collection embodies the apex (or nadir) of the programmed pop sound that flourished in Paris and Abidjan during the 1980s.

influences:
◀◀ The great arrangers of Cuba, producers of American pop in the '60's and '70s

▶▶ Many producers and arrangers working in African pop music today

see also: *Africando, Tshala Muana*

Banning Eyre

Pandit Kamalesh Maitra
North Indian classical
Born 1928, in East Bengal, India. Based in Berlin, Germany.

Pandit Kamalesh Maitra is widely acknowledged as the last living virtuoso of the *tabla tarang,* a rare instrument used in the classical music of North India. A relatively recent addition to the myriad Indian percussion instruments, the tabla tarang consists of 10 to 16 *tablas* (a double-headed drum prominent in Indian music itself), each tuned to the particular notes of the classical *raga*'s scale and set up in ascending order in a semicircle. The word "tarang" means "waves," and that aptly describes the instrument's characteristic sound in the hands of an accomplished performer. Maitra, already a well-known tabla player, was first introduced to the tabla tarang in 1950 when, after boasting that he could learn to play any instrument within six months, he was accepted into the orchestra of the Uday Shankar Ballet on the condition that he learn *this* unusual melodic instrument. Later, after living up to his word and becoming multiply proficient, Maitra was named the group's musical director. Over the course of his lifetime, Maitra has studied and performed with a number of legends in the Indian music community, including Ustad Ali Akbar Khan and Pandit Ravi Shankar (Uday's younger brother), as well as a variety of jazz, folk, rock, and pop groups. In 1980 he formed the Ragatala Ensemble, in which both Indian and Western instruments were integrated, and he has taught Indian classical vocal and instrumental music in Berlin since 1982. But his personal mission remains to keep the tabla tarang from dying out completely, by inspiring younger musicians to take up this rare and valuable art.

what's available: Although probably not recommended for those without a passion for rhythm, *Tabla Tarang—Melody on Drums* 𝄞𝄞𝄞𝄞 (Smithsonian Folkways, 1996, prod. Walter Quintus) is a fascinating recording that shows how tabla tarang masters can combine rhythm, melody, and harmony into one free-flowing whole. Mind-blowing exchanges between Maitra and Trilok Gurtu, especially on the 45-minute "Raag Mia Ki Todi," make this a must-have for fans of virtuosic drumming.

worth searching for: Maitra recorded a number of albums between 1967 and 1994, but nearly all of them are out of print or available only on extremely hard-to-find import labels. Suffice it to say, with the rarity of these recordings, if you find 'em, snap 'em up . . . quickly!

influences:

◀◀ Uday Shankar, Ravi Shankar, Vishnudas Shirali, Pandit Jnan Prakash Ghosh

▶▶ Trilok Gurtu

see also: *Trilok Gurtu*

Bret Love

Miriam Makeba

African vocals

Born on March 4, 1932, in Johannesburg, South Africa. Based in South Africa.

Miriam Makeba is the queen of her country's vocalists. The first South African to be awarded a Grammy—for her participation on Harry Belafonte's 1960 album *An Evening with Belafonte* — Makeba is best known for her million-selling pop single "Pata Pata," recorded in 1959 and released in the U.S. in '67. For much of her career, Makeba was exiled from her birthplace; an April 1991 concert marked the first time she had performed in South Africa in three decades. Makeba's professional singing debut came with the Manhattan Brothers, a popular South African group with whom she performed from 1952 to 1957. After appearing in the documentary *Come Back Africa* in 1959, Makeba came to the attention of Harry Belafonte, who invited her to perform with him during his groundbreaking Carnegie Hall concert the following year. Banned from recording in South Africa the same year, Makeba left her homeland with her then-husband, trumpeter Hugh Masekela, and made a temporary home in New York. Although "Pata Pata" became an international hit, Makeba continued to encounter political problems; following her breakup with Masekela and her subsequent marriage to black activist Stokely Carmichael, many of Makeba's concerts were canceled and her recording contract was dropped. Makeba and Masekela continued to work together musically, with Masekela producing many sessions for his ex-wife. Leaving the United States in 1968, Makeba settled in the West African country of Guinea at the invitation of its president, Sekou Touré. As the Guinean delegate to the United Nations, Makeba twice addressed the General Assembly on the evils of apartheid. She was awarded the Dag Hammarskjöld Peace Prize in 1986. The following year, Makeba was a featured performer on Paul Simon's worldwide *Graceland* tour. In 1988 her autobiography, *Makeba—My Story*, was published in the U.S. and England, and has subsequently been translated into German, French, Dutch, Italian, Spanish, and Japanese. In December 1990, both Makeba and Masekela returned to South Africa; in 1992 Makeba appeared in the filmed apartheid drama *Sarafina!* as the title character's mother. Geographically and artistically, Makeba had come full circle as a leading voice for her people and both a teller and maker of history—come full circle, but certainly not yet come to rest.

what to buy: *The Best of Miriam Makeba* ♫♫♫♫ (Castle, 1993, prod. various) is a memorable retrospective of Makeba's career and includes her original 1959 recording of "Pata Pata."

what to buy next: *Africa* ♫♫♫ (Jive/Novus, 1991) presents 23 of Makeba's best-known songs recorded with sparse arrangements featuring guitar, percussion, and background vocalists.

the rest:
The Many Voices of Miriam Makeba ♫♫♫ (Kapp, 1958)
The Voice of Africa ♫♫♫ (RCA Victor, 1962)
The Magnificent Miriam Makeba ♫♫♫ (Mercury, 1964)
All about Miriam ♫♫♫ (Mercury, 1965)
Keep Me in Mind ♫♫♫ (Reprise, 1966)
The Magic of Makeba ♫♫♫ (RCA Victor, 1966)
Pata Pata ♫♫♫♫ (Esperance, 1970)
Miriam Makeba in Concert! ♫♫♫♫ (Reprise, 1983)
The World of Miriam Makeba ♫♫♫ (RCA, 1985)
Sangoma ♫♫♫ (Warner Bros., 1986)
Makeba Sings ♫♫♫ (RCA Victor, 1988)
Comme Une Symphonie D'Amour ♫♫♫ (Stern's Music, 1991)
Eyes on Tomorrow ♫♫♫ (Polydor, 1991)
Kilimanjaro—Live in Conakry ♫♫♫♫ (Goya, 1994)
A Promise ♫♫♫ (Sonodisc, 1994)
Pata Pata, Vol. 1 ♫♫♫ (Sonodisc, 1994)
Le Monde de Miriam Makeba ♫♫♫ (Sonodisc, 1994)
Click Song, Vol. 1 ♫♫♫ (Sonodisc, 1994)
Sing Me a Song ♫♫♫ (DRG, 1994)
Live Au Palais Du Peuple De Conakry ♫♫♫ (Stern's Music, 1994)
Miriam Makeba & the Skylarks, Vol. 1 ♫♫♫ (Gallo, 1996/1999)
Country Girl ♫♫♫ (Esperance, 1996)
Live from Paris and Conakry ♫♫♫♫ (DRG, 1996)
Pata Pata—Live in Paris ♫♫♫ (Goya, 1996)
Meet Me at the River ♫♫♫ (Goya, 1996)
Malaisha ♫♫♫ (Goya, 1996)
Best of Miriam Makeba & the Skylarks ♫♫♫♫ (Camden, 1997)
Miriam Makeba & the Skylarks, Vol. 2 ♫♫♫ (Gallo, 1997/1999)
Folk Songs from Africa ♫♫♫♫ (A World of Music, 1997)
Click Song N/A (Sonodisc, 1999)
World of Miriam Makeba N/A (Sonodisc, 1999)

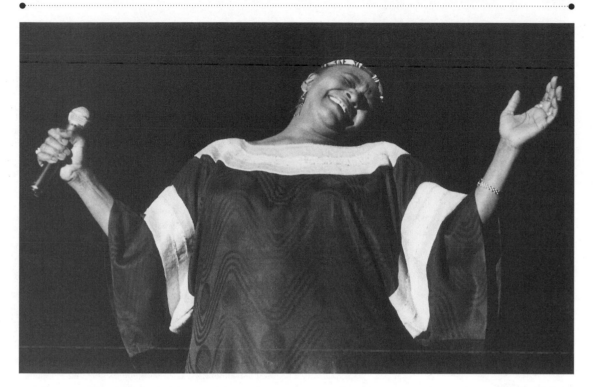

Miriam Makeba

influences:

◀ Harry Belafonte, Dudu Pukwana, Hugh Masekela

▶ Mahotella Queens, Ladysmith Black Mambazo

see also: *Harry Belafonte, Hugh Masekela*

Craig Harris

Tommy Makem

Irish traditional folk

Born 1932, in Keady, County Armagh, Ireland. Based in Ireland.

In the annals of folk, Tommy Makem is generally associated with the Clancy Brothers, the group that gave Irish and Celtic music a face on U.S. soil. However, Makem is an accomplished performer in his own right, a singer and multi-instrumentalist who plays banjo, pennywhistle, piccolo, and guitar. Makem has also embraced several areas of the entertainment world, starring in theatrical productions in New York and even dabbling in management for a time. By the time he was 15, he had already formed his own Irish county dance band. Around the time of

the early 1950s, Pat Clancy had asked his brother Liam to collect material for Tradition Records, a label he was starting. That led Liam to Makem, and, in 1953, the two new-found friends came to the United States. Makem began as a solo act, securing an early break by playing at Greenwich Village's famed Circle in the Square. He also supported himself with theatrical roles on Broadway, *A Hatful of Rain* and the musical *Finian's Rainbow* among them. In 1961, with brothers Liam, Pat, and Tom Clancy all living in New York, Makem was asked to join the Clancy Brothers band. That same year he performed on two albums, the first a solo effort on the Tradition label titled *Songs by Tommy Makem*. The second, *The Clancy Brothers and Tommy Makem,* was made for a much more prestigious label, Columbia, which had signed the Irish boys to a contract. Makem appeared with the Brothers on several more Columbia albums, including *Hearty & Hellish* (1962), *In Person* (1963), *First Hurrah* (1964), and *The Irish Uprising* (1966). The act forged its success through performances on American television, mainly the weekly folk series *Hootenanny* and the *Ed Sullivan Show*. They were also featured in concerts all over the world. From the late 1960s to the early '70s, Makem returned to solo performing and released one album, *Tommy Makem, Love Is Lord of All,* on GWP Records. For a brief period during the late '70s Makem and Liam Clancy formed a duo that reunited for a pair of albums during the mid-'80s. Makem's more recent recordings have been with the Shanachie label. Both on his own and as a member of the Clancy Brothers, Makem has been a welcome, unique addition to the American folk scene; he is certainly among the best-known purveyors of traditional Irish and Celtic music. By helping introduce audiences to the Celtic legacy quite early in the modern era, Makem forged a strong contribution.

what to buy: *Songs of Tommy Makem* 🎵🎵🎵 (Tradition, 1997) is the obvious starting point. It's particularly admired for the depth and quality of recording, considering that Makem was playing most of the instruments in a small studio.

the rest:
(With Liam Clancy) *Tommy Makem & Liam Clancy* 🎵🎵🎵 (Shanachie, 1987)
(With Liam Clancy) *Two for the Early Dew* 🎵🎵🎵 (Shanachie, 1987)
Rolling Home 🎵🎵 (Shanachie, 1990)
Songbag 🎵🎵🎵 (Shanachie, 1991)
Live at the Irish Pavilion 🎵🎵🎵 (Shanachie, 1993)
Lonesome Waters 🎵🎵 (Shanachie, 1993)
Evening With . . . 🎵🎵🎵 (Shanachie, 1993)
From the Archives 🎵🎵🎵 (Shanachie, 1995)
Tommy Makem's Christmas 🎵🎵🎵 (Shanachie, 1997)

influences:
◀◀ Clancy Brothers
▶▶ Irish Rovers, the Chieftains

see also: *The Clancy Brothers*

Bob Paxman

Makgona Tsohle Band
See: Mahlathini & Mahotella Queens

The Ilyas Malayev Ensemble
Classical Uzbeki music, sung in Persian
Formed 1992, in New York, NY, USA. Based in New York, NY, USA.

Ilyas Malayev, vocals, tanbur; Iskhak Katayev, violin; Izra Malakov, vocals; Muhabbat Shamayeva, vocals; Osher Barayev, vocals; Ilyau Khavasov, vocals; Rushel Rubinov, vocals; Abokhai Aminov, vocals; Roman Narkolayev, vocals. (All members are from Uzbekistan.)

The *maqam* is a conceptual and organizational framework for the development of melody and improvisation in a host of musical styles of the Muslim world—Arabian, Turkish, Persian, Egyptian, and North African music included. One of the system's wellsprings was 16th-century Central Asia, where music histo-

rian Kaukaba made a definitive analysis of the *shash maqam,* six lengthy maqams that formed a repertoire of 200 songs and instrumental pieces. These in turn served as the core repertoire of Uzbek and Tadjik classical music—a body of work that was suppressed by the Soviet government during the 20th century. Whereas the music was traditionally performed by individuals, it was now "collectivized"; that is, it had to be performed in ensembles. The lyrical content was "ideologically cleansed"; references to religion or overly sensual sentiments were erased in favor of the correct Marxist doctrine. The original music was heavily ornamented; these "wrong notes" were eliminated to conform with the approved styles of Soviet music—which often sounded suspiciously like 19th-century Russian Romantic music. As state-supported folk orchestras and choruses became the only mode of transmission of Uzbeki music, the shash maqam lost nearly all of its traditional texture. Musician Ilyas Malayev, though Jewish, had long dreamed of reviving the genuine shash maqam, and when he moved from Tashkent, Uzbekistan, to New York in 1992, he gathered a group of professional and amateur players from the Bukharian émigré community in Queens to realize this dream with the recording *At the Bazaar of Love.* Ironically (if miraculously), one of the most important contributions to the performance and preservation of Central Asian classical music is being made in Queens, New York.

what's available: Western sensibilities may find the monophonic musical texture and exotic melodic pitches of the classical shash maqam to be a bit abrasive. Approach the material on *At the Bazaar of Love* 🎵🎵🎵 (Shanachie, 1997, prod. Theodore Levin) in small doses at first. Begin with the "Ufar" and the "Ufarcha." Compare and contrast the maqams to other classical Muslim melodies. The music may not be easily accessible, but it is authentic.

influences:
◀◀ The Uzbeki classical tradition

Aaron Howard

Malika
Tarabu
Born Asha Abdo Suleiman, in Lamu, Kenya. Based in Mombasa, Kenya.

On the East Coast of Africa "Malika" means "Queen," which is fitting, for this artist is the Queen of *tarabu* music (a blending of Arab, African, Indian, and Latin sounds). Malika's specialty is setting the works of the great poets of her region. Her expressive vocal style is as flexible as the sound of a sitar, and she picks the finest musicians in her region to set the exotic rhythmic pace on drums, organ, and bass. Malika began her singing career after her family moved to Somalia during the 1960s. Benefiting from

Ilyas Malayev

sponsorship by both the Somali and Tanzanian governments, her fame quickly spread and led to well-received appearances on Somali television and radio. Upon her return to Kenya during the '70s she began recording with many of the best-known artists in her field, such as Zein L'Abdin and Maulidi. With a whole scene growing around her sound, Malika soon became the most popular artist in Kenya. Her songs of spirituality and political awareness are joyfully embraced and sung by the people of her country, and her recognition has begun to spread worldwide.

what's available: On *Tarabu* 𝅘𝅥𝅘𝅥𝅘𝅥♪ (Shanachie, 1997, prod. Dieter Hauer), Malika sets the poetry of Bakari Omari Abdi, Mjomba Mokte, and Tahareni Bwana Ali to music and brings them to vivid rhythmic life. Aided by *darabouka* drummers Anasi Sheembwana Muhaji and Omar Saleh Al-Abdi, organist Bakari Salim, and Lali Mwalimu Mzamin on bass, Malika sings songs of spirituality ("It Is Not Vain," "Think About It Man," "I Have Seen a Sign," etc.), and the contradictory nature of the human spirit ("Rebellion Will Not Give You Peace," "Darling You Trouble Me"). Though this 10-song disc is recorded entirely in Swahili, English translations and key story points are included in the booklet.

The slick production values and percussive verve should make this outing appeal to Western fans as well as genre purists.

worth searching for: In her U.S. debut, Malika performs "Sibure Nambo" on *Holding Up Half the Sky: Voices of African Women* 𝅘𝅥𝅘𝅥𝅘𝅥♪ (Shanachie, 1997, compilation prod. Randall Graff), a disc also reviewed in this book's Compilations section.

influences:

◀◀ Bakari Omari Abdi, Zein L'Abdin

▶▶ Them Mushrooms

Ken Burke

The Mallet Playboys

See: Terrance Simien

Mama Sana

Malagasy folk music

Born c. 1922, in Antanimora, Madagascar. Died 1998.

Mama Sana played the *valiha,* a zither constructed on a tube of bamboo and played with both hands. Sonically, it suggests a cross between the zither known to the West and the African harp-lute or *kora*. But it's the picking technique used by Malagasy musicians that gives the instrument its unique sound, a combination of rippling arpeggios, slurred bluesy notes, and lightning-fast single-note runs. Mama Sana, once one of the few female musicians in Madagascar, played the instrument from childhood onward. Mama Sana believed she was born around the time the French came to Madagascar in 1882, which would have made her 110 at the time she recorded her only album for Shanachie. That album's notes say differently, but that doesn't make her any less an elder stateswoman of her culture. Mama Sana's songs are all traditional tunes she picked up during her long life, though like most folk musicians, the interpretations are definitely her own.

what's available: *The Legendary Mama Sana* ♫♫♫ (Shanachie, 1992, prod. Henry Kaiser, Dama Mahaleo, Bernhard Ramroth) preserves raw, uncompromising music from one of Madagascar's national treasures. The artist's powerful vocals and technical prowess bring to mind the early Delta Blues 78s made in the U.S. at the dawn of the recording industry. The liner notes, by Kaiser and Mahaleo, give a bit of background, but Mama Sana and her music need no interpretation.

influences:
▶▶ Tarika Sammy, Tarika, D'Gary

j. poet

Cheb Mami

Rai
Born July 11, 1966, in Saïda, Algeria. Based in Paris, France.

Cheb Mami, born Khelifati Mohamed, has been singing *rai*—a combination of Bedouin traditional music and Spanish, Moroccan, French, and black Arabic styles—since he was a teenager. Saïda had a large Bedouin population, and Mami schooled himself in their bedrock traditional styles, which continue to give his music a folksy edge. Mami ("the Mourner") got his stage name because of the soulful quality of his singing, and he made his early reputation by performing at weddings, circumcisions, and other community functions. When he was 15 he won second prize in a talent competition sponsored by *Ihan Wa Chabab,* a popular radio program in Oran. He was immediately deluged with offers from various record companies, including Disco-Maghreb's Boualem, one of the most successful rai labels of the 1980s. Mami began recording cassettes, which sold well although he himself never saw much money. After a brief tour of France, during which he met his future manager Michele Levy, Mami returned to Algeria to fulfill his military duty. After his discharge, he relocated to Paris and began his

international career, touring Canada, the United States, England, and Europe. Mami's band is one of the finest rai outfits extant, a group of young talents who can pace their frontman in his desire to make rai truly international by adding accents of flamenco, Greek and Turkish pop, hip-hop, funk, reggae, and Latin music. Fans have dubbed him "the Prince of Rai," and his popularity is second only to Khaled's.

what to buy: *Saïda* ♫♫♫ (Tinder, 1998, prod. Bobby Summerfield, Nicholas Fiszman, Christian Boissel) is a solid modern rai outing, with about half the tracks sporting smooth, crossover grooves that should appeal to fans of "modern rock" if any of them take the time to listen. The rest of the tracks lean toward the traditional side and will be a bit more appealing to world-music fans. On "Alache Alache," Mami's keyboards mimic the sound of an Arabic string orchestra, while the Afro-Arabic rhythms of "Hay Wadi Hay Galbi" and "Bent Bareh" are guaranteed to put your feet in motion.

what to buy next: The early *Prince of Rai* ♫♫♫ (Shanachie, 1989, prod. Clement Haufman, Bruno Barre) is mostly acoustic, and while traces of reggae-ized funk show up in the basslines, the focus stays on Mami's passionate vocals and the band's fierce groove.

the rest:
Let Me Rai ♫♫♫ (Rhythm Safari, 1990)

influences:
◀◀ Cheikha Remitti, Khaled, Chaba Fadela
▶▶ Cheb Abdelhak

see also: *Khaled*

j. poet

The Mandators /Victor Essiet

African reggae
Formed 1979, in Lagos, Nigeria. Based in Lagos, Nigeria.

Victor Essiet (born c. 1960, Akwa Ibom State, Nigeria), vocals; Frank Martins, guitar; Clement Amarchi, guitar; Peter Freeman, bass; Kwust Ewang, bass; Lemmy Jackson, keyboards, percussion; Lizoma, keyboards; Etienne Kaston, DX7; Mannars Itiene, drums. (All members are from Nigeria.)

The Mandators are the brainchild of Victor Essiet, a guitar player and singer from the Ibibio tribe of southeastern Nigeria. Torn from his comfortable family existence during Nigeria's civil war in 1975, Essiet relocated to Lagos for his high school years. He learned guitar on an instrument he made himself and decided on a career in music when he heard Bob Marley and local reggae stars like Cloud Seven, Sweat, and Sonny Okosun. After two albums for the Tabansi label, *Sunrise* and *Imagination,* Essiet went on tour. His lead guitarist for that first, unsuccessful sojourn was another reggae fan named Majek Fashek. Like Essiet's, Fashek's would one day be a name associated with African reggae stardom. But this would have to wait, as Essiet went from record shop to record shop, self-distributing his first two albums, just to survive. Soon after, he dropped out to meditate and rethink his career. He returned in 1986 with *Crisis,* hailed as a turning point for Nigerian reggae. The album sold 500,000 legitimate copies (and millions of bootlegged albums and cassettes), making Essiet a force to be reckoned with. Since then he has added a bit of dancehall to his basic roots reggae sound and gone from success to success.

what's available: On *Power of the People* 𝄞𝄞𝄞𝄞 (Heartbeat, 1994, prod. Victor Essiet, Lemmy Jackson), Essiet has a gritty tenor that's halfway between Bob Marley and Peter Tosh, and he writes love songs and protest tunes that would do the master proud. The backing band is solid, with a deep one-drop groove that makes their riddims sparkle. This compilation collects tracks from three albums Essiet cut between 1988 and 1992, and it includes a wonderful reworking of Dolly Parton's "Coat of Many Colors."

worth searching for: If the *Power of the People* compilation is any indication, the full albums should be worth tracking down. They include *Storm, Rat Race,* and *Rebel.*

influences:
◀◀ Bob Marley, Sonny Okoson, Storm
▶▶ Majek Fashek

j. poet

Ahdri Zhina Mandiela

Dub poetry
Born in Kingston, Jamaica. Based in Toronto, Ontario, Canada.

Mandiela is a talented second-stringer in the thriving Caribbean arts scene in Toronto that's also home to fellow wordsmiths Lillian Allen, Clifton Joseph, and Michael St. George. But the label "dub poetry" is—as in so many cases these days—simply inadequate to describe her style of performance; her diasporan approach owes as much to Sweet Honey in the Rock, Sonia Sanchez, and Gil Scott-Heron as it does to reggae music and Jamaican Creole. Mandiela's voice is full and confident, intimate and melodic. Her delivery and phrasing favor slow syncopation and internal rhyme; she likes to tease and stretch and stylize natural speech rhythms in a diction that only occasionally slides into artsy affectation.

worth searching for: To date, Mandiela has released only one CD, *Step into My Head* 𝄞𝄞𝄞 (bushooman rag, 1995, prod. Orin

Isaacs, Quammie Williams), available on import from Canada. It's a strong collection of poems, backed by a tight band and wonderful arrangements that draw not just on reggae and ska, but (more often) on jazz and P-Funk, heavy metal and Fulani drumming, hand-clap and tap-step. The subject matter rarely strays from earnest Afrocentrism, lesbian-feminist sisterhood, and the slings and arrows of immigrant life in the wilds of what Mandiela wryly calls the "Toronto bush." Two cuts give those themes a particularly sophisticated spin: "In the Canefields," a sultry but powerful elegy for a plucky immigrant aunt whose early death from diabetes ultimately foils her flight from the canefields of the colonial past; and "Afrikan by Instinct," a brilliant, vibrant, jubilant celebration of the black diaspora that name-checks everyone from C.L.R. James to Ntozake Shange, all in steel-pan/highlife/township-jive double-time. Mandiela's earlier cassettes, *first & last* and *barefoot and black,* are available directly from her independent label, bushooman rag, Box 292, Station B, Toronto, Ontario, Canada M5T 2W2. She is also active as a video producer, theater director, and page poet; her published collections are *Speshal Rikwes* (Sister Vision, 1985) and *dark diaspora . . . in dub* (Sister Vision, 1991).

influences:
◀◀ Lillian Allen

Michael Eldridge

Kanté Manfila

Guitar-based Manding pop
Born 1946, in Farabanah, Guinea. Based in Abidjan, Côte d'Ivoire, and Paris, France.

Kanté Manfila was born a Manding *griot* or hereditary oral historian/troubadour—in other words, a person with ancient music literally in his blood. He spent his early years living the village life, surrounded by the fabulous melodies and rhythms of the *kora* (African harp-lute), the *balafon* (xylophone), and the all-powerful *djembe* drum. Once he left the village, he worked a brief stint with Guinea's Ballets Africains, one of the foremost traditional performance ensembles Africa has produced. By the late '50s Manfila had begun to take an interest in the guitar, which, in the hands of pioneers like Sekou "Docteur" Diabaté, was emerging as a major player in modern griot music.

Manfila mostly learned guitar while living in Abidjan, Côte d'Ivoire, which was becoming a major music center during the '60s. In 1971, he was invited by the great Malian singer Salif Keita to move to that country's capitol of Bamako and form a new band, Les Ambassadeurs du Motel. Keita was leaving the legendary Rail Band de Bamako at the time, and ironically, Manfila's cousin Mory Kanté then took Keita's place as the Rail Band's lead singer. The cousins remained close, but their respective bands entered a period of intense competition. That rivalry came to a dramatic head some years later when Les Ambassadeurs had moved on to Abidjan and Mali's arts-loving dictator, Moussa Tra-oré, invited the two bands to play back-to-back in a stadium show. Though there was no definitive winner, the concert marked a watershed event in the history of Manding pop.

In 1982, Manfila and Keita parted ways. Keita went on to Paris to begin a solo career that would soon rocket him to international fame. Manfila also moved to Paris for a time and began his own solo career, and though he never matched Keita's achievements, he continued to do pioneering work. His all-acoustic release *Tradition* reunited him with Mory Kanté on kora and paved the way for a period of excellent acoustic recordings of Manding griot music by a number of artists. Manfila has stayed active in a variety of settings and remains a powerful force in this music.

what to buy: *Salif Keita & Les Ambassadeurs: Seydou Bathily* ♪♪♪♪ (Stern's Africa, 1997) is perhaps the best of the fine reissues of music from this classic band of the '70s. *N'na Niwalé (Merci les Mères)* ♪♪♪♪ (popular african music, 1990) is a prime acoustic session highlighting Manfila's guitar mastery.

what to buy next: *Ni Kanu* ♪♪♪♪ (Hemisphere, 1995, prod. Patrick Papineau) blends a few acoustic tunes into a mostly electric production showcasing Manfila's contemporary band sound.

worth searching for: *Tradition* ♪♪♪♪ (Celluloid/Melodie, 1989, prod. Tangent, Kante Manfila) is Manfila's seminal back-to-roots recording, well worth tracking down.

influences:

◀◀ Sekou "Docteur" Diabaté, Sekou "Bembeya" Diabaté

▶▶ Ousmane Kouyaté, Mory Kanté

see also: *Mory Kanté, Salif Keita, Rail Band*

Banning Eyre

Sam Mangwana

Soukous

Born 1945, in Kinshasa, Zaire (now Congo). Based in Paris, France.

Mangwana's parents were from Angola, but he was born and raised in the Congo. He sang from childhood and learned formal music during a stint in a Salvation Army choir. By 17 he was fronting Tabu Ley Rochereau's African Fiesta, as well as arranging some of the band's music. Mangwana also moonlighted frequently with other top *soukous* (African rumba) outfits including Negro Band, L'Orchestre Tembo, Vox Afrique, and Tabu Ley's main rival, Franco's TPOK Jazz. In 1976 Mangwana decided to form his own band, which was made easier because of his connections to the top names in Congo's music business. That

band, the African All Stars, toured endlessly, touching down all over Africa, Europe, and the Caribbean. In 1982 he recorded "Maria Tebbo," one of the biggest soukous hits of all time. Mangwana has always been an adventurous composer, adding bits of West African highlife as well as *beguine, zouk,* and other Caribbean rhythms to his melodies. In the past few years he's also been experimenting with the sounds of Cape Verde, Mozambique, Angola, and Cuba.

what to buy: On *Galo Negro* ♪♪♪♪ (Putumayo, 1998, prod. Christian Polloni), Mangwana moves closer to his goal of international domination, with an exciting, eclectic sound. The band, as always, is in top form, shifting easily across numerous geographical and musical boundaries. The title tune is a Cape Verdean *morna* with a zouk backbeat; "Nakupenda" has a pleasing touch of *semba* (Angolan samba); and "Gossip" sounds like the Buena Vista Social Club in Cape Verde and is as sweet as any soukous ballad Mangwana has ever recorded.

what to buy next: Two of Mangwana's early albums go digital for the first time on a single CD, *Maria Tebbo* ♪♪♪♪ (Stern's Classics, 1995, prod. Sam Mangwana). He was already experimenting with other African rhythms as you can tell from such self-explanatory titles as "Tchimurenga Zimbabwe" and "Bana ba Cameroon," and the compilation's own title track was his first Pan-African hit.

best of the rest:

Georgette Eckins ♪♪♪♪ (SAM, 1979/Celluloid France, 1984)
Affaire Video ♪♪♪♪ (Celluloid, 1982)
Les Champions ♪♪♪♪ (Celluloid, 1984)
Aladji ♪♪♪♪ (Shanachie, 1989)
Rumba Music ♪♪♪♪ (Stern's, 1994)

influences:

◀◀ Tabu Ley Rochereau, Franco, Le Grande Kalle

▶▶ Ray Lema, Kanda Bongo Man

see also: *Franco, Tabu Ley Rochereau, Rigo Star*

j. poet

Herbie Mann

World jazz

Born Herbert Jay Solomon, April 16, 1930, in Brooklyn, NY, USA. Based in New Mexico, USA.

Jazz-style improvisation is at the core of Herbie Mann's music. However, a world-spanning range of influences has given it its distinct flavor. Over the past three decades, the New York–born flute player has incorporated everything from African rhythms and Brazilian bossa novas to Memphis-style R&B and Top 40 pop tunes. Mann's childhood dreams to play the drums were altered when his parents took him to see swing clarinet player

Benny Goodman at the Paramount Theater in 1939, hoping to change his mind. Their scheme worked. Two weeks later, Mann had a clarinet of his own. Not long afterwards he was playing saxophone as well. Following a stint in the U.S. Army, Mann planned to become a professional saxophonist. Instead, he found that most of the jobs in jazz bands for sax players were already filled by the likes of Al Cohn, Zoot Sims, and Stan Getz. Switching to the flute, Mann recorded an album with jazz accordionist Matt Mathews and the rhythm section of bassist Percy Heath and drummer Kenny Clarke of the Modern Jazz Quintet. With no previous jazz flute players to serve as models, Mann took his own approach, using the flute more like a trumpet than a classical instrument. Though his playing was initially treated as a novelty, Mann was taken more seriously when he began adding Latin rhythms to his arrangements. With a band that included Chick Corea, Herbie Hancock, Steve Gadd, Tony Levin, and Nana Vasconcelos, Mann became an international success.

In the early 1960s, he toured South America with an all-star jazz band featuring Coleman Hawkins, Roy Eldridge, Al Cohn, Zoot Sims, Wildman Jo Jones, Ronnie Ball, Ben Tucker, David Bailey, Chris Conner, and Kenny Durham. During the tour, Mann's inclusion of a passage from a Brazilian tune during his solo one night earned him a standing ovation and showed him the power of inter-cultural music. Mann later became one of the first American musicians to record with Brazilian ones, including Sergio Mendes and Antonio Carlos Jobim. At the close of the decade, Mann switched to American music and released a jazz-meets-R&B album, *Memphis Underground,* with Muscle Shoals studio musicians including the late Duane Allman. Although his interpretations of songs by the Beatles and Creedence Clearwater Revival upset many jazz traditionalists, the album became an FM hit and introduced his music to a younger audience. Mann's stylistic expeditions abroad were not over, though; the same year he toured with a band that featured jazz greats Cornell Dupree, Chuck Rainey, David Newman, and Les McCann (1992), he launched his own record label, Kokopelli, with the album *Jazil Brazz,* recorded with his Brazilian band of the same name.

what to buy: Recorded during a week-long celebration at the famed New York jazz club in April 1995, *65th Birthday: Live at the Blue Note ♫♫♫♫* (Lightyear, 1995, prod. Herbie Mann) showcases the full spectrum of Mann's legacy. In addition to ultra-funky treatments of "Memphis Underground" and "Dippermouth," Mann leads more than 30 past and present members of his band— including Dave Valentin, Randy Brecker, Tito Puente, and David "Fathead" Newman—through bossa novas like "Sonhos" and reworkings of Ellington's "Jeep's Blues" and Parker's "Au Privau."

what to buy next: Mann upset many of his old jazz fans with his exploration of late-'60s soul music and R&B, *Memphis Un-*

brazil: the northeast

F or over 100 years Quilombo dos Palmares—now the Northeast of Brazil— was an independent nation, formed in the 17th century by escaped slaves. Here the people farmed, practiced the religions of their African ancestors, and ruled by consensus. Their resistance against repeated offensives by the Portuguese and Dutch armies illustrates the gritty strength of the *nordeste* (Northeast) culture.

Luiz Gonzaga (1912–89) was the voice of the nordeste for more than half a century, popularizing his rollicking *baião* style and flaunting clothes reminiscent of bandit folk-hero Lampiao. His best-known song "Asa Branca" tells of a *nordestino* boy who leaves his drought-plagued rural home and goes to the big city to try and earn a living, a story that mirrors millions of lives in Brazil.

Carnival is also a big part of life in the coastal regions (Recife and Olinda in Pernambuco state are especially known for it). Brass bands playing the irrepressible *frevo* music wind through the streets, trailing groups of revelers. The deep, earthy rhythm of *maracatú* pounds out from where the circle dances are taking place. And exhibitions of *caboclo,* or Indian heritage, are theatrically expressed.

Since the 1970s singers Elba Ramalho, Zé Ramalho, Alceu Valença, and Geraldo Azevedo have churned out music with a northeastern twang, heightening the popularity of *forró* (a catch-all term for the myriad northeastern dance-music genres, typically incorporating tambourine, triangle, and accordion). In the '90s the traditional *cóco* and maracatú rhythms have propelled Chico Science and his band Nação Zumbí into funk, acid jazz, and hardcore, resulting in one of the most original sounds to come out of Brazil for some time. The *embolado,* a remarkable rapid-fire improvisational song (which can become an exciting duel of the spoken word if two people are involved), has seen a resurgence through recordings by Chico Science, Daude, and Gilberto Gil. Meanwhile the folkloric heritage of the Northeast has found its champion in Antonio Nobrega, who digs deep to reveal gems of the popular culture.

Mara Weiss and Nego Beto

Manolín, El Médico de la Salsa

dergroud 🎵🎵🎵 (Atlantic, 1969, prod. Herbie Mann). But the album's funky rhythms and pop-minded melodies became a college-radio hit and established Mann with a more youthful following. The album remains a powerful summit meeting of jazz players—including flautist Mann, vibraphonist Roy Ayers, and guitarists Larry Coryell and Sonny Sharrock—and Memphis studio players including the late Duane Allman.

best of the rest:

Bongos, Conga and Flute 🎵🎵🎵 (Atlantic, 1959)
African Suite 🎵🎵🎵🎵 (Atlantic, 1959)
At the Village Gate 🎵🎵🎵🎵 (Atlantic, 1962)
Latin Fever 🎵🎵🎵🎵 (Atlantic, 1962)
Brasil, Bossa Nova & Blues 🎵🎵🎵🎵 (Atlantic, 1962)
Returns to the Village Gate 🎵🎵🎵🎵 (Atlantic, 1963)
(With João Gilberto and Antonio Carlos Jobim) *With Gilberto & Jobim* 🎵🎵🎵🎵 (Atlantic, 1966)
Push Push 🎵🎵🎵🎵 (Atlantic, 1971)
Mississippi Gambler 🎵🎵🎵🎵 (Atlantic, 1972)
Evolution: Anthology 🎵🎵🎵 (Atlantic, 1992)
America/Brasil 🎵🎵🎵🎵 (Lightyear, 1997)

influences:

◀◀ Miles Davis, Dizzy Gillespie, bossa nova, African rhythms, the Beatles

▶▶ Jethro Tull, Hubert Laws

see also: *Maya Angelou*

Craig Harris

Manolín, El Médico de la Salsa

Timba
Born Manuel Gonzales Hernandez, in Havana, Cuba. Based in Havana, Cuba.

In modern Cuba, the only people who (relatively speaking) make big bank legally are musicians. That said, save for OGs Los Van Van, NG La Banda, and the fluky Buena Vista Social Club, new jack *timba* bands like Bamboleo, David Calzado, and Azucar Negra are the top-dollar choices of the people. Though rooted in traditional Cuban *son*, timba's refreshing exuberance, unpredictability, earthiness, and in-ya-grill immediacy come from a worldly synthesis of reggae, '70s funk, electric jazz, hip-hop, and street-smart realness. For certified physician Manuel Hernandez, forming a timba band was a no-brainer: $2,000 annual government salary vs. $40,000-plus rock-star take. Today, smooth-operator tenor pipes intact, white-on-white ensembles in full effect, the re-christened, 30-something Manolín, El Médico de la Salsa is one of Cuba's biggest pop heartthrobs—stage, radio, and television.

what's available: Signed to EMI's Spanish subsidiary Caribe, El Medico's most available release in America is *De Buena Fe* 🎵🎵🎵🎵 (Metro Blue, 1997, prod. Dagoberto Gonzales Jr.). A slightly underwhelming timba album padded with too many mid-tempo ballads (especially when compared with solo timba mack daddy Issac Delgado), *De Buena Fe* does flash sufficient lightning with killer tracks "Yo Tengo Mi Mecánica," "Que Le Llegue Mi Mano," "Pegaito, Peqaito," and "El Que Este Que Tumbé."

influences:

◀◀ NG La Banda, Los Van Van

▶▶ Adalberto Alvarez, Issac Delgado

see also: *Bamboleo*

Tom Terrell

Machanic Manyeruke /Machanic Manyeruke & the Puritans

African gospel
Born in Zimbabwe. Based in Harare, Zimbabwe.

Manyeruke is a gospel singer and guitarist from Zimbabwe with a unique style that's part Pops Staples, part Jonah Sithole. With his backing group, simple piano, and two powerful female singers, he makes a mighty noise unto the Lord, one that's powerful enough to motivate unbelievers too.

what's available: Like many albums released in the early days of the world-music boom, *Machanic Manyeruke & The Puritans* ♫♫♫♫ (Flying Fish, 1986, prod. Bothwell Nyamhondera) has no liner notes, no personnel, no nothin', except for incredible music, great picking, and a big, fat, inspirational vibe.

influences:
◀◀ Ngwara Mpundu, Ephat Mujuru & The Spirit of the People

j. poet

Samba Mapangala & Orchestra Virunga

East African rumba/soukous

Formed 1980, in Nairobi, Kenya. Based in Nairobi, Kenya; Paris, France; London, England; and USA.

Rotating membership in recent years; original lineup featured: Samba Mapangala (born early 1950s, in Matadi, Congo), lead and backing vocals; Risa-Rissa, lead guitar; Mikili Sesti, rhythm guitar; Bavon Masudi, bass guitar; Juma Kachenchy, drums; Rama Athumani, alto sax.

Samba Mapangala epitomizes a major 1970s phenomenon of African pop music—the exodus of talented musicians from the competitive scene in Kinshasa, Zaire (now Congo), and the subsequent spread of the Kinshasa sound to other African cities. Mapangala was born in the Zaire River city of Matadi, but after his parents died, he came to Kinshasa as a teenager and naturally fell into the evolving rumba-rock community there. Mapangala sang with a group called Les Kinois, and in 1975 he took them on the road to East Africa. After a tough run in Uganda, the group landed in Nairobi, Kenya, where they lasted a few years before disbanding. Bringing some Kenyans on board, Mapangala went on to form Orchestra Virunga in 1980. The name referred to a volcano in eastern Zaire, and the music remained loyal to Mapangala's African-rumba roots (a hybrid subsequently known to the world as *soukous*). But now Swahili lyrics sidled up alongside Zairean Lingala, the lingua franca of the form; Virunga had a special identity as a Kenyan rumba outfit. In 1982 they scored an enormous hit with the song "Malako Disco," and their star rose steadily. The music centered around Mapangala's sweet, strong voice and the guitarists' classic, tangling interplay, but Mapangala also used a small saxophone section, which gave his group a unique sound. The band gained worldwide acclaim with the release of *Virunga Volcano* in 1990, and as the new decade wore on they toured in Europe and America, making more fine recordings along the way. The lineup has shifted some, but by now the band has made its mark and their sound keeps steady despite all the changes. Dependably tasty, Virunga's music has held up very well as modernizing trends continue to undermine the impact of recent rumba.

what to buy: *Virunga Volcano* ♫♫♫♫ (Earthworks, 1990, prod. Justus Musyoka Kasoya) defines the original Virunga sound and includes the classic "Malako Disco." *Feet on Fire* ♫♫♫♫ (Stern's Africa, 1991, prod. Charlie Hart) presents the slightly more produced sound of their first U.K. recording, with shorter, more hard-hitting arrangements.

worth searching for: *Vinja Mifupa* ♫♫♫♫ (Disc Makers, 1997, prod. Clifford Lugard) is an excellent, independently produced American recording of the group.

influences:
◀◀ Franco, Zaiko Langa Langa

Banning Eyre

Thomas Mapfumo

Chimurenga

Born 1945, in Marondera, Zimbabwe. Based in Zimbabwe.

"The Lion of Zimbabwe," Thomas Mapfumo is one of his country's most influential musicians, with hard-driving rhythms, politically tinged lyrics, and gutsy vocals. A graduate of a British colonial school in Zimbabwe, Mapfumo was initially inspired by the rock and pop music of Europe and the United States. As a youngster, he performed a version of Elvis Presley's "A Mess of Blues," accompanied by a white band, the Bob Cyclones, in a local talent show. After continuing to sing cover tunes in the short-lived band Cosmic Four Dots, Mapfumo began incorporating the indigenous rhythms associated with Zimbabwe's *mbira* (thumb piano). Accompanied by the Acid Band, a group that he met at a local bar, Mapfumo recorded his first singles in the early 1970s. Inspired by Zimbabwe's move away from the colonial rule of Great Britain, Mapfumo increasingly used his songs to address political issues. Mapfumo's debut album with the Acid Band, *Ho Koyo*, was so politically edged that he was arrested and placed in a prison camp. Although he agreed to perform a concert in exchange for his release, Mapfumo stuck to his political repertoire. In 1976 several of the Acid Band's less talented musicians were replaced by guitarist Jonah Sithole and a new horn section, and the group's name was changed to Blacks Unlimited. In 1978, Mapfumo and Blacks Unlimited celebrated Zimbabwe's independence with the album *Gwindingwe Rine Shumba*. The band's first internationally distributed album, *Corruption*, was released in 1989. Mapfumo's electrically charged style of mbira music is called *chimurenga*, the Shona word for "struggle."

Thomas Mapfumo

what to buy: *Chimurenga Singles* ♫♫♫ (Shanachie, 1984, prod. Thomas Mapfumo & Blacks Unlimited) samples tracks from the band's early albums and documents Mapfumo's updating of the traditional mbira sounds of Zimbabwe.

what to buy next: Focusing on Mapfumo and Blacks Unlimited's early- and late-1970s recordings, *Shumba: Vital Hits of Zimbabwe* ♫♫♫ (Earthworks, 1991, prod. Thomas Mapfumo & Blacks Unlimited) picks up where *Chimurenga* leaves off.

best of the rest:
Ndangariro ♫♫♫ (Hannibal, 1983/Shanachie, 1991)
Corruption ♫♫♫ (Mango, 1989)
Chamunorwa ♫♫♫ (Mango, 1991)
Chimurenga Forever: The Best of . . . ♫♫♫ (Blue Note, 1996)
Chimurenga: Africa Spirit Music ♫♫♫ (WOMAD, 1997)
Hondo ♫♫♫ (Zimbob, 1998)
Chimurenga '98 ♫♫♫ (Stern's USA, 1999)

influences:
◄◄ King Sunny Adé, Stella Chiweshe, Ephat Mujuru & the Spirit of the People

▶▶ Oliver Mtukudzu, Comrade Chinx

see also: *Ephat Mujuru*

Craig Harris

Mariachi Cobre
Mariachi, Tejano, son jalisco
Formed 1971, in Tucson, AZ, USA. Based in Tucson, AZ, USA.

Randy Carrillo, guitarron, guitar; Steve Carrillo, trumpet; Adolfo Roman García, violin (former member); Francisco Grijalva, guitar; Roberto Juan Martínez, vihuela; Israel Gálvez Molina, violin, congas; Antóñio Hernandez Ruíz (Mexico), violin; Mack Ruíz, violin; Carlos Figueroa, violin; Hector Gama (Mexico), violin; Javier Trujillo, guitarra de golpe; Mario Trujillo, violin. (All members are from USA except where noted otherwise.)

In the mid-1960s a young priest in Tucson, Arizona, began encouraging the young people of his church to learn and sing the music of their Mexican heritage. In 1971 Randy Carrillo, a longtime member of the church group, organized Mariachi Cobre with his younger brother Steve, his friend Mack Ruiz, and guitarist Frank

Grijalva. The band expanded, concentrating on the traditional *mariachi* instrumentation of violin, trumpet, and several types of guitar, to bring the sound of Jalisco (the Mexican state from which some members hail) to the world. They founded the first International Mariachi Conference in Tucson in 1981, and since 1982 have played for visitors to EPCOT Center at Walt Disney World in Orlando, Florida. The band members have been able to learn from the seminal Mariachi Vargas, and they've appeared on stage with Linda Ronstadt, Lucha Villa, Lola Beltran, Ana Gabriel, Julio Iglesias, Jose Luis Rodriquez, and other Latin-music leaders.

what's available: *Este Es Mi Mariachi* ♪♪♪♪ (Kuckuck, 1995, prod. Brian Keane) shows the vitality and musicianship that attracted Ronstadt and others to the group. *Mariachi Cobre* ♪♪♪ (Kuckuck, 1991, prod. Brian Keane) captures the band at an earlier stage of evolution, though they'd been playing together for a number of years when it was recorded. *XXV Aniversario* ♪♪♪ (Black Sun, 1996, prod. Brian Keane) is a retrospective celebration of the Mariachi Cobre style.

influences:

◄◄ Mariachi Vargas, Mariachi Reyes del Assaredero

Kerry Dexter

Bob Marley
/Bob Marley & the Wailers

Reggae, ska, rocksteady

Bob Marley born Robert Nesta Marley, February 6, 1945, in St. Ann, Jamaica. Died May 11, 1981, in Miami, FL, USA. The Wailers formed 1963, in Kingston, Jamaica. Disbanded 1981.

Bob Marley, vocals, guitar (1963–81); Peter Tosh (born Winston Hubert McIntosh; died September 11, 1987), vocals, guitar (1963–74); Bunny Wailer (a.k.a. Neville O'Riley Livingston), vocals (1963–74); Junior Braithwaite (died June 2, 1999), vocals (1963–65); Beverley Kelso, vocals (1963–65); Cherry Smith, vocals (1963–65); Constantine "Dream Vision" Walker, vocals (1966); Norma Fraser, vocals (1966); Rita Marley (Cuba), vocals (1966, 1974–81); Aston "Family Man" Barrett, bass (1969–81); Carlton Barrett (died 1987), drums (1969–81); Al Anderson (USA), guitar (1972–76; 1979–81); Earl "Wire" Lindo, keyboards (1972–74); Bernard "Touter" Harvey, keyboards (1974–81); Judy Mowatt, vocals (1974–81); Marcia Griffiths, vocals (1974–81); Julian "Junior" Marvin, guitar (1975–81); Tyrone Downie, keyboards (1975–81); Donald Kinsey (USA), lead guitar (1976). (All members are from Jamaica except as noted otherwise.)

Born in the rural parish of St. Ann to Cedella Malcolm, an 18-year-old black woman, and Captain Norval Marley, a white quartermaster in the British West Indian Regiment, Bob Marley became the Third World's first truly international recording artist and an inspirational Rasta lightning rod—a conduit for "sufferahs" everywhere who let humanity and faith course through him and direct his vision.

As a boy, Marley grew up in the impoverished hamlet of Nine Miles, a country village suffused with the heterodoxy of *obeah* sorcery and *myal* magic. At a very early age he developed a reputation as an eerie, spiritually connected boy—a genuine "natural mystic"—primarily due to his fiercely penetrating gaze, unsettling palmistry skills, and uncanny ability to read and feel "the vibe" of those around him. Barely into his teens, he and his mother moved to the notorious Trenchtown ghettos of Kingston. There Marley became fast friends with fellow youths Peter Tosh and Bunny Wailer. As a teen, Marley was dubbed "Tuff Gong" for his ferocious street-fighting skills, and he eventually earned renown as a fine boxer as well. His first musical instrument was a banjo.

The original Wailers initially coalesced in 1961 as the Teenagers and included Marley, Tosh, Wailer, Junior Braithwaite, Beverley Kelso, and Cherry Smith. The group was then intensively tutored by the great Trenchtown wiseman Joe Higgs. Marley's first solo singles were released by Leslie Kong's Beverley label in 1962: "Terror," "Judge Not," and "One Cup of Coffee," a loose cover of a 1961 Claude Gray country song; all three sold inauspiciously. "Simmer Down" was the Wailers' first release and its popularity was a harbinger of things to come. The record soared to #1 on the Jamaican charts within weeks of its December 1963 issue and remained there for two months, though pre-release sound-system (mobile deejay unit) dub plates had made it a local dancefloor-filler as far back as late 1962. Often backed by the Skatalites, the band recorded numerous tracks for Coxsone Dodd's esteemed Studio One between 1963 and '66, including ska cover versions of U.S. soul and doo-wop songs as well as original pre-rocksteady (proto-reggae) groovers, among them such stand-out singles as "Wings of a Dove," "Destiny," "Freedom Time," "Who Feels It, Knows It," and "Rolling Stone," an adaptation of the Bob Dylan epic. The group also issued the first versions of Marley-penned future sure-shots "One Love" and "Put It On." All of the band's Dodd-produced singles bore the legend "Scorcher!" emblazoned on the labels.

On February 10, 1966, Marley married Rita Anderson, at the time a member of the Soulettes. The next day Marley flew to Wilmington, Delaware, where he worked to earn enough money to finance his own record label and lived with his mother, who had remarried and relocated there. He returned to Jamaica in October of 1966. Early the next year the Wailers, pared down to a Marley/Tosh/Wailer trio, recorded the superb singles "Bend Down Low," "Nice Time" (a nickname for Marley's first child, Cedella), "Hypocrites," and "Stir It Up," a tune written for Rita while Marley was in America that is still one of reggae's most sensual and seductive love songs. Marley's Stateside monetary mission a success, all these tracks were proudly released on the band's own Wail 'N' Soul 'M imprint.

During this period, the Wailers recorded their first Rastafarian hymns, including "Selassie Is the Chapel." However, the group's momentum briefly subsided when Bunny was arrested and imprisoned for marijuana possession. Upon his release in 1969, the band recorded a slew of stellar singles for producer Leslie Kong, who eventually released a compilation album in 1970 called *The Best of the Wailers.* Yet the group continued to struggle financially, and in the summer of '69 Marley again sojourned to Wilmington, where he obtained a job at the city's Chrysler plant.

When he returned to Jamaica later that year, the Wailers' crucial collaboration with Lee "Scratch" Perry began. The songs from this period—1969–71—represent some of the boldest, most inspired reggae music ever made. Rebellion-stoked underdog anthems like "Small Axe," "Duppy Conqueror," "Soul Rebel," and a shamanistic cover of Richie Havens's "African Herbsman," in addition to divinity-imbued remakes of some of the band's Studio One material, were all backed by Perry's organic roots-funk band the Upsetters, which included in its ranks the relentless rhythm section of Aston "Family Man" Barrett (bass) and his "one drop"–wielding brother Carlton (drums). Perry helped convince the Wailers of their status as soul-powered mavericks not only for their shantytown brethren but for oppressed people the world over.

After these stirring sessions, the band was signed by Chris Blackwell's Island Records and released *Catch a Fire,* a brawny reggae/blues/rock album that ignited a crossover Wailers wildfire. The record included organ overdubs by "Stevie" Winwood and a clever Zippo-lighter sleeve, a hip adornment that was targeted toward hippies and white rockers but one which was heedless of the true meaning of the album title—a Jamaican term for "catching hell," not an entreaty to smoke ganja as the marketing implied. The 1973 follow-up *Burnin'* shed all the rockist trappings and is a defiant roots-reggae masterpiece. English rock wanker Eric Clapton's cover of the album's "I Shot the Sheriff" was a #1 U.S. hit, though the Wailers' version is immensely more trenchant and provocative, as Marley testifies with the anger and fear of a real fugitive from (in)justice.

In retrospect, the Wailers' committed and creative triple-threat of Marley, Tosh, and Wailer was both a blessing and a curse, a dynamic that inevitably resulted in the impact of strong personality upon strong personality—a collision that led to the unfortunate implosion of the boyhood triumvirate in mid-1974. Tosh and Wailer decided to pursue solo careers and were replaced with the gorgeous gospel-styled harmonies of the I-Threes—Bob's wife Rita Marley, Marcia Griffiths, and Judy Mowatt. The women lent an exhilarating vocal and visual presence to Marley's live act, with at-once dazzling and dignified dance moves choreographed by Mowatt. In the following years, Marley attained hard-earned international success with the militantly arrayed *Natty Dread* and *Rastaman Vibration,* as well as *Live!,* an astonishing performance recorded at London's Lyceum Ballroom.

On December 3, 1976, on the eve of a much-publicized free Kingston concert, gunmen broke into Marley's home in a blitzing assassination attempt. Marley was shot but survived the hail of bullets; the motive for the shooting is unclear to this day. Undeterred, Marley performed for the massive crowd the following evening, and later released "Ambush in the Night," a song of survival (from the LP also named *Survival*) that entwined calls for brotherhood and integrity among the poor with lyrics that effectively exposed the machinations behind divide-and-conquer political agendas.

Still shaken from the incident, Marley jetted off on an 18-month international tour, which, along with the multi-continent popularity of the *Exodus* LP, further entrenched his image as a revolutionary mystic, an edifying seer, and a contemplative emissary of Rastafari. In July of 1977 Marley entered a hospital in Miami and had surgery to remove cancer cells from his right toe. In 1978, he was awarded the United Nations' Medal of Peace after he brushed off numerous death threats from warring, politically funded tribes to play the One Love Peace Concert in Kingston, where he persuaded Jamaica's bitterly opposed party leaders to clasp hands on stage in a dramatic gesture of national unity and goodwill.

In 1980, Marley's legendary concert in newly liberated Zimbabwe made him forever an apostle of Pan-Africanism. Toward the end of the year, Marley began to grow increasingly frail as his body was ravaged by liver, brain, and lung cancer. In April of 1981, he received one of Jamaica's highest honors, the Order of Merit, for his everlasting gifts to the country's culture. A month later, on May 11th, Marley died in a Miami hospital at the age of 36. He was buried with his time-worn Gibson guitar and a Bible opened to the 23rd Psalm in a sepulcher carved out of hilltop rock high in the Nine Miles countryside. Marley will be remembered as a phenomenon of conviction, rebellion, and conciliation—a man who consistently created inspiring songs alive with gritty, searching cadences, infinite soul, and unwavering hope. His music's unassailable devotion to the downtrodden used the patois, lore, and idioms of Jamaica, yet always strove to establish "One Love"—Marley's term for the space in all of us that is receptive to empathy and redemption. His life, his personality, and his art together are the embodiment of the animating force of reggae music.

what to buy: Possessing a potent amulet's continuous surge of spiritual energy, *Songs of Freedom* ♫♫♫♫ (Island/Tuff Gong, 1992, prod. various) is a truly essential reggae compilation and by far the finest and most comprehensive anthology of Marley's sweeping, sultry body of work. From the very first Leslie Kong singles and kinetic Studio One ska cuts, to the rugged Wailers material with Lee Perry, to the best of the timeless Island classics, all the way to revelatory unreleased tracks, this thoughtfully annotated 4-CD collection captures the essence of the man and the heart-nourishing substance of his legacy. The set also includes a terrific live version of "Redemption Song" and a tremendous collection of photographs that is nearly as revealing as the music. *Burnin'* ♪♪♪♪ (Island, 1973, prod. Chris Blackwell, the Wailers) is a firebrand of closely rising, helix-like three-part harmonies, spellbinding shantytown stories, and unadulterated, utterly arresting roots-reggae music. It includes "I Shot the Sheriff" and "Burnin' and Lootin'," both graphic tales of the ruthlessness of martial law and unmitigated police power. Add tough, distinctive recuts of "Small Axe" and "Duppy Conqueror" and you have one of the Wailers' strongest albums. *Natty Dread* ♪♪♪♪♪ (Island, 1974, prod. Chris Blackwell, the Wailers) is the first album featuring the transcendent gospel-esque harmonies of the I-Threes, but is ultimately catalyzed by the incipient movement-of-Jah-people power of the songs—the title cut, "Them Belly Full (But We Hungry)," "Rebel Music (3 O'Clock Roadblock)," and "Talkin' Blues" emanate both the aura of insurrection and the balmy feel of tropical heat. There are also the definitive versions of "No Woman, No Cry" and "Lively Up Yourself," the latter rendered with a totally wild and unrestrained passion including an ululating war-cry/yodel at the song's outset. *Exodus* ♪♪♪♪♪ (Island, 1977, prod. Bob Marley & the Wailers) is one of Marley's most widely beloved albums and one that successfully commingles songs of exotic cultural convocation ("One Love/People Get Ready" "Natural Mystic," "Jamming") with those based on sweet, imagistic proverbs ("Three Little Birds," "Turn Your Lights Down Low") and beguiling Rasta ritual and history ("Exodus," "The Heathen"). The I-Threes are at their most magical on the title cut's epic tale of exile, and the Barrett brothers' battle-tested rhythms roll, boom, and echo like siege cannons throughout the album. What's more, the sad, serene longing expressed on the beautiful "Waiting in Vain" is an unforgettable moment in the Marley discography.

what to buy next: *African Herbsman* ♪♪♪♪♪ (Trojan, 1973, prod. Lee "Scratch" Perry) and *Soul Revolution I & II* ♪♪♪♪♪ (Upsetter, 1970/Trojan, 1988, prod. Lee "Scratch" Perry) together contain the best of the Wailers' collaborations with the man who made the recording of reggae an art. *Herbsman* mixes the Wailers' gripping unison harmonies with the Tuff Gong's evocatively echoing lyrics on such proverb-wise stone-cold classics as "400 Years," "Duppy Conqueror," "Kaya," "Lively Up Yourself," and of course, "Small Axe," which courageously cuts big, powerful oppressors down to size. The rites and incantations on *Soul Revolution* mix African communion and Babylon-conquering conjury into a potion to rejuvenate the soul; Volume II contains the raw, unceasingly tough dub versions, which accentuate just how mighty and nuanced the Barrett brothers' rhythms truly are.

the rest:
The Wailing Wailers ♪♪♪ (Studio One, 1965)
Marley, Tosh, Livingston & Associates ♪♪♪ (Studio One, 1965/1980)
The Best of the Wailers ♪♪♪♪ (Beverley's, 1970)
Soul Rebels ♪♪♪♪ (Maroon JA/Trojan U.K., 1970)
Catch a Fire ♪♪♪♪♪ (Island, 1973)
The Best of Bob Marley & The Wailers ♪♪♪♪ (Studio One/Coxsone, 1974)
Rasta Revolution ♪♪♪♪ (Trojan, 1974)
Live! Bob Marley & the Wailers ♪♪♪♪ (Island, 1975)
The Best of Bob Marley & the Wailers ♪♪♪ (Studio One/Buddah, 1976)
Rastaman Vibration ♪♪♪♪ (Island, 1976)
Kaya ♪♪♪♪♪ (Island, 1978)
Babylon by Bus ♪♪♪ (Island, 1978)
Survival ♪♪♪♪♪ (Island, 1979)
Uprising ♪♪♪♪ (Island, 1980)
Chances Are ♪♪♪ (Cotillion, 1982)
Marley ♪♪♪ (Phoenix, 1982)
Jamaican Storm ♪♪ (Accord, 1982)
Bob Marley Interviews ♪♪♪ (Tuff Gong, 1982)
Confrontation ♪♪♪♪ (Island, 1983)
In the Beginning ♪♪♪ (Trojan, 1983)
Legend ♪♪♪♪♪ (Island, 1984)
Reggae Greats—Wailers ♪♪♪♪ (Mango, 1984)
Mellow Mood ♪♪ (Topline, 1984)
Bob Marley and the Wailers/Bob, Peter, Bunny & Rita ♪♪ (Jamaica, 1985)
Rebel Music ♪♪♪♪ (Island, 1986)
The Birth of a Legend 1963–1966 ♪♪♪♪ (Epic, 1990)
One Love at Studio One ♪♪♪♪ (Heartbeat, 1991)
Talkin' Blues ♪♪♪♪ (Island/Tuff Gong, 1991)
All the Hits ♪♪♪ (Rohit, 1991)
The Never Ending Wailers **woof!** (RAS, 1993)
Return to Dunn's River Falls ♪♪ (Compose, 1993)
Natural Mystic–The Legend Lives On ♪♪♪♪ (Island/Tuff Gong, 1995)
Power ♪♪♪ (More Music, 1995)
The Rarities, Vol. I & II ♪♪♪ (Jamaican Gold, 1996)
(With Bill Laswell, posthumously) *Dreams of Freedom: Ambient Translations of Bob Marley in Dub* ♪♪♪ (Axiom/Island, 1997)
The Best of Bob Marley **woof!** (Madacy, 1997)
The Complete Wailers, 1968–1972: Part I ♪♪ (JAD, 1998)
Mr. Chatterbox ♪♪♪ (Culture Press, 1998)
Going Back to My Roots ♪♪♪ (M.I.L. Multimedia, 1998)
Simmer Down at Studio One ♪♪♪ (Heartbeat, 1998)
Destiny: Rare Ska Sides from Studio One ♪♪ (Heartbeat, 1999)
1970–71: Upsetter Years ♪♪♪♪ (Cleopatra, 1999)

worth searching for: Several video testaments give you the best way of experiencing Marley's presence in the only way you now can. A Jamaican bush-parish aphorism holds that "when the roots are strong, the fruit is sweet"; on *Live at the Rainbow, 1977* (Island Visual Arts, 1991), the downright invincible roots-reggae music reaches fruition in Marley's singularly possessed performance. Though there are no known quality live videos of the original Wailers, this I-Threes-fortified show is a frenzied yet liberating spiritual spectacle, and the performances of classic Marley meditations are so vital and vivid they make even the outstanding original studio incarnations sound like they were based on tentative charcoal rubbings. Recorded in London just as *Exodus* was entrancing British youth, the atmosphere is decidedly supernatural. *Legend* (Island, 1991) is produced by Big Audio Dynamite's Don Letts—who bites a hefty portion of footage from the *Rainbow* video. Still, there's a lot of concert imagery here that cannot be found elsewhere. As for documentaries on Marley's life as well as work, *Caribbean Nights* (BBC/Island Visual Arts, 1986) and *Time Will Tell* (Island, 1992) will still be rustless a century from now. The former may be familiar from public television, as it was produced by the BBC and won the 1988 ACE Award for programming excellence. The latter is special primarily for its unflinching fidelity to the task of revealing Marley's persona through his own words. There is no narration, just rare, enlightening interviews, fascinating rehearsal footage (which offers insights into the creative impulse behind a number of Marley compositions), and of course, a revolutionary's bandolier of solidarity songs—all performed with the Natural Mystic's mythically healing ardor.

influences:

◄◄ Joe Higgs, Curtis Mayfield and the Impressions, Lee "Scratch" Perry, Fats Domino, the Drifters, Brook Benton, James Brown, Jackie Mittoo, King Sporty, Coxsone Dodd, Bob Dylan, the Skatalites

►► Ziggy Marley & the Melody Makers, Mighty Diamonds, Alpha Blondy, Aswad, Junior Byles, Luciano, Tony Rebel, Culture, the Meditations, the Gladiators, Israel Vibration, Majek Fashek, Johnny Nash, Eric Clapton, Misty in Roots, Itals, Lucky Dube, Apache Indian, Anthony B., UB40, Oku Onuora, Wailing Souls, Linton Kwesi Johnson, Third World

see also: *Cedella Marley Booker, Marcia Griffiths, Joe Higgs, Rita Marley, Ziggy Marley & the Melody Makers, the Meditations, Judy Mowatt, Augustus Pablo, Lee "Scratch" Perry, the Skatalites, Peter Tosh, Bunny Wailer*

Todd Shanker

Rita Marley
Reggae
Born Alpharita Constantia Anderson, 1947, in Cuba. Based in Jamaica.

Rita Marley is one of the most important women in the history of reggae music. The widow of the late Bob Marley and the mother of six of his children including David (Ziggy), Sharon, and Cedella of the Melody Makers, Marley has garnered acclaim for her expressive vocals since the mid-1960s when she led the Soulettes, a light ska trio that was featured on many of the early recordings produced at the storied Studio One in Kingston, Jamaica. As a member of the I-Threes, Marley's vocals were essential to her husband's recordings and performances from the mid-'70s until his death in 1981. A native of Cuba, Marley grew up in Jamaica's Trenchtown. After meeting her future husband in 1964 at the age of 18, Rita fell under the reggae master's influence when she persuaded him to supervise the Soulettes. The Marleys were married on February 10, 1966. Working as a nurse in Delaware in the early '70s, Marley was lured back to music in 1974, when she joined with Marcia Griffiths and Judy Mowatt to form the I-Threes. Although she was at first skeptical of the Rastafarian faith central to reggae, Marley became devoted to the religion after a visit to Jamaica by Ethiopian emperor Haile Selassie I. Marley was working on her debut solo album when her husband died in 1981. Although she completed the album, *Who Feels It Knows It,* and had a minor hit with the single "One Draw," she withdrew from the limelight for most of the 1980s to manage and produce her children's group, the Melody Makers. The absence of a will left by her husband led to a lengthy period of court battles. The situation remained unsettled until 1991, when the Jamaican Supreme Court ruled that control of Bob Marley's multimillion-dollar estate should go to his family. After releasing the album *Harambe (Working Together for Freedom)* in 1983, Marley didn't return to the recording studio until 1990, when she recorded the aptly titled *We Must Carry On.*

what to buy: Marley's debut solo album, *Who Feels It Knows It* ♪♪♪♪ (Shanachie, 1981, prod. Rita Marley, Grub Cooper), remains a reggae masterpiece. Accompanied by many of her late husband's sidemen, including Aston Barrett (bass, guitar), Carlton "Carlie" Barrett (guitar, drums), Tyrone Downie (synthesizers, keyboards), and Julian "Junior" Marvin (guitar), Marley celebrates her commitment to Rastafarianism with such songs as "Jah Jah," "Thank You Jah," "Good Morning Jah," and "Jah Jah Don't Want," and pays homage to the joys of sensimilla with the hit tune "One Draw."

what to buy next: *We Must Carry On* ♪♪♪♪ (Shanachie, 1991, prod. various) includes a reggae-ized version of the Bee Gees' "To Love Somebody" and four Bob Marley tunes, including two that were previously unreleased—"Who Colt the Game" and "So Much Things to Say."

the rest:
Harambe (Working Together for Freedom) ♪♪♪ (Ultrasonic, 1983/ Shanachie, 1987)

worth searching for: A bootleg of a Marley performance with the Melody Makers, *Montego Bay* ♪♪♪♪ (Clinton), was recorded during a November 1992 concert and demonstrates the soulful excitement of her live shows.

Ziggy Marley

influences:

⏪ Bob Marley, Peter Tosh, Bunny Wailer

⏩ Marley's Girls, Ziggy Marley & the Melody Makers

see also: *Bob Marley, Ziggy Marley & the Melody Makers, Pablo Moses, Judy Mowatt, Lee "Scratch" Perry*

Craig Harris

Ziggy Marley & the Melody Makers

Contemporary reggae
Formed 1979, in Kingston, Jamaica. Based in Jamaica.

David "Ziggy" Marley, vocals, guitar; Stephen Marley, vocals, percussion; Cedella Marley, vocals; Sharon Marley Prendergast, vocals. (All members are from Jamaica.)

Bearing a striking resemblance, both physically and vocally, to his father—reggae icon Bob Marley—has likely been as much a burden as a boon to Ziggy Marley. But he's borne it amaz-

ingly well, leading a long-lasting and successful group that includes his brother and two sisters. Early on, their father wrote and produced a single for them, "Children Playing in the Streets," but the Melody Makers' first two albums suffered from the band's general lack of seasoning and from their record company's focus on making Ziggy a solo star. After moving to Virgin, Ziggy was still out front, but his family's influence grew on each successive album. While the group leans decidedly toward the pop side of reggae, with considerable influence from American R&B and hip hop, their lyrics continue in the vein of their late father—cautionary, righteous, but ever optimistic. Still, business is business, and these days the group is perhaps better known for appearing in a Cover Girl makeup commercial and performing the theme song for the cartoon show *Arthur*.

what to buy: The band's years on Virgin, certainly their most fertile period, are well summed up on *The Best Of (1988–1993)* ΔΔΔΔ (Virgin, 1997, prod. various), a 17-track compilation. In terms of individual releases, though, *Conscious Party* ΔΔΔΔ (Virgin, 1988, prod. Chris Frantz, Tina Weymouth) fulfills both parts of its title, with lyrics extolling Rastafarianism and liberation, and grooves that just won't quit. The title track and "Tomorrow People" promote awareness and uplift, while "Lee and Molly" recounts the strife encountered by an interracial couple. The production by Weymouth and Frantz doesn't get in the way of the songs, and the Talking Heads–style keyboard textures—on "Have You Ever Been to Hell," for instance—certainly make some of them more palatable to American ears. The group's reggae/hip-hop/rock synthesis continues on *Free Like We Want 2 B* 𝄞𝄞𝄞𝄞 (Virgin, 1995, prod. the Melody Makers), which finds the family's involvement at an all-time high. Backup vocalists Cedella and Sharon (along with Erica Newell) take the lead on "Today," and Stephen steps to the fore on a number of tunes, including "Tipsy Dazy," "Keep On," and "Bygones." Ziggy's presence is still strong, though, especially on the title track and "Power to Move Ya."

what to buy next: *Jahmakya* 𝄞𝄞𝄞𝄞 (Virgin, 1991, prod. the Melody Makers, Glenn Rosenstein) was perhaps the group's first truly mature album, with a nod to reggae's past but an eye more on creating a sound of their own, incorporating riddim-heavy hip-hop and dancehall influences and adding a harder rock edge to boot. "Raw Riddim," "Kozmik," and "So Good So Right" are standouts.

what to avoid: *Time Has Come . . . The Best of Ziggy Marley & the Melody Makers* 𝄞𝄞 (EMI America, 1988, prod. Rita Marley) captures the best of a formative period, a treat for the devout fan but non-essential for casual listeners.

the rest:
One Bright Day 𝄞𝄞𝄞 (Virgin, 1989)
Joy and Blues 𝄞𝄞𝄞 (Virgin, 1993)
Fallen Is Babylon 𝄞𝄞𝄞 (Elektra, 1997)
Spirit of Music N/A (Elektra, 1999)

worth searching for: Die-hard fans or collectors can scour the used-LP racks for the original Melody Makers releases: *Children Playing* (EMI America, 1984, prod. Steve Levine), *Play the Game Right* (EMI America, 1985, prod. various), and *Hey World* (EMI America, 1986, prod. various). Stephen covers his father's "Rebel Music (3 O'Clock Roadblock)"—with rapper Michael Franti as special guest toaster—on the latter's band Spearhead's *Chocolate Supa Highway* 𝄞𝄞𝄞𝄞 (Capitol, 1997, prod. Michael Franti).

influences:
◄◄ Bob Marley, the Wailers, Curtis Mayfield, Earth, Wind & Fire

►► Fugees, Spearhead, Big Mountain

see also: *Cedella Marley Booker, Bob Marley, Rita Marley, Spearhead*

Daniel Durchholz

Ricky Martin

Latin pop, dance, cumbia, norteña

Born Enrique Martin Morales, December 21, 1971, in San Juan, Puerto Rico. Based in USA.

Ricky Martin first came to the public eye amid the rotating roster of teenage Latin bubblegum institution Menudo, becoming its lead singer and helping bring the group to international celebrity. After Martin outgrew the ensemble he returned to Puerto Rico to finish high school and later spent a brief time in New York. Resuming a childhood enthusiasm for acting, he appeared in small stage roles there and then joined the cast of a Mexican soap opera. Next he turned to the U.S. side of daytime drama, as bartender Miguel Morez on *General Hospital*. This led to the part of Marius in the Broadway production of *Les Miserables*, in which he stayed for about a year. During this time, Martin built a following for his own music with four dance-infused Spanish-language albums, which sold better with each release. His conquest of *el Norte* was already well underway with these albums and his show-stealing 1999 Grammys performance; his first English-language record clinched it with a reign at the top of the singles charts, on the cover of *Time* magazine, and seemingly everywhere else as the new face of Latin pop.

what to buy: *Vuelve* 𝄞𝄞𝄞 (Sony, 1998, prod. Desmond Child) sees Martin fusing the dance-pop, flamenco, *cumbia, norteña,* and rock styles that interest him into a Pan-Latin dance mix that has proved enormously popular to Latin and non-Latin audiences alike. *A Medio Vivir* 𝄞𝄞𝄞 (Sony, 1995, prod. Ian Blake), produced by Martin's fellow Menudo alumnus Ian Blake (a.k.a. Robi Rosa), shows Martin reaching for a harder rock edge than on his two earlier, heavily pop-oriented outings.

what to buy next: No relation to an identically titled predecessor, *Ricky Martin* 𝄞𝄞𝄞 (Sony, 1999, prod. Robi Rosa) was the star's historic crossover dream-come-true, sung mostly in English and featuring the pop-ska mega-seller "Livin' La Vida Loca," a reprise of the career-making 1998 World Cup theme song "The Cup of Life" (which turned the world's head during the '99 Grammys broadcast), and more platinum vouchers where those came from. Critics caveated that ballads weren't really his business, and he may have made more new fans than kept old ones, but overall the album was one of those moment-defining events for which you don't begrudge the messenger.

the rest:
Ricky Martin 𝄞𝄞𝄞 (Sony Discos, 1991)
Me Amarás 𝄞𝄞𝄞 (CBS Discos, 1993)

influences:
◄◄ Los Tigres del Norte, Ricardo Montaner

►► Menudo

Kerry Dexter and Adam McGovern

Narciso Martinez

Conjunto

Born October 29, 1911, in Reynosa, Mexico. Died June 5, 1992, in San Benito, TX, USA.

Though Narciso Martinez was born in Mexico, his family soon moved to the Rio Grande Valley of Texas, where as a young man Martinez took up the accordion and with *bajo sexto* (Tex-Mex 12-string bass) player Santiago Almeida invented the *conjunto* sound, playing lively accordion-led dance tunes with the bajo sexto for rhythm. He became known as "El Huracan del Valle," or "the Hurricane of the Valley." His unique style, his choice to use the accordion as a melodic rather than a rhythm instrument, his willingness to experiment, and the wide distribution of his records over his long career all mark Narciso Martinez as a powerful influence on accordion players and on border music in general.

what's available: *The Father of Tex-Mex Conjunto: El Huracan del Valle* ♪♪♪ (Arhoolie/Folklyric, 1993, prod. Chris Strachwitz) collects 26 tracks from Martinez's extensive and mostly out-of-print catalog. His work often shows up on compilations of accordion, conjunto, and other border music as well.

influences:

◄◄ R. de Leon, Santiago Almeida, Lydia Mendoza

►► Flaco Jimenez, Santiago Jimenez, Tony de la Rosa

see also: *Don Santiago Jimenez*

Kerry Dexter

John Martyn

Folk

Born Iain McGeachy, September 11, 1948, in Surrey, England. Based in Scotland.

Growing up in both Scotland and England, John Martyn was strongly influenced by Scots folkie Hamish Imlach before hitting London in the mid-'6os with a formidable guitar technique already in place. He quickly became the first white solo artist signed to Chris Blackwell's Island label and in 1967 released his first record, *London Conversation*. It was fairly standard singer-songwriter material for the time, tossing in the obligatory blues and Dylan cover, but, considering he was only 19, showed hope for the future. That went some way to being fulfilled the following year on *The Tumbler*, which brought in jazzer Harold McNair on flute and went further to showing Martyn's increasing guitar prowess.

Then came the sidetrack—two albums with his new wife Beverly (née Kutner, who'd been groomed for a solo career and sung uncredited backup on Simon and Garfunkel's "Fakin' It"). Influenced by the rootsiness of the Band, they went to Woodstock to record and came up with a disc, *Stormbringer,* which alternated songs by the pair—Beverly's rather twee, but John's writing skills

accelerating by leaps and bounds. Their next excursion, *Road to Ruin,* was much more English and at the same time jazzier, with saxes and percussion, and altogether more satisfying.

It set the stage for the next (and possibly best) stage of John's solo career, *Bless the Weather,* pairing his guitar with Danny Thompson's bass as an instrumental foil, his voice gone all smoky like a tenor sax. He was also experimenting with an Echoplex unit, the first fruit of which was "Glistening Glyndebourne." This was more a preface than a full work, with everything coming to perfect fruition a couple of years later on *Solid Air.* The title track, written for Nick Drake, was pure night music, connecting the dots between folk and jazz, while his version of Skip James's "I'd Rather Be the Devil" used the Echoplex to weave and repeat lines, offering a very new kind of blues. As far as writing went, Martyn was at the top of his game, with little gems like "May you Never" (later covered by Eric Clapton). Then there came another step sideways: *Inside Out,* more experimental and electric, with the traditional Scots pipe lament "Eibhli Ghail Chiuin Ní Chearbhaill" reproduced on guitar.

Later Martyn became more reflective and in touch with his roots, as he covered both the Copper Family's "Spencer the Rover" and the traditional "Satisfied Mind." The writing, however, remained inspired, as it would through *One World,* which found him diversifying his sound, becoming a little ambient with Steve Winwood and down-and-dirty with reggae producer Lee "Scratch" Perry ("Big Muff"). In between, on the road with Thompson and free-jazz drummer John Stevens, he issued the live disc *Live at Leeds* under his own auspices, immediately selling out the initial pressing of 10,000 copies.

Personal trauma can be good for the creative soul, and when John and Beverly split it resulted in the album *Grace and Danger,* recorded with good friend Phil Collins, himself undergoing a divorce. It was a mix of pleading and anger, with music that veered from the heavily electric to the achingly acoustic and seemed to look in a slightly different direction. Just how different became apparent when he signed with Genesis' Duke label and began his '80s MOR phase. It wasn't that the music was bad, just that the fretless bass and jazz-lite arrangements removed all the fangs, turning it more toward easy listening for the well-heeled. Two albums (*Glorious Fool* and *Well Kept Secret*) began the decline, which continued even when he returned to Island after putting out another live album, *Philenthropy,* which suffered gravely in comparison to its predecessor. *Sapphire* offered his take on "Somewhere over the Rainbow" (a Top Ten single in Sweden), but little more, and a third live record (*Foundations*) served to document the way he was squandering his talent (in part due to ongoing alcohol problems). Perhaps the lowest points came at the beginning of the '90s, with records as mushy and squishy as anyone could imagine. It was his back catalog that saved him. Reinterpreting his old work for money probably wasn't his first choice, but it seemed to offer inspiration and a whole new audience, as did a two-CD compilation of his best Island Records work (*Sweet Little Mysteries*).

The creative juices were obviously flowing again. A new record (*And.*) saw him back in good voice, offering some cutting guitar and experimenting with trip-hop, a genre perfectly suited to his deep velvet vocals. Then a live EP (*Snoo*)—what is it about Martyn and live records, anyway?—was more of a holding action, keeping the name out there until 1998's *The Church with One Bell*. The latter may be all covers but each has a distinct Martyn stamp; whether Randy Newman, Rev. Gary Davis, or Ben Harper, each sounds like a John Martyn tune. Across the years, from blues to jazz to "trad. arr. by," he's pulled the strings together into a whole. And at his best, a very splendid whole it is.

what to buy: *Sweet Little Mysteries* 🎵🎵🎵 (Island Chronicles, 1994, prod. Bill Levenson) rounds up music from his most fertile period. Disc one is perfect; disc two has enough of the later fluff to make a good coaster. The individual albums from 1971 to '73 are the best choice. *Bless the Weather* 🎵🎵🎵🎵 (Island Records, 1971, prod. John Martyn, John Wood) stretches acoustic foundations and is nothing less than pure joy. That it could be eclipsed by *Solid Air* 🎵🎵🎵🎵🎵 (Island Records, 1973, prod. John Martyn, John Wood) is incredible, but true—the perfect John Martyn album, though *The Church with One Bell* 🎵🎵🎵🎵 (Thirsty Ear, 1998, prod. Norman Dayron, John Martyn) is such a return to form you have to love it.

what to avoid: *Glorious Fool* 🎵🎵 (WEA, 1979, prod. Phil Collins) and *Well-Kept Secret* 🎵🎵 (WEA, 1981, prod. Sandy Robertson) find him falling under the Phil Collins spell, a dangerous thing for any human being. It continued throughout the '80s. *Sapphire* 🎵🎵 (Island Records, 1984, prod. John Martyn) and *Foundations* 🎵🎵🎵 (Island Records, 1987, prod. Rob Fraboni) suffered from that syndrome, while *The Apprentice* 🎵🎵 (Permanent, 1990, prod. John Martyn, Brian Young), *Cooltide* 🎵🎵 (Permanent, 1991, prod. John Martyn, Brian Young, Spencer Cozens), and *Live* 🎵 (Permanent, 1995) were the nadir.

the rest:
London Conversation 🎵🎵🎵 (Island Records, 1967)
The Tumbler 🎵🎵🎵 (Island Records, 1968)
Stormbringer 🎵🎵🎵🎵 (Island Records, 1969)
Road to Ruin 🎵🎵🎵🎵 (Island Records, 1970)
Inside Out 🎵🎵🎵 (Island Records, 1973)
Sunday's Child 🎵🎵🎵 (Island Records, 1975)
Live at Leeds 🎵🎵🎵🎵 (Self-released, 1975)
Grace and Danger 🎵🎵🎵 (Island Records, 1977)
BBC 1 Live in Concert 🎵🎵🎵 (Windsong, 1992)
No Little Boy 🎵🎵🎵 (Mesa, 1993)

worth searching for: *And.* 🎵🎵🎵🎵 (Go!Disc, 1996, prod. John Martyn, Stefon Taylor, Spencer Cozens) offers John as trip-hopper, and it works, while *Snoo* 🎵🎵🎵 (Blueprint, 1997) is one of his best live offerings.

influences:
◀◀ Hamish Imlach, Archie Fisher
▶▶ Ben Watt, Gomez

see also: *Lee "Scratch" Perry*

Chris Nickson

Masada
Klezmer-influenced jazz
Formed 1993, in New York, NY, USA. Disbanded 1997.

John Zorn, alto sax, composer; Dave Douglas, trumpet; Greg Cohen, acoustic bass; Joey Baron, drums. Masada Chamber Ensembles (1994–97) also include: Mark Feldman, violin; Erik Friedlander, cello; Marc Ribot, guitar; Anthony Coleman, piano; David Krakauer, clarinets; John Medeski, organ and piano; Mark Dresser, bass; Kenny Wollesen, drums; Chris Speed, clarinet.

Masada (the place and symbol) is the fortress in Israel where besieged Jews chose to commit communal suicide rather than submit to captivity. Masada (the group) is the peak of John Zorn's involvement with jazz. Combining Yiddish music (including but not limited to klezmer) with jazz had been done before. But by specifically emphasizing the parallels between Ornette Coleman's early style and the older, modal Eastern/Central European music of Zorn's Jewish ancestors—and by letting the latter dominate rather than treating it as an ingredient to be added for exotic effect—Zorn came up with something new and distinctive. The band exhibits many jazz aspects not specifically traceable to Coleman, of course; that's just a handy comparison. There are moments when Joey Baron's steady four-beat drumming recalls Tony Williams's pulse on Miles Davis's *In a Silent Way,* and some of the freer explorations suggest the Art Ensemble of Chicago. And Douglas's presence is perfect: his work with Balkan scales and rhythms had him on a parallel path in some of his own music.

what to buy: The extreme coherence of the style Zorn has created—not to mention the incredible artistic consistency of the performers—seems to resist the sort of critical parsing that allows for definable gradations of quality. But certainly many fans retain a special fondness for *One/Alef* 🎵🎵🎵🎵🎵 (DIW, 1994, prod. John Zorn, Kazunori Sugiyama), where the new amalgam first struck them with its startling rightness. "Jair," the opening track, alternates klezmer licks and Ornette phrases in a lead-off that's the perfect proclamation of the new style. Other highlights are "Tzofeh," with its ticking insistence; "Ashnah," with its brooding spontaneity, almost-absent pulse, and focus on subtle instrumental textures; the brief "Delin," with what seem like pure Ornettisms framing a biting bass solo; and the cool-strutting "Janohah." Zorn fans looking for his more extreme playing are directed towards *Five/Hei* 🎻🎻🎻🎻 (DIW, 1995, prod. John Zorn, Kazunori Sugiyama) for the intense "Hobah," which, in the minimal materials of its theme, draws not from early Coleman, but instead sounds like a translation to acoustic instruments of one of the harmolodic themes of his Prime Time period—and which then explodes into collectively improvised energy playing straight out of the post-Coltrane school, with Zorn wailing in the altissimo register and Douglas darting sinuously around Zorn's line, while Baron thunders underneath.

what to buy next: The leader of the Jews at Masada was named Bar Kokhba. The music on the two-CD set *Bar Kokhba* 🎻🎻🎻🎻 (Tzadik, 1996, prod. John Zorn) is performed not by the quartet but by a number of chamber ensembles, sometimes without drums and with Zorn acting as composer and leader but not playing. "Tannaim," for instance, is a contemplative string trio with Mark Feldman, Erik Friedlander, and Greg Cohen. Practically its opposite, the following tune "Nefesh" is swinging piano-trio bop—a lament penned by a depressed Horace Silver, perhaps—with John Medeski (sounding rather Monkish in his solo, with touches of early McCoy Tyner in the second half), Mark Dresser, and Kenny Wollesen. This music is more low-key than the quartet, with a corresponding increase in restful beauty during the strings-only numbers and in plaintive soulfulness when the clarinetists wail.

the rest:
Masada:
Two/Beit 🎻🎻🎻🎻 (DIW, 1994)
Three/Gimel 🎻🎻🎻🎻 (DIW, 1994)
Four/Dalet 🎻🎻🎻🎻🎻 (DIW, 1994)
Six/Nav 🎻🎻🎻🎻 (DIW, 1995)
Seven/Zayin 🎻🎻🎻🎻🎻 (DIW, 1995)
Eight/Het 🎻🎻🎻🎻 (DIW, 1997)
Nine/Tet 🎻🎻🎻🎻 (DIW, 1997)
Live in Jerusalem 1994 🎻🎻🎻🎻🎻 (Tzadik, 1999)
Live in Taipei 1995 🎻🎻🎻🎻🎻 (Tzadik, 1999)

The Masada String Trio/Bar Kokhba Sextet:
The Circle Maker 🎻🎻🎻🎻 (Tzadik, 1998)

worth searching for: Rumor has it that there will be more live Masada albums, and a boxed set of all the studio recordings. The group occasionally reunites.

influences:
◄◄ Ornette Coleman, Yiddish music, Don Byron

►► Hasidic New Wave

see also: *Arto Lindsay*

Steve Holtje

Hugh Masekela
African jazz
Born Hugh Ramapolo Masekela, April 4, 1939, in Witbank, South Africa. Based in South Africa.

Voluntarily exiled from his homeland for 31 years, South African–born trumpet player Hugh Masekela returned in 1991. Masekela's subsequent album, *Hope,* marked the first time he'd worked with South African musicians in three decades.

Masekela was born in Witbank, a small coalmining village 100 miles east of Johannesburg. Although his grandmother was descended from a royal family, her land had been confiscated, and she was forced to live in the township ghettos, where she ran an underground speakeasy. The speakeasy provided Masekela with an understanding of the black South African struggle. Masekela's early memories include listening to Glenn Miller and Benny Goodman records played by sailors stationed in South Africa. By the age of four, he sang along even though he didn't understand the English lyrics. At the age of six, his parents sent him for piano lessons. After seeing the movie *Young Man with a Horn,* featuring Kirk Douglas as influential trumpet player Bix Beiderbecke, Masekela switched to that instrument. By the time he was 15 he was totally absorbed in African American music. Though he initially had only a mild interest in jazz, a turning point came when he heard the playing of Clifford Brown and Miles Davis. Studying for a while at London's Guildhall School of Music, Masekela transferred to the Manhattan School of Music in New York in 1960. He got his greatest encouragement from performers including Harry Belafonte, Louis Armstrong, and Dizzy Gillespie. Vocalist Miriam Makeba, whom he met at the age of 13, had emigrated to America the previous year and provided much support in Masekela's transition. Although they were married only from 1964 to '65, their friendship has remained strong.

Masekela continued to miss his friends and home in South Africa. In 1965 he considered returning and got as far as London; a phone call from Harry Belafonte urging him to remain in the U.S. changed his mind. Belafonte had earlier provided Masekela with one of his first musical jobs in the States, hiring the young trumpet player for several tours and recording sessions. Together with people like Muhammed Ali, Masekela formed a coalition with the civil rights movement and a universal objection to some of the excesses of the Western industrial complex. He performed many anti-war concerts in California with the Doors, the Jefferson Airplane, the Grateful Dead, Janis Joplin with Big Brother and the Holding Company, the Mamas and the Papas, the Byrds, and Buffalo Springfield. At the Monterey International Pop Festival in 1967, Masekela provided an African connection.

Hugh Masekela

A throw-away instrumental provided Masekela with his greatest success the following year. Recorded as an afterthought, "Grazin' in the Grass" reached the top of the charts and sold more than four million copies worldwide. Masekela returned to Africa in 1972. Within 10 years, he had moved to Botswana and founded the Botswana International School of Music. The experience, however, proved heartbreaking when his life was threatened by death squads. Masekela performed for his largest audiences when he joined Paul Simon's *Graceland* tour in 1986. The tour was extremely successful and concerts sold out all over the world. Masekela has remained one of Africa's most outspoken activists. His tune "Mandela (Bring Him Back Home)" become a rallying cry for supporters of the then-jailed African National Congress leader and future South African president.

what to buy: Recorded during a concert at Washington, D.C.'s Blues Alley during the summer of 1993, *Hope* (Triloka, 1994, prod. K.D. Kael, Hugh Masekela) marked the first time Masekela had worked with South African musicians in 30 years. A retrospective covering his entire career, the album included ex-wife Miriam Makeba on a number of tunes.

what to buy next: *Home Is Where the Heart Is* (Blue Thumb, 1972, prod. Hugh Masekela) is a groundbreaking blend of African, jazz, and pop sensibilities.

the rest:
Grrr (Mercury, 1966)
The Promise of a Future (One Way, 1968)
Masekela (UNI, 1968)
Uptownship (Jive/Novus, 1971)
Tomorrow (Warner Bros., 1987)
Stimela (Connoisseur Collection, 1994/1999)
Hugh Masekela & the Union of South Africa (Motown, 1994)
The Lasting Impressions of Ooga Booga (Verve, 1996)
The Boy's Doin' It (Verve, 1998)
Black to the Future (Sony, 1998/Shanachie, 1999)
Home N/A (Stern's, 1999)
The Best of Hugh Masekela N/A (BMG/RCA Victor, 1999)

influences:
◀◀ Miles Davis, Dizzy Gillespie, South African music

▶▶ Randy Weston

see also: *Harry Belafonte, Abdullah Ibrahim, Miriam Makeba*

Craig Harris

Master Musicians of Jajouka

Jibli

Formed in antiquity, in Morocco. Based in Jajouka, in the Jibala hills of Northern Morocco.

Variable, intermittently identified membership over centuries.

An ancient Berber musical clan from a desert village in Morocco, the Master Musicians of Jajouka were first introduced to the outside world by writer, artist, and adventurer Brion Gysin. Gysin had been traveling Morocco with author Paul Bowles in 1950. At a village festival, Gysin was awestruck by the sounds of a local music ensemble, and took the trouble to trace its origin to the village of Jajouka in the hills south of Tangier. Before long, they were playing at his own club in the latter city, the 1001 Nights, which he had established in large part as a means to indulge his infatuation with the group's music.

Morocco had long been a mecca for intellectuals, bohemians, artists, and stoners; notables as diverse as Mark Twain, Henri Matisse, and Jack Kerouac had visited at one time or another. When Brian Jones of the Rolling Stones showed up there in 1970, Gysin accompanied him to Jajouka, where, between generous helpings of the local kif, Jones conducted a recording session capturing the Master Musicians. The resulting album, *Brian Jones Presents the Pipes of Pan at Jajouka,* vaulted the group into international prominence.

The music of the Jajoukans is a blend of Berber (indigenous North African) and Arabic influences. Its potent rhythmic component is provided by double-headed drums, while the main vocal or instrumental melodic line is almost always accompanied by hypnotic drones on *rhaita* double-reed horns, flutes, or *gimbri* three-stringed lutes. A hereditary clan, the Jajoukans have passed their role as musicians from father to son for centuries, playing an important part in the spiritual life of the region through their performances at religious festivals—most notably the ritual of Boujeloud, the "Father of Skins," an awesome half-goat/half-human creature whose story traces its lineage to the Greek myth of Pan and the Roman fertility festival of Lupercalia.

what to buy: *The Master Musicians of Jajouka* ♫♫♫♫ (Delphi, 1972/Genes, 1995, prod. Joel Rubiner), a charming follow-up to the Jones trek, records the group simply, dispensing with the strange effects in favor of an intimate sound. The accompanying text from Robert Palmer's 1971 *Rolling Stone* article, while useful, is amusingly garbled in its translation to liner notes. A more recent release, *Apocalypse across the Sky* ♫♫♫♫ (Island, 1992, prod. Bill Laswell), boasts clean digital multi-track recording and a satisfying sampling of music. It in-

brazil: samba

Samba, a polyrhythm which forms the base of bossa nova and much of Brazilian popular music, has had an enormous impact on jazz and continues to find its way into contemporary music forms worldwide. It is best known as Brazilian Carnival music. Africans who were brought to Brazil during the 17th, 18th, and 19th centuries remembered tribal drum circles and reproduced the rhythms on improvised instruments in their new land. The word samba, according to *The Brazilian Sound* (Temple Univ. Press, 1988), may have originated in Angola as the word *semba,* meaning an invitation to dance. *Samba de roda,* a rhythmic predecessor to today's samba, figured heavily into ceremonies of the Afro-Brazilian spiritist religion *Candomblé.* Samba, as a true musical genre, evolved in Rio de Janeiro around the turn of the century. Free blacks flooded into Rio from Bahia. Music was played at informal gatherings and in bars and dance halls in the growing cosmopolitan city. Legendary composers like Pixinguinha, Donga, Sinho, and Ismael Silva began recording sambas in early sound studios, alongside *chorinhos, maxixes,* and *marchas,* other early forms of popular music. Donga's "Pelo Telefone" (1916) is widely considered to be the first samba ever recorded. By the 1930s and '40s, middle-class whites were embracing samba, and composers Noel Rosa and Ary Barroso, among others, popularized the *samba-canção,* a more refined style, emphasizing melody over rhythm. The *escolas de samba* (samba schools) developed as a Carnival establishment, responsible for lavish parades and general merriment during Carnival week every year, featuring the thunderous *samba-de-enredo* dominated by the *bateria,* or drum section. Today samba is more alive in Brazil than ever before. Popular bands and vocalists enjoy strong record sales, and samba is becoming increasingly popular in Bahia and the Northeastern region. Internationally samba has carved a strong foothold, thanks to thriving escolas in cities throughout Europe, the U.S., and Japan.

Mara Weiss and Nego Beto

The Master Musicians of Jajouka (with Mohamed el-Attar, dancer)

cludes a haunting version of "The Clapping" and a rousing "Boujeloud."

what to buy next: *Brian Jones Presents the Pipes of Pan at Jajouka* ♫♫♫ (Rolling Stones, 1971/Point, 1995, prod. Brian Jones), while not the most accurate musical document, perfectly captures the aura of the music from a stoned perspective. The heavy phasing and echo effects are intense and absorbing, at times like hearing music from the center of a tornado. *Jajouka Black Eyes* ♫♫♫ (Sub Rosa, 1995) is a good collection with some well-known Jajouka tunes heard in relaxed, informal versions and cut with brevity in mind, for those who prefer modest puffs rather than deep drags, as it were.

the rest:
Jajouka between the Mountains (RealWorld/WOMAD)

influences:
◄◄ Centuries of their own tradition

see also: *Bill Laswell*

Jeffrey Muhr

Dave Matthews Band
Cosmopolitan roots rock
Formed 1991, in Charlottesville, VA, USA. Based in USA.

Dave Matthews (born January 9, 1967, in Johannesburg, South Africa), vocals, guitar; Boyd Tinsley, violin; LeRoi Moore, saxophone; Stefan Lessard, bass; Carter Beauford, drums. (All members are from USA except where noted otherwise.)

A transcontinental childhood and a bar-band apprenticeship combined to make Dave Matthews one of the biggest if least likely success stories of '90s rock. There is no precedent for a band as popularly revered in America that draws such a proportion of its influences from outside of rock—including the funky jazz stylings of saxophonist LeRoi Moore, the Celtic/Appalachian fiddle frenzy of Boyd Tinsley, the skipping, almost-*soukous* (African rumba) rhythms of drummer Carter Beauford, and the striving vocals of Matthews himself, who has of late been getting closer and closer to the melisma of Middle Eastern singing and the emotive, non-verbal vocables of the Indian subcontinent. Matthews actually started out on the African continent, a native of racially divided Johannesburg, from which his family moved when he was two. Growing up in the New York City suburb of Yorktown Heights, he relocated to Charlottesville, Virginia, as an adult, eventually picking up Beauford and Moore (regular performers at Miller's, a jazz club where Matthews tended bar), then-16-year-old bass prodigy Stefan Lessard, and Tinsley. The Dave Matthews Band played its first gig in front of 40 people on May 11, 1991, on the roof of a Charlottesville apartment building. After performing as part of an Earth Day Festival that same year, they found regular homes first at the small Eastern Standard restaurant and then a club called Trax—steady work tragically interrupted by world-touring mega-stardom. Ambitious but unpretentious, Matthews's open-minded music found its moment with later-'90s youth's peace-craving outlook and genre-crossing tastes, and the band has been turning arenas and stadia into the intimate clubs of their ascension ever since.

what to buy: *Before These Crowded Streets* 𝄢𝄢𝄢𝄢 (RCA, 1998, prod. Steve Lillywhite), grimmer and more overtly political than the band's previous output, tackles issues of white invasion and rampant progress, but always from a personalized viewpoint that hasn't driven away any of their ardent mass following. Neither has their most challenging compositional effort to date, with Middle Eastern rhythms, jazz intricacies, the well-deployed banjo of Béla Fleck, and singing from Matthews that ranges from anguished vocalese to an almost death-metal hoarseness. A nervy gamble that got the usual chart gold.

what to buy next: The breakthrough album *Under the Table and Dreaming* 𝄢𝄢𝄢 (RCA, 1994, prod. Steve Lillywhite) shows an earlier stage of blending worldbeat, jazz, folk, and pop styles with the group's fierce jamming skills. As would become customary, the experiment yielded a string of hits, including the sweet, acoustic "Satellite," the funk-driven "What Would You Say," and the sprightly "Ants Marching."

the rest:
Crash 𝄢𝄢𝄢 (RCA, 1996)
Live at Red Rocks 8.15.95 𝄢𝄢 (RCA, 1997)
(With Tim Reynolds) *Live at Luther College* 𝄢𝄢𝄢 (RCA, 1999)

influences:
◀◀ The Grateful Dead, Phish, the Samples

▶▶ Agents of Good Roots

Christina Fuoco and Adam McGovern

Maxwell Street Klezmer Band

Klezmer
Formed 1983, in Chicago, IL, USA. Based in Chicago, IL, USA.

Core members: Lori Lippitz, vocals; Lisa Fishman, vocals; Alex Koffman (Russia), violin, balalaika, musical director/arranger; Don Ja-

cobs, clarinet; Shelly Yoelin, saxophone, flute; Ivo Braun, trumpet; Sam Margolis, trombone, vocals; Gail Mangurten, piano; David Rothstein, bass; Steve Hawk, percussion. (All members are from USA except where noted otherwise.)

Maxwell Street is one of the few klezmer groups led by a woman; Lori Lippitz started the outfit as part of a mission to bring Yiddish culture back to Chicago. Like many of the first-generation klezmer revival bands, Maxwell Street learned their repertoire from old Yiddish recordings and films. However, this group has gone much further, with Lippitz's recruitment of Russian Jewish immigrants like Alex Koffman (and acquisition of the first-hand old-country perspective they bring); her teaching of Yiddish dances at the band's concerts; and the incorporation of traditional rituals, including the reenactment of a Russian-Jewish wedding, in the band's performances. In addition to her duties with "Max," as it is affectionately known, Lippitz maintains an amazing schedule of community outreach activities, among them an annual regional klezmer festival and Yiddish music institute, and the Chicago Jr. Klezmer Orchestra, a group of a dozen dedicated kids aged 10–18 who perform locally as school permits. Lippitz and Max have done much to make the perhaps-unlikely American midwest a capitol of the klezmer renaissance.

what to buy: The repertoire on *You Should Be So Lucky* 𝄢𝄢𝄢𝄢 (Shanachie, 1996, prod. Lori Lippitz, Alex Koffman, Paul Smith) is heavy with well-worn Yiddish theater and popular songs, but elevated by inventive orchestral arrangements and strong brass. The group's multiple arrangers are able to find new ways to juxtapose choral structures and different types of ensembles in consistently imaginative ways. Both the core band and its customary guest accomplices distinguish these selections: Jeff Jeziorski's clarinet solo on "Firn Di Mehetonim Aheym" is one of the few that successfully challenges the Naftule Brandwein original, while the Russian flavors added by Alex Koffman and Yuri Bokov enhance the position of the band as keepers of the Eastern European Yiddish tradition.

the rest:
Maxwell Street Days 𝄢𝄢𝄢 (Global Village, 1986)
Maxwell Street Wedding 𝄢𝄢𝄢 (Global Village, 1991)

worth searching for: Maxwell Street is featured on *Jiddisches Lied & Klezmer 4th Internationales Festival,* a recording made at the 1994 German fest of same name and available on the Swiss Pan label.

influences:
◀◀ Abe Schwartz's Orchestra, Dave Tarras, Mickey Katz, the Klezmorim

▶▶ The Cincinnati Klezmer Project, Chicago Jr. Klezmer Orchestra

Aaron Howard

Mazz
Tejano

Formed 1977, in Brownsville, TX, USA. Split into Jimmy González y Grupo Mazz and Joe López y Nuevo Imagen Mazz, 1998. Based in San Antonio, TX, USA.

Original members: Joe Manuel López, vocals; Jimmy González, guitar. (All members are from USA.)

A group of Hispanic teenagers was playing high-energy rock in Spanish in South Texas in the late 1970s. They were good enough to attract the attention of the founders of the fledgling *Tejano* (modern Tex-Mex) label Lado/A Cara, which also soon signed another San Antonio teen, Tish Hinojosa, to a contract. Hinojosa went her own way (and eventually on to stardom) after two now-impossible-to-find recordings, but Mazz stayed and solidified its Tejano chops through the decades and the sale of the record company to EMI Latin. They were a long-lived favorite in the genre, and remain so in two rival incarnations formed by their founding duo in 1998.

what to buy: Over the years, Mazz produced more than 40 CDs, most still in print and most on the EMI Latin label. A good introduction to their evolving sound is the hits retrospective *Reconciliation: 14 Super Exitos* 𝄢𝄢𝄢 (EMI Latin, 1997). They also did a Christmas disc, *Regalo de Navidad* 𝄢𝄢𝄢 (Tejano, 1994), which is an accessible introduction to their style for those who aren't familiar with the Tejano scene.

best of the rest:
Para Nuestra Gente 𝄢𝄢𝄢 (EMI Latin, 1990)
Live! Una Noche Juntos 𝄢𝄢𝄢 (EMI Latin, 1992)
Ten Years of Tejano Music 𝄢𝄢𝄢 (Sony International, 1997)

influences:
◀◀ Tony de La Rosa, Los Tigres del Norte, Laura Canales
▶▶ Chris Perez, Pete Astudillo

see also: *Tish Hinojosa*

Kerry Dexter

Prince Nico Mbarga
Highlife

Born 1950, in Nigeria. Died June 24, 1997.

Prince Nico was perhaps the greatest of the latter-day band leaders in highlife (an influential cosmopolitan dance music). His early-1970s anthem "Sweet Mother" sold over 13 million copies (not counting bootlegs), all over the African continent, making it one of the biggest-selling African records of all time. Mbarga was born in Eastern Nigeria to a Nigerian father and Cameroonian mother, and grew up listening to highlife, *soukous* (African rumba), *makossa* (Cameroonian pop), regional tribal music, and

Western pop. In his desire to reach a Pan-African and perhaps international audience, Mbarga wrote his lyrics in pidgin English, and brought many outside influences to a sound based on the *panko* rhythms of Eastern Nigeria. His guitar playing was always inventive and his rhythms leave no option but to dance. Despite the growing interest in African music in the 1980s, and his large fan base in West Africa, little of Prince Nico's music was ever available in the West. He was killed on June 24th, 1997, when another vehicle smashed into his motorcycle.

what's available: Mbarga's resourceful guitar playing and the non-stop groove of his band make every selection on *Aki Special* 𝄢𝄢𝄢𝄢 (Rounder, 1987) sparkle.

influences:
◀◀ Victor Olaiya, Rex Lawson, African Brothers International, City Boys

j. poet

Jimi Mbaye
Mbalax

Born September 8, 1961, in Dakar, Senegal. Based in Dakar, Senegal, and Paris, France.

Mbaye learned to play on makeshift guitars he built himself and has become internationally known for the guitar licks he's contributed to Youssou N'Dour's Super Étoile band.

what's available: *Dakar Heart* 𝄢𝄢𝄢 (Shanachie, 1997, prod. Jimi Mbaye, Thomas Rome, Brian Cullman), Mbaye's solo debut, is remarkably low-key, bringing to mind a singer/songwriter as much as a guitar god out to strut his stuff. The midtempo grooves have a hint of reggae and funk, and Mbaye's guitar work is impressive, as much for its restraint as for its prowess; he never tries to upstage the rest of the band or his own pleasing vocals.

influences:
◀◀ Youssou N'Dour, Touré Kunda, Lamine Konte

see also: *Youssou N'Dour*

j. poet

Mzwakhe Mbuli
Mbanqanga poetry

Born c. 1958, in Sophiatown, South Africa. Based in Johannesburg, South Africa.

Mzwakhe Mbuli is one of South Africa's most outspoken and popular poets—and, since adding music to his presentations in 1986, is also the country's foremost "dub poet" (a form pioneered by Linton Kwesi Johnson that Mbuli's hybrid recalls). Mbuli was introduced to the power of music and the spoken

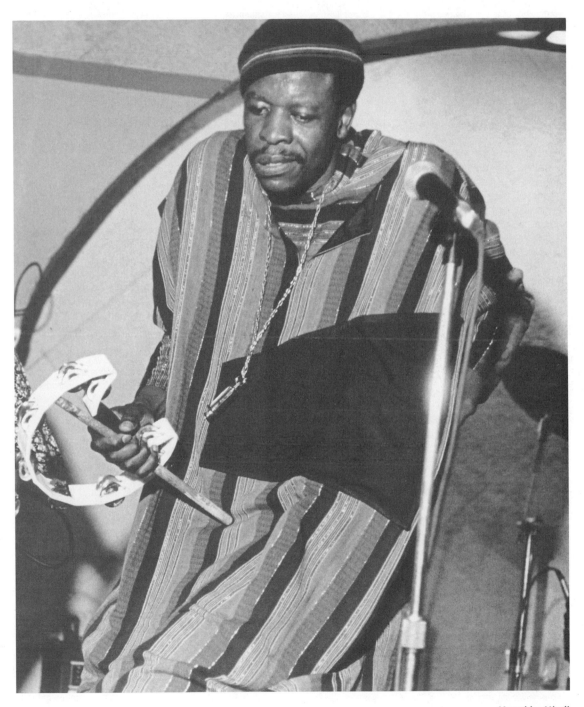

Mzwakhe Mbuli

word by his father, who sang *mbube,* the Zulu *a cappella* style made famous by Ladysmith Black Mambazo. Mbuli's father took the boy to all-night mbube sessions, where he learned traditional singing and dancing. In grammar school Mbuli got interested in drama, and his first role in a school play was as God, perhaps because of his powerful, rumbling baritone. A member of Khuvhangano, a performing troupe that was using poetry and drama to organize resistance to the apartheid government, saw him in the play, and asked him to join; for the next five years Mbuli added his talents to their productions. At that time, Mbuli began writing his own poems, and in 1981, at a funeral for a fellow activist, he recited two of them. The response was overwhelming, and Mbuli began reciting his poems at political rallies and cultural events. In 1985, Mbuli was banned and went underground, staying one step ahead of the security police. He would appear at meetings, weddings, and funerals, recite a few poems, and vanish again. In 1988, in-between detentions, Mbuli recorded his first album *Change Is Pain.* Although backed by session musicians and under intense deadline pressure, the power of Mbuli's voice makes these tracks crackle with energy. *Change Is Pain* was immediately banned, although it was released outside of South Africa to almost universal acclaim. The material on his second album, *Unbroken Spirit,* was composed while he was in prison (Mbuli doesn't write his poems down; he recites them all from memory), and although it too was banned, it went gold. In 1990 a book of his poems entitled *Before Dawn* was published with a foreword written by Nelson Mandela, who was still in prison. At that time Mbuli also organized a band, so that the music and his singing, chanting, and rapping could be honed to a fine point. The first album by the new unit was *Resistance Is Defense.* The end of apartheid hasn't slowed Mbuli down or weakened his outspoken stance. He continues to record regularly, speaking the truth and celebrating the lives of the common people. Recently the Mandela government arrested him for speaking out against government corruption.

what to buy: Mbuli's first album with his own band, *Resistance Is Defense* ⱮⱮⱮⱮ (Earthworks, 1992, prod. Trevor Herman), is full of forceful poetry and kick-ass music. It's easy to see why Mbuli was cast as God; his potent vocals rumble like an earthquake, and his mixture of singing and spoken-word interludes gives his lyrics extra power. The band sizzles and their blend of South African *kwela, marabi,* and jive, as well as Africanized R&B, both supports and amplifies Mbuli's messages.

what to buy next: *Change Is Pain* ⱮⱮⱮⱮ (Rounder, 1998, prod. Lloyd Ross), Mbuli's debut, is a masterpiece of militant fire.

the rest:
Umzwakhe Ubonga Ujehova ⱮⱮⱮ (CCP South Africa, 1997)
Kwazulu Natal ⱮⱮⱮ (CCP South Africa)

influences:
⏮ Moses Mchunu, Linton Kwesi Johnson, SWAPO Cultural Group

j. poet

Andy McGann
Irish traditional
Born 1928, in the Bronx, NY, USA. Based in New York, NY, USA.

Born to parents with roots in Ireland's County Sligo, McGann began playing the fiddle at the ripe old age of seven. His early training came at the hands of fiddler Katherine Brennan, who was a student of Michael Coleman, arguably the most influential figure ever to have played Irish music. A fine fiddler herself, Brennan also had a background in classical music, which influenced McGann as well. Growing up in 1930s New York, the young McGann encountered Irish music everywhere, and he basked in its presence. By the time the '40s rolled around, the city's Irish traditional music scene was flourishing. The Central Opera House became a weekly gathering place for Irish musicians and McGann was more than prominent there. Out of the regular Central Opera House sessions formed the famed New York Ceili Band, of which McGann was a central figure. It also featured fiddlers Paddy Reynolds and Larry Redican, pianist Felix Dolan, Paddy O'Brien on accordion, and Jack Coen on the flute. The music that came from this group is legendary, though they never formally recorded. Even now McGann remains quite active in the New York scene, and if you get lucky and drop by Kate Kearney's on a Saturday night you may hear the sweet strains of his brilliant fiddling first-hand.

what to buy: *It's a Hard Road to Travel* ⱮⱮⱮⱮ (Shanachie, 1995, prod. Richard Nevins, Daniel Michael Collins), with Paul Brady on guitar, is a tour de force of Irish traditional fiddling. McGann's use of rolls and triplets is masterful, and his sweet tone is to die for. One listen is all you'll need to understand why McGann has influenced an entire generation of renowned Irish American musicians.

what to buy next: Originally recorded in 1965, *A Tribute to Michael Coleman* ⱮⱮⱮⱮ (Green Linnet, prod. various) brings McGann together with button accordionist Joe Burke and pianist Felix Dolan, in a now-classic remembrance of arguably the most influential Irish fiddler of all time. *Andy McGann & Paddy Reynolds* ⱮⱮⱮⱮ (Shanachie, 1994, prod. Richard Nevins, Daniel Michael Collins) is a great collection of music by these two fine friends and fiddlers that was recorded and originally released in 1977. Their awe-inspiring duets along with Paul Brady's guitar accompaniment will raise the hair on the back of your neck. The music is simple in its presentation but brilliant in its results.

worth searching for: *Irish Fiddle & Guitar* ♫♫♫ (Shanachie, 1992, prod. Richard Nevins, Daniel Michael Collins) is a cassette-only release of McGann and Paul Brady that is well worth seeking. McGann is also prominently featured in the brilliant documentary film *From Shore to Shore* (Cherry Lane Productions, 1993), which examines the vibrant traditional Irish music scene in New York City past and present. It is a must-have for any fan of this music and paints an extraordinary picture of the social context from which McGann emerged and which he subsequently influenced.

influences:

◀◀ Michael Coleman, Katherine Brennan, Paddy Killoran, James "Lad" O'Bierne

▶▶ Eileen Ivers, Tony Demarco, Brian Conway

see also: *Felix Dolan*

Cliff McGann

Eileen McGann

Celtic/Canadian folk

Born 1959, in Calgary, Alberta, Canada. Based in Canada.

In an age when "folk singers," male or female, tend to be more and more idiosyncratic, postmodern, and unpolished, Calgary's Eileen McGann is that rarest and most welcome of exceptions—a young singer with a keen sense of and pride in the traditional music of her Celtic and British ancestors; an ability to write movingly about the beauties of life and nature around her; and a strong, crystal-clear soprano voice that stops people in their tracks and commands attention. Following the path blazed by fellow Canadian singer/songwriters like Stan Rogers and Gordon Lightfoot, McGann has established herself in the last decade as one of the finest singers, songwriters, and interpreters of traditional music on either side of the Atlantic. A first-generation Irish Canadian, McGann was captivated by the music of Rogers, Lightfoot, and Don McLean in her teenage years. While working toward a degree in medieval history, she was asked by one of her professors to perform at a St. Patrick's Day banquet, and the (by her own description) embarrassing realization dawned on her that despite her Celtic heritage, she didn't know a single Irish song. In listening then to her mother's records of Irish operatic singers doing traditional material, she was drawn to the underlying beauty of the music and the stories it was telling.

Since emerging on the folk scene during the late 1980s, McGann's recordings and live performances have highlighted her stunning ability to deliver traditional fare as well as her own intelligent, finely honed songs. While her melodies are beautiful, she excels at writing thoughtful, well-crafted lyrics

that, as clearly as she sings them, express her thoughts on the environment ("Requiem for the Giants"), politics ("Too Stupid for Democracy"), social justice ("Reservations"), and many other contemporary themes. She can also write ballads ("Isabella Gunn," "The Knight of the Rose") that have a timeless sound, as if they have been around for hundreds of years—the mark of a superior minstrel. Her first three albums feature a solid mix of both traditional and original music, while newer releases have responded to her fans' many requests for an all-traditional recording. More than most singers in the world of folk music today, though, her entire catalog is of top-level quality, making it very difficult to pick favorites. These days, McGann spends much of her time on the road away from her beloved Calgary on the slope of the Canadian Rockies. Traveling and performing as a duo with her long-time musical (and life) partner, David K. (Knutson), she continues to win rave reviews and new fans wherever she goes, still in the early years of what should be a long and fulfilling career. As she sings in one of her most popular songs, "I See My Journey."

what to buy: It's a close call between *Turn It Around* ♫♫♫♫ (Dragonwing, 1991, prod. Eileen McGann) and her 1995 effort *Journeys*, and either will be immensely satisfying. *Turn It Around* features "Requiem for the Giants," "The Knight of the Rose," and the title track, but the real head-turner is her version of the traditional "The Fair Flower of Northumberland." Overall, the album matches four traditional cuts with seven original songs.

what to buy next: *Journeys* ♫♫♫♫ (Dragonwing, 1995, prod. Eileen McGann) opens with "I See My Journey" and includes "Reservations," "Too Stupid for Democracy," and "In the Silence." Traditional songs include "Braw Sailin' on the Sea," "Bonny Portmore," and "Jock O'Hazeldean," and an added bonus is a rendition of Pete Morton's "Another Train."

the rest:

Elements ♫♫♫ (Dragonwing, 1987)
Heritage ♫♫♫ (Dragonwing, 1997)

worth searching for: *Two Thousand Years of Christmas* ♫♫♫ (Dragonwing, 1996, prod. Eileen McGann) features McGann, David K., and Cathy Miller performing as Trilogy, harmonizing on a variety of songs from the Celtic and British Yuletide traditions. This is something unique and a worthwhile addition to the Christmas section of the record collection.

influences:

◀◀ Stan Rogers, Gordon Lightfoot

▶▶ Joan Baez, Janet Russell, Trilogy

John Lupton

Chris McGregor

South African jazz

Born December 24, 1936, in Umtata, South Africa. Died May 26, 1990, in Ager, France.

When Nelson Mandela walked out of South Africa's notorious Robben Island Prison in 1989, that nation's heinous governmental policy of apartheid (institutional racism) was flushed down the toilet. But back in the day—1962—when white South African pianist Chris McGregor put together a band of black countrymen for a gig at the Johannesburg Jazz Festival, the nation was under full-effect apartheid lockdown. The son of a devout Scottish missionary, McGregor was exposed early on to the humanity and spirituality of black folk via Xhosa hymns. Bucking the law, Mc-Gregor formed a permanent sextet the following year. The Blue Notes—Mongezi Feza, trumpet; Dudu Pukwana, alto sax; Nick Moyake, tenor sax; Johnny Dyani, bass; and Louis Moholo, drums—were the absolute fiercest simbas in South African jazz. Straight Art Blakey & the Jazz Messengers (circa Lee Morgan/Wayne Shorter) with a refreshing township-jive chaser, the Blue Notes were only able to record one album (*Live in South Africa 1964*) before leaving—one step ahead of the law—on a European tour. After that, the band woodshedded for a year in Switzerland. In late '65, the Blue Notes (minus Moyake) flipped to London, where they turned jazzbo heads around big-time.

McGregor's rococo blend of Ellingtonian swing, Monkesque spatial dissonance, Cecil Taylor–like clusters of pointillistic abstraction, near-ascetic discipline, business acumen, and leadership skills made him the new Don of London's underground hard-bop/avant-jazz scenes. In addition to the Blue Notes, there was the Chris McGregor Group (trio and quartet), and in 1968, McGregor formed a somewhat twisted big band. Extremely short-lived (six performances!), it nonetheless placed second in Melody Maker's jazz poll (under Duke!). In 1970 McGregor got it even righter with the Mingus Workshop–cum–Sun Ra Arkestra, Limey/Jo'Burg wild-style aggregation Brotherhood of Breath. An inspired pairing of Blue Noters and eight of England's prime players (including Harry Beckett, John Surman, and Alan Skidmore), McGregor's new idea followed up a month of legendary weekly gigs at London's famed jazz club Ronnie Scott's with a debut recording for RCA U.K. (*Chris McGregor's Brotherhood of Breath*). Though this edition of the band split up four years later (final LP: *Live at Willisau*), McGregor was able to cash checks from crucial shots with folk icon Nick Drake (*Bryter Layter,* 1970) and Brit blues godfather Alexis Korner (*Bootleg Him!,* 1972). McGregor then became a permanent resident of southern France in late '74. Between '75 and '88, he pursued a sporadic career of live solo gigs, occasional revivals of the BoB (culminating in '88's *Country Cooking*), and a session date or two. He died of lung cancer in 1990.

worth searching for: Nothing to do with Chris McGregor—be it solo or Brotherhood of Breath—is currently in print in America, though there have been record-store sightings of the excellent Chris McGregor/BoB *Country Cooking ♫♫♫♫* (Venture/Virgin, 1988). The masterpiece they'd always been hinting at, *Country Cooking* is simply loverly. From the exalted jubilance of the title tune (check Annie Whitehead's bumptiously insouciant muted trombone solo) to the Oliver Nelson–by-way-of–James Brown "Thunder in the Mountain," this is one of the best albums you've (probably) never heard. But it's got competition. Recorded by McGregor and the remaining Blue Notes in a nonstop session the week after an impoverished and despondent Mongezi Feza died of pneumonia, *Blues for Mongezi ♫♫♫♫* (Ogun, 1975) is one of the most harrowing and mournful instrumental records ever recorded. An epic, spontaneously improvised outpouring of collective grief, *Blues for Mongezi* is eerily life-affirming.

influences:

◀◀ The Epistles, Sun Ra, Albert Ayler, Art Ensemble of Chicago

▶▶ Centipede, George Gruntz, Jazz Warriors, Pierre Doerge

Tom Terrell

Freddie McGregor

Roots reggae, dancehall reggae

Born 1955, in Clarendon, Jamaica. Based in Kingston, Jamaica.

Freddie McGregor's blessed voice, sophisticated sense of melody, and relentless work ethic have made him one of reggae's most respected artists. From age seven, when he stood on beer crates and tip-toes to voice tracks for the ska band the Clarendonians, he has reached heights seemingly just beyond his grasp. His first full-length record was not released until he had been in the music business for nearly 16 years, despite an excellent series of singles from the late '60s into the '70s with Studio One and producer Coxsone Dodd—including such heavyweight tracks as "Rastaman Camp," "I Am a Revolutionist," "Go Away Pretty Girl," and a cover of the Ethiopians' first hit, "Gonna Take Over Now." All were eventually collected on the extraordinary, faith-endowed *Bobby Bobylon* in 1980. However, before he even released his first full-length record, McGregor was widely respected for his rootsman's vision and lover's heart and was asked by Bob Marley to co-produce and co-write Judy Mowatt's seminal *Black Woman,* the first LP recorded at Marley's Tuff Gong label's Kingston studio. Soon after, a collection of his outstanding singles with the Soul Syndicate band and eccentric producer Niney the Observer finally resulted in his mighty debut, *Mr. McGregor.* Equally as impressive was his work with producer Linval Thompson, which culminated in 1982's *Big Ship,* one of the greatest and most influential albums in reggae's "dancehall" style ever made. McGregor started the Big Ship imprint in 1984 and negotiated an American distribution deal with RAS Records. Though his initial releases with RAS were decidedly overburdened with cheesy synthesizers and an ultimately eye-crossing "worldbeat" vision, McGregor still managed to influence a whole generation of youth when he teamed with Dennis Brown on one of the first *ragga* (digital reggae) hits, the aptly titled "Raggamuffin." In addition, both "Africa Here I Come" (for Studio One) and "Don't Hurt My Feelings" (for George Phang's Powerhouse! label) are bedrocks of the dancehall era. In the late '80s, McGregor toured the world with the Studio One band and scored a huge hit in Colombia with a reggae version of the Sandpipers' "Guantanamera," sung in Spanish. In the '90s, McGregor's best work has been in collaboration with producer Gussie Clarke (*Carry Go Bring Come* and "Rumours," the latter featuring deejay Daddy Rings) and ragga visionaries Steely and Clevie (*Now*). McGregor's catalog is vital in tracing every major change in modern Jamaican music, from ska and rocksteady to roots reggae, all the way to dancehall and ragga. His is truly a voice of Jamaica, past and present.

what to buy: *Bobby Bobylon* ✓✓✓✓ (Heartbeat, 1980, prod. Clement "Coxsone" Dodd) is a masterpiece, even though its encompassment of nearly a decade of singles doesn't afford the most seamless flow. Still, the selection is flawless, ranging from McGregor's dread roots-Rasta anthems (recorded after he became a member of the Twelve Tribes organization in 1975) to some of the earliest examples of the soulful and romantic "lover's rock" style (the moving "Go Away Pretty Girl"). *Big Ship* ✓✓✓✓ (Shanachie, 1982, prod. Linval Thompson) may be his best-sounding album, as his profoundly melodic voice carries killer cuts like the title tune, "Holy Mount Zion," and the riveting "Roots Man Skanking," all backed by the foundation-shaking Roots Radics.

what to buy next: *Reggae Rockers* ✓✓✓✓ (Jamaican Authentic Classics, 1979, prod. Winston "Niney the Observer" Holness) is a budget reissue of the debut, *Mr. McGregor*. The brash and exciting Soul Syndicate band (headed by guitarist Earl "Chinna" Smith) provides a wonderful bottom-end to a string of classics, from "Natural Collie" (which integrates Norman Collins's soul opus "You Are My Starship"), to "Rasta Have Faith" (one of the most dazzling versions of the oft-used "Satta Massa Gana" riddim), all the way to McGregor's surprisingly sincere cover of "Brandy," which is now considered one of the earliest and best lover's rock joints. Of his most recent material, *Sings Jamaican Classics, Volumes 1–3* ✓✓✓ (VP, 1991/1992/1996, prod. Freddie McGregor, Dalton Browne) features his top-notch covers of songs from the island's golden age and collects some of his best-received albums of the '90s. McGregor's renditions of the Gaylads' "Joy in the Morning," the Abyssinians' "Declaration of Rights," and Alton Ellis's "Can I Change My Mind"—to name just one song from each volume—are heartfelt and sublime.

the rest:
Showcase ✓✓✓ (Observer, 1980)
I Am Ready ✓✓✓ (Studio One, 1982)
Come On Over ✓✓✓ (RAS, 1983)
Across the Border ✓✓ (RAS, 1984)
All in the Same Boat ✓✓ (RAS, 1986)
Freddie McGregor ✓✓ (Polydor, 1987)
Live at the Town & Country ✓✓✓ (VP, 1990)
Now ✓✓✓ (VP, 1991)
Hard to Get ✓✓ (Pow Wow, 1992)
Early Days ✓✓✓ (Sonic Sounds, 1993)
(With Dennis Brown and Cocoa Tea) *Legit* ✓✓✓ (Shanachie, 1993)
Carry Go Bring Come ✓✓✓ (Pow Wow, 1994)
Zion Chant ✓✓✓✓ (Heartbeat, 1994)
Push On ✓✓✓ (VP, 1994)
Forever My Love ✓✓✓ (RAS, 1995)
Masterpiece ✓✓ (VP, 1997)
RAS Portraits ✓✓✓ (RAS, 1997)
Rumours ✓✓ (Gone Clear, 1997)

worth searching for: *Jah Jah Dreader Than Dread* ✓✓✓✓ (Munich, 1997) is an exceptional document of the early dancehall recordings produced by Linval Thompson and includes the long-lost McGregor classic "Jah Help the People," along with its even rarer dub counterpart. This is a fabulous compilation loaded with hits from the Wailing Souls, Freddie McKay, and Triston Palmer, plus a trailer-load of deejay versions from the likes of U Brown and Welton Irie.

influences:
◀◀ Ernest Wilson, John Holt, Alton Ellis

▶▶ Judy Mowatt, Triston Palmer, Maxi Priest, Cocoa Tea, Tony Gold

see also: *Dennis Brown, Cocoa Tea, the Ethiopians, Judy Mowatt, the Roots Radics, the Wailing Souls*

Todd Shanker

Loreena McKennitt

New-age folk

Born February 17, 1957, in Morden, Manitoba, Canada. Based in Stratford, Ontario, Canada.

Loreena McKennitt isn't so much a folk artist as a swirling, ethereal musician who uses elements of folk and Celtic to enhance the atmosphere. Though the singer-harpist is more rooted in traditional songcraft than her new-age contemporary Enya, McKennitt's music aims for the spiritual much more than the straightforward. She initially planned a career as a veterinarian but wound up performing in folk clubs and working as a composer, actor,

5
0
2

susan mckeown

musicHound **WORLD**

and singer at the Shakespearean Festival in Stratford, Ontario. (This would account for her dabbling in 19th-century poetry, such as the version of Alfred Lord Tennyson's "The Lady of Shalott" she set to music in 1992.) Soon, she began producing and distributing her own albums, finally catching on during the late-'80s stirrings of new age as a commercial force. McKennitt's soaring voice, and her ability to turn any sort of traditional folk tune into an angelic hymn, launched subsequent albums past gold and platinum level with very little radio or video play. Though she uses her considerable talent to mix all kinds of lofty musical legacies together, McKennitt's music is best experienced while sleeping, having sex, or otherwise trying to avoid distractions.

what to buy: "All Souls Night," the opening track of *The Visit* 𝄞𝄞𝄞 (Quinlan Road/Warner Bros., 1992, prod. Loreena McKennitt), is a spooky Celtic-based and Eastern Europe–tinged tune propelled by rolling percussion and McKennitt's voice blending with a *tambura, balalaika,* cello, and accordion. The album is impeccably crafted and well thought out (including a version of the traditional "Bonny Portmore"), with nary a bump in the road.

what to buy next: McKennitt can sing with emotional power, as on the soft, fragile folk song "The Dark Side of the Soul," which is a nice break from the new-age-isms that otherwise immerse *The Mask and Mirror* 𝄞𝄞𝄞 (Quinlan Road/Warner Bros., 1994, prod. Loreena McKennitt).

what to avoid: "Over a number of years spent ruminating on the distinctive characteristics of the Celts . . ." begins McKennitt's introduction to *The Book of Secrets* 𝄞𝄞 (Quinlan Road/Warner Bros., 1997, prod. Loreena McKennitt), which despite the airy affectations manages to sound pretty good for background music.

the rest:
Elemental 𝄞𝄞𝄞 (Quinlan Road, 1985)
To Drive the Cold Winter Away 𝄞𝄞𝄞 (Quinlan Road, 1987)
Parallel Dreams 𝄞𝄞𝄞 (Quinlan Road, 1989)
A Winter Garden: Five Songs for the Season 𝄞𝄞 (Quinlan Road/Warner Bros., 1995)

influences:
◀◀ Lao Tzu, Johnny Clegg, Peter Gabriel, Alfred Lord Tennyson

▶▶ Enya, Yanni, Erykah Badu, Deep Forest

Steve Knopper

Susan McKeown

Irish singer-songwriter folk
Born February 6, 1967, in Rathfarnham, Dublin, Ireland. Based in New York, NY, USA.

With numerous guest appearances on stage and CD and a deafening buzz in folk circles, Irish chanteuse Susan McKeown

gained attention as a singer and songwriter before she recorded her first solo album. Her success is due in part to her collaborations with other gifted musicians. McKeown's voice has a startling dynamic range that's more evident in concert than on recordings. In composing and covering songs, she is drawn toward stories of women and mysticism, but she doesn't quite fit the "women's music" pigeonhole, nor is she a new-age artist. While she has covered traditional material, including songs in Irish Gaelic, elements of jazz and rock strongly flavor her style. Of late, McKeown has appeared in Johnny Cunningham's production of *Peter and Wendy* and toured as a vocalist with Natalie Merchant's band for several highly successful shows, including an appearance on the PBS series *Sessions at West 54th*. She's done vocal work on albums by rockabilly humorists Five Chinese Brothers, dance-trance project Arthur Loves Plastic, and pop-spiritual writer Thomas Moore. She's adept at slipping into the backing-singer role, but when she's up front, she rules the room.

what's available: McKeown's work is available under various billings, and she hasn't made a bad album yet. *Bones* 𝄞𝄞𝄞𝄞 (Sheila-na-Gig, 1995/PRIME CD, 1996, prod. Jimi Zhivago), credited to Susan McKeown and the Chanting House, is an extraordinary debut, a superb blend of originals and covers that grows in power over time. Traditionally oriented listeners will be drawn to "Westron Wynde/Westlin Winds," which combines a ninth-century anonymous poem with Robert Burns's paean to hunting; and "Gorm," a chilling Gaelic lament. The more adventurous will be tantalized by the erotic "Curiouser" and the spooky title track. "Jericho" and "Snakes" are toe-tappers with spiritual guts, and "I Know I Know" would make Billie Holliday applaud. Augmented by the artful sounds of cello, fiddle, hurdy-gurdy, percussion, bass, guitar, and pipes, McKeown's voice sails, moans, murmurs, and rings through it all like she's been at it for centuries. *Bushes and Briars* 𝄞𝄞𝄞𝄞 (Alula, 1998, prod. Jamshied Sharifi, Akira Satake, Susan McKeown) again gives traditional music the McKeown touch, with brooding vocals and moody instrumentation. *Through the Bitter Frost and Snow* 𝄞𝄞𝄞𝄞 (PRIME CD, 1997, prod. Lindsey Horner, Susan McKeown, David Seitz), a collaboration with Lindsey Horner, is a fine seasonal offering with the Celtic folk-jazz style found on much of *Bones*. The same duo's *Mighty Rain* 𝄞𝄞𝄞𝄞 (Depth of Field, 1998) is a real departure. McKeown's voice and Horner's various bass instruments (bass clarinet, acoustic bass, bass guitar) are the only constants in this spare, haunting collection with more than a hint of torchy blues. "Black Is the Color" will make you shiver.

worth searching for: McKeown's CD single *Snakes* 𝄞𝄞𝄞𝄞 (PRIME CD, 1997, prod. various) contains an in-concert recording of "Daddy's Little Girl" that suggests the passion of her live performances.

influences:

◄ Sandy Denny, Fotheringay, Pentangle, Mary Black, Johnny Cunningham

► Loreena McKennitt, Sarah MacLachlan, Tori Amos, October Project

see also: *Johnny Cunningham, Cathie Ryan, Jamshied Sharifi*

Pamela Murray Winters

Russell Means

"Rap-ajo"
Born 1939, on the Pine Ridge Reservation, SD, USA. Based in USA.

Russell Means is an American Indian renaissance man with a legendary resume (he hates the term "Native American," saying that everyone born in North or South America is a native American). He's an actor (*Last of the Mohicans, Natural Born Killers*); writer (his autobiography *Where White Men Fear to Tread* lays out his personal and political evolution); an activist and founder of the American Indian Movement (AIM); a Libertarian Party spokesperson; founder of KILI (the first radio station owned and operated by Native Americans, located on the Pine Ridge Reservation); and a tireless cultural worker. The *New York Times* once called him "the most famous Indian since Sitting Bull."

what to avoid: In an effort to get his message out to young people, Means created a style he dubbed "rap-ajo," and recorded *Electric Warrior* **woof!** (Warrior, 1993) with the help of vanguard Native rockers Tom and Robby Bee. In July of 1980, Means had spoken at the Black Hills International Survival Gathering, delivering what is considered one of the greatest Indian speeches of the later 20th century, "For America to Live, Europe Must Die." Sad to say, little of this passion and eloquence is in evidence on *Electric Warrior,* a collection of generic music and heavy-handed lyrical clichés that's hard to sit through.

influences:
◄ Robby Bee, Xit

► Natay, Litefoot

j. poet

Meditations

Roots reggae
Formed 1974, in Jamaica. Based in Kingston, Jamaica, and USA.

Ansel Cridland, vocals; Winston Watson, vocals; Danny Clarke, vocals.

One of the all-time great vocal trios, Cridland, Watson, and Clarke first got together in 1974 following the breakup of Cridland's band the Linkers. All three members write, and like their early champion Bob Marley, the Meditations' music imparts the true Rastafarian message of racial harmony and unity. In listening to the trio's sweet tones you can pick up on their inspirations and influences—chief among them American R&B vocal groups the Impressions and Temptations. The Meditations' first hits, "Woman Piabba" and "Babylon Trap," were stand-alone 45s. This success lead to their first album in 1976, *Message from the Meditations*. It contains the roots standards "Running from Jamaica," "Woman Is Like a Shadow," and "Tricked." A second album, *Wake Up,* followed in 1977. Both records deserve their classic status and further qualified the group for backing work with such legends as Marley, Jimmy Cliff, Gregory Isaacs, and the Congos. In the late '80s the Meditations made an amicable split, with Cridland moving back to Jamaica from the United States and Watson and Clarke remaining a duo and retaining the band name. Cridland made several recordings under different identities including Ansel Meditation, Scandal, and the Linkers (again), while Watson and Clarke produced a Meditations album entitled *For the Good of Man*. Cridland rejoined the band in the mid-'90s for the album *No More Friend* and a subsequent tour. The great vocal legacy of groups like the Wailers, the Mighty Diamonds, and Culture once again was living on through the Meditations as well.

what to buy: *Greatest Hits* 𝄞𝄞𝄞𝄞 (Shanachie, 1984/1991, prod. various) has it all, the hits and the classics, showcasing the group at their best with albums cuts and singles such as "Rasta Shall Conquer," "Woman Is Like a Shadow," "Fly Your Natty Dread," "Wake Up," "Running from Jamaica," "Standing on a Corner," and "Tricked." *Reggae Crazy* 𝄞𝄞𝄞𝄞 (Nighthawk, 1998, prod. various) contains many of the same tunes, plus some cuts from *Guidance,* an album cut with the Wailers in 1979 that never saw the light of day. Ansel Cridland made the selections for this CD.

what to buy next: *Deeper Roots: The Best of the Meditations* 𝄞𝄞𝄞 (Heartbeat, 1994, prod. various) is basically a collection of tracks from the Meditation's first two records, *Message from the Meditations* and *Wake Up*. Worthwhile listening, because the originals, both roots classics, are out of print.

the rest:
No More Friend 𝄞𝄞𝄞 (Greensleeves, 1983)
For the Good of Man 𝄞𝄞𝄞 (Heartbeat, 1987)
Return of the Meditations 𝄞𝄞𝄞 (Heartbeat, 1992)

influences:
◄ The Impressions, the Temptations, Jimmy Cliff, Winston Jarrett, the Wailers, Bob Marley

► Gregory Isaacs, the Congos, Culture

see also: *The Congos, Bob Marley*

Andrew BeDell

Doris "D.L." Menard

Cajun
Born April 14, 1932, in Erath, LA, USA. Based in Erath, LA, USA.

Known as the "Cajun Hank Williams," singer and songwriter D.L. Menard has penned some of the most enduring numbers in his genre's canon, including "The Back Door," his biggest hit, which has been covered by countless bands both in and out of Louisiana. Menard's vocal style is nasal, intense, and immediately identifiable. Another of his sobriquets is "the Cajun rhythm machine," referring to his crisp, driving style of rhythm guitar playing.

Menard still lives in Erath, the small town where he was born and raised, and where he and his wife Louella run a chair factory, producing handmade rockers with caned seats. His father Ophy played Cajun music on the harmonica, and, at age 16, D.L. ordered his first guitar from Montgomery Ward. A few months later he began to play in Cajun dancehalls with Elias Badeaux's band, the Louisiana Aces. During the postwar era, Menard says, "Country music was pretty popular and a Cajun band that couldn't play country music with the Cajun music didn't have too many jobs." So the teenage D.L. made a specialty of singing the popular hits of Lefty Frizzell and Hank Williams in addition to traditional Cajun songs.

In the early '50s Menard began to write his own songs in the latter category, starting with "The Jolly Roger Waltz"—a moderate seller directly followed by the huge regional hit "The Back Door." In the '60s Menard began traveling outside southwest Louisiana, eventually touring on five continents. His outgoing, wisecracking performance style combines humorous Cajun anecdotes with excellent traditional music, making him a favorite of festival and concert crowds. In addition, Menard continues to attract brilliant younger musicians as sidemen, including many of the finest accordion and fiddle players in Cajun music: Horace Trahan, Eddie LeJeune, Marc Savoy, Paul Daigle, Dewey Balfa, and Ken Smith. In 1994, Menard won a National Heritage Fellowship, the National Endowment for the Arts' highest honor for a traditional artist.

what to buy: *Under the Green Oak Tree* ♫♫♫♪ (Arhoolie, 1976, prod. Chris Strachwitz) is a model of traditional Cajun music by three undisputed masters of the genre. Marc Savoy's ornate accordion stylings and Dewey Balfa's haunting, soulful fiddling are anchored by Menard on Cajun standards, including great versions of "Lake Arthur Stomp" and "Un Gros Erreur." In addition, Menard sings several of his own hits, including "The Back Door" and the lovely title cut, a beautiful waltz. Relaxed yet intense, this is highly recommended as an introduction to Cajun traditional music. *Cajun Memories* ♫♫♫ (Swallow, 1995, prod. Floyd Soileau) is a compilation of Menard's earliest Swallow recordings, including influential, classic versions of "The Back

Door," "Jolly Roger Waltz," and "She Didn't Know I Was Married," as well as many more of his originals.

what to buy next: *No Matter Where You Are, There You At* ♫♫♫♪ (Rounder, 1989, prod. D.L. Menard, Ken Irwin) offers another traditional treatment of Cajun standards and a few non-Cajun ones as well (such as "Wildwood Flower," usually a guitar showcase but here presented as an exuberant Cajun two-step!). Eddie LeJeune and Blackie Forestier take turns on the Cajun accordion, combining with Ken Smith's Texas-tinged fiddling to provide a perfect foil for Menard's unique vocal style. *Le Trio Cadien* ♫♫♫ (Rounder, 1992, prod. Eddie LeJeune, Ken Irwin) is a second excellent outing featuring the Menard-LeJeune-Smith triumvirate, which unfortunately ended shortly after this album was released. LeJeune's pyrotechnic accordion playing has to be among the hottest in Cajun music, and Smith, with his background in Texas contest-style fiddling, has the chops to match him in speed and virtuosity. As always, Menard provides rock-solid rhythm guitar, requiring neither bass nor drums to be strong and thoroughly danceable.

what to avoid: Out of all Menard's albums, *Cajun Saturday Night* ♫♫ (Rounder, 1989, prod. Jerry Douglas) is probably the least Cajun-influenced. Produced by Nashville whiz Jerry Douglas, the album features Cajunesque honky tonk numbers, sung entirely in English and backed by Nashville sessionmen Buck White, Ricky Skaggs, and Douglas himself. Although *Cajun Saturday Night* is not by any means as traditional as the title suggests, it might serve as a good introduction for those timid listeners reluctant to dive into the heady and strange gumbo that is *real* down-home Cajun.

influences:

◄◄ Hank Williams, Harry Choates, Iry LeJeune, Marc Savoy, Balfa Brothers

►► Eddie LeJeune, California Cajun Orchestra, Savoy-Smith Cajun Band, Steve Riley & the Mamou Playboys, Balfa Toujours

see also: *Balfa Brothers, Eddie LeJeune, Savoy-Doucet Cajun Band*

Suzy Rothfield Thompson

Sergio Mendes

Bossa nova, Latin pop, samba, jazz, lounge
Born February 11, 1941, in Niteroi, Brazil.

Mendes might be considered one of the poster boys of loungedom, so involved was he with the "Blame it on the bossa nova" musical wave that swept through America in the early '60s. But one of his biggest hits was a 1968 easy-listening cover of a Beatles tune, "Fool on the Hill," recorded with his band Brasil '66 (originally named Brasil '65; the year would be updated occasionally). Pianist Mendes first gained fame as the leader of the Bossa Nova Trio. He moved to the States in 1964 and began collaborating with fellow Brazilian Antonio Carlos Jobim and American Art Farmer before creating the band that became Brasil '66, with Jose Soares on vocals and percussion, Bob Matthews on vocals and bass, Jao Palma on drums, and Janis Hansen and Lani Hall on vocals. Hall was the wife of A&M Records co-founder Herb Alpert—no slouch in the area of Latin music reprocessed for the Stateside market himself. The band's debut release—on A&M, naturally—*Sergio Mendes and Brasil '66*, contained the Top 10 hit "Mais Que Nada." With an airy, Latin-laced jazz-pop sound and no pretensions toward making socially relevant or politically pointed music, Mendes and company provided a bit of light escapism during a turbulent time. They released a series of albums filled with catchy originals and savvy covers, including Simon and Garfunkel's "Scarborough Fair," Otis Redding's "(Sittin' On) the Dock of the Bay," and even the Jimmy Webb tune that hit for Glen Campbell, "Wichita Lineman." The band's first few A&M albums fared well, then the Brasil star began to sputter out. By 1975, Mendes had released his first solo disc on Elektra; in 1977, he tried *Sergio Mendes and the New Brasil '77*, to no one's interest. But he did engineer a comeback with 1983's *Sergio Mendes* on A&M, reaching the Top 40 (if abandoning any vestiges of stylistic connection to his old band's title country) with "Never Gonna Let You Go," sung by Joe Pizzulo and Leza Miller. He dropped below the music-world radar again after 1984's *Confetti*, but resurfaced with Brasil '99, another soon-to-be-outdated moniker.

what to buy: Much of Mendes's signature lounge work is no longer in print, but most to the point of this book anyway, you might try *Brasileiro* ✍✍✍✍ (Elektra, 1992, prod. Sergio Mendes), his percussion-drenched exploration of his own musical roots. "Magalenha" is quite catchy in its post–bossa nova way (samba-reggae, to be precise). The disc truly evokes the balmy breezes and intricate rhythms of Brazil, and "Kalimba" is rather funky. *Oceano* ✍✍✍ (Verve, 1996) puts Mendes firmly on Latin soil, musically speaking, with some very nice cuts. But for some reason he felt the need to venture into rap-like territory with "Maracatudo," which proves that genre-jumping is not always a good thing.

what to buy next: *Fool on the Hill* ✍✍✍✍ (A&M, 1968, prod. Sergio Mendes) is the quintessential post–"Girl from Ipanema" sound, using light bossa nova beats and laying lilting female vocals over big strings and Mendes's piano. *Greatest Hits of Brasil '66* ✍✍✍✍ (A&M, 1970, prod. Herb Alpert) showcases Mendes and the band with what's been described as his "winningly sexy blend of American female voices, simplified bossa

brazil: tropicalismo

The samba-rock of Tropicalismo (a.k.a. Tropicalia) coincided with the Brazilian military regime of the late 1960s and early '70s. As the younger generation rebelled against the oppressive government, the electric-guitar-and-Bahian-rhythm mix of Tropicalismo framed their rallying cries, with Caetano Veloso's "Tropicalia" as their anthem. Founders Veloso and Gilberto Gil shrouded their political protest in double entendres; nonetheless considered a threat to the state, they were soon thrown in jail and later forced into exile in England. (This anti-establishment wave converged with an international interest in protest music in the same period, from kindred Latin American movements like the socially conscious *nueva cancion* ["new song"] trend and its Cuban variant *nueva trova* ["new ballad"], to American folk phenoms like Bob Dylan.)

Other Tropicalismo greats include Jorge Ben (now Jorge Ben Jor), Maria Bethânia, and Gal Costa; two good surveys are the Luaka Bop label's *Brazil Classics 1* and *Beleza Tropical 2*. One of the most eccentric and playful of the Tropicalismo bands was Os Mutantes, who received the full reissue treatment in 1999 with a retrospective also on Luaka Bop (*World Psychedelic Classics I: Brazil: The Best of Os Mutantes: Everything Is Possible!*) and the it's-about-time Stateside release of their first three albums (*Os Mutantes, Mutantes,* and *A Divina Comédia Ou Ando Meio Desligado*) on Omplatten.

David Poole

nova rhythms, and lavish Dave Grusin orchestrations." It contains versions of three Beatles compositions ("Day Tripper," "Fool on the Hill," and "With a Little Help from My Friends") alongside Cole Porter ("Night and Day") and Burt Bacharach/Hal David ("The Look of Love"). Also included are "Going Out of My Head," "Scarborough Fair," and other cuts destined for dentists' offices everywhere.

best of the rest:
Four Sider ♫♫♫ (A&M, 1966)

worth searching for: Because many of the albums of Mendes's heyday, such as *Classics* ♫♫♫ (A&M, 1986) and *Crystal Illusions* ♫♫♫ (A&M, 1969), are either out of print or difficult to find, the best way to hear Brasil '66 in the CD era is on a variety of recent compilations. *Cocktail Mix, Vol. 2: Martini Madness* ♫♫♫ (Rhino, 1996, compilation prod. Janet Grey) stacks Mendes's "Mais Que Nada" in context with other Latin-style tinkly instrumentals, including Perez Prado's "Why Wait" and Cal Tjader's "Soul Sauce (Guacha Guaro)." For something completely different, "Mais Que Nada" also shows up on the excellent, rock-heavy soundtrack *I Shot Andy Warhol* ♫♫♫♫ (Tag/Atlantic, 1996, prod. Randall Poster).

influences:

◄◄ Antonio Carlos Jobim, Herb Alpert, Astrud Gilberto, Henry Mancini, the Beatles, Stan Getz, Charlie Byrd, João Gilberto

►► Michael Sembello, Gilberto Gil, David Byrne, Paul Simon

see also: *Antonio Carlos Jobim, Perez Prado*

Lynne Margolis

Mendes Brothers

Funana, morna, coladeira, bandera, Cape Verdean pop
Born early 1950s, in Palonkon, Cape Verde. Based in Brockton, MA, USA.

João Mendes, guitar, vocals; Ramiro Mendes, guitar, keyboards, baixo, drum programs, electric viola, cavaquinho. (Both members from Cape Verde.)

The Mendes Brothers, João and Ramiro, are part of a new generation of U.S.-based Verdeans that have become doctors, lawyers, and professionals in many fields, as comfortable with American culture as with their own. (There is, in fact, a bigger Verdean population in the New England states than in Cape Verde.) In the best spirit of the American dream, the Mendes brothers have gone from penniless immigrants to owners of MB Records, a small label that's recently drawn offers from majors interested in manufacturing and distributing their growing list of Verdean titles. "We were born in the town of Palonkon, on the [Verdean] island of Fogo [fire], where we lived until I was 13," João Mendes recalls. "Our parents had come to the United States a few years before, and we joined them in 1978. We'd never seen snow before and barely spoke the language, so it was quite a shock. The older kids went to work, and I went to school, but right off Ramiro and I had a band that played Cape Verdean and Angolan music all over the East Coast. If we could drive a van there and be back for classes on Monday, we'd go." In 1981 the brothers Mendes added a Haitian keyboard player

named Nono to the lineup. Nono "took over" the band, composing most of the original music and directing the other players. The syncopated Haitian *compas* influence made them a favorite with dancers, and that same year they recorded a Haitian album entitled *Um Novo Metodo,* which João describes as "a blend of compas and Cape Verdean *coladeira* (dance music) with a lot of Angolan influence." The record did well, despite its lack of distribution outside the Verdean community, but the senior Mendeses were not impressed. "To them, music was not an honorable profession." Like parents all over the world, the Mendes' wanted their sons to have "real jobs," even though Ramiro had been taking classical guitar lessons at night while working full-time in a boot factory to support the band. When João finished high school he did get a "real job." Ramiro took his savings and went to Boston to attend the Berklee School, where he graduated with a degree in film scoring and commercial arranging.

Before leaving for Berklee, Ramiro had produced an album entitled *Andorinha Debolta* for Sãozinaha, a woman who sang the traditional style of *morna* ("Cape Verdean blues") that had been popular 100 years before. On the strength of the recording, Sãozinaha was invited to compete in Cape Verde's annual international song contest, "The Whole World Sings." When she won the title, Ramiro's production credentials got a big boost. During his years at Berklee, Ramiro produced more than 20 albums for Verdean, Angolan, and Haitian artists, including *Angola Minha Namorada (Angola My Sweetheart)* for Waldemar Bastos on EMI, and Cesaria Evora's breakthrough album *Mar Azul,* although Ramiro's producing credit didn't make it to the completed CD jacket.

In 1991 the brothers used their savings to buy a 16-track recording studio in Brockton, Massachusetts, and opened the doors of MB Records. "The first thing we did was the title track from our own album *Palonkon.* We wanted to make sure everything worked, so we went in and started playing. We finished it in one day." Their first year of operation saw MB Records putting out *Paranoia* by Mirri Lobo, one of Cape Verde's most popular coladeira singers, and *Simpatia* by Djosinha, the leader of Contratempo, one of the hottest bands in the North American Verdean community. In 1993 the brothers finished *Palonkon,* named in honor of the village of their birth. "Ramiro played most of the instruments on the album, and I sang," João says. "Since we like so many kinds of music, it's more diverse [than most Verdean albums]. 'Helena' and 'Xandinha' are coladeiras; 'Vida' is a mazurka with some touches of *funana* [an older dance rhythm]; 'Angola Beliza Natural' is a coladeira with some Angolan-style samba. The violin and ukulele parts are typical of Angolan music. 'Angola Na Paz' is a morna, and 'Fidju Koitadu,' which means 'Son of the Needy,' is a funana that talks about the political situation back home; how the political system was set up with the settlers owning everything and the workers having nothing. Workers [have to kick back] 50 percent to the landowners, as well as paying a tax out of their share. The song measures the moral integrity of the workers against the owners of the land. The lyrics say 'I am the son of a farmer who was the son of a farmer,' tracing my family line in the African manner. 'We are the people with heart; the people with money and power have no heart.'" Although they've only been in business for a few years, João Mendes is amazed at the impact MB Records has had both in America and back home. "A friend wrote to us from Angola and said that *Palonkon* is a huge seller there. Although it's mostly on pirated cassettes, it's still good to know that people like the music. But the biggest surprise was how open Americans have been. The *Boston Globe* gave us three-and-a-half stars in their music section. I'm beginning to realize that this music isn't just for Verdeans any more. The cliché is true; music is a universal language and everybody wants to learn how to speak it."

what to buy: *Bandera* 𝄞𝄞𝄞𝄞 (MB, 1995, prod. Ramiro Mendes) is pure pop in a Cape Verdean stylee, heavy on the bass and percussion and featuring the soulful vocals of João Mendes. Every track is strong, and the overall sound will appeal to lovers of Brazilian music, although the Mendes Brothers are funkier and a good deal less slick.

what to buy next: Like Trinidad, Cape Verde has a tradition of taking political leaders to task in song. A suite of such pieces with lyrics by Verdean poet Alberto Alves, *Diplomadu* 𝄞𝄞𝄞𝄞 (MB, 1996, prod. Ramiro Mendes) was released just before the 1996 elections in Cape Verde. Some Verdeans hailed it as a masterpiece of political music, others criticized the brothers for "meddling" in Cape Verde's politics, but you don't have to understand the lyrics to catch the album's infectious groove.

the rest:
Palonkon 𝄞𝄞𝄞 (MB, 1995)

influences:
◀◀ B. Leza

▶▶ Mirri Lobo, Djosinha, Cesaria Evora

j. poet

Margareth Menezes
Axe, samba-reggae
Born in Salvador da Bahia, Brazil. Based in Salvador da Bahia, Brazil.

Margareth Menezes's life changed with one phone call. A struggling actress and singer, she had finished a short tour with Gilberto Gil, visiting Rio and Sao Paolo for the first time, when David Byrne called. The former leader of Talking Heads wanted

Menezes to perform with him on his 1989 solo world tour. Menezes's charismatic performance endeared her to American audiences and she soon recorded her debut on Mango Records in 1980, *Elegibo.* Menezes's larger-than-life stage presence, however, belies her in-person shyness. In one interview, she recalled that she was so nervous and homesick rehearsing with Byrne that she could not sing and cried herself to sleep that night. Her sudden success outside of Brazil never quite paralleled her reception within it, and her career has since wobbled. By the time of *Luz Dourada,* her record company barely marketed the album in the United States. Some have said that Menezes's career problems stem from the subtle racism against dark-skinned performers in Brazil. Indeed, Daniela Mercury's subsequent superstardom only highlights the lack of market enthusiasm for Menezes, who performed percussive samba-reggae and axe music similar to that of the light-skinned Mercury.

what to buy: *Elegibo* 𝄞𝄞𝄞𝄞 (Mango, 1990, prod. Nestor Madrid) shows off Menezes's rich alto and infectious energy in a variety of Bahian styles, from samba-reggae to lambada. While this is certainly a pop album, it consistently has more heft and soul than her later releases.

what to buy next: *Luz Dourada* 𝄞𝄞𝄞 (PolyGram, 1995, prod. Nestor Madrid) has a high-energy pop sheen, but there are strong songs and great examples of updated percussive Bahian genres. *Kindala* 𝄞𝄞𝄞 (Mango, 1991, prod. Nestor Madrid) is her sophomore effort and, though it has some great tunes, it also has some lackluster pop cuts.

the rest:
A Novidade Do Movimento (1998)

influences:
◀◀ Olodum, Ile Aiye, Gilberto Gil, Clara Nunes

Marty Lipp

E.T. Mensah
Ghanaian highlife
Born Emmanuel Tettey Mensah, May 31, 1919, in Accra, Ghana. Based in Ghana.

There are few musicians who have almost single-handedly shaped the evolution of a genre, but trumpeter E.T. Mensah is among that select group. Highlife, the Ghanaian pop music that was to have such a big impact on the way Nigerian musicians played, owed its popularity to Mensah and his band the Tempos, who relentlessly toured West African venues. The "high-life" music played by the Tempos had its roots in the formal balls held by the Westernized Ghanaian elite, where tangos, waltzes, and other "high society" dances were performed. Mensah and the Tempos brought African and Caribbean

Margareth Menezes

rhythms to the mix, sang in various tribal dialects, and started using electric guitars, modifications that enabled them to attract a wider demographic than the tuxedo-and-gown set.

Although his father was a guitarist, the young Mensah's musical career actually began in 1924 as a member of his school's band. There he learned how to play fife and flute under the guidance of teacher/bandleader Joe Lamptey. In 1932 Lamptey reorganized the band, making it into a larger ensemble with a new name, the Accra Orchestra. Mensah started out as a roadie for the group before joining its saxophone section. From the late '30s into the mid '40s Mensah and his older brother Yebuah had a spin-off band called the Accra Rhythmic Orchestra. The next group on E.T.'s resume was Jack Leopard's Black and White Spots, an interracial ensemble led by a Scottish sergeant that generally played for foreign troops stationed in Accra. It was during this stint that Mensah picked up the rudiments of playing the alto saxophone and the trumpet.

In 1947 he joined the Tempos, then a seven-piece group with a revolving leadership. Other important members in the initial lineup included Joe Kelly, a tenor saxophonist who had also played in the Accra Orchestra, and Guy Warren, a jazz-oriented drummer later known as Kofi Ghanaba. Warren was particularly important within the fledgling group; he had spent some time in the U.K. and become acquainted with calypso music, a genre that interested some in the band because of its easy adaptability to highlife. Nonetheless, Warren and most of the original Tempos left in 1950 after a dispute over the group's direction in which Mensah (who owned the band's instruments) wanted to blend calypso and Latin rhythms into their highlife, while the dissenting musicians were more interested in jazz and Afro-Cuban music.

As undisputed leader of the Tempos, Mensah made moves that were to further impact other African bands. First of all, he started paying the players, making them the first professional musicians in Ghana. His tours of West Africa (especially the frequent stops in Nigeria) further popularized highlife music and influenced future African greats Victor Olaiya and Rex Lawson to start their own groups modeled on the Tempos. Mensah also became the first chairman of the Ghana Musicians Union in 1961, and under his leadership the union forced the record companies to increase the royalties paid on each record sold. He went on to be a prominent member of the Musicians' Union of Ghana after a government coup forced the previous incarnation to disband because of its ties to the former regime.

Highlife's popularity started to wane in the mid-'60s and Mensah put his career on hold to become a pharmacist for most of the following decade. A resurgence of interest in highlife in the late '70s brought him back into the musical fold. In 1986 a biography of Mensah written by musicologist John Collins, *E.T. Mensah: King of Highlife,* was published by Off the Record

Press in London and the Ghana State Publishing Corporation in Accra. At the end of 1988, Mensah received an honorary Ph.D. and retired from performance once again.

what's available: Mensah's releases from the '50s and early '60s are necessarily cramped by the limitations of 78 rpm records, but they are important documents for understanding the evolution of modern African pop music. *All for You* 𝄢𝄢𝄢𝄢 (Retroafric, 1990, compilation prod. Noel Sidebotham) and *Day by Day* 𝄢𝄢𝄢𝄢 (Retroafric, 1991, compilation prod. Bunt Stafford-Clarke) afford a look at a West African music scene in flux. In addition to instrumentals there are vocals sung in English, Spanish, and pidgin as well as tribal languages (Twi, Fante, and Ga). Amidst entertaining songs like "Tea Samba" and "Day by Day" there are a handful of topical pieces commenting on issues of the day, including "Inflation Calypso" and "Ghana Freedom." Mensah's favorite calypsos and highlife rhythms fill the bulk of these discs but jazz and the Cuban *clave* rhythm have made notable inroads, foreshadowing the styles developed by Victor Uwaifo, Fela Kuti, King Sunny Adé, and other West Africans.

influences:

◀◀ Kwame Asare, Eddie Calvert, Lord Kitchener

▶▶ Victor Olaiya, Rex Lawson, Victor Uwaifo, Jerry Hansen

Garaud MacTaggart

Daniela Mercury

Axe

Born 1965, in Salvador da Bahia, Brazil. Based in Salvador da Bahia, Brazil.

Anyone who has seen Daniela Mercury perform live knows that she has enough energy to light a mid-sized city. With her big voice, indefatigable spirit, and sexy good looks, Mercury is the perfect ambassador for her beloved home state of Bahia. Though Mercury's high-energy repertoire has broadened, it is focused on the exuberant, drum-driven music of Bahia, sometimes called *axe* ("ah-shay"). Indeed, Mercury has done more than anyone to popularize Bahian music, even within Brazil itself, which is why she is sometimes called the "Queen of Axe." Her first connection to music was as a dancer, but it was as a teenager that the former Daniela Mercuri de Almeida Povoas began to recognize her singing ability. Performing in bars she wasn't even old enough to enter otherwise, Mercury soon graduated to belting out crowd-rousing numbers from the back of large flatbed trucks: the *trios eletricos* of Bahia's Carnival celebration. As a solo artist, she scored a hit in 1991 with "Swing Da Cor (Color Swing)," which was one of the first popular songs in the samba-reggae style, a style that built on the drum-corps street music of *afros blocos* such as Olodum and Ile Aiye. Mercury's second album, *O Canto Da Cidade (Song of the City)* was

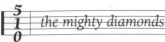
Brazil's first diamond record, with sales surpassing one million copies. With a heavy road schedule, Mercury became one of the top draws in Brazil, and in her wake other Bahian groups such as Banda Eva and E O Tchan have come to post sales that rival her own. For Mercury, Bahia is an inextricable part of her music. "The Bahiano knows how important happiness is," she says. "The human being has to chase happiness. It's necessary for life. Amid all the hardship you have in life, music can bring positive energy—especially when the music is good to dance to—and that is my intention." Further explaining the aim of her relentlessly high-energy music, Mercury says, "When one of us dances, it's beautiful to see. But when we dance together, the earth moves, the ground shakes and we can make a revolution. And today the revolution is to be happy."

what to buy: *Feijão Com Arroz (Beans with Rice)* ♫♫♫♫ (Sony, 1997, prod. Alfredo Moura) is Mercury's most accomplished album to date, one on which each song is done in a different style—from a Rio-style Carnival *samba enredo* to reggae to Northeastern rhythms such as *galope*—and she makes perfect use of many guest artists. A non-stop pace, but every track is excellently arranged.

what to buy next: *O Canto Da Cidade* ♫♫♫ (Sony, 1993, prod. Liminha) has many great cuts too, but some are not as spellbinding.

the rest:
Daniela Mercury ♫♫♫ (Eldor, 1991)
Musica da Rua ♫♫♥ (Sony Discos, 1994)
Eletrica ♫♫♫♫ (Sony Discos, 1999)

influences:
◄◄ Carmen Miranda, Clara Nunes, Olodum, Gilberto Gil

►► Banda Eva, Marcia Freire, E O Tchan, Cheiro De Amor

see also: *Olodum*

Marty Lipp

The Mighty Diamonds

Roots reggae
Formed 1974, in Kingston, Jamaica. Based in Kingston, Jamaica.

Donald Shaw, lead vocals; Bunny Simpson, harmony vocals; Lloyd Ferguson, harmony vocals. (All members are from Jamaica.)

The Diamonds were one of the premier vocal trios of the mid-1970s roots reggae boom, and their first album, *Right Time,* is one of the high water marks of the era. Led by singer/songwriter Donald Shaw, and backed by Sly & Robbie and other Studio One heavies, the first album's brilliant mixture of militant lyrics and smoky, soulful vocals has seldom been matched. The Diamonds have recorded steadily, with the same lineup, for

more than two decades now, though they have never equaled their opening salvo.

what's available: The *Go Seek Your Rights* ♫♫♫♫ (Frontline, 1990, prod. various) compilation, issued during the major-label frenzy of digitalization, contains the entire *Right Time* album, along with tracks from *Deeper Roots* and *Planet Earth.*

worth searching for: As of this writing, there is no plan to release *Planet Earth* ♫♫♫♫ (Virgin, 1978, prod. Karl Pitterson) on CD, although it rivals *Right Time* for its soul and sufferation. It was never officially released in the U.S. either, so if you can find an LP or cassette, snap it up.

influences:
◄◄ Pioneers, Wailers, Heptones

see also: *Sly & Robbie*

j. poet

The Mighty Sparrow /Sparrow

Calypso, soca
Born July 9, 1935, in Grenada. Based in Jamaica, NY, USA, and Port of Spain, Trinidad.

Slinger Francisco, the Mighty Sparrow, is the greatest living singer of calypso, and perhaps the greatest singer and composer the genre has ever produced, although he's extremely modest about his accomplishments. "Your calypso name is given to you by your peers, based on your style," Sparrow says. "In the old days they tried to emulate British royalty; there was Lord Kitchener, Lord Nelson, Duke. When I started, the bands were using acoustic instruments and the singers would stand flat-footed, making a point or accusing someone in the crowd with the pointing of a finger. When I sing, I get excited and move around, and this was new. The older singers said 'Why don't you just sing instead of jumping around like a little Sparrow.' It was said as a joke, but the name stuck." Sparrow had the last laugh, going on to become the most successful calypso singer of all time. If you combined the Beatles' gift for melody, Elvis Presley's hip-shaking showmanship, the lascivious sexuality of Prince, the politically astute observations of Phil Ochs, and the verbal pyrotechnics of Gilbert & Sullivan, and crammed them all into a single compact body, you'd have some idea of Sparrow's impact on the history of Caribbean music. Sparrow's sexually and politically charged compositions and dynamic performances have made him a superstar throughout most of the world, but despite the fact that he lives and works in Jamaica, New York, for six months of every year, he's largely unknown in the United States outside of the West Indian community.

Sparrow was born on the island of Grenada, but his family moved to Trinidad when he was still an infant. Sparrow attended

Daniela Mercury

a Catholic grammar school and traces his love of music to his days as a head choirboy at Newtown Boy's School. A teacher named Carl Jaggermauth held classroom singing contests and rewarded the winner with an extra carton of milk. It may be those early experiences that honed Sparrow's competitive spirit. "I also sang all kinds of American pop music, especially the tunes of Nat 'King' Cole. When I was around 14 I joined a steel band put together by the neighborhood boys for Carnival. That's when I got interested in Calypso." Calypso mixes the rhythmic drive of the West African rhythms the slaves remembered from their homeland with the folk and popular music they heard from their masters on the sugar plantations. Trinidad was conquered by the Spanish and British, and also boasts large populations of French, Indian, Chinese, Portuguese, and Syrian immigrants, so the musical melting pot is brimming over with Latin, Arabic, Asian, and European strains. The West African *griot* tradition of topical song, which granted singers "immunity" for their barbed verses, as well as the tradition of ridiculing rivals or people in positions of power (which may also be the root of the African American practice of "the dozens" or "snaps"), certainly played a part in the evolution of calypso. "It goes back to slavery days," Sparrow explains. "People weren't allowed to learn how to read or write, so the only way the people had to address the issues of the day and find consolation was through music."

Calypso, or *kaiso* as it was called in the early days, was accompanied by drums until the Spanish outlawed the drum. Trinidadians then invented "rhythm sticks," bamboo canes of varying lengths and pitches, to take the place of the drums, but the masters saw the canes as potential weapons and banished them, too. Eventually the music began to integrate European instruments—guitar, bass, piano, etc.—and began a long, slow transformation to respectability. "Under British rule [Trinidad has only been independent since 1961] calypso was considered outlaw music," Sparrow continues. "They called it the 'mouthpiece of the poor,' and since calypsonians were always stepping on the corns of the bigwigs and exposing things that they didn't want exposed, they wouldn't play it on the radio. In the early days there was some risk involved to the singers, but nonetheless, they would stand up and sing out about the problems of the day." Despite, or perhaps because of, official displeasure, calypso became one of Trinidad's major exports, and in the '30s and '40s tourists began flocking to the island each year at Carnival time to hear the latest from Lord Melody, Growling Tiger, and Atilla.

Inspired by these great singers, Sparrow taught himself to play guitar and started writing songs. As a teenager he'd sneak into clubs to sing and play, often missing the last bus home and sleeping on the floor of places like the Dirty Jim Swizzle Club. In young adulthood he entered the yearly calypso competition and won first place with "Jean and Dinah." The prize was the magnificent

sum of 40 dollars. "In those days the competition was corrupt. If you cut a record you didn't get royalties. They acted like they were doing you a favor by letting you record a song." To protest this, Sparrow wrote "Carnival Boycott" and led a strike of about half the singers. "We weren't mad at the strike breakers," Sparrow said. "We understood they were just trying to make a name for themselves, but it would have gone better if we'd all stood together." During the boycott, Sparrow wasn't idle. He cut the first long-playing album of calypsos in 1957, and while he didn't officially compete, songs like "Russian Satellite," "Theresa," and "Post Card to Sparrow" were huge favorites with the crowd.

Despite the lack of unity around the strike, things improved and in 1960 Sparrow returned to the competition. By the end of the decade he had won Calypso King six times, Road March King five times, and both titles three times, making him the most popular calypso performer of all time. So popular, in fact, that in 1974 he formally resigned from competition so "the younger singers would have a chance for exposure." Despite the fact that he didn't enter the yearly calypso jousts, Sparrow's performing and composing skills never got rusty. His world tours were usually sell-out affairs, and he still grappled with the social issues of the day in a forthright manner that combined keen political insights with a bawdy sense of humor. And notwithstanding his hiatus from the annual Carnival competitions, he did compete in the King of Kings show in 1985, a contest between 11 of the performers who'd won the King of Carnival crown including legends like Melody, Kitchener, and Stalin. Sparrow won the grand prize of 100,000 Trinidadian dollars and the title. He has also been awarded an honorary Yoruba title in the wake of his triumphant FESTAC (World Festival of Black Arts and Culture) tour of West Africa in 1977, and in 1988 received an honorary Ph.D. from the University of the West Indies, in observance of all the doctoral candidates who've earned their degrees annotating and deconstructing the lyrics and melodic structure of the master.

For the past 20 years, due to the poor quality of the studios and the high price of recording in Trinidad, most calypso singers, including Sparrow, have spent at least half of their time in Brooklyn, where a large West Indian population supports the music and the artists. The influences of New York City's hip-hop, funk, Haitian, and Salsa scenes have also helped calypso to mutate into its latest incarnation as soca (SOul and CAlypso), a wrinkle that has taken the music into the '90s and kept it vital. "We jumped up the tempo, and simplified the beat somewhat," Sparrow said. "Unfortunately, a lot of the social and political impact of the music has been forgotten. Today most singers talk about dancing and having a good time. In the old days you had to have a large vocabulary, your lyrics had to rhyme, and the words often added a syncopated element to the composition as a whole. With a few exceptions, all you get now is 'wine an' grine.'"

The Mighty Sparrow

Except for a couple of mini-crazes (Harry Belafonte spawned one in the early '50s, and Bing Crosby and Rudy Vallee created a sensation in the mid-'30s by inviting Atilla, Growling Lion, and Gerald Clarke to appear on their NBC Network shows), calypso has kept a remarkably low profile in the United States. While reggae has slowly gained recognition in North America, calypso is still largely unknown even though many of its greatest practitioners live in the States and sing in English. "I think it's mainly a question of promotion," Sparrow says. "Calypso people are eager to embrace all kinds of American music, but they don't realize that their own music is still in its embryonic stages, at least in this market. They want to be assimilated, and sometimes they're oblivious to their own culture. They don't realize that travelers, both musically and culturally speaking, don't want to go where tourists go. They want to see what the natives enjoy. Soca is very infectious music and if you brag about your music, and boast about it, then the Americans will take a chance with it."

what to buy: One of the high points of Sparrow's career, *25th Anniversary* 𝄢𝄢𝄢𝄢 (Charlie's, 1980, prod. Slinger Francisco) celebrated his longevity in calypso and includes "Dead or Alive," a worldwide hit that decried the ruthless dictators of the Third World.

what to buy next: The *Mighty Sparrow, Volume One* 𝄢𝄢𝄢𝄢 (Ice, 1992) compilation gives you 13 early hits, including several tunes that won Sparrow Carnival King titles, like "Jean and Dinah," "Dan Is the Man (in the Van)" and "Congo Man."

the rest:
Mighty Sparrow, Volume Two 𝄢𝄢𝄢 (Ice, 1992)
Mighty Sparrow, Volume Three 𝄢𝄢𝄢 (Ice, 1992)
Sparrow's Dance Party 𝄢𝄢𝄢𝄢 (BLS, 1992)
Dancing Shoes 𝄢𝄢𝄢 (Ice, 1993)
Mighty Sparrow, Volume Four 𝄢𝄢𝄢𝄢 (Ice, 1994)

worth searching for: Any Sparrow album, cassette, or CD will be worth the price; even his "weaker" sets have a classic or two in them, but he hasn't really written a bad song in his entire career.

influences:
◄◄ Growling Tiger, Duke, Melody, Attila the Hun

►► Harry Belafonte, Stalin, Explainer, Shadow

j. poet

Pablo Milanés
Nueva trova, nueva canción
Born 1943, in Bayamo, Cuba. Based in Cuba.

Pablo Milanés uses his music as commentary on revolutionary Cuba and on the emotional life of the Cuban people. Like Silvio Rodríguez and other Cuban artists interested in the politics of change, he studied at film school in Havana in the mid-'60s. With Rodríguez, Milanés is considered by many to have taken on the role of national poet of Cuba, whose work will provide a roadmap to the ideological development of the nation when Fidel's revolution is judged by history.

what's available: *Classicos de Cuba* 𝄢𝄢𝄢 (Simitar Latino, 1997, compilation prod. Thomas Cochran) is a recent example of Milanés's thoughtful originals and covers. Milanés has an extensive discography on Spanish labels, most of which aren't well distributed in the United States. He contributes one track, "Identidad," to the easier-to-find *Cuba: I Am Time,* reviewed in the Compilations section of this volume.

influences:
◄◄ Leo Brouwer, Sindo Garay, Carlos Puebla

►► Carlos Varela, Silvio Rodríguez, Lourdes Perez

see also: *Silvio Rodríguez, Chucho Valdez*

Kerry Dexter

Milladoiro
Spanish folk, Celtic
Formed 1978, in Santiago, Galicia, Spain. Based in Spain.

Rodrigo Romani (1978–present), harp, trompa, ocarina, guitar, bouzouki, vocals; Antón Seoane (1978–present), teclados, accordion, guitar, zanfona; Xosé V. Ferreirós (1978–present), gaita, oboe, bouzouki, mandolin, pandereta, castañolas, uilleann pipes, vocals; Fernando Casal (1978–present), gaita, clarinet, tin whistle, pandereta, vocals; Ramon "Moncho" García Rei (1978–present), percussion, vocals; Xosé A. Fernández Méndez (1978–present), flute, piccolo; Michel Canadá (1981–91), violin, viola, mandola; Laura Quintillén (1979–80), violin; Antonio Seijo (1992–present), violin. (All members are from Spain.)

The University at Santiago de Compostela was a hotbed of music playing and research during the mid-1970s. Xosé A. Fernández Méndez, a jazz musician, was working amongst historical archives, exploring old manuscripts and scores, looking for interesting music. Xosé V. Ferreirós, Fernando Casal, and Ramon García Rei were members of a band of wandering minstrels devoted to playing traditional Galician (Spanish Celtic) music at parties and other functions. Meanwhile Antón Seoane and Rodrigo Romani were playing and researching medieval music, finally recording some of their results on a 1978 album titled *Milladoiro.* The name of their release was taken from the piles of stones left by religious pilgrims on their treks through Galicia. By the end of 1978 all of these musicians had banded together (with violinist Laura Quintillén) to form Milladoiro, the group. After months of practice they unveiled the results in concert and, with the exception of a transient series of violin-

Pablo Milanés

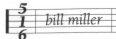

ists, have been performing together as the same unit ever since. The music of Milladoiro has Celtic roots and their biggest initial inspiration was Ireland's pioneering Chieftains, but they also looked to the Celtic music of Brittany in France and the living tradition of their own Galician homeland. Over time Milladoiro have taken their folk sources and blended them with elements lifted from classical music to form a distinctive hybrid. They have toured all over Europe and also traveled to Japan, North America, and South America. They have released 14 albums, counting the one by Seoane and Romani from which they take their name. These include soundtracks and incidental music for various arts-oriented events, but only three of their discs are available in the United States. Milladoiro have also recorded with Paul Winter (on *Solstice Live*) and with their original role models, the Chieftains (on *Celebration*).

what to buy: The band's first American release was *Castellum Honesti* ♫♫♫ (Ion Musica/Green Linnet, 1989/1991, prod. Milladoiro), their eighth album overall. While nine of the ten songs are traditional melodies, the arrangements and instrumentation bring the tunes into the modern age even though nary an electric guitar is present. A truer representation of the band as a concert act can be found on *As fadas de estraño nome* ♫♫♫♫ (Discmedi/Green Linnet, 1995/1997, prod. Milladoiro), recorded in Buenos Aires, Argentina, and in Ortiqueira, Spain. One would never suspect the band's academic background because the performances lack any trace of ivory-tower stiffness. The band bounces, it swings, it can cause uninhibited dancing in the aisles and then, turning on a psychological dime, it can bring tears to the eye with melodies that tug at the heartstrings.

what to buy next: *Galicia no Tempo* ♫♫♫ (Discmedi/Green Linnet, 1991/1992) was written as music for an art exhibition in the band's hometown of Santiago de Compostela, and has a certain restraint that isn't found on their other American releases. It's still a very pleasant project, though it might sound a bit too close to Celtic-influenced new-age music for some listeners.

worth searching for: Probably their most available import, *Iacobus Magnus* ♫♫♫ (Discmedi, 1994, prod. Milladoiro) is a fully realized example of Milladoiro as folklorist/neo-classicists. Recorded with the English Chamber Orchestra and the Orquesta Sinfónica de Galicia, the music is a suite written for the Cathedral of Santiago de Compostela. The body of St. Jacob, one of Jesus's disciples, is supposedly buried there, hence the title.

influences:

◀◀ The Chieftains, the Bothy Band, Alan Stivell, Os Campaneiros

▶▶ Trisquel, Leixaprén, Berroguëtto

see also: *The Chieftains, Bill Whelan, Paul Winter*

Garaud MacTaggart

Bill Miller

Native American, folk, rock
Born 1940, in Wisconsin, USA. Based in USA.

Don't trouble yourself trying to label the music of Native American singer-songwriter Bill Miller; he's happy to do it himself. It's not alternative, he's fond of saying: it's altered-Native. Miller can shift gears rapidly between Neil Young–style folkie reveries and tradition-based Native American chants. On the third hand, his 1996 release was a full-bore rock album, much of which draws on the kind of energy Miller saw when he shared a concert bill with Pearl Jam. Having grown up on a northern Wisconsin reservation, Miller was exposed to the vagaries of racism and all its attendant violence. And while his music occasionally gives in to bitterness and a thirst for revenge, it is mostly about hope, dignity, and compassion. Miller's is an important and genuinely wise voice.

what to buy: On *Raven in the Snow* ♫♫♫ (Reprise, 1995, prod. Richard Bennett), Miller switches from his gentle folk stance to explosive rock arrangements—a good idea since, for the first time, the music reflects the fury behind such songs as "The Final Word" and the title track. Others—such as the defiant "Brave Heart" and "Listen to Me," which pleads for understanding between generations—are more reflective and have an ethereal quality. Altogether, *Raven* is Miller's most fully realized work.

what to buy next: *The Red Road* ♫♫♫ (Warner Western, 1993, prod. Richard Bennett) combines acoustic-based folk music with Native American flutes and chants. It includes the haunting instrumental "Dreams of Wounded Knee" plus "Praises," which is based on a Menominee prayer to the Creator, and "Reservation Road," a gritty memoir of Miller's birthplace.

the rest:

(With Robert Mirabal & the Smokey Town Singers) *Native Suite* ♫♫♫
   (Warner Western, 1996)
Ghostdancer N/A (Sol, 1999)

worth searching for: Miller's earlier, self-released albums, which he sells at shows and by mail order, include a pair of folk outings—*Old Dreams and New Hopes* ♫♫ (Rosebud, 1987) and *The Art of Survival* ♫♫♫ (Rosebud, 1990)—as well as the Native/new-age-leaning *Loon, Mountain and Moon: Native American Flute Songs* ♫♫ (Rosebud, 1991).

influences:

◀◀ Neil Young, Dan Fogelberg, XIT

see also: *Robert Mirabal, Kongar-ool Ondar*

Daniel Durchholz

Áine Minogue

Celtic, harp, new age

Born in Borrisokane, County Tipperary, Ireland. Based in Boston, MA, USA.

Áine Minogue grew up in a musical family, and she found her own instrument at the age of 12 when she began to play the harp. As a teenager she performed with the Bunratty Castle singers and with tenor Sean O'Shay as part of the duo Legacy. In 1990 Minogue moved to the United States, where she became a professor in Boston College's Irish Studies program.

what to buy: Though she plays the harp and sings ethereal vocals, *Circle of the Sun* ♫♫♫♫ (RCA, 1998, prod. Áine Minogue) shows how Áine Minogue differs from Enya. For one thing, Minogue has opened up her sound, albeit with a subtle touch, to music from other sources. There's a *didgeridoo* (Australian Aboriginal drone instrument) on one song, for example, and on another a hymn to Saint Brigid is interwoven with a chant in honor of a Buddhist goddess. Minogue doesn't stop her search at ancient roots, though—on *Between the Worlds* ♫♫♫♫ (RCA, 1997, prod. Áine Minogue) there's the Beatles tune "Across the Universe." Minogue is also interested in exploring the diverse sources of spirituality. Though her Christmas album *To Warm the Winter's Night* ♫♫♫♫ (Evergreen, 1996, prod. Áine Minogue) includes Christian songs as well as winter favorites, and she has a gospel-tinged album, *Were You at the Rock* ♫♫♫ (Beacon, 1994, prod. Áine Minogue), she has a more Celtic view of the interconnection of man and nature, as is shown on *Mysts of Time* ♫♫♫ (North Star, 1996, prod. Áine Minogue).

influences:
◄◄ Turlough O'Carolan

Kerry Dexter

Sugar Minott

Reggae, dancehall, ragga

Born Lincoln Minott, May 25, 1956, in Kingston, Jamaica. Based in Kingston, Jamaica.

In the early 1980s, reggae cognoscenti—both critics and hardcore fans—were ready to anoint Sugar Minott as the next big thing. A pioneer of the dancehall style—bringing DJs to the front to rap (or "toast") over the music—Minott's destiny seemed secure. A star on the reggae horizon in England and the U.S. as well as at home, Minott nevertheless declined to make the jump to superstardom. In the '70s Minott had made the scene as one of the African Brothers, along with Tony Tuff and Derrick Howard. They worked around Kingston and finally ended up at the famed Studio One. With talent as a producer, singer, drummer, and guitarist, Minott quickly rose to the top. He became a celebrity in Britain with his first record, *Hard-Time Pressure*. At this point Minott started a label of his own, Youth Promotion,

with the idea of developing the musical talent from the ghettos of Kingston. When major labels came calling, he would not sign without deals for the Youth Promotion acts. Minott's altruism, though admirable, cost him. While many of the talents he nurtured went on to their own successes, Minott continued recording independently for a variety of producers and labels. Minott still makes good and sometimes excellent records, and to fans and neophytes alike, this versatile artist should rightfully be known as one of the true reggae innovators.

what to buy: Buyer beware: like many reggae artists, throughout his career Minott recorded for a variety of labels, which continue to repackage, remix, and otherwise mess around with the artist's back catalog. *Slice of the Cake* ♫♫♫♫ (PGD/Heartbeat, 1989, prod. Sugar Minott) is arguably Sugar's most solid recent record. His versatility shines through, making the rounds of roots, rockers, dancehall, dub, and more, with Sly and Robbie on rhythm and the Roots Radics in support. This disc includes some of his best: "Nice It Up," "Inna Dance Hall Style," "Slice of the Cake," and "How Could I Let You Get Away." *Musical Murder* ♫♫♫♫ (VP, 1996, prod. Sugar Minott) is more dancehall, even more dub, a little bit of culture, and some of what feels like filler. Highly danceable, however. There's a good take on the minor hit "In the Ghetto," in addition to the grooves of "Slow Rub-A-Dub" and "Ram Jam Session." *20 Super Hits* ♫♫♫♫ (Sonic Sounds, 1993, prod. various), while not exactly a "greatest" hits collection, finds Sugar in a rootsier mood and is not a bad choice if you were to buy only one of his discs. Included are the tasty fun of "Dread Upon Your Head," "Sensimilla," and "Leave Dreadlocks Business," as well as the message songs "Loving Jah," "Stop Fight Rasta," and "Herbman Hustling."

what to buy next: *Ghetto Child* ♫♫♫ (Heartbeat, 1989, prod. Sugar Minott) ranges all over the place from the light ("This Is Reggae" and "Cool and Easy") to the heavy ("Dreadlocks Chalice" and the title track). Dub fans should take note that the second half of the disc—some nine tunes—is a dub version of the first half.

the rest:
Smile ♫♫♫ (VP, 1977)
Good Thing Going ♫♫♫ (Heartbeat, 1981)
Inna Reggae Dance Hall ♫♫♫♫ (Heartbeat, 1987)
Sufferer's Choice ♫♫♫ (Heartbeat, 1988)
Sugar & Spice ♫♫♫ (RAS, 1990)
Happy Together ♫♫♫♫ (Heartbeat, 1991)
Run Things ♫♫♫ (VP, 1993)
Breaking Free ♫♫♫ (RAS, 1994)
Herbman Hustling ♫♫♫♫ (Heartbeat, 1994/1998)
Showdown, Vol. 2 ♫♫♫ (Channel One, 1995)
With Lots of Extra ♫♫♫ (Channel One, 1995)
International ♫♫ (RAS, 1996)
Collector's Collection ♫♫♫ (Heartbeat, 1996)

RAS Portraits ♫♫♫ (RAS, 1998)
Best of Sugar Minott ♫♫♫♫ (VP, 1998)
Mr. Fix It ♫♫ (VP, 1998)
Ghetto Youth Dem Rising ♫♫♫ (Heartbeat, 1998)
African Soldier ♫♫♫♫ (Heartbeat, 1998)

influences:

◀◀ African Brothers, Lee "Scratch" Perry, Sir Coxsone Dodd, Bob Marley, Burning Spear, Toots Hibbert, King Tubby

▶▶ Beenie Man, Yellow Man, Augustus Pablo, Mikey Dread, Buju Banton, Cocoa Tea, Apache Indian

see also: *Mikey Dread, Jackie Mittoo, the Roots Radics, Sister Carol, Sly & Robbie, Super Cat*

Andrew BeDell

Robert Mirabal /Mirabal

Native American, rock, flute

Robert Mirabal born in Taos Pueblo, NM, USA; Mirabal formed 1995, in Taos Pueblo, NM, USA. Based in Taos Pueblo, NM, USA.

Robert Mirabal, vocals, flutes, didgeridoo, keyboards, percussion, harmonica; Reynaldo Lijuan, Native drums and percussion, vocals; Mark Andes, electric and acoustic guitar, bass, percussion, backing vocals (album only); Kenny Arnoo, drums, percussion, loops (album only); Andy York, electric guitar (album only); Matt Andes, slide guitar (album only); Jeff Penderson, keyboards (album only); Michael Wanchic, backing vocals (album only); Eliza Gilkyson, backing vocals (album only); Sue Medley, backing vocals (album only); Bill Miller, backing vocals (album only); Pura Fe Crescioni (a.k.a. Pura Fé), backing vocals (album only); Soni Moreno, backing vocals (album only); Jennifer Kreisberg, backing vocals (album only). (All members are from USA.)

Robert Mirabal has been one of the leaders of the Native Flute renaissance, with a style that's more "traditional" and less commercial than many of his contemporaries. Mirabal came of age in a traditional family that was broken apart by government relocation policies, but he stayed in Taos to help care for his aging grandparents and went to the Indian school at the pueblo. "They had a band there and I learned clarinet, sax, piano, drums, anything I could get my hands on," Mirabal recalls. At 18 he got a flute from Adam Turjillo, a Pueblo flute-maker. "The flute changed my life. As soon as I began playing, people asked me to perform. Since that day I've spent most of my time traveling and playing music."

Mirabal went on to make traditional flute albums for several labels; compose "Land," a suite for the Japanese dancers Eiko and Koma; and have an exhibit of his own handmade flutes at the Smithsonian Institution's National Museum. His music has taken him all over Europe, North America, Russia, and Japan. These travels, and the exposure to the rhythms of other cultures they af-

forded him, had a profound effect on Mirabal's own musical vision. He studied West African drumming, Vodou rhythms from Haiti, and Celtic music, as well as immersing himself in rock, blues, and hip-hop. Those diverse influences came to a head in 1995, when Mirabal met Mark Andes, former bass player for the '60s rock band Spirit. Mirabal and Andes began jamming several times a week, and creative sparks flew. As the melodies came together, Mirabal adapted the poems and stories in his journal for the lyrics. "There was a traditional drummer I knew, Reynaldo Lujan, who has a wide knowledge of indigenous styles from all over the planet," Mirabal says. "We invited him in, and the songs really took shape."

When Mirabal played Warner Bros. (for which he'd done work before) the demo tapes he'd made with Andes and Lujan, they flipped and let him record his new band, playing in a style Mirabal jokingly calls "alter-Native." People familiar with Mirabal's mellow flute work will be surprised, if not shocked, by the sounds he wrenches from the instrument on *Mirabal.* He makes the flute scream with anger, cry with loneliness, shriek with pain. "I wanted to make an album that explores all of the things people experience; love, hate, fear, confusion, and especially the loneliness that seems to be so pervasive in modern society. And I wanted it to have a rock 'n' roll edge. I guess you could say the seed for *Mirabal* was planted when I was living in New York City. For a while I was in a multi-culti band. The keyboard player was from Haiti, the drummer was from Cape Verde, the guitarist from Senegal, and we were surrounded on all sides by hip-hop, funk, and R&B, which really educated me about the groove. With my newest band, what we do is try to create enough syncopation to let my language ride the groove, like a surfer riding the waves."

what to buy: *Mirabal* ♫♫♫♫♫ (Warner Western, 1997, prod. Michael Wanchic) breaks down every American pop and folk style of the last several decades—rock, funk, techno, hip-hop, blues, and singer/songwriter impulses, accented by touches from Aboriginal Australia, Africa, and Celtic music—and reassembles them from a distinctly Native American perspective. It's Robert Mirabal's masterpiece, and may be the best Native rock album ever recorded.

what to buy next: After this collision of many worlds, you can explore some of the others Mirabal has visited in the past. Two of the most hospitable are: *Native Suite* ♫♫♫ (Warner Western, 1996), a mix of classical, traditional Native, and pop impulses; and *Land* ♫♫♫ (Warner Western, 1993), a suite composed for Eiko and Koma (flute without the usual new-age trappings).

influences:

◀◀ R. Carlos Nakai, Tom Ware, Woodrow Hainey, Doc Tate, Neil Young, Bob Dylan, Spirit

see also: *Pura Fé, Bill Miller*

j. poet

Carmen Miranda

Brazilian pop and musicals

Born Maria do Carmo Miranda Da Cunha, February 9, 1909, in Lisbon, Portugal. Died August 5, 1955.

With considerable stage, screen, and radio exposure in Brazil, Miranda was already a popular South American entertainment personality when she came to the States in 1939 to appear in the Broadway musical revue *The Streets of Paris.* A year later, she signed to 20th Century Fox as a contract player. Miranda's timing was nearly perfect—during World War II, American films were not often shown in Europe, and South America dominated the foreign market. As a singer or a dancer, Miranda overpowered any shortcomings in technique with a nearly boundless charisma, not to mention a tolerance for absurd get-ups. In the 1943 musical *The Gang's All Here,* she performed "The Lady in the Tutti Frutti Hat" while wearing said hat—her signature cranially mounted fruit bowl. After the war, Miranda moved out of movies onto the nightclub circuit, and appeared on television regularly. A bad marriage and an exhausting schedule sapped her energy, and a dependence on drugs to make up the difference forced a short retirement in Brazil in the early '50s. Miranda recovered, returned to the States, and continued as a popular performer until 1955, when she died of a heart attack only hours after an appearance on the *Jimmy Durante Show.* Four decades later, Miranda was the subject of an acclaimed 1994 documentary, *Carmen Miranda: Bananas Is My Business.*

what to buy: *Anthology* 🎵🎵🎵 (One Way Records, 1994) collects 20 of the Brazilian Bombshell's most famous performances, including "Bambu-Bambu," "Rebola A Bola," "Chattanooga Choo-Choo," "Chica Chica Boom Chic," and "O Passo Do Kanguru (Brazilly Willy)."

what to buy next: Harlequin Records has released a pair of CDs, *The Brazilian Recordings* 🎵🎵🎵 (Harlequin, 1994) and *Vol. 2: Carmen Miranda, 1930–1945* 🎵🎵🎵 (Harlequin, 1994), which give a good overview of Miranda's entire recording career.

the rest:
South American Way 🎵🎵🎵 (Jasmine, 1993)
Brazilian Bombshell—25 Hits 🎵🎵🎵 (ASV, 1998)

worth searching for: *Maracas, Marimbas, and Mambos: Latin Classics at MGM* 🎵🎵🎵🎵 (WEA/Atlantic, 1997, prod. Will Friedwald, Bradley Flanagan) demonstrates the influence of Latin music on the movies during and just after World War II, with a collection of performances by Xavier Cugat and other bandleaders. Miranda is featured vocalist on three tracks: "Cuanto Le Gusta," "Caroom Pa Pa," and the immortal "Yipsee-I-O."

calypso

alypso, the national music of Trinidad and Tobago, has grandparents in several folk and popular sources, and cousins in similar topical song-forms throughout the Caribbean. Its deepest roots are in Afro-Caribbean slave culture (the name "calypso" seems to point back to an interjection of approval and encouragement in the Hausa language), but its crucible was the barrack-yards of 19th-century Port of Spain, Trinidad, home of poor and working-class Carnival bands. There it bubbled and stewed for decades in relatively raw form until, under pressure from the image-conscious middle and upper classes, it got strained and refined into a more modern and urbane form just before 1900. Since then it's adopted more complex literary structures, absorbed cosmopolitan pop-music influences, and experimented, sometimes wildly, with melody, meter, rhyme, and phrasing. In all its stages of evolution, however, calypso has retained a primary emphasis on verbal ingenuity and virtuosity; calypsonians are equal parts poet, storyteller, and comedian; orator, satirist, and social commentator. The genre's commercial possibilities weren't widely explored until the mid-1930s, when the formal innovations and hard-hitting politics of that decade, as well as the old-fashioned grandiloquence of the era just past, were put on wax in great quantity. The calypsonians of this "Golden Age"—Executor, Atilla (sic), Lion, Tiger, Radio, Invader—are represented on CD by several excellent historical compilations. A younger generation, including Melody, the much beloved Kitchener, and calypso's only real international superstar, the Mighty Sparrow, rose to prominence between World War II and independence. Since the mid-'70s, calypso has been increasingly eclipsed by its livelier stepchild *soca,* much to the chagrin of high-minded purists. But their perennial predictions of calypso's imminent demise have not been borne out by events; Trinidad's annual National Calypso Monarchy competition continues to attract a broad following: though calypso is most closely identified with Trinidad, it is strong in Antigua, Grenada, and Barbados as well.

Michael Eldridge

influences:

◄◄ Edith Piaf, Al Jolson, Cole Porter

►► Patti LaBelle, Madonna

Ben Greenman

Marlui Miranda

Folk, MPB (Brazilian Popular Music)
Born in Brazil. Based in Saõ Paulo, Brazil.

"Brazilian Indian music is a cultural secret, nobody knows it." Marlui Miranda, a singer, musician, and ethnomusicologist, knows the culture she speaks of. Although she lives in Saõ Paulo, her family is descended from a Jesuit priest and his Indian wife, and she's been interested in the indigenous culture of the Amazon basin her whole life. In 1978, she began sorting through compendiums of Indian music and collecting songs on her own, with the idea of producing a series of albums that would introduce this "hidden music" to Brazil and the world. "Compared to Indians in the United States, the Amazon people live in the Stone Age," Miranda has said in many interviews. "They still have their own culture, but they're surrounded by settlers who want their land, so they've had to learn Portuguese, and are struggling to come to terms with the whites. In some areas, with the help of the government, they've been able to hold onto their land, but in other places they were virtually enslaved, until recently, to work the rubber plantations." Miranda's recordings are based on traditional Amazon Indian songs, although, as the artist herself points out, they are the result of "years of attempts, experiments, arrangements, presentations [and] powwowing, until I had a final draft."

what to buy: Miranda's experiments with traditional Indian music will grab your attention from the first track of *Ihu: Todos os Sons* ♪♪♪♪ (Blue Jackal, 1997, prod. Marlui Miranda). The percussion (quite different from Native North American powwow drumming), the vocal stylings of Groupo Beijo (a Brazilian Native women's ensemble), and the arranging of Gilberto Gil take the music in many exciting and unexpected directions. This disc has won several Album of the Year awards, and it's easy to hear why.

what to buy next: The follow-up, *Ihu 2—Kewere: Rezar: Prayer* ♪♪♪♪ (Blue Jackal, 1998, prod. Marlui Miranda), is a slight departure. This time Miranda combines the indigenous music with liturgical music as well as pop to create a mass celebrating the survival of the Amazon's original inhabitants. Once again the music is startling and compelling.

influences:

◄◄ Gilberto Gil, Gal Costa, Maria Bethânia

see also: *Gilberto Gil*

j. poet

Jackie Mittoo

Reggae, rocksteady, ska, dub, dancehall
Born Donat Roy Mittoo, March 3, 1948, in Kingston, Jamaica. Died December 16, 1990, in Toronto, Ontario, Canada.

Jackie "Soul" Mittoo was the fount from which much of Jamaica's culturally distinctive, post-independence music flowed, and the most commanding keyboardist the island has ever known. At age four the gifted Mittoo was already conversant on the piano, thanks to the tutelage of his grandmother, a music teacher. In elementary school he practiced and jammed in a chemistry lab with future reggae luminaries Augustus Pablo and Tyrone Downie, a trio that became known as the Jackie Mittree. At age 13, his music-focused after-school activities included nightclub gigs with bands such as the Vagabonds, the Vikings, and the Rivals. A year later, in 1962, Mittoo earned island-wide recognition as the bantam-sized leader and arranger of the Sheiks, a band that included future Skatalites Johnny "Dizzy" Moore (trumpet) and Lloyd Knibb (drums), as well as singer Dobby "The Loving Pauper" Dobson and the great Lynn Taitt (guitar). After a short hiatus, in August 1963 the Sheiks reemerged as the Cavaliers Orchestra with soon-to-be-Skatalite Lloyd Brevette added on double bass. Producer Clement "Coxsone" Dodd was so impressed with Mittoo's musical gifts that he hired him two months later as his session director for the grand opening of the famed Studio One at 13 Brentford Road. This prestigious position allowed Mittoo to rub elbows with many of Jamaica's finest musicians, including saxophonist Tommy McCook; together they assembled the all-star cast of the Skatalites. At age 16, Mittoo was the youngest member of what is now regarded as history's greatest ska band. He and trombonist Don Drummond quickly became the chief arrangers of the Skatalites' fiery music. Mittoo's pumping piano and groove-oozing organ were featured on some of the band's classic hits, including "Killer Diller" and "Hanging Tree." In 1965, the Skatalites imploded after the mentally ill Drummond stabbed his girlfriend to death during an acute psychotic episode. Mittoo and saxophonist Roland Alphonso broke off on their own under the direction of Dodd and formed the Soul Brothers, who scored immediately with "Dr. Ring A Ding" and "Miss Ska-culation." After a year, this group transmogrified into the unstoppable Studio One house band, the Soul Vendors. In 1966 and '67, as a part of Dodd's Rock Steady Revue, the group became the first to tour beyond the island in support of Jamaican music. Their ambassadorship concluded with the simmering *On Tour* and *Jackie Mittoo in London* LPs.

The self-effacing Mittoo is largely responsible for Studio One's classic rocksteady (proto-reggae) and reggae output from 1966 to 1971, when he was the outfit's chief composer, arranger, talent scout, and keyboardist. His instrumental hits and bone-rattling, earth-tilling rhythms with the Soul Vendors, Sound Dimension, Invaders, New Establishment, and Brentford All-Stars—"Death in the Arena," "Real Rock," "Full Up" (the template for the Mighty Diamonds' "Pass the Kouchie"), "Frozen Soul," "Hot Milk," "Darker Shade of Black" (the rhythm for Frankie Paul's "Pass the Tu-sheng-peng"), "Rockfort Rock," "Peenie Wallie," "Heavy Rock," "One Step Beyond," "Drum Song," and "In Cold Blood," among many others—defined the mid- to late-'60s Brentford Road sound, and provided the accompaniment to hits by the Wailers, the Cables, the Heptones, Burning Spear, and just about every other record emblazoned with the Studio One label. With the help of underrated drummer Bunny Williams, Mittoo constructed the ever-popular "one drop" rhythm for Alton Ellis's "I'm Just a Guy"—the "skanking" beat that ripened into ubiquity during the roots-reggae era. Mittoo also composed the oft-"versioned" (remade in dub) "Ram Jam" rhythm for the Heptones' massive hit "Fatty Fatty," and taught Leroy Sibbles, the group's lead vocalist, how to play bass. During Sibbles's apprenticeship, he and Mittoo gigged in Kingston nightclubs as a jazz trio whenever time permitted. Sibbles is now considered one of Jamaica's greatest bassists.

In the mid-'70s, Mittoo emigrated to Canada and modeled his own Stine-Jac label after Studio One. With producer Bunny "Striker" Lee, he issued a series of dub/instrumental records bolstered by the heavy-duty alloy of Mittoo disciples Sly Dunbar and Robbie Shakespeare as rhythm section. He contributed hot-blooded music and cool-headed sagacity to Sugar Minott's influential Youth Promotion posse—the sound system that created the first music dubbed "dancehall." In the '80s, he imparted his special groove to *Labour of Love,* UB40's homage to reggae's golden era. And toward the end of the decade, he toured with a reconstituted version of the Skatalites.

Mittoo's depth-charged rhythmic instrumentals provided the foundation for the Revolutionaries-led "rockers" era of roots reggae in the mid-'70s and the dancehall era of '79–'85. Even today, his rhythms are endlessly recycled in many of the digital *ragga* hits that currently dominate Jamaican music. Though he succumbed to cancer in 1990, Mittoo's is a vivid and vibrant memory kept alive by the power and inspiration of work that will resound in perpetuity. Befitting the man who composed "Death in the Arena," an ode to valor, Mittoo was eulogized as a hero of Jamaican music before a jam-packed National Arena in Kingston, where his funeral was transformed into a rousing celebration of his life.

what to buy: The double-disc *Tribute to Jackie Mittoo* ♪♪♪♪ (Heartbeat, 1995, prod. various) is the most outstanding overview of his sometimes volcanic, always insinuating instrumentals, with the added bonus of Mittoo's collaboration with Alton Ellis on the mesmerizing "Black Man's Pride" and a few

exceptional previously unreleased cuts—"Jackie's Mood," "Ska Matic," and "Fireball Rock," an inspirational instrumental version of the Gaylads' "There's a Fire." The focus, however, is on legendary hits like "Drum Song," "Ghetto Organ," "Race Track," and "Got My Boogaloo." Also included are funk jewels such as "Hot Tamale," a spicy fusion of New Orleans R&B, spy-flick soundtracks, and greasy Booker T.–influenced grooves; and the amazing "Mission Impossible" and "Freak Out"—both free-flowing conduits for the philosophy that life is intended to be enjoyed rather than endured. "Jericho Skank" is the glaring omission that lops off half a bone. *Downbeat the Ruler: Killer Instrumentals, The Best of Studio One, Volume 3* ♪♪♪♪♪ (Heartbeat, 1988, prod. Coxsone Dodd) is technically not a Jackie Mittoo album, but substantively his magic handiwork is all over this collection, an essential document of the music that moved and grooved the crowds at sound-system (mobile deejay unit) dances throughout the '60s. It includes some of Mittoo's most potent work with Sound Dimension and the Brentford All-Stars (with ska-rhythm inventor Ernest Ranglin on guitar!), including the aforementioned "Rockfort Rock" (a.k.a. "Psychedelic Rock"); the original 10" mix and a surprisingly scorching 1987 remix of "Throw Me Corn"; "Real Rock"; "Heavy Rock"; and "Baby Face"—a cut so damned good the Law of Mittoo dictates you'll wanna hear it at least "(Mit)twice" in a row. "Race Track" and "Freak Out" are the only overlaps with the *Tribute* album. The compilation also includes Tommy McCook's extraordinary "Tunnel One" and Don Drummond's ska-thartic "sufferahs" anthem, "Man in the Street."

what to buy next: *Evening Time* ♪♪♪♪ (Studio One, 1968, prod. Coxsone Dodd) is all elegant, beautiful rocksteady masterpieces like "One Step Beyond" (the prototype of Freddie McGregor's "Bobby Bobylon"), "Drum Song" (versioned on Burning Spear's "Joe Frazier"), "Hot Milk," "Full Charge," and Mittoo's pulse-pounding homage to the '60s spy show *Man from U.N.C.L.E.,* "Napolean Solo." It also includes a compelling cover of Booker T. & the MG's "Hip Hug Her," as well as "Dancing Groove"—the instrumental bed for Delroy Wilson's celebrated "Dancing Mood." Macca fat is a tasty Jamaican fruit that nonetheless can't even touch the flavor of Mittoo's *Macka Fat* ♪♪♪♪ (Studio One, 1970, prod. Coxsone Dodd). The title cut and "Good Feeling" bear the essence of freedom and both "Fancy Pants" (a cover of Marvin Gaye's "What's Going On") and "Ghetto Organ" are quintessential "dread" reggae instrumentals with grooves as deep as Atlantis.

the rest:
On Tour ♪♪♪♥ (Studio One, 1966)
Jackie Mittoo in London ♪♪♪♥ (Studio One, 1967)
Keep On Dancing ♪♪♪♥ (Studio One, 1969)
Now ♪♪♪♪ (Studio One, 1969)
Reggae Magic ♪♪♪♥ (Studio One, 1971)

Hot Blood ♫♫♫ (Third World, 1977)
The Myestro in Cold Blood ♫♫♫ (Third World, 1978)
Keyboard King ♫♫♫ (Weed Beat, 1978)
Show Case ♫♫♫ (Sonic Sounds, 1979)
The Original Jackie Mittoo ♫♫♫♫ (Third World, 1979)
Show Case, Volume 3 ♫♫♫ (Abraham, 1980)
Showcase ♫♫♫♫ (Studio One, 1982)
Wild Jockey ♫♫♫♪ (Wackies, 1989)
Sly & Robbie Present: The Late Great Jackie Mittoo ♫♫♫♫ (Rhino U.K., 1998)
Keyboard King ♫♫♫ (Sonic Sounds, 1998)
In Africa ♫♫♫♪ (Quartz, 1999)

worth searching for: The tough-but-not-impossible-to-find *100% Dynamite* ♫♫♫♫ (Soul Jazz, 1998, prod. various) fulfills the promise of its title. This is a terrific compilation of intensely soulful reggae music that includes three blazingly funk-*aaay* Mittoo performances with Sound Dimension and the Brentford All-Stars that are otherwise rare as hens' teeth. To come across "Stereo Freeze," "Granny Scratch Scratch," and "Greedy G" is to discover long-lost Mittreasures, but add the Upsetters' "Popcorn," the Maytals' "Night and Day," Tommy McCook's lush "Green Mango," and Willie Williams's "Armageddon Time" (which versions Mittoo's "Real Rock" in cool and deadly fashion), and, well, it's time to get your map and compass ready, Magellan.

influences:

◄ Jimmy Smith, Thelonious Monk, Booker T. & the MG's, Art Blakey, the Meters, Oscar Peterson

►► The Revolutionaries, Leroy Sibbles, the Heptones, Augustus Pablo, the Cables, the Wailers, Soul Syndicate, Steely & Clevie (Wycliffe Johnson and Cleveland Brown), the Roots Radics, Third World, Foundation, John Holt, Judy Mowatt, Annette Brissette, Mikey General, Marcia Griffiths, Dennis Brown, UB40, Little Roy, Sugar Minott

see also: *Burning Spear, Alton Ellis, Freddie McGregor, Sugar Minott, Lee "Scratch" Perry, Ernest Ranglin, the Skatalites, Sly & Robbie, the Techniques, Toots & the Maytalls*

Todd Shanker

Mlimani Park Orchestra

East African big-band dance music
Formed 1978, in Dar es Salaam, Tanzania. Based in Dar es Salaam, Tanzania.

Large, mostly undocumented membership; founding members include: Cosmas Tobias, lead vocals; Hassani Bitchuka, lead vocals; Michael Enoch, lead guitar, alto saxophone.

Tanzania's big-band tradition dates back to the 1960s when large dance outfits, complete with guitar sections, horn sections, and a front line of harmonizing singers, were the norm in the more cosmopolitan African cities. Unfortunately, poor economic conditions and an abundance of state control have more recently prevented the tradition from developing. Mlimani Park represents the cream of the remaining Tanzanian crop, a gorgeous, swinging ensemble specializing in tightly interacting horns and guitars; long, generous arrangements; and sensuous vocals. At its prime in the late '80s, the band had 26 members.

Mlimani Park started out as the house band at the Mlimani Club in Dar es Salaam. Star singers Hassani Bitchuka and Cosmas Tobias had two very different styles, the former aggressively passionate and the latter controlled and sweet. That contrast and the band's astounding instrumental chemistry helped to make it one of the strongest forces in Tanzanian pop, perhaps rivaled only by the older Juwata Jazz—in which many Mlimani players began their careers.

The band calls its music *mtindo,* an informal synonym for dancing. While the sound clearly owes something to the rumba-based style that flowed out of the Congolese capitol Kinshasa beginning in the 1950s, there is a distinct Tanzanian character. It has to do with the melodies, the comparatively gentle grooves, and the democratic interaction between the instruments. In all, it is a majestic and seductive sound that, sadly, is disappearing from Africa.

what to buy: *Sikinde* ♫♫♫♫ (Africassette, 1994, prod. Radio Tanzania) offers a generous sampling of tracks from the band's golden years.

the rest:
Tanzanian Dance Bands, Volumes 1 and 2 ♫♫♫♪ (Line Records, 1991)

influences:
◄ Franco, Juwata Jazz

Banning Eyre

Tony Mola

International dance music
Born in Salvador, Brazil. Based in Salvador, Brazil.

Percussionist Tony Mola grew up in Salvador in the Bahia region of Brazil. Moving to New York in 1990, he quickly developed an audience for his percussion-heavy dance music, which also absorbed such non-Brazilian influences as rap, hip-hop, Cuban, and Jamaican flavors. Returning to Brazil, Mola founded Bragadá, a large rotating ensemble that features piano and accordion in addition to percussion and vocals. The group's first performance was a triumphant appearance at the Bahian music festival Lavagem do Bomfim.

what to buy: *Quebra-Mola* ♫♫♫♫ (Blue Jackal, 1998), Mola's second CD with Bragadá, solidifies his distinctive blend of the urban and tribal, with powerful, sweaty dance music driven by

Mola's athletic drumming. Augmented by talented Brazilian guests like saxophonist Leo Gandelman and bassist Arthur Maia, the disc's grooves leap from the CD player. Memorable tracks include the raucous opener "Braga Boy" and "Barabai," which blends a slinky dance groove with the group's always-frenetic wall of percussion.

what to buy next: Mola's first album, *Bragadá* 🎵🎵🎵 (Blue Jackal, 1996), is a strong effort that bursts with energy. The driving blend of smooth vocals, accordion, and drums on "Tribal" is irresistible, as is the Cuban-Bahian fusion of "Abracadabra."

influences:

◄◄ Olodum, Reflexú

►► Daniela Mercury

Michael Parrish

Matt Molloy

Irish traditional

Born January 12, 1947, in Ballaghadreen, County Sligo, Ireland. Based in Westport, County Mayo, Ireland.

Both as a solo artist and a member of the Bothy Band, Planxty, and currently the Chieftains, Matt Molloy has been at the center of Irish traditional music for over 25 years. His instantly recognizable sound, a combination of power and elegance wedded to incredible control of his instrument, has graced many of the most influential recordings in traditional Irish music. Molloy grew up in County Roscommon, an area noted for producing outstanding flute players. He learned his craft from his father, progressing rapidly until he won the senior All-Ireland title at age 17. After a stint with the Siamsa Ceili Band, and a few years as a jet mechanic for Aer Lingus, Molloy helped to found the legendary Bothy Band. Made up of some of Ireland's finest (and wildest) young musicians, the Bothy Band brought a no-holds-barred, rock 'n' roll sensibility to their music both on and off the stage, producing some of the most ferociously beautiful Irish music ever recorded. The lifestyle that went with it came to a halt for Molloy when he contracted tuberculosis in 1977. After a stint in the hospital and the demise of the Bothy Band, he was invited to join a new version of Planxty. He stayed with that band for one album, *After the Break,* and then joined the Chieftains, replacing veteran flute player Michael Tubridy. Molloy continues to tour and record with the Chieftains, while occasionally cutting solo albums and operating his pub in Westport, County Mayo.

what to buy: *Matt Molloy* 🎵🎵🎵🎵 (Green Linnet, 1976, prod. Matt Molloy, Dónal Lunny, Mícheál Ó Domhnaill) is one of the greatest Irish recordings ever made. Cut before his bout with tuberculosis, the album shows a young, driven master at the height of his power. From the first notes of the old favorite "The Boys of the Lough," Molloy demonstrates just how much music can be pulled out of a flute. Highlights include an absolutely killer version of "The Bucks of Oranmore" and the haunting "Lament for Staker Wallace." Molloy's fervid, uninhibited playing is backed by the awesome guitar and bouzouki of Dónal Lunny, his fellow Bothy Band alum and one of the finest accompanists in Irish music.

what to buy next: *Stony Steps* 🎵🎵🎵🎵 (Green Linnet, 1987, prod. Dónal Lunny), along with *Matt Molloy,* is required listening for anyone wanting to hear or play Irish flute music. While the latter is a solo tour-de-force, this album finds Matt sharing the stage with his impressive friends Kevin Burke, Sean Keane, and James Kelly, among others. He lets things stretch out a little further, and explores some more progressive accompaniment under the watchful eye of producer Lunny. *Contentment Is Wealth* 🎵🎵🎵🎵 (Green Linnet, 1985, prod. Brian Masterson) finds Molloy and fellow Chieftain Sean Keane showing off their tasty duet playing. This is a sparse, old-sounding album, with solid, discreet accompaniment by guitarist Arty McGlynn.

what to avoid: Although Molloy's name is in the title of *Music at Matt Molloy's* 🎵🎵 (RealWorld, 1992, prod. Martin Murray, Matt Molloy, Arty McGlynn), he appears on only seven of its 20 tracks. On the rest of the material the performers range from the legendary (Peter Horan, Paul McGrattan) to the competent. A better document of a live Irish session is the import album *Maiden Voyage,* recorded in Clare during the early '90s and released by Celtic Music in England.

the rest:

Matt Molloy, Paul Brady, Tommy Peoples 🎵🎵🎵🎵 (Green Linnet, 1977)
Heathery Breeze 🎵🎵🎵 (Shanachie, 1982)
Matt Molloy, Sean Keane, Liam O'Flynn 🎵🎵🎵 (Claddagh Records, Ireland, 1992)
Shadows on Stone 🎵🎵 (RealWorld, 1996)

influences:

◄◄ Fred Finn & Peter Horan, Michael Coleman, James Morrison

►► Kevin Crawford, Paul McGrattan, Chris Norman

see also: *The Bothy Band, Kevin Burke, the Chieftains, James Keane, Dónal Lunny, Liam O'Flynn, Planxty*

Tony Ziselberger

The Mollys

Celtic conjunto

Formed 1990, in Tucson, AZ, USA. Based in USA.

Catherine Zavala, vocals, mandolin, bodhrán, guitar; Nancy McCallion, vocals, guitar, pennywhistle, harmonica, melodion; Kevin Schramm, accordion, guitar, banjo, bouzouki, vocals (1993–present); Gary Mackender, drums, percussion, vocals (1994–present); Dan

5
2
4

the mollys

The Mollys

Sorenson, bass, guitar (1992–present); **Linda Winkleman, flute (1990–91); Nathan Sady, accordion (1991–93); Michael Faulkner, drums (1991–94).**

The Mollys are an unlikely fusion of Celtic and *conjunto* (Tex-Mex) music from the unlikely town of Tucson, Arizona, where they release their albums on their own label, Apolkalips Now. Implausibility notwithstanding, the band boasts a terrific Irish American songwriter in Nancy McCallion, a great Mexican American singer in Catherine Zavala, a relentless punk 'n' soul rhythm section, and a wild accordionist in Kevin Schramm, who holds the divergent strains together. The result resembles Wynonna Judd singing the Lucinda Williams songbook backed by the Pogues and Los Lobos. McCallion and Zavala met in high school, led Tucson new-wave band Nadine & the Mo-Phonics after graduation, and casually formed the Mollys as a folk trio for a St. Patrick's Day gig. The success of said Pogues and Los Lobos, however, convinced them they could whip up their rootsy traditions into boisterous, bawdy rock 'n' roll, and they became one of the most impressive folk-rock bands of the mid-'90s.

what to buy: *This Is My Round* 🎵🎵🎵🎵 (Apolkalips Now, 1995, prod. Nancy McCallion, Catherine Zavala) served notice that the Mollys were a major new band. Irish folk stars Mick Moloney and Eugene O'Donnell are on hand, but the best songs share the raucous, non-conformist spirit of their protagonists: a Donegal lad in London who does not suffer anti-Irish prejudice quietly, an abused wife who takes imaginative revenge on her husband, and another woman who refuses to apologize for marrying a wealthy older man. Even better is *Hat Trick* 🎵🎵🎵🎵 (Apolkalips Now, 1997, prod. Mollys), which proved that McCallion had blossomed into a major-league songwriter on the order of Gillian Welch or Iris DeMent. She takes much more of a wise-cracking, off-color approach to the world than those two peers, but her songs are no less substantial for it. Just as Welch and DeMent use hillbilly music for their personal stories, so does McCallion use Celtic and *Tejano* (modern Tex-Mex) music for her distinctive take on love and work.

the rest:
Moon over the Interstate 🎵🎵🎵🎵 (Apolkalips Now, 1999)

worth searching for: The Mollys' out-of-print first CD, *Tidings of Comfort and Joy* 🎵🎵🎵 (Apolkalips Now, 1992, prod. Nancy McCallion, Catherine Zavala), features an earlier lineup and tilts the folk-rock equation more to the traditional folk side. *Welt the Floor!* 🎵🎵🎵 (Apolkalips Now, 1995, prod. Kevin Schramm) and *Wankin' Out West* 🎵🎵🎵🎵 (Apolkalips Now, 1997, prod. Mollys) are live albums sold only at the band's gigs. They both capture the irrepressible spirit of the Mollys in action, but the latter especially illustrates how fast and how far they've grown.

influences:

◄◄ The Pogues, Los Lobos, Mick Moloney, Christy Moore, Steve Jordan

►► Gillian Welch, Iris DeMent

see also: *Mick Moloney, Simon Thoumire*

Geoffrey Himes

Mick Moloney

Irish traditional and contemporary
Born November 15, 1944, in Limerick, Ireland. Based in USA.

A Limerick-born singer and player of the guitar, mandolin, and banjo, Mick Moloney got his start doing skiffle songs at about age 14. It wasn't until his exposure to Irish music as a college student in the early '60s, however, that he became a serious musician. After starting on the guitar, he picked up a tenor banjo and seemed to automatically know where his fingers should go. He quickly began attending music sessions in County Clare, an important locus where traditional players from all over Ireland congregated. He devoted a couple of years of his life to fanatical playing and practicing, and tried to incorporate what he learned from each model into his own technique. The end result was a unique style that, years later, would earn him multiple victories as best tenor banjoist in *Frets* magazine's prestigious readers' poll.

During the early '60s, Moloney became a part of the Dublin folk-music scene as a student at University College, Dublin. By 1964, records by the Clancy Brothers and Tommy Makem were forever changing Irish music, and bands of singers with guitars—called "ballad groups"—were becoming the norm. Moloney, who now also played the mandolin, fell in with another student named Dónal Lunny, who would later be a member of both Planxty and the Bothy Band. Armed with mandolins and banjos for playing lead, guitars for accompaniment, and Mick's store of instrumentals and songs, Moloney and Lunny, along with Brian Bolger, formed the Emmet Folk Group. Taking a cue from the Dubliners, they tried to incorporate both ballad group–style singing and traditional playing into their music. Although the band was neither long-lived nor commercially successful, Moloney was soon able to put his talents to work

again. In 1966 he was asked to join a family group from County Meath called the Johnstons. Another future member of Planxty, Paul Brady, joined up with him, and the two applied some of Moloney's ideas from the Emmet Folk Group in their new setting. The Johnstons became one of the most popular groups in Irish music during the 1960s and early '70s, and Moloney was able to tour the world. During a 1971 tour of the United States he met Kenneth S. Goldstein, then-chairman of the department of folklore and folklife at the University of Pennsylvania. With Goldstein's encouragement, Moloney decided to come to the U.S. to get a doctorate in folklore. When he arrived in America, Moloney began to realize what a vast and relatively untapped storehouse of Irish musicians the country was. He took on the role of organizer, putting together festivals and concerts where Irish musicians from different cities could meet and play together. He formed a lasting musical partnership with fiddler Eugene O'Donnell, trained younger players like Seamus Egan, and organized bands including the Green Fields of America; Moloney, O'Connell & Keane; and Cherish the Ladies.

Moloney finally earned his Ph.D. in 1992, 20 years after he moved to the States. He continues to play, both as a solo act and in various groups. He has also become a popular tour guide, organizing and hosting several tours of Ireland every summer that are specifically geared toward traditional music and folklore.

what to buy: Moloney and O'Donnell's *Uncommon Bonds* 🎵🎵🎵🎵 (Green Linnet, 1986, prod. Mick Moloney) may be the best introduction to this artist. Moloney's interest in Irish traditional songs is represented by the moving numbers "Bay of Biscay" and "Bonny Blue-Eyed Nancy." His fascination with the representation of Irishness on the Vaudeville stage compelled him to include such quirky and wonderful songs as "Muldoon the Solid Man" and "Miss Fogarty's Christmas Cake." His love of contemporary material in the Irish tradition is demonstrated by his inclusion of songs by Robbie O'Connell, Tommy Sands, and Seamus MacMathuna. Moloney's mandolin and banjo are perfectly complemented by O'Donnell's sensitive fiddle playing, and the two play their hearts out on several sets of rousing tunes. Also of interest to folk fans is the long list of guest artists on this CD, which includes Norman and Nancy Blake, the Clancy Brothers, and Saul Broudy, as well as some of the top names in Irish instrumental music.

what to buy next: *Mick Moloney with Eugene O'Donnell* 🎵🎵🎵🎵 (Green Linnet, 1978, prod. Mick Moloney) is still one of Moloney's greatest pieces of work. It includes some of Moloney's most appealing songs, including "The Limerick Rake," "The Irish Maid," and "The Bantry Girl's Lament," but it is more focused on instrumentals; numerous sets of jigs and reels show off Moloney's prowess to the fullest. Moloney, O'Connell & Keane's

There Were Roses ♫♫♫ (Green Linnet, 1985, prod. Mick Moloney) teams Moloney with guitarist and singer Robbie O'Connell (also of the Clancy Brothers & Robbie O'Connell) and piano accordion player Jimmy Keane. Fiddler Liz Carroll guests on many tracks as well. The title track, one of Tommy Sands's most moving ballads about the Northern Irish troubles, is a classic, and the rest of the album contains a lot of fine instrumentals and songs. The same band's follow-up, *Kilkelly* ♫♫♫ (Green Linnet, 1988, prod. Mick Moloney), contains a few absolutely indispensable tracks, particularly the title song, which is the definitive version of the most popular recently penned emigration ballad. "Peter Pan and Me," a song about the Northern Irish troubles, is equally affecting. The album's drawback is that half of it is taken up with a single 20-minute medley about the Irish in America that combines serious and silly material. It might have seemed like a good idea at the time, but it doesn't produce a very listenable result. Another quite noteworthy album is *Live in Concert* ♫♫♫ (Green Linnet, 1989, prod. Mick Moloney) by Moloney's all-star Irish American band the Green Fields of America, featuring Moloney, O'Connell & Keane, Seamus Egan, Eileen Ivers, and Donny and Eileen Golden. This contains an alternate version of "Kilkelly" and many more stirring instrumentals and lovely songs. Particularly moving is the tribute to Ed Reavy, one of the greatest composers of Irish traditional tunes.

the rest:
(With Eugene O'Donnell and Seamus Egan) *Strings Attached* ♫♫♫
    (Green Linnet, 1980)
(With Eugene O'Donnell and Seamus Egan) *Three Way Street* ♫♫♫
    (Green Linnet, 1992)
(With Eugene O'Donnell and Seamus Egan) *Out of Ireland Original
    Soundtrack* ♫♫♫ (Shanachie, 1995)

influences:
◄◄ The Clancy Brothers & Tommy Makem, the Dubliners, the
    Flanagan Brothers, Tulla Ceili Band, Willie Clancy, the Johnstons

►► Planxty, Dónal Lunny, Cherish the Ladies

see also: *Liz Carroll, Cherish the Ladies, the Clancy Brothers & Tommy Makem, Eileen Ivers, James Keane, Dónal Lunny, the Mollys, Solas*

Steve Winick

Monks of the Dip Tse Chok Ling Monastery

Tibetan Buddhist prayer chants and songs
Formed in Tibet. Based in Dharamsala, India.

Members unidentified.

The original Dip Tse Chok Ling Monastery was built in the 18th century in Tibet, a few kilometers south of Lhasa and the Potala Palace (residence of His Holiness the Dalai Lama). In 1959, when Tibet was "liberated" by the Chinese army, Dip Tse Chok Ling and over 6,000 other sacred sites were destroyed. A monastery-in-exile was set up in Dharamsala, India. Decades later, in 1992, work commenced on the rebuilding of the original structure. Local volunteers, including the remaining monks, made a request for assistance from the monastery-in-exile, and in September 1992 the site was 25 percent complete and was reopened. Funds are being raised for its full completion, as there has been no assistance from the local Chinese government.

what to buy: *Sacred Ceremonies—Ritual Music of Tibetan Buddhism* ♫♫♫♫ (Fortuna Records/Celestial Harmonies, 1990, prod. Ven. Thupten Nyandak, David Parsons, Kay Parsons) is a straight-up field recording of various notable chants of offering ("The Offerings for General Protectors"), prayer ("Prayer of Kala Rupa"), and praise ("Praises for Guyashamaya"). The monks have the uncanny ability to produce a three-toned chord in their larynxes, and are known for being able to sing at an extremely low pitch—lower than what is normally created by the human voice. A variety of drums, Tibetan oboes, and a pair of *dung chen* (those 12-foot-long horns) accompany the chants. This is approximately an hour's-worth of devotions, recorded during a religious rite.

what to buy next: *Sacred Ceremonies 2—Tantric Hymns and Music of Tibetan Buddhism* ♫♫♫♫ (Fortuna Records/Celestial Harmonies, 1992, prod. Ven. Thupten Nyandak, David Parsons, Kay Parsons) continues the series with hymns and songs of enlightenment. There is wider range of instrumentation this time, including bells and cymbals. Many of the titles explain a lot: "Sounds of the Conch Shell for Remembering Death," "Invocation of Deities through Ritual Instruments," "Hymns & Music for Inviting Deities & Dharma Protectors," "Emanations of Buddha," and "Dissolving the Visualization of the Field of Merit" are a few of the more fascinating examples. *Sacred Ceremonies Volume 3* ♫♫♫♫ (Fortuna Records/Celestial Harmonies, 1996, prod. Ven. Thupten Nyandak, David Parsons, Kay Parsons) includes yet more songs (e.g. "Dham-Chen Choegyal Kala-Rupa") and prayers (e.g. "Neten Chudurk 16 Arahat Prayers") from Dip Tse Chok Ling's busily reverent activities. As with its predecessors, this recording captures quite a bit of the spirit and intensity generated (or is it channeled?) by the monks.

worth searching for: If you prefer a single set, *Sacred Ceremonies'* three volumes are packaged as one on a German import by the same title from Fortuna Records. The monks also appear on the soundtrack *Baraka* (Milan Entertainment, 1992).

Machel Montano

influences:

⏮ Centuries of Tibetan tradition

⏭ David Parsons

Stacy Meyn

Machel Montano

Soca

Born 1975, in Trinidad. Based in Trinidad.

Montano broke all calypso records when he appeared on stage in a giant diaper to sing "Too Young to Soca" in 1986. He was only 11 years old, but his youthful tenor had the fire of a great calypsonian. Becoming a child star is a hard act to follow, but Montano set another record in 1997 when "Big Truck" won him the Road March crown. At 23, he became the youngest Road March King in the history of Trini's Carnival. Machel began singing because his older brother, Marcus, was too shy to perform his own songs. After his 1986 debut, Machel formed a band with other kids his age, but relied on adults like Leston Paul and Winsford Devine for songs, arrangements, and back-

ing musicians when he made his yearly album for Carnival. Since the dawn of the 1990s, though, Machel and his band Xtatik have been controlling their own fate. Today Machel owns his own recording studio and record label, and when the band isn't touring he's in the studio working on remixes of his hits or producing other up-and-coming stars.

what to buy: The hard-hitting party album *Heavy Duty* 𝄞𝄞𝄞𝄞 (Xtatik, 1997, prod. Machel Montano) contains the Road March hit "Big Truck" as well as "Winnerboy," "Music Farm," and "Pretty Gyal."

what to buy next: The four-song mini-album *Too Young to Soca* 𝄞𝄞𝄞𝄞 (Macho Music, 1985, prod. Elizabeth Montano, Winston Montano) introduced Montano to the world, and contains the ultra-catchy title tune that may haunt him for the rest of his adult life.

the rest:

Dr. Carnival 𝄞𝄞𝄞 (Macho, 1988)
Charge 𝄞𝄞𝄞𝄞 (Xtatik, 1998)

Marisa Monte

Marisa Monte

MPB (Brazilian Popular Music)

Born July 1, 1967, in Rio de Janeiro, Brazil. Based in Rio de Janeiro, Brazil.

Marisa Monte has a voice like Marilyn Monroe had curves—with equal parts sweetness and seduction. As the singer tells it, her career began when she was a young girl in Rio and her family and neighbors would plead, "Marisa, sing for us." Since then, Monte has achieved both popular and critical acclaim for the sweet and sophisticated pop around which she wraps her exquisite voice. Monte's father was an important figure within the Portela samba school, but as a teenager she decided to pursue operatic training in Italy. Advised to try her hand at her own country's music, she began playing small clubs in Brazil; her performances gained so much notice that her first disc was a live one. Her eponymous debut displayed Monte's eclectic tastes with a song from *Porgy and Bess* as well as a reggae version of "I Heard It through the Grapevine." On *Mais,* her second album, Monte teamed with producer Arto Lindsay for a sound that borrowed from Brazilian traditions as well as downtown New York's edgy pop. Her third album, *Rose and Charcoal,* was more an exploration of "straight" Brazilian idioms. The album's flawless production and subtle inventiveness mark it as a masterpiece and Monte's high water mark so far. Produced again by Arto Lindsay, the album began Monte's fertile partnership with another brilliant star of Brazil, Carlinhos Brown. While *Rose and Charcoal* is her most Brazilian album, its vision is broad enough that it encompasses a cover of Lou Reed's "Pale Blue Eyes" and Monte's first straight-ahead samba, "Esta Melodia." Monte's fourth album, *A Great Noise,* was a half-live and half-studio compilation. The album's package art became somewhat controversial—consisting as it did of drawings from the underground cartoonist Carlos Zefiro, whose works explored bluntly sexual themes during repressive times in Brazil—and the CD cover was censored by Monte's American distributor. The live section of the CD (the two-disc Brazilian version was put on one disc for the U.S.) culled material from Monte's *Rose and Charcoal* tour, adding a couple of tunes that she had not recorded before. The studio section alternated between dreamy tunes and edgier electrified pop.

what to buy: *Rose and Charcoal* ♫♫♫♫ (Metroblue, 1994, prod. Arto Lindsay) is Monte's most Brazilian album—and her most consistently excellent. It is her attempt to explore various Brazilian styles that use acoustic guitar, percussion, and voice. The album's immaculate production makes a perfect foil for Monte's exquisite voice.

what to buy next: *Mais* ♫♫♫♫ (World Pacific, 1991, prod. Arto Lindsay) is Monte's second album and finds her with one foot each in Brazilian and American pop. Her duet with Ed Motta on "Ainda Lembro" could be a soul classic; the fragile beauty of Pixinguinha's "Rosa" is transcendent. A wonderful album with many highlights, but not quite at the level of the follow-up *Rose and Charcoal. A Great Noise* ♫♫♫ (Metroblue, 1997, prod. Arto Lindsay, Marisa Monte) is half-studio and half-live. The studio section has some great moments, as does the live half, but it seems early for someone of Monte's youth to be revisiting her own catalog. Nevertheless, the studio cuts are alternately beautiful and rocking; the live tracks are exuberant if less manicured than their studio counterparts.

the rest:
Marisa Monte ♫♫♫ (EMI, 1988)

influences:
◀◀ Elis Regina, Antonio Carlos Jobim, Caetano Veloso, Gal Costa

see also: *Arto Lindsay, Timbalada*

Marty Lipp

Christy Moore

Irish traditional rock
Born 1945, in Ireland. Based in Ireland.

Christy Moore is one of Ireland's most influential singer-songwriters. As a founding member of Irish trad-rock bands Planxty and Moving Hearts and as a soloist, Moore has successfully fused the musical traditions of Ireland with an understanding of modern political and social concerns. His original songs, including "Ordinary Man," "Go, Move, Shift," and "City to Chicago," have provided a voice for the working class and have spoken out on violence, war, and economic struggle. The older brother of singer-songwriter Luka Bloom, Moore has been involved with music most of his life. As a child, he sang at home with his mother and with school and church choirs, and learned to play piano. Initially attracted to rock 'n' roll, he shifted his musical direction after hearing a recording by Liam Clancy of the Clancy

Brothers. Moore's knowledge of Ireland's traditional music was expanded when he met Dónal Lunny, the keyboardist of Newbridge band the Liffeysiders. (Lunny has continued to play an important role in Moore's career; in addition to playing together in Planxty and Moving Hearts, the two musicians have collaborated on Moore's solo albums, with Lunny producing several.) Moore was working as a bank official in 1964 when he met and befriended piper Willie Clancy, with whom he would play local pubs for the next year-and-a-half. Moving to London in 1966, he performed several gigs with the Grehans. While recording his debut solo album, *Prosperous,* in 1972, Moore assembled the band that became Planxty. Although he was only with the group for two years, he helped to produce three highly influential albums. In the early 1980s he took the band's energetic approach to modernized tradition a step further and formed Moving Hearts with Lunny, Keith Donald, Davy Spillane, Declan Sinnott, Eoin O'Neill, and Brian Calnan. Combining traditional instruments, including *bodhrán* (Irish frame drum) and uilleann pipes, with contemporary ones, including saxophone and electric guitar, the group brought the musical heritage of Ireland up to date. Since leaving Moving Hearts late in 1982, Moore has largely focused on his solo career.

what to buy: *The Christy Moore Collection, 1981–1991* ♫♫♫♫ (Warner Bros. U.K., prod. Dónal Lunny, Christy Moore) surveys the most influential decade of Moore's solo work and includes such memorable tunes as "Ordinary Man," "Lakes of Pontchartrain," "Biko Drum," and "Lindoosvarna."

what to buy next: Recorded at the Point Theater in Dublin in July 1994, *Live at the Point* ♫♫♫ (Grapevine, 1994, prod. Christy Moore) captures the excitement of Moore's concerts. Accompanying himself on guitar and bodhrán, Moore performs an intimate set that includes traditional folk songs such as "Black Is the Color" and memorable originals including "Fairytale of New York," "Go, Move, Shift," and "Ride On."

the rest:
Prosperous ♫♫♫ (Tara, 1972)
Whatever Tickles Your Fancy ♫♫ (Polydor, 1975)
Christy Moore ♫♫ (Polydor, 1978)
The Christy Moore Folk Collection: 1973–1978 ♫♫♫ (Tara, 1978)
The Iron behind the Gate ♫♫ (Tara, 1978)
Live in Dublin ♫♫♫ (Tara, 1978)
The Time Has Come ♫♫ (Green Linnet, 1983)
Ride On ♫♫♫ (Green Linnet, 1984)
Ordinary Man ♫♫♫♫ (Green Linnet, 1985)
Nice 'n' Easy ♫♫ (PolyGram, 1986)
Unfinished Revolution ♫♫ (Warner Bros., 1987)
Voyage ♫♫ (Warner Bros., 1989)
Smoke & the Strong Whiskey ♫♫ (Warner Bros., 1991)
King Pluck ♫♫ (Columbia/Sony, 1993)
Graffiti Tongue ♫♫♫ (Warner Bros., 1996)

influences:

◀◀ Ewan MacColl, Martin Carthy, the Clancy Brothers, Seamus Ennis

▶▶ Oyster Band, Bothy Band, Rare Air, Luka Bloom

see also: *The Clancy Brothers, the Dubliners, Dónal Lunny, Moving Hearts, Planxty*

Craig Harris

Hamish Moore

Scottish bagpipe
Born in Scotland. Based in Scotland.

Making a name for yourself in two different (albeit related) professions is quite an accomplishment, but that is exactly what Hamish Moore has done. Known as a premier maker of various sorts of bagpipes, Moore has also made a big splash as a practitioner. His work with Scottish small-pipes and Highland Bagpipes, as well as other variants, has opened a whole new frontier to the piping community. Moore is innovative and creative, combining elements of traditional music and modern jazz in a delightful whirlwind. The result leaves the listener filled with anticipation for what is to come next. Moore began playing the Highland Bagpipes at age 10, but his passion was truly kindled when he discovered the "cauld wind" Scottish small-pipes in 1980. His love of the instrument prompted him to promote it in a variety of ways, from handcrafting small-pipes to combining them with other instruments in new and exciting forms of music, thus grabbing a whole new audience for the pipes. His musical credits are numerous, including participation in Scottish festivals of folk and jazz; opening for Van Morrison at Edinburgh Castle; recording a film score with the Montreal Symphony Orchestra; and teaching at a variety of piping schools. He has also established a piping school of his own, with branches in the U.K., North America, and New Zealand.

what to buy: *Stepping on the Bridge* 𝄞𝄞𝄞𝄞 (Greentrax, 1994, prod. Jerry Holland) is a good starting point for those who enjoy well-executed traditional music. Moore plays tunes in the Cape Breton style made popular by such fiddlers as Buddy and Natalie MacMaster. The selection is superb and the playing lively. Liner notes explain Moore's by no means exclusive belief that contemporary fiddling in the emigration tributary of Cape Breton gives a closer picture of 18th-century Scottish music than the styles currently prevalent in Scotland itself.

what to buy next: *Farewell to Decorum* 𝄞𝄞𝄞 (Greentrax, 1993, prod. Michael Marra) is an eclectic montage of creatively presented jazz, folk, and pop. Moore is joined by Dick Lee, a highly acclaimed jazz saxophonist. The two are in turn accompanied by a variety of other musicians, making up an entire jazz band

on some tracks. Moore does a stirring small-pipe solo called "Farewell to Nigg," on which he experiments with an unusual tuning of the drones and chanter, leaving the piece with a decidedly minor feel.

worth searching for: *The Bee's Knees* 𝄞𝄞𝄞 (Green Linnet, 1991, prod. Hamish Moore, Dick Lee) is another noteworthy pairing of Hamish and Lee, resulting in a jazzy selection of traditional and modern tunes.

influences:

◀◀ Alex Currie, Buddy MacMaster, Dick Lee

▶▶ Barbara Dennerlein, Don Patterson, Don Pullen

see also: *Natalie MacMaster*

Jo Hughey Morrison

Beny Moré

Son, mambo, bolero, salsa
Born Bartolome Maximiliano Moré Gutierrez, August 24, 1919, in Santa Isabel de las Lajas, La Villas, Cuba. Died February 19, 1963, in Havana, Cuba.

Nicknamed "El bárbaro del ritmo" (the Barbarian of Rhythm), Beny Moré was the most influential male vocalist to come out of Cuba since Abelardo Barroso's days with the Sexteto Habanero. His forceful yet fluid phrasing propelled his supple tenor past the ordinary and into the legendary, influencing Ruben Blades, Henry Fiol, Oscar D'Leon and a host of other well-known later masters. As a youth Moré played guitar at various local festivals and events, but by 1940 he had moved to Havana and developed a reputation as a singer with various ensembles including the Cuarteto Cordero and the Sexteto Cauto. In 1945 the young vocalist worked with Conjunto Matamoros before moving to Mexico while on a tour with them. Once there Moré worked with the Conjunto de Humberto Cane and Rafael de Paz's group prior to hooking up with Perez Prado's orchestra. This last move propelled Moré into stardom as his powerful, flexible voice wove around Prado's rumbas, mambos, and boleros. Despite the hit records and lucrative movie clips that Prado and Moré forged during the early '50s, the singer moved back home to Cuba in 1953, where he gigged with Ernesto Duarte and Bebo Valdés before forming his big band, the legendary Orquesta Gigante. This group featured a number of great musicians—including trumpeters Alfredo "Chocolate" Armenteros and Alejandro "El Negro" Vivar, timbales player Roland La Serie, ace arranger/trombonist Generoso Jiménez, and pianist Pedro "Peruchín" Justiz—and provided the instrumental backdrop for Moré's greatest recordings. His lifestyle offstage was centered around alcohol and partying, which may have been a factor in his demise at the tragically early age of 43.

what to buy: *Baila Mi Son* ♪♪♪♪ (Caney, 1995, prod. various) is the finest example of Beny Moré's big band available. It might be harder to find than the BMG titles mentioned below, but this set contains more songs (20) than they do (12 and 14), which might tip the scales for folks lucky enough to dig this disc up. The muted, sliding trumpet lines that introduce the *coro* (chorus) on "Santa Isabel de Las Lajas" are almost reason enough to spring for this album, but there are other hits included here. Especially notable are "Que Bueno Baile Usted," "Marianao," "Cienfuegos," and "Maracaibo Oriental." *The Very Best of Beny Moré, Vol. 1* ♪♪♪♪ (BMG, 1995, prod. various) and *The Very Best of Beny Moré, Vol. 2* ♪♪♪♪ (BMG, 1995, prod. various) are fine foundations for a Cuban music collection. Their budget price and the distribution muscle wielded by a major label means that these discs are relatively available (as are most of his BMG recordings), but Moré's historic significance is distilled a tad too much by these anthologies, leaving the novice with the impression that there is nothing else worthwhile in Moré's recorded canon. That may be a nitpicking caveat, but one to consider when building your collection.

what to buy next: *El Bárbaro Del Ritmo* ♪♪♪ (Tumbao, 1992, prod. various) contains almost all of the hits Moré had during his stint with Perez Prado, and the re-mastering lets the dynamic duo's music shine. Smashes include "Babaratiri," "El Suave," and "Guajiro." *Grandes Voces Del Bolero: Beny Moré El Barbaro De La Melodia* ♪♪♪♪ (Caney, 1994, prod. various) concentrates on Moré's skill with boleros, those sensuous bits of balladry that allowed him to display his awesome vocal range and control. The big hits here include the classic "Oh, Vida," plus "Como Fue" and "Corazon Rebelde."

what to avoid: *Ay Mi Cuba!* ♪ (Latino, 1996, prod. various) has incredibly mediocre mastering that negates the musical quality of the performances. Any engineer who renders "Corazon Rebelde," "Marianao," and other gems as if mixed in a sonic dust bowl has committed an audio crime.

best of the rest:
The Most from Beny Moré ♪♪♪♪ (BMG, 1990)
Conjunto Matamoros with Beny Moré ♪♪♪ (Tumbao, 1992)
Maracaibo Oriental ♪♪♪♪ (BMG, 1992)
Y Hoy Como Ayer ♪♪♪♪ (BMG, 1992)
(With Celia Cruz) *Los Originales* ♪♪♪ (Globo/Sony, 1993)

influences:
◄◄ Abelardo Barroso, Israel "Cachao" López

►► Ruben Blades, Henry Fiol, Oscar D'Leon

see also: *Perez Prado, Bebo Valdes*

Garaud MacTaggart

soca

When *soca* broke through in the mid-1970s, skeptics dismissed it as a fad. Its pioneers glossed the term as "soul calypso," and a seminal soca like Shorty's "Om Shanti Om" distinctly echoes African American singers of the day like Marvin Gaye and Donna Summer. But as it happened, soca's propulsive beat—a variant of the *clave* rhythm born (some say) out of the exuberance of oil wealth—inaugurated a lasting revolution in calypso style. Since their snub of Shadow's "Bassman" in the 1974 Calypso Monarchy competition, traditionalists have persistently decried soca for the endless quantities of mindless lyrics and monotonous melodies it seems to have inspired. And yet, like the best radical positions, soca is thoroughly traditional, faithfully carrying on the bacchanalian spirit of Carnival. Its immediate predecessor is the "road march"—an up-tempo tune with simple, catchy lyrics, custom-tailored for street revelry—pioneered by Radio, Lion, and Invader in the late '30s and early '40s, and developed to sublime perfection by Kitchener and Sparrow in the '60s. The road march itself was a makeover of the older *lavway* or *leggo*: brash, unbridled, call-and-response chants sung by carnival masqueraders spoiling for clashes with other bands. These days, calypso and soca have achieved an ambivalent sort of coexistence. The sit-down ambiance of the calypso tent and the Savannah stage allows for leisurely audition and lyrical sophistication, while the jump-up atmosphere of the "Big Truck" (the flatbeds full of deafening P.A. speakers that dominate Carnival parades) demands something less subtle. Still, many of the best contemporary performers—Black Stalin, Calypso Rose, Crazy, Red Plastic Bag, David Rudder, Edwin Yearwood of krosfyah, and even confirmed party people like Super Blue and Colin Lucas—consistently find ways to blend the punchiness and danceability of soca with the verbal wit and melodic *savoir faire* of calypso.

Michael Eldridge

Airto Moreira

Brazilian jazz, African percussion

Born August 5, 1941, in Itaiopolis, Santa Catarina, Brazil. Based in USA.

Airto Moreira is one of the world's best-known percussionists and is largely responsible for introducing Brazilian rhythm into American jazz. His blend of avant-garde Brazilian and contemporary free techniques influenced other musicians of his country who arrived in the United States during the late 1960s and '70s, and his distinctive use of percussion has now become the standard. Infusing jazz with new rhythms, textures, and tone colors, Moreira has appeared as leader and sideman on numerous recordings, often with his wife, Brazilian jazz vocalist Flora Purim. He has been cited as the top percussionist in the readers' and critics' polls of many international magazines.

Moreira grew up in the city of Curitiba and began his musical studies in Brazil from 1948 to 1950 on acoustic guitar and piano. He was performing professionally by his pre-teen years and formed his own groups after playing in the early '60s with the Sambalanço Trio, the Sambrasa Trio, and Quarteto Novo. A multi-talented instrumentalist who didn't fit into a particular niche, he gravitated toward jazz and progressive interpretations of native Brazilian styles, traveling extensively in his native country and studying a wide variety of percussion instruments. In 1968 he and Purim moved to the United States, where Moreira spent several months studying with composer-arranger Moacir Santos before becoming involved with the jazz scene. He played with jazz musicians Paul Winter, Wayne Shorter, Cannonball Adderley, and others, dazzling this community with his prowess on traditional and self-invented instruments. He first gained international notice around 1970 in live performances and recordings with Miles Davis on *Bitches Brew*, *At Filmore*, and *Live-Evil*. In 1971 he worked with Lee Morgan and played percussion on the seminal, eponymous Weather Report album, but he didn't join this group because of his commitment to Davis. His role in the latter's group was to use bells, rattles, and shakers to create colors and sounds more than rhythms, and this experience changed Moreira's musical direction. In between gigs with Davis, he recorded two albums as a leader: *Natural Feelings* and *Seeds on the Ground*, both in 1970. In 1972 he joined Chick Corea's premier version of Return to Forever, recording on the band's first, self-titled fusion LP and leaving the band after their 1973 album, *Light as a Feather*. Moreira had relocated to Berkeley, California, in 1973 and at that time formed and recorded with his own band, Fingers, which lasted for two years. In 1975 he recorded a solo album, *Identity*, which was considered to be one of the decade's best fusion excursions for its dense textures and the multi-tracked, interwoven sound of its myriad instruments. Eventually, Mor-

eira became one of the most in-demand percussionists on the scene, working with a variety of jazz and other artists including the Crusaders, Freddie Hubbard, Carlos Santana, Herbie Hancock, Gil Evans, Mickey Hart, and Babatunde Olatunji. In the 1980s he was a member of the Al Di Meola Project and toured with Dizzy Gillespie's United Nation Orchestra. Moreira has also led another group of his own, Fourth World, which at presstime was scheduled to recorded its final album, *Last Journey to the Fourth World*, for the import label B&W Music.

what to buy: A serendipitous web-surfing session can lead you to some astounding Airto sessions recorded for the British import label B&W Music (check for info on the M.E.L.T. 2000 site at http://www.melt2000.com/). While Moreira has made an indelible mark on jazz, in recent years he's been exploring more world-influenced rhythms. You'll want to investigate three B&W sessions he recorded in Johannesburg and Capetown studios with various South African musicians—Moreira's 1995 tour (two weeks of recordings and three live concerts with over 50 colleagues in that country) was sponsored by the London-based *Straight No Chaser* magazine and documented on three CDs in the *South Africa: Outernational Meltdown* series. Bolstering a team of superb musicians with his colorful percussion, Moreira is featured most prominently on *Outernational Meltdown: Free at Last* 🎵🎵🎵🎵 (B&W Music, 1995, prod. Sipho Gumede), a seven-tune celebration yielding melodically enticing and rhythmically rousing South African jazz from the straight-ahead to the stretched out. It's an ear-expanding journey considerably different from other Airto albums. Singing and playing marimbas, Aboriginal Australian *didgeridoo*, shakers, African drums, additional percussion, and other instruments, an array of South African musicians from Johannesburg and Cape Town join Moreira on the 17-track second release in this series, *Outernational Meltdown: Healer's Brew* 🎵🎵🎵 (B&W, 1995, prod. Airto Moreira). More tribal-sounding than the other two albums in the series, this disc launches with a fervent "Blessing Ceremony," chanted by Susan Hendricks. Moreira often takes a back seat to his partners, playing shakers and, on some tracks, adding to background vocals. Zulu spiritual healers guided by multi-instrumentalist Pops Mohamed and the 17-member vocal choir Intethelelo Yabazalwane enhance this effective African-roots album. Notable selections include the nearly 20-minute rendering of the title track, intriguing songs by the choir, and raw, pulsating drum-laden numbers. More musical and jazz-influenced, the third album in the series, *Outernational Meltdown: Jazzin' Universally* 🎵🎵🎵 (B&W Music, 1995, prod. various), even swings a little bit and contains winning improvisational touches by players such as trumpeter Byron Wallen, pianists Tete Mbambisa and Moses Taiwa Molelekwa, and other gifted South African musicians. Again, Moreira mostly defers to the others, but his presence and inspiration are felt throughout the seven tunes. This venture leans toward the foundations of South African jazz from the 1950s and '60s, with cohesively rendered horn-section arrangements and nationalist themes evoking the contributions of exiled players who never lived to see the election of Nelson Mandela as South Africa's president.

what to buy next: Leading his modern-edged Fourth World band, Moreira recorded three albums for B&W with various lineups. B&W touts itself as "a label without inhibitions, producing music without boundaries," and that's exactly what you can expect on the Fourth World recordings. Airto and Flora are constants, and depending on where their global travels take them, they meld the region's native rhythms to jazz, often with guitarist Neto as a collaborator. You can't go too far astray with any of these albums. *Fourth World* ♪♪♪♪ (B&W Music, 1993, prod. David Garland, Mark St. John) draws inspiration from the Brazilian rainforests. *Fourth World: Live in South Africa, 1993* ♪♪♪♪ (B&W Music/Bootleg.net, 1995) combines Airto and Flora's Brazilian jazz with South African influences to stimulating effect. Recorded during a concert at the Bimhuis Center for Jazz and Improvised Music in Amsterdam, *Encounters of the Fourth World* ♪♪♪♪♪ (B&W Music, 1995, prod. Airto Moreira, Fourth World) continues along the same path, but it's influenced less by Brazilian rhythms and more by jazz-rock fusion. The album features Moreira, Purim, guitarist Neto, bassist/vocalist Gary Brown, keyboardist/flutist Jovino Santos, and special guest Giovanni Hidalgo on congas/percussion. Each Fourth World album offers a distinctive, fresh adventure. Unless you're also an avid jazz fan, you may want to wait to explore the following CDs, though each one is excellent. *The Best of Airto* ♪♪♪♪ (Columbia, 1972–74/1994, prod. Creed Taylor, Billy Cobham, reissue prod. Didier C. Deutsch) draws mostly from Moreira's *Free* and *Fingers* albums, and contains 10 of his best tunes recorded between 1972 and 1974 with an array of jazz artists, including Chick Corea or Keith Jarrett (piano), Ron Carter or Stanley Clarke (bass), Eddie Daniels (flute), George Duke (keyboards), and numerous others. Moreira is superb throughout, demonstrating how mightily he adds fresh percussive flair to each tune. This is one "best of" that lives up to its claim, and it's a good introductory album for new fans to discover Airto's talents with Brazilian-jazz beats, and his pyrotechnic penchant for creating exciting music that holds up decades later. Plenty of Brazilian melodies, scat vocals, and swaying modern-edged beats should also satisfy the experienced listener. Moreira's first album for CTI, *Free* ♪♪♪♪ (CTI, 1972/CBS, 1988, prod. Creed Taylor), was a seminal work that's still immediate and exciting after all these years. Featuring the premier version of Return to Forever with Chick Corea (piano), Stanley Clarke (bass), Joe Farrell (saxophones/flutes), and other jazz luminaries, this was the album that helped spread the word

about this incredibly talented Brazilian percussionist. A satisfying Moreira album that gives an overview of his broad interests, *Three-Way Mirror* ♪♪♪♪ (Reference Recordings, 1987, prod. J. Tamblyn Henderson Jr., Airto Moreira) features him performing eight tunes ranging from native Brazilian numbers to bebop to Return to Forever–type fusion. Vocalist Purim, pianist Kei Akagi, guitarist José Neto, bassists Mark Egan or Randy Tico, and special guest flutist Joe Farrell (in his last performances) contribute to this fine album. While Moreira and Purim perform at their usual best, Farrell's playing is what really makes this expertly produced 1985 date a pleasure trip. If you crave the spontaneity of a jam session among prime innovators, check out *Airto and the Gods of Jazz: Killer Bees* ♪♪♪♪ (B&W Music, 1993, prod. Flora Purim), a unique, modern-sounding set created in California over two weekends in 1989 when percussionist/vocalist Moreira, longing to recreate his NYC loft-session days, assembled a group of all-stars: Hiram Bullock (overdubbed guitars), Stanley Clarke (acoustic/electric bass), Chick Corea (acoustic piano/electronic keyboards), Mark Egan (electric fretless bass), and Gary Meek (tenor/soprano saxophones). Purim makes brief appearances. The album documents one helluva 50-minute jam, with tunes ranging from free-jazz to straight-ahead styles. The title tune grew out of what was initially a beginning soundcheck from Egan. Moreira joins in, playing an Australian bull-roarer, an instrument used by Aboriginals to banish evil spirits (you've probably witnessed its buzzing in the *Crocodile Dundee* films). Corea and Bullock overdub with some nasty, funk-groove beats. The album contains many fine moments and enough variety to appeal to a wide range of jazz lovers.

best of the rest:

Seeds on the Ground ♪♪♪ (One Way, 1971/1994)
The Magicians ♪♪♪ (Concord/Crossover, 1986)
The Sun Is Out ♪♪♪ (Concord/Crossover, 1987/1989)
Struck by Lightning ♪♪♪♪ (Venture, 1989)
The Other Side of This ♪♪♪♪ (Rykodisc, 1992)

influences:

◀ João Parahyba, Téo Lima, Robertinho Silva, Oswaldinho da Cuíca, Cyro Baptista, Paulinho da Costa, Guilherme Franco

see also: *Amampondo, Mickey Hart, Babatunde Olatunji, Orchesta Aragon, Flora Purim, Badal Roy*

Nancy Ann Lee

Morgan Heritage

Reggae
Formed 1992, in Brooklyn, NY, USA. Based in Brooklyn, NY, USA.

Una Morgan, vocals, keyboards; Nakhamya "Lukes" Morgan, vocals, guitar; Roy "Gramps" Morgan, vocals, keyboards; Memmalatel "Mr.

Mojo" Morgan, vocals, percussion; Peter Morgan, vocals. (All members are from USA.)

Originally, Morgan Heritage comprised all eight of underground reggae great Denroy Morgan's children. But by the time their currently available records were made, three members—drummer Denroy Jr., bassist David, and lead guitarist Jeffery—had left, leaving their siblings to work with studio backup. The original octet debuted under their present name in 1992 at the definitive annual Reggae Sunsplash festival, though they had spent some time logging impressive apprenticeship credentials as support for Sister Carol and Judy Mowatt. The Sunsplash appearance got them signed to MCA, though the resulting album, *Miracle,* didn't sell well and was soon deleted. They followed up with several singles that did fairly well (especially in Europe), but those have yet to be compiled on CD. So the siblings moved on to indie reggae powerhouse VP, where they continue to record as a quintet, touring the world.

what to buy: *Don't Haffi Dread* 𝄢𝄢𝄢𝄢 (VP Records, 1999, prod. Bobby "Digital" Dixon) finds Peter Morgan really coming into his own as a vocalist, especially on such tunes as "Earthquake" and the Wailers-like "Reggae Road Block." More important, he's got better songs to sing and better tracks to sing to. Even the weaker ones keep up the groove, and when the pace is changed with the acoustic "Freedom," the harmonies put it over.

what to buy next: When *Protect Us Jah* 𝄢𝄢𝄢 (VP Records, 1997, prod. Bobby "Digital" Dixon) is good, as on "Africa, Here We Come" and "Set Yourself Free," it rocks. However, too much is like the ersatz, bloodless, beatless soul ballad "When You Decide."

the rest:
One Calling 𝄢𝄢𝄢 (VP Records, 1998)

worth searching for: A pop reggae record in the wake of actual reggae hits from Aswad and Inner Circle, *Miracle* 𝄢𝄢 (MCA, 1994, prod. Morgan Heritage, Denroy Morgan) is a mish-mash of new jack swing, rap, dancehall, and other pop grafted onto reggae. Still, tough, poignant tunes like "Unjust World" and "Love Police" make this one worth seeking out.

influences:
◄◄ Denroy Morgan, Bob Marley, Third World

see also: *Judy Mowatt, Sister Carol*

Hank Bordowitz

Pablo Moses

Reggae
Born Pablo Henry, 1953, in Manchester, Jamaica. Based in Jamaica.

With his high-pitched, horn-like vocals set to Eurodisco arrangements, dreadlocked vocalist Pablo Moses has been es-

pousing his Rastafarian-influenced vision of equality and justice for more than two decades. Moses first attracted attention after forming the vocal group the Canaries in the early 1970s. Although he scored a hit with his pro-marijuana anthem "I Man a Grasshopper" in 1975, Moses had little commercial success until the '80s. His debut album *Revolutionary Dream* was such a financial disappointment (if latter-day critical triumph) that Moses withdrew from the public eye for two years, sharpening his skills at the Jamaica School of Music. In 1978 he resumed his career with a vengeance, releasing the powerful *A Song* and remaining a well-respected conscious commentator to this day.

what to buy: Moses's return to the music scene, *A Song* 𝄢𝄢𝄢𝄢 (Mango, 1978, prod. Geoffrey Chung), is still a masterpiece of hard-core Rastafarian lyricism. With such legendary backup as Sly (Dunbar) & Robbie (Shakespeare) as rhythm section, and Bob Marley/I-Threes veterans Rita Marley and Judy Mowatt on vocals, Moses defiantly voices classics like "Revolutionary Step," "Each Is a Servant," and "Protest I/A Song."

what to buy next: The best of Moses's early work, including his first hit "I Man a Grasshopper," is reprised on *I Love I Bring: Anthology of Reggae Collectors' Series, Volume 7* 𝄢𝄢𝄢𝄢 (United Artists, 1978, prod. Geoffrey Chung).

the rest:
Revolutionary Dream 𝄢𝄢𝄢𝄢 (Shanachie, 1975)
In the Future 𝄢𝄢𝄢 (Alligator, 1980)
Reggae Greats 𝄢𝄢𝄢𝄢 (Mango, 1983)
Tension 𝄢𝄢𝄢 (Alligator, 1984)
Live to Love 𝄢𝄢𝄢 (Rohit, 1985)
We Refuse 𝄢𝄢𝄢 (Profile, 1988)
Mission 𝄢𝄢𝄢 (RAS, 1990)
Confession of a Rastaman 𝄢𝄢𝄢 (Musidisc, 1995)
Pave the Way 𝄢𝄢𝄢 (Mango, 1996)
Pave the Way Dub 𝄢𝄢𝄢 (Tabou 1, 1998)
In the Future & Dub 𝄢𝄢𝄢 (Tabou 1, 1998)

influences:
◄◄ Bob Marley, Burning Spear, Peter Tosh
►► Third World, UB40

see also: *Rita Marley, Judy Mowatt, Sly & Robbie*

Craig Harris

Paul Mounsey

Celtic, Scottish, worldbeat
Born April 15, 1959, in Irvine, Scotland. Based in São Paulo, Brazil.

Composer/producer Paul Mounsey has assembled quite a musical mix from his diverse influences and remarkable background. The Scottish native graduated from Trinity College of London with first-class honors in composition, and from London

International Film School in movie scoring. After a short time lecturing at the University of London's Goldsmith's College, he moved to São Paulo, Brazil, in 1983. There he embarked on a successful career producing music for television—commercials, documentaries, and other programs. He also wrote a song that became a three-million-selling single for EMI Mexico and has worked with a number of internationally known performers including soul diva Etta James, reggae great Jimmy Cliff, and the celebrated percussion ensemble Olodum. But Mounsey's career took its most fascinating turn in 1990 and '91, when he heard some Scottish traditional music. Mounsey hadn't listened to any for the first seven or eight years he'd been in Brazil because it "provoked a profound sense of homesickness in me," according to an interview with *Folk Roots* magazine. But by the time he heard it again, "I found that I'd lost the link and it didn't provoke anything in me. It sounded quite foreign and that's why, I think, I decided to start working with it—to try to rediscover my own musical roots and identity." And with the *Nahoo* projects, that's exactly what he has done. The first *Nahoo* recording was released in 1994 by Iona in Scotland and consists mostly of Mounsey's adaptations and re-workings of traditional material. But Mounsey's music is far from conventional folk-rock. He's brought his contemporary pop experience to traditional music, which means ancient Gaelic ballads are given high-tech dance beats with lots of sampling. Mounsey himself sings, plays keyboards and whistle, and is responsible for programming, and the technology is mixed with other actual musicians who play guitar, bass, violin, viola, and percussion. *NahooToo* appeared in 1997 and emphasized original material. The folk base was somewhat less obvious; one track, the bright, catchy, and melodic "Wherever You Go," is as fine a piece of modern pop as you'll ever hear. At the time of writing, Mounsey has begun working on the third installment, which is tentatively titled *Nahoo 3: Notes from the Republic.*

what's available: *Nahoo* 𝄞𝄞𝄞𝄞 (Iona, 1994, prod. Paul Mounsey, João "Janjão" Vasconcelos) is a fine example of the next step in pop/rock/folk fusions—the first wave (Fairport Convention, Steeleye Span) brought the energy of psychedelic rock to folk music; in the 1980s the Pogues, the Men They Couldn't Hang, and Billy Bragg gave folk a punky edge; and in the 1990s traditional sounds are meeting the latest dance/pop and multi-ethnic grooves in the work of Afro Celt Sound System, Talitha MacKenzie, Shooglenifty, and Mounsey. Like his colleagues, Mounsey's specialty is creating whole pieces from all sorts of ingredients—with exciting, listenable results. For instance, the opening track here, "Passing Away," includes a brief spoken-word excerpt lamenting that "Gaelic is on the decline" before you hear ethereal vocals over pulsing dance rhythms and synth washes. On "Alba," Mounsey uses sampled vocals (taken from field recordings made by the School of Scottish Studies in Edin-

burgh) over his electronic beats, the two elements fitting together surprisingly well. Then there's Mounsey's arrangement of the old ballad "Journeyman," which he sings in a straight folk-ish voice to the accompaniment of hard funk/rap drums. He even recites one of the verses as poetry, and that works too. The ancient Scottish music is inherently rhythmic, which is why it adapts so well to these modern treatments. Mounsey broadened his palette for *NahooToo* 𝄞𝄞𝄞𝄞 (Iona, 1997, prod. Paul Mounsey, João "Janjão" Vasconcelos). "North" is an instrumental piece that starts off like a slow air, with violin playing the melody line. Then there's an abrupt shift as loud heavy-metal guitars crash in and make you think you're listening to Black Sabbath. "Turned on the Dog" is loud guitar-rock with sampled bagpipes! Brazilian flutes open up "The Fields of Robert John" while synths provide backing drones; choppy violin bits and strange percussion effects come later in this unique composition. Mounsey even brought in influential Celtic singer Flora MacNeill to sing Gaelic on several cuts, and she's surprisingly at home with all the electronics. Someone else trying to fuse so many different components could easily fail, but the discipline Mounsey underwent as a pop producer and composer undoubtedly gave him the experience to create coherent works from his plethora of sources.

influences:

◄◄ Field recordings, Runrig, Michael Oldfield, Moving Hearts, Peter Gabriel

►► Shooglenifty, Peatbog Faeries, Talitha MacKenzie, Afro Celt Sound System

Ken Roseman

Mouth Music

Celtic world-funk
Formed 1990, in Scotland. Based in Scotland.

Jackie Joyce, vocals; Martin Swan, guitar, whistles, flutes, drums; Michaela Rowan, voice; James MacKintosh, drums; Quee MacArthur, bass; Jeremy Black, percussion.

"All music is singing or drumming," states Mouth Music's Martin Swan, and that is probably the closest you can come to finding a description of this unusual group. Evolving into a whole new sound with each recording, Mouth Music has defied both fans' and critics' expectations with its chameleonic tastes. One moment funky worldbeat, the next new-age with a touch of traditional, quickly followed by techno-pop, this group changes personae at the drop of a song. Which, considering their start, should hardly be a surprise. Formed by Scottish film and TV director Martin Swan and American-born ethnomusicologist Talitha MacKenzie, how could this group help but pull on a variety of styles and traditions, forming a new fusion of sounds at each turn? Feeling that rhythm is the root of any music, they derive such rhythm in the most creative of ways, from bongos and bottles to synthesizers and even the vocal lines themselves.

what's available: Winner of multiple "Best of the Year" awards, *Mouth Music* ✍✍✍✍ (Triple Earth, 1991, prod. Martin Swan, Chic Medley) takes Gaelic tunes to Africa and back, adding a bit of pop culture along the way. Driving rhythms and heavily synthesized vocals and keyboard lines accompany a collection of traditional tunes, bringing them a new sound. Dance-beat meets *waulking* (traditional Scottish washing) songs and *a cappella* mouth music (customarily unaccompanied Scottish dance singing), sometimes all at once, sometimes alternating. Particularly fascinating is "I See the Great Mountains," from the tune better known as "Mist Covered Mountains," which mixes the familiar vocal line with a hypnotic drum beat. *Mo-Di* ✍✍✍ (Triple Earth, 1993, prod. Martin Swan, Stuart Hamilton) is a collection of memorable dance tunes, distinguished by the amazing multi-lingual vocal talents of singer Jackie Joyce. Standout tracks include "Birnam," an ethereal new-age ballad, and "He Mandu," which combines exciting dance rhythms with compelling harmonies. *Shorelife* ✍✍✍ (Triple Earth, 1995, prod. Martin Swan, Chic Medley) has more of a computerized feel, heavy on the synthesizers and drum kits.

influences:

◄◄ David Byrne, Brian Eno, Enya

►► Pink Kross

see also: *Talitha MacKenzie*

Jo Hughey Morrison

Moving Cloud

Irish traditional
Formed 1989, in County Clare, Ireland. Based in Ennis, County Clare, Ireland.

Paul Brock, accordion, melodeon; Maeve Donnelly, fiddle; Manus McGuire, fiddle; Christy Dunne, banjo (1989–93); Kevin Crawford, flute, tin whistle, bodhrán (1993–present); Carl Hession, piano. (Members are from Ireland and England.)

Many groups can play Irish jigs, reels, and hornpipes with fire and energy, but few can do it with the sensitivity and panache of Moving Cloud. Their repertoire is enhanced with a healthy selection of cheeky polkas, lively barndances and flings, memorable mazurkas, and elegant waltzes, setting them in a class by themselves. Moving Cloud's concert-champ status today owes much to their in-the-trenches apprenticeship as an ace dance band. Formed in the late 1980s at a time when set dancing in County Clare was enjoying an enthusiastic revival, the group soon became standard-bearers for that genre. Of course,

it didn't hurt that bandmembers—drawn from Clare, Galway, and Westmeath in Ireland and Birmingham in England—held numerous All-Ireland traditional music titles on their respective instruments. Their aim to move onward and upward to the concert circuit has been realized with the aid of two albums that flawlessly deploy accordion, fiddle, and flute in front of delicately poised piano.

what's available: The debut, *Moving Cloud* ✍✍✍ (Green Linnet, 1995, prod. Moving Cloud), was a breath of fresh air that can never go stale: great dance tunes from Ireland, Scotland, Cape Breton, and French Canada, beautifully presented, with sources duly noted on the sleeve. Two tunes from turn-of-the-century French Canadian melodeon player Alfred Montmarquette, "Virginia Waltz" and "Chinese Polka," are particularly charming. *Foxglove* ✍✍✍ (Green Linnet, 1998, prod. Moving Cloud, Martin Murray) has a more polished and varied sound, making subtle use of some outside guests including Johnny "Ringo" McDonagh on *bodhrán* (Irish frame drum) and Gerry O'Connor on banjo. Generous notes are provided once more, and the way this band plays it, "Swing Waltz," a French *musette* (Gypsy-influenced romantic dance-music) tune from the 1930s, sounds quite at home beside numbers associated with fiddle legend Paddy Fahy and box player Joe Cooley.

influences:

◄◄ Chieftains, Kilfenora Ceili Band, Tulla Ceili Band, Silly Wizard, Cherish the Ladies

see also: *Frankie Gavin*

John C. Falstaff

Moving Hearts

Irish traditional and fusion
Formed 1980, in Dublin, Ireland. Disbanded 1985.

Christy Moore, vocals, acoustic guitar, bodhrán (1980–82); Mick Hanly, vocals, acoustic guitar (1983); Flo Sweeney, vocals (1984); Dónal Lunny, bouzouki, synthesizer, vocals; Davy Spillane, uilleann pipes, low whistle; Declan Masterson, uilleann pipes, low whistle (1985); Keith Donald, saxophone, bass clarinet; Declan Sinnott, guitars, vocals; Eoghan O'Neill, bass, vocals; Brian Calnan, drums, percussion (1980–81); Matt Kelleghan, drums, percussion (1981–85); Noel Eccles, percussion (1985). (All members are from Ireland.)

The sadly overlooked Moving Hearts are clearly the missing link between some of the most innovative Irish groups of the '70s (Horslips, Planxty, Bothy Band) and the *Riverdance* phenomenon of the '90s. Moving Hearts actually co-existed and shared members with Planxty toward the end of the latter band's life (1980 to 1983), playing their unique brand of frequently political Irish-influenced fusion music while Planxty followed a more traditional and certainly less controversial path.

A decade after Moving Hearts broke up, several former members resurfaced together in the *Riverdance* band.

Moving Hearts was first convened in 1980 by prime mover and shaker Dónal Lunny (Planxty, ex–Bothy Band), well-established singer Christy Moore (Planxty), and guitarist Declan Sinnott (ex-Horslips), soon to be joined by Keith Donald (ex-Stagalee) on sax—not to mention future *Riverdance* composer Bill Whelan for a brief moment at the very start. They recruited a brilliant young Dublin piper named Davy Spillane (largely unknown at the time), and started playing live around town. Soon they had developed a reputation for two things: fiery tunes juxtaposing traditional and rock idioms in a startling new way, and often-political songs—anti-nuclear, anti-fascist, pro-republican (in the Irish sense)—sung by Moore in his distinctively soft and deceptively easy-going voice.

"Hiroshima Nagasaki Russian Roulette" (which Planxty also tried live) had been written and recorded in 1975 by Seattle-based protest singer/songwriter Jim Page, who spent some time living in Ireland in the late '70s. Moving Hearts' stunning adaptation of the song was aired on Irish radio at the start of 1981 and electrified many who heard it. It became the band's signature song and was adopted by the (ultimately triumphant) Irish anti-nuclear movement, in which both Christy and his brother Barry (later known to the world as Luka Bloom) were very active.

Expectations were high for the band's self-titled debut album, released in late summer of 1981, and the boys did not disappoint. This was the time of the tragic hunger strikes in Northern Ireland, and in concert the band left absolutely no doubt as to where they stood on that issue. (A rare single from this period includes near-future member Mick Hanly fronting the band live for his own Jackson Browne–soundalike, "On the Blanket.") The follow-up, *Dark End of the Street* (1982), was also very impressive, though it veered even further from traditional Irish music. Moore left at the end of that year to focus on his solo career; he was replaced by Hanly, who as writer had already contributed the best song on *Dark End*.

The only album to feature Hanly as a performer was *Live Hearts,* which includes three previously unrecorded songs—most notably Jimmy McCarthy's "Strain of the Dance"—but is marred by having its weakest track drag on for over 10 minutes. The band then tried out a female singer (Flo Sweeney) in concert before opting for life as a purely instrumental ensemble. They went out on a high note with *The Storm* (1985), recorded with Spillane and Declan Masterson, each on uilleann pipes. Both men, together with ace bassist Eoghan O'Neill and latter-day percussionist Noel Eccles (borrowed at the time from the country's national symphony orchestra), went on to give long service and lend considerable clout to the *Riverdance* project

starting in the mid-'90s. They also kept busy with their own careers—Spillane in particular—as did the more prominent Lunny, Moore, and Hanly. Sinnott found fame backing and arranging for Mary Black and more recently for Sinead Lohan. Donald became the Popular Music Officer for the Irish Arts Council. They have reunited in some shape or form for live gigs on a few occasions.

On a good day, Moving Hearts concocted a uniquely heady brew of swirling pipes (Spillane), sax (Donald), and electric guitar (Sinnott), underpinned with great style by Lunny and O'Neill. Where artists such as Richard Thompson and Dan Ar Braz have used piping techniques as an inspiration for electric guitar playing, Spillane did the exact opposite at times, his piping taking on the role of lead guitar, dueling proudly, passionately, and fearlessly with Sinnott and Donald. Moreover, his soulful low whistle playing brought that once-infrequently heard instrument to a new and wider audience.

In a sense Moving Hearts (the perfect antidote to their contemporaries Talking Heads?) were two different bands: the one with Christy (or Mick) at the helm, belting out songs subtle and not-so-subtle (many of them American); and the other one whose voice needed no words to communicate. This may ultimately have been their undoing, but the fact remains that they considerably expanded the possibilities for the Irish traditional genre as fusion music, and in so doing planted many of the seeds that would later bear fruit as *Riverdance* and the Celtic commercial renaissance it ushered in.

what to buy: *Moving Hearts* ♪♪♪♪ (WEA, 1981, prod. Dónal Lunny) is their best effort, from the explosive "Hiroshima" opener and the instrumental "Category" (jaunty but, despite the title, thoroughly uncategorizable), to the seductive "Irish Ways and Irish Laws" (by John Gibb), "Before the Deluge" (Jackson Browne), and the brilliant "Faithful Departed" (by Irish punk Philip Chevron of the Radiators from Space and later the Pogues), a refreshingly literate look at a rapidly changing Irish society.

what to buy next: *The Dark End of the Street* ♪♪♪ (WEA, 1982, prod. Dónal Lunny) also starts off very strong with Barry Moore's "Remember the Brave Ones," but has a more hybrid, diffuse feel and is less focused than its predecessor. Mick Hanly's hilarious school-days reminiscence "All I Remember" seems tailor-made for Christy Moore, who is also superb on Don Lange's "Allende." The instrumentals range from Spillane's traditional-sounding "Downtown" to O'Neill's Weather Report–inflected "Half-Moon." *The Storm* ♪♪♪ (Tara, 1985, prod. Dónal Lunny) is more coherent and is all instrumental; it's also the only release of the band's to feature two pipers. Eccles's intricate percussion adds depth to Lunny's and O'Neill's rhythm work, and everybody really stretches out on the longer tracks.

Early copies of this came with a free single featuring two otherwise unavailable (but hardly essential) songs recorded with Mick Hanly.

what to avoid: Some early-'80s American copies of *The Dark End of the Street* (same title and artwork as the real thing) actually contain a selection of tracks from the first two albums.

the rest:
Live Hearts ♪♪♪ (WEA, 1983)

worth searching for: Van Morrison's *A Sense of Wonder* ♪♪♪ (Mercury, 1985) has Moving Hearts playing a welcome (if somewhat out-of-place) instrumental called "Boffyflow & Spike," which Van wrote for them. Their flawless backing on some other tracks demonstrates what a consummate bunch of professionals they were.

influences:

◄◄ Planxty, Bothy Band, Weather Report

►► The Pogues, Oyster Band, Rare Air, Bill Whelan, Kila

see also: *Horslips, Dónal Lunny, Christy Moore, Sean Ó Riada, Planxty, Bill Whelan*

John C. Falstaff

Judy Mowatt

Reggae
Born late 1950s, in Jamaica. Based in Jamaica.

"The Queen of Rasta Reggae," Judy Mowatt is one of Jamaica's most influential vocalists. A former member of the I-Threes, background vocalists for Bob Marley from 1974 until his death in 1981, Mowatt has continued to musically address her feminist and Rastafarian philosophies. According to *Newsweek*, Mowatt, whose soulful harmonies can be heard on albums by Peter Tosh, Jimmy Cliff, Big Youth, Pablo Moses, Freddie McGregor, U-Roy, and the Wailing Souls as well as on her own recordings, is "by far reggae's most highly regarded woman vocalist." Mowatt had her initial success as a member of the Gaylettes, a teenage singing group that she formed in 1967. Later lauded as a soloist in the early '70s, Mowatt's popularity reached international proportions when she joined with Rita Marley and Marcia Griffiths to form the I-Threes. Their vocal harmonies on Bob Marley's single "Jah Live" and his album *Natty Dread* marked the beginning of a long collaboration. The I-Threes replaced Marley's original centerpiece trio of himself, Bunny Wailer, and Peter Tosh, and achieved equally historic stature. Mowatt's debut solo album *Black Woman*, released in 1980, was the very first recorded in Marley's Tuff Gong studios. Continuing to perform with the I-Threes following Marley's death in 1981, Mowatt has more recently carried on as a still-acclaimed soloist.

what to buy: With *Black Woman* ♪♪♪♪ (Shanachie, 1980/1987, prod. Judy Mowatt, Freddie McGregor) Mowatt stepped into the limelight as a gifted songwriter and soulful singer. Accompanied by many of the same musicians featured on Bob Marley's recordings, Mowatt sings of strong women and the power of Rastafarian ideologies.

what to buy next: Mowatt's second solo effort, *Only a Woman* ♪♪♪♪ (Shanachie, 1982/1987, prod. Judy Mowatt), further affirms its predecessor's feminist and Rasta themes.

the rest:
Working Wonders ♪♪♪♪ (Shanachie, 1985)
Love Is Overdue ♪♪♪♪ (Shanachie, 1987)
Look at Love ♪♪♪ (Shanachie, 1991)
Rock Me ♪♪♪ (Pow Wow, 1993)

influences:

◄◄ Bob Marley, Dinah Washington, Diana Ross, Rastafarianism

►► Bonnie Raitt, Queen Latifah, Rita Marley

see also: *Marcia Griffiths, Bob Marley, Rita Marley, Pablo Moses*

Craig Harris

Tshala Muana /Tshala Mwana

Mutuashi, soukous
Born 1959, in Lubumbashi, Congo. Based in Congo and Paris, France.

Tshala Muana is regarded, along with Abeti, M'Bilia Bel, and M'Pongo Love, as one of the Congo's great female vocalists. Enormously popular and occasionally controversial in her native continent, Muana is as recognized in many African countries for her sexually suggestive dancing and assertive lyrics and attitude as she is for her impressive vocal range and distinctive rural Congolese yodel. Muana has had her name linked romantically to several African presidents, and her display of a condom in an AIDS public service announcement got the spot banned for a time in Zambia. While Muana's songbook includes plenty of numbers utilizing her country's best-known approach, the fast-tempoed, ringing guitar sound of *soukous* (a.k.a. Congolese rumba), she also sings over equally modern but more percussion-oriented updates of other native rhythms. Raised in a family of singers and dancers in the Southeast portion of the Congo, Muana first received attention for her modernization of traditional dance. Celebrated as "The Queen of Mutuashi" for her updated movements to this folkloric style, Muana relocated to Kinshasa in 1977 where she became a dancer with M'Pongo Love's group Tsheke Tsheke. Taking up professional singing, Muana soon recorded two singles before moving to Côte d'Ivoire in 1979. There in Abidjan, known for its recording stu-

Tshala Muana

dios and an abundance of musicians from around the continent, Muana recorded several more singles and used the coastal town as a base for touring throughout West and Central Africa. She moved to Paris in 1984, where she recorded her debut album and was subsequently voted top African woman vocalist in a number of polls. Since that time Muana has released a number of European- and African-only releases—and sadly only two American efforts—that have further consolidated her acclaim. Muana has worked on these albums with top male arrangers such as Bibi Dens and Souzy Kasseya, but she's never been a mere showpiece. She's written and/or produced much of her material and in her lyrics she's never been less than forthright about discussing the relationships between the sexes.

what to buy: *Mutuashi* 𝄞𝄞𝄞 (Stern's Africa, 1996, prod. Boncana Maiga) is a well-crafted, varied collection that adds Afro-Cuban and acoustic folk accents to Muana's mutuashi and soukous dance rhythms. Producer Maiga brings a number of the Latin musicians he had worked with on the Africando albums, and they add polyrhythmic piano, timbale, and horn sounds to a number of cuts. On the mutuashi song "Tshovo," Muana joy-

ously wails her trademark extended syllable "yoooooh" over a unique blend of xylophone, keyboard, and flute sonics, before engaging in a call-and-response with her backing vocalists. Guitarists Lokassa Ya M'bongo and Daly Kimoko star on the soukous cuts, and Muana's voice takes on a deep, impassioned tone for the melancholy mid-tempo lament "Kabeji."

what to buy next: *Soukous Siren* 𝄞𝄞𝄞 (Shanachie, 1991, prod. Lou Deprijck, Tshala Muana) is a compilation of material Muana recorded between 1985 and 1988 for European labels. Occupying a narrower musical spectrum than *Mutuashi,* the CD still offers a number of scintillating compositions. On "Tshibola" Muana happily exclaims "Mutuashi!" over that style's percussive rhythms, while on "Lwa-Touye" she engages in a jubilant, speedy call-and-response exchange with her supporting singers.

worth searching for: The French import *Dans un Duo pour l'Éternité avec Papa Wemba* 𝄞𝄞𝄞 (Gefraco/Editions Kaluila) may only have Papa Wemba on one song, but Bibi Dens's arrangements, Rigo Star's guitar work, and Muana's vocalizing generally impress. Other albums to look for from Muana's impressive European catalog include *Nasi Nabali* (Sonodisc), *M Bombo* (Kaluila),

La Vie este Belle (Stern's U.K., 1987), *Biduaya* (Celluloid, 1989), *La Divine* (Espera/Sonodisc, 1991), *Yombo* (Sonodisc, 1992), *Elako* (Tamaris, 1993), and *Ntambue* (Sonodisc, 1994).

influences:
◀◀ M'Pongo Love

see also: *Africando, M'Bilia Bel, Boncana Maiga, Rigo Star, Papa Wemba*

Steve Kiviat

Abdel Aziz El Mubarak

Sudanese pop
Born 1951, in Wad Medani, Sudan. Based in Khartoum, Sudan.

Wad Medani is known in Sudan as a center for the arts, and Abdel Aziz El Mubarak is one of its favorite sons. Mubarak comes from a family of noted musicians, and he began singing and composing in elementary school. He went to Khartoum in his early 20s and passed the audition to be a singer on Sudanese Broadcasting, the national radio station. His first hits came in 1975 with "Yah Izzana" and "Laih Ya Galbi Kaih." Soon thereafter he put together a band to play weddings, nightclubs, concert halls, radio, and TV. Mubarak has a pleasingly straightforward tenor that plays neatly off of the band's swinging string section and percolating Arabic rhythms. Mubarak's songs combine classical Arabic music and poetry, and are carefully chosen to avoid musical and lyrical clichés. After the poets write the lyrics Mubarak works with the composers to create the melodies. Sudanese music is highly traditional—there is no musical notation and tunes are not written down, but transmitted directly from musician to musician. After Mubarak has a song ready, the rest of the band learns it, developing new ideas and arrangements as they go along. Before performance a song is submitted to a peer review of leading artists who check to make sure it conforms to tradition and follows the rules of classical Arabic verse and composition.

what to buy: For the past 20 years Mubarak has been Sudan's most popular singer, and one of his innovations was incorporating reggae into his rhythmic repertoire. On *Adbel Aziz El Mubarak* ♫♫♫♫ (Globestyle, 1988, prod. Adam Skeaping, John Haddon) the reggae of "Ahla Eyyoun" and "Bitgooli La" doesn't sound at all Jamaican, but it does have a funky, 12-bar bass line that brings to mind the R&B shuffle of "Night Train."

what to buy next: Recorded live during a performance in London, *Straight from the Heart* ♫♫♫♫ (World Circuit, 1989, prod. John Haddon) includes many of Mubarak's best-known tunes including "Yah Izzana" and "Laih Ya Galbi Kaih," the songs that made his reputation. The reggae influence is more noticeable here—several tunes have the familiar "one drop" riddim in evi-

dence—and the electric guitar is a bit more prominent in the mix, with a raw, twangy quality that brings to mind a late-night 1950s doo-wop recording session.

the rest:
Sounds of Sudan ♫♫♫♪

influences:
◀◀ Khalil Farrah, Ibrahim El Kashif

▶▶ Abdel Gadir Salim, Mustafa Sidahmed

j. poet

Ephat Mujuru

Zimbabwean mbira dzavadzimu ("of ancestral spirits") music
Born August 6, 1950, in Mujuru village, Makoni, Rusape, eastern Zimbabwe. Based in Harare, Zimbabwe.

Ephat Muchandibaya Mujuru specializes in playing the *mbira*, which he makes himself. The hand-forged, iron-keyed portable percussion instrument sits on a small wood base. Sometimes referred to as a "thumb piano" by Western listeners, the thumb and index fingers pluck the keys. A large gourd amplifies the sound and bottle caps add the characteristic timbral buzz. Mujuru often plays while singing or telling a story and he is equally at home vocalizing about animals, ancestors, or answering machines, in English or Shona. His repertoire features traditional material used in religious ceremonies called *biras*, in which the mbira's job is to summon the spirits of forebears. He also composes original pieces; his songs are sometimes political and sometimes popular in their source material.

Mujuru was a strong influence on Thomas Mapfumo, who in defiance of the colonial system brought mbira patterns to the guitar in his *chimurenga* or "struggle" music celebrating Shona culture. Mujuru also influenced and has played with the Balafon Marimba Ensemble, appearing on one track of their eponymous 1990 Shanachie release. The music of Zimbabwe has been passed down to Mujuru through a long, distinguished family line, and he is especially known for his work in spiritual ceremony. Naturally, given this field of expression, he is committed to preserving traditional Shona culture. He spearheaded a revival of it, playing a large part in the foundation of the first National Dance Troupe of Zimbabwe and more recently working with traditional Zimbabwean stories and music in a series of books and cassettes. Mujuru has taught African instruments at the Zimbabwe College of Music and at the University of Washington. The latter occurred while he lived in the U.S. from 1982 to 1985; at that time he also received a Master of Arts degree. Far from a stereotypical academic, he also performs pop songs in his band Spirit of the People.

In addition to his concert work as a soloist and bandleader, the charismatic Mujuru—who is dedicated to introducing the mbira to the whole world—has performed with Mapfumo, Joan Armatrading, Eurythmics, Harry Belafonte, and Fela Kuti. After hearing Mujuru play to a packed house at the Filmore in San Francisco, the famed Fela said, "This is the very first time I have ever listened to an opening act." Mujuru has appeared on television and radio in the U.S., Europe, and Africa, and at festivals in Asia and Australia. His extensive tours throughout North America and Europe have included concerts at Carnegie Hall, Yale University, and the University of Oslo. His first trip to the U.S. was especially memorable for Mujuru, who captured the experience thus: "An iron horse took me to a place with iron beds. I went across the ocean, and the earth and the heaven became one; it was America. When I woke up, I asked: 'Where are the cowboys?' But I was in New York."

what to buy: A recent album featuring Mujuru as a soloist, *Ancient Wisdom* 𝄢𝄢𝄢𝄢 (Music of the World, 1998, prod. Bob Haddad) is a good introduction to the mbira, with a mixture of traditional and original pieces.

what to buy next: *Shona Spirit* 𝄢𝄢𝄢𝄢 (Music of the World, 1996, prod. Bob Haddad), a collaboration with fellow Zimbabwean Dumisani Maraire, is another worthwhile set.

the rest:
Rhythms of Life—Ephat Mujuru 𝄢𝄢𝄢𝄢 (Lyrichord, 1990)

influences:
◀◀ The Mujuru family

▶▶ Thomas Mapfumo and Blacks Unlimited, the Bhundu Boys

see also: *Fela Kuti, Thomas Mapfumo*

Iris Brooks

Hugh Mundell
Reggae, roots reggae
Born 1962, in Kingston, Jamaica. Died 1983, in Kingston, Jamaica.

Hugh Mundell was shot dead at age 21, in a dispute over the ownership of a refrigerator. The shooting took place while Mundell sat in his car, with his close friend Junior Reid watching helplessly from the back seat. Mundell's recorded works were extraordinary for one so young, and we can only guess how he might have developed. Mundell had been making music since the age of 13, when he debuted with the single "Africa Must Be Free by 1983"—still his most famous song and the title track to his first album. The earliest performer in Jamaica to take an anti-apartheid stance, Mundell's gesture soon become a popular sentiment. The subject matter of his music was consistently pacifistic, with a strong roots feel communicated by his breathy alto, the voice audibly breaking with emotion: "Africa must be free/by the year-hear 1983/we have worked for the white man

in the blazing sun/no more slavery, no more brutality." The message is all the more profound coming from someone so young. Along with Junior Delgado, Mundell was the young protégé of producer Augustus Pablo. After working with Pablo, Mundell recorded with Junjo Lawes and Prince Jammy. He even produced Junior Reid's debut single, "Speak the Truth," on his own Muni Music label, after which Reid went on to great commercial success. Mundell's later hits included "That Little Short Man" and "Jah Say the Time Has Come," a tragic prophecy of his bloody end.

what to buy: Mundell's biggest impact was with *Africa Must Be Free by 1983* 𝄢𝄢𝄢𝄢 (RAS, 1978/1989, prod. Hugh Mundell), but at least as compelling is the deeply moving *Blackman's Foundation* 𝄢𝄢𝄢𝄢𝄢 (Shanachie, 1989, prod. Hugh Mundell, Augustus Pablo), nine tracks thick with reverb, words of protest, and prayer to Jah. As Mundell's voice matured his recordings became stronger, though they lacked the endearing quality of his fragile alto. *Blackman's Foundation* features Pablo's famed melodica-playing and spotlights Mundell singing assertive slogans like "Black on black/black some more."

the rest:
Arise 𝄢𝄢𝄢 (Network, 1994)

influences:
◀◀ Bob Marley, Yabby You

▶▶ Buju Banton, Israel Vibration

see also: *Augustus Pablo*

David Poole

Maryam Mursal /Waaberi
Somali jazz
Born 1950, in Galcaio, Somalia. Based in Denmark.

"I love music with a groove," Maryam Mursal says. "My songs start with Somali music; I play out the rhythms on congas or *oud* (prototypical lute), and maintain a traditional style while making it more modern, so young people can dance to it. In Somalia there's no clash between traditional and modern music. I like Dolly Parton, Etta James, Michael Jackson, anyone who puts feeling in the music, but if I borrow from them, I do it in a Somali way." Somalia is Mursal's birthplace, a country best known in the West for the U.S. military's ill-fated intervention in a civil war that dragged on after they left. Although her mother once threatened her with a knife to make her stop singing, Mursal's desire for a music career was fierce. At 17 she joined Waaberi, Somalia's national musical theater; she'd already been singing in nightclubs for three

Maryam Mursal

years, pioneering "Somali jazz," a fusion of international grooves and traditional music. "Our music combined the rhythms of Black Africa and Arabic Africa, India and China," Mursal explains. "I was from a well-to-do family. I knew the Beatles and Ray Charles and put it together with my music." Mursal fled during the civil war, walking her children across Kenya and Ethiopa to Djibouti, where the UN arranged her passage to Denmark. There she met Søren Kjœr Jensen, her collaborator on *The Journey*, an album aimed at the international market, and *New Dawn*, a traditional set recorded with the surviving members of Waaberi. "Peter Gabriel thought traditional music would be a good way to introduce Maryam," Jensen says. "We rounded up the musicians from Waaberi that had escaped the war and moved to Europe, to do *New Dawn* in a traditional style." For *The Journey*, the album that made Mursal a leading world-music diva, Jensen added some digital polish to her Somali jazz sound. "Lie Lei," a traditional children's song, floats Mursal's husky alto over a hip-house track sprinkled with samples from an old Yma Sumac album, and a bouncy Somali rhythm. "It's modern," Mursal admits, "but the core feeling is pure Somali."

what's available: On *The Journey* ♫♫♫♫ (RealWorld, 1998, prod. Simon Emmerson, Martin Rusell, Søren Kjœr Jensen) Mursal's passionate vocals are supported by a stellar cast that includes some of the Arab world's top session players, members of Waaberi, and her Danish touring band. The clash of popular and traditional impulses produces some thrilling moments. *New Dawn* ♫♫♫♫ (RealWorld, 1998, prod. Simon Emmerson, Søren Kjœr Jensen) is the first album of traditional Somalian music released in the West; Mursal's vocals highlight the solid playing of Somalia's top folk musicians, now in exile in Denmark.

influences:
Etta James, Ray Charles, Fairouz, Umm Kulthum

j. poet

Junior Murvin
Roots reggae
Born 1949, in Port Antonio, Jamaica. Based in London, England.

With his trademark eerie, expressive falsetto, Junior Murvin had some minor success in the late '60s covering Curtis Mayfield tunes under the name Junior Soul. In 1972, backed by the excellent Crystalites, he recorded the single "Solomon" for Derrick Harriott, which would later be remade and reconstructed by Lee "Scratch" Perry for the landmark *Police and Thieves* LP. In 1976, after years of struggle with his career, Murvin planted himself outside of Perry's studio—the tiny, magical shack called the Black Ark, a place where many aspiring musicians patiently waited and competed to be recognized by the diminutive sorcerer/producer. One day Perry overheard Murvin singing "Police and Thieves," a tune inspired by the political violence, death, and lawlessness that gripped Jamaica at the time. Perry, who was also known as "The Upsetter," immediately called Murvin into the Ark and conceived a murky, creepy accompaniment for the timely tune. The single was released in a matter of weeks, held the #1 spot in Jamaica for nearly the rest of the year, and became an underground anthem in England, where riots and chaos imploded the Notting Hill Carnival that same year. To be sure, as nations all over the world were gripped by racial tension, the song was recognized as an international plea for peace, rights, and order. Island's Mango subsidiary then signed Murvin with the agreement that Perry would produce his debut. Released in 1977, the *Police and Thieves* LP stands today as a mystical, border-crossing Rasta masterpiece. The record was instantly revered by protest movements across the globe; legendary Brit punk-rockers the Clash even covered the title track on their eponymous '77 debut. Though it is true that *Police and Thieves* depends heavily on Perry's spacey, zero-gravity mix, it is Murvin's singular voice and startling scats that give the album such a compelling, apocalyptic feel. Murvin never again equaled the artistic or popular success of this debut. In the late '70s, he waxed sides for Michael "Mikey Dread" Campbell and scored a minor hit with "Cool Out Son" for Joe Gibbs. Unfortunately, his solid '80s records for the U.K. label Greensleeves—*Muggers in the Street* and *Apartheid*—are currently out-of-print. However, Murvin will forever be remembered in the annals of Jamaican music—and world music—for the foreboding, enigmatic classic that marked the zenith of his career.

what to buy: The centerpiece of *Police and Thieves* ♪♪♪♪ (Mango, 1977, prod. Lee "Scratch" Perry) is, of course, the title cut. Murvin's cool, understated falsetto floats amidst—and subtly cuts through—Perry's skulking, humid, black-cloud atmosphere. But it is Murvin's electrifying, heartstopping mid-song soprano scat which makes this one of the most hypnotic and thrilling reggae songs ever recorded. "Roots Train," "Tedious," "False Teachin'," and "Workin' in the Cornfield" are also standouts on this essential roots reggae document.

the rest:
Bad Man Posse ♪♪♪ (Dread at the Controls, 1982)
Muggers in the Street ♪♪♪ (Greensleeves, 1984)
Apartheid ♪♪♪ (Greensleeves, 1986)
Signs and Wonder ♪♪ (Live and Learn, 1989)

post-soca

The past 10 years or so have seen a plethora of offshoots and upstarts in the *soca* genre (itself a descendent of calypso), many of which—like "ragga soca," with its obligatory gravel-voiced deejay bridge—reflect the Pan-Caribbean popularity of Jamaican dancehall and ragga (digital reggae) music. Other variants include "rapso," a diasporic cousin of U.S. rap and Anglo-Jamaican dub poetry pioneered by Rasta performance poet Brother Resistance; "ring bang," which emphasizes the raw, bottle-and-spoon sound of Carnival's spontaneous "Jouvert" (opening morning) bands; and "binghi," a catch-all form incorporating influences from house, techno, and R&B. Arguably the most significant phenomenon is the emergence of "chutney soca," which inflects the soca beat with *tassa* drumming, *filmi* music, and other traditions of Trinidad's enormous ethnic Indian population—most obviously the earlier "chutney" genre. As its name indicates, chutney is itself a creole blend of folk and popular sources, both sacred and secular, which acquired a name only in the late 1960s. Just as fittingly, it is often spicily risqué. Once associated with female-dominated social occasions, chutney territory is now shared by women and men. Stars in the chutney and chutney-soca firmament include the venerable trailblazers Sundar Popo and Cecil Fonrose, as well as Drupatee Ramgoonai, Sonny Mann, Sally Edwards, Brother Marvin (whose 1996 hit "Jahagi Bhai" signaled chutney soca's breakthrough into the mainstream), and two-time winner of the coveted Chutney Soca Monarch festival title Rikki Jai. A worthy introduction to the genre is *Hot & Spicy Chutney* ♪♪♪♪ (Music Club, 1998).

Michael Eldridge

worth searching for: *Arkology* ♪♪♪♪ (Island, 1997, prod. Lee Perry) is pure dub and reggae lifeblood. Those who submit to this "Scratch" transfusion will have the added benefit of some amazing, previously unreleased Junior Murvin performances coursing through their veins. These include the sizzling "Bad

Weed," the restored mix of "Roots Train" (with a maniacal dee-jay version by Dillinger), an extended mix of "Tedious," and of course, "Police and Thieves," which is presented back-to-back with its instrumental version (Glen DaCosta's "Magic Touch"), deejay version (Jah Lion's #1 Jamaican hit "Soldier and Police War"), and phase-shifter-laden dub version (the Upsetters' stunningly trippy "Grumblin' Dub").

influences:

◀◀ Curtis Mayfield, Alton Ellis, Derrick Harriott, Junior Byles, the Abyssinians

▶▶ Alpha Blondy, the Clash, Lucky Dube, Michael Rose, Triston Palmer, Linton Kwesi-Johnson, African Head Charge, Aswad

see also: *Mikey Dread, Joe Higgs, Lee "Scratch" Perry*

Todd Shanker

Musical Youth

Pop-reggae

Formed 1978, in Birmingham, England. Disbanded 1985.

Junior Waite, lead vocals; Dennis Seaton, lead vocals (1981–85); Patrick Waite, vocals; Kelvin Grant, vocals; Michael Grant, vocals; Frederick Waite, lead vocals (1978–79). (All members are from England.)

Musical Youth formed while four of five original members were attending Duddleston Manor School in Birmingham, England; this first version of the band featured Michael Grant and his brother Kelvin, along with the sibling duo of Junior and Patrick Waite—sons of Frederick Waite, a founding member of legendary Jamaican vocal group the Techniques and, in the beginning, Musical Youth's lead singer. The band's debut single, "Political" b/w "Generals," sparked considerable local interest and led to a career-bolstering appearance on John Peel's famed BBC radio show. In late 1981 the Youth signed a major-label deal with MCA and Dennis Seaton stepped in as lead singer; the senior Waite became the band's manager. In 1982 they released their greatest hit, the truly infectious, pop-smoothed reggae joint "Pass the Dutchie," a version of the Mighty Diamonds' "Pass the Kouchie" on Jackie Mittoo's immortal "Full Up" rhythm. This bowdlerized cover slickly switched the *patois* expression "kouchie" (ganja joint) to the less offensive "dutchie" (a cooking pot). The song reached #1 on the U.K. charts, was Top 10 Stateside, and still stands as one of the best-selling reggae singles ever. The follow-ups—"Youth of Today" and "Never Gonna Give You Up"—lacked the song quality and sales quantity of "Dutchie," but were minor hits, this time just in the U.K. Succeeding singles—"Unconditional Love" with Donna Summer, "Sixteen," and a wretched cover of Desmond Dekker's "Shanty Town (007)"—sold decently in Eng-

land, but nonetheless marked the beginning of the band's descent into virtual anonymity. Seaton left in 1985 to pursue a solo career. In 1993, plans for the now-obligatory "reunion tour" ended when Patrick Waite suddenly died—apparently of natural causes—while in police custody on drug charges. "Pass the Dutchie" was recently resurrected as a prominent selection in the film *The Wedding Singer.*

what to buy: *Anthology* 𝄞𝄞𝄞 (One Way, 1994, prod. various) of course contains the undeniably catchy and zestful "Pass the Dutchie." Little Junior's agile toasting—sprinkled with exclamations like "bim," "oink," and "ribbit," lifted from dancehall acts like Lone Ranger and Papa Michigan & General Smiley—was always the best part of this otherwise weakling reggae band. He gets his due on solid cuts like "Mash It the Youthman, Mash It" and "Children of Zion." This exhaustive single-disc compilation also includes the band's lowlight, "Whatcha Talking 'Bout," a moronic appropriation of the laugh-track inducing catch phrase of Gary Coleman's pint-sized character Arnold on the stomach-spinning sitcom *Diff'rent Strokes.*

the rest:

Youth of Today 𝄞𝄞𝄞 (MCA, 1982)
Different Style 𝄞𝄞 (MCA, 1983)

solo outings:

Dennis Seaton:
Imagine That 𝄞𝄞 (Bellaphon U.K., 1989)

influences:

◀◀ The Techniques, the Mighty Diamonds, Lone Ranger, Papa Michigan & General Smiley, Jackie Mittoo, the Revolutionaries, the Roots Radics

▶▶ New Edition, Hanson

see also: *The Techniques*

Todd Shanker

Musicians of the Nile

Traditional Nile region and Egyptian Gypsy music

Formed in the remote past, in Abu-al-Djud (modern-day Luxor), Egypt. Based in Egypt.

Metqâl Qenâwi Metqâl, rabâbah; Shamandi Tewfiq Metqâl, vocals; Yussef 'ali Bakâsh, vocals; Mohammed Murâd Mejâlî, rabâbah; suffâra, vocals; Yunis al-Hilâli, rabâbah; Mustafâ 'Abd al'-aziz, arghûl; Hanafi Mohamed 'ali, tablah; Qenâwi Bakhit Qenâwi, mizmar; Ramadan Atta Muhammed, mizmar; Jadd al-Rabb Mahmûd, tablah baladi. (All members are from Egypt.)

The Musicians of the Nile are members of a Luxor clan gifted in music, so-called "Charcoal Gypsies" descended from Nubian slaves and Gypsy minorities in Egypt. Veterans of the world-music scene, they made their first international appearance at

France's Chateauvallon Jazz Festival in 1975, and played the inaugural festival of the popularizing WOMAD (World of Music, Arts and Dance) organization in 1983. Their instrumentals and passionate epic ballads, like much music from the Nile valley, feature strong, visceral rhythms played on drums like the clay *tablah,* and pervasive hypnotic drones provided by *mizmar* oboes, *arghûl* double-reed clarinets, or *rabâbah* spike fiddles.

what to buy: The Musicians' first RealWorld CD, *Luxor to Isna* ♫♫♫ (RealWorld, 1989), enchants with mesmerizing ensemble instrumentals such as "Love Is as Vast as a River" and "The Tall Palm Tree," as well as solos like "Everyone Has Had a Broken Heart," on which the arghûl provides both the drone and the melody with the help of its double-reed conformation and the circular breathing technique of soloist Mustafa 'Abd al'-aziz.

what to buy next: Emphasizing the epic vocal ballads over the instrumentals, *Luxor*'s follow-up, *Charcoal Gypsies* ♫♫♫ (RealWorld, 1996), is a good complement to its predecessor. While the music is enjoyable, the accompanying liner notes by Alain Weber tend toward the gratuitous, claiming, for example, that Weber "discovered" the group—one is tempted to ask whether they knew they were musicians prior to Weber's arrival.

worth searching for: Fans of this outfit will also enjoy *The Music of Upper and Lower Egypt* ♫♫♫ (Rykodisc, 1984, prod. Mickey Hart) and *Music of the Nile Valley* ♫♫♫ (Lyrichord, prod. Alain Weber), both field recordings of various ensembles from the region.

influences:

◄ Music of the Nawar, Masalib, and Halab Egyptian Gypsies

► Soundtracks of Peter Gabriel

see also: *Salamat*

Jeffrey Muhr

Sabah Habas Mustapha

Dangdut, kacapi-suling
Born in the town of Szegerely, somewhere in the Balkans. Based in Berlin, Germany.

The youngest brother of the mysterious extended family of musicians known as 3 Mustaphas 3, Sabah is said to have cut his musical teeth playing gigs with them in Szegerely's only club, the Crazy Loquat. Reportedly hidden in refrigerators and spirited into England from Szegerely in 1982, the Mustaphas exploded onto the world-music scene with their tongue-in-cheek, crazy-quilt brand of musical mastery, cutting several hit albums before going into retirement in 1991. Since then, Sabah has performed as a guest musician with various groups, produced albums for the Klezmatics and Ali Hassan Kuban, and traveled to Indonesia, where he recorded two CDs of refined, romantic

Indonesian pop with the help of local musicians. The title song from the first of these, *Denpasar Moon,* was one of the country's biggest pop hits in memory.

what to buy: Drawing upon Sundanese (Western Javanese) *kacapi-suling* (or "zither-flute") and Western pop and jazz idioms, and topped by Sabah's suave vocals, *Jalan Kopo* ♫♫♫ (Omnium, 1997, prod. Sabah Habas Mustapha) provides plenty of delightfully smooth music. A group of top-quality Sundanese musicians Sabah calls the "Jugala All-Stars" provide washes of Indonesian metallophone, flute, and zither that give the music a strong Javanese flavor. Though the CD has a more unique texture than *Denpasar Moon,* one still wishes for something a little less urbane and a bit more impulsive.

what to buy next: *Denpasar Moon* ♫♫♫ (Piranha, 1994, prod. Sabah Habas Mustapha, Kensuke Shiina) brings together shimmering Indonesian *dangdut* pop with some Latin and African touches. Sabah sings on romantic themes and revisits "Singe Tema," a Kenyan *taarab* tune that was covered by the Mustaphas.

influences:

◄ 3 Mustaphas 3, David Sylvian, Bryan Ferry

see also: *3 Mustaphas 3*

Jeffrey Muhr

Mutabaruka

Dub poetry
Born Allen Hope, in Kingston, Jamaica. Based in St. James, Jamaica.

Like Linton Kwesi Johnson, Mutabaruka is among the most respected practitioners of dub poetry—reggae's answer to "spoken word." Muta (as he is widely known) was trained as an electrician and worked for the Jamaican Telephone Company in the early 1970s, but in 1974 he moved from urban Kingston to rural Jamaica and devoted much of his time to writing books of Rastafarian-based poems. Although the artist was combining poetry and music as early as 1973, it wasn't until the early '80s that his recording career really got going. Muta's debut single, "Everytime I 'ear de Soun'," fared well in Jamaica, and he enjoyed much international attention with 1983's *Check It,* his first studio album. Incendiary, angrily socio-political, and influenced by the teachings of Marcus Garvey, *Check It* vehemently spoke out against racial oppression and set the militant tone for subsequent albums Muta recorded in the '80s and '90s. In 1998 he organized and led the Roots All-Stars jam, but the project received a lukewarm response from critics, who didn't seemed to feel it met his solo work's high standards. The dub poet commands a small following in the U.S. and a large one in the Caribbean and Europe, though he has refused to tone his lyrics down to reach pop audiences.

what to buy: Mutabaruka has never recorded a bad album, but his most essential releases are *Check It* 𝄞𝄞𝄞𝄞 (Alligator, 1983, prod. Mutabaruka), *Outcry* 𝄞𝄞𝄞𝄞 (Shanachie, 1984, prod. Mutabaruka), and *The Mystery Unfolds* 𝄞𝄞𝄞𝄞 (Shanachie, 1987, prod. Mutabaruka). Each of these efforts illustrates the uncompromising nature of Muta's lyrics—never one to record fluff, he turns his wrath on capitalists and socialists alike. But even if you don't agree with all of Muta's Rastafarian/Black Nationalist politics, the urgency he brings to these albums makes them quite compelling.

what to buy next: A "best of" anthology, *The Ultimate Collection* 𝄞𝄞𝄞𝄞 (Shanachie, 1996, prod. Mutabaruka), paints an impressive picture of Muta's Shanachie output though it doesn't tell the whole story. Essential tracks such as "Outcry," "Angola Invasion," and "Blacks in America" are missing, but gems like "Bun Dung Babylon," "Walking on Gravel," and "Witeman Country" (Shanachie includes a live version from 1989) are nothing to complain about. *Black Wi Blak . . . k . . . k* 𝄞𝄞𝄞𝄞 (Shanachie, 1991, prod. Mutabaruka) and *Melanin Man* 𝄞𝄞𝄞𝄞 (Shanachie, 1994, prod. Mutabaruka) aren't quite in a class with *Outcry* or *Check It,* but seasoned Muta fans will tell you that they're well worth acquiring nonetheless.

solo outings:
The Roots All-Stars:
Gathering of the Spirits 𝄞𝄞𝄞 (Shanachie, 1998)

influences:
◀◀ U-Roy, I-Roy, Big Youth, King Tubby

see also: *Linton Kwesi Johnson, Ini Kamoze, Oku Onuora*

Alex Henderson

Muzsikás

See: Márta Sebestyén

Mynta

Jazz, Indian classical
Formed 1979, in Sweden. Based in Sweden.

Fazal Qureshi (India), tabla; Nandkishor Muley (India), santoor; Anders Hagberg (Sweden), saxophone, flute; Max Ahman (Sweden), guitar; Mikael Nilsson (Sweden), percussion; Christian Paulin (Sweden), bass.

This exciting group creates a hybrid of jazz and Indian classical music similar to that of John McLaughlin and Shakti. Mynta's four Swedes and two Indians synthesize a kind of chamber-jazz, mixing the exotic sounds of the *santoor* hammered dulcimer and *tabla* drum with standard jazz instruments. The group's most distinctive sonic voice is sax/flute player Anders

Hagberg, and the combination of Fazal Qureshi's tabla and Mikael Nilsson's Western percussion delivers a distinctive rhythmic punch.

what to buy: *Hot Madras* 𝄞𝄞𝄞𝄞 (Miramar, 1995/Blue Flame, 1998) contains some of Mynta's most effective and evocative blendings of East and West. Recommended are the title tune, with its lively flute and tabla textures, and the slow, meditative "Mbira."

what to buy next: *First Summer* 𝄞𝄞𝄞 (Blue Flame, 1998) is Mynta's latest disc, with perhaps a bit more of a new-age feel than their earlier works.

the rest:
Indian Time 𝄞𝄞𝄞 (Intuition, 1997)

influences:
◀◀ Shakti, Ornette Coleman

see also: *Shakti*

Michael Parrish

Naftule's Dream

Modern klezmer
Formed 1993, in Boston, MA, USA. Based in Boston, MA, USA.

Glenn Dickson, clarinet; David Harris, trombone; Michael McLaughlin, piano, accordion; Pete Fitzpatrick, electric guitar; John Manning, tuba; Eric Rosenthal, drums. (All members are from USA.)

Shirim is a Boston-based traditional klezmer orchestra specializing in Yiddish theater music of the 1920s—and Naftule's Dream is Shirim's alter ego. While Shirim continues to play weddings and bar mitzvahs, Naftule's Dream plays cutting-edge klezmer in alternative clubs. The group's front line, clarinetist Glenn Dickson and trombonist David Harris, are two of the more quirky and experimental musicians in their field. Between the moans, shrieks, and horse-laughs of the brass and the vibrato of Fitzpatrick's electric guitar, Naftule's Dream is creating a dramatic new shift in the klezmer landscape.

what to buy: The wildly inventive *Smash, Clap!* 𝄞𝄞𝄞𝄞 (Tzadik, 1998, prod. Glenn Dickson) suggests new directions for collective improvisation in the klezmer genre. The band reminds listeners of the best moments of Lester Bowie's Brass Fantasy on tracks like "Friends of Kafka." The jittery "Free Klez 3 & 4" showcases Dickson's virtuosity on the clarinet. And Michael McLaughlin plays the hippest accordion licks you've ever heard.

what to buy next: *In Search of the Golden Dreydl* 𝄞𝄞𝄞 (Tzadik, 1997) boasts several arresting tracks such as Dickson's "Spin-

Najma

oza of Market Street" and Harris's rave-up of the classic "Oy Tate" by Naftule Brandwein (the klezmer pioneer whose name the band bears). But the rest lacks focus, as if the players are still in the midst of discovering their direction.

worth searching for: Despite its title, *Naftule's Dream* 🎵🎵🎵 (Northeastern, 1993) is a hard-to-find *Shirim* album of Brandwein tunes, some done with a hint of the alternative improvisation that was to come.

influences:
⏪ Naftule Brandwein, John Zorn

Aaron Howard

Najma

Indian pop, Indian light classical, worldbeat
Born in London, England. Based in London, England.

Najma Akhtar is the daughter of Indian immigrant parents and grew up speaking English, although she loved singing along to the *filmi* music (soundtracks of popular Indian movies) her par-

ents played around the house. On an extended visit to her grandparents, the young singer learned Urdu and began investigating *ghazals*—short poems that illuminate the agony and ecstasy of romantic love, some of which date back to the 7th century. Poets recite these lyrics and compose new ones at social gatherings, but the highest form of the art is the sung ghazal, and singers are encouraged to write their own music for these timeless gems. Najma began composing her own tunes, and in 1984 she became the first Asian woman to win a song competition (in England people with roots in India are called Asian, to distinguish them from members of the large West Indian community). Soon after, she was approached about making an album. Although it took three years, *Qareeb* broke new ground for its combination of traditional Indian melodies and Western instruments. This was followed by two more sets that mixed Indian folk and light classical music with Western arrangements and instruments. The singer's latest album is a full-out worldbeat exploration of the filmi songs of S.D. Burman, one of India's great composers of popular music.

what to buy: Najma's vocals are always pleasing on *Qareeb* 🎵🎵🎵 (Shanachie, 1988, prod. Iain Scott, Bunt Stafford Clark), with enough Western influence to make them palatable to those who are put off by the high, keening tones many female Indian vocalists affect. The jazzy sax and keyboard arrangements provide another entry for Westerners.

what to buy next: *Forbidden Kiss* ♪♪♪♪ (Shanachie, 1996, prod. Najma, Chris Rael) is worldbeat with an Indian flavor; Najma collaborates with a trio of British and Austrian rockers to update the tunes of S.D. Burman. Surf guitar, sitar, reggae, swooping Indian string parts played on the synthesizer, and Najma's torchy vocals create an exciting exploration of a form little known outside the Indian community and Western pop-cultists.

the rest:
Pukar ♪♪♪♪ (Mondo Melodia, 1997)

influences:
◄◄ Asha Bhosle, Lata Mangeshkar

see also: *Page & Plant*

j. poet

R. Carlos Nakai

Native flute, jazz, new age, worldbeat
Born April 16, 1946, in Flagstaff, AZ, USA. Based in Tuscon, AZ, USA.

R. Carlos Nakai (Navaho-Ute) has made traditional Native American flute a part of the musical landscape without diluting his spiritual or musical beliefs. "I'm little interested in integrating my culture into the greater American focus," Nakai says. "I'm bringing people into the Native tradition, not taking Native tradition to them."

Nakai was raised in the American West, moving from place to place with his extended family, which included migrant workers and farmers. He'd wanted to play flute since he was a boy, but "when I was forced into the Western music discipline by a teacher in grade school, I was told that men don't play flutes." Nakai was given a trumpet, but he took to the instrument and practiced hard, with an eye toward getting a classical music education at Julliard or Berklee. In 1970, while serving in the navy, he was in a traffic accident and smashed his mouth. After returning home he continued playing. "My lip was in no condition for fine performance, but during that time I remembered a flute song I heard back in 1957 by William Horn Cloud. Soon after, I met a Comanche flute-maker who was trading his flutes for material objects, and that set me on the journey I'm still on."

When Nakai started playing flute in 1982, the tradition was fading. "Doc Tate, Woodrow Hainey and Tom Ware were the only ones playing traditional flute. Later on I discovered Kevin Locke, but what they were doing wasn't getting much atten-

tion, even from Natives. A few non-Native flute-makers were working with the instrument, but they were trying to reconfigure it into a recorder." Nakai researched traditional music and began playing gigs. In 1983 he produced his first recording, which he put out on 250 cassettes, to send to friends and booking agents. Ray Boley, head of Canyon Records, heard the cassette and offered Nakai a recording contract. "Being a Native, and knowing how things work in the white man's world, I decided to bone up on the legalities of the record business. Finally, I decided it wouldn't hurt to let them put it out." The album was called *Changes* and included three traditional songs as well as 12 songs Nakai had composed in a traditional style. "I figured it might sell a few copies for about a year before it died out. I doubted it would be accepted by people outside my own culture, but it's still selling 16 years later. I'm still attempting to understand why it became so popular."

Nakai continues to develop and refine his playing, gradually "using some of the music of the outer culture, when it furthered my own perspective." Nakai began to make a greater impact on the "outer culture" with *Natives,* a collaboration with pianist Peter Kater that topped *Billboard*'s new-age chart in 1990. Since then Nakai has branched out further in almost every musical direction, including new age, classical, jazz, and worldbeat. "African, Latin, and Native styles were impacted by colonialism," Nakai says. "But Don Cherry (Comanche) and Jim Pepper (Kaw) encouraged me to keep taking from the outer culture to revitalize our own." Nakai's excursions have made him traditional Native music's first superstar, and the first artist to earn a gold record for an album of native music without any new-age or rock flavoring, 1989's *Canyon Trilogy.* "The Native flute is made from materials that are part of this land, and its sound seems to reconnect people to the land. Even if your ancestors were European, you are now part of this land, which you may not like to hear coming from a Native, but you have to learn who you now are, so we can come together to honor the land."

what to buy: *Changes* ♪♪♪♪♪ (Canyon, 1983, prod. R. Carlos Nakai) is the album that started Nakai's rise to superstardom, and it is a good first choice for listeners. The simplicity and spiritual power that drives his music is already in place. The purity of his sustained notes and his seemingly endless ability to improvise give the music a tranquil, timeless quality.

what to buy next: Those who think Nakai's music is stuck in a new-age rut will be surprised by *Kokopelli's Cafe* ♪♪♪♪ (Canyon, 1996, prod. R. Carlos Nakai, Will Chipman, J. David Muñiz, Amo Chip, Robert Doyle), credited to the Nakai Quartet. This intercultural group plays world-jazz, with inventive arrangements that mix bits of funk, Afro-Beat, and Native American and Latin rhythms for a smooth, swinging session. Nakai has close to 30 albums out on various labels, ranging from new age to jazz to classical. Take your pick from the rest: *Jackalope* 𝄞𝄞𝄞 (Canyon, 1986) is an early jazz excursion with keyboard player Larry Yañez and guitarist Steve Cheseborough. *Natives* 𝄞𝄞𝄞 (Silver Wave, 1990) introduced Nakai to the new age movement and remains a bestseller. *Winds of Devotion* 𝄞𝄞𝄞 (Earth Sea, 1998) is a collaboration with Tibetan flautist and healer Nawang Khechog, a free-flowing improvisation based on the healing traditions of Native America and Tibet. *Native Tapestry* 𝄞𝄞 (Canyon, 1994) combines African percussion with James Demars's "classical" orchestrations. *How the West Was Lost* 𝄞𝄞𝄞 (Silver Wave, 1993) is the soundtrack to the PBS series, with music by Peter Kater and Nakai.

influences:

⏪ Woodrow Hainey, Doc Tate, Tom Ware

⏩ Kevin Locke, Mirabal, Andrew Vasquez

see also: *Steve Gorn*

j. poet

Milton Nascimento

Brazilian pop, Brazilian jazz
Born 1942, in Rio de Janeiro, Brazil. Based in Brazil.

Milton Nascimento is one of the most significant figures in Brazilian music, both as performer and composer. His vocal abilities are quite phenomenal, gliding from his normal chest voice up to a seamless falsetto. Nascimento's songs have been performed by jazz artists like Sarah Vaughan, Stan Getz, and the Manhattan Transfer. Born in Rio de Janeiro, he was raised in the Brazilian state of Minas Gerais by his adoptive parents. Nascimento played the accordion as a child but had switched to guitar and bass by the time he was a teenager. He also formed an important long-term musical relationship with keyboard player Wagner Tiso when they both played in the same band. Moving to Belo Horizonte, the capital of Minas Gerais, in 1963, Nascimento played area jazz clubs while attending college. His first big break as a songwriter came in 1966 when a tune he wrote called "Cangmo Do Sal" was performed by the popular Brazilian singer Elis Regina. In 1967 Nascimento was voted best performer at the International Song Festival, and one of his compositions, "Travessia" ("Bridges"), copped second place in the writing competition. In addition to writing many of his own songs, Nascimento has been closely involved with a cadre of poets and musicians from Minas Gerais called "Clube da Esquina" or the "Corner Club." As a collective, the club released albums under the names of fellow singer/writer L. Borges and Nascimento that were as important and revolutionary in the early 1970s as the collaboration between Antonio Carlos Jobim and João Gilberto was in the late 1950s. Nascimento has also been heavily involved with the *nueva canción* ("new song") movement that swept Latin America

in the 1960s and 1970s, working with major figures within the genre such as Pablo Milanes, Silvio Rodriguez, and Mercedes Sosa. The socially conscious aspect of that movement is also reflected in Nascimento's non-musical activities; he is a committed political activist speaking for the indigenous peoples of the Amazon, the environment, and Amnesty International. Jazz musicians started becoming aware of his prodigious talents in the late 1960s, when he toured Mexico and the United States in the company of João Gilberto and Art Blakey. Nascimento's first appearance on a U.S. jazz album was on Wayne Shorter's 1974 *Native Dancer*. Shorter returned the favor on Nascimento's 1976 release *Milton*, which also featured appearances by Herbie Hancock and Raul DeSouza in addition to Brazilian stalwarts Airto Moreira and Toninho Horta. Pianist Barry Harris even wrote a lovely ballad called "Nascimento" that has been performed by Harris and Tommy Flanagan, among others. As he consolidates his position as a giant of 20th century music, millions on the other side of the stage continue to sing his praises too.

what to buy: Jazz aficionados will have to hunt for familiar names like Hubert Laws, Pat Metheny, and Steve Slagle on *Encontros e Despedidas* 𝄞𝄞𝄞 (Polydor, 1986, prod. Mazola), but they are there. The personnel is geared more toward Nascimento's favorite Brazilian musicians and the result more than justifies his choice. This album leans further into the jazz spectrum then many of his works, and tunes like "Portal da Cor" and the title song could tempt hard-core jazzers to check out the rest of his catalog. *Minha Historia* 𝄞𝄞𝄞 (PolyGram Latino, 1994, prod. various) and *The Art of Milton Nascimento* 𝄞𝄞𝄞𝄞 (Verve, 1995, prod. various) are both "best of" compilations, featuring many overlapping tunes. The former has "Travessia," perhaps Nascimento's most famous piece; the latter has 20 songs to *Minha Historia*'s 14. Both retail at about the same price and serve as good introductions.

what to buy next: *Clube da Esquina* 𝄞𝄞𝄞 (World Pacific, 1972, prod. Milton Miranda) is a classic album, with L. Borges and the rest of Clube da Esquina. The album blends pop from Lennon and McCartney, folk-song influences from Minas Gerais, and elements of bossa nova for a heady mixture that influenced the direction of much 1970s Brazilian music. *Nascimento* 𝄞𝄞𝄞 (Warner Bros., 1997, prod. Russ Titelman, Milton Nascimento) finds Nascimento making a retreat from some of the pop aspects of his later albums. It opens with "Louva-a-Deus (The Praying Mantis)," a percussion fest à la Olodum with Nascimento's vocals floating and diving with ease. "Cuerpo y Alma (Body and Soul)" (not the jazz classic) and "E Agora, Rapaz (And What Now, Man?)" have that indefinable swing native to the best Brazilian music in general and Nascimento's tunesmithing in particular. *Tambores de Minas—Ao vivo* 𝄞𝄞𝄞 (WEA Brazil, 1998, prod. Paulo Junqueiro, Milton Nascimento) may be the best-recorded

Milton Nascimento

live set Nascimento has ever released, featuring impressive performances from the leader and his band. Nascimento's mature voice is darker in tone than the one heard in his youth—but that doesn't mean over-the-hill, because the control is still there. Reflective moments ("Ponta de Areia") vie for space with gently rolling semi-ballads ("O Rouxinol"), old classics ("San Vincente"), and percussion-heavy audience-rousers like "Janela para o Mundo." There's even a classy duet with Brazilian pop queen Elis Regina, to open up the show. The crowd, while appreciative, never really interferes with the music.

best of the rest:
Sentinela ✍✍✍✍ (Verve, 1980)
Yauaret J ✍✍✍✍ (Columbia, 1988)
Miltons ✍✍✍✍ (Columbia, 1989)
Missa Dos Quilombos ✍✍✍✍ (Verve, 1992)
Amigo ✍✍✍✍ (Warner Bros., 1996)

worth searching for: *Milton* ✍✍✍✍ (A&M, 1976), not to be confused with 1989's *Miltons,* is a marvelous album that keeps going in and out of print. Originally released in the United States, it's the first full-length album by Nascimento that re-

ceived any real distribution. The players include Wayne Shorter and Herbie Hancock, but the songs are the real reason to hunt this album up. "Cravo e Canela" is a classic.

influences:
⏮ João Gilberto, Baden Powell, Yma Sumac, Heitor Villa-Lobos
⏭ Novos Baianos

see also: *João Gilberto, Antonio Carlos Jobim, Pablo Milanes, Airto Moreira, Olodum, Flora Purim, Elis Regina, Silvio Rodriguez, Mercedes Sosa*

Garaud MacTaggart

Johnny Nash
Pop, reggae-influenced pop
Born August 19, 1940, in Houston, TX, USA. Based in England.

The late 1960s and early 1970s pop singles of Texas-born Johnny Nash had a profound effect on the spread of reggae throughout the world. Although he had recorded several Sam Cooke–inspired tunes between 1957 and 1967, Nash left his greatest impression with his reggae-tinged hits "Hold Me

Tight" (1968) and the chart-topping "I Can See Clearly Now" (1972), the latter recorded with Bob Marley and the Wailers. Nash was one of the first North American artists to record songs by Marley, including "Nice Time," "Guava Jelly," "Reggae on Broadway," and "Stir It Up," which was a Top Ten hit in 1973.

Nash had grown up singing gospel in a local church choir. By the age of 13, his talents were so impressive that he became a featured performer on the Houston television show *Matinee*, singing a mixture of country & western, pop, soul, and calypso tunes. From 1956 to 1963, he sang on Arthur Godfrey's nationally broadcast radio and television shows. Nash recorded his debut single "When a Teenager Sings the Blues" in 1957, and he had a minor hit with "A Very Special Love" the following year. In 1959 he collaborated with Paul Anka and George Hamilton IV on the single "The Ten Commandments"; next followed numerous early-'60s singles for Warner Bros., Argo, and Groove, although Nash's only success of the period came as a composer, when his "What King of Love is This" became a Top 20 hit for Joey Dee and the Starlighters. After leaving Godfrey's show in 1963, he performed in supper clubs throughout the United States. In the late 1960s Nash became fascinated with reggae and began recording in Jamaica, first at Byron Lee's studio in Kingston, and eventually at his own newly built studio and on his own record labels, Joda and Jad. He moved to England in 1971, maintaining his ties to his previous adoptive island too.

what to buy: The best of Nash's Jamaican recordings are sampled on *The Reggae Collection* ♪♪♪ (Epic, 1993, prod. Johnny Nash). Although Nash delivered a weakened brand of reggae, the inclusion of many tracks previously unavailable in the United States makes this a historical document. *The Very Best of Johnny Nash* ♪♪♪ (Black Tiger, 1995, prod. Johnny Nash) reprises 16 tunes that span Nash's entire career. In addition to several tracks recorded in Jamaica, the album includes his soulful interpretation of Sam Cooke's "Cupid," which became a hit in England in 1969.

best of the rest:
Johnny Nash ♪♪♪ (ABC, 1958)
I Can See Clearly Now ♪♪♪ (Sony, 1990)

influences:
◀◀ Sam Cooke, Bob Marley

▶▶ Eric Clapton, the Rolling Stones

Craig Harris

Pandit Pran Nath

North Indian classical, Hindustani, khayal
Born 1918, in Lahore, Pakistan. Died June 13, 1996, in Berkeley, CA, USA.

A figure admired for his total commitment to music, *khayal* (classical) singer Pandit ("Teacher") Pran Nath will be remem-

bered primarily for inspiring the American minimalists La Monte Young and Terry Riley. More generally, he made his mark as a sought-after master of the *Kirana* style of North Indian *raga* singing, with its legendary emphasis on perfect intonation. His teacher, Abdul Wahid Khan, gave the languishing khayal a new lease on life at the turn of the century and subsequently made the Kirana *gharana* (school) a great influence on Indian classical music as well as on Western contemporary music. It's primarily due to the commitment of La Monte Young, visual artist Marian Zazeela, and Terry Riley that anything by Nath was ever recorded, and it's a pity more isn't available.

what's available: *Short Stories* ♪♪♪♪ (Nonesuch Records, 1993, prod. Bob Hurwitz, Judith Sherman, Kronos Quartet) is the only recording of Pandit Pran Nath currently in print. This disc has just one track by Nath, but it's a classic. "Aba Kee Tayk Hamaree (It is My Turn, Oh Lord)" is a slow 11-minute raga, with *tambouras* (four-stringed drone instruments) played by Terry Riley and John Constant, *tabla* drum by Krishna Bhatt, and discrete strings by the Kronos Quartet.

worth searching for: *Ragas of Morning and Night* ♪♪♪♪ (Gramavision/Great Northern Arts, 1991, prod. La Monte Young, Marian Zazeela) is a great recording of "Raga Todi" and "Raga Darbari," but it's hard to locate. Notes by La Monte Young make it a valuable find. Nath is accompanied by *sarangi* (bowed string instrument), tabla, and tamboura, and the latter's predominance in the mix show Young's influence.

influences:
◀◀ Ustad Abdul Wahid Khan

▶▶ Rhys Chatham, Don Cherry, Jon Gibson, Michael Harrison, Bhimsen Joshi, Nazakat Khan, Salamat Ali Khan, Lee Konitz, Terry Riley, Yoshimasa Wada, La Monte Young

see also: *Kronos Quartet*

David Paul

Nathan & the Zydeco Cha Chas

See: Nathan Williams

Native Flute Ensemble

Native American flute
Formed 1990, in and around Santa Fe, NM, and San Antonio, TX, USA. Disbanded 1996.

Jessita Reyes, John Martinez, and Lois Little Bear rotated on Native American instruments such as the Native American flute, Taos drum, Yaqui rain stick, log drum, Apache spirit flute, and Hopi rattle, as well as synthesizers. (All members are from USA.)

Drawing on Native American history, culture, and mythology,

the Native Flute Ensemble developed a sound bordering on both the traditional and the new-age. Heavy use of percussion and soaring flute lines characterize their music, with lush synthesizers occasionally creating a backdrop while at other times the unembellished sound of the native instruments stands alone. The melodies, while traditionally inspired, are almost exclusively originals. The ensemble's recordings revolve around themes, such as the influence of the horse in Native American culture (as represented by the rhythmic sound of thundering hooves on *Riding Thunder*).

what to buy: *Gathering of Shamen* ♪♪♪♪ (Talking Taco, 1993) takes the listener on a trance-like journey, exploring several of the popular ritual sites of Native Americans, including the Black Hills of South Dakota, Canyon de Chelly, and Atitlan in Guatemala. Dynamic use of percussion and evocative flute solos make this recording stand out from the rest. Guest percussionist Eric Casias adds a rare flavor to the last cut with the sound of an ocean drum.

what to buy next: On *Enchanted Canyons* ♪♪♪ (Talking Taco, 1990), the Native Flute Ensemble paints a picture of what it might have been like in the society of the ancient Anasazi. Using the drawings of Kokopelli—the mysterious flute-playing figure shown on countless ancient southwestern rock surfaces and now adorning countless new-age trinkets—as the basis of their belief that native flute was an important part of the culture, they explore the sights and sounds of the surrounding canyons and ruins that remain from this fascinating civilization. The musical picture they create is quite compelling.

the rest:
Ritual Mesa ♪♪♡ (Talking Taco, 1990)
Temple of the Dream Jaguar ♪♪ (Talking Taco, 1991)
Riding Thunder ♪♪♡ (Talking Taco, 1994)

solo outings:
Jessita Reyes:
Deer Dancer (Talking Taco, 1991)

influences:
◀◀ Kitaro, R. Carlos Nakai

Jo Hughey Morrison

Emilio Navaira /Emilio

Tejano, conjunto, country, pop
Born August 23, 1963, in San Antonio, TX, USA. Based in USA.

In the Latin music world, Texan Emilio Navaira is known as the King of *Tejano*, a jaunty blend of German polka, folkloric Mexican music, and traditional country styles with a modern, rock-oriented touch. He first stuck to the accordion-fueled *conjunto*

sound—the rootsier predecessor of Tejano—and struck gold. But later, with his George Strait garb, photogenic looks, and penchant for singing English-language country and rock tunes on his albums and in concert, Navaira dropped the last name and recorded a mainstream country album in Nashville, away from the San Antonio, Texas, base he's accustomed to.

what to buy: *SoundLife* ♪♪♪♡ (EMI Latin, 1994, prod. Raul Navaira, Emilio Navaira, Stuart Dill) crosses the boundaries dividing old-school Mexican rhythms and new, pop-edged hybrids. *Quedate* ♪♪♪♡ (EMI Latin, 1996, prod. Michael Morales, Ron Morales, Raul Navaira, Emilio Navaira, Stuart Dill) delivers the familiar stuff, then successfully experiments with 1970s rock elements and flamenco guitar-laced ballads.

what to avoid: *Life Is Good* ♪♪ (Capitol, 1995, prod. Barry Beckett) doesn't do Emilio justice. His robust, raspy voice struggles to remain vital in the midst of gutless production. Singing a batch of middle-of-the-road songs safely aimed at mainstream country radio, Emilio sounds like he walked into the studio and followed every order given by the producer, not once offering an original idea.

influences:
◀◀ Little Joe, Roberto Pulido, George Strait
▶▶ Rick Orozco, Rick Trevino

Mario Tarradell

Youssou N'Dour

Mbalax
Born 1959, in Dakar, Senegal. Based in Senegal.

Youssou N'Dour is one of West Africa's leading singers. The originator of *mbalax*, a dance-inspiring mixture of African, Caribbean, and Western pop, N'Dour has transformed the music of Senegal into an international phenomenon. Descended from a long line of *griots* (oral historians), N'Dour has sung all of his life. As a youngster, he performed at local gatherings in the impoverished Medina section of Dakar. Shortly after making his professional singing debut—at the age of 12—N'Dour joined the Star Band, one of Senegal's most popular groups. In 1979 he left the band and formed the Étoile de Dakar to play his newly conceived mbalax style. Although the term "mbalax" came from the Wolof language's description of the rhythm traditionally played by the *mbung mbung* drum, N'Dour's approach called for this rhythm to be played on guitar, and for that of the *sabar* drum to be played on guitar and keyboards. Following his first visit to Paris in 1983, N'Dour wrote a tune, "Immigres," that was heard by British vocalist Peter Gabriel. Gabriel was so moved by it that he had N'Dour sing harmony on his recording "In Your Eyes" in 1986, and chose

Youssou N'Dour

N'Dour as the opening act for his worldwide tour the following year. In 1988 N'Dour joined with Gabriel, Bruce Springsteen, Sting, and Tracy Chapman on Amnesty International's Human Rights Now tour, thus advancing his stature as one of the earliest "world music" artists whose success bore out the scope of the term. In the 1990s N'Dour cut down on touring to focus on studio recordings. His apex to date came in 1994 with the hit duet with Nenah Cherry, "7 Seconds," from his album *Wommat—The Guide,* and his internationally broadcast set at the 25th-anniversary Woodstock Festival that same year.

what to buy: *Wommat—The Guide* ♫♫♫ (Chaos, 1994, prod. Boogie Bear) remains N'Dour's most commercially successful album, with the hit "7 Seconds," a unique interpretation of Bob Dylan's "Chimes of Freedom," and several tunes featuring the saxophone playing of Branford Marsalis. The best of N'Dour's late-1980s recordings are reprised on *Hey You: The Essential Collection* ♫♫♫ (Nascente, 1998, prod. Youssou N'Dour).

the rest:
Immigres ♫♫♫♪ (Earthworks, 1988)
Nelson Mandela ♫♫♫♪ (Verve, 1988)
The Lion ♫♫♫♪ (Virgin, 1989)
Set ♫♫♫♪ (Virgin, 1990)
Eyes Open ♫♫♫♪ (40 Acres & A Mule, 1992)
Djamil ♫♫♫♪ (Celluloid, 1997)

worth searching for: Released only in his native Senegal, the two-cassette set *Live '93* ♫♫♫♪ (Studio 2000, 1994, prod. Youssou N'Dour) captures the excitement and dynamic rhythms of N'Dour's live shows.

influences:
◀◀ Star Band, Super Diamono
▶▶ Ismael Lô, Baaba Maal, Orchestre Baobab

see also: *Manu Dibango, Étoile de Dakar, Cheikh Lô, Jimi Mbaye, Alan Stivell*

Craig Harris

Nelson
/Lord Nelson

Soca

Born c. 1930, in Tobago, Trinidad and Tobago. Based in Brooklyn, NY, USA.

Nelson has been a major calypso (and *soca*) artist for almost 40 years, and one of the artists credited with introducing the latter genre (a contraction of SOul and CAlypso) to the world. "I lived in New York City, so it was natural that R&B and Latin music would creep into my songs," Nelson says, "but I don't think any one person invented soca. We all did it together."

After finishing high school in Tobago, Nelson came to the United States to seek his fortune, but six weeks after entering the country, he was drafted and sent to Korea. "I started singing and performing comedy in Army shows," Nelson recalls. "I found out I had a gift for it." After coming back home, Nelson sang with local steel bands in Brooklyn. "We did covers of the popular calypsos of the day. Since I hadn't been back to the islands in years, I had my own way of doing things." Nelson's unique style made him a favorite in Brooklyn's Caribbean community, but he didn't consider composing his own material until he became friends with the Mighty Duke. "Duke was encouraging. He taught me how to compose music, how to write a tight lyric, and encouraged me to continue to develop my style." Nelson's early hits, including "La La," "Stella," and "King Liar," electrified the calypso community with their funky beat. Since Nelson lives in the U.S., he isn't allowed to compete in the Carnival King contests in Trini, but in 1989 he won the title of Uncrowned King in a special competition for calypsonians from off-island. "There is a lot of jealousy in Trinidad," Nelson says. "They don't let singers from other countries compete, but in the long run, it's worked in my favor. I took calypso all over the world—South America, Canada, England, Europe, places the other singers seldom go."

Nelson became one of the few soca artists to get his music distributed in mainstream America when he signed with Shanachie in 1990. They put out two albums that helped introduce him to worldbeat fans, and on his first American release *When the World Turns Around* he added a bit of rap and reggae, as well as some African rhythms, to his international potpourri. "I find all black music inspiring, anything with a good backbeat. I make sure every song has a story, and love to play with words and use double entendres. That way the children can always understand it, while their parents can listen to it on a whole other level."

what to buy: *When the World Turns Around* ♫♫♫♫ (Shanachie, 1990, prod. Granville Straker), a digital remake of *Love You Forever* (originally on the Joker label), is a solid soca outing from one of the music's best practitioners. Nelson's tenor has a unique, gritty quality that's especially effective on his love songs, where he can purr like a kitten or growl like a lion before sliding up to a thrilling falsetto. The band is solid and the tempos are kicking.

what to buy next: The production on *Bring Back the Voodoo* ♫♫♫♫ (Shanachie, 1991, prod. Nelson, Mojah, Eddie Bullen, Michael Gould) is more stripped-down, but the music still sizzles. The set includes a re-make of "Mi Love," one of Nelson's big hits from the mid-1980s.

best of the rest:
We Like It ♫♫♫♫ (B's, 1982)

Hotter Than Hot 🎝🎝🎝 (B's, 1983)
The Chief 🎝🎝🎝 (Shanachie, 1990)

influences:

◄◄ Lord Melody, Mighty Duke, Roaring Lion, Sparrow

►► Machel Montano

j. poet

The New Orleans Klezmer All Stars

Rock-funk klezmer
Formed 1991, in New Orleans, LA, USA. Based in New Orleans, LA, USA.

Ben Ellman, soprano and tenor saxophones, tambourine; Robert Wagner, clarinet, bass clarinet, percussion; Rick Perles, violin (1991–98); Glenn Hartman, accordion, piano, organ, toy piano, prepared piano; Johnathan Freilich (England), acoustic and electric guitars, sleigh bells; Arthur Kastler, acoustic and electric bass, slide whistle, bicycle horn; Stanton Moore, drums; Kevin O'Day, drums. (All members are from USA unless otherwise noted.)

The most rockin' klezmer outfit around, the New Orleans Klezmer All Stars, started out when musicians from several "Big Easy" bands met and jammed. As the group learned more tunes and became a more cohesive unit, they began playing in public. They did the expected wedding and bar mitzvah gigs, but also appeared at bars and night clubs, attracting a diverse crowd ranging from hippies to Jewish grandparents. Their first, eponymous CD was released in 1994, and they won the Big Easy Award for Best Folk Artist in 1994 and 1995. Wider recognition came after successful appearances at the New Orleans Jazz and Heritage Festival; the band hit clubs and concert venues in many major U.S. cities and even played at the Barbican Centre in London, England. But undoubtedly one of All Stars' most special gigs is their annual "unofficial" Mardi Gras parade, the manic "Juloo" parade. Recordings have continued to appear on a regular basis, with later releases showing an increasing emphasis on original material. *Manichalfwitz* was released in 1996, followed by *The Big Kibosh* in 1997. *Fresh Out the Past*, the boys' wildest recording yet, was released in March 1999.

what to buy: *The Big Kibosh* 🎝🎝🎝🎝 (Shanachie, 1997, prod. Joe Ferry, the New Orleans Klezmer All Stars) is the most balanced of the band's four recordings, with a good mix of fast, frantic tunes and slower pieces. It's also the last N.O.K.A.S. album to feature violinist Rick Perles. *Manichalfwitz* 🎝🎝🎝🎝 (Gert Town, 1996, prod. Lizz Farrakhan) was the group's second recorded offering, and the faster tracks sound like klezmer played by a rock/funk band. The roots are there, but the rhythms are speeded up, noisy electric guitar riffs jump in and out, and the sax and clarinet blowing will make the listener think of any-

thing from a rough 'n' ready 1950s rock 'n' roll band to an avant-garde jazz combo.

the rest:
The New Orleans Klezmer All Stars (Stretchy, 1994)
Fresh Out the Past 🎝🎝🎝 (Shanachie, 1999)

influences:

◄◄ Boiled in Lead, Brave Combo, the Neville Brothers, 3 Mustaphas 3

►► The Klezmatics

Ken Roseman

NG La Banda /Nueva Generación (New Generation)

Cuban son, rumba, guaracha, timba, salsa
Formed 1988, in Cuba. Based in Cuba.

Extensive and changeable membership has included: José Luis Cortés, producer, arranger, flute; José Miguel Crego, trumpet; Calixto Oviedo Mulens, drums; Issac Delgado, vocals (1989–91); Mariano Mena Pérez, vocals; Miguel Angel de Armas, keyboards; Feliciano Arango Noa, bass; Rolando Pérez Pérez, alto saxophone; Elpido Chapotín Delgado, trumpet; Pablo Cortéz, bongos; Roldolfo Argudin Justiz, piano; Francisco Antonio (Tony) Calá, vocals; Juan Nogueras Jordan, percussion; Rafael Jenks Jiménez, tenor saxophone; Guillermo Amores Silveiras, guiro. (All members are from Cuba.)

In 1988 a group of graduates from Havana's state conservatory formed the ground-breaking *timba* (contemporary salsa) band Nueva Generación (New Generation)—since known as NG (pronounced "enna-hey") La Banda—to explore Cuban dance music and Latin jazz. Led by José Luis Cortés, known in Cuba as "el Tosco" (the Coarse One), these players had received their classical training during a time when jazz was not wholly accepted and serious musicians did not play dance music in the streets. They originally formed the band to play concert music that would take advantage of their conservatory training, a very precise kind of dance music that was meant to please musicians, critics, and intellectuals. It was a flop.

So, opting for the music of the people, they decided to play what they felt—music for dancers—and that decision led to their great success and their launching the whole timba movement, which builds on the rhythms of *son, guaracha,* and rumba; the same roots as the New York–bred salsa. But with its pronounced syncopation, timba is even easier to dance to. According to Cortés, a flutist who had played with such seminal Cuban outfits as Los Van Van (from 1970 to 1980) and Irakere (from 1980 to 1987), NG La Banda set out to establish a middle ground between the two styles, melding any international rhythms with

Afro-Cuban music. They polished their sound in the barrios of Havana, acquiring a following of thousands and a slew of radio hits, including "La Expresiva," an ode to the barrio which has endured as an anthem of Cuban pride. Cortés continued to write songs the people could relate to, drawing from social and political themes of his country. His often vulgar lyrics, filled with street slang, sexual innuendo, and references to racism, prostitution and the economy, have gotten him into frequent trouble with government censors. Since its inception, NG La Banda has become one of the most popular groups on Cuba's dance-music scene and is becoming the Band That Launched a Thousand Careers—over the past decade such outstanding young talents as singers Issac Delgado, Paulito FG, and Manolín, and drummer Giraldo Piloto, among others, have stinted with the group before successfully venturing out on their own.

NG La Banda's blend is a frenzied, crowd-pleasing mix. Yet because of the U.S. embargo against Cuba, their discography is in disarray and their music is hard to find in this country, especially outside of large metropolitan areas. Still, the band has recorded or appeared on about 40 albums and continues to tour, perform, and gain international fans.

what to buy: A compilation of their best early material, *En la Calle* 𝄞𝄞𝄞𝄞 (Qbadisc, 1992, prod. José Luis Cortés) collects nine tracks recorded in Havana in 1989 and 1990 as the band's reputation was growing. With their danceable grooves, impeccable arrangements, provocative lyrics, and jazz-based instrumental solos, they generate plenty of excitement on this recording, which spotlights vocalist Issac Delgado before he left the band in 1991 to launch his phenomenal solo career. While their music is laden with percussion and focuses on vocals, the horn section is prominently featured in melody leads and call-and-response segments as they navigate some intricate Cortés arrangements. Cortés's own flute playing adds sweet sonorities as he soars above horns and percussion on some tunes. This is joyful, party-atmosphere music that will have even the most recalcitrant listeners up and moving.

what to buy next: *Veneno* 𝄞𝄞𝄞 (Metro Blue, 1998) is a sophisticated, 12-tune album incorporating Pan-Caribbean musical influences and various Latin rhythms. Translated, the album title means "venom" or "poison." Perhaps a dose of their music is so infectious you're forever changed; it sure is hard to sit still during these 52 minutes. Updated for the late 1990s, rhythms remain danceable, some tunes being infused with straight-ahead jazz solos, funk-rap beats ("Cucalambé"), NYC salsa ("Verano habanero"), and smooth-jazz tinges ("Veneno"). Vocal choruses are dense and arrangements are slicker and more intricate. Cortés has crafted alluring compositions that provide for spontaneous collective and individual performances, but you don't hear much of his flute playing on this

disc. The major difference of this album from their others is the appearance of a talented, passionate female vocalist on three ballads (unfortunately, musicians are not listed). The driving rhythms, the bold, brassy horns, and the confident and expressive Spanish vocals that stand out even if you don't understand them—all make this a compelling recording.

best of the rest:

Best of NG La Banda 𝄞𝄞𝄞𝄞 (BMG/Milan Latino, 1997)

influences:

◄◄ Bailar con Cuba, Mario Bauzá, Juan Formell y Los Van Van, Irakere, Israel "Cachao" López, Mongo Santamaria, Chico O'Farrill

►► Issac Delgado y Su Orquesta, Arturo Sandoval & the Latin Train

see also: *Issac Delgado, Manolín, El Médico de la Salsa*

Nancy Ann Lee

Mbongeni Ngema

Mbanqanga

Born 1955, in Verulam, South Africa. Based in Johannesburg, South Africa.

Ngema is best known in the United States as a playwright; with his partner Percy Mtwa, he co-wrote and starred in the award-winning *Woza Albert!,* an anti-apartheid comedy/drama of uncommon power. He also wrote and produced *Asinamali* and *Sarafina!,* works that helped keep the political struggle of black South Africans in the minds of Americans. Ngema was born in a township and was working to support his family before he finished high school, sometimes as a musician playing background music for theatrical productions. One night the lead in Lucky Mavundla's *Isigcino* took sick and Ngema filled in, which led to his successful theatrical career. In 1979 he moved to Soweto and joined Gibson Kente's theater for *Mama and the Load.* In 1981 he met Mtwa and they created *Woza Albert!,* which went on to tour the world for more than five years, garnering rave reviews wherever it played. Ngema returned home and wrote *Asinamali,* which opened in New York in 1986. Next up was his debut album, *Stimela Sase-Zola,* which featured the talents of the Soul Brothers and the Music Unlimited Orchestra; and then the dramatic musical *Sarafina!,* for which Ngema provided book, music, and lyrics. While he was in New York with *Sarafina!,* Ngema also recorded *Time to Unite,* his first international release.

what to buy: In *Sarafina!* 𝄞𝄞𝄞𝄞 (RCA, 1988, prod. Mbongeni Ngema), Ngema's tale follows Sarafina and her classmates at Morris Isaacson High School during the bloody anti-apartheid riots of 1976. The subject matter is serious, a matter of life and death for some students, but Ngema manages to find hope and humor in this epic struggle. The music is remarkably low-key for such a charged subject, but the message comes through loud and clear: even in the most dire of circumstances, the human soul will rise up and sing.

what to buy next: Like *Sarafina!, Time to Unite* 𝄞𝄞𝄞𝄞 (Mango, 1988, prod. Mbongeni Ngema) is given an understated performance that intensifies its tales of life under apartheid. The cast of *Sarafina!* provides spirited backing vocals on most tracks.

influences:

◄◄ Rupert Bopape, Mahlathini & Mahotella Queens, Soul Brothers

j. poet

Samba Ngo
Afropop, worldbeat
Born 1950, in Zaire (now Congo). Based in Santa Cruz, CA, USA.

Ngo, like many of his African contemporaries, is interested in transforming the music of his youth into a pop sound that will captivate the sophisticated international listener. Since 1986 Ngo has been based in Santa Cruz, California, where he has gradually put together a powerhouse band he calls the Ngoma Players, a unit that combines *soukous* (African rumba), jazz, rock, and pop into a smooth multicultural confection. Ngo was born in Congo and was playing *kalimba* (thumb piano) in the village orchestra by the time he was six. He began teaching himself guitar at age 15, after hearing the legendary Franco's TPOK Jazz group. In 1964 he moved to Brazzaville, Congo, where he joined Echo Noire. Echo Noire moved to Paris in the early 1970s. After settling in Paris himself, Ngo joined M'Bamina, an international unit that toured the world and recorded nine albums. In 1985 he decided to start his own band, and chose California as its home base, so he wouldn't be tempted into session work in the booming Paris world-music scene. Ngo has made two solo albums since coming to the United States, and the second, *Metamorphosis,* was just picked up by Compass Records, the eclectic Nashville label run by progressive bluegrass star Allison Brown.

what's available: As heard on *Metamorphosis* 𝄞𝄞𝄞𝄞 (Compass, 1998, prod. Samba Ngo, Steve Carter), Ngo's jazzy Afropop fusion is both multicultural and ear-friendly. His eclectic guitar style slips from the smooth, rippling single-note leads of soukous, to the muted staccato picking of Zimbabwean *chimurenga,* to the ringing chords of jazzman Wes Montgomery, while the funky bass lines and sharp horn parts add a pleasing pop sheen to the proceedings.

worth searching for: *Introspection* 𝄞𝄞𝄞 (Elingo, 1990, prod. Samba Ngo, Steve Carter), Ngo's first solo outing on his own

india, north and south

The classical music of India can be divided into two main categories: the *Hindustani* style of North India and the *karnatak* style of South India. The two sounds are similar in their general outlook and theoretical background, but differ in a variety of details, due mainly to the more prominent Islamic influence on the music of the North. To Western ears, karnatak music may seem more emotionally direct than the usually serene, restrained characteristics of Hindustani. While the *alaap*—the opening segment, in which the soloist introduces the primary musical theme—of many North Indian classical *raga* pieces proceeds in a refined, stately manner, karnatak musicians are more liberal in adding decorative flourishes. Where Hindustani players then veer off into abstract, almost jazz-like improvisations (albeit within certain traditional confines), karnatak music places greater importance on compositional structure. But the most obvious way to tell a Hindustani recording from a karnatak one is simply by looking at the instruments used. In the classical music of North India, the most important melodic instrument is the *sitar,* a lute with six or seven main strings (two or three of which are used for drones) and anywhere from 11 to 19 sympathetic strings. South India's version, the *veena,* has no sympathetic strings, as karnatak musicians appear not to like the somewhat hollow tone they give the instrument. For percussion, Hindustani music features the *tabla*—actually a pair of drums, one with a high ringing tone, the other with a bendable bass tone—almost exclusively, while karnatak music tends to favor percussion ensembles comprising a variety of drums, the *mridangam* being the most prominent. And though the North Indian classical ethic is notoriously traditional, accepting the introduction of new instruments like the *santoor* hammered dulcimer only slowly over time, karnatak musicians seem eager to experiment with new sounds—guitars, mandolins, and saxophones all having been embraced in recent years.

see also: Indian percussion (sidebar), the Sitar (sidebar), the Tabla (sidebar)

Bret Love

small label, already shows him on the path to the bubbly Afropop of *Metamorphosis*.

influences:

◀◀ Fela Kuti, Franco, Thomas Mapfumo

▶▶ Alpha Yaya Diallo, Angélique Kidjo

j. poet

Maire Ní Chathasaigh

Celtic harp

Born April 21, 1956, in County Cork, Ireland. Based in England.

Until recently the harp had, for the most part, fallen out of the world of traditional Irish dance music. While there were a few scattered players and a harp category remained at the All-Ireland competition, the rarity and expense of the instrument meant that there were few harpers in the rural countryside where traditional music survives most strongly. During the last 30 years, artists like Derek Bell of the Chieftains, Antoinette McKenna, and even Mary O'Hara had helped to start a harp revival, but it wasn't until the 1980s and the arrival of Maire Ní Chathasaigh's recordings that harpers began to use the techniques and ornamentation common to Irish dance music. Her precise, technically proficient style is based on the playing of the fiddlers and pipers she heard as a child in County Cork in the west of Ireland. Her first recording, *The New Strung Harp,* introduced audiences to her use of traditional ornamentation—including the rolls, cuts, and slurs common to fiddles, accordions, and pipes—and served as a revelation to harpers all over the Celtic world. The album forced harpers everywhere to raise their playing standards and changed forever the role of the harp in dance music. Born into a musical family (her sister is fiddle player Nollaig Casey) and brought up speaking both Irish and English, Ní Chathasaigh began playing the harp at age 12, having already learned whistle and piano. She attended University College, Cork, where she spent time collecting songs and music from traditional players in the area and received an honors degree in Celtic studies. Having won numerous harp competitions in her youth, Ní Chathasaigh is now a fixture as a judge and teacher at those same competitions. She has toured and taught throughout the United States and Europe, both as a solo performer and with her long-time musical partner, guitarist Chris Newman. She currently lives in England and is also president of Old Bridge Records, her own label.

what's available: *The New Strung Harp* ♫♫♫♫ (Temple, 1985/1997, prod. Robin Morton) is a classic. When released in 1985, the recording showed a new way to play Irish jigs and reels on the harp. Modeled on the playing of fiddlers and pipers, Ní Chathasaigh's playing mimics those instruments in her style of ornamentation, allowing her music to fit as closely as possible into the dance-music idiom. She shows off her awesome

technique on the set of reels "The Volunteer" and "The Pullet" and on the jig "Gander in the Pratie Hole," and she also sings a few traditional Irish songs in a sweet, clear voice. Although other harpers have in the intervening years raised their level of playing to Ní Chathasaigh's, she was the first to play in this modern style, and for that reason she is important listening. *The Carolan Albums* ♫♫♫♫ (Old Bridge, 1994) is an essential compilation of the music of Turlough O'Carolan, a blind 18th-century itinerant considered to be the last of the great traveling Irish harpers. His compositions have become a major part of the traditional Irish repertoire and Ní Chathasaigh's precise, confident performances set a new standard for this important material.

worth searching for: Ní Chathasaigh's other recordings, all with guitarist Newman, are available on the import Old Bridge label. They are: *The Living Wood* ♫♫♫ (Old Bridge, 1995); *Out of Court* ♫♫♫ (Old Bridge, 1991); and *Live in the Highlands* ♫♫♫ (Old Bridge, 1995).

influences:

◀◀ Antoinette McKenna, Grainne Yeats

▶▶ Aine Minogue, Sue Richards, Carol Thompson

Tony Ziselberger

Maighread Ní Dhomhnaill

Celtic

Born in County Donegal, Ireland. Based in Ireland.

Maighread Ní Dhomhnaill sings in Gaelic and English in a manner known as *sean-nós* ("old style"), a tradition believed to be descended from the bardic singers of ancient Ireland. Other singers who use this heritage in some of their popular work include Dolores Keane and Mary Black. Maighread was a member of the group Skara Brae with her brother Mícháel Ó Domhnaill and her sister Tríona Ní Dhomhnaill, both of whom have gone on to musical careers as solo artists and producers, as well as members, at various points, of such groups as the Bothy Band and Nightnoise.

what's available: *No Dowry* ♫♫♫♫ (1991, Gael-Linn, prod. Dónal Lunny) is a confident and engaging production of music in the old style. Perhaps easier to locate is the compilation *A Woman's Heart 2,* which contains a cut from this album (and is reviewed in this book's Compilations section). Her first album—with a different spelling of her name—*Mairead Ní Dhomhnaill* (Gael-Linn, 1976), is difficult to find.

influences:

◀◀ Seán Ó Riada

see also: *Mary Black, the Bothy Band, Dolores Keane, Tríona Ní Dhomhnaill, Nightnoise, Trian*

Kerry Dexter

Tríona Ní Dhomhnaill

Irish folk

Born late 1940s, in Donegal, Ireland. Based in Portland, OR, USA.

With her expressive, heavily brogued soprano vocals and melodic harpsichord playing, Tríona Ní Dhomhnaill has been at the forefront of modern Celtic music for more than two decades. Although her solo outings have been limited to a single album, *Tríona*, released in Ireland in 1976 and the United States in 1983, Ní Dhomhnaill has showcased her vocal warmth in such influential Celtic bands as Skara Brae, the Bothy Band, Touchstone, Relativity, and Nightnoise. Many of Ní Dhomhnaill's recordings have been in collaboration with her brother, Mícháel Ó Domhnaill, a virtuosic Celtic guitar player. In the early 1970s, she and Mícháel joined with their sister, Maighread, and multi-instrumentalist Dáithí Sproule to form the tradition-rooted Gaelic band Skara Brae. Their introduction to most American audiences, however, came when they became founding members of the Bothy Band, a group formed by ex-Planxty bouzouki player Dónal Lunny in 1975 that combined Ireland's musical traditions with a modern sensibility. Emigrating to the United States in 1979, Ní Dhomhnaill recorded two albums of Irish, American, and Nova Scotian music as a member of the Chapel Hill, North Carolina–based band Touchstone. After moving to Portland, Oregon, Ní Dhomhnaill reunited with her brother, who had preceded her to the United States. After she'd toured and recorded two albums with Scottish brothers John and Phil Cunningham (of Silly Wizard fame) as Relativity, the reunion with Mícháel became musical too, with both she and he (as well as John Cunningham and others) playing in the Celtic new-age band Nightnoise.

what to buy: Ní Dhomhnaill's only solo album, *Tríona* ♪♪♪♪ (Gael-Linn, 1976/Green Linnet, 1983, prod. Mícháel Ó Domhnaill), combines traditional Irish tunes in Gaelic with songs sung in English, including the memorable gender-switching ballad "When I Was a Fair Maid."

influences:
◄◄ Planxty, Jean Redpath

►► Mary Black, Maura O'Connell

see also: *The Bothy Band, Johnny Cunningham, Dónal Lunny, Nightnoise, Maighread Ní Dhomhnaill, Silly Wizard, Trian*

Craig Harris

Nightnoise

Celtic fusion

Formed 1983.

Billy Oskay, violin, viola, keyboards (1983–90); Mícheál Ó Domhnaill, guitar, whistles, synthesizers, vocals; Tríona Ní Dhomhnaill, keyboards, vocals, whistles, accordion (1986–present); Brian Dunning, flutes, panpipes (1986–present); John Cunningham, fiddle, vocals (1991–present). (Members are from Ireland and Scotland.)

Familiarity with French Impressionist painters like Monet might help an unfamiliar listener understand the group Nightnoise. Calling on backgrounds from the classical to the traditional Irish, this group has assembled a mist-covered image from a series of brightly colored impressions. Pulling their various backgrounds together, they have created a soft, romantic mood with the music they play. Nightnoise has a distinct and unusual sound, with a new-age feel to the instrumentation, but with more of a jazz-like rhythm to the music. Unquestionably Celtic in background, the group never exactly attempts to be traditional, yet it never loses the sense of the traditional either. Definitely not rock, but far too varied to be new age, this group is just plain hard to classify. There is a chamber-folk quality to them, but the music also borders on pop and still maintains an Irish feel. Perhaps they are the closest thing the Irish have to American jazz. The band was started by Billy Oskay, who wanted to record some tracks and asked Mícheál Ó Domhnaill to join him. The resulting music soon became the album known as *Nightnoise*, and they decided to take their show on the road. They added a piano player and a second fiddler for the tour, and by the time they were ready to record again, they had added Ó Domhnaill's sister Tríona (from Touchstone and the Bothy Band) and Brian Dunning to the mix. When Oskay decided to leave, they quickly filled his position with John Cunningham (of Silly Wizard fame). What appealed to these top-notch performers with busy solo schedules was the loose-knit structure of the group, which does ample touring but allows the members plenty of time to pursue other projects during the course of the year. This may be key to their success as a unit, with exploration of other creative outlets keeping the songwriting juices flowing and resulting in highly evocative and creative music from Nightnoise.

what to buy: *Shadow of Time* ♪♪♪♪ (Windham Hill, 1993, prod. Dawn Atkinson, Nightnoise) contains a delightful mix of traditional and new material, sporting soaring flute lines, rhythmic piano accompaniment, and melodic fiddle. Exciting rhythms highlight "Silky Flanks," a wonderful instrumental track, and amazing Gaelic vocals create rhythm, melody, harmony, and texture in the mouth music (unaccompanied Scottish dance song) "Fionnghuala." This is new-age folk at its best.

what to buy next: *A Different Shore* ♪♪♪♪ (Windham Hill, 1995, prod. Nightnoise) is also filled with new age–style music in a slightly more exotic vein. The arrangements include wonderful fiddle, flute, and vocal lines, brilliantly performed. The melodic piano line on the song "Falling Apples" and the throaty bass flute line on the title track are particularly lovely.

what to avoid: Both *At the End of the Evening* ♫♫ (Windham Hill, 1988, prod. Nightnoise) and *Something of Time* ♫♫ (Windham Hill, 1987, prod. Billy Oskay, Mícheál Ó Domhnaill) seem to have more new-age material and less folk substance to them than Nightnoise's other albums. A lack of tension in the music keeps these albums from living up to the group's overall standard.

the rest:
Oskay & Ó Domhnaill: Nightnoise ♫♫♫ (Windham Hill, 1984)
Parting Tide ♫♫♫ (Windham Hill, 1990)
Nightnoise: A Windham Hill Retrospective ♫♫♫ (Windham Hill, 1992)
The White Horse Sessions ♫♫♫ (Windham Hill, 1997)

influences:
◄◄ Jethro Tull, Relativity, Silly Wizard, Touchstone

►► Enya

see also: *The Bothy Band, John Cunningham, Tríona Ní Dhomhnaill, Silly Wizard*

Jo Hughey Morrison

West Nkosi

See: Mahlathini & Mahotella Queens

Noa

Jazz, pop
Born Achinoam Nini in Tel Aviv, Israel. Based in Israel and USA.

Although she now reigns as one of Israel's primary pop stars, Achinoam Nini's route to stardom was surprisingly circuitous. Born in Tel Aviv to a Yemenite family, Nini grew up in New York City, but was constantly kept mindful of her cultural heritage. In New York, she attended the famed High School for the Performing Arts, but fell in love with an Israeli boy (now her husband) who convinced her to move back home. There she was drafted into the army, where she became a singing sergeant assigned to an entertainment unit. Following her stint in the service, Nini caught a break when she teamed with guitarist Gil Dor, a former student of jazz guitarist Pat Metheny. With her name shortened to Noa to avoid pronunciation woes and to emphasize her pop/jazz leanings over ethnic expectations—Noa is no Ofra Haza, nor does she attempt to be—Metheny co-produced her first American album, which led to a second, but with pop producer Rupert Hine at the helm. Noa's music does contain elements of Eastern exotica, and she frequently sings in Hebrew, but this Yemenite thrush is more intent on becoming Israel's answer to Joni Mitchell, or maybe even Madonna. With both folky and pop leanings at which she is equally adept and ambitious, she's already well on her way to doing just that.

what to buy: Noa's two U.S.-released major-label efforts are equally fine. *Noa* ♫♫♫♫ (Geffen, 1994, prod. Pat Metheny, Steve Rodby) is somewhat dominated by Metheny and Rodby's production, which sounds of a piece with Metheny's own group albums. Still, Noa shines on the sparkling "Wildflower," and numbers sung in Hebrew such as "Mishaela" and "Uri." The showstopper, though is "Ave Maria"—not the age-old hymn, but an original plea for "beauty, gentleness, and laughter." *Calling* ♫♫♫♫ (Geffen, 1996, prod. Rupert Hine) gets the edge, however, thanks to a terrific batch of songs including the enchanting "U.N.I," the slow-building release of "By the Light of the Moon," and the hard-rocking "Lama," which contains the immortal couplet "Every day that passes/Proves that God has lost his glasses."

what to buy next: An effort to expose some of Noa's Israeli-released work in the United States, *Both Sides of the Sea* ♫♫♫ (Mondo Melodia, 1998, prod. Yossi Fine, Noa, Gil Dor) combines tracks from *Achinoam Nini* and *Achinoam Nini Gil Dor.* Highlights include songs such as "Nisayon," "Nocturno," "Three Days," and "Me," featuring lyrics by Israeli poets Leah Goldberg and Rachel. The songs here are solidly in the pop realm, but use more exotic instrumentation than allowed on her American albums.

worth searching for: Fans of *Both Sides of the Sea* may want to tap their friendly import dealer for Noa's entire catalog of Israeli albums. They include *Achinoam Nini Gil Dor Live* (NMC, 1991); *Achinoam Nini Gil Dor* (NMC, 1993); *Achinoam Nini* (NMC, 1997); and *Achinoam Nini and the Israel Philharmonic Orchestra* (NMC, 1998).

influences:
◄◄ Leah Goldberg, Pat Metheny, Joni Mitchell, Rachel

Daniel Durchholz

Nocy

Spanish guitar
Born in Lebanon. Based in Los Angeles, CA, USA.

Nocy Karkour began his infatuation with classical Spanish guitar music in the unlikely setting of his native Lebanon. He developed his technique first at the Paris Conservatory for Spanish Guitar and then under the tutelage of Betho Davezac, Segovia's top protégé. Nocy has played with a diverse and impressive roster of musicians, including jazz guitarist Larry Coryell, blues-rock drummer Buddy Miles, and Gypsy swing guitarist Manitas de Plata. Since moving to Los Angeles in the early 1990s, Nocy has continued to broaden his commercial appeal, working with pop notables such as Rod Stewart, Kenny G, and Jon Anderson of Yes. He performed at the opening ceremonies for the 1994 Olympic Games and now regularly appears at the Mirage Hotel in Las Vegas. Although traditionalists might bemoan the commercial path Nocy has taken (and the success he has met with it), his technique remains impressive and his playing inventive and emotional.

what's available: The slick but passionate *Flames of Spain* 🎵🎵🎵 (Earthtone, 1997, prod. Carol Horvsepian) puts Nocy's fiery playing in a new-age/light-jazz setting, augmented by bass, percussion, and backing vocals.

influences:

◀◀ Gipsy Kings, Andres Segovia

▶▶ Craig Chaquico, Kenny G

Michael Parrish

Nomos

Irish folk

Formed 1990, in County Cork, Ireland. Based in County Cork, Ireland.

Niall Vallely (1990–present), concertina, low whistle, piano, drones; Liz Doherty (1990–96), fiddle; Vince Milne (1996–present), fiddle; Gerry McKee (1990–present), mandocello; Frank Torpey (1990–present), bodhrán, drones; John Spillane (1992–98), vocals, guitar, bass; Eoin Coughlan (1998–present), vocals, bass. (All members are from Ireland.)

Nomos has its roots in the University of County Cork, where Niall Vallely and Frank Torpey were students. Gerry McKee joined the duo after moving to Cork from County Antrim via County Clare and the United States. Original fiddler Liz Doherty joined the lineup shortly thereafter, and Nomos expanded to a quintet a few years later with John Spillane. This lineup recorded *I Won't Be Afraid Any More* in 1994. Doherty left the group in 1996, replaced by Milne, who had previously played in traditional Irish folk groups and with bluegrass bands. This was the ensemble that recorded *Set You Free* in 1996, an album that *Folk Roots* magazine considered one of the best of that year. While the essential sound of the band remained unchanged through both releases, they'd been tweaking their concept to include more original material. This adjustment was pretty natural since Spillane was proving to be a talented composer, Vallely is one of the better concertina players around these days, Torpey has developed an interesting approach to rhythm and harmony, and Milne has a kinetic stage presence. In addition to jaunts throughout Ireland, Nomos has played in Great Britain, North America, and Denmark, with a short 1997 tour of the United States playing to sold-out houses. In 1998, during another North American tour, Spillane was replaced by bassist Eoin Coughlan.

what's available: The group's debut release *I Won't Be Afraid Any More* 🎵🎵🎵 (Solid/Green Linnet, 1995/1996, prod. Nomos) hews fairly close to tradition, with danceable reels and jigs leading the way. It also serves to introduce Spillane as a songwriter worth watching, with beautifully constructed gems like "All the Ways You Wander" and the title track. Nomos's next album *Set You Free* 🎵🎵🎵🎵 (Green Linnet, 1997, prod. Nomos) introduced a new fiddler (Milne) and more assured tune-smithing from Spillane. The rock-

ish feel of the title song fits well with the many reels and jig medleys on the project, but Spillane's reflective "Poor Weary Wanderer" and Vallely's beautiful instrumental "Súile Shuibhne (Sweeney's Eyes)" are closer to the album's basic ambiance.

influences:

◀◀ Dónal Lunny, Mícheál Ó Súilleabháin, Alan Stivell

▶▶ Reeltime

Garaud MacTaggart

Nordan Project

Improvisational folk music, jazz

Formed 1992, in Stockholm, Sweden. Based in Stockholm, Sweden.

Ale Möller, mandola, flutes, harp, shawm, cow's horn trumpet, hammered dulcimer, accordion; Lena Willemark, vocal, fiddle; Palle Danielsson, bass; Mats Edén, hardanger fiddle, kantele; Per Gudmundson, fiddle, Swedish bagpipes; Tina Johansson, percussion; Jonas Knutsson, sax, percussion; Björn Tollin, percussion. (All members are from Sweden.)

If American audiences are at all familiar with Swedish folk music, it is because of the Nordan Project, one of the few Swedish groups that have undertaken an extensive tour of the United States—although the musicians hasten to point out that the Nordan Project isn't a group, since all the members are involved in other bands or solo careers. Lena Willemark, who has an interest in medieval Swedish folk music, met multi-instrumentalist Ale Möller at a fiddler's convention in 1984. They hit it off and have played together ever since in various formats, including their trio Frifot and a quintet called Enteli. The duo met ECM Records head Manfred Eicher in 1992 and suggested putting together an album that would combine the improvisational traditions of folk music and modern jazz. *Nordan* was recorded as a one-off project, but the enthusiastic reception of the disc led to a tour and to a second album, *Agram*.

what's available: Möller's fretwork on a variety of instruments, Knutsson's melancholy sax, Johanssen's Afro-Arabic hand drumming, the droning fiddle of Mats Edén, and Willemark's astonishing vocals have produced a unique hybrid on *Nordan* 🎵🎵🎵🎵 (ECM, 1993, prod. Manfred Eicher); a powerful kind of international folk/jazz that's dark, deep, and dreamy. *Agram* 🎵🎵🎵🎵 (ECM, 1996, prod. Manfred Eicher) is another excursion into the subliminal psyche of Scandinavia—perfect music for long, cold winter nights; alternately chilling and heartwarming.

influences:

◀◀ Enteli, Frifot, Groupa, Simon Simonsson

see also: *Groupa*

j. poet

Nordan Project

Clara Nunes

Samba, MPB (Brazilian Popular Music), tropical
Born 1943, in Brazil. Died 1989, in Brazil.

Clara Nunes became a force in samba singing with the release of her breakout recording *Alvorecer* in 1964, when she was 21. A vocalist of sensuality and power, many of Nunes's lyrics drew from her belief in *Candomblé*, an Afro-Brazilian relative of *Santería* which reveres spirits of nature and admits the presence of such spirits in everyday life. Despite this less-than-mainstream source material, Nunes's vocal presence was such that she scored many popular hits and is still, despite her tragic early death, regarded as one of samba's enduring artists.

what's available: For an idea of the range of Nunes's music, look for *The Best of Clara Nunes* ♫♫♫ (World Pacific, 1992, prod. Gerald Seligman).

influences:

◄◄ Ismael Silva

►► Alcione, Beth Carvahlo

Kerry Dexter

Sven Nyhus

Norwegian folk
Born 1932, in Norway. Based near Oslo, Norway.

Sven Nyhus is the towering figure in folk music of the Røros district of Norway. He is a master of the fiddle and *hardanger* fiddle, an ornate instrument with almost magical properties. Its "sympathetic" strings produce an unusual drone effect that lingers after each tune. Besides instrumental *gammeldans* or old-time dance music, Nyhus also plays classical violin and viola, soloing with the Oslo Philharmonic Orchestra and a string quartet. Nyhus was folk music director at Norway's public radio for more than a decade and curator of the national folk archives. He has written books on traditional music and produced many recordings. Nyhus founded a four-piece band in 1969, which has through the years grown to a sextet, with more than a dozen albums to its credit. Central to the group's sound is accordionist Tore Løvgreen, who's been playing with Nyhus since the mid-1960s. The brightest recent addition is his daughter, Åshild Breie Nyhus. Born in 1975, she's carrying the family fiddle tradition into at least a fourth generation. The Røros music championed by Nyhus is often melancholy. But he always tosses in a few jaunty numbers, even some with bluegrassy and jazzy lilts. Meanwhile, his elfish grin on the album covers suggests these are more than just funeral dirges for Norwegian bachelor farmers.

what to buy: A good place to start is *Skuddårslek* 𝄞𝄞𝄞 (Callisto, 1988, prod. Jan Erik Kongshaug), credited to the Sven Nyhus Kvartett & Åshild Breie Nyhus. Barely a teen when this was recorded, Åshild has no trouble keeping up with the seasoned veterans in dad's band. More fun and varied than the later *Grimen,* this set includes some real toe-tappers with jolly accordion solos. About half are originals, including a *pols* based on a Bach melody, written for the master's 300th birthday. With Åshild all grown up, the Sven Nyhus Sekstett's *Grimen* 𝄞𝄞𝄞 (Heilo, 1997, prod. Hallvard Kvåle) features a fuller, six-piece sound, but still no percussion except for an occasional tapping (on a fiddle?). These 20 tunes range from sad waltzes to sprightly dances such as the asymmetrical *pols* and self-explanatory *galopp.* Some Sven learned from his Swedish grandfather (Sven Paulsson Nyhus); others are re-recordings of his originals from the 1970s and 1980s. Sometimes the album bogs down in drone and groan. Lest things get too samey, though, there's a sprightly whistle solo and some uncredited bird-calls after the last track—a touch of suitably dry humor.

the rest:
Traditional Norwegian Fiddle Music (Shanachie, 1992)

worth searching for: Nyhus is all over Arne Nordskaug's album *Portrett av en spellmann* 𝄞𝄞𝄞 (Heilo, 1985, prod. Ivar Stranger, Sven Nyhus, Jan Erik Kongshaug). On half of it, his quartet backs this fellow Norwegian fiddle legend; the remainder consists of charming duets between Nyhus and Nordskaug, who was 68 at the time. To hear three generations of Nyhus fiddlers, seek out *Folkemusikk frå Trøndelag 9* 𝄞𝄞𝄞 (Grappa, 1995, prod. Leiv Solberg), a compilation in a handsome package with booklet. Among some 30 tracks there are five by Nyhus, one solo by Åshild, and one by Sven's father Peder Nyhus—a tad quavery at age 86, yet thoroughly charming. Finally, there's a live tune by all three, recorded a few years before Peder's death.

influences:
◀◀ Arne Nordskaug, Peder Nyhus, Sven Paulsson Nyhus

▶▶ Annbjørg Lien, Åshild Breie Nyhus

Wif Stenger

Sally Nyolo
Afropop
Born c. 1969, in Eyen-Meyong, Cameroon. Based in Paris, France.

Nyolo began singing at the same time she began talking. Her aunt Mamterry was a traditional singer and healer, who taught Nyolo many songs and rituals, some of which she has used in her own compositions. Nyolo was known for her dancing at an early age, and she moved to Paris when she was 13. She began her professional career singing backup and dancing with Afropop groups like Sixun and Touré Kunda. In 1993 she put together her first band and became a local star in Paris. She composed music for French radio dramas and contributed a tune to the soundtrack of a French film, *Ashakara.* After an appearance at one of Peter Gabriel's WOMAD (World of Music, Arts and Dance) Festivals, Gabriel invited her to record for a possible album. The songs turned up on the RealWorld compilation *Around the World in 20 Tracks* and *Strictly Worldwide* for the German Piranha label. In 1993 Nyolo met Marie Daulne, who invited her to join Zap Mama. Nyolo stayed with the band until 1996, when she parted ways to pursue her own international crossover dreams.

what's available: *Multiculti* 𝄞𝄞𝄞 (Tinder, 1998, prod. Sally Nyolo) is a mini masterwork from Nyolo and a fine supporting cast, which includes a few Zap Mamas and a small army of Afro-Parisian regulars. The pop and African elements are perfectly balanced, creating tunes that are at once commercial and deeply rooted in Nyolo's traditional past. Her first effort at forging her own sound, *Tribu* 𝄞𝄞𝄞 (Tinder, 1997, prod. Sally Nyolo, Lusafrica), is spotty, but interesting as a document of an artist trying to find her individual voice.

influences:
◀◀ Manu Dibango, Les Tetes Brulées, Sam Fan Thomas, Zap Mama

see also: *Zap Mama*

j. poet

Ebenezer Obey
Juju
Born 1942, in Idogo, Western Region, Nigeria. Based in Nigeria.

"Chief Commander" Ebenezer Obey is a pioneer of Nigeria's dance-inspiring *juju* music. Although King Sunny Adé was the first juju musician to perform in the Western world, Obey remains the genre's most prolific and best-selling artist, with more than 50 albums since 1969. Obey's musical talents were evident from the days of his Methodist primary school, where he was invited to lead his first band. After moving to the capitol city of Lagos he went professional with several outfits, including the Fatayi Rolling Dollars from 1958 until 1963. A year later he

Sally Nyolo

started recording with his own band, the International Brothers. Their first single, "Ewa Wo Ohun Ojuri," was also released in 1964, with the debut album, *Late Oba Gbadelo II,* following five years later. Although Obey's group was initially a small ensemble, it continued to expand with the addition of more drummers, guitarists, pedal steel players, and background vocalists. By the time Obey reorganized the band as the International Reformers in the early 1970s, it featured more than 20 musicians—and Obey's compositional ambitions continued to grow in proportion, with expanded arrangements and half-hour tunes. Set to intricate guitar melodies and the polyrhythms of multiple drums, Obey's songs remained jubilant and uplifting. His style of juju has come to be known as *miliki,* an African word meaning "joy and happiness." Many of the songs celebrate his ties to Christianity, linking his music back to that primary school where the teachers knew he was just beginning.

what to buy: Recorded in Seattle in late 1987, *Get Your Jujus Out* ✦✦✦✦ (Rykodisc, 1990, prod. Keith Keller) demonstrates the polyrhythmic intensity of Obey's concerts. His first American release, *Juju Jubilee* ✦✦✦✦ (Shanachie, 1985, prod. various), samples the best of Obey's early singles and album cuts.

best of the rest:
Late Oba Gbadelo II ✦✦✦ (Soundpoint, 1969)
And His Miliki Sound ✦✦✦ (Decca, 1973)
Inter-Reformers a Tunde ✦✦✦ (Decca, 1974)
Late Great Murtara Murtala Ramat Muhammed ✦✦✦ (Decca, 1976)
Operation Feed the Nation ✦✦✦ (Decca, 1977)
In the Sixties Vol. 1 ✦✦✦ (Decca, 1979)
In the Sixties Vol. 2 ✦✦✦ (Decca, 1979)
There Is No Friend Like Jesus ✦✦✦ (Decca, 1979)
Leave Everything to God ✦✦✦ (Decca, 1980)
Current Affairs ✦✦✦✦ (Decca, 1980)
Celebration ✦✦✦ (Decca, 1982)
Austerity ✦✦✦ (Decca, 1982)
Precious Gift ✦✦✦ (Decca, 1983)
Ambition ✦✦✦ (Decca, 1983)
Singing for the People ✦✦✦ (Decca, 1983)
Greatest Hits Vol. 3 ✦✦✦✦ (Decca, 1983)
The Only Condition to Save Nigeria ✦✦✦ (Obey, 1984)
Solution ✦✦✦ (Obey, 1984)
Peace ✦✦✦ (Obey, 1985)
Security ✦✦✦ (Obey, 1985)
My Vision ✦✦✦ (Obey, 1986)
Patience ✦✦✦ (Obey, 1988)
Determination ✦✦✦ (Obey, 1988)
Vanity ✦✦✦ (Obey, 1989)
Womanhood ✦✦✦ (Obey, 1993)
The Legend (Evergreen Songs) ✦✦✦ (Obey, 1996)

influences:
◄◄ Babatunde Olatunji, I.K. Dairo

▶▶ King Sunny Adé, Fela Anikulapo Kuti, Segun Andawale

see also: *King Sunny Adé*

Craig Harris

Maura O'Connell

Celtic country, singer-songwriter
Born September 16, 1958, in Ennis, County Clare, Ireland. Based in Nashville, TN, USA.

Maura O'Connell is a quality example of the singer as freewheeling interpreter, unfettered by any genre in particular. Her soulful eclecticism is only fitting from an Irish-born artist who scored her first big musical successes by recording pop albums in Nashville. After starting out singing in clubs for Galway college kids, O'Connell hooked up with the Celtic traditional group De Dannan for two years. She split in 1983, trekked to Nashville on her manager's advice, and recorded three solo albums that became huge hits in her home country. O'Connell's signing to Warner Bros. sparked a string of meticulously produced albums distinguished by her warm, flexible mezzo and adventuresome song selections from John Hiatt, Tom Waits, and Shawn Colvin, mixed with second looks at standards from Tin Pan Alley and the Beatles. These efforts earned critical raves but only modest U.S. sales, though her incandescent live performances have solidified her Stateside audience while her star status in Ireland remains assured. Still, Warners opted not to renew her contract in 1994, so O'Connell launched her own Permanent Records imprint for her 1995 album *Stories,* which was released through Hannibal/Rykodisc, where at last check she's been living happily ever after.

what to buy: *Helpless Heart* ✦✦✦✦✦ (Warner Bros., 1989, prod. Béla Fleck) probably is the closest O'Connell has flirted with country, but Fleck's thoughtful arrangements deftly blend bluegrass and mountain influences with traditional Irish touches—and in "You'll Never Know," O'Connell demonstrates her authority with standards.

what to buy next: The smokier *A Real Life Story* ✦✦✦✦ (Warner Bros., 1990, prod. Greg Penny) continues O'Connell's great sense of song selection for grownups, with such meaty items as Hiatt's "When We Ran" and Hugh Prestwood's "A Family Tie"—a wrenching, ambivalent look at an alcoholic husband.

what to avoid: You won't get burned with any of O'Connell's stuff—it's all at least interesting—but you can skip some of the completist's items, such as the folky, low-key *Just in Time* ✦✦✦ (Philo, 1988, prod. Béla Fleck), until after you've bought the Warner Bros. and Hannibal albums.

the rest:
(With De Dannan) *The Star-Spangled Molly* ✦✦✦ (Shanachie, 1981)

Maura O'Connell ♫♫♫ (Third Floor Music, 1983)
Blue Is the Colour of Hope ♫♫♫♫ (Warner Bros., 1992)
Stories ♫♫♫♫ (Rykodisc/Hannibal, 1995)
Wandering Home ♫♫♫♫ (Rykodisc/Hannibal, 1997)

worth searching for: *A Woman's Heart* (Dara, 1992, prod. various) is a collection of works by Irish female singers that includes O'Connell's "Trouble in the Fields" and "Western Highway" (and is reviewed in this book's Compilations section).

influences:

◀◀ Dolores Keane, Linda Ronstadt, New Grass Revival, Bonnie Raitt, Little Feat

▶▶ Eleanor McEvoy, Niamh Parsons, Mary Black, Mary Coughlan, Dolores O'Riordan

see also: *De Dannan, Kukuruza*

Elizabeth Lynch

Robbie O'Connell

See: The Clancy Brothers

Sinéad O'Connor

Experimental Celtic-influenced multi-genre pop
Born December 8, 1966, in Dublin, Ireland. Based in London, England.

The eternal infamy of Sinéad O'Connor's early-'90s Pope-ripping episode has eclipsed the distinctly world-music moment that preceded it—a Gregorian chant-like reading of Bob Marley's "War." It was a musical mix to match her personal one, as a recent Rastafari convert who's unshakably associated with another island culture through her recurrent Irish-liberation lyrical agenda ("Irish Ways and Irish Laws," "Famine," "This IS a Rebel Song"). That theme is not often echoed in O'Connor's musical settings, which aren't as interested in Celtic roots as new shoots of late-20th-century avant-pop. But the relatively few exceptions are doozies, which not only keep her hand in tradition but also keep one foot in the future, including the spoken-word Gaelic guest-shot by Enya ("Never Get Old") on O'Connor's 1987 debut *The Lion and the Cobra* (well in advance of the music 'n' poetry market niche), and the ominous Irish-fiddle-infused hip-hop backdrop of "I Am Stretched on Your Grave" on 1990's *I Do Not Want What I Haven't Got* (way ahead of the late-'90s' Gaelic-funk and Afro Celt trends). You'll also find O'Connor in the mix wherever there's a high-impact media project on Ireland's trials and triumphs, from the Catholic/Protestant cultural exchange initiative "Peace Together," to the soundtracks for *In the Name of the Father* and *Michael Collins,* to several of the Chieftains' with-a-lotta-help-from-our-friends concept CDs. But perhaps most importantly, you'll hear the figurative and literal voice of Ireland in O'Connor's extreme repertoire of vocal embellishments, inextricably tied—however innovative its variations or unfamiliar its audiences—to the ornamented improvisational *sean-nós* ("old-style") genre of traditional Gaelic singing.

what to buy: Celtic or no Celtic, you want O'Connor's first two shots heard 'round the world, *The Lion and the Cobra* ♫♫♫♫♫ (Ensign/Chrysalis, 1987, prod. Sinéad O'Connor) and *I Do Not Want What I Haven't Got* ♫♫♫♫♫ (Ensign/Chrysalis, 1990, prod. Sinéad O'Connor), both phenomenal declarations of artistic uniqueness, the former edgy and arty, the latter subtle and smoldering. "Scarlet Ribbons" is given a satisfying tin whistle and uilleann pipes treatment on the largely lounge-y and lackluster *Am I Not Your Girl?* ♫♫♫ (Ensign/Chrysalis, 1992, prod. Phil Ramone, Sinéad O'Connor), and with the folky *Gospel Oak* ♫♫♫♫ (Chrysalis/EMI, 1997) EP's structures and instrumentation O'Connor ventured decisively into the Celtic Lite marketplace—though the disc's best song, the Rwandan orphan dedication "Petit Poulet," offers a rolling rhythm and accordion-driven arrangement that also give the track a vaguely Franco-African feel. (These way-too-tame recordings were all given killer treatments in concert, so find a live bootleg if you can . . . not that there's anything right with that!) O'Connor's most acclaimed and easy-to-find classically Celtic material has been rendered with the Chieftains, the acknowledged best-of being "He Moved Through the Fair" and "The Foggy Dew" on *The Long Black Veil* ♫♫♫♫ (RCA/BMG, 1995, prod. Paddy Moloney). Keep up with all the directions of O'Connor's widely traveled muse at the exhaustive website http://sinead-oconnor.com.

the rest:
Universal Mother ♫♫♫♫ (Ensign/Chrysalis, 1994)
So Far . . . The Best of Sinéad O'Connor ♫♫♫♫ (Chrysalis/EMI, 1997)

influences:

◀◀ In Tua Nua, Enya, Clannad, Dónal Lunny, Kate Bush, Peter Gabriel

▶▶ The Cranberries, Alanis Morissette, Ashley MacIsaac, Mary Jane Lamond

see also: *Afro Celt Sound System, the Chieftains, Manu Dibango, Abdel Ali Slimani*

Adam McGovern

Odadaa!

See: Yacub Addy

Liam O'Flynn /Liam Ó Floinn

Irish traditional
Born 1950, in Kill, County Kildare, Ireland. Based in Dublin, Ireland.

Having first gained renown as a member of the 1970s Irish

group Planxty, but more recently associated with orchestral works like *The Brendan Voyage*, Liam O'Flynn is widely recognized as one of Ireland's finest performers on the uilleann pipes. Born into a musical family, O'Flynn started playing the whistle at an early age and enjoyed his first taste of the pipes through the playing of Tom Armstrong. O'Flynn, however, credits Leo Rowsome, Willie Clancy, and Séamus Ennis as his main musical influences. As the folk boom was taking Ireland by storm in the early 1970s, O'Flynn was asked by singer Christy Moore to participate in the making of the album *Prosperous*, featuring Andy Irvine, Dónal Lunny, and a few others as accompanists. After the album came out in 1972, the foursome decided to perform together under the name Planxty. Over the next 10 years the band went on to record six albums, each featuring O'Flynn's piping prominently. By the time Planxty broke up in the early 1980s, O'Flynn had become involved in performing the compositions of his good friend Shaun Davey, who was experimenting with bringing together uilleann pipes and symphony orchestra. Recorded in 1980, the first and still the best-known of these pieces is *The Brendan Voyage*, evoking the legend of St. Brendan, Abbot of Clonfert's sixth-century sea voyage to North America. In 1988 O'Flynn finally recorded his first, eponymous solo album, released on his own label and featuring Seán Keane and Lunny. *The Fine Art of Piping*, produced for the British company Celtic Music, followed in 1989, and the fine trio album *The Fire Aflame*, with Keane and Matt Molloy, in 1992. Some of O'Flynn's more recent albums like *Out to an Other Side* (1993) and *The Given Note* (1995), which clearly show the influence of the piper's collaboration with Davey, are no match for his earlier output. However, his latest recording, *The Piper's Call* (1998), while again showing a tendency towards rather full accompaniments, is a masterpiece of classical piping and reunites him with Keane and Molloy. Even more compelling perhaps is the video release by the same title, beautifully shot and featuring fascinating interviews of the artist and others.

what to buy: Although the somewhat inflated accompaniments can at times overwhelm his masterful piping, O'Flynn's latest album, *The Piper's Call* ♪♪♪♪ (Tara, 1998, prod. Liam O'Flynn, Arty McGlynn), is also the best choice among his recent solo releases. The pieces performed are perfect vehicles for O'Flynn's deliberate and expressive style of piping. Notable tracks include wonderful duets with Irish masters like Seán Keane (fiddle) and Matt Molloy (flute), as well as with the Galician piper Carlos Núñez, who has come to prominence through his collaboration with the Chieftains.

what to buy next: While O'Flynn's piping is immaculate throughout, his recent albums, *Out to an Other Side* ♪♪♪ (Tara, 1993, prod. Shaun Davey) and *The Given Note* ♪♪♪ (Tara, 1995, prod.

indian/jazz fusion

World music is a genre replete with cultural cross-pollinations, but no fusion has proven quite so artistically rewarding as the collaboration between Western jazz and Indian classical musicians. That the concept works so well makes sense, as both forms consist primarily of standard compositions within which musicians are free to improvise in order to demonstrate their technical prowess. The movement owes a great debt to Ravi Shankar, who broke with the restraints of Hindustani tradition to collaborate with Western classical violinist Yehudi Menuhin and the Beatles in the 1960s. This opened the door for two Indian/jazz fusion supergroups, Shakti and Oregon, whose music set the standards that persist to this day. Shakti, the more influential of the two, featured John McLaughlin on guitar, L. Shankar (no relation to Ravi) on violin, Zakir Hussain on *tabla* drum, and Vikku Vinayakram on *ghatam* percussion. Oregon was co-founded by one of Ravi Shankar's students, Collin Walcott, an American considered among the finest non-Indian tabla practitioners. That instrument always seems to play a prominent role in this hybrid genre, and three tabla virtuosos—Hussain, Badal Roy, and Trilok Gurtu—can be found at the heart of many excellent fusion projects. In addition to Shakti, Hussain is a crucial ingredient in Mickey Hart's Planet Drum ensemble and Bill Laswell's cross-stylistic experiments; Roy has played with jazz legends ranging from Miles Davis and Ornette Coleman to Pharoah Sanders; and, in addition to replacing the late Walcott in Oregon, Gurtu has worked with Don Cherry, Joe Zawinul, Pat Metheny, and Material. For an introduction to the wondrous sounds these inspired unions can create, check out *The Best of Shakti* ♪♪♪♪ (Moment, 1994) and *The Essential Oregon* ♪♪♪♪ (Vanguard, 1981/1987), two impressive compilations from the genre's most influential groups. Beyond that, look for albums featuring any of the above-mentioned names, or those of masters like guitarist Vishwa Mohan Bhatt, violinist L. Subramaniam, and American *bansuri* bamboo flutist Steve Gorn.

Bret Love

Shaun Davey), would hardly meet with the approval of traditional music lovers. The influence of O'Flynn's collaboration with Shaun Davey is clearly heard in the overwhelmingly busy and pop-ish arrangements. Although only distantly related to traditional music, Davey's orchestral suites like *The Brendan Voyage* ♫♫♫ (Tara, 1980, prod. Shaun Davey), *The Pilgrim* ♫♫♫ (Tara, 1983, prod. Shaun Davey), *Granuaile* ♫♫♫ (Tara, 1985, prod. Shaun Davey), and *The Relief of Derry Symphony* ♫♫♫ (Tara, 1990, prod. Shaun Davey) have been successful in their own way. On *The Seville Suite* ♫♫♫ (Tara, 1992, prod. Bill Whelan, Dónal Lunny), O'Flynn performs with Andy Irvine and Lunny on "Timedance '92," the piece that was to evolve into co-producer Whelan's award-winning show *Riverdance.*

worth searching for: Unfortunately, O'Flynn's best recordings of traditional music remain his earlier ones, which are the hardest to find. During his Planxty heyday, he appeared on Mick Hanly and Mícheál Ó Domhnaill's beautiful *Celtic Folkweave* ♫♫♫♫ (Polydor, 1974, prod. Dónal Lunny). Although O'Flynn experimented with the accompaniment on his first solo LP, *Liam O'Flynn* ♫♫♫ (LOF, 1988, prod. Dónal Lunny), Lunny's production avoided the excesses of the later, Davey-produced albums. *The Fine Art of Piping* ♫♫♫♫ (Celtic Music, 1989) is just that, excellent solo piping by a master of the instrument. On *The Fire Aflame* ♫♫♫♫ (Claddagh, 1992, prod. Seán Keane, Matt Molloy, Liam O'Flynn) O'Flynn collaborated with Matt Molloy (flute), Séan Keane (fiddle), and Arty McGlynn (guitar) to produce a remarkable album of deftly played traditional music.

influences:

◀◀ Tom Armstrong, Leo Rowsome, Seamus Ennis, Willie Clancy

▶▶ Mick O'Brien, Jimmy O'Brien-Moran

see also: *Patrick Cassidy, Shaun Davey, Frankie Gavin, James Keane, Dónal Lunny, Matt Molloy, Sean Ó Riada, Planxty, Áine Uí Cheallaigh, Bill Whelan*

Philippe Varlet

Ayub Ogada

Luo folk and fusion
Born in Mombasa, Kenya. Based in London, England.

A member of the Luo tribe, Ayub Ogada was inducted into the world of music at the tender age of six, when he accompanied his father, who was studying medicine in the U.S., and his mother, as they began playing Luo songs on the U.S. college circuit. Later, Ogada's education and uncanny knack for percussion led to a position with the French Cultural Centre in Nairobi, where he composed modern and traditional music for various productions. These two formative periods provided the yin and yang of Ogada's musical spirit, which combines a healthy re-

spect for tradition with a hunger to nourish his own progressive creativity. A sophisticated urbanite, Ogada absorbed a variety of musical legacies, including soul, jazz, and the gorgeous, guitar-based sounds of *benga,* a Luo-derived rhythm popular in the '70s and '80s—but his love for traditional sounds led him to co-found the African Heritage Band in 1979. Six years and two albums later, Ogada followed the African musical exodus to Europe, where, after a time spent playing in the promising rumba band Taxi Pata Pata, he was discovered busking in England's subways and signed to Peter Gabriel's RealWorld label.

what's available: Ogada's only solo album available in the States is *En Mana Kuoyo* ♫♫♫♫ (RealWorld, 1993, prod. Ayub Ogada, Richard Evans), a fantastic outing on which the buoyant melodies of Ogada's lyre-like *nyatiti* are matched only by the lilting beauty of his rich tenor. With Ogada on nyatiti, percussion, and flutes, former Taxi Pata Pata bandmate Zak Sikobe on guitars, and Alex Gifford on double bass and Hammond organ, the album is a seamless blending of the traditional and the modern, with jubilant Afropop numbers like "Ondiek (Hyena)" offset by the haunting ambience of chilling songs like "Kothbiro (It's Going to Rain)." Ogada collaborated with a cast of dozens in RealWorld's pan-cultural supergroup Jam Nation, whose *Way Down Buffalo Hell* ♫♫♫ (RealWorld, 1993, prod. Mark Rutherford, Sugar J) features Ogada's distinctive vocal style to great effect, as does the aptly named Afro Celt Sound System, whose *Volume 1: Sound Magic* ♫♫♫ (RealWorld, 1996, prod. Simon Emmerson) presented a surprisingly fluid blending of two seemingly disparate cultural traditions.

influences:

◀◀ D.O. Misiani, Shirati Jazz, Osibisa, Victoria Jazz

see also: *Afro Celt Sound System*

Bret Love

Helen O'Hara

Celtic, Irish fiddle
Born in Bristol, England. Based in the British Isles.

From childhood onward, Helen O'Hara just couldn't help being impressive. At age nine she began simultaneous study of violin and piano, first at the Birmingham School of Music with Felix Kok (leader of the Birmingham Symphony Orchestra), then with James Coles (leader of the Bournmouth Symphony) and Andrew Watkinson (leader of the Endellion Quartet). Her highly identifiable violin sound brought her attention and acclaim as the featured soloist in Dexys Midnight Runners, with whom she was awarded four gold records for sales of the album *Too-Rye-Ay* and international #1 hit single, "Come On Eileen." O'Hara also basked in the success of the group's follow-up, *Don't Stand Me Down,* when it was rereleased and rediscovered by radio in the late '90s. But her triumphs with Dexys are not her only ones; O'Hara also scored a Top 10 English hit with "Because of You," the theme-song for the BBC television series *Brush Strokes*; helped Mark Isham arrange brass and violin sections for Tanita Tikaram's *Everybody's Angel* ; and contributed as a session violinist to a lengthy list of recordings including the 1990 Irish World Cup single. As dedicated out of the spotlight as in it, O'Hara notes that she's a member of Greenpeace and a "keen" recycler.

what to buy: While Celtic music has rapidly become a staple in the international marketplace, Irish fiddlers remain predominantly male, with players like Johnny Cunningham, Kevin Burke, Hugh Gillespie, John Doherty, and the Chieftains' Seane Keane taking up most of the limited limelight. Women are usually relegated to vocals or the harp—with a few bold souls like accordionist Sharon Shannon claiming new ground. This leaves O'Hara, Natalie MacMaster, and lamentably few other female violin soloists to pave the way for others. Of the two, O'Hara has sold more records because her unique cross of Celtic and skiffle stylings helped power Dexys Midnight Runners around the world; but her solo recordings find O'Hara hewing closer to her Irish roots, though in an expansive way. *A Night in Ireland* ♪♪♪♪ (New World Music, 1999, prod. Helen O'Hara) finds the violinist at her best in a refreshing, impromptu, concert-like atmosphere put across with state-of-the-art production that showcases special guest performances by the late Rolling Stones pianist Nicky Hopkins, harpist Skaila Kanga, and accordion player Eddie Hession. In addition to moving instrumental treatments of traditional Celtic favorites like "Danny Boy" and "Three Captains," you'll discover rarer traditional Irish and English tunes like "Mountains of Mourne," "The Curragh of Kildaire," and "The Mason's Apron." O'Hara also contributes several outstanding originals, including "Hills of Calheiros" and the charming "Irish Lullaby." While perhaps not as technically proficient as the legendary Keane—who has recorded more than 50 albums—O'Hara demonstrates an equal measure of the emotive quality that is so vital to Celtic interpretation. Her ability to manipulate melody while soloing or laying back is impressive, and her compositional style is sublime.

what to buy next: Not to be confused with music from the land of Dixie, *Southern Hearts* ♪♪♪♪ (New World Music, 1998, prod. Helen O'Hara) features O'Hara as she focuses on the music of Ireland's south, along with such stellar guest artists as pedal steel guitarist B.J. Cole, pianist Hopkins, Celtic harpist Kanga, percussionist Woody Woodmansey, and the legendary Robin Williamson on Celtic harp, pennywhistle, and acoustic guitar.

the rest:
(With Dexys Midnight Runners) *Too-Rye-Ay* ♪♪♪♪ (PolyGram, 1982)
(With Dexys Midnight Runners) *Jackie Wilson Said* ♪♪♪ (PolyGram, 1982)

(With Dexys Midnight Runners) *Let's Get This Straight from the Start* ♪♪♪♪ (PolyGram, 1982)
(With Dexys Midnight Runners) *Celtic Soul Brothers* ♪♪♪♪ (PolyGram, 1983)
(With Dexys Midnight Runners) *This Is What She's Like* ♪♪♪ (PolyGram, 1985)
(With Dexys Midnight Runners) *Don't Stand Me Down* ♪♪♪♪ (PolyGram, 1985/1997)
(With Dexys Midnight Runners) *Because of You* ♪♪♪ (PolyGram, 1986)
(With Dexys Midnight Runners) *The Way You Look Tonight* ♪♪ (PolyGram, 1988)
(With Dexys Midnight Runners) *Kevin Rowlands 13th Crime* ♪♪ (PolyGram, 1988)
(With Tanita Tikaram) *Everybody's Angel* ♪♪♪ (Warner Bros., 1988)
(With Tanita Tikaram) *The Sweetkeeper* ♪♪♪ (Warner Bros., 1988)
(With Tanita Tikaram) *Ancient Heart* ♪♪♪ (Warner Bros., 1988)
(With the Adventures) *Trading Secrets with the Moon* (Warner Bros., 1990)
(With Mary Coughlin) *Uncertain Pleasures* ♪♪♪♪ (Warner Bros., 1990)

influences:
◄◄ Seane Keane, Johnny Cunningham, skiffle

PJ Birosik

Sonny Okosun /Sonny Okosuns

African funk, highlife, reggae, "ozzidi"
Born 1947, in Benin City, Nigeria. Based in Lagos, Nigeria.

Okosun got his start as an actor with the Eastern Nigerian Theater and began playing in bands in 1966, at the age of 19. He was originally inspired by Western artists like Elvis and Cliff Richard, and played Western pop until he was hired by Sir Victor Uwaifo as second guitarist in 1969. Uwaifo became a star by adapting "palm-wine" (acoustic) guitar to various traditional styles, and giving them a contemporary spin. Perhaps he inspired Okosun, because after he left Uwaifo, Okosun developed his own combination of funk, reggae, and traditional music and gave it the label "ozzidi." His first albums with his Ozzidi band were still a bit ragged—the seams of his rock/funk fusion still showed— but by the time he cut *Fire in Soweto* the sound was his own. The title track of that album became a Pan-African hit, selling millions of copies. When it was released on the British OTI label, it caused a sensation in Europe too, making Okosun an international star. From the late 1970s to the mid-1980s Okosun released a string of hit albums that combined reggae, rock, highlife, funk, and, increasingly, a heavy disco/house backbeat. The fact that he sang in English, and tended to address the social and economic problems of Nigeria and South Africa, made him a cause celebre—especially in the U.S., where he was briefly compared to Bob Marley for his militant lyrics and highly melodic tunes.

what's available: *Liberation* ♫♫♫♫ (Shanachie, 1991, prod. Sonny Okosun) is a solid compilation of the smashes from Okosun's heyday, although it inexplicably leaves out "Fire in Soweto" and "Tell Papa," his biggest hits of the time. The funky, chattering guitars, reggae-ized basslines and relentless percussion give listeners a fine example of one era's state-of-the-art Afropop.

worth searching for: Most of Okosun's music is currently out of print, although you may be able to turn up some anthologies on import. EMI, which put out Okosun's hits in the 1980s, no longer has a distribution deal with its Nigerian partners, which will probably make much of Okosun's best stuff hard to find. The ones to look for are *Fire in Soweto* ♫♫♫♫ (Oti, 1978), *3rd World* ♫♫♫♫ (Oti, 1980), and *Togetherness* ♫♫♫♫ (EMI, 1983). *African Soldiers* ♫♫♫♫ (Profile, 1991) was released on CD in 1991, but the recording went out of print within a year.

influences:

◀◀ Bob Marley, Fela Kuti, Sir Victor Uwaifo

▶▶ Alpha Blondy, Majek Fashek

j. poet

Victor Olaiya

Highlife
Born c. 1920, in Ijebu, Nigeria. Based in Lagos, Nigeria.

Known as "The Evil Genius of Highlife" ("evil" being synonymous with "bad" in 1960s black American slang), Olaiya is one of the few highlife musicians who have managed to keep making a living after the music's heyday. Highlife (a cosmopolitan dance music) was the day-to-day soundtrack for a generation of African youth that grew up in the heady times of early post-colonialism. When Ghana ousted the British in 1957 to became the first democratically ruled black African nation, West Africa witnessed an explosion of cultural pride and artistic expression. Kwame Nkrumah's government actively encouraged cultural expression and cooperation between ethnic groups, and supported the music of the highlife bands that ruled Ghana (and later Nigeria) and gave that pride "feet." Highlife swept through West Africa and England, preparing ears for what we now call "worldbeat" music, and piquing curiosity about the many rich varieties of African music in its less commercial forms.

In the 1920s, colonial contact with Europeans introduced the people of Sierra Leone and Ghana to a variety of new styles that included sea chanteys (which were similar to African religious chants), Christian church music, brass marching bands, and European popular songs. These forms were quickly "Africanized," and since they weren't the property of a single ethnic group, they provided a means for instant musical cross-pollination. The introduction of Western instruments—guitars,

horns, and trap drums—also sparked the African imagination. By the mid-'30s these forms had combined into a new dance craze that was popular from Congo in the south to the border of Mali in the north, where Muslim forms predominated.

Olaiya, who is a singer, composer, and trumpet player, got his start in the band of Bobby Benson playing the European and Latin dance charts that were popular with African audiences in the early 1950s. But after catching E.T. Mensah and the Tempos on their first Nigerian tour, Olaiya left Benson and started a highlife group, the Cool Cats. He retained his popularity throughout the 1950s and 1960s with a series of hit singles, and gave many young musicians their first taste of fame, including Fela Kuti, Victor Uwaifo, and Sonny Okosuns (a.k.a. Okosun). He continues to lead his International Stars band to this day, playing a mix of new material and rearrangements of his back catalog at his Stadium Hotel Club and selected live concerts.

worth searching for: Not much by this pioneer is available in the States, so you'll have to do dig through the import bins to find his work. His greatest-hits compilations are probably the best bet; try *In the '60s* (Polydor Nigeria), *Highlife Reincarnation* (Polydor Nigeria), and *Highlife Giants, Vol. 1* (Polydor Nigeria).

influences:

◀◀ Bobby Benson, E.T. Mensah

▶▶ Rex Lawson, Pat Thomas, African Brothers International

see also: *Fela Kuti, E.T. Mensah, Sonny Okosun*

j. poet

Babatunde Olatunji

African drumming, Afro-jazz
Born 1927, in Ajido, Nigeria. Based in New York, NY, USA.

The sounds of West Africa come alive through the music of Babatunde Olatunji. In the 40 years since the release of his groundbreaking debut album, *Drums of Passion,* the Nigeria-born and New York–based drummer, vocalist, and bandleader has taken the spirited rhythms of his homeland to stages around the globe. Although the West African tradition of drumming is vital to Olatunji's playing, he has consistently explored and adapted the rhythms of Earth's many cultures. In the 1960s and '70s, he performed and recorded with such jazz giants as Max Roach and John Coltrane. In the early '90s, he and many others joined with the Grateful Dead's Mickey Hart to record and tour as the percussion supergroup Planet Drum.

Olatunji's upbringing matched his destiny. In Ajido, the small fishing and trading village where he grew up, music was viewed as a necessary accompaniment for every aspect of life. The son of a fisherman, Olatunji was fascinated by music from earliest

Babatunde Olatunji

memory. At the age of six he was already watching and studying the musicians he saw at village festivals. Despite this enthusiasm, Olatunji didn't imagine a professional music career until coming to the United States, in 1950, to study political science at Morehouse College in Atlanta. While there, he produced a popular multi-media show based on the music and culture of his homeland. Moving to New York in 1954 to attend the New York University Graduate School of Public Administration, he continued to balance his academic studies with musical performances. A turning point came during an extended engagement at Radio City Music Hall in 1957. Performing a medley of African songs with a 66-piece orchestra, Olatunji was heard by Columbia Records' John Hammond (a legendary jazz producer who later produced Bob Dylan and Bruce Springsteen), and was invited to record. The resulting album, *Drums of Passion,* went on to sell more than five million copies and became not only the first album of African music ever recorded in the Western world, but, to this day, one of the most successful.

Much of the money that Olatunji and his band earned on their early tours was used to open an Institute of African Cultural Studies in Harlem. The Institute, however, was plagued by financial instability and closed after two years. But never tiring in efforts for his people both on the continent and among the diaspora, in the early '60s Olatunji and Drums of Passion became actively involved with the Civil Rights movement, performing at NAACP rallies and traveling with Martin Luther King. Despite his influence, Olatunji faced great obstacles in his creative quest. Although he composed the score for the Broadway and Hollywood productions of *A Raisin in the Sun,* he was paid only $300 for his efforts. He suffered similarly when he assisted fellow Morehouse alumni Bill Lee with the music for *She's Gotta Have It,* the hit film debut by Lee's son, Spike. When Olatunji's contract with Columbia Records expired in 1965, he was unable to interest another label in his music. By the '80s, he had practically faded into obscurity. Things began to change in 1985, when Grateful Dead drummer Hart came backstage after Olatunji performed at a San Francisco club. "I had played at his high school," Olatunji said during a 1996 interview. "He told me that I was responsible for his interest in drums." The meeting led Hart to produce and secure Rykodisc's release of two new Olatunji albums, *Drums of Passion: The Beat* and *Drums of Pas-*

**5
7
2**

sion: *The Invocation*. These discs further widened Olatunji's sound, with 11 percussionists and seven vocalists, and the master drummer again increased his following when he and his band opened the Dead's New Year's Eve show at the Oakland Coliseum on December 31, 1985.

Over the past decade, Olatunji and Drums of Passion have remained active. Their performances have included "Earth Celebration '95" in Japan; the "One World, One Music Celebration" of the United Nations' 50th anniversary at Madison Square Garden; the opening ceremonies of the International Peace University in Berlin; the International Transpersonal Association Conference in Czechoslovakia; and the New Orleans Jazz and Heritage Festival. In 1997, Sony issued a four-CD collection of Olatunji's recordings for Columbia from 1959–65, and Olatunji recently completed an autobiography, *The Beat of My Drum,* for Temple University Press. Although it's been more than four decades since he gave up his dream of becoming an ambassador, Olatunji has continued to promote an increased understanding of his native continent. In addition to teaching at the Esalen Institute in Big Sur, California, and the Omega Institute in Rhinebeck, New York, the "grand old man of the African drum" has conducted workshops in Italy, Japan, Canada, Switzerland, and Ghana, and set more future music in motion than we can yet conceive.

what to buy: The first album of African music to be recorded in the United States, *Drums of Passion* 🎵🎵🎵🎵 (Columbia, 1957, prod. John Hammond Sr., Teo Macero) was a phenomenal success—selling more than five million copies and sparking an interest in African music that continues today.

what to buy next: *Drums of Passion: The Beat* 🎵🎵🎵🎵 (Rykodisc, 1988, prod. Mickey Hart) is a musical exploration of West Africa's traditional chants and songs, with Olatunji's band augmented by (among many others) Brazilian percussionist Airto Moreira and bassist Bobby Vega of Sly and the Family Stone.

best of the rest:
Zungo! 🎵🎵🎵 (CBS, 1960)
Drums of Passion: The Invocation 🎵🎵🎵 (Rykodisc, 1989)
Love Drum Talk 🎵🎵🎵 (Chesky, 1997)

influences:
◀◀ The West African drumming tradition

▶▶ Mickey Hart, Airto Moreira, Carlos Santana

see also: *Mickey Hart, Airto Moreira, Randy Weston, Stevie Wonder*

Craig Harris

Olodum
Samba-reggae
Formed 1979, in Salvador, Bahia, Brazil. Based in Salvador, Bahia, Brazil.

Vast and varied membership throughout the years, prominently featuring president and founder João Jorge and co-founder Neguinho do Samba.

With their much-heralded participation in the song "The Obvious Child" on Paul Simon's *Rhythm of the Saints* album and its subsequent tour, Olodum launched their heavily percussive sound—a Latin rhythm so unlike others—into the international arena. The rise over the last 20 years of the *blocos afros*—cultural organizations promoting race-consciousness and artistic expression—on Brazil's Atlantic Coast, mainly in Salvador, Bahia, has transformed both Carnival and day-to-day life. With the blocos, Carnival gained a strong black focus. The polyrhythms of *ijexa, aluja,* and *samba-de-roda* departed from the three *atabaque* drums of the local *Candomblé* religion and found strength in numbers through the percussion instruments already associated with samba—the giant *surdo,* the *repenique,* and the *tamborim.* The fusion of these Afro-Brazilian rhythms with Caribbean influences resulted in *samba-reggae,* the dominant bloco sound. To see the expansive bloco ensemble Olodum up close, in the street, 3,000 strong, every step and drumbeat synchronized, is to feel the raw power of music.

Since its inception as a small Carnival group, Olodum has built itself into a powerful institution of cultural production and community rejuvenation in the Pelourinho district of Salvador. Olodum operates music and dance schools, theater groups, shops, and restaurants, as well as programs for underprivileged youth. (Some of the banner performers of late-20th century Brazil, including Virginia Rodrigues, have gone from impoverished obscurity to the world stage thanks largely to initial aid from Olodum's operations.) Olodum's earlier recordings are gems, rough-hewn on very little technology, featuring thundering drums and traditional call-and-response vocals. Today the structure includes guitar, bass, keyboards, and a horn section, and the sound leans more toward pop arrangements and melodic vocals. Either way, good music remains as much their hallmark as good works.

what to buy: There are three versions of the album *The Best of Olodum* 🎵🎵🎵🎵 (Continental, 1991, prod. Max Pierre). One is the original Brazilian release, which recaps the first phase of the group's development. Then there are two same-named Japanese variations, from 1993 and '94, that pop up from time to time and are also excellent collections.

what to buy next: *Sol E Mar* 🎵🎵🎵 (Continental, 1995, prod. Mauro Almeida) is a live set from the Montreux Jazz Festival.

Olodum

The quality of the recording is not 100 percent, but the renditions are fresh, and the repertoire goes from the very beginning to their most modern numbers.

best of the rest:

Nubia/Axum Etiopia 𝄢𝄢𝄢𝄢 (Continental, 1988)
Do Deserto do Saara ao Nordeste Brasileiro 𝄢𝄢𝄢𝄢 (Continental, 1989)
Da Atlantica a Bahia, o Mar e o Caminho 𝄢𝄢𝄢𝄢 (Continental, 1990)
A Musica do Olodum 𝄢𝄢𝄢𝄢 (Continental, 1992)
O Movimento 𝄢𝄢𝄢𝄢 (Continental, 1993)
Os Filhos do Sol 𝄢𝄢𝄢𝄢⁺ (Continental, 1994)
Roma Negra 𝄢𝄢𝄢 (Continental, 1996)
Liberdade 𝄢𝄢𝄢 (Continental, 1997)

worth searching for: Olodum's first album *Egito/Madagasgar* 𝄢𝄢𝄢𝄢 (Continental, 1987, prod. Max Pierre) is a piece of history, an impassioned paean to Africa and affirmation of Brazil that stirs something deep inside.

influences:
◀◀ Ile Aye

▶▶ Carlinhos Brown, Daniela Mercury, Caetano Veloso, Gilberto Gil, E O Tchan

see also: *Timbalada*

Mara Weiss and Nego Beto

OMC

Pacific pop
Formed 1995, in Auckland, New Zealand. Based in New Zealand.

Rotating accompanists led by Pauly Fuemana, vocals, guitars, drums, bass.

OMC, essentially, is Pauly Fuemana, even though at least eight people accompany him on tour. Best known for the worldwide smash single "How Bizarre" but with more where that came from—especially in concert—this group has the ability to give any rave or late-night party a second wind with its funkified, Polynesian-influenced sound. OMC was born after the Otara Millionaires Club disbanded in 1995. The original group formed in a poor section of Auckland and adopted the name to show naysayers that these kids bred on the tough streets were smart enough to create a unique sound and survive. Thus far, what "How Bizarre" may have given OMC a shot at is being a one-hit wonder. However, with Fuemana's strong vision of musical success, OMC may just be around for a while.

what's available: OMC's debut album *How Bizarre* 𝄢𝄢𝄢 (Mercury, 1997, prod. Alan Jansson) combines Fuemana's Polynesian roots-flair with hip-hop, jazz, funk, and runaway rock. Although Fuemana is credited with playing the majority of the instruments on the album, he enlisted a host of musicians to

contribute their expertise on the likes of pedal steel, violin, cello, piano, trumpet, accordion, French horn, Dobro, and sax.

influences:
◀◀ Marvin Gaye, Prince, Grandmaster Flash, David Bowie, New Order

Ari Bendersky

Kongar-ool Ondar

Tuvan throat-singing
Born 1962, in Chadaana, Tuva. Based in Chadaana, Tuva.

One of the most intriguing figures in world music, Ondar is considered the world's finest master of the art of Tuvan throat-singing, a phenomenal technique that enables a vocalist to sing as many as four distinctly audible notes at once. After graduating from high school, Ondar was drafted into the Soviet Navy, where he eventually suffered a broken neck while unloading cargo. Fortunately, he returned to Tuva with his throat intact, and by 1992 had been crowned world champion in the *sygyt* style of throat-singing, which is said to emulate the songs of birds. He holds the title of "People's Throat-Singer" in Tuva, and was named "National Artist of Russia" after serenading Boris Yeltsin during the Russian President's historic visit to Tuva in 1994. But the most eventful year for Ondar proved to be 1998, during which he founded a school for throat-singing in Tuva's capital, Kyzyl; was elected to the Tuvan Parliament representing his home district of Chadaana; and became the first Tuvan throat-singer signed to a major label, Warner Bros.

what's available: Its questionable title aside, Ondar's major-label debut, *Back Tuva Future* 𝄢𝄢𝄢𝄢 (Warner Bros., 1999, prod. David Hoffner, Jim Ed Norman), is a brilliantly innovative fusion of styles that puts the somewhat alien sounds of Tuvan throat-singing in a variety of familiar contexts. "Tuva Groove" is a downright funky jam matching danceable rhythms, Ondar's mind-boggling vocals, and otherworldly chants from scientist/long-time Tuva enthusiast Richard P. Feynman, while "Two Lands, One Tribe" smartly pairs Ondar with Native American flutist/vocalist Bill Miller, pointing out the similarities between their traditions. Willie Nelson and Randy Scruggs drop by to make an East-West connection (strangely enough, Tuva is also known for its cowboys), while "Kargyraa Rap" draws comparisons between the Tuvan affinity for rapidly spoken tongue-twisters and . . . well, you figure it out.

worth searching for: Ondar's debut CD, *Echoes of Tuva*, and his strangely effective collaboration with San Franciscan bluesman Paul "Earthquake" Pena, *Genghis Blues*, are available by mail-order only from Friends of Tuva, Box 182, Belvedere, CA 94930; but several selections from each can be found on the excellent throat-singing anthology *Deep in the Heart of Tuva* 𝄢𝄢𝄢𝄢 (ellipsis arts . . . , 1996, prod. various), which is also very highly recommended (and is reviewed in this book's Compilations section).

influences:

◄◄ Oorzhak Khunashtaar-ool, Bilchi-Maa Davaa, Sainkho Namtchylak, Huun-Huur-Tu

►► Paul "Earthquake" Pena

see also: *Bill Miller*

Bret Love

Remmy Ongala

Ubongo, soukous fusion
Born 1947 in Kivu, Congo. Based in Dar Es Salaam, Tanzania.

Like many Africans, Ongala began his musical education as a drummer; he joined the band Bantu Success while still in his teens. Later on, after teaching himself guitar and playing in several local *soukous* (African rumba) groups, he traveled to Tanzania to join Orchestra Makassy. When Makassy moved to Kenya after their big hit "Mamba Bado," Ongala stayed behind and joined Orchestra Super Matimila, a band owned by a local businessman. Ongala's tenure with Super Matimila lifted them to superstar status, mainly on the strength of his songwriting, which deals with the day-to-day tribulations of ordinary citizens, and his creative arrangements, which combine Congolese soukous with Tanzanian rhythms and sizzling horn charts. In 1988 Peter Gabriel brought Ongala and his band to Bath, England, to record in the RealWorld studios and play several dates at various WOMAD (World of Music, Arts and Dance) festivals. Because of the expense involved, Ongala had to leave about half of the band in Tanzania, and some critics claim that the reduced band relies too much on Ongala's guitar, and arrangements that are considerably less adventurous than those he was cutting for his Tanzanian albums.

what's available: On *Songs for the Poor Man* ♪♪♪ (RealWorld, 1988, prod. Remmy Ongala, Basil Anderson, David Bottrill) Ongala, one of Africa's finest protest singers, reprises some of his Tanzanian hits in a stripped-down style featuring his smooth vocals and inventive guitar work, and the complex rhythms of drummers Lawrence Linbanga and Saidi Salum. Ongala's second international album *Mambo* ♪♪♪ (RealWorld, 1992, prod. Rupert Hine) sounds more Congolese and less eclectic than his RealWorld debut, but it's still filled with sparkling musicianship; a few tunes are even sung in English to give Westerners a better idea of Ongala's impassioned songwriting.

influences:

◄◄ Orchestra Makassy, Franco and TPOK Jazz, Juwata Jazz Band, DDC Mlimani Park

j. poet

Oku Onuora

Dub poetry
Born Orlando Wong, 1952, in East Kingston, Jamaica. Based in Kingston, Jamaica.

Onuora is one of the originators of "dub poetry" (a reggae-influenced form of spoken-word) who's since fallen out of the limelight, eclipsed by fellow pioneers Mutabaruka and Linton Kwesi Johnson. Like some other revolutionaries, Onuora came to writing via prison, and his particular road to literary epiphany is the stuff of folk legend. While still a teenager, he was working as a community activist and agitator when he purportedly robbed a post office (a charge he denies) in order to help an underfunded literacy program for ghetto youth. Arrested and convicted, he was shot five times in two escape attempts. He eventually served five-and-a-half years of hard labor, during which time he changed his name and took up Rastafarianism—and the pen. Once his poems were smuggled out and gained some exposure (they were collected and published as *Echo* in 1977), a public campaign led in part by PEN International first won him limited "work release" (to give poetry readings), then ultimately parole. Like several of his dub-poet contemporaries, he sharpened his performance skills at the Jamaican School of Drama, and released his first single ("Reflections in Red" on the 56 Hope Road label) in 1979. Onuora's classic poems are strong, spare, and simple, written—in keeping with his longstanding program of democratizing literary language—almost exclusively in Jamaican creole. Out of his mouth, the compact, pared-down, stutter-step cadences and couplets that lesser dub poets have exhausted from overwork still seem fresh, taut, and clean, perfectly suited to the mix of fervor and desperation he's trying to convey. And whether he's incanting a catalog of outrages or a call to action, his urgent bass-baritone can jump from a low, guttural monotone to a high, keening wail in the space of a single line.

what's available: Most of Onuora's oeuvre is hard to find and only intermittently in print. *I a Tell . . . Dubwize and Otherwise* ♪♪♪♪ (ROIR, 1991, prod. Oku Onuora) was one attempt to remedy this with a vital collection of Onuora's seminal work—singles and remixes, both previously released and unreleased, from 1979 to 1983. On the title track he adopts his trademark persona: what Trinidadian scholar Gordon Rohlehr calls the "tribal 'I,'" the voice of the community who sees it and calls it on behalf of the "sufferah" in the street. It's that same persona who speaks "Wat a Situashan," a minimalist though impassioned adaptation of Mikey Smith's famous litany of local indignities, "Mi Cyaan Believe It." Onuora's version connects the local to the global, and finishes with a menacing promise of international conflagration. Most of the arrangements are true to the dub aesthetic of the day, making ample use of echo and reverb.

worth searching for: Though it adds hardcore funk and R&B to Onuora's musical bag of tricks, *Pressure Drop* ♫♫♫♪ (56 Hope Road, 1984/Heartbeat, 1986/Zola & Zola, 1993)—released under the name "Oku+AK7"—continues in the vein of his early material, documenting "downpression" and shouting away the shackles of colonial mentality, from the screeching manifesto "A Slum Dweller Declares" to the fortifying anthem "Change Yes Change." Heartbeat has deleted this title, but Dutch label Zola & Zola has gallantly filled the gap. *New Jerusalem Dub* ♫♫♫ (ROIR, 1990, prod. Oku Onuora)—available on cassette only—is a sort of "ambient" concept album in the tradition of Lee "Scratch" Perry, which Onuora describes as "poetry without words." Though American labels have largely decided that dub poetry doesn't sell, European audiences apparently haven't heard the news; Onuora's recent import releases include *Bus Out* (Zola & Zola, 1993, prod. Oku Onuora) and *Yesterday, Today, Tomorrow: 20th Anniversary Collection* (Who Done It/Jamma, 1998). Two albums are forthcoming: the self-explanatory *OverDub: A Tribute to King Tubby* (ION), and *A Movement*, which features roots-reggae legends Sly & Robbie and Jamaican-born jazz pianist Monty Alexander. While this album moves Onuora onto some new musical ground (namely smooth jazz and hip-hop), lyrically it takes him back to his beginnings; "Education," for example, is an exhortatory sermon for youth literacy and scholarship. Among his noteworthy guest appearances, Onuora—along with Chuck D, John Trudell, Augustus Pablo, and others—contributed several numbers to the Afro-Native-Anarchist "The Fire This Time" collective's second compilation, *Dancing on John Wayne's Head* (Extreme/Dub Systems, 1995, prod. various). Selected published poems are collected in *Echo* (Sangster's, 1977) and *Fuel for Fire* (Frontline, 1998). Onuora maintains a website at www.escape.com/~dred/ which includes both sound and video clips.

influences:

⏮ Big Youth

⏭ Jean Binta Breeze

see also: *Jean Binta Breeze, Linton Kwesi Johnson, King Tubby, Mutabaruka, Augustus Pablo, Lee "Scratch" Perry, Sly & Robbie, John Trudell*

Michael Eldridge

Open House

Celtic, folk

Formed in 1992. Based in Washington, Oregon, and California, USA.

Kevin Burke (Ireland), fiddle; Mark Graham, vocals, harmonica, clarinet; Paul Kotapish, guitar, cittern, mandolin; Sandy Silva, dancing (foot percussion). (All members are from USA unless noted otherwise.)

Kevin Burke's reputation as an Irish fiddle player can be both a boon and a bane. The upside of his celebrity is the hoardes of devotees coming to see him in concert as a solo act; the downside comes when those same fans attend a show by his band Open House expecting to hear only Celtic material. It just isn't going to happen. The band started off as a studio project and gradually grew into a touring entity. Burke and Paul Kotapish were the first to meet and perform together, when guitarist Kotapish substituted for Burke's usual accompanist (an ailing Míchaél Ó Domhnaill) during a brief tour of the American Northwest. Mark Graham and Sandy Silva, who were doing gigs as Hoof and Mouth, were friends of Kotapish and would sometimes appear on the same bill as the other two folks. In 1992 all four of them formed Open House and went into the studio to lay down some tracks before arranging a brief tour of the American West Coast. The first album was loaded with Irish-inflected material, but by the time the second disc was released the other members were starting to influence the group's sound. Graham's songwriting and Kotapish's bluegrass roots made the biggest impact, but Central European modes also surfaced in the arrangements.

Open House is still somewhat of a side project for the various members. Burke continues working on his solo career and playing with groups like the Celtic Fiddle Festival, while Kotapish has pursued his involvement with the Rodney Miller Band, the Hillbillies from Mars, and the Moving Cloud Orchestra in addition to a career as a graphic designer. Silva is heavily involved in the California folk dance scene, and Graham, who used to perform with the Chicken Chokers, continues to demonstrate his harmonica prowess and impish, punning way with lyrics in various ensembles.

what to buy: The band's first album, *Open House* ♫♫♫♪ (Green Linnet, 1992, prod. Míchaél Ó Domhnaill), was initially billed as a Kevin Burke project. Most of the songs stride with an Irish folk slant to their gait, with Burke's fiddle featured prominently, which may be a nod to fans expecting that approach. The vocals featured on the later albums are absent here, while Silva's feet provide an interesting (and unusual) pulse for many of the pieces. Together Burke and Graham prove to be a formidable songwriting duo, auguring well for future outings in which Graham provided even more material for the group's repertoire.

what to buy next: Following up their debut release, Open House unveiled more of a band sound with *Second Story* ♫♫♫♪ (Green Linnet, 1994, prod. Tim O'Brien). This revealed most of Burke's associates as strong contributors in their own right, as the members sought to forge a group identity. Graham's witty songs, supple baritone, and fluid artistry with harmonica and clarinet are more up-front on this album, but Silva's unique contributions aren't as evident as in a concert situation. Burke's showpiece is "The Moth in the Lantern/Take No Prisoners," a Balkan-based tour de force. By the time *Hoof and Mouth* ♫♫♫♫ (Green Linnet, 1997, prod. Ged Foley) was realized, Open House and their new producer had solved the mystery of how to fit Silva's contributions into the recorded sound.

influences:

◀◀ Bill Monroe, Christy Moore, Roger Miller, Walter Horton

see also: *Kevin Burke*

Garaud MacTaggart

Orchestra Baobob

African pop

Formed 1970, in the Plateau district of Dakar, Senegal. Disbanded late 1980s.

Abdoulaye Laye M'Boup (died 1974), vocals, maracas; Balla Sidibé, vocals, timbales; Thione Seck, vocals, timbales; Ndiouga Dieng, vocals, percussion; Rudolphe Gomis, vocals, percussion; Médoune Diallo, vocals, maracas; Bartélémy Attiso, lead guitar; Ben Geloum, guitar; Charles Ndiaye, bass; Pape Bâ, guitar; Issa Cissokho, tenor, alto saxophones; Peter Udo, clarinet, alto saxophone; Montaga Kouyate, drums, percussion. (All members are from Senegal.)

Caribbean music had already made a substantial impact on African bands by the time Orchestra Baobob was created in 1970. The rhythms of Trinidad had inflected E.T. Mensah's groundbreaking highlife groups over in Ghana and Nigeria, but the Cuban *clave* was king throughout much of West Africa, as bands absorbed the horn-driven rumba arrangements of Beny Moré, Bebo Valdés, Machito, and Mario Bauza, among others. At first the various ensembles duplicated the playing of their Cuban influences, but gradually native instruments and rhythms came into the music. Many of the West African bands were singing in Spanish without understanding a word of what they were voicing; in Senegal this changed drastically with the advent of Orchestra Baobob, who created Creole, Wolof, and Mandinka lyrics for their songs.

The Orchestra evolved as the house band for the Baobob Club in Dakar. Most of the members were recruited from the Star Band de Dakar, one of Senegal's most important bands. It was an amazing confluence of talent and vision. Togo native Attiso was one of the most inventive African guitarists ever, and singers M'Boup and Theck were to make the Wolof and Mandinka languages the lyrical cornerstone of the group's repertoire. Baobob still performed songs in other languages, with Sidibé and Diallo covering most of the Creole, Spanish, and French vocals, but M'Boup's charismatic performances of Wolof and Mandinka lyrics attracted much of the initial attention. This talented but somewhat undependable vocalist died as the result of a car accident in 1974, whereupon Theck, who later left the group in 1979 to lead his own influential bands, fi-

nally stepped into the vocal spotlight along with Sidibé and Diallo. Orchestra Baobob went to the Djandeer club after the Baobob was sold in 1977. They became the house band at a couple of other clubs after that, but then left for Paris, France, in the summer of 1978, hoping to tour Europe and make more money than they could at home. It was by all accounts a fiscal disaster, with poorly attended concerts almost everywhere. While they were in Paris, Orchestra Baobob went into the studio and recorded some material that later showed up on two cassettes after a move back to Senegal in the winter of 1978.

The majority of material performed prior to the 1980s had a Latin tinge to it (despite the efforts of M'Boup and Seck), but the public's taste was beginning to change, sliding toward more local content with young bands like Étoile 2000. Seck had left to pursue his vision and Sidibé became the leader of Orchestra Baobob. By mid-decade, under Sidibé's guidance, the band started including tribal instruments in the arrangements and added a pair of female singers to the lineup. This revamped edition of the group didn't make it out of the 1980s, but many of the personnel have gone on to perform in other outfits.

what to buy: The band's frustrating journey to Paris, France, still resulted in the best recorded sound of their career to that time. *On Vera Ça!: The 1978 Paris Sessions* ♫♫♫♫ (World Circuit/ Ledoux-Melodie, 1992/1997, prod. Abou Ledoux) finds Orchestra Baobob playing a lot of Spanish-language material, angling towards the vocal strengths of Diallo and Sidibé. Still, Attiso's "Wane Ma Maguiss," and the group's arrangement of the traditional tune "Digon Gama," demonstrate how they started bringing tribal elements into the Caribbean/Cuban formula.

what to buy next: The songs heard on *N'Wolof* ♫♫♫ (Dakar Sound, 1998, compilation prod. Ted Jaspers) were recorded in the Baobob Club (but not in concert) at the beginning of the band's career. M'Boup is vocalist on most of these tracks, and his rough-hewn voice cries and moans with expressive power. He wrote the beautiful ballad "N'Diaye"—which has become a classic tune performed by both Touré Kunda and Ismael Lô— and his rendition on this album is forceful, if not as polished as the other two versions. The sound is rather cavernous, knocking half a bone off the results, but the excitement of this recording lies in hearing the band work out its signature sound. Attiso's guitar playing is already pretty advanced and Seck is still in the chorus, ready to step out if the charismatic and somewhat erratic M'Boup doesn't show up for the gig. *Bamba* ♫♫♫♫ (Jambaar/Stern's Africa, 1980/1993, prod. Ibrahima Fall, Ibrahima Sylla) is a blend of two albums released in 1980— *Mouhamadou Bamba* and *Sibou Odia* —that were credited to "Orchestra Baobab-Gouye-Gui de Dakar." Seck's use of traditional tunes within an electrified setting reached a zenith with

"Mouhamadou Bamba" and "Doomou Baaye." His expressive tenor vocals soar over Attiso's chiming guitar leads and a percolating percussion squad. The title tune was a fairly big hit in Senegambia, as was Diallo's "Autorail." Sidibé, Dieng, Attiso, and Gomis also contributed well-crafted songs to these sessions, further enhancing the band's legend as a font of talent.

worth searching for: World Circuit's license to distribute *Pirates Choice: The Legendary 1982 Session* 🎵🎵🎵 (World Circuit, 1989) had expired as this book went to press, and it is uncertain when this wonderful disc will be back on the market. It contained some well-chosen selections originally found on 1982's *Senegambie* and *Ngalam* cassettes. (These tunes had been cobbled together for an MCA album called *Ken Dou Werente* before appearing under the World Circuit imprint.) If this were still in print, picking between it and *On Vera Ça!* would be very difficult.

influences:

◀◀ Star Band de Dakar, Rio Band de Dakar

▶▶ Youssou N'Dour, Super Diamono, Sahel de Dakar, Ismael Lô, Africando

see also: *Africando*

Garaud MacTaggart

Orchestra Marrabenta Star de Moçambique /The Marrabenta Star Orchestra /Marrabenta Star

Traditional southern Mozambiquan pop music
Formed 1984, in Maputo, Mozambique. Disbanded c. 1995.

Variable membership from the mid-'80s to the mid-'90s, including: Wazimbo, lead vocals; Dulce, lead vocals; Mingas, lead vocals; Guimarães, lead vocals, rhythm guitar; Sox, lead guitar; Milagre, bass; Xico, trumpet; Leman, trumpet; Matchoti, trumpet; Stewart, percussion; Zeca Tcheco, drums; Carlos Fernandes, bass; Mario Fernandes, saxophone, guitar; Manuel Miranda, drums; José Barata, keyboards; Joâo Maibasse, trumpet; Issufo Mussa, percussion. (All members are from Mozambique.)

The Marrabenta Star Orchestra is the proverbial thistle in the battlefield, something beautiful that thrived in the harshest of environments. Following its independence from Portugal in 1974, Mozambique slid into 15 years of brutal civil war, mostly driven by neighboring South Africa's inability to accept the new nation's overtly socialist government. With its generous ranks of singers, percussionists, horns, and guitars, the Marrabenta

Star Orchestra was one of the only Mozambiquan bands to work during these years, in no small part because it enjoyed the favor of the governing party, Frelimo, and was the National Radio Station's house band. *Marrabenta* is also the name of the music that came out of Mozambiquan towns and into the capitol, Lourenco Marques (now Maputo), beginning in the 1950s, roughly simultaneous with the emergence of *kwela* music in South Africa. Some marrabenta was smooth and polished and encouraged by the Portuguese colonialists. Other varieties, especially the heavier sound coming from the Gaza province in the south, were seen as subversive. Nevertheless, prior to independence, many itinerant marrabenta singers operated throughout much of this vast East African country. But by 1980, with the civil war heating up, it became impossible for them to continue.

The Marrabenta Star Orchestra brought together veterans of the defunct marrabenta scene into a supergroup. The band revved traditional rhythms to high gear and set them in hard-hitting arrangements, always working around the transcendent, horn-like vocals of lead singer Wazimbo. After recording two releases and touring abroad, the band came on hard times in post-war Mozambique. Though the early '90s brought peace, there were no venues, recording studios, or touring opportunities for bands within the country. Since the group disbanded, ex-members have pursued solo recording careers, in particular Wazimbo and singer Stewart Sukuma, who have both released highly produced CDs.

what's available: *Independence* 🎵🎵🎵🎵 (Mapiko/Piranha, 1989) delivers the excitement of a classic African big band. Rough, lively, and full of glorious vocal work and surprising grooves, this is a must-own Mozambiquan release. *Marrabenta Piquenique* 🎵🎵🎵 (Piranha, 1996) is a somewhat slicker followup, including an electric remake of the powerful ballad "Nwahulawana."

influences:

◀◀ Lisboa Mathavel, Fanny Mfumo, Alberto Mula, Dilon Djinji, Xidiminguani

▶▶ Wazimbo, Stuart Sukuma, Jose Guimaraes

Banning Eyre

Orchestra Virunga

See: Samba Mapangala

Orchestre National de Barbès

Traditional North African, pop, dance
Formed mid-1990s, in Paris, France. Based in Paris, France.

Youcef Boukella, bass, vocals, *chef d' orchestre*; Larbi Dida, vocals; Aziz Sehmaoui, percussion, vocals; Fateh Benlala, vocals, mandolin;

Toufik Mimouni, claviers; Olivier Louvel, guitar; Jean-Baptiste Ferr, keyboards; Fathella Ghoggal, guitar; Alain Debiossat, saxophone; Karim Ziad, karkabous; Michel Petry, drums; Ahmed Bensidhoune, bendir, derbouka; Kemel Tenfiche, percussion, vocals. (All members are from North Africa.)

Barbès is a North African "nation" composed of a few streets in the middle of the Montmartre district of Paris. It is home to a style of hypnotic dance music mined from funk, calypso, jazz, and rock and fused into Moroccan, Algerian, and French pop and traditional forms. Orchestre National de Barbès puckishly describe what they play as the "national music" of this multi-cultural milieu. Like many other "world" musicians, ONB inverts the meanings of that term and "neighborhood," taking in influences from every music that wafts into their area and creating sounds that express the spirit of a particular place. As if to complete the circle, this "local" music is rapidly gaining a global following.

what's available: *En Concert* ♫♫♫♫ (Tinder, 1998, prod. Taj-maat) was recorded live in 1996 at the Théatre de l'Agora in Paris. Every track is superb, executed with technical exuberance and almost flippant mastery of a wide range of instruments. Soaring vocals, wistful lyrics, and joyous, passionate grooves make this album music for the head, heart, and feet. *En Concert* is one of the most critically acclaimed world-music releases ever, and so beloved by the Rolling Stones (true story!) that they play it at the end of their shows to send the paying customers out in the proper festive mood.

influences:
◄◄ North African tradition, contemporary pop

Ron Garmon

Peadar Ó Riada

Irish traditional, choral, chamber, and orchestral
Born December, 1954, in Dublin, Ireland. Based in Cúil Aodha, Cork, Ireland.

The oldest of visionary Seán Ó Riada's seven children, composer and traditional musician Peadar Ó Riada inherited his father's influential role as director of the Cúil Aodha choir at the young age of 16, following the elder Ó Riada's untimely demise in 1971. Founded by Sean in a tiny church in a remote Irish-speaking pocket of west Cork in the early '60s, the all-male, 20-member choir included Peadar from its formative years; the tradition of fathers and sons singing together continues to this day. Over the three decades he has directed the choir, Peadar has written a large body of mostly liturgical music for it. A more recent graduate of the choir is singer Iarla Ó Lionáird. Ó Riada recorded two albums for Gael-Linn in the '70s, and obtained a music degree from University College Cork. He's worked exten-

indian percussion

As the primary percussion instrument of the North Indian classical tradition, the *tabla* is the drum most people think of when they think of Indian music (and rightfully so). But there are a host of other fascinating instruments in the pantheon of Indian percussion that deserve wider recognition, particularly in the South Indian (or *karnatak*) style. The two-headed *mridangam,* for instance, is a smaller version of the *pakhavaj*—the ancient Indian drum from which the tabla evolved—with the same paste on its heads which gives the tabla its ringing tone. The *ghatam* is a large, cylindrical clay pot that is played with the fingers, wrists, and palms on the side of the instrument, and which produces a distinctive low pitch when the opening is slapped with the hand. The *morsing* is a fantastic Indian jaw harp which, in skilled hands, emits a variety of textural sounds like nothing you've ever heard. The *tavil* is a large, booming drum used primarily in outdoor ceremonies, while the *dholak* is a traditional folk drum made of clay that makes a distinctive ringing sound. The *kanjira,* which has recently been banned from exportation, is a tambourine made from a wood frame and lizard skin. But perhaps the most unique percussion used in South Indian music, *konnakkol,* isn't technically an instrument at all, but an incredibly complex vocalization system Indian students learn to help them memorize rhythmic compositions. With dozens of different sounds delivered at lightning speed, konnakkol makes hip-hop's human beat-boxing sound like baby talk. For a great introduction to all of these wonderful instruments and techniques, check out the Karnataka College of Percussion's dazzling album *River Yamuna* ♫♫♫♫ (Music of the World, 1997).

see also: Karnataka College of Percussion, the Tabla (sidebar), Vadya Lahari, T.H. "Vikku" Vinayakram

Bret Love

sively in traditional music—and music for church, film, TV, and radio—and his compositions incorporate classical, avant-garde, and Indian elements as well as Irish ones. While German writer Herman Hesse is a particular influence, much of Ó

Riada's output is provincial in the best sense of the word: his biggest inspirations often come from local poet Dónal Ó Liatháin, neighboring musicians, and the natural wonders he finds in abundance both inside his home and outside in the semi-tamed wilds of west Cork.

An accomplished musician on button accordion, concertina, tin whistle, and piano, Ó Riada also accompanies the Cúil Aodha choir on pump organ. He is a firm believer in the culture of the individual rather than the culture of the masses, and it shows in his recent highly personal releases. Unlike so many albums issued today, which target some combination of the dance hall, the concert hall, and radio, Ó Riada's projects give the impression of being carefully crafted creations of a keen, dynamic intellect with little or no regard for market expectations. Poetry, reverie, compassion, intelligence, and a sense of fun and adventure exist side-by-side in his music. Ó Riada displays a wonderful feel for pace, space, and mood. Breaking with modern convention, he preserves, rather than suppresses, natural sounds (birds, sheep, coughing, laughter, children) heard in his home and in the recording studio—which are often the same place.

what to buy: *Amidst These Hills* 𝄫𝄫𝄫𝄫 (Bar/None, 1994, prod. Peadar Ó Riada) is a carefully woven tapestry featuring the Cúil Aodha choir singing one of his earliest pieces, a setting of a poem about bees (another of Ó Riada's fascinations) by Ireland's first president; some reels for concertina and bones; meditative piano pieces taped at home with blackbird and peacock adding their contributions from outside the window; and an extended suite commemorating a key 1647 battle that took place not far from the Ó Riada homestead. *Winds—Gentle Whisper* 𝄫𝄫𝄫𝄫 (Bar/None, 1996, prod. Peadar Ó Riada) includes guests Kevin Glackin (fiddle) and Nigel Warren-Green of the London Chambre Orchestra (cello), each of whom shines on a large-scale work written specifically with them in mind. On a 15-minute tribute to Ireland's Sulan river, which flows past Ó Riada's door, Glackin plays hypnotically alongside Indian drones. "Shadows and Darkness with a Glimmer of Light"—set down in an inspired first take—is a moving piano and cello duet dedicated to young orphans of war across the world. Neighbor Connie O'Connell then lightens the mood with some lively reels on fiddle. The Cúil Aodha choir sing "The Road of Peace" (by Ó Liatháin) in Irish, which Peadar set to music in the summer of 1995, when glimmers of light first started to appear in Northern Ireland.

influences:

◀ Seán Ó Riada, Mícheál Ó Súilleabháin

▶ Chieftains, Mícheál Ó Súilleabháin, Iarla Ó Lionáird

see also: *Seán Ó Riada*

John C. Falstaff

Seán Ó Riada

Irish traditional, choral, chamber, and orchestral
Born John Reidy, August, 1931, in Cork, Ireland. Died October 1971, in London, England.

If the Chieftains are the most visible product of the traditional music revival that has shaped the music scene in Ireland for the past 30 years, then composer, arranger, and revivalist Seán Ó Riada was the catalyst whose own extraordinary vision and accomplishments made their formation and rise to fame possible. In fact, most of the members of the original Chieftains got their first taste of playing together in Ó Riada's groundbreaking Ceoltóirí Chualann ensemble in the early 1960s. Ó Riada's star burned bright and fast, his career including periods as jazz pianist; European classical composer; Irish traditional music enthusiast, revivalist, and innovator; radio broadcaster; writer of film and theater music; founder and leader of Ceolteori Chualann; and finally a long, self-imposed exile far from the spotlight, where he wrote in many different genres at a furious pace.

Born John Reidy in Cork City of parents who were both traditional players, he grew up in Adare, County Limerick, surrounded by music. Reidy graduated from University College Cork with a music degree in 1952, by which time he'd gone through jazz and European classical music phases. The following year he was named Assistant Director of Music for Ireland's state radio in Dublin. He soon felt bored there, however, and uprooted to Paris for a while, where he met seminal Greek composer and hellraiser Mikis Theodorakis, and kept body and soul together by translating pornography by day and playing jazz piano in clubs by night. Back in Dublin, Reidy adopted the Irish form of his name, and the culture that went with it. The whole family—including his half-Italian wife—were obliged to follow suit, and to speak only Irish at home. Seán Ó Riada then wrote his first film score, the very successful and much lauded *Mise Eire* ("I Am Ireland"), and found himself appointed Director of Music at the Abbey Theatre. There, in 1959, he hired young Paddy Moloney and Sean Potts as part of a small band of traditional musicians who would appear on stage during a particular play. This radical idea proved to be very popular with both critics and theater-goers, and set Ó Riada to thinking about setting up his own folk orchestra. What some credit as the first-ever concert by a group of traditional Irish musicians—on stage rather then as a *ceilidh* (communal dance) band—took place in Dublin's Shelbourne Hotel later that year: Ó Riada on harpsichord leading a group of musicians that included Paddy Moloney, Sean Potts, Martin Fay, and Michael Tubridy, collectively dubbed Ceoltóirí Chualann ("Musicians of Chualann"). They soon found themselves with live radio exposure and more work at the Abbey. Ó Riada and his troupe—now including his distant cousin, the distinctive singer Seán Ó Sé—courted the concert-going classes in Dublin over the next four years, and issued numerous popular singles and albums.

Around 1963, Ó Riada disbanded Ceoltóirí Chualann as a recording unit (though they still played the occasional concert) and retreated to the remote Irish-speaking village of Cúil Aodha in west Cork, where his own mother had come from. There he founded an all-male choir in the local church; his setting of the old poem "Ag Críost an Siol" ("To Christ the Seed") as an offertory hymn for this choir in now common currency in Ireland and beyond. (The Cúil Aodha Choir still sing on Sundays and holidays under the direction of Seán's son Peadar Ó Riada, their repertoire including seldom-heard Irish secular and church music, as well as a large body of work specially written for them by both Ó Riadas.) During this village period, the elder Ó Riada also served as Lecturer in Irish Music at University College Cork, and was arguably the earliest such academic appointee in Ireland. By the time he died in 1971, at the far-too-young age of 40, he had produced well over 500 works—including three Masses—only a fraction of which have been published to date. His "Mná na hÉireann" ("Women of Ireland") is undoubtedly his best-known tune; later popularized by the Chieftains, it has also been recorded by Phil Coulter & James Galway, Sinéad O'Connor, Scottish group Macalla, Breton (French Celtic) singer and harper Alan Stivell, and English artists Davy Graham, Mike Oldfield, and Kate Bush.

Ó Riada's resurrection and championing of Irish music, including the works of 18th-century harper Turlough O'Carolan (1670–1738), created a deep and lasting effect on the traditional revival scene in Ireland. In some ways, his efforts paralleled what Ewan MacColl and A.L. "Bert" Lloyd were doing at around the same time in Britain. Like Lloyd, Ó Riada was not above passing off as "traditional" some of his own compositions, e.g. the ever-popular "Carrigfergus." Many of the tunes we now associate with the Chieftains date back to their pioneering years as members of Ceoltóirí Chualann, and can be heard on the few Ó Riada CDs available today from the dozen albums in diverse styles he issued during his lifetime. His film scores were among the very earliest orchestral works to incorporate Irish traditional tunes, and have been hugely influential on the writing of the generation that followed: Shaun Davey, Míchéal Ó Súilleabháin, Bill Whelan, Patrick Cassidy, and others. In 1987 an important Ó Riada retrospective concert in Dublin, with musical director Dónal Lunny, resulted in a live double album. A re-united Ceoltóirí Chualann of sorts, including Ó Sé, de Buitléar, Potts, Tubridy, Kelly, and Mercier, was joined by Lunny, Paddy Glackin, Liam O'Flynn, Julia and Billy Clifford, Tony MacMahon, Éamon Kelly, Mary Bergin, and Peadar Ó Riada and the Cúil Aodha Choir.

what to buy: Both *Ó Riada sa Gaiety* 𝄞𝄞𝄞𝄞 (Gael-Linn, 1969) and *Ó Riada* 𝄞𝄞𝄞𝄞 (Gael-Linn, 1972) feature Cork singer Seán Ó Sé fronting a 10-member, reconvened Ceoltóirí Chualann in exciting, historic live recordings. The first and half of the second were recorded at Dublin's Gaiety Theatre in 1969; the rest of the second album is from the Carolan Tercentenary Concert in Cork in 1970. Ó Sé's piercing, strident voice may not be to everybody's liking today, but it was he who first put Ó Riada's "Mná na hÉireann" ("Women of Ireland") and "Carrigfergus" on the map. Add tunes like "O'Neill's March," "The West Wind," "March of the King of Laois," "Tabhair Dom Do Lámh" ("Give Me Your Hand"), "Si Bheag, Si Mhor," "Planxty Maguire," "Fanny Power," and "Planxty Irwin"—all standards today—and you can't go wrong.

what to buy next: *Mise Eire* 𝄞𝄞𝄞𝄞 (Gael-Linn, 1969) brings together three masterful film scores from 1959–66, a period of emerging national pride and new cultural aspirations in Ireland as the 50th anniversary of the 1916 Rising approached. *Mise Eire* ("I Am Ireland") was the first, and like its successors, it effortlessly encompassed Irish melodies both known and obscure in a seamless Mahlerian cloak of strings and horns.

worth searching for: Fans of Seán Ó Sé's voice may want to hunt down *Heritage* (Harmac, 1986/Outlet, 1988), recorded under the watchful eye of Dónal Lunny. The years have softened the contours of Ó Sé's nasal voice, and the tracks include a remake of his signature song "Carrigfergus" and the odd nod to the Moving Hearts sound (the latter due to Davy Spillane's presence in addition to fellow Hearts alum Lunny's). The two-disc live *Ó Riada Retrospective* (Gael-Linn, 1987) is a fine tribute to the man and his music, and reprises many Ó Riada favorites, including his son and choir singing "Mo Ghile Mear," as they had done at his funeral. The all-orchestral *Romantic Ireland* (Marco Polo, 1996) includes Ó Riada's "The Banks of Sullane" from 1956, which was based on the very first piece of music he ever wrote as a college student, and inspired by a similarly titled song his mother used to sing. Ó Riada lived the last eight years of his life right on the banks of this river.

influences:

◀◀ Turlough O'Carolan, Gustav Mahler, Jean Sibelius

▶▶ The Chieftains, Peadar Ó Riada, Alan Stivell, Dónal Lunny, Shaun Davey, Míchéal Ó Súilleabháin, Bill Whelan, Patrick Cassidy

see also: *Mary Bergin Patrick Cassidy, the Chieftains, Shaun Davey, Dordan, Paddy Glackin, A.L. "Bert" Lloyd, Dónal Lunny, Ewan MacColl, Moving Hearts, Tríona Ní Dhomhnaill, Nightnoise, Turlough O'Carolan (sidebar), Liam O'Flynn, Peadar Ó Riada, Mikis Theodorakis, Bill Whelan*

John C. Falstaff

Oriental Brothers
/Orientals
/Dr. Sir Warrior and the (Original) Oriental Brothers International
/Goodwin Kabaka Opara's Oriental Brothers International

Highlife
Formed 1971, in Owerri, Nigeria. Based in Lagos, Nigeria.

Core band: Warrior Opara, vocals; Dan Satch Opara, guitar; Goodwin Kabaka Opara, guitar. All members are from Nigeria.

The Oriental Brothers (the name refers to a birthplace in Eastern Nigeria, not the Far East)—vocalist Warrior Opara and twin guitar masters Dan Satch Opara and Goodwin Kabaka Opara—formed their band in 1971, just as the heyday of highlife (a cosmopolitan dance music) was being eclipsed by juju (a more Yoruba-influenced form). Their style was more Nigerian and less international than the highlife groups from Ghana, and for much of the 1970s the Oriental Brothers were one of Nigeria's most popular bands. Despite this popularity, the band's personnel was unstable, allegedly due to the constant sibling rivalry of the principals. In 1977 Goodwin Kabaka left the band to form Kabaka International, later known as Kabaka Opara's Oriental Brothers International. His version of the band included Ghanaian and Congolese accents in the rhythms and guitar lines. In 1980, Warrior left to form Dr. Sir Warrior and the (Original) Oriental Brothers International; Dan Satch continued playing with his own version under the original name. All three are still releasing records successfully, leading many to believe that the inter-familial warfare was a marketing ploy.

worth searching for: The various incarnations of the Oriental Brothers have released more than 50 albums in Nigeria, but, with few exceptions, they are not available outside West Africa. Credited to Dr. Sir Warrior and the Oriental Brothers International, *Heavy on the Highlife!* ♪♪♪♪ (Original Music, 1990) is an excellent compilation put together by Afrophile John Storm Roberts, and contains hit singles by the early Oriental Brothers, Dan Satch Opara, and Dr. Sir Warrior. The incredible guitar work, non-stop groove, and Warrior's gritty vocals make this a must-have. *Do Better If You Can* ♪♪♪♪ (Original Music, 1995) is another John Storm Roberts compilation, this time by Goodwin Kabaka Opara's Oriental Brothers International. The guitar work and overall feel is as much Congolese as Nigerian, with a smoother groove and bubbly, almost reggae-like basslines. Unhappily, Roberts' Original Music

label is presently in limbo, so these titles are collector's items for now, with *Heavy on the Highlife!* being offered for 50 dollars or more. If you can find these albums any cheaper, snap them up. Vinyl and cassette versions may be available in world-music collector's stores.

influences:

◀◀ Peacocks Guitar Band International, Prince Nico Mbarga, Victor Olaiya

▶▶ Super Negro Bantous, Highlife International, Osibisa

j. poet

Orquesta Aragon

Charanga
Formed 1939, in Cienfuegos, Cuba. Based in Cuba.

Extensive and varying membership across six decades, led first by Rafael Ley Sr. (died 1989), and currently by Rafael Ley Jr.

Charanga is a style of Cuban music in which the rhythms are played on violin and flute rather than the more usual horn section. This resulted in an elegant and perhaps more European-oriented style when Orquesta Aragon began playing in the late 1930s. It was one of the first groups to set the model for this method of performing, and produced hit dance tunes for decades—and still does, under the leadership of the band's founder's son, Rafael Ley Jr. Aragon's music is said to have inspired the New York mambo scene of the 1950s, but they are by no means a retro band, having continued to infuse their sound and styles with lively Caribbean influences.

what's available: *Cha-Cha-Charanga* ♪♪♪♪ (Tinder, 1997) is Aragon's first new recording in several years, and gives a vibrant snapshot of the group's strong sense of instrumentation, combining elegant dance style with lively island rhythm. *50 Anos de Oro* ♪♪♪♪ (EGREM, 1989) is the best historical compilation of Aragon's extensive discography, and one of its most popular recordings. With more than 700 songs in its repertoire, the band enjoys an extensive international recording history. For a look at their style at the height of their popularity in the 1950s, seek out *Riverside Years* ♪♪♪ (RCA), which, with guest artists like singer Beny Moré and pianist Perez Prado, showcases them in quintessential Latin ballroom-dance mode.

influences:

◀◀ Beny Moré, Perez Prado

▶▶ Irakere, Los Van Van

see also: *Beny Moré, Perez Prado*

Kerry Dexter

A. Paul Ortega

Native American traditional, singer/songwriter
Born in Albuquerque, NM, USA. Based in Albuquerque, NM, USA.

A. Paul Ortega is a Mescalero Apache artist and spiritual leader. He is also a well-known singer/songwriter, one of the first Native artists to adapt traditional music for non-Native ears. Ortega plays guitar and traditional Native drums, and his fusion of Native forms with American folk music has created a style all his own. Ortega performs as a solo artist and is a generous benefactor to young artists. He has collaborated with singers such as Sharon Burch and Joanne Shenandoah, giving them their first recording opportunities.

what's available: *Loving Ways* ♪♪♪ (Canyon, 1991), a collection of Indian love songs performed with Joanne Shenandoah, is the only album of Ortega's on CD, and is a good example of his Native folk style. His spoken interludes, while undoubtedly sincere, often sound embarrassingly amateurish, which is strange given the power and melodic beauty of his music.

worth searching for: Most of Ortega's music is only available on cassette. Look for *The Blessing Ways* ♪♪♪ (Canyon, 1984), a collaboration with Sharon Burch; and Ortega's solo albums *Two Worlds* ♪♪♪ (Canyon) and *Three Worlds* ♪♪♪ (Canyon).

influences:

◄◄ Buffy Sainte-Marie, Floyd Westerman

►► Joanne Shenandoah, Sharon Burch, Bill Miller

see also: *Sharon Burch, Joanne Shenandoah*

j. poet

Geffery Oryema

Worldbeat, singer/songwriter
Born 1953, in Kampala, Uganda. Based in Paris, France.

Oryema grew up during the worst days of Ugandan tyrant Idi Amin's regime, and after his father was assassinated, Oryema was smuggled into Kenya in the trunk of a car. Before Oryema's father passed, however, he had taught his son to play the *nanga* (harp) and introduced him to African folk, ritual, and pop music. Oryema had also studied Western music in school, and, after making his way to Paris, set about combining these influences into his own special brand of music, a moody style informed by European melodies, African harmonies, and Uganda's unique traditions. Oryema's rich, supple voice combines a growling lower register with a clear, high tenor that often slides effortlessly into falsetto.

what to buy: Who woulda thunk that electronica godfather Brian Eno would provide the perfect balance between tradi-

tion and the ambient dreams of the African future? On the lush *Exile* ♪♪♪♪ (RealWorld, 1990, prod. Brian Eno) half the tracks benefit from Eno's soothing atmospherics, and the other five feature Oryema's majestic open-hearted vocals and his work on traditional instruments, chiefly harp and thumb piano.

what to buy next: Oryema's slick African pop never loses its soul or its musicality on *Night to Night* ♪♪♪♪♪ (RealWorld, 1977, prod. Lokua Kanza, Jean-Pierre Alarcen, Nicolas Fiszman, Daniel Lanois), a perfect blend of Anglo-American and African pop instincts, sung mostly in English. Proof that African pop can embrace the West without being watered down or produced to death.

the rest:
Beat at the Border ♪♪♪♪♪ (RealWorld, 1993)

influences:

◄◄ Jimmy Katumba and the Ebonies, Sammy Kasule, Maria Wadaka

►► Samite

j. poet

Chief Steven Osita Osadebe

Highlife
Born 1936, in Nigeria. Based in Nigeria.

One of the true legends of the popular and influential Nigerian highlife genre, Osadebe has played the music since 1959. His stellar career as a bandleader with the Soundmakers International has been running strong since 1964, and he's parlayed his classic highlife style into a sustained following, as well as Nigerian gold records well into the '80s. Unfortunately, U.S. listeners have only one album to choose from — but it's a good choice.

what's available: *Kedu America* ♪♪♪♪ (Green Linnet/ Xenophile, 1996, Prod. Andrew C. Frankel) presents Osadebe as one of the few contemporary highlife acts left (kind of equivalent to playing surf music in the States). Nonetheless, this album shows how influential the sound is. Osadebe fuses heavy rumba rhythms and Ezikel Uti's monumental guitar work with long jams, large percussion sections, and big, circular horn arrangements. The roots of later revolutions like Fela Kuti's Afro-Beat are well-traceable in this Pan-African-flavored project.

influences:

◄◄ Steven Amache, Cardinal Rex Lawson

►► Fela Kuti, Sonny Okosums

Hank Bordowitz

Osibisa

Afropop

Formed 1969, in London, England. Based in England.

Teddy Osei, tenor sax, flute, African drums, vocals; Sol Amarfio, drums, percussion, fontonfrom; Mac Tontoh, trumpet, flugelhorn, percussion; Spartacus R., bass, percussion; Wendell Richardson, lead guitar, vocals; Robert Bailey, organ, piano, timbales; Loughty Lasisi Amao, tenor/baritone sax, flute, congas, fontonfrom.

The world's first true Afropop band, Osibisa emerged out of London's African expatriate underground scene. A veritable Middle Passage crew composed of cats from Ghana, Nigeria, Antigua, Grenada, and Trinidad, Osibisa was a hothouse of hip-shaking, polyrhythmic flow. Their unique mix of Fela Kuti beats, jazz atmospherics, griot-wisdom soundbites, Carnival mas, and skydog guitars secured them a recording contract with Decca—the first such band to be signed to a major British label. At the beginning of 1971, Osibisa released its self-titled debut album; before the year was out, the band also released *Woyaya*. On a roll, Osibisa toured the U.K. and Europe extensively. In 1972, they brought out *Heads,* which proved so popular among black college students that the band played several successful shows on that circuit during its 1972 U.S. tour. Since that high point, Osibisa has drifted from label to label, and further away from prominence. The band still exists today, gigging in the U.K. and Europe, sadly overlooked in the world-music boom. Nonetheless, their page in history is guaranteed.

what to buy: *Woyaya* ♫♫♫♫ (MCA, 1971/AIM, 1993, prod. Tony Visconti) is Osibisa's masterpiece. From the ancestral spirits channeling through "Beautiful Seven" to the Nevilles-meet-War-at-the-intersection-of-Horace Silver take on Rahsaan Roland Kirk's "Spirit Up Above," *Woyaya* is a worldpop fusion that no one—not even Osibisa itself—has equaled since.

the rest:

Celebration: The Best of Osibisa ♫♫♫ (AIM, 1993)
Ojah Awake ♫♫♫♩ (AIM, 1995)
African Flight ♫♫♩ (AIM, 1995)
Welcome Home ♫♫♫ (Songhai Empire, 1995)
Best of Osibisa N/A (Cleopatra, 1999)

worth searching for: The out-of-print LP versions of *Osibisa* (Decca, 1971), *Woyaya,* and *Heads* (Decca, 1972) all feature great gatefold cover art, the first two with surreal flying elephant imagery by Roger Dean and the latter with humorous elephant imagery by Mati Klarwein.

influences:

⏪ E.T. Mensah, Guy Warren, Fela Kuti, Rahsaan Roland Kirk

⏩ Mandrill, O.J. Ekomede, Santana, Touré Kunde

Tom Terrell

Ossian

Scottish folk

Formed 1976, in Glasgow, Scotland. Disbanded 1991; re-formed 1997. Based in Scotland.

Billy Ross, vocals, guitar, dulcimer, whistle (1976–80, 1997–present); George Jackson, cittern, mandolin, fiddle, whistle, flute, guitar, vocals (1976–91); John Martin, fiddle, cello, vocals (1976–91); William Jackson, harp, uilleann pipes, whistles, vocals, bass, synthesizer, piano, bodhrán (1976–91, 1997–present); Tony Cuffe, vocals, guitar, tiple (1980–91); Iain MacDonald, bagpipes, flute, whistle, jew's-harp, vocals (1982–91); Stuart Morison, fiddle, cittern, mandolin, vocals (1997–present); Iain MacInnes, Scottish smallpipes, whistles (1997–present); other intermittent touring members, including Maggie MacInnes, harp, vocals; Norman Chalmers, concertina, harp, whistles, vocals. (All members are from Scotland.)

Named after the Bard of the Fianna in Celtic mythology (and the title of one of Scotland's most renowned and infamous works of literature), the folk band Ossian was a gentler alternative to the fiery Tannahill Weavers and the electrified Battlefield Band for the entire 1980s and a couple of years more. Ossian grew out of the Glaswegian folk-rock group Contraband, which included John Martin, George Jackson, and William "Billy" Jackson. These three, plus singer Billy Ross, comprised Ossian's original lineup, which formed in 1976 and established the band's trademark sound: a soft, classically informed, and subtle style that could nonetheless burn with intensity. In 1980 Ross was replaced by singer and guitarist Tony Cuffe, a veteran of such groups as Alba and Jock Tamson's Bairns. Cuffe's voice and full, round guitar-playing became further hallmarks of the group. To complete its growth, Ossian added one final distinctive ingredient in 1982: the sensitive highland pipe and flute playing of Iain MacDonald.

Apart from one tour on which William Jackson was replaced by Maggie MacInnes because of a broken hand, this classic Ossian lineup remained constant until 1990, when Jackson and Cuffe both moved to the United States. At that point, although Ossian did not break up right away, several of its members sought new opportunities and, as a result, both George and William Jackson were sometimes not available for tours. They were replaced on those occasions by multi-instrumentalist Norman Chalmers. Although Ossian remained together for a short time after that, the pressures on a band based in two countries ultimately won out and they broke up. After a short time Martin was recruited into the Tannahill Weavers and MacDonald into the Battlefield Band, while Cuffe and William Jackson performed as solo artists. Ossian was reborn in 1997, when the group Smalltalk, composed of Ross, Iain MacInnes, and Stuart Morison, added William Jackson, who had since moved back to Scotland, to its membership. Although only Jackson and Ross were former members of Ossian (MacInnes and Morison having passed through the ranks of that other Scottish musical institution, the Tannahill Weavers), they decided to play music in the spirit of Ossian's work during the '70s and '80s. Smalltalk changed its name to Ossian and recorded an album. Whether this new version of Ossian will be as successful and long-lived as the previous incarnation remains to be seen.

what to buy: *The Best of Ossian* 🎵🎵🎵🎵 (Iona, 1994, prod. Ossian) is undoubtedly the place to start for the uninitiated. It contains tracks from all of Ossian's recordings for the Iona label, which means all but the first of the original group's albums. The selection of tracks is terrific, and manages really to capture what was best about each Ossian lineup: Ross's beautiful Gaelic vocal on "S Gann Gunn Dirich Mi Chaoidh," Cuffe's equally affecting singing in Scots on songs like "The Road to Drumleman" and "I Will Set My Ship in Order," and piper MacDonald's rousing playing on several sets of tunes. Of course, the contributions of stalwart members John Martin, William Jackson, and George Jackson, the founders who remained with the group through almost its entire life, are without peer in Scottish music. There would be only one way to make *The Best* better: more tracks. At 56 minutes it's not exactly skimpy, but there's room on a CD for considerably more.

what to buy next: *Borders* 🎵🎵🎵🎵 (Iona, 1984, prod. Ossian) was the best of Ossian's original albums. It was produced after the band had been together for some time, and had really learned what worked best about their sound. The combination of highland pipes and harp, right from the start of the album, is more compelling than it had been on the predecessor, *Dove across the Water*. The arrangements are unusual, confident, and quite lovely. Cuffe mined several collections of songs, especially John Ord's *Bothy Songs and Ballads*, to find unusual and beautiful traditionals to sing, composing melodies where none existed and writing extra verses when necessary. In short, this was both their most traditional and their most original album. *Seal Song* 🎵🎵🎵🎵 (Iona, 1981, prod. Ossian) comes in a close second. Ossian did not yet benefit from the highland bagpipes, which were to be an important part of Ossian's later palette, but this album nonetheless offers a full and rich sound, due in part to new member Cuffe. Cuffe's strong guitar playing—influenced by Martin Carthy and by Nic Jones—added melodic, harmonic, and percussive dimensions to the band, and his voice is magnificent. Even so, the band was already excellent without Cuffe, as is evident on *St. Kilda Wedding* 🎵🎵🎵🎵 (Iona, 1978, prod. Ossian). The group's deft handling of many and diverse instruments gives this album a light, airy, and appealing feeling. Despite the repertoire of entirely Scottish material, the band at this stage sounded more like an Irish group in the mold of Planxty than like contemporary Scottish acts,

with uilleann pipes, cittern, whistle, and guitar taking center stage. Nonetheless, Martin's fiery fiddling and Ross's undeniably Scottish singing in both Gaelic and Scots made the band's Scottish identity quite evident. Ross's singing Is also a major ingredient on the re-formed Ossian's debut, *The Carrying Stream* 🎵🎵🎵 (Greentrax, 1997, prod. Ossian). On this CD, the new band does not quite succeed in reproducing the classic Ossian sound, but they do come close; MacInnes's Scottish smallpipes are a sort of compromise between the highland and uilleann pipes featured on the original band's albums. Jackson's harp takes a more dominant role, and his piano fills out the sound in places. Ross's voice, guitar, and dulcimer sound as delicate and practiced as they did 20 years ago, and Morison's strong fiddling, while not identical to Martin's, is nonetheless stirring. Of the many solo and duet albums produced by Ossian's members, the best is Cuffe's *When First I Went to Caledonia* 🎵🎵🎵🎵 (Iona 1988, prod. Tony Cuffe). Cuffe's firm, sure guitar playing gets much more of a chance to shine on solo tunes like "The Lass o' Patie's Mill," and his singing is never more lovely than on the title track. It is one of the best solo albums of a Scottish singer/guitarist ever.

the rest:
Dove across the Water 🎵🎵🎵 (Iona, 1982)
Light on a Distant Shore 🎵🎵🎵 (Iona, 1986)

worth searching for: The band's self-titled debut LP *Ossian* 🎵🎵🎵 (Springthyme, 1976) featured the same lineup as *St. Kilda Wedding*. Offering some nice songs and tunes, the effort is somewhat tentative overall.

influences:
◀◀ Planxty, Battlefield Band, Jock Tamson's Bairns, Alba, Contraband

▶▶ Tony Cuffe, William Jackson, Smalltalk

see also: *Battlefield Band, Martin Carthy, Tannahill Weavers*

Steve Winick

Ottopasuna

Modern and traditional folk
Formed 1990, in Helsinki, Finland. Based in Helsinki, Finland.

Petri Hakala, mandolin, mandocello, guitar; Kurt Lindblad, flute, tin whistle, bagpipes, clarinet (1990–1995); Kimmo Pohjonen, melodeon, harmonica, marimba; Kari Reiman, violin; Kristiina Ilomonen, flute, percussion (1995–present); Janne Lappalainen, bouzouki, bass clarinet, tin whistle (1996–present). (All members are from Finland.)

Ottopasuna's name is derived from that of a Finnish folk fiddler, but their take on traditional music isn't very traditional. The group is mainly a recording unit, since the members maintain ongoing careers with bands that include Värttinä, Helsinki

Mandoliners, and Pinnin Pojat. Their first eponymous album drew from venerable sources and was played with some interesting Afro Celtic flavors, while the followup is more Finnish—though even less traditional, since all the material was composed by the group.

what's available: *Ottopasuna* 𝄞𝄞𝄞𝄡 (Xenophile, 1993) is one of the original albums in the prestigious Xenophile label's "Finnish Invasion" series, a quirky platter full of fancy picking. The material is traditional, taken from early recordings and old manuscripts, but the renditions are thoroughly modern.

worth searching for: *Suokaasua (Swamp Gas)* 𝄞𝄞𝄞𝄡 (Amigo, Finland, 1996, prod. Tom Nyman) is a solid, quirky instrumental outing, well worth searching for, by turns sprightly and moody.

influences:
◄◄ Värttinä, Karelia, JPP
►► Pinnin Pojat

j. poet

Orlando "Doctor Ganga" Owah /Orlando Owah with his Omimah Band /Orlando Owah and his Young Kenneries

Toye
Born c. 1940, in Owo, Nigeria. Based in Lagos, Nigeria.

In Nigeria, Orlando Owah is a legendary singer, guitarist, and bandleader, known for his unpretentious, deeply African style of music. He started out playing percussion in local bands, but soon moved to Lagos and hooked up with Fatai Rolling Dollar, who taught him to play guitar. Owah formed his first Omimah Band in the late 1960s, launching a career that continues to this day. In 1976 he renamed the band the Young Kenneries. Owah based his music on the "palm wine" (acoustic) guitar styles of Sierra Leone, with a heavy *juju*/highlife influence. Owah's music is called *toye* by his fans, who appreciate its earthy lyrics and wild polytonality—the two guitars and the bass each play in a different key, giving the music a slightly jarring quality to non-Africanized ears. The band's rhythmic shifts and unexpected changes of key and tempo undoubtedly keep dancers, and listeners, awake. Owah was jailed for drug use in the 1980s, which may explain his nickname.

worth searching for: The clashing tempi and conflicting keys make Owah's music challenging, and fun. The four track compilation *Dr. Ganga's Polytonality Blues* 𝄞𝄞𝄞𝄡 (Original Music, 1995, compilation prod. John Storm Roberts) features ex-

tended jams and dazzling guitar work. The collection features two tracks by the Omimah Band from 1974 and two by the Young Kenneries from 1981. More than 60 albums of Owah's work have been released in Nigeria, most on the Decca West Africa label.

influences:
◄◄ I. K. Dario, Tunde Nightengale
►► Music Makers, Okukuseku

j. poet

O'Yaba
Reggae
Formed 1990, in Welkom, South Africa. Based in South Africa.

Botiki Letsi, drums; **Tsietsi Koetle**, bass; **Edward Mphatsang**, percussion, backing vocals; **Tshidiso "Alexis" Fako**, lead and backing vocals; **Andrew Dlamini**, electric piano, backing vocals; **Bernard Themba**, lead and rhythm guitar; **Sidney Makoni**, lead and rhythm guitar, backing vocals. (All members are from South Africa.)

The number of quality rocksteady outfits in Africa testifies to the power of reggae as an international force. One of the better non-Jamaican bands, O'Yaba, came together in the wake of two local predecessors, Sebela and Comedy. O'Yaba's sound recalls the more mainstream pop reggae of Third World and later Steel Pulse, with vocal and lyrical overtones of gospel. Produced by the late, great West Nkosi (better known for his work in *mbaqanga,* the "township jive" style popularized in the West by Paul Simon's *Graceland*), the group blends modernism and roots, pop smarts and upfull messages. They seemed to drop out of sight in the mid-'90s, but reunited for one of Nkosi's last productions, *Crazy Love,* a recording that has yet to receive wide distribution outside of Africa.

what's available: *Game Is Not Over* 𝄞𝄞𝄞𝄡 (Shanachie, 1992, prod. West Nkosi), brings together choice material from the group's first two South African albums, *Tomorrow Nation* and *Caught Up.* Their pop leanings are clear from the opening lick of the first disc's title track, a tip of the hat to the Beatles' "Let It Be." Their synth-powered rhythms and killer harmonies are best displayed in tunes like "Rootsman Soul." Tshidiso Fako's powerhouse voice just erupts out of the record. Whether it's the band's idea or Nkosi's, some home-township licks slip into the guitar part on "Rootsman Story" and even into the pennywhistle hook in "Tsalane." While most of the songs are in English, "Thube" and the aforesaid "Tsalane" show that reggae works just as well in the mother tongues.

influences:
◄◄ Bob Marley, Peter Tosh, the King's Messengers, Lucky Dube

Hank Bordowitz

The Oyster Band

Expansive English folk-rock
Formed 1981, in England. Based in England.

John Jones, lead vocals, melodeon, accordion, piano; Ian "Chopper" Kearey, bass, cello, tiple, vocals; Ian Telfer, fiddle, viola, tenor concertina; Russell Lax (a.k.a. Lee), drums, percussion, hammer, vocals; Alan Prosser, guitar, banjo, mandolin, violin, vocals; Cathy LeSurf, vocals (1981); Chris Taylor (1981–84).

The Oysters are a one-of-a-kind punk band whose master musicians lean on Celtic and English dance traditions while rocking harder than most of the mainstream. Criminally underappreciated, they explore the political and personal landscape with intensity and consistency, generating high-spirited power-folk led by the assertive vocals of Welshman John Jones and the incisive electric fiddle of Telfer. The band is frequently transcendent on disc, though no release has ever approached their incendiary live performances. The Oyster Band owes its genesis to two others, the Whitstable Oyster Co. Ceilidh Band (later the Oyster Ceilidh Band), which first took the stage in 1975; and Fiddler's Dram, founded in 1972 by violinist David Arbus, known for his work with East of Eden and the Who. Fiddler's Dram, then also consisting of Prosser, Telfer, Taylor, and LeSurf, made the album *To See the Play*, notable for a "posthumous" hit novelty single in 1979, "Day Trip to Bangor." The song's success forced the band to make another album, on which they were joined by Kearey, among others. Meanwhile, much of Fiddler's Dram enjoyed a parallel existence in the Oyster Ceilidh Band, with LeSurf, Prosser, Kearey, Telfer, and Taylor joining Jones on the dancehall circuit. In 1981 the band dropped "Ceilidh" from its name, LeSurf departed, and the Oyster Band became essentially the unit that exists today. The Oysters have occasionally collaborated with English folk singer June Tabor, and earned a higher profile for their work—if, again, not for themselves—with buzz-binned Newfoundland folk-rockers Great Big Sea's recent cover of "When I'm Up I Can't Get Down."

what to buy: *Ride* ♫♫♫♫ (PolyGram, 1989, prod. Dave Young) comes closest to the glorious assault of their live show. Cuts range from the rollicking "New York Girls" to the pensive "This Year, Next Year," closing with the itchy fiddle cover of New Order's "Love Vigilantes." *The Shouting End of Life* ♫♫♫ (Cooking Vinyl, 1995, prod. Pat Collier) is highlighted by the fiddle-and-guitar pyrotechnics of "Blood-Red Roses" and a pulsating reworking of Bruce Cockburn's "Lovers in a Dangerous Time." *Deserters* ♫♫♫ (Rykodisc, 1992, prod. John Ravenhall) is a hard-edged beauty that includes the reeling "All That Way for This" and the working-class anthem "Fiddle or a Gun."

what to buy next: The band's one full-fledged experiment with June Tabor, *Freedom and Rain* ♫♫♫ (Rykodisc, 1990, prod. Oyster Band), is an atmospheric near-masterpiece that in-

cludes tunes by Shane MacGowan, Richard Thompson, and Billy Bragg.

what to avoid: Though a poor Oyster recording is not to be had, *Little Rock to Leipzig* ♫♫♫ (Rykodisc, 1991, prod. Oyster Band, Dave Young) is a less compelling collection of studio and live odds-and-ends best left to die-hard fans.

the rest:
Step Outside ♫♫♫ (Cooking Vinyl, 1986)

---

the sitar

The best-known instrument of India, and perhaps in all of world music, is the sitar. Created by the 13th-century musicologist Amir Khusrau, the sitar's strings are plucked with a pick or *plectrum*. The instrument can have six or seven main strings, along with 11 to 19 sympathetic strings on a different bridge; together these strings provide both melody and accompanying drone. The body of the sitar is historically made from half a dried mature gourd. The sitar's most prominent performer is Ravi Shankar. When George Harrison of the Beatles discovered the instrument at an Indian restaurant during the filming of *Help,* the seeds of one of the earliest and highest-profile world-music crossovers were sown. After his tutelage with Shankar, Western ears were suddenly "hip" to the East when Harrison played the sitar on 1965's "Norwegian Wood." Once famed session-man Vince Bell discovered the sitar's potential to create an "in" sound, it became not only the instrument of choice for spiritually enlightened hippies, but also easy-listening swingers who discovered sitar-lite through Gabor Szabo and Lord Sitar. Shankar, at once disappointed and galvanized by the superficial level on which most of these fans were approaching his centuries-old tradition, would alternately retreat to India and tour the world, collaborating with Western classical ensembles and heading music schools and programs in the U.S. Both perspectives seem to have won out; today the sitar is equally well regarded as a tool of the Indian classicism Shankar exemplifies, and the crossover pop of hip favorites like Cornershop.

Sam Wick

Wild Blue Yonder 𝄞𝄞𝄞 (Cooking Vinyl, 1987)
Holy Bandits 𝄞𝄞𝄞𝄞 (Rykodisc, 1993)
Trawler 𝄞𝄞𝄞 (Cooking Vinyl, 1996)
Deep Dark Ocean 𝄞𝄞𝄞 (Cooking Vinyl, 1997)

worth searching for: Several early Oyster recordings were released on the band's own Pukka label, and are not readily available: *English Rock 'n' Roll—The Early Years 1800–1850, Lie Back and Think of England, 20 Golden Tie Slackeners,* and *Liberty Hall.* The CD single "Cry Cry" (Rykodisc, 1994) from the *Holy Bandits* album collects three previously unreleased tunes, including an astonishing "Star of the County Down." The Putumayo label's engaging survey of the Celtic-music world's expanding and porous borders, *Dublin to Dakar* 𝄞𝄞𝄞𝄞 (Putumayo, 1999, executive prod. Dan Storper), features a track from Oysterband (as they are now referring to themselves) not yet otherwise available in the U.S.

influences:

◀◀ Fairport Convention, Pentangle, the Clash

▶▶ The Pogues, Spirit of the West

see also: *Great Big Sea, the Pogues/Shane MacGowan, Richard Thompson*

Martin Connors

Talip Ozkan

Traditional Turkish folk
Born 1939, in Acipayam, Turkey. Based in Paris, France.

Ozkan began his formal training as a student of classical music in the 1940s, studying a variety of Western and Turkish forms. Although it was becoming increasingly popular at the time for Turkish musicians to join orchestras or nightclub bands, Ozkan instead decided to focus on "pure" traditional music, studying Turkish scales, modal systems, and instrumental technique. After graduating from school, Ozkan went to work for Turkish national radio, where he eventually became director of folkloric music and dance programs, arranging and orchestrating performances by musicians from all across the country. By 1977, however, he'd become so tired of the constant lack of funds and the bureaucratic red tape that he moved to Paris, where he earned a doctorate in ethnomusicology. Now widely considered the world's finest living master of the *saz,* the popular lute instrument traditionally associated with Ottoman music and culture, Ozkan currently concentrates on teaching music theory, and instruction in various instruments and voice, in Paris.

what's available: *Mysteries of Turkey* 𝄞𝄞𝄞𝄞 (Music of the World, 1990, prod. Bob Haddad), originally released in Europe in 1987 by Goasco Music as *Talip Ozkan,* is a delightfully hyp-

notic introduction to Ozkan's warm, rich baritone and masterfully intricate saz solos. Although he is unaccompanied and the production values are minimal, Ozkan is spellbinding, tapping out simple rhythms with his foot as the mystical melodies build to rousing crescendi. Romantic, poetic, and voluptuous, this is the Turkish tradition at its finest. Although not quite as stirring, *The Dark Fire* 𝄞𝄞𝄞𝄞 (Axiom, 1992, prod. Bill Laswell, Nicky Skopelitis) is another vigorous effort, with a brilliant performance by Ozkan showcased through Laswell's typical crystal-clear production. The necessity of Mahmut Demir's appearance on saz and percussion seems questionable at times, as it occasionally detracts slightly from the purity of Ozkan's performance, but on majestic songs like "Karsilama," his drums do lend the proceedings a suitably monolithic air.

worth searching for: Ozkan has recorded a number of albums released only in Europe (most notably *L'Art Viviant de . . .*), some of which you may be able to order on import through his French label, Ocora. But expect to pay a pretty penny, and understand that not all may be available on CD.

influences:

◀◀ Nayi Osman Dedl, Kul Nesimi, Ashik Veysel, Emrah

▶▶ Nicky Skopelitis, Velkis Akkale, Besir Kaya, Turku

see also: *Bill Laswell*

Bret Love

Ozomatli

Latin-funk-hip-hop-rock
Formed 1995, in Los Angeles, CA, USA. Based in Los Angeles, CA, USA.

Wil-Dog Abers, vocals, bass; Raúl Pacheco, guitar, lead vocals; Asdru Sierra, trumpet, lead vocals; Jose Espinoza, alto sax; Jiro Yamaguchi, tabla, percussion; Cut Chemist, turntables; Chali 2na, rap vocals; Justin "Niño" Porée, percussion; William Marrufo, drums, vocals; Ulises Bella, tenor sax, guitar, clarinet, bass clarinet, vocals. (All members are from USA.)

Ozomatli smashed onto the scene in Los Angeles almost by accident. Founder Wil-Dog Abers began writing songs during a month-long strike protesting conditions at his workplace, a local youth jobs agency called the Los Angeles Conservation Corps. During the downtime, he hooked up with an old friend, Raúl Pacheco, who had just moved back to town. Together, they started putting together material that reflected the increasingly hot and spicy ethnic, political, social, and musical stew that is Southern California. More musicians were added until Ozomatli, named after the Aztec god of dance, became a veritable UN of multi-culti rhythms. Its members claim Cuban, Mexican, African, Japanese, and European ancestry; its instrumental lineup includes turntables and tablas; and its style covers funk, salsa, hip-hop, and rock. The group's weekly residency at the tiny Opium Den sparked such word-of-mouth crowds that the engagements had to be moved to a larger, 400-capacity club. A year later, to satisfy the growing fan base, Ozomatli issued a four-track EP, *Ya Llego!,* which included one of their most popular songs, "Como Ves." In addition to its packed, sweaty club dates, the band began dazzling large audiences by opening for the likes of Santana and playing at stops on the multi-act Warped and H.O.R.D.E. festival tours. A recording deal with Almo Sounds soon followed, and an eponymous debut album was issued in 1998, fully documenting Ozomatli's pan-global pop style. Take-no-prisoners touring brought them to every town in the land while the album got them on seemingly every critic's Top Ten list, with ubiquitous soundtrack incursions like *EdTV* inching them ever closer to world domination.

what's available: Go with the full-length debut album, *Ozomatli* &&&& (Almo Sounds, 1998, prod. T-Ray, Ozomatli), as all of the band's swinging strengths are evident. Then backtrack and pick up *Ya Llego!* &&& (self-released, 1997, prod. various), where it *really* all began.

influences:
◀◀ Santana, Tower of Power, Azteca, Malo

Cary Darling

Augustus Pablo
Reggae, dub

Born Horace Swaby, 1953, in Kingston, Jamaica. Died May 18, 1999, in Kingston, Jamaica.

Augustus Pablo was a master of the melodica, a mouth-blown keyboard instrument, and one of the originators of dub, an offshoot of reggae that utilizes the recording studio to remix tunes beyond recognition. Pablo's musical approach blended reggae rhythms with minor-key melodica and organ melodies in a style that he called "Far Eastern."

The former Horace Swaby's first instrument was piano, which he taught himself to play while attending the Kingston College School. But after borrowing a melodica from a girlfriend, Swaby became fascinated with that instrument, adapting to it so quickly that he was invited to play on several tunes recorded by Bob Marley & the Wailers be-

tween 1969 and 1970. He later appeared on recordings by Jimmy Cliff and Burning Spear, and performed as a member of Sly Dunbar's Skin, Flesh & Bones Band. During one recording session, the not-yet-pseudonymous artist met the original Augustus Pablo (Glen Adams), who played keyboard (and, coincidentally, melodica) for the Upsetters. When Adams emigrated to the United States in 1971, producer Herman Chin-Loy suggested that Swaby adopt the name. Although he recorded his first hit, "Java," in 1972, Pablo's greatest period came when he joined forces with producer King Tubby in 1973. His own triumphs as a producer would follow, including Junior Delgado's groundbreaking *Raggamuffin Year* in 1986. Pablo died of the nerve disorder myasthenia gravis in 1999, leaving behind a legacy far out of proportion to his tragically young age.

what to buy: There were dub albums prior to the release of *King Tubby Meets Rockers Uptown* &&& (Shanachie, 1976, prod. King Tubby), but none had the impact of this recording featuring Augustus Pablo. Accompanied by Robbie Shakespeare (bass) and members of Bob Marley's band, including Aston "Family Man" Barrett (bass), Carlton "Carlie" Barrett (drums), and Earl "Chinna" Smith (guitar), Pablo mellifluously blows his melodica through such dub classics as "Keep on Dubbing," "Young Generation Dub," "Each One Dub," "Brace's Tower Dub," and "Skanking Dub."

what to buy next: The follow-up to *King Tubby Meets Rockers Uptown, East of the River Nile* &&& (Shanachie, 1977, prod. Augustus Pablo) continues to explore the possibilities of dub.

best of the rest:
Rebel Rock Reggae: This Is Augustus Pablo &&&& (Heartbeat, 1973/1997)
Ital Dub &&& (Trojan, 1975)
Meet King Tubby Inna Fire House &&&& (Shanachie, 1981)
Original Rockers &&& (Shanachie, 1979)
Thriller &&& (Echo Jazz, 1983)
Earth's Rightful Ruler &&& (Shanachie, 1983)
Rebel Rock Reggae &&& (Heartbeat, 1986)
Rockers Story &&& (RAS, 1989)
Rockers International Showcase &&& (Rykodisc, 1991)
Presents Rockers Dub Store '90s &&& (Rockers, 1993)
Pablo & Friends &&& (RAS, 1997)
Valley of Jehosaphat &&& (RAS, 1999)

influences:
◀◀ Bob Marley, the Skatalites, the Upsetters
▶▶ The Clash, Sly & Robbie, Burning Spear

see also: *Joe Higgs, King Tubby, Hugh Mundell, Oku Onuora, Sly & Robbie*

Craig Harris

Johnny Pacheco

Johnny Pacheco

Salsa

Born March 25, 1935, in Santiago de los Caballeros, Dominican Republic. Based in New York, NY, USA.

Think of it in terms of the word-association exercises you had in school: James Brown is to soul as Johnny Pacheco is to . . . salsa. That's right. Pacheco is the godfather—maybe even the father—of what has arguably been the most popular Latin music in the United States over the past 50 years. Pacheco, who plays flute, saxophone, and percussion, moved from the Dominican Republic to New York City as a teen in the late 1940s. He joined the legendary Charlie Palmieri's Latin orchestra and played with them for a number of years, leaving in 1959 to form his own band. With his own outfit, Pacheco began experimenting with new sounds, blending African, Cuban, Puerto Rican, and other Latin music into what was soon to be called salsa. In 1964 Pacheco and attorney Gerald Masucci launched the Fania record label, giving birth to this new musical form in earnest. Pacheco and Fania continue to crank out the salsa, under Pacheco's own name as well as

that of the Fania All-Stars and other aggregations. The label has been home at one time or another to many Latin superstars, including Willie Colon and the legendary queen of salsa, Celia Cruz. Throughout his lengthy career Pacheco has turned out more than 60 records, with still more tunes appearing on numerous compilations. Although many of his groundbreaking 1960s recordings are out of print or darn hard to find, several can be located in stores with large Latin selections.

what to buy: The reissue *Compadres* 𝄞𝄞𝄞 (Fania, 1995, prod. Johnny Pacheco) might be scarce, but it's the record that put the hot in 1970s "tipico"-style salsa. Pacheco leads the band and plays flute and percussion, while Pete "El Conde" Rodriguez belts out the vocals. Fania put out more than 15 of Pacheco's recordings in 1992—reissues, remixes, some old, some new. One of them, *Demanda Popular* 𝄞𝄞𝄞 (Fania, 1992, prod. Johnny Pacheco), includes Pacheco's "Suarilo" as well as a—needless to say—surprising cover of Donovan's "Sunshine Superman." El Conde, Elliot Romero, and Pete Podriguez handle the vocals.

Artist ♫♫♫ (Fania, 1992)
El Maestro ♫♫♫ (Fania, 1992?)

influences:

◀◀ Charlie Palmieri, Noro Morales, Tito Puente

▶▶ Willie Colon, Celia Cruz, Ruben Blades, Joe Cuba, Yomo Toro, Gloria Estefan

see also: *Willie Colon, Celia Cruz, Charlie Palmieri*

Andrew BeDell

Page & Plant

Rock 'n' roll
Formed 1994, in London, England. Based in England.

Jimmy Page (born January 9, 1944, in Heston, Middlesex, England), guitar; Robert Plant (born August 20, 1948, in Bromwich, Staffordshire, England), vocals.

Most people know and love Jimmy Page and Robert Plant as half of the iconic granddaddy of all metal bands, Led Zeppelin. However, it is doubtful that anybody immersed in world music in the purist sense would recognize these former paragons of excess to be true "world" artists. And rightfully so. But the guys must be given their due. In their youth as Zep, Page and Plant's tunes borrowed certain elements from abroad—a kind of pseudo-Celtic, middle-brow Middle Eastern lilt—not typically found in the blues-based rock being played by so many bands of the 1970s. Today, they're not exactly giving the oldies circuit what it wants either, having reunited after 14 years of post-Zep wanderings for a world-heavy *MTV Unplugged* concert and subsequent second act, still in progress as we speak.

what to buy: *No Quarter* ♫♫♫♫ (WEA/Atlantic, 1994, prod. Jimmy Page, Robert Plant) is the energetic live recording from the MTV special. To their credit, Page & Plant assembled an outstanding supporting cast for this gig, including Porl Thompson on guitar and banjo, Jim Sutherland on mandolin and *bodhrán* (Irish frame drum), Nigel Eaton on hurdy-gurdy, and Charlie Jones on bass. Notable Middle Eastern (and Indian) musicians include Najma Akhtar on vocals, Hossam Ramzy and Ibrahim Abdel Khaliq on percussion, and Abdel Salam Kheir on *oud* (Arabic lute). And we can't leave out the London Metropolitan Orchestra. The proceedings, recorded in Marrakesh, Morocco; Bron-Y-Aur, Wales; and London, include several Led Zeppelin chestnuts and a few new numbers. Page & Plant's decidedly world-music approach lends an exotic air to "The Battle for Evermore," "Kashmir," and "Gallows Pole," while they give a more classic *Houses of the Holy* treatment to "Nobody's Fault but Mine" and "Friends." The newer tracks, "Yallah" and "City Don't Cry," are both laced with hypnotic chanting by Najma

Akhtar and others from the assembled chorus. *Walking into Clarksdale* ♫♫♫ (WEA/Atlantic, 1998, prod. Jimmy Page, Robert Plant) is a slightly less worldly effort. Though there are decided nods to Middle Eastern instrumentation, the disc is more Celtic in flavor, with Plant's pagan lyrical imagery in full swing. The song list is all new, albeit with an acoustic Zeppelin feel, again paying homage to *Houses of the Holy* and *Physical Graffiti*.

influences:

◀◀ Willie Dixon, the Beatles, Chuck Berry, Sonny Boy Williamson, Howlin' Wolf, Robert Johnson, Led Zeppelin, Hossam Ramzy

▶▶ AC/DC, Aerosmith, Bad Company, Black Sabbath, Bonham, Whitesnake, Van Halen, and a host of others

see also: *Najma, Hossam Ramzy*

Andrew BeDell

Gabby Pahinui

Slack-key guitar
Born Charles Philip Pahinui, 1921, in HI, USA. Died October 13, 1980, in Honolulu, HI.

Gabby Pahinui was one of Hawaii's great slack-key guitarists, and the one who introduced many mainlanders to the style (known for its open-tuned finger-picking). He ushered in the modern slack-key era when he made his first recordings in 1947, and continued recording and performing—both as a frontman and a sideman—until his death more than 30 years later. His many recordings, along with his virtuosic playing style and evocative falsetto singing, forever distinguished him as the father of his style in its modern form. Pahinui played In many well-known Hawaiian bands, including the Sons of Hawaii and the Hawaiian Serenaders. During the 1970s he led his own outfit, the Gabby Pahinui Hawaiian Band, which featured four of his children. World-music patron and guitar master Ry Cooder helped bring Pahinui's talents to mainland attention, but within the Hawaiian islands, there probably was and is not one guitarist who's not already directly influenced by Pahinui's music.

what's available: Though Pahinui recorded often throughout his career, most of his albums are no longer in print or are very difficult to find outside Hawaii. Fortunately, his watershed album *The Gabby Pahinui Hawaiian Band, Volume 1* ♫♫♫♫ (Edsel, 1975/1987, prod. Panini) is readily available as a British import. It features a band including Sonny Chillingworth, Cyril and James "Bla" Pahinui, and Ry Cooder. It's an outstanding recording—made with a generator-driven studio in a remote section of the island of Hawaii in 1974. This is probably the best place to start for someone who's just getting interested in

Hawaiian music. Pahinui and Atta Isaacs, who often played together, can be heard in duo fronting a five-piece band on *Two Slack-Key Guitars ♫♫♫* (Tradewinds, 1996, prod. Margaret Williams). The age of the recording shows, but the playing is exceptional.

influences:

◀◀ Sonny Chillingworth, Atta Isaacs

▶▶ James "Bla" & Cyril Pahinui, George Kuo, the Kahumoku Brothers, Ozzie Kotani, Keola Beamer, Rev. Dennis Kamakahi, Ledward Kaapana

see also: *Sonny Chillingworth, Ry Cooder, the Pahinui Brothers*

Brian Mansfield

The Pahinui Brothers /Cyril Pahinui /James "Bla" Pahinui

Slack-key guitar
Formed in HI, USA. Based in HI, USA.

Cyril Pahinui (born April 21, 1950, in Waimanalo, HI, USA), guitar, ukulele, vocals; James "Bla" Pahinui (born 1942, in Waimanalo, HI, USA), guitar, ukulele, vocals; Martin Pahinui (born in Honolulu, HI, USA), bass, vocals.

As sons of one of Hawaii's musical legends, the Pahinui Brothers have had big shoes to fill. Though they had performed on their own, they came to the forefront of Hawaiian music when they and another sibling joined their father in the Gabby Pahinui Hawaiian Band during the early 1970s, shortly after Gabby left the Sons of Hawaii. Since the elder Pahinui's death in 1980, the brothers have continued performing and recording, both separately and together. Cyril, James (usually called "Bla"), and Martin recorded an album for Private Music in 1992, and Cyril and Bla have each recorded solo for Dancing Cat.

what's available: *The Pahinui Bros. ♫♫* (Private Music, 1992, prod. Steve Siegfried, Witt Shingle, Ry Cooder) takes a mainstream, mainland approach to Hawaii's distinctive, open-tuned slack-key guitar style, mixing songs by John Lennon ("Jealous Guy") and Steve Earle ("My Old Friend the Blues") with otherwise largely traditional fare. The session band includes lap-steel player David Lindley, drummer Russ Kunkel, and guitarist Ry Cooder. Both Cyril and James subsequently signed with George Winston's Dancing Cat Records and released solo albums. Cyril Pahinui, the ninth of Gabby's 10 children, made his solo debut with *6 & 12 String Slack Key ♫♫♫* (Dancing Cat, 1994, prod. George Winston) after a many-band apprenticeship. Half instrumental and half vocal, *6 & 12 String Slack Key* offers exactly what its title suggests, with Cyril playing each in-

strument solo in a variety of tunings. James "Bla" Pahinui has recorded more often, though his early solo albums are out of print. Bla's *Mana ♫♫♫* (Dancing Cat, 1997, prod. George Winston, Howard Johnson) shows the influence of his interest in both Latin music and doo-wop—he does a vocal medley including "Silhouettes (On the Shade)," "Goodnight My Love," and "Can't Help Falling in Love (With You)." That's a little odd, but, like the rest of the album, it has an endearing quality to it. James is a left-handed guitarist who plays his instrument upside-down and backwards; he plays all the songs here in a "Dropped D" tuning that runs D-A-D-G-B-E from the highest-pitched string to the lowest.

worth searching for: Cyril and Bla both play guitar on their dad's classic *The Gabby Pahinui Hawaiian Band, Volume 1 ♫♫♫♫♫* (Edsel, 1975/1987, prod. Panini).

influences:

◀◀ Gabby Pahinui, Sonny Chillingworth, Ry Cooder

▶▶ George & Moses Kahumoku, Ozzie Kotani, George Kuo

see also: *Gabby Pahinui, Ry Cooder*

Brian Mansfield

Charlie Palmieri

Salsa, Latin jazz
Born 1927, in New York, NY, USA. Died 1988, in England.

Although not as well known as his younger brother Eddie, Charlie Palmieri was one of the most influential piano players in the history of salsa and Latin jazz. Classically trained, Palmieri is best remembered for his heavily percussive approach to the keyboards.

Palmieri began his musical career very young. Studying piano from the age of seven, he became a professional musician at 16. Though he formed his own band, El Conjunto Pin Pin, in 1948, it was short-lived and he went on to become a sideman in bands led by Tito Puente, Tito Rodriguez, and Pupi Campo. Palmieri's second attempt as a leader was more successful. Formed in 1958, his Charanga Dubonney was one of the best Latin bands to feature flute and violin. In its mid-1960s incarnation, the Dubonney Orchestra, Palmieri replaced the flute and violin with trumpets and trombones. Also during that decade, Palmieri served as music director of the Alegre label's Alegre All-Stars in New York.

But Palmieri's hard work came with a price. In 1969 he suffered severe emotional problems. Following a lengthy recovery period, he was hired as music director of Tito Puente's television show, *El Mambo De Tito Puente.* In an attempt to slow down his touring schedule, Palmieri became a teacher and lecturer on

Latin music and history. He then moved to Puerto Rico in 1980, and remained on the island until 1983. Although he subsequently planned to perform a concert with his brother, he suffered a massive heart attack and stroke after traveling to New York to help plan the event. Still, he resumed his career in 1984 with a small ensemble. Together with Jimmy Sabater, he served as co-leader of the aptly named Combo Gigante, and in 1987 played piano on an album by a fellow giant, percussionist Mongo Santamaria. The following year, Palmieri traveled for the first time to England. While there, he suffered a second heart attack, which would take his life.

what to buy: *Impulsos* 🎵🎵🎵 (Mpl, 1975, prod. Charlie Palmieri) documents a historic jazz and Latin music session with Palmieri's piano and organ-playing accompanied by such top-notch Latin players as Tito Puente and Jerry Gonzalez.

what to buy next: *Gigante Hits* 🎵🎵🎵 (Alegre, 1994, prod. Charlie Palmieri) samples tracks from throughout his recording career.

the rest:
Tribute to Noro Morales 🎵🎵🎵 (Alegre, 1956)
Charanga 🎵🎵🎵 (United Artists, 1960)
Pachanga at the Caravana Club 🎵🎵🎵 (Alegre, 1961)
Latin Bugalu 🎵🎵🎵 (Atlantic, 1968)
The Giant of the Keyboard 🎵🎵🎵 (Alegre, 1972)
Adelante Gigante 🎵🎵🎵 (Alegre, 1975)
Perdido 🎵🎵🎵 (Alegre, 1977)
A Giant Step 🎵🎵🎵 (Tropical Budda, 1984)
Hay Que Estar En Algo 🎵🎵🎵 (Alegre, 1992)
Heavyweight 🎵🎵🎵 (Alegre, 1995)
Echoes of an Era 🎵🎵🎵 (PolyGram, 1996)

influences:
◀◀ Tito Puente, Mongo Santamaria, Dizzy Gillespie

▶▶ The Fort Apache Band, Ray Barretto, Gato Barbieri

see also: *Jerry Gonzalez & the Fort Apache Band, Eddie Palmieri, Tito Puente, Mongo Santamaria*

Craig Harris

Eddie Palmieri

Latin jazz
Born December 15, 1936, in New York, NY, USA. Based in USA.

Eddie Palmieri started playing the piano when he was eight years old, picking up the rudiments of performance from his older brother Charlie. It was Charlie who introduced Eddie to his first formal teacher in 1949, even though the younger Palmieri was starting to gravitate toward the *timbales*. This interest in percussion was to remain with him after he switched back to playing the piano a few years later. During the mid- and late 1950s Palmieri worked with a variety of bandleaders, the

Cyril Pahinui

best-known of whom were vocalists Vincentico Valdez and Tito Rodriguez. When Palmieri finally went out on his own in 1960, he formed a *charanga* (violin-and-flute-heavy Cuban ensemble) called La Perfecta, which was similar to the groups led by his brother Charlie. Jazz elements started creeping into Eddie's playing and writing in the mid-1960s, just in time for the band to break up in 1968. Palmieri continued exploring his own personal fusion of Latin music and jazz during the 1970s, with an emphasis on the newer electronic gadgets being brought into the market. His later material shows an increased growth in both arranging and composition (although his electronic experimentation appears less often these days), and he, along with Cachao and Tito Puente, can now be considered among the most popular elder statesmen in the world of Latin jazz.

what to buy: *Palmas* 🎵🎵🎵🎵 (Elektra/Nonesuch, 1994, prod. Eddie Palmieri) shows the jazz influences in Palmieri's music more than anything he had done before it. His association with trumpeter Brian Lynch, trombonist Conrad Herwig, and alto saxophonist Donald Harrison was to continue past this release, but the formidable front line created by these three expert jazzmen here adds an improvisational punch to the awesomely talented Latin rhythm section already on hand. There are no weak tunes in the entire set, making this the Palimeri album jazz fans should start with. On *Arete* 🎵🎵🎵🎵 (RMM/Tropijazz, 1995, prod. Eddie Palmieri), listeners should go right to "Definitely In," where Palmieri's slightly skewed arrangement and McCoy Tyner-esque piano voicings blend Latin and jazz elements as well as anyone ever has. "Waltz for My Grandchildren" has a pleasant Monk/Brubeck-goes-Latin feel to it, and the rhythm-fest at the front end of "Sixes in Motion" is a pulsating delight. The one caveat for this release concerns Palmieri's vocal groans and moans (à la Keith Jarrett, Oscar Peterson, and Glenn Gould) when he plays piano on the otherwise commendable "Sisters." For some folks, it's an annoyance that might detract from the overall quality of the album.

what to buy next: *El Rumbero del Piano* 🎵🎵🎵🎵 (RMM, 1998, prod. Eddie Palmieri) features the usual batch of jazzers, but the slant aims straight at the salsa market. The tunes are relatively compact and to the point, with hot vocals from Wichy Camacho and Hermán Olivera. Folkloric group Los Pleneros De La 21, an outfit specializing in Puerto Rico's native *plena* rhythms, appears on "Dónde Está Mi Negra," and there is a splendid cover of Arsenio Rodríguez's "Oiga Mi Guaguancó," with a *tres* (small Cuban guitar) solo from Nelson González that echoes the original. *Lucumi, Macumba, Voodoo Leyendas* 🎵🎵🎵🎵 (Sony Discos, 1978/1995, prod. Eddie Palmieri) was a groundbreaking recording for Palmieri in the same way that 1979's *Rican/Struction* was for Ray Barretto, yet it sold poorly. On many levels, this is more a pop album than a jazz album, but the skillful arrangements incorporating both Brazilian and R&B elements are better than what one would hear on a rock session from the same period. "Colombia Te Canto" and the *Santería*-inflected percussion (reflecting that Afro-Caribbean religion's ritual) of "Mi Congo Te Llama," as well as the title tune, make this one of Palmieri's more interesting experiments. A solid album throughout, *Vortex* 🎵🎵🎵 (RMM/Tropijazz, 1996, prod. Eddie Palmieri) is marred slightly by a useless if clever Latinized arrangement of Beethoven's "Minuet in G," and Palmieri's distracting vocal rumbles and wheezes. Noteworthy tunes include "Iriaida," with its surprisingly tasteful use of electronic sounds, and "Vanilla Extract," an extended version of Palmieri's earlier hit, "Chocolate Ice Cream."

best of the rest:
Mozambique 🎵🎵🎵 (Tico, 1965/1992)
Champagne 🎵🎵🎵 (Tico, 1968/1992)
Live at Sing Sing, Vol. 1 🎵🎵🎵 (Tico, 1974/1994)
Palo Pa Rumba 🎵🎵🎵 (Fania, 1984/1992)

worth searching for: Search for two rousing concert albums by the Tropijazz All-Stars that feature long works by Palmieri: *Tropijazz All-Stars: Volume One* 🎵🎵🎵🎵 (Tropijazz, 1996, prod. Ralph Mercado) contains "Suite 925-2828" and *Tropijazz All-Stars: Volume Two* 🎵🎵🎵 (Tropijazz, 1997, prod. Ralph Mercado)

features "Nobel Cruise." Other personnel on these albums include Tito Puente, Giovanni Hidalgo, David Valentin, Charlie Sepulveda, J.P. Torres, and David Sanchez.

influences:

⏮ Tito Puente, Charlie Palmieri, Thelonious Monk, McCoy Tyner, Bud Powell, Benny Golson

⏭ Michel Camilo, Hilton Ruiz

see also: *Ray Barretto, Cachao, La India, Los Pleneros De La 21, Charlie Palmieri, Tito Puente*

Garaud MacTaggart

The Pan-African Orchestra
African orchestral
Formed in Accra, Ghana. Based in Accra, Ghana.

Nano Danso Abiam, director; Baba Ayombila, wia (notched flute); Anthony Awingura, wia; Thomas Segkura, gyile (xylophone); Yaw Asiedu Kwakye, gyile; Mahmadu Susso, kora (harp-lute); Lamine Susso, kora; Abukari Alhassan, gonje (African violin); Gruma Muhamah, gonje; Emmanuel Nana Kwesi Ansong, Antenteben flute; Zorkie Nelson, Antenteben flute; Yaw Della Botri, Antenteben flute; Eric Yemoh Mensah, Antenteben flute; Kotey Amon, Antenteben flute; Vida Koranteng Opare, Antenteben flute; Kweku Sakyeama Kwakye, Antenteben flute; Yaw Asumadu, Antenteben flute; Boateng Kodua Acheampong, Antenteben flute; John Lartey Ayisi, Antenteben flute; David Okoe Nunoo, drums/percussion; Robert Tawiah Nunoo, drums/percussion; Ibrahima Abukari, drums/percussion; Kwabena Kwakye, drums/percussion; Charles Ofei Odametey, drums/percussion; Stanley Baidoo, horns; Ebenezer Bortey, horns; Edward Sackey, horns; Yaw Adjei, horns; Kofi Sarkwa, horns; Kofi Dei, horns; Samuel Ofori, horns. (All artists are from Ghana.)

Just as the Third Stream movement in jazz synthesized that genre and classical music, the Pan-African Orchestra's *Opus 1* represents perhaps the first truly African symphonic work. Persuading the French horn player of the Ghanaian National Symphony Orchestra to bin his brass and use an elephant tusk had been a losing battle. Nano Danso Abiam was struggling with a colonial mentality by which classical music was well funded and taken seriously, and the musicians' own heritage was not. Abiam formed his own group, rejecting European culture and reclaiming African music as a serious pursuit for a large ensemble. His long struggle to finance this project originally aimed for 108 musicians, the amount that might be in a Western orchestra; 30 was the final figure. Pan-African in spirit more than specific source material, Abiam's symphonies are composed from a synthesis of mainly Ghanaian village music.

what's available: The nine compositions on *Opus 1* 🎵🎵🎵 (RealWorld, 1995, prod. Nano Danso Abiam, Andy Summers) have been edited from full concert length. The title of the first track,

"Wia Concerto No. 1: First Movement, in Four Parts," reinforces Abiam's intent to have *Opus 1* compared directly with classical music. It does not sound like an African take on Mozart by any means, and rather than simply amplifying traditional music, the larger ensemble plays at a much more complex level, with carefully plotted interactions between the instrumentalists.

influences:

Ghanian musical tradition, Duke Ellington

David Poole

Ivo Papasov

Stambolovo (Bulgarian wedding-band music)
Born 1952, in Kurdzhali, Bulgaria. Based in Bulgaria.

Ivo Papasov is a living legend in Bulgaria, where he is considered the superstar of Bulgarian wedding music, also known as *stambolovo* (named after the city where various wedding bands hold an annual festival). It's a feast of swirling sound set in motion by clarinet, saxophone, electric guitar, accordion, bass, and drums. Papasov leads the way on robustly played clarinet, blending in Gypsy, klezmer, and jazz influences with a snake-charmer's sensibility. There's metric zaniness afoot in Papasov's hold-your-breath music, propelled by such wonderfully odd time signatures as 11/16, 5/8, 7/8, and 9/8.

Legend has it that the hefty Papasov, of Turkish Rom (Gypsy) ancestry, had his umbilical cord tied with a thread from his father's *zurna* (double-reeded horn) at birth. And indeed, not long after, at the age of nine, Papasov switched from accordion to clarinet and got his first gig at a local restaurant when the house orchestra took its breaks. Early on, he began tinkering with Bulgarian folk traditions—an act frowned upon by communist government officials—by experimenting with jazz, blues, and rock influences. He even did some prison time in 1982 for his far-flung musical ideas. Yet this new rocket-fueled brand of Bulgarian folk—a whirlwind of asymmetrical rhythms, accelerating tempos, and staccato melody lines—eventually made Papasov the highest-paid wedding musician in the country. It's been said that he and his band are so popular some couples even resort to scheduling their marriages mid-week to hire him.

Even though Papasov's celebratory music is played brilliantly, its sheer power, beauty, and joy override any concern with virtuosic excesses. Saxophonist Youri Younakov once commented on why Papasov's band never looks at its audience when it plays: "There's no time. Have you ever seen how a hunted rabbit runs? It . . . zig-zag[s], stops, returns, does 8's and 16's . . . . That's how Ivo plays. And we chase him like hounds with our tongues hanging out." Papasov also has a reputation for getting so involved in the intensity of his music that he sometimes flies into a rage. In an interview, he admitted: "I am like a wild animal almost. If somebody makes a small mistake, I will shout at him. But my musicians are used to it. Some musicians are actually afraid of me; not just my musicians, but other musicians as well. But that's my temperament. When I'm onstage I could kill everybody." Papasov's popularity has spread to the concert circuit in Europe, where he fills stadia and inspires youth to spray-paint "Ivo Rules!" on walls. Figuratively, at least, he seems poised to knock 'em dead across the continent for some time to come.

what's available: *Orpheus Ascending* ⅏⅏⅏⅏ (Hannibal, 1989, prod. Joe Boyd, Rumyana Tzintzarska) is a remarkable introduction to Papasov's vigorous Bulgarian wedding-band music. Its unusual vocal and instrumental loops, dissonant notes, and shifting rhythms assault you with waves of brilliant colors and fascinating textures. An even more fiery outing by Ivo and company is found on *Balkanology* ⅏⅏⅏⅏ (Hannibal/Rykodisc, 1991, prod. Joe Boyd). There's plenty of ecstatic playing, with a Turkish dance number and Macedonian and Greek material tossed into the mix. As if that weren't enough (and what for this band is?), there's also a gorgeous vibrato vocal appearance by Papasov's wife, Maria Karafezieva, on the delicate ballad "Istoria Na Edna Lyubov," the only respite in this entire collection of fast dance frenzy.

influences:

Benny Goodman, Charlie Parker, David Sanborn, Petko Radev

Dan Ouellette

Niamh Parsons

Irish folk
Born 1959, in Dublin, Ireland. Based in Dublin, Ireland.

Niamh (pronounced "Neeve") Parsons is a good person to be carrying on the role created by Mary Black, Dolores Keane, and Sandy Denny. Her voice is by turns lustrous and austere, a Celtic aesthete's dream. Music was a prominent feature in Parsons's home life, and her early listening patterns included Irish folk pioneers Boys of the Lough and Planxty. Life as a musician was sketchy at first, when Parsons began singing with a variety of groups in a local scene where day jobs were an accepted part of being in a band. The blooming of her career started about the time she finally went into the studio to record her first album. With her husband Dee Moore and a batch of musicians handpicked to cut the disc, Parsons laid down the tracks for 1992's *Loosely Connected*. In relatively short order she was invited to join Arcady (replacing no less than the acclaimed Frances Black), and *Loosely Connected* was critically hailed. While she was singing with Arcady, Parsons and Moore put together a band called the Loose Connections as a vehicle for her

Abida Parveen (center)

performances and his songs. The second album, *Loosen Up*, featured this band, with Moore, Parsons, and the splendid piper John McSherry being the only holdovers from the first album's sessions. Parsons left Arcady in 1997.

what to buy: While Parsons has been a steady, reliable singer ever since her debut, her work on *Blackbirds and Thrushes* ♪♪♪♪ (Green Linnet, 1999, prod. Niamh Parsons, Gavin Ralston, Alan Whelan) is a quantum leap in quality. All the promise held in anything she had done before has been fulfilled in this stunningly lovely disc of traditional tunes. From solo voice to sextet settings, there are moments of wonder to be heard.

what to buy next: Parsons's first album, *Loosely Connected* ♪♪♪ (Greentrax, 1992/Green Linnet, 1995, prod. Vinnie Kilduff), contains a fair number of tunes that were written by established writers, or are arrangements of traditional folk songs. Her voice is strong throughout and the project was nominated as Album of the Year in Great Britain's prestigious *Folk Roots* magazine. It still holds up well, but the second album, *Loosen Up* ♪♪♪ (Green Linnet, 1997, prod. Dee Moore), has more of a band feel to it, with most of the songs coming from Moore's

pen—though the standout cut is Parsons's moving, *a cappella* rendering of Ron Kavana's "Reconciliation."

worth searching for: Arcady's *Many Happy Returns* ♪♪♪♪ (Shanachie, 1995, prod. Johnny McDonagh) shows that Parsons was a happy choice for the band. Her singing on "The Boys of Barr Na Sraide" and "The Rambling Irishman" is absolutely wonderful.

influences:
◀◀ Boys of the Lough, Planxty, Dolores Keane, Mary Black

see also: *Arcady*

Garaud MacTaggart

Abida Parveen
Qawwali, ghazal
Born 1957, in Larkana, Pakistan. Based in Larkana, Pakistan.

While Nusrat Fateh Ali Khan made Pakistan's spiritual *qawwali* music famous worldwide through extensive touring and recording (and Western hybrid hits like his soundtrack work on *Dead*

Man Walking), little is known of the style's female practitioners outside of Pakistan. But if Nusrat was the undisputed king of "qawwals" then Abida Parveen is the reigning queen. Her messages of love are uplifting, her soprano soars with divine grace, and the love she sings of in Urdu needs no translation, for in every breath her words communicate a deep devotion. Parveen excels equally at qawwali and the Persian-derived light-classical song form *ghazal*. Her music transports an audience into a state of *marifat*, or inner knowledge, in which repeated phrases lose their meaning to gain a wordless greater truth.

what to buy: *The Best of Abida Parveen* 𝄞𝄞𝄞𝄞 (Shanachie, 1997) was compiled from Parveen's industrious stint with EMI Pakistan. Her exquisite voice chimes several octaves above the drums, yet beneath the plucking sound of the sitar, as she scats captivatingly to vigorous rhythms. All 10 songs are a delight.

what to buy next: Longer improvisations can be heard on Parveen's most recent album, *Devotional Journey* 𝄞𝄞𝄞 (Shalimar, 1998), which was recorded live in New York.

worth searching for: *Pakistani Sufi Songs* (Inedit, 1995) is available as a French import.

influences:

◀◀ Ustad Ghulam Haider, Ustad Salamat Ali Khan, Umm Kulthum

▶▶ Sheila Chandra, Natacha Atlas

David Poole

Margareta Paslaru

Romanian folklore–influenced mainstream and experimental pop
Born July 9, 1943, in Bucharest, Romania. Based in Summit, NJ, USA.

Few suburban New Jerseyans suspect that there's a Madonna in their midst. But in her home country of Romania, Margareta Paslaru carries that kind of stature—to begin with. Take the hit-making instincts the comparison implies, and combine it with the sustained and illuminating experimentation of a David Bowie or Yoko Ono, the unflagging and uplifting commitment to home-grown folklore of a Pete Seeger, the staying power of a child-star-turned-national-treasure like Stevie Wonder, and the timelessly hip sophistication (not to mention smoky lower-register vocal presence) of a Marlene Dietrich, and you're closer to the mark.

Paslaru's screenplay-like story begins with her discovery at age 15 and instant embrace by an escape-hungry national audience, whose country had lived under an authoritarian regime from the year she was born. Margareta, as she is simply known to her generations of admirers, moved through big-band, pop, folkloric, avant-garde, and other styles over a decades-long career, softening the human toll of strongman Nicolae

Ceauçescu's communism—both for her fans and herself—even as she too chafed under its restrictions, eventually sacrificing the only life she'd ever known to be free of it.

Margareta's sound, while at one time or another having encompassed all the major stylistic movements of the 20th century both popular and rarefied, is centered on a flamboyant interpretation of Romanian traditional music for contemporary listeners. In her homeland, those listeners span several generations and every taste, supplied not only by Margareta's many recordings, but also her pioneering and longstanding prominence in Romanian television, her prolific and wide-ranging Elvis-like movie career, and her celebrated performances in theatrical works like a long-running *Three-Penny Opera*. Her concert tours throughout the communist world and in virtually every Western democracy but the U.S. only magnified her legend both at home and abroad, but it was a small, human concern that would change the course of that saga more profoundly than any artistic triumph.

By the early 1980s Margareta longed to reunite herself and her young daughter with her husband, a businessman then operating in the U.S. Family came first for Margareta, but, unsurprisingly, not for the regime, which obstructed her and little Anna's emigration for a year before mother and child moved on to an unfamiliar new home, and left behind the undying but now underground adoration of the masses in their old one. The family settled into a quiet life in Summit, New Jersey, with the parents attending to the financing of their daughter's upbringing and education—and providing what relief they could to many other relatives who hadn't made the trip. Margareta retired from performance, seeing this time philosophically as an introduction to the common life of the many who'd once supported her. But as Anna entered adulthood and one revolution overturned another in Romania, a broader kind of family concern drew Margareta back to the public arena.

Distraught by reports of Romanian orphans' abject state in the aftermath of political turmoil, Margareta began to record songs which sometimes detailed and always benefited the cause of humanitarian relief. Compilations of new and old favorites electrified post-communist Romania, and, upon the country's election of an opposition government for the first time in her life, Margareta made a triumphant homecoming which riveted the nation's attention, brought out mass crowds, and saturated nightly newscasts. Though timed to coincide with another "best of" release, Margareta's accompanying tour was not of concert halls but orphanages, to raise her countrymen and women's awareness of one of the ongoing crises within their borders. She received honors from UNICEF and UNESCO, and returned in two subsequent years as a distinguished arts–awards presenter (at the kinds of festivals where she herself had long been a recipient)—each time using the opportunity to press her cause. Equally triumphant reunions with the expatriate Romanian community in North America followed, with a sold-out tour throughout the U.S. and Canada (her return to the stage after an almost unbroken 16-year absence) in honor of her 40th anniversary in show business.

Today, Margareta divides her performing time between the Romanian-American oldies circuit continent-wide, and the avant-garde Eastern European–fusion underground in downtown New York City. At this writing, she was preparing for another tour to benefit the children and elderly displaced by the war over Kosovo, and looking forward to another anniversary, that of her 40th year in recording. Her work is hard to find in her adoptive country, but like the human potential she strives to preserve, it's a treasure worthy of the quest.

worth searching for: The definitive survey of either Margareta's folkloric or experimental-pop highpoints has yet to be compiled, and for now its appearance in your record collection faces some obstacles. First, the sound quality of what's extant is widely variable, since many masters were destroyed by the Ceauçescu regime after the artist's departure, and post-communist compilations are often transferred from vinyl once hoarded by reprisal-risking fans. Second, at this point Margareta has several different generations (and nations) of fans to accommodate, and the most general crowd-pleasers dominate the more rootsy and visionary stuff on her available releases. But for the hearty album-winnower there's still a lot of worthy material to sift for. The second and fourth volumes of her cassette-only "Suita Nostalgiilor" ("Nostalgic Suite") of archival tracks, self-released in the U.S. for Romanian and American charitable causes, feature the best batches of her traditional material you can find. *De La Suflet La Suflet (From Soul to Soul)* ♪♪♪♪ (M. Soul Productions, 1994, prod. various) includes such Romanian folkloric classics as the rousing, rapid-fire, fiddle-driven "Tarina"; the stately, swooping "Ouas"; and the hushed, haunted "Doina," a song of lamentation given a stark timpani-and-voice treatment (with metallic Japanese percussion sparingly deployed to memorably eerie effect). These three tracks are from before Margareta's emigration and are relatively well preserved. From the '90s and clear as a bell is "Collinde," an impeccably arranged and beautifully sung medley of Romanian Christmas carols (and one of Margareta's many Stateside collaborations with the talented Adrian Antonescu and Anthony Petosa). The album *40 de ani de la debut (40 Years from the Debut)* ♪♪♪♪ (M. Soul Productions, 1998, prod. various) includes two stunning *a cappella* folk songs, "Saraca Inima Mea (Oh, My Poor Heart)" and "Balada lui Iancu Jianu (The Ballad of Iancu Jianu)," recorded live at the surprise mini-concert in Queens, New York (a large Romanian-American enclave), with which Margareta re-

turned to public performance after more than a decade. Each is a life-affirmingly melodious yet achingly lamentational soliloquy quaking with drama. The tape also surveys the cream of Margareta's recent radio smashes and hybrid innovations. "Sarbarori Fericite (Happy Holidays)," from 1996, merges the African American gospel and Romanian choral traditions in an infectious pop sheen, while 1997's measured but insistently rhythmic "Bucuria de a Cinta (The Joy of Singing)," at once percussive and solemn, adds rollicking rock-roadhouse piano to an ancient ethnic beat, with world-class vocal belting punctuated by swooning peasant cries; all dynamic elements in an unforgettable whole. *Un Pod Peste Ocean (A Bridge Across the Ocean)* ♪♪♪♪ (Electrecord, 1993, prod. various), the comeback CD from after the fall of communism, compiles many Margareta favorites while introducing the four American recordings with which she'd broken her long silence. The forlorn, flute-driven "Un Copil Uitat (The Unknown Child)" (a prime collaboration with fellow Romanian émigré Alex Adrian) is a plea for abandoned and alone children the world over, and is the new song most evocative of Romanian stylistic tradition on this album. It's complemented by the affecting mid-tempo ballad "Am Cântat (I Sang)"; the rhythmically acrobatic "Septembrie (September)," a state-of-the-art European techno-disco number with an unexpected poignancy; and the moody, orchestra-sampling title track, whose rhythmic, raspy vocals deliver an inventive and respectful take on rap. All of these standouts on all of these albums are well worth having, and listeners 60 and up—not to mention lounge hipsters of all ages—may even find the dated but always exuberant material that fills out each collection enjoyable too. *Source* ♪♪♪♪ (Knitting Factory, 1999), a CD by Matt Darriau's Paradox Trio, features Margareta on a strong new reading of "Doina," and is the first recorded document of her ongoing collaboration with this adventurous offshoot project of the Klezmatics' clarinetist. Margareta's "Nostalgic Suite" cassettes are available from M. Soul Productions, P.O. Box 301, Summit, NJ 07902-0301, and through her Web site at www.margareta.com.

influences:

◀◀ Romanian folkloric tradition, international pop

▶▶ Generations of contemporary Romanian entertainers

see also: *The Klezmatics*

Adam McGovern

Patato

Son, salsa

Born Carlos Valdés, November 4, 1926, in Havana, Cuba. Based in New York, NY, USA.

"Patato" Valdés is a master *conguero* who has played with every giant in the history of salsa and jazz, including Beny

Moré, Machito, Cachao, Mario Bauzá, Dizzy Gillespie, Art Blakey, Tito Puente, and Quincy Jones. He was the first musician to tune the congas to a song's dominant chord, a fact of which he's justifiably proud. "Before I invented the tuning keys, you had to heat the drum head with fire, but because of the humidity in Cuba, they would always tune down," Patato says. "I asked Ramon Bragerra to put keys on the conga, like on the bongo, to keep a true tuning. I'm the only harmonic and melodic conga player around," he laughs, and at 73 he still plays with more energy than a roomful of men half his age. Patato's father was a musician who "played *tres* [small guitar] with Los Apaches, and piano with Sexteto Habanero. I started on tres, but when the piano took over in the 1940s, the tres was unnecessary, so at 18 I went to the congas." Patato also mastered *cajones* (wooden boxes played with wooden spoons, similar to the cajones in Afro-Peruvian music), *shekere* (rattles), washtub bass, and *marimbula,* a large Cuban thumb piano that's used for bass lines in traditional rumba groups. At 19 he joined La Sonora Matancera, the most popular and influential Cuban band of its day. After playing with Perez Prado, Beny Moré, and Conjunto Azul (with Chano Pozo), he left for New York in 1954. He's lived there ever since. Patato's incredible showmanship—he gave Brigitte Bardot a mambo lesson in *And God Created Woman* and invented new dances like the yoyo and the penguin—is the perfect complement to his innate rhythmic sense. He was one of the first Cuban congueros to make a name for himself in the United States, and his early contributions to the bands of Mario Bauzá and Dizzy Gillespie helped write the book for several generations of jazz and salsa percussionists. In-between regular gigs with Herbie Mann, Tito Puente, and Mario Bauzá, Patato did sessions with J.J. Johnson, Willie Bobo, Machito, Cal Tjader, and others. His free-flying rhythmic sense and high energy have always been in demand. "I don't like to be a mechanical player," Patato says. "I play whatever comes into my mind, bossa nova, Cuban, African. Nobody can imitate me, because I never play the same way twice. When the [producer] counts it off, I pick it up and go after it."

what to buy: Although Patato has been present on some of the greatest recordings of Afro-Cuban jazz, bugaloo, and salsa ever recorded, *Masterpiece* 𝄽𝄽𝄽𝄽 (Messidor, 1993, prod. Jorge Dalto, Patato) is only his second set as a bandleader. With Argentinean pianist/composer/arranger Jorge Dalto lending an able hand, Patato and company turn in a scorching set. Not unexpectedly, all tracks feature stellar drumming, with the two tunes based on Cuban traditional music ("Felice Navidad" and "Tonan Che Cabaldo a Ochún") particular standouts.

what to buy next: *Ritmo y Candela* 𝄽𝄽𝄽𝄽 (Round World, 1998, prod. Greg Landau) is a reissue of the Grammy-nominated *descarga* (jam session) first released on Redwood Records in

the tabla

The most important percussion instrument in the North Indian classical tradition, the *tabla* is actually a pair of drums that evolved around 450 years ago from the *pakhavaj,* a two-headed drum played on its sides with the hands. Details of how the tabla developed from the pakhavaj are debated, but one theory involves an anecdotal incident in which two percussionist brothers were involved in a battle of skills. Out of frustration, one of the brothers threw his pakhavaj to the ground, splitting it in two and thereby creating a new instrument. Of the tabla's two units, the higher-toned one, called the "tabla" itself, is cylindrical, made of wood, and tuned by sliding wooden pegs beneath the straps that tighten the head. The lower-pitched *bayan* is larger, kettle-shaped, and usually made of brass. The head of the bayan is kept relatively loose, allowing players to alter its pitch by applying pressure with the palm as it is struck with the fingertips. These components and techniques, along with the *gab* (the black circle of paste in the center of the heads, which is made from rice powder and iron or magnesium filings), give the tabla its characteristic sounds: a bendable bass tone and a harmonic, ringing high tone. It all makes up one of the world's most distinctive, complex percussion instruments. The tabla has more than 50 different *bols*—spoken syllables assigned to the various sounds the instrument can produce—and students spend years learning to connect these syllables to form "words" that complete a rhythmic sentence. In the hands of tabla masters like Zakir Hussain and Badal Roy, who introduced the tabla to Western audiences back in the early '70s as a sideman with Miles Davis, these sentences are joined together to form a gorgeously poetic rhythmic language.

see also: Bikram Ghosh, Trilok Gurtu, Zakir Hussain, India, North and South (sidebar), Indian/Jazz Fusion (sidebar), Indian Percussion (sidebar), Badal Roy, Talvin Singh

Bret Love

1995, and features Patato, *timbalero* Orestes Vilato, and Jose Luis "Changuito" Quintana, the man who reinvented the use of the trap-drum set in Cuban jazz during his tenure with Los Van Van. This is a flat-out masterpiece: great tunes; sharp, down-to-earth production; and one of the most powerful and innovative Cuban rhythm sections ever put together.

the rest:

Ritmo y Candela II: African Crossroads ♪♪♪♪♪ (Round World, 1998)

influences:

◄◄ Machito, Chano Pozo

see also: *Mario Bauzá, Celia Cruz, ¡Cubanismo!, Paquito D'Rivera, Los Van Van, Machito, Herbie Mann, Beny Moré, Perez Prado, Tito Puente, Sexteto Habanero*

j. poet

Patrick Street

Modern Irish folk
Formed 1986, in Dublin, Ireland. Based in Ireland.

Andy Irvine, vocals, bouzouki, mandolin, harmonica (1986–present); Kevin Burke, fiddle (1986–present); Jackie Daly, button accordion (1986–present); Arty McGlynn, guitar (1986–94); Ged Foley, guitar, Northumbrian smallpipes (1995–present).

Imagine Woody Guthrie singing with the Bothy Band, and you get some idea of the heady mix achieved by Ireland's all-star folk group Patrick Street. Andy Irvine is a lifelong Guthrie devotee and sings songs charged with political passion, irreverent humor, and sharp-eyed detail—with the requisite harmonica and roughened baritone. He is backed, however, by two of Ireland's finest instrumental soloists, fiddler Kevin Burke and accordionist Jackie Daly. As a result, Patrick Street's albums and concerts bounce back and forth between moving songs and dazzling dance tunes—sometimes fusing the two into wonderful medleys. Irvine, Burke, Daly, and guitarist Gerry O'Beirne first toured together as the Legends of Irish Music in the United States in 1986. They enjoyed the experience so much that they returned in 1987 with a new name, Patrick Street; a new guitarist, Arty McGlynn; and an eponymous debut album. The quartet had ties to some of the finest Irish folk bands of the post-Beatles era. Irvine was a co-founder of Sweeney's Men in 1966 and of Planxty in 1972, and has also played with Paul Brady, De Dannan, and others. Burke played with Christy Moore before replacing the legendary Tommy Peoples in the Bothy Band in 1976. He later formed his own band, Open House, in his adopted home of Portland, Oregon. Daly was a member of De Dannan and Kinvara before joining Patrick Street. McGlynn had been the rhythm guitarist of choice for everyone from Christy Moore and Tommy Makem to Paul Brady

and Van Morrison. Moreover, Dónal Lunny, who produced and played on Patrick Street's first album, had played with Planxty and the Bothy Band. The liner notes of that album claim the band was named after an old fiddler named Patrick Street, but the band later admitted that was a shaggy-dog story. Ultimately, however, Patrick Street outshone its many famous real-life predecessors by staying together longer than any of them, and growing tighter and brighter as a result.

what to buy: For *Irish Times* ♪♪♪♪ (Green Linnet, 1990, prod. Gerry O'Beirne, Patrick Street), Patrick Street grew from a quartet to an octet with the temporary addition of fiddler James Kelly, keyboardist Bill Whelan, piper Declan Masterson, and guitarist Gerry O'Beirne. This little-big-band enables the group to achieve an astonishing density of sound on five songs and five instrumental medleys. Especially effective is their *ceili* (traditional communal dance-band) version of the Penguin Café Orchestra's "Music for a Found Harmonium." By the release of *All in Good Time* ♪♪♪♪ (Green Linnet, 1993, prod. Bill Whelan), Patrick Street had achieved a longevity and a corresponding cohesiveness known to no other Irish band but the Chieftains. The payoff came in the exquisite arrangements and well-earned rapport of tracks on this album. The highpoint is the seven-and-a-half-minute medley, "Lintheads," which threads together two songs about textile mills with evocative instrumentals. The instrumental highlights of *No. 2 Patrick Street* ♪♪♪♪ (Green Linnet, 1988, prod. Patrick Street) include the jigs and reels written by Jackie Daly for his effortlessly flute-like accordion figures. Vocal highlights include Andy Irvine's revamping of Woody Guthrie's "Tom Joad" to the tune of "John Hardy," and Irvine's own stirring song about Sacco and Vanzetti. Arty McGlynn was replaced by Battlefield Band guitarist Ged Foley on *Corner Boys* ♪♪♪♪ (Green Linnet, 1996, prod. Patrick Street), and he helped Kevin Burke and Daly forego all tentative and ornamental notes to carve out confident, surprising melodic variations. And whether accompanying each other's solos or Irvine's vocals, these pickers know how to push without shoving.

what to buy next: Even on their debut album, *Patrick Street* ♪♪♪ (Green Linnet, 1988, prod. Dónal Lunny), the promise of this illustrious band was already obvious. Burke's fiddle and Daly's accordion improvise grand leaps over the pulsing rhythms of McGlynn's guitar and Irvine's bouzouki. The highlights, though, are the three ballads which Irvine sings with a whispery intimacy that brings a genuine affection to his themes of loss. On *Made in Cork* ♪♪♪ (Green Linnet, 1997, prod. Patrick Street), the group seem content to rely on proven methods rather than push forward with any innovations. These methods prove as pleasurable as ever, however. To further demonstrate how, for this band, staying put in no way means standing still, there's the vigorous—and remarkably, given how long they've been together, the first—live album, *Live from Patrick Street* 🎵🎵🎵🎵 (Green Linnet, 1999, prod. Patrick Street).

influences:

◀◀ The Bothy Band, Planxty, De Dannan

▶▶ Celtic Thunder, Solas

see also: *Battlefield Band, the Bothy Band, Kevin Burke, the Clancy Brothers/Tommy Makem, Jackie Daly, De Dannan, the House Band, Andy Irvine, Dónal Lunny, Christy Moore, Open House, Tommy Peoples, Planxty, Sweeney's Men, Bill Whelan*

Geoffrey Himes

Jim Payne
Newfoundland folk

Born in Notre Dame Bay, Newfoundland, Canada. Based in St. John's, Newfoundland, Canada.

As owner of the St. John's, Newfoundland–based SingSong Music, Payne has been at the forefront of a movement to promote that province's rich heritage. Since 1990 his label has released more than 10 recordings of Newfoundland music, story, and song. Three of those releases have been solo outings by Payne himself, a talented singer-songwriter whose voice and original compositions bring home the reality of life in maritime Canada. Payne is also highly active in the theater community, and has directed, performed in, and written music for many of Newfoundland's finest stage productions of the last two decades. He has at one time or another been linked with every major Newfoundland folk artist, and his longtime association with Rufus Guinchard, grand master of Newfoundland fiddle, has had much effect on his own career. Payne plays guitar, accordion, mandolin, and tin whistle in addition to violin, and his frequent trips throughout the world to teach the traditional folk dances of his province have led many to dub him Newfoundland's ambassador of culture.

what to buy: *Wave over Wave—Old and New Songs of Atlantic Canada* 🎵🎵🎵🎵 (SingSong Music, 1995, prod. Jim Payne, Fergus O'Byrne) is a phenomenal collection of traditional and contemporary songs featuring Payne and Irishman Fergus O'Byrne. Both possess strong voices, and they interweave them effortlessly on traditional chanteys like "Heave Away" and newly composed but traditionally based songs like "Rig Workers Alphabet." Payne's own composition, "Wave over Wave," has already become a classic in the Newfoundland tradition.

what to buy next: *State of the Nation* 🎵🎵🎵🎵 (SingSong Music, 1992, prod. Jim Payne) is a collection of songs written by Payne specifically for Newfoundland's Rising Tide Theater, six of whose annual revues he has toured in as both musician and actor. This is folk music as it should be: touching, socially conscious, and,

most importantly, heartfelt. Payne's voice is at times rough-edged, but it is an edge that gives his music just the immediacy and poignancy his important topics deserve. *Empty Nets* 🎵🎵🎵🎵 (SingSong Music, 1992, prod. Jim Payne) is a great mix of Jim Payne originals and songs in the traditional idiom by other Newfoundland writers. Selections like the bluegrass/country & western–tinged "Work Work Work" survey Payne's diverse influences, while the title track, concerning the plight of Newfoundland's diminishing fishing industry, is pure folk brilliance.

worth searching for: *The Southern Cross* 🎵🎵🎵🎵 (SingSong Music, 1989, prod. Jim Payne) is Payne's first solo outing and is only available on cassette. It contains some great songs about Newfoundland's sealing industry.

influences:

◀◀ Rufus Guinchard, Emile Benoit, Minnie White

▶▶ Arthur O'Brien, Great Big Sea, the Punters

Cliff McGann

Peatbog Faeries
Ambient Scottish folk-dance fusion

Formed 1993, on the Isle of Skye, Scotland. Based on the Isle of Skye, Scotland.

Peter Morrison, pipes, whistles; Ben Ivitsky, fiddle; Ali Pentland, guitar; Innes Hutton, bass, bodhrán; Iain Copeland, drums, percussion; Norman Austin ("Nurudin"), synthesizer, keyboards. (All members are from Scotland.)

The Peatbog Faeries—along with their colleagues and fellow Greentrax-label alums Shooglenifty—represent the avant-garde of the '90s Scottish folk/roots scene. But while Shooglenifty presents a very in-your-face Scottish/funk/groove fusion, the Peatbog Faeries veer off in a slightly different direction. Like Shooglenifty, the Peatbog Faeries start from a base in Scottish folk-dance music. And they also funk up the rhythms. But the band shows they've been listening to the likes of Fripp & Eno and Kraftwerk as well. The tempos are slowed down and the whole sound is very dense. So far the Peatbog Faeries have only played live in Scotland and England, but when word gets further out—as they've tried to arrange with a recent U.S. label jump—their unique Gaelic groove thing is sure to become a world party.

what to buy: *mellowosity* 🎵🎵🎵🎵 (Greentrax, 1996, prod. Iain Copeland, Peatbog Faeries) is the Peatbogs' only CD in release as we go to press, but it's a perfect showcase for their special brand of ambient Celtic funk. The rhythm section puts down a steady pulse while pipes, whistles, or fiddle handle the main melodies. Then other sounds—brief electric-guitar riffs, keyboard-created effects—are layered on top. Synth washes also provide a bed for everything else to sit in. Pete Morrison's title track displays a quintessential Peatbog Faeries arrangement: the basic rhythm is that of a dramatically slowed folk dance, slightly syncopated. Then guitar and keyboard effects appear, with whistle joining in for a bit of the melody line, which is soon taken over by bagpipes. An eerily distorted fiddle is heard throughout. Spooky, but brilliant.

the rest:

Faerie Stories N/A (Astor Place, 2000)

influences:

◀ Fripp & Eno, Kraftwerk, Mouth Music, Moving Hearts

▶ Shoopglenifty, Talitha MacKenzie, Afro Celt Sound System

see also: *Shooglenifty*

Ken Roseman

Gnonnas Pedro

Afro-Cuban rumba

Born in Benin. Based in Cotonou, Benin.

Although Benin has a rich store of musical tradition, its music business is fairly underdeveloped, forcing many artists to relocate to Nigeria, Congo, and Ghana in order to make a living. The sound of Benin's biggest pop bands has also been dominated by Cuban music, to the detriment of their own traditions. Pedro was one of the leading bandleaders of the early '70s, when his African take on Cuban music made him a big star. There are some nice African touches, especially in the spare guitar parts, but most of his music doesn't sound too different from the Cuban bands he was emulating.

what's available: *La Compilation* ♪♪♪ (Ledoux France, 1991, prod. Abou Sylla) collects Pedro's hits from the '70s. Though the recording isn't great, there are touches of brilliance—the rippling guitar lines on "La Musica en Verite," for example—but most of this is fairly generic.

influences:

◀ Alpha Jazz, Black Santiagos

▶ Wally Badarou, Angélique Kidjo

see also: *Africando*

j. poet

Paco Peña

Flamenco

Born in Córdoba, Spain. Based in England and the Netherlands.

When Paco Peña began his performing career in the mid-1960s, he decided to do it in England rather than his native Spain. The warmth of the audiences and the sold-out clubs and concert venues he soon found told Peña that he could make a musical home there. He set out to carve a niche between then-popular showman and pseudo-flamenco stylist Manitas de Plata and rising-star flamenco innovator Paco de Lucia. Peña had something different to say—with fine and fluid technique, he presented music that stayed close to the canon of flamenco while breaking new ground in vigor, grace, and style of performance. His international base made him especially influential in bringing traditional flamenco to British and American audiences in the '60s and '70s. During that time he also started a company of flamenco dancers, singers, and musicians that tours worldwide. In the '80s, Peña returned to his native Córdoba to found a prestigious guitar festival. He is currently professor of flamenco at the University of Rotterdam in the Netherlands.

what to buy: *Azahara* ♪♪♪♪ (Nimbus, 1988, prod. Paco Peña) is a journey through the four main modes of flamenco— *soleares, seguitiyas, tientos,* and *fandangos*—with several folk-influenced and South American–inspired pieces thrown in to give a complete picture of the music's current sources. The album as a whole illustrates both traditional forms and more contemporary influences. Brief yet instructive liner notes about the structure and origins of the songs make this disc especially valuable for those new to the genre. *Misa Flamenca* ♪♪♪♥ (Nimbus, 1991, prod. Paco Peña) is a collaboration between Peña, several well-known flamenco vocalists, and the chorus of England's Academy of St. Martin in the Fields, resulting in a mass-like presentation that illuminates both the flamenco style and the traditional liturgy.

the rest:

Flamenco ♪♪♪ (Verve, 1978)
Paco Peña Plays Montoya ♪♪♪ (Nimbus, 1987)
Encuentro ♪♪♪♥ (Nimbus, 1989)
The Art of Paco Peña ♪♪♪♪ (Nimbus, 1993)
Fabulous Flamenco ♪♪♪ (Alex, 1993)
Flamenco Puro Live ♪♪♪♥ (Nimbus, 1996)

influences:

◀ Sabicas

▶ Inti-Illimani

Kerry Dexter

Tommy Peoples

Irish traditional

Born September 20, 1948, in Letterkenny, County Donegal, Ireland. Based in County Clare, Ireland.

In his book *Notes from the Heart,* Irish record producer P.J. Curtis writes about taking an American friend to a session in a Clare pub, and of his friend's disbelief when it was revealed that the fiddler playing there was none other than Tommy Peoples. One of the few true masters of Irish traditional fiddle playing, one whose sound can be instantly identified, Peoples remains an unassuming man, generous with his music and happy to lead a simple life in the countryside of County Clare—he doesn't even have a phone at home. Peoples grew up in a musical family in the village of St. Johnston, in the eastern part of County Donegal that borders Northern Ireland. His father, Tom, who was a fiddle player himself, and especially his cousin Joe Cassidy, were Tommy's first sources of inspiration and instruction on the fiddle. By all accounts, he was already an impressive player by the time he'd reached his teenage years. After leaving school, Peoples moved to Dublin where he soon joined in the growing traditional music scene, playing at sessions with the likes of Matt Molloy, Liam O'Flynn, James and Seán Keane, and Mary Bergin.

By the early 1970s, Peoples was living in Clare, where he had married the daughter of Kitty Linnane, piano player for the famed Kilfenora Ceili Band. He became a member of that band, and participated in a 1974 recording of them produced by Mick Moloney for the American label Tradition. During that same period, Peoples was also involved for a time with 1691, a short-lived group that toured and recorded in Brittany. Among other members of the band were singer and clavinet player Tríona Ní Dhomhnaill and flute player Matt Molloy, with whom Peoples would soon become a member of the legendary Bothy Band in 1975. The band's debut album, which remains a revered classic, prominently features Peoples's fiery fiddle-playing. However, the pressures of the road did not agree with Peoples, who parted company with the band in 1976 and settled in Clare once again. That same year, Comhaltas Ceoltóiríéireann Éireann (the Irish Musicians' Association) released a collection of live recordings of Peoples made between 1974 and 1976. That album is still regarded as an essential document. In 1976 the fiddler also made a brand new album, *The High Part of the Road,* with guitarist Paul Brady as his accompanist, for the New York label Shanachie. Out of Peoples's participation in informal sessions in Dublin came the exhilarating *Matt Molloy, Paul Brady, Tommy Peoples,* recorded for Dónal Lunny's Mulligan label in 1977 and released the following year. At the same time, Peoples appeared on Paul Brady's celebrated *Welcome Here Kind Stranger.* In 1985 Peoples renewed his ties with Shanachie and recorded *The Iron Man,* with Dáithí Sproule providing the guitar accompaniment. More recently, Peoples released a self-produced solo album, *The Quiet Glen,* which instantly became one of the most sought-after new CDs of Irish music, and he was the first recipient of the Teilif ís na Gaeilge Traditional Music Award, presented to him in Galway's Town Hall. Tommy Peoples continues to appear in concert and teach for workshops. His daughters Siobhán and Gráinne carry on the family tradition with distinction, as does his nephew Séamus Gibson,

who strives with great success to emulate his uncle's playing style. And if you are ever in Ennis or Kilfenora, County Clare, you may well run into Tommy Peoples at a local session.

what's available: *The High Part of the Road* ♪♪♪♪ (Shanachie, 1976, prod. Richard Nevins, Daniel Michael Collins) was Peoples's first album to be distributed in the United States. His playing has its characteristic urgency and rough edge, even with Paul Brady's guitar lending an air of civility. There are some great tunes here associated with Donegal, including the reels "The Oak Tree" and "The Pinch of Snuff." *Matt Molloy, Paul Brady, Tommy Peoples* ♪♪♪♪ (Mulligan, 1978/Green Linnet, 1985, prod. Dónal Lunny, Paul Brady), sounding much as if the three musicians were having a bit of a session in a Dublin pub, is an album that belongs at the top of any list of Irish recordings. It is pure energy and a thrilling listening experience, which daunts attempts to cite highlights only because each track is a highlight. *The Iron Man* ♪♪♪♪ (Shanachie, 1985, prod. Daniel Michael Collins, Richard Nevins), with Dáithí Sproule contributing his usual stellar guitar backing, recaptures the atmosphere of Peoples's 1976 album, with some of the rougher edges smoothed over. Once again, most of the dance selections are reels, but the medley of strathspeys, including the title tune, and the hornpipe "Kitty O'Shea," are things of wonder.

worth searching for: Even though it is only available from Peoples's own Web site and through a few specialized stores, *The Quiet Glen* ♪♪♪♪♪ (self-released, 1998, prod. Tommy Peoples) is a must for any lover of Irish traditional fiddle music. Discretely and tastefully backed by Alph Duggan on guitar, Peoples performs a mixture of old tunes and his own compositions, all played with that unmistakable Peoples touch. Peoples appears with his daughter Siobhán, also a fiddler, on several tracks of the wonderful live recording *Maiden Voyage* ♪♪♪♪ (Celtic Music, 1991, prod. Páraic MacDonnchadha, Kevin Crawford), made on location at Peppers Bar in Feakle, County Clare. There are other local performers involved, the music is varied and excellent throughout, and it retains the live-session atmosphere with fidelity and verve. If you are very lucky, you may come across Peoples's original solo LP, *Tommy Peoples* ♪♪♪♪♪ (Comhaltas Ceoltóirí Éireann, 1976, prod. Séamus MacMathúna). Do not let it pass; it is one of the most exciting records of Irish fiddle playing ever made. Paul Brady's *Welcome Here Kind Stranger* ♪♪♪♪ (Mulligan, 1978, prod. Dónal Lunny, Paul Brady), an outstanding album recently reissued on CD in Ireland and worth looking for in any case, happens to feature the playing of Peoples on several tracks, including the spectacular set of reels "The Boys on the Hilltop/Johnny Goin' to Céilidh."

influences:

◄◄ Matt Peoples, Joe Cassidy, Vincent Campbell, Frank Kelly, Jimmy Hueston

▶▶ Siobhán Peoples, Gráinne Peoples, Séamus Gibson, Mairéad Ní Mhaonaigh, Paddy Glackin, Paul O'Shaughnessy

see also: *Mary Bergin, the Bothy Band, James Keane, Dónal Lunny, Matt Molloy, Mick Moloney, Tríona Ní Dhomhnaill, Liam O'Flynn, Planxty*

Philippe Varlet

Percussion Incorporated

Worldbeat

Formed 1990, in New Orleans, LA, USA. Based in New Orleans, LA, USA.

Kenyatta Simon, drums; Kufaru Mouton, vibes, drums; Luther Gray, drums; Harold Brown, drums; Lloyd Daily, synthesizer; Amura Frezell, synth bass; Rick Nick, guitar; Amon Sheriff, vocals, flute, gongs; Wayne Bennett, guitar; David Barard, bass; Gabriel Cousins, trumpet; Jawara Atiba Simon, vocals; Kalamu Ya Salaam, vocals, drums; Issa Gray, vocals, piano; Congo Square Percussion Workshop, drums. (All members are from USA.)

Percussion Incorporated grew out of the Congo Square Percussion Workshop program, a project that was put together to celebrate the history of Congo Square, the only spot in North America where slaves and freemen could mingle equally. Around 1730 one of the open-air markets in New Orleans got the nickname Congo Square. Sunday was considered a "free day" based on the Black Code, a French law that made forced labor illegal on Sundays and religious holidays. Musicologists now believe that the unique New Orleans style of music was born as Native Americans, Africans, and Europeans began mixing and playing music in Congo Square. When the Spanish took over in 1769 they continued to honor the tradition, and the next influx of West African slaves added more elements to the musical and cultural melting pot. One of the dances that evolved was the Bamboula, a rhythm that may have laid the foundation for New Orleans–style jazz. On their one album, the players of Percussion Incorporated attempt to recreate the vibe of Congo Square with a session that combines jazz, African hand drumming, spoken word, and N'awlins-style funk.

what's available: The music on *Congo Square* ♪♪♪♪♪ (Repercussion, 1991, prod. Percussion Incorporated, Richard Bird) is percussive, symphonic, jazzy, and highly improvisational in nature, a suite to a time and place that has undoubtedly influenced the entire musical history of North America. The album is available direct from: Repercussion, 6913 W. Barrington Ct., New Orleans, LA 70128.

influences:
◀◀ Louis Armstrong, Lee Dorsey, Wild Tchoupitoulas

j. poet

Chris Perez

Rock, Tejano

Born 1969, in San Antonio, TX, USA. Based in Corpus Christi, TX, USA.

Chris Perez grew up in central Texas with his hands on an electric guitar, listening to the mainstream rock stars of the '70s and '80s and the border dance bands of his home region. He had a band of his own as a teenager, and played guitar with *Tejano* (modern Tex-Mex) artist Shelly Lares. In 1990 Perez was hired as lead guitarist for the genre's soon-to-be-queen Selena Quintanilla, bringing a harder-rocking edge to her rise to the top of Tejano. Two years later they were married. As their success grew in the studio and on the road, the future seemed bright for the couple, but Selena was murdered by a disturbed employee in 1995. In the resultant firestorm of publicity, Perez has preferred to keep his grief private while he works out his musical future.

what's available: On *Resurrection* ♪♪♪♪ (Hollywood, 1999, prod. Julian Raymond), Chris Perez and bandmates John Garza and Joe Ojeda know how to rock in both English and Spanish. They mix in border flavor—horns, guitars, and rhythm patterns—in contrast to the tropical-pop brand of Latin music climbing the charts around them. Although the group is still looking for a completely coherent voice, they're a good way toward crafting one—and toward reaching out to audiences who've sampled the Latin-pop flavor of the moment and are ready to try the stronger stuff.

influences:
◀◀ Eric Clapton, Selena

see also: *Selena*

Kerry Dexter

Lourdes Perez

Singer-songwriter, nueva canción, nueva trova

Born Hato Arriba, in San Sebastian, Puerto Rico. Based In Austin, TX, USA.

Lourdes Perez grew up in a family of children who loved to sing. It was also a family aware of social justice and involved in the Puerto Rican independence movement, so when Perez first chose a career it was as a social worker, and she kept her music as a sideline. In the early 1990s, having relocated to Austin, Texas, Perez attended a concert by one of her musical heroes, Argentinean singer and political activist Mercedes Sosa. That proved a turning point. Perez decided to make music her main career focus, and began building up her performing opportunities in Austin and throughout the Southwest. The next time Mercedes Sosa played Austin, Lourdes Perez was her opening act, and Sosa was so impressed by the singer that she invited her to open her next concert, in Boston, beginning the exposure of

Perez to a wider audience. Recently, Perez has toured with the Indigo Girls' high-profile, all-star Suffragette Sessions revue.

what to buy: *Vestigios* 🎵🎵🎵🎵 (VivaVoce, 1997, prod. Cathy Ragland, Annette D'Armata, Lourdes Perez) is a powerful expression of Perez's songwriting skills, as well as her command of voice and guitar. The album contains several examples of both her live and studio artistry, and in each is the strength and sensibility of the poet and the insight of the *trovadora* (all songs are in Spanish). Particularly outstanding is a duet with Irene Ferrara on "Tengo la Vida." *Recuerdate por Mi* 🎵🎵🎵🎵 (CheeWee, 1994, prod. Peg Miller, Lourdes Perez) is a snapshot of Perez in concert at an intimate Austin club, performing nine originals, two Puerto Rican *plenas,* and two songs of social justice by other writers, all of which offer evidence that her voice transcends language, which explains why she has many fans who do not understand Spanish.

worth searching for: Her now-rare debut release, *Lourdes Perez* 🎵🎵🎵🎵 (VivaVoce, 1993, prod. Lourdes Perez), is a five-song collection that hints at the bases of Perez's work—it contains original songs, Puerto Rican traditional tunes, and socially conscious *nueva canción.*

influences:

◀◀ El Topo, Silvio Rodriguez, Violetta Parra, Mercedes Sosa

see also: *Mercedes Sosa*

Kerry Dexter

Perfect Thyroid

Ska, punk, funk
Formed 1991, in Hudson Valley, NY, USA. Based in Ulster County, NY, USA.

Chris "Skunk" Hanson, lead vocals, trumpet, baritone horn, slide whistle, percussion; Shane Kirsch, tenor sax, vocals, percussion; Chris "Cornball" Snykus, drums, vocals; Jason Foster, guitar, vocals; Joe Cuchelo, four- and six-string bass; Dean "Lazy Bones" Jones, trombone, vocals, keyboards, percussion, xylophone. (All members are from USA.)

Perfect Thyroid blends the ska beat with horn arrangements and funk 'n' punk guitar energy to forge a musical style they refer to as "skunk." At their best, this band delivers punchy sounds and danceable rhythms with a big beat, which appeal to both fans of third-wave ska and those on the cusp of the neo-swing movement. Originally called Cat Butt (the title of one of their more popular club jams), Perfect Thyroid embellishes their songs and performances with humor of the Bonzo Dog Band variety, and more than a hint of social commentary. Their wild onstage antics, unusual look, and non-stop energy have made them quite popular in the college towns of upstate New York, and they have played major shows with such genre stars

as Reel Big Fish and the Toasters. Their first national release, *Musical Barnacles,* made the *Alternative Press* list of "Ska-Punk's Top Ten Essential Albums" and garnered much airplay on college stations throughout the Northeast.

what's available: On their only major independent label release, *Musical Barnacles* 🎵🎵 (Shanachie, 1997, prod. Joe Ferry, Perfect Thyroid), Perfect Thyroid brings something fresh and vibrant to a few original tunes ("Marella," "Take Care," "Blah, Blah, Blah") as well as a Joe Jackson cover ("Got the Time"), but too often they let their sense of parody run rampant at the expense of the music. As a result, a few promising (and not-so-promising) tracks run far too long or dissolve into self-indulgent, silly in-jokes. A little bit of creative discipline could go a long way with a band this talented. Though Perfect Thyroid was recently dropped from Shanachie's roster of artists, this disc is still available through some online services and catalogs.

worth searching for: Perfect Thyroid has put out a few discs on their own label, including *That's Good Enough, Let's Go Home* (Skunkjam, 1993, prod. Perfect Thyroid), *Kiss the Mammoth and Run!!!* (Skunkjam, 1993, prod. Perfect Thyroid), and *Which One of Us Is Me?* (Skunkjam, 1995, prod. Rick Slater). All are available through the band's Web site at www.perfectthyroid.com.

influences:

◀◀ Parliament-Funkadelic, Joe Jackson, the Specials, Fishbone, 311

▶▶ Yolk

Ken Burke

Itzhak Perlman

Classical, klezmer
Born August 31, 1945, in Tel Aviv, Israel. Based in USA.

Itzhak Perlman is a classical violinist of outstanding power and virtuosity who has been on the world musical stage since his debut as a child prodigy in the 1950s. Long after he was well-established in the academic tradition of Europe as a whole, Perlman began to explore his own cultural roots in klezmer, the sometimes soulful, sometimes frenetic jazz-like folk music of Eastern European Jews. Both alone and in collaboration with artists such as Andy Statman, Brave Old World, and the Klezmatics, Perlman has created several albums based in this form, which have lent it a fresh take while encouraging his mostly classical audience to listen to roots music. In addition to his klezmer explorations, Perlman has an extensive catalog of classical recordings (most of them on the Angel/EMI label), and has recently begun composing for film.

what to buy: *In the Fiddler's House* 🎵🎵🎵🎵 (Angel, 1995, prod. Steven Paul) is Perlman's first recorded venture into klezmer and it remains the freshest, with input from old-line and up-start experts like Andy Statman, the Klezmatics, Brave Old World, and the Klezmer Conservatory Band. *Live in the Fiddler's House* ♪♪♪ (Angel, 1996, prod. Steven Paul), *Itzhak Perlman Plays Popular Jewish Melodies* ♪♪♪ (Angel, 1998), and *Tradition: Popular Jewish Melodies* ♪♪♪ (Angel, 1998) continue Perlman's voyage of rediscovery.

influences:

◄◄ Isaac Stern, Ivan Galamian

►► Sarah Chang, Andre Previn, Anne Akiko Myers

see also: *Brave Old World, the Klezmatics, the Klezmer Conservatory Band, Andy Statman*

Kerry Dexter

Lee "Scratch" Perry /The Upsetter

Reggae, dub

Born Rainford Hugh Perry, March 20, 1936, in Kendal, Jamaica. Based in Zurich, Switzerland.

Lee "Scratch" Perry is one of reggae's most influential characters. As a producer and record label executive, Perry oversaw seminal recordings by Bob Marley & the Wailers, Junior Murvin, the Heptones, Max Romeo, Gregory Isaacs, and even the Clash. As a songwriter, he penned hits for the Wailers, including "Duppy Conqueror," "Small Axe," "Kaya," and "The Sun Is Shining." And as a performer in his own right, Perry has recorded numerous tunes, including the #5 British hit "Return of Django."

Born to a poor family in the small Jamaican village of Kendal, Perry began his climb to international fame after moving to Kingston in the late 1950s. As a teenager, Perry chose records for the weekly ska parties run by Coxsone Dodd's Downbeat Sound Systems. After recording his debut single, "The Chicken Scratch," in the early '60s, Perry became an A&R director and producer for Dodd's Studio One label. Leaving Dodd in 1966, Perry teamed with producer Joe Gibbs to record a single, "I Am the Upsetter," and to run Gibbs's label, Amalgamated Records. His early production projects in this capacity included the Pioneers' "Long Shot," one of the first singles to utilize the rhythms that were later dubbed "reggae."

In 1968, Perry set up his own label, Upsetter Records, and formed a flagship studio band, the Upsetters. The original group, however, soon left Perry to become Toots Hibbert's band, the Maytals. Recruiting members of an outfit called the Hippy Boys, Perry formed his second version of the Upsetters. The reorganized band quickly became one of Jamaica's most respected. When Bob Marley & the Wailers teamed with the

group, Perry agreed to become their executive producer. The enlarged ensemble remained with Perry until 1971, when the Wailers, with the Upsetters' rhythm section—Aston "Family Man" Barrett (bass) and his brother Carlton "Carlie" Barrett (drums)—signed with Island Records. Although he and the Wailers had initially agreed to share all profits from their recordings together, Perry took all the money and ignited a lengthy battle that lasted until Bob Marley's death in 1981.

Shortly after moving to Washington Gardens, a wealthy suburb of Kingston, in 1973, Perry built a studio, Black Ark, in his backyard. That studio became one of the most influential recording facilities in Jamaica, producing such albums as the Heptones' *Party Time,* Max Romeo's *War in a Babylon,* the Upsetters' *Super Ape,* and Junior Murvin's *Police and Thieves.* The studio was also home to many of the first recordings in the instrumental, sonically manipulated, proto-electronica reggae variant known as "dub." In 1975, Perry signed a worldwide distribution deal with Island.

Despite his growing success, Perry was beset by personal demons. After his wife left him, taking their two children, he set fire to the studio, shot himself in the foot, and began displaying very bizarre behavior. Halting his production activities, Perry recorded a string of unsuccessful singles on his own. Traveling between Europe and Jamaica for a couple of years, he temporarily settled in Amsterdam. In 1980, he assumed the name Pipecock Jackxon, and though he planned to reopen Black Ark Studios and ordered new equipment, he cut all the wires and dug a duck pond in the studio. Perry toured the United States in 1981 with a white reggae band from New York, the Terrorists. The following year, he toured with another white reggae band, the Majestics, and recorded his first album since torching Black Ark, *Mystic Miracle Star.* His problems, however, persisted. After accusing Chris Blackwell, then-president of Island Records, of being a vampire and blaming him for Marley's death, Perry's distribution agreement with Island was canceled.

Though he released another album, *Battle of Armagideon,* in 1986, Perry didn't show signs of resurrecting his career until joining with British producer Adrian Sherwood to record the apparently prophetically titled *Time Boom X De Devil Dead* that same year. Perry then relocated to Switzerland with his second wife, Mireille Ruegg, in 1989. A year later, he reunited with Sherwood and Island Records to release *From the Secret Laboratory.* A retrospective of Perry's recording career, *Arkology,* appeared in 1997—barely keeping pace with his still-prolific contemporary activities.

what to buy: With 52 tracks on three CDs, *Arkology* ♪♪♪♪ (Island, 1997, prod. Lee "Scratch" Perry) spans Perry's full career and offers a history lesson in the evolution of reggae and dub.

The collection includes many remixes and previously unreleased dub tracks.

what to buy next: *Chicken Scratch* 𝄞𝄞𝄞 (Heartbeat, 1989, prod. Coxsone Dodd) collects recordings produced by Coxsone Dodd at Studio One between 1963 and 1966, and features musical accompaniment by the Skatalites, Bob Marley & the Wailers, and Rita Marley with her singing group, the Soulettes.

best of the rest:
Super Ape 𝄞𝄞𝄞 (Mango, 1976)
The Upsetter Collection 𝄞𝄞𝄞 (Trojan, 1981)
The Best of Lee Perry & the Upsetters 𝄞𝄞𝄞 (Pama, 1984)
Reggae Greats 𝄞𝄞𝄞 (Mango, 1984)
The Upsetter Box Set 𝄞𝄞𝄞 (Trojan, 1985)
Some of the Best 𝄞𝄞𝄞 (Heartbeat, 1986)
Battle of Armagideon (Millionaire Liquidator) 𝄞𝄞𝄞 (Trojan, 1986)
Time Boom X De Devil Dead 𝄞𝄞𝄞 (On U Sound, 1987)
The Upsetter Compact Set 𝄞𝄞𝄞 (Trojan, 1988)
All the Hits 𝄞𝄞𝄞 (Rohit, 1989)
Mystic Warrior 𝄞𝄞𝄞 (RAS, 1989)
Shock of the Mighty, 1969–74 𝄞𝄞𝄞 (Attack, 1989)
From the Secret Laboratory 𝄞𝄞𝄞 (Mango, 1990)
Heavy Manners: Reggae's Best 𝄞𝄞𝄞 (Lagoon, 1993)
Kung Fu Meets the Dragon 𝄞𝄞𝄞 (Lagoon, 1995)
Super Ape Inna Jungle 𝄞𝄞𝄞 (RAS, 1995)
Black Ark Experryments 𝄞𝄞𝄞 (RAS, 1995)
Experryments at the Grassroots of Dub 𝄞𝄞𝄞 (RAS, 1995)
The Best of Lee Perry 𝄞𝄞𝄞 (Upsetter, 1996)
Technomajikal 𝄞𝄞𝄞 (Roir, 1997)
Archive 𝄞𝄞𝄞 (Rialto, 1998)
The Mighty Upsetter 𝄞𝄞𝄞 (Roir, 1998)
Live at Maritime Hall 𝄞𝄞𝄞 (Maritime Hall, 1998)
Africa Blood 𝄞𝄞𝄞 (Trojan, 1998)

influences:

◀◀ Coxsone Dodd, King Tubby, the Skatalites

▶▶ Bob Marley, the Upsetters, Max Romeo, Junior Murvin

see also: *Black Uhuru, the Congos, Wasis Diop, Gregory Isaacs, Mad Professor, Bob Marley, Rita Marley, John Martyn, Jackie Mittoo, Junior Murvin, the Skatalites, Toots & the Maytals*

Craig Harris

Sir Shina Peters

Afro-juju

Born 1958, in Nigeria. Based in Nigeria.

Along with the "Yo-pop" (Yoruba pop) sensation Segun Adewale, Shina Peters worked as a backing musician for *juju* (Yoruba dance music) veteran Prince Adekunle. Both sidemen left the band, forming Shina Adewale & the Superstars International in 1977. However, their ambitions differed. Adewale

wanted to make the music more mainstream while Peters wanted to delve deeper into the roots of Nigerian pop. So they split so each could pursue their own directions. An impressive showman, Peters mixed juju with *fuji* (another popular Yoruba voice-and-percussion-dominated sound) and even Afro-Beat (Fela Kuti's big-band tribal/jazz style) to create music totally new yet totally Nigerian. His self-dubbed "Afro-juju" took West Africa by storm in 1989, sparking the movement that quickly became known as "Shinamania." Peters's popularity soared, and he earned Nigerian Juju Musician of the Year honors in 1989 and '90. The phenomenon lasted until he released the album that bore its name, *Shinamania,* in 1991. Sales were good, but this further synth-heavy evolution got critically panned and the fervor dampened. Nonetheless, Peters's prophetic juju visions played an important and lasting role in opening up the music dominated by King Sunny Adé and Ebenezer Obey to younger artists.

what to buy: *Shinamania* 𝄞𝄞𝄞 (Stern's, 1991) leans heavily on the fuji/juju percussion, but also throws in guitars and keys that sound vaguely like *soukous* (Congolese rumba) or even Kenyan music. Peters also tosses in a reggae lick to start off "Omo Mbo," and the call-and-response vocals that begin "Pelemo" go so far as to recall Cab Calloway. However, the bulk of the vocals and talking drums are pure Yoruba.

what to buy next: *Experience* 𝄞𝄞𝄞 (Stern's/Sony Music Nigeria, 1992, prod. Laolu Akins) once again blends the heavy percussion with juju guitars in a nearly seamless group of songs. The album is short—less than 40 minutes—but powerful.

worth searching for: *Afro-Juju 1* (Sony Nigeria, 1989) is not available outside of Nigeria. For the intrepid import-searcher Peters has 20 others like it to choose from, but this is the one that shook the world.

influences:

◀◀ Prince Adekunle, King Sunny Adé, Fela Kuti, Sikiru Ayinde Barrister

▶▶ Dele Taiwo, Fabulous Olu Fajemirokum

see also: *Fela Kuti, King Sunny Adé, Ebenezer Obey*

Hank Bordowitz

Cornel Pewewardy
/Oyate Ump Moni

Native American

Born 1952, in OK, USA. Based in Lawrence, KS, USA.

There are so many exciting styles of Native American vocal music available today, and the field is growing phenomenally. From the powwow style of the Black Lodge Singers (Blackfeet) to the peyote chants of Sioux and Navajo Native American Church members Primeaux & Mike, from the delicate bird songs of Keith Mahone (Hualapai) to the legendary Natay-Navajo vocalist Ed Lee Natay, there has evolved a dazzling assortment of ballad, "chicken scratch," dance-accompaniment, and even rap recordings. One of the names that always comes up when discussing distinctive singers of great heart is that of Cornel Pewewardy. Oyate Ump Moni is Dr. Pewewardy's Dakota name. Meaning "the one who stands out as a leader in a large gathering of people," he received it through a Dakota name-giving ceremony while living in Minnesota, USA. He is Comanche and Kiowa, and an enrolled member of the Comanche tribe of Oklahoma, USA.

Growing up in the southwestern part of that state, Pewewardy closely heeded the talents of an artistic extended family. From this exposure, he learned at an early age of his cultural ancestry and rich tribal background. Brought up, as he says, "on the drum," the young man encountered the internal appreciation and luminescent spirituality that comes from spending long hours with master singers of the southern plains. Currently, Pewewardy is an assistant professor in the teaching and leadership department at the University of Kansas's School of Education. He gives courses in multicultural education and Indian education, and has taught Native American music and dance at the University of New Mexico and Navajo Community College. Dr. Pewewardy also keeps a busy professional speaking schedule for diverse audiences. His music has been widely performed throughout the United States and Canada, and he continues to stretch his horizons through practicing, composing, and teaching. "Working with students," he says, "helps me clarify the important and often subtle nuances that make a good song."

Dr. Pewewardy's honors include a doctorate in education from Pennsylvania State University. He was named the 1988 National Indian Student of the Year and 1991 National Indian Educator of the Year by the National Indian Education Association in Omaha, Nebraska; the 1992 Indian of the Year by the American Indian Exposition and Fair in Anadardo, Oklahoma; and the 1997 Musician of the Year by the Wordcraft Circle of Native Writers & Storytellers. He also received the 1992 Minnesota Transformational Leadership Award from the Minnesota Administrator's Academy in Minneapolis, Minnesota, and the 1998 Phoenix Award for Music by the Lawrence Arts Commission of Kansas. Pewewardy dedicates his music to the memory of the many prominent southern plains singers and composers from Oklahoma and the Southwest. He hopes to promote and perpetuate their songs so the younger generation will be able to hear, understand, and love their cultural celebrations.

what to buy: On *Spirit Journey* ♪♪♪♪ (SOAR, 1992, prod. Tom Bee), Pewewardy combines creative narration, nature sounds, and a unique musical ear to create an album appealing to a broad range of tastes. Whether playing his native flute or singing southern plains songs on the "big drum," Pewewardy's music conveys a wistful sense of serenity, beauty, and harmony between nature and humanity that is timeless and poignant. His voice is incredibly warm; sweet as a sigh when used softly, yet retaining that warmth even in his most powerful expressions. He describes the album's title as "a path of reclaiming or perhaps rediscovering elements about yourself: who you are, what you are, why you are as you are, and where you're heading. [It's about] learning to take control of your life and consciously fashioning your own path."

what to buy next: *Comanche Hymns from the Prairie* ♪♪♪ (SOAR, 1996, prod. Tom Bee) presents Christian-inspired songs, dating back as early as 1895, from two Comanche Indian Churches, Baptist and Mennonite, in the native language as presented in the *Numuhuviyanuu Songbook*—a compilation of 116 songs by the late Elliot Canoge, a linguist who conducted and recorded music among the Comanche in the 1940s and '50s. The roots of chorales like "Follow On" and "Only Trust Him" stretch back to the days when tribal men were drafted to fight in World War I. The classic church organ and male-female choral arrangements are easily recognizable as liturgical.

the rest:
Dancing Buffalo ♪♪♪ (Music of the World, 1992)

worth searching for: Look for performances by Pewewardy on the various-artists compilations *The Rough Guide to Native American Music* ♪♪♪♪♪ (World Music Network, 1998) and *Between Father Sky and Mother Earth* ♪♪♪♪ (Narada, 1995) (each reviewed in this book's Compilations section), and on Robbie Robertson's *Contact from the Underworld of Red Boy* ♪♪♪♪♪ (Capitol, 1998).

influences:
◄◄ Woody Big Bow (Kiowa), Woogie Watchetaker (Comanche)

see also: *Black Lodge Singers, Primeaux & Mike, Southern Scratch*

PJ Birosik

Peter Phippen
Contemporary flute
Born in WI, USA. Based in USA.

Peter Phippen spent most of his musical career as a bass guitarist for rock bands—and then, he says, the Native American flute found him. His first flute was a bamboo whistle, and others, including handcrafted Native American flutes, South American vertical notch flutes, and transverse bamboo flutes, soon joined his growing cache. As Phippen has learned the instrument's techniques he has also learned about its history, and often gives talks in which he demonstrates authentic ancient specimens.

what's available: *Book of Dreams* ♫♫♫ (Canyon, 1996, prod. Robert Doyle) is a meditative collection of original tunes (with the exception of "Scarborough Fair") that offers a haunting variation on contemporary flute music based in Native American ideas.

influences:

◄◄ The ancient Native American flute tradition

Kerry Dexter

Astor Piazzolla

Nuevo tango
Born March 11, 1921, in Argentina. Died July 5, 1992, in Paris, France.

Argentina's tango was combined with jazz and classical influences to create *nuevo tango* ("new tango") by *bandoneón* player and composer Astor Piazzolla. Although he was initially scorned in his homeland as "asesino del tango"—"the assassin of the tango"—Piazzolla's unique approach successfully brought the once-forbidden dance music to concert stages around the world. In addition to recording on his own, Piazzolla collaborated with such stellar jazz musicians as Gerry Mulligan and Gary Burton. Piazzolla's compositions have been featured in numerous films, including Roman Polanski's *Frantic,* and have been performed by such ensembles as the Kronos Quartet and the Santa Fe Chamber Music Festival Orchestra.

Piazzolla's involvement with music was sparked shortly after moving to the United States with his parents at the age of three, temporarily settling in New York's Little Italy. Presented with a bandoneón that his father had purchased at a pawn shop, Piazzolla was sent for lessons. By the age of nine, he had mastered the instrument and begun playing professionally. From a similarly young age Piazzolla was fascinated by American jazz, and would often sneak into nightclubs in Harlem to hear masters like Cab Calloway and Duke Ellington. Classical music was equally influential, and Piazzolla developed an interest in the compositions of Mozart, Chopin, and Bach. A concert pianist who lived next door, Bela Wilder, helped Piazzolla transpose classical compositions to the bandoneón.

When tango master Carlos Gardel came to the United States in 1934, Piazzolla became his tour guide and translator, and had a bit role in Gardel's film, *El Dia Que Me Quieres.* Although he was invited to record and tour with Gardel, Piazzolla's parents refused to grant permission. Their decision proved pivotal when Gardel's plane crashed in Colombia the following year. Returning to Argentina in the late 1930s, Piazzolla performed in local tango clubs. A meeting with classical conductor Arturo Rubinstein, then touring Argentina, resulted in Piazzolla becoming a student of Alberto Ginastera, who, in addition to

jamaican music 1: rastafarianism

Rastafarianism (a.k.a. Rastafari) is a widespread millennial religion and cultural movement that includes a small minority of Jamaicans. The reggae sound associated with it gives rise to a common perception of Rastas as defiant black men with natty, unshorn locks and a plenitude of ganja, oft-ingested as an aid to meditation. In reality, the practice of Rastafari varies among its diverse adherents, who do share a fundamental belief in the brotherhood of man and a vision of Africa as the spiritual homeland and future promised land.

Rastafarians view themselves as the Israelites of the West—abducted from their motherland and transported in chains to foreign territory ruled by oppressors ("Babylon"). To overcome this ignorance and cruelty, the displaced believe the dream of returning to their true home in Africa ("Zion") will one day come to fruition.

The Universal Negro Improvement Association, founded by Jamaica's Marcus Garvey in 1914, helped create this kind of kinship, based on common ancestral bonds, among African-descended men and women wherever they resided. Garvey's 1916 prophecy of a "divine black King" in Africa would eventually help Rastafari itself coalesce as a faith and a program   Rastafarians view the 1930 coronation of Ras Tafari (Amharic for "Prince of Peace") Makonnen as Ethiopian Emperor Haile Selassie (Amharic for "Power of the Trinity") as the arrival of the everliving God.

Rastafarianism incubated through the economic depression of the '30s and the anti-colonial riots of 1938; in the '50s, Rastafarian communes began to widely incorporate variations of the 17th-century renegade-slave Maroons' religious ritual into a method of socially conscious worship called *nyahbingi.* In the volatile '60s, after independence failed to bring much improvement for ghetto "sufferahs," Rastafari went from a means of afterlife redemption to a spiritual protest movement aimed at uplift in *this* life—often through the soul-stirring music created by its followers.

Todd Shanker

teaching the young prodigy orchestration, harmony, and music theory, instructed him in art, film, and literature.

Although Piazzolla's biggest break thus far came when he was invited to join Anibal Troila's top-notch Tango Orchestra, he remained with the group for only a few years. By 1944, Piazzolla was so frustrated with traditional tango that he left to form his own ensemble, Orquesta Del 46. He continued to write classical pieces as well, under conductor Herman Scherchen. Piazzolla's composition "Sinfonia Buenos Aires" placed first in the International Fabien Sevitsky Competition. A further honor for these efforts came when, in 1954, Piazzolla received a grant from the French government to study classical composition in Paris. Although he had a few lessons with Nadia Boulanger, Piazzolla was directed away from classical music and instructed to be faithful to his own cultural roots. As a result, he began writing tangos. With the help of Lalo Schifrin, Piazzolla hired musicians from the Orchestra of the Paris Opera and recorded his first album.

Inspired by the octet led by jazz saxophonist Gerry Mulligan, Piazzolla formed Octeto Buenos Aires in 1955. Although he returned to New York for three years, commercial success continued to elude him. After moving back to Argentina, Piazzolla formed Quinteto Nuevo Tango and regularly performed at his own club, Jamaica. Together with poet Horacio Ferrer, Piazzolla composed a tango-based folk opera that premiered in 1968; it would not be the last of his attempts to confer high-art respectability upon this traditionally lowly form.

Although he tried to slow down following a massive heart attack in 1973, Piazzolla continued to work at a feverish pace. His efforts finally paid off as his modern approach to the tango achieved acceptance in his native country in the mid-1980s. Among other triumphs, Piazzolla's music was featured in the Broadway hit *Tango Argentina* in 1986. But Piazzolla's inability to scale down his activities resulted in his suffering a cerebral hemorrhage in 1989, shortly after he had arrived in Paris to work on a full-scale opera. Piazzolla's final performance came in July 1990, when he appeared with the Athens Colours Orchestra under the direction of Manos Hidjidakis. A recording of the concert was released as *Bandoneón Sinfonico*. Piazzolla died two years later.

what to buy: Piazzolla's artistic approach to the tango is best showcased on *Tango: Zero Hour* ♫♫♫♫ (American Clave, 1986/1998, prod. Kip Hanrahan). Accompanied by Fernando Suarez Paz (violin), Pablo Ziegler (piano), Horacio Malvicino Sr. (guitar), and Hector Console (bass), Piazzolla and his bandoneón offer a performance marked by sensuous passion.

what to buy next: Piazzolla traces the development of the tango, from the brothels of Buenos Aires to the international concert stage, on *The Rough Dancer and the Cyclical Night* ♫♫♫♫ (American Clave, 1987/1993, prod. Kip Hanrahan, Astor Piazzolla).

best of the rest:
Suite for Vibraphone and New Tango Quintet ♫♫♫ (Atlantic Jazz, 1987)
Astor Piazzolla: The Central Park Concert ♫♫♫ (Chesky, 1987)
Concierto Para Bandoneón ♫♫♫ (Nonesuch, 1988)
The Vienna Concert ♫♫♫♫ (Messidor, 1992)
Ballet Tango ♫♫♫♫ (Milan, 1992)
Piazzolla Classics ♫♫♫♫ (RCA, 1993)
The Lausanne Concert ♫♫♫♫ (Milan, 1993)
Collection ♫♫♫♫ (Alex, 1994)
Tangamente: 1968–73 ♫♫♫♫ (Just A Memory, 1994)
Piazzolla Clasico II ♫♫♫♫ (Milan, 1995)
Tango Piazzolla: Key Works, 1984–1989 ♫♫♫♫ (Music Club, 1995)
Astor Piazzolla Plays Piazzolla ♫♫♫♫ (EPM Musique, 1995)
Concerto for Bandoneón ♫♫♫♫ (Capriccio, 1996)
Bandoneón Sinfonico ♫♫♫♫ (Milan, 1996)
Golden Collection ♫♫♫♫ (Leader Music, 1996)
Paris 1955 ♫♫♫♫ (Wotre Music, 1997)
Live at the BBC 1989 ♫♫♫♫ (Intuition, 1998)

influences:
◀◀ Vicente Greco, Roberto Firpo, Carlos Gardel
▶▶ Litto Nebbia, Siglo XXX, Sexteto Mayor

see also: *Carlos Gardel*

Craig Harris

Pixinguinha
Chorinho
Born Alfredo da Rocha Vianna Jr., April 23, 1897, in Rio de Janeiro, Brazil. Died February 17, 1973, in Rio de Janeiro, Brazil.

In 1922, the great Brazilian flautist and composer Pixinguinha and his band Os Oito Batutas were summoned for a European tour. There was an outcry in conservative circles and the media. Editorials called the musicians "savage" and "barbaric blacks." Even members of white society who had considered themselves friends of Pixinguinha now turned against him when it became a question of representing Brazil to the "civilized world."

Os Batutas played *chorinho,* an instrumental genre derived from polka, waltz, and Portuguese music, but with a strong link to Afro-Brazilian rhythms and an improvisational current that likened it to ragtime and the budding jazz movement in the United States. It proliferated in the "becos" and "botiquins" of Rio (small bohemian bars), later spreading to dancehalls, theaters, and redoubts of the upper classes. However, in the 1920s percussive instruments like the *reco-reco* and *pandeiro* were considered ignoble by the musical establishment; the Batutas not only incorporated them but featured them prominently, in a hybrid style which drew from northeastern *maxixe* and *frevo* and the frowned-upon samba. This mix caught fire in Europe, titillating the Week of Modern Art festival in Paris and obliging the group to stay long past their scheduled term.

But, notwithstanding the percussion for which his band was most notorious, Pixinguinha's first love was the flute. On it he composed some of his greatest works, including "Rosa" (1917), "Um a Zero" (1919), and his most famous song, "Carinhoso" (1923). On his return from overseas, Pixinguinha began playing more saxophone as well. His run with Benedito Lacerda's band in the 1940s, plus many recordings, solidified his identity as a woodwind icon; his soulful renditions, masterful technique, and joyful, irrepressible virtuosity endeared him to all of Brazil. As an arranger Pixinguinha continued to flourish, and his compositions were recorded by countless musicians across the musical spectrum. He brought serious instrumentalism to Brazilian popular music, and introduced popular elements to the orchestra. Over the course of his fruitful career he penned some 600 tunes. In 1997, the centennial of Pixinguinha's birth gave rise to research, commemorative recordings, and a well-deserved celebration of the life and work of this remarkable artist.

what to buy: An apt 100th-birthday present is the two-CD set *Pixinguinha 100 Anos* ♫♫♫♫ (RCA/BMG, 1997). Featuring stellar sessions by Pixinguinha, ranging from vintage 1920s material to recordings done in the early '70s, this slick but user-friendly package is a quality intro to the world of chorinho. Paulo Moura, one of Brazil's premier contemporary musicians, revisits Pixinguinha's repertoire with *Paulo Moura e Os Batutas/Pixinguinha* ♫♫♫♫ (Blue Jackel, 1998, prod. Gabi Leib). On this live album, Moura suffuses the melodies with his charisma, recreating the big-band atmosphere of mid-century *gafieira* dancehalls.

what to buy next: Kuarup Records, a Brazilian indie label, has worked hard to raise awareness about the king of chorinho. *Sempre Pixinguinha* ♫♫♫♫ (Kuarup, 1997, prod. Henrique Cazes, Mario de Aratanha), with Paulo Sergio Santos on clarinet and Odette Ernest Dias on flute, soars on taut tempos and crisp, acoustic flair. *Orquestra Brasilia* ♫♫♫♫ (Kuarup, 1997, prod. Henrique Cazes, Mario de Aratanha) brings to light a trove of never-before-recorded Pixinguinha arrangements accidentally discovered in the National Library of Brazil. Old-guard *sambistas* share the mike with the younger generation and memorable renditions ensue.

best of the rest:
Orchestra Pixinguinha ♫♫♫♫♫ (Kuarup, 1977)
Pixinguinha no Tempo dos Oito Batutas ♫♫♫♫ (Revivendo)

worth searching for: The "Os Originais" series from EMI-Odeon Brazil is out of print. Lucky scavengers may find the series's *São*

Pixinguinha ♫♫♫♫ (EMI-Odeon Brazil, 1977) in a store or catalog. You've really hit the jackpot if you unearth a record called *Gente da Antiga* ♫♫♫♫ (EMI-Odeon), featuring Pixinguinha along with Clementina de Jesus and João da Baiana.

influences:

◄◄ Donga, Noel Rosa

►► Cartola, Jacob do Bandolim, João Gilberto, Antonio Carlos Jobim, Paulo Moura

Mara Weiss and Nego Beto

Planxty

Irish traditional
Formed 1972, in Dublin, Ireland. Disbanded 1983.

Christy Moore, vocals, guitar (1972–74); Andy Irvine, vocals, mandolin, bouzouki, hurdy-gurdy (1972–75, 1979–83); Dónal Lunny, bouzouki, guitar (1972–73, 1979–83); Liam O'Flynn, uilleann pipes, tin whistle (1972–75, 1979–83); Paul Brady, vocals, guitar (1974–75); Johnny Moynihan, vocals, bouzouki, fiddle, tin whistle (1973–75); Matt Molloy, flute (1979–80); Bill Whelan, keyboards (1983); James Kelly, fiddle (1983); Nollaig Casey, fiddle (1983); Eoghan O'Neill, bass guitar (1983). (All members are from Ireland.)

The emergence of Planxty during the early 1970s marked the beginning of an Irish traditional music revival that is still going strong today. The band also ushered in a new era in which Irish music was no longer seen as the exclusive domain of ballad groups like the Clancy Brothers and the Dubliners. Other bands before Planxty, Sweeney's Men in particular, had experimented with arranging traditional material for modern folk audiences, but Planxty's unique stroke of genius—and luck—was to secure the services of brilliant uilleann piper Liam O'Flynn. As the story goes, it all came about as singer Christy Moore and producer Bill Leader put their heads together to plan the album *Prosperous,* featuring Andy Irvine, Dónal Lunny, O'Flynn, and a few other accompanists. After the album came out in 1972 on Leader's Trailer label, the foursome decided to perform together under the name Planxty, a term found in titles of 17th-century harp tunes composed in praise of patrons. The immediate success of their single "The Cliffs of Dooneen" was followed by the 1973 release of their eponymous first album, known as the "black album" for its mostly black cover with an eerie shot of the musicians caught in the beam of a stage projector. Planxty's following grew rapidly and the band's success continued, despite Lunny's departure after the completion of *The Well below the Valley,* also in 1973. Replacing Lunny was singer and bouzouki player Johnny Moynihan, a former accomplice of Irvine's in Sweeney's Men. Moynihan was featured on the band's third album, *Cold Blow and the Rainy Night,* which was named *Melody Maker* magazine's folk album of the year for 1974. However, by the time the album was released, Moore had left the band to return to a quieter life in Ireland. Singer and multi-instrumentalist Paul Brady, formerly with the vocal group the Johnstons, was asked to replace Moore, a move frowned upon by Planxty fans at the time as Brady was involved in the California rock scene. As it turned out, Brady embraced this opportunity to return to his roots with enthusiasm, and the Planxty of 1975, although never recorded and short-lived, was at least as good as the original lineup. Not until 1979, with Lunny's Bothy Band on its way out, did Lunny and the three other original members decide to try it again, this time with the addition of the great Roscommon flute player Matt Molloy.

The reunited Planxty made a smashing comeback, despite a power outage interrupting their set, at the Ballysadare festival in August 1979 (an event also marked by the Bothy Band's final appearance), and released the powerful *After the Break.* Molloy, who unfortunately was soon gone to join the Chieftains, also appeared on the band's next album, *The Woman I Loved So Well,* released in 1980. During the early '80s, Lunny was once again distracted by other projects, namely an experimentation in folk-rock out of which came the great Moving Hearts, and Planxty began winding down slowly but surely. They released their final album, *Words and Music,* in 1983, with the participation of fiddler James Kelly and keyboard player Bill Whelan, well known today as the man behind *Riverdance.* However, all former members of the band continue to participate actively in the Irish music scene, Moore and O'Flynn as solo performers, Irvine with Patrick Street, and Lunny as one of the busiest producers and session musicians in Ireland today.

what to buy: The band's official first album, *Planxty* 🎵🎵🎵🎵 (Polydor, 1973/Shanachie, 1979, prod. Phil Coulter), remains one of its best. The famous opening song, "Raggle Taggle Gypsy," is left practically unchanged from *Prosperous,* though the fidelity of the studio recording allows a better appreciation of the intricacies of the arrangement, in particular the brilliant transition into the old harp tune "Tabhair Dom Do Lámh (Give Me Your Hand)." Other classic songs on the album include "Arthur McBride," later made into a hit by Paul Brady; "The Jolly Beggar"; "Follow Me up to Carlow," celebrating a rare Irish victory against the Crown; "The Blacksmith," with its Balkan-tinged instrumental conclusion; and Andy Irvine's own "West Coast of Clare." Liam O'Flynn's masterful piping is heard on the lovely reel medley "Junior Crehan's Favorite," the multi-part slide "Merrily Kissed the Quaker," and a couple of harp compositions by the legendary Turlough O'Carolan. Much in the same vein, *The Well below the Valley* 🎵🎵🎵🎵 (Polydor, 1973/ Shanachie, 1979, prod. Phil Coulter) features Christy Moore and Irvine equally as lead singers, performing such classics as "Cúnla" and the two versions of "As I Roved Out." O'Flynn con-

tributes some of the great pieces of the piping repertoire, including the slip jig "An Phis Fhliuch" and the reels "The Dogs among the Bushes" and "Jenny's Wedding." Despite Dónal Lunny's departure (he actually participated in the recording), *Cold Blow and the Rainy Night* 🎵🎵🎵🎵 (Polydor, 1974/ Shanachie, 1979, prod. Phil Coulter) remains true to the earlier Planxty sound. New member and ex–Sweeney's Men vocalist Johnny Moynihan is the featured singer on "'P' Stands for Paddy," one of the memorable songs on the album. Others include Irvine's "Johnny Cope" and Moore's "The Lakes of Pontchartrain." Among the instrumental highlights are a set of polkas now universally known among Irish session-goers, and the exotic Balkan tune "Mominsko Horo," which immediately follows Irvine's own Romanian-themed (though not Romanian-sounding) song, "Baneasa's Green Glade." With *After the Break* 🎵🎵🎵🎵 (Tara, 1979, prod. Dónal Lunny), Planxty made a stunning comeback. Lunny's "blarge" (five-course bouzouki) brings new depth to the sound, while the sophistication of the mandolin-and-bouzouki arrangements reaches new heights, particularly on "The Good Ship Kangaroo" and "The Pursuit of Farmer Michael Hayes." The addition of Matt Molloy's expert flute playing makes the instrumentals that much richer—one of them is a spectacular Bulgarian dance tune titled "Smeceno Horo." The CD reissue of the album includes two additional tracks that had been previously released on the LP sampler *High Kings of Tara.*

what to buy next: Although not officially a Planxty album, Moore's *Prosperous* 🎵🎵🎵 (Trailer, 1972/Tara, 1972, prod. Bill Leader) gives a glimpse at a prototypical form of the band, as Moore gathered Lunny, O'Flynn, Irvine, and a few others to record the album. It features two songs, "Raggle Taggle Gypsy" and "The Cliffs of Dooneen," which Planxty would continue to perform with great success, along with other, equally interesting selections like Bob Dylan's "Tribute to Woody" and Woody Guthrie's "Ludlow Massacre." *The Planxty Collection* 🎵🎵🎵🎵 (Polydor, 1974/Shanachie, 1979, prod. Phil Coulter) is an excellent sampler based on Planxty's first three albums, to which is added the enormously successful "The Cliffs of Dooneen" from the band's 1972 single. Although not as exciting an album as *After the Break, The Woman I Loved So Well* 🎵🎵🎵🎵 (Tara, 1980, prod. Dónal Lunny, Brian Masterson) contains some fine songs, like Irvine's "Kellswater," learned from the Sam Henry collection, and Moore's epic "Little Musgrave." The instrumental tracks benefit from the presence of guest musicians, particularly the great Clare duo of Noel Hill (concertina) and Tony Linnane (fiddle). *Words and Music* 🎵🎵🎵 (WEA, 1983/Shanachie, 1983, prod. Dónal Lunny) was Planxty's swan song. The influence of Lunny's experiments with Moving Hearts can be clearly heard on this album, especially in some of the accompaniments featuring electronic keyboards and electric bass—although the marriage of high technology and traditional music works rather well on the beautiful piping air "Táimse Im' Chodlach." On other instrumental tracks, O'Flynn's pipes are combined with the twin fiddles of James Kelly and Nollaig Casey.

worth searching for: Three live Planxty tracks, one being a set of jigs not appearing on any of their studio albums, were included on the Breton-produced *2e Festival Pop' Celtic Kertalg 73* ♫♫♫ (Barclay, 1973, prod. Gwenn Le Goarnic, Hughes de Courson). *High Kings of Tara* ♫♫♫♫ (Tara, 1980, prod. Dónal Lunny) contains three Planxty tracks left over from the *After the Break* sessions, two of which were later included in the CD reissue of that album. *Arís* ♫♫♫ (Polydor, 1984) is another anthology drawn from the band's first three albums, with the added interest being the inclusion of "Yarmouth Town" from the B-side of Planxty's famous first single. You will be truly lucky if you can find a copy of the two-cassette self-released bootleg *The Best of Planxty Live* ♫♫♫♫ (Planxty, c. 1986, prod. Kevin Flynn, Michael Germaine), recorded live at the Olympia Theatre by the original quartet with Nollaig Casey (fiddle) and Bill Whelan (keyboards). The numbers performed span the complete recorded output of the band and its members, from the black album's "The Jolly Beggarman" to Andy Irvine's "Plains of Kildare," first recorded with Paul Brady, to "Pity the Poor Immigrant" and "The Irish March" from the band's final album.

influences:

◀◀ Ceoltóirí Cualann, Sweeney's Men

▶▶ The Bothy Band, Touchstone, Moving Hearts, Patrick Street, Dónal Lunny, Dervish

see also: *The Bothy Band, Patrick Cassidy, Andy Irvine, Dónal Lunny, Matt Molloy, Christy Moore, Moving Hearts, Liam O'Flynn, Sweeney's Men, Bill Whelan*

Philippe Varlet

The Pogues
/Shane MacGowan

Celtic punk
Formed 1982, in London, England. Disbanded 1997.

Peter "Spider" Stacy, vocals, pennywhistle; **Jeremy "Jem" Finger,** banjo, guitar; **Shane MacGowan,** vocals (1982–91); **Joe Strummer,** vocals, guitar (1991–93); **James Fearnley,** accordion (1982–93); **James McNally,** accordion (1993–present); **Philip Chevron,** guitar (1984–93); **Jamie Clarke,** guitar (1993–97); **Andrew Ranken,** drums; **Cait O'Riordan,** bass (1982–86); **Darryl Hunt** (1986–97).

The Pogues injected the bile of punk rock into traditional Celtic folk music. At their best—with the brilliant gutter-

poet Shane MacGowan on lead vocals—they were one of England's most original rock acts. But MacGowan, a career alcoholic, became increasingly unstable and left the band in 1991. With Spider Stacy handling lead vocals, the Pogues became a decent Celtic rock outfit, but hardly the revolutionary group they were in the past. The magic was gone without MacGowan, and the band split up after one lackluster album.

what to buy: *Rum, Sodomy & the Lash* ♫♫♫♫ (MCA, 1985, prod. Elvis Costello) is MacGowan and the Pogues at their peak, thrashing through punk workouts such as "The Sock Bed of Cuchulainn" and switching easily into ballads like "And the Band Played Waltzing Matilda."

what to buy next: MacGowan was still in fine form on *If I Should Fall from Grace with God* ♫♫♫♫ (Island, 1988, prod. Steve Lillywhite), especially on his brawling duet with Kirsty MacColl, "Fairy Tale of New York." But you could practically smell the whiskey in his slurred vocals on *Peace and Love* ♫♫♫ (Island, 1989, prod. Steve Lillywhite), a still-strong effort that nonetheless foreshadowed the downhill stumble to follow.

what to avoid: *Pogue Mahone* ♫♫ (Mesa, 1995, prod. Steve Brown) is a pleasant but all-too-safe post-MacGowan effort.

the rest:
Red Roses for Me ♫♫♫ (Enigma, 1984)
Poguetry in Motion ♫♫♫ (MCA EP, 1986)
Hell's Ditch ♫♫♫ (Island, 1990)
Yeah, Yeah, Yeah, Yeah ♫♫ (Island, 1990)
Essential Pogues ♫♫♫ (Island, 1991)
Waiting for Herb ♫♫♫ (Chameleon, 1993)

worth searching for: The soundtrack *Straight to Hell* (Enigma Classics, 1987) features the Pogues' version of Ennio Morricone's theme from the Clint Eastwood film *The Good, the Bad, and the Ugly,* as well as the traditional "Danny Boy."

solo outings:
Shane MacGowan & the Popes:
The Snake ♫♫♫ (ZTT/Warner Bros., 1995)
The Crock of Gold ♫♫♫♫ (Phantom, 1998)

influences:

◀◀ The Clancy Brothers, the Clash, the Chieftains, the Sex Pistols

▶▶ The Drovers, the Levellers, the Cranberries

see also: *The Dubliners, the Oyster Band, Alan Stivell, Sweeney's Men*

Thor Christensen

Martti Pokela

Finnish folk, classical

Born January 23, 1924, in Haapavesi, North Ostrobothnia, Finland.
Based in Finland.

Martti Pokela has done more to promote the use of Finland's national instrument, the *kantele* (a form of zither), than just about any other performer. Although the kantele was honored in Finnish tradition as the main instrument played within Finland's national epic poem, the *Kalevala*, by the 20th century it had been superseded by the fiddle and the accordion in folk groups. Pokela just happened to grow up in an area where kantele playing was still a living tradition, and he became captivated by its sound. Originally a hollowed-out piece of wood strung with five pieces of twisted horse hair, the kantele evolved over time into a finely crafted wooden zither with 9, 25, 32, or 36 copper or steel wire strings, and a tuning mechanism that lets the player modulate between keys and beyond the pentatonic scale to which it was originally confined. By the late 1940s Pokela was traipsing around the country collecting folk songs, which he then arranged and performed with his wife Marjatta. He has since joined the staff of the world-renowned folk music department at the Sibelius Academy, where, along with the department's director Heikki Laitinen, he has taught many of the musicians prominent in the new Finnish folk movement, including Maria Kalaniemi, Anna-Kaisa Liedes, and Timo Väänänen (Finland's 1997 Young Artist of the Year).

what to buy: *Old & New Kantele* 𝆏𝆏𝆏𝆏 (Finnlevy/Arc, 1978, prod. Martti Pokela, Matti Kontio) includes 16 pieces played on a variety of kanteles by a trio that includes Pokela, his daughter Eeva-Leena Pokela-Sariola, and Matti Kontio. There are plenty of sprightly tunes on this disc, but what's most notable is that some of the most affecting work is done using the older 5-string kanteles instead of the more modern 36-string instruments. Pokela shows that he is not just a folk artist on albums in which he takes the kantele into the classical world, including *Sonata for Kantele* 𝆏𝆏𝆏𝆏 (Finlandia, 1995, prod. Martti Pokela, Matti Kontio) and the more recent *Snow Kantele/Sami Suite* 𝆏𝆏𝆏𝆏 (Finlandia, 1998, prod. Martti Pokela, Matti Kontio), a series of variations on *joiks* (the compelling music of the Sami, an indigenous people of Scandanavia once known as Laplanders).

what to buy next: The bulk of *Finnish Kantele Music, Vol. 2* 𝆏𝆏𝆏𝆏 (Finlandia, 1993, compilation prod. Jari Tiessalo) comes from sessions that Pokela recorded in 1965 and 1969 for the Scandia label. They include a lot of traditional tunes, plus some material that he composed using joiks as a base. Included alongside Pokela's recordings are some pieces performed by Ulla Katajavuori, another influential kantele player, in 1957.

worth searching for: The young Finnish quartet Loituma consists of four kantele players (including Timo Väänänen), and on *Things of Beauty* 𝆏𝆏𝆏𝆏 (Kansanmusiikki-institutti/NorthSide, 1998, prod. Timo Alakotila, Timo Väänänen) they perform the Pokela composition "Suo," as well as a fine mix of originals and traditional arrangements.

influences:

◀◀ Paul Salminen

▶▶ Matti Kontio, Anna-Kaisa Liedes, Eeva-Leena Pokela-Sariola, Timo Väänänen

Garaud MacTaggart

The Police /Sting

Rock/reggae

Formed 1977, in London, England. Disbanded 1984.

Sting (born Gordon Sumner, October 2, 1951, in Newcastle, England), bass, vocals, saxophone, keyboards; Stewart Copeland (Egypt), drums; Henri Pandovani, guitar (1977); Andy Summers (born Andrew Somers, in England), guitar.

Arriving amid the fury of England's punk revolution, the members of the Police, while not actual punks themselves, played them on TV. By bleaching their hair so they could appear in a bubblegum commercial, the band may have called their credibility into question from the very beginning, but the fact is, their ability to write songs and actually play their instruments wouldn't have curried much favor in the DIY era anyway. With musical pasts ranging from jazz (Sting) to prog-rock (Copeland) to all manner of session work (Summers), the Police collectively focused on white reggae—*Regatta de Blanc,* as their second album's title proclaimed—coating it with a pop sheen that soon enough brought the world to their punky reggae party. Sting's middle-to-highbrow lyrics included some serious pretensions—namechecking novelist Vladimir Nabokov here, attempting to explain Jungian concepts there. But give the guy credit: if he helped move a few extra copies of *Lolita* or *Psychology of the Unconscious* along the way, then so much the better. The group splintered in 1984 with all three members going on to solo success of varying degrees, led of course by Der Schtingle, who has become one of the world's most famous rock superstars, retaining his reggae "roots" while mixing Latin, Celtic, English-folk, and other genres' elements into his jazzy, cinematic pop.

what to buy: The Police's *Zenyatta Mondatta* 𝆏𝆏𝆏𝆏 (A&M, 1980, prod. the Police, Nigel Gray) is the album on which the group's grasp first matched its outsized reach. Moody, murky dub sonics and reggae-rhythmic digressions abound on just-happen-to-be monster hits like "Don't Stand So Close to Me," "De Do Do Do, De Da Da Da," "Driven to Tears," and "When the World Is Running Down, You Make the Best of What's Still

Around," while "Canary in a Coalmine"'s beat qualifies it for, let's say, the second-and-a-half wave of ska. Dauntingly verbose, Sting's . . . *Nothing Like the Sun* ✻✻✻✻✻ (A&M, 1987, prod. Neil Dorfsman, Sting) scores on the basis of its joyous polyrhythmic groove, thanks in large part to drummer Manu Katché. Sting's broad stylistic palette is most tasteful on the Latin-jazzy "Straight to My Heart," the Brazilian-balladic "Fragile," and the synth-Andean "They Dance Alone (Gueca Sola)" (with spoken-word accompaniment from Ruben Blades). To frame a semi-autobiographical tale of working-class struggle and his father's demise, Sting swerved from Afro/Latin/Caribbean sources to Celtic and English-folk ones for his masterwork, *The Soul Cages* ✻✻✻✻ (A&M, 1991, prod. Hugh Padgham, Sting). British-Isles superstars like Northumbrian piper Kathryn Tickell evoke the home ground, while pan-rhythmic regulars like Katché keep the horizons wide.

what to buy next: The well-drawn blueprints for the Police's reggae-lite can be viewed on *Outlandos d'Amour* ✻✻✻ (A&M, 1978) and *Regatta de Blanc* ✻✻✻✻ (A&M, 1979, prod. the Police, Nigel Gray). It's the supernaturally talented Sting's special curse that he can commercially overachieve even when he's artistically undertrying. The high point of his lush-but-facile post–*Soul Cages* work is the Celtic-lament-into-Brazilian-pop stunner "I Was Brought to My Senses" on *Mercury Falling* ✻✻✻✻ (A&M, 1996, prod. Hugh Padgham, Sting). The song is doubly search-worthy for its writer's well-advised reunion with sax genius Branford Marsalis. Sting's justly chart-climbing solo debut, *The Dream of the Blue Turtles* ✻✻✻✻✻ (A&M, 1985, prod. Pete Smith, Sting), has among its lesser moments the reggae-ish "Love Is the Seventh Wave," and among its greater moments the African-inspired melodic percussion loop anchoring the poignant "We Work the Black Seam."

the rest:
The Police:
Ghost in the Machine ✻✻✻✻ (A&M, 1981)
Synchronicity ✻✻✻✻✻ (A&M, 1983)
Every Breath You Take: The Singles ✻✻✻✻ (A&M, 1986)
Message in a Box: The Complete Recordings ✻✻✻✻ (A&M, 1993)
The Police Live! ✻✻✻✻ (A&M, 1995)
Every Breath You Take: The Classics ✻✻✻✻ (A&M, 1995)

Sting:
Bring on the Night ✻✻✻✻ (A&M, 1986)
Ten Summoner's Tales ✻✻✻✻ (A&M, 1993)
Demolition Man ✻✻✻ (A&M EP, 1993)
Fields of Gold: The Best of Sting, 1984–1994 ✻✻✻✻✻ (A&M, 1994)
The Very Best of Sting & the Police ✻✻✻✻ (A&M, 1997)

worth searching for: Depending on where your tastes fall on the purist-ometer, the Police's popularization of reggae was either the best thing that ever happened to the genre or the worst. Many reg-

gae stars themselves seem to cast their vote for the former on a two-volumes-and-counting series of various-artists tributes, starting with *Regatta Mondatta: A Reggae Tribute to the Police* (MVP, 1997) and *Regatta Mondullu: A Reggae Tribute to the Police, Volume II* (EMD/Ark 21, 1998). Among the top-notch artists featured on these albums are Steel Pulse, Maxi Priest, Freddie McGregor, Toots & the Maytals, and recent Sting collaborators Aswad. Meanwhile, a later, Latin American generation of reggae synthesists and style-splicers (King Changó, Plastilina Mosh, et al) pay their respects on *Outlandos d'Americas: A Rock en Español Tribute to the Police* (EMD/Ark 21, 1998). Also, from the same sessions that produced Sting's . . . *Nothing Like the Sun, Nada Como el Sol* (A&M EP, 1991, prod. Neil Dorfsman, Sting) offers Spanish-language versions of "We'll Be Together," "Little Wing," and "Fragile," plus a version of "Fragile" sung in Portuguese.

influences:

◄◄ Bob Marley, the Beatles, Miles Davis, Wayne Shorter, Gilberto Gil

►► Wang Chung, Men at Work, the Samples, Rancid, Goldfinger, Dave Matthews Band

see also: *Aswad, the Chieftains*

Daniel Durchholz and Adam McGovern

Perez Prado
Mambo

Born Damaso Perez Prado, December 11, 1916, in Matanzas, Cuba. Died September 14, 1989, in Mexico City, Mexico.

Jazzman Tito Puente got his due in the 1992 film *The Mambo Kings*, but where was Perez Prado? Some say the native Cuban invented the mambo rhythm circa 1942, and his nickname throughout his career was "El Rey del Mambo," or—you guessed it—"The Mambo King." Whether he was the pioneer or not, it's indisputable that when Prado moved from Cuba to Mexico in 1948, he set off the international mambo craze with his mixture of Afro-Cuban rhythms and American swing.

In Mexico City, Prado immediately set up shop at Club 1-2-3, earning the supplemental nickname "The Glenn Miller of Mexico" and using this notoriety to tour the U.S. and act in Mexican movies. His orchestra's mambo songs—built on a steady, tinny Latin rhythm and using an incredibly catchy, playful horn or whistle melody—became big hits in the late 1940s and led to an RCA Victor recording contract. His American tours, beginning in the early 1950s, gave him a massive audience, especially in such prominent New York City nightclubs as the Palladium. (Always a great showman, Prado's trademark cry was "Dilo!" which means "give it!") Though snooty jazz fans preferred Puente and Tito Rodriguez above Prado's unashamed hit-making style, Prado's influence flowed in unexpected directions. Singer Rosemary Clooney, inspired by Prado and the 1954 mambo craze, recorded her wonderful "Mambo Italiano"; Perry Como, Dizzy Gillespie, and the Crows also adapted his style. Prado's first #1 American hit, 1955's "Cherry Pink and Apple Blossom White," cemented his long-term popularity. He recorded until the 1970s, then retired to live with his family in Mexico City. As with many musicians who thrive on whimsical public crazes, Prado's body of work is rarely taken seriously; but he was a major talent, and instrumentals like "Why Wait" still sound fresh and catchy.

what to buy: The hard part about navigating Prado's multi-album career is determining which Spanish imports overlap with the original studio albums, and which of those are out of print. *Mondo Mambo! The Best of Perez Prado & His Orchestra* 🎜🎜🎜 (Rhino, 1995, prod. various) focuses on Prado's glory years—and, not coincidentally, the height of the mambo craze—and includes such classics as "Cherry Pink and Apple Blossom White" and "Patricia."

what to buy next: Prado's best-known studio album remains *Havana 3 A.M.* 🎜🎜🎜 (BMG, 1956/1990), in which jazzman Maynard Ferguson contributes the lead trumpet parts and a big Latin swing band supplies the supernaturally catchy pop melodies. Other noteworthy studio albums, handily reissued on CD, include the breakthrough *Prez* 🎜🎜🎜 (RCA, 1958) and *Que Rico Mambo!* 🎜🎜🎜 (BMG, 1982).

what to avoid: Like most pop musicians of his era, Prado was prolific, putting out a few albums every year during the height of his popularity; as a result, much of his stuff sounds like much of his other stuff, not to mention the other Latin-influenced easy-listening music of the same period. Among the examples of bland pop product are *The Mambo King* 🎜🎜 (RCA International, 1957) and the Spanish reissue *Cuba, Grandes Idoles de Siempre* 🎜🎜 (Orfeon, 1997).

best of the rest:
King of Mambo 🎜🎜 (BMG, 1967/1989)
Concierto Para Bongo 🎜🎜🎜 (PolyGram Latino, 1993)
Dance Date with . . . Perez Prado 🎜🎜 (Polydor, 1994)
Esta Si Viven 🎜🎜 (PolyGram Latino, 1996)
Sinfeonola Tropical, Vol. II 🎜🎜🎜 (RCA, 1997)
15 Grandes Exito de Perez Prado, Vol. 2 🎜🎜🎜 (RCA, 1997)

worth searching for: Don't ignore the Latin import repackages, including *Go Go Mambo* 🎜🎜🎜 (Tumbao, 1992) and *Perez Prado and Benny Moré: Mambos* 🎜🎜🎜 (Saludos Amigos, 1994)—although novices are advised to stick with the Rhino compilation.

influences:
◀ Tito Puente, Arsenio Rodriguez, Orestes Lopez, Tito Rodriguez, Xavier Cugat

▶ Rosemary Clooney, Herb Alpert, Sergio Mendes, Dizzy Gillespie

see also: *Benny Moré, Orchesta Aragon*

Steve Knopper

Maxi Priest
Reggae
Born Max Elliot, June 10, 1962, in London, England. Based in London, England.

Maxi Priest is perhaps the most popular international reggae singer since the earth-shaking Robert Nesta Marley. However, while Marley rallied people across the globe with songs of protest and struggle, Priest has crossed borders with a sweet, lissome tenor and nary a trace of defiance or controversy. He changed his surname after sighting the Rastafarian religion as a young man, redefining himself after Priest Levi, a figurehead of the 12 Tribes of Israel.

Notwithstanding his superb voice, Priest's music career initially sprung from his talent as a carpenter. In the early 1980s, while building speaker cabinets for Saxon Sound International—at the time the most massive of the U.K.'s dancehall sound systems (mobile deejay units)—Priest was moved by the nimble, rap-like "ragamuffin" toasting styles of deejays like Tippa Irie, Smiley Culture, and Peter King. But his favorite music was that of Jamaican roots singers Beres Hammond and Dennis Brown, and U.S. soul legend Marvin Gaye.

The Saxon crew eventually coaxed Priest out from the woodwork and onto the stage alongside them. Using the same rough-and-tough backing rhythms as the MCs (as U.K. deejays preferred to be called), Priest performed at a variety of south London dancehall shows, and brought a silky soulfulness to a place usually dominated by gritty high-speed chat. Priest's versatile fusion of "lover's-rock" romanticism, dancehall energy, and subtle roots-reggae touches led to a recording contract with Virgin in the U.K. The series of albums that followed exhibit little originality or lyrical substance, but damn do they sound good! With the song "Close to You," Priest even seized the #1 spot on the *Billboard* charts in 1990.

But what really cemented Priest's international rep was his perfectly timed revisitation of his rugged dancehall roots just as hip-hop exploded into the Top 40 in America. His collaborations with ragga-rappers Shabba Ranks ("Housecall") and, more recently, Shaggy ("That Girl") crossed over to the pop and R&B charts and significantly expanded his fan base. Ironically, even while Priest has helped popularize reggae as much as any living artist on the global stage, his music is generally unappreciated back home in Jamaica, where jaded dancehall fans pelted him with oranges at the 1988 edition of their annual Woodstock, the Sting Concert.

what to buy: *Bonafide* ♪♪♪ (EMD/Capitol, 1990, prod. Geoffrey Chung) includes the aforementioned #1 single with Soul II Soul, "Close to You," and, more importantly, demonstrates Priest's versatility better than any of his other releases. Modern reggae, pop, roots, lover's rock, soul—it's all warmly cocooned in this fine release. Priest's debut, *You're Safe* ♪♪♪ (EMD/Capitol, 1985, prod. Barry Boom), stands as his purest reggae album, and is bolstered with tight, spongy backing from the all-star band Caution, which included Fashion Records founder Chris Lane and the great Barry Boom (a.k.a. singer Paul Robinson), who doubled as producer.

what to buy next: *Intentions* ♪♪♪ (EMD/Capitol, 1986, prod. various) is a sleek, quality collaboration with fellow U.K. reggae-poppers Aswad. On Priest's first U.S. release, *Maxi* ♪♪♪ (EMD/Capitol, 1987, prod. Sly & Robbie), he performs a scintillating duet with his hero Beres Hammond on "How Can We Ease the Pain." This album benefits from production by Sly (Dunbar) & Robbie (Shakespeare), indisputably among Jamaica's greatest rhythm sections and session masterminds, and includes Priest's hit cover of Cat Stevens's "Wild World." *Best of Me* ♪♪♪ (EMD/Capitol, 1991, prod. various) is a serviceable greatest-hits package with a whopper bonus cut—the white-hot "Housecall" with Shabba Ranks.

what to avoid: *Fe Real* ♪♪ (EMD/Capitol, 1992, prod. various) is lightweight and uneven, though it does contain the marvelous soul cut "Groovin' in the Midnight." *The Man with the Fun* ♪ (Virgin, 1996, prod. various) is cluttered with detritus like Priest's practically catatonic cover of the Police's "Message in a Bottle." But it does include the irresistible single "That Girl," with some tough toasting from Shaggy.

the rest:
Live in Concert (BBC Session) ♪♪♪ (Strange Fruit, 1999)
So What If It Rains N/A (Virgin, 1999)

influences:
◀◀ Alton Ellis, Beres Hammond, Dennis Brown, Marvin Gaye
▶▶ Princess Sharifa

see also: *Aswad, Shabba Ranks, Shaggy, Sly & Robbie*

Todd Shanker

Primeaux & Mike

Intertribal peyote music
Formed 1987, in Kitsili, AZ, USA. Based in Kitsili, AZ, USA.

Verdell Primeaux, vocals; Johnny Mike, vocals. (Both members are from USA.)

Verdell Primeaux is the son of Francis Primeaux Sr., a well-known peyote singer. Verdell is from the Oglalla Sioux Reservation, where he began singing at the age of five. He has com-

jamaican music 2: nyahbingi

The hypnotic and intricate rhythms of *nyahbingi* drumming descended from traditional West African dance beats brought to Jamaica by Ashanti slaves. There are essentially three different types of drums used in the music. First, a large bass drum, approximately three feet in diameter, keeps time in deep, resonant thumps intended to mimic the heartbeat. These drums are usually struck with the padded mallet-head of a wooden staff. The smaller *funde* is a hand drum that fleshes out the rhythm. Finally, the "repeater," also a smaller hand drum, improvises and embroiders beats over the top. Handmade percussion, bottle horns, and occasionally brass instruments like the saxophone and trumpet are also worked into the celebratory "nyah" mix.

The seemingly infinite nyah rhythms are churned out for many consecutive hours at spiritual "grounation" sessions, supplemented with *ganja* (marijuana) smoked from communal chalices, and enlivened by *kumina* (Ashanti Twi for "possessed by an ancestor") dancing and chanting. The ritual's participants aim to obliterate time, escape the harsh reality of the present, sojourn with the proud spirits of ancestors, and use the wisdom acquired to form a clearer vision of the future.

The Ashanti Africans were known as Maroons in Jamaica, and they carried on the worship of their god *Nyankopong*—one theorized source of the rite's name. In any case, the Maroons were the first to rebel against Jamaica's slave system in the mid-17th century, establishing the defiant foundation of the Rastafarian movement of nearly three centuries later. The first recognized nyah sessions occurred in the wild Wareika Hills outside Kingston in the 1950s. The most famous nyah drummers—Count Ossie and Ras Michael—emerged from this "Rastaman camp." Count Ossie & the Mystic Revelation of Rastafari's *Grounation* ♪♪♪♪ (Ashanti, 1988) and Ras Michael & the Sons of Negus's *Rastafari* ♪♪♪♪ (Greensleeves, 1975) are two of the greatest recorded documents of the rhythms that would become the beating heart of roots reggae.

Todd Shanker

posed songs since 1983. Johnny Mike has been involved with the Native American Church all his life. He has been singing "healing songs" with Primeaux since 1987. Healing songs are sung without drum and rattle, to teach younger people how to sing the traditional songs and to provide a soothing healing environment for the sacred peyote ceremony, a spiritual communion controversial with the white authorities because of its use of a natural hallucinogen. By using harmonies that are similar to Christian church music, Primeaux & Mike have created a new style of peyote singing, although it is still very rooted in Native tradition.

what to buy: On *Walk in Beauty* ♫♫♫♫ (Canyon, 1991, prod. Robert Doyle), Primeaux & Mike's voices blend their wonderful harmonies with almost no production, save a bit of echo to add depth of field. The result is a soothing and energizing effort that makes the melody of Indian music plain to white ears.

what to buy next: *Sacred Path* ♫♫♫♫ (Canyon, 1997, prod. Robert Doyle) adds a bit of new-agey synthesizer drone to the voices. It's unobtrusive, but unnecessary. The vocals are compelling enough on their own.

best of the rest:
Healing and Peyote Songs of the Native American Church ♫♫♫♫♫ (Canyon, 1994)

influences:
◀◀ The Primeaux Family

see also: *Robbie Robertson*

j. poet

Maddy Prior
/The Silly Sisters
/Maddy Prior & Tim Hart
/Maddy Prior
& the Carnival Band

British folk-rock
Born late 1940s, in St. Albans, England. Based in England.

Maddy Prior is one of British folk-rock's leading vocalists. A founding member of Steeleye Span, Prior has also recorded as a soloist, as leader of the Carnival Band, and, together with June Tabor, as the Silly Sisters.

Initially inspired by American folk songs, Prior was introduced to traditional British folk music by a friend who steered her toward the songs of Ewan MacColl and the British folk-song archives at the Cecil Sharpe House. Meeting multi-instrumentalist and vocalist Tim Hart in the late 1960s, Prior joined with him to form a tradition-rooted duo.

Although they recorded three albums—*Folk Songs of Old England, Volume 1* and *Folk Songs of Old England, Volume 2* in 1968, and *Summer Solstice* in 1971—Prior and Hart were little-known outside of St. Albans, England. The first break for the duo came when they met bassist Ashley Hutchings at the Keele Folk Festival in 1969. Hutchings, who had recently left Fairport Convention, was seeking musicians to form a band that would play an electrified version of traditional British folk. Prior and Hart were quickly recruited along with Gay and Terry Woods (formerly of Sweeney's Men) for the project, which became known as Steeleye Span. The group, which initially concentrated on 17th- and 18th-century songs that they found in journals of the English Folk Dance and Song Society, released their debut album, *Hark! The Village Wait,* in 1970. Although the Woodses left a few months later, Prior and Hart continued to perform in the group, with folk guitarist Martin Carthy added to its lineup. After the departure of Hutchings and Carthy in 1971, lead guitarist/vocalist Bob Johnson and bassist/vocalist Rick Kemp signed up in their place (Prior and Kemp were later married).

Prior and Steeleye Span had their first hit, "Gaudete"—an old Latin chant that the band performed *a cappella*—the following year. The band had an even bigger hit in 1976 with "All Around My Hat," one traditional song that Prior reworked with verses from another, "Farewell He." Although she also teamed with folksinger June Tabor to record the duo's first album as the Silly Sisters in 1976, Prior continued to perform with Steeleye Span until March 7th, 1978, when the group disbanded. Shortly afterwards, she released her debut solo album, *Woman in the Wings,* produced by Ian Anderson of Jethro Tull. While Prior reunited with Steeleye Span in 1980, her focus remained on raising her two children. The band failed to record another studio album until 1986, when they released *Back in Line*. After Prior experienced voice problems in 1993, Gay Woods returned to Steeleye as a second vocalist. Prior had become involved with a variety of outside projects in the late 1980s. In addition to recording a second Silly Sisters album with Tabor, *No More to the Dance,* she formed the Carnival Band, which has subsequently recorded four albums.

what to buy: *Momento: The Best of Maddy Prior* ♫♫♫♫ (Park, 1995) surveys Prior's recordings as a soloist and with June Tabor as the Silly Sisters. Prior's songwriting talents are showcased on 15 of the album's 18 tracks.

what to buy next: The changing seasons are thematically explored on *Year* ♫♫♫♫ (Park, 1993), with such tunes as "Swimming Song," "Harvest Home," "Winter Wakeneth," and "Snowdrops/Birth." In addition to six original songs, the album includes tunes by Loudon Wainwright III and Nick Jones.

the rest:
Maddy Prior:
Woman in the Wings 🎵🎵🎵 (Chrysalis, 1978)
Changing Winds 🎵🎵🎵 (Chrysalis, 1978)
Flesh and Blood 🎵🎵🎵 (Park, 1997)
Ravenchild N/A (Park, 1999)

Maddy Prior & Tim Hart:
Folk Songs of Old England, Volume 1 🎵🎵🎵 (Mooncrest, 1968)
Folk Songs of Old England, Volume 2 🎵🎵🎵 (Mooncrest, 1968)
Summer Solstice 🎵🎵🎵 (Mooncrest, 1971/Shanachie, 1988)

Maddy Prior & the Carnival Band:
A Tapestry of Carols 🎵🎵🎵 (Saydisc, 1987)
Sing Lustily with Good Courage 🎵🎵🎵 (Saydisc, 1990)
Carols & Capers 🎵🎵🎵 (Park, 1991)
Hang Up Sorrow and Care 🎵🎵🎵 (Park, 1995)

worth searching for: With Prior's soprano and June Tabor's deeper contralto accompanied by some of England's best acoustic musicians (including Martin Carthy, Nick Jones, Andy Irvine, Johnny Moynihan, and Danny Thompson), *The Silly Sisters* 🎵🎵🎵🎵 (Chrysalis, 1976/Shanachie, 1988, prod. Maddy Prior, Robin Black) remains one of the historic artifacts of modern British folk music. *No More to the Dance* 🎵🎵🎵🎵 (Shanachie, 1988, prod. Andrew Cronshaw) is a fitting follow-up, with accompaniment by guitarist Dan Ar Braz, harp duo Sileas, and Prior's husband, Rick Kemp, on bass.

influences:
◀◀ Sandy Denny, Ewan MacColl

▶▶ June Tabor, Connie Dover, the New St. George

see also: *Dan Ar Braz, Frankie Armstrong, Martin Carthy, Fairport Convention, Ashley Hutchings, Andy Irvine, Ewan MacColl, Cecil Sharp (sidebar), Steeleye Span*

Craig Harris

Willis Prudhomme
Zydeco
Born September 22, 1931, in Kinder, LA, USA. Based in Oberlin, LA, USA.

Willis Prudhomme typifies many of the zydeco performers who work the circuit and rarely become known outside the Cajun triangle of South Louisiana. Prudhomme is a rice farmer who started performing in public only in 1975. A solid but not flashy accordionist, he was recruited by drummer and singer Leo Thomas to play with his group. Prudhomme's apprenticeship with Thomas lasted 10 years before he was ready to strike out on his own. His band, Zydeco Express, is a lot like its leader:

unassuming, but steady. They play an honest rural zydeco sound, nothing fancy and no frills. That means there is a bounce in the beat that distinguishes it from the crunch of the doubling, clutching sound popularized by Beau Jocque. Dancers always know that they will get their money's worth when Prudhomme is on the marquee.

what to buy: Prudhomme & Zydeco Express share *Zydeco Live! Volume II* 🎵🎵🎵 (Rounder, 1989, prod. Scott Billington) with John Delafose & the Eunice Playboys. Prudhomme works exclusively on the one-row button accordion with an internal pickup, which produces a gritty sound similar to that of a good Chicago blues harpist. The band shines on the waltzes in particular, something of a dying art among zydeco groups.

what to avoid: Live, with a dance floor, these guys pack a lot of excitement. Their style of zydeco is about playing evenly, not about the kind of climaxes that are such a part of rock music. As exhibited on *Willis Prudhomme & Zydeco Express* 🎵🎵🎵🎵 (Maison De Soul, 1990, prod. Floyd Soileau), this doesn't translate well into the studio, where the band fails to catch fire or a great groove without an audience. Prudhomme is an average singer, so you're not able to get much from focusing in on his voice.

influences:
◀◀ John Delafose, Roy Carrier

▶▶ Geno Delafose, Keith Frank, Chubby Carrier

see also: *John Delafose & the Eunice Playboys*

Jared Snyder

Tito Puente
Latin jazz
Born Ernest Anthony Puente Jr., April 20, 1923, in New York, NY, USA. Based in USA.

When the rock group Santana covered "Oye Como Va," a classic Latin hit that Tito Puente had written and recorded, the composer was slightly outraged that such a band would dare sully his music. As soon as the royalty check came (based on massive sales of Santana's first album), Puente discovered the upside of having other people perform his songs. He has prefaced the playing of "Oye Como Va" with that little story many times since then, and come to realize that his music has done as much to promote Latin jazz for current audiences as Machito's did for an earlier generation. Puente's musical career began with Latin groups such as the Cuarteto Caney and, after World War II, Xavier Cugat's band.

In the mid-1940s, after serving in the United States Navy during World War II, Puente came back to New York, where Noro Morales and Machito gave the budding percussionist work.

By the early 1950s he had formed his own ensemble, the Piccadilly Boys, and played the Palladium, New York's cultural mecca for Latin bands. His outfit mutated into the Tito Puente Orchestra and, with lead vocalist Vincentico Valdes, proceeded to change the face of Latin music. Puente took the Cuban *charanga* form and arranged its flutes and violins in more of a big-band jazz context, punching up the brass and reeds for a more powerful sound. He also started using a lot of non-Latin jazz artists, like Doc Severinsen, in his bands, and playing arrangements of jazz standards with a Latin beat. During the 1960s and 1970s Puente recorded albums for GNP, Tico, and Fania with large and small groups, continuing the heavy schedule of touring he had developed in the 1950s. By the 1980s Puente's popularity was even stronger than it had been in the early '50s due to a base of fans that included not only the hard-core Latin music lovers, but a fair number of jazz musicians and enthusiasts as well. It was in 1983 that the multi-talented Puente (timbales, drums, marimba, vibraphone, percussion, vocals, arranging) won the first of his many Grammy Awards, for the album *Tito Puente and His Latin Ensemble on Broadway*. With over 100 releases to his credit, Puente has recorded with most of the major names in Latin music, and has been a leading force in the Latinization of jazz during the last half of the 20th century.

what to buy: The three-CD compilation set *50 Years of Swing* 𝄞𝄞𝄞𝄞𝄞 (RMM, 1997, prod. various) is a perfect starting place for anyone wanting a well-conceived, albeit abridged, introduction to Tito Puente's music. The 50 songs cover his stints with the major pop labels like MCA and RCA, in addition to sampling material from Latin specialty companies like Tico and Westside Latino. His big hits "Para Los Rumberos" and "Oye Como Va" are included, along with distinguished covers of tunes made famous by Machito ("Tanga" and "Babarabatiri"), renditions of jazz classics like "Lullaby of Broadway" and "Moody's Mood for Love," and distinctly cheesy remakes of pop favorites ("Crystal Blue Persuasion"). The two previously unreleased songs— "Llegue" and "I'm Going to Go Fishing"—are adequate performances at best, adding little of real value for non-completists. From the mid-1950s through the early 1960s Puente had one of the hottest bands around, jazz or Latin. The lineup on *The Best of Dance Mania* 𝄞𝄞𝄞𝄞 (BMG/International, 1957–60/1994, prod. Fred Reynolds, Marty Gold) features his second great vocalist (after Vincentico Valdes), Santitos Colon; the remarkable bassist Bobby Rodriguez; and a host of stellar percussionists, including Ray Barretto and Jose Mangual. This CD has 23 cuts, including some previously unreleased outtakes that showcase the care Puente took to craft the perfect performance of a song. His unwillingness to make changes in an arrangement once he had things in place can be heard prior to take number six of "Estoy Siempre Junto a Ti," when he chides a sideman for wasting time "while the light is on" (signifying that the tape was rolling). *Mambo Beat, Vol. 1* 𝄞𝄞𝄞𝄞 (BMG/International, 1956–57/1994, prod. various) is a well-chosen collection (compiled by Domingo Echevarria) featuring performances of jazz material—with a Latin kick—by Puente and his Afro-Cuban Jazz All-Star Orchestras. The arrangers include Puente, Marty Holmes, and one of Machito's ace writers, A.K. Salim. The personnel includes jazz musicians Doc Severinsen, Eddie Bert, Gene Quill, and Jimmy Cobb, plus a bevy of Latin percussion kings like Puente (on timbales and vibes), Mongo Santamaria, Willie Bobo, Candido, and Patato Valdes. Standards like "Yesterdays" by Jerome Kern and Oscar Pettiford's "Bohemia after Dark" (renamed "Birdland after Dark") share space with Puente's own wonderful "Night Ritual" and the percussion-fest "Ti Mon Bo." On *Live at the Village Gate* 𝄞𝄞𝄞𝄞 (RMM, 1992, prod. Alfredo Cruz), Puente leads an all-star group, including Mongo Santamaria, Giovanni Hidalgo, Paquito D'Rivera, and Hilton Ruiz, through a well-selected program of jazz favorites and another hip arrangement of his "Oye Como Va." Especially noteworthy are Miles Davis's "Milestones" and Santamaria's "Afro Blue."

what to buy next: With the exception of the big-band mini-suite "Night Ritual," *Top Percussion* 𝄞𝄞𝄞𝄞 (BMG/International, 1957/1992) is one of the most subversive Latin albums—given the time it first appeared—ever released. *Santería* (controversial Afro-Cuban religion) practitioner Puente released this album of polyrhythmic percussion honoring the *orishas* (deities) decades before Milton Cardona's classic *Bembe*. Alongside Mongo Santamaria, Willie Bobo, and a quartet of Cuban vocalists (including the great Mercedita), Puente went for percussion heaven, conducting a textbook example of how exciting and challenging his music can be. Constructed mainly for people with a minimal budget who want to start exploring Puente's voluminous catalog, *El Rey Del Timbal! The Best of Tito Puente & His Orchestra* 𝄞𝄞𝄞𝄞 (Rhino, 1997, prod. various) is a good single-disc sampler of Puente's material, covering the period from 1949 to 1987. Production is very good but this compilation still does not replace *50 Years of Swing*. *Special Delivery* 𝄞𝄞𝄞𝄞 (Concord Picante, 1996, prod. John Burk, Tito Puente) is a big-band jazz album surveying the bebop and post-bop composers whom Puente is most comfortable with—Dizzy Gillespie, Thelonious Monk, and Horace Silver. Puente features trumpeter Maynard Ferguson on Gillespie's "Be-Bop" and on the classic tune "On Green Dolphin Street," but his normal complement of players, like trumpeters Michael Philip Mossman, Bobby Shew, and Ray Vega, are just about as good. Solid playing throughout makes this a satisfying choice for those who want Puente in a "pure" jazz setting. In addition to his talents on timbales and other assorted percussion instruments, Puente is a gifted vibes player, and *Mambo of the Times* 𝄞𝄞𝄞𝄞

Tito Puente

(Concord Picante, 1992, prod. John Burk, Allen Farnham, Tito Puente) displays some of his best work in that regard. His playing on Fats Waller's "Jitterbug Waltz" is firmly within the jazz camp even as his supporting cast flits about his melodic statement like Latin fireflies. Puente's vibes on Billy Strayhorn's beautiful ballad "Passion Flower" cut another gem. *The Mambo King* 𝄞𝄞𝄞 (RMM, 1991, prod. Sergio George) is Puente's 100th album, marking a significant milestone in his career. More of a Latin recording than a straight jazz session, the album features Puente joined by major Latin vocal stars like Oscar D'Leon, Celia Cruz, Ismael Miranda, and Tito Nieves. The performance standard is suitably high and the playing is professional yet relaxed. The discography included in the negligible liner notes leads the reader through the honor roll of Puente's albums prior to this one. And then there is *Live at Birdland: Dancemania '99* 𝄞𝄞𝄞 (RMM, 1998, prod. Tito Puente), an attempt to capture the magic of a night at the Palladium, New York City's Latin music headquarters during the 1950s. Sonny Bravo, Puente's longtime pianist, leads an amazing band of players, including saxophonists Mario Rivera and Bobby Porcelli, trombonist J.P. Torres, and special guest flautist Dave Valentin. The performances are exciting, with remakes of "Babarabatiri" and "Complicación" leading the pack.

best of the rest:

Goza Mi Timbal 𝄞𝄞𝄞𝄞 (Concord Picante, 1990)
Out of This World 𝄞𝄞𝄞 (Concord Picante, 1991)
In Session 𝄞𝄞𝄞𝄞 (RMM, 1994)
Tito's Idea 𝄞𝄞𝄞 (RMM, 1996)
Concord Jazz Heritage Series 𝄞𝄞𝄞 (Concord Picante, 1998)
Oye Como Va: The Dance Collection 𝄞𝄞𝄞𝄞 (Concord Picante, 1998)

influences:

◄◄ Machito, Mario Bauzá, Dizzy Gillespie, Gene Krupa

►► Guilherme Franco, Cal Tjader, Carlos Santana

see also: *Ray Barretto, Milton Cardona, Celia Cruz, Xavier Cugat, Paquito D'Rivera, Oscar D'Leon, Machito, Charlie Palmieri, Patato, Poncho Sanchez, Arturo Sandoval, Mongo Santamaria*

Garaud MacTaggart

Roberto Pulido

Tejano
Born 1940s, in Edinburg, TX, USA. Based in Edinburg, TX, USA.

Roberto Pulido lost some of his hearing in a truck accident when he was two years old. Like many in his family he also grew up working in the fields, picking produce in California during harvest season. Pulido managed to graduate from Edinburg High School, cop a music scholarship at Pan American University, and get a degree that would let him earn a living teaching music in high schools. While his day job brought in some cash, Pulido still wanted to perform, and he played gigs in area clubs to that end. In the early 1970s he took a big step towards Tex-Mex stardom when he finally opted to concentrate on his music-making. He started putting together the band Los Clásicos in 1973 as a deliberate blend of the *conjunto* style popularized by accordionist Narciso Martinez and the *orquesta tejana* style typified by Beto Villa's saxophone-laden lineup. Pulido's first recordings were with the San Antonio–based company GCP, but he found more success in 1976 with Falcón, a label that developed Pulido and Los Clásicos into one of the top acts on the *Tejano* (contemporary Tex-Mex) circuit. His more recent albums have started blending synthesizers into the arrangements, thus keeping up with trends and maintaining his position in the marketplace. Pulido and his band have also turned into cultural icons, routinely honored at the Tejano Music Awards and constantly working to broaden their fan base. Pulido's sons and daughters have proven to be talented musicians as well—Bobby is a budding Tejano star, Alma is often Roberto's duet partner, Roel and Joel once anchored the saxophone section, and Leonel is quite a classy accordionist in his own right—adding yet another dimension to the influence their dad has had on the genre.

what to buy: Some of Pulido's Falcón hits show up on *Roberto Pulido Y Los Clásicos* 𝄞𝄞𝄞𝄞 (Rounder/Easydisc, 1997, compilation prod. Louisa Hufstader). Most of the album features *rancheras* (sentimental songs) and *cumbias* (dance numbers), with the accordion weaving through saxophone lines while Pulido's vocals soar over the mix. The "Schottische"—both the name of a track here and of a style passed on to Tex-Mex culture, much the same as polkas and waltzes were—is an interesting legacy of the time when Texas's German and Czech settlers hired Tejano musicians for their social functions. *Através de los Año* 𝄞𝄞𝄞𝄞 (EMI Latin, 1996, prod. Roberto Pulido) is one of the most interesting things the artist has done in years—perhaps in spite of itself. Pulido isn't really working the "authenticity" angle as defined by Santiago Jimenez Jr., and while the stylistic innovations that Pulido helped pioneer are all here, the arrangements almost make this a pop album. It's almost too slick; a kind of Tejano Abba. But the melodies and the danceable pulse are very seductive.

what to buy next: A very good budget collection of Pulido's early 1990s work for EMI Latin, *12 Super Exitos* 𝄞𝄞𝄞𝄞 (EMI Latin, 1994, prod. Roberto Pulido) has some fine performances, but also includes a move towards the Anglo market with a conjunto version of Hank Williams's "Jambolaya" (sic). *Toro Prieto* 𝄞𝄞𝄞𝄞 (EMI Latin, 1995, prod. Roberto Pulido, Hugo Rodriguez, Brando Mireles) was a big hit with fans. During the 16th Annual Tejano Music Awards it secured nominations for Vocal Duo of the Year (for "Me Desperto La Realidad" with his daughter Alma), Male Entertainer of the Year, Tejano Video of the Year (for the title song), and Album of the Year/Conjunto Progressive. Synthesizers, harps, and nylon-string guitars blend in with the accordion/sax sound Pulido helped pioneer, but they almost gild the lily. Luckily the vocals are wonderful.

best of the rest:
Roberto Pulido y Los Clásicos Live 𝄞𝄞𝄞𝄞 (EMI Latin, 1993)
Te Vi Partir 𝄞𝄞𝄞 (EMI Latin, 1994)

worth searching for: An admirable, wide-ranging introduction to Tejano music can be found in *¡Conjunto! Texas-Mexican Border Music, Volume 3* 𝄞𝄞𝄞𝄞 (Rounder, 1990, compilation prod. Carl Finch). Pulido's "Accordeones alegres de Irineo Torres" (an atypical hit of his for the Freddie label) is his sole contribution here, but it provides a taste of how good the early stuff from his band was when it hugged the tradition instead of tinkering with it. Other legendary performers included on this set are Valeria Longoria, Tony de la Rosa, and Steve Jordan. Even though it's now out of print, *Si Te Decides* 𝄞𝄞𝄞𝄞 (EMI Latin, 1992, prod. Roberto Pulido) contains some wonderful material that makes hunting it up worthwhile. Included are an updated version of Salome Gutierrez's classic "Vagar Sin Esperanza," and Leonel Pulido's swinging accordion showpiece "Griselda."

influences:
◀◀ Beto Villa, Narciso Martinez, Valeria Longoria, Conjunto Bernal

▶▶ Bobby Pulido, Alma Pulido, La Tropa F

Garaud MacTaggart

Flora Purim

Brazilian jazz, jazz fusion
Born 1942, in Rio de Janeiro, Brazil. Based in USA.

With a soulful, six-and-a-half-octave range, Flora Purim is one of contemporary jazz and world music's most distinctive vocalists. Her collaborations with Chick Corea in the early 1970s were influential on the early development of jazz fusion, and her solo albums and recordings with her husband, percussionist Airto Moreira, have spotlighted her unique instrument-like approach to vocalizing.

The daughter of amateur classical musicians, Purim was exposed to the jazz recordings of pianist Erroll Garner and vocalists Billie Holiday and Ella Fitzgerald as a youngster. Studying guitar at the age of 14, Purim made her professional debut six years later, singing a mixture of jazz standards and songs by leading Brazilian composers like Antonio Carlos Jobim and Egberto Gismonti. After meeting and falling in love with Moreira,

Purim was introduced to the African-influenced music of Brazil's Bahia region.

Moving with Moreira to New York in 1968, Purim became a frequent singer at late-night jam sessions at bassist Walter Booker's home, where she and Moreira temporarily resided. During one session, she sang with saxophonist Stan Getz and pianist Chick Corea; Getz subsequently hired her to tour with his band. Purim later recorded with pianist Duke Pearson and performed with pianist-composer Gil Evans, in whose band she met tenor saxophonist Joe Henderson and bassist Stanley Clarke. Purim's biggest break to this point came when she joined a band that Corea was forming with Clarke, flute player Joe Farrell, and her husband. The band recorded two seminal albums in this configuration: the eponymous *Return to Forever* in 1972 and *Light As a Feather* in 1973. Purim continued to evolve after studying the Stanislavsky method, which helped her to expand her vocal range even further, and working with voice coach and mentor Hermeto Pascoal.

Purim's first American solo album, *Butterfly Dreams,* was released in 1973, and it included her rendition of Corea's tune "Light As a Feather." Together with Moreira, Purim turned out a number of memorable albums on the Milestone label in the mid-1970s. In 1974, she received prestigious recognition from *Down Beat* magazine as Best Female Vocalist. The same year, however, she was arrested for possession of cocaine and placed in a California prison for 18 months. Following her release, Purim resumed her solo career. Signing with Warner Bros. in 1977, Purim and Moreira took a more commercial approach to their music. The pair have also had a long association with Grateful Dead percussionist and world-music impresario Mickey Hart. In addition to collaborating with him on the atmospheric cross-cultural album *Däfos,* released in 1985, they have more recently recorded and toured with Hart's percussionist supergroup, Planet Drum.

what to buy: Purim and Moreira reached their peak with *500 Miles* 𝄞𝄞𝄞𝄞 (Milestone, 1976, prod. Orrin Keepnews). Recorded during their performance at the Montreux Jazz Festival on June 6, 1974, the album is a memorable fusion of Brazilian and jazz influences. Its high point comes during "Cravo e Canela," featuring the song's composer, Milton Nascimento, on guitar and vocal harmonies.

what to buy next: Recorded in the studio a month after their Montreux performance, *Stories to Tell* 𝄞𝄞𝄞𝄞 (Milestone, 1974/Fantasy, 1988, prod. Orrin Keepnews) was one of Purim's last true jazz masterpieces. In addition to her husband's expressive percussion playing, Purim's vocals are ably backed by such stellar jazz musicians as pianists McCoy Tyner, Hemeto Pascoal, and George Duke, and tenor saxophonist Joe Henderson.

best of the rest:

Flora E M.P.M. ♫♫♫ (RCA, 1964)

Butterfly Dreams ♫♫♫ (Milestone, 1974/Fantasy, 1988)

Open Your Eyes, You Can Fly ♫♫♫ (Milestone, 1976)

Encounter ♫♫♫ (Milestone, 1977/Fantasy, 1994)

That's What She Said ♫♫♫ (Milestone, 1978)

Love Reborn ♫♫♫ (Milestone, 1980)

Brazilian Heatwave ♫♫♫ (Accord, 1982)

(With Mickey Hart and Airto Moreira) *Däfos* ♫♫♫♫ (Reference, 1985/Rykodisc, 1988)

(With Airto Moreira) *Humble People* ♫♫♫ (George Wein Collection/Concord, 1985)

(With Airto Moreira) *The Magicians* ♫♫♫ (Crossover/Concord, 1986)

(With Airto Moreira and Joe Farrell) *Three Way Mirror* ♫♫♫ (Reference, 1987)

Milestone Memories ♫♫♫ (BGP, 1988)

(With Airto Moreira) *The Colours of Life* ♫♫♫ (In + Out, 1988)

Midnight Sun ♫♫♫ (Venture/Virgin Records, 1988)

(With Airto Moreira) *The Sun Is Out* ♫♫♫ (Crossover/Concord, 1989)

Queen of the Night ♫♫♫ (Sound Wave, 1992)

Now Go Ahead and Open Your Eyes ♫♫♫ (B&W, 1994)

Speed of Light ♫♫♫ (B&W, 1995)

influences:

◀◀ Billie Holiday, Ella Fitzgerald, Erroll Garner, Antonio Carlos Jobim, Milton Nascimento, Egberto Gismonti

▶▶ Rachelle Ferrell, Carla Bley

see also: *Mickey Hart, Airto Moreira, Milton Nascimento, Badal Roy*

                                                    Craig Harris

Queen Ida
/Ida Guillory

Zydeco

Born January 15, 1929, in Lake Charles, LA, USA. Based in CA, USA.

Born in Lake Charles, Louisiana, Ida Guillory's family followed the exodus of many Creole families to the San Francisco Bay region. She brought the music of her childhood with her to the West Coast but performed exclusively at social functions. While raising her children and driving a bus part-time, she borrowed brother Al Rapone's accordion and started practicing. With the encouragement of brothers Al and Wilbert Lewis, Ida began to perform in the Bay Area. The rarity of her stature as a female accordion player has overshadowed her talent on the three-row accordion, but increased the demand for her. Ida's music has a less intense

beat than the music of bands working southwest Louisiana, and the English lyrics are easier to make out than those of most zydeco bands, but when the band breaks down to the drums, *frattoir* (washboard), and Ida's accordion, there is no denying the roots of her music. Ida, who is known to fans as "Queen," should be proud of the number of female zydeco performers following in her footsteps, including Rosie Ledet and Anne Goodley.

what to buy: *Cookin' with Queen Ida* ♫♫♫♫ (GNP, 1989, prod. Neil Norman) demonstrates the Queen Ida sound: zydeco mixed with rock and blues, with a lot more backing and harmony vocals than you'll probably ever hear from a Louisiana zydeco band (except maybe Double Clutchin'). Her son, Myrick "Freeze" Guillory, contributes accordion, frattoir, and vocals.

what to buy next: *Band on Tour* ♫♫♫♫ (GNP, 1982, prod. Neil Norman), winner of the 1982 Grammy Award for Best Ethnic/Traditional Folk Album, finds Ida's sound geared toward an audience that is mostly English-speaking and from the lands outside of southwest Louisiana. The mix is lighter and more rock-oriented.

best of the rest:

Zydeco ♫♫ (GNP, 1976)

In New Orleans ♫♫♫ (GNP, 1980)

Caught in the Act ♫♫♫ (GNP, 1985)

Zydeco a la Mode (GNP, 1987)

Play the Zydeco (GNP, 1987)

On a Saturday Night ♫♫♫ (GNP, 1987)

In San Francisco ♫♫♫ (GNP, 1988)

Mardi Gras ♫♫♫♫ (GNP, 1994)

worth searching for: The cookbook *Cookin' with Queen Ida: "Bon Temps" Creole Recipes (and Stories) from the Queen of Zydeco Music* (Prima Publishing, 1990), by Queen Ida Guillory and Naomi Wise, is full of stories about Queen Ida and Creole music. The food is great, as are the stories.

influences:

◀◀ Amédée Ardoin, Boozoo Chavis, Canray Fontenot, Clifton Chenier

▶▶ Beau Jocque, Zachary Richard

                                                    Jared Snyder

Radio Tarifa

Pan-Mediterranean/International

Formed 1993, in Madrid, Spain. Based in Madrid, Spain.

Rotating lineup; core members include: Faín Sanchez Dueñas (Spain), guitar, percussion, bass, keyboards, vocals, banjo, bouzouki,

Queen Ida

arrangements, musical director; Vincent Molino (France), crumhorn, ney, Poitou oboe, flute; Benjamin Escoriza (Spain), vocals, jaleos.

Radio Tarifa exemplifies what "world" music is all about. The group's name comes from Tarifa, a port on the strait of Gibraltar in southern Spain, from which you can actually see Africa. And the music Radio Tarifa produces—a blend of flamenco, Middle Eastern, North African, and medieval European styles with a solidly contemporary feel; just check out the funk bass on several tracks of their second CD, *Temporal* —is exactly what you might hear on a radio station based in Tarifa. The band evolved from musical activities group-leader Faín Sanchez Dueñas was involved with in the 1980s. He and Vincent Molino played in Ars Antiqua Musicalis, an outfit that specialized in music from 12th-century France, Italy, and Spain. Dueñas also played in flamenco groups and had a trio playing rumbas in Madrid bars. Dueñas, Molino, and Benjamin Escoriza came together as the core of Radio Tarifa in 1993. They're augmented by other musicians for recording and live dates, but Dueñas is definitely the boss. As he explained to journalist Lois Darlington in an article for the English magazine *Folk Roots*: "I plan everything. First I choose the songs. Then I ask my colleague if he likes it or wants to sing it—he says 'yes' or 'no' and so on until I choose the right song for him. Then I work out all the instruments and who is going to play them. Normally on the record I play nearly everything—strings, bass, percussion, and keyboards. When we record, it is usually me and the individual musicians—never the whole group. Most of the songs are for Benjamin but I also choose other songs for other singers"; some of those others can be heard in concert. As Dueñas pointed out to Patricia Garcia-Rios of the U.S. folk publication *Dirty Linen,* "Our live lineup doesn't necessarily match the one we use when we record. Radio Tarifa live is very different; more imperfect, but also more alive." To date Radio Tarifa has released only two full-length recordings, *Rumba Argelina* and *Temporal,* but work on a third has begun.

what's available: *Rumba Argelina* 🎵🎵🎵🎵 (World Circuit/Nonesuch, 1995, prod. Juan A. Arteche) consists of traditional lyrics set to new music, traditional music with new lyrics, or completely original (though tradition-based) compositions. Many people will think "Middle East," but that's just one flavor in Radio Tarifa's musical smorgasbord. For instance, "Soledad," an original Dueñas composition, is very trance-like but also uses flamenco-ish runs and snatches of loud electric guitar. "La Canal," with music by Dueñas and lyrics from Escoriza, sounds like a fusion of belly-dancing and medieval music. There are elegant choral vocals (reminiscent of Steeleye Span's interpretation of "Gaudete"), and the crumhorn gives the arrangement its distinctive medieval flavor. On *Temporal* ☝☝☝☝ (World Circuit/Nonesuch, 1997, prod. Faín S. Dueñas, Vincent Molino), Radio Tarifa delves more into flamenco, but there are still lots of other soundscapes to explore. Particularly satisfying is their arrangement of "El Mandil de Carolina," a traditional Castilian and Galician (Spanish Celtic) piece. This number rocks, with fast rhythms and a wild melody line played on Poitou oboe. There's also a stately 12th-century "processional" from France played on the definitely different array of Poitou oboe, *ney* (Turkish reed flute), tenor saxophone, *oud* (Arabic lute), electric bass, and percussion.

influences:

◄◄ Blowzabella, 3 Mustaphas 3, Gryphon, Malicorne, flamenco, Ofra Haza

►► Tayfa, Yosefa, Adaro

Ken Roseman

Rail Band /Super Rail Band of Bamako

Big-band Malian dance music, pop arrangements of Manding classics
Formed 1970, in Bamako, Mali. Based in Bamako, Mali.

Large, evolving membership over the years. In the early '70s, star members included: Salif Keita, lead vocals; Mory Kanté, lead vocals; Djelimady Tounkara (still current), lead guitarist. Most recent recorded lineup also includes: Kabiné Keita, saxophones; Mamadou Ouedraogo, saxophones; Fotigui Keita, bass; Ali Dembelé, rhythm guitar; Maguette Diop, drums; Lassana Bagayogo, percussion; Bamba Dembelé, percussion; Damory Kouyaté, lead vocals; Samba Sissoko, vocals; Adama Fomba, vocals.

In 1970, Mali's Ministry of Information decided to sponsor a cultural big band to operate in the capital of Bamako at the train-station hotel, the Buffet Hôtel de la Gare. It was a time when the government was cutting back on more ambitious means of promoting Malian musical culture. The great national ensembles launched by Mali's first president, Modibo Keita, were on the way out. From the start, the Rail Band preserved the best of the old vision: to take Mali's proud traditions and make them relevant as modern pop music. The band also did something that would have been hard to envision—they became a commercial success.

That was largely due to the sensational musicians involved. To name only the most significant ones, singers Salif Keita and

Mory Kanté (of neighboring Guinea) were both destined to become international superstars in the era of Afropop a decade or more later; each got his start in the Rail Band. And Djelimady Tounkara, arguably the greatest living guitarist in Africa, remains the solid center of the modern Rail Band to this day. In every era, though, the lineup has had a genius for taking classics from the repertoire of the Manding *griots* (oral historians) and arranging them for present-day electric guitars, horns, bass, drums, percussion, and vocals. In the Rail Band's hands, the epic of the 13th-century Manding king Soundiata became a half-hour dancefloor extravaganza.

Over the years, the outfit has undergone many changes. When Salif Keita left in 1972 to create Les Ambassadeurs, Mory Kanté stepped in to sing lead for the Rail Band, and the two ensembles riveted West Africa with their spirited competition. After both singers had moved on, the Rail Band came to rely more on its instrumental prowess and band chemistry than on star vocalists. Reggae, funk, jazz, and rumba entered the mix. But Manding music has always been the band's mainstay. Tounkara's ability to harness the fleet delicacy of griot music as roaring electric-guitar bravado remains one of the wonders of modern African music.

what to buy: *Mali Stars, Vol. 1: Salif Keita & Mory Kanté* ☝☝☝☝ (Melodie) is the only recording you're likely to find of the original Rail Band. Though not exactly hi-fidelity, this is a classic, especially for its back-to-back presentations of Keita's and Kanté's versions of the Malian epic "Soundiata." *Mansa* ☝☝☝☝ (Indigo, 1995) shows the band in its modern glory.

the rest:
New Dimensions in Rail Culture ☝☝☝☝ (GlobeStyle, 1985)

influences:

◄◄ Orchestre Nationale du Mali

►► Les Ambassadeurs du Motel, virtually all Malian bands formed since 1975

see also: *Mory Kanté, Salif Keita, Talking Heads*

Banning Eyre

RAM

Vodou rock
Formed 1990, in Port-au-Prince, Haiti. Based in Port-au-Prince, Haiti.

Richard Morse (USA), leader, lead vocals; Lunise Morse, lead vocals; Wilson Theluce, drums; Jean Mary Brignol, drums; Robert Wood Romain, drums; Jose Modelus, bass; Onito Parfait, guitar; Emmanuel Marcelin, keyboards; Yonel Justin, Roland Octapad; Sylvain Jean, backing vocals; Patau Lindor, backing vocals; Jonas Jean, horns; Pierre Jules, horns. (All members are from Haiti except where noted otherwise.)

Richard Morse grew up in New Haven, Connecticut, where

his father was a retired professor of Latin American studies. His mother was born in Haiti, and his maternal grandfather, Candido, wrote "Yellow Bird" for Harry Belafonte. After graduating from Princeton, Morse played in a series of punk bands but at the same time was becoming curious about his Haitian heritage. In 1985 he moved to Haiti and became manager of the Oloffoson Hotel. One of his duties was booking bands to perform there, and he began getting acquainted with the local musicians, including a singer named Lunise who eventually became his wife. Morse investigated *Vodou* and after a time was welcomed into the religion. In 1990 he decided to combine the Afro-Haitian music he was learning with the rock 'n' roll of his youth and formed RAM. Having the hotel as a springboard helped the new band achieve instant credibility. Their first album, *Aïbobo,* was a hit, with the single "Labonit (Banging Drums)" hitting #1 on Haitian radio. The band was included on the soundtrack of *Philadelphia* thanks to director Jonathan Demme's love of Haitian culture. Jimmy Buffett saw them perform at the New Orleans Heritage and Jazz Festival in 1996 and signed them to his Margaritaville label.

what's available: Singing in English may give Morse and company a slight edge in cracking a large world-music market share, but it's doubtful that Boukman Eksperyans are staying up late worrying about the competition. RAM may be a kickin' live band, but on *Puritan Vodou* 𝄞𝄞𝄞 (Margaritaville, 1998, prod. Richard Morse) only the extended cut "Zanj" builds up any steam; most of this sounds like worldbeat custom-made for AOR programmers.

influences:

◀◀ Boukan Ginen, Boukman Eksperyans, Manno Charlemagne

▶▶ Tropicana, Foula

j. poet

Hossam Ramzy

Egyptian folk music, Arabic jazz, worldbeat
Born 1954, in Cairo, Egypt. Based in London, England.

Ramzy is acknowledged as a master percussionist throughout the Arabic and world-music communities. He has played sessions with a wide cross-section of international musicians including Peter Gabriel, Rachid Taha, Maryam Mursal, Loreena McKennitt, Boy George, E.L.O., and the Rolling Stones. Ramzy's highest-profile rock gig (so far) came when Jimmy Page and Robert Plant asked him to put together and lead a band for their historic "No Quarter" reunion tour of 1995.

Ramzy began playing the Egyptian *tabla*—not to be confused with the Indian drum of the same name, and known in the

jamaican music 3: mento

From the 1930s to the early '50s, *mento* was Jamaica's primary pop-cultural music. Like its forebear calypso and its progeny reggae, mento is a rhythm-propelled sound that incorporates the passions, concerns, and speech patterns of an African-descended people into a distinctive and rich indigenous culture. In mento, antiphonal call-and-response vocals are accompanied by instruments including the bamboo fife (popularized by perhaps the greatest mento artist, Sugar Belly Walker), banjo, bass drum, fiddle, rumba box (a large thumb piano), guitar, piccolo, and occasionally saxophone, along with a panoply of hand-made percussion instruments—such as shakers and scrapers built from bamboo, calabash, various organic seeds, metal graters, and sardine cans.

Mento used humor more prominently than previous Jamaican genres, and its lyrics were often unabashedly loaded with double-entendre. The first commercially recorded song in Jamaica's history was Lord Fly's "Whai! Ay!," a mento tune he wrote after experiencing a series of flat tires in the desolate Jamaican countryside, and a quintessential example of this easygoing form's framework for being able to laugh at yourself and your sorry plight. Other important mento artists included Lord Lebby, Count Lasher, Baba Motta, Lord Power, and Harold Richardson & the Ticklers.

Sadly, as with the Delta blues in America, the vibrancy and relevance of the music faded when severe economic hardship spurred country dwellers to migrate *en masse* to the urban centers. Though the style persists primarily as a cultural artifact, later musics' roots in it run deep to this day—to name but one vital vein, the rhythm for the mento song "Dog War a Matches Lane" was later used by the Maytals on their ska classic "Dog War," and now finds valuable currency in the digital "riddims" of ragga. There are also still a few mento artists devoted to reviving the form, including the Blue Glades, the Lititz Mento Band, and the peerless Jolly Boys, who have been happily performing the music for nearly 50 years.

see also: The Jolly Boys

Todd Shanker

West as a *dumbek*—at the age of three. He came from an artistic family, and they recognized his talents and arranged for him to study with Cairo's leading percussionists. As a young man he traveled throughout Saudi Arabia, where he learned traditional Bedouin drumming and singing. In the mid-1970s, Ramzy moved to England to begin a professional career as a jazz drummer, but he soon returned to the traditional music of his youth. He put together a band, and his first album, *Introduction to Egyptian Dance Rhythms,* became an instant classic, with both Arabic and European fans praising the music for its melodic and rhythmic innovations. In 1987 Peter Gabriel asked Ramzy to help with the soundtrack to Martin Scorsese's *The Last Temptation of Christ.* This led to work on Gabriel's *Us* as well as gigs and recording dates with Joan Armatrading, Ann Dudley, Big Country, Marc Almond, and others. Between pop sessions, Ramzy leads his own band, Hossam Ramzy & His Egyptian Ensemble, a group that plays slick arrangements of traditional Arabic music aimed at dancers.

what to buy: *Egyptian Rai* ♫♫♫ (ARC U.K., 1994, prod. Hossam Ramzy) is one of Ramzy's hottest albums, a set of "Arabic fusion" in which he weaves together elements of music from Algeria, Morocco, Egypt, Lebanon, Kuwait, Saudi Arabia, and more, to give listeners what he calls "an eagle's eye view of the Arabic world." The music is full of hard-driving rhythms and stunning musicianship, including the Pan-Arabic hit "Wah Wah."

what to buy next: *Ahlamy* ♫♫♫ (ARC U.K., 1996, prod. Hossam Ramzy) is a collaboration with Rafat Misso, a virtuoso on the quarter tone saxophone, an instrument not widely used in Arabic music. Misso is the most in-demand sax player in Egypt, and he jumped at a chance to collaborate with Ramzy. The set includes several *baladi* (a type of urbanized folk dance) composed by Misso, some favorite Egyptian pop tunes, and folk songs. The tempos are slower than on *Egyptian Rai,* to highlight Misso's inspired improvisations.

best of the rest:

Best of Umm Kulthum ♫♫♫ (ARC U.K., 1994)
Source of Fire ♫♫♫♫ (ARC U.K., 1995)
Gamaal Rawhany—Soulful Beauty ♫♫♫♫ (ARC U.K., 1996)
Best of Baladi & Saaidi ♫♫♫♫ (ARC U.K., 1997)
(With Phil Thornton) *Immortal Egypt* ♫♫♫ (New World Music, 1998)

influences:

◄◄ Umm Kulthum, Sheikh Sayed Darweesh, Abd el-Halim Hafez, Mohamed Abdel Wahab

see also: *Farid al-Atrash, Page & Plant, Rachid Taha*

j. poet

Ernest Ranglin

Reggae, jazz

Born June 19, 1932, in Robin's Hall, Jamaica. Based in Kingston, Jamaica.

Ernest Ranglin has an international reputation as a jazz guitarist and arranger, but it's his work in the field of popular music that will probably secure his place in history. In 1959 Ranglin cut an instrumental called "Shuffling Bug" for Clement "Coxsone" Dodd's Federal Records. It was an attempt to cash in on the New Orleans shuffle rhythm then so popular with Jamaican dancers, but when Ranglin and his fellow band members tried to "imitate" American black music, the rhythms came out "wrong." Jamaican folk and roots music share a strong 4/4 foundation with their American counterparts, but the emphasis is on the second and fourth beats, not the first and fourth as it is up north. When Ranglin played the shuffle, the result was ska, a loping riddim that laid the foundation for rocksteady, reggae, dancehall, ragga, and all the other Jamaican forms that have been so influential in world music.

When ska exploded and began replacing American R&B in Jamaica's dancehalls, Ranglin was in constant demand. He backed up Prince Buster and Baba Brooks on their early hits and in 1962 traveled to London at the request of Chris Blackwell, who had recently launched Island Records. Ranglin recorded "My Boy Lollipop" with a singer named Millie. The tune hit #2 on the British pop charts and went on to introduce the rhythms of ska to the world. As ska transformed itself into reggae, Ranglin continued to be in demand. He arranged the Melodians' "Rivers of Babylon" and added lead guitar to Bob Marley's "Hurts to Be Alone" and "I'm Still Waiting."

But despite his pop credentials, Ranglin's true love is jazz. Two uncles had taught him the basics, and hearing the recordings of Charlie Christian had set his course. At 15 he moved to Kingston from his country home of Robin's Hall allegedly to go to school, but he was soon playing in the Eric Deans Orchestra, one of the island's top hotel bands. He learned tunes by Benny Goodman, Stan Kenton, and Duke Ellington, as well as popular Cuban hits and Broadway show tunes. At the same time Ranglin was burning up the pop charts with "My Boy Lollipop," he was in residence at Ronnie Scott's famed jazz club, wowing the critics and topping *Melody Maker*'s annual jazz poll. Ranglin returned to Jamaica in the late '60s, hoping to get on with his jazz career, but pop music came calling again. He worked with Johnny Nash on his reggae-influenced pop hits and joined Jimmy Cliff's touring band until 1973, when he returned to his first musical love, making his Newport Jazz Festival debut with Randy Weston in 1974. Since the '70s Ranglin has toured and recorded with such notables as Stanley Jordan, Charlie Byrd, Tal Farlow, and Jamaica's other jazz giant, pianist Monty Alexander.

Ernest Ranglin

what to buy: Baaba Maal's band, with Maal himself on a couple of lead vocals, sits in with Ranglin on the Afro-Jamaican fusion effort *In Search of the Lost Riddim* 🎵🎵🎵🎵 (Palm Pictures, 1998, prod. Ernest Ranglin, Baaba Maal). On most of his albums, Ranglin's relaxed playing tends to bland out, but when he has someone to play off of, things get interesting—his battle with *tama* (talking drum) player Assane Diop on "Cherie" and the interplay between his guitar and the *kora* (harp-lute) played by Kawding Cissokho (a.k.a. Kaouding Cissoko) on "Nuh True" shows his laid-back style can shoot off sparks in the right setting.

best of the rest:
Ranglin Roots 🎵🎵🎵 (Island, 1977)
Below the Bassline 🎵🎵🎵 (Island Jamaica, 1996)
Memories of Barber Mack 🎵🎵🎵 (Island Jamaica, 1997)

influences:
◄◄ Cecil Houdini, Charlie Christian, Wes Montgomery, Les Paul
►► Bob Marley

see also: *The Congos, Alton Ellis, Baaba Maal, Jackie Mittoo, Sister Carol, the Skatalites*

j. poet

Shabba Ranks
Reggae
Born Rexton Rawlston Fernando Gordon, January 17, 1966, in St. Ann's Parish, Jamaica. Based in Jamaica.

The reigning sex symbol of Jamaican dancehall swing and self-proclaimed "Mr. Loverman," Shabba Ranks—the first reggae artist ever to win a Grammy Award—exploded on the international music scene with a series of crossover hits in the early 1990s, powered by his ragged, booming vocals. Developing his uniquely raunchy rap-and-reggae style for a decade before becoming an overnight sensation, Ranks sang and recorded in small Jamaican clubs and studios under the name "Co-Pilot," enjoying considerable success regionally and in the Caribbean sections of major cities like New York and London. Choosing "Shabba" after two local gangsters with the same name died, Ranks developed a musical variation all his own, combining the sounds of reggae, dancehall, and hip-hop with blatantly sexual lyrics (the latter known as "slackness," though not by Shabba, who beats reformers to the punch by calling his music "X-rated"). During the peak of his stardom from 1989 to '91, he released 50 singles, made a now-legendary helicopter-

Shabba Ranks

drop entrance at the 1989 Reggae Sunsplash festival, won his first of two Grammys for the 1991 LP *As Raw As Ever,* and signed a major three-album deal with Epic/Sony. Immodestly releasing a greatest-hits album the following year, Shabba's meteoric rise was blunted by an accusation of rape (for the fourth time in his life) by a woman who appeared in his "Trailer Loada Girls" video; he compounded the controversy around him with an interview on British television in which he said gays "deserve to be crucified," making him a target of GLAAD protesters. Nonetheless, Ranks claimed a string of crossover U.S. hits, including the Top 10 R&B tunes "Housecall (Your Body Can't Lie to Me)," "Mr. Loverman," "Slow and Sexy," and the #1 remake of Sly & the Family Stone's "Family Affair" off the *Addams Family Values* movie soundtrack. He continues to be an extremely popular attraction outside the U.S., particularly in Japan and Europe.

what to buy: Though he released not one but two "greatest hits" packages called *Rough & Ready* in the early 1990s, the subsequent 1995 double-disc set *Caan Dun: The Best of Shabba ⚞⚞⚞⚞* (VP, 1995, compilation prod. David Sanguinetti,

Derrick Moo-Young), graced with the gift of perspective, stands as a much more fulfilling overview of a dynamically unique performer. The Caribbean hits that spurred his breakout, like "Live Blanket" and "Wicked in Bed," are prominent here, as are the majority of his international victories, led by "Mr. Loverman" and "Best Baby Father." A fine introduction to Shabba in all his guttural, gritty glory.

what to buy next: His second Grammy-winning LP, *X-tra Naked ⚞⚞⚞⚞* (Epic, 1992, prod. Wycliffe Johnson), finds the singer maximizing the style that propelled him to fame while giving the people what he believes they want: all his creativity is concentrated below the waist. Featuring his hit duet with Johnny Gill, "Slow and Sexy," and contributions from rappers Queen Latifah and Chubb Rock, the Shabba beats are fresh, challenging, nasty, and definitely not for the pure of spirit.

what to avoid: A rehashing of Shabba's best tunes repackaged without enhancement, *Shabba Ranks/J.C. Lodge ⚞⚞* (Pow Wow, prod. various) adds nothing significant to his body of recordings, appearing to be more a device to place second-biller Lodge within the fringe of his spotlight.

the rest:

Rappin' with the Ladies 𝄢𝄢𝄢𝄿 (VP, 1988)

Just Reality 𝄢𝄢𝄢𝄢 (VP, 1990)

Best Baby Father 𝄢𝄢 (VP, 1990)

Golden Touch 𝄢𝄢𝄢 (VP, 1990)

As Raw As Ever 𝄢𝄢𝄢𝄢 (Epic, 1991)

Mr. Maximum 𝄢𝄢𝄢 (Pow Wow, 1992)

Rough & Ready, Vol. 1 𝄢𝄢𝄢𝄢 (Epic, 1992)

Rough & Ready, Vol. 2 𝄢𝄢𝄢 (Epic, 1993)

No Competition 𝄢𝄢𝄢 (Critique, 1993)

A Mi Shabba 𝄢𝄢𝄢𝄢 (Epic, 1995)

Get Up Stand Up 𝄢𝄢𝄢𝄢 (Artists Only!, 1998)

Shabba & Friends 𝄢𝄢𝄢𝄿 (Sony, 1999)

worth searching for: A brilliant roster of reggae, funk, and jazz talents—including Sly & Robbie, Bootsy Collins, Herbie Hancock, and Bernie Worrell, with Fred Wesley and Maceo Parker in the horn section—surrounds fellow guest-artist Shabba on the future-pop album from Bill Laswell's Material, *The Third Power* 𝄢𝄢𝄢𝄢 (Axiom, 1991). Ranks isn't the whole show here, but he steals it when he appears.

influences:

◀◀ Yellowman, Josey Wales, General Echo, King Jammy, Brigadier Jerry

▶▶ Maxi Priest, Buju Banton

see also: *Cocoa Tea, Bill Laswell, Maxi Priest*

Andre McGarrity

Enzo Rao

World-jazz fusion

Born in Sicily, Italy. Based in Sicily, Italy.

Born Vincenzo Rao Camemi, this Sicilian violinist/bassist/programmer is best known in the West for his fusion of jazz improvisation and the folk traditions of Italy and the Middle East with his group Shamal, which also features frame drum virtuoso Glen Velez and Sicilian saxophonist Gianni Gebbia. Like many children raised in Europe after World War II, Rao grew up divided between a respect for the deep-rooted traditions of his native land and a love for the modern music of the times, especially jazz and funk. After years of performing professionally in these genres in Italy, he formed Shamal in the early 1990s to, as he says, "sow the seeds of world music throughout the earth."

what's available: Rao's only U.S. release, *Ettna* 𝄢𝄢𝄢𝄢 (Music of the World, 1996, prod. Bob Haddad), showcases Shamal's multitude of talents, with a timeless fusion of styles that seem to know no geographical boundaries. The title track, named after a majestic Sicilian volcano, sets the stage, with funky jazz interludes led by Gebbia's reedy sax solos interspersed between rhythmically invigorating passages driven by Velez's Arabic percussion sounds. Mediterranean references abound, with elements of traditions running from Eastern Europe through the Middle East and down to Morocco. A few songs were directly inspired by Sicilian sources, but Rao's hypnotic violin solo on "Waiting for You" is as specifically traditional as this wide-rangingly inventive album gets. A solid set that leaves you hungry for more.

influences:

◀◀ Shakti, John Zorn's Masada, Oregon

see also: *Glen Velez*

Bret Love

Rara Machine

Mizik rasin (Haitian "roots music"), rara

Formed late 1980s, in Port-au-Prince, Haiti. Based in Port-au-Prince, Haiti.

Clifford Sylvain, lead vocals, percussion, hand drumming, drum programming, leader; Jephte Guillaume, bass, hand drumming, vocals; Welmir J. Pierre, keyboards, piano; Donald Guillaume, drum kit, vocals; Gerald Sylvain, hand drumming, vocals; Bonga Jean Baptiste, hand drumming, vocals; Kenya, dancing, choreography; Nadia, dancing, choreography; Smitty, dancing, choreography; Sheila Degraff, lead vocals; Nadege Bowens, lead vocals; Robert Miller, sax. (All members are from Haiti.)

Clifford Sylvain started making his own drums and playing music at age 12. A few years later he formed a neighborhood band with friends, but his father didn't appreciate his interest in music and gave him a beating; the band broke up. Clifford's older brother was already playing in Boffa Combo, a band that played *compas*, Haiti's "upper class" music (a style the African roots of which had been considerably watered down over the years). Boffa was a favorite of the Duvalier family, and at one of their state parties, Clifford sat in on congas. The enthusiastic reaction of the crowd earned him a place in Boffa Combo's lineup. After finishing high school he played with the Ambassadors, Scorpio Band, and Accolade. In the mid-1980s Clifford moved to New York City to further his studies and started taking classes at the Latin Rhythm School with Mongo Santamaria, Frankie Mabali, and other samba and salsa masters. He played briefly with another New York–based compas band, Ska Shah—who had a hit with his "Min Numerou"—but was generally dissatisfied with their laid-back style. He returned to Haiti after the overthrow of the Duvalier regime, and, inspired by the success of the groundbreaking Boukman Eksperyans, put together Rara Machine. Like the Boukmans, Sylvain based his sound on traditional *Vodou* rhythms with a healthy dose of *rara,* a street-level dance music played at Carnival.

what's available: *Voudou Nou* ✍✍✍ (Shanachie, 1994, prod. Clifford Sylvain) is an album of high-energy Haitian roots music featuring lilting female vocals, swooping basslines, and relentless drumming, topped off by Sylvain's enthusiastic vocals. Solid production, with a taste of dancehall reggae and a couple of semi-traditional tunes that feature the band's drummers and singers. Rara Machine's debut, *Break the Chain* ✍✍✍ (Shanachie, 1991, prod. Clifford Sylvain), is a stunner, with a touch of funky bass, some propulsive horn charts, and a slight Latin rhythmic accent here and there. But mostly it's straight-ahead Carnival music, with a kick drum that'll push any party into overdrive.

influences:

◄ Boukman Eksperyans, Boukan Ginen

j. poet

Rasha

North African and Iberian traditional and pop
Born in Khartoum, Sudan. Based in Madrid, Spain.

Rasha is determined to acquaint the world with the music and culture of her native Sudan, though ironically, due to civil strife, gender inequality, and religious strictures, she finds it safer and more possible to do so outside of Sudan itself. Some of her Sufi Muslim songs would not be allowed by the current orthodox regime, and some would be forbidden to women—as was an education, which Rasha went to Spain to get, soon switching from a literary career to a musical one as her possibilities opened up and her potentials came into view. She has transmitted Sudanese musical tradition to great acclaim and branched out into stylistic hybrids inspired by her adoptive country. (A taste for cultural convergence seems to run in the family; one of Rasha's brothers has played with star Arabic/flamenco fusionists Radio Tarifa.) Rasha has a serene demeanor that belies her rebellious spirit, but which says a lot about how she's attained her considerable goals. That calm is reflected on her debut CD, in a still, sublime, intimately organic sound that may be familiar to fans of Malian diva Oumou Sangare. But the similarities are purely atmospheric; the style is all Rasha's own. She's come far through a quiet confidence in her talents, and in the worthiness of giving expression to the unique voices in her head—and her audiences never need much convincing either.

what's available: Rasha's first release, *Sudaniyat* ✍✍✍✍ (NubeNegra/Alula, 1997), is a gourmet blend of Sufi, Sudanese, Nubian, and even some Jamaican sounds, with sultry sax, swooning strings and woodwinds, and rhythms by turns lilting and languid all shimmering beneath Rasha's subtle siren voice. You need Rasha's songs on *La Sal de la Vida (The Spice of Life)* ✍✍✍✍ (NubeNegra/Alula, 1998), an album of trios, duos, and solos centered around Our Heroine, Galician (Spanish Celtic)/Portuguese vocalist Uxía, and Castilian singer María Salgado. The Iberian influence is in the ascendant throughout the album, and after Rasha's restraint on *Sudaniyat* you'll skip a breath at her commanding, vivacious delivery here. Xesús Pimentel's chiming flamenco guitar arrangements are priceless, Rasha's percussion arrangements are endlessly inventive and energizing, Salgado is a rising star to watch, and Uxía matches Salgado's passion if not always her full timbre.

worth searching for: The two albums above are well available in the U.S., but perhaps not as ubiquitously as Putumayo World Music's fine *Romantica* compilation and even finer *Women of Spirit* one, each of which has a song from *Sudaniyat* and much more from a number of important and often hard-to-find artists. (*Women* is also reviewed in this book's Compilations section.)

influences:

◄ Abed Azrié, Radio Tarifa

Adam McGovern

Ravel

Merengue
Born in Sabana Grande de Boya, Dominican Republic. Based in New York, NY, USA.

Ravel is a multi-talented singer, artist, and actor who emigrated to the U.S. when he was still a boy. His first singing gig, in his teens, was with Los Reyes del Caribe Orchestra. He formed his own band, Los Bravos, soon after, and recorded three albums with them. In 1993 the singer started his own label, Camino, and produced two hit-filled albums for it; the second, *Llego El Tipo*, won two Estrellas del Merengues (an award in his field), for Most Popular Orchestra and Most Distinguished Artist. He recently signed a worldwide deal with RMM, which should gain him a considerably higher profile.

what to buy: Ravel's smooth tenor and the band's intense, energetic attack makes *Llego El Tipo* ✍✍✍ (Camino, 1995, prod. Victor Waill, Ravel) swing from start to finish. Includes the hits "El Meneo," "Dondé Están Las Mujeres," and "Celosos."

what to buy next: Ravel's first major-label offering, *Alma, Ritmo y Pueblo* ✍✍✍ (RMM, 1997, prod. various), continues his winning formula—high-energy arrangements, catchy tunes, and inspired vocals, which have acquired a pleasingly sensuous mid-range as he's matured.

the rest:

Como Tu Lo Querias ✍✍✍ (Camino, 1993)
Ravel ✍✍✍ (J&N)
Amor de Verdad ✍✍✍ (J&N)
El Tercero ✍✍✍ (J&N)

influences:

◀◀ Johnny Ventura, Wilfrido Vargas, Juan Luis Guerra

j. poet

Red Plastic Bag

Calypso, soca
Born Stedson Wiltshire, c. 1960, in Barbados. Based in Barbados.

Those who've only just discovered Bajan (Barbadian) music through the red-hot soca ("SOul-CAlypso") group krosfyah may not know that the island's flourishing calypso scene has long rivaled that of Trinidad and Tobago. Red Plastic Bag (or RPB), a perennial crowd-pleaser who belongs to the generation of accomplished veterans that includes Gabby, Grynner, and Ras Iley, proves this axiom with a vengeance. His lyrical and melodic wit and agility (not to mention his characteristically piercing diction) have won him four "Pic-O-De-Crop" titles (Barbados's equivalent of Trinidad's National Calypso Monarchy), the first in 1982—he was then the youngest ever to win the crown—and the most recent in 1996. Since his reputation as a serious-minded calypsonian is secure, his recent makeover from "De Lyrical Master" to "De Ragga Soca King" (ragga soca indicating the presence of "raggamuffin"-style dancehall chat and a languorous *tassa*-drum beat), far from being some career-resuscitating gimmick, only adds to his standing and versatility.

Red Plastic Bag (the name is a kind of anti-sobriquet that pokes fun at calypsonians' traditionally grandiose titles) first came to the notice of U.S. listeners on Shanachie's out-of-print 1988 compilation *When the Time Comes: Rebel Soca* with the irresistible "Cannot Find Me Brother." This punchy party tune about a famously unlocatable desperado clearly demonstrated RPB's strong suit: a shrewd ability to cross the high-energy with the hard-hitting, producing party soca that eschews the prefix "mindless." His penchant for clever and sophisticated verse—especially for subtle innuendo and extended metaphorical conceits—also applies to the slower-paced, more lyrically complex traditional calypso, though you'd scarcely know it from any of his releases currently available in the U.S.

what to buy: Not that there's anything wrong with those Stateside releases: the superlative *One More* ⫘⫘⫘⫘ (WIRL, 1996, prod. Nicholas Brancker, Mac Fingall, Stedson Wiltshire) culls six of the best tunes (including the atomic-powered, flag-waving road march "Hittin de Front" and the gleeful ragga soca "One More") from RPB's two previous LPs—*Hittin de Front* (Bayfield, 1994) and *Someting in de Music* (Bayfield, 1995)—and combines them with an equal number of compatriot-sidekick Mac Fingall's hits from the same period (including the Pan-Caribbean novelty-soca smash "Big Belly Man"). *Bajan Invasion* ⫘⫘⫘ (WIRL, 1996, prod. various) exploits both the proven

commercial success of the RPB-Mac pairing and Bajan road march composers' overrunning of Trinidad's 1996 Carnival. It's a weaker album overall, even though it comprises all of Red Plastic Bag's LP of the same year, *Riding de Riddim* (Bayfield, 1996)—which featured the prize-winning, anti-downsizing soca "Give It to Me" and the topical calypso on confusing notoriety with heroism, "Issue of de Day."

worth searching for: It's in the nature of calypso albums to disappear within a year or two of their release, and this means that much of RPB's work on LP is long gone. (We can only hope for a greatest-hits anthology!) That said, you won't go wrong with anything out of the RPB back catalog that happens to fall into your hands. Most recently out of print is the first joint effort with Mac Fingall, *Happiness* ⫘⫘⫘ (WIRL, 1993, prod. Nicholas Brancker, Mac Fingall), which again blends the contents of RPB's solid LP of the same name (Bayfield, 1993) with good-naturedly raunchy novelty songs by Mac. RPB's most recent releases—the buoyant *plastic@calypso.com* ⫘⫘⫘ (Bayfield, 1997, prod. Nicholas Brancker, Stedson Wiltshire), whose anchor tune "On Line" metaphorically questions national priorities; and last year's *Unlimited* (Bayfield, 1998)—haven't found national distribution in the U.S., but should be available from record shops that specialize in Caribbean music. A thorough scouring of the same shops might turn up an old copy of *De Heat Is On* ⫘⫘⫘ (Bayfield, 1989/Rohit, 1989, prod. Kenny Wallace, Mac Fingall), whose "Pluck It" (a double-entendre about a local poultry-processing scandal) and "The Country En Well" (which diagnoses and anatomizes the state of the nation, body part by body part) won Pic-O-De-Crop.

Influences:

◀◀ Grynner, Ras Iley

see also: *krosfyah*

Michael Eldridge

Red Tail Chasing Hawks

Traditional flute, new age, Latin jazz
Formed c. 1992, in Phoenix, AZ, USA. Based in Denver, CO, USA and Phoenix, AZ, USA.

Calvin Standing Bear, flutes; James Torres, piano. (Both members are from USA.)

Calvin Standing Bear is a Rosebud Sioux who began singing in the church choir as a youth. He has played traditional flute for almost a decade and teaches traditional drumming, singing, and flute-playing in Denver. James Torres is Chiricahua Apache and Mexican American; he has been a professional musician most of his life, playing with Tito Puente, Willie Colon, Celia Cruz, Airto Moreira, and Flora Purim. Standing Bear says the duo came together in the early 1990s to "share music with the world. I pray this music will touch the hearts and spirits of all people; we are all related."

what's available: *Eagle Dances with the Wind* 🎵🎵🎵 (Canyon, 1995, prod. Calvin Standing Bear, James Torres) offers pleasant powwow jazz, meditative flute, and free-form improvisations for flute and piano, with a bit of Native percussion. *Brother Hawk* 🎵🎵🎵 (Canyon, 1996, prod. Robert Doyle) is another soothing album, with some chanting and percussion on two tracks and the usual new-agey nature sounds.

influences:
◀◀ R. Carlos Nakai

j. poet

Jean Redpath

Celtic
Born April 28, 1937, in Edinburgh, Scotland. Based in USA.

Jean Redpath's unaffected, crystalline mezzo-soprano is an excellent instrument for Scottish songs. A university lecturer, she is as much a scholar as she is a performer. Nevertheless, her delivery is never dry; her heart is in every syllable, perhaps in part because she learned many of the songs she sings, and the stories behind them, from her mother, who was a scholar of Scots oral history. Redpath emigrated to New York and spent time in Greenwich Village in the 1960s. There she became a widely respected champion of the folk music revival that was then underway in the U.S., impressing her audiences with the size of her repertoire. Her best-known undertaking is the complete songs of Robert Burns. Seven volumes of a projected 22 in this series were recorded before the death of her producer, Serge Hovey, put the plan on hold. Another of Redpath's well-known endeavors is a compilation of Scottish songs written by women.

what to buy: *Lowlands* 🎵🎵🎵🎵 (Philo, 1994, prod. Jean Redpath) is an excellent mix of songs. Two of the best are "Faraway Tom" (with cello accompaniment by Abby Newton) and the *a cappella* "Gallowa' Hills." Equally strong is *Jean Redpath* 🎵🎵🎵🎵🎵 (Philo, 1975/1989), which includes "I Live Not Where I Love," one of Redpath's most requested songs.

what to buy next: *The Songs of Robert Burns, Volumes I and II* 🎵🎵🎵🎵🎵 (Philo, 1976/1980/1996, prod. Serge Hovey) contains the best of Redpath's versions of Burns's songs, including "Auld Lang Syne," "A Red, Red Rose," and "Nine Inch Will Please a Lady."

best of the rest:
The Songs of Robert Burns, Volumes III and IV 🎵🎵🎵🎵 (Philo, 1982/1983/1996)

The Songs of Robert Burns, Volumes V and VI 🎵🎵🎵🎵 (Philo, 1985/1987/1996)
Lady Nairne 🎵🎵🎵🎵 (Philo, 1986)
First Flight 🎵🎵🎵🎵 (Philo, 1989)
The Songs of Robert Burns, Volume VII 🎵🎵🎵🎵 (Philo, 1990)
Song of the Seals 🎵🎵🎵🎵 (Philo, 1994)

influences:
◀◀ Robert Burns, Jeannie Robertson

Pamela Murray Winters and Kerry Dexter

Elis Regina

MPB (Brazilian Popular Music), bossa nova, Brazilian jazz
Born Elis Regina Carvalho Costa, 1945, In Porto Algre, Brazil. Died January 19, 1982.

Along with such leading lights as Milton Nascimento and Caetano Veloso, the late Elis Regina remains one of Brazil's most popular and talented singers. Born to a working-class family, Regina began singing professionally at age 12 on a children's television show, gaining local fame during two years of regular performances. She signed her first recording contract at age 13 and made three records, returning home after each junket to Rio de Janeiro. Her superb voice, full of spellbinding, full-throated soulfulness and polished technique, gained her distinction as the queen of MPB, and she rose to fame while still in her teens. As the family's main breadwinner, Regina relocated to Rio with her father in 1963, about the time that a military junta took control of the country. By the age of 21, she was the most revered (and handsomely paid) singer in Brazil. Not as overtly political as her contemporaries but still openly critical of Brazil's military rule, her enormous popularity probably kept her out of jail and exempt from exile. Still, she was forced to sing the Brazilian national anthem at an "independence" ceremony, an act that was criticized by leftist performers who felt her public, pro-government display was inappropriate. She would not learn until years later that her husband had been threatened with jail had she not complied with the government's demand. Regina's career continued full-blast into the 1970s, and she recorded some of her best albums during this decade. Songwriters sought her out as an interpreter with impeccable taste, and she helped introduce such Brazilian composers as Nascimento, João Bosco, Ivan Lins, Joyce, Renato Teixeira, and many others. However, a temperamental and moody artist, her personal life was in disarray. Her two marriages ended in divorce, leaving her to provide not only for three children but her parents as well. She secretly started using cocaine in the late 1970s, after the collapse of her second marriage. She began 1982 by signing a new recording contract, marrying for the third time, and making future plans. But on January 19 of that year, she was found dead of an accidental overdose of drugs and alcohol. Nearly two decades later, the musicians she inspired continue to pay tribute to her with songs and whole albums dedicated to her memory. If you're just getting acquainted with Regina, it's important to note that her style is quite different than what you might expect. Rather than the soft, mellow vocal style of other Brazilian singers known to American audiences, she exudes a raw power that is often compared to Janis Joplin's. On her many albums Regina sings with untamed gusto and heat, leaning mostly to the pop side of modern Brazilian music centered in São Paulo.

what to buy: *Vento De Maio (May Wind)* 𝄞𝄞𝄞𝄞 (EMI/Hemisphere, 1997), a collection of tunes split between ballads and up-tempo MPB pop numbers, is the only recording Elis Regina made for EMI, but it ranks among her best. While she fervently mines the samba tradition, Regina delivers a diverse, modern-sounding session. Joining forces on some tracks with other popular Brazilian singer-songwriters, she kicks off with a lush version of the title song, elegantly performed with Lô Borges, and flirtatiously sings "Tiro Ao Alvaro (Hit the Bull's Eye)" with its composer Adoniran Barbosa. Highlights of this 13-track set are Regina's collaboration with Milton Nascimento on the captivating scorcher "O Que Fol Feito Devera (What Was Really Done)," and her version of Gilberto Gil's reverent, gospel-tinged "Rebento (Explode)." Three rare tracks are added to the CD version, and throughout, Regina artfully maintains a delicate balance between old and new. A collection of songs by Milton Nascimento, *Nada Sera Como Antes (Nothing Will Be As It Was)* 𝄞𝄞𝄞𝄞 (Verve, 1972/1984), demonstrates why Regina became one of the most cherished singers in Brazil and why so many of her colleagues still mourn her loss. Well chosen, these 10 songs convey not only Nascimento's artistry, but Regina's inventiveness at transforming his works, backed with gorgeous arrangements and support from unnamed instrumental soloists. Liner notes contain only Portuguese lyrics, but Regina sings with such fervent longing and undiminished skill, words don't matter.

what to buy next: If you want the most value for your money, check out either of two compilation albums released in 1990 that feature Regina in both studio and live performances. *A Arte De Elis Regina* 𝄞𝄞𝄞𝄞 (Verve, 1975/1990) contains 21 songs—more than 68 minutes' worth—compiled for Verve's "The Best of Brazil" series. Communicating a spectrum of moods, Regina sings MPB classics by composers Gilberto Gil, Milton Nascimento, Ivan Lins, Ary Barrosa, Antonio Carlos Jobim, Ed Lopo, and others. Some tracks include (synthesized) orchestral backing; others pair Regina with small, intimate combos. From start to finish, whether the material is up-tempo or stretched out, her performances sizzle with earthy passion. Portuguese lyrics, without English translations, are included in the liners. Reissued the same year, *Fascination: The Best of Elis Regina* 𝄞𝄞𝄞𝄞 (Verve,

1990) is slightly more appealing than the other disc, though it duplicates about a third of that disc's tracks. The 20 songs here include powerful performances like the kicking opener, "Meninho Das Laranjas (The Orange-Selling Boy)"; Baden Powell's "Lapinha (A Neighborhood of São Paulo)," on which Elis is supported by a community chorus; the funky pop piece "Como Nossos Pais (Like Our Parents)"; and Regina's laughter-laced "Vou Deitar E Rolar (I'll Do It to the Hilt)." These songs and a gorgeous version of the classic American standard title tune heighten the charm of *Fascination,* giving it a slim edge over *A Arte De Elis Regina* —but if you're a completist, buy both.

what to avoid: While the performances are competent and die-hard Regina fans may want to devour everything she's recorded, be forewarned that most of the 16 songs on *Personalidade: Elis Regina* 𝄞𝄞𝄞𝄞 (Verve, 1987) are repeated on other, more engaging Verve albums.

best of the rest:
Brazilian Collection from A to Z: Elis Regina 𝄞𝄞𝄞𝄞 (Mercury, 1998)

worth searching for: Regina's album with Antonio Carlos Jobim, *Elis & Tom* 𝄞𝄞𝄞𝄞 (PolyGram Brazil, 1974/Verve, 1990, prod. Aloysio de Oliveira), is a delightful way to experience two Brazilian legends at once. It includes their classic duet "Águas de Março."

influences:

◀◀ Antonio Carlos Jobim, Ary Barroso

▶▶ Milton Nascimento, João Bosco, Ivan Lins, Joyce, Renato Teixeira

see also: *Gilberto Gil, Antonio Carlos Jobim, Joyce, Milton Nascimento, Caetano Veloso*

Nancy Ann Lee

Cheikha Remitti

Oranese folklore, rai
Born May 8, 1923, in Tessala, Algeria. Based in Paris, France, and Oran, Algeria.

The mother of *rai* (Algerian pop music), Cheikha Remitti was born with the name Saâdia, but that, like her peaceful village life and so much else in her country, was not to last. Orphaned at an early age, she settled in Relizane under protection of a patron. Her difficult life became all the more so with the onset of World War II and its attendant food shortages and other hardships. Young Saâdia fell in with musicians, dancing and singing the nights away as a kind of escape from the suffering around her. "Misfortune has been my teacher," says Remitti now. Her next misfortune was the plague that ravaged Oran in the 1940s and inspired Camus's famous novel. The resulting horrors also inspired Saâdia to begin writing songs of her own, something she has continued to this day.

Under the tutelage of a great flutist, Saâdia started recording her songs at Radio Algiers. She earned the name Remitti while entertaining French soldiers during the war. After attempting the French expression for "another round" ("remettez"), her heavily accented utterance inspired fans to shout "Remitti, the singer! Remitti!" They have never stopped. She began recording under this name in the early '50s.

Remitti's works trace their roots to the *sh'ir al-malhun,* sacred Arabic poetry rendered as song. Once this music began to be recorded early in the 20th century, it started appearing in more popularized forms that appealed to common folk. As a girl, Remitti adapted these idioms, especially the form called *gharbi.* Singing for mostly male audiences, Remitti laid the groundwork for modern rai with her suggestive wordplay and sexual double entendres. As young male rai singers—most notably Khaled—came onto the scene in the 1970s, their rebellious style enraged Islamic fundamentalists and riveted youth, making the music a massive pop phenomenon for the first time.

Remitti's star rose with rai's, though she tends to dismiss rai stars as unoriginal and overrated. Her prolific cannon of songs has expanded to explore friendship, love, alcohol dependency, prostitution, and the problems of immigrants and nomadic people. In violence-stricken Algeria, Remitti cannot perform publicly, yet she now enjoys worldwide renown.

what to buy: *Aux Sources du Rai* ♫♫♫♫ (Blue Silver, 1994, prod. L'Institute du Monde Arab) features Remitti's robust voice in a live recording with simple percussion and deep-toned *gasba* flute backing. *Sidi Mansour* ♫♫♫♫ (Absolute Records, 1994, prod. Houari Talbi, JBV, Geza X) marks Remitti's first adventure into rai rock. With support from Robert Fripp and others, she turns out a hard-hitting, even majestic production, not at all like the slick dance tracks of more commercial rai artists.

what to buy next: *Rai Roots* ♫♫♫♫ (Buda Musique) provides more of Remitti's sultry traditional sound.

influences:

◀ *sh'ir al-malhun,* malhun-derived Oranese folk music

▶ Chaba Fadela, Chaba Zahouania, Cheb Mami, Cheb Hasni, Cheb Khaled, and many others

see also: *Khaled*

Banning Eyre

Zachary Richard

Cajun, swamp pop, rock
Born September 8, 1950, in Lafayette, LA, USA. Based in Lafayette, LA, USA.

Zachary Richard started out as a folky after graduating from Tu-

lane University. Looking for something to make him stand out from all the other guitar-playing singers, he took up the Cajun accordion and learned from the great Felix Richard (who also mentored Horace Trahan) and by playing along to Aldus Roger records. Richard's style now is not often based on traditional Cajun music or the accordion, but on a blend that weighs more towards zydeco and New Orleans music, with a strong rock sensibility. There is a continuing thread of social activism in his work—about Cajun culture and the struggle to maintain the French language in Louisiana—that is juxtaposed with the music's danceable, good-times sound.

what to buy: *Snake Bite Love* ♫♫♫♫ (A&M, 1992, prod. Jim Wray) represents the mature Richard sound: a zydeco beat with elements of rock, country, swamp pop, and R&B built on top, all filtered through a Cajun sensibility. Richard's songwriting owes more to the singer-songwriter genre than to Lawrence Walker or Dewey Balfa, but the passion found in his vocals is clearly inspired by those Cajun legends.

what to buy next: On *Women in the Room* ♫♫♫♫ (A&M, 1990, prod. Zachary Richard, Jim Scott), Richard's songwriting began to match the major-label quality of his live performances. He struck the perfect synthesis of his social commentary and folk-rock style with "No French, No More," and mixed a south Louisiana dance groove and nonsense lyrics in "Who Stole My Monkey."

the rest:
Mardi Gras Mambo ♫♫♫ (Rounder, 1980)
Zack's Bon Ton ♫♫♫ (Rounder, 1989)
Zack Attack ♫♫♫♫ (Arzed, 1989)
Bayou des Mystées ♫♫♫ (Arzed, 1991)
Vent d'Eté ♫♫♫ (Arzed, 1996)

worth searching for: *Looking Back* ♫♫♫♫ (Arzed, 1985, prod. Zachary Richard) is a retrospective of Richard's early work.

influences:

◀ Aldus Roger, Jimmy C. Newman

▶ Tasso, Steve Riley

see also: *Horace Trahan, Aldus Roger*

Jared Snyder

Mike Richmond

World jazz
Born in Philadelphia, PA, USA. Based in New York, NY, USA.

Bassist Mike Richmond has played with a who's who of musicians as diverse as Ravi Shankar, Stan Getz, and Richie Havens. He took over the bass slot when Charles Mingus's band became the Mingus Dynasty upon the leader's demise. Richmond played with Miles Davis and Quincy Jones on Davis's last live concert recording and worked with other jazz notables including Gil Evans, Dizzy Gillespie, and Stan Getz. Today, Richmond teaches music at New York University and has been developing a fusion of acoustic styles with a group of innovative young musicians including percussionists Glen Velez and Joe Passaro, *oud* (lute) player Simon Shaheen, and harpist Lois Colin.

what's available: Although he has long done session work, *Basic Tendencies* 𝄞𝄞𝄞 (Nomad, 1996) represents Richmond's debut as a solo act. Working with a diverse slate of artists including percussionist Glen Velez and harpist Lois Colin, this album blends Richmond's classic jazz chops with his global music perspective. Although the other musicians provide tasty accents (notably Velez's Middle Eastern percussion touches), Richmond's lean, elegant bass lines are the principal focus on this fine first effort.

influences:

◀◀ Charles Mingus, Gil Evans

▶▶ Glen Velez, Todd Phillips

see also: *Glen Velez, Badal Roy, Simon Shaheen*

Michael Parrish

Bonnie Rideout

Scottish

Born December 18, 1962, in Saline, MI, USA. Based in USA.

Bonnie Rideout started playing violin at age eight and went on to study music and fine arts at the University of Michigan, graduating in 1985. As she was growing up, her family often played music together. Her mother was a concert pianist and was also her accompanist on her first recording, *Soft May Morn*. Rideout served as musician-in-residence at Armadale Castle on the Scottish Isle of Skye, where she had access to an unpublished 18th-century music manuscript of traditional tunes collected by Patrick McDonald. These rare tunes appear throughout her recordings. She is best known for her trademark *piobrachs*—highly ornamented Highland bagpipe tunes—and a style that borrows from such Highland bagpipe ornamentation. She has also been the National Scottish Fiddle champ three times. In 1996 Rideout became the first American ever invited to the prestigious Edinburgh International Festival in Scotland to demonstrate Highland-style fiddling. She took the gathering by storm and is influencing the next generation of young Scottish fiddlers. On both violin and viola, this tiny woman produces one of the biggest, fieriest sounds in Scottish music today.

what to buy: Rideout's recordings are all well researched, beautifully arranged, and masterfully performed. *Celtic Circles* 𝄞𝄞𝄞𝄞𝄞 (Maggie's Music, 1994, prod. Charlie Pilzer) has the theme of a day's cycle from sunset to nighttime. Starting with a distant drum that leads into a driving march, the music makes

a memorable statement. Braveheart piper Eric Reigler adds drive. Chris Caswell on nylon- and wire-strung harps and Carolyn Surrick on viola da gamba add delicacy and a haunting bass. The *Washington Post* describes Rideout's performance on this album best: "She transforms a lonely melody into utter desolation . . . then effortlessly switches gears from languorous ballad to virtuoso exercise." *Kindred Spirits* 𝄞𝄞𝄞𝄞 (Maggie's Music, 1996, prod. Bonnie Rideout, Bill McElroy) is devoted to music for, by, and about women. Highlights include the heartbreaking eulogy written by Robert Burns at the death of his first wife and the soaring, uplifting "Aldavaloch" and "Roy's Wife" (who was reputed to be a fickle lass). Rideout is joined by her usual brilliant crew of Eric Rigler, Al Pettaway, Chris Caswell, Abby Newton, and Maggie Sansone.

the rest:

Soft May Morn 𝄞𝄞𝄞𝄯 (Atholl Brose Recordings, 1990/Maggie's Music, 1994)
A Scottish Christmas 𝄞𝄞𝄞𝄞 (Maggie's Music, 1996)
Gi'me Elbow Room 𝄞𝄞𝄞𝄞 (Maggie's Music, 1998)

influences:

◀◀ Rideout's musical family, Dr. John Turner, an old northeast Scottish farmer named Jim Falconer

see also: *Maggie Sansone*

Karen Ashbrook

Steve Riley & the Mamou Playboys

Cajun, zydeco

Formed 1990, in Mamou, LA, USA. Based in Mamou, LA, USA.

Members have included: Steve Riley, fiddle, accordion, vocals; Peter Schwarz, fiddle, bass, vocals; David Greeley, fiddle, saxophone, vocals; Jimmy Domengeaux (died January 25, 1999), guitar, vocals; Kevin Dugas, drums; Kevin Berzas, guitar. (All members are from USA.)

In Philip Gould's collection of photographs, *Cajun and Zydeco Music,* he juxtaposes an image of a very young Steve Riley wedged against the stage at a music festival in Mamou, his eyes locked in on the musicians, with a picture of a 20-year-old Riley playing on the same stage. The look of determination in the young boy's eyes sums up the intensity of Riley's development as a player and performer. Riley taught himself to play the accordion, taking as a model his cousin, master accordion maker and player Marc Savoy. His prodigious skills brought him to the attention of Dewey Balfa, who took Riley out on the road with him. It was under Balfa's eye that he learned to fiddle, and it was also in Balfa's sphere that he met Peter Schwarz, son of Tracy Schwarz and fellow fiddle student of the great Mr. Balfa. One of the master's final tours featured a band that included Riley, Schwarz, Christine Balfa (now of Balfa Toujours), and Kevin Barzas, a young guitarist from Mamou, whose grandfather Maurice had for years led one of the best Cajun bands around: the Mamou Playboys. With the addition of Baton Rouge–area fiddler David Greeley, the new Mamou Playboys were formed. Riley is a monster on both accordion and fiddle. He has expanded his talents to include three-row and piano accordion. The band uses complicated modulating arrangements, three-part harmony, and the occasional presence of Greeley's saxophone to vary the sound. Riley can play everything from the toughest, fastest two-steps, to solid zydeco, to the oldest of fiddle tunes from the Balfa Brothers repertoire.

what to buy: Titled after the French version of All Souls' Day, when people tend to the graves of their ancestors, *Toussaint* 𝄞𝄞𝄞𝄞𝄞 (Rounder, 1995, prod. Scott Billington) shows off the strengths of the Mamou Playboys and keeps their excesses in check. The three-part harmonies are here, but used for accenting ("T'es Parents Veulent Plus Me Voir" and "La Valse D'Amitié"); the same can be said for the modulations the band sometimes can't resist jumping through ("Between Eunice and Opelousas"). "La Toussaint" may be the best Cajun composition of the '90s, a moving piece written by Schwarz with words by Greeley. Placing it as the centerpiece of the CD gives the recording a kind of thematic quality that isn't all that common in Cajun releases. Around it you have dancehall originals like "Katherine," complete with guest Issac Miller on steel, and archaic pieces based on seminal song-collector Alan Lomax's fiddle recordings. There are also two zydeco numbers with Riley showing his chops on three-row button accordion and C.J. Chenier contributing alto sax. Overall the record captures the essence of this group and makes for great listening you don't have to be a Cajun fan to enjoy.

what to buy next: While *Bayou Ruler* 𝄞𝄞𝄞𝄞 (Rounder, 1998, prod. C.C. Adcock, Tarka Cordell) shows you where the Mamou Playboys come from—the Balfa Brothers, Clifton Chenier, blues, and swamp pop—it is more about the contemporary tastes of their loyal fans in Louisiana. That means more English lyrics and more pronounced rock and zydeco influences. In this music, the Playboys are coming closer to Los Lobos than Beausoleil in the way they express their roots. There is less of the reverential updating of traditional tunes; here they use their understanding of their sources as a springboard for creating a modern sound embracing all their musical influences. *Bayou Ruler* is not their *Kiko*, but it shows they have the potential to make a record that distinctive. These are also sadly the last recordings with guitarist Jimmy Domengeaux, who died in a motorcycle crash on January 25, 1999. The enthusiastic playing and singing on *Trace of Time* 𝄞𝄞𝄞𝄞 (Rounder, 1993, prod. Al

Tharp) are marred only by murky and bottomless production. Otherwise all the traits of the band are there: the modulations and the three-part harmonies that are their signature, and the Balfa Brothers tune "Parlez-Nous a Boire," played with respect for tradition.

the rest:
Steve Riley and the Mamou Playboys 𝄞𝄞𝄞 (Rounder, 1990)
Tit' Galop Pour Mamou 𝄞𝄞𝄞 (Rounder, 1992)
Live! 𝄞𝄞𝄞 (Rounder, 1994)
Friday Night at Last 𝄞𝄞𝄞𝄞 (Swallow, 1997)

influences:

◀◀ The Balfa Brothers, Savoy-Doucet Cajun Band, Tracy Schwarz, D.L. Menard, Dewey Balfa

▶▶ Horace Trahan, Balfa Toujours

see also: *Alphonse "Bois Sec" Ardoin, the Balfa Brothers, Balfa Toujours, C.J. Chenier, Clifton Chenier, Savoy-Doucet Cajun Band, Tracy Schwarz*

Jared Snyder

Archie Roach
Folk, rock
Born 1955, in Framlingham, Victoria, Australia. Based in Australia.

For proof of the healing power of music, look no further than the story of Archie Roach. An Aboriginal with the misfortune to be born in the days of a moronic government program bent on forcing Australia's indigenous population to assimilate, Roach was removed from his family at the age of four and raised in an orphanage. He was told that his family was killed in a fire. At 14, he discovered the lie, but not in time to see his real mother alive again. He became alcoholic and lived for years on the streets. Eventually, he channeled his rage into music and wrote the song "Took the Children Away," which dealt with the plight of Australia's "stolen generation." He has returned to the subject several times across his trio of albums, but he also writes passionately about other things he's seen throughout a life of hardship and disappointment. Over and above his fine material, which ranges from folk and country-tinged numbers to blazing rock, Roach is possessed of an unusual vocal timbre, more or less that of an Outback Sam Cooke.

what to buy: Roach's debut, *Charcoal Lane* 𝄞𝄞𝄞𝄞 (HighTone, 1990, prod. Paul Kelly, Steve Connally), is often painful to listen to as the singer opens old wounds and sprinkles them liberally with salt. *Jamu Dreaming* 𝄞𝄞𝄞𝄞 (HighTone, 1993, prod. David Bridie) has its share of grim tales as well, such as "From Paradise" and "Tell Me Why." But overall, the atmosphere here is more cleansing and redemptive, and the arrangements are more fleshed out than on the debut. That's even more true on

Looking for Butter Boy ♪♪♪♪ (HighTone, 1997, prod. Malcolm Burn), which rocks with forthright energy as it rages against injustice. Highlights include the righteous "A Child Was Born Here" and the aching "Louis St. John," which features a guest vocal by Roach's wife, Ruby Hunter, an acclaimed singer-songwriter in her own right.

influences:

◄◄ Sam Cooke, Ray Charles, Paul Kelly

Daniel Durchholz

Steve Roach

Ambient/world fusion

Born 1955, in La Mesa, CA, USA. Based in Tucson, AZ, USA.

Steve Roach is an incredibly prolific multi-instrumentalist/producer who seems equally comfortable performing live on Aboriginal *didgeridoo* and percussion or crafting futuristic soundscapes on synthesizers in his home studio. Initially inspired by Tangerine Dream and Can, Roach began composing experimental electronic music in the early '80s, meticulously assembling albums that seem in retrospect to be a little too influenced by the ambient synth sounds pioneered by Brian Eno. Roach's artistic breakthrough came in the late '80s when, on a trip to Australia, he met a young Aboriginal didgeridoo virtuoso named David Hudson. This meeting not only would be the start of an enduring friendship and musical partnership, but also spawned the album *Dreamtime Return,* which signaled the beginning of Roach's fascination with the music of Australian and other indigenous cultures. He went on to produce all of Hudson's albums, including the solo debut *Woolunda,* which was one of the first traditional didgeridoo recordings available in the U.S. (By now, the droning, organically constructed yet electronic-sounding instrument has gained much popularity Stateside and around the world.) Since then, although he has collaborated with a broad variety of musical talents, his work can be loosely divided into three categories—non-traditional world-music excursions; atmospheric electronic experiments; and, most prominently, fusions between the two—all of which work fairly well thanks to an appealingly timeless quality that brings music's ancient past and unforeseeable future together in a meditative present. Relocated to the desert of Arizona to commune with his muse, Roach has recently realized what would seem to be his destiny, composing music used for soundtracks (the films *Rapa Nui* and *Heat,* and the PBS series *The Way West*). His older electronic stuff may get a bit too new-agey at times, but with nearly 40 albums to his credit in the last 17 years, his batting average remains surprisingly high.

what to buy: Because Roach's vast output has been so stylistically diverse, you'll probably want to start with his two-CD

jamaican music 4: deejay style

In the late 1950s Jamaica's neighborhood dances, held by competing "sound systems," became the primary way most of the island enjoyed music. The sound system was essentially a mobile, massively amplified stereo. "Selectors" moved the crowd by spinning the hottest records of the day; Count Machuki and King Stitt were unique in that they stoked the fire of the dance by introducing the "scorchers" with short, punchy flurries of rhythmic word patter—making them widely considered to be the forebears of the deejay style of reggae (and the rap beyond).

By the late '60s bass-bolstered instrumental B-sides, called "versions," were the rage of record at sound-system dances. When King Tubby decided to add U-Roy's funky patois jive over his own crafty remixes of these versions, it ignited a phenomenon called "deejaying" or "toasting." U-Roy's roller coaster timbre and staccato braggadocio masterfully slalomed through the rhythms of the mix, and he was the first to establish deejaying as a popular art form—in 1969 he held the top three chart positions in the country, and from that point onward deejaying would be an integral part of Jamaican music.

The deejay's slang-peppered commentary on both the personal and the political over raw, heavy beats bestowed the bloodline that led to the birth of hip-hop in late-'70s New York, with the ruling deejays (like the Stateside MCs) attaining their often briefly assumed thrones by captivating the crowds with creative catchphrases and imaginative, intensely rhythmic rhyme flows. The immortal U-Roy's *Version Galore, Words of Wisdom, Dread in a Babylon,* and *Natty Rebel* are outstanding examples of the deejay form, as are the John Coltrane–inspired Big Youth's seminal *Screaming Target, Dread Locks Dread,* and *Natty Cultural Dread.* Other slippery-tongued microphone maestros include Prince Jazzbo, Dennis Alcapone, Trinity, Dillinger, Prince Far I, Yellowman, and I-Roy.

Todd Shanker

greatest-hits collection, *Dreaming . . . Now, Then: A Retrospective 1982–1997* 𝄢𝄢𝄢 (Celestial Harmonies, 1998, prod. Steve Roach), a 21-track overview of his 15-year association with the Fortuna label that charts his artistic evolution from promising synth-noodler to one of America's finest ethno-ambient fusionists. For a more cohesive creative statement, try *Halcyon Days* 𝄢𝄢𝄢𝄢 (Fathom, 1996, prod. Steve Roach), his gorgeously produced collaboration with the similarly talented Stephen Kent and Kenneth Newby, both of Trance Mission fame. Also well worth a listen is David Hudson's *Gunyal* 𝄢𝄢𝄢𝄢 (Black Sun, 1998, prod. Steve Roach), a gloriously transcendental Australian Aboriginal concept album teaming Roach with his friend and significant artistic influence.

what to buy next: Although Roach has always been fairly well received by critics, few of his solo projects have gotten the same adulation as Suspended Memories, his group with multi-instrumentalist Jorge Reyes and guitarist Suso Saiz. *Earth Island* 𝄢𝄢𝄢𝄢 (Fathom, 1994, prod. Steve Roach) is a captivating patchwork of surreal soundscapes navigating heretofore uncharted territories of time, space, and mind. Likewise, *Kiva* 𝄢𝄢𝄢𝄢 (Fathom, 1995, prod. Steve Roach), a collaboration with ambient composer Michael Stearns and Native American musician Ron Sunsinger, builds hallucinogenic mirages of sound around source recordings made at Native ceremonies fueled by the natural mind-alterers peyote and ayahuasca.

what to avoid: Although not altogether bad, some of Roach's early offerings are likely to prove dangerous to those without a natural immunity to the sound of new-age synth-wanking. If this sounds like you, stick primarily with his post-1990 efforts.

the rest:
Now/Traveler 𝄢𝄢 (Fortuna, 1982/1983/1992)
Structures from Silence 𝄢𝄢 (Fortuna, 1984)
Empetus 𝄢𝄢𝄢 (Fortuna, 1986)
(With Kevin Braheny) *Western Spaces* 𝄢𝄢𝄢 (Fortuna, 1987)
Quiet Music 𝄢𝄢𝄢 (Fortuna, 1988)
Dreamtime Return 𝄢𝄢𝄢𝄢 (Fortuna, 1988)
(With Kevin Braheny and Michael Stearns) *Desert Solitaire* 𝄢𝄢𝄢 (Fortuna, 1989)
(With David Hudson and Sarah Hopkins) *Australia: Sound of the Earth* 𝄢𝄢𝄢 (Fortuna, 1990)
(With Robert Rich) *Strata* 𝄢𝄢𝄢𝄢 (Hearts of Space, 1990)
(With Robert Rich) *Soma* 𝄢𝄢𝄢𝄢 (Hearts of Space, 1992)
World's Edge 𝄢𝄢𝄢 (Fortuna, 1992)
(With Suspended Memories) *Forgotten Gods* 𝄢𝄢𝄢𝄢 (Hearts of Space, 1993)
The Lost Pieces 𝄢𝄢𝄢 (Projekt, 1993)
Origins 𝄢𝄢𝄢𝄢 (Fortuna, 1993)
Artifacts 𝄢𝄢𝄢𝄢 (Fortuna, 1994)
(With Vidna Obmana) *Well of Souls* 𝄢𝄢𝄢𝄢 (Projekt, 1995)
The Magnificent Void 𝄢𝄢𝄢𝄢 (Fathom, 1996)

(With Vidna Obmana) *Cavern of Sirens* 𝄢𝄢𝄢 (Projekt, 1996)
On This Planet 𝄢𝄢𝄢𝄢 (Fathom, 1997)
(With Roger King) *Dust to Dust* 𝄢𝄢𝄢𝄢 (Projekt, 1998)
(With Vir Unis) *Body Electric* 𝄢𝄢𝄢𝄢 (Projekt, 1999)

worth searching for: Like any good prolific artist, Roach has released a number of albums that are difficult to find or are long out of print, but only a few merit the effort to track them down. His 1994 solo effort, *The Dream Circle* (Soundquest, 1994), and his three-CD collaboration with Vidna Obmana, *Ascension of Shadows* 𝄢𝄢𝄢𝄢 (Projekt, 1998), were both limited-edition runs of 2,000 copies. And there are two ambient albums available only through Roach's Web site at www.steveroach.com, *Slow Heat* (Timeroom Editions, 1998) and *Truth & Beauty: The Lost Pieces, Volume Two* (Timeroom Editions, 1999).

influences:
◄◄ Tangerine Dream, Brian Eno, Can, David Hudson

►► Dead Can Dance, Trance Mission, Soma, Lights in a Fat City

see also: *David Hudson, Ron Sunsinger, Takadja, Omar Faruk Tekbilek, Trance Mission*

Bret Love

Roaring Lion

Calypso
Born Rafael de Lion, 1909, in Trinidad. Based in Port of Spain, Trinidad.

At 90, Roaring Lion is the last surviving member of calypso's first golden age in the 1930s. He began singing in 1927, at a time when singers were expected to improvise a lyric on the spot, and many of his most famous tunes, like "Mary Ann" and "Ugly Woman," evolved out of lyrics he composed during various impromptu battles with other singers.

In the early 1930s, when islanders realized people would pay to see calypso singers perform, the first "tents" were created, and Lion became star of the Victory tent. In 1933, Lion, Atilla the Hun, King Radio, and Lord Beginner became the first singers to perform throughout the Caribbean, and in 1934 Lion and Atilla became the first calypsonians to record, when they cut sides for New York's Brunswick Records. Lion also sang for President Roosevelt, appeared on Broadway at Rudy Vallee's Hollywood Café, and became the first calypso singer to make a movie when he sang his famous "Ugly Woman" in the film *Happy Go Lucky,* the first Hollywood movie made in Trinidad.

Lion was an early Carnival favorite and won the Road March Crown from 1933 to 1938. He entertained the British and American troops stationed in Trinidad during WWII and opened Calypsoville, one of the original calypso nightclubs. After the war he lived in England for 11 years, constantly touring the continent and founding the Coloured People's Accommodation Bureau, an organization that helped West Indians and Africans settle into their new immigrant life. As he nears the century mark, the Lion still performs regularly and composes new material.

what's available: The 25 tracks on *Sacred 78's* 𝄞𝄞𝄞𝄞𝄞 (Ice, 1994, prod. various) are from the Lion's heyday in the 1930s, and the digital remastering is remarkable. Lion has an impish quality; you can almost hear him smirk as he sings of love, politics, and sex. Included are the original recordings of "Mary Ann" (later a hit for the Easy Riders), "Bananas," and "Ugly Woman," a sexist standard the world over ("If you wanna be happy the rest of your life, never make a pretty woman your wife"). The music has a stronger Cuban influence than modern *soca* (the descendant of calypso), and the big band arrangements are full of spunk.

influences:

▶▶ Sparrow, Kitchener, Arrow, Calypso Rose

j. poet

Kim Robertson

Celtic harp
Born in WI, USA. Based in USA.

To many, the first name in Celtic harp is Kim Robertson. Her sensuous arrangements have become a hallmark of the folk harp community, the tunes she plays magically woven into a tapestry of ethereal threads. Her touch on the strings is firm, yet delicate, her expression evocative, and her arrangements perfectly suited for the instrument. Robertson plays a wide variety of styles, from Celtic tunes to original works, from American folk favorites to new-age sounds. One of her greatest skills is improvisation, in which she soars to the height of her expression. Robertson's dedication extends to spending much of her time running harp workshops, both in the U.S. and abroad. She has written several books on music and published two instructional videos as well. Robertson began playing in her senior year of high school, learning the pedal harp. She enjoyed the instrument but had no desire to join a symphony, so she did not pursue it as a career. Instead she entered college as a piano major. Her background in that field included jazz improvisation, a skill that she translated beautifully to the harp in general and to the Celtic harp in particular; she discovered that instrument during the mid-'70s while attending a retreat for its practitioners. She soon fell in love with the instrument, exploring its many voices and experimenting with its possibilities. The result was her own unique sound, capturing the spirit of the harp itself and carrying it to the listener in music. Some of her more recent work has also included her equally unique vocals.

what to buy: Displaying her talent for evocative arrangements of traditional tunes, Robertson plays an array of delightful works on *Wind Shadows II* 𝄞𝄞𝄞𝄞 (Invincible, 1987, prod. Liv Khalsa). Her arrangements of "Arise and Get Dressed," "Black Nag," "Star of County Down," and "Bridget Cruise" display her work at its very best. The selection will please fans of traditional Celtic music. *Celtic Christmas II* 𝄞𝄞𝄞𝄞 (Invincible, 1990, prod. Liv Khalsa) is among the best Christmas albums around. A broad collection of well-known and lesser-known carols, this recording combines the delicate strains of Robertson's harping with the haunting voice of a cello, played by Virginia Kron. Special selections include a delightful Spanish carol, "A la Nanita Nana"; the American folk song "As Joseph Was a Walking"; and a wonderful 13th-century French "Pastourelle."

what to buy next: On *Treasures of the Celtic Harp* 𝄞𝄞𝄞𝄞 (Dargason Music, 1995, prod. Joemy Wilson, Scott Fraser), Robertson returns to arranging traditional material after a period of largely original work. Such gems as "Glenlivet" and "The Water Is Wide" sparkle on this fresh recording, along with four of her own compositions. Incorporating haunting flute by Bettine Clemen and an occasional cello or percussion accompaniment, *Love Song to a Planet* 𝄞𝄞𝄞𝄞 (Invincible, 1994, prod. Bettine Clemen, Kim Robertson) is an uplifting collection of traditional tunes and new material, all expressing the love and joy the musicians have for this earth. A moving rendition of the "New World Symphony" theme launches this album, followed by several choice Robertson originals. There are also stirring arrangements of "Mist-Covered Mountains," "The Dark Island," and "Amazing Grace." *Joy! Joy! Joy!* 𝄞𝄞𝄞𝄞 (Invincible, 1989, prod. Liv Khalsa), another Christmas recording, features remarkable reworkings of familiar carols. Sometimes bordering on jazz, as in the stirring rendition of "Joy to the World," sometimes soft and romantic, as in the gentle "Jesus Lullaby," Robertson and flautist Steve Kujala paint a highly evocative Christmas picture.

what to avoid: If you are looking for active-listening music, avoid all of the Crimson Collection series: *Crimson Collection, Volumes I and II* 𝄞 (Invincible, 1991, prod. Liv Khalsa); *Crimson Collection, Volumes IV and V* 𝄞 (Invincible, 1991, prod. Liv Khalsa); and *Crimson Collection, Volumes VI and VII* 𝄞 (Invincible, 1991, prod. Liv Khalsa). These recordings each contain two half-hour-long chants, featuring Liv Khalsa's voice and Robertson's harp. Although the original themes are all strong, they are very repetitive, meant to be used as a background for deep meditation or prayer, and promoted for their healing powers. Although excellent for their intended purpose, they will not excite a listener looking for more than background sound.

the rest:
Wind Shadows 𝄞𝄞𝄞 (Invincible, 1983)
Water Spirit 𝄞𝄞𝄞𝄞 (Invincible, 1987)
Moonrise 𝄞𝄞 (Invincible, 1987)
Celtic Christmas 𝄞𝄞𝄞 (Invincible, 1987)

Wild Iris ♫♫ (Invincible, 1989)
Angels in Disguise ♫♫♪ (Invincible, 1990)
Gratitude ♫♫♫ (Invincible, 1990)
Tender Shepherd ♫♫♫ (Gourd Music, 1992)
Wood, Fire, and Gold ♫♫♫ (Dargason Music, 1996)
Spiral Gate N/A (Narada, 1999)

influences:

◄◄ Virginia Kron, Singh Kaur

►► Knodel & Valencia, Sunita Staneslow

Jo Hughey Morrison

Robbie Robertson

Classic rock, modern Native American, electronica

Born Jaime Robbie Robertson, July 5, 1943, in Toronto, Ontario,
Canada. Based in Los Angeles, CA, USA.

Contemporary audiences probably know Robbie Robertson
most as a driving force behind classic rockers The Band, or as a
hit-making musical director for big-budget movies (most recently masterminding Eric Clapton and Babyface's double-
Grammy-winning "Change the World" as executive soundtrack
producer for *Phenomenon*). But history may regard him best
for his riveting explorations of his Native American heritage. At
this writing it's a relatively recent phase of his career, which has
produced just two albums, but each one is a landmark. Robertson's introspective odyssey began with the score to the Turner
Broadcasting documentary series *The Native Americans,* and
continued with his Grammy-nominated *Contact from the Underworld of Redboy*. On each, he employed that most modern
of forms, electronic music, to evoke not the trendy but the
timeless, pursuing a more ambient sound on the former album
and a more syncopated techno-dance one on the latter. These
sets are all-star affairs in which the communal voice of Native
tradition and the multi-perspectival aesthetic of postmod-
ernism converge. True to a culture that doesn't partition art
and life the way the European one has—and to an embattled
people that doesn't have the luxury of differentiating the personal and political as the dominant society may—Robertson's
definition of "all-star" ranges from Native American musical luminaries (Ulali), to healers (Primeaux & Mike), to imprisoned
activists (Leonard Peltier). Like the "keepers of the ancient future" in one of his lyrics, this rock icon—and the proud civilization he helps speak for—has only begun to fight.

what to buy: The former Band leader creates a new kind of
classic for the age of electronica with *Contact from the Underworld of Redboy* ♫♫♫♫ (Capitol, 1998, prod. various). Alternately ethereal and frenetic, Robertson collages a groundbreaking synthesis of Native rhythm and computerized bpm, of
venerable belief and futuristic sound textures. The non-confor-

mity of popular musics past is revived in deadly earnest by
guest vocals from framed American Indian Movement advocate
Leonard Peltier (taped by phone from super-max incarcera-
tion); golden-voiced but controversial peyote-ceremony healers Primeaux & Mike; and, sampled from an old ethnographic
field recording, the unquiet ghost of 16-year-old Leah Hicks-
Manning, who grew up to become Native activist John Trudell's
mother-in-law before perishing with his wife and their children
in a suspicious arson the U.S. government refused to investigate. When not yielding the spotlight to his honored guests,
Robertson sings/narrates the tracks in a hushed and measured
rasp by turns mystically reverent and smolderingly indignant.
Historically significant (if a bit sonically out of place) is the
bonus inclusion of Robertson's surprise gay club hit, "Take
Your Partner by the Hand." *Music for the Native Americans*
♫♫♫♫ (Capitol, 1994, prod. Robbie Robertson) was credited to
Robbie Robertson and the Red Road Ensemble, an impressive
honor roll of Native performers, including Jim Wilson, Ulali,
Douglas Spotted Eagle, the Silvercloud Singers, Kashtin, and
Coolidge (the last-named being a prototypical version of the
well-received trio Walela). Wilson's stirring "Coyote Dance" appears on his own innovative Little Wolf project's debut album,
and Ulali's ethereal harmonies on "Mahk Jchi (Heartbeat Drum
Song)" will recur in your dreams. Wilson and Robertson's
"Ghost Dance" uses affecting MOR funk (and a striking babble-
drone intro and outro) to deliver a stinging account of 19th-cen-
tury religious persecution. Coolidge matches Ulali revelation
for revelation on the dream-like "The Vanishing Breed." The
steady but ominous beat of "It Is a Good Day to Die" finds
Robertson exactly half-way on his road from the tribal rhythm
to the techno pulse, while Kashtin's anthem "Akua Tuta" breaks
it all down to the most striking folk-rock being produced today.
An exhilarating chant from a Manhattan skyscraper by Ulali and
the Silvercloud Singers, and a bizarrely beautiful insect-and-
opera-singer prototype of Little Wolf's "Twisted Hair," are the
set's benediction. Even in electro-classic-rock mode Robertson's playing is impeccable, and the lyrics are among the best
of his career. The gifted Wilson, who doubled as musical director, has become more well known in this technology-rich genre
by virtue of having started his career with it, but Robertson remains a late-blooming master as well.

best of the rest:

(With The Band) *Music from Big Pink* ♫♫♫♫ (Capitol, 1968)
(With The Band) *The Band* ♫♫♫♫ (Capitol, 1969)
(With The Band) *Rock of Ages* ♫♫♫♫ (Capitol, 1972)
Robbie Robertson ♫♫♫ (Geffen, 1987)

influences:

◄◄ Ronnie Hawkins, Bob Dylan, Tom Bee, Buffy Sainte-Marie,
Jim Wilson, Leonard Peltier

Tabu Ley Rochereau

▶▶ Walela, Little Wolf

see also: *Kashtin, Primeaux & Mike, Douglas Spotted Eagle, John Trudell, Pura Fé, Walela, Jim Wilson (sidebar)*

Adam McGovern

Tabu Ley Rochereau /Tabu Ley /Pascal Tabu Rochereau

Soukous, Afropop
Born 1940, in Bandundu, Congo. Based in Paris, France.

If Congolese music has one living legend, it is Tabu Ley Rochereau. With more than 200 albums and 2,000 songs to his credit, Rochereau still tours and records prolifically with his large ensemble, adapting new trends and keeping his style fresh. Many stars of Congolese music started their careers or enjoyed their earliest success in Rochereau's band Afrisa, including Sam Mangwana, Faya Tess, and M'Bilia Bell. It was the extension of a great musical dynasty in which

Rochereau himself had apprenticed with Joseph "Le Grand Kalle" Kabasele's epic African Jazz band. Congo rules African pop, and Tabu Ley Rochereau is its king (a title for which he long vied good-naturedly with the late, legendary Franco). Rochereau has sung all his life, as a child finding a focus for his skills in the hymns at Catholic school before writing his first hit, "Besama Muchacha," at the age of 14 with African Jazz. The year was 1954, and the band dominated the Congolese music scene, with much more to come. In an interview the artist explained how he got his name—all of it: "Tabu is my father's name; Ley is my father's name. Rochereau is a name I got in grammar school. During a French history lesson I was the only one who knew the names of Napoleon's generals; the rest of the class was punished because of it. They teased me and called me Rochereau, but I liked the sound of it and kept it as my artistic name." A fitting enough overture to the history he himself would make.

what to buy: *Africa Worldwide* ♪♪♪♪ (Rounder, 1996, prod. Scott Billington) is a 35th-anniversary live recording of Rochereau and his excellent ensemble. The songs provide a retrospective of his long career, while showing that this powerhouse of ideas is anything but a nostalgia act.

best of the rest:
Babeti Soukous ♫♫♫ (RealWorld, 1989)
Man from Kinshasa ♫♫♫ (Shanachie, 1991)
Muzina ♫♫♫♫ (Rounder, 1994)

worth searching for: Rochereau is a superstar in the French-speaking world, a fact reflected by the more than 30 recordings available on French label Sonodisc and obtainable through Stern's USA, (212) 964-5455.

influences:

◄◄ Joseph "Le Grand Kalle" Kabasele, Manu Dibango, Dr. Nico, Franco/OK Jazz

►► Sam Mangwana, Papa Wemba

see also: *Africando, M'Bilia Bel, Dr. Nico, Franco, Sam Mangwana*

David Poole

Rock en Español

There's always been a truism in rock 'n' roll: sing it in English or don't bother to sing it at all. Despite fervent cults for German art-rock, French cabaret, and Japanese noise, native English speakers have relegated most foreign-language pop to the back of the musical bus. But the Spanish-language world is fighting back and it has a potent weapon: rock en Español. As with so much of the globe, many pop/rock musicians in Spain and Latin America (as well as Latino players in the U.S.) merely imitated their Anglo-American counterparts from the '50s through the '70s. There were exceptions, of course. From Ritchie Valens through Santana and Los Lobos, the West Coast began exporting a unique Latino rock subculture—though much of it was in English. That started to change during the '80s, when musicians across Spain, Latin America, and the United States—raised on rock and *ranchera,* beatbox and *bolero*—began mixing it all up and singing about things that mattered to them, in Spanish—global commercialism be damned. Unsurprisingly, rock en Español got its initial start in countries with the closest ties to the United States or Europe, namely Mexico, Argentina, and Spain. Despite disdain or outright hostility from local authorities, "los roqueros" flocked around such acts as El Tri, a smoky-voiced Mexican blues-rock outfit whose roots go back to the '60s and Mexico City's working class, and Charly Garcia, a musical rebel with a cause in a clamped-down Argentina. It wasn't until the early '90s, though, that this movement bubbled up from the underground and became a force with which the English-speaking world has had to reckon. Spanish folk-rock duo Duncan Dhu signed to Sire and

teamed with Argentinian rocker Miguel Mateos for a small-scale U.S. tour that proved there was an audience outside their home countries. Meanwhile, back home, the socially aware salsa/punk/*cumbia*/Afropop of Maldita Vecindad (Mexico); sassy alternative rock of Soda Stereo (Argentina); dreamy, swirling rock of Caifanes (Mexico); electro-dance grooves of Los Prisioneros (Chile); punk folklorico of Café Tacuba (Mexico); punk-funk-ska of Los Fabulosos Cadillacs (Argentina); sublime, quirky pop of Fobia (Mexico); beautiful, post-McCartney pop of Fito Paez (Argentina); lightweight pop-reggae of Mana (Mexico); and heavy, Doors-like rock of Heroes del Silencio (Spain) began filling clubs and stadiums. No doubt the movement has been helped along by the collapse of the region's military regimes, the introduction of MTV Latino, and the large Spanish-speaking population in los Estados Unidos. By the mid- to late '90s, there was cool stuff coming out of Panama (Los Rabanes); Venezuela (Desorden Publico, Los Amigos Invisibles); Colombia (Aterciopelados); Peru (Pedro Suarez-Vertiz); and the United States (Maria Fatal, Los Olvidados, King Chango, Yeska). In fact, rock en Español could end up being a victim of its own success. With a Grammy category to itself, at least two slick California-based fanzines (*Retila, La Banda Elastica*), specialty record labels (Aztlan, Grita!), and increased media exposure, the young genre could find its unique, fiery cross-cultural musical and political attitudes crushed by hype and a broader, mainstream audience. However, until then, rock en Español—with its often ferocious, soccer game–style live shows, musicians who can skillfully play both sides of the rhythmic border, and lyrics honed by culturally divergent situations—proves that rock's innate spirit doesn't talk only in English and can speak to everyone.

what to buy: Two compilations are absolute musts—*Silencio = Muerte: Red Hot + Latin* ♫♫♫♫ (PolyGram/Hola, 1996, prod. various) and *Reconquista! The Latin Rock Invasion* ♫♫♫♫ (Rhino/Zyanya, 1997, prod. various). The former, a high point in the anti-AIDS "Red Hot" benefit discs, pairs leading Latin lights with cutting-edge English-language performers: Los Lobos with Money Mark; Café Tacuba with David Byrne; and Los Fabulosos Cadillacs with Fishbone. The latter disc is more of a historical sampler of the genre, though compiler Ruben Guevara keeps things on the punk and political end of the spectrum.

what to buy next: In terms of individual acts, here's the essential list: Maldita Vecindad, *El Circo* ♫♫♫♫ (BMG Latin, 1991, prod. Gustavo Santaolalla), a perfect introduction to the genre with its heady blend of cross-continental styles and social observation; Fito Paez, *Circo Beat* ♫♫♫♫ (WEA Latina, 1994, prod. Phil Manzanera, Fito Paez), the Beatles meet Elvis Costello in Buenos Aires; Plastilina Mosh, *Aquamosh* ♫♫♫ (Capitol, 1998, prod. Tom Rothrock, Rob Schnapf, Plastilina Mosh), Beck meets the Beastie Boys meets Esquivel in Mexico; Aterciopelados, *La Pipa de la Paz* ♫♫♫♯ (BMG Latin, 1996, prod. Phil Manzanera), inventive, intelligent rock fronted by the charismatic Andrea Echeverri; Los Fabulosos Cadillacs, *Rey Azucar* ♫♫♫♯ (Sony Discos, 1995, prod. Chris Frantz, Tina Weymouth), a propulsive pastiche of ska, reggae, and punk with some top-shelf guest stars (Mick Jones, Deborah Harry, Big Youth); Caifanes, *El Silencio* ♫♫♫♯ (BMG Latin, 1992, prod. Adrian Belew), moody yet hooky Cure-like art-rock; Soda Stereo, *Cancion Animal* ♫♫♫♯ (CBS Discos, 1990, prod. Gustavo Cerati, Zeta Bosio), muscular pop-psychedelia alt.rock; Los Amigos Invisibles, *The New Sound of the Venezuelan Gozadera* ♫♫♫♯ (Warner Bros./Luaka Bop, 1998, prod. Andres Levin), a party-rocking blend of disco, acid jazz, and bossa-nova lounge; Todos Tus Muertos, *Dale Aborigen* ♫♫♫♯ (Grita!, 1996, prod. Todos Tus Muertos, Guillermo Picolini), ultra-political Bad Brains-ish punk-funk from a group fronted by two Afro-Argentinians; Fobia, *Amor Chiquito* ♫♫♫♯ (BMG Latin, 1995, prod. Gustavo Santaolalla, Fobia), clever and quirky pop-rock; Café Tacuba, *Café Tacuba* ♫♫♫ (WEA Latina, 1992, prod. Gustavo Santaolalla) and *Avalancha de Exitos* ♫♫♫ (WEA Latina, 1996, prod. Gustavo Santaolalla, Anibal Kerpel), both fun stylistic hodgepodges, ranging from Mexican traditionalism to Beck-ish post-modernism, marred only by the sometimes screeching vocals of Cosme (who changes names every album); and Mana, *Donde Jugaran Los Ninos?* ♫♫♯ (WEA Latina, 1992, prod. Fher, Alex Quintana, Jose Quintana), the best album from the Guadalajara outfit whose mix of Police-lite reggae, environmentalism, and suave good looks has made it a major act at home and the first rock en Español band to move to the arena level in the States. Finally, rock en Español is as diverse as its English counterpart. There's ska, rap, and even Celtic-Hispano rock. One of the best of the ska-influenced bands is Desorden Publico, whose two U.S. albums—*Canto Popular de la Vida y Muerte* ♫♫♫♯ (Sony Discos, 1995, prod. Carlos Savalla) and *Plomo Revienta* ♫♫♫♯ (Sony Latin, 1997, prod. K.C. Porter)—are breezy and infectious. *Pura Eskañol: Latin Ska Underground* ♫♫♫ (Aztlan, 1997, prod. various) is a solid compilation of U.S.-based acts. Rap en Español exploded in the mid-'90s thanks to albums such as Molotov's *Donde Jugaran Las Ninas?* ♫♫♯ (Universal, 1997, prod. Gustavo Santaolalla)—whose title is a take-off on the popular Mana album mentioned above—and Control Machete's *Mucho Barato* ♫♫♯ (PolyGram Latino, 1996, prod. Jason Roberts, Antonio Hernandez), both Mexican acts very much influenced by Cypress Hill and the Beastie Boys. The best, though, may come from Spain's Latino Diablo, whose *El Mundo No Es de la Gente Humilde* ♫♫♫♯ (Grita, 1998, prod. Latino Diablo) pounds hard yet has subtle touches. Also from Spain, Celtas Cortos combine a love of both Celtic and Spanish cultures on the knockout *En Estos Dias Inciertos . . .* ♫♫♫♯ (WEA Latina, 1996, prod. Eugenio Munoz, Celtas Cortos).

worth searching for: Some of the most striking music in the genre doesn't get released by American labels, and Latin divisions of U.S. companies are notoriously dim-witted about promoting rock en Español. That means seeking out mom-and-pops or small chains in Latino neighborhoods that carry imports from Latin America to find such gems as Spain's Los Planetas, whose *Super 8* (BMG Mexico, 1995) is an explosion of Replacements/Nirvana–style riff-o-rama.

influences:

⏪ Santana, Los Lobos, War, Los Brazos, Ritchie Valens

⏩ Ozomatli, Maria Fatal, Bloque, Los de Abajo

Cary Darling

Rockin' Dopsie
Zydeco

Born Alton Rubin, February 10, 1932, in Carencro, LA, USA. Died August 26, 1993, in Lafayette, LA, USA.

Most people will know Rockin' Dopsie from "That Was Your Mother" on Paul Simon's *Graceland,* but that was just a footnote to a long and successful career playing zydeco. The former Alton Rubin was born in Carencro, Louisiana, and spent much of his childhood working the land, either picking cotton or cutting cane. He started playing the accordion at 14, encouraged by his father, who was an accordionist himself. Being a lefty, Rubin had to flip over the accordion and play it upside down—the same way Jimi Hendrix played the guitar. He taught himself by learning tunes heard over the radio. His local reputation soon surpassed that of his father, but his career really took off when he moved to Lafayette and began to play the clubs with his cousin Chester Zeno on washboard. Rubin moved up to the three-row button accordion and got the moniker "Dopsie" from an out-of-town dancer who performed in Lafayette. The "Rockin'" was for the drive in his playing, and his bands throughout the '60s and '70s cooked. His sons Alton Jr. and David joined him on drums and *frattoir* (washboard) respectively. There is always a respect for Creole music in his records, and, in turn, a lasting admiration for his legacy among the artists who are carrying it on.

what to buy: *Louisiana Music* ♫♫♫♯ (Atlantic, 1991, prod. Shane Keister, Ahmet Ertegun) was Dopsie's major-label debut, and he got to keep it gritty while having the production values he deserved. This does what a good zydeco record should—it sizzles and then cools into an occasional Ivory Joe Hunter tune like "Since I Lost My Baby" to let you catch your breath.

what to buy next: *Big Bad Zydeco* ♫♫♫♯ (Sonet, 1988, prod. Sam Charters) is worth buying just to hear how a zydeco band

Rockin' Dopsie

reshapes "Jambalaya"—a tune Hank Williams reshaped from the Cajun two-step "Grand Texas"—and brings it home in cooking fashion. Dopsie could drive a dance floor all night with his accordion alone, but this band likes being driven. The production is sparse, but it suits the sound well.

the rest:
Crowned Prince of Zydeco 𝄞𝄞𝄞𝄞 (Maison de Soul, 1987)
Saturday Night Zydeco 𝄞𝄞𝄞𝄞 (Maison de Soul, 1988)
Good Rockin' 𝄞𝄞𝄞 (GNP, 1988)
Zy-De-Co-In' 𝄞𝄞𝄞𝄞 (Gazell, 1989)
Feets Don't Fail Me Now 𝄞𝄞𝄞𝄞 (Aim, 1994)

worth searching for: *French Style* (Sonet, 1982, prod. Sam Charters) brings Dopsie together with Cajun fiddler Dewey Balfa with mixed results. Sometimes it works very well, sometimes it's a little odd—sometimes even in the same tune. Still, a team-up of two legends is worth finding.

influences:
◀◀ Boozoo Chavis, Clifton Chenier, Amédée Ardoin
▶▶ John Delafose, Roy Carrier, Chubby Carrier

see also: *Balfa Brothers, Clifton Chenier*

Jared Snyder

Rockin' Sidney
Zydeco, swamp pop
Born Sidney Simien, April 9, 1938, in Lebeau, LA, USA. Died February 25, 1998, in Lafayette, LA, USA.

Sidney Simien began playing guitar and harmonica before discovering accordion (he also played organ in Lake Charles lounges). He started playing professionally in his late teens and had his first regional hit in 1957. His 1962 chart record "No Good Woman" was backed with "You Ain't Nothin' but Fine," which would eventually be covered by Rockpile. During his days on the soul circuit he was "Count Rockin' Sidney," complete with turban. Like Lynn August, he also worked the Lafayette circuit as an organist. Starting in the 1970s he began to work more in a zydeco vein that owed much to Clifton Chenier, but it was in 1985 that he struck gold with the unlikely hit "My Toot Toot." This song is loosely based on a French term of endearment, "my special all and all." "Toot Toot" won a Grammy and received radio airplay far outside of the normal spectrum for zydeco recordings. As is to be expected, Sidney's sound is much more soul- and R&B-influenced than most other zydeco performers. His recordings are almost always a mixed bag.

what to buy: *My Toot Toot* 𝄞𝄞𝄞 (Maison de Soul, 1986, prod. Sidney Simien) includes the more band-oriented version of the title hit, probably the most well-known zydeco song there is. Sidney covers his hits with a good solid ensemble that includes Katie Webster, Warren Storm, and Marcus Miller, but this is still missing the level of passion and excitement found on most zydeco records.

what to buy next: On *My Zydeco Shoes Got the Zydeco Blues* 𝄞𝄞𝄞 (Maison de Soul, 1984, prod. Sidney Simien), Sidney plays all the instruments. Sometimes this works, sometimes it doesn't. Many tunes from *My Toot Toot* also appear here.

the rest:
Give Me a Good Time Woman 𝄞𝄞𝄞 (Maison de Soul, 1987)
Mais Yeah Chere! 𝄞𝄞𝄞 (Maison de Soul, 1992)
Zydeco Is Fun 𝄞𝄞 (Maison de Soul, 1992)
Boogie, Blues, and Zydeco 𝄞𝄞𝄞 (Maison de Soul, 1995)

worth searching for: Forget about "Toot Toot"; *They Call Me Rockin'* 𝄞𝄞𝄞𝄞 (Flyright, 1974, prod. Floyd Soileau) is the record you want to check out. It's not zydeco or Cajun music, it's the R&B you could find in the same area in the 1960s and 1970s. This is what Sidney is really known for, and *They Call Me Rockin'* brings together his hits and his B-sides. The most famous track here is "You Ain't Nothin' but Fine," but there are plenty of excellent tunes to go around.

influences:
◀◀ Clifton Chenier

⏩ Nathan Williams, Lynn August, Zydeco Force, John Delafose

Jared Snyder

Rocky Boy Singers

Traditional Chippewa-Cree drum group
Formed 1980s, in Rocky Boy, MT, USA. Based in Rocky Boy, MT, USA.

Lloyd Top Sky, lead vocals, drum; Kenny Standing Rock, vocals, drum; Athan Standing Rock, vocals, drum; Clinton Standing Rock, vocals, drum; William Standing Rock, vocals, drum; Merle Tendoy, vocals, drum. (All members are from USA.)

The Rocky Boy Singers are a drum group that use the old Chippewa-Cree rhythms in an attempt to preserve the music of their tribal traditions.

what to buy: The music and drumming on *Montana Homeland* 𝄞𝄞𝄞 (SOAR, 1995, prod. Spotted Eagle) is well recorded and very traditional in style. Some tracks were composed by Lloyd Top Sky, others were given to him by elders like Hector Winnepeg and Alfred Driver.

the rest:
Rocky Boy Chippewa-Cree Grass Dance Songs 𝄞𝄞𝄞 (Indian House cassette, 1982)
Grass Dance and Jingle Dress Songs, Vol. 1 𝄞𝄞𝄞 (Indian House, 1993)
Grass Dance and Jingle Dress Songs, Vol. 2 𝄞𝄞𝄞 (Indian House, 1993)

influences:
◀◀ Ponemah Chippewa Singers, Pigeon Lake Singers

j. poet

Amália Rodrigues

Fado
Born 1920, in the Alfama district of Lisbon, Portugal. Based in Portugal.

Amália Rodrigues is to *fado* what Celia Cruz is to salsa, Umm Kulthum is to Egyptian music, and Edith Piaf is to the art of French cabaret: a queen in her realm. Fado in Portugal, like tangos in Argentina and jazz in America, arose from the lower classes to become an art form associated with the country as a whole. It is a mournful sound, and its poetry is filled with resignation to the inevitability of fate. The classic fado group generally includes a singer and two *guittarras* (a pair of long-necked guitars with a sound approximating Greece's *bouzouki*). The legendary Maria Severa was evidently the first singer to bring fado from the rough-and-tumble environs of the impoverished, desperate Alfama district into society at large, but her reign took place in the mid-1800s. When Rodrigues started her career in 1939 most of the better-known fado singers were men, including Edmundo de Bettancourt and Lucos Junot—but she has since eclipsed all other fado artists in the eyes of her country and be-

come the leading proponent of this art in the eyes of the world. Rodrigues, like Severa, came from the Alfama and rose from these humble beginnings by virtue of her amazingly powerful voice, the force of her personality, and her striking beauty. Rodrigues has toured Europe (with France proving to be especially receptive) and journeyed to various Portuguese-speaking communities around the world. Fado, as sung by Rodrigues, has also had an impact on *morna,* the style of singing most closely associated with Cape Verde and its best-known vocalist, Cesaria Evora.

what to buy: Fado as "fun" is not really a Portuguese concept, but *Amália Rodrigues Sings Portugal* 𝄞𝄞𝄞𝄞 (Celluloid, 1990, prod. Jean-Jacques Lafaye) is packed with energy, almost begging the listener to dance. The guittarras ring and the vocals chime in this well-recorded recital, with "Fadinho Da Ti Maria Benta" and "Malhao De Cinfaes" taking pride of place. This may be the best starting point for newcomers to Rodrigues's art. *The First Recordings* 𝄞𝄞𝄞𝄞 (EPM, 1997, compilation prod. Philippe Zani) shows the power of Rodrigues's young voice in the stripped-down settings of pure fado.

what to buy next: On *Obsessão* 𝄞𝄞𝄞𝄞 (DRG, 1990, compilation prod. Joao Belchlor Viegas), Rodrigues is backed by a quartet— two guittarras, one guitar, and a bass guitar—that puts the emphasis on her voice, where it belongs. Her remake of "Alma Minha" proves that Rodrigues can still sing with power, and the title tune is an admirable example of the kind of paean to puzzlement and acceptance that the best *fadistas* can bring forth at the drop of a hat. *Fado Lisboeta* 𝄞𝄞𝄞𝄞 (BCD, 1992) samples her material from the 1950s and 1960s, which means the traditional format is augmented with full orchestration on some of the songs. The short, mournful clarinet and oboe solos heard during "Que Deus Me Perdoe" could have served as inspiration for the misguided sessions with Don Byas referred to below. The stripped-down, roots-oriented sound of "Disse Mal de Ti" and "Sem Razão" is far more interesting.

what to avoid: The concept of blending American jazz with Portuguese fado is at the heart of *Fado* 𝄞 (Celluloid, 1990, prod. Jean-Jacques Lafaye), but the results just aren't that good. Rodrigues is still in fine voice throughout, but the great jazz saxophonist Don Byas had his playing grafted onto the basic tracks and sounds surprisingly nondescript.

best of the rest:
Amália Rodrigues at the Olympia Theatre 𝄞𝄞𝄞𝄞 (Monitor, 1960)
Queen of the Fado 𝄞𝄞𝄞𝄞 (Sounds of the World, 1992)
Amália Rodrigues 𝄞𝄞𝄞𝄞 (DRG, 1997)
Amália Rodrigues 𝄞𝄞𝄞𝄞 (Pharoah, 1997)

worth searching for: Hearing Rodrigues's potent alto on *American Songs* 𝄞𝄞𝄞 (Celluloid, 1992, prod. Jean-Jacques Lafaye), in arrangements by Norrie Paramor, is a guilty pleasure. Her renditions of "Who Will Buy" and "Blue Moon" won't replace other, better-known versions, but once heard they won't be forgotten either. There are only eight songs here, but the disc's likely cutout-bin price should be worth the experiment.

influences:

◀◀ Maria Severa

▶▶ Bévinda, Dulce Pontes, Marta Dias

Garaud MacTaggart

Virginia Rodrigues

MPB (Brazilian Popular Music), samba, Candomblé, Christian devotional

Born 1964, in Salvador de Bahia, Brazil. Based in Brazil.

Had Virginia Rodrigues been born in Europe, she might have become one of history's all-time-great opera singers—so thank God she was born in Brazil. Gifted with a voice that's a new wonder of the world but coming from humble origins, Rodrigues brings a classical insight and excellence to a thoroughly modern variety of expression. The overused, opera-derived term "diva" ceases to be a cliché when the name "Virginia Rodrigues" appears after it; she goes beyond the triple-underlined belting of a Celine Dion to convey an emotional range as wide as her vocal range. And the Three Tenors have nothing on this one contralto, who avoids the mismatched overkill of a Pavarotti pop song by coming to her material from her own roots rather than from on high. Rodrigues calls upon the spirits of the Afro-Brazilian *Candomblé* religion for her phenomenal talents, and her concerts are enough to make a believer of anyone—they're not-of-this-earth events in which Rodrigues starts and finishes each song as if entering and waking from a trance. Rodrigues wants her voice to sing the realities of black Brazilians, whose recognition lags behind that of the dominant classes in her country as in the rest of the hemisphere (well whaddya know). In finding a fittingly stunning aural environment for her arresting vocals, it was Rodrigues's fortune to encounter wunderkind-cum–elder statesman Caetano Veloso and secure him as her debut album's artistic director. Rodrigues's drop-dead-gorgeous music with the ethnic-pride subtext must have struck a chord with Veloso, whose own *Tropicalismo* style was a good-time sound with metaphorically political lyrics that got him and others exiled from the Brazil of not too long ago. Of course, with lyrics all in Portuguese, the "message" of Rodrigues's music will remain subtextual to many listeners, and it is indeed best accessed through that wondrous voice, a testament to the artistic wealth that can be robbed from the world because some of its artists are born to material poverty. Rodrigues's story has a happily-ever-after, and whatever rewards she now reaps can't compare with her gift to the world.

what's available: You'd need the Jaws of Life to pry *Sol Negro (Black Sun)* ♪♪♪♪ (Hannibal/Rykodisc, 1998, prod. Celso Fonseca) off my stereo. Though it's Rodrigues's only album to date, it's like an advance "best of," with no two songs alike and not a bad one in the bunch. Recorded in an improvised home-studio setting, the album's immaculately intimate sound puts nothing between you and Rodrigues's heavenly voice, though an understated yet substantial array of sparing instrumentation complements it impeccably. Rodrigues makes a trove of treasures from the Brazilian canon her own with interpretive gifts second to none, while this literally millennial event in the music of their country invites inspired cameos by three of Brazil's other very-living legends, Djavan, Gilberto Gil, and Milton Nascimento. The vocals and arrangements swoop and sway from the lilting to the sultry to the reverent, taking in everything from samba to liturgical chant. Forty minutes that changed the course of world-music history. Just wait and see.

influences:

◀◀ Marcio Meireles, Milton Nascimento, Caetano Veloso, Djavan, Gilberto Gil, Maria Bethânia, Candomblé and Christian chant

see also: *Djavan, Gilberto Gil, Milton Nascimento, Olodum, Caetano Veloso*

Adam McGovern

Arsenio Rodríguez

Son montuno

Born August 30, 1911, in Güira de Macurije, Matanzas Province, Cuba. Died December 31, 1970, in New York, NY, USA.

When a horse kicked eight-year-old Arsenio Rodríguez in the head, the young lad's eyesight became history, but he wasn't deprived of a bright musical future. When he was 15 Rodríguez learned how to play the *tres* (a small guitar with three sets of paired strings), bass, maracas, and bongos from Victor Feliciano, a local musician. A few years later Rodríguez started composing tunes and playing tres with his own group, Sexteto Boston. By 1937 he was ready to move on to bigger things, joining the Conjunto Bellamar and the Casino De La Playa before forming his own first classic *conjunto* (a general term for Latin-music bands) in 1940. With his new group, Rodríguez reconfigured the classic *sexteto* and *septeto* lineups (by adding two more trumpets, a piano, and congas), and—because of the band's subsequent popularity—influenced the way many future Cuban outfits would be structured. This new group and Rodríguez's new songs became the foundation of both the mambo and what we know today as "salsa." In 1947 Rodríguez was in New York City, where a doctor told him there was no way to surgically restore his sight. While he was in the States, Rodríguez became involved in a recording session for Chano Pozo that included vocalists Miguelito Valdés and Tito Rodríguez (no relation), and members of Machito's orchestra. The communion with such formidable names must have had an impact on him, for upon returning to Cuba, Rodríguez ended up turning his group over to the legendary trumpeter Felix Chappotin just before moving back to New York City to live. Rodríguez continued to record and perform with various groups through the '60s, experimenting with lineup changes and different formats, including a musical hybrid that he called "quindembo." Even though the music he recorded during the '40s and '50s was influential in the Latin "roots revival" that took place in the late '60s and '70s, Rodríguez died in near obscurity.

what to buy: *Dundunbanza* 𝄞𝄞𝄞𝄞 (Tumbao Cuban Classics, 1994, prod. various) contains a whole slew of hits that Rodríguez recorded in Cuba from 1946 to 1951 with his awesome conjunto. In addition to the leader and a healthy fistful of his compositions (including the title tune and the majestic "Ta Benito Eh"), the ensemble also featured the magical trumpet section of Felix Chappotin, Carmelo Alvarez, and Alfredo "Chocolate" Armenteros. After Rodríguez moved to New York City he hooked up with vocalists René Scull (his cousin, who was in Rodríguez's conjunto on the previous disc) and Candido Antomattei for the sessions found on *Como Se Goza En El Barrio* 𝄞𝄞𝄞𝄞 (Tumbao Cuban Classics, 1992, prod. various). The opening strains of "Esclavo Triste," with its subtle, swaying tres chords rubbing up against a pulsating piano line and understated trumpets, is almost an open invitation to licentious behavior.

what to buy next: *Quindembo: Afro Magic—La Magia de Arsenio Rodríguez* 𝄞𝄞𝄞 (Epic/Sony Tropical, 1963/1995) was an experiment in what Rodríguez called "quindembo," a Congolese-based amalgam that substituted saxophones for the trumpets usually found in Cuban conjuntos. He even sings on "Canto Abacoa" and "Bruca Maniguá," and his tres solo on "Oración Lucumí" is absolutely marvelous. One of the landmark Latin music sessions of all time took place in 1947 at a New York City studio, and the results can be heard on *Legendary Sessions: 1947–53* 𝄞𝄞𝄞 (Tumbao Cuban Classics, 1992, prod. Gabriel Oller). The CD revolves around the marvelous conga player Chano Pozo and finds him in the spotlight with various groups, including a healthy handful of tunes with Rodríguez's conjunto.

best of the rest:

Arsenio Dice . . . 𝄞𝄞𝄞 (Tico, 1968)
A Todos Los Barrios 𝄞𝄞𝄞 (Cariño/BMG, 1974/1992)
Montuneando: 1946–50 𝄞𝄞𝄞 (Tumbao, 1993)
Clasicas De Un Sonero 𝄞𝄞𝄞 (Seeco, 1998)

worth searching for: Tributes to Arsenio Rodríguez abound! One of the first, *Arsenio Rodríguez* 𝄞𝄞𝄞 (Artex, 1993, prod.

jamaican music 5: ska

The charging horns and intensely percussive rhythms of *ska* soared from the heart of downtown Kingston bands to the bull's-eye of the tiny nation's search for the first distinctively Jamaican sound—a search that was intensified in the wake of its new-found independence from Britain in 1962. Ska is the umbilical cord for all Jamaican cultural music, and was conceived from a combination of New Orleans R&B, traditional *mento,* big-band jazz, and sheer indigenous creativity.

The raw, ghetto sound of the amazing Skatalites is the style's archetype. Formed in 1963, the band produced vital, brassy music, which implemented a jerky riff on the offbeat, resulting in more hit songs than any other group in the nation's history. The band also provided superb backup for the top vocalists of the era, including the young Wailers; the Rasta-tinged Justin Hinds & the Dominoes; Lord Creator; and the sanctified Jamaican gospel of the Maytals. Led by the furnace-eyed Bob Marley, the Wailers' own string of ska hits was so popular that on the 7-inch dub plates for their singles the name of the group was replaced by the simple appellation "Scorcher!" Prince Buster developed a variation of ska that highlighted the piano and guitar instead of the brass on the accented beat, along with uniquely integrated hand claps and horn honks; it earned him monster hits as well. On New Year's Day 1965, Skatalite Don Drummond's murder of his girlfriend and subsequent institutionalization and suicide tragically portended the temporary demise of both the Skatalites and ska, as the cooler rhythms of the "rocksteady" style were soon to sway the island. But ska would rise again—and again, during the "two-tone" English revival of the late '70s, and a "third wave" in the U.S. in the '90s. Proudly resounding from a one-time slave depot, the jubilant horns and frenzied rhythms of ska announced a nation's freedom, a people's celebration, and—perhaps most important—the mostly poor and black "sufferahs'" unbridled optimism for a brighter future.

see also: The Skatalites

Todd Shanker

various), mixes classic Rodríguez performances with versions of his tunes by such artists as Chucho Valdés, Irakere, and Grupo Manguaré. There is also a recent, rather whacked-out album by avant jazz guitarist Mark Ribot, *Mark Ribot y los Cubanos Postizos* ♫♫♫ (Atlantic, 1998, prod. J.D. Foster), with strange yet loving renditions of eight songs associated with Rodríguez and one written by Alfredo Boloña, the founder of Sexteto Boloña. The best of all the tributes, though, is probably the one that Sierra Maestra did, *Dundunbanza!* ♫♫♫♫ (World Circuit, 1994, prod. Nick Gold, Marcos González), an album that smokes from beginning to end.

influences:

◀◀ Isaac Oviedo, Victor Feliciano

▶▶ Sierra Maestra, Conjunto Casino, Conjunto Matamoros

see also: *Mario Bauzá, Irakere, Machito, Tito Rodríguez, Sexteto Boloña, Sierra Maestra, Chucho Valdés*

Garaud MacTaggart

Silvio Rodríguez

Nueva trova
Born 1946, in San Antonio de los Baños, Havana Province, Cuba. Based in Havana, Cuba.

The songs of Silvio Rodríguez bear little resemblance to most Cuban music, where rhythm is king. He is the best known of the island's *nueva trova* ("new ballad") artists who emerged in the 1970s. A homegrown variant of the Latin American *nueva canción* ("new song") movement, nueva trova eschewed mainstream Cuban pop and its trappings. Rodriguez's best work is set to acoustic guitar with little or no percussion. That said, he has an amazingly broad palette of sound. He also has a gift for indelible, almost supernatural melodies and arrangements—as catchy as any capitalist ad jingles. His trademark is the easy-listening ballad with offbeat, subversive lyrics.

Rodríguez has been erroneously tagged "the Bob Dylan of Cuba." Sure, he's a folkie whose political tunes became anthems for a generation throughout the region. Yet Rodríguez is no protest singer. On the contrary he was—and is—an enthusiastic supporter of the Castro government, which took power when he was 12. Like the nueva canción singers elsewhere in Latin America, Rodríguez and fellow *neuva trovadore* Pablo Milanés wrote plenty of tender love songs while "protesting" against colonialism, machismo, and tyranny. Their early music was often anti-American—though partly inspired by U.S. folk. Still, Rodríguez's sound is miles from Dylan. With his sweet tenor voice, lilting melodies, and flexible song structures, he is closer to the European troubadour tradition: Rodríguez was influenced by French *chanson* and has often toured and recorded

in Spain, beginning in 1976 when his international debut was released there.

Since then, Rodríguez has embraced more traditional Latin musical forms. In the mid-'80s he began collaborating with the groups Los Van Van and Afrocuba, and in 1990 he taped a live album with Irakere in Chile. Now a musical elder statesman and national hero with more than 20 releases under his belt, Rodríguez has remained active through the '90s. He returned impressively to acoustic music and then launched an ambitious four-part trilogy (!) contemplating his parents and his own maturation.

what to buy: *Cuba Classics 1: Canciónes urgentes* ♫♫♫♫ (Sire/Luaka Bop, 1991, prod. various) is the best place to start. This compilation on David Byrne's label plucks accessible tracks from the first decade-and-a-half of Rodríguez's career, from pop-, rock- and jazz-oriented work to the trademark acoustic ballads. Rodríguez's debut, *Dias y Flores (Days and Flowers)* ♫♫♫ (EGREM, 1975/Carthage/Hannibal, 1976, prod. Frank Fernandez), is uneven, ranging from the irresistible pop opener "Como esperando Abril" to some cheesy period production. But on *Silvio* ♫♫♫♫ (Fonomusic, 1992, prod. Silvio Rodríguez), Rodríguez makes a triumphant return to acoustic ballads after 14 years. He recorded all the music, voices, and sound effects—including champagne pouring and demented yodeling—alone in Havana between 1989 and 1992. This launched a trilogy that continued with *Rodríguez* ♫♫♫ (Fonomusic, 1994, prod. Silvio Rodríguez) and *Dominguez* ♫♫♫ (Fonomusic, 1996, prod. Silvio Rodríguez), dedicated to his father and mother respectively. *Descartes* ♫♫♫♫ (Fonomusic, 1998, prod. Silvio Rodríguez), the fourth installment of the "trilogy," is made up of outtakes from the previous three albums.

what to buy next: *Triptico, Vols. 1–3* ♫♫♫♫ (Areito, 1984, prod. Eduardo Ramos) is a treasure-chest of 25 songs written between 1968 and 1983, dedicated to the 25th anniversary of the revolution. The set ranges from sparse acoustic ballads and instrumental fragments to fully orchestrated seven-minute epics, before ending with a painfully dated 1976 duet with Milanés about the Angolan war. *Causas y azares* ♫♫♫ (Fonomusic, 1986, prod. Silvio Rodríguez) includes music for two films and his first recordings with Afrocuba, recorded in Madrid.

what to avoid: Misleadingly labeled as a Silvio Rodríguez album, *El hombre extraño* ♫ (Iris, 1995) is actually by a mediocre group called Sintesis, with Rodríguez guesting briefly.

the rest:

Mujeres ♫♫♫♫ (EGREM, 1978)
Oh melancolía ♫♫♫♫ (Fonomusic, 1988)
Silvio Rodríguez en Chile ♫♫♫ (Fonomusic, 1991)

worth searching for: Rodríguez sings two songs on *April in Managua* 🎵🎵 (Varagram/Fonomusic, 1984, prod. various), a politically charged live album featuring many of his Latin American cohorts from Chico Buarque to Mercedes Sosa. *Mano a mano* 🎵🎵🎵 (Fonomusic, 1994) is another live album, with Luis Eduardo Aute.

influences:

◀ Violeta Parra, Victor Jara, the Beatles, Bob Dylan

▶ David Byrne, Juan Luís Guerra, Carlos Varela, Los Van Van

see also: *Pablo Milanés*

Wif Stenger

Tito Rodríguez

Latin beat, salsa

Born January 4, 1923, in San Juan, Puerto Rico. Died February 28, 1972, in New York, NY, USA.

As a young teenager, Tito Rodríguez moved to New York from Puerto Rico to sing with the band formed by his brother, Johnny Rodríguez. He also sang with the orchestras of Xavier Cugat, Noro Morales, and Jose Curbelo. In 1947 he started a trumpet quintet of his own. His 1963 recording of "Inolvidable (Unforgettable)" sold over a million copies in Latin America.

what's available: *The Best of Tito Rodríguez and His Orquesta* 🎵🎵🎵 (RCA, 1992) offers a portrait of Rodríguez's music as singer and bandleader in salsa style.

influences:

◀ Xavier Cugat, Jose Curbelo, Johnny Rodríguez

Kerry Dexter

Aldus Roger

Cajun

Born February 10, 1916, in Carencro, LA, USA. Died April 4, 1999. Based in Scott, LA, USA.

Aldus Roger was an accordionist and band leader whose groups set the standard for performance of Cajun music from the late 1950s to the 1970s. He emulated his hero, Lawrence Walker, until his own success finally eclipsed Walker's popularity. Roger was a full-time carpenter, but he was so in-demand that he played every night. His band, the Lafayette Playboys, served as a proving ground for many important young musicians, including swamp-pop singer and historian Johnnie Allan, steel players Phillippe Alleman and Rodney Miller, fiddler Doc Guidry, and Cajun singer Belton Richard. Roger developed a syncopated, energetic style on the accordion, which he played standing and using a shoulder strap (a configuration some credit him with inventing). His bands swung hard through two-steps, with the bass percolating and the steel player coming in on the off-beats. A number of his records feature twin fiddle in a style influenced by western swing, but at their heart there's always pure Cajun singing and Roger's distinctive accordion. Their unique quality is what caused later luminary Zachary Richard to spend two hours a day playing along with Roger's recordings.

what to buy: Roger was known to say that his band would often walk into the studio in the afternoon after appearing on a morning TV or radio show and record. Listen to *A Cajun Legend* 🎵🎵🎵🎵 (La Louisiana, 1995, prod. Carol Rachou Sr.) and see if you can hear any mistakes. This band is so tight and so on-the-music that they make it sound easy. Cajun culture is built around a love of dancing, and you can tell from the effect of this music why the Lafayette Playboys packed the clubs. *Legend* brings together two earlier Roger albums, *Plays the French Music of South Louisiana* and *King of the French Accordion Plays His Old Hits.*

what to buy next: *Plays the French Music of South Louisiana* 🎵🎵🎵🎵 (La Louisiana, 1995, prod. Carol Rachou Sr.) was Roger's biggest seller, and although it's folded into the previously mentioned disc, it stands on its own as a classic of the time. On the two-steps the instruments seem to be chasing each other, with Roger's accordion being followed by Phillip Alleman's steel and then Doc Guidry's fiddle.

worth searching for: *Marie/Be Careful, You're Breaking My Heart* 🎵🎵🎵🎵 (Swallow, c. 1966, prod. Floyd Soileau) is the only 45 rpm record that Roger cut for Swallow, but it has stayed in print on the power of the A-side, which continues to be performed by both Cajun and zydeco bands.

influences:

◀ Lawrence Walker, Sundown Playboys

▶ Zachary Richard, Mark and Ann Savoy, Paul Daigle, Bruce Daigrepont

see also: *Zachary Richard*

Jared Snyder

S.E. Rogie
/Sooliman E. Rogie

Palm wine guitar

Born 1926, in Freetown, Sierra Leone. Died 1994, in Catford, England.

Rogie was just a boy when he heard his first guitar music. He lived out in the country with his uncle, and the music was coming from the local bar. "It was what they call palm wine music," Rogie once said. "It's like folk music or the blues, and probably influenced calypso when they heard it in Trinidad." Rogie got himself a guitar and began playing, partially influenced by the Jimmie Rodgers records he heard. "Highlife [a modern, danceable form] was popular back then, but I liked the more traditional style of acoustic guitar." In the early 1960s, however, Rogie heard rock 'n' roll and shifted over to a more electric sound. He put together a small studio in his home, and began making demos with his friends. One of those tunes, "My Lovely Elizabeth," became a hit, and was picked up by EMI. It then became an even bigger smash and allowed Rogie to put together an African rock 'n' roll band that he called the Morningstars. They had a modest hit of their own, "Twist with the Morningstars," in 1965.

Rogie moved to Oakland, California, in 1973 and was around for the Bay Area's worldbeat boom of the mid-1980s. He put together a small combo to play his old hits and the new material he was writing, but as soon as he'd train a guitarist in the intricacies of his style, that musician would split and form another worldbeat band. During his stay in Oakland Rogie started his own small label and released *African Lady,* a beautiful example of his sparkling playing and gruff, Jimmie Rodgers–style vocals. He was also smart enough to retain the masters of his African sides and released *The '60s Sound of Sooliman E. Rogie,* a collection of his hits from Sierra Leone.

In 1990 BBC Radio asked Rogie to play a few dates in England. Rogie liked the vibe and stayed on, eventually getting signed to Peter Gabriel's RealWorld label. He cut *Dead Men Don't Smoke Marijuana,* a return to the acoustic style of his youth, in 1994, and was putting together a tour to support the album when he died of a heart attack.

what's available: Rogie's mellow vocals and relaxed guitar stylings give the folky tunes on *Dead Men Don't Smoke Marijuana* ♪♪♪♪ (RealWorld, 1994, prod. Tchad Blake) a timeless beauty. You can almost feel the palm wine bubbling in your veins as you surrender to Rogie's soothing, soulful crooning.

worth searching for: *The '60s Sound of Sooliman E. Rogie* gives you a good idea of what African rock 'n' roll sounded like in the 1960s, but the album had limited distribution, even in the Bay Area where Rogie was based when he released it. If you can find it, grab it.

influences:
◀◀ Ticklers, Police Orchestra, Ebenezer Calebdar
▶▶ Karma Kanix, Jungular Grooves, Looters

j. poet

Ruben Romero & Lydia Torea

Flamenco
Formed in Santa Fe, NM, USA. Based in Santa Fe, NM, USA.

Ruben Romero, guitar; Lydia Torea, dance.

Ruben Romero began playing the guitar as a child, eventually

studying both classical and flamenco styles in Spain. He has recorded more than a dozen solo albums and his work appears in a number of contemporary guitar collections. Lydia Torea is a flamenco dancer who began her international career touring with the Jose Greco Dance Company. Currently she heads her own dance conservatory in Phoenix, Arizona.

what's available: *Flamenco Fantasia* ♪♪♪♪ (Canyon, 1993, prod. Ruben Romero, Lydia Torea, Robert Doyle) offers an unusual chance to visit a side of flamenco performance rarely displayed to the public, the *juerga*. That's a sort of jam session in which the intricate relationships between guitarist, dancer, and singer, later to be played out in public presentation, are explored and formed. Romero, the guitarist; Torea, the dancer; singer Chaytto; singer/guitarist Guytano; percussionists Carlos Calleros, Step Raptis, and Jaime Betancourt; and bassist Demetri Sahnas have created a unique picture of that point of creativity. It's an especially well-engineered record that makes clear the percussive role of the flamenco dancer's feet in the music.

influences:
◀◀ Sabicas, Jose Greco

Kerry Dexter

Linda Ronstadt

Mexican, Mexican American, tropical, country, rock, pop
Born July 15, 1946, in Tucson, AZ, USA. Based in Tucson, AZ, USA.

Tucson, Arizona, where Linda Ronstadt grew up, is about an hour's drive from Mexico. It's a border town, an area of the United States that used to be Mexico, and part of that unique mix of cultures that characterizes Mexican American life. Ronstadt found this mix in her own family: her father is Mexican and her mother is Anglo. Though she did not grow up speaking the Spanish language, she grew up singing harmony in Spanish to the *rancheras* and *corridos* her father and brothers enjoyed playing, and trailing around fascinated behind mariachi musicians on family visits to Mexico. As she made her rise through folk-rock and country to pop stardom, Ronstadt didn't make a point of being Mexican American, but neither did she conceal her heritage. In fact, she has said, she tried to incorporate ideas she'd absorbed from listening to her father's records of famous Mexican vocalist Lola Beltrán into her rock singing: "You can hear it most clearly on my earlier records like *Different Drum* in which I made a conscious effort to recreate her vocal tone," she told an interviewer for the biography *Linda Ronstadt: It's So Easy!* "Later, in my version of 'Blue Bayou,'" she continued, "I used falsetto in the end, which is a Mexican vocal trick. Unfortunately, the English language can only accommodate these sounds to a certain extent."

As early as 1978, Ronstadt began to express the desire to record an all-Spanish record, only to have her record company remind her that Joan Baez had done that at the height of her popularity and the record hadn't sold well. Ronstadt kept the idea in the back of her mind, though, and it resurfaced in a way that would lead to the project she had envisioned when she was invited to perform at the Tucson Mariachi Festival in 1985. The organizers of the festival that year knew of the Ronstadt family's Spanish-singing background, and asked her father if performing at the festival was something Linda would like to do. "I said, 'You bet!'" she recalls, "because I knew I would get a chance to meet Mariachi Vargas de Tecalitlan and Ruben Fuentes." In fact, Ronstadt persuaded Fuentes to assist her in arranging and learning songs for the festival, as she discovered that singing lead was quite different than singing harmony on the songs she'd chosen, ones from her father's repertoire that she'd learned as a child. Fuentes, a famous Mexican folksinger who at that time had retired from performing, agreed to help Ronstadt because he saw her devotion to the music. "Even though I had sung these songs when growing up at home," Ronstadt has said, "I had to practice each song 15 to 20 hours just to get the pronunciation, not to mention the intricate Indian rhythm, which is just not the same as our African-based rock 'n' roll." Ronstadt brought her father up on stage with her because "I figured if I was going to embarrass myself then we'd all be embarrassed together," but the performance was a success. It convinced the singer to pursue her plans of making a record of all Spanish songs, a project which eventually turned into three discs, an appearance on public television, and a touring show with a mariachi band, which was, Ronstadt said at the time, "the first time I really felt comfortable and at home on the stage." Ronstadt's appetite for vocal challenge has led her to expand her repertoire of English recordings since doing the Spanish albums, but with them she brought Mexican music and Mexican American culture more firmly to the attention of the mainstream pop audience in the United States.

what to buy: *Canciones de Mi Padre* ♪♪♪♪ (Elektra/Asylum, 1987, prod. Peter Asher, Ruben Fuentes) and *Mas Canciones* ♪♪♪♪ (Elektra/Asylum, 1991, prod. George Massenburg, Ruben Fuentes) show Linda Ronstadt doing what she does best, wringing every drop of vocal power, emotion, and intensity from the tunes she chooses to interpret. Since these are songs—rancheras, corridos, *huapangos,* and *danzas habaneras*—of the border regions and northern Mexico, which have been part of Ronstadt's life since childhood, the emotional connection is powerful. That may explain why *Frenesi* ♪♪♪ (Elektra/Asylum, 1992, prod. George Massenburg, Peter Asher), despite its Grammy for Best Tropical Latin Performance, just doesn't resonate with quite the same intensity. It was a product of Ronstadt's investigation into music of the islands in connection with her work on the film *The Mambo Kings.* Most of Ronstadt's output since *Frenesi* has been in English, but her version of fellow Mexican American Tish Hinojosa's "Donde Voy" on *Winter Light* ♪♪♪♪ (Elektra/Asylum,

1994, prod. Steven Tyrell) is worth seeking out. Of her English-language discs, *Trio* ♪♪♪♪ (Warner Bros., 1987, prod. George Massenburg), *Heart Like a Wheel* ♪♪♪♪ (Capitol, 1974, prod. Peter Asher), *Feels Like Home* ♪♪♪ (Elektra/Asylum, 1995, prod. George Massenburg), and *We Ran* ♪♪♪ (Elektra/Asylum, 1998, prod. George Massenburg) give the most varied and complete picture of Ronstadt as a vocalist of power, emotion, and imagination. Ronstadt has an extensive discography of pop, rock 'n' roll, country-rock, Broadway, and even children's music, and in early 1999 she released a sequel to her Grammy-winning *Trio* country project with Emmylou Harris and Dolly Parton, *Trio 2* ♪♪♪♪ (Asylum, 1999, prod. George Massenburg).

influences:

◄◄ Lola Beltrán, Hank Williams Sr., Mariachi Vargas de Tecalitlan, Emmylou Harris

►► Terri Clark, Lone Justice, Rosanne Cash, Trisha Yearwood, Tish Hinojosa

see also: *The Chieftains, Tish Hinojosa*

Kerry Dexter

The Roots Radics

Roots dancehall
Formed 1978, in Kingston, Jamaica. Based in Kingston, Jamaica.

Vast and varying membership over many years, prominently including: Eric "Bingy Bunny" Lamont (died December 31, 1993), rhythm guitar, vocals; Errol "Flabba" Holt, bass; Lincoln Valentine "Style" Scott, drums; Noel "Sowell Radics" Bailey, lead guitar; Dwight "Brother Dee" Pinkney, lead guitar; Roy Hamilton, lead guitar; Eric "Fish" Clarke, drums; Tony Greene, saxophone; Carlton "Santa" Davis, drums; Wycliffe "Steely" Johnson, keyboards; Earl Fitzsimmons, keyboards. (All members are from Jamaica.)

The mighty Roots Radics laid the molten rhythmic substratum for the entire dancehall era of reggae music. Founded by two former members of the Morwells, vocalist Eric "Bingy Bunny" Lamont and bassist Errol "Flabba" Holt—along with ex–Hippy Boys lead guitarist Noel "Sowell Radics" Bailey and drummer Lincoln Valentine "Style" Scott—the Radics dethroned the Revolutionaries as the island's most in-demand session band in the late '70s, and rhythmically ruled Jamaica until the digital revolution of the mid-'80s. Indeed, it was Lamont's initial baptism as a rhythm guitarist with the Revolutionaries, at the height of the "rockers" era in the mid-'70s, that convinced him to pursue a career as an instrumentalist rather than as a singer/songwriter. The quartet was briefly dubbed the Roots Rock Band during some sinewy sessions with the great toaster and producer Jah Thomas in 1977 and 1978. As the Roots Radics, however, they went on to transform the whole vibe and groove of reggae on subsequent recordings with producers Don "Jah Bible" Mais, Linval Thompson, and Henry "Junjo" Lawes. The Radics slowed the beat down to a sensual, well-oiled skank and at the same time stripped down the instrumental backing to raw, rippling drum-and-bass, punctuated by Bingy Bunny's distinctively stinging, reverb-embellished "skeng" guitar sound. The Radics' genius was to alchemize familiar rhythms (many from the seminal Studio One) into something both texturally inventive and brutally visceral. The Radics were so predominant from 1978 to 1985 that it's almost easier to list the artists they *didn't* back. Suffice it to say that the Radics' menacing rhythms power Barrington Levy's *Bounty Hunter,* Bunny Wailer's *Rock 'N' Groove,* Gregory Isaacs's *Night Nurse,* Freddie McGregor's *Big Ship,* the Wailing Souls' *Fire House Rock,* nearly all of the terrific Scientist dub albums, Johnny Osbourne's *Never Stop Fighting,* John Holt's *Police in Helicopter,* Eek-a-Mouse's *Skidip,* Josey Wales & Yellowman's titanic deejay album *Two Giants Clash,* Papa Michigan & General Smiley's "Diseases," and Triston Palmer's "Entertainment," to name just one far-too-long sentence's worth. In the mid-'80s, the Radics began a long and prosperous association with the roots-harmony trio Israel Vibration, both on record and on tour. Their bond culminated with a coruscating concert in the holy city of Jerusalem in 1993, a performance of tremendous spiritual significance to the ailing Bingy Bunny, who died of prostate cancer that New Year's Eve. At the height of their powers the Roots Radics were one of Jamaica's greatest rhythm sections. Their roiling, rising current of rhythm consistently induced the soul-connected trance state that most of this decade's electronic music only aspires to.

what to buy: Spin your choice of any of the aforesaid albums to hear the Radics' Richter-scale riddims in their prime. But to hear their innovative early grooves—which boldly experiment with spatial contrast and state-of-the-art drum-and-bass topography—check *Roots Tradition from the Vineyard* ℐℐℐℐ (Majestic Reggae, 1997, prod. Don Mais), an invaluable document of the conception, if not the birth, of the deejay-driven dancehall style. This is a collection of outstanding and rare singles from producer Don Mais's Roots Tradition imprint between 1977 and 1980, the majority of which cascade, ebb, and swell due to dramatically propulsive Radics rhythms. The sound and subject-matter are still deeply rootsy, but you can feel the vibe reviving itself into something fresh and new. Highlights include Rod Taylor's prideful "True History," nine-year-old Little John's "Robe," and Peter Ranking & General Lucky's "Housing Scheme," a pulse-quickening protest against both segregation of the poor and the scarcity of safe, affordable shelter. *King Tubby Meets Roots Radics: Dangerous Dub* ℐℐℐℐ (Greensleeves U.K., 1981, prod. Jah Screw, Ranking Joe) and *Jah Thomas Meets King Tubby inna Roots of Dub* ℐℐℐℐ (Rhino U.K., 1982, prod. Nkrumah "Jah" Thomas) are both wonderful oppor-

tunities to hear the inventor of dub himself—the massive King Tubby—magically manipulate a cauldron of hot, surging Radics rhythms. The results are a thing of beauty . . . and dread.

what to buy next: *Jah Jah Dreader Than Dread* ℐℐℐℐ (Majestic Reggae, 1997, prod. Linval Thompson) collects early roots-dancehall rub-a-dub from the Thompson Sound label between 1979 and 1983. This one just drips with the fast-changing, kinetically charged musical atmosphere of the time, and features thick, heavy, simmering rhythms by the Radics behind such great singers, toasters, and roots-harmony groups as Freddie McGregor, Freddie McKay, U-Brown, Triston Palmer, the Wailing Souls, and the Viceroys, all of whom stand atop the mountain and let themselves be heard. Awesome! On *Dubbin' with Horns* ℐℐℐℐ (Burning Sounds, 1981, prod. Nkrumah "Jah" Thomas), the mad beat-chemist known as Scientist mixes the Radics' formidable subterranean boom with a brimming beakerful of some of Jamaica's finest hornsmen—including Dean Frazier, "Deadly" Headley Bennett, Bobby Ellis, and Vincent "Don Drummond Junior" Gordon. Scientist's crafty application of reverb to alternate drumbeats and keyboard chords, and nuanced horn-section fusillades, result in an extraordinarily lively three-dimensional mix.

the rest:
Radical Dub Session ℐℐℐℐ (Solid Groove, 1982)
Radification ℐℐℐ (Cha Cha, 1982)
Scientist and Prince Jammy Strike Back ℐℐℐ (Greensleeves, 1983)
Freelance ℐℐℐ (Kingdom, 1985)
Hot We Hot! ℐℐ℣ (RAS, 1988)
Hot We Hot Dub ℐℐ℣ (Roir, 1989)
Forwards Ever, Backward Never ℐℐℐ℣ (Heartbeat, 1990)
World Peace Three ℐℐℐ℣ (Heartbeat, 1992)
Live at Channel One ℐℐℐ (Live & Love, 1995)
Radically Radics ℐℐ℣ (RAS, 1996)
King Tubby's Rockers ℐℐℐ (Trojan, 1998)

solo outings:
Eric "Bingy Bunny" Lamont:
Me and Jane ℐℐℐ (Cha Cha, 1982)
Kingston 12 Toughie: A Tribute to Bingy Bunny ℐℐℐℐ (RAS, 1996)

Errol "Flabba" Holt:
Vision of Africa ℐℐℐ (Dread & Dread, 1982)

The Morwells (with Lamont & Holt):
Presenting the Morwells ℐℐℐ (Mor-well Esq., 1975)
Dub Me: Morwell Unlimited Meets King Tubby ℐℐℐℐ (Mor-well Esq., 1975/Blood & Fire, 1997)
Crab Race ℐℐℐ (Burning Sounds, 1978)
Cool Runnings ℐℐℐ (Bushays, 1979)
Kingston 12 Toughie ℐℐℐ (Carib Gems, 1980)
The Best of Morwells ℐℐℐℐ (Nighthawk, 1981)

influences:

⏮ The Revolutionaries, Soul Vendors, Sound Dimension, the Morwells, Bongo Herman, Derrick Harriott, Brentford All-Stars, Jah Thomas, Linval Thompson, Henry "Junjo" Lawes, King Tubby, Scientist, Don Mais, Israel Vibration, Hippy Boys, Prince Far I, Zap Pow, Mikey Dread

⏭ Prince/King Jammy, Jah Lion, Prince Hammer, Adrian Sherwood, African Headcharge, Creation Rebel, Singers & Players, Steely & Clevie, Barrington Levy, Eek-a-Mouse, Freddie McGregor, Gregory Isaacs, Congo Ashanti Roy, Triston Palmer, Yellowman, Josey Wales, Papa Michigan & General Smiley, John Holt, Israel Vibration, Wailing Souls, Eberhard Schoener, Cabaret Voltaire

see also: *Black Uhuru, Cocoa Tea, Culture, Eek-a-Mouse, Gregory Isaacs, Israel Vibration, the Itals, King Tubby, Barrington Levy, Freddie McGregor, Sugar Minott, Bunny Wailer, Wailing Souls, Yellowman*

Todd Shanker

Lazaro Ros

Cuban folk music

Born May 11, 1925, in Havana, Cuba. Based in Havana, Cuba.

Lazaro Ros began singing as a child and was initiated into the oral traditions of the Yoruban religion at an early age. At the time of his birth, many Cubans considered African music to be low-class and unsophisticated, but Ros persevered in his musical and religious beliefs. In his early teens, Ros attended the Afro-Cuban rituals at the house of Otilia Mantecón, where he learned from the older drummers and singers whose parents and grandparents had come from, and still remembered, Africa. In 1950 Ros was initiated into La Regla de Osha—the Rule of the Orisha (African deities)—and worked with the master singer Eugenio de la Rosa to learn the pronunciation of the Nigerian language and better preserve the songs, chants, and rhythms of Africa. After the revolution in 1959, Castro encouraged the preservation of Afro-Cuban culture. In 1962 Ros became a founding member of the Conjunto Folklórico Nacional and since then has been tireless in his efforts to preserve and protect traditional forms. He has collaborated with the National Ballet and National Symphony of Cuba and written many theatrical and musical works based on the Afro-Cuban tradition, including *Alafin de Oro* and *Arara,* considered the two most important plays in the repertoire of the Cuban Folk Theater. He has toured widely, taking Afro-Cuban roots music to Europe, North America, South America, and back to Africa. He has arranged tunes for the Cuban rock band Sintesis, recorded "modern" versions of African songs with the Cuban world-music band Mezcla, and created Groupo Olorún, a group of young singers he is training to pass this tradition on to future generations.

what to buy: Credited to Ros and Mezcla, *Cantos* 🎵🎵🎵🎵 (Intuition, 1992, prod. Rachel Faro, Sammy Figueroa) shows what happens when rock 'n' roll, Cuban style, meets its African roots. Mezcla is a "rock" band, but their rock draws as much on the music's African and Latin American sources as it does on the more familiar Anglo/American pop hybrid. The band pulls out the stops, peppering their crunchy guitar explorations with traces of rumba and its African cousin *soukous,* as well as jazz and funk, while Ros cuts through the mix with a simple yet forceful vocal style that's equal parts sandpaper and sugar. No matter what you expect from an album of Cuban music, this set will surprise you.

what to buy next: *Olorún* 🎵🎵🎵🎵 (Ashe/Xenophile, 1994, prod. Rachel Faro, Sammy Figueroa) is a more folkloric outing, beautifully recorded, with Ros and Groupo Olorún backed only by a handful of drummers. The material is traditional, prayers and chants full of stark beauty and uncommon power.

the rest:

Asoyi 🎵🎵🎵♪ (Discmedi, 1993)

influences:

⏮ Pablo Roche, Jesús Peerez, Argelier León

⏭ Sintesis, Mezcla, Los Muñequitos de Matanzas

see also: *Sintesis*

j. poet

Doudou N'Diaye Rose

Wolof drumming

Born 1928, in Senegal. Based in Dakar, Senegal.

They call Doudou N'Diaye Rose the father of modern *sabar* drumming. While *djembes* are played throughout West Africa, the sabars are the royal drums of Senegal and are unique to it. Similarly, Rose himself has largely remained unique to Senegal. Although you can find hundreds of tapes of his work in that country, only two releases are in print worldwide. Rose and his family (including 38 children) often perform together as a percussion orchestra, another concept he introduced to Senegal. He has worked with Western artists including Peter Gabriel, and he contributed to *Four World Songs,* choreographer Kathryn Posin's award-winning entry in the Sarasota Ballet's competition.

what to buy: On *Djabote* 🎵🎵🎵♪ (RealWorld, 1992, prod. Eric Serra), rivaling such ensemble drum classics as the legendary Drummers of Burundi recordings and the holy rhythm of Olatunji, Rose creates an audio sea of percussion with some 50

Lazaro Ros

drummers playing sabar, djembe, and other drums. The album flows on a riptide of cross-rhythms, with tunes like "Khine Sine" sporting a traditional *griot* call-and-response. Pieces like "Walo" get super-intense, with some purely amazing rhythms. The traditional tune "Diame," with the 50 drummers augmented by an 80-voice choir, may be one of the most awe-inspiring pieces of music ever committed to tape.

the rest:
Sabar 𝄞𝄞𝄞 (Melodie France)

influences:
▶▶ Mapathe Diop, Doudiabay N'Diaye, Omar Thiam

see also: *Drummers of Burundi, Babatunde Olatunji*

Hank Bordowitz

Anders Rosén

Folk, classical

Born September 8, 1946, in Malung, Dalarna, Sweden. Based in Sweden.

Anders Rosén was born in Dalarna, Sweden's most famous folk-music province, but due to his father's job with the postal service, the family moved frequently. Rosén took up fiddle at 11, but briefly switched to sax when he got interested in American jazz. "I rediscovered folk music in the mid-1960s," Rosén says. "Swedish jazz musicians, like the piano player Jan Johansson, had done jazz versions of Swedish folk tunes, showing the great possibilities of this music." In 1970 Rosén moved back to Malung in Dalarna and stayed with his grandparents. He introduced himself to Willie Toors, who took him under his wing, teaching him fiddle and introducing him to many of the old fiddlers who still knew the traditional music. Although Toors was a great teacher, Rosén felt the need to develop his own style. With Kalle Almlöf he formed a duo that became quite an influence on the younger folk fiddlers. Rosén also started his own independent folk label, which was unprecedented for the genre in Sweden.

Rosén achieved a breakthrough with his third album, *Forsens låt (Tune of the Rapid),* on which he recruited soprano saxophonist Roland Keijser and featured, for the first time on record, a Swedish kind of fiddle with resonant strings that he had seen in a museum collection. The label was now called "Hurv" after "Hurven," a family of *polska* (triple-time dance) tunes from western Sweden and eastern Norway. In 1976 Rosén made *Stamp, tramp and långkut (Stamp, Tramp and Long-Run)* with Almlöf, in front of a live audience, dancing the polska, a tradition that had almost died out. Rosén and Almlöf supplied free dancing lessons before the concert, and free food and drink during. The evening and album were so successful that the dances

became a weekly event, slowly spreading across the country to create a new generation of traditional dancers.

After Rosén married and had a child, he retired from the indie music business to raise his family; he taught violin and went to school to study baroque music and musicology. He also investigated the historical origins of the polska, but instead of a dissertation, presented the results on a couple of albums, *The History of the Polska I and II.* In 1989 came Utdansbandet (Outdance Band), a contemporary folk ensemble; Rosén also began producing other artists, including Ulf Störling (on *I polskatagen (In a Polska Turn)*). "In the '90s I switched back to the fiddle and concentrated on the traditional local styles from Dalarna," Rosén says. "My goal is to reconstruct old repertoire and playing techniques from my part of Sweden. Young players today learn folk fiddling at courses and music schools—the old fiddlers are gone. There is a risk that original folk playing is substituted with a simplified classical playing technique, because the old-fashioned folk style isn't accepted if one is going to be a teacher. That would be a great loss for Swedish folk music, because genuine folk playing has many secrets and technical specialties, making it quite different from modern classical playing. There is also a risk in the demand of the 'market' for a folk-music style adapted to 'world music'—creating a mishmash of different unrelated elements that don't blend harmoniously." Rosén's most recent projects include producing Willie Toors's first album, *Från skogar, logar, zigenarläger och cirkustält (From forests, barn dances, gypsy camps and circus tents),* and planning a seven-CD archival series called *Historical Recordings of Swedish Folk Music.* He's also continued his own recording as a solo artist and as a member of duos and trios.

what to buy: *Dance Minuets, 1731–1801* 𝄞𝄞𝄞𝄞 (Hurv, 1998, prod. Mats Hellberg) is a trove of folk archaeology that unearths some of the earliest known dance tunes from the song books of the 1700s, a time when Swedish folk and baroque fiddle styles were hard to separate. Rosén and second fiddler Ulf Störling give us a spirited example of the music that was rocking the house in 1732. Both play gut-stringed fiddles, tuned as they were in the 1700s, which gives the music a rounder, more full-bodied tone.

what to buy next: The solo fiddle outing *Hurv!* 𝄞𝄞𝄞 (Hurv, 1991, prod. Anders Rosén) has a lonesome, haunted quality. Rosén's playing is full of passion, and the music weaves a dark, deeply somber spell.

best of the rest:
(With Kalle Almlöf) *Västerdalton (Sound of West Dalarna)* 𝄞𝄞𝄞 (Hurv, 1972)
(With Kalle Almlöf) *Troskari Tunes* 𝄞𝄞𝄞 (Hurv, 1992)
(With Kalle Almlöf and Per-Olof Moll) *Hopp Tussilunta (Jump Tussilunta)* 𝄞𝄞𝄞𝄞 (Hurv, 1994)

worth searching for: Kristina Ståhl Cedervall's *Horsehair Strings, Tunes from Älvdalen* 🎻🎻🎻 (Hurv, 1996), with Rosén on second fiddle, features traditional tunes from Älvdalen, Sweden's "wildest" musical "dialect."

influences:

◀◀ Willie Toors, Olmorts Erik Olsson

see also: *Willie Toors*

j. poet

Rossy
Malagasy pop

Born Paul Bert Rahasimanana, in Antananarivo, Madagascar. Based in Antananarivo, Madagascar.

Rossy was born in a poor section of Antananarivo, Madagascar's capital city. He got hold of an accordion when he was seven and taught himself how to play. He had a band while he was still in high school, but it was a trip to visit his father, who lived in northeastern Madagascar, that inspired his desire to be a professional musician. The pop music of the northeast is called *salegy*, a bouncy 6/8 dance rhythm that combines Malagasy roots music and some Western influences, notably rock, into a style that has been popular since the late 1960s. ("Malagasy" is the adjectival form of "Madagascar.") Northeast port cities like Diego Suarez and Mahajanga had thriving music scenes and two record labels (Discomad and Kaiamba) that fed this madness. Rossy had never heard electric instruments or experienced such a scene before. When he returned to Antananarivo he acquired a guitar and began playing it, as well as the *valiha* (zither) and flute. He also began borrowing from Madagascar's many folk traditions, as well as rock, funk, reggae, and South African jive, for his new compositions. Rossy's style made him the toast of Antananarivo, successful enough to buy instruments and equipment for his band as well as a bus to have them travel all over the island. In 1986 Globestyle Records sent an expedition to Madagascar to record its pop and folkloric music, though drawing the line between the two is increasingly hard on an island where almost everyone sings and plays an instrument. They recorded two Rossy tunes, which brought him to the attention of Peter Gabriel, who signed Rossy to his RealWorld label. Henry Kaiser and David Lindley fell under Rossy's spell when they recorded their Malagasy hootenannies *A World out of Time, Volumes 1 and 2* (reviewed in this book's Compilations section). They arranged for the Shanachie label to ship a 16-track studio to Madagascar so Rossy could record an album for that label, the acclaimed *One Eye on the Future, One Eye on the Past*. Studio Rossy is the only such facility on the island run by Malagasy musicians and has since become a center for Madagascar's blossoming local folk and world-music scenes.

what's available: *One Eye on the Future, One Eye on the Past* 🎻🎻🎻🎻 (Shanachie, 1992, prod. Rossy) is Malagasy music recorded for the home market, but its vitality and verve can be felt by anyone with ears, or feet that want to dance. As befits an island that lies in the path of ancient trade routes between Asia, Europe, the Pacific, and Africa, the music is complex and multifaceted. There are hints of Hawaiian slack-key guitar, Latin percussion, and Malagasy folk music, and traces of rock, funk, reggae, *soukous* (African rumba), and South African jive, but Rossy and band manage to shamelessly incorporate most of it into their own smooth, rockin' style. *Island of Ghosts* 🎻🎻🎻 (RealWorld, 1991, prod. Vic Coppersmith-Heaven, David Hickman) is another fine collection, although the dance rhythms and synth added by the producers make it sound as much world-beat as Malagasy.

influences:

◀◀ Roger Georges, Tianjamani, Les Smockers

▶▶ Tarika, D'Gary

j. poet

Badal Roy
World/jazz fusion

Born Amerendra Roy Choudhury, 1944, in Bangladesh. Based in NJ, USA.

The two-headed *tabla* drum is one of the most important instruments in Indian music, and one of the most versatilely expressive ones in *all* world music. Although he began learning to play the tabla from his uncle, Dwijendra Bhattacharya, at an early age, percussionist Badal Roy was still an amateur when he came to America in 1968 with a pair of tablas and eight dollars in his pocket. Three days later he took a job as a waiter at an Indian restaurant in New York, and was soon studying with tabla master Alla Rakha by day and performing for diners by night. The story of Roy's discovery is the stuff showbiz myths are made of: a few months after the tabla player began entertaining audiences at New York's A Taste of India restaurant, a young man with a guitar approached him and asked if he could sit in. After playing together for six months, Roy learned that the guitarist was John McLaughlin, who later became a jazz legend, and the next thing Roy knew he was in the studio performing on *My Goals Beyond,* a seminal album in the jazz fusion movement. Shortly thereafter, Roy was asked to record with, and eventually join, Miles Davis's band, and he thus began his long courtship with the cream of America's jazz musicians. Over the years, Roy has recorded with hundreds of stellar artists in the jazz and world-music fields, including Pharoah Sanders, Lonnie Liston Smith, Herbie Mann, Nana Vasconcelos, Babatunde Olatunji, and Purna Das Baul. But perhaps his biggest

Badal Roy (third from left) with Steve Gorn, Amit Chatterjee, and Adam Rudolf

break came in 1988, when he was asked to join Ornette Coleman's Prime Time band, a fruitful partnership that continues today. Strangely enough, although Roy has collaborated with a wide variety of musicians and appeared as a sideman on hundreds of recordings, his first headlining project to be widely available in the U.S. didn't appear until 1997—but he's confident that it is the first of many more to come. "Honestly," he told this writer, "I feel now that I should've done it a long time ago . . . but it's never too late!"

what to buy: For a showcase of Roy's stellar tabla skills, there's no better place to start than his "solo" recording, *One in the Pocket* 𝄠𝄠𝄠𝄠 (Nomad, 1997, prod. Bob Haddad), which features appearances by frequent collaborators like Indian guitarist Amit Chatterjee, Brazil's Duofel, jazz bassist Mike Richmond, and master percussionist Glen Velez. This one's worth owning just for "Rinpoche's Rag," a *Deliverance*-gone-to-India track featuring Jim Bowie's Bengali-style banjo dueling with Mike Richmond's basslines, as Roy's nimble tabla rhythms drive the track to a frenzied crescendo. Whew! For a kinder, gentler Indian music experience, try *Yantra* 𝄠𝄠𝄠𝄠 (Latitudes,

1987, prod. Bob Haddad), Roy's collaboration with American-born *bansuri* bamboo flute master Steve Gorn, which features five gorgeous *ragas* that showcase Roy's largely self-taught classical skills.

what to buy next: Although Roy's tabla is featured less prominently, *Asian Journal* 𝄠𝄠𝄠𝄠 (Nomad, 1988, prod. Bob Haddad) is a brilliant cross-cultural fusion featuring Roy, Gorn, Richmond, Nana Vasconcelos, Turkish saxophonist Ismet Siral, and Turkish percussionist Murat Verdi. Songs like the title track present a seamless marriage of many seemingly disparate musical styles, while tunes like "Bombay Boogie" and "Badal" play to Roy's considerable percussive strengths. Of course, most of Roy's work with jazz fusionists like Pharoah Sanders, Miles Davis, and John McLaughlin is in the same league, but since the list of albums on which Roy has appeared as a sideman is so extensive, the absolute best of the bunch are simply highlighted in the section below.

best of the rest:
John McLaughlin:
My Goals Beyond 𝄠𝄠𝄠𝄠 (Douglas, 1971)

David Rudder

Miles Davis:
On the Corner ♫♫♫♫ (Columbia, 1972)
Miles Davis in Concert ♫♫♫ (Columbia, 1973)
Get Up with It ♫♫♫♫ (Columbia, 1974)

Mike Richmond:
Basic Tendencies ♫♫♫♫ (Nomad, 1989)

Ornette Coleman & Prime Time:
Tone Dialing ♫♫♫ (Harmolodic, 1995)

Ustad Sultan Khan:
Festival of India ♫♫♫♫ (Music of the World)

Steve Turre:
Sanctified Shells ♫♫♫♫♫ (Antilles, 1997)

Pharoah Sanders:
Wisdom through Music ♫♫♫♫ (Impulse!)

worth searching for: Roy has released a number of superb collaborations that are either available only as imports or are currently out of print, including *Endless Radiance* with Amit Chatterjee, *Espelho das Aguas* with Duofel, *Global Brazilians* with Airto Moreira and Flora Purim, and the cassette-only *Songs for Sitar & Tabla* with Indian sitar virtuoso Arooj Lazewal. If you find any of these, buy one for yourself and send one to me!

influences:
◀◀ Alla Rakha, Ravi Shankar, Dwijendra Bhattacharya
▶▶ Zakir Hussain, Bikram Ghosh, Talvin Singh

see also: *Purna Das Baul, Steve Gorn, Bill Laswell, Herbie Mann, Airto Moreira, Babatunde Olatunji, Flora Purim, Mike Richmond, Shakti, Nana Vasconcelos, Glen Velez*

Bret Love

David Rudder

Soca, calypso
Born September 8, 1961, in Port of Spain, Trinidad. Based in Trinidad.

Each year at Carnival time the streets of Port of Spain, Trinidad, explode with music as the island's calypso singers vie for the title of Calypso King, among other honors. In 1986, the first time David Rudder entered the fray, his tune "The Hammer" won him the title of Young King of Carnival (best new performer), Calypso King (best performer), and Road March King (best song). Another of his compositions, "Bahia Girl," took second place in the Road March competition. Capturing four of Carnival's top honors made Rudder the most successful calypso singer and composer Trinidad and Tobago had seen in 30 years. His quadruple crown caused so much jealousy that in 1988 the singer announced his intention to refrain from further Carnival competition, saying, "My job now is to take calypso to the rest of the world.

"To people in the States, calypso means Harry Belafonte," Rudder explains, "but the tradition goes back to slavery days. Calypso makes use of African rhythms, jazz, British and French folk music, rock 'n' roll, and popular styles from neighboring islands like Haiti and Guadeloupe. In the early days, before people could read, calypsos were the newspapers of the black community. The singers commented on politics, made up satirical songs about the slavemasters, and helped keep resistance alive."

Rudder was originally inspired by soul musicians. He says Sly & the Family Stone and Stevie Wonder were early idols. "I admired Sly because of the radical things he did with rhythm, and Stevie Wonder because he was physically handicapped. [Rudder has a slight limp from a childhood bout with polio.] He overcame his blindness with music, so I decided I shouldn't let anything stand in my way." This love of American soul music stayed strong until "I heard some of the early calypsonians, men like Attila the Hun, then of course Kitchner and the Mighty Sparrow. That's when I realized that calypso could make use of soul, jazz, salsa, or whatever I wanted. And calypso has a lyrical freedom you don't find [in other music]." That freedom can be puzzling to people who weren't raised in the calypso tradition. Singers often make comments about the political or sexual lives of public figures that would be considered libelous elsewhere (at least in the pre–Kenneth Starr era). On occasion, governments have been toppled because of the overwhelming public response to a vicious parody, but because of their popularity, the singers remained immune to prosecution. "Men in Trinidad are very macho," Rudder explains. "If you're a public figure and someone makes fun of you, you've got to take it 'like a man' or you'll lose face. In the '30s and '40s the ruling class did attempt to censor the singers. They had to take their songs to the police station to be approved, but the singers would take a false song to the police and sing the real lyrics later on. Once or twice the police tried to stop the shows where the libelous songs were being sung, but riots broke out so they had to give up and accept it.

"People in Trinidad are open to all kinds of music," Rudder continues, "salsa, [Haitian] *compas,* reggae, mambo. In the last couple of years *zouk,* the music from Guadeloupe, has made an impact in Trinidad, and calypso is starting to gain in popularity on the other Caribbean islands as well. It's creating a kind of international musical outlook that's very attractive." Once Rudder was attracted to the music of Trinidad, he taught himself guitar and began writing songs for Charlie's Roots, a band fronted by his friend Tambu (Chris Herbert). Rudder explains that the band took its name from influential calypso label-head Rawlston Charles, for whom they used to do session work, becoming "like the Sly & Robbie of calypso. Chris was an old friend of mine, and when he got a case of writer's block he asked me for a few songs. Then in '86 he had laryngitis, so he asked me to sing for Carnival." The rest is history, though it's far from over. Dropping out of the Carnival competition has allowed Rudder and the band (with he and Herbert now sharing lead vocals) to pursue their own destiny. They tour the world bringing calypso's message of racial unity and political awareness to people from North America to Southeast Asia, and the band is constantly searching for ways to make their music as international as their lyrics. Still, Rudder's outlook has its critics. Some claim that Rudder's music is being diluted by his worldbeat approach, but he discounts that notion. "We grew up in Trinidad listening to all kinds of music: rock, jazz, African music—but we know our own culture inside and out. So instead of losing our roots, listening to these other musics makes our love of calypso stronger. After all, zouk is African Guadalupian music, jazz is African American music, calypso is African Trinidadian. So when we bring these sounds to our music we're not trying to cross over, we're crossing back, bringing these African forms back and reclaiming them. This way we can reach out to the whole diaspora."

what to buy: *Haiti* 🎧🎧🎧🎧 (Sire, 1987, prod. Joe R. Brown) is one of the best calypso albums of the modern generation. It contains the monster hits "Haiti" and "The Hammer," plus the usual solid party grooves.

jamaican music 6: rocksteady

In 1965, the seminal Skatalites broke up. Maybe it was the legendary ska band's demise or maybe it was simply that the post-independence frenzy had calmed a bit, but in 1966, when Hopeton Lewis released the steady-rockin' "Take It Easy," a whole new wave of cooler, more elegant Jamaican music was ushered in." The electric bass superseded the stand-up acoustic version, and slow, strutting basslines overtook the music, as did more emphatic melodicism in general. One of Jamaica's great musicians, Leroy Sibbles of the Heptones, described the change in the book *Reggae Routes*: "Ska is more up-tempo—'uh UH uh UH uh UH'—and we brought it down to 'gidgy gidgy boom, gidgy gidgy boom.' And that's rocksteady." The emphasis on bass and drums has remained vital to all future genres of Jamaican music. But with its deep space between notes and its seductive pacing, rocksteady cast the spotlight on the singers. It was Jamaica's soul sound, and the voices that carried it were unforgettably sophisticated and expressive.

Duke Reid was the king of the rocksteady era, producing a veritable chest-full of booty in the Treasure Isle studio above his wife's liquor store in Kingston. Coxsone Dodd's sound was rougher and tougher than Reid's; he produced a number of "rudeboy"-oriented rocksteady hits about the rebellious and at times violent youth of Kingston's ghettos—though arguably, the two greatest rudeboy achievements were Desmond Dekker's "007 (Shanty Town)" and the Slickers' "Johnny Too Bad," each for Leslie Kong.

It was also in the rocksteady era that nationalistic pride and the Rastafarian faith started coming to the fore in life and music, nourished by outspoken professor Walter Rodney and visits from Martin Luther King Jr. and Emperor Haile Selassie in 1965 and '66. In 1968, the graceful grooves and beautiful vocal virtuosity of rocksteady were about to change with Jamaica's people, as poverty still gripped the island and racial tension and war ravaged the world. The reign of reggae was at hand.

Todd Shanker

the rest:

1990 🎵🎵🎵 (Sire, 1990)

Frenzy 🎵🎵🎵 (Lypsoland, 1992)

worth searching for: Sire Records was at one point going to sink big money into Rudder and calypso, hence the two-CD *This Is Soca* 🎵🎵🎵🎵 (Sire, 1987, prod. Joe Brown), which contains Rudder's *Bahia Girl* album plus a bonus disc of Carnival hits from 1987, including work by Duke, Stalin, Shadow, Gypsy, and others.

influences:

◀◀ Sparrow, Duke, Sly & the Family Stone, Stevie Wonder, Kassav'

▶▶ Chris Herbert (Tambu), Taxi, WCK

see also: *Tambu/Chris Herbert*

j. poet

Adam Rudolph

World-influenced jazz

Born September 12, 1955, in Chicago, IL, USA. Based in Los Angeles, CA, USA.

Adam Rudolph is a world-music drummer who often works in jazz-related contexts. His most famous jazz associations have been with Yusef Lateef (eight albums), Don Cherry, Herbie Hancock, and Kevin Eubanks, and his most jazz-oriented project as a leader, with his group Moving Pictures, appeared on Soul Note. He specializes in hand drums—congas, *djembe, bendir, dumbek, tabla,* talking drum, *udu*—but also plays bamboo flutes, *kalimba* (African thumb piano), *didgeridoo* (Aboriginal Australian blown drone instrument), and synthesizers, with multiphonic singing also ranking among his talents. He draws on music literally from around the world (Bali, Cuba, Ghana, Haiti, India, and Morocco), and has seen more of it than many musicians. He lived in Ghana in 1977 and later spent time with the Gnawa musicians of Morocco, as has pianist Randy Weston. Another major contribution to Rudolph's style was his study of North Indian *tabla* drums with Ravi Shankar's tabla player, Pandit Taranath Rao. Rather than playing in imitation of the styles he studies, however, Rudolph synthesizes them into a cross-cultural melting pot that has a jazz/improvisation sensibility at its core. Rudolph's other groups include the percussion quintet Vashti, with Chicago jazz drummer Hamid Drake, Poovalur Srinivasan (South India), Souhael Kaspar (Egypt), and I Nyomen Wenten (Bali); and the Mandingo Griot Society (co-founded with Jali Foday Musa Suso), which blends traditional African music with R&B and jazz. Moving Pictures uses a variable lineup that has included guitarists Wah Wah Watson and Kevin Eubanks, double violinist L. Shankar, harpist Susan Allen, multi-windplayer Ralph Jones III, and many others, and overlaps somewhat with another Rudolph band, Eternal Wind.

what to buy: Recorded with Yusef Lateef, *The World at Peace: Music for 12 Musicians* 🎵🎵🎵🎵 (YAL/Meta, 1996, prod. Yusef Lateef, Adam Rudolph) is a two-CD dual release on Lateef's and Rudolph's labels. It is a major work full of innovative writing that so far is the crowning achievement of Rudolph's career. Rudolph and Lateef follow unusual processes that include splitting the parts of a given piece between the two composers, who then write independently and put the two halves together after the fact. Lateef was one of the pioneers of the multiculturalism Rudolph has built his sound around, and this compositional method produces not clashes but rather complementary cogs in meshing wheels. There are more normally composed pieces as well on a CD that brings jazz, blues, and world music together in a gloriously coherent whole. A number of musicians from Moving Pictures are included in the ensemble, with Ralph Jones and trumpeter Charles Moore making especially valuable contributions and Lateef excelling like the venerable master he is.

what to buy next: Credited to Moving Pictures, *Skyway* 🎵🎵🎵 (Soul Note, 1994, prod. Adam Rudolph) includes Jones, Allen, Eubanks, and multi-instrumentalist Jihad Racy on *ney* and *salamiyyah* (reed flutes), *oud* (Arabic lute), *kaman* (Arabic violin), *mijwiz* (double clarinet), and *rababah* (Egyptian fiddle). The sheer variety of timbres, textures, and rhythms is a delight, but there is nothing cut-and-paste about the way it all comes together; the music seems to grow organically, with a pervading feeling of ritual throughout the project.

the rest:

(With Hassan Hakmoun and Don Cherry) *Gift of the Gnawa* 🎵🎵🎵 (Flying Fish, 1991)

Adam Rudolph's Moving Pictures 🎵🎵🎵 (Flying Fish, 1992)

Contemplations 🎵🎵🎵 (Meta, 1997)

worth searching for: *The Dreamer* 🎵🎵🎵 (Meta, 1995, prod. Adam Rudolph) was Rudolph's first release on his Meta label, and uses Moore, guitarist G.E. Stinson, Allen, violinist Jeff Gauthier, Jones, vocalist Kimball Wheeler, narrator Robert Wisdom, and Rudolph's young daughter, Hannah, on vocals. It's an opera of sorts, and comes as part of a gorgeous package with 12 paintings accompanying texts (inspired by Nietzsche and Schopenhauer) by Nancy Jackson, with each musical piece matched to a painting. Perhaps because the 32-page spiral-bound booklet is nearly the size of two CDs laid top-to-bottom, and thus an awkward size for chain-store bins, this release may be easiest to obtain by ordering it directly from Rudolph through his Web site, www.metarecords.com, where his other Meta albums are available as well. The suite, as one might guess from its title, often has the floating quality of a dream. The music's more composed nature and the texture of Rudolph's synthesizers and Gauthier's violin combine with

Wheeler's classically trained singing to project a more formal feeling than Rudolph's other recordings.

influences:

◀◀ Don Cherry, Yusef Lateef, Fred Anderson, Malawi Nurdurdin, Charles Moore, Pandit Taranath Rao

▶▶ Kevin Eubanks, Hassan Hakmoun

see also: *Hassan Hakmoun, L. Shankar, Foday Musa Suso, Randy Weston*

Steve Holtje

Runrig

Scottish folk-rock
Formed 1973, in Scotland. Based in Scotland.

Rory MacDonald, bass, vocals, accordion (1973–present); Calum MacDonald, percussion, vocals (1973–present); Blair Douglas, accordion (1973–74, 1978–79); Donnie Munro, vocals (1973–97); Robert MacDonald (died 1986), accordion; Malcolm Jones, guitars, accordion, pipes, hurdy-gurdy, whistle, jew's-harp (1979–present); Richard Cherns, keyboards (1981–86); Iain Bayne, drums, percussion, timpani (1984–present); Peter Washart, keyboards, keyboard programming (1986–present); Bruce Guthro (Canada), vocals (1998–present). (All members are from Scotland except where noted.)

Beginning as a university band playing traditional dance tunes, Runrig has come a long way in 25 years. Their Gaelic folk-rock anthems (with emotional lyrics commenting on social and political conditions past and present) have won them a huge following in Scotland, where their concerts fill large stadium-like venues. Late in the summer of 1997, longtime vocalist Donnie Munro left Runrig to pursue a career in politics. The first album with his successor, Bruce Guthro, was released in 1999 (*In Search of Angels*), with the band carrying on Munro's social consciousness in its own way—Runrig released a special, limited-edition CD single of "May Morning" to commemorate the formation of a Scottish Parliament.

what to buy: Although Runrig's 1988 release, *The Cutter and the Clan,* was issued in the United States by Chrysalis, it is only available now as an import. The one all-original Runrig album presently licensed to a U.S.-based label is *Maral* 𝄞𝄞𝄞𝄞 (Chrysalis, 1995/Avalanche Communications, 1996, prod. Brian Young, Runrig). It's pretty standard late-period Runrig, with Munro's charismatic voice leading the charge over the instrumentalists' energetic, rocked-up march rhythms. "Lighthouse" is a particularly effective track, not as bombastic as several others, but with a melody that lingers long in your mind even after the first time you hear it. The thoughtful lyrics use the metaphor of lighthouse as refuge to relate modern feelings of alienation and confusion.

the rest:
BBC Session/Live at the Royal Concert Hall, Glasgow '96 N/A (BBC Music/EMI, 1999)
Long Distance—The Best of Runrig N/A (BBC Music/EMI, 1999)

worth searching for: If you can find it as an import, *The Cutter and the Clan* 𝄞𝄞𝄞𝄞 (Chrysalis, 1988) is worth picking up. It contains two singularly strong songs with environmental themes: "Protect and Survive" and "Our Earth Was Once Green."

influences:

◀◀ Dick Gaughan, Battlefield Band, Tannahill Weavers, Fairport Convention, Bruce Springsteen, Five Hand Reel

▶▶ Capercaillie, the Oyster Band, Billy Bragg, Rawlins Cross, Wolfstone

Ken Roseman

Rurutu Choir

Polynesian
Formed in Rurutu. Based in Rurutu.

Individual members not identified.

The small, isolated island of Rurutu, roughly 250 miles southeast of Tahiti, has produced a polyphonic *a cappella* choral style with a pentatonic origin in the island's ancient pagan chants. Swooping intonation by the lead voice and the sort of high, wailing head tone heard in traditional Chinese singing have been augmented (some might say corrupted) by the chordal influence of Protestant hymns. The resulting hybrid suggests nothing so much as an independently developed gospel style, with the communal fervor of the group and the individual expression of the high voice perfectly balanced. Sometimes the choir is co-ed, but most often it seems exclusively female, or at least dominated by the treble voices.

what's available: *Polynesian Odyssey* 𝄞𝄞𝄞𝄞 (Shanachie, 1996, prod. Pascal Nabet-Meyer) was the third album produced by scholar/preservationist Pascal Nabet-Meyer in his exploration of Polynesian music, and as the only current record of this group it is a very valuable document. Veteran or open-minded world-music listeners will quickly hear past the variable tuning and (probably deliberately) inexact group intonation (compared to Western choral standards, so intolerant of individual variation) and luxuriate in the fullness of the sound, the diversity of the arrangements, and the passion the singing exudes at every point. It's especially chordal (and thus accessible for first-time listeners) on "Ietu Te Ea," "Pure," and "Faatata," the latter sounding uncannily like "Bringing in the Sheaves." The liner notes are over-romantic and vague, but one Ngatokorua Patia has songwriting credit for all tracks; whether that's merely for publishing purposes or involves either arranging of

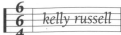

traditional materials or actual composition is not specified. Texts of songs are provided, but not translations, though each lyric is summarized.

influences:
◄◄ Tahitian Choir, Tubuai Choir

see also: *Tahitian Choir*

Steve Holtje

Kelly Russell

Newfoundland folk
Born 1956, in St. John's, Newfoundland, Canada. Based in St. John's, Newfoundland, Canada.

A professional musician since 1974, Kelly Russell was born into a well-known Newfoundland family. His father, Ted Russell, was familiar to Newfoundland audiences through his role as Uncle Mose on CBC radio. Many of the humorous stories the elder Russell used in his radio show were culled from ones local fisherman had told him during his travels around Newfoundland's tiny outport communities as a district magistrate. The deep love for Newfoundland traditional arts that was passed from father to son led to the establishment of Pigeon Inlet Productions in 1979. Since its inception, the record label, owned and operated by Kelly Russell, has produced more than 30 recordings of Newfoundland's rich and diverse musical and storytelling traditions. In addition, Russell was an original member of landmark Newfoundland groups Figgy Duff and the Wonderful Grand Band. But his most fruitful musical relationships were with Newfoundland's late great fiddle masters Rufus Guinchard and Emile Benoit. While primarily known as a fiddler, Russell also plays concertina, bouzouki, mandolin, tin whistle, dulcimer, and harp.

what to buy: It is a testament to Russell's immense talent that no single recording best encompasses his music. This is partly because he has yet to produce a definitive solo recording, all his work having been within band settings. The Plankerdown Band was formed by Russell and accordion player Fran Maher after the demise of Figgy Duff. Their only recording, *The Jig Is Up* 𝄞𝄞𝄞𝄞 (Pigeon Inlet Productions, 1993, prod. Plankerdown Band), is a great collection of traditional music that is in much the same traditional-roots vein as early Figgy Duff. Russell's fiddle and Maher's accordion are front-and-center while the other members provide a steady beat on bass, guitar, and drums—but the core is always acoustic. The playing is excellent and arrangements superb. The ensemble Bristol's Hope features an all-star cast of Newfoundland's finest musicians and is the closest thing to a traditional supergroup you will find in the province. Their only recording, *Lately Come Over* 𝄞𝄞𝄞𝄞 (Pigeon Inlet Productions, 1997, prod. Sandy Morris, Kelly Rus-

sell), is a highly successful combination of Newfoundland's folk instrumental and vocal traditions. This group was formed specifically to celebrate the 500th anniversary of John Cabot's arrival in what was to become Newfoundland, and this album is the best collection of the area's music released since the heyday of Figgy Duff.

what to buy next: Following the demise of the Plankerdown Band, Russell joined forces with St. John's–based alternative outfit Drive to form the Planks. *Smashed Hits* 𝄞𝄞𝄞𝄞 (Pigeon Inlet Productions, 1998, prod. Tom Ronan, Kelly Russell) is the Planks' debut, successfully combining an alternative-music sensibility with the traditional music of Newfoundland. The band convincingly emulates the sounds of Led Zeppelin, Pearl Jam, and Black Sabbath while Russell works his fiddle magic. Guest appearances by the grand master of the Newfoundland accordion, Frank Maher, and a nice version of the traditional song "Arthur McBride," make for a truly diverse and innovative listening experience. The Planks definitely aren't for everyone, but their combination of two seemingly irreconcilable musical forms turns out to be a match made in heaven.

worth searching for: *Tall Are the Tales* 𝄞𝄞𝄞 (Pigeon Inlet Productions, 1995, prod. Kelly Russell) features narratives from seven of Newfoundland's finest storytellers, including Russell and his late father. While there is no music, the stories are entertaining and paint a splendid picture of the island's vibrant tradition in this field.

influences:
◄◄ Emile Benoit, Rufus Guinchard, Ted Russell, Noel Dinn
►► Patrick Moran, Glen Hiscock

Cliff McGann

Rustavi Choir

Georgian Polyphony
Formed 1968, in Georgia, U.S.S.R. Based in Georgia.

Variable and seldom-identified membership over 30+ years, directed by Anzor Erkomaishvili.

Established during the Cold War, this all-male choir is typical of the type of ethnic ensembles once supported by the Soviet regime. Though the basis of the group's material lies in folk music, it is not stylistically "pure." However, the choir's structure sensibly gives the lead vocals in songs from different parts of Georgia to vocalists who hail from those regions. Though use of the term "Georgian Polyphony" is standard, it's something of a misnomer. As noted above, it's not really one style, but several, from various regions of the former Soviet republic. Nor is it usually polyphonic in the strict sense of the word. Most often it's in three parts, a drone bass and two upper parts

The Rustavi Choir

that frequently move in parallel motion. These upper parts sometimes are ornate, or flutter in wide intervals in a style between ululation and yodeling, often on nonsense syllables. Too much has been made of the group's maleness, overemphasizing the singers' robust tones and dissonant harmonies. Not only do female choirs from Eastern Europe tend to exhibit the same qualities, but such stereotyping obscures the great versatility of this group, which excels equally in quiet, mellifluous repertoire.

what to buy: By its very title, *Oath at Khidistavi: Heroic Songs and Hymns from Georgia* ♫♫♫♫ (Shanachie, 1998, prod. Ted Levin) plays into the testosterone stereotype, but two of the highlights are the hushed "Romelni Kerubinta (Those Who Are like the Cherubim)" and the lullaby "Batonebo." There are plenty of rousing tunes, though, with a nice mix of work songs, wedding songs, tales of battle, and the so-called "table songs"—which allow for bravura virtuosity. The liner notes include an interview with choir director Anzor Erkomaishvili and complete lyrics and translations.

what to buy next: Recorded live (in good sound) in Germany in 1986, *2: Georgia* ♫♫♫ (World Network, 1995) gets its title from being the second in a series of World Network releases proceeding by country (some references call this album *Georgian Polyphony*). There are 18 tracks by the Rustavi Choir and six by the instrumental Duduki Trio. There are also two Rustavi tracks with light instrumental accompaniment. Again, there is a well-programmed mix of styles, including some religious material. *Georgian Voices* ♫♫♫ (Nonesuch, 1989, reissue prod. Ted Levin) was this group's introduction to the West. Nonesuch compiled it from 1980s recordings made by the official Soviet record label, Melodiya. It lags slightly behind the group's other albums, but only in recording quality.

worth searching for: *Global Voices: A Vox Set* ♫♫♫♫ (Music of the World, 1998, prod. Bob Haddad) is a three-CD collection of vocal music from around the world. It includes a previously unreleased Rustavi Choir track, "Tsmida Dedoplis Sagalobeli," a liturgical song from the Guria region for four vocal parts. *Voices* ♫♫♫♫ (Alula, 1996, prod. Ulrich Balss) is a compilation of eight modern vocal groups that includes two rare solo tracks by the late singer Hamlet Gonashvili, a Rustavi Choir member who died in 1986.

influences:

◄◄ Red Army Chorus, Bulgarian State Radio & Television Female Vocal Choir (a.k.a. Le Mystère des Voix Bulgares, a.k.a. Angelite)

►► Tsinandali Choir, Ensemble Georgika

Steve Holtje

Cathie Ryan
Celtic
Born November 26, 1959, in Detroit, MI, USA. Based in USA.

In recent years there has been a resurgent interest in female performers of Celtic music. No wonder: with voices as haunting and mystical as that of harpist Aine Minogue, Canadian songstress Loreena McKennitt, or the ever-present Celtic/new-age performer Enya, the sound is stunningly beautiful and captivating. One of the latest upon the scene is Detroit native Cathie Ryan, formerly the lead singer of the renowned New York group Cherish the Ladies. Ryan's parents were from Kerry and Tipperary, Ireland, and Ryan gained much of her Irish musical influence from her grandmother and her father, a singer at the Gaelic League and Irish American Club. They taught her the value of choosing the right songs. From age seven she learned the *sean-nós* unaccompanied singing style and participated in All-Ireland competitions. Eventually Ryan moved to New York, where she studied under legendary sean-nós singer Joe Heaney. She acquired other influences on her music, however, from friends who were fans of country music, Motown, and traditional blues. Eventually, Cherish the Ladies' director and flutist, Joanie Madden, who had heard Ryan sing at a party, asked her to join the troupe. Ryan spent seven years with them, singing and playing *bodhrán* (Irish frame drum), before moving on to a solo career with respected roots/world label Shanachie Records.

what to buy: The artist is nothing less than phenomenal on her self-titled debut *Cathie Ryan* ♫♫♫♫ (Shanachie, 1997, prod. Seamus Egan). She sings in a variety of Celtic styles, from traditional Gaelic to contemporary, her voice gracing melodies by Dougie MacLean, Dave Swarbrick, and Ralph McTell, in addition to the steady, buoyant rhythms of her own "Eveline," inspired by James Joyce. Particularly good is the sadly affecting love poem by John Frazier and Sean Tyrrell, "The 12th of July (Lament for the Children)," which calls for unity among people: "Your badge my patriot brother/It's the everlasting green for me/And we for one another." Though the sean-nós singing she is known for is present here, so are Ryan's American influences, the rhythms and styles that have shaped the rest of her career. *The Music of What Happens* ♫♫♫♫ (Shanachie, 1998, prod. Seamus Egan) continues in Ryan's poignant but affirmative fashion with an astute selection of songs on the traditional-to-contemporary spectrum and impeccable yet flexible vocal technique. Tasteful, sometimes haunting acoustic and *a cappella* settings do Ryan's singular voice great justice. Ryan joins singer Susan McKeown and new-age pianist Robin Speilberg for *Mother: Songs Celebrating Mothers and Motherhood* ♫♫♫ (North Star, 1999), a collection of lullabies, Celtic traditionals, and new compositions exploring the cycles of life and family.

worth searching for: Recorded during her tenure with Cherish the Ladies, *The Back Door* ♪♪♪ (Green Linnet, 1992, prod. Gabrielle Donohue, Eileen Ivers) is titled for Ryan's song, a tribute to Irish immigrants in the United States. Another effort worthy of a concerted search is the Ladies' *Out and About* ♪♪♪ (Green Linnet, 1993, prod. Johnny Cunningham).

influences:
◀◀ Hank Williams, Emmylou Harris, Joe Heaney, Dolores Keane, her grandparents

see also: *Cherish the Ladies, Johnny Cunningham, Susan Mc-Keown*

Stephen Ide

The Sabri Brothers
Qawwali
Formed 1946, in East Punjab, India (now Pakistan). Based in Pakistan.

Ghulam Farid Sabri (died 1994), harmonium, vocals; Maqbool Ahmed Sabri, harmonium, vocals; Haji Kamal Sabri, chirya trana, vocals; Mehmood Ghazanavi Sabri, bongo, vocals; Fazal Islam, vocal; Azmat Farid Sabri, vocals; Sarwat Farid, vocals; Javed Kamal Sabri, vocals; Haji Abdul Karim, dholak; Haji Mohammed Anwar, tabla. (All members are from Pakistan.)

The Sabri Brothers were taught the technique of *qawwali* (the devotional music first known to the world through Nusrat Fateh Ali Khan) by their father and began singing in public when they were still children. They helped modernize the form with a more forceful percussion attack, and the call-and-response between the brothers made their performances especially memorable.

what to buy: *The Greatest Hits* ♪♪♪ (Shanachie, 1997), a compilation of extended performances from the Sabri's Indian albums, is a tour de force with its powerful vocals, relentless percussion, and accompaniment that includes hammered dulcimer and violin. The opening interlude of "Tajdar-E-Harman" sounds strangely similar to the opening notes of Joaquin Rodrigo's "Concerto de Aranjuez" as played by Miles Davis on his *Sketches of Spain* album, raising interesting questions about who influenced whom.

what to buy next: *Ya Habib* ♪♪♪♪ (RealWorld, 1990, prod. Richard Evans), the album that introduced most Westerners to the Sabris, mixes the incredible vocals and percussion way up front, adding to the overall impact.

the rest:
Ya Mustapha ♪♪♪ (Xenophile, 1996)
Qawwali ♪♪♪ (Nonesuch, 1998)

worth searching for: Like many artists, the Sabris have turned out hundreds of cassettes for the Indian market. If you live in or near a city with a large Indian population, you'll be able to find their work in any cassette shop or food store.

influences:
◀◀ Minshi Razi-ud-din Ahmed, the Nazami Brothers, Farid Ayaz Brothers
▶▶ Badar Ali Khan

j. poet

G.S. Sachdev
Indian classical music
Born in India. Based in India.

Gurbachan Singh Sachdev is one of the world's best-known and most accomplished players of the Indian *bansuri* bamboo flute. Sachdev has worked with a who's-who of musicians in his genre, including Ravi Shankar and Ali Akbar Khan. The flute is less familiar as a lead instrument in Indian classical music than the stringed *sarod* and sitar, but Sachdev's impeccable technique makes the *ragas* he plays sound as if they were written for wood instruments. The combination of Sachdev's round, fluid tones with the contemplative nature of the classical pieces he performs has made his music a favorite in meditation/Yoga circles. He frequently appears in a duet format, usually with one of the two leading younger *tabla* drum players, Zakir Hussain or Swapan Chaudhuri.

what to buy: *The World of G.S. Sachdev* ♪♪♪ (Lyricord, 1996, prod. various) is a box set compiling three of Sachdev's best recordings, *Solo Bansuri* (1992), *Live in Concert* (1994), and *Flights of Improvisation* (1996). The concert disc finds Sachdev paired with Swapan Chadhuri and *Flights of Improvisation* is just that, a virtuoso duo performance with Zakir Hussain. *Solo Bansuri* emphasizes unaccompanied pieces, though occasional guests, including *tambura* (stringed drone instrument) player Gay Kagy, also appear.

best of the rest:
Amar Sangit ♪♪♪ (Relaxation Company, 1996)

influences:
◀◀ Ravi Shankar, Vijay Ragh Rao
▶▶ Zakir Hussain, Hari Prasad Chaurasia

see also: *Zakir Hussain, Ali Akbar Khan*

Michael Parrish

G.S. Sachdev

Balwinder Safri /The Safri Boys

Bhangra
Born December 15, 1965, in Blehar Khanpur, the Punjab, India. Based
in London, England.

Balwinder Safri is one of the most influential vocalists in
bhangra, the musical style that developed in the U.K. from roots
in the Punjab region of India. An energetic dance music, bhangra
blends traditional Punjabi music with Western influences, including reggae, hip-hop, rock, soul, and other dance forms. The son
of a *ragi* (religious singer), Safri initially sang Punjabi folk songs.
Emigrating to England in 1981, he switched to bhangra and performed with such popular bands as Azaad, Ashoka, and Geet
Sangeet. With his debut solo album, *Reflections,* released in
1991, Safri became one of the genre's leading performers. Safri's
single "Par Lingarde (Legends)" was one of the first in the style
and became a major hit. Together with his band the Safri Boys (a
rotating ensemble with Safri as the focus), he attained international recognition with the 1994 album *Get Real.* The Safri Boys'
second album, *Off the Record,* followed in 1995.

what to buy: A collection of 10 very diverse bhangra tunes, *Get
Real* ♪♪♪♪ (Multitone/BMG, 1994, prod. Harjinder Bopara)
spent eight weeks at the top of the charts and includes the hits
"Chan Meray Makhna" and "Rehaye Rehaye."

what to buy next: Balwinder and the Safri Boys continued to
weave their infectious Punjabi-inspired dance music on *Off the
Record* ♪♪♪ (Multitone/BMG, 1995, prod. Harjinder Bopara).

influences:
◄◄ Kuldip Manak, Charanjit Ahiya, Gerdes Maan
►► Golden Star, Apache Indian, Bally Sagoo

Craig Harris

Bally Sagoo

Bhangra, Hindi remix, ragga
Born 1964, in New Delhi, India. Based in Birmingham, England.

Bally Sagoo is the man who almost single-handedly changed
the global face of Indian music with his remixes of popular
bhangra and Hindi movie hits. Sagoo grew up like many immigrant children, slightly embarrassed by the music his parents
liked. Sagoo's father, Saminder, was in the Musafirs, a band
that played bhangra, a style of percussion-heavy folk music
from the Punjab, while Sagoo Jr. was into funk, rock, reggae,
and later techno. By the early 1980s the younger Sagoo was a
well-known club and party DJ.

Meanwhile, a new generation of Asian youth had taken
bhangra and made it their own (in England people with roots in

India are called Asian to differentiate them from the large West
Indian immigrant community). When bands like Alaap, the Safri
Boys, and XLNC realized the bhangra beat fit neatly into the
4/4 of rock, reggae, and hip-hop, they began adding Western
drum kits and electric instruments to the traditional percussion
lineup of *dohls* and *tablas.* The result was an explosion of creativity that eventually led to new beats like jungle.

Since he was a musician himself, Sagoo's father had friends at
Oriental Star, one of the new bhangra labels, and helped his
son get a crack at remixing Malkit Singh's "Hey Jamalo," which
was already a big hit. When the younger Sagoo's remix exploded worldwide, the label asked him to do his own remix
album. The result, *Wham Bam, Vol. 1,* caused another sensation, and Sagoo joined the staff of Oriental Star as a producer.
One of his first projects was *Magic Touch,* a collaboration with
Nusrat Fateh Ali Khan that transformed the latter's *qawwali*
style into a dancefloor flavor of the month. Dozens of remix albums followed, including *Star Crazy,* another monster hit.

By 1992 Asian dancers were complaining about the generic
quality of the bhangra beat, and Sagoo put on his thinking cap.
When Jackson Heights DJ Magic Mike suggested doing a remix
job on the latest Hindi soundtrack hits, Sagoo jumped on it.
Bombay, called "Bollywood" in India, produces thousands of
movies a year, and every film includes several extravagant song
and dance numbers—music videos from before the age of television. Films often rise and fall with the popularity of their
soundtrack cassettes, and several generations of Asians are familiar with the biggest soundtrack hits. By this time, Sagoo had
signed to Sony Music U.K., the first Asian artist on their roster.
His inaugural effort for the label was *Bollywood Flashback,* a
collection of Hindi soundtrack tunes given a big fat house 'n'
techno remix treatment. The success of *Bollywood Flashback* —
"Chura Liya," the lead-off single, became the first Indian song
ever played on London's Radio One—created a new industry.
Almost overnight every Asian DJ on the planet was remixing
Bollywood hits and raking in the bucks, but few had the taste
to turn out the kind of smooth dancefloor pop that is Sagoo's
trademark.

what to buy: House, techno, hip-hop, and smooth R&B rub up
against sumptuous Indian vocals by Ranjana Joglekay and
Ireen Perveen to produce *Bollywood Flashback* ♪♪♪♪ (Tristar,
1996, prod. Bally Sagoo), one of the most innovative club albums of the 1990s, regardless of genre.

what to buy next: *Wham Bam* ♪♪♪♪ (Oriental Star, 1990, prod.
Bally Sagoo), Sagoo's first remix album and his first megahit,
includes the smash "Hey Jamalo." This album knocked Asian
club music for a loop, and many people have yet to recover
from its effects.

Balwinder Safri

best of the rest:
Star Crazy ♪♪♪ (Oriental Star, 1991)
Wham Bam, Volume 2 ♪♪♪ (Oriental Star, 1992)
On the Mix ♪♪♪ (Mango U.K., 1993)
Rising from the East ♪♪♪ (Tristar, 1996)

worth searching for: Sagoo has hundreds of cassettes (legit and bootlegged) available. Even the poorest are full of innovative beats and can produce unexpected cultural meltdowns. Check you nearest Indian market or music store.

influences:
◀ Malkit Singh, Mohammed Raffi, Asha Bholse, Alaap, Heera, the Safri Boys, Detroit techno

see also: *Nusrat Fateh Ali Khan*

j. poet

Yan Kuba Saho

Traditional Mandinka kora music
Born mid-1940s, in Danhunhi, Gambia. Based in Serrekunda-Bandung, Gambia.

Yan Kuba Saho was born to a family of Mandinka *griots* (musical oral historians) in Gambia, the heartland of the *kora,* the 21-string harp-lute. He received a traditional griot's education, part kora and part Koran, and after 10 years he began to practice his ancestral art. This involved traveling throughout Gambia and Senegal, performing at ceremonies such as weddings and baptisms, using his music and his dry, powerful voice to praise patrons by evoking the great deeds of their ancestors. This tradition remains strong throughout the Mande (including Mandinka) lands of Mali, Guinea, Senegal, Gambia, Côte d'Ivoire, and Burkina Faso. A person who is being "sung" by a griot experiences a palpable sense of grounding in ancient events. The subject then feels inspired to proceed in the (presumably) honorable and courageous ways of his or her better ancestors. The griots of Africa may be equated with the historians of the West, but in a real sense they act as preemptive psychotherapists as well.

Saho lived in the Gambian capital, Banjul, during the 1960s and '70s before moving to his current family dwelling in the countryside. He has traveled in Europe and North America to perform but has remained a traditional musician rather than pursuing pop fusions of griot music as have so many of his kora counterparts, especially in Mali and Guinea. Saho is undeniably a master, and to compare his solo playing to, say, that of Toumani Diabaté of Mali is to understand the distinctive character of the Gambian kora style. Its sometimes-oblique harmonies and moody stop-and-dash rhythms are among the wonders of African music.

what's available: *Kora Music from Gambia* ♪♪♪ (Music of the World, 1998, prod. Bob Haddad) presents Saho's renditions of

newer songs in the griot repertoire; not the classics, but his playing is absolutely in the tradition, and quite sublime.

influences:
◀ Alhaji Bai Konteh, Amadu Bandang Jobarteh

see also: *Toumani Diabaté*

Banning Eyre

Sainkho

Tuvan, improvisational
Born Sainkho Namtchylak, 1957, in Kyzyl, Tuva. Based in Vienna, Austria; Moscow, Russia; Amsterdam, Holland; and Milan, Italy.

Sainkho stands out in a style where men dominate and women have actually been discouraged from practicing—the phenomenal "throat singing" of the small central Asian Republic of Tuva, a form in which two or more tones are created at once by a single voice. The rarity of her gender gives Sainkho special novelty in a genre that is enjoying widespread novelty appeal overall, but Sainkho herself eschews specific labels, and it is indeed by incorporating these techniques into a broader avant-garde vocabulary that she has most distinguished herself.

Born to schoolteacher parents in a small gold-mining village near the Tuva/Mongolia border, Sainkho studied music at both a local college and in Moscow. Outside of this schooling, she also studied Tuvan and Mongolian throat singing, as well as lamaistic and shamanistic traditions of Siberia. Her professional singing career began as a member of Sayani, the Tuvan State Folk Ensemble. Moving to put her music into a broader context, she began working with improvisational musicians, first in what was then the Soviet Union and later in Europe and the U.S. She joined the ensemble Tri-O (which more or less translates not as "trio" but as "three holes"), with Sergej Letov (sax), Arkadij Kiritschenko (tuba), and Alexander Alexandrov (bassoon), and was noticed in the West. She has frequently collaborated in ad-hoc, free-form performances with horn players; a CD with New York saxophone/woodwind player Ned Rothenberg documents a sterling example. Sainkho seems determined not to be pigeonholed as a "world-music" artist, yet has not abandoned her roots—a difficult balancing act that doesn't please purists of either the world or jazz camps, yet broadens her appeal in the populous space between musical extremes. Gradually, other Tuvan artists are starting to record outside traditional boundaries, following Sainkho's lead, though not necessarily going in her avant-garde direction.

what to buy: *Naked Spirit* ♪♪♪♪ (Amiata, 1998, prod. Marc Eagleton, Matteo Silva) is at press time Sainkho's most recent release, and her most "produced," on a label with new-age leanings. But fear not; this actually works in her favor—she has freedom to explore new sound-combinations, and in a more

Sainkho

structured and focused context than some of her other projects. The title track features the *duduk* (Armenian oboe) playing of Djivan Gasparyan, while on the haunting "Midnight Blue" Sainkho sings over Roberto Cacciapaglia's heavily pentatonic piano. Elsewhere she is joined by percussionists, and the mouth harp is a frequently heard texture. German Popov adds low vocals as well as indigenous Tuvan instruments. Some especially hypnotic tracks seem to utilize tape loops. This is a very approachable album, yet it retains musical depth on repeated listenings.

what to buy next: *Amulet* 𝄞𝄞𝄞 (Leo, 1995) is a duo album with Ned Rothenberg, who gets equal billing. Sainkho and Rothenberg (on saxophone, bass clarinet, and Japanese *shakuhachi* flute) sometimes build off of pre-existing songs, but largely seem to start from scratch and intertwine in imaginative free improvisations where variety of timbre is paramount. Sainkho, though she comes from a different tradition, will on many tracks here remind Western listeners of the more avant-garde moments of Yoko Ono; other possible references could be Joan LaBarbara or even Patty Waters. Much of the album was

recorded in concert, and Tuvan roots are present but hardly predominant—this is music created in the heat of the moment, and valuable for representing the context in which the singer has made the greatest impression on Western listeners.

the rest:
Out of Tuva 𝄞𝄞𝄞 (Crammed Discs, 1993)
Letters 𝄞𝄞𝄞 (Leo, 1995)

influences:
⏮ Bilchi-Maa Davaa, Okna Zam Tasgan, Oorzhak Khunashtaar-ool, Yoko Ono

see also: *Djivan Gasparyan*

Steve Holtje

Buffy Sainte-Marie
International folk, hybrid pop, experimental music
Born February 20, 1941, in Saskatchewan, Canada. Based in HI, USA.

A sizable early output followed by a 25-year low profile has made Buffy Sainte-Marie one of those artistic icons who's more respected than known, but she beat everyone to some of the most fertile and enduring trends in contemporary music. Though most remembered as a folkie, you'll hear the very earliest stirrings of worldbeat, goth, electronica, and new age on her albums, as well as explorations in almost any other style you can name. The folk revitalizations heralded by such artists as Suzanne Vega and Tracy Chapman during the 1980s and Ani DiFranco in the 1990s were actually resumptions of the uncompromising and borderless music movement Sainte-Marie had begun before most of them were born. Her unique, melismatic vocal style introduced a histrionic, revelatory extremity that has revolutionized rock every time it has been expanded on, from Yoko Ono and Patti Smith to John Lydon and Sinéad O'Connor. With her *Illuminations* album, she also ushered in the era of electronic rock, a year before Kraftwerk. The secret is an absolute disregard of limits, which sometimes takes her music over the top but overall has sustained her as a Native American woman in a white male–dominated field and yielded a contribution to the 20th-century musical canon that few have paralleled.

what to buy: Sainte-Marie's debut, *It's My Way!* ✍✍✍✍ (Vanguard, 1964, prod. Buffy Sainte-Marie), takes the gloves right off with the Native rights anthem "Now That the Buffalo's Gone" and never stops slugging, through prime blues-gospel and Hindi standards, window-rattling feminist laments, joyous Americana, and the exhilarating, iconoclastic title track. *The Best of Buffy Sainte-Marie* ✍✍✍✍ (Vanguard, 1970, compilation prod. Maynard Solomon) and *The Best of Buffy Sainte-Marie, Vol. 2* ✍✍✍✍ (Vanguard, 1971, compilation prod. Maynard Solomon) are solid, satisfying collections that rescue many great songs from her out-of-print albums and salvage what's good from her lesser in-print ones.

what to buy next: Even were its ambitious folk/Scottish/Muzak instrumental track to be erased, *Little Wheel Spin and Spin* ✍✍✍✍ (Vanguard, 1966, prod. Buffy Sainte-Marie) would stand as one of the most harrowing and virtuosic vocal performances of the rock era. On *Moonshot* ✍✍✍ (Vanguard, 1972, prod. Buffy Sainte-Marie, Norbert Putnam), Sainte-Marie's damn-the-torpedoes experimentation results in perhaps the most enigmatically bizarre pop album of all time. Recently back in print, *Fire & Fleet & Candlelight* ✍✍✍ (Vanguard, 1967, prod. Maynard Solomon) teeters on the genius/madness razor's edge and often falls over into the latter. The album's cream has already been skimmed for the *Best Of*s—including orchestral art-song numbers conducted by Peter Schickele (soon to become the highbrow prankster PDQ Bach) that surpass most "classical pop" that's been attempted since—but if you want to hear it in its full messy glory, now's your chance.

what to avoid: The quasi-Nashville approach of *I'm Gonna Be a Country Girl Again* ✍✍✍ (Vanguard, 1968, prod. Bob Lucie, May-

jamaican music 7: reggae

At its roots, reggae music encompasses the experiences and aspirations of the "sufferah"— giving formidable voice to the downtrodden, whether in articulating the Rastafarian's spiritual quest, as with Burning Spear's mystical, hypnotic chanting on *Marcus Garvey,* or in crying out the pain of the poor with a survivor's sense of purpose, as on Jimmy Cliff's reggae cornerstone *The Harder They Come*. It is a music with immense humor, as in Lee "Scratch" Perry's gut-busting slap at his former employer, "People Funny Boy." The funky-ass instrumental organ sure-shots of Jackie Mittoo and the Upsetters—that's reggae too, kid! And, as vivified in the mighty sounds of Bob Marley & the Wailers, and in the very image of the imposing "stepping razor" Peter Tosh, reggae is music of fist-pumping rebellion against "Babylon": the system of powerful, often white-skinned oppressors who have devised and implemented the iniquitous institutions of racism, colonialism, and police brutality. Reggae plants its feet on the foundation—earthy rhythms from the African ancestral core, including *nyahbingi, mento,* and *kumina* cultural music. Reggae is that same diminutive sorcerer named Lee "Scratch" Perry, blowing ganja smoke onto his master tapes as a spiritual blessing after creating dense, eerie works of art. Reggae too is the Revolutionaries—the band that updated classic "rocksteady" rhythms with unsurpassed skill, and provided the heart-stopping backup on such classic "rockers" albums as the Mighty Diamonds' *Right Time* and the Wailing Souls' *Wild Suspense,* not to mention their own self-titled masterpiece. The goose-bump-raising roots harmonies of vocal groups like the Abyssinians, Israel Vibration, and Culture—damn right that's reggae. Ditto for Toots & the Maytals' ecstatic "Reggae Got Soul," an ode to joy brought on by music. And perhaps this is the ultimate goal of all reggae—to uplift. As the Wailers sing on "Trenchtown Rock": "One good thing about music/When it hits you, you feel no pain."

Todd Shanker

Buffy Sainte-Marie

nard Solomon) ranges from pedestrian to gauche, with little in between. *She Used to Wanna Be a Ballerina* ♫♫ (Vanguard, 1971, prod. Jack Nitzsche, Buffy Sainte-Marie) is a strained and dated attempt at commerciality. *Up Where We Belong* ♫♫♫ (Angel, 1996, prod. Chris Burkett, Buffy Sainte-Marie) has a few moments of bracing powwow pop that aren't worth its many listless hits remakes, though the better tracks would make a great EP.

worth searching for: Inexplicably out of print, *Illuminations* ♫♫♫♫ (Vanguard, 1969, prod. Buffy Sainte-Marie) electronically processed Sainte-Marie's vocals and guitar to add a kind of proto-sampling and eerie instrumental atmosphere to her haunting folk balladry, prescient worldbeat, and banshee-wail psychedelia. Three decades ahead of its time, it's still a striking listen. On *Coincidence and Likely Stories* ♫♫♫ (Ensign, 1992, prod. Rick Marvin, Chris Burkett, Buffy Sainte-Marie), also revolutionary and out of print, Sainte-Marie synthesized pissed-off political pop with a radical, powwow-influenced singing style that yet again expanded the horizons of what the rock vocal could be. The singer's pronounced tremolo, often misidentified as the tragic flaw that makes her the anti-Baez, is in fact di-

rectly traceable to this rich ritual form of singing, and *Coincidence* is the album on which she started making the connection literal. Its hard-edged version of "Starwalker" (also given a good reading on *Up Where We Belong*) can be found on the must-have anthology *Heartbeat: Voices of First Nations Women,* which is reviewed in this book's Compilations section. Sainte-Marie spent some of her years away from the recording studio, guest-starring on *Sesame Street* with her son and becoming a certified teacher; she has now developed an acclaimed educational program, the Cradleboard Teaching Project. This course links mainstream and Native schools in yearlong distance-learning partnerships, in which the two communities gain understanding of each other through video, telephone, and online exchanges of knowledge. The project's Web site is at www.cradleboard.org.

influences:

◄◄ Woody Guthrie, Pete Seeger, Bob Dylan, Joan Baez, Ben Blackbear

►► Yoko Ono, Patti Smith, Suzanne Vega, Sinéad O'Connor, Tracy Chapman, Diamanda Galas, John Lydon, Morrissey,

Ani DiFranco, Mary Ann Farley, Jim Wilson/Little Wolf, Robbie Robertson

Adam McGovern

Ryuichi Sakamoto

World synth-pop

Born January 17, 1952, in Nakano, Japan. Based in Japan.

Along with Peter Gabriel and Brian Eno, Ryuichi Sakamoto occupies an extremely rare position in contemporary popular music: that of a world-class artist who has created a unique, truly global form of music and whose every move is viewed with excitement and trepidation by fans all over the planet. Schooled in Western classicism but influenced by both Japanese music and Western pop, Sakamoto is an international leader in the melding of synth-pop and dance music with folk elements from not only Japan, but also Africa, Brazil, India, and even (gulp) North America. After an initial solo album in 1978 (*Thousand Knives*), the keyboardist-composer formed the Yellow Magic Orchestra (YMO) with drummer-vocalist Yukihiro Takahashi and bassist-producer Haruomi Hosono. The three took Japan by storm with their arty and sometimes downright silly disco-ish synth-pop. Sakamoto left the trio in 1983 and immediately placed himself squarely on the map with his lovely, synth-inflected score to the film *Merry Christmas, Mr. Lawrence*, the first of close to a dozen such works. In 1984, he took the first step toward the extraordinary synthesis of styles that now characterizes his music, releasing *Illustrated Musical Encyclopedia*. By 1987's *Neo Geo*, he had developed his concept to a level that still stands as a benchmark for world-music fusion, and a year later his portion of the score to Bernardo Bertolucci's *The Last Emperor* won him both an Oscar and a Grammy for best motion picture soundtrack. Since then he has furthered his pop and film-scoring careers, honing the advancements of *Neo Geo* on *Heartbeat* and re-working themes from his scores on *Playing the Orchestra* and the chamber-music album *1996*. Given his interest in using technology to serve the creative process, it's not surprising that his latest release, *Discord*, is also a "CD Extra," with visual tracks and a hyperlink to a special *Discord* Web site. But the music on *Discord*, a four-movement tone poem leading from "Grief" to "Salvation," continues his shift back towards orchestral writing. No matter where Sakamoto's interests lead, however, he will certainly keep on producing quirky, dazzling, beautiful, and ultimately meaningful music of lasting value.

what to buy: From start to finish, *Neo Geo* ♪♪♪♪♪ (Epic, 1987, prod. Bill Laswell, Ryuichi Sakamoto) is a knockout. Framed by gentle, Satie-like instrumental pieces, the album shifts through Okinawan/hip-hop combinations, rocketing dance-funk, and cool 'n' jazzy alternative rock ("Risky," sung by collaborator Iggy Pop). Of Sakamoto's soundtracks, *Merry Christmas, Mr. Lawrence* ♪♪♪♪ (London/Milan, 1983) is the best starting point, as the main theme illustrates his singular ability to mix Asian modality with a rather French, impressionistic style of classical music.

what to buy next: *Heartbeat* ♪♪♪♪ (Virgin, 1991, prod. Ryuichi Sakamoto, David Sylvian) is in many ways a more listenable affair than *Neo Geo*, although it seems more of a stylistic grab bag. Still, no matter what genres he dances through, Sakamoto's composing, arranging, and producing skills are in tip-top form here. The best-known cut from *Illustrated Musical Encyclopedia* ♪♪♪♪ (Midi, 1984) is the bouncy Thomas Dolby collaboration "Field Work," but that track doesn't begin to reveal the cross-cultural wonders hidden within this disc, which ties together big-band jazz lines, Asian beats, rugged classical passages, light funk, and Japanese and Brazilian motifs.

what to avoid: Because Sakamoto has never been much of a singer, he (like Carlos Santana) has often been at the mercy of the vocalists with whom he's collaborated. On *Media Bahn Live* ♪♪♪ (Midi, 1986, prod. Ryuichi Sakamoto), he depends on Bernard Fowler to carry most of the melodies, and Fowler is little more than a middle-of-the-road R&B singer. Even the band seems rather stiff on this double album worthy of dismissal.

the rest:
Thousand Knives ♪♪♪ (Alfa, 1978)
Miraiha Yaro ♪♪♪ (Midi, 1985)
(With David Byrne and Cong Su) *The Last Emperor (Soundtrack)* ♪♪♪♪ (Virgin, 1988)
The Handmaid's Tale (Soundtrack) ♪♪♪ (GNP Crescendo, 1989)
Beauty ♪♪♪♪ (Virgin, 1990)
The Sheltering Sky (Soundtrack) ♪♪♪ (Virgin, 1991)
High Heels (Soundtrack) ♪♪♪♪ (Island, 1992)
Little Buddha (Soundtrack) ♪♪♪♪ (Milan, 1993)
(With Yosuke Yamashita and Bill Laswell) *Asian Games* ♪♪♪♪ (Verve, 1993)
Sweet Revenge ♪♪♪♪ (Elektra, 1994)
1996 ♪♪♪♪ (Milan, 1996)
Smoochy ♪♪♪ (BMG/Milan, 1997)
Discord ♪♪♪♪ (Sony Classical, 1998)

worth searching for: *Playing the Orchestra* (Virgin, 1988, prod. Aki Ikuta, Ryuichi Sakamoto) features a suite of material from the score to *Merry Christmas, Mr. Lawrence* and one from *The Last Emperor*, performed live by an orchestra. The music is gripping, poignant, and marvelously played. Rarity seekers may want to search for the special promo-only boxed version of this album, which includes an extra three-song CD single highlighted by an orchestral version of "Before Long," the opening cut from *Neo Geo*.

Ryuichi Sakamoto

influences:

◀ Brian Eno, Bill Nelson, Prince, David Byrne, Material, Sergio Mendes, Erik Satie, Maurice Ravel, Japanese, African, and Arabian folk music

▶ Pizzicato Five, Deee-Lite, Soul Coughing, Air

see also: *Farafina, Bill Laswell, Talvin Singh, Caetano Veloso*

Bob Remstein

Salala
/Ricky & Mbasalala

Beka (traditional Malagasy funeral music)

Formed 1983, in Taolanaro, Madagascar. Based in Taolanaro, Madagascar.

Mbasalala, lead vocals; Senegemana, vocals, percussion; Christian Andrianjanaka, vocals, Malagasy violin; Ricky Randimbiarison, vocals (recording only, 1995). (All members are from Madagascar.)

Although many people on Madagascar are Christian, many pre-Christian religious practices still survive as well. One is a funeral ritual in which singers known as *mpibeko* improvise a song to soothe the passage between worlds. The songs include details of the departed's life and incantations to calm the spirits of the survivors. These songs are also sung at *famadiahana* ceremonies—where the dead are disinterred and carried to the home of their children to be wrapped in clean sheets before reburial—and at healing ceremonies, where the music is said to enter into the deepest part of the soul and persuade evil spirits to assume a more positive form. Mbasalala and his trio draw on this tradition, but they have also trained in Western music, and use Western ideas of composition and harmony in their music. Mbasalala met Ricky at the German Institute for the Arts in Antananarivo, a school that supports and promotes Malagasy music. ("Malagasy" is the adjectival form of "Madagascar.") Although they both sing with their own groups, Ricky and Mbasalala decided to team up for the disc that bears their name.

what's available: The production on *Ricky & Mbasalala* ✍✍✍✍ (Weltmusik, 1995, prod. Sender Freies) is cleaner than on Mbasalala's earlier *Salala* album, but the music is just as amazing. The singers mix African doo-wop, deep churchy harmonies, rhythmic grunts and pants that could be from Zululand or the mid-Pacific, soaring falsetto flights of ecstasy, and call-and-response vocals that bob and weave like a flock of hummingbirds courting a field of honey-dripping jungle flowers. Another of many world-music styles that display the incredible flexibility of the human voice. The sound on *Salala* ✍✍✍ (Cobalt, 1994, prod. Philippe Conrath) is a bit dry, but it's a minor distraction. Everything mentioned above applies here too; another brilliant low-key gem.

influences:

◀ Bessa

▶ Lazan' Amtanifosty

j. poet

Salamat

Nubian pop

Formed c. 1992, in Cairo, Egypt. Based in Cairo, Egypt.

Fathi Abou Greisha, vocals; Mahmoud Fadl, conga, dohopla, tar; Hassan Meky, accordion, keyboards; Ahmed El Saidy, sax; Salma Abd Rady, vocals. (All members are from Egypt.)

Young players who cut their teeth in Ali Hassan Kuban's Nubian Band strike out on their own, with a Pan-Arabic and Pan-African sound that will rock the casbah, no matter what language you speak.

what's available: *Salam Delta* ✍✍✍✍ (Piranha, 1995, prod. Hijaz Mustapha) is more traditional than their debut, and quite impressive. Salamat joins the Musicians of the Nile for an Egyptian super-session. The aforesaid debut, *Mambo El Soudani* ✍✍✍✍ (Piranha, 1994, prod. Mahmoud Fadl), offers Nubian pop that balances traditional drumming and vocals with African rhythms and a hint of European musical theory. The recording isn't the best, but the muddy mix adds to the music's power. The yearning R&B-flavored sax of Ahmed El Saidy is particularly impressive.

influences:

◀ Ali Hassan Kuban, Hamza El Din

see also: *Ali Hassan Kuban, Musicians of the Nile*

j. poet

Dino Saluzzi

Tango, classical, jazz

Born Timoteo Saluzzi, May 20, 1935, in Campo Santa, Argentina. Based in Argentina.

Dino Saluzzi has a deep and abiding interest in the folk-music traditions of his native country, acquiring them through his membership in a clan of musicians. He learned the *bandoneón* (an accordion-like instrument) from his father and, despite an academic background in avant-garde classical music acquired through later studies, he has always used folk elements as the basis for his compositions. In that regard Saluzzi is a lot like fellow countryman Astor Piazzolla, whose interest in the tango spurred him to experiment with the form. Saluzzi uses the same elements in combination with *milóngas* (Argentinean cowboy songs), *Camdomblé* (Afro-Brazilian ritual) rhythms, and music from the Andean Indian tradition to make a whole new hybrid. Saluzzi has entered the world-music market in the company of jazz performers like Charlie Haden, Edward Vesala, and George Gruntz, adding piquant, folk-rooted improvisations and colors to their music. Despite this, he is best known in South America for his membership in an experimental ensemble called Musica Creativa.

what to buy: *Cite de la Musique* 𝄢𝄢𝄢𝄢 (ECM, 1997, prod. Manfred Eicher) provides an introduction to Saluzzi's jazzier side. Along with bassist Marc Johnson and his son/guitarist, Jose M. Saluzzi, the senior Saluzzi's wizardly bandoneón playing has reached the synthesis of jazz and Argentine tango that was only hinted at in earlier recordings. Despite some quick pattering percussion on songs like "El Rio y el Abuelo," the overall impression is still sensuous and reflective rather than raucous. For *Mojotoro* 𝄢𝄢𝄢𝄢 (ECM, 1992, prod. Manfred Eicher), Saluzzi hired three other talented Saluzzis and a trio of outsiders. The blend of two bandoneóns by Dino and Celso with reed work by Felix (Saluzzis all!) swings in the same lush yet ascetic fashion as many ECM albums. Dino has some of the same stylistic conceits as Astor Piazzolla and Gato Barbieri, but the collective combination of Argentine passion and classical training doesn't take away from anyone's individuality.

what to buy next: With *Rios* 𝄢𝄢𝄢𝄢 (Intuition, 1995, prod. Lee Townsend), Saluzzi is first among equals in a trio with bassist Anthony Cox and vibes/marimba player David Friedman. The interplay between bandoneón and marimba is especially pleasing to the ear, but the music owes more to the vibrant folk roots of Argentina than it does to the traditional jazz bastions of New Orleans, Chicago, or New York. On *Andina* 𝄢𝄢𝄢𝄢 (ECM, 1988, prod. Manfred Eicher), Saluzzi makes his bandoneón jump and mourn through intense, folk-based melodies, much as Piazzolla, Billy Strayhorn, and Zoltan Kodaly did for their respective cultures. Another worthwhile hybrid from Saluzzi is the album he made with the Rosamunde Quartet, *Kultrum: Music for Bandoneón and String Quartet* 𝄢𝄢𝄢𝄢 (ECM, 1998, prod. Manfred Eicher). Where the first *Kultrum* (released in 1983) featured Saluzzi's bandoneón with overdubbed voice, percussion, and flutes (all played by him), this new version combines his instrument with forces more closely aligned with the avant-garde aspects of his earlier training. The resultant blend of folk, jazz, tango, and European-based classical idioms, while heady, may not necessarily be the place for new listeners to start.

the rest:
Kultrum 𝄢𝄢𝄢 (ECM, 1983)
Once upon a Time—Far Away in the South 𝄢𝄢𝄢 (ECM, 1986)

influences:
◀◀ Astor Piazzolla

▶▶ Celso Saluzzi

Garaud MacTaggart

Sam-Ang Sam Ensemble

Mohori (Cambodian folk music)
Formed in Newington, CT, USA. Based in Newington, CT, USA.

Sam-Ang Sam, khloy (flute), thaun-rumanea (drums), roneat (Cambodian folk xylophone) vocals; Pok Van, tror so tauch (mid-range fiddle), tror ou (low-pitch fiddle), krapeu (zither); Yan Van, vocals; Chan Moly Sam, chhing (cymbals); Ra Khlay, vocals; Ngek Chum, roneat ek (high xylophone), roneat thung (low xylophone), khimm (hammered dulcimer). (All members are from Cambodia.)

With the help of some like-minded friends, Sam-Ang Sam and his wife, Chan Moly, formed this group in their adoptive land to play the secular folk music of their original one.

what to buy: *Mohori* 𝄢𝄢𝄢𝄢 (Latitudes, 1997, prod. Sam-Ang Sam) is one of the few albums of Khmer (Cambodian) music available in the States. A *mohori* is a small group composed of string and percussion players; songs are performed alternately—the singer sings a verse, then the band echoes the verse and adds improvisations. The music has a pleasing, percolating quality.

influences:
◀◀ Cambodian folk music

j. poet

Samite

Traditional Ugandan
Born in Uganda. Based in Ithaca, NY, USA.

Samite, like most Africans, lives in many worlds: traditional and contemporary, urban and rural, African and Western, introspective and wildly ebullient. Although he came of age in Uganda during Idi Amin's dictatorship and lost a brother to the reign of terror, his outlook remains positive and he continues to make music that's deeply spiritual; full of love, compassion, and hope.

Samite grew up surrounded by music, some of it literally coming out of the ground. "My mother played a traditional instrument she made by selecting a young supple tree and digging a trench around it. Then she'd fasten a section of tin roofing or a lid from a big metal can to the ground, tie one end of a string to the metal and the other to the tree. By pulling on the tree and plucking the string, she would make the most beautiful sound; music that made the earth sing."

Samite's uncle and grandfather both played flute and exposed him to the recordings of Miriam Makeba, Harry Belafonte, and Barry White, and when the family began renting rooms, he spent hours with the boarders learning to play drums and *kalimba* (thumb piano). Samite's first professional experience was in a band called the Mixed Talents, a group that played

Sam-Ang Sam

covers of tunes by Bob Marley, Kenny Rogers, and Rod Stewart. "We tried to be as Western as possible, and got quite popular." Samite didn't begin to explore his own cultural background until he settled in Kenya and joined the African Heritage Band. "I replaced the flute player, and when I began missing Uganda, I got my own kalimba and amazed myself, because I remembered how to play it." Around the same time, Samite met and befriended an old *litungu* (Kenyan harp) player. The old man taught him how to play litungu, and that instrument led Samite further back to his roots and his home.

By 1982 life in Uganda was unbearable. "Everyone was totally paranoid. The police took my brother away, and since we were very close, I felt that it would be my turn next." Samite fled and landed in a refugee camp back in Kenya, an experience that changed his life. "It is easy to look down on people less fortunate than you. I had always had material things, and didn't realize people who lived on the streets had lives too. In the camp beggar and bank president became equal, all of us in the same desperate situation." Samite remembers one man in particular, a beggar, "who became popular with his amazing stories of the things he'd seen while living on the street. He led a hard life, but he made jokes about everything." Samite came out of the camp a new man. "I learned that despite class or education, we all share the same feelings. There are many differences and complexities, but in the end we all share our common humanity."

After leaving the refugee camp, Samite had musical success in Kenya, both with the African Heritage Band and as a solo act. He emigrated to the United States in 1987 and, thanks to an opening spot on an early Ladysmith Black Mambazo tour, began building a reputation as a traditional African musician. In an unlikely coincidence, a tune he wrote for the African Heritage Band while he was in Kenya came to the attention of the producers of *Good Morning America*. They used it for a segment on the show and the royalties paid for Samite's first home studio. For the past several years Samite has made his living as Uganda's unofficial musical ambassador to the United States. When he's not busy in his studio working on the songs that come to him "in dreams, or through the grace of the instrument," he's constantly performing. "I really enjoy doing shows for young children, especially kids from rural America who have never met an African or been exposed to African music, and young African American children. Children often seem embarrassed about Africa, perhaps from seeing too many Tarzan movies, but by the end of the show they're all singing and dancing. And when the black children see the white kids enjoying it, they develop a real sense of pride about their own culture. After eight years of living and traveling throughout the world, performing in temple courtyards in Japan, music festivals in East Berlin, and at Woodstock '94, the similarities of the human spirit overwhelmingly occupy my thoughts. I am convinced that we are all moved by the same desires, needs, and emotions, regardless of the language in which those feelings are expressed."

Samite's soothingly energetic music may sound jazzy to Western ears, but, as he points out, "Ugandan music, like jazz, is highly improvisational. In my music I use everything I've ever heard, traditional African music, jazz, classical, American country music. When an idea comes to me, I play it over and over again, till it arranges itself into a melody. My music, whether traditional or of my own composition, celebrates the common threads of human concern—love, friendship, the value of family, respect for the elderly, peace, prosperity, and pride in the planet that gave us birth. From the cradle to our last days, we all need to be valued, protected, challenged, and loved."

what's available: *Silina Musango* ♫♫♫♪ (Xenophile, 1996, prod. Samite, Tony Cedras) is a collection of jazzy African praise songs, lullabies, and gently rhythmic ballads. Samite's traditional style is complemented by his jazzy improvisations on drums, kalimba, flute, and harp, with help from the guitar of Tony Cedras and occasional touches of cello, bass, accordion, and backing vocals. Samite recorded the deep, meditative work *Dance My Children Dance* ♫♫♫♪ (Shanachie, 1989, prod. Samite, Al Butterfield) in his home studio; simpler and folkier than *Silina Musango*, but equally as charming.

influences:
◀◀ Sammy Kasule, Maria Wandaka, Jimmy Katumba & the Ebonies

j. poet

Poncho Sanchez

Latin jazz
Born October 30, 1951, in Laredo, TX, USA. Based in TX, USA.

Along with his former boss, Cal Tjader, Poncho Sanchez is one of the two great non-Caribbean Latin-jazz bandleaders. A virtuoso *conguero* (conga player), Sanchez leads one of the most consistent and versatile (not to mention employed) Latin bands in jazz. Growing up in Norwalk, California, in a large Mexican-American family (he was the youngest of 11 kids), Sanchez taught himself flute, guitar, and percussion before learning the congas at age 18. Though it took him a while to break into the close-knit Latin percussion circles, he soon began working with local southern California bands. Hired by Tjader in 1975, he played a central role in that leader's popular group until Tjader's death in 1982. Sanchez formed his own band the same year and recorded two albums for Discovery, then signed on with Concord Picante. His band has become one of the label's staples, recording a series of consistently well-crafted albums, often featuring special guests. Part of the band's strength is its stability—the Banda brothers (Tony on bass and Ramon on *timbales*) have been with Sanchez since the beginning. With his large book of Latin and modern jazz charts, Sanchez fits easily into any musical context, working regularly at clubs, festivals, and concerts.

what to buy: As the title says, *Para Todos* ♪♪♪♪♪ (Concord Picante, 1994, prod. Carl E. Jefferson, John Burk) has something for everyone, including a very funky dose of tenor saxophonist Eddie Harris, who fits right in with Sanchez's typically well-played Latin jazz. Sanchez puts an Afro-Cuban twist on modern jazz tunes by Gerry Mulligan, Harold Land, J. J. Johnson, and Art Farmer, and spurs Harris to some very satisfying low-down tenor work on his great theme "Cold Duck Time." Sanchez's formula of tight, swinging arrangements, strong improvisers, and a mixed program of jazz and Latin themes reaches a perfect balance on *Papa Gato* ♪♪♪♪ (Concord Picante, 1987, prod. Carl E. Jefferson), one of his better sessions. Saxophonist Justo Almario, trumpeter Sal Cracchiolo, and trombonist Art Velasco all take advantage of their solo space, and the band is in excellent form on Horace Silver's "Señor Blues," Dizzy Gillespie's "Manteca," and "Tania," a lovely tune by the band's pianist, Charlie Otwell. A meeting of two Latin jazz giants, *Chile Con Soul* ♪♪♪♪♪ (Concord Picante, 1990, prod. Frank Marrone, Allen Farnham) features one of the best versions of Sanchez's band, with the great timbales player Tito Puente sitting in on two tracks, including one of the most emphatic versions of "Lover, Come Back to Me" ever recorded. Other highlights include pianist Charlie Otwell's title track, Eddie Palmieri's "Con Migo," and Cal Tjader's "Soul Burst."

what to buy next: An excellent Latin jazz session by one of the best bands in the business, *Fuerte!* ♪♪♪♪ (Concord Picante, 1994, prod. Chris Lang) features spirited solos by trumpeter Sal Cracchiolo, trombonist Art Velasco, and tenor saxophonist Kenny Goldberg, who also contributes two strong tunes. Sanchez keeps things interesting by varying the mood with a *bolero* piece and the West African–derived "Alafia" by pianist Charlie Otwell, as well as a smoking Latin version of Clifford Brown's "Daahoud" to close the album. In some sense every album Sanchez has made is a tribute to Cal Tjader, but for *Soul Sauce* ♪♪♪♪ (Concord Picante, 1995, prod. Carl E. Jefferson, John Burk) he recreates the great bandleader's sound by bringing vibraphonist Ruben Estrada into the band. Sanchez picked out a host of tunes associated with Tjader, including Clare Fischer's "Morning" and Mongo Santamaria's "Tu Crees Que." Sanchez's love and respect for his former boss comes through on every track. A must for Latin percussion fans, *Conga Blue* ♪♪♪♪♪ (Concord Picante, 1996, prod. John Burk, Nick Phillips) features the great conguero Mongo Santamaria sitting in on

five tracks, including a brief but blazing version of Herbie Hancock's "Watermelon Man." The band is in fine form, with many solo opportunities for trombonist Alex Henderson, saxophonist Scott Martin, and trumpeter Stan Martin.

the rest:
Sonando ♪♪♪♪ (Concord Picante, 1983)
El Conguero ♪♪♪♪ (Concord Picante, 1987)
Bien Sabroso ♪♪♪♪♪ (Concord Picante, 1988)
La Familia ♪♪♪♪♪ (Concord Picante, 1988)
Cambios ♪♪♪♪ (Concord Picante, 1991)
El Mejor ♪♪♪♪ (Concord Picante, 1992)
A Night with Poncho Sanchez Live: Bailar ♪♪♪♪ (Concord Picante, 1993)
Baila Mi Gente—Salsa ♪♪♪♪ (Concord Picante, 1996)
Freedom Sound ♪♪♪♪ (Concord Picante, 1997)
Concord Jazz Heritage Series ♪♪♪♪ (Concord Jazz, 1998)
Afro-Cuban Fantasy ♪♪♪♪ (Concord Jazz, 1998)

influences:
◄◄ Mongo Santamaria, Cal Tjader, Tito Puente

see also: *Tito Puente, Mongo Santamaria*

Andrew Gilbert

Arturo Sandoval

Afro-Cuban, Afro-Caribbean, jazz
Born November 6, 1949, in Artemisa, Havana, Cuba. Based in USA.

Called "Cubop" when it arose in the 1940s with the late Dizzy Gillespie as its prime innovator, Afro-Cuban jazz is alive today partly through Gillespie's protégé, multi-talented Cuban trumpeter Arturo Sandoval. Much like Gillespie carried on from his models Mario Bauzá and Chano Pozo, Sandoval continues that legacy, merging Afro-Cuban polyrhythms with bebop harmonies and lines. With his band Latin Train, formed in the mid-1990s, Sandoval strives to infuse jazz with Afro-Cuban rhythms instead of merely tacking Latin percussion onto a jazz tune.

Sandoval began playing music at age 13 in a village band, where he learned the rudiments of theory and percussion. He selected the trumpet after playing many instruments, and in 1964 started three years of classical trumpet studies at the Cuban National School of the Arts. By age 16 he'd earned a place in an all-star national band and had his first exposure to jazz recordings by Dizzy Gillespie, who would become his idol and mentor. After a stint in the military (during which he continued to play with the Orquesta Cubana de Música Moderna), Sandoval co-founded Irakere, a Grammy-winning group that melded traditional Cuban music, jazz, classical, and rock into an explosive mixture. This band quickly became a worldwide sensation, and their appearance at the 1978 Newport Jazz Festival in New York introduced them to American audiences and resulted in a recording contract with Columbia. Sandoval left Irakere in 1981, formed his own international touring band, and captured honors as Cuba's best instrumentalist in 1982, 1983, and 1984. He also performed as a classical trumpeter with the BBC Symphony in London and with the Leningrad Symphony in the former Soviet Union.

Sandoval was thrilled to finally meet his muse in 1977 when Dizzy Gillespie was in Cuba to perform. Though Sandoval couldn't speak a word of English, he chauffeured Gillespie into the black neighborhoods to hear musicians play *guaguanco* and rumba in the streets. Gillespie was surprised when his "driver" performed that evening with Irakere. Impressed with the young musician, Gillespie took him under his wing. Sandoval recorded and toured internationally with Gillespie's United Nation Orchestra and appeared on the 1992 recording *Live at Festival Hall.* In fact, it was while touring with this Grammy Award-winning group in Rome in July 1990 that Sandoval requested political asylum. With help from Gillespie and then–Vice President Dan Quayle, Sandoval resettled with his family in Miami, where he now teaches full–time at Florida International University. Although there were problems in the late 1990s with Sandoval's status in the U.S., they have been resolved and he continues to tour extensively, performing jazz, of course, but also classical music with symphony orchestras. He has lectured in the U.S. and overseas and has written and performed on several film soundtracks, including *The Perez Family, The Mambo Kings,* and *Havana.*

what to buy: After Sandoval established his wide-ranging talents on a few GRP albums, he hit big with the one his fans had been waiting for: *Arturo Sandoval & the Latin Train* 𝄞𝄞𝄞𝄞 (GRP, 1996, prod. Arturo Sandoval), an album of 11 Afro-Cuban jazz classics featuring one of Sandoval's hottest bands. Their Cuban grooves and Sandoval's soaring solos could shake dust from club rafters and coax fans to dance in the aisles. Augmented by vocalists and a host of percussionists, the Latin Train band simmers with the expert musicianship of director Kenny Anderson (saxophones), Otmaro Ruiz (piano), David Enos (bass), Aaron Serfaty (drums), and Manuel "Equi" Castrillo (percussion). Sandoval's clean, crisp tone and polished technique are astounding. You'll be reminded of Dizzy, especially when Sandoval hits those shrieking high notes. The energetic tunes are balanced by beautiful Latin ballads such as "Waheera," sweetened with "strings" briefly before the tempo shifts. The band embraces danceable grooves that include mambo, *danzón, son montuno, guajira, guaracha, songo,* and *cha cha cha.* If you can't discern one style from another, just let your head and feet feel the beat. Sandoval soon followed up with *Hot House* 𝄞𝄞𝄞𝄞 (N2K, 1998, prod. Arturo Sandoval), an appropriately titled album that deservedly won him a 1999

Grammy Award for Best Latin Jazz Performance. Influenced by Gillespie's Afro-Cuban jazz bands and by memorable gigs with Cuban outfits including La Orquesta Cubana de Música Moderna, Sandoval brilliantly fronts a Latin big band, playing fiery upper-register solos on tunes that are mostly his originals. Guests Patti Austin, Michael Brecker, Ed Calle, Tito Puente, Rey Ruiz, Charles McNeill, and Rene Toledo add much to the success of this 11-tune album that magnificently builds on the tradition of Sandoval's main mentor, the late Gillespie. Sandoval creatively takes things a few steps ahead with lusciously thick, colorful arrangements and hearty, blended rhythms.

what to buy next: *Danzón* 𝄞𝄞𝄞𝄞 (GRP, 1994, prod. Arturo Sandoval, Richard Eddy) is full of exciting rhythms, soaring solos, and plentiful surprises (for one, Bill Cosby sings). A fun-filled celebration of Afro-Cuban music in the style of the legends, late and living, this 11-rack album shows the full range of Sandoval's talents as player of trumpet, flugelhorn, piano, timbales, and other percussion, as well as singer and composer/arranger. In addition to playing some high-note trumpet, Sandoval sings scat vocals on a hot version of "Groovin' High." A vast powerhouse of talented guest artists maintains the matchless vitality of the album. Joining Sandoval on various tracks are vocalist Gloria Estefan, pianist Danilo Perez, guitarist Rene Toledo, flutist Dave Valentin, percussionist Giovanni Hidalgo, and saxophonist Ed Calle. Highlights are many on this must-own disc of danceable rhythms. For an earful of Sandoval's combustible high-register trumpet playing, check out *The Best of Arturo Sandoval* 𝄞𝄞𝄞 (Milan Latino, 1997, prod. various), an eight-tune compilation of Sandoval's Bernstein-to-bop-to-Latin-fusion performances, along with some originals. You may have to adjust the treble-bass controls on your audio setup, but you'll appreciate the trumpeter's open and muted virtuosity on the diverse mixture of tunes. Unless you hanker for reeling bebop, you may want to pass on the spectacular all-jazz tribute to the late trumpeter Clifford Brown, *I Remember Clifford* 𝄞𝄞𝄞𝄞 (GRP, 1992, prod. Papito, Carl Griffin, Rudy Perez, Arturo Sandoval)—not necessarily "world music," but still stunning. Sandoval's second album as leader after emigrating from Cuba to the U.S. in 1990, it showcases his mastery of the post-bop tradition with racing lines and controlled technique, as well as a warmly compassionate take on the title tune. Although Sandoval is superbly backed by a top-notch rhythm crew and guests including keyboardist Felix Gomez, tenor saxists Ernie Watts, David Sanchez, and Ed Calle, he steers clear of his native rhythms.

the rest:
Tumbaito 𝄞𝄞𝄞 (Messidor, 1986/1991)
Flight to Freedom 𝄞𝄞𝄞 (GRP, 1991)
En Concerto 𝄞𝄞𝄞 (Habacan, 1992)

Dream Come True ♫♫♫♪ (GRP, 1993)
The Classical Album ♫♫♫♫♫ (RCA Victor/Red Seal, 1994)
Swingin' ♫♫♫♫ (GRP, 1996)

worth searching for: A date that brings Sandoval back together with leader Paquito D'Rivera, *Reunion* ♫♫♫♫ (Messidor, 1991, prod. Götz A. Wörner, Uwe Feltens) features the former members of the groundbreaking Orquesta Cubana de Música Moderna and the innovative Irakere. With accomplices fluent in Afro-Cuban rhythms—bassist David Finck, guitarist Fareed Haque, percussionist Giovanni Hidalgo, pianist Danilo Perez, and drummer Mark Walker—Sandoval sizzles in solos, especially when he slows things down for his rendition of "Body and Soul" with Perez and Finck. A totally engaging album from start to finish.

influences:
◀◀ Dizzy Gillespie, Clifford Brown

see also: *Paquito D'Rivera, Gloria Estefan, Irakere, Tito Puente*

Nancy Ann Lee

Tommy Sands

Irish folk
Born in Rostrevor, County Down, Ireland. Based in Ireland.

Tommy Sands is a singer, guitarist, and one of Ireland's truly great songwriters. His songs deal most often with questions of reconciliation, personal and political, and it's no surprise; the small farm in war-torn Northern Ireland where he grew up with his parents and six siblings was often the locus where Catholics and Protestants got together in friendly, intimate circumstances for music, dancing, and fun. His father and six uncles all played the fiddle, his mother played the accordion, and his six aunts lilted for dances—so there was never an absence of music. His first recollections of instrumentals and songs are from a time when he was too young to participate; he would hear the music of the session coming in under the bedroom door. Catholics and Protestants making music together demonstrated to the young Sands children that the lines drawn by political allegiance are artificial, and that they can be transcended by ordinary people.

The sessions also gave Sands his start as a musician and songwriter. After taking up the fiddle for a while, he became more interested in singing, and eventually in songwriting, which he initially saw as a direct outgrowth of traditional music, marking a continuity of traditional creativity. Sands left the farm to go to college, where he studied philosophy and theology. He was nearing home on his final return from university, unsure of his future, wondering if he'd end up working in the ditches like the men he passed along the way, when a black taxi filled with his siblings passed him going in the opposite direction. It stopped, and his brother Colum rolled the window down. "We're going to play a concert," he said. "We've got your guitar in the back of the car." Tommy hopped into the taxi, and became a professional musician. The Sands Family, composed of siblings Tommy, Eugene, Ben, Colum, and Ann Sands, became one of the great groups of the 1960s and '70s Irish folk revival. Tommy remembers feeling the influence of the Clancy Brothers, as well as that of American folk music greats like Pete Seeger and Joan Baez. A first-place award in a national ballad-group contest won the Sandses a concert trip to New York City in 1970; eventually they were playing Carnegie Hall. But the political troubles at home made the family want to stay closer to Ireland, so most of their touring over the years was in Europe. During one of those tours, in 1975, tragedy struck; the youngest brother, Eugene (or Dino, as he was known), was killed in an auto accident going from gig to gig. After that, the family's professional life underwent some major changes. Ann didn't have the heart to tour Germany anymore, so any family tours there were restricted to the three brothers. Meanwhile, Tommy had started a weekly radio program, which continues to this day. The Sands Family, after 14 albums and numerous tours, was reunited as a professional group only once a year for the summer music festivals in Ireland, and Tommy started to tour the world on his own. He can be seen in the U.S. often as a solo act, and occasionally with Mick Moloney's Green Fields of America or with accordion player Mairtin O'Connor.

what to buy: *Singing of the Times* ♫♫♫♫ (Green Linnet, 1989, prod. Colum Sands) features two of Tommy's best-known political songs, "There Were Roses" and "Daughters and Sons." The first of these is probably his most powerful of all; it recalls a sad event in Sands's youth when two of his friends, a Catholic and a Protestant, were murdered in the Northern Irish "troubles." Another nice touch is the inclusion of some old Sands Family tracks, two of which feature the late Dino Sands. Backing musicians, in addition to the Sands family, include Dónal Lunny (bouzouki), Arty McGlynn (guitar), Nollaig Casey (fiddle), and Desi Wilkinson (flute).

what to buy next: *Beyond the Shadows* ♫♫♫♪ (Green Linnet, 1992, prod. Tommy Sands, Colum Sands, Kieran Goss) has several challenging songs on it. "1999" is a call for peace in Northern Ireland, as urgent today after the cease-fire as it was in 1992. "Dresden" explores the feelings of people who have suffered years of oppression. From the Nazis to the allied bombardment to occupation to the Iron Curtain, and finally to the toppling of the Berlin wall, the song follows the story of one small family. Like "There Were Roses," both are quiet and sad songs that don't preach. Also featured is Sands's rollicking emigration ballad, "When the Boys Come Rolling Home." Guests this time include Steve Cooney (guitar, bass, keyboards), Mairtin O'Connor (button accordion), and Tao Seeger (voice and percussion). Sands's third album, *The Heart's a Wonder* 🎵🎵🎵 (Green Linnet, 1995, prod. Tommy Sands), explores similar themes. Like everyone in Northern Ireland, he views the recent cease-fires as a reason to hope for the future. He knows, however, that a solution will only be reached by hard work. "No matter what the eventual solution is to be," he says, "ordinary people have to learn to live together." To that end, he has written "The Music of Healing," his most celebrated song since "There Were Roses." It is a plea for understanding, for love, and for peace, crystallizing the prayers of many Irish people.

worth searching for: Apart from Sands's albums, there are currently no CDs by the Sands Family available in the United States. However, keep a lookout in the used record bins; the Sands family recorded 14 albums for companies in Ireland and Germany, and any one of them is a collector's item today.

influences:

◀◀ Pete Seeger, Joan Baez, the Clancy Brothers & Tommy Makem

▶▶ Colm Sands, Ben Sands, Sean Tyrrel

see also: *Dónal Lunny, Mick Moloney*

                                                                    Steve Winick

Oumou Sangare

Afropop, wassoulou
Born 1968, in Mali. Based in Bamako, Mali.

Oumou Sangare is a singer, songwriter, feminist, and international phenomenon. At the age of six, she made her debut at Mali's Omnisports Stadium to a huge crowd. Her performance was good enough to earn her a place in the National Ensemble of Mali, where she was trained in traditional singing and performance. In 1986 she joined Djoliba, a traditional percussion troupe led by Bamba Dambele, for a world tour. On her return to Mali she was determined to start her own band, and write and perform her own songs. Sangare began working with Amadou Ba Guindo, a noted Malian arranger and producer, and put together a band with Boubacar Diallo on guitar and Aliou Traore on violin (replacing the traditional horse-hair fiddle). After two years of rehearsing they went into a studio in Côte d'Ivoire and cut *Moussolou (Women)*. On its release the cassette sold over 200,000 copies, not to mention the millions of pirated ones. When Britain's World Circuit label released the album internationally, Sangare became a contender for divahood.

Sangare's parents came from the Wassoulou region of Mali, home to an extraordinary number of women singers. The area has a distinct style based on the popular traditional dances everyone knows, including the *sogonikun,* a ritual performed mainly by young women at harvest time. It was this rich musical heritage Sangare would draw upon, and with *Moussolou* she and her collaborators did something remarkable for Africa: they made modern-sounding music using traditional instruments, without synthesizers or heavy pop production. Sangare also outraged traditionalists by singing about the status of women in a country that's dominated by longstanding Muslim beliefs. *Ko Sira (Marriage Today),* Sangare's second album, consolidated her position as a star and spokesperson for the common people. While much of Mali's music is based on the *jali* tradition—songs composed to honor powerful personages and their deeds—Sangare's lyrics address the daily joys and sorrows of the working class. "I am not trying to change the whole society," Sangare recently told the *Boston Globe.* "Just look how I dress. I am a traditional woman, but I do not like the injustice between men and women. I don't like that men can marry many women, and the women suffer. I write about what I see around me, and the young people hear what I'm saying, especially the women. Men with many wives don't like me, but the young men understand. And the music is very traditional, which is very respectful. Then when they listen to the music, I launch my words at them." Sangare recently lent her talents to the soundtrack of the film *Beloved.* Her performance of the "ancestor vocals" is brief, barely four minutes long in total, but introduces her powerfully to mainstream American listeners, showing how much her singular sound warrants even wider international exposure.

what to buy: On *Worotan (Ten Cola Nuts)* 🎵🎵🎵🎵 (World Circuit, 1996, prod. Oumou Sangare), Sangare takes her music to another level by adding a horn section led by Pee Wee Ellis, late of James Brown's band and the Horny Horns. It's a credit to both musicians that the horn charts remain understated, adding texture to the arrangements rather than overwhelming the music with obviously funky moves. The main attraction remains Sangare's forceful vocals. The title refers to the price a man must pay to secure a bride in Mali.

what to buy next: *Moussolou* 🎵🎵🎵🎵 (World Circuit, 1991, prod. Bientou Musique) is one of the classics of modern African music; a deeply traditional showcase for Sangare's voice and the skillful interplay between Boubacar Diallo's guitar, Aliou Traore's violin, and the subtle percussion of Benogo Diakite.

the rest:
Ko Sira 🎵🎵🎵🎵 (World Circuit, 1993)
Beloved (Soundtrack) 🎵🎵🎵 (Epic, 1998)

influences:

◀◀ Coumba Sidibe, Sali Sidibe, Flan Saran

                                                                    j. poet

Oumou Sangare

Trichy Sankaran

Trichy Sankaran

South Indian (karnatak) classical drumming, gamelan, percussion, chamber music

Born Tiruchi Sankaran, July 27, 1942, in Puvalur, Madras State, India. Based in Toronto, Ontario, Canada.

Trichy Sankaran is a virtuoso percussionist from South India who has performed traditional and original works on four continents. He plays with precision and a polished delicacy while expressing intricate rhythmic patterns on the *mridangam,* a tunable, double-headed wooden barrel drum. Both of the skin-derived heads are held to the body by leather thongs, and a dark spot in the center of the skin is made of iron filings and rice paste. Sankaran sits cross-legged, holding the instrument over his lap, playing the centuries-old classical music of South India as well as original compositions and collaborations with other contemporary, jazz, and world-music artists. He also plays the lizard-skinned *kanjira,* a small single-headed tambourine from South India. "Trichy is my home town but it has become my name," explains Sankaran. "Many artists are known by their home town. They started printing this name—Trichy Sankaran—on concert posters; it wasn't my decision. Then I started receiving checks from All-India Radio and I had to sign that name!" Sankaran's public debut was at age 13, and since then he has performed

widely throughout Asia, Europe, and North America. He is the founding director and professor of Indian Music Studies at York University in Toronto, Ontario, Canada, where he is currently based. It is one of many teaching posts he has held, and his method has been influential on other music educators. His awards and titles are numerous, as are his collaborations with a range of artists in diverse genres, while his impact reverberates even further through his thorough manual on how to play the mridangam, *The Rhythmic Principles and Practice of South Indian Drumming* (Lalith Publishers, Toronto, 1994).

what to buy: *Lotus Signatures* 𝄞𝄞𝄞𝄞 (Music of the World, 1997, prod. Trichy Sankaran, Bob Haddad) was recorded in India with a full percussion ensemble as well as violin and flute. This excellent album features the virtuosity of Sankaran paired with the melodic mastery of bamboo flutist Dr. N. Ramani.

what to buy next: *Laya Vinyas* 𝄞𝄞𝄞 (Music of the World, 1990, prod. Bob Haddad)—whose title translates literally as "rhythmic elaborations"—pulses forward with a dazzling display of South Indian drumming on the mridangam. Sankaran overdubs several tracks, and there is also a kanjira solo.

the rest:
Sunada 𝄞𝄞𝄞 (Music of the World, 1993)
(With Paul Plimley) *Ivory Ganesh Meets Dr. Drum* 𝄞𝄞𝄞 (Songline, 1998)

influences:
⏮ Palani Subramania Pillai, Palghat Mani Iyer, Kishan Maharaj
⏭ Sal Ferraras & Drum Heat, Nexus, Glen Velez

Iris Brooks

Maggie Sansone

Celtic hammered dulcimer

Born in Miami, FL, USA. Based in Annapolis, MD, USA.

Maggie Sansone has been a pivotal force in heightening the profile of Celtic music in the U.S.—from both sides of the stage and studio. As a hammered dulcimer player, she has done much to popularize that instrument in Celtic music, through her recordings and through her performances at Celtic, Renaissance, and folk festivals. As a teacher, she has published an innovative music-book series for the hammered dulcimer, among several other music books from Mel Bay Publications. As an independent label executive, she has released nearly 25 albums for worldwide distribution, most focusing on the music of the Celts. The label has received four "Wammie" Record Label of the Year awards from the Washington, D.C., Area Musicians Association, while Sansone's own albums have received "Indie" awards from the Association for Independent Music. She has taken her musical cause to CBS-TV's *Sunday Morning* and National Public Radio's *All Things Considered, Performance Today,* and *Thistle and Shamrock*. Her albums ring with a Renaissance spirit, a fusion of ancient sounds and modern sensibility, fueled by rich arrangements and innovative use of instruments old and new.

what to buy: On *A Scottish Christmas* 🎵🎵🎵🎵 (Maggie's Music, 1996, prod. Charlie Pilzer), Sansone teams up with Scottish fiddler Bonnie Rideout and guitarist Al Petteway for one of the best seasonal albums ever. Featuring pipes, bells, hammered dulcimer, fiddle, and cello, it lifts you away to castle banquet halls with roaring fires and to desolate snow-filled forests, in a celebration of Christmas, Hogmanay, and the New Year. Sansone's newest release, *A Traveler's Dream* 🎵🎵🎵🎵 (Maggie's Music, 1999, prod. Bobby Read), is perhaps her best "solo" album yet and only adds luster to her growing reputation. The album's theme is one of the hammered dulcimer following the migration of ancient civilizations across Asia Minor and onto the European continent from the Black Sea to the North Atlantic shores. It also reflects Sansone's own journey from her childhood in Florida to her first exposure to folk music and her later infatuation with both Celtic and world music. Again featuring the likes of Al Petteway on guitar, Bonnie Rideout on fiddle and viola, Aran Olwell on Irish flute, David Sheim on Celtic harp, and producer Bobby Read on some 23 different instruments, this is a lush production, but one that never overwhelms the dulcimer. Sansone's playing is impeccable, often taking advantage of the pedal dampers on her Nick Blanton instrument to produce rhythmic variations that are both compelling and perfectly in keeping with the music. Petteway and Rideout are also just about the best at what they do. A landmark album. On *Ancient Noels* 🎵🎵🎵 (Maggie's Music, 1993, prod. Charlie Pilzer), Sansone teams with Ensemble Galilei, Rideout, percussionist Ben Harms, and guitarist and citternist Zan McLeod to deliver an unusual and special holiday recording that you'll want to have available all year long. Renaissance rhythms and haunting medieval hymns bring to life images of desert landscapes, stone monasteries, and the origins of Christmas.

what to buy next: *Dance upon the Shore* 🎵🎵🎵 (Maggie's Music, 1994, prod. Charlie Pilzer) finds Sansone in a jazzy crossover into what she calls a "cool Celtic voyage to Ireland, Scotland, Brittany, and the Isle of Man." It features her hammered dulcimer, but also adds Bob Read's soprano saxophone, clarinet, and alto flute; Steve Bloom's excellent percussion; and the stringed wizardry of both Robin Bullock and Petteway.

the rest:
Sounds of the Season 🎵🎵🎵🎵 (Maggie's Music, 1988)
Traditions 🎵🎵🎵 (Maggie's Music, 1989)
Mist and Stone 🎵🎵🎵 (Maggie's Music, 1990)
Sounds of the Season II 🎵🎵🎵 (Maggie's Music, 1991)
(With Sue Richards, Bonnie Rideout, and Ensemble Galilei) *Music in the Great Hall* 🎵🎵🎵 (Maggie's Music, 1992)

jamaican music 8: dub

In the 1970s context of Afrocentric and liberation-oriented reggae lyric-content, the coronation of dub was even more phenomenal than it might have been. For the most part, dub used only ghostly, floating vocal snatches from hit records of the time, and focused on dismantling and resculpting the rhythms with complex studio sorcery. Dub is a kind of psychedelic reggae, with the "trip" ignited by the imaginative and magical use of modern technology—in particular, mixing devices such as reverb, echo, delay, and equalization, and jarring sound effects. The recording engineer moved to the forefront with dub, as visionaries like its inventor King Tubby (Osbourne Ruddock) and the confounding Lee "Scratch" Perry developed adventurous and intuitive ways of manipulating, treating, and disintegrating sound. Basslines with jet-engine power would suddenly echo and fade into infinity, only to come flying back out of nowhere like a renegade sound boomerang. The vocals, horns, and drums could also instantly disappear and reappear, in wholly different combinations and places. Occasionally, the music was completely eviscerated except for the faint *a cappella* echoes of the vocalist suspended in solitude. Dub creates a sizzling tension between the missing elements and their inevitable yet unpredictable reappearance, which often occurs with stunning amplification and/or metamorphosis. Like the best hip-hop deejays, dub engineers were able to break down a song to its essence with a third-eye focus on rhythm, and dub is an undeniable ancestor of later dance musics including ambient, house, acid jazz, techno, drum 'n' bass, and jungle. Dub is thrilling, wall-shaking, floor-rumbling, (mostly) instrumental roots-reggae that recalls Bob Marley's on-target line from "Bad Card": "Turn the speakers up, I want to disturb my neighbor."

see also: Mikey Dread, King Tubby, Mad Professor, Lee "Scratch" Perry

Todd Shanker

influences:

⏮ Bonnie Rideout, Malcolm Dalglish

⏭ Ceoltoiri, Karen Ashbrook

see also: *Bonnie Rideout*

Neal Walters

Mongo Santamaria

Latin jazz

Born Ramon Santamaria, April 7, 1922, in Jesus Maria, Havana, Cuba. Based in USA.

Born in a poor district of Havana known for its Afro-Cuban culture, Mongo Santamaria originally studied the violin, but switched to drums before dropping out of school to become a professional musician. Santamaria was 28 years old and already established in this career path in Havana when he traveled to the U.S. via Mexico, arriving in New York City with fellow congo player Armando Peraza. Billed as the Black Cuban Diamonds, they were performing during a time when Latin music was changing course and spawning an array of mambo groups, from big bands to small combos. Perez Prado led probably the biggest crossover band to reach non-Latin audiences, and master *conguero* Santamaria worked with Prado before joining Tito Puente for six years. Santamaria recorded with Dizzy Gillespie in 1954, then relocated to the West Coast where he joined San Francisco–based vibist Cal Tjader (somewhat of a pacesetter himself in Latin jazz) from 1958 to 1961. While on the West Coast Santamaria began recording his own albums with a straight-Latin *charanga* band (a style known for the prominence of violin and flute in its instrumental lineup), debuting with *Mongo* and *Yambu*. His popular composition "Afro Blue" from this early period eventually became a jazz standard, recorded by countless musicians. But his biggest hit would be the Herbie Hancock tune "Watermelon Man," which the pianist brought to a New York nightclub one night in 1962 where Santamaria's band was performing to an audience of about three people. Hancock began to demonstrate his new tune, the musicians gradually joined in, and the tune became part of Santamaria's repertoire. Producer Orrin Keepnews heard it, and had it recorded as a single for the Battle label that same year. It became a huge hit, topping pop charts in 1963. It remains Santamaria's theme song and the tune that most fans remember him by. Throughout the 1960s Santamaria led his own groups including both jazz and Latin players, among them Brazilian Joao Donato on piano. Santamaria became tremendously popular running long-lasting bands that combined traditional charanga with jazz brass sections, wind instruments, and piano solos. His lineups in the early '60s included pianist Chick Corea and flutist Hubert Laws, as well as Brazilian and Cuban musicians.

Santamaria formed a New York–based group in 1961, and, between 1965 and '70, made a series of recordings for Atlantic and Columbia that combined R&B and soul tunes with Latin rhythms and jazz—a hot, danceable combination that brought him greater fame. Santamaria continued to mix musical genres in the 1960s and '70s, and has since returned to his Afro-Cuban roots, recording for Vaya, Pablo, Concord Picante, Chesky, Milestone, and other labels.

what to buy: The two-CD set *Skin on Skin: The Mongo Santamaria Anthology (1958–1995)* 𝄞𝄞𝄞𝄞 (Rhino, 1999, compilation prod. Miles Perlich, Ted Myers) scans Santamaria's 40-year career and, from a world-music perspective, contains some of his earliest and best recordings, when he was less influenced by jazz. The set collects 34 exemplary tracks from the Fantasy, Riverside, Battle, Atlantic, Columbia, and Concord Picante labels. Santamaria's sides of the late 1950s, and into the early '60s, lean more toward his musical roots, and disc one kicks off with a beautiful, simply layered version of his classic "Afro Blue." The set is chronologically arranged so that you begin to hear the growing influence of jazz creeping into Santamaria's varied Afro-Cuban rhythms. It's a pleaser from start to finish. If you're a fan of Latin rhythms or just want to hear a single album of the music that started Santamaria's career, check out *AfroRoots* 𝄞𝄞𝄞𝄞 (Prestige, 1958/1989, prod. various), which combines 12 tunes from Santamaria's 1959 session for Fantasy (originally released as *Mongo*) with nine selections recorded in 1958 (originally released as *Yambu*). Just as the title implies, these 21 percussion-laden tunes cut to the quick, with Santamaria playing native rhythms based on venerable chants and rituals. One track features vibist Cal Tjader and pianist Vince Guaraldi, hinting at the leader's more jazz-oriented albums to come. Willie Bobo appears on *Timbalero,* creating some of the most exciting Afro-Cuban rhythmic exchanges fans at the time had ever heard. On *Sabroso!* 𝄞𝄞𝄞𝄞 (Fantasy, 1993), Santamaria leads a band based on the classic Latin charanga format, as well as the *pachanga,* a pulsing variant that was briefly the rage among New York's Latin teenagers around 1961. The 13 tunes capture a performance recorded in San Francisco in the early '60s. The danceable rhythms and instrumentation of this CD are most attractive. *Our Man in Havana* 𝄞𝄞𝄞𝄞 (Fantasy, 1960/1993), which compiles recordings made in the title city in early 1960 with Willie Bobo and other percussionists, vocalists, and instrumentalists from Cuba, is equally enticing, and you can hear how this music had begun to influence the development of Latin jazz. With *Mongo Returns* 𝄞𝄞𝄞𝄞 (Milestone, 1995, prod. Todd Barkan), the then 73-year-old percussionist comes home to the label that issued his 1963 Top Ten hit "Watermelon Man." Santamaria maintains a palatable, diverse mix of nine modernized Afro-Cuban jazz tunes laced with smatterings from his '70s fusion days. The session features a tight, melodic horn section and solo improvisations from Eddie Allen (trumpet and flugelhorn), Robert DeBellis (alto and baritone saxes and flute), and Roger Byam (tenor and soprano saxophones and flute). Mongo is on the spot, illustrious and supportive as conguero and leader. Conductor Marty Sheller contributes three modern-edged tunes. Highlights include a seductive version of Ary Barroso's "Bahia" that features Allen's pretty muted-trumpet solos, and a Latinized interpretation of Marvin Gaye's "When Did You Stop Loving Me, When Did I Stop Loving You." Allen also proves his prowess as composer with two funky originals—"Ol' School Groove" and "Slyck 'n' Slyde." Most of the 12 musicians comprise Santamaria's regular working group of the past decade (guest pianist Hilton Ruiz and bassist John Benitz excluded). Pianist Oscar Hernandez, an array of percussionists (Louis Bauzo, Greg Askew, Steve Berrios), and the horn team generate spacious, fresh Latin-jazz grooves that are enriched by fine solos. The euphonious melodies and easy rhythms will charm you. *Live at Jazz Alley* ♫♫♫♫ (Concord Picante, 1990, prod. Carl E. Jefferson, Allen Farnham) captures conguero Santamaria in a magnificent, 10-tune, roots-rich Afro-Cuban jazz performance at Dimitriou's Jazz Alley in Seattle, Washington, in March 1990. By this time, some of his 12 musicians had been with him for a while and, navigating mostly Santamaria or Marty Sheller arrangements, they deliver polished performances. Santamaria's original "Bonita," a funk *guajira* (peasant rhythm), is a catchy number spotlighting a splendid solo from Ray Vega (trumpet, flugelhorn). Dizzy Gillespie's "Manteca" features top-notch, expansive solos from Bobby Porcelli on baritone sax and Mitch Frohman on tenor sax, not to mention a lengthy solo from Mongo. "Afro Blue," a popular minor blues/jazz melody combined with 6/8 African rhythm, was one of the first songs to be included in Santamaria's band book when he formed his outfit in 1961. As the finale here, it's a saucy ending made splendiferous by improvisations from Mongo, vocalist/percussionist Eddie Rodriguez, tenor saxman Mitch Frohman, and pianist Bob Quaranta. This disc is perhaps less fiery but more danceable than some of his earlier Concord Picante releases, and that's its major appeal.

what to buy next: If you're more interested in hearing overt jazz influences, pick up *Skins* ♫♫♫♫ (Milestone, 1962/1976/1990, prod. Orrin Keepnews), which features 10 tunes by a 1964 version of Santamaria's band first documented on the Riverside recording *Mongo Explodes!*, and nine tunes recorded by the 1962 version of "the Mongo Santamaria Afro-Latin Group" (originally issued as *Go, Mongo!*). The 1964 band included jazz players such as Hubert Laws (piccolo, flute, tenor sax) and guesting soloists Nat Adderley (cornet) and Jimmy Cobb (drums), in addition to Santamaria's regular lineup. Capers and Sheller were writing some great tunes by then, and this album has numerous highlights and catchy beats that tried to recap-

ture the success of "Watermelon Man." (They come close with the instrumental track "Corn Bread Guajira.") The band performing the tunes for the first Riverside date in 1962 was originally thrown together by Santamaria and his manager (because Santamaria at the moment of signing had no band), and includes a young Armando Corea at the piano (before he became known by his nickname "Chick"), and Chicago musicians Paul Serrano (trumpet), Pat Patrick (flutes, saxophones), and others. Obviously, this CD offers historical value as well as some good music. Riding on the success of his 1963 hit "Watermelon Man" (and his album of the same name), Santamaria appeared at the Village Gate in New York City with his band on September 2, 1963, and made the live-recorded *Mongo at the Village Gate* ♫♫♫♫ (Riverside, 1963/OJC, 1990, prod. Orrin Keepnews). By now the up-front horns feature musical director Marty Sheller (trumpet), and Bobby Capers and Pat Patrick (flutes, saxes), with a rhythm section that includes Santamaria, Rodgers Grant (piano), Victor Venegas (bass), and Frank Hernandez (drums), plus two other Latin percussionists. Along with originals by Santamaria (including the bonus track "Para Ti"), there are tunes by band members and others. Highlights are many, but especially notable are Sheller's trumpet solos. Santamaria performs a skin-against-skins solo on "My Sound" that's a knockout. His mastery as a conguero was long established, but this recording documents his continuing growth and the rigor of his new music, which would pave the way for ensembles of today such as Jerry Gonzalez & the Fort Apache Band. *Brazilian Sunset* ♫♫♫♫ (Candid, 1992, prod. Alan Bates, Mark Morganelli) features Santamaria with an array of prime musicians conversant in Afro-Cuban jazz for a 1992 live-recorded performance at Birdland, New York City. Likely owing to the appreciativeness of the audience, these tunes really kick, spurred by the leader's colorful percussion. Santamaria remains in the forefront on the 12 selections (seven of them originals), laying down great rhythms for his soloists—musical director Eddie Allen (trumpet, flugelhorn), Jimmy Crozier (alto and baritone saxes, flute), and Craig Rivers (tenor sax, flute)—with support from the fine rhythm players Ricardo Gonzalez (piano), Guillermo Edgehill (bass), Johnny Almendra (drums, timbales), and Eddie Rodriguez (percussion). The version of Marty Sheller's "Gumbo Man" maintains distinctive '70s funk flair tinged with shifting Latin rhythms. Mongo's original "Sofrito" features an excellent baritone sax solo (either by Rivers or Crozier; liner notes vary). Another take on Santamaria's most memorable hit, "Watermelon Man," adds to the festive atmosphere.

best of the rest:
Arriba! ♫♫♫♫ (Fantasy, 1959/1996)
At the Blackhawk ♫♫♫♫ (Fantasy, 1962/1994)
Mongo Introduces La Lupe ♫♫♫♫ (Riverside, 1963/Milestone, 1993)

Afro Blue 🎵🎵🎵🎵 (Concord Picante, 1987/1997)
Soy Yo 🎵🎵🎵 (Concord Picante, 1987)
Soca Me Nice 🎵🎵🎵🎵 (Concord Picante, 1988)
Olé Ola 🎵🎵🎵 (Concord Picante, 1989)
Mambo Mongo 🎵🎵🎵 (Chesky Records, 1993)
Mongo's Greatest Hits 🎵🎵🎵🎵 (Fantasy, 1995)

influences:

◄◄ Luciano "Chano" Pozo y Gonzales, Willie Bobo

►► Carlos Santana, Jerry Gonzalez, ¡Cubanismo!

see also: *Jerry Gonzalez & the Fort Apache Band, Charlie Palmieri, Perez Prado, Tito Puente, Poncho Sanchez*

Nancy Ann Lee

Santana
/Carlos Santana

Latin rock, jazz rock, classic rock, hybrid rock
Formed 1967, in San Francisco, CA, USA.

Variable membership throughout the years, including: Carlos Santana (born July 20, 1947, in Autlan de Navarro, Mexico), guitar; Gregg Rolie, organ, vocals; David Brown, bass; Michael Shrieve, drums; Jose "Chepito" Areas, timbales; Michael Carabello, congas.

Unknowns who took Woodstock by storm—literally, since the band played during a downpour—Santana could have stopped recording after their third album and their legacy would still be secure. Leader Carlos Santana is the musician who launched a thousand would-be and actual guitar heroes (Vernon Reid is one of many worshippers), and Santana's legacy in mainstream rock is matched by his elder-statesman status in world music. His band was one of the earliest battering rams at the door of general acceptance for Latin sounds, and he went on to become an in-demand session guest with such artists as Beninese diva Angélique Kidjo, Nigerian percussion giant Babatunde Olatunji, Malian superstar Salif Keita, and others, as well as a devotee of Sri Chinmoy and a student of Indian classical virtuoso Ali Akbar Khan. Santana's earliest inspiration came from his mariachi-violinist father, and was then fleshed out by an infatuation with Stateside blues players. His supergroup style and later aspirations to jazz would follow. Though his solo projects and numerous editions of Santana the band may have failed to quite equal the power and sweep of those first three historic albums, Santana the man's historical stature is assured.

what to buy: On the heels of the original band's 1998 induction into the Rock and Roll Hall of Fame, Columbia Legacy gave the cornerstone first three albums a complete going over, with previously unreleased bonus tracks that weren't even part of the exemplary box set *Dance of the Rainbow Serpent* 🎵🎵🎵🎵 (Columbia, 1995, compilation prod. Bob Irwin). That collection re-

mains essential, and you'll also want the refreshed first testaments: the sparkling debut, *Santana* 🎵🎵🎵🎵 (Columbia, 1969, prod. Brent Dangerfield); *Abraxas* 🎵🎵🎵🎵🎵 (Columbia, 1970, prod. Fred Catero); and *Santana III* 🎵🎵🎵🎵🎵 (Columbia, 1971, prod. Santana).

what to buy next: The band's initial attempt at recording the debut album—a December 1968 show at the Fillmore West—is featured on *Live at the Fillmore '68* 🎵🎵🎵🎵 (Columbia Legacy, 1998, prod. David Rubinson, Bill Irwin), and why this wasn't released in the first place is an utter mystery. Confident to the point of being cocky, these strutting, menacing newcomers manhandle their fiery fusion of blues, Latin, jazz, and rock like masters.

what to avoid: The so-called *Lotus* **woof!** (Columbia, 1973, prod. various), a three-record set recorded live in Japan but unreleased in this country for nearly 20 years, finds the guru guitarist's jazz-fusion pretensions at their teetering height.

the rest:
Carvanserai 🎵🎵 (Columbia, 1972)
Welcome 🎵 (Columbia, 1973)
Greatest Hits 🎵🎵 (Columbia, 1974)
Borboletta 🎵 (Columbia, 1974)
Amigos 🎵 (Columbia, 1976)
Festival 🎵 (Columbia, 1977)
Moonflower 🎵 (Columbia, 1977)
Marathon 🎵🎵 (Columbia, 1979)
Zebop! 🎵🎵 (Columbia, 1981)
Shango **woof!** (Columbia, 1982)
Havana Moon 🎵🎵🎵🎵 (Columbia, 1983)
Beyond Appearances 🎵 (Columbia, 1985)
Freedom **woof!** (Columbia, 1987)
Viva Santana! 🎵🎵🎵 (Columbia, 1988)
Spirits Dancing in the Flesh 🎵 (Columbia, 1990)
Milagro 🎵🎵🎵🎵 (Polydor, 1992)
The Best of Santana 🎵🎵🎵 (Columbia Legacy, 1998)
Supernatural 🎵🎵🎵🎵 (Arista, 1999)

worth searching for: The only time the most ferocious version of Santana ever performed the Miles Davis classic "In a Silent Way" happened to also be the final time this illustrious lineup played together, closing night at the Fillmore West in 1971. This serene benediction was recorded live and included on the box set *Fillmore: The Last Days* 🎵🎵🎵🎵 (Epic, 1972/Legacy, 1995).

solo outings:
Carlos Santana:
Love, Devotion and Surrender 🎵🎵🎵 (Columbia, 1973)
Illuminations **woof!** (Columbia, 1974)
Oneness, Silver Dreams—Golden Reality **woof!** (Columbia, 1979)
The Swing of Delight 🎵 (Columbia, 1980)
Blues for Salvador 🎵🎵 (Columbia, 1987)

Savoy-Doucet Cajun Band

Sacred Fire: Live in South America ♪♪♪ (Polydor, 1993)
Brothers ♪♪ (Island, 1994)

influences:

◀◀ Willie Bobo, Tito Puente, Babatunde Olatunji, John Coltrane, Miles Davis, Peter Green

▶▶ Malo, Azteca, Journey

see also: *Salif Keita*

Joel Selvin and Craig Harris

Henry Sapoznik

See: Kapelye, Klezmer Plus!

Savoy-Doucet Cajun Band

Cajun
Formed 1978, in Lafayette, LA, USA. Based in USA.

Marc Savoy, accordion, vocals; Ann Savoy, guitar, vocals; Michael Doucet, fiddle, vocals. (All members are from USA.)

This occasional band is dedicated to the perpetuation of tradi-
tional Cajun music; their material is rooted in the sound of the Gulf Coast Cajun culture. They record and tour whenever member Michael Doucet's busy schedule allows—he is the leader of Cajun supergroup Beausoleil. Though well-known for his inventive fiddle forays with that band, Doucet's playing with Savoy-Doucet is firmly within the tradition; he is conversant with and mindful of the work of his fiddling forebears at all times. He has been particularly influenced by Dennis McGee and two great Creole fiddlers, Canray Fontenot and Amédée Ardoin. Marc Savoy is probably the most accomplished accordionist in traditional Cajun styles and is also celebrated as an accordion builder. His wife, Ann, born in St. Louis and raised in Virginia, is Cajun by marriage and has embraced the musical traditions of the culture enthusiastically as a forceful rhythm guitarist and singer. The trio's work in both instrumentalism and voice is exemplary.

what to buy: *Home Music with Spirits* ♪♪♪♪♪ (Arhoolie, 1992, prod. Chris Strachwitz) contains classic waltzes, two-steps, stomps, and blues from the Cajun repertoire. It also includes a wonderful version of the "Cajun national anthem," "Jolie

Blonde." *Two-Step d'Amédée* 🎵🎵🎵 (Arhoolie, 1988, prod. Chris Strachwitz, Savoy-Doucet Cajun Band) is a studio set just as good as *Home Music with Spirits,* with the added excitement of seven live cuts. *Live! At the Dance* 🎵🎵🎵 (Arhoolie, 1994, prod. Chris Strachwitz) effectively captures the palpable excitement of traditional Cajun dance music in its natural live setting.

what to buy next: On *Now and Then* 🎵🎵🎵 (Arhoolie, 1996, prod. Scott Ardoin), Ken Smith, another outstanding fiddler—if less adventurous and more melodic than Doucet—sits in on a typically excellent batch of Cajun classics with the Savoys.

worth searching for: *Cajun Jam Session* 🎵🎵🎵 (Arhoolie, 1989, prod. Chris Strachwitz) features Doucet along with guitarist Alan Senauke and accordionist Danny Poullard in an impromptu recording of a live radio show from 1983. It's an enjoyable, if occasionally ragged, set of traditional Cajun music.

solo outings:
Marc Savoy:
(With Dewey Balfa and D.L. Menard) *Under a Green Oak Tree* 🎵🎵🎵🎵 (Arhoolie, 1977)
(With Wallace Read) *Cajun House Party* 🎵🎵🎵 (Arhoolie, 1979)
Oh, What a Night 🎵🎵🎵 (Arhoolie, 1981)

influences:
⏪ Iry LeJeune, Harry Choates, Cleoma Falcon, Canray Fontenot, Amédée Ardoin, Dewey Balfa, Nathan Abshire, Dennis McGee

⏩ Steve Riley, Balfa Toujours, California Cajun Orchestra

see also: *Amédée Ardoin, Bayou Seco, Beausoleil, Canray Fontenot, Steve Riley & the Mamou Playboys*

Randy Pitts

Tracy Schwarz /Tracy Schwarz Cajun Trio

Cajun
Born September 13, 1938, in New York, NY, USA. Based in West Virginia, USA.

Born and raised in New York City, Tracy Schwarz began working with the New Lost City Ramblers as a replacement for Tom Paley in 1962, and shortly thereafter met a young Dewey Balfa at the Newport Folk Festival. The two men hit it off, and thus began a long friendship. Schwarz's development as a Cajun fiddler and accordionist is chronicled on individual tracks of various New Lost City Ramblers albums. His first collaboration with Balfa was the Folkways LP *How to Play Cajun Fiddle,* released in 1976. The two worked together at many festivals and workshops. You can hear the Balfa family influence in the plain, lonesome quality of Schwarz's style, along with some hint of the Appalachian music mined by the New Lost City Ramblers.

what to buy: *Mes Amis!* 🎵🎵🎵 (Swallow, 1996, prod. various) delivers consistent quality. Schwarz is never going to overwhelm with emotions like Beausoleil's Michael Doucet, or leap through syncopated modulation like Steve Riley; instead you'll get something that's steady and dignified.

what to buy next: *Les Quatre Vieux Garçons* 🎵🎵🎵 (Folkways, 1984, prod. Quatre Vieux Garçons) brings together Tracy and Peter Schwarz with Dewey and Tony Balfa to play some old favorites. Peter had been studying with Dewey and the project gave them a chance to record their fiddle interplay. Papa Tracy adds accordion and fiddle to the mix. Tony is Rodney Balfa's son and plays guitar in the same driving, percussive way.

the rest:
(With Dewey Balfa) *How to Play Cajun Fiddle* 🎵🎵🎵 (Folkways, 1976) (cassette only)
Louisiana and You 🎵🎵🎵 (Marimac, 1990) (cassette only)
Tracy Schwarz Cajun Trio 🎵🎵🎵 (Swallow, 1993)

worth searching for: *Souvenirs* 🎵🎵🎵🎵 (Swallow, 1985, prod. Tracy Schwarz) was made under Dewey Balfa's name, but features the same group as on *Les Quatre Vieux Garçons,* with the addition of superb accordionist Robert Jardell. Recapturing some of the old Balfa magic, this album consists primarily of Dewey Balfa originals played on three fiddles, with Dewey in the lead, Peter Schwarz an octave below, and Tracy playing the tenor parts in the middle. The record also contains "Bienvenue Au Paradis," a Tracy Schwarz original written after the tragic death of Dewey's brothers, Rodney and Will, in an automobile accident.

influences:
⏪ Balfa Brothers, Lawrence Walker, Nathan Abshire
⏩ Balfa Toujours, Horace Trahan, Steve Riley

see also: *Balfa Brothers, Balfa Toujours, Beausoleil, Steve Riley & the Mamou Playboys*

Jared Snyder

Sean Nua

Irish traditional
Formed in Dublin, Ireland. Based in Dublin, Ireland.

Joe McKenna, accordion, uilleann pipes, vocals, whistle; Gerry O'Donnell, whistle, flute, vocals, clarinet; Antoinette McKenna, harp, vocals; Joe McHugh, uilleann pipes, bouzouki, vocals, keyboards; Jo Partridge, vocals, guitar; Mario N'Gomo, percussion.

At the heart of Sean Nua is the husband and wife team of Joe and Antoinette McKenna. Both hail from Dublin and grew up entrenched in Ireland's rich musical heritage. Joe began studying the uilleann pipes at a young age at the famed Pipers Club in Dublin. It was there that he came under the tutelage of Leo Rowsome, one of the piping world's most respected and imitated players. Antoinette came from a musical family; her sister Mary Bergin (of the band Dordan) is one of the finest exponents of the Irish tin whistle. Growing up, Antoinette and her family would make frequent excursions to Galway, where she was exposed to the traditional songs of Ireland. At the same time, she was taking harp lessons—and excelling—back home in Dublin. Another once-and-future prodigy, Joe McHugh, who'd already won an All-Ireland championship on the uilleann pipes by the age of 18, provides more of Sean Nua's impressive instrumental interplay—and even that hardly exhausts the band's supply of exceptional musicianship.

what to buy: *The Open Door* 𝄞𝄞𝄞 (Shanachie, 1993, prod. Jo Partridge, Joe McKenna) is a vehicle for the piping of Joe McKenna and the fine flute playing of Gerry O'Donnell. Antoinette McKenna's harp, Jo Partridge's guitar, and Mario N'-Gomo's percussion provide the canvas on which the two other talented artists paint a beautifully vibrant picture. Joe McHugh adds some graceful bouzouki playing as well as joining McKenna on some blistering pipe duos. The exquisitely poignant numbers "Ó Ró Song of the Sea" and "Tá Mé 'Mo Shui," each sung by Antoinette McKenna, provide some welcome juxtaposition to the sprightly instrumental sets.

what to buy next: Although Sean Nua has only recorded one album, the group's core, Joe and Antoinette McKenna, have recorded together for the Shanachie label for years. *The Best of Joe and Antoinette McKenna* 𝄞𝄞𝄞𝄞 (Shanachie, 1997) gives a great overview of the duo. Their unique combination of uilleann pipes and harp is featured prominently, as is Joe's fabulous tin whistle playing. Joe's style of piping is brilliant both visually and aurally; his use of the instrument's regulators to frame his playing is great to watch and even better to listen to. Antoinette and Joe are each wonderful singers, too, and their talents are well represented on "Willie Archer" and "Fill Fill a Run O."

worth searching for: *Offshore* 𝄞𝄞𝄞 (Brambus Records, 1996) is a Swiss release by Sean Nua piper and bouzouki player Joe McHugh and Swiss *hackbrett* (hammered dulcimer) player Gilbert Paeffgen. The album is all instrumental, except one song featuring Irish vocalist Shirley Grimes. It is indeed heavily reliant on the Irish tradition for its contemporary tunes, and features a host of instruments played by these two fine talents.

influences:

◀◀ Leo Rowsome, Seumas Ennis, Willie Clancy

▶▶ Danu, Todd Denman

see also: *Mary Bergin*

Cliff McGann

Márta Sebestyén /Muzsikás /Vujicsics

Hungarian folk music

Muzsikás formed 1972, in Budapest, Hungary. Based in Budapest, Hungary.

Muzsikás: Márta Sebestyén, vocals, recorder (1980–present); Sandor Csoóri, bagpipe, hurdy-gurdy, viola, vocals; Mihaly Sipos, violin, zither, vocals; Peter Eri, bouzoúki, Turkish horn, cello, viola, vocals; Daniel Hamar, bass, hurdy-gurdy, vocals. (All members are from Hungary.)

When she recorded two songs for the Oscar-winning movie *The English Patient,* Márta Sebestyén broke out of the world-music ghetto and became internationally famous, at least for the next 15 minutes. It would be wonderful to believe that a talented folk singer of Hungarian, Transylvanian, and Carpathian music could become a star on her own merits, but in the current musical climate, it's probably not meant to be.

Sebestyén was born and raised in Budapest, Hungary. Her mother had not only studied with one of Hungary's great modern composers and folk-music preservationists, Zoltan Kodaly, but taught music herself. Before Sebestyén was a teen, she was singing in a *tanchez* (dance house), a club where the students of the Communist era were trying to keep their own culture alive by playing folk music—particularly the music of Transylvania, a part of Hungary that had been absorbed by Romania. Although singing folk music is the kind of wholesome activity the Communists would ordinarily promote, there was a nationalistic element to this movement that bothered the regime. People were followed, phones were tapped, and the music was banned for a short time by the powers that be—probably making it all the more appealing.

Sebestyén went on to become a well-known singer on the folk scene from an early age, and sang with Sebö & Halmos and Vujicsics before joining Muzsikás in 1980. Muzsikás got started in the early 1970s when Mihaly Sipos, Peter Eri, Daniel Hamar, and Sandor Csoóri left behind their classical training to play folk music. They joined the tanchez movement as a reaction to the Russian music that was dominating Hungary at the time. The band began learning their repertoire the same way Sebestyén had, by listening to recordings, but as they grew in confidence as individuals and as an ensemble, they started making trips to Transylvania and other outlying regions to record and collect songs that were in danger of vanishing. Since they signed with Hannibal Records in 1986, they've become one of the best-known international folk bands on the world-music circuit. In 1991 Sebestyén became the first folk singer to win the country's top musical award, the Liszt Prize, and has had an equally successful solo career since 1992.

Márta Sebestyén of Muzsikás

what to buy: The band is at its best on the recent *Morning Star* 𝄢𝄢𝄢𝄢 (Hannibal, 1997, prod. Daniel Hamar, Muzsikás); jaunty rhythms, incredible virtuosity from the fiddlers, and Sebestyén's solitary vocal style drift through the mix like the forlorn echo of a primeval mother drowning in the world's sorrows.

what to buy next: *The Prisoner's Song* 𝄢𝄢𝄢𝄢 (Hannibal, 1986, prod. Levente Szörényi) is the album that introduced Sebestyén and Muzsikás to the West. The dance tunes grip you with their lively energy, and while Sebestyén's voice lacks the confidence it exhibits today, it's still a haunting instrument. Includes an early *a cappella* recording of "Szerelem, Szerelem," later re-recorded for the *English Patient* soundtrack.

best of the rest:
Muzsikás:
Blues for Transylvania: The Lost Jewish Music of Transylvania 𝄢𝄢𝄢𝄢
(Hannibal, 1990)
Maramaros 𝄢𝄢𝄢𝄢 (Hannibal, 1993)
Márta Sebestyén with Muzsikas 𝄢𝄢𝄢𝄢 (Hannibal)

Márta Sebestyén:
Apocrypha 𝄢𝄢𝄢𝄢 (Hannibal)
Kismet 𝄢𝄢𝄢𝄢 (Hannibal, 1996)
Best of Márta Sebestyén: The Voice of the English Patient 𝄢𝄢𝄢 (Hannibal, 1997)

influences:
◄◄ Zoltan Kodaly, Bogiszió Folk Orchestra, Vujicsics

►► Sebo Ensemble, Eva Fábián, András Berecz

see also: *Deep Forest, Bill Whelan*

j. poet

Mansour Seck
Afropop
Born 1955, in Podor, Senegal. Based in Dakar, Senegal, and Paris, France.

Mansour Seck's father was the *griot* (oral historian) of the Maal family; Senegalese superstar Baaba Maal and Seck have been best friends since boyhood. Griots in Fouta (Seck's home re-

Mansour Seck

gion) usually don't sing, but Seck began singing as a boy, and in addition to the *kora* (harp-lute), taught himself guitar. In 1972, Maal, Seck, and another boyhood friend, Bassou Niang, joined a group of actors, singers, and dancers under the direction of Ousegnu Gueye. Later on, the three friends moved to Dakar and performed as a trio before hooking up with Lasly Fouta, a well-known folkloric group. When Maal decided to become a professional musician, he went on a long trek through Mauritania, Mali, Gambia, Côte d'Ivoire, and Senegal with Seck, playing for food and collecting songs from the various ethnic groups. Since Seck came from a griot family, he was able to win the trust of other traditional musicians, and the duo received a priceless education from the people they met. At this time, Seck also began going blind as the result of a hereditary disease, and Maal became his eyes. In 1981 Maal and Seck were in Paris, where they first formed a small folkloric group. In 1984 the duo recorded *Djam Leelii,* a tour de force that featured the twin vocals and guitars of Maal and Seck, and introduced some subtle electric guitar playing to the mix. The cassette version of this album was a hit, both on the European world-music scene and in Senegal. Later that year, Mall and Seck returned

to Senegal and recruited musicians for Daande Lenol ("Voice of the People"), which has since become the world's premiere African pop band, due in part to the incredible guitar playing and vocals of Mansour Seck. In 1994, with Daande Lenol and Maal well-established as stars, Seck began a solo recording career that has so far produced three albums of breathtaking, mostly acoustic music.

what to buy: On *Yelayo* ♫♫♫♫ (Stern's, 1997, prod. Mansour Seck), Seck continues to work his quiet magic on the guitar, playing off of the sparkling kora rhythms of Niumoukunda Cissoko. The subtle backing vocals of Izabel Gonzales and Cathy Renoir give the set a deep, almost religious feeling.

what to buy next: *Djam Leelii* ♫♫♫♫ (Mango, 1989, prod. Mansour Seck, Baaba Maal), released for the Senegalese cassette market in 1985, became a surprise hit in Europe, launching the careers of Maal and Seck. The gorgeous guitar playing and Maal's incredible vocals in a quiet, almost traditional setting made this one an instant classic. Interestingly, the original master tapes of this session were lost, but Maal was able to find tapes of another earlier session during which they'd cut some of the same tunes. After a brief absence from the market, this album has again become widely available as *Djam Leelii: The Adventurers* (Palm Pictures, 1998). This version contains three worthwhile bonus tracks from the same era.

the rest:
N'der Fouta Tooro, Vol. 1 🎵🎵🎵🎵 (Mango, 1989)
N'der Fouta Tooro, Vol. 2 🎵🎵🎵🎵 (Mango, 1989)

influences:
◄◄ Idrissa Diop, Star Band de Dakar, Youssou N'Dour

see also: *Baaba Maal*

j. poet

Peggy Seeger
See: Ewan MacColl

Seelyhoo
See: Anam

The Selecter
Two-tone, ska
Formed 1979, in Coventry, England. Disbanded 1981. Re-formed 1992. Based in England.

Noel Davies, guitar; Charley Anderson, bass (1979–81); Pauline Black, vocals; Charley "H" Bembridge, drums (1979–81); Compton Amanor, guitar (1979–81); Arthur Hendrickson, vocals (1979–81); Desmond Brown, keyboards (1979–81); Perry Melius, drums (1992–present); Martin Stewart, keyboards (1992–present); Nick Welsh, bass (1992–present).

In an effort to get its ska brew heard, the Selecter band started its own company, 2-Tone, a label that went on to considerable success with kindred spirits such as the Specials. Like most of its ska-revivalist peers, the Selecter focused mainly on brittle and propulsive tunes with a political edge, highlighted by the jumpy drama of Pauline Black's vocals. The Selecter wrongly played second fiddle as England embraced the Specials and Madness. Black and Noel Davies regrouped in 1992 to no greater recognition, just a bit too early for the new ska movement in the U.S.

what to buy: *Selected Selecter Selections* 🎵🎵🎵🎵 (Chrysalis, 1989, prod. Errol Ross) is a potent reminder of the band's best work, culled from its first two albums, *Too Much Pressure* and *Celebrate the Bullet*. Selections such as "Too Much Pressure," "Murder," "On My Radio," "Three Minute Hero," and "Celebrate the Bullet" all reveal, again, that the Selecter was indeed an unjustly neglected part of the early '80s ska scene.

the rest:
Out on the Streets 🎵🎵 (Triple X, 1992)

The Happy Album 🎵🎵 (Triple X, 1994)
Back out on the Streets 🎵🎵 (Triple X, 1996)
Collection 🎵🎵🎵 (Cleopatra, 1997)
Cruel Britannia N/A (Madfish, 1999)

influences:
◄◄ Bob Marley, Jimmy Cliff, Skatalites, Delroy Wilson, Derrick Morgan, Desmond Dekker

▶▶ Smash Mouth, Chumbawamba, Sublime, 311, Sugar Ray

Allan Orski

Selena
Tejano
Born April 16, 1971, in Lake Jackson, TX, USA. Died March 31, 1995, in Corpus Christi, TX, USA.

The five Hispanic-American women who have reached international prominence in music have each gone about it with a different emphasis: Joan Baez, passionate storyteller and political activist; Linda Ronstadt, who delights in the sheer vocal challenge of singing the Mexican music she grew up with; Tish Hinojosa, visionary songwriter whose work crosses genres and borders; Gloria Estefan, who moves her music to island dance rhythms; and Selena Quintanilla Perez, the entertainer, who drew her joy in music from sharing it with her audiences. Selena had the chance to discover the thrill—and the work—of connecting with people from behind a microphone while she was still in elementary school. Her father, Abraham Quintanilla Jr., had worked in the band Los Dinos, and he recognized his daughter's developing vocal talent. The young Selena sang on stage at the family's restaurant, and when the restaurant had to close, the family decided to take the band (which included Selena's brother and sister) on the road to make a living. Though Selena hadn't grown up speaking Spanish, her father insisted that she learn songs in the language, and the band began to work its way up through the fairs, clubs, and bars of the Texas *Tejano* (modern Tex-Mex music) circuit. Though there were hard times in this life, by the time she was 14, the singer had established an engaging stage presence, the beginnings of a following in the male-dominated Tejano market, and an adult voice of power and sensibility. The band recorded several singles on regional labels that were heard on Tejano stations and, with Selena's growing maturity, caught the ear of record company executives as well as radio listeners. In 1986 she won her first Tejano Music Awards, as Female Vocalist and Entertainer of the Year. In 1989, she signed with EMI Latin, a move that was predicted to break Selena and the band both internationally and in the crossover market at home. She was still building up unprecedented popularity for a woman in the Tejano community itself. The 1991 release *Entre a M Mundo* produced what would become Selena's signature song, "Como La Flor." This was followed by the Grammy-winning *Selena Live!* and the best-selling *Amor Prohibido.* During this time Selena performed in Mexico, receiving a warm reception that was striking, for Mexican-American musicians are generally regarded with disfavor across the border. Her lively, sexy stage show; her down-to-earth personality; her family-oriented outlook (her brother AB wrote many of her songs, her sister Suzette played the drums in her band, her father produced her records, and she had married her lead guitarist, Chris Perez); and her ability to connect with audiences and draw them into her songs had enchanted the established listeners of Texas and the wary crowds of Mexico. It seemed that she was ready to make the move, one she had long wished for, to success in the crossover market alongside her early idols Paula Abdul and Madonna. Along the way Selena, who loved to design clothes, had achieved another dream, that of opening her own fashion boutique. While she was recording tracks for an English-language album, questions arose about the integrity of her business and fan-club manager, Yolanda Saldivar. Saldivar was fired, and when Selena went to meet her to collect business records, the star was shot in the back upon leaving. Saldivar was convicted of Selena's murder in November, 1995.

what to buy: *Selena: An Anthology* 𝄢𝄢𝄢𝄢 (EMI Latin, 1998, prod. Abraham Quintanilla Jr.) is a 30-song career retrospective. The three discs are arranged stylistically, with one devoted to pop (including songs in both English and Spanish), one to ballad-infused *ranchera,* and one to danceable *cumbia* tunes. It's a good portrait of Selena's oeuvre (and of her brother AB's flexible songwriting). Though some of the music has been remixed and remastered, her vocals are all original, including several songs she recorded when she was 14. It's not a greatest-hits collection. Several of those had been issued or planned at the time *Anthology* was put together, so the decision was made to favor earlier or less widely available songs. *Dreaming of You* 𝄢𝄢𝄢 (EMI Latin, 1995, prod. Abraham Quintanilla Jr.) is the music most of the non-Hispanic world associates with Selena, though it's not her strongest disc. *Amor Prohibido* 𝄢𝄢𝄢𝄢 (EMI Latin, 1994, prod. Abraham Quintanilla Jr.) and the above-mentioned *Anthology* would qualify for that designation. *Dreaming of You* consists of tracks Selena had recorded for her projected English-language release together with several of her Tejano best-sellers such as "Techno Cumbia," "Bidi Bidi Bom Bom," and "Como la Flor." A particularly strong track is the bilingual duet with David Byrne, "God's Child/Balia Conmigo." For the most part what *Dreaming of You* illustrates is that, in English or Spanish, Selena favored light, hook-laden danceable pop, and that she could, through the power of her voice and personality, connect with the listener through even the most insubstantial song. It also offers a good survey of her popular styles and may be the best entry point to Selena's music for those who don't speak Spanish.

what to buy next: *Entre a Mi Mundo* 𝄢𝄢𝄢𝄢 (EMI Latin, 1992, prod. Abraham Quintanilla Jr.) is best-selling Tejano/pop as Selena began her rise to national stardom. *Ven Conmigo* 𝄢𝄢𝄢𝄢 (Capitol, 1990, prod. Abraham Quintanilla Jr.) was the first Tejano recording to go gold, which it did in 1991. *Selena!* 𝄢𝄢𝄢 (EMI Latin, 1997, prod. Abraham Quintanilla Jr.), the soundtrack to the motion picture of the singer's life, gives a taste of several styles of her music and includes two songs in tribute to her as well.

the rest:
Entertainer of the Year 𝄢𝄢𝄢 (Capitol, 1992)
Mis Mejores Canciones: 17 Super Exitos 𝄢𝄢𝄢 (Capitol/EMI Latin, 1993)

worth searching for: Because of the dramatic circumstances of Selena's murder at a young age, several photo books, celebrity biographies, and videos were produced to satisfy the desire for information about her. A commonly available video to avoid is *Selena: The Final Notes,* which is a poorly edited and—especially disturbing in a piece about a musician—poorly mixed collection of news clips woven together with a badly written script. Despite the title, the producers clearly didn't obtain permission to use Selena's recordings. The only time she is heard singing in this video is on a tape within a tape, as actresses auditioning for a role in the movie about her practice lip-synching to the music. A much better choice, though it veers a bit toward the iconographic side in its introduction, is *Selena Remembered.* As might be expected in a video issued by her record company, there is much well-shot and well-recorded concert footage, interspersed with informal interviews with the singer, her family, and others who worked with her. It ends, however, without making clear the circumstances of her death. The best understanding of the singer's life on video can be gained by watching the theatrical film *Selena!.* In the title role, Jennifer Lopez provides insight into the personality of the young girl who grew up both Mexican and American, seeking pop stardom and a balanced life on her own terms.

influences:

◀◀ Madonna, Paula Abdul, Rocío Dúrcal

▶▶ Jennifer y los Jets

see also: *David Byrne, Jennifer Lopez, Chris Perez*

Kerry Dexter

Seven Nations
Celtic rock
Formed 1994, in USA. Based in Windermere, FL, USA.

Kirk McLeod, vocals, guitars, keyboards, bagpipes; Struby, bass, vocals; Neil Anderson, bagpipes, uilleann pipes, whistles (1994–98);

Nick Watson, drums (1995–96); Ashton Geoghagan, drums (1996–present); Scott Long, bagpipes, mandolin (1999–present); Dan Stacey, fiddle, step dancing (1999–present). (All members are from USA.)

Billing themselves as a "Celtic rock" band, Seven Nations purvey an increasingly loud brand of undistinguished plain-old rock spiced up with raucous bagpipes. Their main Celtic credentials seem to be electrified medleys of traditional tunes—which suggest too much listening to Boiled in Lead and bad Wolfstone—and their stage presence: bandmembers often appear in kilts. Showing a little bare knee never lost the Spice Girls any fans, and so far it seems to be paying off for Seven Nations as well. They've started to play at Scottish Highland Games festivals with some regularity, where they have been known to drown out performers on other stages with over-the-top amplification. Formerly trading under the "Clan na Gael" moniker, in 1994 the band adopted their current name, invoking the ancient Celtic lands of Ireland, Scotland, Wales, Isle of Man, Cornwall, Brittany, and Galicia. Their music is less ambitious, however, rarely straying from the Irish and Scots domains when it does draw on the old traditions. They seem equally content working the crowds with all the polish and finesse of the average boogie band, and rushing out albums before they have much to say; their musical abilities have a long way to go to catch up with their marketing and publicity skills. The recent loss of their greatest asset, piper Neil Anderson, cast a shadow over their future, but his replacement with not one but two new members showed they'd rather light a candle than curse the obvious.

what to avoid: *Rain and Thunder* 🎵🎵 (Seven Nations, 1994, prod. J. Melville) and *Old Ground* 🎵🎵 (Seven Nations, 1995, prod. Seven Nations, Grant Austin) display a confused sense of purpose, mixing bar-band quality playing —some spirited piping notwithstanding—of Irish/Scottish tune medleys and non-Celtic cover songs, with largely characterless compositions of McLeod's. On the first album they cover "Faithful Departed" by former Irish punk Philip Chevron (later of the Pogues), though the Seven Nations take is faithful to Christy Moore's version with Moving Hearts, a band whose sound is briefly echoed elsewhere in the Seven Nations catalog. With *Big Dog* 🎵🎵🎵 (Seven Nations, 1996, prod. Seven Nations) the band gets a bit more focused, though exactly what on is not clear; it doesn't seem to be Celtic music. Opening with a straight cover of the Church's late-'80s hit "Under the Milky Way," cleverly used as an excuse for some feisty bagpipe solos, they continue with a decent attack on Dominic Behan's "Crooked Jack," some group originals with a little more bite to them, and a handful of the obligatory jigs-and-reels medleys. The band turns up the volume even more for the pointless live *Roadkill—Volume One* **woof!** (Seven Nations, 1998, prod. Kirk McLeod), whose claim to

be an accurate representation of the in-concert Seven Nations experience ("totally us, totally live, warts and all") is a troubling thought indeed. Some of the between-tracks "Gee, guys" patter is as indulgent as it gets and raises serious questions about their credibility. Which doesn't make the recent rumors of a *Roadkill—Volume Two* any less ominous. . . .

influences:

📻 Boiled in Lead, Moving Hearts, Christy Moore, Wolfstone

John C. Falstaff

Sexteto Boloña

Son

Formed 1923, in Havana, Cuba. Disbanded 1935.

Alfredo Boloña Jimenez, bongos, tres; Manuel Menocal, tres; Manuel Corona, guitar; Victoriano López, maracas; Joaquín Velázquez, bongos; Hortensia Valerón, vocals; Tata Gutiérrez, vocals, maracas; José Manuel "El Chino" Incharte, bongos; Abelardo Barroso, vocals, claves; Mario Rosales, vocals; José Interián, trumpet; Loreto Zequeira, bongos; José Vega Chacón, guitar, vocals; Tabito, bass. (All members are from Cuba.)

Out of the ashes of the Cuarteto Oriental came two sextets that helped change the direction Cuban music would take. The more famous of the two was the Sexteto Habanero while the other, the Sexteto Boloña, lasted for a dozen years before splitting up when two of the members (Tata Gutiérrez and José Vega Chacón) left to form the Septeto Bolero. Both sextets were famous for the music they played and the personnel that passed through them on the way to other groups. The leader of the Sexteto Boloña was Alfredo Boloña Jimenez, a classy *tres* (small guitar) player with fairly decent compositional chops. A few years after the group formed they went on a tour that took in Venezuela and New York City, and it was during the Big Apple visit that the group recorded 17 songs for posterity. Luckily they were pretty memorable, and this was due in no small part to the golden throat of Abelardo Barroso and the percussion of the superb *bongosero* "El Chino" Incharte (both of whom also passed through the Sexteto Habanero).

what's available: The Sexteto Boloña didn't record much material. On CD the main choice is *Echale Candela* 🎵🎵🎵 (Tumbao Cuban Classics, 1995, prod. various), which has all 17 tunes that were recorded in NYC. The sound is not that spectacular but the performances are well worth searching out. The alternative is the cassette of *La Historia Del Son Cubano (The Roots of Salsa 1)* 🎵🎵🎵 (Folk Lyric, 1985, compilation prod. Chris Strachwitz), which duplicates the now out-of-print vinyl and lacks three of the songs heard on the Tumbao CD.

worth searching for: *Sones-Vol. II, Original Recordings from 1926–1928* 🎵🎵🎵 (Arhoolie, 1996, compilation prod. Chris Strachwitz) may be the best all-around buy for folks looking to explore this musical territory. It duplicates 12 of the 17 tunes found on the Tumbao CD, but makes up for that by including six songs by the Sexteto Occidente, four by the Sexteto Nacional, and two from the Sexteto Matancero (featuring Cuban music legend Isaac Oviedo).

influences:

◀◀ Cuarteto Oriental

▶▶ Septeto Bolero, Sierra Maestra

see also: *Arsenio Rodríguez, Sexteto Habanero*

Garaud MacTaggart

Sexteto Habanero /Septeto Habanero

Son

Formed 1920, in Havana, Cuba. Based in Cuba.

Membership variable; see below. (All members are from Cuba.)

Sexteto Habanero set the timer on the salsa explosion when they brought Cuban *son*'s crossfire rhythms and African-rooted call-and-response vocal patterns from Oriente Province—including the country around Guantánamo, Baracoa, and Santiago de Cuba—into metropolitan Havana. By challenging the entire *tipico* style of performance that Cuba's high-society dance bands were used to playing, the Sexteto Habanero revolutionized the island's popular music forever. They were also the first band to have "hit" records in Cuba and, when they mutated into a septet in 1927 with the addition of a trumpet player, laid down the stylistic blueprint for other groups to build upon.

The sextet evolved from two earlier bands (the Trio Oriental and the Cuarteto Oriental) whose core members also sang with the popular choral group Los Apaches. Their initial lineup included Gerardo Martínez (leader, vocals, and *marimbula*), Carlos Godínez (*tres*—a small guitar), Felix Neri Cabrera (vocals and maracas), José "Cheo" Jiménez (vocals and *claves*—wooden sticks), Guillermo Castillo (vocals and guitar), Antonio Bacallao (*botija*) and either Agustín Rodríguez, José María "El Chino" Incharte, or Oscar Satolongo (sources vary on this point) on bongos. Martínez's marimbula and Bacallao's botija were both percussive instruments that held down the musical bottom for the group and later gave way to the string bass (also played by Martínez).

In 1927 the group added trumpeter Enrique Hernández, who left soon after and was replaced by one of the giants of Cuban music, Felix Chapottin. Other major figures to pass through the band during its late-'20s heyday were the vocalist/claves player

jamaican music 9: dancehall

Dancehall music emerged in the late 1970s, when political instability and a further declining economy swayed Jamaica's people and music away from roots-reggae's Pan-African perspective to one more focused on recreational escape and fulfillment of desire. After nearly a decade of U.S.-encouraged turmoil and nearly a thousand killings between the election of slain pseudo-socialist Prime Minister Michael Manley and successor Edward Seaga—the "CIA-ga" of Kingston graffiti—the people no longer wanted to meditate on idealistic visions of liberation from oppression; instead, they wanted to forget these problems altogether. The lyrical topics turned to funky dance moves, gun-fortified empowerment, and sexually explicit microphone chat called "slackness," a term first coined by deejay General Echo on his influential 1979 LP *Ranking Slackness*. With Tenor Saw's "Ring the Alarm" providing the theme song, boastful deejay "sound clashes" became dancehall "sporting" events as popular as soccer matches. Producers rarely constructed new rhythms; to save studio time and cash, they recycled classic rocksteady and reggae tracks for the dancehalls on "dub plates." Nonetheless, the rhythms rarely sounded retread, as the best session bands (Roots Radics, Soul Syndicate) and producers (Prince Jammy, Junjo Lawes, Linval Thompson) were able to make vintage beats sound explosively new. *A Deejay Explosion inna Dancehall Style ♪♪♪♪* (Heartbeat), recorded at Kingston's famed Skateland venue in 1982, is perhaps the best approximation of the visceral energy of live dancehall music, and a stellar example of the improvisational art of deejaying. Despite the preeminence of microphone motormouths, singers were still a critical element of the dancehall, and chants of "respect due!" were showered on such fine vocalists as Sugar Minott (actually the first artist to earn the "dancehall" tag), Barrington Levy, Freddie McGregor, Frankie Paul, Cocoa Tea, and Half Pint. For its followers—the dedicated downtown "massive"—dancehall music is a rhythmic hailstorm, its venues a site of temporary but cathartic communion.

Todd Shanker

Abelardo Barroso (oftimes referred to as "Caruso" for his clear tenor and impeccable phrasing), and the "bongosero" Agustin Gutierrez, whose later career included stints in the Septeto Agabama (alongside the legendary Machito) and in the Conjunto de Matamoros. The group has gone through various lineups over the years, breaking up only to reform later. Septeto Habanero is still playing gigs but all of the original personnel have died, leaving Manuel Furé (vocals and clave) as the longest-tenured member, dating from the Martínez era in 1952.

what to buy: With 24 tunes, *Las Raices del Son* 🎧🎧🎧🎧 (Tumbao Cuban Classics, 1992, prod. various) serves as a perfect audio introduction to the Sexteto Habanero. The selections include a fair number of originals but they also contain works by Ignacio Piñeiro, whose Septeto Nacional was the main competition for the Septeto Habanero, and by the great Latin composer Ernesto Lecuona. The mastering has reduced the noise considerably, though there is a slight loss in the upper ranges.

what to buy next: A companion volume to the above-mentioned album, *Son Cubano* 🎧🎧🎧 (Tumbao Cuban Classics, 1991, prod. various) is much shorter, but the performances are still worth checking out. *75 Years Later* 🎧🎧🎧 (Corason, 1995, prod. Eduardo Llerenas) marks the recording comeback of the Septeto Habanero under Manuel Furé's direction. The production is very clean and the tunes and playing do honor to the group's progenitors.

the rest:
Sexteto Habanero, Vol. 1 🎧🎧🎧 (Bongo Latino, 1994, prod. various)
Sexteto Habanero, Vol. 2 🎧🎧🎧 (Bongo Latino, 1994, prod. various)
Sexteto Habanero, Vol. 3 🎧🎧🎧 (Bongo Latino, 1995, prod. various)
1926–1931 🎧🎧🎧🎧 (Harlequin, 1995, prod. various)
1926–1948 🎧🎧🎧🎧 (Harlequin, 1996, prod. various)
Sones Cubanos Vol. 2, 1926–1931 🎧🎧🎧🎧 (Folk Lyric cassette, 1983, compilation prod. Chris Strachwitz)

influences:
◀◀ Trio Oriental, Cuarteto Oriental

▶▶ Arsenio Rodriguez y su Conjunto

see also: *Machito, Sexteto Boloña*

Garaud MacTaggart

Shadow
Soca, calypso
Born c. 1942, in Tobago, Trinidad and Tobago. Based in Port of Spain, Trinidad, and Brooklyn, NY, USA.

Shadow (a.k.a. Winston Bailey) is a giant of *soca* (the phenomenally popular hybrid named as a contraction of "soul" and "calypso"), both as a singer/composer and as a musician. His masterful electric bass playing has redefined the instrument's role in calypso and soca, and added an extra element of rhythmic excitement to the music. Shadow was born on Tobago, a small island near Trinidad, and grew up poor, dreaming of a career in music, one of the few ways out of the ghetto for a hungry young man. He began his career by joining Sparrow's tent (calypso organization) as a backup singer, but soon moved on to form his own band. In 1974 he won his first Road March Crown (given to the composer of the most-covered song of the current Carnival season) with "Bassman," the tune that introduced his remarkable style on the instrument. It was the first time in years that anyone but Sparrow or Kitch (Lord Kitchener) had won the Road March Crown, and signaled an end to their domination of Carnival music. Like Sparrow and Kitch, Shadow can compose a mordant political lyric, but he is also welcomed by the younger generation for his ability to build a tune around a phat party groove.

what to buy: *The Best of Shadow, Vol. 1* 🎧🎧🎧🎧🎧 (Straker's, 1995, prod. Granville Straker) is a collection of hits in their original versions, starting with "Bassman," the tune that made Shadow a force to be reckoned with. It only duplicates one track from the almost-as-good compilation *Columbus Lied*.

what to buy next: *Columbus Lied* 🎧🎧🎧🎧 (Shanachie, 1991, prod. Granville Straker) is a retrospective featuring re-recordings of some of Shadow's biggest carnival hits including "Tan Tan," "Bad Boy Peter," and the title track, a scathing indictment of colonial mentality and racism.

best of the rest:
Return of De Bassman 🎧🎧🎧🎧 (Straker's)
High Tension 🎧🎧🎧🎧 (Straker's)
Mystical Moods 🎧🎧🎧🎧 (MRS, 1984)
Sweet Sweet Dreams 🎧🎧🎧🎧 (CCP, 1984)
Raw Energy 🎧🎧🎧🎧 (B's, 1986)

influences:
◀◀ Sparrow, Lord Kitchener, Growling Lion, Atilla

▶▶ David Rudder, Tambu, Machel Montano, Taxi

see also: *Lord Kitchener, the Mighty Sparrow*

j. poet

Shaggy
Dancehall
Born Orville Richard Burrell, October 22, 1968, in Kingston, Jamaica. Based in Brooklyn, NY, USA.

Dancehall was in the doldrums around 1993, having taken hits from Snow, the Vanilla Ice of reggae, and Buju Banton, an influential star who earned lots of bad press for slurring gays in public. Then came "Oh Carolina," Shaggy's clinking, clanking, brightly hoarse remake of a 1960 reggae song by the Folkes

Brothers, and the genre revitalized itself. Nicknamed, as you might expect, for the hippie character on the *Scooby Doo* cartoon, Orville Burrell moved with his mother from Kingston to a West Indian section of Brooklyn when he was 18. Like his reggae forebears, he worked as a deejay in local clubs and started "toasting," making up lyrics to rap over songs by Super Cat and other established dancehall stars. He recorded a few singles with the big-name producer Sting (no relation to a certain other big name who's dabbled in reggae), but had decided to join the U.S. Marines—and, to his chagrin, served in the Persian Gulf—before anything happened. Upon his return friends called to say his singles, such as "Big Up," were taking off. Ditching the Marines for his pop career, he scored a huge hit with "Oh Carolina"—his first of several. One of reggae's few mainstream Stateside success stories, Shaggy's sunny hits about love and partying are rarely as political as, say, Bob Marley, or as ponderous as Maxi Priest's heavy crooning.

what to buy: "Oh Carolina" is the centerpiece of *Pure Pleasure* 𝄢𝄢𝄢 (Virgin, 1993, prod. J. Ralf Allen), but the rest of the album, most notably "Soon Be Done," is almost as irresistible. In addition to his catchy, superlow vocals and jittery dancehall production, there's an underlying devotion to old-school soul and reggae melodies; even on his debut album Shaggy reveals he's far more Marvin Gaye than Eek-a-Mouse.

what to buy next: *Boombastic* 𝄢𝄢 (Virgin, 1995, prod. Robert Livingston, Gemma Corfield) recaptures the feel of "Oh Carolina" on several standout cuts, including the bouncy title track, a version of Ken Boothe's reggae classic "The Train Is Coming," and the snappy opener "In the Summertime."

what to avoid: Though *Midnite Lover* 𝄢𝄢 (Virgin, 1997, prod. various) features fun, upbeat songs like "Sexy Body Girls" and Percy Sledge's "Warm and Tender Love," it's less spry than the singer's earlier material, with more heavy-handed production.

the rest:
Original Doberman 𝄢𝄢𝄢 (Greensleeves, 1990)

worth searching for: *Tougher Than Tough: The Story of Jamaican Music* 𝄢𝄢𝄢𝄢 (Mango/Island, 1993, prod. Chris Blackwell) is a four-disc chronology that contains just one Shaggy tune. But it nicely shows the progression from the Folkes Brothers' original "Oh Carolina" (produced by the great Prince Buster) to Shaggy's wonderful revamp, with Bob Marley, Dennis Brown, Desmond Dekker, Junior Murvin, Culture, and Shabba Ranks in between. (The disc is also reviewed in this book's Compilations section.)

influences:
◄ Prince Buster, Shabba Ranks, Super Cat, Lee "Scratch" Perry, Wilson Pickett, James Brown, Ken Boothe, Bob Marley, Boogie Down Productions

▶▶ Red Rat, Beenie Man

see also: *Maxi Priest*

Steve Knopper

Simon Shaheen
Traditional Arabic folk
Born 1955, in Tarshiha, Galilee/Israel. Based in Brooklyn, NY, USA.

Most artists would be content with being considered a master of one instrument, but Shaheen is equally adept at two. World-renowned as a virtuoso of the *oud*—the short-necked, pear-shaped Arabic precursor of the European lute—Shaheen's skill as a violinist is somewhat overlooked. Born in a small village in Galilee to a family rich in musical talent, Shaheen began studying the oud with his father, Hikmet, a well-known composer and teacher of Arabic music, at the age of five, and at seven entered the Rubin Conservatory, where he studied violin and Western classical music. After graduating from the Academy of Music in Jerusalem in 1978 with a double degree in performance and Arabic literature, but feeling limited in his career opportunities, Shaheen moved to New York in 1980, where he studied musicology, music education, and violin performance. In 1982 he formed the Near Eastern Music Ensemble, and has since become highly respected in the U.S. as a teacher, giving lectures and workshops at prominent institutions like Harvard, Princeton, and Juilliard. Just as Shaheen had mastered two instruments, he soon earned recognition as an expert in the musical traditions of two worlds, the Middle East and the West, through collaborations with a variety of European and American artists and groups, including Bill Laswell's fusion project Material. But even as he explores styles ranging from jazz and flamenco to film scores (*The Sheltering Sky* and *Malcolm X*) and theater, Shaheen continues to promote Arab musical traditions, producing the annual Arab Arts Festival, Mahrajan Al-Fan, in New York. He is currently in the process of establishing an Arab Art Institute in that same city.

what to buy: If you're looking to learn more about Arabic music but don't know where to start, *The Music of Mohamed Abdel Wahab* 𝄢𝄢𝄢𝄢 (Axiom, 1990, prod. Bill Laswell, Simon Shaheen) is as great an introduction as you'll find. An homage to Egyptian composer Wahab, this sultry masterpiece features a massive orchestra of more than 20 musicians and singers, including Shaheen's brother on oud and his sister on vocals. Beautifully recorded and filled with dazzling rhythms and spellbinding melodies, this blissful excursion is world music at its absolute finest. For a more in-depth examination of Shaheen's own compositional skills and instrumental prowess, try *Saltanah* 𝄢𝄢𝄢𝄢 (Water Lily

Simon Shaheen

Acoustics, 1996, prod. Kavichandran Alexander), Shaheen's brilliant collaboration with Indian slide guitarist Vishwa Mohan Bhatt. Impossibly complex improvisations by both musicians converge on five wondrous tracks that point out the inherent similarities between Indian *ragas* and Arabic *maqams*.

what to buy next: *Taqasim* ♪♪♪♪ (Lyrichord, 1991, prod. Phillip D. Schuyler) is a more sublime, stripped-down outing featuring Shaheen trading extended improvisations with Lebanese musician Ali Jihad Racy, a master of the *buzuq*, a Near Eastern variation on the Greek bouzouki. Although the compositions on *Turath* ♪♪♪♪ (CMP, 1992, prod. Bill Laswell, Simon Shaheen) fit the more stereotypical idea of traditional belly-dancing music, it's still an album well worth having for Shaheen's virtuosic picking and some maddeningly infectious rhythms.

influences:
◄◄ Mohamed Abdel Wahab, Hikmet Shaheen
►► William Nakhly, Bill Laswell, Najib Shaheen

see also: *V. M. Bhatt, Bill Laswell, Mike Richmond, Mohamed Abdel Wahab*

Bret Love

Shakira

Latin pop
Born Shakira Isabel Mebarak Ripoll, February 9, 1977, in Barranquilla, Colombia. Based in Miami, FL, USA.

Shakira was born into a poor family in Barranquilla, Colombia. At 13 she left her home for Bogotá, seeking success as a model. Her voice attracted interest from Sony Discos and at 14 she released what proved to be an unsuccessful collection of self-penned tunes, *Magia.* A second album, *Peligro,* also did not do well, so the teenager pursued her modeling career and began acting in *telenovelas* (soap operas), including the Colombian *El Oasis.* Still, having not completely abandoned her interest in music and having earned a touch more maturity in the entertainment business, she went back to Sony in 1996 and put out what at first appeared to be another unsuccessful project, *Pies Descalos.* But this time singles slowly began getting airplay in South American countries and eventually made the *Billboard* Latin charts, building the album's popularity and opening doors for the even more successful *Donde Estan Los Ladrones?.*

what to buy: *Donde Estan Los Ladrones?* ♪♪♪ (Sony International, 1998, prod. Shakira Mebarak R.) and *Pies Descalos* ♪♪♪ (Sony International, 1996, prod. Shakira Mebarak R.) hit a balance of danceable tunes and angry-young-woman-rock attitude. There are acoustic guitar touches that recall the artist's Latin origins and she sings in Spanish, but Shakira's music moves in the direction of dance pop's globalization rather than the expression of Latin culture. She's been called the Latin Alanis Morissette and has attracted the attention of Gloria and Emilio Estefan, at whose Miami studio *Donde Estan Los Ladrones?* was recorded, and who are said to be assisting Shakira with English adaptations of her songs.

the rest:
Magia ♪♪♪ (Sony, 1991)
Peligro ♪♪♪ (Sony, 1992)
Megamixes ♪♪♪ (Sony, 1997)

influences:
◄◄ Beck, Alanis Morissette, the Estefans

Kerry Dexter

Shakti

World, jazz-fusion, Indian jazz
Formed 1975, in London, England. Disbanded 1978.

John McLaughlin (England), acoustic guitar; Zakir Hussain, percussion; T. H. "Vikku" Vinayakram, percussion; L. Shankar, violin. (All members are from India except where noted otherwise.)

After attracting international acclaim for his lightning-fast playing with the electric jazz-fusion groups the Miles Davis Band

and the Mahavishnu Orchestra, British guitarist John McLaughlin turned his focus toward the acoustic guitar. Teaming with virtuoso Indian violinist L. Shankar, *tabla* drum player Zakir Hussain, and *ghatam* (clay pot) player T. H. "Vikku" Vinayakram to form an acoustic group, Shakti, McLaughlin used Indian classical *ragas* as a springboard for lengthy improvisations and created one of the first true world jazz-fusion bands. Although they were only together for two years, the band recorded three memorable albums and spurred the growth of world music as we know it today—a much-transformed cultural climate into which McLaughlin and Hussain set out on a "Remember Shakti" tour in 1999.

what to buy: The debut, *Shakti with John McLaughlin* ♫♫♫♫ (Columbia, 1975, prod. John McLaughlin), was recorded during a concert at South Hampton College. A true East/West summit meeting, the album showcases McLaughlin's fiery playing balanced by the rest of the band's tradition-rooted arrangements. The highpoint comes with a longer-than 29-minute improvisation.

what to buy next: Though recorded in a studio and thus not quite matching the intensity of their live album, the six-tune follow-up *Natural Elements* ♫♫♫ (Columbia, 1978/Sony, 1997, prod. John McLaughlin) finds its potency through subtlety and instrumental lyricism.

the rest:
Handful of Beauty ♫♫♫ (Tristar Music, 1977)
The Best of John McLaughlin and Shakti ♫♫♫ (Moment, 1995)

influences:
◀◀ Ravi Shankar, the Paul Winter Consort, Oregon
▶▶ Bill Meyers, Trilok Gurtu

see also: *Hari Prasad Chaurasia, Zakir Hussain, L. Shankar, T. H. "Vikku" Vinayakram*

Craig Harris

Anoushka Shankar

Indian classical
Born 1981, in London, England. Based in England.

So what do you do when you're the child of sitar master Ravi Shankar? It ain't roller blading, that's for sure. The daughter of Ravi's second wife, Sukanya, Anoushka was born in London and grew up splitting time between Southern California and her father's native India. As the only player ever trained completely by the elder Shankar, Anoushka started learning at age nine on a "baby" sitar built especially for her and made her performing debut when she was 13, sharing the stage with her father in New Delhi and, by all accounts, blowing him off it

(which we find a bit hard to believe). Still, she seems well set up to be Ravi's successor, having recorded with him and George Harrison on the former's 1997 release *Chants of India* and becoming the youngest (and first female) recipient of a House of Commons Shield from the British Parliament in 1998—all before the release of her self-titled debut album.

what's available: *Anoushka* ♫♫♫ (Angel/EMI Classics, 1998, prod. Ravi Shankar), given her laudable credentials, is not really all it should be. She's clearly a gifted technician, but at this young age Anoushka's playing tends to be more skillful than emotional. She is also quite clearly the daughter of Ravi, and while that close tie has obviously given her a leg up on the instrument and in the marketplace, it has somewhat hampered the development of her independent voice.

influences:
◀◀ Ravi Shankar

see also: *Ravi Shankar*

Gary Graff

L. Shankar
/Shankar

Indian classical and jazz, world fusion
Born 1953, in Madras, India. Based in Los Angeles, CA, USA.

The classical *ragas* and drones of India are combined with a multitude of world-music influences by India-born violinist and vocalist Larshinarayana "L." Shankar. In addition to many solo recordings, Shankar has recorded albums with his wife, Caroline, a former British vocalist whom he met during recording sessions with Peter Gabriel in 1980; and in a rock band, the Epidemics. Shankar has also been featured on albums by such performers as Gabriel, Bruce Springsteen, Yoko Ono, and Talking Heads. His 1979 recording *Touch Me There* was produced by Frank Zappa, who wrote lyrics to several tunes. Since 1980 Shankar has played a special, 10-string, double violin that he designed with guitar builder Ken Parker. The instrument has given Shankar much flexibility, with five strings that sound like a double bass or cello, and five strings on the upper neck that sound like a violin or viola.

Shankar grew up in a musical family. Both of his parents were professional vocalists, and his father was also one of the country's premier violinists and operated his own music school. Shankar himself began studying music at the age of five. He was exposed to a mixture of traditional Indian sounds and the pop, rock, and classical music of the Western world. In the early 1960s Shankar performed with his brothers, L. Subramaniam and L. Vaidhyanathan, as the Violin Trio. Shankar came to the United States to teach Indian music at Wesleyan University and to study for a Doctorate in Ethnomusicology. His most influential learning, however, came in the clubs of New York, where he was befriended by many musicians. Shankar's earliest recording sessions in the U.S. were with such jazz artists as Archie Shepp and Jan Garbarek. In 1976 he formed a groundbreaking acoustic band, Shakti, with fusion guitarist John McLaughlin of the Mahavishnu Orchestra. He has since become a much-in-demand session player. In 1989, he joined with such artists as Bruce Springsteen, Sting, Lou Reed, and Tracy Chapman for the Amnesty International-sponsored "Human Rights Now!" tour. Shankar's music has been featured in several films, including *The Last Temptation of Christ, Robin Hood,* and *Jennifer 8.* He had his greatest success to date in 1991, when his *Pancha Nadai Pallavi* became the first Indian classical music album to make the Top Ten on *Billboard*'s World Music chart.

what to buy: The musical traditions of India are blended with jazz fusion and rock rhythms on Shankar's album *Touch Me There* 𝄢𝄢𝄢𝄢 (Barking Pumpkin, 1979, prod. Frank Zappa). In addition to such imaginative instrumentals as "No More Mr. Nice Girl," the album includes the memorable song "Dead Girls of London," featuring Zappa on guitar and Mothers of Invention vocalist Ike Willis.

what to buy next: Although *Raga Aber* 𝄢𝄢𝄢 (Music of the World, 1995, prod. Shankar) is more rooted in classical Indian music than the above disc, the energetic drive of Shankar's playing adds a contemporary touch. His violin is enhanced by the percussive rhythms of Caroline on tambourine and Zakir Hussain on *tabla* drum.

the rest:
Who's to Know 𝄢𝄢𝄢 (ECM/Polydor, 1979)

influences:
◄◄ Ravi Shankar, V. Shankar

►► Zakir Hussain, Mickey Hart

see also: *Zakir Hussain, Bill Laswell, Shakti, Dr. L. Subramaniam, T. H. "Vikku" Vinayakram*

Craig Harris

Lakshmi Shankar

Indian classical
Born late 1920s, in India. Based in India.

One of India's top female vocalists, Lakshiminarayan or "Lakshmi" Shankar joined one of India's leading musical families when she married sitar player Ravi Shankar's older brother Rajendra Shankar (a scriptwriter) in the early 1940s. Although she began her career as a dancer in the troupe organized and managed by Uday Shankar (another of Ravi's brothers), she turned

to music when health problems prevented her from practicing her first artistic love. She then garnered acclaim for her work on the ballet *Discovery of India* in 1946 and '47. In addition to singing on the soundtracks of several movies including the Academy Award-winning *Gandhi,* Shankar has been featured on several of Ravi's albums. The mother-in-law of Indian jazz violinist L. Subramaniam, Shankar is a master of *khayal,* a light classical style of Indian singing.

what to buy: Shankar's talents for singing classical Indian music are obvious on the live album *Evening Concert* 𝄢𝄢𝄢 (Ravi Shankar Music, 1986, prod. Richard Bock).

what to buy next: Shankar's vocals are strengthened by the innovative playing of Norwegian jazz saxophonist Jan Gabarek on *Vision* 𝄢𝄢𝄢 (1983, ECM, prod. Jan Gabarek).

the rest:
Who's to Know 𝄢𝄢𝄢 (ECM, 1980)
Song for Everyone 𝄢𝄢𝄢 (ECM, 1984)
Les Heurs Et Les Saisons 𝄢𝄢𝄢 (Ocara, 1987)
Nobody Told Me 𝄢𝄢𝄢 (ECM, 1990)
Soul Searcher 𝄢𝄢𝄢 (Axiom, 1991)

influences:
◄◄ Ravi Shankar, Lata Mangeshkar, Begum Akhtar

►► Peter Gabriel, Jan Garbarek, L. Subramaniam, Najma Akhtar

see also: *Ali Akbar Khan, Ravi Shankar, Dr. L. Subramaniam*

Craig Harris

Ravi Shankar

Indian classical
Born Rabindra Shankar Chowdery, April 7, 1920, in Uttah Pradesh, India. Based in India.

A master of the sitar, India's best-known stringed instrument, Ravi Shankar attracted international acclaim when he gave lessons to the Beatles' George Harrison in the mid-1960s. Shankar later became one of the few non-rock performers at the Monterey Pop Festival in 1967 and the Woodstock Music Festival in 1969. Together with Harrison, Shankar helped organize, and performed at, the Concert for Bangladesh in 1971. The event and subsequent three-disc album helped raise more than $15 million for that war-ravaged country. *Billboard* named Shankar its Recording Artist of the Year and Musician of the Year in 1967; in a 1995 interview Harrison referred to Shankar as "the godfather of world music."

The son of Shyam Shankar, a Minister for the Maharajah of Jhalawar, Shankar made his professional debut, at the age of 13, as a dancer in the Compaigne de Danse et Musique Hindou, a troupe that included his older brother Uday Shankar. A turning

Ravi Shankar with his daughter Anoushka

point came after meeting influential multi-instrumentalist Al-laudin Kahn, father of Indian percussionist Ali Akbar Khan, at the All-Bengal Music Conference in December of 1934. Shankar apprenticed himself to the elder Kahn, who toured with the dance troupe as a featured soloist from 1935–36. In 1938, Shankar left the troupe to spend six years studying music under Kahn.

Performing his first public recital at a Music Conference in Alla-habad in 1939, Shankar toured throughout India in the late '40s. In 1945 his composition "Sare Jahan Se Accha" became one of the country's most popular songs. Shankar served as music director and launched the chamber orchestra Vadya Vrinda for All-India Radio in New Delhi from 1949 until 1956, when he performed his first solo concerts in Europe and the United States.

Shankar's music has been featured in such films as *Charlie, The Flute and the Arrow, Kabuliwala,* and *Ghandi.* Shankar has com-posed many pieces for ballets, including "Samanya Ksnati," "India Immortal," "The Discovery of India," and "Ghyanshyam: The Broken Branch." The first Indian musician ever commis-

sioned by a major Western orchestra—"A Concerto for Sitar and Orchestra," performed by the London Philharmonic in 1970—Shankar has also composed material for the New York Philharmonic under the direction of Zubin Mehta, the Baltimore Symphony Orchestra, and French flute player Jean-Pierre Ram-pal. In 1979, Shankar performed on an *East Greets East* tour with Japanese flute player Hosan Yamamoto and *koto* (classical zither) player Musumi Miyashita. In 1988, Shankar was com-missioned by the Palace of Culture of the Soviet Union to com-pose a piece, "Swar Milan," to be performed by 140 musicians and singers. Two years later, he collaborated with minimalist composer Philip Glass on the recording *Passages.*

Shankar has been extremely generous in sharing his under-standing of Indian music. In 1967, he founded the Kinnara School of Indian Music in Bombay. He later opened a branch in Los Angeles. Shankar also served as chairperson of the depart-ment of Indian music at the California Institute of Arts.

Shankar reached his lowest point in 1975 when he suffered a near mental breakdown during a tour with Harrison and the Festival of India. Following his recovery, he vowed to perform only in classical or ethnic music venues. In 1997, he established the Ravi Shankar Foundation in Encinitas, California; his autobiography, *My Music, My Life,* was published in 1969.

what to buy: A four-CD set, *In Celebration* ♪♪♪♪ (Angel, 1996, prod. various) is a thorough retrospective of Shankar's career and includes several cuts with the London Symphony Orchestra and the Chamber Orchestra of the Moscow Philharmonic.

what to buy next: *Ravi Shankar* ♪♪♪♪ (Deutsche Grammaphon, 1993, prod. various) unites four of Shankar's most influential albums—*East Greets East, Ragas Hameer & Gara, Raga Jogeshwari,* and *Homage to Mahatma Ghandi and Baba Allauddin.*

the rest:
Ragas ♪♪♪♪ (Fantasy, 1973)
Raga Paramsehwari ♪♪♪♪ (Capitol, 1976)
Shankar Project: Tana Mana ♪♪♪♪ (Private Music, 1987)
The Genius of Ravi Shankar ♪♪♪♪ (Sony, 1987)
The Sounds of India ♪♪♪♪♪ (Sony, 1987)
Inside the Kremlin ♪♪♪♪ (Private Music, 1988)
Golden Jubilee Concert ♪♪♪♪ (Chandra Dhara, 1990)
Farewell, My Friend ♪♪♪♪ (EMI India, 1992)
At the Monterey International Pop Festival ♪♪♪♪ (One Way, 1993)
Live at Monterey, 1967 ♪♪♪♪♪ (Ravi Shankar Music Circle, 1993)
Concert for Peace ♪♪♪ (Moment, 1995)
The Music of Ravi Shankar ♪♪♪♪ (Ocara, 1995)
Genesis Soundtrack ♪♪♪♪♪ (BMG/Milan, 1995)
In San Francisco ♪♪♪♪♪ (One Way, 1995)
In Celebration: The Highlights ♪♪♪♪ (Angel, 1996)
The Genius of Ravi Shankar ♪♪♪♪♪ (SPM, 1997)
Raga Tala ♪♪♪♪♪ (Interra, 1997)
Mantram: Chants of India ♪♪♪♪♪ (Angel, 1997)

worth searching for: *The Concert for Bangladesh* ♪♪♪♪♪ (Apple, 1972/Capitol, 1991, prod. Phil Spector) includes Shankar's expressive *raga,* "Bangla Dhun."

influences:
◀◀ Allaudin Khan

▶▶ George Harrison, Ashwan Batish, Anoushka Shankar

see also: *V. M. Bhatt, Tarun Bhattacharya, George Harrison, Zakir Hussain, Ali Akbar Khan, Anoushka Shankar, Lakshmi Shankar*

Craig Harris

Sharon Shannon

Irish traditional
Born June 8, 1967, in Ruan, County Clare, Ireland. Based in Ireland.

Sharon Shannon is at the top of a stellar crop of young Irish musicians bringing traditional music to the attention of a new generation in Ireland and the United States. An amazing talent with a

firm grasp of traditional music and killer chops on both button accordion and fiddle, Shannon has taken her solid foundation in Irish music and expanded upon it, adding influences from the world of pop and from other cultures to whose music she is drawn. Growing up in North Clare, one of the hotbeds of Irish traditional music and the home turf of the legendary Kilfenora Ceili Band, Shannon was surrounded by dancers and musicians from an early age. Her brother Gary, a fine flute player, and sister Mary, the banjo player with the Irish band the Bumblebees, were early influences, as was Frank Custy, a local music teacher credited with giving many of Clare's young musicians the right start. Shannon was performing professionally at an early age as a member of Disirt Tola, a group that also counted Gary and Mary Shannon, piper Ronan Browne, and concertina player Gearoid O'hAllmhurain among its members. They were active through the '80s and released one album in 1984. Shannon was also active in Comhaltas Ceoltoiri Eireann tours during the 1980s, where she met the great piano accordion player Karen Tweed, whose repertoire and style were very influential on Shannon's development. After a short period with the group Arcady during the late '80s, Shannon was asked by Mike Scott to join the Waterboys. She spent a year and a half touring and recording with the band and being exposed to a whole host of new musical ideas and styles. After Scott changed the band's direction to a less folk-oriented one, Shannon left to pursue a solo career. Her first album, recorded in 1990, mixed traditional tunes with a somewhat pop-oriented acoustic backing and featured appearances by Liam O'Maonlai of Hothouse Flowers and Adam Clayton of U2, as well as many of her former Waterboys bandmates. Their support put her name in front of the Irish popular music press and made her a star to young Irish audiences. Her appearance on the 1992 *A Woman's Heart* anthology, the best-selling album in Irish history, cemented her status as one of Ireland's leading young artists. Since then she has toured throughout the U.S. and Europe and recorded two more albums. Shannon is a dynamite musician on both fiddle and accordion; her playing is firmly rooted in Irish heritage; and she has a great store of traditional tunes. She is also an artistic explorer completely at home in a pop-music idiom. As a result, her arrangements are often more adventurous than on many Irish traditional albums, employing drum machines, synthesizers, saxophones, and other instruments rarely heard in her chosen genre. While this approach often irritates hard-core traditionalists, it's gained a wider ear for the music and helped give it a future—Shannon's credentials are impeccable, and her debt to the music of her forbears is definitely mutual.

what to buy: *Each Little Thing* ♪♪♪♪♪ (Green Linnet, 1997, prod. Dónal Lunny), Shannon's third album, is her most cohesive and self-assured. Working with a crack crew of musicians including guitarist Steve Cooney and fiddler Winnie Horan, Shannon has produced an album that combines traditional and contemporary influences in a completely personal musical statement. From the audacious version of Grace Jones's "Libertango," featuring vocalist Kirsty MacColl, and a cover of Fleetwood Mac's "Never Going Back Again," to a sweet version of Junior Crehan's "With Her Lovely Long Hair," Shannon mixes her sources into a tasty musical stew, with the steady hand of producer Lunny keeping things from boiling over. While not everything works (the hooked-on-classics-sounding programming on "Bag of Cats," for instance), everything bears the stamp of an artist exploring fresh ideas and synthesizing new music out of old.

what to buy next: *Sharon Shannon* ♫♫♫ (Philo, 1991, prod. John Dunford) was Shannon's debut album, and her most musically conservative. While her playing is astounding as always, the arrangements are spare and subdued, with less of the daring of her later recordings. Highlights include the slow air "Marbhna Luimni," and a killer set of box tunes from the pen of Phil Cunningham. If you're a hard-core traditional Irish music fan, this would be the album to purchase—though Shannon's adventurousness in repertoire is still displayed with an imaginative pairing of a Kerry slide and a Cajun dance tune, as well as a Portuguese number.

what to avoid: *Out the Gap* ♫♫ (Green Linnet, 1995, prod. Dennis Bovell, John Dunford) is an album by an artist searching for a style; the control and sophistication developed by Shannon for *Each Little Thing* were not yet there. As usual, her taste in tunes is tremendous, and her playing is great, but saxophonist Richie Buckley has little feel for traditional music and producer Dennis Bovell's tracks seem too restrained. All in all, the pieces just don't fit together.

the rest:
Spellbound—Best of Sharon Shannon ♫♫♫ (Green Linnet, 1999)

worth searching for: One of Shannon's first recorded appearances was on *Ceol Tigh Neachtain* ♫♫♫ (Gael-Linn, 1989, prod. Brendan O'Regan), a sampler featuring many of the fine young musicians in Galway at the time. Other highlights include appearances by fiddler Sean Smyth and *sean-nós* (Irish "old-style") singer Deirbhile Ní Bhrolchain. Good luck finding the eponymous *Disirt Tola* album; you'll have to search used record stores in Ireland. However, *A Woman's Heart* is very much available and reviewed in this book's Compilations section.

influences:
◄ Tommy Peoples, Karen Tweed, Mairtin O'Connor

► Ashley MacIsaac, Mary Custy Band, Natalie MacMaster, Eileen Ivers

see also: *Arcady, Máire Breatnach, Phil Cunningham, Dónal Lunny, the Waterboys*

Tony Ziselberger

Jamshied Sharifi

Middle Eastern jazz
Born October 17, 1960, in Kansas City, MO, USA. Based in New York, NY, USA.

His name suggests his Middle Eastern background, but Jamshied Sharifi was born in Kansas City, and that town's jazz tradition is equally strong in his music. Sharifi studied at Boston's prestigious Berklee College of Music, and then reacquainted himself with the music of his childhood as well. Sharifi draws from Middle Eastern, Ghanaian, and other African music in his compositions and arrangements, and has played all over the world with artists as disparate as John Lurie, Phyllis Hyman, Leon Russell, and Babatunde Olatunji. Irrespective of his leanings toward tradition and the organic ethic of jazz, he is known for his synthesizer work. "Because I've always had a lot of contact with acoustic instruments and players," Sharifi explains, "I have tried to hold the synthesizer up to an 'acoustic' standard; in other words, to try and play it with the depth, detail, and richness of articulation that come naturally to an acoustic instrumentalist." In addition to performance, Sharifi has gained a name in recent years for production and film work. To name one notable example, he coproduced Irish chanteuse Susan McKeown's acclaimed 1998 album *Bushes and Briars* with McKeown and Akira Satake.

what's available: *A Prayer for the Soul of Layla* ♫♫♫ (Alula, 1997, prod. Jamshied Sharifi, Akira Satake) is a masterful blend of bells, handclaps, drones, and the slicker sounds of synthesized jazz. It doesn't have the earthy power of a field recording or even a Nusrat Fateh Ali Khan album, but it's a fusion work that still contains the spices of another world. The listener is drawn into an almost cinematic landscape with Sharifi's arrangements. No wonder, then, that his other major album credit is for a film score. *Harriet the Spy* ♫♫♫ (Castle, 1996, prod. Graham Walker, Jamshied Sharifi) boasts one of the hippest soundtracks ever found in a kid flick, with music that frames and backs selections by James Brown, Jill Sobule, and Les Negresses Vertes. Sharifi brings a true melting-pot sensibility to the jazz-based proceedings.

influences:
◄ Salif Keita, Lyle Mays, Pat Metheny

Pamela Murray Winters

Shiv Kumar Sharma

North Indian classical
Born 1939, in Jammu, Kashmir, India. Based in India.

Before Shiv Kumar Sharma began playing the 100-string *santoor,* a distant relative of the hammered dulcimer, the instrument had only been associated with Kashmiri folk. Sharma changed the tuning system and the number of strings, replaced brass strings with steel ones, and separated the instrument from its traditional wooden stand. The result was a new santoor that could play all 12 notes of the Indian musical scales in three octaves with clarity, readying it for a loftier application. Purists scoffed at the idea that a lowly regional folk instrument could be used in Hindustani classical music, even though the santoor had long played a role in the Persian classical tradition. But with the huge critical and financial success of his *Call of the Valley* album in 1967, Sharma silenced all doubters. He is unsurpassed in his mastery of delicate opening *alaap* movements and the complicated rhythms of fast-tempo climaxes. Taking his artistry full-circle to popular forms, Sharma has followed his success in the classical field by introducing the santoor into film music as well.

what to buy: *Call of the Valley* 𝄞𝄞𝄞𝄞 (Hemisphere/EMI, 1967, prod. G. N. Joshi) was a kind of concept album that portrayed a day in the lives of two lovers in a Kashmiri valley. In addition to the santoor, the album featured two other instruments not previously associated with Indian classical music—the *bansuri* flute and the guitar—also to an enthusiastic public reception. Hard-core classical fans were wowed by the new possibilities these sounds opened up for Hindustani music, and won over by the interplay between the talented musicians, while the album's accessible folk melodies and direct storytelling struck a cord with non-classical listeners. The album remains one of the greatest in Hindustani music.

what to buy next: *Santoor* 𝄞𝄞𝄞𝄞 (Moment, 1993, prod. Zakir Hussain) is the live performance of a popular evening *raga* (an Indian classical piece synched to the varied moods of the times of day), "Rag Rageshri." Sharma has recorded a large number of albums with percussionist Zakir Hussain to amazing effect, and this is no exception. Since the santoor is struck with curved sticks made of walnut, it is an ideal rhythm instrument in the right hands; when these two musicians are in synch, as here, the rhythmic interplay is unbelievable. *The Valley Recalls* 𝄞𝄞𝄞𝄞 (Navras, 1996, prod. Vibhaker Baxi) is a two-volume *jugalbandi* or duet between Sharma and Hari Prasad Chaurasia, his partner on the landmark *Call of the Valley*. Their 1995 reunion, recorded at Delhi's Nehru Centre, is not only a historic occasion but a showcase for two of India's top musicians at the peak of their talent.

worth searching for: Any album that features Sharma and *tabla* drum virtuoso Zakir Hussain is a good bet. Among the dozens of Sharma releases available at better Indian music stores are: *Hundred Strings of Santoor* 𝄞𝄞𝄞𝄞 (Navras, 1986) with Zakir Hussain; *Megh Malhar* 𝄞𝄞𝄞𝄞 (Music Today, 1991) with vocalist Pandit Jasrae; *The Pioneer of Santoor* 𝄞𝄞𝄞𝄞

(Chhandra Dhara, 1991), also with Hussain; *Shiv Kumar Sharma: Maestro's Choice* 𝄞𝄞𝄞𝄞 (Music Today, 1991); *Gurjari Todi* 𝄞𝄞𝄞𝄞 (Navras, 1993); and *Shiv Kumar Sharma Plays Santoor in Osho's Samadhi* 𝄞𝄞𝄞𝄞 (Meditation, 1994).

influences:
◀◀ Uma Dutt Sharma

see also: *Tarun Bhattacharya, Hari Prasad Chaurasia, Zakir Hussain*

Aaron Howard

Joanne Shenandoah
Native American, pop
Born in the Oneida Nation, NY, USA. Based in the Oneida Nation, NY, USA.

Shenandoah, one of the country's most prolific Native musicians, doesn't use any tricks to coax the muse. "Whenever I need a song, I sit down and write one," Shenandoah says, "although I don't take personal credit for my songs; they're all ancestrally inspired. When I'm working on a song, I can hear the voices of the past and future coming through." A member of the Oneida Nation, Shenandoah was born in Iroquois territory and was given the name Takalihwa kwha—She Sings. Shenandoah has performed at both Clinton inaugurals; contributed music to the soundtracks of *Northern Exposure,* PBS's *How the West Was Lost,* and the feature film *The Indian in the Cupboard;* been nominated for a Pulitzer Prize in music for her symphonic composition *Ganondagan;* written books; performed at powwows, clubs, and music festivals in France, Canada, and the United States; and recorded six albums including her latest, *All Spirits Sing,* a coming-of-age story for children that she calls "a mythical journey that all ages can relate to—a tale to raise children's self-esteem." Shenandoah has been performing since her own childhood, and her father, Clifford Shenandoah, played jazz guitar with Duke Ellington's band. She started playing piano as a child, going on to guitar, clarinet, cello, flute, and more. In college, Shenandoah discovered computers and considered a career in systems management, but music always called out to her. After doing commercials and background singing, she finally decided to see how far she could go with her own music and signed with Canyon Records in 1989. Since then she's followed her heart and produced a body of work that combines all her interests—pop, symphonic, folk, and her own Native roots.

what to buy: On *Matriarch* 𝄞𝄞𝄞𝄞 (Silver Wave, 1996, prod. Tom Wasinger, Joanne Shenandoah) Shenandoah performs 13 traditional Iroquois women's songs as a tribute to the women in her family. The tracks were recorded *a cappella* at various sites sacred to the Oneida; the sounds of the birds and wind are all natural. It's one of Shenandoah's most powerful and deeply felt recordings.

what to buy next: On *Life Blood* 𝄞𝄞𝄞 (Silver Wave, 1995, prod. Peter Kater) producer Kater, a new-age keyboard star, provides sympathetic settings for a collection of traditional Haudenosaunee-Iroquois songs. This album prompted *Billboard* to call Shenandoah a "Native American Enya."

the rest:

Joanne Shenandoah 𝄞𝄞 (Canyon, 1989)
(With A. Paul Ortega) *Loving Ways* 𝄞𝄞𝄞 (Canyon, 1991)
Once in a Red Moon 𝄞𝄞 (Canyon, 1994)
All Spirits Sing 𝄞𝄞𝄞 (Music for Little People, 1995)

influences:

◀◀ Willie Nelson, A. Paul Ortega, Jackson Brown, Rita Coolidge

▶▶ Sharon Burch, Mishi Donovan

see also: *A. Paul Ortega*

j. poet

Shinehead

Reggae/rap

Born Edmund Carl Aiken, April 10, 1962, in London, England. Based in England.

Raised in both the center of reggae (Jamaica) and the birthplace of rap (the Bronx), it's no wonder Shinehead became one of the first artists to fuse the two genres. Less evident, however, is why he began remaking old pop, rock, and soul songs—though it's hard to quibble with most of the results. Still, hearing Boston's rock hit "More than a Feeling" in a reggae-fied hip-hop context is a bit jarring.

what to buy: On his expertly produced major-label debut, *Unity* 𝄞𝄞𝄞𝄞 (Elektra, 1988, prod. Claude Evans, Jam Master Jay, Davy D.), the even-keeled toaster-of-the-town gets a little help from the Beatles, using "Come Together" as the foundation for the self-explanatory title track. Even better, though, is "Chain Gang (Rap)," a warm, funky, and funny update of the Sam Cooke song. Shinehead gets topical, too, serving up a sort of dancehall "White Lines" for the hubba era with "Gimme No Crack."

the rest:

The Real Rock 𝄞𝄞𝄞 (Elektra, 1990)
Sidewalk University 𝄞𝄞 (Elektra, 1992)
Troddin' 𝄞𝄞 (Elektra, 1994)

influences:

◀◀ Don Baron, Asher D & Daddy Freddy

▶▶ Snow

see also: *Sly & Robbie*

Josh Freedom du Lac

jamaican music 10: ragga

As it did everywhere else, the digital age radically transformed the music of Jamaica. The realization that session bands and studio time were no longer a necessity led to a deluge of computer-generated rhythms and releases. Even the poorest would-be producer could create music for the price of a toy Casio keyboard, the instrument King Jammy used to construct the immortal "Sleng Teng" rhythm— the 1985 drum-roll that announced the arrival of Jamaica's digital era. This renewed populism in the dancehall inspired Junior Delgado's "Raggamuffin Year," a tune which purged the negative connotations of the term and transformed an abbreviation of it—"ragga"—into a proud emblem of the new music being made by and for Jamaica's ghetto youth. The hottest producers included the aforesaid Jammy, Donovan Germain, Dave Kelly, Gussie Clarke, Bobby Digital, and Sly (Dunbar) & Robbie (Shakespeare). Interestingly, though the digital sound was far more pulverizing than its analog forebear, and so clean it bordered on sterile, the rhythms it drew on were more traditionally Jamaican than in any then-recent genre.

The boisterous atmosphere of the dancehall swiftly intensified; in the "arena," guns were fired in appreciation, bottles hurled in denunciation, and orgasmic shouts unleashed in the midst of lascivious wind-and-grind dancing. But when a profusion of bullets and cocaine flowed into the current of dancehall culture, and the government countered with the automatic weaponry of the "Eradication Squad," it led to much tragedy and death—the legendary King Tubby and Peter Tosh; former Wailers drummer Carlton Barrett; talented deejays Pan Head, Major Worries, Dirtsman, General Echo, and Flux; and the sonorous singer Nitty Gritty were among those who didn't survive the era. Slowly but surely the '90s have seen spiritual and cultural themes return to the dancehall. Nonetheless, it will always be energized to some extent by the hellfire-intense rhythms, sweaty sexuality, and fierce competition meant to transport the "arena" from the realities that once intruded upon it with such impact.

Todd Shanker

Shooglenifty

Experimental folk
Formed 1994, in Edinburgh, Scotland. Based in Edinburgh, Scotland.

Iain MacLeod, mandolin, tenor banjo; Angus R. Grant, fiddle; Garry Finlayson, banjo, banjax; Malcolm Crosbie, acoustic guitar, electric guitar; Conrad Ivitsky, bass; James MacKintosh, drums, percussion, piano. (All members are from Scotland.)

At the forefront of Scotland's '90s generation of "roots" bands is Shooglenifty. Given their exploratory bent the term is used loosely—the group itself describes its music as "hypno-funkadelic ambient trad" or "acid croft." If that doesn't help, think of a buzzing fusion of traditional Scottish dance music with modern-pop rhythm grooves. Equally at home playing on a folk/world-music festival stage or at urban concert halls and dance clubs, the band has traveled extensively, thrilling audiences in the United Kingdom, Poland, Spain, Denmark, and as far afield as Hong Kong and Malaysia. Shooglenifty has recorded two studio albums and one live set, and members of the band also participated in the groundbreaking Afro Celt Sound System project.

what's available: The group's first album, *Venus in Tweeds* ♫♫♫♫ (Greentrax, 1994, prod. Jim Sutherland), is a bit softer than its successor, *A Whiskey Kiss* ♫♫♫♫ (Greentrax, 1996, prod. Jim Sutherland). On the latter the rhythms are tougher; drums are more prominent and much better used to become a fully integrated part of the band. The ensemble as a whole plays with more confidence and their music acquires an exciting edge.

the rest:
Live at Selwyn Hall (WOMAD Select/RealWorld, 1996)

influences:
◀ Mouth Music, Capercaillie, Moving Hearts, Edward II

▶▶ Afro Celt Sound System, Peatbog Faeries, Old Blind Dogs, Talitha Mackenzie, Mary Jane Lamond

see also: *Afro Celt Sound System*

Ken Roseman

Shu-De

Throat singing/overtone singing/höömeï
Formed in Tuva. Based in Tuva.

Oleg Kuular, throat-singing, igil, khomus; Mergen Mongush, throat-singing, limbi, vocals; Leonid Oorzhak, throat-singing, igil, doshpuluur, vocals; Nadezhda Shoigu, vocals; Boris Salchak, vocals, percussion. (All members are from Tuva.)

"Throat-singing," also known as overtone singing or *höömeï*, is an astonishing vocal technique employed by the peoples of such Asian regions as Mongolia, Tibet, and Tuva, in the last of which the art has been refined to its highest level. Throat-singers are able to utter two or more tones at one time, producing what is in essence an entire chord without the aid of an instrument; this is accomplished by carefully forming the mouth and tongue into certain configurations. The resulting sounds range from low abdominal growls to unearthly, whistling overtones. Shu-De is a traditional throat-singing ensemble from Tuva. They back their vocals with *igil* (two-stringed fiddle), *doshpuluur* (lute), *khomus* (jew's-harp), and other instruments of their homeland.

what's available: The band's only CD available to date, *Shu-De: Voices from the Distant Steppe* ♫♫♫♫ (RealWorld, 1994, prod. Stephen Pritchard), contains some pretty intense music-making. "Throat Singing and Igil," for example, showcases impressive soaring and wobbling in the *sygyt* sub-style, and on "Khomus Solo," Oleg Kuular creates some wild, pulsating effects as he combines his khomus playing with a resonant vocal line. Also included is a recording of the *kham* shamanic ritual. The liner notes put perhaps too much emphasis on the shamanic component of Tuvan music, however; it seems a bit hyperbolic to contend that throat-singers are in a "trance" when they perform. In addition to the questionable text, there are some annoying discrepancies between the track listing and the CD's actual running order—but these lapses of perspective and organization fall happily short of preventing one's enjoyment of often-remarkable music.

influences:
◀ Tuvan tradition

Jeffrey Muhr

Sierra Maestra

Son
Formed 1976, in Havana, Cuba. Based in Havana, Cuba.

Alejandro Suárez, musical director, cata, claves; Eduardo Himely, bass, guitar, marímbula; Juan de Marcos González, tres, vocals; Carlos González, bongos, congas; Bárbaro Teuntor Garcia, trumpet; Jesús Alamañy, trumpet (1976–1992), vocals; Carlos Puisseaux, güiro; Alberto "Virgilio" Valdés, maracas; José Antonio "Maceo" Rodriguez, vocals, guitar; Luis Barzaga, vocals, claves. (All members are from Cuba.)

Son is one of Cuba's main musical exports, the basic building block of New York and Miami salsa. This folkloric form grew out of the religious rituals of the African slave population in Oriente province, when they combined it with European and possibly Native American forms. Around 1800 refugees from Haiti's revolutionary violence brought their music, which mixed with the already potent brew of Afro-Cuban, Spanish, and French styles. For a while in the late '60s and early '70s, the more folkloric forms of son were supplanted by salsa and rock 'n' roll from the U.S. (despite the American embargo), and the Cuban *neuva trova,* a singer/songwriter movement that was concerned with poetic representations of everyday life. Irakere and Los Van Van had begun to revitalize the son in the early 1970s, but they were playing in a more modern style, to appeal to the younger generation. When Sierra Maestra got together, they decided to concentrate on the music's classic style: they played acoustically and their instrumentation was heavily traditional, including *tres,* guitar, trumpet, bongos, *güiro,* maracas, *clave,* and vocals. Juan de Marcos González, one of Sierra Maestra's founders, decided in favor of this approach because, as he says, "Son is the essence of all Cuban dance music. We wanted to prove that this traditional music was still a living thing, a vibrant musical force." "Sierra Maestra was both classical and nostalgic," concurs Jesus Alamañy, who honed his trumpet skills with a 10-year apprenticeship in the band before striking out on his own with ¡Cubanismo!. "The son is the root of Cuban music, but it had been forgotten. In Sierra Maestra we kept the original ideas and rhythms, but opened it up, creating a new era of dancing music."

what to buy: *Dundunbanza!* 🎵🎵🎵🎵 (World Circuit, 1994, prod. Nick Gold, Marcos González), the album that introduced Sierra Maestra to the international audience, is a stunner; it includes many hits written by the blind tres (small guitar) player Arsenio Rodríguez, whose innovations set the standard for son in the 1940s and 1950s. The piano of special guest Bernardo Sassetti is particularly tasty.

what to buy next: On the band's latest international offering, *Típiri Tábará* 🎵🎵🎵 (World Circuit, 1998, prod. Nick Gold, Alejandro Suárez, Eduardo Himely), the production is slicker, but the pumped-up sound of the percussion serves the music well. Bernardo Sassetti returns to add his keyboard magic to the session.

the rest:
Criolla Carabali 🎵🎵🎵 (Soni Do France, 1995)

influences:
◀◀ Sexteto Habanero, Beny Moré, Orquesta Aragon

▶▶ NG La Banda, ¡Cubanismo!

see also: *Arsenio Rodríguez, ¡Cubanismo!*

j. poet

Garnett Silk
Dancehall reggae, ragga
Born Garnet Smith, 1967, in Manchester, Jamaica. Died December 10, 1994, in Manchester, Jamaica.

With a rare open-hearted certitude, Garnett Silk's sleek, impassioned tenor brought the topics of peace and love—physical and spiritual, corporeal and divine—to the ragamuffins of the nihilistic dancehall. Silk began his career as a teenager under the name DJ Bimbo, recording "Problems Everywhere" and "See Bimbo Ya" for Delbert "Callo" Collins in the mid-'80s. He then developed his vocal craft and vision at Destiny Outernational Sound System, where he worked with his Manchester homey, Tony Rebel. Rebel introduced him to Anthony "Fire" Rochester, a young songwriter who shared Silk's conscientious idealism. After some lean, rough years, their collaboration resulted in Silk's 1992 debut, *It's Growing,* an album of depth and beauty that briefly shifted the attention of the dancehall "massive" away from lyrics of gun-glamorizing violence and disrespectful, sexually explicit "punany" slackness. A year later, Silk became a nationwide sensation in Jamaica with his follow-up *100% Silk,* a set of thoughtful songs with cultural substance and melodic sweetness to spare, including "Nothing Can Divide Us," "Necessity," and "Zion in a Vision." The same year he signed a recording contract with Atlantic, and plans were made to issue his substantial back catalog of fine singles for producers such as Steely & Clevie, King Tubby, King Jammy, Jack Scorpio, and Donovan Germain. The intensity of Silk's conviction moved many reggae fans to compare him with the late Bob Marley after his inspirational performance at the 1994 Reggae Sunsplash festival. Unfortunately, like Marley, Silk was to be taken from this earth far too soon. In late '94, Silk's mother's home in the Manchester community of Brumalia was robbed. After receiving ongoing threats, the peaceful Silk resorted to borrowing a gun from his attorney. While at home, one of his brothers was demonstrating how to use the weapon when it accidentally fired, striking a gas canister and igniting an explosion and fire. Amidst the flames, Silk attempted to carry his mother out of the home, but to no avail. He and his mother—to whom he gave moving tribute in his early hit single "Mama"—perished in each other's arms on December 10, 1994.

what to buy: A perfect place to begin your exploration of Silk's revelatory vocal power is the budget-priced 20-track compilation *Jet Star Reggae Max* 🎵🎵🎵🎵 (Jet Star, 1996, prod. various), which features a prime selection of singles from a variety of producers, including the magnificent "Lion Heart" (Donovan Germain), the #1 Jamaican single "Zion in a Vision" (Jack Scorpio), the previously hard-to-find U.K. hit "Hello Africa" (Startrail), and for Courtney Cole's Roof International, the aforementioned "Mama," an earnest paean to the person most responsible for Silk's kind-hearted spirituality. *It's Growing* 🎵🎵🎵🎵 (V.P., 1992, prod. Bobby Digital) is Silk's masterful debut, and there is no overlap with the fine Jet Star disc. Soul-restoring cuts like "I Am Vex," "A Friend," and "Commitment" are only the highlights of this cohesive dancehall classic.

what to buy next: Released posthumously, both *Silky Mood* 🎵🎵🎵🎵 (V.P., 1995, prod. various) and *Journey* 🎵🎵🎵 (V.P., 1998, prod. various) have much to offer Silk's dignified legacy. The former features the Silky One's excellent singles with King Jammy, including the essential "Lord Watch Over Our Shoulders"—a grooving plea to Jah for guidance in tough times— and "So Divine," an uplifting hymn in praise of women that was so out-of-place in the dancehall at the time it was recorded (late '80s) it's no wonder it wasn't released until now. The latter includes early singles interspersed with insightful interviews with Silk from Jamaica's IRIE-FM and JBC Television. These interviews prove that Silk was every bit the vulnerable, culture-proud nobleman his fans believed him to be.

the rest:

100% Silk ♫♫♫ (V.P., 1993)
Live in Concert ♫♫♫ (Power Play, 1994)
Garnett Silk Meets Tony Rebel Inna Dancehall Conference ♫♫♫ (Heartbeat, 1994)
Love Is the Answer ♫♫♫ (V.P., 1995)
Nothing Can Divide Us ♫♫♫ (V.P., 1995)
Collector's Series ♫♫♫ (Penthouse, 1998)

worth searching for: The rare "Silk Chant," an earthy, nyabinghi-charged psalm, is one of the treasures on the superb *Digital B Presents Kette Drum* ♫♫♫♫ (Digital B, 1995, prod. Bobby Digital). With every song utilizing the classic Kette Drum beat, this is a "one-rhythm" album in the tradition of Rupie Edwards's historic *Yamaha Skank* LP from 1975, and includes stellar contributions from Beenie Man and Determine ("Kette Drum"), Bounty Killer ("Seek God"), and dub poet Mutaburuka.

influences:

◄◄ Bob Marley, Horace Andy, Sugar Minott, Alton Ellis, Jackie Edwards, Delroy Wilson, the Abyssinians, the Ethiopians, Tony Rebel, Yasus Afari, Anthony "Fire" Rochester

►► Luciano, Tony Rebel, Yasus Afari, Richie Stephens

Todd Shanker

Silly Wizard

Scottish folk
Formed 1972, in Edinburgh, Scotland. Disbanded 1988.

Andy M. Stewart, vocals, banjo; **Phil Cunningham,** accordion, keyboards, whistle; **John Cunningham,** fiddle, vocals; **Gordon Jones,** acoustic guitar, bodhrán, vocals; **Martin Hadden,** bass, guitar, vocals.

Characterized as one of the most traditional of all folk bands, Silly Wizard were known for their electric playing of mostly acoustic instruments. John Cunningham's flying fiddle, his brother Phil's amazing accordion, Andy Stewart's stirring vocals, and Gordon Jones's accompanying guitar helped define the band's sound. Rivaling the best of contemporary folk groups, Silly Wizard brought a unique chemistry to the stage, through its members' good-natured humor and technically brilliant musicianship, not to mention a passion for the material and performance themselves. Rivaling Steeleye Span in their focus and aim, Silly Wizard's music was distinctly different from anything else popular on the folk circuit of the day. This was largely due to the group's unquestionably Scottish sound and Stewart's powerful sense of song and ballad. The group's history was tumultuous. It started as a trio (Gordon Jones, Bob Thomas, and John Cunningham), working around Cunningham's schedule, as he was only 14(!) at the time. These three recorded an album with singer Maddy Taylor, but it was never released. Soon after, Stewart joined the group, along with John's younger brother Phil, on accordion. Living in squalid digs and fighting to keep their heads above water, they finally had a major breakthrough with a huge recording offer from a London firm. However, the deal fell through, leaving them to find their own way to the top. They eventually recorded 10 albums and toured all over Europe and America, building a reputation as solid as their musicianship. Despite their ultimate demise, their fiery dance tunes and soulful ballads live on in their excellent recordings.

what to buy: Widely considered the definitive Silly Wizard set, *Live Wizardry* ♫♫♫♫ (Green Linnet, 1988, prod. Phil Cunningham) captures the scope and spirit of the band in concert, playing their most-loved tunes. Live performance definitely brings out the best in this group, as shown through such tracks as the moving "The Valley of Strathmore" and the energetic "The Queen of Argyll." Another excellent collection of the band's work is *The Best of Silly Wizard* ♫♫♫ (Shanachie, 1985, prod. Silly Wizard), which includes a number of its most popular songs.

what to buy next: With a delightful selection of tunes, *So Many Partings* ♫♫♫ (Highway, 1978/Shanachie, 1989, prod. Archie Fisher, Silly Wizard) may show the top mix of ballads and dance pieces in the band's catalog. Standout tracks include Andy Stewart's "The Highland Clearances," a heartfelt lament about the loss of natural landscape in Scotland, and the stirring "Donald McGillavry/O'Neill's Cavalry March." *Caledonia's Hardy Sons* ♫♫♫ (Highway, 1978/Shanachie, 1989, prod. Silly Wizard, John Zollman) displays the excellent accordion work of Phil Cunningham and includes two of the group's best ballads, "Fhear a Bhata" and "Broom o' the Cowdenknowes."

what to avoid: *Golden, Golden* and *Silly Wizard: Live in America* are the two albums from which *Live Wizardry* was compiled; as the single set is missing only one track from the original pair, it's the better choice for most fans.

the rest:

Wild and Beautiful ♫♫♫ (Highway, 1981/Shanachie, 1982)
Glint of Silver ♫♫ (Green Linnet, 1986)
Kiss the Tears Away ♫♫ (Highway, 1983/Shanachie, 1987)

influences:

⏪ Dougie MacLean, Boys of the Lough, Whistlebinkies, Planxty

⏩ Capercaillie, Tannahill Weavers

see also: *Altan, Kevin Burke, Johnny Cunningham, Phil Cunningham, Connie Dover, Tríona Ní Dhomhnaill, Nightnoise, Solas, Andy M. Stewart, David Wilkie*

Jo Hughey Morrison

J. Reuben Silverbird

Native American flute and chant
Born in the southwestern USA. Based in the southwestern USA.

J. Reuben Silverbird is a Navajo Apache best known for his album celebrating Native American creation legends, *The World in Our Eyes,* and as producer and percussionist on the works of his son, flutist Perry Silverbird.

what's available: *The World in Our Eyes* 🎵🎵🎵 (Celestial Harmonies, 1991, prod. J. Reuben Silverbird, Ron Russo) combines the venerable (ancient flute melodies and the age-old instrument of human voice raised in chant) with the modern (synthesizer and other more contemporary sounds) to create an intricate aural tapestry. A double CD, it allows pure instrumental listening on one disc, and music interwoven with chant and narration by Silverbird on the other.

influences:

⏪ Early Apache flute players and singers

⏩ Perry Silverbird

see also: *Perry Silverbird*

Kerry Dexter

Perry Silverbird

Native American flute and chant
Born in the southwestern USA. Based in the southwestern USA.

Perry Silverbird is a Navajo Apache flute player, performing most often on small wooden flutes that he augments with drumming, chant, and sounds from nature.

what's available: *The Blessing Way* 🎵🎵🎵 (Celestial Harmonies, 1992, prod. J. Reuben Silverbird) is a meditative collection of original music incorporating natural sounds from the southwest with drumming and chant in flute-based melodies.

worth searching for: The harder-to-find *Spirit of Fire* 🎵🎵🎵 (Celestial Harmonies) focuses on the image of purity, with flute melodies inspired by Native American conceptions of the title element.

influences:

⏪ J. Reuben Silverbird, Steve Roach

see also: *J. Reuben Silverbird*

Kerry Dexter

Terrance Simien /The Mallet Playboys

Zydeco, New Orleans R&B
Born September 3, 1965, in Mallet, LA, USA. Based in Lousiana, USA.

A fast-paced, hard-driving approach has made accordion player and vocalist Terrance Simien a leader in the new breed of southwest Louisiana's zydeco music. Best known as co-writer of two songs performed with his band the Mallet Playboys in the film *The Big Easy,* Simien has continued to attract attention with his dance-inspiring style. Inheriting his love of music from his mother, who sang with the choir at St. Ann's Catholic Church, Simien studied jazz and classical trumpet at Lawtell Elementary School. However, his interests in zydeco didn't develop until he attended dances as a teenager. Acquiring a single-row diatonic accordion for his 15th birthday, Simien taught himself to play the squeezebox. Forming the Mallet Playboys in 1981, Simien sharpened his skills by playing church dances and zydeco clubs including Slim's Y-Ki-Ki in Opelousas, Louisiana. A turning point came when the band was chosen to perform at the 1984 World's Fair in New Orleans. That led to a booking in Washington, D.C., and before long Simien and the band were touring throughout the U.S. When Paul Simon came to Louisiana in search of zydeco musicians to provide a stylistic counterpoint to the African sounds on his album *Graceland,* Simien and the Mallet Playboys were one of the outfits he auditioned. Although Simon chose Rockin' Dopsie instead, he produced and sang harmony on a recording session for the group, a single from the session, "You Used to Call Me," was later released. An appearance at the Lone Star Cafe in New York, on the eve of the Live Aid concert in 1985, attracted an audience that included Simon, Bob Dylan, and Mick Jagger. Two other Rolling Stones, Keith Richard and Ron Wood, took the stage to play with the group. Despite their ongoing popularity, Simien and the Mallet Playboys remain less than prolific as recording artists: Though their first two albums were separated by a relatively reasonable three years, it took nine years from their formation for the initial one to come out, and there has yet to be a third.

what to buy: Terrance Simien and the Mallet Playboys' long-overdue debut album, *Zydeco on the Bayou* 🎵🎵🎵 (Restless, 1990, prod. Dick Landry), was well worth the wait, with Simien reinventing the zydeco of Louisiana's Cajun country as turbocharged dance music.

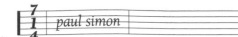

what to buy next: With guest appearances by pianist Art Neville and the Meters, *There's Room for Us All* 𝄞𝄞𝄞 (Black Top, 1993, prod. Daryl Johnson) further showcases Simien's eclectic approach.

influences:

◀◀ Clifton Chenier, Boozoo Chavis, the Neville Brothers

▶▶ Filé, The Basin Brothers, C. J. Chenier

see also: *Rockin' Dopsie, Paul Simon*

Craig Harris

Paul Simon

American pop, folk, world-music fusion
Born October 13, 1941, in Newark, NJ, USA. Based in New York, NY, USA.

With an infusion of African rock and roots music on his 1986 album *Graceland,* Paul Simon rejuvenated a career dulled by too much reliance on the then-tired California session musician scene. As stunning as the album was, Simon was criticized for being a post-colonial exploiter of Third World music, a charge similar to what George Gershwin faced when he used black American music as the inspiration for works such as *Porgy and Bess.* Unlike Gershwin, Simon gave credit to the musicians who helped him write the songs. In turn, the musicians who played with Simon, particularly Joseph Shabalala, leader of Ladysmith Black Mambazo, expressed gratitude to him for opening doors to the lucrative American market. Ladysmith most likely would never have had the opportunity to record a Life Savers commercial without *Graceland.* (Okay, that's a dubious distinction; but the album and its tours—spotlighting South African acts not just as backup players but as artists in their own right—got and held Stateside attention for world music like never before.) Coming as it did in the waning days of apartheid, the popularity of *Graceland* helped Americans put a face on the struggle in South Africa; even Nelson Mandela eventually complimented Simon on his work.

In fact, a quick look at Simon's career shows that *Graceland* was no sudden gimmick from a fame-deprived former hitmaker, but was the result of years of interest in other music besides American pop. On their first album in 1966, Simon & Garfunkel's arrangement of "Benedictus," an ancient church chant, anticipated the kind of genre-bending that defines today's world music. Simon's English lyrics to "El Condor Pasa" helped turn that 18th-century Peruvian melody into a hit on the pop charts and introduced many Americans to Andean sounds. His solo career, which began in 1972, continued this fascination with such tunes as the Peruvian-inflected "Duncan" and a venture into reggae with "Mother and Child Reunion." Later, his blandest period was redeemed by jump-out tracks with a "world" view, like the strongly Latin-influenced "Late in the Evening." Even the gospel stylings of "Love Me Like a Rock" and "Slip Sliding Away," though deriving from these shores, are part of his round-the-world mentality. Musicians are influenced by what they hear, and Simon's ears apparently had been wide open for a long time.

what to buy: *Graceland* 𝄞𝄞𝄞𝄞 (Warner Bros., 1986, prod. Paul Simon) captures the golden moment of an aging pop veteran being inspired and uplifted by the sounds of Africa. The rhythms and melodies provided by the Pan-African group of musicians loosened Simon's tongue for some of the best lyrics of his career. For a world-music novice, this is the jumping-off point to albums by the likes of Ladysmith Black Mambazo, King Sunny Adé, Hugh Masekela, and Miriam Makeba. Remember, a back-and-forth interchange between American and African pop has been one of the driving forces of world-music growth.

what to buy next: *Rhythm of the Saints* 𝄞𝄞𝄞 (Warner Bros., 1990, prod. Paul Simon) and *Songs from the Capeman* 𝄞𝄞𝄞 (Warner Bros., 1997, prod. Paul Simon, Oscar Hernandez, Roy Halee) aren't at all as revelatory as *Graceland* and don't hold up as well. Simon's intellectualism takes over and saps the energy of the music—a promising fusion with Brazilian sounds in the case of *Saints* and a less-satisfying blend of theater and Puerto Rican music on *Capeman.* Better to pick up *Paul Simon* 𝄞𝄞𝄞𝄞 (Columbia, 1972, prod. Paul Simon, Roy Halee), which features "Mother and Child Reunion," "Duncan," and the Latin-flavored "Me and Julio Down by the Schoolyard," or *Live Rhymin'* 𝄞𝄞𝄞𝄞 (Columbia, 1974, prod. Phil Ramone), which includes instrumental support by the Peruvian group Urubamba and vocals by the Dixie Hummingbirds, to hear a lively precursor of the spirit of collaboration that made *Graceland* a joy.

what to avoid: From the perspective of a world-music buyer, the rest of Simon's mostly solid catalog would be of little interest except for occasional flashes of international influence. However, if you enjoy Simon as a pop star, the listless *Hearts and Bones* 𝄞 (Warner Bros., 1983, prod. various) is the nadir, followed closely by *One-Trick Pony* 𝄞𝄞 (Warner Bros., 1980, prod. Paul Simon, Phil Ramone), even though it contains the wonderful Latin-tinged hit "Late in the Evening," one of Simon's best numbers ever.

the rest:
There Goes Rhymin' Simon 𝄞𝄞𝄞𝄞 (Columbia, 1973)
Still Crazy After All These Years 𝄞𝄞𝄞𝄞 (Columbia, 1975)
Negotiations and Love Songs 𝄞𝄞𝄞𝄞 (Warner Bros., 1980)
Paul Simon's Concert in the Park 𝄞𝄞𝄞𝄞 (Warner Bros., 1991)
1964/1993 𝄞𝄞𝄞𝄞 (Warner Bros., 1993)

worth searching for: *Paul Simon: The Collection* 𝄞𝄞𝄞𝄞 (Warner Bros., 1991, prod. various), a three-volume Japanese survey, includes a live set from the *Graceland* tour in addition to Simon's hits.

influences:

⏪ Joseph Shabalala, Tao Ea Matsekha, Clifton Chenier, Milton Nascimento, Youssou N'Dour, Everly Brothers, Bob Dylan

⏩ James Taylor, Jackson Browne, Mary Chapin Carpenter

see also: *Marc Anthony, Ruben Blades, Ladysmith Black Mambazo, Los Incas, Miriam Makeba, Hugh Masekela, Olodum, Rockin' Dopsie, Terrance Simien*

Salvatore Caputo

Talvin Singh

Ethno-techno fusion
Born 1970, in London, England. Based in London, England.

Born in London to Indian parents, Singh's music is a product of both nature and nurture. He began studying Indian classical music at the age of six, and by the age of eight had begun serious study on the *tabla* drum. However, growing up in Leytonstone, the young musician was surrounded by the sounds of electro-funk, punk, and hip-hop, and was soon accompanying a local Asian breakdancing crew by playing tablas along with programmed drum-machine beats. Singh left for India at the age of 16 to study tabla in earnest, but soon rebelled again the strict, closed-minded attitudes of the classical community. Returning to Britain in the late '80s, Singh soon found himself in high demand as a sideman, working with a diverse cast of artists ranging from Sun Ra and the Indigo Girls to Massive Attack and Future Sounds of London, and backing Siouxsie & the Banshees on the first Lollapalooza tour in 1991. In 1995 Singh founded "Anokha," a club in London where techno DJs and Asian punk bands mixed comfortably with Singh's blend of Indian *bhangra* dance music, drum 'n' bass, and tabla breakbeats. Singh has been a sought-after remixer and producer ever since (Björk's "Possibly Maybe" from the remix album *Telegram* being one high-profile example), and he recently started his own label, Omni Records.

what's available: Although slightly overrated on the whole, Singh's compilation *Anokha: Sounds of the Asian Underground* 🎵🎵🎵 (Quango, 1997, prod. Talvin Singh) was an imaginative introduction to an exotic techno subculture few outside of London even knew existed. Singh is only credited with composing two tracks, but one of those, "Jaan," soon found its way into the mainstream via its use in a highly visible TV commercial for Philips recordable CD players. His proper solo debut, *OK* 🎵🎵🎵🎵 (Island, 1998, prod. Talvin Singh), was far more impressive for its seamless fusion of styles ranging from drum 'n' bass and ambient techno to Indian classical. Here, Singh's formidable

tabla talents are on fine display, giving the album a distinctly ethnic feel whose appeal is only enhanced by appearances from Japanese avant-gardist Ryuichi Sakamoto on flute, *sarangi* (bowed string instrument) master Ustad Sultan Khan, and the stirring strings of the Madras Philharmonic Orchestra, which are put to great use on the dazzling opener, "Traveler."

influences:

⏪ Zakir Hussain, Ravi Shankar, Transglobal Underground, Pandit Kamalesh Maitra

⏩ State of Bengal, Asian Dub Foundation

see also: *Michael Brook, Ryuichi Sakamoto*

Bret Love

Sintesis

Afrocubano, ethno-rock
Formed 1976, in Cuba. Based in Cuba.

Carlos Alfonso, lead vocals, bass; Ele Valdés, lead vocals, keyboards; Fidel García, lead vocals, percussion, keyboards; Equis Alfonso, keyboards; Esteban Puebla, keyboards; Victor Navarrete, guitar; Raul Pineda, drums. Past members have included: José Bustillo, guitar; Frank Padilla, drums; Roberto Vincaino, bata drums; Lazaro Ros, vocals; Lucia Huergo, vocals, flute, sax, keyboards; Joel Drich, percussion; José Leonardo Angel, percussion; Oney Cumbá, percussion; Madonna Alonso, vocals. (All members are from Cuba.)

Evolved out of vocal group Tema IV, Sintesis fuses traditional *Santería* (Afro-Cuban ritual) chanting and drumming with synthesized rock and pop textures. The combination has made them one of Cuba's most popular bands and kept individual members in session demand, lead singers Carlos Alfonso and Ele Valdés turning up on salsa star Adalberto Alvarez's 1993 hit "Dale Como E." Though they've toured internationally, Sintesis had the embargo to thank for not visiting the U.S. until 1997, when they cut the album *Orishas* in California.

what to buy: Highly acclaimed though it may be, *Ancestros* 🎵🎵🎵 (QbaDisc, 1987, prod. Carlos Alfonso, Lucia Huergo) doesn't date well due to its tired '80s production and reliance on synthesized textures. Nevertheless, the band's songs are rather special, chants and prayers sung in the Nigerian Yoruba language to Santería deities such as Yewa, mistress of the world of death, and Elegua, lord of the crossroads (and you thought all this time it was Robert Johnson). Playing not so much world music as netherworld music, Sintesis finds the right balance on the excellent follow-up *Ancestros 2* 🎵🎵🎵🎵 (QbaDisc, 1994, prod. Carlos Alfonso), structured from beginning to end as an *oru,* or rite, for their pagan gods. Whatever their subject matter the songs are quite catchy, leaving little chance these gods will come knocking, since the music's sweet temperament is a perfect talisman.

what to buy next: *Orishas* 🎵🎵🎵 (Milan Latino, 1997, prod. Carlos Alfonso) continues the band's formula, a highly integrated fusion of devotional and dancefloor rhythms.

worth searching for: *El Hombre Extraño* 🎵🎵🎵 (Artex, 1993, prod. Carlos Alfonso) is a collaborative effort with lyrics and vocals by pioneer of the socially conscious *nueva trova* ("new ballad") movement Silvio Rodríguez.

influences:
◀◀ Tito Puente, Santería, Tema IV

see also: *Silvio Rodríguez, Lazaro Ros*

Bill Ellis

Sister Carol

Reggae

Born Carole Theresa East, 1959, in Kingston, Jamaica. Based in Brooklyn, NY, USA.

Though as notable as an actress—particularly in some of Jonathan Demme's late-'80s comedies—as for her work in reggae, Sister Carol's music career predated her acting by a good 10 years. Hooking up with the star of reggae's "dancehall" variant, Brigadier Jerry, she adopted his style of toasting (reggae rapping) . . . for a while. She eventually grew tired of the dancehall scene, telling Tom Weber in *Reggae Island* (Da Capo Books, 1998), "People taking off their clothes on stage—it got to that point where it was getting unbearable to everybody." As a musical postscript, she would add in her own song "Sellout" from the *Lyrically Potent* album, "I'm not one of these and I'm not one of those/Can't pay me fi go take off mi clothes/My body parts should not be exposed." She came to Brooklyn and started to work on a hybrid, splicing the roots and righteousness of the proto-reggae "rocksteady" with the riddims of dancehall. Demme saw her performing with the legendary Judy Mowatt and cast her to act in several of his films, including "Married to the Mob" and "Something Wild." This raised her profile enormously—with her parallel appearances on the soundtracks not hurting what would become her signature career.

what to buy: On *Jah Disciple* 🎵🎵🎵🎵 (RAS, 1989), one of her livest-sounding albums, Carol plays to her strengths and avoids the weaknesses that plague some of her other releases. Said strengths are a combination of toasting and singing over the roots grooves, a winning way that starts with "Ram the Party" and runs through her tribute to Bob Marley, "Get It Straight Africans." Even the tunes straight off the dancehall tip, like "Lost in Space," have a conscious charm. "Potential" reworks "Reggae Gone International" from *Black Cinderella* (see below). And how can you not be amazed by any record with a song like "Intelligence," whose inspirational verse instructs, "They taught me trigonometry to find the content/Studied algebra to find the coefficient"?

what to buy next: Again proving as able a singer as she is a toaster—especially when she moves effortlessly between the two on "Lovers Rock Style"—Sister Carol successfully works both sides of the old and new sounds of Jamaica on *Mother Culture* 🎵🎵🎵🎵 (RAS, 1991, prod. Carol East, D. Wauchope). She even borders on mainstream R&B with "B Who U R," a tune that might have mainstreamed her on a label with promotion muscle in that world. Some of the backing tracks, though, do not have as much muscle as Carol's performances. On the somewhat-earlier *Black Cinderella* 🎵🎵🎵 (Heartbeat, 1984, prod. Hyman "Papa Life" Wright, Percy Chin) Carol mixes her roots and rap, and a pretty good singing voice as well. What weighs this record down are tunes like "No Way No Better Than Yard," with its somnolent band and reliance on the old dancehall cadence. At about 15 beats-per-minute faster, "Reggae Gone International" would be inspirational, not a drag. On the other hand, "Dedicated to Bob Marley," with little snippets from his catalog done inna dancehall stylee, is fun, as is "My Children," a toast based approximately on the children's ditty "This Old Man." Casting from children's traditional to adult contemporary, she lifts the nice, sprightly little tune of "Jah Is Mine" from the Carpenters' "On Top of the World." Carol earned a Best Reggae Record Grammy nomination for *Lyrically Potent* 🎵🎵🎵 (Heartbeat, 1996, prod. Carol East, Dean Wauchope/Kariang Productions). Here she toasts far more than she sings. "Can't Stop Reggae" wanders into hip-hop, but most of the album comes off more like dub poetry (reggae's spoken-word form) than dancehall. It helps that the recording has spank and spunk, with a punchier band and mix than any of her others. With guest artists like ska pioneer Ernest Ranglin and dancehall groundbreaker Sugar Minott, and production that falls just short of dub, this album is not only lyrically potent, but musically potent too. In fact, one track is just dub (the sonically manipulated reggae mutation), a move Sister Carol had yet to make despite her dancehall background. "Milk and Honey" fuses reggae and acid jazz for its backing track. No slackness there. *Call Mi Sister Carol* 🎵🎵🎵 (Heartbeat, 1994, prod. various) mostly features Carol toasting, continuing to avoid slackness (dancehall slang for sexual explicitness) by stressing values of education, universal suffrage, and of course Jah Rastafari. She still takes opportunities like the "Human Nature" riff in "Ital Jacuzzi" to show off her singing voice.

what to avoid: *Potent Dub* 🎵🎵 (Shanachie, 1997, prod. Carol East), the dub version of *Lyrically Potent,* has tracks like "Natty

Congo Dub" that show what made the album so successful. On the other hand, such selections as "Strong and Fit Dub" are merely repetitive. Only "Ras Dub" and "Who the Dub Fit" really make interesting use of the echo and effects that are the genre's trademark.

the rest:
Isis—The Original Womb-Man N/A (Tuff Gong International, 1999)

influences:
◄◄ Brigadier Jerry, Linton Kwesi Johnson

see also: *Sugar Minott, Judy Mowatt, Ernest Ranglin*

Hank Bordowitz

Six Nations Women Singers

Traditional Native American (Seneca, Onondaga, Cayuga)
Formed 1968, in the Six Nations Community, NY, USA. Based in the Six Nations Community, NY, USA.

Charlene Bomberry, vocals; Sadie Buck, vocals; Betsy Buck, vocals; Pat Hess, vocals; Janice G. Martin, vocals; Jaynane Burning, vocals. (All members are from USA.)

The Six Nations Women Singers are members of the Seneca, Onondaga, and Cayuga tribes of upper New York state, and have been singing together at dances and religious and social functions for more than 30 years. According to acclaimed singer-songwriter Joanne Shenandoah of the Oneida Nation, women have always been the spiritual backbone of the Six Nations, and much of the tribes' teachings have been passed down by their female members.

what's available: Native music poses unique problems for listeners unfamiliar with its underlying culture. Like the *qawwals* (devotional singers) of Pakistan, Native Americans use vocables—syllables that are "meaningless" on a conscious level—in an attempt to express the inexpressible, usually the unity of the human spirit with the greater spirit some call God. On *We Will All Sing* 𝄢𝄢𝄢 (SOAR, 1996, prod. Tom Bee) the Six Nations Women Singers touch that spirit, with rousing social songs that feature a powerful lead singer backed by the slightly dissonant harmonies of the ensemble, in the manner of the well-regarded Bulgarian Women's Choir. All the melodies are strong, and one—"Yo Ho O Ho"—sounds uncannily like Steven Foster's "Camptown Races," which raises intriguing questions about that better-known song's possible origins.

influences:
◄◄ Traditional Native singing styles of the Six Nations
►► Yoko Ono, Don Cherry

j. poet

Sixteen Ninety-One
See: The Bothy Band

SKAndalous All-Stars
Ska
Formed 1996, in New York, NY, USA. Based in New York, NY, USA.

Vic Ruggiero, keyboards, vocals; T. J. Scanlon, guitar; Marcus Geard, bass; Joe Ferry, guitar, percussion; Ara Babajian, drums; Greg Robinson, trombone; Doug Dubrosky, saxophone, vocals; Donna Lupie, vocals; Nathan Breedlove, trumpet; Dan Dulin, trumpet; Brendog, guitar; Britt Savage, vocals; Chris "Skunk" Hanson, vocals.

Members of such punk and ska bands as the Skatalites, Mephiskapheles, Ruder Than You, and the Slackers converge for a clever if thin concept: interpret rock hits as ska tunes.

what to buy: *Hit Me* 𝄢𝄢𝄢 (Shanachie, 1997, prod. Joe Ferry) has a few clever adaptations—Nirvana's "Lithium" and Radiohead's "Creep" work best—but the gimmick wears quickly. Living Colour fans take note: guest vocalist Corey Glover sings not on the All-Stars' rendition of "Cult of Personality" but on the Stevie Wonder classic "Higher Ground."

what to buy next: *Punk Steady* 𝄢𝄢 (Shanachie, 1998, prod. Joe Ferry) is more of the same, with the Camper Van Beethoven parody "Take the Skinheads Bowling" not even mildly ironic. Better than hearing a wedding band cover such material, but not by much.

the rest:
Age of Insects N/A (Shanachie, 1999)

influences:
◄◄ Dread Zeppelin, Perfect Thyroid

Bill Ellis

Skara Brae
See: The Bothy Band

The Skatalites
Ska
Formed 1963, in Kingston, Jamaica; several disbandings and reunions since.

Variable membership over many years, including: Tommy McCook, trumpet, tenor sax; Roland Alphonso, tenor sax; Don Drummond (died 1969), trombone; Jackie Mittoo, keyboards; Jah Jerry Haines, guitar; Lloyd Brevette, bass; Ernest Ranglin, guitar; Johnny "Dizzy" Moore, flugelhorn, trumpet; Lester Sterling, alto sax; Lloyd Nibbs, drums, percussion.

Seldom have so many done so much for so short a time as the Skatalites. The prototypical band of the prototypical Jamaican sound, their very name heralded the galloping ska rhythm that

The Skatalites

would mutate in due course into reggae and resurface in its original form to fire youth-music movements of its own, from the late-'70s "two-tone" British invasion of bands like the Specials and Madness, to the '90s "third wave" skaquake of Stateside punk bands like Rancid, Goldfinger, and too many more to mention.

Formed in 1963, this all-star congregation of Jamaica's top musicians had more hit songs than any other group in the nation's history, leaving behind such classics as "Guns of Navarone," "Man in the Street," "Don Cosmic," "Yard Broom," "Don D Lion," "Confucious," "Lucky Seven," and "Musical Communion" for starters. Tenor saxophonists Tommy McCook and Roland Alphonso teamed up with the brilliant but mad musical genius trombonist Don Drummond, and 16-year-old keyboard wonder Jackie Mittoo, to form this legendary group that also included Jah Jerry Haines on guitar and the great Lloyd Brevette on bass. The outfit's almost telepathic tightness goes back to an earlier apprenticeship of most members in the Eric Deans Orchestra in the 1950s, not to mention a common musical tutelage at the esteemed Alpha Boys School a decade before that.

The Skatalites' 18-month existence was a force of nature that left nary a major venue of the time untouched—legend even had it that one young lady became so enthralled by the band's miracles of invention she literally danced herself to death at a concert. Sadly, there was nothing apocryphal about Drummond's murder of his girlfriend in 1965, after which he was institutionalized until his death by suicide four years later. The crime also signaled the first end of the Skatalites, whose members split into a number of illustrious successor bands and solo careers. The outfit's first reunion came on July 7, 1984, when they performed at the definitive annual Reggae Sunsplash festival. Since their most recent rebirth in the early '90s, the Skatalites have resumed touring and recorded such albums as *Ska-Voovie, Hi-Bop Ska,* and *Greetings from Skamania.* Ska and its namesake live on.

what to buy: With 32 tracks spread over two CDs, the early recordings of the Skatalites are sampled on *Foundation Ska* ♫♫♫ (Heartbeat, 1996, prod. Clement "Coxsone" Dodd, Arthur "Duke" Reid). In addition to instrumental tracks, the album includes several songs by Jackie Opel and the Wailers, two of many equally historical names with which the Skatalites shared stage and studio.

what to buy next: *Ska after Ska after Ska* ♫♫♫ (Heartbeat, 1998, prod. Arthur "Duke" Reid) includes more early recordings by the Skatalites in a variety of incarnations.

best of the rest:
Ska-Voovie ♫♫♫♫ (Shanachie, 1993)
Hi-Bop Ska ♫♫♫♫ (Shanachie, 1994)
Greetings from Skamania ♫♫♫♫ (Shanachie, 1996)
Authentic Ska ♫♫♫♫ (Musicrama, 1997)
Ball of Fire ♫♫♫♫ (Island, 1998)
Stretching Out ♫♫♫ (ROIR, 1998)

influences:
◀◀ Dennis "Ska" Campbell, the Upsetters

▶▶ The Wailers, the Maytals, the Melodians

see also: *Alton Ellis, Bob Marley, Jackie Mittoo, Lee "Scratch" Perry, Ernest Ranglin, the Techniques*

Todd Shanker and Craig Harris

Skyedance

See: Alasdair Fraser

Abdel Ali Slimani

Rai, worldbeat
Born in El Anasser, Algeria. Based in London, England.

Abdel Ali Slimani is Algeria's unofficial musical ambassador to England. Khaled and others have made quite an impact with the large Algerian expatriate community in Paris, but Slimani is our man in London. Slimani's extended hollers and deep-chested elisions of notes will be familiar to fans of Jah Wobble's Invaders of the Heart, on whose records he sings in French and Arabic. Slimani first performed in Algeria—playing guitar at local soccer matches—but was not able to make a living as a musician until he moved to Paris, and later London, where he was discovered by Wobble, the British post-punk bassist and world-music impresario.

what's available: Slimani has only recorded one album under his own name: *Mraya* ♫♫♫♫ (RealWorld, 1995, prod. John Reynolds, Jah Wobble), which features Wobble's heavy bass and vocals by Sinéad O'Connor and Middle Eastern diva Natacha Atlas (of Transglobal Underground fame). "Mraya" means "mirror," and the album is Slimani's self-portrait, expressing his devotion to his family on "Laziza," "Habibti," and "Yasmin"; his country on "Alger"; and its soccer team on "Hadi." As a member of Jah Wobble's Invaders of the Heart, Slimani can be heard singing on *Take Me to God* ♫♫♫ (Island, 1994, prod. Jah

Wobble, Mark Ferda), most notably on "I'm an Algerian," from which his resonant, nasal tenor is not soon forgotten.

influences:
◀◀ Khaled

see also: *Khaled, Sinéad O'Connor, Transglobal Underground*

David Poole

Sly & Robbie

Reggae
Formed 1974, in Kingston, Jamaica. Based in Kingston, Jamaica.

Lowell Fillmore "Sly" Dunbar (born May 10, 1952, in Kingston, Jamaica), drums; Robbie Shakespeare (born September 27, 1953, in Kingston, Jamaica), bass.

Sly & Robbie—aptly a.k.a. "the Riddim Twins"—are not only reggae's leading rhythm section, but have been the genre's most important producers and record executives since the mid-1970s. In addition to cutting several albums of their own, the duo has overseen scores of influential recordings for other artists. While the best known are those for such reggae names as Jimmy Cliff, Gregory Isaacs, Black Uhuru, Max Romeo, and Desmond Dekker, the duo's credits outside the usual reggae realm include Bob Dylan, Carly Simon, Mick Jagger, Joan Armatrading, Joe Cocker, Robert Palmer, Grace Jones, and Ian Drury.

Dunbar, whose first drum kit was composed of empty food cans, performed in the late-'60s reggae bands the Yardbrooms and the Collins Brothers, and the early-'70s group Skin, Flesh & Bones. Shakespeare had studied bass under Aston "Family Man" Barrett, then a member of the Hippy Boys and later of the Upsetters and the Wailers. Shakespeare in fact replaced Barrett in the Hippy Boys and played bass on Bob Marley's recordings "Concrete Jungle" and "Stir It Up."

Although they had met each other while playing at different clubs in downtown Kingston, Dunbar and Shakespeare didn't play together until the mid-1970s, when they performed on several sessions produced by Bunny Lee. Their first break came in 1976, when they played on Peter Tosh's album *Legalize It* and toured with Tosh's band. They remained with him until 1979, contributing to four additional albums—*Equal Rights, Bush Doctor, Mystic Man,* and *Wanted Dread and Alive* —and enjoying their global breakthrough as producers with Tosh's 1978 collaboration with Mick Jagger "(Keep on Walking) Don't Look Back."

During this time Dunbar and Shakespeare had stayed active in a variety of outside projects. After Dunbar toured England with the Mighty Diamonds, he and Shakespeare formed a dub band, the Revolutionaries. In 1978, the pair launched their own company, Taxi Productions, and formed a studio band, the Taxi All-Stars. Their first production effort under the new banner resulted in the chart-topping hit "Soon Forward" by Gregory Isaacs. Then, shortly after signing a worldwide distribution deal with Island Records, they produced their first albums—*Red* by Black Uhuru and *Nightclubbing* by Grace Jones. They subsequently toured with Black Uhuru and produced the band's albums *Showcase, Sinsemilla, Chill Out,* and *The Dub Factor.* Later came work on Dylan's album *Infidels* in 1983, and collaborations with producer Bill Laswell including another Mick Jagger project, his solo album *She's the Boss.* Dunbar and Shakespeare would then work with such hip-hop artists as KRS-One, Queen Latifah, and Young MC. The duo continued to record albums of their own as well, including the hip-hop disc *Silent Assassin* and *Murder She Wrote,* which featured a new style of reggae that they dubbed "bam bam." In 1999 they loomed large in a later-generation form of Caribbean-influenced sonic manipulation through a collaboration with British electronica auteur Howie B.

what to buy: *Rhythm Killers* ♫♫♫ (Island, 1987, prod. Sly Dunbar, Robbie Shakespeare, Bill Laswell) is a super-funky session with guests including Shinehead (vocals), Bernie Worrell (piano), Bootsy Collins (guitar, vocals), and Henry Threadgill (flute, sax, vibraphone, and melodica). In addition to several originals, the album features steaming-hot renditions of the Ohio Players "Fire" and Allen Toussaint's "Yes We Can Can."

what to buy next: Dunbar and Shakespeare's first production collaboration with Bill Laswell, *Language Barrier* ♫♫♫ (Island, 1985, prod. Sly Dunbar, Robbie Shakespeare, Bill Laswell) is a dub masterpiece with guest appearances by Bob Dylan, Herbie Hancock, and Afrika Bambaataa.

best of the rest:
Sly, Wicked and Slick ♫♫♫ (Virgin, 1979)
Sly and Robbie Present Taxi ♫♫♫ (Island, 1981)
Sly-go-ville ♫♫♫ (Island, 1982)
Kings of Reggae ♫♫♫ (Keystone, 1983)
Crucial Reggae Driven by Sly and Robbie ♫♫♫ (Mango, 1983)
A Dub Experience ♫♫♫ (Island, 1983)
Electro Reggae Vol. 1 ♫♫♫ (Island, 1986)
Taxi Connection: Live in London ♫♫♫♫ (Island, 1987)
Sly & Robbie Present Gregory Isaacs ♫♫♫♫ (RAS, 1988)
The Summit ♫♫♫♫ (Greensleeves, 1988)
Silent Assassin ♫♫♫ (Island, 1989)
DJ Riot ♫♫♫ (Island, 1990)
Murder She Wrote ♫♫♫ (Island, 1992)
1978–90—Sly & Robbie Hits ♫♫♫ (Sonic Sounds, 1993)
Sly & Robbie Present Mykall Rose ♫♫♫ (Taxi, 1995)
The Punishers ♫♫♫ (Island, 1996)

Hail Up the Taxi ♫♫♫ (Island, 1996)
Mambo Taxi ♫♫♫ (VP, 1997)
Friends ♫♫♫♫ (WEA/Elektra Entertainment, 1998)
Reggae Dance Hall ♫♫♫♫ (CAS Records, 1998)
Sly & Robbie Present: The Late Great Jackie Mittoo ♫♫♫♫ (Rhino U.K., 1998)
Drum & Bass Strip to the Bone by Howie B ♫♫♫♫ (Palm Pictures, 1999)

influences:

◀◀ King Tubby, Clement "Sir Coxsone" Dodd, Arthur "Duke" Reid

▶▶ Roots Radics, Big Audio Dynamite

see also: *Abyssinians, Black Uhuru, Johnny Clarke, the Congos, Culture, Manu Dibango, Gregory Isaacs, Ini Kamoze, Bill Laswell, Barrington Levy, Luciano, Mighty Diamonds, Sugar Minott, Jackie Mittoo, Pablo Moses, Maxi Priest, the Techniques, Toots & the Maytalls, Peter Tosh, Shinehead*

Craig Harris

Christina Smith & Jean Hewson

Newfoundland fiddle and song
Formed 1995, in St. John's, Newfoundland, Canada. Based in Newfoundland, Canada.

Christina Smith, fiddle, cello, viola da gamba, backing vocals; Jean Hewson, lead vocals, guitar. (Both members are from Canada.)

Christina Smith and Jean Hewson both bring classical training and extensive experience with other styles to the music of their home region, the windswept Atlantic coast of Canada. Influenced by the French, Scots, Breton, Irish, and English peoples who settled in its harbors and rocky landscapes and by the sailors who flowed through its ports, Newfoundland music is the very definition of fusion. It is a distinct tradition though, and one that Hewson and Smith, each of whom are qualified music teachers and maintain extensive schedules of festival workshops and individual music instruction, are committed to sharing with the next generation.

what's available: *Like Ducks!* ♫♫♫ (Borealis, 1998, prod. Sandy Morris, Jean Hewson, Christina Smith) is a lively and engaging album that includes instrumental and vocal works of Newfoundland style and a version of Hank Williams Sr.'s "I'm So Lonesome I Could Cry" that makes it seem right at home among its Celtic-based neighbors.

influences:

◀◀ Emile Benoit, Rufus Guinchard, Fairport Convention, Bothy Band, Kevin Burke, Shin'ichi Suzuki

Kerry Dexter

Leo Soileau

Cajun

Born January 19, 1904, in Ville Platte, LA, USA. Died August 2, 1980, in
Ville Platte, LA, USA.

Leo Soileau was one of the most popular bandleaders and
recording artists in Cajun music from the late 1920s to 1940s.
He grew up learning fiddle from Dennis McGee and Sady
Courville, performed old-time fiddle duets with his cousin, and
made two records that show him in command of this traditional form. He was also a visitor at the home of master accordionist Adam Fontenot, father of Canray Fontenot and good
friend of Amédée Ardoin. Soileau's recordings with accordionists Moise Robin and Mayuse LeFleur from this period are regarded as classics, and many of the songs continue to be performed. But Soileau is remembered for neither the old-style
fiddle tunes nor the accordion duets. Instead, he began to follow the string-band style that was being popularized by the
Hackberry Ramblers. His band, the Three Aces (later the Four
Aces and finally the Rhythm Boys), played Cajun tunes in an
almost hillbilly style, with Soileau's fiddle never quite escaping its roots in the countryside outside of Ville Platte. This
music and the rolling quality of Soileau's fiddle-bow strokes
captivated younger practitioners like Dewey Balfa, who would
carry the mark Soileau made even further in canonical contributions of their own.

what to buy: *Early American Cajun Music: The Early Recordings
of Leo Soileau* ♪♪♪♪ (Yazoo, 1999, prod. Richard Nevins)
brings together almost all of Soileau's formative sides on one
CD. The sound quality is as good as you can expect from remastered 78s, the notes by Ann Savoy are superb, and the
music is classic. Included are all four of Soileau's recordings
with accordionist Mayuse LaFleur—who was shot dead shortly
after the session—as well as all those with accordionist Moise
Robin. An extra bonus is the two tracks Soileau made with his
cousin Alius Soileau, which harken back to the classic fiddle
duets of Dennis McGee and Sady Courville.

what to buy next: *Pioneer Cajun Fiddler (1929–37)* ♪♪♪♪
(Arhoolie, 1993, prod. Chris Strachwitz) includes a couple of
the classic Soileau and Robin tunes ("La Valse de Josephine"
and "Demain c'est pas Dimanche"), but the rest of this release
is all the rough and smoking string-band sound of Soileau and
his Rhythm Boys. What's amazing is the interplay between his
guitar players and the drummer, which sounds at times more
like a Caribbean or African band than a hillbilly group.

worth searching for: The anthology *Cajun String Bands: Cajun
Breakdown* ♪♪♪♪ (Arhoolie, 1997, prod. Chris Strachwitz) includes four great cuts by Leo and his musical Aces. This includes the definitive version of the "Port Arthur Blues."

jamaican music 11: sonia pottinger

Sonia Pottinger was not only Jamaica's first
female music producer, but, until the
1980s, its only one. She is also one of its
all-time finest and most successful producers,
period, her coveted catalog on many labels
sanctified with an unmatched stateliness and
rapture. She may trail the great Coxsone Dodd
and Duke Reid in historical impact and output,
but her slow-cooked productions were always
suffused with feeling and unbroken in quality.
Her vision was beholden to no one, as she all
but ignored the trends sweeping the sound-sys-
tems and dancehalls; her simple axiom was to
produce only music she loved.

In 1966, "Mrs. Pottinger" opened the Tip Top
Record Shop in Kingston and released her first
single. With the advent of rocksteady, Mrs. P.
let loose with a batch of sure-shots that are essential listening for any reggae lover—or anyone interested in just feeling fine. Many of her
charges' classics can be found on the priceless
compilation *Musical Feast: Mrs. Pottinger's
High Note and Gayfeet Labels* ♪♪♪♪ (Heartbeat). Albeit with a little overlap and inferior
sound quality, *Put On Your Best Dress: Sonia
Pottinger's Rocksteady 1967–68* ♪♪♪♪♪ (Attack) adds some glittering gems that are otherwise rare as the Hope Diamond. Nearly all of
her rocksteady output is backed by Lynn Taitt &
the Jets, an outstanding studio band with a full,
blooming sound that was often unfairly overshadowed by the Supersonics and the Soul Vendors. In the '70s Pottinger produced vintage,
lilting, fundamentally positive reggae music
mixed by one of the most subtle engineers of
the time, Errol Brown. *The Reggae Train: More
Great Hits from the High Note Label* ♪♪♪♪♪
(Heartbeat) is a flawless and inspiring collection of landmarks, extended mixes, and rarities.
When Duke Reid died in 1974, Mrs. P. was chosen to inherit his historic Treasure Isle studios
and catalog. She retired in 1985, but will forever ring in history herself.

Todd Shanker

influences:

◄◄ Dennis McGee, Hackberry Ramblers

►► Wallace "Cheese" Reed, Michael Doucet, Dewey Balfa, Harry Choates

see also: *Amédée Ardoin, Balfa Brothers, Canray Fontenot, Savoy-Doucet Cajun Band*

Jared Snyder

Sol y Canto

Latin

Formed 1994, in Boston, MA, USA. Based in Boston, MA, USA.

Rosi Amador, vocals; Brian Amador, guitar, vocals; Edilio Bermudez, bass, vocals (1994); Eugenio Huanca, quena, zampona, vocals (1994); Renato Thomas, conga, bongos, percussion, vocals; Jon Weeks, sax, flute; Eduardo Tancredi, keyboards, accordion, piano; Fernando Huergo, bass.

Sol y Canto is among the best of the worldbeat/Latin fusion groups to emerge from the vibrant northeastern U.S. international music scene. Fueled by the mixing of dreams and cultures from immigrants and their children, the big cities of New England have become a source for new explorations of heritage music. Husband and wife Brian and Rosi Amador founded Sol y Canto after the breakup of another well-known Latin fusion band to which they both belonged, Flor de Caña.

what's available: *Sendero del Sol* ♩♩♩♩ (Rounder, 1996, prod. Danilo Perez Jr.) and *Sancocho* ♩♩♩♩ (Rounder, 1994, prod. Brian Amador) show Sol y Canto exploring influences from Venezuela and other regions of the Latin world as well as the Afro-Antillean chain and other island rhythms. Lead vocalist Rosi Amador is featured on most of the tracks. She has a strong voice and rhythmic sense that anchors the band, whether she's singing in English or Spanish, but these are really ensemble works, with every musician contributing to the sound.

influences:

◄◄ Violetta Para, Flor de Caña

Kerry Dexter

Liu Sola

Avant-garde Chinese fusion

Born in China. Based in New York, NY, USA.

Liu Sola, whom one critic has described as "the only Chinese artist who'd qualify to play the New Orleans Jazz Festival," is an eclectic musician whose radically distinctive sound successfully melds seemingly incongruous influences, including Chinese opera, free jazz, funk, blues, and the in-between-notes singing style common to Japanese Noh theater. A graduate of the Composition Department at the Central Conservatory of Music in Beijing, Sola was among China's first generation of university students to emerge during the Cultural Revolution of the mid-'70s. In addition to being an incredibly original vocalist, Sola is also an accomplished composer and author; her song "Shu Li" and her first novella *You Have No Choice* each won national awards in 1985 and '88, respectively. After representing China at the Seoul Song Festival for the 1988 Olympics, Sola moved to London in response to the massacre in Tiananmen Square and the artistic repression that followed. Embracing the blues on a trip to America in 1989, she collaborated with Memphis-based musicians on what may be the world's first Chinese blues song, "Reborn." By the early '90s she had moved to America full time, collaborating with Bill Laswell, Wu Man, and a variety of jazz, blues, and world-music artists on her groundbreaking debut album *Blues in the East*. Since then, Sola has divided her time between recording, literary endeavors, and film-, theater-, and dance-scoring activities, with several critically acclaimed books and albums to her credit. A rock opera based on her novella *Blue Sky Green Sea* was recorded in 1988 with the Chinese Central Symphony Orchestra and a rock band from Hong Kong, but remains unreleased for political reasons.

what to buy: Sola's truly unforgettable singing style, which can range from free-form vocalizing and animated nonsensical emoting that make Yoko Ono look reserved by comparison, to simple folk-like melodies, is definitely an acquired taste. *Haunts* ♩♩♩♩ (ALSO Productions, 1998, prod. Liu Sola, Fernando Saunders) is easily her most accessible and compelling album to date; an artsy outing on which she largely eschews Chinese traditions in favor of an evocative sound so joyously original it's almost impossible to resist. True to the title, this is a haunting, stripped-to-the-bone album, with varying moods and methods that show Sola exercising considerable restraint. The lack of vocal histrionics allows the subtle textures in her versatile voice to come to the fore on gorgeous tunes like "Witch's Beads" and the title track.

what to buy next: Her debut Western release, *Blues in the East* ♩♩♩♩ (Axiom, 1994, prod. Bill Laswell), is equally memorable but not quite as consistent. With a stellar lineup of musicians that includes organist Amina Claudine Myers, guitarist James Blood Ulmer, bassist Fernando Saunders, drummer Jerome "Bigfoot" Brailey, and saxophonist Henry Threadgill, plus storytelling from the Last Poets' Umar Bin Hassan, the album is a typically eclectic Bill Laswell fusion experiment, but one that doesn't always hit the bullseye. Still, when it does work, on songs like "Boya's Adventures," this radical collusive concept piece is as refreshingly original as anything you're likely to hear.

the rest:

(With Wu Man) *China Collage* ♩♩♩♩ (Avant, 1996)

influences:

◄◄ Chinese Opera, Japanese Noh Theater, Yoko Ono, Junior Wells

see also: *Bill Laswell, Wu Man*

Bret Love

Solas
/Seamus Egan

Irish traditional

Formed 1995, in New York, NY, USA. Based in New York, NY, USA.

Seamus Egan, flute, tres, nylon-string guitar, tin whistle, low whistle, uilleann pipes, bodhrán, background vocals; Karan Casey, lead vocals; John Doyle, acoustic guitar, background vocals; Winifred Horan, fiddle, .background vocals; John Williams, accordion, concertina, background vocals.

Solas has established itself as one of the top Irish folk groups on either side of the Atlantic. Following the example of Washington's Celtic Thunder, Solas balances male and female contributions as well as instrumental and vocal traditions. Providing the male influence in the New York-based quintet are two All-Ireland champions, accordionist John Williams and multi-instrumentalist Seamus Egan, as well as hard-driving rhythm guitarist John Doyle. Providing the female flavor are fiddler Winifred Horan from Cherish the Ladies and the Sharon Shannon Band and singer Karan Casey, born in Ireland's County Waterford. On the instrumental numbers, Egan and Horan lead the way, pushed through the up-tempo jigs, reels, and hornpipes by Doyle and Williams. On the songs, Casey takes the foreground with her supple soprano, which is framed by her four bandmates, who play with such sympathy they might as well be harmony singers. The linchpin of Solas is Egan, the kid from Philadelphia who won All-Ireland Junior Championships on flute, tenor banjo, tin whistle, and uilleann pipes by the time he was 16—which is also how old he was when his debut solo album appeared in 1985. By age 27 he had released four solo albums, contributed to four soundtracks, recorded with Eileen Ivers, John Whelan, and Living Colour's Vernon Reid, and co-founded Solas. In 1996 he became the youngest musician ever to win the Irish Echo's Traditionalist of the Year award.

what to buy: *Solas* ♫♫♫♫ (Shanachie, 1996, prod. Johnny Cunningham), guided through its paces by Silly Wizard's Johnny Cunningham, immediately established this new American quintet as a major force in Celtic music. The dance tunes combine rhythmic verve and melodic invention, and the songs give the instruments as much expressive room as the vocals. The group proved the best possible setting for Egan's special gifts. On the even better follow-up, *Sunny Spells and Scattered Showers*

♫♫♫♫ (Shanachie, 1997, prod. Johnny Cunningham), Casey manages to make an ancient song, "The Wind that Shakes the Barley," sound as if it had been ripped from today's headlines, and to make a modern feminist anthem, "Vanished Like the Snow," sound as if it had been handed down for generations. The instrumental medleys gallop along with the aggressive energy only a young band can muster.

what to buy next: Egan's debut solo album, *Traditional Music of Ireland* ♫♫♫ (Shanachie, 1985, prod. Mick Moloney), showcased the prodigious skills of the 16-year-old multi-instrumental whiz but lacked emotional heft. That would come with the second all-instrumental album, *A Week in January* ♫♫♫♫ (Shanachie, 1990, prod. Mick Moloney, Seamus Egan), whose title track is one of the classics of modern Irish-American folk music. The co-producers achieved a chamber-folk intensity in their arrangements. *The Brothers McMullen: Original Motion Picture Soundtrack* ♫♫♫♫ (Arista, 1995, prod. Mick Moloney, Seamus Egan) may be the best introduction to Egan's work as it includes the half-dozen best tracks from *A Week in January* and the five best tracks from *When Juniper Sleeps*. It also features "I Will Remember You," a song with lyrics and a vocal by Sarah McLachlan based on Egan's "Weep Not for the Memories." The latter tune can also be found on the aforesaid *When Juniper Sleeps* ♫♫♫♫ (Shanachie, 1996, prod. Michael Aharon, Seamus Egan), an album that found Egan collaborating with Horan, Doyle, and Williams, and thus laying the groundwork for Solas. *Three Way Street* ♫♫♫ (Green Linnet, 1993, prod. Mick Moloney) is a trio album that matches Egan with his two Philadelphia mentors, Moloney and Eugene O'-Donnell, in a lovely session of mutual admiration and affection. Egan also produced Karan Casey's debut solo album, *Songlines* ♫♫♫♪ (Shanachie, 1997, prod. Seamus Egan). Though four-fifths of Solas are represented on it, this is very much a solo album, with Casey singing in the spare, understated style of her hero, Dolores Keane. Like her, Casey delivers the lyrics' story with crisp articulation and genuine empathy, and carries the melody in a flush tone with little embellishment. This puts the emphasis where it should be—on the song, not the singer.

the rest:

Words That Remain ♫♫♫♫ (Shanachie, 1998)

influences:

◄◄ Cherish the Ladies, Celtic Thunder

►► Trian, Eileen Ivers, Sharon Shannon

see also: *Cherish the Ladies, Johnny Cunningham, Dolores Keane, Mick Moloney, Sharon Shannon, Silly Wizard, Paul Winter*

Geoffrey Himes

Songhai

See: Toumani Diabaté

Jo-El Sonnier

French-Cajun accordion
Born October 2, 1946, in Rayne, LA, USA. Based in Louisiana, USA.

Jo-El Sonnier is an internationally known French-Cajun accordionist. He started playing the instrument at the age of three, and by the time he was 13 had already cut his first record—"Tes Yeaux Blues" ("Your Blue Eyes"), which became a regional hit. From 1972–80 Sonnier bounced between Nashville and Los Angeles, establishing himself as a songwriter and studio musician. In 1975 he signed with Mercury Records and scored a few minor hits with "I've Been Around Enough to Know," "Always Late (With Your Kisses)," and "He's Still All Over You." In 1980 he returned to his roots and recorded *Cajun Life,* which was sung entirely in Acadian French. Sonnier recorded a similar album, *Cajun Roots,* in 1994. Keeping up his country connections, during the '80s Sonnier penned songs for George Strait, Johnny Cash, Conway Twitty, Loretta Lynn, Emmylou Harris, and John Anderson, and he backed new wave rock icon Elvis Costello on his critically acclaimed country outing *King of America.* In 1987 Sonnier signed with RCA and cracked the country Top 40 with "Come on Joe." The following year, his "No More One More Time" and Cajun-inflected "Tear-Stained Letter" hit the country Top 10.

what to buy: *Cajun Roots* ♫♫♫♫ (Rounder, 1994, prod. Michael Doucet), which is sung entirely in old-world French, shows Sonnier covering the music of his native Louisiana with style, grace, and expert musicianship—especially when it comes to the artist's accordion playing and powerful tenor. Standout tracks include "Huppes Taiauts" and "La Chere Toute-Toute," which features dazzling guitar/fiddle interplay between Sonnier and Beausoleil's Michael Doucet.

what to buy next: *Cajun Life* ♫♫♫♫ (Rounder, 1980, prod. Earl Ball, Alex Broussard) shows Sonnier reveling in the traditional Acadian sounds of Louisiana's bayou country.

the rest:
The Complete Mercury Sessions ♫♫♫ (Mercury, 1992)
(With Eddy Raven) *Cookin' Cajun* ♫♫♫ (K-Tel, 1996)
Cajun Pride ♫♫♫ (Rounder, 1997)

worth searching for: *Come On Joe* ♫♫♫♫ (RCA, 1988, prod. Bill Halverson, Richard Bennett) and *Have a Little Faith* ♫♫♫♫ (RCA, 1990, prod. Bill Halverson, Richard Bennett, Josh Leo) were Sonnier's two best major-label albums. *Come On Joe* contains his biggest hits, "No More One More Time" and "Tear-Stained Letter." The hits from *Have a Little Faith,* "(Blue, Blue, Blue) Blue, Blue" and "If Your Heart Should Ever Roll This Way Again," didn't chart as high, but the album has excellent covers of John Hiatt's "Have a Little Faith in Me" and "I'll Never Get Over You."

influences:
◀◀ Iry LeJeune, Amédée Ardoin

▶▶ Michael Doucet, Beausoleil, Wayne Toups, Zachary Richard

see also: *Beausoleil*

Rick Petreycik

Sorten Muld

Danish techno-folk
Formed September, 1995, in Denmark. Based in Aarhus, Denmark.

Ulla Bendixen, vocals; Martin Ottosen, keyboards; Henrik Munch, sound effects; Søren Bendixen, guitar; Thomas Holm, jew's-harp, pipes, frame drum (1995–97); Martin Seeberg, pipes, jew's-harp, frame drum (1997–present); Niels Kiele, percussion; Tommy Nissen, percussion; Johannes Hejl, double bass. (All members are from Denmark.)

Just as Steeleye Span, Fairport Convention, and their colleagues fused traditional British folk styles with psychedelic rock, so does Denmark's Sorten Muld fuse their Scandanavian heritage with modern electronic dance pop. The band's repertoire consists of original treatments of Danish folk ballads; their arrangements surround Ulla Bendixen's breathy soprano voice with a striking blend of keyboards and other electronic effects, for a metallic sheen that's colored by effective use of hurdy-gurdy, various kinds of pipes, and guitars. Sorten Muld's only full CD to date is *Sorten Muld Mark II,* but at presstime another was planned for release late in 1999. The band has appeared at festivals in Denmark, Germany, and Sweden; they were also nominated in eight categories for the 1998 Danish Grammys, winning the Producer of the Year and Techno Release of the Year prizes.

what's available: *Sorten Muld Mark II* ♫♫♫♫ (Sony/Pladecompagniet, 1997, prod. Sorten Muld) is definitely not your father's folk rock, even though Ulla Bendixen's vocals will remind some of Maddy Prior, Loreena McKennitt, and Enya. Her voice carries most of the melody lines, while electronic keyboards and percussion provide the high-tech rhythm pulse fundamental to late-'90s dance pop. Hurdy-gurdies (unfortunately uncredited) and bagpipes add all sorts of sharp buzzing noises to the overall sound. While that may seem rather avant-garde, the combination works quite well. A very distinctive blend of pretty folk melodies and singing with edgy cyber-rhythms.

worth searching for: Tanz & Folkfest Rudolstadt is a major world/folk/roots festival held annually in Germany. Festival organizers produce a sampler CD from each year's events, and *Tanz & Folkfest Rudolstadt '97* (hei-deck, 1997) includes a live version of Sorten Muld's "Venelite" with a slightly different arrangement than the studio track. A bit less high-tech, but with a little more electric guitar riffing and improvisation.

influences:

◄◄ Steeleye Span, Hedningarna, Loreena McKennitt, Värttinä

►► Garmarna, Afro Celt Sound System, Holderlin Express

Ken Roseman

Mercedes Sosa

South American folk

Born July 9, 1935, in San Miguel de Tucuman, Argentina. Based in Argentina.

Mercedes Sosa has a warm, honeyed alto that conveys pathos, power, and passion in every song she sings. It is one of the most impressive interpretive tools in the world of song, a tonal palette filled with such richness and conviction that Sosa can easily stand in comparison with Cesaria Evora, Edith Piaf, and Ella Fitzgerald. She has used this instrument to sing about love, rural poverty, and politically sensitive topics, earning her the enmity of the generals who ran Argentina during the '60s and '70s. Sosa started her career by winning an amateur talent contest sponsored by the local radio station while still a teenager. By 1962 she was an important member of the loosely organized *nueva cancíon* ("new song") movement that combined a knowledge of folk forms with a roots-based political stance at odds with the repressive governments in power throughout Latin America. In 1978 Sosa was arrested during a concert where she sang a song condemning powerful land barons and their relationship to their tenant farmers ("When They Have the Land"). The government also enforced a ban on the performance and distribution of Sosa's music within Argentina, forcing the singer to leave her homeland for exile in Europe. After living in Spain and France she returned to Argentina in 1982, and once more took up her career as artistic gadfly and spokesperson for the campesinos. She retired from active performance in 1997.

what to buy: If you could have only one Sosa album then *30 Años* 𝄢𝄢𝄢𝄢 (PolyGram Latino, 1994), a 20-song set covering some of her finest material, would be the place to start. In addition to such Sosa standards as "La Maza" and "Al Jardin de la Republica," there is her incredibly moving version of Violeta Parra's "Gracías a la Vida," the tune that became the cornerstone of Sosa's repertoire. When she returned from her exile in Europe Sosa scheduled and performed at the concert memorialized on *Mercedes Sosa En Argentina* 𝄢𝄢𝄢𝄢 (Philips, 1983/PolyGram Latino, 1992). The result is a stunning portrayal of audience and artist glorying in each other's presence.

what to buy next: Despite the strings that float "Quiero amar mi pais" and "Madre de madres" into easy listening territory,

the balance of *Vengo A Ofrecer Mi Corazon* 𝄢𝄢𝄢𝄢 (Philips, 1992) features Sosa in arrangements that enhance the singer's efforts to wring every last possible bit of emotion from the lyrics without getting sappy. The title tune became one of her most-requested songs in concert. *Sino* 𝄢𝄢𝄢𝄢 (Philips, 1992, prod. Fito Paez, Mercedes Sosa) is from the same vintage and mixes relatively upbeat material like Milton Nascimento's "Encuentros y Despedidas" and the title tune with powerful yet reflective songs including "Honrar la Vida" and "Caruso." Sosa interprets the work of Argentine rocker Charly García on *Alta Fidelidad* 𝄢𝄢𝄢𝄢 (Mercury, 1998, prod. Say No More), stepping outside the usual folk trappings of her career. Despite her having recorded García's songs on other albums, some listeners may find it a bit weird to hear Sosa within a rock setting. Still, most of these tunes are anthemic responses to the same political repression she faced, and she relates well to the composer's lyrical vision. The result puts Sosa in a more comfortable context for her magnificent voice than would a batch of Chuck Berry-inspired riffs, but it is sometimes an awkward fit no matter how commendable the effort. The *charanga*-charged "El tuerto y los ciegos" with its echoes of Andean rhythms is probably the most successful arrangement on the album.

what to avoid: In the late '60s and early '70s there were a batch of albums, by a number of artists, that sought to blend Catholic ritual with folk rhythms, including *Missa Luba, Misa Criolla,* and Sosa's own *Cantata Sudamericana* 𝄢 (PolyGram Discos, 1972/Polydor, 1992, prod. Ariel Ramírez). Sosa's vocals are the most interesting thing about this recording; the score attempts to mine elements from all over South America's folk landscape but the composer, Ariel Ramírez, tries too hard to model the piece on the architecture of classical Western European music. Part of the problem is the harpsichord and cheesy organ playing, which bring a touch of Esquivel to the proceedings without the requisite sense of humor. Strictly for Sosa completists.

best of the rest:

Gracías a la Vida 𝄢𝄢𝄢 (PolyGram Latino, 1994)
Será Posible El Sur 𝄢𝄢𝄢 (PolyGram Latino, 1994)
Gestos De Amor 𝄢𝄢𝄢 (PolyGram Latino, 1995)
Oro 𝄢𝄢𝄢 (PolyGram Latino, 1996)
Mi Historia 𝄢𝄢𝄢 (PolyGram Latino, 1997)
Al Despertar 𝄢𝄢𝄢 (PolyGram Latino, 1998)

worth searching for: Some of Sosa's finest material has never been released in the United States, including her stunning *Mercedes Sosa Interpreta a Atahualpa Yupanqui* 𝄢𝄢𝄢𝄢 (PolyGram Ibérica, 1977). Her haunting voice covers a dozen songs closely associated with fellow nueva canción giant Yupanqui, accompanied only by acoustic guitars, bass, and her own drumming. Included in this recital are a wonderful "Piedra y Camino," a poignant "Los Hermanos," and a classic rendition of "Duerme Negrito" that compares favorably with the master's own version.

influences:

◄◄ Atahualpa Yupanqui, Violeta Parra, Victor Jara, Milton Nascimento, Pablo Neruda

►► Lourdes Perez, Beatriz Montes

see also: *Lourdes Perez, Atahualpa Yupanqui*

Garaud MacTaggart

Soto Koto Band /Super Eagles /Ifang Bondi

Gumbay, Afropop
Formed 1977, in Bangul, Gambia. Based in Eindhoven, Holland.

Adbel Kabirr, vocals, keyboards, (1977–1991); Ousman Beyai, guitar, bass, keyboards, keyboards; Alain Eskinasi, keyboards, synthesizer, guitar; Musa Mboob, percussion; Sankung Jobarteh, guitar, percussion; Gerald Valdor, guitar; Paps Touray, vocals (1993–present).

The Gambia is a tiny country on the West African coast, almost completely surrounded by Senegal. Senegalese music tends to dominate Gambian pop, but there are a few Gambian styles that are holding their own, including the eclectic approach of Foday Musa Suso and the "gumbay" of the Soto Koto Band, founded by Abdel Kabirr in 1977 as the Super Eagles (later known as Ifang Bondi). The Super Eagles were the first Gambian band to "go electric" and combine Western influences with traditional *jali* music. Although the band was widely popular in the Gambia, making a living was hard, prompting a relocation to Holland in the mid-1980s. The band has gone through extensive personnel shifts over the years, with only a small core of the original members remaining.

what to buy: Solid dance tunes, stellar playing, and impassioned vocals distinguish *Gumbay Dance!* ♪♪♪♪ (Higher Octave, 1991, prod. M. Oko Drammeh), a solid, uplifting set from a band that has retained its African roots despite the use of Western instruments.

what to buy next: *Mandingo Beat* ♪♪♪ (Higher Octave, 1994, prod. M. Oko Drammeh) is a definite move to generate a bit of crossover action, with a touch of R&B in the vocals and a Latin funk influence to some of the rhythms.

the rest:
Soto Koto Band ♪♪♪♪ (Higher Octave, 1993)

worth searching for: Before moving to Europe, the band put out a number of albums under the name Ifang Bondi; titles include *Saraba* and *Mantra*.

influences:

◄◄ Ifang Bondi, Manding Kelepha, Guelewar

see also: *Foday Musa Suso*

j. poet

Soul Brothers

Mbaqanga
Formed 1974, in Hammersdal, South Africa. Based in Johannesburg, South Africa.

Studio band: David Masondo (died 1984), vocals; Moses Ngwenya, keyboards, vocals; Zenzele Mchunu, bass; Tuza Mthethwa (died 1984), vocals; Maxwell Mngadi, guitar; Sicelo Ndlela, bass; Thomas Phale, saxophones. Live band: All the above plus Bongani Nxele, drums; Javas Magubane, sax; Ernest Smith, percussion; Japan Sidoyi, vocals; Sipho Bhengu, vocals; Mbongelele Dladla, vocals; Vusi Mabuza, vocals. (All members are from South Africa.)

The original Soul Brothers vocal trio—David Masondo, Zenzele Mchunu, and Tuza Mthethwa—met while they were working in a factory in Hammersdale. To blow off steam they formed a band to play Motown, jazz, *marabi* (South African piano music, urbanized with electric guitars), and *mbaqanga* (the South African township music popularized by Paul Simon's *Graceland*). In 1974 they were signed to a small label, which convinced them to quit their day jobs and move to Johannesburg in search of fame. They arrived in the big city penniless, and for a while made a living backing up other groups under a series of assumed names, on a number of labels. By the late '70s they'd developed their own sound by slowing down the tempos, adding jazzy sax lines, mixing up the keyboards, and featuring a disco-fied, thumping bass/kick drum backbeat that complemented the lead vocals of the band's front line. They also introduced slang lyrics and sang to the fans in the streets. The band's new sound electrified the black population and made the Soul Brothers South Africa's best-selling band.

what to buy: *Jive Explosion* ♪♪♪♪ (EarthWorks, 1988, compilation prod. Trevor Herman) is a compilation of the tunes that made the Soul Brothers stars. The tracks are crammed with inventive organ parts that bring to mind the 1960s garage-band Farfisa mania of the United States, and a relentless beat, complemented by the sweet, soul-stirring harmonies of the band's three vocalists. Some of these singles probably inspired the genesis of *Graceland*.

what to buy next: The band is still going strong on the mid-'90s compilation *Jump & Jive* ♪♪♪♪ (EarthWorks, 1995, compilation prod. Trevor Herman). The production is more refined, but the earth-shaking Zulu stomp that made them favorites is still in evidence.

the rest:

Soul Mbaqanga—The Remixes 𝄢𝄢𝄢 (Riverboat, 1994)

influences:

◀◀ Philip Tabane, Zacks Nkosi, Boyoyo Boys

▶▶ Johnny Clegg, Brenda Fasse & the Big Dudes, Paul Simon

j. poet

Southern Scratch

Chicken scratch

Formed 1990, in Tucson, AZ, USA. Based in Tucson, AZ, USA.

Ron Joaquin, sax, bass; Sara Joaquin, cowbell; Alex Cruz, bass, drums, accordion; Angie Joaquin, maracas; Brandis Joaquin, drums, accordion; Richard Garcia, accordion; Jesse Puentes, bajo sexto. (All members are from USA.)

The kick drum cracks like a whip, the sax and accordion dance rings around each other, the bass thumps like an excited jackrabbit, and the people in the audience go spinning across the floor, laughing, shouting, and kicking up clouds of dust. Southern Scratch is on the scene, and the party won't wind down until the sun comes up.

Southern Scratch plays the traditional dance music of the Tohono O'odham tribe called *waila* ("why-la") or chicken scratch; it sounds similar to the Tex-Mex style *norteño*, but has a faster tempo and is performed without vocals or keyboard instruments. "Chicken scratch grew out of the fiddle bands that were formed down around El Presidio, which is now known as Tucson, in the 1860s," says Ron Joaquin, the band's leader. "The missionaries taught Indian people how to play European instruments so they could play for church fiestas." As the Tohono O'odham came into contact with Mexican, German, and Yaqui Indian musicians, they evolved their own unique style of playing. In the '50s players started using guitars, accordions, and saxophones instead of fiddles, but the basic elements of the music remained. There are no solos, no lyrics, little improvisation, and few newly composed tunes.

"Most bands play by ear," Joaquin continues. "I learned from my father, who played with the Joaquin Brothers Band, the first group to take the music off of the res. When I was starting he'd stand by the stage and shout out the chord changes for me. I passed the music on to my son, Brandis, but I think he gets most of his talent from my father. When he started playing the drums, his time was always a bit off, but two weeks after my dad died, he started nailing the rhythm. I believe he received my father's musical spirit." Like his father, Ron Joaquin wants to make chicken scratch available to all people. "We played at WOMAD (World of Music, Art and Dance—the border-breaking organization associated with Peter Gabriel) in Canada and a bunch of folk festivals on the East Coast, and people loved it." The Tohono O'odham word "waila" comes from the Spanish "bailer" ("dance"), so why do white people call the music chicken scratch? "The story they usually tell is that when you dance to this music, which is usually played outdoors, you kick up dust like a chicken scratching," Joaquin says. "But an old man just told me that when Anglos tried to imitate Indian dancing, the Indians said that they looked like chickens scratching for corn." Joaquin laughs, "I don't know which version is true."

what to buy: Chicken Scratch is bouncy dance music, and *Piast Tas* 𝄢𝄢𝄢 (Canyon, 1997, prod. Stephen Butler) will surely get you moving, though the style's relative subtlety within that framework—no solos, no lyrics, no grandstanding—may take some getting used to by mainstream American ears attuned to the pop cult of personality.

the rest:

Southern Scratch, Volume 1 𝄢𝄢𝄢 (Canyon, 1991, cassette)
Southern Scratch, Volume 2 𝄢𝄢𝄢 (Canyon, 1993, cassette)
Southern Scratch, Volume 3 𝄢𝄢𝄢 (Canyon, 1994, cassette)

influences:

◀◀ Gu Achi Fiddlers, Joaquin Brothers Band, El Conjunto Murrietta, Mike Enis & Company

▶▶ Simon & Friends, Friends, Pima Express

j. poet

Sparrow

See: The Mighty Sparrow

Spearhead

Hybrid hip-hop

Formed 1993, in Oakland, CA, USA. Based in California, USA.

Michael Franti, vocals; Mary Harris, vocals (1993–95); Le Le Jamison, keyboards (1993–96); Keith McArthur, bass (1993–96); David James, guitar; James Gray, drums (1993–96); Sub Commander Ras I Zulu, chant; Trinna Simmons, vocals (1996–present); Carl Young, bass, keyboards, string and horn arrangements (1996–present).

The best band you don't know where to find in a record store, Spearhead's handlers aren't sure if they should be marketed as hip-hop, R&B, or alterna-rock—so you might as well add "world music" to the list. Underrated but unsurpassed, Spearhead is an innovative and articulate ensemble that varies the known textures of rap into subtle but startling areas of reggae, acoustic folk, and art-rock, not to mention a foundation of classic soul and old/new/next-school hip-hop. The brainchild of musical frontiersman and recent Rasta Michael Franti—who previously shocked the system with the industro-punk Beatnigs and the agit-hop Disposable Heroes of Hiphoprisy—Spearhead is nonetheless a boisterous group effort, in both extended-family size and political bent very much the Stateside counterpart of Caribbean sound-armies like Haiti's Boukman Eksperyans. They suffer a little guilt by association as the rap group most likely to appear in an "alternative" magazine, and get grudging-to-no respect from a white critical establishment for whom hip-hoppers who don't cash in on thug-life stereotypes don't register as "authentically" black. But for those who'd rather listen to music than read about it (sorry ya had to read it here!), Spearhead throw the most visionary party in millennial pop. They may have to wait a bit while the fuses run out on the dynamite sticks they've placed in the market's myriad niches—but when the fire catches they're gonna blow up good.

what's available: The debut *Home* &&&& (Capitol, 1994, prod. Michael Franti, Joe "The Butcha" Nicolo) is the unsung fulcrum of late-century hip-hop, most notable to world-music fans for the running commentary of resident Rasta wiseman Sub Commander Ras I Zulu and the sorta-salsa "Red Beans & Rice"—but with whole other worlds of listening to be had, from the dreamy but disturbed "Of Course You Can" to the rap-folk of "Hole in the Bucket" to the political soul of "Positive" and "Runfayalife" and beyond. Franti adds convincing Jamaican dialect to his full-time roster of vocal characters on *Chocolate Supa Highway* &&&& (Capitol, 1997, prod. Michael Franti), with some of the most smile-evoking, self-effacing odes to the herb you're likely to find in the Rasta cannon. One of these goes all the way with a guest-star duet vocal by Stephen Marley on his dad Bob's "Rebel Music (3 O'Clock Roadblock)," suitably updated for the hip-hop generation by the usual frontman. Two other guests show Spearhead more corners of the world—Joan Osborne, with a stunning North American roots-folk interpolation into "Wayfarin' Stranger," and Zap Mama's Marie Daulne, with otherworldly African vocal revelations in the midst of the sitar-reggae of "Comin' to Gitcha." Franti returns the favor with raps both insightful ("Baba Hooker") and otherwise ("Poetry Man") on Zap's own *7* &&&& (Luaka Bop, 1997, prod. various). Meanwhile, future-vintage hip-hop rounds out *Supa Highway,* with the master storytelling of "Gas Gauge"; the party-political vibe of "Keep Me Lifted" and "Food for tha Masses" (featuring South African toaster Ishmael from Prophets of Da City); and the superlative eulogy-rap (sorry, Puffy) of "Why Oh Why."

worth searching for: Franti's world travels also lead him to a duet with Senegalese superstar Baaba Maal on "Yelle Jam (Hamady Boiro)" from *Reggae on the River: The 10th Anniversary Part 1* &&&& (Earthbeat!, 1995, prod. various).

influences:
◄ Gil Scott-Heron, Last Poets, Public Enemy, Bob Marley

see also: *Baaba Maal, Ziggy Marley & the Melody Makers, Zap Mama*

Adam McGovern

The Specials
Two-tone, ska

Formed 1977, in Coventry, England. Disbanded 1981. Re-formed 1994. Based in England.

Jerry Dammers, keyboards (1977–81); Lynval Golding, guitar; Sir Horace Gentleman (born Horace Panter), bass; Terry Hall, vocals (1978–81); Neville Staples, vocals, percussion; Roddy "Radiation" Byers, guitar; Siverton, drums (1977–78); John Bradbury, drums (1979–81); Mark Adams, keyboards, vocals (1994–present); Adam Birch, horns (1994–present); Aitch Hyatt, drums (1994–present).

A ska revival group, the Specials were the showpiece band of the U.K.'s short-lived two-tone movement of the late '70s and early '80s. Two-tone referred to the racially mixed groups that formed partly as a reaction to emerging skinhead racial violence in England. Evolving from various bands known as Coventry, the Coventry Specials, and the Specials AKA, the group had a number of U.K. singles and EP hits with their bouncy, party-friendly ska songs. The band shattered in 1981, when Neville Staples, Terry Hall, and Lynval Golding formed Fun Boy Three and Roddy Byers formed Roddy Radiation & the Tearjerkers. Jerry Dammers led a revamped lineup known as Specials AKA, then re-formed the band under its original moniker in 1994. Today, ska fans refer to the Specials' peak period as the genre's "second wave"—the first being the originals, Jamaicans such as the Skatalites, and the third being recent hit modern rock bands such as the Mighty Mighty Bosstones and No Doubt.

what to buy: *The Specials* &&&&♪ (Chrysalis, 1979, prod. Elvis Costello) is the group's peak, with party favorites such as "A Message to You, Rudy," "Monkey Man," "Gangsters," and "Too Much, Too Young." The best set in print is *Singles Collection* &&&& (Capitol, 1991, prod. various), which includes "Ghost Town" and "Free Nelson Mandela," two of the group's best songs.

what to buy next: After the band regrouped, *Today's Specials* &&&& (Virgin, 1996, prod. various) gets back on the ska track with a number of covers—particularly a scorching version of "Take Five"—but doesn't quite match the unbridled exuberance of the first album.

what to avoid: *More Specials* &&♪ (Chrysalis, 1980/Alliance, 1986, prod. Jerry Dammers, Dave Jordan), the follow-up to *The Specials,* lost the beat as the group veered into lounge music.

the rest:
(With Desmond Dekker) *King of Kings* &&&♪ (Trojan, 1994)
(With Desmond Dekker) *King of Ska* &&& (Trojan, 1991/Varèse Sarabande, 1998)
Guilty 'til Proved Innocent &&♪ (MCA, 1998)
Blue Plate Specials Live &&&& (Big Ear, 1999)

influences:

◄◄ The Skatalites, the Wailers, Madness

►► No Doubt, Mighty Mighty Bosstones

see also: *Desmond Dekker*

Lawrence Gabriel

Davy Spillane
See: Moving Hearts

Splash
See: Daniel Tshanda

Douglas Spotted Eagle
Native flute, world, new age
Born in Valley Junction, IA, USA. Based in Stockton, UT, USA.

Douglas Spotted Eagle was working at Native Restoration, the recording studio he owns and operates in the peaceful country near Stockton, Utah, when the president of Windham Hill Records called. *Closer to Far Away,* Spotted Eagle's first album for Windham Hill, had only been out for three weeks, but it was already #9 on *Billboard* magazine's new-age chart. Still, the record executive hadn't called to congratulate Spot (as he is nicknamed) on his accomplishment. "He told me 'There's too much "Hey yah, hey yah" stuff on the album,'" Spot says, laughing. "He had no idea how culturally insensitive he was being. He told me they didn't want any traditional stuff on the next album." Not unexpectedly, there was no next album for Windham Hill. The company restructured and jettisoned many of their artists, including Spotted Eagle.

For Spot, who composes, produces, and plays Native flute, keyboards, and traditional percussion, the label's disinterest was a blessing in disguise. It enabled him to finish work on *Tenaya,* the soundtrack to a film by documentary-maker Sterling Johnson that lets viewers sample the four seasons at Yosemite National Park. "Most of that music was recorded live in Yosemite," Spot says. "We lugged some recording equipment up there, and I played, sometimes freezing my butt off while I sat on a frosty river bank, but I wanted to capture the feel of the place." The music Spotted Eagle makes today has a deeply spiritual content, but that was not always the case. "In high school I was in a metal band. I was experimenting with the flute, but it didn't become a spiritual force in my life until I was a lot older." While Spot has some Native blood, he plays down that aspect of his life. "I was raised the Native way, and speak the language and practice the religion, but I tell people 'I'm a white guy that makes music based on the Native music I love.'"

His bloodline notwithstanding, Spot has had a major impact on Native music. He has produced almost 300 albums of Native music for pop, powwow, and traditional artists; recorded 11 albums of his own; starred in the flute instruction video *Learning to Play the Native American Flute with Spotted Eagle;* and written two books, *Voices of Native America,* an overview of Native music with a large section on how to play and make flutes, and *Making Indian Bows and Arrows.* Spot also created a CD-ROM for Q-Up Arts called *Voices of Native America.* The disc is a diverse collection of Native instrumental and vocal samples. "Every time a Native person came on screen on TV or in the movies, you heard a *shakuhachi,* a Japanese flute," Spot says. "I got tired of that, and put together a sampler of drumming, chanting, singing, flute-playing and other musical cues that filmmakers could use that would be more authentic." Spike Lee, Michael Jackson, and the *X-Files* TV series are just a few of the clients who have made use of Spot's digital dictionary of Native sounds. "Music is a bridge between the visible and invisible world" Spot says. "It doesn't matter if you're looking out to a higher power, or into your own core; the principle is the same. Music is my prayer to, and for, the world."

what to buy: Spotted Eagle contributes another laid-back combination of Native and worldbeat influences on *Pray* ♫♫♫ (Higher Octave, 1998, prod. Spotted Eagle), with guests Marion Meadows, an African American/Native American sax player; Wil Numkena, the Hopi singer who was sampled for the *Sacred Spirits* ethno-techno disc; Native singers Herman Begay and Frank Warren from the Indian Creek Singers; and Samantha Rainbow, a contemporary and traditional Lakota singer.

what to buy next: Despite the opinion of the Windham Hill marketing department, *Closer to Far Away* ♫♫♫ (Windham Hill, 1996, prod. Brian Keane) is a solid new-age/world instrumental album.

the rest:
Sacred Feelings ♫♫♫ (Natural Visions, 1989)
Legend of the Flute Boy ♫♫♫ (Natural Visions, 1990)
Stand at Center ♫♫♫ (Natural Visions, 1992)
Ultimate Collection ♫♫♫ (Natural Visions, 1993)
Human Rites ♫♫♫ (Natural Visions, 1993)
Common Ground ♫♫♫ (Natural Visions, 1994)
Tenaya ♫♫♫ (Natural Visions, 1997)

influences:

◄◄ Tom Ware, R. Carlos Nakai

►► Gary Stroutsos, Raven

see also: *Robbie Robertson*

j. poet

Dáithí Sproule

See: Altan, Trian

U. Srinivas

Karnatak mandolin

Born Upalappu Srinivas, February 28, 1969, in Palakol, Andhra Pradesh, India. Based in Madras, India.

Upalappu Srinivas (better known by his first initial) pioneered the use of the mandolin in *karnatak* (South Indian classical) music; a match that seems natural in retrospect, but was revolutionary for its time. Srinivas's first public performance at the age of nine garnered him a reputation as a child prodigy. "I thought that it's common to hear people playing classical music on the violin or *veena* [plucked stringed instrument], so why don't I try something new?" he recalls. "Of course, I never dreamed I would become so well-known or that the mandolin would become so popular." Inspired, his clarinet-playing father taught his son what little he knew—though with no experience in the mandolin, he had to sing karnatak music, which Srinivas would then play. In any case the artist's talent transcended his training: Srinivas currently draws diverse crowds of as many as 10,000, including *rasikas,* fanatical concert-goers able to detect the slightest mistake. Even in settings where the stakes aren't quite so high, he doesn't disappoint.

what to buy: For traditional Hindustani karnatak music try *Rama Sreerama* ♪♪♪♪ (RealWorld/Caroline, 1994, prod. Michael Brook), recorded live in one evening. Srinivas's latest is *Dawn Raga* ♪♪♪♪ (WOMAD, 1996), another satisfying exploration of the fresh interpretations to be coaxed from a venerable tradition.

what to buy next: Producer Michael Brook describes *Dream* ♪♪♪ (RealWorld/Caroline, 1995, prod. Michael Brook) as "very much 'see what happens' with Srinivas as the focus." Expect a modern mix of samples, ambiance, avant-popper Jane Siberry's voice on the title track, and Brazilian percussion phenom Nana Vasconcelos's drumming for a multicultural menu.

worth searching for: Confusions abound among Srinivas's many hard-to-find import recordings, as they nearly all have "mandolin" in the title. These releases will tend toward more traditional composition and production, compared to the three slicker ones cited above. Keep in mind that Srinivas only recently turned 30, and has improved with age, so pick the more recent recordings where possible: *Mandolin* (Magnasound, 1986), *Magic Mandolin* (Chhanda Dhara, 1989), *Music on Mandolin* (Super Cassette, 1990), *Modern Mandolin Maestro* (Globestyle U.K., 1991), *Double Mandolin* (Magnasound/San, 1991), *Trio Mandolin* (Sangeetha/Koel, 1992), *Mandolin Duets*

(EMI, 1994), *Prodigy* (Sangeetha/Koel, 1994), and *Mandolin Ecstasy* (Oriental, 1996).

influences:
◄◄ Ravi Shankar

see also: *Michael Brook, T. H. "Vikku" Vinayakram*

David Poole

Sunita Staneslow

Jewish, Celtic, jazz, classical

Born April 21, 1962, in Ithaca, NY, USA. Based in St. Paul, MN, USA.

Truly an international performer, Sunita Staneslow's mastery of the harp grows from many roots. Calling on an extensive background in a variety of musical styles—and her travels to countries such as Israel, France, and Scotland to learn their music first-hand—Staneslow embraces a broad palette, with a versatile mastery rare to traditional harpers. Beyond sheer technical command, Staneslow also truly conveys an empathy with the joy or sorrow expressed in each piece of music. Although she plays Celtic, classical, and jazz beautifully, her artistry in her own heritage in particular has brought about a revival of Jewish music on the harp. Staneslow's credentials are many, including a master's degree from the Manhattan School of Music. She studied harp under Lucile Lawrence at Boston University, and in France with Lilly Laskine and Jaqueline Borot. She also studied privately with Judith Liber in Israel from 1985–87, meanwhile playing principal harp with the Jerusalem Symphony Orchestra and busking on the street with traditional harp music! Staneslow's resume is as long as her training is broad; she has played with the Minnesota Opera, the Des Moines Opera, and the Chicago Chamber Orchestra, as well as the jazz ensemble Vida and the Celtic group Northern Gael.

what to buy: The best showcase of Staneslow's diversity is *Sunita: Solo Harp* ♪♪♪♪ (Maxemillian Productions, 1991, prod. Frederick Schlomka). This unique recording displays an uncommon technical range and emotional depth—exclusively on solo harp. Traditional Polish, Irish, English, Greek, Sephardic, Ladino, and other Jewish tunes are all passionately delivered. On *City of Gold* ♪♪♪♪♪ (Maxemillian Productions, 1996, prod. Shelley Hanson), Staneslow further displays her rich understanding of Jewish music, joined by excellent musicians on violin, cello, oboe, clarinet, and English horn. This beautiful collection of 12 tunes ranges from the elegantly traditional "On the Rivers of Babylon" to the hauntingly modern "Theme from Shindler's List," capturing the very essence of Jewish music at its best. *Mist Covered Mountains* ♪♪♪♪ (Excelsior, 1996, prod. Sunita Staneslow, Bobby Schnitzer) features some stirring Celtic harp solos in a wide selection, including a very moving version of "Bridget Cruise." Staneslow is joined by fiddle, flute, guitar, pipes, concertina, and other instruments, although the harp takes center stage throughout.

what to buy next: Vida's *Acoustic Passion* ♪♪♪♪ (Maxemillian Productions, 1994) is truly world music, with a mixture of jazz, traditional, and classical strains covering a wide variety of old and modern music. This electric trio of cello, harp, and percussion is exotic and exciting. Staneslow appears with Northern Gael on *Crossing the Shannon: A Musical Portrait of Ireland* ♪♪♪♥ (Excelsior, 1996, prod. Laura MacKenzie, Sunita Staneslow). This upbeat recording features flutes, pipes, concertina, fiddle, and a few vocals in a fine collection of Irish tunes. *Romantic Harp II: A Musical Portrait of France* ♪♪♪♪ (Excelsior, 1997, prod. Sunita Staneslow) displays the beauty of the harp on French romantic music by such greats as Debussy, Bizet, and Ravel.

the rest:
The Romantic Harp: Music for Quiet Times ♪♪♪ (Excelsior, 1996)

influences:

◄◄ Kim Robertson, Deborah Henson-Conant, Sileas, Sue Richards, Laura MacKenzie, Laura Sewell, Akiva Ben-Horin

Jo Hughey Morrison

Rigo Star
Soukous
Born in Kinshasa, Zaire (now Congo). Based in Paris, France, and Oakland, CA, USA.

Rigo Star is one of the world's great guitarists, a *soukous* (Congolese rumba) master who has been able to perform the delicate balancing act of maintaining a strong fan base in both the Congo and abroad. "People in the Congo are like Americans," Star says. "They're loyal to their own music; they don't like it to change too much. Because my soukous has a strong traditional foundation, people accept my innovations, like using distortion to emulate the sounds I heard Jimi Hendrix making. I did that when I played for Papa Wemba in Viva La Musica, and people flipped. That's how we stayed fresh; when inspiration came, we let it take us forward."

Star's risk-taking made him a favorite sideman, producer, and songwriter; he's added his scorching licks to more than 300 albums playing soukous, *makossa* (Cameroonian pop), *zouk* (Antillian dance-pop), and more. He's written and produced for M'Bilia Bel and Kofi Olomide, helped pioneer the "zoukous" hybrid of the '80s by adding his guitar to projects by zouk luminaries like Kassav' founder Jacob Desvarieux and Ronald Rubinel, and worked his magic for Paul Simon and Kanda Bongo Man. Star says he keeps his music fresh by producing albums of classically flavored material for the Congolese market while exploring the possibilities of fusing soukous with other forms,

especially American jazz. To that end, he came to California in 1997 to record *Got the Feeling*, a smooth jazz set that has drawn some flack from critics for its mellow, AOR sound.

"Since I was a young man, I've dreamed of making a record in America," Star says. "In Paris, we had to make soukous the French could understand, so maybe I will get people in America to listen by mixing jazz with soukous. I think mixing styles produces good music. Soukous came from playing Cuban music in an African style, so maybe something new will come of this." At the time of writing Star was putting together a band that he planned to tour America, then the world, with what he says will be a new soukous sound. "I don't want to say too much, because I don't want another musician to steal my ideas," he says, only half joking. "I'm going to use jazz musicians, if I can teach them to play soukous, because we'll only be playing a few jazz tunes in the show. I'm also looking for a female singer who can sing soukous in English."

He won't go into too much more detail on this, but as far as his "almost" famous nom de guitar goes, the explanation was pretty straightforward. "My name is Rigobart Bamundele," he says. "In my language 'bamundele' means 'star,' and since everybody knows Ringo the Beatle, I though it would make a good stage name."

what to buy: *Attention* ♪♪♪♪ (IMA, 1997, prod. Rigo Star) is killer modern soukous, with plenty of Star's incendiary guitar licks and guest vocals by Sam Mangwana.

what to buy next: Star helped make singer M'Bilia Bel famous by writing, playing, and producing on her early solo albums. She returns the favor by adding her sultry vocals to the stellar *Yalowa* ♪♪♪♪ (IMA, 1996, prod. Rigo Star).

what to avoid: *Got the Feeling* ♪♪♪ (IMA, 1997, prod. Rigo Star, Jennifer Kreltzer, Kincaid Miller) isn't as bad as most smooth jazz; there's a hint of North Africa in the rhythms and Star's guitar is always interesting, but if you're looking for fireworks, this isn't the place to find them.

worth searching for: As mentioned above, Star has produced and played on more than 300 albums in the past 15 years, most for Parisian or Congolese labels. The pick of the litter includes: *Phénomene* ♪♪♪♪ (IMA, 1996), a reissue of M'Bilia Bel's first solo album from 1988, produced and written by Star; *Sang Bleu Aziza* ♪♪♪♪♥ (IMA, 196), by vocalist Luciana Demingongo, arranged and produced by Star, who met Demingongo when both were featured players in Papa Wemba's Viva La Musica; *Papa Wemba* ♪♪♪♪ (Stern's U.K., 1988), one of Wemba's biggest hits, due in part to Star's guitar wizardry; *Amour Fou* ♪♪♪♪ (Ryko, 1988), a compilation of the three albums Kanda Bongo Man put out on his own Bongo Man label, with excellent guitar work by Diblo Dibala and Rigo; and a couple of early Star projects, *Jotongo* &&&& (Mayala France, 1986), credited to "Rigo and Josky"; and *Ai, Ai* &&&& (Mayala France, 1986), by "Rigo and Koffi."

influences:

◄◄ Zaiko Langa Langa, Franco, Tabu Ley Rochereau

►► Kanda Bongo Man, Diblo Dibala, Loketo

see also: *M'Bilia Bel, Diblo Dibala, Kanda Bongo Man, Kassav', Sam Mangwana, Tshala Muana, Papa Wemba*

j. poet

Andy Statman

Klezmer, bluegrass, jazz, classical Jewish music
Born in New York, NY, USA. Based in New York, NY, USA.

One of the most versatile of contemporary traditional musicians, Andy Statman is a world-class bluegrass mandolin player, and an equally gifted clarinetist who is both a jazz cat and one of the shining lights of contemporary Hasidic music. New Yorker Statman's explorations of klezmer led him into the spiritual reaches of the Bill Monroe sound.

what to buy: *Between Heaven and Earth: Music of the Jewish Mystics* &&&&& (Shanachie, 1997) is a spectacular recording on which Statman and his quartet (also featuring pianist Kenny Werner, bassist Harvie Swartz, and drummer Bob Weiner) use *Niggunim* (18th- and 19th-century Chassidic liturgical vocal pieces) as springboards for soaring, free-jazz improvisations in the spirit of the transcendent work of '60s players like John Coltrane and Albert Ayler. Always an expressive musician, this work brings out new emotional depths in Statman's extraordinary clarinet playing; his note-bending on the opener "Maggid" is particularly remarkable.

what to buy next: *Songs for Our Fathers* &&&& (Acoustic Disc, 1996, prod. David Grisman, Andy Statman), a wonderfully reverent, sentimental exploration of traditional Jewish melodies by two masters of contemporary acoustic music—Statman and fellow mandolin virtuoso David Grisman—features a splendid supporting cast including bassists Edgar Meyer and Jim Kerwin, percussionist Hal Blaine, tuba player Zachariah Spellman, and guitarist Enrique Coria. The second release by Statman's devout jazz quartet, *The Hidden Light* &&&& (Sony Classical, 1998, prod. A. Statman), is the equal of the first. On a mixture of familiar Yiddish melodies and new instrumental pieces, Statman and company again mine the blend of spiritual questing and improvisational elegance that made their debut such a powerful and moving work.

the rest:
Andy Statman:
Flatbush Waltz &&&& (Rounder, 1980)

(With David Grisman) *Mandolin Abstractions* &&&& (Rounder, 1982)
(With David Grisman) *Nashville Mornings, New York Nights* &&& (Rounder, 1986)
Andy's Ramble &&& (Rounder, 1994)

Andy Statman Klezmer Orchestra:
Klezmer Music &&&▽ (Shanachie, 1992)
Jewish Klezmer &&& (Shanachie, 1994)

influences:

◄◄ Bill Monroe, Dave Tarras

►► Klezmatics, New Orleans Klezmer All-Stars

see also: *De Dannan, Itzhak Perlman*

Michael Parrish

Steel Pulse

Reggae
Formed 1975, in Birmingham, England. Based in Birmingham, England.

David Hinds, vocals, rhythm guitar; Ronald McQueen, bass (1975–83); Basil Gabbidon, lead guitar, vocals (1975–81); Selwyn Brown, keyboards, vocals, percussion; Steve "Grizzly" Nisbett, drums (1976–present); Michael Riley, vocals, percussion (1976–78); Alphonso Martin, vocals, percussion (1976–present); Alvin Ewan, bass (1983–present); Carlton Bryan, guitar (1983–present). (All members are from England.)

Steel Pulse was among the first of England's reggae bands to achieve international attention. With their heavily political lyrics and righteous rhythms the group has continued to project their commitment to justice, economic freedom, and racial equality. *Trouser Press Record Guide* called the band "one of the world's very best self-contained reggae units." Steel Pulse came together in the Handsworth ghettos of Birmingham, England, at the suggestion of bass player Ronald McQueen. Although none of the other original members initially knew how to play their instruments, three years of intensive rehearsals led to a more refined sound. Shortly after performing their first gig at the Compton Pub in Birmingham, the group recorded their debut single, "Nyah Love." With the arrival of Phonso Martin and Michael Riley in 1976 and Steve Nisbett the following year, Steel Pulse continued to polish their musical skills.

Beginning in 1977, the band aligned itself with punk's Rock Against Racism movement. After opening shows for Generation X, the Adverts, the Stranglers, and the Slits, the group secured a prestigious gig as opening act for Burning Spear at the Rainbow Theater in London. Their highly charged performance resulted in a contract with Island Records. Steel Pulse's first single for the label, "Klu Klux Klan," was followed by their debut album *Handsworth Revolution* and a tour of the U.K. and Europe as opening act for no less than Bob Marley & the Wailers.

Though their next two albums—*Tribute to the Martyrs* and *Caught You*—were released by Island, they conflicted with the label and their contract was dropped in 1980, shortly before their first tour of the United States. The following year, Steel Pulse became the first British reggae band to perform at the definitive annual Reggae Sunsplash festival in Jamaica. Their fourth album, *True Democracy,* was released on their own label, Wise Man Doctrine, in England, and on Elektra in the U.S.

The latter label released Steel Pulse's fifth album, *Earth Crisis,* as well. Friction was sparked, however, when the band recorded the live *Babylon the Bandit* and Elektra refused to print song lyrics. Although Steel Pulse went on to receive a Grammy for the album—which included a lyric sheet financed by the band—they terminated their contract with Elektra. Three years passed before they were able to convince another label (MCA) to sign them. Their relationship with that label, however, was short-lived too. Releasing two blatantly commercial albums, *State of Emergency* in 1988 and *Victims* in 1991, which nonetheless failed to generate sales, the band became disillusioned with MCA's demand for mainstream material. After releasing a second live album, *Rastafari Centennial,* in 1992, and a rootsier studio album, *Vex,* in 1994, the group left to reactivate their own Wise Man Doctrine label. Released in 1997, *Rage and Fury* re-established the band's earlier roots-conscious sound.

Steel Pulse has been featured on several tribute albums including *Fire on the Mountain: Reggae Celebrates the Grateful Dead* in 1986, and *Regatta Mondatta: A Reggae Tribute to the Police* in 1997. Their song "Can't Stand the Heat" was featured in the Spike Lee film *Do the Right Thing* in 1989. Four years later, they became the first reggae band to perform at an American presidential inauguration.

what to buy: The two-CD set *Rasthanthology* 𝄞𝄞𝄞𝄞 (Wise Man Doctrine, 1996, prod. various) is a 17-song retrospective covering the band's entire recording career.

what to buy next: *Sound System: The Island Anthology* 𝄞𝄞𝄞𝄞 (Island, 1997, prod. various) samples tunes from Steel Pulse's first three albums and includes several previously unreleased live tracks.

the rest:
Handsworth Revolution 𝄞𝄞𝄞𝄞 (Island, 1978)
Tribute to the Martyrs 𝄞𝄞𝄞 (Island, 1979)
Caught You 𝄞𝄞𝄞 (Island, 1980)
True Democracy 𝄞𝄞𝄞 (Elektra, 1982)
Earth Crisis 𝄞𝄞𝄞 (Elektra, 1983)
Babylon the Bandit 𝄞𝄞𝄞 (Elektra, 1985)
State of Emergency 𝄞𝄞 (MCA, 1988)
Victims 𝄞𝄞 (MCA, 1991)
Rastafari Centennial 𝄞𝄞𝄞 (MCA, 1992)

chris blackwell

Arguably no figure is more important than Chris Blackwell in the realization of world music as a commercial genre. While his Island Records was not the first label in the West to release what we now call "world music," none brought as many world artists to as high and lasting mainstream prominence. Though Blackwell was born in London, much of his early life was spent in Jamaica. This cultural crossroads, a hotbed of world-musical creativity, would forever influence Blackwell's tastes and guide his professional decisions. Settling there after his British schooling, Blackwell started Island, which early on hit the country's #1 chart spot with Laurel Aiken's "Little Shells." However, Blackwell soon realized that his ska singles were selling more on the burgeoning mod teen scene in England than in the style's native country. Relocating to London in 1962, Island then had one of the biggest world-music hits of the decade with "My Boy Lollipop" by 15-year-old sensation Millie. But it was the '70s that provided Island with perhaps its most history-making connection to world music: the signing of superstar-to-be Bob Marley, which would establish reggae's global presence like never before. The company later helped spur the worldwide acceptance of African pop, especially by licensing Senegalese Parisian Mamadou Konte's phenomenal festival, Africa Fête, as a North American package tour in the '90s. During Island's ascent with general-interest pop giants like U2, the groundbreaking world-music imprint Mango was also formed. But long before this subdivision, Island was unique in being the first major label with world music as its foundation rather than an afterthought. As a white man who's made at least as much of a fortune from his world acts as they have, Blackwell's motives have been questioned by some. But his results, putting artists from all over the geographical map on the musical one, are above reproach. Now parted with Island, his Palm Pictures label guarantees more success for world music's best and brightest well into the new century.

Sam Wick and Adam McGovern

Andy Statman

Vex ♫♫♫ (MCA, 1994)

Rage and Fury ♫♫♫♪ (Wise Man Doctrine, 1997)

influences:

◄◄ Burning Spear, Peter Tosh

►► The Police, Aswad, Culture

Craig Harris

Steeleye Span

British folk-rock

Formed 1969, in England. Based in England.

Maddy Prior, vocals (1969–97); Tim Hart, vocals, guitar, dulcimer, harmonium, five-string banjo, fiddle (1969–82); Ashley Hutchings, electric bass, vocals (1969–71); Terry Woods (Ireland), electric guitar, five-string banjo, mandola (1969–70); Gay Woods (Ireland), vocals, bodhrán (1969–70, 1994–present); Peter Knight, violin, vocals (1971–76, 1980–present); Martin Carthy, vocals, guitar, banjo, organ (1971–72, 1977–78); Bob Johnson, vocals, guitar (1972–76; 1980–present); Rick Kemp, bass, vocals (1972–87); Nigel Pegrum, drums, (1974–89); John Kirkpatrick, vocals, accordion (1977–78); Tim Harries, bass, keyboards, vocals (1989–present); Liam Genocky, drums (1989–98). (All members are from England except where otherwise noted.)

Steeleye Span was and is one of the most important and influential British folk-rock bands. Ashley Hutchings had developed a serious interest in traditional music after working on the seminal *Liege and Lief* as a member of Fairport Convention. He wanted to form a group devoted exclusively to creating new interpretations of traditional ballads and tunes, and Steeleye Span was born. Their first line-up—Hutchings, Maddy Prior, Tim Hart, Gay Woods, and Terry Woods—was short-lived, recording one album, *Hark! The Village Wait,* before the Woods duo left. They were replaced by Martin Carthy (already a star on the British folk scene) and Peter Knight. With this incarnation the famous Steeleye Span sound—characterized by Prior's crystal-clear soprano and the ensemble's precise choral harmonies over electric instrumental backing led by fiddle and electric guitar—began to develop. The second configuration both played live and recorded two remarkable albums, *Please to See the King* and *Ten Man Mop or Mr. Reservoir Butler Rides Again.* After those projects, Carthy and Hutchings departed. Hutchings began his life-long career of producing English-rooted contemporary music, which has included leading all the various permutations of the Albion Country Band and being involved with many special one-off projects. Carthy returned to solo work, but his résumé since has also impressively included membership in the Albion Country Band, the Watersons, Brass Monkey, and Waterson:Carthy. Stepping in for Hutchings and

Carthy were Bob Johnson and Rick Kemp. With these new members, Steeleye Span was in for its headiest period yet, which included hit singles in Britain and regular concert tours of that country, North America, and continental Europe. The group's style became definitive upon this incarnation, with even tighter vocal harmonies and rhythms derived from rocked-up courtly dances. Drummer Nigel Pegrum came on board in time to record *Now We Are Six,* which cemented the group's "medieval Jefferson Airplane" sound. The next big changes came when Johnson and Knight left in 1977 after producing an outside recording, *The King of Elfland's Daughter.* Carthy rejoined, bringing with him accordionist/vocalist John Kirkpatrick. Kirkpatrick's accordion in turn brought a different color to Steeleye Span's music, and on *Storm Force Ten,* the group's only studio recording in this version, they presented distinctive arrangements of "The Black Freighter" (from *The Threepenny Opera*) and "The Wife of the Soldier." For several years after that, Steeleye Span rested until reforming in 1979 with its mid-'70s membership: Prior, Hart, Johnson, Knight, Kemp, and Pegrum. In 1976 Prior had taken some time off to record an acoustic album with June Tabor—the celebrated *Silly Sisters*—and in 1978 she used the break from Steeleye Span to release two albums of contemporary songs: *Woman in the Wings* and *Changing Winds.* Then, in 1980, Steeleye Span released *Sails of Silver.* After that, Hart left for good; he worked as a producer and issued one solo album. The next Steeleye studio album, *Back in Line,* appeared in 1986 and then came another "Silly Sisters" set (produced by avant-garde folkie Andrew Cronshaw), *No More to the Dance,* in 1988. Steeleye Span's 20th anniversary album, *Tempted and Tried,* appeared the following year, after which the live collection *Tonight's the Night* was released in 1992. In addition to all this Steeleye activity, Prior teamed with "early music" folk ensemble the Carnival Band for a series of tours and recordings that continues to this day. Gay Woods returned to the Steeleye fold in 1994, and her distinctive vocals (just a little rougher and lower than Ms. Prior's) can be heard on Steeleye Span's 1995 release *Time.* In late 1997 Prior officially left Steeleye Span to pursue other projects. That same year saw the release of another solo project, *Flesh and Blood,* which included a mini song-cycle titled "Dramatis Personae." Two years later *Ravenchild* appeared, with two more sets of related songs: the historical "With Napoleon in Russia"; and "In the Company of Ravens," inspired by Prior's work on a documentary about the title beast. *Horkstow Grange,* the first Steeleye Span album without Prior—albeit retaining the group's distinctively elegant folk-rock style—was also released in 1999.

what to buy: Some of Steeleye Span's best-loved songs ("Boys of Bedlam," "False Knight on the Road"), along with fiery instrumentals featuring Martin Carthy on electric guitar (a rare sight now!) and Peter Knight on fiddle, appear on *Please to See the King* 𝄢𝄢𝄢𝄢 (B&C, 1971/Shanachie, 1990, prod. Sandy Roberton). *Below the Salt* 𝄢𝄢𝄢𝄢 (Chrysalis, 1972/Shanachie, 1988, prod. Steeleye Span, Jerry Boys) includes a number of songs that have also become Steeleye classics: the grim supernatural ballad "King Henry"; the more pastoral "Spotted Cow" and "Rosebud in June"; and the band's unforgettable interpretation of "Gaudete," a 16th-century religious piece sung entirely in Latin. The lineup that recorded *Storm Force Ten* 𝄢𝄢𝄢𝄢 (Chrysalis, 1977/BGO, 1996, prod. Steeleye Span, Mike Thompson) only lasted a short time but produced remarkable music. They never toured North America, which makes this album essential for U.S. and Canadian fans. (However, a short reunion set by this configuration was one of the special treats for those who attended "Steeleye Span: The Journey," an eight-hour mega-concert held September 2, 1995, at the Forum in London, England, featuring almost everyone who'd ever been a member of the band.) *Spanning the Years* 𝄢𝄢𝄢𝄢 (Chrysalis, 1995, prod. various) is a compilation sampling tracks from all periods of Steeleye Span's by-then 25-plus year history. The CD booklet includes an informal, informative essay by Prior with John Tobier and Lynda Morrison.

best of the rest:
Hark! The Village Wait 𝄢𝄢𝄢 (RCA, 1970/Shanachie, 1991)
Parcel of Rogues 𝄢𝄢𝄢 (Chrysalis, 1973/Shanachie, 1987)
Live at Last 𝄢𝄢𝄢 (Chrysalis, 1978/BGO, 1997)
Back in Line 𝄢𝄢𝄢 (Shanachie, 1986/Park, 1991)
Tempted and Tried 𝄢𝄢𝄢 (Shanachie, 1989)
Time 𝄢𝄢𝄢 (Shanachie, 1995)
Horkstow Grange 𝄢𝄢𝄢 (Park, 1999)

worth searching for: There have been two Steeleye Span concert videos released in the United States: *A 20th Anniversary Celebration* (Shanachie, 1989) and *Steeleye Span 25 Live* (Teal Entertainment/Wienerworld Limited/Anchor Bay Entertainment, 1995).

solo outings:
Maddy Prior:
Woman in the Wings 𝄢𝄢𝄢𝄢 (Chrysalis, 1978/BGO, 1994)
Changing Winds 𝄢𝄢𝄢 (Chrysalis, 1978)
Year 𝄢𝄢𝄢𝄢 (Park, 1993)
Memento: The Best of Maddy Prior 𝄢𝄢𝄢𝄢 (Park, 1995)
Flesh and Blood 𝄢𝄢𝄢𝄢 (Park, 1997)
Ravenchild N/A (Park, 1999)

Tim Hart:
Tim Hart 𝄢𝄢𝄢 (Chrysalis 1979/BGO, 1997)

Peter Knight:
Ancient Cause 𝄢𝄢𝄢 (Shanachie, 1991)

Maddy Prior & Tim Hart:
Folk Songs of Old England Volume I 𝄢𝄢𝄢 (Mooncrest, 1968)
Folk Songs of Old England Volume II 𝄢𝄢𝄢 (Mooncrest, 1968)
Summer Solstice 𝄢𝄢𝄢 (Mooncrest, 1971/Shanachie, 1991)

Maddy Prior & June Tabor:
Silly Sisters 𝄢𝄢𝄢𝄢 (Chrysalis, 1976/Shanachie, 1988)
No More to the Dance 𝄢𝄢𝄢𝄢 (Shanachie, 1988)

Maddy Prior and the Carnival Band:
A Tapestry of Carols 𝄢𝄢𝄢 (Saydisc, 1987)
Sing Lustily and with Good Courage 𝄢𝄢𝄢 (Saydisc, 1990)
Carols and Capers 𝄢𝄢𝄢 (Park, 1991)
Hang Up Sorrow and Care 𝄢𝄢𝄢𝄢 (Park, 1995)

Rick Kemp:
Escape 𝄢𝄢𝄢 (Fellside, 1997)

influences:
◀◀ The Copper Family, Young Tradition, Jefferson Airplane, Fairport Convention, the Watersons, Mr. Fox

▶▶ Connie Dover, Clarion, Garmarna, Värttinä, Blyth Power, Pyewackett, Spriguns, Hedgehog Pie, the New St. George (USA), the Klezmatics, Polly Bolton, Iron Horse

see also: *Martin Carthy, Shirley Collins, Andrew Cronshaw, Fairport Convention, Ashley Hutchings, Trevor Lucas, Ewan MacColl, Maddy Prior, Sweeney's Men*

Ken Roseman

Stellamara
Worldbeat
Formed 1997, in San Francisco, CA, USA. Based in San Francisco, CA, USA.

Sonja Drakulich, voice, bendir, riqq, zills, keyboard samples; Jeffery Stott, oud, darabouka, bendir, hammered dulcimer, guitar, bells, keyboard samples. (Both members are from USA.)

Worldbeat duo Stellamara have fashioned their alternative earth-pop from familiar sources—the choral music of medieval Europe, the rhythms of North Africa, the polyphonic vocal styles of Eastern Europe, and new-age/electronica textures—but they give these elements their own uniquely melancholy spin.

what to buy: *Star of the Sea* 𝄢𝄢𝄢 (City of Tribes, 1997, prod. Sonja Drakulich, Jeffery Stott) shows how, unlike many ethno/ambient groups, Stellamara always place the soothing synth tones in service of the music. Dead Can Dance is the obvious reference for lazy critics, but Stellamara's sound is more organic and down-to-earth.

influences:
◀◀ Madredeus, Popul Vuh, Dead Can Dance

j. poet

Andy M. Stewart

Scottish and Irish traditional

Born 1952, in Perthshire, Scotland. Based in Scotland.

Andy M. Stewart is one of the greatest living interpreters of traditional Scottish and Irish songs. As a member of the historically crucial band Silly Wizard, and later as a solo singer and as part of several duos, Stewart has taken his rich, sweet voice and produced definitive versions of some of the gems of the traditions he preserves. He has also been an important interpreter of the works of poet Robert Burns and of other folk-revival songwriters, and the author/composer of some of his own that have become revival standards. Although Stewart comes from a well-known extended family of singers, his experiences as a professional musician began in high school, in Blairgowrie, the town where he was raised. He and several schoolmates, including Dougie MacLean and Martin Hadden, formed a folk band called Puddock's Well. They gigged around the Scottish Highlands and served as the house band at their local folk club. They were happy to be playing music, and upon finishing school they all got day jobs and kept at the band in the evenings. One of the gigs Puddock's Well landed in the early 1970s was as the opening act for a trio called Silly Wizard. The two groups hit it off, and when the chaps in Silly Wizard found themselves short a few members, they called Stewart and Hadden to fill their ranks. After a few more reorganizations, the lineup stabilized with Stewart on voice and tenor banjo, Hadden on bass, Gordon Jones on voice and guitar, Phil Cunningham on accordion and keyboards, and Johnny Cunningham on fiddle. They were a powerhouse band, one of the most successful acts the Scottish folk scene ever produced. In addition to packing as much fun as he could into his years with the legendary band, Stewart made use of his association with Silly Wizard to cement his reputation as a consummate performer and songwriter. In his time with them he supplied many staples of both Silly Wizard's repertoire and the modern folk canon, including "The Queen of Argyll," "The Ramlin' Rover," "The Blackbird," "Golden, Golden," and "A Lover's Heart." In 1985, during a break from the band, Stewart was slated to go on tour with Phil Cunningham when the latter got into a bad car accident. Stewart called Irish guitarist and bouzouki player Manus Lunny. Lunny agreed to fill in, and a new partnership emerged that lasted six years and carried Stewart beyond the breakup of Silly Wizard in 1988. The two toured many times and released four albums; one as a trio with Phil Cunningham, one credited as a Stewart solo disc, and the other two as "Andy M. Stewart and Manus Lunny." By 1991 Lunny's main gig was with Scottish folk-pop band Capercaillie, and he was no longer able to be Stewart's touring partner. Another Irish guitarist, Gerry O'Beirne, stepped in to fill his shoes, and still regularly tours with Stewart today. The pair has released two CDs, credited as Stewart solo discs but arranged and produced largely by O'Beirne.

what to buy: *Dublin Lady* 🎵🎵🎵🎵 (Green Linnet, 1987, prod. Manus Lunny, Andy M. Stewart), recorded with Lunny, is a classic of the genre, on which Stewart interprets some fine old songs. Tracks include Stewart's lovely version of "Bogie's Bonnie Belle" as well as the hilarious Irish drinking song "The Humours of Whiskey," both of which are definitive performances. "Dinny the Piper," a great ballad from the 1798 rebellion in Ireland, tells of a misunderstanding involving a soldier, a bagpipe player, and an apparently carnivorous cow—perhaps the first recorded case of Mad Cow Disease? Two of the original songs on this album, "Take Her in Your Arms" and "Where Are You (Tonight I Wonder)," have become favorites on the folk revival circuit, with numerous cover versions on the market. In addition to the fine singing by Stewart, Lunny contributes vocals to one song and guitar and bouzouki accompaniment throughout the disc. Other accompanists include Phil Cunningham (accordion, keyboards), Aly Bain (fiddle), and Sean Og Potts (uilleann pipes and whistles).

what to buy next: *Donegal Rain* 🎵🎵🎵🎵 (Green Linnet, 1997, prod. Gerry O'Beirne) is another refreshing album of folk standards and new treasures. Some of the traditional ballads recorded here will stand as the authoritative versions of magnificent songs; Stewart's version of "Matt Hyland," a rare Scottish ballad with a happy ending, hasn't been outdone on record, and his treatment of "The Banks of Sweet Dundee" is absolutely beautiful. "The Irish Stranger" is given an appropriately solemn treatment, as is "Ramblin' Irishman"; both are sad songs of emigration, but with glimmers of hope and perseverance. More lighthearted material is here as well, mostly songs of sexual dalliance like "Tibbie Fowler o' the Glen" and "Queen Amangst the Heather." Three Stewart originals fill out the album's 11 selections. The arrangements are a nice blend of the Celtic and acoustic with a touch of rock 'n' roll here and there. *Man in the Moon* 🎵🎵🎵🎵 (Green Linnet, 1994, prod. Gerry O'Beirne) features accompaniments by O'Beirne as well as other top names in Irish and Scottish music, but the focus is on Stewart's resonant voice. Several well-known traditional songs are given the Stewart treatment, including "The Echo Mocks the Corncrake," "The Gaberlunzie Man," and "The Lakes of Ponchartrain." In addition, he has adapted words by Thomas Moore, Sir Walter Scott, and others. There are two songs in particular that will stand out in the memories of Stewart's fans. "The Errant Apprentice" was written by Bill Watkins and set to music by Stewart and O'Beirne. It's a clever, if somewhat bizarre, ballad about a failed love affair, and its hilarious words and simple tune will remind fans of "The Ramblin' Rover," one of Stewart's best-loved songs from Wizard days. "The Land of the Leal" appeared on Silly Wizard's very first (and now very hard-to-find) LP. Like that album, *Man in the Moon* ends with this sweet and moving song about heaven. *By the Hush* ♪♪♪♪ (Green Linnet, 1983, prod. Phil Cunningham), released at the height of Silly Wizard's popularity, was Stewart's first album without the band. It features two songs, "The Ramblin' Rover" and "The Parish of Dunkeld," that were highlights of the Wizards' early repertoire, and these versions suffer a bit in comparison with the band's arrangements. The other songs, mostly slow sad ballads, are lovingly arranged and performed—the painful tales of Patrick Sheehan's enlistment and of an unnamed Irishman's emigration to a Civil War-torn America get a silky-smooth treatment by Stewart rather than the usual harder-edged arrangements of angrier singers. Stewart's originals deal with unhealed wounds, both personal and political. In all, this is Stewart's darkest and most melancholy album, with unfulfilled longings haunting almost all the songs; his honeyed voice is the perfect vehicle for them. As a testament to its quality, the collection was named *Melody Maker*'s Folk Album of the Year in 1983.

the rest:

(With Manus Lunny and Phil Cunningham) *Fire in the Glen* ♪♪♪
   (Shanachie, 1985)
(With Manus Lunny) *At It Again* ♪♪♪ (Green Linnet, 1990)
Songs of Robert Burns ♪♪♪ (Green Linnet, 1991)

influences:

◄◄ Archie Fisher, Lucy Stewart, Silly Wizard

►► Ed Miller, Tony Cuffe

see also: *Boys of the Lough, Capercaillie, Phil Cunningham, Dougie MacLean, Silly Wizard*

Steve Winick

Alan Stivell

Harp, Celtic rock, fusion
Born Alan Cochevelou, January 1944, in Riom, Auvergne, France.
Based in Paris, France.

Alan Cochevelou (who later took the pseudonym Stivell) made his public debut playing the Breton (French Celtic) harp in 1953, at age nine. The harp had been built by Jord Cochevelou, his father, based on the plans of the famous medieval Irish "Brian Boru" harp, and was the first of this ancient type in Brittany. So Stivell can justifiably lay claim to having been the first person to play the "Breton Harp," but only with the qualifying explanation that it was built from Irish plans—a distinction not incompatible with the much wider cultural fusions he would attempt in his music later on. In time, Stivell learned to play the *bombarde* (Breton bagpipes); the double-reeded *shawm* or oboe; and the Scottish bagpipes. He joined the Bagad Bleimor, or Bleimor Pipe Band, in 1954; became the band's *pen-sonneur*, or

head piper, in 1961; and won the 1966 pipe-band championships (also winning championships for his duo piping with friend Youenn Sicard). During the same period, he made the first-ever recordings of Breton harp music, beginning with a few singles and EPs in 1959. Still not creatively complacent after proving himself in all these ways, he set out to innovate in the fields of Breton folk, Celtic rock, and world music. Stivell's groundbreaking albums of the early 1970s chronicle his explorations of Breton music for ensembles. These albums, including *Reflets* (1970), *Renaissance de la Harpe Celtique* (1971), *A l'Olympia* (1972), *Chemins de Terre* (1973), and *E Langonned* (1974), revolutionized the music of his native region. They introduced the Celtic harp to the Breton recording scene, and admitted influences from the folk music of Ireland, Scotland, Wales, and the United States, as well as from classical, pop, and rock 'n' roll. The resultant catalog resembled, in Stivell's words, "an inventory of the possibilities for untried marriages of instruments." As the years progressed Stivell indeed tried everything from orchestral arrangements to new-age soundscapes to rock, all in the context of the Celtic melodies of Brittany. He is undoubtedly the single most influential figure on the Breton music scene: his ideas about arranging this music for ensembles have affected every band since his own during the early '70s, and his introduction of the harp to Brittany influenced a whole generation of performers on that instrument.

what to buy: *70/95 ZOOM* ♪♪♪♪♪ (Dreyfus, 1997, prod. Alan Stivell) is a two-CD compilation of Stivell's most influential recordings from his 1970 full-length debut to 1995. It features all the styles in which Stivell has played, from early, simple harp arrangements of traditional dance tunes; through mid-period compositions evoking Breton folk stories as well as exploring acoustic ensemble playing, gentle new-age music, and fiery folk-rock; and beyond to quasi-symphonic compositions. In accordance with Stivell's Pan-Celtic idealism, there is a lot of Irish and Scottish music here alongside the more purely Breton traditionals and newer compositions. This set can serve not only as an introduction to Stivell's music, but also as a road map to his many albums; he has played in so many styles it's hard to guide listeners to any one that's definitive.

what to buy next: *70/95 ZOOM* is the best point of departure, but as a rule, practically all of Stivell's LPs are worth hearing. *Renaissance of the Celtic Harp* ♪♪♪♪ (Rounder, 1972/Dreyfus, 1994, prod. Franck Giboni) stands up remarkably well after more than 25 years, and shows the seeds of many of Stivell's future ideas: orchestral arrangements, proto-new-age flourishes, and rock 'n' roll influences are beginning to make their way into his music. The second side of the original LP—and last track on the CD—is a 19-minute foray into Gaelic music from Scotland, Ireland, and the Isle of Man, ingeniously compiled and boldly arranged. *Live in Dublin* 🎵🎵🎵 (Dreyfus, 1975/1994, prod. Alan Stivell, Peter Rice) captures an important Stivell folk-rock band. A couple of years after electric guitarist Gabriel Yacoub (himself quite influential) had left to form the group Malicorne, this lineup still packed a great deal of punch when it was captured live in '75. The album's excellent players of bagpipe, bombarde, fiddle, flute, organ, bass, drums, and harp are capable of a wide variety of textures and a rich, full sound— and they deliver all they promise, from gentle harp airs to bouncy Irish dance tunes to fairly heavy rockish arrangements. Electric guitarist Dan Ar Braz (who played briefly with the *English* folk innovators Fairport Convention) and piper Patrick Molard have gone on to two of the most important solo and band careers in Brittany. *Again* 🎵🎵🎵 (Dreyfus, 1993, prod. Alan Stivell, Kate Bush) includes new renditions of some of Stivell's seminal mid-'70s hits, with more of a world-music/pop flavor this time around—not surprising with guests like Kate Bush and the Pogues' Shane MacGowan. *Harpes du Nouvel Age* 🎵🎵🎵 (Rounder, 1985) is an album of harp music arranged by someone who should know: Stivell's father, the harpmaker Jord Cochevelou. It's got a lot of Irish and Scottish music on it, as well as the many requisite Breton tunes. Mostly low-key, it would be appropriate for new-age fans, as its translated title suggests. For those who share Stivell's love not only of new-age sounds but also Celtic mythology, choral arrangements, and complex compositions, *Celtic Symphony* 🎵🎵🎵 (Dreyfus, 1979) should fit the bill, though it's impressive more for its scope and atmosphere than for electrifying performances. This exploration of Stivell's most grand ambitions is contrasted intriguingly by his earliest creative stirrings. *Telenn geltiek— Harpe celtique* 🎵🎵🎵🎵 (Dreyfus, 1994) is a reissue of the very first, all-instrumental sides the young Alan Cochevelou cut in 1959 and 1961, long out of print and forgotten until their recent resurrection. These 40-year-old recordings sound amazingly clear, and show the precocious teenage harper playing mostly Irish and Scottish material, with just a smattering of Breton. Tunes like "The Wearin' of the Green," "The Derry Air," "Ye Banks an' Braes," and "Loch Lomond" would become well-known to a much larger audience in the ensuing years, as popularized by other performers. An almost-lost revelation from before all that, *Telenn geltiek* is a fascinating glimpse into the pre-'60s Celtic revival period, and shows just how far ahead of the curve Stivell was at such a tender age. From there it was on to more landmarks: *Chemins de Terre* 🎵🎵🎵🎵 (Mercury, 1973/Dreyfus, 1994, prod. Franck Giboni) was one of Stivell's first forays into Celtic rock with an all-star band. It's a brilliant album, which was fittingly released in the U.K. as *From Celtic Roots*. The live album *A l'Olympia* 🎵🎵🎵🎵 (Mercury, 1972/Dreyfus, 1988, prod. Franck Giboni) features many of the same players as *Chemins de Terre,* but on a different set of songs, and is equally impressive. *E Langonned* 🎵🎵🎵🎵 (Mercury, 1974, prod.

Philippe Lerichomme), one of Stivell's most underrated albums, was a sort of antidote to the previous two, with completely acoustic renditions of Breton, Irish, Scottish, and Welsh folk music. The sleeve notes, a manifesto explaining Stivell's ideas about music and life, are as interesting as the album itself. Much later, for *1 Douar (One World)* 🎵🎵🎵 (Dreyfus, 1998, prod. various), Stivell finally went the whole hog worldbeat-wise, roping in stars Youssou N'Dour (Senegal) and Khaled (Algeria) as well as Paddy Moloney of the Chieftains (Ireland), Jim Kerr of Simple Minds (Scotland), and John Cale (Wales). Stivell's titular message of global harmony is matched by its stylistic subtext of international synthesis. A fascinating Afro Celtic connection is forged with N'Dour, his and the headliner's rather different voices intertwining as effortlessly—on two different renditions of the same song—as do the Breton harp and the West African harp-like *kora* backing them up.

the rest:

Reflets 🎵🎵🎵 (Mercury, 1970/Dreyfus, 1994)
Journée à la maison 🎵🎵🎵 (Dreyfus, 1978)
Legende 🎵🎵 (Celtic Music, 1983)
The Mist of Avalon 🎵🎵 (Dreyfus, 1991)
Brian Boru 🎵🎵🎵 (Dreyfus 1995)

influences:

⏪ Sean Ó Riada, the Chieftains, Bagad Bleimor, Goadec Sisters, Afro Celt Sound System

⏩ Malicorne, Gabriel Yacoub, Dan Ar Braz, Kornog, Gwerz, Afro Celt Sound System

see also: *Dan Ar Braz, the Chieftains, Khaled, Youssou N'Dour, the Pogues*

Steve Winick

Strunz & Farah

World, new age, flamenco fusion
Formed 1979, in Los Angeles, CA, USA. Based in Los Angeles, CA, USA.

Jorge Strunz, guitar; Ardeshir Farah, guitar; Luis Conte, percussion (1980–present); Guillermo Guzman, electric bass (1990–93); Juanito "Long John" Oliva, Afro-Cuban percussion, cajon (1990–94); Luis Perez Ixoneztli, pre-Columbian winds and percussion, vocals (1990–93); Paul Tchounga, drums (1990–present); Eliseo Borreo, electric bass, vocals (1993–present); Cassio Duarte, percussion (1994–present).

While they often get pegged as flamenco or new age, this fiery worldbeat combo falls into neither pigeonhole. Led by the acoustic guitar pyrotechnics of Jorge Strunz and Ardeshir Farah, the six-piece band assimilates Afro-Latin, Arabic, and Spanish influences into a melting pot that transcends easy categorization. The group's sound has progressed and matured since its inception, moving from the raw power of *Mosaico,* to the nocturnal moods of *Misterio,* to the fascinating world fusion sounds of *Primal Magic.* Each album offers its own trademark, whether it's the progressive structures of *Guitarras* or the primal worldbeat of *Americas.* What keeps their music fresh is that Strunz & Farah have played in other formats. Strunz recorded four albums with the 1970s Latin/jazz fusion group Caldera, and Farah played pop music with Iranian musicians in the late 1970s. Although many world-music groups do not tend to sell in large numbers, this one has done very well over the years. *Primal Magic* and *Americas* are both close to gold status, with the latter being nominated for a Grammy as Best World Music album in 1992.

what to buy: *Live* ♫♫♫♪ (Selva, 1997, prod. Strunz & Farah, Kathlyn Powell) nicely captures the band's inspiring energy. Songs from their previous three recordings are played, and the musicians really get to display their chops, from the powerful rhythm section to the extended solos of the guitarists themselves, who sound like they could race across the frets all night long. *Primal Magic* ♫♫♫♫ (Mesa/Blue Moon, 1990, prod. Strunz & Farah) started a new trend among young flamenco/Spanish guitar wannabes. While Flamenco stylings certainly play a part in the music, the exotic pre-Columbian winds of Luis Perez and the band's Afro-Latin rhythm section flesh out a sophisticated sound that is both mystical and uplifting, yielding an inspired recording. *Americas* ♫♫♫♪ (Mesa/Blue Moon, 1992, prod. Strunz & Farah) followed this path and is also quite noteworthy. *Mosaico* ♫♫♫♫ (Mesa/Blue Moon, 1982) features some truly blistering guitar work that will not fail to move you. There is no such thing as a bad Strunz & Farah record, but fans of their other 1990s material will probably find *Misterio* ♫♫♫ (AudioQuest, 1991) very mellow; it consists of the headline duo and guitarist Ciro Hurtado (on three tracks) without a rhythm section. But it still stands on its own, and offers romantic guitar musings perfect for late-night listening.

the rest:
Frontera ♫♫♫♪ (Milestone, 1984)
Guitarras ♫♫♫♪ (Milestone, 1985)
Heat of the Sun ♫♫♫♪ (Selva, 1995)
Wild Muse ♫♫♫♪ (Selva, 1998)

see also: *Dr. L. Subramaniam*

Bryan Reesman

Dr. L. Subramaniam

Indian classical/fusion

Born 1947, in Madras, India. Based in India, Europe, and Los Angeles, CA, USA.

Violin playing seems to run strongly in Dr. L. Subramaniam's family. At the age of five he began studying the South Indian

karnatak style of the instrument with his father, master violinist V. Lakshminarayana—who also taught his brothers, L. Shankar and L. Vaidyanathan, both later distinguished in this area as well. It seems fitting that Subramaniam would eventually become famous in the West for his excursions in East-West fusion, as the Indian violin was itself the result of such a fusion at the beginning of the nineteenth century. Subramaniam's interest in the music of other cultures began at an early age, when he heard elements of Indian classical music in a composition by Bach. His father encouraged him to keep "an open ear and an open mind." After establishing himself as a respected karnatak musician in his native land, Subramaniam came to Los Angeles, and by the late '70s and early '80s was collaborating with jazz legends like Stanley Clarke, Herbie Hancock, and Tony Williams on recordings that fused Indian classical influences with jazz, rock, funk, and even flamenco. Since the mid-'80s he has primarily concentrated his energies on commissioned orchestral pieces, and soundtrack work for the films of Indian director Mira Nair (*Mississippi Masala* and *Salaam Bombay!*). He also continues to head an annual fusion-music festival started in India in 1991, but has released no new material since the tragic death of his wife. An unfinished reunion project with former collaborator and fellow violinist Stephane Grapelli, featuring Herbie Hancock and guitarist Larry Coryell, currently remains unmixed on the shelf.

what to buy: Although Subramaniam has performed extensively in a variety of East-West contexts, much of this work falls short of that by contemporaries like Zakir Hussain, Trilok Gurtu, and even his brother, L. Shankar, as it fails to utilize Subramaniam's Indian musical background to its full potential. For a pure, unadulterated glimpse of this phenomenal violin virtuoso at his finest, check out *Raga Hemavati* ♫♫♫♫ (Nimbus, 1990), a masterful, 64-minute epic classical *raga* featuring Subramaniam's hypnotic melodic runs on violin and deft accompaniment by percussionist K. Shekar, all building to an invigorating crescendo that will leave you breathless. Only slightly less rewarding is the more melancholy *Three Ragas for Solo Violin* ♫♫♫♫ (Nimbus, 1991), which was dedicated to his father and guru, who had recently passed away. The tone of these three unaccompanied ragas is somber and reflective, but the mesmerizing melodies delicately explored therein are possibly even more gorgeous than those on *Raga Hemavati.*

what to buy next: Though none of Subramaniam's fusion recordings are absolute must-haves, *Spanish Wave* ♫♫♫♪ (Milestone, 1983, prod. L. Subramaniam) is a compelling experiment mixing elements of jazz, rock, funk, Indian classical music, and flamenco into a uniquely distinctive sonic smorgasbord. The tracks featuring Spanish guitarist Jorge Strunz, *tabla* drum legend Alla Rakha, and karnatak percussionist Guruvayoor Dorai work best, standing out among a relatively tepid batch of tunes that occasionally border on the wanky sort of noodling that gives jazz fusion a bad name.

the rest:

Indian Express 🎝🎝 (1984, Milestone)

(With Stephane Grapelli) *Conversations* 🎝🎝🎝 (1984, Milestone)

Mani & Co. 🎝🎝🎝 (1986, Milestone)

Sarasvati (Water Lily Acoustics, 1990)

Kalyani (Water Lily Acoustics, 1990)

worth searching for: Thankfully, in the '90s Subramaniam has steered away from jazz fusion and stuck more toward the traditional side of his sound, with brief but enjoyable excursions into soundtrack work as well. Two of his most brilliant Indian classical recordings, *South Indian Strings* and *The Virtuoso Violin of South India,* only recently went out of print, but you may still be able to locate copies on cassette if you start looking *now,* and look you should. On the soundtrack side, his original scores for the films *Mississippi Masala* and *Salaam Bombay!* are both impressive, with the former exploring an intriguing East-West hybrid far more rewarding than any of his mid-'80s work.

influences:

◀◀ V. Lakshminarayana, Oregon, Shakti, Ravi Shankar

▶▶ Material, Cornershop, Talvin Singh

see also: *L. Shankar, Strunz & Farah, T. H. "Vikku" Vinayakram*

Bret Love

Sukay

Andean

Formed 1975, in San Francisco CA, USA. Based in San Francisco, CA, USA.

Quentin Howard (a.k.a. Quentin Howard Navia, USA), vocals, wind instruments; Eddy Navia (Bolivia), charango, guitar, bass, mandolin (1989–present); Gabriel Navia (Bolivia), charango (1993–present); Isaac Lopez, wind instruments (1995–present); Enrique Coria (Argentina), guitar, bass (1990–93); Alcides Mejia (Bolivia), wind instruments, percussion (1990–94); Yuri Ortuño (Bolivia), vocals (1986–87, 1995); Mauricio San Martin (Bolivia), wind instruments (1991–93); Omar Sepulveda (Chile), charango (1985–88, 1992–94); Carlos Crespo (Bolivia), wind instruments (1985–88); Edmond Badoux (USA), (1975–85); Javier Canelas (Bolivia) (1978–81); Gonzalo Vargas (Bolivia) (1978–84). (Instruments of some members unspecified; some members exchange listed instruments.)

Andean music derives much of its aural impact from the timbral qualities of its ancient wind instruments. One of these is the Andean pan-pipe, called the *siku* or *zampoña,* a closed-end set of pipes that produces a pungent, sibilant sound (and which can range in size from 7 inches to 54 inches for the largest, bass variety). Another is the *kena,* a simple flute with a plaintive tone. The oldest scales played on these wind instruments were pentatonic, and the traces of these mournful patterns still shape Andean music today. A more modern addition to the Andean ensemble is the *charango,* a 12-stringed treble guitar with a body often fashioned from an armadillo shell. The arrangement of the strings into pairs gives the charango a sound that is quite akin to that of a mandolin, and the rapid strumming often employed on charango provides a rhythmic complement to the melody of the sikus and flutes.

Sukay was formed by Quentin Howard, a graphic artist from Brooklyn, New York. Upon hearing Andean traditional music for the first time in the 1970s at a folk festival in upstate New York, Howard felt a strong attraction to its spiritual, mysterious quality; as Howard describes it, "that sound went right to the heart of me." Soon she was heading to South America, where she spent 15 months traveling with musician and folklorist Edmond Badoux in Peru, Bolivia, and Ecuador, studying the music and culture of the Andean region and digging up traditional songs. Along with Badoux and a pair of musicians they met in Bolivia, she formed the first incarnation of Sukay in 1975, releasing an album, *Music of the Andes,* in 1978, and eventually making a flurry of recordings with a newly configured group in the mid-1980s. With the addition of famed Bolivian charango master Eddy Navia in 1989, Sukay took a turn toward refined arrangements and musical experimentation. But the group has never strayed too far from direct (albeit urbane) interpretations of various traditional genres known to its chosen region's Aymara and Quechua peoples. Perennially in demand as leading ambassadors of Andean music and culture, the members of Sukay appear at conferences, workshops, and concerts worldwide.

what to buy: Of Sukay's recent releases, *Return of the Inca* 🎝🎝🎝🎝 (Sukay World Music, 1991, prod. Sukay) is the finest. Recorded with help from bluegrass legend David Grisman, *Inca* adds a degree of sophistication to the typical raw Andean sound, with Navia and Grisman providing masterful string flourishes. *The Sukay Workbook* 🎝🎝🎝🎝 (MelBay Publications, 1998) is a delightful book-and-CD combination, written and beautifully designed by Howard. The book includes sheet music for various Sukay songs; lessons on kena, zampoña, and charango technique; and even a set of instructions on how to build a kena. The disc, *Instrumental Music of the Andes,* compiles cuts from Sukay's years on the Flying Fish label and more recent releases, with the whole package costing only a few dollars more than the CD would alone.

what to buy next: While most Sukay albums are largely instrumental, *Love Songs of the Andes* 🎝🎝🎝🎝 (Sukay World Music, 1995, prod. Eddy Navia, Quentin Howard) presents an appealing variety of vocal selections.

the rest:

Instrumental Music of the Andes 𝄢𝄢𝄢 (Flying Fish, 1989/Sukay World Music, 1996)

Cumbre (The Summit) 𝄢𝄢𝄢 (Sukay World Music, 1990/1995)

Naivdad Andina 𝄢𝄢𝄢 (Sukay World Music, 1993)

Encueritros (Meetings) 𝄢𝄢𝄢 (Sukay World Music, 1995)

worth searching for: The out-of-print Flying Fish releases culled on *The Sukay Workbook* are all worth having in whole if you can find them; scan the used record shops for: *Music of the Andes* 𝄢𝄢𝄢 (Flying Fish, 1978), *Socavon* 𝄢𝄢𝄢 (Flying Fish, 1985), *Tutayay* 𝄢𝄢𝄢 (Flying Fish, 1986), *Mama Luna* 𝄢𝄢𝄢 (Flying Fish, 1987), and *Huayrasan* 𝄢𝄢𝄢𝄢 (Flying Fish, 1988).

solo outings:

Eddy Navia:

En Charango (Sukay World Music)

Mozart en Machu Picchu 𝄢𝄢𝄢 (Sukay World Music, 1995)

influences:

◀◀ Village music of the Andes

Jeffrey Muhr

Yma Sumac

Incan and South American folk

Born Zoila Emperatriz Charrari del Castillo, c. 1921–28, in Ichocan, Peru. Based in Los Angeles, CA, USA.

The woman North America came to know as Yma Sumac developed a phenomenal voice with what is often reported to have been a five-octave range. (Granted, this sounds unlikely, but objective observers documented that she could indeed span four-and-a-half octaves.) She was discovered at an early age and performed on radio and in movies throughout South America. In the 1940s she came to the U.S., and in 1950 signed with Capitol Records, where she was paired with the incomparable Les Baxter as arranger. Sumac made a career singing Americanized versions of Incan and South American folk songs, until leaving the label in 1959. She continued performing regularly and recording whenever there was interest—just as she does today.

what to buy: *Voice of the Xtabay* 𝄢𝄢𝄢 (The Right Stuff, 1996, prod. Les Baxter) is a reissue compiling Sumac's original *Voice of the Xtabay* and *Inca Taqul* albums, her most popular releases; the former includes some great work by Baxter. *Mambo! Yma Sumac* 𝄢𝄢𝄢 (The Right Stuff, 1996, reissue prod. Tom Cartwright) is exactly what the title advertises, with tracks such as "Bo Mambo," "Goomba Boomba," "Malambo No. 1," and "Five Bottle Mambo."

the rest:

Sampler Exotica 𝄢𝄢𝄢 (EMD/Capitol, 1996)

Legend of the Sun Virgin 𝄢𝄢𝄢 (The Right Stuff, 1996)

Legend of the Jivaro 𝄢𝄢𝄢 (The Right Stuff, 1996)

Fuego Del Ande 𝄢𝄢𝄢 (The Right Stuff, 1996)

worth searching for: *Miracles* 𝄢𝄢𝄢 (London, 1972) is an uncommon rock outing. Sumac also cut a track for *Stay Awake: Interpretations of Vintage Disney Films* 𝄢𝄢𝄢 (A&M, 1988), an homage to the mouse factory by various modern artists.

influences:

◀◀ Les Baxter, Perez Prado, Xavier Cugat, Martin Denny, Juan Garcia Esquivel, Rosemary Clooney

▶▶ Combustible Edison, Love Jones

Jim DeRogatis

Ron Sunsinger

Traditional Native American, electronic, ambient

Born 1957, in California, USA. Based in Albuquerque, NM, USA.

An adopted grandson of the Cheyenne, Lakota, and Hopi tribes, Sunsinger is a musician, studio-owner, ceremonial artist, and craftsman (he makes ritual objects used by tribal shamans). A collaboration with studio wizard Michael Stearns resulted in 1994's *Singing Stones,* an exploration of the aural and spiritual mysteries of Native American religious practice. Use of ceremonially decorated "singing stones" struck on granite outcroppings at certain ritual sites in the Southwest was discovered to produce chimes of the utmost clarity and depth. Archaeological evidence indicates such places were sacred at a time long before recorded history. Sunsinger and Stearns got permission from tribal elders to bring recording equipment to one site, and captured sonic phenomena of an almost eerie beauty and power. The two later collaborated with Steve Roach on *Kiva.*

what to buy: *Singing Stones* 𝄢𝄢𝄢𝄢 (Fathom/Hearts of Space, 1994, prod. Michael Stearns, Ron Sunsinger), with its resonant title implements backed by traditional Native American singers and instrumentation, as well as synths, tape-loops, a Tibetan singing bowl, and the ambient coyotes and crickets of the Apache Ridge, is a brilliant achievement. Soaring, rippling, indeed hallucinogenic tones combine with the elemental dignity and simplicity of the subject matter to produce a music evocative of ghosts and ancient belief. It is majestic, visionary work, and a must-have for lovers of world music and psychic innerspace.

what to buy next: Musical world explorer Steve Roach joined the pair for *Kiva* 𝄢𝄢𝄢 (Fathom/Hearts of Space, 1995, prod. Steve Roach, Michael Stearns, Ron Sunsinger). A "kiva" is described as "an unbroken circle of the Earth . . . the church within her womb," and the album attempts to capture the ecstasies of four types of Native American ceremony. Sunsinger's

"Mother Ayahuasca" is a 15-minute meditation inspired by a psychedelic sacrament made from the bark of a South American jungle vine. All three artists collaborate on the ethereal closing track, "Trust and Remember." The album is a very worthy follow-up to *Singing Stones,* but without the former's free-fall spaciness.

influences:

◄◄ Tangerine Dream, Mother Earth

see also: *Steve Roach*

Ron Garmon

Super Rail Band of Bamako

See: Rail Band

Super Cat

Dancehall, ragga

Born William Maragh, 1963, in Kingston, Jamaica. Based in Kingston, Jamaica.

Born of mixed African and East Indian descent, William Maragh's surname is Hindi for "great king" or "king of kings," though his music has always championed the pauper. Maragh was dubbed Super Cat while serving a term in Jamaica's General Penitentiary in the early '80s—mainly because of his ability to always land on his feet. Once free, Super Cat approached the microphone with a new ferocity, and became the top deejay at Stereo Mars and Kilimanjaro Sound Systems. At the latter, fellow deejay Early B gave him the second half of his nickname—"The Wild Apache"—in punning reference to his heritage. Super Cat first distinguished himself on wax in 1985 with "Trash & Ready," an excellent toast (reggae rap) over the famed "Sleng Teng" rhythm. A year later, with former Technique Winston Riley producing, he released "Boops," a memorably humorous rant about wealthy sugar daddies and their sweet-toothed young female companions. The song is now considered a deejay classic in Jamaica and at the time spawned a string of sequels from other artists. Blessed with an international perspective, his superb "Mud Up" single featured some extraordinary hip-hop scratching and turntablism. In the late '80s, Super Cat founded the Wild Apache imprint and subsequently released the 12-inch "Too Greedy," an excoriating insider depiction of the ravages of crack cocaine, which had just made a deadly incursion onto the island. In 1991, he teamed with Jamaican-born rapper Heavy D. and dancehall singer Frankie Paul on the compelling "combo" single "Big and Broad." However, rumors swirled when he was pummeled with beer bottles after a poor performance at that year's Sting concert (an annual reggae showcase not related to the gentleman riddim-dabbler of same name) and responded by threatening

to draw a gun on the audience. Mere months later, Super Cat was arrested for the murder of deejay Nitty Gritty, who was shot dead just outside the Super Power record shop in Brooklyn. The Cat was cleared in 1992, though the murder remains unsolved. Wasting no time, Super Cat instantly claimed redemption on the hip-hop–influenced *Don Dada,* the title cut a Godfather-wise microphone rebuke to newly rising deejays Shabba Ranks and Ninjaman. 1995's *The Struggle Continues* sustained Super Cat's place as a deejay elder with a keen and eloquent ability to express the realities of the "sufferah"'s life. His description of *ragga* (digital reggae) music in the book *Reggae Routes* (Kevin Obrien Chang, Temple University Press) could just as easily be an assessment of his own spellbinding microphone excursions: "It's from people coming out of the street. Out of the ghetto. And these are not people that live soft. They live hard. Suffer hard. So what they got to sing about is nothing too soft. They singing about everyday living. Sufferation. What's going on in the ghetto."

what to buy: *The Good, the Better, the Best* ⅊⅊⅊⅊ (Sony, 1999, prod. various) is armed to the hilt with many of Super Cat's greatest and edgiest microphone adventures, including "Ghetto Red Hot," "Too Greedy," "Forgive Me Jah," a wicked hip-hop remix of "Don Dada," the marauding "Scalp Dem" (with Wu-Tang Clan's Method Man), and the old-school dancehall reminiscence "A-Class Rub-a-Dub," a terrific collaboration with deejay originator U-Roy and dancehall progenitor Sugar Minott—from the roots to the fruits, kid! Also included is much of Super Cat's work with his Wild Apache crew, most notably the Jamaican smash "Cabin Stabbin'," which is not a tale about a remote murder, but rather ragga slang for a particularly voracious version of the wild thing. It's a pity that "Boops" and many of the original Jamaican mixes of the above singles were not included.

what to buy next: Available as an import from Ernie B's Reggae (P.O. Box 5019, El Dorado Hills, CA 95762, phone: (916) 939-0578, e-mail: ErnieB@calweb.com), *Si Boops Deh* ⅊⅊⅊⅊ (Techniques, 1986, prod. Winston Riley, Prince Jammy) is a nice companion to the compilation above, as it does include "Boops"—the prized, dancehall-ruling single that showcases Super Cat's aggressive, tongue-rolling style and shrewd, imaginative lyrical flow over Steely & Clevie's digital renovation of the glorious rocksteady rhythm from Marcia Griffiths's "Feel Like Jumping." The album also features Super Cat's excellent take on the "Sleng Teng" riddim, "Trash & Ready," and one of his most dramatic, thoughtful and socially conscious ragga-raps, "Cry Fi De Youth." *Don Dada* ⅊⅊⅊⅊ (Columbia, 1992, prod. various) contains the original mixes of both the sage title cut and "Ghetto Red Hot," along with the first U.S. release of the rare "Mud Up" single.

Foday Musa Suso

the rest:

Sweets for My Sweet ♪♪♪ (VP, 1990)

(With Nicodemus, Junior Cat, and Junior Demus) *The Good, the Bad, the Ugly & the Crazy* ♪♪♪ (Columbia, 1994)

(With Nicodemus and Junior Demus) *Cabin Stabbin'* ♪♪♪ (VP, 1994)

The Struggle Continues ♪♪♪ (Columbia, 1995)

influences:

⏪ Winston Riley, Buro Banton, Tenor Saw, Nicodemus, Lone Ranger, U-Roy, Sugar Minott, Chaka Demus

⏩ Apache Indian, Shabba Ranks, Lukie D., Junior Cat, Cutty Ranks, Mad Cobra, Bounty Killer, Merciless

see also: *Marcia Griffiths, Sugar Minott, Shabba Ranks, the Techniques*

Todd Shanker

Foday Musa Suso

Traditional and experimental Manding griot kora music
Born 1950s, in Gambia. Based in Chicago, IL, USA.

Foday Musa Suso spans the ancient world of Gambia's Manding *griots* (oral historians) and the most modern of musical settings, from jazz and techno to new age and even the contemporary clas-

sical of Philip Glass. Suso was raised to play the 21-string harp/lute called the *kora,* and to recite the ancient glories of the Manding people. But from his childhood, when he first saw an airplane flying overhead and wondered whence it came, he was destined to do far more than that. Suso went to Ghana to teach kora in 1974, and a couple of years later, during the hubbub surrounding the publication of Alex Haley's *Roots,* Suso got the idea that Americans might be interested in his traditional music. He moved to Chicago in 1977, and wound up playing music for the famed book's filmed version. Once in the U.S., Suso made connections, including Don Cherry—a partner in Suso's first American group, Mandingo Griot Society—and Herbie Hancock, with whom Suso went on to make a number of recordings. Suso's 1984 release *Watto Sitta* revealed him as an early innovator in the area of Manding electric pop. He has continued to collaborate and innovate, including memorable sessions with Bill Laswell, Philip Glass, and the Kronos Quartet. In 1995, during one of his frequent visits to Gambia, Suso helped to create a landmark recording, *Jali Kunda,* which reunites the wandering adventurer with the ongoing rituals and settings of griot music back home.

what to buy: *Jali Kunda* ♪♪♪♪ (ellipsis arts . . . , 1996, prod. Bill Laswell) has Suso returning to his ancestral home for an intimate series of sessions in the field. The release comes with a beautiful book of photographs and text (and is reviewed at greater length in the Compilations section of this volume). *Dreamtime* ♪♪♪♪ (CMP, 1990, prod. Bill Laswell, Foday Musa Suso) is a fine example of Suso's work in America, featuring the acoustic side of his music.

what to buy next: *Village Life* ♪♪♪ (Columbia, 1985, prod. Bill Laswell, Herbie Hancock) captures the early and promising moments of Suso's fruitful collaboration with Herbie Hancock.

what to avoid: *New World Power* ♪♪♪ (Axiom, 1991, prod. Bill Laswell) puts Suso in a driving but drab electronic context.

influences:

⏪ Jali Nyama Suso, Malamini Jobarteh

see also: *Kronos Quartet, Bill Laswell, Adam Rudolph*

Banning Eyre

Dave Swarbrick

British folk and folk-rock
Born April 5, 1941, in New Malden, Surrey, England. Based in Coventry, England.

Dave Swarbrick's friend Beryl Marriott deserves the thanks of music fans everywhere—she is the one believed to have persuaded the young "Swarb" to switch instruments from piano to fiddle. Swarbrick made the fiddle his lover; he made it sing and groan, he danced and crooned with it, he wore out his instruments and, in turn, let them nearly wear him out. Swarbrick began as a "straight" folk artist with the Ian Campbell Folk Group. After guesting on folk-rock institution-to-be Fairport Convention's *Unhalfbricking,* he joined the group for its seminal *Liege and Lief.* Fairport, which transformed so many who passed through it, changed Swarbrick into a singer and composer as well as a fiddler. He remained with the group until 1979, and his departure ended the band, however briefly. Years of electrified fiddling had left him nearly deaf, but he continued working—mostly in acoustic settings—with fellow Fairport alum Simon Nicol, with Martin Carthy (a duet partner going back to 1968), and in the group Whippersnapper with Chris Leslie (who would join Fairport in 1997). He was also in the Keith Hancock Band with Ruari MacFarlane and Carthy. Swarbrick has suffered some health problems of late, which seem to be what led to an impressive, albeit premature, obituary in the London *Daily Telegraph* of April 20, 1999. ("It's not the first time I've died in Coventry," he later quipped.) He still performs in small groups and shows up at Fairport's reunion festivals from time to time. His imprint on that band—as a performer and as a personality—is its most consistent characteristic. As a solo artist and in his other projects, Swarb is likewise full of fire and passion, romanticism and rough-hewn minstrelsy.

what to buy: *Smiddyburn/Flittin'* 🎻🎻🎻🎻 (Raven, 1981/1996) is the essential Swarb starter kit. Swarbrick says in the liner notes that both of the collected albums were recorded within a two-week period in July 1981. Joining Swarbrick are Simon Nicol, Dave Pegg, Dave Mattacks, Richard Thompson, Beryl Marriott, Bruce Rowland, John McCormick, and Roger Marriott in various configurations. Aside from the marvelous instrumentals, Swarb sings Sandy Denny's "It Suits Me Well"—and it does indeed. *Folk on 2* 🎻🎻🎻🎻 (Cooking Vinyl, 1996), recorded for the BBC in 1991 as a commemoration of Swarb's 50th birthday, is an excellent collection of solo and group recordings, including several with Fairport Convention.

what to buy next: *Swarbrick/Swarbrick II* 🎻🎻🎻🎻 (Transatlantic, 1976–77/Castle, 1996, prod. Bruce Rowland), a re-release of Swarbrick's first two solo albums on one CD, features many of his cronies, including Carthy. The 1991 performance released as *Live at Jackson's Lane* 🎻🎻🎻 (Gadfly, 1996) is rather spare—just voice and fiddle—but it's a rare chance to hear Swarb in concert, droll comments and all.

influences:

◄◄ Beryl Marriott, Ian Campbell, Martin Carthy

►► Sandy Denny, Ric Sanders, Eliza Carthy, Ashley MacIsaac

see also: *Ian Campbell Folk Group, Martin Carthy, Fairport Convention, A.L. Lloyd*

Pamela Murray Winters

turlough o'carolan

One of Ireland's greatest composers and poets, Turlough O'Carolan (1670–1738) was born in County Nobber, Ireland, to a poor farm family. When O'Carolan lost his sight, he was taught how to play the harp by his patron, Màire MacDermott Roe, and took up the vocations of wandering minstrel, composer, and music tutor. Of the over 200 O'Carolan tunes that survive today, the bulk were written in honor of friends, patrons, or those who offered him hospitality during his travels. O'Carolan's heavily ornamented compositions form the backbone of traditional Irish music as we know it. Although he wrote for the harp, his tunes have been widely performed on other instruments, notably fiddle, guitar, and pipes. O'Carolan's works were profoundly influenced by Italian classical composers of his day, including Vivaldi, Corelli, and Gemaniani. Indeed, O'Carolan's lush, vivid melodies would probably be considered classical music today if they had been written in a salon in Italy rather than in a series of farms and estates in Ireland.

Michael Parrish

The Swedish Sax Septet

Jazz, folk, traditional Swedish
Formed 1990, in Sweden. Based in Sweden.

Roland Keijser, tenor and soprano saxophone; Kjell Westling, soprano saxophone, clarinet; Anders Rosén, alto saxophone; Jonas Simonsson, bass; Sten Källman, baritone saxophone, soparino; Thomas Ringdahl, soprano saxophone; Jonny Wartel, tenor saxophone, soparino.

Combining a love of American jazz idioms with traditional Scandinavian forms and a wickedly subtle sense of humor, the Septet's music is an astringent and bracing melange of jazz and world influences. Starting from a commitment to honor and preserve such classical genres as the *polska* (polka) and the *halling* (a traditional male dance demanding great acrobatic skill and endurance), their music blends such vastly divergent influences as Thelonious Monk, Miles Davis, the European avant-garde, and Moroccan and Afro-Caribbean horn styles. All seven members are multi-instrumentalists who have been active in the Scandinavian recording scene for decades.

what's available: *Riff-Ola* ♫♫♫ (NOMAD, 1996, prod. Anders Rosén) is the Septet's only release to be had in the U.S. at this writing, and is well worth seeking out for those interested in the farther reaches of jazz. With spare production, biting performances, and arrangements that veer brilliantly from the haunted to the hilarious, the band effortlessly achieves a high-modernist "shock of the new" within the context of an unflagging folkie classicism. Tracks like "Limping Waltz," "Thaw Tune," "When the Devil Danced on the Ruins of Fredrikshad," and the title piece attain incredible levels of aural beauty. The soloists work the simple tunes into delicate and spidery shapes, with the whole taking on an at-once austere and good-humored dignity that approaches Miles Davis or Rashaan Roland Kirk. One longs for the outfit's next release (or even a live album), and *MusicHound* recommends it unheard.

influences:

◀◀ Greig, Scoenberg, Miles Davis, Theolonious Monk

Ron Garmon

Sweeney's Men

Irish folk

Formed 1966, in Galway, Ireland. Disbanded 1969.

Andy Irvine, mandolin, harmonica, guitar; Johnny Moynihan, bouzouki, tin whistle; Terry Woods, six- and 12-string guitar. Other members included Joe Dolan, guitar; Henry McCullough, guitar.

During the late 1960s in Ireland, a new kind of folk group began to emerge. Influenced by the head-on ballad-singing style of the Clancy Brothers and Tommy Makem, by the urban grit of the Dubliners, by the English folk club scene, and by Sean Ó Riada's ideas as expressed by the Chieftains, young people began to blend sensitive singing, basic accompaniment, and arranged instrumental passages in a totally new way. Among the first of these groups to make recordings was Sweeney's Men. Usually remembered as the great Irish folk group of the '60s, Sweeney's Men was formed in Galway in 1966, but spent much of its time on the Dublin and London folk scenes in the late '60s. The group consisted on its recordings of Andy Irvine (later of Planxty and Patrick Street), Johnny Moynihan (later of Planxty and De Dannan), and Terry Woods (later of Steeleye Span and the Pogues), who replaced original member Joe Dolan. Rock guitarist Henry McCullough, later of the Grease Band, was a member in between their two LPs and greatly influenced the later one. Indeed, many have contended that McCullough's period in Sweeney's Men was one of the earliest manifestations of folk-rock in either Britain or Ireland.

what's available: The compilation *Time Was Never Here 1968–69* ♫♫♫ (Transatlantic/Demon, prod. Bill Leader) features almost all the music from the band's two LPs, *Sweeney's Men 1968* and 1969's *The Tracks of Sweeney,* and echoes with historic moments. You'll hear, among other landmarks, the first time that most beloved of Greek imports, the bouzouki, was used in Irish music; it was Moynihan who started that trend. There's also the first time "Willy O' Winsbury" was sung to its now-familiar tune, as popularized by Ann Briggs, Pentangle, and other artists; Irvine erred when cross-referencing a ballad collection with its tune index, and connected the wrong melody to these words. It's a fabulous combination, and Irvine's sweet voice never sounded better than it does on this simple solo track. Still, *Time Was Never Here* isn't a history lesson, but a vibrant recording of contemporary Irish folk. Listened to as such, it has many other pleasures to offer. Woods's banjo and singing sound remarkably Appalachian, while Irvine's guitar, mandolin, and harmonica and Moynihan's bouzouki and whistle clearly foreshadow the Planxty/De Dannan style of playing that was yet to develop. Overall the originals haven't held up as well as the traditionals (heck, they were already a century old in 1968, so how were a few more years going to matter?), but most of the goods are wonderfully played, if quirkily sung, and still quite fresh. Another bonus here is the sleeve notes, which contain a lot of information taken from interviews with band members and friends. Everything adds up to a rare and wonderful glimpse of a remarkable band and a pivotal moment in history—this is an absolute must for serious Irish music fans.

worth searching for: *Sweeney's Men 1968* ♫♫♫ (Transatlantic, 1969), now out of print, contained mostly traditional material that stands the test of time.

influences:

◀◀ The Clancy Brothers & Tommy Makem, the Dubliners, the Chieftains

▶▶ Planxty, De Dannan, Patrick Street, East Wind, Steeleye Span, the Pogues, Horslips

see also: *De Dannan, Andy Irvine, Patrick Street, Planxty, the Pogues, Steeleye Span*

Steve Winick

Sweet Honey in the Rock

International folk

Formed November 1973, in Washington, DC, USA. Based in Washington, DC, USA.

Variable membership over many years, most recently including: Bernice Johnson Reagon, vocals; Nitanju Bolade Casel, vocals; Aisha Kahlil, vocals; Ysaye Maria Barnwell, vocals; Shirley Childress Johnson, vocals; Evelyn Maria Harris, vocals.

Growing out of a theater workshop that Bernice Johnson Reagon hosted at the Black Repertory Company in Washington, D.C., in the early 1970s, Sweet Honey in the Rock have surpassed even their founder's vision. Performing mostly *a cappella* and using tradition-rooted harmonies, the women sing out against racism, economic struggle, and sexual oppression. From their inception, Sweet Honey's mixture of spirituals, gospel, jazz, blues, rap, and traditional African songs has made them one of the top-ranked contemporary folk groups. They were nominated for a Grammy for their song "Emergency" in 1990, and got one the next year for their interpretations of two Leadbelly compositions, "Sylvie" and "Gray Goose." One of the first groups to feature a full-time American Sign Language interpreter (Shirley Childress Johnson), Sweet Honey celebrated their 20th anniversary with the book *We Who Believe in Freedom,* published by Anchor/Doubleday in 1993. The group has been showcased in numerous films and television documentaries; a performance in celebration of Martin Luther King Day was broadcast nationally on PBS, and their version of Sojourner Truth's tribute to the Colored Michigan regiment, set to the music of "John Brown's Body," was heard in the acclaimed historical series *The Civil War.* Noways tired, they run on as an institution of international folk and of "world" music from right where they are.

what to buy: With 34 tracks covering Sweet Honey's first dozen years on record, the double CD *Selections 1976–1988* ♪♪♪♪♪ (Flying Fish, 1997, compilation prod. Bernice Johnson Reagon) is a masterpiece of inspiring harmonies, African-American hand percussion, and politically conscious lyricism.

what to buy next: Recorded during a November 1987 performance, *At Carnegie Hall* ♪♪♪ (Flying Fish, 1988) captures the dynamic energies and awareness-raising of the band's concerts. The first of Sweet Honey's albums to be produced by a member other than Reagon, *25* ♪♪♪ (Rykodisc, 1998, prod. Ysaye M. Barnwell) not only celebrates the group's first quarter-century, but signals a new direction with the addition of drums and percussion. The album ranges from the church-like tunes "Greed" and "Sound Bite from Beijing," to the wordless "Chant" (inspired by an African Ituri rainforest Pygmy tribe), a harmony-filled rendition of Bob Marley's "Redemption Song," and a re-make of Reagon's "Sometime," which first appeared on the group's album *Good News.*

the rest:
Sweet Honey in the Rock ♪♪♪ (Flying Fish, 1976)
B'lieve I'll Run On . . . See What the End's Gonna Be ♪♪♪ (Redwood, 1978)
Good News ♪♪♪ (Flying Fish, 1982)
The Other Side ♪♪♪ (Flying Fish, 1986)
Feel Something Drawing Me On ♪♪♪ (Flying Fish, 1989)
Breaths ♪♪♪♪ (Flying Fish, 1989)
All for Freedom ♪♪♪ (Music for Little People, 1989)
In This Land ♪♪♪ (Earthbeat!, 1992)

I Got Shoes ♪♪♪ (Music for Little People, 1992)
We Who Believe in Freedom ♪♪♪ (Earthbeat!, 1993)
Still on the Journey ♪♪♪♪ (Earthbeat!, 1993)
Sacred Ground ♪♪♪ (Earthbeat!, 1995)

worth searching for: A live version of "Crying for Freedom" is included on *Ben & Jerry's Newport Folk Festival: Turn of the Decade* ♪♪♪ (Red House, 1991, prod. Bob Feldman).

influences:
◄◄ Odetta, Paul Robeson, the Freedom Singers, Pete Seeger

►► Tracy Chapman, Toshi Reagon, Casselberry-Dupree, Kim & Reggie Harris

Craig Harris

Synergy

World-flavored, classically influenced percussion music
Formed 1974, in Sydney, Australia. Based in Sydney, Australia.

Core membership (since 1987): Michael Askill, artistic director, percussion; Ian Cleworth, drums, koto; Rebecca Lagos, percussion, timpani, cimbalom, piano; Colin Piper, percussion, piano. (All members are from Australia.) The group is joined by three associate percussionists/assistants for 12 month periods each.

Not Larry Fast's pioneering electronic project, *this* Synergy was dreamed up by founding member Michael Askill during rehearsals with the Sydney Symphony Orchestra. Combining the "elements of Sydney and energy," the ensemble (also known from time to time as Sydney Percussion, the Sydney Percussion Ensemble, and Synergy Percussion Limited) debuted in 1974 when experimental musician David Ahearn presented their first performance as part of his *A-Z Music* series. Their first official appearance as "Synergy" was in 1978 at the Art Gallery of New South Wales. Michael Askill, Colin Piper, Ian Bloxsom, and Ron Reeves were the founders, and David Clarence, Graeme Leak, and Richard Miller have been part of the group. Synergy's repertoire includes works by Béla Bartók, Pierre Boulez, Benjamin Britten, John Cage, Maki Ishii, Red Norvo, Somei Satoh, and Steve Reich; they have performed everything from fife and drum music of the American Revolution to percussion music of West Africa. Numerous guest musicians, choirs, dance companies, actresses—even an Indonesian *gamelan* ensemble—have performed with Synergy all over Australia, as well as in Paris, Taipei, Hong Kong, the U.K., and New Zealand. Synergy is one of its country and region's preeminent forces in new music, promoting the works of composers from Asia and the Pacific Rim. Michael Askill himself has become one of Australia's most important musical figures, working with such other ensembles as Southern Crossings and John Williams's septet, and also celebrated as a composer and soloist. Synergy is Australia's longest-running contemporary music group, and while percussion remains at the heart of its performances, Askill, Cleworth, Lagos, and Piper also include elements of music-theater and electronics in their repertoire.

what to buy: *Matsuri* ♫♫♫♫ (Celestial Harmonies, 1994, prod. Synergy) demonstrates the incredible influence Japanese music has had on the core quartet.

what to buy next: *Taiko* ♫♫♫♫ (Celestial Harmonies, 1996, prod. Synergy) is inspired by the philosophy and sounds of Japan's *taiko* drumming tradition. The quartet joins with Japanese flutist/composer Sen Amano and *shakuhachi* flute master Riley Kelly Lee in a series of musical dialogues. The sounds range from the traditional Japanese flute called *shinobue* to the taiko and gongs of the ensemble Arahan. Cleworth contributes a composition utilizing percussion instruments, shells, and found objects.

the rest:
Impact ♫♫♫ (ABC Classics, 1996)

worth searching for: *Fata Morgana* ♫♫♫♫ (Celestial Harmonies, 1995, prod. Michael Askill) is the collaboration between Michael Askill and Turkish virtuoso instrumentalist Omar Faruk Tekbilek. Ghassan Barakat, Ian Cleworth, and Rebecca Lagos also lend their talents to this musical exploration of the Middle East, Asia, and West Africa, as well as Western jazz and classical. *Salomé* ♫♫♫♫ (Black Sun, 1998, prod. Michael Askill) is the duo's traditional soundtrack to the Bible story. Askill is on Black Sun's *Heinrich Schütz Der Schwanengesang (The Swan-Song)* —performed by Roland Peelman and the Song Company in the Sydney Opera House—and is credited with the superb production of *Tango* ♫♫♫♫ (Black Sun, 1996, prod. Michael Askill), featuring Daniel Binelli and his self-titled septet recorded in Buenos Aires. *Free Radicals: Voice Percussion & Didgeridoo* ♫♫♫♫ (Black Sun, 1997, prod. Michael Askill) is the combined force of Michael Askill/David Hudson/Alison Low Choy/Alison Addington. This is the soundtrack to the stage production *Free Radicals* by Graeme Murphy of the Sidney Dance Company. Fine experimental work with the title components (including the last-named Australian Aboriginal drone instrument).

solo outings:
Michael Askill:
Australian Percussion (Black Sun, 1995)
(With Riley Lee and Michael Atherton) *Shoalhaven Rise* ♫♫♫♫ (Black Sun, 1995)
Rhythm in the Abstract N/A (Black Sun, 1999)

Ian Cleworth:
Yarrageh: Nocturne for Percussion and Orchestra (ABC/PolyGram)

influences:
⏪ Classical, Japanese, avant-garde, Australian Aboriginal repertoire

see also: *David Hudson, Omar Faruk Tekbilek*

Stacy Meyn

Philip Nchipe Tabane /Malombo
South African jazz fusion
Born 1930s, in Mamelodi, Pretoria, South Africa. Based in Mamelodi, Pretoria, South Africa.

The respect guitarist Philip Tabane commands among his fellow musicians has never been mirrored in his treatment by record labels, although he has shared stages with such jazz legends as Miles Davis, Herbie Hancock, and Ella Fitzgerald in the United States and Europe, and toured extensively during the 1970s and 1980s. Not by design, Tabane's performances today take place principally in the vicinity of his Mamelodi township home, near Pretoria. His trio Malombo—the Venda language's word for "spirits"—was formed in the early 1960s; it has united Tabane with two dynamic percussionists, Oupa Mahapi Monareng on Malombo drums and Raymond Mphune Motau on various hand percussion, since 1976. Considered South Africa's preeminent guitar hero by many, Tabane (who also sings and plays flute, drums, bass, and pennywhistle) works in a style strongly rooted in traditional idioms from the Sotho, Amandebele, and Venda cultures of the northern Transvaal province. On this foundation he has built a style of freeform acoustic jazz based on soft percussion and intricate chords, resulting in the unique Malombo sound.

Tabane turned professional after winning the 1964 Castle Lager Jazz Contest and, since that time, has produced one of the smaller—but more significant—catalogs in world music. Although he left school at age 12, Tabane was awarded an honorary doctorate of music by the University of Venda in 1998, presented by Chancellor Cyril Ramaphosa, former secretary general of the African National Congress. "Ke A Bereka," from Tabane's recent CD of the same name, won the award for best single at the 1998 South African Music Awards. A 1986 Montreux Jazz Festival video provides a rare look at Tabane, and a film about the three original band members—Tabane, Abbey Cindi, and Julian Bahula—has been planned for South African television. Recently, Malombo's music was heard on *Facing the Truth,* Bill

Philip Nchipe Tabane

Moyers's PBS special examining personal implications of South Africa's Truth and Reconciliation Commission hearings.

what's available: In this instance, buy anything you can get your hands on. *Unh!* 𝄞𝄞𝄞𝄞 (WEΛ/Elektra/Nonesuch, 1989) is generally available in the States. Malombo also has tracks on both *Thunder before Dawn: Indestructible Beat of Soweto, Vol. 2* (Earthworks/Caroline, 1987) and *Freedom Fire: Indestructible Beat of Soweto, Vol. 3* (Earthworks/Caroline, 1990), each of which is reviewed in this book's Compilations section. To experience Tabane's undiminished artistic vitality from several perspectives within his long career, you'll thank yourself for digging up his most recent South African recording, *Ke A Bereka* 𝄞𝄞𝄞𝄞 (Tusk, 1996), and the older *Pele Pele* 𝄞𝄞𝄞𝄞 (Tusk, 1976, prod. Peter Davidson, Philip Tabane), as well as a 1997 re-release of *Malombo* on the German label Kijim.

influences:
◄◄ Wes Montgomery, John McLaughlin

►► Sakhile, Bayete, Amampondo, Malopoets

Linda Vartoogian

Tabou Combo

Compas

Formed 1968, in Port-au-Prince, Haiti. Re-formed 1971, in Brooklyn, NY, USA. Based in Brooklyn, NY, USA.

Roger Eugene (Haiti), lead vocals; Yvon Andre (Haiti), percussion, vocals; Yves Joseph (Haiti), congas, vocals, songwriter; Herman Nau (Haiti), drum kit, vocals; Elysee Pyronneau (Haiti), lead guitar; Jean Claude Jean (Haiti), rhythm guitar; Albert Chancy Jr. (Haiti), guitar (1968–69); Gary Resil (Haiti), rhythm guitar; Yves Albert Abel (Haiti), bass guitar; Adolph Chancy (Haiti), bass (1968–69); Raynald Valme (Haiti), congas; Daniel Pierre (Haiti), keyboards; Tom Mitchell (USA), sax (early 1990s); David Weeks (USA), sax; Ken Watters (USA), trumpet (early 1990s); Curtis Ebe (USA), trumpet; Jason Forsythe (USA), trombone (early 1990s); Andre Atkins (USA), trombone; Ernst Crepsac (Haiti), keyboards, (1987–90).

Although they've been playing together for more than 30 years, the five-man core of Tabou Combo—Roger Eugene, Yvon Andre, Yves Joseph, Herman Nau, and Elysee Pyronneau—remains the same, an almost unheard-of feat in popular music, "world" or otherwise. Tabou Combo bases its sound on *compas*, a Haitian folk form that grew out of the collision of African rhythms with the French dance music of the slavemasters. In the early 1960s sax man Nemours Jean-Baptiste created "compas-direct" by adding Cuban music, especially the mambo, to the mix, and supercharging it with a hot horn section. In the mid-1960s younger bands began adding rock and salsa to the stew, scaling down the lineup to guitar, keys, bass, and drums. The result was dubbed "mini-jazz." (The mini refers to the mini skirt, a popular craze at the time, and in Haiti all bands play "jazz.")

Tabou Combo started as Nau's band, Los Incognitos de Petionville. Nau was already an influential musician; his use of traditional rhythms—he played the *kata* on his ride cymbal—had boosted the western drum kit to a position of prominence in compas bands. After a series of personnel shifts, the core of today's Tabou Combo came together in 1968. They began adding hints of James Brown, the Rolling Stones, and Sly Stone to the mix, and their first album, *Haiti,* was an immediate sensation. In 1969 one of the founding members, Albert Chancy Jr., quit the band, and things fell apart. The country, under the dictatorship of Papa Doc Duvalier, was also falling apart, and one by one the Tabous drifted up to New York City, which has the biggest Haitian population of any city outside of Port-au-Prince.

When the band members rediscovered each other in Brooklyn, they began playing again, hooked up with Fred Paul, who had just started Mini Records to service the growing needs of New York's Haitian fans, and began recording. Their second album, *8th Sacrament,* took off like a shot behind the single "New York City," a catchy tune that included French, Spanish, and English lyrics. When the album was released in France it quickly rose to the top of the charts on the strength of that single, which remains one of the band's most-requested tunes. The album went gold in France and made Tabou Combo international stars.

In the late 1970s the band added an American horn section and began writing charts with an R&B flavor, hoping to crack the African American market and become some sort of Caribbean Earth, Wind & Fire. They also changed their logo, using heavy metal/sci-fi funk lettering, and began dressing in "space suits" a la Funkadelic. Luckily, they didn't try to change their sound to go with the new image, and the hits kept coming. In the 1980s the band got political and began asking people to consider the problems of racism and poverty, although the music's energy and groove remained constant. As general interest in world music intensifies, the Combo has begun to pick up more non-Haitian fans. Their yearly summer concerts in New York City's Central Park draw upwards of 20,000 people, and they've become a regular attraction at the New Orleans Jazz and Heritage Festival.

what to buy: *8th Sacrament* 🎵🎵🎵🎵 (Mini, 1974) is the album that rocketed Tabou Combo to the top of the world-music

charts, and contains their monster hit "New York City." Every track is strong; it's almost a greatest hits package all on its own.

what to buy next: Once you get bitten by the Tabou bug you may not be able to get enough, so *Best of Tabou Combo, Volumes 1–5* 🎵🎵🎵🎵 (Sonodisc, 1995), a French release that collects most of the hits the band has cut over the past 30 years, should give you a good start into the back catalog. But be warned: Tabou Combo is a very popular band throughout the French-speaking world and, as with any group with a spectacular three-decades-and-counting history, their hits and their "best of" albums have been packaged and repackaged many times, by many labels, in many countries. Read the track listings and take note of copyright dates to make sure you're not buying the same songs in a different wrapper.

best of the rest:
Haiti 🎵🎵🎵🎵 (Ibo, 1969)
The Music Machine 🎵🎵🎵🎵 (Mini, 1978)
Superstars 🎵🎵🎵🎵 (Disques Esperance, 1988)
Aux Antillies 🎵🎵🎵🎵 (Zafem, 1989)
Live au Zenith 🎵🎵🎵🎵 (Mini, 1990)
Zap Zap 🎵🎵🎵🎵 (Zafem, 1991)

influences:
◀◀ Nemours Jean-Baptiste, Ibo Combo, Coupé Cloué, Shleu Shleu

▶▶ Boukman Eksperyans, Ra Ra Machine, Zin, Zéklé

j. poet

Rachid Taha
Rai, Arabic pop, world-dance
Born 1958, in Oran, Algeria. Based in Paris, France.

Rachid Taha got his first taste of show business spinning records at African and Arabic clubs in his adoptive home of Lyons, France. "I played a real patchwork: Arabic, salsa, rap, funk, anything you could dance to," Taha recalls. The crowd's reaction to his international smorgasbord made Taha want to make his own music. He started a band called Carte de Sejour ("Green Card"). Like many immigrants, Taha was torn between his Algerian roots and the French and European culture that now surrounded him: Carte de Sejour played Arabic music in the manner of the Clash, very loud, almost metal." The band's first—and only—album was produced by former Gong guitarist Steve Hillage, who had become interested in the music of Egyptian pop diva Umm Kulthum. Hillage and Taha continued their collaboration after Carte de Sejour broke up, blending Arabic, pop, and dance music with Taha's radical, politically charged lyrics. *Diwân,* Taha's forth solo effort and his fifth project with Hillage, is also the most Arabic record of his career, an album Taha has characterized as "my version of John Lennon's

Rock 'n' Roll album; covers of the Arabic singers and writers that inspired me to make music when I was young. I chose songs for their strong rhythms and the political poetry of their lyrics. Arabs in France are like blacks in the U.S., integrated yet separate. Music may be the best way we have to come to a real understanding of each other."

what's available: In Arabic, "Diwân" means a collection of poetry or songs. *Diwân* 𝄢𝄢𝄢𝄢 (Island, 1998, prod. Steve Hillage) is Taha's most pleasing and most traditionally Arabic album; the vocals are full of passion, and the players include Egyptian master percussionist Hossam Ramsy. On *Olé Olé* 𝄢𝄢𝄢 (Mango, 1995) Taha mixes Arabic and club-friendly beats for an entertaining but not essential collection.

influences:

◄◄ Khaled, Mohammed El Anka, Dahmane El Harrachi, Nasa El Ghiwane

see also: *Hossam Ramzy*

j. poet

Tahitian Choir

Traditional Polynesian vocal music
Based in Oparo, Tahiti.

The music of remote Rapa Iti would still be unknown were it not for the efforts of French record producer Pascal Nabet-Meyer. He visited Tahiti in 1981, inspired by the paintings of the French artist Gaugin, and heard about Rapa, an island 1,000 miles southeast of Tahiti that, with its 300 residents, was the last inhabited land before Antarctica. Told about a vocal group on Rapa that sang in quarter-tonal voices, he was determined to visit and record their singing. The recording trip took place in 1991, on Nabet-Meyer's return to Tahiti. When Nabet-Meyer finally arrived on Rapa he met Tetaria, the island's pastor, who introduced him to the people who practice *himene,* which is Tahitian for "song." Nabet-Meyer recorded the choir singing their oldest songs, those written before the arrival of the first European missionaries centuries before, as *Rapa Iti.* He returned again in 1994, to both record the native music and document native Rapa culture. "Within the choir, each group has its own melodic part," explains Nabet-Meyer, "and as there can be up to 16 groups, a complex web of voices develops. They sing a micro-tonal scale that has so far resisted the attempts of ethnomusicologists to chart it. We will need a new system to represent the drops between notes that give the glissando effect and polyphonic structure to the songs. The myths of Rapa tell us chants were once used to enter into other worlds; with these recordings I hope to let people step into the world of the Rapa."

what's available: *Rapa Iti* 𝄢𝄢𝄢𝄢 (Triloka, 1992, prod. Pascal Nabet-Meyer) is a magical recording of what may be the only Oceanic vocal music to remain uncontaminated by Western influences, full of odd meters, shifting time signatures, rhythmic grunts, and falsetto cries of ecstasy. *Tahitian Choir, Vol. II* 𝄢𝄢𝄢𝄢 (Shanachie, 1994) is slightly underproduced, but that only adds to its other-worldly charm.

see also: *Rurutu Choir*

j. poet

Takadja

West African traditional and traditional-based music
Formed 1989, in Montréal, Canada. Based in Montréal, Canada.

Francine Martel (Canada), djembé, djallé, wassakhumbas, berimbau; Oumar N'Diaye (Guinea), lead vocals, kenkeni, dundumba, djembé, boloï, cowbell, kirin, m'beng, gongoma; Robert Lépine (Canada), balafon, djembe, dundumba, kenkeni, vocals; Youssou Seck (Senegal), vocals, kenkeni, dundumba, m'beng, lamb, xin, n'der, gongoma; Nathalie Dussault (Canada), cora, vocals; Alassane Fall (Senegal), vocals, guitar, m'beng, balafon, taman, lamb, wassakhumbas (1996–present); Naby Camara (Guinea), balafon, vocals (1989–96).

Some white folks catch the vibe of Third World music and then just steal back across the border and revel in the rewards; others cross the culture line without ever double-crossing. Francine Martel is one of the latter, a French Canadian scholar and musician who's immersed herself in the discipline of West African drumming with seriousness and good faith. Upon returning to Canada from her first trip to Africa in 1980, she remembers, "a part of me had decided to stay"—so, over the subsequent two decades she would return regularly to Africa, managing to bring the continent home to North America as well by founding the ensemble Takadja. Aptly named after the Côte d'Ivoirian Guéré language's term for "to vibrate while dancing," Takadja is in many ways the world's most modest supergroup, its members quietly devoted to their craft while counting among them some of the most impressive credentials in international music. The group's Canadian members have all studied under African master drummers in the Motherland itself, and Takadja's African contingent has ancestral or professional roots in *griot* (musical/oral historian) lineages, the revered cultural preservation institution Koteba Ensemble of Abidjan, and the blockbuster worldbeat band Fatala (from which fellow African-in-Canada Alpha Yaya Diallo launched his acclaimed solo career). Takadja's sound is based around a flexible and formidable arsenal of drums, soulful vocals, and the delicate yet dynamic intertwine of the chiming *balafon* (African xylophone) and *kora* (African harp-lute). The repertoire is ritualistic and traditional, featuring some ancient pieces but actually many more originals, written with both fidelity to the old ways and strikingly new imagination. The music sparked by this meeting of cultures and bridging of centuries is irresistible: a rare and magical mix most Western listeners will find totally unfamiliar but instantly engaging.

what's available: Takadja has but two albums to show for a rigorous and wide-ranging touring history, but the competing demand for the group's live spectacle must be served, and most bands would be thankful to accomplish in an entire career what this band has in its earliest recordings. The life-affirming *Takadja* ♫♫♫♫ (Celestial Harmonies, 1995, prod. Steve Roach) and *Diyé* ♫♫♫♫♫ (Black Sun, 1996, prod. Steve Roach) are two of the finest West African–oriented releases, and together represent one of the most listenable and legitimate Afro-Euro music fusions ever recorded. The first album's rhythms are by turns celebratory, sober, and stately, with rich choral vocals and duet interplay; spontaneous but precision musicianship; and sophisticated, attention-holding drumming in a spectrum of textures. The crystalline kora and balafon settings are interspersed with expert drum-ensemble workouts which are themselves downright melodious in their range of resonances, varied in tempo and mood like a symphonic suite—actually more so, as the elementality of the instrumentation forces an ingenuity on the ensemble that Western classical players need not engage. Drum groups highlight the second album too, which introduces even more melody through the prominent use of the traditional *serdou* flute. There are joyous rhythms; beautiful asymmetrical interweaves of vocals; structures epic in depth as well as length; and surprising but well-considered accompaniment from outside the native African musical sphere, including drones on the Australian Aboriginal *didgeridoo* and Brazilian *berimbau*. Both albums welcome the listener even further with informative and readable liner notes on song origins, group members, and instruments used—everything this captivating music will make you want to know.

influences:

◀◀ Sékou Camara Cobra, L'Ensemble Koteba d'Abidjan

▶▶ Frå Senegal Til Setesdal

Adam McGovern

Talking Heads

Pop, experimental
Formed 1975, in New York, NY, USA. Disbanded 1992.

David Byrne (Scotland) vocals, guitar; Tina Weymouth (USA) bass, synth; Chris Frantz (USA) drums; Jerry Harrison (USA) keyboards, guitar (1977–92).

Many current world-music fans were first turned on to African rhythms and Latin beats by Talking Heads. Encouraged by the eclectic listening habits of their producer, Brian Eno, David Byrne was checking out Fela Kuti, guitarist Jerry Harrison was

experimenting with a fusion of American country and western and African highlife finger-picking, and Chris Frantz adapted African polyrhythmic drumming styles. By their last album *Naked* the band recorded with a full, international ensemble including the star of Mali's Rail Band Mory Kanté on *kora* (African harp-lute), and lesser-known session players like Abdou M'Boup on congas and talking drums, Yves N'Djock on guitar, and Manolo Badrena on percussion. Byrne's distinctive vocal expression and the band's knack for tight pop tunes belied the exotic origins of much of their music, but not so much that a new audience for international sounds wasn't inspired to go to the sources for more of what they'd enjoyed about Talking Heads.

what to buy: The band's fullest exploration of world music is on the ensemble performance of *Naked* ♫♫♫♫ (Sire, 1988), particularly on "Blind" with M'Boup's talking drums, N'Djock's highlife guitar, and Wally Badarou's synthesized conga drums. Riding in on the wave of his international success, Kanté made a guest appearance with his agile kora playing on "Mr. Jones" and "The Facts of Life."

what to buy next: You'll hear a gospel choir on "Road to Nowhere," the twang of country guitar, a hint of zydeco, blues, samba beats, and quirky U.S. pop on the best-of compilation *Popular Favorites 1976–92: Sand in the Vaseline* ♫♫♫♫ (Sire, 1992, prod. various). *Fear of Music* ♫♫♫ (Sire, 1979, prod. Brian Eno, Talking Heads) is noteworthy for "I Zimbra," based loosely on a track by legendary Nigerian bandleader Fela Kuti.

what to avoid: While the collaboration between Byrne and producer Eno on *My Life in the Bush of Ghosts* **woof!** (Sire, 1981) is often cited as the template for their subsequent ambient/worldbeat experiments, it has not aged well, and at best is an interesting piece of conceptual art.

the rest:

Talking Heads: 77 ♫♫♫ (Sire, 1977)
More Songs about Buildings and Food ♫♫♫ (Sire, 1978)
Remain in Light ♫♫♫♫ (Sire, 1980)
The Name of This Band Is Talking Heads ♫♫♫♫ (Sire, 1982)
Speaking in Tongues ♫♫♫ (Sire, 1983)
Stop Making Sense ♫♫♫ (Sire, 1984)
Little Creatures ♫♫♫♫ (Sire, 1985)
True Stories ♫♫ (Sire, 1986)

influences:

◀◀ Fela Kuti, the Rail Band, Brian Eno, Silvio Rodriguez, Caetano Velozo, Gilberto Gil, Los Van Van, David Bowie

▶▶ Peter Gabriel, Arto Lindsay

see also: *David Byrne, Brian Eno, Mory Kanté, Fela Kuti, Rail Band*

David Poole

Tam Tam 2000

Funana, coladeira, zouk

Formed c. 1980, in Cape Verde. Based in Paris, France.

Belmiro Moniz, drums, percussion; Manuel Fernandez, percussion; Manuel Brito, bass, vocals; Adolphe Pauloby, lead guitar, vocals; Isidro Dominguez Bands, rhythm guitar, vocals; Edouard Moniz, lead vocals, percussion; Jean-Luc Lemble, keyboards. (All members are from Cape Verde.)

The dance band Tam Tam 2000 formed in Cape Verde, but is now based in Paris, where its members mix eclectic African and Caribbean strains with their Verdean rhythms. The group landed a track on the early Earthworks sampler, *Afric Typic Collection,* which gave them a big international boost.

what's available: The *Best of Tam Tam 2000* ♫♫♫♫ (Melodie France) compilation has no info. on the label, but features "Zouk en Avant," which was included on *Afric Typic Collection,* and showcases the band's credible attempts at *zouk* (Antillean hybrid pop), *soukous* (African rumba), and *son* (Afro-Cuban folk), as well as Verde's own dance styles *funana* and *coladeira* (which sounds a bit like Trinidadian *soca*) and its bluesy *morna.* *Sintia* ♫♫♫♫ (Melodie France) has another blank label, but the recording quality and raw, unpolished performances would indicate it as an early effort, a down-home collection of morna, funana, and coladeira. No liner info on *Sabe Cabo Verde* ♫♫♫♫ (Melodie France) either, but this compilation is slickly produced and includes remakes of a couple of tunes from *Sintia.* Less international, with great interplay between the guitars and the keyboards and plenty of live (not programmed) percussion.

influences:

◄◄ Bulimundo, Finaçon

►► Mendes Brothers

j. poet

Tambu

Soca

Born Chris Herbert, in Trinidad. Based in Port of Spain, Trinidad.

Tambu was the lead singer and main songwriter of Roots, a session band that backed up many famous *soca* singers in the studios of famed calypso label Charlie's Records. (Soca is a hugely popular modern variant of calypso.) When label-head Rawlston Charles told Roots members they should think of doing gigs as a live band, they agreed. Charlie bought them their equipment and, as a tribute to his generosity, they became "Charlie's Roots." The group began its career with a regular Thursday night gig at the Atlantis Club in Port of Spain, where members added a bit of funk and pop

david parsons

D avid Parsons and his tape recorder have traveled the world to capture exotic sounds for mass consumption. A series of culture-specific surveys has set a new, high standard for world-music projects. The quality sonics, dogged research, and handsome presentation make each one a coveted artifact and an infinite source of pleasure and learning. The world owes David Parsons a vast reward for his years of patiently preserving—conveniently boxed and annotated for posterity—ethnic music traditions from Armenia, Cambodia, Vietnam, Bali, and across the Islamic world.

Beginning as a jazz-rock drummer, Parsons first made his name as a composer of new-age synthesizer music melded with field recordings of chants and nature sounds. Luckily he had the good sense to apply his ear for the uncommon to recording other musicians, as his own albums are conceptually interesting but actually rather dull. "The sound of the River Ganges in India" looks good on paper, but funneled through Parson's arsenal of nine synths and displaced from its original setting it loses any power it might have possessed a clear case of you-had-to-be-there.

In contrast, Parsons's scholarly yet anything-but-academic compilations *put* you there. Inspired by the sitar music of Ravi Shankar, his first trips abroad were to study the culture of India. He recorded Tibetan chants for the *Sacred Ceremonies* CDs (Celestial Harmonies, 1994), and has produced such historic collections—all reviewed in this book's Compilations section—as *The Music of Armenia* (1997), *The Music of Bali* (1994), *The Music of Cambodia* (1994), *The Music of Islam* (1998), and *The Music of Vietnam* (1994), all on the Celestial Harmonies label as well.

When not living a nomadic existence, Parsons resides in his native New Zealand. The Celestial Harmonies projects have absorbed most of his time in recent years, but Parsons's bread and butter comes from his second life as a composer for New Zealand's TV, radio, and film industries. Now *that's* unusual.

David Poole

to the group's mix. Now that they were playing on their own they needed material, and Tambu began writing tunes. He also asked his friend David Rudder to contribute, and in 1986, when Tambu had laryngitis, he asked Rudder to sing during Carnival. Rudder's "The Hammer" swept all Carnival titles that year, and he and Tambu have been sharing lead vocals ever since. Tambu's tunes tend to be less political than Rudder's, but they're just as catchy. He won the Road March title in 1987 with "This Party Is It," a tune that became an instant standard.

what's available: The rhythm-heavy *Culture* 𝄞𝄞𝄞𝄞 (Sire, 1997, prod. Joe R. Brown) is a classic. After the rave-up of "This Party Is It," the band shifts into a mid-tempo groove that accents the drumming and Tambu's celebrations of Trini culture. "How Many More Must Die," one of the first calypso ballads, surprises with its strong political lyric and decidedly Stax/Volt groove.

influences:
◀◀ Sparrow, Arrow, Super Blue

see also: *David Rudder*

j. poet

Tannahill Weavers

Scottish traditional
Formed 1968, in Paisley, Scotland. Based in Scotland.

Roy Gullane, guitar, vocals; Phil Smillie, flute, bodhrán, whistles, vocals; Leslie Wilson, guitar, bouzouki, keyboards, bass pedals, vocals; John Martin, fiddle, cello, mandolin, viola, vocals; Duncan Nicholson, Highland bagpipes, Scottish small-pipes, whistles, keyboards. (All members are from Scotland.)

Ever since their earliest years, the Tannahill Weavers have established their niche deep in the heart of traditional music, staying almost purely acoustic in nature, and using predominantly traditional Celtic tunes, or new material that sounds so traditional it is indiscernible from the old. This has made them virtually unique in the field of Celtic music, where most groups that start with their feet firmly rooted on traditional soil soon find themselves wandering into new territory, usually to stay. Combining this solidly anchored tradition with skilled instrumentalists, tight harmonies, an intensity of rhythm, and a well-rounded sound, the band has defined a new voice in Celtic music. Boasting a cast of more than 20 members during nearly three decades as a group, the Tannahill Weavers have seen a variety of talent come and go while always managing to maintain the integrity of their sound. The signature of the Tannies has to be the use of the Highland bagpipes in their music. The first professional Scottish folk group to include full-sized pipes on stage, they

quickly drew the attention of music-lovers and critics alike. The various pipes, combined with hearty vocals, soaring flute lines, and a fiery violin, carry the group through a wide variety of traditional tunes, keeping listeners humming along. The cast of pipers has included Alan MacLeod, Iain MacInnes, Kenny Forsyth, and Duncan Nicholson. Phil Smillie's flute lines and Roy Gullane's work on guitar and mandolin combine to add to the depth of the music, and their vocal work is the essential icing on the cake. The Tannahill Weavers have been creating hearty, enjoyable music for so much longer than most bands can be expected to, there can't be any end in sight.

what to buy: The group reached a musical peak with *The Mermaid's Song* 𝄞𝄞𝄞𝄞 (Green Linnet, 1992) and *Capernaum* 𝄞𝄞𝄞𝄞 (Green Linnet, 1994). Both albums display top-of-the-line piping by Kenny Forsyth and some amazing fiddle work by John Martin. The choice of material on these albums is particularly wonderful, mixing delightful dance tunes and heartfelt ballads, perfectly distributed throughout. In the States *Capernaum* won the National Association of Independent Record Distributors' 1994 Indie Award for Celtic Album of the Year.

what to buy next: Their latest release, *Epona* 𝄞𝄞𝄞 (Green Linnet, 1998), is representative of the current lineup and shows the group's depth of musical passion and their excellent taste in track selection. Although it lacks the pipe sound characteristic of the Tannies during the rest of their career, their first album, *Are Ye Sleeping Maggie* 𝄞𝄞𝄞𝄞 (Plant Life, 1976/Hedera, 1993), contains a wonderful assortment of tunes passionately performed by the group. The thunderstorm sound that begins the opening title track, "Are Ye Sleeping Maggie," is indicative of the highly charged performance to come. Also from their early days, *Tannahill Weavers* 𝄞𝄞𝄞𝄞 (Plant Life, 1979/Green Linnet, 1982/Hedera, 1993) won the group the Scotstar Award for Best Folk Group in 1980. *Tannahill Weavers IV* 𝄞𝄞𝄞𝄞 (Plant Life, 1982/Green Linnet, 1982/Hedera, 1993) rounds out the "top of the Tannies" set, with a collection of exciting and memorable dance tunes.

what to avoid: *Passage* 𝄞𝄞𝄞 (Green Linnet, 1984) was a definite diversion for the group, in which they toyed with electric instruments and a more modern sound. It contains some excellent numbers, but doesn't stand out like the rest of their work. Their two "favorites" albums, *The Best of the Tannahill Weavers 1979–89* 𝄞𝄞𝄞 (Green Linnet, 1989) and *Choice Cuts 1987–96* 𝄞𝄞𝄞 (Green Linnet, 1997), are both good collections, but true fans will want the rest of the material on the original albums. Since neither compilation contains anything unreleased elsewhere, they are somewhat superfluous.

Taraf de Haïdouks fiddler Pasolan

the rest:
Old Woman's Dance ♫♫♫♪ (Plant Life, 1978/Hedera, 1993)
Land of Light ♫♫♫♪ (Green Linnet, 1985)
Dancing Feet ♫♫♫ (Green Linnet, 1987)
Cullen Bay ♫♫♫ (Green Linnet, 1990)
Leaving St. Kilda ♫♫♫♪ (Green Linnet, 1996)

influences:
◀◀ Davy Spillane, Alan MacDonald
▶▶ Silly Wizard, Capercaillie

see also: *Ossian*

Jo Hughey Morrison

Taraf de Haïdouks
Traditional Romanian wedding and folk music
Formed 1990, in Clejani, Romania. Based in Clejani, Romania.

Ion Manole, violin, vocal; Nicolae Neacsu, violin, vocal; Dumitru Baicu, cymbalum, vocal; Ilie Iorga, vocal; Paul Giuclea, vocal, violin, accordion; Marin P. Manole, accordion; Anghel Gheorghe, violin; Constantin Lautaru, violin, vocal; Ionel Manole, accordion; Marin Manole, accordion; Gheorghe Falcaru, flute; Ion Tanase, small and big cymbalum; Marinel Sandu, cymbalum; Viorel Vlad, bass; Pasolan, fiddle. (All members are from Romania.)

Nicolae Neacsu, fiddle player, singer, and storyteller, is a walking encyclopedia of Gypsy and Romanian folklore and one of the leaders of the Romanian Gypsy band Taraf de Haïdouks. The two albums the Haïdouks have cut for Belgium's Crammed Discs label have brought Neacsu and his band of self-proclaimed brigands international superstardom. This unexpected interest in his music came at exactly the right time. A few years ago Neacsu was living alone in a one-room sod house in the village of Clejani, his fiddle set aside, doing little more than watching the spring thaw and waiting to die. That same spring Stéphane Karo, a Hungarian musician based in Brussels, and Michel Winter, an Israeli of Hungarian origin, were in the CD library at Brussels' Mediatech, looking for material for their band, which played classical Arabic music. They discovered a CD containing Romanian Gypsy ballads, and Karo decided to seek out people still playing this music. While Romania was in political turmoil under the waning years of the Ceausescu regime, Karo journeyed to Clejani and met Neacsu, who was surprised to find someone from Belgium interested in his music. Karo recorded Neacsu, with a few younger players, on a Walkman. "It was a bad recording," Winter recalls, "but you could feel the madness of this music. We talked about going back to make a real recording, but then the revolution started."

In 1990, after the political climate cooled, Karo and Winter went to Clejani and discovered 200 professional musicians, all of them Gypsies. After a summer listening to the village's music, they decided to organize a European tour for their new friends. The group settled on the name Taraf de Haïdouks, a *haïdouk* being a Robin Hood–like brigand from Romanian folklore, a rogue who defeats powerful lords with quick thinking and craftiness, while *taraf* is Turkish for a loose band of musicians. Winter and Karo picked six of the best performers, including Neascu and Ion Manole, a singer with a style of guttural modulations that may well die when he does. Under pressure from the village, the first touring band grew to 11 members, the youngest being 13-year-old cymbalum (Middle Eastern hammered dulcimer) player Marinel Sandu. That initial outing led to a recording contract with Crammed Discs, which released *Musique des Tziganes de Roumanie* in 1991. The band went on to knock out crowds at the WOMAD (World of Music, Arts and Dance), Montreux, and other festivals, as well as at concert halls and clubs all over Europe. The mix of young and old satisfied audiences, Winter explained, because "The old people do more ballads, the young like to play at 200 miles per hour, and are open to different styles, including Bulgarian, Yugoslavian, and Turkish influences. The old men are more traditional, but they like the music of the young. They're happy to see traditional music evolve and love the way children are changing it."

what to buy: The Haïdouks are irresistible. On the dance tunes, the band's rhythms are pumped out by a couple of accordions and anchored by a slappin' bass that rocks like some kind of mutant Arabic rockabilly, while the fiddles and cymbalum soar off on dizzying flights of fancy. On the ballads Manole's vocal pyrotechnics and melancholy violin take you back to the times of flickering campfires, when Gypsy tears twinkled as bright as the stars in the sky. The raw, driving music on *Musique des Tziganes de Roumanie* ♫♫♫♫ (Crammed Discs, 1991), from a band that lives the tradition, is one of the most exciting folk albums ever recorded. The second collection, *Honourable Brigands, Magic Horses, and Evil Eye* ♫♫♫♫ (Crammed Discs, 1994), is just as primal and exhilarating as the first; you probably need 'em both.

the rest:
Dumbala Dunba ♫♫♫♩ (Crammed Discs, 1998)

influences:
◀◀ Fanica Luca, Trio Pandelescu, Sandor Fodor, the Szazcsavas Band

j. poet

Tarika
/Tarika Sammy

Malagasy folk music, Afropop

Tarika formed in London, England, 1993. Tarika Sammy formed 1982, in Antananarivo, Madagascar. Tarika based in London, England; Tarika Sammy based in Madagascar.

Tarika (1993–present): Hanitra Rasoanaivo, korintsana, ambio, tsikadraha, vocals; Tina Norosoa Raharimalala, korintsana, ambio, tsikadraha, vocals; Dieudonné Randriamanantena, marovana, valiha, accordion, jejy voatavo; Victor Randrianasolomalala, kabosy, drums, vocals. Tarika Sammy #1 (1982–91): Sammy Andriamalalaharijaona, kabosy, marovana, kaiambarambo, valiha, fiddle, harmonica, percussion, vocals; Tiana Ratianarinaivo, kabosy, guitar, valiha, vocals; Hanitra Rasoanaivo, korintsana, ambio, tsikadraha, vocals; Tina Norosoa Raharimalala, korintsana, ambio, tsikadraha, vocals. Tarika Sammy #2 (1994–present): Sammy Andriamalalaharijaona, kabosy, marovana, kaiambarambo, valiha, fiddle, harmonica, percussion, vocals; Tiana Ratianarinaivo, kabosy, guitar, valiha, vocals; Johnny Andriamamahirana Zafimahery, guitar, bass, kabosy, valiha, n'lapa, vocals; Claudia Marie Noëll Ramasimanana, vocals; Hanitra Razaonialimiarina, vocals. (All members are from Madagascar.)

When Hanitra Rasoanaivo, band leader of Tarika, walks on stage, people gasp. She has a supermodel's looks and an elegant charisma that wakes up the crowd even before the music starts. When the band finally does launch into a high-energy Malagasy rave-up, the air becomes electric. "Ironically, Malagasy music is more popular outside Madagascar," Rasoanaivo says. "In Madagascar you're surrounded by people playing music—your family, all your friends—so we take it for granted, like the lemurs or the forest."

In 1983 London's Globestyle label led an expedition to Madagascar to record the local folk and pop music. The result was four stunning CDs of Malagasy music. Rasoanaivo had studied English at university and acted as the group's translator, introducing the Globestyle gang to musicians like Sammy Andraimanahirana. "Sammy was about to give up music, because folkloric musicians can't make a living. I convinced him to make a group for the Globestyle sessions, then joined the band." Tarika Sammy, fronted by Rasoanaivo, her sister Norosoa, and Andraimanahirana, got several tracks on Globestyle's *Current Modern Music of Madagascar,* as well as Henry Kaiser's *A World out of Time* compilations. Eventually Tarika Sammy signed to Green Linnet's Xenophile imprint and went on to become Madagascar's most well-known musical export. "I'm ambitious," Rasoanaivo says. "There are 12 ethnic groups in Madagascar, all with different styles that I'd like to reconcile. I also want to use other African rhythms." Andraimanahirana wanted

Hanitra Rasoanaivo of Tarika

to stay true to traditional rhythms, and left the band in 1991 to play folk music again.

Andraimanahirana's version of the band's ups and downs is considerably different from Rasoanaivo's, and in concert he often talks about the women who "stole" his band from him. It's difficult to choose sides in this disagreement, especially since both bands are producing compelling—and completely different—styles of Malagasy pop. Tarika Sammy's latest, *Beneath Southern Skies,* is a collection of traditionally flavored originals, while Tarika's current project is *Son Egal,* an attempt to meld Malagasy music with other African forms. Senegalese drumming, provided by members of Baaba Maal's band, gives Rasoanaivo's new compositions a sharp Pan-African edge. "In Madagascar when people get money, they go buy Western music," Rasoanaivo says. "I want to bring Malagasy music to the West, so our people will realize we have something unique to contribute to the world."

what to buy: In 1947 the Malagasy people tried to throw out the French colonials, who responded by hiring Senegalese mercenaries to put down the revolt. Ever since, there has been enmity between the people of Madagascar and Senegal. With *Son Egal* ♫♫♫♫ (Xenophile, 1997, prod. Simon Emmerson, Martin Russell) Rasoanaivo attempts a musical and spiritual healing by having Senegalese and Malagasy musicians play a set of politically charged tunes. The result won the Indie Label Grammy for World Music Album of the Year in 1998.

what to buy next: On *Beneath Southern Skies* ♫♫♫♫ (Xenophile, 1996) Tarika Sammy returns in fine form with a set that mixes instrumental prowess and sparkling vocals.

the rest:
Tarika Sammy:
Fanafody ♫♫♫♫ (Xenophile, 1992)
Balance ♫♫♫♫ (Xenophile, 1994)

Tarika:
Bibiango ♫♫♫♫ (Xenophile, 1994)

influences:
◀◀ Rakotofra, Tsimialona Volambita, Ny Sakelidalana, Rossy

▶▶ D'Gary, Les Smockers

see also: *Baaba Maal*

j. poet

Dave Tarras
Klezmer
Born 1897, in Russia. Died 1989, in New York, NY, USA.

Clarinet player Dave Tarras was one of the greatest influences on the U.S. revival of klezmer, the dance music of Eastern Euro-

pean Jews. His enthusiastic melodies, heard in cartoons and films, as well as with big bands including Joseph Cherniavsky's Yiddish-American Jazz Band, had a profound effect on such other influential jazz clarinetists as Benny Goodman and Don Byron. According to Henry Sapoznik, founder of the Archive of Recorded Sound at the Institute for Jewish Research in New York, Tarras's recordings were like "three-minute Rosetta Stones." A native of Russia, Tarras escaped religious persecution and emigrated to the United States in 1921. A highly trained musician, he became a regular performer in Yiddish theaters and the vaudeville circuit. First recording in 1925, he remained active until the mid-1950s.

what's available: *Yiddish-American Klezmer Music* ♫♫♫ (Yazoo, 1992, prod. Henry Sapoznik) features cuts from old 78s, radio transcriptions, and commercials recorded between 1925 and 1956. Although covering a shorter period, *1929–49: Master of Klezmer Music* ♫♫♫ (Global Village, 1995) further documents the strength and range of Tarras's music.

influences:
◀◀ Abe Schwartz's Orchestra, Naftule Brandwein

▶▶ Benny Goodman, Ziggy Elman, the Andrews Sisters, Klezmorim, the Klezmer Conservatory Band, Klezmatics, Don Byron's Bug Music

see also: *Kapelye, Klezmer Plus!*

Craig Harris

Tau Moe Family
Hawaiian traditional group falsetto singing with steel guitar
Formed 1934, in Hawaii (now USA). Disbanded 1980s.

Tau Moe (Samoa), steel guitar; Rose Kaohu Moe (Hawaii; died December 18, 1998), vocals; Lani Moe (Japan), vocals, ukulele; Dorian Moe (India), vocals and guitar.

The story of the Tau Moe Family is one of the most amazing in all of show business. Tau and Rose left Hawaii as teenagers to work for Madame Riviere, a woman sent by the French government to Tahiti, then a French colony. Mme. Riviere's Hawaiians, as their troupe was known, visited the colonial outposts of Europe and performed for the wealthy for seven years. After the group broke up, the Moes struck out on their own to tour the world for another 50 years, bringing the joy of Hawaiian music to the finest venues in dozens of countries. In the later years of World War II, Tau Moe led a big band in Bombay, India, with musicians from China, Russia, and Hawaii. The entire family finally returned home to Hawaii in the early 1980s, and continued to perform well into that decade, when Hawaiian music practitioner/preservationist Bob Brozman connected with them and recorded a wonderful retrospective album in 1988. It appeared in 1989, and 10 years later, even without Rose, Tau is carrying on with recording as he enters his 90s.

what's available: The recordings of this group are rare, and *The Tau Moe Family with Bob Brozman: Ho'omana'o I Na Mele O Ka Wa U'i (Remembering the Songs of Our Youth)* 𝄞𝄞𝄞𝄞 (Rounder, 1989, prod. Bob Brozman) is a better-than-the-originals recreation of those old songs. Every effort was made to get the exact instrumentation, timbre, rhythm, and harmony of the 1920s and 1930s. Tau played rhythm guitar in his uncle's old style, Rose sang, and Brozman played steel guitar with the intent of getting Tau's old 1929 sound.

worth searching for: Tau Moe Family completists will want to seek out two compilations showcasing rare recordings by related bands. *Vintage Hawaiian Music: The Great Singers 1928–34* 𝄞𝄞𝄞𝄞 (Rounder, 1989, prod. Bob Brozman) includes three tracks from Mme. Riviere's Hawaiians along with other first-class cuts by Kalama's Quartet, Sol Hoopii, and other unforgettable Hawaiian vocalists. Two 1952 songs recorded by Tau Moe and His Original Hawaiians appear on *Tickling the Strings 1929–52: Music of Hawai'i* 𝄞𝄞𝄞 (Harlequin, 1993, prod. Bruce Bastin). In general, anything on the Harlequin label is a winner, but this particular release lacks the fire of the Rounder compilation, no doubt because Brozman was not involved.

influences:

◀◀ Joe Kekuku, M.K. Moke, John Almeida, David Kaili, Sol Hoopii

▶▶ Bob Brozman, Robert Armstrong, Allen Dodge

Sandy Miranda

Te Vaka

Tokelauan folk and popular music
Formed in Auckland, New Zealand. Based in Auckland, New Zealand.

Opetaia Foa'i, lead vocal, guitar, percussion, log drum; Neil Forrest, log drum, percussion, electric guitar, vocals; Andrew Dukeson, drum kit, log drums; Luavasa Foa'i, bass, vocals; Lutila Kalolo, vocals; Nick Prater, wooden flute; Auburn, didgeridoo. (All members are from New Zealand.)

Opetaia Foa'i was born in Samoa and raised in New Zealand, but his parents are from Tokelau and Tuvalu, small islands in the mid-Pacific. Foa'i grew up in New Zealand's Tokelauan community, where he learned music from his uncles and stayed close to his people's traditional cultural expressions, particularly the log drum that provides the basic rhythm for his compositions. The band also uses Pacific *conga* and *tumba* drums, which were traditionally headed with sharkskin, though cow and goat are more commonly used today. Foa'i sings in the Tokelauan language, which has managed to retain its own

unique character despite years of contact with other Polynesian and European dialects.

what's available: Foa'i's compositions are based on Tokelauan folklore, but on *Original, Contemporary Pacific Music* 𝄞𝄞𝄞𝄞 (ARC England, 1997, prod. Malcolm Smith, Opetaia Foa'i) he blends this music with elements from all over the Pacific and the world. The most stirring thing about the album, aside from its strong melodies and the gorgeous harmonies of the singers (including a guest appearance by the Auckland Tokelauan Choir), is the drumming. The log drums have a sharp, exciting sound, and the driving polyrhythms are on a par with the work of the best Afropop bands.

influences:

◀◀ Bob Marley, Auckland Tokelauan Choir, Yothu Yindi

j. poet

The Techniques

Rocksteady, reggae, ska
Formed 1962, in Kingston, Jamaica. Disbanded 1972; re-formed 1982; disbanded 1983.

Keith "Slim" Smith, vocals (1962–66); Winston Riley, vocals (1962–72, 1982); Franklin White, vocals (1962–64); Frederick Waite, vocals (1962–66); Junior Menz, vocals (1964–66); Pat Kelly, vocals (1967–68); Bruce Ruffin, vocals (1967–69); Morvin Brooks, vocals (1967–70, 1982); Lloyd Parks, vocals (1968–69); Jackie Parris, vocals (1968–70); Dave Barker, vocals (1968–69); Tyrone "Don" Evans, vocals (1982). (All members are from Jamaica.)

The Techniques sported many fine vocalists in their storied heyday. Most of them ventured into successful solo careers; one suffered a lonely and premature demise. In 1962, under the leadership of founding members Winston Riley and Slim Smith, the fresh-scrubbed Techniques began performing their dramatic, refined Jamaican soul music at Kingston Senior School and future Jamaican Prime Minister Edward Seaga's Chocomo Lawn Youth Club. The combination of an inspirational performance at the 1964 Jamaica Festival, their first single, "No One," and their first *hit* single, the ska-charged "Little Did You Know," sent the Techniques' reputation soaring across the musical hotbed of Kingston. Popular ska singer Stranger Cole set up a meeting with Treasure Isle Studio honcho Duke Reid, who immediately produced the band's classic 1965 debut *Little Did You Know,* an LP that spotlighted Smith's quavering-with-emotion lead vocals in tandem with the group's chilling, sophisticated harmonies. Smith left in 1966 and released a number of hits on his own and with his next band, the Uniques, essentially a clone of the Techniques in style and substance. Pat Kelly, a subtler vocalist with a rapturous sense of phrasing and a distinctive falsetto, moved into the lead spot for a string of famed rocksteady singles, including "You Don't Care" (a #1 hit in Jamaica), "Queen Majesty" (a soul-nourishing and novel interpretation of the Impressions' "Minstrel and Queen"), a cover of the Temptations' "I Wish It Would Rain," "Run Come Celebrate," and the extraordinarily sublime "It's You I Love." All are now regarded as exemplars of vocal mastery in the rugged, electric bass-driven, rocksteady groove. Also added to the group at this time was the deeper-voiced Bruce Ruffin, who added guts to the existing vocalists' glory. In 1968 Riley formed his own Techniques label with his brother Buster, who was a member of the Sensations. Riley self-produced the Techniques on songs that were every bit the equal of their eminently sensitive work for Duke Reid, including "Man of My Word," "One Day," "What's It All About," and "Go Find Yourself a Fool." Ex-Termites vocalist Lloyd Parks then joined the group, which by now was considered an academy for elite vocalists. But as Riley focused more on production and rhythm-creation during the reggae era, the Techniques separated and pursued solo careers. In 1970 Riley produced former-Technique Dave Barker's U.K. #1 hit single "Double Barrel" and the follow-up smash "Monkey Spanner," a song also notable as the first recording session of Sly Dunbar (of now-legendary rhythm section/production team Sly & Robbie). Ruffin recorded some unjustly neglected singles for Leslie Kong, including "Dry Up Your Tears," "Free the People," and a dynamite cover of the Five Stairsteps' "Ooh Child." Pat Kelly had a #1 single in 1969 with "How Long Will It Take," the first Jamaican record to feature a string arrangement. Original Technique Frederick Waite managed and fathered two members of Musical Youth, whose 1982 hit "Pass the Dutchie" (based on the Mighty Diamonds' "Pass the Kouchie") still stands as one of reggae's biggest international hits. Riley went on to become a prominent architect of dancehall music and one of the most important deejay producers in the land, launching the careers of General Echo and Super Cat in addition to the great dancehall singers Frankie Paul and Tenor Saw. Riley also created the wicked "Stalag" riddim, which would thrive in and at times dominate the dancehall over the next two decades. In 1982 Riley briefly revived the Techniques with Brooks and Tyrone "Don" Davis (formerly of the Paragons) and released *I'll Never Fall in Love*. Slim Smith overcame recurring mental illness to become one of Jamaica's most memorable vocalists. However, in 1973, he was locked against his will in a poorly run mental asylum. In a desperate attempt to escape, Slim severed a vein when he punched his bare fist through a small glass window. Unfitting and unfair as it may seem for a man who contributed so much to Jamaica's culture, Smith bled to death alone in his sanitarium cell.

what to buy: The yearning beauty of the Techniques' seductive harmonizing is demonstrated on *Run Come Celebrate:*

Their Greatest Reggae Hits 𝄢𝄢𝄢𝄢 (Heartbeat, 1994, prod. Duke Reid, Winston Riley), which includes the utterly alchemical title cut, "Queen Majesty," and the wise and mellifluous "Love Is Not a Gamble," along with previously unreleased rarities like "Festival '68." *Rock Steady Classics* 𝄢𝄢𝄢𝄢 (Rhino U.K., 1994, prod. Duke Reid) fills in the gaps on the Heartbeat collection with must-have groove-de-forces "You Don't Care," "There Comes a Time," and the thoroughly intoxicating "Drink Wine," which will leave you feeling buzzed and ecstatic without even a drop of the title sauce. *Little Did You Know* 𝄢𝄢𝄢𝄢 (Treasure Isle, 1965, prod. Duke Reid) contains early Techniques gems "Don't Leave Me," "When You Are Wrong," and the title cut, all of which showcase Smith's striking, passion-packed falsetto and somewhat frenzied edginess. The peerless Don Drummond (trombone) and Lynn Taitt (guitar) provide stunning instrumental moments as well.

the rest:
Unforgettable Days: 1965–72 𝄢𝄢𝄢𝄢 (Techniques, 1981)
I'll Never Fall in Love 𝄢𝄢𝄢 (Techniques, 1982)
Classics, Vols. I & II 𝄢𝄢𝄢𝄢 (Techniques, 1991)

worth searching for: *Techniques in Dub* 𝄢𝄢𝄢𝄢 (Pressure Sounds, 1997, prod. Winston Riley) is a re-release of the classic 1976 *Meditation Dub* LP with a number of previously unreleased tracks. This is a pleasantly woozy and spacious dub album that, unlike most other recordings in the sometimes heavy-handed genre, contains an abundance of lovely melodic elements—primarily because the melodies and rhythms originate from vintage Techniques sides. These no-frills instrumentals are bolstered by top-rank musicians like Jackie Mittoo, Sly & Robbie, "Chinna" Smith, and ex-Skatalites Roland Alphonso and Tommy McCook. While it still packs a rhythmic knockout punch that ranks with even the most heavyweight dub, this is also one of the most listenable and soothing albums of its kind you will find, perfect for those hesitant but curious dub novices out there.

influences:

◄◄ Sam Cooke, Nat King Cole, the Impressions, Curtis Mayfield, the Temptations, the Blues Busters, Jackie Edwards, Owen Gray

►► The Uniques, the Mighty Diamonds, the Chosen Few, Chain Reaction, Joseph Cotton, Sanchez, Nora Dean, Tenor Saw, Cutty Ranks, General Echo, Frankie Paul, Lone Ranger, Super Cat, Sons of Jah, Papa San, Admiral Tibet, Musical Youth

see also: *Jackie Mittoo, Musical Youth, the Skatalites, Sly & Robbie, Super Cat*

Todd Shanker

Omar Faruk Tekbilek /Omar Faruk Tekbilek & the Sultans

Turkish and Middle Eastern folk, classical, and religious music
Born in Istanbul, Turkey. Based in Rochester, NY, USA.

Born to a Turkish father and Egyptian mother in Istanbul, Faruk (as he prefers to be called) began his career at age nine while working in a music store. He credits the owner of the store for giving him the opportunity of a lifetime. "It is he who taught me to read music and told me to work there as a salesman, to play and watch. And I would absorb everything," says Faruk. Indeed he did, learning to play an incredible variety of Turkish instruments and becoming especially known for his work on the *ney,* a long, end-blown flute made of cane. By age 12 Faruk was gigging professionally in Istanbul with the great Turkish musicians of the time, such as flute and saxophone player Ismet Siral and famous percussionist Burhan Tonque. At 17 Faruk was working with the great teacher and jazzist I. Siral (no relation to Ismet). During the '60s Faruk made a name for himself as one of the world's foremost performers of Middle Eastern music. In 1971, also established as one of the top Turkish studio musicians, he began touring Europe and the States, relocating to New York state in 1971, where he settled and married an American woman. Faruk has recorded and performed with many internationally known musicians, including arranger Arif Mardin, jazz notables Don Cherry and Karl Berger, and rock drummer Ginger Baker. He has made prestigious concert appearances worldwide, including the Kool Jazz Festival and the Israeli Music Festival. Introduced to the Celestial Harmonies label by accomplished composer and guitarist Brian Keane, Faruk went on to collaborate with him on several projects. Label owner Eckart Rahn then offered Faruk an opportunity to compose solo works for Celestial Harmonies. Rahn is also credited with introducing Faruk to one of Australia's leading percussionists, Michael Askill of the ensemble Synergy, thus setting Faruk on yet another rewarding path in his always-eventful creative journey.

what to buy: *Süleyman the Magnificent* ♪♪♪♪ (Celestial Harmonies, 1988, prod. Briane Keane) is the soundtrack for the film about the life of the great Sultan of the Ottoman Empire. Süleyman reigned from 1520–66 and was known as a reformer of law and administration. The album features Turkish melodies and Keane's original ones on a combination of authentic Turkish instruments, including the *tanbur* (long-necked lute), *daire* (drum), *kanun* (plucked boxed zither), and *kaval* (rim-blown flute, a pastoral instrument associated with shepherds and nomads). The film aired on PBS and was a winner of the American Film Festival and Ohio State Film Festival awards.

Although the U.S. guitarist and Turkish multi-instrumentalist hail from different backgrounds, they developed a close musical rapport and an ongoing collaboration. *Fire Dance* ♪♪♪♪♪ (Celestial Harmonies, 1990, prod. Briane Keane) is a natural progression from *Süleyman,* blending a plethora of Middle Eastern and North African instruments with synthesizers, guitar, and sophisticated orchestrations. The compositional focus of *Fire Dance* also expands beyond Turkey to include music from Egyptian and other North African, Middle Eastern, and Arabic sources. Selections feature the *oud* (similar to the lute), the *zurna* (like an oboe), and a wide array of percussion instruments. *Beyond the Sky* ♪♪♪♪♪ (Celestial Harmonies, 1992, prod. Briane Keane) has Faruk and Keane joined by Ara Dinkjian, one of the foremost oud players in the world, and Armenian percussionist Arto Tuncboyaciyan, a bandmate of Dinkjian's in the ensemble Night Ark, which is well known in Greece, Turkey, and the Middle East. Also joining the project in his recording debut is Hassan Isikkut, with a unique and dazzling style of playing the kanun.

what to buy next: *Whirling* ♪♪♪♪ (Celestial Harmonies, 1992, prod. Briane Keane) is Faruk's debut as a solo artist, reuniting him with Dinkjian (oud), Isikkut (kanun), and Tuncboyaciyan (percussion). Brian Keane adds guitar and his subtle, atmospheric orchestrations. *Whirling* is a musical tribute to Sufi religious music, and references the dervishes, who enter trancelike states of reverence while whirling in place. The various-artists compilation *Gypsy Fire* ♪♪♪♪ (Traditional Crossroads, 1995, prod. Richard A. Hagopian) incorporates the influence of Gypsy music from around the world with traditional Turkish sounds and instruments. *Mystical Garden* ♪♪♪♪ (Celestial Harmonies, 1996, prod. Brian Keane) has Keane, Isikkut, Tuncboyaciyan, Dinkjian, and Dan Pickering joining Faruk to explore the garden theme important in the Turkish Sufi mythos. *Crescent Moon* ♪♪♪♪♪ (Celestial Harmonies, 1998, prod. Brian Keane) gets Faruk and Keane at it again, along with guest Steve Roach, to offer homage to the history of the crescent moon, an important Islamic religious symbol. *Fata Morgana* ♪♪♪♪ (Celestial Harmonies, 1995, prod. Michael Askill) is a collaboration between Michael Askill and Faruk, suggested by Celestial Harmonies-head Rahn, preceded by phone exchanges of ideas between the two artists, and recorded in two days right after their first actual face-to-face meeting. Ghassan Barakat, Ian Cleworth, and Rebecca Lagos also lend their talents to 15 selections reflecting the musical cultures of the Middle East, Asia, West Africa, and Western jazz and classical music. In *Salomé* ♪♪♪♪ (Black Sun, 1998, prod. Michael Askill), Askill and Faruk provide a traditional soundtrack for the Bible story.

worth searching for: *The Best of the Sultans* ♪♪♪♪ (Dynamic, 1997) is a compilation of tunes by Omar Faruk Tekbilek & the

Sultans. Originally named the Sultans Middle Eastern Band, the group was formed in 1976 by Faruk and his brother-in-law Ibrahim Turmen, a *darbuka* (Turkish percussion instrument) master. Other members included Egyptian Sherif Sarakby performing on keyboards and accordion and Greek Nick Mouganis playing bouzouki, guitar, and bass. The Sultans released five dynamic recordings; this collection, which captures and enhances their best performances, was remastered for CD. *World Resonance* ♪♪♪♪ (DRK, 1998) is a collaboration between Faruk (ney, *bendir* drum, and darbuka), Mitzie Collins (Celtic hammered dulcimer), and Al Saint John (Caribbean steel drums) of the Trinidad & Tobago Steel Band. The CD insert contains photos detailing the instrumentation and its history, as well as personal anecdotes about the musicians and the way they came together for this four-year project.

influences:
◀◀ I. Siral

see also: *Steve Roach, Synergy, Vas*

Stacy Meyn

Terem Quartet

Russian folk music
Formed 1986, in St. Petersburg, Russia. Based in St. Petersburg, Russia.

Andrei Konstantinov, soprano domra, vocal; Igor Ponomarenko, alto domra, vocal; Andrei Smirnov, accordion, vocal; Mikhail Dziudze, bass balalaika, vocal. (All members are from Russia.)

St. Petersburg has a reputation for being a bohemian city, and the "punk folk" of the Terem Quartet might not have happened anywhere else in Russia. This quartet of classically trained musicians met at the then Leningrad Conservatory and play Russian folk music that includes Gypsy dance tunes, traditional ballads, pop songs arranged as "traditional" material, and even a bit of Tchaikovsky. The Quartet has astonishing technique; their playing is energetic and totally devoid of the academic stodginess that can often make listening to traditional music a chore. They've been credited with re-energizing interest in Russian folk music among the younger generation.

what's available: *Terem* ♪♪♪♪ (RealWorld, 1992, prod. Tony Berg) is a wild Russian hootenanny that never lets up. The *domra* is a small three-stringed guitar plucked like a mandolin that produces a rippling shower of arpeggios to carry the music forward at breakneck speed.

influences:
◀◀ Theodore Bikel, Sasha Polinoff, Vladimir Vysotsky

j. poet

Texas Tornados

Tex-Mex, country, rock 'n' roll
Formed 1989, in San Francisco, CA, USA. Based in Texas, USA.

Doug Sahm, vocals, guitar; Freddy Fender, vocals, guitar; Flaco Jimenez, accordion, vocals; Augie Meyers, keyboards, vocals. (All members are from USA.) ,

For those seeking encyclopedic knowledge of Texas music over the past three decades or so, you could do a lot worse than to begin your search with a serious study of the Texas Tornados. From the Anglo side come rockers Doug Sahm and Augie Meyers, who brought arid border breezes to the rest of the nation in the '60s with the Sir Douglas Quintet and songs like "She's about a Mover" and "Mendocino." From the Latino side come balladeer non pareil Freddy Fender, who charted with "Wasted Days and Wasted Nights" and "Before the Next Teardrop Falls," and accordionist Flaco Jimenez, who has enjoyed crossover success by rocking up traditional Mexican *conjunto* and *norteño* styles. The Tornados play party music, pure and simple, with an occasional Fender ballad or Sir Douglas oldie thrown in like a couple of swigs of cerveza between bites of hot Texas chili. Given how mercurial the individual members of the group are, that they can get together to make music this engaging—aw, hell, just plain fun—is nothing short of awe-inspiring.

what to buy: The Tornados' best album is their debut, *Texas Tornados* ♪♪♪♪ (Reprise, 1990, prod. Bill Halverson, Texas Tornados). Featuring songs sung in Spanish and English, the group scores with the Sir Douglas–style "Who Were You Thinkin' Of" and the high-stepping conjunto number "(Hey Baby) Que Paso." Fender contributes the heart-tugging ballad "A Man Can Cry," and Sahm takes an admirable run at Butch Hancock's brilliant "She Never Spoke Spanish to Me." The album is also available in a Spanish-only version, *Los Texas Tornados* ♪♪♪♪ (Reprise, 1990, prod. Bill Halverson, Texas Tornados).

what to buy next: *The Best of Texas Tornados* ♪♪♪♪ (Reprise, 1994, prod. Bill Halverson, Texas Tornados) is just that, collecting tunes from each of their albums, including updates of Fender's "Wasted Days and Wasted Nights" and Sahm's "Is Anybody Goin' to San Antone."

what to avoid: *The Nada Mixes* **woof!** (Reprise, 1997) contains dance remixes of "A Little Bit Is Better Than Nada" from 1995's *4 Aces*. In this case, nada would have been better.

the rest:
Hangin' on by a Thread ♪♪♪♪ (Reprise, 1991)
Zone of Our Own ♪♪♪ (Reprise, 1992)
4 Aces ♪♪♪♪ (Reprise, 1995)

(l to r) Doug Sahm, Augie Meyers, and Freddy Fender of the Texas Tornados

influences:

◄◄ Don Santiago Jimenez, the Dave Clark Five, Ritchie Valens, Bob Dylan

►► Emilio, Los Lobos, Santiago Jimenez Jr., Los Super Seven

see also: *Flaco Jimenez, Los Super Seven*

Daniel Durchholz

Mikis Theodorakis

Greek modern and classical
Born 1925, on Chios Island, Greece. Based in Athens, Greece.

Mixing Greek *bouzoukis,* modern classical, and a heavy dose of Marxist politics, the music of Mikis Theodorakis is not everyone's cup of ouzo. His career as a political firebrand—which has gotten him tortured, imprisoned, and exiled—has attracted as much attention as his music. Theodorakis wrote his *Symphony No. 1* in 1945 in the heat of the Greek civil war, while engaged in street fighting against the royalists and the British. He was also jailed and tortured during World War II, yet managed to lead his

first concert of choral music and publish a poetry chapbook, both at age 17. He has continued to write lyrics since, while his brother Yannis has also written words to many of his compositions. Many of Theodorakis's best-known works are musical settings of poetry by Pablo Neruda, George Seferis, Yannis Ritsos, and others. He has composed much choral music since his first symphony, considering the human voice to be the most beautiful instrument—though his own thin vocal performances stand in contrast to the powerful female singers who have interpreted his work best, including Maria Farandouri and Agnes Baltsa.

Theodorakis studied composition at Athens Conservatory in the '40s, and in Paris under Olivier Messiaen in the '50s. He rose to prominence in the mid-'60s as founder of the Greek Communist Youth Organization and the Patriotic Front, and as composer of the hit film soundtrack *Zorba the Greek.* When a military dictatorship seized power in 1967 Theodorakis was imprisoned in a concentration camp and then banished until 1970; sale or performance of his music was illegal during that period. While in exile he scored the films *Z* and *Serpico.* After the junta fell in 1974 he returned home triumphantly to resume an active musical and political life, closely entwined as ever. These activities included finding time to compose several symphonies and involvement in controversial work with Turkish protest singer Zülfü Livandi. A heavyset bear of a man, Theodorakis suffered a heart attack in 1980 while conducting his own work at the Kennedy Center in Washington, D.C. He recovered to become a communist Member of Parliament the following year, a seat he held off and on until 1993, spending two of those years as a government minister as well. At the same time he directed the Greek Radio Symphony Orchestra and composed theme music for the Barcelona Olympics—seemingly with his left hand. On the cusp of the Millenium this dynamo had composed at least 1,000 songs, seven symphonies, seven ballets, four operas, and 13 soundtracks . . . and counting.

what to buy: For an introduction to Theodorakis's traditional folk side, *Opyavikó* ♫♫♫♫ (Minerva, 1987) is bouncy bouzouki music that transforms any room into a Greek coffee shop or taverna. For his heavier, artier side, *To Axion Esti* ♫♫♫♫ (Minos/EMI, 1988) brings it all together: a double CD of haunting bouzouki melodies, Turkish-tinged sounds, majestic orchestral work, and singing, intercut with poems by Nobel Prize winner Odysseus Elytis.

what to buy next: *The Ballad of Mauthausen/Six Songs* ♫♫♫ (Fidelio/Sound-Products) is about as heavy as you can get; bitter songs based on an Austrian concentration camp and similarly grim subject matter. Vocalist Maria Farandouri is at the height of her powers, while the composer conducts.

what to avoid: *Theodorakis Sings Theodorakis* ♫♫ (Intuition, 1991, prod. Wolfgang Loos) is for fans only; at age 66 his voice is well past its prime. Still, songs like "Repudiation" are haunting despite the thin, uncertain vocals. Another completists-only disc is *Canto General* ♫ (RCA/BMG/Ariola, 1975/1991): massive settings of Neruda poems recorded live before huge stadium crowds in Greece shortly after the fall of the junta. Today it sounds badly dated and pompous. Even Maria Farandouri is strident and histrionic, though male vocalist Petros Pandis delivers moving solos. The audience is riotous with excitement; guess you had to be there.

the rest:
PANTAP ♫♫♫ (Minos, 1981)
Symphony No. 4 (of the Choral Odes) ♫♫♫♫ (Athens Symphony Orchestra, cond. Lukas Karytinos) (Intuition, 1984/98)
Alexis Zorbas Ballet Suite ♫♫♫ (Hungarian State Orchestra, cond. Theodorakis/Lukas Karytinos) (Intuition, 1989)
Canto Olympico ♫♫♫ (Greek Radio Symphony Orchestra) (Intuition/Lyra, 1992)
Zorba: The Ballet (excerpts) ♫♫♫ (Intuition, 1992/96)

worth searching for: Greek mezzo-soprano Agnes Baltsa's collection *Songs My Country Taught Me* ♫♫♫♫ (Deutsche Gramo-

phone, 1986) includes several Theodorakis elegies backed by bouzouki and orchestra—a wonderful entry gate. *The Very Best of Maria Farandouri* ♫♫♫♫ (Minos, 1987) is a fascinating mix, featuring tunes by Theodorakis along with other Greek and international heavy-hitters. *Arja & Mikis—Paijaa mua* ♫♫♫ (MTV Musiikki/AXR, 1993) is an oddity, with Theodorakis conducting live performances of his poppier tunes sung in Finnish by tango vocalist Arja Saijonmaa.

influences:

◀◀ Olivier Messiaen, Wolfgang von Beethoven, *rembetiko* music

▶▶ Maria Farandouri, Agnes Baltsa

see also: *Stavros Xarhakos & Nicos Gatsos*

Wif Stenger

Third World

Reggae, pop
Formed 1973, in Kingston, Jamaica. Based in Jamaica.

Stephen "Cat" Coore, guitar; Michael "Ibo" Cooper, keyboards; William "Bunny Rugs" Clark, vocals (1977–present); Milton "Prilly" Hamilton, vocals (1973–77); William "Willie" Stewart, drums (1977–present); Cornel Marshall, drums (1973–77); Richard Daley, bass; Irvin "Carrot" Jarrett, percussion (1973–89). (All members are from Jamaica.)

When classical cellist/guitarist Cat Coore (son of Jamaica's Minister of Finance) and keyboardist Ibo Cooper formed Third World in response to the dearth of live reggae music in 1973, they had no idea that they would still be meeting the need over 25 years later. Barnstorming the island with other cohorts Richard Daley, Cornel Marshall, and Prilly Hamilton, Third World soon became the buzz of Jamaica with their original tunes and covers of U.S. R&B hits. Aided by a loan of £4,000, they traveled to London with one thing in mind—securing a contract with Island Records, home of Bob Marley & the Wailers. Within weeks, they signed and opened for Marley at the legendary Lyceum concert preserved on his *Live* LP. In late 1976 the label released Third World's groundbreaking, self-titled debut. Neither in the roots nor militant styles of reggae that predominated at the time, Third World was an audacious, decidedly pop-rock version of the form; more Santana, Kool & the Gang, and Beatles than Abyssinians or Burning Spear. Unfortunately, the album also revealed the band's weakness: inconsistency. The next year Third World replaced Hamilton and Marshall with Bunny Rugs Clark and Willie Stewart and created their masterwork, *96 Degrees in the Shade*. A killah mix of anthemic originals ("Jah Glory," "Rhythm of Life," the title tune) with an inspired, almost definitive version of Bunny Wailer's "Dreamland," this is a triumph of reggae genre expansion. Nonetheless, *96 Degrees in the Shade* was not well received—but its follow-up, *Journey to Addis,* was. Propelled by the radio/club smash "Now That We Found Love," the album crossed Third World into the pop mainstream. Now a truly global reggae band, Third World slipped into a long-term strategy of diminishing returns: they would reduce their touring to select venues and make records with one or two blockbusters and cool but underachieving filler tracks. The hits—"Try Jah Love," "Sense of Purpose," "Lagos Jump"—followed (albeit sporadically), but by the mid-1980s the band was relegated to nostalgia-act status. They continue with their salad-days membership intact, but seem sadly past their time.

what to buy: *96 Degrees in the Shade* ♪♪♪♪ (Mango, 1977/1996, prod. Third World) is ground zero for reggae-pop. Sure, Bob Marley is the King, but this album is fighting for a corner of his throne. Essential.

what to buy next: *Reggae Ambassadors: 20th Anniversary* ♪♪♪ (Island Chronicles, 1993, prod. various) is not the definitive Third World anthology. Although it contains a few songs from the band's Columbia and later Mercury tenures, this is basically a by-the-numbers hits package. There's just not enough from crucial out-of-print Island discs *Prisoner in the Streets, Third World,* and *Arise in Harmony* or the Columbia stuff. Hopefully, someday justice will be done.

what to avoid: Early in the 1990s the group self-released its albums, but *Live It Up* ♪♪ (Third World, 1995) leaves you wondering if they'd have been able to get another label interested anyway.

the rest:
Reggae Greats ♪♪♪♪ (Mango)
Rock the World ♪♪♪ (Columbia, 1981/1989)
You've Got the Power ♪♪♪ (Columbia, 1982)
Sense of Purpose ♪♪♪ (Columbia, 1985)
Hold on to Love ♪♪ (Columbia, 1987)
All the Way Strong ♪♪ (Columbia, 1989)
Serious Business ♪♪♪ (Mercury, 1989)
Committed ♪♪♪ (Mercury, 1992)
The Best of Third World ♪♪♪ (Legacy, 1993)
Generation Coming ♪♪♪ (Gator, 1999)

worth searching for: *Aiye Keta* ♪♪♪ (Edsel U.K., 1973/1997) is an interesting if intermittently successful collaboration with Steve Winwood.

influences:
◄◄ Bob Marley, Santana, the Paragons

►► Foundation, Steel Pulse, UB40, 311

see also: *Bob Marley, Bunny Wailer*

Tom Terrell and Gary Graff

Eric & Suzy Thompson
See: California Cajun Orchestra

Richard Thompson
/Linda Thompson
/Richard & Linda Thompson
Rock, Anglo-Celtic folk-rock

Formed 1972, in England; discontinued work as duo, 1982. Richard Thompson based in London, England, and Los Angeles, CA, USA. Linda Thompson based in London, England.

Richard Thompson (born April 3, 1949, in London, England), vocals, guitar; Linda Thompson (born Linda Pettifer, 1948, in London, England), vocals.

Richard Thompson, an original member of the innovative folk-rock band Fairport Convention, has in the intervening years carved out a niche as a supremely gifted songwriter and guitarist. With his deep, burnished vocals and generally dark songs, he has modernized the British folk idiom in several ways; his expressive, often baroque fretwork conjoins a number of different traditions—imagine a Celtic Hendrix in Morocco—and has hugely influenced Mark Knopfler of Dire Straits, among many others. It was Richard Thompson's fellow Fairport Convention alum Sandy Denny who first introduced him to her friend Linda Peters (born Pettifer), who sang in folk clubs and recorded commercial jingles. They married during the early '70s, converted to Islam in 1974, and divorced in 1982 (Richard subsequently married Nancy Covey). Richard began his solo career first, with 1972's *Henry the Human Fly,* then joined forces with Linda for some of the most emotionally bare music ever produced in the pop idiom. After they split up Richard reactivated his solo career; worked with avant-gardists Fred Frith, Henry Kaiser, and John French; was a busy gun-for-hire (Nick Drake, J.J. Cale, Robert Plant, Bonnie Raitt, Crowded House, Suzanne Vega, the Golden Palominos, Syd Straw); and wielded enough influenced to inspire a 1994 tribute album featuring a bevy of cutting-edge acts. Linda moved into theater before releasing a solo album in 1985 and a retrospective in 1996.

what to buy: The couple's *Shoot out the Lights* ♪♪♪♪♪ (Hannibal, 1982, prod. Joe Boyd), the release of which barely preceded their divorce, is a devastating, virtually flawless set of performances and the last of their collaborations. Their first release, *I Want to See the Bright Lights Tonight* ♪♪♪♪ (Hannibal, 1974/Rykodisc, 1991, prod. Richard Thompson, John Wood), is an equally gripping and somewhat happier dialogue.

what to buy next: Richard's first solo album, *Henry the Human Fly* ♪♪♪♪♪ (Warner Bros., 1972/Rykodisc-Hannibal, 1991, prod. Richard Thompson, John Wood) is saturated with his fondness for English roots music. Richard's best solo work is collected in the hefty but consistently engaging three-disc set *Watching the Dark: The History of Richard Thompson* 𝄞𝄞𝄞 (Rykodisc/Hannibal, 1993, prod. various). Linda's *Dreams Fly Away* 𝄞𝄞𝄞 (Rykodisc/Hannibal, 1996, prod. various) is a 20-track overview of her career, from before Richard to her post-divorce work.

the rest:
Richard Thompson:
(Guitar, Vocal) 𝄞𝄞𝄞 (Island, 1976/Rykodisc-Hannibal, 1991)
Strict Tempo! 𝄞𝄞𝄞 (Hannibal, 1981)
Hand of Kindness 𝄞𝄞𝄞 (Hannibal, 1983/Rykodisc-Hannibal, 1991)
Small Town Romance 𝄞𝄞𝄞 (Hannibal, 1984)
Across a Crowded Room 𝄞𝄞𝄞 (Polydor, 1985)
Daring Adventures 𝄞𝄞𝄞 (Polydor, 1986)
Mirror Blue 𝄞𝄞𝄞 (Capitol, 1994)
You? Me? Us? 𝄞𝄞𝄞 (Capitol, 1996)
(With Danny Thompson) *Industry* 𝄞𝄞𝄞 (Hannibal/Carthage, 1997)
(With Philip Pickett and the Fairport Rhythm Section) The Bones of All Men 𝄞𝄞 (Hannibal, 1998)

French, Frith, Kaiser & Thompson:
Live, Love, Larf, and Loaf 𝄞𝄞𝄞 (Rhino, 1987)
Invisible Means 𝄞𝄞𝄞 (Windham Hill, 1990)

Richard & Linda Thompson:
Hokey Pokey 𝄞𝄞𝄞 (Hannibal, 1975/Rykodisc-Hannibal, 1991)
Pour down like Silver 𝄞𝄞𝄞 (Hannibal, 1975/Rykodisc-Hannibal, 1991)
First Light 𝄞𝄞𝄞 (Carthage, 1978/Rykodisc, 1992)
Sunnyvista 𝄞𝄞𝄞 (Carthage, 1979/Rykodisc, 1992)

Linda Thompson:
One Clear Moment 𝄞𝄞𝄞 (Warner Bros., 1978)

worth searching for: Two of Richard's best albums are out of print at the moment. *Rumor and Sigh* 𝄞𝄞𝄞 (Capitol, 1991, prod. Mitchell Froom) reveals his passionate concerns about the global condition. A solid set of compositions includes the anti-imperialist "Yankee, Go Home"; the Dylanesque "Jerusalem on the Jukebox," about the media trivialization of religion; and "Pharaoh," where "Maggie's Farm" meets "Go Down Moses." *Amnesia* 𝄞𝄞𝄞 (Capitol, 1988, prod. Mitchell Froom) attacks former British Prime Minister Margaret Thatcher with a blistering "Mother Knows Best," but it's also a showcase for his gift for musical mimicry, with a Scottish polka for record collectors ("Don't Sit on My Jimmy Shands") and a ballad about motorcycle-based romance ("1952 Vincent Black Lightning"). The Kurt Weill–influenced "God Loves a Drunk" is one of Richard's masterpieces. The Richard & Linda Thompson disc *Strange Affair* 𝄞𝄞𝄞 (Silver Rarities, 1994) offers Thompson followers a chance to hear selections from the couple's 1977 concerts, featuring long, mystical electric guitar solos and lyrics influenced by Sufi devotional poetry. The two-disc set also includes some of the couple's best unreleased material from 1978 and 1980. Henry Kaiser's album *Hope You'll Like*

Our New Direction 𝄞𝄞𝄞 (Reckless, 1991, prod. various) includes Kaiser's buddy Richard on two tracks: "Kanaka Wai Wai," a Hawaiian slack-key guitar piece with Raymond and Elodea Kane; and "Annihilation in Allah," a traditional Muslim song movingly sung by Richard in the original Arabic.

influences:
◀◀ Wes Montgomery, Django Reinhardt, Jimi Hendrix, Nick Drake, Van Morrison, Bob Dylan

▶▶ Dire Straits, Elvis Costello, Jeff Buckley, Womack & Womack, Billy Bragg

see also: *Sandy Denny, Fairport Convention, Home Service, Ashley Hutchings, Ray Kane, Trevor Lucas, Oyster Band*

Simon Glickman, Gary Graff, and Pamela Murray Winters

Simon Thoumire /Seannachie

Scottish folk
Born July 11, 1970, in Edinburgh, Scotland. Based in Scotland.

Based upon the volume of work he's done in such a relatively short period of time, Simon Thoumire could be labeled the "Mark O'Connor" of the concertina. Just as O'Connor—a former bluegrass fiddle prodigy from the States—was a perennial prizewinner in his youth before developing into the mature artist we know today, Thoumire's early career as a concertina player foreshadowed his current remarkable skills. His precocious triumphs included BBC Radio 2's Young Tradition Award and kudos from the British magazine *Folk Roots* for the year's "most innovative performance," both in 1989. To add to these distinctions he has toured all over Europe and North America; played with such well-regarded elder statesmen as Aly Bain, Phil Cunningham, and Dónal Lunny; taught the art of concertina playing in both the U.K. and the United States; appeared on various radio and television shows; and worked with Yehudi Menuhin's "Live Music Now!" program bringing high-quality performances into a variety of communities. With the exception of *March, Stratspey & Surreal* none of Thoumire's material is readily available in the U.S., although the rest can probably be ordered through the Internet. A self-taught musician, Thoumire started playing the bagpipes when he was nine years old and moved on to the concertina when he was 12, supposedly after hearing a broadcast that featured Hamish Bain. His first professional gigs occurred in 1989 as a member of the tradition-oriented group Seannachie, with whom he was later to make a pair of well-received albums. But Thoumire has actually done his most interesting work as a band leader, or co-leader, with the guitarist Ian Carr and keyboard player Fergus MacKenzie. As the force behind the Simon Thoumire Three, he has forged a spirited blend of traditional Scottish folk-roots with high-flying jazz riffs. Their first album, *Waltzes for Playboys,* only set the stage for the wonders of their second release, *March, Stratspey & Surreal.* Thoumire has also kept himself busy with a series of often ad hoc ensembles, including Simon Thoumire's Reel Life Ceilidh and the Simon Thoumire Orchestra. Perhaps his most quirky project has been the pseudonymous "Hamish MacGregor and the Blue Bonnets" album *Trip to Scotland.*

what's available: *March, Strathspey & Surreal* 𝄞𝄞𝄞𝄞 (Green Linnet, 1996, prod. Simon Thoumire) is probably the finest blend of traditional Scottish folk tunes and jazz ever played on a concertina. Kevin MacKenzie's guitar and Simon Thorpe's bass lines provide much of the disc's jazz feel, but Thoumire has a flair for improvisation as well. Rhythmic flexibility is the key phrase here, but not the kind of willy-nilly beat sure to confound dancers; rather a pulse that ebbs and flows with a virtuosic naturalness.

the rest:
(With Ian Carr) *Hootz* 𝄞𝄞𝄞𝄞 (Black Crow, 1990)
Waltzes for Playboys 𝄞𝄞𝄞𝄞 (Celtic Music, 1993)
(With Fergus MacKenzie) *Exhibit A* 𝄞𝄞𝄞 (Iona, 1995)

worth searching for: *Trip to Scotland* 𝄞𝄞𝄞 (Tartan Tapes, 1997, prod. Hamish MacGregor) is a hoot because it features Thoumire with a few members of the Mollys on a disc created specifically for the tourist trade. The group calls itself Hamish MacGregor & the Blue Bonnets for this set, but nowhere on the jacket is there any information that would connect Thoumire with the project. Fiddle and pipes are the main instruments on the album, and the players whip through a set of traditional folk melodies.

solo outings:
Seannachie:
Take Note 𝄞𝄞𝄞 (Raven, 1988)
Devil's Delight 𝄞𝄞𝄞𝄞 (Raven, 1992)

influences:
⏪ Hamish Bain

see also: *The Mollys*

Garaud MacTaggart

3 Leg Torso

Eastern European cabaret-tango
Formed 1996, in Portland, OR, USA. Based in Portland, OR, USA.

Béla Balogh, violin; Gabe Leavitt, cello; Courtney Von Drehle, accordion. (All members are from USA.)

3 Leg Torso was formed in early 1996 when a cellist, a violinist, and an accordionist discovered their common musical cause. Béla Balogh is a third-generation violinist whose grandfather was the leader of a Hungarian gypsy orchestra. Gabe Leavitt turned to the cello after years as a guitarist and electric bassist.

cecil sharp

At the close of the 19th century, British folk songs and dance were passed down almost entirely in the oral tradition. Late in his life and early in the subsequent century, Cecil Sharp (1859–1924) undertook a vigorous campaign to preserve and document the traditions of British folk culture. Traveling around England on his bicycle, Sharp began writing down the songs and dances of different regions of the country and released a series of books, beginning with *Folk Songs from Somerset* in 1904, that made the fruits of his collections available to the masses. In 1911 Sharp founded the English Folk Song and Dance Society, an organization that remains a potent force in preserving British folk traditions. In 1916 Sharp traveled to America, where he spent two years in rural areas of southern Appalachia and collected nearly 2,000 songs and dances that reconfirmed the strong links between the folk cultures of that region and those of Great Britain. Today, Sharp's archives are kept at the Cecil Sharp House in North London, a mecca for traditional and contemporary folkies that served as a wellspring of material and inspiration for revivalists like Ashley Hutchings (who presented a one-man tribute to Sharp in the mid-1980s) and Richard Thompson.

see also: Appalachia (sidebar), Ashley Hutchings, Maddy Prior, Richard Thompson

Michael Parrish

The trio's primary composer, Courtney Von Drehle, has scored music for dance, theater, television, and radio. Their work is a natural mix of serious compositional forms with a populist bent. Not surprisingly they bring to mind others who have sought to make similar leaps, such as Kurt Weill and Astor Piazolla. Since their inception the Portland, Oregon-based trio have become key participants in their hometown's International Performance Festival, and have had works commissioned by the Portland Institute for Contemporary Arts. And yes, they take a firm stand on using the digit, rather than the word "three."

what's available: *3 Leg Torso* 𝄞𝄞𝄞𝄞 (3 Leg Torso, 1997, prod. 3 Leg Torso, Jim Greve) is a perfect debut, making a gentle but forceful declaration of the group's arrival. Von Drehle is a deft composer, writing the bulk of the work on this set. Never strident, the melodies and their arrangements turn from humor to romance with ease. This is not an easily classifiable album or outfit, but then new and original voices never are.

influences:

◄◄ Astor Piazolla, the Kronos Quartet, Kurt Weill

David Greenberger

3 Mustaphas 3

Worldbeat

Formed August 6, 1982, in Szegerely, somewhere in the heart of the Balkans. Disbanded early 1990s.

Hijaz Mustapha, guitar, bouzouki, violin; Daoudi Mustapha, sax, clarinet; Houzam Mustapha, drums, vocals; Kemo Mustapha, keyboards, accordion; Niaveti 3 Mustapha, flute, accordion; Sabah Mustapha, bass, vocals; Uncle Patrel Mustapha, saz; Expen$ive Mustapha, trumpet.

3 Mustaphas 3 amazed international audiences with their uncanny grasp of world music from the moment they landed in London in 1982. The number of people on stage would fluctuate from gig to gig, but the revolving troupe of family members was informally led by brothers Hijaz, Houzam, and Sabah, the three Mustaphas of the group's title. "In our country," says Hijaz Mustapha in lightly accented English, "people do not think of music as a way of making a living. It's like Ireland, or Louisiana. If you say 'I play music' they answer 'Yes, so do we, but what do you do for a living?' So for many years we played at a club in our hometown of Szegerely called the Crazy Loquat Club, even though we didn't know we were musicians. We learned to excel on our instruments by playing tunes from the radio, local tunes, and the requests of the truck drivers who came there from all over the world. It is very good to play requests from the audience, because it makes you aware of many kinds of music. We like our own Balkan music, starting with wedding music and going on from there, because it has interesting tempos; 7/8, 9/8, 11/8, 13/14—it's very irregular and good for circle dancing or dancing in a line." Hijaz says that the transformation of the Mustaphas from "local" players to professional musicians had a lot to do with the jukebox at the Crazy Loquat. "They don't keep music on records in our town, they just play it for today. So the first records we heard were in the jukebox at the Crazy Loquat Club bar. A man came and filled the machine with records, so we didn't have to buy any. We heard African music, American country music, and your Elvis who is very good."

Since the Mustaphas came West, many legends have grown up around the band, including one that says they were smuggled out of Szegerely in refrigerators. "I have read that story, yes," says Hijaz. "I'd like to believe it was true in fact, but it is only true in fiction. There are not so many political problems in our homeland as people believe. We left because it is good to travel, to expand your awareness of other people." No matter how they got to London, the Mustaphas' worldbeat bag caused a sensation. "Mustaphas like expansive music, pleasing music—music with the local touch still left in." When pressed for a definition of "local" music, Hijaz says, "Local music is authentic, played by musicians for an audience of local people. We like Indian film music, like the soundtrack to the movie *Pren Tapasya,* and records by Sunya Ganguly, who is an Indian man that plays your American steel guitar for Indian films; the *vallenato* music of the Colombian accordion; the Black Sea music called *Kara Demiz;* bands like Select from Haiti. They are local musicians because they don't want to be national music like your Bobby Rydell or Pat Boone. We don't like that kind of music because there's no local feeling; the next day you don't remember you were in a concert. There's nothing there for local people to enjoy—they make it for as many people as possible, like an appliance that you take home and never use."

what to buy: *Heart of Uncle* ♫♫♫♫ (Rykodisc, 1989, prod. David Young), released at the height of Mustapha mania, showcases the band's excellent international chops with grooves from Kenya, India, Greece, and Santa Domingo, as well as a few inspired originals.

what to buy next: *Soup of the Century* ♫♫♫ (Rykodisc, 1990) was the band's swan song, with another crazy mixed-up excursion to Japan, Greece, India, Spain, Bulgaria, Albania, and London.

the rest:

Shopping ♫♫♫ (Globestyle, 1987)
Friends, Fiends & Fronds ♫♫ (Globestyle, 1991)

influences:

◄◄ D.O. Misiani, Foday Musa Suso, Mohammad Rafi, Olatunji, Harry Belafonte

►► Paul Simon, Annabouboula, Boiled in Lead, Baka Beyond

see also: *Abana Ba Nasery, Stella Chiweshe, Pépé Kallé, Sabah Habas Mustapha*

j. poet

Tianjin Buddhist Music Ensemble

Buddhist devotional music

Formed 1983, in Tianjin, northeast China. Based in Tianjin, China.

Li Jinwen, gu, guanzi, nao, chazi; Wang Fenrui, sheng, guanzi, dangzi, yunluo; Zhang Shicai, sheng, nao; Zhang Shenglu, dizi, gezi; Pan Shizong, yunlao, guanzi, bo, dizi; Zhang Yuije, go, sheng. (All members are from China.)

During the Chinese cultural revolution, Buddhist ritual was suppressed, including any performances of Buddhist music. In the 1980s interest in pre-revolutionary culture resulted in the appearance of some outfits reviving Buddhist traditions. The Tianjin Buddhist Music Ensemble was founded by Li Jinwen, a former Buddhist priest who is one of the country's leading masters of the *guanzi* (Chinese oboe). The ensemble also consists of three other musicians who, like Li, are in their 70s, along with two younger players. The group's music is primarily an instrumental blend of reed instruments, gongs, and other percussion.

what's available: The group's single CD, *Buddhist Music of Tianjin* ♪♪♪ (Nimbus, 1994), documents their 1993 European tour. Beautifully recorded, the ensemble's exotic blend of wind instruments with a variety of reeds, gongs, and drums makes for a profoundly moving, ethereal listening experience.

influences:

◀◀ Gyuto Monks

▶▶ Tan Dun

Michael Parrish

Kathryn Tickell

British folk, Celtic

Born June 8, 1967, in Wark, North Tyne Valley, Northumberland, England. Based in Northumberland, England.

Kathryn Tickell has almost single-handedly brought the Northumbrian smallpipes to international fame, establishing herself as an outstanding folk musician along the way. Tickell's technique on the bellows-blown pipes is only excelled by her general musicianship, allowing emotion to flow through the pipes as she plays. From hard-driving, almost rocking reels and hornpipes to evocative airs and waltzes, Tickell covers a broad spectrum of musical colors while performing. She is not only an excellent piper, but has also distinguished herself as an award-winning fiddler.

Tickell grew up in a family of musicians: her father is a ballad singer, her mother a concertina player, and both grandfathers were musicians as well. She began on piano at the age of six and started learning both the smallpipes and the fiddle by the age of nine. At 13 Tickell was winning piping competitions and appearing at major folk music festivals. A local radio station encouraged her to make her first recording while she was still in high school, which resulted in *On Kielder Side,* a brilliant debut. That same year, Tickell was named official piper to the Lord Mayor of Newcastle-upon-Tyne. Through the ensuing years she has become a musical force to be reckoned with, having five more albums under her belt and a long list of self-authored tunes. She has collaborated with numerous fine musicians as well, including Sting, John Surman, and the Chieftains. She also works to encourage new folk players, both through personal appearances and through a charity she established to assist lower-income children in receiving music lessons.

what's available: Tickell's most recent release, *The Northumberland Collection* ♪♪♪♪ (Park, 1998, prod. Kathryn Tickell), is a beautifully crafted recording featuring Tickell's brilliant pipe and fiddle work and the skills of a variety of Northumberland musicians on melodian, harp, vocals, and other instruments. This is a well-rounded overview of music from the Northumberland region, with the traditional and the modern each represented. Both the music selection and the recording quality are impeccable. *The Gathering* ♪♪♪♪ (Park, 1997, prod. Kathryn Tickell) also showcases a mix of traditional and original music. Tickell's own tunes are soulful, playful, and, while traditional in nature, sometimes branch out rebelliously towards rock 'n' roll. This recording displays Tickell's mature understanding of music, her highly developed expert technique, and the fiery passion typical of her work.

worth searching for: *On Kielder Side* ♪♪♪♪ (Saydisc, 1984, prod. Keith Proud), Tickell's debut, features traditional music from Northumberland, Ireland, and Scotland, all brilliantly played when she was only a teenager. From the lively full-band sound on "The Peacock Followed the Hen," featuring pipes, fiddle, keyboards, and guitar, to the exciting smallpipe solo "Jean's Reel," Tickell shows her versatility and virtuosity. Other highlights include a moving Shetland tune, "Da Slockit Light," and an uplifting air-and-hornpipe set, "Border Spirit/A.B. Hornpipe/Billy Pigg's Hornpipe."

influences:

◀◀ Alistair Anderson, Tom Anderson, Will Atkinson, Joe Hutton, Willy Taylor, Mike Tickell

▶▶ Chris Ormston, Billy Bragg, the Pogues, the Oyster Band

Jo Hughey Morrison

Timbalada

Axe

Formed 1993, in Salvador Da Bahia, Brazil. Based in Salvador Da Bahia, Brazil.

Carlinhos Brown, leader, percussionist (1993–present); a large roster of other musicians.

The brainchild of percussionist Carlinhos Brown, Timbalada represents the next generation of Bahia's *blocos afros* cultural organizations like Ile Aiye and Olodum. The group took the rolling thunder of the blocos' Carnival drumming groups and successfully re-created it in a pop format, with electric guitars, horns, and keyboards. The group has listed as many as 60 people as members on its albums, and during Carnival time thousands of Salvadorans march as part of Timbalada's parade. But the group does have a more compact touring ensemble—of about 20 members.

While Brown has written some of Timbalada's songs and produced all of its albums, he does not sing with the group, relinquishing those duties to an extensive bullpen of vocalists including Patricia Gomes, Xexeu, and the gray-haired Ninha. Now their trademark, the group's members always appear shirtless with white-painted lines, swirls, dots, and circles decorating their bodies, a practice that reputedly began because they had no money for costumes. Since those lean beginnings, though, Timbalada has been able to achieve critical and popular success, even raising enough money to establish a combination recording studio/education center in its home base, the neighborhood of Candeal. Despite its occasional rhythmic experimentation, the group's albums increasingly have a sameness to them—especially in contrast to the diverse sounds on leader Brown's 1997 solo album, *Alphagamabetizado*. Perhaps it was timely, then, that with the release of Timbalada's *Mae de Samba* the following year, Brown told reporters the group was a three-act concept of three albums each, and would dissolve after its ninth release in 2001.

what to buy: *Timbalada* 𝄞𝄞𝄞𝄞 (PolyGram, 1993, prod. Carlinhos Brown, Wesley Rangel) is the group's raw, powerful debut. The drum-and-chant format sounds surprisingly full, even without additional instrumentation, and the excitement and exuberance is palpable. What the follow-up, *Cada Cabeça é um Mundo* 𝄞𝄞𝄞𝄞 (PolyGram, 1994, prod. Carlinhos Brown, Wesley Rangel), may lack in power, it makes up for with more sophisticated arrangements and production. This second effort basically established the template for the rest of the group's output, and has not been equaled yet.

what to buy next: *Andei Road* 𝄞𝄞𝄞 (PolyGram, 1995, prod. Carlinhos Brown, Wesley Rangel) maintains its predecessor's format, but does it with strength and consistency almost all the way through.

what to avoid: *Timbalada Dance* 𝄞𝄞 (PolyGram, 1996) is an ill-advised collection of remixes, adding heavy electronic beats to what already was wonderfully polyrhythmic music.

the rest:
Mineral 𝄞𝄞𝄞 (PolyGram, 1996)
Mãe do Samba 𝄞𝄞𝄞 (PolyGram, 1998)
Timbalada Live (1998)

solo outings:
Carlinhos Brown:
Alphagamabetizado 𝄞𝄞𝄞 (Emd/Blue Note, 1997)
Omelete Man N/A (Emd/Blue Note, 1999)

influences:
◀ Ile Aiye, Olodum

▶▶ Bragadá

see also: *Daude, Olodum, Caetano Veloso*

Marty Lipp

Willie Toors
Folk, modern folk
Born 1921, in Mobyn, Sweden. Based in Malung, Sweden.

Willie Toors began playing fiddle at age nine, and learned from many living legends of Swedish folk. In his 20s Toors studied and played classical music, but also kept playing folk music at weddings, public dances, and Forest Balls—parties put on by farmers in Sweden's back country, away from cities and police. After his military service, Toors wandered the country playing with small groups and picking up many different styles from Swedish Gypsies. He composed most of the music on his long-overdue debut disc, *Från Logar, Skogar, Zigenarläger, och Cirkustält,* though the tunes are often based on traditional themes. On some tracks Toors is backed by a small acoustic group—keyboards, bass, and guitar—but the main attraction is his fiddle. He has a full-bodied, lyrical style, full of smoldering Gypsy soul. There's something timeless and magical about this music, and since Toors makes his bread and butter by playing at social events, the tunes have a sprightly feeling that recalls dancing snowflakes and flickering bonfires.

what's available: *Från Logar, Skogar, Zigenarläger, och Cirkustält* 𝄞𝄞𝄞𝄞 (Hurv, 1997, prod. Anders Rosén) is one of the best albums of tradition-based Swedish fiddling ever. Toors is an amazing technician, but his chops are always in the service of his passionate playing. Even if you think you hate instrumental music, this album will win you over. In the CD booklet (English translation included), Toors gives his recollections of each tune, where he heard it, or how he came to compose it, and his stories add an extra dimension to the music—especially "Wedding Banquet," a tribute to a woman he loved and lost, and "Forest Hymn," an ode to the whistling of the wind through the trees.

influences:
◀ Rudolf Sundqvist

▶▶ Mats Edén

see also: *Anders Rosén*

j. poet

Toots & the Maytals
Reggae
Formed 1962, in Kingston, Jamaica. Based in Kingston, Jamaica.

Frederick "Toots" Hibbert (born 1946, in Maypen, Jamaica); various collaborators.

Toots & the Maytals were one of the pioneers of reggae. In fact, it was their 1968 recording "Do the Reggay" that gave the genre its name. Initially known in the United States for their songs "Sweet and Dandy" and "Pressure Drop," included on the soundtrack of the 1972 film *The Harder They Come,* the group continued to make its presence felt throughout the world with a soulful mixture of Jamaican rhythms and American R&B. Enigmatic lead vocalist and songwriter Frederick "Toots" Hibbert has been called "the Otis Redding of Reggae." The son of a Revival Zion preacher, Hibbert grew up singing in a church choir. Shortly after moving to Kingston in 1962 he formed a trio with Nathaniel "Jerry" Mathias and Ralphus "Raleigh" Gordon. As the Vikings, they recorded several singles for Clement "Sir Coxsone" Dodd's Studio One label, including "Hallelujah" and "Six and Seven Books of Moses." In 1964 the by-now rechristened Maytals left Dodd and began working with rival producer Prince Buster. Under Buster's supervision, the group performed and recorded with Byron Lee & His Ska-Kings Band from 1964 to 1966.

The success of Hibbert's song "Bam Bam," which earned him the first of three first-place songwriting awards at the Jamaican Song Festival, was overcast by his arrest and 12-month imprisonment for possession of marijuana. The experience resulted in the classic "54–46 (That's My Number)," recorded with producer Leslie Kong. This partnership continued until Kong's death in 1971, when the band began recording with Kong's former partner, Warrick Lyn. Tracks produced by Kong and Lyn included all-time-favorites like "Do the Reggay," "Monkey Man" (their first single to chart in England), and "Sweet and Dandy," which won the Jamaican Song Festival competition in 1969. Shortly after the release of *The Harder They Come* the group, now performing as Toots & the Maytals, earned its third Jamaican Song Festival award with Hibbert's tune "Pomp and Pride."

Signing a contract with Island in 1975, Toots & the Maytals released their first album in the United States, *Funky Kingston,* which combined two previous albums—*Funky Kingston* and *In the Dark* —and included a reggae rendition of John Denver's "Country Roads." They first toured the country as an opening act for the Who. Although the original group disbanded in 1981 Toots continued to work as soloist with famed producers and rhythm section Sly Dunbar and Robbie Shakespeare. A new version of the Maytals was formed in the early 1990s, with a late-decade Grammy nomination for *Ska Father* cementing the act's historical status and verifying its continued vitality.

what to buy: *Time Tough: Anthology* ♫♫♫♫ (Island, 1996, prod. various) spans the full recording career of Toots & the Maytals. The 40-song, two-CD set includes many rare singles and previously unreleased tunes.

what to buy next: The first American release by Toots & the Maytals, *Funky Kingston* ♫♫♫♫ (Island, 1975, prod. Warrick Lyn, Chris Blackwell, Dave Bloxham) remains one of reggae's greatest albums. Accompanied by the driving horn section Sons of the Jungle, the band offer a soulful set that includes their Ja-

maican hits "Pomp and Pride," "Pressure Drop," and the title track, as well as reggae-fied versions of John Denver's "Country Roads" and Richard Berry's "Louie Louie."

the rest:
Reggae Got Soul ♫♫♫♫ (Island, 1976)
Reggae Greats ♫♫♫ (Island, 1984)
Toots in Memphis ♫♫♫ (Island, 1988)
Ska Father ♫♫♫♫ (Artist Only!, 1998)

influences:
◄◄ The Wailers, the Skatalites, the Upsetters

►► Third World, UB40

see also: *Joe Higgs, Jackie Mittoo, Sly & Robbie*

Craig Harris

Yomo Toro
Salsa
Born July 26, 1933, in Ensenada, Puerto Rico. Based in the Bronx, NY, USA.

Yomo Toro is a master of the *cuatro,* a small Puerto Rican folk guitar descended from the *viheula* of Spain. Since emigrating to New York in 1956, Toro has been an influential presence in the Latin-music community. In addition to recording as a soloist, he has toured and recorded with the Fania All Stars and guested on albums by Willie Colon, Daniel Ponce, Eddie Palmieri, Tito Puente, and Hector LaVoe, as well as Harry Belafonte, Paul Simon, the Barry Sisters, and Linda Ronstadt. The son of an amateur guitarist and cuatro builder, Toro began playing his father's instruments at the age of five. Making his first trip to the United States in 1953, Toro performed eight shows a week at the Puerto Rican Theater in New York and created a stir with his unique approach to the *Jibaro* folk music of Puerto Rico. He teamed with Larry Harlow's Orchestra to record the influential album *Tribute to Arsenio* in 1969, and reunited with Harlow to form the Latin Legends Band in 1994.

what to buy: *Funky Jibaro* ♫♫♫♫ (Island, 1988, prod. Robert Musso) is a successful balance of Toro's traditional approach and more modern sensibilities.

what to buy next: Toro's lightning-fast cuatro melodies are accompanied by members of Puerto Rican group Batacumbele and Ruben Blades's Seis del Solar, and vocalists Jerry Medina and Dalia Silva, on the joyous tribute to the yuletide season *Celebramos Navidad* ♫♫♫ (Ashe/Rounder, 1996, prod. Rachel Faro, Sammy Figueroa).

the rest:
Gracias ♫♫♫ (Island/Mango, 1990)
Manos de Oro (Hands of Gold) ♫♫♫ (Crepuscule, 1994)

Yomo Toro

influences:

◄◄ Eddie Palmieri, Tito Puente

▶▶ Fania All Stars, the Latin Legends Band, Ruben Blades

see also: *Ruben Blades, Willie Colon, Larry Harlow, Eddie Palmieri, Tito Puente*

Craig Harris

Roberto Torres

Salsa, vallenato, charanga, son
Born c. 1948, in Güines, Cuba. Based in Miami, FL, USA.

Miami-based Roberto Torres is, above all else, a great *sonero*, a master of Cuban song. Torres has that rare combination of voice and improvisatory chops that mark the great singer in this style. His flexibility as a performer comes from a singing career that began when he was 16, and from working with legendary outfits like Orquesta Aragón and bandleaders like Beny Moré. Torres left Cuba in 1959 and headed straight for Miami. He was soon making his own records, eventually founding his own label, Güajiro. Outside the Latin music scene, Torres is known for having created a sound called *charanga/vallenato*. Perhaps only in Miami could a musician combine the rather elegant charanga tradition from Cuba—which features percussion, strings, and flute—with the rural sound of vallenato from Colombia, which features percussion, electric bass, and button accordion. Bringing these two divergent styles together to create a new one is no easy task, but Torres was up to it. The sound is much lighter than any vallenato records, but the reedy accordion changes the dynamic of the traditional orchestral charanga, giving it a thicker quality. In some ways Torres's innovations foreshadowed the movement of vallenato from a rural music to one with almost a pop following now in Colombia.

what to buy: *El Rey del Montuno* 𝄢𝄢𝄢𝄢𝄢 (SAR, 1996, prod. Roberto Torres) is Torres in real Cuban form. No fusion here, just a very solid band, good songwriting, and Torres's great voice.

what to buy next: Though Torres's Cuban recordings are better than his charanga/vallenato fusion, *Y La Charanga Vallenato* 𝄢𝄢𝄢𝄢 (SAR, 1992, prod. Roberto Torres) is pretty good music.

You can here how the two divergent styles are brought together under Torres's watchful ear.

the rest:
Con el Sabor de . . . Roberto Torres 🎵🎵🎵 (SAR 1992)
Exclusivamente Lo Mejor 🎵🎵🎵⅞ (Sony, 1992)
Homenaje a Beny Moré 🎵🎵🎵🎵 (SAR, 1992)
Y La Charanga Vallenato, Vol. 3 🎵🎵🎵⅞ (SAR, 1992)
Corazon de Pueblo 🎵🎵🎵 (SAR, 1992)
Recuerda a La Sonora 🎵🎵🎵🎵⅞ (SAR, 1994)
Y Su Charanga Vallenato 🎵🎵🎵 (SAR, 1994)
Castigador 🎵🎵🎵🎵 (Salsoul, 1996)
La Fiesta 🎵🎵🎵 (SAR, 1996)
Vallenatos a Mi Estilo, Vol. 1 🎵🎵🎵🎵 (SAR 1996)
Juntos 🎵🎵🎵🎵 (Salsoul, 1997)
Viva el Bolero 🎵🎵🎵🎵 (SAR, 1998)

worth searching for: *Recuerda al Trio Matamoros* 🎵🎵🎵🎵 (SAR, 1993, prod. Roberto Torres) is not a fusion, but an homage to one of the great trios of Cuban music, in which Torres brings his wit and talent to these classics.

influences:
◀◀ Benny Moré, Trio Matamoros, Mario Rivera

see also: *Benny Moré, Orquesta Aragón*

Jared Snyder

Peter Tosh
Reggae
Born October 9, 1944, in Westmoreland, Jamaica. Died September 11, 1987, in Barbican, St. Andrew, Jamaica.

Of the three original Wailers—along with Bunny Livingston and Bob Marley—Peter Tosh was certainly the most limited vocally, his gruff baritone being no match for Livingston's mystical warmth or Marley's sage-like delivery. But as the reggae supergroup became Marley's show, the street-wise tenacity in Tosh erupted. A swaggering bravado, which would provide backup to no man, took over, and the solo work he had dabbled with in the Wailers became a full-time endeavor. And perhaps not so surprisingly, his career brimmed with a rebellion and staunch Rastafarian ideology that neither Marley nor Livingston (commonly known as Bunny Wailer by the 1970s) approached in their respective romantic noodlings and murky spirituals. The same man who announced "I'm the Toughest" in the 1960s charged into the 1970s championing marijuana, simultaneously butting heads with the police (who nearly beat him to death in 1978) and releasing deep-rooted reggae albums that were as gritty as they were uncompromising. Though his work waned during the 1980s, Tosh remained a strident mouthpiece against the Jamaican government, which some feel led to his murder in 1987. To this day accusations fly that the three pistol-waving men who killed the singer were carrying out a political execution. Two other people were fatally shot and four more wounded in the course of the robbery (as it was officially reported) of Tosh's home.

what to buy: Tosh's first two efforts, *Legalize It* 🎵🎵🎵🎵 (Columbia, 1976, prod. Peter Tosh) and *Equal Rights* 🎵🎵🎵🎵 (Columbia, 1977, prod. Peter Tosh), stand as defiant cornerstones of both reggae and Tosh's refusal to be eclipsed by Marley's stardom. *Legalize It* hoists ganga up the topical flagpole while *Equal Rights* blisters with both political and personal warnings, as in the sharp " Stepping Razor."

what to buy next: A decidedly more mainstream album, complete with a Motown-like duet, *Wanted Dread and Alive* 🎵🎵🎵⅞ (EMI, 1981, prod. Peter Tosh) makes up for Tosh's Marvin Gaye flip-out with the captivating "Reggae Mylitis"; this ode to reggae "disease" is an unexpected playful peak, while the more typically defiant title track and "Cold Blood" stand among his best work.

what to avoid: Since it's out of print, *Mystic Man* 🎵🎵⅞ (Rolling Stones, 1979) is easy to avoid. It suffers mostly from uneven material and an abundance of murk.

the rest:
Bush Doctor 🎵🎵🎵 (Rolling Stones, 1978)
The Toughest 🎵🎵🎵 (Capitol, 1988)
Dread Don't Die 🎵🎵⅞ (FMI, 1995)
Honorary Citizen 🎵🎵🎵🎵 (Legacy, 1997)

influences:
◀◀ The Wailers, Bob Marley, Bunny Wailer, Desmond Dekker

see also: *Bob Marley, Bunny Wailer*

Allan Orski

Ali Farka Touré
African blues
Born 1939, in Gourmararusse, Mali. Based in Mali.

The blues of the Mississippi Delta are fused with the musical traditions of West Africa by guitarist and vocalist Ali Farka Touré. Though often compared to U.S. bluesmen like John Lee Hooker and Muddy Waters—already the best company imaginable—Touré, who mostly sings in his native language, has created his own musical legacy. Touré began playing guitar at age 10 and mastered the instrument by age 17, yet he worked as a sound engineer until 1980. He had recorded his first single in France in 1976, but wasn't known in the United States until the 1988 release of his impressive self-titled debut album—after which he had a steady ascent as one of the all-time most successful world-music artists on the U.S. charts and the global stage.

Ali Farka Touré

what to buy: Touré's collaboration with born-in-the-U.S.A. guitar virtuoso and world-music patron Ry Cooder, *Talking Timbuktu* ♫♫♫♫ (World Circuit, 1994, prod. Ali Farka Touré), is a groundbreaking meeting of two cultures. The album held the top slot on *Billboard*'s world-music charts for 32 weeks—a still-unbroken record—and won a Grammy as best world-music album. Guests include guitarist Clarence "Gatemouth" Brown and drummer Jim Keltner.

what to buy next: Touré's unique approach to the blues makes *The Source* ♫♫♫♪ (Hannibal, 1991, prod. Ali Farka Touré) a memorable fusion of his West African-inspired playing and U.S.-based style. Famed genre-crossing blues guitarist Taj Mahal is featured on two cuts.

the rest:
Ali Farka Touré ♫♫♫ (Island, 1988)
The River ♫♫♫ (Island, 1990)
African Blues ♫♫♫ (Shanachie, 1990)
La Drogue ♫♫♫ (Sonodisc, 1994)
Timbarma ♫♫♫ (World Circuit, 1996)
Radio Mali ♫♫♫ (World Circuit, 1996)

Niafunke N/A (World Circuit/Hannibal, 1999)

worth searching for: To hear other artists on each end of the African/blues connection Touré has come to personify, enjoy the superb collection *Mali to Memphis: An African-American Odyssey* ♫♫♫♫ (Putumayo, 1999, compilation prod. Dan Storper), which is also reviewed in this book's Compilations section.

influences:

⏮ John Lee Hooker, Lightnin' Hopkins, Muddy Waters, West African musical tradition

⏭ Ry Cooder, Taj Mahal

see also: *Ry Cooder, Taj Mahal*

Craig Harris

Touré Kunda
International Senegalese pop
Formed 1981, in Paris, France. Based in Paris, France.

Amadou Tilo Touré (died 1983), drums, percussion, vocals; **Ismaila Touré,** drums, percussion, vocals; **Sixu Tidiane Touré,** drums, percussion, vocals; Ousmane Touré (1983–90), drums, percussion, vocals. (All members are from Senegal.)

Touré Kunda loosely translates as "Family of Elephants," and during their long career they've certainly laid down a strong, stomping beat. Touré was the first African band to make an impression on the U.S. market, and its mix of African and Caribbean beats has made group members major stars in France and most of West Africa.

Diaby Touré, the father of the Touré brothers, had five wives, each from different tribal backgrounds. The four brothers hit it off from an early age, and began traveling around with local *griots* (oral historians), learning drumming and the *kora* (African harp-lute). After their father died, Amadou, Ismaila, and Sixu joined a theatre group where they learned stagecraft, dance, costume design, music, and theatrical presentation, all of which would later inform their shows. By the late 1960s the brothers were playing in bands that ranged from folkloric troupes to Congolese-style rumba groups, but the corruption of the music business in Africa convinced Ismaila that Paris would be better suited to his talents.

By 1981 all three brothers had relocated to Paris and put together a band of their own. Ismaila had lived briefly in London and discovered the reggae beat, which reminded him of *djabdong*, a ritual rhythm from the brothers' native Senegal. When the band began writing tunes based on a fusion of the two forms, it hit a winning combination. The title track of the group's first album, *Em'ma,* was a worldwide smash, and Touré was soon signed to Celluloid, a pioneering Paris-based world-music label. In 1983, during a stage show, Amadou died of a heart attack. The brothers asked Ousmane to come to Paris, and Touré Kunda continued, releasing the stunning, folkloric album *Casamance au Clair de Lune.* By the mid-1980s Touré Kunda was a major draw in Africa and Europe. After experimenting with a new African-based international style the brothers recorded *Natalia,* with Bill Laswell producing and Funkadelic keyboard player Bernie Worrell adding his intergalactic funk to the mix. Touré was one of the first Afropop bands to tour the United States, and with each new release continued to explore and diversify its music. In 1987 there was another disaster; most of the backing band jumped ship to join the dance-craze cash-in group Kaoma, and for a while Touré's future looked grim. During long, drawn-out litigation with their former label over this breach, Ousmane got fed up and left the band. Eventually the dust cleared; Ismaila and Sixu found new backing musicians and carried on. Although some of the creative spark is lacking in more recent releases, the brothers continue to forge ahead with their groundbreaking Afropop sound.

what to buy: Few live albums live up to their name, but *Touré Kunda Live—Paris—Ziguinchor* 𝄞𝄞𝄞𝄞 (Celluloid, 1983, prod.

Touré Kunda) delivers, with extended versions of some of the band's best tunes from its early period. There were two editions of this CD released; make sure to get the reissue with all 10 tracks on it. It's right up there with Otis Redding's *Live in Europe* and James Brown's *Live at the Apollo.*

what to buy next: Every Touré Kunda album from the 1980s is solid, but the 18-track overview of the band's landmark Celluloid recordings, *Dance of the Leaves* 𝄞𝄞𝄞𝄞 (Restless, 1993), is the best introduction to its back catalog. The group is still making compelling music in the 1990s, but the early stuff gives off a heat that some of the more recent discs lack. The French compilation *Best Of* 𝄞𝄞𝄞𝄞 (Celluloid, 1984) only duplicates two tracks from the Restless collection, and may be easier to find.

best of the rest:
Natalia 𝄞𝄞𝄞𝄞 (Celluloid, 1985)
Karadindi 𝄞𝄞𝄞𝄞𝄞 (Celluloid, 1989)
Touré Kunda—1981–82 𝄞𝄞𝄞𝄞 (Celluloid, 1990)
Touré Kunda—1983–84 𝄞𝄞𝄞𝄞 (Celluloid, 1990)
Salam 𝄞𝄞𝄞𝄞 (Trema France, 1990)
Touré Kunda Collection 𝄞𝄞𝄞𝄞 (Putumayo, 1996)
Mouslaï 𝄞𝄞𝄞𝄞𝄞 (Mesa, 1996)

influences:
◀◀ Pascal Diatta, Kassav'

▶▶ Mory Kante, Ismael Lo, Baaba Maal

see also: *Kaoma, Bill Laswell*

j. poet

Horace Trahan
Cajun
Born June 12, 1976, in Lafayette, LA, USA. Based in Ossun, LA, USA.

Horace Trahan is a Cajun traditionalist, a student both of Cajun music and Cajun culture. Perhaps only Eddie LeJeune or Cory McCauley play a more traditional style of Cajun accordion. Though only in his early 20s, Trahan sings with great sincerity and authority. He wasn't born until the third year of the Festival Acadian, which had only one performer under 40 in its first year. Like most of the kids of his generation he started out on guitar wanting to play rock 'n' roll. Once that had lost its romance, he started playing country music. When he became interested in the accordion, he went to his father for guidance. The elder Trahan took Horace to visit his cousin Felix Richard, an accomplished Cajun accordionist who had taught Zachary Richard. "Mr. Felix" tutored Trahan almost daily after school. It was not just music, but an appreciation for Cajun culture that the teacher imparted to the impressionable young man. Trahan was frustrated by his limited mastery of the language that went with it, and made a pact with family and friends to speak only French so he could improve—in the process becoming aware of how important the culture is to the music, and of how easy a thing it is to lose. As Trahan's career took shape, he honed his skills on his own and by touring and recording with D.L. Menard and Kristi Guillory.

what to buy: *Ossun Blues* ♫♫♫♫ (Swallow, 1996, prod. Terry Huval) is as good a Cajun record as has been made since *The Balfa Brothers Play Traditional Cajun Music*. While Trahan's accordion playing is truly something special (the best comparison may be Eddie LeJeune), his singing is his most impressive talent. He also has a true, unaffected Cajun voice; there are no hints of rock 'n' roll or country in his style, and comparisons can certainly be made to a very young Dewey Balfa or Iry LeJeune in his full-throated sound. Trahan has picked a mix of classics from these two, Nathan Abshire, and D.L. Menard, and mixed in originals of his own that fit into the style seamlessly.

what to buy next: *Reveille: The New Cajun Generation* ♫♫♫ (Swallow, 1994, prod. Terry Huval) is billed as a Kristi Guillory and Bill Grass album, but it features Trahan playing rhythm guitar and sharing lead vocals with Guillory. Each member of this band was under 20 at the time of the recording, but the only way you'd know it is from the friskiness of their playing. Trahan's rich voice evokes the great historical Cajun singers on traditional tunes like "T'en a Eu, T'en Auras Plus" and "L'Anse aux Pailles." His and Guillory's deep vocals intertwine on "Les Veuves de la Coulée" and "Les Flammes d'en Fer" a bit like Marc and Ann Savoy's duets.

worth searching for: *The American Fogies, Vol. I* ♫♫♫♫ (Rounder, 1996, prod. Ray Alden), an anthology of U.S. bands playing roots music, includes a track of Trahan playing Douglas Belair's "Les Barres de la Prison" with the Mamou Prairie Band and Mitch Reed of Tasso.

influences:

◀◀ Nathan Abshire, Balfa Brothers, Iry LeJeune

▶▶ Tasso, Balfa Toujours

see also: *Balfa Brothers, Eddie LeJeune, Iry LeJeune, D.L. Menard, Zachary Richard, Savoy-Doucet Cajun Band*

Jared Snyder

Trance Mission

World-jazz, ambient
Formed 1991, in San Francisco, CA, USA. Based in San Francisco, CA, USA.

Beth Custer (USA), Bb, alto and bass clarinet, vocals, percussion; Stephen Kent (U.K.), didgeridoo, vocals, percussion; John Loose (USA), tar, bodhrán, morsing, kanjire, riqq, percussion, vocals; Kenneth Newby (USA), suling, p'iri, khaen, gongs, sampling, klunting, percussion.

Didgeridoo player Steven Kent—born in England, raised in Uganda, and a frequent traveler to Java, Australia, and Vancouver in western Canada—kept running into Kenneth Newby, a composer and Javanese music fanatic who specializes in exotic (at least to U.S. ears) wind instruments like the *suling, p'iri,* and *khaen*. After they both landed in the Bay Area in the early 1990s, they began collaborating on their own version of a world-music-meets-free-jazz combo. They enlisted the help of Beth Custer, a well-known avant garde player and founding member of the Club Foot Orchestra and John Loose, who'd played with Rhythm & Noise and the Blue Rubies, and Trance Mission was born. The expert chops and innate musicality of the group keep their free-form explorations lively as they bounce from chamber-jazz swing, to outback ambient drone, to the tribal stomp of "Bo Didgeley," the track that introduced them to the world with its mixture of rock, funk, and good humor.

what to buy: One of the first "world jazz" discs, *Trance Mission* ♫♫♫♫ (City of Tribes, 1992, prod. Oliver DiCicco) stands out because of Kent's immense talent on the Aboriginal Australian didgeridoo—he plays the instrument with more innate musicality than anyone else today—and the sterling support of the rest of the band. Every track shines, with each player providing an amazing depth of textures, rhythms, and timbres.

what to buy next: *Meanwhile* ♫♫♫ (City of Tribes, 1993, prod. Simon Tossano) has better production values, but the band's enigmatic vibe remains compelling and its deep, tribal jazz still swings.

the rest:
Head Light ♫♫♫ (City of Tribes, 1996)

influences:

◀◀ Lights in a Fat City, Yothu Yindi, Club Foot Orchestra

▶▶ Deep Forest, Loop Guru

see also: *Steve Roach*

j. poet

Transglobal Underground /Natacha Atlas

Ethno-techno fusion
Formed 1991, in London, England. Based in London, England.

Members have included: Alex Kasiek, keyboards, vocals, flute, melodica, programming; Count Dubulah, bass, guitar, programming; Hamid Mantu, drums, percussion, keyboards, programming; T.U.U.P., vocals, congas; Natacha Atlas, vocals; Coleridge, vocals, djembe; Johnny Kalsi, dhol.

Transglobal Underground is a loose-knit multicultural collective that has involved numerous musicians over the years, and describing their eclectic sound is even more difficult than defining their ever-evolving line-up. Some have called Transglobal's music "world techno," but that only begins to scratch the surface of the influences at work in their trance-like style, which splices inspirations ranging from hip-hop, dub reggae, and drum 'n' bass to African drumming and Middle Eastern chants. The tie that binds this fusionist mish-mash is a penchant for exotic yet accessible grooves whose hypnotic repetition makes them perfect for dancefloors from New York City to Marrakesh. The group's most powerful secret weapon is the entrancing Arabic vocals of Natacha Atlas, whose more traditional solo albums, each produced by the Transglobal collective, delve even deeper into her Middle Eastern roots. All politically correct debates about the co-opting of traditional forms aside, Transglobal Underground is providing the instant heritage of the next millennium's musical mix-and-match.

what to buy: For such an enigmatic ensemble, Transglobal's output has been surprisingly consistent, but *Rejoice, Rejoice* ♫♫♫ (Nation/MCA, 1998, prod. Transglobal Underground) seems like the definitive fruition of their experimental efforts. Atlas is in top form, weaving spellbinding melodic tapestries with her voice, and collaborations with Bapi Das Baul and especially *qawwali* (Pakistani devotional) group Musafir (on "Ali Mullah," which is dedicated to Nusrat Fateh Ali Khan) lead the group to ecstatic creative heights.

what to buy next: *Psychic Karaoke* ♫♫♫ (Nation/MCA, 1996, prod. Transglobal Underground) is almost as fully realized, albeit with a slightly less organic approach that relies more heavily on layered world-ly samples and ambient house loops than live instrumentation. Still, Atlas carries the day, her sublimely lovely voice at times proving transcendent.

the rest:
Dream of 100 Nations ♫♫♫ (Nation/Beggars Banquet, 1993)
International Times ♫♫♫ (Nation/Beggars Banquet, 1994)
Interplanetary Meltdown ♫♫♫ (Nation, 1995)

solo outings:
Natacha Atlas:
Diaspora ♫♫♫ (Nation/Beggars Banquet, 1995)
Halim ♫♫♫ (Nation/Beggars Banquet, 1997)
Gedida ♫♫♫ (Beggars Banquet, 1999)

influences:
◀◀ Nusrat Fateh Ali Khan, Peter Gabriel, Ofra Haza, Yma Sumac
▶▶ Talvin Singh, Loop Guru, Trance Mission, Banco De Gaia

see also: *Abdel Ali Slimani*

Bret Love and Barry M. Prickett

jim wilson

Jim Wilson is a prolific musician and producer who's done much to advance the artform of ambient techno and the cause of Native American recognition. Dispelling rustic stereotypes with state-of-the-art electronics even as he draws heavily on the rhythms and found voices of his own and other indigenous cultures, Wilson is at the forefront of emphasizing the First Peoples' contemporary presence while preserving their ancient heritage. Helping ex-Band leader Robbie Robertson fashion the textural soundscapes for the groundbreaking 1994 TV documentary score *The Native Americans,* Wilson next invested the electronic genre with uncommon personality and nuance—while sacrificing none of its cybernetic edge—with his Little Wolf project's two landmark suites of atmospheric ancient-futurism, *Dream Song* ♫♫♫♫ (Triloka, 1995) and *Wolf Moon* ♫♫♫♫ (Triloka, 1997). As cultural impresario, Wilson assembled a collection surveying the breadth of contemporary Native devotional musics, *Songs of the Spirit* ♫♫♫ (Triloka, 1996), a characteristically substantive take on new-agey material. Bringing many traditional artists to mainstream attention on that anthology, Wilson also helped connect another mainstream icon with her roots: his production of former chart-ruler Rita Coolidge's vocal trio with her sister and niece, Walela, played a major role in making the group favorites of both the Native and non-Native world-music audiences immediately upon the release of their debut album, *Walela* ♫♫♫ (Triloka, 1997). As interested in the convergence of cultures on the social level as he is in the convergence of styles on the artistic one, Wilson has helped guide American musical mystic Krishna Das, and gave sonic life to Russian psychiatrist Olga Kharitidi's odyssey into the world of Siberian shamanism on the haunting *Entering the Circle* ♫♫♫♫ (Triloka, 1996), which accompanies her book of same name. Wilson's world-wide all-star project Tulku is more standard-issue ethno-techno, but from time to time he's entitled to fall back on the conventions of a genre he helped pioneer. With Jim Wilson at the controls, silenced societies are patched into the system and wired for sound.

Adam McGovern

Natacha Atlas with Transglobal Underground

Trebunia Family Band

Polish dance music

Formed in Zakopane, Tatra Mountains region, Poland. Based in Zakopane, Tatra Mountains region, Poland.

Whadislaw Trebunia, fiddle, flutes, vocals; Kryzsztof Trebunia, fiddle, vocals; Stanislaw Trebunia Sr., fiddle, vocals; Stanislaw Trebunia Jr., basy, vocals, dance; Hania Trebunia, fiddle, vocals; Jas Trebunia, fiddle; Helena Trebunia Sr., vocals; Helena Trebunia Jr., vocals; Janina Czernik, vocals; Katarzyna Trebunia, vocals, dance; Andrez Chowaneic, dance. (All members are from Poland.)

The 11-member Trebunia Family Band spans three generations of musicians from Zakopane, a cultural center and resort area high in the Tatra Mountains region of Poland. Their single recording is a field session done in Poronin, Poland, in 1994. The group's sound is dominated by fiddles, four or five of which are played simultaneously, augmented by the *basy* (three-stringed, cello-sized bass), one or more vocalists, and several dancers.

what's available: The 10 tracks on *Music of the Tatra Mountains* 𝄞𝄞𝄞 (Nimbus, 1995, prod. R. Broadbank, K. Cwizewicz)

capture the ebullient sound of this venerable family band performing a variety of styles of Polish dance music including waltzes and, of course, polkas.

influences:
◀◀ Polish regional tradition
▶▶ Brave Combo

Michael Parrish

Trian

Irish traditional

Formed 1987, in Baltimore, MD, USA. Based in USA.

Billy McComiskey (USA), button accordion, concertina; Dáithí Sproule (Ireland), guitar, vocals ; Liz Carroll (USA), fiddle.

Trian easily ranks among the best traditional Irish groups in North America. Indeed, only top acts from abroad, like Altan, even come close to their superb musicianship. All of the group's members were renowned before forming Trian, and, as with many groups on the North American Irish music scene, they had played together in various formations for years before coming together as a touring ensemble. Raised in an exclusively Irish neighborhood, Billy McComiskey was exposed to the country's music very early in his life. He began to play accordion during the 1960s, influenced first by Bobby Gardiner and then by the great Sean McGlynn. In 1970 he came in second in the all-Ireland accordion championships, becoming the first American to place so highly. In 1975, having moved to Baltimore, he formed the Irish Tradition, in its day the most successful traditional Irish music group in the Baltimore/Washington, D.C., area. After that band's members went their separate ways in the 1980s McComiskey remained active in the traditional music scene. He reckons it was about 1987 when he formed Trian with Liz Carroll and Dáithí Sproule. Carroll took up the fiddle when she was nine years old, and honed her technique in sessions with Chicago musicians like Johnny McGreevy, Joe Shannon, and Jimmy Keane. In 1974 she won the junior all-Ireland fiddle championship, and returned the following year to capture the senior title. She has been a member of some of the outstanding lineups of traditional Irish music in the States, including the Green Fields of America and Cherish the Ladies. She is currently known not only as a member of Trian, but also as a solo fiddler and a composer of magnificent tunes. Dáithí Sproule's early musical influences were mostly from U.S. and British folk artists like Joan Baez and Bert Jansch. He combined this love of folk music with his strong interest in Celtic culture when he formed the Irish-language singing group Skara Brae with the three siblings Tríona and Maighread Ní Dhomhnaill and Mícheál Ó Domhnaill in the early 1970s. When Skara Brae broke up, Tríona and Mícheál went on to found the Bothy Band, while Sproule went south to Dublin. During the late 1970s he emigrated to the United States, where he quickly became part of the nationwide Irish music community by joining forces with fiddler James Kelly and accordionist Paddy O'Brien. This trio appeared regularly and recorded two LPs, cementing Sproule's reputation as one of the foremost guitar accompanists and bilingual singers in the Irish-music world. He is currently a member of two of the top Irish traditional bands in existence, Trian itself and the aforementioned Altan, and is in heavy demand as an accompanist, arranger, and solo artist. The trio of McComiskey, Carroll, and Sproule did not immediately settle on the name Trian as a moniker for the band. They first used it as the title of their 1991 debut album, which is credited to them under their individual names. In the next few years, as their reputation grew and demand for them increased, they settled on Trian, the signature of their first triumph, as the banner for their subsequent ones.

what to buy: *Trian* 🎵🎵🎵🎵🎵 (Flying Fish, 1991, prod. Liz Carroll, Dáithí Sproule, Billy McComiskey) is truly one of the landmark Irish CDs of the 1990s. Most of the album is made up of dance tunes played by all three musicians. In these trio arrangements McComiskey's accordion and Carroll's fiddle entwine effortlessly, sounding like one instrument, while Sproule's guitar keeps the rhythm with interesting and precise picking. Listen closely to McComiskey's accordion and you'll hear ornamentation you never would have thought possible from 10 fingers. Carroll's fiddle playing is equally impressive, and Sproule's guitar makes sure your feet keep tapping. In addition, McComiskey and Carroll each give us a few solo tunes to prove their mettle, and leave the listener in awe, if not in tears. Sproule's lovely, shrill singing voice graces four songs, two in Gaelic and two in English; of these, Peggy Seeger's "My Dearest Dear" stands out as the best.

what to buy next: *Trian II* 🎵🎵🎵🎵 (Green Linnet, 1995, prod. Billy McComiskey, Liz Carroll, Dáithí Sproule), the unimaginatively named follow-up to *Trian*, is another brilliant recording featuring McComiskey and Carroll's tight melodic duets accompanied by Sproule's bright, quick guitar work. A bit less flashy and ferocious, more subtle and controlled, than its predecessor, it takes the collaboration a step further, featuring more original compositions and more challenging arrangements. Sproule's songs on this outing include his melodic setting of the old ballad "The Death of Queen Jane," which he had given to Mícheál Ó Domhnaill in the early 1970s; Ó Domhnaill recorded it with the Bothy Band, but this is Sproule's own first crack at it.

solo outings:
Liz Carroll:
(With Tommy Maguire) *Kiss Me Kate* 🎵🎵🎵 (Shanachie, 1978)
A Friend Indeed 🎵🎵🎵 (Shanachie, 1979)
Liz Carroll 🎵🎵🎵🎵 (Green Linnet, 1988)

Billy McComiskey:
Makin' the Rounds 🎵🎵🎵🎵 (Green Linnet, 1981)

Dáithí Sproule:
(With Tommy Peoples) *The Iron Man* 🎵🎵🎵🎵🎵 (Shanachie, 1985)
A Heart Made of Glass 🎵🎵🎵 (Green Linnet, 1993)

influences:
◀◀ Skara Brae, the Irish Tradition, Green Fields of America, Sean McGlynn, Johnny McGreevy, John Healy

▶▶ Altan, Cherish the Ladies

see also: *Altan, the Bothy Band, Liz Carroll, Ceoltoiri, the Irish Tradition, Maighread Ní Dhomhnaill, Tríona Ní Dhomhnaill*

Steve Winick

John Trudell
Native American, rock, spoken-word
Born February 15, 1946, in Omaha, NE, USA. Based in USA.

Not many musicians can claim that they've garnered enough

notoriety to warrant a hefty FBI file, but John Trudell can. Granted, the Feds' interest in Trudell relates not to his poetry or music, but to his involvement with the Indians of All Tribes organization, which occupied Alcatraz Island in 1969, and the American Indian Movement, which he chaired from 1973 to 1979. A Santee Sioux from Nebraska, Trudell has suffered for his militancy—in the late '70s, his three children, wife, and mother-in-law were killed in a suspicious fire that authorities refused to investigate, leading Trudell to conclude the government may have been behind the blaze. Eventually, Trudell channeled his rage into art, resulting in books of poetry and albums with lyrics that he speak-sings over rock music. He hooked up with Jackson Browne to produce his debut, which Bob Dylan praised extravagantly. Still intensely political, Trudell continues to struggle for Native American rights. He's recorded infrequently, which is a shame.

what to buy: *AKA/Grafitti Man* ♪♪♪♪ (Rykodisc, 1992, prod. Jackson Browne) contains some material Trudell recorded with his friend and guitarist Jesse Ed Davis (who later died) for a mail-order cassette, plus some new tracks as well. Songs range from the opening statement of purpose, "Rockin' the Res," to "Bombs over Baghdad," an angry screed against the Gulf War, to "Baby Boom Ché," which posits Elvis as America's most potent revolutionary. Trudell reads in a clear, confident voice while the blues-tinged rock and native chants thunder behind him. It's a fine, fiery combination. With "Rant and Roll," the first track on *Johnny Damas and Me* ♪♪♪♪ (Rykodisc, 1994, prod. Terry Becker, Ricky Eckstein, Mark Shark), Trudell puts a name on his style of music and poetry. The album also addresses women's rights ("See the Woman," "Shadow over Sisterland") and social inequity ("All There Is to It"). Friends and admirers Jackson Browne and Jennifer Warnes sit in on a couple of tracks.

the rest:
Blue Indians ♪♪♪ (Dangerous Discs, 1999)

worth searching for: In addition to poetry and music, Trudell has added acting to his repertoire of skills, performing in films such as *Thunderheart, On Deadly Ground, Extreme Measures,* and *Smoke Signals.* His latest book of poems is *Stickman* (Inanout Press, 1995).

influences:
◀◀ Bob Dylan, Russell Means, Leonard Peltier

▶▶ Jackson Browne, Bob Dylan, Robbie Robertson

see also: *Oku Onuora, Robbie Robertson*

Daniel Durchholz

Daniel Tshanda /Dalom Kids /Splash
Bubblegum
Formed mid-1980s, in Johannesburg, South Africa. Based in Johannesburg, South Africa.

South African "bubblegum" is a more commercial style of *mbaqanga* (the "township jive" music first popularized among U.S. listeners through Paul Simon's *Graceland*) that features synthesizers and drum machines in place of guitars and drums. It began its ascent during the turbulent days preceding majority rule, and is now one of the dominant forms of black pop music in South Africa. The vocal styles and the use of countermelodies continue, but to the untrained ear this music sounds similar to any international pop based on rock and disco beats. With his groups Splash and the Dalom Kids, Daniel Tshanda was one of the main architects of this new sound. Like hit pop producers all over the world, Tshanda composes all his bands' music and controls all aspects of their careers, their many spin-off projects, and their ever-changing personnel.

what's available: *A Dalom Kids and Splash Collection* ♪♪♪ (Putumayo, 1996, prod. Daniel Tshanda) is a serviceable compilation of the most popular groups from Tshanda's stable of stars. Reggae, R&B, and disco pop up in the arrangements and the vocals are smooth and slick, often in English rather than Zulu.

worth searching for: Both bands have at least half-dozen albums available on import, but they're mostly interchangeable. A greatest-hits compilation like the one above is probably the way to go.

influences:
◀◀ Mahlathini, Boyoyo Boys, Soul Brothers

▶▶ Yvonne Chaka Chaka, Brenda Fassi, Stello "Chicco" Twala

j. poet

23 Skidoo
Proto-ethno-techno
Formed early 1980s, in England. Disbanded late 1980s.

Fritz Haaman, bandleader; numerous other performers.

Fritz Haaman headed up the enigmatic 23 Skidoo, considered one of England's most experimental avant-dance ensembles. Fond of tape loops and various styles of ethnic percussion, 23 Skidoo created a unique dance/funk style that became even more experimental and ethnically influenced with each release. Their catalog has not been released on CD. The curious will have to dig for LPs, but 23 Skidoo's work is well worth hearing.

worth searching for: In quirky 23 Skidoo manner, the EP *Seven Songs* ♫♫♫♫ (Fetish, 1982/Illuminated, 1985, prod. Fritz Haaman) lists eight tracks, actually has nine, and was re-released with 12. It's a brilliant mix of loops, funk, and African percussion. The *Tearing Up the Plans* ♫♫♫♫ (Pineapple-Fetish, 1982, prod. Fritz Haaman) EP is more of the same. The first side of *The Culling Is Coming* ♫♫♫ (Operation Twilight, 1983/Bel. Laylah, 1988, prod. Fritz Haaman) features 23 Skidoo live at the WOMAD (World of Music, Arts and Dance) Festival and is almost too experimental, with its traffic-jam of tape loops and undisciplined percussion. Side two contains the more soothing sounds of the Balinese *gamelan*. In that vein, *Urban Gamelan* ♫♫♫ (Illuminated, 1984, prod. Fritz Haaman) uses glass jugs and carbon-dioxide cylinders to mimic the signature tuned-percussion sounds. For a taste of everything up to that point, *Just Like Everybody* ♫♫♫ (Bleeding Chin, 1986, prod. Fritz Haaman) is a collection of previously released tracks.

influences:

◀◀ Nurse with Wound, Death in June

see also: *Paban Das Baul & Sam Mills*

Stacy Meyn

The Twinkle Brothers

Reggae
Formed 1962, in Falmouth, Jamaica. Based in London, England.

Norman Grant, vocals, drums (1962–present); Ralston Grant, vocals, rhythm guitar (1962–81); Derrick Brown, bass (1977–81); Eric Barnard, piano (1962–81); Karl Hyatt, vocals, percussion (1962–81); Albert "Bongo Asher" Green, congas, percussion (1962–81). (All members are from Jamaica.)

To say it is a crime that the Twinkle Brothers' finest releases are scarcely available domestically is to emphasize just how impressive these extraordinary proto-Rasta roots-reggae albums really are. *Rasta Pon Top, Love,* and *Countrymen* provide definitive thrills and chills in the studied art of "steppers" music, a ferociously rhythmic and "dread" serious form of reggae popular from the late '70s into the early '80s. The magical harmonizing on these records emerges from the thunderous riddims like a sunbeam through a cloudburst. All of the original members of the band were born in Falmouth, Jamaica, and throughout the '60s and into the early '70s, their music retained a softer, sunnier, North Coast drift that contrasted with the knife-edged toughness of the sounds emanating from Kingston. During these years the Twinkles wore matching outfits and toured the northern hotel circuit. In 1975, after Norman Grant had saved enough money from his work as a solo artist to finance a truly independent project, the Twinkle Brothers waxed the intrepid *Rasta Pon Top,* which includes potent hymns like "Beat Them

Jah Jah" and "Barabas." This led to a deal with Virgin Front Line and a series of heavyweight rootical classics, including "Since I Threw the Comb Away," "Never Get Burn," "Jah Kingdom Come," and "Watch the Hypocrites." In the early '80s the band was dropped from Virgin, and Grant briefly joined Inner Circle after lead singer Jacob "Killer" Miller died in a car accident. He then moved his base of operations to England, and has since recorded prolifically on his own Twinkle label, with results as varied as the rotating cast of musicians and singers. The Twinkle imprint is widely esteemed as an assiduously ethical label and has introduced such artists as Aisha, Princess Sharifa, Sista Rebeka, and Steve Santana. Of the Twinkles' more recent releases, perhaps most intriguing are Grant's beautiful and distinctive recordings with the Tribunia-Tutee Family—a Polish wedding band based in Warsaw. Ultimately, under Grant's direction, the Twinkle Brothers have all but ignored the evolution of dancehall reggae and digital *ragga,* and instead have steadfastly adhered to creating and exploring culture-rich roots and dub music, much to the satisfaction of their loyal fans in the U.K. and Eastern Europe.

what to buy: The Twinkle Brothers' greatest sets—*Rasta Pon Top* ♫♫♫ (Twinkle, 1975, prod. Norman Grant), *Love* ♫♫♫♫ (Virgin Front Line, 1977, prod. Norman Grant), and the stone-cold classic *Countrymen* ♫♫♫♫ (Virgin Front Line, 1980, prod. Terry Barham, Paul Smykle)—are all long overdue for reissue in America. However, the import-only *Free Africa* ♫♫♫♫ (Virgin Front Line, 1990, prod. various) collects the very best from *Love* and *Countrymen* and the cream of the crop from the otherwise spotty *Praise Jah* ♫♫♫ (Virgin Front Line, 1979, prod. Norman Grant). This titanic compilation and *Rasta Pon Top* are available from ErnieB's Reggae, Box 5019, El Dorado Hills, CA, 95762; e-mail: ErnieB@calweb.com; phone: (916) 939-0691.

what to buy next: *Enter Zion* ♫♫♫ (Twinkle, 1983, prod. Norman Grant) is one of the best of the post-Virgin Twinkle Brothers albums. The title cut is an underground Rasta masterpiece that showcases some heavenly harmonies. Interested in sampling some honest-to-God international reggae? Then check the sometimes gleeful, sometimes sorrowful, always unique collaborations between Norman Grant and Warsaw's Tribunia-Tutee Family. *Don't Forget Africa* ♫♫♫ (Twinkle, 1992, prod. Norman Grant), *Dub with Strings* ♫♫♫ (Twinkle, 1992, prod. Norman Grant), *Higher Heights (Twinkle Inna Polish Stylee)* ♫♫♫ (Twinkle, 1993, prod. Norman Grant), and *Comeback Twinkle 2* ♫♫♫ (Ryszard, 1994, prod. Norman Grant) feature the Family T.T. enthusiastically singing Polish folk songs over a double-take-inducing mix of fat steppers rhythms and evocative violins and cellos.

the rest:
Me No You, You No Me ♫♫♥ (Twinkle, 1981)

Underground 🎵🎵🎵 (Twinkle, 1982)
Dub Massacre, Parts 1-5 🎵🎵🎵 (Twinkle, 1982–90)
Burden Bearer 🎵🎵🎵 (Twinkle, 1983)
Live from Reggae Sunsplash (Sunsplash, 1984)
Right Way 🎵🎵🎵 (Shaka Music, 1985)
Kilimanjaro 🎵🎵🎵 (Twinkle, 1985)
Anti-Apartheid 🎵🎵🎵 (Twinkle, 1985)
Respect and Honour 🎵🎵🎵 (Twinkle, 1987)
Twinkle Love Songs 🎵🎵 (Twinkle, 1987)
All the Hits from 1970–88 🎵🎵🎵🎵 (Twinkle, 1988)
New Songs for Jah 🎵🎵🎵 (Twinkle, 1989)
Rastafari Chant 🎵🎵🎵 (Twinkle, 1989)
All Is Well 🎵🎵🎵 (Twinkle, 1990)
Live in Warsaw 🎵🎵🎵 (Twinkle, 1990)
Unification 🎵🎵 (Twinkle, 1990)
Wind of Change 🎵🎵🎵 (Twinkle, 1990)
Old Cuts (in Dub) 🎵🎵🎵 (Twinkle, 1991)
Twinkle Love Songs Vol. 2 🎵🎵 (Twinkle, 1992)
Babylon Rise Again 🎵🎵🎵 (Twinkle, 1992)
Rasta Surface 🎵🎵 (Twinkle, 1993)
Dub Feeding Program 🎵🎵🎵 (Twinkle, 1994)
DJ's Selections 🎵🎵🎵 (Twinkle, 1994)
Other Side 🎵🎵 (Twinkle, 1995)
Dub Plate 🎵🎵🎵 (Twinkle, 1995)
Chant Down Babylon 🎵🎵🎵 (Twinkle, 1998)

influences:

◄◄ The Abyssinians, the Melodians, the Mighty Diamonds, Morwells, Jah Shaka

►► Bim Sherman, African Head Charge, Dub Syndicate

Todd Shanker

UB40

Pop reggae
Formed 1978, in Birmingham, England. Based in England.

Ali Campbell, guitar, vocals; Robin Campbell, lead guitar; Astro, vocals; Earl Falconer, bass; Mickey Virtue, keyboards; Brian Travers, saxophone; James Brown, drums; Norman Hassan, percussion.

UB40 widened the audience for reggae by blending the rhythm-heavy, traditional Caribbean music with a British pop sensibility. Taking its name from the English unemployment form (something with which the eight band members were quite familiar), UB40 received its first major exposure opening for the Pretenders during that band's first U.S. tour. UB40

rapidly became a college radio favorite, and its 1983 rendition of Neil Diamond's "Red, Red Wine" scored with the masses. Socially conscious on- and off-record, UB40 was particularly proud to be one of the first Western acts to perform in the Soviet Union. With its lineup remarkably intact, the band enjoys a true worldwide following, taking its typical tours to no less than six continents. One tip: you can find UB40's albums in the reggae rather than the pop sections in more than a few record stores.

what to buy: Sitting squarely in the middle of the discography, the self-titled *UB40* 🎵🎵🎵🎵 (Virgin, 1988, prod. UB40) finds the band at a career peak with pointed songs like "Come Out to Play," "Where Did I Go Wrong," and "Breakfast in Bed," a duet with early benefactor Chrissie Hynde of the Pretenders. The band's first album, *Signing Off* 🎵🎵🎵🎵 (Virgin, 1980/1994, prod. Roy Falconer, Bob Lamb, UB40), features its first U.K. hit, "King," as well as the standouts "Food for Thought" and "Tyler." *Labour of Love* 🎵🎵🎵🎵 (Virgin, 1983, prod. Roy Falconer, UB40) showcases the band applying its reggae-pop flavoring to 10 covers, including "Red, Red Wine" and "Please Don't Make Me Cry."

what to buy next: Two strong best-of compilations were released simultaneously. *Volume One* 🎵🎵🎵 (Virgin, 1995, prod. various) features earlier, edgier work, while *Volume Two* 🎵🎵🎵 (Virgin, 1995, prod. UB40) features more radio-friendly fare from the recent past.

what to avoid: *Little Baggaridm* 🎵🎵 (A&M EP, 1985, prod. Ray Falconer, UB40) is an unsatisfying winnowing of the *Baggaridm* album that went unreleased in the U.S.

the rest:
Present Arms 🎵🎵🎵 (Virgin, 1981/1992)
Present Arms in Dub 🎵🎵 (A&M, 1981)
Live 🎵🎵🎵 (Virgin, 1983)
1980–83 🎵🎵🎵🎵 (A&M, 1983)
Geoffrey Morgan 🎵🎵🎵 (A&M/Virgin, 1984)
Rat in the Kitchen 🎵🎵🎵🎵 (A&M/Virgin, 1986)
CCCP—Live in Moscow 🎵🎵🎵 (A&M, 1987)
Labour of Love II 🎵🎵 (Virgin, 1989)
Promises and Lies 🎵🎵🎵 (Virgin, 1993)
Guns in the Ghetto 🎵🎵🎵 (Virgin, 1997)
Labour of Love III N/A (Virgin, 1999)

worth searching for: The import *Best of UB40, Volume 1* (Virgin U.K., 1987, prod. various) is a thorough representation of the group's prime period.

solo outings:
Ali Campbell:
Big Love 🎵🎵🎵 (Virgin, 1995)

influences:

◀◀ Bob Marley, Gregory Isaacs, Bim Sherman

▶▶ Rancid, Big Mountain, Chrissie Hynde

see also: *Ian Campbell Folk Group*

Gary Plochinski

Udi Hrant

Turkish/Armenian classical

Born Hrant Kenkulian in 1901, in Adapazar, Turkey. Died August 29, 1978, in Istanbul, Turkey.

Hrant Kenkulian was considered blind from birth, but didn't give up the idea of having his eyes repaired until very late in life. In 1915 his family fled Adapazar because of a pogrom against ethnic Armenians, finally settling in Konya where the young Kenkulian started learning how to play the *oud* (lute). The style he picked up is one that differs considerably from the kind heard throughout the bulk of the Islamic world. (The instrument used in Turkish music is somewhat shallower-bodied than the variety of oud preferred in Egypt or other Middle Eastern countries, with a brighter, higher-pitched sound affecting the way Turkish virtuosi—whose ranks would eventually include Kenkulian—attack the strings.) By the 1920s Kenkulian was playing in cafes and selling musical instruments. It was also during this time that he made the first of many foreign journeys to fix his eyesight, traveling to Vienna, Austria, for an unsuccessful treatment. Even though his skills were constantly improving and he had already recorded a series of 78 rpm discs, Kenkulian found no regular jobs with any of the day's performing ensembles until after his marriage in 1937. He finally caught the ear of Serif Içli, a musician/composer whose connections led to Kenkulian playing concerts on Ankara Radio. It was there that he started to build and solidify his reputation as an oud virtuoso and composer. Soon Kenkulian was so admired that he became known as Udi Hrant, the "Udi" being an honorific for "Master of the Oud." He went to the United States in 1950 in another failed attempt to gain his eyesight, and while there was convinced to undertake a concert tour of the country. He then returned to Turkey to teach and perform on the radio, both as a soloist and with the Radio Istanbul Orchestra. His final international tour took place in 1963, hitting France, Greece, Lebanon, Armenia, and the United States. He died from cancer mere months after performing his last concert in Istanbul.

what to buy: Start at the beginning. *The Early Recordings, Volume 1* ♪♪♪♪ (Traditional Crossroads, 1995, compilation prod. Harold G. Hagopian) and *The Early Recordings, Volume 2* ♪♪♪♪ (Traditional Crossroads, 1995, compilation prod. Harold G. Hagopian) contain exquisitely re-mastered performances from the cream of Kenkulian's early 78s. There are examples of his singing, his violin artistry, and, above all, his way of playing the improvisational *taqâsîm* technique on the oud. *Volume 2* contains "Hastayim Yasiyorum," his most famous song, while *Volume 1* has the lovely "Siroon Aghcheek," written for his wife Agavini.

what to buy next: During his 1950 tour of the United States, Kenkulian taped some pieces that were probably not meant for general release. Still, *Udi Hrant* ♪♪♪♪ (Traditional Crossroads, 1994, compilation prod. Harold G. Hagopian) is a wonderful document of his mature style, including some fine examples of taqâsîm.

influences:

◀◀ Tanburi Cemil Bey, Udi Yorgo Bacanos, Udi Krikor Berberian

▶▶ Richard Hagopian, Münir Nurettin Beken, Mutlu Torun

see also: *Richard Hagopian*

Garaud MacTaggart

Áine Uí Cheallaigh

Irish traditional

Born Ann McPartland in Belfast, Northern Ireland. Based in Ring, County Waterford, Ireland.

In 1995, *sean-nós* ("old-style") singer Áine Uí Cheallaigh was catapulted from near obscurity to relative fame in Ireland thanks to her single contribution to the *Riverdance* stage show and its Grammy-winning soundtrack: her exquisite vocals on "Lift the Wings," a tender song of emigration and longing for the homeland. In fact, her performance turned many a head at home *and* abroad, even before it was adopted by Aer Lingus, Ireland's national airline, as their piped-in music for U.S. callers put on hold. Unlike the other performers who found themselves enjoying the spotlight that *Riverdance* shone on them, Uí Cheallaigh was, strictly speaking, neither a young hopeful looking for her first break, nor a seasoned career artist lending her talents and name recognition to the project; she was a schoolteacher who was just beginning to get noticed as a singer. One person who'd been impressed when he heard her on the radio was Bill Whelan, who wrote "Lift the Wings" especially for her.

Born Ann McPartland in her father's native Belfast, she grew up there listening to his renditions of the Ulster singing tradition. By 1982 she was using her married name and had relocated to her mother's original home: the tiny Irish-speaking community of Ring, near Dungarvan, County Waterford. There she immersed herself in the Munster province's sean-nós tradition of delicately ornamented, unaccompanied singing, and started competing nationally. She won the coveted Corn Uí Riada prize in 1990 and again in 1992. The bilingual *Idir Dhá Chomhairle/In Two Minds* is her only solo release to date. Following her *Riverdance* success, Uí Cheallaigh opted to return to her school-teaching job in Ring rather than tour the world with the show, but the interest in and demand for her voice has lead to more appearances: a recording for another Bill Whelan project and some songs on an album commemorating the 1798 rebellion. Tracks from her solo release are starting to surface on compilations in the U.S., and you don't have to be a school child to experience her teaching skills. She gives master classes in sean-nós singing at festivals around Ireland. Uí Cheallaigh's modest recording career to date belies her considerable abilities.

what to buy: *Idir Dhá Chomhairle/In Two Minds* ✍✍✍✍ (Gael-linn, 1992) is a wonderful showcase of both the Munster sean-nós style (in Irish) and the Ulster singing style (in English). While largely unaccompanied, some understated contributions are made here and there by piper Liam O'Flynn and a few others. One highlight is "Peace in Erin," a plea for reconciliation as relevant today as it was when it was written in the 1830s by schoolmaster Hugh McWilliams from County Antrim.

worth searching for: Bill Whelan's *The Roots of Riverdance* (Celtic Heartbeat, 1997) includes Uí Cheallaigh singing the otherwise unavailable "Cill Liadáin," a new setting of a well-known Irish-language poem by the blind 18th-century folk poet Raftery. *Who Fears to Speak—The Official 1798 Bicentenary Commemorative Album* (RTE, 1997) sees Uí Cheallaigh take turns with guest singers Liam Clancy and Len Graham.

influences:

◄ Nioclás Tóibín, Labhrás Ó Cadhla, Paddy Tunney

►► Liam O'Flynn, Bill Whelan, Liam O Maonlai, Karen Casey

see also: *The Clancy Brothers, Liam O'Flynn, Bill Whelan*

John C. Falstaff

The Ukrainians

Alternative Ukrainian folk-rock
Formed 1988, in Leeds, England. Based in Leeds, England.

Peter Solowka, guitars, mandolin, backing vocals; Len Liggins, vocals, violin; Stepan Pasicznyk, accordion, vocals; Dave Lee, drums; Paul Dino Briggs, bass; Roman Remeynes, mandolin. (All members originally from England.)

Leeds, England, has always been remarkably multi-ethnic, with small but active populations from various Central European countries to complement the English, Indian, West Indian, Pakistani, and Irish segments of the city. But about the last place anyone would have expected Ukrainianism to raise its head was with The Wedding Present, the Energizer Bunnies of the post-punk scene. Solowka was a guitarist with the band, and

persuaded leader Gedge to do some traditional Ukrainian material. The idea took off, and very soon the Ukrainians were a separate, established identity, with their own personnel and recording contract. Their eponymous first album debuted in 1991 to excellent reviews. Basically, they charged headlong into traditional music, or self-composed tunes that seemed traditional enough. It was close-to-the-edge, someone's-gonna-get-their-babushka-kicked-in-tonight style, more fun than an evening swilling vodka. From there they took a slight musical detour, an EP of the Smiths covers (*Pisni Iz the Smiths*) that was nothing less than a delight—an unlikely but perfect marriage. A second album, *Vorony,* includes one track from that EP, as well as a cover of the Velvets' "Venus in Furs." It's more of the same, but played with even more confidence and enjoyment. This is just as true of their third (and so far seemingly final) effort in 1996, *Kultura.* As the real Ukraine's former Soviet dominators would ruefully agree, all good things must come to an end . . . .

what to buy: *Kultura* ✍✍✍ (Cooking Vinyl, 1996, prod. Ukrainians) is the *ne plus ultra* of the catalog, and with the Smiths EP appended, their work doesn't come any better.

the rest:
The Ukrainians ✍✍✍ (Omnium, 1991)
Vorony ✍✍✍ (Green Linnet, 1993)

influences:

◄ The Smiths, the Velvet Underground

Chris Nickson

Ulali
See: Pura Fé

Urubamba
See: Los Incas, Paul Simon

Jai Uttal

World pop/jazz
Born Doug Uttal, in New York, NY, USA. Based in Los Angeles, CA, USA.

This talented vocalist/multi-instrumentalist studied classical piano as a child before also learning to play banjo, harmonica, and electric guitar. His diverse musical abilities were reflected in his picking up a wide range of styles and absorbing everything from Jimi Hendrix to John Coltrane to modern classical. By age 19 he became entranced by the work of world famous Indian musician Ali Akbar Khan, and was compelled to move to California to study voice and the 25-string *sarod* under Khan's guidance. Uttal was later able to apply his Indian classical training to the other forms of music he played during the 1970s and 1980s, including reggae, punk, Motown, and blues. Also during the 1970s (after changing his name to Jai), he made many pilgrimages to India, while still studying music in California under various tutors. One of those Indian treks was incredibly influential—he lived and played amongst the Bengali street musicians known as *Bauls,* communicating with them entirely through music, and the lessons learned there would permanently alter his musical course. Uttal has been categorized both as a world and jazz musician, but his work blends those elements with pop and jazz-fusion to form a signature sound that is full of warmth and romanticism. He began his recording career with the 1990 debut *Footprints,* an album that found him taking his inspirational journeys to India (particularly his time spent with the Bauls) and applying them to his Western heritage. In other words, the improvisational nature of certain Indian styles was appropriated into more structured forms such as pop and electronic music. Uttal then formed the Pagan Love Orchestra (which includes multi-instrumentalist Peter Apfelbaum and keyboardist Kit Walker) to interpret his early works live—and when he saw the greater possibilities of working with a live band, there was never another of his albums on which the outfit didn't appear. Their sound includes guitar, trombone, violin, bass, and percussion. The electronic influences of his debut gave way to more pop-based ones, which later led to fusion and even a few reggae inflections. Uttal's main instrument is the *dotar,* which sonically resembles a sitar but possesses a crisper sound with less twang. It dominates his first two albums, but as his music has matured, he has let the other contributions of the Pagan Love Orchestra become stronger and more independent. No matter what album you listen to, though, the sound of Uttal and his orchestra is very distinct. Uttal has also performed on albums by the Hieroglyphics Ensemble, Tulku, the Peter Apfelbaum Sextet, and Gabrielle Roth & the Mirrors, and has produced two albums for Ali Akbar Khan.

what to buy: While his latter two releases are more orchestrated and quite sonically rich, his debut has more of an immediate, and lasting, visceral impact. *Footprints* ♫♫♫♫ (Triloka, 1990, prod. Jai Uttal) is primarily a solo project and features a larger amount of electronic-based pieces. The intense trance sounds of "Madzoub (God Intoxicated)" and "Bus Has Come" are engrossing, as is the Tangerine Dream–like sequencer freefall of "Snowview." Trumpeter Don Cherry and vocalist Lakshmi Shankar lend their talents to some of the tracks. Jai Uttal and the Pagan Love Orchestra's latest, *Shiva Station* ♫♫♫♫ (Triloka, 1997, prod. Jai Uttal), was mixed by Bill Laswell, and it features songs with lyrics and chants in Sanskrit, Hindi, Bengali, and English. It shows the group getting tighter and more cohesive, with the album possessing a more lush and orchestrated feel than previous works. While not as groundbreaking as the other releases, it is a warm, passionate affair. Some of it rocks, a couple tunes get jazzy, and Uttal's romantic lyrics are more personal and less conventional this time.

what to buy next: Uttal's second outing, *Monkey* ♫♫♫ (Triloka, 1992, prod. Jai Uttal), is the first disc with the Pagan Love Orchestra and features some well-done pop ballads with intriguing Eastern twists. Uttal's impassioned singing elevates them above standard world-pop fare. There are also plenty of catchy world instrumentals featuring Uttal's dotar-playing at their center, and while the sound here is sparser than subsequent works, it's engaging. *Beggars and Saints* ♫♫♫ (Triloka, 1995, prod. Jai Uttal) is another good release, which grows on you with each listen. The Pagan Love Orchestra is given more of a chance to shine, integrating Indian instruments with Western rock and brass arrangements. The album leans more towards a fusion and less towards a pop sound than before, and subliminal ambient touches weave into different spots.

influences:

◀◀ Ali Akbar Khan

▶▶ Tulku

see also: *Peter Apfelbaum, Krishna Das, Ali Akbar Khan, Bill Laswell, Lakshmi Shankar, Jim Wilson (sidebar)*

Bryan Reesman

Vadå

Folk-rock
Formed 1995, in Sweden. Based in Sweden.

Christer Suneson, vocals, guitar; David Kronlid, bass, keyboards; Stefan Brisland-Ferner, violin, hurdy gurdy, jew's-harp; Gotte Rinqvist, lute, flute, jew's-harp; Lars Forslund, drums; Björn Eriksson, bass. (All members are from Sweden.)

Suneson and Kronlid met in the mid-1980s and began playing a punk-edged folk music, but they weren't satisfied with the sound until Brisland-Ferner and Rinqvist, who also play with Garmarna, signed up in 1995. Under the name Jezebel they recorded two singles, then broke up. After rethinking their direction, they re-formed as Vadå, emphasizing a crunching, metallic guitar approach with lots of droning industrial background noise. The Swedish press flipped over their first, and so far only, album. Some said it was the best folk-rock album ever, others hated it. In 1996 they recorded an English-language version called *Red White and Gray.* It was released in North America by the Canadian Phyrric label and, strangely enough, when it reached Sweden, did better than the original.

what to buy: *Vadå* ♪♪♪ (Massproduktion, 1995, prod. Sank) is a loud, dark, dirty album crammed with grinding guitars, rumbling bass, deadly plodding drumbeats, and lots of ambient noise; think Nine Inch Nails in a sauna on belladonna. This is more rock than folk, and more grindcore than rock.

influences:
◄◄ Garmarna, Hedningarna, Hoven Droven

see also: *Garmarna*

j. poet

Vadya Lahari
South Indian karnatak music
Formed 1987, in South India. Based in South India.

A. Kanyakumari, violin; Mannargudi A. Easwaran, mridangam; Kumari N. Vijayalakshmi, vina; Mambalam K.S. Siva, nadaswaram; Yarpanam K. Ganesh Pillai, tavil. (All members are from southern India.)

Formed by noted female violinist A. Kanyakumari, Vadya Lahari is an unusual experiment within South India's deep tradition of karnatak music that could only have taken place in the modern era. Until recently, it would have been nearly impossible to conceive of an ensemble pairing the delicate, sitar-like sound of the *vina* with the piercing roar of the *nadaswaram,* an enormous oboe-like reed instrument primarily used in outdoor ceremonies. In a world without amplification, the subtleties of the vina and the violin would be drowned out by the intrusion of any percussion instrument, let alone the booming of the *tavil* drum (also used by this group) and the nadaswaram, whose sounds are meant to penetrate every corner of the neighborhood. To most Indian listeners Vadya Lahari must seem like a bold experiment indeed, but for Kanyakumari, who once played a 29-hour non-stop recital, it is an opportunity to open minds and ears to a whole new world of karnatak music.

what's available: *Vadya Lahari: South Indian Instrumental Ensemble* ♪♪♪ (Music of the World, 1992, prod. Bob Haddad) is a thrilling introduction to the surprisingly accessible karnatak style, which in general is much livelier and more focused on the ensemble than the classical music of northern India. The interweaving of melodic lines on violin, vina, and nadaswaram is particularly engrossing, as the three musicians trade off on solos, diverge in harmony, and then reunite in unison to great effect. The rhythmic exchanges are also impressive, especially on the 24-minute "Rāma Kathā Sudhārasa," where Easwaran shows why he's considered one of the finest *mridangam* masters in the world today with jaw-droppingly complex beat cycles that will leave percussion fans in awe. The album is also notable for its closing track, "Ragupati Rāghava Rājarām," a

devotional song Mohandas K. Gandhi used to open all his political meetings.

influences:
◄◄ L. Shankar, Sri. K. Swaminatha Pillai, Dr. M.L. Vasantha Kumari

Bret Love

Bebo Valdes
Cuban jazz
Born October 9, 1918, in Quivican, Cuba. Based in Sweden.

Bebo Valdes is the father of renowned Cuban pianist Chucho Valdes, but he deserves to be considered on his own merits. Certainly by the time he left Quivican for Havana in 1936, the senior Valdes had already acquired an impressive keyboard technique, enabling him to find a series of jobs in many local bands. In addition to his work as musical director at Havana's famous Tropicana Night Club, Valdes can also be credited as one of the primary forces in the Cuban jam session (known as a *descarga*) alongside bassist Cachao (Israel Lopez). He also appeared in many radio and television concerts during the late 1950s with his group, Sabor de Cuba. Valdes left Cuba in 1960 for Mexico, where he became associated for a short time with a record label as a musical director and pianist. He then lived in Spain, touring with a reconstructed version of the legendary Lecuona Cuban Boys, before moving to Stockholm, Sweden.

what to buy: *Bebo Rides Again* ♪♪♪♪ (Messidor, 1995, prod. Paquito D' Rivera), the first album Bebo Valdes had recorded in 35 years, finds the pianist/arranger in fine form. Amid an impressive array of Latin talent, the master finds room for a solo spot ("Oleaje"), on which he trips lightly through a lovely fantasia with impeccable elan.

what to buy next: The 20 songs on the collection *Mayajigua* ♪♪♪ (Caney, 1995, prod. various) were recorded in Havana in 1957 and 1960, documenting one of the best Cuban ensembles of the day, Bebo Valdes y Su Orquesta Sabor de Cuba. There is a nice array of rhythms displayed in the program, from *montunos,* mambos, and boleros to rumbas, *guarachas,* and *danzones.* The big band's playing and arranging are all quite good, especially a tremendous trumpet section featuring Alejandro "El Negro" Vivar and "Chocolate" Armenteros on the classic "El Manisero," to name one highlight. Valdes also recorded for the Panart label, and some of those sides appear on *Todo Ritmo* ♪♪♪ (T.H. Rodven, 1992). The packaging is muy cheesy but the performances are classic and, at times, witty. "Persian Shah" is a bit of a novelty, with a clarinet echoing a stereotypical Ottoman style, proving that title and atmosphere don't have to have anything to do with reality.

the rest:
Descarga Caliente 𝄞𝄞𝄞𝄾 (Caney, 1995)

influences:
◄◄ Rene Hernandez, Ernesto Lecuona, Arsenio Rodriguez

►► Gonzalo Rubalcaba, Chucho Valdes

see also: *Cachao, Paquito D'Rivera, Chucho Valdes*

Garaud MacTaggart

Carlos "Patato" Valdes

See: Patato

Chucho Valdes

Cuban jazz
Born Jesus Valdes, October 9, 1941, in Quivican, Cuba. Based in USA.

Chucho Valdes has been one of the major forces on the Cuban jazz scene since the late 1960s, when he formed Orquesta Cubana de Musica Moderna with trumpeter Arturo Sandoval and reed player Paquito D'Rivera. From there the trio helped the acclaimed Irakere outfit get off the ground in 1973. Son of Cuban music legend Bebo Valdes, Chucho is a formidable pianist in his own right and a composer of some repute. As a jazz piano player, he owes much to Art Tatum and McCoy Tyner, but leavens that with roots sunk deep in the rhythms of his homeland.

what to buy: The finest album available by Valdes is *Bele Bele en la Habana* 𝄞𝄞𝄞𝄞 (Blue Note, 1998, prod. Réne López). The music is alive and the pianist is supported by a trio of young-bloods with bright futures. Raúl Piñeda Roque, the drummer, is a particular find, as demonstrated from the very first tune, "Son Montuno." The last song on the disc, the rhythmic *guaguancó* (modern rumba rhythm) "Los Caminos," was composed by the great Cuban songwriter Pablo Mllanés. *Cuba Jazz* 𝄞𝄞𝄞𝄞 (TropiJazz, 1996, prod. Ralph Mercado, Eddie Rodriguez), one of the strongest Latin-jazz albums of the 1990s, is billed as "Paquito D'Rivera presents Cuba Jazz featuring Bebo and Chucho Valdes," but it is Chucho's album more than anyone else's. His piano playing and arranging touches are all over the album, and his duet with the senior Valdes (on "Peanut Vendor") is marvelous.

what to buy next: Listening to Valdes's performances on *Lucumi: Piano Solo* 𝄞𝄞𝄞 (Messidor, 1988, prod. Gotz A. Worner) makes one realize where Cuban players like Gonzalo Rubalcaba and Hilario Diaz got their roots. He wrote all the material, and his playing is superb, with supple ballads like "Jica" acting as wonderful counterweights to dance-inflected tunes like "Mambo Influenciado" and "Osun." Valdes has created a solo piano album for Latin jazz fans that may serve as a touchstone for future generations.

the rest:
Solo Piano 𝄞𝄞𝄞𝄾 (World Pacific, 1993)
Pianissimo 𝄞𝄞𝄞 (Molito, 1994)
(With Omara Portuondo) *Desafios* 𝄞𝄞𝄞𝄞 (Nubenegra/Alula, 1997/1998)
Chucho Valdes Live 𝄞𝄞𝄞 (RMM, 1998)

worth searching for: Valdes composed and arranged all the material on Irakere's *Live at Ronnie Scott's* 𝄞𝄞𝄞𝄞 (World Pacific, 1993, prod. Pete King, Chris Lewis), which offers a good sense of Valdes's perspective on his long-standing ensemble. Of particular note is his playing on "Cuando Canta el Corazon," while the greatest workout is the nearly 13-minute "Flute Notes."

influences:
◄◄ Ernesto Lecuona, Horace Silver, Art Tatum, McCoy Tyner, Bebo Valdes

►► Hilario Diaz, Gonzalo Rubalcaba

see also: *Paquito D'Rivera, Irakere, Pablo Milanés, Arsenio Rodríguez, Arturo Sandoval, Bebo Valdes*

Garaud MacTaggart

Ritchie Valens

Latino Rock
Born Richard Valenzuela, May 13, 1941, in Pacoima, CA, USA. Died February 3, 1959, in Clear Lake, IA, USA.

Best known for his updating of the traditional Mexican folk song "La Bamba," Ritchie Valens was the first Chicano rock star. Only 17 when he died along with Buddy Holly and J.P. Richardson ("The Big Bopper") in a plane crash outside of Clear Lake, Iowa, Valens had become a regular presence on the charts with such self-penned hits as "Donna" and "Come on, Let's Go." Valens's career lasted a brief two years. After performing with a high school band, the Silhouettes, he was signed to a record contract with the Del-Fi label by producer Bob Keene in the spring of 1958. That year, he nearly reached the top 40 with "Come on, Let's Go," later covered by Tommy Steele and Los Lobos. His biggest hit came with a song inspired by a girlfriend, "Donna," the A-side of the single that included "La Bamba"—which itself reached #2. In 1959 Valens was in the film *Go Johnny Go* and made several appearances on Dick Clark's nationally broadcast *American Bandstand* TV show. Valens's short life was memorialized in the 1987 film *La Bamba*. A recording of the title track by his phenomenal Latin-rock descendants Los Lobos became a #1 hit.

what to buy: *Rockin' All Night: The Best of Ritchie Valens* 𝄞𝄞𝄞𝄞 (Del-Fi, 1995, compilation prod. Bob Perry, Rob Santos) is a thorough examination of Valens's brief career. In addition to the hits, the 22-song collection includes nearly every tune he recorded.

Chucho Valdes

what to buy next: Released after Valens's death, *In Concert at Pacoima Jr. High* ♫♫♫ (Del-Fi, 1960, prod. Bob Keene) was the first live rock 'n' roll album and documents a time when rock shows were relegated to school sock hops. The six-song set includes Valens's hits and a memorable rendition of Eddie Cochran's "Summertime Blues." The album is rounded out by demos of five songs Valens planned to release but never finished.

influences:

Little Richard, Elvis Presley, Mexican folk music

Los Lobos, Chris Montez

Craig Harris

Justin Vali

Malagasy folk and popular music
Born October 1964, in Fierenana, Madagascar. Based in Paris, France.

Justin's actual last name is Rakotondrasoa, but he's called "Vali" after the *valiha* (Madagascar's zither), of which he is the master. Vali was born into a musical family—his father and grandfather both knew hundreds of folk melodies. The family was also noted for the instruments they made. Vali began developing his own style as a youth; he picked the strings with his fingernails, rather than the pads of his fingers, giving the instrument a brittle, chiming quality. He also began fingerpicking long, single-note interludes with a jazzy improvisational quality that astounded listeners. In 1982 he joined a folkloric group and toured the world. When he reached Paris, he relocated there and formed his trio. The success of his first two albums, *Rambala* and *Bilo,* led to worldwide tours that included dates at Woodstock '94 and a gig serenading Nelson Mandela at the French Embassy in South Africa.

what's available: *Ny Marina—The Truth* ♫♫♫♫ (RealWorld, 1995, prod. Tchad Blake) is easier to find than *Rambala* and *Bilo,* but it's decidedly less traditional in style. There are flamenco handclaps, waltzes, "raps" in Malagasy (the language of Madagascar), more percussion—some of it with a decidedly Latin feel—and plenty of opportunities to experience Vali's incredible fingerpicking technique. If you can locate it, *Rambala* ♫♫♫♫ (Silex France, 1991, prod. Sir Ali) offers stripped-down Malagasy folk music, with abundant fancy picking and rumbling harmonies from the three male principals.

influences:

Martin Rakotoarimanana, Rokotofra, Tsimialona Volambita

Les Smockers, Tarika

j. poet

Carlos Varela

Nueva trova, nueva canción
Born c. 1969, in Cuba. Based in Havana, Cuba.

Carlos Varela is following in the tradition of Cuban poet José Martí and political singers Silvio Rodriguez and Pablo Milanés. Sometimes appearing with an acoustic guitar and sometimes with heavily rocked-up backing, he offers thoughtful lyrics from the perspective of a young Cuban looking at the politics and emotions of his home country. However, his work has not been released in Cuba itself. Despite this, Varela intends to stay in his homeland, finding there his subject matter and muse.

what's available: *Jalisco Park* ♫♫♫♫ (Eligeme, 1993) is Varela's debut disc, recorded in Spain, which brought his music to the world and marked him as a presence in the *nueva trova* or "new ballad" movement, a personalized take on Latin America's folk-inspired, activist *nueva canción* ("new song") genre. *Monedas del Aire* ♫♫♫♫ (Qbadisc, 1994) and *Como Los Peces* ♫♫♫♫ (RCA International, 1995) show the further development of his lyrical commentary and musical style. These discs aren't the easiest to find, but are worth seeking out.

influences:

Victor Jara, Pablo Milanés, Silvio Rodriguez

Kerry Dexter

Värttinä

Modern Finnish folk
Formed 1983, in Finland. Based in Finland.

Sari Kaasinen, Mari Kaasinen, Kirsi Kähkönen, Sirpa Reiman, all vocals, with various backing musicians. (All members are from Finland.)

Our story starts in 1983, in Rääkkylää, in the Karelia area of southeastern Finland, near the Russian border. Fifteen girls and six boys, singing and backed by the *kantele* (zither), whistle, saxophone, bass, flute, and possibly kitchen sink, began exploring the folk music of the area, with its irregular rhythms and strong vocal tradition. They even traveled into the then-Soviet Union to collect songs from the Mari and Setu peoples—all part of the Finno-Ugric (linked Finnish, Siberian, and Hungarian) tradition. What made the band so distinctive was the fact that it was led by women, with an instinctively feminist approach, and that there was also no attempt to be cute by donning traditional costume. This was exuberant and young; quite punk in its own little way. The group issued one record in 1989 (*Musta Lindu*) before thinning the ranks a couple of years later for its second album *Oi Dai,* which became one of Finland's all-time best-sellers. These girls could be bad, dallying 'round the corner with the boys and asking them to spend the night—but more than lyrical content, it was the harmonies that thrilled,

Carlos Varela

dangerous and taken at high speeds. The trip continued on the next two albums, *Värttinä* and *Seleniko,* but they really hit top gear a couple of years later with *Aitara,* which saw them negotiating edgy vocal turns that left awed spectators wondering if it would all spin out of control. By now, they'd garnered a world audience through their energetic performances and were ready to move on to bigger and better things. In 1996 there was a new label, Nonesuch, and a new record, *Kokko,* that was mature and . . . disappointing. To an extent, they'd gone pop. It was like hearing the girls from Abba singing folk; not particularly inspiring. Nonetheless, sales were good and critical reception respectable, but in spite of this, they switched labels again in 1998 to Wicklow, the Chieftains' Paddy Moloney's new label, with the stunning return to form *Vihma* and renewed progress toward world domination.

what to buy: *Aitara* 𝄢𝄢𝄢 (Xenophile, 1994, prod. Janne Haavisto) shows that voices can be dangerous—don't try this at home, or you could end up rupturing your vocal cords. *Vihma* 𝄢𝄢𝄢 (Wicklow, 1998, prod. Janne Haavisto, Richard Horowitz) has all the trademark vocal qualities interlocking like jigsaw

puzzles, plus some fantastic rhythms that offer a very modern edge without resorting to the drum machine.

what to avoid: *Kokko* 𝄢 (Nonesuch, 1996) is a lackluster attempt to go pop that fizzles like a wet Helsinki Monday morning.

the rest:
Oi Dai 𝄢𝄢𝄢 (Green Linnet, 1991)
Seleniko 𝄢𝄢𝄢 (Green Linnet, 1992)

worth searching for: *Musta Lindu* 𝄢𝄢𝄢 (Olarin Musiikki Oy, 1989) and *Värttinä* 𝄢𝄢𝄢 (Mipu Music, 1992/Finlandia, 1998) are two choice items that, surprisingly, have yet to find an American-label home—though, happily, the latter's Finlandia reissue is one of many fine offerings on the powerhouse Warners subsidiary that are making their way into American record bins.

solo outings:
Sari Kaasinen and Mari Kaasinen:
Can We Have Christmas Now? 𝄢𝄢𝄢 (NorthSide, 1998)

influences:
◄ Traditional Finnish folk music

see also: *Maria Kalaniemi*

Chris Nickson

Vas
Ambient vocal worldbeat
Formed 1995, in Los Angeles, CA, USA. Based in Los Angeles, CA, USA.

Azam Ali (Iran), voice, hammered dulcimer, bendir; Greg Ellis (USA), percussion (including udu, dumbeck, madal, nagara, bendir, bowls, bells, shakers, tambura), vocal drones, keyboards.

Many artists collected here lament the broadness of the "world music" label. But Vas would probably jump at the chance to switch labels with them. The unearthliness of Azam Ali's pipes, the cyclical, devotional quality of her and Greg Ellis's compositions, and the understated temperament of their sound gets Vas tagged as "new age," but this is anything but background music, and anything but anonymous. The band seeks as many audiences as it has influences, and those influences are wide—Vas means "vessel," and this particular chalice is deep enough to contain the sensibilities Ali gained from her Iran-to-India-to-the-U.S. upbringing, and which Ellis acquired from casting beyond his suburban American one. Yet what flows back out from the vessel is measured and well blended, a stream of mostly Middle Eastern-sounding chants from Ali (although Mediterranean, Eastern European, and other influences occasionally bubble through it), in a remarkable yet restrained range of percussive textural settings from Ellis. Vas take a novel approach to one of America's main fears of world music: You don't have to worry about not speaking the language of the singer, because she doesn't either. Ali prefers an improvised vocalese that she feels more flexibly meets her expressive needs, and broadcasts under the babble of mere words to communicate on a universal emotional frequency. The band's style is one which, like Ali's lyrical feelings, defies naming. They may not get to be called "world," but Vas's music is out of it in the way that counts the most.

what's available: Vas's unassuming material doesn't demand repeated listenings, but it does welcome and reward them. Like the mysteries it implicitly celebrates, this music reveals its wealth to you with persistence and patience. The band's sound will evolve thoughtfully over time, so if you like one of their thus-far two albums you'll probably like the other. Each has its surprises, but start with the slightly tighter debut, *Sunyata* 𝄞𝄞𝄞𝄞 (Narada, 1997, prod. Azam Ali, Greg Ellis). Ali's entrancing vocals and Ellis's formidable yet subtle musicianship get the band off to a great beginning. Sophisticated but sensual, theirs is a spiritual sound that takes as much joy in this life as the next. *Offerings* 𝄞𝄞𝄞 (Narada, 1998, prod. Azam Ali,

Greg Ellis) may stretch out a bit, but anything it lacks in directness it makes up for in experimentation. Although Vas still plays live as a duo, a Who's Who of accompanists joins them here, including Ellis's former Billy Idol bandmate Steve Stevens (true story!) and sought-after Turkish flutist Omar Faruk Tekbilek. But to say that this album's arrangements are expanded is not entirely accurate—you'll hear instruments you didn't on *Sunyata,* but even at its most minimal the music has always been rich.

worth searching for: Ellis wrote the introductory liner notes and contributed "Minus One," a solo percussion variation on *Sunyata*'s title track, to the compilation *Mondo Beat: Masters of Percussion* (Narada, 1998, executive prod. Dan Harjung), a stellar survey of rhythm's reigning talents including Tito Puente, Airto Moreira, the Musicians of the Nile, Babatunde Olatunji, Mongo Santamaria, and Mickey Hart.

influences:
◄ Dead Can Dance, Glen Velez

see also: *Omar Faruk Tekbilek*

Adam McGovern

Nana Vasconcelos
Brazilian folklore, jazz, and fusion
Born August 2, 1944, in Recife, Brazil. Based in Brazil.

Along with Airto Moreira, Nana Vasconcelos is one of the most important purveyors of the colorful and polyrhythmic percussion style that is a treasure of his native Brazil. What makes him especially valuable is his ability to adapt his multicultural approach to a variety of musical genres. Making an early debut with his father's band while still in his teens, Vasconcelos would work for a time with the celebrated Milton Nascimento before coming to the United States in the 1970s as a member of Gato Barbieri's band. Later that decade, the percussionist teamed with fellow Brazilian Egberto Gismonti before helping to form the group Codona, which combined a variety of world-music styles and featured trumpeter Don Cherry. Throughout this period, Vasconcelos recorded for the ECM label with various ensembles, including a memorable early-1980s stay with the Pat Metheny Group. His most recent efforts have found him performing with, among others, Jan Garbarek and Scottish percussionist Evelyn Glennie. The foundation of Vasconcelos's multilayered sound, which often includes vocals, guitar, and hand percussion, is the *berimbau*. This native instrument includes a hollow gourd and attached, bowed piece of wood which stretches a wire strand, its resonance closely resembling that of a slack guitar string. As a proponent of the rich musical legacy that Brazil has to offer, Vasconcelos remains one of the country's most valuable exports.

what to buy: *Saudades* ♫♫♫♫ (ECM, 1979, prod. Manfred Eicher) is a great place to experience Vasconcelos's talent; a tour de force of his resplendent approach. *Duas Vozes* ♫♫♫♫ (ECM, 1984, prod. Manfred Eicher) is a session co-led with Egberto Gismonti that finds the pair exploring a variety of traditional songs and spontaneous duets with fascinating results.

what to buy next: *Storytelling* ♫♫♫♫ (EMI, 1995, prod. Nana Vasconcelos) has Vasconcelos utilizing a more contemporary approach. The overall effect is still one of multilayered textures, yet electronics have a more prominent role.

the rest:
Lester ♫♫♫♪ (Soul Note, 1985)
Bush Dance ♫♫♫♪ (Antilles, 1986)
Rain Dance ♫♫♫ (Antilles, 1988)
Fragments: Modern Tradition ♫♫♫ (Tzadik, 1997)

worth searching for: Egberto Gismonti's *Danca das Cabecas* ♫♫♫♫ (ECM, 1976, prod. Manfred Eicher) features several lengthy pieces for percussion and Gismonti's guitar that highlight the unique rapport shared by these two major talents. Pat Metheny and Lyle Mays's *As Falls Wichita, So Falls Wichita Falls* ♫♫♫♫ (ECM, 1980, prod. Manfred Eicher) is one of the three sets that Vasconcelos recorded with Metheny, and it's the best of the bunch due to the expansive title track, which benefits greatly from Vasconcelos's uncanny percussion work. Codona's *Codona 3* ♫♫♫ (ECM, 1983, prod. Manfred Eicher) summarizes the chamber-music approach of this atypical group, which owed much of its vitality and rhythmic variety to Vasconcelos.

influences:
◄◄ Brazilian folk tradition

see also: *Michael Brook, Eliane Elias, Egberto Gismonti, Milton Nascimento, Flora Purim, Badal Roy, Caetano Veloso*

Chris Hovan

Väsen

Traditionally influenced Swedish folk
Formed 1990, in Sweden. Based in Sweden.

Olov Johansson, nyckelharpa; Mikael Marin, viola; Roger Tallroth, guitar; Andre Farrari, percussion.

Take the tradition of Uppland in Sweden, a world-champion *nyckelharpa* (keyed fiddle) player, a manic guitarist, a violist who's written a piece for the Kronos Quartet, and a percussionist with a taste for Native American costume, and you've got something a little different. Johansson, who'd been the nyckelharpa world champ after taking up the instrument at 14, played the traditional score for the performance of *Hamlet* that inspired fellow ground-breakers Garmarna to form in 1990. Teaming up with Marin and Tallroth, Johansson founded Väsen, performing not

only music from the Uppland tradition, but also a number of original compositions. The group was quickly noticed, and between 1990 and 1996 released four albums on Sweden's Drone label—*Väsen, Vilda Väsen, Essence,* and the live *Levande Väsen* —tracks from all of which were compiled on their first U.S. release in 1997, *Spirit.* Although resolutely acoustic, that's hardly dampened the musical adventures, or the wit of the sounds. Johansson in particular was singled out by appreciative critics, fans, and colleagues alike for his instrumental expertise, and has performed with the Kronos Quartet, playing the nyckelharpa on a piece written by Marin. The roots have remained a part of the band's sound, but on their most recent album, *Whirled,* where they added percussionist Farrari, they show themselves more than capable of tackling anything with grand style, from *polska* dances to tangos and jigs. Far from being academic, everything is done with a sly (and sometimes not-so-sly) humor. The band has grown slowly and steadily, building up audiences across Europe and now America. Accessible, skilled, exciting, they're the cream of an acoustic crop.

what to buy: *Spirit* ♫♫♫♫ (NorthSide, 1997, prod. Väsen, Olle Paulsson, Magnus Dahlberg) collects tracks from their first four releases and shows the growth of their sound, which wasn't tentative even in the beginning. This is a band that knows how to rock without playing rock music. *Whirled* ♫♫♫♫ (NorthSide, 1998, prod. Väsen) introduces the percussionist as a full and vital member of the band, expanding their sound and showing that they've moved from being merely exceptional to world-class. It all seems effortless, and every note is a delight.

worth searching for: *Väsen* ♫♫♫ (Drone, 1990, prod Väsen) is the start of the story, while *Levande Väsen* ♫♫♫♫ (Drone, 1995, prod. Magnus Dahlberg) captures the live experience—truly the best way with a band like this. If you want a Hendrix of the nyckelharpa, it has to be Johannson (okay, so there aren't too many candidates), as evidenced on his 1998 solo album *Storvarten* ♫♫♫♫ (NorthSide, 1998).

influences:
◄◄ Swedish folk tradition

see also: *Dervish, Garmarna, JPP*

Chris Nickson

Glen Velez

Worldbeat, jazz
Born in Dallas, TX, USA. Based in New York, NY, USA.

Velez is internationally recognized as a master musician, with a specialty in frame drums—the large tambourine-like hand drums that include the Egyptian *riq* and the Irish *bodhrán.* Glen's father was a trumpet player who made his living in Latin

Glen Velez

dance bands, but it was through an uncle that Velez got interested in drumming. He had his first kit at age 10, and by 14 he was exploring jazz and improvisation. After a stint in the army playing in the army band, Velez studied percussion at the Manhattan School of Music and became a member of the Steve Reich Ensemble in 1972. He added the Paul Winter Consort to his résumé in 1983. Although Velez is widely recognized as a hand drummer, he also plays steel drums, *mbira* (thumb piano), drum kit, and world percussion. He has a large collection of drums—more than 300—which allows him to produce a never-ending variety of textures, timbres, and rhythms. Velez has an eclectic style that makes him a highly desired session musician for pop, jazz, and world-music dates, and he's added his talents to more than 150 recordings by Suzanne Vega, Eddie Gomez, Glen Moore, Rabib Abou-Khalil, and many others. Velez has also recorded about a dozen albums under his own name, as well as a number of well-received instructional videos on hand drumming.

what to buy: *Hand Dance* 🎵🎵🎵🎵 (Latitudes, 1996, prod. Bob Haddad) is a digital reissue of the 1985 album that introduced Velez to world-music buffs; his first outing as a leader, with music that's subtle, driving, and thoroughly intoxicating.

what to buy next: On *Rhythmcolor Exotica* 🎵🎵🎵🎵 (ellipsis arts . . . , 1996, prod. Jamey Hadad) Velez leads his Handance Frame Drum Ensemble through a percussive world-music travelogue that touches down in Brazil, North Africa, India, and other uncharted inner ports of call.

best of the rest:
Internal Combustion 🎵🎵🎵🎵 (CMP, 1985)
Assyrian Rose 🎵🎵🎵🎵 (CMP, 1989)
Doctrine of Signatures 🎵🎵🎵🎵 (CMP, 1991)
Pan Eros 🎵🎵🎵🎵 (CMP, 1994)
Rhythms of the Chakras 🎵🎵🎵🎵 (Sounds True, 1998)

influences:
◀◀ Diga Rhythm Band, Zakir Hussain, Oregon

see also: *Steve Gorn, Enzo Rao, Mike Richmond, Badal Roy, Paul Winter*

j. poet

Caetano Veloso

MPB (Brazilian Popular Music)
Born August 7, 1942, in Santo Amaro da Purificacao, Bahia, Brazil.
Based in Brazil.

At once as gentle as a rainbow and as powerful as equatorial sun-shine, Caetano Veloso neatly sums up the Brazilian musical per-sonality. While his music can be melodic, beguiling, and sweetly sublime, it can also be "dangerous" enough to get him exiled from his homeland, as it did in the late 1960s. But the story of Veloso, one of the most influential Brazilian musicians of this cen-tury because he helped launch the "Tropicalismo" or "Tropicalia" movement, begins several years earlier, when the budding musi-cian and filmmaker discovered the bossa nova of João Gilberto. Totally smitten by music, he put his other artistic ambitions aside. Later, while at university, he and his sister, Maria Bethânia (soon to be a noted singer in her own right), began playing around Sal-vador, Bahia's big city. In 1964 Veloso hooked up with a team of would-be ground-breakers—Gilberto Gil, Gal Costa, Tom Zé, and Carlos Coqueijo—to mount the stage production *Nos, por Ejem-plo*. He subsequently moved to Rio de Janeiro and slowly began to gain fame with such songs as "Um Dia," but it was his mixing of rock with native Brazilian forms—as on the 1967 song "Alegria Alegria"—that made Veloso a revolutionary. Influenced by the quick-shifting cultural currents of the day, Veloso and other mem-bers of the *tropicalista* vanguard shocked Brazilians with their musical mix-and-match. *Fado* and funk, samba and soul were blended together, as on the album *Tropicalia*, recorded with Costa, Zé, Gil, and others. It's hard to believe now, but what would later be hailed as a step forward for Brazilian music was derided by the military dictatorship of the time as "chaos." In 1968 Veloso was thrown in jail for four months and then fled to exile in Eng-land for two years. Upon returning to Brazil, he was still as experi-mental as ever. In concert, he danced like Carmen Miranda, alarming observers on all points of the political spectrum be-cause of his androgyny. However, ordinary Brazilians began to take him to their hearts, and in the 1980s he became a national star. It helped that he was doing some of his best work, such as the stirring *Estrangeiro* in 1989. Also during this period Veloso's American reputation began to grow, thanks to exposure from compilations on former head Talking Head David Byrne's Luaka Bop label. A 1997 U.S. tour brought Veloso to the West Coast for the first time, while he also scored the soundtrack for the Brazil-ian film *Tieta do Agreste*. After more than 30 years, Veloso is fi-nally getting his due. With his heavily percussive 1999 *Livro* album and acclaimed North American journey in support of it the same year, he proves that just because he's getting older doesn't mean he's growing any less vital.

what to buy: For Americans weaned on rock who are just wak-ing up to the brilliance of Brazilian music, Veloso's 1980s and 1990s material is the best place to start. The edgy yet graceful *Estrangeiro* ♪♪♪♪ (Elektra/Musician, 1989, prod. Peter Scherer, Arto Lindsay) is a knockout display of Veloso's musical and lyrical skills. His poetic fire even comes through to those who don't understand a word of Portuguese. He's helped here by some of Brazil's best musicians, including percussionists Nana Vasconcelos and Carlinhos Brown, not to mention such other noted names as Bill Frisell and Marc Ribot. On *Circulado* ♪♪♪♪ (Elektra/Nonesuch, 1991, prod. Arto Lindsay), even Japanese ground-breaker Ryuichi Sakamoto helps out on a couple of tracks.

what to buy next: Veloso's career has spanned such a long time and he has recorded so many albums—more than 30— that it's hard to pinpoint a couple of discs that sum up what he's about. That's where compilations come in, offering hints of each of Veloso's eras. *Without Handkerchief without Docu-ment—The Best of Caetano Veloso* ♪♪♪♪ (PolyGram/Verve, 1990, prod. various) is one of the best, featuring 19 tracks and intelligent liner notes written by Gerald Seligman, who later went on to found the respected worldbeat label Hemisphere. All the early breakthrough songs are here: "Alegria, Alegria," "Soy Loco por Ti, America," "Tropicalia," and "Atras do Trio Electrico."

the rest:
Livro ♪♪♪♪ (Nonesuch, 1999)

worth searching for: The four-CD box set *Caetano* ♪♪♪♪♪ (Poly-Gram Brasil, 1994, prod. various) is available as an import in the United States, and it has just about everything a Veloso-raptor could want, including bilingual sleeve notes. An album with Gilberto Gil, *Tropicalia 2* ♪♪♪♪ (Elektra/Nonesuch, 1994, prod. Liminha, Gilberto Gil, Caetano Veloso), reunites these two giants of Brazilian music and finishes a story interrupted by oppression and closed-mindedness in the 1960s.

influences:
◄◄ Astrud Gilberto, João Gilberto, Antonio Carlos Jobim

►► Carlinhos Brown, Marisa Monte, Paralamas, Chico Science & Nacao Zumbi

see also: *Maria Bethânia, Gal Costa, Celia Cruz, Gilberto Gil, João Gilberto, Virginia Rodrigues, Ryuichi Sakamoto, Timbal-ada, Nana Vasconcelos, Tom Zé*

Cary Darling

Veritas

Croatian folk music
Formed 1987, in Hamburg, Germany. Based in Hamburg, Germany.

Mile Spejar, first lead tamburica; Gordana Grgie, second lead tam-burica; Kristina Spejar, harmony tamburica; Robert Spejar, harmony

Caetano Veloso

tamburica; Zoran Zavrski, rhythm tamburica; Drago Spejar, bass tamburica; Marica Perinic, vocals. (All members are from Croatia.)

Veritas is a *tamburica* (eastern European lute) ensemble that plays traditional folk and dance music from Croatia; the group was formed by a Croatian family (now living in Germany) to preserve their musical culture. For most of us in the West, Croatia is merely a trouble spot in the former Yugoslavia, plagued by genocide and civil war. Perhaps the music of Veritas will help put a more human, and considerably more happy, face on the Croatians.

what's available: The tamburica is a small guitar-like stringed instrument that sounds like a cross between a Greek *bouzouki* and a mandolin, with a high-pitched, cheery timbre. There are several types of tamburica: small instruments, *samica,* which play the leads; medium-sized *bugarijas,* which play chords and melody; and the *berde* or *bas,* for the bass parts. The tunes on *Folk Music from Croatia* 🎵🎵🎵🎵 (ARC, 1997, prod. Robert Spejar)—mostly merry, up-tempo jigs—sound similar to Greek folk music, but they're more sprightly and less melancholy. The tamburica picking is exhilarating throughout, and Marica Perinic's vocals are always heartwarming.

influences:

◄◄ P. Ilic, M. Von Farkash

j. poet

T.H. "Vikku" Vinayakram
South Indian percussion
Born 1932, in Madras, India. Based in Madras, India.

One of the foremost percussionists in the South Indian *karnatak* style, Vikku Vinayakram is also acknowledged as the world's greatest master of the *ghatam,* a large clay water pot that is stroked with the fingers, slapped, and sometimes tossed into the air in a burst of high spirits. Initially trained under his father, Harihara Sarma, at his renowned school of percussion, Vikku gave his first public performance at the age of 13, and was immediately touted as a rising star. Vinayakram's career in the West started to take off in the late 1960s, when he began touring Europe extensively with artists such as violin virtuosos L. Subramaniam and L. Shankar and mandolin prodigy U. Srinivas. In 1974 he began teaching at the Centre for World Music at Berkeley, where he eventually joined forces with jazz guitarist John McLaughlin, *tabla* drum master Zakir Hussain, and L. Shankar to create Shakti, an influential ensemble that combined elements of jazz and Indian classical to create a new East-West hybrid. But this was just the beginning of Vikku's involvement in the burgeoning Indian/jazz fusion movement, and the two decades since Shakti's dissolution have seen him recording with artists ranging from Mickey

Hart's Grammy Award–winning Planet Drum ensemble to Bill Laswell's ever-evolving Material. Although he has yet to make much of a mark in the United States as a bandleader in his own right, Vinayakram remains in high demand as a sideman, and as a ghatam teacher at his own school in Madras, recording classical albums in India whenever his busy schedule permits. Indian newspapers reported that he performed with Sankara, a new fusion group led by karnatak percussionist Subhas Chandran, in early 1999, but there is no word yet on whether the ensemble plans to record.

what to buy: Vinayakram's only solo Western release is *Together* 🎵🎵🎵🎵 (Magnasound/OMI, 1996, prod. G. Suresh), a percussion-heavy venture that showcases Vikku's formidable talents alongside those of his sons, *kanjira* (tambourine) specialist Selva Ganesh and rising ghatam master Uma Shankar. The album's centerpiece, "Family Matter," is a 30-minute epic that may turn off non-percussion fans, but the other four songs use Rikhi Ray's pastoral guitar textures to great effect, creating a strangely enjoyable, non-traditional vibe perfect for weekend afternoons spent lounging in the sun. Every Indian music fan should own a copy of *The Best of Shakti* 🎵🎵🎵🎵 (Moment/Sony, 1994, prod. John McLaughlin), a nine-song masterpiece that captures four instrumental wizards at their mind-blowing peak. Although there have been hundreds of Indian/jazz fusion experiments since Shakti recorded its last album, none have quite captured the breathtaking passion that seems to explode from every single song on this 76-minute classic. A definite must-have!

what to buy next: L. Shankar's *Raga Aberi* 🎵🎵🎵🎵 (Music of the World, 1995, prod. the Epidemics) is a brilliant recording featuring three-fourths of Shakti—Shankar, Vikku, and Zakir Hussain. Far more traditional in nature than their work with John McLaughlin, this 48-minute *raga* composed by Shankar allows each of these masterful musicians ample room to show off his dazzling improvisational skills, with Vikku and Zakir trading remarkably complex percussive riffs that build to an earth-shattering climax.

the rest:
(With L. Shankar) *Soul Searcher* 🎵🎵🎵🎵 (Axiom, 1990)
(With L. Shankar) *M.R.C.S.* 🎵🎵🎵 (ECM, 1991)
(With Mickey Hart) *Planet Drum* 🎵🎵🎵🎵 (Rykodisc, 1991)
(With Material) *Hallucination Engine* 🎵🎵🎵🎵 (Axiom, 1994)

worth searching for: Vinayakram has recorded a number of albums in India, many of which can be found in Indian specialty stores. *Generations* is especially worth searching for, as it features some of the karnatak style's most prominent musicians, including Vikku, his two sons, and, on the 30-minute "Tidal Waves," some magnificent drumming and *konnakkol* (spoken percussion) from Subhas Chandran.

influences:

influences:

◀◀ Harihara Sarma

▶▶ Subhas Chandran, Selva Ganesh, Uma Shankar

see also: *Mickey Hart, Zakir Hussain, Bill Laswell, Shakti, L. Shankar, U. Srinivas, L. Subramaniam*

Bret Love

Vinx

Soul, drum ensemble, jazz, funk, Afropop fusion
Born Vincent De'Jon Parrette, in Kansas City, MO, USA. Based in Watertown, MA, USA.

For all of Vinx's achievements—including scoring the second-best triple jump in the world to qualify for the 1980 Moscow Olympics (the games the United States boycotted)—it's amazing that he's not more renowned as a multidimensional performer, athlete, author, visual artist, and even diplomat. A singer and percussionist who started his career playing with Taj Mahal in 1978, Vinx continued to pursue his Olympic goals, moving to Los Angeles in 1984. Sidelined by an injury at the trials, however, he turned his attention to music. His first recording session, with saxophonist Ernie Watts (*Musician*), earned a Grammy in 1986. The following year, crooner Tom Jones recorded a Vinx tune, "Touch My Heart." Vinx's reputation grew when he appeared in 1988 commercials for Levi's 501 jeans and Sprite. That year also saw him touring with Rickie Lee Jones, Teena Marie, the Bus Boys, and Toni Childs. But just as his own career was taking off, Vinx experienced a brutal loss: his father was murdered during a mugging while visiting family in Detroit. Despite losing his biggest musical influence, Vinx continued performing and touring, heading to Europe with his drum band, the Barkin' Feet, and appearing on Herbie Hancock's Showtime *Coast to Coast* program with Donnie Raitt, Bruce Hornsby, B.B. King, Lou Reed, and Woody Harrelson.

After he joined Sting on the latter's *The Soul Cages*, Sting and I.R.S. Records head Miles Copeland (brother of ex-Police drummer Stewart) signed Vinx to Sting's own short-lived I.R.S. imprint, Pangea—whose very name invokes a one-world concept (it's the geological term for the hypothetical single landmass that broke apart to form the modern continents). Vinx's debut release was *Rooms in My Fatha's House*, with Taj Mahal, Herbie Hancock, Sting, Sheryl Crow, Branford Marsalis, and other guests. A baritone compared vocally to Al Jarreau, Bobby McFerrin, Donny Hathaway, and Nat King Cole, Vinx proved a commanding (and funny) stage act as the opener and percussionist/backing vocalist for Sting's Soul Cages tour. He also performed with Peter Gabriel, Sinéad O'Connor, Elton John, and Zucchero. His song "While the City Sleeps" became the soundtrack to the opening dance segment of the Fox TV show *In Living Color*. In 1992 Vinx headed to Santa Fe, where he sold his first painting and released his next CD, *I Love My Job,* with a jazz/soul approach and internationally influenced guests such as Patrice Rushen, Zap Mama, and Hiroshima's Don Kuromoto. Another Vinx composition, "There I Go Again," was heard on TV's *Northern Exposure* and became the subject of so many inquiries it wound up on a compilation of the show's most-requested songs. Among the artists Vinx opened for in 1992 were Steel Pulse, Third World, Drummers of Burundi, Richard Elliot, Big Country, and Manhattan Transfer. During 1993 Vinx released his third album, *The Storyteller,* with Stevie Wonder and Cassandra Wilson, and moved to Boston to be near his future wife. The following year, he turned out a pilot for Oprah Winfrey's Harpo Productions, and played and co-emceed at Woodstock '94. He also hit the road with the Spin Doctors, Cracker, and the Gin Blossoms.

In 1995 Vinx's multitalented, multicultural leanings earned him an appointment as a U.S. State Department cultural attaché on a four-month tour of Africa as part of a drum trio. He then toured with renowned bassist Me'Shell Ndegéocello, and opened for such renowned world acts as Baaba Maal, Yothu Yindi, and King Sunny Adé. His fourth CD, *Lips Stretched Out,* was released in 1996 on his own Internet label H.O.E. (Heroes of Expression) Records. He also wrote a children's book and made a belated appearance at the Olympics—this time as a performer at the summer games in Atlanta. In 1997 he took his own band, Jungle Funk (with Will Calhoun and Doug Wimbish of Living Colour and Bernie Worrell of Parliament/ Funkadelic), on a tour of Europe. Not a bit afraid to genre-jump, his eclectic abilities allow him to cross over in a broad range of categories, from worldbeat, reggae, salsa, and pop to funk, R&B, jazz, soul, and blues. A true man of the world, Vinx is always likely to turn up exactly where he might least be expected—as he did at the 1997 NFL playoff game between the New England Patriots and the Pittsburgh Steelers, where he sang "The Star-Spangled Banner."

what to buy: *Rooms in My Fatha's House* ✍✍✍ (Pangea/I.R.S., 1991, prod. Sting, John Eden, Greg Poree, Vinx) is an inviting place—subtle, passionate, witty, never overdone, and filled with charisma. Among the friends hanging out are Taj Mahal, Herbie Hancock, Sheryl Crow, and Branford Marsalis.

what to buy next: *The Storyteller* ✍✍✍ (Pangea/I.R.S., 1993, prod. Greg Poree, Vinx) features a huge list of contributors, including Stevie Wonder (piano), Harvey Mason (drums), and Cassandra Wilson (vocals). It's sometimes categorized as rock, but is full of eclectic fusions and non-categorizable, uniquely Vinx sounds. *I Love My Job* ✍✍✍ (Pangea/I.R.S., 1992, prod. Greg Poree, Vinx) is equally offbeat, soulful, and clever.

the rest:
Lips Stretched Out ✍✍✍ (H.O.E., 1996)

worth searching for: You'll thank yourself for seeking out Cassandra Wilson's *Blue Light til Dawn* (Blue Note, 1993), on which Vinx delivers percussion and vocals, and Sting's *The Soul Cages* (A&M, 1991), on which he plays percussion.

influences:

[◄◄] Gerald Albright, Nat King Cole, Herbie Hancock, Al Jarreau, Bobby McFerrin, Leslie Jackson Parrette Sr., Prince, Sting, Stevie Wonder

[►►] Bobby McFerrin, Cassandra Wilson

Lynne Margolis

Viva la Musica

See: Papa Wemba

Carlos Vives

"Techno vallenata"

Born Carlos Alberto Vives Restrepo, 1964 or 1965 (sources vary), in Santa Marta, Valle de Upar, Colombia. Based in Colombia.

There was a time when you could say that Carlos Vives wasn't a *vallenata* musician but he played one on TV. He had received some early musical training on the piano from his grandmother, and his father used to make him sing at family reunions, but music took a back seat to acting when Vives enrolled at the School of Dramatic Art in 1979. By 1982 he was making his mark as an actor in a Colombian television series called *Tiempo sin Huellas*. Vives later went on to be a fixture in the Hispanic soap opera world, culminating with his starring role as the title character in *Escalona,* as in "Raphael," a series based on the life of the legendary vallenata figure. Combining Vives's handsome, charismatic screen presence with his persuasive tenor delivered unheard-of demographics to the show's producers, and inspired national pride in one of Colombia's native musics. The corresponding soundtrack album, released in 1990, helped point the direction for Vives's future career. The accordionist on these projects was Egidio Cuadrado, a superb musician whose impeccable roots-oriented credentials provided the traditional base for Vives's music for the rest of the 1990s.

Vallenata revolves around the trinity of accordion, bongos, and *guiro* (a rhythmic scraped instrument), while the lyrics tell tales of love and civic pride. Unlike *cumbia,* Colombia's other major musical export, vallenata had remained a bit more rural and rootsy, giving it a slightly more transparent "feel." These characteristics were tweaked in 1993 with Vives's release of *Clasicos de la Provincia,* an album that was to change the face of the music with sales of over a million copies worldwide. Vives and his band La Provincia embraced a traditional genre only to weave in electric instruments and a drum kit, taking the form into the future even as they were paying tribute to composers

of its past. In many ways this is an accomplishment in Colombian music that ranks with what Fairport Convention and Milton Nascimento's Clube da Esquina did in their respective countries. If vallenata has been dragged into the late 20th century, then *Clasicos de la Provincia* (along with Gloria Estefan's album *Abriendo Puertas*) played a major role in making the music relevant to a younger demographic. Vives's variation has been labeled by some critics as "techno vallenata," but from the viewpoint of the performer himself, it is an ever-evolving hybrid. *Tengo Fe,* Vives's latest album, adds cumbia and *jíbara* rhythms to the basic mix, although Cuadrado's accordion always anchors the music.

what to buy: Vives's most influential album is an unqualified pop masterpiece, *Clasicos de la Provincia* ♪♪♪♪ (Sonolux/PolyGram Latino, 1993, prod. Eduardo De Narvaez), propelled to multi-platinum sales by the Emiliano Zuleta–penned hit "La Gota Fria." Egidio Cuadrado's notable interpretations of vallenata style are almost as experimental with the form as some of Dino Saluzzi's tangos. Ditto for Luis Angel Pastor, one of the most interesting bassists in the Western Hemisphere.

what to buy next: While not as big a seller as *Clasicos de la Provincia, La Tierra del Olvido* ♪♪♪♪⁷ (Sonolux/PolyGram Latino, 1995, prod. Carlos Vives, Richard Blair) still makes some interesting choices as Vives blends the music of Colombia's Andean slopes with his "techno vallenata." Most of the material is generated from La Provincia, including tunes either written or co-written by Vives, guitarist Ernesto Ocampo, and accordion wizard Egidio Cuadrado. Rock also starts to make a strong appearance with this album, as Ocampo whips a few lines from the Stax/Volt rhythm catalog on "La Cachucha Bacana" before traditional percussion riffs and Andean pan flutes drive the music back toward its roots. Drifting ever closer to mainstream Latin pop, Vives released *Tengo Fe* ♪♪♪♪ (EMI/Latin, 1997, prod. Carlos Vives). There are moments of melodrama seemingly aimed at the same demographic that goes nuts for Luis Miguel, but Vives usually manages to spring the vallenata card and make routine tunes rise above expectations. He had a hand in writing all the songs except "Caballito," a hard-charging arrangement of a Colombian folk song that is almost a throwback to *Clasicos*. Much of the original La Provincia is gone but Cuadrado and Pastor are still with Vives, and key to his sound.

worth searching for: Before there was *Clasicos de la Provincia,* there was *Escalona un Canto a la Vida* ♪♪♪♪ (Sony Discos, 1992, prod. Josefina Severino). This is more of a traditional vallenata album, with less prominent roles for the bass guitar and drum kits. Everything was written by Rafael Escalona, one of the genre's most honored songwriters, and the musicians play the music sans anything but the most traditional of embellishments. Vives's vocals are catchy and Cuadrado's accordion playing does the past justice while doing the future proud. This album was the follow-up to the *Escalona* soundtrack.

influences:

⏪ Leandro Diaz, Rafael Escalona, Charlie García

⏩ Amparo Sandino, Shakira, Tulio Zuluaga

see also: *Bloque*

Garaud MacTaggart

Vocal Sampling

Son

Formed 1990, in Havana, Cuba. Based in Havana, Cuba.

Members have included: René Baños, vocals, musical director; Sergio Pereda, vocals; Reinaldo Sanler, vocals; Abel Sanabria, vocals; Carlos Díaz, vocals; Luis Alzaga, vocals; José Rolando Duran, vocals; Renato Mora, vocals. (All members are from Cuba.)

Vocal Sampling replicates the sound of a salsa band using nothing but their vocal chords and a few well-placed hand claps. The six singers, who have all played in traditional Cuban bands, met while studying music and began refining their unique vocal take on the *son* (Afro-Cuban folk music) during after-class vocal jam sessions. In 1992 Poney Gross of the Belgian company Zig Zag Productions brought them to Europe and convinced them to make their "hobby" their career. The band's "vocalese salsa" may sound like a gimmick, but when they start singing they make it obvious they're musicians as well as entertainers. Abel Sanabria's vocal congas and José Duran's deep booming basslines lay down a groove so deep a dinosaur couldn't climb out of it. Carlos Diaz and Reinaldo Sanler add a faux horn section of trumpet and trombone while Luis Alzaga and René Baños, the group's founder, share lead vocals, adding incredible ornamentation to the end of each line. Your ears tell you there's an orchestra on stage, but your eyes confirm the fact that everything you hear, including the fat, swooping sound of a fretless bass, is coming from the mouths of the six singers. And despite the "gimmick," Vocal Sampling writes solid original material. If they were fronting a traditional band and singing these songs, they'd still be an impressive outfit. The fact that they do it all vocally is nothing short of astonishing.

what to buy: *Live in Berlin* ♪♪♪♪ (Ashé, 1998, prod. Zig Zag, René Baños) includes some of the band's strongest material, recorded before an adoring—and amazed—crowd. The "bass solo" on the doo-wop-flavored *bolero* "Sueño Contigo" gives you a good idea of the band's vocal and improvisational chops.

what to buy next: The merengue "Eso Está Bueno" on *De Vacaciones* ♪♪♪ (WEA Latina, 1996, prod. Vocal Sampling, Rachael Faro) is another example of the vocal prestidigitation the band is becoming famous for.

WOMAD

Celebrating diversity was WOMAD's goal long before it was a corporate buzzword. By the time Peter Gabriel released his third self-titled solo album in 1980, he'd begun to break out of the U.S./Anglo rock continuum and into world music—a landmark for-instance being the South African drums and chants (not to mention bagpipes) of the anti-apartheid anthem "Biko." So it's not surprising that in the same year Gabriel catalyzed a group of people to create WOMAD—World of Music, Arts & Dance. The effort was conceived as a meeting ground of the traditional and the modern from cultures around the world. The primary venue for this vision would be an annual festival, though WOMAD also supports cross-cultural educational efforts and recordings. The first WOMAD gathering, held in England in 1982, succeeded artistically but left a pile of debt, which Gabriel was able to pay off by holding a benefit reunion concert with his old band Genesis. After that dodgy start, the organization grew in strength. The WOMAD Foundation was established in 1983 to support multicultural education, and it runs workshops in schools, colleges, and community centers throughout England. In 1988, WOMAD enhanced its international scope by offering festival programs in Denmark and Canada. It has since held more than 90 events in 20 countries. The format acted as a template for such American touring festivals as Lollapalooza and H.O.R.D.E.—performances take place on two or three stages, surrounded by participatory workshops in music, arts, and dance, as well as vendors of globe-spanning crafts and foods. Today, WOMAD boasts a family-oriented atmosphere featuring activities to keep children happy in their parents' spirit of cultural adventure. The week-long festival in Reading, England remains the cornerstone of the organization's worldwide year-round schedule; WOMAD's outpost in Seattle, Washington, puts on an annual event that keeps the former capital of Alternative Nation a full-time mecca of world music.

see also: Peter Gabriel

Salvatore Caputo

Vocal Sampling (with Renato Mora, front)

the rest:

Una Forma Mas ♪♪♪♪ (Sire, 1995)

influences:

 Juan Luis Guerra, Bobby McFerrin, Beny Moré, Orquesta Aragón

j. poet

W

Waaberi

See: Maryam Mursal

Mohamed Abdel Wahab

Arabic pop

Born March 13, 1907, in Cairo, Egypt. Died May 3, 1991, in Cairo, Egypt.

The Big Four of Egyptian music during the first half of the 20th century were the legendary singers Umm Kulthum and Abd el-

Halim Hafez, the flamboyant *oud* (lute) virtuoso Farid al-Atrash, and the meticulous composer, musician, singer, and actor Mohamed Abdel Wahab. While it was al-Atrash's unfulfilled wish to write material for Kulthum (the most-loved vocalist in Arabic music history), Wahab did write one of her biggest hits, "Enta Omri," in 1964. By the time he died, Wahab was the most honored musician in the Arab world, with a backlist of over 1,500 songs and a secure reputation as one of the finest, most imaginative oud players to emerge from the early days of the 20th century.

His career spanned an era of turbulence in Arabic society as a whole and Egyptian society in particular. As a child Wahab was just starting his life as an entertainer, singing in a theater, as Egypt was swaying under the burden of a dual occupation, by the Ottoman Empire and the British Empire. After years spent studying music in the classical Arab tradition, Wahab was introduced to the music of Western Europe. Coincidentally, the British and French governments had effectively strengthened their control of the Middle East, and King Farouk I was sitting on the Egyptian throne. This last fact was important for

Wahab's future, since he was to become friends with Farouk's poet laureate—and Wahab's first major mentor—Ahmad Shawky. When the monarchy finally bit the dust in 1952, Wahab—who had previously played up to royalty and the monied classes and done well by it—proved that he could adapt to the times as he churned out a regiment of patriotic songs glorifying life in the new republic. Wahab's reputation had spread all over the Middle East by this time, due in part to Egypt's cultural primacy within the region, and since he was the most famous Arab composer of his day, it seemed only natural that Wahab write music for the national anthems of Egypt, Oman, and the United Arab Republic.

In many ways the region's budding nationalism sought to blend traditional ways with modern ones; the resulting cultural climate was a bubbling cauldron of contrasting ideas and Wahab was one of the major alchemists. Overlayed on his traditional training he wove Western elements into his music, especially the scores for movies that he starred in. He meshed flamencos, waltzes, and tangos with Arabic themes in much the same way his compatriot Farid al-Atrash did, even including the electric guitar in his later aural palette. Despite breaking new ground for future Arab composers, Wahab often retreated into traditionalism in his own '50s-era recordings, and by the mid-'60s had ceased singing, choosing to concentrate on writing for others. This album drought lasted until 1988, when Wahab was moved to enter the studio for one last recording.

what to buy: *Kollina Nehib Elquamar: 1920–1935* ⅃⅃⅃⅃ (Mélodie/CMM Productions, 1996, compilation prod. Philippe Zani) is a fine historic overview of Wahab's early career, when his singing and playing were solidly within the classical Arab tradition. "Ya Tara Ya Nesma (I Ask the Wind)" is a true gem, featuring Wahab's fluid tenor set against his accomplished solo oud playing. This set also includes a recording of Wahab at the precocious age of 13, "Waylahou ma hilati (God, what can I do?)." *Min Gheyr Leh* ⅃⅃⅃⅃ (EMI Arabia, 1989, prod. John G. Deacon) was the last recording session for Wahab, but his first studio date as a singer in over 20 years. Essentially a two-part suite with lyrics by Morsi Gameel Aziz, the title work "Min Gheyr Leh" upset quite a few religious conservatives who thought the song mocked man's place in the universe, a direct assault on the teachings of the Koran. Wahab was cleared in a religious court and the album went on to be one of his biggest hits.

what to buy next: While most of Wahab's recordings feature his performance within the context of an orchestra, *Besoto Ala El Aoud* ⅃⅃⅃⅃ (Soutelphan, c. 1960) reveals the master singing and playing his oud in a solo setting, with a small studio audience occasionally voicing their approval of Wahab's prowess. While not necessarily as important historically as the other two

recommended albums, this may be the perfect disc for novices to hunt up and listen to.

best of the rest:
Les Archives, Vols. 1-10 ⅃⅃⅃⅃ (Club des Disque Arabes, 1991–93)
Abdel Wahab Plays Abdel Wahab ⅃⅃⅃⅃ (EMI Music Arabia, 1997)

worth searching for: Simon Shaheen's tribute album *The Music of Mohamed Abdel Wahab* ⅃⅃⅃⅃ (Axiom, 1991, prod. Bill Laswell, Simon Shaheen) is a succinct condensation of Wahab's career, with Shaheen playing oud and violin in front of an Arabic orchestra and chorus.

influences:
◀◀ Said Darwish, Ahmad Shawky

▶▶ Simon Shaheen, Hossam Ramzy, Saad M. Hassan

see also: *Farid al-Atrash, Umm Kulthum, Simon Shaheen*

Garaud MacTaggart

Bunny Wailer
Reggae
Born Neville O'Riley Livingston, April 10, 1947, in Kingston, Jamaica. Based in Kingston, Jamaica.

The last surviving member of the Wailers, Bunny Wailer has continued the group's legacy with several solo albums of Rastafari-inspired reggae. In addition, he has explored such post-reggae styles as dub, dancehall, and rap-reggae. Wailer was raised as Bob Marley's step-brother from the age of nine, when his father, Thaddeus "Toddy" Livingston, became Marley's mother Cedella's live-in lover in 1957. After Wailer and Marley met Peter Tosh (Winston Hubert McIntosh) in Joe Higgs's Third Street Year, the three vocalists formed a trio, the Teenagers. Changing their name to the Wailing Wailers, the group recorded their first single, "Simmer Down," in 1963. The song became a number-one hit in Jamaica. Although Marley temporarily moved to Delaware in 1966 to raise money for his own record label, Wailer continued to perform in the group (which had shortened its name to the Wailers), with Rita Marley's cousin Constantine "Dream Vision" Walker taking Marley's place. While the original lineup was reorganized after Marley's return in 1967, Wailer was arrested for possession of marijuana and imprisoned for a year and a half. Following his release in September 1968, the original Wailers recorded two albums produced by Lee Perry—*Soul Rebels* in 1970 and *African Herbsman* in 1973—and two albums for the Island label—*Catch a Fire* and *Burning* (which included Wailer's composition "Pass It On")—also within just two months in 1973.

Wailer's aversion to flying kept him from accompanying the group on an early-'73 tour of the United States. Although he then agreed to tour England in November of that year, he and Tosh soon left the band and returned to Jamaica. Wailer had been considering a solo career as early as 1972, when he launched his own record label, Solomonic, and released a solo single, "Search for Love." After his departure from the group, however, Wailer maintained his association with Marley and Tosh. His 1976 debut album, *Blackheart Man*, features guest appearances by both vocalists. In 1984, three years after Marley's death, Wailer joined with Tosh, Junior Brathwaite, and Walker to record an album featuring vocals of Marley taken from a tape recorded between 1968 and 1971. The resulting album was released in 1993 as *The Never Ending Wailers*. Wailer later received Grammy awards for his own album-length tributes to Marley's songs, *Time Will Tell* in 1991 and *Hall of Fame: Tribute to Bob Marley's 50th Anniversary* in 1995. Wailer finally performed his first show in the U.S. in 1986. His subsequent tours have featured accompaniment by Sly Dunbar, Robbie Shakespeare, the Roots Radics, and members of the Skatalites. Wailer has also toured and recorded with Tosh's eldest son, Andrew. His future plans include the publication of an autobiography, *Old Fire Sticks*.

what to buy: With his first solo album, *Blackheart Man* 𝄞𝄞𝄞𝄞 (Mango, 1976, prod. Bunny Wailer), featuring guest vocals by Bob Marley and Peter Tosh and musical accompaniment from members of Bob Marley's Wailers including Aston "Family Man" Barrett (bass), Carlton "Carlie" Barrett (drums), and Tyrone Downie (keyboards), Wailer stepped out of Marley and Tosh's shadows and showcased his strengths as a lead vocalist and songwriter.

what to buy next: Wailer is at his best singing the songs of his late step-brother, deservedly winning Grammy Awards with his two Marley tributes, *Time Will Tell* 𝄞𝄞𝄞𝄞 (Shanachie, 1991, prod. Bunny Wailer) and *Hall of Fame: Tribute to Bob Marley's 50th Anniversary* 𝄞𝄞𝄞𝄞 (RAS, 1995, prod. Bunny Wailer).

the rest:
Struggle 𝄞𝄞𝄞 (Solomonic, 1980)
Bunny Wailer Sings the Wailers 𝄞𝄞𝄞𝄞 (Mango, 1981)
Rock 'n' Groove 𝄞𝄞𝄞 (Solomonic, 1983)
Live 𝄞𝄞𝄞𝄞 (Solomonic, 1985)
Marketplace 𝄞𝄞𝄞 (Shanachie, 1987)
Protest 𝄞𝄞𝄞 (Mango, 1987)
Roots Radics Rockers Reggae 𝄞𝄞𝄞 (Shanachie, 1987)
Rootsman Skanking 𝄞𝄞𝄞 (Shanachie, 1987)
Rule Dance Hall 𝄞𝄞𝄞 (Shanachie, 1989)
Liberation 𝄞𝄞𝄞 (Shanachie, 1990)
Gumption 𝄞𝄞𝄞 (Shanachie, 1992)
Dance Massive 𝄞𝄞𝄞 (Shanachie, 1993)
Just Be Nice 𝄞𝄞𝄞 (RAS, 1995)

influences:
◀◀ Joe Higgs, Clyde McPhatter, Curtis Mayfield
▶▶ Ziggy Marley, Andrew Tosh

see also: *Cedella Marley Booker, Joe Higgs, Bob Marley, Rita Marley, Lee "Scratch" Perry, the Roots Radics, the Skatalites, Sly & Robbie, Peter Tosh*

Craig Harris

Wailing Souls
Roots reggae, dancehall reggae
Formed 1968, in Trenchtown, Jamaica. Based in Kingston, Jamaica.

Winston "Pipe" Matthews, vocals; Lloyd "Bread" McDonald, vocals; George "Buddy" Haye, vocals (1968, 1974–85); Oswald Downer, vocals (1969–74); Norman Davis, vocals (1969–74); Joe Higgs, vocals (1974); Rudolph "Garth" Dennis, vocals (1976–85); Winston "Ziggy" Thomas, vocals (1985–present). (All members are from Jamaica.)

The Wailing Souls are one of Jamaica's greatest vocal harmony groups, anchored throughout their long and fruitful career by the impassioned voices and conscious songs of "Pipe" Matthews and "Bread" McDonald. After being tutored in their native Trenchtown by Bob Marley–mentor Joe Higgs on the art of imaginative harmonizing and songwriting, the group recorded a stunning series of singles for Studio One, later collected on two albums released in the '70s—their self-titled debut and *Soul & Power*. They also provided stirring background harmonies on the Wailers' "Trenchtown Rock" single. Joined by original Black Uhuru vocalist "Garth" Dennis in 1976, the Souls re-recorded tempestuous "rockers" versions of some of their previous triumphs including "Back Out with It" (a Jamaican #1 single), "Fire Coal Man," and the amazing and chilling "War" at Channel One, all backed by the thunderous rhythms of the Revolutionaries. They also seized artistic and financial independence by launching the Massive label and releasing such stone-cold classics as "Bredda Gravalicious," "Feel the Spirit," and "Very Well," all collected on the essential *Wild Suspense*. In the dancehall era, the Wailing Souls proved their majestic harmonies could flourish in any musical environment. They joined forces with producer "Junjo" Lawes and the unstoppable Roots Radics band on *Fire House Rock*, with the title cut and "Kingdom Rise Kingdom Fall," now universally regarded as prime examples of roots harmony songcraft. The follow-up was another quality collaboration with Lawes and the Radics, the unjustly overlooked *Inchpinchers*. On Sly & Robbie's Taxi label, the Souls released "Old Broom," a song that is still beloved in Jamaica nearly 20 years later and was reworked by Tony Rebel on his big 1992 hit "Sweet Jamdown." In the '90s, the band tried to cross over with a more generic "worldbeat" sound, with a modicum of success—namely "Shark Attack," which briefly hit the U.S. pop charts in 1992. Though often compared with the Wailers, the Wailing Souls maintain a musical legacy that stands alone as one of sustained originality, astonishingly spiritual vocal expression, and songwriting that oozes wisdom and common sense.

what to buy: The magnificent *Wild Suspense* 𝄞𝄞𝄞𝄞 (Mango, 1979, prod. Wailing Souls) is a Wailing Souls primer, loaded with classics like "Very Well," "Feel the Spirit," and "Bredda Gravalicious," and the CD version adds the Revolutionaries' thrilling, plunging, echo-embellished dubs. The band's revelatory self-titled debut LP *Wailing Souls* 𝄞𝄞𝄞𝄞 (Studio One, 1971, prod. Clement "Coxsone" Dodd) unabashedly explores their rural, "country-reggae" roots. It includes the first glorious versions of "Back Out," "Row Fisherman Row," "Walk, Walk, Walk," and "Mr. Fire Coal Man," and showcases the group's words of wisdom voiced in soul-based harmonies with a gospel-like fervor. *Fire House Rock* 𝄞𝄞𝄞𝄞 (Greensleeves U.K., 1981, prod. Henry "Junjo" Lawes) is also chock full of treasures, including the aforementioned "Kingdom Rise Kingdom Fall" and the beautiful, criminally neglected gems "A Fool Will Fall" and "See Baba Joe."

what to buy next: *Psychedelic Souls* 𝄞𝄞𝄞 (Pow Wow, 1998, prod. Wailing Souls) is easily the wildest album in the group's catalog, consisting entirely of their interpretations of rock and psychedelic anthems from 1962 to 1972. The Who's "My Generation," Jimi Hendrix's "May This Be Love (Waterfalls)" and the Beatles' "Tomorrow Never Knows" are a few of the top-notch relics soulfully refashioned into reggae sure-shots.

the rest:
Face the Devil 𝄞𝄞𝄞 (Hitbound, 1979)
Inch Pinchers 𝄞𝄞𝄞𝄞 (Greensleeves U.K., 1983)
On the Rocks 𝄞𝄞𝄞 (Shanachie, 1983)
Stranded 𝄞𝄞𝄞 (Greensleeves U.K., 1984)
Best Of 𝄞𝄞𝄞𝄞 (Hit Bound, 1984)
Lay It on the Line 𝄞𝄞𝄞 (Live & Learn, 1986)
Kingston 14 𝄞𝄞 (Live & Learn, 1987)
Very Best Of 𝄞𝄞𝄞𝄞 (Shanachie, 1987)
Stormy Night 𝄞𝄞𝄞 (Rohit, 1989)
All Over the World 𝄞𝄞𝄞𝄞 (CBS/Sony, 1992)
Tension 𝄞𝄞 (Pow Wow, 1997)

influences:
◀◀ Joe Higgs, the Abyssinians, the Wailers, Alton Ellis, the Techniques, Ken Boothe, the Heptones

▶▶ Garnett Silk, Tony Rebel, Wayne Wonder

see also: *Black Uhuru, Joe Higgs, Barrington Levy, Freddie Mc-Gregor, the Roots Radics*

Todd Shanker

Walela
Pop, gospel, Native American
Formed 1994, in Hollywood, CA, USA. Based in Los Angeles, CA, USA.

Rita Coolidge, vocals; Priscilla Coolidge, vocals; Laura Satterfield, vocals. (All members are from USA.)

Walela—the Cherokee word for "hummingbird"—is an appropriate name for the close-harmony trio of Rita Coolidge, her sister Priscilla Coolidge, and Priscilla's daughter Laura Satterfield. Their harmonies, like those of many family singing groups, blend into a single mystical voice, greater than the sum of its parts, and their music, a seamless fusion of Native, pop, and gospel influences, produces a profoundly spiritual and deeply moving effect. Rita, Priscilla, and Laura have been singing together for years, but it's only recently that they became a professional unit. "It was natural," Satterfield says. "When you're with family, you don't edit yourself, you just let it fly. We first got together on one of Rita's albums, doing a song called 'Cherokee.' Robbie Robertson heard it, and asked us to sing on his *Music for the Native Americans* album. That was the real beginning of the group." Walela recorded their eponymous debut with producer Jim Wilson, a Native musician known for his groundbreaking work with his own band, Little Wolf. "Jim's a wonderful arranger," Rita Coolidge says. "He's easy-going, knowledgeable about Native music, and strong enough to stand back and let us put our stamp onto the music."

what's available: On *Walela* 𝄞𝄞𝄞 (Triloka, 1997, prod. Jim Wilson), Wilson's understated production perfectly complements the strong vocals of the group's three principals. Players include keyboardist Mike Utley from Jimmy Buffet's band, Geoffrey Gordon—Jai Uttal's percussionist—and Native flautist Andy Vasquez, but the instrumental layer stays in the background, a faint echo that supports the women's voices without overwhelming them.

influences:
◀◀ Rita Coolidge, Booker T. Jones, Delaney & Bonnie, Bonnie Raitt

see also: *Robbie Robertson, Jim Wilson (sidebar)*

j. poet

The Waterboys
Celtic rock
Formed 1981, in London, England. Disbanded 1993.

Mike Scott, vocals, guitar, piano, Hammond organ; Steve Wickham, fiddle, Hammond organ, vocals; Anthony Thistlethwaite, saxophone, mandolin, organ, harmonica; Colin Blakey, whistle, flute, Hammond organ, piano; Noel Bridgeman, drums, percussion; Jay Dee Daugherty, drums; Sharon Shannon, accordion, fiddle; Trevor Hutchinson,

bass, bouzouki; **Karl Wallinger**, bass, keyboards; **Roddy Lorimer**, trumpet.

The history of the Waterboys is the story of Mike Scott's ever-evolving musical and spiritual quest. "I've always followed my heart or where my latest musical fascination is, which is rarely where popular trends have been going," says Scott. True to these wanderings, the band was known for a continually changing cast of characters supporting Scott, with one anchor being the musical versatility of Anthony Thistlethwaite. The Waterboys originated the "Big Music," an epic, sprawling, feverish sound of layered acoustic guitars, ecstatic horns, and charging, obscure, expansive poetics reminiscent of the myth-making of William Butler Yeats and William Blake. At its best, the music was transcendent, leading the listener into a new, exotic land brimming with imagery and feeling, and owed a debt to the earlier work of fellow shamans Patti Smith, Van Morrison, and Bruce Springsteen, as well as the Beatles. Scott then changed tactics for the band's fourth album, the astounding *Fisherman's Blues,* bringing his Celtic passions to the forefront and toning down the Big Music. That particular "raggle taggle" version of the band broke up after two albums; the Waterboys became Scott and a slew of session players, and the music returned to harder guitar riffs, with disappointing results. A recent solo outing by Scott is much closer to the spiritual essence he sought with *Fisherman's Blues,* and on the tour supporting that album Scott promised that next time around, he'd return with a band. So perhaps a new generation of the Waterboys is just around the corner.

what to buy: Different eras of the Waterboys produced distinctly different music. Early Waterboys is best sampled on *A Pagan Place* ✶✶✶✶ (Chrysalis, 1984, prod. Mike Scott), featuring the strumming acoustic majesty of the title cut. *This Is the Sea* ✶✶✶✶✶ (Chrysalis, 1985, prod. Mike Scott, Mick Glossop) is a fully realized epic that showcased the Scott-Wallinger partnership and included the shimmering "This Is the Sea," "The Whole of the Moon," "Spirit," and "Old England." Late Waterboys is captured in all its glory on *Fisherman's Blues* ✶✶✶✶✶ (Chrysalis, 1988, prod. John Dunford, Mike Scott) with its embrace of the Celtic tradition. Commencing with the luminous title cut (recently resurrected for the film *Waking Ned Devine*), the album includes a stirring cover of Van Morrison's "Sweet Thing" and the last recorded song written by Scott and Wallinger (with Hutchinson), "World Party." A masterpiece from start to finish.

what to buy next: *Best of the Waterboys* ✶✶✶✶ (Chrysalis, 1991, prod. Mike Scott) is a good retrospective of the band, with the addition of "Killing My Heart," an early electric version of "When Ye Go Away," and a live "Old England." *The Secret Life of the Waterboys* ✶✶✶✶ (Chrysalis, 1994, prod. Mike Scott) is a

collection of unreleased studio recordings, radio sessions, live tracks, and "lost" B-sides recorded between 1981 and 1985.

what to avoid: *Dream Harder* ✶✶ (Geffen, 1993, prod. Mike Scott, Bill Price) is a lackluster attempt to do the Waterboys without the Waterboys, and is hopefully Scott's last attempt to become a guitar god.

the rest:
The Waterboys ✶✶✶✷ (Ensign, 1983)
Room to Roam ✶✶✶ (Ensign, 1990)
Pagan Place ✶✶✶✷ (Alliance, 1997)
Best of '81–'90 ✶✶✶✶ (Alliance, 1997)
The Live Adventures of the Waterboys ✶✶✶✶ (Pilot, 1999)

worth searching for: A variety of CD singles and 12-inch releases dates most prominently from the *Fisherman's Blues* era onward. They include: *And a Bang on the Ear/Raggle Taggle Gipsy* (1989); *The Whole of the Moon/Golden Age Medley* (1991); *Fisherman's Blues/Medicine Bow* (1991); and *Bring 'Em All In* (with three previously unreleased songs), all on Chrysalis; and *The Return of Pan/Karma/Mister Powers* (Geffen, 1993).

solo outings:
Mike Scott:
Bring 'Em All In ✶✶✶✶ (Chrysalis, 1995)
Still Burning ✶✶✶ (Minty Fresh, 1998)

Anthony Thistlethwaite:
Aesop Wrote a Fable ✶✶✶ (Rolling Acres, 1993)

influences:
◄◄ Bob Dylan, Patti Smith, the Beatles, Bruce Springsteen, Van Morrison, the Chieftains

►► U2, Sinéad O'Connor, World Party

see also: *Sharon Shannon*

Martin Connors

Waterson:Carthy
See: Eliza Carthy, Martin Carthy

The Watersons
See: Eliza Carthy, Martin Carthy

Papa Wemba
Soukous, African pop
Born Shungu Jules Wembadia, 1953, in Kasai province, Zaire (now Congo). Based in Paris.

Papa Wemba is one of the most towering and controversial figures to emerge from the musical colossus of Congo. Not content with his status as a mere superstar of *soukous* (African rumba), Wemba went on to break the sacred rules of that, the

Papa Wemba

most influential dance-music style Africa has produced, and forge new ground on his own terms. His father was a village chief and his mother was a "pleureuse," a woman who sang and wept at funerals. The makings of a royal crooner with a bold streak and a soft touch were all there in those remote, rural beginnings.

Wemba moved to the capital of Congo, Kinshasa, just as the rumba-rock revolution was swinging into high gear. He gained instant celebrity in the front line of the hottest band in the city, Zaiko Langa Langa, formed in 1969. Wemba lavished Zaiko's guitar-intensive soukous sound with spinning-saw-blade tenor vocals and loose-limbed dancing. A stylish dresser from the start, he also helped to pioneer the phenomenon of the "sapeur"—part eccentricity, part expression of modern African freedom; in this case the freedom to wear Italian designer clothing. As is the pattern for star singers in Congolese bands, he broke off to form his own group, Viva la Musica, in 1974.

Rootsy rhythms from the Kasai region found their way into Wemba's pumped-up Congolese rumba, all right in step with President Mobutu's call for "authenticity" in the country's society and arts. But by the mid-1980s, when African pop was winning worldwide acceptance, Wemba was itching to veer from the strict regimen of his style. His eponymous 1988 release used non-Zairean musicians, song forms, and stylistic touches, and established him as a world-class African singer. At the same time, Wemba was chosen to be the pop act in a touring extravaganza of African traditional music, Africa Oyé. Many saw this as a strange choice, given Wemba's desire to break with even his country's more modern traditions. On the other hand, Wemba has always stayed faithful to those funky Kasai rhythms, no matter how fused and electronic his sound has become.

In the ensuing decade-plus Wemba has maintained a difficult balancing act, performing and recording both with Viva la Musica and his international band. His star may have fallen with Congolese traditionalists, but it has definitely risen worldwide. Ten years after Africa Oyé, Wemba returned to America as part of Africa Fête, a who's-who wherein none could question his presence. With one of the sweetest and most evocative voices of any African singer, and no shortage of innovative ideas, Wemba remains the only artist to successfully move beyond the soukous sphere into the larger arena of international pop.

what to buy: Viva la Musica's *Pole Position* ♪♪♪♪ (Sonodisc, 1995, prod. Papa Wemba) shows the sophistication and class Wemba brought to straight-ahead soukous. *Papa Wemba* ♪♪♪♪ (EMI, 1988, prod. Papa Wemba), the moment when Wemba moved away from soukous, stands up very well. *Emotion* ♪♪♪♪ (RealWorld, 1995, prod. Stephen Hague) is his most polished international release.

best of the rest:
Le Voyageur ♪♪♪♪ (EarthBeat!, 1992)
Molokai ♪♪♪♪ (RealWorld, 1998)

worth searching for: Three old Viva la Musica records, *Love Kilawu* ♪♪♪♪♪ (Sonodisc, 1987), *Nouvelle Generation à Paris* ♪♪♪♪ (Sonodisc, 1988), and *La Naissance de L'Orchestre Viva la Musica, 1977, 1978* ♪♪♪♪ (Répartition Ngoyarto, prod. Bella Bella), are especially good finds. *Foridoles* ♪♪♪♪♪ (Sonodisc, 1994) is a fine recent release from the band.

influences:
◀◀ Tabu Ley Rochereau, Franco

▶▶ Reddy Amisi, Lokua Kanza, Dominic Kanza

see also: *Cheikh Lô, Zaiko Langa Langa*

Banning Eyre

Floyd Red Crow Westerman
Native American folk
Born 1936 or 1940 (sources vary), in SD, USA. Based in Palm Springs, CA, USA.

Floyd Red Crow Westerman has made a major contribution to the increasing pride and self-awareness of Native Americans. A country folksinger in the early 1970s, Westerman has focused most of his recent attention on acting. In addition to playing the role of Ten Bears in the 1990 Oscar-winner *Dances with Wolves,* Westerman appeared in such films as *Renegade* in 1989 and *Clearcut* in 1992, and narrated the TV documentaries *Legends of the West* in 1993 and *Lakota Woman—Siege at Wounded Knee* in 1994. He also appeared as Jim Morrison's spiritual guide in the biopic *The Doors,* and has guested on such shows as *MacGyver, Hardball, The X-Files, Roseanne, Dharma and Greg, L.A. Law,* and *Northern Exposure.* A committed political activist, Westerman has spoken numerous times on Native American and environmental concerns. In 1992, he was a featured speaker at the World Uranium Hearing in Salzburg.

Born on the Sisseton-Wahpeton Sioux Reservation in northeast South Dakota, Westerman, whose Indian name is Kanghi Duta, attended an Indian boarding school 80 miles away. After returning to the reservation for high school, he left again to study speech, theater, and art at Northern State University in Aberdeen, South Dakota, and graduated with a degree in secondary art education. Westerman traveled to New York in the late 1960s, and signed a record contract in '69. His debut album, *Custer Died for Your Sins,* was released shortly after the publication of the book of same name by Vine Deloria Jr. His second album, *The Land Is Your Mother,* was released in 1982. Westerman has performed often in Europe, making more than

50 trips overseas. One of his first worldwide tours was a benefit for the Rain Forest Foundation Project, and also featured Sting and Raoni, the chief of the Kayapo Indian Nation from the Zingu River region of the Amazon.

what's available: Although neither of Westerman's albums is currently available in the United States, they were recently combined and reissued on CD in Germany as *Custer Died for Your Sins/The Land Is Your Mother* (Tritont, 1997).

influences:

◀◀ Traditional Native American music, Buffy Sainte-Marie, Patrick Sky

▶▶ Bill Miller, R. Carlos Nakai, John Trudell

Craig Harris

Randy Weston

Jazz, world-jazz

Born April 6, 1926, in Brooklyn, NY, USA. Based in USA.

Randy Weston has been a pioneer in emphasizing the African roots of jazz, something he was doing even before he lived in Africa for six years. In addition, he is a superb pianist and composer whose jazz waltz "Hi-Fly" has become a standard. Weston is greatly respected by his fellow musicians and by hard-core jazz fans, but has not received the mainstream acclaim a creator of his accomplishments would seem to merit, which has resulted in too much of his catalog lapsing from availability.

Weston grew up in Brooklyn, where his father operated a West Indian restaurant frequented by jazz musicians. Weston has often commented on the sense of community he felt growing up in that environment, and many of his sidemen, such as Cecil Payne, were childhood friends. It was Weston's father who first taught him about African history and who encouraged his piano studies. He started his professional career later than many, at age 23, and then not in a jazz context but rather as accompanist to blues singer Bull Moose Jackson. Subsequent jobs were with Eddie "Cleanhead" Vinson, trumpeter Kenny Dorham, and drummer Art Blakey, and Weston became friends with Thelonious Monk, studying informally with him. In 1954 Weston became the first modern musician to record for the fledgling Riverside label, and it was his albums for that company that first gained him a nationwide reputation. "Hi-Fly," "Little Niles," and a number of other jazz waltzes became popular vehicles for other musicians, establishing him as an important writer.

In 1960 Weston recorded an influential album for Roulette, the five-movement suite *Uhuru Afrika*. It used large-group arrangements by trombonist Melba Liston, who had previously arranged for Weston's quintet, and with whom he has worked off and on ever since. *Uhuru Afrika* showcased an all-star ensemble that prominently featured the percussion of Babatunde Olatunji, Candido, and Armando Peraza, plus drummers Max Roach, Charli Persip, and G.T. Hogan, along with 13 star horn players. It was the strongest expression yet of Weston's interest in Africa. By this time he was regularly featuring drummer Big Black in his groups, emphasizing the African element even outside of such special projects. The following year Weston visited Nigeria, returning in 1963. A similar album was recorded that year, *Highlife,* which has been combined with *Uhuru Afrika* on a limited-edition CD. Weston and his sextet also spent a year touring New York City elementary schools with a History of Jazz program, giving 40 concerts that traced the history of the genre from Africa through the Caribbean, the black church, New Orleans jazz, and so on. The program was sponsored by Pepsi Cola and the players worked for union scale.

Weston toured North Africa in the beginning of 1967, sponsored by the U.S. State Department, and decided to settle there. He spent most of his time until 1973 on the continent, opening his African Rhythms Club in Tangier, Morocco. In that period he released no records, a drought broken by the atypical 1972 album *Blue Moses,* which found Weston pressured into playing electric piano—which he continued to do for a few tracks on his followup record, the much better *Tanjah,* where he once again worked with Melba Liston. He continued to release records during subsequent sojourns in France and Africa, and eventually returned to the United States in the early 1990s, beginning a fruitful association with the Verve label that has yielded Weston's most mature statements. He still works in Morocco on occasion, and recorded an album with some of the Gnawa musicians whose style has had the strongest influence on his own, as heard in the magnificent "Blue Moses" and "The Healers." Weston's small ensemble African Rhythms, which works as a sextet or septet, was his touring group for much of the 1990s.

what to buy: Recommendations will concentrate on albums that include world-music elements. The bold, questing two-CD set *The Spirits of Our Ancestors* 𝄢𝄢𝄢𝄢 (Antilles, 1992, prod. Randy Weston, Brian Bacchus, Jean-Philippe Allard) explores jazz's Africanicity, with Weston's angular piano style set jewel-like amidst Melba Liston's arrangements for an almost-big band. Guests Pharoah Sanders, on tenor sax and *gaita* (a high-pitched African horn), and trumpet legend Dizzy Gillespie show how expansive the parameters of Weston's vision are, but everything's grounded in loping rhythms that swing no matter how far-out the playing gets. The CD set contains a number of classic Weston tunes, from "Blue Moses," "The Healers," and "African Cookbook" to "African Village Bedford-Stuyvesant" (heard in two versions), "African Sunrise," and "A Prayer for Us All"—10 tracks total, and though there's a one-CD selection available, the entire original album is a must-own. On his most recent

Randy Weston

work, *Khepera* 🎵🎵🎵🎵 (Verve, 1998), Weston looks at the common links between jazz and music from Africa and China. His compositions are simple but richly layered, elegant but earthy, ritualistic but spontaneous, hypnotic but rhythmically exciting. Guest artists include trombonist Benny Powell, saxophonist Pharoah Sanders, and *pipa* (Chinese lute) player Min Xiao Fen.

best of the rest:

Uhura Africa/Highlife 🎵🎵🎵 (Roulette, 1961/1964, Capitol, 1990)
Blues to Africa 🎵🎵🎵 (Freedom, 1975)
Splendid Master Gnawa Musicians of Morocco & Randy Weston 🎵🎵🎵 (Antilles, 1994)
Marrakech in the Cool of the Evening 🎵🎵🎵🎵 (Verve, 1994)

influences:

◀◀ Thelonious Monk, Art Tatum, Duke Ellington

▶▶ Rodney Kendrick

see also: *Yacub Addy, Babatunde Olatunji*

Steve Holtje

Bill Whelan

Irish traditional and neo-traditional

Born May 22, 1950, in Limerick, Ireland. Based in Dublin and Galway, Ireland.

Composer Bill Whelan has put traditional Irish music on the worldwide map even more than the Chieftains, Clannad, and Enya have in long years of recording, and he's done it with just one album: the Grammy-winning soundtrack to the phenomenal *Riverdance* stage show. The keyboardist and percussionist did not spring out of nowhere; his long apprenticeship included two years with Planxty in their later period, a brief stint in a prototype Moving Hearts, extensive experience with musicals (from Gilbert & Sullivan to Andrew Lloyd Webber & Tim Rice), five years as the Yeats Festival's composer-in-residence at Dublin's famed Abbey Theatre, and arranging and production work for Paul Brady, Andy Irvine, the Dubliners, U2, Van Morrison, Kate Bush, Elvis Costello, and many more.

The seeds of *Riverdance* can certainly be traced back to the early '90s, when the cascading cross-rhythms of Whelan's percussive keyboards joined forces with bouzouki player Andy

Irvine, piper Davy Spillane, accordionist Mairtin O'Connor, saxophonist Ken Edge, percussionist Noel Eccles, Bulgarian multi-instrumentalist Nikola Parov, and Hungarian singer Márta Sebestyén for *East Wind*. Though the release was credited to Irvine and Spillane only, all arrangements and production were by Whelan. The album incorporated Irvine's trademark Balkan-influenced playing with the passion and excitement of Moving Hearts (with whom both Spillane and Eccles had served many years) and the exotic sounds of Sebestyén and Parov. Spillane, O'Connor, Edge, and Parov resurfaced together alongside Whelan on the *Riverdance* score.

Whelan's main efforts in the years immediately prior to *Riverdance* were dedicated to two large-scale works: *The Seville Suite,* scored for full orchestra and soloists Spillane, O'Connor, and members of Milladoiro from the Celtic area of Galicia in Spain; and *The Spirit of Mayo,* featuring an 85-piece orchestra, Spillane, violinist Máire Breatnach, a female soprano, and over 200 singers, including the choral group Anúna. (Only part of the latter has been recorded and released so far.) One thing was clear from all of these projects: Whelan possesed big ambitions, a broad vision, a great affinity for both Irish and orchestral writing, and a deep understanding of music as a force to move people.

Riverdance took Ireland—and then the U.K. and U.S.—by storm following its explosive stage debut in Dublin in early 1995. A dance extravaganza spearheaded by two charismatic Irish-American champion dancers, Michael Flatley and Jean Butler, the show overhauled an old (and oft-ridiculed) cultural artifact with such style and panache that all but the most jaded were immediately captivated by it. Suddenly Irish dancing was all the rage among young and old alike, thanks to the show's sensuous take on this traditionally staid form. Central to the project's unparalleled and ongoing worldwide success is the all-original score by Bill Whelan. A dynamic new blend of Irish styles forms the basis for much of the instrumental music, mixed with haunting vocal pieces, and distinctive and convincing nods to Spanish and Balkan traditions. Soundtracks for two films prove that while the world waits to see what Whelan will follow *Riverdance* with, he has not been idle. Neither has Michael Flatley: his spin-off show *Lord of the Dance* may have been a box-office hit, but the mediocre and derivative score he commissioned from Irish jingle-writer Ronan Hardiman is destined to be soon forgotten.

what to buy: *Riverdance* ♫♫♫♫♫ (Celtic Heartbeat, 1995, prod. Bill Whelan) is a stunning snapshot of a musical culture in transition: every tune on it is original, yet within a short time half a dozen of the pieces had entered the consciousness of Irish people at home and abroad as quintessential expressions of a proud, vibrant, multi-dimensional, and thoroughly modern

Irishness. With this album, more than any that preceded it, Irish music truly took the world stage, while the accompanying show helped feed a growing international hunger for all things Celtic. *Riverdance* rose from modest enough beginnings: its title track debuted as the interval song-and-dance number during the 1994 Eurovision Song Contest, broadcast live to a vast TV audience around the continent. The extraordinary reception that telecast met with eventually prompted thoughts of a full stage show the following year; that too was a hit on a scale undreamed of. Variety is an essential ingredient here, in the writing, playing, and presentation. From the nouveau-Irish "Countess Cathleen" and "Slip into Spring," which are distinguished by Máire Breathnach's flawless fiddle and Mairtin O'Connor's exquisite accordion, respectively, to the refreshing choral contributions from Anúna; the surprisingly convincing Spanish and Balkan pieces; Davy Spillane's heart-stopping slow piping on "Caoineadh Cu Chulainn (Cu Chulainn's Lament)"; Áine Uí Cheallaigh's sublime singing on the touching "Lift the Wings"; and "The Harvest," a high-energy tour-de-force written for Irish-American fiddling sensation Eileen Ivers when she joined the production in mid-1995—this is an album without peer.

what to buy next: *The Roots of Riverdance* ♫♫♫ (Celtic Heartbeat, 1997, prod. Bill Whelan) is in essence a Bill Whelan sampler, including tracks from all of his 1990s projects, from *East Wind* to *Riverdance* itself and a 1996 film score. Two items released here for the first time are excerpted from the otherwise-unrecorded *Spirit of Mayo* suite: a setting of a well-known poem in the Irish language by the blind 18th-century Mayo folk poet Raftery, sung by the incomparable Áine Uí Cheallaigh; and another fine slow air for pipes, played by Declan Masterson. The orchestral *Seville Suite* ♫♫♫♫ (Tara, 1992/Celtic Heartbeat, 1997, prod. Bill Whelan), subtitled "Kinsale to La Coruqa," was commissioned by the Irish government as part of Ireland's National Day at *Expo '92* in Spain. (Who says good art can't be state-sponsored?) It tells the story of the flight to Spain of the defeated forces of Red Hugh O'Donnell after the disastrous Battle of Kinsale in 1601. Spillane's piping is gorgeous, especially on the slow "O'Donnell's Lament," and O'Connor's graceful and stylish accordion is the perfect counterfoil for the orchestra on "Father Conroy's Jig," which also features wonderfully mournful low whistle from Spillane. The string writing is impressionistic, assured, and powerful. Galician harp, whistles, and pipes (played by members of Milladoiro) join in for a joyous conclusion. Inevitably, an Irish work about a sea journey, featuring orchestra and pipes, invites comparison to Shaun Davey's landmark *The Brendan Voyage* (1980), but amazingly Whelan largely manages to steer a clear course for himself in the treacherous waters of musical influence. Included as a bonus is a new version of "Timedance," a non-LP track from Planxty during Whelan's tenure with them in 1981 (this recording sees the original band—minus Christy Moore—reunited). While lacking in cohesion, *East Wind* ✹✹✹✹ (Tara, 1992, prod. Bill Whelan) offers some great moments, and as a precursor to *Riverdance* it has earned its place in history. In one sense it's an Eastern European variation on what Moving Hearts achieved, including pieces in time signatures such as 5/16, 7/16, 11/16, and 15/16 (which are not normally attempted by Irish musicians!), all driven along with consummate skill by Whelan on keyboards, Irvine on bouzouki, and Parov on *gadulka, kaval,* and *gaida.* Two vocal pieces are included, both sung by Sebestyén (Irvine's distinctive voice is silent); despite their Macedonian and Bulgarian origins, Sebestyén's delicate ornamentations make the pieces sound almost Irish.

the rest:
Some Mother's Son ✹✹✹♥ (Celtic Heartbeat, 1996)
Dancing at Lughnasa ✹✹✹♥ (Sony Classical, 1998)

worth searching for: The first Irish release of *Riverdance* (Celtic Heartbeat/K-Tel, 1995, prod. Bill Whelan)—distinguished by an orange sleeve rather than the more familiar blue version—contains fewer tracks but is notable for the inclusion of two songs (unavailable elsewhere) that Whelan wrote for the Atlanta gospel group the Deliverance Ensemble, led by Rev. James Bignon, which formed an integral part of the initial stage production. One of these songs, "Freedom," is still featured in the show.

influences:
◄◄ Seán Ó Riada, Planxty, Andy Irvine, Moving Hearts, Dónal Lunny, Davy Spillane, Shaun Davey, Jimmy Webb, Fairport Convention

►► Anúna, Eileen Ivers, Ronan Hardiman, Leahy, Phil Coulter, Shaun Davey, William Jackson

see also: *Anúna, Máire Breathnach, Shaun Davey, Andy Irvine, Eileen Ivers, Milladoiro, Moving Hearts, Patrick Street, Planxty, Márta Sebestyén, Áine Uí Cheallaigh*

John C. Falstaff

Fredrick Whiteface
Jazz, Native American
Born 1922, in Martin, SD, USA. Based in Rapid City, SD, USA.

Like many Native people, Whiteface grew up bi-cultural, and after learning guitar as a young man played in "white" dance bands (Native bands that covered pop tunes), jazz combos, and swing bands. But his first love was always the traditional Lakota songs of his youth. For most of his life Whiteface worked non-musical day jobs and played jazz at night, while working on a system to create formal scales for Lakota music. He finally wrote some charts, based on the changes of Lakota songs, that his jazz combo could play, and went into the studio

with both the combo and some traditional singers and drummers to create *Mato Hota.* "My approach is tri-cultural," Whiteface says. "I use the melodic structure of European music, the improvisational spirit of the African American jazz tradition, and the freedom of Lakota melodies that have been handed down for centuries. By using all three cultures, hopefully I've made something that all cultures can listen to and enjoy."

what's available: On *Mata Hota* ✹✹✹✹ (Natural Visions, 1996, prod. Tom Bee), Whiteface's melodic and mellow sax explorations are anchored in the Kansas City style he grew up listening to, while the traps of Chuck Childs mesh perfectly with the Lakota rhythms of the singers and drummers, making the tunes instantly accessible to non-Native ears.

influences:
◄◄ Count Basie, Duke Ellington, Harry James, 1930s swing bands

j. poet

David Wilkie
"Cowboy Celtic"
Born 1948, in San Francisco, CA, USA. Based in Turner Valley, Alberta, Canada.

It looks like a shotgun wedding at first sight: cowboy and Celtic musics reluctantly joining hands by the camp fire. But don't judge too soon. David "Mandoline Kid" Wilkie's Scottish grandmother had exposed him to Scots dancing and piping early in life at family gatherings in California, but it was cowboy culture that really grabbed him by the scruff of the neck. Following a move to Canada in the fall of 1966, Wilkie issued his first western album there in 1977, and was soon hosting a country/cowboy radio show in Calgary and playing for Ian Tyson and Diamond Joe White. He visited the U.K. in 1981 as part of the Calgary Stampede Wild West Show, and in 1985 founded the Great Western Orchestra back in Alberta. This provided, er, stable work over the next eight years, and several albums resulted.

Following a tour of Ireland in 1993, Wilkie realized that many of the rugged adventurers who took possession of western Canada and America starting in the mid-19th century were displaced Celts, and in 1994 he decided the time was right to assemble a collection of Celtic-based cowboy tunes. He rounded up members of Edmonton's esteemed McDade musical family (Terry McDade on Irish harp, Jeremiah McDade on tin whistle and pipes, Solon McDade on bass, and Shannon Johnson on fiddle), and soon unleashed the *Cowboy Celtic* album upon an unsuspecting world. Thus a genre was born, re-hitching the Old West and the Auld Sod and played with grace and charm. Wilkie's vision is a sort of counterpoint to bluegrass, that more eastern assimilation of Irish and Scots music into Americana.

For many of the tracks on the follow-up, *Cowboy Ceilidh* (the latter term a Gaelic word for communal dances), Wilkie recorded in Ireland and Scotland. He enlisted fiddler Matt Cranitch, flute and whistle player Johnny McCarthy, and harper Laoise Kelly for the Irish sessions, and accordionist Phil Cunningham and singer Arthur Cormack for the Scottish sessions. With Denise Withnell deputizing for Wilkie on vocals at times, a wider range of material was also possible.

Where can Wilkie take it from here? That remains to be seen. Has he really launched a trend? Perhaps, but hardly a stampede—and compared to his imitators thus far, Wilkie still rides tall in the saddle. Whatever lies around the bend, his gift to world music has been to eloquently remind us of a forgotten role Celtic music played for the hardy settlers out there on the western prairies all those years ago.

what's available: *Cowboy Celtic* ♫♫♫ (Red House, 1996, prod. David Wilkie), like its successor, takes the listener on a delightful romp through the plains of Alberta and Montana, with some tunes that are familiar ("Shenandoah," "The Colorado Trail," "The Gal I Left behind Me"), and others that sound it but aren't ("Custer Died a Runnin'" and "Tempting the Salmon to Come to the Fly," each doing the 19th century proud by way of their 20th-century author, Wilkie). The playing and production are both seamless. *Cowboy Ceilidh* ♫♫♫ (Red House, 1997, prod. David Wilkie) sounds just as cohesive, despite having being recorded in installments in four different countries. Great notes on the choices are provided, and the instrumentals include "The Water Is Wide" and the staple "Bridget Cruise" (by the seminal 18th-century Irish harper Turlough O'Carolan), but it's the songs that really shine here. Michael Martin Murphy contributes a wonderful vocal recorded in New Mexico on "The Cowboy's Song," whose Irish origin ("The Bard of Armagh") is better known to Americans in its "Streets of Laredo" incarnation. Two more of Wilkie's historical re-creations, "Wind in the Wire" (also covered by Randy Travis) and "The Ballad of Nate Champion," again show what a careful student of his sources—and what a fine songwriter by any measure—Wilkie is. Two of the tracks here drive home this music's surprising resonance for folks on both ends of the diaspora. While Withnell was preparing to sing Badger Clark's "Border Affair" in the studio, the Irish musicians recognized the tune as "Níl Sé Ina Lá"—and of course the band ended up recording both. The album finishes with Arthur Cormack singing the moving "Farewell to Coigach" from 1911, which is probably the only Scots Gaelic song written in Montana in this century. Thanks to Wilkie, it's back in circulation in Scotland.

influences:

◄◄ Jethro Burns, Tiny Moore, Dash Crofts, Levon Helm, Bill Monroe, Turlough O'Carolan, Phil Cunningham, Four Star Trio (Johnny McCarthy, Pat Ahern, Con Ó Drisceoil)

see also: *Silly Wizard*

John C. Falstaff

Nathan Williams /Nathan & the Zydeco Cha Chas
Zydeco

Born March 24, 1963, in Lafayette, LA, USA. Based in Lafayette, LA, USA.

With Buckwheat Zydeco out on the road playing to an international audience, Nathan Williams has hung back to champion the blues- and R&B-inflected zydeco sounds of both artists' native Lafayette. Williams plays the full-size piano accordion with a vigor and skill equal to all but the great Clifton Chenier. His bands are tight and tend to have stinging guitar solos as well as sweaty zydeco grooves. Although Williams's covers can range far, like Stevie Wonder's "Isn't She Lovely," his music doesn't sway off into the rock-dominated sound that appears too readily in the work of other young zydeco performers. While the diatonic-accordion, minor-riff fashion seems to dominate at the moment, Nathan remains true to the Creole blues of Chenier and the traditional Creole French culture.

what to buy: *Creole Crossroads* ♫♫♫♫ (Rounder, 1995, prod. Scott Billington) works as an unintentional tribute to the great Clifton Chenier by two artists whom he greatly influenced: Nathan Williams and Michael Doucet. Chenier recorded "Black Girl" with his uncle Morris on fiddle, and Williams and Doucet provide an update. Two of the album's duet pieces echo another great Creole/Cajun pairing (that of Creole Amédée Ardoin and Cajun Dennis McGee). Elsewhere, it is a joy to hear Doucet solo over the Cha Chas' crackerjack rhythm section instead of the sometimes-porous Beausoleil. Doucet is at his bluesiest here, emulating Canray Fontenot and Bradford Gordon, the black fiddlers with whom he studied. While not the perfect example of Williams's sound, this CD is his most entertaining work.

what to buy next: It's almost impossible to capture the excitement of a live zydeco band on record, but *I'm a Zydeco Hog* ♫♫♫ (Rounder, 1997, prod. Scott Billington) comes close. You'll just have to imagine the heat of a full house and the way the band plays off the dancers and the dancers in turn inspire the musicians. Williams and the band deliver one crushing dance groove after another, from the start of "Tante Rose" to the closing notes of "Zydeco Road," only pausing for the "Grand Prix" waltz. The guitar and bass drop out for "Hey Bebe Bebe" when Nathan trades licks with "Cat Roy" Broussard's saxophone, sounding a bit like a *merengue* band lost in the Achafalya swamp. Mostly you get a really tight zydeco outfit in

Nathan Williams of Nathan & the Zydeco Cha Chas

a current version of the classic Clifton Chenier sound. This record is the perfect example of the Nathan Williams experience, but lacks the diversity that will make *Creole Crossroads* more appealing to those less familiar with zydeco.

the rest:
Steady Rock ♪♪♪ (Rounder, 1989)
Your Mama Don't Know ♪♪♪♪ (Rounder, 1990)
Follow Me Chicken ♪♪♪♪ (Rounder, 1993)

influences:
◄◄ Clifton Chenier, Rockin' Sidney, Buckwheat Zydeco

►► Geno Delafose, Lynn August

Jared Snyder

Willie & Lobo

New age, nuevo flamenco, polyglot world music
Formed 1991, in Puerto Vallarta, Mexico. Based in USA (Willie), and Mexico (Lobo).

Willie Royal (USA), violin; Wolfgang "Lobo" Fink (Germany), guitar.

Willie Royal and Wolfgang "Lobo" Fink create the sort of music that seems to be from everywhere and nowhere at once. That's not surprising when you consider that Royal grew up a U.S. Air Force brat, living all over the world and picking up various musical influences along the way. Fink is a German classical guitarist who studied flamenco music in France. The two met while playing in different sections of the same bar, Mama Mia's, in San Miguel de Allende, Mexico. They jammed together for nearly a decade before formally joining forces in 1991. Once playing and recording together, the duo wasted no time in becoming a new-age/world-music sensation. The diverse elements in their style include jazz, flamenco, Cajun, Celtic, and Middle Eastern influences among the new-age musing. More so than is true of most groups, the world is Willie and Lobo's oyster.

what to buy: There's a certain sameness to the duo's offerings, which isn't necessarily a bad thing since they're operating at a relatively high level. You can feel confident that any of their albums you pick up will be just fine. On that basis, *Caliente* ♪♪♪ (Mesa/Bluemoon, 1997, prod. Rick Braun, George Nauful) is as good a place to start as any, with the searching, Middle Eastern–flavored "Desert Sun," the flamenco guitar showcase "Lunada," and the sweet reverie "Napali."

what to buy next: *Between the Waters* ♪♪♪ (Mesa/Bluemoon, 1995, prod. Dom Camardello, George Nauful) kicks off with the lively title track and features the jazzy "Vallarta Boogie" and the contemplative "Ola Mistica."

what to avoid: There's certainly nothing wrong with Willie and Lobo's contributions to *Music from Puerto Vallarta Squeeze: The Novel by Robert James Waller* ♪♪ (Mesa/Bluemoon, 1996,

prod. Rick Braun, George Nauful, Robert James Waller), which is primarily a compilation of their earlier material. The involvement of hack novelist Robert James Waller spoils the fun, though. Waller, a fan of their music, wrote them into the first chapter of his novel *Puerto Vallarta Squeeze,* which he reads here before offering a selection of his favorite Willie and Lobo tracks. *You* can program Waller out, of course, but for Willie and Lobo, there's the remaining guilt by association. With friends like these, who needs critics?

the rest:
Gypsy Boogaloo ♪♪♪ (Mesa/Bluemoon, 1993)
Fandango Nights ♪♪♪ (Mesa/Bluemoon, 1994)

worth searching for: If you know anyone who vacationed in Puerto Vallarta in the early '90s, check their record collection for Willie and Lobo's self-released live album, *Playing Hard* (1991), which the duo sold from the stage at Mama Mia's.

influences:
◄◄ Stephane Grappelli, Jean-Luc Ponty, Paco de Lucia

Daniel Durchholz

Joemy Wilson

"Baroque Irish chamber music"
Born September 1, 1945, in Fort Worth, TX, USA. Based in CA, USA.

Joemy Wilson has been hailed by critics on both sides of the Atlantic as one of the world's foremost interpreters of the music of Turlough O'Carolan, the legendary blind 18th-century Irish harper and composer. Raised in a musical family in New Haven, Connecticut, Wilson studied piano and violin as a child and began voice lessons in high school. While attending Barnard College in New York, she received her first fretted dulcimer, using it to accompany her singing, and then she took up the hammered dulcimer in 1979. She toured for several years as the musical half of Mime Musica, a performing duo with her husband, Jon Harvey. In 1984, they created their independent label, Dargason Music. "Dargason," an English country dance tune, is the title track of Wilson's debut album, *Dargason: A Dulcimer Sampler,* which features fretted dulcimer and vocals. Her subsequent recordings showcase her brilliant hammered dulcimer playing, with a splendid ensemble of Celtic harp, classical guitar, flute, violin, and *bodhrán* (Celtic frame drum). As one of the pioneers of the dulcimer renaissance and the Celtic revival of the early 1980s, Wilson calls her style "Baroque Irish chamber music." Irish critic John Paddy Browne writes, "Now, at last, we have a new interpreter who has converted the great man's exquisite music to the hammered dulcimer and restored it to its natural classical setting." In addition to four Celtic titles, Wilson has recorded three Christmas albums, a collection of

Beatles tunes, and a collection for children—*Dulcimer Lullabies* was showcased on the ABC special *In a New Light* starring Arsenio Hall and Paula Abdul.

what to buy: *Carolan's Cup* 🎵🎵🎵🎵 (Dargason Music, 1984, prod. Joemy Wilson, Scott Fraser) is the first in a series of Celtic recordings and exclusively features the works of Turlough O'Carolan, from the well-known "Sheebeg and Sheemore" to the less-familiar "Number 171," which is from a collection of numbered O'Carolan tunes without titles. The Carolan Consort of musicians that accompanies Wilson's hammered and fretted dulcimer includes Anisa Angarola (guitar), Valarie King (flute, piccolo, alto flute, bass flute), Miamon Miller (violin), and Sylvia Woods (Celtic harp). *Carolan's Cottage* 🎵🎵🎵🎵 (Dargason Music, 1986, prod. Joemy Wilson, Scott Fraser) is Wilson's second recording devoted to the music of O'Carolan and includes a beautiful version of "Morgan Megan." *Celtic Dreams* 🎵🎵🎵🎵 (Dargason Music, 1989, prod. Joemy Wilson, Scott Fraser) is the third Wilson recording devoted to O'Carolan, but also includes other tunes from Ireland, Scotland, and Wales, such as "Coilsfield House." *Celtic Treasures* 🎵🎵🎵🎵 (Dargason Music, 1994, prod. Joemy Wilson, Scott Fraser) includes four O'Carolan pieces as well as works by two other Irish harpers, Cornelius Lyons and Rory Dall O'Cahan. The assortment of jigs, reels, airs, and a hornpipe makes this recording a treasure-chest of Celtic delights. The liner notes on each collection are exceptionally well presented, with the complete historical background of every tune.

what to buy next: *Beatles on Hammered Dulcimer* 🎵🎵🎵 (Dargason Music, 1989, prod. Joemy Wilson, Scott Fraser) is a fun collection of 12 Lennon-McCartney masterpieces played on the hammered dulcimer as instrumentals. Wilson is accompanied by the same talented musicians as in her Celtic recordings. *Dulcimer Lullabies* 🎵🎵🎵 (Dargason Music, 1991, prod. Joemy Wilson, Scott Fraser) is subtitled "Quiet-time Music for Children on Hammered Dulcimer." These lullabies come from Ireland, Scotland, Wales, Holland, Germany, and the U.S., and include a lovely Wilson original, "Naya's Song." All of the above recordings are available from Dargason Music, P.O. Box 189, Burbank, CA 91503 or through e-mail at dargason@earthlink.net. (Some of Wilson's and the label's offerings are also reviewed in this book's Compilations section.)

the rest:
Gifts 🎵🎵🎵 (Dargason Music, 1985)
Gifts, Volume II 🎵🎵🎵 (Dargason Music, 1987)
Gifts III 🎵🎵🎵 (Dargason Music, 1990)

worth searching for: Joemy Wilson's debut recording, *Dargason: A Dulcimer Sampler* 🎵🎵🎵 (Back Lot Recordings, 1982/Dargason Music, 1986, prod. Joemy Wilson, Scott Fraser), a cassette-only release, features her fretted dulcimer skills and also includes some nice vocals, which are not heard on any of her subsequent recordings.

influences:
◀◀ The Chieftains, Derek Bell, Seán Ó Riada, Wolfgang Amadeus Mozart

▶▶ Madeline MacNeil, Carrie Crompton

Heidi Cerrigione

Wimme

Late 20th-century joik
Born Wimme Saari, 1959, in Finland. Based in Finland.

The *yoik,* or *joik,* has nothing to do with eggs or Brooklynites. It's a singing style of the Saami people (once known as Laplanders), and can be found in their cultures all across the north of Scandinavia. Of the three distinct joiking dialects, Wimme was raised in the North Sami Luohti tradition, probably the most widely known; it's a form that uses a pentatonic scale (no halftones), and the joik centers on a specific subject. However, Wimme is far from traditional in his approach to joiking, using accompaniment that often includes samples, loops, and a band. His mother was from a joiking family, but by Wimme's days those links to the past had been broken. In fact, it wasn't until 1986, while working at the Finnish Broadcasting Company, that Wimme discovered tapes of his uncle joiking, and from them learned the older vocal techniques. These he incorporated into his music—though that music was far more impressionistic than its models, featuring lyrics about fog or even the Milky Way. Essentially, Wimme gave new life to the tradition by putting it in a new context. Many were impressed by what he was doing, including producer Hector Zazou, with whom he recorded for the collection *From the Cold Seas.* In 1995 Wimme released his own eponymous debut, accompanied by musicians from the well-known Finnish band Rinneradio. This debut was voted Folk Music Album of the Year in his home country, and the following year Wimme's muse took him further afield. He'd recorded a joik titled "Texas," and suddenly found himself invited to appear at the South by Southwest festival in Austin—which much impressed his bandmates, who urged him to record another called "Hawaii." "Texas," along with other tracks by Wimme and Rinneradio, appeared on a subsequent record, *File Under: Finnish Ambient Techno Chant.* Wimme became a fixture on the Scandinavian Festival scene, often sitting in with Hedningarna, and in early 1999 he released another new album to instant acclaim.

what to buy: *Wimme* 🎵🎵🎵🎵🎵 (NorthSide, 1997, prod. Tapani Rinne) is as atmospheric and soaring as anything in the new-age bins, but with the added bonus of real substance. The human voice—at least Wimme's voice—can evoke fog, thunder, and boiling springs. What more can you ask from one man? On the electrifying *Gierran* 𝄢𝄢𝄢𝄢 (NorthSide, 1999), Wimme's voice aims for the stratosphere while his and Rinneradio's music heads in multiple stylistic directions but never loses sight of its Saami home base. From mesmerizing solo tracks that will remind Stateside ears of Native American chants, to full-band flirtations with art-rock and avant-jazz, each one of this sometimes sublime, sometimes whimsical album's experiments pays off.

the rest:

File Under: Finnish Ambient Techno Chant 𝄢𝄢𝄢 (Catalyst/BMG, 1997)

influences:

◀ The Finnish joiking tradition

see also: *Hedningarna*

Chris Nickson

Paul Winter

Jazz, new age, world music

Born Paul Theodore Winter Jr., August 31, 1939, in Altoona, PA, USA. Based in Litchfield, CT, USA.

Soprano saxophonist Paul Winter is one of the pioneers of world music. In addition to combining elements of African, Asian, Latin, and Russian music with American jazz, Winter was one of the first to incorporate the sounds of nature and wildlife into his compositions. Winter, who studied saxophone from the age of nine, was initially rooted in the jazz tradition. After performing with school-age bands including the Little German Band and the Silver Liners, he went on his first tour at the age of 17. Although he majored in English composition at Northwestern University in Chicago, he frequented the city's jazz clubs. With the Paul Winter Sextet, he won the Intercollegiate Jazz Festival competition in 1961 and, at the invitation of Jacqueline Kennedy, became the first jazz musician to perform at the White House. Signed by John Hammond to Columbia Records, Winter and the sextet recorded a self-titled debut album the same year. A 23-country cultural exchange tour of Latin America, sponsored by the U.S. State Department in 1962, inspired Winter to add the bossa nova of Brazil to his musical vision. The music so captivated him that he remained in the Ipanema section of Rio for nearly a year recording with Brazilian musicians. In 1967, Winter formed the Paul Winter Consort, naming the group in the manner of the house bands of the Elizabethan Theater. Their first studio album, *Icarus,* was released in 1970 and produced by former Beatles mentor George Martin. Shortly afterwards, original members Ralph Towner, Paul McCandless, Colin Wollcott, and David Darling left to start the experimental acoustic jazz band Oregon.

The sounds of nature fascinated Winter, who first heard the songs of humpback whales in 1968. After hosting a whale-watching/music-making workshop in Baja, California, in 1977, Winter and the Consort combined the sounds of whales, wolves, and birds with their acoustic improvisations on their next album, *Common Ground.* In 1980, Winter and the group became artists-in-residence at the Cathedral of St. John the Divine, the world's largest Gothic cathedral, in New York, and launched their own record label, Living Music. While most of their albums have been recorded in a studio that Winter built in a barn, the Paul Winter Consort has recorded in such locales as the cathedral, the General Assembly of the United Nations, and the Grand Canyon. They have earned numerous awards for their albums—in 1983 *Sun Singer* was named "Best Jazz Album" by the National Association of Independent Record Distributors, and the Consort received their first Grammys back-to-back, for *Spanish Angel* in 1994 and for *Prayer for the Wild Things* the following year. Winter has collaborated with a variety of artists. He toured the United States with Russian poet Yevgeny Yevtushenko in 1985, and joined with a Russian chorus, the Dmitri Pokrovsky Ensemble, to record *Earthbeat* three years later—each groundbreaking artistic achievements and risky social statements during the Cold War. Winter collaborated with marine biologist Roger Payne and actor Leonard Nimoy to record an album of humpback whale songs, *Whales Alive!,* in 1986. He provided musical accompaniment for beat poet Gary Snyder on the 1991 album *Turtle Island,* and produced Pete Seeger's *Pete,* which received the "Best Traditional Folk Album" Grammy in 1996. His own most recent albums are squarely in the world-music canon: the self-explanatory *Brazilian Days* and *Celtic Solstice.*

what to buy: Producer George Martin called *Icarus* 𝄢𝄢𝄢𝄢𝄢 (Epic, 1970, prod. George Martin), the first studio album by the Paul Winter Consort, "the best album I've ever been associated with." Considering that Martin produced nearly all the albums of the Beatles, the remark carried much importance. With Winter's soprano sax accompanied by the musicians who went on to form the innovative jazz band Oregon, the album is a masterpiece that serves as a bridge between small-combo jazz and world music. *Common Ground* 𝄢𝄢𝄢𝄢 (A&M, 1977, prod. Paul Winter) was the first album to blend musical influences from around the globe with the natural sounds of humpback whales, wolves, and eagles. *Brazilian Days* 𝄢𝄢𝄢𝄢 (BMG/Living Music, 1998) is a collaboration with Oscar Castro-Neves, the Brazilian guitarist who first inspired Winter's interest in the bossa nova nearly 40 years before. *Celtic Solstice* 𝄢𝄢𝄢𝄢 (BMG/Windham Hill, 1999) draws from the stellar Celtic musicians who have played at Winter's annual Winter Solstice Celebration at the Cathedral of St. John the Divine. Many of the album's tracks were recorded in the cathedral, and it's a cornucopia for Celtic fans, including appearances by uilleann piper Davy Spillane, singer Karan Casey from Solas, tin whistle player and flutist Joanie Madden from Cherish the Ladies, and fiddler Eileen Ivers of *Riverdance* fame, not to mention a full Irish, African, and South American percussion ensemble.

the rest:

Road: 1968–1970 𝄞𝄞𝄞𝄞 (Columbia, 1971)
Wintersong 𝄞𝄞𝄞𝄞 (Living Music, 1979)
Callings 𝄞𝄞𝄞 (Living Music, 1980)
Missa Gaia/Earth Mass 𝄞𝄞𝄞 (Living Music, 1982)
Sun Singer 𝄞𝄞𝄞𝄞 (Living Music, 1983)
Concert for the Earth 𝄞𝄞𝄞𝄞 (Living Music, 1985)
Canyon 𝄞𝄞𝄞⅞ (Living Music, 1985)
Whales Alive! 𝄞𝄞𝄞 (Living Music, 1987)
Canyon Lullaby 𝄞𝄞𝄞𝄞 (Living Music, 1988)
Wolf Eyes 𝄞𝄞𝄞𝄞 (Living Music, 1988)
Earthbeat 𝄞𝄞𝄞⅞ (Living Music, 1988)
Retrospective 𝄞𝄞𝄞 (Living Music, 1989)
Earth: Voices of a Planet 𝄞𝄞𝄞 (Living Music, 1990)
(With Gary Snyder) *Turtle Island* 𝄞𝄞𝄞 (Living Music, 1991)
Anthems 𝄞𝄞𝄞𝄞 (Living Music, 1992)
Spanish Angel 𝄞𝄞𝄞𝄞 (Living Music, 1994)
Prayer for the Wild Things 𝄞𝄞𝄞𝄞 (Living Music, 1995)

influences:

◀◀ American jazz, African, Asian, Latin, and Russian music, whales, wolves, and birds

▶▶ Oregon, Will Ackerman, Shadowfax

see also: *Cherish the Ladies, Eileen Ivers, Joanie Madden, Solas*

Craig Harris

Jah Wobble

See: Abdel Ali Slimani

Wolfstone

Celtic rock
Formed 1988, in Scotland. Disbanded 1997.

Duncan Chisholm, electric fiddle; Ivan Drever, vocals, acoustic guitar; Stuart Eaglesham, acoustic and electric guitars, vocals; Struan Eaglesham, keyboards; Mop Youngson, drums; Wayne MacKenzie, bass; Stevie Saint, bagpipes, whistles. (All members are from Scotland.)

Sounding like a collision between a traditional dance band and a grungy rock outfit, Wolfstone merged the old with the new, the acoustic with the electric, and in so doing breathed new life into old tunes, energized their fans, and made traditional music accessible to rock and pop audiences. The seven members of Wolfstone were from the highlands of Scotland, but eschewed the commonly romanticized version of their homeland, pre-senting a more realistic picture of the everyday joys and struggles of a resilient and musically rich people. Wolfstone began during the late '80s when Duncan Chisholm and some friends formed a professional band to play music for *ceilidhs* (public dances). The potent combination of fiddle, bagpipes, and a rock rhythm section played well to an audience wanting more from traditional music. The original Wolfstone, including Struan Eaglesham on keyboards and brother Stuart Eaglesham on guitar, subsequently welcomed accomplished guitarist and songwriter Ivan Drever into the fledgling group. Wolfstone's first album, *Unleashed,* released on Iona Records in Scotland, quickly became the label's biggest seller, earning the band a Silver Disc Award from the Scottish Music Industry Association. With the release of *The Chase* in 1992, Wolfstone's touring schedule expanded to include Europe and North America. Their success at the international Tonder Festival in Denmark made them the only band ever invited to perform for three consecutive years. The excitement generated at Wolfstone concerts was almost legendary; unfortunately, due to a combination of management problems and record-company squabbles, the band called it quits at the end of 1997.

what to buy: *The Chase* 𝄞𝄞𝄞𝄞 (Iona, 1992/Green Linnet, 1994, prod. Phil Cunningham), the group's groundbreaking second album, garnered rave reviews from critics all over the world. "Tinnie Run," opening with an in-your-face electric guitar riff and segueing into a set of pumped-up traditional tunes, perhaps best exemplifies the Wolfstone sound. *The Chase* also includes one of the band's most-requested songs, "The Prophet." Stuart Eaglesham rocks passionately as he sings of a mysterious sage of Scottish legend. "The Appropriate Dipstick" is a showcase for guest piper Dougie Pincock. The album ends with "Cannot Lay Me Down," a set that ranges from the title song, written and sung by Drever, to the gorgeous finale "Lady of Ardross," written by Eaglesham.

what to buy next: Guided by Chris Harley, a producer for bands like Runrig, *The Half Tail* 𝄞𝄞𝄞𝄞 (Green Linnet, 1996, prod. Chris Harley) shows a more rocked-up and polished Wolfstone, with more emphasis on the rhythm section. Included is the standout "Bonnie Ship the Diamond," which exquisitely combines a well-known traditional whaling song with "The Last Leviathan," a newer song from the dying whale's point of view. The track begins with an ethereal wash of synthesizer and percussion followed by the exuberant piping of Stevie Saint. Other notable numbers are "Gillies," one more pipe-infused stomper, and "Glenglass," a bit more laid-back mix of keyboards and fiddle. From the opening drum roll to the final pipe drone, *Year of the Dog* 𝄞𝄞𝄞𝄞 (Green Linnet, 1994, prod. Phil Cunningham) kicks with frenetic fiddling, sparkling piano, and spirited flutes, whistles, and pipes, paired with a grungier background than the two albums that preceded it. *Year of the Dog* broke the band out of their earlier, more acoustic mode while still appealing to Celtophiles; hard-core traditionalists could be found dancing along with rock fans to the tunes from this album. The original numbers range from pithy social and political commentary to tender love songs. Producer Phil Cunningham once again contributes several tunes and places his well-regarded sonic stamp on the project.

what to avoid: *Wolfstone I* and *Wolfstone II* are very early versions of the band that even they would rather not have in circulation. The owner of the master tapes began rereleasing them when Wolfstone started getting worldwide attention.

the rest:
Unleashed ♪♪♪♪ (Iona, 1991/Green Linnet, 1992)
Burning Horizons EP ♪♪♪♪ (Iona, 1993)
Pick of the Litter ♪♪♪♪ (Green Linnet, 1997)
This Strange Place (Green Linnet, 1998)

worth searching for: The 68-minute video *Wolfstone: Captured Alive Video* (Grampian Television/Wolfstone Partnership, 1992), shot at a concert in Aberdeen, Scotland, is a good look at the band's live shows and gives a sense of their storied energy.

influences:
◄◄ Silly Wizard, Battlefield Band, Runrig, Bothy Band, Planxty
►► Burach, Paperboys, Rock Salt and Nails, Rawlins Cross

see also: *Phil Cunningham, Runrig*

Denise Sofranko

Wolga Balalaika Ensemble

Russian folk music
Formed in Koblenz, Germany. Based in Koblenz, Germany.

Mischa Taschenkow, alto balalaika, vocals; Nicolai Malinow, bass balalaika, vocals; Ivan Nesterow, prime (lead) balalaika, vocals. (All members are from Russia.)

This trio of Russians, based in Germany, play Russian folk music with plenty of fire and brimstone, providing the perfect soundtrack for an evening of vodka sipping and borscht-fueled joviality.

what to buy: *In the Land of the Tsarevitsch* ♪♪♪♪ (ARC England, 1992, prod. Wolga) is set up like a typical evening's revels; each tune is faster, crazier, and more energetic than the last. Like the blues, Russian music displays a deeply plaintive quality, even when the band is playing at a breakneck pace. This set includes "Padmoskownyije Wjetschera," which Kenny Ball "borrowed" for his hit "Midnight in Moscow."

what to buy next: *Kalinka* ♪♪♪♪ (ARC England, 1998, prod. Wolga) is another energetic outing from these balalaika virtu-

osos. Includes some incendiary accordion playing by an unaccredited cohort.

the rest:
Songs from the Taiga ♪♪♪♪ (ARC England, 1996)

influences:
◄◄ Theodore Bikel, Dmitri Pokrovsky Ensemble

j. poet

Stevie Wonder

Universal pop synthesis
Born Steveland Morris, May 13, 1950, in Saginaw, MI, USA. Based in USA.

Stevie Wonder's *Secret Life of Plants* is part of the secret history of world music. Released the same year as David Bowie and Brian Eno's proto-worldbeat album *Lodger* —and surely no less financially successful at the time—*Plants* cultivated the same global grab-bag approach that bloomed into some of the most familiar excesses and singular accomplishments of later world-music, and was no doubt equally influential on future waves of culture-crossing artists. Wonder had dabbled in international styles before—and has since—but this commercially obscure album was the one on which he most intensively pursued the we-are-the-world vibe with which, interestingly, he became more associated in the popular imagination somewhat later.

what to buy: For purposes of this book, you want to start with the recording most people pass up. *Stevie Wonder's Journey through the Secret Life of Plants* ♪♪♪♪ (Tamla/Motown, 1979, prod. Stevie Wonder), partially begun as the soundtrack to an instantly forgotten environmentalist documentary, was Wonder's paean to all of Mother Earth's species and cultures . . . and styles, including not only the attempts at Japanese, Indian, and West African forms that land it in the world-music column, but also a sometimes-kitschy, often-visionary spectrum of jazz, scat, ambient, lounge piano, church organ, muzak ragtime, baroque funk, neo-classical, karaoke medley, proto-sampling, and prophetically early techno, not to mention some of his most overlooked smooth-soul balladry. Wonder duets with a Japanese children's choir on "Ai No Sono," and performs live in Africa (an interesting choice for a concept album) on "A Seed's a Star and Tree Medley." He doesn't even come close to *raga* on "Voyage to India" (though for better or worse he anticipates new-age mall music more clearly than Eno ever did), but he nails a West African kora-and-talking-drum trad-pop sound on "Kesse Ye Lolo De Ye"; there's been nothing like it on any mainstream American album since.

what to buy next: Justly famed as a stylistic omnivore, Wonder has, throughout the mature phase of his career, touched on world-music textures as regularly as on those of any other genre. "Don't You Worry 'Bout a Thing" from *Innervisions* ♪♪♪♪ (Tamla/Motown, 1973, prod. Stevie Wonder) has become a salsa standard, and the less-known "Bird of Beauty" from *Fulfillingness' First Finale* ♪♪♪♪ (Tamla/Motown, 1974, prod. Stevie Wonder) merits a similar honorary place in the annals of MPB (Brazilian Popular Music). Wonder has dabbled more or less convincingly in reggae and associated forms over the years: "Master Blaster (Jammin')" from *Hotter Than July* ♪♪♪♪ (Motown, 1980, prod. Stevie Wonder) and the *Characters* ♪♪♪ (Motown, 1987, prod. Stevie Wonder) album's "You Will Know" in the "more" category; *Fulfillingness*'s "Boogie On, Reggae Woman" and "Tomorrow Robins Will Sing" from *Conversation Peace* ♪♪♪ (Motown, 1985, prod. Stevie Wonder) in the "less" category. On *Songs in the Key of Life* ♪♪♪♪♪ (Tamla/Motown, 1976, prod. Stevie Wonder) Wonder and a small army give "Another Star" a memorable Latin jazz feel, while all by himself he achieves an interesting synth-flamenco sound on "Ngiculela/Es Una Historia/I Am Singing" (delivered in Zulu, Spanish, and English). Also on the hybrid side, Wonder offers intriguingly electronicized takes on Caribbean rhythm and African polyrhythm, respectively, with "Chemical Love" from *Jungle Fever* ♪♪♪♪ (Motown, 1991, prod. Stevie Wonder) and "It's Wrong" from *In Square Circle* ♪♪♪ (Motown, 1985, prod. Stevie Wonder)—to say nothing of *Fever*'s hit title track, assisted by African drum master Babatunde Olatunji.

influences:

◄◄ Marvin Gaye, Duke Ellington, Babatunde Olatunji, Bob Marley, Woody Guthrie

►► Boyz II Men, Sting, every soul and pop artist since the beginning of the 1970s

Adam McGovern

Gary Wright

Rock, African/Brazilian worldbeat
Born April 26, 1943, in Creskill, NJ, USA. Based in California, USA.

Best known for his '70s smash hits "Dream Weaver" and "Love Is Alive," Gary Wright has spent three decades exploring the world of music and searching for his niche. Wright's distinctive vocal style and authoritative use of keyboards and synthesizers distinguish his music from the morass of '70s flashes-in-the-pan. Wright began his career with a tour of Germany as a singer/songwriter, and soon joined the rock band Spookytooth. He has collaborated with the likes of George Harrison, Eric Clapton, Phil Collins, Jeff Lynne, and Ringo Starr, and has worked on a variety of movie scores. His all-keyboard album *Dream Weaver* was considered groundbreaking for the pop genre at the time. Wright discovered the lure of Brazilian per-

cussion on a visit to that country, coming home with a recording of several of the best percussionists in the area. Years later, while working with Sayuka from South Africa, he heard the call of African vocal music. These influences eventually combined to drastically change the direction of Wright's own work. The result, a mix of mainstream pop with tribal rhythms and chants, was released in 1995 as *First Signs of Life* —though at presstime there were some doubts as to the second sign, as Wright's upcoming *Human Love* album was reported to be a return to his pre-worldbeat style.

what to buy: Wright's one world-music album is *First Signs of Life* ♪♪♪ (Triloka Records, 1995, prod. Franz Pusch, Gary Wright). Wright explores a fusion of pop/rock with African vocals and Brazilian rhythms, creating a fascinating blend of driving beat, rich but simple vocals, and modern keyboards. This recording evokes a wonderful tribal feeling with a modern edge. Nigerian Singer Ayo Adeyeni and Brazilian guitarist Ricardo Silviera add sparkle, pizzazz, and authenticity.

what to buy next: Considered a classic by many, *Dream Weaver* ♪♪♪ (Warner Bros., 1975, prod. Gary Wright) contains the hits "Dream Weaver" and "Love Is Alive," which are its two standouts. Wright's pioneering keyboard style is also well showcased on *Headin' Home* ♪♪ (Warner Bros., 1979, prod. Gary Wright) and *Touch and Gone* ♪♪ (Warner Bros., 1977, prod. Gary Wright).

influences:

◄◄ Traffic, George Harrison, Paul Simon

Jo Hughey Morrison

Wu Man

Chinese classical and fusion
Born 1963, in Hangzhou, China. Based in Boston, MA, USA.

Wu Man, one of the most outstanding masters of the *pipa* (a four-stringed Chinese lute), is equally comfortable playing traditional Chinese music, more contemporary sounds, and even unprecedented stylistic fusions. She began her professional training at the age of nine and in 1977 won first place in the national entrance exam to the Central Conservatory of Music in Beijing. There she studied the *Pudong* school of playing under a number of pipa masters. After winning the First National Academic Competition for Chinese Instruments and earning China's first master's degree in the pipa, she took her place among an exciting new generation of Chinese composers, though, as much as any of them, she found her expression restrained by the ruling regime. Moving to the U.S. in the '80s, she joined Music from China, a New York ensemble formed in that decade to promote both the traditional and modern work of her people. In more than 300 concert appearances around

Wu Man

the world, she has collaborated with the Kronos Quartet, the Boston Symphony Orchestra, the Los Angeles Philharmonic New Music Group, the New York New Music Consort, the Pittsburgh New Music Ensemble, and the Vienna Radio Symphonic Orchestra. A recent invitation to play at the White House with famed cellist Yo-Yo Ma underscored her success, while by no means culminating her eclectic and ambitious musical quest.

what to buy: For a brilliant overview of traditional and contemporary Chinese music at its finest, check out Wu Man's Western recording debut, *Chinese Music for the Pipa* ♪♪♪♪ (Nimbus, 1993), a virtuosic solo performance of seven compositions that highlight her extraordinarily emotive playing. From lively folk suites and plaintive ballads to modern works by composers like Chen Yi, Wu Man handles each song with equal aplomb, creating a wonderful showcase for the myriad sounds one can create with ten fingers and four strings. *Chinese Traditional & Contemporary Music* ♪♪♪♪♭ (Nimbus, 1996) is even better; a more mature effort that places Wu Man in a chamber-music setting alongside Liu Qi-Chao on flute, Yang Yi on plucked zither, and Tien-Juo Wang on bowed violin. The quartet works exceptionally well together on songs like "Niao Tou Lin (Birds in the Forest)" and "Xiyang Xiaogu (Flute & Drum at Sunset)," crafting lush, exotic melodies packed with vivid imagery evoking playful wildlife and gorgeous Eastern landscapes. A captivatingly accessible introduction to the music of China.

what to buy next: Far more unusual is Wu Man's first album with the Kronos Quartet, *Ghost Opera* ♪♪♪♪ (Nonesuch, 1997, prod. Judith Sherman), a fascinatingly inventive conceptual piece composed by Tan Dun. Pipas, violins, one-stringed lutes, and cellos merge with drums, cymbals, stones, gongs, bells, and haunting, spectral vocals to tell the story of a little girl (voiced by Wu Man) who has lost her parents. The tradition of ghost opera is thousands of years old, but in keeping with its dominant theme of dialogue between past and future, spirit and nature, Tan Dun and the quintet of musicians have fashioned a timeless treasure, poignant across languages and beyond words.

the rest:
(With Liu Sola) *Blues in the East* ♪♪♪♭ (Axiom, 1994)
(With Liu Sola) *China Collage* ♪♪♪♭ (Avant, 1996)
(With Martin Simpson) *Music for the Motherless Child* ♪♪♪♪ (Water Lily Acoustics, 1997)

worth searching for: In addition to recording a number of albums available only in China, Wu Man also composed the scores for two Ang Lee films, 1993's *The Wedding Banquet* and 1994's *Eat Drink Man Woman*. Both soundtrack albums are now long out-of-print but are worth snapping up if you can track them down. You also won't regret seeking out Wu Man's performances on other artists' albums, including *T.A.Z.* ♪♪♪♪ (Axiom,

1994) with Hakim Bey, *Carry the Day* ♪♪♪ (Columbia, 1995) with Henry Threadgill, and *Early Music* ♪♪♪♪ (Nonesuch, 1997) with the Kronos Quartet.

influences:

◄◄ Lin Shicheng, Liu Dehai, Chen Zemin, Kuang Yuzhong

▶▶ Kronos Quartet, Liu Sola

see also: *Kronos Quartet, Bill Laswell, Liu Sola*

Bret Love

Stavros Xarhakos & Nicos Gatsos
Rembetiko
Formed 1964, in Athens, Greece. Based in Athens, Greece.

Stavros Xarhakos; Nicos Gatsos. (Both artists are from Greece.)

Rembetiko is the outlaw music of Greece. It first flourished in the 1930s when sailors returned to their homeland with tales of drinking, exotic women, and opium dens. The lyrical themes came to include political oppression during the Greek civil war in the 1950s, and again mirrored the country's angst during a dictatorship in the 1970s. For most of its history rembetiko had remained underground due to censorship, but with the fall of the dictatorship it was rediscovered by some of the most prominent Greek songwriters and composers, elevating this once-taboo form into one of the most popular Greek genres today. Along with respected composer Mikis Theodorakis, the songwriting team of Stavros Xarhakos and Nicos Gatsos not only rediscovered rembetiko, but redefined it. Xarhakos and Gatsos are widely credited with bringing rembetiko to Greek cinema. Their beautiful arrangements and dramatic music made them the perfect team for the medium, and they have written songs for the most beloved movie stars of Greece, including Aliki Vouyouklaki. And along with the *music* of rembetiko comes the *dances*. The *hasapiko* or Greek sailor dance and the *tsefeli* or belly-dance became integral parts of Greek cinema, thanks to the music of Xarhakos and Gatsos. Their contributions expanded their country's and the world's perception of one of Greece's richest cultural offerings, and made them, now and forever, the Rodgers and Hammerstein of Greece.

what to buy: *Ta Rembetika* ♪♪♪♪ (CBS, 1983, prod. G. Kostandopoulo) is Xarhakos and Gatsos's seminal album. Written for the movie of same name by Kostas Ferri, the music follows the lives of main characters Marika Nikou and Vassilis Titsanis, reflecting on estrangement and redemption. With memorable choruses and the primal wailing of singer Xorodia, this album reflects the turmoil of post-war Greece. The later flourishing of rembetiko was largely due to this enormously successful soundtrack. Following its success, Xarhakos and Gatsos released *Hrises Epitihies* 𝄢𝄢𝄢𝄢 (EMI Minos), a collection of some of the most significant rembetiko songs released from 1962 to 1974. The album is filled with Xarhakos's trademark style of bouzouki playing and Gatsos's keen lyrics.

what to buy next: While the 1970s and '80s were the most important years of Xarhakos and Gatsos's career, they still continue to compose and arrange albums of a high caliber. *6+6* 𝄢𝄢𝄢𝄢 (Xenophone Records, 1996) and *Spiti Mou, Spitaki Mou* 𝄢𝄢𝄢𝄢𝄢 (Xenophone Records) reaffirm that rembetiko music has taken a central place in the heart and soul of Greece. Nana Mouskouri's appearances on the latter collection are not to be missed. That disc also marks a shift in lyrics from broad political and social matters to more personal ones, concerning the family life, which is a vital part of Greek culture.

worth searching for: Since Xarhakos and Gatsos have done so much of their work as the compositional masterminds behind other artists, the discography of their releases on their own is minuscule in comparison. Nonetheless there have been many reissues of these recordings, though most of them are hard to find in America. Labels such as EMI Minos, CBS, and Mercury will assure clarity of sound, and all three labels have done a good job of selecting vital songs from the composers' repertoire. If you enjoy the kind of music you hear on any of the releases mentioned above, you'd like to check out the various-artists Greek import double CD *Flying with Greek Music Vol. 1 & 2: The Best Instrumentals* 𝄢𝄢𝄢𝄢 (Eros, 1998). This compilation is not easy to find, but it does a wonderful job of showcasing important composers and bouzouki players.

influences:

◄◄ Manos Hadjiahis, Mikis Theodorakis

►► Stevros Kokostas, George Dalaras

see also: *Mikis Theodorakis*

Helen Giano

Xit

Native American rock

Formed 1969, in Albuquerque, NM, USA. Disbanded 1976; re-formed 1977; disbanded 1981.

Xit #1: Tom Bee, leader, songwriter, guitar, Native percussion; Lee Herrera, drums; Mac Suazo, bass; R.C. Gariss Jr., lead guitar; A. Michael Martin, vocals, lead guitar (1968–72); Obie Sullivan, keyboards (1973–76); Tyrone King, backing vocals, Native percussion, dancing (1973–76); Chili Yazzie, backing vocals, Native percussion, dancing (1973–76). **Xit # 2:** Tom Bee, leader, songwriter, guitar, Native percussion; Mac Suazo, bass; various other sidemen.

Today Tom Bee is president of Sound of America Records (SOAR), the country's most aggressive marketer, distributor, and promoter of Native music, but his history in the biz stretches back to the late '60s, when he put together the first all-Native rock band. Xit (Exit) started out like most bands, playing cover versions of Top 40 hits in local clubs and bars, but then Bee had a vision: a Native band that would combine traditional music and militant lyrics, and deliver them with the clout of a full-tilt rock 'n' roll outfit. Bee began writing tunes and shopping the band's demo tape; one of those demos got to Motown Records, which used one of Bee's songs, "(We've Got) Blue Skies," for a Jackson 5 album. When Motown started the Rare Earth imprint in 1971 as a venue for non-black acts, Xit became the first all–Native American rock group to get a label deal with a company that had access to the cultural mainstream. While signed to Motown, Bee also wrote and produced tunes for the Jackson 5 and Smokey Robinson. Xit eventually splintered; their militant lyrics and support of the American Indian Movement (AIM) led to a noticeable lack of bookings outside of reservation gigs and the odd college folk festival. After the original band fell apart, Bee and bass player Mac Suazo carried on with various other musicians sitting in, playing their last gig in Lucerne, Switzerland, in 1981. Bee went on to work as a record salesman and concert promoter before starting SOAR in 1988. "The lyrics I wrote for Xit are pretty tame by today's standards," Bee says, "but at the time, nobody had ever heard the story from the Indian's side. We had some good times, and I think we opened up the doors for today's generation of Red Rockers." Xit's albums had all gone out of print, but after starting SOAR Bee bought back the masters and began reissuing the band's catalog. At press time a collector's edition of *Plight of the Redman*, completely remastered and with new art work, was due in mid-1999.

what to buy: *Silent Warrior* 𝄢𝄢𝄢𝄡 (SOAR, 1991, prod. Tom Bee) is a time-machine back to the many popular styles of 1973, when this album was first released. Pop-rock, proto-metal, and singer/songwriter are all here, and all drenched with powwow drums and orchestral strings. It's also one of the first albums to deal with the growing ecological disasters being brought on by advancing technology, way before environmentalism moved from activist cause to pop vogue.

what to buy next: Most tracks on *Plight of the Redman* 𝄢𝄢𝄢𝄢 (SOAR, 1988), originally released in 1970, start with Native drumming and singing in Native languages—a remarkably anti-commercial move despite the Hendrix-drenched guitar stylings and Motown-on-the-reservation rhythm tracks. A bit over-earnest at times, but forgivable, especially in light of the self-pity the average white singer/songwriter was putting down at the time.

the rest:
Drums across the Atlantic—Live ♬♬♬ (SOAR, 1988)
Relocation ♬♬♬ (SOAR, 1990)
Entrance ♬♬♬ (SOAR cassette, 1993)

solo outings:
Tom Bee:
Color Me Red ♬♬♬ (Rare Earth, 1979)

influences:
◀◀ A. Paul Ortega, Buffy Sainte-Marie

▶▶ Redbone, John Trudell, Indigenous, Clan/Destine

see also: *Robby Bee & the Boyz from the Rez*

j. poet

Yabby You
Roots reggae, dub
Born Vivian Jackson in 1945, in Kingston, Jamaica. Based in Kingston, Jamaica.

When Vivian Jackson, a.k.a. Yabby You, sings about suffering, he sings from experience. By the time he was 17, Jackson was so malnourished that he had to be hospitalized. The side effects were terrible—severe arthritis and crippled legs. Jackson couldn't work, but he had a remarkably pure voice, and in 1972—through divine inspiration, as he describes it—performing with the aid of crutches, he formed the Prophets, one of Jamaica's foremost harmony trios. The Prophets' first single (and, eventually, the title track of their debut album) was "Conquering Lion," the first hit of many on Jackson's own Prophets record label. King Tubby mixed B-side dubs to most of Jackson's singles, and also gave Jackson his nickname, Yabby You. In addition to his own band, Jackson launched the careers of Michael Prophet, Wayne Wade, and Tony Tuff, as well as Willie Williams, Ras I-buna, and Half Pint. The hallmarks of his production technique were a distinctive bass line mixed with organs, horns, and an emphasis on beautiful vocal harmonies for a spiritual feel. Jackson appeared to have retired between 1985 and 1991; in fact, he had still been recording, and got firmly back in business with new material like *Fleeing from the City* and "old" releases from during his hiatus.

what to buy: *One Love, One Heart* ♬♬♬♬ (Shanachie, 1983, prod. Yabby You, Randall F. Grass) is hit after hit with no filler. The rootsy *Fleeing from the City* ♬♬♬ (Shanachie, 1991, prod. Yabby You) is a strong return from retirement, with a good balance of Christian hymns ("Praise Jahovia") and love songs ("Love Me, Love Me Girl"). Updating the mix with the notorious Mad Professor at the controls, *Yabby You Meets Mad Professor* ♬♬♬ (ARIWA Sounds, 1993) is a more light-hearted record. Jackson cut five dub albums with King Tubby; the first (and currently the only one available) is *King Tubby's Prophesy of Dub* ♬♬♬ (Prophets, 1976/Blood & Fire, 1995, prod. Vivian Jackson), with deep rhythms and mind-bending mixes of "Conquering Lion," "Jah Vengeance," and "Born Free."

what to avoid: From the same period, *Jesus Dread (1972–1977)* ♬♬♬ (Blood & Fire, 1997, prod. various) is an example of reissue overkill. While the packaging is a work of art, there are too many versions of each track—an original vocal mix, a dub version, a deejay version, and sometimes an utterly redundant instrumental version featuring saxophonist Tommy McCook. The material is first-rate, but hampered by exhaustive duplications.

worth searching for: Only recently deleted is Jackson's third collaboration with King Tubby, *Beware Dub* (Prophets, 1978/Shanachie, 1995).

influences:
◀◀ Bob Marley

▶▶ Buju Banton

see also: *King Tubby, Mad Professor*

David Poole

Stomu Yamash'ta
World jazz-fusion
Born March 15, 1947, in Kyoto, Japan. Based in Japan.

Percussionist, keyboardist, and composer Stomu Yamash'ta is one of Japan's most internationally acclaimed contemporary musicians. In addition to touring with the Chicago Chamber Orchestra and the jazz-rock trio Come to the Edge, Yamash'ta has composed for theatrical works, including *Red Buddha* and *The Man from the East*; film soundtracks, including *The Devils* and *The Man Who Fell to Earth*; and ballet scores, including the British Royal Ballet's *Shukumei*. In the mid-1970s, Yamash'ta toured and recorded with Go, an international all-star band featuring British keyboardist Stevie Winwood, German synthesizer player Klaus Schulze, and Americans Al Di Meola on guitar and Michael Shrieve on drums. Yamash'ta studied percussion at the Berklee College of Music in Boston, and then returned to Japan and formed the Red Buddha Theater in 1971. A 35-member collective of actors, dancers, and musicians, the Theater toured Europe during the summer of 1972. Establishing residency at the Carre Thorigney, a then-new theater in Paris, the ensemble performed Yamash'ta's lengthy compositions "Red Buddha" and "The Man from the East" nightly until January 1973. After leaving the Red Buddha Theater, Yamash'ta continued to work with Come to the Edge, a jazz-rock band featuring drummer Morris Pert, electric pianist Peter Robinson, and bassist Alyn Ross, and also performed with Red Buddha. Yamash'ta reached his commercial peak after forming the jazz-fusion group Go in 1976. They recorded three albums before disbanding the following year: Go, Go Live from Paris, and, after Winwood left, Go Too. Although he temporarily withdrew from music in 1980 and moved into a Buddhist temple, Yamash'ta recorded the cosmic-minded album Sea and Sky in 1983, featuring synthesizers, taped sound effects, orchestral instruments, and percussion.

what to buy: A summit meeting of innovative musicians from throughout the world, *Go Live from Paris* ♫♫♫ (Island, 1976, prod. Stomu Yamash'ta) was recorded during a concert performance on June 12, 1976.

what to buy next: The soundtrack *Red Buddha* ♫♫♫ (Vanguard, 1974, prod. Stomu Yamash'ta) best illuminates Yamash'ta's unique blending of Japanese traditions and Western influences.

the rest:
Contemporary ♫♫ (L'oiseau, 1972)
The Man from the East ♫♫♫ (Island, 1973)
Freedom Is Frightening ♫♫♫ (Island, 1973)
One by One ♫♫ (Island, 1974)
Raindog ♫♫ (Island, 1974)
Go ♫♫♫ (Island, 1976)
Go Too ♫♫♫ (Arista/One Way, 1977)
Sea and Sky ♫♫♫ (Kuckuck, 1984)
Solar Dream, Vol.1: The Eternal Present ♫♫ (Kosei, 1993)
Solar Dream, Vol. 2: Fantasy of Sanukit ♫♫ (Kosei, 1993)

influences:
◀◀ Tangerine Dream, Pink Floyd, Karlheinz Stockhausen

▶▶ Airto Moreira, Nana Vasconcelos

Craig Harris

Yat-Kha
Tuvan folk-rock
Formed 1991, in Tuva. Based in Tuva.

Albert Kuvezin, vocals, guitar, shanzi, yat-kha, khomuz, bass; Aldyn-ool Sevek, vocals, morin-huur; Alexei Saaia, bass shanzi, morin-huur; Zhenya Tkach'v, drums, vocals. (All members are from Tuva.)

Named for a zither-like instrument featured in its music, Yat-Kha is a unique group that combines the ancient folk traditions of Tuva—the Central Asian republic best known for its distinctive, unearthly style of "throat-singing"—with Western pop and rock sounds. Yat-Kha was formed by Albert Kuvezin, a founding member of unlikely throat-singing supergroup Huun-Huur-Tu, who sought to break free from the narrow folkloric interpretations of Tuvan music imposed by the Soviet Union, which controlled the republic from 1944 until its own collapse in the early '90s. To that end, Kuvezin made the somewhat radical decision to include rock instruments like electric guitars, bass, and trap drums in the band's eclectic sound, adopting a rebellious, politically charged ethos that favors lyrics about pride, freedom, and independence. After winning the prestigious Grand Jury Prize from Radio France Internationale's "Rock and Pop in the East" competition in 1996 and performing at Austin's South by Southwest music conference in 1997, a copy of the group's album *Yenisei-Punk* (which had risen as high as #2 on the European world-music charts) found its way into the hands of Chieftains leader Paddy Moloney, who quickly signed them to a multi-album deal with his label, Wicklow Records.

what's available: The band's only Stateside release, *Dalai Beldiri* ♫♫♫♫ (Wicklow, 1999, prod. Lu Edmonds), is a mesmerizing piece of work that takes Tuva's ancient shamanic roots several daring steps into the future, subtly mixing in elements of pop, rock, dub, and (yikes!) even funk to create a wholly original, almost surrealistically exotic sound that somehow manages to work. Kuvezin and Sevek both prove adept masters at a variety of throat-singing styles, including *sygyt, kargiraa,* and *khöömei,* with Kuvezin's impossibly low-pitched drones standing in impressive contrast to the rich, warm tenor of Sevek (whose fitting name literally means "Golden Boy"). But however deep this rooting in ancient ways, nearly every song here offers an interesting modern twist, from the hypnotically echoing guitar of "Khemchim" to the funky groove of "Kazhan Toren Karam Bolur." Along with the similarly inventive *Back Tuva Future* from Yat-Kha's sensational countryman Kongar-ool Ondar, *Dalai Beldiri* is evidence of a unique musical community increasingly unwilling to rest on tradition.

worth searching for: The band released two albums in Europe before they were signed to Wicklow. *Antropofagia* (1991) may be impossible to hunt down, but, due to its popularity, the critically acclaimed *Yenisei-Punk* (1995) may still be available in Europe.

influences:
◀◀ Huun-Huur-Tu, Oorzhak Khunashtaar-ool, Sainkho Namtchy-lak

see also: *Huun-Huur-Tu, Kongar-ool Ondar*

Bret Love

Eva Ybarra

Conjunto

Born in San Antonio, TX, USA. Based in San Antonio, TX, USA.

Conjunto is dance-band music, the accordionist and the *bajo sexto* guitarist leading the dancers in a lively evening's entertainment. Sometimes the singers with the band are women, but the band *leader*? Never—until Eva Ybarra. She's developed that prime requirement of conjunto stars, a distinctive style on the accordion, and proven herself in a still male-dominated realm. She also composes most of her own music in a field whose artists usually make their reputations as interpreters of traditional tunes. At press time she was set to build on an already burgeoning legacy with a new album on the Viva Voce label in 1999.

what to buy: Ybarra is adept at various strains of Tex-Mex music, which crosses more than a geographical border to meld the styles of Mexico's Spanish-influenced culture and immigrant Texas's Eastern European–derived one. *A Mi San Antonio* ♪♪♪♪ (Rounder, 1994, prod. Cathy Ragland) is a fine example of her lively way with *ranchera, huapago,* and polka.

the rest:
A Bailar con Eva ♪♪♪ (Hacienda, 1995)
Pobre Palomita ♪♪♪ (Hacienda, 1995)
Romance Inolvidable ♪♪♪♭ (Rounder, 1996)

influences:
◀◀ Narciso Martinez, Flaco Jimenez

Kerry Dexter

Yellowman

Dancehall, toasting

Born late 1940s, in Jamaica. Based in Jamaica.

Vocalist/deejay Yellowman (so nicknamed for his albino complexion) is an originator of toasting, the fast-talking, pre-rap style that developed in Jamaica alongside reggae. With his rapid-fire words weaving in and out of instrumental dub versions of reggae tunes or pop hits, Yellowman took toasting from the "sound systems" of Jamaica's ghettos to the international stage. Raised in a state-run orphanage, Yellowman turned to performing as an escape from the teasing he experienced for his ultra-light skin. A prolific recording artist, Yellowman has released more than 50 albums. On the downside for many listeners, he's also been at the forefront of toasting's increasing use of sexist and anti-gay themes.

what to buy: Yellowman's talent for mesmerizing an audience is evident on *Live at Reggae Sunsplash, '83* ♪♪♪ (Genes, 1983, prod. Yellowman), as he espouses his views about sex with

"Me Too Sexy," "Me Have Too Much Women," and "Get Me to the Family Court on Time"; violence with "Gunman"; and his commitment to Rastafarianism with "Jah Jah Made Us for a Purpose."

what to buy next: On *King Yellowman* ♪♪♪ (Columbia, 1984, prod. Yellowman) the title monarch tempered the sexism of "Girls Can't Do What the Guys Do" with classic tunes like "Reggae Calypso" and unique covers of Frankie Ford's "Sea Cruise" and John Denver's "Take Me Home, Country Roads."

best of the rest:
Party ♪♪♪ (RAS, 1991)
Prayer ♪♪♪ (RAS, 1994)
Divorced (For Your Eyes Only) ♪♪♪ (Burning Sounds, 1996)
Meets the Paragons ♪♪♪ (House of Reggae, 1996)
Live at Maritime Hall ♪♪♪ (Artists Only, 1998)

influences:
◀◀ Clement "Sir Coxsone" Dodd, Arthur "Duke" Reid, General Echo
▶▶ Shabba Ranks, Lavindeer

Craig Harris

Yosefa

International Middle Eastern–influenced pop

Born Yosefa Dahari in 1951, in Eilat, Israel. Based in Israel.

While Israel has produced its share of pop/rock stars whose music is just like that of the U.S. or Western Europe but for its Hebrew lyrics, other performers have emerged whose style reflects Israel's multi-ethnic character. Vocalist Yosefa Dahari is one of those artists. Born to parents of Yemenite and Moroccan descent, Yosefa's music fuses modern, high-tech dance-pop with Middle Eastern roots. She began singing while in the Israeli army, and at one performance near Lebanon had a remarkable experience. "I sang a few Yemenite songs. People on the other side of the fence heard me and understood the words. They didn't know what to think. When the song ended, there was a silence and then they began clapping. It was so very moving." Yosefa's first album, *Yosefa,* topped the European Broadcasting Union's world-music chart in May 1994. In June 1995, she appeared at Sofia, Bulgaria's International Festival Golden Orpheus, and won the audience over with "Compassion" from her second album *The Desert Speaks*; that same performance earned Yosefa a UNESCO International Music Council prize.

what's available: The singer's debut *Yosefa* ♪♪♪ (Triloka, 1993, prod. Zvika Kagan) is an homage to her Yemenite and Moroccan heritage. Several of the album's most memorable songs were written by Yemenite composer Aharon Amram, whom Yosefa cites as a major influence. There are also two traditional Moroccan songs and a traditional Yemenite one. But *Yosefa* is no simple acoustic folk recording. Yosefa and producer Kagan went for the latest high-tech rhythm grooves; many of the tracks have an aggressive dance-pop beat. The ethnic elements come from Yosefa's own singing style, from the melodies, and from the use of regional instruments like the *oud, kanoon,* and various hand drums sprinkled throughout the arrangements. *The Desert Speaks* 🎵🎵🎵 (EMI Hemisphere/metro blue, 1995, prod. Zvika Kagan) is different. It's a great fusion of pop song construction and contemporary dance-music production with Middle Eastern accents. Most of the songs are contemporary and were contributed by several songwriting teams. All of the tracks are sung in Hebrew (except for a brief English interlude in "Before the Night Is Gone"), and Yosefa does seem more comfortable in that language. In addition, the arrangements seem better fitted to Yosefa's voice than on the previous effort; the rhythm tracks are not so dominant and the other instruments—keyboards, guitars, bass, drums, percussion, violin, soprano sax, clarinet, flute, Arabic flute, accordion—are used in a more supportive way.

influences:

◀◀ Aharon Amram, Peter Gabriel, Ofra Haza

▶▶ Natacha Atlas

Ken Roseman

Masakazu Yoshizawa

Traditional Japanese folk, new age
Born in Japan. Based in Los Angeles, CA, USA.

Masakazu Yoshizawa is probably the world's best-known player of the various styles of Japanese flutes, particularly the beloved *shakuhachi.* Trained at the Tokyo University of Fine Arts, Yoshizawa now resides in California and works in numerous areas of the music industry. In addition to composing for himself, he has played on a diverse roster of soundtracks including *Jurassic Park* and *Teenage Mutant Ninja Turtles III.* He performs as a soloist, and also works with the innovative trio Kokin-Gumi, which features Hirio Hashibe on *koto* (13-string flat harp) and vocals, and Tateo Takahashi on *shamisen* (a three-stringed traditional Japanese lute). Yoshizawa has had sessions with a variety of Western musicians as well, including the Crusaders, R. Carlos Nakai, and Berlin.

what to buy: *Kyori (Innervisions)* 🎵🎵🎵 (Fortuna, 1998, prod. Masakazu Yoshizawa), Yoshizawa's American major label debut, is a fusion of traditional sounds and more contemporary explorations, featuring two solo tracks and two collaborations with new age keyboardist Osamu Kitajima.

the rest:

Yu (Play) 🎵🎵🎵 (Soundcastle)

solo outings:

Kokin Gumi:

Sorin 🎵🎵🎵 (Sound Castle, 1995)

Wakyo (Sound of Japan) 🎵🎵🎵 (Sound Castle, 1997)

influences:

▶▶ R. Carlos Nakai

Michael Parrish

Yothu Yindi

Aboriginal rock, worldbeat
Formed 1986, in Yolngu homelands, Arnhem Land, Australia. Based in Sydney, Australia.

Mandawuy Yunupingu, guitar, vocals; Witiyana Marika, bilma, dance, vocals; Makuma Yunupingu, yidaki, vocals, bilma; Stuart Kellaway, bass; Mangatjay Yunupingu, dance; Banula Marika, vocals, dance; Bunimbirr Marika, yidaki; Cal Williams, guitar; Natalie Gillespie, vocals; Galarrwuy Yunupingu, vocals, bilma, clan leader; Milkayngu Munuggurr, yidaki; Gurrumul Yunupingu, guitar, vocals, keyboards; Jodie Cockatoo, vocals. (All members are from Australia.)

Yothu Yindi was created by singer/guitarist Mandawuy Yunupingu to explore a fusion of Yolngu (Aboriginal Australian) and Balanda (non-Aboriginal) music and introduce the world to the beauties of an Aboriginal culture, which can trace itself back about 60,000 years. Yunupingu is from Northeast Arnhem Land and the band's name means "child and mother," which refers to the kinship relations between various segments of the Yolngu people. Many of the tunes the band performs are based on the traditional songs of the Gumati and Rirratjingu clans of Northeast Arnhem Land, and incorporate *bilma* (clapsticks that sound similar to Cuban *claves*) and *yidaki* (or *didgeridoo,* the mesmerizing blown instrument whose synthesizer-like sounds have increasingly captivated the West). The band's choreography is also based on traditional dances that mimic crocodiles, wallabies, brolga, and other indigenous animals. "We operate on two levels of reality," says Mandawuy, who's also the band's leader and spokesperson. "One is restricted (sacred); the other is unrestricted (public). That's why I can come into the white man's world, then go back to my world without fear of losing it. I'm using white skills and Yolngu skills to make a new beginning."

what's available: *Tribal Voice* 🎵🎵🎵 (Hollywood, 1992, prod. Mark Moffatt) is a pleasing folk/rock excursion with some Aboriginal flavoring. The most interesting tracks are the four examples of traditional singing and didgeridoo playing, which open non-Aboriginal ears to a startling beauty. Recorded after their amazing success down under, *Freedom* 🎵🎵🎵 (Hollywood, 1996, prod. Lamar Lowder) takes a slightly more mainstream approach, but the didgeridoo and tribal vocals are still evident.

influences:

◀◀ Midnight Oil

▶▶ Alan Dargin

j. poet

Mary Youngblood

Native American flute
Born in Seattle, WA, USA. Based in USA.

"I believe these songs came from those who walked before me. I am simply a vessel between the creator and this sacred instrument," says Mary Youngblood of her work on the Native American flute. In Native American culture and in contemporary Native recordings, the flute is typically played by men, but Youngblood did not let that deter her from exploring the instrument. Of Seminole and Aleut ancestry, she did not start out on the Native variety, however—she was classically trained on several others including the transverse flute, and also developed as a singer, finding inspiration in the voices of James Taylor, Ella Fitzgerald, and Karen Carpenter. Youngblood's compositions on the Native American flute were first introduced to nationwide audiences in the United States on the PBS special *American Indian Circles of Wisdom* and in the film *Naturally Native.*

what's available: *The Offering* ✍✍✍✍ (Silver Wave, 1998, prod. James Marienthal, Tom Wasinger, Mary Youngblood) is Native American flute stripped to the essence; just the instrument, the breath, and the ideas of the composer. Youngblood's 17 original compositions were recorded deep inside the Moaning Caverns in California, and the resonances and subtle water sounds add just enough atmosphere to allow you to imagine being there. She employs several types of flutes to express her ideas on such subjects as first love, the gift of music, the places and people in her life, and the winds of change. This is the first disc a Native American woman has recorded on Native flutes for national distribution, and as such, Youngblood's work has been compared to that of the premier male Native American flutist, R.Carlos Nakai—and it meets the comparison.

influences:

◀◀ Buffy Sainte-Marie, Wolfgang Amadeus Mozart, James Taylor, Ella Fitzgerald, Karen Carpenter

Kerry Dexter

Atahualpa Yupanqui

South American folk, nueva canción
Born Héctor Chavero on January 31, 1908, in El Campo de la Cruz, Argentina. Died 1992, in Paris, France.

Along with Antonio Pantoja, Victor Jara, and Violetta Parra, Atahualpa Yupanqui can be counted as one of the founders of the *nueva canción* ("new song") movement that promoted an awareness of South American folk culture through research, composition, and performance. It was in doing such research that Yupanqui and others experienced the richness of Andean folk music and the poverty of the people living in the Andes. This led to writing and concertizing songs rooted in the modes and lives of Andean peoples, inspiring the careers of musicians like Inti-Illimani and Mercedes Sosa. It also led to exile, voluntary and otherwise, for some of these performers as the military juntas in power at the time took umbrage at the lyrical content of songs describing the conditions of the downtrodden.

Born Héctor Chavero, Yupanqui took his stage name from the last of the Inca kings. He learned how to play the violin and guitar before he was 10, wrote his first serious poems at the age of 14, and composed his landmark "Caminito del Indio (The Path of the Indian)" when he was only 19. Yupanqui first tried getting work as a journalist, despite having little in the way of formal education. When that didn't work out he traveled around South America, visiting Argentine provinces along the Andean spine before exploring Bolivia, Peru, Venezuela, Ecuador, Columbia, and Chile, documenting the musical traditions of rural peoples. Their rhythms, the *zamba,* the *chacarera,* and the *milonga,* inspired his music while their lives helped inform his poetry. Yupanqui made himself into a regular renaissance man, publishing his first book of poetry (*Piedra Sola*) in 1940 and unveiling his first play (*Cerro Bayo*) in 1943. He would later write books in a variety of idioms, including many volumes of poetry, an autobiographical sketch (*El Canto del Viento*), and essays on Japan (where he toured in 1968), the music of the Andes, and the French writer LaFontaine. Yupanqui's first trip to France took place in 1948, when he appeared on stage with Edith Piaf prior to touring around Europe in 1949. He was so impressed with his reception by the French during the course of his frequent European treks that he finally moved to Paris in the early 1960s. In 1986, the French government bestowed upon Yupanqui the title of Knight of the Order of Arts and Letters for his life's work as a musician and voice of social conscience. Looking back during an interview that took place a few days before he died (with Manuel Osorio for the *UNESCO Courier*), Yupanqui noted that "I contribute what I have—my songs, a touch of atmosphere, of color, the sufferings and the hopes of my native land, that immense continent we know as Latin America."

what to buy: *Thirty Years of Singing* ✍✍✍✍✍ (Chant du Monde, 1992, prod. Robert Prudon) is the best place to start exploring Yupanqui's catalog. Everything heard here is distilled from the monumental five-disc set *L'Integrale Atahualpa Yupanqui*, and it serves as a superb career sampler that will leave you hungering for more. The classic "Duerme Negrito" is worth the price alone. *Camino del Indio: Sus Primeros Exitos, 1942–1944* ✍✍✍

(Blue Moon, 1995, prod. various) is well recorded and mastered, revealing early versions of understated musical masterpieces (the title tune, "Viento, Viento" and "Me Voy"). Yupanqui was just starting to unveil his political agenda during these years, but there was still time for a few instrumentals ("Malambo," "Vidala del Silencio," and "Huajra") based on Andean folk melodies and emphasizing his skills as a guitarist more than his wordplay.

what to buy next: Be careful! There is a Yupanqui album out there, *La Zamba Perdida* (Blue Moon, 1996), which contains the same performances as *El Poeta* ♫♫♫ (ANS, 1997), and in the same order, but at a higher price. That said, this is a good companion for either of the albums listed above, and the singing and playing is fine. The sonics of these Argentinean recordings are a tad constricted when compared to the later Paris ones, but not enough to affect a listener's enjoyment.

the rest:
Don Ata ♫♫♫ (Tropical Music, 1992)
Y Su Guitarra ♫♫♫ (Legacy Latino, 1996)
(With Antonio Pantoja y su Conjunto) *Se poblaban de musica los Andes...* ♫♫♫♫ (Blue Moon, 1996)
Amistad ♫♫♫♫ (ANS, 1996)

worth searching for: *L'Integrale Atahualpa Yupanqui* ♫♫♫♫ (Chant du Monde, 1992, prod. Robert Prudon) is a five-disc set that covers all the material Yupanqui recorded with Prudon during the years 1968–1980. You will never find another batch of recordings that so fully documents his genius. It even includes the remarkable 726-verse poem/song "El payador perseguido," which times out at over 41 minutes!

influences:
◄◄ Antonio Pantoja
►► Mercedes Sosa

see also: *Mercedes Sosa*

Garaud MacTaggart

Zaiko Langa Langa
Congolese rumba-rock, soukous
Formed 1969, in Kinshasa, Zaire (now Congo). The two groups now using this name work between Kinshasa, Congo, and Brussels, Belgium.

Enormous, often undocumented membership over the years. Some key members have included: N'Yoka Longo, vocals; Lengi-Lenga, vocals; Papa Wemba, vocals; Bimi Ombale, vocals; J.P. Buse, vocals; Matima, lead guitar; Manuaku Waku, lead guitar; Beninko Poli, lead guitar; Petit Poisson, lead guitar; Zangilu Beniko, lead guitar; Enoch Zamuangana, guitar; Jimmy Yaba, guitar; Avedila, guitar; Popolipo, guitar; Muaka "Oncle" Bapius, bass; Kabama Vonvon, bass; Meri-Jo, drums; Belobi, drums; Bakunde, drums. (All members are from Congo.)

In 1969, electric African rumba had become the most widely disseminated dance music on the continent. Rumba's epicenter was the city of Kinshasa, the bustling, sleepless capital of Zaire, now the Democratic Republic of Congo. In Kinshasa's musical quarter, Matonge, rumba blared from clubs and record shops 24 hours a day. That was the year that a group of high school students decided to weigh in with a rougher, readier take on the sound. The new group paid its dues to rumba giants like Franco and Le Grand Kalle, but also took into account international forces like the Rolling Stones and American soul. They called the band Zaiko Langa Langa, which roughly translates as "Zaire of our ancestors." Zaiko's rumba-rock shook the Kinshasa music colossus at its roots, and for the next 15 years—the very years when the Zaire sound would travel all over the world under the name *soukous*—Zaiko remained the standard by which all others were measured.

Theirs was an inclusive sound that amalgamated the best of older rumba with strong folkloric elements and aggressive modernity. It was also tremendously disciplined music. Zaiko's songs began with slow rumba, but turned on sharp arranging points, moving first to a mid-tempo section with interactive, harmonized vocals involving up to five singers, and then to the diabolical *seben* section, where the snare drum snapped out a propulsive beat, guitars tangled ecstatically, and the singers chanted clever phrases of "animation" and rallied club audiences with outrageous choreography. Guitars came to the fore in the Zaiko sound, while horns went by the wayside. Indigenous rhythms fit with then-President Mobutu's doctrine of "authenticity," while designer clothes reflected a desire to appropriate foreign fashion. Most of all, dancers demanded the Zaiko seben style in clubs all over Africa.

Driven by fierce competition for better songs, better dances, better chants, better clothes, and more surprises in the musical arrangements, Zaiko's sound led the way into a period of rich innovation by all Kinshasa bands. Inevitably, the competition took its toll on Zaiko. Singing star Papa Wemba was one of the first to leave and make his own band, Viva la Musica. Lead guitarist Manuaku Waku followed suit by creating Grand Zaiko Wawa, and Langa Langa Stars became another spinoff. Coming into the 1990s, the core band split, with singer-composer N'Yoka Longo keeping the original name and singers J.P Buse and Lengi-Lenga creating Zaiko Langa Langa Familia Dei. All of this bifurcation makes the mountains of Zaiko-related recordings something of a puzzle, but it's a puzzle well worth grappling with. For Zaiko is more than a band. It is a sub-genre of Zairian music, and it represents one of the most creative and influential movements in modern African dance pop.

what to buy: *L'Authenticite* ✍✍✍✍ (Disques Esperance/Sonodisc, 1992) is a particularly excellent example of the full-force early-'80s Zaiko magic. *Zaire-Ghana 1976* ✍✍✍✍ (Retroafric, 1993, prod. Henri Bowane) goes back even further with a powerful, raw snapshot of the original band live in the studio.

what to buy next: *Out of Africa* ✍✍✍ (Sabam), by the Familia Dei Zaiko, and *Jetez L'Eponge* ✍✍✍ (Carrere, prod. Prozal), by N'Yoka Longo's Zaiko, are fine examples of the two bands' slicker, more high-tech 1990s sounds. Turn-on-a-dime arranging, lush vocals, and deep grooves still put the Zaiko stamp on the music.

influences:

◀◀ Franco/OK Jazz, Thu Zaina

▶▶ All modern soukous acts

see also: *Franco, Papa Wemba*

Banning Eyre

Zamfir

Romanian folkloric, international popular instrumental
Born 1941, in Romania. Based in Romania.

Zamfir, master of the panpipe (or pan flute) and star of constant late-night television commercials hawking his proto-new-age albums, has a first name—it's Gheorghe. He has a nationality—he's Romanian. He even has a long history as a recording artist, first charting in Britain with the 1976 hit "Doina De Jale," the melody of which was lifted from a traditional eastern European funeral piece. Most important, Zamfir has a following as one of the world's premier easy-listening artists, integrating folk melodies and classical compositions into his soothing soundscapes. He has also recorded a significant amount of film music, most notably the compositions of soundtrack innovator Ennio Morricone (*The Good, the Bad, and the Ugly*).

what to buy: On *Lonely Shepherd* ✍✍✍ (Mercury, 1984, prod. Jean-Pierre Hebrard, Will Hoebee, James Last), Zamfir turns his flute magic on a collection of pop standards new and old, including the Bee Gees' "Run to Me," Charles Chaplin's "Theme from Limelight," and Andrew Lloyd Webber's "Don't Cry for Me, Argentina."

what to buy next: Zamfir is still plying his panpipe trade on *Gypsy Passion* ✍✍✍ (Special Music, 1995), which is something of a departure from his romantic standards into a more focused

folk-music setting. Also of particular interest for readers of this book are two other more traditionally based releases, *Folksongs from Rumania* ✍✍✍ (Laserlight, 1991) and *Midsummer Night Dreams* ✍✍✍ (Foulane, 1996), which revisit his roots both culturally (they're heavy on the Romanian folk tunes) and commercially (several of the mournful *doinas* with which he first made his name are included).

what to avoid: *Romance of the Pan Flute* ✍✍ (Philips, 1982) isn't abysmal, but you can get better quality Zamfir elsewhere. And who really needs to hear pan flute covers of the Beatles' "Yesterday," Elton John's "Your Song," or Billy Joel's "Just the Way You Are"?

the rest:

Fantasy: Romantic Favorites for Pan Flute ✍✍✍ (Laserlight, 1985)

worth searching for: *The Ennio Morricone Anthology: A Fistful of Film Music* ✍✍✍✍ (Rhino/BMG, 1995, prod. David McLees) features Zamfir's magic flute in the context of the film composer's work, along with other Morricone themes and songs performed by artists such as Joan Baez, Baldo Maestri, and Alessandro Allessandroni.

influences:

◀◀ Gandalf, Paul Winter

▶▶ Vangelis, Yanni, John Tesh

Ben Greenman

Zap Mama

Folkloric worldbeat, international roots-pop
Formed 1990, in Brussels, Belgium. Based in Brussels, Belgium.

Varying membership on record and stage throughout the years, including: Marie Daulne, vocals, percussion; Cécilia Kankonda, vocals (1990–94); Céline 'T Hooft, vocals (1990–93); Sabine Kabongo, vocals (1990–96); Sylvie Nawasadio, vocals (1990–96); Marie Cavanaile, vocals (1993–94); Sally Nyolo, vocals, percussion (1994–96); Marie Afonso (1994–96); Tanya Saw, vocals (1997–present); Angelique Wilkie, vocals (1997–present); Wahtanga Rema, vocals (1997–present); Lene Norgaard Christensen, vocals (1997–present); Manou N'Guessan, bass, vocals (1997–present); Bilo Donneux, drums (1997–present). (Members are from countries throughout Africa and Europe.)

You think you've got problems? Everybody does, and for those who suspect they don't have enough there's always the American rock 'n' pop industry, where lovelorn longing and teenage angst are permanent best-sellers. The figurative blues-singing of suburbanites finds its doppelganger in the music of Zap Mama, whose founder, Marie Daulne, has morphed the most traumatic of childhoods into the most spirit-lifting of songs.

When her Belgian father perished in the civil strife and anti-European backlash that followed her homeland of Zaire (now

Congo)'s liberation from his, Daulne's Bantu mother (then pregnant with Marie) and her three other children fled to the forest Pygmy communities for sanctuary. There the young Marie learned ways of social and environmental harmony against formidable odds, and was introduced to ways of making stunning art with humble means. Going on to spend much of her upbringing in Belgium, Daulne remembers that it was ironically her mother who encouraged her and her siblings' integration with European society, while the white side of the family inspired her to explore her African heritage, which she did on later return visits to the Pygmies while also establishing a music career. Eventually the cultural convergences in her own makeup, in the bi-continental life she led, and in the cosmopolitan surroundings where she lived most of it, were personified by the multiracial (and often mixed-race) ensemble with which she changed the international pop landscape: Zap Mama. Their eponymous debut, released Stateside as volume one in the Luaka Bop label's Adventures in Afropea series, is one of the all-time best-selling and most critically acclaimed world-music albums in the U.S. With it, Zap Mama became the standard to which every subsequent culture-crossing band would be compared.

Aiming from the start to dynamically mix African and European influences in art as they had in life, the outfit chose a name that conjured both the telecommunications age and humanity's origins. Sticking to a phenomenal *a cappella* sound for much of their career, Zap Mama's music often evoked technology (sometimes enthusiastically, sometimes satirically) while always announcing their independence from it (a statement that persisted even after their sparing adoption of mostly acoustic instruments). All they ever needed were their ideas—astonishingly varied in both concept and sonics on disc, and on stage rivaling the most blockbuster pyrotechnics with nothing but smart choreography and costuming. Zap Mama's optimistic polyglot groove was an instant and deserved hit, drawing on the musics of Africa, Jamaica, Cuba, the Middle East, India, Aboriginal Australia, medieval and contemporary Europe, African America, and beyond, and singing to nearly every conceivable audience in its own language at one time or another—but in any case communicating a buoyant energy that needed no translation. The band has an unerring instinct for global-jukebox rainbows of sound that go straight to your subconscious Top 10, and its members' multitude of cultural backgrounds—and Daulne's educational one as a degreed ethnomusicologist—have allowed them to touch a striking breadth of bases with authority and discretion; awesome but never overwhelming, eclectic but never perfunctory. Daulne's considerable talents as a leader of women prompted a reconfiguration of Zap Mama into much more of a solo project for the third (and, at this writing, most recent) release, and the music suffered from the decrease in communal

input. But the album still had its share of gems, and there's no reason not to expect at least as many from the 1999 follow-up and others to come.

what to buy: Zap Mama showed an entire generation of world-beaters how it's done, and *Adventures in Afropea 1: Zap Mama* ♫♫♫♫ (Luaka Bop, 1993, prod. Vincent Kenis) was too prescient to not sound as fresh now as the day it was released. Whether in the service of sublime song or jaw-dropping sound effects, the Mamas' vocal abilities amaze from start to finish, showing an equal command of chant, madrigal, Cuban *son,* African reggae, swing, and soul balladry. The band is particularly impressive—moving, even—on the Congolese folkloric material (which rescues ethereal women's worksongs from archival obscurity) and the Pygmy chants—one of the *original* "ambient" styles, invoking the forest's animal and elemental sounds and evoking its eternal calm, which must have come as a comfort to Daulne in her literal wilderness years, and which she and her band do great justice. Throughout the album the Mamas recreate an orchestra of instruments and innovate a spectrum of ryhthms, oddly effective vocalese, and, on one memorable occasion, the sputters, honks, and crashes of a traffic jam and pileup. Infectious grooves, one-world positivity, jokes, and a car chase—what more could you ask for? *Sabsylma (What's Your Name?)* ♫♫♫♫ (Luaka Bop, 1994, prod. Marie Daulne) provided an answer, and yet another forehead-smiting for anyone who'd thought the band was out of surprises. An exhilarating musical-chairs of Islamic, Aboriginal, and Indian explorations; airborne continental pop; African folk; and the two English-language smashes, "Mr. Brown" (a backhanded organic hip-hop homage to James) and the title tune, the album cemented Zap as a many-hit wonder. A tendency towards overwrought political laments starts here, but not for many minutes of the overall running time. And in addition to opening numerous ears to a whole 'nother planet-full of music, with the aforesaid title track the band anticipates—and outdoes—the neo-swing craze by half a decade.

what to buy next: On *7* ♫♫♫♫ (Luaka Bop, 1997, prod. various), the now ostensibly solo Daulne's academic leanings sometimes dry out her songwriting, while political overstatement pounds some other songs flat. Of the album's two bids for single-dom, a cutesy reading of Phoebe Snow's "Poetry Man" is unforgivable, but an impassioned rendition of the blues standard "Damn Your Eyes" is unforgettable. Which, though it's the song that closes the album, is as good a way as any of leading into this set's many other strengths. Daulne's stylistic sweeps bring in some of the most astonishing inter-genre innovations on any Zap album, including the rap-in-Morocco masterwork "Baba Hooker" (one of many fruits of Daulne's recurrent collaborations with world-hop leader Michael Franti of Spearhead);

Zap Mama

the riveting Afro-Caribbean-Islamic footrace of "Jogging a Tombouctou"; the stark, atonal cabaret jazz of "Timidity"; the dazzling rhythmic complexity, tribal scat, and horror drone of the suite-like "Warmth"; and much more. Daulne's voice alone can't do as much as she thinks it can, but she still gets a lot of good help; and the instruments aren't really needed, but sure don't get in the way.

the rest:
A Ma Zone N/A (Luaka Bop, 1999)

worth searching for: Both as a unit and as a pseudonym for Daulne, Zap Mama has guided a number of like-minded pioneers—most notably Spearhead, Vinx, and the Roots—across stylistic borders. A fine example of the results can be heard on Spearhead's *Chocolate Supa Highway* 🎵🎵🎵🎵 (Capitol, 1997, prod. Michael Franti), on which Daulne lends distinctive and unearthly vocals to "Comin' to Gitcha."

influences:
◀◀ Miriam Makeba, Mahotella Queens

▶▶ Les Go de Koteba, Sally Nyolo

see also: *Sally Nyolo, Spearhead, Vinx*

Adam McGovern

Hukwe Zawose

Tanzanian traditional

Born 1940, in Doduma, Tanzania. Based in Bagamoyo, Tanzania, and London, England.

Hukwe Zawose is a national treasure of mythic proportions in his homeland of Tanzania. With a voice that can freely range five octaves and virtuoso marimba and thumb-piano playing, not to mention his academic work, Zawose is a vital force in the traditional music of his country. Somehow he also managed to find time to father 15 children by four wives. A larger-than-life character, Zawose performs with his son Charles in a bright costume of coral-bead jewelry, headdress, feathered skirt, and ankle bells. Zawose and his son hold their thumb pianos at waist height and jangle their ankle bells as they dance in time to the music. The *kalimba,* or thumb piano, is a wooden box whose stiff metal keys are plucked to effect a clockwork plunk amplified by the wooden casement. The piano can be played very rapidly with only two thumbs. This is Zawose's most distinctive sound, though his resonant throat singing is matched only by traditions in Tuva.

Zawose is not modest about his reputation, as he writes in the liner notes to the album *Chibite* : "As a young man my voice was so sweet that people would often cry when I sang. In fact, sometimes I would hear myself and even I would cry," he boasts, redeeming himself in conclusion, "wondering what I had done to deserve such a precious gift." Zawose grew up as a cattle herder and that background imbues his music with a love of the land and a profound connection to folk traditions, unlike the pop stars of Dar Es Salaam. Inspired by his older brother, Zawose originally took up the marimba, then switched to the stringed *izeze*, an instrument favored by his father, adding nine extra strings to suit his rapid-fire finger picking. Tanzania's first president, Julius Nyerere, heard of the boy's reputation, and called him to the state residence in Dar Es Salaam. Mixing traditional stories with political celebration (no wonder the president took a liking to him), his style is called *wagogo*. While Tanzanian pop music can sound similar to tunes from Kenya and the Congo, the traditional music is unique. Zawose has only one release available in the U.S., and at most record stores it will be the only example of his country's rich folkloric tradition.

what's available: On *Chibite* ♪♪♪♪ (RealWorld, 1996, prod. Richard Evans), the lyrics to "Sisitizo La Amani Duniani" reflect on the lessons from the horror of Hiroshima, but Zawose's music is not all grand statements. "Nyangawuya" is a macabre tale of a man whose sister-in-law so calms his baby that he beheads her so as to always be able to use the familiar face to stop the baby's crying. The gruesome subject matter is belied by the upbeat music. Other tracks have no particular meaning, like the polyphony of "Chilumi," which recalls Pygmy chants.

worth searching for: The Master Musicians of Tanzania's two albums, *The Art of Hukwe Zawose* ♪♪♪♪ (JVC/Victor Japan) and *Tanzania Yetu and Mateso* ♪♪♪♪ (Triple Earth U.K.), both spotlight Zawose's resonant thumb-piano playing. The group is also referred to as the National Musical Ensemble of Tanzania.

influences:

◀◀ Remmy Ongala, Nuta Jazz Band

▶▶ Vijana Jazz Band

David Poole

Tom Zé

MPB (Brazilian Popular Music)

Born Antonio José Santana Martins, 1937, in Irara, Brazil. Based in Sao Paulo, Brazil.

Tom Zé ("zee-ay") is one of Brazil's most unique—and some say oddest—singer-songwriters. He has used electric blenders, manual typewriters, and floor-polishers as rhythm instruments, and his surrealistic lyrics, unique vocal phrasing, and disjointed sense of rhythm place him far outside the mainstream of Brazilian music; a strange but compelling mixture of John Cage, Villa-Lobos, Brecht, and Frank Zappa.

Zé was born in a small town in Bahia, which is one of Brazil's poorest provinces, though it's also known for the richness of its Afro-Brazilian culture. He had to move to Salvador as a teenager because there was no high school in his hometown. He wasn't a good student, but when a guitar-playing friend showed him a song he'd written himself, Zé saw the light. He bought his own instrument and began composing. One of Zé's first public performances set the tone for his coming career. He appeared on a pop TV show called *Escada Para O Sucesso*—"Stairway to Success." He composed a song for the occasion, "Rampa Para O Fracasso"—"Ramp to Failure"—and followed it up with others satirizing the city's political realities. The show provided entrée to a group of young, radical performers and songwriters, including future stars like Gilberto Gil, Gal Costa, and Caetano Veloso. In addition, Zé entered the College of Music at the University of Bahia and studied composition, counterpoint, harmony, piano, guitar, and cello.

Zé was preparing for his finals in 1967, and was on the verge of becoming established as a classical player of note, when Veloso suggested they go to Sao Paulo and try their hand at pop music. In the next few years Zé and his friends created the *Tropicalismo* movement, which incorporated rock 'n' roll and Afro-Brazilian folkloric music in a reaction against the smooth bossa nova sound (they called their style the "intellectual samba"). He began recording his highly original compositions in 1968 on an album called *Tom Zé*, which he followed with . . . *Tom Zé* in 1970 and, um, *Tom Zé* in 1972. By the time he cut *Todos os Olhos (All the Eyes)* a few years later, he'd become interested in experimental music, and his albums began selling less and less. Although Zé was able to survive due to a strong cult following, and by writing jingles for leftist politicos, he dropped off the map as his music became more and more bizarre. By the time David Byrne released the *Best of Tom Zé* compilation in 1990, Zé was laboring in relative obscurity, even in Brazil. Zé still dislikes travel, and although he's played some European dates to support his recent Luaka Bop albums, he prefers to stay at home with his family, working on music that continues to confound and delight his listeners.

what to buy: On *Brazil Classics, Vol. 4: Best of Tom Zé* ♪♪♪♪♪ (Luaka Bop, 1990), David Byrne runs through Zé's back catalog to produce a streamlined introduction to this unique musical maverick. The album, ironically subtitled *Massive Hits,* is sparse, poetic, rhythmically challenging, and totally original,

8
3
2
benjamin zephaniah

Tom Zé

possessing all the assets great music should have. The quirks that sound odd at first begin making sense on repeated listings. Like Thelonious Monk, Zé has his own unique perception, one that makes perfect sense once you set aside your preconceptions.

what to buy next: Zé's 1998 offering, *Com Defeito de Faricaçño (Fabrication Defect)* 𝄞𝄞𝄞𝄞 (Luaka Bop, 1998, prod. Brian Martin), is his most accessible Luaka Bop outing, but that said, it still has quirks to spare. Songs can clock in at a minute or go on for five, but they're always exploring interesting territory from *farro* to *musique concrète* to the samba and the tango. The "effects" David Byrne adds to some tracks often take the music to the edge of Talking Heads territory, but Zé's skewed vision always prevails.

the rest:

The Hips of Tradition 𝄞𝄞𝄞𝄞 (Luaka Bop, 1998)

worth searching for: From the evidence of these three American albums, Zé's Brazilian work should be worth tracking down. The titles are: *Tom Zé* (1969), *Tom Zé* (1970), *Tom Zé*

(1972), *Todos os Olhos (All the Eyes)* (1974), *Estudando o Samba (Studying the Samba)* (1976), *Correio da Estação do Brás* (1978), and *Nave Marie* (1979).

influences:

◀◀ Agusto de Campos, Villa-Lobos, Jackson do Panderio

see also: *Gal Costa, Gilberto Gil, Caetano Veloso*

j. poet

Benjamin Zephaniah
Dub poetry
Born 1958, in Handsworth, Birmingham, England. Based in London, England.

Zephaniah, the U.K.'s *other* famous dub poet, is both a household name and a one-man cottage industry in England—a prolific and loquacious foil for Linton Kwesi Johnson's measured taciturnity. What sets him apart first and foremost from his more dour compatriot, though, is a highly wrought sense of the farcical and the absurd. Zephaniah prefers to document the outrages of Babylon's Albion branch in comic doggerel that's often howlingly, scathingly funny.

Like many black Britons of his generation, Zephaniah spent much of his childhood in the Caribbean (Jamaica, in his case), returning just in time for the national epidemic of racist paranoia of the late 1960s and '70s. Falling temporarily into his typecast role (the public discourse of the time criminalized all young blacks), he became a juvenile delinquent and functional illiterate. While serving a jail sentence for burglary, he underwent a spiritual epiphany, and left prison both a writer and a Rasta. Though he began his poetic career as the dreadlocked bard of neighborhood events and political rallies, the gregarious performance style he adopted for his motormouth "rants" soon gained him an appreciative national audience. He quickly developed a canny flair for self-promotion and media celebrity, and before long he was appearing on the popular soap *Eastenders* (to this day he's a dedicated community activist in East London) and writing radio plays for the BBC. By 1989, he found himself shortlisted for a poetry professorship at Oxford—prompting a virulent outbreak of tabloid bigotry of the "would-you-let-your-coed-near-this-man?" variety. These days, he's more likely to be found writing children's books for Penguin or doing commercial spots for the Vegan Council—though at press time he was also considered a long shot (or, in the incorrigibly racist parlance of the gutter press, "dark horse") for successor to Ted Hughes as Poet Laureate.

Zephaniah's poems are determinedly democratic and unapologetically oral. Composing for the most part in his head, he relies on an aesthetic that's immutably metrical and relentlessly rhyming, propelled as much by the bounciness of the English ballad stanza and the plummy inflections of white working-class speech as by the relaxed rhythms of reggae or the clipped tones of black British Pan-Caribbean Creole. While some critics mistake Zephaniah for a kind of "clown prince" of dub poetry, "court jester" would be more accurate. His mischievous, singsongy delivery belies a d(r)ead seriousness: in the middle of a genial rant, his booming bass-baritone can turn on a dime and—as befits his prophetic name—take on the roaring, declamatory sonority of an Old Testament harangue. Under cover of disarming humor, Zephaniah is always conveying some more sober critique.

worth searching for: Call it an anti–dub poetry conspiracy: since 1995, none of Zephaniah's recordings have been in print in the U.S. Though it's more slickly produced (and perhaps more commercially oriented) than much of his work, the first album to seek out is the excellent *Us an Dem* 𝄢𝄢𝄢𝄢 (Mango, 1990, prod. Paul "Groucho" Smykle). It ranges adroitly from a didactic riff on Bob Marley's call to historical literacy ("History") to an unabashed love letter to an immigrant ma ("Me Love Me Mud-

der"). In between is a wry, ska-powered reconsideration of the relative iniquity of owning and robbing banks ("Big Time Gangsters"). The show-stopper (CD version only) is the album's final cut, "Green"—an epic, *a cappella,* stentorian rail against Johnny-come-lately bourgeois environmentalists: "Fe years/Yu hav been fighting wars an destroying the scene/An now dat yu dying/Yu start turn Green." Zephaniah's early singles are difficult to find, but readily available as imports are: his first complete album, *Rasta* 𝄢𝄢𝄢𝄢 (Upright, 1983/Workers Playtime, 1990, prod. Benjamin Zephaniah), which includes the grim-humored "Dis Policeman Keeps on Kicking Me to Death," and whose CD reissue adds cuts from the 12-inch single "Free South Africa/Stop De War" (Upright, 1986), featuring the original Wailers; *Back to Roots* (Acid Jazz, 1995), which Zephaniah describes as "done the old way" with live musicians, where "once again you can hear the fingers on the strings"; and *Belly of de Beast* 𝄢𝄢𝄢𝄢 (Ariwa, 1996, prod. Mad Professor), whose thudding, bass-heavy mix will likewise satisfy reggae traditionalists. Zephaniah has also appeared on (and produced) several compilations, including the soundtrack to his television special *Dread Poets Society* 𝄢𝄢𝄢 (T'Bwana, 1993, prod. T'Bwana Sound), with Levi Tafari and Lillian Allen. In many respects his best work—where his voice really shines—is his "poetry without music": *Radical Rapping* 𝄢𝄢𝄢𝄢 (African Arts Collective, 1988/BZ Associates, 1993, prod. Benjamin Zephaniah), *Overstanding* 𝄢𝄢𝄢𝄢 (BZ Associates, prod. Benjamin Zephaniah), and *Reggae Head* 𝄢𝄢𝄢𝄢𝄢 (57 Productions, 1997), the first two being cassette-only releases. These and other items, along with audio clips of Zephaniah's work, are available at his website: www.oneworld.org/zephaniah/. His numerous books include *The Dread Affair* (Arena, 1985), *City Psalms* (Bloodaxe, 1992), and *Propa Propaganda* (Bloodaxe, 1996).

influences:
◀◀ Linton Kwesi Johnson

see also: *Lillian Allen, Linton Kwesi Johnson*

Michael Eldridge

Zimbabwe Legit
Zimbabwean rap

Akiro Ndlovu, vocals; Dumisani Ndlovu, vocals. (Both members are from Zimbabwe.)

The hook with this duo was that its members were natives of Zimbabwe who rapped in their native tongue. What Zimbabwe Legit turned out to be, though, was an exercise in whimsy by their label, Hollywood BASIC.

what's available: Their only release, *Zimbabwe Legit* 𝄢 (Hollywood BASIC, 1992, prod. various), is a tough call. The EP's lead song, "Doin' Damage in My Native Language," is completely forgettable, as are the different vocal and instrumental mixes from such producers as Black Sheep's Mista Lawnge. But the EP is completely worth the money—and might even have collector-type value, too—because of "Shadow's Legitimate Mix," a seven-minute opus that marks the official recording debut of DJ Shadow. This instrumental cut, based on Idris Muhammad's version of Grover Washington Jr.'s "Loran's Dance," was actually supposed to have vocals, but BASIC head Dave Funkenklein was so enamored of Shadow's version that he left it as is. A year later, Mo Wax's James Lavelle heard the song and was inspired to track Shadow down and sign him.

influences:

◀◀ Fab 5 Freddy, Last Poets

▶▶ DJ Shadow

Jazzbo

Jalal Zolfonun

Persian classical music

Born 1937, in Abadeh, Iran. Based in Tehran, Iran.

Jalal Zolfonun is considered a master of the *setar* (not to be confused with the North Indian sitar), a four-stringed, long-necked lute descended from the ancient Iranian *tambur,* which is credited as the ancestral form of nearly all Eastern lutes. Born into a musical family, Zolfonun studied violin with his brother before taking up the *tar* (a Middle Eastern lute) at the Tehran School of Art, and later taught himself to play setar with some instruction from the late Mousa Khan Maroufi. Inspired by early recordings of the great Persian masters, Zolfonun went on to learn from such leading heirs to the tradition as Nour Ali Khan Boroumand and Dr. Dariush Safvat. Upon completion of his university studies, he became involved with the Center for the Preservation and Propagation of Iranian Music, and soon began teaching traditional Persian music at Tehran University. Now considered among the world's finest Persian musicians, Zolfonun has apparently passed down the family legacy to his son Soheil, who has developed into a fine setar virtuoso in his own right, accompanying his father on his albums and at his international performances.

what's available: There are few recordings of authentic Persian classical music available in the U.S., which makes an album like *Kord Bayat* 𝄞𝄞𝄞𝄞 (Music of the World, 1995, prod. Gholamhosain Janati-Ataie, Bob Haddad) an absolute treasure. Accompanied by his son and percussionist Bijan Zangeneh, Zolfonun delivers dazzlingly complex melodies ripe with mysticism and magic. Much of the music has no steady beat, but rather proceeds with a pacing closely related to the rhythms of Persian poetry. Traditional Persian music is almost always devo-

tional, and one can feel a deep sense of spirituality resonating in these stately compositions. *Mystic Journey* 𝄞𝄞𝄞𝄞 (Music of the World, 1999, prod. Bob Haddad) is slightly less traditional, with significant reliance on folk motifs and a number of original compositions that utilize harmony, which is rarely found in traditional Persian music. With more significant input from Soheil and the addition of Neel Murgai on percussion, this album truly establishes the Zolfonuns as a musical force to be reckoned with.

influences:

◀◀ Mousa Khan Maroufi, Nour Ali Khan Boroumand, Dr. Dariush Safvat

▶▶ Soheil Zolfonun

Bret Love

Soheil Zolfonun

See: Jalal Zolfonun

Tappa Zukie /Tapper Zukie

Reggae, dub, toasting

Born David Sinclair, July 2, 1955, in Kingston, Jamaica. Based in Kingston, Jamaica.

A devotee of the local sound systems in Kingston's ghettos from an early age, Tappa (a.k.a. Tapper) Zukie was performing publicly, improvising his own lyrics over the latest dance tunes, by the time he was 12. He was also quickly wanted by the law, so his mother packed him off to England to steer him away from the trouble both she and he associated with the reggae scene. But once there, Zukie began his recording career at age 16. Unknown outside London's Caribbean community, his break came with a mid-'70s invitation to the Hammersmith Odeon from proto-punk singer Patti Smith. When the already-revered Smith introduced Zukie from the stage as a major influence, he became headline news overnight. Smith released Zukie's debut album on her own MER label in 1976, and his hits have kept on coming ever since, both under his own name and on his production jobs for such artists as Beres Hammond and Gregory Isaacs. Hugely influential on current dancehall rap, Zukie now heads a retail store, record-pressing plant, and label (Stars), from which he launches the latest by his own heroes like U-Roy.

what to buy: To hear Zukie's early hits check out the excellent *From the Archives* 𝄞𝄞𝄞𝄞 (RAS, 1995, prod. Tappa Zukie), which contains the classics "M.P.L.A.," "Don't Get Crazy," "Pick Up the Rocker," and the anthem to herb "Chalis to Chalis." For dub versions of those songs and more buy *In Dub* 𝄞𝄞𝄞𝄞 (Frontline, 1976/Blood & Fire, 1995, prod. Tappa Zukie), whose vibrant packaging is as award-worthy as its music. *If Deejay Was Your*

Trade: The Dreads at King Tubby's, 1974–1977 🎵🎵🎵🎵 (Blood & Fire, 1994) is worth purchasing for Zukie's one early track alone. "Jah Is I Guiding Star" is one of the most moving tracks in reggae—Zukie toasts an avowal of his Rastafarianism closer to the beat-poem confessional of Allen Ginsberg's "Howl" than any typical DJ rap. When he sings "Been down in'a Babylon a very long time/time to go home now," you can hear him choking back tears with a strong conviction behind his words.

what to buy next: Zukie's gritty voice graces roots classics on both *Deep Roots* 🎵🎵🎵 (RAS, 1996, prod. Tappa Zukie) and the latest installment on the Zukie plan, *Man from Bosrah* 🎵🎵🎵 (Stars, 1996, prod. Tappa Zukie).

worth searching for: The Zukie discography is woefully peppered with deletions, even including his fine debut *Man Ah Warrior* 🎵🎵🎵🎵 (Klik, 1974/MER, 1977). The following were printed in small runs of vinyl LPs, and would be a lucky find: *M.P.L.A.* (Klik, 1976/Frontline, 1976), *Peace in the Ghetto* (Frontline, 1979), *Tapper Roots* (Frontline, 1979), *Black Man* (Mobiliser, 1979), *Raggy Joey Boy* (Mobiliser, 1982), *Earth Running* (Mobiliser, 1983), and *Ragamuffin* (World Enterprises, 1986).

influences:

◀◀ U-Roy, I-Roy, Dennis Alcapone

▶▶ Patti Smith, Beenie Man, Josey Wales

see also: *King Tubby*

David Poole

Zulu Spear

Worldbeat, Zulu pop
Formed 1983, in Oakland, CA, USA. Based in Oakland, CA, USA.

Sechaba Mokoena, vocals, founder (South Africa); Gideon Bendile, bass, vocals; Motome Somo, vocals, percussion; Babatunde Garaya, keyboards, vocals; Paajoe Amissah, bass (South Africa); Jerome Leonard, drums, vocals (USA); Mathew Lacques, guitars; Ron Van Leewaarde, guitars, vocals (Holland).

Sechaba Mokoena, Zulu Spear's founder, main songwriter, and exuberant frontman, came to the United States from South Africa during the days of apartheid in 1981. He was one of the leads in *Ipi Tombi*, a government-sponsored South African musical that was supposed to show the world how happy black South Africans were. When the troupe played in Berkeley, California, after an eight-month run in Las Vegas, Mokoena led a mass defection and obtained political asylum in the United States. His first project thereafter was the U-Zulu Dance Theater, which combined drama, music, and dance to portray the *real* everyday lives of black South Africans. O.J. Ekemode, an expatriate superstar from Nigeria, hired the U-Zulus to sing and dance with his band, but soon after Mokoena met keyboardist Sergi

Shkurkin, an American who had played in Swahili Top 40 bands in Kenya. They formed the first version of Zulu Spear in 1983, at a time when the Bay Area's worldbeat scene was beginning to draw national attention. But despite their energetic live shows, the band's personnel remained unstable, with several mass defections of its own breaking the momentum at critical points. Zulu Spear settled down, with most of the musicians listed above, in 1990, the sole survivor of the regional worldbeat movement that had looked so promising only five years before. In one of those once-in-a-lifetime music-industry quirks of fate, Jimmy Bowen, president of Capitol Records' country music division, saw the band in a Nashville club and signed them to Liberty Records, home of Garth Brooks. They cut their debut, *Welcome to the USA,* and received the full promo treatment, but even in the post-*Graceland* era American radio still didn't have a clue about South African pop. After this brush with success the band splintered yet again: one faction continued on as Spear, while Mokoena still perseveres under the Zulu Spear banner.

what's available: *Welcome to the USA* 🎵🎵🎵 (Liberty, 1992, prod. Ron Terry, Zulu Spear) is a worthy worldbeat debut (and finale?) led by Mokoena's Otis-meets-Toots vocals, solid songwriting, and the chiming twin guitars of Mathew Lacques and Ron Van Leewaarde.

influences:

◀◀ Malathini, Boyoyo Boys, West Nkosi

▶▶ Paul Simon, Spear

j. poet

Zydeco Force

Zydeco
Formed 1987, in Lawtell, LA, USA. Based in Lawtell, LA, USA.

Jeffery Broussard, one-row and three-row accordions; Shelton Broussard, guitar; Kent Perre August, guitar; Robby "Mann" Robinson, bass; Herbert Broussard, frattoir; Raymond Thomas, drums. (All members are from USA.)

Robby "Mann" Robinson, originally from Opelousas, Louisiana, honed his chops working the northern California blues circuit with acts like Etta James. When he relocated back to his home state, he worked with local performers like Roy Carrier in Lawtell. It was there that he met Jeffery Broussard, the son of late, great Creole accordionist Delton Broussard. The two joined to create Zydeco Force in 1987. While their best playing tends to emphasize one-chord vamps and solid grooves similar to the great Lawtell Playboys, with which Delton Broussard played for years, Robinson has fueled the transition to a slicker, urban brand of zydeco that distinguishes the Force from most other rural groups in their genre.

what to buy: *It's La La Time* 𝄞𝄞𝄞 (Flat Town, 1995, prod. Robby "Mann" Robinson) shows the almost schizo nature of Zydeco Force. The traditional tunes are here, including Leo Thomas's updating of Canray Fontenot's "Tit Monde" as "Why You Wanna Make Me Cry?," and "Broken Hearted" from the repertoire of John Delafose. But the band sways between this sound and a more urban one almost cut by cut.

what to buy next: The flip between the urban and rural strains of zydeco is what makes Zydeco Force unique. On *Zydeco Push* 𝄞𝄞𝄞 (Maison de Soul, 1993, prod. Robby "Mann" Robinson), it's the more urban sound that dominates. Maybe it's just that Robinson's originals, which make up most of the set, lack the grit and funk of the more rural side this group shows in live performance.

the rest:
The Sun's Going Down 𝄞𝄞𝄞 (Maison de Soul, 1995)

worth searching for: *Zydeco Shootout at El Sid O's* 𝄞𝄞𝄞𝄞 (Rounder, 1991, prod. Scott Billington), a sampler of zydeco bands live at the famous title club, features two classics by Zydeco Force. "Madeline" is a tune made popular by Cajun fiddler and songwriter Adam Hebert, and it's syncopated into a hard-driving zydeco dance number by the group. Meanwhile, "I'm on My Way" has that odd, old, blues waltz feel that shows up in Creole music like Canray Fontenot's "Bonsoir Moreau" or Beau Jocque's "Moreau." It's a hypnotic kind of groove that is alone worth the price of the recording.

influences:
◀◀ Rockin' Dopsie, Clifton Chenier, John Delafose
▶▶ Keith Frank, Geno Delafose, Chris Ardoin

see also: *Roy Carrier, John Delafose and the Eunice Playboys, Canray Fontenot, Beau Jocque*

Jared Snyder

Zydeco Hurricanes
Zydeco, blues, R&B
Formed 1992, in Lafayette, LA, USA. Based in Lafayette, LA, USA.

Selwyn Cooper, guitar, vocals; John Wilson, accordion, vocals; Alonzo Johnson Jr., bass; Nathaniel Jolivette, drums; Adam "Razor Blade" Robinson, washboard. (All members are from USA.)

Fans of the zydeco genre know this group's pedigree well. Drummer Nathaniel Jolivette has played extensively behind Buckwheat Zydeco. Bassist Alonzo Johnson and guitarist Selwyn Cooper have both worked for Clifton Chenier and Rockin' Dopsie. A popular session man and touring pro, Cooper has also played behind such luminaries as C.J. Chenier, Lynn August, Fernest Arceneaux, and the aforementioned Buckwheat

Zydeco. The group's sound accentuates the R&B and blues side of zydeco, with Cooper's riffs running hot and free alongside John Wilson's light, soulful vocals. Though scarcely known in the Americas, the Zydeco Hurricanes have become a popular attraction at folk and blues festivals worldwide.

what's available: It's not exactly groundbreaking work, but *Louisiana Zydeco* 𝄞𝄞𝄞 (Mardis Gras, 1994, prod. Jerry Embree) is a pretty entertaining mix of guitar-based blues and churning, squeezebox zydeco. Selwyn Cooper pays tribute to his old boss Clifton Chenier on a few numbers ("I'm Coming Home," "Tante Na Na," "Do Right Sometime," "Hot Tamale Baby"), and attempts to liven up some genre standards ("Big Mamou," "The Night Time Is the Right Time") in hit-and-miss fashion. However, the finest moments on this disc are the sans-accordion straight-blues performances ("Do You Love Me," "I Woke Up This Morning"), which are rendered with heart and style.

worth searching for: Those who dig Selwyn Cooper's fluid blues guitar work and soul-oriented vocals should check out *Louisiana Swamp Blues* (The Sound of New Orleans, 1999, prod. Gary Edwards), the session wizard's first solo effort.

influences:
◀◀ Clifton Chenier, Buckwheat Zydeco, Rockin' Dopsie

see also: *Buckwheat Zydeco, C.J. Chenier, Clifton Chenier, Rockin' Dopsie*

Ken Burke

musicHound WORLD

Resources and Other Information

Compilation Albums

Books and Magazines

Web Sites

Record Labels

Concert Venues

Radio Stations

AFRICA

Adventures in Afropea 3: Telling Stories to the Sea
♪♪♪♪ (Luaka Bop/Warner Bros., 1995, compilation prod. David Byrne, Yale Evelev)

Angola, Cape Verde, São Tomé et Príncipe
genre: Coladeira, morna, funaná, Luanda merengue, bonga

Bonga (Angola); Vum Vum (Angola, Germany); Cesaria Evora (Cape Verde); André Mingas (Angola); Africa Negra (São Tomé); Waldemar Bastos (Angola); Tulipa Negra (Cape Verde, Portugal); Bana and Paulino Vieira (Cape Verde); Livity (Netherlands, Cape Verde); Pedro Ramos (Cape Verde); Jacinta Sanches (Cape Verde); Dany Silva (Cape Verde, Portugal).

The third CD in David Byrne's series of musical meetings between African and European cultures, *Telling Stories to the Sea* is a marvelous assortment of Afro-Portuguese music from Angola and two island groups just off the western coast of Africa, Cape Verde and São Tomé et Príncipe. All three nations were once Portuguese territories, and the similarities between their musical cultures reflect this common colonial heritage. Yet the exact blend of influences heard in the music of each country is unique, as if strains of melody had echoed from Portugal to Brazil and Cuba, back to the African mainland in Angola and then on to the islands, mixing with native forms and innovations along the way. Ironically, the driving force behind some of this musical diffusion was Portugal's trade in slaves and goods spanning both sides of the Atlantic, as well as a bloody war in Angola that brought thousands of Cuban troops there in the 1970s and '80s. The cultural cross-pollination set in motion by those events has made the music of "Afro-Portugal" elusive, refreshing, and sometimes baffling if you're trying to make guesses about what you're listening to. Taking São Tomé as an example, Africa Negra's dance romp "You Let the Dog Bite You"

sounds like it came straight out of Central Africa, while the lush melancholy of Cape Verdean Cesaria Evora's gorgeous "Sodade (Homesick)" displays an unmistakable debt to Brazilian music. The sultry echoes of Brazil can also be heard in Angolan Waldemar Bastos's "N Gana," and it's a delightful surprise to discover that the merengue-cum–South African jive of "Tulipa Negra" (both band name and song title) comes from Cape Verde. David Byrne once again shows his skill as a compiler, culling an exciting variety of tracks and wrapping them in a clever, amusing package, including a booklet crafted as a miniature work of art. What's more, *Telling Stories to the Sea* is one of a relatively few available discs with music from Cape Verde and São Tomé, making it an essential buy.

Jeffrey Muhr

Africa Never Stand Still ♪♪♪♪ (ellipsis arts . . . , 1994, compilation prod. Brooke Wentz)

International
genre: Tuku, krio, salegy, iscathamiya, rai, fuji, taarab, mbaqanga, marrabenta, soukous, mbira, semba, chimurenga, Luo benga, kwassa kwassa, mbalax, highlife, juju, benga

Oliver Mtukudzi (Zimbabwe); Robson Banda and the New Black Eagles (Zimbabwe); Thomas Mapfumo and the Blacks Unlimited (Zimbabwe); Stella Chiweshe and the Earthquake (Zimbabwe); Remmy Ongala and Orchestre Super Matimila (Tanzania); Zuhura Swaleh with Maulidi Musical Party (Tanzania); Abdul Tee-Jay's Rokoto (Sierra Leone); Tarika Sammy (Madagascar); Ladysmith Black Mambazo (South Africa); Lulu Masilela (South Africa); Soul Brothers (South Africa); Bellemou and Gana El Maghnaoui (Algeria); Ali Farka Touré (Mali); Oumou Sangare (Mali); Salif Keita (Mali); Mandinka Musicians (Gambia); Les Têtes Brulées (Cameroon); Chief Dr. Sikiru Ayinde Barrister and Africa's International Music Ambassadors (Nigeria); Sir Shina Peters (Nigeria); Dulce and Orchestra Marrabenta Star de Mozambique (Mozambique); Pierre Akendengue (Gabon); Baaba Maal (Senegal); Youssou N'Dour (Senegal); Pépé Kallé and Nyboma (Congo); Aurlus Mabele and Loketo (Congo); Le Zagazougou (Ivory Coast); Mendes Brothers (Cape Verde); Abdel Gadir Salim All-Stars (Sudan); Papa Wemba (Congo); Kanda Bongo Man (Congo); Ndere Troupe (Uganda); Khalifa Ould Eide and Dimi Mint Abba (Mauritania); Kapere Jazz Band (Kenya); Gabriel Omolo and His Apollo Komesha (Kenya); Farafina (Burkina Faso); Seleshe Demassae (Ethiopia); Gnawa Musicians of Marrakesh (Morocco); Martin K. Obeng (Ghana); Bonga (Angola).

There may be no better place to begin a serious study or lifelong love of African music than right here, with this marvelously eclectic, 192-minute, three-disc collection juxtaposing the continent's circa mid-'90s superstars with relatively unsung performers. Nearly all the usual suspects are here (King Sunny Adé and Fela Kuti are notable exceptions), and the selected tracks are duly representative of them. Tarika Sammy's "Eh Zalahy" thrives on call-and-response vocals, urgent rhythms, and lovely acoustic instrumental textures, while *a cappella* favorites Ladysmith Black Mambazo turn in a rising and falling tide of lush harmonies, fluttering lead singing, and clicking mouth sounds on "Ngingenwe Emoyeni," and Ali Farka Touré offers haunting guitar blues on the reggae-tinged "Heygana." Name acts from the second CD include Baaba Maal, with the flickering *kora* (African harp-lute) and expressive wailing of "Mariama"; Papa Wemba, with the liquid six-string lines, *soukous* (African rumba) rhythms, and wall of vocals and percussion on "M'Fono Yami"; and Thomas Mapfumo, with the throaty singing and tricky *chimurenga* beat of "Mhondoro." The final disc offers such favorites as the sparkling electric-acoustic instrumental textures and hybrid *kwassa kwassa* dance groove of Kanda Bongo Man's "Sai"; the exotic funk punch of Salif Keita's "Nyanafin" (with keyboard support from Weather Report founder Joe Zawinul); and the beehive of swirling sonics on Youssou N'Dour's "Fakastalu." Contributions from other justly or should-be-famous artists like Oliver Mtukudzi; Les Têtes Brulées; Dulce and Orchestra Marrabenta Star de Mozambique; Pépé Kallé and Nyboma; Robson Banda and the New Black Eagles; the Mendes Brothers; the Gnawa Musicians of Marrakesh; Martin K. Obeng; Sir Shina Peters; and Aurlus Mabele and Loketo number among the other highlights of this 39-song spectacular. Food for the soul and fuel for the feet are to be found everywhere on the beautifully packaged set, accompanied by an informative 48-page booklet packed with musician biographies and revealing photos.

Philip Booth

African Tranquility ♫♫♫ (Shanachie, 1996, compilation prod. Al Evers)

Senegal, Uganda, Algeria, Mali, Madagascar, South Africa, Sudan, Guinea
genre: Folk/traditional

Musa Dieng Kala (Mawahibou); Samite of Uganda (Uganda); Vieux Diop (Senegal); Baly Othmani & Steve Shehan (Algeria/USA); Tunde Jegede (Mali/UK); Mahaleo (Madagascar); Geoffrey Oryema (Uganda); Rossy (Madagascar); Ladysmith Black Mambazo (South Africa); Tarika Sammy (Madagascar); Hamza El Din (Sudan); Sona Diabate (Guinea).

"The Contemplative Soul of Africa," this is subtitled, and if you just want to mellow out, here you go. But if you're looking for something not just tranquil but involving, this compilation shoots blanks half the time. Its first half is mostly boring (exception: "Jali," an arresting trance-out by Senegal's Vieux Diop), crossing the wrong side of the fine line between meditative calm and dull new-age noodling—it's sure to make some listeners feel Culturally Significant, but it doesn't do jack for the rest of us. The second half is better, starting with Ugandan Geoffrey Oryema's "Makombo," a drop-dead gorgeous blues surrounded by pools of subtle echo, and peaking (of course) with a Ladysmith Black Mambazo hymn. But if you're really looking to bliss out Motherland-style, skip *African Tranquility* and buy Ladysmith's *Classic Tracks*, one of the loveliest albums ever assembled. And if you get *Tranquility* as part of Shanachie's *African Heartbeat* box set, the tracks to include on your mix tape are 3-7-8-9-10. Got that? Good.

Michaelangelo Matos

The Arthur S. Alberts Collection: More Tribal, Folk, and Café Music of West Africa ♫♫♫♫ (Rykodisc, 1998)

International
genre: African folk music

Performers from the following tribes: Malinke (Guinea); Mano (Liberia); Igbo (Nigeria); Ashanti (Ghana); Baule (Ivory Coast); Fanti (Ghana); Loma (Liberia); Bindendela (Congo); Bobo-Dioulasso (Burkina Faso).

Listening to this batch of vintage field recordings—released as part of the *Library of Congress Endangered Music Project* series (reviewed in its entirety on page 916)—conjures the feeling of passing through a series of African communities where music is being made informally with skill, passion, and playfulness. In that sense, it is an accurate representation of the journey from which the recordings emerged, a 4,000-mile trek through West Africa that aficionado Alberts and his wife made by jeep in 1949. In their travels they encountered, for example, Mano men cutting stone for a building; the workers took a break to sing for Alberts, striking their hammers and chisels for percussion. Like most of the people he recorded, Alberts was a musical amateur, but if his notes are stunted his ears are open and fresh. His approach must have been easy on the musicians, who sound unanimously liberated and at peace in performance, none more than the Congolese people we hear making a percussive symphony by slapping the surface of a river. And the acoustic rumba also recorded in Congo offers an irresistible snippet of village *soukous* (the Cuban style's African variant)—here is the music that shook the disco, unplugged and backstage, loping along as if there were no tomorrow.

Chris King

Bayaka: The Extraordinary Music of the BaBenzélé Pygmies ♫♫♫♫ (ellipsis arts . . . , 1995, prod. Bernie Krause)

International
genre: African folk

Unidentified BaBenzélé Pygmy groups who roam an area in West and Central Africa.

By mixing ambient sounds from the Congo basin—the audio backdrop of rainforest life—with recordings of the BaBenzélé Pygmies, producer Bernie Krause and author/explorer Louis Sarno have come up with a fascinating audio document and an equally worthy tome. The ellipsis arts . . . label has bound the two formats into a package deal, with the hardback, 96-page book containing its companion CD in a little pouch on the inside back cover. Even though polychoral writing has a long and honorable history in the Western world, this project demonstrates that a seemingly simple society like that of the Pygmies may have a similar tradition predating the work of composers like Gabrielli and Palestrina, whose experiments in the 16th century with space and multiple voicings were considered groundbreaking. The album showcases the Pygmy use of song in everyday life; echoing, yodeling, and bouncing sound off the rain forest canopy without a thought to the complex, forward-thinking musicality of what they've been doing. The Pygmies play counterpoint with arboreal rhythms of life: the click, whir, and ratcheting of insects; the hooting and howling of primates; the calls and songs of avians. The results are beautiful and awe-inspiring.

Garaud MacTaggart

Black Star Liner ♫♫♫ (Heartbeat, 1992)

Nigeria, Sierra Leone, Liberia
genre: Reggae

Sonny Okosun (Nigeria); Sabanoh 75 (Sierra Leone); Cloud "7" (Nigeria); Bongos Ikwue and the Groovies (Nigeria); Victor Uwaifo and his Titibitis (Nigeria); Miatta Fahnbulleh (Liberia).

Reggae in Africa (much like Cuban forms on the continent) is an interesting example of the reverse flow of music back to the Motherland, and has produced several world-class exponents. Even though many of the acts here include reggae as part of a wider repertoire, the explorations of the genre on this collec-

tion are exceptionally good and mostly of the "roots" persuasion, as these recordings date from the mid-'70s to early '80s. Aptly named after early-20th-century black nationalist Marcus Garvey's "back to Africa" Black Star Line shipping company, this compilation illustrates the cultural rather than physical migration that has eventually transpired. A close listen will reveal the African elements present to a lesser or greater extent on all tracks, especially Victor Uwaifo's composition from 1978. Of interest is how completely and naturally reggae has lodged in the hearts of Africans from many countries, as has the spiritual message of the Ethiopian-inspired Rastafarian belief. In this sense of kinship with its Western cousin, African reggae often concerns itself with social and political matters, as on Sonny Okosun (a.k.a. Okosuns)'s two vital recordings here. The sound quality, with plenty of vinyl clicks and scratches, leaves something to be desired, but it is more than made up for by the quality of the music itself, and compiler Ken Bilby's excellent liner notes make this a keystone collection in a still-evolving genre.

Derek Rath

Desert Blues ♫♫♫♫ (Network, 1995, compilation prod. Christian Scholze, Jean Trouillet)

Nubia, Mali, Algeria, Ethiopia, Sudan, Gambia, Senegal, Guinea, Morocco, Mauritania
genre: African folk, American blues, African/blues hybrids

Hamza El Din (Nubia); Oumou Sangare (Mali); Baly Othmani/Steve Shehan (Algeria/USA); Ali Farka Touré/Ry Cooder (Mali/USA); Aster Aweke (Ethiopia); Baaba Maal (Senegal); Abdel Gadir Salim (Sudan); Mahmoud Ahmed (Ethiopia); Tata Dindin (Gambia); Abou Djouba (Senegal); Kanté Manfila (Guinea); Hassan Hakmoun/Adam Rudolph (Morocco/USA); Dimi Mint Abba (Mauritania); Ali Farka Touré/Taj Mahal (Mali/USA); Ensemble El Moukhadrami (Mauritania); Sali Sidibe (Mali); Sona Diabate (Guinea).

Beautifully packaged and drawing from the catalogs of many labels, *Desert Blues* is an in-depth, two-CD exploration of the tangible, visceral connections between the music of Western and Northern Africa and the blues of America. Rather than instrumental or structural similarities, the focus is on the voice and the role of singers as repositories of news, stories, and tradition (like the *jalis* or *griots* of West Africa), as well as their soulful evocation of the human spirit and desires. Highlights abound among impeccably chosen selections from a wealth of major talent, showcasing myriad styles from Ethiopia to Gambia, along with some interesting contemporary fusion experiments. The recordings of Malian singer-guitarist Ali Farka Touré and American Ry Cooder are perhaps the best-known and most obvious example, but other pairings like Baly Othmani and Steve Shehan show equally inventive respect for roots and possibilities for new expression. Many of the individual men and women represented here (such as, notably, Malian rising star Oumou Sangare) are major vocal talents regardless of specific style or culture. Well annotated in German, French, and English and with plenty of bibliographic information, *Desert Blues* is an essential collection that should be on anyone's world-music Top 10 list.

Derek Rath

Electric and Acoustic Mali ⅃⅃⅃⅃ (Hemisphere, 1994, compilation prod. Gerald Seligman)

Mali
genre: Folk, pop

Sekouba "Bambino" Diabaté (Guinea); Kagja Tangara; Lobi Traore; Dounanke Koita; Bougouniere Diarrah Sanogo; Les Soeurs Sidibe; Issa Bagayogo; Djeneba Diakite; Kagbe Sidibe; Wassolon Fenin; Ami Koita; Kerfala Kante (Guinea). (All artists are from Mali, except where noted otherwise.)

As in many African countries, in Mali there is no conflict between folk and pop styles. You might call the music here "evolving folk" just as well as "pop." The main traditional instruments—*balafon* (xylophone) and *kora* (harp-lute)—play side-by-side with drum kit, electric guitar (if often played in a style that closely mimics the rhythms and tonalities of the kora), and synthesizers. Although most artists on this disc are unknown outside of Mali, their music has a non-stop groove and exuberant energy that wouldn't be out of place on dancefloors anywhere in the world. Highlights include Dounanke Koita's funky mix of electric guitars and traditional percussion; the acoustic "blues" of Issa Bagayogo; and the searing vocal prowess of Ami Koita. The two artists from Guinea share common cultural roots with Mali's Malinke people, and their music fits easily into the album's mosaic.

j. poet

Ethiopian Groove: The Golden Seventies ⅃⅃⅃⅃ (Abyssinian, compilation prod. Francis Falceto)

Ethiopia
genre: Eskita, R&B

Alemayehu Eshete; Hirut Bekele; Tamrat Ferendji; Aster Aweke; Bzunesh Bekele; Wallias Band; Ayalew Mesfin; Asseletetch Ashine/Getenesh Kebret. (All artists are from Ethiopia.)

Taken from the roster of Kaifa Records, these 16 cuts were all recorded in the 1970s period considered a golden age in Ethiopian music. A curious melange of traditional Ethiopian sounds and imported grooves from American R&B, jazz, and European pop, this is a hybrid that has never been emulated anywhere else. The local vocal styles, redolent of the Middle East and Africa in equal amounts, seem at first listen to be at odds with the churning funk and jazz grooves laid down by police and military bands—the wellspring for virtually all musicians of the period—but once accustomed to the sound it is easy to recognize some extremely soulful performances. The recordings were done in rudimentary circumstances, often in hotels or clubs with just one or two microphones, but what they lack in fidelity they make up for in immediacy and vitality. Some landmark sides are contained herein, including the first outings from Aster Aweke, probably Ethiopia's best-known star internationally, and support from some of the best back-up outfits including Shebelle's, Wallias, Dahlak, and the Black Lion Band. Soon after these tracks were made the military cracked down and the nightlife that spawned this music was snuffed out, leaving a tiny legacy of historically important and highly entertaining recordings such as those preserved here.

Derek Rath

Holding Up Half the Sky: Voices of African Women ⅃⅃⅃⅃⅃ (Shanachie, 1997, compilation prod. Randall Grass)

International
genre: Popular African music

The Mahotella Queens (South Africa); Angélique Kidjo (Benin); Kiné Lam (Senegal); Äicha Koné (Ivory Coast); Stella Chiweshe (Zimbabwe); M'Bilia Bel (Congo), Ami Koita (Mali); Malouma Mint Miadeh (Mauritania); Miriam Makeba (South Africa); the Lijadu Sisters (Nigeria); Malika (island of Naum in Kenya); Tshala Muana (Congo); Netsanet Mellesse (Ethiopia); Dorothy Masuka (Zimbabwe).

Often restricted in both classic and current roles, on this album—part of a series also spotlighting women in reggae (reviewed on page 914) and Celtic and Asian music (page 913 and 856, respectively)—African female performers get to stretch out. Some have an advantage, such as those in the *griot* (oral historian) culture of West Africa, where women have great involvement in the music-making, while others jam in the increasing number of nightclubs as much of the old conservatism dissipates from region to region. The Mahotella Queens, gigging since the early 1960s, have been hitmakers longer than any other female African group. Angélique Kidjo (très moderne, with her French production team) offers a standout performance of her international hit "Batonga"—a story of a young woman who annoys the rich by dancing like a princess. Stella Chiweshe is the only prominent female player of *mbira* (thumb piano) music—a style usually reserved for males. The influence of Miriam Makeba is so significant that her nickname is "Mama Africa." Malika (meaning "queen"), whose birth name is Asha Abdo Suleiman, is a master of the East African (particularly Swahili) *tarabu* style. Dorothy Masuka has sung with Makeba and is known as "Queen of Zimbabwe Blues and Jazz." *Holding*

Up Half the Sky: Voices of African Women helps these and the other stellar performers continue to prove that sisters are indeed doin' it for themselves—and for us.

Stacy Meyn

The Igede of Nigeria: Drumming, Chanting and Exotic Percussion ♫♫♫♫ (Music of the World, 1991, prod. Robert Nicholls, Bob Haddad)

Nigeria
genre: Igede traditional

Ainu Center Choir, soloist Eje Onminyi; Etuh Ensemble; Ijege Ensemble; Obohu villagers; Onyeweh Children's Ensemble; Ogirinye Ensemble; Aitah Ensemble of Obohu; Aitah Ensemble of Andibla. (All artists are from Nigeria.)

The Igede people of Benue State are far removed from the Yoruba culture of Nigeria's capital Lagos and from the legacy of Nigerian pop stars like King Sunny Adé or Fela Kuti. It is hard to assess how musically significant the Igede are, being just one of more than 400 ethnic groups in Nigeria, yet music plays a central and highly regarded role in their traditional life. Igede men join an ensemble so that a group exists to play at their own funeral (funerals are not sorrowful events but a celebration of that person's achievements). These groups will play at all ceremonies from births and marriages to social dances or worship. A wide range of their improvised tunes are represented in this collection, including wakes, Christian hymns sung polyphonically by children's choirs, and songs reflecting the Igede's own beliefs. The sound quality of these 1978 recordings is clear, though the voices are given priority over instruments in the mix. As to the latter, the album features choirs from various villages chanting as they play percussion. They hammer an iron spear, or *ijachi*, into the ground, where clappers attached to the spear vibrate and clatter. The chime of the *ojeh*, a metal gong; the rattle of *icheche* (pebble-filled shakers); and the beat of the *ubah* (skin drum) are accompanied by the high-pitched *aji* (tin whistle) and bellowing *oko* (gourd trumpet) for a raw and lively experience.

David Poole

The Indestructible Beat of Soweto ♫♫♫♫♫ (Shanachie, 1986, compilation prod. Trevor Herman)
Thunder before Dawn: The Indestructible Beat of Soweto, Volume Two ♫♫♫♫ (Earthworks, 1987, compilation prod. Trevor Herman)
Freedom Fire: The Indestructible Beat of Soweto, Volume Three ♫♫♫♫ (Earthworks, 1990, compilation prod. Trevor Herman)
The Kings & Queens of Township Jive: Modern Roots of the Indestructible Beat of Soweto ♫♫♫♫♫ (Earthworks, 1990, compilation prod. Trevor Herman)

Jive Soweto: The Indestructible Beat of Soweto, Volume Four ♫♫♫ (Earthworks, 1992, compilation prod. Trevor Herman)
A Taste of the Indestructible Beat of Soweto ♫♫♫ (Earthworks, 1993, compilation prod. Trevor Herman)

South Africa
genre: Mbaqanga

Udokotela Shange Namajaha; Nelcy Sedibe; Umahlathini Nabo; Amaswazi Emvelo; Mahlathini Nezintombi Zomgoashiyo; Moses Mchunu; Nganeziyamfisa No Khambalomvaleliso; Johnson Mkhalali; Ladysmith Black Mambazo; Dilika; Abafakasi; Jozi; Makgona Tshole Band; Malombo; Mahotella Queens; Inkunzi Emdaka; J.J. Chauke & the Tiyimeleni Young Sisters; Isaac Sibiya; Bra Sello; Abafana Baseqhudeni; Lulu Masilela; Mbazo; Thomas Phale; Soul Brothers; West Nkosi; Ihashi Elimhlophe; Sipho Mabuse; Amadoda Ahlangene; Mbongeni Ngema; Steve Kekana; Mzwakhe Mbuli. (All artists are from South Africa.)

The single most important series of world-music albums ever put out in England or the U.S. is also the best. Thirteen years after its initial release, *The Indestructible Beat of Soweto* still carries the kind of knockout punch its title promises: if I may put it mildly, this is a perfect album, one of the greatest compilations of any style ever assembled, and in particular perhaps the single best African pop release of all time. From the pinched, spellbinding electric-guitar twang of Udokotela Shange Namajaha's "Awungilobolele," which opens the album, to the keening violin of the same band's instrumental "Sobamba," which brings it to its mid-point climax, to Ladysmith Black Mambazo's haunting *a cappella* "Nansi Imali," which closes it, *Indestructible* doesn't step wrong for a minute. Anyone unconvinced of the *mbaqanga* style's majesty after hearing this has tin ears.

That first *Indestructible* fostered a series of titles in its image, and although none of the numbered volumes that followed quite lives up to the original (how could they?), each is worthy enough on its own terms. *Thunder before Dawn* hews closest to the first album's formula, and had it not followed such a masterpiece it might have been accorded a bit more of the respect it deserved. Highlights include Johnson Mhhalali's joyous instrumental "Sunshine Boots" and a trio of cuts by the great goat-voiced "groaner" Mahlathini. *Freedom Fire* stretches out, going for an hour and slackening a bit on selection. Titles like Mahlathini & Mahotella Queens' "Thuto Kelefa" and J.J. Chauke & the Tiyimeleni Young Sisters' "Madyisa Mbitsi" are still pretty indestructible, but also pretty slick—in step with changing times in South Africa, but still disappointing to fans of the rougher earlier editions. *Jive Soweto* is longer still (67 minutes), and while the series ensures brand-name quality, it's a rather sad sign when the best cut on the album (Mahlathini &

the Queens' "Jive Makgona") is a glossed-up remake of a readily available, far superior track from the same series.

The original "Jive Makgona" is on *The Kings & Queens of Township Jive*, which for my money is every bit as enjoyable as the 1986 album, if not quite as galvanic. This is a straight-up party record, and pity any gathering that can't groove to it: Abafana Baseqhudeni's "Mubi Umakhelwane" leads it off angular and in-the-pocket, while instrumental gems like Thomas Phale's sax-led "Platform 14" and West Nkosi's "Chillis 500" (featuring the best wah-wah guitar part this side of Hendrix's "Voodoo Child") raise the roof of any building you play them in. Absolutely essential.

The *Indestructible* series wasn't the original's only legacy: Earthworks spawned a minor cottage industry in its wake, highlighting artists featured on the compilations by giving them their own albums. The company therefore released *A Taste of the Indestructible Beat of Soweto*, a sampler volume of all but the first in the series plus related titles. While many find the album as classic as the first *Indestructible* and *Kings & Queens*, it's actually rather stiff. There's great stuff here, but the sequencing—a key element of the other albums' success—is indifferent: *Taste* doesn't flow, leaving it flat and disappointing. Besides, who just wants a taste when you can eat the whole meal?

Michaelangelo Matos

Jali Kunda: Griots of West Africa & Beyond 🎵🎵🎵🎵 (ellipsis arts . . . , 1996, prod. Bill Laswell, Foday Musa Suso)

International
genre: West African folk

Hundreds of musicians, all from the Senegambia region.

The *griots* (a.k.a. *jali*) of West Africa are oral historians and troubadours who have passed down and preserved their region's culture for more than 800 years. The music on this magnificent CD, which was selected and arranged by legendary griot Foday Musa Suso and produced by his frequent collaborator, the ever-prolific first-world fusionist Bill Laswell, is gloriously vibrant, collecting songs performed by some of West Africa's most outstanding talents. The majority of the tunes prominently feature the lyrical beauty of the *kora*, the 21-stringed harp-lute favored by many griots, but you'll also hear the *balafon* (a wooden xylophone with gourd resonators); the *kutiro* drums; the *newo* (metal percussion played exclusively by women); and the *nyanyer* (a one-stringed fiddle). Coming in a box including a 96-page book filled with gorgeous photos and extensive background on the tracks and the region, this package provides a great overview of West African musical history—but collaborations with the likes of Laswell, experimental composer Philip Glass, and jazz saxophonist Pharoah Sanders show that this is not a culture content with resting on that history, however illustrious.

Bret Love

Juju Roots: 1930s–1950s 🎵🎵🎵🎵 (Rounder, 1985, prod. Chris Waterman)

Nigeria
genre: Juju

Irewoloede Denge and Dickson Oludaiye; Tunde King and His Group; Ayinde Bakare and His Group; Ojo Babajide and His Ibadan Juju Group; Jolly Orchestra; S.S. Peters and His Group; Lagos Mozart Orhestra; Julius Olofin and His Group; Rafiu Bankole and His Group; Ojoge Daniel and His Juju Band; C.A. Balogan and His Abalabi Group; J.O. Araba and His Rhythm Blues; J.O. Oyesiku and His Rainbow Quintette; Irewolede Denge and His Group. (All artists are from Nigeria.)

Juju Roots traces the growth and diversity of a style of Nigerian music that has been popularized around the world by stars King Sunny Adé and Ebenezer Obey. Arising from a soup of influences in Lagos around the late 1920s and early '30s, *juju* developed chiefly in the Yoruba community, serving as entertainment, political commentary, and social ritual at weddings, funerals, and naming ceremonies. At the same time, juju's broad audience—traders, clerks, and sailors from many nations—reflected the "melting pot" nature of Lagos. Following the lead of juju pioneer Tunde King, many early ensembles made use of four people: a guitar- or banjo-playing singer, a tambourine player, a gourd rattle player, and a triangle player doubling on vocals. The first half of the CD presents some songs from these early groups, showing their debt to the simple verse-chorus *palm-wine* guitar-and-percussion ensembles that preceded them. The guileless charm of "Ojo Davies" and "Abasi Olubadan," for instance, derives from the melody of British folk music filtered through a palm-wine aesthetic. The remainder of the CD follows juju through the postwar period, presenting several progressive styles as well as one called *toy motion,* which revisits the old palm-wine with renewed energy. Notable are "Sowemimo" by Rafiu Bankole, with its funky interplay of guitar and percussion, and "Egan Mik Ko Ye O" by C.A. Balogun, a very bluesy example of the *Abalabi* style. Also included to give a sense of context are several cuts from other genres that were popular at the time, such as the brass-band sound of the Lagos Mozart Orchestra. As with the *Mbube Roots* CD (reviewed on page 846), the detail of the liner notes makes the listening better by pointing out instrumental or melodic details that might otherwise pass unnoticed. Overall, a great sonic and scholarly success!

Jeffrey Muhr

Madagasikara One: Current Traditional Music of Mada-gascar ♫♫♫♫ (Ace/Globestyle, 1986, prod. Ben Mandelson, Roger Armstrong)

Madagasikara Two: Current Popular Music of Madagas-car ♫♫♫♫ (Ace/Globestyle, 1986, prod. Ben Mandelson, Roger Armstrong)

Madagascar

genre: Gorodao, Hira-Gasy, salegy, waltz, sova, vakisova, jijy, zana kira, tromba, sigaoma

Rakotofra; Martin Rakotoarimanana; Daniel Tombo; Marceline Vaviroa; Georges Norbert; L. Honore Rosa; Rabenaivo Group; David Andriamamonjy; Tsimialona Volambita; Zeze (Rabenja Ravelonandro); Groupe "Son"; Rossy; Mahaleo; Trio "Fa"; Ny Sakelidalana; Les Smockers; Tarika Sammy; Nonot Kidza. (All artists are from Madagascar.)

This pair of CDs presents a broad cross-section of styles, played by some of Madagascar's finest musicians. Like the island's culture as a whole, Malagasy (the adjectival form of "Madagascar") music absorbs elements from many other places. The *valiha*, for example, a Malagasy zither with strings stretched around a central bamboo shaft, closely resembles an instrument found in New Guinea, while the *jejo vaotavo* stick zither looks quite like a monochord used in Southeast Asia. Indeed, Madagascar's first inhabitants are thought to have journeyed across the Indian ocean from as far away as Southeast Asia and the Polynesian islands to the African mainland before arriving on their island home of today. Following these original pioneers were Bantus and other mainland Africans, Arab traders, and the inevitable Portuguese, British, and French colonial settlers. While Malagasy music forges elements from all of these peoples, it is absolutely unique. It has an unmistakable jauntiness and sense of rhythm that are difficult to pin down, but immediately set it apart from other African music. These features are readily apparent on tracks like "Kilalao" by valiha master Zeze and Groupe "Son," which incorporates delicate melodic passages, unusual percussive punctuation, and cascading runs on the valiha.

Though the set consists of a "traditional" and a "popular" CD, the distinction between the two is somewhat ambiguous. Malagasy musicians seem to have resisted succumbing to Western pop music all at once. Instead, many have modernized their ensembles a bit with electric instruments, and experimented with or "stretched" tradition without abandoning it altogether. Often the inspiration for new forms of Malagasy pop still comes not from Western music but from traditional regional styles. For instance, Rossy and his eight-piece band, who kick off the second CD, play a music called *sova* or *vakisova*, which is intended to unite the music of all six of Madagascar's provinces. Such forms of fusion are at once a testament to the creativity of Malagasy musicians and to the vitality

of the traditional forms they have drawn upon. Yet Malagasy artists are certainly not averse to cross-pollinating their music with other influences. Rossy, it might be argued, despite his regard for native genres, contributes the most glossy pop-oriented songs on the set. Les Smockers, a working band around the capital Antananarivo's clubs, plays a cut called "Sarotra" that, like many on the second volume, is undeniably infused with mainland African pop. On the traditional (but still otherwise-influenced) end of the spectrum, Andriamamonjy contributes "Nilentika/Tazana Kely," a lovely medley of waltzes on solo accordion that was written "by a lady in Tamatave" but undoubtedly owes a debt to the sea chanteys of colonial times. With its spectrum of some of the island's most important performers, this set is a great starting point for a collection of Malagasy music. The informal text and storytelling of the liner notes by compiler Ben Mandelson (a secret member of mad worldbeat fusionists 3 Mustaphas 3) are an excellent complement to the relaxed variety of music found here.

Jeffrey Muhr

Makossa Connection: The Best Of, Volumes 1–4 ♫♫♫ (Sonodisc, 1993, prod. Aladji Toure)

Cameroon

genre: Makossa

Prince Eyengo; Guy Lobe; Emile Kangue; Manulo; Moni Bille; Ben Decca; J.C. Mbimbe; Salle John; Lapiro De Mbanga; Ndidy Dibango; Petit Pays; Gilly Doumbe; Hoigen Ekwalla. (All artists are from Cameroon.)

Those familiar with the *makossa* style only through Manu Dibango's '70s hit "Soul Makossa" will be plenty surprised by this series. Drawing from the collection of Paris-based T.J.R. Music, it showcases some of the bigger names in the genre, many of whom are relatively unknown outside of it. The sound is close to *soukous* (African rumba) from neighboring Congo, but less strident. Perhaps because of the Paris connection it also shares a production quality with the late-'80s sound of *zouk* from Guadalupe and Martinique's expatriates in France. Stylistically it has some of zouk's tropical sway, with just a little of its own inherent Cuban influence, as much *Oriente* as rumba. The best cuts are those that feature more live musicians than synthesizers, and many of these extended opuses swing inventively and hard. But the aforesaid lackluster and cheesy electronic sound mars several offerings, and the low-budget packaging contains absolutely no information on the artists or the music, rendering this less than satisfactory as an introduction to the genre.

Derek Rath

Master Drummers of Dagbon: Drumming from Northern Ghana, Vols. 1–2 ♪♪♪♪ (Rounder, 1992, prod. John Miller Chernoff)

Ghana
genre: African drumming

Alhaji Ibrahim Abdulai, group leader; individual members not identified. (All artists are from Ghana).

Ethnomusicologist John Miller Chernoff began his studies in Africa with the ambitious hope of learning about the continent's entire panorama of music. Realizing, after a year in Ghana, that he could not hope to master even a fraction of that one nation's traditions, he settled on documenting a musical form that inspired him—the percussion music of the Dagbamba people of Dagbon in northern Ghana. Drumming has a central place in Dagbamba society—drummers perform for festivals, dances, and ceremonies; to honor neighboring peoples by learning their beats; to drum the "praise-names" of great chiefs or ancestors; even to drum episodes from the history of Dagbamba culture. As Chernoff describes it, Dagbamba drumming blends "the clarity of the music of the savannah cultures with the driving power of the music of the forest cultures." Indeed, the 36 drum beats compiled on this two-volume set exhibit plenty of emotional power and driving force. What's more, their intricate polyrhythmic patterns, made with ensembles composed of two types of drums, are performed with exhilarating virtuoso musicianship. Chernoff, though a careful scholar in his liner notes, is not afraid to let us cut loose and enjoy the music—in fact, he suggests that the visceral impact of the live ensemble is best reproduced "by using headphones at high volume."

Jeffrey Muhr

Mbube Roots: Zulu Choral Music from South Africa, 1930s–1960s ♪♪♪♪♪ (Rounder, 1987, prod. Veit Erlmann)

South Africa
genre: Mbube

Bantu Glee Singers; Crocodiles; Fear No Harm Choir; African Zulu Male Voice Choir; Solomon Linda's Original Evening Birds; Solomon Linda and Evening Birds; Shooting Stars; Morning Light Choir; Dundee Wandering Singers; Natal Champions; Durban Crocodiles; Scorpions; King Star Brothers; Ladysmith Black Mambazo. (All artists are from South Africa.)

Mbube Roots documents the growth and development of a style of South African *a cappella* music popularized internationally by the group Ladysmith Black Mambazo in recent decades. *Mbube*, or "lion" music, gets its name from a classic song of the genre recorded by Solomon Linda's Original Evening Birds in the late 1930s and included on the compilation. This song would later become a hit in the U.S. as "The Lion Sleeps Tonight" by the Tokens. Mbube arose from a blend of influences that included traveling American minstrel music, local wedding music, and hymns from rural missionary churches, and it moved in several stylistic directions. One of the earliest styles, *isikhunzi*, was based on minstrel songs, and can be heard here on "Ina Ma Wala" by the Fear No Harm Choir. A more strident style with loud vocals, called *ibombing*, is heard on "Yek Emarabini" by the Shooting Stars. Groups in the 1960s would react against this trend, creating *isicathamiya*, the "walk softly" style, which reached a pinnacle in the sweet, tightly harmonized, imploring sound typified by tracks like the King Star Brothers' "Ukuqubuda" and Ladysmith Black Mambazo's "Umama Lo." Originally, mbube performances and singing contests drew an audience consisting chiefly of Zulu migrant workers in cities such as Durban and Johannesburg, but the music garnered a wider following throughout South Africa when it began to receive airplay on the South African Broadcasting Service (SABC) in the late '60s. Around the same time, Ladysmith Black Mambazo would bring the vocal art to a higher level of refinement, fueling its popularity both at home and abroad. This CD features superbly illuminating liner notes, and the track selection includes a number of songs from the archives of the SABC that were never released commercially. The soulful sound of the recordings and the attention to historical detail in the text make this a valuable acquisition for those interested in the development of African popular music, or lovers of vocal music in general. Anyone who enjoys this CD will no doubt savor its companion, *Juju Roots*, which is reviewed on page 844.

Jeffrey Muhr

The Moon and the Banana Tree: New Guitar Music from Madagascar ♪♪♪♪♪ (Shanachie, 1996, prod. Paul Hostetter)

Madagascar
genre: Guitar

Ralanto; Johnny; D'Gary; Dama Mahaleo; Haja; Colbert; Germain Rakotomavo; Solo Razaf; Etienne Ramboatiana; Dédé. (All artists are from Madagascar.)

This outstanding compilation of Malagasy guitar music features chiefly lesser-known musicians, along with a few stars like D'Gary and Mahaleo whose work has been released outside of Madagascar. With over 20 cuts, there's plenty of good music to listen to, with influences from funk, jazz, and even country & western, ranging from the Kottke-esque fingerstyle of Johnny on "Manina," to the classical symmetry of Germain Rakotomavo's contributions. While all the artists show impressive instrumental skills, perhaps a more important strength of these guitarists is their ability to avoid modern homogeneity by keeping one foot planted in native traditional music. Whether by playing recognizably traditional melody and rhythm, or by re-creating the timbre and tone of native instruments, the musicians here imaginatively adapt the guitar to traditional styles. Haja and Johnny, for example, damp their strings by stuffing a fragment of foam rubber or leather under the bridge, creating a sound much like that of the *marovany,* a native harp similar to the *valiha,* Madagascar's "national instrument." Haja uses this technique, called *guitare etouffee,* to produce a bright, staccato tone that highlights his expert runs on "Fiainana," while Johnny's "Mailaka," equally skillful, creates a softer, mellower sound. Some of the artists featured here also appear on the compilation series *A World Out of Time*, reviewed on page 852.

Jeffrey Muhr

Morocco: Crossroads of Time ♫♫♫♫ (ellipsis arts . . . , 1995, compilation prod. Randall Barnwell, Bill Lawrence)

Morocco
genre: Traditional Moroccan folk

Abdelkrim Rais Ensemble; Rais Najib Ensemble; Binizi-Zoughari; Jilala; Isaac Ouanounou; Guedra; Ganawa; Halima Chedli Ensemble; Najat Aatabu; Nouamane Lahlou. (All artists are from Morocco).

Morocco has one of the world's richest cultural traditions, inspiring creative geniuses including artist Henri Matisse, writers Paul Bowles and William S. Burroughs, and musicians ranging from jazz legends like Ornette Coleman and Pharoah Sanders to rock stars like Jimi Hendrix and the Rolling Stones (whose member Brian Jones, coincidentally, first introduced the Western world to the country's acclaimed Master Musicians of Ja-Jouka). Listening to *Morocco: Crossroads of Time*, it's easy to see why these artists were so fascinated with this mystical culture whose geographical location on ancient trade routes led to its incorporation of elements from the musical traditions of Asia, Africa, Europe, and the Middle East. Through 10 songs and two ambient sound recordings made in the *medinas* (or marketplaces) of Fez and Marrakesh, the listener is taken on an aural tour of this magical land, from Bowles's 1959 recording of Abdelkrim Rais's Andalusian orchestral ensemble, to Binizi-Zoughari's hypnotic *Ganawi* (a.k.a. *Gnawa*) rhythms, to Isaac Ouanounou's spiritual Jewish folksong and Guedra's syncopated Sufi-style healing chants. Including a mixed-media book with 64 pages of gorgeous photos, enlightening cultural insights, and detailed track listings, this album is the cheapest ticket to an enriching Moroccan cultural experience you're likely to find.

Bret Love

Music from Rwanda ♫♫♫♫ (Rounder, 1999)

Rwanda
genre: Rwandan folk

Hutu, Tutsi, and Twa tribal ensembles and individuals, not all credited.

Rwanda spells genocide in the 1990s, and given that unshakable connotation, you will hear war in these songs. There is a song in praise of an army corps, sung to a hand-clapped martial rhythm, though it comes from the Twa ethnic group, which was marginal to the 1994 Rwandan tragedy. A Hutu man sings "The War Cry is Long," accompanying himself on a musical bow, which sounds like a lute strummed by a pair of clacking scissors. Actually, the track here that will curdle your blood has nothing to do with war: it's a late-night drinking song improvised by Tutsi cowherds, pierced by ululations that probably mean something like "yeah buddy!" but sound exactly like a scream from a slit throat. These field recordings were made in the mid-'50s when genocide still had a Nazi ring (with American undertones, given Hiroshima). The liner notes are skimpy, but still suggest the cultural divisions—a massive Hutu peasant majority ruled by a tiny Tutsi royalty—that have erupted periodically in warfare, none more devastating than the 1994 Hutu-led genocide. Perhaps we can enjoy the driving Tutsi royal drums, though, without imagining the peasant cowherds they terrified, and the Tutsi court bards have charm regardless of their attachment to power. It's the Hutu, however, who sound most ordinary in these selections. They sing a wedding anthem with hand-clapping that ranks among the classics of African choral song. There are two Hutu flute pieces; one, called "Difficult Woman" and intended to drive away cattle marauders, imitates its title and is sure to do its job. The real beauty here, though, is a hummable, Afropop-ready Hutu ditty sung against a thumb piano, the title of which is demurely translated as "Too Old to Procreate." From the same mouth issues love, gripes, and war cries; the same hands strum strings, finger flute holes, and slide machetes across the throats of neighbors. This paradox is not Rwandan, nor African, but human, hideously human.

Chris King

Music of the !Kung Bushmen ♫♫♫♫ (Smithsonian Folkways, 1962)

Botswana
genre: !Kung music

Artists unidentified.

This legendary field recording has the feel of a relic. Part of its mystique is that its performers and recording location are nameless. The technician, a young Canadian mining engineer named John Phillipson, was not even sure in what country he made the recording. He gives the location in the vast Kalahari Desert only by approximate longitude and latitude—apparently Botswana. As explained in the fascinating field notes, his interaction with the subjects was completely non-verbal. The Bushmen, now preferably referred to as the San or !Kung San, had—and to some degree still maintain—one of the oldest lifestyles in the world. These nomads have lived in much the same way in southern Africa for at least 4,000 years, long before the now-dominant Bantu herding tribes migrated into the region, let alone any palefaces. As nomads in an extremely dry, hot climate, the San traditionally took next to nothing with them as they traveled, even weak or handicapped members of the tribe. Yet music is an almost continual part of their lives, so their few possessions include light, compact instruments. These include a *kalimba*-like thumb piano, which produces a wavery plucking sound, and a one-stringed bamboo "fiddle." Its reedy screeching sound suggests that of a virtuoso cricket. The third instrument included here is the voice: giggles, hums, nursery rhymes, and the characteristic San tongue click (represented by the exclamation point in "!Kung"). The sound quality is good considering the conditions and equipment—Phillipson was backpacking alone. Tracks stop and start abruptly, adding to the eeriness. The overall effect is rhythmic, soothing, hypnotic, almost psychedelic. This is the sound of a dry, harsh garden of Eden.

Wif Stenger

The Nairobi Beat (Kenyan Pop Music Today) ♫♫♩
(Rounder, 1989, compilation prod. Douglas B. Patterson)

Kenya
genre: Afropop

D.O. 7 Shirati Jazz; Mbiri Young Stars; Super Bunyore Band; Original Kilimambogo Stars; Maroon Commandos; Gatundu Boys; Migori Super Stars; Kalambya Sisters; Bana Likasi; Mayanja Bungoma Jazz Band. (All artists are from Kenya.)

Nairobi, Kenya's capital city, is far more than a national musical hub; it is a crossroads for musicians from across the continent. And although Swahili is the most widespread language in African music, this album spotlights a variety of tongues, from the Kikuyu of the Gatundu Boys and the Mbiri Young Stars' Luo, to songs in languages including Kamba, Bukusu, and Luhya. While *The Nairobi Beat* is a good overview of Kenya's sounds of the '80s, it is no longer exactly "Kenyan Pop Music Today." These musicians are obviously enjoying the novelty of drum machines and synthesizers, but their music sounds dated.

David Poole

Ngoma: Music from Uganda ♫♫♫ (Music of the World, 1997, compilation prod. Wade Patterson, Bob Haddad)

Uganda
genre: Folk music

Wat-mon Cultural Group; Edukut William; Tebifaanana Abifuna Cultural Group; Nebbi Community Adungu Group; Nsawo Mbaire Group; Ndere Troupe; Sande, Peter Kabodha, and Musee Kasata. (All artists are from Uganda.)

Ngoma—which means both "drum" and "dance" in many Bantu languages—is the savory first fruits of a wonderful initiative: Uganda's premier folkloric group, the Ndere Troupe, traveling their nation's rural areas with top-notch documentary technology, recording grass-roots performance. We can't see the dancing on a CD, of course, but the drumming (always accompanied by rich, raw choral singing) is feisty and dynamic, even when the drum is the earth, beaten by sticks to drive out termites for collection and consumption. The material ranges from that humble endeavor to a traditional royal dance, the *Baksimba,* which also has a gastronomic aspect, since the drum pattern imitates a king's praise song upon drinking the kingdom's first batch of banana beer. This record feasts the ear with more than percussion and singing: the charming tones of the *akogo* (thumb piano) accompany a song admonishing a drunkard; an *adungu* (harp) and *rigurigi* (fiddle) drive a youth protest song; and the *enanga* (zither) backs a bard's epic musings and the stomping feet of a communal dance. This record is as full of life as the seven ethnic groups represented.

Chris King

Queens of African Music ♫♫♫♫ (Music Club, 1997, compilation prod. Rick Glanvill)

International
genre: World music

Angélique Kidjo (Benin); Mahotella Queens (South Africa); Soukous Stars (Congo); Tarika (Madagascar); Nahawa Doumbia (Mali); Oumou Diobate (Mali-Guinea); Ami Koita (Mali); Oumou Sangare (Mali); Yvonne Chaka Chaka (South Africa); M'Bilia Bel (Congo); Tshala Muana (Congo); Nayanka Bell (Ivory Coast).

Hearing this record is like standing on a street corner in an African hub city, catching brief sights and sounds from travelers bringing new stories with them. In this case most of the travelers are women, and most are those whose music is evolving using contemporary percussion techniques. They also share concerns of identity, both as individuals in relationships and citizens in the midst of change in their nations. A track that brings these elements (and many of the singers) together is Yvonne Chaka Chaka's "Legends," a celebration of the pioneers of African consciousness in music.

Kerry Dexter

Resting Place of the Mists: New Valiha and Marovany Music from Madagascar 🎵🎵🎵🎵 (Shanachie, 1996, compilation prod. Paul Hostetter)

Madagascar
genre: Folk music

Akombaliha; Tiana and Sammy; Trio Ratovo; Sylvestre Randafison; Rajery; Lemaditsy; Done and Dede. (All artists are from Madagascar.)

The *valiha* and *marovany* are Malagasy harps that produce some of the warmest tones on earth. ("Malagasy" is the adjectival form of "Madagascar.") The valiha, recognized as Madagascar's national instrument, is a bamboo tube with strings stretched lengthwise all around it; the marovany is a box-like wooden adaptation of the valiha with its origins most likely in bamboo scarcity. The instruments have a vast traditional repertoire, and there are many contemporary masters conversant with it, as well as with modern compositions and borrowings from other traditions (waltzes, for one). This album documents Madagascar's greatest valiha and marovany players plucking a superlatively pleasant, lush set of traditional and modern tunes. The playing is consistently at the level of, say, Leo Kottke at his most melodic, and the occasional accompanying vocals and flutes add gorgeous new tonal dimensions. This and the companion volume of Malagasy guitar tunes, *The Moon and the Banana Tree* (reviewed on page 846), are essential listening for lovers of melody.

Chris King

The Rough Guide to the Music of Kenya & Tanzania 🎵🎵🎵🎵🎵 (World Music Network, 1996, compilation prod. Phil Stanton)

Kenya, Tanzania
genre: Benga, Islamic taarab, ngoma

Simba Wanyika (Kenya); Victoria Kings (Kenya); Samba Mapangala (Kenya); D.O. Misiani & Shirati Jazz (Kenya); Abana Ba Nasery (Kenya); Henry Makobi (Kenya); Ogwang Lelo Okoth with Paddy J. Onono (Kenya); Master Musicians of Tanzania (Tanzania); "Moheme" Dance Tanzania (Tanzania); Mlimani Park Orchestra (Tanzania); Juwata Jazz Band (Tanzania); Zein Musical Party (Tanzania); Culture Musical Club (Tanzania).

The *Rough Guide* travel books and their conjugal CD series devote themselves to exposing every worthwhile nook and cranny for the novice traveler to explore. For the CDs, this means that, while every volume has at least a few gems, most sacrifice flow for completism. The greatest exception to that rule is *The Rough Guide to Kenya & Tanzania* —partly because East Africa is so rich with great music, and partly because this *Rough Guide* moves through its terrain so expertly. The album leads off with four breathlessly exuberant *shirati* grooves (Victoria Kings' "V.B. Pod Wamol" is on my

short-list of favorite Afropop cuts ever). These are followed by three similar-sounding tracks—same rhythms; same pretty, gritty guitar playing; just as melodically indelible— which ease up the drums and slow things down. Then the album's centerpiece: a hypnotic, traditional-sounding song by the Master Musicians of Tanzania, and an astonishing field recording of a Wagogo initiation dance, taped in Dodoma in the early '90s. The music's Islamic influences slowly push their way forward on these cuts, and blossom in the last four songs, which feature keener vocals and slower grooves than the four that opened the album. This disc moves you from A to B with extraordinary grace, which is what a tour guide is supposed to do.

Michaelangelo Matos

The Rough Guide to the Music of Zimbabwe 🎵🎵🎵🎵 (World Music Network, 1996, compilation prod. Phil Stanton)

Zimbabwe
genre: Mbira, chimurenga, jit, rumba

Thomas Mapfumo & the Blacks Unlimited; the Bhundu Boys; the Four Brothers; Stella Rambisai Chiweshe; Oliver Mtukudzi & the Black Spirits; Machanic Manyeruke & the Puritans; Black Umfolosi; Biggie Tembo; the Mbira Masters of Zimbabwe; the Real Sounds. (All artists are from Zimbabwe.)

This 69-minute disc offers a good cross-section of the current scene in Zimbabwe, from traditional *mbira* thumb-piano music, to its updating in the *chimurenga* style, to the more modern *jit* sound and African rumba variants. The music's polyrhythms develop at length; only one track here is shorter than five minutes. Leading off the album is the most famous Zimbabwean musician in the West, Thomas Mapfumo, a pivotal figure in the country's music for his band's adaptation of mbira figures to guitar, the basis of his chimurenga ("liberation war") style. Showing its acoustic origins are Stella Chiweshe and the Mbira Masters of Zimbabwe. Followers of Mapfumo's style heard here include the Four Brothers and Oliver Mtukudzi & the Black Spirits. The four-piece Machanic Manyeruke & the Puritans operate outside the mainstream with their gentle electric gospel. Sounding quite South African, Black Umfolosi is an *a cappella* vocal group. Originally from Zaire (Congo), the Real Sounds speed up their rumba style to fit the Zimbabwean norm. The most overtly pop-oriented group here are the Bhundu Boys, whose jit style is also evident in the track by sometime-member Biggie Tembo. Though this CD's selection is good, no texts, translations, or even lyric summaries are included, and the liner notes are incomplete.

Steve Holtje

Singing in an Open Space: Zulu Rhythm and Harmony 1962–1982 ♪♪♪♪ (Rounder, 1990, prod. Rob Allingham)

South Africa
genre: Zulu traditional, mbaqanga

Mhleneleni Mtambo; Frans Msomi; Raymond Mbele; Aaron Nezimtobi; Amos Mkhiza; John Bhengu; M. Shezi Nezimtombi Za Kwazulu; Norman Sibisi & Izintombi Zakwa Zulu; Ishoba Lembongolo; Moses Mchunu Nezintombi Zengoma; Amagugu; Phuzushukela; Philemon Mchunu; Abafana Bomdabu. (All artists are from South Africa.)

Traditional Zulu music has evolved from acoustic guitar to a full band and the sophisticated choral productions of Ladysmith Black Mambazo or the *mbaqanga* style of stars like Mahlathini. This album surveys the early artists who laid the foundations for today's South African music. Their uplifting voices and guitars lilt magically; lyrics deal with the troubles of the new urban life in Durban and Johannesburg: the loneliness of separation from rural relatives is evoked in "Write Home," as are the dangers of warring Zulu gangs in "The Crooks Are Coming." Royalties were rare when a number of these recordings were made, and the flat fee paid instead meant that many of these talented musicians did not even consider a career in music, and only recorded once or twice. Some were killed in tribal conflict; some preferred to concentrate on their taxi business or return to cattle herding. On the other hand, Zululand's greatest star was John Bhengu, whose acoustic guitar blues can be heard here on "Diki Diki" and "Isidwaba." Bhengu influenced many of those who followed him, particularly the high-voiced Frans Msomi (also on this collection), who went on to form the traditional group Phuzushukela.

David Poole

The Soul of Cape Verde ♪♪♪♪ (Tinder, 1996, prod. François Post)

Cape Verde
genre: Morna, coladeira

Cesaria Evora; Humbertona & Piuna; Maria Alice; Djoshina; Luis Morais; Tito Paris; Ana Firmino & Travadinha; Teofilo Chantra; Bau; Chico Serra; Bana; Titina; Mindel Band; Simentere; Voz de Cabo Verde; Amandio Cabral; Cenina Pereira; Paulino Vieira. (All artists are from Cape Verde.)

A few years ago, most people didn't even know what continent Cape Verde was considered part of. Since Cesaria Evora has become an international star, they know Cape Verde is a collection of islands off the coast of Africa, but are still probably unaware of the archipelago's rich Creole culture, a combination of West African and European influences that has produced an amazing variety of styles. These include *coladeira,* a politically charged dance music likened to the calypso of Trinidad; *fu-*

nana, a fractured (to American ears) dance rhythm that could be the Verdean cousin of Haitian *compas*; and *mazurka,* a kind of Africanized waltz music; as well as the blues-like *morna* that Evora has made popular. This compilation was originally released on Lusafrica (a company that specializes in the music of Portuguese Africa), and includes a constellation of Verdean stars playing their trademark selections. Highlights include Humbertona & Piuna's gentle instrumental version of "Miss Perfumado," an Evora hit from the pen of one of Cape Verde's master composers, B. Leza; the horn-heavy sound of Teofilo Chantra's bouncy "Pais di Mel"; Bana's mellow vocals on "Serpentina"; Amandio Cabral's seductive "Cutch Cutch"; "Galo Bedjo" by Titina, another singer of morna with a style that contrasts nicely with Evora's; and "Suade" by Cenina Pereira, a singer with a more traditional morna approach.

j. poet

The Spirit of Cape Verde ♪♪♪♪♪ (Tinder, 1998)

Cape Verde
genre: Morna, funana, coladeira, batuco, tabanca

Cesaria Evora; Ildo Lobo; Tito Paris; Boy Gé Mendes; Fantcha; Bau; Maria Alice; Simentera; Mindel Band; Katchupa Rica; Mobafuco; Téofilo Chantre; Luis Morais; Celina Pereira; Vox de Cabo Verde. (All artists are from Cape Verde.)

The Cape Verde Islands, on the Atlantic trade route from Africa to South America, have evolved a unique musical tradition in which West African and Brazilian motifs coalesce with the *fado* of colonial Portugal to produce one of the world's richest musical heritages, the most well-known form of which is the blues-like *morna.* Morna's reigning queen, Cesaria Evora, starts off this 16-track compilation, setting the stage for an astonishing variety of singers and styles. As astonishing is the uniformly high standard of performance, with many of these singers primed to lose their "unknown" status. Like Brazil, a lot of the music is light and acoustically driven with the vocals sung in Portuguese, but you can also hear occasional echoes of Caribbean *zouk* or even a suggestion of Colombian *cumbia.* The music swings, even at the often-slow tempos, and the exquisite melancholy of the morna vocal styles in particular only heightens the romantic appeal. Most of the selections are less than five years old, making this both an extremely valid introduction for beginners and a valuable update for aficionados.

Derek Rath

Super Guitar Soukous ♪♪♪♡ (Tinder, 1996, prod. Gerald Seligman)

Congo
genre: Soukous

Kanda Bongo Man; Dave Depeu (Ivory Coast); Patience Dabany; Tabu Ley Rochereau; Dindo Yogo; Gueatan System (Ivory Coast); Joyce Delly; Zoukunion (Ivory Coast); Olives Guede (Ivory Coast); General Defao; Pépé Kallé and Empire Babuka; Seliko. (All artists are from Congo, except where noted otherwise.)

When *soukous* (a form inspired by Cuban rumba) came roaring out of Zaire (now Congo) in the late '70s, it swept Africa, and later much of the Francophone world, with its mixture of breakneck tempos and wild guitar pyrotechnics. The music's instrumental approach—the lead and tenor guitars usually play different but interlocking lead lines—set off sparks that made the style irresistible to both dancers and musicians. In the early '80s many of the genre's strongest players, led by Kanda Bongo Man and his legendary guitarist Diblo Dibala, moved to Paris, where they began adding the international touches to their sound that helped create the current interest in world music. As the global profile and commercial fortunes of soukous rose, bands all over Africa and Europe began playing it, although the compilation at hand centers on Congolese practitioners and an Ivory Coast hybrid of the style called *polihet*. Every track is solid, with standouts being Kanda Bongo Man and Seliko's exceptional contributions; the simmering horn charts on Dave Depeu's "Africa"; the staccato guitar work of Zoukunion's T. Matilene on "N'Nanele"; and the beautiful vocals of the late Pépé Kallé on "Soso Na Ngai."

j. poet

Township Jazz 'n' Jive: 18 South African Urban Swing Classics from the Jivin' '50s ♫♫♫♫ (Gallo Africa/Music Club, 1997, compilation prod. Graeme Ewens)

South Africa
genre: Jazz, jive

The Four Yanks; Kippie Moeketsi & the Marabi Kings; Spokes Mashiyane; the Jazz Dazzlers; the Royal Players; the Solven Whistlers; the Skylarks; the Father Huddlestone Band; Nacy Jacobs & Her Sisters; Dolly Rathebe; Orlando Seven; the Manhattan Brothers; Lemmy "Special" Mabuse; Dorothy Masuka; Solomon Linda's Original Evening Birds; Reggie Msomi's Hollywood Jazz Band. (All artists are from South Africa.)

South Africa's record industry blossomed during the 1950s to the sound of *marabi*, a swinging blend of township dance beats and American jazz. Eric Gallo recorded the emerging stars of Johannesburg, like Hugh Masekela on "Ndenzeni Na?" Masekela performed with Father Huddlestone's band, who generously donated Masekela's first trumpet at a time when brass instruments were in short supply. As a member of the Skylarks you can hear one of Miriam Makeba's first recordings on "Holilili," prior to the outspoken black nationalism that became her trademark in the '60s. Makeba also appears here on a couple of songs with the Manhattan Brothers. Listen for the bridge be-

tween these marabi dance tracks and the later crop of *mbaquanga* pop in the pennywhistle *kwela* melodies of songs by the Solven Whistlers or Lemmy Mabuse's "Kwela Blues." All together, *Township Jazz 'n' Jive* is an upbeat overview of the evolution of South African music, and the beginnings of some of its still-greatest stars.

David Poole

Viva Zimbabwe ♫♫♫♫ (Earthworks, 1983, prod. D.A. Vanrenen)

Zimbabwe
genre: African pop

Deverra Ngwena Jazz Band; the Four Brothers; Thomas Mapfumo and the Blacks Unlimited; the New Black Montana; Super Sounds; Nyami Nyami Sound; Patrick Mukwamba; James Chimombe and the O.K. Success; Elijah Madzikatire and the Brave Sun. (All artists are from Zimbabwe.)

This intense dance music from the 1980s makes even South African jive sound sluggish in comparison. While the melodic instinct and style of adept guitar riffing found on this CD have much in common with Central African pop music of the period, the lyrical content is sometimes spiced with the kind of revolutionary zeal found in Zulu jive from the South. Indeed, Thomas Mapfumo, with his *chimurenga* music (heard here on "Drums Have Woken Me Up"), made his name and galvanized Zimbabwe by incorporating pointed political statements against the white Rhodesian regime into songs built around Shona folk music. But most of the bands found here play straight three-chord African pop with adroit guitar fills, and cover lighter fare lyrically. The common thread of these tracks is a powerful dance rhythm. The Four Brothers follow the frenetic opening cut ("Solo and Mutsai" by the Deverra Ngwena Jazz Band) with the bass-driven celebratory romp "Congratulations," and by the fourth track, "Fatty," by the New Black Montana, the pace has elevated to a fever pitch—one is almost grateful that "He Refuses Advice," a song by Super Sounds exhorting a street drunk to change his ways, slows the tempo down a bit despite its pile-driving drums. The remainder of the disc continues in much the same buoyant vein, and will provide plenty of satisfaction for listeners in search of a party-starter or in need of a mood lift.

Jeffrey Muhr

The Wassoulou Sound: Women of Mali ♫♫♫♫ (Stern's)

Mali
genre: Wassoulou

Sali Sidibe; Oumou Sangare; Coumba Sidibe; Dienaba Diakité; Kagbe Sidibe. (All artists are from Mali.)

Women comprise 90 percent of the singers in *wassoulou*, a genre based in songs of praise to the hunt (to which the men dance), but more recently encompassing songs of love and passion. The Arabic heritage is apparent both vocally and instrumentally, but this south-Mali style boasts its own elliptical rhythms and graceful vocals. Although the artists heard here collectively represent 30 years of popularity in the genre, it is the younger generation, such as Sali Sidibe and especially the startling Oumou Sangare, who have brought it to the foreground of world music. Every artist featured here exhibits great feminist self-confidence and vocal strength; singing in English they would be the equal of any soul songstress. Though the traditional roots are very visible, the album's nine tracks benefit from a contemporary production that heightens the magical web these trance-like performances weave on the listener. Traditional *kamal ngoni* lute and *djembe* drum are variously combined with keyboards and electric bass in a very natural and harmonious manner, respecting ancient and modern sensibilities alike. The brief liner notes give a concise background to the music while providing no details on the individual tracks, but nonetheless this album will appeal to both novice and advanced listener.

Derek Rath

A World Out of Time: Henry Kaiser and David Lindley in Madagascar, Vols. 1–3 🎵🎵🎵🎵 (Shanachie, 1992/1993/1996, prod. Birger Gesthuisen, Henry Kaiser, Paul Hostetter)

Madagascar
genre: Kabary; vakisoava; salegy; kalon 'ny fahiny; Dama picking; Hira-Gasy; guitarre etouffee

Ramilison; Tarika Ramilison group; Paul Bert Rahasimanana (Rossy); Rossy group; Sameola Andriammalalahanjaona (Sammy); Sammy group; Dama Mahaleo; Mahaleo group; Rakoto Frah; Tarika Rakoto Frah group; Voninavoko group; Roger Georges; Sylvestre Randafison; Germain Rakotomavo; Ernest Randrianasolo (D'Gary); Ratovonirina Ranaivovololona (Tovo); Tovo group; Mama Sana; Johnny; Lemaditsy. (All artists are from Madagascar.)

Considering the amazing diversity, charm, and accessibility of the music heard on this set of CDs, it's hard to believe that, prior to 1991, no Malagasy music (music from Madagascar) had been released in the U.S. Late that year, guitarists David Lindley and Henry Kaiser brought the recording team of Birger Gesthuisen and Bernhard Ramroth (of the German Feuer und Eis label, which had recently released a series of CDs of Malagasy music called *Madagaskar*) to Antananarivo, the capital of the island, to help them sample the country's music and record jams with the local artists. Their collaboration yielded spectacular results—three excellent CDs, a Grammy nomination for the sec-

ond one, and an explosion of interest in Malagasy music. In fact, *A World Out of Time* helped lift a number of Malagasy performers to prominence on the world-music circuit. Lindley, a virtuoso string player best known as a backing guitarist for artists such as Jackson Browne, Warren Zevon, and Linda Ronstadt; and Kaiser, reputed for his quirky forays into jazz and the avant-garde, deserve praise for staying out of the spotlight. Most of the time they wisely avoid using the musicians as a backing group to showcase their own ideas, instead serving as quiet catalysts to the musical process. Much of the time, the listener is not even aware of their presence. When they do emerge from the mix, it feels just right, as when Kaiser's peculiar, psychedelic solo closes "Tsaiky Mboly Hely," a *salegy* dance tune. Yet Lindley provides some of the most charming moments on the CDs by throwing old Western tunes in the direction of the Malagasy musicians to see how they will be transformed. For instance, the accordion-driven "I Fought the Law" delightfully defies pigeon-holing with its Irish jig-cum-Zulu jive shape, while "I'm a Lonesome Fugitive," with Lindley on the lead vocal, redeems its tepid pop synthesizer opening when the lead guitar line is taken by a *valiha* bamboo zither player, with a totally endearing result. Any sense of dislocation caused by hearing these songs out of their familiar instrumental context is wiped out by the positive energy of the musicians, who seem totally relaxed working with major chord changes not that different from their own. The Malagasy artists consistently shine. High points include the remarkable valiha jam "Lemavo" by Mama Sana, which has the intensity of a gritty blues; the crystalline flute, zither, and vocal song "O Isa" by Rossy and Rakoto Frah; the country oldie "You Done Me Wrong," which begins as a Lindley slide guitar solo and is spontaneously transformed into a soulful, beckoning call by flutist Rakoto Frah; and the dignified "classical" form of the choral-and-guitar song "Ralanto," sung by Ralanto and Tarika Sammy. The first two CDs are compiled exclusively from the original field recordings of 1991, while the third combines some remaining 1991 tracks with new ones made by Paul Hostetter in 1995, as well as some live and studio tracks recorded in the U.S.

Jeffrey Muhr

The World's Musical Traditions 8: Yoruba Drums from Benin, West Africa 🎵🎵🎵 (Smithsonian/Folkways, 1996, compilation prod. Marcos Branda Lacerda)

Benin
genre: African drumming

The Bata Repertoire for Egungun in Pobe; Rhythm for Shango in Pobe; the Bata Repertoire for Shango in Sakete; Three Rhythms of the Dundun Ensemble from Adjarra; Two Rhythms of the Dundun Ensemble from Atchoukpa; Repertoire for Gelede in Ketou; Repertoire for Oro and Ifa in Ketou. (All artists are from Benin.)

How politically incorrect is it to criticize music that's an important part of a Third World culture? No matter how you see it, drum solos can be tedious, in rock or any type of music. But techno or hip-hop mavens should definitely check out the *real* beatmasters here—extensive, comprehensive liner notes (though not really for the layperson) and pictures come along with what turns out to be an instructive history lesson (other volumes in the series, and their reviews, are sprinkled across the globe and the Compilations section of this book). Still, even African music fans who dig Adé, Fela, or Ladysmith will be thrown for a loop by the minimal repetitive rhythms. This style of music is very spare and almost cries out for the visuals that are a part of its presentation. Great pains were taken to provide a very authentic recording of ancient rituals (with clear, clean audio no less)—so much so that Western ears may have a hard time getting a hold of this music. Although somewhat amelodic, the interweaving polyrhythms create depth and some variety, usually with fast tempos. The problem is that it's not varied enough for the different ensembles and tracks to be easily told apart. Seekers of African drum music might instead want to look up Avant's *Drums of Death* compilation, which has more detailed, complex, and exciting drum sounds, though it's not as well-recorded or educational. For raw field recordings, the less scholarly minded Westerner may prefer the Pygmies of Cameroon (on *Heart of the Forest* from Hannibal) and Congo (*Mbuti Pygmies of the Ituri Rainforest* from Smithsonian).

Jason Gross

Zulu Jive: Umbaqanga (Urban and Rural Zulu Beats from South Africa) 𝄢𝄢𝄢𝄢 (Carthage, 1984)

South Africa
genre: Mbaqanga, jive

Aaron Mbambo; Joshua Sithole; the Rainbows; Shoba. (All artists are from South Africa.)

This CD features the relentless energy, frenetic riffing, and tight rhythmic musicianship of several South African *mbaqanga* bands (a genre identified slightly differently in the album's title). Mbaqanga, a word meaning "dumpling" or "homemade," is applied to a raw style of South African "jive" or popular music that features choral call-and-response vocals; thick, driving dance rhythms; strident guitar playing; and three-chord melodic structures. Often thrown into the mix are instruments such as pennywhistle, accordion, and electric organ. Included here are several cuts from the early 1980s by each of three artists: Aaron Mbambo, Shoba, and Joshua Sithole, with additional tracks by Sithole's band, the Rainbows. All of the contributions make delightful listening. The blissful instrumental cuts by the Rainbows, with their driving accordion and chicken-scratch guitars,

are wonderful ("Mashonisa" is particularly noteworthy for its hypnotic beat), while the buoyancy of Mbambo's "We Have Caught the Chairman" belies its ominous title. The only small complaint about this collection is that it seems to be a little on the short side—indeed, some of the tracks seem to fade out prematurely, though it's hard to tell whether this is a result of overzealous editing or the compelling quality of the music. Those who enjoy this CD will probably also like two other Carthage compilations: *Viva Zimbabwe*, reviewed on page 851, and *Phezulu Eqhudeni* 𝄢𝄢𝄢𝄢, a collection of classic (and slightly more understated) jive tracks from the mid-1970s.

Jeffrey Muhr

ASIA

Bali: Gamelan and Kecak 𝄢𝄢𝄢𝄢𝄢 (Elektra/Nonesuch, 1989, prod. David Lewiston)

Indonesia
genre: Gamelan, kecak, gong kebyar

Gamelan Gong Sekaha Sadha Budaya, directed by I Wayan Rai S, Chokorda Raka, and I Made Sadia; I Nyoman Artika; I Made Meji; Genggong Batur Sari, Batuan, directed by I Nyoman Artika; Gamelan Salunding, Tenganan, directed by Nyoman P. Gunawan; Sadha Budaya Gamelan Gong Suling, directed by Anak Agung Raku Cameng; Gender Wayang, Sukawatl, directed by I Wayan Loceng; I Wayan Sarga; I Wayan Nartha; I Ketut Balik; Sekaha Ganda Sari, Bona, directed by Gusti Putu Putra; Gamelan Gong Kebyar Sekolah Tinggi Seni Indonesia, Denpassar, directed by Dr. I Made Bandem. (All artists are from Bali.)

Twenty years after recording the famed Balinese LP *Music from the Morning of the World* (reviewed on page 859), producer David Lewiston returned to the island to compile further recordings and assess changes in Bali's musical culture. The CD that came out of this return journey, *Bali: Gamelan and Kecak*, captures the breadth and vitality of Balinese music perhaps even better than its predecessor did. As on that album, Lewiston selects a variety of *gamelan* (tuned percussion) styles, including the *kecak* chant; *gong kebyar* gamelan such as the exquisitely tense "Gending Kebyar Kosalya Arini"; *gamelan sunding*, a very ancient form played on an equally ancient, sacred ensemble of metallophones forged from iron rather than the typical bronze; and the important *gender wayang* ensemble, a stripped-down gamelan that backs the Balinese shadow-puppet performance. Several non-gamelan styles are also represented. The astringent "Genggong Duet" for bamboo jew's-harps and the yearning flute ensemble of "Tabuh Teleh" show a laid-back side of Balinese musical culture that, while quite pleasing, is sometimes passed over by compilers in favor of the more dramatic gamelan pieces. Lewiston's liner notes recount some interesting episodes from his return to Bali and provide commentary on each track. While deploring the negative changes that have swept through Bali, he makes it clear that the Balinese have not lost touch with their culture and their past. Indeed, the performances serve as clear evidence that, even under the pressure of tourism and Westernization, the Balinese continue to produce profound and vital music. With its diverse track selection, great musicianship, sparkling digital sound, and intriguing accompanying text, this disc has just about everything an excellent world-music compilation could need. The only thing missing here is a performance of the stunning *jegog* bamboo ensemble, and those hooked by this delightful recording will find one on the *Music of Bali* set reviewed on page 860.

Jeffrey Muhr

Bukhara: Musical Crossroads of Asia ♪♪♪♫ (Smithsonian, 1991, prod. Theodore Levin, Otanazar Matykubov)

Uzbekistan
genre: Sozanda, mavrigi, shashmaqam, liturgical chant

Tofakhon; Ensemble Nozanin—Gulmira Rakkhimova; Tamara Kandova; Gunchekhra Mamedova, Raya Borukhova, Saifullah Abdullaev; Hussein Kasimov; Madhi Ibodov; Ochil Ibragimov; Suleiman Takhalov; Izro Malakhov; Mahmudjan Tojiboev; Zakir Bobotonov; Saifullajan Musaev; Orif Bobo Hamro; Rakhamim Yakutelov; Yakub Meer Ochildiev; Muhammad Aminjon Nasriddinov (Tajikistan, Uzbekistan); Isaac Kataev. (All artists are from Uzbekistan except where otherwise noted.)

Since before the time of Alexander the Great, the city of Bukhara, located along the ancient "Silk Route" in Central Asia's Uzbekistan, served as a trading post and cultural center for peoples from a vast number of lands, and the diversity of people still living here, including Persians, Turko-Mongolians, even Persian-speaking Jews, is reflected in the wealth of Bukharan music. In this compilation, musicologists Levin and Matykubov select four genres from the Bukharan canon: *sozanda* social music; *mavrigi* music; the *shashmaqam* repertory of central Asian "classical" music; and liturgical chant. *Sozanda,* which takes its name from the professional female musicians who traditionally played it, is a style for performance at social occasions, such as births, weddings, veiling ceremonies, or any of the *toy* (celebration) events that are put on for almost any reason in Bukhara. Essentially, the music is designed to provide pure entertainment. Rousing and rhythmic, it makes for invigorating listening. Heard between the sozanda suites are a pair of *mavrigi* tunes. This style, traditionally performed by males who trace their ancestry to Iranian Shiite Muslim slaves brought into Bukhara, parallels sozanda in being

played for similar occasions and having similarities in its structure and accompaniment. Next heard are a pair of *shashmaqam* songs. These "art" songs prospered in the Muslim court from the late 1700s until the Soviet revolution swept into the region. Played on the Uzbek *tambur* (an ancestor of the Indian sitar), or the Kashgar *rabab* (spike fiddle), these melodies, set to classical verse, seem to hybridize the music of the Islamic Middle East and Asia with that of the Indian subcontinent. Finally we hear a set of liturgical chants, such as the Muslim "call to prayer" and readings from Jewish kabbalistic texts. The minutely detailed annotation provided by Levin and Matykubov will be a goldmine of information for those with a specific interest in this region, but probably a bit too scholarly for the more casual listener. Those who want to explore Central Asian music in even greater depth will want to take a look at Levin's book and CD, *The Hundred Thousand Fools of God.*

Jeffrey Muhr

Burmese Music Series ♪♪♪♪♪ (Shanachie, 1997, prod. Rick Heizman, Henry Kaiser)

Burma (Myanmar)
genre: Pat waing, saing waing, saung gauk

Kyaw Kyaw Naing; U Phone; U Yee Nwe; Daw Yi Yi Thant; U Ohn Lwin; U Tin Yi; Ko Ba Htay; Zaw Win Maung; Kko Kyaw Swe; Ko Thien Htay; Ko Yint Sein; U Kyi; U Tin Maung. (All artists are from Burma.)

Consisting of three CDs, grouped here for review purposes but available separately—*White Elephants and Golden Ducks: Enchanting Musical Treasures from Burma*, *Pat Waing: The Magic Drum Circle of Burma*, and *Sandaya: The Spellbinding Piano of Burma*—this wonderful series captures an unforgettably rich musical canon. Like much music from Southeast Asia, Burmese music puts an emphasis on percussion such as tuned drums or gongs, and often uses seven-note (heptatonic) scales—yet its frenetic, intricate sound is absolutely unique. Burmese melodies, broken into unusual phrases, flow in directions that don't sound intuitive to the Western ear, yet feel exquisitely refreshing. The most common ensemble in Burmese music is the *saing waing,* a group consisting of two sets of gongs called the *kyi waing* and *maung zaing*; a double-reed oboe called the *hne*; two sets of tuned drums called the *chauk lon bat* and *pat waing*; *siwa* finger cymbals; and a few other instruments. Various instruments from this group can be played solo or combined in different permutations. The Burmese have also made several Western adoptions, including the piano, slide guitar, and mandolin.

The *White Elephants* disc summarizes the basic Burmese sounds, with quite a variety of ensembles presented. One of the many highlights is the pair of tracks featuring the *saung gauk,* a gorgeous harp that is one of the classic instruments of Burma. On "Phu Pwae Lat Tin (The Hug)" it accompanies a delicate vocal, and on "Nan Bhon Thi Har Bway (Distinguished Palace for Royalty)" it trades masterful solos with a *pattala* bamboo xylophone. Another astonishing moment is "Ar Kar Na Ban (Heavenly Space)," a mandolin solo of staggering beauty. The *Pat Waing* and *Sandaya* discs focus more tightly on specific instruments, but also offer a variety of music. The piano, featured on *Sandaya,* was first imported to Burma around the late 1800s, and has come to play an important part in the nation's music. It is played solo, with a vocalist, or with various ensembles. Burmese pianists have learned to play heptatonic music in the style of the saung gauk on the diatonic keyboard using the "extra" notes as embellishment. On tracks like "Than Yoe (Simple Melody)," a learning melody, we gain a bit of insight into how root melodies are used as "skeletons" upon which elaborate improvisations are built. Yet these melodies remain wonderfully evasive, giving the songs a mysterious flavor and fostering the illusion that they are completely improvised on the spot, like some kind of traditional Asian free jazz. While each CD is well worth having, those on a limited budget can start with the fine overview provided by *White Elephants* without missing too much. At presstime two more volumes, *Saung Gauk: The Enchanting Harp of Burma* and *Silver Strings of the Golden Land: Slide Guitar, Mandolin, Banjo, Violin, and Zither of Burma* are planned for release and eagerly awaited.

Jeffrey Muhr

China: Time to Listen ♪♪♪♪ (ellipsis arts . . . , 1998, compilation prod. Josef Bomback)

China
genre: Chinese classical

The Huaxia Chamber Ensemble; Shan Wen Tong; Thundering Dragon; Sisi Chen; Wu Man. (All artists are from China.)

It is indeed "time to listen" to Chinese music, the traditions of which predate Western music by thousands of years. Its principles are quite different from what Westerners expect, but perhaps all the more fascinating for this. Every song comes from a story, which provides an essential historical or folkloric subtext for Chinese listeners. Composition relies on melody rather than Western-style harmony, which can sound jarring or lacking in progression and resolution to Western ears. Chinese instrumentalists will play with little concern for harmonizing with fellow musicians, their melodies operating independently—yet within strict rules and traditions. In China, professional musicians tend to be highly educated and receive a paycheck from the state, with little pressure to meet commercial demands as

in the West. This cultivates confident musicianship and stable lifestyles, while also offering little incentive for musicians to push the limits of their art form. So, while this three-volume set showcases a wide variety of styles, there is little sense of an avant-garde or of rapid evolution in the music. But that music's tradition is rich enough as is, especially to unfamiliar Western listeners. It is absurd that so little Chinese music is available in the USA when China contains one-fifth of the world's population, so it is a pleasure to have this collection's window on the current state of the art.

David Poole

Deep in the Heart of Tuva: Cowboy Music from the Wild East ♪♪♪♪ (ellipsis arts . . . , 1996, prod. Ralph Leighton)

Tuva
genre: Throat-singing, overtone singing, höömeï

Oleg Kuular; Oorzhak Khunashtaar-ool; Bilchi-Maa Davaa; Shaktar Shulban; Kongar-ool Ondar; Kaigal-ool Khovalyg; Nadezhda Kuular; the Tuvan State Ensemble Sayani; Sainkho Nahchylak; Mikhail Alperin (Russia); Huun-Huur-Tu; the Bulgarian Women's Choir Angelite (Bulgaria); Albert Kuvezin; Yat-Kha; Paul "Earthquake" Pena (USA). (All artists are from Tuva except where noted otherwise.)

Largely unknown to Westerners just a few years ago, the remote corner of Asia known as Tuva is now a popular destination on the world-music map. The exotic sound of Tuvan "throat-singing," or *höömeï,* can be heard on a spate of CDs, and Tuvan musicians such as the group Huun-Huur-Tu now tour the world regularly. The manner in which this state of affairs came to pass is as strange and intriguing as the music itself.

The story begins with the Nobel Prize–winning physicist Richard Feynman. Feynman had been fascinated with the idea of Tuva since he came across some odd-looking postage stamps from the nation as a child. Sitting over dinner with friend Ralph Leighton in the late 1970s, Feynman proposed a trip there on a whim, even though neither of them knew a thing about Tuva. Since it was under the domination of the Soviet Union at the time, getting there turned out to be insanely difficult, even for a man of Feynman's stature. Along the way, Feynman and Leighton obtained some records of Tuvan music from a professor in Moscow, which they passed on to a local world-music DJ after recovering from the shock of the strange vocalizations they had heard. They even set up a little club they dubbed "The Friends of Tuva." Ironically, musical scholar Theodore Levin made it there (and recorded *Tuva: Voices from the Center of Asia*) while Feynman was still struggling to get official clearances from the Soviets. In a final twist of fate, a letter from Soviet authorities granting Feynman approval to travel in Tuva arrived just days after he died of cancer, but his efforts helped to establish a solid relationship between Tuva and the American academic community. The road paved, Tuvan music would burst onto the scene in the U.S. following the demise of the Soviet Union.

Produced by Leighton, *Deep in the Heart of Tuva* is a pleasurable tour through the Tuvan music scene, with an emphasis on some of the cross-cultural experimentation that has taken place in the wake of Tuva's world-music popularity. The album assembles cuts from a number of CDs in wide release, as well as some rare tracks previously available only on imports or "Friends of Tuva" editions. The first section of the CD contains several examples of "primal" or "pure" höömeï (see the review of *Tuva: Voices from the Center of Asia*, on page 865, for more on the technique). Included here are two tracks from the legendary singer Oorzhak Khunashtaar-ool that boggle the mind with their bizarrely resonant, flowing, robotic sound. The next part highlights songs with instrumental accompaniment such as the *khomus* mouth harp or the *igil* two-stringed fiddle. Notable here is the touching "Shamanic Prayer for Richard Feynman," sung to the beat of a *dungur* animal-skin drum. The final portion documents a number of cross-cultural experiments between Tuvans, Russians, Bulgarians, and Americans, like the *kargyraa* style throat-song by American blues singer "Earthquake" Pena. Some of these efforts work better than others, but the nobility of the attempt is what counts here. The CD is accompanied by a pleasantly designed booklet; Leighton's text, a bit of an amble through Tuvan culture, is nicely illustrated with color photographs. In all, *Deep in the Heart of Tuva* is a nice place for the curious to start the same voyage of discovery made by Leighton and Feynman themselves.

Jeffrey Muhr

Holding Up Half the Sky: Voices of Asian Women
🎵🎵🎵🎵 (Shanachie, 1999, compilation prod. Randall Grass)

International
genre: Asian traditional and contemporary

Liu Sola (China); Najma Akhtar (India/England); Shizura Ohtaka (Japan); Euis Komariah (Java); Nenes (Okinawa); Yulduz Usmanova (Uzbekistan); Nasida Ria (Indonesia); Yungchen Lhamo (Tibet); Idjah Hadidjah (Java); Sainkho Namchilak (Tuva); Chawiwan Damnoen (Thailand); Aidysmaa Kandan and Chirgilchin (Tuva); Daw Yi Yi Thant (Burma/Myanmar); Choying Drolma and Steve Tibbetts (Tibet).

In Asia, the only regular outlet for female musicians is the voice, which the women wield as storytellers of traditional ways and advocates against patriarchal societies. This album (one of a series whose African, Celtic, and reggae volumes are reviewed on pages 842, 913, and 914, respectively) is the first representative collection of Asian female vocalists, offering up 14 tracks representing

13 nations. The classically trained Liu Sola teams up with über-producer Bill Laswell to create "The Broken Zither (Introduction)," a jazzy, experimental collaboration about seeking adventure that ranges from Chinese opera to Japanese *Noh* theater. The English-born Najma (who usually goes by her first name) was to be a chemical engineer before discovering her Indian background through the *ghazal*—a short devotional lyric poem. She has worked with contemporary artists ranging from Jah Wobble to Page & Plant. Shizuru Ohtaka rose to fame via backup singing (Kyu Sakamoto's hit "Sukiyaki") and TV commercials, making her known as "the voice of seven colors." Having joined forces with Mott the Hoople's Morgan Fischer and Nubian luminary Hamza El Din, she has a unique style combining singing, speaking, vocal effects, and, in 1997's "Lovetune," an imaginary language. Euis Komariah and Idjah Hadidjah came up through the Indonesian *gamelan* (tuned percussion ensemble) and puppet theater respectively, and are now demonstrating the incredible range and emotion in their own music and vocals. Yulduz Usmanova had the honor of authoring a national anthem for Uzbekistan—here, she escapes former Soviet repression with a 1995 Euro-pop/Uzbeki lament entitled "Ona." Yungchen Lhamo's name translates to "goddess of song," and she fulfills this role to make the world aware of the plight of Tibetan exiles like herself. Sainkho (another usually one-name artist) is better known in avant-garde and jazz circles than traditional, but she pays attention to her Tuvan roots with the danceable 1992 "Tanola Nomads," which is produced by Belgian avant-garde/jazz impresario Hector Zazou. Also collaborating with "outside" producers, this time Rick Heizman and Henry Kaiser, Daw Yi Yi Thant delivers the sweet "Kyar Chi Yan," a Burmese royal court solo piece. Tibetan Buddhist nun Choying Drolma and American guitarist Steve Tibbetts released *Cho* in 1997; from that album, "Kyema Mimin" includes the nuns of the Nagi Gompa Buddhist Nunnery in Nepal. There are even more tracks here by artists and ensembles from Indonesia and Tuva, as well as Okinawa (featuring *shima uta,* a.k.a. island songs) and Thailand (the poetic *mor lam* from the Laos and Isan regions). With resourcefulness and resiliency, this album's lineup has talent to burn and not a woman to spare.

Stacy Meyn

Homrong: Musicians of the National Dance Company of Cambodia 🎵🎵🎵 (RealWorld, 1991, prod. Richard Evans, Richard Blair, Bill Lobban)

Cambodia
genre: Pinpeat

But Channa; Chap Siphat; Em Theay; Hun Sarath; Keo Snguon; Kreal Chan Thol; Meas Saem; Nol Mech; Sin Samadekcho; Sok Mom; Sok Torng; Yem Dong. (All artists are from Cambodia.)

Homrong features the music of a *pinpeat* ensemble, a type of percussion-based orchestra heard in Cambodia, Thailand, and Laos. Traditionally, such orchestras functioned within the royal courts of the region, playing for ceremonies and backing refined classical dance performances that were held to entertain the nobility. During the reign of the Khmer Rouge in Cambodia, the pinpeat, "classical" dance, and the culture they stood for were wiped out. Only recently have these arts begun to grow anew in Cambodia, and in the process to be recognized as a cultural treasure rather than a royal vestige. The lively, busy sound of the pinpeat is oriented rhythmically toward reflecting the intricate, elegant movements of the dancers that it often accompanies. But on *Homrong*, the full ensemble, which includes the *ranat* wooden xylophone, *khong* gong row, *srlay* oboe, and several strings and drums, only comes into play on a couple tracks such as "Preah Chinnavong" and the "Tep Monorom Dance." On most of the cuts, various portions of the orchestra are used to back vocal folk songs, as on "Nor Kor Reach," in which the three-stringed *chappay* opens the piece with an elegant modal solo, then settles in to accompany the vocal. Though the tracks are quite endearing and crisply recorded, the CD suffers from poor liner notes, which make mention of the horrors of the Khmer Rouge era but say next to nothing about the pinpeat, its instruments, or other details that might help to draw unfamiliar listeners into the music. For a more thorough treatment, you might want to check out any of the three volumes of Celestial Harmonies' *Music of Cambodia* series, reviewed on page 860.

Jeffrey Muhr

The Hugo Masters: An Anthology of Chinese Classical Music 𝄢𝄢𝄢𝄢 (Celestial Harmonies, 1992, prod. Aik Yew-goh)

China
genre: Chinese classical

Members of the Beijing Opera; Shanghai Chinese Orchestra; Shanghai Film Chinese Orchestra; Xinhai Music Conservatory of Guang; Conservatory of Music Shanghai; Frontline Dance and Music Group. Soloists: Li Ming-Xiong; Deng Jian-Dong; Yun He-Yun; Hua Yan-Jun; Shen Feng-Quan; Zeng Jia-Qing; Liu Tian-Hua; Min Hui-Fen; An Zhi-Shun; Zhu Kan-Fu; Yang Wei; Ma Mei Ye; Wu Jiang; Liu Bo; Han Zhi Ming; Li Yi; Xu Feng Xia; Du Chong; Rao Ning Xin; Wang Wei; Cheng Gong Liang; Wu Zhao Ji; Li Bian. (All artists are from China.)

This is the most comprehensive single collection of Chinese classical music, selected from engineer Aik Yew-goh's Hugo record label. Aik traveled across China to record traditional music as played by artists old enough to have performed prior to the revolution and therefore still be part of the oral tradition that has been passed down for the last 3,000 years. Chinese classical music was transformed in the 20th century by the introduction of Western instruments by the Russians and the Chinese state's use of music as propaganda. The music is rarely found in a written form, and as the bearers of the oral tradition pass away, documentation such as this album is crucial to its survival. *The Hugo Masters* is divided into four volumes, each spotlighting, though not exclusive to, a particular category of instrument. The lutes and zithers of *Volume 1: Bowed Strings* and *Volume 2: Plucked Strings* vary greatly in their number of strings, frets, and overall size. These can be heard in group and solo settings on soothing songs about nature. One of the "stars" of *Volume 3: Wind Instruments* is the *xun,* an egg-shaped instrument that is blown at the tip and played along the side. The oldest of these to be found thus far is made of stone and dates back 7,000 years; others have been made of bone or ivory. The most widespread wind instrument of course is the flute, of which there are many varieties in China. Percussion instruments serve the same effect in this music as harmonies do in Western music, that is to form an underlying expression, set a contrast, and propel the music forward. *Volume 4: Percussion* features drums, gongs, and cymbals of varying sizes and tones, always as part of an ensemble, evoking "The Rumbling Ocean," the march of "The General's Victory," and the grandeur of "Flying Dragons and Jumping Tigers."

David Poole

Istanbul 1925 𝄢𝄢𝄢𝄢 (Traditional Crossroads, 1994, compilation prod. Harold G. Hagopian)

Turkey
genre: Turkish classical (fasil), Arabesk

Sükrü Tunar; Mahmut Celalettin; Münir Nurettin Selçuk; Udi Hrant Kenkulian; Deniz Kizi; Kanuni Artaki Candan-Terzian (Armenia/Turkey); Sadettin Kaynak; Kemani Haydar Tatliyay (Greece/Turkey); Suzan Yakar (Armenia/Turkey); Udi Marko Çolakoglu; Kuçuk Nezihe Hanim (Greece/Turkey); Kemani Nubar Tekay-Çömlekçiyan; Perihan Altindag; Rakim Elkutlu; Hanende Agyazar Efendi. (All artists are from Turkey except where noted otherwise.)

The Ottoman Empire was headquartered in Constantinople and covered a large portion of the eastern Mediterranean including Turkey, Armenia, and Greece. After the decline of the empire and the installation of Kemal Atatürk as president of the Turkish republic in 1923, Constantinople became Istanbul. The city, just as in the heyday of the Empire, was a cultural magnet, attracting artists from all over Asia Minor. During the '20s Istanbul became fertile territory for record companies seeking to document and sell the work of the country's leading musicians. In addition, Mohamed Abdel Wahab's experiments in Egypt with Western musical instruments were beginning to make an impression with some of the more adventuresome performers in Turkey, though not enough to displace the still-strong Turkish classical tradition. Kanuni Artaki Candan-Terzian was a renaissance figure within this musical ferment. He was a scholarly musician and composer who played the zither-like *kanun,* but he also managed a recording studio for the Turkish branch of HMV and supervised all the music heard on this album. Each of the performers here (especially Udi Hrant Kenkulian, a.k.a. Udi Hrant) was very popular in his or her day, and these recordings document a bygone era the impact of which is still being felt by modern Turkish musicians.

Garaud MacTaggart

Japanese Noh Music: The Kyoto Nohgaku Kai ♪♪♪♪
(Lyrichord, prod. Katsumasa Takasago)

Japan
genre: Noh

Mitsuharu Morita; Hiroshi Sowa; Katsuxo Taniguchi; Kinichi Kodera. (All artists are from Japan.)

Japanese court theater or *gagaku* is divided between the popular *kabuki* and the highbrow *noh,* in which Buddhist stories are underscored with shrill flute playing (*nohkan*) and drummers who call to each other, chanting a drawn out "yoh" to mark time between beats. Noh music colors the symbolic gestures of the dancers, who wear grotesque carved masks to denote demon, deity, warrior, or noble lady. Like a soundtrack isolated from its movie, noh music lacks the plot and visual impact of the complete performance, yet for Westerners it still evokes medieval Japan, Kurosawa films, and the exotic qualities of Buddhist culture. These nine compositions were recorded in Kyoto and offer a taste of the *Nohgaku* school of noh theater, one of five existing in Japan today.

David Poole

The King Records World Music Library: Indonesian Music Titles, Vols. 1–31 ♪♪♪♪ (King Records, 1991–97, prod. various)

Indonesia
genre: Gamelan

Diverse artists and ensembles over many volumes, including: Gamelan Selonding Guna Winangun; Langen Praja Mankunegaran, directed by R. M. Mg. Rana Suripta; Amag Sip; Amag Sanep; Rebana Desa Nyelot; Gamelan Telek Desa Batu Tulis. (All artists are from Indonesia.)

The 31 Indonesian titles from Japanese label King Records' massive "World Music Library" are one of the largest collections of CDs dedicated to Indonesian music. Beautifully digitally recorded, they cover a huge swath of musical ground, mainly

through the islands of Java and Bali, and include many of the major styles of *gamelan* music. Gamelan is the name given to an ensemble of instruments composed chiefly of metal gongs and metallophones (xylophones with metal keys). The roots of the gamelan extend into Asian prehistory. The earliest proto-gamelan instrument was the "gong-chime," a kind of metal gong bossed with a central nipple and suspended on a rack horizontally. This instrument apparently originated in Java in the Asian Bronze Age around the third century B.C. From there, the gong-chime spread across Southeast Asia, eventually to play a significant role in music throughout the region, from Burma to the Philippines. In Java, a variety of other bronze instruments came to be developed, and by A.D. 347 the first known gamelan ensemble, the *gamelan munggang,* had been created.

Today, a typical gamelan consists of several hanging gongs of various sizes, several types of kettle-gongs or gong-chimes, and as many as six types of keyed metallophones suspended over different types of resonators. Stringed zithers, a two-stringed fiddle called the *rebab,* bamboo flutes, drums, and vocalists might be included. The sound of gamelan, whether played in rapid and frenetic or slow and meditative style, is shimmering and reverberant. Based on elaboration around a repeating series of beat cycles, gamelan music is typically "stratified"—the lowest-pitched instruments play the slow skeletal framework, while the highest in pitch play rapid melodic elaborations. The major centers of gamelan today are the islands of Bali and Java, and the King Records series covers both extensively. Also covered are a number of other genres of Balinese ensemble music, along with a few musical forms from Lombok and Sumatra. A few of the many highlights from the series:

The Gamelan of Cirebon presents a unique gamelan style heard on the coast of Java northeast of Sunda. More cheerful than the stately central Javanese court ensembles, Cirebonese gamelan often backs a local improvisational dance called the *tayuban,* a masked dance known as *wayang topeng,* or a puppet show called *wayang golek.* Played on iron instruments rather than the more common bronze, the performances on the CD have a soft, pleasing tone, and the big, low gongs come through with much force. As they follow the flow of the dance or puppet performance, the musicians control the dynamics of volume and tempo expertly, alternating between lively passages that make use of what sound like *kecer* cymbal clappers to punctuate the beat, and smooth, meditative interludes. On *Gamelan Selonding "Guna Winangun," Tenganan* we hear an iron gamelan once again, this time from Bali. The instruments for this type of sacred ensemble are said to have dropped from the heavens in the form of thunder, and few recordings of *gamelan selonding* have been permitted. Oddly, selonding ensembles have no gongs, using only several sets of metallophones and a *ceng-ceng,* a small cymbal. Lacking the frenetic quality of much modern Balinese gamelan, the music is measured, delicate, and sparkling, and its use of pauses to create a "roaring silence" is particularly striking. *Music of Mangkunegaran Solo I* presents the classic gamelan of Surakarta or "Solo" in central Java. A deeply meditative and stately style, Solonese gamelan has been recorded often, but seldom this beautifully. Arguably as atmospheric as the classic LP *Javanese Court Gamelan Vol. 2* 𝄞𝄞𝄞𝄞 (Nonesuch, 1977, prod. by Robert E. Brown), this disc has a gorgeous ambient sound, capturing many thunderous lows, yet clearly resolving the individual character of the instruments. The music of the ancient "Rain of Love" and "Rain of Perfume" ensembles heard here seems to transcend time and geography altogether, leaving the listener enraptured. Finally, *The Music of Lombok* takes us to an island just east of Bali with a distinctly different musical culture. Unlike their Hindu neighbors in Bali, the native Sasaks of Lombok were Islamicized in the 1500s and their music naturally takes some of its inspiration from the Muslim world. An important musical instrument here is the *rebana,* a single-headed drum that came from the Arabic peoples and is associated symbolically with the spread of Islam. Pentatonic gamelan-like melodies are pounded out with sticks on tuned groups of these drums, and we hear three such rebana tracks on the disc. Also featured are a set of duets for *genggong* or jew's-harp. These recordings, made in a hut during a strong rain, radiate a beautiful sense of peace. Finally, we hear the *gamelan telek,* a rapid and rhythmically simple style that includes plenty of embellishments from the drum accompaniment. While a few King titles are usually available in record stores, most will have to be special-ordered (King Record Co., Ltd., 1-2-3, Otowa, Bunkyo-ku, Tokyo 112-0013 Japan; telephone: 81-3-3945-2134; fax: 81-3-3945-4806; e-mail: kokusai@kingrecords.co.jp). It's worth the extra effort to obtain them, because they provide a broad insight into one of the most complex and rewarding musical cultures in the world.

Jeffrey Muhr

Music from the Morning of the World 𝄞𝄞𝄞𝄞𝄞
(Elektra/Nonesuch, 1966/1988, prod. David Lewiston)

Indonesia
genre: Gamelan, kecak, gong kebyar

Artists not identified. (All artists are from Bali.)

Probably one of the first albums of Balinese music to appear on a non-academic label in the U.S., this disc showcases a broad spectrum of the island's *gamelan* (tuned percussion) music and includes excerpts from the spine-chilling *kecak* performance. This dance, which opens and closes the CD, has an odd history. Created by Dutch expatriate artist Walter Spies in the 1930s, the kecak took the *a cappella* vocal element from the ancient exorcism trance ritual called the *sanghjang,* placing it in the context of the Hindu *Ramayana* epic. The result was a new style of music for performance, driven by spooky cries of "chak" from a male chorus as they play the part of the armies of the monkey-god Hanuman in battle with the demon Ravana. Between these kecak excerpts can be heard examples of several gamelan styles, the best known being the *gamelan gong kebyar.* Set to dances or played as a pure instrumental, the gong kebyar features a shimmering gamelan orchestra of metallophones with bronze keys, bronze gongs, drums, and other instruments. Kebyar, which means "bursting into flame," accurately describes the dramatic, explosive sound produced as the gamelan players interweave their notes using a technique called *kotekan.* This "interlocking" instrumental practice allows pairs of metallophone players to perform single melodic lines with incredible speed. The wonderfully strident dynamics on the *baris* dance performed here sound like a giant clockwork gone wild or a musical thunderstorm, while the *barong* dance, played on the five-note *pelog* scale (like much of the gamelan music on the CD), carries a powerfully hypnotic resonance—a characteristic of many styles of Balinese music. The recording also includes several non-gamelan tracks, including flute solos, vocal solos, and the *sekehe gambuh* flute ensemble. These selections, generally sedate and gentle, constitute a nice counterpoint to the overwhelming power of the gamelan ones. In all, this is one of the best short compilations of Balinese music available—and best starting points for the curious. In 1987, Lewiston returned to record the follow-up, *Bali: Gamelan and Kecak,* reviewed on page 853.

Jeffrey Muhr

The Music of Armenia Vols. 1–6 𝄞𝄞𝄞𝄞 (Celestial Harmonies, 1995, prod. David Parsons, Kay Parsons)

Armenia
genre: Armenian traditional

The Haissmavourk Choir; Shoghaken Ensemble; Sharakan Early Music Ensemble; Gevorg Dabagian; Gregor Takushian; Eduard Harutunian; Kamo Khachaturian; Karineh Hovhannessian. (All artists are from Armenia.)

Armenia has a history of poor luck, sandwiched between Russia and Iran, persecuted by the Turks, suffering a devastating earthquake in 1988 and an ongoing war with neighboring oil-rich Azerbaijan. Armenian music is appropriately melancholy, as is well documented in this six-volume survey. Excommunicated along with all the Near Eastern Christian churches in A.D. 451,

Armenia's Christian hymns developed their own unique timbre. *Volume One: Sacred Choral Music* will appeal to fans of Gregorian chant, albeit sung in Armenian Grabar. Given the country's location, the familiar harmonies of a European-style church choir are mixed with modal melodies that evoke Asian forms. The acoustics are tremendous in the Holy Echmiadzin Cathedral and the Geghard Monastery. Rather than an *a cappella* choir, *Volume Two: Sharakan* features many of the same songs arranged for the soloist Armenuhi Seiranian and a chamber ensemble. The hymns, and the volume's title, are all drawn from an early Christian songbook. The last four volumes survey Armenian "folk" song, though the sophistication of the troubadour's compositions place them within the classical tradition. Vocalists are accompanied by *duduk* (oboe), *kanon* (zither), and various other traditional instruments on *Volume Five: Folk Music/ Shoghaken Ensemble* and *Volume Six: Nagorno/Karabakh,* while vocal-less versions spotlight these settings themselves on *Volume Three: Duduk* and *Volume Four: Kanon. Volume Six* was recorded in the Nagorno/Karabakh war zone, and it is extraordinary to hear the artists sing with such vigor during such strife. Indeed, the overall tone of this survey is meditative and oddly calming, evoking an ancient and sophisticated civilization. While the stories behind the songs are often tragic or somber, the music itself is soothing and graceful—a fusion of styles unique to this vibrant yet ill-fated country.

David Poole

The Music of Bali, Vols. 1–3 ♪♪♪♪ (Celestial Harmonies, 1997, prod. David Parsons)

Indonesia
genre: Gamelan, jegog, kecak, tektekan

Swara Cipta Priyanti; Tojan; Rama Budaya; Gamelan Tirta Sari. (All artists are from Bali.)

The Music of Bali is notable for its clear sound and its attention to styles that have not often been recorded. The first disc is devoted entirely to *jegog,* an ensemble of marimba-like bamboo instruments that produces melodies of earth-shattering impact. The largest of these instruments, called *jegogan,* consist of eight enormous bamboo tubes, and are so massive that their players must straddle atop them as they strike the tubes with rubber mallets. The primary melody is played by these and several other lower-octave instruments, and enlarged on by several higher-octave ones. Jegog is chiefly played for entertainment rather than ritual, and exhausting competitions are often held in which the rival ensembles beat the living daylights out of their instruments and even attempt to drown one another out by playing at the same time. (The style's throbbing low harmonics give it a visceral and spooky

ambience that belies the light-hearted manner in which it is most often performed.)

The second disc presents *legong gamelan* (a dance form of the well-known gamelan tuned-percussion genre), which merges aspects of the ancient seven-tone *semar pegulingan* ("gamelan of the Love God") with the frenetic modern *gong kebyar.* Though in general its sound is very familiar to those who have heard Balinese gamelan before, it has certain specific characteristics, such as a trebly note range, that suit its use as dance music. A notable track from this disc is the *kebyar*-styled "Ujan Mas," which opens with a lightning-quick interlocking melody, then moves into a watery solo for *reyong,* a row of small upturned gongs balanced in a wooden frame. The piece closes in rousing fashion as the full ensemble and drums kick into action.

The most intriguing music heard on the final disc is *tektekan,* a ritual form that is used to dispel malevolent spirits or employed as a means of purification. Derived from *beleganjur,* a marching music played widely in religious processions throughout Bali, tektekan adds the use of bamboo slit-drums. The repetition of the main rhythm, occasionally punctuated with accelerated passages in which crashing cymbals and shrieks from the musicians bring the music to a crescendo, is ominous and absolutely riveting. Illustrated booklets with each disc provide clear, brief summaries of the styles covered. With 70 minutes of music per disc, this set is a good value as a follow-up to introductory collections of the island's music such as *Music from the Morning of the World* (reviewed on page 859).

Jeffrey Muhr

The Music of Cambodia, Vols. 1–3 ♪♪♪♪♪ (Celestial Harmonies, 1993, prod. David Parsons)

Cambodia
genre: Pi phat, pinpeat, mahori, taam ming

Diverse artists and ensembles, not all identified. Vol. 3: Yeum Sang; Prach Chhuon; Sok Duch; Khan Heuan; Yon Khien. (All artists are from Cambodia.)

This path-breaking set of CDs surveys many important musical styles of Cambodia, some of them for the first time. Recorded at the ancient Angkor Wat temple complex, the first volume, called *Nine Gong Gamelan,* includes several tracks of the unusual *taam ming* funeral ensemble, an orchestra consisting of a set of nine gongs, another large gong, an oboe-like instrument called the *srlay,* and drums. While calling this ensemble a *gamelan* (Indonesia's famed tuned-percussion ensemble) is a misnomer (a fact readily admitted by producer Parsons in his text), its somber sound does resemble the form; the cyclic rhythmic structure is strongly reminiscent of Javanese-style gamelan, with the srlay filling the melodic role that the *rebab* fiddle handles in the Indonesian ensemble. The remainder of the first disc records the *trot,* a dance music of the Samreh people of Cambodia's northern border, and a rural *pinpeat* ensemble. Like the pinpeat of Thailand, the Cambodian variant includes wooden xylophones called *ranak,* a keyed metallophone, and numerous gong-chimes (knobbed gongs that are set horizontally into circular frames). The lively music of the pinpeat is captured with a notably clear sound; the shimmering of the gongs seems to come through more than that on most such recordings.

The second disc, *Royal Court Music,* covers a delightful variety of genres, including a courtly, "professional" version of the pinpeat ensemble, as well as a "popular music orchestra" known as the *mahori,* which combines the pinpeat lineup with several wind and string instruments. This yields a smoother texture, as on the bright "Laang Preah Poun Leah," in which the flutes, fiddle, and hammered dulcimer seem to reveal a Chinese melodic influence. Perhaps the most intriguing music on this disc is the *arak,* a tribal form with roots in shamanism that is used chiefly for healing and magic. One of the strangest arak tracks, "Craen," features a bizarre reed instrument that sounds like a cross between a clarinet and a flute, embellishing the melodic line of a vocalist with wild note-bending and trills.

The final disc covers several unusual instruments in solo settings, such as the *kse diev,* a monochordal string instrument said to be the oldest in Khmer culture. Its soundbox is a halved hollow gourd that is pressed against the player's chest, producing an amazing visceral resonation that sounds something like a jew's-harp. Another unique sound comes from the *pey or,* a bamboo reed; when a piece of paper is applied to one of its sound holes it emits, in Parson's words, a "peculiar buzzing." Beautifully digitally recorded and supplemented with plenty of descriptive text, *The Music of Cambodia* is easily the best widely available survey of Cambodian music. Each of the discs is available separately, or the entire set can be purchased in a slip case.

Jeffrey Muhr

The Music of Indonesia, Vols. 1–17 ♪♪♪♪♪ (Smithsonian, 1991–99, prod. Philip Yampolsky)

Indonesia (Sumatra, Java, Bali, Lombok, Sumba, Sumbawa, Timor, Borneo, Kalimantan, Celebes, Sulawesi, Flores, Riau, Mentawai, New Guinea, Irian Jaya)
genre: Gandrung Bayuwangi, kroncong, dangdut, langgam Jawa, gambang kromong, lagu lama, lagu sayur, hoho, gendang Karo, gondang Toba, topeng Betawi, tanjidor, ajeng, saluang, rabab pariaman, dendang pauah, wor, yospan, zapin, mak yong,

mendu, ronggeng, talempong, didong, kulintang, salawat dulang, wayang Sasak, jemblung, wayang Banjar, topeng Banjar

Diverse artists and ensembles over many volumes.

Stunning in its breadth and unsurpassed in its detail, the *Music of Indonesia* series is one of the most ambitious regional world-music compilations ever attempted. Begun in 1991 and nearly complete as of mid-1999, the series was conceived by Anthony Seeger, the Director of Smithsonian Folkways Records, and musicologist Philip Yampolsky, as a collaborative effort with Indonesian researchers to document a wealth of music never heard before outside that nation. Stretching between mainland Asia and Australia, Indonesia's diverse and sprawling territory consists of 13,000-odd islands, including portions of some of the largest in the world such as Sumatra, Borneo, and New Guinea, and is home to several hundred unique cultures. Musically, much of Indonesia outside of Java and Bali has remained *terra incognita* even to many within the country. Seeger and Yampolsky comment: "Of the hundreds of distinct genres and styles of national and regional or ethnic music in Indonesia, only a handful have been represented on commercial recordings available in the West. Commercial releases have concentrated on . . . only a few genres (mainly the classical *gamelan* traditions)."

The *Music of Indonesia* series fills this void in spectacular fashion, covering vocal, choral, solo instrumental, and ensemble music made by scores of cultures from more than a dozen of Indonesia's major islands. While the sheer unfamiliarity and strangeness of the music will be enough to scare off the casual or average listener, the series will reward patient and careful attention with all manner of discoveries. The listening experience is guided and enhanced by marvelously detailed liner notes. Humbly described by Yampolsky as "initial forays into uncharted territory," the notes go far beyond mere track descriptions, exploring the musical and cultural context of the recordings. If the dozen or so pages of text and bibliographic material included with each volume are not enough, errata, additional commentary, and lyric transcriptions are available on the Smithsonian Institution's web site at http://www.si.edu/folkways/Indonesia/indonesia_start.htm. The site also has sound samples for each volume if you want to get an impression of the music before you buy. With three more volumes planned to complete the series, here is a rundown of the 17 titles released as of this writing:

Vol. 1: Songs before Dawn introduces to the West an entertainment genre called *gandrung Bayuwangi* from an isolated region of Eastern Java. The *gandrung* is a night-long affair in which a female dancer and singer performs a kind of stylized erotic dance with paying male guests. The sultry music, featuring vocals backed by an ensemble of drums, several gongs, and a *biola* violin, sounds a little bit like the better-known *jaipongan* of Sundanese West Java.

Vol. 2: Indonesian Popular Music includes three styles with mass appeal in Indonesia, *kroncong, dangdut,* and *langgam Jawa.* Dangdut, a music popular among youth from lower economic classes, combines elements of Middle Eastern, Indian, and Western pop. Kroncong makes use of Western instruments such as guitar, ukulele, flute, violin, and even Hawaiian guitar. While it is strongly rooted in Portuguese music from the colonial era, it has developed a distinctive gentle and rhythmic twist. And langgam Jawa twists kroncong a bit further by using the Indonesian seven-tone *pelog* scale as its melodic palette.

Vol. 3: Music from the Outskirts of Jakarta presents an ensemble music called *gambang kromong* with a sound that can only be described as bizarre to the Western ear. Combining Chinese, Indonesian, and Western instruments, the gambang kromong has a dual repertoire: the old *lagu lama,* which synthesizes Chinese and Indonesian folk music, and the *lagu sayur,* which incorporates pre–World War II American jazz. Both are played in a loose organization that grants a lot of freedom to the individual instruments as they dance around the core melody. The juxtaposition of styles and instruments is quite novel, as when Indonesian gongs play rhythm alongside brass and a riffing Hawaiian guitar on "Stambul Bila."

Vol. 4: Music of Nias and North Sumatra features several genres from the island of Nias and the area surrounding Lake Toba in North-Central Sumatra: the *gendang karo* of the Karo people, with its simple gong cycles overlaid with oboe riffs and elaborate rhythms on sets of tiny drums; the *hoho* chorus of the Oho Niha people; and two types of *gondang toba,* a frenetic and complex ensemble of tuned drums, oboes, and bossed gongs that is propelled like a runaway train by the dense melodicism of the *taganing* tuned drums and *sarune* oboe.

Vol. 5: Betawi and Sundanese Music of the North Coast of Java returns to the area surrounding Jakarta to sample more of the region's diverse musical riches. Notable are the *ajeng,* a full-blown *gamelan* (ensemble dominated by tuned percussion) that uses a double-reed instrument called the *tarompet* in place of the typical *rebab* violin and plays with the jagged rhythmic sensibility of Balinese gamelan; and the surreal, languid strains of the brass *tanjidor* ensemble.

Vol. 6: Night Music of West Sumatra documents the music of the Minangkabau of West Sumatra and includes *saluang,* a spooky and claustrophobic vocal poetry backed with flute; *rabab pariaman,* a similar form that replaces the flute with rebab; and a storytelling song style called *dendang Pauah.* Given the narrative nature of the music, complete translations of the lyrics would have been helpful.

Vol. 7: Music from the Forests of Riau and Mentawai compiles music from the central Sumatran province of Riau and from the nearby island group of Mentawai. It's a well-rounded variety of music, with highlights including the energetically ornamented xylophone and gong-row music of the Petalangan people of Riau; a percussive shamanic healing ritual; and a vocal curing song from Mentawai that sounds like the shadow of a spiritual song from the American South.

Vol. 8: Vocal and Instrumental Music from East and Central Flores and *Vol. 9: Vocal Music from Central and West Flores* are landmark volumes collecting an incredible proliferation of vocal music from the island of Flores. Yampolsky elaborates on its variety: "there is singing in parallel intervals, harmony based on thirds (like standard Western-music harmony), harmony not based on thirds, melody with drone, unison and multi-part choruses, and occasional instances of true counterpoint." A veritable feast for students and fans of vocal music.

Vol. 10: Music of Biak, Irian Jaya presents the music of an island on the northwest coast of Irian Jaya. Notable are some beautifully harmonized informal hymns sung by a women's choir in Sor, and a series of *wor* choral-and-percussion songs that serve to entertain, provide social commentary, and challenge the ability of the singers as they carry out a sort of vocal "battle."

Vol. 11: Melayu Music of Sumatra and the Riau Islands compiles several dance and theater genres of the ethnic Malay residents of the Riau islands off Singapore and Malaysia (administratively linked to the Riau province covered on Volume 7), as well as adjoining areas of Sumatra. Two of these styles are *zapin,* a distinctly Middle Eastern form with possible roots in Yemen; and *ronggeng,* a dance similar to jaipongan or gandrung Bayuwangi in its performance structure. A notable example is "Damak," which presents an elegant and amusing urbane take on ronggeng that incorporates an accordion to carry the melodic line.

Vol. 12: Gongs and Vocal Music from Sumatra revisits the Minangkabau and introduces us to the music of the Gayo and Melinting people. Beaten out on rows of shimmering gongs, the beautifully sophisticated cyclical melodies of the *talempong* and *kulintang* seem to induce a perfect balance between stimulation and relaxation in the listener.

Vol. 13: Kalimantan Strings takes us to the Indonesian portion of the island of Borneo, where stringed lutes such as the Melayu *gambus* and the Dayak *kacapi* or "boat lute" play an important musical role. On the kacapi (also known as the *sampeq* in certain regions), melodies are played against one or two drone strings, using scales that have a "sharpness" to the Western ear. They can move along with plenty of rhythmic attack, as on the violin-driven "Karangut Saritan Nampui Kambang," or bring one to the verge of tears, as on the gentle duet "Sampeq Urau," played by Kenyah musicians originally from the interior jungle. The song, said to be about a lone survivor returning from a Japanese prison after World War II, sounds to romanticizing Western ears almost like a requiem for the Dayak themselves. Transcendental listening.

Vol. 14: Lombok, Kalimantan, Banyumas: Little Known Forms of Gamelan and Wayang is the only CD in the series covering Indonesia's best-known music, the percussive *gamelan* ensemble, but it seeks to document the unconventional. We hear *Wayang Sasak* from Lombok, played by an ensemble closely resembling a Balinese *gambuh*. Spiced with metallic clappers, the gong, drum, and flute ensemble, sounding like a diminutive blacksmith shop, backs the action of the all-night *wayang kulit* puppet show. Also heard is the ingenious Central Javanese *jemblung,* a form of theater presented by a group of "actor-singers" who perform a wayang and imitate the backing gamelan with vocals only! Included as well is some refreshingly raw and amateur village wayang gamelan from Kalimantan.

Vol. 15: South Sulawesi Strings provides diverse and exciting examples of entertainment music of the Bugis, Makasar, Kajang, Mandar, and Toraja peoples of Sulawesi (the Celebes). A notable highlight is the rubbery, rapid-fire, virtuoso performance of Abdul Halim's kacapi lute ensemble. This includes songs, stories, and even parodies of Indonesian pop stars, and in the live setting is fronted by a sort of contortionist-buffoon who writhes, dances, and carries on while the real musicians play behind him.

Vol. 16: Music from the Southeast: Sumbawa, Sumba, Timor is a whirlwind tour through the island region known as Nusa Tenggara. There's plenty to enjoy, such as the tracks from Sumba featuring funerary gong ensembles that sound a bit like muted Caribbean steel bands; the snaky note-bending of a drone lute player; and the modal howling of a Timorese vocalist backed by a drone string band.

Vol. 17: Kalimantan: Dayak Ritual and Festival Music returns to the indigenous people of Borneo, covering choral music, gong ensembles, and a bamboo-tube ensemble akin to the gambang group of Bali without the metallophones. One of the many delights is the chunky, hypnotic gong-and-drum ensemble of the Benuaq people of East Kalimantan, which is played in the context of community and shamanic rituals such as the 24-day *nguguq tautn* harvest ceremony.

Jeffrey Muhr

The Music of Vietnam, Vols. 1–3 🎵🎵🎵🎵 (Celestial Harmonies, 1994–95, prod. David Parsons, Kay Parsons)

Vietnam
genre: Traditional and contemporary Vietnamese music

Phan Kim Thanh; Le Tu Cuong; Trieu Tien Vuong; The Dan; Pham Van Ty; Dang Xuan Khai; Nguyen Thi Hong Phuc; Leu Kim Thu; Thao Giang; Nguyen Xuan Hoach; Dinh Quang Huan; Lai Thi Cam Van; Nguyen Quac Ngu; Tran Dai Dung; Tran Bo; Nguyen Tan Hong; Cao Chanh Giau; Huynh Anh Tuan; La Nguyen; Duong Van Lan; Vo Minh Thanh; Nguyen Ngoc Lam; Nguyen Thi Thanh Binh; Tran Thi Nguyet Nga; Phan Thi Bach Hac; Phan Thi Thu Thuy; Phan Thi Bach Hoa; Tran Thi Thu Van; Le Thi Dieu Hy; members of the Hue Traditional Art Troupe. (All artists are from Vietnam.)

Recorded by composer and musical adventurer David Parsons and his life/artistic partner Kay Parsons, *The Music of Vietnam* is not so much an overview of Vietnamese music as a snapshot of a couple of its aspects. The first two volumes, recorded in Hanoi, bring together a sort of "supergroup" of 15 of Vietnam's greatest traditional musicians and set them to playing all kinds of traditional ensemble music. But instead of producing slavishly faithful renditions learned by rote, the group shines with creativity, verve, virtuosity, and innovation. As John Schaefer points out in his commentary to these volumes, the Vietnamese think of their traditional music as a living, evolving entity worth building upon as well as preserving. In some cases they have adopted Western styles and instruments, but always in a measured, thoughtful manner that adds to the music while maintaining its integrity. The resulting hybrid generates much excitement with its variety, novel combinations, and delicate textures. Some notable moments of this aesthetic expansion are when traces of Western harmony suddenly emerge, then disappear, as in the traditional "Dance of the Tay Nguyen Highlands," and when the sounds of neighboring Thailand and China simultaneously echo through "Stream of the T'rung." The most incredible moment may be when Le Tu Cuong adroitly coaxes a host of startling textures from a tribal Hmong *lam kep* reed-flute on "Calling Sounds of the Khen (sic) Pipe," sounding in turn like a saxophone, a shawm, a Thai *khaen* mouth organ, and a traffic jam.

The third disc, recorded in the ancient Vietnamese capital of Hue and performed by members of the Hue Traditional Art Troupe, compiles ceremonial music and kingly dances from the days of the Imperial Court. The music here is strictly traditional, showing two faces—the majesty and pomp of the *Dai Nhac,* or "great music," and the exuberance and cheer of the *Tieu Nhac,* or "elegant music." While the disc is greatly enjoyable, as a sort of historical retrospective it has to be listened to with different expectations than the first two. By the same token, the notes for the Hue volume are quite different from those of the others; written by a pair of Vietnamese experts, they are scholarly and thorough, but a bit dense and dry in comparison to the conversational commentary by Schaefer on the Hanoi discs.

In sum, *The Music of Vietnam* does an admirable job of covering both progressive and historical aspects of Vietnamese traditional music. While it should not be taken as a comprehensive anthology, since it leaves a lot of territory (like tribal music, vocal music, and the less-sophisticated regional ensembles) uncovered, the revelatory Hanoi discs alone make the set a bargain.

Jeffrey Muhr

New Music Indonesia, Vols. 1–3 ♪♪♪♪♥ (Lyrichord, 1992, prod. Jody Diamond, Larry Polansky)

Indonesia
genre: Musik murni, musik total, komposisi baru

Suhendi Afryanto; Dody Satya Ekaghustdiman; Harry Roesli; Nano S.; Pande Made Sukerta; Otok Bima Sidarta; B. Subono; I Wayan Sadra. (All artists are from Indonesia.)

This series highlights the efforts of a group of experimental musicians from West Java (Sunda), Central Java, and Bali who are creating fresh and unique sounds in a musical culture that typically focuses on its ancient traditions. Produced by Jody Diamond, a veteran researcher of Indonesian music, and Larry Polansky, the disc grew from an idea that Diamond had while documenting the state of new music, or *komposisi baru,* in Indonesia. To give financially strained composers the freedom to create, Diamond and Polansky decided to go beyond mere research and commission new compositions from pioneering artists, carrying out recording sessions in Bandung, West Java, and Surakarta, Central Java.

The first disc, *Asmat Dream*, covers the Bandung session. Featuring six fascinating pieces by four Sundanese composers, it is an inventive explosion in terms of both compositional technique and spontaneous energy. The opening piece, the free-form "Diya," summarizes some of the musical ideas that recur through the series, including the use of minimalist textures; the stringing together of contrasting loose sections or "movements" called *merangkai*; a sense of musical discovery in the use of found objects such as sandpaper, tin cans, bottles, and woks; and a random feel à la John Cage that paradoxically builds drama despite its spontaneity. "Galura," by the veteran classical and pop composer Nano S., sticks to more familiar and traditional elements—such as the Sundanese combination of *kacapi* zither and *suling* flute—but puts them in a different context to create a tense sound not unlike that of Philip Glass.

The second disc, *Mana 689*, recorded in Surakarta, features another group of four composers. Like *Asmat Dream*, it merges a sense of adventure with a respect for tradition. We hear, for example, a composition for treble *gamelan* (tuned metallic percussion) instruments called "Griting Rasa," which, in its overall sound and alternation of instrumental "overtures" with narrative passages, resembles the music of a Javanese *wayang kulit* puppet-show (so it is no surprise to find out that its composer, Blacius Subono, is also a *dalang* or puppet-master). Likewise, "Stay a Maverick," played on a conventional gamelan array, shows a healthy regard for traditional structures, yet violates them by combining the *slendro* and *pelog* scales, which are not typically used together.

The final disc, *Karya*, spotlights a single composer, the Javanese-born I Wayan Sadra. On "O-A-E-O," Sadra, who is also a visual artist, uses repetition to build tension, a method that is deeply rooted in traditional Indonesian gamelan music with its *colotomic* rhythmic cycles. Sadra also makes use of electronic and multi-tracking studio techniques on "Snow's Own Dream," which builds a rich, ghostly drone, and he draws from other cultures with his use of Sufi *zikir* (a.k.a. *zikr*) devotion and Buddhist chant on "Miba." Affirming Indonesia's continued musical vitality, *New Music Indonesia* is an exciting, surprising, and rewarding listen.

Jeffrey Muhr

The Sultan's Pleasure: From the Palace of Yogyakarta ♪♪♪♥ (Music of the World, 1989, prod. Roger Vetter)

Indonesia
genre: Gamelan

Musicians of the palace of Sultan Hamangku Buwana IX, Yogyakarta, Java. (All artists are from Indonesia.)

Though long-since politically powerless, the Javanese sultans hold an important place in the artistic life of Indonesia, specifically in Yogyakarta and Surakarta, two of the country's key cultural centers. In Yogyakarta, for example, the sultan's palace, or *kraton,* holds a large number of ancient and venerated *gamelan* ensembles. These lovingly preserved sets of instruments, some of which are several hundred years old, are composed chiefly of gongs, metallophones, and drums, and have even been given names like "Tempting to Love" or "The Torrent of Honey." Such names aptly describe the flowing, elegant sounds these instruments make as they are played by large groups of musicians using five- and seven-note scales. *The Sultan's Pleasure* excerpts a group of special performances made on three of these historical gamelans. Each year in celebration of the Sultan's birthday or *Seitu-Paing,* a set of selections called *Uyon-Uyon Hadiluhung* ("Glorious and Beautiful Game-lan Playing") is performed. This set comprises six full gamelan compositions and two vocal performances. It includes a couple of unusual pieces like "Ladrang Mares Kumencar," a *mares* or march that adds a set of marching-band tenor drums to the ensemble to punctuate the beat; and the closing track, "Ladrang Sri Kondur," a nice example of the archaic "loud" style, which is played in a vigorous fashion, typically on old gamelans with massive instruments. All told, this is a worthwhile recording; if the sound were a bit better and the descriptive notes a little longer, it might warrant a higher recommendation.

Jeffrey Muhr

Tibet: The Heart of Dharma 𝄞𝄞𝄞𝄞 (ellipsis arts . . . , 1996, prod. David Lewiston)

Tibet
genre: Chant

Monks of Drepung; Monks of Khampagar. (All artists are from Tibet.)

Some 40 years ago the Chinese communists destroyed or shut down Tibet's 6,500 monasteries. This album records the prayer chants of Tibetan monks who have taken refuge in monasteries in India. Many recordings of Buddhist prayer are available, yet the basis for musical comparison is hard to establish. The prayer is not intended as music, although the mesmeric effect of listening to the droning bass voices intoning their mantras certainly has musical properties. On the criteria of recording quality at least, it is clear that this disc meets the highest standards. The accompanying book offers evocative photography of the monasteries, background information on Buddhist tradition, and the stories behind these specific prayers. The Drepung Monastery prayers were selected by the abbot, who hand-picked 25 monks adept at *Jokkhah,* or chordal chanting, in which up to three notes are sounded simultaneously by one voice, not unlike the Tuvan style of "throat-singing." The monks also employ an *arda* or crescendo—a style in which melodies open softly, at a very low pitch, rising gradually to a full, high-pitched hum. At their peak a distinctive cadence is introduced by the addition of a deep vocal drone. At Khampagar Monastery the ritual of *Tsedrup* features chants spiced up with the ringing of the *drilbu* (handbell) and the clash of the *rolmo* (cymbal); a foghorn blast comes from a pair of *dung* (eight-foot-long trumpets). The ritual is intended to bless the participants with long life and robust health, and the monks get to knock back a little beer, which they refer to as the very "liquor of life."

David Poole

Tibetan Invocations 𝄞𝄞𝄞𝄞 (Music Club, 1998, prod. Huan Tung Sun)

Tibet
genre: Chant, spiritual, religious

Song Huei Liou; Ya Ging Ging; Sheng Horng; Sheng Yan. (All artists are from Tibet.)

Recently chants from Native American religions, medieval Catholic liturgies, and Bulgarian Easter services have found their way into world-music prominence. Here is an entry in that category from the mountain fastness of Tibet. The primary religion of that country is Buddhism, and part of its spiritual discipline involves the repetition of words to aid meditation. Three such songs comprise this disc; music of unusual—and for much of the Western world, still unfamiliar—beauty.

Kerry Dexter

Tuva: Voices from the Center of Asia 𝄞𝄞𝄞𝄞 (Smithsonian, 1990, prod. Ted Levin, Eduard Alexeev, Zoya Kirgiz)
Tuva: Among the Spirits 𝄞𝄞𝄞𝄞 (Smithsonian, 1999, prod. Ted Levin, Joel Gordon)

Tuva
genre: Throat-singing, overtone singing, höömeï

Fedor Tau; Mergen Mongush; Anatolii Kuular; Sundukai Mongush; Tumat Kara-ool; Andrei Chuldum-ool; Anchimaa Sonat; Anchimaa Khert; Anchimaa Targin; Mikhail Dopchun; Marzhimal Ondar; Ensemble Amirak; Vasili Chazir; Vasilii Khuurak; Shozhul Salchak; Polina Ore-ool; Doluma Lopsanchap; Khuren Oorzhak; Shimet Soyan; Alexander Davakai; Tatyana Sat; Balgan Kuzhuget; Bilchit-Maa Davaa; Kok-ool Khovalig; Saskur-ool Mongush; Dosumaa Mongush; Valentina Kulaar; Raisa Mongush; Lenmaa Kuular; Soskul Mongush; Kazak Sandak. (All artists are from Tuva.)

Recorded and annotated by eminent musicologist Theodore Levin, these are perhaps the two most important releases of Tuvan music, and they are without a doubt two of the most remarkable world-music issues in recent years. Though they are not sold as a set and were recorded years apart, their contents are perfectly complementary. *Voices from the Center of Asia*, made in the late 1980s, is a straightforward effort to survey styles of Tuvan music that had not yet been displaced or transformed by pop introduced from elsewhere or standardized Soviet "folk" imposed from within. *Among the Spirits*, on the other hand, attempts to recapture the primal sound-world of the Tuvans using more adventurous recording techniques and performances.

Isolated by its remote, mountainous location between Mongolia and Siberia, and by decades of domination by the Soviet Union, Tuva has, to some extent, managed to escape the cultural homogenization suffered by much of the world at the hands of the West. Like their ancestors for centuries, many of the inhabitants of this wild, windswept region are still nomadic pastoralists, hunting, raising cattle and horses, and following the contours of the landscape in search of the best pastures through the seasons. Essentially, the music of the Tuvans is a direct outgrowth of their physical environment and of a timeless lifestyle that includes an animistic respect for nature and the practice of shamanism. As described by Levin, their "music forms a discourse with nature that reinforces their sense of place, purpose and self." At the simplest level, the sonic palette that Tuvans draw upon to make music is derived from the landscapes and living creatures that surround them. Levin calls this process "sound mimesis," from the Greek word for imitation. On *Voices from the Center of Asia*, for example, musicians can be heard making masterful imitations of reindeer, wolves, birds, or domestic animals with simple vocalizations as well as instruments like the *amirge* hunting horn.

But the real heart of Tuvan music is an astonishing vocal technique called throat-singing, overtone-singing, or *höömeï*. By holding the mouth, tongue, and lips in certain configurations while vocalizing, the throat-singer can produce two or more pitches at the same time, creating, in effect, a chord. The tones generated can range from a low, earthy growl emanating from the voice box and chest, to a piercing whistle emerging from the roof of the mouth, depending on the specific technique used. Examples of all five important throat-singing styles are heard on *Voices*, including the throbbing, whipping *borbangnadyr,* said to resemble the gallop of a horse; and the soaring, flute-like *sigit*.

Though it sounds unearthly to the urbanized listener, in *Among the Spirits* Levin shows that the inspiration for throat-singing (as with other Tuvan musical expression) can be found, not surprisingly, in such natural phenomena as animal sounds, rushing brooks, waterfalls, wind, and caves, and even in other musical instruments used by Tuvans, especially the *khomus,* a kind of jew's-harp used throughout Central Asia for centuries. On cuts like "Höömeï on Horseback" and "Borbangnadyr with Stream Water," the interactive character of the music and its deep connection with nature are revealed with exhilarating clarity. More recent styles of Tuvan music place throat-singing in the context of folk song structures with backing from instruments like the *igil* two-stringed fiddle and the *doshpuluur* lute. A few examples of such songs are presented on these discs, but listeners who want to hear that aspect of Tuvan music will be better served by listening to groups like Huun-Huur-Tu and Shu-De, profiled in this book's main section.

Jeffrey Muhr

Women of Istanbul ♫♫♫ (Traditional Crossroads, 1998, compilation prod. Harold G. Hagopian)

Turkey
genre: Cabaret music

Faide Yildiz; Zehra Bilir; Fahriye Hanim; Safiye Ayla; Suzan Yakar Rutkay; Roza Eskenazi; Müzeyyen Senar; Saadet Hanim; Hamiyet Yüceses; Müserref Hanim; Mahmur Handam Hanim; Perihan Altindag Sözeri; Necmiye Ararat Hanim; Kücük Nezihe Uyar; Nedime; Nezihe; Sabite Tur Gülerman. (All artists are from Turkey.)

In the 1920s, the new secular Turkish republic turned against Ottoman court music, diverting many generations of intense musical development into the nightclubs of Istanbul, and opening space for women singers. Women from the marginalized ethnic minorities (Armenians, Greeks, Jews) took the spotlight, though in many cases they did not actually perform live but only recorded for the radio, which provided a kind of veil, hiding them from shame. This collection brings those recordings brilliantly to life through expert remastering and detailed notes. These are the outpourings of deep and responsive souls, registered in rich voices: Saadet Hanim running trills that make your tonsils hurt in empathy; Mahmur Handam Hanim singing like a Turkish dove sprung from a French cabaret; Nezihe keeping breathless pace with some nervy runs on the *oud* (Arabic lute) fretboard; and Perihan Altindag Sözeri lilting like Billie Holiday on her way to a savage breakdown. If one suspects menace and danger in the life of an Istanbul cabaret singer, it certainly appears in the songs. In an anguished moan Nedime sings, "I have had enough torture and poison from you." I loaned this album to an Egyptian chef friend, but he returned it, saying, "I love this record, it makes me weep, but if I play this in my restaurant, the food will taste like death."

Chris King

The World's Musical Traditions 6: Song Creators in Eastern Turkey ♫♫♫ (Smithsonian, 1993, prod. Ursula Reinhard)

Turkey
genre: Âşik

Şeref Taşliova; Murat Çobanoglu; Mevlut Şafak Ihsani; Rahim Saglam. (All artists are from Turkey.)

Song Creators in Eastern Turkey, the third CD in a fine series released by the Smithsonian Institution (see the review of *Bunggridj-bunggridj* on page 867 for the series' convoluted history), documents the music of four poet-singers from the towns of eastern Turkey. These bards, originally called *ozan*, traditionally wandered through Central Asia singing songs of, among other things, shamanic religion and praise to rulers or tribal leaders. After the Turkic peoples of Asia adopted Islam, ozan music came to incorporate the Shiah system of Islamic belief and aspects of Sufi thought. It was at this time that ozan singers were given the name *âşik,* which means "singer of love songs," in reference to their passionate devotional songs. The âşik have also played the role of social critics, singing on behalf of the poor and oppressed. But with the emergence of a modernized and Westernized middle class in Turkey, not to mention an oppressive government fearful of their polemics, the âşik have found it necessary to tone down this aspect of their presentation. Today epic stories are a common source for song material, because they contain elements of entertainment and traditionalism, and because social criticism can be veiled in the narrative. Episodes from the epic of Köroglu, a legendary renegade poet-singer of the 16th century, are frequently drawn upon. Often sung today in teahouses in the towns of eastern Turkey, âşik songs are performed with accompaniment only on the *saz* lute. Sometimes âşik will sing in groups, but solo singing is most common. Because of their timbral homogeneity, and because Turkish structures and scales are so different from those of European music, the 20 songs heard here might sound indistinct at first. But repeated listening is richly rewarded as the wonderful subtleties of the music start to emerge; one begins to notice more clearly, for instance, the diverse coloring provided by the lute on different tracks. The accompanying booklet of commentary is a big help in this regard, as the listener can follow along with detailed descriptions of the songs and full translations of the lyrics. At presstime *Song Creators in Eastern Turkey* was sadly out of print, but worth a search and, like so much world music in the States, likely not far from its next reissue.

Jeffrey Muhr

***The World's Musical Traditions 10: Tabla Tarang:
Melody on Drums*** ♪♪♪♪ (Smithsonian, 1996, prod. Walter Quintus)

India
genre: Raag

Pandit Kamalesh Maitra, Trilok Gurtu. (Both artists are from India.)

This CD, the seventh in a special series released by the Smithsonian Institution (see the review of *Bunggridj-bunggridj* on this page for the series' convoluted history), compiles sparkling performances for the *tabla tarang,* a set of tuned *tabla* drums. Unlike a typical tabla set, which consists of a treble drum called, confusingly, the tabla, and a bass drum called the *bayan,* the tabla tarang uses from 10 to 16 treble drums, each tuned to a specific pitch falling within a two-octave range.

Tuning is accomplished by applying a paste of rice, iron powder, and water to the center of the drum heads. In order to play specific scales, drums are added or removed from the set. The tabla tarang is a relatively recent innovation dating to the late 1800s, and its use is still rare, perhaps due to the high level of skill required to perform on it. Indeed, Pandit Kamalesh Maitra, who plays the tracks on this CD (with backing from Trilok Gurtu on tabla), is probably the only person ever to perform full-length *raags* (improvisations based on specific melodic frameworks) on tabla tarang. The CD consists of four raags of differing lengths; all are variations on the raag called *Todi,* a melodic pattern considered to invoke moods of "quietness and devotion" and also associated with the morning (raags are typically tied to times of day and their feelings). Maitra plays these in truly scintillating fashion, by turns subtle, relaxed, and forceful. The recording quality is also outstanding; the unique method used by producer Walter Quintus, which involves miking the instruments from the performers' perspective, results in a sound that is both intimate and incredibly clear. The CD includes a 54-page booklet with brief notes on tabla history and construction, biographies of the performers, a discussion of raag music theory, and descriptions of each track.

Jeffrey Muhr

AUSTRALIA

***The World's Musical Traditions 4: Bunggridj-bunggridj:
Wangga Songs by Alan Maralung*** ♪♪♪♪ (Smithsonian, 1993, prod. Allan Marett)

Australia
genre: Wangga songs

Alan Maralung, vocals and click-sticks; Peter Manaberu, didgeridoo. (Both artists are from Australia.)

Bunggridj-bunggridj is the first volume of an excellent world-music series released by the Smithsonian Institution. The odd numbering of the CD calls for a bit of historical explanation: the now defunct International Institute for Traditional Music in Berlin, Germany, had released three volumes of a series called "Traditional Music of the World" when they asked the Smithsonian to pick up the series starting with the fourth volume. After the Smithsonian had issued six of the volumes in a beautiful slip-case format under the same name as the German releases, they were threatened with legal action by another record label for using the phrase "Music of the World." Forced, at great expense, to reprint all of the existing packaging to read "The World's Musical Traditions," the Smithsonian had to take a couple volumes out of print for lack of money. As it stands, all of the existing volumes, numbered 4–6 and 8–10, are reviewed in this book; the seventh volume, *Ritual Music of Brazil*, is out of print.

In any case, *Bunggridj-bunggridj* archives a series of *wangga* songs by the late Aboriginal song master Alan Maralung. Performed both for ceremonial and non-ceremonial purposes, these songs are unusual in a number of respects. First, they are not composed, but dreamed! Aboriginal musicians receive the songs from *wahru*, or spirits, while asleep or in altered states of consciousness. In Maralung's case, the two spirits Bunggridj-bunggridj, who is a small bird, and Balandjirri, the ghost of a dead musician, "gave" him the songs recorded here, usually in dreams. Another peculiarity of the songs is that their vocal portions do not contain ordinary lyrics, but rather are sung using "special song words" that are only sometimes given symbolic meanings. The vocals are also filled out with "nonsense-syllables" that act to enhance the rhythmic flow of the song.

Accompanied by Peter Manaberu on the blown drone instrument the *didgeridoo*, Maralung sings and plays a set of clicksticks. Many of his songs are inspired by nature, wildlife, or supernatural phenomenon, like the strange "Minmin Light," which is named for a frightening illuminated spirit that appeared to him in a dream. Though careful research by producer Allan Marett clearly documents the structural complexities of the music, one need not intellectualize anything to experience the poignant simplicity in the songs' spirit. This humble spirit is embodied in Maralung's intonation of the name of his wahru Bunggridj-bunggridj at the end of each song, which serves as an affirmation that the power of his music is not primarily his own.

Jeffrey Muhr

CARIBBEAN

Afro-Cuba: A Musical Anthology ♫♫♫♫ (Rounder, 1994, prod. Morton Marks)

Cuba
genre: Afro-Cuban

Intermittently identified artists in field and studio recordings. (All artists are from Cuba.)

Cuba's sugar plantations demanded a vast influx of slaves between the years 1835 and 1864. These 400,000 Africans made up 40 percent of Cuba's population and had a profound effect on Cuban culture. Rather than focus on the well-documented and explosive mix of African and Hispanic styles, this collection examines the four dominant communities of African descent—the Lucumi, Arara, Abakua, and Kongo—whose music has remained relatively intact. African traditions were maintained by the societies

or *cabildos* these communities formed to pursue their own religious rituals. Most influential were the Lucumi, who sang in Yoruban. Their style was adapted by singers like Celia Cruz and Mercedes Valdes; one adaptation can be heard here with Gina Martin's "Song for Ogun." Known as the "white queen of black rhythms," Martin sings accompanied by a bell, a single drum, and the percussive playing of the piano. This album's recordings of various cabildos' performance groups range from simple chanting and drumming—as with the Yoruban song of praise for the god of creation, Ododua—to more sophisticated harmonies and varied percussion. The rumbas and Carnival music of the second half of the collection are sung in Spanish, yet the rhythms are still distinctly African. By focusing on Cuban music's African roots, the album unravels elements that today appear to be a seamless whole, but which in fact represent a fortunate meeting of two vibrant cultures under unfortunate circumstances.

David Poole

Angels in the Mirror: Vodou Music of Haiti ♫♫♫♫ (ellipsis arts . . . , 1997, compilation prod. Holly Nicolas, Y.M. David Yih, Elizabeth McAlister)

Haiti
genre: Vodou

Mapou Fo; Gwoup Premye Nimewo; Sanba Zawo and Djakata; Lakou Badjo; Rara La Fraicheur de L'Anglade. (All artists are from Haiti.)

Vodou (voodoo) is often misunderstood as black magic—in fact it is a way of life for the people of the Caribbean island nation of Haiti. "Vodou" means "spirit," and Haitians see a spiritual element in everything; as the title of this compilation suggests, they perceive this essence as existing just below the surface of everyday life. Vodou music is a way to communicate with spirits by singing, drumming, and dancing, with lyrics in Creole or the African Yoruba language. *Angels in the Mirror* is a field recording of traditional drumming styles and Vodou ceremonies by a variety of Haitian musicians. The accompanying guidebook provides thorough historical and photographic background on Vodou culture. Elements of this music can be heard in more commercial recordings like the Vodou/rock fusion of Boukman Eksperyans.

David Poole

Best of Straker's: Ah Feel to Party ♫♫♫♫ (Rounder, 1996, prod. Granville Straker)

Trinidad & Tobago
genre: Calypso

Shadow; Lord Melody; Count Robin; Squibby; Chalkdust; Black Stalin; Ken "Professor" Philmore; Lord Nelson; Singing Francine; Cro Cro; Protector; Marcia Miranda; Nappy Mayers; Bill Trotman; Calypso Rose; Blakie; Winston Soso (St. Vincent); Machel Mon-

tano; Poser; Duke; Brother Ebony; Explainer. (All artists are from Trinidad and Tobago except where noted otherwise.)

The Brooklyn-based Straker's label was created by Trinidadian expatriate Granville Straker in the early 1970s, and quickly established itself with a string of hits from the best calypso talent available, most of whom are featured on this two-CD set. Curiously, it was the Mighty Sparrow, arguably the most famous calypsonian ever, who gave Straker his break when he offered his old friend the chance to record a live album at no charge—yet he is about the only artist not represented here. Starting with Shadow's classic "Bass Man" from 1974, this is a high-quality excursion through an interesting point in calypso's evolution, more or less in chronological order. Consequently the first cuts tend to have a rootsier feel with echoes of earlier stars like Lord Kitchener, but already the style was shifting toward the party sound of calypso's successor, *soca*. The Straker's sound itself was strong, echoing the vitality and exuberance of its "live" origins, and due in large part to the participation of ace steel drum maestro Frankie McIntosh and the Equitables as house band for more than half of the 25 selections here, taken mostly from the mid-'80s to early '90s. Lyrically the songs tend to be less specifically political than the time-honored calypso norm, save for universal themes such as streaking, AIDS, or raising families, centering instead on partying, sexual innuendo, and dancing as per the soca legacy. This collection is a sure sign of Straker's' persistence at the forefront of promoting must-hear Trinidadian music.

Derek Rath

By the Rivers of Babylon: Timeless Hymns of Rastafari
𝄞𝄞𝄞𝄞 (Shanachie, 1997, compilation prod. Randall Grass)

Jamaica
genre: Reggae

Ras Michael & the Sons of Negus; the Abyssinians; the Melodians; Yabby You & the Prophets; Joe Higgs; Culture; Judy Mowatt; the Ethiopians; Maxie, Niney & Scratch; Rita Marley; Augustus Pablo; Mutabaruka; Winston Jarrett; Count Ossie & the Mystic Revelation of Rastafari. (All artists are from Jamaica.)

Named after Ras Tafari Makonnen, a.k.a. Ethiopian emperor Haile Selassie, the Rastafarian religion views the political leader—crowned in 1930—as a spiritual savior for the black race, notably those Africans relocated by the slave diaspora to the Caribbean and America. These 14 well-chosen tracks from the 1960s–'90s document the importance of Rastafarian hymns (many with melodies borrowed from Western Christian ones) on the development of reggae. The most familiar is the classic title number by the Melodians (featured on the seminal soundtrack to *The Harder They Come*), but every song hits home with pointed grace, including "New Name" by Ras Michael; "Black-

man Know Yourself" by Joe Higgs (who goes into a South Africanesque "Lion Sleeps Tonight" falsetto); Winston Jarrett's cover of the Wailers' great "Selassie Is the Chapel"; "So Long" by the pivotal Mystic Revelation of Rastafari; and—the highlight in a disc of highlights—a super-session version of "Babylon Burning (Fire, Fire)" by Lee "Scratch" Perry, Niney the Observer, and Max Romeo. A fantastic collection.

Bill Ellis

Calypso Breakaway 𝄞𝄞𝄞𝄞 (Rounder, 1990, compilation prod. Dick Spottswood, Keith Warner)

Trinidad & Tobago
genre: Calypso

Keskidee Trio; King Radio; Felix and his Krazy Kats; Growler; Lion; Lord Executor; Al Philip Iere Syncopators; Tiger; Lord Beginner; Atilla the Hun; Lord Invader; Lionel Belasco's Orchestra; Lion and Atilla the Hun; Wilmouth Houdini; Caresser; Codello's Top Hatters Orchestra. (All artists are from Trinidad and Tobago.)

These 20 songs are representative of an extremely musically sophisticated period in the evolution of calypso. Transcribed from vintage recordings, the songs are politically and socially topical to their period, yet there is plenty of humor, wisdom, and wit inherent in the calypsonians' lyrics to relate to the human condition in any age. Calypso has always acted as a kind of bulletin board of the times, with politics, weather, and news stories intermixed with racy double entendres on love and relationships, and these tunes are no exception, save being from a slower, more naïve period of history. The music, with overt influence from American jazz, Cuba, and (more distantly) Africa, is, if anything, richer and more musically informed than today's counterpart stylings, and although the instrumentation has changed over the years, much of this music swings hard and will stand the test of time long after the overly synthesized *soca* variant of our time has been forgotten. Many of these artists were performing in cabarets and night clubs in New York and London at the time, and several went on to international acclaim. *Calypso Breakaway* is both a great introduction for the newcomer and a priceless, carefully mastered document for the aficionado, though its liner notes are not very specific or informative about the artists.

Derek Rath

Calypsos from Trinidad: Politics, Intrigue & Violence in the 1930s, Including the Butler Calypsos 𝄞𝄞𝄞𝄞 (Arhoolie/Folklyric, 1991, compilation prod. Chris Strachwitz)

Trinidad
genre: Calypso

Atilla the Hun; Lord Beginner; Growling Tiger; Roaring Lion; Lord Caresser; Lord Executor; the Growler; King Radio. (All artists are from Trinidad.)

Of the many historical anthologies of calypso assembled by Rounder, Matchbox, Folkways, et. al, this augmented reissue of *Where Was Butler?: A Calypso Documentary from Trinidad* (Folklyric, 1987) is simply one of the best. Amply annotated by discographer Dick Spottswood, it documents one of the most active and innovative periods in the modern history of calypso, when the ostentatious oratorical style of the 20th century's first two decades had been thoroughly played out, and when—bolstered by the success of their triumphant recording trips to New York—established names like Lion and Atilla and talented newcomers like Tiger were experimenting wildly with melody, meter, rhyme, and phrasing; absorbing influences from American jazz and popular song; and preparing the way for (among other things) the first, now-forgotten, U.S. calypso fad in the late 1930s. But modern-day Americans expecting to hear popular calypsos of that time—light-hearted ditties about the virtues of marrying ugly women or quaint dirges about the abdication of the lovelorn Edward VIII—will be in for a surprise. For in the context of widespread depression and unemployment, stunning economic inequity, and violent labor riots, one of the calypsonians' principal innovations was thoroughly backward-looking: a revival, albeit more radical and sophisticated, of the form's folk tradition of acute social commentary on topical issues. (If rap in the '80s, as Chuck D used to claim, was black America's CNN, then calypso in the '30s was Trinidad's *Daily News*.) Included among the 23 selections are Tiger's classic lament "Money Is King" (if you're rich, you can get away with murder; if you're poor, "a dog is better than you"); Lion's dryly ironic "Send Your Children to the Orphan Home"; and Atilla's withering assessment of a government investigation into the causes of social unrest, "Commission Report"—whose casual mention of "capitalistic oppression" was too much for the censors.

Michael Eldridge

Caribbean Island Music ♫♫♪ (Nonesuch, 1972/1998, prod. John Storm Roberts)

Haiti, the Dominican Republic, Jamaica
genre: Merengue, bolero, mento

Los Congos del Espiritu Santo (Dominican Republic); Odalicia Ventura (Dominican Republic); Orchestre Jazz Corondo (Haiti); Benjamin Reid (Jamaica); Charles Welsh (Jamaica); Valerie Walker (Jamaica); Theophilus Chiverton (Dominican Republic).

Caribbean music is known internationally for calypso and reggae, yet these urban styles are relatively new phenomena. The

learned musicologist John Storm Roberts recorded examples of traditional Caribbean music in casual street settings during 1971, replete with the sounds of passing cars and barking dogs. Evident in both the music and the dialects are strong links with culture from Africa, England, Spain, and France, with flavors of folk, flamenco, and Cajun music. This disc, however, is more interesting than entertaining. The largely amateur musicians offer endearing performances, yet the collection is best enjoyed by musicologists concerned with tracing the evolution of Caribbean music; Storm's informative liner notes are the CD's most intriguing aspect.

David Poole

Caribbean Revels: Haitian Rara and Dominican Gaga
♫♫♫♫ (Smithsonian/Folkways, 1978/1991)

Haiti, Dominican Republic
genre: Rara, gaga

Artists uncredited. (All artists are from Haiti and the Dominican Republic.)

In Haiti, *rara* is the pre–Lenten Carnival time when the Christian saints and Vodou *iwa* sleep, leaving the more corporeal elements of the population to exhausting pleasures and excesses. Haitian migrants, pushed by destitution into the Dominican Republic's sugar-cane industry, celebrate the officially discouraged *gaga* holiday in an effort to maintain cultural identity under oppressive conditions. They march through the streets and fields playing a raucous party music that is part religious celebration and part social protest, mixed with a liberal dose of bawdiness and satire. During the festivals of 1976–78, music scholars Verna Gillis and Ramon Perez went to the streets, plazas, and graveyards of both countries to record the tracks on this splendid compilation. The music is a joyous, ribald blend of local percussion and wind instruments that has a subtly hypnotic effect, almost as if the listener had imbibed the *kleren* (a cheap and potent sugar-cane liquor) fueling the musicians. The audio quality is excellent throughout and the performances are enthusiastic, even riotous. The disc comes with excellent, scholarly liner notes that provide social and political context to the music.

Ron Garmon

The Churchical Chants of the Nyahbingi ♫♫♫♫ (Heartbeat, 1983, prod. Elliott Leib)

Jamaica
genre: Ritual Rastafarian music

Various uncredited members of the Church Triumphant of Jah Rastafari and Haile Selassie I Theocracy Government (Jamaica).

For those interested in the roots of reggae and other popular Afro-Caribbean musical forms, these rare field recordings of the chants of the Nyahbingi order of the Rastafarian religion provide an invaluable cultural history lesson. The album was recorded during Ronald Reagan's 1982 visit to Jamaica. As Reagan carried out affairs of state and enjoyed the attention of "establishment" Jamaica, the hills of Trelawney rang out with the pulsating sounds of Nyahbingi drums while the Rastafari Judgement fire blazed all through the night. Simple songs like "Got to Move" and "Keep Cool Babylon" feature repetitive polyphonic chants accompanied only by trance-like drumming and rattles, providing the missing link between ancient African musical forms and modern reggae. But the righteous anger of lyrics criticizing Reagan, Pope John Paul II, and other oppressive forces of Babylon stand in stark contrast to conscious reggae's more positive and uplifting sociopolitical messages. This is raw, primal stuff, but undeniably powerful.

Bret Love

Cuba Classics 1: Silvio Rodríguez 𝄢𝄢𝄢 (Luaka
Bop/Warner Bros., 1991, prod. David Byrne)
Cuba Classics 2: Incredible Dance Hits of the '60s &
'70s 𝄢𝄢𝄢𝄢 (Luaka Bop/Warner Bros., 1991, prod. Ned Sublette, executive prod. David Byrne)
Cuba Classics 3: New Directions in Cuban Music—Diablo Al Inferno 𝄢𝄢𝄢 (Luaka Bop/Warner Bros., 1992, prod. Ned Sublette, executive prod. David Byrne)

Cuba
genre: Nueva trova, son, rumba, blues, speed metal

Silvio Rodríguez; Celeste Mendoza; María Tereza Vera; Orquesta Original de Manzanillo; Orquesta Riverside; Chappotín y Sus Estrella; Los Van Van; Conjunto Rumbavanna; Orquesta Revé Changiií '68; Caridad Hierrezuelo y Conjunto Caney; Los Zafiros; Orquesta Pancho el Bravo; El Jiguero de Cienfuegos; Los Papines; Irakere; Sintesis; Pio Leyva; Lazaro Ros with Mezcla; Los Blues; Grupo Vocal Sampling; Dan Den; NG La Banda; Pablo Milanés; Carlos Varela; Zeus. (All artists are from Cuba.)

Producer David Byrne's three *Cuba Classics* compilations were for many Americans the first opportunity to hear any of the new sounds in Cuban music since the beginning of the U.S. economic blockade in 1961. In the late '60s, protest songs in the mold of Bob Dylan and John Lennon were popularized by Silvio Rodríguez, and the movement was termed *nueva trova* (new ballad), a close cousin of the *nueva canción* (new song) trend elsewhere in Latin America. The first volume here gathers Rodríguez's material from 1975 to '86, in which he voices social statements in a seamless fusion of avant-garde lyrics and popular melodies. His songs are steeped in cryptic metaphors and poetry influenced by Pablo Neruda. While troubadours like Rodríguez struggled with pressing political issues, Havana's nightclubs throbbed to the *son* and rumba of Los Van Van, Ce-

leste Mendoza, and the other excellent Afro-Cuban dance bands collected on Volume 2 of this series. Volume 3 explores the fusion of styles popular in the '80s, including Los Van Van again; the *Santería*-techno of Sintesis; and Pablo Milanés, singing an updated version of nueva trova. These are well-chosen compilations with enthusiastic and intelligently written liner notes—Americans, find out what you've been missing!

David Poole

Cuba Fully Charged 𝄢𝄢𝄢 (Earthworks, 1993, compilation
prod. Trevor Herman)

Cuba
genre: Son, rumba, guaguanco, son montuno, guaracha son

Son 14; Adalberto Alvarez; NG La Banda; Carlos Embale; Conjunto Chappotin Y Sus Estrellas; Sierra Maestra; Conjunto Rumbavana; Conjunto Los Bocucos; Conjunto Los Magnificos; Pello El African. (All artists are from Cuba.)

Released just prior to the boom of interest in all things Cuban, this 14-track compilation offers a well-rounded overview of the island's music, featuring many famous names from the past alongside some of the newer movers and shakers. Immediately apparent is the energy and vitality of some of the elders, including Felix Chappotin and Carlos Embale, well into his 70s and singing like a teenager. Current big names like NG La Banda prove that the roots of Cuban music are alive and well, regardless of how the instrumentation may change, while Sierra Maestra, for all their dedication to tradition, remain both relevant and contemporary. Cuba is still producing great composers and bandleaders, and one of today's best, Adalberto Alvarez, gets three cuts, alone and with his first group, Son 14. As the somewhat verbose liner notes point out, Afro-Cuban music has a long and complex pedigree, and it is this heritage, along with the high musical expertise fostered by the music, that have inspired players and audiences alike to stick with this sensual and sophisticated celebration of life over many generations and evolutions. The clarity of the recordings indicates that they are all relatively modern, though the sleeve notes offer no information on dates. But in any circumstances, this music speaks eloquently for itself.

Derek Rath

Cuba: I Am Time 𝄢𝄢𝄢 (Blue Jackel Entertainment, 1997,
compilation prod. Jack O'Neil)

Cuba
genre: Afro-Antillean, Cuban, Cuban jazz

Over 50 artists on four discs. (All artists are from Cuba.)

Ancient mysteries, forgotten rhythms, obscure religious ideas—they don't seem at first glance to have a great deal to do with contemporary Latin jazz and pop music. From the first disc of this four-album compilation, though, you'll be taken to a darker, more tropical world than you had imagined, where chants from the Yoruban peoples transported to Cuba from Africa intertwine with indigenous rhythms and borrowings from Spanish religious music. The first disc is called *Cuban Invocations*, and as the music moves into the second disc, *Cantar en Cuba*, the voice of the singer and the idea of Cuba as a world crossroads emerge. Then the Cuban people show the world how to dance with them in the third album, *Bailar con Cuba*. The music makes its full transition to the world stage with artists such as Gonzalo Rubalcaba, Chico O'Farrill, and Grupo AfroCubano playing *Cubano Jazz*. But there's still the underlying sound of the ancient invocations where cultures first began to meet . . . that's what you learn from listening to this collection. You can also learn from reading the 112-page book that comes with the set. It's well-researched and well-designed, filled with information about the artists, the history of Cuban music, and the story of Cuba.

Kerry Dexter

Cuban Counterpoint: History of the Son Montuno &&&&
(Rounder, 1992, compilation prod. Morton Marks)

Cuba
genre: Son

Los Tutankamen; Sexteto Habanero; Sexteto Boloña; Sexteto Nacional; Septeto Nacional; Conjunto Tipíco Habanero; Arsenio Rodriguez y su Conjunto; Cachao All Stars; Celia Cruz with the Sonora Matancera; Miguel Cuní with the Conjunto Modelo; Abelardo Baroso with the Orquesta Sensación; Félix Chapotín; Beny Moré. (All artists are from Cuba.)

The "Cuban counterpoint" of the title is the mix of African and Hispanic cultures that forms the rhythms of Cuban music as we know it. The *son montuno* style combined these sounds more successfully than any other and went on to influence the immensely popular salsa genre. This collection surveys the evolution of *son montuno* dance music in recordings from the 1920s to the '70s, including the upbeat, jazz-influenced sound of the '50s.

David Poole

Cuban Dance Party: Roots of Rhythm Volume 2 &&&&
(Rounder, 1990, prod. Howard Dratch, Eugene Rosow, Rene Lopez)

Cuba
genre: Son

Grupo Irakere; Los Van Van; Estrellas Cubanas; Septeto Nacional De Ignacio Piñero; Orquesta Orestes Lopez; Isaac Oveido and His Family; Son De La Loma. (All artists are from Cuba.)

Intended as a companion to the three-hour television series *Roots of Rhythm with Harry Belafonte*, *Cuban Dance Party* is 11 foot-stomping examples of prime *son* (Cuba's seminal rhythmic song form), recorded live in Cuba for the state-owned label EGREM. The stars of this collection are the veteran Septeto Nacional De Ignacio Piñero, founded in 1927 and still performing. Their three traditional songs are led by vocalist Carlos Embale in a style that has changed little since their heyday in the '30s. The distinctive growl of Juan Formell and his funky rhythm section in Los Van Van are captured while playing to an audience of 50,000. Formell's herky-jerky vocal style as heard on "Que Palo" was a strong influence on Talking Heads. All of these tracks were laid down live at Carnival and community dances, catching an excitement and vivacity guaranteed to fuel your own dance parties.

David Poole

Cuban Gold, Volumes 1–5 &&&&& (Qbadisc, 1995–97, compilation prod. Harry Sepulveda)

Cuba
genre: Son, bolero, charanga, son montuno, rumba-son, son-cha, guaracha, cha cha cha, guaguanco, guajira, mambo, danzon, bachata son, pachanga, montuno

Vol. 1: Los Van Van; Orquesta Original de Manzanillo; Estrella de Areito; Son 14; Groupo Manguare; Francisco Fellove; Orquesta Ritmo Oriental; Orquesta Aliamen; Conjunto Rumbavana; Irakere. Vol. 2: Orquesta Aragon con Los Papines; Estrellas de Chocolate; Estrellas Cubanas; Estrellas de Areito; Ritmo Oriental; Adalberto Alvarez y su Son; Reve y su Charangon; Los Van Van; Orquesta Original de Manzanillo. Vol. 3: Orquesta Melodias del 40; Orquesta Riverside con Tito Gomez; Orquesta Sensacion con Abelardo Barroso; Estrellas de Chocolate; Orquesta Neno Gonzalez; Orquesta Aragon; Pio Leyva; Chappotin y sus Estrellas con Miguelito Cuni; Orquesta Ideal; Orquesta Estrellas Cubanas; Orquesta Novedades con Miguelito Cuni. Vol. 4: Las Maravillas de Florida; Conjunto Bolero; Orquesta Aragon; Chappotin y sus Estrellas con Miguelito Cuni; Orquesta Riviera; Ritmo Oriental; Nino Rivera con Miguelito Cuni; Los Mravillas de Mali con Boncana Maiga; Orquesta Aragon con Elena Burke; Chappotin y sus Estrellas con Laito; Orquesta America; Reyes '73; Los Van Van. Vol. 5: Adalberto Alvarez y su Son; La Maravilla de Florida; Irakere; Conjunto Rumbavana; Estrellas Cubanas; Orquesta Enrique Jorrin con Bobby Carcasses; Los Van Van. (All artists are from Cuba.)

Taken from the vaults of Cuba's EGREM records, this series is indispensable in understanding the evolution of Cuban popular music since the revolution isolated the island from neighboring America. As thorough a study as it is, there is nothing academic about these swinging and very musical cuts, many of which were chart-toppers in their times. The vibrancy of the bands can be seen by how many names pop up time and time again throughout this often chronologically sequenced set, albeit sometimes with fresh lineups as musicians fled Cuba for a better life. The 1960s (Volume 3), for instance, were interesting for the overlap of musicians from the '40s and a new breed formulating future developments (including salsa) from these roots; Volume 4 reveals yet further modernization in the '70s, but even here classic Cuban music is omnipresent both rhythmically and harmonically. Volume 5 has the hardest extended jams (especially from Irakere and Adalberto Alvarez), but this series is first-class dance music throughout, with the much-liked *charanga* sound of violins and flutes often softening or replacing the brass that became customary in salsa from New York. Major names both familiar and unfamiliar abound with too many highlights to mention; this is essential, deep, and fun listening for anyone interested in Latin music. The liner notes are brief or sometimes nonexistent, but the artist bibliography is a valuable who's-who in itself.

Derek Rath

Duke Reid's Treasure Chest 🎵🎵🎵🎵 (Heartbeat, 1992, prod. Duke Reid)
Ska after Ska after Ska 🎵🎵🎵🎵 (Heartbeat, 1998, prod. Duke Reid)

Jamaica
genre: Rocksteady, ska

The Paragons; the Melodians; Alton Ellis; Phyllis Dillon; U-Roy; Justin Hinds & the Dominoes. (All artists are from Jamaica.)

Albert "Duke" Reid, the studio auteur and gun-lover who didn't hesitate to intimidate the groups that recorded for him but extracted some of the best performances of their careers, had an ear for the definitive singers of the proto-reggae "rocksteady" era. He stands alongside Clement "Coxsone" Dodd as one of Jamaica's great producers of hit songs. Reid's secret weapon was his engineer Byron Smith, who captured the intimate sound at the Treasure Isle studios on countless well-preserved masters. Over two classic-packed discs, *Duke Reid's Treasure Chest* collects gems like the Paragons' original recording of "The Tide Is High" (later famously covered by Blondie) and versions of '60s American soul landmarks like "My Girl," performed here by the Techniques. *Ska after Ska after Ska* offers more virtuosity from the Silvertones, Justin Hinds, and other Duke Reid staples, though from slightly earlier than on *Treasure Chest*. You'll hear the signature ska beat, doo-wop, other vocal harmony, and hints of the flowering of reggae music to come.

David Poole

Konbit: Burning Rhythms of Haiti 🎵🎵🎵 (A&M, 1989, compilation prod. Jonathan Demme, Fred Paul, Edward Saxon)

Haiti
genre: Compas (a.k.a. konpa), mini-jazz, rara

Ensemble Nemours Jean-Baptiste; Magnum Band; Skah Shah; Sakad; Neville Brothers (USA) with Les Freres Parents; Manno Charlemagne; Sanba Yo; Tabou Combo; Mini All-Stars; D.P. Express. (All artists are from Haiti, except where noted otherwise.)

At the time this album came out, somewhat before Boukman Eksperyans became a world-music household word, Haitian sounds were largely unknown in the U.S.—even though the harrowing political situation on the island had driven many of its top bands to seek stateside exile, mainly in Brooklyn and Miami, where groups like Magnum Band, Skah Shah, and Tabou Combo maintain a busy schedule playing for the large expatriate community. Most of this compilation covers *compas,* the slick, modern dance music most loved by the Haitian community, as performed by the best artists on the genre's scene. The two tracks by Sakad and Sanba Yo in the *Vodou/rara* style (an Afro-Haitian ritual/street-festival form later made famous by the aforesaid Boukman) are marked by breakneck percussion and frenzied singing, while people's troubadour Manno Charlemagne gives a brief example of Haitian acoustic balladry. The two tracks pairing the Neville Brothers with Les Freres Parents are funky anomalies, perhaps meant to boost the album's commercial appeal.

j. poet

Mambo Mania: The Kings and Queens of Mambo 🎵🎵🎵 (Rhino, 1995, compilation prod. Laura Canellias, Alan Geik)

Cuba
genre: Mambo

Celia Cruz Con La Sonora Matancera; Pérez Prado & His Orchestra; Tito Rodriguez; Mongo Santamaria Orchestra; Hector Rivera & His Orchestra; Beny Moré Y Su Orquesta; Desi Arnaz & His Latinos (Cuba/USA); Ray Barretto (USA); La India De Oriente; Tito Puente & His Orchestra (Cuba/USA); Machito & His Orchestra (Cuba/USA); Cachao Y Su Ritmo Caliente; Cal Tjader Mambo Quintet (Cuba/USA); Xavier Cugat & His Orchestra (Spain/USA); Septeto Nacional De Ignacio Pinero. (All artists are from Cuba except where noted otherwise.)

Mambo is more than a musical genre or a dance style. It might be more useful to think of it as a force—something that starts in the feet, shoots up to make the head spin, and then results in a pronounced hip disturbance. For certain purists the form was at its peak in the 1950s and '60s, when mambo's exotic rhythms crossed over to worldwide popularity. That's exactly the period covered on this single-disc compilation from the reissue gurus at Rhino Records. The "golden age" of the Cuban craze saw a host of artists realize their crossover dreams in the U.S. pop charts (and, in the case of Desi Arnaz, beyond). The amusing liner notes offer a bit of history, artist background, and even basic dance instruction. But the music will get you moving before you have a chance to practice. From the trademark blast of

Pérez Prado's Orchestra on "Pachito E-Ché" to the liquid groove of Tito Puente & His Orchestra on "Guaguanco Margarito," this is all quality product with great sound and excellent programming. While licensing restrictions kept the label from including artists like Noro Morales and Johnny Pacheco, it would still be hard to find a better introductory compilation.

Tim Sheridan

Merengue: Dominican Music and Dominican Identity
🎵🎵🎵🎵 (Rounder, 1997, compilation prod. Paul Austerlitz)

Dominican Republic
genre: Merengue

Antonio Morel y su Orquesta; Belkis Concepcion. (All artists are from the Dominican Republic.)

The merengue is the national music of the Dominican Republic, a vibrant dance rhythm combining African and Spanish styles. Merengue's roots are in the Caribbean ballrooms of the mid-19th century. Eventually rejected by the Eurocentric middle class as being too African and lascivious, merengue managed to find a devoted following among rural Dominicans, who emphasized the African elements and added regional flavors. Everyone can merengue—just shuffle to the beat. The ease and fun of this dance style have made it a hit across the world. For the unadulterated source, no collection could be better than this one. You'll hear everything from peppy 1930s recordings to contemporary grooves like accordionist Domingo Azolo's 1991 "Merengue Redondo." As a companion to Paul Austerlitz's book of the same name (Temple University Press, 1996), this is a serious study, but the vitality and friendly rhythms of merengue make it anything but stuffy.

David Poole

Reggae Jamdown: The RAS Tapes 🎵🎵🎵🎵 (Rykodisc, 1990, compilation prod. Steven Jurgensmeyer)

Jamaica
genre: Reggae

Pinchers; Frankie Paul; Half Pint; Charlie Chaplin; Ini Kamoze; Edi Fitzroy; Sugar Minott; Brigadier Jerry; Admiral Tibet; Hugh Mundell; Dennis Brown; Peter Broggs; Don Carlos; Freddie McGregor; Gregory Isaacs; Jacob Miller; Ijahman; Israel Vibration. (All artists are from Jamaica.)

Once upon a time, hang out on the beach at Negril and with a couple of decent-quality tapes you could trade for one mixtape of the trader's favorite songs. This compilation has that air, right down to the typewritten back cover. Fortunately it has far better fidelity. *Reggae Jamdown* crystallizes the moment when reggae had yet to thoroughly give in to the subsequent "dancehall" style. At least RAS Records, the source of all these

sides, hadn't. The mix does feature some early dancehall landmarks like Brigadier Jerry's "Three Blind Mice," Charlie Chaplin's classic "Cool the Violence" (complete with its sample of Scott Joplin's "The Entertainer"), and Frankie Paul's half-toasted, dubwise "Tato." It also presents some of reggae's better contemporary vocalists, like the hero of "lovers' rock," Gregory Isaacs, doing something other than "Night Nurse" (here, "Red Rose for Gregory"). This record is highly recommended, especially if your taste in reggae stopped in the '70s with *Rastaman Vibration* and *The Harder They Come.*

Hank Bordowitz

Septetos Cubanos: sones de Cuba 🎵🎵🎵🎵
(Corason/Música Tradicional, 1990, compilation prod. Eduardo Llerenas)

Cuba
genre: Son

Septeto Tipico Oriental; Tipicos del Son; Septeto Soneros San Luis; Cuarteto Patria; Septeto Tipico Spirituano; Estudiantina Invasora; Septeto Nacional; Agrupación Cucalambé; Guitarras y trovadores. (All artists are from Cuba.)

The tradition started by such marvelous groups as the Trio Matamoros, the Cuarteto Oriental, and the Sexteto Habanero is still alive and documented in this double-disc package. While the rhythmic *son* style lies at the heart of the Afro-Cuban musical revolution, the format for groups playing it is more flexible than the septet lineup of this album's title would lead you to believe—quartets, octets, and nonets are included, a slight caveat that fades when listening to such a superb set. There is even a recording by the pivotal Septeto Nacional here (though the historic lineup with Ignacio Piñero is long defunct). Comprehensive, reader-friendly liner notes by the producer are printed in Spanish and English and detail the history of *son* and its various elements. If they want, though, listeners can skip over the text and dig right into some of the liveliest acoustic music on the planet.

Garaud MacTaggart

Sextetos Cubanos Vols. I & II 🎵🎵🎵🎵 (Arhoolie, 1991, compilation prod. Chris Strachwitz, Michael Ivan Avalos)

Cuba
genre: Son

Sexteto Munamar; Sexteto Machin; Sexteto Nacional; Sexteto Matancero; Sexteto Occidente; Sexteto Bolona. (All artists are from Cuba.)

Each of Havana's sextets in the Golden Age of the 1920s and '30s vied competitively for the prestige of foreign tours, radio spots, and record deals, and had its own distinct style. The Sexteto Munamar emphasized its Afro-Cuban heritage; the romance, the most popular theme of Cuba's seminal *son* form, was perfected by the Sexteto Nacional; the suggestive stories in Sexteto Machin's *son* were notorious, as with "Mama Yo Quiero Un Yoyo"'s mother-daughter admonition, "I've already told you child leave your yoyo alone!" *Sextetos Cubanos* will appeal to fans of the best-selling *Buena Vista Social Club* albums, whose retro style recalls this period.

David Poole

Soca Gold 1998 ♪♪♪ (VP Records, 1998)

Trinidad, Jamaica, USA
genre: Soca

Ronnie McIntosh; krosfyah; Super Blue; Nigel Lewis; Poser; Osha; Onyan; Square One; Iwer George; Chinese Laundry; Bud; Allison Hinds; Beenie Man; Technic Band; Johnny King. (Artists are from Trinidad, Jamaica, and USA.)

Old-time calypso purists may blanch at the techno/dancehall direction of '90s *soca* (the form's more modern variant), but under the electronic surface many of the old traditions flourish. Social commentary and current affairs each get their turn, along with sexual innuendo and the rampant slackness (sexual explicitness) found in dancehall reggae. In fact the presence of Jamaican giant Beenie Man shows how the genres are merging, with steel drums and Rastafarian beliefs alternately showcased on his two contributions. Elsewhere the legacy of erstwhile soca legend Arrow shows up in the stylings on several tracks, while Poser's "Deyar" harks back to the more traditional songs of the '70s. The Asian contingent is represented by Iwer George's "Bottom in de Road," delivered in the Indian-influenced "chutney soca" style that is now a major force in Trinidad. These 16 tracks of high-power party music, if naturally inclined toward assimilation with other contemporary trends, contain some fine performances from some top contenders In the current soca arena. Hopefully the paucity of information in the sleeve notes will be addressed for future volumes.

Derek Rath

Soca Music from Trinidad: Heat in De Place ♪♪♪
(Rounder, 1990, prod. Gene Scaramuzzo)

Trinidad
genre: Soca

Johnny King; Shadow; Bally; All Rounder; Singing Francine; Chalkdust. (All artists are from Trinidad.)

"Lyrics don't stand a chance/man want to dance," sang Chalkdust, bemoaning the seeming demise of calypso, which served as a form of social commentary expressing popular discontent with the government and local affairs in Trinidad. Under the in-

fluence of disco and a booming economy in the mid-1970s, calypso evolved into soul-calypso or "soca," with drum machines, party lyrics, and smoother production. Every year around December, in good time for Trinidad's famous Carnival, a new set of colorful, libidinous soca tunes is released. This album's seven long jams were in heavy rotation in Trinidadian music's various venues—on the sound-system trucks on the "road march," in the calypso tents, and at the outdoor fetes. Culled from the highlights of the '88 season, this collection provides an equal quota of calypso, in which satirical lyrics are as crucial as a good beat. Either way, this vibrant disc makes for great party music.

David Poole

Solid Gold, Coxsone Style ♪♪♪♪♪ (Studio One, 1972/
Heartbeat, 1992, prod. Clement "Coxsone" Dodd)

Jamaica
genre: Reggae

John Holt; Alton Ellis; Sound Dimension; the Abyssinians; the Helpers; the Beltones; the Freedom Singers; Jackie Mittoo; Delroy Wilson; Wayne McGie; Ernest Ranglin; Dennis Brown; Ruddy Thomas. (All artists are from Jamaica.)

Featuring many of Jamaica's greatest reggae singers and instrumentalists at their best, *Solid Gold, Coxsone Style* also displays the kind of lush magic producer Clement Dodd conjured with striking consistency during reggae's golden age. The Abyssinians' "Declaration of Rights" is one of the most important songs in the history of Jamaican music—or even world music for that matter. Its graceful yet rousing call to "get up and fight for your rights" is rendered with the kind of uncommon passion that uplifts the spirit *and* the hairs on the back of the neck. Ex-Paragon John Holt, who would eventually become one of the most popular singers in the land, oozes the groove with a subtle, cool, and deadly vocal approach on "Strange Things" and two gospel-styled Neil Diamond covers, "Holly Holy" and "Soolaimon." On "I'll Be Waiting," the legendary Alton Ellis's bewitchingly soulful vocals carry a tune with substandard lyrics to the promised land. The crack Studio One house band Sound Dimension also gloriously delivers on the instrumental version, "Park View," with guitarist Ernest Ranglin's amazing solo beautifying the vista considerably. One of Ranglin's true original masterpieces is included here as well, the pristinely melodic and surprisingly psychedelic "Surfing." But what makes this collection superior to others out there is Dodd's inclusion of superb rarities from relative shadow-dwellers, the Helpers and the Beltones. The Beltones have at least a claim to the first true reggae song: "No More Heartaches" for Harry J. in 1968. Whether you buy that claim or not, the searing piece included here—"Let Him Live"—proves that this was a harmony group capable of entrancing alchemy. The Helpers' "Help Me" was the band's only hit—but what an unforgettable sure-shot it is! Jackie Mittoo just wrecks shop on the keyboard-driven riddim, and the singing is majestic and beautiful. The late Mittoo—one of the greatest, funkiest keyboardists this side of Jimmy Smith and Groove Holmes—is a secret to far too many. One listen to "Ironside" and you'll be scouring record shops for Mittoo's dynamite catalog. As if all this weren't enough, the disc also contains an extended mix of the great Delroy Wilson's version of "Love You Madly." Wilson's voice is reminiscent of the Chi-Lites' Eugene Record and he just lays everything out on this heavy soul cut. *Solid Gold, Coxsone Style* is as fine a single-disc compilation of reggae as is available.

Todd Shanker

The Story of Jamaican Music: Tougher Than Tough
♫♫♫♫ (Mango, 1993, compilation prod. Steve Barrow)

Jamaica
genre: Reggae

Laurel Aitken; the Folkes Brothers; Jimmy Cliff; the Skatalites; Prince Buster; Desmond Dekker; the Maytals; the Wailers; Burning Spear; Buju Banton. (All artists are from Jamaica.)

Steve Barrow is one of the world's great reggae experts, and there are few better starting points than his compilation *The Story of Jamaican Music* and his book *Reggae Music—The Rough Guide.* Jamaican musicians have released an unfathomable quantity of records, yet the scene is based in one town, Kingston; the same group of session musicians crops up on most of the records for years on end; there is a relative handful of studios and producers; and the same rhythm will be used in many different recordings, in varying versions and under different names. Given these facts, the variety and imagination of Jamaican music is as much a wonder as its sheer volume. This album spans from the *mento* of the 1950s; to the ska and rocksteady of the '60s; to the roots, reggae, dub, and deejay toasting of the '70s. The '80s are represented by the hip-hop–influenced dancehall style, but much has happened since the collection was completed in 1993, so top off these four discs with a sampler of recent *ragga* (digital reggae). Barrow's picks well survey the landmarks and the lesser-known gems, inspiring further exploration. The accompanying booklet makes this a stylish precursor to the Blood & Fire label's reinvention of the reggae reissue, brimming with atmospheric photos and historic album covers. Nothing else comes close to covering all the bases or belongs more in your collection.

David Poole

West Indies: An Island Carnival ♫♫♫♫ (Caprice Records, 1977/Elektra/Nonesuch, 1983/1991, prod. Krister Malm)

Lesser Antilles
genre: Afro-Caribbean, vintage calypso

Unidentified musicians from Dominica, Young Island, Grenada, St. Lucia, Trinidad, Tobago, St. Vincent, Guadeloupe.

Recorded originally for a Swedish label by Krister Malm between 1969 and '71 in the Lesser Antilles, these 12 songs in 39 minutes reflect the various influences on the region of colonialism by the Spanish, French, British, Dutch, Portuguese, Danish, Swedish, and other European nations. West African slaves were brought to the area to work on sugar plantations until 1806, when the British banned the slave trade. The resultant lack of agricultural workers led to a wave of immigration from then-British colonies such as India, China, and Lebanon-Syria. In addition, large numbers of Scots, Irish, Venezuelans, Colombians, Portuguese (from Madeira), and Indonesians came to the islands. On this disc you'll hear all of these cultural influences, but with the greater emphasis on African traditions in instrumentation, musical arrangement, and social purpose. Most of the songs have a charming, rustic quality. The more percussive tunes, made for dancing or spiritual ceremonies (Hindu, Muslim, and Afro-Trinidadian Shango), are performed with vocals and accompanied by instruments including the *guiro,* a scraped instrument that could be a hard fruit with grooves in it, an ordinary tin grater, or another rough object; the *boom boom,* a bamboo cane without finger-holes, blown like a tuba; the maracas or *shak shak*; the cocoa lute, a stringed instrument plucked with the mouth using the same technique as a jew's-harp; and African hand piano (*mbira, zana*). The informative 20-page booklet describes in considerable detail the origins of each song. Don't expect the album to reflect the Afro-Caribbean rhythms Americans are used to hearing today; this is roots stuff, somewhat raw and unpolished.

Nancy Ann Lee

Wind Your Waist ♫♫♫♫ (Shanachie, 1991, compilation prod. Randall Grass)

Trinidad
genre: Soca

Arrow (Montserrat); Shadow (Trinidad); Burning Flames (Antigua); Drupatee (Trinidad); Spice (Barbados); Tambu (Trinidad); Organiser (Trinidad); Kitchener (Trinidad).

Soul and calypso are the basic elements of *soca,* a tastefully modernized version of the joyous and erotic dance music made famous at Trinidad's Carnival. *Wind Your Waist* is a particularly interesting and enjoyable soca compilation because it demonstrates the African, Indian, Latin, Jamaican, and American influences in this culture-rich music. For instance, Drupatee, a Trinidadian of East Indian descent, displays a fascinating mixture of Indian textures and soca beats on "Mr. Bissessee," in a style known as "curry-tabanca." Arrow is from the tiny but music-drenched island of Montserrat and is perhaps best known for his crossover soca anthem "Hot, Hot, Hot!" The Bacchanalian-spirited "Long Time" appropriately segues for one hot minute into that international hit, but throughout uses subtle touches of West African syncopation and American-soul vocal embellishment. David Rudder is one of the more internationally revered soca stars. His band Charlie's Roots teams with the equally popular Tambu on the Road March winner (Carnival favorite) "This Party Is It." The title says everything about the sound of this classic soca scorcher, which integrates pummeling Jamaican-*ragga*-like digital beats and bright, distinctly salsafied horn charts. Old-school calypso legend Lord Kitchener proves he distinctly comprehends both the modern soca sound and its global impact on the huge 1990 hit "Parkway," a jubilant reminiscence of the annual Labor Day Carnival on Brooklyn's Eastern Parkway. And Shadow, a Carnival favorite with a uniquely deep-toned singing voice and a riveting vibrato, unleashes one of his many hits, the decidedly frisky "Tension," which alone is worth the price of the disc. This insightful compilation is a superb document of modern soca and one that fully lives up to its subtitle—"The Ultimate Soca Dance Party."

Todd Shanker

Word Soun' 'Ave Power: Reggae Poetry 🎵🎵🎵🎵 (Heartbeat, 1983, prod. Mutabaruka)

Jamaica
genre: Dub poetry

Breeze; Mutabaruka; Malachi Smith; Tomlin Ellis; Glenville Bryan; Navvie Nabbie; Oliver Smith. (All artists are from Jamaica.)

While the first Jamaican deejays in the 1960s toasted over records with a patter to spur on the dance crowd, they would not have considered their words to be poetry, and rarely did they have an agenda beyond keeping their sound-system audience at capacity. But by the late '70s the "dub poets" crafted this patter into poetry, soon to be extended over whole albums of deep dub rhythms. As reggae music for a time lost some of the revolutionary zeal and drive that had made performers like the late Bob Marley so popular, the dub poets urgently sought a forum to voice strongly held opinions and relevant social commentary. They reveled in the power of language and rhythm to hammer home their points, with clever wordplay as their stock in trade. In 1983 dub poet Mutabaruka helped document this movement in nine tracks of heavy reggae bass lines

and positive, empowering messages. A second, all-women volume—*Woman Talk: Caribbean Dub Poetry* 🎵🎵🎵 (Heartbeat cassette, 1986, prod. Mutabaruka)—followed. The most notable omission from the first disc was Linton Kwesi Johnson, foremost among dub poets, who can be best heard on *Independant Intavenshan: The Island Anthology* 🎵🎵🎵🎵 (Island, 1998, prod. Jerry Rappaport, Bill Levenson). This collects material from four of Johnson's powerful albums, from the same era as *Word Soun'*.

David Poole

CENTRAL AMERICA

Calypsos: Afro-Limonese Music of Costa Rica 🎵🎵🎵 (Lyrichord, 1988, prod. David Petrosino)

Costa Rica
genre: Calypso

Artists not identified. (All artists are from Costa Rica.)

Unlike Trinidadian calypso, Costa Rican calypso is sung in Spanish and serves less as social commentary than Carnival dance music. Maracas, harmonica, and guitar add a Latin flavor. Instead of large steel drums, the small steel *timbaletas*, bass drum, snare drum, and congas offer a riveting percussion section. Costa Rican Carnival takes place in Puerto Limon on the Caribbean coast. Historically calypso was performed by *shatwels* (singers) to accompany *kalendas* (wrestling matches) where fighters battered each other with wooden clubs, often killing an opponent. The shatwels chanted phrases to which the crowd responded to incite the combatants. These kalendas gradually evolved into non-violent dances performed throughout Carnival, as heard on this upbeat 1988 recording.

David Poole

EUROPE

Arte Flamenco, Vols. 1–15 🎵🎵🎵🎵 (Mandala/Harmonia Mundi, 1999, prod. Juan Barral)

Spain
genre: Flamenco

El Niño de Marchena; Pepe Martínez; La Niña de los Peines; Román El Granáino; Juan Breva; Aurelio de Cádiz; El Niño de Almadén; Canalejas de Jerez; Pepe Soler; M. Torre; Escancena; Gordito de Triana; Cojo Luque; Niño de Priego; Rebollo; Luis Caballero; Luis Maravilla; La Niña de Linares; El Niño de Cabras; El Americano; Angelillo; Cojo de Malaga; Guerrita; El Niño de la Huerta; Josélito de Cádiz; Ramon Montoya; Manuel Vallejo; El

Chocolate; Juan Varea; Canalejaz de Puerto-Real; Estebán de Sanlúcar. (All artists are from Spain.)

In this excellent 15-volume survey of flamenco history, Mandala revives long-deleted LPs and previously unheard performances by the early greats. Indeed, this exhaustive but fascinating series unearths gems from the 1890s through the 1970s. Of particular note are the recordings dating from the 1930s to the late '50s, during which time flamenco was already undergoing dramatic changes. Reviled by purists then, the innovations have since become mainstream, from vocal flourishes to the establishment of flamenco guitar as a solo instrument rather than always accompaniment for a singer. About half of the tracks from the '30s and '40s, especially Volumes 12 and 13 (but also volumes 4, 5, 7, 9, 10, 14, and 15), are slightly marred by a hissing surface noise—yet all the performances in the series are of an unusually high standard, and even these volumes offer great insight into some of Spain's greatest flamenco guitarists and singers. Standouts with clearer recording are the super-fast yet intricate guitar picking of Román El Granáino on Volume 6; Niño de Almadén's beautifully doleful voice on Volume 3; and, with a slight hiss, the ubiquitous guitar of early innovator Ramon Montoya accompanying the forthright tenor of Aurelio Selles on Volume 4.

David Poole

A Celebration of Scottish Music ♫♫♫♪ (Temple, 1988, compilation prod. Robin Morton)

Scotland
genre: Scottish Traditional

Battlefield Band; Cilla Fisher; Hamish Moore; Alan Reid; Alison Kinnaird; Brian McNeill; Shotts & Dykehead Caledonia Pipe Band; Christine Primrose; Jim Johnstone Band. (All artists are from Scotland.)

Since its establishment in 1978 by Robin Morton—Irishman and founding member of the well-known Pan-Celtic group Boys of the Lough—Temple Records has dedicated itself to the promotion of the traditional music of Scotland. This recording is an exceptional example of the vibrant variety that exists in Scottish music today, thanks in no small part to Temple's preservationist efforts. The Gaelic songs of Christine Primrose and Hamish Moore's brilliant Scottish smallpiping can be found alongside Allison Kinnaird's splendid harp and Scottish fusion stalwarts the Battlefield Band. Scotland's traditional sounds have long taken a back seat to other traditional Celtic-based music, due in part to much of Scotland's willingness to promote the kilt-and-haggis mentality so popular with tourists. One listen to this collection will help set the record straight and do much to bring back the nobility and charm of Scottish folk culture, separating the pure article from the pastiche.

Cliff McGann

Duende: From Traditional Masters to Gypsy Rock
♫♫♫♫ (ellipsis arts . . . , 1994, compilation prod. Angel Romero)

Spain
genre: Flamenco

Over 40 artists and ensembles, including: Paco de Lucia; La Nina de los Peines; Sabicas; Tomatito; Eduardo Rodriguez; Ramon Montoya; Camarón de la Isla; Pata Negra; Duquende. (All artists are from Spain.)

The rapid style of the flamenco guitarist and the heel-tapping and finger-clicking of the dancer in her blood-red dress are icons of Spanish culture. The 41 tracks of this three-disc set exhibit a great variety within the genre. The common thread is the guitar, and an underlying melancholic passion or *duende*. The focus of a performance is the tension between the dancer and the guitarist; their chemistry can reflect either a courtship or a battle. As flamenco has evolved, the male vocal has maintained its moaning, almost bluesy sadness. Beginning with current flamenco's roots in the traditionalist revival of the 1950s, *Duende* also follows the subsequent fusions with jazz and rock. Its "Explorations" disc maintains only tenuous links to flamenco—the rumba of Willi Giménez; the Andalusian blues of Radio Tarifa's "La Canal"; the sitar-like guitar quality of Pata Negra. But the set's accompanying 48-page book provides informative notes on the music's history and the stories behind its stars.

David Poole

Early Cante Flamenco ♫♫♫♫ (Arhoolie, 1990, compilation prod. Chris Strachwitz)

Spain
genre: Flamenco

Antonio Mairena; Tomás Pavón; Pepe Pinto; Manolita de Jerez; Niña de los Peines; Manuel Vallejo; Monolo Caracol. (All artists are from Spain.)

It's hard to imagine a musical style more closely associated with Spain than flamenco. But according to the liner notes for this collection of rare 78 rpm recordings from the 1930s, the style was developed by Gypsies who were driven into hiding by the Spanish Inquisition in the 1500s. So in addition to the tourist attraction it is known as by many in the West, this is truly a music of struggle, hardship, and passion. Perhaps that is why it has such a painful beauty, as evidenced on these sides. There are fine examples of what some would consider the purer form of flamenco, before pop sensibilities were infused into the style for broader appeal. Forget the Gipsy Kings, try listening to Tomás Pavón's high-flown tenor, beautifully offset by Melchor de Marchena's fragile guitar lines, on "Bulerias." Then experience the spirit of flamenco dance, nicely realized here by Manolita de Jerez on "Soleares." While the recordings are over 60 years old, the sound quality is quite good and all the performances are arresting.

Tim Sheridan

El Sonido de Flamenco 🎵🎵🎵🎵 (Music Club, 1998)

Spain
genre: Flamenco

Pepe Pinto; Pepe Marchena; Niña de la Puebla; Perlita de Huelva; Juanito Valderrama; Canaléjas de Puerto Real; Fosforito; Porrina de Badajoz; Antoñita Peñuela; Naranijito de Triana; Juanito Maravilla; LaPaquera de Jerez. (All artists are from Spain.)

This disc offers 16 vintage tracks from a time when recorded and club-performed flamenco was the most popular music in Spain, around the middle of the 20th century. The emphasis here is on the flamenco vocalist, and superstars of the day from several styles, ranging from the operatic to the more light-hearted *fandango,* are heard. It's a solid introduction to and record of this part of the music's history, and a useful background for exploring later evolutions of it.

Kerry Dexter

Flamenco: Fire & Grace 🎵🎵🎵🎵 (Narada, 1996, prod. Michael Sullivan, Jesse Cook)

Spain
genre: Flamenco

Miguel de la Bastide (Trinidad); Tomatito; Enrique Morente; Moraito; Rafael Riqueni; El Viejín; Diego Carrasco; Jesse Cook (Canada). (All artists are from Spain except where otherwise noted.)

This album is almost a counterpoint to another Narada compilation, *Gypsy Passion* (reviewed on page 912). On this disc, the focus is on guitar and modern expansions of flamenco; on this one, while the approach is contemporary, the flamenco triumvirate of guitar, singer, and dancer is the center of attention, resulting in music that is closer to *flamenco puro* than to "new flamenco."

Kerry Dexter

Folk 'n' Hell 🎵🎵🎵🎵 (EMI Hemisphere/Metro Blue, 1996, compilation prod. Gerald Seligman)

Scotland
genre: Scottish folk-rock and fusion

Jim Sutherland; Burach; Bongshang; Shooglenifty; Paul Mounsey (Scotland/Brazil); the Colour of Memory; Coelbeg; Seelyhoo; Dougie MacLean; Fergus MacKenzie/Simon Thoumire; the Humpff Family; Rock, Salt & Nails; the Poozies (Scotland, England); the

Iron Horse; Tannas; Khartoum Heroes; Old Blind Dogs. (All artists are from Scotland except where otherwise noted.)

Rather than encompassing a panoramic view of the Scottish folk scene, this collection focuses on its cutting edge, circa 1995 to 1996. And although there have been even further permutations since it was released—such as Peatbog Faeries' fusion of ambient/techno production with folk dance music—this is still pretty adventurous stuff. Seelyhoo brings a jazzy swing to its arrangements of two original instrumentals, for instance, and the Iron Horse offers a rendition of "The Burning of Auchindoun" in which it sounds like an acoustic (if pumped-up and slightly syncopated) incarnation of British folk-rock trailblazers Steeleye Span. Farther edges are reached by producer/auteur Paul Mounsey, whose "Passing Away" blends all sorts of studio wizardry with a melodic Scottish base, and Shooglenifty, which puts modern pop rhythm grooves behind ancient Gaelic dance tunes.

Ken Roseman

Greek-Oriental Rebetica: Songs & Dances in the Asia Minor Style, 1911–1937 🎵🎵🎵🎵 (Arhoolie, 1991, prod. Chris Strachwitz)
Mourmourika: Songs of the Greek Underworld, 1930–1955 🎵🎵🎵🎵 (Rounder, 1999, prod. Charles Howard)
My Only Consolation: Classic Pireotic Rembetica, 1932–1946 🎵🎵🎵🎵 (Rounder, 1999, prod. Charles Howard)

Greece
genre: Rebetica, mourmourika

Greek-Oriental Rebetica: Marika Papgika; Yorghos Papasidheris; Dhimitrios Semsis; Stratos Payumdzis; Rita Abadsi; Andoni Dalgas; Marika Kanaropulu; Roza Eskenazi; Haralambos Panayis; Yanis Oghdhondakis; Yangos Psamatyalis. *Mourmourika*: Ioannis (Jack) Halikias; A. Kostis; Spachanis; Yeorgios Kamvisis; Stell. Perpiniadhis; V. Mesolongitis; Yeorgios Katsaros; Tassos Eleftheriadhis; K. Kostis; Konst. Dhoussas; Z. Kasimatis; Stellakis Perpiniadhis; Marika Kanaropoulou; Tourkalista; Kostas Roukounas; F. Zouridhakis; Harilaos Kritikos; N. Poupourakis. *My Only Consolation*: Markos Vamvakaris; Y. Batis; An. Dhelias; Stellakis Perpiniashis; Stratos Payioumdzis; M.Stellios Keromitis; M. Yennitsaris; Hadzichristos-Stamoulis; K. Roukounas; I. Papaioannou; Y. Kavouras; A. Hadzichristos; S. Payioumidzis; K. Kaplanis. (All artists are from Greece.)

Rebet means "gutter" in Turkish, and it was the life of slum-dwelling Greeks and Turkish refugees (themselves ethnic Greeks) living in Greek port towns like Piraeus that inspired the *rebetica,* or urban folk music, of the early 20th century (a.k.a. *rembetica* and *rembetiko*). It bears comparison with American blues—invented by an underclass using improvised couplets; picked up by record labels in the 1930s as it became popular in urban markets; falling into obscurity until a revival in the '60s and '70s; then revitalized once again in the '90s. The links with hash smoking and rebellion were key to its series of rediscoveries. Stars like Roza Eskenazi sang "Why I Smoke Cocaine," and others sang about their experiences in an underworld of drugs, brothels, gambling, theft, and even prison. They brought instruments from Turkey like the *oud* (lute), zither, and hammered dulcimer, incorporating them with the more local arrangements of clarinet, accordion, and violin. These are three outstanding collections of the genre's first wave. The crackly 78s on the Arhoolie disc have not transferred as clearly as those compiled from Charles Howard's collection for the Rounder albums; Howard's liner notes are also more comprehensive. However, Arhoolie covers earlier material, and the sonic quality is naturally a little rough. First-class musicianship and entertaining lyrics are evident on all three volumes, with no tracks repeated and only two instances of the same artist appearing on more than one disc, a testament to the wealth of material available. Also featured is the rural *mourmourika* style, a precursor to rebetica just as country blues preceded urban blues. The dignified singing here is often at odds with the seedy, saucy subject matter, from *Greek-Oriental Rebetica*'s explicit "Bordello Blues" to the same album's invitation in "Hashish Harem" to "light your joint/and have a smoke/and have a ball with us."

David Poole

New Electric Muse: The Story of Folk into Rock 🎜🎜🎜🎜♥
(Essential/Castle Communications, 1996)
New Electric Music II: The Continuing Story of Folk into Rock 🎜🎜🎜🎜♥ (Essential/Castle Communications, 1997, compilation prod. Laurence Aston)

England, Scotland, Ireland
genre: Anglo-Celtic folk and folk-rock

New Electric Muse: Steeleye Span (England); Ian Campbell Folk Group (Scotland); Dave Swarbrick (England); the Copper Family (England); Ray & Archie Fisher (Scotland); Ewan MacColl (Scotland); Shirley Collins & Davey Graham (England); the Dubliners (Ireland); the Johnstons (Ireland); Sweeney's Men (Ireland); Finbar & Eddie Furey (Ireland); Gryphon (England); Fairport Convention (England); Morris On Band (England); John Martyn (Scotland); Davey Graham (England); Bert Jansch (Scotland); John Renbourn (England); Pentangle (England); Martin Carthy (England); John & Beverley Martyn (Scotland); the Young Tradition (England); Martin Carthy & Dave Swarbrick (England); Shirley Collins (England); Sandy Denny/Fotheringay (England); Traffic (England); Bob & Carole Pegg (England); Mr. Fox (England); Sandy Denny (England); Lindisfarne (England); Jack the Lad (England); Richard Thompson (England); Steve Ashley (England); Mike & Lal Waterson (England); Albion Country Band (England); Robin & Barry Dransfield (England); the Battlefield Band (Scotland); Richard & Linda Thompson (England); Dick Gaughan (Scotland); June Tabor (England); Martin Simpson (England); Capercaillie (Scotland); Andrew Cronshaw (England); June Tabor & the Oyster Band (England); the Oyster Band (England); Four Men & a Dog (Ireland); Energy Orchard (Ireland); Sharon Shannon (Ireland); Eliza Carthy (England); Lal Waterson & Oliver Knight (England). *New Electric Music II*: The Watersons (England); the Young Tradition (England); the Young Tradition

with Shirley & Dolly Collins (England); John Renbourn (England); Steeleye Span (England); Shirley Collins & the Albion Country Band (England); Morris On (England); Gryphon (England); John Kirkpatrick & Ashley Hutchings (England); the City Waites (England); Bob Pegg (England); Dave Swarbrick (England); the Albion Band (England); Brass Monkey (England); John Kirkpatrick Band (England); Jacqui McShee (England); Kate Rusby (England); the Johnstons (Ireland); Anne Briggs (England); June Tabor (England); Nic Jones (England); the Cock and Bull Band (England); Home Service (England); Oyster Band (England); the Barely Works (England); Mouth Music & Mairi MacInnes (Scotland); Shooglenifty (Scotland); Oige (Ireland); Burach (Scotland); Fairport Convention (England); the Ian Campbell Folk Group (Scotland); Sweeney's Men (Ireland); the Humblebums (England); Fotheringay (England); Anne Briggs (England); Cyril Tawney (England); Richard & Linda Thompson (England); Dransfield (England); Linda Thompson (England); Richard Thompson (England); June Tabor & Oyster Band (England); Billy Bragg (England); Oyster Band (England); Jez Lowe & the Bad Pennies (England); Ralph McTell (England); Norma Waterson (England).

New Electric Muse is a revised and expanded reissue of the very similarly titled *The Electric Muse: The Story of Folk into Rock*, originally a four-LP box set released in 1975 to document the evolution of Anglo-Celtic music from its acoustic/traditional roots to what came to be called electric folk or folk-rock. Performers from England, Scotland, and Ireland are represented on both of the album's incarnations, the most recent of which is a three-CD set. Its first two CDs contain most of the material from the original, and are organized by the same themes: "From the Acoustic Roots," surveying modern yet acoustic-based arrangements of traditional tunes; "Blues, Baroque and Beyond," documenting the "folk baroque" fusion of jazz, classical, and folk elements pioneered by guitarist Davey Graham (which received its fullest expression in the work of Pentangle); "Roll over Cecil (and Tell Vaughan Williams the News)," containing more contemporary (yet still acoustic) treatments of traditional material; "The Electric Adventure," featuring some of the first electric adaptations of traditional ballads; and "A New Tradition," showcasing the different strains of folk-rock being practiced by 1975, from electric adaptations of folk dance tunes to original songs—written and performed by the likes of Richard Thompson, Steve Ashley, and Mr. Fox—that were clearly inspired by traditional ballad styles. The third CD is called "The Muse Revisited, the Continuing Story: Folk into Rock into Folk," and covers the two decades since the original box was released. There's acoustic and electric material, showing that both approaches continue to evolve—and the first burst from Anglo-Celtic folk's next generation is well represented by tracks from vocalist/fiddler Eliza Carthy and Irish accordionist Sharon Shannon.

A year after this set's release producer Laurence Aston expanded its concept for *New Electric Muse II: The Continuing Story of Folk into Rock*. Each of this second box's CDs focuses on the evolution of a particular sub-genre of Anglo-Celtic folk and folk-rock. Disc one, "King Arthur's Children," focuses on artists who were heavily influenced by medieval and "early" music, such as the Young Tradition, Gryphon, and Steeleye Span. Disc two, "The Wild Beasts in the Forest," presents a fascinating array of treatments of traditional source material, ranging from the more acoustic performances of the Watersons, Pentangle, and June Tabor to the '90s multi-culti, punk-folk, and dance-pop fusions explored by Mouth Music & Mairi McInnes, the Barely Works, and Shooglenifty. Disc three, "Songs of Experience," offers up original songs with traditional flavors by Richard Thompson ("Devonside"), Oyster Band ("Granite Years"), Jez Lowe ("Bede Weeps"), Billy Bragg ("Moving the Goalposts"), and others.

Suffice it to say that if you were stuck on the proverbial desert isle and wanted to have a definitive souvenir of the recent musical history of the British, these two boxes would do it, offering as comprehensive an overview of Anglo-Celtic folk and folk-rock as is presently available.

Ken Roseman

Nordic Roots: A NorthSide Collection ♪♪♪♪ (NorthSide, 1998)

Sweden, Norway, Finland
genre: Contemporary tradition-based Scandinavian music

Chateau Neuf Spelemannslag (Norway); Den Fule (Sweden); Garmarna (Sweden); Groupa (Sweden); Hoven Droven (Sweden); Hedningarna (Sweden, Finland); Olov Johansson (Sweden); Loituma (Finland); Hege Rimestad (Norway); SWÅP (Sweden, U.K.); Triakel (Sweden); Troka (Finland); Väsen (Sweden); Tapani Varis (Finland); Wimme (Finland).

NorthSide is a U.S.-based label specializing in roots music from the Scandinavian countries. This compilation is not only an easy introduction to the label and its artists, but also serves as a great jumping-off point for those wanting to learn more about the dynamic Scandinavian scene. The avant-garde/hybrid side is well-represented by Hedningarna's heavy, high-tech Swedish/Finnish balladry; Den Fule's noisy roots-funk; and the lush sounds of Chateau Neuf Spelemannslag—an 18-piece folk-rock orchestra with choral-style vocals accompanied by horns, fiddles, woodwinds, electric bass, and drums. Meanwhile, Loituma, which features full multi-part vocal harmonies over strummed *kanteles* (a unique zither which is the Finnish national instrument), and the instrumental groups Troka and Väsen, show off the potential of acoustic formats. As a special bonus, three of the tracks here are available on no other releases.

Ken Roseman

Rembetica: Historic Urban Folk Songs from Greece ♪♪♪♪ (Rounder, 1992, compilation prod. Charles Howard, Dick Spottswood)

Greece
genre: Rembetica

Adonis Dalgas (Turkey/Greece); Agapios Tomboulis (Turkey/Greece); Yiannis Tsanakas (Turkey/Greece); Roza Eskenazi (Turkey/Greece); Markos Vamvakaris (Greece); Apostolos Hatzichristos (Greece); Vassilis Tsitsanis (Turkey/Greece); Efstratios Pagioumitzis (a.k.a. Stratos) & Stelios Keromitis (Greece); Ioannis Papaioannou (Turkey/Greece); Rita Abatzi (Turkey/Greece); Ioannis Halikas (a.k.a. Jack Gregory) (Greece/USA); Ioannis Dhragatsis (a.k.a. Ogdhondakis) (Turkey/Greece); Marika Papagika (Greece/USA); George Macreyannis (Greece); Marika Kanaropoulou (Greece/USA); George Theologitis (a.k.a. George Katsaros) (Greece/USA); Adonis Kalivopoulos (Turkey/Greece) & Yiovan Tsaous (Turkey/Greece); Stratos Pagioumitzis (Greece); Lambros Leondaridhis (Turkey/Greece); Yiangos Psamatianos (Turkey/Greece).

After the breakup of the Ottoman Empire in 1922, Kemal Atatürk kicked many of the ethnic Greeks out of Turkey, and some of them migrated to Greece's coastal cities. When they came to their ancestral homeland, these immigrants found little favor with the entrenched upper classes. Mixing with the indigenous proletariat, the new arrivals took elements of the Ottoman musical tradition and blended them with more mainstream Greek components to create *rembetica* (a.k.a. *rebetica* or *rembetiko*). The results have been likened to American blues and Portuguese *fado,* music associated with criminals and other undesirables. Lyrics celebrated love, sex, and drugs in an open and unabashed manner, but also told tales of loss and alienation. Within decades rembetica became somewhat tamer, as government censorship banned the racier lyrics and the first generation of performers died off. The period covered on this album is 1906 to 1946, with most of it recorded during the '30s. The collection gives a good picture of rembetica's evolution and includes some of the biggest names in the genre, including the matchless singer Roza Eskenazi and the bouzouki virtuoso Ioannis Halikias, who later moved to New York City and adopted the name Jack Gregory.

Garaud MacTaggart

The Rough Guide to Scottish Music ♪♪♪♪ (World Music Network, 1996, compilation prod. Phil Stanton)

Scotland
genre: Scottish folk

Wolfstone; Catherine-Anne MacPhee; Capercaillie; the Iron Horse; Talitha MacKenzie; Ring 'O' Steall; the Cast; Dick Gaughan; the Tannahill Weavers; the Boys of the Lough; Heather Heywood; Tannas; Ceolbeg; the Battlefield Band; Bert Jansch; Old Blind Dogs. (All artists are from Scotland.)

This collection is an excellent introduction to the contemporary Scottish folk/roots music scene, from veteran performers like the Tannahill Weavers, the Battlefield Band, and Bert Jansch, to younger acts like the Iron Horse, Tannas, and Old Blind Dogs; from straightforward and acoustic interpretations of traditional folk, to all sorts of eclectic and electric fusions. In the former category, Catherine-Anne McPhee sings a lovely Gaelic ballad accompanied by harp, the Boys of the Lough offer an original waltz, and vocalist Heather Heywood gives a clear, powerful rendition of the well-known ballad "Down by the Sally Gardens." Those who prefer more rough-edged stuff will enjoy Wolfstone's kick-ass bagpipe-and-fiddle-led rock 'n' reel. Yet another take on Scottish heritage is provided by Talitha MacKenzie, who marries a bit of traditional "mouth music" (usually unaccompanied dance singing) with high-tech electronic percussion; the steady Gaelic rhythms adapt well to a bit of funky syncopation. "Claire in Heaven," written by Capercaillie's Manus Lunny, splendidly mixes pop song construction with a folkish melody, modern rhythm grooves, and what sound like bits of ancient jigs and reels—now that, like the album as a whole, just about ties it all up in one snazzy package.

Ken Roseman

The Rough Guide to the Music of Eastern Europe ♫♫♫♫
(World Music Network, 1998, compilation prod. Phil Stanton)

International
genre: Folk music

Márta Sebestyén (Hungary); Taraf de Haïdouks (Romania); Apparatschik (Machorka Tabakistan); Kocani Orkestar featuring Naat Veliov (Macedonia); Trio Bulgarka (Bulgaria); Ferus Mustafov (Macedonia); Kálmán Balogh & the Gipsy Cimbalom Band (Hungary); Trebunia Family Band (Poland); Vízönto (Hungary); Mystery of Bulgarian Voices Choir (Bulgaria); "Horo" Orchestra (Bulgaria); Ivo Papasov & His Bulgarian Wedding Band (Bulgaria); Zsarátnok (Hungary); Mark Pashku (Albania); Nikola Parov (Hungary).

This CD offers a 73-and-a-half-minute survey of current trends in Eastern European music, with better liner notes than is the norm for this series and a pleasing amount of stylistic and textural variety. Traditional styles are well-represented: the Gypsy music of Taraf de Haïdouks (whose name translates as "Orchestra of Honorable Brigands"); a rebel song of Thrace sung by the Trio Bulgarka; the exotic sound of the *cimbalom* (a large dulcimer) as played by Kálmán Balogh in a dance context; the Trebunia Family Band's string-band-and-vocals evocation of Poland's Górales culture; and more. There are striking hybrids such as the Macedonian Gypsy oriental brass band Kocani Orkestar, which (with plenty of military drums) performs the Tito-era Yugoslavian pop hit "The Orient Is Red," based on a

Communist Chinese song. And then there are relatively schooled, even slick productions, which blend the ancient and the up-to-date, from Vízönto's mix of Hungarian music with a pop-folk chord progression and jazzy touches; to the practically postmodern exuberance of Ivo Papasov; to the "Horo" Orchestra's use of contemporary instruments; to Nikola Parov's new-age leanings. Last but not least, world-music superstars like the Mystery of Bulgarian Voices Choir and Márta Sebestyén transcend all such categories. The recordings are for the most part relatively recent, even if the musical styles sometimes aren't, so sound quality is never an issue.

Steve Holtje

The Rough Guide to the Music of Portugal ♫♫♫♫ (World Music Network, 1998)

Portugal
genre: Portuguese folk/roots

Jose Afonso; Dulce Pontes; Realejo; Teresa Silva Carvalho; Carlos Paredes; Amália Rodrigues; Vai De Roda; Terra A Terra; V Império; Lendas & Mitos; Anabela; Maria Da Fe; Margarida Bessa; Vitorino; Maria Teresa de Noronha; Lenita Gentil; Carlos Zel; Manuel De Almeida; Ronda Dos Quatro Camhinos; Grupo Cantadores Do Redondo. (All artists are from Portugal.)

Not much Portuguese music has been exported to U.S. audiences, but this collection offers a brief sampling of what's available. *Fado*, the distinctive bluesy-jazzy ballad style, is well-represented, and from this disc you'd definitely get the impression that Portugal has great female vocalists on every street corner. But what is most impressive here are the instrumental tracks from Realejo and V Império. Realejo has a singular chamber-folk sound based around the hurdy-gurdy's buzzing tone over softer strings and woodwinds. V Império takes such a style in a different direction; their approach fuses "classical" textures (violins, cellos, violas, woodwinds) and melodies with a pulsing dance-pop energy. Elsewhere on the disc, Ronda Dos Quatros Caminhos unite vocal harmony with driving percussion, and those who enjoy Welsh choirs or Ladysmith Black Mambazo will get a kick out of the massed voices of Grupo Cantadores Do Redondo.

Ken Roseman

Sacred Treasures: Choral Masterworks from Russia
♫♫♫♫ (Hearts of Space, 1998, prod. Leyla R. Hill)

Russia, Bulgaria, Belgium
genre: Sacred choral music

Russian State Symphony Capella (Russia); Leningrad Glinka State Academic Choir (Russia); Bulgarian National Choir (Bulgaria); USSR Ministry of Culture Chamber Choir (Russia); Men's

Chamber Choir of Sofia (Bulgaria); Chevetogne Monastery Choir (Belgium); Bulgarian Radio & Television Choir (Bulgaria).

If you're one of the millions of people who fell in love with the sacred sounds of Gregorian chant when it exploded into the mainstream a few years back, you're bound to enjoy this powerfully moving compilation. The Russian Orthodox Church is nearly unparalleled for the beauty of its choral traditions, due primarily to the fact that *a cappella* singing has been its central form of worship for more than 1,000 years. The church's divine liturgy has become more complex and refined over that time, evolving from simple Gregorian-style, Byzantine-inspired chants sung by all-male choirs, to mixed choirs singing compositions rich with Western harmonies, varied dynamics, and layered textures. *Sacred Treasures* compiles 17 aptly described masterworks from this tradition, many of them written by luminous composers like Sergei Rachmaninov and Peter Tchaikovsky. Individually, each track is a spiritual revelation of surprising emotional impact. But when taken as a whole, the songs flow together into a glorious tapestry of haunting beauty and sublime, transcendent peace.

Bret Love

Silvana Licursi: Far from the Land of Eagles ♪♪♪♪ (Sud-Nord, 1989/Lyrichord, 1991, prod. Erasmo Treglia)

Italy
genre: Albanian

Silvana Licursi (Italy).

Albanians fleeing Turkish invaders in the 15th century settled in Italy, and to this day their descendants have maintained the Albanian language and traditions despite living across the Adriatic Sea from their homeland. Silvana Licursi has been gathering Albanian-Italian folk music and performs it with great feeling and melancholy, singing her pastoral love songs in Albanian while gently picking the strings of her lute, accompanied by Celtic harp, sax, guitar, flute, and tambourine. The result is a mellow and soothing collection, one of the only recordings from Italy's Albanian community.

David Poole

Song of the Crooked Dance: Early Bulgarian Traditional Music, 1927–42 ♪♪♪♪♪ (Yazoo/Shanachie, 1998, prod. Lauren Brody)

Bulgaria
genre: Ballad, dance song, funeral music, wedding music

Boris Mashalov; Mita Stoicheva; Masha Byalmustakova; Georgi Stanev; Parush Parushev; Gudi Gudev; Vulkana Stoyanova; Stanil Payakov; Ivan Hristov Kavaldzhiev; Boris Karlov; the Bistrishkata Chetvorka; Tsvyatko Blagoev; Ramadan Lolov. (All artists are from Bulgaria.)

Many world-music listeners have come to know the music of Bulgaria through the melancholy choral arrangements of "Le Mystère des Voix Bulgares," the catch-all name for what is in Bulgaria a number of official choirs. Selected from discs issued between the First and Second World Wars, *Song of the Crooked Dance* reveals a far more spontaneous, guileless, and energetic aspect of Bulgarian music. It includes a variety of ballads and dance tunes, with an emphasis on instrumentals and male vocals that were less commonly recorded at the time. One notable feature of the folk tunes heard here is the frequent use of odd time signatures, such as 7/8, 5/16, or 11/16, that lend the tracks that wonderful jumpy quality familiar to listeners of Balkan music. Though we're never told in the CD text, this might be the origin of the term "crooked dance." Another common thread is a highly developed sense of the tragic. "Kapitan," for instance, tells of a military commander who falls ill and asks his comrades to "write a letter for me/to my wife/and tell her that I've perished here," while the ballad "Three Brothers, Master Builders" recounts a morbid folk tale of three bridge builders who seal the wife of the youngest brother into the bricks as a macabre sacrifice.

Positioned at a cultural and historical crossroads between Europe, Asia, and the Middle East, Bulgaria embodies a fantastic collision of civilizations, which is of course reflected in its multifaceted music. The disc provides many illustrations: "Tsonka's tune," an intricate solo on the *gaida* (bagpipe), uses a scale reminiscent of a Middle Eastern mode; "Kopano horo" features a *tambura* (long-necked lute) melody played in clearly Greek style; and "Georgi Sugarev," a ballad on *oud* (Arabic lute), has a distinct Turkish flavor. In the words of producer Lauren Brody, *Crooked Dance* serves as an "antidote to those floral, complex arrangements of 'Mystère' fame" which have mistakenly come to stand for Bulgarian folk music. Half a bone has to be deducted only because the same song is accidentally included twice, as tracks 9 and 21. But the CD is clearly a labor of love, with clean disc transfers, interesting selection, illuminating text, and transcribed lyrics.

Jeffrey Muhr

The Story of Flamenco ♪♪♪ (Hemisphere, 1997, compilation prod. Rafael Pastor)

Spain
genre: Flamenco

Pepe De La Matrona; Perla De Cadiz; Pericon de Cadiz; Sernita de Jerez; Paco Isidro; Manolo Caracol; Fernanda de Utrera; Gabriel Moreno; Flores de Gaditano; La Nina de la Puebla; Terremoto de Jerez; Romerito; El Borrico; Diamante Negro; Sordera; Sernita; Carmen Linaresa; El Pali; Hermanos Toronjo; Enrique Morente; Pepe Marchena. (All artists are from Spain.)

Flamenco is the calmest, most tranquil music on God's green Earth. Just kidding. Actually, how much you get into it depends on how far you're willing to follow its practitioners' frenzy—flamenco vocals are passion personified; the unvarnished feeling takes getting used to for Western ears, and can grate when you're not in the right mood. The cuts on this compilation are well-wrought, and serve as a nice introduction to the style. Which is okay, but I can't help but feel cheated: when flamenco is on it really KICKS, and none of the flamenco that's knocked me on my ass with its unbridled vigor is equaled here. Not all that exciting, but a fairly nice package makes it worth owning for the curious.

Michaelangelo Matos

Sult: Spirit of the Music 𝅘𝅥𝅮𝅘𝅥𝅮𝅘𝅥𝅮𝅘𝅥𝅮 (The Bottom Line Record Co., 1997, prod. Dónal Lunny)

Ireland
genre: Irish Traditional

John McSherry; Van Morrison; Máire Brennan; Nollaig Casey; Mark Knopfler (England); Sharon Shannon; Laoise Kelly; Paul Brady; Máirtin O'Connor; Maighréad Ní Dhomhnaill; Iarla Ó Lionáird; Nomos; Matt Molloy; Máire Breatnach; Brian Kennedy; Anúna; Steven Cooney (Australia/Ireland); Seamus Begley; John Spillane; Liam O'Flynn; Mary Black; Dónal Lunny; Richard Bennett; Noel Bridgeman; Richie Buckley; Pat Crowley; Keith Donald; Glenn Worf; Brendan Power (Australia); Frank Torpey; Sean Keane; Niall Vallely; Mairead Nesbitt. (All artists are from Ireland except where otherwise noted.)

Recorded especially for a 13-part series on Dublin-based Irish-language television station TnaG, *Sult* was produced by Dónal Lunny, one of the foremost interpreters of Irish music. Lunny has brought together an odd group of musicians to create a diverse recording that has its roots firmly planted in Irish tradition but goes well beyond that into the realms of pop and rock. Van Morrison and Mary Black duet on the funky "St. Dominic's Preview," while Irish Gaelic singers Maighréad Ní Dhomhnaill and Iarla Ó Lionáird give a spirited rendition of the traditional "Siul a Ruin." Lunny is ever-present, playing on nearly every track and imbuing most with a modern Irish sensibility. "Sult" literally translates from Irish to English as "fun" or "amusement," and the fun that the musicians are obviously having translates into a spirited recording.

Cliff McGann

Sweet Sunny North 𝅘𝅥𝅮𝅘𝅥𝅮𝅘𝅥𝅮𝅘𝅥𝅮 (Shanachie, 1994, prod. Birger Gesthuisen, Henry Kaiser)
Sweet Sunny North, Vol. II 𝅘𝅥𝅮𝅘𝅥𝅮𝅘𝅥𝅮𝅘𝅥𝅮 (Shanachie, 1996, prod. Birger Gesthuisen, Henry Kaiser)

Norway
genre: Folk and pop music

Sweet Sunny North: Kirsten Bråten Berg; Ailu Gaup (Norwegian Sami); Tiriltunga; Susanne Lundeng; Paolo Vinaccia; Annbjørg Lien; the Brazz Brothers; Deepika (Pakistan/Norway); Chateau Neuf Spelemannslag; Halvard T. Bjørgum; Knut Reiersrud; Steinar Ofsdal; Berit Nordland (Norwegian Sami); Gabriel Fliflet; Ole Hamre; Bjørgulv Straume; Tone Hulbækmo; Hans Fredrik Jacobsen; Hans Brimi; Rolv Brimi; Farmers Market; Elisabeth Kværne; Henry Kaiser (USA); David Lindley (USA). *Sweet Sunny North, Vol. II*: All the above artists, plus Jon Faukstad. (All artists are from Norway, except where otherwise noted.)

Musical omnivore/impresarios Henry Kaiser and David Lindley take their instruments and recording rigs up to Norway to introduce U.S. audiences to a rich musical tradition that's almost unknown in this country—although it's fairly certain that immigrant fiddlers must have added something to the American song bag (as Kaiser points out in his liner notes, "Jack of Diamonds" has the same tune as a Norwegian folk song called "Drunken Hiccups"). For these sessions Kaiser & Lindley gathered together some of Norway's finest traditional players, both old-timers and upstarts who are continuing to work within the folk tradition to create their own music. The sound has a Celtic ring to it, at least to non-Norwegian ears, but it's bluesier and more melancholic. The 28 tracks on the first album include unique Pakistani/Norwegian fusion by Deepika; hootenannies by the big folk band Chateau Neuf Spelemannslag; folk-jazz from the Brazz Brothers and Farmers Market; virtuosic *hardanger* (Norwegian fiddle) playing from then-newcomer/now-star Annbjørg Lien and master *spelemann* (folk musician) Hans Brimi; dissonant dances from Gabriel Fliflet and Ole Hamre; *joiks* (the distinctive song form of Scandinavia's indigenous Sami people) by Berit Nordland and Ailu Gaup; and more. The second volume, recorded at the same time, is a sequel but no afterthought. Once again the performers range over a wide array of styles, though this collection sounds slightly more traditional than the first. There are stunning vocal pieces by Tiriltunga; some quasi-swing jazz from the Brazz Brothers; a sheep-calling song from Tone Hulbækmo; joiking that sounds similar to the African American field hollers of the rural South; and a dozen fiddlers who play blue, eerie, and/or sprightly music that weaves its own unique magic.

j. poet

Taraf: Romanian Gypsy Music 𝅘𝅥𝅮𝅘𝅥𝅮𝅘𝅥𝅮𝅘𝅥𝅮 (Music of the World, 1996, prod. Martha Lorantos, Bob Haddad)

Romania
genre: Gypsy folk

Various musicians from the villages of Mârşa, Clejani, Albeşti, and Dobroteşti. (All artists are from Romania.)

The diverse music of the Romanian Gypsies is compelling, if not exactly easy listening. In Romania, the performance of festive folk music is not a recreational affair but largely relegated to professional musicians—usually Gypsies from the local village. Because of this "outsider" profession and their ethnic origin, Gypsy musicians are considered "foreign" by the Romanian peasant class and are often treated with contempt, though when performing they're invested with a special authority, treated like beloved friends, and lavishly rewarded for their talents (an acceptance as entertainers but not as individuals, not uncommon to disfavored nationalities in the United States and elsewhere). There has (not coincidentally) been much debate in Romania as to whether the country's musical traditions are accurately represented by Gypsy interpretations, and the nine songs presented here do show elements of influence from all around the Mediterranean, especially Italy and Greece. The music's primary features are violin, accordion, dulcimer, double bass, and, of course, the fiery, passionate vocals Gypsy music is best known for, which often drive the songs to rapturous crescendos. Its narrow geographical focus limits this compilation's musical scope in comparison with an all-encompassing album like *Latcho Drom* (reviewed on page 916), but if you want an in-depth listen to the traditional music of a specific Gypsy community, this is not a bad choice.

Bret Love

Tulikkulkku 𝄞𝄞𝄞𝄞𝄞 (Kansanmusiikki Instituutti, 1993, compilation prod. Kurt Lindblad, Hannu Saha)

Finland
genre: World music

Me Naiset; Väinönputki; Etnopojat; Hedningarna; Pohjantahti; Arja Kastinen; Tuulenkantajat Septet; Virpi Forsberg; Niekku; Primo; Martti Pokela; Suomussalmi-ryhmä. (All artists are from Finland.)

This collection documents the cutting edge of Finnish folk music as performed by some of the foremost students, instructors, and fellow travelers of the Folk Music Institute in Kaustinen and the Sibelius Academy's Folk Music Department in Helsinki. It is a richly cross-pollinated musical community, as evidenced by some of the "big names" covered in this book's main section who appear in different settings here: accordion wizard Maria Kalaniemi is a member of Niekku, for instance, while JPP's Arto Järvelä can be heard playing fiddle with Primo. The disc was prepared in honor of Heikki Laitinen, perhaps the leading force behind Finland's acceptance of folk music as a strong, viable form still worthy of study and performance. Some of the tunes on this collection are very traditional in ori-

entation, while others use what has gone before as a springboard for experimentation.

Garaud MacTaggart

Two Girls Started to Sing: Bulgarian Village Singing
𝄞𝄞𝄞𝄞 (Rounder, 1990, prod. Martha Forsyth, Dick Forsyth)

Bulgaria
genre: Bulgarian traditional singing

Names of the artists are not provided; all artists are from Bulgaria.

These Bulgarian women sing in pairs, with one voicing the melody while the other creates a drone. This two-part style is typical of southwest Bulgaria, where these amateur singers were recorded. Most were in their 50s or older, having lived long enough to have used these songs for every aspect of village life—while harvesting, dancing in the village square, gathered with the family, or at ceremonies. Traditionally in Bulgaria women sang while men played instruments, but more often women sang unaccompanied, as on this collection. Their performances are not professional, simply an instinctive part of their everyday life, a far cry from the honed polyphony of Le Mystère Des Voix Bulgares. Yet the raw, intimate, and natural quality of this music is greatly compelling.

David Poole

Village Music of Bulgaria/Bulgarian Folk Music 𝄞𝄞𝄞𝄞 (Elektra/Nonesuch, 1970/1971/1988, prod. Ethel Raim, Martin Koenig)

Bulgaria
genre: Folk music

Vasilka Andonova; Kremena Stancheva; Shtiliyan Tihov; Nadezhda Georgieva Klicherova; Gena Ivanova Bodenova; Nadezhda Georgieva Palestova; Bitov Orchestra; Lina Gekova Gergova; Menka Ilieva Aronova; Bozhurka Tupankova; Borislav Vassilev; Smolyan Folk Ensemble; Stephan Zahmanov; Valya Balkanska; Lazar Konevski; Sandanski Folk Ensemble; Magda Beorgieva Mavrikova; Magda Borisova Belluhova; Penka Nikolova Chukarinova; Vesa Atanasova Zinkova; Yana Hristova Stankova; Elena Petrova Kefalova; Magda Georgieva Visheva; Fatme Mehmedova Kelesheva; Nezife Salieva Musarlieva; Ismail Kurtov Limanov; Asen Kurtov Limanov; Abidin Kurtov Dzhaferov; Linka Stoyanova Dimcheva; Stanka Krumova Dimcheva; Sandanski Folk Ensemble; Boyana Kirilova Georgieva; Hadezhda Kostadinova Doneva. (All artists are from Bulgaria.)

Located between Asia Minor and western Europe, the small country of Bulgaria has felt the influences of many cultures on its music, and the aural proof is on this album. The tempos, harmonies, patterns, and vibrato-style singing of the country date back to the Ottoman Turks and others who occupied Bulgarian lands until the latter part of the 19th century. Albeit in a conquered nation, the Bulgarian folk culture flourished, and evidence of its tradition is heard here in strong, self-assured vocal performances and skillful instrumentals. An earmark of Bulgarian music is its odd meters (to Western ears, at least), displayed here in lively traditional dance tunes usually performed for social ceremonies and harvest rituals. Originally recorded in 1968, the 37 tracks on this compilation combine the two 1970s LPs of its dual title. Featured are songs mostly in two vocal styles, the single-voice melodies of the Rhodope region in the south, and the two-voice (diaphonic) melodies of the Pirin-Macedonia and Shope regions in the southwest. The first 13 tracks are from these regions and also Thrace in the southeast; the remaining cuts, all of short duration, feature songs and dances only from Pirin-Macedonia. Robust songs, executed by piercing, "open-throated" female singers and various folk instrumentalists, are often dissonant and formed on tonal clusters. They contrast singer against small chorus, regional instruments against solo singer, and singer against singer in an *a cappella* call-and-response format. Some pieces feature solo instruments native to the area such as the *kaval* (seven-hole, woody-toned reed pipe), *kaba gaida* (a droning bagpipe), and *gadulka* (a stringed, bowed, viola-toned instrument). Liner notes provide English translation, describe the music, and include a history of each piece.

Nancy Ann Lee

A Woman's Heart 𝄞𝄞𝄞𝄞 (Dara, 1992)
A Woman's Heart 2 𝄞𝄞𝄞 (Dara, 1995, prod. Mary Black, Frances Black, Declan Sinnot)

Ireland
genre: Singer/songwriter, Celtic, pop

A Woman's Heart: Mary Black; Eleanor McEvoy; Dolores Keane; Sharon Shannon; Frances Black; Maura O'Connell. *A Woman's Heart 2*: Sinéad Lohan; Frances Black; Mary Coughlan; Mary Black; Dolores Keane; Sharon Shannon; Maura O'Connell; Sinéad O'Connor; Maighread Ní Dhomhnaill. (All artists are from Ireland.)

The women whose music appears on these albums work in styles ranging from rock (O'Connor) to country (O'Connell) to pop (the Black sisters) to more traditional Irish forms (Keane, Shannon). What they've put together is a collection that emphasizes their Celtic sensibilities in these diverse styles. Some chose to include their own songs, while others picked standards from varying traditions (including songs by Nanci Griffith and Billie Holiday), and these work well together. A particular strength of these discs is that some of the singers have chosen to record music by contemporary Celtic songwriters. For example, several artists pay tribute to Eleanor McEvoy's songwriting talent, and indeed the title of the series was taken from a tune she wrote, and which she sings on the first album as a duet with Mary Black. Other Celtic songwriters represented include Dougie McLean and Noel Brazil. These two collections offer an attractive and accessible introduction to many of the best contemporary Irish voices; they hold enough power and quality to make them important listening for experts in the genre as well.

Kerry Dexter

The World's Musical Traditions 9: Musical Traditions of Portugal 𝄞𝄞𝄞𝄞 (Smithsonian, 1994, prod. Max Peter Baumann, Tiago de Oliveira Pinto)

Portugal
genre: Dances, chants, ballads, guitarradas, folk songs

Paulino Pereira João; Paulino José Raposo; Domingos Alfredo Flacão; Grupo Instrumental de Constantim; Marta dos Anjos Martins Fidalgo; Rancho de Monsanto; Grupo Coral 'Os Ceifeiros de Cuba; Quarteto de Guitarras de Coimbra; Rancho folclórico 'Os Camponeses de Riachos; Grupo folclórico de Viana do Castelo. (All artists are from Portugal.)

Musical Traditions of Portugal, the sixth CD in an excellent series released by the Smithsonian Institution (see the review of *Bunggridj-bunggridj* on page 867 for the series' convoluted history), samples a few of the diverse musical genres to be found in the title country. Traditionally one of the great seafaring nations, Portugal's contacts over the centuries with Africa, the Americas, and Asia are reflected in the breadth of its music. The CD includes five traditional genres: dances from the northeast; ritual songs and chants from the central east; choral songs from the south; *guitarrada* instrumentals from Coimbra; and songs and dances performed by folklore societies called *ranchos folclóricos*. While the simple, plaintive quality of the chants and vocal songs makes them difficult to grab onto, the energetic guitarradas and folkloric ensemble performances are more satisfying as a listening experience. Guitarradas are instrumentals performed by one or two *guitarras* accompanied by one or two *violas*. The guitarras are pear-shaped *citterns,* or proto-guitars, with six double strings, while the violas are simply six-string Spanish guitars with metal strings. The overall sound created by these ensembles is bright and jaunty with more than a little vibrato; it sounds a lot like what the uninitiated listener might expect Portuguese music to sound like. The waltzes, *fandangos,* and merry vocal songs made by the ranchos folclóricos carry as much energy to the listener as the guitarradas, even if their sound also isn't unexpected. But a few surprises do spring up, such as the "stick dances" that open the CD. These feature a Portuguese goatskin bagpipe called the *gaita de foles* accompanied by drum. Included with the CD is an impressive 76-page booklet with extensive notes and lyrics.

Jeffrey Muhr

NORTH AMERICA

American Warriors: Songs for Veterans 🎵🎵🎵 (Rykodisc, 1996, prod. Thomas Vennum Jr.)

USA, Canada
genre: Native American

Identified artists are: Richard la Ferneier (Ojibway); Black Lodge Singers (Blackfeet); Kiowa War Mothers Chapter (Kiowa); Sioux Valley Singers (Sioux); Fort Kipp Singers (Sioux); Winnebago Sons (Winnebago); the Smokey Town Singers (Menominee). (All artists are from USA.)

Somewhere in historical imagination, there's an image of the Native American warrior—maybe noble in defeat, maybe vicious in victory—but it's an idea having very little to do with the actual place of the warrior among Native American cultures. This disc offers music to illuminate that place, presenting recordings of chants and war songs from the days of Custer up through Desert Storm. Music held (and still holds) an important role in preparing the warrior for battle; in sending him from and reuniting him with the community; in celebrating victory and in surviving defeat. This is an uncommon thematic collection of chants and spoken-word selections on this subject as expressed by Native American tribes of the upper Midwest. It's not a disc for casual listening, but if you are interested in the evolution of cultural ideas, you'll want to check it out.

Kerry Dexter

Americanos: Latino Life in the United States: A Celebration 🎵🎵🎵🎵 (Atlantic, 1999, prod. Steve DeBro)

USA
genre: Hispanic, Latin jazz, rock, Tejano

Ruben Blades; Lhasa; Los Lobos; Willie Bobo; Ozomatli; War; Pedro Luis Ferrer; Santana; Frankie Negron; Celia Cruz; Mark Ribot y los Cubanos Postizos; Eddie Palmieri; Tito Puente; Flaco Jimenez (with Ry Cooder); Ayuda a los Pueblos; Paquito D'Rivera with the Orchestra of Saint Luke's. (All artists are from Latin countries or from the USA of Latino descent. Most are currently based in USA.)

This collection of 13 tracks is part of an interlocking film, traveling photo exhibit, and book of same name (Little, Brown & Co., 1999) intended to take a portrait of Latino life in the USA at the turn of the millennium. The project was spearheaded by well-known actor and activist Edward James Olmos. The disc does give a glimpse of certain aspects of Latino music, skewed more toward the urban Latino who listens to rock and Latin jazz than to his cousin who might prefer country, folk, and Tejano. There must have been contractual as well as stylistic considerations that directed the choice of musicians on this disc, and all of those chosen are excellent. Their fellow artists—ranging from classical guitarist Manuel Barrueco, to pop superstar Gloria Es-

tefan, to Tejano crossover hitmaker Selena, to country & western favorite Emilio, to visionary songwriter Tish Hinojosa—would seem to deserve a place at this table as well, though. *Americanos* is a lively slice of Latino music in the U.S. today; just don't let it be your only sample.

Kerry Dexter

Ballinasloe Fair: Early Recordings of Irish Music in America 🎵🎵🎵 (Traditional Crossroads, 1998)

USA
genre: Irish Traditional

Packie Dolan and the Melody Boys; Dan Sullivan's Shamrock Band; Dinny "Jimmy" Doyle; Larry Griffin; Frank Murphy; John Sheridan; Neil Nolan; Dan Sullivan; Murty Rabbett; Mike Hannifin; Connie Hannifin; John McGettigan and His Irish Minstrels; Michael Cashin. (All artists are from USA.)

This collection provides the listener with a view of Irish music in America during the 1920s, one of that genre's most vibrant periods. While most reissues of Irish music have dealt with the instrumental tradition, this one aims at providing the listener with a holistic view of Irish music in a certain place and time. It does so by including not only the tradition-based fiddle, flute, and accordion music popular with the Irish community, but also music representative of the strong Irish presence in the dance halls and vaudeville stages of New York, Boston, and Chicago—a form that won favor with a wide array of ethnic groups at the time, despite its often-stereotypical view of the Irish people. Great pains have been taken in remastering these old recordings, and the liner notes written by Irish folklorist Mick Moloney are highly informative.

Cliff McGann

Between Father Earth and Mother Sky 🎵🎵🎵🎵🎵 (Narada, 1995, executive prod. Michael Sullivan, Mabel Bensen)

USA, Canada, Mexico
genre: Native American

Douglas Spotted Eagle (Navajo/Lakota); Primeaux, Mike, & Attson (Dine/Yankton/Oglala); Perry Silverbird (Navajo/Apache); Tsa'ne Dose'e (Saponi/Tuscarora); Cornel Pewewardy (Comanche/Kiowa); the Native Flute Ensemble (U.S. Southwestern tribes); R. Carlos Nakai (Navajo/Ute); Bill Miller (Mohican); Chester Mahooty (Zuni Pueblo); Charles Jefferson (Cherokee/African American). (Artists are from USA, Canada, and Mexico.)

Whether a reworking of a traditional tribal melody or a new composition drawn from spiritual inspiration, the tracks on *Between Father Earth and Mother Sky* fulfill one of music's most ancient purposes: offering the listener a connection between history and the now, between present time and the space of the spirit. Though it conveys a strong sense of the beliefs in which it is based, it is music to be appreciated regardless of tradition.

Kerry Dexter

Borderlands: from Conjunto to Chicken Scratch 🎵🎵🎵🎵
(Smithsonian Folkways, 1993, prod. Texas Folklife Resources, Austin, Texas)

USA, Mexico
genre: Conjunto, Mexican American, Native American

Narciso Martinez; Jesus Maya; Timoteo Cantu; Lydia Mendoza; Beto Villa y su Orquesta with Carmen y Laura; Los Donneños; El Conjunto Bernal; Rubén Vela y su Conjunto; Ramón Ayala y los Bravos del Norte; Los Invasores de Nueva Leon; Los Cachorros de Juan Villareal; Los Dos Gilbertos with Beatriz Llama; Oscar Hernández; Roberto Pulido y los Clásicos; Franciso Molina and Marcelina Valencia; Gu-Achi Fiddlers; the Molinas; Southern Scratch; El Conjunto Murietta. (Artists are from USA and Mexico.)

Borderlands is about negotiation, in a sense—the changes and adjustments that take place when cultures, beliefs, ways of living, politics, and music come up against each other in daily life. The music on this disc explores those circumstances in an area that has been intimately familiar with cultural exchange for centuries, the Rio Grande Valley along the Texas/Arizona/ northern Mexico border. Here, in an illuminating chronological sequence, appear the *corrido* ballads and *conjunto* dance tunes popular on both sides of the river, merging and changing and holding their own identity with Native American fiddle tunes, country-rock, chicken scratch (a Native polka-based style), and *Tejano* (modern Tex-Mex). The way the songs are organized makes this a good introduction for the beginner, and will likely provoke lively discussion among those already informed about the region.

Kerry Dexter

Cajun & Creole Masters 🎵🎵🎵🎵 (World Music Institute, 1987/1996)

USA
genre: Cajun

Dennis McGee; Alfonse "Bois Sec" Ardoin; Canray Fontenot; Sady Courville; Michael Doucet; Billy Ware. (All artists are from USA.)

Four grandfathers of Cajun music, two white and two African American, show off the reels, waltzes, and nasal French singing that still define the Louisiana country tradition. Featuring music from before the great 1950s color break that sent African American musicians toward the R&B of zydeco and left white musicians (including host Michael Doucet) to stand as neo-conservative guardians of what was once a vital Saturday-night tradition, this disc brims with foot-stomping, triangle-ringing life. It is also an important historical document: accordionist "Bois Sec" Ardoin, a nephew of the great Amédée Ardoin, and his late partner, fiddler Canray Fontenot, were both recipients of National Heritage Fellowships and, until Fontenot's death in 1995, entertained thousands at the New Orleans Jazz and Heritage Festival with their endless, ornate variations on the

"chanky-chank" style rhythmic waltzes and blues sampled here. The late fiddling team of Dennis McGee and his brother-in-law Sady Courville also learned their music from family and community, reflecting the intricate two-violin harmonies that predate the accordion's introduction into South Louisiana. In addition to the live tracks (several with Doucet on guitar and Billy Ware on triangle), this disc features short interviews (in English), which are transcribed in the CD booklet. McGee also sings a short vocal solo that could be from a century ago, complete with cowboy yelps and elongated vowels that would still ring across the prairie.

Clea Simon

Conjunto! Texas-Mexican Border Music, Vols. 1–5 🎵🎵🎵🎵 (Rounder, 1988–90, compilation prod. Carl Finch)

USA, Mexico
genre: Conjunto

More than three dozen conjunto musicians, individuals and groups, the best-known including: Flaco Jimenez; Tony de la Rosa; David Lee Garza; El Conjunto Bernal. (Artists are primarily from the *frontera,* the Texas-Mexico border region.)

Conjunto is, fundamentally, a dance music, a rhythm that sends partners whirling across the sawdust floor. It's grounded in the sound of the accordion and the *bajo sexto* (12-string bass guitar), added to by singers and perhaps drums or other bass and guitar. It's a very atmospheric music, calling up images of South Texas, a place where German, Mexican, Native American, and the southern and western U.S. cultures met, converged, clashed—and eventually joined on the dance floor. Its listeners are most often bilingual and multicultural, so the music keeps changing as they do to meet their interests. In these five discs Rounder has collected and annotated 68 recordings, most of which had only been available on regional labels. It's a cohesive and interesting program for those who want to learn about conjunto (though the liner notes are sometimes repetitive). It's also fun for those who just want to dance.

Kerry Dexter

Conjuntos Norteños 🎵🎵🎵 (Arhoolie, 1989, compilation prod. Chris Strachwitz)

USA
genre: Tex-Mex

Los Pinguinos Del Norte; Conjunto Trio San Antonio. (All artists are from USA.)

Tex-Mex music, due in large part to the Hollywood image factory and the films of John Ford, evokes rugged country, dusty barrooms, and the heat of the western sun. One can almost picture the camera panning across a cowboy tableau: a gunfighter rides into town, tumbleweeds roll past. But in reality, the *conjuntos norteños* were popular groups that utilized vocal duets, accordion, *bajo sexto* (12-string bass guitar), bass, and drums, performing in plazas and at parties in northern Mexico and southern Texas. The two groups featured on this disc run through a host of traditional *corridos* (story ballads) with great skill. The trademark of Los Piguinos Del Norte is the contrast of Ruben Castillo Juarez's high nasal voice with Hilario Gaytan Moreno's smoother baritone. Conjunto Trio San Antonio is set apart by the nimble accordion of leader Fred Zimmerle. Unfortunately the ambience is rather staid, as if the disc were an academic exercise rather than a living document. Many tracks seem too restrained, with occasional obligatory vocal exclamations that sound like an afterthought. Conjunto Trio San Antonio does begin to loosen up late in the disc with a lusty "Borracho Perdido," complete with a winning slap-back bass rhythm and dancing accordion solo. If more of the material matched this buoyancy, it could be more recommendable for your next party than for your next ethnographic symposium.

Tim Sheridan

Corridos y Tragedias de la Frontera: First Recordings of Historic Mexican American Ballads, 1928–1937 𝄞𝄞𝄞𝄞
(Arhoolie, 1994, compilation prod. Chris Strachwitz)

USA, Mexico
genre: Corrido

Pedro Rocha & Lupe Martinez; Los Madrugadores; Hermanos Bañuelos; Hernández & Sifuentes; Ramos & Treviño; Silvano Ramos & Daniel Ramírez; Trio Matamoros; Dúo Latino; Los Cancioneros Alegres; Nacho & Justino; Dúo El Arte Mexicano; Francisco Montalvo & Andrés Berlanga; Silavano Ramos & Ortega; Trinidad & María López; Sifuentes y Guzman; Hermanos Chavarría; Salas y Mendoza; Cancioneres Picarescos; Antonio Flores & Manuel Valdéz. (All artists are from the Texas-Mexico border region.)

The *corrido* was—and in some cases still is—both the newspaper and the storybook of the border, a song-form relating the conflicts and exploits of daily life as well as extraordinary events. Many corridos are based in fact, but fictional tales also abound. Though it remains a vital form along the *frontera* (Texas-Mexico border) today, the heyday of the corrido was during the decade early in the century when these recordings were made. The musicians featured here were among the best and most widely known throughout the region. This two-disc set—and its extensive booklet—are invaluable both for appreciating the historical recordings themselves and for understanding the roots of contemporary Latin-based musics like *Tejano*, *conjunto*, and *nueva canción*.

Kerry Dexter

Cuarteto Coculense: Mexico's Pioneer Mariachis, Vol. 4
𝄞𝄞 (Arhoolie, 1998, compilation prod. Chris Strachwitz)

Mexico
genre: Mariachi

Cuarteto Coculense (Mexico).

One of the first Mariachi bands, the Cuarteto Coculense left their native town of Cocula for Mexico City in 1908 to make the records collected on this representative look at the genre's origins. In those pre-tech days the sound traveled through a horn and was etched directly onto a cylinder. The results are a struggle to listen through, with no bass and much hiss and distortion. Hearing beyond the recordings' limitations requires the dogged patience of a musical historian, yet proves rewarding. The wealth of Cocula at the turn of the century gave rise to much leisure time and a demand for groups like the Cuarteto. With the bass rendered inaudible the singers sound like altos, though they no doubt had rich tenor voices. They sing charming stories about their daughters, lost cattle herds, a motherless goat, and their courting of an Indian woman. The guitar playing is straightforward, alternating between only two or three chords with additional harmonies on the two violins. Now that the mariachi band has become synonymous with Mexican culture, it is interesting to listen back in time to the very first of their kind.

David Poole

Fifteen Tex-Mex Conjunto Classics 𝄞𝄞𝄞𝄞 (Arhoolie, 1996, compilation prod. Chris Strachwitz, Tom Diamant)

USA, Mexico
genre: Conjunto

Flaco Jimenez; Conjunto Bernal; Lydia Mendoza; Santiago Jimenez Jr.; Don Santiago Jimenez; Los Pavos Reales; Tony de la Rosa; Valerio Longoria; Los Pinguinos del Norte; Juan Lopez; Fred Zinnerle and Trio San Antonio; Narciso Martinez; Los Cenzontles; Steve Jordan. (Artists are from USA and Mexico.)

Conjunto is a music that grew out of the mixture of cultures that came to South Texas. The duet ballad style of Mexican *norteño*; the polka and accordion of German and Czech settlers; the country-music subjects of dancing, drinking, and dying: these and more mixed together in a way that all these cultures could relate to—and dance to. Conjunto is above all a dance music, and on this disc of 15 historic recordings are tunes by the pioneers of the style like the Jimenezes, and those who took it in new directions, like Tony de la Rosa (who electrified the band and added drums) and Lydia Mendoza (who brought a woman's perspective to the lyrics). It's an excellent collection for introduction or review of the roots of conjunto. Unlike Arhoolie's regular-priced discs, though, the budget series of which this is part (and which is drawn from those CDs) does not come with the label's characteristically extensive liner notes.

Kerry Dexter

Fire in the Kitchen ♫♫♫♫ (BMG Classics, 1998, prod. Paddy Moloney)

Canada
genre: Anglo-Celtic/Quebecois folk

Leahy; the Rankins; Great Big Sea; Laura Smith; Ashley MacIsaac; Rita MacNeil; Natalie MacMaster; Mary Jane Lamond; the Barra MacNeills; the Ennis Sisters; La Bottine Souriante; the Chieftains (Ireland). (All artists are from Canada except where noted otherwise.)

In the grand tradition of the Chieftains' all-star invitationals (like the best-selling Celtic/rock project *The Long Black Veil*) and musical ambassadorships (like the exploration of Celtic Spain on *Santiago*), *Fire in the Kitchen* (named after a famed form of domestic jam session, the "kitchen party") is a guide to the folk/roots music of eastern Canada with the Chieftains as your friendly hosts—a generous cross between a collaboration and a compilation, with the Canadian stars often taking the spotlight and the Chieftains not even named on the CD cover. But they do join sensational Ontario family band Leahy to become a grand folk orchestra swingin' their way through a set of traditional dance tunes on the album's opening track—which sets the tone of top-rank backing for the other household-names-to-be on this disc, including Cape Breton's Gaelic singing queen Mary Jane Lamond on "A Mhairi Bhoidheach." On "Fingal's Cave" the Chieftains and Cape Breton fiddle phenom Natalie MacMaster jell so nicely you'd think they'd been playing together for years. And although most of the performers selected for this collection come from Canada's Anglo-Celtic traditions, *Fire* finishes off with a blast from fantastic Quebecois band La Bottine Souriante (fiddle, accordion, foot percussion, acoustic guitar, mandolin, piano, bass, jew's-harp, and a full horn section of bass trombone, saxophone, trumpet, and trombone!). The Chieftains once again sit in and rock out like they never have before—now there's a team-up to be wished for on the Chieftains' long concert trail!

Ken Roseman

Folksongs of the Louisiana Acadians ♫♫♫♫ (Folklyric, 1959/Arhoolie, 1994, reissue prod. Chris Strachwitz)

USA
genre: Cajun

Chuck Guillory; Wallace "Cheese" Read; Mrs. Odeus Guillory; Mrs. Rodney Fruge; Savy Augustine; Isom J. Fontenot; Bee Deshotels; Shelby Vidrine; Austin Pitre; Milton Molitor. (All artists are from USA.)

Most of the players on this collection of traditional Cajun dance tunes and ballads have deep roots in the flatlands and bayous of southwestern Louisiana; the ancestors of Chuck Guillory, Isom Fontenot, and Bee Deshotels were among the first settlers of Mamou and Eunice, where these field recordings were made by ethnomusicologist Dr. Harry Oster between 1956 and 1959. The songs here reflect the dual nature of Acadian (colloquially known as "Cajun") culture as both a proud French enclave and an American-style melting-pot; traditionals from Northern France bear shades of Anglo-Saxon folk that other area settlers brought with them; Guillory's fiddling is deeply influenced by country and western; and Mrs. Rodney Fruge plays the hillbilly-style guitar that began to seep into Cajun music via radio in the '30s and '40s. Other tracks reveal hints of Louisiana's regional music: Wallace "Cheese" Read's "Colinda" was inspired by a rural *Vodou* ("voodoo") dance brought to the area by slaves, while Mrs. Odeus Guillory's version of "Tu Peux Cogner Mais Tu Peux Pas Rentrer (Keep a Knockin' but You Can't Come In)" has roots in New Orleans' red-light district. But while some of the selections reflect outside influences, this compilation is distinctly Cajun in tone, with no-nonsense songs about hard work, hard love, and hard drinking sung in a provincial French dialect. The traditional Acadian instruments—fiddle and Cajun accordion (which plays in only one key)—are embellished here with guitar, harmonica, spoons, and a triangle to create an upbeat backdrop for the high-lonesome vocals, illustrating yet another paradox of Cajun culture—the contrast between the Acadians' sad, nomadic history and their unabashed love of partying (whoops and hollers are audible throughout the disc). This is earthy, beautiful music that comes straight from the heart.

Meredith Ochs

Heartbeat: Voices of First Nations Women ♫♫♫♫ (Smithsonian Folkways, 1995/1998, prod. Howard Bass, Reyna Green)
Heartbeat 2: Voices of First Nations Women ♫♫♫♫ (Smithsonian Folkways, 1995/1998, prod. Howard Bass, Reyna Green)

USA, Canada
genre: Native American

Thirty Native American women musicians (individuals and groups), from tribes across the USA and Canada, are recorded on these discs. Some are professional musicians while others sing only for tribal and family occasions. Among the best known are: Buffy Sainte-Marie; Joy Harjo; Ulali; Sharon Burch; Joanne Shenandoah; Mary Youngblood.

For most Native American tribes, music—at least the public performance of music—has traditionally been the job of men. Women have had their own songs for family rituals and for teaching, and in some cultures have shared dancing and courting songs in public with men. It is only in recent years, though, that Native American women have come forward in public to sing and play instruments, to share their native languages and family songs, and in some cases to add to those traditions, pass them on, and follow the common tribal practice of using music to comment on contemporary life and events as "songcatchers." All of these aspects of the music of Native American women are shown here, accompanied by liner notes that put faces and lives with the voices of the singers, and offer useful suggestions for further listening and reading.

Kerry Dexter

Hearts, Hands, & Hides ♫♫♫ (Talking Taco, 1997, prod. Jennifer Jones)

USA
genre: Native American

Peter Wyoming Bender; Mesa Music Consort; Marilyn Rife with Alice Gomez; Native Flute Ensemble; Eric Casillas. (All artists are from USA.)

Talking Taco is a small San Antonio record label that specializes in the musics of the southwest. Here they've collected percussion-driven tracks from several of their discs; music framing Native American drums with sounds of nature, for example, or pairing hand drums with Latin guitar. It's a tasteful introduction to the variety of uses of the drum in contemporary Native music.

Kerry Dexter

Honor the Earth Powwow: Songs of the Great Lakes Indians ♫♫♫ (Rykodisc, 1991, prod. Mickey Hart)

USA
genre: Native American

Little Otter Singers; LCO Soldiers' Drum; Smokeytown Singers; Bad River Singers; Winnebago Sons; Bear Claw Singers; Three Fires Society Singers. (All artists are from USA.)

Recorded in a natural amphitheater within a Wisconsin forest, three tribes—the Ojibway, Menominee, and Winnebago—gather for the Honor the Earth Powwow to pay tribute to nature, recorded here by Grateful Dead drummer Mickey Hart. As the groups sing accompanied by drums, their dancing can be heard in the bells attached to their ankles and dresses. Technically the music is simple, perhaps even dull to some Western ears, yet it aptly evokes distinctive and ancient Native American ceremonies and occasionally transcends its limited structure, as with the polyphony of the Smokeytown Singers' "We're the People." The generation of Native Americans who took part in these ceremonies in July 1990 were reviving traditions that had been neglected for many years, and in these songs there is

an audible pleasure at rediscovering a spiritual connection uniquely their own.

David Poole

J'ai Été Au Bal (I Went to the Dance) ♫♫♫♫ (Arhoolie, 1990, compilation prod. Chris Strachwitz, Les Blank)

USA (Southwest Louisiana)
genre: Cajun, zydeco

Volume I: Walter Mouton & the Scott Playboys; Queen Ida & the Bon Ton Zydeco Band; Lionel LeLeux; Michael Doucet; Canray Fontenot; Dennis McGee; Amédée Ardoin; Bois Sec Ardoin & Sons; Nathan Abshire; Marc and Ann Savoy; Joe Falcon & Cleoma Breaux; Odile Falcon; Solange Falcon; Luderin Darbone & the Hackberry Ramblers; Leo Soileau & His Four Aces; Chuck Guillory with Preston Manuel & the Rhythm Boys; Harry Choates; Iry LeJeune. Volume II: Joseph Jones; Jimmy Peters & the Ring Dane Singers; Sidney Babineaux; Clifton Chenier; D.L. Menard with the Louisiana Aces and the California Cajuns; Belton Richard; Johnny Allan; Dewey Balfa; Balfa Brothers Band; Rodney Balfa; Michael Doucet & Beausoleil; Paul Daigle & Cajun Gold; John Delafose & the Eunice Playboys; Boozoo Chavis; Rockin' Sidney; Wayne Toups & Zydecajun. (All artists are from USA.)

Whether you've only recently discovered the modern Cajun rock sound of Beausoleil or are a serious drinker at the wellspring of Louisiana music, this extraordinary two-volume compilation (and its companion film/video) is indispensable for *anyone* interested in American roots music. This is no dusty historical museum piece; the heartfelt music jumps right out and drags the listener into a passionate world of dancing, feasting, family, and over 200 years of rich musical history. Virtually every major Cajun and zydeco artist appears here, along with many equally skillful if more obscure musicians. These recordings were made in every decade from the late 1920s onward, in every imaginable setting from Cajun dance halls, to recording studios, to a zydeco picnic, to a folk festival, to a country kitchen in Eunice, Louisiana, to (full disclosure!) my own California living room. Each cut is a gem, highlighting the different facets of this rich musical tradition to brilliant advantage.

Volume I revolves mostly around Cajun music (but includes a track from zydeco's ever-popular Queen Ida) while Volume II features some more incredible zydeco as well. There is plenty of unaccompanied fiddle music, masterfully played by heroes of the form like Dewey Balfa, Michael Doucet, Canray Fontenot, Dennis McGee, and Lionel LeLeux. Dennis McGee and Sady Courville playing the "Happy One-Step" in 1929 is as psychedelic a session as you'll ever find, and it's fascinating to hear Mr. McGee's older track back-to-back with one made nearly 60 years later! Both he (who died in 1989, at the age of 96) and Lionel LeLeux were mentors to Michael Doucet, now probably the most well known living Cajun fiddler. Doucet can be heard backing up LeLeux on guitar (in addition to the aforesaid solo fiddle cuts, and several with Beausoleil); the inclusion of some of the old and new masters' banter and laughter brings the listener right into the living room where the recording was made. Fiddler Harry Choates had the first "crossover" Cajun hit with "Jolie Blonde" in 1946; this highly influential record had been commercially unavailable for decades, but it's here on Volume I, along with Iry LeJeune's passionate 1949 rendering of "Valse Des Grands Chemins," not to mention the very first Cajun 78: the 1928 recording of "Allons à Lafayette" by accordionist Joe Falcon and his vocalist-guitarist wife Cleoma Breaux. These seminal works influenced, either directly or indirectly, virtually every Cajun musician who came after. Accordion giants showcased include Clifton Chenier, Boozoo Chavis, Iry LeJeune, Marc Savoy, Nathan Abshire, and the original trailblazer, Amédée Ardoin. The Western swing/Cajun string-band style is well-represented by Luderin Darbone of the Hackberry Ramblers (as well as by the Harry Choates cut). Swamp pop songs by Belton Richard and Johnny Allan (Joe Falcon's great-nephew!) provide a taste of '50s and '60s Cajun rock 'n' roll. Southwest Louisiana pop music is brought right up to the '90s with Rockin' Sidney's huge zydeco hit "My Toot Toot," but it's not the Grammy-winning version you've probably heard. This down-home reading was recorded live by Sidney at the Soul Brothers picnic near Laureville, Louisiana, complete with background noise from what sounds like a wild party!

Besides the familiar fiddle-accordion Cajun and zydeco sounds, *J'ai Été Au Bal* showcases some astonishing older musical styles that are now nearly extinct, such as the unaccompanied ballad tradition, which was practiced only in the home, mainly by women; the charming octogenarian Odile Falcon, in her kitchen, sings a saucy rendition of "La Reine De La Salle." *Juré* singing, an archaic unaccompanied black vocal and dance style that is the direct antecedent of zydeco, is beautifully represented with a phenomenal 1934 Library of Congress recording of Jimmy Peters & the Ring Dance Singers sounding very African as they deliver the song from which zydeco takes its name: "Zydeco Sont Pas Salés." Next is Creole accordion pioneer Sidney Babineaux's solo accordion version of the same song, followed by Clifton Chenier's full-blown treatment, which launched zydeco as a popular music style.

J'ai Été Au Bal includes several rarities that alone would be worth the price of the compilation. Among these are two songs by the legendary accordionist and singer Walter Mouton (with the Scott Playboys), in all likelihood his only commercially available recordings. Mouton, who has refused to make another record since the one 45 from which these songs derive was released in the '60s, earns his living as a truck driver—

while continuing to hold forth every Saturday night with his band, which at the time of the historic single included several of Cajun music's most renowned dance hall figures. Randall Foreman's sinuous steel playing harmonizes with Dick Richard's classic Cajun fiddling to create a unique texture that instantly transports one to the smoky atmosphere of La Poussiere, the Breaux Bridge dance hall where the cuts were recorded. In addition to these finds, Joseph Jones's gut-wrenching 1934 recording of "Blues De Prison" is a superb unaccompanied version of what was later to become one of fiddler Canray Fontenot's signature tunes—the song was originally recorded even earlier by the legendary Creole fiddler Douglas Bellard, but that 78 is so rare no copies have ever been found!

The delights of this collection are too numerous to describe further; you should waste no more time reading about this essential chronicle of Cajun and zydeco's history and future, and obtain one to enjoy yourself!

Suzy Rothfield Thompson

Klezmer 1993—New York City ⅃⅃⅃⅃ (Knitting Factory Works, 1993, compilation prod. Michael Dorf)

USA
genre: Klezmer

Billy Tipton Saxophone Quartet; New Klezmer Trio; John Zorn's Masada; Klezmatics; Hassidic New Wave; Paradox Trio; Shvitz All-Stars; Alollo Trehorn with Klezmatics. (All artists are from USA.)

By the early 1990s, the klezmer revival had been underway for two decades; Jewish musicians had gone back to their roots to revive traditional East European Yiddish music. Going back, for some, meant playing more "traditionally" and more "authentically." But other Jewish musicians argued that "tradition" is not a fixed reference point, but a continuum; Jewish music must live in the present and move toward the future, they said. Some of these musicians began experimenting with forms that blended jazz, rock, Balkan, and radical lyrical material with klezmer. The Knitting Factory, a progressive club on New York City's Lower East Side, began booking cutting-edge klezmer bands. Most of the important artists in the "Radical Jewish Culture" movement that ensued are here. This anthology, taken from a series of performances at "the Knit," documents the emergence of a Jewish musical phenomenon that feels comfortable reinterpreting Yiddish culture through a postmodern sensibility. Six years after the release of this album, Radical Jewish Culture continues to bring in new and exciting elements.

Aaron Howard

Lullaby Journey 🎵🎵🎵 (Dorian, 1996, prod. Douglas Brown, Chris Norman, Custer LaRue)

Canada, USA
genre: Lullaby, meditation

Custer LaRue (USA), Chris Norman (Canada), Kim Robertson (USA).

The harp, the flute, and the human voice are three of the most ancient instruments, and the impulse of the lullaby, a bridge between the conscious and the dreaming mind, is one of music's oldest purposes. Soprano Custer LaRue, flutist Chris Norman, and harper Kim Robertson explore these ideas in a collection that begins with the connection between music, dreaming, and magic (the traditional Welsh lullaby "Hwi-Hwi"), and comes to a conclusion with the elegant reflection of the sleeper observed in Stephen Foster's "Beautiful Dreamer." Along the way they visit traditional and more recently composed lullabies from the English, Celtic, and other canons. The music is structured somewhat in three song-cycles that, the artists say, act as a metaphor for the time we spend traveling through sleep, dreaming into waking. While the music is suitable for children, it's far more complex and challenging than most children's albums. It will appeal to adult listeners in search of meditative sounds and could be a bridge not only between slumber and wakefulness but between the simpler music of childhood and more sophisticated material to share with a growing youth.

Kerry Dexter

The Mexican Revolution Corridos 🎵🎵🎵🎵 (Arhoolie, 1996, compilation prod. Chris Strachwitz)

Mexico, USA
genre: Corrido

More than 40 individuals and groups in 59 tracks on four CDs, including: Augustín Lara; Lydia Mendoza; Conjunto Tamaulipas. (Artists are from Mexico and USA.)

The *corrido* is a ballad, a four-minute movie whose characters are drawn, usually, from current events. As with all good drama, the favorite stories are of heroes surviving against the odds, and along the Mexico/USA border, those odds most often meant the wealthy landowner, the "rinches" or rangers, and the government. Then, in 1910, the odds really changed—the Mexican Revolution began. The battles, tragedies, and social and political shifts of this continuing struggle immediately became the subject of corridos—corridos intended for Mexicans living across the border in the United States. Not only were they at a distance and thus craving news of their homeland in this time of change, but they were the ones with access to the phonographs on which to play the music. Most people

living in Mexico (at least those who would listen to revolutionary corridos) couldn't afford or obtain the machines. This compilation contains corridos from the era of 1910 to 1940, although many would argue that the best corridos of the revolution in Mexico have yet to be written—or have been ones that were not chosen for recording and commercial marketing. In any case, this is a fascinating musical and historical document, which includes a 175-page booklet with more historical information and English versions of the lyrics. There are four discs in the set: *Outlaws and Revolutionaries*; *The Francisco Villa Cycle* (Villa was a revolutionary leader who rose through the ranks and was later assassinated); *Local Revolutionary Figures*; and *Post-Revolutionary Corridos and Narratives*, which contains a numbers of songs commenting on the fate of the common person in the wake of revolutionary change. The set is compiled from a historical perspective, and it also works as a tracing of musical evolution and as an example of how the less-powerful groups in society have often used music as a way to express the otherwise-unwritten history of *their* perspective.

Kerry Dexter

Mexico: Fiestas of Chiapas & Oaxaca 🎵🎵🎵🎵 (Elektra/Nonesuch, 1976/1991, compilation prod. David Lewiston)

Mexico
genre: Mexican festival music

More than 26 musicians in various configurations, including: Lol Gomez Gomez; Xun Perez Perez; Mariano Santis Hernandez; Juan Hernandez Lopez; Marian Gonzales Vasquez; Victor Gomez Senestino; Rominko Lopez de la Cruz; Rominko Patixtan Patixtan; Pegro Ruiz Ruiz; Pegro Lunes Tak'il Bek'et; the Jimenez family. (All artists are from Mexico.)

Though torn by violent citizen unrest and alleged government reprisal in recent years, there are other sides to the south of Mexico, and some are heard here. Those expecting the ubiquitous brass band in this collection of Mexican fiesta music will find a rambunctious Christmas Eve procession where horns vie with carol-singing students and the whoosh of fireworks (an appeal for rain). Yet these field recordings—made in the states of Oaxaca and Chiapas and originally released on LP in 1976—have surprising diversity: fife and drum music that shares stylistic traits with that found in the West Indies and the Mississippi hill country; polyphonic singing that recalls the complexity of Balinese *kechak*; carefree marimba; frantic horn-and-guitar *conjunto*; and the percussive *coup de grace*—a tortoise shell played with deer antlers. The region's mix of Spanish, Mayan, and Afro-Caribbean cultures gives plenty of referential pleasure; all that's missing is a video companion to these highly colorful performances.

Bill Ellis

The Music of Arab Americans ♫♫♫♫ (Rounder, 1997, compilation prod. Anne K. Rasmussen)

USA
genre: Arabic

Alexander Maloof (Syria/America); Constantine Souse (Syria/America); Amer Khadaj (Lebanon/America); Sana Khadaj (Lebanon/America); Na'im Karakand (Syria/America); Hanan Harouni (Lebanon/America); Tony Abdel Ahad (America); Danny Thomas (America); Russell Bunai (Syria/America); Kahraman (Lebanon/America); Jalil Azzouz (Palestine/America).

Early in the 20th century there was a plethora of small record companies targeting immigrants who clamored for the music of their homelands. During that time the Arab community in America was one of the less-populous segments seeking reminders of the culture they'd left behind. Most of them came from Greater Syria (consisting of territories we now know as Syria, Lebanon, and Palestine) and, to some extent, were under the cultural sway of Egypt. All of these facts are well documented in the liner notes of this remarkable collection by producer Anne K. Rasmussen. Her text is a marvel of clear, concise commentary that gives the reader all the facts necessary to approach the music with an open mind. Some of this material is surprisingly forward-looking for its time. Alexander Maloof and the Maloof Oriental Orchestra's "Fatima" dates from the early 1930s and mixes Western instruments like the piano and the saxophone into the music, prefacing an approach that Mohamed Abdel Wahab would later pioneer in Egypt. Also of interest is a medley of Arabic folk songs performed by Danny Thomas as a benefit for the St. Jude Hospital Foundation. People who only know Thomas as a comedian or the father of Marlo will be pleasantly surprised by his warm, fluid singing.

Garaud MacTaggart

Music of New Mexico: Native American Traditions ♫♫♫♫ (Smithsonian Folkways, 1992, prod. Howard Bass)
Music of New Mexico: Hispanic Traditions ♫♫♫♫ (Smithsonian Folkways, 1992, prod. Howard Bass)

USA
genre: Native American, Hispanic

More than 40 musicians working in the Hispanic and Native American traditions in contemporary New Mexico.

New Mexico has long been a place for confluence of cultures. Three Native American tribes have lived in the region: the Pueblo, the Apache, and the Navajo. On *Native American Traditions*, music from each of these groups is recorded, but it's not intended as a historical document. The project (like its companion, *Hispanic Traditions*) was prepared in celebration of the 500th anniversary of the Western Hemispheric cultural meeting exemplified by the area (however uncelebratory its beginnings

often were), so the producers have chosen both tribal songs that are still current in daily life, and music by contemporary Native musicians.

Though disparate societies have encountered each other in New Mexico, the rough and dramatic landscape of the place has allowed them to develop at a distance from mainstream influence as well. The Hispanos, as descendants of the first Hispanic immigrants to the area call themselves, had a lifestyle that evolved (and still does) in connection with but at a remove from the influence of Spain and Mexico. *Hispanic Traditions* offers examples of this in both religious and secular music, presenting versions of tunes in the folk tradition that are still in common use today.

Kerry Dexter

Navajo Songs ♫♫♫ (Smithsonian Folkways, 1992, prod. Laura Boulton, Charlotte Frisbie, David McAllester)

USA
genre: Native American, chant

Navajo musicians from the 1930s and '40s (not all identified), including Ben Hudson Begay and Pablo Huerito. (All artists are from USA.)

This is a collection of historic recordings compiled by Laura Boulton in the 1930s and '40s. The Navajo are the largest Native tribe in the United States, and Boulton was one of the foremost researchers involved in preserving their traditional music. She collected songs of daily life such as "moccasin game" and "corn-grinding" songs, as well as recording the intricate multi-voiced chants of the spiritual *Yeibichei* or "nightway ceremonial." This is an important document of the music before outside influences brought by radio and record-player had been added to it; the album also provides interesting material for comparing Navajo chant to that of other tribes and cultures.

Kerry Dexter

Norteño and Tejano Accordion Pioneers 1929–1939 ♫♫♫♫ (Arhoolie, 1995, compilation prod. Chris Strachwitz)

USA, Mexico
genre: Norteño, Tejano

Narciso Martinez; Roberto Rodriguez; Clemente Mendoza; R. deLeon; L. Villalobos; Estanislado Salazar; Hnos. Mier; Pas Flores; Francisco Montalvo; Bruno Villareal; Jésus Casiano; Santiago Jimenez; José Rodriguez; Lolo Cavazos. (All artists are from the *frontera,* the Texas/Mexico border region; historical specifics uncertain.)

The historical recordings on this album comprise a portrait of music at a time of change. In the decade covered by these tracks, the duet singing style of northern Mexico was mixing with the polka and waltz dance music of South Texas—and both the *norteño* (Mexican) and *Tejano* (Texan) styles were themselves blends of other musical influences. Into this mix came the button accordion, whose unique sweetness and vibrato and choppy squeezebox style of bending notes both complemented and encouraged the development and joining of these musical genres. On this disc are featured the better-known pioneers of the new hybrids—Narciso Martinez, Bruno Villareal, and Santiago Jimenez—as well as several vital musicians whose work is less widely heard. They play polkas, *valses,* and two-steps as well as *canciones, huapangos,* and mazurkas. This is a great document of historic music that remains vibrant in its own right while illuminating the source upon which much of today's Tex-Mex music draws.

Kerry Dexter

Plains Chippewa/Metis Music from Turtle Mountain
𝄞𝄞𝄞𝄞 (Smithsonian Folkways, 1984/1992, prod. Nicholas Curchin Peterson Vrooman)

USA, Canada
genre: Native American

Members of the Plains Chippewa/Metis communities around Turtle Mountain, ND, USA.

This is, as the producer describes it, a cultural fingerprint put on disc, and like the impression of a finger tip, there are many whorls and ridges to examine. The Turtle Mountain reservation stands in North Dakota at almost the geographical center of the North American continent. It is an isolated location, and that has caused the residents to maintain a strong tradition of both Native American drum songs from the Pembina Chippewa Tribe, and *chansons* (ballads) and story-songs handed down from the French traders who intermarried with the Chippewa to form the Metis community. An instrumental tradition was passed on as well, and the results of that can be heard in seven tracks of fiddle dance songs. To conclude the disc, the continuing evolution of this culture is shown in recordings of contemporary songs from Turtle Mountain in fiddle, country, and rock 'n' roll styles.

Kerry Dexter

The Rough Guide to Native American Music 𝄞𝄞𝄞𝄞
(Rough Guide/World Music Network, 1998, prod. Phil Stanton)

Canada, USA
genre: Native American

Chester Mahooty (Zuni); Walela (Cherokee); Sharon Burch (Navajo); Primeaux & Mike (Oglalla-Yankton Sioux-Ponca & Navajo, respectively); Southern Scratch (Tohono O'odham); Judy Trejo (Paiute); Garcia Brothers (San Juan); R. Carlos Nakai (Navajo-Ute); Robert Tree Cody & Rob Wallace with Will Clipham (Maricopa-Dakota); Without Rezervation (Pitt River-Paiute, Navajo, Pima-Papago-Cree); Cornel Pewewardy & Alliance West Singers (Comanche-Kiowa); Joanne Shenandoah (Oneida); Blackstone Singers (Cree); Black Lodge Singers (Blackfeet); Burning Sky (Navajo-Ute, Navajo); Ed Lee Natay (Navajo); Bill Miller (Mohican). (Artists are from Canada and USA.)

To truly understand a culture, one must become immersed in its music. Native American music is reaching ever greater heights of creativity and popularity, with some artists transcending tradition while others hold fast to their roots. The soothing, healing peyote ceremonial songs of Primeaux & Mike, polka-like rhythms of Southern Scratch, urban street rap of Without Rezervation, and pretty warbling of female trio Walela are presented here along with dances, ballads, hymns, victory songs, and over a dozen other styles that hint at the broad diversity of indigenous Northern American music today. One of the best tracks is "Mickey Mouse" by the famed powwow performers Black Lodge Singers; it demonstrates how modern influences can positively impact a very traditional art form. While some powwow songs use vocables (words without meaning, or "speech from the soul"), this tune is sung in English, replete with references to Disneyland. Representing 18 artists at their peak, this newest edition in the popular Rough Guide series (a number of whose other volumes are reviewed elsewhere in this Compilations section) is a joyful collision of culturally affirming styles in a thriving genre. If you thought Native American music begins with solo flute and ends with percussion, this is your ticket to ride.

PJ Birosik

Songs of Earth, Water, Fire & Sky 𝄞𝄞𝄞𝄞 (New World Records, 1976, prod. Charlotte Heth)

USA
genre: Native American music

More than 50 singers, dancers, and musicians, including: the Garcia Brothers; the Los Angeles Northern Singers; Archie Sam; Luman Wildcat; Aileen Figueroa; Frankie Jishie Jr.; Raymond K. Yazzie; Sam Yazzie Jr.; Sam Yazzie Sr.; Jack Anquoe. (All artists are from USA.)

What's remarkable about this first album in a six-CD series produced by Charlotte Heth for New World Records is the sincerity of the ancient and diverse music preserved here from the oral tradition. Heth, a member of the Cherokee nation of Oklahoma and an Associate Professor of Music and director of the American Indian Studies Center at UCLA, has authored and edited numerous articles, books, records, and videotapes on Native culture. Captured on-location, this album's nine tracks document ceremonial and social dance music from various regions. Excellent sound quality makes it seem as though you're right there, and a wide selection of styles and traditions throughout the entire series and this edition of it makes for always enjoyable and intriguing listening.

Nancy Ann Lee

Songs of the Spirit ♪♪♪♪ (Triloka/Mercury, 1996, prod. Jim Wilson, Al Evers, Mitchell Markus)

USA

genre: Native American

Coyote Oldman; Little Wolf; Joanne Shenandoah; R. Carlos Nakai; Kashtin; Way West; Native Flute Ensemble; Michael Stearns & Ron Sunsinger; Primeaux & Mike; 500 Nations; Rita Coolidge. (All artists are from USA.)

This is a collection of songs celebrating the ancient Native American spiritual reverence for, and connection with, nature and the cycles of the seasons. The styles vary with the artists, from R. Carlos Nakai's wooden flutes, to the chant of 500 Nations, to the call-and-response form of Rita Coolidge's music. It's a thoughtful group of songs, which, although most have appeared elsewhere, benefit from being heard in this context.

Kerry Dexter

Talking Spirits ♪♪♪♡ (Music of the World, 1992, prod. James Lascelles, Bob Haddad)

USA

genre: Native American

Many Native American singers and musicians from the southwestern USA, including the Garcia Brothers (San Juan Pueblo); the Laguna Singers & Dancers (Laguna); the Zuni Olla Maidens (Zuni); Chester, Dorothy, and Brenner Mahooty (Zuni); the Hopi Singers from Second Mesa (Hopi); Roger Mase (Hopi).

This is a collection of social dance music from four pueblos of the American southwest: music used to celebrate community occasions, to ask for blessings, and as a public part of otherwise private religious observations. Rather than a historic re-creation, the works are sung and played here by people who still use them as an integral part of their lives.

Kerry Dexter

Tejano Roots/Raices Tejanos: The Roots of Tejano and Conjunto Music ♪♪♪♪♡ (Arhoolie, 1991, reissue prod. Chris Strachwitz)

USA, Mexico
genre: Tejano

Conjunto Bernal; Narciso Martinez; Lydia Mendoza; Tony de la Rosa; Carmen y Laura; Beto Villa y si Orquesta; Jesus Maya y Timoteo Cantu; Trio San Antonio; Hermanas Mendoza; Juan Lopez; Chelo Silva; Freddie Fender/Eddie con los Shades; Isidro Lopez y Conjunto Ideal; Isidro Lopez y su Orquesta; Agapito Zuniga; Wally Almendarez. (All artists are from the Texas/Mexico border region.)

This is a collection of two-dozen jukebox hits from the Texas/Mexico border popular from the early 1940s to the late 1960s. The biggest stars of the region—the Mendozas, Narciso Martinez, Freddie Fender, Tony de la Rosa—are here, and it's a lively set that shows off the fine voices and styles of these performers. It's also a document of how more traditional forms of border music evolved by incorporating elements of rock and country from the Anglo side of the jukebox. This album is enjoyable in its own right and insightful as a snapshot of contemporary border music's historical beginnings. There are several other volumes in the Tejano Roots series, including *Compeones de Conjunto: Conjunto Champs* and *Tejano Roots: the Women*.

Kerry Dexter

Tribal Fires ♪♪♪♪ (Earthbeat!, 1997, prod. Agnes Patak, Leib Ostrow)

USA, Canada
genre: Native American, singer/songwriter

Walela; Jerry Alfred; Jani Lauzon; Robert Mirabal; Joy Harjo and Poetic Justice; Keith Secola; Ulali; Lunar Drive; Quiltman; Joanne Shenandoah; Andrew Vasquez; Songcatchers; Brulé. (Artists are from USA and Canada.)

Native American musicians live in the same world the rest of us do, but far too often they are expected only to sing ancient chants or perform ethereal melodies on the flute. The music on this album shows another side of that equation: Native American singers and composers using—and fusing—contemporary and ancient musical styles and viewing contemporary issues through tribal perspectives. If you're from the non-Native community, prepare to be surprised.

Kerry Dexter

Tribal Voices ♪♪♪♪ (Earthbeat!, 1996, prod. Leib Ostrow, David Swenson, Agnes Patak)

USA
genre: Native American, chant

Quiltman; Walela; Kevin Locke; Sharon Burch; Joseph FireCrow; Ulali; Jerry Alfred; Andrew Vasquez; Six Nations Women Singers; Primeaux & Mike; Sissy Goodhouse; Joanne Shenandoah; Robert Tree Cody & Rob Wallace; Spirit of Song Singers. (All artists are from USA.)

The producers of this collection have emphasized the chant style of Native American singing, which across cultures and tribes appears in both religious and secular music as prayer, preparation, as celebration. Chant as duet, as the song of an individual, as harmony and chorus, and as call-and-response are all present in this multi-tribal exploration, which makes it a fine introduction to this aspect of Native American music.

Kerry Dexter

Tribal Winds 𝄞𝄞𝄞𝄞 (Earthbeat!, 1995, prod. David Swenson)

USA, Canada
genre: Native American

Bryan Akipa (Dakota); Keith Bear (Mandan/Hidatsa); Fernando Cellicion (Zuni); Joseph FireCrow (Northern Cheyenne); William Guitierrez (Southern Ute/Dineh); Hawk Henries (Nipmuc); Toya Inajin/Kevin Locke (Lakota); Tom Mauchaty-Ware (Kiowa/Comanche); R. Carlos Nakai (Navajo/Ute); Andrew Vasquez (Kiowa/Apache). (Artists are from USA and Canada.)

Native American peoples have honored the spirit of the winds, and their traditions of communicating with that force, through the music of the flute for many generations. As the tribes became involved in dealing with conquest and expansion by other cultures in the Americas, flute players became less common, until recent years when many Native American artists have explored, studied, revived, and created new music for this ancient instrument. *Tribal Winds* is unusual not for its high quality—there are many fine Native American flute recordings available now—but for the scope of the disc, the collaboration of musicians of many tribes that made it come together. Cedric Goodhouse, who was involved in developing the concept for the album, captures the image that became the title: " . . . I watched the prairie grasses move . . . not just to one song, but to many. I realized I was hearing the song of all time—I was listening to tribal winds."

Kerry Dexter

Under the Green Corn Moon 𝄞𝄞𝄞𝄞 (Silver Wave, 1998, prod. Tom Wasinger)

USA, Mexico, Canada
genre: Native American, children's songs

Lorain Fox (Aztec); Dorothy White (Kiowa); Robert Mirabal (Taos Pueblo); Julia Begaye (Navajo); Micki Pratt (Cheyenne); Joanne Shenandoah (Onieda Iroquois); Alph Secakuku (Hopi); Mary Philbrook (MicMac); Tzó Kam (Salish/Lillooet); Dorothy Hunting Horse Gray (Kiowa); Tom Wasinger (Pawnee); Myra Aitson (Comanche); Jerry Garret (Oglala Sioux); Laughing Woam (Masantucket Pequot); Ann Shadlow (Cheyenne); Kelly White (Salish/Coast). (Artists are from USA, Mexico, and Canada.)

The emotions in lullabies sung to children remain the same across cultures and nations: warmth, joy, playfulness, comfort, and love. This disc brings together both traditional nighttime songs and newly composed pieces by members of tribes from the Mexican *frontera* to the northern plains, from the Pacific Coast to the eastern woodlands. Though the songs are sung in many languages, the love and respect for children comes through clearly in them all.

Kerry Dexter

Zydeco: The Early Years 𝄞𝄞𝄞 (Arhoolie, 1989/1996, compilation prod. Chris Strachwitz)

USA
genre: Zydeco

McZiel & Gernger; Sidney Babineaux; Albert Chevalier; George Alberts; Peter King & Hebert; Willie Green; Herbert Sam; Clifton Chenier; Clarence Garlow. (All artists are from USA.)

Forget all the horn arrangements, electric guitar solos, and drum sets that have marked zydeco over the past two decades. As explained by C.J. Chenier, the son of zydeco originator Clifton Chenier, during an early-1980s interview with this writer, true zydeco music was only produced by an accordion and a washboard. That claim is substantiated on this 19-track CD, which chronicles the beginnings of this lively southwest Louisiana dance music. Mostly recorded in that state and Texas in 1961 and '62, the album demonstrates how Louisiana's Cajun music combined with Texas blues to create the Creole hybrid known as zydeco. Especially revealing are zydeco-ized treatments of classic Cajun tunes including "Allons à Lafayette" (here by McZiel & Gernger) and "Jole Blon" (here by Willie Green). The high points of the album are the oldest tracks— "Clifton's Blues" and "Louisiana Stomp," both performed by Clifton Chenier. Although zydeco has increasingly achieved international acclaim, the rawness of this album's tracks may prevent it from being much more than a musicological artifact to most listeners. Collectors will appreciate the field-like quality of these recordings, but the novice may be better served by newer artists like Buckwheat Zydeco, Terrance Simien, and Nathan & the Zydeco Cha Chas.

Craig Harris

PACIFIC

Australia: Songs of the Aborigines and Music of Papua New Guinea 𝄞𝄞𝄞 (Lyrichord, prod. Wolfgang Laade)

Australia, Papua New Guinea
genre: Aboriginal

Aboriginals of Cape York peninsula, North Queensland, and Elcho Island, Arnhem Land; musicians of Waidoro, Papua New Guinea. (Artists are from Australia and Papua New Guinea.)

Unique to Australian Aboriginal culture (in this album's title referred to by the previously preferred "Aborigine") is the *didgeridoo,* a long tube of eucalyptus wood that is blown to emit a deep, vibrating hum. Popularized by Aboriginal rock groups like Yothu Yindi, electronic artists like Dr. Didg, and movies like *Crocodile Dundee* and *The Rescuers Down Under,* this distinctive instrument can be heard in its original setting on this album. Complimenting the solo and ensemble "didg" pieces is non-didg music from Papua New Guinea (once administered by Australia as suggested in the album title, but now independent). The Aboriginals of Elcho Island sing and clap sticks together for a beat while the didg resonates. The group recorded in Waidoro, Papua New Guinea, uses more complex instrumentation, including the *darumbere* (a bamboo jew's-harp), *gora* (a rattle made of nut shells), *walep* (wooden hourglass-shaped drums), *pat* (bamboo slit drum), and *tatarore* (bamboo flute), with a chorus. The album's most rudimentary (and unfortunately longest) section, recorded in Cape York, Australia, is little more than a beat hammered on a tobacco tin or log to monotonous chanting and didg cycling. Listeners accustomed to the sophisticated use of the didgeridoo might be disappointed by this elementary collection, the highlight of which is not the Australian section but the more multi-faceted ensemble from Papua New Guinea.

David Poole

Hawaiian Drum Dance Chants: Sounds of Power in Time
🎵🎵🎵🎵 (Smithsonian Folkways, 1989, compilation prod. Elizabeth Tatar, Bishop Museum, Honolulu, HI)

Hawaii (USA)
genre: Hawaiian drum dance chants

Kau'i Zuttermeister; Hau'oli Lewis; Noenoe Lewis; Brenda Lehua Hulihe'e; Anthony La'akapu Lenchanko; Charles Albert Manu'aikohanaiki'ilili Boyd; James Kapihe Palea Kuluwaimaka; Samuel Pua Ha'aheo; Keahi Luahine; Kawena Pukui; Hoakalei Kamau'u; Keakaokalo Kanahele; Ka'upena Wong; Tom Hiona. (All artists are from Hawaii, USA.)

This recording was produced during the Smithsonian Institution's "Festival of American Folklife" focus on Hawaii in 1989. Packaged with a booklet that provides the historical details, this disc is an excellent introduction to Hawaiian chants, dances, drumming, and the individuals who have performed and taught the *mele hula pahu* form, which involves all three. The *pahu* is a wooden sharkskin drum considered a sacred ritual instrument of great power, linking today's Hawaiians with the rich culture of their Polynesian ancestors. The traditions of mele hula pahu have been kept alive by a handful of masters, many of whom appear here. Restored recordings from the 1930s through 1950s are included, as well as chants by contemporary masters recorded in 1989 at the historic Hawaiian Hall of the Bishop Museum in Honolulu. The texts and translations were prepared by the influential scholar and teacher Mary Kawena Pukui, author of the definitive *Hawaiian Dictionary* and many other important Hawaiian volumes. Only the most enthusiastic researcher could listen to this entire recording in one sitting, but individual performances are very moving. Some

chants are so powerful they give one the feeling that Pele herself is speaking from the steaming volcanic vents at Kilauea.

Sandy Miranda

Vintage Hawaiian Music: The Great Singers, 1928–1934
🎵🎵🎵🎵 (Rounder, 1989, compilation prod. Bob Brozman, Chris Strachwitz)
Vintage Hawaiian Music: Steel Guitar Masters, 1928–1934 🎵🎵🎵🎵 (Rounder, 1989, compilation prod. Bob Brozman, Chris Strachwitz)

Hawaii (USA)
genre: Hawaiian

Mme. Riviere's Hawaiians; Coral Islanders; Waikiki Stonewall Boys; Sol K. Bright Hollywaiians; Kalama's Quartet; Sol Hoopii Trio; George Ku Trio; Tamari Tahiti; Sam Alama; Hilo Hawaiian Orchestra; King Benny Nawahi; Tau Moe; Sam Ku West Harmony Boys; S. Cortez y sus Hawaiianos; Charlie Wilon; Kanui & Lula; Walter Kolomoku; Jim & Bob the Genial Hawaiians. (All artists are from Hawaii, USA.)

Set aside any vestige of the easy-listening stereotype that has handicapped Hawaiian music—these records have all the credibility of Jelly Roll Morton's proto-jazz piano, Robert Johnson's blues guitar, or Scott Joplin's ragtime piano rolls. From the 1830s on, a large influx of cowboys from California and Mexico introduced the guitar and falsetto singing style which became trademarks of Hawaiian music. The cultural exchange persisted, as the songs on these two albums bear strong similarities to the yodeling and guitar popular in American country music at the time they were recorded. Despite the old technology, the vibrant music collected here projects clearly, full of the warmth and optimism and performed at the mellow pace that characterizes Hawaiian culture. On *The Great Singers, 1928–1934*, Mme. Riviere's Hawaiians yodel in harmony while superstar Rose Moe sings in an emotionally affecting falsetto. The Sol K. Bright Hollywaiians sing "Tomi Tomi" in a tempo that reflects the swinging jazz of that era, the tongue-twister Hawaiian vocals sounding like a verbal pastiche of the *hula* dancing style. *Steel Guitar Masters, 1928–1934* features virtuoso guitar-picking accompanied by vocal groups. The sharp twang of the steel guitar and the slide effect evoke ragtime, blues, early jazz guitar, and even ballroom dance.

David Poole

SOUTH AMERICA

Andean Legacy 🎵🎵🎵🎵 (Narada Media, 1996, executive prod. Michael Sullivan)

Bolivia, Ecuador, Peru, Chile
genre: Andean

Savia Andina (Bolivia); Alturas (Bolivia); Viento de los Andes (Ecuador); Echoes of Incas (Mexico, Cuba, Peru); Rumillaita (Bolivia); Inkuyo (Bolivia); Imbaya (Ecuador); Inti-Illimani (Chile); Andes Manta (Ecuador); Ancient Winds (Ecuador); Sukay (Bolivia, Peru); Caliche (Chile).

When the ritual flute and drum of the native musicians of the central Andes met the guitar, harp, and mandolin of the Spanish conquistadors, the Andean legacy was begun. As this connection spread through the mountains, the stringed instruments grew smaller and higher-pitched, and were sometimes made of armadillo shells in a region where wood was scarce. As the developing style began to incorporate rhythms from neighboring areas, such as *joropos* from Venezuela and Bolivian *huyanosas,* it evolved into the Pan-Andean music on this disc. It's a lively collection of the vocal and instrumental styles of the region, which are still distinguished by the sound of mountain breezes represented through the pan pipes or vertical flutes.

Kerry Dexter

Argentina: The Guitar of the Pampas 🎵🎵🎵 (Lyrichord, prod. Rev. Jorge Alfano)

Argentina
genre: Milonga, Argentinean folkloric, classical guitar

Roberto Laro (Argentina).

Just as Argentina's Astor Piazzolla incorporated the tango into his classical music, Abel Fleury uses the *milonga,* another indigenous dance style, for his classical guitar pieces. Both compose art music by appropriating folk traditions. Fleury discards the lyrics and danceable rhythms in favor of intricate and cerebral guitar solos. The title and cover of the album are thus misleading. This is not authentic *gaucho* (cowboy) music of the Pampas, Argentina's central grasslands. This is highbrow music from Buenos Aires, Argentina's cultural capital, though certain gaucho song forms provided inspiration for Fleury's complex, classical, European-reminiscent compositions. The guitarist is Roberto Laro, whose soothing style is milder than the "real" thing, which has a rhythm section for dancing and lyrics that tell melancholy love stories. However, Laro's skillful and tender picking will suit new-age gauchos seeking dinner music in their Buenos Aires loft.

David Poole

The Best of Latin America: Change the Rules 🎵🎵🎵🎵 (World Music Network, 1997, compilation prod. Phil Stanton)

Colombia, Cuba, Brazil, Peru, Bolivia, Argentina
genre: Salsa, tango, Latin jazz, Andean folk, bossa nova, samba, mariachi

Joe Arroyo (Colombia); the Latin Brothers (Colombia); Jesus Alemany (Cuba); Fruko Y Sus Tesos (Colombia); Nico Saquito (Cuba); Sierra Maestra (Cuba); Moleque de Rua (Brazil); A. Reiner, F. Menendez, M. Candeias, L. Gazineu (Brazil); Os Ingenuos (Brazil); Susana Baca (Peru); Julie Freundt (Peru); Kjarkas (Bolivia); Emma Junaro (Bolivia); Los Nemus Del Pacifico (Colombia); Estudiantina Invasora (Cuba); La Sonora Dinamita (Colombia); Maximo Jiminez (Colombia); Juan Jose Mosalini & His Tango Orchestra (Argentina); Adriana Varela (Argentina).

The Best of Latin America, eh? Yeah, *suuurrre* it is. But while any album with that title will correctly arouse suspicion, the good people at World Music Network have gone and fashioned a flawless introduction to one of global pop's most enticing regions. So it's not as heavy on Brazilian styles as I'd like. So it smooths over or ignores completely some of the more specifically raucous sounds of the region. It doesn't matter, because the 19 cuts on *Change the Rules* effortlessly outline the pleasures to be had within the album's genre-based or geographic mini-categories, the better to indicate an endlessly varied musical vein you'll be inspired to explore and more equipped to encounter thanks to this album. An icebreaker as wonderful as the late, lamented Original Music's amazing *Africa Dances,* and nearly as good.

Michaelangelo Matos

Brazil Classics 1: Beleza Tropical 🎵🎵🎵🎵 (Luaka Bop/Warner Bros., 1989, compilation prod. Todo Mundo, executive prod. David Byrne)
Beleza Tropical 2: Novo! Mais! Melhor! 🎵🎵🎵🎵 (Luaka Bop/Warner Bros., 1998, compilation prod. Todo Mundo, executive prod. David Byrne)
Brazil Classics 2: O Samba 🎵🎵🎵🎵 (Luaka Bop/Warner Bros., 1989, compilation prod. Todo Mundo, executive prod. David Byrne)
Brazil Classics 3: Forró etc. 🎵🎵🎵🎵 (Luaka Bop/Warner Bros., 1991, compilation prod. Todo Mundo, executive prod. David Byrne)

Brazil
genre: Tropicalismo, samba, forró

Jorge Ben; Maria Bethânia; Gilberto Gil; Caetano Veloso; Chico Buarque; Lô Borges; Milton Nascimento; Nazare Pereira; Clara Nunes; Zeca Pagodinho; Alcione; Ciro Monteiro; Beth Carvalho; Neguinho da Beija Flor; Chico da Silva; Almir Guineto; Agepê; Martinho da Vila; Paulinho da Viola; Luiz Gonzaga; Gal Costa; Jackson do Pandeiro; Dominguinhos; Anastácia; Nando Cordel & Amelinha; Gonzaguinha; Clemilda; Jorge de Altinho; Marinalva; Genival Lacerda; Trio Nordestino; João do Vale; Elba Ramalho. (All artists are from Brazil.)

Producer David Byrne's *Brazil Classics* series is a well-packaged overview of that nation's musical output from the 1970s to '80s, the slick design and intelligent liner notes only enhancing the music's hip cache. *Brazil Classics 1: Beleza Tropical* contains the cream from the *Tropicalismo* movement of the '70s, a psychedelic spin on indigenous Brazilian forms influenced by English-language rock of a rebellious era. The military coup of 1964 led to a restrictive Brazil in which protest music had to be hidden beneath double entendres to avoid censorship. These subtle and gentle-sounding songs actually landed Tropical-ismo's heroes Caetano Veloso and Gilberto Gil in jail—but those key figures, along with Maria Bethânia, Jorge Ben, and the internationally acclaimed Milton Nascimento, continue to dominate Brazilian popular music. Skipping ahead a bit to commemorate and expand upon this groundbreaking anthology, *Beleza Tropical 2: Novo! Mais! Melhor!* celebrates Luaka Bop's 10th year, showcasing both new talent and new recordings by the old guard. Veloso's "O Estrangeiro," Gil's "Madalena," and Tom Ze's "Curiosiade" vie with newer kids on the block Margareth Menezes, Lenine, and the Carnival music of Nacao Zumbi. *Brazil Classics 2: O Samba* captures the essence of the samba's Afro-Brazilian dance music. Some say the word is indeed derived from the Angolan *semba,* "to touch belly buttons while dancing," and the music works best in close-contact festive dancing. *O Samba* covers the genre's key figures, including Beth Carvalho, Martinho Da Vila, and Clara Nunes, all whom have been playing since the '60s. *Brazil Classics 3: Forró etc.* includes Gal Costa from the Tropicalismo volume, and lesser-known practitioners of the distinctive northeastern style known as *forró*, like Luiz Gonzaga and Dominguinhos. Forró is Brazilian cowboy party music, an upbeat sound somewhere between polka, zydeco, and samba.

David Poole

Brazilliance: The Music of Rhythm ♪♪♪♪ (Rykodisc, 1990, compilation prod. Gerald Seligman)

Brazil
genre: Samba

Beth Carvalho; Martinho da Vila; Maria Bethânia; Paulinho da Viola; Joanna; Gal Costa; João Bosco; Chico Buarque; Alcione; Bezerra de Silva. (All artists are from Brazil.)

The sheer variety of styles in Brazilian music is well represented on this collection, all united by danceable rhythms and the undeniable influence of the samba. Many listeners will already be familiar with the seductive whisper of Astrud Gilberto's "Girl from Ipanema"; this is a great opportunity to hear other great Brazilian vocalists, from the deep blues of Maria Bethânia's "Noite de Cristal," to the sophisticated jazzy soprano of Gal Costa, to the uplifting spirit and tempo of Beth Carvalho's assured and cheerful singing on "Enquanto a Gente Batuca," perfectly reflective of the shimmying percussion. Selected from a period between 1977 and 1989, this album covers similar territory to *Brazil Classics 1* and *Brazil Classics 2* (reviewed on page

899), but there is happily no overlap. Whether or not you understand Portuguese, the language sounds beautiful when sung well—and you can be assured of that here, with songs that evoke humor, tragedy, yearning, and celebration in a bubbly mix of hip-shaking rhythms and delightful voices.

David Poole

Brazil Samba Roots ♪♪♪♪♪ (Rounder, 1989, prod. Katsunori Tanaka)

Brazil
genre: Samba

Wilson Moreira; Nelson Sargento; Velha Guarda De Portela. (All artists are from Brazil.)

With *Brazil Samba Roots* listeners are treated to traditional samba music of the highest order. For some the samba has come to refer to anything even faintly Brazilian, but it is strictly Carnival music in 2/4 time, developed in the *favelas,* or slums, where it was the only brief escape from a dead-end system. The samba is the sound of Brazil; when the squeaking laugh of the *cuica* opens a track, it transports the listener to Carnival in Rio and gets them dancing. Culled from Kuarup Discos' *Grandes Sambistas* series of classic samba recordings, these 19 tracks are the real thing.

David Poole

Festival of the Andes ♪♪♪♪ (Music of the World, 1996, prod. Bob Haddad)

Peru
genre: Andean

Unidentified groups and individuals involved in the celebration of the Fiesta Mamacha Carmen in Paucartambo, Peru.

The earliest record of a festival in Peru in honor of the Virgin of Mount Carmel is from the 17th century. Even then, at the beginning of the interaction and blending of Hispanic and indigenous ways of life, it appears to have been a multicultural event. In the centuries following, with ever-closer connections between the two communities resulting in the development of the mixed-race *mestizo* population, the evolution has continued. What comes through most clearly in this recording is the sense of joy and celebration, whether framed in the flute-based music of the Native tribes, the string styles brought by the Hispanics, or a fusion of the two.

Kerry Dexter

Fiesta Vallenata ♪♪♪♪♪ (Shanachie, 1989, compilation prod. Ben Mandelson)

Colombia
genre: Vallenatan dance music

Rusbell Chimenti & Orlando Jimenez; Julio De La Ossa; Morgan Blanco; Jimmy Pedrozo; Franklin Ariza; Joaquin Sanchez y Su Conjunto; Luis Tobio & Vincente Iguita; Miguel Duran y Su Conjunto; Barranquilla Vallenata (All artists are from Colombia).

In the Vallenata region of northern Colombia, drug kingpins live in Fantasy Island–like splendor alongside culturally proud common folk entangled in abject poverty. It is a land of joyous all-night music festivals, cockfights, and one of the world's strongest concentrations of organized crime. Given the contrasts, it is no wonder that Peruvian, Incan, Cordoban, and Bolivian Indians, along with musicians of Spanish and African descent, have all contributed to the hot, jumpy, button-accordion-pumped dance music of this Caribbean coastal region. While the heaving button accordion provides an irresistible percussive drive and a sweet, honest melody, other traditional indigenous instruments—such as the *gaita* (a flute made from cane and turkey quills) and the *cana de millo* (a cane pipe blown like a saxophone)—add tensile rhythmic textures and subtle yet surprising melodic flourishes. Simultaneously, the *caja* (a tiny, hand-played drum) and *guiro* (scraper) zig-zag cross-rhythmically against alarmingly free bass lines, which roll, stutter, and echo in defiance of the other beats. The exuberant Spanish vocals tell universally understood stories of village heroes and historic events alongside biting, humorous social commentary and, perhaps most importantly, convincing expressions of love and celebration. The music on this distinctive, comprehensively annotated compilation is uniformly fiery and insinuates itself into your soul almost immediately. This is not music that is difficult to appreciate and savor on the first spin. In fact, it is virtually impossible not to move while listening to this breathtaking, wild-grooved musical documentary of Vallenata.

Todd Shanker

Flutes & Strings of the Andes ✍✍✍✍ (Music of the World, 1990, prod. Bob Haddad)

Peru
genre: Andean

Members of the Quechua and Aymara tribes of the Peruvian Andes.

It's common to hear Andean music transformed by new-age styling or enhanced by instruments and influences from other cultures. This, however, is the real thing—members of Andean tribes singing in their native languages and playing traditional instruments, including harp, *charango* (mandolin), and *quena* (bamboo flute). It's not an exhaustive ethnomusicological document, but rather a vivid snapshot of a vibrant culture.

Kerry Dexter

Forró: Music for Maids and Taxi Drivers ✍✍✍✍✍
(Rounder, 1989, prod. Ze da Flauta, Ben Mandelson, Gerald Seligman)

Brazil
genre: Forró

Toinho Dé Alagoas; Duda Da Passira; José Orlando; Heleno Dos Oito Baixos. (Are all artists from Brazil.)

Forró is the music of the rugged *Nordestino* people of Brazil's arid northeast. Gritty, hyperactive, and dance-oriented, forró is played by small ensembles and fueled mercilessly by manic button accordion, giving it a sound that's a little bit like zydeco, South African jive, or Mexican polka. On the surface, forró embodies the same working-class spirit of, say, rockabilly or honky-tonk country music, with songs typically involving love, sex, or simple moralizing, with an emphasis on the concerns and tribulations of farmers and common people. When the disc's producer told a Brazilian friend that he was compiling a forró record, the shocked friend replied, "Forró! You're kidding, that's what maids listen to, what taxi drivers listen to!" Indeed, forró is the kind of simple music that provides release, a music made for those who need to unwind and dance after a weeks' hard work. Yet to pass it off as "party music" would be to sell it short, for forró songs also serve as connections to Nordestino history and culture. One such tie is provided by the booklets of folk poetry sold around the northeast, containing political commentary, stories of folk heroes, and local fairy tales, from which forró musicians often cull ideas or lyrics. The compilation covers four of forró's more vigorous practitioners. Notable tracks include two cuts by Duda—the peculiarly African "De Pernambuco Ao Maranhão" and the white-hot "Casa De Tauba"—as well as a raw instrumental by Heleno, rudely entitled "Entra E Sai (In and Out)." Once again, Rounder has put great care into the overall package, with invigorating music, superb liner notes composed by Gerald Seligman, and a charming woodcut on the cover by Nordestino artist Marcelo Soares.

Jeffrey Muhr

Kingdom of the Sun: Peru's Inca Heritage ✍✍✍✍ (Elektra/Nonesuch, 1969/1988, prod. David Lewiston)

Peru
genre: Huayno

Artists not identified. (All artists are from Peru.)

The spectrum of musical emotion is nowhere more apparent than in the *huayno* songs of the Andes. These waltz-like dances have lively tempos and energetic tunes that are somehow melancholy and joyful at the same time. *Kingdom of the Sun*, one of the earlier releases of rural Inca music to appear on a non-academic label, contains several of these delightfully wistful huaynos, as well as a variety of other music made in the mountain villages of Peru. Recorded in the highland towns of Ayacucho, Chuschi, and Paucartambo by journeyman musicologist David Lewiston in 1968, albums like this one opened the ears of many a budding world-music listener. It documents a body of traditional music that developed in the ancient Inca empire and has come to incorporate some instruments and musical forms of Spanish colonial culture, yet still retains a uniquely Incan purity of expression. Featured are solo and ensemble recordings, with instruments including Andean harps, bamboo flutes called *quena, charango* mandolins, and the well-known panpipes called *siku*. All of the tracks, made at village festivals or by street musicians, exert a tremendous pull on the listener with their lack of pretense and deeply felt authenticity. For example, the poignant "Flute Solo from Apurimac," played by a blind beggar, and the mysterious flute duet "Mauca Zapotoyke (Old Shoes)" convey directly the spirit of an era when no distinction between musical performance and immediate emotional expression seemed to exist. While this album sticks to the "purer" styles of Peruvian mountain music, the growth of the music as a commercial form can be heard on CDs such as *Peru: Huayno Music, Vol. I (1949–1989)*, *Peru: Huayno Music, Vol. II: The Discos Smith Recordings*, and *Music of Peru: From the Mountains to the Sea* (all reviewed below). *Kingdom of the Sun*'s CD reissue also includes four tracks from *Fiestas of Peru*, collected by Lewiston during the same field-recording session.

Jeffrey Muhr

Peru: Huayno Music, Vol. I (1949–1989) ♫♫♫♫ (Arhoolie, 1989, compilation prod. Chris Strachwitz)
Peru: Huayno Music, Vol. II: The Discos Smith Recordings ♫♫♫♫ (Arhoolie, 1991, compilation prod. Chris Strachwitz)
Music of Peru: From the Mountains to the Sea ♫♫♫♫ (Arhoolie, 1996, compilation prod. Chris Strachwitz)

Peru
genre: Huayno

La Pallasquinita; Conjunto Los Chankas Apurimac; Julia Illanes; Juan Rosales; Conjunto Los Luceros Del Cuzco. (All artists are from Peru.)

Huayno singers are the Peruvian equivalent of Appalachian "hillbillies." They sing in Spanish or Native Quechua about the beauty of their country, their latest romance, or local politics. The instrumentation is a mix of the Spanish Colonial with the Incan, in which violins, trumpets, and flutes can be heard alongside Andean harp, pan-pipes, and *charango* (Andean mandolin). The melody is distinctly Peruvian, with a rhythm

stressing the first beat followed by two short beats. On a visit to Peru, Arhoolie's label head rescued master tapes of 500 such tunes from the 1960s and '70s just before their previous owner taped over them. The tapes' engineer had recorded the latest trends in Lima, using excellent equipment and an ear for original sounds; the cream of this work is collected on these three volumes.

David Poole

The Rough Guide to the Music of Brazil ♫♫♫♫♪ (Rough Guide/World Music Network, 1998, compilation prod. Phil Stanton, Sandra Alayon-Stanton)

Brazil
genre: MPB (Brazilian Popular Music), samba, bossa nova, axe, regional

Ivan Lins; Dominguinhos; Ze Paulo; Adil Tiscatti; Rita Ribeiro; Marlui Miranda; Uakti; Paulo Freire; Dinho Nascimento; Muzenza; Gilberto Monteiro; Renato Braz; Tobias do Vai-Vai; Leny Andrade; Guinga; Rosa Passos; Papete; Cristaldo Souza; Pena Branca & Xavantinho; Joel Nascimento; Radames Gnattali. (All artists are from Brazil.)

The Rough Guides have always prided themselves on being the travel guides of roads less traveled. And their accompanying CDs fill the tall orders of demanding musical tourists. This disc makes a leisurely expedition from the north of Brazil to the south, with an uncanny knack for delving straight to the roots of each regional genre. Many selections are acoustic; all thankfully exclude the brash keyboards that choke much of the music produced for Brazil's internal consumption. The artist selection is intelligent, refusing to sell out to fads or to rest on the laurels of the country's brightest stars. Samba is well represented, with tight, uptempo numbers from Ivan Lins, Rosa Passos, and Guinga, culminating in a dazzling *samba-enredo* (carnival theme song) from *Manguiera*, Rio's most popular samba school. Of the Bahian tracks, by far the most outstanding is Muzenza's slamming rap 'n' percussion rendition of Jorge Ben Jor's "Charles Anjo 45." The insert provides comprehensive liner notes and mini-biographies of all of the contributors, as well as photographs of many of the albums from which the tracks were gleaned—overall a discerning choice for those seeking an astute overview of Brazilian music.

Mara Weiss and Nego Beto

The Soul of Black Peru ♫♫♫♫ (Luaka Bop, 1995, compilation prod. David Byrne, Yale Evelev)

Peru
genre: Afro-Peruvian pop

Susana Baca; Manuel Donayre; Cecilia Barraza; Lucia Compos; Roberto Rivas & el Conjunto Gente Morena; Eva Ayllon;

Abelardo Vasquez & Cumanana; Chabuca Granda; Peru Negro; Nicomedes Santa Cruz; David Byrne (USA). (All artists are from Peru except where otherwise noted.)

This is the compilation that introduced Afro-Peruvian music to the rest of the world—and, to an extent, to Peru, where the music of black Peruvians is still looked upon with suspicion, not unlike the way white Americans viewed "race" records in the 1920s and rock 'n' roll in the '50s. The main attractions here are Susana Baca, who has gone on to become an internationally acclaimed world-music diva as a result of this album; and Peru Negro, whose two percussion-driven tracks brim over with uncontainable energy. The Afro-Peruvians have an arsenal of unique rhythm instruments, including the *cajón,* a large wooden box that the player sits upon and pounds with both hands, and the *cajita,* a small wooden box that is played by opening and shutting the lid (different tones can be obtained by placing the hands around or under the box). The Afro-Peruvian population is not very large, but they produce a vital music that is making large waves in the world community.

j. poet

The Story of Tango ♫♫♫♫ (Hemisphere, 1997, compilation prod. Roli Hernandez, Gerald Seligman)

Argentina
genre: Tango

Jose Basso; Sexteto Mayor; Hector Varela; Anibal Troilo; Raul Garrelo; Osvaldo Pugliese; Carlos Gardel; Mariano Mores; Francisco Canaro; Florindo Sassone. (All artists are from Argentina.)

Tango may be the least "world music"–like of world musics, especially if you're a Westerner who grew up watching Bugs Bunny cartoons, which frequently utilize the genre's popular hits to great parodic effect. With its roots in the classical tradition, tango's blatant sensuousness is still shocking to modern ears, and, as advertised, this album is as good a place as any to start exploring the genre. You'll recognize melodies aplenty here, from pianist Jose Basso's version of "La Cumparsita" (probably the most famous work in the tango canon), to Francisco Varela's sweeping, beautiful arrangement of "De Vuella Y Media," to the Sexteto Mayor orchestra's brooding rendition of Astor Piazzolla's classic "Adios Nonino." Though the pivotal Piazzolla himself doesn't make an appearance here, the artists included more than make up for his absence, with a couple of scratchy, vocal-led 1930s cuts by the legendary Carlos Gardel spicing the otherwise cleanly recorded, up-to-date proceedings. As fun as a Bugs Bunny cartoon, and way more seductive.

Michaelangelo Matos

The World's Musical Traditions 5: Bandoneón Pure: Dances of Uruguay ♫♫♫♫ (Smithsonian, 1993, prod. Tiago de Oliveira Pinto)

Uruguay
genre: Tango, milonga, ranchera, polca, vals

René Marino Rivero (Uruguay).

Bandoneón Pure, the second CD in a special series from the Smithsonian Institution (see the review of *Bunggridj-bunggridj* on page 867 for the series' convoluted history), compiles 24 performances for bandoneón, a type of button accordion, by virtuoso René Marino Rivero. With its classy slip-case format, exhaustive 80-page booklet, and wonderfully performed music, this is a great example of what a world-music release can be. Rivero chooses to present his performances in a simple way without recording embellishments, hence the CD's title. His repertoire consists of several dance styles as they are traditionally played in Uruguay, including the tango, *ranchera, milonga,* foxtrot, and waltz. But his masterful, intricate technique elevates the music far beyond ordinary dance accompaniment. The consistent beauty of the music makes picking standouts difficult, but one might take a stab at it by selecting a tune like "Corazón de Oro," a miniature *vals oriental* (a popular pre-tango dance style) by F. R. Canaro in which Rivero varies the tempo, rhythms, and dynamics with subtlety, and closes with an elegant melodic verse graced with touches of arpeggio. Listening to "Milonga que peina canas," on the other hand, is like watching leaves blow in a dust devil; here Rivero throws melodic twists over a Gordian knot of rhythmic variation in the bass. The booklet, written by Maria Dunkel, is remarkably meticulous; an accordion fanatic might well purchase this disc for the text alone, which details, in a Uruguayan context, bandoneón history, construction, playing technique, and song interpretation—complete with illustrations, footnotes, a bibliography, and an appendix! Though quite daunting to the casual listener, it's still fun to browse, if only to glance at the archival photos or to notice an interesting connection: the transcription of a passage from the tune "El Choclo" was made by Argentinean bandoneón and tango giant Astor Piazzolla.

Jeffrey Muhr

INTERNATIONAL

Afro-Latino ♫♫♫♫ (Putumayo World Music, 1998, compilation prod. Dan Storper)

Senegal, Cape Verde, Congo, Angola, Cuba, Peru
genre: Son, mambo, salsa

Tam-Tam 2000 (Senegal/Cape Verde); Ricardo Lemvo (Congo); Africando (Senegal); Orchestre Baobab de Dakar (Senegal); Sam Mangwana (Congo/Angola); Papi Oviedo (Cuba); Julian Avalos and Afro-Andes (Peru); Cuarteto Oriente (Cuba); 4 Etoiles (Congo); Ruy Mingas (Angola); Vieja Trova Santiaguera (Cuba); Conjunto Cespedes (Cuba).

Although nothing will ever induce me to love Putumayo's cover illustrations—which depict an icky PC multiculti la-la land that could make a faith-healer retch—their albums are getting better and better, and *Afro-Latino*, an incredibly rich collection of 12 Cuban-based tracks performed by a cast of top-flight African, South American, and Cuban musicians, is their best to date. The album's concept—an exploration of the give-and-take between the Congo and its slave-descendants in Cuba—is smart and beautifully executed, with an intelligently sequenced selection of grooves that get under your skin and stay there. Ricardo Lemvo & Makina Loca's "Mambo Yo Yo," Orchestre Baobab's "El Son de Llama," and Cuarteto Oriente's "Mueve la Cintura Mulata" establish deep, relaxed, powerful rhythms and then float gorgeous, incremental, sometimes-jarring embellishments atop them for four, six, eight minutes at a time. Every song is unhurried, and most are instantly classic: if these aren't the definitive renditions of traditional songs like "Aideu" and "El Son de Llama," they're close enough that you won't care. Last word goes to the liner notes' Charlie Palmieri quote: "If you can't dance to this, you died last week." Amen.

Michaelangelo Matos

Anthology of Chant 🎵🎵🎵🎵 (Celestial Harmonies, 1995, prod. various)

International
genre: Worldwide chant

Saad Ullah Khan (India); the Madrigal Choir of the Munich Academy of Music (Germany); H.Hafiz Hüseyin Erek; H.Hafiz Kâni Karaca; the Haissmavourk Choir (Armenia); the Students' Choir and Students' Chamber Choir Utrecht (Holland); the Augsburg Ensemble for Early Music (Germany); Perry Silverbird (USA); Monks of the Dip Tse Chok Ling Monastery of Dharmasala (Tibet/India); David Hudson (Australia); David Hykes; Timothy Hill; Karineh Avetissian (Armenia); Oxford Camerata and Jeremy Summerly (England); Perry Silverbird & Steve Roach (USA); Omar Faruk Tekbilek & Brian Keane (Turkey/USA).

Thousands of years before the push-button atmospherics of the synthesizer, the ethereal arrangements of chant were evoking the infinite. Its phenomenal recent popularity stems from the way it simultaneously gives us a sense of something beyond ourselves, and of a capability within ourselves. This compilation also gives us a sense of each other, branching beyond the European world from which chant has charted most to recognize the reverent voices of Aboriginal Australia, Native America, Tibet, India, and Islam as well as Germany, Armenia, and

France. Divorced from the utilitarian yet inspired purpose of the traditional versions, Western neo-chanter David Hykes's entry sounds artificial and slight despite its 12-minute length. But otherwise, bravura performances make this a collection not of background noise but of compelling foreground music, and insightful selection of a cohesive spectrum of song makes this not a skim, but a complete work in its own right.

Adam McGovern

Anthology of World Music, Vols. 1–18 🎵🎵🎵🎵 (Rounder, 1998–99, reissue prod. Scott Billington)

India, China, Iran, Laos, Morocco, Liberia, Rwanda, Ivory Coast, Vietnam, Cameroon, Tibet, Albania
genre: Raga, tala, alaap, dhamar, khyal, thamri, ibitaramo, amahamba, imbyino, ngoma drums, ta, mokombi, pi phat, pinpeat, khene, loi tuang, nha nhac, dai nhac, nieu noi, tolba, adhan, tehlil, tejwid, derdeba, jedba, al-milhun, Buddhist chant, kaba, çam dance

Diverse artists and ensembles from many countries, over many volumes.

The reissue of the *Anthology of Traditional Music of the World* is a watershed event in the field of world music. Consisting of 50 albums, the *Anthology* was Alain Daniélou's visionary attempt to document musical ways of life across a broad sweep of cultures, and make available for study a wealth of non-Western music. The *Anthology* was originally released between 1968 and 1987 in three series—*A Musical Anthology of the Orient*, *An Anthology of North Indian Music*, and *An Anthology of African Music*—with the help of UNESCO and the International Institute for Comparative Music Studies and Documentation in Berlin, Germany (an organization founded by Daniélou himself). Until Rounder began reissuing the series in 1998 under the current title listed above, the albums were available in the U.S. only as imports.

Born in 1907 in Paris, France, Daniélou became known for his writings on Indian religion and culture, as well as pathbreaking efforts in world music and controversial works on music theory. A talented musician, he had learned piano, vocal technique, and composition in his teens, and would later study the stringed *veena* for six years while a resident of India. Obtaining an early portable tape recorder around the late 1950s, Daniélou traveled through many Asian countries searching out traditional music. After his return to Europe, he created his Institute in Berlin with the aim of promoting the understanding of traditional musics in the West. The first volume of the *Anthology* series was released in 1968 on the Bärenreiter Musicaphon label; when Daniélou left the organization the series was carried on by Ivan Vandor and Paul Collaer through 1987.

Daniélou's study of musical forms led him to develop a complex, metaphysical theory of the interaction of musical intervals on which he elaborated in works such as *Introduction to the Study of Musical Scales* (1943) and *Musical Semantics* (1967). In the first of these books, reissued as *Music and the Power of Sound* (Inner Traditions, 1995), he carried out a detailed analysis of the scales and systems of the Chinese, Indians, and Greeks and compared them to the European "equal temperament" scale, ultimately making an argument for dividing the octave into 53 "microtonal" intervals. In the service of this conception he enlisted the help of instrument makers such as the famed Maurice Martenot, who had created a "tunable electronic keyboard" for him in 1936, and Stephan Kudelski, who created an instrument in 1979 that can sound 52 precise intervals per octave.

A converted Hindu who lived in India for nearly 30 years, Daniélou took a broad, ecological view of human civilization that stressed continuity, harmony, and mutual respect between cultures, a view that informed both his recordings and writings. By the time he died in 1994, he had written and translated over 30 books on various topics; published several series of traditional music recordings; and served with a host of academic, cultural, and musical organizations in Europe and Asia.

Rounder has so far rereleased 18 volumes of the *Anthology*, with attractive new graphics and careful digital remastering of the original music, much of which was recorded in the field for the series. In a few cases, tracks that could not be fit onto the LPs have been added back. The original liner notes, which often reflected Daniélou's abiding interest in musical scales, have also been reproduced. With its rerelease, the *Anthology of World Music*, which has always been a primary resource for traditional music, can reach a new generation of listeners while playing a small part in slowing the decline of cultural diversity in the face of rampant Westernization. The available volumes at this time are: *North Indian Classical Music, Vols. 1–4*; *Africa: Music from Rwanda*; *Africa: The Dan*; *Africa: The Ba-Benzele Pygmies*; *The Music of Laos*; *Iran, Vols. 1–2*; *The Music of Vietnam, Vols. 1–2*; *The Music of Islam and Sufism in Morocco*; *China*; *The Music of Tibetan Buddhism, Vols. 1–3*; and *Albania*.

Jeffrey Muhr

The Big Bang: In the Beginning Was the Drum 🎵🎵🎵🎵🎵
(ellipsis arts . . . , 1994, compilation prod. Angel Romero)

International
genre: World music

Tumuenua Dance Group (Cook Islands); Giovanni Hidalgo (Puerto Rico); Mino Cinelu & George Jinda (Martinique & Hungary); Suwa-Daiko Hozonkai (Japan); Mustapha Tettey Addy (Ghana); Glen Velez (USA); Terry Bozzio (USA); Mickey Hart (USA); Zakir Hussain & U.K. Sivaraman (India); Nurudafina Pili Abena (USA); Tommy Hayes (Ireland); Gasper Lawal (Nigeria); Reinhard Flatischler & Samul Nori (Germany & Korea); Funhouse (USA); Bernie Krause (USA); Baka Forest People (Congo); Fatala (Guinea); Dudu Tucci (Brazil); Michael Shrieve (USA); the Voodoo Gang (Cameroon); Sekehe Gong Windu Karya Putpa (Bali); Carl Palmer (Great Britain); Airto Moreira (Brazil); Carlos "Patato" Valdés (Cuba); Juan Mari Beltran & Joxan Goikoetxea (Spain); Stella Rambisai Chiweshe (Zimbabwe); Avo Chakhlasyan (Armenia); Ming-Chun Puppet Troupe (Taiwan); Misri Khan (Pakistan); Babatunde Olatunji (Nigeria); Tamborito Del Norte (Panama); Karnataka College of Percussion & Dr. Raghavendra (India); Farafina (Burkina Faso); Jorge Reyes (Mexico); Amampondo (South Africa); Orchestra Of Chinese Central Music College (China); Ladji Camara (Guinea); LCO Soldier's Drum (Lac Court Oreilles Reservation, USA); Jack DeJohnette (USA); Hossain Tehrani (Iraq); Malang & Mohammad Akram Rohnawaz (Afghanistan).

Three discs-full of varying styles of percussive rhythms, combined with an informative booklet of short summaries of the music heard, sounds like an awful lot of information to digest. There are so many different kinds of meters, rhythms, and settings within which to experiment and play with time that the mind boggles. But that's why this collection is so valuable; the folks at ellipsis specialize in taking a vast field and sampling it for a primer that's fun to listen to. They still don't cover every rhythmic possibility, but with all this work that's beside the point and it *is* the point—the styles presented here range from jazz to rock to *gamelan* and beyond.

Garaud MacTaggart

Big Noise (A Mambo Inn Compilation) 🎵🎵🎵🎵 (Hannibal, 1995, compilation prod. Gerry Lyseight)
Big Noise 2 (A Mambo Inn Compilation) 🎵🎵🎵🎵 (Hannibal, 1997, compilation prod. Gerry Lyseight)

International
genre: World dance music

Big Noise: Numerous artists including: Nusrat Fateh Ali Khan (Pakistan); Khaled (Algeria); Sweet Talks (Ghana); Tchando (Guinea-Bissau); Mambomania (France); Andy Montañez (Puerto Rico); Airto Moreira (Brazil); Kanda Bongo Man (Zaire); Ramsey Lewis (USA); Luther Barnes & the Red Budd Gospel Choir (USA). *Big Noise 2*: Numerous artists including: Timbalada (Brazil); Gal Costa & Caetano Veloso (Brazil); Baaba Maal (Senegal); Dorothy Masuka (Zimbabwe/South Africa); Hamid Baroudi (Algeria/Germany); Jephte Guillaume (Haiti/USA); Africando (Senegal/Cuba/Puerto Rico/USA); Jazz Jamaica (UK); iCubanismo! (Cuba); krosfyah (Barbados); Israel "Cachao" Lopez (Cuba).

Big Noise is one hot worldbeat dance album, packed, like the English club in Brixton that inspired it, with irresistible, joyous tracks—here ranging from a magnificently mambo-fied 1991 remix of Pakistani *qawwali* legend Nusrat Fateh Ali Khan by UK dancefloor *bhangra* master Bally Sagoo, to the infectious groove of Airto and friends on "Samba de Flora." Khaled, Kanda Bongo Man, and Andy Montañez have never sounded more seductive. A personal favorite is the unstoppable "Mango Mango Mangue" by France's leading mambo practitioners, Mambomania. This alternately soaring and sizzling number from the pen of Francisco Fellove—cheekily interpolated here with "Take the 'A' Train"—originally found fame in 1962 as a hit for salsa queen Celia Cruz. *Big Noise 2* manages to match its predecessor for sheer excitement and energy, thanks to impeccable selections and superior sequencing. From the samba-reggae and straight-ahead bossa nova of Brazilian openers Timbalada and Gal Costa & Caetano Veloso respectively, through Senegalese superstar Baaba Maal's funky reggae-like *yele* and the distinctive *marabi* of Zimbabwe's Dorothy Masuka and beyond, the pace and the fun never let up. The cross-pollination that characterized the Mambo Inn philosophy is exemplified by "African Soul" from Algeria's Hamid Baroudi, former member of Germany's world-fusion band Die Dissidenten. Here Baroudi melds Arabic trance music with an African dance beat to great effect. New York–based Jephte Guillaume's slinky "Lakou-A" blends music of his native Haiti with Nuyorican house rhythms, while UK-based Jazz Jamaica's terrific "skazz" rendition of Duke Ellington's "Caravan" is listed, appropriately enough, as "Skaravan." Like the best compilations, this one leaves the listener gasping for more, and poring over the sleeve notes trying to figure out where else this stuff can be found.

John C. Falstaff

B'ismillah 🎵🎵🎵🎵 (Sounds True, 1997, prod. Joel Davis, Tami Simon)
Hamdulillah 🎵🎵🎵🎵🎵 (Sounds True, 1998, prod. Joel Davis, Tami Simon)

Bosnia-Herzegovina, Syria, Morocco, Egypt, Pakistan, Spain, India, Azerbaijan, France, Uzbekistan, Iraq, Java, Iran, Konya (Turkey)
genre: Sacred world music

B'ismillah: Radio and Television Symphony Orchestra (Bosnia-Herzegovina); Hamza Shakour and the Al Kindi Ensemble (Syria); Al-Iman Al-Busiri Association (Morocco); Tagmout of Zagora (Morocco); Sheikh Ahmed Barrayn (Egypt); Mehr Ali and Sher Ali (Pakistan); Said Chraibi (Morocco); Diego de Los Santos (Spain); Ahaidous (Morocco); Ustad Gulam Hassan Shagan (Pakistan). *Hamdulillah*: Ahmed Piro Ensemble with Amina Alaoui (Morocco); Taqtouqa Al Iabaliyya (Morocco); Ustad Zia Fariduddin Dagar (India); Begonia Olavide and Mudeiar Ensemble (Spain); Children of Abraham (Israel, France, & Morocco); Alim Qassimov (Azerbaijan); Francoise Atlan (France); Albert Bouhadanna (Morocco); Sidi Thami Mdaghri (Morocco); Mona-iat Yulcheva (Uzbekistan); Hussayn Al Azanu with Ensemble Al Kindi (Syria); El Suspiro del Moro (Morocco & France); Wacana Budaya Gamelan (Java); Sharam Nazeri and Dastan Ensemble (Iran); The Whirling Dervishes of Konya (Konya, Turkey).

I can still remember when local Boulder, Colorado, radio personality Joel Davis told me he was going to make some field recordings at the Fes Festival of World Sacred Music in Morocco; man, was I green with envy. Until, at least, he gave me a copy of *B'ismillah* hot off the press a few months later; that original CD of ethnic spirituals blew me away with an unparalleled in-your-face grittiness that no Western chant album ever engendered. My mind melted as my soul soared on whirling dervish dance rhythms until my aesthetic appetite cried out for more. It was the first compilation of its kind. Luckily, many listeners shared my passion for this music; so, a year and many thousands of miles later, we can all now savor Joel's latest triumph, the joyful *Hamdulillah* (roughly translated from the Arabic as "Oh, you make noise!"), a more elegant but still stirring double-disc compilation of Arabian, Sufi, Hindu, Sephardic Jewish, and other exotic cultural devotionals; mystical texts accompanied by music; and enticing instrumentals. From Sharam Nazeri's Iranian spiritual songs, to dizzyingly delightful Javanese *gamelan* music, to Moorish Muslim melodies dating back to medieval Andalusia, there is a breathtaking array of non-stop spiritual celebration that imbues the listener with an overwhelming feeling of ecstatic universality. The terrific Whirling Dervishes of Konya—a group of 26 musicians, singers, and dancers of Turkey's Mevlevi sect—close this exceptional anthology with a reading from the Qur'an, reminding us of the literally divine power of music.

PJ Birosik

Bliss 🎵🎵🎵🎵 (RealWorld, 1998, prod. various)

International
genre: World music, ambient, ethno-techno

Nusrat Fateh Ali Khan (Pakistan); Peter Gabriel (England); Sarmila Roy (India); the Grid (England); Ayub Ogada (Kenya); Jam Nation (England); the Tsinandali Choir (Georgia); Sheila Chandra (India/England); Afro Celt Sound System (International); U. Srinivas (India) & Michael Brook (Canada); the Guo Brothers & Shung Tian (China); Iarla Ó Lionáird (Ireland).

It was RealWorld Records founder Peter Gabriel who first exposed much of the Western world to phenomenal talents like Pakistani *qawwali* legend Nusrat Fateh Ali Khan and Senegalese superstar Youssou N'Dour back in 1988 with his outstanding fusion recording, *Passion*. So it seems only natural that 10 years later, RealWorld would release a compilation that ties together songs by artists from a variety of cultures, pointing out the inherent similarity in humanity's seemingly disparate musical traditions. Fused seamlessly by Russell Kearney, 13 mesmerizing tracks are connected with the same sort of ambient soundscapes that made *Passion* such a groundbreaking conceptual piece. Opening, appropriately enough, with songs by Khan and Gabriel himself, the album is a transcendent journey into the hypnotic power of music, with spellbinding ambient/techno tracks like the Grid's "Angel Tech" blended beautifully with traditional tunes like Ayub Ogada's "Kothbiro" to create entrancing global-village chill-out music. The fusion of musical traditions has long seemed the future of pop music; leave it to Peter Gabriel and RealWorld to lead the way.

Bret Love

Brave Hearts 𝄞𝄞𝄞𝄞𝄞 (Narada, 1998, compilation prod. Michael Sullivan)

International
genre: Celtic

Blair Douglas (Scotland); Ashley MacIsaac (Canada); Mary Jane Lamond (Canada); Karen Matheson (Scotland); Leahy (Canada); Anna Murray (Scotland); Tannas (Scotland); Capercaillie (Scotland); Old Blind Dogs (Scotland); Alisdair Fraser (Scotland); Dougie MacLean (Scotland).

Ireland is usually the first country that comes to mind when one speaks of Celtic music. As the artists on this disc make clear, Scotland has a vibrant contemporary/traditionalist music community of its own, infused by contributions from the Scots who took the music to the Atlantic coast of Canada. From Blair Douglas's spin on the Scots parade march "Nelson Mandela's Welcome to the City of Glasgow" through Dougie MacLean's thoughtful presentation of "Auld Lang Syne" (itself an example of new traditionalist music when Robert Burns first wrote it), this is an intriguing and lively collection. It's a fine survey of current Scots music by artists of high quality, a good blend of musicians well known worldwide and regionally famous.

Kerry Dexter

Bringing It All Back Home 𝄞𝄞𝄞𝄞 (BBC, 1991, compilation prod. Bruce Talbot, Dónal Lunny)

England, Ireland, USA
genre: Irish folk roots

Dónal Lunny (Ireland); Dolores Keane (Ireland); Rita and Sara Keane (Ireland); the Lee Valley String Band (Ireland); Mick Moloney (Ireland/USA); Jimmy Keane (Ireland/USA); Robbie O'Connell (Ireland/USA); Philip Chevron (Ireland); the Hughes Band (Ireland); the Everly Brothers (USA); Hothouse Flowers (Ireland); De Dannan (Ireland); Emmylou Harris (USA); Mary Black (Ireland); Paul Brady (Ireland/England); Sharon Shannon (Ireland); Mary Custy (Ireland); Eoin O'Neill (Ireland); Luka Bloom (Ireland/USA); Peadar Ó Riada and Cór Cúil Aodh (Ireland); Máire Ní Chathasaigh (Ireland); Noirin Ní Riain and the Monks of Glenstall Abbey (Ireland); Micheál Ó Súilleabháin and the Irish Chamber Orchestra (Ireland); Elvis Costello (England); Mary Coughlan (Ireland); Davy Spillane (Ireland); An Emotional Fish (Ireland); Ricky Skaggs (USA); Paddy Glackin (Ireland); Mark O'Connor (USA); Richard Thompson (England); Sonny

Condell (Ireland); Seamas Glackin (Ireland); Kevin Glackin (Ireland); Catherine Ennis (Ireland); Liam O'Flynn (Ireland); Pierce Turner (Ireland/USA); Roger Sherlock (Ireland/England); Maura O'Connell (Ireland/USA); the Waterboys (Ireland); the Voice Squad (Ireland).

This two-CD set contains 37 performances heard in the BBC TV series of same name. Documenting the travels of Irish music in diaspora, that program sought to bring together classical, rock, country, and traditional folk artists, illustrating the power of the Celtic muse to bridge oceans and influence cultures. The list of musicians recruited for the project is an impressive one and the performances are equally so. A number of artists in this set were born in Ireland but left for the U.S. or England to pursue careers; this gives an added authenticity to songs detailing the breaking apart of families and a longing for the home country such as "My Love Is in America" (by Dolores Keane), "Western Highway" (featuring Maura O'Connell), and "Kilkelly" (from Mick Moloney, Jimmy Keane, and Robbie O'Connell). Cross-cultural blends include trios featuring American country stars Emmylou Harris, Ricky Skaggs, and Mark O'Connor along with various Irish compatriots. By taking traditional Irish folk melodies and arranging them for larger ensembles, Peadar Ó Riada and Micheál Ó Súilleabháin bring a classical approach to ancient material, while rockers Hothouse Flowers and An Emotional Fish meld contemporary sounds with ancestral modes.

Garaud MacTaggart

Celtic Christmas 𝄞𝄞𝄞𝄞 (Windham Hill, 1995, prod. Mícheál Ó Domhnaill)

International
genre: Contemporary Celtic, Christmas, spiritual

Phil Cunningham and Manny Lunny; Tríona Ní Dhomhnaill; Mícheál Ó Domhnaill and Kevin Burke; Liam O'Flynn; Luka Bloom; Cromac Breatnach; Maighread Ní Dhomnaill and Dónal Lunny; Nightnoise; Carlos Nuñez; Altan; Johnny Cunningham; Loreena McKennitt; Jeff Johnson and Brian Dunning. (Artists are from Ireland or other countries of the Celtic diaspora.)

Central to Celtic music is its exploration of spirituality, and that's the not-too-heavy focus of this Christmas album—you won't find rowdy holiday drinking songs, but neither will you find much in the way of hymns or ancient chants. The music here is varied, though, from Scotsman Johnny Cunningham's "King Holly, King Oak" to Galician (Spanish Celtic) piper Carlos Nuñez's "Carol." Canadian harper and vocalist Loreena McKennitt's meditation on "Snow" may best represent the theme of this disc: a quiet celebration of the Celtic spirit of winter. (As of this writing, three subsequent volumes in the same vein are available.)

Kerry Dexter

Celtic Legacy 🎵🎵🎵🎵 (Narada, 1995, prod. various)

Ireland, Scotland, Spain, Canada, USA, Wales, Belgium, France
genre: Celtic and Celtic diaspora

William Coulter (USA); Orion (Belgium); the Barra MacNeils (Canada); 4Yn Ybar (Wales); Natalie MacMaster (Canada); Milladoiro (Spain); the Poozies (Scotland); Máire Breatnach (Ireland); Maighread Ní Dhomnaill (Ireland); William Jackson (Scotland); John Whelan/Eileen Ivers (Ireland/USA); Altan (Ireland); Déanta (Ireland); Deiseal (Ireland); Dominig Bouchaud (France); Talitha MacKenzie (USA/Scotland).

The idea of journeys—life's journey through time; the leaving of and returning to a loved one; the longing for a homeland—is an emotional theme basic to Celtic music. Though this isn't strictly a thematic album, that emotion forms the connection among the musicians, who themselves come from or live in the Celtic homelands of Ireland, Scotland, Wales, Galicia, and Brittany as well as the areas of Celtic dispersion in Europe and North America. It's a tasteful collection well suited as an introduction to what contemporary Celtic artists are doing with the reflective aspect of their musical heritage.

Kerry Dexter

Celtic Lullaby 🎵🎵🎵 (ellipsis arts . . . , 1996, compilation prod. Michel Shapiro)

Canada, Ireland, Isle of Man, New Zealand, Scotland, USA, Wales
genre: Celtic

Tommy Sands (Ireland); Plethyn (Wales); Jean Redpath (Scotland); Margie Butler (USA); Dafydd Iwan (Wales); Garry ÓBriain (Ireland); Pádraigin Ní Uallacháin (Ireland); Ann Mayo Muir (USA); Chris Norman (Nova Scotia); Parson's Hat (Ireland); Moira Craig (Scotland); Jill Rogoff (New Zealand); Alison Kinnaird (Scotland); Emma Christian (Isle of Man); Tudor Morgan (Wales); Margo Carruthers (Nova Scotia); Mac-talla (Scotland).

The lullaby is a song form common to almost every musical tradition on the planet. Lullabies represent a distinct and prolific body within the oral tradition of the Celtic world in particular. This is a beautifully evocative collection of mellow music performed by some of the world's finest exponents of the Celtic song and instrumental. Unlike similar compilations *called* "Celtic," this selection comes closest to representing the full range of its topic by surveying so many of the Celtic countries and so much of their diaspora. With over 60 minutes of wonderful music, this disc will lull any child to sleep, and, truth be told, worked pretty well on this adult as well.

Cliff McGann

Celtic Odyssey 🎵🎵🎵🎵 (Narada, 1993, compilation prod. Eric Lindert)

Ireland, Scotland
genre: Celtic

Northern Lights (USA); Orison (USA); Altan (Ireland); Alisdair Fraser/Paul Machlis (Scotland); Scartaglen (USA); John Whalen/Eileen Ivers (Ireland/USA); Moving Hearts (Ireland); Relativity (Ireland); Capercaillie (Scotland); Sileas (Scotland); Gerald Trimble (USA); Laurie Riley & Bob McNally (USA); Simon Wynberg (Scotland/Canada).

One of the constants of Celtic music is a sense of place—the green, misty windswept European lands where the music was born, and the similar places that Celts around the world have called home, from the mountains of North Carolina to the shores of Cape Breton Island. It's also a basic idea communicated by the songs on this compilation, most of them either traditional or composed in a style that draws on tradition.

Kerry Dexter

Celtic Spirit 🎵🎵🎵 (Narada Media, 1996, executive prod. Michael Sullivan)

Ireland, France, Scotland, USA
genre: Celtic, religious/spiritual

Connie Dover (USA); Aoife Ní Fhearraigh (Ireland); Aine Minogue (Ireland); the Anjali Quartet (USA); William Jackson (Scotland); Groupe Vocal Jef le Penven (France); William Coulter (USA); the Baltimore Consort (USA); Sheena Wellington (Scotland); Therese Schroeder-Sheker (USA).

The strength of this collection is that the artists take traditional spiritual songs in languages from within the Celtic tradition (Gaelic, Breton) and outside it (English, Latin), and perform them with instrumentation and styles embedded in that tradition. It's a side of Celtic culture and history not often explored by contemporary artists, and it's refreshingly handled here. The meditative tone is set with Connie Dover's opening arrangement of the Gregorian chant "Ubi Caritas," and continues throughout the selections, which evoke the mist-covered hills and the longing for home, as well as the search for understanding, at the heart of so much music in this genre. If your experience with Celtic music has been fighting, drinking, or political songs, or new-age interpretations of ancient melodies, you'll find this album fits none of those categories and will expand your knowledge of the interaction between old and new in Celtic tradition.

Kerry Dexter

Celtic Treasure: The Legacy of Turlough O'Carolan 🎵🎵🎵 (Narada, 1996, executive prod. Michael Sullivan)

International
genre: Celtic, O'Carolan

Shelley Phillips; Orion; Déanta; Deiseal; Ann Heymann; Dordán; William Coulter; Séamus McGuire; Maíre Ní Chathasaigh and Chris Newman; Donna Long; Dominig Bouchaud and Cyrille Colas; El McMeen; John Whelan; Jerry O'Sullivan. (All artists are from Ireland or the Celtic Diaspora in Europe and the New World).

None of Turlough O'Carolan's compositions were written down during his lifetime. It is a testament to the power of his music that more than 200 of his tunes have survived three centuries, both in their original form as songs for the harp and as transcriptions for instruments from the hammered dulcimer to the guitar. Carolan took up the career of itinerant musician when he was blinded by smallpox at age 18. He began composing shortly thereafter when one of his hosts challenged him to start writing music to add to his less-than-spectacular playing skills. It was a wise challenge, and a wise acceptance. Carolan was able to blend the folk tunes of his youth with the classical ideas of the growing Baroque style in Europe (represented, for example, by Bach, Telemann, Corelli, and Vivaldi). Carolan's music seemed immediately accessible to all those who heard it, bridging the gap between simple songs of the street and complex melodies of the mansion. That is still true today and is one aspect of his work that attracts artists of the caliber heard on *Celtic Treasure*. This is a lively presentation of the music of Ireland's most important composer by a group of accomplished Celtic musicians who bring varied influences to the task.

Kerry Dexter

Dancing with the Dead 🎵🎵🎵🎵 (ellipsis arts . . . , 1999, prod. various)

International
genre: World memorial music

Pastor Ediemae Layne (USA); the Eureka Brass Band (USA); the Tlanjin Buddhist Music Ensemble (China); Asif Ali Khan (Pakistan); Los Nani (Cuba); Nasioi People of Papua New Guinea (Papua New Guinea); Janet Leuchter (USA); Los Camperos de Valles (Mexico); Antanosy & Mahafaly Peoples of Madagascar (Madagascar); Fong Naam (Thailand); the Lileh Choir of Dmanisi (Georgia); Sanjukta Sen (India); Koo Nimo & the Kumasi Ensemble Adadam Agofomma (Ghana); Gabriel Souza Carvalho (Brazil); Keith Mahone (Native America); Seka Gamelan Angklung (Bali); Central African Republic Bokoto Music (Central African Republic).

Death ain't what it used to be. The ravages of AIDS and the controversial ability of modern medicine to prolong life seemingly beyond reason have moved the West to confront death with less squeamishness and stigma than ever before. In this, the "developed" world is finally developing up to the cultural standards of the *rest* of the world, where the reality of death is incorporated into people's understanding of the processes of life, and departure from the living is celebrated as a graduation

to the infinite. Consequently, the music collected on this fascinating and tasteful disc, while never seeming festive, always feels affirmative, replacing the dirges expected by Western (and Western-bred) ears. While at no time abandoning an air of gravity, these pieces don't convey a sense of tragedy but one of wonder. A Mardi Gras–style brass band sends the deceased off in style (significantly, the only geographically Western selections are from traditions influenced by Africa and Native America), and the delicate bell-like percussion of a Balinese *gamelan* ensemble is like a gentle rain upwards toward heaven. Death unifies us all, and this collection shows how connected we are in life, too: the choral updraft of melodious mourners in the Republic of Georgia could almost be mistaken for a spiritual from the *other* Georgia; a spoken/sung eulogy from a Southern Baptist church locates the exact half-way mark in the journey from West African *griot* storytelling to the urban legends of rap. The set's beautifully designed, digest-size hardcover companion book introduces the subject in an engaging and low-pressure way, while protecting your CD and providing the best antidote yet to the environmentally unfriendly jewel box and the alleged demise of album art. Mirroring the book's fascinating overview, the CD's music is insightfully sequenced and judiciously excerpted to avoid the archival overkill that can defeat the purpose of a survey and obscure the bigger picture. In the buoyant tones of this album you'll literally hear spirits being lofted to another plane—and won't feel nearly so earthbound yourself.

Adam McGovern

Dargason Music Sampler 🎵🎵🎵 (Dargason Music, 1996, compilation prod. Joemy Wilson)

International
genre: Celtic, world music

Kim Robertson; Joemy Wilson; John Bullard; Anisa Angarola; Miamon Miller; Valeriu Apan; Gremoli. (All artists are based in USA.)

Dargason Music is a small label founded several years ago by hammered dulcimer player Joemy Wilson and her husband Jon Harvey. At first they intended it just to be a vehicle for helping them answer requests for Wilson's music fostered by her active performing career. That became no insignificant task—Wilson's recordings of the complex music of 17th-century Irish harper Turlough O'Carolan, which she had transcribed for the hammered dulcimer, quickly became so well respected that they were sought after for the collection of the Irish National Archives and became staples on the playlists of many classical music stations. These developments allowed Wilson and Harvey to consider producing and distributing music by other artists, and in the beginning they focused mainly on Celtic-oriented musicians, like classical guitarist Anisa Angarola and world-renowned Celtic harpist and vocalist Kim Robertson. Later, they expanded to offer a group of holiday-music albums from different cultures, some with Wilson playing and some with the work of panflutist Valeriu Apan and violinist Miamon Miller. As the label has developed it has begun to venture in wider directions, with the music of John Bullard, who plays Bach on the five-string banjo, and Gremoli, a New Orleans–style jazz group. The individual tunes on this disc are all of high quality and stand well on their own. Taken as a whole they give an intriguing portrait of the musical tastes of the founders of this small but influential labor-of-love label.

Kerry Dexter

Ethno Punk: Around the World with Attitude ♪♪♪♪℣
(EMI Hemisphere/Metro Blue, 1996, compilation prod. Gerald Seligman)

Israel, Spain, Greece, Scotland, Sweden, France, Japan, Poland, USA/Ireland, Brazil, China
genre: Unorthodox contemporary world music

Yehuda Poliker (Israel); Ciudad Jardin (Spain); Pyx Lax (Greece); Rock, Salt, & Nails (Scotland); Den Fule (Sweden); Mano Negra (France); Parsha Club (Japan); Raz, Dwa, Trzy (Poland); Mau Mau (Italy); Black 47 (Ireland/USA); Paralamas do Sucesso (Brazil); Ciu Jian (China); Shooglenifty (Scotland); Hedningarna (Sweden); Wilmer X (Sweden).

This collection gives the adventurous listener a good summary of the more avant-garde exponents of world/roots music. Some of the tracks, such as Black 47's Irish-rap tale of the band's history, "Rockin' the Bronx," and Mano Negra's rendition of the traditional Arab song "Sidi H'Bibi," which brings together Middle Eastern, French, and Latin American sounds, are forward-rushing multicultural fusions. Other selections, such as Den Fule's "Det Är Jag," Shooglenifty's "Waiting for Conrad," and Hedningarna's "Aivoton," are contemporary expressions of more specific ethnic/folk traditions. English translations of all song lyrics are included, but if you're up for the challenges and rewards of the unexpected, these artists are speaking your language already.

Ken Roseman

Faces of the Harp: Celtic & Contemporary ♪♪♪℣ (Narada, 1997, executive prod. Dan Harjung)

International
genre: Harp, Celtic, contemporary

Dennis Doyle (USA/Ireland); Thomas Loefke (Germany); Kim Robertson (USA); Laurie Riley and Michael McBean (USA); Sileas (Scotland); Sylvia Woods (USA); Sedren (Greece/Brittany, France); Katie LaRaye Waldren and Candace Kreitlow

(USA); Derek Bell (Ireland); Ani Williams (USA); Julia Haines; Northern Lights (USA/Holland/Ireland); Ann Heymann and Alison Kinnaird (USA/Scotland); Judith Pintar (USA); Riley Lee and Andy Riley (Australia/USA).

The harp is one of humankind's oldest instruments. It's also one of those that contemporary composers and players have the most fun taking in new directions. The majority of musicians represented here play the Celtic or folk harp, but draw on traditions and studies as diverse as African *kora* and Latin *marimba,* as well as the diversity of Celtic styles, to inform their compositional choices. This disc is both a good introduction to the current state of the Celtic harp and a compendium of unexpected melodic choices for those who enjoy contemporary instrumental music in general.

Kerry Dexter

Festival of Light ♪♪♪♪♪ (Island, 1996, compilation prod. Robert Dusjis, Bob Appel)

International
genre: Religious/spiritual

Marc Cohn; the Mels featuring Jon Leventhal; Flairck; Don Byron; the Covenant; Rebbe Soul; John McCutcheon; the Klezmatics; Masada String Trio; Alistut; Jane Siberry; Peter Himmelman & David Broza. (Artists are from USA, Canada, and Israel.)

This collection honors the Jewish holiday of Hanukkah by affording contemporary artists the freedom either to compose their own music on the ideas of the holiday or to reinterpret traditional songs. This results in a disc that is both contemporary and timeless, and allows the handing on of tradition to stand side-by-side with the exploration and creation of it. An outstanding example of the latter is Peter Himmelman and David Broza's "Lighting Up the World," and of the former, the Covenant's "Kiddush Le-Shabbat." This is a set that will appeal equally to those versed in and new to the music and culture from which it springs.

Kerry Dexter

Folk Roots Magazine Presents Roots: 20 Years of Essential Folk, Roots & World Music (Britain, Ireland and North America) ♪♪♪♪♪ (Nascente, 1999, prod. various)
Folk Roots Magazine Presents Routes: 20 Years of Essential Folk, Roots & World Music (Africa, Europe, Asia and the World) ♪♪♪♪♪ (Nascente, 1999, prod. various)

International
genre: International

Roots: Ry Cooder (USA); Afro Celt Sound System (England); Nic Jones (England); the McGarrigles (Quebec, Canada); Billy Bragg (England); Peter Rowan (USA); Fernhill (Wales); Corey Harris (USA); the Mekons (England); Loudon Wainwright III (USA); the

Pogues (England); Spider John Koerner (USA); Eliza Carthy (England); Rory Block (USA); Kathryn Tickell & Rory McLeod (England); Robin & Linda Williams (USA); Alias Ron Kavana (England); Brave Combo (USA); Shooglenifty (Scotland); Richard Thompson (England); Ani DiFranco (USA); Elvis Costello (England); Taj Mahal (USA); Jumpleads (England); Kate Rusby (England); Guy Clark (USA); Tiger Moth (England); Cordelia's Dad (USA); Oysterband (England); Emmylou Harris (USA); Dick Gaughan (Scotland); Chris Smither (USA); June Tabor & Martin Simpson (England); Bruce Cockburn (Canada); Altan (Ireland); John Hammond (England); Brass Monkey (England); La Bottine Souriante (Quebec, Canada). *Routes*: Youssou N'Dour (Senegal); Cuarteto Patria (Cuba); Tarika (Madagascar); Re Niliu (Italy); Maryam Mursal (Somalia); Márta Sebestyén & Muzsikás (Hungary); Nenes featuring Ry Cooder (Okinawa/USA); Ali Farka Touré (Mali); Kepa, Zabaleta & Motriku (Basque Country); Abdel Aziz El Mubarak (Sudan); Filarfolket (Sweden); Dembo Konte & Kausu Kuyateh (Gambia/Senegal); Ali Akbar Khan & Asha Bhosle (India); Trans-Global Underground (England); Mahlathini & Mahotella Queens (South Africa); Buena Vista Social Club (Cuba); Baaba Maal & Mansour Seck (Senegal); Eleftheria Arvanitaki with Stavros Logarides (Greece); Garmarna (Sweden); Kanda Bongo Man (Congo); Bob Brozman & Ledward Kaapana (USA/Hawaii); Jali Musa Jawara (Guinée); Najma (England); 3 Mustaphas 3 (Szegerely); Hijas Del Sol (Equatorial Guinea); Euis Komariah & Yus Wiradiredja (Indonesia); Thomas Mapfumo (Zimbabwe); Los Camperos De Valles (Mexico); Les Negresses Vertes (France); Virunga (Kenya).

England's *Folk Roots,* America's *Rhythm* magazine, and the Web's *RootsWorld* are the *Time, Newsweek,* and *U.S. News & World Report* of world music, and this phenomenal, two-volume/four-disc set commemorates the first-named's 20th anniversary. The real phenomenon is that *"fROOTS"* has the inclination or, especially, the time, to stand still for a portrait—but this revelatory collection maintains the forward momentum of preserving traditions from the past and propelling them into the future that the magazine has pledged its existence to, and the portrait is of course not of the entity itself but of the myriad artists it has always bowed out of the picture to spotlight. Split between the extended family of Anglo musics in whose epicenter of England the magazine is headquartered, and the staggering remainder of the world over which *fROOTS* has spread its observation branches, this anthology, insightfully selected by *fROOTS* editor Ian Anderson (no, not *that* one), the kind of look-no-further crash course novice world-music adventurers dream of. You may, of course, have to look a *bit* far, since at this writing the collection is available only as an import—but an important one indeed, with a range that could be overwhelming but is merely breathtaking, and a sequence that could dizzy but merely awes. The menu is so full that Native America and Aboriginal Australia aren't as conspicuous by their absence as they might be; scout elsewhere in this book to fill those crucial gaps, but otherwise, fall in step behind the album-covers' mascot—an anonymous, determined man crossing the world

seemingly on foot in search of its sonic wealth—pack an extra empty suitcase, and get rooting!

Adam McGovern

Folkstyles of Mexico and Colombia ♪♪♪♪ (Music of the World, 1994, prod. Bob Haddad, Robert Browning)

Mexico, Colombia, USA
genre: Jarocho, bambuco, pastillo, corrido, ranchera

Los Pregoneros del Puerto (Mexico); Maria Olga Piñeros & Aires Colombianos (Colombia); Lydia Mendoza (USA).

This disc offers an interesting juxtaposition of artists and styles. Los Pregoneros del Puerto are from the Mexican state of Veracruz and play the *jarocho* style, which developed in that coastal area, influenced by strong regional ties to Spain and by the music brought to its shores by African slaves. Maria Olga Piñeros & Aires Colombianos are from the *altiplano,* the high plains of Colombia in South America, and formed in 1983 to perform the traditional love songs and dances of that region. Lydia Mendoza is an artist of almost legendary reputation along the Texas/Mexico border, not only for the quality of her singing and playing of the 12-string guitar, but also because when she began her solo career in the 1930s she was one of the earliest female singers to rise to prominence in the music of the *frontera,* as the border region is known. This somewhat unusual combination of musics on one disc works well and illuminates crosscurrents among the styles and musicians.

Kerry Dexter

Global Meditation ♪♪♪♪ (The Relaxation Company, compilation prod. Brooke Wentz)

International
genre: World music, meditative music, healing music

Numerous artists including: Anonymous 4 (USA); Master Musicians of Jajouka (Morocco); Kecak Ganda Sari (Bali); Nusrat Fateh Ali Khan (Pakistan); Bibayak Pygmies of Minvoul (Gabon); U. Srinivas (India); Shartse College of Ganden Monastery (Tibet); Soliman Gamil (Egypt); Farafina (Burkina Faso); Zakir Hussain (India); Gnawa Musicians of Marrakesh (Morocco); Glen Velez (USA); Milton Cardona (Cuba); Guo Brothers (China); Philip Boulding (Ireland); Kudsi Erguner & Suleyman Erguner (Turkey); Djivan Gasparyan (Armenia).

Meditational music has gotten a bad rap in the wake of the new-age phenomenon, but this fabulously diverse collection shows that contemplative reflection is a universal practice that goes much deeper than merely sitting in a lotus position and chanting a few "om"s. Although well worth purchasing in its boxed form, the set is broken down stylistically into four CDs, each of which is also available separately. *Voices of the Spirit* explores the many ways in which the human voice is used around the world, from Balinese monkey chants and the polyphonic singing of Gabonese Pygmies to Anonymous 4's glorious English Ladymass (another song form usually involving *a cappella* vocal polyphony, sung exclusively by females). *Harmony and Interplay* features a variety of impressive ensemble efforts, including the trance-like repetition of the Gnawa Musicians of Marrakesh's "Chabako," the serene gentility of mandolin virtuoso U. Srinivas's "Ghananayakam," and the rapturous crescendos of Nusrat Fateh Ali Khan's "Haq Ali Ali Haq." *The Pulse of Life* showcases master percussionists like Zakir Hussain, Glen Velez, and Milton Cardona, pointing out the transcendental healing powers of rhythm, while *Music from the Heart* is the most peaceful of the bunch, focusing primarily on meditative melodies designed to elevate the listener to a higher plane of consciousness. Whether you choose just one or two CDs or the entire inspired set, this is one compilation you'll want to share with your friends—though you may have trouble letting it out of your sight!

Bret Love

Global Voices 🎵🎵🎵🎵 (Music of the World, 1998, compilation prod. Bob Haddad)

International
genre: World vocal music

Numerous artists including: Purna Das Baul (India); Seleshe Damessae (Ethiopia); the Garcia Brothers (Native America); Anatoli Kuular (Tuva); Dumisani Maraire (Zimbabwe); Ganden Monastery Monks (Tibet); Hassan Hakmoun (Morocco); the Sterling Jubilee Singers (USA); Folk Scat (Bulgaria); Tico da Costa (Brazil); Boukan Ginen (Haiti); the Dagar Brothers (India); Bayram Bilge Toker (Turkey); Ora Sittner (Yemen); Orlando "Puntilla" Rios and Nueva Generación (Cuba); Maria Olga Piñeras (Colombia); Karnataka College of Percussion (India); Zvonimir Croatian Choir (Croatia); SoVoSó (USA).

This fabulous three-CD box set collects songs from a variety of world-music traditions, all of which celebrate the awesome emotive power of the human voice. Divided into three categories—traditional songs, sacred songs, and contemporary vocal music—each disc is a remarkable journey of discovery. The traditional tracks are a delight, with Maria Olga Piñeras's simple Colombian folk-song standing in stark contrast to the Karnataka College of Percussion's dazzlingly complex *konakkol* (or spoken rhythms). The contemporary music is also exceptional, with *a cappella* groups like Folk Scat and SoVoSó showing the directions vocal music may be heading in the future. But perhaps best of all is the disc of sacred songs, which only reinforces the ancient, widely held belief that singing is the closest one can get to God. Whether it's the Zvonimir Croatian Choir's captivating harmonies or Hassan Hakmoun's riveting Moroccan meditations, this incredibly spiritual CD

will take you higher than anything this side of Sly Stone. With 43 songs, nearly half of which were either previously unreleased or available only on hard-to-find labels, this outstanding "Vox Set" is a must-have for those enraptured by the sound of the human voice.

Bret Love

Gypsy Passion 🎵🎵🎵🎵 (Narada, 1997, executive prod. Michael Sullivan)

International
genre: Flamenco, new flamenco, guitar

Oscar Lopez (Chile); Jesse Cook (Canada); Armik (USA); Lara & Reyes (Mexico/USA); Ottmar Liebert (Germany); Strunz & Farah (Costa Rica/Iran); Eric Tingstad (USA); Romero & Torea (USA); Govi (Germany/India); Bruce Becvar (USA); Miguel de la Bastide (Trinidad); Willie & Lobo (USA/Germany).

In *flamenco puro,* the ancient Gypsy music of Andalusia in southern Spain, the guitarist, the singer, and the dancer form the structure of the song, each playing a part as the drama unfolds. In "new flamenco," which has come out of the caverns to the stages, clubs, and streetcorners of the world, the guitarist must find other partners. For the artists on this disc, that has meant exploring different world musics and bending them to support the voice of flamenco; it has meant finding kinship in instruments far removed from the landscape of southern Spain; it has meant finding new ways to relate to dancers and other guitarists as the music evolves. These artists come from diverse backgrounds, which the listing of countries above only begins to suggest. Most have traveled the world to study and perform this art that fascinates them, and they have backgrounds ranging from traditional flamenco dance to American rock 'n' roll. It's not really necessary to know any of that, or anything about flamenco, to appreciate this album as a vigorous and fresh Latin-based instrumental collection, but for those who wish to delve, this disc is an excellent starting place for learning about the best of the ways this tradition is evolving.

Kerry Dexter

Harpestry 🎵🎵🎵🎵 (Imaginary Road, 1997, prod. Diana Stork, Dawn Atkinson)

International
genre: Harp, Latin, Celtic, contemporary, new-age

Rudiger Oppenheim (Germany); Maureen Brennan (USA); Ann Heyman (USA); Deborah Henson-Conant (USA); Michele Sell (USA); Janet Harbison (Scotland); Cynthia Mowrey (USA); Luis Felipe Gonzales (Venezuela); Geist (USA); Derek Bell (Ireland); Patrick Ball (USA); Andrea Piazza (Italy); Andreas Vollenweider (Switzerland).

In ancient times, the idea of the harp began when someone plucked the string of a hunting bow and liked the sound. From that grew different sizes, styles, strings, and playing arrangements over the centuries. Each of the artists on this disc was drawn to the magical and musical diversity of the instrument, and that's a theme the producers have chosen to emphasize by selecting work in many styles played on variations of the harp from the grand (the kind you usually see in the orchestra) to the Celtic (usually small and sometimes portable), as well as the Tyrolean harp, the Venezuelan version of the instrument, and the electro-harp.

Kerry Dexter

Harvest Song: Music from around the World Inspired by Working the Land ♫♫♫♫ (ellipsis arts . . . , 1995, compilation prod. Larry Blumenfeld, Jeffrey Charno)

International
genre: Harvest songs

Expresión (Peru); Lazaro Ros (Cuba); Ali Farka Touré (Mali); Shanghai National Music Orchestra (China); Fiddlers 5 (Scotland); Gnawa Musicians of Morocco (Morocco); Nico Saquito (Cuba); Mississippi John Hurt (USA); Efe Pygmies (Congo); Alison Kinnaird & Christine Primrose (Scotland); Pueblo Indians (USA); Pena Branca & Xavantinho (Brazil); Ona Hanako & Kamata Kansui (Japan); Dagarti Musicians (Ghana); Tsinandali Choir (Georgia).

This eclectic compilation of harvest songs was a smart idea. The exoticism of "world music" makes it easy to overlook the common ground—in both senses of the term—and functionality that folk traditions share, the oldest being prayer for a good harvest and gratitude if it is delivered. Most of the human race still works the land, so songs related to farming are utterly relevant to their everyday lives. Bluesman Mississippi John Hurt labored most of his life as a farm hand. As with many in this trade, Hurt's tenuous sustenance depended on the changeable forces of nature and the whims of a master, so when he sings "What will the harvest bring?" on "Blue Harvest Blues," although he sang for his amusement, the message is full of uncertainty. Harvest songs are falling into disuse as farming becomes increasingly mechanized and its practitioners work in solitude rather than as a group. Japanese farmers' thousand-year-old tradition of singing while scything grass was no doubt an uplifting pastime, but is now no more than a dimly remembered tradition. Thankfully this mesmerizing chant can be heard on "Akita Kusakira Uta" ("A Mowing Song of Akita"). Similarly, when the Efe Pygmies sing "Meli-e Estele-u Odu-Ene" ("The Forest That Was Producing Gold"), it is with nostalgia for the abundance of what used to be their Ituri rainforest. *Harvest Song* reminds us of the central role farming once played in all our lives. Recipes

for hulled corn soup seem tangential, but overall the accompanying book of photos and information is superb.

David Poole

Her Song: Exotic Voices of Women from around the World ♫♫♫ (Shanachie, 1996, compilation prod. Bette Timm)

India, Ireland, Hungary, Norway, Israel, Czechoslovakia, USA
genre: World music

Ofra Haza (Israel); Najma (England); Talitha MacKenzie (USA); Flesh and Bone (USA); Pura Fé (Native America); Jai Uttal featuring Lakshmi Shankar (India); Kirsten Bråten Berg (Norway); Irén Lovász (Hungary); Joanne Shenandoah (Native America); Etti Ankri (Israel); Solas featuring Karan Casey (Ireland, USA); Nada Shakti (Czechoslovakia).

This compilation of female artists isn't too diverse, just too inconsistent. While Israeli star Ofra Haza and Indian chanteuse Najma deliver fine performances (culled from Shanachie albums that fans will already have), others simply don't cut it: the new-age approach of Native troubadour Joanne Shenandoah; the overly synthesized track with Indian singer Lakshmi Shankar, composer Jai Uttal, and late trumpeter Don Cherry; Pura Fé's Native American/scat hybrid. Still, Karan Casey shines, confirming her stature as a new Irish diva. And the idea of a truly "world" music comes into view with Talitha MacKenzie's Gaelic and Middle Eastern blend, as well as the Tibet-inspired chant of Czech singer Nada Shakti.

Bill Ellis

Holding Up Half the Sky: Voices of Celtic Women ♫♫♫♫ (Shanachie, 1997, compilation prod. Edward Haber)

Ireland, Scotland, USA
genre: Celtic

Máire Ní Bhraonáin (County Donegal, Ireland); Cilla Fisher (Scotland); Tríona Ní Dhomhnaill (County Donegal, Ireland); Niamh Parsons (Ireland); Gay Woods (Ireland); Talitha MacKenzie (USA); Mary Black (Ireland); Dolores Keane (Ireland); Karan Casey (County Waterford, Ireland); Maura O'Connell (Ireland); Cathie Ryan (USA); Maighread Ní Dhomhnaill (Ireland); Cathy Jordan (Ireland); Sylvia Barnes (Scotland); Karen Matheson (Scotland).

Most of the recognized (and recorded) Celtic singers of the LP age were men, but as Irish and Scottish music went worldwide and the technology changed, the women got to rightly strut their stuff. Some of the most gorgeous voices of any style stem from the Celtic female tradition. Part of a series whose African, Asian, and reggae volumes are reviewed on pages 842, 856, and 914, respectively, *Voices of Celtic Women* is a who's who of many of this century's finest female vocalists in their field. Máire Ní Bhraonáin (a.k.a. Maire Brennan, Enya's sister) has been singing for almost three decades and is one of the most visible Irish voices today, both with Clannad and as a solo artist. Starting with the Fisher Family in 1965, Cilla Fisher continues to add her Scottish brogue successfully to Irish traditional lyrics. Tríona Ní Dhomhnaill, meanwhile, adds harmonium and clavinet to her voice (for over ten years now featured in Nightnoise, after a stint with seminal Irish group the Bothy Band and other illustrious résumé-builders). A student of Scottish Gaelic *puirt-a-beal* (instrumental music), Talitha MacKenzie uses her voice as the instrument; she was part of the experimental duo Mouth Music before going solo. In common with most of the women mentioned above, Mary Black and Dolores Keane are two artists carrying on the traditions of renowned Irish singing families. Likewise, Maighread Ní Dhomhnaill sings here alongside her sister Tríona; their father was famous song collector Aodh Ó Domhnaill, and aunt Neillí Ní Dhomhnaill had much to do with getting women singers to the forefront. The voice of Capercaillie, Karen Matheson sings Gaelic songs of the Scottish Highlands, and it runs in the family with her too, as her grandmother was a well-known singer from the Gaelic-speaking island of Barra in the Outer Hebrides. Bubbling over with folk songs, laments, epic tales, and new interpretations of tradition—not to mention many more fine vocalists than are even cited here—*Voices of Celtic Women* enables every one of these artists to be heard at her best. Always and forever, Celtic vocal music is an earthly treasure, rendered delightfully unearthly by the female voice.

Stacy Meyn

Holding Up Half the Sky: Women in Reggae: Roots Daughters ♫♫♫♫ (Shanachie, 1996, compilation prod. Randall Grass)

Jamaica, USA
genre: Roots reggae

Marcia Griffiths (Jamaica); Judy Mowatt (Jamaica); Althea and Donna (Jamaica); Rita Marley (Jamaica); Hortense Ellis (Jamaica); The I-Threes (Jamaica); Sister Carol (Jamaica); Barbara Paige (USA); Dhaima (USA); Marcia Aitken (Jamaica); Joy White (Jamaica); Nadine Sutherland (Jamaica); Senya (Jamaica); Shan-I Benjamen (Jamaica); the Mad Professor (England).

The 1970s are considered to be the "golden" period for female reggae performers, as they finally were able to start establishing their own careers outside of rumored (and often actual) romantic links to studio owners and male reggae successes. *Roots Daughters* (part of a series whose African, Celtic, and Asian volumes are reviewed on pages 842, 913, and 856, respectively) arrays the jewels of roots reggae and Rastafarian vocals. The famed I-Threes triumvirate and even non-Jamaican singers are included in this required reading of reggae. Marcia

Griffiths (of said I-Threes) demonstrates why she has collected just about every Jamaican music award there is, with her mighty "Steppin' out of Babylon." Judy Mowatt (also an I-Three), the "Rasta Queen" with a 30-year music career, delivers the reggae "dawtas" anthem "Black Woman." Rita Marley, while known primarily for her marriage to and work with Robert Nesta "Bob" Marley, started out as one of Coxsone Dodd's Soulettes in the early 1960s, before helping to complete, you guessed it, the I-Threes. She delights us with the pro-spliff stance of "One Draw," a deserved solo hit in the aftermath of Bob's untimely death in 1981. Rocksteady immortal Alton Ellis's sister Hortense checks in with "Jah Mysterious Works," mixed by Scientist at King Tubby's and backed by an early version of the Roots Radics—reggae royalty all. Called the "Black Cinderella," social activist and actress Sister Carol bases herself in New York and raises consciousness with such songs as "International Style." Nashville native Dhaima was the first Rasta woman to have her own TV show in Jamaica in the 1970s, and she expresses the importance of new generations in "Ina Jah Jah Children." With "Narrow Minded Man" Marcia Aitken takes a feminist turn on the nearly misogynistic "Woman Is Like a Shadow" by the Meditations. Even with all the headiness (political, spiritual, and herbal) of the tracks, "Sister" Shan-I Benjamen reminds you to "Look After Your Structure" (i.e. eat right and exercise). The Mad Professor's "Structure Dub" is a male-created bonus track, and there are even more gems in the collection proper. Forget that "behind every great man" adage—the ladies of *Roots Daughters* are right out front.

Stacy Meyn

Invocations: Sacred Music from World Traditions ♫♫♫♫ (Music of the World, 1998, prod. Martha Lorantos, Richard Klecka, Bob Haddad)

International
genre: Sacred world music

Hassan Hakmoun (Morocco); Dumi Maraire & Ephat Mujuru (Zimbabwe); Etuh Ensemble (Nigeria); Karnataka College of Percussion (India); Cornel Pewewardy (Native America); Qhapaq Negros (Peru); K. Subramaniam & Trichy Sankaran (India); Nueva Generación (Cuba); Bayram Bilge Toker (Turkey); Tadashi Tajima (Japan); Alliance West Singers (Native America); Jalal Zolfonun (Iran).

Interested in world music but just don't know where to start? You could do a lot worse than this fine compilation of sacred and spiritual music, which includes songs from the Afro-Cuban, Muslim, Hindu, Sufi, Buddhist, African, Syncretic Christian, and Native American traditions. Opening with "Sala Alla 'Alik Dima Dima," a rhythmically rapturous song from Morocco's Gnawa tradition by Hassan Hakmoun, the album includes healing music, sacred hymns, meditational pieces, devotional songs, and trance-inducing melodies that all hold an important place in their respective cultures. Whether it's K. Subramaniam's dazzling *veena* melodies on "Sarasasamadana," the throbbing pulse of the Alliance West Singers' haunting "Memorial Song," or the peaceful serenity of Tadashi Tajima's *shakuhachi* flute on "Sagari Ha (Falling Leaf)," all of the music here has one thing in common—a remarkable propensity for lifting your spirits to ecstatic new heights.

Bret Love

Islands ♫♫♫ (Putumayo World Music, 1997, compilation prod. Dan Storper)

International
genre: Coladeira, zouk, bomba, morna, bolero, hapa haole, reggae

Tito Paris (Cape Verde); Kali (Martinique); José González y Banda Criolla (Puerto Rico); Maria Alice (Cape Verde); Los Tradicionnales de Carlos Puebla (Cuba); D'Gary and Jihé (Madagascar); Tarika (Madagascar); Bobby and Angelo (Tahiti); Hapa (Hawaii); Quito Rymer (Tortola).

With no other linkage than the title, this 10-song compilation contains a diverse range of musical styles from Pacific, Atlantic, and Indian Ocean islands. All of the selections have a gentle island sway to them, and if the album lacks adventurousness it does present a very pleasurable listen to a variety of cultures that have evolved in very insular and thus somewhat unique ways. Not that they are immune from influences—Jamaica (perhaps the major island omission, though amply covered elsewhere) is latently represented by the Bob Marley–tinged songs of Quito Rymer from tiny Tortola, and José González exhibits the multicultural ingredients that form Puerto Rico's *bomba* style. On the other hand, Madagascar's two entries reflect a culture only recently joining the international scene. Distinctive packaging and informative artist notes make this a useful CD for the budding world-music enthusiast, but, with the constraints inherent in a roster of only 10 tracks, veteran music globetrotters may find the range a little shallow and too easy-listening in nature. In either case, though, this makes a pleasantly tropical background for the cocktail hour or daydreaming in the hammock.

Derek Rath

Klezmania: Klezmer for the New Millennium ♫♫♫ (Shanachie, 1997, prod. Henry Sapoznik)

USA, Germany
genre: Klezmer

Aufwind (Germany); Ahava Raba (Germany); Boiled in Lead; the Klezmatics; Don Byron; the Paradox Trio; Nathanson and Coleman; Frank London; Kapelye; New Orleans Klezmer All-Stars; New Klezmer Trio; Godchildren of Soul; Twistin' the Freylakhs. (All artists are from USA except where noted otherwise.)

Klezmer is a music of both identity and incorporation—in the five centuries of its existence it has served as a rallying point for the preservation of Jewish heritage as well as adding ideas and styles from the nations and cultures with which it has come into contact. As a dance music, it's also been a way to share the culture with others and encourage them to join in. This is a collection of what producer Henry Sapoznik calls "edge klezmer," a snapshot of the state of explorations in the style near the end of the 20th century. These range from the jazz-influenced music of Don Byron to the beach-klezmer of Twistin' the Freylakhs and the fusion of funk, rap, and old-time *freylich* rhythms by Godchildren of Soul.

Kerry Dexter

Klezmer Music: A Marriage of Heaven and Earth ♫♫♫♫ (ellipsis arts . . . , 1996, compilation prod. Michal Shapiro)

USA, Hungary, Germany, Canada
genre: Klezmer

Alicia Svigals (USA); the Chicago Klezmer Ensemble (USA); Di Naye Kapelyen (Hungary); La'om (Germany); Andy Statman (USA); Budowitz (USA); Deborah Strauss and Jeff Warschauer (USA); the Klezmatics with Ray Musiker (USA); the Flying Bulgar Klezmer Band (Canada); Naftule's Dream (USA); Brave Old World (USA).

As with other fine releases on the ellipsis arts . . . label, this disc is clearly a labor of love and does a great job of capturing the richness of its subject's living spirit, from folk-based roots to swing and rock influences. As the lengthy (64 pages!) and entertaining liner notes explain, the klezmer band is traditionally heard at Jewish weddings. For Jews this celebration is filled with both joy and remembrance: joy at lives being joined, and remembrance of the hardships that have come before (the smashing of the glass at the end of the ceremony commemorates the destruction of the original temple). The music on *Heaven and Earth* embodies this complex character. The better-known, clarinet-centric brand of klezmer is represented here by such crack outfits as the Chicago Klezmer Ensemble ("Mazeltov") and Budowitz ("Behusher khusid"), while the more daring Naftule's Dream stretches the boundaries with the jazzy musical narrative "The Black Wedding." The inclusion of marvelous pieces by violinists Alicia Svigals and Deborah Strauss illustrates that the clarinet does not have to be the predominant instrument in the klezmer band, and the sound can be reflective as well as boisterous. Without a doubt, an excellent introduction to wonderful music.

Tim Sheridan

***Klezmer Pioneers: European and American Recordings,
1905–1952*** 𝄞𝄞𝄞𝄞 (Rounder, 1993, compilation prod. Henry
Sapoznik, Dick Spottswood)

USA, Poland, Hungary
genre: Klezmer

Art Shryer's Orchestra (USA); Abe Elenkrig's Yidishe Orchestra
(USA); Sam Musiker and His Orchestra (USA); Belf's Rumanian
Orchestra (Romania); Mishka Tsiganoff (USA); Abe Schwartz's
Orchestra (USA); Joseph Cherniavksy and His Yiddish-American
Jazz Band (USA); Kandel's Orchestra (USA); Mihal Viteazul (Ro-
mania); Alexander Olshanetsky Und Zein Orkester (USA); Josef
Solinski (Poland); Israel J. Hochman's Jewish Orchestra (USA);
Joseph Moskowitz (USA); Dave Tarras (USA); Abe Katzman's
Bessarabian Orchestra (USA).

After World War II, only a handful of European klezmer musicians remained alive to play the old Jewish instrumental music.
Almost none of the Jewish generation born in the United States
had taken up the old styles, preferring jazz and other forms of
American popular music. By the 1960s, it appeared that
klezmer had disappeared. Then, in the '70s, a small group of
Jewish musicians in the folk music scenes of New York, Boston,
and San Francisco became interested in their own roots. Because little of the music had been written down and there was
scarce source material, the discovery of caches of 78-rpm
records in Jewish archives was like striking gold. It allowed a
new generation of musicians to learn the klezmer modes, performance styles, ornamentation, and rhythms. Henry Sapoznik
was probably the most important figure in the klezmer revival
because of his access to the YIVO Institute for Jewish Research's musical collections, his knowledge of Yiddish, and his
career in researching, recording, and performing traditional
music. Although this compilation came out in 1993, too late to
play a role in that first klezmer revival, it's guided by one of the
movement's mainstays, Sapoznik himself, and is an important
document of the richness and diversity of this music in the
early part of the 20th century.

Aaron Howard

Latcho Drom (Soundtrack) 𝄞𝄞𝄞𝄞 (La Bande Son/Virgin
France, 1993, prod. Alain Weber, Armand Amar)

**India, Egypt, Turkey, Romania, Hungary, Yugoslavia,
France, Spain**
genre: Gypsy music

Talob Khan Barna (Rajasthan/India); Daoud Langa
(Rajasthan/India); Gazi Khan Manghaniyar (Rajasthan/India);
Musicians of the Nile (Egypt); Nicolas Naegelen (Turkey);
Hasam Yarim Dunya & His Ensemble (Turkey); Taraf de Haïdouks
(Romania); Nicolas Naegelen (Turkey); Rostas Szabina (Hun-
gary); Kek Lang Ensemble (Hungary); Marichka (Yugoslavia);
Dorado et Tchavolo (France); the Gypsies of Badojoz (Spain); La
Caita (Spain).

The Rom people, know as Gypsies in the West because of the
mistaken idea that they originated in Egypt, left Rajasthan,
India, over 2,000 years ago. No one knows why this mass migration took place. Some theorize that the Rom were employed
as mercenaries by the ancient Indian empire, and as they
fought their way West, they forgot their original mission. Be
that as it may, the Rom language never developed a written
form, and their traditions and myths were passed down as
lyrics, making music an important part of their cultural identity.
Everywhere the Rom go they are welcomed as musicians, while
at the same time they are stereotyped and persecuted as
thieves, fortune tellers, prostitutes, and ne'er-do-wells. When
French Rom director Tony Gatlif set out to film a history of his
people's migrations, he decided to use music rather than words
to tell the story, and in the process created as great a film (and
album) for listeners as for historians. The musicianship on the
disc is all world-class, and despite the divergent traditions represented, a strong thread of Rom rhythm and melancholy runs
throughout this excellent collection.

j. poet

***The Library of Congress Endangered Music Project,
Vols. 1–6*** 𝄞𝄞𝄞𝄞 (Rykodisc, 1993–98, prod. Mickey Hart,
Alan Jabbour)

**Brazil, Belize, French Guiana, Suriname, Peru,
Jamaica, Colombia, Panama, Bali (Indonesia), Madura
(Indonesia), Kangean Islands (Indonesia), Senegal,
Mali, Liberia, Ghana, Nigeria, Ivory Coast, Guinea,
Zaire (Congo), Burkina Faso, Haiti, Trinidad, Cuba**
genre: Abaimahani, arumahani, berusu, punta, aleke, songe,
lonsei, mato, awasa, kumanti, susa, papa, tambu, gamelan
semar pegulingan, gender wayang, gamelan gong, gamelan
gong kebyar, kecak, côco, rojão, congos, maracatú, waltz,
catopê, viçungos, xangô, Tambor de Mina, babacuê, pajelança,
praiá, samba, carimbú, bumba-meu-boi, Santería, Candomblé,
Shango, Vodou

Dozens of individuals and ensembles, only intermittently credited.

Begun in 1993 and still in progress today, *The Endangered
Music Project* series aims to dig out archival recordings of
global traditional music and bring them to light for study and
enjoyment. An ideal locus for such work can be found at the
American Folklife Center of the Library of Congress, where the
Archive of Folk Culture holds 50,000 recordings of traditional
music, spanning both the globe and the entire history of
recording. The producers of the series, Alan Jabbour and Grateful Dead percussionist/world-music patron Mickey Hart, have
clearly pulled off a coup by combing this archive, blowing the
dust from some forgotten gems of ethnomusicology, and bringing them back to life with classy graphics and engrossing liner
commentary by experts in the field.

The discs released at this writing are as follows: *The Spirit Cries: Music from the Rainforests of South America and the Caribbean*, which samples the chants and songs of several peoples bound by their common ways of rainforest life; *Music for the Gods: The Fahnestock South Sea Expedition, Indonesia*, the recordings of two adventuring brothers who traveled the Indonesian archipelago on a schooner outfitted with two Presto 16-inch disc-cutting machines and several miles of microphone cable for remote recording; *The Discoteca Collection: Missão de Pesquisas Folclóricas*, a selection from a field expedition carried out by a Brazilian folkloric archive; *L.H. Corrêa de Azevedo: Music of Ceará and Minas Gerais*, from the field recordings of a Brazilian composer who collected music in remote parts of his country with the help of the Library of Congress; *The Yoruba/Dahomean Collection: Orishas across the Ocean*, which compiles the work of several seminal researchers into the trans-Atlantic religious diaspora rooted in the West African Yoruba people's belief in *orisha* deities (a faith known by such names as *Vodou* and *Santería* in the West); and *The Arthur S. Alberts Collection: More Tribal, Folk, and Café Music of West Africa*, music from recordist Alberts's legendary 1949 whirlwind tour through West Africa in a customized Jeep. (The last-named album is reviewed on its own on page 840.)

The series is appealing in its diversity. Perhaps its high-water mark so far is the *Yoruba/Dahomean Collection*, with its chants, songs, and trance beats from the Caribbean and South America, which trace the importation and evolution of West African orisha worship since the era of the slave trade. This diaspora is documented in thrilling fashion. From the strikingly percussive attack and bitonal drum interlock of the Brazilian rites to the melodic pause that heralds the arrival of possession in Trinidad, the album's intensity is breathtaking. While the brevity of the cuts may in some cases be an artifact of the crude recording technology available to the original researchers, this suits the modern attention span nicely, and those not satiated can check out the "Suggested Reading and Listening" notes included in the liner text.

Jeffrey Muhr

Mali to Memphis: An African American Odyssey ♫♫♫♫
(Putumayo World Music, 1999, compilation prod. Dan Storper)

Mali, USA
genre: American blues, Malian Bambara, Malian Fulani and Songhai traditions

Amadou et Mariam (Mali); Habib Koíte (Mali); Rokia Traoré (Mali); Boubacar Traoré (Mali); Lobi Traoré (Mali); Baba Djan (Guinea); Jesse Mae Hemphill (USA); Muddy Waters (USA); Eric Bibb (USA); Guy Davis (USA); John Lee Hooker (USA); Taj Mahal (USA).

This carefully constructed set, half by musicians from Mali and Guinea and the other by American bluespeople of several generations, celebrates the African *griot* (musical storyteller) tradition that all 12 tracks seem to share. There's certainly the same fiery presence of spirit in Amadou Bagayoko's guitar solo during "Mon Amour, Ma Cherie" as you find in the trance riffs of John Lee Hooker, who follows with "I'm in the Mood," or Jessie Mae Hemphill, represented by the eerie tones of "Standing in My Doorway Crying." The real payoff comes as you begin to discern traces of American blues in the music of the contemporary African groups. Who's influencing whom? Does it matter? Perhaps it's as Malian guitarist Lobí Traoré explains, that when he first heard American blues on the radio he made an instant connection with the music of his ancestors. With musical genres being chopped into ever tighter, more restrictive compartments, it's nice to run across a concept compilation that suggests otherwise.

Leland Rucker

Men with Guns (Hombres Armadas) ♫♫♫ (Rykodisc, 1998, prod. Mason Daring)

International
genre: Pan-Latin, Afro-Antillean

El General; Jeanie Stahl; Lito Barrientos; El Chane; Ramon Ropain; Toto la Momposina; Banda Once de Enero; Les Miserables Brass Band; Susana Baca; and an ensemble band whose members are: Duke Levine, Nancy Zeltzman, Jamey Haddad, Billy Novick, Gus Sterling, Frank London, Arturo Offarill, Lewis Kahn, Bobby Sanabria, Andrew Gonzalez, and Evan Harlan.

Create music for a Latin American country that doesn't exist—that was the challenge posed by director John Sayles when he envisioned the soundtrack for his film *Men with Guns (Hombres Armadas)*. He wanted to suggest Latin America in general rather than anchor the story in any one culture. The result is a Latin mix that, while giving brief nods to the music of Mexico and the *frontera* (Texas-Mexico border), returns again and again to Afro-Antillean musical figures, rhythms, and vocal styles. Does it succeed? As a Pan-Latin fusion, no—it's too rooted in one aspect of the music. As an atmospheric collection that supports the film and is strong enough to stand on its own as well, though, it works.

Kerry Dexter

The Music of Islam, Vols. 1–15 ♫♫♫♫♫ (Celestial Harmonies, 1997, prod. David Parsons, Prof. Margaret Kartomi)

International
genre: Arabic

Saleh Abdul Baqi (Yemen); H. Hafiz Kani Karaca (Turkey); Al-Sheikh Nail Kesova (Turkey); Fawzy Fawzy and the Aswan Troupe for Folkloric Arts (Egypt); Ahmed Baqbou (Morocco); Lotfi Jormana (Tunisia); Agha-Ye Sadjadifard (Iran); Ustad Bary Ali Khan (Pakistan).

The Music of Islam is the crowning achievement of engineers David and Kay Parsons' career, and the most outstanding release on the Celestial Harmonies label. It is a joy to own, with beautiful calllgraphy on velum, extensive liner notes, and a wood box to hold the 15 volumes. The scope of the project is vast: a survey of the sacred, folk, and classical music of the Islamic world, which comprises one-fifth of the earth's population, and a stretch of countries that begins in North Africa and sweeps across the Middle East through South Asia and into the Pacific. What unites these countries is their common faith in one god, Allah, and their use of the Arabic holy book the *Qur'an* (Koran).

Volume 10: Qur'an Recitation is the best starting point if you want to buy a single volume. It opens with the "Ezan" or call to prayer, a chant that will be familiar to anyone who has visited an Islamic country or been to a mosque. The volume continues with recitations of *surahs,* or chapters, from the Qur'an. Each surah is sung in richly embroidered chants firmly grounded by strict rules. In fact, as with other spiritual practices associated with music by modern Westerners (i.e. Tibetan prayer or Gregorian chant), the reciters themselves do not consider this music, but devotion. However, one of the reciters, Nail Kosova, is an excellent composer as well as singer. He can be heard with his ensemble of whirling dervish musicians on *Volume Nine: Mawlawiyah Music of the Whirling Dervishes* and *Volume 14: Mystic Music through the Ages.* Through repeatedly chanting the many names of God the dancers whirl themselves into an ecstatic trance. Similarities to the Dervish tradition can be heard in the ceremony of the Aissaoua brotherhood on *Volume Five: Aissaoua Sufi Ceremony,* recorded live in a Moroccon courtyard. As the men go into a trance, they call out, while the women make high-pitched ululations called *zgharit,* which punctuate the steady music by invoking the prophet. Another recording of trance music, made in Marrakesh, *Volume Six: Al-Maghrib/Gnawa Music* features members of the Gnawa brotherhood, Morocco's black African population. They believe that the trance state helps the audience exorcise the *jinn* (spirits) that afflict them.

Morocco's musical connections with neighboring Spain are explored in *Volume Seven: Al-Andalus/Andalusian Music*; Andalusia is a region of the latter nation once occupied by the former. The resultant fusion of Arab and European styles has since been adopted as the court music of Morocco. Its elaborate

melodies are played here on *oud* (lute), violin, flute, *tabla* (a goblet drum not to be confused with the double-headed Indian percussion instrument of same name), and tambourine. Moving East past Algeria, to Tunisia, on *Volume Eight: Folkloric Music of Tunisia* we hear the *mizwid* (bagpipe), which provides a constant drone above the percussion (including a variety of drums and a tambourine), while flowing melodies interact with leader Lotfi Jormana's voice. *Volume 13: Music of Pakistan* spotlights Ustad Bary Fateh Ali Khan singing classical *ragas* accompanied on string instruments and drums. The raga predates Islam; in Pakistan the lyrics have been adapted from Sanskrit to Urdu and the subject has been modified to praise of Allah. As is a genre custom, the three ragas here are intended to complement the mood of different times of day—"Early Morning," "Early Evening," and "Evening." *Volume 15: Muslim Music of Indonesia*, a two-disc set, surveys a variety of ensembles from the Indonesian island of Sumatra which play music dramatically different from the more familiar Indonesian *gamelan* (tuned percussion) orchestra. Disc One explores prayer and drumming in the West of the island, including a "Tiger capturing song." Disc Two visits the North to record a female chorus of body percussionists and a clan of male frame-drum players.

Ofra Haza popularized Yemenite folk song, and those familiar with her fast-paced pop music might imagine traditional folk outfits to be more sedate. Far from it—on *Volume 11: Music of Yemen*, Nizar Ghanem's ensemble of singers armed with ouds pick up the beat fueled by *qat* (a leaf that when chewed serves as a stimulant). The classical traditions of Sana'a, the town where these songs were recorded, are close to Andalusian music—the oud sounds similar to a Spanish guitar, and the virtuosity of the finger-picking recalls flamenco. Most arresting are the variety of rhythms displayed: a limping beat offset from the central rhythm; the brittle skittering of the *reqq* (tambourine); and the drive of the tabla—Yemenite music is nearly always accompanied by dancing, and it is easy to hear why. Fans of Haza will also not be disappointed by Iman Ibrahim's powerful soprano.

Volume One: Al-Qahirah explores Egyptian classical music, while *Volume Two: Music of the South Sinai Bedouins* features desert nomads, a Bedouin chorus recorded in a dry river-bed in the South Sinai desert under a full moon, accompanied by oil drums and *rababah* (one-stringed fiddle). The Bedouin love songs reflect the local landscape and culture—unrequited love is characterized as extreme thirst, while a lover is compared to a gazelle, and women are addressed in song as "he" to preserve their reputation. *Volume Three: Music of the Nubians* records another dislocated Egyptian ethnic group, with its own distinct language, whose homeland of Nubia was flooded by the Aswan dam. A soloist or chorus is accompanied by hand-claps, *tambura* (lyre), and *tar* (frame-drum). These folk songs are the roots for Ali Hassan Kuban's popular Nubian blues.

Volume 12: Music of Iran was recorded with some trepidation—a fear fueled by the Western media's negative portrayal of Iran—but turned out to be the engineers' most positive experience of this musical odyssey. A trio perform classical Persian *dastgah-ha* (suites) on *santur* (zither), *kemenche* (lute), and frame-drum. The dastgah-ha are in two styles, the love poetry of the *shur* and the bittersweet *homayoun*. The smallest Arab country, Qatar, is represented on *Volume Four: Music of the Arabian Peninsula* by a duo of expatriate Iraqis who perform on oud and tabla.

The Parsons' *Music of Islam* joins Jean Jenkins and Poul Rovsing Olsen's earlier, hard-to-find, and similarly vast *Music in the World of Islam* as a tremendous cultural resource. It should dispel some of the misunderstanding and animosity that has lingered between the Western and Islamic worlds for many centuries, and introduce many Western ears to the joys of both music in praise of God and the folk song that co-exists with it in these cultures.

David Poole

Musica de la Tierra ♪♪♪♪ (Music of the World, 1992, prod. Bob Haddad)

Ecuador, Haiti, Brazil, Colombia, Mexico, Argentina
genre: Latin

Tahuantinsuyo (Ecuador/Peru); Marc Ribot (Haiti); Tico da Costa (Brazil); Atahualpa Poalasin (Colombia); Los Pregoneros del Puerto (Mexico); Maria Olga Piñeros (Colombia); Aires Colombianos (Colombia); Los Troveros Cuyanos (Argentina).

This is a tasteful sampler from Mexico, Haiti, and South America that provides an introduction to vocal and instrumental music beyond the mainstream. Both contemporary and traditional songs are included.

Kerry Dexter

Musical Instruments of the World ♪♪♪♪♪ (Le Chant Du Monde/Harmonia Mundi, 1990)
Voices of the World: An Anthology of Vocal Expression
♪♪♪♪♪ (Le Chant Du Monde/Harmonia Mundi, 1996, prod. Hugo Zemp)

International
genre: Vocal, traditional

Musical Instruments of the World: 36 artists or ensembles, most uncredited, but including: Nicolas Masemokombo (Central African Republic); Chatur Lal (India); Monks of Dharmsala (Tibet); Kammu Khan (India); Aurelio Porcu (Italy); Sadiq

(India). *Voices of the World*: 103 artists or groups, including: Imas Permas (Indonesia); Kondé Kouyaté (Guinea); Bac Nam Ngu (Vietnam); Aïcha Redouane (Saudi Arabia); Salah el-Din Mohammed (Saudi Arabia); Pepe de la Matrona (Spain); Roman el Granaino (Spain); Erik Marchand (France); Marcel Guillou (France); Zhang Junqiu (China); Aldubin Garcia (Honduras); Takni Dance Group (USA); Moinuddin Dagar (India); Aminuddin Dagar (India); Namsir (Mongolia); Afsâne Ziâ'i (Iran); Hoseyn Omumi (Iran); Yûsuf al-Tâj (Lebanon); Wiriyi (Australia); Buwai-jigu (Australia); Non'ikeni (Solomon Islands); Sherha Mahamad (India); Nang Suy (Laos); Cerenamid (Mongolia); Mary Travers (Canada); Mbenzele Pygmies (Central African Republic); Mabu (Papua New Guinea); Mahamat Chaïmi (Chad).

Musical Instruments of the World began as an LP, kicking off the most exemplary and essential series in world music. Expanded for this CD reissue and featuring extensive liner notes, the collection covers the four major categories of instruments: chordophones (plucked or bowed strings), membranophones (drums), aerophones (blown instruments), and idiophones (solid percussion), offering virtuoso solo performances to spotlight the tone and potential of each. There is no more useful introduction for understanding the nuts and bolts of world music. Listeners will be able to distinguish between a box zither and board zither, how the lute is played in Chad, and the nuances of lute playing in Azerbaijan. Often in ensemble music it is hard to distinguish particular instruments and familiarize oneself with their sound, but here are isolated examples of the harp-lute, goblet drum, wooden trumpet, and more, which allow the listener space to make sense of each instrument. Likewise, for anyone interested in the sheer variety of vocal expression, the 103 cultures represented on the three-CD companion volume *Voices of the World* provide the best starting point bar none. Its first two discs examine vocal techniques like calls, cries, and clamors, while the third covers polyphony under themes like "echoes and overlapping" or "drones and ostinati." The accompanying book offers a crash course in the science of song and details about the performers. *Voices of the World* stands above almost any other world-music album as a must-have, celebrating the glorious qualities of the human voice. Together with *Musical Instruments of the World* it draws from humankind's greatest archives of ethnic music to provide the widest range of traditional styles ever presented on one compilation. Look out for *Dances of the World*, forthcoming at presstime.

David Poole

Narada World: A Global Vision ♪♪♪♪♪ (Narada, 1997, prod. various)

International
genre: World music, contemporary instrumental

Connie Dover (USA); Alasdair Fraser (Scotland); Mary McLaughlin (Ireland); Orion (Belgium); Shelley Phillips; Scartaglen

(USA); John Whelan (Ireland/USA); Jesse Cook (Canada); Miguel de la Bastide (Canada); Carlos Guedes (Venezuela); Nando Lauria (Brazil); Oscar Lopez (Canada); Bernardo Rubaja (Argentina); Rumillayta (Bolivia); Tomas San Miguel; Bill Miller (Mohawk/USA); R.Carlos Nakai (Navajo/Ute/USA); Ayub Ogada (Kenya); Michael Pluznick (USA); Samite (Uganda); Michael Whalen (USA); Hans Zimmer (USA); Ancient Future (USA); Riley Lee (Australia); Vas (Iran/USA); Richard Warner (USA).

Listening to this collection is like wandering the streets of a crossroads market town—here a vibrant splash of color, a strange pattern, there a familiar word, just ahead an enticing smell and a lively conversation. The music was selected to mark the 15-year anniversary of recording company Narada Media, and it does indeed show how the taste and vision of the people of this organization have led them to seek out and combine unusual and perhaps unclassifiable music talents and give them a place to be heard. It's a good starting point to learn about what thoughtful, mostly melodically oriented artists of many traditions are doing to connect their music with contemporary life. It's also an interesting survey of the choices one recording company has made.

Kerry Dexter

A Native American Odyssey ♫♫♫♫ (Putumayo World Music, 1998, compilation prod. Dan Storper)

Canada, USA, Mexico, Brazil, Peru, Bolivia
genre: Native American

Kashtin (Montagnais/Canada); Tudjaat (Inuit/Canada); Andrew Vasquez (Apache/USA); Bill Miller (Mohican/USA); Burning Sky (Navajo-Ute/USA); Jerry Alfred & the Medicine Beat (Techone/Canada); Jaramar (Huave/Mexico); Binni Gula'za (Zapotec/Mexico); Marlui Miranda (Amazon/Brazil); Regional Vermelho e Branco (Amazon/Brazil); Los Incas (Andean/Peru); Bolivia Manta (Andean/Bolivia); Expresión (Andean/Peru).

"Brazilian Indian music is a cultural secret, nobody knows it," states featured South American singer Marlui Miranda, but her comment could accurately describe much of the music presented on *A Native American Odyssey*, an exceptionally well-researched collection of indigenous American styles. From Northern Canada's Inuit throat singers to the poignant harmonies of Peruvian panpipe-*charango* (Andean mandolin) duets, this anthology documents the fresh-sounding complexities of both traditional and contemporary Native repertoire. Helping to preserve Zapotec-language ballads, the vocal-guitar trio Binni Gula'za demonstrates that lover's quarrels are timeless on "Ni'bixi Dxi Zina (The Tantrum)," while the tornado-like force of Montagnais duo Kashtin is completely current, as the Robbie Robertson–arranged "Akua Tuta" melds crooning violin with thunderdrums to potent effect. Sensational soulsters Burning Sky ignite on "Native Funk," while the flute-laced guitar musings of Bill Miller on "Ghost Dance" are positively haunting. In the end, this

compilation succeeds because it embraces artists who are essentially influenced by the positive contributions of other cultures, rather than relying on strictly traditional tunes; this makes for much more compelling listening.

PJ Birosik

The New Feeling ♫♫♫♫ (Celestial Harmonies, 1996, executive prod. Eckart Rahn)

International
genre: International

Marcio Montarroyos (Brazil); Michael Askill (Australia); Omar Faruk Tekbilek (Turkey); Takadja (Senegal, Guinea, Canada); R. Carlos Nakai (Native America); David Hudson (Aboriginal Australia); Fong Naam (Thailand); Inkuyo (Bolivia); Paul Horn (Australia); Pham Van Ty (Viet Nam); Mariachi Cobre (Mexico); Coolangubra (Australia); Rafael Jimenez (Spain); Synergy (Australia); Perry Silverbird (Native America).

This stunning compilation offers not only an ideal world-music starter kit, but a welcome way of spotlighting a world-music patron whose contributions make her as significant as any artist in this volume. As a major broadcaster in Australia, Jaslyn Hall is a pioneer popularizer of world music; her personal track selection and encyclopedic but lively liner notes make *The New Feeling* more than a mere label sampler—even though Celestial Harmonies' thoughtfully adventurous catalog makes it hard to go wrong. With the seasoned instincts of the top alternative radio programmer she is, Hall maintains interest and balances diversity across the collection's multi-continent roster and its 79 minutes. You can find almost every track here on other Celestial Harmonies albums, but the compilation stands alone as an exceptionally eye-opening (while not overwhelming) intro to many timeless traditions and daring recombinations.

Adam McGovern

Planet Soup ♫♫♫♫ (ellipsis arts . . . , 1995, compilation prod. Angel Romero)

International
genre: International

Numerous artists including: Oleg Fesov (Tajikistan); Kongar-ool Ondar (Tuva) & Paul Pena (USA); La Cucina (England); Bustan Abraham (Israel); Akira Satake (Japan); Astor Piazzolla (Argentina); Värttinä (Finland); Ali Hassan Kuban (Nubia); Aisha Kandisha's Jarring Effects (Morocco); Enzo Rao (Italy); Mynta (Sweden); Gualberto (Spain); Aquarela Carioca (Brazil); Bolot Bairyshev (Mongolia); Wolfstone (Scotland); Tananas (South Africa); Jim Bowie & Badal Roy (USA/India).

If you're at all interested in a fusing of the world's traditions to create some forward-thinking theme-music for the global village, this eye-opening three-CD box set is custom-made for you. Living up to its highly appropriate title, this scrumptious sonic stew uses a dash of folksy, traditional melodies and a pinch of the most modern, dance-floor-pounding grooves to create a simmering 40-song collection without a single lame ingredient to spoil the broth. Inspired collaborative recipes abound, from the matching of Paul Pena's Delta-blues riffing with Kongar-ool Ondar's masterful Tuvan throat-singing on "The Ballad of Cher Shimjer (What You Talkin' About?)," to the marriage of Jim Bowie's Bengali-style banjo with Badal Roy's nimble *tabla* drum rhythms on the remarkably inventive "Rinpoche's Rag." But this groovy stylistic gumbo also features a number of self-contained musical hybrids, including Wolfstone, which blends traditional Scottish music with elements of jazz fusion and rock; and Aisha Kandisha's Jarring Effects, a band that creates a riotous mix of Moroccan pop, dub reggae, and hip-hop. One of the best world-music collections ever whipped up, this delicious dish proves that it really is a small world after all.

Bret Love

Polish Village Music 𝄢𝄢𝄢𝄢 (Arhoolie, 1995, compilation prod. Dick Spottswood)

Poland, USA
genre: Folk music

Orkiestra Majkuta; Stefan Skrabut; Bruno Rudzinski; Karol Stoch Muzyka Góralska; Tarnowska Orkiestra Stasiaka; Stefan I Wladyslaw Macón; Frank P. Kawa; Wladyslaw Dombkowski; Aleksander Brokowski; Józef Brangel; Ignaci Podgórski; Józef Kallini; Piotr Kopacz; Orkiestra Jana Dranki; Wiejska Ork. Kmiecia; Makowska Ork. Dzialowego; Waclaw Turchanowicz; Stanislaw Mermel; Baczkowski Wiejska Orkiestra; Wladyslaw Polak; Jan Wanat; Polska Orkiestra Pod Bialem Orlem; Frank Dukla. (All artists are from Poland.)

Back in the 1920s and '30s, when these recordings were made in New York and Chicago, sound technology was still in its infancy. But because of its novelty it was in time to capture remarkably honest performances of music before American pop aesthetics overtook the world. That's why whatever these tracks lack in fidelity (despite the producers' commendable job of removing excess surface noise) is a small price to pay considering the priceless music they preserve. The wonder and genuineness of these performers, many of them new arrivals to the United States, still comes through. Take for example Karol Stoch's throaty bellow on the ballad "Ostatki No Podhalu (Last Evening in Podhale)." It's a unique listening experience as it skitters across a pulsing melody. Also impressive is the range of styles and forms featured on the disc: waltzes, mazurkas, polkas, and various other dances keep the music consistently interesting. Listen for the klezmer flavors in Frank P. Kawa's polka "Pijal Ojciec, Pije Ja (Father Drinks, So Do I)," with its lighthearted clarinet line. But of particular note are unusual curios like Alek-

sander Brokowski's comic song "Cialy do Boxy (Charlie in Jail)." While the compilation is not for all tastes, with screechy orchestras and unusual tonal ranges, the songs are surely a treasure trove of oral history and storytelling for those who speak Polish—or are intrigued to experience a rich cultural tradition as close to its source as modern technology will allow.

Tim Sheridan

Ramble to Cashel: Celtic Fingerstyle Guitar, Volume 1
𝄢𝄢𝄢𝄢 (Rounder, 1998, prod. Stefan Grossman, Pat Kirtley)
The Blarney Pilgrim: Celtic Fingerstyle Guitar, Volume 2
𝄢𝄢𝄢𝄢 (Rounder, 1998, prod. Stefan Grossman, Pat Kirtley)

International
genre: Celtic fingerstyle guitar

Martin Simpson (UK); Steve Baugman (Malaysia/USA); Pierre Bensusan (Algeria/France); Duck Baker (USA); Tom Long (USA); Pat Kirtley (USA); El McMeen (USA).

Fiddle, pipes, flutes, button accordion, harp, and whistle are all instruments found in Celtic music. Until less than a century ago, the guitar—especially the solo acoustic guitar—was rarely heard in the genre. Inspired variously by the folk-music revival in the United States and Britain, the style of blues player Big Bill Broonzy, the bluegrass and string-band music of the Appalachian South, and their own quest for exploring how music works, the seven men who play on these discs have become pioneers in creating a voice for Celtic ideas on the solo guitar. The tracks collected here represent the several major groups of Celtic song: the march or martial music; the ballad; the dance tune; and, in a category by itself, the complex folk and classical mix found in the compositions of Turlough O'Carolan. Within the context of melody and rhythm basic to Celtic music, each man creates his own strong instrumental signature.

Kerry Dexter

The Secret Museum of Mankind, Vols. 1–8 𝄢𝄢𝄢𝄢𝄢
(Shanachie/Yazoo, 1995–99, prod. Pat Conte)

International
genre: World music

Hundreds of artists and ensembles from over 100 countries, including every continent except Australia and Antarctica.

Delightfully turning the conventional wisdom of sober folkloric study on its head, *The Secret Museum of Mankind* series, with its antique photography, sketchy and cryptic notes, and unorthodox track sequencing, is a chaotic and exhilarating throwback to the days of pure exoticism in "ethnic" music listening. Compiled by inveterate record collector, musician, and philosopher Pat Conte from his own library of rare 78s, the series gathers global traditional and popular music that was recorded at a time when world music was not taken seriously by many scholars as a topic worthy of study. Ironically, such music was preserved chiefly by mavericks and record companies in search of marketable "ethnic" sounds for niche audiences such as expatriate communities and armchair adventurers.

Conte was led to his role as compiler of the series by his own unabashed attraction to exotica. As a child, he collected stamps, listened avidly to shortwave radio, and was fascinated by distant countries. Soon he was collecting records as well, and eventually he got together with Shanachie Records founder Richard Nevins to propose remastering rare 78s of global artists onto CD. Apparently everything truly coalesced for Conte when he ran across a strange tome called *The Secret Museum of Mankind*. A coffee-table book of foggy provenance, originally published in the early 1940s, it contains odd antique photos of "primitive" peoples culled from postcards, journals, and who-knows-where, captioned with quaint and slightly lurid descriptions. It was from this book that Conte drew the specific concept for the CD series.

The music on that series' five numbered volumes is organized not by country, region, or even theme, but is instead ordered, as Conte put it in an interview for *Sing Out* magazine in 1999, "purely for enjoyment, purely for listening." Conte arranged the tracks to provide continuities and surprises in the listening experience, a process he describes as "trying to sequence these elements into a little journey." Though the series violates some of the "rules" of academic folkloric study by valuing aesthetics over objective presentation and by giving wonderment priority over understanding with regard to traditional peoples, no one can say that listening to *The Secret Museum* isn't exciting and joyful, like discovering an old travel journal or a dusty pile of weird records in the attic.

To date, the series includes the following: five general volumes called *The Secret Museum of Mankind: Ethnic Music Classics 1925–48, Vols. 1–5*; and, in a concession to logical organization, three excellent regional volumes, *The Secret Museum of Mankind: The Music of Central Asia: Ethnic Music Classics 1925–48*, *The Secret Museum of Mankind: The Music of North Africa: Ethnic Music Classics 1925–48*, and *The Secret Museum of Mankind: The Music of East Africa: Ethnic Music Classics 1925–48*. In addition, a proto-*Secret Museum* album of Malagasy music, *The Music of Madagascar* (Shanachie/Yazoo, 1995, prod. Pat Conte), was released prior to the start of the series proper.

From his cluttered basement in suburban New York City, Conte continues to champion the preservation of recorded global music. He also hosts the weekly *Secret Museum of the Air* on the area's WFMU radio station, which is available in Real Audio on the web at www.wfmu.org. For those interested in the *Secret Museum* book, a new black-and-white edition is available from Gibbs Smith Publishing.

Jeffrey Muhr

Shaman, Jhankri and Néle: Music Healers of Indigenous Cultures 𝄞𝄞𝄞𝄞 (ellipsis arts . . . , 1997, prod. Pat Moffitt Cook)

International
genre: Shamanism, ritual healing

Babaji (India); Koshalya (India); Ram Tmapa (Nepal); Suni Ram (Nepal); Don Agustin Rivas-Vasquez (Peru); Micheline Forestal (Haiti); Kanucas Littlefish (Native North America); Maestro Demosdenes Ramirez Hurtas (Panama); Darkiking Don Alejandro (Peru); Alexander Tavakay (Tuva); Pointing Father (St. Vincent); Mara'akame (Native North America); Jorge K'in (Mexico); Nele Buna Inayenikidili (Panama); Anselmo Palma Cruz (Mexico); Kangsinmu (Korea); Steve Old Coyote (Native North America); Simon Eliet (Panama); Phawo Nyidhon (Tibet).

This box set, containing a 96-page book and CD, surveys the key role of music in rituals of healing around the world. Much healing music has its deepest roots in the practice of *shamanism,* an ancient form of religion in which a visionary adept, called a *shaman,* mediates with the spiritual world on behalf of a community, curing disease, healing social dislocation, insuring success in hunting and farming, or performing other civic services by invoking and harnessing cosmic forces. One of the shaman's most important tools is music; the drum beat, chant, or song is used as a vehicle to travel into ecstatic states of consciousness in which these forces may be contacted. In the case of the healing ritual conducted by Peruvian shaman Don Agustin Rivas-Vasquez, for instance, a complex sequence of music (with a bit of help from hallucinogenic *ayahuasca*) brings the participants to deep, healing changes in consciousness. In the opening of this ceremony, called "Anticuna" (also the title of the album's corresponding track), Don Agustin's soothing "whooshing" and tuneful chant powerfully convey a sense of gentle compassion. During a Nepalese healing ritual (and recording here) called "Giving Energy to a Dying Woman," *jhankri* shaman Ram Tmapa, transported by the sound of clattering bells and cymbals as well as his own "intense vocalizations," becomes possessed and issues instructions to a patient on how to carry out a cure. Eighteen other tracks touch upon musical healing practices in locations as diverse as India, Haiti, the Caribbean, South America, and Korea. The accompanying book, written by cross-cultural music scholar Pat Moffit Cook, expands on each track, and stands on its own as interesting reading.

Jeffrey Muhr

Trance 1 & Trance 2 *ⅢⅢ* (ellipsis arts . . . , 1995, prod. Jeffrey Charno, David Lewiston)

International
genre: Trance, religious, ganawi, odalan, dhrupad

Sadreddin Özçimi (Turkey); Necati Çelik (Turkey); Arif Erdebil (Turkey); Kemal Karaöz (Turkey); Monks of the Shartse Dratsang Garden Monastery (Tibet); Ustad N. Zahiruddin Dagar (India); F. Wasifuddin Dagar (India); Naqshbandi Sufis (Turkestan); Halima Chedli Ensemble (Morocco); Abdenbi Binizi Ensemble (Morocco); unidentified temple festival musicians (Bali).

While the recent profusion of "trance" CDs may scare off listeners who wisely wish to steer clear of superficial marketing fads, they need not shy away from *Trance 1* and *Trance 2*, which offer genuinely exciting music. Produced by veteran world-music archivist David Lewiston, the CDs are packaged with a hardcover mini-book that supplements the music nicely with pleasant coffee-table design, color photographs, and entertaining and well-researched text. While the title "Trance" might not do justice to the profuse experiences encompassed by the music—which include religious ecstasy, meditation, and possession—the text does a good job of making the tracks intelligible by putting them into their cultural context.

The first disc contains music from a Mevlevi rite, a Tibetan chant, and an Indian *dhrupad* song. The best of these may be "Perde Kaldirma," a song of Turkey's Mevlevi order of Sufis, also known as the "whirling dervishes" for their ecstatic spinning dances. Based on an ancient Sufi ceremonial vocal form, the track layers a wailing *ney* flute over a lusciously repetitive backing sounded out by *oud* and *tambour* lutes and a frame drum. The soaring, passionate flute lines, which "play between the notes" in imitation of the human voice, really put the listener's hair on edge. The second volume includes music of the Naqshbandi Sufis of Central Asia; a pair of excerpts from Moroccan ritual songs called *ganawi* (a.k.a. *Gnawa*); and a final track made up of excerpts from a Balinese *odalan* temple festival. A standout is "Touhami Dikr," which consists of music for a ritual called the *hadra ganawi*. This ritual is notable for the fact that it is held by and for women only. Its purpose is to drive out *jinn* or evil spirits from a person or household; those attending the ritual are often propelled into a trance by the music. The track begins with a vocal chant over an insistent drum rhythm, but soon intensifies as an additional set of drums kicks into action, augured by a shrill exclamation from one of the vocalists. One can clearly sense how dancing to this driving music for an hour or more could send participants into another state of consciousness. *Trance 1* and *Trance 2*, with their generous 70-minute CDs, clever design, and enjoyable text, offer the listener a similar divergence from the ordinary.

Jeffrey Muhr

Trance Planet Vols. I–IV *ⅢⅢ* (Triloka, 1995–98, compilation prod. Tom Schnabel)

International
genre: World music, meditative music, trance music

Numerous artists including: Orchestra Marrabenta Star de Moçambique (Mozambique); Zakir Hussain (India); Nusrat Fateh Ali Khan (Pakistan); Jai Uttal (USA); Cesaria Evora (Cape Verde); Sainkho (Tuva); Hassan Erraji (Morocco); Ayub Ogada (Kenya); Madredeus (Portugal); Loop Guru (England); Rachid Taha (Algeria); Tulku (Native America); Djivan Gasparyan (Armenia); Ali Akbar Khan (India); Vox (International); Radio & Television Symphony Orchestra of Bosnia-Herzegovina (Bosnia-Herzegovina); Muzsikas featuring Márta Sebestyén (Hungary).

This extensive four-CD series, released over the course of as many years, is perfectly suited for fans of the ellipsis arts . . . label's *Global Meditation* and *Planet Soup* box sets (reviewed on page 911 and 920, respectively). The premise is virtually the same: collect hypnotic tracks by a variety of celebrated and lesser-known world-music artists from countries spanning the globe, then compile them on CDs that flow rather seamlessly from start to finish. Unfortunately, although *Trance Planet* features a number of brilliant songs over the course of its 53 total tracks, it ultimately fails to match the thematic unity of the aforementioned classic collections. There seems to be little rhyme or reason to the way in which these CDs were sequenced, and the remarkably flimsy liner notes (which in most cases only offer one or two sentences about each track) fail to add any clarification. Fortunately for Triloka, the music is generally spectacular, and the fact that each CD is sold separately may be a blessing in disguise. The most consistent of the bunch is Volume I, which opens with the Orchestra Marrabenta's gorgeous, plaintive lament "Nwahulwana" and goes on to include powerfully moving tracks from Indian *tabla* drum master Zakir Hussain, Pakistani *qawwali* legend Nusrat Fateh Ali Khan, Cape Verdean vocalist Cesaria Evora, and Moroccan fusionist Hassan Erraji. An admirable effort, and though it's hardly the best in its class, it's still a great introduction for world-music novices.

Bret Love

Voices *ⅡⅡ* (Alula, 1996, prod. Ulrich Balss)

International
genre: Vocal

The Bulgarian Voices Angelite (Bulgaria); Huun-Huur-Tu (Tuva); Hamlet Gonashvili (Georgia); Saraband (Europe, Middle East); Mikhail Alperin and Sergey Starostin (Ukraine); Trinovox (Italy); Tam Echo Tam (France, Guayana, Morocco, Congo); Yoon & Bunka Earborn (Korea, Germany).

The suggestion on *Voices*' packaging to "File under World & New Age" is unfortunately apt for one-half of the recording—

Trinovox manipulates its Gregorian chant with synthesizers and contributes to a mess of styles on the syrupy "Scolopendra"; Saraband claims to unite East and West, but offers little more than poorly executed medieval repertoire. What saves *Voices* from the new-age waste pile is the distinctive sustained high notes of the Bulgarian Voices Angelite meshing superbly with the deep rumble of the Tuvan throat-singers Huun-Huur-Tu on the collaborative "Fly, Fly My Sadness." More throat-singing (the phenomenal style in which a single vocalist can emit more than one note at a time) is provided by Ukrainian Sergey Starostin, whose voice creates overtones for a traditional Russian chorus. The late Hamlet Gonashvili, from the Georgian Rustavi Choir, also solos on a very slow-tempo hymn rising over the hum of a chorus. The Afro-Belgian *a cappella* quartet Tam Echo Tam succeeds where counterpart Zap Mama fails in providing a compelling fusion of European and African vocal styles.

David Poole

Women of Spirit ♫♫♫♫ (Putumayo World Music, 1998, prod. various)

International
genre: International

Capercaillie with Sibeba (Scotland/Guinea); Fortuna (Brazil); Groupe Oyiwan (France/Sudan); Coco Mbassi (Cameroon); Susana Baca (Peru); Cassandra Wilson (USA); Tarika (Madagascar); Sibongile Khumalo (South Africa); Rasha (Sudan); Ani DiFranco (USA); Ima Galguen (Spain); Savina Yannatou (Greece); Toshi Reagon/Bernice Johnson Reagon (USA).

It begins with "Inexile," a life-giving collaboration between Scotland's Capercaillie and Guinea's Sibeba that could single-handedly get America's budding imported-music market more enthused about sounds from outside the majority Celtic culture. Indeed, opening eyes to natural if unexpected musical connections is the overriding theme here. Brazil's Fortuna fortuitously exposes more of us to Latin Jewish music (it exists!). Sudan's Groupe Oyiwan will pleasantly remind the casual world-music listener of the popular Oumou Sangare from across the same continent. The contribution from Cameroon's Coco Mbassi stacks up to the best of New World balladry, while the urgency of Tarika's startling Malagasy rap speaks louder than language. Statesiders will know the deep drama of Cassandra Wilson, and welcome the lofting loveliness of Sibongile Khumalo from South Africa. Ani DiFranco and the extended family of Sweet Honey in the Rock need no introduction, but this collection performs that much-deserved service for Peru's Susana Baca, Sudan's Rasha, and the Mediterranean's Ima Galguen and Savina Yannatou. Every compilation from the prolific Putumayo contains at least a few gems, but this one's a goldmine from start to finish. And with proceeds benefiting

grass-roots women's empowerment groups worldwide, it continues a company tradition of making you feel good in more ways than one.

Adam McGovern

Women of the World: International ♫♫♫♫♫ (Putumayo World Music, 1995, compilation prod. Dan Storper)
Women of the World: Celtic ♫♫♫♫♫ (Putumayo World Music, 1995, compilation prod. Dan Storper)
Women of the World: Celtic II ♫♫♫♫♫ (Putumayo World Music, 1997, compilation prod. Dan Storper)

International
genre: International

International: Amoya (Mozambique); Margareth Menezes (Brazil); Angélique Kidjo (Benin); Des'ree (England); Karen Matheson (Scotland); Jacqueline Farreyrol (Reunion Islands); Sophia Arvaniti (Greece); Toni Childs (USA); Yehudit Ravitz (Israel); Amina (Tunisia); Riské (Haiti); the Dalom Kids (South Africa). *Celtic*: Máire Brennan (Ireland); Máighread Ní Dhomhnaill (Ireland); Mary Black (Ireland); Karen Matheson (Scotland); Connie Dover (USA); Máire Breatnach (Ireland); Maura O'Connell (Ireland); Fiona Joyce (Island of Jersey); Nancy McCallion (USA); Máiread Ní Mhaonaigh (Ireland). *Celtic II*: Natalie MacMaster (Canada); Christina Crawley & Kerstein Blodig (Ireland/Germany); Eileen Ivers (USA); Mary Jane Lamond (Canada); Susan McKeown & the Chanting House (Ireland); Marcy D'Arcy & the Prodigal Sons (Scotland, Ireland, England); Eithne Ní Uallachain (Ireland); Pamela Morgan (Canada); Annie Grace & Lynn Morrison (Scotland); Karen Matheson (Scotland); Julie Murphy (England); Sharon Murphy with Whisp (Ireland).

The temptation is always there for international compilations to try and take in everything in one gulp, rather than just select out everything that works in an introductory taste. *Women of the World: International*, however, is secure enough in its conversance with its subject matter to be able to pick and choose, sounding much more like a cohesively conceived album than a disjointed sampler. Great sensitivity and savvy is shown in weaving a consistent whole from some widely divergent sources. Standouts are a matter of thoughtful pacing rather than hasty mismatch, and they include Margareth Menezes's reeling fanfares of festivity, Angélique Kidjo's slow-burning tribal techno-soul, and Des'ree's deeply grooved trans-oceanic reggae, as well as the relaxed grandeur of Toni Childs's processional chant/anthems, the gathering power of Amina's slinking Arabic rhythms and after-echoed future-synth textures, and the crystalline lilt of Riské's and the Dalom Kids' polychromatic chorales. Meeting the challenge of leaving you wanting more without leaving something to be desired is what distinguishes this compilation from many of its counterparts. Its own partner, *Women of the World: Celtic*, came at a time of Celtic rule on the U.S. world-music charts—a situation that would undermine the point of that umbrella genre if it only extended listeners' horizons to what sounds most familiar to the Euro majority. But this collection enjoyably and intriguingly accentuates the distinctive. There's a handful of artists who try too hard to preempt typecasting through MOR melodrama and world-mush of the piped-in Pier One Imports variety (one of Máire Brennan's tracks and all of Mary Black's and Fiona Joyce's, to name names). Otherwise, the music soars, most often when it retains the courage of its characteristics, as in the sonic modernism and timeless melancholy of Máighread Ní Dhomhnaill's mid-19th-century melody or Karen Matheson's anthemic semi-plugged roots-rock; the never-outdated energy of Connie Dover's, Nancy McCallion's, and Máiread Ní Mhaonaigh's spirited jigs, reels, and nursery tunes; and the proto-ambient, indomitable homeland spirituality of the spectral choirs on Brennan's other track, the majestic "Mighty One." Perhaps not coincidentally, many of these highlights are sung in native tongues. But traditionalism needn't become another

formula; the endearing Country & Caribbean Celtic of Maura O'Connell's "Stories" has an unaffected internationalism that branches out while escaping the small-world-after-all syndrome in its own way. Just as the *International* volume of the series shows how compatible a world of music can be, this one shows how diverse a single corner of it can be, and matches the companion volume's high quality. The *Celtic* sequel busted other category confines, at the height of Lilithmania giving disc-space to some of the "Women in Music" who don't fit male major-label execs' pre-existing pigeonholes and stereotypes. The results are refreshing, matching up jazz, hip-hop, Latin, and ambient flavors of Celtic to straighter strains of one of Europe's truly thriving tribal musics. Influenced but never diluted, the Putumayo catalog consistently leads the way while remembering the origin.

Adam McGovern

Books

Now that you've seen the world with this guide, you can visit some of its places and learn more about some of its people with the following books on specific cultures', countries', and artists' music. Below you'll also find many of the best general-interest guides, which include good world-music reading.

Africa (The Garland Encyclopedia of World Music, Vol. 1)
Ruth M. Stone and James Porter, ed. (Garland Publishing, 1997)

Africa O-Ye!: A Celebration of African Music
Graeme Ewens (Da Capo Press, 1992)

African American Music; A Chronology: 1619–1995
Hansonia Caldwell (Ikoro Communications, Inc., 1996)

African Rhythm: A Northern Ewe Perspective
V. Kofi Agawu (Cambridge University Press, 1995)

African Rhythm and African Sensibility
John Chernoff (University of Chicago Press, 1981)

African Stars: Studies in Black South African Performance
Veit Erlmann (University of Chicago Press, 1991)

Afropop! An Illustrated Guide to Contemporary African Music
Sean Barlow, Banning Eyre, and Jack Vartoogian (Chartwell Books, 1995)

All-Music Guide: The Experts' Guide to the Best CDs, Albums & Tapes
Michael Erlewine, Vladimir Bogdanov, Chris Woodstra, and Stephen Thomas Erlewine, ed. (Miller Freeman, 1997)

All-Music Guide to Rock
Michael Erlewine, Vladimir Bogdanov, and Chris Woodstra, ed. (Miller Freeman, 1995)

Ancient Echoes: The Anasazi Book of Chants
Mary Summer Rain (Hampton Roads Publishing Co., 1993)

And the Beat Goes On: An Introduction to Popular Music in America, 1840 to Today
Michael Campbell (Schirmer Books, 1996)

Angels in the Mirror: Voodoo Music of Haiti
Elizabeth A. McAlister (Relaxation Co., 1997)

The Arabesk Debate: Music and Musicians in Modern Turkey
Martin Stokes (Clarendon Press, 1992)

Australia and the Pacific Islands (The Garland Encyclopedia of World Music, Vol. 9)
Adrienne L. Kaeppler and Jacob W. Love, ed. (Garland Publishing, 1998)

Bachata: A Social History of Dominican Popular Music
Deborah Pacini Hernandez (Temple University Press, 1995)

Balinese Music
Michael Tenzer (Periplus Editions, 1998)

Barrio Rhythm: Mexican American Music in Los Angeles
Steven Loza (University of Illinois, 1993)

The Big Drum Ritual of Carriacou: Praise-songs for Rememory of Flight
Lorna McDaniel (University Press of Florida, 1998)

The Billboard Guide to Progressive Music
Bradley Smith (Watson-Guptill Publications, 1998)

Black Music of Two Worlds, Revised Second Edition
John Storm Roberts (MacMillan Library Reference, 1998)

Bob Marley: A Rebel Life: A Photobiography, 1973–1980
Dennis Morris (Plexus Publications, 1999)

Bob Marley: An Intimate Portrait by His Mother
Cedella Booker with Anthony Winkler (Penguin, 1997)

Bob Marley: Conquering Lion of Reggae
Stephen Davis (Schenkman, 1990)

Bob Marley in His Own Words
Ian McCann (Omnibus Press, 1997)

Bob Marley: Songs of Freedom
Adrian Boot and Chris Salewicz (Penguin Studio, 1995)

Bob Marley: Spirit Dancer
Bruce W. Talamon (W.W. Norton & Co., 1994)

The Brazilian Sound: Samba, Bossa Nova, and the Popular Music of Brazil
Chris McGowan and Ricardo Pessanha (Temple University Press, 1998)

Brian Eno: His Music and the Vertical Color of Sound
Eric Tamm (Da Capo Press, 1995)

Brown Girl in the Ring: An Anthology of Song Games from the Eastern Caribbean
Alan Lomax, ed. (Pantheon Books, 1997)

Caribbean Currents: Caribbean Music from Rumba to Reggae
Peter Manuel, Kenneth Bilby, and Michael Largey (Temple University Press, 1995)

Carnival, Canboulay and Calypso: Traditions in the Making
John Cowley (Cambridge University Press, 1996)

Catch a Fire: The Life of Bob Marley
Timothy White (Henry Holt & Co., 1989)

Chanting Down Babylon: The Rastafari Reader
Nathaniel Samuel Murrell, William David Spencer, and Adrian Anthony McFarlane, ed. (Temple University Press, 1998)

Choctaw Music and Dance
James H. Howard (University of Oklahoma Press, 1997)

Comparative Musicology and Anthropology of Music: Essays on the History of Ethnomusicology
Bruno Nettl, ed. (University of Chicago Press, 1991)

The Complete Guide to the Music of Bob Marley
Ian McCann (Omnibus Press, 1995)

Dancing in Your Head: Jazz, Blues, Rock, and Beyond
Gene Santoro (Oxford University Press, 1994)

Dancing Prophets: Musical Experience in Tumbuka Healing
Steven M. Friedson (University of Chicago Press, 1996)

The Dave Matthews Band: Step into the Light
Morgan Delancey (ECW Press, 1998)

A Day for the Hunter a Day for the Prey: Popular Music and Power in Haiti
Gage Averill (University of Chicago Press, 1997)

Didgeridoo: Ritual Origins and Playing Techniques
Dirk Schellberg (Samuel Weiser, 1996)

The Drummer's Path: Moving the Spirit with Ritual and Traditional Drumming
Sule Greg Wilson (Inner Traditions International Ltd., 1992)

Engendering Song: Singing and Subjectivity at Prespa Albanian Weddings
Jane C. Sugarman (University of Chicago Press, 1997)

Excursions in World Music
Bruno Nettl, ed. (Prentice Hall, 1996)

Fairportfolio—Personal Recollections of Fairport Convention from the 1967–1969 Era
Kingsley Abbott (Abbott)

Fiddling for Norway: Revival and Identity
Chris Goertzen (University of Chicago Press, 1997)

Flamenco: Gypsy Dance and Music from Andalusia
Claus Schreiner, ed. (Amadeus Press, 1996)

Folk Music of China: Living Instrumental Traditions
Stephen Jones (Clarendon Press, 1999)

From Cakewalks to Concert Halls: An Illustrated History of African American Popular Music from 1895 to 1930
Thomas L. Morgan and William Barlow (Elliott & Clark Publishing, 1993)

From Swing to Soul: An Illustrated History of African American Popular Music from 1930 to 1960
William Barlow and Cheryl Finley (Black Belt Press, 1994)

Gamelan: Cultural Interaction and Musical Development in Central Java
Sumarsam (University of Chicago Press, 1995)

Global Pop: World Music, World Markets
Timothy Dean Taylor (Routledge, 1997)

Griots and Griottes: Masters of Words and Music
Thomas Hale (University of Indiana Press, 1998)

The Hako: Song, Pipe, and Unity in a Pawnee Calumet Ceremony
Alice C. Fletcher (University of Nebraska Press, 1996)

The Heartbeat of Irish Music
Peter Woods (Roberts Rinehart Publishing, 1997)

A History of Arabian Music to the XIIIth Century
Henry George Farmer (Weatherhill, 1996)

A History of European Folk Music
Jan Ling (University of Rochester Press, 1997)

The Hundred Thousand Fools of God: Musical Travels in Central Asia (And Queens, New York)
Theodore Levin (Indiana University Press, 1997)

Imaging Sound: An Ethnomusicological Study of Music, Art, and Culture in Mughal India
Bonnie C. Wade (University of Chicago Press, 1998)

In Griot Time: An American Guitarist in Mali
Banning Eyre (Temple University Press, 2000)

In the Course of Performance: Studies in the World of Musical Improvisation
Bruno Nettl, ed. (University of Chicago Press, 1998)

Island Sounds in the Global City: Caribbean Popular Music & Identity in New York
Ray Allen, Lois Wilcken, and Peter Manuel, ed. (University of Illinois Press, 1998)

Jewish Musical Traditions
Amnon Shiloah (Wayne State University Press, 1992)

Juju: A Social History and Ethnography of an African Popular Music
Christopher Alan Waterman (University of Chicago Press, 1990)

Keeping Together in Time: Dance and Drill in Human History
William H. McNeill (Harvard University Press, 1997)

The Kingdom of Zydeco
Michael Tisserand (Arcade Publishing, 1998)

Knowing Music, Making Music: Javanese Gamelan and the Theory of Musical Competence and Interaction
Benjamin Brinner (University of Chicago Press, 1995)

Land Where Two Streams Flow: Music in the German-Jewish Community of Israel
Philip V. Bohlman (University of Illinois Press, 1989)

Last Night's Fun: In and out of Time with Irish Music
Ciaran Carson (North Point Press, 1997)

The Latin Tinge: The Impact of Latin American Music on the United States
John Storm Roberts (Oxford University Press, 1998)

Leaving Everything Behind: The Songs and Memories of a Cheyenne Woman
Bertha Little Coyote (University of Oklahoma Press, 1998)

Let Jasmine Rain Down: Song and Remembrance among Syrian Jews
Kay Kaufman Shelemay (University of Chicago Press, 1998)

Let the Good Times Roll! A Guide to Cajun & Zydeco Music
Pat Nyhan, Brian Rollins, and David Babb (Upbeat Books, 1998)

Let Your Voice Be Heard! Songs from Ghana and Zimbabwe
Dumisani Maraire and Judith Cook Tucker (World Music Press, 1997)

The Life of Music in North India: The Organization of an Artistic Tradition
Daniel M. Neuman (University of Chicago Press, 1995)

Listening to Salsa: Gender, Latin Popular Music, and Puerto Rican Cultures
Frances R. Aparicio (Wesleyan University Press, 1997)

May It Fill Your Soul: Experiencing Bulgarian Music
Timothy Rice (University of Chicago Press, 1994)

Meet Me on the Ledge: Fairport Convention—The Classic Years
Patrick Humphries (Virgin Publishing, 1997)

The Mirror of the Sky: Songs of the Bauls of Bengal
Deben Bhattacharya, trans. (Hohm Press, 1999)

Music Cultures of the Pacific, the Near East, and Asia
William P. Malm (Prentice Hall College Div., 1995)

Music in Latin American Culture: Regional Traditions
John M. Schechter, ed. (Schirmer Books, 1999)

Music in the World of Islam: A Socio-Cultural Study
Amnon Shiloah (Wayne State University Press, 1995)

Music, Modernity, and the Global Imagination: South Africa and the West
Veit Erlmann (Oxford University Press, 1999)

The Music of Africa
J.H. Kwabena Nketia (W.W. Norton & Company, 1974)

Music of Hindu Trinidad: Songs from the India Diaspora
Helen Myers (University of Chicago Press, 1998)

The Music of Israel: From the Biblical Era to Modern Times
Peter E. Gradenwitz (Amadeus Press, 1996)

The Music of the Arabs
Habib Hassan Toouma (Amadeus Press, 1996)

Music of the Common Tongue: Survival and Celebration in African American Music
Christopher Small (Wesleyan University Press, 1998)

Music of the Warao of Venezuela: Song People of the Rain Forest
Dale A. Olsen (University Press of Florida, 1996)

Music of the Whole Earth
David Reck (Da Capo Press, 1997)

The Music, Songs, & Instruments of Ireland
Karen Farrington (Thunder Bay Press, 1998)

Musica Tejana: The Cultural Economy of Artistic Transformation
Manuel H. Pena (Texas A&M University Press, 1999)

MusicHound Blues: The Essential Album Guide
Leland Rucker, ed. (Visible Ink Press, 1998)

MusicHound Country: The Essential Album Guide
Brian Mansfield and Gary Graff, ed. (Visible Ink Press, 1997)

MusicHound Folk: The Essential Album Guide
Neal Walters and Brian Mansfield, ed. (Visible Ink Press, 1998)

MusicHound Jazz: The Essential Album Guide
Steve Holtje and Nancy Ann Lee, ed. (Visible Ink Press, 1998)

MusicHound Lounge: The Essential Album Guide to Martini Music and Easy Listening
Steve Knopper, ed. (Visible Ink Press, 1998)

MusicHound R&B: The Essential Album Guide
Gary Graff, Josh Freedom du Lac, and Jim McFarlin, ed. (Visible Ink Press, 1998)

MusicHound Rock: The Essential Album Guide
Gary Graff and Daniel Durchholz, ed. (Visible Ink Press, 1998)

MusicHound Swing: The Essential Album Guide
Steve Knopper, ed. (Visible Ink Press, 1999)

Musics of Many Cultures
Elizabeth May, ed. (University of California Press, 1983)

Musics of Multicultural America: A Study of Twelve Musical Communities
Kip Lornell and Anne K. Rasmussen, ed. (Schirmer Books, 1997)

My Music Is My Flag: Puerto Rican Musicians and Their New York Communities, 1917–1940
Ruth Glasser (University of California Press, 1997)

The Mystery of Samba: Popular Music and National Identity in Brazil
Hermano Vianna (University of North Carolina Press, 1999)

National Anthems from Around the World: The Official National Anthems, Flags, and Anthem Histories from 56 Countries
Hal Leonard, ed. (Hal Leonard Publishing Corp., 1996)

The New Age Music Guide
PJ Birosik, et al. (Macmillan/Collier, 1989)

New Perspectives on Vietnamese Music: Six Essays
Phong T. Nguyen (Yale Center, 1995)

Nightsong: Performance, Power, and Practice in South Africa
Veit Erlmann (University of Chicago Press, 1995)

On Racial Frontiers: The New Culture of Frederick Douglass, Ralph Ellison and Bob Marley
Gregory Stephens (Cambridge University Press, 1999)

A Passion for Polka: Old-Time Ethnic Music in America
Victor Greene (University of California Press, 1992)

Passport to Jewish Music
Irene Heskes (Greenwood Publishing Group, 1994)

The Political Calypso: True Opposition in Trinidad and Tobago
Louis Regis (University Press of Florida, 1999)

Popular Musics of the Non-Western World: An Introductory Survey
Peter Manuel (Oxford University Press, 1990)

The Power of Black Music: Interpreting Its History from Africa to the United States
Samuel A. Floyd, Jr. (Oxford University Press, 1995)

The Power of Kiowa Song: A Collaborative Ethnography
Luke E. Lassiter (University of Arizona Press, 1998)

Raga Mala: The Autobiography of Ravi Shankar
Ravi Shankar (Intl. Book Marketing, 1999)

Reggae Bloodlines: In Search of the Music and Culture of Jamaica
Stephen Davis, Peter Simon, and Simon Peter (Da Capo Press, 1992)

Reggae Island: Jamaican Music in the Digital Age
Brian Jahn, ed. (Da Capo Press, 1998)

Reggae, Rasta, Revolution: Jamaican Music from Ska to Dub
Chris Potash, ed. (Schirmer Books, 1997)

Reggae Routes: The Story of Jamaican Music
Kevin O'Brien Chang and Wayne Chen (Temple University Press, 1998)

Reggae: The Rough Guide
Steve Barrow and Peter Dalton (Rough Guides/The Penguin Group, 1997)

Rhythm Planet: The Great World Music Makers
Tom Schnabel (Universe Publishing, 1998)

Rolling Stone Album Guide
Anthony DeCurtis and James Henke, ed., with Holly George-Warren (Random House, 1992)

Roots and Branches: A Legacy of Multicultural Music for Children
Patricia Sheehan-Campbell, Ellen McCullough-Brabson, and Judith Cook-Tucker (World Music Press, 1994)

Roots of Black Music: The Vocal, Instrumental, and Dance Heritage of Africa and Black America
Ashenafi Kebede (Africa World Press, Inc., 1995)

Roots Rock Reggae: An Oral History of Reggae Music from Ska to Dancehall
Chuck Foster (Billboard Books, 1999)

Rumba: Dance and Social Change in Contemporary Cuba
Yvonne Daniels (University of Illinois Press, 1994)

Santeria: An African Religion in America
Joseph M. Murphy (Original Publications, 1951)

Sardinian Chronicles
Bernard Lortat-Jacob (University of Chicago Press, 1995)

Silent Temples, Songful Hearts: Traditional Music of Cambodia
Sam-Ang Sam and Patricia Sheehan-Campbell (World Music Press, 1991/1998)

Stir It Up: Musical Mixes from Roots to Jazz
Gene Santoro (Oxford University Press, 1997)

The Soul of Mbira: Music and Traditions of the Shona People of Zimbabwe
Paul F. Berliner (University of Chicago Press, 1993)

Sound Alliances: Indigenous Peoples, Cultural Politics and Popular Music in the Pacific
Philip Hayward, ed. (Cassell Academic, 1998)

South America, Mexico, Central America, and the Caribbean (The Garland Encyclopedia of World Music, Vol. 2)
Dale A. Olson and Daniel E. Sheehy, ed. (Garland Publishing, 1998)

Southeast Asia (The Garland Encyclopedia of World Music, Vol. 4)
Terry E. Miller and Sean Williams, ed. (Garland Publishing, 1998)

Southern Cheyenne Women's Songs
Virginia Giglio and David P. McAllester (University of Oklahoma Press, 1994)

Spanish Music in the Twentieth Century
Tomas Marco (Harvard University Press, 1993)

Spirit of the First People: Native American Music Traditions of Washington State
Willie Smyth and Esme Ryan, ed. (University of Washington Press, 1999)

Sufi Music of India and Pakistan: Sound, Context and Meaning in Qawwali
Regula Burckhardt Qureshi (University of Chicago Press, 1995)

Swamp Pop: Cajun and Creole Rhythm and Blues
Shane K. Bernard (University Press of Mississippi, 1996)

Tejano and Regional Mexican Music
Ramiro Burr (Billboard Books, 1999)

Teton Sioux Music and Culture
Frances Densmore (University of Nebraska Press, 1992)

Tito Puente and the Making of Latin Music
Steven Loza (University of Illinois Press, 1999)

Traditional Songs of Singing Cultures: A World Sampler
Patricia Shehan Campbell, Sue Williamson, and Pierre Perron (Warner Brothers Publishing, 1997)

The Virgin Encyclopedia of Popular Music
Colin Larkin (Virgin Books, 1997)

The Voice of Egypt: Umm Kulthum, Arabic Song, and Egyptian Society in the Twentieth Century
Virginia Danielson (University of Chicago Press, 1997)

Voices in Bali: Energies and Perceptions in Vocal Music and Dance Theater
Edward Herbst and Judith Becker (Wesleyan University Press, 1998)

West African Pop Roots
John Collins (Temple University Press, 1992)

The World Centre for Jewish Music in Palestine, 1936–1940: Jewish Musical Life on the Eve of World War II
Philip Vilas Bohlman (Oxford University Press, 1992)

The World Music CD Listener's Guide: The Best on CD
Howard Blumenthal (Billboard Books, 1998)

World Music: The Rough Guide
Simon Broughton, Mark Ellingham, David Muddyman, and Richard Trillo, ed. (Rough Guides/The Penguin Group, 1995)

World Musicians
Clifford Thompson, ed. (H.W. Wilson, 1999)

World of African Music
Ronnie Graham (Pluto Press, 1995)

Worlds of Music: An Introduction to the Music of the World's Peoples
Jeff Todd Titon, Linda Fujie, David P. McAllester, Mark Slobin, and David Locke (Schirmer Books, 1996)

Zouk: World Music in the West Indies
Jocelyne Guilbault, Gage Averill, and Edouard Benoit (University of Chicago Press, 1993)

Zydeco
Ben Samdel (University Press of Mississippi, 1999)

Magazines

Check out the following publications for the best writing on recent and classic releases, news about concerts and resources, and profiles of the personalities and cultures behind the sounds. Some cover the world, some specialize in a corner of it, and some are general-interest publications with frequent world-music reporting.

WORLD AND FOLK

The Beat
Bongo Productions
P.O. Box 65856
Los Angeles, CA 90065 USA
E-mail: GETTHEBEAT@aol.com

Crossroads
3054 N. First Ave.
Tucson, AZ 85719 USA
E-mail: crossroads@xrm.com

Dirty Linen
P.O. Box 66600
Baltimore, MD 21239-6600 USA
Tel: (410) 583-7973
Fax: (410) 337-6735

E-mail: office@dirtylinen.com
Web site: http://www.dirtylinen.com

Folk Roots
Southern Rag Ltd.
P.O. Box 337
London N4 1TW
England
Tel: (020) 8340-9651
Fax: (020) 8348-5626
E-mail: froots@froots.demon.co.uk
Web site: http://www.froots.demon.co.uk

Irish Music Magazine
11 Clare St.
Dublin 2
Ireland
Tel: (01) 6624887
Fax: (01) 6624886
E-mail: irishmusic@mayo-ireland.ie
Web site: http://www.mayo-ireland.ie/IrishMusic.htm

Latin Beat Magazine
15900 Crenshaw Blvd., Ste. 1-223
Gardena, CA 90249 USA
Tel: (310) 516-6767
Fax: (310) 516-9916

Reggae & Global Music Report
P.O. Box 2722
Hallandale, FL 33008-2722 USA
Tel: (305) 933-1178
Fax: (305) 933-1077
E-mail: ReggaeRprt@aol.com

Rhythm Magazine
World Marketing Inc.
928 Broadway, Ste. 204
New York, NY 10010-6008 USA
Tel: (212) 253-7102

Sing Out!
P.O. Box 5253
Bethlehem, PA 18015-0253 USA
Tel: (610)-865-5366
E-mail: info@singout.org
Web site: http://www.singout.org

Songlines
c/o Gramophone Publications Ltd.
135 Greenford Rd.
Sudbury Hill
Harrow, Middlesex HA1 3YD
England
Tel: (0181) 422-4562
E-mail: songlines@gramophone.co.uk
Web site: http://www.gramophone.co.uk

World Music
AASA Publications
P.O. Box 14123
London W12 9WW
England

GENERAL

Billboard
1515 Broadway
New York, NY 10036 USA
Tel: (212) 764-7300
Web site: http://www.billboard.com

CMJ New Music Report
11 Middle Neck Rd., Ste. 400
Great Neck, NY 11021-2301 USA
Tel: (516) 466-6000
Fax: (516) 466-7159
E-mail: cmj@cmjmusic.com
Web site: http://www.cmj.com

ICE
P.O. Box 3043
Santa Monica, CA 90408
Tel: (800) 647-4ICE

NAPRA ReVIEW
P.O. Box 9
6 Eastsound Sq.
Eastsound, WA 98245 USA
Tel: (360) 376-2702
E-mail: napra@napra.com

Pulse!
2500 Del Monte St.
West Sacramento, CA 95691 USA
Tel: (916) 373-2450
Web site: http://www.towerrecords.com/pulse

Raygun
2110 Main St., Ste. 100
Santa Monica, CA 90405-2276 USA
Tel: (310) 452-6222

Request
10400 Yellow Circle Dr.
Minnetonka, MN 55343 USA
Tel: (612) 931-8740

The Rocket
2028 Fifth Ave.
Seattle, WA 98121 USA
Tel: (206) 728-7625

Rolling Stone
1290 Avenue of the Americas, 2nd Fl.
New York, NY 10104 USA
Tel: (212) 484-1616
Web site: http://rollingstone.com

Spin
6 W. 18th St., 8th Fl.
New York, NY 10011-4608 USA
Tel: (212) 633-8200

Vibe
205 Lexington Ave., 3rd Fl.
New York, NY 10016 USA
Tel: (212) 522-7092

The virtual world provides an extensive map to the real one, and the global chat-room is one of the best ways for cultures to cross and fans to keep up with the far-flung rewards of world music. The Web is ever-changing and ever-expanding, but here's a good list of sites—on specific artists and bands, styles and regions of music, or general-interest information with a strong world-music component—to get you started. You'll find recreational, research, and commercial content—as with any topic on the Web, there are as many kinds of sites as there are subjects to be enthused about. Don't forget to check for additional URLs (Web site addresses) of record labels and publications in our other Resources lists!

Artists

King Sunny Adé
http://www.mediaport.net/Music/Artistes/king_sunny_ade/index.en.html

Alabina
http://www.alabina.com/

Albita
http://www.yuca.com/albita.htm

Herb Alpert
http://www.almosounds.com/herbalpert/

Altan
http://www.altan.ie/

Robin Adnan Anders
http://quantumweb.com/robin/

Laurie Anderson
http://agape.trilidun.org/la/
http://www.cc.gatech.edu/~jimmyd/laurie-anderson/

Anggun
http://www.anggun.com/anggun/c_une_e.html

Marc Anthony
http://www.marcanthonyonline.com/
http://albertos.com/bands/MarcAnthony/MarcAnthony.html
http://members.aol.com/merenbooty/Marc.html

Dan Ar Braz
http://www.execpc.com/~henkle/fbindex/a/arbras_dan.html

Arcady
http://publish.uwo.ca/~eegraing/arcady/

Ray Barretto
http://www.bluenote.com/barretto.html

Battlefield Band
http://www.rootsworld.com/temple/battlefield/index.htm

Mario Bauzá
http://www.waypages.com/music/jazz/legends/B/Mario_Bauza.HTM

Keola Beamer
http://www.kbeamer.com/

Beausoleil
http://www.rosebudus.com/beausoleil/

Francis Bebey
http://www.uflib.ufl.edu/hss/africana/bebey.html

Maria Bethânia
http://www.dnai.com/~emc/pryngo/brasil/bahia2.htm
http://www.so-brazil.com/bio/bethania.html
http://www.gilbertogil.com.br/bio/eb2bet.htm

Frances Black
http://house-of-music.com/frances/index.shtml

Mary Black
http://www.celts.dk/mblack/

Black 47
http://www.black47.com/
http://www.geocities.com/SunsetStrip/Frontrow/2794/

Ruben Blades
http://www.amherst.edu/~dshender/ruben.html

Alpha Blondy
http://www.alphablondy.com/

Boom Shaka
http://www.boomshaka.com/

Boukan Ginen
http://miloz.com/artist/b/boukan_ginen.cfm

Boukman Eksperyans
http://www.boukman.com

Robin Huw Bowen
http://www.ceolas.org/artists/
Huw_Bowen.html

David Bowie
http://www.davidbowie.com/
http://www.algonet.se/~bassman/
BOWIE.html
http://www.bowiefans.com/
http://www.bowiewonderworld.com/
http://www.users.cts.com/crash/p/phil/
bowielps.html

Boys of the Lough
http://www.ceolas.org/artists/
Boys_of_the_Lough.html

Brave Old World
http://braveoldworld.com/

Michael Brook
http://the-fringe.com/brook/

Buckwheat Zydeco
http://www.buckwheatzydeco.com/

David Byrne
http://www.talking-
heads.net/davidbyrne/

Cachao
http://www.geocities.com/TheTropics/
Cabana/9683

Café Tacuba
http://www.cafetacuba.com.mx/

Capercaille
http://www.capercaillie.co.uk/

Hari Prasad Chaurasia
http://www.aoe.vt.edu/~boppe/MUSIC/
GM/HI/Hariprasad.html

C.J. Chenier
http://www.thefuturenow.com/ce/
chenier

The Chieftains
http://www.escape.ca/~skinner/
chieftains/chief.html
http://www.cybercomm.net/~executor/
chieftains.html

**The Clancy Bros and Tommy
Makem/Liam Clancy**
http://www.clancymusic.com/

Clannad
http://www.jtwinc.com/clannad/

Willie Colon
http://www.williecolon.com/

Ry Cooder
http://www.geocities.com/BourbonStreet/
Delta/7969/

Cornershop
http://www.wbr.com/cornershop/

Coyote Oldman
http://www.coyoteoldman.com/

Celia Cruz
http://members.aol.com/Salsoso/index.
html

¡Cubanismo!
http://www.rosebudus.com/cubanismo/
http://www.sastom.demon.nl/cubanismo/

De Dannan
http://www.ceolas.org/artists/
De_Dannan.html

Dead Can Dance/Lisa Gerrard
http://www.nets.com/dcd/
http://www.meniscusdesign.com/
dcdold.html
http://members.aol.com/midevlman/
dcd.htm
http://www.lisa-gerrard.com/cmp/
d-index-ns-alt.htm

Deep Forest
http://members.xoom.com/_XOOM/
deepforest/index.html
http://home.sol.no/~perta/dforest/
dforest.html
http://www.spikes.com/worldmix/

Sandy Denny
http://www.informatik.uni-hamburg.
de/~zierke/sandy.denny/

Dervish
http://www.geocities.com/Paris/Metro/
3858/dervish.html

Diblo Dibala
http://www.mediaport.net/Music/
Artistes/diblo_dibala/index.en.html

Dr. Loco's Rockin' Jalapeño Band
http://www.drloco.com/

Connie Dover
http://www.celticmusic.com/
connie_dover/

The Dubliners
http://www.astro.durge.org/dubliners.
html

The Dynatones
http://www.dynatones.com/

Brian Eno
http://www.hyperreal.org/music/artists/
brian_eno/
http://www.spies.com/Eno/Enohome.
html

Enya
http://www.celts.dk/enya/

http://homepages.enterprise.net/kbb/
EnyaLinks.html

Gloria Estefan
http://www.estefan.net/
http://www.epiccenter.com/EpicCenter/
custom/56/
http://www.gloriafan.com/
http://www.almetco.com/estefan/
gloria-1.html

Cesaria Evora
http://www.caboverde.com/evora/
evora.htm
http://www.there1.com/cesaria.html

Jose Feliciano
http://www.fantasticfeliciano.com/

Fortuna
http://www.rahul.net/hrmusic/discos/
fdisc.html

Peter Gabriel
http://www.geffen.com/gabriel/
http://www.biggben.com/pg/home.html
http://www.intercenter.net/~jnu/pg/

Gamelan Son of Lion
http://members.aol.com/gsol1/main.
html

Carlos Gardel
http://www.lvd.com.ar/Gardel/
principal.htm

Gilberto Gil
http://www.GilbertoGil.com.br/

Astrud Gilberto
http://www.gregmar.com/astrud.htm

The Gipsy Kings
http://www.gipsykings.com/
http://www.treefort.org/~bish/gkings/

Great Big Sea
http://www.greatbigsea.com/

Juan Luis Guerra
http://www.sdhumo.com/

Joy Harjo & Poetic Justice
http://www.hanksville.org/PJ/

George Harrison
http://web.mit.edu/scholvin/www/
harrison/harrison.html
http://www.bekkoame.or.jp/~garp/hari/
george.htm

Mickey Hart
http://grateful.dead.net/band_members/
mickey/index.html

Ofra Haza
http://www.ofrahaza.com/

Hedningarna
http://memberstheglobe.com/
hedningarna/

Tish Hinojosa
http://www.io.com/~dsmith/tish/
frames.html

Sol Hoopii
http://www.well.com/user/wellvis/
hoopii.html

The House Band
http://www.ceolas.org/artists/
House_Band.html

Huun-Huur-Tu
http://www.huunhuurtu.com/

Indigenous
http://www.indigenousrocks.com/

Andy Irvine
http://www.ceolas.org/artists/
Andy_Irvine.html

Israel Vibration
http://incolor.inetnebr.com/cvanpelt/
IVibes.html
http://www.outersound.com/band/
israel/bio.htm

Antonio Carlos Jobim
http://nortemag.com/tom/
http://photoshoptips.i-us.com/Estrada.
htm

Beau Jocque
http://www.iei.net/~drifter/blues/
beaujocque.html

Junoon
http://www.junoon.com/
http://www.angelfire.com/pa/junoonie/

Maria Kalaniemi
http://www.hoedown.com/html/mariak.
html

Pépé Kallé
http://www.mediaport.net/Music/
Artistes/pepe_kalle/index.en.html

Mory Kanté
http://www.mediaport.net/Music/
Artistes/mory_kante/index.en.html

Doug Kershaw
http://www2.dougkershaw.com/
dougkershaw/

Nusrat Fateh Ali Khan
http://www.nfak.com/

Khenany
http://www.khenany.com

Angélique Kidjo
http://wwwusers.imaginet.fr/~kidjo/

Kíla
http://www.kila.ie/www/home/

King Changó
http://www.wbr.com/kingchango/

King Tubby
http://www.furious.com/perfect/
kingtubby.html

Klezmer Conservatory Band
http://www.aaronconcert.com/acm/kcb.
htm

Kodo
http://www.sme.co.jp/Music/Info/
KODO/

Kronos Quartet
http://www.kronosquartet.org/
http://www.lochnet.com/client/gs/kq.
html

Fela Kuti
http://www.ccnet.com/~caldeira/fela.
html

La Mafia
http://www.lamafia.com/

Ladysmith Black Mambazo
http://www.mambazo.com/
http://www.singers.com/ladysmith.html

Mary Jane Lamond
http://www.chatsubo.com/mjlamond/

Daniel Lanois
http://www.sfbayconcerts.com/lanois/
home.html

Bill Laswell
http://www.hyperreal.org/music/labels/
axiom/

Leahy
http://www.geocities.com/~leahynet/
http://www.openface.ca/~congo/leahy1.
html

Dan Levenson & Kim Murley
http://www.folknet.org/dan

Yungchen Lhamo
http://realworld.on.net/rwr/release/
lhamo/yungchen1.html
http://tibet.cyborganic.com/yungchen

Kevin Locke
http://www.kevinlocke.com/

Jennifer Lopez
http://www.jenniferlopez.com/
http://www.jenlopezfan.net/
http://jenniferlopez.toocool.com/

Los Lobos
http://www.mindspring.com/~krazyfish/
loslobos/index.htm
http://www.wbr.com/loslobos/

Baaba Maal
http://members.home.net/baaba/

Dougie MacLean
http://www.ceolas.org/artists/
Dougie_MacLean.html
http://home.wish.net/~nisto/index.html
http://www.samusic.com/pro-macl.
shtml

Natalie MacMaster
http://nataliemacmaster.com/

Mad Lion
http://www.jetpack.com/lounge02/
beats/mad_prof/index.html

Madness
http://www.madness.co.uk/
http://www.jabba.demon.co.uk/
madness/

Taj Mahal
http://www.hawaiian.net/~sparrow/taj.
htm
http://www.taj-mo-roots.com/

Mahlathini & Mahotella Queens
http://www.gallo.co.za/gmi/mahlat.htm
http://www.mediaport.net/AeS/4/
4_95_39.en.html

Bob Marley
http://www.bobmarley.com/
http://www.aramagic.com/lounge/
bob_marley.html
http://www.livemarley.com/index.htm
http://members.aol.com/travisnd/page/
index.htm
http://www.bobmarley-foundation.
com/main.html
http://www.geocities.com/SunsetStrip/
9162/
http://www.angelfire.com/al/tuffsframe/
indexOLD.html

Ziggy Marley
http://www.melodymakers.com/

Ricky Martin
http://www.rickymartin.com/
http://www.rickymartinymasintl.com/
http://members.tripod.com/
~Maria_Lajos/rickring.html

Dave Matthews Band
http://www.dmband.com/
http://www.geocities.com/~bestofwa/
http://dancies.simplenet.com/

Maxwell Street Klezmer Band
http://members.aol.com/maxwellst/
index.htm

Eileen McGann
http://www.canuck.com/~jscown/
mcgann/index.html

Loreena McKennitt
http://www.quinlanroad.com/
http://www.geocities.com/Vienna/2044/
http://www.wbr.com/mckennitt/

Milladoiro
http://www.ceolas.org/artists/
Milladoiro.html

Mick Moloney
http://www.ceolas.org/artists/
Mick_Moloney.html
http://www.irishfolkloretours.com
http://www.geocities.com/
BourbonStreet/3034/Mick.html

Marisa Monte
http://www.marisamonte.com/

Christy Moore
http://www.christymoore.net/
http://www.ceolas.org/artists/
Christy_Moore/

Sabah Habas Mustapha
http://members.aol.com/sabahhabas

Youssou N'Dour
http://www.khm.de/~oblaum/youssou/
http://w3.to/youssou-ndour

Nightnoise
http://www.ceolas.org/artists/
Nightnoise.html

Nordan Project
http://www.bahnhof.se/~kario/nordan.
htm

Clara Nunes
http://www.slipcue.com/music/brazil/
nunes.htm
http://www.asahi-net.or.jp/~uh6k-ogr/
clara/disc.html

Sinéad O'Connor
http://www.engr.ukans.edu/~jrussell/
music/sinead/sinead.html
http://www.geocities.com/SunsetStrip/
Backstage/9922/
http://www.sinead-oconnor.com/

Oku Onuora
http://www.escape.com/~dred/

Oyster Band
http://www.sussex.ac.uk/Users/kcci1/
Oysterband/

Ozomatli
http://home.earthlink.net/~phatbass/
Ozomatli/index.html
http://www2.crosswinds.net/
los-angeles/~ozogirl/

Eddie Palmieri
http://www.berkeleyagency.com/
palmieri.html
http://home.dti.net/warr/palmieri.html
http://www.lamusica.com/eddiep.htm

Margareta Paslaru
http://www.margareta.com

Peatbog Faeries
http://www.peatbog-faeries.com/

Perfect Thyroid
http://www.perfectthyroid.com
http://www.rpi.edu/~uedad/PT/
http://www.isc.rit.edu/~rrso682/skunk.
html

Itzhak Perlman
http://www.geocities.com/Vienna/1066/
perlman.html

Lee "Scratch" Perry
http://www.leeperry.com/
http://homepage.oanet.com/sleeper/
scratch.htm

Astor Piazzolla
http://www.rootsworld.com/rw/feature/
astor.html
http://www.piazzolla.org/

Planxty
http://www.ceolas.org/artists/Planxty.
html

The Pogues/Shane MacGowan
http://www.pogues.com/
http://users.terabit.net/todea/
http://www.ferrie.demon.co.uk/pogues/
index.htm
http://www.csc.liv.ac.uk/~laurence/
macgowan.html
http://www.dzm.com/pogues/

The Police/Sting
http://www.sting.demon.nl/
http://www.stingchronicity.co.uk/
http://stingetc.com/index.html
http://www.concentric.net/~donsden/
http://www.newwave.net/~ghawk/
sting/sting.html

Tito Puente
http://home.earthlink.net/
~spaceagepop/puente.htm
http://www.onlinetalent.com/
Puentes_Allstars_homepage.html

Shabba Ranks
http://www.epiccenter.com/EpicCenter/
docs/artistupdate.qry?artistid=137

Steve Riley & the Mamou Playboys
http://lafourche.k12.la.us/teymard/
steveriley/

Steve Roach
http://www.steveroach.com/

Robbie Robertson
http://theband.hiof.no/band_members/
robbie.html

Tabu Ley Rochereau
http://www.chl.ca/JamMusicArtistsR/
rochereau.html

Silvio Rodríguez
http://spin.com.mx/~hvelarde/Cuba/
Silvio/

Linda Ronstadt
http://users.powernet.co.uk/skeyes/
dedicatedtolinda/index.html
http://www.ais-gwd.com/~tpartridge/
http://ourworld.compuserve.com/
homepages/eric_herni/guest.htm
http://suzann.com/music/ronstadt.htm

Adam Rudolph
http://www.metarecords.com

Runrig
http://www.mockett.net/runrig.html
http://www.netspace.org/~ehane/runrig.
html

Buffy Sainte-Marie
http://www.aloha.net/~bsm/
http://www.vanguardrecords.com/
buffy/
http://www.cradleboard.org

Samite
http://www.samite.com/

Poncho Sanchez
http://www.ponchosanchez.com/

Mongo Santamaria
http://www.onlinetalent.com/
Mongo_Santamaria_homepage.html

Santana
http://www.santana.com/
http://www.csv.warwick.ac.uk/~amuet/
santana.html
http://www.geocities.com/SunsetStrip/
Palms/6009/santana.html

Selena
http://www.selenaetc.com/
http://sourcetribute.com/
http://sophie.allan.org/roseanne/
selena.html

http://www.caller.com/selena/selena.htm

http://www.geocities.com/SunsetStrip/Stage/2192/

http://www.hotshotdigital.com/WellAlwaysRemember/Selena.html

Seven Nations
http://www.sevennations.com/

Shaggy
http://users.iafrica.com/p/pa/pantsula/shaggy.htm

L. Shankar
http://www.geocities.com/BourbonStreet/6789/shankar.html

Ravi Shankar
http://www.ravishankar.org/
http://www.gl.umbc.edu/~achatt1/Bio/ravisankar.html
http://www.datanet.hu/bau-dok/rimpa/
http://users.aol.com/tiedyejr/life/ravi/ravi.html

Sharon Shannon
http://www.ceolas.org/artists/Sharon_Shannon.html

Shiv Kumar Sharma
http://www.santoor.com/

Joanne Shenandoah
http://www.joanneshenandoah.com/

Paul Simon
http://www.wbr.com/paulsimon/
http://www.best.com/~rlai/Paul-Simon.html
http://paulsimon.org/

The Skatalites
http://www.skatalites.com/

Sly & Robbie
http://slyrob.3va.net/

Spearhead
http://hollywoodandvine.com/spearhead/

The Specials
http://www.thespecials.com/

Steeleye Span
http://ourworld.compuserve.com/homepages/RichardHollis/

Alan Stivell
http://www.ceolas.org/artists/Stivell.html

Strunz and Farah
http://www.strunzandfarah.com/

Yma Sumac
http://www.accesscom.com/~pc/sumac/

Dave Swarbrick
http://ourworld.compuserve.com/homepages/sjsheldon/swarb.htm
http://hum2mac1.murdoch.edu.au/watersons/swarb.html

Sweeney's Men
http://www.ceolas.org/artists/Sweeneys_Men.html

Sweet Honey in the Rock
http://www.sweethoney.com/

Philip Nchipe Tabane
http://www.music.org.za/artists/malombo.htm

Talking Heads
http://www.talking-heads.net/
http://penguin.cc.ukans.edu/Heads/Talking_Heads.html
http://www.xs4all.nl/~hornstra/hilmusic.htm

Tannahill Weavers
http://www.ceolas.org/artists/Tannies/
http://ourworld.compuserve.com/homepages/tannahill_weavers/

Tarika
http://www.froots.demon.co.uk//tarika.html

Texas Tornados
http://www.borderfest.com/texas.htm
http://www.xanadu2.net/rrogers/tornados.html

Mikis Theodorakis
http://members.aol.com/gwagner373/mikihome/index.htm

Third World
http://www.thirdworldband.com/

Richard & Linda Thompson
http://www.thebeesknees.com/bk-rt-bi.html
http://www.amug.org/~deeg1225/
http://www.alphalink.com.au/~sfy/RT/
http://people.netcom.co.uk/r.kendrick/rt/

3 Mustaphas 3
http://www.lochnet.com/client/gs/3m3.html

Trance Mission
http://www.cot.com/Trance.mission/index.html

John Trudell
http://www.planet-peace.org/trudell/

Värttinä
http://www.hoedown.com/html/varttina.html

Walela
http://www.Walela.com/

The Waterboys/Mike Scott
http://www.ceolas.org/artists/Waterboys.html
http://bath.future.easyspace.com/

Paul Winter
http://www.livingmusic.com/

Stevie Wonder
http://student-www.uchicago.edu/users/jrgenzen/stevie.html
http://darkwing.uoregon.edu/~thierry/wonder/wonder.html
http://www.xmission.com/~dan_nan/wonder/stevie.html

Gary Wright
http://www.thedreamweaver.com/

Stomu Yamash'ta
http://www.geocities.com/Tokyo/7011/sy.html

Yothu Yindi
http://www.yothuyindi.com/

Benjamin Zephaniah
http://www.oneworld.org/zephaniah/

Other World Music–Related Sites (Styles, Regions, Schools, Stores, and More!)

Accretions
http://www.accretions.com/

Africa
http://biochem.chem.nagoya-u.ac.jp/~endo/africa.html

African Music Archive
http://www.uni-mainz.de/~bender/

African Music Encyclopedia
http://africanmusic.org/

Afro-Caribbean Musics
http://www.mediaport.net/Music/index.en.html

Afropop Worldwide
http://www.afropop.org

Ali Akbar College of Music
http://www.nbn.com/~aacm/

All Music Guide
http://www.allmusic.com

Amazon.com
http://www.amazon.com/music

Ancient Music of Ireland
http://services.worldnet.net/~pybertra/
ceol/

Appalachian Music and Arts
http://www.whistlepig.com

Appalachian Music Archives
http://www.pitt.edu/~gebanks/pers/
oldtime.html

Arabic Music Info Source
http://members.aol.com/amisource/

Asia CD
http://www.asiacd.com/

Australian Institute of Eastern Music
http://www.ozemail.com.au/~dukewalk/

Balkan Tunes
http://deepthought.armory.com/~cope/
balkantunes

barnesandnoble.com
http://www.bn.com

Bembe Records
http://www.bembe.com/

Billboard Magazine
http://www.billboard.com

BMG Music Service
http://www.bmgmusicservice.com

Borders.com
http://www.borders.com/music

BrazilianMusic.com
http://brazilianmusic.com/

Broadcast.com
http://www.broadcast.com

Cajun French Music Association
http://www.cajunfrenchmusic.org/

Cajun/Zydeco Music & Dance
http://www.bme.jhu.edu/~jrice/cz.html

Cathals Irish Music
http://indigo.ie/~chick/

CD Universe
http://www.cduniverse.com

CDnow
http://www.cdnow.com

Celtic Christian Music Index
http://www.open.org/~curtis/celtxian.
htm

Celtic Connections
http://www.celticconnections.co.uk/

Celtic Peak
http://www.collins-peak.co.uk/celtic/

Celtic Resources
http://www.geocities.com/SunsetStrip/
Palladium/7358/

Celtic Wonder
http://w3.to/celticwonder/

CelticMusic.com
http://www.celticmusic.com/artists.html

Celts.dk
http://www.celts.dk/celts/

Ceol
http://www.ceol.ie/

Ceolas
http://www.ceolas.org/ceolas.html

Columbia House Music Club
http://www.columbiahouse.com

Comhaltas Ceoltóirí Éireann
http://cce.irish-music.net/CCE.htm

Compact Disc Connection
http://www.cdconnection.com

Culburnie Records
http://www.culburnie.com/

Dancehall Reggae Productions
http://www.dancehallreggae.com/

Alain Danielou
http://www.alaindanielou.org/

Ari Davidow's Klezmer Shack
http://www.well.com/user/ari/klez/

Dirty Linen
http://www.dirtynelson.com/linen/

Driftweb
http://www.wnur.org/drift/

Dub and Reggae Music
http://usuarios.intercom.es/grgsvi/
index.htm

East African Music
http://hometown.aol.com/dpaterson/
eamusic.htm

East Asian Music
http://www.medieval.org/music/world/
asia.html

Ejaness Reggae Comprehensive
http://www.reggaecd.com

Flamenco World
http://www.flamenco-world.com/

400 Years
http://incolor.inetnebr.com/cvanpelt/
Years.html

Global Beat
http://www.globalbeat.com/

Global Dragon
http://www.globaldragon.com/

Global Music Centre
http://www.globalmusic.fi/index.html

Guide to Classical Indian/Jazz Fusion
http://www.nitehawk.com/alleycat/
indyjazz.html

Hoobellatoo (Beautiful People)
http://www.hoobellatoo.org

Hot Salsa
http://www.chez.com/abri/a/index.htm

ICE Magazine
http://www.icemagazine.com

Interceltique
http://www.azimut-com.fr/interceltique/

International Music Archives
http://www.eyeneer.com/World/index.
html

Ireland Music List
http://home.wirehub.nl/~taco/

Irish Music Box
http://www.dojo.ie/musicbox/

Irish Music Net
http://www.imn.ie/

Irish Music Page
http://www.geocities.com/SouthBeach/
Marina/4870/music.html

Irish Traditional Music Archive
http://www.itma.ie/home/itmae1.htm

Irish World Music Center
http://www.ul.ie/~iwmc/HomePage.html

Isle of Music Festival
http://www.manxradio.com/

Jammin Reggae Archives
http://niceup.com/

LaMusica.com! (Latin Music On-Line)
http://209.73.224.4/index.htm

LatinoLink
http://www.latinolink.com

Mizik
http://www.unik.no/~robert/mizik/
mizik.html

Motion Records
http://www.motionrecords.com/

The MPB Zone: Musica Popular Brasileira
http://members.aol.com/thempbzone/index.html

Music Web Ireland
http://www.musweb.com/

NahenaheNet
http://www.interpac.net/~nahenahe/

Netropolis Records
http://www.motor-city.com/tomb/NetropolisRecords.html

New Native
http://www.wcpworld.com/native/sounds.htm

Northern Journey Online (Canadian Folk Music)
http://www.interlog.com/~njo

Oasis Salsero
http://www.chez.com/abri/a/index.htm

Peace through World Music
http://rhythmweb.com/peace/

Pierre's Cajun Record Shop
http://www.winningways.com/pierre/

Planet Ireland
http://www.geocities.com/Broadway/Alley/8686/index.html

RAS Records
http://www.erols.com/hwilliam//ras1.html

RealAudio
http://www.real.com

A Recorded Anthology of Indonesian Music
http://www.inform.umd.edu/EdRes/ReadingRoom/Newsletters/EthnoMusicology/Archive/cdindo-project

Reggae Ambassadors Worldwide
http://www.coolcrew.com/RAW/index.html

Reggae.com
http://www.reggae.com/

Reggae Links
http://www.ireggae.com/reggae.htm

Reggae Ring
http://www.reggaering.org/

Reggae Web
http://www.reggaeweb.com/

Riddim Music
http://www.riddim.com/

Riggadig Records
http://www.riggadig.com/

Robi Droli New Tone Records
http://web.inrete.it/robidroli/home.html

Rootsworld
http://www.rootsworld.com

Russian Reggae Rasta Roots Review
http://www.zhurnal.ru:8083/music/rasta/links.html

Salsa Mundo
http://www.salsamundo.com/

Salsa-Music
http://www.telebyte.nl/~ramirez/index.htm

Salsa Stories
http://www.si.umich.edu/CHICO/MHN/Salsa/index.html

Salsa Talks
http://www.digido.com/salsatalks.html

Salsaweb
http://www.salsaweb.com/

Scotdisc
http://www.scotdisc.co.uk/

Scotmusic
http://www.chased.demon.co.uk/

Scottish Music Index
http://www.netreal.co.uk/music/index.htm

Scottish Music Information Centre
http://www.music.gla.ac.uk/HTMLFolder/Resources/SMIC/homepage.html

Secret Museum of the Air
http://www.wfmu.org

Skuntry
http://www.skuntry.com/home.cfm

Sonic Safaris
http://www.jonkey.com/

SummerStage
http://www.SummerStage.org

Talking Drum Reggae
http://www.erols.com/hwilliam/

Tejano Home Page
http://www.ondanet.com/tejano/tejano.html

Tim's World Music Info
http://www.duke.edu/~td/music.htm

To Didgeridoo or not Didgeridu
http://mail.cruzio.com/~cosker/didgerido.htm

Total E
http://www.totalE.com

Tower Records
http://www.towerrecords.com

Triloka
http://www.triloka.com/

Trojan Records
http://www.trojan-records.com/

Tunes.com
http://www.tunes.com

Ultimate Band List
http://www.ubl.com

unfURLed
http://www.unfurled.com

Wall of Sound
http://www.wallofsound.com

World Flamenco
http://www.Flamenco.org/

World Music Forum
http://one-rbs-plaza.com/220wmusic/

World Music Fusion Music Links
http://www.ancient-future.com/links/index.html

World Music Institute
http://www.HearTheWorld.org

World-Wide Samba Home Page
http://www.worldsamba.org/

Zyde.com
http://members.aol.com/zydecom/page1.htm

The Zydeco Road
http://frontpage.erie.net/tex/zydeco.htm

Zydeco Underground
http://www.zydecomusic.com/

ZydE-Magic Cajun/Zydeco Web Page
http://www.nmaa.org/member/ghayman

The following are just some of the record labels that let you hear the world: labels that specialize in international music outside the mainstream, or focus on one or a few particular cultures, or are industry giants with strong world-music divisions and offerings. You may want to contact some of these labels if you have questions regarding specific releases. It's good to keep up with resources like the publications and organizations in our other appendixes, to keep track of what albums are being released by which companies—some world artists have scores or even hundreds of albums, not all on the same label, not all released in this country, and not all in print at a given time. This list will get you off to a good start! (If one item below refers you to another, it means that the first label is affiliated with the second.)

A&M Records
1416 N. La Brea Ave.
Hollywood, CA 90028 USA
Tel: (213) 469-2411
Fax: (213) 856-2600
Web site: www.amrecords.
   com

Ace Records
F-mail: info@acerecords.co.uk
Web site: www.acerecords.
   co. uk

Acoustic Disc
PO Box 4143
San Rafael, CA 94913 USA
Tel: (800) 221-DISC (3472)
E-mail: cmmang@idt.net
Web site: www.dawgnet.com

Africassette Music
PO Box 24941
Detroit, MI 48224 USA
Tel: (313) 881-4108
Fax: (313) 881-0260
E-mail: rsteiger@africassette.
   com
Web site: www.africassette.
   com

akku disk
Music Contact
Musikverlag
Saarstr. 8
D-72070 Tübingen
Germany
Tel: 49 7073 2250
Fax: 49 7073 2134
E-mail: zellner@musiccontact.
   com
Web site: www.musiccontact.
   com

Alam Madina Music Productions
74 Broadmoor Ave.
San Anselmo, CA 94960 USA
Tel: (415) 456-5963
E-mail: info@ammp.com
Web site: www.ammp.com/
   records.html

Allegro
14134 NE Airport Way
Portland, OR 97230-3443 USA
Tel: (800) 288-2007
Fax: (503) 257-9061
Web site: www.allegro-music.
   com

Alligator Records
PO Box 60234
Chicago, IL 60660 USA
Tel: (773) 973-7736
Fax: (773) 973-2088
E-mail: info@allig.com
Web site: www.alligator.com

Almo Sounds
360 N. La Cienega Blvd.
Los Angeles, CA 90048-1925
   USA
Tel: (310) 289-3080
Fax: (310) 289-8662
Web site: www.almosounds.
   com

Al Sur/Media 7
15, Rue des Goulvents
92000 Nanterre
France

Alula Records
PO Box 62043
Durham, NC 27715-2043 USA
Tel: (919) 416-9454

Fax: (919) 286-1788
E-mail: alulamedia@aol.com
Web site: www.alula.com

American Clave
See: Rounder Records

Amiata Media
PO Box 405
Chappaqua, NY 10514 USA
Tel: (914) 238-5943
Fax: (914) 238-5944
E-mail: audio@computer.net
Web site: www.amiatamedia.it

Angel Records
810 Seventh Ave., 4th Fl.
New York, NY 10019 USA
Tel: (212) 603-8700
Fax: (212) 603-8648

Antilles Records
555 West 57th St., 10th Fl.
New York, NY 10019 USA
Web site: www.antillesnet.com

Appleseed Recordings
PO Box 2593
West Chester, PA 19380 USA
E-mail: folkradicl@aol.com
Web site: www.appleseedrec.
   com

ARC Music Productions International
PO Box 111
East Grinstead
West Sussex RH 19 4FZ
England
Tel: 44 1342 312161
Fax: 44 1342 325209
E-mail: robert@arcmusic.co.uk
Web site: www.arcmusic.co.uk

ARC Music US
PO Box 2453
Clearwater, FL 34617-2453
USA
Tel: (813) 447 3755
Fax: (813) 447 3820
E-mail: arcamerica@ij.net
Web site: www.arcmusic.co.uk

Arhoolie Productions, Inc.
10341 San Pablo Ave.
El Cerrito, CA 94530 USA
Tel: (510) 525-7471
Fax: (510) 525-1204
E-mail: mail@arhoolie.com
Web site: www.arhoolie.com

Arista Records
6 W. 57th St.
New York, NY 10019 USA
Tel: (212) 489-7400
Fax: (212) 830-2238
E-mail: info@aristarec.com
Web site: www.aristarec.com

Ariwa
34 Whitehorse Ln.
London SE25 6RE
England
Tel: 44 208 6537744
Fax: 44 208 7711911
E-mail: info@ariwa.com
Web site: www.ariwa.com

Artists Only! Records
477 Madison Ave., 10th Fl.
New York, NY 10022 USA
E-mail: aor@artistsonly.com
Web site: www.artistsonly.com

Astor Place Recordings
740 Broadway
New York, NY 10003
E-mail: Astorinfo@aol.com
Web site: www.astorplace.com

Atlantic Recording Corporation
1290 Avenue of the Americas
New York, NY 10104 USA
Tel: (212) 707-2000
Fax: (212) 405-5507
E-mail: web@atlantic-records.com
Web site: www.atlantic-records.com

Avant
See: Koch International

Axiom Records
400 Lafayette St., 5th Fl.
New York, NY 10003 USA
Web site: www.hyperreal.org/music/labels/axiom

Bar/None Records
PO Box 1704
Hoboken, NJ 07030 USA
Tel: (201) 795-9424
Fax: (201) 795-5048
E-mail: info@bar-none.com
Web site: www.bar-none.com

Barking Pumpkin Records
PO Box 5265
North Hollywood, CA 91616-5265 USA
Tel: (818) 755-3700
Fax: (818) 761-7773

Beautiful Jo Records
86 Marlborough Rd.
Oxford OX1 4LS
England
Tel: 44 1865 249194
Fax: 44 1865 792765
E-mail: info@bejo.co.uk
Web site: www.bejo.co.uk

Black Top Records
PO Box 56691
New Orleans, LA 70156 USA
Tel: (504) 895-7239
Fax: (504) 891-1510

Blind Pig Records
PO Box 2344
San Francisco, CA 94126 USA
Tel: (415) 550-6484
Fax: (415) 550-6485
E-mail: blindpigs@aol.com
Web site: www.blindpigrecords.com/

Blix Street Records
11715 Blix St.
N. Hollywood, CA 91607-4004
USA
E-mail: blixstreet@aol.com
Web site: www.blixstreet.com/

Blood and Fire
Ducie House
37 Ducie St.
Manchester M1 2JW
England
E-mail: info@bandf.u-net.com
Web site: www.bloodandfire.co.uk

Blue Flame Records
parlerstrasse 6
70192 Stuttgart
Germany
Tel: 49 711 2567671
Fax: 49 711 2567674
E-mail: 100646.2257@compuserve.com
Web site: www.blueflame.com

Blue Jackel Entertainment
PO Box 87

Huntington, NY 11743-0087
USA
Tel: (516) 423-7879
Fax: (516) 423-7875
E-mail: bluejackel@earthlink.net
Web site: www.bluejackel.com

Blue Note Records
304 Park Ave. S., 3rd Fl.
New York, NY 10010 USA
Tel: (212) 253-3000
Web site: www.bluenote.com

Blue Thumb Records
555 W. 57th St., 10th Fl.
New York, NY 10019 USA
Tel: (212) 424-1000
Fax: (212) 424-1007

BMG/BMG Classics
1540 Broadway, 41st Fl.
New York, NY 10036 USA
Tel: (212) 930-4941
Web site: www.bmgclassics.com

Borealis Recording Company
67 Mowatt Ave., Ste. 233
Toronto, ON M6K 3E3 Canada
Tel: (416) 530-4288
Fax: (416) 530-0461
E-mail: brc@interlog.com
Web site: www.interlog.com/~brc

Bottom Line Record Company
740 Broadway, 6th Fl.
New York, NY 10003 USA

Buda Musique
See: Allegro

Bushooman Rag
Box 292, Station B
Toronto, Ontario
Canada M5T 2W2

Canyon
4143 N. 16th St., Ste. 6
Phoenix, AZ 85016 USA
Tel: (800) 268-1141
Fax: (602) 279-9233
E-mail: canyon@canyonrecords.com
Web site: www.canyonrecords.com

Capitol Records
See: EMI-Capitol Records

Caroline Records
104 West 29th St., 4th Fl.
New York, NY 10001 USA
Tel: (212) 886-7500
Web site: www.caroline.com

Castle Communications
29 Barwell Business Park
Leatherhead Rd.
Surrey KT9 2NY
England

Celestial Harmonies
Div. of Mayflower Corp.
4549 E. Fort Lowell Rd.
Tucson, AZ 85712-1182 USA
Tel: (520) 326-4400
Fax: (520) 326-3333
E-mail: celestial@harmonies.com
Web site: www.harmonies.com

Celtic Heartbeat
Universal Records
1755 Broadway, 7th Fl.
New York, NY 10019 USA
E-mail: celtic@numb.ie
Web site: www.celticheartbeat.com

Celtic Music
CM Distribution
2/4 High St.
Starbeck, Harrogate, North Yorkshire
HG1 7HY England

Chesky Records
PO Box 1268
Radio City Station, NY 10101
USA
Tel: (800) 331-1437
E-mail: feedback@chesky.com
Web site: www.chesky.com

Claddagh Records
Dame House
Dame St.
Dublin 2 Ireland
Tel: 353 1 6778943
Fax: 353 1 6793664
E-mail: claddagh@crl.ie
Web site: indigo.ie/~claddagh

Columbia Records
550 Madison Ave.
New York, NY 10022-3211 USA
Tel: (212) 833-8000
Fax: (212) 833-7731
Web site: www.columbiarecords.com

Comhaltas Ceoltóirí Éireann
Belgrave Square
Monkstown
Co. Dublin
Ireland
Tel: 353 1 2800295
Fax: 353 1 2803759
E-mail: enquiries@comhaltas.com
Web site: www.mayo-ireland.ie/CCE.htm

Compass Records
117 30th Ave. S.
Nashville, TN 37212-2507 USA
Tel: (615) 320-7672
Fax: (615) 320-7378
E-mail: info@compassrecords.
    com
Web site: www.
    compassrecords.com

Cooking Vinyl America
PO Box 311
Port Washington, NY 11050
USA
Tel: (516) 484-2863
Fax: (516) 484-6179
E-mail: info@cookingvinyl.com
Web site: www.cookingvinyl.
    co.uk

Corasón/Música Tradicional
See: Rounder Records

Crammed Discs
43, rue General Patton
1050 Brussels
Belgium
E-mail: crammed@crammed.be
Web site: www.crammed.be

Dancing Cat
PO Box 639
Santa Cruz, CA 95061 USA
Tel: (408) 429-5085
Fax: (408) 423-7057
E-mail: ml@dancingcat.com
Web site: www.dancingcat.com

Dara Records USA
207 E. 84th St., Ste. 32
New York, NY 10028 USA
Tel: (800) 714-3272
Fax: (212) 628-7224
Web site: www.dararecords.
    com

Dargason Music
PO Box 189
Burbank, CA 91503 USA
Tel: (818) 502-2021
Fax: (818) 502-1017
E-mail: dargason@earthlink.
    net
Web site: www.dargasonmusic.
    com

Deutsche Grammaphon
Alte Rabenstrasse 2
20148 Hamburg
Germany
E-mail: dgclassics@dgclassics.
    com
Web site: www.dgclassics.com

Distribution North America (DNA)
1280 Santa Anita Ct.

Woodland, CA 95776 USA
Tel: (732) 530-5879

Domo Records, Inc.
2211 Corinth Ave., Ste. 100
Los Angeles, CA 90064 USA
Tel: (310) 966-4414
Fax: (310) 966-4420
E-mail domo@domo.com
Web site: www.domo.com

Dunkeld Records
Cathedral St.
Dunkeld
Perthshire PH8 0AW
Scotland
Tel: 44 1350 727686
Fax: 44 1350 728606
E-mail: admin@dunkeld.co.uk
Web site: www.dunkled.co.uk

Earache Records
295 Lafayette St., Ste. 915
New York, NY 10012 USA
Tel: (212) 343-9090
Fax: (212) 974-9314
E-mail: EaracheRec@aol.com
Web site: www.earache.com

Earth Beat Music
1 Shilpa Ct.
Nanda Patkar Rd.
Vile Parle (E)
Mumbai, India 400 057
Tel: 91 22 6148060
Fax: 91 22 6109082
E-mail: mail@earthbeatmusic.
    com
Web site: earthbeatmusic.com

EarthBeat!
PO Box 1460
Redway, CA 95560-1460 USA
Tel: (707) 923-3991
Fax: (707) 923-3241
E-mail: musicforlittlepeople
    @mflp.com
Web site: st6.yahoo.com/
    melody/earthbeat.html

EarthSea Records
PO Box 1109
Warrenton, VA 20188 USA
Tel: (540) 351-6191
Fax: (540) 351-6193
E-mail: info@earthsearecords.
    com
Web site: www.
    earthsearecords.com

EarthWorks
See: Stern's Music

Earwig Music Co.
1818 W. Pratt Blvd.
Chicago, IL 60626 USA
Tel: (773) 262-0278
Fax: (773) 262-0285

ECM Records
1540 Broadway
New York, NY 10036-4098
    USA
Web site: www.ecmrecords.
    com

Elektra Entertainment Group
75 Rockefeller Plaza
New York, NY 10019-6907 USA
Tel: (212) 275-4000
Fax: (212) 956-2270
Web site: www.elektra.com

ellipsis arts . . .
PO Box 305
Roslyn, NY 11576 USA
Tel: (800) 788-6670
Fax: (516) 621-2750
E-mail: contacts@ellipsisarts.
    com
Web site: www.ellipsisarts.com

EMI-Capitol Records
1750 N. Vine St.
Hollywood, CA 90028 USA
Tel: (213) 462-6252
Fax: (213) 467-6550
Web site: www.
    hollywoodandvine.com

Enja
PO Box 190333
D-80603 Munich
Germany
Fax: 49 89 1678810
E-mail: info@enjarecords.com
Web site: www.enjarecords.
    com

Epic Records
550 Madison Ave.
New York, NY 10022-3211 USA
Tel: (212) 833-8000
Fax: (212) 833-5134
E-mail: Epic_Records
    @sonymusic.com
Web site: www.epiccenter.
    com/EpicCenter/docs/
    index.qry

Ernie B's Reggae
PO Box 5019
El Dorado Hills, CA 95762 USA
Tel: (916) 939-0578
E-mail: ErnieB@calweb.com

Fellside Recordings
15 Banklands
Workington
Cumbria CA 14 3EW
UK
E-mail: info@fellsiderecords.
    demon.co.uk

Finlandia Records
PO Box 169

FIN-02101
Espoo, Finland
Tel: (358) 9-435-011

Fledg'ling Records
PO Box 547
London SE26 4BD
England
Web site: www.thebeesknees.
    com

Flying Fish Records
See: Rounder Records

Folk-Legacy Records
PO Box 1148
Sharon CT 06069 USA
Tel: (800) 836-0901
Fax: (860) 364-1050
E-mail: folklegacy@snet.net
Web site: folklegacy.com/

Fonomusic
E-mail: fonomusic
    @fonomusic.es
Web site: www.fonomusic.com

Fonovisa
7710 Haskell Ave.
Van Nuys, CA 91406 USA
Tel: (818) 782-6100
Fax: (818)782-6162
E-mail: usradio@icnt.net
Web site: www.fonovisa.com

Fortuna Records
PO Box 32016
Tucson, AZ 85751 USA

4AD Records
PO Box 46187
Los Angeles, CA 90046 USA
Tel: (310) 289-8770
Fax: (310) 289-8680
E-mail: 4AD@almaroad.co.uk
Web site: www.4ad.com

Gadfly Records
PO Box 5231
Burlington, VT 05402 USA
Tel: (802) 865-2406
E-mail: gadfly1@aol.com
Web site: www.gadflyrecords.
    com

Gael-Linn Records
26 Merrion Sq.
Dublin 2
Ireland

Geffen Records/DGC Records
9130 Sunset Blvd.
Los Angeles, CA 90069-6197
    USA
Tel: (310) 278-9010
Fax: (310) 273-9389
Web site: www.geffen.com

GlobeStyle Records
48-50 Steele Rd.
London NW10 7AS
England

Globetrotter
550 Madison Ave., Ste. 1956
New York, NY 10022 USA
E-mail: Globetrotter
@sonymusic.com
Web site: www.sonymusic.
com/globetrotter

Great Northern Arts
80 Gordon Rd.
Middletown, NY 10941 USA
Tel: (888) 641-5600
E-mail: gna@warwick.net

Green Linnet Records
43 Beaver Brook Rd.
Danbury, CT 06810 USA
Tel: (203) 730-0333
Fax: (203) 778-4443
E-mail: glr@mags.net
Web site: www.greenlinnet.
com

Greensleeves
Unit 14 Metro Centre
St Johns Rd., Isleworth
Middlesex TW7 6NJ
England
Tel: 44 181 7580564
Fax: 44 181 7580811
E-mail: greensleeves
@easynet.co.uk
Web site: www.easynet.co.uk/
greensleeves

Greentrax Recordings Ltd.
Cockenzie Business Centre
Edinburgh Rd., Cockenzie
East Lothian EH32 0HL, Scot-
land
Tel/Fax: 44 1875 813545
E-mail: greentrax@aol.com
Web site: members.aol.com/
greentrax/greentrx.htm

GRP Recording Company
555 W. 57th St., 10th Fl.
New York, NY 10019 USA
Tel: (212) 424-1000
Fax: (212) 424-1007
Web site: www.
vervemusicgroup.com/grp/
index.html

Hannibal Records
See: Rykodisc

Harmonia Mundi USA
2037 Granville Ave.
Los Angeles, CA 90025 USA
Tel: (310) 478-1311
Fax: (310) 996-1389

E-mail: infousa
@harmoniamundi.com
Web site: harmoniamundi.com

Harmony Ridge
PO Box 995
El Granada, California 94018
USA
Tel: (800) 611-4698
Fax: (415) 726-6660
E-mail: hrmusic@hrmusic.com
Web site: www.hrmusic.com

Heartbeat
See: Rounder Records

Hearts of Space
PO Box 31321
San Francisco, CA 94131 USA
Tel: (415) 331-3200
Fax: (415) 331-3280
Web site: www.hos.com

Hemisphere
See: Metro Blue

Higher Octave Music
23852 Pacific Coast Highway,
Ste. 2C
Malibu, CA 90265 USA
Tel: (310) 589-1515
Fax: (310) 589-1525
E-mail: info@higheroctave.
com
Web site: www.higheroctave.
com

HighTone Records
220 Fourth St., Ste. 101
Oakland, CA 94607 USA
Tel: (510) 763-8500
Fax: (510) 763-8558
E-mail: htrecords@aol.com
Web site: www.hightone.com

Hollywood Records
500 S. Buena Vista St.
Burbank, CA 91521 USA
Tel: (818) 560-5670
Fax: (818) 841-5140
E-mail:
Web site: hollywoodrecords.
go.com

Hurv, Sweden
Nordanåker 1789
S-782 91 Malung
Sweden
Tel: 46 280 60089
Fax: 46 280 60089
E-mail: hurv@hurv.com
Web site: www.hurv.com/
index-eng. html

India Archive Music
2124 Broadway, Ste. 343
New York, NY 10023 USA
Tel/Fax: (212) 740-1508

E-mail: indarcmus@aol.com

Indian House
PO Box 472
Taos, New Mexico 87571 USA
Tel: (505) 776-2953
Fax: (505) 776-2804
E-mail: music@indianhouse.
com
Web site: www.indianhouse.
com/music

Indigena Records
PO Box 62043
Durham, NC 27715-2043 USA
Tel: (919) 416-9454
Fax: (919) 286-1788
E-mail: indigena99@aol.com

International Soul
PO Box 3444
Oakland, CA 94609-3444 USA

Interscope Records
10900 Wilshire Blvd.
Los Angeles, CA 90024 USA
Tel: (310) 208-6547
Fax: (310) 208-7343
Web site: www.
interscoperecords.com

Interworld Music
30 S. Main St.
Concord, NH 03301 USA
Tel: (800) 698-6705
E-mail: interworld
@interworldmusic.com
Web site: www.
interworldmusic.com

Iona Records
27-29 Carnoustie Pl.
Scotland St.
Glasgow G5 8PH
Scotland
E-mail: lismor@lismor.co.uk
Web site: www.lismor.co.uk

Iris Musique
Qualiton Imports Ltd.
24-02 40th Ave.
Long Island City, NY 11101 USA
Web site: www.qualiton.com

Island Records
825 8th Ave., 24th Fl.
New York, NY 10019 USA
Tel: (212) 333-8000
Fax: (212) 603-3965
Web site: www.island.co.uk/

**Jive Records/Silvertone
Records**
137–139 W. 25th St., 11th Fl.
New York, NY 10001 USA
Tel: (212) 727-0016
Fax: (212) 645-3783

Juna
121 Thunder Lake Rd.
Wilton, CT 06897 USA
Tel: (888) 286-JUNA (5862)
E-mail: juna@junamusic.com
Web site: www.junamusic.com

JVC Music
3800 Barham Blvd., Ste. 305
Los Angeles, CA 90068 USA
Tel: (213) 878-0101
Fax: (213) 878-0202

Kells Music
64 New Hyde Park Rd.
Garden City, NY 11530-3909
USA
Tel: (800) 854-3746
Fax: (516) 354-7768
E-mail: kellsmus@pipeline.com

Keltia Musique
1 Place Au Beurre
29000 Quimper
France
E-mail: keltia@eurobretagne
Web site: web.bagadoo.tm.fr/
uk/culture/keltia/index.
html

King Record Co., Ltd.
1-2-3
Otowa
Bunkyo-ku
Tokyo 112-0013 Japan
Tel: 81 3 39452134
Fax: 81 3 39454806
E-mail: kokusai@kingrecords.
co.jp

Knitting Factory Records
74 Leonard St.
New York, NY 10013 USA
Tel: (212) 219-3006
Fax: (212) 219-3401
Web site: www.knittingfactory.
com

Koch International
2 Tri Harbor Ct.
Port Washington, NY 11050-
4617 USA
Tel: (516) 484-1000
Fax: (516) 484-4746
E-mail: koch@kochint.com
Web site: www.kochint.com

Kuarup
Rua México, 3/2°
CEP 20031-144
Rio de Janeiro - RJ
Brazil
Tel: 55 021 2201623
Fax: 55 021 2200494
E-mail: kuarup@uninet.com.br
Web site: www.kuarup.com.
br/ing.htm

La Louisianne Records
PO Box 52131
Lafayette, LA 70505 USA

Laserlight Digital
Delta Music Company
1663 Sawtelle Blvd.
Los Angeles, CA 90025 USA
Tel: (310) 268-1205
Fax: (310) 268-1279
E-mail: info@deltamusic.com
Web site: www.deltamusic.com

Le Chant du Monde
See: Harmonia Mundi USA

Legacy Recordings
550 Madison Ave.
New York, NY 10022-3211 USA
Tel: (212) 833-8000
Fax: (212) 833-7731
Web site: www.
   legacyrecordings.com

Loco
PO Box 410023
San Francisco, CA 94141-0023
   USA
E-mail: locoline@drloco.com

London Records
825 Eight Ave., 23rd Fl.
New York, NY 10019 USA
Tel: (212) 333-8000
Fax: (212) 333-8030

Luaka Bop
PO Box 652, Cooper Station
New York, NY 10276 USA
Tel: (212) 255-2714
Fax: (212) 255-3809
Web site: www.luakabop.com

Lyrichord Discs
141 Perry St.
New York, NY 10014 USA
Tel: (212) 929-8234
Fax: (212) 929-8245
E-mail: info@lyrichord.com
Web site: www.SkyWriting.
   com/Lyrichord

M. Soul Productions
PO Box 301
Summit, NJ 07902-0301 USA
Web site: www.margareta.com.

Macmeanmna
Quay Bray
Portree
Isle of Skye IV51 9DB
Scotland
Tel: 44 1478 612990

Maggie's Music
PO Box 4144
Annapolis, MD 21403 USA
Tel: (410) 268-3394

Fax: (410) 267-7061
E-mail: mail@maggiesmusic.
   com
Web site: www.maggiesmusic.
   com

Maison de Soul
238 E. Main St.
PO Drawer 10
Ville Platte, LA 70586 USA

Mardis Gras Records
3331 St. Charles Ave.
New Orleans, LA 70115 USA
Tel: (504) 895-0441
Fax: (504) 891-4214

MCA Records
70 Universal City Plz.
Universal City, CA 91608 USA
Tel: (818) 777-4000
Fax: (818) 733-1407
Web site: www.mcarecords.
   com/

MCD World Music
R. General Jardim, 618 cj 51
Sao Paulo, SP-Brazil
01223-010

MCG Records/Curb Records
3907 W. Alameda Ave., Ste. 101
Burbank, CA 91505 USA
Tel: (818) 843-1616
Fax: (818) 843-5429
Web site: www.curb.com

Mélodie
E-mail: info@melodie.fr
Web site: www.melodie.fr

M.E.L.T. 2000
6C Littlehampton Rd.
Worthing
West Sussex BN13 1QE
Tel: 44 1903 260033
Fax: 44 1903 261133
E-mail: info@melt2000.com
Web site: www.melt2000.com/

Mercury
World Wide Plaza
825 Eighth Ave.
New York, NY 10019 USA
Tel: (212) 333-8000
Fax: (212) 333-1093
Web site: www.
   MercuryRecords.com

Mesa/Bluemoon Recordings
9229 Sunset Blvd.
Los Angeles, CA 90069 USA
Tel: (310) 205-7445
Fax: (310) 205-5911

Messidor
See: Rounder Records

Metro Blue Records
1290 Avenue of the Americas
New York, NY 10104 USA
Web site: www.metroblue.com

Miramar Recordings
200 2nd Ave. W.
Seattle, WA 98119 USA
Tel: (206) 284-4700
Fax: (206) 286-4433
E-mail: info@miramarupx.com
Web site: www.miramarupx.
   com

Mobile Fidelity Sound Lab
105 Morris St.
Sebastopol, CA 95472 USA
Tel: (707) 829-0134
Fax: (707) 829-3746
E-mail: mofi@mofi.com
Web site: www.mofi.com

Moon Ska NYC
84 E. 10th St.
New York, NY 10003 USA
Tel: (212) 673-5538
Fax: (212) 673-5571

Mopiato
PO Box 3503
South Pasadena, CA 91031
   USA

Motown Records
825 Eighth Ave., 29th Fl.
New York, NY 10019 USA
Tel: (212) 294-9516
Fax: (212) 946-2615
Web site: www.motown.com

Music Club
Music Collection International
76 Dean St.
London W1V 5HA
England
E-mail: info@mcimusic.co.uk
Web site: www.musicclub.com

Music for Little People
PO Box 1460
Redway, CA 95560 USA
Tel: (800) 346-4445
E-mail: musicforlittlepeople
   @mflp.com

Music of the World
PO Box 3620
Chapel Hill, NC 27515-3620
   USA
Tel: (888) 264-6689
Fax: (919) 932-9700
E-mail: motw@mindspring.com
Web site: www.
   musicoftheworld.com

Narada Media
4650 N. Port Washington Rd.

Milwaukee, WI 53212-1063
   USA
Tel: (414) 961-8350
Fax: (414) 961-8351

Nascente
Music Collection International
   Ltd.
76 Dean St.
London W1V 5HA
England
Tel: 44 171 3968899
Fax: 44 171 3968900
E-mail: info@mcimusic.co.uk
Web site: www.vci.co.uk

Naxos of America, Inc.
416 Mary Lindsay Polk Dr.,
   Ste. 5
Franklin, TN 37067 USA
Web site: www.hnh.com/hnh.
   htm

New World Records
701 Seventh Ave.
New York, NY 10036 USA

Nimbus
609 E. Market St., Ste. 203
Charlottesville, VA 22902 USA
Tel: (804) 985-8555
Fax: (804) 985-3953
E-mail: nimbuscd@aol.com
Web site: www.nimbus.ltd.uk/
   nrl/index.html

Nonesuch Records
75 Rockefeller Plaza
New York, NY 10019 USA
Tel: (212) 275-4000
Fax: (212) 956-2270
Web site: www.nonesuch.com

North Star Music
22 London St.
Providence, RI 02818-3628
   USA
E-mail: info@northstarmusic.
   com
Web site: www.
   northstarmusic.com

NorthSide
530 North Third St.
Minneapolis, MN 55401 USA
Tel: (612) 375-0233
Fax: (612) 359-9580
E-mail: chill@noside.com
Web site: www.noside.com

N2K Encoded Music
55 Broad St., 18th Fl.
New York, NY 10004 USA
Tel: (212) 378-6100
Fax: (212) 742-1775
Web site: www.
   n2kencodedmusic.com

NubeNegra
See: Alula Records

Palm Pictures
4 Columbus Circle, 5th Fl.
New York, NY 10019 USA
Tel: (212) 506-5800
Fax: (212) 506-5809
Web site: www.palmpictures.
com

Pandisc Records
6157 NW 167th St., Ste. F-9
Miami, FL 33015 USA
Tel: (305) 557-1914
Fax: (305) 557-9262

Park Records
678 Massachusetts Ave.
Cambridge, MA 02139 USA
Web site: www.parkrecords.
com

Philips
See: PolyGram

Philo
See: Rounder Records

Pigeon Inlet Records
Box 1202
St. John's, Newfoundland
Canada
A1C 5M9
Tel: (709) 754-7324
Fax: (709) 722-8557
E-mail: krussell@pigeoninlet.
nfnet.com
Web site: www.pigeoninlet.
nfnet.com/

Point
825 Eighth Ave., 26th Fl.
New York, NY 10019 USA
Tel: (212) 333-8000
Fax: (212) 333-8402
Web site: www.pointmusic.com

Polydor Records
1416 N. La Brea Ave.
Hollywood, CA 90028 USA
Tel: (213) 856-6600
Fax: (213) 856-6610
E-mail: polydor@us.polygram.
com
Web site: www.polydor.com

PolyGram/PolyGram Latino
PolyGram Holding, Inc.
825 Eighth Ave.
New York, NY 10019 USA
Tel: (212) 333-8357
Fax: (212) 333-8203
E-mail: comm-us@PolyGram.
com
Web site: www.polygram.
com/polyindex.html

Prestige/Folklore
10th and Parker
Berkeley, CA 94710 USA

1-800-PRIME CD
111 E. 14th St., Ste. 300
New York, NY 10003 USA
Tel: (212) 366-5982
Fax: (212) 366-0615
E-mail: mail@primecd.com
Web site: www.primecd.com

Priority Records
6430 Sunset Blvd., 9th Fl.
Hollywood, CA 90028 USA
Tel: (213) 467-0151
Fax: (213) 856-0150
Web site: www.priorityrec.com

Private Music
8750 Wilshire Blvd.
Beverly Hills, CA 90211 USA
Tel: (310) 358-4500
Fax: (310) 358-4520

Putumayo World Music/Putu-mayo Artists
324 Lafayette St., 7th Fl.
New York, NY 10012 USA
Tel: (212) 625-1400
Fax: (212) 460-0095
Web site: www.putumayo.com

Qbadisk
PO Box 1256
Old Chelsea Station
New York, NY 10011 USA

Qwest Records
3800 Barham Blvd., Ste. 503
Los Angeles, CA 90068 USA
Tel: (213) 874-7770
Fax: (213) 874-5049
E-mail: info@qwestrecords.
com
Web site: www.qwestrecords.
com

RAS Records
PO Box 42517
Washington, DC 20015 USA
Tel: (301) 588-9641
Fax: (301) 588-7108
Web site: www.rasrecords.com

RCA Records
1540 Broadway
New York, NY 10036 USA
Tel: (212) 930-4000
Fax: (212) 930-4468
Web site: www.bmg.com

RealWorld
4650 N. Port Washington Rd.
Milwaukee, WI 53212 USA
Tel: (414) 961-8350
Fax: (414) 961-8351

Web site:
www.realworld.on.net/

Red House Records
PO Box 4044
St. Paul, MN 55104 USA
Tel: (800) 695-4687
Web site: www.
redhouserecords.com/

Reference Recordings
580 Crespi Dr., Unit 1
Pacifica, CA 04044 USA
Tel: (650) 355-1892
Fax: (650) 355-1949
E-mail: rrec@aol.com
Web site: www.
referencerecordings.com

Rego Irish Records and Tapes
64 New Hyde Park Rd.
Garden City, NY 11530 USA
Tel: (516) 328-7800
Fax: (516) 354-7768
E-mail: kellsmus@pipeline.com

Repercussion
6913 W. Barrington Ct.
New Orleans, LA 70128 USA

Reprise Records
3300 Warner Blvd.
Burbank, CA 91505-4694 USA
Tel: (818) 846-9090
Fax: (818) 953-3211
E-mail: ToReprise@aol.com
Web site: www.RepriseRec.
com/

Restless Records
1616 Vista Del Mar Ave.
Hollywood, CA 90028 USA
Tel: (800) 573-7853/
Tel: (213) 957-4357
Fax: (213) 957-4355
Web site: www.restless.com/

Rhino Records
10635 Santa Monica Blvd.
Los Angeles, CA 90025 USA
Tel: (310) 474-4778
Fax: (310) 441-6575
E-mail: drrhino@rhino.com
Web site: www.rhino.com

RMM Records
568 Broadway, Ste. 806
New York, NY 10012 USA
Tel: (212) 925-2828
Fax: (212) 925-6154
E-mail: rmmrecords@aol.com
Web site: www.rmmrecords.
com

Rounder Records
1 Camp St.
Cambridge, MA 02140 USA

Tel: (617) 354-0700
Fax: (617) 491-1970
E-mail: info@rounder.com
Web site: www.rounder.com

Rykodisc
Shetland Park
27 Congress St.
Salem, MA 01970 USA
Tel: (978) 825-3200
Fax: (978) 825-3290
E-mail: info@rykodisc.com
Web site: www.rykodisc.com

Sain Records
Llandwrog, Caernarfon
Gwynedd
Wales LL54 5TG
UK
Web site: www.sain.wales.com

Scamp Records
See: Caroline Records

Shanachie Entertainment Corp.
37 E. Clinton St.
Newton, NJ 07860 USA
Tel: (201) 579-7763
Fax: (201) 579-7083
E-mail: contact@shanachie.
com
Web site: www.shanachie.com

Silver Wave Records
2475 Broadway
Boulder, CO 80304 USA
Tel: (303) 443-5617
Fax: (303) 443-0877
E-mail: info@silverwave.com
Web site: www.silverwave.com

SingSong Inc.
PO Box 6371
St. John's, Newfoundland
Canada
A1C 6J9
Tel: (709) 726-3570
Fax: 726-3533
E-mail: singsong@nfld.com
Web site: www.singsong.nfld.
com/

Sire Records
75 Rockefeller Plz., 17th Fl.
New York, NY 10019 USA
Tel: (212) 275-2500
Fax: (212) 275-3562
Web site: www.sirerecords.
com

Six Degrees Records
PO Box 411347
San Francisco, CA 94141-1347
USA

Web site: www.
 sixdegreesrecords.com

Slash Records
7381 Beverly Blvd.
Los Angeles, CA 90036 USA
Tel: (213) 937-4660
Fax: (213) 933-7277

Slask Sweden
Box 27
S-430 84 Styrsö
Sweden

**Smithsonian Folkways
Recordings**
Center for Folklife Programs
 and Cultural Studies
955 L'Enfant Plaza, Ste. 7300,
 MRC 953
Smithsonian Institution
Washington, DC 20560 USA
E-mail: folkways@aol.com
Web site: www.si.edu/folkways

**SOAR (Sound of America
Records)**
PO Box 8606
Albuquerque, NM 87198 USA
Tel: (505) 268-6110
Fax: (505) 268-0237
E-mail: soar@rt66.com
Web site: www.
 soundofamerica.com

Solar Records
1635 N. Cahuenga Blvd.
Los Angeles, CA 90028 USA
Tel: (323) 461-0390
Fax: (323) 461-9032

Sonodisc
85 rue Foundary
75015 Paris
France
E-mail: sonodisc
 @club-internet.fr

Sony Music
550 Madison Ave.
New York, NY 10022 USA
Tel: (212) 833-8000
Fax: (212) 833-7120
Web site: www.sonymusic.com

Sounds True
413 S. Arthur Ave.
Louisville, CO 80027 USA

Stern's Music
71 Warren St.
New York, NY 10007 USA
Tel: (212) 964-5455
Fax: (212) 964-5955
E-mail: infonyc@sternsmusic.
 com

Straker's
242 Utica Ave.
Brooklyn, NY 11213 USA
Tel: (718) 756-0040

Sugar Hill Records
PO Box 55300
Durham, NC 27717 USA
Tel: (919) 489-4349
Fax: (919) 489-6080

Sukay World Music
3450 Sacramento St., Ste. 523
San Francisco, CA 94118 USA
Tel: (415) 751-6090
Fax: (415) 752-3559
E-mail: sukay@sirius.com

Tamizdat
PO Box 20618
New York, NY 10009 USA
Tel/fax: (212) 780-0287
E-mail: info@tamizdat.org

Temple Records
See: Rounder Records

Thirsty Ear Recordings
274 Madison Ave., Ste. 804
New York, NY 10016 USA
Tel: (212) 889-9595
Fax: (212) 889-3641
E-mail: thirstye@aol.com
Web site: www.thirstyear.com

Tinder Records
619 Martin Ave. Unit 1
Rohnert Park, CA 94928 USA
Tel: (800) 900-4527
Fax: (707) 588-9229
E-mail: tinder@worldmusic.com
Web site: www.worldmusic.
 com/tinder

Topic Records
50 Stroud Green Rd.
London N4 3EF
England
Tel: 44 171 2631420

Tradition Records
See: See Rykodisk

Traditional Crossroads
PO Box 20320, Greeley
 Square Station
New York, NY 10001-9922 USA
Tel: (800) 422-6282
E-mail: tradcross@aol.com
Web site: www.rootsworld.
 com/crossroads/

Triloka Records
6399 Wilshire Blvd., Ste. 404
Los Angeles, CA 90048 USA
Tel: (800) 578-4419
Web site: www.triloka.com

Triple Earth
24 Foley St.
London W1P 7LA
England
E-mail: iain@triple-earth.co.uk

TriStar/Sony Music
79 5th Ave.
New York, NY 10003 USA
Tel: (212) 337-5454
Fax: (212) 337-5453

Tuff Gong International
350 5th Ave., Ste. 5101
New York, NY 10118 USA
Tel: (212) 563-5173
Fax: (212) 594-1594

TVT Records
23 E. 4th St., 3rd Fl.
New York, NY 10003 USA
Tel: (212) 979-6410
Fax: (212) 979-6489
Web site: www.tvtrecords.com

Universal Records
1755 Broadway, 7th Fl.
New York, NY 10019 USA
Tel: (212) 373-0600
Fax: (212) 247-3954

Uptown Records
1755 Broadway, 7th Fl.
New York, NY 10019 USA
Tel: (212) 841-8114
Fax: (212) 841-8142

Vanguard Recording Society
A Welk Music Group Company
2700 Pennsylvania Ave.
Santa Monica, CA 90404-4000
 USA
Tel: (310) 829-WELK (9355)
Fax: (310) 315-9996
E-mail: info
 @vanguardrecords.com
Web site: www.
 vanguardrecords.com

Varèse Sarabande Records
11846 Ventura Blvd., Ste. 130
Studio City, CA 91604 USA
Tel: (818) 753-4143
E-mail: info
 @varesesarabande.com
Web site: www.
 varesesarabande.com

Varrick Records
See: Rounder Records

Verve Music Group
555 W. 57th St., 10th Fl.
New York, NY 10019 USA
Tel: (212) 333-8000
Fax: (212) 333-8194

Web site: www.
 vervemusicgroup.com

Virgin Records
338 N. Foothill Rd.
Beverly Hills, CA 90210 USA
Tel: (310) 278-1181
Fax: (310) 278-6231
Web site: www.virginrecords.
 com

VP Record Distributors
89-05 138th St.
Jamaica, NY 11435 USA
Tel: (718) 291-7058
Fax: (718) 658-3573
Web site: www.vprecords.com

Warner Bros. Records
3300 Warner Blvd.
Burbank, CA 91505-4694 USA
Tel: (818) 846-9090
Fax: (818) 846-8474
E-mail: wbrepinc@wbr.com
Web site: www.wbr.com

Water Lily Acoustics
PO Box 91448
Santa Barbara, CA 93190 USA
E-mail: music
 @waterlilyacoustics.com
Web site: www.
 waterlilyacoustics.com

Watermelon Records
1201 W. 24th, Ste. 204
Austin, TX 78765-9056 USA
Tel: (512) 472-6192
Fax: (512) 472-6249

WEA Latina
5201 Blue Lagoon Dr., Ste.
 200
Miami, FL 33126-2065 USA
Tel: (305) 266-6077
Fax: (305) 266-8771

Wicklow Entertainment
1540 Broadway
New York, NY 10036-4098
 USA
Tel: (212) 930-4547
Fax: (212) 930-6663
Web site: www.
 wicklowrecords.com

Windham Hill Records
c/o Sound Delivery
PO Box 1862
Woodland, CA 95776-1862
 USA
Tel: (310) 358-4800
Fax: (310) 358-4805
E-mail: whinfo@bmge.com
Web site: www.windham.com

The WORK Group
2100 Colorado Ave.

Santa Monica, CA 90404 USA
Tel: (310) 449-2666
Fax: (310) 449-2095
Web site: www.epiccenter.
    com/EpicCenter/work/
    index.qry

World Circuit
8-14 St. Pancras Way
London, NWI 0QG
England
Tel: 44 171 3879943
Fax: 44 171 3834908

World Music Network
6 Abbeville Mews
88 Clapham Park Rd.
London SW4 7BX
England
Tel: 44 171 4985252
Fax: 44 171 4985353
E-mail: post@worldmusic.net
Web site: www.worldmusic.net

Xenophile Records
See: Green Linnet Records

Yazoo Records
See: Shanachie Records

More than most forms of music, you have to see the "world"—in-person is the way that so many world musics have been experienced for centuries in their own cultures, with the spectacular live presentation you'd expect. But knowing where to find the world is also not as easy as with other forms of music, so here's a list of some of the U.S. establishments that regularly feature world-music artists. Check local concert listings for the whole picture, and consult the publications in our Books and Magazines list for the most up-to-date information on the many world-music festivals held each year—but on the list below, find some of the best places to start!

Alabama

The 22nd Street Jazz Cafe
710 22nd St. S.
Birmingham, AL 35233-3114
(205) 252-0407

Arizona

Fiddler's Dream Coffee House
1702 E. Cactus Wren
Phoenix, AZ 85020-5516
(602) 997-9795

Rhythm Room
1014 E. Indian School Rd.
Phoenix, AZ 85014-4810
(602) 265-4842

California

Ashkenaz
1317 San Pablo Ave.
Berkeley, CA 94702-1021
(510) 525-5054

Bahia Cabana
1600 Market St.
San Francisco, CA 94102-5910
(415) 626-3306

Blarney Stone
5701 Geary St.
San Francisco, CA 94121-2111
(415) 386-9914

Cafe du Nord
2170 Market St.
San Francisco, CA 94114-1319
(415) 861-5016

El Rio
3158 Mission St.
San Francisco, CA 94110-4560
(415) 282-3325

The Elbow Room
647 Valencia
San Francisco, CA 94110-1150
(415) 552-7788

House of Blues
8430 Sunset Blvd.
Los Angeles, CA 90069-1910
(213) 650-0247

Jack's Sugar Shack
1707 N. Vine St.
Hollywood, CA 90028-5248
(213) 466-7005

Luna Park
665 N. Robertson Blvd.
West Hollywood, CA 90069-5016
(310) 652-0611

Maritime Hall
450 Harrison St.
San Francisco, CA 94105-2640
(415) 974-0674

Moguls
1650 N. Schrader St.
Hollywood, CA 90028-6214
(213) 465-7449

Pat O'Shea's
2848 Geary St.
San Francisco, CA 94118-3408
(415) 752-3148

Ventura Theatre
26 S. Chestnut St.
Ventura, CA 93001-2800
(805) 648-1888

Colorado

Bentley's at the Broker Inn
555 30th St.
Boulder, CO 80303-2397
(303) 444-3330

Los Cabos II
1512 Curtis St.
Denver, CO 80202-2342
(303) 571-0007

Maximilian's
2151 Lawrence St.
Denver, CO 80205-2032
(303) 297-0015

District of Columbia

Bravo! Bravo!
1001 Connecticut Ave. NW
Washington, DC 20036
(202) 223-5330

Coco Loco
810 7th St. NW
Washington, DC 20001-3718
(202) 289-2626

Cities
2424 18th St. NW
Washington, DC 20009
(202) 328-7194

Diversite
1526 14th St. NW
Washington, DC 20005-3746
(202) 234-5740

Kala Kala
2439 18th St. NW
Washington, DC 20009-2042
(202) 232-5433

Kilimanjaro
1724 California St. NW
Washington, DC 20009-2681
(202) 328-3838

Latin Jazz Alley
1721 Columbia Rd. NW
Washington, DC 20009-2803
(202) 328-6190

Takoma Station
6914 Fourth St. NW
Washington, DC 20012-1904
(202) 829-1999

Florida

Brazilian Delight
154 SW 1 Ave.
Miami, FL 33130-1620
(305) 374-0032

Cafe Azucar
740 SW 8th St.
Miami, FL 33130-3311
(305) 858-4224

Cafe Nostalgia
2212 SW 8th St.
Miami, FL 33135-4914
(305) 541-2631

Cafe 165
16509 NW 27 Ave.
Opa Locka, FL 33054-6406
(305) 621-5323

Centro Vasco
2235 SW 8th St.
Miami, FL 33135-4913
(305) 643-9626

Club Tamarind
3900 NW 21st St.
Miami, FL 33142-6704
(305) 220-7115

Hungry Sailor
3426 Main Hwy.
Coconut Grove, FL 33133-5916
(305) 444-9359

Respectable Street Cafe
218 Espanola Way
Miami Beach, FL 33139-4106
(305) 672-1707

Georgia

Chili Peppers
208 Pharr Rd.
Atlanta, GA 30305-2204
(404) 812-9266

Kaya
1068 Peachtree St.
Atlanta, GA 30309-3963
(404) 874-4460

Sanctuary International
128 E. Andrews Dr.

Atlanta, GA 30305-1315
(404) 262-1377

Tongue & Groove
3055 Peachtree Rd.
Atlanta, GA 30305-2221
(404) 261-2325

Illinois

Bossa Nova
1960 N. Clybourn
Chicago, IL 60614-4924
(312) 248-4800

El Jardin's Fiesta Cantina
3407 N. Clark St.
Chicago, IL 60657-1605
(773) 327-4646

Green Dolphin
2200 N. Ashland
Chicago, IL 60614-3026
(773) 395-0066

Hot House
31 E. Balbo
Chicago, IL 60605-2121
(312) 362-9707

La Piramide Azteca
3661 S. Archer Ave.
Chicago, IL 60609-1058
(312) 523-8020

720 Club
720 N. Wells St.
Chicago, IL 60610-3510
(312) 397-0600

Vinyl
1615 N. Clybourn
Chicago, IL 60614-5507
(312) 587-8469

Maryland

Phantasmagoria
11319 Elkin St.
Wheaton, MD 20902-4609
(301) 949-8886

Massachusetts

Club Passim
47 Palmer St.
Harvard Sq.
Cambridge, MA 02138-3718
(617) 492-7679

House of Blues
96 Winthrop St.
Harvard Sq.
Cambridge, MA 02138-4930
(617) 491-BLUE (2583)

Mama Kin
36 Lansdowne St.
Boston, MA 02215-3411
(617) 536-2100

Phoenix Landing
512 Massachusetts Ave.
Central Sq.
Cambridge, MA 02139-4029
(617) 576-6260

Rhythm and Spice
315 Mass Ave.
Cambridge, MA 02139-4151
(617) 497-0970

Ryles Jazz Club
212 Hampshire St.
Inman Sq.
Cambridge, MA 02139-1333
(617) 876-9300

Michigan

Parabox
1927 Michigan Ave.
Detroit, MI 48216-1347
(313) 965-3333

Sierra Afrique
19325 Plymouth Rd.
Detroit, MI 48228-1359
(313) 838-3833

New York

Cafe Remy
104 Greenwich St.
New York, NY 10006-1801
(212) 267-4646

The Knitting Factory
74 Leonard St.
New York, NY 10013-3437
(212) 219-3006

Nell's
246 W. 14th St.
New York, NY 10011-7201
(212) 675-1567

Night Owls at Club Morocco
1036 2nd Ave.
New York, NY 10022-4006
(212) 715-0668

SOB's
204 Varick St.
New York, NY 10014-4809
(212) 243-4940

Oregon

Atwater's Restaurant
111 SW 5th Ave.
Portland, OR 97204

(503) 275-3629

Dublin Pub
6821 SW Beaverton Hillsdale Hwy.
Portland, OR 97225-1407
(503) 297-2889

Texas

Club Babalu
2912 McKinney Ave.
Dallas, TX 75204-2431
(214) 953-0300

Elephant Room
315 Congress
Austin, TX 78701-4023
(214) 473-2279

Ruta Maya
218 W. Fourth St.
Austin, TX 78701-3917
(214) 472-9637

Shaggy's
1600 S. Congress Ave.
Austin, TX 78704-3522
(214) 447-5375

Utah

Cinegril
344 S. 300 E.
Salt Lake City, UT 84111-2504
(801) 328-4900

Gepetto's
230 S.1300 E.
Salt Lake City, UT 84102-2609
(801) 583-1013

Oasis Cafe
151 S. 500 E.
Salt Lake City, UT 84102-1906
(801) 322-0404

Virginia

Outbacks
917 Preston Ave.
Charlottesville, VA 22903-4421
(804) 979-7211

The Prism Coffee House
214 Rugby Rd.
Charlottesville, VA 22903-1878
(804) 977-7476

Trax
120-X 11th St. SW
Charlottesville, VA 22903-3408
(804) 295-8729

Washington

Beso Del Sol
4468 Stone Way N.
Seattle, WA 98103-7439
(206) 547-8087

Black Bean Coffee House
3801 E. Mercer Way
Mercer Island, WA 98040-
3805
(206) 232-7115 x254

Dimitrion's Jazz Alley
2033 6th Ave.
Seattle, WA 98121
(206) 441-9729

This list was excerpted from Rhythm *magazine. All rights reserved. For more information about a subscription to* Rhythm *call: 1-800-464-2767.* Rhythm *is a monthly world music magazine featuring music, film, food, and travel. Every issue includes a 10-track complimentary world-music CD with a subscription.*

The following are some of the U.S. stations that feature world-music programming. Radio formats are always subject to change, and the world-music offerings are likely to be just one part of a diverse selection; your best bet is to check the local radio listings in your area or those you visit. There is always a good chance of catching strong world-music programming on the nearest outlet of National Public Radio (http://www.npr.org), the Pacifica network (http://www.pacifica.org), and other listener-sponsored or college stations.

Alaska

Anchorage
KNBA (90.3 FM)

Fairbanks
KSUA (91.5 FM)

Arizona

Tucson
KXCI (93.1 FM)

Window Rock
KTNN (660 AM)/KWRK (96.1 FM)

California

Berkeley
KPFA (94.1 FM)

Cupertino
KKUP (91.5 FM)
WAZU (90.3 FM)

Davis
KDVS (90.3 FM)

Fresno
KFRF (102.3 FM)

Los Angeles
KXLU (88.9 FM)

Nevada City
KVMR (89.5 FM)

Pacific Grove
KAZU (90.3 FM)

Sacramento
KSSU (1580 AM)
KXJC/KXPR (90.9 FM)
KXJZ (88.9 FM)

San Jose
KVCH (104.1 FM)

San Luis Obispo
KGUR (105.3 FM)

Santa Clara
KSCU (103.3 FM)

Santa Cruz
KUSP (89.9 FM)

Santa Monica
KCRW (89.9 FM)

Santa Rosa
KBBF (89.1 FM)

Tahoe City
KKTO (80.5 FM)

Colorado

Grand Junction
KAFM (88.1 FM)

Connecticut

New London
WCNI (91.1 FM)

Storrs
WHUS (91.7 FM)

West Hartford
WWUH (91.3 FM)

Georgia

Atlanta
WREK (91.1 FM)
WRFG (89.3 FM)

Iowa

Davenport
KALA (88.5 FM/105.5 FM)

Louisiana

Eunice
KEUN (1330 AM)

Lafayette
KRVS (88.7 FM)

New Orleans
WWOZ (88.7 FM)

Washington
KNEK (1190 AM)

Maryland

Towson
WTMD (89.7 FM)

Massachusetts

Amherst
WMUA (91.1 FM)

Boston
WERS (88.9 FM)
WZBC (90.3 FM)

Cape Cod
WOMR (92.1 FM)

Michigan

Ann Arbor
WCBN (88.3 FM)

Detroit
CJAM (91.5 FM)
WDET (101.9 FM)
WDTR (90.9 FM)

Minnesota

Minneapolis
KUOM (770 AM)

Missouri

Florissant
KCFV (89.5 FM)

Kansas City
KKFI (90.1 FM)

Montana

Missoula
KBGA (89.9 FM)

New Hampshire

Keene
WKNH (91.3 FM)

New Jersey

East Orange
WFMU (91.1 FM)

Newark
WBGO (88.3 FM)

Pemberton
WBZC (88.9 FM)

Trenton
WTSR (91.3 FM)

New Mexico

Albuquerque
KUNM (89.9 FM)

Santa Fe/Albuquerque
KBAC (98.1/95.9 FM)

New York

Brooklyn
WBCR (590 AM)

Ithaca
WICB (91.7 FM)

New York
WBAI (99.5 FM)
WLIB (1190 AM)
WPAT (AMOR) (93.1 FM)
WRTN (93.5 FM)
WSKQ (MEGA) (97.9 FM)

Poughkeepsie
WVKR (91.3 FM)

North Carolina

Durham
WXDU (88.7 FM)

Ohio

Cleveland
WRUW (91.1 FM)

Dayton
WDPS (89.5 FM)

Oberlin
WOBC (91.5 FM)

Yellow Springs
WYSO (91.3 FM)

Oklahoma

Stillwater
KSPI (93.7 FM)

Oregon

Portland
KBOO (90.7 FM)

Pennsylvania

Carlisle
WDCV (88.3 FM)

State College
WKPS (90.7 FM)

Texas

Austin
KOOP/KVRX (91.7 FM)

Houston
KTRU (91.7 FM)

Utah

Salt Lake City
KRCL (90.9 FM)

Vermont

Plainfield
WGDR (91.1 FM)

Wisconsin

Beloit
WBCR (90.3 FM)

musicHound
WORLD

Indexes

The following albums achieved the highest rating possible — ♪♪♪♪♪ — from our discriminating MusicHound *World writers. You can't miss with any of these recordings. (Note: Albums are listed under the name of the entry (or entries) in which they appear and are not necessarily albums by that individual artist or group. The album could be a compilation album, a film soundtrack, an album on which the artist or group appears as a guest, etc. Consult the artist or group's entry for specific information. Albums that appear in sidebars are listed under the title of the sidebar. Albums that appear in the Compilations section are listed at the end of this index under "Compilations.")*

Abana Ba Nasery
Abana Ba Nasery (Globestyle, 1989)

Nathan Abshire
French Blues (Arhoolie, 1993)
Le Grand Mamou: A Cajun Music Anthology: The Historic Victor/Bluebird Sessions 1928–1941 (Country Music Foundation, 1990)
Les Haricots Sont Pas Salés: Legendary Masters of Cajun and Creole Music (Cinq Planetes, 1998)

The Abyssinians
Forward (Alligator, 1982/Musidisc, 1996)
Forward on to Zion (Blue Moon, 1976)

Satta Massa Ganna (Heartbeat, 1993)

King Sunny Adé
Juju Music (Mango, 1982)

Africando
Vol. 2 — Tierra Tradicional (Stern's, 1994)

Afro Celt Sound System
Kora Revolution (Palm Pictures/Yoff, 1999)

Pierre Akendengue
Lambarena (Celluloid/Melodie France, 1993)

Haris Alexiou
Laika Tragoudia (Mercury, 1975)
Mikra Asia (Asia Minor) (1973)
To Pehnidi tis Kardias (Games of the Heart) (Mercury, 1988)

Altan
Horse with a Heart (Green Linnet, 1989)

Alphonse "Bois Sec" Ardoin
Allons Danser (Rounder, 1998)
The Ardoin Family Band with Dewey Balfa: A Couple of Cajuns (Sonet, 1987)
La Musique Creole (Arhoolie, 1997)
Les Blues du Bayou (Melodeon, 1967)
Les Haricots Sont Pas Salés: Legendary Masters of Cajun and Creole Music (Cinq Planetes, 1998)

Amédée Ardoin
Cajun Music: Fais Do-Do (Columbia, 1994)
I'm Never Comin' Back: The Roots of Zydeco (Arhoolie, 1995)

Frankie Armstrong
Till the Grass O'ergrew the Corn (Fellside, 1996)

Arrow
Knock Dem Dead (Mango, 1988)
Soca Savage (Arrow Records, 1984)
Zombie Soca (Arrow, 1991)

Abed Azrié
Aromates (Nonesuch, 1990)
Suerte (Harmonia Mundi France, 1994)

Susana Baca
Del Fuego y Del Agua (Tonga, 1997)
The Soul of Black Peru (Luaka Bop, 1995)
Susana Baca (Luaka Bop, 1997)

Bad Brains
Bad Brains (ROIR, 1982/1996)

Badawi
The Heretic of Ether (Asphodel, 1999)

The Balfa Brothers
The Balfa Brothers Play Traditional Cajun Music, Vols. 1 & 2 (Swallow, 1987)
Les Haricots Sont Pas Salés: Legendary Masters of Cajun and Creole Music (Cinq Planetes, 1998)

Balfa Toujours
Allons Danser (Rounder, 1998)

Carlos Barbosa-Lima
Music of the Brazilian Masters (Concord Picante, 1989)

Mario Bauzá
Messidor's Finest, Volume One (Messidor, 1997)
My Time Is Now (Messidor, 1993)
Tanga (Messidor, 1992)

Francis Bebey
Akwaaba (Original Music, 1986)
Dibiye (Pee Wee, 1998)

Nandolo: Works 1963–1994 (Original Music, 1995)

M'Bilia Bel
Phenomene (IMA, 1996)

Harry Belafonte
All-Time Greatest Hits, Vols. 1–3 (RCA, 1987)
Belafonte at Carnegie Hall (RCA, 1959)
Calypso (RCA, 1956)

Jorge Ben
A Tabua Da Esmeralda (Philips, 1974)
Ben (Philips, 1972)
Gil e Jorge (Verve, 1994)
Live in Rio, Vols. I and II (Warner-Latin, 1992)

Mary Bergin
Feadoga Stain (Gael-Linn, 1976/Shanachie, 1992)

V.M. Bhatt
Guitar a la Hindustan (Magnasound/OMI, 1992)
Saltanah (Water Lily Acoustics, 1996)

Asha Bhosle
Legacy (AMMP, 1996)

Bhundu Boys
Shabini (DiscAfrique France, 1986)
Tsvimbodzemoto (DiscAfrique, 1987)

Tony Bird
Sorry Africa (Rounder, 1991)

Black Stalin
In Ah Earlier Time (Makossa, 1981)
Roots, Rock, Soca (Rounder, 1991)
To De Master (WB, 1989)
You Ask for It (CCP, 1984)

Luiz Bonfá
The Bossa Nova Years (Verve, 1964/1989)
Jazz Samba (Verve, 1963)

The Bothy Band
The Bothy Band 1975 (Mulligan, 1975/Green Linnet, 1983)
Old Hag You Have Killed Me (Mulligan, 1976/Green Linnet, 1982)

Boukan Ginen
Jou a Rive (Xenophile, 1995)

Boukman Eksperyans
Kalfou Danjere/Dangerous Crossroads (Mango, 1992)
Libète (Pran Pou Pran'l!)/Freedom (Let's Take It!) (Mango, 1995)

Robin Huw Bowen
Kiss of Fire (Fflach, 1992/Firebird, 1994)

David Bowie
"Heroes" (RCA, 1977/Rykodisc, 1991)

Low (RCA, 1977/Rykodisc, 1991)

The Boys of the Lough
The Boys of the Lough (Shanachie, 1973)

Anouar Brahem
Barzakh (ECM, 1991)

Brave Old World
Blood Oranges (Pinorrek Records, 1997)

Máire Breatnach
Riverdance (Celtic Heartbeat, 1995)

Kevin Burke
Andy Irvine, Paul Brady (Mulligan, 1976/Green Linnet, 1981)

Cachao
Master Sessions, Vol. 1 (Crescent Moon/Epic, 1994)

Calypso Rose
Trouble (Straker's, 1984)

Eliza Carthy
Norma Waterson (Rykodisc, 1996)

Martin Carthy
Life and Limb (Topic/Green Linnet, 1991)
The Martin Carthy Collection (Green Linnet, 1993)

John Carty
At the Racket (Racket, 1997)
Last Night's Fun (Shanachie, 1996)

Hari Prasad Chaurasia
Call of the Valley (Hemisphere/EMI, 1967)

Clifton Chenier
60 Minutes with the King of Zydeco (Arhoolie, 1988)
Zydeco Dynamite: The Clifton Chenier Anthology (Rhino, 1993)

The Chieftains
Chieftains 3 (Claddagh, 1971/Shanachie, 1980s)
Chieftains 4 (Claddagh, 1973/Shanachie, 1980s)
Ó Riada sa Gaiety (Gael-Linn, 1969)

Chinese Classical Music (sidebar)
Various Artists: *The Hugo Masters: An Anthology of Chinese Classical Music* (Celestial Harmonies, 1992)

Stella Chiweshe
Ambuya? (Globestyle, 1988)
Chisi (Piranha, 1988)
The Healing Tree (Shanachie, 1998)
Kumusha (Piranha, 1989)
Shungu (Piranha, 1990)

Clannad
Dulaman (Blackbird, 1976/Shanachie, 1988)

Johnny Clarke
Authorized Rockers (Virgin Frontline, 1991)

Jimmy Cliff
The Harder They Come (Island, 1972)

Shirley Collins
Etchingham Steam Band (Fledg'ling, 1995)
For As Many As Will (Topic, 1978/Hokey Pokey, 1993)
Love, Death, and the Lady (EMI, 1974)
Morris On (Island, 1972/Hannibal)
No Roses (BBC, 1971/Mooncrest, 1991)

The Congos
Arkology (Island, 1997)
Heart of the Congos (Black Art, 1977/Blood & Fire, 1996)

Gal Costa
Acustico (BMG Brazil, 1997)
Domingo (PolyGram Brazil, 1967)
India (PolyGram Brazil, 1973)
Rio Revisited (PolyGram Brazil, 1992)

Celia Cruz
100 Percent Azucar: The Best of Celia Cruz con la Sonora Matancera (Rhino, 1997)

¡Cubanismo!
Jesús Alamañy's ¡Cubanismo! (Hannibal, 1996)
Reencarnacion (Hannibal, 1998)

Culture
Baldhead Bridge (Shanachie, 1993)
Two Sevens Clash (Shanachie, 1988)

George Dalaras
Mikra Asia (1973)
Ta Rembetika (EMI/Minos, 1975)
Y Ta Tragoudia K' Ego Fteo (EMI/Minos, 1993)

Jackie Daly
Music from Sliabh Luachra (Topic, 1977/Green Linnet, 1992)

Olu Dara
In the World: From Natchez to New York (Atlantic, 1998)

Paco de Lucia
Guitar Trio (PolyGram, 1996)

Dead Can Dance
Spiritchaser (4AD, 1996)

Geno Delafose
La Chanson Perdue (Rounder, 1998)
That's What I'm Talking About! (Rounder, 1996)

John Delafose & the Eunice Playboys
Blues Stay Away from Me (Rounder, 1993)
Joe Pete Got Two Women (Arhoolie, 1988)

Sandy Denny
The BBC Sessions 1971–73 (Strange Fruit, 1997)
Sandy (Island, 1972)
Who Knows Where the Time Goes? (Island, 1985)

D'Gary
Mbo Loza (Indigo, 1992)

Toumani Diabaté
Kaira (Hannibal/Rykodisc, 1988)
Kulanjan (Hannibal, 1999)

Diblo Dibala
Amour Fou (Hannibal, 1988)
Matchatcha (AfricMusic France)

Manu Dibango
Logozo (Mango, 1991/1992)

Diga Rhythm Band
Diga Rhythm Band (Rykodisc, 1988)

John Doherty
The Floating Bow—Traditional Fiddle Music from Donegal (Claddagh, 1996)

Felix Dolan
Warming Up (Green Linnet, 1993)

Mikey Dread
African Anthem Dubwise (Dread at the Controls, 1978/Big Cat, 1997)

Paquito D'Rivera
Come on Home (Columbia, 1995)
Havana Café (Chesky, 1992)
Reunion (Messidor, 1991)

The Dubliners
Original Dubliners, 1966–1969 (EMI, 1993)

The Dynatones
Live Wire (World Renowned Sounds, 1982)
Vintage Dynatones (World Renowned Sounds, 1995)

Hamza El Din
Escalay—The Water Wheel (Nonesuch, 1968)
Muwashshah (JVC, 1996)

Eliane Elias
Eliane Elias Sings Jobim (Blue Note, 1998)
The Three Americas (Blue Note, 1997)

Alton Ellis
Cry Tough (Heartbeat, 1993)

The English Beat
I Just Can't Stop It (Sire, 1980)

Enya
Watermark (Reprise, 1989)

Epstein Brothers Band
Kings of Frelekh Land (Wergo/Weltmusik, 1995)

Kudsi Erguner
Fasl: Musique de l'Empire Ottoman (Auvidis Ethnic, 1990)
Sufi Music of Turkey (CMP, 1990)

Cesaria Evora
Miss Perfumado (Lusafrica, 1992/Nonesuch, 1998)

Chaba Fadela
Hana Hana (Mango, 1989)
You Are Mine (Mango, 1988)

Fairport Convention
House Full (Hannibal, 1986)
Liege and Lief (A&M, 1969)
Unhalfbricking (Hannibal, 1969)
What We Did on Our Holidays (Hannibal, 1968)

Joseph Falcon & Cleoma Breaux Falcon
Abbeville Breakdown (Columbia, 1990)
Cajun Dance Party: Fais Do Do (Columbia, 1994)
Cleoma B. Falcon: A Cajun Music Classic (Jadfel, 1983)

Jose Feliciano
Court and Spark (Asylum, 1974)

Fernhill
Llatai (Beautiful Jo, 1998)

Alec Finn
Feadóga Stáin (Shanachie, 1992)

Frank Emilio Flynn
A Tiempo de Danzón (Milan Latino, 1998)

Folk Scat
Folk Scat (Nomad, 1996)

Canray Fontenot
La Musique Creole (Arhoolie, 1997)
Les Blues du Bayou (Melodeon, 1965)
Les Haricots Sont Pas Salés: Legendary Masters of Cajun and Creole Music (Cinq Planetes, 1998)
Louisiana Hot Sauce, Creole Style (Arhoolie, 1992)

Juan Carlos Formell
Songs from a Little Blue House (Wicklow/BMG, 1999)

Fortuna
Cantigas (Fortuna Produções Artísticas, 1994)
La Prima Vez (Fortuna Produções Artísticas, 1993)

Franco
A L'Ancienne Belgique (Grace, 1984)
Attention na SIDA (Sonodisc, 1987)

Cooperation: 1980–1982 (Sonodisc, 1982)
Disques d'Or et Maracas d'Or (Sonodisc)
En Colere: 1979/1980 (Sonodisc)
For Ever (Melodie)
Franco Joue avec Sam Mangwana (Grace)
Le Grande Maitre Franco (Celluloid, 1991)
Lettre à Monsieur le Directeur Général (Melodie)
Live in Europe (Sonodisc)
Merveilles du Passé 1957-1958-1959 (Sonodisc)
Originalité (RetroAfric, 1990)
Tres Impoli (Sonodisc, 1984)
20e Anniversaire (Sonodisc)

Carlos Gardel
The Best of Carlos Gardel (Hemisphere, 1998)

Dick Gaughan
Handful of Earth (Green Linnet, 1981)

Frankie Gavin
Frankie Goes to Town (The Bee's Knees, 1989/Green Linnet, 1991)
A Tribute to Joe Cooley (Gael-Linn, 1986)

Ghazal
As Night Falls on the Silk Road (Shanachie, 1998)
Lost Songs of the Silk Road (Shanachie, 1997)

Astrud Gilberto
Getz/Gilberto (Verve, 1963/1987)

João Gilberto
Getz/Gilberto (Verve, 1963/1987)
The Legendary João Gilberto (World Pacific, 1990)

The Gipsy Kings
The Best of the Gipsy Kings (Columbia, 1995)

Gjallarhorn
Ranarop—Call of the Sea Witch (Finlandia, 1997)

Paddy Glackin
The Whirlwind (Shanachie, 1995)

Ben Goldberg
Here by Now (Music and Arts, 1997)
Junk Genius (Knitting Factory Works, 1996)
Masks & Faces (Nine Winds, 1991/Tzadik, 1996)
Twelve Minor (Avant, 1997)

Jerry Gonzalez & the Fort Apache Band
Crossroads (Milestone, 1994)

Steve Gorn
Luminous Ragas (Interworld, 1994)

Marcia Griffiths
Best of 1969–1974: Put a Little Love in Your Heart (Trojan, 1993)

Mary Jane Lamond
Suas e! (A&M, 1997/Wicklow, 1998)

La Muscagña
En Concierto (Resistencia, 1997)

La Sonora Dinamita
Cumbia, Cumbia: Cumbias de Oro de Colombia (World Circuit, 1989)
Cumbia, Cumbia, Vol. 2 (World Circuit, 1993)

La Sonora Meliyara
La India Meliyara (Riverboat, 1992)

Bill Laswell
Ekstasis (Axiom, 1993)

Le Mystère des Voix Bulgares
Le Mystère des Voix Bulgares (Nonesuch, 1987)

Eddie LeJeune
It's in the Blood (Rounder, 1991)

Iry LeJeune
Cajun's Greatest: The Definitive Collection (Ace, 1994)

Les Têtes Brulées
Hot Heads (Shanachie, 1990)

Lhasa
La Llorona (Atlantic, 1998)

Arto Lindsay
Big Gundown (Nonesuch, 1984)

Little Joe
15 Exitos de Oro, Vol. II (SRP, 1984)
16 de Septiembre (Sony, 1991)

Cheikh Lô
Ne l a Tiasse (World Circuit/Nonesuch, 1997)

Lord Kitchener
Kitch—King of Calypso (Melodisc Reissue)
Kitchener Goes Soca (Charlie's, 1980)
Klassic Kitchener, Volume One (Ice, 1992)
Klassic Kitchener, Volume Two (Ice, 1993)
Klassic Kitchener, Volume Three (Ice, 1993)
Lord Kitchener (Melodisc Reissue)
Master at Work (Kalico, 1987)
Roots of Soca (Charlie's, 1983)

Lord Melody
Lola (B's, 1982)
Precious Melodies (Ice, 1994)

Los Camperos de Valles
El Triunfo (Corasón/Música Tradicional, 1992)

Los Lobos
Kiko (Slash/Warner Bros., 1992)

Los Pleneros de la 21
Somos Boricuas—We Are Puerto Rican (Henry Street, 1996)

Los Super Seven
Just Another Band from East L.A.: A Collection (Warner Bros., 1993)

Los Van Van
Los Van Van: La Colección Cubana (Music Club, 1998)

Trevor Lucas
Fotheringay (Island, 1970)

Baaba Maal
Baayo (The Orphan) (Mango, 1991)
Djam Leelii: The Adventurers (Palm Pictures, 1998)
Firin' in Fouta (Mango, 1994)
Kora Revolution (Palm Pictures/Yoff, 1999)
Lam Toro (King of Toro) (Mango, 1993)
Live at the Royal Festival Hall (Palm Pictures, 1999)
Nomad Soul (Palm Pictures, 1998)
Wango (Syllart, 1985/Stern's, 1988)

Sipho Mabuse
Burn Up (Columbia, 1985)

Ashley MacIsaac
Suas e! (A&M, 1997/Wicklow, 1998)

Talitha MacKenzie
Sólas (Shanachie, 1994)
Spiorad (Shanachie, 1996)

Dougie MacLean
Putamayo Presents the Dougie MacLean Collection (Putamayo, 1995)
Singing Land (Dunkeld Records, 1986)

Mad Professor
No Protection (Circa/Gyroscope, 1994)
Who Knows the Secret of the Master Tape? Dub Me Crazy Part Five (Ariwa, 1990)

Taj Mahal
Kulanjan (Hannibal, 1999)

Mahlathini & Mahotella Queens
The Lion of Soweto (Earthworks, 1987)
The Lion Roars (Shanachie, 1989)
Thokozile (Earthworks, 1988)

Kante Manfila
N'na Niwalé (Merci les Mères) (popular african music, 1990)
Tradition (Celluloid/Melodie, 1989)

Sam Mangwana
Maria Tebbo (Stern's Classics, 1995)
Rumba Music (Stern's, 1994)

Samba Mapangala & Orchestra Virunga
Feet on Fire (Stern's Africa, 1991)

Bob Marley
African Herbsman (Trojan, 1973)
Exodus (Island, 1977)
Natty Dread (Island, 1974)
Songs of Freedom (Island/Tuff Gong, 1992)

Ziggy Marley & the Melody Makers
Chocolate Supa Highway (Capitol, 1997)

John Martyn
Solid Air (Island Records, 1973)

Masada
Bar Kokhba (Tzadik, 1996)
Eight/Het (DIW, 1997)
Five/Hei (DIW, 1995)
Nine/Tet (DIW, 1997)
One/Alef (DIW, 1994)
Seven/Zayin (DIW, 1995)
Six/Vav (DIW, 1995)
Three/Gimel (DIW, 1994)
Two/Beit (DIW, 1994)

Prince Nico Mbarga
Aki Special (Rounder, 1987)

Andy McGann
It's a Hard Road to Travel (Shanachie, 1995)

Eileen McGann
Turn It Around (Dragonwing, 1991)

Chris McGregor
Blues for Mongezi (Ogun, 1975)
Country Cooking (Venture/Virgin, 1988)

Susan McKeown
Bones (Sheila-na-Gig, 1995/PRIME CD, 1996)
Bushes and Briars (Alula, 1998)

Daniela Mercury
Feijao Com Arroz (Beans with Rice) (Sony, 1997)

The Mighty Diamonds
Go Seek Your Rights (Frontline, 1990)

The Mighty Sparrow
Mighty Sparrow, Volume One (Ice, 1992)
25th Anniversary (Charlie's, 1980)

Robert Mirabal
Mirabal (Warner Western, 1997)

Marlui Miranda
Ihu: Todos os Sons (Blue Jackal, 1997)
Ihu 2—Kewere: Rezar: Prayer (Blue Jackal, 1998)

Jackie Mittoo
Downbeat the Ruler: Killer Instrumentals, The Best of Studio One, Volume 3 (Heartbeat, 1988)
100% Dynamite (Soul Jazz, 1998)

T.H. "Vikku" Vinayakram
The Best of Shakti (Moment/Sony, 1994)

Carlos Vives
Clasicos de la Provincia (Sonolux/Poly-Gram Latino, 1993)

Vodou (sidebar)
Various Artists: *Rhythms of Rapture: Sacred Music of Haitian Voudou* (Smithsonian Folkways, 1995)

Wailing Souls
Wild Suspense (Mango, 1979)

The Waterboys
Fisherman's Blues (Chrysalis, 1988)
This Is the Sea (Chrysalis, 1985)

Randy Weston
The Spirits of Our Ancestors (Antilles, 1992)

Bill Whelan
Riverdance (Celtic Heartbeat, 1995)

Wimme
Gierran (Northside, 1999)
Wimme (Northside, 1997)

Paul Winter
Celtic Solstice (BMG/Windham Hill, 1999)
Icarus (Epic, 1970)

Wolfstone
The Chase (Iona 1992/Green Linnet, 1994)

Stavros Xarhakos & Nicos Gatsos
Ta Rembetika (CBS, 1983)

Atahualpa Yupanqui
Thirty Years of Singing (Chant du Monde, 1992)

Zaiko Langa Langa
L'Authenticite (Disques Esperance/Sonodisc, 1992)

Zap Mama
Adventures in Afropea 1: Zap Mama (Luaka Bop, 1993)
Chocolate Supa Highway (Capitol, 1997)

Tom Zé
Brazil Classics, Vol. 4: Best of Tom Zé (Luaka Bop, 1990)

Benjamin Zephaniah
Reggae Head (57 Productions, 1997)

Jalal Zolfonun
Mystic Journey (Music of the World, 1999)

Tappa Zukie
From the Archives (RAS, 1995)

Compilations
Anthology of Chant (Celestial Harmonies, 1995)
Anthology of World Music, Vols. 1–18 (Rounder, 1998–99)
The Arthur S. Alberts Collection: More Tribal, Folk, and Café Music of West Africa (Rykodisc, 1998)
Bayaka: The Extraordinary Music of the BaBenzélé Pygmies (ellipsis arts . . . , 1995)
Between Father Earth and Mother Sky (Narada, 1995)
The Big Bang: In the Beginning Was the Drum (ellipsis arts . . . , 1994)
B'ismillah (Sounds True, 1997)
Bringing It All Back Home (BBC, 1991)
Burmese Music Series (Shanachie, 1997)
By the Rivers of Babylon: Timeless Hymns of Rastafari (Shanachie, 1997)
Calypsos from Trinidad: Politics, Intrigue & Violence in the 1930s, Including the Butler Calypsos (Arhoolie/Folklyric, 1991)
Cuban Gold, Volumes 1–5 (Qbadisc, 1995–97)
Desert Blues (Network, 1995)
Duende: From Traditional Masters to Gypsy Rock (ellipsis arts . . . , 1994)
Duke Reid's Treasure Chest (Heartbeat, 1992)
Festival of Light (Island, 1996)
Folk Roots Magazine Presents Routes: 20 Years of Essential Folk, Roots & World Music (Africa, Europe, Asia, and the World) (Nascente, 1999)
Folk Roots Magazine Presents Roots: 20 Years of Essential Folk, Roots & World Music (Britain, Ireland, and North America) (Nascente, 1999)
Folksongs of the Louisiana Acadians (Folklyric, 1959/Arhoolie, 1994)
Forró: Music for Maids and Taxi Drivers (Rounder, 1989)
Global Meditation (The Relaxation Company)
Global Voices (Music of the World, 1998)
Holding up Half the Sky: Voices of Celtic Women (Shanachie, 1997)
Holding up Half the Sky: Voices of Asian Women (Shanachie, 1999)
The Hugo Masters: An Anthology of Chinese Classical Music (Celestial Harmonies, 1992)
The Indestructible Beat of Soweto (Shanachie, 1986)
J'ai été Au Bal (I Went to the Dance) (Arhoolie, 1990)
Jali Kunda: Griots of West Africa & Beyond (ellipsis arts . . . , 1996)
Javanese Court Gamelan Vol. 2 (Nonesuch, 1977)
The Kings & Queens of Township Jive: Modern Roots of the Indestructible Beat of Soweto (Earthworks, 1990)
Latcho Drom (Soundtrack) (La Bande Son/Virgin France, 1993)

The Moon and the Banana Tree: New Guitar Music from Madagascar (Shanachie, 1996)
Mourmourika: Songs of the Greek Underworld, 1930–1955 (Rounder, 1999)
The Music of Armenia, Vols. 1–6 (Celestial Harmonies, 1995)
The Music of Indonesia, Vols. 1–17 (Smithsonian, 1991–99)
The Music of Islam, Vols. 1–15 (Celestial Harmonies, 1997)
Musical Instruments of the World (Le Chant Du Monde/Harmonia Mundi, 1990)
Narada World: A Global Vision (Narada, 1997)
The New Feeling (Celestial Harmonies, 1996)
Planet Soup (ellipsis arts . . . , 1995)
Rembetica: Historic Urban Folk Songs from Greece (Rounder, 1992)
Resting Place of the Mists: New Valiha and Marovany Music from Madagascar (Shanachie, 1996)
The Rough Guide to the Music of Kenya & Tanzania (World Music Network, 1996)
Sacred Treasures: Choral Masterworks from Russia (Hearts of Space, 1998)
The Secret Museum of Mankind, Vols. 1–8 (Shanachie/Yazoo, 1995–99)
Septetos Cubanos: sones de Cuba (Corason/Música Tradicional, 1990)
Solid Gold, Coxsone Style (Studio One, 1972/Heartbeat, 1992)
The Soul of Black Peru (Luaka Bop, 1995)
The Spirit of Cape Verde (Tinder, 1998)
The Story of Jamaican Music: Tougher Than Tough (Mango, 1993)
Tibet: The Heart of Dharma (ellipsis arts . . . , 1996)
Tulikkulkku (Kansanmusiikki Instituutti, 1993)
Tuva: Among the Spirits (Smithsonian, 1999)
Vintage Hawaiian Music: The Great Singers, 1928–1934 (Rounder, 1989)
Voices of the World: An Anthology of Vocal Expression (Le Chant Du Monde/Harmonia Mundi, 1996)
Women of Spirit (Putumayo World Music, 1998)
A World out of Time: Henry Kaiser and David Lindley in Madagascar, Vols. 1–3 (Shanachie, 1992/1993/1996)

Can't remember what band a certain musician or vocalist is in? Wondering if a person has been in more than one band? The Band Member Index will guide you to the appropriate entry (or entries).

Abel, Yves Albert *See* Tabou Combo

Abers, Wil-Dog *See* Ozomatli

Abhissira, Michel *See* Kaoma

Abiam, Nano Danso *See* The Pan-African Orchestra

Aboltynsh, Alexeui *See* Kukuruza

Abreu, Luis A. *See* Bamboleo

Abruzzo, Tommy *See* Klezmer Plus!

Abshire, Nathan *See* The Balfa Brothers/Freres Balfa

Abukari, Ibrahima *See* The Pan-African Orchestra

Acheampong, Boateng Kodua *See* The Pan-African Orchestra

Adama, Paco Yé *See* Farafina

Adams, Mark *See* Dominic Kanza & the African Rhythm Machine

Adams, Mark *See* The Specials

Adamu, Danjuma *See* Kotoja/Ken Okulolo

Adelin, Mbazumutima *See* The Drummers of Burundi

Adepoju, Sikiru *See* Kotoja/Ken Okulolo

Adioa, Maxidilick *See* Adioa

Adjei, Yaw *See* The Pan-African Orchestra

Adolphi, Klaus *See* Horch

Afata, André *See* Les Têtes Brulées

Afonso, Marie *See* Zap Mama

Agard, Michael *See* krosfyah

Agudelo, Nestor *See* La Sonora Meliyara

Aguilar, Juan *See* Julian Avalos & Afro-Andes

Aguilar, Michael *See* La Mafia

Ahanda, Jean-Marie *See* Les Têtes Brulées

Ahmad, Salman *See* Junoon

Ahman, Max *See* Mynta

al'-aziz, Mustafâ 'Abd *See* Musicians of the Nile

al-Hilâli, Yunis *See* Musicians of the Nile

Al Kobary, Raid *See* El-Funoun

Al-Tawil, Thafer *See* El-Funoun

Alakotila, Timo *See* JPP/Järvelän Pikkupe-limannit

Alalos, Pedro *See* Julian Avalos & Afro-Andes

Alamañy, Jesús *See* ¡Cubanismo! Sierra Maestra

Alamañy, Luís, Jr. *See* ¡Cubanismo!

Albareda, Fernando *See* Los Fabulosos Cadillacs

Albert, Laurent *See* Gazoline

Alchedes, Congera *See* The Drummers of Burundi

Aldar, Tamdyn *See* Chirgilchin

Alesi, Tommy *See* Beausoleil

Alfonso, Carlos *See* Sintesis

Alfonso, Equis *See* Sintesis

Alfonso, Jesus *See* Los Muñequitos de Matanzas

Alfonso, Jorge "El Nino" *See* Irakere

Alfred, Jerry *See* Jerry Alfred & the Medicine Beat

Alhassan, Abukari *See* The Pan-African Orchestra

Ali, Azam *See* Vas

'ali, Hanafi Mohamed *See* Musicians of the Nile

Allamuradovm, Khakberdy *See* Ashkabad

Allcock, Martin *See* Fairport Convention

Allen, Michael *See* Coyote Oldman

Allmond, Peck *See* Kotoja/Ken Okulolo

Almendros, Enrique *See* La Muscagña

Almo, Michael *See* Kid Creole & the Coconuts/Dr. Buzzard's Original Savannah Band

Alonso, Madonna *See* Sintesis

Alpert, Michael *See* Brave Old World

Alphonso, Roland *See* The Skatalites

Birch, Adam *See* The Specials

Bird, David *See* Eden's Bridge

Bitchuka, Hasani *See* Mlimani Park Orchestra

Bjorling, Kurt *See* Brave Old World

Black, Frances *See* Arcady; The Black Family/Shay, Michael, and Martin Black

Black, Jeremy *See* Mouth Music

Black, Martin *See* The Black Family/Shay, Michael, and Martin Black

Black, Mary *See* The Black Family/Shay, Michael, and Martin Black; De Dannan/De Danann

Black, Michael *See* The Black Family/Shay, Michael, and Martin Black

Black, Pauline *See* The Selecter

Black, Shay *See* The Black Family/Shay, Michael, and Martin Black

Blake, Tchad *See* Latin Playboys

Blakey, Colin *See* The Waterboys

Blanco, Luís Eduardo *See* King Changó

Blanquito Man *See* King Changó

Blom, Pedro *See* Hoven Droven

Blythe, Geoffrey *See* Black 47

Bobadilla, Gregorio *See* Echoes of Incas

Bohan, Gary *See* Klezmer Conservatory Band

Bolander, Pelle *See* Abel & Kaninerna

Bold Eagle, Al *See* Arawak Mountain Singers

Bomberry, Charlene *See* Six Nations Women Singers

Bonaventure, Jean-Claude *See* Kaoma

Bonilla, Don Armando *See* Kid Creole & the Coconuts/Dr. Buzzard's Original Savannah Band

Bonnar, John *See* Dead Can Dance

Bonne, Angel *See* Los Van Van

Boond, Peter *See* Ceolbeg

Boone, Michael *See* Kid Creole & the Coconuts/Dr. Buzzard's Original Savannah Band

Borges, Vannia *See* Bamboleo

Borreo, Eliseo *See* Strunz & Farah

Bortey, Ebenezer *See* The Pan-African Orchestra

Bortnick, Avi *See* Kotoja/Ken Okulolo

Botri, Yaw Della *See* The Pan-African Orchestra

Bouchiki, Jahloul "Chico" *See* The Gipsy Kings

Boukella, Youcef *See* Orchestre National de Barbès

Boura, Jerico *See* Gazoline

Bourke, Ciaran *See* The Dubliners

Bovell, Margaret *See* krosfyah

Bowen, Robin Huw *See* Crasdant

Bowens, Nadege *See* Rara Machine

Boyoyo *See* Boyoyo Boys

Boysen, Dean *See* Dr. Loco's Rockin' Jalapeño Band

Bradbury, John *See* The Specials

Brady, Paul *See* Planxty

Braithwaite, Junior *See* Bob Marley/Bob Marley & the Wailers

Brand, Dollar *See* Abdullah Ibrahim/Dollar Brand

Bråten Berg, Kirsten *See* Frå Senegal Til Setesdal

Braun, Ivo *See* Maxwell Street Klezmer Band

Braz, Loalwa *See* Kaoma

Breaux, Jimmy *See* Beausoleil

Breedlove, Nathan *See* SKAndalous All-Stars

Brendog *See* SKAndalous All-Stars

Brennan, Ciaran *See* Clannad

Brennan, Enya *See* Clannad

Brennan, Máire *See* Clannad

Brennan, Paul *See* Clannad

Brennan, Pól *See* The Guo Brothers & Shung Tian

Bressler, Judy *See* Klezmer Conservatory Band

Brevette, Lloyd *See* The Skatalites

Briceno, Julio *See* Los Amigos Invisibles

Bridgeman, Noel *See* The Waterboys

Brigandi, Joe *See* Dr. Loco's Rockin' Jalapeño Band; Kotoja/Ken Okulolo

Briggs, Paul Dino *See* The Ukrainians

Brignol, Jean Mary *See* RAM

Brisland-Ferner, Stefan *See* Garmarna; Vadå

Brisset, Donovan *See* The Itals

Brito, Manuel *See* Tam Tam 2000

Brock, Paul *See* Moving Cloud

Broderick, Patsy *See* Arcady

Brody, David *See* Klezmer Conservatory Band

Brody, Lauren *See* Kapelye

Brooks, Brian *See* The House Band

Brooks, Ken *See* Kotoja/Ken Okulolo

Brooks, Mark Steven *See* Gamelan Son of Lion

Brooks, Morvin *See* The Techniques

Brotman, Stuart *See* Brave Old World

Brousard, Kevin *See* Roy Carrier/Roy Carrier & the Night Rockers

Broussard, Bobby *See* Chris Ardoin & Double Clutchin'

Broussard, Herbert *See* Zydeco Force

Broussard, Jeffery *See* Zydeco Force

Broussard, Shelton *See* Zydeco Force

Browder, Dr. Buzzard, Jr. 's Original Savannah Band: Stoney *See* Kid Creole & the Coconuts/Dr. Buzzard's Original Savannah Band

Brown, Carlinhos *See* Timbalada

Brown, David *See* Santana/Carlos Santana

Brown, Derrick *See* The Twinkle Brothers

Brown, Desmond *See* The Selecter

Brown, Harold *See* Percussion Incorporated

Brown, James *See* UB40

Brown, Selwyn *See* Steel Pulse

Bruce, Jo *See* Afro Celt Sound System

Bryan, Carlton *See* Steel Pulse

Buck, Betsy *See* Six Nations Women Singers

Buck, Sadie *See* Six Nations Women Singers

Bulgrin, Lascelles "Wiss" *See* Israel Vibration

Clancy, Liam *See* The Clancy Brothers & Tommy Makem/Tommy Makem & Liam Clancy/Robbie O'Connell

Clancy, Pat *See* The Clancy Brothers & Tommy Makem/Tommy Makem & Liam Clancy/Robbie O'Connell

Clancy, Tom *See* The Clancy Brothers & Tommy Makem/Tommy Makem & Liam Clancy/Robbie O'Connell

Clark, Brian *See* Ian Campbell Folk Group/Ian Campbell

Clark, Jenny *See* Battlefield Band

Clark, William "Bunny Rugs" *See* Third World

Clarke, Chris Gonzalez *See* Dr. Loco's Rockin' Jalapeño Band

Clarke, Danny *See* Meditations

Clarke, Eric "Fish" *See* The Roots Radics

Clarke, Jamie *See* The Pogues/Shane MacGowan

Claudio *See* Alaap

Clegg, Johnny *See* Johnny Clegg & Savuka/Juluka

Clement, José Mari *See* La Muscagña

Cleworth, Ian *See* Synergy

Coakley, John *See* The Boys of the Lough

Cockatoo, Jodie *See* Yothu Yindi

Coco *See* Alabina

Coffey, Aidan *See* De Dannan/De Danann

Coffy, Jean Paul *See* Boukman Eksperyans

Cohen, Greg *See* Masada

Coleman, Anthony *See* Masada

Coleridge *See* Transglobal Underground/Natacha Atlas

Collado, Alvaro *See* Los Van Van

Collins, Bernard *See* The Abyssinians

Collins, Shirley *See* Shirley Collins/Shirley & Dolly Collins/Etchingham Steam Band

Côme, Ntirandekura *See* The Drummers of Burundi

Comeaux, Tommy *See* Beausoleil

Comén, Jens *See* Hoven Droven

Connally, Jennifer *See* Black Uhuru

Conneff, Kevin *See* The Chieftains

Connolly, Brian *See* Craobh Rua

Connolly, John *See* Anam

Conrad, David *See* Black 47

Conte, Luis *See* Cuba L.A.; Strunz & Farah

Conyngham, Phillip *See* Alan Dargin/Reconciliation

Coogan, Mary *See* Cherish the Ladies

Coolidge, Priscilla *See* Walela

Coolidge, Rita *See* Walela

Cooper, Adrienne *See* Kapelye

Cooper, Chris *See* Conjunto Céspedes

Cooper, Michael "Ibo" *See* Third World

Cooper, Selwyn *See* Zydeco Hurricanes

Coore, Stephen "Cat" *See* Third World

Copado, Heliodoro *See* Los Camperos de Valles

Copeland, Iain *See* Peatbog Faeries

Copeland, Stewart *See* The Police/Sting

Corbett, Michael *See* Jungular Grooves

Córdoba, Emilio Córdoba *See* Conjunto Alma Jarocha

Coria, Enrique *See* Inkuyo; Sukay

Corona, Manuel *See* Sexteto Boloña

Cortés, José Luis *See* NG La Banda/Nueva Generación (New Generation)

Cortez, Carlos *See* Los de Abajo

Cortez, Jose Luis *See* Irakere

Cortéz, Pablo *See* NG La Banda/Nueva Generación (New Generation)

Coughlan, Eoin *See* Nomos

Coulibaly, Soungalo *See* Farafina

Coulon, Jorge *See* Inti-Illimani

Coulon, Marcelo *See* Inti-Illimani

Cousins, Gabriel *See* Percussion Incorporated

Covarrubias, Jesus *See* Dr. Loco's Rockin' Jalapeño Band

Covarrubio Soto, Rafael *See* Khenany

Cradick, Martin *See* Baka Beyond

Craig, Albert "Apple" *See* Israel Vibration

Craig, Shaun *See* Capercaillie

Crawford, Kevin *See* Moving Cloud

Crego, José Miguel *See* NG La Banda/Nueva Generación (New Generation)

Crepsac, Ernst *See* Tabou Combo

Crespo, Carlos *See* Sukay

Cridland, Ansel *See* Meditations

Cros, Jean-Louis *See* Ad Vielle Que Pourra

Crosbie, Malcolm *See* Shooglenifty

Cruz, Alex *See* Southern Scratch

Csoóri, Sandor *See* Márta Sebestyén/Muzsikás/Vujicsics

Cuao, Enrique *See* La Sonora Meliyara

Cuchelo, Joe *See* Perfect Thyroid

Cuervo, Armando *See* Irakere

Cuevas, Carlos *See* Los de Abajo

Cuffe, Tony *See* Ossian

Cullen, Maria *See* Alan Dargin/Reconciliation

Cumbá, Oney *See* Sintesis

Cumbo, Jorge *See* Los Incas/Urubamba

Cunningham, John *See* Nightnoise; Silly Wizard

Cunningham, Martín Adrian *See* King Changó

Cunningham, Phil *See* Silly Wizard

Curran, Ciarán *See* Altan

Custer, Beth *See* Trance Mission

Cut Chemist *See* Ozomatli

Cutting, Andy *See* Blowzabella; Fernhill

Czernik, Janina *See* Trebunia Family Band

D., Michael *See* Robby Bee & the Boyz from the Rez

Daily, Lloyd *See* Percussion Incorporated

Dalera, Juan *See* Los Incas/Urubamba

Daley, Richard *See* Third World

Daly, Jackie *See* Arcady; De Dannan/De Danann; Patrick Street

Daly, Mick *See* Four Men & a Dog

Damant, Jean-Louis *See* Gazoline

Dambele, Dedougou *See* Farafina

Dammers, Jerry *See* The Specials

Danielsson, Palle *See* Nordan Project

Jules, Pierre *See* RAM

Juncaj, Djeto *See* Immigrant Suns

Jungney, Lobsang *See* The Gyuto Monks

Justin, Yonel *See* RAM

Justiz, Roldolfo Argudin *See* NG La Banda/Nueva Generación (New Generation)

Juvénal, Mpitabavuma *See* The Drummers of Burundi

Kaapana, Ledward *See* Hui Ohana/Ledward Kaapana

Kaapana, Nedward *See* Hui Ohana/Ledward Kaapana

Kaasinen, Sari *See* Värttinä

Kabirr, Adbel *See* Soto Koto Band/Super Eagles/Ifang Bondi

Kabongo, Sabine *See* Zap Mama

Kachenchy, Juma *See* Samba Mapangala & Orchestra Virunga

Kada *See* The Itals

Kaewkramon, Suwit *See* Fong Naam

Kagona, Rise *See* Bhundu Boys

Kahlil, Aisha *See* Sweet Honey in the Rock

Kalama, William *See* Kalama's Quartet

Kalhor, Kayhan *See* Ghazal/Kayhan Kalhor

Källman, Sten *See* The Swedish Sax Septet

Kalolo, Lutila *See* Te Vaka

Kalsi, Johnny *See* Transglobal Underground/Natacha Atlas

Kandan, Aidysmaa *See* Chirgilchin

Kaneko, Ryutaro *See* Kodo

Kaneva, Radostina *See* Bŭlgari

Kangwena, Shakespear *See* Bhundu Boys

Kangwena, Shakie *See* Bhundu Boys

Kankonda, Cécilia *See* Zap Mama

Kano, Yasukazu *See* Kodo

Kanta, Alpha Senyni *See* Étoile de Dakar

Kanté, Mory *See* Rail Band/Super Rail Band of Bamako

Kante, Naima *See* Les Go de Koteba

Kanyakumari, A. *See* Vadya Lahari

Kanza, Dominic *See* Dominic Kanza & the African Rhythm Machine

Karim, Haji Abdul *See* The Sabri Brothers

Kasiek, Alex *See* Transglobal Underground/Natacha Atlas

Kastler, Arthur *See* The New Orleans Klezmer All Stars

Kaston, Etienne *See* The Mandators/Victor Essiet

Katayev, Iskhak *See* The Ilyas Malayev Ensemble

Katz, Mike *See* Battlefield Band; Ceolbeg

Kavana, Ron *See* Abana Ba Nasery

Kavhai, Washington *See* Bhundu Boys

Kazidonna, Mimi *See* Diblo Dibala/Loketo/Matchatcha

Keane, Conor *See* Arcady

Keane, Dolores *See* De Dannan/De Danann

Keane, Sean *See* The Chieftains

Kearey, Ian "Chopper" *See* The Oyster Band

Keenan, Paddy *See* The Bothy Band

Keijser, Roland *See* The Swedish Sax Septet

Keita, Fotigui *See* Rail Band/Super Rail Band of Bamako

Keita, Kabiné *See* Rail Band/Super Rail Band of Bamako

Keita, Maate *See* Les Go de Koteba

Keita, Tiawara *See* Farafina

Kellaway, Stuart *See* Yothu Yindi

Kelleghan, Matt *See* Moving Hearts

Kellner, Jean-Francois *See* Gazoline

Kelly, James *See* Planxty

Kelly, Liam *See* Dervish

Kelly, Luke *See* The Dubliners

Kelly, Mark *See* Altan

Kelly, Pat *See* The Techniques

Kelso, Beverley *See* Bob Marley/Bob Marley & the Wailers

Kemp, Rick *See* Steeleye Span

Kennedy, Frankie *See* Altan

Kent, Stephen *See* Trance Mission

Kenton, Johnny *See* Los Pleneros de la 21

Kenya *See* Rara Machine

Keppeler, Ken *See* Bayou Seco/Bayou Eclectico

Kershaw, Doug *See* Doug Kershaw/Rusty & Doug

Kershaw, Rusty *See* Doug Kershaw/Rusty & Doug

Ketkhong, Boonyong *See* Fong Naam

Khan, Shujaat Hussain *See* Ghazal/Kayhan Kalhor

Khavasov, Ilyau *See* The Ilyas Malayev Ensemble

Khlay, Ra *See* Sam-Ang Sam Ensemble

Khovalyg, Kaigal-ool *See* Huun-Huur-Tu

Kicking Woman, Keith *See* Black Lodge Singers

Kiele, Niels *See* Sorten Muld

Kikusui, Kofu *See* The Japanese Koto Consort

Kilbride, Pat *See* Battlefield Band

Kilpatrick, Charles *See* Bio Ritmo

Kim, Harry *See* Cuba L.A.

Kimball, Jim *See* Firewater

King, Sherwin *See* krosfyah

King, Steve *See* Home Service

King, Tyrone *See* Xit

Kinsey, Donald *See* Bob Marley/Bob Marley & the Wailers

Kinzaki, J.P. *See* Diblo Dibala/Loketo/Matchatcha

Kirkpatrick, John *See* Steeleye Span

Kirsch, Shane *See* Perfect Thyroid

Kirwan, Larry *See* Black 47

Kitch *See* Lord Kitchener/Kitch

Klein, Marlon *See* Dissidenten

Knight, Peter *See* Steeleye Span

Knockwood, Brian *See* Eastern Eagle Singers

Knockwood, Gary *See* Eastern Eagle Singers

Knockwood, Ivan *See* Eastern Eagle Singers

Knosi, Vusi *See* Boyoyo Boys

Malayev, Ilyas *See* The Ilyas Malayev Ensemble

Malinow, Nicolai *See* Wolga Balalaika Ensemble

Mamedov, Gassan *See* Ashkabad

Mancini, Gus *See* Hawk Project

Mangurten, Gail *See* Maxwell Street Klezmer Band

Mangxola, Mildred Faith *See* Mahlathini & Mahotella Queens/Makgona Tsohle Band

Mani, T.A.S. *See* Karnataka College of Percussion

Mankaba, David *See* Bhundu Boys

Mankwane, Marks *See* Mahlathini & Mahotella Queens/Makgona Tsohle Band

Manning, Donald *See* The Abyssinians

Manning, John *See* Naftule's Dream

Manning, Lynford *See* The Abyssinians

Manole, Ion *See* Taraf de Haïdouks

Manole, Ionel *See* Taraf de Haïdouks

Manole, Marin *See* Taraf de Haïdouks

Manole, Marin P. *See* Taraf de Haïdouks

Mansikka-aho, Tommi *See* Gjallarhorn

Mantu, Hamid *See* Transglobal Underground/Natacha Atlas

Mapangala, Samba *See* Samba Mapangala & Orchestra Virunga

Mapika, Gordin *See* Bhundu Boys

Marc, Habonimana *See* The Drummers of Burundi

Marc, Mpitabakana *See* The Drummers of Burundi

Marcelin, Emmanuel *See* RAM

Marcovich, Alejandro *See* Caifanes/Jaguares

Margolis, Sam *See* Maxwell Street Klezmer Band

Marika, Banula *See* Yothu Yindi

Marika, Bunimbirr *See* Yothu Yindi

Marika, Witiyana *See* Yothu Yindi

Marin, Mikael *See* Väsen

Marley, Bob *See* Bob Marley/Bob Marley & the Wailers

Marley, Cedella *See* Ziggy Marley & the Melody Makers

Marley, David "Ziggy" *See* Ziggy Marley & the Melody Makers

Marley, Rita *See* Bob Marley/Bob Marley & the Wailers

Marley, Stephen *See* Ziggy Marley & the Melody Makers

Marley Prendergast, Sharon *See* Ziggy Marley & the Melody Makers

Marquinei, Mandosini *See* Amampondo

Marrufo, William *See* Ozomatli

Marshall, Cornel *See* Third World

Marshall, Jonathan *See* Eastern Eagle Singers

Martel, Francine *See* Takadja

Marthely, Jean Philippe *See* Kassav'

Martin, A. Michael *See* Xit

Martin, Alphonso *See* Steel Pulse

Martin, Janice G. *See* Six Nations Women Singers

Martin, John *See* Ossian; Tannahill Weavers

Martín, Rafa *See* La Muscagña

Martinez, Alex *See* Bloque

Martinez, Aris *See* Los Pleneros de la 21

Martinez, Christian *See* Gazoline

Martinez, Daniel *See* Dr. Loco's Rockin' Jalapeño Band

Martinez, Gilbert *See* Bloque

Martinez, Ray *See* Los Pleneros de la 21

Martínez, Roberto Juan *See* Mariachi Cobre

Martinez, Rolo *See* ¡Cubanismo!

Martins, Frank *See* The Mandators/Victor Essiet

Marvin, Julian "Junior" *See* Bob Marley/Bob Marley & the Wailers

Mashinini, Vusi *See* Boyoyo Boys

Masondo, David *See* Soul Brothers

Masterson, Declan *See* Moving Hearts

Masudi, Bavon *See* Samba Mapangala & Orchestra Virunga

Matas, Héctor *See* Los Pleneros de la 21

Matchoti *See* Orchestra Marrabenta Star de Moçambique/The Marrabenta Star Orchestra/Marrabenta Star

Matheson, Colin *See* Ceolbeg

Matheson, Karen *See* Capercaillie

Matima *See* Zaiko Langa Langa

Matimba, Kuda *See* Bhundu Boys

Matole, Simpiwe *See* Amampondo

Matotiyane, Mantombi *See* Amampondo

Matsu, Bob *See* Kalama's Quartet

Mattacks, Dave *See* Fairport Convention

Matthews, Ceri Rhys *See* Fernhill

Matthews, Dave *See* Dave Matthews Band

Matthews, Iain *See* Fairport Convention

Matthews, Winston "Pipe" *See* Wailing Souls

Mattson, Hallbus Totte *See* Hedningarna

Mavuso, Steve *See* Johnny Clegg & Savuka/Juluka

Mayr, Johannes *See* Hoelderlin Express/Hölderlin Express

Mazibuko, Abedrigo *See* Ladysmith Black Mambazo

Mazibuko, Albert *See* Ladysmith Black Mambazo

Mbasalala *See* Salala/Ricky & Mbasalala

Mbida, Jacques Douglas *See* Kassav'

Mbizela, Blackie Zandisile *See* Amampondo

Mboob, Musa *See* Soto Koto Band/Super Eagles/Ifang Bondi

M'Boup, Abdoulaye Laye *See* Orchestra Baobob

McAleer, Shane *See* Dervish

McArthur, Keith *See* Spearhead

McCabe, Desy *See* Craobh Rua

McCallion, Nancy *See* The Mollys

McCann, Jim *See* The Dubliners

McCann, Séan *See* Great Big Sea

McCarlos, Don *See* Black Uhuru

McChesny, Bill *See* Groupa

McColeman, Andrea *See* Jerry Alfred & the Medicine Beat

White, Franklin *See* The Techniques

White, Kevin *See* The English Beat/General Public

White Grass, William *See* Black Lodge Singers

Wickham, Steve *See* The Waterboys

Wieczorek, Stefan *See* Horch

Wiggins, Graham *See* Dr. Didg

Wilhelms, Jenny *See* Gjallarhorn

Wilkie, Angelique *See* Zap Mama

Willemark, Lena *See* Groupa; Nordan Project

Williams, Babatunde *See* Kotoja/Ken Okulolo

Williams, Cal *See* Yothu Yindi

Williams, Huw *See* Crasdant

Williams, John *See* Solas/Seamus Egan

Williams, John L. *See* Joy Harjo & Poetic Justice

Williams, Roger *See* Home Service

Williams, Susan M. *See* Joy Harjo & Poetic Justice

Willington, Rupert *See* Burning Spear

Willis, Larry *See* Jerry Gonzalez & the Fort Apache Band

Wilson, Cam *See* Mad Pudding

Wilson, John *See* Zydeco Hurricanes

Wilson, Leslie *See* Tannahill Weavers

Wilson, Roger *See* The House Band

Wilson, Shade *See* Bio Ritmo

Wimmer, Kevin *See* Balfa Toujours; California Cajun Orchestra

Winkleman, Linda *See* The Mollys

Winter, Charly *See* Adioa

Wishnefsky, Brian *See* The Klezmorim

Wollesen, Kenny *See* Masada

Wongwirojruk, Prasarn *See* Fong Naam

Woodgate, Dan *See* Madness

Woods, Gay *See* Steeleye Span

Woods, Terry *See* Steeleye Span; Sweeney's Men

Xhosa, Vusi *See* Boyoyo Boys

Xico *See* Orchestra Marrabenta Star de Moçambique/The Marrabenta Star Orchestra/Marrabenta Star

Ya Salaam, Kalamu *See* Percussion Incorporated

Yaba, Jimmy *See* Zaiko Langa Langa

Yacoub, Mohammed *See* El-Funoun

Yamaguchi, Jiro *See* Ozomatli

Yamaguchi, Motofumi *See* Kodo

Yamba, Miguel *See* Diblo Dibala/Loketo/Matchatcha

Yanagi, Michiko *See* Kodo

Yarwood, Chip *See* Ashkaru

Yazzie, Chili *See* Xit

Yearwood, Edwin *See* krosfyah

Yerry, Dennis *See* Hawk Project

Yoelin, Shelly *See* Maxwell Street Klezmer Band

York, Andy *See* Robert Mirabal/Mirabal

Young, Carl *See* Spearhead

Young, Jimmy *See* The House Band

Youngson, Mop *See* Wolfstone

Yttrehus, Ronny *See* Chateau Neuf Spelemannslag

Yunupingu, Galarrwuy *See* Yothu Yindi

Yunupingu, Gurrumul *See* Yothu Yindi

Yunupingu, Makuma *See* Yothu Yindi

Yunupingu, Mandawuy *See* Yothu Yindi

Yunupingu, Mangatjay *See* Yothu Yindi

Zach, Ingar *See* Chateau Neuf Spelemannslag

Zafimahery, Johnny Andriamamahirana *See* Tarika/Tarika Sammy

Zalba, Javier *See* ¡Cubanismo!

Zamorra, Danile *See* Inkuyo

Zamuangana, Enoch *See* Zaiko Langa Langa

Zavala, Catherine *See* The Mollys

Zavrski, Zoran *See* Veritas

Zeliazov, Georgi *See* Bŭlgari

Zequeira, Loreto *See* Sexteto Boloña

Zhang Shenglu *See* Tianjin Buddhist Music Ensemble

Zhang Shicai *See* Tianjin Buddhist Music Ensemble

Zhang Yuije *See* Tianjin Buddhist Music Ensemble

Zhao Zheng Ren *See* The Guo Brothers & Shung Tian

Ziad, Karim *See* Orchestre National de Barbès

Zon, Seydou *See* Farafina

Zorn, John *See* Masada

Zulu, Dudu *See* Johnny Clegg & Savuka/Juluka

Looking to explore the music of a certain country? The Country Index arranges the artists and groups covered in MusicHound World *according to the country they were born (for artists) or formed in (for bands). Please note that the country designation may not reflect the ethnicity of an artist or the nationality of a group's members.*

Algeria
Abdelli
Djur Djura
Chaba Fadela
Khaled
Cheb Mami
Cheikha Remitti
Abdel Ali Slimani
Rachid Taha

Angola
Bonga

Antigua
Burning Flames

Argentina
Los Fabulosos Cadillacs
Dino Saluzzi
Mercedes Sosa

Armenia
Djivan Gasparyan

Australia
Alan Dargin
David Hudson
Trevor Lucas
Archie Roach

Synergy
Yothu Yindi

Austria
Theodore Bikel

Bangladesh
Ali Akbar Khan
Ustad Vilayat Khan
Badal Roy

Barbados
krosfyah
Red Plastic Bag

Belgium
Dr. Nico
Zap Mama

Benin
Angélique Kidjo
Gnonnas Pedro

Brazil
Leny Andrade
Badi Assad
Carlos Barbosa-Lima
Jorge Ben
Maria Bethânia
Luiz Bonfá
Dori Caymmi
Gal Costa
Daude
Djavan
Eliane Elias
Fortuna
Gilberto Gil
Astrud Gilberto
João Gilberto
Egberto Gismonti
Gonzaguinha
Joyce
Sergio Mendes
Margareth Menezes

Daniela Mercury
Marlui Miranda
Tony Mola
Marisa Monte
Airto Moreira
Milton Nascimento
Clara Nunes
Olodum
Pixinguinha
Flora Purim
Elis Regina
Virginia Rodrigues
Timbalada
Nana Vasconcelos
Caetano Veloso
Tom Zé

Bulgaria
Bŭlgari
Folk Scat
Le Mystère des Voix Bulgares
Ivo Papasov

Burkina Faso
Farafina
Cheikh Lô

Burundi
The Drummers of Burundi

Cameroon
Baka Beyond
Francis Bebey
Manu Dibango
Henri Dikongué
Les Têtes Brulées
Sally Nyolo

Canada
Ad Vielle Que Pourra
Jerry Alfred & the Medicine Beat
Ashkaru
The Barra MacNeils
Michael Brook

Jane Bunnett
J.P. Cormier
Eastern Eagle Singers
Great Big Sea
Irish Rovers
Kashtin
Mary Jane Lamond
Daniel Lanois
Leahy
Laurel MacDonald
Ashley MacIsaac
Natalie MacMaster
Mad Pudding
Eileen McGann
Loreena McKennitt
Jackie Mittoo
Jim Payne
Robbie Robertson
Kelly Russell
Buffy Sainte-Marie
Christina Smith & Jean Hewson
Takadja

Cape Verde
Bana
Cesaria Evora
Fantcha
Mendes Brothers
Tam Tam 2000

Chile
Inti-Illimani
Victor Jara

China
Jie-Bing Chen
Sisi Chen
Dadawa
Film Orchestra of Shanghai
The Guo Brothers & Shung Tian
Liu Sola
Tianjin Buddhist Music Ensemble
Wu Man

Colombia
Joe Arroyo
Bloque
Carlos Gardel
La Sonora Dinamita
La Sonora Meliyara
Shakira
Carlos Vives

Congo
Waldemar Bastos
M'Bilia Bel
Diblo Dibala
Franco
Pépé Kallé
Kanda Bongo Man
Ray Lema
Sam Mangwana
Tshala Muana
Samba Ngo
Remmy Ongala
Tabu Ley Rochereau
Rigo Star

Papa Wemba
Zaiko Langa Langa

Cote d'Ivoire
Alpha Blondy
Les Go de Koteba

Cuba
Albita
Bamboleo
Cachao
Celia Cruz
¡Cubanismo!
Issac Delgado
Paquito D'Rivera
Gloria Estefan
Frank Emilio Flynn
Juan Carlos Formell
Celina González
Rubén González
Irakere
Los Muñequitos de Matanzas
Los Van Van
Manolín, El Médico de la Salsa
Rita Marley
Pablo Milanés
Beny Moré
NG La Banda
Orquesta Aragon
Patato
Silvio Rodríguez
Lazaro Ros
Arturo Sandoval
Mongo Santamaria
Sexteto Boloña
Sexteto Habanero
Sierra Maestra
Sintesis
Roberto Torres
Bebo Valdes
Chucho Valdes
Carlos Varela
Vocal Sampling

Denmark
Sorten Muld

Dominican Republic
Juan Luis Guerra
Johnny Pacheco
Ravel

Egypt
Hamza El Din
Ali Hassan Kuban
Umm Kulthum
Musicians of the Nile
Hossam Ramzy
Salamat
Mohamed Abdel Wahab

England
Afro Celt Sound System
Alaap
Apache Indian
Frankie Armstrong
Aswad

Blowzabella
Robin Huw Bowen
David Bowie
Kevin Burke
Ian Campbell Folk Group
Eliza Carthy
Martin Carthy
John Carty
Sheila Chandra
Emma Christian
Johnny Clegg & Savuka
Shirley Collins
Cornershop
Steven Cragg
Andrew Cronshaw
Paban Das Baul & Sam Mills
Dead Can Dance
Sandy Denny
Dr. Didg
Eden's Bridge
The English Beat
Brian Eno
Fairport Convention
John Faulkner
Alec Finn
Peter Gabriel
George Harrison
Home Service
The House Band
Ashley Hutchings
Andy Irvine
Femi Anikulapo Kuti
A.L. Lloyd
Machito
Mad Lion
Madness
John Martyn
Musical Youth
Najma
Helen O'Hara
Seán Ó Riada
Osibisa
The Oyster Band
Page & Plant
Charlie Palmieri
The Pogues
The Police
Maxi Priest
Maddy Prior
S.E. Rogie
The Selecter
Shakti
Anoushka Shankar
Shinehead
Talvin Singh
The Specials
Steel Pulse
Steeleye Span
Dave Swarbrick
Richard Thompson
Kathryn Tickell
Transglobal Underground
23 Skidoo
UB40
The Ukrainians
The Waterboys

COUNTRY INDEX

The Contributor Index makes it easy for you to locate MusicHound World entries by your favorite writers. Under each contributor's name, the entries they have written for this volume are listed alphabetically. Artist (or group) entries and sidebars can be found in the main section of the book; entries with the "compilation" designation can be found in the Compilations section.

Karen Ashbrook
The House Band
Bonnie Rideout

Robert Baird
Beausoleil

Andrew BeDell
Leny Andrade
Luiz Bonfá
Phil Coulter
Olu Dara
John Delafose & the Eunice Playboys
Don Santiago Jimenez
Esteban "Steve" Jordan
Meditations
Sugar Minott
Johnny Pacheco
Page & Plant

Ari Bendersky
OMC

Nego Beto
Jorge Ben
Brazil: Bahia (sidebar)
Brazil: Samba (sidebar)

Brazil: The Northeast (sidebar)
Gal Costa
Olodum
Pixinguinha
The Rough Guide to the Music of Brazil (compilation)

PJ Birosik
Robin Adnan Anders
Robert Tree Cody
Steven Cragg
The Didgeridoo (sidebar)
Echoes of Incas
Film Orchestra of Shanghai
Hamdulillah (compilation)
A Native American Odyssey (compilation)
Helen O'Hara
Cornel Pewewardy
The Rough Guide to Native American Music (compilation)

Philip Booth
Africa Never Stand Still (compilation)

Hank Bordowitz
Yami Bolo
Coupé Cloué
Nemours Jean-Baptiste
Habib Koité & Bamada
Magnum Band
Morgan Heritage
Chief Steven Osita Osadebe
O'Yaba
Sir Shina Peters
Reggae Jamdown: The RAS Tapes (compilation)
Doudou N'Diaye Rose
Sister Carol

Iris Brooks
Steve Gorn
Ephat Mujuru
Trichy Sankaran

Ken Burke
Maya Angelou
Clifton Chenier
Irish Rovers
Malika
Perfect Thyroid
Zydeco Hurricanes

Salvatore Caputo
David Byrne
Gamelan Son of Lion
Paul Simon
WOMAD (sidebar)

Heidi Cerrigione
Hammered Dulcimers Worldwide (sidebar)
Joemy Wilson

Thor Christensen
The Pogues

Martin Connors
Black 47
The Oyster Band
The Waterboys

Cary Darling
Ozomatli
Rock en Español
Caetano Veloso

Jim DeRogatis
Yma Sumac

Kerry Dexter
American Warriors: Songs for Veterans (compilation)
Americanos: Latino Life in the United States: A Celebration (compilation)
Andean Legacy (compilation)
Joe Arroyo
Badi Assad
Mary Bergin

Between Father Earth and Mother Sky (compilation)
Frances Black
The Blarney Pilgrim: Celtic Fingerstyle Guitar, Volume 2 (compilation)
Borderlands: from Conjunto to Chicken Scratch (compilation)
Brave Hearts (compilation)
Irving Burgie
Celtic Christmas (compilation)
Celtic Legacy (compilation)
Celtic Odyssey (compilation)
Celtic Spirit (compilation)
Celtic Treasure: The Legacy of Turlough O'Carolan (compilation)
Chayanne
Conjunto! Texas-Mexican Border Music, Vols. 1–5 (compilation)
Jesse Cook
J.P. Cormier
Corridos y Tragedias de la Frontera: First Recordings of Historic Mexican American Ballads, 1928–1937 (compilation)
Coyote Oldman
Elvis Crespo
Joe Cuba
Cuba: I Am Time (compilation)
Dargason Music Sampler (compilation)
Tony de la Rosa
Oscar D'Leon
Eden's Bridge
El Sonido de Flamenco (compilation)
Faces of the Harp: Celtic & Contemporary (compilation)
Pura Fé
Festival of Light (compilation)
Festival of the Andes (compilation)
Fifteen Tex-Mex Conjunto Classics (compilation)
Flamenco: Fire & Grace (compilation)
Flutes & Strings of the Andes (compilation)
Folkstyles of Mexico and Colombia (compilation)
Juan Carlos Formell
Celina Gonzaléz
Gypsy Passion (compilation)
Harpestry (compilation)
Heartbeat 2: Voices of First Nations Women (compilation)
Hearts, Hands, & Hides (compilation)
Tish Hinojosa
Inkuyo
Victor Jara
Klezmania: Klezmer for the New Millennium (compilation)
The Kronos Quartet
Kukuruza
Dan Levenson & Kim Murley
Jennifer Lopez
Los de Abajo
Los Tigres del Norte
Lullaby Journey (compilation)
Mariachi Cobre
Ricky Martin
Narciso Martinez
Mazz

Men with Guns (Hombres Armadas) (compilation)
The Mexican Revolution Corridos (compilation)
Pablo Milanés
Áine Minogue
Music of New Mexico: Hispanic Traditions (compilation)
Musica de la Tierra (compilation)
Narada World: A Global Vision (compilation)
Navajo Songs (compilation)
Maighread Ní Dhomhnaill
Norteño and Tejano Accordion Pioneers 1929–1939 (compilation)
Clara Nunes
Orquesta Aragon
Paco Peña
Chris Perez
Lourdes Perez
Itzhak Perlman
Peter Phippen
Plains Chippewa/Metis Music from Turtle Mountain (compilation)
Queens of African Music (compilation)
Jean Redpath
Tito Rodríguez
Ruben Romero & Lydia Torea
Linda Ronstadt
Selena
Shakira
J. Reuben Silverbird
Perry Silverbird
Christina Smith & Jean Hewson
Sol y Canto
Songs of the Spirit (compilation)
Talking Spirits (compilation)
Tejano Roots/Raices Tejanos: The Roots of Tejano and Conjunto Music (compilation)
Tibetan Invocations (compilation)
Tribal Fires (compilation)
Tribal Voices (compilation)
Tribal Winds (compilation)
Under the Green Corn Moon (compilation)
Carlos Varela
A Woman's Heart 2 (compilation)
Eva Ybarra
Mary Youngblood

Josh Freedom du Lac
Shinehead

Daniel Durchholz
Michael Brook
Wyclef Jean
Latin Playboys
Madness
Ziggy Marley & the Melody Makers
Bill Miller
Noa
The Police
Archie Roach
Texas Tornados
John Trudell
Willie & Lobo

Michael Eldridge
Jean Binta Breeze
Calypso (sidebar)
Calypsos from Trinidad: Politics, Intrigue & Violence in the 1930s, Including the Butler Calypsos (compilation)
krosfyah
Ahdri Zhina Mandiela
Oku Onuora
Post-Soca (sidebar)
Red Plastic Bag
Soca (sidebar)
Benjamin Zephaniah

Bill Ellis
By the Rivers of Babylon: Timeless Hymns of Rastafari (compilation)
Her Song: Exotic Voices of Women from around the World (compilation)
Mexico: Fiestas of Chiapas & Oaxaca (compilation)
Sintesis
SKAndalous All-Stars

Banning Eyre
Dimi Mint Abba
Camara Aboubacar
Dr. Sikuru Ayinde Barrister
Bembeya Jazz
Black Umfolosi
Dark City Sisters
Abdoulaye Diabaté
Sékouba "Bambino" Diabaté
Toumani Diabaté
Cheikh Lô
Boncana Maiga
Kante Manfila
Samba Mapangala & Orchestra Virunga
Mlimani Park Orchestra
Orchestra Marrabenta Star de Moçambique
Rail Band
Cheikha Remitti
Yan Kuba Saho
Foday Musa Suso
Papa Wemba
Zaiko Langa Langa

John C. Falstaff
Anúna
Waldemar Bastos
Big Noise 2 (A Mambo Inn Compilation) (compilation)
Máire Breatnach
Ian Campbell Folk Group
Carreg Lafar
Patrick Cassidy
The Chieftains
Emma Christian
Craobh Rua
Crasdant
Shaun Davey
Horslips
Kíla
Moving Cloud
Moving Hearts

Peadar Ó Riada
Seán Ó Riada
Seven Nations
Áine Uí Cheallaigh
Bill Whelan
David Wilkie

Christina Fuoco
Jose Feliciano
Dave Matthews Band

Lawrence Gabriel
Ruben Blades
Kid Creole & the Coconuts
The Specials

David Galens
Daniel Lanois

Ron Garmon
Bonga
*Caribbean Revels: Haitian Rara and Do-
    minican Gaga* (compilation)
Andy Cooney
Orchestre National de Barbès
Ron Sunsinger
The Swedish Sax Septet

Helen Giano
Haris Alexiou
George Dalaras
Stavros Xarhakos & Nicos Gatsos

Andrew Gilbert
Poncho Sanchez

Simon Glickman
Richard Thompson

Gary Pig Gold
Herb Alpert

Alex Gordon
Desi Arnaz
Harry Belafonte

Gary Graff
Bloque
Manu Dibango
Gloria Estefan
Anoushka Shankar
Third World
Richard Thompson

David Greenberger
3 Leg Torso

Ben Greenman
Jose Feliciano
Carmen Miranda
Zamfir

Jason Gross
The Pygmies (sidebar)
*The World's Musical Traditions 8: Yoruba
    Drums from Benin, West Africa* (compi-
    lation)

William Hanson
The English Beat

Craig Harris
Chava Alberstein
Marc Anthony
Dan Ar Braz
Ar Log
Aswad
Ashwan Batish
Theodore Bikel
Tony Bird
Mary Black
Black Uhuru
Alpha Blondy
Jimmy Bosch
Dennis Brown
Burning Spear
Camarón de la Isla
Willie Colon
I.K. Dairo
Paco de Lucia
Desmond Dekker
Lucky Dube
Eek-a-Mouse
Brian Eno
Filé
Gilberto Gil
The Gipsy Kings
George Harrison
Mickey Hart
Ofra Haza
Joe Higgs
Zakir Hussain
Abdullah Ibrahim
Inti-Illimani
Gregory Isaacs
The Itals
Kanda Bongo Man
Kapelye
Salif Keita
Ladysmith Black Mambazo
Miriam Makeba
Herbie Mann
Thomas Mapfumo
Rita Marley
Hugh Masekela
Christy Moore
Pablo Moses
Judy Mowatt
Johnny Nash
Youssou N'Dour
Tríona Ní Dhomhnaill
Ebenezer Obey
Babatunde Olatunji
Augustus Pablo
Charlie Palmieri
Lee "Scratch" Perry
Astor Piazzolla
Maddy Prior
Flora Purim
Balwinder Safri
Santana
Shakti
L. Shankar
Lakshmi Shankar

Ravi Shankar
Terrance Simien
The Skatalites
Sly & Robbie
Steel Pulse
Sweet Honey in the Rock
Dave Tarras
Toots & the Maytals
Yomo Toro
Ali Farka Touré
Ritchie Valens
Bunny Wailer
Floyd Red Crow Westerman
Paul Winter
Stomu Yamash'ta
Yellowman
Zydeco: The Early Years (compilation)

Alex Henderson
Dori Caymmi
Gonzaguinha
Mutabaruka

Geoffrey Himes
Eileen Ivers
The Mollys
Patrick Street
Solas

Steve Holtje
Jie-Bing Chen
Jin Hi Kim
Masada
*The Rough Guide to the Music of Eastern
    Europe* (compilation)
*The Rough Guide to the Music of Zim-
    babwe* (compilation)
Adam Rudolph
Rurutu Choir
Rustavi Choir
Sainkho
Randy Weston

Chris Hovan
Nana Vasconcelos

Aaron Howard
Hari Prasad Chaurasia
Richard Hagopian
Klezmer 1993 — New York City (compila-
    tion)
*Klezmer Pioneers: European and Ameri-
    can Recordings, 1905–1952* (compila-
    tion)
Klezmer Plus!
La Mafia
The Ilyas Malayev Ensemble
Maxwell Street Klezmer Band
Naftule's Dream
Shiv Kumar Sharma

Stephen Ide
Cathie Ryan

Jazzbo
Mad Lion
Zimbabwe Legit

Hamza El Din
Electric and Acoustic Mali (compilation)
Luis Enrique
Epstein Brothers Band
étoile de Dakar
Chaba Fadela
Fantcha
Majek Fashek
Frå Senegal Til Setesdal
Franco
Garcia Brothers
Djivan Gasparyan
Gazoline
Ghazal
Girls of Angeli
Gladiators
Eddy Grant
Grayhorse Singers
Sylvan Grey
Groupa
Gu-Achi Fiddlers
Juan Luis Guerra
Hassan Hakmoun
Hawk Project
Sol Hoopii
Hoven Droven
Linton Kwesi Johnson
Jolly Boys
Jungular Grooves
Mory Kanté
Kaoma
Karnataka College of Percussion
Kashtin
Kassav'
Khac Chi Ensemble
Khaled
Badar Ali Khan
Nusrat Fateh Ali Khan
Shoukichi Kina
Konbit: Burning Rhythms of Haiti (compilation)
Kotoja
Ali Hassan Kuban
Forward Kwenda
Latcho Drom (Soundtrack) (compilation)
Le Mystère des Voix Bulgares
Ray Lema
Ricardo Lemvo & Makina Loca
Les Têtes Brulées
Annbjørg Lien
Little Joe
Ismaël Lô
The Looters
Lord Kitchener
Lord Melody
Los Fabulosos Cadillacs
Los Incas
Los Muñequitos de Matanzas
Los Pleneros de la 21
Luciano
Sipho Mabuse
Mahlathini & Mahotella Queens
Mama Sana
Cheb Mami
The Mandators
Sam Mangwana

Machanic Manyeruke
Prince Nico Mbarga
Jimi Mbaye
Mzwakhe Mbuli
Russell Means
La Sonora Meliyara
Mendes Brothers
The Mighty Diamonds
The Mighty Sparrow
Robert Mirabal
Marlui Miranda
Machel Montano
Abdel Aziz El Mubarak
Maryam Mursal
Najma
R. Carlos Nakai
Native American Pop (sidebar)
Nelson
Mbongeni Ngema
Samba Ngo
Nordan Project
Sally Nyolo
Sonny Okosun
Victor Olaiya
Remmy Ongala
Oriental Brothers
A. Paul Ortega
Geffery Oryema
Ottopasuna
Orlando "Doctor Ganga" Owah
Patato
Gnonnas Pedro
Pépé Kallé
Percussion Incorporated
Primeaux & Mike
RAM
Hossam Ramzy
Ernest Ranglin
Rara Machine
Ravel
Red Tail Chasing Hawks
Roaring Lion
Rocky Boy Singers
S.E. Rogie
Lazaro Ros
Anders Rosén
Rossy
David Rudder
The Sabri Brothers
Bally Sagoo
Salala
Salamat
Sam-Ang Sam Ensemble
Samite
Oumou Sangare
Scandinavian Folk and Beyond (sidebar)
Márta Sebestyén
Mansour Seck
Shadow
Joanne Shenandoah
Sierra Maestra
Six Nations Women Singers
Soto Koto Band
Soul Brothers
The Soul of Black Peru (compilation)
The Soul of Cape Verde (compilation)

Southern Scratch
Douglas Spotted Eagle
Rigo Star
Stellamara
Super Guitar Soukous (compilation)
Sweet Sunny North, Vol. II (compilation)
Tabou Combo
Rachid Taha
Tahitian Choir
Tam Tam 2000
Tambu
Taraf de Haïdouks
Tarika
Te Vaka
Terem Quartet
3 Mustaphas 3
Willie Toors
Touré Kunda
Trance Mission
Daniel Tshanda
Vadå
Justin Vali
Glen Velez
Veritas
Vocal Sampling
Walela
Fredrick Whiteface
Wolga Balalaika Ensemble
Xit
Yothu Yindi
Tom Zé
Zulu Spear

David Poole

Afro-Cuba: A Musical Anthology (compilation)
Angels in the Mirror: Vodou Music of Haiti (compilation)
Argentina: The Guitar of the Pampas (compilation)
Arte Flamenco, Vols. 1–15 (compilation)
Australia: Songs of the Aborigines and Music of Papua New Guinea (compilation)
Bollywood (sidebar)
Brazil Classics 2: O Samba (compilation)
Brazil Samba Roots (compilation)
Brazil: Tropicalismo (sidebar)
Brazilliance: The Music of Rhythm (compilation)
Calypsos: Afro-Limonese Music of Costa Rica (compilation)
Caribbean Island Music (compilation)
China: Time to Listen (compilation)
Chinese Classical Music (sidebar)
Cuarteto Coculense: Mexico's Pioneer Mariachis, Vol. 4 (compilation)
Cuba Classics 3: New Directions in Cuban Music—Diablo Al Inferno (compilation)
Cuban Counterpoint: History of the Son Montuno (compilation)
Cuban Dance Party: Roots of Rhythm Volume 2 (compilation)
Alpha Yaya Diallo
Mikey Dread

musicHound **SERIES INDEX**

This index is a guide to all of the artists and groups included in the Music-Hound series of books (MusicHound Rock, MusicHound Country, MusicHound Blues, MusicHound R&B, Music-Hound Lounge, Music-Hound Folk, MusicHound Jazz, MusicHound Swing, and MusicHound World). Following the artist or group's name you'll find the book (or books) they appear in.

a-ha
See MH Rock

A House
See MH Rock

A. Robic and the Exertions
See MH Folk

A+
See MH R&B

A3
See MH Rock

Aaliyah
See MH R&B

Najat Aatabou
See MH World

Abana Ba Nasery
See MH World

Greg Abate
See MH Jazz

ABBA
See MH Lounge, MH Rock

Dimi Mint Abba
See MH World

Gregory Abbott
See MH R&B

ABC
See MH Rock

Abdelli
See MH World

Paula Abdul
See MH R&B, MH Rock

Ahmed Abdul-Malik
See MH Jazz

Ahmed Abdullah
See MH Jazz

Abel & Kaninerna
See MH World

John Abercrombie
See MH Jazz

Rabih Abou-Khalil
See MH World

Camara Aboubacar
See MH World

Above the Law
See MH R&B

Colonel Abrams
See MH R&B

Muhal Richard Abrams
See MH Jazz

Rick Abrams
See MH Folk

Nathan Abshire
See MH Folk, MH World

Absolute Zeros
See MH Rock

The Abyssinians
See MH World

AC/DC
See MH Rock

The Accelerators
See MH Rock

Ace
See MH Rock

Johnny Ace
See MH Blues, MH R&B, MH Rock

Ace of Base
See MH R&B, MH Rock

The Aces
See MH Blues

Acetone
See MH Rock

Barbara Acklin
See MH R&B

Acoustic Alchemy
See MH Jazz

Acousticats
See MH Folk

Roy Acuff
See MH Country, MH Folk

Ad Vielle Que Pourra
See MH World

Adam & the Ants
See MH Rock

Bryan Adams
See MH Rock

George Adams
See MH Jazz

Johnny Adams
See MH Blues, MH Jazz, MH R&B

Oleta Adams
See MH R&B

Pepper (Park) Adams
See MH Jazz

Barry Adamson
See MH Lounge, MH Rock

Adaro
See MH World

C.C. Adcock
See MH Rock

Eddie Adcock
See MH Country, MH Folk

Julian "Cannonball" Adderley
See MH Jazz, MH Lounge

Obo Addy
See MH World

Yacub Addy
See MH World

King Sunny Adé
See MH Rock, MH World

Adioa
See MH World

Hasil Adkins
See MH Rock

Trace Adkins
See MH Country

Helen Folasade Adu
See MH Lounge

The Adverts
See MH Rock

Aengus
See MH Folk

Aerosmith
See MH Rock

Ron Affif
See MH Jazz

The Afghan Whigs
See MH Rock

A.F.I.
See MH Rock

Africando
See MH World

The Afro Blue Band
See MH Jazz

Afro Celt Sound System
See MH World

Afro Rican
See MH R&B

Agent Orange
See MH Rock

Agents of Good Roots
See MH Rock

Agnes Gooch
See MH Rock

Eden Ahbez
See MH Lounge

Ahmad
See MH R&B

Mahmoud Ahmed
See MH World

Caroline Aiken
See MH Folk

Air
See MH Jazz, MH Rock

Air Miami
See MH Rock

Air Supply
See MH Rock

Kei Akagi
See MH Jazz

David "Stringbean" Akeman
See MH Country, MH Folk

Pierre Akendengue
See MH World

Garfield Akers
See MH Blues

Rhett Akins
See MH Country

Akinyele
See MH R&B

Toshiko Akiyoshi
See MH Jazz

Farid al-Atrash
See MH World

Alaap
See MH World

Alabama
See MH Country

Alabina
See MH World

Scott Alarik
See MH Folk

The Alarm
See MH Rock

Joe Albany
See MH Jazz

Chava Alberstein
See MH World

Albion Band
See MH Folk

Albion Country Band
See MH Rock

Albita
See MH World

Gerald Albright
See MH Jazz, MH R&B

Alcatrazz
See MH Rock

Howard Alden
See MH Jazz, MH Swing

Ronnie Aldrich
See MH Lounge

Brian Ales
See MH Jazz

Alessi
See MH Lounge

Alger Alexander
See MH Blues

Arthur Alexander
See MH R&B, MH Rock

Eric Alexander
See MH Jazz

John Marshall Alexander Jr.
See MH Blues

Monty Alexander
See MH Jazz

Texas Alexander
See MH Blues

Haris Alexiou
See MH World

Jerry Alfred & the Medicine Beat
See MH World

Pat Alger
See MH Country, MH Folk

Alice in Chains
See MH Rock

Alien Fashion Show
See MH Swing

Tha Alkaholiks
See MH R&B

All
See MH Rock

All-4-One
See MH R&B

The All Girl Boys
See MH Folk

All Saints
See MH Rock

Gary Allan
See MH Country

Carl Allen
See MH Jazz

Fulton Allen
See MH Blues

Geri Allen
See MH Jazz

Harley Allen
See MH Country

Harry Allen
See MH Jazz

Henry "Red" Allen
See MH Jazz, MH Swing

Lillian Allen
See MH World

Peter Allen
See MH Lounge

Red Allen
See MH Country, MH Folk

Rex Allen
See MH Country

Rex Allen Jr.
See MH Country

Steve Allen
See MH Jazz, MH Lounge

Terry Allen
See MH Country, MH Folk

Red Allen & Frank Wakefield
See MH Country

Jenny Allinder
See MH Folk

Amy Allison
See MH Country, MH Rock

Ben Allison
See MH Jazz

Luther Allison
See MH Blues, MH Folk

Mose Allison
See MH Blues, MH Folk, MH Jazz, MH Lounge

The Allman Brothers Band
See MH Blues, MH Rock

Alloy Orchestra
See MH Jazz

Karrin Allyson
See MH Jazz

Laurindo Almeida
See MH Jazz, MH Lounge

Almighty RSO
See MH R&B

Herb Alpert
See MH Jazz, MH Lounge, MH World

Alphaville
See MH Rock

Peter Alsop
See MH Folk

Gerald Alston
See MH R&B

Alt
See MH Rock

Altan
See MH Folk, MH Rock, MH World

John Altenburgh
See MH Jazz

Altered Images
See MH Rock

Joey Altruda with the Cocktail Crew
See MH Lounge

Barry Altschul
See MH Jazz

Dave Alvin
See MH Blues, MH Country, MH Folk, MH Rock

Phil Alvin
See MH Blues, MH Country, MH Rock

Amampondo
See MH World

Amazing Blondel
See MH Folk

The Amazing Rhythm Aces
See MH Country, MH Folk

Eric Ambel
See MH Rock

Ambitious Lovers
See MH Rock

Franco Ambrosetti
See MH Jazz

Ambrosia
See MH Rock

America
See MH Folk, MH Rock

The American Breed
See MH Rock

The American Cafe Orchestra
See MH Folk

American Flyer
See MH Rock

American Music Club
See MH Rock

The Ames Brothers
See MH Lounge

The Amidons
See MH Folk

Amina
See MH World

aMiniature
See MH Rock

Albert Ammons
See MH Jazz, MH Swing

Gene "Jug" Ammons
See MH Jazz

Tori Amos
See MH Rock

The Amps
See MH Rock

Anam
See MH World

Robin Adnan Anders
See MH World

Eric Andersen
See MH Folk, MH Rock

Andersen, Danko, Fjeld
See MH Rock

Al Anderson
See MH Country

Bill Anderson
See MH Country

Chris Anderson
See MH Jazz

Clifton Anderson
See MH Jazz

Ernestine Anderson
See MH Jazz

Fred Anderson
See MH Jazz

Ian Anderson
See MH Rock

John Anderson
See MH Country

Laurie Anderson
See MH Rock, MH World

Leroy Anderson
See MH Lounge

Little Willie Anderson
See MH Blues

Lynn Anderson
See MH Country

Pete Anderson
See MH Country

Pink Anderson
See MH Blues, MH Folk

Ray Anderson
See MH Jazz

Wessell Anderson
See MH Jazz

Leny Andrade
See MH World

Leah Andreone
See MH Rock

Ernie Andrews
See MH Jazz

Julie Andrews
See MH Lounge

Molly Andrews
See MH Folk

The Andrews Sisters
See MH Lounge, MH Swing

Horace Andy
See MH Rock

Angel
See MH Rock

Maya Angelou
See MH Lounge, MH World

The Angels
See MH Rock

Anggun
See MH World

The Animals
See MH Blues, MH Rock

Anitas Livs
See MH World

Paul Anka
See MH Lounge, MH Rock

Ann-Margret
See MH Lounge

Annabouboula
See MH World

Anotha Level
See MH R&B

Another Girl
See MH Rock

Adam Ant
See MH Rock

Antenna
See MH Rock

Marc Anthony
See MH World

Ray Anthony
See MH Lounge, MH Swing

Anthrax
See MH Rock

Bok, Muir & Trickett
See MH Folk

Tommy Bolin
See MH Rock

Zuzu Bollin
See MH Blues

Claude Bolling
See MH Jazz

Yami Bolo
See MH World

The Bolshoi
See MH Rock

Michael Bolton
See MH Rock

Polly Bolton
See MH Folk

Bomb Bassetts
See MH Rock

Bomb the Bass
See MH Rock

Bon Jovi
See MH Rock

James Bonamy
See MH Country

Eddie Bond
See MH Country

Johnny Bond
See MH Country

Gary U.S. Bonds
See MH R&B, MH Rock

Bone Thugs-N-Harmony
See MH R&B

Luiz Bonfá
See MH World

Bonga
See MH World

Bongwater
See MH Rock

Bonham
See MH Rock

Tracy Bonham
See MH Rock

Joe Bonner
See MH Jazz

Juke Boy Bonner
See MH Blues

Simon Bonney
See MH Country

Karla Bonoff
See MH Country, MH Folk, MH Rock

The Bonzo Dog Band
See MH Rock

The Boo Radleys
See MH Rock

Boo-Yaa T.R.I.B.E.
See MH R&B

Boogie Down Productions
See MH R&B

Boogiemonsters
See MH R&B

Roy Book Binder
See MH Blues, MH Folk

Cedella Marley Booker
See MH World

Chuckii Booker
See MH R&B

James Booker
See MH Blues, MH Jazz, MH R&B, MH Rock

Booker T. & the MG's
See MH R&B, MH Rock

Boom Crash Opera
See MH Rock

Boom Shaka
See MH World

The Boomtown Rats
See MH Rock

Pat Boone
See MH Country, MH Lounge, MH Rock

Boone Creek
See MH Country, MH Folk

Laura Boosinger
See MH Folk

Victor Borge
See MH Lounge

Jimmy Bosch
See MH World

Bo$$
See MH R&B

Boss Hog
See MH Rock

Earl Bostic
See MH Jazz, MH R&B

Boston
See MH Rock

Boston Pops Orchestra
See MH Lounge

The Boswell Sisters
See MH Lounge

Libbi Bosworth
See MH Country

The Bothy Band
See MH Folk, MH World

The Bottle Rockets
See MH Country, MH Rock

Boukan Ginen
See MH World

Boukman Eksperyans
See MH World

Phil Boulding
See MH Folk

The Bouncing Souls
See MH Rock

Jean-Paul Bourelly
See MH Jazz, MH R&B, MH Rock

Bob Bovee and Gail Heil
See MH Folk

Bow Wow Wow
See MH Rock

Jimmy Bowen
See MH Country

Robin Huw Bowen
See MH Folk, MH World

Bryan Bowers
See MH Folk

David Bowie
See MH R&B, MH Rock, MH World

Lester Bowie
See MH Jazz

Ronnie Bowman
See MH Country

The Box Tops
See MH R&B, MH Rock

Boxcar Willie
See MH Country

Boy George
See MH Rock

Boy Howdy
See MH Country

Pat Boyack
See MH Blues

Eddie Boyd
See MH Blues

Ronnie Boykins
See MH Jazz

Boymerang
See MH Rock

Boyoyo Boys
See MH World

The Boys from Indiana
See MH Country, MH Folk

The Boys of the Lough
See MH Folk, MH World

Boyz II Men
See MH R&B

Ishmon Bracey
See MH Blues

Charles Brackeen
See MH Jazz

JoAnne Brackeen
See MH Jazz

Brad
See MH Rock

Don Braden
See MH Jazz

Bobby Bradford
See MH Jazz

Carrie Bradley
See MH Folk

Robert Bradley's Blackwater Surprise
See MH Rock

Tiny Bradshaw
See MH Swing

Paul Brady
See MH Folk, MH World

The Brady Bunch
See MH Country

Ruby Braff
See MH Jazz, MH Swing

James Brown
See MH Blues, MH R&B, MH Rock

Jeri Brown
See MH Jazz

Jim Ed Brown
See MH Country

J.T. Brown
See MH Blues

Junior Brown
See MH Country, MH Swing

Les Brown
See MH Jazz, MH Lounge, MH Swing

Marion Brown
See MH Jazz

Marty Brown
See MH Country

Maxine Brown
See MH R&B

Nappy Brown
See MH Blues

Paul Brown
See MH Folk

Ray Brown
See MH Jazz

Rob Brown
See MH Jazz

Robert Brown
See MH Blues

Roy Brown
See MH Blues, MH R&B, MH Swing

Ruth Brown
See MH Jazz, MH R&B, MH Rock, MH Swing

Shirley Brown
See MH R&B

T. Graham Brown
See MH Country

Willie Brown
See MH Blues

Roger Brown & Swing City
See MH Country

Milton Brown and the Musical Brownies
See MH Folk

Chuck Brown & the Soul Searchers
See MH R&B

Jackson Browne
See MH Folk, MH Rock

Jann Browne
See MH Country

Tom Browne
See MH Jazz

The Browns
See MH Country

Brownsville Station
See MH Rock

Bob Brozman
See MH Folk

Dave Brubeck
See MH Jazz, MH Lounge, MH Swing

Ed Bruce
See MH Country

Jack Bruce
See MH Rock

Bill Bruford
See MH Jazz

Jimmy Bruno
See MH Jazz

Brush Arbor
See MH Country

Brute
See MH Folk

Stephen Bruton
See MH Country

David Bryan
See MH Rock

James Bryan
See MH Folk

Ray (Raphael) Bryant
See MH Jazz

Bryndle
See MH Country, MH Folk, MH Rock

Jeanie Bryson
See MH Jazz

Peabo Bryson
See MH R&B

bt
See MH Rock

B.T. Express
See MH R&B

Roy Buchanan
See MH Blues, MH Rock

Rachel Buchman
See MH Folk

The Buckets
See MH Folk

The Buckhannon Brothers
See MH Folk

Lindsey Buckingham
See MH Rock

The Buckinghams
See MH Rock

Jeff Buckley
See MH Folk, MH Rock

Lord Buckley
See MH Swing

Tim Buckley
See MH Folk, MH Rock

Milt Buckner
See MH Jazz, MH Swing

Richard Buckner
See MH Country, MH Folk, MH Rock

Buckshot Lefonque
See MH R&B

Buckwheat Zydeco
See MH Folk, MH World

Harold Budd
See MH Lounge

Buena Vista Social Club
See MH World

Norton Buffalo
See MH Blues

Buffalo Springfield
See MH Folk, MH Rock

Buffalo Tom
See MH Rock

Jimmy Buffett
See MH Country, MH Folk, MH Rock

George "Mojo" Buford
See MH Blues

The Buggles
See MH Rock

Alex Bugnon
See MH Jazz

Buick MacKane
See MH Rock

Built to Spill
See MH Rock

LTJ Bukem
See MH Rock

Bukken Bruse
See MH World

Bŭlgari
See MH World

Sandy Bull
See MH World

Luke & Jenny Anne Bulla
See MH Country, MH Folk

Bulletboys
See MH Rock

Robin Bullock
See MH Folk

The Bum Steers
See MH Country

Bumble Bee Slim
See MH Blues

The B.U.M.S.
See MH R&B

John Bunch
See MH Jazz

William Bunch
See MH Blues

Alden Bunn
See MH Blues

Jane Bunnett
See MH Jazz, MH World

Sharon Burch
See MH World

John Burgess
See MH World

Sonny Burgess
See MH Country, MH Rock, MH Swing

Irving Burgie
See MH World

Kevin Burke
See MH Folk, MH World

Solomon Burke
See MH Blues, MH R&B

Guy Clark
See MH Country, MH Folk

Petula Clark
See MH Lounge, MH Rock

Roy Clark
See MH Country

Sonny Clark
See MH Jazz

Terri Clark
See MH Country

W.C. Clark
See MH Blues

Doug Clark & the Hot Nuts
See MH Lounge

The Dave Clark Five
See MH Rock

The Clark Sisters
See MH R&B

Gilby Clarke
See MH Rock

Johnny Clarke
See MH World

Kenny Clarke
See MH Jazz

Stanley Clarke
See MH Jazz

William Clarke
See MH Blues

The Clarks
See MH Rock

The Clash
See MH Rock

Classics IV
See MH Rock

Claudia
See MH World

Clawgrass
See MH Folk

James Clay
See MH Jazz

Otis Clay
See MH Blues, MH R&B

Richard Clayderman
See MH Lounge

Philip Claypool
See MH Country

Buck Clayton
See MH Jazz, MH Swing

Clayton-Hamilton Orchestra
See MH Jazz

The Clean
See MH Rock

Cleaners from Venus
See MH Rock

Eddy Clearwater
See MH Blues

The Cleftones
See MH R&B

Johnny Clegg & Savuka
See MH Rock, MH World

Albert Clemens
See MH Blues

Vassar Clements
See MH Country, MH Folk

Clarence Clemons
See MH Rock

Clever Jeff
See MH Jazz, MH R&B

Jimmy Cliff
See MH R&B, MH Rock, MH World

Bill Clifton
See MH Country, MH Folk

Alex Cline
See MH Jazz

Charlie Cline
See MH Country

Nels Cline
See MH Jazz

Patsy Cline
See MH Country

George Clinton
See MH R&B, MH Rock

Rosemary Clooney
See MH Jazz, MH Lounge, MH Swing

Clouds of Joy
See MH Swing

The Clovers
See MH R&B, MH Rock

Club Nouveau
See MH R&B

Clusone 3
See MH Jazz

Clutch
See MH Rock

The Coasters
See MH R&B, MH Rock

Arnett Cobb
See MH Jazz, MH Swing

Willie Cobbs
See MH Blues

Billy Cobham
See MH Jazz

Anita Cochran
See MH Country

Eddie Cochran
See MH Rock, MH Swing

Jackie Lee Cochran
See MH Rock

Bruce Cockburn
See MH Folk, MH Rock

Joe Cocker
See MH R&B, MH Rock

Cockeyed Ghost
See MH Rock

Cocoa Tea
See MH World

Cocteau Twins
See MH Rock

Phil Cody
See MH Rock

Robert Tree Cody
See MH World

David Allan Coe
See MH Country

Leonard Cohen
See MH Country, MH Folk, MH Rock

Al Cohn
See MH Jazz

Marc Cohn
See MH Rock

Pat Coil
See MH Jazz

Coldcut
See MH Rock

Freddy Cole
See MH Jazz

Holly Cole
See MH Jazz, MH Lounge, MH Rock

Jude Cole
See MH Rock

Khani Cole
See MH Jazz

Lloyd Cole
See MH Rock

Nat "King" Cole
See MH Jazz, MH Lounge, MH R&B, MH Swing

Natalie Cole
See MH Lounge, MH R&B

Paula Cole
See MH Folk, MH Rock

Richie Cole
See MH Jazz

Cecilia Coleman
See MH Jazz

Cy Coleman
See MH Lounge

Deborah Coleman
See MH Blues

George Coleman
See MH Jazz

Jaz Coleman
See MH Rock

Michael Coleman
See MH Folk

Ornette Coleman
See MH Jazz

Steve Coleman
See MH Jazz

William "Bill" Coleman
See MH Jazz

Johnny Coles
See MH Jazz

Collective Soul
See MH Rock

Buddy Collette
See MH Jazz

Mark Collie
See MH Country

Gerald Collier
See MH Rock

Albert Collins
See MH Blues, MH Folk

Bootsy Collins
See MH R&B, MH Rock

Edwyn Collins
See MH Lounge, MH Rock

Jay Collins
See MH Jazz

Judy Collins
See MH Folk, MH Lounge, MH Rock

Lui Collins
See MH Folk

Mitzie Collins
See MH Folk

Paul Collins
See MH Rock

Phil Collins
See MH Rock

Sam Collins
See MH Blues

Shirley Collins
See MH Folk, MH World

Tommy Collins
See MH Country

The Collins Kids
See MH Country, MH Swing

Christine Collister
See MH Folk, MH Rock

Willie Colon
See MH World

Colony
See MH Rock

Color Me Badd
See MH R&B

The Colourfield
See MH Rock

Jessi Colter
See MH Country

Anita Belle Colton
See MH Lounge

John Coltrane
See MH Jazz

Turiya Alice Coltrane
See MH Jazz

Russ Columbo
See MH Lounge, MH Swing

Shawn Colvin
See MH Folk, MH Rock

Combustible Edison
See MH Lounge, MH Rock

Come
See MH Rock

Amle Comeaux
See MH Country

Commander Cody & His Lost Planet Airmen
See MH Country, MH Folk, MH Rock, MH Swing

Commissioned
See MH R&B

The Commodores
See MH R&B

Common
See MH R&B

Communards
See MH Rock

Perry Como
See MH Lounge

Con Funk Shun
See MH R&B

Concrete Blonde
See MH Rock

Ray Condo & His Ricochets
See MH Country, MH Swing

Eddie Condon
See MH Jazz, MH Swing

Confederate Railroad
See MH Country

Congo Norvell
See MH Rock

The Congos
See MH World

Conjunto Alma Jarocha
See MH World

Conjunto Bernal
See MH World

Conjunto Céspedes
See MH World

John Conlee
See MH Country

Arthur Conley
See MH R&B

Earl Thomas Conley
See MH Country

Graham Connah
See MH Jazz

The Connells
See MH Rock

Chris Connelly
See MH Rock

Connemara
See MH Folk

Harry Connick Jr.
See MH Jazz, MH Lounge, MH Swing

Ray Conniff
See MH Lounge

Rita Connolly
See MH Folk

Chris Connor
See MH Jazz, MH Swing

Joanna Connor
See MH Blues

Bill Connors
See MH Jazz

Norman Connors
See MH Jazz, MH R&B

Stompin' Tom Connors
See MH Country, MH Folk

Patricia Conroy
See MH Country

Conscious Daughters
See MH R&B

Consolidated
See MH Rock

Continental Divide
See MH Country

The Continental Drifters
See MH Rock

The Contours
See MH R&B

Ry Cooder
See MH Blues, MH Country, MH Folk, MH Rock, MH World

Barbara Cook
See MH Lounge

Jesse Cook
See MH World

Junior Cook
See MH Jazz

Sam Cooke
See MH R&B, MH Rock

The Cookies
See MH R&B

Spade Cooley
See MH Country, MH Folk, MH Swing

Rita Coolidge
See MH Country

Coolio
See MH R&B

Andy Cooney
See MH World

Alice Cooper
See MH Rock

Bob Cooper
See MH Jazz

Dana Cooper
See MH Folk

Roger Cooper
See MH Country, MH Folk

Wilma Lee & Stoney Cooper
See MH Country, MH Folk

Cop Shoot Cop
See MH Rock

Cowboy Copas
See MH Country

Julian Cope
See MH Rock

Johnny Copeland
See MH Blues

Stewart Copeland
See MH Rock

Marc Copland
See MH Jazz

Jeff Copley
See MH Country

The Copper Family
See MH Folk

Cordelia's Dad
See MH Folk

Larry Cordle
See MH Country, MH Folk

Joey Dee
See MH Rock

Lenny Dee
See MH Lounge

Dave Dee, Dozy, Beaky, Mick & Tich
See MH Rock

Deee-Lite
See MH R&B, MH Rock

The Deele
See MH R&B

Barrett Deems
See MH Jazz

Deep Forest
See MH Rock, MH World

Deep Purple
See MH Rock

Def Jam
See MH R&B

Def Jef
See MH R&B

Def Leppard
See MH Rock

Joey DeFrancesco
See MH Jazz

Buddy DeFranco
See MH Jazz

deftones
See MH Rock

Defunkt
See MH R&B

Jack DeJohnette
See MH Jazz

Desmond Dekker
See MH R&B, MH World

Del Amitri
See MH Rock

Del Fuegos
See MH Rock

The Del Lords
See MH Rock

Dan Del Santo
See MH World

Del tha Funkee Homosapien
See MH R&B

Geno Delafose
See MH Folk, MH World

John Delafose
See MH Folk

John Delafose & the Eunice Playboys
See MH World

Delaney & Bonnie
See MH Rock

Peter Delano
See MH Jazz

Paul DeLay
See MH Blues

The Delevantes
See MH Country

The Delfonics
See MH R&B

Issac Delgado
See MH World

Delinquent Habits
See MH R&B

The Dells
See MH R&B

The Delmore Brothers
See MH Country, MH Folk, MH Swing

Victor DeLorenzo
See MH Rock

Iris DeMent
See MH Country, MH Folk, MH Rock

Barbara Dennerlein
See MH Jazz

Bernardo Dennis
See MH Blues

Cathy Dennis
See MH Rock

Wesley Dennis
See MH Country

Martin Denny
See MH Lounge

Sandy Denny
See MH Folk, MH Rock, MH World

John Denver
See MH Country, MH Folk, MH Lounge, MH Rock

Depeche Mode
See MH Rock

The Derailers
See MH Country

Derek & the Dominos
See MH Blues, MH Rock

Joe Derrane
See MH Folk

Rick Derringer
See MH Rock

Dervish
See MH Folk, MH World

Descendents
See MH Rock

The Deseret String Band
See MH Folk

The Desert Rose Band
See MH Country, MH Rock

Jackie DeShannon
See MH Rock

Paul Desmond
See MH Jazz, MH Lounge, MH Swing

Des'ree
See MH R&B

Jimmy Destri
See MH Rock

Det Syng
See MH World

Marcella Detroit
See MH Rock

William DeVaughn
See MH R&B

Willy DeVille
See MH Rock

The Devlins
See MH Folk, MH Rock

Devo
See MH Lounge, MH Rock

Howard DeVoto
See MH Rock

Dexy's Midnight Runners
See MH R&B, MH Rock

Dennis DeYoung
See MH Rock

D'Gary
See MH World

Dharma Bums
See MH Rock

Al Di Meola
See MH Jazz

Abdoulaye Diabaté
See MH World

Sékouba "Bambino" Diabaté
See MH World

Toumani Diabaté
See MH World

The Diablos
See MH R&B

Alpha Yaya Diallo
See MH World

Neil Diamond
See MH Country, MH Lounge, MH Rock

Diamond D
See MH R&B

Diamond Rio
See MH Country

The Diamonds
See MH Rock

Diblo Dibala
See MH World

Manu Dibango
See MH R&B, MH World

Dick & Dee Dee
See MH Rock

Hazel Dickens
See MH Country, MH Folk

Little Jimmy Dickens
See MH Country

Walt Dickerson
See MH Jazz

Whit Dickey
See MH Jazz

The Dickies
See MH Rock

Bruce Dickinson
See MH Rock

The Dictators
See MH Rock

Bo Diddley
See MH Blues, MH Folk, MH R&B, MH Rock

Marlene Dietrich
See MH Lounge

Skip Ewing
See MH Country

Exile
See MH Country

Extreme
See MH Rock

Fabian
See MH Lounge, MH Rock

Bent Fabric
See MH Lounge, MH Lounge

The Fabulous Thunderbirds
See MH Blues, MH Rock

Face to Face
See MH Rock

The Faces
See MH Rock

Jon Faddis
See MH Jazz

Chaba Fadela
See MH World

Eleanora Fagan
See MH Blues, MH Lounge

Donald Fagen
See MH Lounge, MH Rock

John Fahey
See MH Folk, MH Rock

Barbara Fairchild
See MH Country

The Fairfield Four
See MH Folk

Fairground Attraction
See MH Rock

Fairport Convention
See MH Folk, MH Rock, MH World

Adam Faith
See MH Rock

Percy Faith
See MH Lounge

Th' Faith Healers
See MH Rock

Faith No More
See MH Rock

Marianne Faithfull
See MH Folk, MH Lounge, MH Rock

Joseph Falcon & Cleoma Breaux Falcon
See MH Folk, MH World

The Falcons
See MH R&B

Jason Falkner
See MH Rock

The Fall
See MH Rock

Charles Fambrough
See MH Jazz

Georgie Fame
See MH Lounge, MH Rock

Fania All-Stars
See MH World

Fantcha
See MH World

Farafina
See MH World

Donna Fargo
See MH Country

Richard and Mimi Fariña
See MH Folk

Mary Ann Farley
See MH Rock

Tal Farlow
See MH Jazz

Chris Farlowe
See MH Rock

The Farm
See MH Rock

Farm Dogs
See MH Rock

Art Farmer
See MH Jazz

Farmer Not So John
See MH Rock

Farmer's Daughters
See MH Folk

Allen Farnham
See MH Jazz

Joe Farrell
See MH Jazz

Dionne Farris
See MH Rock

Farside
See MH Rock

Majek Fashek
See MH World

Fastbacks
See MH Rock

Fastball
See MH Rock

Zusaan Kali Fasteau
See MH Jazz

Fat Boys
See MH R&B

Fat Joe Da Gangsta
See MH R&B

Fatala
See MH World

Fatback Band
See MH R&B

John Faulkner
See MH World

Faust
See MH Rock

Pierre Favre
See MH Jazz

Pura Fé
See MH World

Fear
See MH Rock

Stephen Fearing
See MH Folk

Charlie Feathers
See MH Country, MH Rock, MH Swing

John Fedchock
See MH Jazz

Danny Federici
See MH Rock

The Feelies
See MH Rock

Michael Feinstein
See MH Lounge

Jerome Felder
See MH Blues

Lee Feldman
See MH Rock

Jose Feliciano
See MH Lounge, MH World

Narvel Felts
See MH Country

Freddy Fender
See MH Country

Mike Fenton
See MH Folk

H-Bomb Ferguson
See MH Blues

Jay Ferguson
See MH Rock

Maynard Ferguson
See MH Jazz

Fernhill
See MH World

Ferrante & Teicher
See MH Lounge

Rachelle Ferrell
See MH Jazz, MH R&B

Melissa Ferrick
See MH Rock

Glenn Ferris
See MH Jazz

Ferron
See MH Folk

Bryan Ferry
See MH Lounge, MH Rock

Garrison Fewell
See MH Jazz

Fiddle Fever
See MH Folk

Arthur Fiedler
See MH Lounge

Dale Fielder
See MH Jazz

The Fifth Dimension
See MH Lounge, MH R&B

54.40
See MH Rock

Fig Dish
See MH Rock

The Figgs
See MH Rock

Figgy Duff
See MH Folk

Fight
See MH Rock

Fiji Mariners
See MH Rock

Greg Ginn
See MH Rock

The Gipsy Kings
See MH World

Girls Against Boys
See MH Rock

Girls of Angeli
See MH World

Regis Gisavo
See MH World

Egberto Gismonti
See MH Jazz, MH World

Jimmy Giuffre
See MH Jazz

Gjallarhorn
See MH World

Paddy Glackin
See MH World

Gladhands
See MH Rock

Gladiators
See MH World

Glass Eye
See MH Rock

Jackie Gleason
See MH Lounge

Gary Glitter
See MH Rock

Glitterbox
See MH Rock

Globe Unity Orchestra
See MH Jazz

The Glove
See MH Rock

Corey Glover
See MH Rock

The Go-Betweens
See MH Rock

The Go-Go's
See MH Rock

Go West
See MH Rock

Goats
See MH R&B

God Street Wine
See MH Rock

The Godfathers
See MH Rock

The Goins Brothers
See MH Country

Julie Gold
See MH Folk

Barry Goldberg
See MH Blues

Ben Goldberg
See MH Jazz, MH World

Samuel Goldberg
See MH Lounge

Golden Earring
See MH Rock

Golden Gate Orchestra
See MH Swing

Golden Gate Quartet
See MH Folk

The Golden Palominos
See MH Rock

Golden Ring
See MH Folk

Golden Smog
See MH Country, MH Rock

Goldfinger
See MH Rock

Goldie
See MH Rock

Larry Goldings
See MH Jazz

Vinny Golia
See MH Jazz

Mac Gollehon
See MH Jazz

Benny Golson
See MH Jazz

Eddie Gomez
See MH Jazz

Paul Gonsalves
See MH Jazz

Gonzaguinha
See MH World

Celina González
See MH World

Rubén González
See MH World

Jerry Gonzalez & the Fort Apache Band
See MH Jazz, MH World

Goo Goo Dolls
See MH Rock

Good Ol' Persons
See MH Country, MH Folk

Goodie Mob
See MH R&B

Cuba Gooding
See MH R&B

Benny Goodman
See MH Jazz, MH Lounge, MH Swing

Steve Goodman
See MH Country, MH Folk, MH Rock

Mick Goodrick
See MH Jazz

Ron Goodwin
See MH Lounge

Bobby Gordon
See MH Jazz

Dexter Gordon
See MH Jazz, MH Lounge

Robert Gordon
See MH Country, MH Rock, MH Swing

Berry Gordy Jr.
See MH R&B

Lesley Gore
See MH Lounge, MH Rock

Martin Gore
See MH Rock

John Gorka
See MH Country, MH Folk, MH Rock

Gorky's Zygotic Mynci
See MH Rock

Skip Gorman
See MH Country, MH Folk

Eydie Gorme
See MH Lounge

Steve Gorn
See MH World

Vern Gosdin
See MH Country, MH Folk

Danny Gottlieb
See MH Jazz

Susan Gottlieb
See MH Folk

Barry Goudreau
See MH Rock

Morton Gould
See MH Lounge

Robert Goulet
See MH Lounge

Gov't Mule
See MH Rock

Lawrence Gowan
See MH Rock

Dusko Goykovich
See MH Jazz

The GP's
See MH Folk

Davey Graham
See MH Folk

Graham Central Station
See MH R&B

Lou Gramm
See MH Rock

Grand Daddy I.U.
See MH R&B

Grand Funk Railroad
See MH Rock

Grandmaster Flash & the Furious Five
See MH R&B

Grandpa Jones
See MH Country

Jerry Granelli
See MH Jazz

Amy Grant
See MH Rock

Bill Grant
See MH Folk

Darrell Grant
See MH Jazz

Eddy Grant
See MH World

Grant Lee Buffalo
See MH Rock

Grant Street
See MH Folk

Syl Johnson
See MH Blues, MH R&B

Tommy Johnson
See MH Blues

Johnson Mountain Boys
See MH Country, MH Folk

Daniel Johnston
See MH Rock

Freedy Johnston
See MH Folk, MH Rock

Phillip Johnston
See MH Jazz

Randy Johnston
See MH Jazz

Tom Johnston
See MH Rock

The Johnstons
See MH Folk, MH World

Jolene
See MH Country

Jolly Boys
See MH World

Al Jolson
See MH Lounge, MH Swing

Casey Jones
See MH Blues

Curtis Jones
See MH Blues

Eddie Lee Jones
See MH Blues

Edward Jones
See MH Blues

Elvin Jones
See MH Jazz

Etta Jones
See MH Jazz, MH Lounge

Floyd Jones
See MH Blues

George Jones
See MH Country, MH Folk

Glenn Jones
See MH R&B

Grace Jones
See MH R&B

Grandpa Jones
See MH Folk

Hank Jones
See MH Jazz

Howard Jones
See MH Rock

Isham Jones
See MH Swing

Jack Jones
See MH Lounge

Jo Jones
See MH Jazz, MH Swing

Johnny Jones
See MH Blues, MH Blues, MH Swing

Linda Jones
See MH R&B

Little "Sonny" Jones
See MH Blues

Marti Jones
See MH Rock

Mick Jones
See MH Rock

Oliver Jones
See MH Jazz

Paul "Wine" Jones
See MH Blues

"Philly" Joe Jones
See MH Jazz

Quincy Jones
See MH Jazz, MH Lounge, MH R&B, MH Swing

Rickie Lee Jones
See MH Folk, MH Rock

Robert Lewis Jones
See MH Blues

Ruth Lee Jones
See MH Blues

Sam Jones
See MH Jazz

Spike Jones
See MH Jazz, MH Lounge, MH Swing

Steve Jones
See MH Rock

Thad Jones
See MH Jazz, MH Swing

Tom Jones
See MH Lounge, MH Rock

Tutu Jones
See MH Blues

Diane Jones and Hubie King
See MH Folk

Carol Elizabeth Jones & James Leva
See MH Folk

Betty Joplin
See MH Jazz

Janis Joplin
See MH Blues, MH R&B, MH Rock

Scott Joplin
See MH Jazz

Al Jordan
See MH Lounge

Charley Jordan
See MH Blues

Clifford Jordan
See MH Jazz

Duke Jordan
See MH Jazz

Esteban "Steve" Jordan
See MH World

Louis Jordan
See MH Blues, MH Jazz, MH Lounge, MH R&B, MH Swing

Marlon Jordan
See MH Jazz

Montell Jordan
See MH R&B

Ronny Jordan
See MH Jazz

Sheila Jordan
See MH Jazz

Stanley Jordan
See MH Jazz

Margie Joseph
See MH R&B

Pleasant "Cousin Joe" Joseph
See MH Blues

Scott Joss
See MH Country

Journey
See MH Rock

Joy Division
See MH Rock

Joyce
See MH World

JPP
See MH World

JT the Bigga Figga
See MH R&B

Judas Priest
See MH Rock

Cledus "T." Judd
See MH Country

Wynonna Judd
See MH Country

The Judds
See MH Country

Judybats
See MH Rock

Jules & the Polar Bears
See MH Rock

Juluka
See MH Rock

Jump with Joey
See MH Lounge

Jumpin' Jimes
See MH Swing

Jungle Brothers
See MH R&B

Jungular Grooves
See MH World

Junior
See MH R&B

Junior M.A.F.I.A.
See MH R&B

Junk Monkeys
See MH Rock

Junoon
See MH World

Vic Juris
See MH Jazz

Just Ice
See MH R&B

Barbara K
See MH Rock

Paul K
See MH Rock

Klezmer Conservatory Band
See MH Folk, MH World

Klezmer Plus!
See MH World

The Klezmorim
See MH Folk, MH World

Earl Klugh
See MH Jazz, MH R&B

KMD
See MH R&B

KMFDM
See MH Rock

The Knack
See MH Rock

Knapsack
See MH Rock

Jimmy Knepper
See MH Jazz

The Knickerbockers
See MH Rock

Cheri Knight
See MH Folk, MH Rock

Jean Knight
See MH R&B

Gladys Knight & the Pips
See MH Lounge, MH R&B

The Knitters
See MH Rock

Mark Knopfler
See MH Blues

Buddy Knox
See MH Country, MH Rock

Chris Knox
See MH Rock

Cub Koda
See MH Rock

Kodo
See MH World

Ray & Glover Koerner
See MH Blues

"Spider" John Koerner
See MH Folk

Koerner, Ray & Glover
See MH Folk

Charlie Kohlhase
See MH Jazz

Habib Koité & Bamada
See MH World

Walt Koken
See MH Country, MH Folk

Steve Kolander
See MH Country

Fred Koller
See MH Country, MH Folk

Ken Kolodner
See MH Folk

Lee Konitz
See MH Jazz

Alhaji Bai Konteh
See MH World

Kool & the Gang
See MH R&B

Kool Ass Fash
See MH R&B

Kool G Rap and D.J. Polo
See MH R&B

Kool Keith
See MH R&B, MH Rock

Kool Moe Dee
See MH R&B

Al Kooper
See MH Blues, MH Rock

Peter Koppes
See MH Rock

KoRn
See MH Rock

Kornog
See MH World

Kenny Kosek
See MH Country

Andre Kostelanetz
See MH Lounge

Ozzie Kotani
See MH Folk

Kotoja
See MH World

Leo Kottke
See MH Folk, MH Rock

Peter Kowald
See MH Jazz

Dave Koz
See MH Jazz

Jake Krack
See MH Folk

Kraftwerk
See MH Rock

Diana Krall
See MH Jazz, MH Lounge, MH Swing

Wayne Kramer
See MH Rock

Billy J. Kramer & the Dakotas
See MH Rock

Alison Krauss
See MH Country, MH Folk

Phil Krauth
See MH Rock

Lenny Kravitz
See MH R&B, MH Rock

Chantal Kreviazuk
See MH Rock

Kris Kross
See MH R&B

Kris Kristofferson
See MH Country, MH Folk

Ernie Krivda
See MH Jazz

The Kronos Quartet
See MH Jazz, MH World

krosfyah
See MH World

Gene Krupa
See MH Jazz, MH Lounge, MH Swing

K's Choice
See MH Rock

K7
See MH R&B

Ali Hassan Kuban
See MH World

Smokin' Joe Kubek Band with Bnois King
See MH Blues

Ed Kuepper
See MH Rock

Joachim Kuhn
See MH Jazz

Steve Kuhn
See MH Jazz

Kukuruza
See MH World

Kula Shaker
See MH Rock

Umm Kulthum
See MH World

George Kuo
See MH Folk, MH World

Tuli Kupferberg
See MH Rock

Kurious
See MH R&B

Fela Kuti
See MH Jazz, MH World

Femi Anikulapo Kuti
See MH World

Leonard Kwan
See MH Folk, MH World

Forward Kwenda
See MH World

Jim Kweskin & the Jug Band
See MH Folk

Kwest Tha Madd Lad
See MH R&B

Kay Kyser
See MH Lounge, MH Swing

Kyuss
See MH Rock

The L.A. Four
See MH Lounge

L.A. Guns
See MH Rock

La India
See MH World

Lá Lugh
See MH Folk, MH World

La Mafia
See MH World

La Muscagña
See MH World

La Sonora Dinamita
See MH World

La Sonora Matancera
See MH World

Sleepy LaBeef
See MH Country, MH Swing

Patti LaBelle
See MH R&B

Abraham Laboriel
See MH Jazz

Rube Lacy
See MH Blues

Steve Lacy
See MH Jazz

Lady Bianca
See MH Blues

Lady of Rage
See MH R&B

Ladysmith Black Mambazo
See MH World

Scott LaFaro
See MH Jazz

Jimmy LaFave
See MH Country, MH Folk

Francis Lai
See MH Lounge

Laika
See MH Rock

Cleo Laine
See MH Jazz, MH Lounge

Frankie Laine
See MH Lounge, MH Swing

Greg Lake
See MH Rock

Oliver Lake
See MH Jazz

Tim Lake
See MH Folk

Lakeside
See MH R&B

Lamb
See MH Rock

Barbara Lamb
See MH Country, MH Folk

Lambchop
See MH Country, MH Rock

Lambert, Hendricks & Ross
See MH Jazz

Mary Jane Lamond
See MH Folk, MH World

Nancy LaMott
See MH Lounge

Major Lance
See MH R&B

Harold Land
See MH Jazz

Art Lande
See MH Jazz

Sonny Landreth
See MH Blues, MH Rock

Hollis Landrum
See MH Folk

James A. Lane
See MH Blues

Mary Lane
See MH Blues

Ronnie Lane
See MH Rock

Mark Lanegan
See MH Rock

Jonny Lang
See MH Blues, MH Rock

k.d. lang
See MH Country, MH Folk, MH Lounge, MH Rock

Jonboy Langford & the Pine Valley Cosmonauts
See MH Country, MH Rock

Lester Lanin
See MH Lounge, MH Swing

Daniel Lanois
See MH Rock, MH World

Lard
See MH Rock

Largo
See MH Rock

Patty Larkin
See MH Folk

Ellis Larkins
See MH Jazz

Nick LaRocca
See MH Jazz

Mary LaRose
See MH Jazz

Nicolette Larson
See MH Country

The La's
See MH Rock

Denise LaSalle
See MH R&B

Grit Laskin
See MH Folk

James Last
See MH Lounge

Last Exit
See MH Jazz, MH Rock

Last Poets
See MH Jazz, MH R&B

The Last Roundup
See MH Country, MH Rock

Bill Laswell
See MH R&B, MH Rock, MH World

Yusef Lateef
See MH Jazz

Latimore
See MH R&B

Latin Playboys
See MH Rock, MH World

Stacy Lattisaw
See MH R&B

Jim Lauderdale
See MH Country

Laughing Hyenas
See MH Rock

Cyndi Lauper
See MH Rock

The Laurel Canyon Ramblers
See MH Country, MH Folk

Andy LaVerne
See MH Jazz

Christine Lavin
See MH Country, MH Folk

The Law
See MH Rock

Azar Lawrence
See MH Jazz

Tracy Lawrence
See MH Country

Steve Lawrence & Eydie Gorme
See MH Lounge

Hubert Laws
See MH Jazz

Johnny Laws
See MH Blues

Ronnie Laws
See MH Jazz

Doyle Lawson
See MH Country, MH Folk

Hugh Lawson
See MH Jazz

Lawson Square Infirmary
See MH Rock

Lazy Lester
See MH Blues

Bernadette Lazzaro
See MH Lounge

Le Mystère des Voix Bulgares
See MH World

Leadbelly
See MH Blues, MH Folk

The Leaders
See MH Jazz

Leaders of the New School
See MH R&B

The League of Crafty Guitarists
See MH Rock

Leahy
See MH World

Paul Leary
See MH Rock

The Leaves
See MH Folk, MH Rock

Led Zeppelin
See MH Blues, MH Rock

Chris LeDoux
See MH Country

Arthur Lee
See MH Folk, MH Rock

Brenda Lee
See MH Country, MH Lounge, MH Rock

Bryan Lee
See MH Blues

Frankie Lee
See MH Blues

Irma Lee
See MH Blues

Lost Boyz
See MH R&B

The Lost Continentals
See MH Swing

Lothar & the Hand People
See MH Rock

Lotion
See MH Rock

Loud Family
See MH Rock

John D. Loudermilk
See MH Country, MH Folk

Joe Hill Louis
See MH Blues

Louisiana Red
See MH Blues

The Lounge Lizards
See MH Jazz, MH Lounge, MH Rock

Louvin Brothers
See MH Country, MH Folk

Joe Lovano
See MH Jazz

Love
See MH Folk, MH Rock

Darlene Love
See MH R&B, MH Rock

Laura Love
See MH Folk

Willie Love
See MH Blues

Love & Rockets
See MH Rock

G. Love & Special Sauce
See MH Blues, MH Rock

Love Delegation
See MH Rock

The Love Dogs
See MH Swing

Love Jones
See MH Lounge

Love Spit Love
See MH Rock

Love Tractor
See MH Rock

Love Unlimited Orchestra
See MH R&B

Patty Loveless
See MH Country

Lovemongers
See MH Rock

Loverboy
See MH Rock

Lyle Lovett
See MH Country, MH Folk, MH Rock

Ruby Lovett
See MH Country

Lene Lovich
See MH Rock

The Lovin' Spoonful
See MH Folk, MH Rock

Frank Lowe
See MH Jazz

Jez Lowe
See MH Folk

Nick Lowe
See MH Rock

L7
See MH Rock

L.T.D.
See MH R&B

L'Trimm
See MH R&B

Albert Luandrew
See MH Blues

Norman Luboff Choir
See MH Lounge

Lucas
See MH Jazz, MH R&B

Trevor Lucas
See MH World

Luciano
See MH World

Jon Lucien
See MH Jazz

Steve Lucky & the Rhumba Bums
See MH Swing

The Lucky Strikes
See MH Swing

Lulu
See MH Rock

Luna
See MH Rock

Jimmie Lunceford
See MH Jazz, MH Swing

Carmen Lundy
See MH Jazz

Luniz
See MH R&B

Dónal Lunny
See MH Folk, MH World

Bascom Lamar Lunsford
See MH Country, MH Folk

Evan Lurie
See MH Rock

John Lurie
See MH Lounge, MH Rock

Luscious Jackson
See MH R&B, MH Rock

Lush
See MH Rock

Luxuria
See MH Rock

L.V.
See MH R&B

Annabella Lwin
See MH Rock

John Lydon
See MH Rock

Arthur Lyman
See MH Lounge

Frankie Lymon & the Teenagers
See MH R&B, MH Rock

Brian Lynch
See MH Jazz

Claire Lynch
See MH Country, MH Folk

George Lynch/Lynch Mob
See MH Rock

Cheryl Lynn
See MH R&B

Loretta Lynn
See MH Country

Jeff Lynne
See MH Rock

Shelby Lynne
See MH Country

Lynyrd Skynyrd
See MH Country, MH Rock

Jimmy Lyons
See MH Jazz

The Lyres
See MH Rock

Johnny Lytle
See MH Jazz

Paul Lytton
See MH Jazz

M-Base Collective
See MH Jazz

Baaba Maal
See MH World

Harold Mabern
See MH Jazz

Willie Mabon
See MH Blues

Mabsant
See MH Folk, MH World

Joel Mabus
See MH Folk

Sipho Mabuse
See MH World

Margaret MacArthur
See MH Folk

Ewan MacColl
See MH Folk, MH World

Kirsty MacColl
See MH Rock

Jeanette MacDonald
See MH Lounge

Laurel MacDonald
See MH World

Pat MacDonald
See MH Folk, MH Rock

Rod MacDonald
See MH Folk

Shane MacGowan & the Popes
See MH Rock

Machito
See MH Jazz, MH World

Ashley MacIsaac
See MH Folk, MH Rock, MH World

Mannheim Steamroller
See MH Lounge

Manolín, El Médico de la Salsa
See MH World

Joseph "Wingy" Manone
See MH Jazz

Ray Mantilla
See MH Jazz

Mantovani
See MH Lounge

Machanic Manyeruke
See MH World

Phil Manzanera
See MH Rock

Samba Mapangala & Orchestra Virunga
See MH World

Thomas Mapfumo
See MH World

The Mar-Keys
See MH R&B

The Marcels
See MH R&B

Steve Marcus
See MH Jazz

Rick Margitza
See MH Jazz

Bob Margolin
See MH Blues, MH Folk

Kitty Margolis
See MH Jazz

Tania Maria
See MH Jazz

Mariachi Cobre
See MH World

Charlie Mariano
See MH Jazz

Teena Marie
See MH R&B, MH Rock

Marillion
See MH Rock

Marilyn Manson
See MH Rock

The Mark-Almond Band
See MH Rock

Marky Mark
See MH R&B

Rita Marley
See MH World

Ziggy Marley & the Melody Makers
See MH R&B, MH Rock, MH World

Bob Marley & the Wailers
See MH R&B, MH Rock, MH World

Marley Marl
See MH R&B

Marley's Ghost
See MH Folk

Marmalade
See MH Rock

Dodo Marmarosa
See MH Jazz

Marry Me Jane
See MH Rock

Chris Mars
See MH Rock

Johnny Mars
See MH Blues

Branford Marsalis
See MH Jazz

Delfeayo Marsalis
See MH Jazz

Ellis Marsalis
See MH Jazz

Wynton Marsalis
See MH Jazz

Warne Marsh
See MH Jazz

Amanda Marshall
See MH Rock

Evan Marshall
See MH Folk

Mike Marshall
See MH Folk

The Marshall Tucker Band
See MH Country, MH Rock

Martha & the Vandellas
See MH R&B, MH Rock

Claire Martin
See MH Jazz

Dean Martin
See MH Lounge, MH Swing

Freddy Martin
See MH Lounge, MH Swing

Jimmy Martin
See MH Country, MH Folk

Mel Martin
See MH Jazz

Ricky Martin
See MH World

Tony Martin
See MH Lounge

Narciso Martinez
See MH World

Al Martino
See MH Lounge

Pat Martino
See MH Jazz

John Martyn
See MH World

The Marvelettes
See MH R&B, MH Rock

Richard Marx
See MH Rock

Masada
See MH Jazz, MH World

Steve Masakowski
See MH Jazz

Miya Masaoka
See MH Jazz

Hugh Masekela
See MH World

Dave Mason
See MH Folk, MH Rock

Mila Mason
See MH Country

Nick Mason
See MH Rock

David Massengill
See MH Folk

Cal Massey
See MH Jazz

Zane Massey
See MH Jazz

Massive Attack
See MH R&B, MH Rock

Masta Ace
See MH R&B

Master Musicians of Jajouka
See MH World

Master P
See MH R&B

Matchbox 20
See MH Rock

Material
See MH Jazz, MH Rock

Material Issue
See MH Rock

Johnny Mathis
See MH Lounge, MH R&B

Jas. Mathus & His Knock-Down Society
See MH Rock

Kathy Mattea
See MH Country, MH Folk

Eric Matthews
See MH Lounge, MH Rock

Iain Matthews
See MH Folk, MH Rock

Dave Matthews Band
See MH Rock, MH World

Matthews Southern Comfort
See MH Folk

June Maugery
See MH Folk

The Mavericks
See MH Country

Maxwell
See MH R&B

David Maxwell
See MH Blues

Maxwell Street Klezmer Band
See MH World

Billy May
See MH Lounge, MH Swing

Brian May
See MH Rock

John Mayall
See MH Blues, MH Rock

Curtis Mayfield
See MH R&B, MH Rock

Percy Mayfield
See MH Blues, MH R&B

Maypole
See MH Rock

Bill Mays
See MH Jazz

Lyle Mays
See MH Jazz

Maze
See MH R&B

Mazz
See MH World

Mazzy Star
See MH Rock

Prince Nico Mbarga
See MH World

Jimi Mbaye
See MH World

M'Boom
See MH Jazz

Mzwakhe Mbuli
See MH World

MC Breed & the DFC
See MH R&B

MC Eiht
See MH R&B

M.C. Hammer
See MH R&B

MC Lyte
See MH R&B

MC 900 Ft. Jesus
See MH R&B, MH Rock

M.C. Shan
See MH R&B

MC Solaar
See MH Jazz, MH R&B

Mac McAnally
See MH Country, MH Folk

Kimberly M'Carver
See MH Folk

Christian McBride
See MH Jazz

Martina McBride
See MH Country

McBride & the Ride
See MH Country

Jerry McCain
See MH Blues

Edwin McCain Band
See MH Rock

Cash McCall
See MH Blues

C.W. McCall
See MH Country

Darrell McCall
See MH Country

Les McCann
See MH Jazz

Cormac McCarthy
See MH Folk

Paul McCartney
See MH Rock

Kathy McCarty
See MH Rock

Mary McCaslin
See MH Country, MH Folk

Scott McCaughey
See MH Rock

Charly McClain
See MH Country

Mighty Sam McClain
See MH Blues

Debby McClatchy
See MH Folk

Tommy McClennan
See MH Blues

Delbert McClinton
See MH Blues, MH Country, MH Rock

Carol McComb
See MH Folk

David McComb
See MH Rock

Billy McComiskey
See MH Folk

Rob McConnell
See MH Jazz

Marilyn McCoo
See MH Lounge

Susannah McCorkle
See MH Jazz

Maureen McCormick
See MH Country

The Del McCoury Band
See MH Country, MH Folk

Neal McCoy
See MH Country

Van McCoy
See MH R&B

The McCoy Brothers
See MH Blues

Jimmy McCracklin
See MH Blues

Larry McCray
See MH Blues

Mindy McCready
See MH Country

Rich McCready
See MH Country

Ian McCulloch
See MH Rock

Robert Lee McCullum
See MH Blues

John McCutcheon
See MH Folk

Ellas McDaniel
See MH Blues

Floyd McDaniel
See MH Swing

Mel McDaniel
See MH Country

Michael McDermott
See MH Rock

Country Joe McDonald
See MH Folk, MH Rock

Michael McDonald
See MH Rock

Megon McDonough
See MH Folk

Mississippi Fred McDowell
See MH Blues, MH Folk

Ronnie McDowell
See MH Country

Jack McDuff
See MH Jazz

Reba McEntire
See MH Country

John McEuen
See MH Country, MH Folk, MH Rock

Eleanor McEvoy
See MH Country, MH Folk, MH Rock

McFadden & Whitehead
See MH R&B

Bobby McFerrin
See MH Jazz

MC5
See MH Rock

Andy McGann
See MH World

Eileen McGann
See MH Folk, MH World

Kate & Anna McGarrigle
See MH Country, MH Folk, MH Rock

Dennis McGee
See MH Folk

Sam & Kirk McGee
See MH Folk

Sterling McGee
See MH Blues

Brownie McGhee
See MH Blues, MH Folk

Howard McGhee
See MH Jazz

Stick McGhee
See MH Blues

Maureen McGovern
See MH Lounge

Tim McGraw
See MH Country

Chris McGregor
See MH World

Freddie McGregor
See MH World

Jimmy McGriff
See MH Jazz

Roger McGuinn
See MH Folk, MH Rock

McGuinn, Clark & Hillman
See MH Country

Barry McGuire
See MH Rock

Kalaparusha Maurice McIntyre
See MH Jazz

silverchair
See MH Rock

Shel Silverstein
See MH Country, MH Folk

Terrance Simien
See MH World

Kim Simmonds
See MH Rock

Patrick Simmons
See MH Rock

Sonny Simmons
See MH Jazz

Carly Simon
See MH Folk, MH Lounge, MH Rock

Joe Simon
See MH R&B

Paul Simon
See MH Folk, MH Rock, MH World

Simon & Garfunkel
See MH Folk, MH Rock

Nina Simone
See MH Jazz, MH Lounge

Mark Simos
See MH Folk

Simple Gifts
See MH Folk

Simple Minds
See MH Rock

Simply Red
See MH R&B, MH Rock

Martin Simpson
See MH Folk, MH Rock

Martin & Jessica Simpson
See MH Folk

Frankie Lee Sims
See MH Blues

Zoot Sims
See MH Jazz

Frank Sinatra
See MH Jazz, MH Lounge, MH Swing

Frank Sinatra Jr.
See MH Lounge, MH Swing

Nancy Sinatra
See MH Lounge, MH Rock

Singers Unlimited
See MH Lounge

Talvin Singh
See MH World

Daryle Singletary
See MH Country

Sintesis
See MH World

Siouxsie & the Banshees
See MH Rock

Sir Douglas Quintet
See MH Rock

Sir Julian
See MH Lounge

Sir Mix-a-Lot
See MH R&B

Noble Sissle
See MH Swing

Sister Carol
See MH World

Sister Hazel
See MH Rock

Sister Sledge
See MH R&B

Sister Souljah
See MH R&B

Sisters of Mercy
See MH Rock

Six Nations Women Singers
See MH World

Six Shooter
See MH Country

6 String Drag
See MH Rock

16 Horsepower
See MH Rock

Sixteen Ninety-One
See MH Folk, MH World

The 6ths
See MH Rock

Roni Size
See MH Rock

Ricky Skaggs
See MH Country, MH Folk

SKAndalous All-Stars
See MH World

Skara Brae
See MH World

The Skatalites
See MH World

Skee-Lo
See MH R&B

Skeeter & the Skidmarks
See MH Folk

The Skeletons
See MH Country, MH Rock

Skid Row
See MH Rock

The Skillet Lickers
See MH Country, MH Folk

Skinny Puppy
See MH Rock

Skunk Anansie
See MH Rock

Patrick Sky
See MH Folk, MH Rock

Sky Cries Mary
See MH Rock

Sky King
See MH Rock

Skyedance
See MH Folk, MH World

Skylark
See MH Folk

Skyy
See MH R&B

Slade
See MH Rock

Steve Slagle
See MH Jazz

Slash's Snakepit
See MH Rock

Slave
See MH R&B

Slayer
See MH Rock

Sleater-Kinney
See MH Rock

Percy Sledge
See MH Blues, MH R&B

Sleeper
See MH Rock

Sleeping Bag/Fresh Records
See MH R&B

Grace Slick
See MH Rock

Slick Rick
See MH R&B

Abdel Ali Slimani
See MH World

The Slits
See MH Rock

Sloan
See MH Rock

P.F. Sloan
See MH Rock

Carol Sloane
See MH Jazz

Slowburn
See MH Rock

Slowdive
See MH Rock

Sly & Robbie
See MH World

Sly & the Family Stone
See MH R&B, MH Rock

Drink Small
See MH Blues

Fred Small
See MH Folk

Judy Small
See MH Folk

Small Faces
See MH Rock

Smash Mouth
See MH Rock

Smashing Pumpkins
See MH Rock

Smif-N-Wessun
See MH R&B

Arthur "Guitar" Smith
See MH Country

Barkin' Bill Smith
See MH Blues

Bessie Smith
See MH Blues, MH Folk, MH Jazz, MH R&B

Betty Smith
See MH Folk

The Strawbs
See MH Rock

Stray Cats
See MH Rock, MH Swing

Billy Strayhorn
See MH Jazz, MH Swing

Mel Street
See MH Country

Chic Street Man
See MH Folk

Sarah Streeter
See MH Blues

Barbra Streisand
See MH Lounge

Strength in Numbers
See MH Country, MH Folk

The String Trio of New York
See MH Jazz

Stringbean
See MH Country, MH Folk

Strings & Things
See MH Folk

John P. Strohm & the Hello Strangers
See MH Rock

Percy Strother
See MH Blues

Frank Strozier
See MH Jazz

Joe Strummer
See MH Rock

Strunz & Farah
See MH Jazz, MH World

Dave Stryker
See MH Jazz

Dan Stuart
See MH Rock

Marty Stuart
See MH Country

John Stubblefield
See MH Jazz

Studebaker John
See MH Blues

Cinderella G. Stump
See MH Lounge

Rolf Sturm
See MH Jazz

Style Council
See MH Lounge, MH R&B, MH Rock

The Stylistics
See MH R&B

Styx
See MH Rock

The subdudes
See MH Folk, MH Rock

Sublime
See MH Rock

Dr. L. Subramaniam
See MH World

Subrosa
See MH Rock

Suede
See MH Rock

Sugar
See MH Rock

Sugar Blue
See MH Blues

Sugar Hill Records
See MH R&B

Sugar Ray
See MH Rock

Sugarcubes
See MH Rock

The Sugarhill Gang
See MH R&B

Suicidal Tendencies
See MH Rock

The Suicide Machines
See MH Rock

Sukay
See MH World

Sukia
See MH Rock

Ira Sullivan
See MH Jazz

Jerry & Tammy Sullivan
See MH Country

Joe Sullivan
See MH Jazz

Maxine Sullivan
See MH Jazz

Yma Sumac
See MH Lounge, MH World

Hubert Sumlin
See MH Blues

Donna Summer
See MH R&B

Andy Summers
See MH Rock

Elaine Summers
See MH Rock

Sun Ra
See MH Jazz, MH Rock

The Sundays
See MH Rock

Sundown Playboys
See MH Folk

Sunny Day Real Estate
See MH Rock

Sunnyland Slim
See MH Blues

Sunshine Skiffle Band
See MH Folk

Ron Sunsinger
See MH World

Super Cat
See MH World

Super Chikan
See MH Blues

Super Deluxe
See MH Rock

Super Furry Animals
See MH Rock

Super Rail Band of Bamako
See MH World

Superchunk
See MH Rock

Supergrass
See MH Rock

Doug Supernaw
See MH Country

Supersax
See MH Jazz

Supertramp
See MH Rock

The Supremes
See MH R&B, MH Rock

Al B. Sure!
See MH R&B

Surf Music
See MH Rock

Surface
See MH R&B

John Surman
See MH Jazz

Foday Musa Suso
See MH World

Susquehanna String Band
See MH Folk

Pete Sutherland
See MH Folk

Kirk Sutphin
See MH Folk

Ralph Sutton
See MH Jazz

Steve Swallow
See MH Jazz

Swamp Dogg
See MH Rock

Billy Swan
See MH Country, MH Rock

Swans
See MH Rock

Dave Swarbrick
See MH Folk, MH World

Keith Sweat
See MH R&B

The Swedish Sax Septet
See MH World

Sweeney's Men
See MH Folk, MH World

The Sweet
See MH Rock

Matthew Sweet
See MH Rock

Rachel Sweet
See MH Rock

The Sweet Baby Blues Band
See MH Jazz

Sweet Honey in the Rock
See MH Folk, MH World

Sweet 75
See MH Rock

Sweethearts of the Rodeo
See MH Country, MH Folk

Steve Wariner
See MH Country

Jennifer Warnes
See MH Folk, MH Rock

Warrant
See MH Rock

Baby Boy Warren
See MH Blues

Robert Henry Warren
See MH Blues

The Warrior River Boys
See MH Country

Wartime
See MH Rock

Dionne Warwick
See MH Lounge, MH R&B

Was (Not Was)
See MH R&B, MH Rock

Washboard Sam
See MH Blues

Dinah Washington
See MH Blues, MH Jazz, MH
Lounge, MH R&B, MH
Swing

Grover Washington Jr.
See MH Jazz, MH R&B

Isidore "Tuts" Washington
See MH Blues

Keith Washington
See MH R&B

**Walter "Wolfman" Washing-
ton**
See MH Blues

Rob Wasserman
See MH Jazz

The Waterboys
See MH Folk, MH Rock, MH
World

Linda Waterfall
See MH Folk

Benny Waters
See MH Jazz, MH Swing

Crystal Waters
See MH R&B, MH Rock

Ethel Waters
See MH Blues, MH Jazz, MH
Swing

Muddy Waters
See MH Blues, MH Folk, MH
R&B, MH Rock

Patty Waters
See MH Jazz

Roger Waters
See MH Rock

Jack Waterson
See MH Rock

Norma Waterson
See MH Folk

Waterson:Carthy
See MH Folk, MH World

The Watersons
See MH Folk, MH World

Jody Watley
See MH R&B

Bill Watrous
See MH Jazz

Bobby Watson
See MH Jazz

Dale Watson
See MH Country

Doc Watson
See MH Country, MH Folk

Gene Watson
See MH Country

Johnny "Guitar" Watson
See MH Blues

Mike Watt
See MH Rock

Charlie Watts
See MH Jazz

Ernie Watts
See MH Jazz

Noble "Thin Man" Watts
See MH Blues

Eunice Waymon
See MH Lounge

WC and the MAAD Circle
See MH R&B

Weather Report
See MH Jazz, MH Rock

Carl Weathersby
See MH Blues

Curley Weaver
See MH Blues

"Boogie" Bill Webb
See MH Blues

Chick Webb
See MH Jazz, MH Swing

Harry Roger Webb
See MH Lounge

Jimmy Webb
See MH Lounge, MH Rock

Eberhard Weber
See MH Jazz

Ben Webster
See MH Jazz, MH Lounge, MH
Swing

Katie Webster
See MH Blues

Dave Weckl
See MH Jazz

The Wedding Present
See MH Rock

Ted Weems
See MH Swing

Ween
See MH Rock

Weezer
See MH Rock

Scott Weiland
See MH Rock

Kurt Weill
See MH Lounge

George Wein
See MH Jazz

The Weirdos
See MH Rock

Bob Welch
See MH Rock

Gillian Welch
See MH Blues, MH Country,
MH Folk

Kevin Welch
See MH Country, MH Folk

Casey Bill Weldon
See MH Blues

Lawrence Welk
See MH Lounge, MH Swing

Paul Weller
See MH Rock

Valerie Wellington
See MH Blues

Junior Wells
See MH Blues, MH R&B

Kitty Wells
See MH Country, MH Folk

Mary Wells
See MH R&B, MH Rock

Dick Wellstood
See MH Jazz

Paula Joy Welter
See MH Folk

Papa Wemba
See MH World

Wendy & Lisa
See MH Rock

Kenny Werner
See MH Jazz

Susan Werner
See MH Folk

Pete Wernick
See MH Swing

Paul Wertico
See MH Jazz

Kelly Werts
See MH Folk

Fred Wesley
See MH Jazz, MH R&B

Frank Wess
See MH Jazz

Camille West
See MH Folk

Dottie West
See MH Country

Leslie West
See MH Rock

Mae West
See MH Lounge

Speedy West & Jimmy Bryant
See MH Country

West, Bruce & Laing
See MH Rock

Floyd Red Crow Westerman
See MH World

Western Flyer
See MH Country

Joe Williams
See MH Jazz, MH Swing

John Williams
See MH Lounge

Larry Williams
See MH R&B

Lee "Shot" Williams
See MH Blues

Lucinda Williams
See MH Country, MH Folk, MH Rock

Mars Williams
See MH Jazz

Mary Lou Williams
See MH Jazz, MH Swing

Mason Williams
See MH Folk, MH Lounge

Nathan Williams
See MH Folk, MH World

Robert Pete Williams
See MH Blues

Robin & Linda Williams
See MH Country, MH Folk

Roger Williams
See MH Lounge

Tex Williams
See MH Country, MH Swing

Tony Williams
See MH Jazz

Vanessa Williams
See MH R&B

Victoria Williams
See MH Folk, MH Rock

Walter Williams
See MH Blues

Maurice Williams & the Zodiacs
See MH R&B

Cris Williamson
See MH Folk

Homesick James Williamson
See MH Blues

Robin Williamson
See MH Folk

Sonny Boy Williamson I
See MH Blues

Sonny Boy Williamson II
See MH Blues

Steve Williamson
See MH Jazz

Willie & Lobo
See MH Jazz, MH World

Aaron Willis
See MH Blues

Chick Willis
See MH Blues

Chuck Willis
See MH Blues, MH R&B

Kelly Willis
See MH Country

Larry Willis
See MH Jazz

Little Sonny Willis
See MH Blues

The Willis Brothers
See MH Country

Bob Wills
See MH Country, MH Folk, MH Swing

Mark Wills
See MH Country

Michelle Willson
See MH Blues, MH Swing

Al Wilson
See MH R&B

Brian Wilson
See MH Lounge, MH Rock

Cassandra Wilson
See MH Jazz, MH Lounge

Chris Wilson
See MH Rock

Gerald Wilson
See MH Jazz

Hop Wilson
See MH Blues

Jackie Wilson
See MH R&B, MH Rock

Joemy Wilson
See MH Folk, MH World

Murry Wilson
See MH Lounge

Nancy Wilson
See MH Jazz, MH Lounge, MH R&B

Smokey Wilson
See MH Blues

Steve Wilson
See MH Jazz

Teddy Wilson
See MH Jazz, MH Swing

U.P. Wilson
See MH Blues

Wilson Phillips
See MH Rock

Marty Wilson-Piper
See MH Rock

Wimme
See MH World

Angie & Debbie Winans
See MH R&B

BeBe & CeCe Winans
See MH R&B

The Winans
See MH R&B

Vickie Winans
See MH R&B

Angela Winbush
See MH R&B

Jesse Winchester
See MH Country, MH Folk, MH Rock

Lem Winchester
See MH Jazz

Kai Winding
See MH Jazz

Winger
See MH Rock

Wings
See MH Rock

George Winston
See MH Lounge

Edgar Winter
See MH R&B, MH Rock

Johnny Winter
See MH Blues, MH Rock

Paul Winter
See MH World

Hugo Winterhalter
See MH Lounge

Steve Winwood
See MH Rock

The Wipers
See MH Rock

Wire
See MH Rock

Wire Train
See MH Rock

Reverend Billy C. Wirtz
See MH Country

Chubby Wise
See MH Country, MH Folk

Mac Wiseman
See MH Country, MH Folk

Wishbone Ash
See MH Rock

Bill Withers
See MH R&B

Jimmy Witherspoon
See MH Blues, MH Jazz, MH Lounge, MH Swing

Jah Wobble
See MH Rock, MH World

Kate Wolf
See MH Folk

Peter Wolf
See MH R&B, MH Rock

Wolfgang Press
See MH Rock

Wolfstone
See MH Folk, MH World

Wolga Balalaika Ensemble
See MH World

The Wolverines
See MH Swing

Bobby Womack
See MH R&B, MH Rock

Lee Ann Womack
See MH Country

Womack & Womack
See MH R&B

Stevie Wonder
See MH R&B, MH Rock, MH World

Hear no evil, see no evil!
These Hounds won't monkey around with your leisure time.

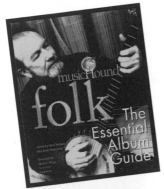

MusicHound Folk

The original buyer's guide to the entire folk genre will satisfy both baby boomers and younger fans just discovering folk music. The 1,120 artists whose work is critiqued in these pages include the legends and the lesser knowns, current acts as well as up-and-comers. This all-inclusive coverage, with a band's influences and the acts they've inspired, will have fans adding to their collections. For each artist you'll find suggestions for what to buy, what to avoid and why. *MusicHound Folk* also offers a substantial resource section, packed with information on folk music publications, Web pages, record labels and more. A free music CD sampler is included.

Neal Walters and Brian Mansfield • 1998 • 1,030 pp. • ISBN 1-57859-037-X

MusicHound Jazz

Following the format that MusicHound has made famous, collectors and fans alike can enjoy jazz like never before. *MusicHound Jazz* reviews the works of nearly 1,300 prominent performers and is unparalleled in its comprehensiveness. This guide rates the recordings of the artists and recommends what to buy and what to avoid. One hundred photos, resource information, indexes and a free music CD sampler make this an essential album guide.

Steve Holtje and Nancy Ann Lee • 1998 • 1,400 pp.• ISBN 1-57859-031-0

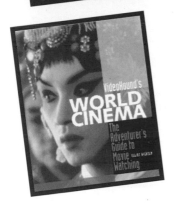

VideoHound's World Cinema
The Adventurer's Guide to Movie Watching

World Cinema wanders the globe in search of great moviemaking and wonderful viewing. More than 800 significant movies are reviewed. Coverage spans Asia, Australia, Britain, France, Italy, Africa, Europe, Russia, Canada and everywhere else films are made outside of the U.S. *World Cinema* is the only foreign film guide geared toward the increasingly adventurous video renter. It is also the only one offering 9 indexes, including director, cast, title translation, country of origin, writer and others.

Elliot Wilhelm • 1999 • 550 pp. • ISBN 1-57859-059-0

VISIBLE INK PRESS

Available at fine bookstores everywhere,
or at your favorite online bookseller.

FREE MUSIC
from **Wicklow Records**

1. ALPHA YAYA DIALLO "DUNIYA"
(From *The Message,* Wicklow 09026-63407-2)
Originally from Guinea, Diallo's own unique hybrid of West African idioms and modern world influences is definitive world music for the millennium, and is perfectly captured on this infectious opening track, driven by the sublime *kora* (African harp-lute).

2. JUAN CARLOS FORMELL "PALO DE GUAYABA"
(From *Songs from a Little Blue House,* Wicklow 09026-63452-2)
This Cuban expatriate and son of Juan Formell (leader of the legendary Los Van Van) has re-invigorated the roots of Cuban music with modern compositions, a distinct world view, breathtaking melodies, and thoughtful lyrics—often, as here, concerning humans' troubled relationship with nature (and by implication, with each other).

3. MARY JANE LAMOND "A MHAIRI BHOIDHEACH"
(From *Fire in the Kitchen,* Wicklow 09026-63133-2)
Lamond's youthful discovery of the ancient Gaelic spinning songs that crossed the sea to her native Cape Breton aboard immigrant ships from Ireland and Scotland are what inspired her to become a singer. Performing here with members of the Chieftains, her passion and dedication to the Gaelic language comes shining through on every note.

4. VÄRTTINÄ "NEITONEN"
(From *Vihma,* Wicklow 09026-63262-2)
Ten members and seven albums strong, Värttinä have always been at the forefront of Nordic neo-folk. Based largely on the ancient folk music of Finland's storied Karelia region, Värttinä's style is ever evolving. With dense vocal harmonies and masterful playing, their sound is surprising, yet filled with infectious and instantly familiar melodies.

5. YAT-KHA "KALDAK-KAMAR"
(From *Dalai Beldiri,* Wicklow 09026-63351-2)
The strange and beautiful "throat-singing" of Tuva has only recently found its way into the West, but even those familiar with its otherworldly tones will find something unique in the sound of Yat-Kha. Started in 1991 by Albert Kuvezin (a founder of Tuvan sensation Huun-Huur-Tu), the band has emerged as a brave new voice on the world-music scene.

6. LAUREL MACDONALD "ÒRAN NA H-EALA"
(From *Chroma,* Wicklow 09026-63270-2)
With influences that run from avant-garde composition to medieval liturgical poems, Canada's MacDonald conjures up sounds that speak of the future but are rooted deeply in the past. Her cinematic journeys into Celtic mysticism have made her a favorite of modern dance groups and contemporary audiences alike.

7. SACRED SYSTEM "BLACK LOTUS"
(From *Nagual Site,* Wicklow 09026-63263-2)
The brainchild of New York dub producer and bassist Bill Laswell, Sacred System was conceived to explore the deep roots of Sufi mysticism in a thoroughly modern context. Featuring luminaries like Gulam Mohamed Khan of Pakistan's devotional *qawwali* tradition, and the inimitable Zakir Hussain on Indian *tabla* drums, this track is a sonic odyssey across worlds seen and unseen.

8. ALPHA YAYA DIALLO "BADENMA"
(From *The Message,* Wicklow 09026-63407-2)
Growing up in Guinea, Diallo had the chance to study under some of West Africa's finest *griots* (oral historians and troubadours)—and guitarists. Featured here on both *balafon* (African xylophone) and guitar, his rock-solid rhythm playing shines through on this infectious Mandinka-culture workout.

9. VÄRTTINÄ "LAULUTYTTÖ"
(From *Vihma,* Wicklow 09026-63262-2)
This song catches the Finns at their high-flying best, as the band's crackerjack playing and jazz-influenced arrangements provide the perfect counterpoint for the singers' incomparable four-part harmonies and classic good-time message.

10. THE BULGARIAN VOICES ANGELITE
"HEI LASSIE" (From *Christmas in Rome,* Wicklow 09026-63250-2)
From Grammy nominations to the world's greatest stages, this phenomenal choir has defined its own unique voice and made an indelible mark on the world of music. Their lilting Christmas carol here was specially commissioned for the album *Christmas in Rome* in collaboration with Paddy Moloney and the Vatican Choir and Orchestra.

11. BILL LASWELL "DÉJALA EN LA PUNTICA/ HABANA TRANSMISSION #2: CUBAN EVOLUTION" (From *Imaginary Cuba: Deconstructing Havana,* Wicklow 09026-63514-2)
Leave it to jack-of-all-styles Laswell to turn the recent American/Cuban music explosion on its head. Starting with a series of field recordings with the likes of Clave Guaguanco, Tat Guinnes, and Frank Emilio, Laswell took his tapes home to New York and emerged five months later from his Orange Studios with a totally cutting-edge take on Cuban rhythms.

12. JUAN CARLOS FORMELL "MANGO MANGÜEY"
(From *Songs from a Little Blue House,* Wicklow 09026-63452-2)
With his instantly recognizable style, Formell has no problem making this Latin classic his very own—he even re-wrote the verse lyrics.

13. LA BOTTINE SOURIANTE "LE LYS VERT"
(From *Fire in the Kitchen,* Wicklow 09026-63133-2)
Without losing any of their distinct French-Canadian flare, this legendary Quebecois show band combines big-band jazz, Celtic reels, Cajun stomps, and even polkas into an unstoppable and heady musical stew. Joined here by members of the Chieftains, the resulting worldbeat big bang is a force that can't be denied.

WICKLOW RECORDS
www.wicklowrecords.com

Launched in the summer of 1997, Wicklow Records has a vision of a world brought closer together through music. Centered on the creative instincts of eminent musician/ producer/composer Paddy Moloney, the label present artists from around the world, giving them the opportunity to reach a broader audience. By developing a roster of both new and established artists performing traditional and contemporary styles, Wicklow is committed to breaking down barriers and bringing fans a wider world of music.